HORTICA

COLOR CYCLOPEDIA
of GARDEN FLORA

in all Climates
— Worldwide —
and Exotic Plants Indoors

*8,100 Photographs
in Living Color*
with Hardiness Zone Maps

ALFRED BYRD GRAF, D.Sc.

FIRST EDITION

ROEHRS COMPANY — Publishers
East Rutherford, N.J. 07073, U.S.A.

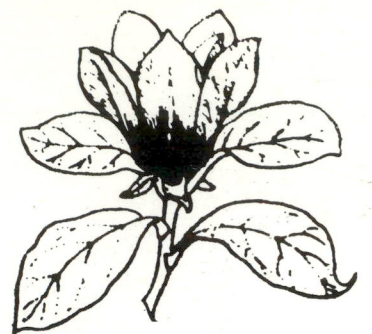

**International
Standard Book Number
ISBN 0-911266-25-9**

**Library of Congress
Card No. 92-060464**

**©Copyright 1992
by Dr. A. B. GRAF**

Art Director
Philip Grushkin
Englewood, New Jersey

Typography
DATCO Design & Typography
Oakland, New Jersey

Map Maker
C. S. Hammond & Co.
Maplewood, New Jersey

Printing and Binding
Horowitz/Rae
Book Manufacturers
Fairfield, New Jersey

Published by
Roehrs Company
P.O. Box 125
E. Rutherford, New Jersey 07073
Tel. (201) 939-0090

First Edition 1992

CONTENTS

*Cover: Geodesic Dome Solarium, at
University Botanic Garden, Duesseldorf, Germany*

In Bermuda Botanic Gardens

Working on Hortica

On this map Chinese names are spelled in the traditional manner. The list below indicates their equivalents in the new Pinyin spelling system.

Traditional	Pinyin	Traditional	Pinyin
Canton	Guangzhou	Peiping	Beijing
Chengtu	Chengdu	Si	Xi
Chungking	Chongqing	Sinkiang	Xinjiang
Foochow	Fuzhou	Tientsin	Tianjin
Hwang Ho	Huang He	Tihwa	Urümqi
Mukden	Shenyang	Tsinan	Jinan
Nanking	Nanjing	Yangtze Kiang	Chang Jiang
Ningsia	Yinchuan		

This map of the world shows the tropic belt, an area 3,200 miles wide, with the countries and islands which, together with the subtropics, an area of varying breadth with long summers and mild winters, are the native habitat of most of the exotic plants used for indoor decoration. The Tropics of Cancer and Capricorn border the tropic zone at 23.5 degrees north and south of the equator. This region between or near these parallels is marked by its warm climate and luxuriant vegetation, modified of course by altitude, prevailing winds and precipitation. Guided by the lines of latitude on this map, and the tables on elevations, temperature and rainfall under 'Plant Geography', a fair idea can be formed about climatic background and geographical distribution of plants, which in turn gives us a clue to their requirements.

Longitude 80° East of 100° Greenwich

11/92

'Our doubts are traitors
and make us lose the good
we oft might win
by fearing to attempt'

... Shakespeare

ABOUT THE AUTHOR

Alfred Graf ranks with the great botanists and horticulturists of all time. His scholarly pursuits, carried out with much courage, determination and pioneering spirit, have opened new horizons for understanding our universe and for practical application of this knowledge in horticulture.

Dr. Graf is probably the most widely travelled plant explorer of the world's Tropics and Subtropics. Horticulturist, botanist and professional photographer, he has roamed the earth in the spirit of von Humboldt, Darwin, and David Fairchild earlier in the 20th and 19th centuries, in search of exotic botanicals to add to the enlarging horticulture of the world. From his headquarters at the Exotic Nurseries of the Roehrs Company, where he has presided over one of the world's most complete plant collections, Alfred Graf during the past fifty years journeyed into the remote regions of the two hemispheres where tropical and subtropical plants abound.

Central and South America, the West Indies, Africa, India and Sri Lanka, China, Southeast Asia, Indonesia, New Guinea, and the South Pacific have yielded to his painstaking search hundreds of new introductions to our ornamental horticulture. During this time he has created a vast and comprehensive collection of botanical photographs of plants in cultivation or in habitat, the best of which have been gathered in his horticultural books on ornamental plants, particularly the renowned and universally known Pictorial Cyclopedia EXOTICA, and in his comprehensive Colorama TROPICA.

While the Tropics and Subtropics may seem more romantic, as the home of most of our ornamental indoor plants, the world's colder zones are no strangers to Dr. Graf. Being of German roots, he is well acquainted with European gardenflora, and has spent extended periods in northern Asia, from Turkey to the Caucasus, the Himalayas, China, Korea and Japan.

Amongst the honors received by the author are the award of the Large Gold Medal of the Massachusetts Horticultural Society, the Certificate of Merit of the Pennsylvania Horticultural Society, the Distinguished Service Award of the Horticultural Society of New York, a Citation Award of the American Horticultural Society, and the Tercentenary Medallion of the State of New Jersey, presented 1964 at the New York Coliseum. In 1967 he was invested with the Sarah Chapman Francis Medal of the Garden Club of America for outstanding literary achievement. During the National Convention in Pittsburgh 1972, Alfred Graf was elected to Horticulture's Hall of Fame, the highest distinction of the Society of American Florists, for his contributions to the advancement of floriculture in America. He is also a contributor to Encyclopedia Britannica. In cognizance of his research and published reference works on exotic plants, Fairleigh Dickinson University of New Jersey conferred on him the honorary degree of Doctor of Science. In Portland, Oregon, 1979, he was awarded the treasured Medal of his mentor, Dr. Libery Hyde Bailey of Cornell University, New York, the highest honor of the American Horticultural Society.

Tulip Time at Keukenhof, Lisse, Holland.

INTRODUCTION to HORTICA

With continuing interchange amongst the world's people, more and more interesting and beautiful ornamentals, as well as useful fruiting plants have been discovered in distant habitats, or developed in Horticulture. The possibilities to add to botanical collections, and to our gardenflora are endless, provided the climatic environment is suitable.

HORTICA is a wide-ranging pictorial assemblage, intended to show our floral wealth in living color, as seen and recorded by the author, with note-book and camera, taking some 150,000 polychrome photos in nearly every inhabited region on earth.

While the companion Colorama TROPICA presents essentially the fantastic flora of warm climate and tropical latitudes, HORTICA extends into the colder zones, to include the widest possible selection of attractive ornamentals, and of edible fruit, found in gardens or in habitats experiencing frigid winters. The pictorial part of HORTICA is divided into 16 distinct categories, from Exotic Plants Indoors, to Perennials, and Trees planted outdoors. When plants shown in TROPICA are also listed in HORTICA, these are usually of different photos to avoid duplications. This kaleidoscope of color should be of great help as reference to visual plant identification. In the area of cool climate perennials, I had the capable assistance of Pamela Harper, of England and Virginia, which helped to cover this section in HORTICA more comprehensively. Filled with detailed information, each plant is described as to character and generally its use; its family and origin; synonym if any, and common name where determined. Dimension and measurements are given in International Metric Terms, along with conversion scales to relate to the English system. Flowering seasons cited are usually those of the Northern hemisphere, normally governed by day-length, but are reversed by six months in southerly latitudes of the Southern hemisphere.

I have been privileged to visit botanical collections worldwide, and to spend time on expeditions into remote areas, and all floristic regions. Thus I had the opportunity to study various climates, from the cool zones of North America, Europe and northern Asia, to species-rich Central America, the rainforest of the Amazon, and the humid jungles of Malaysia, contrasting with the xerophytic vegetations of northern Mexico, and Africa. Many strange and handsome plants and trees from Australia and New Zealand have found a new home north of the equator, in regions of similar climate. As a guide to optimum use in gardens, all plants have been assigned a cold-hardiness zone, or a range for best performance, scaled from zone 2 cold-temperate, to 12 humid-tropical.

HORTICA however is essentially not a "how-to" book on practical gardening of which there are many excellent works available; nor could it attempt to record all the periodic novelties, which are adequately shown in annual nursery catalogs. It does, however, to the widest possible extent, portray the basic species, as well as cultivars known and tested in horticulture worldwide, emphasizing in each their individual merits or use.

Botanical nomenclature has experienced a series of revisions in recent years, and to determine a name currently valid, is often difficult. My principal reference has been HORTUS 3, updated by the periodical 'Baileya' (Cornell University New York). Further important sources are the Royal Hort. Soc. Dictionary of Gardening, and the new European Garden Flora; from Germany we have the carefully edited Zander, Dictionary of Plant names, 13th Edition. Our own extensive library is replete with regional Floras world-wide, in 5 languages. Also at my disposal were the most important works in specialized horticulture or on various plant families (see condensed Bibliography pg. 1211). In addition, we constantly receive the journals and papers of botanic gardens, and numerous plant societies, reporting on continuing research, and names newly mandated.

My thanks and appreciation are due to those honored taxonomists and plant specialists, who assisted me by dialogue, in meticulously bringing together this far-flung international cyclopedia. A constant resource in the New York area were the vast plant collections of Julius Roehrs Co. Exotic Nurseries, founded in 1869. With her knowledge of the gardenflora of our Southwest, daughter Doris Matthews of California has focused her contribution on this principally arid region. I am especially grateful to Lieselotte Graf, my learned spouse, for her 25 years of recording and research, and final typing of the often difficult manuscripts, of both TROPICA and HORTICA.

In a Reference work such as HORTICA, which endeavors to form a bridge between botanical science and practical usage in horticulture, discrepancies and errors can probably not be avoided, especially since pertinent parallel literature often does not agree. However, I have diligently tried to reach for perfection, and feel reassured in knowing, that lovely flowers will smile at us with happy faces, regardless of any name adopted.

First Edition, June 1992

P.O. Box 125
East Rutherford, N.J. 07073
Phone (201) 939-0090

Pacific Coast
856 Mason Road
Vista, Calif. 92084

ALFRED B. GRAF, D.Sc.

ESSAYS on CONTENTS

PLANTS INDOORS *(570 photos)*

Usually Exotics from Warm climate regions of the world which find our comfortably warm, hospitable homes and interiors of business offices very similar in temperature to the environment of their homelands. Ornamental plants are not only decorative against stark walls, but also bring the beauty of nature and their romance to live with us in harmony. Favorite indoor subjects are found amongst Araliads, Aroids, Begonias, Bromeliads, Gesneriads, Cacti and other Succulents, but most require attention to adequate moisture and sufficient light needed for their happiness and well-being.

ORCHIDS — Queen of Flowers *(180 photos)*

This primarily tropical family of aristocrats, creations of great beauty and strange shapes, comprises some 35,000 species in 800 genera, growing as epiphytes on forest trees, or also as terrestrials. In addition, there are countless hybrids, initiated by orchid fanciers, and their culture is most interesting and rewarding as a hobby. In temperate climates they would respond best within the controlled and hospitable condition of a greenhouse which can provide needed humidity and comfortable temperatures.

PALMS and Palm-like plants *(215 photos)*

Palms have always been the noble family signifying the Tropics, with some genera extending into subtropical climates as well. To see a palmtree conjures up visions of romance in South Seas islands, areas where the Coconut palm is also an important source of food, as is the Date palm in North Africa and the Near East. The decorative value of palms has long been appreciated, and they have been grown in containers for ages. Similar in appearance is the family of Cycads. From arid regions are the Palm-lilies or Yuccas.

FERNS and their Allies *(147 photos)*

Botanically termed FILICES, ferns belong to the series of non-flowering plants collectively known as CRYPTOGAMS. They are of all plant groups the most widely distributed, from the Arctic to the Tropics and on South to Alpine New Zealand. Their history goes back 400 million years, to an era before dinosaurs roamed the earth, long before the first flowering-plants appeared. In close to 12,000 species, from dainty moss-like miniatures to palm-like treeferns 25 m high; some genera such as Platycerium, or Staghorns, and the Birdsnest, Asplenium nidus, prefer to grow on rainforest trees as epiphytes. Usually, ferns inhabit the humid environment of the Tropics. Ferns adapt well to interior decorative use provided their moisture needs are carefully watched. In their greenery they create a cool and refreshing ambience. Propagation is from spores forming on the underside of fronds, or by division of rhizome clusters.

CACTI and other SUCCULENTS *(512 photos)*

Because of their unique oddity or strange beauty of color in their flowers, succulents are highly prized by hobbyists and decorators. They are generally very durable, and accustomed to privation because most have emerged as children of the sun, struggling for survival in hostile arid regions of wide temperature variation, with day-time heat to chilly nights. Cacti especially, of which there are thousands of species and varieties, in 2 cm miniatures to desert giants 10 m high, have developed a special capacity to store water in thick fleshy bodies or leaves, which enables them to exist in dry locations. There are exceptions such as the orchid-cactus, dwelling epiphytically in tropical rainforest, resplendent with their showy flowers in vivid colors. The Cactaceae are native to the American hemisphere but there are Cactus-like succulents such as Euphorbias in the Eastern hemisphere, especially Africa.

CARNIVORES and other CURIOS *(65 photos)*

One of the great mysteries of Plant life is the often unexplained ability of 450 species of insectivorous plants, to act like animals by setting in motion parts of their bodies, or thinking up means of trapping moving or flying insects and small animals. There are several methods used by these "flesh-eaters" having ferocious jaw-like toothed traps as in Dionaea, the Venus fly-trap, that snap shut on inquisitive bugs seeking nectar; then there is Pinguicula, having fleshy fly-catcher leaves which are sticky with a digestive fluid attracting insects to hold and gradually absorb them. Droseras, the Sundews, have sensitive sweet-sticky hairs curving inward on touch to catch their victims. Lastly, there is death by drowning; the long funnels of the pitcher plants are equipped with nectar glands, enticing bugs and even small animals to fall into an urn of pepsin-charged water.

BULBS and TUBERS *(491 photos)*

Bulbs indoors or in the garden are amongst the most rewarding blooming plants, and their beauty and versatility has made them popular worldwide. What we know as "Bulbs" is a horticultural term to include true bulbs, tubers, and corms. Genuine bulbs consist of a central growth bud sheathed in graded layers of scales and include Amaryllis, Lilies, Narcissus, and Tulips. The tuber is generally a thickened subterranean stem of irregular shape, and has no tunic nor basal plate, but a rough leathery skin and forms widespread roots; on its surface are the latent buds, so well known in the potato. Other tuberous plants are Caladium, Colocasia, Cyclamen, Sinningia. Tuberous rhizomes are elongate thickened underground branches bearing buds, found in such as Anemone, Cannas, Iris, and Zantedeschia; also the Gesneriads Achimenes and Smithiantha. Tuberous roots are true swollen roots which have no buds except at stem-base around which they congregate, so typical in Dahlias and Ranunculus. Corms are very bulb-like but solid, consisting of the swollen base of a stem, and which stores food. Cormous plants are Crocus, Freesia, Gladiolus, Ixia, Tritoma, and Kohleria.

What "Bulbs" have in common is an underground food reserve. Also, during their built-in period of dormancy, bulbs may be taken up to be dried and cured for storage, to be planted again in due time, in the garden or into pots, preparing for a new awakening.

TRAILERS, CLIMBERS and CREEPERS *(552 photos)*

Most vines and trailers are actually creeping plants with stems too weak to support themselves. The climbing kinds reach out with their lengthening stems for any possible support, to which they cling by tendrils or suction cups, or twining spirally. Outdoors there are many opportunities to utilize slender wiry climbers such as Clematis and Bignonias, or scandent woody flowering shrubs; Roses and showy Bougainvilleas. Bougainvilleas can be trained on wires against walls and fences, or draped over curving pergolas. Good groundcovers will form durable matted areas even in difficult locations as under trees or on dry slopes. Good chocies are broadleaf genera such as Ivy (Hedera), and many other perennials, also prostrate forms of Conifers such as Cupressus and Juniperus; in warm areas various succulent Ice plants including Carpobrotus, Delosperma and Lampranthus.

WATER PLANTS and NEAR-AQUATICS *(114 photos)*

"Water plants" may be living under water, float on its surface, or merely grow along the edge of a pond or stream. Some are with roots anchored in the bottom, the leaves and flowers floating, as do most water-lilies (Nymphaea); others swim completely free as true aquatics; this includes Water ferns, Water lettuce (Pistia), Floating moss, Duckweed and some Waterhyacinths (Eichhornia). Then there are the underwater aquatics that are most appreciated in tropical aquariums, since they act as oxygenators to keep standing water clean and healthy for the fishes; amongst the best are Cryptocoryne and Echinodorus.

PERENNIALS and ANNUALS in the garden *(1662 photos)*

Perennials technically are enduring herbaceous plants that persist year after year, increasing in size by spreading from a rhizomatous rootstock which may be divided for propagation. Hardy perennials are common in cold climate gardens, having ample rainfall, and where the tops freeze down in Winter for a period of dormancy, with new growth commencing in Spring, providing an array of color in succession of blooms throughout the season. Some short-lived herbaceous perennials are grown as Biennials such as Pansies (Viola tricolor hort.), Wallflower (Erysimum), Hollyhock (Alcea), or Stock (Matthiola). Seeds are sown one year, and will usually bloom the second year and then normally die. Annuals from seed bloom within the year, planted in cool-climate gardens.

HERBS and SPICES *(217 photos)*

A collection of aromatic herbs in pots on a window sill or planted in a special garden patch, continues a tradition familiar in European home gardens since the Middle Ages, brought to America by early colonists, and grown for culinary use and as household remedies. The Greek physician Hippocrates taught the use of herbs in the 5th century B.C. In medieval times, herbs were treasured by monasteries and in castle gardens. "Herbs" as popularly known, are a gathering of herbaceous and shrubby plants, selected for their usefulness and purpose, and the aromatic properties of roots, stems, leaves, flowers, or seeds. True spices are the berries or bark of aromatic shrubs or trees such as Peppercorns, Nutmeg and Cinnamon.

BAMBOOS and GRASSES *(197 photos)*

Bamboos are long-lived woody grasses, ranging from dwarfs 10 cm high to tropical giants like Dendrocalamus giganteus, forming culms 25 cm thick and to 35 m tall. Native of every continent except Europe, they fall into two categories — the clump forms and the running types. The "Clumpers" are tropic and subtropic, so-named because each new rhizome promptly turns upward, developing a junctured hollow stem or culm which together form a dense cluster. In the "Running" bamboos the underground rhizomes continue their horizontal development, and culms come up at intervals from lateral buds, spreading wide, in time forming thickets.

Success with Grasses used in lawn depends largely on environments, whether cool climate or tropical. From experience we know that in moist-temperate regions the Blue-grass (Poa) and the Perennial rye (Lolium) will provide refreshing greenery; also Creeping Bentgrass on such as golf courses much used in California is most satisfactory. In subtropic hot weather areas the fine-textured Korean grass (Zoysia) is frequently planted. In tropical regions the aggressive, silky-leaved Bermuda grass (Cynodon) is widely established, also the broad-leaved St. Augustine grass (Stenotaphrum) is very popular from Florida to Brazil. See TROPICA p. 12.

CONIFEROUS EVERGREENS *(329 photos)*

Conifers means cone-bearers, known as needle-trees, mostly evergreen and of striking habit, having balsamic resin typified by Fir and Spruce. Though lacking showy flowers, they are recognized instead by their various woody or fleshy ornamental cones. The Coniferae are a distinct order in the Gymnosperms, plants bearing free or unprotected seeds, thus differing from the great Angiosperms or true flowering plants which carry their seed enclosed in ovaries. These two divisions comprise the phanerogamic or seed-bearing plants. All gymnosperms bear "flowers", but without petals and sepals, better described as cones, both pollen cones and seed cones.

HEDGES, TOPIARY, BONSAI *(108 photos)*

Topiary is the art of trimming plants or shearing them into fancy or imaginative sculptured shapes most often resembling animals, practiced since ancient times. Their origin can be traced to the 4th Century B.C., reaching its peak in the 17th Century, when Privet (Ligustrum) was pruned by gardeners to form beasts, birds and men. Today, most topiaries are evergreen vines trained on moss-filled frames of wire. These may be of gigantic dimensions, but they must be kept steadily moist.

Bonsai are dwarfed trees, grown in shallow stoneware containers, an art evolved out of China in the 12th Century, trimmed and shaped with patience and loving care by hobbyists in Japan. The aim is to create replicas in miniature of normally large, majestic trees by constant skillful thinning, pinching and pruning. In Japan, I have seen Bonsai trees only 60 cm high, yet more than 300 years old. "Penjing" in China, are miniature landscapes grown in fine porcelain bowls holding small evergreens arranged with Liliputian, oddly shaped rocks imitating the fantastic mountain scenery such as along the Li-river near Kweilin, made famous in China paintings.

Flowering TREES and SHRUBS *(2408 photos)*

Broad-leaved trees are of greatest importance to life on earth. The true flowering trees belong to the great order ANGIOSPERMS, which carry their seeds enclosed in ovaries. They produce oxygen, essential to life, through their foliage. The leaves will trap harmful carbon-dioxide from the atmosphere, and when dropping, are decomposed forming humus to benefit the earth. As a forest, they are the home of animals and birds, they attract and hold the clouds that invite rain to bless the soil; many of them bring us the beauty of flowers and bountiful fruit on which we live, not to forget their valuable timber. Where forest is destroyed, life and fertility cease to exist, and soils burn out and become barren and stone-hard in the sun.

FRUITS and NUTS *(341 photos)*

Fruit or Nut-bearing trees and shrubs have been planted in tropical, subtropic and temperate climate regions since the beginning of civilization. We know that date palms were cultivated in ancient Babylon in 3500 B.C., and olives in Minoan Crete since 3000 B.C. For the ancient Hebrews the fig tree was a symbol of abundance. Many venerable old Mango trees spread through tropical Eastern Africa owe their existence to Arab traders, who were commanded by Mohammed never to throw away a seed but plant it every time. However, it was the Citron tree, first reported in China in 2200 B.C., as a fruit, that took the fancy of Royal gardeners and wealthy aristocrats in Europe, causing them to grow Lemon trees and Oranges in containers, housed in Winter in orangeries, and displayed outside in formal gardens during Summer. Smaller oranges, in Terracotta jars, were popular in every Italian garden, and, inspired by the Moors, in Spain since the 11th century.

Most important fruit of temperate climate are Apples, Pears, and Plums. The apple has been cultivated since prehistoric times in Western Asia, sacred to Aphrodite in classical mythology, treasured for its cold-hardiness, good storage qualities and tart-sweet taste. Also, wine grapes can be traced back to Greek and Roman times, in whose legends Bacchus was the God of Wine.

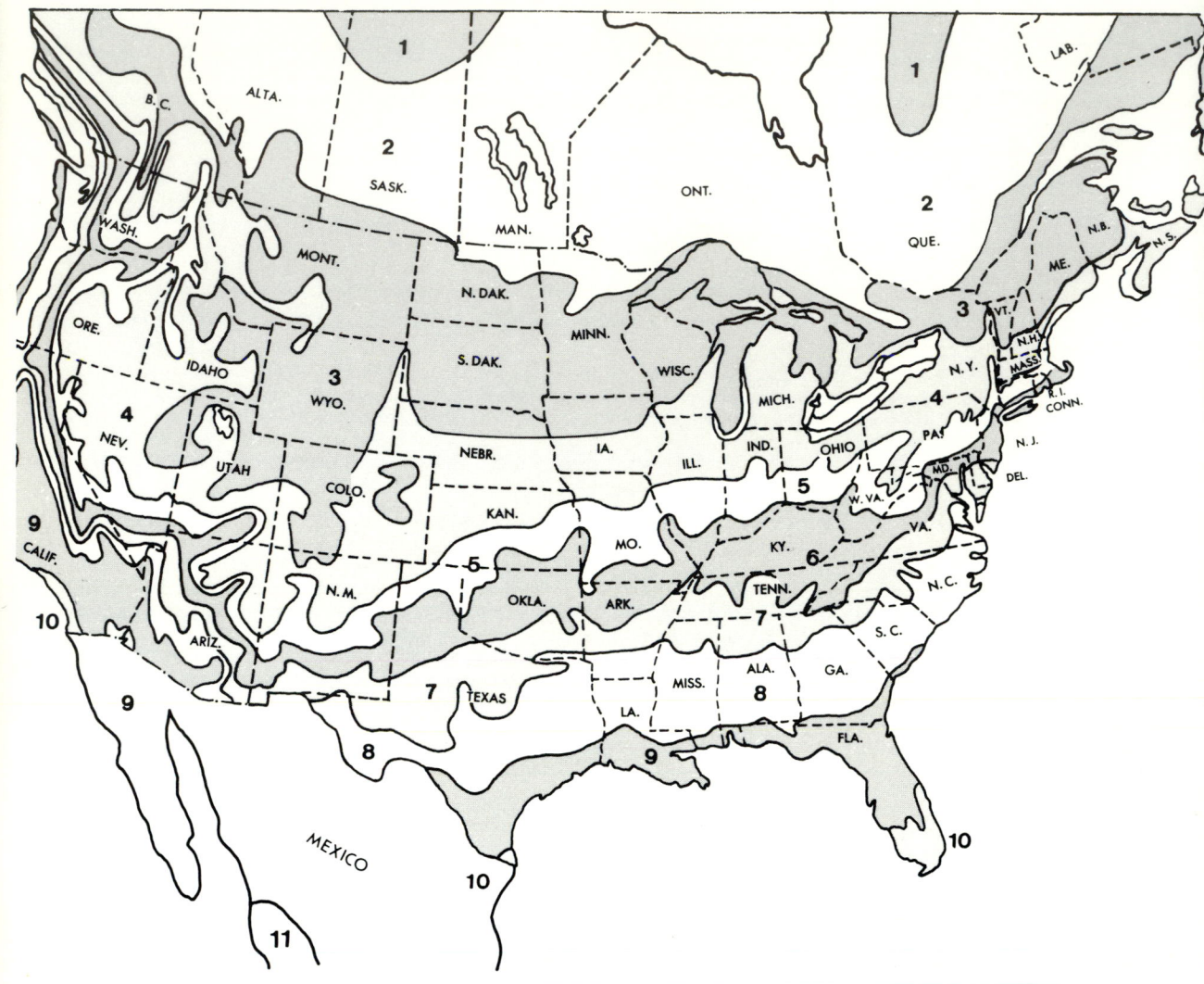

CLIMATE ZONES
for PLANT HARDINESS.

The use of a Climate map is very much disputed. Gardeners know that the actual extremes in freezing weather can kill a living plant—unless protected by snow or otherwise. However, practically every garden book and nursery catalog includes such maps, which may be useful in HORTICA also, if only as a general guide.

The Hardiness Zone rating indicates the limit of probable cold tolerance of plants. Zones follow isothermal lines of EXTREME minimum temperatures as recorded or expected each winter across the country, modified by factors such as elevation, wind-chill, snowcover or the lack of it, and degrees of precipitation.

Minimum Temperatures possible

ZONE	down to
1	− 52° C (− 58° F)
2	− 46° C (− 50° F)
3	− 40° C (− 40° F)
4	− 34° C (− 30° F)
5	− 29° C (− 20° F)
6	− 23° C (− 10° F)
7	− 18° C (0° F)
8	− 12° C (10° F)
9	− 7° C (20° F)
10	− 1° C (30° F)
11	8° C (46° F)
12	18° C (64° F)

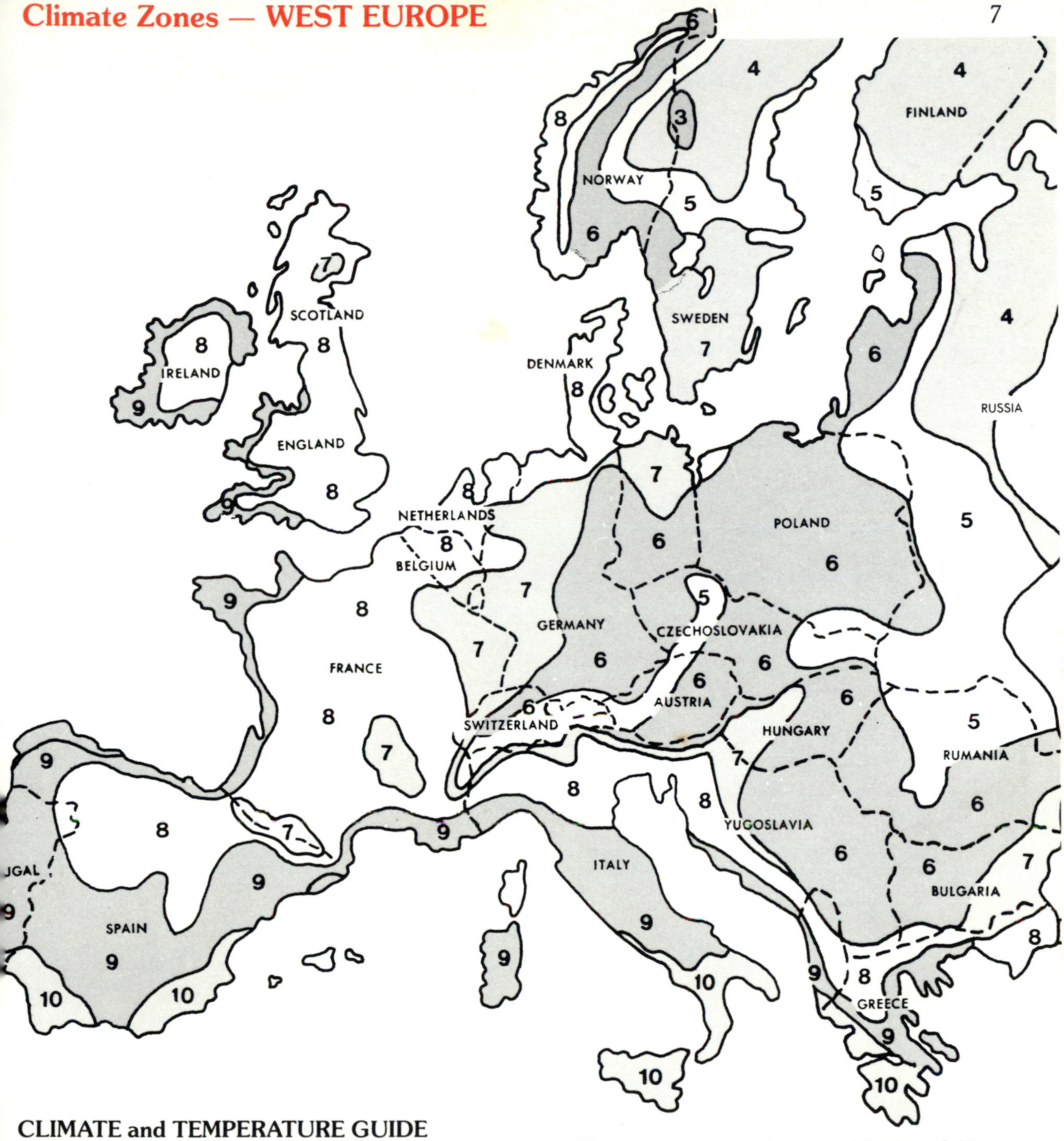

The map shows climate zone numbers across Western Europe:

NORWAY — 6, 8, 3, 5, 6
FINLAND — 4, 5
SWEDEN — 4, 7, 6
DENMARK — 8
RUSSIA — 4, 5
SCOTLAND — 7, 8
IRELAND — 8, 9
ENGLAND — 8, 8
NETHERLANDS — 8
BELGIUM — 8, 7
POLAND — 6, 5
FRANCE — 9, 8, 7, 7, 8
GERMANY — 7, 6, 6
CZECHOSLOVAKIA — 5
AUSTRIA — 6, 6
HUNGARY — 6, 7
SWITZERLAND — 6
RUMANIA — 5, 6
SPAIN — 9, 8, 9, 9, 10, 10
PORTUGAL — 9, 9, 8
ITALY — 8, 9, 10, 9, 10
YUGOSLAVIA — 8, 6, 6
BULGARIA — 6, 6, 7, 8
GREECE — 8, 9, 10

CLIMATE and TEMPERATURE GUIDE

Plants in the text designated TROPICAL, SUBTROPIC, WARM-TEMPERATE, and TEMPERATE indicate the environment of their native habitat, or that which they would prefer to best succeed in gardens or indoors. However, most living beings are very tolerant and flexible, and experience has shown that a suggestion of temperature preferences does not necessarily mean that plants would not adapt to different living conditions—cold tolerant subjects to warmer climate, or tropicals to more rigorous and cooler regions—once they are acclimated and reasonably sheltered.

TROPICAL: warm surroundings, with hot or humid-warm days 21-28°C (70-85°F), and balmy nights, where temperature should normally not go below a minimum of 15°C (60°F), never with frost. Primary tropical climates are found round the world, except at higher elevations, in Central and No. South America, West Indies, West and East Africa, India, Malaysia, Philippines, Indonesia, South Pacific, Hawaii (zones 11-12).

SUBTROPIC: the mild climate typical of Southern California, Florida, Mediterranean Region, South Africa, Southern So. America, Southern Australia, with warm to hot sunny days, the nights with temperatures down to 10°C or 8°C (50°F or 45°F) but sometimes with frost in winter. (U.S. Hardiness zones 9-10).

WARM-TEMPERATE: climate as prevailing in the Southern U.S., Oregon, England to S.E. Europe, Asia Minor, Japan, So. New Zealand; warm and often rainy in daytime, minimums at night generally down to 5° Celsius (40°F), with some frost and soil freezing occasionally in winter (U.S. Hardiness zones 7-8).

TEMPERATE: cool climate, such as in the Northern United States, Southern Chile and Argentina, Northern Europe, Eastern China. Frigid winter temperatures dropping to under zero deg. Celsius (32°F or lower), with heavy snow and hard freezes, especially nights. This chilling causes perennials and bulbous plants to go dormant, and to initiate flower buds and fruit wood in deciduous trees. (U.S. Hardiness zones 4 to 6).

COMMON NAMES INDEX

Some descriptive — Others humorous

Of nearly 6,000 vernacular names listed in HORTICA, the most widely known are shown under their botanical binomials in this photo index. Where referred to a generic name only, this may indicate a group of several species, which can be located in the alphabetical text on pages 946 to 1211.

Acanthus mollis
"Artists", or "Greek acanthos"

Aphelandra chamissoniana
"Yellow Pagoda" from Brazil

Aphelandra sinclairiana
"Coral aphelandra" (C. America)

Aphelandra tetragona
(West Indies, So. America)

Aphelandra squarrosa var. louisae
"Zebra plant" from Brazil

Crossandra infundibuliformis
"Firecracker-flower" from India

Hypoestes phyllostachya
(sanguinolenta hort.) "Freckleface"

Jacobinia (Justicia) carnea
"Flamingo plant" (Brazil)

Pachystachys lutea, from *Perú*
(Beloperone 'Super-Goldy')

Catharanthus roseus 'Bright Eyes' *(AP.)*
(Vinca rosea), "Madag. periwinkle"

Porphyrocoma pohliana *(ACANTH.)*
from tropical Brazil

Pseuderanthemum alatum *(ACANTH.)*
"Chocolate plant" in Mexico

Strobilanthes dyerianus *(ACANTH.)*
"Persian shield" from Burma

Fittonia verschaffeltii *(ACANTH.)*
"Mosaic plant" from Perú

Graptophyllum pictum *(ACANTH.)*
in Kew Gardens; from S.E. Asia

Nerium oleander 'Petite Pink' *(APOC.)*
"Dwarf oleander"; Los Angeles Arboretum

Nerium oleander 'Carneum fl. pl.' *(AP.)*
('Mrs. Roeding' in hort.), double-fl.

Nerium oleander *(APOC.)*
"Rose-bay" (Asia Minor)

Aglaon. x commut. 'White Rajah' *(left)*
Aglaonema commut. 'Treubii' *(right)*

Aglaonema marantifolium
in Kota Kinabalu, North Borneo

Aglaonema crispum *of Malaya*
(Schismatoglottis roebelinii)

Aglaonema commutatum
"Silver evergreen" (Philippines)

Aglaonema 'Silver King'
(Curtisii hybrid)

Aglaonema 'Silver Queen'
(Florida hybrid)

Aglaonema modestum 'Medio-pictum'
"Mandalay plant" in Bermuda

Aglaonema modestum *with inflor.*
"Chinese evergreen" from Kwangtung

Aglaonema 'Pseudobracteatum'
"Golden evergreen"

Aglaonema 'Whorl'
in Los Baños, Philippines

Agl. philippinense stenophyllum
'White lance' *in Makati, Philippines*

Aglaonema commutatum picturatum
at Sarian's Nursery, Manila

Aglaonema pictum, *from Sumatra*
by J. Bogner, Munich Botanic Garden

Aglaonema commutatum 'Medio-pictum'
in Munich Botanic Garden

Aglaonema philippinense 'Nocturne'
Los Baños Arboretum, Philippines

Aglaonema linearifolium
Sarian Nursery, Manila

Agl. costatum 'Foxii magnificum'
in Bermuda Botanic Gard., Hamilton

Alocasia cuprea 'Vera'
green form, in Manila

Alocasia korthalsii *(thibautiana)*
from tropical Borneo

Alocasia macrorrhiza *of S.E. Asia*
in Bien Hoa, Vietnam

Alocasia micholitziana 'Cherie Darian'
with satiny foliage, in Vista, California

Alocasia sanderiana
the beautiful "Kris plant" (Philippines)

Aglaonema simplex metallica
at Mandai's Nursery, Singapore

Aglaonema comm. pictur. 'Fat Jade'
Sarian Nursery, Makati, Manila

Aglaonema philippinense 'Cebu'
Los Baños Arbor., Philippines

Amorphophallus titanum
giant "Titan arum" of Sumatra

Amorphophallus rivieri *(Hydrosme)*
"Devil's tongue", inflorescence

Amorphophallus rivieri
of Vietnam, foliar growth

Anthurium brownii *(Colombia)*
at New York Flower Show

Anthurium hookeri *(huegelii hort.)*
"Birdsnest" from Guyana

Anthurium pariense
from Venezuela (J. Bogner)

Anubias afzelii *(lanceolata)*
"Water aspidistra" of Cameroon

Anthurium andraeanum rhodochlorum
in Honolulu, Hawaii

Anthurium huegelii, *of Venezuela*
at Bermuda Bot. Gard., Hamilton

Anthurium x ferrierense
"Oilcloth flower"

Anthurium scherzerianum
"Flamingo flower" (Costa Rica)

Anthurium andraeanum
"Tail flower" from Colombia

Anthurium crystallinum
"Crystal anthurium" (Perú)

Anthurium clarinervium *(Mexico)*
"Hoja de Corazon" in Vera Cruz

Anthurium bakeri
from Costa Rica, C. America

Anthurium macrolobum
from Mato Grosso, Brazil

Anthurium veitchii *(Colombia)*
"King anthurium" in San Francisco

Anthurium warocqueanum *(Colombia)*
"Queen anthurium" in Longwood G.

Arum italicum, *"Italian arum"*
(Europe, No. Africa to Syria)

Arum palaestinum *(sanctum)*
"Solomon's lily" in Israel

Biarum tenuifolium (abbreviatum)
from Greece (J. Bogner, Munich)

Ariopsis peltata
tuberous plant from India

Arisaema flavum
(Mediterranean to Himalayas)

Arisaema triphyllum *(E. No. America)*
"Jack-in-the-pulpit"

Caladium lindenii *(Xanthosoma)*
"Yautia" from Colombia

Caladium macrotites
(Brazil, Bolivia)

Cercestis taiensis
from Ivory Coast, West Africa

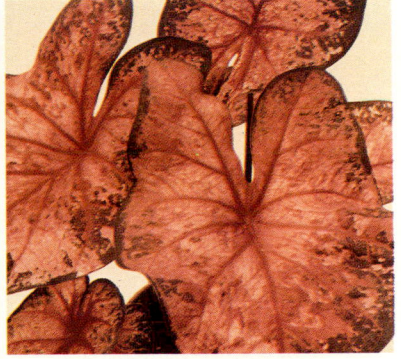

Caladium x hortulanum
'Ace of Hearts'

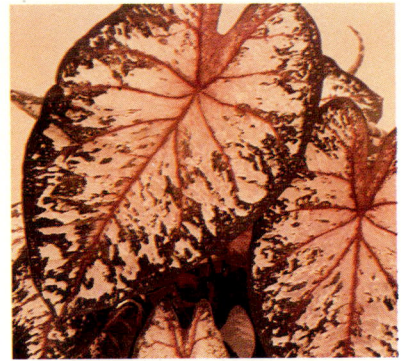

Caladium x hortulanum
'Elizabeth Dixon'

Caladium x hortulanum
'E.O. Orpet'

Caladium x hortulanum
'Marie Moir'

Caladium x hortulanum
'Hortulania'

Caladium x hortulanum
'Macahyba'

Caladium x hortulanum
'Frieda Hemple'

Caladium x hortulanum
'Mrs. F. M. Joyner'

Caladium x hortulanum
'Scarlet Beauty'

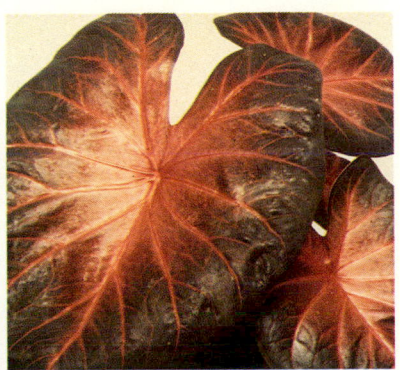

Caladium x hortulanum
'Triomphe de l'Exposition'

Caladium x hortulanum
'Scarlet Pimpernelle'

Caladium x hortulanum
'White Queen'

Colocasia esculenta 'Illustris'
(antiquorum hort.) "Black caladium"

Colocasia esculenta, *(Pacific Isl.)*
"Taro" cultivated in Trinidad

Cyrtosperma merkusii chamissonis
in tropical Malaysia

Ulearum viridispadix *(Brazil)*
in Munich Bot. Garden, Germany

Cryptocoryne albida
from tropical Burma

Cryptocoryne pontederiifolia
from West Sumatra

Dracontium changuango
"Serpent cup" of Venezuela

Dracunculus vulgaris *(Arum)*
"Dragon arum" (Mediterr. reg.)

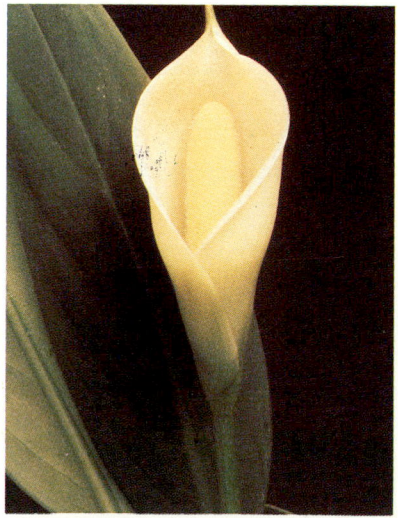

Heteroaridarum annae *(Aridarum)*
collected in Sarawak, Borneo

Dieffenbachia amoena
in El Panama Hotel, Panama

Dieff. amoena 'Tropic Snow'
on Park Avenue, New York

Dieffenbachia 'Wilson's Delight'
(Fantastic Gardens, Miami)

Dieffenbachia maculata *(picta). "Spotted dumbcane"*
at home along the Amazon, Brazil

Dieffenbachia maculata 'Rudolf Roehrs'
"Gold dieffenbachia" (Roehrs cultivar, 1936)

Dieffenbachia 'Camilla'
compact Danish mutation

Dieffenbachia 'Exotica Perfection'
Florida cultivar of compact habit

Dieffenbachia 'Candida'
handsome cultivar from Holland

Philodendron 'Pluto'
New Jersey Flower Show, 1985

Monstera deliciosa *juv. form*
Philodendron pertusum in hort.

Monstera deliciosa borsigiana
small-leaved, from Cordoba, Mexico

Philodendron selloum, *of Paraná, S. W. Brazil*
"Lacy Tree philodendron"

Epipremnum aureum (syn. Scindapsus aureus)
"Devil's ivy", or "Pothos", in hort.

Philodendron leyvae
(serratum of hort.) (Colombia)

Philodendron undulatum
(Mato Grosso, Brazil)

Philodendron laciniatum (pedatum)
(Guianas and Venezuela)

Monstera deliciosa, *the "Mexican bread-fruit", or "Ceriman"* *with maturity-stage character leaves, in Puerto Rico*

Philodendron tweedianum *(Argentina to Paraguay)* *by Dr. E. Pingatore, Jardin Botanico, Buenos Aires*

Philodendron x evansii *(selloum x speciosum)* *in San Pasqual Animal Park, California*

Philodendron selloum, *the "Lacy Tree philodendron"* *at Iguassu Falls of Paraná, near border of Paraguay*

Philodendron seidelii
col. in Mucuje, Bahia, Brazil

Philodendron bipennifolium 'Variegatum'
(panduraeforme cv.) Bermuda Bot. G.

Philodendron rugosum *(Ecuador)*
in Munich Botanic Garden

Montrichardia linifera
Jardim Botanico, Rio de Janeiro

Montrichardia arborescens *(Guyana)*
col. Munich Botanic Garden

Homalomena wallisii *(Curmeria)*
"Silver shield" from Colombia

Zamioculcas zamiifolia
from Zanzibar, East Africa

Lagenandra lancifolia
col. in Sri Lanka by J. Bogner

Lagenandra insignis *(ovata)*
waterside plant from Sri Lanka

Philodendron scandens oxycardium
(P. cordatum of hort., Trop. America)

Philodendron melanochrysum
"Velour philodendron" (Colombia)

Philodendron sellowianum
in Cristobal, Panama

Philodendron pinnatifidum
from Venezuela and Amazonas

Philodendron bipinnatifidum
tree philodendron from C. Brazil

Philodendron verrucosum
"Velvet-leaf" (Costa Rica, Colombia)

Monstera pertusa, *"Windowleaf"*
in Foster Bot. Garden, Honolulu

Raphidophora decursiva *(Monstera)*
(Sri Lanka to Indochina)

Epipremnum pinnatum
in Kebun Raya, Bogor, Java

Spathiphyllum 'Londonii'
Florida cv. with undulate foliage

Spathiphyllum floribundum
"Snow-flower" from Colombia

Spathiphyllum 'Clevelandii' *(kochii)*
"White flag" or "Peace lily"

Spathiphyllum patinii
from Colombia

Spath. floribundum 'Mini-variegata'
(Tropicana Nursery, Florida)

Spathiphyllum wallisii
compact species of Venezuela

Rhektophyllum mirabile
collected in Ibadan, Nigeria

Spathiphyllum blandum
Longwood Gardens, Penna.

Spathiphyllum 'Mauna Loa'
robust California hybrid, Los Angeles

Zantedeschia 'Green Goddess'
at Los Angeles Arboretum

Zantedeschia 'Striped hybrids'
at the Zapotec market, Oaxaca, Mexico

Zantedeschia aethiopica
"White calla" (Southern Africa)

Zantedeschia elliottiana
"Yellow calla", from So. Africa

Zantedeschia albo-maculata
"Spotted calla" (So. Africa, Angola)

Zantedeschia rehmannii
"Pink calla", from Natal

Urospatha sagittifolia, *in habitat
Rio Caroni, Canaima, Venezuela*

Xanthosoma robustum
"Palma yautia", of Guatemala

Syngonium steyermarkii
(Venezuela)

Spathicarpa sagittifolia gardneri
"Fruit-sheath plant" in Munich Bot. G.

Scindapsus pictus argyraeus
"Satin pothos" (Borneo)

Syngonium podophyllum 'Imperial'
"Arrowhead vine"

Synandrospadix vermitoxicus
Andean aroid from Salta Prov., No. Argentina

Xanthosoma plowmanii *(Brazil)*
in Nymphenburg Botanic Garden, Munich

Xenophya lauterbachiana, *w. fruit*
(Schizocasia) from New Guinea

Symplocarpus foetidus
"Skunk cabbage" (E. North America)

Xanthosoma atrovirens
Quail Botanic Gardens, California

Schefflera (Brassaia) actinophylla
"Queensland umbrella tree" in New York

Schefflera arboricola
"Hawaiian Elf" of Taiwan

Schefflera pueckleri
(Tupidanthus calyptratus in hort.)

Hedera canar. 'Arbor. variegata'
in maturity stage

Polyscias guilfoylei 'Victoriae'
"Lace aralia" from Polynesia

Polyscias balfouriana 'Pennockii'
"White aralia" in Puerto Rico

Hedera canariensis
'Arborescens variegata' *("Ghost tree")*

Fatsia japonica 'Marginata'
Essen Botanic Garden, Germany

Schefflera arboricola 'Variegata'
"Variegated Elf"

Radermachera sinica *(BIGN.)*
"China doll" in Amsterdam

Nothopanax filicifolia (ARAL.)
"Fernleaf aralia" in Polynesia

Polyscias balfouriana *(ARAL.)*
"Dinner-plate aralia" in Cartagena

Polyscias guilfoylei 'Marginata' *(ARAL.)*
Singapore World Trade Center

Polyscias guilf. 'Quercifolia' *(ARAL.)*
"Oakleaf panax" in Brooklyn Bot. G.

Pseudopanax lessonii 'Gold splash'
(ARAL.) colorful California cultivar

x Fatshedera lizei *(ARAL.)*
"Ivy tree", or "Miracle plant"

Dizygotheca elegantissima *(ARAL.)*
"False aralia" (New Hebrides)

Araucaria heterophylla *(CONIF.)*
(excelsa) "Norfolk Island pine"

Impatiens walleriana 'Futura'
"Patient Lucy" in W. Chicago

Impatiens walleriana 'Elfin'
"Elfin miniature" in California

Impatiens 'New Guinea hyb.' *(BALS.)*
in New York Botanical Garden

Impatiens walleriana 'Variegata'
"Variegated Sultana" in Brooklyn Bot. G.

Begonia 'Christmas Candy'
hanging basket in Vista, Calif.

Begonia chlorosticta
('Kew species') from Sarawak

Begonia conchifolia rubrimacula
"Zip begonia" from Costa Rica

Begonia longimaculata (Perú)
in Munich Bot. Garden, Germany

Begonia coccinea *(BEG.)*
"Angelwing begonia" (Organ Mts., Brazil)

Begonia grandis *(evansii)*
"Hardy begonia" in New Jersey

Begonia hemsleyana
rhizomatous species from China

Begonia sutherlandii
semi-tuberous, from Natal

Begonia manicata 'Aureo-maculata'
"Leopard begonia" at Logee's, Conn.

Begonia x margaritae
(echinosepala x metallica)

Begonia thelmae, *in Rio de Janeiro*
('Brazil species')

Begonia 'Orange rubra'
in New York Botan. Garden

Begonia peltata *(incana)*
from Mexico (rhizomatous)

Begonia metallica, *(Bahia)*
"Metallic-leaf begonia"

Beg. rex 'Comtesse Louise Erdoedy'
"Corkscrew begonia" (Logee, Conn.)

Begonia rex 'Princess of Hannover'
at Logee's, Danielson, Conn.

Begonia rex 'Curly Fireflush'
"Spiral begonia"

Begonia decora *(rhizomatous)*
(Assam, Vietnam, Malaya)

Begonia 'Exotica' *(brevirimosa)*
along Baiyer River, New Guinea

Begonia olsoniae *(Brazil)*
(velozoana hort.) in Munich Bot. G.

Begonia paulensis *(Brazil)*
handsome rhizomatous species

Begonia x sementacea *(Brazil)*
Kartuz Greenhouses, Vista, Calif.

Begonia rufosericea, *from Brazil*
with Tovah Martin (Logee's, Conn.)

Begonia rex 'Helen Teupel'
(rex x diadema)

Begonia rex 'Yuletide'
(from Man Nurseries, Holland)

Begonia rex 'His Majesty'
(English hybrid, 1903)

Begonia semperflorens 'Fiesta'
green-leaved "Wax begonia"

Begonia semperflorens 'Luminosa'
red-brown foliage in full sun

Begonia semperfl. fl. pl. 'Lady Frances'
"Rose-begonia"

Begonia x cheimantha 'Lady Mac'
"Christmas begonia" at Roehrs

Begonia x cheimantha 'Marina'
"Scandinavian winter-begonia"

Begonia x cheimantha 'Dark Lady Mac'
"Dark rose Christmas begonia"

Begonia x erythrophylla 'Bunchii'
"Curly kidney begonia"

Begonia heracleifolia nigricans
"Star begonia" from Mexico

Begonia 'Cleopatra'
"Maple-leaf begonia"

Begonia x tuberhyb. pendula fl. pl.
(B. lloydii), "Basket begonia"

Begonia x tuberhybrida 'Triumph'
in Wellington, New Zealand

Begonia x tub. multiflora 'Maxima'
dwarf tuberous, in Ghent, Belgium

Begonia x hiemalis
'Rieger's Yellow', *in Germany*

Begonia x hiem. 'Schwabenland'
for Christmas bloom indoors

Begonia 'Tom Ment'
Florida angel-wing (cane-stem)

Begonia goegoensis
"Fire king begonia" (Sumatra)

Begonia rajah *(Malaya)*
col. Dahlem Bot. Garden, Berlin

Begonia masoniana *(Indochina)*
"Iron cross begonia"

Begonia floccifera
miniature from India

Begonia x richmondensis
(fuchsioides x semperflorens)

Begonia limmingheiana *(glaucophylla)*
"Shrimp begonia" from Brazil

Begonia vareschii *(Venezuela)*
col. Botanic Garden Munich

Begonia foliosa var. miniata
(B. fuchsioides in hort.) (Mexico)

Begonia platanifolia *(Brazil)*
col. Essen Bot. Garden, Germany

Begonia scharffiana
true species from Brazil

Begonia scharffii *(haageana)*
"Elephant-ear begonia" (Brazil)

Begonia schmidtiana *(Brazil)*
fibrous-rooted miniature

Aechmea tillandsioides 'Marginata'
in Escondido, California

Aechmea fasciata
"Silver vase" (Rio de Janeiro)

Aechmea chantinii
"Amazonian Zebra plant" (Perú)

Aechmea mulfordii *(Brazil)*
in Durban Bot. Garden, So. Africa

Aechmea mertensii *(So. America)*
"China berry" in Bermuda Bot. Gard.

Aechmea dichlamydea trinitensis
Andromeda Garden, Barbados

Aechmea nudicaulis
(Mexico, W. Indies, to Brazil)

Aechmea pineliana
Bermuda Bot. Garden, Hamilton

Aechmea phanerophlebia
Prof. W. Rauh, Heidelberg Bot. G.

Aechmea caudata var. variegata
(Billbergia forgetii hort.) Brazil

Aechmea fulgens
"Coral berry" from Pernambuco

Aechmea mariae-reginae
"Queen aechmea" (Costa Rica)

Aechmea fernandae
in Amazonas, Brazil

Aechmea miniata discolor
from Bahia, Brazil

Billbergia nutans, *"Queen's tears"*
(So. Brazil, Uruguay, Argentina)

Cryptanthus zonatus 'Zebrinus'
"Zebra plant"

Cryptanthus bivittatus minor
(C. roseus-pictus hort.), Brazil

Cryptanthus beuckeri
"Marbled spoon" (Brazil)

Guzmania sanguinea
(C. America to Ecuador)

Guzmania lingulata 'Major'
"Scarlet star" (Ecuador)

Guzmania zahnii
from Colombia and Panama

Ananas bracteatus tricolor
"Variegated Wild pineapple"

Ananas comosus (sativus)
"Pineapple" in Puerto Rico

Ananas comosus 'Porteanus'
"Golden rocket" on St. Thomas, V.I.

Bromelia karatas *(West Indies)*
large armed terrestrial rosette

Canistrum cyathiforme, *of So. Brazil*
collected by Alvim Seidel, Corupá, Santa Catarina

Bromelia pinguin *(West Indies)*
"Wild pineapple" in Virgin Isl.

Bromelia balansae *(Brazil, Argent.)*
"Piñuela", a formidable terrestrial

Bromelia serra 'Variegata'
"Heart of Flame" (Argentina)

Billbergia pyramidalis concolor
"Summer torch" in Encinitas, Calif.

Billbergia venezuelana
"Giant urn-plant" (Venezuela)

Guzmania conifera
from Rainforest of Ecuador

Fosterella penduliflora *(Perú)*
col. Bermuda Botanic Garden

Guzmania monostachia
"Striped torch" (C. America)

Vriesea (Guzmania) zamorensis
in Rainforest of Tingo Maria, Perú

Guzmania zahnii 'Tricolor'
Denver Botanic Garden, Colorado

Aechmea sphaerocephala *(Brazil)*
in Quail Bot. G., Encinitas, Calif.

Hohenbergia stellata
from cloud forest of Martinique

Hechtia glomerata *(Mexico)*
in Munich Bot. Garden, Germany

Navia splendens, *a xerophyte*
on Guayana Highlands, Venezuela

Pseudananas sagenarius *(Brazil)*
Royal Bot. Garden Sydney, Australia

Neoregelia carolinae 'Tricolor'
Blushing bromeliad" in Del Mar, Calif.

Neoregelia olens
variable epiphyte from Brazil

Neoregelia carolinae 'Meyendorffii'
(Karatas) at flowering time

Pitcairnea flammea var. floccosa
col. Alvim Seidel, Paraná, Brazil

Portea petropolitana
from Coastal S.E. Brazil

Neoregelia ampullacea
Espirito Santo and Guanabara

Fascicularia pitcairniifolia
large spiny rosette from Chile

Navia arida, *mountain xerophyte
of the "Lost World" of Venezuela*

Streptocalyx biflorus, *from Andes of Ecuador
col. by J. Bogner, Munich Botanic Garden*

Neoregelia concentrica *(Nidularium)
Botanic Garden Rio de Janeiro*

Tillandsia aeranthos *(dianthoidea)
Rainforests of Argentina and Brazil*

Pitcairnea bifrons, *terrestrial rosette
on St. Vincent, West Indies*

Neoregelia compacta *(Col. A. Seidel, Corupá)
from the Restinga of Rio de Janeiro*

Greigia sphacelata, *of Valdivia, Chile
col. by Dr. W. Rauh, Heidelberg, Bot. Garden*

Tillandsia flabellata
"Red fan" from Guatemala

Tillandsia imperialis
"Christmas candle" (Oaxaca, Mex.)

Tillandsia crispa
from Panama to Perú

Tillandsia leiboldiana
So. Mexico to Guatemala

Tillandsia utriculata
"Big Wild pine" (Florida, W. Indies)

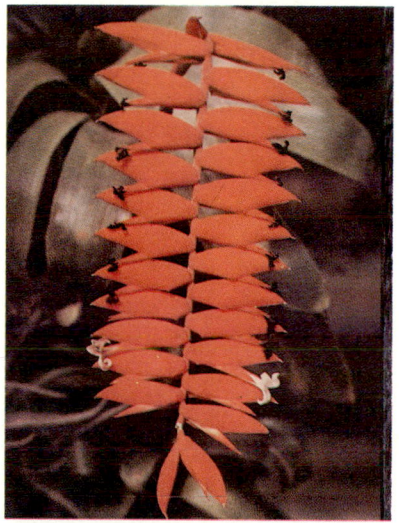

Tillandsia dyeriana *(fragrant fl.)*
col. by Prof. W. Rauh in Ecuador

Cryptanthus bivittatus tricolor
"Rainbow star" in Longwood Gard.

Tillandsia streptophylla
"Twist plant" from Jamaica

Tillandsia fasciculata
"Wild pine" in Florida Everglades

Vriesea heterostachys
from Espirito Santo, Brazil

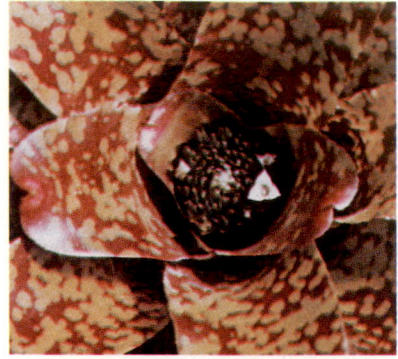

Neoregelia marmorata
in coastal São Paulo, Brazil

Nidularium innocentii
"Black birdsnest" (So. Brazil)

Tillandsia lindenii
"Blue-flowered torch" of Perú

Tillandsia cyanea
"Pink quill" (Ecuador)

Pitcairnia andreana
from the Choco of Colombia

Tillandsia flexuosa
"Spiralled airplant" in Chiriqui, Panama

Tillandsia ionantha
"Sky plant" in Nicaragua

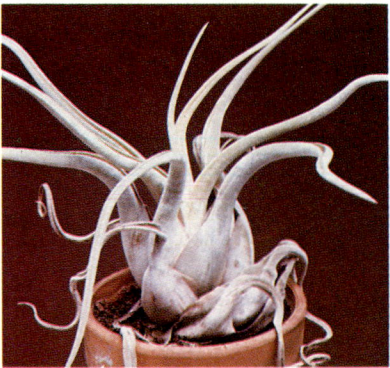

Tillandsia caput-medusae
in San Jose, Costa Rica

Tillandsia crocata, *rockdweller
from Bolivia to Argentina*

Tillandsia usneoides, *"Spanish moss"
(S.E. United States to Argentina)*

Vriesea fenestralis *(S. Brazil)
in Tijuca Forest, Rio de Janeiro*

Vriesea sintenisii *(Thecophyllum)*
El Yunque rainforest, Puerto Rico

Vriesea splendens
"Flaming sword" from Guayana

Vriesea splendens 'Variegata'
col. Botanic Garden Essen, Germany

Vriesea imperialis, *"Giant vriesea"*
Organ Mts., Estado do Rio, Brazil

Vriesea heliconioides
in Turrialba, Costa Rica

Vriesea hieroglyphica *(Brazil)*
"King of bromeliads" in Paraná

Vriesea fosteriana 'Seideliana'
Botanic Garden Frankfurt, Germany

Vriesea regina *(S.E. Brazil)*
Jardim Botanico, Rio de Janeiro

Nidularium fulgens
"Blushing cup" (S.E. Brazil)

Callisia repens *(Trop. America)*
miniature "Turtle vine"

Tradescantia fluminensis 'Variegata'
"Wandering Jew" from Argentina

Zebrina pendula *(Mexico)*
"Silvery Wandering Jew" in Calif.

Tradescantia sillamontana
"White velvet" from N.E. Mexico

Palisota barteri
from Fernando Po, West Africa

Siderasis fuscata *(Tradescantia)*
"Brown spiderwort" (Brazil)

Palisota pynaertii 'Elizabethae'
Palmengarten Frankfurt, Germany

Rhoeo spathacea 'Vittata'
"Moses-in-the-cradle" (Mexico)

Cochliostema odoratissimum 'Striatum'
variegated form of Ecuador species

Cyclamen persicum 'Pearl of Zehlendorf' *(right)*
Cyclamen persicum *(left) (PRIM.) in Aalsmeer*

Senecio x cruentus, *(hybridus) (COMP.)*
"Florist's cinerarias" at Roehrs greenhouses, N.J.

Pelargonium x hortorum 'New Porter' *(GERAN.)*
Los Angeles Plant Co. Vista, California

Sinningia speciosa fyfiana *(GESNER.)*
"Gloxinia" of hort. at Roehrs Nursery, N.J.

Tulipa x gesneriana 'Apeldoorn' *(LIL.)*
"Darwin hybrid" forced for Easter

Astilbe japonica, *florist's "Spiraea" (SAX.)*
in the flower market of Oslo, Norway

Tulipa x gesneriana 'Red Giant'
"Triumph tulip" forced for Easter

Tulipa x gesneriana 'Ursa Minor'
"Single Early tulip" (LIL.)

Kalanchoe grandiflora 'Marginata'
spring-blooming in Rhineland (CRASS.)

Hyacinthus orientalis 'Delft Blue'
"Dutch garden hyacinth" (LIL.)

Lilium longiflorum 'Nellie White'
Florist's early "Easter lily" (LIL.)

Scilla peruviana *(LIL.)*
"Cuban lily" (Mediterranean reg.)

Sinningia spec. fyfiana 'Defiance'
Florist's gloxinia (GESN.)

Saintpaulia rupicola *(GESN.)*
"African violet" from Kenya

Gardenia jasminoides 'Veitchii'
"Everblooming gardenia" (RUB.)

Fuchsia hybrida
'Winston Churchill' *(ONAGR.)*

Senecio x cruentus 'Multifl. nana'
small-fl. florist's "Cineraria" (COMP.)

Calceolaria crenatiflora 'Grandiflora'
"Pocketbook plant" (SCROPH.)

Rosa x multiflora 'Mother's Day'
late-blooming "Baby rose" (ROS.)

Rosa x multiflora 'Margo Koster'
Polyantha rose for Easter

Rosa x odorata 'Mrs. W. C. Miller'
old Hybrid Tea-rose 1909

Rosa (Grandiflora) 'Queen Elizabeth'
(Hybrid-tea x Floribunda)

Rosa x borboniana 'Magna Charta'
"Hybrid-perpetual" rose

Rhododendron
'Jean Marie de Montague' *(ERIC.)*

Pelargonium x domesticum
'Easter Greeting' *(GERAN.)*

Hydrangea macroph. 'Chaperon Rouge'
"French hortensia" (SAX.)

Hydrangea macrophylla 'Kuhnert'
blue-flowered "Snowball"

Petunia x hyb. grandiflora 'Bingo'
huge bicolor (SOLAN.)

Petunia x hyb. fl. pl. 'Caprice'
double pot petunia

Petunia x hyb. 'California Giant'
giant pot petunia

Cyclamen x persicum 'Swiss Dwarf'
miniature, in San Diego, Calif.

Narcissus pseudon. 'King Alfred'
"Daffodil" for Easter (AMARYLL.)

Hippeastrum 'Leopoldii hyb.' *(AMAR.)*
"Amaryllis" in Mitla, Oaxaca, Mex.

Rhododendron 'Coral Bells' *(ERIC.)*
Azalea Kurume cv. in hort.

Rhododendron x simsii 'Ambrosiana'
early-fl., Azalea indica in hort.

Hydrangea macroph. 'Sensation' *(SAX.)*
German Garden Show Duesseldorf 1987

Pelargonium x hort. 'Irene' *(GERAN.)*
excellent commercial "Geranium"

Primula obconica *(PRIM.)*
"German primrose" in Rhineland

Pelargonium x hort. 'Mrs. Strang'
"Tricolor geranium" in Maine

Pelargonium peltatum 'Amethyst'
as standard in Berlin (GERAN.)

Chrysanthemum x morifolium
garden indicum in California

Chrys. x morif. 'Decorative incurved'
in Vaduz, Liechtenstein (COMP.)

Chrysanthemum x morifolium 'Bonaffon'
incurved "pot-mum" of florists

Solanum pseudo-capsicum *(SOLAN.)*
"Jerusalem cherry" for Christmas

Capsicum annuum 'Fips' *(SOLAN.)*
"Christmas pepper" at Ball's, Chicago

Erica gracilis *(So. Africa)*
"Rose heath" in Aalsmeer, Holland

Erica melanthera *(ERIC.)*
winter-blooming at Roehrs

Schlumbergera truncata 'Delicatus'
flowers white in shade (CACT.)

Crassula ovata *(argentea hort.)*
"Jade plant" flowering in Calif.

Rhipsalidopsis x graeseri 'Rosea'
"Easter cactus" in Rutherford, N.J.

Skimmia japonica 'Teufel's Dwarf'
female plant, in Oregon (RUTAC.)

Nertera granadensis *(N. Zealand)*
"Coral-bead plant" in Germany

Pernettya mucronata *(ERIC.)*
"Chilean myrtle" (female plant)

Kalanchoe blossfeldiana 'Tom Thumb'
"Flaming Katy" for Christmas

Fortunella margarita *(RUT.)*
"Nagami kumquat" (Kwangtung)

x Citrofortunella mitis *(RUT.)*
"Calamondin" in Florida

Chrysanthemum x morif. 'Princess Ann'
excellent "decorative" pot-mum

Chrysanthemum x morifolium
'Yellow Princess Ann' *(COMP.)*

Chrys. x mor. 'Peggy Ann Hoover'
"Spider-mum" or "Fuji"

Euphorbia pulch. 'Henrietta Ecke'
"Double poinsettia" (EUPH.)

Euphorbia pulcherr. 'Annette Hegg'
compact Christmas poinsettia

Euphorbia pulcherrima 'Eckespoint'
in tree-form, Roehrs Nursery, N.J.

Euphorbia pulcherrima 'Alba' *('Ecke white')*
poinsettia with creamy-white bracts, in N.J.

Rhipsalidopsis gaertneri *(So. Brazil)*
"Easter cactus", Los Angeles Plant Co., Calif.

Exacum affine *(GENTIAN.)*
"Persian violet", Socotra, Arab. Sea

Schlumbergera truncata *(Zygocactus)*
"Thanksgiving cactus" in California

Schlumbergera bridgesii *(CACT.)*
"Christmas cactus" from Bolivia

Codiaeum variegatum 'Apple leaf'
"Croton" of hort. (EUPH.)

Codiaeum variegatum 'Craigii'
Philadelphia croton 1910

Codiaeum variegatum 'Gloriosum'
"Autumn croton"

Aucuba japonica 'Variegata'
"Gold-dust tree" (CORN.)

Gynura x sarmentosa *(aurantiaca hyb.)*
"Purple passion vine" (COMP.)

Euphorbia 'Giant Christthorn'
superb California hybrid

Euphorbia grandicornis
"Cowhorn euphorbia" from Kenya

Euphorbia mammillaris 'Variegata'
"Indian corn-cob"

Euphorbia lactea 'Cristata'
"Crested elk-horn"

Pelargonium peltatum 'Variegatum'
"Variegated Ivy-geranium"

Pelargonium x hortorum 'Velma'
"Tricolor geranium" (GERAN.)

Pelargonium x domest. 'Mrs. Mary Bard'
"Martha Washington geranium"

Acalypha wilkesiana 'Tricolor'
Peradeniya Bot. Gard., Sri Lanka

Acalypha hispida 'Pendula'
"Firetails" from Haleiwa, Hawaii

Acalypha wilkesiana 'Macafeana'
"Copper leaf" in Borneo (EUPH.)

Achimenes cettoana *(GESNER.)*
from Southern Mexico

Coleus blumei *(Java) (LAB.)*
"Painted nettle" in variety

Gynura aurantiaca *(COMP.)*
"Velvet plant" in Veracruz, Mex.

Capanea grandiflora *(GESNER.)*
tropical Chiriqui, Panama

Columnea brenneri
(Trichantha) from Ecuador

Columnea hirta *(GESNER.)*
"Goldfish plant" (Costa Rica)

Columnea microphylla
"Goldfish vine" in Auckland, N.Z.

Columnea arguta hyb. 'Merkur'
by Haualand, Stavanger, Norway

Columnea arguta
trailing epiphyte from Panama

Briggsia muscicola *(Yunnan to Tibet)*
by J. Bogner, Munich Botanic Garden

Columnea arguta hyb. 'Sirius' *(Norway)*
of erect growth, by Haualand, Stavanger

Chrysothemis pulchella *(cv. 'Amazon')*
succulent from Trinidad to Amazonas

Corytoplectus capitatus
"Velvet alloplectus" (Colombia)

Aeschynanthus obconicus *(Malaya)*
at Bermuda Botanic Garden

Eucodonia andrieuxii *(Achimenes)*
col. by A. Lau in Oaxaca, Mexico

Gasteranthus atratus *(Besleria)*
Selby Bot. G., Sarasota, Florida

Chirita lavandulacea
"Hindustan gentian" (Malaya)

Episcia reptans *(fulgida)*
"Flame violet" (Brazil to Surinam)

Episcia cupreata
"Carpet plant" from Colombia

Episcia lilacina *('Fannie Haage')*
"Blue-flowered Teddy-bear"(Costa Rica)

Haberlea ferdinandi-coburgii
from cool-climate Bulgaria

Haberlea rhodopensis
from mountains of Greece and Turkey

Ramonda myconii *(pyrenaica)*
in Cold Spring Harbor, New York

Nematanthus fissus
(Hypocyrta selloana) of Brazil

Pentadenia zapotalana (Ecuador)
col. J. Bogner, Munich Bot. Garden

Niphaea oblonga (Chiapas)
"Snow-wort", Bailey Hortorium, N.Y.

Petrocosmea kerrii
"Hidden violet" of Thailand

Monopyle grandiflora (So. America)
in col. Kartuz, Vista, Calif.

Phinaea multiflora, a miniature
at Bailey Hortorium, Ithaca, N.Y.

Kohleria 'Eriantha hybrid'
(Isoloma hirsutum multiflorum hort.)

Rehmannia elata (angulata)
"Foxglove gloxinia" from C. China

Kohleria bogotensis
(Isoloma pictum hort.) of Colombia

Achimenes erecta *(coccinea hort.)*
in habitat at Xochicalco, Mexico

Columnea minor *(Ecuador)*
(Trichantha teuscheri hort.)

Columnea purpureovittata *(Trichantha)*
wide-spreading gesneriad from Perú

Saintpaulia ionantha
original "African violet" from Tanzania

Saintpaulia 'Pixie Blue'
true miniature, in tea cup

Kohleria x sciadotydaea
(Sciadocalyx x Tydaea)

Saintpaulia 'Morning Glow'
delicate soft-pink

Saintpaulia 'Delaware'
Holtkamp Optimara series

Saintpaulia 'Loretta'
quilted leaves, double flowers

Saintpaulia 'Blue 'Peak'
double flowers w. fringed petals

Saintpaulia 'Savannah Sweetheart'
holly-leaf; double-flowered

Saintpaulia 'Pocono'
with giant 5 cm flowers

Sinningia cardinalis *(Rechsteineria)*
"Cardinal flower" from Brazil

Saintpaulia 'Elfriede' *in Winter*
(German Rhapsodie strain)

Saintpaulia rupicola, *in Kenya*
in habitat on rocks of Marakaya

Sinningia guttata *(Brazil)*
col. Munich Botanic Garden

Gesneria cuneifolia *(Cuba, Hispaniola)*
at Longwood Gardens, Pennsylvania

Sarmienta scandens *(repens hort.)*
charming creeper from Chile

Streptocarpus phyllanthus
mono-leaved "Cape primrose"

Streptocarpus x hybridus
"Cape primrose" at Roehrs, N.J.

Titanotrichum oldhamii
from South China and Taiwan

Sinningia 'Tom Thumb'
charming "Miniature gloxinia"

Sinningia spec. fyfiana 'Chicago'
"Double gloxinia" with frilled petals

Didissandra morganii
in Bot. Garden Darmstadt

Sinningia hirsuta
miniature from Brazil

Sinningia pusilla *(Brazil)*
"Miniature slipper plant"

Sinningia macropoda *(Rechsteineria)*
"Vermillion helmet flower" (So. Brazil)

Sinningia canescens *(Brazil: Paraná)*
(Rechsteineria leucotricha hort.)

Sinningia regina
"Cinderella slippers"

Sinningia concinna
miniature from Brazil

Smithiantha hyb. 'Orange King'
"Orange temple-bells"

Streptocarpus saxorum *(Tanzania)*
"False African violet"

Streptocarpus rexii
"Cape primrose" of So. Africa

Chlorophytum comosum 'Vittatum'
"Spider plant" with runners

Chlorophytum comos, 'Variegatum'
"Green-lily" at Roehrs, N.J.

Chlorophytum comosum 'Mandaianum'
"Walking anthericum" (LIL.)

Dracaena sanderiana *(AGAV.)*
"Ribbon plant" from Cameroun

Dracaena godseffiana hort.
(surculosa) "Gold-dust dracaena"

Dracaena marginata 'Tricolor'
"Rainbow plant" in Puerto Rico

Sansevieria trifasciata 'Laurentii'
"Variegated snake plant" (AGAV.)

Yucca aloifolia 'Tricolor'
"Red daggers" (AGAV.)

Aspidistra elatior *(LIL.)*
"Cast-iron plant" from China

Dracaena fragrans 'Massangeana'
"Corn plant" canes at Roehrs, N.J.

Dracaena marginata *(AGAV.)*
"Madagascar dragon tree"

Beaucarnea recurvata *(Nolina)*
"Pony tail" from Mexico (AGAV.)

Dracaena goldieana *(Nigeria, West Africa)*
"Queen of dracaenas" at Roehrs Exotic Nurseries, N.J.

Dracaena deremensis 'Souv. de Aug. Schryver'
in bed of Erica gracilis, in Ghent, Belgium

Cereus 'Peruvianus hybrid' *(CACT.)*
"Peruvian apple" in California

Agave angustifolia 'Marginata'
"Variegated Caribbean agave"(AGAV.)

Euphorbia canariensis *(EUPH.)*
"African cereus" in Tenerife

Cordyline terminalis 'Lilliput'
"Dwarf Red dracaena" of Hawaii

Dracaena deremensis 'Warneckii'
"Striped dracaena" at Roehrs, N.J.

Pleomele reflexa 'Variegata' *(AGAV.)*
"Song of India" in Sri Lanka

Drimiopsis kirkii *(LIL.)*
bulbous plant from Zanzibar

Rohdea japonica 'Marginata' *(LIL.)*
"Sacred Manchu lily"

Dracaena deremensis 'Skunky' *(AGAV.)*
pat. mutation (Krieser, Wisconsin)

Dracaena deremensis 'Compacta'
"Calypso Queen" in Brooklyn Bot. G.

Pleomele reflexa 'Song of Jamaica'
in Metro Manila, Philippines

Dracaena deremensis 'Janet Craig'
Roehrs Exotic Nurseries, N.J.

Abutilon x hyb. 'Souvenir de Bonn'
"Variegated flowering maple" (MALV.)

Hibiscus rosa-sin. 'Santana'
dwarf beauty in Vista, Calif.

Hibiscus rosa-sin. 'White Wings'
profuse with blooms, in Calif.

Calathea zebrina *(MARANT.)*
"Zebra plant" of São Paulo, Brazil

Calathea lancifolia *(insignis hort.)*
"Rattlesnake plant" of Brazil

Calathea ornata 'Roseo-lineata'
colorful form of Ecuador heritage

Calathea veitchiana
"Peacock plant" from Ecuador

Maranta leuconeura erythroneura
"Red-veined prayer plant" of Rio

Calathea roseo-picta
decorative low plant from Brazil

Calathea makoyana
"Brazilian peacock plant"

Calathea lindeniana
from Amazonas, Brazil

Maranta leuconeura kerchoveana
Brazilian "Prayer plant"

Donax grandis *(Arundo)*
in tropical Malacca, Malaya

Calathea metallica 'Undulata'
col. Alvim Seidel, Corupá, Brazil

Calathea ecuadoriana *(tigrina hort.)*
col. Longwood Gardens, Pennsylvania

Calathea picturata 'Argentea'
in Brooklyn Bot. Garden, N.Y.

Ctenanthe stromata *(Calathea)*
from tropical Brazil

Ctenanthe oppenheimiana 'Tricolor'
"Never-never plant" of Brazil

Calathea warscewiczii *(Costa Rica)*
in New York Botanical Garden

Ctenanthe species 'Burle Marx'
(Stromanthe amabilis in Calif. hort.)

Calathea bella *(kegeliana hort.)*
in Dahlem Botanic Garden, Berlin

Ficus benjamina, *the "Weeping fig" (MORAC.)*
in Rockefeller Center, New York City

Ficus benjamina 'Exotica', *"Java fig"*
for indoor decoration, Guggenheim Museum, New York

Laurus nobilis, *the "Roman laurel" (LAUR.)*
along Theatinerstr., Munich, Bavaria

Ficus retusa, *the "Chinese banyan"*
featured at the Art Museum, Los Angeles

Ficus elastica 'Decora'
"Wide-leaf rubber plant"

Ficus elastica 'Decora tricolor'
at Rochford Nurs. near London

Ficus benjamina 'Variegata'
"Variegated weeping fig"

Ficus pumila 'Marginata'
"Variegated creeping fig"

Ficus triangularis 'Variegata'
"Sweetheart tree" in Germany

Ficus microcarpa nitida 'Hawaii'
"Variegated Indian laurel"

Ficus benjamina, *semi-standard
with braided stems, in Florida*

Ficus retusa 'Variegata'
"Varieg. Chinese banyan" in Calif.

Ficus microcarpa nitida, *with fruit*
"Indian laurel", from Malaya

Ficus elastica, *"India rubber"* container-grown in Calif.

Ficus retusa, *"Chinese banyan"* as standard, New York Bot. Garden

Ficus lyrata *(pandurata hort.)* *"Fiddle-leaf"* in Florida nursery

Citrus sinensis *(RUT.)* *"Sweet orange"* in flower

Pandanus veitchii *(PAND.)* *"Varieg. screwpine" (Polynesia)*

Gardenia jasminoides 'Fortuniana' *"Cape jasmine" from So. China (RUB.)*

Ligustrum japonicum *(OLEAC.)* *(lucidum in hort.) "Waxleaf privet"*

Bletilla striata *(ORCH.)* *"Hyacinth orchid"*, Kwangchow, China

Bougainvillea x buttiana *(NYCT.)* *pot grown in the Rhineland*

Peperomia argyreia (sandersii)
"Watermelon peperomia" from Brazil

Peperomia verschaffeltii
"Sweetheart pep." in Amazonas

Peperomia puteolata
"Parallel peperomia" of Perú

Peperomia clusiifolia (PIP.)
"Red-edged pep." from W. Indies

Peperomia caperata
"Emerald ripple" of Brazil

Peperomia magnoliifolia 'Rainbow'
"Tricolor Pepperface" in Florida

Peperomia fraseri 'Variegata'
"Variegated Mignonette" in Calif.

Peperomia pernambucensis, (juv.)
Dahlem Botanic Garden, Berlin

Peperomia obtusifolia 'Variegata'
"Variegated peperomia"

Peperomia arifolia litoralis
in São Paulo, Brazil

Pellionia pulchra (URTIC.)
"Satin pellionia" of Vietnam

Bertolonia marmorata (MELAST.)
in Tuebingen Bot. Gard., Germany

Phoenix canariensis, *"Canary date"*
in terracotta jar, Tijuana, Mex.

Howea forsteriana *in tub*
"Paradise palm" in New York

Chrysalidocarpus lutescens
"Butterfly palm" in Acapulco, Mex.

Trachycarpus fortunei *(juv.)*
Chamaerops excelsa of hort.

Phoenix roebelenii *(Vietnam)*
juvenile "Pigmy date palm"

Chamaedorea metallica *(tenella)*
"Miniature fishtail" of Mexico

Chamaedorea erumpens
"Bamboo palm" (Honduras)

Chamaedorea elegans *(Mexico)*
"Parlor palm" at Roehrs, N.J.

Chamaedorea seifrizii, *"Reed palm"*
Roehrs Exotic Nurs., N.J.

Ardisia crenata *(MYRS.)*
"Coral berry" of Japan

Pittosporum tobira 'Variegatum'
"Variegated mock-orange" (PITT.)

Medinilla magnifica *(MELAST.)*
"Rose grape" of the Philippines

Barbacenia elegans *(Vellozia)*
from tropical Africa (VELLOZ.)

Ixora macrothyrsa 'Superking'
"King ixora" (RUB.)

Lantana camara *(VERB.)*
"Shrub verbena" of West Indies

Pilea mollis *(URTIC.)*
"Moon Valley green" (Costa Rica)

Pilea cadierei 'Minima'
"Aluminum plant" of Vietnam

Pilea forgetii
"Angel-wings" from Perú

Pilea involucrata
"Panamiga" of South America

Pilea 'Silver Tree'
"Silver and bronze" (Caribbean)

Nymphaea x chromatella
in Chinese picklejug

Camellia sasanqua 'Shishi-Gashira'
"Sunlight camellia" in Calif. (THEAC.)

Pittosporum tobira *(PITT.)*
"Mock orange" in San Diego

Sparmannia africana *(TILIAC.)*
"Indoor linden" from So. Africa

Tetranema roseum *(Allophyton)*
"Mexican foxglove" (SCROPH.)

Portulaca oleracea cv. 'Belgica'
"Flowering purslane" in Florida

Cissus rhombifolia 'Ellen Danica'
introduced from Denmark (VIT.)

Hoffmannia ghiesbreghtii 'Variegata'
"Variegated taffeta plant"

Adenia olabuensis *(Madagascar)*
"Spider tree" in Vista, Calif. (PASS.)

Hoffmannia refulgens *(RUB.)*
"Quilted taffeta plant" of Chiapas

Piper magnificum *(PIP.)*
"Lacquered pepper tree" of Perú

Miconia calvescens *(magnifica)*
"Velvet tree" from Mexico (MEL.)

Coccoloba uvifera *(POLYGON.)*
"Sea grape" of the West Indies

Costus malortieanus *(ZING.)*
"Stepladdder plant" (Costa Rica)

Hedychium gardnerianum *(ZING.)*
"Kahili ginger" from India

Musa x paradisiaca 'Koae' *(MUS.)*
variegated Hawaiian banana

Costus ignaeus
"Fiery costus" from Brazil

Costus pulverulentus *(sanguineus)*
"Violet spiral flag" of C. America

Kaempferia galanga
"Ginger lily" from India

Kaempferia pulchra *(ZING.)*
"Pretty resurrection lily" (Burma)

Kaempferia roscoeana
"Tropical crocus" of Burma

Kaempferia grandiflora
"Resurrection lily" of Kenya

Angraecum superbum *(eburneum)*
by Marcel Lecoufle, Paris, France

Bletilla striata
in Kwangchow, China

Bletia reflexa
from Sonora, Mexico

Acriopsis javanica *(Spathoglottis)*
epiphyte from Sumatra

Bulbophyllum ornatissimum
(Cirrhopetalum) from Sikkim

Arachnis flos-aeris
"Spider orchid" of Java

Anguloa clowesii
"Tulip orchid" (Andes of Colombia)

Anguloa uniflora 'Rosea'
"Cradle orchid" of Perú

x Aranda 'Christine'
(Aranda x Vanda) in Singapore

Aerides odorata var. major
"Foxtail orchid" of Java

Bifrenaria harrisoniae
fragrant epiphyte from Brazil

Brassavola digbyana
"Lady of the Night" in Honduras

Calanthe x vestita
'William Murray'

Brassavola nodosa
"Lady of the Night" (Guatemala)

Brassavola glauca
(Mexico, Guatemala)

Brassia allenii
epiphyte of Panama

Brassia maculata
(Cuba to Guatemala)

Brassia verrucosa
"Queen's umbrella" (C. America)

x Aranthera 'Ann Black'
at Mandai Nurs., Singapore

Catasetum roseum
of Oaxaca, So. Mexico

Cattleya citrina *(Encyclia)*
"Tulip-cattleya" of Mexico

x Brassocattleya lehmannii
typical bearded flower

Cattleya 'Enid'
(warscewiczii x mossiae)

Cattleya intermedia
(Paraguay to Uruguay)

Cattleya labiata punctata
col. A. Seidel, Corupá, Paraná

Cattleya mossiae
"Easter orchid" of Venezuela

Cattleya 'Priscilla alba'
('Enid' x lueddemanniana)

Cattleya granulosa
from Guatemala

Cattleya rex
(Perú to Brazil)

Chysis aurea
(Mexico to Venezuela)

Coelogyne dayana
"Necklace orchid" from Borneo

Coelogyne flaccida
(Nepal Himalayas)

Coelogyne pandurata
"Black orchid" from Sumatra

Cattleya forbesii
"Cocktail orchid" of Brazil

Cattleya trianaei
"Christmas orchid" (Colombia)

Coelogyne cristata
(Himalayas of Nepal)

Calanthe x vest. 'Baron Schroeder'
in Longwood Gard., Pennsylvania

Calanthe furcata *(veratrifolia)*
terrestrial from Pacific Islands

Cleisostoma paniculatum
dwarf orchid in Teipei, Taiwan

Cymbidium x insigne *(Hybrid)*
at New York Flower Show 1984

Cyrtopodium andersonii
in habitat near Santos, Brazil

Cymbidium 'Show Girl The Bride'
large-flowered hybrid in New York

Cypripedium cordigerum
in the Nepal Himalaya

Cypripedium calceolus *(Europe)*
wire-protected from plant thieves

Cypripedium acaule *(No. America)*
"Pink ladyslipper" in New York

Cypripedium candidum
"Small white ladyslipper"

Cypripedium reginae
"Showy ladyslipper" (E. No. America)

Cypripedium speciosum
(macranthon), from Japan

Dendrobium bigibbum
"Cooktown orchid" in Queensland

Chiloschista lunifera *(Burma)*
Munich Bot. Garden, Germany

Cypripedium japonicum
from China and Japan

Coelogyne parishii
from Moulmein, Southern Burma

Cochlioda rosea
(Andes of Perú)

Cycnoches ventricosum
"Swan orchid" from Guatemala

Cymbidium lancifolium
(Japan, India, Malaysia)

Cymbidium 'Flirtation'
miniature terrestrial

Cymbidium pumilum
dwarf species, in Taiwan

Dendrobium densiflorum
(Himalayas to Indochina)

Dendrobium fimbriatum
(Himalayas to Malaya)

Dendrobium infundibulum
(Burma and Thailand)

Dactylorhiza foliosa
(Orchis maderensis) on Madeira

Dendrobium nobile 'Albiflorum'
of Southeast Asia parentage

Dendrobium johnsoniae
epiphyte of New Guinea Mountains

Encyclia baculus
(Epidendrum pentotis) (C. America)

Encyclia cordigera *(Epid. atropurp.)*
"Spice orchid" (Mexico, Brazil)

Encyclia prismatocarpa *(Epid.)*
"Rainbow orchid" (Costa Rica)

Encyclia cochleata *(Epidendrum)*
tropical Cuba to Brazil

Encyclia radiata *(Epidendrum)*
(Mexico to Venezuela)

Encyclia mariae *(Epidendrum)*
(Sierra Madre, So. Mexico)

Encyclia fragrans *(Epidendrum)*
(West Indies to Perú)

Encyclia oncidioides *(Epid.)*
from Mexico to Brazil

Elleanthus capitatus *(W. Indies)*
in Kew Bot. Gardens, England

Epigeneium lyonii *(Sarcopodium)*
from mountains of Luzon

x Epiphronitis veitchii
(Epidendrum x Sophronitis)

Cryptostylis arachnites
terrestrial of Malaya to Java

Epidendrum ciliare
(Mexico, West Indies, Brazil)

Epidendrum stamfordianum
(Honduras to Colombia)

Dendrochilum glumaceum
"Foxbrush" of the Philippines

Habenaria clypeata
"Rein orchid" of Chihuahua, Mexico

Herschelia graminifolia
"Blue Disa" on Table Mountain, So. Afr.

Galeandra stangeana
col. by A. Seidel, Corupá, Brazil

Kingiella philippinensis
miniature in the Philippines

Laelia anceps *(Mexico, Honduras)*
epiphytic "Amalia"

Laelia rubescens *(acuminata)*
"Flor de Jesú, in Mexico

Laelia purpurata oculata
in Corupá, Santa Catarina, Brazil

Laelia cinnabarina
charming epiphyte from Brazil

Laelia tenebrosa alba
rare variety from Brazil

Dendrobium farmeri albiflorum
from the Himalayan region

Dendrobium phalaenopsis
(Queensland and New Guinea)

Disa uniflora *(So. Africa)*
"Pride of Table Mountain"

Epidendrum brassavolae
collected by A. Lau, in Mexico

Epidendrum x o'brienianum
"Scarlet baby-orchid" in Honolulu

Epidendrum parkinsonianum
pendulous epiphyte from Mexico

Haemaria discolor dawsoniana
(Ludisia) "Jewel orchid" of Burma

Grammatophyllum scriptum
tropical epiphyte in Bogor, Java

Cymbidiella rhodochila *(Madagascar)*
col. Marcel Lecoufle, Paris, France

Laeliocattleya hassallii
alba 'Majestica'

Laeliocattleya canhamiana alba
(Laelia purpurea x Catt. mossiae)

Odontoglossum williamsianum
(Rosioglossum) from Costa Rica

Liparis lilifolia
"Tway blade" (Eastern U.S.)

Lockhartia acuta
"Braided orchid" of Costa Rica

Macroplectrum sesquipedale
(Angraecum) "Star of Bethlehem"

Lycaste aromatica
(Mexico to Honduras)

Lycaste cruenta
(Mexico, Guatemala, El Salvador)

Lycaste skinneri *(virginalis)*
"Nun orchid" of Guatemala

Malaxis latifolia
terrestrial from Malaysia

Gastorchis luteus
(Phaius luteus) of Madagascar

Neofinetia falcata *(Angraecum)*
fragrant miniature of Japan, Korea

Masdevallia veitchiana
Andes of Perú, to 4000 metres

Masdevallia infracta
of Brazil and Perú

Masdevallia militaris *(ignea of hort.)*
from Andean cloud forests, Colombia

Maxillaria tenuifolia
(Mexico to Nicaragua)

Maxillaria punctata
small epiphyte of Brazil

Maxillaria picta
fragrant Brazil epiphyte

x Miltonidium 'Aristocrat'
(Miltonia x Oncidium)

Ophrys speculum
"Mirror of Venus" on Rhodos

Orchis morio, *"Salep orchid"*
(Europe, Asia Minor to Siberia)

Miltonia vexillaria 'Volunteer'
of Ecuador parentage

Miltonia candida *(Brazil)*
fragrant-flowered epiphyte

Miltonia 'Storm'
lovely "Pansy orchid"

Odontoglossum laeve reichenheimii
large epiphyte from Mexico

Odontoglossum crispum
from Cordillera Oriental, Colombia

Odontoglossum insleayi
noble epiphyte of South Mexico

Odontoglossum pulchellum
"Lily of the Valley" of Guatemala

Odontoglossum rossii
(Oaxaca to Nicaragua)

Odontoglossum 'Alispum'
(Alorcus x crispum)

Oncidium papilio
"Butterfly orchid" of Colombia

Oncidium splendidum
from Guatemala and Honduras

Oncidium sphacelatum
"Golden shower" of C. America

Oncidium flexuosum
"Dancing-doll orchid" (Argentina)

Oncidium concolor
small epiphyte of Rio de Janeiro

Oncidium lanceanum
"Leopard orchid" of Guyana

Odontoglossum grande *(Rosioglossum)*
"Tiger orchid" (Mexico, Guatemala)

Miltonia schroederiana
bold epiphyte from Costa Rica

Cattleya dowiana
"Queen cattleya" of Costa Rica

Ophrys fuciflora *(arachnites)*
"Bee orchid" of So. Europe

Phalaenopsis equestris *(Philippines)*
miniature epiphyte

Paphiopedilum insigne
"Lady-slipper" from Nepal

Paphiopedilum x maudiae
(callosum x lawrenceanum)

Phalaenopsis 'Doris' *(amabilis hyb.)*
magnificent tetraploid

Peristeria elata
"Dove orchid" of Costa Rica

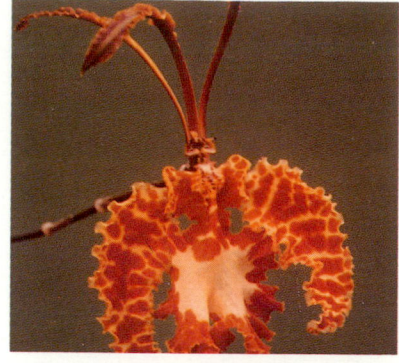

Oncidium longipes
small epiphyte in Paraná

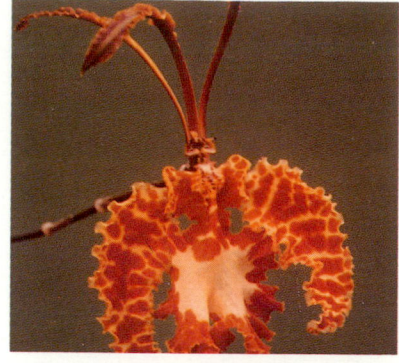

Oncidium kramerianum
beautiful epiphyte (Ecuador)

Oncidium uniflorum
small species from Brazil

Oncidium forbesii
from Organ Mts. of E. Brazil

Paphiopedilum callosum
colorful terrestrial in Vietnam

Paphiopedilum irapeanum *(Cyprip.)*
in Mitla, Oaxaca, Mexico

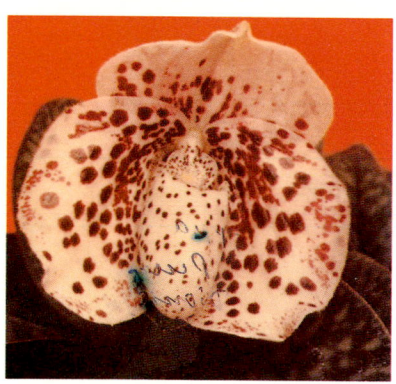

Paphiopedilum bellatulum
dwarf terrestrial of Burma

Paphiopedilum harrisianum
(villosum x barbatum)

Paphiopedilum fairrieanum
(Himalayas to Assam)

Paphiopedilum lawrenceanum
terrestrial of North Borneo

Paphiopedilum insigne 'Sanderae'
primrose "Ladyslipper" of England

Paphiopedilum lowii
large epiphyte of Sarawak

Ornithocephalus bicornis
"Mealybug orchid" in Panama

Phaius tankervilleae
"Nun orchid" in Sikkim, Himalaya

Phalaenopsis x rothschildiana
(schilleriana x amabilis)

Phalaenopsis schilleriana
"Rosy Moth orchid" of Luzon

Phalaenopsis amabilis
"Moth orchid" (Malaya to Queensland)

Phalaenopsis lueddemaniana
epiphytic in the Philippines

Phragmipedium x grande *(Selenip.)*
"Spiralled ladyslipper"

Phragmipedium vittatum
"Mandarin orchid" of Brazil

Pleione bulbocodioides
(yunnanensis) of W. China

Renanthera monachica
"Fire orchid" of Burma

Rodriguezia secunda
"Coral orchid" (Panama to Surinam)

Restrepia guttulata
from the Andes of Colombia

Schomburgkia undulata
large epiphyte of Venezuela

Sobralia decora
"Reed orchid" in Oaxaca, Mexico

Sobralia macrantha
"Zapatitos" in Mexico and Costa Rica

Sophronitis cernua
epiphytic in Eastern Brazil

Sophronitis coccinea *(Brazil)*
on the Serra do Mar, São Paulo

Sophronitis coccinea rosea
in col. Seidel, Corupá, Brazil

Spathoglottis plicata
on Moorea, French Polynesia

Stanhopea wardii
epiphyte in Vera Cruz, Mexico

Stanhopea tigrina
"El Toro" of Mexico

Thunia alba, *terrestrial*
North India to Thailand

Trichocentrum tigrinum
small epiphyte (Ecuador)

Trichopilea suavis
epiphyte of Costa Rica

Polystachya affinis
epiphyte (West Africa to Uganda)

Polystachya pubescens
(Cape Prov. to Transvaal)

Restrepia elegans
curious epiphyte of Venezuela

Solenangis aphylla
climbing in Madagascar habitat

Stenoglottis fimbriata
tuberous species in Natal

Spiranthes aurantiaca
(Stenorrhynchus) in Jalisco, Mexico

Zygopetalum mackayi
as terrestrial in São Paulo

Vanda teres *(N.E. India)*
a corsage orchid, in Barbados

Vanda coerulea
"Blue orchid" of Burma

Vanda cristata
curious epiphyte of Nepal

Vanda 'Miss Agnes Joaquim'
"Corsage orchid"in Hawaii

Vanda lamellata
(Philippines, North Borneo)

Vanda tricolor
spectacular epiphyte in Java

Vanda tricolor suavis
fragrant waxy flowers on Bali

Vanilla planifolia *(fragrans)*
"Vanilla" flowering in Mexico

Vanilla planifolia 'Marginata'
ornamental scandent epiphyte

Vanilla pompona *with beans*
secondary source of "Vanillon"

Vanilla pompona *(lutescens)*
"West Indian vanilla"

Vanilla tahitensis *(Tahiti)*
in col. Marcel Lecoufle, France

Zygosepalum labiosum
(Guyana to Amazonas)

Bulbophyllum purpureorhachis
"Cobra orchid" of Zaire

Acrocomia intumenscens, *in Fairchild Gardens*
tall feather palm from Brazil

Archontophoenix cunninghamiana, *"Piccabeen palm"*
(Seaforthia elegans in Calif. hort.)

Arenga pinnata, *of Malaya*
"Sugar palm" at Foster Botanic Gardens, Honolulu

Caryota urens, *"Fishtail palm" (Sri Lanka)*
in San Diego Zoo, California

Borassodendron machadonis *(Malaya)*
in Singapore Botanic Garden

Ceroxylon quindiuense
"Wax palm" in Cartagena, Colombia

Calamus fasciculatus
showing spiny stems, in Malaya

Calamus fasciculatus
spiny palm in Singapore Bot. G.

Calamus scipionum
"Malacca rattan cane"

Pinanga geonomaeformis
Makiling Arboretum, Philippines

Brahea brandegeei *(juvenile)*
"Daughter of the West"

Brahea brandegeei *(Erythea)*
in Baja California, Mexico

Brahea dulcis *(Erythea)*
"Rock palm" (Mexico, Guatemala)

Areca catechu, *"Betel-nut palm"*
in Medan, Sumatra, Indonesia

Arenga obtusifolia *(Java)*
in Queens's Park, Barbados

Syagrus romanzoffiana, *"Queen palm"*
(Arecastrum romanzoffianum in hort.)

Borassus flabellifer *(India)*
"Palmyra palm" near Madras

Butia capitata *(Cocos australis)*
"Jelly palm" in Montevideo, Uruguay

Brahea armata *(Erythea)*
"Mexican Blue palm" in Calif.

Caryota mitis *"Tufted fishtail"*
in San Juan, Puerto Rico

Caryota urens, *"Wine palm"*
showing fishtail fronds

Caryota urens 'Nepal variety'
"Mountain fishtail" in California

Ravenea rivularis, *feather palm from rainy East Madagascar*

Chamaedorea metallica *(tenetta)* *"Miniature Fishtail" (Mexico)*

Chamaedorea seifrizii *"Reed palm" of Yucatan*

Chamaedorea stolonifera *"Climbing Fishtail" (So. Mexico)*

Chamaedorea elegans *(Collinia)* *"Parlor palm" (Guatemala)*

Chamaedorea erumpens *"Bamboo palm" of Honduras*

Bismarckia nobilis *Fairchild B. Garden, Miami*

Euterpe edulis, *"Assai Palm" juvenile plant, in San Diego*

Chamaedorea costaricana *"Showy Bamboo palm"*

Chrysalidocarpus lutescens *(Areca of hort.)*
in ceramic bowl, Royal Palace, Bangkok

Cocos nucifera, *"Coconut palms"*
on Nuku Hiva, Marquesas, South Pacific

Chamaerops humilis, *arborescent form*
"European Fan palm", in Valencia, Spain

Elaeis oleifera, *from Costa Rica to Venezuela*
"American oil palm", in Singapore Bot. Garden

Corypha umbraculifera, *"Talipot palm"*
Pamplemousse Gardens, Mauritius

Cyrtostachys lakka
"Sealing-wax palm" on Barbados

Dictyosperma album *(rubrum)*
"Princess palm" (Bermuda Bot. Garden)

Cocos nucifera 'Dwarf Samoan'
in the Marquesas, French Polynesia

Elaeis quineensis
"African Oil-palm", Lagos, Nigeria

Chamaerops humilis *with fruit*
in El Centro, So. California

Copernicia prunifera *(cerifera)*
"Carnauba wax palm" in N.E. Brazil

Hydriastele microspadix *(Australia)*
cane-palm in Singapore Bot. Garden

Iguanura wallichiana *(juv.)*
from Malaysian rainforest

Jubaeopsis caffra
"Cliffhangers" in E. So. Africa

Jubaea chilensis *(spectabilis)*
"Syrup palm" from Chile

Howea forsteriana *(Kentia)*
bearing seeds, in New Zealand

Kerriodoxa elegans
fan-leaf and seed, in Thailand

Latania lontaroides *(borbonica)*
"Red latan" in Mauritius

Licuala grandis *(Vanuatu)*
"Ruffled Fan-palm" in Singapore

Kentiopsis oliviformis
elegant palm from New Caledonia

Licuala peltata *(Bengal)*
beautiful fan-palm, in Penang

Licuala spinosa
"Spiny Licuala palm" in Singapore

Livistona benthamii
(Queensland)

Livistona australis *(S.E. Australia)*
"Australian Cabbage palm"

Livistona chinensis *(borbonica hort.*
"Chinese fan palm"

Phoenix canariensis
20 years old, in Vista, California

Phoenix canariensis, *with fruit*
"Canary Island date palm"

Phoenix sylvestris
"Wine palm" near Madras, India

Phoenix roebelenii
"Pigmy date palm" in Hong Kong

Latania loddigesii
"Blue Latan palm" at Kew Bot. G.

Hyophorbe lagenicaulis *(Mauritius)*
"Bottle palm" in Singapore

Phoenix reclinata, *"Senegal date palm"*
Casa del Prado, Balboa Park, San Diego

Phoenix dactilifera, *"Date palms"*
bearing fruit in Elche, Alicante, Spain

Hyphaene thebaica, *the "Dhoum palm"*
typically branching, in Tanzania

Trachycarpus fortunei *"Windmill palms" in tubs*
for decoration, Forbidden City, Beijing, China

Metroxylon sagus *(Malaysia)*
commercial "Sago" in Peradeniya

Pigafetta filaris *(Celebes)*
in Dr. Darian's Palmarium, Calif.

Prestoea montana *(Euterpe)*
"Palma de Sierra" in Puerto Rico

Howea belmoreana *(Kentia)*
"Sentry palm" (Australia)

Rhopaloblaste ceramica *(Solomon Is.)*
Melanesian collecting fruits

Acoelorrhaphe wrightii *(Paurotis)*
"Everglades palm" in Florida

Lodoicea maldivica, *"Double coconut"*
"Coco de Mer" in the Seychelles

Rhopalostylis sapida
"Nikau palm" of New Zealand

Rhopalostylis baueri, *with fruit*
in Sydney Botanic Garden, Australia

Ptychosperma elegans *(Seaforthia)*
"Solitaire palm" (Queensland)

Ptychosperma macarthurii
"Hurricane palm" of New Guinea

Ptychosperma caryotoides
in Port Moresby, New Guinea

Rhapis subtilis
miniature from Thailand

Rhapis excelsa *(flabelliformis)*
"Lady palm" in Kobe, Japan

Rhapis humilis
"Slender Lady palm" (So. China)

Pseudophoenix sargentii
in Yucatán, Eastern Mexico

Mauritia flexuosa, *"Ita palm"*
at Lake Canaima, Guayana

Mauritia flexuosa, *in Amazon forest*
Parque Nacional Canaima

Roystonea oleracea, *"Cabbage palms"*
Jardim Botanico, Rio de Janeiro

Roystonea regia *(Oreodoxa)*
"Royal palms" in Bombay

Roystonea elata, *"Florida Royal palm"*
Everglades Nat'l. Park, Florida

Sabal bermudana
"Bermuda palmetto" in Hamilton

Sabal mexicana, *"Texas palmetto"*
in Chitzen-Itza, Yucatán

Roystonea venezuelana
"Chaguaramo palm" in Caracas

Sabal minor, *"Dwarf palmetto"*
(Carolina to Florida and Texas)

Serenoa repens, *"Scrub palmetto"*
Daytona Beach, Florida

Sabal palmetto, "Cabbage palmetto"
on Atlantic Coast of Florida

Raphia australis
in Botanical Garden Singapore

Trithrinax acanthocoma
"Webbed trithrinax" (So. Brazil)

Thrinax radiata, *in Florida*
"West Indian thatch palm"

Nypa fruticans, *"Nypa palm"*
growing in water, Perak, Malaya

Thrinax parviflora
"Palmetto thatch" (Bahamas)

Thrinax morrisii *(ekmanii)*
"Key palm" in South Florida

Siphokentia beguinii, *juvenile pl.*
in Los Baños, Philippines

Trachycarpus fortunei *(excelsa)*
young "Windmill palm" in California

Trachycarpus takil *(wagnerianus)*
of Western Himalayas

Veitchia joannis *(Adonidia)*
in Fiji, Melanesia

Pritchardia pacifica
"Fiji fan palm" in Rarotonga

Veitchia merrillii *(Adonidia)*
"Christmas palm" in Philippines

Verschaffeltia splendida
"Stilt-root palm" in Seychelles

Orbignya martiana *of So. America*
in Foster Botanic Garden, Honolulu

Salacca edulis *(Malaysia)*
"Snakeskin fruit"

Washingtonia filifera, *"Pettycoat palm"*
at Pala Indian Mission, California

Washingtonia filifera
young plant with foliar filaments

Washingtonia robusta *in habitat*
Cabo San Lucas, Baja Cal., Mexico

Cycas circinalis, *"Fern palm"*
from India and New Guinea

Cycas revoluta, *"Sago palm"*
(Southern Japan to Java)

Cycas media, *"Australian nut-palm"*
in North Queensland habitat

Encephalartos villosus, *in Natal, So. Africa*
spreading from underground trunk

Encephalartos woodii, *from Zululand*
massive trunk with spreading crown

Dioon purpusii, *w. bluish leaves*
in Oaxaca, So. Mexico

Dioon edule, *"Virgin's palm"*
in Fortin, Veracruz, Mexico

Dioon spinulosum *(Mexico)*
"Giant dioon" in Yucatán

Encephalartos lehmannii
"Blue-leaved cycad" in So. Africa

Cycas taiwaniana *with male cone*
in Teipei, Taiwan

Ceratozamia mexicana
"Mexican horn-cone" (Mexico)

Encelphalartos arenarius
blue form, in So. Africa

Macrozamia communis
(New South Wales, Australia)

Macrozamia moorei, *(Queensland)*
female cone with seeds

Stangeria eriopus *(So. Africa)*
in Del Dios, California

Zamia fisheri, *fern-like*
caulescent cycad from Mexico

Zamia pumila *(furfuracea)*
"Jamaica sago tree" (C. America)

Dracaena draco *(AGAV.), Canary Isl. "Dragon tree"*
in Quail Botanic Garden, Encinitas, California

Cordyline australis *(AGAV.) (Dracaena indivisa hort.)*
overlooking Wellington, New Zealand

Aloe bainesii *(LIL.) of So. Africa*
handsome tree blooming in Vista, California

Yucca rostrata *(AGAV.), from South Texas*
in desert landscape, Escondido, California

Carludovica palmata *(CYCLANTH.)*
"Panama hat plant" in Ecuador

Dasylirion serratifolium *(AGAV.)*
in Montevideo, Uruguay

Cordyline fruticosa *(AGAV.)*
on Moorea, Polynesia

Cordyline indivisa
"Palm lily" of New Zealand

Cordyline rubra 'Bruantii'
Botanic Garden Munich

Cordyline stricta
(Dracaena congesta) in Los Angeles

Cordyline terminalis
"Red dracaena" in Tahiti, Polynesia

Cordyline terminalis 'Ti'
"Tree of Kings" of Hawaii

Dracaena americana *(AGAV.)*
in Botanic Garden, Rio de Janeiro

Dracaena marginata
"Madagascar Dragon tree"

Beaucarnea stricta
from arid Tehuacan, Mexico

Beaucarnea recurvata *(Nolina)*
Mexican "Pony-tail" in Los Angeles

Dracaena fragrans 'Victoriae'
Paradeniya Bot. Garden, Sri Lanka

Dracaena fragrans 'Massangeana'
"Cornstalk plant" in Puerto Rico

Dracaena draco, *bearing fruit*
"Dragon tree" in So. California

Phormium tenax 'Yellow Wave'
at New York Flower Show 86

Phormium tenax, *"N.Z. flax"*
on South Island, New Zealand

Phormium colensoi 'Tricolor'
"Mountain flax" in Wellington, N.Z.

Pleomele angustifolia honoriae
from Solomon Islands, Melanesia

Pleomele reflexa *(Dracaena) (AGAV.)*
"Malaysian dracaena" in Bermuda

Pleomele reflexa 'Variegata'
in Mahabalipuram, South India

Yucca aloifolia
"Spanish bayonet" in Tenerife

Yucca aloifolia 'Tricolor'
"Red dagger" in California

Yucca baccata, *"Datil yucca"*
in Mesa Verde, Colorado

Yucca filamentosa
"Adam's needle" (Carolina to Florida)

Yucca filamentosa 'Variegata'
in Wellington Bot. Garden, N.Z.

Yucca flaccida *(filamentosa in hort.)*
(No. Carolina to Alabama)

Yucca brevifolia, *"Joshua tree"*
on the Mohave Desert, California

Yucca elata
"Soaptree yucca" in Arizona

Yucca elephantipes *(Guatemala)*
Sultan's Garden, Tangier, Morocco

Yucca carnerosiana
Jardin Botanico, Mexico City

Yucca gloriosa, *"Spanish dagger"*
shores of Carolina to Florida

Yucca recurvifolia, *(pendula)*
"Lord's candle" in California

Yucca glauca
"Soapweed" of New Mexico

Yucca schidigera, *in habitat*
Mohave Desert, California

Yucca schottii, *stem-forming*
with showy flowers, Arizona

Yucca thompsoniana *(AGAV.)*
in Coahuila, Mexico

Yucca torreyi, *tree-forming*
(New Mexico, Texas, No. Mexico)

Yucca whipplei, *"Lord's candle"*
in Sequoia National Park, Calif.

Heliconia marginata *(MUSAC.)*
on Dominica, West Indies

Heliconia bihai
"Firebird" in Brazil

Heliconia bihai 'St. Vincent'
at Andromeda Gardens, Barbados

Heliconia caribaea
"Wild plantain" in St. Vincent, W.I.

Heliconia psittacorum
"Parrot flower" in Guyana

Heliconia lanceana
from Southern Brazil

Heliconia pendula *(collinsiana)*
with pendant inflorescence (Guatemala)

Heliconia mariae, *"Beefsteak heliconia"*
in Andromeda Gardens, Barbados

Heliconia rostrata
"Hanging Lobster-claw" in Perú

Heliconia lingulata *in habitat*
Cordillera Oriental, Santa Cruz, Bolivia

Heliconia longiflora *"Coral plantain"*
in Panama rainforest habitat

Heliconia wagneriana
(Costa Rica, Panama)

Heliconia brasiliensis
"False Bird-of-Paradise" on Maui

Heliconia humilis
"Lobster-claw" (Trinidad)

Musa coccinea
"Flowering banana" in Vietnam

Musa velutina *(Assam)*
"Ornamental banana" on Hilo, Hawaii

Strelitzia nicolai, *inflorescence*
"Bird-of-Paradise tree" (So. Africa)

Musa sumatrana
"Blood banana" in Java

Heliconia spectabilis 'Edwardus Rex'
Nymphenburg Bot. Garden, Munich

Heliconia subulata *(Argentina)*
(Pingatore, Bot. G. Buenos Aires)

Ensete maurelii
"Black banana" (Ethiopia)

Ensete ventricosum *(Musa ensete)*
"Abyssinian banana" container-grown

Heliconia schiedeana *(Mexico)*
in Fortin de las Flores, Veracruz

Strelitzia reginae
"Bird-of-Paradise" (South Africa)

Strelitzia nicolai *(MUS.)*
"Bird-of-Paradise tree" in California

Musa x paradisiaca 'Champa'
"Lady's fingers" in Kew G., Richmond

Ravenala madagascariensis *(MUS.)*
"Traveler's tree" in Northern Madagascar

Trachycarpus fortunei *(PALM.) (Chamaerops excelsa in hort.)*
at entrance to Temple of Heaven, Beijing, China

Musa basjoo *(MUS.)*
"Japanese fiber banana" (So. Japan)

Musa acuminata *(cavendishii, nana)*
"Dwarf Chinese banana" on Madeira

Musa x paradisiaca *(sapientum)*
"Common banana" in Puerto Rico

Pandanus tectorius novo-caledonicus *female tree with edible seeds*

Pandanus lamprocephalus *in Lae Bot. Garden, New Guinea*

Pandanus leram, *with edible nuts* "Nicobar breadfruit" in Sri Lanka

Pandanus utilis, *female tree* "Screw pine" in Madagascar

Pandanus pygmaeus (graminifolius) *from Mauritius and Madagascar*

Pandanus pristis (Madagascar) *male rosette in flower*

Pandanus tectorius sanderi *Bot. Garden Peradeniya, Sri Lanka*

Pandanus veitchii (tectorius var.) *in Mahe Bot. Garden, Seychelles*

Pandanus baptistii (tectorius var.) "Blue Screw pine" in New Guinea

Pandanus papuanus *(PAND.), "Papua Crewpine"*
stilted trees in Lae Botanic Garden, New Guinea

Ravenala madagascariensis *(MUS.)*
"Traveler's palm" in Kuala Lumpur, Malaysia

Strelitzia alba *(augusta) (MUS.) (Natal, So Africa)*
"Great white strelitzia" in Rosarito, Baja California

Pandanus odoratissimus *"Walking tree"*
by Dr. B. Stone, Pulau Besar, Malacca, Malaya

Cibotium schiedei *(DICKSON.)*
"Mexican treefern" (So. Mexico)

Dicksonia antarctica *(DICKSON.)*
"Tasmanian treefern" (Australia)

Cyathea spinulosa *(CYATH.)*
in Kwangtung Prov., So. China

Sphaeropteris cooperi *(Alsophila autralis) (CYATH.)*
overlooking Opera House, Sydney, Australia

Dicksonia squarrosa, *the "Westland treefern"*
near Franz-Joseph Glacier, New Zealand

Osmunda regalis *(OSMUND.)*
"Royal fern" (No. America, Europe)

Osmunda claytoniana
"Interrupted fern" (No. Am. to China)

Osmunda cinnamomum
"Cinnamon fern" (America, E. Asia)

Dicksonia antarctica, *"Tasmanian treeferns"*
in Golden Gate Park, San Francisco

Cyathea arborea, *"West Indian treeferns"*
in habitat, Luquillo Nat'l. Forest, Puerto Rico

Cibotium chamissoi *(menziesii hort.)*
"Hawaiian treefern", in California

Sphaeropteris medullaris *(Cyathea)*
"Black treefern", in Wellington, New Zealand

Angiopteris erecta *(MARATT.)*
"Mules-foot fern" (Australia)

Botrychium dissectum obliguum
"Grape-fern" in Sparta, N.J.

Acrostichum danaeifolium *(POLYP.)*
"Swamp fern" (Trop. America)

Marsilea vestita *(MARSIL.)*
"Water clover" (West Indies)

Cystopteris bulbifera v. crispa
"Bladder-fern" in New Jersey

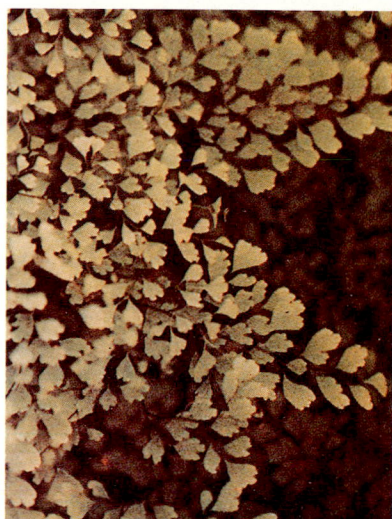

Adiantum capillus-veneris
"Venus-hair" (Temp. to Tropics)

Adiantum hispidulum *(POLYP.)*
"Australian maidenhair"

Adiantum macrophyllum
"Showy maidenhair" (Trop. America)

Blechnum capense *(POLYP.)*
from South Africa

Adiantum pedatum *(No. America)*
"American maidenhair" in N. Jersey

Adiantum raddianum *(cuneatum)*
"Delta maidenhair" of Brazil

Adiantum tenerum
"Brittle maidenhair" (W. Indies)

Adiantum trapeziforme
in Brooklyn Bot. Garden, N.Y.

Adiantum venustum
from Himalayas of Nepal

Asplenium simplicifrons
epiphytic in No. Queensland

Asplenium antiquum *(So. Japan)*
at San Diego Fern Soc., Del Mar

Asplenium bulbiferum
"New Zealand mother fern"

Asplenium daucifolium *(viviparum)*
"Mother fern" of Mauritius

Blechnum penna marina
"Sea feather" in Rotorua, N.Z.

Blechnum spicant, *"Deerfern"*
(Alaska to Calif., Europe)

Camptosorus rhizophyllus
"Walking fern" in Sparta, N.J.

Cystopteris fragilis
"Fragile bladder-fern" in N. York

Asplenium monanthemum
in Madeira habitat

Belvisia platyrhynchos
from the Philippines

Ceterach officinarum *(Chile)*
"Scale fern" on Easter Island

Asplenium platyneuron
"Ebony spleenwort" in Colorado

Asplenium trichomanes
"Maidenhair spleenwort" in N. Jersey

Athyrium filix-femina
"Lady-fern" (North Temperate reg.)

Asplenium nidus, *"Birdsnest fern"*
(India to Queensland)

Asplenium nidus 'Fimbriatus'
"Fringed birdsnest" in Germany

Cryptogramma crispa, *"European parsley-fern"*
from the Arctic to England and North Asia

Cheilanthes lanosa *(tomentosa)*
"Hairy Lip-fern" (Connecticut to Arizona, Mexico)

Athyrium niponicum pictum
(goeringianum) "Silver fern" (Japan)

Blechnum gibbum*(Lomaria)*
from New Caledonia

Blechnum brasiliense
in Jardim Botanico, Rio de Janeiro

Cheilanthes gracillima
"Lip fern" in Brit. Columbia

Cyrtomium falcatum 'Rochfordianum'
"Fringed Holly fern" (English cv.)

Cyrtomium falcatum, *"Holly fern"*
(Japan, China, India to Hawaii)

Davallia griffithiana, *from India and So. China*
"Rabbit's-foot fern" in hanging pot

Davallia fejeensis *(Melanesia)*
"Fiji Rabbit's-foot" with furry rhizomes

Davallia mariesii *(bullata)*
"Ball fern", popular in Japan

Davallia trichomanoides *(canariensis)*
"Squirrel's-foot fern" (Malaya)

Davallia fejeensis 'Plumosa'
epiphytic in Polynesia

Dennstaedtia punctilobula
"Hay-scented fern" (Nova Scotia)

Didymochlaena truncatula
col. at Iguassu, Paraná

Diplazium pycnocarpon *(Athyrium)*
"Silvery spleenwort" (Québec)

Drynaria quercifolia, *epiphytic*
"Oakleaved fern" in New Guinea

Dryopteris austriaca *(dilatata)*
"Shield fern" in Sparta, N. Jersey

Dryopteris erythrosora
"Autumn fern" (China, Japan)

Dryopteris filix-mas, *"Male fern"*
(No. America, Europe to Asia)

Dryopteris filix-mas crispa
in Oxford Bot. Garden, Britain

Dryopteris marginalis *(spinulosa)*
"Marginal Shield fern" (Eastern U.S.)

Dryopteris goldiana
"Giant wood fern" in N. Jersey

Dryopteris wallichiana
"Wood fern" (Japan to Nepal)

Matteuccia orientalis
"Oriental Ostrich" (Japan to Himalayas)

Gymnocarpium dryopteris *(Currania)*
"Oak fern" in Ketchikan, Alaska

Matteuccia struthiopteris
"Ostrich fern" in England

Matteuccia pensylvanica
"American Ostrich fern" in Springtime

Microlepia strigosa *(speluncae)*
(Polynesia to Trop. Asia)

Nephrolepis duffii *(cordifolia var.)*
"Pigmy sword fern" (New Zealand)

Nephrolepis cordifolia
"Erect sword fern" in Jamaica

Nephrolepis cordifolia pendula
at Selby Bot. Gard. Sarasota, Florida

Nephrolepis exalt. 'Bostoniensis'
"Boston fern" in Brooklyn Bot. G.

Nephrolepis exaltata
"Sword fern" in Florida Everglades

Nephrolepis exaltata 'Bostoniensis compacta'
"Dwarf Boston fern" of florists at Roehrs, N.J.

Nephrolepis exaltata 'Whitmanii'
sturdy "Lace fern" with feathery fronds

Nephrolepis biserrata 'Furcans'
"Fishtail fern" on Barbados

Onoclea sensibilis, *"Sensitive fern"*
in Skylands Arboretum, N.J.

Hemionitis palmata *(Tectaria incisa)*
"Strawberry fern" in São Paulo

Pellaea viridis macrophylla
(Pteris adiantoides of hort.)

Pellaea rotundifolia
"Button fern" (New Zealand)

Pellaea bridgesii
"Cliff brake" of Oregon

Phyllitis scolopendrium
"Hart's-tongue fern" in Munich

Phyllitis scolopendrium 'Crispum'
"Crisped deer-tongue" in E. Germany

Pityrogramma chrysophylla
"Gold fern" in Puerto Rico

Platycerium stemaria
"Triangle staghorn" in Nigeria

Platycerium holtumii *(Thailand)*
in Botanic Gardens, Singapore

Platycerium ridleyi
(Malaya, Borneo, Sumatra)

Platycerium wandae *(wilh. reginae)*
"Queen elkhorn" of New Guinea

Platycerium superbum *(grande hort.)*
"Regal elkhorn" (E. Australia)

Platycerium grande *(Philippines)*
in Leiden Bot. Garden, Holland

Platycerium bifurcatum *(alicorne hort.)*
the "Common staghorn fern" from Eastern Australia

Platycerium bifurcatum cv. 'Netherlands'
cultivar of Dutch origin with broad fronds

Platycerium andinum
"American staghorn" from E. Perú

Platycerium willinckii
"Silver staghorn" of Java

Platycerium coronarium
"Crown staghorn" in Sarawak, Borneo

Polypodium aureum *(Phlebodium)*
"Hare's-foot fern" in Mexico City

Polypodium aureum 'Mandaianum'
"Crisped blue fern"

Polypodium interjectum
"Lacy wall-fern" in England

Polypodium phyllitides
"Strap fern" in Bermuda Bot. Gard.

Polypodium polypodioides
"Resurrection fern" in Texas

Polypodium scouleri *(B. Columbia)*
"Leathery polypody" in Vancouver

Polypodium punctatum *(Polynesia)*
"Climbing birdsnest", in Kew Bot. G.

Polypodium punctatum 'Grandiceps'
"Crested fishtail" on Barbados

Polypodium subauriculatum 'Knightiae'
"Lacy pine-fern" in Brooklyn Bot. G.

Polypodium virginianum
"American wall fern" (E. No. America)

Polypodium vulgare *(Eur., No. America)*
"Common polypody" or "Adder's fern"

Polystichum acrostichoides
"Christmas fern" in New Jersey

Polystichum aculeatum
"Prickly shield fern" in England

Polystichum braunii
in Foster col., Sparta, N. Jersey

Dryopteris arguta *(Polystichum)*
"Wood fern" in Del Mar, Calif.

Polystichum lonchites *(Aspidium)*
"Northern hollyfern", in Germany

Polystichum munitum *(Alaska)*
"Western swordfern" in Ketchikan

Polystichum tsus-simense *(Japan)*
"Tsus-sima holly fern"

Polystichum setiferum
"Hedgefern" in Edinburgh, Scotland

Polystichum setiferum 'Proliferum'
"Filigree fern" in Australia

Pteridium aquilinum *(Worldwide)*
"Bracken" or "Eagle fern"

Pteris cretica 'Childsii'
at San Diego Garden Show

Pteris ensiformis 'Victoriae'
silvery "Victoria fern"

Pteris tremula
"Australian bracken"

Pyrrosia lingua *(Diplazium)*
"Tongue fern" in Kew Bot. G., England

Rumohra adiantiformis
(Polystichum) "Leather fern"

Pyrrosia longifolia cristata
epiphytic in Malaysia

Solanopteris bifrons *(Polypodium)*
curious epiphyte of Perú

Stenochlaena tenuifolia *(palustris)*
"Liane fern" in St. Petersburg, Fla.

Doodia caudata
"Hacksaw fern" in New Zealand

Sadleria cyatheoides, *a tree fern*
"Pygmy cyathea", or "Mau-Mau fern" in Hawaii

Thelypteris hexagonoptera
"Beech fern" in Montreal Bot. Garden, Quebec

Gymnocarpium robertianum
"North. oak-fern" in Oxford Bot. G.

Thelypteris noveboracensis
"New York fern" at Lake Mohawk, N.J.

Thelypteris phegopteris
"Long beechfern" in Washington

Woodsia obtusa *(POLYPOD.)*
"Blunt-lobed woodsia" in Vermont

Woodwardia areolata
"Netted chain fern" in Sussex, N.J.

Woodwardia fimbriata *(POLYP.)*
"Giant chain fern" in Brit. Columbia

Lycopodium clavatum *(LYCOPOD.)*
"Staghorn clubmoss" in Oregon

Lycopodium obscurum
"Princess pine" (Alabama to Alaska)

Lycopodium squarrosum
"Rock tassel" in Cairns, Queensland

Lygodium japonicum *(SCHIZ.)*
"Climbing fern" in Kew Bot. Gardens

Lycopodium complanatum
"Ground cedar" in Ontario

Tmesipteris tannensis *(PSILOT.)*
primitive epiphyte in New Zealand

Asparagus retrofractus *(LIL.)*
"Zigzag asparagus" in So. Africa

Asparagus densiflorus cv. 'Myers'
"Plume asparagus" in San Diego

Asparagus densiflorus 'Sprengeri'
"Sprengeri fern" in Vista, Calif.

Selaginella lepidophylla *(SEL.)*
"Resurrection plant" in Texas

Selaginella kraussiana 'Brownii'
"Dwarf clubmoss" from Azores

Selaginella martensii *(Mexico)*
in col. Botanic Garden Munich

Selaginella kraussiana *(denticulata)*
"Spreading clubmoss" (Cameroon)

Selaginella tamariscina
in Ikeda Park, Tokyo

Selaginella emmeliana *(pallescens)*
"Sweat plant" in Colombia

Aptenia cordifolia 'Red Apple'
"Baby sunrose" (So. Africa)

Carpanthea pomeridiana
(Mesembryanthemum) (Cape Prov.)

Carpobrotus acinaciformis
on the Algarve coast, Portugal

Carpobrotus edulis
"Hottentot fig" (Cape to Karroo)

Astridia herrei
from Namaqualand, So. Africa

Carruanthus ringens *(Cape Prov.)*
in Bermuda Botanic Garden

Cephalophyllum alstonii
"Red spike" in Escondido, Calif.

Delosperma 'Alba'
"Disneyland ice-plant" in California

Delosperma tradescantioides
in the Transvaal

Delosperma sutherlandii
(So. Africa: Transvaal, Natal)

Delosperma cooperi
in Jena Bot. Garden, Thuringia

Dorotheanthus bellidiformis
"Livingstone daisy" in variety

Drosanthemum hispidum *(true species)*
showy shrub in habitat, Namibia, Southwest Africa

Drosanthemum speciosum *of the Transvaal*
in Stellenbosch Botanic Garden, So. Africa

Delosperma aberdeenensis *(Cape)*
in Duesseldorf Bot. G., Germany

Drosanthemum hispidum *(close-up)*
in Kirstenbosch Bot. G., So. Africa

Drosanthemum floribundum
"Rosea ice-plant" in California

Fenestraria aurantiaca
"Window plant" at H. Johnson, Calif.

Frithia pulchra
"Purple Baby-toes" (Transvaal)

Glottiphyllum fragrans *(Cape)*
in Bermuda Botanic Garden

Glottiphyllum linguiforme
"Green tongue-leaf" (So. Africa)

Malephora latipetala
in San Diego, California

Malephora luteola *(Hymenocyclus)*
"Yellow trailing ice-plant"

Lampranthus aureus
in Mexico City Bot. Garden

Lampranthus conspicuus
(Mesembryanthemum) (Cape)

Lampranthus multiradiatus *(roseus)*
on Table Mountain, Cape Town

Lampranthus productus
"Purple ice-plant" in So. Calif.

Oscularia deltoides *(Mesembryanth.)*
"Pink fig-marigold" in Vista, Calif.

Lampranthus spectabilis
"Red ice-plant" (Cape Prov.)

Lampranthus tricolor, *on the Transvaal Veld*
"Copper ice-plant", flowers open to the warming sun

Lampranthus haworthii, *from the Cape, So. Africa*
col. Botanic Garden Essen, W. Germany

Mesembryanthemum crystallinum
"Ice plant" naturalized in California

Pleiospilos purpusii *(Cape Prov.)*
"Living-rock cactus", Fallbrook, Calif.

Pleiospilos magnipunctatus
spreading "Stone-plant" (So. Africa)

Lithops dorotheae *(AIZ.)*
"Living stones" from Cape Prov.

Ruschia karrooica *(AIZ.)*
Karroo Desert, So. Africa

Rhombophyllum nelii *(AIZ.)*
"Elkhorns" of South Africa

Agave schidigera *(AGAV.)*
"Feather agave" of Mexico

Agave cerulata *(Baja California)*
San Diego Floral Exhibition

Agave filifera, *"Thread agave"*
in Botanic Garden, Mexico City

Agave franzosinii
in Bermuda Botanic Garden

Agave parryi huachucensis
from Southern Arizona

Agave parviflora, *of Sonora*
"Little princess agave"

Agave americana 'Marginata'
"Variegated Century plant" in Vista, California

Agave sebastiana, *with inflorescence
on Isla Cedros, Baja California, Mexico*

Agave attenuata, *with arching inflorescence*
"Dragon tree agave" in Funchal, Madeira

Agave americana, *"Century plant" or "American aloe"*
in view of the Acropolis, Athens, Greece

Agave atrovirens, *inflorescence*
"Pulque agave" in Oaxaca, So. Mexico

Agave ferdinandi-regis
"King agave" (N.E. Mexico)

Agave victoriae-reginae
"Queen agave" (Nuevo Leon, Mexico)

Doryanthes excelsa *(E. Australia)*
the "Spear lily" above Funchal, Madeira

Agave barbadensis
on Antigua, West Indies

Agave neglecta *(Florida)*
large rosette in San Diego Zoo

Agave sisalana, *"Sisal hemp"*
on plantation in Tanzania, E. Africa

Agave angustifolia 'Marginata'
"Variegated Caribbean agave"

Adenium obesum *(APOC.)*
"Desert rose" grafted on oleander

Adenium swazicum flore pleno
"Dble. Impala lily" in Vista, Calif.

Adenium swazicum
"White Impala lily" in Mozambique

Pachypodium succulentum *(APOC.)*
in Botanic Gard. Essen, W. Germany

Pachypodium lamierei
"Madagascar palm"

Ceropegia haygarthii *(ASCLEP.)*
"Wine-glass vine" of Natal

Huernia reticulata *(ASCLEP.)*
in Cape Prov., South Africa

Hoodia rosea *(ASCLEP.)*
"African hat plant" (Botswana)

Caralluma praegracilis *(ASCLEP.)*
in Pretoria, the Transvaal

Hechtia glomerata *(BROMEL.)*
in Dahlem Bot. Garden, Berlin

Furcraea selloa 'Marginata'
"Variegated false agave" on Madeira

Furcraea macdougallii *(Oaxaca)*
with Dave Grigsby, Vista, Calif.

Furcraea foetida 'Striata'
(gigantea) "Mauritius hemp"

Stapelia gigantea
"Giant toad plant" of Zululand

Stapelia hirsuta *(ASCLEP.)*
"Hairy starfish flower" (Cape Prov.)

Stapelia nobilis
(Transvaal and Mozambique)

Stapelia semota var. lutea
(Orbea) from Tanzania

Stapelia variegata *(Orbea)*
"Carrion flower" (Cape Prov.)

Lithops bella *(AIZ.)*
"Pretty stone-face" (So. Africa)

Fenestraria rhopalophylla
"Baby toes" (Namibia) (AIZ.)

Faucaria tigrina *(AIZ.)*
"Tiger-jaws" (Cape Prov.)

Gibbaeum dispar *(AIZ.)*
from Cape Prov., So. Africa

Ophthalmophyllum schlechteri
(So. Africa: Namaqualand)

Conophyllum auriflorum *(AIZ.)*
(aureum in hort.)

Astrophytum capricorne *(CACT.)*
"Goat's-horn" (No. Mexico)

Stapeliopsis neronis *(ASCLEP.)*
rare species of S.W. Africa

Dyckia fosteriana *(BROMEL.)*
"Silver and Gold dyckia" (Paraná)

Astrophytum myriostigma
"Bishop's cap" (C. Mexico)

Astrophytum asterias
"Sand dollar" (No. Mexico)

Astrophytum ornatum
"Monk's hood" of Hidalgo

Astrophytum 'ornatum x asterias'
col. New York Botanical Garden

Borzicactus madisoniorum *(Perú)*
(syn. Matucana, Submatucana)

Borzicactus celsianus, *grafted pl.*
"Cotton tree" in Kwangchow, China

Borzicactus tuberculatus
of the Rio Maranon, Perú

Carnegiea gigantea
flowers of the "Saguaro"

Borzicactus hendriksenianus ssp.
densilatus *(Oreocereus ritteri)*

Ariocarpus trigonus elongatus
"Living rock" of Mexico

Buiningia aurea
col. in Brazil by Glass & Foster

x Aporophyllum 'Star-fire'
(Aporocactus x Epiphyllum)

Cereus peruvianus 'Monstrosus'
"Curiosity plant" in California

Cereus peruvianus *of So. America*
in Tegelberg col., California

Cereus 'Peruvianus hybrid'
popular "Column cactus" in Calif.

Cephalocereus palmeri
"Woolly torch cactus" in E. Mexico

Cleistocactus strausii
"Silver torch" of Bolivia

Chamaecereus sylvestri
"Peanut cactus" of No. Argentina

Cleistocactus jujuyensis
"Argentine silver torch"

Cleistocactus smaragdiflorus
"Firecracker cactus" (Uruguay)

Cleistocactus baumanii
"Scarlet bugler" of Paraguay

Coryphantha laredoi
of Coahuila, Mexico

Coryphantha cornifera
in Hidalgo, Mexico

Mammillaria longimamma
(Dolichothele), "Finger-mound"

Discocactus silicicola *(grafted)*
(Brazil: Mato Grosso)

Echinopsis multiplex, *with quail*
"Easter-lily cactus" in Vista, Calif.

Cleistocactus hyalacanthus *of hort.*
at Del Mar Floral Exh., California

Echinocereus pentalophus
in Munich Bot. Garden, Germany

Echinofossulocactus arrigens
"Brain cactus" of Central Mexico

Echinocereus fasciculatus
"Pitaya" in So. Arizona

Echinocer. pectinatus neomexicanus
"Rainbow cactus" decorated with eyes

Cephalocereus senilis
"Old Man cactus" of Hidalgo, Mexico

Cochemiea poselgeri
"Long-hook cactus" (Baja California)

x Chamaelopsis 'Firechief' *(Chamaecereus x Lobivia)*
Harry Johnson bigeneric hyb. in California

Echinocereus reichenbachii perbellus
"Lace cactus" at Abbey Gardens, Carpinteria, Calif.

Echinocer. pectinatus neomexicanus
(dasyacanthus hort.) "Yellow pitaya"

Espostoa lanata, *"Soroco",*
"Peruvian Old man" in California

Echinocereus pamanesiorum
in Zacatecas habitat, Mexico

Echinocactus grusonii, *with flowers*
"Golden barrel" in C. Mexico

Ferocactus diguetii carmenensis
on Isla Cerralvo, Gulf of California

Ferocactus stainesii var. pringlei
(Central Mexico)

Ancistrocactus uncinatus
"Hook cactus" in Arizona

Ferocactus macrodiscus *(Oaxaca)*
"Visnaga" in Bermuda Bot. Garden

Ferocactus peninsulae (horridus)
"Fish-hook cactus" of Baja California

Epithelantha micromeris, *crested*
grafted on Trichocereus trichogonus

Ferocactus wislizenii *(emoryi)*
with Zapotec Indian in Sonora

Ferocactus glaucescens
"Blue barrel cactus" (C. America)

Carnegiea gigantea, *"Giant Saguaro"*
along the highway, near Gila Bend, Arizona

Cephalocereus alensis, *"Woolly torch cactus"*
at Lawrence Welk Village, Escondido, Calif.

Espostoa lanata, *"Soroco" of the Indians*
in the Cordilleras of Northern Perú

Backebergia militaris, *curious tree cactus*
with Mazateco Indian in Michoacan, Mexico

Escobaria bella *of Texas
in Bermuda Bot. Garden*

Gymnocalycium guerkeanum
with green flowers (Bolivia)

Leuchtenbergia principis
"Prism cactus" of Mexico

Gymnocalycium mihanovichii
"Plain chin cactus" (Paraguay)

Gymnocalycium mihanov. friedr. 'Rubra'
"Red-cap" grafted on Hylocereus

Gymnocalycium denudatum
"Spider cactus" (Brazil, Argentina)

Lophophora williamsii, *"Peyote"
"Sacred mushroom" of Mexico*

Harrisia martinii *(Eriocereus)
nocturnal "Moon cactus" (Argentina)*

Erythrorhipsalis pilocarpa
"Bristle-tufted twig cactus"

Cephalocereus royenii
on Curacao, West Indies

Lophocereus schottii, *"Senita"*
"Totem-pole" in Sonora, Mexico

Myrtillocactus geometrizans
"Blue myrtle" near Oaxaca, Mexico

Stenocereus thurberi *(Lemaireocereus),* "Pitahaya"
"Organ-pipe cactus" near Tucson, Arizona

Corryocactus krausii, *in habitat*
near Cochabamba, in the Andes of Bolivia

Melocactus intortus
"Turk's cap" in the West Indies

Lophocereus schottii 'Monstrosus'
"Monstrose totem" in California

Hylocereus undatus
night-blooming "Honolulu Queen"

Coryphantha potosiana *(clavata)*
(San Luis Potosi, Mexico)

Copiapoa laui
Esmeralda, Chile

Coryphantha henricksonii
of Chihuahua, Mexico

Coryphantha vivipara
"Spiny stars" (Alberta to Texas)

Espostoa melanostele
(Pseudoespostoa) of W. Perú

Ariocarpus scapharostrus
"Rock cactus" of Nuevo Leon

Gymnocactus subterraneus
var. zaragosae *(Mexico)*

Echinocereus nivosus
clustering sp. (Coahuila, Mexico)

Eriosyce ceratistes aurea
near Santiago de Chile

Mamillopsis senilis
in the Sierras of W. Mexico

Lobivia cylindrica
from Cordoba, Argentina

Gymnocactus viereckii
of Tamaulipas, Mexico

Melocactus matanzanus
"Melon cactus" of Cuba

Lobivia famatimensis nigricans
from Northern Argentina

x Lobiviopsis 'Red Riding Hood'
Pygmy Paramount hyb., California

Lobivia marsoneri, *from No. Argentina*
col. Chas. Glass, Santa Barbara, California

x Lobiviopsis 'Aurora' *(Lobivia x Echinopsis)*
Paramount hybrid by H. Johnson, California

Mammillaria elegans
of Distrito Federal, Mexico

Mammillaria cerralboa
on Isla Cerralvo, Baja California

Mammillaria louisae
in Bermuda Botanic Garden

Mammillaria elongata 'Cristata'
"Brain cactus" in Escondido, Calif.

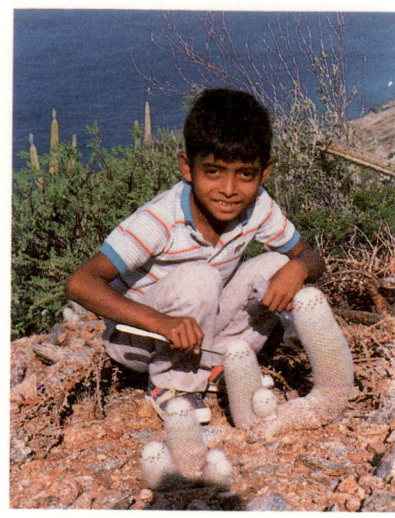

Mammillaria albicans *in Baja Calif.*
Mazateco Indian collecting seed

Mammillaria eriacantha *(C. Mexico)*
col. A. Lau, Fortin de las Flores

Mammillaria parkinsonii
"Owl's-eyes" (C. Mexico)

Mammillaria camptotricha
"Birdsnest" of Querétaro, Mexico

Mammillaria candida *(Mexico)*
"Snowball cactus" in Bermuda Bot. G.

Mammillaria aureilanata *(C. Mexico)*
col. Botanic Garden Bermuda

Mammillaria bachmanii *(Mexico)*
Bermuda Bot. Garden, Hamilton

Mammillaria baxteriana *(pacifica)*
from Baja California Sur

Mammillaria hahniana
"Old Lady cactus" (Mexico)

Mammillaria brauneana (N.E. Mexico)
col. Bermuda Botanic Garden

Mamm. centricirrha (magnimamma hort.)
"Bird's-foot pincushion"

Mammillaria longicoma
col. in San Luis Potosi, Mexico, by Chas. Glass

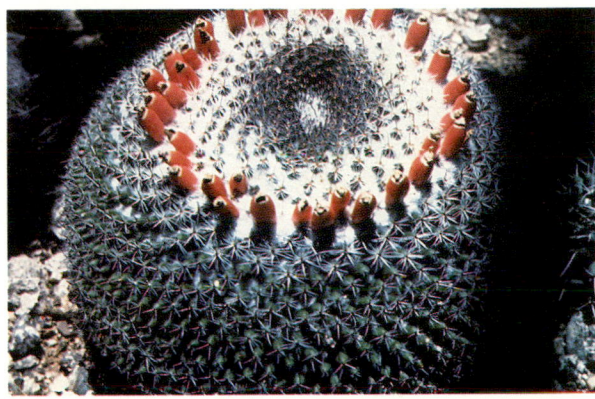

Mammillaria chionocephala, ringed with seed
from Coahuila, Mexico

Mammillaria gracilis pulchella
collected in Hidalgo, Mexico

Mammillaria bucareliensis (C. Mex.)
in Bermuda Botanic Garden

Sulcorebutia rauschii
at Abbey Gardens, Carpinteria, Calif.

Mammillaria saboae var. saboae
miniature from Chihuahua, Mexico

Mammillaria fragilis *(gracilis var.)*
"Thimble cactus" of Hidalgo

Mammillaria geminispina *of Veracruz*
"Whitey" in Bermuda Bot. G.

Mammillaria glassii nominis dulcis
of Nuevo Leon, Mexico

Mammillaria herrerae
(C. Mexico: Querétaro)

Mammillaria bravoae
(Mexico: Guanajuato)

Mammillaria longiflora *(Krainzia)*
from Durango, Mexico

Mammillaria huizilipochtli fa.
in Tomellin Canyon, Mexico, by A. Lau

Mammillaria ebenacantha *(Mexico)*
in col. Bermuda Bot. Garden

Mammillaria martinezii
of South Mexico

Mammillaria melanocentra
in Coahuila, No. Mexico

Mammillaria oteroi, *by Glass & Foster*
col. in Alta Mizteca, Oaxaca

Mammillaria verhaertiana
(Baja California, Mexico)

Mammillaria tegelbergiana
from Chiapas, So. Mexico

Mammillaria winteriae
in col. Bermuda Bot. Garden

Mammillaria glassii ascensionis
col. Glass & Foster in Nuevo Leon

Mammillaria pennispinosa
collected in Coahuila, Mexico

Mammillaria spinosissima
of Southern Mexico

Mammillaria prolifera haitiensis
clustering sp. from Haiti

Mammillaria multiseta
of Puebla, Mexico

Mammillaria zeilmanniana
"Strawberry cactus" of Guanajuato

Neolloydia unguispina v. laui
collecting of seed in Zacatecas

Neolloydia conoidea
in Fortin de las Flores, Veracruz

Melocactus maxonii
of Guatemala, C. America

Neoporteria nidus fa. senilis
"Birdsnest" grafted on Cereus

Neoporteria islayensis
(Islaya flavida) of So. Perú

Neoporteria rapifera *(Chile)*
in col. Bermuda Botanic Garden

Notocactus crassigibbus
"Ball cactus" from So. Brazil

Notocactus mammulosus
"Lemon ball" of Argentina

Oroya peruviana *(C. Perú)*
from the Andes at 3800 m alt.

Notocactus leninghausii *(So. Brazil)*
"Golden ball" in Fallbrook, Calif.

Nyctocereus serpentinus
a "Queen of the Night" of Mexico

Notocactus magnificus
(Eriocactus) of So. Brazil

Opuntia erinacea ursina, *"Grizzly bear"*
in habitat on the high Mohave Desert, California

Carnegiea gigantea, *the "Giant Saguaro"*
in habitat, near Tucson, Sonoran Desert of Arizona

Notocactus herteri
north of Montevideo, Uruguay

Notocactus scopa
"Silver ball of Paraguay"

Notocactus uebelmanianus
in col. Bermuda Bot. Garden

Opuntia bergeriana, *tree-type
naturalized in Italy*

Opuntia arbuscula, *"Pencil cholla"
of Arizona and Sonora*

Opuntia basilaris
"Beaver-tail" on Sonoran Desert

Opuntia chrysacantha
of Hidalgo, Mexico

Opuntia subulata
"Eve's-pin" with artificial berries

Opuntia dillenii, *"Tuna"
Southeast U.S. to West Indies*

Opuntia elata
"Orange tuna" in Paraguay

Opuntia humifusa *(compressa)
Ontario to Montana; Texas*

Opuntia imbricata
"Chain-link cactus" (Colorado to Mex.)

Opuntia cholla, *in Mexican habitat on Isla Cerralvo, Gulf of California*

Opuntia rubescens *(Consolea) ornamental Nopal, in Puerto Rico*

Opuntia galapageia *(Galapagos Islands, Ecuador)*

Opuntia falcata *in flower* Tree opuntia from Haiti

Opuntia ficus-indica, *"Nopal tree" "Indian fig" of Trop. America*

Op. ficus indica 'Burbank spineless' *bearing edible Tuna fruit*

Opuntia phaeacantha *"Prickly pear" of Southwest deserts*

Opuntia juniperina *"Apache Prickly pear" of Arizona*

Opuntia fulgida *"Jumping cholla" in Arizona*

Opuntia microdasys, *"Bunny-ears"*
with Helichrysum straw-flowers

Opuntia microdasys rufida
"Cinnamon cactus", in Texas

Opuntia schickendantzii
"Lion's-tongue" of Argentina

Opuntia violacea Santa Rita
"Blue blade" in Arizona

Opuntia fragilis, *"Pigmy tuna"*
in Teton Nat'l. Park, Wyoming

Opuntia vulgaris *(monacantha)*
"Irish mittens" in Argentina

Opuntia brasiliensis
"Tropical tree Opuntia" in Tonga

Opuntia polyacantha
from Alberta, Western Canada

Opuntia tuna, *in Madeira*
(West Indies to Jamaica)

Parodia borealis
from La Paz area, Bolivia

Parodia ayopayana
of Puente Pilatos, Bolivia

Parodia ocampoi
in Cochabamba, Bolivia

Parodia mairanana
from Santa Cruz, E. Bolivia

Parodia sanguiniflora
"Red Tom Thumb" from No. Argentina

Parodia echinus *(Bolivia)*
from the Cordilleras at 3600 m alt.

Parodia penicillata
in Salta, No. Argentina

Parodia ritteri *(Bolivia)*
col. A. Lau, Fortin de las Flores

Parodia nivosa *(No. Argentina)*
col. Harry Johnson, California

Parodia subtilihamata
rare sp. from Salitre, Bolivia

Quiabentia chacoensis
in Quail Bot. Gard. Encinitas, Calif.

Mammillaria elongata
"Golden stars" of Hidalgo

Rebutia albiflora *(Aylostera)*
in col. Bermuda Bot. Garden

Rebutia cajasensis *(Bolivia)*
col. H. Johnson, Fallbrook, Calif.

Rebutia calliantha
(krainziana var.) (No. Argentina)

Rebutia spegazziniana
(No. Argentina)

Rebutia senilis, *"Fire crown"*
near Salta, No. Argentina

Rebutia heliosa, *in Escondido, Calif.*
grafted on Myrtillocactus

Rebutia nivea *(Bolivia)*
H. Johnson col., Bonsall, Calif.

Rebutia marsoneri
in Jujuy, No. Argentina

Rebutia minuscula
"Red crown" of Tucuman, Argentina

Rebutia narvaecense, *in Carpinteria, Calif.*
from border area of Bolivia-Paraguay-Argentina

Rebutia glomeriseta *(Sulcorebutia)*
from Cochabamba, Bolivia (Glass & Foster photo)

Rebutia fiebrigii *(Aylostera)*
"Crown cactus" (Bolivia)

Rebutia violaciflora
"Rosy crown cactus"

Sulcorebutia albo-pectinata
from Cochabamba, Bolivia

Nopalxochia phyllanthoides
epiphytic "German Empress" (Mexico)

Nopalxochia phyll. 'Pink Nightie'
in De Luz, Fallbrook, California

Nopalxochia ackermannii
"Orchid cactus" of Chiapas, Mex.

Cryptocereus anthonyanus *of Chiapas*
"Anthony's rick-rack" basket plant

Epiphyllum laui *(So. Mexico)*
from Tumbala jungle of Chiapas

Selenicereus grandiflorus *(Jamaica)*
"Queen of the Night" or "Moon cactus"

Epiphyllum 'Grace Ann'
"Orchid cactus" in Santa Barbara

Epiphyllum chrysocardium *(Marniera)*
"Corazon de Oro" of Chiapas

Epiphyllum oxypetalum *(Mexico)*
night-blooming "Pond-lily cactus"

Stenocereus marginatus
"Organ pipe" near Mexico City

Pachycereus pringlei, *"Mexican giant"*
on Isla Cerralvo, Gulf of California

Stenocereus thurberi *(Lemaireocereus)*
"Arizona organ pipe", Baja California

Cereus hexagonus, *"Blue columns"*
in coffee country, Cali, Colombia

Thelocactus lophothele longispina
from Chihuahua, Mexico

Stenocereus gummosus, *"Dagger cactus"*
on Isla Cerralvo, Baja California

Trichocereus spachianus
nocturnal "Torch cactus" (Argentina)

Uebelmannia pectinifera
black-spine species of Brazil

Trichocereus huaschua rubriflorus
(Helianthocereus) (Catamarca, Argentina)

Thelocactus McDowellii
of Coahuila, No. Mexico

Weingartia hediniana
(Gymnocalycium) of Bolivia

Trichocereus peruvianus
"Peruvian torch" (Perúvian Andes)

Turbinicarpus laui
(Mexico: San Luis Potosi)

Turbinicarpus pseudomacrochele
(Toumeya) miniature of Mexico

Weingartia longigibba
from Oropeza Prov., Bolivia

Wilcoxia poselgerei
(So. Texas to Coahuila)

Wilcoxia albiflora *of Mexico*
at Abbey Gardens, Carpinteria, Calif.

Wittia panamensis
epiphytic in Venezuela

Pereskia grandifolia *(Brazil)*
"Rose cactus" in Cape Town

Schlumbergera truncata
(Zygocactus) "Thanksgiving cactus"

Schlumbergera orssichiana
"Christmas Countess" by Dr. Ira Slade

Rhipsalis capilliformis
"Old man's head" of Brazil

Heliocereus speciosus
"Sun cactus" (C. Mexico)

Rhipsalis quellebambensis
"Red Mistletoe"

Rhipsalis baccifera *(cassutha)*
"Mistletoe cactus" in Kenya

Rhipsalis paradoxa
"Chain cactus" in São Paulo

Rhipsalis houlletiana
"Snowdrop cactus" (S.E. Brazil)

Aeonium haworthii *(CRASS.)*
in "Chiquito" of Mexico

Senecio articulatus 'Variegatus'
"Candle plant" in De Luz, California

Aeonium arboreum 'Variegatum'
at Rancho Verde, San Diego

Senecio rowleyanus *(COMP.)*
"String of beads" (Namibia)

Senecio deflersii
"Cucumber plant" of Arabia

Senecio jacobsenii
(Notonia petraea) of Namaqualand

Aeonium arboreum 'Schwarzkopf'
Duesseldorf Bot. Garden, Germany

Senecio kleinia
(Kleinia neriifolia) Canary Isl.

Senecio scaposus
"Silver coral kleinia" (So. Africa)

Aeonium tabuliforme
"Saucer plant" (Tenerife)

Aeonium percarneum
of Gran Canaria

Aeonium hierrense, *with flowers
from the Canary Islands*

Chiastophyllum oppositifolium
"Moss-rose" showing inflorescence

Cotyledon ladismithiensis
"Cub's paws" of the Karroo

Cotyledon macrantha
(East Cape Province)

Crassula portulacea 'Gollum'
P. Hutchison mutation in California

Crassula arta *(Cape Prov.)*
in Fallbrook, Calif.

Crassula falcata *(Rochea)*
"Scarlet paintbrush" in California

Aichryson x domesticum 'Variegatum'
"Youth and Old Age" (Aeonium)

Adromischus festivalis *(cooperi)*
"Plover eggs" (Cape Prov.)

Adromischus maculatus *(rupicola)*
"Calico hearts" (So. Africa)

Aeonium undulatum *(Gran Canaria)*
"Saucer plant" or "Green platters"

Senecio serpens (Kleinia repens)
"Blue chalk sticks" (Cape Prov.)

Cotyledon undulata
"Silver crown" (So. Africa)

Crassula hemisphaerica
"Arab's turban" (Namibia)

Crassula grisea
from Namaqualand, So. Africa

Crassula alstonii, *in De Luz, Calif.*
(Cape Prov. and Namibia)

Crassula 'Morgan's Beauty'
in Oceanside, California

Crassula perforata 'Marginata'
"Variegated necklace vine"

Crassula ovata 'Minima variegata'
in Old Town, San Diego

Crassula lactea
"Taylor's patch" of Natal

Crassula arborescens *(So. Africa)*
"Silver dollar" in California

Crassula ovata *(argentea) in bloom*
(arborescens of hort.), "Jade plant"

Crassula streyi
from Natal, So. Africa

Crassula lycopodioides
"Toy cypress" of Namibia

Crassula pseudolycopodioides
"Princess pine" of Southwest Africa

Crassula corymbulosa 'Campfire'
Quail Bot. Gard., Encinitas, Calif.

Crassula 'Jade Necklace'
at Los Angeles Flower Show

Crassula teres *(barklyi)*
"Rattlesnake" of Southern Africa

Aeonium lindleyi *in hort.*
miniature in California trade

Crassula picturata
from Cape Prov., So. Africa

Dudleya candida
on Coronado Isl., Baja California

Cremnophila nutans *(Sedum)*
from Moretos, Mexico

Dudleya brittonii
at Del Mar Floral Expo., Calif.

Dudleya greeneae *(Isles off Calif.)*
in Bermuda Botanic Garden

Dudleya pachyphytum *(Dr. A. Lau)*
on Cedros Island, Mexico

Dudleya virens, *"Alabaster plant"*
on coast of Southern California

Dudleya farinosa
on Point Lobos, No. California

Echeveria 'Doris Taylor'
"Woolly rose" (setosa hyb.)

Echeveria lindsayana *(Mexico)*
col. Tegelberg's, Lucerne, Calif.

Echeveria listida *(prob. Mexico)*
(New Jersey Cactus Soc.)

Echeveria crenulata 'Valentine'
"Scallop echeveria" in Fallbrook, Calif.

Echeveria crenulata *'Pettycoat'*
frilled hyb. at De Luz, Calif.

Echeveria derenbergii
"Painted lady" in Oaxaca

Echeveria gibbiflora 'Mauna Loa'
on the Island of Hawaii

Echeveria 'Festival', *(harmsii hyb.)*
for cut flowers, in So. California

Echeveria gibbiflora
in Jardin Botanico, Mexico City

Echeveria 'Haageana'
"Fruit cups" in Bermuda Bot. Garden

Echeveria 'Desmetiana' *hort.*
in Villach, Austria carpet bed

Echeveria peacockii
"Peacock echeveria", So. Mexico

Echeveria elegans
"Mexican snowball" of Hidalgo

Echeveria x imbricata
popular "Hen-and-chicks" in California

Echeveria chihuahuaensis
Northwestern Mexico

Echeveria pulidonis *(E. Mexico)*
col. Bermuda Botanic Garden

Echeveria agavoides *(Urbinia)*
"Lipstick" of San Luis Potosi

Echeveria x kirchneriana
(carmicolor x derenbergii)

Echeveria secunda glauca
"Blue hen-and-chicks" in Germany

Echeveria shaviana
col. Merry Gardens, Camden, Maine

Graptopetalum paraguayense
(Sedum weinbergii) "Ghost plant"

Kalanchoe 'Grandiflora hybrid'
in 6 cm pot, Aalsmeer, Holland

Kalanchoe manginii
"Madagascar wax-bells"

Kalanchoe blossfeldiana 'Tom Thumb'
"Flaming Katy" for Christmas

Kalanchoe fedtschenkoi
"Purple scallops" (Madagascar)

Kalanchoe teretifolia *(bentii)*
from India and Arabia

Kalanchoe beharensis
"Elephant-ears" in Vista, California

Kalanchoe daigremontiana
with plantlets along margins

Kalanchoe pinnata *(Bryophyllum)*
"Miracle-leaf" of India

Kalanchoe laciniata *(glaucescens)*
"Christmas tree kalanchoe" in Calif.

Kalanchoe tomentosa
"Panda plant" in California

Orostachys iwarenge fa. 'Fuji'
highly variegated Japan cultivar

Kalanchoe gastonis-bonnieri
"Life plant" w. plantlets on leaves

Kalanchoe marmorata
"Pen-wiper" from Ethiopia

Kalanchoe fedtschenkoi 'Marginata'
"Aurora Borealis" in Santa Barbara

Kalanchoe tubiflora *(Bryophyllum)*
"Chandelier plant" tipped w. plantlets

Pachyphytum werdermannii *(Mexico)*
col. Quail Bot. Garden, Encinitas

x Pachyveria haagei
bigeneric "Jewel plant"

Sedum suaveolens
tropical Durango, W. Mexico

Sedum adolphi *in bloom*
"Golden sedum" (Mexico)

Sedum pachyphyllum
"Jelly-beans" of Oaxaca

Sedum dendroideum praealtum
flowering in Funchal, Madeira

Sedum aizoon, *in bloom*
from Siberia to Japan

Sedum cauticola *(Japan)*
in the Mountains of Honshu

Sedum sordidum *of C. Japan*
Chanokideira Alpine Gard., Nikko

Sedum rubrotinctum *(guatemalense)*
"Christmas cheer" in Nice, France

Sedum kamtschaticum
in Duesseldorf Bot. Garden, Germany

Sedum makinoi
in Fallbrook, California

Sedum sempervivoides
(Asia Minor to Caucasus)

Sedum reflexum
in Bergen, So. Norway

Sedum spathulifolium pruinosum
"Capa Blanca" in Vancouver, B.C.

Sedum morganianum, *"Burro-tail"*
basket at Kew Gardens, England

Sedum sieboldii 'Medio-variegatum'
at Garden Center in Germany

Sedum sieboldii *(Japan)*
"October plant" in West Los Angeles

Sedum pluricaule 'Rose Carpet'
colorful spreader from Sakhalin and Hokkaido

Sedum pilosum *(Umbilicus pubescens)*
biennial from the mountains of Asia Minor to Caucasus

Rochea coccinea *(So. Africa)*
(Crassula rubicunda of hort.)

Sedum spectabile
"Live-forever" in Seoul, Korea

Sedum telephium 'Autumn Joy'
Scandinav. Hort. Expo., Lund, Sweden

Orostachys japonicus
(South Korea to Japan)

Sempervivum albidum 'Oddity'
curious Oregon mutation

Sedum telephioides
(No. Carolina to Illinois)

Sempervivum arachnoideum
"Cobweb houseleek" in Florence, Italy

Sempervivum tectorum
"Hen and chickens" (Europe)

Aeonium ciliatum 'Rubrum'
in Orotava, Tenerife

Jovibarba arenaria *(Sempervivum)*
in Alps near Salzburg, Austria

Jovibarba hirta *(Sempervivum)*
near Bratislava, Czechoslovakia

Jovibarba heuffelii *(S.E. Europe)*
in Jena Bot. Garden, E. Germany

Euphorbia milii var. imperatae
"Mini-Christthorn" (Madagascar)

Euphorbia milii 'Albiflora'
"White crown-of-thorns" in Germany

Euphorbia 'Giant Christ-thorn'
in Carlsbad, California

Tacitus bellus *(CRASS.)*
"Chihuahua flower" of Mexico

Euphorbia tirucalli
"Elephant bush" of Uganda

Euphorbia ammak 'Variegata'
col. Exotic Botanic Garden, Monaco

Umbilicus rupestris *(CRASS.)*
"Pennywort" (Britain to Asia Minor)

Euphorbia grandicornis
"Cowhorn euphorbia" (Natal to Kenya)

Euphorbia caput-medusae
"Medusa's head" near Cape Town

Euphorbia aeruginosa *(Transvaal)*
Johnson Cact. Gard., Fallbrook, Calif.

Euphorbia neohumbertii
colorful column of Madagascar

Euphorbia canariensis
"African cereus" on Tenerife

Euphorbia fianarantsoae *(Madagascar)*
by J. Bogner, Munich Botanic Garden, Germany

Euphorbia punicea *of Jamaica and Cuba*
in col. Jardin Botanique 'Les Cèdres' French Riviera

Didierea trollii *(DIDIER.)*
of arid S.W. Madagascar

Euphorbia candelabrum (erythraea)
from Eritrea, East Africa

Euphorbia ingens *"Candelabra tree"*
with floral cephalia, in Vista, Calif.

Euphorbia xantii *(Baja California)*
as hedge in Fallbrook, Calif.

Euphorbia lactea 'Cristata'
crested "Elkhorn" or "Frilled fan"

Euphorbia lactea
"Dragonbone" in Madras, So. India

Euphorbia loricata *(Cape Prov.)*
at Lindemann, Fallbrook, Calif.

Monadenium torreyi *(Tanzania)*
Grigsby's Cact. Gard., Vista, Calif.

Euphorbia squarrosa
of Albany, Cape Prov.

Euphorbia paralias
"Seaside spurge" on Madeira

Alluaudia comosa *(DIDIER.)*
flowering in S.W. Madagascar

Euphorbia xylophylloides
Nymphenburg Bot. Garden, Munich

Pedilanthus tithymaloides 'Varieg.'
"Zigzag plant" on Dominica, W. Indies

Beaucarnea gracilis *(AGAV.)*
young "Pony-tail" of Yucatán

Idria columnaris *(FOUQ.)*
"Boojum tree" of Baja California

Hesperaloe parviflora *(AGAV.)*
"Western aloe" in Van Horn, Texas

Fouquieria splendens *(FOUQ.)*
"Ocotillo" near Palm Springs, Calif.

Fouquieria diguetii *(Mexico)*
near Hermosillo, Sonora

Pelargonium crassicaule *(GERAN.)*
"Succulent geranium" of Namibia

Sarcocaulon pennicillatus *(GERAN.)*
from Southwest Africa

Calibanus hookeri *(AGAV.)*
caudiciform "Mexican boulder"

Aloe divaricata *(S.W. Madagascar)*
col. Munich Botanic Garden

Aloe acutissima antanimorensis
in Bermuda Bot. Garden

Aloe aculeata *(Transvaal)*
in col. New York Bot. Garden

Aloe ciliaris *(Cape Prov.)*
"Climbing aloe"

Aloe dorotheae *(Tanzania)*
col. Wright, De Luz, California

Aloe rauhii *(Tuléar, Madagascar)*
col. H. Johnson, Fallbrook, Calif.

Aloe bellatula, *in California*
from Central Madagascar

Gasteria rawlinsonii *(Cape Prov.)*
in Grigsby col., Vista, California

Aloe elgonica *(Kenya)*
in Munich Bot. Garden

Aloe thraskii, *in Vista, Calif.*
showy tree from Zululand

Aloe bainesii, *giant tree*
in Cape Town Bot. Garden

Aloe bainesii, *flowering*
on Sunset Ranch, Vista, California

Aloe arborescens *(So. Africa)*
"Candelabra aloe" in San Diego

Aloe dichotoma *(Cape to Namibia)*
"Dragon tree aloe", Encinitas, Calif.

Aloe africana *(Transvaal)*
"Spiny aloe" in Los Angeles Bot. Garden

Aloe camperi *(eru)*
in Eritrea, N.E. Africa

Aloe ferox, *"Ferocious aloe"*
flowering in Worcester, Cape Prov.

Aloe wickensii, *flowering*
in North Transvaal habitat

Haworthia setata var. major
from the Karroo, Cape Prov.

Aloe striata
"Coral aloe" (Cape Prov., Namibia)

Aloe saponaria (LIL.)
"Soap aloe" in No. Transvaal

Aloe polyphylla (So. Africa)
"Spiral aloe" of the Drakensberg

Aloe variegata (Cape Prov.)
"Partridge breast" of the Karroo

Gasteria gracilis 'Variegata'
at Del Dios, Escondido, Calif.

Gasteria liliputana (LIL.)
miniature "Ox-tongue" (Cape Prov.)

Haworthia fasciata (LIL.)
"Zebra haworthia" (So. Africa)

Haworthia cooperi
"Window haworthia"

Peperomia columella (columnaris)
snake-like succulent from Perú

Peperomia asperula (PIP.)
interesting succulent from Hawaii

Portulacaria afra 'Macrophylla'
"Giant elephant bush" of So. Africa

Aloe haworthioides aurantiaca
Johnson Cact. Gard., Fallbrook, Calif.

Aloe marlothii *(LIL.)*
flowering in Kenya habitat

Aloe barbadensis *(vera hort.)*
"Medicine plant" in San Diego, Calif.

Aloe plicatilis *(So. Africa)*
"Fan aloe" on Cape of Good Hope

Aloe nobilis *(Cape Prov.)*
"Gold tooth aloe" in Vista, Calif.

Haworthia limifolia *(LIL.)*
"Fairy washboard" of Swaziland

Peperomia graveolens *(PIP.)*
in Wright Nursery, De Luz, Calif.

Haworthia truncata *(Cape Prov.)*
"Clipped window plant" of the Karroo

Aloe harlana *(Ethiopia)*
at Seaborn Del Dios, Escondido, Calif.

Brighamia citrina *(Hawaii)*
"Alula" or "Tree lobelia" of Kauai

Dorstenia crispa *(MORAC.)*
curious xerophyte of Somalia

Yucca valida *(AGAV.) (Mexico)*
at Del Mar Hort. Expos., California

Sansevieria pinguicula *(AGAV.)*
agave-like, from N.E. Kenya

Sansevieria trif. 'Golden Hahnii'
"Variegated birdsnest"

Sansevieria ehrenbergii
in habitat, Teita Hills, Tanzania

Lewisia cotyledon *(PORT.)*
in Cold Spring, New York

Portulaca grandiflora *(PORT.)*
"Rose moss" of Brazil

Portulaca oleracea 'Wildfire'
"Flowering purslane" in Vista, Calif.

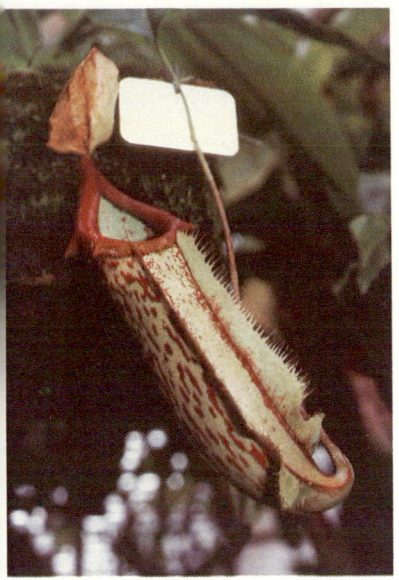

Nepenthes x mixta *(NEPENTH.)*
tropical "Pitcher plant"

Nepenthes rafflesiana
from rainforest in Malaya

Nepenthes x coccinea
in Dahlem Botanic G., Berlin

Neoregelia carolinae 'Marechalii'
center cup insect trap (BROM.)

Sarracenia purpurea *(SARR.)*
"Sweet pitcher plant" in N. Jersey

Nepenthes 'Superba'
in col. Marcel Lecoufle, France

Nepenthes madagascariensis
in Tolagnaro, S.E. Madagascar

Nepenthes ampullaria *(NEP.)*
terrestrial in Malaysia

Nepenthes maxima
tropical pitcher plant of Celebes

Drosera capensis (DROS.)
"Daily dew" of South Africa

Drosera pedata, (E. Australia)
in col. Munich Botanic Garden

Drosera binata (dichotoma)
"Twin-leaved sundew" (New Zealand)

Utricularia inflata (LENTIB.)
aquatic "Bladderwort" in Louisiana

Drosera rotundifolia
"Common sundew" (insectivorous leaf)

Heliamphora nutans (SARRAC.)
"Sun pitcher" of Roraima, Guayana

Byblis gigantea (BYBL.)
from Swan River, West Australia

Pinguicula caudata (moranensis)
"Tailed butterwort" of Mexico

Pinguicula vulgaris (LENTIB.)
hardy "Butterwort" in Alberta, Canada

Dionaea muscipula *(DROS.)*
"Venus fly-trap" of the Carolinas

Sarracenia flava *(SARR.)*
"Yellow pitcher plant" (Virginia)

Darlingtonia californica *(SARR.)*
"Cobra plant" in Oregon

Sarracenia rubra *(S.E. U.S.)*
"Red pitcher plant" in Japan

Sarracenia psittacina *(Louisiana)*
"Parrot pitcher plant" in St. Louis

Sarracenia minor
"Hooded pitcher plant" (Florida)

Sarracenia alata
"Yellow trumpets" (Alabama to Texas)

Drosera aliciae *(DROS.)*
"Daily dew" of So. Africa

Sarracenia leucophylla
"Fiddler's trumpet" in Mississippi

Solanum integrifolium
"Tomato-fruited eggplant" in California

Solanum mammosum (SOLAN.)
"Nipple fruit" in Indonesia

Jatropha cathartica (EUPH.)
"Jicamilla" of the Rio Grande

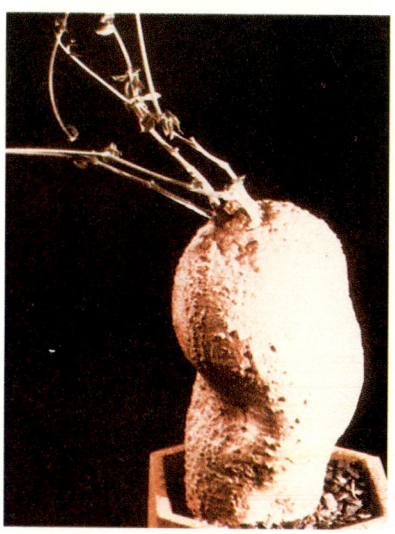

Fockea edulis (ASCLEP.)
forms edible caudex (So. Africa)

Bowiea volubilis (LIL.)
"Climbing onion" of So. Africa

Fouquieria fasciculata (FOUQ.)
"Teocotillo" of Durango, Mexico

Dioscorea elephantipes (DIOSC.)
"Elephant-foot" of the Transvaal

Dioscorea macrostachys (Testudinaria)
weird "Tortoise plant" of Mexico

Ipomoea holubii (CONVOLV.)
with massive caudex (So. Africa)

Amorphophallus rivieri (ARAC.)
"Devil's tongue" of Vietnam

Amorphophallus campanulatus
giant inflorescence, in New Guinea

Rhododendron macgregoriae (ERIC.)
on Goroka Highlands, New Guinea

Mammillaria parkinsonii, crested
"Sadsack" in Encinitas, California

Mammillaria nejapensis, crested
"Smiling Jack", 25 cm across, in San Diego

Brassica oleracea acephala
"Flowering cabbage" w. cabbage doll

Ruscus hypoglossum (LIL.)
"Mouse-thorn" bearing small flowers

Tolmiea menziesii (SAXIFR.)
"Piggy-back plant" in Alaska

Phoradendron juniperinum *(LORANTH.)*
"Mistletoe" at Grand Canyon, Arizona

Phoradendron californicum
"Calif. mistletoe" on the Mohave

Viscum album *(Europe, Asia Minor)*
"Mistletoe" in Black Forest, Germany

Mimosa pudica *(LEGUM.)*
"Sensitive plant" of Brazil

Sequoia sempervirens *(TAXOD.)*
"Redwood" burl of No. California

Kalanchoe pinnata *(CRASS.)*
"Miracle leaf" of India

Solanum melongena ovigerum
"Egg tree" of Asia

Schlumbergera bridgesii *(CACT.)*
grafted on Hylocereus, in China

Rafflesia tuan-mudae
parasite on Mt. Kinabalu, Borneo

Schinus molle, *"California pepper tree"*
first in California, Mission San Luis Rey, 1830

Cocos nucifera, *"Coconut palm"*
seven trunks from one seed, Rarotonga, South Pacific

Adansonia digitata, *giant "Baobab"*
upside-down tree in Kruger Park, Transvaal

Dracaena draco *(AGAV.), ancient "Dragon tree"*
at Icod, Tenerife, Canary Islands

Psittacanthus americanus
"Parrot flower", parasitic in Yucatán

Sarcodes sanguinea, *"Snow plant"*
in Sequoia National Park, California

Bugula species, *a moss-animal*
"Air-fern" or "Neptune plant"

Adansonia digitata *(BOMB.)*
African "Baobab" planted in Barbados, 1795

Cordyline terminalis 'Ti' *(AGAV.)*
Polynesian dancers wearing skirts of "Ti" leaves at Waikiki

Yucca aloifolia, *"Mata Rosa Blanca"*
good luck egg shells, Puerto Rico

Prunus persica, *old peach tree*
at Imperial Palace, Kyoto, Japan

Euphorbia pulcherrima, *"Poinsettia"*
flowering from hard wood, Madeira

Chlidanthus fragrans
"Perfumed fairy-lily" of Perú

Amaryllis belladonna
"Belladonna lily" (So. Africa)

x Amarcrinum memoria-corsii
(Amaryllis x Crinum)

Clivia nobilis, *"Cape clivia"*
"Green-tip Kafir lily" (So. Africa)

Clivia miniata *(Imantophyllum)*
"Kafir lily" of Natal

Clivia miniata 'Citrina'
at Chelsea Flower Show, London 1984

Clivia x cyrtanthiflora
col. Munich Bot. Garden, Germany

Dichelostemma pulchellum
(Brodiaea pulchella) in Oregon

Eucharis grandiflora *(Urceolina)*
"Amazon lily" in Cuernavaca, Mexico

Eurycles sylvestris *(Pancratium)*
"Brisbane lily" in Tahiti

Curculigo latifolia
"Palm grass" of Malaya

Brodiaea elegans
"Harvest brodiaea" in California

Habranthus tubispathus
from Argentina

Crinum macowanii
(Transvaal, Natal, Zimbabwe)

Ixiolirion tataricum
"Tartar lily" of So. Russia

Crinum erubescens
(So. Mexico to Brazil)

Leucocoryne ixioides
"Glory-of-the-sun" of Chile

Hypoxis mexicana *(HYPOX.)*
"Gold-eye grass" (Durango, Mex.)

Leucojum autumnale
"Autumn Snowflake" (Mediterr. reg.)

Leucojum vernum
"Spring snowflake" of C. Europe

Leucojum aestivum
"Summer snowflake" (Europe)

Crinum bulbispermum *(capense)*
Cape of Good Hope, So. Africa

Crinum amabile
"Giant spider lily" in Sumatra

Crinum moorei
"Longneck spider lily" of Natal

Crinum americanum
"Swamp lily" in South Florida

Crinum asiaticum
"Poison bulb" on Oahu, Hawaii

Crinum x powellii 'Roseum'
in Botanic Garden Hamburg

Crinum x powellii
(bulbispermum x moorei)

Cyrtanthus mackenii, *in plastic bags*
"Ifafa lily" in Taipo, China

Crinum augustum *(amabile hort.)*
"Queen Emma lily" in Mauritius

Galanthus nivalis 'Flore pleno'
"Double snowdrops" in N. Jersey

Galanthus nivalis, *"Snowdrop"*
spring-blooming in New Zealand

Galanthus elwesii
"Giant snowdrop" (Asia Minor)

Haemanthus multiflorus *(Scadoxus)*
in Kirstenbosch Bot. Gard., So. Africa

Haemanthus katherinae *of Natal*
"Catherine Wheel" in Durban

Haemanthus katherinae 'King Albert'
(Scadoxus) "Blood flower"

Haemanthus albiflos
"White paintbrush" (So. Africa)

Ipheion uniflorum
"Spring-star flower" in Argentina

Ipheion uniflorum 'Wisley Blue'
spring-blooming in Britain

Hippeastrum retic. 'Striatifolium'
"Stripeleaf amaryllis" in Singapore

Hippeastrum 'Leopoldii hybrid'
giant-flowered "Dutch amaryllis"

Hippeastrum puniceum *(equestre)*
"Barbados lily" in West Indies

Hippeastrum vittatum
'King of the Striped' *in Holland*

Hippeastrum 'Vittatum hybrid'
commercial amaryllis of florists

Hippeastrum 'Papilio' *of Argentina*
"Butterfly amaryllis" (Wayside 1986)

Hippeastrum vittatum
from the Peruvian Andes

Lycoris radiata
"Red spider lily" of China

Lycoris squamigera
"Resurrection lily" in Japan

Hymenocallis caribaea
"Spider lily" in Aruba, Antilles

Hymenocallis expansa
Taj Mahal Gardens, Agra, India

Hymenocallis x festalis *(Ismene)*
(narcissiflora x longipetala)

Hymenocallis littorialis
"Crown beauty" in Singapore

Hymenocallis narcissiflora
(Ismene calathina), "Peruv. daffodil"

Hymenocallis speciosa
"Winter spice" in W. indies

Pancratium maritimum
"Sea daffodil" (Spain to Syria)

Phaedranassa carmiolii
"Queen lily" of Costa Rica

Narcissus triandrus
'Silver Chimes' *in Bermuda*

Narcissus 'Gold Medal', *"Pot daffodil"*
for Easter bloom at Roehrs, New Jersey

Narcissus jonquilla 'Minnow'
fragrant "Jonquils" in Spring

Narcissus tazetta orientalis
"Chinese sacred lily" in Shanghai

Narcissus poeticus 'Praecox'
large-flowered cv., in Germany

Narcissus poeticus
fragrant "Poet's narcissus" in Spain

Narcissus tazetta papyraceus
"French Paper-white"

Narcissus pseudonarcissus
"Trumpet narcissus" of W. Europe

Narcissus jonquilla 'Tittle-tattle'
at German Garden Show, Duesseldorf

Narcissus cyclamineus
'February Silver', *in Bermuda*

Narcissus bulbocodium
"Petticoat daffodil" in So. France

Narcissus asturiensis
"Miniature trumpet" of Spain

Narcissus cyclamineus
(Spain and Portugal)

Narcissus dubius
in Southern France

Narcissus x incomparabilis
'Gustav Mahler', *large-cupped*

Narcissus jonquilla 'Baby Moon'
floriferous miniature in Lisse, Holland

Narcissus tazetta 'Geranium'
"Polyanthus narcissus"

Narcissus poeticus 'Actaea'
"Pheasant's eye"

Narcissus tazetta *(canaliculatus)*
(Mediterranean region)

Narcissus jonquilla *miniature*
"Common jonquil" in Spain

Narcissus tazetta 'Ziva strain'
large-flowered "Paper white" from Israel

Narcissus triandrus
"Angel's tears" from Spain

Polianthes tuberosa *(AGAV.)*
sweet "Tuberose" of Mexico

Polianthes tuberosa flore pleno
"Double-flowered tuberose"

Vallota speciosa *(AMARYLL.)*
"Scarborough lily" of So. Africa

Urceolina peruviana *(AMAR.)*
"Urn flower" (Boliva, Perú)

Triteleia hyacinthina *(AMARYLL.)*
"Wild hyacinth" (Brit. Columbia)

Triteleia laxa *(Brodiaea)*
"Triplet lily" of California

Zephyranthes lindleyana *(AMAR.)*
"Zephyr lily" (San Luis Potosi, Mex.)

Zephyranthes grandiflora
"Rain lily" of Guatemala

Zephyranthes candida
"Fairy lily" in Argentina

Nerine undulata
November flowering in Virginia

Nerine bowdenii
"Spider lily" of So. Africa

Nerine sarniensis
"Guernsey lily" (Cape Prov., So. Africa)

Sprekelia formosissima
"Aztec lily" in Guatemala

Zephyranthes atamasco
"Atamasco lily" in Virginia

Tulbaghia violac. 'Tricolor'
"Tricolor garlic" in California

Zephyranthes citrina
a "Rain lily" of Guyana

Sternbergia lutea
"Winter daffodil" (Asia Minor)

Stenomesson variegatum
from Ecuador to Chile

Paramongaia weberbaueri
"Cojomaria" of Perú

Zephyranthes tubispatha
"Zephyr lily" of the W. Indies

Zephyranthes rosea
"Cuban Zephyr lily" near Havana

Amorphophallus koratensis
curious tuber of Thailand

Amorphophallus rivieri *(Hydrosme)*
"Devil's tongue" of Vietnam

Amorphophallus campanulatus
"Telingo potato" of New Guinea

Arisaema dracontium
"Green dragon" (Québec to Texas)

Caladium lindenii 'Magnificum'
fancy "Yautia" from Colombia

Arum maculatum
"Lords and ladies" (Britain)

Caladium bicolor, *inflor.*
"Heart of Jesus" (Guyana, Brazil)

Caladium x hortul. 'Candidum'
"White caladium"

Caladium x hort. 'Mrs. Halderman'
"Fancy-leaved caladium"

Zantedeschia aethiopica *(ARAC.)*
"White calla" in Cape Prov.

Zantedeschia elliottiana
"Yellow calla" of So. Africa

Zantedeschia 'Green Goddess'
in Escondido, California

Zantedeschia 'Albo-maculata'
"Spotted calla" in Calif. hort.

Xanthosoma atrovirens *(ARAC.)*
"Yautia" of So. America

Arum italicum *(ARAC.)*
"Italian arum" (Europe, No. Africa)

Begonia grandis *(evansiana)*
"Hardy begonia" (China, Japan)

Begonia tuberhybrida
'Rubro-marginata', *"Tuberous beg."*

Begonia tuberhybrida pendula
"Basket begonia" in Norway

Dahlia pinnata, *Decorative type*
in ceramic pot, in Hong Kong

Dahlia pinnata 'Casey'
"Formal decorative" in Denver, Colo.

Dahlia pinnata 'Figaro'
"Single-fl." in Berlin Bot. Garden

Dahlia coccinea, *"Acocotli"*
in Oaxaca, So. Mexico habitat

Dahlia pinnata 'Fairie'
"Pompon dahlia"

Dahlia pinnata 'Collarette'
semi-double bicolor type

Dahlia pinnata 'Mignon'
"Dwarf single-flowered"

Dahlia pinnata 'Schweizerland'
"Formal decorative type"

Dahlia pinnata 'Unwin's Dwarf'
colorful dwarf strain

Dahlia pin. 'Siegerland' *(COMP.)*
"Cactus-type" in Germany

Dahlia pin. 'Summer Smile'
"Formal decorative type"

Dahlia pin. 'Garnet Spoon'
showy "Anemone class"

Ipomoea batatas *(CONVOLV.)*
"Sweet potato" or "Yam" in water

Ipomoea holubii *(Merremia)*
with caudiciform base (So. Africa)

Sinningia speciosa fyfiana
'Emp. Frederick', *florists' "Gloxinia"*

Babiana purpurea
"Baboon flower" (Cape Prov.)

Babiana rubrocyanea *(So Africa)*
striking "Winecup babiana"

Babiana stricta *(IRID.)*
"Upright Cape flower" of So. Africa

Acidanthera murieliae
"Peacock orchid" of Ethiopia

Chasmanthe floribunda
"Pennants" in Bermuda Bot. Garden

Chasmanthe aethiopica
on Island of Madeira

Crocosmia x crocosmiiflora
"Montbretia" in hort.

Crocosmia masoniorum
"Golden swan tritonia" (Transvaal)

Crocosmia pottsii *(Tritonia)*
"Slender tritonia" on Malta

Crocus vallicola
"Autumn crocus" of the Caucasus

Curtonus paniculatus
"Pleated leaves" (Transvaal)

Ferraria crispa *(undulata)*
"Orchid iris", Cape Prov., So. Africa

Crocus chrysanthus 'Blue Pearl'
late winter-blooming "Snow crocus"

Crocus etruscus in Spring
in the Toscana, No. Italy

Crocus medius, *autumn blooming
in Maritime Alps of France*

Crocus speciosus albus, *flowering through variegated
ivy at home in S.E. Europe to Turkey and Iran*

Crocus niveus
autumn-flowering in mountains of So. Greece

Crocus tommasinianus
at home from Hungary to Dalmatia, Yugoslavia

Crocus vernus 'Pickwick'
spring-blooming, striped "Dutch crocus"

Crocus vernus 'Giant Purple' *(neapolitanus)
March-blooming in New York Botanic Garden*

Crocus flavus *(aureus)*
March-blooming in New Jersey

Crocus vernus 'Orange'
early spring-blooming

Crocus vernus 'Purpureus'
purple "Dutch crocus"

Crocus sieberi
winter-flowering in Greece

Crocus sativus *in Spain*
"Saffron crocus" or "Flor de Oro"

Crocus tournefortii
"Autumn crocus" of Greek Isl.

Crocus speciosus, *autumn fl.*
in Royal Botanic Gardens Kew

Dierama pendulum
"Angel's fishing rods" in Transvaal

Dierama pulcherrimum, *"Wandflower"*
Strybing Arboretum, San Francisco

Freesia x hybrida 'Stockholm Red'
in Bergianska Garden, Sweden

Freesia refracta
"Common freesia" in So. Africa

Freesia x hyb. 'Czardas'
at Los Angeles Hort. Show, Arcadia

Homeria breyniana 'Aurantiaca'
"Cape tulip" on Cape of Good Hope

Freesia x hybrida
various cultivars, in Bermuda

Freesia x hybrida 'White Swan'
in Botanic Garden, Bermuda

Moraea ramosissima
"Branching moraea" (So. Africa)

Moraea huttonii *(spathacea)*
"Butterfly iris" of Transvaal

Homeria breyniana *(collina)*
in New York Bot. Garden

Gladiolus x hortulanus
"Garden gladiolus"

Gladiolus x colvillei
"Coronado hybrid"

Gladiolus x hortulanus nanus
'D'Artagnan' *(Butterfly hyb.)*

Gladiolus byzantinus
of the Mediterranean region

Gladiolus communis
on Mallorca, Spain

Gladiolus segetum *(italicus)*
"Corn flag" in Gibraltar

Gladiolus tristis
"Marsh Afrikander" of Natal

Watsonia beatricis, *"Bugle lily"*
in Kirstenbosch Bot. G., Cape Town

Watsonia pyramidata 'Alba'
on the Cape Peninsula, in April

Iris 'Wedgwood', *"Dutch iris"*
U.S. Exper. Sta., Beltsville, Maryland

Gynandriris sisyrinchium *(Iris)*
on the Algarve, Portugal

Iris bucharica *(Juno sect.)*
Duesseldorf Bot. Garden, Germany

Iris xiphioides
'Queen of the Blues'

Iris xiphioides *(latifolia hort.)*
in the Pyrenées of Spain

Iris xiphium, *"Spanish iris"*
in Oxford Bot. Garden, England

Iris histrioides 'Major'
from Armenia (Reticulata sect.)

Iris aucheri *(Juno sect.)*
(Turkey to Syria, Iran)

Iris xiphioides 'Montblanc'
an "English iris" of hort.

Iris xiphium hyb. 'Ideal'
bulbous "Dutch iris" in Maryland

Iris tingitana *(xiphium var.)*
from Tangiers, Morocco

Iris cycloglossa *(Juno section)*
in temple of Miletus, Turkey

Iris reticulata 'Cantab'
with scented flowers, in England

Iris pumila, *with tuber-like rhizome*
(C. Europe to So. Russia, Asia Minor)

Iris reticulata
bulbous dwarf iris from Russia to Iraq

Iris reticulata 'Joyce'
of dwarf habit, with large scented flowers

Freesia x hybrida 'Ballerina'
large-flowered Dutch hybrid

Hesperantha vaginata
"Evening flower" of So. Africa

Geissorhiza rochensis
"Wine-cups" near Cape Town

Ixia polystachya hybrid
"Corn-lily" in Madeira

Ixia maculata ornata 'Nelson'
in Funchal, Portugal

Ixia maculata *(yellow form)*
"Golden ixia" of S.W. Cape Prov.

Ixia speciosa *(So. Africa)*
"Red corn lily" in New Zealand

Sparaxis tricolor 'Harlequin'
"Harlequin flower" on Madeira

Sparaxis tricolor 'Firebrand'
"Scarlet wand-flower" in N. Zealand

Tritonia crocata 'McKenzie'
October-blooming in New Zealand

Tritonia crocata 'Incomparabile'
"Flame freesia" on Madeira

Tritonia rubrolucens *(rosea)*
in England

Lapeirousia laxa *(cruenta)*
"Woodland painted petals" (Transvaal)

Tigridia pavonia *(IRID.)*
"Tiger-flower" in Mexico

Tigridia bicolor
"Mexican shell flower" in Oaxaca

Agapanthus africanus *(LIL.)*
"African lily" in Kirstenbosch

Agapanthus africanus 'Minor'
"Peter Pan lily" in California

Trimeza caribaea *(Neomarica)*
"Fan iris" of Brazil (IRID.)

Agapanthus orientalis
"Common agapanthus" of the E. Cape

Agapanthus campanulatus
"Bell agapanthus" of Natal

Albuca nelsonii *(LIL.)*
"Sentry-in-the-box" in San Diego

Allium aflatunense *(LIL.)*
"Ornamental onion" of C. Asia

Allium cepa, *"Garden onion"*
in Bern Bot. Garden, Switzerland

Allium cernuum
"Wild onion" (New York to Calif.)

Allium christophii
"Stars of Persia" in Thuringia

Allium fistulosum
"Spanish onion" from Siberia

Allium flavum, *"Yellow onion"*
(S.W. Europe to Western Asia)

Allium giganteum *(Himalayas)*
"Giant ornamental onion"

Allium karataviense *(Turkestan)*
in Kew Botanic Gard., England

Allium moly, *"Lily leek"*
at Chelsea Flower Show, London

Allium obliquum
from Tien Shan Mts., China

Allium narcissiflorum *(Italy)*
in Botanic Garden Munich

Allium neapolitanum *(Mediterr. reg.)*
"Daffodil garlic" in Kew Bot. Gard.

Allium oreophilum *(ostrowskianum)*
(Caucasus to C. Asia)

Allium pulchellum *(carinatum)*
of So. Europe to W. Asia

Allium rosenbachianum
"Showy onion" from Turkestan

Allium sativum, *bearing bulbils*
"Garlic" of S.W. Asia, India

Allium senescens *(tuberosum)*
"Chinese chives" (Nepal to China)

Allium senescens glaucum
curve-leaf form in England

Allium schoenoprasum
culinary "Chives" in Germany

Allium sphaerocephalum
"Round-head garlic" of No. Africa

Allium suworowii *(C. Asia)*
Royal Bot. Gardens Kew, England

Allium subhirsutum
at Kew Bot. Gardens, England

Allium stipitatum
giant onion of Central Asia

Allium triquetrum
"Triangle onion" of So. Europe

Allium tuberosum, *"Oriental garlic"*
in Somerset Arboretum, New Jersey

Allium unifolium
of California coastal mountains

Allium ursinum
"Bear's garlic" of Siberia

Watsonia pyramidata *(IRID.)*, *"Pink watsonia"*
in Hottentot-Holland Mountains, South Africa

Allium giganteum *(LILIAC. or AMARYLL.)*
"Giant Ornamental onion", Botanic Gardens, Berlin

Dahlia pinnata hybrid 'Informal decorative' *(COMP.)*
dwarfed in terracotta pots, Beijing, China

Vallota speciosa *(Cyrtanthus) (AMARYLL.)*
"Scarborough lily", Bot. Garden, Duesseldorf, Germany

Asphodelus cerasiferus *(ramosus)*
"Asphodel" in Spain

Asphodelus albus
"Greek asphodel" (Greece)

Asphodelus microcarpus
Kew Botanic Gardens, England

Camassia cusickii
"Camass" of N.E. Oregon

Camassia quamash *(esculenta)*
"Beargrass" or "Common camass"

Camassia leichtlinii
(Brit. Columbia to No. California)

Camassia quamash alba
"Indian hyacinth" in New Jersey

Camassia scilloides alba
"Wild hyacinth" in Arizona

Camassia scilloides
"Indigo squill" (Penna. to Texas)

Calochortus ambiguus
"Mariposa lily" of Arizona

Calochortus kennedyi
"Desert mariposa" (Arizona to Sonora)

Calochortus venustus *in var.*
"Butterfly tulip" of California

Calochortus gunnisonii
"Sego lily", Tucson, Arizona

Calochortus splendens *(California)*
"Lilac mariposa" near Monterey

Calochortus caeruleus
"Cat's ears", Sierra Nevada, Calif.

Calochortus weedii
"Mariposa" in Encinitas, Calif.

Calochortus lyallii
"White mariposa" of Pacific N. West

Calochortus nuttallii
"Lilac Sego lily" in Utah

Cardiocrinum giganteum *(Tibet)*
"Heart lily"in Bern Bot. G., Switz.

Convallaria majalis
"Lily of the Valley" in Spring

Amianthium muscitoxicum
"Fly poison" in Pennsylvania

Chionodoxa luciliae
"Glory of the snow"in Crete

Chionodoxa sardensis
"Blue Glory of the Snow" (Asia Minor)

Chionodoxa nana *(cretica)*
Mountains of Crete

Colchicum autumnale
"Autumn crocus" in Germany

Colchicum cilicicum *(byzantinum)*
from Taurus Mts. of Turkey

Colchicum speciosum
"Showy autumn crocus" (Caucasus)

Hyacinthoides hispanica
(Endymion) "Spanish bluebell"

Hyacinthoides non-scripta
"English bluebell" in London

Galtonia candicans
"Giant summer hyacinth" (So. Africa)

Lachenalia aloides (tricolor)
"Cape cowslip" of So. Africa

Lachenalia pustulata
col. New York Bot. Garden

Gloriosa superba
"Crisped glory-lily" (Transvaal)

Eucomis autumnalis (undulata)
Kirstenbosch Bot. Garden, So. Afr.

Eucomis bicolor
"Pineapple lily" of Natal

Eucomis comosa (punctata)
"Pineapple flower" from Transvaal

Erythronium americanum
"Trout lily" (Nova Scotia to Florida)

Erythronium 'Golden Torch'
at Keukenhof Show in Holland

Erythronium grandiflorum
"Glacier lily"in Montana snow

Erythronium montanum
"Dog-tooth violet" in Oregon

Erythronium 'Pagoda'
(tuolumnense x revolutum)

Erythron. revolutum 'White Beauty'
"Great Fawn lily"

Erythronium tuolumnense
"Coast Fawn lily" of California

Fritillaria verticillata
(C. Asia to China, Japan)

Fritillaria pudica
"Yellow bell" in Wyoming

Fritillaria amoena
in Duesseldorf Alpine Garden

Fritillaria imperialis 'Aurora'
in Keukenhof Gardens, Holland

Fritillaria imperialis
"Crown Imperial" (W. Himalayas)

Fritillaria atropurpurea
in the Sierra Nevada, California

Fritillaria imperialis 'Lutea'
"Yellow Crown-imperial" in Penna.

Fritillaria imperialis
'Lutea maxima', *in Holland*

Fritillaria involucrata
from Maritime Alps of France

Fritillaria meleagris
"Checkered lily" in Britain

Fritillaria persica *(Turkey)*
at New York Flower Show

Hyacinthus orientalis
'Blue Jacket' *for spring bloom*

Hyacinthus orientalis
'Pink Pearl' *(early hyacinth)*

Hyacinthus orientalis 'Ostara'
early, very fragrant

Hyacinthus orientalis
'Delft Blue' *(midseason)*

Hyacinthus orientalis
'Carnegie' *(late blooming)*

Hyacinthus orientalis
'Lady Derby' *(midseason)*

Lilium pumilum *(tenuifolium)*
"Coral lily" of China

Lilium cernuum
from Korea and No. China

Hyacinthus orientalis
'Anne Marie,' *for early forcing*

Lilium x hollandicum *(umbellatum)*
"Candlestick lily"

Lilium 'Prosperity'
(Mid-century hybrid)

Gloriosa rothschildiana
"Glory lily" of Uganda

Lilium auratum
"Goldband lily" of Japan

Lilium amabile 'Enterprise'
"Korean lily" in San Francisco

Lilium regale
"Regal lily" of Szechwan, China

Lilium concolor, *miniature*
"Star lily" (Manchuria to Japan)

Lilium candidum
"Madonna lily" in Berlin Bot. Garden

Lilium hansonii *(Japan, Korea)*
"Japanese Turk's-cap"

Lilium martagon
"Turban lily" in Stockholm, Sweden

Lilium lancifolium *(tigrinum)*
"Tiger lily" of China

Lilium x aurelianense
"Aurelian lily" in Germany

Lilium martagon album
"Turk's cap"in Germany

Lilium monadelphum
"Caucasian lily"

Lilium pensylvanicum *(dauricum)*
"Candlestick lily" in Japan

Lilium superbum *(E. No. America)*
"American Turk's cap"

Lilium maritimum
"Coast lily" near San Francisco

Lilium henryi
from Yunnan, W. China

Lilium 'Connecticut King'
Mid-century Asiatic hybrid

Lilium 'Enchantment'
Mid-century hybrid in Oregon

Lilium 'Limelight' *(Aurelian hyb.)*
Longwood Gardens in Penna.

Lilium 'Imperial Crimson' *(Oriental hyb.)*
"Empress lily" in Gresham, Oregon

Lilium parvum
"Sierra lily" in So. Oregon

Lilium canadense
"Meadow lily", from Nova Scotia to Alabama

Lilium washingtonianum var. minus
"Shasta lily" from Mt. Shasta, California

Lilium speciosum rubrum
"Japanese lily" from Japan

Lilium parryi, *"Lemon lily"*
on Mt. San Jacinto, near Palm Springs, Calif.

Lilium szovitsianum *(monadelphum var.)*
"Caucasus lily" along the Black sea

Lilium longiflorum 'Ace', *florists' "Easter lilies"*
blooming at Roehrs Exotic Nurseries, New Jersey

Littonia modesta
"Climbing lily" of So. Africa

Hesperocallis undulata
"Desert lily" in Arizona

Lloydia serotina
"Alp lily" in Alaska

Milla biflora
"Mexican star flower" (C. America)

Melanthium virginicum
"Bunch flower" (New York to Texas)

Muscari armeniacum
"Grape hyacinth" in Holland

Muscari botryoides *(So. Europe)*
"Common grape hyacinth" in Virginia

Muscari comosum
"Tassel hyacinth", Delos, Greece

Muscari racemosum *(neglectum)*
"Meadow hyacinth" in France

Ornithogalum arabicum
"Star of Bethlehem" in Portugal

Ornithogalum caudatum
"False sea-onion" in New York Bot. G.

Ornithogalum montanum
"Snow-flake" in Oxford Bot. Garden

Ornithogalum nutans
"Nodding Star of Bethlehem"

Ornithogalum saundersiae
"Giant chincherinchee" (So. Africa)

Ornithogalum thyrsoides
"Chincherinchee" or "Wonder-flower"

Puschkinia scill. libanotica
in Keukenhof Gardens, Holland

Puschkinia scilloides
"Striped squill" (Asia Minor)

Ornithogalum umbellatum
"Summer snow-flake" in England

Sandersonia aurantiaca
"Christmas bells" of Natal

Scilla mischtschenkoana
"Persian blue bell" (N.W. Iran)

Scilla peruviana *(Mediterr. reg.)*
"Peruvian jacinth" in Calif.

Scilla siberica 'Spring Beauty'
in Keukenhof Gard., Holland

Scilla siberica
"Blue squill" of Russia

Tulbaghia fragrans
"Pink agapanthus" (Transvaal)

Thysanotus tuberosus
"Fringed lily" in Australia

Tulbaghia violacea
in Los Angeles Arboretum

Ledebouria socialis *(So. Africa)*
(Scilla violacea) "Silver squill"

Dutch Tulip Festival *in May*
Keukenhof Gardens, Lisse, Holland

Narcissus poeticus, *"Pheasant's eye" narcissus*
naturalized in Botanic Garden, Brooklyn, New York

Easter display *of lilies, hyacinths and tulips*
in Park Avenue bank lobby, Manhattan

Planting of tuberous begonias, Beg. tuberhybrida
for summer bloom at City Hall, Oslo, Norway

Tulipa gesneriana
'Princess Irene' *(single early)*

Tulipa gesneriana
'Olympic Flame' *(Darwin hyb.)*

Tulipa gesneriana 'Paris'
(Triumph tulip)

Tulipa gesner. 'Rose Tendre'
(Darwin) at Brooklyn Bot. G.

Tulipa gesner. 'Robinea'
(Triumph tulip)

Tulipa gesner. 'Rose Beauty'
(Triumph tulip)

Tulipa gesner. 'Topscore'
multi-flowered Triumph

Tulipa gesner. 'Blenda'
(Triumph tulip)

Tulipa ges. 'Karel Doorman'
(Parrot tulip)

Tulipa gesner. 'Makassar'
(Triumph tulip)

Tulipa gesner. 'Eros' *(Peony)*
in Salt Lake City, Utah

Tulipa gesner. 'Balaleika'
(single late, Cottage tulip)

Tulipa gesn. 'Duc van Tol'
early scarlet, since 1850

Tulipa 'Duc van Tol Aurora'
(early flowering single)

Tulipa 'Duc van Tol Violet'
in Keukenhof, Holland

Tulipa 'Couleur Cardinal'
grown since 1845

Tulipa 'Double early' *mixed*
Keukenhof Festival, Holland

Tulipa gesn. 'Peachblossom'
early double flowered

Tulipa gesn. 'Thule'
(Triumph tulip)

Tulipa 'Overdale' *(Triumph)*
Duke Gardens, Somerville, N.J.

Tulipa gesn. 'Kees Nelis'
mid-season Triumph tulip

Tulipa gesn. 'Ace of Spades'
mid-season Darwin tulip

Tulipa gesn. 'Bartigon'
popular pot plant since 1898

Tulipa gesn. 'Black Forest'
(Darwin) Brooklyn Bot. Garden

Tulipa 'Merry Widow' *(Triumph)*
'Lustige Witwe' in Germany

Tulipa gesn. 'Sweet Harmony'
(Darwin) in Brooklyn Bot. Garden

Tulipa gesn. 'Flying Dutchman'
early May-bl. in New York

Tulipa 'Princess Elizabeth'
(Darwin), May-blooming

Tulipa ges. 'Cream Delight'
mid-season Darwin tulip

Tulipa 'Queen of Bartigons'
(Darwin) May-fl. in Brooklyn

Tulipa gesn. 'Elsie Eloff'
(Cottage tulip) May-fl.

Tulipa gesn. 'Firebird'
Parrot tulip in Holland

Tulipa gesn. 'Georgette'
(Cottage-type) multi-flowered

Tulipa 'Princess Rose'
(Cottage) Brooklyn Bot. G.

Tulipa gesn. 'Ivory Gem'
Cottage tulip in Hillegom, Holland

Tulipa 'Jeanette Heath'
(Single late, Cottage)

Tulipa 'Evening Song'
(Lily-flowered) in New York

Tulipa gesn. 'Westpoint'
(Lily-flowered) in Germany

Tulipa gesn. 'Mariette'
(Lily-type) New York Fl. Show

Tulipa 'Queen of Sheba'
(Lily-flowered) in Brooklyn

Tulipa gesn. 'China Pink'
(Lily-flowered) in May

Tulipa gesn. 'Burgundy Lace'
(Fringed-cottage tulip)

Tulipa gesn. 'Fringed Beauty'
(Double early) in Holland

Tulipa gesn. 'Rembrandt'
(Rembrandt-flamed) late-fl.

Tulipa 'Flaming Parrot'
at Missouri Botanic Garden

Tulipa gesn. 'Nizza'
(Double-late Peony)

Tulipa 'Vincent van Gogh'
(Double-late Peony)

Tulipa saxatilis
fragrant "Cliff tulip" on Crete

Tulipa kaufmanniana
"Waterlily tulip" (Turkestan)

Tulipa kaufmann. 'Corona'
March-blooming, Haarlem, Holland

Tulipa acuminata
"Turkish tulip" of W. Asia

Tulipa fosteriana
(early-fl.) from Central Asia

Tulipa fosteriana 'Juan'
Keukenhof, Holland in May

Tulipa montana
"Mountain tulip" of Iran

Tul. greigii 'Oriental Splendor'
Bot. Gard. Duesseldorf, Germany

Tulipa greigii 'Plaisir'
at New York Flower Show

Tul. greigii 'Red Riding Hood'
Chelsea Flower Show, London

Tulipa batalinii
from Bokhara, So. Cent. Asia

Tulipa dasystemon
Tien Shan Mts., C. Asia

Tulipa chrysantha *(Iran)*
"Golden tulip" in Holland

Tulipa clusiana
"Candy-stick tulip" (Afghanistan)

Tulipa clusiana chrysantha
"Lady tulip" of India

Tulipa kolpakowskiana
miniature of Turkestan

Tulipa linifolia
low species of Bokhara

Tulipa patens *(Siberia)*
in Duesseldorf Bot. G., Germany

Tulipa biflora *(polychroma)*
"Two-flowered tulip" in Turkey

Tulipa praestans 'Unicum'
at Keukenhof, Holland (fl. removed)

Brimeura amethystina
from the Pyrenees of Spain

Tulipa sylvestris
"Florentine tulip" in Italy

Tulipa tarda (dasystemon hort.)
Duesseldorf Bot. G., Germany

Tulipa pulchella (humilis)
"Red crocus tulip" in Brooklyn B. G.

Tulipa urumiensis
of Northwest Iran

Urginea maritima
"Sea onion" in Cyprus

Veltheimia viridifolia
"Forest lily" of So. Africa

Zigadenus fremontii
"Star lily" on Oregon coast

Oxalis deppei *of So. Mexico*
"Lucky clover", during Floriade, Amsterdam

Oxalis adenophylla, *of Chile*
bulbous "Shamrock" in New Zealand

Oxalis acetosella
"European wood sorrel" near St. Petersburg, Russia

Oxalis braziliensis
"Brazilian shamrock" in Montreal Botanic Garden

Oxalis oregana, *in Monterey habitat*
florists' "Irish shamrock"

Oxalis enneaphylla alba
"Scurvy grass" of the Falklands and Patagonia

Oxalis purpurea 'Grand Duchess' (variabilis)
showy bulbous plant in Leucadia, California

Oxalis crassipes
"Lady's sorrel" in Strybing Arboretum, San Francisco

Bletilla striata *(ORCHID.)*
(Bletia hyacinthina) of Vietnam

Oxalis hedysaroides 'Rubra'
"Fire-fern" in Honolulu

Oxalis hirta
winter-blooming in Escondido, Calif.

Oxalis pescaprae
"Bermuda buttercup" in Gibraltar

Oxalis bowiei *(purpurata)*
"Giant pink clover" in New Zealand

Oxalis regnellii
as rubra alba in hort. (So. America)

Oxalis purpurea *(variabilis)*
"Cape oxalis" in So. Africa

Oxalis rubra *(rosea)*
winter-blooming, from Brazil

Oxalis purpurea 'White Duchess'
Quail Bot. Garden, Encinitas, Calif.

Cyclamen repandum *(PRIM.)*
habitat So. France to Rhodos

Cyclamen x pers. 'Rose of Marienthal'
in Aalsmeer, Holland

Cyclamen pers. 'Perle of Zehlendorf'
"Florists' cyclamen" in Berlin

Cyclamen hederifolium
"Baby cyclamen" in New York Bot. G.

Cyclamen purpurascens *(europaeum)*
"Alpine violet" (Europe: Alps)

Cyclamen coum *(PRIM.)*
near Dubrovnik, Croatia

Claytonia virginica *(PORT.)*
"Spring beauty" in Virginia

Narthecium ossifragum *(LIL.)*
"Bog asphodel" in England

Anemone blanda 'Radar' *(RAN.)*
in Keukenhof Gardens, Holland

Anemone blanda *"Greek anemone"*
in Brooklyn Bot. Garden, New York

Anemone blanda 'Atrocaerulea'
"Blue wind flower" in Turkey

Anemone coronaria coccinea
in ancient Pergamon, Asia Minor

Anemone coronaria 'DeCaen hyb.'
superior florists' strain

Anemone canadensis
"Meadow anemone" in Québec

Anemone x fulgens *(annulata)*
"Flameanemone", Chelsea Show, London

Anemone coronaria 'St. Brigid'
in Bermuda Botanic Garden

Anemone halleri, *with fruitheads*
in the Alps of Switzerland

Anemone pulsatilla *(vulgaris)*
"Pasque flower" with whiskered fruit

Anemone tuberosa *(RANUNC.)*
"Tuber anemone" in Arizona

Ranunculus asiaticus
"Persian buttercup" in Nepal

Anemonella thalictroides
"Rue anemone" in Virginia

Ranunculus aconitifolius
"Aconite buttercup" at Kew Bot. G.

Ranunc. asiaticus 'Sakata Dwarf'
superb Japanese double-flowered

Ranunculus ficaria
"Lesser celandine" (Europe, W. Asia)

Eranthis hyemalis *(RANUNC.)*
"Winter aconite" in Hungary

Solanum tuberosum *(SOLAN.)*
"Potato" in flower, Peruvian Andes

Tecophilaea cyanocrocus *(TEC.)*
"Chilean crocus" (Andes of Chile)

Thunbergia gregorii *(gibsonii)*
"Golden glory climber" (E. Africa)

Thunbergia alata *(ACANTH.)*
"Black-eyed Susan" (S.E. Africa)

Thunbergia mysorensis
in San Diego Zoo

Thunbergia grandiflora
"Clock-vine" in the Seychelles

Thunbergia laurifolia
"Laurel clockvine" in Miami

Thunbergia battiscombei
Quail Bot. G., Encinitas, Calif.

Allamanda cathartica fl. pleno
double-flowered, in Singapore

Allamanda violacea *(APOC.)*
"Purple allamanda" in Florida

Allamanda cath. 'Hendersonii'
"Golden trumpet vine" in Tahiti

Mandevilla sanderi *(APOC.)*
"Rose dipladenia" in Vista, Calif.

Mandevilla 'Alice Dupont'
in Longwood Gardens, Pennsylvania

Mandevilla x amabilis
Roehrs Exotic Nurs., New Jersey

Mandevilla boliviensis
in Bot. Garden, Los Angeles

Mandevilla splendens
in Bot. Garden Rio de Janeiro

Mandevilla laxa *(suaveolens)*
"Chilean jasmine" in Argentina

Artabotrys siamensis *(ANNON.)*
"Climbing ylang-ylang"

Beaumontia grandiflora *(APOC.)*
"Herald's trumpet" in Calcutta

Chonemorpha penangensis *(APOC.)*
in Botan. Garden Singapore

Philodendron erubescens (ARAC.)
"Blushing philodendron" in Venezuela

Monstera deliciosa (juv.)
in Ciudad Rodrigo, Spain

Philodendron x evansii
in San Pasqual, California

Syngonium podoph. 'Imperial White'
"Varieg. African evergreen"

Philod. scandens oxycardium
"Cordatum vine" of C. America

Epipremnum aureum (ARAC.)
(Scindapsus) "Pothos" (So. Pacific)

Odontadenia speciosa (APOC.)
in Singapore Botanic Garden

Trachelospermum jasminoides
"Star jasmine" in Encinitas, Calif.

Trachelospermum lucidum (APOC.)
in Portland, Oregon

Bignonia capreolata (BIGN.)
"Cross vine" in Louisiana

Strophanthus gratus (APOC.)
"Climbing oleander" (Trop. W. Africa)

Strophanthus speciosus
"Corkscrew flower" in Sydney Bot. G.

Alyxia ruscifolia (APOC.)
"Sea box" from Queensland

Aristolochia elegans (littoralis)
"Calico flower", in Brazil

Beaumontia fragrans (APOC.)
"Trumpet flower" in Vietnam

Hoya bella (ASCLEP.)
"Miniature wax plant" of India

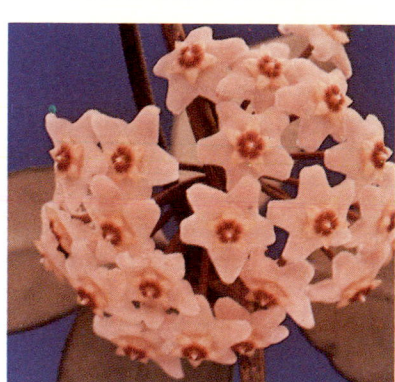

Hoya carnosa
"Wax plant" of South China

Hoya carnosa 'Variegata'
"Varieg. wax vine", in flower

Hoya lacunosa
in Bermuda Bot. Garden

Rhabdadenia biflora (APOC.)
"Rubber vine" of C. America

Pyrostegia venusta (Bignonia)
"Flame vine" in Sri Lanka

Aristolochia trilobata *(ARIST.)*
"Dutchman's pipe" (West Indies)

Aristolochia chessmanniana
in Botanic Gardens Singapore

Hedera canariensis 'Variegata'
on pergola, Del Mar, California

Aristolochia clematitis
"Birthwort" in New York

Araujia sericifera *(ASCLEP.)*
"Bladder flower" in Auckland, N.Z.

Cryptostegia grandiflora
"India rubber vine" on Mauritius

Hoya polyneura *(ASCLEP.)*
"Fishtail hoya" from the Himalayas

Hoya multiflora
"Shooting stars" from Malacca

Hoya carnosa 'Variegata'
"Varieg. wax vine" in California

Stephanotis floribunda *(ASCLEP.)*
fragrant "Madagascar jasmine"

Anemopaegma chamberlaynii *(BIG.)*
in Mogul Gardens, New Delhi, India

Campsis x tagliabuana 'Mad. Galen'
in Auckland Bot. G., New Zealand

Campsis grandiflora *(BIGNON.)*
"Chinese trumpet creeper" in Los Angeles

Distictis buccinatoria *(Bignonia)*
"Trompetilla grande" in Mexico

Cydista aequinoctialis *(BIGN.)*
"Garlic vine" in Oaxaca, Mexico

Distictis x riversii *(BIGN.)*
Nickersen Nurs., Fallbrook, Calif.

Macfadyena unguis-cati *(BIGN.)*
"Cat's claws" on St. Thomas, Virgin Isl.

Campsis radicans
"Trumpet vine" in Florida

Podranea ricasoliana *(So. Africa)*
"Port St. John's creeper" in Mexico

Pyrostegia venusta
"Flaming trumpet" in Sri Lanka

Clytostoma callistegioides
Bignonia violacea in Calif. hort.

Tecomaria capensis
"Cape honeysuckle" in So. Africa

Pseudocalymma alliaceum
"Garlic-scented vine" in Guyana

Pandorea jasminoides
"Bower-of-beauty" in Queensland

Saritaea magnifica
on St. Thomas, Virgin Islands

Tecomanthe dendrophylla
on Cap Ferrat, French Riviera

Tecoma alata *(smithii)*
in Chula Vista, California

Distictis buccinatoria *(Bignonia cherere)* of Mexico
"Scarlet trumpet vine" on Sunset Ranch, Vista, California

Aristolochia grandiflora var. sturtevantii
"Pelican flower" with Chinantego Indian, Oaxaca, Mexico

Dischidia rafflesiana *(ASCLEP.)*
"Malayan urn vine" in Sogeri jungle of Papua

Dischidia nummularia
epiphytic climber in Borneo rainforest

Linnaea borealis *(CAPRIF.)*
"Western twin-flower" (Brit. Columbia to California)

Eccremocarpus scaber *(BIGN.)*
"Glory flower", scrambling bush of Chile

Tecomanthe speciosa *(BIGN.)*
Three-kings Isl. of N.W. New Zealand

Lonicera x tellmanniana *(CAPR.)*
"Coral honeysuckle" in the Rhineland, Germany

Lonicera x americana
Essen Botanic G., Germany

Lonicera x brownii
"Scarlet trumpet honeysuckle"

Lonicera x brownii
'Dropmore Scarlet', *in Canada*

Lonicera x brownii
'Fuchsioides', *in East Germany*

Lonicera sempervirens
"Coral honeysuckle"

Lonicera caprifolium
"Italian woodbine" in Europe

Lonicera dioica
fruiting in Québec

Lonicera x heckrottii
"Goldflame honeysuckle" in Berlin

Lonicera flava
"Yellow honeysuckle" in Georgia

Lonicera japonica
"Jap. honeysuckle" in Fatima, Portugal

Lonicera japonica 'Variegata'
"Gold and silver flower"

Lonicera jap. 'Aureo-reticulata'
"Yellow-net honeysuckle"

Lonicera periclymenum
"English woodbine" in Sydney, Australia

Lonicera pericl. serotina
in Strybing Arboretum, San Francisco

Lonicera periclymenum
serotina 'Winchester'

Lonicera pericl. 'Belgica'
"Dutch woodbine" in New Zealand

Lonicera hildebrandiana
"Burmese honeysuckle" in San Diego

Lonicera japonica 'Halliana'
in Portland, Oregon

Argyreia nervosa *(CONV.)*
"Silver morning-glory" in Florida

Quisqualis indica *(COMBR.)*
"Rangoon creeper" in Myanmar

Senecio confusus *(COMP.)*
"Mexican Flame-vine" in San Diego

Ipomoea carnea fistulosa
in Rarotonga, South Pacific

Calonyction album *(Ipomoea)*
"Moon flower"in New Guinea

Exogonium bracteatum *(CONV.)*
"Jicama" in Sonora, Mexico

Ipomoea carnea fistulosa alba
(crassicaulis) Trop. So. America

Quamoclit coccinea *(CONV.)*
"Star ipomoea" in New Mexico

Ipomoea cairica *(CONV.)*
Kew Botanic Gardens, England

Ipomoea digitata (*mauritiana*)
in Singapore Bot. Garden

Ipomoea horsfalliae
"Princess vine" in New Zealand

Ipomoea x multifida
"Cardinal climber"

Ipomoea nil (*Pharbitis*)
"Japanese morning glory"

Ipomoea quamoclit
"Cypress vine" of Trop. America

Ipomoea tricolor 'Heavenly Blue'
at Geo. Ball, West Chicago, Illinois

Ipomoea purpurea, *"Morning glory"*
on the Algarve coast, Portugal

Ipomoea purpurea kermesina
(*Pharbitis*) *on Madeira*

Ipomoea purpurea caerulea
Kew Botanic Gardens, England

Maripa passifloroides *(CONV.)*
(Asystasia) in Rio de Janeiro

Merremia tuberosa, *ornamental pods*
known as "Wood-rose" in Hawaii

Merremia tuberosa *(Ipomoea)*
"Ceylon morning-glory" in flower

Merremia umbellata *(CONV.)*
from Sinaloa, Mexico

Mina lobata *(Quamoclit)*
"Star-glory" of Mexico

Actinidia kolomikta *(DILL.)*
"Kolomiktavine" from Japan

Actinidia arguta
"Tara" or "Saru Nashi" in Japan

Actinidia chinensis, *"Kiwi-vine"*
"Chinese gooseberry" in California

Hibbertia scandens *(DILLEN.)*
"Guinea goldvine" in Queensland

Cucurbita ficifolia
"Malabar gourd" (Trop. America)

Lagenaria siceraria 'Clavata'
"Calabash gourd" in Frankfurt Bot. G.

Cucurbita pepo 'Pyriformis'
"Ornamental gourd" in Germany

Ibervillea sonorae (Maximowiczia)
of the Sonoran Desert, in Calif.

Ibervillea sonorae peninsularis
on Isla Cerralvo, Baja California

Ibervillea lindheimeri
"Balsam gourd" (Texas to Sonora)

Thladiantha punctata
ornamental fruit in Taiwan

Trichosanthes cucumeroides
"Snake gourd" in Osaka, Japan

Luffa aegyptiaca (cylindrica)
"Vegetable sponge" in El Salvador

Dioscorea elephantipes
"Hottentot-bread" of So. Africa

Dioscorea discolor *(DIOSC.)*
"Ornamental yam" in Surinam

Dioscorea quaternata
"Wild yam" of Southeast U.S.

Adlumia fungosa *(FUMAR.)*
"Mountain fringe" (E. No. America)

Macleania insignis *(ERIC.)*
Mts. of Veracruz to Guatemala

Lygodium japonicum *(FILIC.)*
"Climbing fern" (Japan to Australia)

Apios americana *(LEG.)*
"Ground-nut" (E. No. America)

Centrosema virginianum *(LEG.)*
"Conchita pea" (E. No. America)

Clianthus puniceus *(LEG.)*
"Parrot's bill" in New Zealand

Clitoria ternatea *(LEG.)*
"Butterfly pea" in Fiji

Derris involuta *(LEG.)*
"Jewel vine" of Queensland

Dolichos lablab *(LEG.)*
"Hyacinth bean" in Egypt

Milletia reticulata *(LEG.)*
"Evergreen wisteria" in California

Glycine clandestina *(LEG.)*
"Twining glycine" of Australia

Hardenbergia comptoniana *(LEG.)*
"Sarsaparilla" of West Australia

Kennedia rubicunda *(LEG.)*
"Coral-pea" in New Zealand

Schisandra rubriflora *(MAGN.)*
"Magnolia vine" at Kew, England

Phaseolus coccineus *(LEG.)*
"Scarlet runner bean" (So. America)

Lathyrus grandiflorus
"Everlasting pea" of So. Europe

Lathyrus clymenum articulatus
"Wild pea" on Delos, Greece

Lathyrus latifolius
"Perennial pea" in So. California

Lathyrus rotundifolius
"Persian everlasting pea" (Anatolia)

Lathyrus tuberosus
"Earth-nut-pea" of W. Asia

Lathyrus latifolius 'Albus'
"White everlasting pea" (So. Europe)

Lathyrus odoratus carnea
"Salmon pea" in Benares, India

Lathyrus odoratus
"Sweet pea" in Lisbon, Portugal

Lathyrus odor. 'Rosea' *winter-fl.*
in Longwood Gard., Pennsylvania

Wisteria floribunda *(Glycine)*
"Japanese wisteria" in Kyoto

Wisteria sinensis
"Chinese wisteria" in Bermuda

Strongylodon macrobotrys
"Jade vine" of the Philippines

Wisteria frutescens nivea
"White Southern glycine" in Virginia

Wisteria frutescens
"Southern wisteria" in Alabama

Wisteria venusta *(China)*
"Silky wisteria" in Kew Gardens

Vigna caracalla *(Phaseolus)*
"Snail vine" in Encinitas, Calif.

Pueraria phaseoloides
"Tropical Kudzu" on Moorea

Swainsona galegifolia
"Swan flower" from Queensland

Wisteria sinensis *(LEG.)*, *"Chinese wisteria"*
in Royal Botanic Gard. Kew, England

Wisteria floribunda, *May-blooming*
in Giardini Gard., Venice, Italy

Bougainvillea spectabilis 'Rubra plena' *(NYCT.)*
"Double bougainvillea" on Samosir, Sumatra

Gloriosa superba *(LIL.)*
"Malabar glory lily" on St. Kitts, West Indies

Gloriosa superba
"Crisped lily" in Mysore, India

Gloriosa simplex, *"Glorylily"*
in Munich Bot. Garden, Germany

Gloriosa rothschildiana
"Kenya glory lily" in Mombasa

Smilax laurifolia
"Bamboo vine" in New Jersey

Asparagus falcatus
"Sickle-thorn" of Sri Lanka

Smilax glauca
"Wild sarsaparilla" in Virginia

Asparagus setaceus *(plumosus hort.)*
"Fern asparagus" of florists

Asparagus asparagoides myrtifolius
florists "Smilax" or "Medeola"

Asparagus retrofractus *hort.*
"Zigzag shrub" in California

Tristellateia australasiae
"Galphimia vine" in Sumatra

Gelsemium sempervirens *(LOG.)*
"False jasmine" (Virginia to Texas)

Lapageria rosea *(LIL.)*
"Chile bells" in the Cordilleras

Senna nitida *(LEG.)*
"Climbing senna" in Sumatra

Abutilon megapotamicum *(MALV.)*
"Trailing Chinese lantern" in S. Paulo

Stigmaphyllon ciliatum *(MALP.)*
"Golden vine" in Brazil

Marcgravia rectiflora *(MARC.)*
"Shingle plant" maturity stage (Cuba)

Marcgravia paradoxa
in Luquillo Forest, Puerto Rico

Mirabilis jalapa *(NYCT.)*
"Four-o'clock" of Perú

Humulus lupulus, *male flower*
"European hops" in Germany

Humulus lupulus, *"Hops"*
female cones used for brewing

Humulus japonicus 'Variegatus'
"Japanese hops" (Temp. E. Asia)

Ficus sagittata 'Variegata'
"Varieg. rooting fig" of E. Asia

Ficus pumila *(repens) (MOR.)*
"Creeping fig" in Brooklyn Bot. G.

Freycinetia javanica expansa
in Sumatra, by J. Bogner, Munich

Freycinetia cumingiana (PAND.)
climbing screwpine in Philippines

Freycinetia funicularis
with fruit-cones in Java

Freycinetia multiflora
"Climbing pandanus" (Philippines)

Wisteria floribunda 'Alba' *(Glycine) (LEG.)*
"White Japanese wisteria" in New York state

Wisteria floribunda 'Macrobotrys' *(multijuga)*
blooming in Pretoria, Transvaal

Cucurbita pepo 'Lageniformis' *(CUCURB.)*
"Bottle gourds" on trellis in Hakone, Japan

Wisteria sinensis 'Alba'
"White Chinese wisteria" in Virginia

Ipomoea tricolor *(CONVOLV.)*
"Blue morning glory" on Oahu, Hawaii

Phanera kockiana *(syn. Bauhinia) (LEG.)*
trop. climber of Sarawak, Borneo (by J. Bogner)

Bougainvillea brasiliensis *in hort.*
in Cuernavaca, Morelos, Mexico

Bougainvillea x buttiana
on St. Thomas, Virgin Islands

Bougainvillea x butt. 'Barbara Karst'
in San Diego, California

Bougainvillea glabra
in Botanic Garden Singapore

Boug. x buttiana 'Gerry's Orange'
in Encinitas, California

Bougainvillea spectabilis
"Paper flower" in Brazil

Boug. spect. 'Manila Magic Pink'
double-fl., Diamond Head, Hawaii

Bougainvillea spectabilis 'Rosea'
in Tiger Balm Garden, Singapore

Bougainvillea spect. 'Louis Wathen'
Peradeniya Bot. Garden, Sri Lanka

Bougainvillea spectabilis
'Raspberry Ice', *in Vista, Calif.*

Bougainvillea spect. flore pleno
"Double bougainvillea" in Thailand

Boug. spect. 'Cherry Blossom'
charming double in So. California

Jasminum polyanthum *(OLEAC.)*
"Pink jasmine" of W. China

Jasminum sambac
"Arabian jasmine" (Arabia, India)

Jasminum mesnyi *(primulinum)*
"Primrose jasmine" in Nepal

Piper betle *(PIP.)*
"Betel-leaf" in Sri Lanka

Piper porphyrophyllum
"Velvet cissus" of Indonesia

Piper sylvaticum
"Silver cissus" from Borneo

Passiflora aurantia *(Tacsonia)*
in New Guinea habitat

Passiflora amethystina *(Brazil)*
in Napoleon's garden, St. Helena

Passiflora x alato-caerulea
(syn. pfordtii) "Showy passion fl."

Passiflora ornithoura *(Costa Rica)*
at Kartuz Greenh., Vista, Calif.

Passiflora caerulea
"Blue passion flower" in Brazil

Passiflora alata
col. Alvim Seidel, Corupá, Brazil

Passiflora edulis flavicarpa
"Granadilla" in Waimanalo, Hawaii

Passiflora coriacea
"Batleaf vine" of So. Mexico

Passiflora seemannii *(Trop. America)*
Waimanalo Exper. Stat., Hawaii

Passiflora manicata *(ignea)*
"Scarlet passion flower", in California

Passiflora mollissima
"Banana passion fruit"

Passiflora coccinea
"Red passion flower" (So. America)

Passiflora 'Coral Glow'
col. Kartuz Greenh., Vista, Calif.

Passiflora platyfolia
with edible fruit, El Salvador

Passiflora palmeri sublanceolata
"Sandia de la pasion" in Mexico

Passiflora quadrangularis
"Giant granadilla" (Trop. America)

Passiflora racemosa *(princeps)*
"Red passion vine" of Brazil

Passiflora 'Imperatrice Eugenie'
in Essen Bot. Garden, Germany

Passiflora suberosa *(Costa Rica)*
Sydney Botanic Garden, Australia

Passiflora trifasciata
"Three-banded passionvine" of Perú

Passiflora violacea *(PASS.)*
"Purple passionflower" of Bolivia

Billardiera longiflora *(PITT.)*
"Purple apple-berry" in Sydney

Passiflora vitifolia
"Crimson passion flower" in Perú

Cobaea scandens *(POLEMON.)*
"Monastery bells" of Mexico

Polygonum aubertii *(POLYG.)*
"Fleece vine" at Rutgers, N. Jersey

Antigonon guatimalense *(POLYG.)*
"Coronilla" in Oaxaca, Mexico

Antigonon leptopus *(Mexico)*
"Flor de Mayo" on Cabo San Lucas

Clematis x jackmanii
"Virgin's bower" in San Diego

Clematis x jackmanii 'Purpurea'
in Duesseldorf-Grafenberg

Clematis hyb. 'Ernst Markham'
in Dortmund Bot. Garden, Germany

Clematis hyb. 'Mrs. N. Thompson'
in Auckland, New Zealand

Clematis hybrida
'Etoile de Malicorne'

Clematis hyb. 'Ville de Lyon'
(French viticella hybrid)

Clematis lanuginosa
'President' in England

Clematis lanuginosa
'Ville de Paris' in Oregon

Clematis lanuginosa 'Nelly Moser'
at Wayside Gardens, So. Carolina

Clematis montana 'Tetrarose'
"Anemone clematis", in Boskoop

Clematis hybrida
'Duchess of Edinburgh' *(double fl.)*

Clematis hyb. 'Proteus'
double-flowered, in Germany

Clematis hybr. 'Perry Picton'
in Romberg Arboretum, Dortmund

Clematis x lawsoniana 'Henryi'
at Anderson Nursery, San Diego

Clematis hyb. 'M. Koster'
Romberg Arboretum, Germany

Clematis lanuginosa
'Mad. Moser', *July-blooming*

Clematis hyb. 'Titania'
Dortmund Botanic Garden

Clematis hyb. 'Andrew'
floriferous with small flowers

Clematis alpina
"Alpine clematis" in Austria

Clematis armandii *(China)*
evergreen in Pacific Northwest

Clematis crispa, *with seed head*
"Blue jasmine" in Virginia

Clematis macropetala
"Downy clematis" in Virginia

Clematis hybrida *(patens)*
'Countess of Lovelace' *(double)*

Clematis tangutica
"Golden clematis" with plumed fruit

Clematis hyb. 'Alice Fisk'
Bot. Garden, Dortmund, Germany

Clematis hyb. 'Voluceau'
in Southern France

Clematis hyb. 'Barbara Dibley'
(patens group) floriferous

Clematis lanuginosa 'Nelly Moser'
summer-blooming in Delaware

Clematis macropetala
"Downy clematis" of No. China and Siberia

Clematis paniculata *hort. (maximowicziana)*
with spidery seed heads

Clematis paniculata *hort.*
"Sweet autumn clematis", of Korea

Clematis paniculata *(true species)*
"Puawhananga" of the Maoris, N. Zealand

Clematis virginiana, *"Virgin's bower"* or
"Woddbine" from Nova Scotia to Kansas

Clematis chrysocoma, *"Gold-wool clematis"*
in Kew Botanic Gardens, England

Clematis florida bicolor
attractive form of hardy Chinese species

Rosa 'American Pillar' *(1902)*
Dahlem Bot. Garden, Berlin

Rosa x noisett. 'Maréchal Niel'
delicately scented "Noisette rose"

Rosa 'Paul's Scarlet Climber'
in Munich Botanic Garden

Rosa 'Crimson Rambler'
"Ten sisters rose" of China

Rosa 'Double Paul's Scarlet'
Roehrs mutant 1943

Rosa banksiae
"Lady Banks rose" in Dallas, Texas

Rubus reflexus *(moluccanus)*
"Trailing velvet-pl." in Hong Kong

Rosa rubininosa *(eglanteria)*
"Sweet-brier", in England

Rosa 'Mad. Eugene Jacquet'
"Rambler rose" as Easter basket

Hydrangea anomala petiolaris
"Climbing hydrangea" (Japan)

Pilostegia viburnoides *(SAX.)*
self-clinging climber of Taiwan

Decumaria barbara *(SAX.)*
"Wood-vamp" in Virginia

Manettia inflata *(RUB.)*
"Firecracker plant" (Paraguay)

Clerodendrum splendens *(VERB.)*
(Senegambia to Angola)

Clerodendrum thomsoniae
"Bleeding heart vine" (W. Africa)

Asarina antirrhinifolia *(Maurandya)*
from Texas to California

Asarina barclaiana *(SCROPH.)*
(Maurandya) in Mexico

Congea tomentosa *(VERB.)*
"Shower orchid" in Singapore

Solandra grandiflora *(SOLAN.)*
"Golden Chalice" in Puerto Rico

Solandra maxima *(nitida)*
"Cup of Gold" in Bermuda

Solandra longiflora
"Copa de Oro" in Havana, Cuba

Solanum wendlandii
"Climbing potato" of Costa Rica

Solanum jasminoides
"Jasmine night-shade" of Brazil

Solandra maxima 'Warrimoo'
colorful cv. in New South Wales

Rhodochiton volubile *(SCROPH.)*
"Purple bell-vine" in Oaxaca

Solanum jasmin. 'Grandiflorum'
in Los Angeles Botan. Garden

Solanum seaforthianum
"Star potato vine" of So. America

Oxera pulchella *(VERB.)*
"Royal climber" in So. France

Hillia parasitica *(RUB.)*
scandent epiphyte in Jamaica

Petrea volubilis *(Mexico) (VERB.)*
"Purple wreath" in Uganda, Africa

Ampelopsis brevipedunc. 'Elegans'
"Colored grape-leaf" of Manchuria

Ampelopsis brevipedunculata
"Porcelain berry" of Mongolia

Ampelopsis aconitifolia *(VIT.)*
"Monks-hood vine" in New Jersey

Cissus hypoglauca *(VITAC.)*
"Water vine" in Melbourne

Cissus discolor
"Rex begonia vine" in Cambodia

Cissus antarctica
"Kangaroo vine" in Sydney

Cissus rhombifolia *(Rhoicissus)*
"Grape ivy" in Caracas, Venezuela

Cissus rhomb. 'Ellen Danica'
"Danish grape ivy" (Denmark)

Rhoicissus capensis *(So. Africa)*
"Evergreen grape vine" in San Diego

Parthenocissus inserta
in Zona Rosada, Mexico City

Parthenocissus quinquefolia
"Virginia creeper" in Ogden, Utah

Parthenoc. quinquef. 'Engelmannii'
in the Rhineland, Germany

Parthenocissus tricuspidata
"Woodbine" in autumn color

Parthenocissus tricuspidata
"Boston ivy" in Virginia

Parthenocissus tricusp. 'Lowii'
"Butterfly ivy" in England

Parthenocissus henryana
from China, in autumn color

Parthenocissus henryana
"Silver-vein creeper" in London

Parthenocissus tric. 'Veitchii'
juvenile form "Japanese ivy"

Vitis thunbergii *(Japan)*
in Botanic Garden, Copenhagen

Vitis coignetiae
"Crimson glory vine" in Kew Gard.

Tetrastigma voinierianum
"Chestnut vine" in San Diego

Vitis riparia *(vulpina)*
"Riverside grape" of No. America

Cissus striata *(Chile)*
"Miniature grape ivy" at Roehrs, N.J.

Vitis rotundifolia
"Muscadine grape" in Delaware

Lampranthus aureus *(AIZ.)*
"Orange ice plant" in San Diego

Lampranthus productus
"Purple iceplant" of the Karroo

Aptenia cordifolia 'Red Apple'
"Baby sun rose" (So. Africa)

Drosanthemum floribundum *(AIZ.)*
"Rosea iceplant" in California

Dorotheanthus bellidiformis
"Livingstone daisy" of Cape Prov.

Carpobrotus edulis *(AIZ.)*
"Hottentot fig" in So. Africa

Vinca minor *(APOC.)*
"Periwinkle" in New Jersey

Vinca major
"Greater periwinkle" in California

Vinca major 'Variegata'
"Band plant" ideal in baskets

Hedera canariensis
"Algerian ivy" (No. Africa)

Hedera canar. 'Variegata'
"Variegated Canary ivy"

Hed. colchica 'Dentato-variegata'
"Variegated Persian ivy"

Hedera helix
'Abundance'

Hedera helix 'Albany'
"Albany ivy"

Hedera helix
'Chicago variegated'

Hedera helix cristata
'Curlilocks' *in Brooklyn Bot. G.*

Hedera helix 'Heise-Denmark'
Danish varieg. miniature

Hedera helix 'Deltoidea'
juvenile stage "Sweetheart ivy"

Hedera helix 'Discolor'
"Marmorata ivy"

Hedera helix
'Garland' *(small-leaved)*

Hedera helix 'Hahn's variegated'
miniature, in California

Hedera canariensis
'Arborescens variegata', *"Ghost tree"*

Hedera canar. 'Gloire de Marengo'
in European horticulture

Hedera colchica
"Persian ivy" (Asia Minor)

Hedera helix
"English ivy" in New Jersey

Hedera helix fa. 'Arborescens'
arborescent maturity stage

Hedera helix 'Zorgvlied'
at Floriade 1982, Amsterdam

Hedera helix
'California Fan'

Hedera helix 'Deltoidea'
in maturity stage

Hedera helix 'Fluffy Ruffles'
with crested foliage

Hedera helix 'Erecta' *(congesta)*
non-climbing Japanese clone

Hedera helix 'Baltica' *(Latvia)*
"Baltic ivy" on Bornholm, Denmark

Hedera helix 'Triton'
curious palmate foliage, in South Carolina

Hedera helix 'Conglomerata'
"Japanese ivy", with contorted stems

Hedera helix 'Adam', *variegated miniature*
at Rochford Nurseries, near London, England

Hedera helix 'Diamant'
variegated miniature at German Nat'l. Show, Hamburg

Hedera helix 'Telecurl'
self-branching, with deeply lobed leaves

Hedera helix 'Shamrock'
"Shamrock ivy" with trilobed leaves

Hedera helix 'Glacier'
"Glacier ivy", in California

Hedera helix 'Harald'
"White and green ivy" in Denmark

Hedera helix 'Goldheart' *(Italy)*
on Isola Bella, Lago Maggiore

Hedera helix 'Hahnii'
in California horticulture

Hedera helix 'Ivalace'
self-branching

Hedera helix 'Mandaiana variegata'
in Rhineland Nursery

Hedera helix
'Manda's Crested' *(New Jersey)*

Hedera hel. 'Pittsburgh Patricia'
"Philadelphia self-branching ivy"

Hedera helix '238th Street'
arborescent, in the Bronx, New York

Hedera helix 'Maculata' *(ARAL.)*
"Variegated English ivy"

Hedera helix 'Jubilee'
tiniest variegated

Hedera helix
hibernica 'Variegata'

Hedera helix hibernica
"Irish ivy" at Kew Gardens

Hedera helix "Needlepoint'
dwarf self-branching, in Calif.

Hedera hel. 'Parsley crested'
"Parsley ivy" in England

Hedera helix 'Schafer'
German miniature

Hedera helix 'Ripples'
Brooklyn Botanic Garden

Hedera helix 'Star'
small star-ivy in Brooklyn

Hedera nepalensis
"Nepal ivy" in adult stage

Asystasia gangetica *(ACANTH.)*
"Coromandel" in Singapore Bot. G.

Hemigraphis alternata *(ACANTH.)*
(colorata), "Red ivy" in Java

Lampranthus aureus *from Cape Prov. (AIZOAC.)*
"Orange iceplant", March-blooming in Vista, California

Lampranthus spectabilis *(Mesembryanthemum)*
"Red iceplant" at Tropic World, Escondido, California

Osteospermum fruticosum *from So. Africa (COMP.)*
"Trailing African daisy" in San Diego, California

Lampranthus productus *from the Karroo (AIZOAC.)*
"Purple ice plant", winter blooming in So. California

Pelargonium peltatum *of Eastern So. Africa (GERAN.)*
"Ivy geraniums" on Sunset Ranch, California

Juniperus horizontalis 'Blue Chip' *(CONIF.: CUP.)*
"Creeping juniper" in Missouri Bot. Garden, St. Louis

Setcreasea pallida 'Purple Heart'
(purpurea hort.) of Mexico

Callisia repens, in New York
"Turtle vine" (Bailey Hortorium)

Callisia repens 'Bolivian Jew'
"Mini turtle plant" in Kew Bot. G.

Callisia fragrans (Tradescantia)
in St. Thomas, Virgin Islands

Zebrina pendula (Mexico)
"Silvery wandering Jew" in N.Y. Bot. G.

Tradescantia flumin. 'Variegata'
"Wandering Jew" of Argentina

Gibasis schiedeana (Tradescantia)
"Tahitian Bridal veil"

Cyanotis somaliensis
"Pussy ears" of East Africa

Tradescantia virginiana
"Spiderwort" in New Jersey

Begonia limmingheiana *(BEG.)*
"Shrimp begonia" of Brazil

Alternanthera ficoidea
'Bettzickiana', *"Calico plant"*

Pachysandra terminalis *(BUX.)*
"Japanese spurge" in New Jersey

Campanula elatines garganica
"Adriatic bellflower" (CAMP.)

Campanula elatines
garganica 'Major' *(So. Italy)*

Euonymus fortunei 'Gracilis'
"Silver-edge creeper" in New York

Euonymus fortunei 'Colorata'
"Purple-leaf winter creeper"

Euonymus fortunei 'Kewensis'
in England (CELAST.)

Euonymus fortunei radicans
in Dahlem Bot. Garden, Berlin

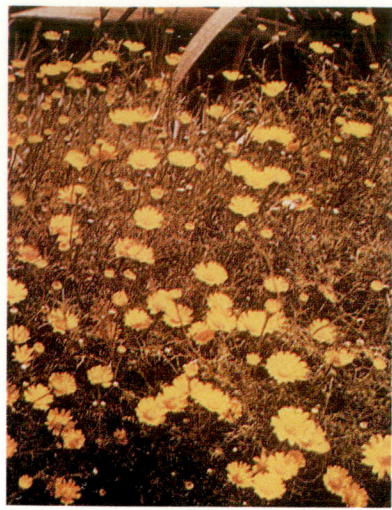

Dyssodia tenuiloba *(Thymophylla)*
"Dahlberg daisy" in Texas

Chamaemelum nobile 'Lutea' *(COMP.)*
"Chamomile"in Calif. herb garden

Senecio macroglossus 'Variegatum'
"Variegated waxvine" (Cape Prov.)

Mutisia spinosa *(COMP.)*
shrubby vine of Chile

Ballya zebrina *(COMMEL.)*
from tropical E. Africa

Haplopappus glutinosa *(COMP.)*
"Chilean daisy"

Arenaria grandiflora *(CARYOPH.)*
"Sandwort" in Austrian Alps

Herniaria glabra *(CARYOPH.)*
"Green carpet" (So. Europe, Asia)

Sagina subulata 'Aurea' *(CARYOPH.)*
"Scotch moss" in California

Juniperus communis 'Prostrata'
in Munich Botanic Garden

Juniperus chinensis
'Procumbens nana' *in California*

Junip. conferta 'Blue Pacific'
"Shore juniper" in San Diego

Junip. horizontalis 'Bar Harbor'
Somerset Arboretum, New Jersey

Junip. horizont. 'Prince of Wales'
at Los Angeles Arboretum

Juniperus sabina 'Tamariscifolia'
"Tamarix juniper" in San Diego

Juniperus squamata 'Prostrata'
in col. New York Bot. Garden

Juniperus squamata 'Blue Carpet'
in Monrovia Nurs., California

Junip. communis 'Hornibrookii'
in Munich Bot. Garden, Germany

Osteospermum fruticosum
"Trailing African daisy" (COMP.)

Gazania rigens 'Fiesta Red'
"Treasure flower" in California

Gazania rigens leucolaena
"Creeping gazania" (Los Angeles Arb.)

Ipomoea pes-caprae *(CONVOLV.)*
"Beach morning glory" in Aruba

Wedelia trilobata *(COMP.)*
"Creeping daisy" in So. Florida

Arctotheca calendula *(COMP.)*
"Cape weed" in San Diego Viejo

Raoulia australis *(COMP.)*
"Silver-mat" (New Zealand)

Artemisia schmidtiana 'Nana'
"Silver mound" of Japan (COMP.)

Dichondra micrantha *(repens)*
"Lawn-leaf" in California

Sempervivum arachnoideum
"Cobweb hen-and-chicks" (Alps)

Sedum kamtschaticum
var. middendorfianum *(E. Siberia)*

Sedum sieboldii *(CRASS.)*
"October plant" of Japan

Sedum hyb. 'Immergruenchen'
in Saalfeld, East Germany

Sedum acre *(CRASS.)*
"Golden carpet" in Swiss Alps

Sedum laconicum
of Greece and Asia Minor

Sedum oreganum
"Oregon stonecrop" in Alaska

Sedum spurium
"Dragon's blood" (Caucasus)

Sedum spurium 'Purple Carpet'
in Munich Botanic Garden

Aurinia saxatilis *(Alyssum)*
"Basket of gold" in Austrian Alps

Aubrieta deltoidea *(CRUC.)*
"Purple rock-cress" of Sicily

Arabis caucasica *(CRUC.)*
"Wall rock-cress" in Greece

Erodium petraeum *(GERAN.)*
in the Pyrenées of Spain

Erodium chamaedryoides
"Alpine geranium" of Corsica

Iberis sempervir. 'Snowflake'
"Edging candytuft" in California

Pelargonium peltatum 'Amethyst'
"Giant ivy geranium" in Berlin

Akebia quinata *(LARD.)*
"Chocolate vine" in New Jersey

Baccharis pilularis 'Twin Peaks'
"Coyote brush" in Calif. (COMP.)

Aeschynanthus radicans *(GES.)*
"Lipstick vine" in San Francisco

Columnea microphylla 'Variegata'
"Variegated Goldfish vine"

Impatiens walleriana 'Minima'
creeping, in Brooklyn Bot. Garden

Scaevola microc. 'Mauve Clusters'
"Fan flower" in California

Ajuga reptans 'Variegata'
Oxford Botanic Garden, England

Ajuga reptans *(LAB.)*
"Carpet bugleweed" in New Jersey

Hypericum calycinum *(HYP.)*
"Rose of Sharon" in Liechtenstein

Glechoma hederacea *(LAB.)*
"Gill-over-the-ground" in Madeira

Glechoma hederacea 'Variegata'
"Ground ivy" in Denver, Colorado

Meehania urticifolia *(LAB.)*
creeping mint (Japan, Korea)

Lamium maculatum *(LAB.)*
"Dead nettle" of No. Europe

Lamiastrum galeobd. 'Variegatum'
"Yellow archangel" in Germany

Plectranthus australis *(LAB.)*
"Swedish ivy" in Brooklyn Bot. G.

Limnanthes douglasii *(LIMN.)*
"Meadow-foam" in Oregon

Rosmarinus offic. 'Prostratus'
"Creeping rosemary" (Mediterr.)

Bomarea multiflora *(AMAR.)*
"Tetona" in New Zealand

Fuchsia procumbens *(ONAGR.)*
"Trailing fuchsia" (New Zealand)

Coleus pumilus, *"Trailing Queen"*
at New Jersey Flower Show (LAB.)

Thymus serpyllum *(LAB.)*
"Creeping thyme" in Germany

Myoporum parvifolium *(MYOP.)*
prostrate evergreen from Australia

Lotus berthelotii *(LEG.)*
"Winged pea" of Canary Islands

Lobelia erinus 'Pendula' *(LOB.)*
"Balcony lobelia" in planter box

Laurentia fluviatilis *(Isotoma)*
"Blue star creeper" in California

Pratia angulata *(LOBEL.)*
"Creeping half-flower" (New Zealand)

Abronia wootonii *(NYCT.)*
"Sand-verbena" of Arizona

Abronia villosa *(Mexico)*
"Desert verbena" in Baja Calif.

Abronia umbellata *(California)*
"Pink sand-verbena" in Anza Borrego

Phlox subulata *(POLEMON.)*
"Moss-pinks" in New Jersey

Armeria maritima 'Vindictive'
"Sea pinks" at Kew Bot. Gardens

Armeria juniperifolia *(PLUMB.)*
"Juniper-thrift" of Spain

Jasminum parkeri *(OLEAC.)*
prostrate shrub of N.W. India

Peperomia scandens 'Variegata'
variegated "Philodendron peperomia"

Sollya heterophylla *(PITT.)*
"Bluebell creeper" in Perth, W. Austr.

Polygonum capitatum *(POLYG.)*
"Knot-weed" in Escondido, Calif.

Polygonum vacciniifolium
"Rose carpet knotweed" (Himalayas)

Muehlenbeckia complexa *(POLYG.)*
"Maidenhair vine" (New Zealand)

Portulaca oleracea 'Belgica'
"Salmon purslane" in Florida

Portulaca oleracea 'Wildfire'
"Rose-red purslane" (California)

Lysimachia nummularia *(PRIM.)*
"Creeping Jennie" of Britain

Cotoneaster microphyllus
"Rockspray cotoneaster" in Sikkim

Cotoneaster microphyllus 'Cochleatus'
fruiting in Munich Bot. Garden

Cotoneaster dammeri radicans
"Dwarf bearberry" in bloom (China)

Duchesnea indica *of India*
"Mock strawberry" with flowers

Duchesnea indica *(fruit insipid)*
as groundcover in California

Fragaria chiloensis (ROS.)
"Sand strawberry" in Los Angeles

Cotoneaster horizontalis
"Rock cotoneaster" of Western China

Potentilla tridentata *(ROS.), as groundcover*
"Wine-leaf cinquefoil" (Greenland to Wisconsin)

Cotoneaster divaricatus
"Spreading cotoneaster" in California

Berchemia racemosa *(RHAM.)*
"Supplejack" or "Rattan vine" of Japan and Taiwan

Cotoneaster dammeri *(ROS.)*
"Bearberry cotoneaster" in Rhineland cemetery

Cotoneaster dammeri 'Skogholm'
in Skogsholmen Arboretum, Malmoe, Sweden

Cotoneaster congestus *(pyrenaicus hort.)*
"Pyrenées cotoneaster" in the Himalayas

Cotoneaster apiculatus, *"Cranberry cotoneaster"*
at Rutgers Univ. Exper. Sta., New Brunswick, N.J.

Potentilla verna *in hort.*
"Spring cinquefoil" in California

Potentilla fruticosa *(ROS.)*
"Shrubby cinquefoil" in Berlin Bot. G.

Waldsteinia ternata *(ROS.)*
"Barren strawberry" in California

Rubus calycinoides *(ROS.)*
"Chinese bramble" of Taiwan

Coprosma x kirkii variegata
"Silvery birdnest" (New Zealand)

Mitchella repens *(RUB.)*
"Partridge berry" (E. No. America)

Asarina erubescens *(SCROPH.)*
"Creeping gloxinia" of Trop. Mexico

Saxifraga stolonifera *(SAX.)*
"Strawberry geranium" in England

Soleirolia soleirolii *(Helxine)*
"Baby tears" or "Irish moss"

Mazus reptans *(SCROPH.)*
"Wart flower" of the Himalayas

Cymbalaria pallida *(Linaria)*
Royal Bot. Gardens Kew, England

Cymbalaria muralis *(SCROPH.)*
"Kenilworth ivy" in Ontario

Nierembergia hippoman. violacea
"Cupflower" in Argentina

Veronica persica *(SCROPH.)*
"Persian speedwell" in Germany

Sibthorpia peregrina *(SCROPH.)*
"Hera terrestre" of Madeira

Phyla nodiflora rosea *(VERB.)*
"Cape weed" in California

Pilea depressa *(URTIC.)*
"Miniature peperomia" of Puerto Rico

Pilea nummulariifolia
"Creeping Charley" (West Indies)

*Balconies of "Ivy geranium", Pelargonium peltatum
at Zellerhof Inn, in the Alps of Bavaria*

*Carpet bed of Alternanthera, Begonia, Echeveria
in Dahlem Botanic Garden, Berlin*

*Summer planting of Begonias, Tagetes, Salvias, Centaureas
Tapestry garden in Rhineland, Germany*

*English ivy, Hedera helix, Begonias and Ilex
in stoneware container on Fifth Avenue, New York*

*Parthenocissus tricuspidata, the Japanese ivy, in autumn color
covering walls of Fort Montjuich, Barcelona, Spain*

*Groundcover carpet of Pelargonium, Tagetes, Begonias
in Queen Elizabeth Arboretum, Vancouver, Canada*

Tropaeolum tricolor *(TROP.)*
"Tricolored Indian cress" of Chile

Tropaeolum tuberosum
"Tuber nasturtium" of the Andes

Tropaeolum pentaphyllum
climber, from Bolivia to Brazil

Tropaeolum polyphyllum
"Wreath nasturtium" (Argentina)

Tropaeolum speciosum
"Vermillion nasturtium" (Chile)

Verbena peruviana *(VERB.)*
in Wellington Bot. G., New Zealand

Lantana camara 'Festival'
at Pala Indian Mission, California

Lantana montevidensis *(VERB.)*
"Trailing lantana" in San Diego

Viola hederacea *(VIOL.)*
"Trailing violet" in Melbourne

Sagittaria latifolia *(ALIS.)*
"Arrowhead" (No. America)

Echinodorus macrophyllus
"Sword plant" of Colombia

Echinodorus palaefolius *(ALIS.)*
"Mexican sword plant"

Acorus gramineus *(ARAC.)*
"Japanese sweet flag"

Acorus calamus
"Sweet-flag" growing in water

Acorus calamus 'Variegatus'
ornamental aquatic in Germany

Colocasia esculenta *(ARAC.)*
"Taro" or "Yam", in Tonga

Calla palustris *(ARAC.)*
"Water arum" (No. Amer. to Siberia)

Lysichiton americanum *(ARAC.)*
Western "Skunk-cabbage"

Cryptocoryne cordata 'Rosanervis'
in col. Munich Bot. Garden

Lasia concinna *(ARAC.)*
tropical bog plant of Borneo

Aponogeton distachyus
"Cape pondweed" of So. Africa

Azolla filiculoides *(FIL.)*
floating "Fairy-moss" in Oregon

Orontium aquaticum *(ARAC.)*
"Golden club" of No. America

Peltandra virginica *(ARAC.)*
"Arrow arum" (Maine to Florida)

Marsilia drummondii *(FIL.)*
"Water clover" of W. Australia

Symplocarpus foetidus *(ARAC.)*
"Eastern skunk-cabbage" in New York

Typhonodorum lindleyanum *(ARAC.)*
Jardim Botanico, Rio de Janeiro

Ludwigia sedioides *(ONAGR.)*
"False loosestrife" in Munich Bot. G.

Ariopsis peltata *(ARAC.)*
small tuberous swamp plant of India

Cryptocoryne aponogetifolia *(usteriana) (ARAC.)*
freshwater aquatic in Luzon, Philippines

Montrichardia arborescens *(ARAC.)*
Waterside plant in tropical Surinam

Neptunia plena *of Trop. Asia (LEG.)*
"Sensitive water mimosa" in St. Petersburg, Russia

Typhonium divaricatum *(ARAC.)*
tuberous waterside plant of Indonesia

Paepalanthus costaricensis *(ERIOCAUL.)*
tropical bog plant of Costa Rica

Paepalanthus itatiaiensis
rush-like "Pipewort" in Brazil

Hydrocleys nymphoides
"Water poppy" in Argentina

Hydrocleys martii *(BUTOM.)*
"Water-key" in Munich Bot. Garden

Butomus umbellatus *(BUTOM.)*
"Flowering rush" of Eurasia

Rorippa sylvestris *(Nasturtium)*
"Swamp cress" in Duesseldorf Bot. G.

Eriophorum vaginatum *(CYP.)*
"Arctic cotton grass" in Norway

Eriophorum angustifolium
"Cotton grass" in Scotland

Cyperus alternifolius *(CYP.)*
"Umbrella plant" in California

Cyperus albostr. 'Variegatus'
"Striped umbrella palm"

Cyperus albostriatus *(diffusus)*
"Broad-leaf umbrella plant"

Carex riparia *(CYPER.)*
waterside sedge in Germany

Rhynchospora alba *(CYPER.)*
"Star grass" in Florida

Cliftonia monophylla *(CYRILL.)*
"Buckwheat bush" in Louisiana

Equisetum hyemale *(EQUIS.)*
"Scouring rush" in California

Equisetum maximum
"Dutch rush" in Holland

Equisetum giganteum
"Giant horsetail" in Argentina

Donatia novae-zelandiae *(DON.)*
"Cushion plant" in Tasmania

Equisetum arvense
"Horsetail" in Munich Bot. Garden

Ceratopteris cornuta *(FIL.)*
"Floating staghorn" (Monsoon Asia)

Gunnera tinctoria *(chilensis) "Chilean rhubarb"*
in Strybing Arboretum, San Francisco, California

Gunnera manicata, *"Prickly rhubarb"*
in Queen Elizabeth Arboretum, Vancouver, Canada

Gunnera magellanica, *mat-forming*
from Patagonia and Falklands

Thalia dealbata *(MAR.)*
"Water canna" (Carolina to Texas)

Juncus effusus 'Spiralis' *of Eurasia*
"Corkscrew rush" for tatami mats in Japan

Pistia stratiotes, *"Water-lettuce"*
afloat on the White Nile, in Uganda

Menyanthes trifoliata *(GENT.)*
waterside *"Bog-bean" in Sweden*

Nymphoides humboldtiana
"Floating heart" of Trop. America

Nymphoides peltata *(GENT.)*
"Yellow floating heart" (Eurasia)

Myriophyllum aquaticum *(HAL.)*
"Parrot's feather" in California

Hippuris vulgaris *(HIPP.)*
"Mare's tail" (North. hemisphere)

Hydrocharis morsus-ranae *(HYD.)*
"Frog's-bit" (Europe to Siberia)

Salvinia auriculata *(FIL.)*
in Munich Bot. Garden, Germany

Salvinia natans
"Floating fern" of Eurasia

Lemna minor *(LEMN.)*
"Duck-weed" of No. hemisphere

Iris graminea *(IRID.)*
"Plum iris" in Germany

Iris x ensata *(kaempferi of hort.)*
beardless "Japanese iris"

Iris x ensata 'Violet' *(kaempferi)*
in Palmengarten Frankfurt

Iris laevigata 'Alba'
"Japanese swamp-iris" (white cv.)

Iris laevigata 'Albo-variegata'
in Kew Bot. Gardens, England

Iris pseudacorus
"Yellow flag" (Europe to Asia)

Neptunia oleracea *(LEG.)*
"Water mimosa" in Bogor, Java

Hydrophyllum capitatum *(HYDROPH.)*
"Cat's-breeches" (Brit. Columbia)

Thalia dealbata, inflor. *(MAR.)*
"Water canna" (Southeast U.S.)

Victoria cruziana, *from Paraná (NYMPH.)*
"Santa Cruz lily" on the Riviera of France

Victoria amazonica *(regia)*
"Royal water lily" on Rio Negro, Amazonas

Nymphaea odorata
"Fragrant water-lily" in E. North America

Euryale ferox, *"Gorgon" (NYMPH.)*
"Prickly water lily" from India to Japan

Rhizophora mangle *(RHIZ.)*
"American mangrove" in Florida Keys

Brugiera conjugata *(RHIZ.)*
"Oriental mangrove" along Kaneohe Bay, Hawaii

Luronium nat. *"Floating spoons" (small)*
Potamogeton nat. *"Pond-weed" (large fol.)*

Nuphar advena *(NYMPH.)*
"Cow lily" (New England to Texas)

Nuphar luteum
"Europ. pond lily" in Switzerland

Nymphaea lotus dentata
"White lotus of Egypt" (No. Africa)

Nymphoides indica *(GENT.)*
"Water snowflake" in Frankfurt Bot. G.

Nymphaea 'Director G. Moore'
tropical water lily in St. Louis

Nymphaea callicantha
in Lake Victoria, Uganda

Nymphaea rubra
trop. night bloomer of India

Nymphaea gigantea *(Nymph.)*
"Australian water lily"

Nymphaea candida
Botanic Garden Munich, Germany

Nymphaea caerulea
"Blue lotus of Egypt" in Kenya

Nymphaea capensis
"Cape blue waterlily" (So. Africa)

Nymphaea x virginalis
hardy white, excellent bloomer

Nymphaea alba *(winter-hardy)*
"European white water-lily"

Nymphaea 'Pink Sensation'
day-bloomer at Lilypons, Maryland

Nymphaea stellata
"Blue lotus of India"

Nymphaea x daubeniana
viviparous "Pygmy waterlily"

Nymphaea colorata *(Tanzania)*
pigmy-lily of Dar-es-Salaam

Eichhornia crassipes *(PONT.)*
floating "Waterhyacinth" in Florida

Eichhornia azurea
"Peacock hyacinth" in Brazil

Heteranthera dubia *(PONT.)*
"Water star-grass" in Cuba

Pontederia lanceolata *(PONT.)*
"Pickerel-weed" in So. Carolina

Hydrothrix gardneri *(PONT.)*
submerged aquatic of Brazil

Heteranthera reniformis
"Mud plantain" in Munich Bot. Garden

Pontederia cordata
"Heartleaf pickerel" (E. Canada)

Spiranthes cernua *(ORCH.)*
"Ladies-tresses" (Nova Scotia)

Leptocarpus similis *(REST.)*
rush-like, in Rotorua, New Zealand

Caltha palustris *(RAN.)*
"Marsh marigold" in Alaska

Caltha leptosepala
"Meadow-bright" (Alberta to N. Mex.)

Caltha palustris ssp. minor
in Kew Bot. Gardens, England

Ranunculus lingua *(RAN.)*
"Greater spearwort" in Britain

Rhizophora mucronata *(RHIZ.)*
"Mangrove" (inflor.) in Taiwan

Cephalanthus occidentalis *(RUB.)*
"Button bush" near Detroit, Michigan

Peltiphyllum peltatum *(SAX.)*
"Umbrella plant" in Oregon

Typha latifolia *(TYPH.)*
"Cat-tail" of No. America, Eurasia

Typha angustifolia, *in Germany*
"Narrow-leaf cat-tail"

Nelumbo nucifera, *the "East Indian lotus"
exotically fragrant, in Balboa Park, San Diego*

Montrichardia linifera, *tropical aroid
along Rio Caroni, Canaima, Venezuela*

Zantedeschia aethiopica, *"White calla"
in tropical lake, Kebun Raya, Bogor, Java*

Cyperus papyrus, *the "Egyptian paper plant"
on the shore of Lake Victoria, Uganda*

Acanthus balcanicus *(ACANTH.)*
"Bear's breech" in Greece

Acanthus mollis
"Greek acanthos" in Lisbon Bot. G.

Hypoestes aristata *(ACANTH.)*
"Ribbon bush" of So. Africa

Amaranthus caudatus *(AMAR.)*
"Love-lies-bleeding" of So. Africa

Celosia arg. plumosa 'Flame'
in Domain of Auckland, N. Zealand

Amaranthus cruentus
on Rhodos, Greece

Celosia cristata *(AMAR.)*
"Cocks comb" in Bogor, Java

Celosia arg. plumosa 'Apricot Beauty'
Somerset Arboretum, New Jersey

Celosia argentea plumosa
"Feathered amaranth" in California

Gomphrena globosa *(AMAR.)*
"Globe amaranth" in Denver, Colo.

Amaranthus tricolor *(AMAR.)*
"Joseph's-coat" in Sydney Bot. G.

Coleus pumilus
'Red Trailing Queen' *(LAB.)*

Alternanthera ficoidea 'Amoena'
"Parrot-leaf" of Brazil

Alternanthera ficoidea 'Aurea'
"Yellow calico plant"

Alternanthera fic. 'Bettzickiana'
"Red calico plant"

Iresine lindenii 'Formosa'
"Yellow blood-leaf"

Iresine herbstii *(AMAR.)*
"Beafsteak plant" in San Francisco

Aerva persica *(AMAR.)*
in Arta Mountains, Somalia

Amsonia hirtella *(APOC.)*
"Western Blue star" in Arizona

Rhazya orientalis *(APOC.)*
from Greece to Anatolia

Alstroemeria aurantiaca 'Cyprus'
at Keukenhof Festival, Holland

Alstroemeria aurantiaca
"Peruvian lily" of W. So. America

Alstroemeria pelegrina
"Lily of Lima" from Perú

Alstroemeria ligtu
"Inca lily" in Berkeley, Calif.

Dionysia involucrata *(PRIM.)*
from Pamir Mts., C. Asia

Amsonia tabernaemontana *(APOC.)*
"Blue star" of Southeast U.S.

Apocynum androsaemifolium *(APOC.)*
spreading "Dogbane" (Canada to Mexico)

Veronicastrum virginicum *(SCROPH.)*
"Culver's-root" in Ontario

Catharanthus roseus *(APOC.)*
"Madagascar periwinkle" in Tahiti

Catharanthus roseus 'Purple Eyes'
Vinca rosea hort. in California

Asarum europaeum (ARIST.)
"Wild ginger" of No. Europe

Asarum europaeum variegatum
as niponica in Kew Bot. Gardens

Asarum hartwegii
"Asarabacca" in No. California

Asarum shuttleworthii
"Mottled wild ginger" in Virginia

Anchusa capensis (BORAG.)
"Cape forget-me-not" of So. Africa

Anchusa azurea
"Italian alkanet" in New Jersey

Anchusa caespitosa
"Alkanet" of Crete

Lithodora diffusa 'Grace Ward'
(Lithospermum hort.) in Maryland

Buglossoides purpureo-caeruleum
of Europe to Russia, Asia Minor

Borago officinalis (BORAG.)
"Borage" (So. Europe, No. Africa)

Brunnera macrophylla (BORAG.)
"Siberian bugloss" in Russia

Arnebia pulchra (BORAG.)
"Prophet flower" of Asia Minor

Aralia nudicaulis *(ARAL.)*
"Sarsaparilla" (No. America, E. Asia)

Panax pseudoginseng *(ARAL.)*
"Ginseng" in Taiwan

Aristolochia tricaudata *(ARIST.)*
curious long-tailed fl., in Mexico

Asclepias syriaca *(ASCLEP.)*
"Milkweed" (Canada to Kansas)

Cynanchum vincetoxicum *(ASCLEP.)*
"Cruel plant" (Europe, to Himalaya)

Oxypetalum caeruleum *(ASCL.)*
(Tweedia) from Argentina, Brazil

Asclepias curassavica
"Blood flower" in San Diego

Asclepias tuberosa
"Butterfly weed" (Maine to Arizona)

Asclepias incarnata
"Swamp milkweed" (Québec to Texas)

Impatiens bals. rosea plena
"Rose balsam" of Malaya

Impatiens glandulifera
"Jewel-weed" from India

Impatiens oliveri *(BALS.)*
"Giant touch-me-not" (E. Africa)

Impatiens repens
"Creeping impatiens" in Colombo

Incarvillea mairei *(BIGN.)*
in the Himalayas of Nepal

Incarvillea delavayi
"Hardy gloxinia" in New Jersey

Begonia grandis *(evansiana)*
"Hardy begonia" of China

Begonia semperflorens
planted in the Kremlin, Moscow

Begonia semp. 'Susie' *(red-leaved)*
in Palmengarten Frankfurt, Germany

Impatiens walleriana *cultivars*
"Sultanas" in Duesseldorf, Germany

Impatiens walleriana, *in habitat*
on Mt. Kilimanjaro, Tanzania

Impatiens 'New Guinea Lollipop'
by Longwood Gardens, Pennsylvania

Impatiens walleriana 'Rosette'
"Rose impatiens" or "Sultana"

Impatiens walleriana 'Red Ripple'
"Star sultana" of dwarf habit

Impatiens walleriana 'Elfin'
"Liliput miniatures" in California

Impatiens 'New Guinea variegata'
at Del Mar Exposition, San Diego

Impatiens 'New Guinea Starfire'
by Iowa State University

Impatiens hawkeri, *in habitat*
Chimbu, Highlands of New Guinea

Podophyllum hexandrum *(emodi)*
woodland herb with white waxy flowers

Podophyllum hexandrum *(BERB.)*
"May-apple" w. edible berry, from the Himalayas

Epimedium x youngianum *(BERB.)*
(diphyllum x grandiflorum), in Virginia

Epimedium grandiflorum
"Bishop's hat" of Japan and Korea

Vancouveria hexandra *(BERB.)*
"American barrenwort" in Redwood forest, Oregon

Epimedium x rubrum
(alpinum x grandiflorum), in South Carolina

Cynoglossum amabile
"Chinese forget-me-not" of W. China and Tibet

Cynoglossum nervosum *(BORAG.)*
"Great hounds-tongue" from the Himalayas

Epimedium grandiflorum album
in New York Botanical Garden

Epimedium grandifl. 'Rose Queen'
"Longspur epimedium"

Lindelofia longiflora *(BOR.)*
close-up of inflorescence

Epimedium x youngianum 'Niveum'
"Snowy epimedium" in Germany

Epimedium alpinum var. roseum
"Alpine epimedium" in England

Lithospermum canescens *(BOR.)*
"Indian paint" in Oklahoma

Podophyllum peltatum *(BERB.)*
"American Mandrake" in Vermont

Eritrichium elongatum *(BORAG.)*
"Alpine forget-me-not" in Wyoming

Lithodora diffusa 'Heavenly Blue'
(Lithospermum diffusum in hort.)

Lindelofia longiflora *(BORAG.)*
hairy perennial of the Himalayas

Hackelia floribunda *(BORAG.)*
"False forget-me-not" in Glacier Park, Montana

Moltkia x intermedia *(BORAG.)*
(M. petraea x suffruticosa)

Mertensia virginica *(BORAG.)*
"Virginia bluebells" in Great Smoky Mts., Tennessee

Pentaglottis sempervirens *(Anchusa hort.)*
"Evergreen alkanet" in the Pyrenées of Spain

Symphytum grandiflorum *(BUX.)*
"Groundcover comfrey" from the Caucasus

Pachysandra procumbens *(BUX.)*
"Alleghany spurge" of Kentucky to Louisiana

Pachysandra terminalis
"Japanese spurge" from China and Japan

Echium simplex *(giganteum)*
"Tower of jewels" in Orotava

Echium wildpretii
"Pride of Tenerife" on Pico Teide

Echium fastuosum
"Pride of Madeira" in California

Mertensia longiflora
"Lungwort" in Montana

Echium lycopsis *(plantagineum)*
purple "Viper's bugloss" (Mediterr.)

Echium vulgare
"Blue devil" in England

Omphalodes verna
"Creeping forget-me-not" in Austria

Omphalodes cappadocica
"Navel-seed" of Asia Minor

Omphalodes nitida
"Navelwort" in Portugal

Myosotis sylvatica *(BORAG.)*
"Wood forget-me-not" in Britain

Myosotis alpestris
"Alpine forget-me-not" in Bavaria

Myosotis sylvatica 'Blue Globe'
(alpestris of hort.) in Germany

Heliotropium arborescens *(BORAG.)*
fragrant *"Heliotrope" of Perú*

Myosotis scorpioides
"Water forget-me-not" in Arizona

Ipomoea batatas *(CONVOLV.)*
"Sweet potato" in fl. on Madeira

Onosma tocuensis *(BORAG.)*
"Hungarian gold-drops"

Onosma albo-roseum
"Pink gold drops" of Turkey

Onosma echioides
"Golden drops" in New York Bot. G.

Pulmonaria angustifolia
"Blue cowslip" (Europe to Caucasus)

Pulmonaria longifolia *(BORAG.)*
"English lungwort" of Isle of Wight

Pulmonaria saccharata
"Bethlehem sage" at Kew, England

Pulmonaria sacchar. 'Mrs. Moon'
"Lungwort" in East Germany

Symphytum orientale *(BORAG.)*
"Comfrey" near Istanbul, Turkey

Symphytum x uplandicum
"Russian comfrey" in New Jersey

Symphytum asperum
"Prickly comfrey" in Munich Bot. G.

Symphytum caucasicum
"Blue comfrey" of So. Russia

Campanula isophylla *(CAMP.)*
"Falling stars" of Liguria, Italy

Adenophora bulleyana
"Lady-bell" of W. China

Adenophora takedae (howozana)
"Japanese ladybell"

Adenophora confusa
"Purple lady-bells" in Connecticut

Campanula aucheri
in Duesseldorf Bot. Gard., Germany

Campanula bellidifolia
"Caucasus bellflower"

Campanula calamenthifolia
"Greek bellflower"

Campanula carpatica 'Alba'
"Tussock bellflower" in California

Campanula carpatica
"Carpathian harebell" in Hungary

Campanula isophylla 'Alba'
"Star of Bethlehem" in Holland

Campanula medium
'Calycanthema caerulea' *in Colorado*

Campanula medium
"Canterbury bells" in England

Campanula medium 'Calycanthema'
"Cup-and-saucer bells" in Italy

Campanula medium 'Rosea'
"Pink Canterbury bells"

Campanula glomerata *(CAMP.)*
"Clustered bellflower" in Thuringia

Campanula medium 'Alba'
"Mary's bells" in Berlin

Campanula lactiflora ('Molyneux')
"Milky bellflower" of the Caucasus

Trilisa paniculata *(Comp.)*
"Vanilla plant" in Virginia

Campanula elatines garganica
"Robust Adriatic bellflower"

Campanula persicifolia
"Peachbells" in California

Campanula trachelium
"Nettle-leaf bellflower" in Holland

Campanula rotundifolia
"Bluebells-of-Scotland" in N. Jersey

Campanula thyrsoides
Kew Botanic Gardens, England

Campanula punctata
Duesseldorf Bot. Garden, Germany

Campanula patula
(Carpathian Mts. to So. Europe)

Campanula hegielia
in habitat at Priene, Turkey

Jasione perennis *(laevis)*
Int'l. Garden Show, Munich

Jasione perennis 'Rosea'
"Shepherd's scabiosa" in Italy

Campanula portenschlagiana *(muralis in hort.)*
"Dalmatian bellflower" of Croatia

Campanula rupestris *(tomentosa)*
"Silky bellflower" in Turkey

Campanula elatines
"Star of Bethlehem" in No. Italy

Campanula poscharskyana
"Serbian bellflower" of No. Yugoslavia

Campanula sarmatica
"Sarmatian bellflower" of the Caucasus Mts.

Campanula cochleariifolia
low groundcover of European mountains

Codonopsis ovata *(CAMP.)*
"Bonnet bellflower" from Kashmir Himalayas

Jasione montana *(CAMP.)*
"Sheeps-bit scabious" (Europe to Asia Minor)

Platycodon grandifl. 'Mariesii'
"Japanese bellflower"

Platycodon grandiflorus
"Balloon flower" in California

Platycodon grand. 'Semi-plenus'
"Double balloon flower" in Carolina

Cannabis sativa *(CANNAB.)*
true "Hemp" of India

Trachelium caeruleum *(CAMP.)*
"Throat-wort" (Amsterdam Floriade)

Symphyandra hoffmannii
"Ring bellflower" of Croatia

Phyteuma comosum *(Physoplexis)*
"Horned rampion" (Dolomites)

Phyteuma humile *(CAMP.)*
"Dwarf horned rampion" (So. Alps)

Phyteuma nigrum
"French rampion" in Strasbourg

Echium wildpretii *(bourgeanum)* (BORAG.)
"Tajinaste" with Pico Teide, on Tenerife

Canna x generalis 'Hercules' *(CANN.)*
in Botanic Garden Tjibodas, Java, Indonesia

Campanula isophylla, *"Falling Stars"* (CAMP.)
in hanging baskets, Hammerfest, Arctic Norway

Canna x generalis 'President' *(indica cv.)*
with Mt. Pelegrino, on sunny Sicily

Canna edulis *(CANNAC.)*
"Edible canna" of West Indies

Canna indica, *"Indian shot"*
at Kew Bot. Gardens, England

Canna iridiflora
"Iris-flowered canna" of Perú

Cleome spinosa *(pungens) (CAPP.)*
"Spiny spider flower" (W. Indies)

Cleome hassleriana *(arborea)*
Joshua Tree Park, Arizona

Gypsophila repens 'Rose Beauty'
German Hort. Show, Duesseldorf

Triosteum rosthornii *(CAPR.)*
"Horse gentian" from China

Triosteum perfoliatum
"Wild coffee" (Mass. to Kansas)

Triosteum pinnatifidum
"Tinker's weed" of N.W. China

Canna x generalis 'President'
Quail Bot. G., Encinitas, Calif.

Canna x generalis 'King Humbert'
in Cape Town, So. Africa

Canna x generalis 'Striata'
in Bot. Garden Durban, Natal

Canna x generalis 'Felix Ragout'
Bot. Garden Tuebingen, Germany

Canna x generalis 'Lucifer'
in tropical Bombay, India

Canna x generalis 'Rosamond'
San Diego Animal Park, S. Pasqual

Canna generalis 'Cleopatra'
in Hilo Lagoon, Hawaii

Canna x generalis
'Pfitzer Dwarf Salmon'

Canna x generalis
'Pfitzer Dwarf Scarlet' *in Calif.*

Arenaria montana (CARYOPH.)
"Mountain sandwort" of France

Arenaria rigida
"Bulgarian sandwort"

Arenaria tetraquetra 'Granat.'
"Sandwort" in the Pyrenées

Cerastium arvense
"Field chickweed" in England

Cerastium alpinum lanatum
"Mouse-ears" of the Arctic

Cerastium boissieri *of Spain
in Kew Bot. Gardens, England*

Cerastium tomentosum
"Snow-in-summer", in Sicily

Cerastium arvense 'Compactum'
"Starry grasswort" in Germany

Dianthus knappii (CARYOPH.)
from Hungary and Bosnia

Dianthus sylvestris
"Wood-pinks" (Spain to Greece)

Dianthus deltoides
"Maiden pink" in Austria

Herniaria glabra (CARYOPH.)
"Green carpet" in San Diego, Calif.

Dianthus x allwoodii
"Allwood pinks" in England

Dianthus barbatus
"Sweet William" in California

Dianthus armeria
"Deptford pink" in Rhineland

Dianthus plumarius 'Her Majesty'
"Feather carnation" in New York B.G.

Dianthus caryophyllus chorus
"Hanging carnation" in Norway

Dianthus plumarius
"Cottage pink" (Italian Alps)

Dianthus caryoph. 'Mini Queen'
in Malmoe, Sweden

Dianthus caryoph. 'Pink Sim'
florist's "Carnation" in Delaware

Dianthus caryophyllus
"Clove pinks" in Honolulu

Dianthus chinensis
"Rainbow pinks" in Benares, India

Dianthus pungens *hort.*
from the Pyrenées of Spain

Dianthus alpinus
"Alpine pink" in Austrian Alps

Dianthus chinensis 'Heddewigii'
biennial "Chinese pink"

Dianthus chinensis 'Snowfire'
in col. Geo. Ball, W. Chicago

Dianthus chinensis
'Heddewigii Baby Doll'

Dianthus chinensis 'Pink Charm'
in Bot. Garden, Duesseldorf, Germany

Dianthus chin. 'Queen of Hearts'
in Leucadia nursery, California

Dianthus seguieri
"Bearded pink" in Spain

Dianthus gratianopolitanus
"Cheddar pink" at Hort. Expo. Munich

Gypsophila paniculata
"Chalk flower" or "Baby's-breath"

Gypsophila panic. 'Bristol Fairy'
"Florists double baby's breath"

Gypsophila elegans
"Annual baby's breath" (Caucasus)

Gypsophila repens
"Creeping baby's breath" in Europe

Gypsophila paniculata fl. pl.
"Double baby's breath" in California

Lychnis alpina
"Catch-fly" in Arctic Norway

Lychnis x arkwrightii
in Essen Bot. Garden, Germany

Lychnis chalcedonica
"Maltese cross" in Stockholm

Lychnis flos-jovis
"Flower of Love" in Swiss Alps

Lychnis coeli-rosa 'Loyalty'
"Blue viscaria" in Berlin Bot. G.

Lychnis coeli-rosa *(Silene)*
"Rose of heaven" on Tenerife

Lychnis coronaria
"Mullein pink" in California

Lychnis x haageana
"Haage's campion"

Lychnis visc. 'Splendens Plena'
"Double German catchfly"

Minuartia stellata *(Alsine)*
"Greek sandwort" (S.E. Europe)

Lychnis viscaria
"German catchfly" in Scotland

Petrorhagia saxifraga fl. pl.
double "Tunic flower" in Virginia

Paronychia kapela serpyllifolia
"Nailwort" in Austrian Alps

Saponaria caespitosa
"Soapwort" from the Pyrenées

Sagina subulata 'Aurea'
"Pearlwort" in San Diego

Saponaria officinalis
"Bouncing bet" in Pennsylvania

Saponaria officinalis alba
"White soapwort" in England

Sagina subulata
"Irish moss" in California

Saponaria x olivana
"Rose sandwort" in Rhineland

Saponaria lutea
"Yellow soapwort" in Swiss Alps

Saponaria ocymoides
"Rock soapwort" in Italy

Silene maritima
"Sea campion" in California

Silene colorata
"Catchfly" on Delos, Greece

Silene compacta
Munich Bot. Garden, Germany

Silene acaulis
"Moss campion" in Montana

Silene californica
"Indian pink" in Arizona

Silene caroliniana
"Wild pink" in Pennsylvania

Silene dioica
"Morning campion" in Germany

Silene laciniata
"Fringed Indian pink" in N. Mexico

Silene pendula
"Nodding catchfly" of So. Russia

Kochia scoparia *(CHENOPOD.)*
"Summer cypress" of S.E. Europe

Kochia scoparia trichophylla
"Burning bush" at Rutgers, N. Jersey

Kochia scoparia 'Childsii'
"Bold summer cypress" in Germany

Stellaria holostea *(CAR.)*
"Stitchwort" or "Moon flower"

Scleranthus uniflorus *(CAR.)*
moss-like "Knawe" of New Zealand

Atriplex hortensis 'Rubra' *(CHENOP.)*
"Mountain spinach" in Amsterdam

Baileya multiradiata *(COMP.)*
"Desert marigold" in Arizona

Gillenia trifoliata *(CLETH.)*
"Indian physic" in New York

Beta vulgaris cicala *(CHENOP.)*
"Ornamental Swiss chard" in Calif.

Dichorisandra thyrsiflora
"Blue ginger" in Brazil

Commelina coelistis *(COMM.)*
"Mexican day-flower"

Tradescantia x andersoniana
in Munich Botanic Garden

Cuthbertia rosea *(Tripogandra)*
(Coastal Carolina to Florida)

Ageratum houston. 'Nordmeer'
compact cv. in Germany

Ageratum houstonianum *(COMP.)*
"Floss flower" of Mexico

Chrysanthemum coccin. 'Rubrum'
"Red painted daisy" in Munich

Anacyclus depressus
from the mountains of Morocco

Anacyclus radiatus *(COMP.)*
in Lisbon Bot. Garden, Portugal

PERENNIALS - ANNUALS

Arctotheca calendula
"Cape weed" in South Africa

Achillea filipendulina
"Fernleaf yarrow" (Asia Minor)

Achillea filip. 'Coronation Gold'
in Botanic Garden Hamburg

Achillea ageratum
"Sweet yarrow" in Croatia

Achillea nobilis
"Thessaly yarrow" of No. Greece

Achillea millefolium
"Milfoil", cut flower in Germany

Achillea taygetea
from the mountains of Greece

Achillea ptarmica 'The Pearl'
double "Sneeze-wort" in Virginia

Achillea tomentosa
"Woolly yarrow" in California

Anaphalis yedoensis
"Japanese everlasting"

Anaphalis margaritacea
"Pearly everlasting" in Arizona

Anaphalis triplinervis
"Everlasting" of the Himalayas

Anthemis tinctoria
"Golden marguerite" in Scotland

Anthemis sancti-johannis
"St. John's camomile" of Bulgaria

Anthemis arvensis
"Corn chamomile" in England

Antennaria dioica ('Nyewood')
"Pussy-toes" in West Ireland

Arctotis acaulis
"African daisy" in Cape Prov.

Venidium fastuosum (Arctotis)
"Namaqualand daisy" in So. Africa

Arnica chamissonis foliosa
"Leafy arnica" in Wyoming

Arctotis venusta *(stoechadifolia)*
"Blue-eyed African daisy"

Arctotis breviscapa
"Yellow African daisy" in Lisbon

Artemisia lanata *(pedemontana)*
"Woolly wormwood" in the Dolomites

Artemisia ludoviciana
"Silver King artemisia"

Venidium fastuosum 'Exotic'
"Monarch of the Veldt"

Artemisia arborescens
"Wormwood" in Kew Gardens

Artemisia lactiflora
"White sagebrush" of China

Artemisia stelleriana
"Beach wormwood" in Virginia

Aster ericoides
"Heath aster" in So. Dakota

Aster ageratoides
"Noyama-kingiku" in Japan

Aster x alpellus
"Michaelmas daisy"

Aster alpinus
"Rock aster" in Colorado

Aster amellus
"Italian aster" in Meran

Aster dumosus 'Prof. A. Kippenberg'
"Pillow aster" in Rhineland

Aster radula
"Atlantic aster" in New York

Aster x frikartii
in California nursery, Vista

Aster linariifolius
"Savoryleaf aster" in Montréal

Aster novi-belgii
"New York aster" (E. No. America)

Aster novae-angliae
"New England aster" in California

Aster novae-angl. 'Harringt. Pink'
in Essen Bot. Garden, Germany

Asteriscus sericeus
"Canary Islands star"

Bellis perennis flore pleno
double flowers, in Hangchow, China

Aster spectabilis
"Seaside aster" in Virginia

Bellis perennis
"English daisy" in Britain

Brachycome multifida *hort.*
"Rock daisy" in Melbourne

Brachycome iberidifolia
"Swan River daisy" in W. Australia

Bidens ferulifolia
"Fern-leaved beggar-ticks"

Buphthalmum salicifolium
"Ox-eye" in Austria

Balsamorhiza sagittata
"Oregon sunflower" in So. Dakota

Callistephus chinensis
annual *"China aster" in Chicago*

Boltonia asteroides 'Snowbank'
"White boltonia" in New York

Bidens aristosa
"Bearded beggar-ticks" in N. Jersey

Centratherum muticum
"Brazil button-flower" on Dominica

Celmisia prorepens
"New Zealand Alpine daisy"

Catananche caerulea
"Cupid's dart" in Spain

Balsamorhiza sagittata, *"Balsam-root"*
in Grand Teton National Park, Wyoming

Chrysanthemum x morifolium 'Spoon type'
on wire frame, Chosun Hotel, Seoul, Korea

Carlina acaulis, *"Silver thistle"*
in University Botanic Garden, Lund, Sweden

Chrysanthemum coronarium, *"Crown daisy"*
in the ancient port of Catania, Sicily

Centaurea cineraria *(candidiss.)*
"Dusty miller" (So. Italy)

Centaurea gymnocarpa
"Velvet centaurea" of Capri

Senecio cineraria
(Cineraria maritima 'Diamond')

Centaurea dealbata
"Persian centaurea"

Chrysanthemum x morifolium
"Exhibition type mum"

Centaurea regusina
"Dalmatian dusty miller"

Chrysanthemum x morif. 'Carnelia'
"Anemone-type mum"

Chrysanthemum x morif. 'Delaware'
"Incurved formal mum"

Chrys. x morif. 'Illini Bonbon'
"Cushion anemone mum"

Chrysanthemum x morifolium
'Indianapolis-yellow' *(incurved)*

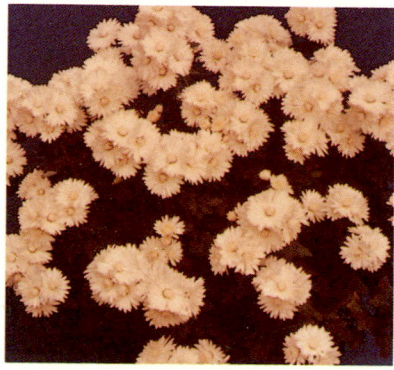

Chrys. x morif. 'Shimo-Bashira'
Japanese *"Cascade mum"*

Chrysanthemum x morif. 'Bonaffon'
popular *"Incurved pot mum"*

Carlina acaulis
"Silver thistle" in the Dolomites

Calendula officinalis
"Pot marigold" at Ball's, W. Chicago

Calendula officinalis 'Pacific'
"Pacific Beauty" in California

Carlina vulgaris
"Gold thistle" in England

Silybum marianum compactum
"St. Mary's thistle" in Rhineland

Carlina acaulis simplex
"Weather-thistle" (caulescens hort.)

Carlina acanthifolia
"Acanthus thistle"

Celmisia hookeri
"Otago daisy" of So. Island, N.Z.

Celmisia coriacea
on Mt. Cook, New Zealand

Centaurea cyanus purpurea
"Bachelor button" in Bavaria

Centaurea scabiosa
in So. England

Centaurea cyanus
"Blue cornflower" in Germany

Centaurea montana
"Mountain bluet" in Austrian Alps

Centaurea macrocephala
"Globe centaurea" of Armenia

Centaurea triumfettii
"Knapweed" (C. and So. Europe)

Chrysanthemum carinatum
"Tricolor mum" of Morocco

Chrysanthemum cinerariifolium
"Dalmatian pyrethrum"

Chrysanthemum indicum
"Chinese mum" in Hong Kong

Chrysanthemum coccineum
"Painted daisy" in Munich Bot. G.

Chrysanthemum coronarium
"Crown daisy" in Sardinia

Chrysanthemum corymbosum
(Tanacetum) from the Caucasus

Chrys. frutescens 'Mary Wootton'
"Tree marguerite" in Wellington, N.Z.

Chrys. frutescens chrysaster
"Boston yellow daisy"

Chrysanthemum frutescens
"Marguerite" in Canary Isl.

Chrysanthemum leucanthemum
"Oxeye daisy" (Europe to Caucasus)

Chrysanthemum x maximum 'Aglaya'
"Double Shasta daisy" in Calif.

Chrysanthemum maximum
"Daisy mum" in Cologne, Germany

Chrysanthemum x morif. 'Songster'
"Spider mum" by Yoder

Chrys. x morif. 'Golden Cascade'
on wire frame, in Seoul, Korea

Chrys. x morifolium 'Turner'
at Rochford greenhouses, England

Chrys. multicaule *(Algeria)*
as annual bedder in California

Chrys. x morif. 'Daisy White'
"Garden mum" at Roehrs, N. Jersey

Chrysanthemum argenteum
in Kew Bot. Gardens, England

Chrysanthemum hosmariense
(Leucanthemum) of Morocco

Chrysanthemum macrophyllum
"Tansy mum" in Hungary

Chrysanthemum ptarmiciflorum
"Silver lace" of Gran Canaria

Chrysanthemum myconis
"Yellow marguerite" in France

Chrysanthemum paludosum
"Miniature Shasta daisy" in Calif.

Chrysanthemum x spectabilis
Munich Botanic Garden

Aster pringlei *(ericoides hort.)*
"September-kraut" in Germany

Chrysanthemum parthenium fl. pl.
"Double feverfew" in Sparta, N.J.

Chrysanthemum parthenium 'Roseum'
"Pink button-flower" in Holland

Chrysanthemum segetum *('Prado')*
"Yellow Boy" in Britain

Chrys. segetum 'Orient Star'
"Corn marigold" in Cologne Bot. G.

Chrysanthemum weyrichii
"Japanese daisy" in Kyoto

Chrysogonum virginianum
"Golden star" in So. Carolina

Chrysopsis mariana
"Maryland gold aster"

Chrysopsis villosa
"Golden aster" (Southwest U.S.)

Parahebe lyallii *(SCROPH.)*
of Milford Sound, New Zealand

Cirsium japonicum
"Japan thistle"

Cirsium edule
"Edible thistle" in Arizona

Cirsium spinosissimum
"Alpine thistle" in Switzerland

Cnicus benedictus
"Blessed thistle" in Israel

Cladanthus arabicus *(Anthemis)*
aromatic plant in Spain

Coreopsis auriculata
"Eared tickseed" in Virginia

Coreopsis grandiflora 'Sun baby'
in Munich Bot. Garden, Germany

Coreopsis lanceolata
"Lance tickseed" (Mich. to N. Mex.)

Coreopsis maritima
"Sea dahlia" on California coast

Coreopsis verticillata
"Threadleaf coreopsis" in Arkansas

Coreopsis tinctoria
"Calliopsis" in Missouri

Cosmos sulphureus
"Mexican aster"

Cosmos atrosanguineus
"Black cosmos" of Mexico

Cosmos bipinnatus
"Garden cosmos"

Crepis aurea
Kew Botanic Gardens, England

Crepis rubra
"Pink hawksbeard" (S.E. Europe)

Cynara cardunculus
"Cardoon" of So. Europe

Cynara scolymus
"Globe artichoke" in California

Cynara scolymus glauca
ornamental "Blue artichoke"

Dahlia imperialis
"Tree dahlia" in Mexico

Heracleum sphondylium *(UMB.)*
"Cow-parsnip", in the Ukraine

Dimorphotheca sinuata
"Rain Cape marigold" in California

Encelia californica
"Brittle bush" in Mexico

Doronicum cordatum
"Leopard's bane" in Austria

Doronicum plantagineum
"Plantain leopard's bane" in Oxford

Dyssodia tenuiloba
"Dahlberg daisy" in California

Dracopis amplexicaulis
"Cone flower" (Kansas to Texas)

Echinops ritro
"Globe thistle" in Russia

Echinaceae purpurea
"Purple coneflower" (Louisiana)

Emilia javanica *(sagittata)*
"Flora's paintbrush"

Erigeron unalaskensis
from the Aleutians off Alaska

Erigeron speciosus
"Ray-aster" (Western U.S.)

Erigeron alpinus
in Jena Bot. Garden, Germany

Erigeron danelium
Botanic Garden Bermuda

Erigeron glabellus
"Alaska fleabane" (N.W. No. America)

Erigeron flettii
"Olympic fleabane" of Washington

Erigeron glaucus
"Seaside daisy" in California

Erigeron x hybridus
Cologne Bot. Gard., Germany

Erigeron x hybridus roseus
in Munich Bot. Gard., Germany

Erigeron pinnatisectus
"Rocky Mountain fleabane"

Erigeron pulchellus
"Robin's plantain" in Georgia

Eriophyllum lanatum
"Woolly sunflower" of Montana

Eupatorium coelestinum
"Hardy ageratum" in New Jersey

Eupatorium purpureum
"Sweet Joe-Pye weed" in Virginia

Eupatorium riparium
"Mistflower" of Mexico

Euryops acraeus *(evansii)*
"Silver euryops" in California

Euryops pectinatus
"Resin bush" in So. Africa

Felicia amoena *(So. Africa)*
in Munich Botan. Garden

Felicia amell. 'Variegata'
"Variegated blue daisy" in Calif.

Felicia amelloides
"Blue marguerite" of Cape Prov.

Gazania maritima
in Botanic Garden Munich

Gazania pinnata
of Cape Prov., So. Africa

Gazania rigens *(So. Africa)*
"Treasure flower" in Kirstenbosch

Gazania rigens 'Aztec Queen'
in San Diego, California

Gazania rigens 'Copper King'
(splendens of hort.)

Gazania rigens 'Gold Nugget'
in San Diego

Lactuca plumieri *(Cicerbita)*
"Mountain lettuce" in Switzerland

Gazania pavonia hirtella
in the Little Karroo, So. Africa

Gazania nivea *hort. (krebsiana)*
Cologne Bot. Gard., Germany

Gaillardia x grandifl. 'Mandarin'
in Encinitas, California

Gaillardia aristata
"Blanket flower" in Wyoming

Gaillardia x grandiflora
"Monarch strain" in Virginia

Gazania rigens 'Aztec'
"Goldband treasure flower"

Gazania rigens 'Fiesta Red'
(splendens in Calif. hort.)

Gazania rigens leucolaena
creeping in Durban, Natal

Gazania rigens 'Sun Gold'
in Los Angeles Arboretum

Gerbera jamesonii *(So. Africa)*
"Transvaal daisy" in Pretoria

Gerbera x jamesonii hybrida
"Giant African daisy"

Gamolepis chrysanthemoides
"Daisy bush" in California

Gamolepis tagetes *(Psilothonna)*
"Golden daisy" near Cape Town

Grindelia chiloensis
"Gum-plant" of Argentina

Helenium autumnale
"Sneeze weed" in Montréal

Helenium big. 'Moerheim Beauty'
"California sneezewort"

Helenium autumnale 'Waltraut'
in Botanic Garden Munich

Gazania rigens fa. splendens
Nymphenburg Bot. G. Munich

Helenium hoopesii
"Orange sneezeweed" of Wyoming

Jurinea alata
interesting Caucasus perennial

Helianthus salicifolius
"Willow-leaf sunflower" of Kansas

Helianthus laetiflorus
"Showy sunflower" in Nebraska

Helianthus x multiflorus
double "Cut-and-come-again"

Helianthus grosseserratus
"Sawtooth sunflower" in Texas

Helianthus annuus
"Sunflower" of Western U.S.

Helianthus ann. 'Russian Giant'
in Salzburg, Austria

Helianthus annuus nanus
"Dwarf sunflower" in Trinidad

Helianthus annuus flore pleno
"Double sunflower" in Germany

Helianthus ann. 'Autumn Beauty'
bicolored, in England

Helichrysum roseum
"Immortelle" of W. Australia

Helichrysum bracteatum
"Strawflower" in Perth, Australia

Helichrysum bellidioides
"Immortelle" of New Zealand

Helichrysum graveolens
on the Crimea, Black Sea reg.

Helichrysum milfordiae
"Lesotho immortelle" (So. Africa)

Helichr. orientale 'Sulphur Light'
in Dahlem Botanic G., Berlin

Helichrysum lanatum
"Flannel everlasting" of So. Africa

Helichrysum petiolare
"Licorice plant" in Rhineland

Helichrysum arenarium
"Northern everlasting" in Finland

Heliopsis hel. 'Incomparabilis'
"Double oxeye" in Cologne Bot. G.

Heliopsis helianthoides scabra
"Rough oxeye" in New York

Heliopsis helianthoides
"False sunflower" in Ontario

Heliopsis helianthoides scabra
'Golden plume', *in Munich Bot. G.*

Helipterum manglesii *(Australia)*
"Swan River everlasting" in Perth

Helipterum roseum (Acroclinium)
"Rose sunray" in W. Australia

Hymenoxys acaulis glabra
"Actinea" of Ontario to Illinois

Hymenoxys grandiflora
in snow of Alpine Colorado

Layia platyglossa
"Tidy-tips" of California

Hieracium bombycinum
"Hawkweed" of Spain

Hieracium villosum
"Shaggy hawkweed" (So. Europe)

Hieracium maculatum
"Devil's paintbrush" (W. Europe)

Inula britannica
"English elecampane"

Hieracium aurantiacum
"Orange hawkweed" in Stockholm

Inula ensifolia
"Swordleaf inula" in Germany

Inula helenium
"Elecampane" in Arnold Arbor., Boston

Inula orientalis
"Caucasian inula" in New York

Inula hookeri
in the Himalayas of Sikkim

Inula magnifica
from Eastern Caucasus

Inula macrocephala
Turkey to Armenia

Leucogenes leontopodium
"New Zealand edelweiss"

Leontopodium stoechas *(China)*
in Munich Bot. G., Germany

Leontopodium souliei
"Chinese edelweiss" of Yunnan

Leontopodium alpinum
"Edelweiss" in Tirol, Austria

Liatris elegans
"Blue blazing star" in Texas

Liatris aspera
"Gay-feather" in Virginia

Leuzea centauroides
(Centaurea) of So. Europe

Liatris punctata
"Western gay-feather" in Kansas

Liatris spicata 'Alba'
"White gay-feather" in Germany

Liatris spicata
"Gay feather" on Long Island, N.Y.

Ligularia dentata
"Golden-ray" in Essen Bot. Garden

Ligularia hodgsonii
"Togebuki" in Hokkaido

Ligularia wilsoniana
"Giant groundsel" of China

Ligularia przewalskii *(China)*
in Tivoli Gardens, Copenhagen

Ligularia tussilaginea
'Aureo-maculata', *"Leopard plant"*

Ligularia stenocephala
in Fukuoka, Kyushu

Lindheimera texana
"Star daisy" in West Texas

Onopordum nervosum
"Ornamental thistle" in New Jersey

Onopordum acanthium
"Scotch thistle" (Chelsea Fl. Show)

Lonas annua
"Yellow ageratum" in Italy

Osteospermum ecklonis 'Buttermilk'
at Chelsea Flower Show, London

Osteospermum ecklonis 'Whirligig'
Notcutt's Nurs., Suffolk, England

Osteospermum ecklonis
"Cape marigold" in Madeira

Osteospermum fruticosum 'Album'
"Freeway daisy" in California

Osteospermum frut. 'Burgundy mound'
"Trailing African daisy" (Cape)

Othonna parviflora
in Stellenbosch, So. Africa

Machaeranthera tanacetifolia
"Tahoka daisy" of Alberta

Oyedaea verbesenioides
U. of Calif. Bot. G. Los Angeles

Perityle crassifolia *(Mexico)*
on Isla Cerralvo, Baja Calif.

Petasites hybridus
"Butter-bur" (Europe to Asia)

Piqueria trinervia *(Mexico)*
"Stevia serrata" of florists

Scolymus hispanicus
"Golden thistle" of S.W. Europe

Scorzonera humile
"Viper's grass" in Kew Gardens

Santolina chamaecyparissus
"Lavender cotton" (Mediterr. reg.)

Rudbeckia fulgida
"Orange coneflower" (Southeast U.S.)

Rudbeckia fulgida sullivantii
in Botanic G. Krefeld, Germany

Coreopsis grandiflora
"Tickseed", in St. Louis, Missouri

Rudbeckia hirta 'Gloriosa'
"Gloriosa daisy" in California

Rudb. hirta 'Double Gloriosa'
February blooming in Cape Town

Rudbeckia laciniata
"Cutleaf cone-flower" in Virginia

Rudbeckia triloba *(Southeast U.S.)*
"Brown-eyed Susan" in Delaware

Rudbeckia nitita 'Autumn Sun'
in Botanic Gard. Essen, Germany

Sanvitalia procumbens
"Hussar's heads" in Guatemala

Senecio adonidifolius
"Pyrenées groundsel" of Spain

Senecio cineraria
Cineraria maritima of hort.

Senecio grandifolius (So. Mex.)
in Bot. Garden, Auckland, N.Z.

Senecio leucostachys (vira-vira)
"Dusty miller" of Argentina

Senecio webbii
in Gran Canaria, Spain

Silybum marianum
"Holy thistle" in Miletus, Turkey

Scorzonera hispanica
"Black salsify" in Segovia

Silphium perfoliatum
"Cup-plant" in Missouri

Stokesia laevis
"Stoke's aster" in Louisiana

Solidago altissima
"Golden rod" (Québec to Arizona)

Solidago canadensis
"Canada golden rod" in Manitoba

Solidago nemoralis
"Dyersweed goldenrod" in Penna.

Solidago virgaurea minuta
"Miniature goldenrod" of Kyushu

Solidago spathulata
in Ketchikan, Alaska

Solidago serotina *(No. America)*
Botan. Gard. Duesseldorf, Germany

Telekia speciosa
"Oxeyes" in Munich Bot. Gard.

x Solidaster luteus
"Hybrid golden rod" (France)

Sclerocarpus divaricatus
near Puntarenas, Costa Rica

Tagetes patula 'Naughty Marietta'
single "French marigold"

Tagetes patula 'Gold Rush'
dwarf double, at Ball's, W. Chicago

Tagetes lemmonii
"Arizona marigold" in Calif.

Tagetes patula 'Pascal'
"Rose of India" in Munich

Tagetes patula 'Petite Orange'
"Petite marigold" (Geo. Ball)

Tagetes tenuifolia 'Orange Gem'
"Striped Mexican marigold"

Tithonia diversifolia
along roadside in Sumatra

Tithonia rotundifolia
"Mexican sunflower"

Taraxacum officinale
"Dandelion" or "Blowballs"

Tripleurospermum maritimum
"Matricary" in Berlin-Dahlem

Tolpis barbata
annual in So. France

Townsendia parriyi
Rocky Mountains of Wyoming

Tragopogon dubius, *with seeds*
"Goat's beard" in Austria

Tragopogon porrifolius
"Oyster plant" in California

Ursinia anethoides *(So. Africa)*
Nymphenburg Bot. G. Munich

Venidium fastuosum 'Phantom'
at Temple of Luxor, Egypt

Chrysanthemum parthenium
Tanacetum praealtum in Munich Bot. G.

Senecio bicolor, *"Silver cineraria"*
in Duesseldorf Bot. G., Germany

Urospermum dalechampii
on Mallorca, Spain

Verbesine encelioides
in Missouri Bot. Garden, St. Louis

Convolvulus althaeoides
"Bindweed" of Mediterranean reg.

Vernonia noveboracensis
"Ironweed" in Virginia

Wedelia trilobata *(COMP.)*
"Creeping daisy" in Moorea

Xeranthemum annuum *(COMP.)*
"Immortelle" of S.E. Europe

Wyethia angustifolia *(COMP.)*
"Narrow-leaf mules-ears" in Oregon

Wyethia amplexicaulis
"Mules-ears" in Wyoming

Evolvulus arbuscula *(CONV.)*
hanging plant of Brazil

Zinnia elegans 'Cherry Ruffles'
with ruffled florets

Zinnia angustifolia *(Mexico)*
in Bot. Gard. Duesseldorf, Germany

Zinnia elegans 'Cactus strain'
at Los Angeles Flower Show

Zinnia elegans 'Peter Pan'
dwarf strain, in California

Zinnia elegans 'Thumbelina'
Minis at Geo. Ball's, W. Chicago

Zinnia elegans 'Yellow Ruffles'
at Ball Trial Gard., W. Chicago

Convolvulus mauritanicus
"Ground morning-glory" of Spain

Convolvulus tricolor *(CONV.)*
"Dwarf morning-glory" in Sicily

Convolv. tricolor 'Royal Ensign'
"Purple glorybind"

Aethionema coridifolium
"Stone-cress" of Lebanon

Cornus canadensis, *in fruit (CORN.)*
"Bunch berry" in New Mexico

Cornus canadensis *with flowers*
of No. America to Alaska, Korea

Aurinia saxatilis *(Alyssum sax.)*
"Basket of gold" of So. Europe

Alyssum serphyllifolium
"Thymian madwort" of Spain

Aethionema grandiflorum *(CRUC.)*
"Persian stonecress" of Iran

Alyssum heldreichii *(CRUC.)*
"Greek stonecress" in Kew Gardens

Alyssum markgrafii
"Madwort" of Albania

Alyssum wulfenianum *(S.E. Alps)*
in New York Bot. Garden

Arabis alpina 'Variegata'
in Auckland Domain, N. Zealand

Arabis caucasica
"Rock cress" (S.E. Europe)

Arabis ferdinandi-coburgii
'Variegata' *of Bulgaria*

Aubrieta deltoides *(CRUC.)*
"Purple rock-cress" in California

Aubrieta kotcheviana
on Oregon coast

Aubrieta deltoidea 'Cobalt'
in Royal Botanic Gardens, Kew

Aubrieta deltoides 'Variegata'
in Botanic Gard. Oxford, England

Aubrieta deltoidea 'Red Cascade'
(Van Tubergen, Holland)

Arabis alpina rosea
"Mountain rock-cress" (Europe)

Fibigia clypeata
in Merano, So. Tyrol, Italy

Brassica oler. acephala crispa
ornamental "Kale" in Oaxaca, Mex.

Brassica oleracea laciniata
"Miniature flowering kale"

Cheiranthus cheiri lutea *(CRUC.)*
"Yellow wall flower" in Oregon

Cheiranthus cheiri *(Erysinum)*
"Wall flower" in Andalusia, Spain

Cheiranthus cheiri flore pleno
"Double wallflower" in England

Cardamine trifolia
"Cuckoo flower" in Italian Alps

Crambe cordifolia
"Colewort" in Vermont

Crambe maritima
"Sea kale" in Sweden

Brassica oleracea acephala *(CRUC.)*
"Flowering cabbage" at Nijo Castle, Kyoto, Japan

Brassica oleracea acephala crispa, *"Flowering Kale"*
in West Lake garden, Hangchow, Chekiang, China

Zinnia elegans *(COMP.)*
"Youth-and-old-age" in romantic Bali, Indonesia

Chrysanthemum x morifolium 'Cascade' *in variety*
at the Music Hall on Sejong Blvd., Seoul, Korea

Erysimum x allionii 'Aurantium'
"Golden wallflower" in Pennsylvania

Erysimum linifolium
"Alpine wallflower" of Spain

Erysimum x allionii *(Cheiranthus)*
"Siberian wallflower" in Brooklyn

Draba arabisans
from E. Canada to New York

Draba sibirica
in Bergianska Bot. G., Sweden

Draba carinthiaca *(siliquosa)*
in New York Bot. Garden

Dentaria diphylla
"Toothwort" in South Carolina

Hesperis matronalis
"Dame's violet" in Somerville, N. Jersey

Hutchinsia alpina
"Alpen-cress" in Bavarian Alps

Iberis sempervirens
"Evergreen candytuft" in Brooklyn B.G.

Iberis umbellata
"Globe candytuft" in California

Iberis amara
"Rocket candytuft" in Germany

Isatis tinctoria
"Dyer's wood" in England

Ionopsidium acaula
"Diamond flower" of Portugal

Lepidium fremontii
"Desert alyssum" in Arizona

Lobularia mar. 'Oriental Nights'
in Botanic Garden Munich

Lobularia maritima
"Sweet alyssum" in Amsterdam

Lobularia marit. 'Royal Purple'
in San Diego, California

Lunaria annua, *flowering*
"Honesty" or "Satin flower"

Lunaria annua *(seedpods)*
"Money-plant" in Gotland, Sweden

Lunaria rediviva
"Perennial honesty" in Oxford Bot. G.

Malcolmia maritima
"Virginian stock" in Greece

Matthiola incana *(double-fl.)*
"Imperial stocks" on Capri, Italy

Matthiola incana 'Rosea'
"Imperial stocks" in Cologne

Matthiola incana 'Rubra'
"Stocks" in Durban, So. Africa

Matthiola sinuata
"Greek gilliflower" on Delos

Alyssum montanum
"Mountain alyssum" in Lebanon

Schivareckia podolica *(Alyssum) (CRUC.)*
mat-forming "Geese cress" in Carpathians of Rumania

Petrocallis pyrenaica *(Draba) (CRUC.)*
alpine perennial from Spain and Switzerland

Galax urceolata *(aphylla) (DIAPENS.)*
"Beetle-weed" of Virginia to Alabama

Shortia galacifolia *(DIAPENS.)*
"Oconee bell" in Great Smoky Mts. of Carolina

Pterocephalus parnassi *(perennis) (DIPSAC.)*
"Teasel winghead" on mountains of Greece

Corydalis lutea *(FUMAR.)*
"Yellow corydalis" in the Dolomites of Italy

Dicentra eximia *(FUMAR.)*
"Fringed bleeding heart" in Adirondack Mts. of New York

Dicentra formosa
"Western bleeding heart" in the Sierra Nevada, California

Pyxidanthera barbulata *(DIAP.)*
"Flowering moss" in New Jersey

Shortia soldanelloides *(DIAP.)*
"Fringed galax" in New York Bot. G.

Cephalaria alpina *(DIPSAC.)*
"Alpine cephalaria" in No. Italy

Dipsacus sylvestris *(DIPSAC.)*
"Teasel" (France to Ukraine)

Morina longifolia *(DIPSAC.)*
"Whorl-flower" in Munich Bot. G.

Knautia arvensis *(DIPSAC.)*
"Blue buttons" (Europe to Siberia)

Corydalis aurea *(FUMAR.)*
"Golden corydalis" in E. Canada

Corydalis cava *(FUMAR.)*
"Hollow-tuber fumewort" in Vienna

Corydalis ochroleuca *(Balkans)*
in Kew Bot. Gardens, England

Scabiosa atropurpurea
"Sweet scabiosa" in California

Scabiosa graminifolia
"Grassleaf scabious" of So. Europe

Scabiosa caucasica *(DIPSAC.)*
in Dahlem Bot. Gard. Berlin

Scabiosa ochroleuca
"Cream scabious" (Europe to Asia)

Scabiosa lucida
"Pincushion flower" in Thuringia

Centaurium scilloides *(GENT.)*
"Centaury" of Portugal

Dicentra eximia 'Alba'
"White Turkey corn" in Germany

Dicentra spectabilis *(FUM.)*
"Bleeding heart" of Japan

Dicentra spectabilis 'Alba'
"White bleeding heart"

Gentiana asclepiadea
"Willow gentian" of So. Alps

Gentiana angustifolia
"Gentian" near Zermatt, Switzerland

Gentiana bavarica
"Bavarian gentian" near Garmisch

Gentiana clusii *(acaulis var.)*
near Cortina, Dolomites, Italy

Gentiana cruciata
"Cross gentian" (C. Europe to Siberia)

Gentiana cruciata phlogifolia
in Carpathian Mts. of Hungary

Gentiana parryi
"Rocky Mtn. gentian" in Montana

Gentiana scabra
"Rough gentian" of Manchuria

Gentiana sept. lagodechiana
from the Eastern Caucasus

Gentiana sino-ornata
"Chinese gentian" (Yunnan, Tibet)

Gentiana acaulis *(kochiana)*
"Blue gentian" in Swiss Alps

Gentiana germanica, *autumn. fl.*
in the Dolomites, No. Italy

Eustoma grandiflorum
"Prairie gentian" in Nebraska

Gentianopsis thermalis
"Fringed gentian" in Arizona

Gentiana septemfida
"Crested gentian" of Turkestan

Gentiana farreri
"Kansu gentian" of N.W. China

Exacum affine flore pleno
"Dble. Persian violet" in Calif.

Exacum affine
"Persian violet" from Socotra

Gentiana tibetica
from the Himalaya mountains

Gentiana verna *(Switzerland)*
"Spring gentian" in Zermatt

Gentiana lutea
"Yellow gentian" in the Pyrenées

Geranium argenteum
"Silver-leaved cranesbill" (Italy)

Geranium grandiflorum *hort.*
from the Himalayas of Sikkim

Geranium maculatum
"Spotted geranium" in Maine

Geranium macrorrhizum
from Italian Alps to Balkans

Geranium cinereum
from the Pyrenees of Spain

Geranium subcaulescens
(Italy to Balkans and Lebanon)

Geranium renardii
from the Caucasus region

Geranium psilostemon
of Armenia, Asiatic Turkey

Geranium endressii *(Pyrenées)*
in Palmengarten Frankfurt

Swertia perennis *(GENT.)*
alpine of Europe, Asia, Alaska

Geranium wallichianum
from temperate Himalayas

Erodium manescavii *(GERAN.)*
"Heron's-bill" of the Pyrenées

Erodium x kolbianum
Botanic Garden Kew, England

Geranium platypetalum
in Frankfurt, Germany

Geranium sylvaticum
on Gudvangen Fjord, Norway

Geranium dalmaticum
in Escondido, California

Erodium pelargoniflorum
from Anatolia, Asia Minor

Geranium maderense
on Island of Madeira

Geranium sanguineum
"Blood geranium" in New Jersey

Geranium malviflorum
of Mediterr. reg., at Kew Gardens

Geranium palmatum
on Tenerife Isl., Spain

Pelargonium x hortorum 'Velma'
"Tricolor geranium"

Pelargonium x hort. 'Mr. Wren'
striking bicolor geranium

Pelargonium tricolor
(violareum hort.) in So. Africa

Pelarg. x hort. 'Mad. Salleron'
"Carpet-bed geranium" in France

Pelargonium tomentosum
"Peppermint geranium"

Pelarg. 'Prince Rupert varieg.'
"French lace", lemon-scented

Pelargonium x hortorum
'Salmon Supreme'

Pelargonium x hort. 'Olympic Red'
"Florist 's geranium" at Roehrs

Pelargonium x hortorum
'Carefree Scarlet' *(from seed)*

Pelargonium x domesticum
'Circus Day'

Pelargonium x domesticum
'Gay Nineties'

Pelargonium x domest. 'MacKay'
"Martha Washington geranium"

Gentiana lutea *(GENT.), "Yellow gentian"*
on Rigi, Bernese Alps, Switzerland

Pelargonium x hortorum. *"Zonal geraniums"*
overlooking Millstadt Lake, Carinthia, Austria

Pelargonium peltatum 'Amethyst', *"Ivy Geranium"*
as standard tree, Charlottenburg Castle, Berlin

Pelargonium x hortorum, *"Zonal geraniums"*
with historic Conservatory, Copenhagen Bot. Garden

Pelargonium x hortorum
'Salmon Irene' *in Germany*

Pelargonium x hort. 'Happy Thought'
"Butterfly geranium"

Pelarg. x domest. 'Frilly Aztec'
in Vista, California

Pelargonium graveolens
"Rose geranium" at Logee, Conn.

Pelargonium crassicaule
"Succulent geranium" of Namibia

Pelargonium peltatum 'Mexico'
"Bicolor ivy geranium"

Pelargonium 'Lumière du Matin'
"Strasbourg geranium" in Rhineland

Pelargonium 'Ville de Paris'
(peltato-zonale hyb.) in France

Pelargonium x glaucifolium
"Black-flowered geranium"

Anigozanthos pulcherrimus
"Golden kangaroo paw"

Anigozanthos manglesii
"Kangaroo paw" in W. Australia

Anigozanthos flavidus
"Yellow kangaroo paw" in Calif.

Anigozanthos rufus (HAEMOD.)
"Red kangaroo paw" near Perth

Anigoz. flavidus rubrum
in Western Australia

Anigozanthos viridis
"Green kangaroo paw"

Globularia cordifolia (GLOB.)
"Heart leaf globularia" in Florida

Globularia nudicaulis
"Globe daisy" at Kew, England

Globularia trichosantha
"Syrian globularia"

Hypericum formosum
"St. John's-wort" in Montana

Hypericum cerastoides
"Rhodope St. John's-wort" of Greece

Hypericum hirsutum *(HYPER.)*
"Hairy St. John's-wort" in England

Nemophila menziesii *(HYDR.)*
"Baby-blue-eyes" in Oregon

Phacelia campanularia *(HYDR.)*
"California bluebell"

Gentianella diemensis *(GENT.)*
Australian Alps, New So. Wales

Hypoxis angustifolia
"Star flower" in the Transvaal

Hypoxis stellata *(Spiloxene)*
"White star-grass" of Cape Prov.

Hypoxis hirsuta *(HYPOX.)*
"Star grass" (Maine to Texas)

Schizostylis coccinea
"Crimson flag" of So. Africa

Belamcanda chinensis *(IRID.)*
"Leopard flower" in Sumatra

Gunnera tinctoria *(HALORAG.)*
"Chilean rhubarb" in Munich Bot. G.

Rhodohypoxis baurii platypetala
at Tropic World, Escondido, Calif.

Rhodohypoxis baurii *(HYPOX.)*
"Red star", Kirstenbosch, So. Africa

Rhodohypoxis baurii pictus
at Chelsea Flower Show, London

Libertia chilensis *(IRID.)*
Bot. Gard. Duesseldorf, Germany

Libertia pulchella
from Tasmania to New Guinea

Libertia grandiflora
"New Zealand iris"

Iris graminea
(beardless) of So. Europe

Iris sibirica 'Perry's Blue'
"Siberian iris" (beardless)

Iris ensata (true species)
kaempferi of hort., in Japan

Iris pumila hybrid, "Dwarf bearded iris"
spring-blooming in Arnold Arboretum, Boston

Iris tectorum, "Roof iris"
grown on thatched roofs in Japan

Iris gracilipes (Japan)
"Slender iris" in Hillsdale, New Jersey

Iris melitta (bearded)
"Toad iris", miniature of Greece

Dietes vegata (Moraea)
"African iris" in Vista, California

Dietes grandiflora (So. Africa)
"Large wild iris" in Kirstenbosch

Dietes bicolor (IRID.)
"Yellow moraea" in Los Angeles

Iris x germanica 'Lilacina'
"Bearded iris" in Germany

Iris x germ. 'Beverly Sills'
pink beauty in Maryland

Iris x germanica 'Old Melodies'
bearded iris in New Zealand

Iris x germanica *(bearded)*
"German iris" in Bot. G., Essen

Iris x germ. 'Wiener Walzer'
Mirabelle Gard., Salzburg, Austria

Iris chamaeiris *(pumila hort.)*
"Crimean iris" of No. Italy

Iris flavissima *(humilis)*
"Gold-beard iris" in Hungary

Iris x ensata 'Housah' *(kaempferi)*
"Japanese iris" (beardless)

Iris x ensata 'Better Yet'
fancy beardless (Pamela Harper)

Iris x fulvala
"Louisiana iris" in New Orleans

Iris japonica *(China, Japan)*
"Fringed iris" (crested)

Iris spuria *(beardless)*
"Butterfly iris" in Sweden

Iris douglasiana *(beardless)*
dwarf *"Douglas iris" of Oregon*

Iris cristata, *"Crested iris"*
dwarf, *of Maryland to Missouri*

Iris crocea *(spuria aurea)*
in Munich Botanic Garden

Iris orientalis *(ochroleuca)*
"Oriental iris" from Syria

Iris orientalis sulphurea
"Yellow-banded iris"

Iris gracilis *(goniocarpa)*
miniature, in Kew Bot. Gardens

Iris laevigata 'Regal'
"Rabbit-ear iris" in Virginia

Iris macrosiphon *(beardless)*
miniature "Tube iris" *(California)*

Iris laevigata 'Variegata'
in Japan. temple garden, Kyoto

Iris sibirica *(beardless)*
"Siberian iris" in Moscow

Iris pallida 'Variegata'
"Orris" in Oxford Bot. Garden

Iris tectorum 'Alba' *(crested)*
Willowwood Arboretum, New Jersey

Iris verna, *"Dwarf iris"*
of Pennsylvania to Georgia

Iris versicolor, *"Blue flag"*
(Labrador to Manitoba, Virginia)

Iris pallida *(odoratissima)*
"Sweet iris" in South Tyrol

Neomarica bicolor *(IRID.)*
"Walking iris" of Brazil

Neomarica caerulea
"Twelve apostles" in São Paulo

Neomarica northiana
(Bot. Cabinet, London 1824)

Sisyrinchium arizonicum
in Cochise County, Arizona

Sisyrinchium bellum *(IRID.)*
"Blue-eyed Susan" of California

Sisyrinchium bermudiana
in Botanic Gard. Kew, England

Petersonia glabrata
"Australian native iris"

Orthrosanthus laxus *(IRID.)*
"Morning iris" in W. Australia

Orthrosanthus multiflorus
"Purple morning flag" (W. Australia)

Sisyrinchium californicum
"Gold-eyed grass" in Monterey

Sisyrinchium angustifolium
"Blue-eyed grass" in Virginia

Melittis melissophyllum *(LAB.)*
"Bastard balm" (Europe to Ukraine)

Sisyrinchium striatum *(IRID.)*
"Rush lily" of Argentina

Sisyrinchium macrocephalum
at Kew Bot. Gardens, England

Sisyrinchium macounii
"Blue-eyed grass" of Brit. Columbia

Ajuga pyramidalis *(LAB.)*
"Bugle weed" in California

Ajuga reptans
"Carpet bugle" in Pennsylvania

Clinopodium coccineum *(LAB.)*
"Calamint" in Alabama

Coleus scutellarioides *(LAB.)*
in Munich Bot. Garden, Germany

Coleus blumei 'Brilliancy'
"Flame nettle" in San Francisco

Coleus blumei 'Verschaffeltii'
"Painted nettle"

Dracocephalum nutans
"Dragonhead" at Kew Bot. G., England

Plectranthus 'Variegated mintleaf'
in Valley of 1000 Hills, Natal

Lavandula dentata
"French lavender", in Spain

Dracocephalum prattii
"Chinese dragonhead"

Iboza riparia *(Transvaal)*
"Misty plume bush" in New York B.G.

Lavandula viridis
"Green Fire" of Madeira

Lamiastrum galeobdolon 'Varieg.'
"Varieg. archangel" in Germany

Lamium maculatum
"Spotted deadnettle" in N. Jersey

Leonotis leonurus
"Lion's-ear" in Escondido, Calif.

Monarda didyma 'Croftway Pink'
"Bee-balm" in Cologne, Germany

Monarda didyma
"Oswego tea" in San Francisco

Monarda fistulosa
"Wild bergamot" in Virginia

Monardella linoides
Sierra Nevada of California

Monarda punctata
"Horse-mint" in Germany

Moluccella laevis
"Bells of Ireland" from Syria

Perilla frutescens
annual "Shiso" of Japan

Perilla frut. 'Atropurpurea'
"Black nettle" in Hangchow, China

Perilla frut. 'Atropurp. crispa'
"Frilled nettles" in California

Perovskia abrotanoides
"Russian sage" in Jena, Thuringia

Perovskia atriplicifolia
"Azure sage" in Longwood, Penna.

Plectranthus ecklonii
"Purple spur-flower" in Zululand

Marrubium incanum
"Silver horehound" in Sicily

Orthosiphon stamineus
in Singapore Botanic Garden

Phlomis chrysophylla
"Jerusalem sage" in Lebanon

Nepeta x faassenii
"Persian ground-ivy" in Copenhagen

Nepeta mussinii *(racemosa)*
"Catmint" of the Caucasus

Calamintha grandiflora
"Calamint" in Lyon, France

Phlomis russeliana *(Anatolia)*
"Sticky Jerusalem sage"

Rhexia mariana, *(MELAST.)*
"Maryland meadowbeauty"

Phlomis fruticosa
"Jerusalem sage" in California

Phlomis tuberosa
"Lion's heart" in Munich Bot. G.

Physostegia virgin. 'Violacea'
"Obedience" in Bot. G. Sydney

Physostegia virginiana
"False dragonhead" (E. No. America)

Plectranthus ciliatus
in Botanic Gard. Cape Town

Plectranthus coleoides 'Marginatus'
"Candle plant" of So. India

Plectranthus 'Varieg. Mintleaf'
in Escondido, California

Prunella grandiflora
"Self-heal" in New England

Prunella vulgaris
"Heal-all" of Eurasia

Salvia argentea
"Silver sage" in Athens, Greece

Salvia pratensis
"Meadow sage" in So. England

Salvia azurea, *"Blue sage"*
in Duesseldorf Bot. G., Germany

Salvia farinacea
"Mealy-cup sage" of N. Mexico

Salvia fruticosa
"Greek sage" (S.E. Europe)

Salvia azurea grandiflora
"Pitcher's sage" in California

Salvia viridis 'Oxford Blue'
Nymphenburg Bot. G., Munich

Salvia blepharophylla
"Red sage" of Mexico

Salvia x superba *(nemorosa)*
striking hybrid, in Munich

Salvia splendens
"Scarlet sage" of Brazil

Salvia greggii
"Autumn sage" in Texas

Salvia guaranitica *(ambigens)*
from Brazil and Paraguay

Salvia gesneriiflora *(Colombia)*
Kew Bot. Gardens, England

Salvia canariensis *(Tenerife)*
in Chula Vista, California

Salvia coccinea
"Texas sage" (Carolina to Mex.)

Salvia farinacea 'Blue Bedder'
in San Diego, California

Salvia farinacea 'Catima'
at New York Botanical Garden

Salvia involucrata
"Roseleaf sage" in Auckland, N.Z.

Salvia farinacea 'Victoria'
at Floriade 82 in Amsterdam

Salvia leucantha purpurea
"Mexican purple sage"

Salvia lavandulifolia
"Spanish sage" in Granada, Spain

Salvia leucantha
"Mexican sage" in San Diego

Salvia patens 'Cambridge blue'
"Gentian sage" in England

Salvia mexicana
"Ramona" in Encinitas, California

Pycnanthemum virginianum
"Mountain mint" of Eastern U.S.

Stachys officinalis
"Betony" in England

Scutellaria costaricana
"Scarlet skullcap" of C. America

Scutellaria indica parvifolia
"Lilac skullcap" of China

Stachys byzantina
"Lamb's ears" in California

Stachys grandiflora *(macrantha)*
"Big betony" of Anatolia

Stachys grandiflora 'Superba'
in Bot. Garden Munich, Germany

Teucrium scorodonia
"Wood-sage" (Norway to Poland)

Teucrium betonicum
"Germander" on Madeira

Teucrium fruticans
"Tree germander" in Portugal

Anthyllis montana
in Kew Bot. Gard. England

Coronilla varia
"Crown vetch" in New England

Indigofera gerardiana
"Himalayan indigo" (India)

Baptisia perfoliata
"Catbells" in Savannah, Georgia

Baptisia tinctoria
"Wild indigo" or "Rattleweed"

Baptisia australis
"Blue false indigo" in Tennessee

Crotalaria juncea
"Bengal hemp" near Calcutta

Galega officinalis
"Goat's-rue" in Turkey

Senna marilandica *(Cassia)*
"Wild senna" of Southeast U.S.

Lupinus polyphyllus hyb.
"Washington lupine" in Oregon

Lupinus x regalis 'Castellan'
Russell hybrid, in Germany

Lupinus polyphyllus *(No. America)*
in Oxford Bot. Garden, England

Lupinus arboreus
"Tree lupine" in California

Lupinus luteus
"Yellow lupine" in Portugal

Lupinus hartwegii
Strybing Arboretum, S. Francisco

Pedicularis groenlandica *(SCROPH.)*
"Elephant heads" in Canada

Lupinus texensis
"Texas blue bonnet" near Dallas

Lupinus perennis
"Sundial lupine" in Pennsylvania

Melilotus alba *(LEG.)*
"White sweet clover" in Holland

Lathyrus luteus aureus *(Turkey)*
in Botanic Gard. Kew, England

Lathyrus vernus 'Roseum'
"Spring vetchling" in Belgium

Lotus tetragonolobus
"Winged pea" of So. Europe

Lotus corniculatus *(LEG.)*
"Birdsfoot trifoil" in Ontario

Vicia faba *(LEG.)*
"Broad-bean" in Germany

Trifolium repens *(LEG.)*
"White clover" in New Jersey

Trifolium pratense
"Red clover" in Thuringia

Trifolium procumbens *(dubium)*
"Irish shamrock" in Longwood, Penna.

Trifolium incarnatum
"Italian clover" in Texas

Asparagus officinalis, *in flower*
"Garden asparagus" in California

Asparagus densiflorus 'Myriocladus'
"Zigzag asparagus" in Rio Bot. G.

Thermopsis divaricarpa
"Golden pea" in Rocky Mts., Utah

Thermopsis montana *(LEG.)*
"False lupine" in Colorado

Thermopsis caroliniana *(villosa)*
"Carolina lupine" in Rawleigh

Anthericum liliago *(LIL.)*
"St. Bernard lily" in Copenhagen Bot. G.

Elsholtzia stauntonii *(LAB.)*
"Mint-shrub" of No. China

Hedysarum coronarium *(LEG.)*
"French honeysuckle" in Monaco

Asparagus densiflorus 'Myers'
"Plume asparagus" in flower

Asparagus densifl. 'Sprengeri'
"Sprengeri fern" of Natal

Asphodeline lutea *(LIL.)*
"Jacob's rod" (Mediterr. reg.)

Bulbinella floribunda *(LIL.)*
"Florist's bulbinella" (So. Africa)

Bulbinella hookeri
"Maori onion" of New Zealand

Blandfordia grandiflora *(LIL.)*
"Christmas bells" in E. Australia

Bulbinella gibbsii
"Cat's-tail" (New Zealand)

Calochortus gunnisonii *(LIL.)*
"Mariposa lily" near Denver, Colo.

Chamaelirium luteum *(LIL.)*
"Fairy-wand" of E. No. America

Chlorophytum comosum 'Varieg.'
"Ribbon plant" at Roehrs, N. Jersey

Dianella caerulea (LIL.)
"Blue flax lily" in New So. Wales

Lagotis stolonifera *(SCROPH.)*
Bergianska Bot. Garden, Sweden

Eremurus himalaicus
"Himalayan desert-candle"

Eremurus x isabellinus
Int'l. Hort. Exhib., Munich

Eremurus elwesii
"Desert candle" in New York

Heloniopsis orientalis
"Shojobakama" near Nikko, Japan

Eremurus olgae
"King's spear" of Turkestan

Eremurus stenophyllus
"Afghan desert candle", (S.W. Asia)

Convallaria majalis
"Lily-of-the-valley" in Germany

Clintonia umbellulata
"Speckled wood-lily" in Virginia

Clintonia uniflora
"Bride's bonnet" in No. California

Hemerocallis aurantiaca
"Golden day lily" in New Jersey

Hemerocallis citrina *(nocturnal)*
"Citron daylily" in Rhineland

Hemerocallis forrestii *(S.W. China)*
"Day lily" in Kew Bot. Gardens

Hemerocallis fulva
"Orange daylily" in California

Hemerocallis lilioasphodelus
"Tall yellow daylily"

Hemerocallis lilioasph. 'Ewen'
in Fortin de las Flores, Mexico

Hemerocallis hybrida 'Bonanza'
spectacular "Bicolor daylily"

Hemerocallis minor
"Grass-leaf daylily" in Sydney, Austr.

Hemerocallis hyb. 'Royal Flare'
tetraploid with rounded flowers

Disporum sessile 'Variegatum'
"Japanese fairy bells" in Kyoto

Disporum flavum
"Fairy bells" in Virginia

Arthropodium cirrhatum
evergreen per. of New Zealand

Hesperaloe parviflora *(AGAV.)*
"Western aloe", El Paso, Texas

Hosta amanuma *(Japan)*
miniature in Bot. G. Frankfurt

Hosta decorata 'Marginata'
Strybing Arboretum, San Francisco

Hosta lancif. 'Albo-Marginata'
"White-rim plantain lily"

Hosta lancifolia *(LILIAC.)*
"Narrowleaf plantain lily" in Tokyo

Hosta plantag. 'Honey-bells'
in Royal Bot. Gard. Kew, England

Hosta fortunei *(gigantea)*
"Giant plantain lily" on Honshu

Hosta elata 'Praeflorens'
in Palmengarten Frankfurt

Hosta crispula
Nymphenburg Bot. G., Munich

Hosta fortunei 'Albo-picta'
in Kew Botanic Gardens

Hosta fortunei 'Aureo-marginata'
in Auckland Domain, N. Zealand

Hosta fortunei 'Rugosa'
"Crinkled plantain-lily"

Hosta plantaginea
"Fragrant plantain-lily" in New York

Hosta 'Thomas Hogg' *(decorata)*
(Funkia hort.) in England

Hosta tardiflora
"Autumn-lily" in New York Bot. G.

Hosta sieboldiana 'Viridis'
in Botanic Garden Cologne

Hosta sieboldiana *(Japan)*
Bergianska Bot. Gard., Stockholm

Hosta sieboldiana 'Elegans'
"Giant blue hosta" in Wisconsin

Hosta rectifolia
"Giant funkia" of Japan

Hosta sieboldiana 'Williams'
"Gold circle hosta" in Connecticut

Hosta undulata 'Univittata'
"Wavyleaf shade lily" in Germany

Hosta tokudama
"Tokudama" of Honshu, Japan

Hosta ventricosa *(China)*
"Blue plantain lily" in California

Hosta venusta *(Japan, Korea)*
"Pretty plantain lily" in New York

Maianthemum kamtschaticum
"False lily-of-the-Valley"

Maianthemum bifolium *(Eurasia)*
"Two-leaf Solomon's seal" in England

Maianthemum canadense
"Canada mayflower"

Polygonatum multiflorum
"Solomon's seal" in Germany

Leucocrinum montanum
"Sand-lily" in New Mexico

Paris polyphylla
from the Himalayan region

Polygonatum commutatum
"Great Solomon's seal" (New England)

Polygonatum jacquinii
in Kew Botanic Gard., England

Polygonatum odoratum 'Varieg.'
"Varieg. Solomon's seal" in Chicago

Kniphofia uvaria
"Torch lily" in So. Africa

Kniphofia 'Royal Standard'
"Poker plant" in Oxford Bot. Garden

Kniphofia tuckii
"Dwarf torch lily", Munich Bot. G.

Kniphofia uvaria praecox
"Red hot poker" in San Francisco

Rohdea japonica, *with berries*
"Sacred lily of China" in Yokohama

Speirantha gardenii *(China)*
in Kew Bot. Gardens, England

Tofieldia glutinosa
"False asphodel" (E. No. America)

Smilacina stellata
"Star-fl. valley lily" in Boston

Smilacina racemosa
"False Solomon's seal" in Montréal

Tricyrtis macranthopsis
"Toad lily" of Honshu, Japan

Tricyrtis hirta
"Hairy toad lily" from Kyushu

Veratrum viride
"American hellebore" in N.Y. Bot. G.

Uvularia grandiflora
"Big merry bells" in Québec

Uvularia perfoliata
"Straw-bells" at Chelsea, London

Uvularia sessilifolia
"Little merry bells" in Arkansas

Trillium chloropetalum
"Wake-robin" in Seattle, Washington

Trillium undulatum
"Painted trillium" in Virginia

Trillium erectum albiflorum
"Squawroot" in Bot. Garden Kew

Trillium sessile, *"Toad-shade"*
in Missouri Bot. Gard. St. Louis

Trillium decumbens
"Birth-root" in Mobile, Alabama

Trillium viride var. luteum
"Yellow wood trillium" at Kew G.

Trillium viride
"Wood trillium" at New York Bot. G.

Trillium grandiflorum
"Eastern wake-robin" in New York B.G.

Trillium grandifl. florepleno
at Kew Botanic Gard., England

Trillium cernuum
"Nodding trillium" in Montreal Bot. G.

Trillium erectum
"Purple trillium", Longwood G., Penna.

Trillium ovatum
"Coast trillium" in Oregon

Xerophyllum asphodeloides
"Turkey-beard" in New York B.G.

Xerophyllum tenax *(LIL.)*
"Beargrass" in Glacier, Montana

Linum grandiflorum 'Rubrum'
"Scarlet flax" in Delhi, India

Linum arboreum *(LIN.)*
"Greek flax" in Heraklion, Crete

Linum austriacum
"Austrian flax" in Carinthia

Linum capitatum
"Flax" in Duesseldorf Bot. Garden

Linum perenne
"Blue flax" in Monterey, California

Linum grandiflorum
"Flowering flax" of No. Africa

Linum flavum
"Golden flax" in Germany

Mentzelia asperula *(LOAS.)*
"Stickleaf" in Tucson, Arizona

Loasa acanthifolia
in Santiago Bot. G., Chile

Limnanthes douglasii *(LIM.)*
"Meadow-foam" of Oregon

Lobelia cardinalis *(LOBEL.)*
"Cardinal flower" (E. No. America)

Lobelia erinus 'Sapphire'
"Edging lobelia" in England

Lobelia erinus
Cape of Good Hope, So. Africa

Lobelia erinus 'Rosamonde'
in Aalsmeer, Holland

Lobelia siphilitica
"Blue Cardinal flower" in Boston

Pratia angulata *(LOBEL.)*
"Creeping half-flower" in Calif.

Spigelia marilandica *(LOG.)*
"Indian pink" in Texas

Lobelia splendens *(fulgens)*
"Mexican lobelia" as cut flower

Lythrum salicaria 'Flame'
in Dahlem Bot. Garden, Berlin

Hibiscus cannabinus *(MALV.)*
"Indian hemp" in Mexico

Hibiscus trionum *(So. Europe)*
"Flower of an hour" in N. Zealand

Anoda cristata *(MALV.)*
"Snow cup" in San Antonio, Texas

Lobelia tupa *(LOBEL.)*
in Santiago Bot. Garden, Chile

Hibiscus coccineus
"Scarlet rose-mallow" in Savannah

Callirhoe involucrata *(MALV.)*
"Poppy mallow" in Jackson, Wyoming

Alcea rosea *(Althaea)*
"Garden hollyhock" in Copenhagen

Alcea rosea 'Rubra'
"Red hollyhock" in California

Alcea rosea plena
"Double hollyhock" in England

Althaea officinalis
"Marsh-mallow" in Darmstadt, Germany

Hibiscus moscheutos 'Disco Belle'
"Dwarf rose mallow" (Sakata, Japan)

Hibiscus mosch. 'Southern Belle'
"Giant mallow" in Brooklyn Bot. G.

Gossypium herbaceum
"Cotton" with bolls of fleece

Anisodontea capensis *hort.*
"Busy Lizzie" in Frankfurt

Malva alcea *(Europe)*
"Hollyhock mallow" in Berlin

Lavatera arborea
"Tree mallow" (Mediterr. reg.)

Lavatera cachemiriana
"Kashmir tree mallow"

Lavatera olbia 'Rosea'
"Tree lavatera" in Portugal

Lavatera trimestris 'Silver Cup'
in Botanic Garden Munich

Malva sylvestris
"Algiers mallow" in Malaga, Spain

Lavatera thuringiaca
"Saxon mallow" in Weimar

Malva verticillata crispa
"Curled mallow" in New York

Malope trifida *(grandiflora)*
from Spain and No. Africa

Malva moschata
"Musk mallow" in Wisconsin

Maranta arundinacea 'Variegata'
at Temple of Borobudur, Java

Maranta leuconeura erythroneura
"Red-veined prayer plant"

Calathea makoyana *(MAR.)*
"Peacock plant" from Brazil

Dorstenia argentata *(MOR.)*
from Santa Catarina, Brazil

Dorstenia yambuyaensis, *in fruit*
fig relative of Zaire, C. Africa

Triolena pustulata *(Bertolonia)*
from cloudforest of Ecuador

Heliconia bihai *(MUS.)*
"Firebird" on Maui, Hawaii

Ensete ventricosum *(MUS.)*
"Abyssinian banana" in Kenya

Strelitzia reginae *(MUS.)*
"Bird-of-paradise" in California

Sidalcea malviflora 'Brilliant'
"Checker mallow" in Oregon

Sphaeralcea coccinea *(MALV.)*
"Prairie mallow" in Texas

Nolana paradoxa *(acuminata)*
"Chilean bellflower" in England

Abronia villosa *(NYCT.)*
"Sand verbena" in Baja Cal., Mexico

Abronia umbellata
"Coast sandverbena" in California

Lopezia hirsuta *(ONAG.)*
"Mosquito flower" of Mexico

Epilobium hirsutum *(ONAG.)*
"Willow-weed" in Germany

Mirabilis multiflora *(NYCT.)*
"Umbrellawort" in Arizona

Mirabilis jalapa
"Four-o'clock" of Perú

Clarkia purpurea viminea
"Orchid godetia" in Oregon

Dissotis rotundifolia *(MEL.)*
of Trop. West Africa

Oenothera caespitosa *(West U.S.)*
"Twisted evening primrose"

Gaura lindheimeri, *of Louisiana*
at Chelsea Flower Show, London

Oenothera brevipes (Camissonia)
in the desert of Nevada

Oenothera clavaeformis
in Death Valley, E. California

Clarkia amoena whitneyi
"Satin flower" (Calif. coast)

Clarkia amoena *(Godetia)*
"Farewell-to-spring" in San Diego

Clarkia amoena plena
"Dble. satin flower" in Bonn Bot. G.

Clarkia unguiculata *(elegans)*
"Mountain garland" of California

Epilobium angustifolium
"Fireweed" in Edinburgh, Scotland

Oenothera laciniata *(mexicana)*
"Pale evening primrose" in Texas

Oenothera biennis *(E. No. America)*
"Common evening primrose"

Oenothera speciosa
"Showy white sundrops" in Kansas

Oenothera deltoides *(Arizona)*
"Desert evening primrose"

Oenothera speciosa grandiflora
"Great white sundrops"

Oenothera erythrosepala
in Munich Bot. Garden, Germany

Oenothera pilosella
"Prairie sundrops" in Ohio

Oenothera neomexicana
day-blooming in arid Arizona

Oenothera hookeri
"Night-candle" in San Diego, Calif.

Oenothera perennis *(pumila)*
"Canada sundrops" in Québec

Oenothera fruticosa *(ONAGR.)*
"Common sundrops" (N. Eng. to Okla.)

Oenothera berlandieri
"Mexican evening primrose"

Oenothera missouriensis
"Ozark evening primrose"

Oenothera tetragona fraseri
in Botan. Gard. Jena, Thuringia

Zauschneria californica latifolia
"Hummingbird trumpet" in Arizona

Zauschneria californica *(ONAG.)*
"California fuchsia" in Monterey

Argemone corymbosa *(PAPAV.)*
"Argemony" at Grand Canyon, Ariz.

Argemone platyceras
"Prickly poppy" in Mexico

Mirabilis longiflora *(NYCT.)*
"Sweet four o'clock" (Mexico)

Cypripedium acaule *(ORCH.)*
"Pink ladyslipper" (E. No. America)

Cypripedium calceolus
"Moccasin flower" (Eurasia, N. America)

Cypripedium calceolus pubescens
"Yellow ladyslipper" (No. America)

Cyclanthus bipartitus
"Splitleaf" inflorescence

Cypripedium cordigerum
in the Himalayas of Nepal

Cypripedium reginae *(ORCH.)*
"Showy lady-slipper" in Minnesota

Paeonia mascula *(PAEON.)*
"Southern peony" in France

Paeonia mascula arietina
"Turkish peony" at Kew G., England

Paeonia mlokosewitschii
"Caucasia peony"

Paeonia lact. 'Edmund Steichen'
"Garden peony" in New York

Paeonia lact. 'Festiva Maxima'
"Double Chinese peony" in Germany

Paeonia lactiflora *(albiflora)*
"Chinese peony" in Philadelphia

Paeonia mollis
"Siberian peony" in Kew Gardens

Paeonia lact. 'Grace Root'
in Brooklyn Botanic Garden

Paeonia lactiflora 'Requiem'
in Williamsburg, Virginia

Paeonia officinalis
"Peasant's peony" in Salzburg, Austria

Paeonia tenuifolia
"Fern-leaved peony" in Rumania

Paeonia suffuticosa *(Moutan)*
"Tree peony" of N.W. China

Chelidonium majus *(PAP.)*
"Celandine" in Willowwood, N. Jersey

Eomecon chionantha *(PAP.)*
"Snow poppy" of E. China

Glaucium corniculatum *(PAP.)*
"Sea poppy" in Berkely, Calif.

Hylomecon japonica *(PAP.)*
"Japanese poppy" in England

Meconopsis cambrica *(PAP.)*
"Welsh poppy" (W. Europe)

Meconopsis betonicifolia
"Blue poppy" in Edinburgh, Scotland

Stylophorum diphyllum *(PAP.)*
"Celandine poppy" in Illinois

Meconopsis grandis
"Asiatic poppy" in Nepal

Platystemon californicus *(PAP.)*
"Cream cup" in Tucson, Arizona

Polemonium carneum *(amoenum)*
in Strybing Arbor., San Francisco

Ipomopsis multiflora *(Gilia)*
"Sky rocket" in Arizona

Gilia capitata *(POLEM.)*
"Globe gilia" in Portland, Oregon

Asteriscus maritimus *(COMP.)*
"Gold coins" in Portugal

Monardella macrantha *(LAB.)*
in San Diego, California

Glaucium flavum *(PAP.)*
"Horned poppy" in Toledo, Spain

Hunnemannia fumariifolia *(PAP.)*
"Mexican tulip poppy"

Macleaya cordata *(PAPAV.)*
"Coral plume poppy" in Stockholm

Macleaya microcarpa
"Plume poppy" in Pennsylvania

Meconopsis napaulensis
"Satin poppy" in Virginia

Meconopsis regia *(PAPAV.)*
"Royal poppy" in Khatmandu, Nepal

Mecon. x sheldonii 'Branklyn'
(betonicifolia x grandis)

Eschscholtzia californica
"California poppy" near San Diego

Papaver burseri *(alpinum)*
"Alpine poppy" near Lucerne, Switz.

Papaver anomalum
in Munich Bot. Garden, Germany

Papaver aurantiacum
near Interlaken, Switzerland

Papaver radicatum, *"Arctic poppy"*
at Arctic Circle in Spitzbergen

Romneya coulteri
"Matilija" in Coronado, Calif.

Papaver nudicaule
"Iceland poppy" in Nara, Japan

Papaver orientale
"Oriental poppy" in Kew Bot. Gard.

Papaver orientale 'Flore pleno'
in Bot. Garden Oxford, England

Papaver orientale, *"Oriental poppies"*
at Lake Louise, in view of Victoria Glacier, W. Canada

Papaver nudicaule, *"Iceland poppies"*
Banff National Park, Canadian Rockies

Alcea rosea, *old-fashioned "Hollyhocks"*
at Andersen's birthplace, Odense, Denmark

Papaver dubium, *"Greek Poppy"*
on Isle of Delos, birthplace of Apollo

Papaver somniferum 'Danebrog'
"Fringed opium poppy" in Munich

Papaver somniferum
"Opium poppy" in Turkey

Papaver somnif. paeoniaeflorum
in Bot. Garden Lisbon, Portugal

Papaver rhoeas
"Corn poppy" in Thuringia

Papaver orientale 'Mary Finan'
fringed beauty in Berlin Bot. Garden

Sanguinaria canadensis *(PAP.)*
"Blood-root" in Pennsylvania

Rivina humilis *(PHYTOL.)*
"Rouge plant" in Nassau, Bahamas

Phytolacca americana *(PHYT.)*
"Poke-weed" (Eastern U.S.)

Armeria maritima 'Alba' *(PLUMB.)*
"Ladies cushion" in Berlin Bot. G.

Armeria juniperifolia 'Ardenholme'
"Rose thrift" in Copenhagen

Armeria maritima *(PLUMB.)*
"Sea pink" (Europe to Asia)

Armeria pseudarmeria
"Pinkball thrift" of Portugal

Ipomopsis aggreg. macrosiphon
"Skyrocket" in Tucson, Arizona

Ipomopsis aggregata *(Gilia)*
"Scarlet gilia" in Bryce, Utah

Ipomopsis rubra *(POLEM.)*
"Texas plume" in San Francisco

Plantago major rosularis
"Rose plantain" in England

Plantago major *(PLANT.)*
"Cart-track plant" in Germany

Plantago major 'Rubrifolia'
"Redleaf plantain" in Virginia

Limonium sinuatum (PLUMB.)
perennial "Statice" in Italy

Psylliostachys suworowii (Limonium)
"Annual sea-lavender" in Cologne

Limonium latifolium 'Violetta'
"Violet sea lavender" in California

Limonium latifolium
"Wideleaf sea-lavender" in Penna.

Goniolimon tataricum (Statice)
"Shore lilac" in Berlin Bot. Garden

Ceratostigma plumbaginoides
"Blue plumbago" in Virginia

Collomia grandiflora (POL.)
in Sierra Nevada of California

Linanthus androsaceus (Gilia)
Coast range of California

Linanthus montanus (POLEM.)
Sequoia Nat'l. Park, California

Phlox austromontana
prostrate form, in Arizona

Phlox douglasii 'Crackerjack'
at Chelsea Flower Show, London

Phlox drummondii
"Annual phlox" in California

Phlox ovata *(Penna. to Alabama)*
"Mountain phlox" in Pittsburgh

Phlox paniculata 'Starfire'
"Garden phlox" in Munich Bot. G.

Phlox paniculata
"Summer phlox" in New Jersey

Phlox nivalis *(subulata var.)*
"Trailing phlox" in Virginia

Phlox subulata
"Moss pink" in San Francisco

Phlox subulata 'Atropurpurea'
red "Creeping phlox" in Rhineland

Phlox carolina 'Miss Lingard'
"Carolina phlox" in No. California

Phlox divaricata
"Wild Sweet William" in Ontario

Phlox bifida
"Sand phlox" in Kansas

Phlox diffusa
in Rocky Mountains of Utah

Phlox stolonifera
Willowwood Arboretum, N. Jersey

Phlox stansburyi
in Kanab, So. Utah

Phlox lutea
yellow phlox of Mexico

Phlox douglasii, *of Montana*
at Kew Bot. Gardens, England

Phlox woodhousei
at Grand Canyon, Arizona

Polemonium caeruleum
"Jacob's ladder" in England

Polemonium reptans *(POLEM.)*
"Creeping polemonium" in New York

Polemonium pulcherrimum
"Skunkleaf" in Ketchikan, Alaska

Polemonium foliosissimum
"Greek valerian" in Wyoming

Eriogonum ovalifolium
"Wild buckwheat" in Arizona

Eriogonum umbellatum *(POLYG.)*
"Sulphur flower" (Sierra Nevada)

Parnassia fimbriata *(SAX.)*
"Bog-stars" in Denver Bot. Garden

Polygonella americana
"Jointweed" in So. Carolina

Polygonum affine *(POLYG.)*
"Himalayan fleece-flower"

Polygonum bistorta
"Snake weed" in Bergianska, Sweden

Polygonum orientale
"Prince's feather" of India

Polygonum campanulatum
"Alpine bistort" (Himalayas)

Polyg. cusp. compact. 'Femina'
bearing fruit, from Japan

Polygonum cuspidatum
in Ketchikan, Alaska

Polygonum viviparum
Mt. McKinley Nat'l. Park, Alaska

Polygonum weyrichii
"Sakhalin knotweed" (Japan)

Polygonum carneum *hort.*
at Alan Bloom's, Suffolk, England

Rumex acetosa *(POLYG.)*
"Garden sorrel" in Europe

Lewisia nevadensis *(PORTUL.)*
in the Sierra Nevada, California

Lewisia cotyledon howellii
along Columbia River in Oregon

Anemopsis californica *(SAURUR.)*
"Yerba Mansa" in the Sierras

Lewisia rediviva
"Sand rose" in Nevada desert

Lewisia milleri hyb.
in Bot. Gard. Duesseldorf, Germany

Lewisia tweedyi
on Mount Rainier, Washington

Portulaca pilosa 'Hortualis'
on St. Thomas, Virgin Islands

Portulaca grandiflora
"Rose-moss" of Brazil heritage

Portulaca oleracea 'Wildfire'
"Purslane hyb." in Florida

Dodecatheon pulchellum
"Southern shooting star"

Dodecatheon meadia *(PRIM.)*
"Shooting star" in London

Dodecatheon hendersonii
"Sailor caps" of Brit. Columbia

Montia sibirica *(PORT.)*
at Chelsea Flower Show, London

Cortusa matthiola *(PRIM.)*
Edinburgh Bot. G., Scotland

Anagallis monelli *(PRIM.)*
"Pimpernel" in Spain

Androsace sarmentosa *(PRIM.)*
"Rock jasmine" in No. California

Androsace strigillosa
in Darjeeling Himalaya

Androsace primuloides 'Chumbyi'
Royal Bot. Gard. Kew, England

Douglasia laevigata
in Olympic Mts. of Washington

Lysimachia barystachys
in Mts. of Honshu, Japan

Lysimachia clethroides
"Goose-neck loosestrife" (China)

Lysimachia ephemerum
from So. France to Spain

Lysimachia punctata
"Yellow loosestrife" in New York

Lysimachia vulgaris
"Garden loosestrife" in Munich

Primula alpicola
"Moonlight primrose" in Sikkim

Primula aurantiaca
"Candelabra primrose" in Yunnan

Primula bulleyana
"Yunnan candelabra"

Primula auricula hyb.
"Auricula primrose" of gardens

Primula auricula
"Alpine auricula" in San Francisco

Primula capitata
"Purplehead primrose" of Sikkim

Primula burmanica
in Portland, Oregon

Primula cockburniana
in Longwood Gard., Pennsylvania

Primula beesiana *(China)*
Bergianska Bot. Garden, Stockholm

Primula frondosa
"Balkan primrose" in Bulgaria

Primula florindae
"Giant cowslip" in Pennsylvania

Primula x briscoei *hort.*
col. Essen Bot. G. Germany

Primula x polyantha 'Pacific'
"Polyanthus" hyb. in California

Primula malacoides
"Fairy primrose" at Roehrs, N. Jersey

Primula x polyantha 'Crescendo'
German Garden Expo. Duesseldorf

Primula elatior
"Oxlip primrose" in England

Primula juliae
dwarf primrose of the Caucasus

Primula helodoxa
"Amber primrose" of Myanmar

Primula odorata
Bot. Garden Duesseldorf, Germany

Primula elatior pallasii
(Ural Mts.) in Kew Bot. Gard.

Primula japonica
"Japanese candelabra primrose"

Primula vulgaris (acaulis)
"English primrose" (Europe)

Primula vulgaris 'Rubra'
in New Jersey garden center

Primula pulverulenta
"Silverdust primrose" at Chelsea

Primula melanops (S.W. China)
in Kew Bot. Gardens, England

Primula denticulata
"Globe primrose" in Pennsylvania

Primula kisoana
"Kakko-so" in Honshu, Japan

Primula sieboldii
"Sakkura-so" of Kyushu

Primula rosea
"Kashmir primrose"

Primula sikkimensis
"Sikkim primrose" in Oregon

Primula secundiflora
"Sideflower primrose" of Yunnan

Primula veris *(PRIM.)*
"Cowslip primrose"in England

Primula vialii
"Orchid primrose" in San Francisco

Soldanella alpina *(PRIM.)*
"Glacier Alpenclock" (Alps)

Primula obconica
"German primrose" in Rhineland

Pyrola asarifolia *(PYROL.)*
"Pink wintergreen" in Canada

Pterospora andromedea *(PYROL.)*
"Giant bird's-nest" (No. America)

Actaea pachypoda *(RANUNC.)*
"Gull's eyes" in New Jersey

Actaea rubra *with berry-fruit*
"Baneberry" in South Dakota

Aconitum fischeri
"Monk's head" in Connecticut

Aconitum lycoctonum
"Wolf's bane" (No. Europe)

Aconitum henryi
"Autumn monk's-hood" of China

Aconitum napellus
"Helmet flower" in Sweden

Adonis annua
"Pheasant's-eye" (Mediterr. reg.)

Adonis vernalis
"Spring adonis" in Denmark

Anemone alpina *(Pulsatilla)*
"Alpine windflower" in the Dolomites

Adonis flammea
"Flame adonis" in Lebanon

Adonis amurensis
"Amur adonis" in Osaka, Japan

Anemone hupehensis
"Dwarf Japan anemone" in N. Jersey

Anemone hupehensis 'Splendens'
in Leyden Bot. Garden, Holland

Anemone hupenhensis japonica
"Japanese anemone" in So. California

Anemone sylvestris
"Snow drop anemone" in New York

Anemone multifida
in Kew Bot. Gardens, England

Anemone magellanica
"South American windflower"

Aquilegia saximontana
from Rocky Mts. of Colorado

Anemone occidentalis
near Lake Agnes, Alberta, Canada

Anemone nemorosa 'Allenii'
"Wood anemone" in Europe

Anemone pulsatilla *(Pulsatilla)*
"Pasque flower" in Britain

Anemone rivularis
"Wind flower" of No. India

Anemone vitifolia 'Robustissima'
from Nepal Himalayas

Aquilegia caerulea
"Colorado columbine" in Denver Bot. G.

Anemonopsis macrophylla
"False anemone" in Nikko, Japan

Aquilegia chrysantha
"Golden columbine" in New Mexico

Aquilegia flavescens *(canadensis)*
at Lake Moraine, Alberta

Aquilegia vulgaris
"European columbine"

Aquilegia formosa
"Sitka columbine" in San Diego

Cimicifuga racemosa
"Snake-root" in St. Louis, Missouri

Clematis integrifolia
"Solitary virgin's-bower"in Austria

Clematis recta
"Ground clematis" in Spain

Consolida orientalis *(Delphinium)*
"Oriental larkspur" in California

Consolida regalis *(Delphinium)*
"Regal larkspur" in England

Consolida ambigua *(Delphinium)*
"Rocket larkspur" in Boston, Mass.

Delphinium elatum
"Candle larkspur" in So. France

Delph. elatum 'Pacific Hybrid'
giant strain of California

Delphinium elatum 'Klingsor'
in Munich Botanic Garden

Nigella damascena
"Love-in-a-mist" (So. Europe)

Nigella hispanica
'Persian Jewels' *in England*

Nigella sativa
"Nutmeg flower" in Israel

Hepatica americana
"Liver-leaf" (Canada to Florida)

Glaucidium palmatum
"Shirane" of Hokkaido, Japan

Hepatica nobilis
"European liver-leaf"

Delphinium exaltatum
"Tall larkspur" in Ohio

Delph. grandiflorum 'Blue Mirror'
"Siberian larkspur", in California

Delphinium nelsonii
from So. Dakota to Arizona

Coptis occidentalis
"Gold-thread" in Montana

Hydrastis canadensis
"Golden seal" at New York Bot. G.

Hydrastis canadensis, *in fruit*
in Munich Bot. G., Germany

Helleborus foetidus
"Bear's-foot hellebore" in Germany

Helleborus cyclophyllus
stemless hellebore, in Greece

Helleborus viridis occidentalis
"Green hellebore" in Kew Bot. G.

Helleborus niger
"Christmas rose" in New York

Helleborus orientalis 'Atropurp.'
"Lentenrose" in England

Helleborus lividus corsicus
"Corsican hellebore"

Ranunculus gramineus
"Grassy buttercup" in Kew Bot. G.

Ranunculus eschscholtzii
near Lake Louise, Alberta

Ranunculus acris flore pleno
"Meadows buttercup" in Brooklyn Bot. G.

Ranunculus lanuginosus
"Bachelor's-buttons" in Copenhagen

Ranunculus aconitifolius
"Fair maids of France"

Ranunculus montanus *(geraniifol.)*
on Mt. Jungfrau, Swiss Alps

Ranunculus repens
"Creeping buttercup", Oxford Bot. G.

Thalictrum aquilegifolium
"Columbine meadow-rue" in England

Thalictrum dipterocarpum
"Yunnan meadow-rue" in California

Thalictrum kiusianum
"Meadow-rue" of Japan

Thalictrum rochebrunianum
"Lavender-mist" from Honshu

Thalictrum speciosissimum
"Dusty meadow-rue" of Spain

Trollius europaeus *(RAN.)*
"Globe flower" in Arctic Norway

Trollius asiaticus
"Siberian globeflower" at Kew Gard.

Trollius chinensis
"Chinese globeflower" in Denmark

Trollius ledebourii
in Pennsylvania

Trollius x cult. 'Orange Globe'
superb hybrid, in Virginia

Acaena buchananii *(ROS.)*
"Spine-nuts" in New Zealand

Reseda luteola *(RESED.)*
"Dyer's rocket" on Tenerife

Reseda odorata
"Mignonette" in Egypt

Acaena microphylla *(ROS.)*
"Red-spine sheepburr" (N.Z.)

Alchemilla mollis
"Lady's mantle" in Berlin Bot. G.

Aruncus dioicus 'Kneiffii'
"Goat's-beard", dwarf form

Dryas octopetala, *"Mountain avens"*
on Spitzbergen, Arctic Norway

Dryas x suendermannii
Visby Bot. Gard., Gotland, Sweden

Filipendula palmata
"Meadow-sweet" in Milwaukee, Wis.

Filipendula rubra
"Queen of the prairie" in Illinois

Filipendula vulgaris fl. pl.
in Longwood Gard., Pennsylvania

Filipendula ulmaria 'Plena'
"Queen of the meadow" in Virginia

Waldsteinia geoides
Duesseldorf Bot. Gard., Germany

Geum triflorum
"Avens" on Nebraska prairie

Geum coccineum
"Scarlet avens" in Dalmatia

Geum quellyon *(chiloense)*
"Chilean avens"

Potentilla alba
"Five-fingers" in Germany

Potentilla atrosanguinea
"Himalayan cinquefoil" in Thuringia

Potentilla fragiformis
"Strawberry cinquefoil" (N.E. Asia)

Potentilla fruticosa
"Golden hardhack"

Potentilla heptaphylla
Bot. Gard. Duesseldorf, Germany

Potentilla nepalensis
at Milford Sound, New Zealand

Potentilla x tonguei
"Tormentilla cinquefoil"

Potentilla verna *(ROS.)*
"Spring cinquefoil" in California

Potentilla rupestris
"Rock cinquefoil" in Britain

Potentilla recta 'Warrenii'
"Sulphur cinquefoil" in New York

Sanguisorba canadensis *(ROS.)*
"Burnet" (Labrador to Michigan)

Sanguisorba obtusa
"Japanese burnet" of Honshu

Asperula nitida puberula *(RUB.)*
from mountains of C. Greece

Coprosma x kirkii variegata *(RUB.)*
"Silver birdsnest" of N. Zealand

Crucianella stylosa 'Rubra' *(RUB.)*
"Cresswort" from Asia Minor

Galium schultesii *(RUB.)*
"Bedstraw" in Duesseldorf B.G.

Pentas lanceolata *(RUB.)*
"Egyptian star-cluster"

Hedyotis caerulea *(RUB.)*
"Bluets" in Virginia

Phuopsis stylosa *(RUB.)*
pungent herb from E. Turkey

Dictamnus albus 'Rubra'
"Burning bush" in Munich B. G.

Dictamnus albus *(RUT.)*
"Gas plant" of Palestine

Houttuynia cordata *(SAUR.)*
in Somerset Arb., New Jersey

Astilbe glaberrima *hort.*
of dwarf habit, from Kyushu

Astilbe simplicifolia *(SAX.)*
"Star astilbe" of Honshu, Japan

Astilbe x arendsii 'Fanal'
brilliant hybrid, in Sweden

Astilbe chinensis
"Chinese astilbe" in Holland

Astilbe chinensis 'Pumila'
Strybing Arboretum, San Francisco

Astilbe chinensis taquetii
striking giant in So. Carolina

Astilbe fortunei, *"Goat's-beard"*
in Duesseldorf Bot. G., Germany

Astilbe thunbergii
"Ostrich feather" of Japan

Astilbe japonica
"Silver sheaf" of Japan

Astilbe x japonica 'Deutschland'
in Dortmund Bot. G., Germany

Astilbe x japonica 'Koblenz'
charming cultivar in Rhineland

Bergenia cordifolia
"Heartleaf bergenia" in New York

Bergenia crassifolia
"Winter begonia", Mexico City B. G.

Bergenia purpurascens
"Himalaya bergenia" (W. China)

Francoa ramosa
"Maiden's wreath" of Chile

Heuchera x brizoides
hybrid coralbells in Germany

Heuchera cylindrica
"Alum-root" in Kew Bot. Gard.

Heuchera rubescens *(alpicola)*
rock dweller in the Sierra Nevada

Heuchera sanguinea *in pots*
"Coral bells" in Swiss Alps

x Heucherella tiarelloides
(Heuchera x Tiarella)

Rodgersia aesculifolia
resembling chestnut (C. China)

Rodgersia pinnata
in Essen Bot. Garden, Germany

Kirengeshoma palmata
in forests of Kyushu, Japan

Rodgersia podophylla *(Korea)*
waterside plant in Brooklyn

Rodgersia sambucifolia *(Yunnan)*
at Int'l. Hort. Exhib. Munich

Rodgersia tabularis *(Astilboides)*
"Umbrella leaf" at Kew G., England

Saxifraga umbrosa aurea
"Golden London pride"

Saxifraga x boydii
"Yellow hind" in Britain

Saxifraga rotundifolia
Essen Bot. Garden, Germany

Saxifraga oppositifolia
in Arctic Spitzbergen 79 deg. No.

Saxifraga longifolia *(encrusted)*
"Longleaf saxifrage" (Pyrenées)

Saxifraga rosacea 'Kumomaso'
Hibiya Park Exhib. in Tokyo

Saxifraga x arendsii
in Wuppertal-Ronsdorf, Germany

Saxifraga hostii
in Kew Bot. Gard., England

Saxifraga rhomboidea
in the Colorado Rocky Mts.

Saxifraga paniculata *(aizoon)*
"Encrusted saxifrage" in Switzerland

Saxifraga stolonifera 'Tricolor'
"Magic Carpet" at Roehrs, N. Jersey

Saxifraga hirculus
in Arctic Spitzbergen, Norway

Saxifraga trifurcata *(SAX.)*
"Threefork saxifrage" of N. Spain

Saxifraga x urbium
"London-pride" in England

Saxifraga umbrosa
"Porcelain flower" (W. Pyrenées)

Saxifraga x geum
"Kidneyleaf saxifrage"

Saxifraga hirsuta *(geum)*
at Kew Bot. Gard., England

Saxifraga hypnoides
"Mossy rockfoil" of N.W. Europe

Saxifraga bronchialis
near Lake Louise, Alberta

Saxif. cortusifolia fortunei
woodlands of Honshu, Japan

Tellima grandiflora *(SAX.)*
"Fringe-cups" (Alaska to Calif.)

Tiarella trifoliata *(SAX.)*
"False miterwort" in Oregon

Asarina roseiflora *(Maurandya)*
in Zacatecas, Mexico (SCROPH.)

Tolmiea menziesii *(SAX.)*
"Piggy-back plant" in Oregon

Tiarella cordifolia
"Foam flower" in Boston, Mass.

Tiarella wherryi *(SAX.)*
"False miterwort" in Virginia

Alonsoa warscewiczii *(SCROPH.)*
"Mask flower" in Germany

Antirrhinum majus 'Royal Carpet'
"Dwarf snapdragon" in California

Antirrhinum majus *(SCROPH.)*
in Bot. Gard. Kwangchow, China

Chelone lyonii *(SCROPH.)*
"Turtlehead" of Carolina

Calceolaria crenatiflora 'Maxima'
"Pocketbook plant" for Easter pots

Calceolaria integr. 'Gold Bouquet'
"Chilean pouch flower" for outdoors

Calceolaria crenat. 'Multifl. nana'
"Lady's pocket book" of florists

Digitalis purpurea alba
Longwood Gard. Pennsylvania

Digitalis purpurea
"Foxglove" in Saalfeld, Thuringia

Digitalis grandiflora
"Yellow foxglove" in Austria

Digitalis lutea
"Straw-foxglove" in Dortmund Arb.

Digitalis purpurea 'Excelsior'
Longwood G., Kennett Square, Pa.

Digitalis purpurea 'Rosea'
in Nymphenburg Bot. Garden

Digitalis x mertonensis
in England

Digitalis sibirica
in Palmengarten, Frankfurt

Chelone obliqua
"Snakehead" in Maryland

Castilleja coccinea *(parasitic)*
"Scarlet paint brush" in Colorado

Castilleja chromosa
"Indian paintbrush" in Wyoming

Melampyrum nemorosum
"Cow-wheat" in Thuringia forest

Diascia rigescens *(So. Africa)*
annual "Twin spur" in England

Linaria purpurea 'Canon Went'
"Toadflax" of So. Europe

Linaria maroccana 'F. Bouquet'
in Missouri Bot. G., St. Louis

Jovellana violacea
tender perennial of Chile

Diascia barberae
"Twin-spur" in California

Erinus alpinus
"Alpine liver-balsam"

Mimulus cupreus
"Chilean monkey flower"

Mimulus guttatus
"Monkey flower" in Germany

Mimulus guttatus 'Malibu Orange'
in Southern California

Mimulus lewisii
Glacier Nat'l. Park, Montana

Mimulus luteus
"Golden monkey-flower" of Chile

Mimulus cardinalis
"Scarlet monkey-flower" in Utah

Mimulus moschatus
"Musk plant" in Montana

Mimulus bigelovii
in Mojave County, Arizona

Mimulus tilingii
in the Sierra Nevada of Calif.

Nemesia strumosa
"Cape jewels" in Fallbroock, Calif.

Nemesia versicolor
"Spurred nemesia" of Namibia

Otacanthus coeruleus *(Brazil)*
at Tropic World, Escondido, Calif.

Penstemon x glox. 'Fire King'
hartwegii hyb. (Wayside G.)

Penstemon hartwegii
(gentianoides hort.) at Wisley Gard.

Penstemon x gloxinioides
"Garden penstemon" in Germany

Penstemon smallii
in Great Smokies of Tennessee

Penstemon barbatus
"Scarlet beard-tongue" of Utah

Penstemon fruticosus
in Kew Bot. Gard., England

Penstemon rupicola
"Cliff penstemon" in Washington

Penstemon campanulatus 'Evelyn'
popular cv. in England

Penstemon eriantherus *(young pl.)*
"Dakota beard-tongue"

Penstemon parryi
near Tucson, So. Arizona

Penstemon heterophyllus
"Chaparral penstemon" in California

Penstemon campanulatus
from Mexico and Guatemala

Penstemon hirsutus 'Pygmaeus'
"Hairy beard-tongue"

Penstemon fendleri
in arid region Arizona

Ourisia macrophylla
"Mountain foxglove" of N. Zealand

Nemesia strumosa *(SCROPH.)*, *"Cape jewels" of So. Africa in colorful planting on Emerald Lake, Canadian Rockies*

Chrysanthemums and Salvias in Autumn at Temple of Heaven, Beijing, China

Autumn planting of Chrysanth. with topiary Taxus at Rockefeller Center, Fifth Avenue, New York

Scenic Rockgarden plantings in Queen Elizabeth Arboretum, Vancouver, Brit. Columbia

Plants and Shrubs at Flower market in the harbor area of historic Bergen, Norway

Perennials and Alpines at Chelsea Flower Show by Royal Horticultural Society, in May, London

Phygelius capensis 'Moonbells'
"White Cape fuchsia" in Germany

Phygelius aequalis, *"River bells"*
in Strybing Arbor., San Francisco

Phygelius capensis
"Cape fuchsia" in Kirstenbosch

Synthyris reniformis
along San Francisco Bay

Rehmannia elata *(GESNER.)*
"Foxglove gloxinia" in New Jersey

Torenia fournieri
"Wishbone plant" in Vietnam

Veronica filiformis
'Creeping veronica" in New York

Wulfenia carinthiaca
in Carinthia, Austrian Alps

Gratiola officinalis
"Herb-of-grace" in Holland

Verbascum bombiciferum *(broussa)*
in Dortmund Bot. G. (from Turkey)

Verbascum thapsiforme
"King's candle" in Sweden

Verbascum thapsus
"Flannel mullein" in Boston, Mass.

Verbascum caesareum
Royal Bot. Gard. Kew, England

Verbascum pulverulentum
"Hoary mullein" in Britain

Verbascum nigrum
"Dark mullein" in Germany

Verbascum chaixii 'Album'
"Nettle-leaf mullein" in Virginia

Verbascum olympicum
"Olympic mullein" in Greece

Verbascum bomb. 'Arctic Summer'
in San Francisco, California

Veronica austriaca
"Austrian speedwell" in Salzburg

Veronica gentianoides
"Gentian speedwell" (Asia Minor)

Veronica incana
"Woolly speedwell" in California

Veronica longifolia
"Speedwell" in Stockholm, Sweden

Veronica prostrata
"Creeping speedwell" in California

Veronica bachofenii *(grandis)*
in Vienna, Austria

Veronica sibirica *(virginica)*
in Munich Bot. Gard., Germany

Veronica spicata
"Cat's-tail speedwell" in Delaware

Veronica pectinata 'Rosea'
"Comb-speedwell" in San Francisco

Browallia speciosa
"Amethyst flower" of Colombia

Browallia viscosa
"Bush violet" in Perú

Atropa belladonna
"Deadly nightshade" in Greece

Datura inoxia *(meteloides)*
in Zion Nat'l. Park, Utah

Datura metel flore pleno
"Horn-of-plenty" (S.W. China)

Datura stramonium *(No. America)*
"Thorn-apple" in Texas

Capsicum annuum 'Holiday Cheer'
ornamental "Spanish pepper"

Capsicum ann. conoides 'Fiesta'
"Cone pepper" in Chicago

Capsicum annuum 'Holiday Time'
at Geo. Ball's, in Illinois

Nicotiana tabacum
"Tobacco" flowering in Virginia

Nicotiana tabacum macrophylla
commercial "Tobacco" in Cuba

Nicotiana alata 'Nicki White'
"Jasmine tobacco" in Chicago

Nicandra physalodes
"Apple of Perú" in New York

Nierembergia hippomanica
"Cup flower" of Argentina

Nicotiana africana
from Namibia, S.W. Africa

Nierembergia hippomanica
violacea 'Purple Robe', *in Calif.*

Nierembergia scoparia
"Tall cupflower" of Uruguay

Nierembergia repens
"White cupflower" in California

Petunia x hybrida 'Caprice'
"Double Grandiflora petunia"

Petunia x hybrida 'All-Star'
"Garden petunia" (Ball, W. Chicago)

Petunia x hyb. 'Royal Cascade'
blue "Balcony petunia"

Petunia x hybrida multiflora
'Summer Fun', *for bedding*

Petunia violacea *(Argentina)*
in Munich Bot. Gard., Germany

Petunia x hybrida 'Happiness'
large-flowered Grandiflora strain

Schizanthus x wisetonensis
"Poor man's orchid"

Schizanthus pinnatus
"Butterfly flower" of Chile

Schizanthus retusus
in Longwood Gardens, Penna.

Salpiglossis sinuata *(SOL.)*
"Painted tongue" from Perú

Stylidium adnatum *(STYL.)*
"Trigger plant" of S.E. Australia

Physalis alkekengi *(SOL.)*
"Lantern plant" in Kyushu

Solanum sisymbriifolium
"Sticky nightshade" (Trop. America)

Tacca chantrieri *(TACC.)*
"Bat-flower" of Malaya

Solanum marginatum
prickly perennial of Ethiopia

Tropaeolum majus *(TROP.)*
"Indian cress" of Perú

Tropaeolum majus fl. pl.
"Double nasturtium" in Conn.

Tropaeolum majus coccineum
"Red nasturtium" on Rhodes Isl.

Eryngium agavifolium
in Bot. Garden Essen, Germany

Eryngium giganteum
"Ivory-thistle" in Munich Bot. G.

Eryngium bromeliifolium
Bot. Gard. Strasbourg, France

Eryngium bourgatii
"Eryngo" of Spain

Eryngium alpinum
"Alpine thistle" in Austria

Eryngium planum
"Noble bristle" in Kashmir

Ferula chiliantha *(Turkey)*
"Gold giant fennel" near Ephesus

Heracleum laciniatum
"Cow parsnip" of the Caucasus

Heracleum mantegazzianum
"Cartwheel flower" in New York

Ferula communis
"Giant fennel" in Greece

Aegopodium podograria 'Varieg.'
"Bishop's-weed" in Massachusetts

Astrantia major *(UMB.)*
"Masterwort" in Sochi, Caucasus

Lomatium martindalei *(UMB.)*
in the Cascade Mts., Oregon

Turnera ulmifolia elegans
"Sulphur alder" in Edinburgh Bot. G.

Thapsia villosa *(UMBELL.)*
on the Algarve, Portugal

Patrinia triloba *(VAL.)*
from Mts. of Honshu, Japan

Valeriana globulariifolia
fragrant per. at Kew Bot. G., England

Plectritis congesta *(VAL.)*
in Vancouver, Brit. Columbia

Centranthus ruber *(VAL.)*
at Meteora Cloisters, Greece

Centranthus ruber 'Albus'
in Munich Bot. G., Germany

Centr. ruber 'Atrococcineus'
"Foxbrush" in Saalfeld, Thuringia

Verbena bipinnatifida
"Dakota vervain" of Midwest U.S.

Verbena bonariensis *(VERB.)*
from So. Argentina to Brazil

Verbena canadensis
"Rose verbena" in Chicago

Verbena laciniata
"Moss verbena" in Santiago, Chile

Verbena peruviana
"Peruvian vervain" in Tucson, Arizona

Verbena x hybrida 'Springtime'
"Garden verbena" in California

Verbena rigida *of Brazil*
"Vervain", natural. in So. U.S.

Verbena tenera *(pulchella)*
at Pala Indian Mission, Calif.

Verbena tenera 'Aphrodite'
in Bot. Gard. Munich, Germany

Verbena tenera var. maonettii
along Rio La Plata, Argentina

Verbena tenuisecta *(VERB.)*
"Creeping moss-vervain" in Calif.

Viola calcarata *(VIOL.)*
slopes of Jungfrau, Swiss Alps

Viola canadensis
"Canada violet" in Montreal

Viola sororia *(papilionacea)*
"Butterfly violet" in Minnesota

Viola sororia 'Immaculata'
"Pentecost violet", in Germany

Viola odorata
"Sweet violet" in Switzerland

Viola cornuta
"Horned violet" in Spain

Viola canina
"Dog violet" in Rutherford, N. Jersey

Viola tricolor
"Johnny-jump-up" in Scotland

Viola x wittrockiana 'Bambini'
"Whiskered faces" (Thompson-Morgan)

Viola x wittr. 'Majestic Giants'
at Ball Seeds, W. Chicago

Viola cornuta hybrid
"Tufted pansy" in Rhineland

Viola x wittr. 'Illumination'
Bot. Gard. Duesseldorf, Germany

Viola x wittrockiana
"Pansies" in Keukenhof, Holland

Alpinia purpurata
"Red ginger" in Tahiti

Alpinia haenkei
"Erect shellginger" in Luzon

Alpinia purpurata 'Rosea'
"Jungle Queen" on Moorea, So. Pacific

Alpinia sanderae
"Variegated ginger" (New Guinea)

Alpinia zerumbet *(speciosa)*
"Shell ginger" in Taiwan

Costus speciosus
"Crepe ginger" in Malaya

Costus stenophyllus
in Turrialba, Costa Rica

Costus speciosus 'Marginatus'
"Varieg. spiral ginger" on Luzon

Costus spicatus
"Indian-head ginger" in Haiti

Curcuma roscoeana
"Hidden lily" of Myanmar (Burma)

Hedychium coronarium
"Butterfly lily" in Florida

Hedychium coccineum
"Scarlet ginger-lily" in Hawaii

Hedychium flavum
"Yellow ginger" in Jamaica

Hedychium gardnerianum
"Kahili ginger" in California

Hedychium flavescens
"Cream ginger" in Melbourne Bot. G.

Hedychium greenei *of Bhutan*
in Sydney Bot. Gard., Australia

Zingiber spectabile
giant ginger of Malaya

Nicolaia elatior *(Phaeomeria)*
"Torch ginger" in Bogor, Java

Roscoea humeana
low ginger of Yunnan, China

Roscoea cautleoides *(W. China)*
in Kew Bot. Gard., England

Tapeinochilus ananassae
"Giant spiral ginger" of Malaysia

Roscoea purpurea
from Sikkim Himalayas

Thaumatococcus daniellii
of Trop. West Africa

Roscoea alpina
from Himalayas of Nepal

Curcuma aeruginosa
in Northern Thailand

Kaempferia brachystemon
"Dwarf ginger-lily" (Tanzania)

Zingiber zerumbet 'Variegata'
in Trinidad Botanic Gardens

Bixa orellana *(BIX.)*
"Annatto-tree" in Jamaica

Ilex paraguariensis *(AQUIF.)*
"Yerba-de-Maté" in Paraguay

Asclepias tuberosa *(ASCL.)*
"Butterfly milkweed" in Arizona

Panax quinquefolius *(ARAL.)*
"American ginseng" in Georgia

Panax pseudoginseng
"Ginseng" of Korea

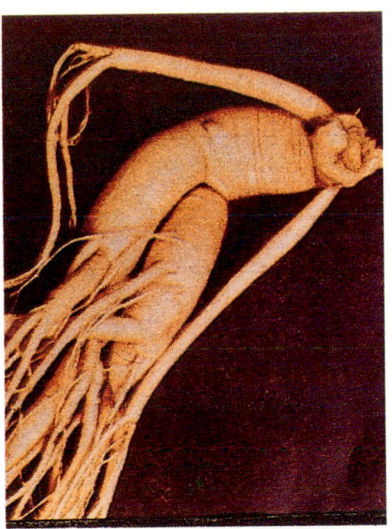

Panax pseudoginseng *roots,*
used for medicinal purposes

Canarium album *(BURS.)*
"Chinese white olive"

Capparis spinosa *(CAPP.)*
"Caper-bush" of So. Europe

Simmondsia chinensis *(BUX.)*
"Jojoba" with fruit, in California

Tanacetum vulgare
"Tansy", bitter herb of Britain

Tussilago farfara
medicinal "Coltsfoot" in England

Helichrysum angustifolium
aromatic "Curry plant" in Italy

Arnica montana *(Europe)*
"Mountain arnica" in Germany

Anthemis tinctoria *(Europe)*
aromatic "Golden marguerite"

Chrysanthemum coccineum
"Pyrethrum" in Munich Bot. G.

Chamaemelum nobile *(Anthemis)*
"Roman camomile" in France

Matricaria recutita
"Sweet false camomile" in New Jersey

Tripleurospermum maritimum
(Matricaria maritima of gardens)

Symphytum officinale *(BOR.)*
"Healing herb" in Germany

Pulmonaria officinalis *(BOR.)*
"Blue lungwort" in Sweden

Symphytum x uplandicum
"Russian comfrey" in New Jersey

Armoracia rusticana *(CRUC.)*
"Horseradish" in Brooklyn Bot. G.

Acorus calamus *(ARAC.)*
"Sweet flag" with spicy roots

Lychnis coronaria *(CARYOPH.)*
"Rose campion" in Vista, California

Achillea filipendulina *(COMP.)*
"Fernleaf yarrow" in New York

Artemisia schmidtiana *in N. Jersey*
"Silver-mound", name in braille

Calendula officinalis *(COMP.)*
"Pot-marigold" in Madeira

Colchicum autumnale *(LIL.)*
"Autumn crocus" in N. Jersey

Chenopodium ambrosioides *(CHEN.)*
"Epazote" or "Mexican tea" in Calif.

Achillea millefolium 'Rosea'
"Pink yarrow" in Vista, Calif.

Saponaria ocymoides *(CAR.)*
"Soapwort" in Bordeaux, France

Artemisia frigida *(COMP.)*
"Fringed sage" in Alaska

Hesperis matronalis *(CRUC.)*
"Sweet rocket" in Somerville, N.J.

Artemisia camphorata
camphor-scented, in Italy

Artemisia vulgaris, *"Mugwort"*
Hop substitute in England

Artemisia absinthium
"Absinthe" in Dortmund Bot. G.

Artemisia abrotanum
"Southernwood" in California

Artemisia ludoviciana
"White sage" in Vancouver, B.C.

Artemisia dracunculus
"Estragon" in Budapest, Hungary

Symphytum x uplandicum *(BOR.)*
"Russian comfrey" (Caucasus)

Borago officinalis *(BOR.)*
"Borage" at German Hort. Expo.

Achillea filipendulina
at Taylor Herbs, Vista, Calif.

Achillea millefolium *(COMP.)*
"Milfoil" in Arnold Arbor., Boston

Chrysanthemum balsamita
"Costmary" or "Mint geranium"

Helichrysum angustifolium
"Whiteleaf everlasting" in Calif.

Lepidium sativum *(CRUC.)*
"Garden cress" from Egypt

Tanacetum vulgare crispum
"Bitterherb" or "Fernleaf tansy"

Nasturtium officinale *(CRUC.)*
aquatic "Water Cress"

Helianthus tuberosus *(COMP.)*
"Jerusalem artichoke" in Louisiana

Euphorbia lathyris *(EUPH.)*
"Gopher purge" in San Diego

Matricaria recutita *(COMP.)*
"Sweet false chamomile" in Calif.

Cornus mas *(CORN.)*
"Cornelian cherry" in Virginia

Ricinus communis *(EUPH.)*
"Castor-oil plant" of Trop. Africa

Juniperus communis *(CON.)*
"Common juniper" with fruit

Ephedra distachya *(EPHED.)*
"Joint fir" in Duesseldorf Bot. G.

Crocus sativus *(IRID.)*
"Saffron crocus" on La Mancha

Taraxacum officinale *(COMP.)*
"Dandelion" in English meadow

Brassica hirta *(CRUC.)*
"White mustard" in Russia

Barbarea verna *(CRUC.)*
"Winter cress" in Brooklyn Bot. G.

Brassica napus *(CRUC.)*
oil producing "Rape"

Pelargonium x nervosum
"Lime geranium" of England

Pelargonium crispum *(GER.)*
"Lemon geranium" in California

Pelarg. grav. 'Lady Plymouth'
"Variegated rose-geranium"

Cichorium intybus *(COMP.)*
"Chicory" on European roadside

Santolina chamaecyparissus *(COMP.)*
"Lavender cotton" in Berlin Bot. G.

Lamium maculatum *(LAB.)*
"Spotted deadnettle" in Scotland

Boswellia hildebrandtii *(BURS.)*
"Frankincense" of Kenya

Lavandula angustifolia
"English lavender" in Virginia

Lavandula stoechas *(LAB.)*
"Spanish lavender" in Portugal

Coix lacryma-jobi *(GRAM.)*
"Job's-tears" in California

Cymbopogon citratus *(GRAM.)*
"Lemon-grass" of So. India

Glycyrrhiza glabra *(LAB.)*
"Licorice", from Spain

Lavandula lanata *(LAB.)*
"Woolly lavender" of Andalucia

Agastache foeniculum *(LAB.)*
"Licorice mint" in Dakota

Hyssopus officinalis *(LAB.)*
"Hyssop" (Spain to Balkans)

Lavandula dentata 'Vera'
"Green toothed lavender"

Lavandula angustifolia
at Taylor Herbs, Vista, Calif.

Lavandula dentata
"French lavender" (So. France)

Pelargonium graveolens
"Rose geranium" (Cape Prov.)

Pelargonium graveolens x tomentosum
"Lemon rose-geranium"

Pelargonium tomentosum *(GER.)*
"Peppermint geranium" (So. Africa)

Iris x florentina *(x. germanica var.)*
"Florentine iris" or "Orris"

Marrubium vulgare *(LAB.)*
"Horehound" in Arnold Arbor. Boston

Melittis melissophyllum *(LAB.)*
"Bastard balm" in Gdansk, Poland

Mentha x piperita *(LAB.)*
"Peppermint" in Britain

Tilia x europaea
Linden blossoms for tea

Mentha spicata
"Spearmint" in New Jersey

Monarda didyma *(LAB.)*
"Bee-balm" in Montréal, Québec

Nepeta cataria *(LAB.)*
"Catnip" in Dortmund Herb Garden

Nepeta x faassenii
"Persian ground-ivy" or "Catmint"

Melissa officinalis
"Lemon balm" in Cologne, Germany

Mentha piperita
"Peppermint" in California

Mentha piperita citrata
"Orange bergamot"

Mentha pulegium
"Penny-royal" or "Flea mint"

Mentha spicata 'Variegata'
"Variegated spearmint"

Mentha suaveolens 'Variegata'
"Pineapple mint" in England

Perilla frutescens 'Crispa'
"Crisped nettle" in France

Ocimum basilicum
"Sweet basil" in California

Mentha x gentilis 'Variegata'
"Scotch mint" in Edinburgh Bot. G.

Cunila origanoides
"American dittany" in Maryland

Mentha requienii
"Corsican mint"

Origanum vulgare 'Aureum'
"Golden marjoram"

Ocimum basilicum
"Basil" blooming in N. Jersey

Ocimum basilicum 'Purpurascens'
"Dark opal basil" in Calif.

Ocimum sanctum
"Sacred basil" of India

Ocimum gratissimum
Herb garden, Brooklyn Bot. G.

Origanum pulchellum
"Showy marjoram" (Asia Minor)

Origanum majorana *(hortensis)*
"Sweet marjoram" on Delos, Greece

Origanum vulgare *(onites)*
"Pot marjoram" or "Oregano"

Rosmarinus offic. majorica
"Pink rosemary" of Portugal

Rosmarinus officinalis
"Rosemary" in San Francisco

Salvia officinalis *(LAB.)*
"Garden sage" in Spain

Salvia officinalis 'Tricolor'
"Variegated sage" in California

Salvia officinalis latifolia
"Mammoth sage" in Italy

Salvia officinalis 'Icterina'
"Golden sage" in San Diego

Salvia elegans
"Pineapple-scented sage" of Mexico

Salvia sclarea
"Clary sage" of Spain

Cinnamomum camphora
"Camphor tree" in Hong Kong

Cinnamomum cassia *(LAUR.)*
"Cassia-bark tree" in Vietnam

Aloe barbadensis *(vera) (LIL.)*
"Medicine plant" on St. Héléna

Satureja douglasii *(LAB.)*
"Yerba buena" in California

Satureja hortensis
"Summer savory" in N. Jersey

Satureja montana
"Winter savory" of So. Europe

Stachys olympica *hort.*
"Woolly betony" in Darmstadt Bot. G.

Stachys officinalis
"Betony" in San Diego, California

Stachys byzantina *(LAB.)*
"Lamb's ears" in Munich Bot. G.

Teucrium chamaedrys *(LAB.)*
"Germander" in Vista, California

Galega officinalis *(LEG.)*
"Goat's rue" in Meran, Italy

Thymus vulgaris *(LAB.)*
"Garden thyme" in Palermo, Sicily

Thymus capitatus
"Thymian" in Priene, Turkey

Thymus x citriodorus 'Aureus'
"Golden thyme" in California

Thymus glabrescens
"Loevyanus thyme" in Vienna, Austria

Thymus herba-barona
"Caraway thyme" in Sardinia

Thymus pannonicus *(marshall.)*
Kew Bot. Gardens, England

Thymus pulegioides 'Coccineus'
"Coconut thyme" in California

Thymus serpyllum
"Mother-of-thyme" in Germany

Thymus vulgaris 'Argenteus'
"Silver thyme" from Italy

Thymus villosus *(Portugal)*
in New York Botan. Garden

Cinnamomum zeylanicum *(LAUR.)*
"Cinnamon tree" in Sri Lanka

Laurus nobilis, *with fruit*
"Sweet bay" in Barcelona, Spain

Tamarindus indica *(LEG.)*
"Tamarind tree" at U.S.D.A. Miami

Syzygium aromaticum *(MYRT.)*
"Clove" flowers from Indonesia

Olea europaea, *"Common olive"*
ripe olive fruit in California

Osmanthus fragrans *(OLEAC.)*
"Sweet olive" in Kweilin, China

Myrtus communis *(MYRT.)*
"Greek myrtle" fruited in Calif.

Myristica fragrans *(MYRIST.)*
"Nutmeg tree" in Trinidad

Pimenta dioica *(MYRT.)*
"All-spice" in Jamaica

Allium sativum *(LIL.)*
"Garlic" in German herbgarden

Allium schoenoprasum
"Chives" in Oceanside, California

Allium cepa, *of Persian origin*
"Garden onion" in New York Bot. G.

Allium tuberosum
"Chinese chives" in Somerset Arb., N.J.

Allium ascalonicum
"Shallots" in Escondido, Calif.

Allium ampeloprasum *(porrum)*
blanched "Leek" in Switzerland

Tulbaghia violacea *(LIL.)*
"Society garlic" in Quail B.G., Calif.

Papaver somniferum *(fruit)*
seed pods yielding opium

Papaver somniferum *(flower)*
"Opium poppy" in W. Asia

Cinchona officinalis *(RUB.)*, "Jesuit's bark" or "Quinine"
on plantation in Chicacao, Pacif. slope of Guatemala

Areca catechu *(PALM.)*, "Betel-nut palm"
bearing fruit, near Kuala Lumpur, Malaya

Boswellia carteri *(sacra) (BURS.)*
treasured "Frankincense tree" in Oman, Arabia

Knotgarden of intertwining borders
of Rosemary and Santolina at New York Botan. Garden

Vanilla planifolia *(ORCH.)*
"Vanilla" with fruit, in Mexico

Piper nigrum *(PIP.)*
"Black pepper" in Sri Lanka

Humulus lupulus *(MOR.)*
"Hops", cones on female plant

Reseda odorata 'Goliath'
"Giant mignonette" in Cologne

Fagopyrum esculentum *(POL.)*
"Buckwheat" in Pennsylvania

Alchemilla vulgaris *(ROS.)*
"Lady's mantle" in Germany

Rheum palmatum *(POLYG.)*
"Chinese rhubarb" in W. China

Rheum officinale
"Medicine rhubarb" of Tibet

Rheum rhabarbarum, *"Rhubarb"*
Bergianska Bot. Gard., Stockholm

Rosa rugosa *(ROS.)*
"Turkestan rose" in Kobe, Japan

Sorbus aucuparia *(ROS.)*
"European mountain ash"

Rosa canina
"Dog rose" with fruit (Europe)

Aloysia triphylla *(VERB.)*
"Lemon verbena", from Argentina

Citrus aurantium *(RUT.)*
"Seville orange" in Sevilla, Spain

Coffea canephora *(RUB.)*
"Robusta coffee" in New Guinea

Polygala senega *(POLYG.)*
"Seneca snake-root" in Québec

Murraya paniculata *(RUT.)*
"Satinwood" on Tonga, So. Pacific

Atropa belladonna *(SOLAN.)*
"Deadly night-shade" of India

Sesamum indicum *(PEDAL.)*
"Sesame-oil plant" in India

Nigella sativa *(RAN.)*
"Fennel flower" (Mediterran.)

Rumex scutatus *(POLYG.)*
"French sorrel" in California

Portulaca oleracea *(PORT.)*
"Purslane" in South Carolina

Poterium sanguisorba *(ROS.)*
"Burnet" in Vista, California

Anthriscus cerefolium *(UMB.)*
"Salad chervil" of So. Europe

Asperula tinctoria *(RUB.)*
"Dyer's woodruff" in England

Carum carvi, juvenile pl. *(UMB.)*
"Caraway" (Europe to Mongolia)

Foeniculum vulgare *(UMB.)*
"Fennel" or "Sweet anise"

Pimpinella anisum *(UMB.)*
"Anise" of Greece

Viola odorata *(VIOL.)*
"Sweet violet" October bl. in Calif.

Verbascum blattaria *(SCROPH.)*
"Moth mullein" in New England

Solanum dulcamara *(SOL.)*
"Deadly nightshade" in Germany

Mandragora officinarum *(SOL.)*
"Mandrake" on Delos, Greece

Capsicum chinensis *(SOL.)*
"Papaya chile" of Honduras

Capsicum annuum 'Longum'
"Cayenne pepper" (Trop. America)

Capsicum frut. var. Tabasco
"Tabasco pepper" of Mexico

Capsicum frut. 'Wirri-wirri'
at Andromeda Gard., Barbados

Ruta graveolens *(RUT.)*
"Common rue" of So. Europe

Angelica archangelica *(UMB.)*
"Archangel" in Munich Bot. Garden

Anethum graveolens *(UMB.)*
piquant "Dill" in California

Bunium bulbocastanum *(UMB.)*
"Ground chestnut" in Dalmatia

Coriandrum sativum *(UMB.)*
"Coriander" in England

Carum carvi *(UMB.)*
"Caraway" flowering, in Germany

Levisticum officinale *(UMB.)*
"Lovage" in Virginia

Myrrhis odorata *(UMB.)*
"Myrrh" in Pyrenées of Spain

Foeniculum vulgare *(UMB.)*
"Fennel" in bloom (Asia Minor)

Petroselinum crispum *(UMB.)*
"Parsley", an ideal kitchen herb

Apium graveolens dulce *(UMB.)*
"Celery", at N. Jersey supermart

Galium odoratum *(RUB.)*
"Sweet woodruff" or "Waldmeister"

Valeriana officinalis *(VAL.)*
"Valerian" in Edinburgh, Scotland

Scandix pecten-veneris *(UMB.)*
"Venus-comb" in Brooklyn Bot. G.

Tropaeolum majus *(female pl.)*
"Nasturtium" or "Indian cress"

Urtica dioica, *female plant*
"Stinging nettle" in Scotland

Pimpinella major 'Rosea' *(UMB.)*
"Rose anise" in Virginia

Sium sisarum *(UMB.)*
"Skirret" in Duesseldorf Bot. G.

Elettaria cardamomum *(ZING.)*
"Malabar cardamom" of India

Zingiber zerumbet *(ZING.)*
"Bitter ginger" in Munich Bot. G.

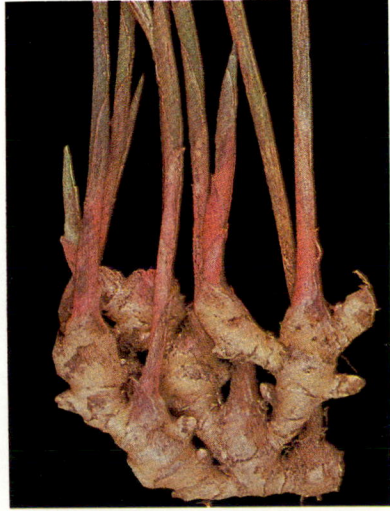

Zingiber officinale
"Ginger" of commerce (Trop. Asia)

Arundinaria alpina, *"Mountain bamboo"*
bamboo forest in Gorilla country, Kigezi, Uganda

Arundinaria amabilis, *the "Tonkin cane bamboo"*
grown commercially in Kwangtung Prov., So. China

Bambusa arundinacea, *with edible shoots*
"Giant thorny bamboo" in Quail Bot. G., Encinitas, Calif.

Bambusa beecheyana *(Dendrocalamus latiflorus hort.)*
"Beechey bamboo" of Kwangtung, Southeast China

Bambusa textilis, *along Li River*
at Jangshuo, Kwangsi Prov., Western China

Bambusa textilis, *"Wong Chuk"*
used commercially, at Guilin, S.W. China

Bambusa tuldoides, *"Punting pole bamboo"*
in col. American Bamboo Soc., Encinitas, Calif.

Bambusa oldhamii, *"Giant timber bamboo"*
in California hort. as Dendrocalamus latiflorus

Arundinaria falconeri
from the Nepal Himalayas

Arundinaria pumila *(Sasa)*
in Bot. Garden Munich, Germany

Arundinaria pygmaea
"Pygmy bamboo" (Honshu, Kyushu)

Fargesia nitida *(Sinarundinaria)*
"Hardy blue bamboo" in Copenhagen

Arundinaria viridistriata
Bambusa argentea hort. (So. Japan)

Arundinaria anceps
Indian Himalayas to 2400 m

Fargesia murielae *(Sinarundinaria)*
"Umbrella bamboo" in the Rhineland

Bambusa dolichoclada
"Chosihi-chiku" of Taiwan

Bambusa dolichoclada 'Stripe'
in Quail Bot. G., Encinitas, Calif.

Bambusa glaucescens *(multiplex)*
"Hedge bamboo" in Los Angeles

Bambusa glauc. 'Alphonse Karr'
"Fernleaf bamboo" (Japan)

Bambusa glauc. 'Silver Stripe'
Quail Bot. G., Encinitas, Calif.

Bambusa longispiculata
in tropical Puerto Rico

Bambusa nananae, *"Dwarf fernleaf"*
in Botanic Gardens Singapore

Bambusa malingensis *(China)*
Quail Bot. G., Encinitas, Calif.

Arundinaria variegata *(Sasa)*
Finca Burle-Marx, Rio de Janeiro

Arundinaria amabilis
"Tonkin cane" in Encinitas, Calif.

Chimonobambusa marmorea
at Int'l. Hort. Exhib. Munich

Bambusa tuldoides
Quail Bot. G., Encinitas, Calif.

Bambusa tulda *of India*
bamboo used for paper pulp

left: Bambusa beecheyana
right: B. vulgaris, *in Kweilin, China*

Bambusa vulgaris 'Vittata'
"Greenstripe bamboo" in Hawaii

Bambusa ventricosa
"Buddha's belly" at German Hort. Expo

Bambusa oldhamii, *"Male bamboo"*
inscribed culms, San Diego Zoo

Hakonechloa macra 'Variegata'
in Bot. Gard. Munich, Germany

Dendrocalamus latiflorus
"Sweet bamboo" in Hong Kong

Bambusa guadua, *in Jamaica*
largest American bamboo

Bambusa textilis, *"Wong Chuk"*
in People's Botanic Garden, Kwangchow, China

Arundinaria amabilis, *the noble "Tonkin cane"*
in Bamboo Exper. Garden, Savannah, Georgia

Bambusa ventricosa, *"Buddha's belly bamboo"*
with Fu-lion, at Ming Palace, Kwangchow, China

Bambusa vulgaris, *"Feathery bamboo"*
in Sierra Luquillo rainforest, Puerto Rico

Chusquea coronalis
at Tropic World, Escondido, Calif.

Dendrocalamus asper
"Rebong" of Myanmar (Burma)

Dendrocalamus pendulus
in Botanic Gardens Singapore

Chimonobambusa quadrangularis
"Square bamboo" in Hong Kong

Gigantochloa verticillata
timber bamboo of Java

Gigantochloa apus *(India)*
Quail Bot. G., Encinitas, Calif.

Phyllostachys makinoi
"Taiwan madake"

Sasa palmata, *(No. Japan)*
"Palmate bamboo" inflorescence

Phyllostachys aurea
"Fishpole bamboo" in New York

Bambusa guadua, *largest American bamboo*
in Montego Bay, Jamaica, W. Indies

Phyllostachys nigra henonis, *"Hachiku"*
Atrium planting at 56 and Madison Ave., New York

Phyllostachys bambusoides 'Allgold' *(sulphurea hort.)*
in Jardin Botanique Cap Ferrat, French Riviera

Dendrocalamus giganteus, *the "Giant bamboo"*
in Peradeniya Botanic Garden, Sri Lanka

Phyllostachys bambusoides *(China)*
showing typical grooved culm

Phyllostachys bambusoides
"Madake" in Quail Gardens, Calif.

Otatea acuminata *(Yushania)*
"Weeping bamboo" of So. Mexico

Phyllostachys nigra
"Black bamboo" from So. China

Arundinaria viridistriata 'Aurea'
"Gold bamboo" in Encinitas, Calif.

Phyllorhachis sagittata
"Aquatic bamboo" of Trop. Africa

Phyllostachys vivax
giant hardy bamboo in Calif.

Phyllostachys vivax
"Elegant bamboo" of China

Phyllostachys viridi-glaucescens
in Kew Bot. Gardens, England

Phyllostachys bambusoides, *a running "Timber bamboo"*
at the Shogun's Nijo Castle (1603), Kyoto, Japan

Phyllostachys nigra, *"Blackstem bamboo"*
at Tiger Springs near Hangchow, China

Phyllostachys pubescens, *the "Moso bamboo"*
Hakone Nat'l. Park, Honshu, Japan

Semiarundinaria fastuosa, *"Narihira bamboo"*
at a Kyoto Inn, a hooded monk soliciting food

Pogonatherum paniceum
"Mini-bamboo" or "Catgrass" in Germany

Otatea acuminata, *"Weeping bamboo"*
(Yushania aztecorum) in San Diego

Pseudosasa japonica, *"Arrow bamboo"*
blooming in New Jersey

Sasa palmata
in Longwood Gard., Pennsylvania

Arundinaria pumila *(Sasa in hort.)*
hardy dwarf bamboo of Japan

Sasa tessellata, *in Sri Lanka*
in col. Peradeniya Bot. Garden

Bambusa vulgaris, *"Feathery bamboo"*
in Victoria Bot. Garden, Hong Kong

Schizostachyum zollingeri
"Golden bamboo" in Philippines

Phyllostachys aureosulcata
"Yellow-groove bamboo" in Vermont

Bambusa vulgaris 'Vittata', *"Greenstripe bamboo"*
with handsome striped culms, in California

Fargesia spathacea *(Thamnocalamus),* "Umbrella bamboo"
Panda feeding on bamboo, in Kweilin, S.W. China

Schizostachyum brachycladum
decorated for New Year, in Chinese Garden Singapore

Schizostachyum sp. 'Finisterre' *in New Guinea*
bamboo filled with water carried by Kikiepa villager

Carex conica 'Variegata'
"Miniature varieg. sedge" in Korea

Carex foliosiss. 'Albo-mediana'
(elegantissima) of No. Japan

Carex morrowii 'Variegata'
"Varieg. sedge grass" in California

Carex plantaginea *(CYP.)*
"Plantain sedge" (E. No. America)

Cyperus alternifolius
"Umbrella plant" in Florida

Eriophorum latifolium *(CYP.)*
"Broad cotton grass" in Sweden

Scirpus cernuus *(CYP.)*
(Isolepis gracilis in hort.)

Scirpus lacustris albescens
"White bulrush" in England

Arrhenatherum elatius bulbosum *(GRAM.)*
"Tuber oatgrass" in Brooklyn Bot. G.

Briza maxima *(GRAM.)*
"Rattlesnake grass" in California

Briza media
"Quaking grass" in Berlin, Germany

Cortaderia selloana *(GRAM.)*
"Pampas grass" in Argentina

Calamagrostis x acutiflora *(GRAM.)*
"Feather reed grass" (Karl Foerster)

Acorus gram. 'Variegatus' *(ARAC.)*
"Miniature sweet flag" of Japan

Bouteloua gracilis *(GRAM.)*
"Mesquite grass" in Texas

Deschampsia caespitosa *(GRAM.)*
"Tufted hair grass" (No. America)

Danthonia decumbens *(GRAM.)*
"Oat grass" of Europe, No. Africa

Cortaderia richardii *(GRAM.)*
"Plumed tussock grass" (N. Zealand)

Hystix patula
"Bottlebrush grass" in Québec

Festuca cinerea 'Blue-silver'
"Silver fescue" in Germany

Festuca ovina
"Sheep fescue" in So. France

Koeleria glauca
"Blue hair grass" (Eurasia)

Festuca scoparia
"Bearskin grass" (Pyrenées)

Glyceria maxima 'Variegata'
aquatic "Manna grass" in Munich

Helictotrichon sempervirens
"Blue oatgrass" in Rhineland

Melica nutans *(uniflora)*
"Pendant pearlgrass" in Holland

Holcus mollis 'Variegatus'
"Velvet grass" in Oxford Bot. G.

Imperata cylindrica 'Rubra'
"Japanese blood grass" in Oregon

Lamarckia aurea
"Goldentop" (Mediterran. reg.)

Miscanthus sinensis
"Japan silver grass" in Penna.

Miscanthus sinensis 'Variegatus'
"Variegated eulalia" (Brooklyn Bot. G.)

Miscanthus sinensis 'Zebrinus'
"Zebra grass" (P. Harper photo)

Miscanthus floridulus
"Giant miscanthus" of Japan

Molinia altissima
"Tall moor grass" (Europe, Asia)

Molinia caerulea 'Variegata'
"Variegated moor grass" in Virginia

Molinia caerulea
"Moor grass" in Duesseldorf Bot. G.

Chlorophytum comosum 'Vittatum' *(LIL.)*
"Spider plant" in hanging basket, from Cape of Good Hope

Ophiopogon jaburan *(LIL.)*
"White lily turf" from Honshu to Kyushu

Lagurus ovatus *(GRAM.)*
"Rabbit-tail grass" from Mediterranean to Canary Islands

Pennisetum alopecuroides *(GRAM.)*
"Chinese fountain grass" in Longwood Gardens, Pennsylvania

Elymus arenarius *(GRAM.)*
"European dune grass" on South coast of Britain

Uniola latifolia *(Chasmanthium latifolium) (GRAM.)*
"Wild oats" or "Spike grass" (Manitoba to New Mexico)

Spartina pectinata 'Aureo-marginata' *(GRAM.)*
"Prairie cord grass" from New England to Texas

Milium effusum 'Aureum' *(GRAM.)*
"Millet grass" or "Bowles golden grass"

Pennisetum setaceum 'Cupreum'
"Red fountain grass" in Fiji garden

Pennisetum setaceum
"Fountain grass" in So. Arabia

Pennisetum orientale
"Orient fountain grass" of Asia Minor

Setaria italica
"Foxtail millet" (So. Europe)

Phalaris arundinacea picta
"Canary grass" in Holland

Pennisetum villosum
"Feathertop" in Madeira

Panicum clandestinum
"Panic grass" (N. England to Texas)

Panicum virgatum *(Oplismenus)*
"Switch grass" in Jackson, Wyoming

Pennisetum setac. 'Atrosanguinea'
"Blood grass" in Fallbrook, Calif.

Uniola paniculata *(GRAM.)*
"Sea oats" on Virginia coast

Stenotaphrum secund. 'Varieg.' *(GRAM.)*
"Variegated St. Augustine grass"

Stipa gigantea *(GRAM.)*
"Feather grass" of Portugal

Reineckia carnea 'Variegata' *(LIL.)*
"Fan grass" as pot plant in Ohio

Luzula nivea *(JUNC.)*
"Snowy wood-rush" (Alps, Pyrenées)

Stipa pennata *(GRAM.)*
"Maidenhair grass" in Thuringia

Arundo donax *(GRAM.)*
"Giant reed" on Madeira Is.

Dianella caerulea *(LIL.)*
"Blue flax lily" of E. Australia

Arundo donax 'Versicolor'
"Varieg. giant reed" of So. Europe

Liriope platyphylla
"Lily turf" in Bermuda Bot. G.

Ophiopogon intermed. 'Arg.-marg.'
"Silvery mondo grass" in Bermuda

Liriope spicata
"Creeping lily-turf" (Vietnam)

Liriope muscari 'Variegata'
"Silvery lily-turf" in San Diego

Liriope muscari
"Big blue lily-turf" of China

Liriope graminifolia
"Grassy lily-turf" in Germany

Ophiopogon japonicus
"Snake's-beard" in California

Ophiopogon jap. 'Kyoto Dwarf'
"Dwarf mondo grass" in Hawaii

Ophiop. planiscapus nigrescens
"Black dragon" in Bot. G. Frankfurt

Dasylirion longissimum *(AGAV.)*
"Junquillo", Bot. Gard. Mexico City

Dasylirion serratifolium
at City Hall, Oslo, Norway

Xanthorrhoea preissii *(LIL.)*
"Blackboy" near Perth, W. Australia

Nolina bigelovii *(AGAV.)*
"Beargrass" in Del Dios, Calif.

Phormium tenax *(AGAV.)*
"Flax lily" in Wellington, N.Z.

Phormium tenax 'Variegatum'
"Variegated flax" in N. Zealand

Pandanus pygmaeus *(PAND.)*
"Dwarf pandanus" in Manila

Yucca glauca *(AGAV.)*
"Soapweed" in South Dakota

Yucca filamentosa *(AGAV.)*
"Adam's needle" in Carolina

Elymus racemosus
"Volga wild rye" in Munich Bot. G.

Avena sativa
"Common oats" (Mediterranean reg.)

Secale cereale *(S.W. Asia)*
"Common rye" for bread

Hordeum vulgare, *annual*
"Barley grain" in Germany

Hordeum nodosum, *perennial*
"Barley grass" in Alaska

Oryza sativa
"Common rice" in Thailand

Triticum dicoccon *(durum group)*
"German wheat" for breakfast cereal

Triticum aestivum *(sativum)*
"Common wheat" for bread flour

Triticum durum *(turgidum)*
"Hard wheat", for noodles

Agrostis tenuis *(GRAM.)*
"Bent grass" in San Luis Rey, Calif.

Saccharum officinarum *(GRAM.)*
"Sugar cane" in Cuba

Cynodon dactylon *(GRAM.)*
Taj Mahal gardens, Agra, India

Sagina subulata *(CARYOPH.)*
"Scotch moss", Los Angeles Arbor.

Sorghum dochna *(GRAM.)*
"Sugar moor-millet"

Zea diploperenne
"Perennial corn" of Oaxaca

Zea mays gracillima
"Decorative maize" in California

Zea mays indurata 'Rainbow'
"Indian flint corn" in So. California

Zea mays *(GRAM.)*
"Indian corn" or "Maize"

Arenaria verna *(caespitosa) (CARYOPH.)*
"Irish moss" in California

Carex pendula *(CYPER.)*
"Drooping sedge" in Britain

Sagina subulata *(CARYOPH.)*
"Scotch moss" in W. Europe

Dichondra micrantha *(CONV.)*
"Lawn-leaf" of W. Indies

Agrostis tenuis *(capillaris) (GRAM.)*
"Colonial bent grass" in Calif.

Cynodon dactylon *(GRAM.)*
"Bermuda grass" in Bombay

Oplismenus hirtellus 'Variegatus'
"Basket grass" in Brooklyn Bot. G.

Paspalum notatum *(GRAM.)*
"Bahia grass" in Sarasota, Florida

Zoysia japonica 'Meyeri' *(GRAM.)*
"Korean grass" w. Plumeria, Cordia

Agrostis capillaris *in flower*
"Tall bent" in Duesseldorf Bot. G.

Agrostis stolonifera palustris
"Creeping bent" in Alaska

Lolium perenne *(GRAM.)*
"Perennial rye grass" in Calif.

Festuca rubra *(GRAM.)*
"Red fescue" in Toronto, Ontario

Festuca elatior
"Reed fescue" in Washington

Festuca ovina glauca
"Blue sheep fescue" in California

Poa pratensis *(GRAM.)*
"Kentucky blue grass" in Oregon

Eremochloa ophiurides *(GRAM.)*
"Centipede grass" in Savannah, Ga.

Muehlenbeckia axillaris *(POL.)*
"Wire plant" of New Zealand

Stenotaphrum secundatum *(GRAM.)*
"St. Augustine grass" in Florida

Zoysia tenuifolia 'Emerald'
"Velvet grass" for Southern lawns

Zoysia tenuifolia *(GRAM.)*
"Temple grass" in San Diego

Araucaria araucana *(imbricata), the "Monkey-puzzle"*
mature tree in Royal Bot. Gardens Kew, England

Araucaria bidwillii, *"Bunya-Bunya" pine*
in Quail Botanic Garden, Encinitas, California

Araucaria heterophylla *(excelsa)*
"Norfolk Island pine" in Petropolis, Brazil

Araucaria cunninghamii, *the "Hoop pine"*
in Botanic Gardens Sydney, Australia

Araucaria bidwillii *(ARAUC.)*
"Bunya-Bunya" of Queensland

Araucaria araucana *(imbricata)*
"Hardy monkey-puzzle" from Chile

Araucaria angustifolia
"Paraná-pine" (So. Brazil)

Agathis robusta *(ARAUC.)*
"Queensland kauri" in Sydney

Cephalotaxus fortunei *(CEPH.)*
"Chinese plum-yew" in Auckland, N.Z.

Agathis australis *(New Zealand)*
"Kauri pine" with female cone

Cephalotaxus harringtoniana
"Plum-yew" in Maplewood, New Jersey

Araucaria cunninghamii *in Sydney*
"Hoop pine" with male cones

Araucaria columnaris
with female cones, in California

Callitris columellaris
"White cypress pine" (W. Australia)

Callitris rhomboidea
"Cypress pine" of S.E. Australia

Calocedrus macrolepis
"Incense cedar" of So. China

Calocedrus decurrens
"California incense cedar"

Calocedrus formosana
"Formosa incense cedar" (Taiwan)

Chamaecyparis funebris
"Mourning cypress" in Brisbane

Chamaecyparis lawsoniana 'Lanei'
"Golden false cypress" in England

Chamaecyp. lawsoniana 'Glauca'
"Blue false cypress" in Holland

Chamaecyp. nootkatensis 'Pendula'
"Weeping Alaska cedar" in Bavaria

Chamaecyparis lawson. 'Stewartii'
with golden foliage, in England

Chamaecyparis lawsoniana
'Columnaris glauca' *in Duesseldorf*

Chamaecyparis lawsoniana
"Port Orford cedar" in Munich

Chamaecyparis obtusa 'Compacta'
Somerset Arboretum, N. Jersey

Cham. obtusa 'Tetragona aurea'
"Dwarf golden Retinispora" in N. York

Chamaecyparis obtusa
"Hinoki cypress" in Longwood G., Penna.

Chamaecyparis obtusa 'Aurea'
golden form in Brooklyn Bot. G.

Chamaecyparis obtusa 'Nana'
"Dwarf Hinoki cypress"

Chamaec. obtusa 'Nana Gracilis'
in Botanic Garden Munich

Chamaecyparis pisifera 'Boulevard'
blue "Sawara cypress" in N. Jersey

Chamaecyparis pisifera 'Squarrosa'
"Moss cypress" (Retinispora hort.)

Chamaec. pisif. 'Filifera aurea'
"Golden threadleaf cypress" in Germany

Chamaec. pisif. 'Plumosa aurea'
"Plume false cypress" of Japan

x Cupressocyparis leylandii
"Leyland cypress" in California

x Cupressocyp. leyl. 'C. Wellan'
"Golden Leyland cypress"

Cupressus glabra
"Smooth Arizona cypress"

Cupressus arizonica
"Arizona cypress" in California

Cupressus arizonica columnaris
in Sonora, Mexico

Cupressus cashmeriana
"Kashmir cypress" (Himalayas)

Cupressus goveniana
"Gowen cypress" in California

Cupressus macrocarpa
"Monterey cypress" with cones

Cupressus macrocarpa 'Aurea'
"Golden Monterey cypress"

Cupressus sempervirens 'Glauca'
"Blue Italian cypress"

Cupressus macrocarpa 'Goldcrest'
as standard, in Nordwijk, Holland

Cupressus sempervirens *(on right)*
C. semp. 'Stricta' *(left) on Rhodes*

Cupressus sempervirens
"Mediterranean cypress" with cones

Cupressus sempervirens 'Stricta'
"Columnar Ital. cypress" in Calif.

Cedrus libani, *"Cedar of Lebanon"*
in original habitat on Mount Lebanon

Cupressus macrocarpa, *"Monterey cypress"*
windblown on Point Lobos, No. California

Cupressus sempervirens 'Fastigiata' *hort.*
cypress pyramids in Thessaly, Northern Greece

Thuja orientalis *(Platycladus), "Oriental arborvitae"*
at Chongmyo Royal Shrine, Seoul, Korea

Araucaria heterophylla, *the "Norfolk Isl. pine"*
Summer planting at Rockefeller Center, New York

Plantings of Pinus, Juniperus, Chamaecyparis, etc.
at terraced condominiums, Duesseldorf, Germany

Juniperus chinensis 'Torulosa'
"Hollywood juniper" of Japan

Juniperus chinensis 'Blue Point'
"Tear-drop juniper" in California

Juniperus chinensis 'Emerald Green"
Roehrs Nurs., Franklin Lakes, N.J.

Juniperus chinensis 'Hetzii'
"Hetz blue juniper" in Germany

Juniperus chinensis 'Pfitzeriana'
broad-spreading "Pfitzer juniper"

Junip. chin. 'Pfitzeriana aurea'
"Gold Pfitzer juniper" in Rhineland

Juniperus chin. 'Pfitzer. glauca'
"Blue Pfitzer juniper" in California

Juniperus chin. 'Procumbens nana'
in Oceanside Gard. Center, California

Juniperus chinensis, *w. cones*
"Chinese juniper" at Roehrs, N. Jersey

Juniperus chinensis 'Torulosa', *"Hollywood juniper"* *in Disney World, near Orlando, Florida*

Juniperus osteosperma, *"Utah juniper"* *gnarled tree at Grand Canyon, Arizona*

Cupressus sempervirens, *"Mediterranean cypress"* *at the Alcazar, Ciudad Rodrigo, Spain*

Juniperus horizontalis 'Blue chip', *as border* *at Climatron, Missouri Bot. Garden, St. Louis*

Juniperus communis, *w. berries*
"Common juniper" in Vancouver, B.C.

Juniperus communis, *as column*
at German Hort. Show, Duesseldorf

Juniperus excelsa 'Stricta'
"Greek juniper" of S.E. Europe

Juniperus communis hibernica
"Irish juniper" in New Jersey

Juniperus communis alpina
"Mountain juniper" in Austrian Alps

Juniperus comm. 'Echiniformis'
col. New York Botanical Garden

Juniperus comm. depressa 'Aurea'
"Rheingold juniper" in Germany

Junip. conferta 'Blue Pacific'
"Blue Shore juniper" in California

Junip. davurica 'Expansa varieg.'
"Daurian juniper" in Illinois

Junip. horizont. 'Bar Harbor'
Somerset Arboretum, New Jersey

Juniperus horizontalis
'Andorra compact' *in Munich Bot. G.*

Juniperus horizontalis 'Glauca'
Arnold Arboretum, near Boston

Juniperus horizont. 'Wiltonii'
"Blue rug juniper" on stake

Juniperus recurva, *prostrate form*
"Himalayan juniper" (Sikkim)

Juniperus recurva coxii
"Drooping juniper" of Myanmar

Juniperus rigida
"Needle juniper" in Seoul, Korea

Junip. sabina 'Tamariscifolia'
"Tamarix juniper" in San Diego

Junip. scopulorum 'Blue Heaven'
"Rocky Mountain juniper" in New York

Junip. scopulorum 'Gray Gleam'
silvery "Colorado red-cedar"

Juniperus scopulorum repandens
at Los Angeles Arboretum, Arcadia

Juniperus scopulorum
'Tolleson's weeping' *in Santa Fe*

Juniperus squamata
"Singleseed juniper" in Munich Bot. G.

Juniperus squamata 'Blue Star'
from a witches broom, in California

Juniperus squamata 'Prostrata'
mat-forming at New York Bot. G.

Juniperus virginiana 'Skyrocket'
Indiana cv. of Eastern red-cedar

Juniperus virginiana 'Canaertii'
popular Belgian pyramid (1865)

Juniperus virginiana
"Eastern red-cedar" in Somerset, N.J.

Microbiota decussata
choice spreader from E. Siberia

Juniperus virginiana 'Columnaris'
"Pyramid red-cedar" in New Jersey

Tetraclinis articulata
"Sandarak wood" of Morocco

Thuja occidentalis 'Emerald'
"Emerald arborvitae" from Denmark

Thuja occidentalis
"American arborvitae"

Thuja occidentalis
female plant with young cones

Thuja occidentalis 'Filiformis'
"Threadleaf arborvitae" in Calif.

Thuja occidentalis 'Gold Tip'
"Gold-tip arborvitae" in N. Jersey

Thuja orientalis 'Elegantissima'
"Golden arborvitae" in Germany

Thuja orientalis *(Platycladus)*
"Oriental arborvitae" with cones

Thuja orientalis 'Aurea nana'
"Dwarf gold arborvitae" in Calif.

Thuja plicata *(CUP.)*
"Giant cedar" in Rhineland

Abies bracteata *w. male flowers*
"Bristle-cone fir" in California

Thujopsis dolabrata *(CUP.)*
"Broadleaf arborvitae" of Japan

Abies alba *(PIN.)*
"Silver fir" in Thuringia

Abies balsamea, *in Québec, Canada*
aromatic leaves whitish beneath

Abies balsamea
"Balsam fir" used as Christmas tree

Abies concolor
"White fir" (Colorado to Ariz.)

Abies alba, *the "Silver fir"*
in Alpine forest of Bavaria

Abies concolor, *"Colorado fir"*
in Rocky Mountains habitat

Abies concolor 'Violacea'
with striking silver-blue needles

Abies koreana, *"Korean fir"*
with bluish purple cones

Abies koreana, *from Korea*
col. Arnold Arboretum, Boston

Abies procera (nobilis)
"Noble fir" of Yosemite, California

Abies pinsapo 'Glauca'
"Blue Spanish fir" in Somerset, N.J.

Abies veitchii *(Japan)*
"Shirabe fir" of Honshu

Abies nordmanniana
"Caucasus fir" (Armenia)

Abies pinsapo
"Spanish fir" in Andalucia

Abies procera 'Glauca'
at Floriade in Amsterdam

Cedrus atlantica 'Glauca'
"Blue Atlas cedar" in England

Abies nordmanniana
resinous cones in New York Bot. Gard.

Abies magnifica
"Red fir" of Oregon and California

Cedrus deodara
"Deodar cedar" in Sydney Bot. Garden

Abies grandis
"Grand fir" in Vancouver

Larix decidua, *"Europ. larch"*
in Bot. Gard. Bern, Switzerland

Cedrus libani,
"Cedar of Lebanon" in New York

Abies balsamea, *the "Balsam fir" of Canada*
as long-lasting Christmas tree in United States

Abies lasiocarpa, *"Alpine forest fir"*
in Grand Teton National Park, Wyoming

Cedrus atlantica 'Glauca', *"Blue Atlas cedar"*
in Atlas Mountains, near Marrakech, Morocco

Cedrus atlantica 'Glauca pendula'
of French origin, in col. New York Bot. Garden

Cedrus deodara compacta
"California Christmas tree" in Vista

Cedrus atlantica 'Aurea'
"Golden Atlas cedar" in Holland

Cedrus atlantica
"Atlas cedar" of No. Africa

Keteleeria fortunei, *w. cones*
of Taiwan and S.E. China

Keteleeria fortunei
in Bot. Gardens Sydney, Australia

Cedrus libani 'Nana'
"Dwarf Lebanon cedar" in New York

Larix laricina
"American larch" (Canada to Alaska)

Larix decidua *(europaea)*
"European larch", in Swiss Alps

Larix kaempferi, *with cones*
"Japanese larch" in Honshu

Picea pungens 'Koster', *"Koster's blue spruce"*
handsome cultivar, in Somerset Arboretum, New Jersey

Picea pungens, *"Colorado spruce"*
forest along Snake River, Teton N. Park, Wyoming

Picea abies *(excelsa), "Common spruce"* of C. Europe
in forest planting of Southern Bavaria

Larix kaempferi *(leptolepis), "Japanese larch"*
beautiful tree in Darmstadt, Germany

Picea abies *(excelsa)*
"Common spruce" with pendant cones

Picea abies, *"Norway spruce"*
young tree in nursery near Munich

Picea abies acrocona
"Dwarf weeping spruce" in Uppsala

Picea abies 'Diffusa'
in col. New York Bot. Garden

Picea abies 'Columnaris'
"Columnar spruce" in Boskoop, Holland

Picea abies 'Nidiformis'
"Bird's-nest spruce" in N. Jersey

Picea abies 'Pendula'
"Weeping spruce" in Somerset Arbor.

Picea alcoquiana
'Howell's Dwarf' *in Holland*

Picea breweriana
"Siskiyou spruce" of Oregon

Picea x omorika 'Gnome' *(x mariorika)*
in Bot. Garden Dortmund

Picea glauca 'Conica'
in Kew Bot. Gardens, near London

Picea glauca albertiana 'Pyramidalis'
"Dwarf Alberta spruce" in Germany

Picea glauca 'Densata'
"Black Hills spruce" in So. Dakota

Picea engelmannii
"Engelmann spruce" in Oregon

Picea glauca, *w. young cones*
"White spruce", across Canada

Picea glauca 'Echiniformis'
"Hedgehog spruce" in 15 cm pot

Picea glehnii *(Japan)*
"Sakhalin spruce", in Osaka

Picea omorika
"Serbian spruce" of Yugoslavia

Picea orientalis 'Aurea'
Skylands Arboretum, New Jersey

Picea orientalis 'Aureospica'
gold-spike "Oriental spruce"

Picea pungens
"Colorado spruce" in New York

Picea pungens 'Glauca'
"Blue spruce" with cones

Picea pungens *w. male flowers*
in Bryce Canyon, Utah

Picea pungens argentea
"Silver spruce" in N. York Bot. G.

Picea abies 'Echiniformis'
"Prickly hedgehog" in Germany

Picea pungens 'Glauca'
in Boskoop nursery, Netherlands

Picea sitchensis, *"Sitka spruce"*
in Ketchikan, Alaska

Pinus aristata, *w. resin drops*
"Bristle-cone pine" of Colorado

Pinus armandii, *"Armand pine"*
in Hangchow Bot. Garden, China

Pinus bungeana
"Lacebark pine" (N.W. China)

Pinus canariensis *with male candle*
"Canary Islands pine" (Tenerife)

Pinus cembra
"Swiss stone-pine"

Pinus cembra 'Aurea'
with yellow needles, in Holland

Pinus cembroides
"Mexican stonepine"

Pinus contorta *(California to Alaska)*
"Shore pine" with male inflor.

Pinus densiflora 'Umbraculifera'
"Tanyosho", "Japan umbrella pine"

Pinus coulteri
"Big-cone pine" in San Diego

Pinus edulis
"Pinyon pine" in So. Utah

Pinus echinata
"Yellow pine" in South Carolina

Pinus densiflora 'Pendula'
Botan. Garden Hangchow, China

Pinus x eldarica *(Afghanistan)*
in San Marcos, California

Pinus elliottii
"Slash pine" in Mississippi

Pinus glabra
"Cedar pine" in Morristown, N.J.

Pinus halepensis
"Aleppo pine" in Syria

Pinus halepensis
living Christmas tree in Calif.

Pinus canariensis, *"Canary Island pine"*
on the Montaña Grande, Tenerife

Pinus taeda, *the "Loblolly pine"*
in habitat, near Greenwood, So. Carolina

Pinus thunbergiana, *"Japanese black-pine"*
at Nijo Castle, Kyoto, Japan

Pinus pinea, *the "Italian stone pine"*
at Balaia, Algarve coast, South Portugal

Pinus nigra var. nigra
typical "Austrian pine"

Pinus nigra
"Black pine" of S.E. Europe, W. Asia

Pinus nigra 'Hornibrookiana'
dwarf form in Brooklyn Bot. Gard.

Pinus maximinoi *(W. Mexico)*
in Chula Vista, California

Pinus maximinoi *(tenuifolia)*
San Pasqual Arboretum, Calif.

Pinus jeffreyi
"Jeffrey pine" in Oregon

Pinus mugo *(montana)*
"Swiss mountain pine"

Pinus mugo 'Compacta'
"Dwarf mountain pine" in Brooklyn

Pinus leucodermis *(heldreichii)*
"Bosnian red-cone pine"

Pinus halepensis, *"Jerusalem pine"*
in ancient Olympia, So. Greece

Pinus edulis, *wind-blown "Pinyon-nut pine"*
on South Rim of Grand Canyon, Arizona

Pinus strobus 'Witches broom'
at Arnold Arboretum, Jamaica Plain, Mass.

Pinus pinea, *"Italian stone-pine"*
in Vatican Gardens, with St. Peter's Basilica, Rome

Tsuga sieboldii, *"Japanese hemlock"*
in mountains of Honshu, Japan

Picea abies, *living "Norway spruce" in New Jersey*
sprayed with artificial snow for Christmas

Pinus kochiana
"Turkish Scotch pine" in Calif.

Pinus pinaster
"Maritime pine" in So. France

Pinus montezumae *(So. Mexico)*
"Montezuma pine" in Oaxaca

Pinus palustris
"Longleaf pine" of Southeast U.S.

Pinus palustris, *in Alabama*
"Southern pine" yields turpentine

Pinus palustris
"Longleaf yellow pine" in Virginia

Pinus parviflora *(Honshu, Kyushu)*
"Japanese white pine"

Pinus parviflora 'Glauca'
in Boskoop nursery, Holland

Pinus pinea, *with juvenile growth*
"Italian stone pine", in California

Pinus ponderosa, *"Western yellow pine"*
in Bryce Canyon National Park, Utah

Pinus pseudostrobus, *"Guatemala pine"*
Mirov Arboretum, San Pasqual, California

Pinus radiata, the *"Monterey pine"*
near Carmel, Monterey Bay, California

Pinus resinosa, *"American red pine"*
in E. Rutherford, Bergen County, New Jersey

Pinus radiata, *sheared column*
living Christmas tree in Calif.

Pinus radiata *(close-up)*
"Monterey pine" in Escondido

Pinus sabiniana
"Digger pine" of California

Pinus ponderosa
"Ponderosa pine" in Texas

Pinus pseudostrobus
"False Weymouth pine" (So. Mexico)

Pinus pungens
"Prickly pine" in No. Carolina

Pinus resinosa
"Red pine" in New Jersey

Pinus rigida
"Pitch pine" in New York Bot. G.

Pinus roxburghii
"Indian longleaf pine" in Nepal

Pinus monticola
"Western white pine" in California

Pinus strobus, *pendant cones*
"Eastern white pine" in Boston

Pinus strobus 'Nana'
"Dwarf white pine" in Brooklyn B.G.

Pinus strobus 'Pendula'
Somerset Arboretum, New Jersey

Pinus strobus 'Variegata'
"Tiger pine", in England

Pinus torreyana
"Torrey pine" in La Jolla, Calif.

Pinus virginiana
"Jersey pine" (Southeast U.S.)

Pinus thunbergiana, *w. male fl.*
"Japanese black pine" in Germany

Pinus monophylla
"Single-leaf pinyon" in Utah

Pinus sylvestris 'Nana'
"Dwarf Scotch pine" in Brooklyn

Pinus sylvestris *as young tree*
"Scots pine" (No. Europe, Asia)

Pinus sylvestris, *close-up*
at Rutgers Univ., N. Brunswick, N.J.

Pinus sylvestris 'Watereri'
col. Somerset Arboretum, N.J.

Pinus torreyana
in La Jolla, California

Pinus wallichiana *(griffithii)*
"Bhutan pine" with young growth

Pseudolarix amabilis *(kaempferi)*
showing leaves in clusters

Pseudolarix amabilis
"Golden larch" of E. China

Pseudolarix amabilis *in Autumn*
Cologne Hort. Expos., Germany

Tsuga canadensis, *the "Canada hemlock"*
under January snow, E. Rutherford, New Jersey

Picea sitchensis, *"Sitka spruce"*
in habitat near Ketchikan, Alaska

Pseudotsuga menziesii, *"Douglas fir"*
between spiral rock of Bryce Canyon, Utah

Pinus thunbergiana, *shaped "Japanese black pine"*
at 13 Cent. Daibutsu shrine, Kamakura, Japan

Pseudotsuga menziesii
young "Douglas fir" in N. Jersey

Pseudotsuga menziesii
showing cone, in Brit. Columbia

Pseudotsuga menziesii, *close-up
in Nordpark, Duesseldorf, Germany*

Tsuga mertensiana
at National Arboretum, Washington

Tsuga canadensis
"Hemlock spruce" in New Jersey

Tsuga canadensis
"Eastern hemlock" with cones

Tsuga canadensis 'Prostrata'
"Cole's prostrate hemlock"

Tsuga caroliniana
"Carolina hemlock"

Tsuga heterophylla
"Western hemlock" (Pacific Coast)

Podocarpus gracilior *(Kenya)*
"African fern-pine" in San Diego

Podocarpus henkelii *(Transvaal)*
"Longleaf-yellowwood" in Kirstenbosch

Podocarpus elongatus
"African yellowwood" (W. Africa)

Podocarpus macrophyllus 'Maki'
"Southern yew" in New Orleans

Podocarpus macrophyllus
in Hangchow Bot. G., China

Podocarpus macrophyllus
"Buddhist pine" in San Diego

Podocarpus milanjianus
"Yellowwood" in Uganda

Podocarpus wallichianus
in Botanic Garden Singapore

Podocarpus wallichianus
handsome tropical "Yellowwood"

Dacrydium franklinii
"Huon pine" of Tasmania

Dacrydium cupressinum *(POD.)*
"Rimu" of the Maoris, N. Zealand

Thujopsis dolabrata, *w. cones*
"Lizard tree" of Japan (PIN.)

Podocarpus neriifolius
at University of Hawaii

Podocarpus salignus *(PODOC.)*
"Willowleaf pine" of Chile

Podocarpus latifolius *(S. Africa)*
in Vista nursery, California

Podocarpus nagi *(Japan, Taiwan)*
"Broadleaf podocarp" in Los Angeles

Podocarpus totara
"Totara" in Marlborough, N.Z.

Podocarpus falcatus
"Oteniqua yellow-wood" (So. Africa)

Cryptomeria japonica, *the "Japanese cedar"*
in Shiroyama Park, Kagoshima, Kyushu

Sequoia sempervirens, *"Coast redwood"*
along Redwood Highway, Northern California

Taxodium distichum, *"Swamp cypress"*
hung with Tillandsia, in Cypress Gardens, Florida

Taiwania cryptomerioides
a sacred temple tree from mountains of Taiwan

Taxus cuspidata 'Capitata'
"Upright Japanese yew"

Taxus cuspid. 'Green Mountain'
by Bobbink Nurseries, in New Jersey

Taxus baccata 'Fastigiata'
"Irish yew" in Bavaria

Taxus baccata, *female tree*
"English yew" with fruit

Taxus baccata, *90 years old*
as tree, in Duesseldorf, Germany

Taxus x media 'Hicksii'
"Hicks yew", branch w. berries

Taxus x media 'Hatfieldii'
"Hatfield yew" in Wayne, N. Jersey

Taxus cuspidata *(Japan)*
female plant, bearing fruit

Taxus cuspidata
"Japanese yew", as sheared bush

Taxus cuspidata 'Densiformis'
"Dense yew" in Princeton, N.J.

Taxus x media *(TAXAC.)*
pyramidal "Anglo-Japanese yew"

Taxus baccata 'Repandens'
"Flat-top yew" in Holland

Torreya californica
"California nutmeg"

Torreya nucifera *(TAXAC.)*
"Jap. torreya" w. aromatic leaves

Torreya taxifolia
crushed leaves malodorous

Torreya taxifolia
"Stinking cedar" of Florida

Cunninghamia lanceolata
"Mao Chia" in Taiwan

Cunninghamia lanceolata *(TAXOD.)*
"China fir" in Virginia

Taxodium distichum
juvenile "Bald cypress"

Taxodium distichum
in Longwood Gardens, Pennsylvania

Taxodium distichum
in Kew Bot. Gardens, England

Metasequoia glyptostroboides
"Dawn redwood" of C. China

Metasequoia glybtostroboides
"Fossile age conifer", in N. Jersey

Taxodium mucronatum
"Montezuma cypress" (So. Mexico)

Sequoiadendron giganteum
"Redwood" in Calif. nursery

Sequoia sempervirens 'Adpressa'
"Dwarf redwood" in Germany

Athrotaxis laxifolia
"Tasmanian cedar"

Sequoiadendron giganteum, *the "Giant redwood"*
Tunnel tree, in the Sierra Nevada, Calif. (TAXOD.)

Sequoiadendron giganteum, *General Sherman tree*
3000 yrs. old, Sequoia Nat'l. Park, California

Taxus baccata, *sheared "English yew"*
in Versailles gardens of Louis XIV of France

Podocarpus macrophyllus, *sheared globe*
in West Lake garden, Hangchow, China

Taxodium macronatum, *"Montezuma cypress"*
est. 4000 yrs. old, El Tule, Oaxaca, So. Mexico

Pinus thunbergiana, *"Japanese black pine"*
in Temple gardens of Heian Shrine, Kyoto, Japan

Cryptomeria japonica *(Japan)*
in Kagoshima Park, Kyushu

Cryptomeria japonica
"Japanese cedar", branch w. cones

Glyptostrobus lineatus, *in Autumn*
"Chinese water pine" (S.E. China)

Cryptomeria japonica 'Dacrydioides'
in juvenile shrub stage

Cryptomeria japonica 'Dacrydioides'
as tree in New York Bot. Garden

Cryptomeria jap. 'Bandai Sugi'
in Somerset Arboretum, New Jersey

Cryptomeria japonica 'Lobbii'
"Lobb cryptomeria" on Long Island

Sciadopitys verticillata *(Japan)*
"Umbrella pine" in Winterthur, Delaware

Taxodium distichum nutans
"Pond cypress" in Alabama

Buxus sempervirens, *"English boxwood"* in topiary
in Governor's garden, Williamsburg, Virginia

Carpinus betulus, *"European hornbeam"*
trimmed into hedges and arches, Bot. G. Essen, Germany

Chamaecyparis obtusa 'Pygmaea', *"Pygmy Hinoki cypress"*
as low hedge, in Brooklyn Bot. Garden, New York

Begonia x semperflorens, *colorful "Wax begonias"*
planted into mossed wire fence, Hamburg, Germany

Tilia platyphyllos, *"Big-leaf linden"*
as windbreak in Rondel, GRUGA Expos. Essen, Germany

Buxus microphylla var. japonica, *"California boxwood"*
in Monastery garden, Pala Indian Mission, California

Cotoneaster divaricatus
low hedge in Brooklyn Bot. Garden

Berberis thunb. 'Atropurpurea'
"Redleaf Jap. barberry" in Germany

Hedera helix, *"English ivy"*
trained into hedge, in Rhineland

Picea abies, *"Norway spruce"*
hedge near Garmisch, Bavarian Alps

Mahonia aquifolium
"Oregon grape" along city street

Picea abies, *3 m high*
spruce as windbreak, near Munich

Carpinus betulus, *"Hornbeam"*
hedge in suburban Duesseldorf

Buxus microphylla japonica
boxwood in Balboa Park, San Diego

Carissa grandiflora *(macrocarpa)*
"Natal plum" in San Diego Zoo

Buxus sempervirens 'Angustifolia' *in artistic patterns*
Parque Eduardo VII, Lisbon, Portugal

Hibiscus rosa-sinensis 'Cooperi', *"Checkered hibiscus"*
as hedging at hotel in Colón, Panama

Ilex crenata, *box-leaf "Japanese holly"*
as curving, moulded hedge, Brooklyn, Bot. Garden

Bougainvillea x buttiana 'Barbara Karst'
as natural hedge in Vista, California

Thuja occidentalis, *"Arborvitae"*
as windbreak hedge, in Ruhrland

Buxus sempervirens 'Suffruticosa'
"Edging box", Williamsburg, Virginia

Thuja occidentalis, *low hedge*
in Herrsching village, near Munich

Taxus cuspidata, *"Japanese yew"*
sheared hedge in E. Rutherford, N.J.

Thuja plicata, *close-sheared*
in Nymphenburg Bot. Garden

Chaenomeles japonica
"Japanese quince" as hedge

Cupressus sempervirens
windbreak in Fallbrook, Calif.

Ligustrum lucidum
"Glossy privet" hedge in S. Diego

Syzygium paniculatum
"Brush cherry" in San Diego Zoo

Myrtus communis, *hedge of the classic myrtle,* *in the Alhambra, Granada, Andalucia*

Syzygium paniculatum *(Eugenia myrtifolia hort.)* *hedge at Palacio Jai Alai, Tijuana, Mexico*

Ligustrum japonicum *(L. lucidum hort.)* *"Japanese privet" hedge, in Vista, California*

Myrtus communis, *well-groomed hedge of myrtle* *in garden of Moorish Alcazar, Sevilla, Spain*

Ligustrum japonicum *(lucidum)*
"Creole privet" hedge in Miami

Ligustrum ovalifolium
"California privet" of Japan

Lampranthus productus, *"Ice plant"*
as low hedging in Vista, California

Prunus laurocerasus 'Otto Luyken'
compact form "English laurel"

Ixora coccinea *as hedge*
Zihuatanejo, Guerrero, Mexico

Rosmarinus officinalis
hedge on the Algarve, Portugal

Lonicera pileata
"Privet honeysuckle" of China

Myoporum laetum *(N. Zealand)*
on the Balaia coast, Portugal

Crataegus monogyna
"English hawthorn" in Grafenberg

Thuja occidentalis 'Fastigiata' *in low hedging 11th century cemetery in Vallentuna, Sweden*

Carpinus betulus, *the "Hornbeam" of No. Europe as sheared hedge and arbor, in Bot. Garden Essen*

Euphorbia xantii, *"Liga" of Mexico as dense hedge in Fallbrook, California*

Cupressus lusitanica, *"Mexican cypress" shaped by jardineiros in Coimbra, Portugal*

Pyracantha koidzumii, *"Formosa firethorn" espaliered on wall at Lake San Marcos, Calif.*

Topiary forms at Disneyland, Anaheim, California giraffe of Lingustrum jap., hedge and topiary of Taxus

Pittosporum tenuifolium, *the "Tawhiwhi" of N. Zealand very dense evergreen hedge in Coastal Virginia*

Rosa rugosa, *"Ramana roses" as informal hedge in University Botanic Garden, Duesseldorf, Germany*

Forsythia x intermedia, *hedge of "Golden bells" flowering in early Spring, Wood Ridge, New Jersey*

Nandina domestica 'Compacta' *"Dwarf Heavenly bamboo", informal hedge in California*

Euonymus alata 'Compacta', *"Winged euonymus" as mound hedge, in Brooklyn Botanic Garden, New York*

Tsuga canadensis, *"Hemlock spruce" of No. America as sheared hedge-wall in Rhode Island*

Buxus sempervirens 'Suffruticosa', *"True dwarf box"*
as edging in Missouri Botanic Garden, St. Louis

Photinia x fraseri, *"Redleaf photinia"*
hedge in colorful young growth, Seaford, Virginia

Ilex vomitoria, *the "Yaupon holly"*
low hedge in garden of Colonial Williamsburg, Virginia

Berberis thunbergii 'Crimson Pygmy', *"Miniature red barberry"*
in N.J. Knotgarden; Lavandula and Teucrium as herbs

Syzygium paniculatum, *"Brush cherry eugenia"*
with young red foliage, in Santa Monica, California

Pyracantha fortuneana, *the "Chinese firethorn"*
as spiny barrier hedge, in Norfolk Virginia

Cereus hexagonus, *"So. American blue column" cactus as coffee finca fence, in Cali, Colombia*

Stenocereus marginatus, *"Organ pipe cactus" as village fence, in Mitla, Oaxaca, So. Mexico*

Trichocereus chilensis *as cattle fence in arid Atacama Province of Chile*

Hibiscus rosa-sin., *living fence of hardwood cuts Hacienda Fortin de las Flores, Veracruz, Mexico*

Tilia platyphyllos, *sheared linden standards along Giants avenue, Castle Herrenhausen, Hannover*

Ilex aquifolium 'Balearica', *"Mallorca holly" in hedge tests, Brooklyn Bot. Garden, New York*

*Floral Carpet with edging of Lavandula and Santolina
with spring tulips, at Duke Garden, Somerville, New Jersey*

*Taxus baccata, "English yew", sheared pyramids
Castle Belverede gardens in Vienna, Austria*

*Modernistic Garden, designed by Roberto Burle-Marx
at Petropolis, in the Organ Mountains of Brazil*

*Platanus x acerifolia, "Sycamore" or "London plane"
pollarded tree along shore of Lake Lucerne, Switzerland*

*Bamboo w. revered Tai Hu stone, symbol of long life
in the Botanic Garden of ancient Hangchow, So. China*

*Olea europaea, an Olive tree 130 years old
patiently trimmed into topiary form, in Vista, Calif.*

Cupressus sempervirens
in spiral column, Coimbra, Portugal

Thuja orientalis *(Platycladus)*
topiary elephant, Disney World, Florida

Buxus sempervirens, *"Boxwood"*
topiary twist, in Germany

Cedrus atlantica 'Glauca pendula'
"Weeping cedar" with curly stem

Podocarpus macrophyllus
topiary giraffe, Disney World

Podocarpus macrophyllus 'Maki'
shaped as swan, Orlando, Florida

Laurus nobilis, *"Bay tree"*
spiral standard, in Rhineland

Ficus benjamina, *"Weeping fig"*
with braided stems, in California

Buxus sempervirens, *"Boxwood"*
grown as standard, in Holland

Tamarindus indica, *shaped "Tamarind" trees
in Royal Grand Palace, Bangkok, Thailand*

Prunus mume 'Alboplena', *"Dble. Flowering Jap. apricot"
dwarfed as Penjing, in Bot. Garden Hangchow, China*

Ficus pumila, *"Creeping fig" on mossed wire frame
as topiary bird, Longwood Gard., Kennett Square, Penna.*

Dinosaur, alive with Ficus pumila, on 5th Avenue
Rockefeller Center New York, by J. Roehrs Co.

Ficus pumila, *"Creeping fig"* topiary at New York Flower Show

Buxus microphylla japonica *as topiary deer, in Los Angeles*

Ficus religiosa, *dwarfed "Sacred fig"* Temple of Emerald Buddha, Bangkok

Juniperus chinensis 'Torulosa' *as topiary, Corona del Mar, California*

Zelkova serrata, *"Sawleaf zelkova"* *as bonsai 60 years old, in Germany*

Pinus thunbergiana, *sheared trees* *in Deer Park, Nara Shrine, Japan*

Acer palmatum, *"Japanese maple"* *as dwarfed tree, in Osaka, Japan*

"Ming tree" of moss and wood imitating Penjing, in San Francisco

Acer palmatum 'Atropurpurea' *dwarfed "Red Jap. maple" in Tokyo*

Juniperus chinensis 'Sargentii'
as weathered bonsai, at Osaka Expo.

Junip. chin. 'Globosa' *as Penjing
Beijing-Hangchow Express, China*

Pinus parviflora, *"Jap. White pine"
as dwarfed Bonsai in Bot. G. Essen*

Diospyros kaki, *"Jap. persimmon"
Bonsai w. fruit (Yamada, Hiroshima)*

Osmanthus fragrans, *"Sweet olive"
as Penjing in Kweilin, S.W. China*

Chaenomeles speciosa, *"Flow. quince"
Bonsai miniature in Brooklyn Bot. G.*

Pinus nigra, *"Austrian pine"
Bonsai 65 yrs. old, Essen Bot. Garden*

Fagus crenata, *"Jap. beech"
Lilliput forest in GRUGA col.*

Juniperus rigida, *"Needle juniper"
Bonsai 150 yrs. old, in Japan*

Clerodendrum inerme, *"Indian privet"*
trained into water buffaloes, Hanging Gardens, Bombay

Racing horses of seasonal flowers
jumping Thuja barrier, in Meran, Italian Tyrol

Cryptomeria japonica, *"Japanese cedar"*
miniature forest 60 yrs. old, Osaka Expo., Japan

Rhododendron indicum 'Shinnyo-no-tsuki'
"Satsuki" (Fifth moon) azalea as bonsai, Nikko, Japan

Laurus nobilis, *the classical laurel, as Patio trees*
some with twisted stems, grown in Belgium

Conifers such as Pinus, grown as dwarfed trees
in ceramic bonsai dishes along Kyoto street, Japan

Acanthus spinosus
"Classic acanthos" in Greece

Dicliptera suberecta *(Jacobinia)*
in San Diego Zoo

Duvernoia adhatodoides *(So. Afr.)*
in Botanic Garden Sydney

Graptophyllum pictum
"Caricature plant" in Cape Town

Jacobinia carnea *(Justicia)*
"Flamingo plant" (Brazil)

Jacobinia carnea 'Alba'
at Posada Lomas, Fortin, Veracruz

Justicia aurea *(Mexico)*
Quail Bot. Gard., Encinitas, Calif.

Justicia betonica
"White shrimp plant" on Rarotonga

Justicia ghiesbreghtiana *(Mexico)*
in Brooklyn Botanic Garden

Beloperone guttata *(Justicia)*
"Shrimp plant" of Mexico

Beloperone guttata lutea
Botanic Gardens Sydney, Australia

Megakepasma erythrochlamys
"Red justicia" in Honolulu

Pseuderanthemum graciliflorum
at Andromeda Gardens, Barbados

Pseuderanth. atropurp. 'Variegatum'
in Bermuda Botanic Garden

Pseuderanthemum kewense
Solomon Islands, South Pacific

Pseuderanthemum reticulatum
"Yellow-vein eranthemum" (Polynesia)

Ruellia ciliosa
(South Carolina to Texas)

Ruellia macrantha *(Brazil)*
"Christmas pride" in California

Ruspolia seticalyx *(Trop. Africa)*
in Royal Botan. Garden, Sydney

Sanchezia speciosa *(nobilis)*
in Botanic Garden of Tahiti

Schaueria flavicoma *(Justicia)*
tropical subshrub of Brazil

Strobilanthes anisophyllus
in Mahé Bot. Garden, Seychelles

Thunbergia battiscombei *(Trop. Afr.)*
Quail Bot. Gard., Encinitas, Calif.

Thunbergia erecta
"King's mantle", in Sénégal

Whitfieldia elongata *(Ruellia)*
of Trop. West Africa

Pseuderanthemum sinuatum *hort.*
Pacific Hort. Show, Los Angeles

Hypoestes aristata
"Ribbon bush" of So. Africa

Acer barbatum
"Southern sugar maple" in Florida

Acer buergerianum
"Trident maple" of China

Acer campestre
"Hedge maple" in England

Acer davidii
"David maple" of C. China

Acer palmatum 'Laciniatum'
in Arnold Arboretum, near Boston

Acer ginnala
"Amur maple" or "Fire maple"

Acer griseum
"Paperbark maple" of W. China

Acer griseum
cinnamon paperbark trunk

Acer pensylvanicum
"Striped maple" (Québec to Georgia)

Acer japonicum 'Aconitifolium'
"Fernleaf moon-maple"

Acer japonicum 'Aureum'
"Golden fullmoon maple"

Acer palmatum 'Bloodgood'
in Somerset Arboretum, N. Jersey

Acer negundo 'Odessanum'
"Gold box-elder" of the Ukraine

Acer negundo 'Variegatum'
"Silverleaf box-elder"

Acer negundo 'Flamingo'
at Floriade Expo., Amsterdam

Acer x neglectum, *in Germany*
(campestre x lobelii)

Acer palmatum 'Sango Kaku'
North Haven Gardens, Dallas, Texas

Acer palmatum 'Sango Kaku'
"Coral bark maple" without foliage

Acer palmatum
"Japanese maple" in New Jersey

Acer palmatum
fruiting branch in Autumn

Acer palmatum 'Atropurpureum'
"Red cutleaf Japanese maple"

Acer palmatum 'Dissectum' *('Viride')*
"Threadleaf Japanese maple"

Acer platanoides 'Crimson King'
along Lake Lucerne, Switzerland

Acer palmatum 'Crimson Queen'
Somerset Arboretum, New Jersey

Acer pseudoplatanus
"Sycamore maple" w. winged fruit

Acer pseudoplatanus
pendulous flowers in Spring

Acer platanoides 'Schwedleri'
"Schwedler Norway maple" in Germany

Acer platanoides
"Norway maple" in California

Acer platanoides 'Columnare'
in autumn color, Rutherford, N.J.

Acer platan. 'Albo-marginatum'
"Varieg. Norway maple" in Holland

Acer pseudoplatanus 'Purpureum'
"Purple sycamore" in Thuringia

Acer rubrum, *"Red maple"*
at Rutgers University, New Jersey

Acer rubrum *(E. and C. No. America)*
scarlet flowers before foliage.

Acer tataricum *(Eur. to W. Asia)*
"Tatarian maple" w. winged fruit

Acer saccharum
"Sugar maple" in Autumn

Acer saccharinum 'Laciniatum'
"Silver maple", cutleaf form

Dipteronia sinensis *(ACER.)*
with cupped fruit, in China

Actinidia kolomikta *(Japan)*
"Kolomikta-leaf" in Kew Bot. Gardens

Anacardium occidentale
"Cashew-nut tree" in Madras, India

Cotinus coggygria *(So. U.S.)*
"Smoke tree" w. plumy inflor.

Cotinus obovatus *(ANAC.)*
"Amer. smoke tree" in autumn color

Cotinus coggygria 'Rubrifolius'
"Venetian sumac" of So. Europe

Mangifera indica *(ANAC.)*
"Mango tree" flower in Sénégal

Harpephyllum caffrum *(ANAC.)*
"Kaffir plum" in San Diego

Spondias mombin *(ANAC.) in Hawaii*
"Spanish plum" in flower

Schinus molle, *first "California pepper" planted 1830 at Franciscan Mission San Luis Rey, California*

Anacardium occidentale, *"Cashew-nut tree" at Hindu temple of Mahabalipuram, South India*

Polyalthia longifolia pendula, *"Asoka tree" of India planted in temple area, Chinese Garden, Singapore*

Rhus chinensis 'September Beauty' *(ANAC.) "Chinese sumac" cv. by Rutgers University, New Jersey*

Pistacia chinensis *(ANAC.)*
"Chin. pistache", San Pasqual, Calif.

Pistacia chinensis
in autumn color, in Georgia

Pistacia atlantica
"Mastic tree" in Bonsall, California

Schinus molle *(ANACARD.)*
female tree on St. Helena Isl.

Schinus therebinthifolius
"Brazilian pepper tree" in San Diego

Rhus radicans *(ANAC.)*
"Poison ivy", as climbing shrub

Polyalthia longifolia pendula
"Mast tree" in Delhi, India

Polyalthia longifolia pendula
with delicate star-like flowers

Asimina triloba, *in New Jersey*
"Paw-paw" or "Northern banana" (fl.)

Rhus glabra
"Vinegar tree" of E. No. America

Rhus copallina
"Shining sumac" in Virginia

Rhus copallina, *in autumn fruit*
Blue Ridge Mts. of No. Carolina

Rhus chinensis 'September Beauty'
autumn bloom, New Brunswick, N.J.

Rhus aromatica *(E. No. America)*
"Fragrant sumac" in Ontario

Rhus diversiloba
"Poison oak" on Pacific Coast

Rhus typhina *(N.E. No. America)*
"Staghorn sumac"

Rhus typhina 'Laciniata'
"Lacy velvet-sumac" in Germany

Rhus ovata *(Arizona to Mexico)*
"Sugar bush" of Southwest deserts

Carissa grandiflora *(macrocarpa)*
"Natal plum" in Durban

Carissa grandiflora 'Fancy' *(APOC.)*
"Dwarf Natal plum" in California

Cananga odorata *(ANNON.)*
"Ylang-ylang" on Tonga, So. Pacific

Acokanthera oblongifolia *(APOC.)*
"Wintersweet" in Gran Canaria

Pagiantha dichotoma *(APOC.)*
"Forbidden fruit" of India

Kopsia singaporensis *(APOC.)*
in Botanic Gard. Singapore

Tabernaemontana divaricata
"Crape jasmine" in No. India

Tabernaemontana corymbosa *(APOC.)*
"Pinwheel flower" in Calcutta, India

Tabernaemontana divaricata plena
"Flower-of-Love" in Agra, India

Nerium oleander, *"Rose-bay"*
in habitat, Aden, So. Arabia

Nerium oleander 'Roseum'
at Amon temple in Luxor, Egypt

Nerium oleander 'Petite Pink'
South Coast Bot. G. Los Angeles

Nerium oleander 'Cherry'
in San Marcos, California

Nerium oleander 'Album'
"Sister Agnes oleander" in Florida

Nerium oleander 'Sealy Pink'
large pink, in Escondido

Plumeria obtusa
"Temple tree" in Benares, India

Plumeria rubra
"Frangipani" on Rarotonga

Plumeria rubra acutifolia
"Flor de Mayo" in Mexico

Strophanthus gratus *(APOC.)*
"Clambering oleander" in Nigeria

Rauvolfia tetraphylla *(APOC.)*
medicinal shrub in Trinidad

Rauvolfia caffra, *"Quinine tree"*
at Tropic World, Escondido, Calif.

Thevetia ovata, *in flower*
in San Blas, Nayarit, Mexico

Thevetia ovata, *with fruit*
"Huevo de gato" or "Egg tree"

Wrightia religiosa *(APOC.)*
"Jasmine tree" in Singapore

Thevetia thevetioides
"Narciso amarillo" in Mexico

Thevetia peruviana *(APOC.)*
"Yellow oleander" in Tahiti

Ilex amelanchier *(AQUIF.)*
"Sarvis holly" in Virginia

Ilex x altaclarensis
"Altaclara holly" in Germany

Ilex x altaclar. 'Lawsoniana'
Royal Bot. Gardens, Kew

Ilex x meserveae 'Blue Girl'
Ag. Exper. Sta. N. Brunswick, N.J.

Ilex aquifolium *(female)*
"English holly" in New Jersey

Ilex aquifolium 'Marginata'
"Variegated English holly"

Ilex x attenuata 'Fosteri'
"Topel holly"in Virginia

Ilex cassine
"Dahoon holly" (Southeast U.S.)

Ilex crenata 'Microphylla'
"Small-leaved Jap. holly"

Ilex crenata
"Japanese holly" in New Jersey

Ilex crenata 'Helleri'
"Heller's Jap. holly" in California

Ilex crenata 'Hetzii'
"Hetz's Japanese holly"

Ilex crenata 'Mariesii'
miniature, popular in Japan

Ilex cornuta, *"Horned holly"*
in Hangchow Bot. Gard., China

Ilex cornuta 'Burfordii'
in Strybing Arboretum, San Francisco

Ilex cornuta 'Rotunda'
"Dwarf holly" in Santa Ana, Calif.

Ilex decidua, *in Illinois*
deciduous stage with fruit

Ilex decidua *(Southeast U.S.)*
"Possum haw" with foliage

Ilex glabra, *"Ink-berry"*
female plant with black fruits

Ilex x koehneana
at Rutgers, New Brunswick, N.J.

Ilex laevigata
"Smooth winterberry" in Maine

Ilex latifolia
"Luster-leaf holly" (E. China)

Ilex opaca *(Mass. to Texas)*
"American holly"

Ilex pernyi, *female plant*
"Perny holly" of China

Ilex pedunculosa
"Long-stalk holly" (Japan)

Ilex rotunda *(E. Asia)*
in Disney World, Orlando, Fla.

Ilex paraguariensis
"Yerba de Maté" (Paraguay)

Ilex verticillata
"Winter-berry" in New York

Ilex wilsonii *(AQUIF.)*
at Anderson's, San Diego, Calif.

Ilex serrata, *female plant*
"Jap. winter-berry" (deciduous)

Ilex vomitoria
"Yaupon holly" (Virginia to Texas)

Nemopanthus mucronatus
"Cat-berry" of E. No. America

Alocasia macrorrhiza
"Elephant's-ear" on Timor

Alocasia macrorrhiza 'Variegata'
in Andromeda Gardens, Barbados

Alocasia plumbea *(ARAC.)*
at Montego Bay, Jamaica

Acanthopanax trifoliatus *(ARAL.)*
(Philippines to So. China)

Acanthopanax sieboldianus
"Five-leaf aralia" (Japan)

Aralia chinensis
"Chinese angelica" (So. China)

Aralia elata
"Japanese angelica" (E. Asia)

Aralia elata 'Variegata'
"Variegated angelica tree"

Aralia spinosa, *in New Jersey*
"Devil's walking-stick"

Cussonia spicata *(Transvaal)*
"Spiked cabbage tree" in Calif.

Dendropanax trifidus
"Kakure mino" of Japan

Cussonia holstii *(Kenya)*
"Cabbage tree" in Los Angeles

Dizygotheca elegant. 'Castor'
handsome European introduction

Dizygoth. veitchii *(mature stage)*
"False aralia" in New Caledonia

Fatsia japonica (Aralia)
"Japanese aralia" in San Diego

Fatsia japonica 'Variegata'
in Sydney, N.S.W., Australia

x Fatshedera lizei
"Ivy tree" or "Miracle plant"

Hedera canar. 'Arbor. variegata'
"Ghost-tree ivy" in California

Hedera helix 'Arborescens'
"English ivy" in flowering stage

Kalopanax pictus (China)
in Brooklyn Botanic Garden

Meryta sinclairii
"Puka tree" in New Zealand

Osmoxylon boerlagei
floral display on Mindanao

Osmoxylon 'Miagos'
Los Baños Arboretum, Philippines

Polyscias balfouriana
"Dinner-plate aralia" in Penang

Polyscias fruticosa
"Ming aralia" in Honolulu

Polyscias paniculata
"Wild coffee" in Panama

Polyscias guilfoylei 'Laciniata'
"Laceleaf papua" in Hemet, Calif.

Polyscias guilf. 'Quercifolia'
"Oakleaf panax" in Brooklyn Bot. Garden

Polyscias guilf. 'Quinquefolia'
"Celery-leaf panax" in Bombay, India

Polyscias guilfoylei 'Variegata'
in New York Botanical Garden

Polyscias crispatum
"Chicken gizzard" (Brazil)

Polyscias guilfoylei, *"Wild coffee"*
in old Cartagena, Colombia

Polyscias paniculata 'Variegata'
"Variegated rose-leaf" in Acapulco

Polyscias paniculata 'Aurea'
Longwood Gardens, Pennsylvania

Polyscias filicifolia
"Fern aralia" in Java

Polyscias scutellaria
"Saucer panax" in So. Mexico

Polyscias ornata 'Wavy Pam'
in Hemet, California

Polyscias ornata 'Aurea'
in Surabaya, Java

Polyscias guilfoylei 'Crispa'
"Blackie" with crinkly leaves

Polyscias filic. 'Golden Prince'
Foster Botanic Garden, Honolulu

Nothopanax filicifolia hort.
"Fern angelica" in Singapore Bot. G.

Oreopanax capitatus
U. of Calif. Bot. G., Los Angeles

Pseudopanax 'Adiantifolius'
at Harrison Nursery, New Zealand

Pseudopanax ferox
"Lance-wood" in New Zealand

Pseudopanax lessonii
"False panax" (North Isl., N.Z.)

Pseudopanax laetus
(North Isl., New Zealand)

Pseudopanax arboreus
"Five fingers" in Auckland, N.Z.

Tetrapanax papyriferus
"Rice-paper plant" of China

Trevesia palmata 'Micholitzii'
"Snowflake plant" at Kew Bot. G.

Cussonia paniculata
"Cabbage tree" of Natal

Schefflera angustifolia
Los Baños Arboretum, Philippines

Schefflera actinophylla *(Brassaia)*
"Queensland umbrella" in California

Schefflera albido-bracteata
"Starshine" of Mindanao

Schefflera digitata *(N. Zealand)*
"Seven fingers" at Milford Sound

Schefflera elliptica *(odorata)*
Makiling Arboretum, Philippines

Schefflera insularum
on Luzon, Philippines

Schefflera octophylla 'Variegata'
in Botanic Garden, Bermuda

Scheffl. venulosa erythrostachys
"Star-leaf" in Kew Bot. Gardens

Schefflera polybotrya
from tropical Java, Indonesia

Schefflera actinophylla *(Brassaia)*
"Octopus tree" in Sogeri, Papua

left: Schefflera actinophylla
right: Schefflera pueckleri

Schefflera pueckleri, *in fruit*
(Tupidanthus calyptratus hort.)

Schefflera venulosa
"Starleaf" in New South Wales

Schefflera minutifolia *hort.*
(from Mindanao) in California

Schefflera volkensii
on Mt. Kilimanjaro, Tanzania

Schefflera arboricola 'Variegata'
in San Diego, California

Schefflera arboricola *w. fruit*
in Taiwan habitat

Aralia californica
"Elk clover" in Oregon

Barklya syringifolia, *(LEG.)*
"Gold-blossom tree" in Sydney Bot. G.

Asclepias physocarpa *(ASCL.)*
"Butterfly flower" in Transvaal

Calotropis gigantea *(ASCL.)*
"Crown plant" in Hyderabad

Berberis amurensis *(BERB.)*
"Manchurian barberry" in N. Jersey

Berberis darwinii
in Duesseldorf Bot. Garden, Germany

Berberis empetrifolia
from Cordilleras of Chile

Berberis koreana *(Mahonia)*
in Skylands, New Jersey

Berberis julianae
"Wintergreen barberry" (China)

Berberis linearifolia *hort.*
in Bot. Garden Essen, Germany

Berberis x mentorensis
"Mentor barberry" in Ohio

Berberis x notabilis
in Botanic Garden Essen, Germany

Berberis x stenophylla
"Rosemary barberry" in England

Berberis thunb. 'Atropurpurea'
"Purple Japan barberry"

Berberis thunbergii
"Japan barberry" in Autumn

Berberis verruculosa *(Mahonia)*
"Warty barberry" (China)

Berberis vulgaris
"Barberry" with edible fruit

Berberis vulgaris
"European barberry" in flower

Berberis vulgaris 'Atropurpurea'
"Redleaf barberry" in Munich

Mahonia aquifolium
"Oregon grape" with fruit

Mahonia aquifolium
"Holly mahonia" in flower

Mahonia bealei *(China)*
"Leatherleaf mahonia" in Calif.

Mahonia lomariifolia *(Yunnan)*
"Chinese holly-grape" in Holland

Mahonia lomariifolia
flowering in New Zealand

Mahonia x media
Royal Bot. Gardens, Kew, England

Mahonia repens
in Grand Canyon Nat'l. Park, Arizona

Mahonia pinnata
"Cluster mahonia" in California

Mahonia trifoliolata
"Tri-leaved holly-grape" in Texas

Nandina domestica *(BERB.)*
"Heavenly bamboo" in So. China

Nandina domestica filamentosa
"San Gabriel nandina" in Calif.

Nandina domestica 'Nana'
autumn color in Auckland, N.Z.

Alnus glutinosa 'Laciniata'
"Cutleaf alder" in Dortmund Bot. G.

Alnus glutinosa *(BETUL.)*
"Black alder" in Moscow, Russia

Alnus hirsuta
"Manchurian alder"

Alnus incana 'Laciniata'
in Krefeld Bot. Garden, Germany

Alnus incana
"Grey alder" (Europe, Asia)

Alnus rhombifolia *(BETUL.)*
"White alder" in Escondido, Calif.

Alnus cordata
"Italian alder" in Palermo

Alnus oregona *(rubra)*
"Red alder" in Ketchikan, Alaska

Betula alleghaniensis
"Yellow birch" (E. No. America)

Betula albo-sinensis
"Chinese paperbirch"

Betula nigra
"Black birch" in New England

Betula nigra
"River-birch" w. flaking bark

Betula ermanii
"Gold birch" in Seoul, Korea

Betula raddeana *(Caucasus)*
in Botanic Garden, Duesseldorf

Betula lenta
"Cherry birch" (Maine to Ala.)

Betula papyrifera *(syn. alba)*
"Paper birch" in the Kremlin, Moscow

Betula populifolia
"Gray birch" at Capitol, Washington, D.C.

Betula papyrifera fa. grandis
large tree in Botanic Garden, Munich

Betula pendula 'Gracilis' *('Laciniata')*
"Cutleaf European birch" in Saalfeld, Thuringia

Betula pendula 'Dalecarlica'
"Cutleaf white birch" in Sweden

Betula papyrifera, *"Canoe birch"*
used by Indians to make boats

Betula papyrifera *(close-up)*
Royal Bot. Gardens Kew, England

Betula pendula *(verrucosa)*
with female catkins

Betula pendula, *"Silverbirch"*
or "European white birch"

Betula pendula 'Gracilis'
"Cutleaf European birch"

Betula pendula 'Purpurea'
"Purple European birch" in Calif.

Betula pendula 'Tristis'
"Slender European birch"

Betula pendula 'Tristis'
"Weeping birch" in Germany

Betula pubescens, *with catkins*
"English white birch" in Denmark

Betula pubescens
Brooklyn Botanic Gard., New York

Betula pendula 'Youngii'
"Weeping birch" in Germany

Betula platyphylla japonica
"Japanese white birch"

Betula populifolia 'Pendula'
in Springfield, Missouri

Betula maximowicziana
"Monarch birch" of Japan

Bet. populifolia *w. male catkins*
"Gray birch" in New Jersey

Betula pumila
"American swamp birch"

Betula nana, *in Hammerfest, Norway*
"Arctic dwarf birch"

Carpinus betulus, *with fruit*
"European hornbeam"

Carpinus caroliniana
"Iron-wood" in Virginia

Carpinus caroliniana
"American hornbeam"

Carpinus betulus 'Quercifolia'
"Oakleaved ironwood" in M. Gladbach

Carpinus japonica
"Japanese hornbeam" with fruit

Corylus avellana *(BETUL.)*
"Hazelnut" in Oregon

Corylus maxima 'Purpurea'
"Purple filbert" in Greece

Corylus avellana 'Contorta'
"Twisted hazel" in N.Y. Bot. G.

Catalpa ovata *(BIGN.)*
"Chinese catawba" with pods

Ostrya carpinifolia *(BET.)*
"European hop-hornbeam"

Catalpa bignonioides
"Southern catawba" or "Indian-bean"

Catalpa speciosa *(BIGN.)*
"Western catawba" in Los Angeles

Ostrya virginiana, *w. fruit*
"American hop-hornbeam"

Crescentia cujete (BIGN.)
"Calabash tree" in Sri Lanka

Crescentia cujete
flowering in Florida

Chilopsis linearis *(BIGN.)*
"Desert willow" in Van Horn, Texas

Chilopsis linearis
flowering in Escondido, California

Cybistax donnell-smithii *(BIGN.)*
"Primavera" in Guatemala

Tecomaria capensis 'Aurea'
"Gold Cape honeysuckle" in Calif.

Campsis x tagliabuana
in Auckland Bot. G., N. Zealand

Tecomaria capensis
"Cape honeysuckle" in So. Africa

Radermachera sinica
"China doll" in container

Radermachera sinica
flowering in Kweilin, So. China

Millingtonia hortensis
"Indian cork-tree" in Singapore

Tabebuia serratifolia
"Yellow pui" in Puerto Rico

Kigelia pinnata
"Sausage tree", Brisbane Bot. G.

Parmentiera cereifera
"Candle tree" in Panama

Spathodea campanulata
"African tulip tree" in Uganda

Markhamia lutea *(Dolichandrone)*
in Los Angeles Arboretum

Tabebuia heterophylla
in Moghul Garden, Agra, India

Jacaranda obtusifolia
"Green ebony" of Venezuela

Tabebuia chrysotricha
"Gold trumpet tree" in Cali, Colombia

Tabebuia avellanedae *(ipe)*
in Asuncion, Paraguay

Tabebuia palmeri
in Sonora, Mexico

Tabebuia roseo-alba *(pallida)*
in Durban Bot. Garden, Natal

Tabebuia impetiginosa
Jardim Botanico, Rio de Janeiro

Tabebuia rosea *(pentaphylla)*
Caracas Bot. Garden, Venezuela

Tabebuia pallida *hort.*
Nassau Bot. Garden, Bahamas

Tabebuia argentea *(BIGN.)*
"Golden bells" of Paraguay

Stereospermum chelonoides
"Yellow snake tree" in Java

Tecoma stans *(BIGN.)*
"Yellow-bells" in San Diego

Ceiba rivieri *(BOMB.)*
"Silk cotton" in Rio de Janeiro

Bixa orellana *(BIX.)*
"Lipstick tree" in Tahiti

Chiranthodendron pentadactylon
"Mexican hand-flower"

Jacaranda mimosifolia *(BIGN.)*
Quail Bot. Garden, Encinitas, Calif.

Bombax ceiba *(malabaricum)*
"Red Kapok" at Angkor, Kampuchea

Adansonia digitata *(foliage)*
"Baobab" at Fairchild G., Florida

Cavanillesia platanifolia
"Quipo" in Cartagena, Colombia

Bombax ceiba, *flowering*
"Red silk cotton" in Mandalay

Pseudobombax ellipticum
"Shaving brush" in Yucatán

Bombax buonopozense
"Gold Coast bombax" in Nigeria

Chorisia insignis
"White floss-silk tree" in Perú

Chorisia spec. 'Majestic Beauty'
at Monrovia Nursery, California

Chorisia speciosa, *"Floss-silk"*
in Montevideo, Uruguay

Cordia elaeagnoides
"Bocote" near Ixtapa, So. Mexico

Cordia sebestena *(BORAG.)*
"Geiger tree" on Barbados

Ehretia tinifolia *(BORAG.)*
"Capulin" in Chichen Itza, Yucatán

Lithodora rosmarinifolia
"Rosemary-leaf puccoon" in Sicily

Boswellia carteri *(BURS.)*
"Frankincense tree" (Arabia)

Kigelia pinnata *(BIGN.)*
flowering in the Transvaal

Bursera microphylla *(Mexico)*
"Elephant tree" of Sonora

Bursera simaruba *(BURS.)*
"Gumbo limbo" in Florida

Bursera simaruba
"West Indian birch"

Canarium vulgare *(BURS.)*, "Java almond"
in Peradeniya Bot. Gardens, Sri Lanka

Adansonia digitata *(BOMB.)*
ancient "Baobab" near Mt. Kilimanjaro, Tanzania

Jacaranda mimosifolia *(background) and Date palms*
Plaza de España, Sevilla, Spain

Cordia elaeagnoides *(BORAG.) "Bocote tree"*
in Zihuatanejo, Guerrero, So. Mexico

Buxus harlandii *(China)*
Brooklyn Bot. Garden, New York

Buxus microphylla koreana
"Korean boxwood" in New Jersey

Buxus balearica
"Spanish boxwood" on Mallorca

Buxus microphylla 'Compacta'
"Dwarf littleleaf box" in Brooklyn

Buxus microphylla japonica
"Japan boxwood" in Oceanside, Calif.

Buxus microph. japonica 'Nana'
"Dwarf Calif. box" in San Marcos

Buxus sempervirens
"English boxwood" in New Jersey

Buxus sempervir. 'Suffruticosa'
"Hedge box" in New York

Buxus sempervir. 'Angustifolia'
in Parque Eduardo, Lisbon

Simmondsia chinensis *(BUX.)*
"Jojoba" in Tucson, Arizona

Sarcococca hookeriana humilis
"Sweet box" in Kew Bot. G., England

Sarcococca ruscifolia *(BUX.)*
"Fragrant box" in California

Chimonanthus praecox *(CALYC.)*
"Winter-sweet" in New Zealand

Reevesia thyrsoidea *(BYTT.)*
(South China to Java)

Calycanthus floridus
"Carolina all-spice"

Crateva roxburghii *(CAPP.)*
"Garlic pear" in Vietnam

Capparis floribunda
"Caper bush" of Taiwan

Capparis micracantha *(CAPP.)*
"Caper-thorn" in Singapore

Abelia x grandiflora *(CAPP.)*
"Glossy abelia" in San Diego

Abelia x grand. 'Edward Goucher'
at U.S.D.A. Beltsville, Maryland

Abelia chinensis
"Chinese abelia" in Brisbane

Abelia floribunda
"Mexican abelia" in New Zealand

Diervilla sessilifolia *(CAPR.)*
"Bush honeysuckle" in Rhineland

Dipelta floribunda *(CAPR.)*
Oxford University Bot. Garden

Maerua kirkii *(CAPPAR.)*
on the Tsavo Desert, Kenya

Kolkwitzia amabilis *(CAPR.)*
"Beauty bush" of Hupeh, China

Lonicera fragrantissima *(CAPR.)*
"Winter honeysuckle" in California

Lonicera korolkowii 'Zabelii'
"Blue-leaf honeysuckle" in California

Lonicera maackii *(Manchuria)*
"Amur honeysuckle" in Germany

Lonicera morrowii
"Morrow honeysuckle" (Japan)

Lonicera nitida 'Elegant'
"Box honeysuckle" in Duesseldorf B.G.

Lonicera nit. 'Baggersen's Gold'
yellow summer foliage, in England

Lonicera pileata
"Privet honeysuckle" (China)

Lonicera rupicola
"Rock cherry" of Tibet

Lonicera tatarica
"Tatarian honeysuckle" in N. Jersey

Lonicera tatarica
with berry-fruits in So. Russia

Lonicera xylosteum
"Fly honeysuckle" in Sochi, Caucasus

Lonicera xylosteum
"Hedge cherry" in Rhineland

Lonicera standishii
in Hangchow Bot. Garden, China

Sambucus nigra, *in bloom*
"European elderberry" or "Holunder"

Sambucus ebulus
"Dwarf elder" in Britain

Sambucus callicarpa
"Pacific red elder" in Oregon

Sambucus racemosa
"European red elder"

Sambucus rac. 'Plumosa-aurea'
"Golden elder" in England

Sambucus pubens
"American red elder" in Vermont

Leycesteria formosa
"Himalaya honeysuckle" in Munich Bot. G.

Symphoricarpos albus
"Snowberry" (Alaska to Québec)

Symphoricarpos orbiculatus
"Indian current" in Denver, Colorado

Viburnum acerifolium
"Mapleleaf viburnum" in Virginia

Viburnum burejaeticum
in Brooklyn Bot. Garden, N.Y.

Viburnum x burkwoodii
(carlesii x utile) in England

Viburnum x carlcephalum
Willowwood Arboretum, New Jersey

Viburnum carlesii 'Compactum'
in Rest Area Highway 80, in Ohio

Viburnum cassinoides
"Appalachian tea" in Carolina

Viburnum alnifolium *with showy flowers*
"American wayfaring tree" in Virginia

Viburnum alnifolium, *bearing edible fruit*
"Hobble-bush" on mountains of Northeast U.S.

Viburnum davidii, *from Western China*
evergreen with white fl. and bright blue fruit

Viburnum dentatum *(Southeastern U.S.)*
"Southern arrowwood" in autumn foliage and fruit

Viburnum dilatatum *(Mts. of Japan)*
"Linden viburnum" or "Gamazumi"

Viburnum japonicum, *from Japan and Taiwan*
evergreen "Japanese viburnum" in Santa Ana, California

Viburnum odoratissimum *(Japan to India)*
"Sweet viburnum", evergreen for Southern gardens

Viburnum sargentii 'Onondaga'
clonal hybrid of "Sargent Cranberrybush"

Viburnum grandiflorum
blooming before foliage, in England

Viburnum henryi *(China)*
in Palmengarten, Frankfurt

Viburnum farreri 'Candidissimum'
earliest bloomer, in New York Bot. G.

Viburnum x hillieri
Oyster Bay, Long Island

Viburnum x juddii
Arnold Arboretum, Mass.

Viburnum lantana *(Europe)*
"Woolly snowball" in Brooklyn Bot. G.

Viburnum x bodnantense
National Arboretum, Washington

Viburnum lantana rugosum
"Wayfaring tree" in Denver Bot. G.

Viburnum macrocephalum
"Chinese snowball"

Viburnum opulus, *with fruits*
"Cranberry bush" in Amsterdam

Viburnum opulus roseum
"European snowball" in Edinburgh

Viburnum odoratissimum 'Irvinii'
"Redleaf sweet viburnum" in San Diego

Viburnum plicatum
"Japanese snowball" in N. Jersey

Viburnum x pragense
in Prague nursery, Chechoslovakia

Viburnum prunifolium
"Sheepberry" (Conn. to Texas)

Viburnum rhytidophyllum
"Leatherleaf viburnum" in Philadelphia

Viburnum rigidum
"Canary-Island viburnum"

Viburnum setigerum
"Tea viburnum" of China

Viburnum setig. 'Aurantiacum'
bearing coppery berry-fruits

Viburnum sieboldii
"Goma-ki" of So. Japan

Viburnum plicatum 'Roseum'
in Longwood, Kennet Square, Penna.

Viburnum suspensum *(Japan)*
"Sandankwa viburnum" in California

Vib. tinus 'Aureo-variegatum'
in Warrimoo, N.S.W., Australia

Viburnum tinus
"Laurentinus" in Encinitas, Calif.

Viburnum japonicum
"Hakusan-boku" in Japan

Viburnum trilobum
"American cranberry bush"

Viburnum wrightii *(Japan)*
"Leather-leaf" in New Jersey

Weigela floribunda 'Variegata'
at *Floriade in Amsterdam*

Weigela florida *(Diervilla)*
"Old-fashioned weigela" in Germany

Weigela florida 'Aureo-variegata'
"Gold-leaved weigela" in Australia

Weigela florida 'Bristol Ruby'
Edinburgh Bot. Garden, Scotland

Weigela florida 'Eva Ratke'
Brooklyn Bot. Garden, New York

Weigela florida 'Folii purpuriis'
"Purple-leaf weigela" in Rhineland

Weigela florida 'Variegata'
Chelsea Flower Show, London

Weigela maximowiczii *(CAPR.)*
greenish-yellow flowers (C. Japan)

Catha edulis *(CELAST.)*
"Khat tree" in Foster Bot. G. Honolulu

Casuarina cunnighamiana
"River she-oak" in Florida

Casuarina nobilis *(CASUAR.)*
"Borneo Ru-tree" in Singapore

Casuarina equisetifolia
"Australian pine" on Tahiti

Celastrus orbiculatus
"Oriental bittersweet" in New Jersey

Celastrus scandens *(CEL.)*
"American bittersweet"

Euonymus alata *(CELAST.)*
"Bursting heart" in California

Euonymus americana
"American spindle-tree"

Euonymus europaea
"European spindle-tree"

Euonymus fortunei *(China)*
"Winter-creeper" with fruit

Euonymus fortunei 'Colorata'
"Purple-leaf winter creeper"

Euonymus fortunei vegeta
"Bigleaf winter creeper"

Euonymus fortunei 'Elegans'
in Saalfeld, Thuringia

Euonymus fort. 'Emerald n' Gold'
Dortmund Botanic Garden, Germany

Euonymus fortunei 'Gracilis'
adult form, climbing on a poplar tree

Euonymus fortunei 'Gracilis'
"Silver-edge creeper" juvenile stage

Euon. fort. 'Minima variegata'
at New York Bot. Garden

Euonymus fortunei 'Kewensis'
miniature, in England

Euonymus hamiltoniana yedoensis
Chinese tree w. orange fruits

Euonymus japonica 'Microphylla'
miniature in Palmengarten, Frankfurt

Euonymus japonica
"Japan spindle" in San Marcos, Calif.

Euonymus jap. 'Argenteo-variegata'
with silvery leaves, in San Diego

Euonymus jap. 'Aureo-marginata'
in San Marcos, California

Euonymus jap. 'Aureo-marginata'
container standard in Germany

Euonymus jap. 'Argenteo-marginata'
"Silver Queen" in Frankfurt Bot. G.

Euonymus jap. 'Albo-marginata'
Nurseryland in Oceanside, Calif.

Euonymus japonica 'Medio-picta'
"Gold-heart" in Tuebingen Bot. Gard.

Euonymus japonica 'Yellow Queen'
in Escondido, California

Euonymus latifolia *(CELAST.)*
"Broadleaf euonymus" (Iran)

Euonymus phellomana
from North and Western China

Euonymus sachalinensis
in Arnold Arboretum, Mass.

Maytenus boaria *(Chile)*
"Mayten tree" in Escondido, Calif.

Maytenus dryandri *(Catha)*
"Madeira bittersweet"

Maytenus pittieri *(CELAST.)*
"Zapatero" of Venezuela

Tripterygium regelii *(CELAST.)*
"Kurozuru" in Japan

Cercidiphyllum japonicum *(CERC.)*
"Katsura tree" in Kyoto, Japan

Atriplex hymenelytra *(CHEN.)*
"Desert holly" in Death Valley

Cistus incanus *(villosus)*
"Rock rose" on Mallorca

Cistus x purpureus
"Orchid rock-rose" in California

Cistus ladanifer *(Portugal)*
"Gum cistus" in Kew Bot. Gardens

Cistus monspeliensis
Oxford Bot. Garden, England

Cistus salviifolius
on Algarve coast of Portugal

Cist. nummularium 'Wisley Pink'
"English rock-rose"

Helianthemum apeninnum roseum
"Apeninne sunrose" in Kew Gardens

Helianthemum canum
"Sunrose" in England

Helianth. nummul. 'Rubro-plenum'
"Double sun-rose"

Clethra alnifolia *(CLETH.)*
"Sweet pepper-bush" (Maine to Florida)

Paxistima canbyi *(CELAST.)*
"Cliff-green" of Virginia mountains

x Halimiocistus sahucii *(CIST.)*
(Cistus x Halimium) in So. France

Halimium lasianthum *(Helianthemum) (CIST.)*
in Strybing Arboretum, San Francisco, Calif.

Halimium ocymoides *(Cistus algarvensis)*
on the Algarve coast of Portugal

Helianthemum nummularium 'Cupreum' *(CIST.)*
"Red sun-rose" in Los Angeles Arboretum, California

Hudsonia ericoides *(CIST.)*
"Golden heather" (Nova Scotia to Carolina)

Cistus x hybridus *(x corbariensis) (CIST.)*
"White rock-rose" of Mediterranean parentage

Clethra arborea *(CLETH.)*
"Lily-of-the-valley tree" in Calif.

Clethra barbinervis
"Japanese clethra" in England

Clethra monostachya
"Chinese summersweet" in Germany

Clethra acuminata
"Cinnamon clethra" in Virginia

Clethra alnifolia 'Rosea'
"Summersweet" in Brooklyn Bot. Garden

Terminalia catappa *(COMBR.)*
"Tropical almond" on Tahiti, So. Pacific

Helianthemum nummularium *(CIST.)*
"Yellow sun-rose" (Kew Bot. G.)

Cochlospermum vitifolium
"Buttercup tree" in Costa Rica

Cochlospermum religiosum *(COCHL.)*
"Silk-cotton tree", in Burma (Myanmar)

Bucida buceras *(COMBRET.)*
"Black olive" in Florida

Bucida buceras
inflorescence developing fruits

Conocarpus erectus *(COMBRET.)*
"Buttonwood" in So. Florida

Encelia farinosa *(COMP.)*
"Brittlebush" in Death Valley

Athanasia crithmifolia *(COMP.)*
on Table Mountain, Cape Town

Chrysocoma coma-aurea *(COMP.)*
in Cape habitat, So. Africa

Baccharis glomeruliflora
male plant in Carolina swamp

Baccharis pilularis *(COMP.)*
"Coyote brush" in California

Cassinia fulvida *(COMP.)*
"Yellow cassinia" (New Zealand)

Chrysothamnus nauseosus
"Rabbit-bush" in Utah

Calocephalus brownii *(COMP.)*
"Cushion-bush" (Australia)

Combretum fruticosum *(COMB.)*
"Burning-bush" in Los Angeles Arbor.

Dymondia margaretae *(COMP.)*
Kirstenbosch Bot. G., So. Africa

Felicia fruticosa *(COMP.)*
"Aster-bush" in Encinitas, Calif.

Pachystegia insignis *(COMP.)*
"Marlborough rock-daisy" in N. Zealand

Montanoa speciosa *(mexicana)*
"Daisy-tree" in San Francisco Arboretum

Montanoa grandiflora *(COMP.)*
"Teresita" in Honduras

Osteospermum ecklonis *(COMP.)*
"Cape marigold" on Madeira

Ozothamnus rosmarinifolius
"Rosemary-everlasting" (Tasmania)

Helichrysum selago
curious "Everlasting" of N. Zealand

Phoenocoma prolifera
"Pink everlasting" in Cape Prov.

Olearia nummulariifolia
"Daisy bush" of New Zealand

Psiadia trinerva *(Mauritius)*
Sydney Bot. Garden, Australia

Olearia albida
"Coastal tree daisy" (New Zealand)

Olearia ilicifolia
"Hakeke" of the Maori (N.Z.)

Olearia stellulata 'Pink form'
"Tasmanian daisy-bush"

Olearia stellulata
in Oxford Univ. Botanic Garden

Sclerocarpus frutescens *(CONV.)*
in Xochicalco, Morelos, Mexico

Senecio petasitis *(COMP.)*
"California geranium" in Los Angeles

Stifftia chrysantha *(COMP.)*
showy evergreen of Brazil

Ipomoea woolcottiana *(CONV.)*
U.S.D.A. Gardens, So. Miami

Ipomoea carnea fistulosa
"Flor de la Mañana" on Bequia, W.I.

Ipomoea pauciflora *(So. Mexico)*
"Casahuate" on Monte Alban

Corokia cotoneaster *(CORN.)*
"Golden koroko" (New Zealand)

Ipomoea carnea 'Goodetlii'
in Encinitas, California

Ipomoea murucoides *(CONV.)*
"Morning-glory tree" in Oaxaca

Aucuba japonica *(CORN.)*
"Japanese laurel" in Germany

Elaeagnus angustifolia
"Russian olive" on the Crimea

Aucuba japonica 'Variegata'
"Gold-dust tree" with fruit

Aucuba japonica 'Dentata'
Royal Bot. Gardens Kew

Aucuba japonica 'Picturata'
"Golden laurel" in California

Cornus alba 'Argenteo-marginata'
"Tatarian dogwood" in Utrecht, Holland

Cornus controversa
"Giant dogwood" in Hangchow, China

Cornus alba 'Albo-marginata'
"Red-bark dogwood" in Munich Bot. G.

Cornus alternifolia
"Pagoda dogwood" in Virginia

Cornus kousa, *in flower*
"Japan dogwood" in Korea

Cornus kousa, *bearing fruit*
N.J. Exper. Sta., N. Brunswick

Cornus florida 'Welchii'
"Tricolor dogwood" at Rutgers, N.J.

Cornus florida 'Sweetwater'
N.J. Exper. Sta., N. Brunswick

Cornus florida 'Rubra'
"Pink dogwood" in England

Cornus florida
"Flowering dogwood" in New York

Cornus florida 'Welchii'
foliage green, white, pink

Cornus capitata *(Himalayas)*
"Evergreen dogwood" in N. Zealand

Cornus florida 'Rainbow'
autumn colors in So. Carolina

Cornus florida 'Cloud Nine'
clouds of white, in Dallas, Texas

Cornus suecica
"Dwarf cornel" in Flam, Norway

Cornus mas *(Europe to Asia)*
"Cornelian cherry" flowering

Cornus hessei *(N.E. Asia)*
in Rhineland Bot. Garden

Cornus macrophylla
"Largeleaf dogwood" (China)

Cornus officinalis
"Japan Cornelian cherry"

Cornus sanguinea
"Blood-twig dogwood" in Britain

Cornus sericea *(E. No. America)*
"Red Osier dogwood" in Boston

Cornus nuttallii
"Pacific dogwood" on Sierra Nevada

Griselina littoralis *(CORN.)*
"Kupuka tree" (New Zealand)

Corynocarpus laevigata *(CORYN.)*
"New Zealand laurel" in Marlborough

Erysimum scoparium *(CRUC.)*
"Teide wallflower" on Tenerife

Cunonia capensis *(CUN.)*
"African red alder" (So. Africa)

Weinmannia trichosperma *(CUN.)*
from the Andes of Chile

Cyrilla racemiflora *(CYR.)*
"Leatherwood" in Texas

Dillenia indica *(DILL.)*
"Elephant apple" in Panama

Hibbertia cuneiformis *(DILL.)*
"Button-flower" of W. Australia

Hippophae rhamnoides *(ELAEAG.)*
"Sea-buckthorn" in Austria

Elaeagnus x ebb. 'Gilt-edge'
Chelsea Flower Show, London

Elaeagnus x ebbingei
in Boskoop nursery, Holland

Elaeagnus x ebbingei
close-up, in San Diego, California

Elaeagnus multiflora
"Cherry elaeagnus" of Japan

Elaeagnus commutata
"Silverberry" (Canada to Utah)

Elaeagnus pungens 'Variegata'
leaves margined cream

Elaeagnus umbellata
"Autumn elaeagnus" in fruit

Elaeagnus umbellata
fragrant flowers, in Japan

Elaeagnus angustifolia
"Russian olive" (W. Asia)

Elaeagnus pungens *(ELAEAG.)*
at the Serail, Istanbul, Turkey

Elaeagnus pungens 'Maculata'
in Cologne Bot. Garden

Hernandia bivalvis
in Brisbane, Queensland

Crinodendron hookerianum
Botanic Garden Duesseldorf

Crinodendron patagua *(ELAEOC.)*
"White lily-tree" in San Francisco

Crinodendron patagua
with fruit capsules

Elaeocarpus hainanensis
in Botanic Garden Hong Kong

Elaeocarpus grandiflorus
with silky flowers, in Java

Elaeocarpus kirtonii *(Australia)*
"Illawara ash" in Sydney Bot. G.

Dracophyllum secundum *(EPAC.)*
"Dragon heath" (New So. Wales)

Epacris impressa *(EPAC.)*
"Victoria heath" in Melbourne

Epacris longiflora
"Australian fuchsia"

Elaeocarpus reticulatus
"Blueberry ash" in Queensland

Dracophyllum traversii
"New Zealand grass-tree"

Acrotriche aggregata *(EPAC.)*
evergreen of Queensland

Richea scoparia *(EPAC.)*
"Austral heather" (Tasmania)

Ephedra distachya *(EPHED.)*
"Joint fir" in Italy

Agapetes serpens *(ERIC.)*
on Cap Ferrat, France

Andromeda polifolia *(ERIC.)*
"Bog rosemary" at New York Bot. G.

Andromeda glaucophylla
"Downy andromeda" in Québec

Damnacanthus indicus *(RUB.)*
New York Flower Show 1987

Arctostaphylos manzanita *(ERIC.)*
"Manzanita" flowering in Calif.

Rhodothamnus chamaecistus *(ERIC.)*
"Dwarf Alpine-rose" in Switzerland

Arctostaph. uva-ursi, *in bloom*
"Bear-berry" on Pacific Coast

Enkianthus cernuus rubens
in Edinburgh Bot. G., Scotland

Enkianthus perulatus, *w. fruit*
"White enkianthus" of Japan

Enkianthus campanutalus *(ERIC.)*
"Redvein enkianthus" in Los Angeles

Arctostaphylos edmundii, *"Little Sur manzanita"*
on the coast of Monterey, California

Arctostaphylos insularis var. pubescens
"Island manzanita" of Santa Cruz Is., Calif.

Cassiope lycopodioides
forming mats, at home from Japan to Alaska

Cassiope mertensiana, *"White heather"*
at Lake Agnes, Banff National Park, Alberta, Canada

Bruckenthalia spiculifolia
"Spike-heath", in habitat from Romania to Asia Minor

Daboecia cantabrica 'Purpurea' *and* 'Alba'
"Irish heath" (Portugal to Ireland)

Enkianthus perulatus, *in flower*
in University Botanic Garden Osaka, Japan

Chamaedaphne calyculata
"Leatherleaf" from the Arctic regions

Befaria glauca *(Colombia)*
"Rose of the Andes"

Befaria racemosa
"Fly-catcher" in Cuba

Calluna vulgaris
"Heather" of Scotland

Epigaea repens *(E. No. America)*
"Trailing arbutus" in New York Bot. G.

Erica gracilis *(So. Africa)*
"Rose heath" in Aalsmeer, Holland

Corallobotrys acuminatus
Himalayas of Bhutan

Erica arborea
"Tree heath" on Tenerife

Erica carnea
"Spring heath" in Southern France

Erica carnea 'Alba'
"White heath" in New Jersey

Erica hyemalis
"Winter heather" (So. Africa)

Erica 'Felix Faure'
"French heather" in San Diego

Erica cinerea
"Bell heather" in Dortmund Bot. G.

Erica cerinthoides
in Johannesburg, Transvaal

Erica carnea 'Springwood White'
Brooklyn Botanic Garden, N.Y.

Erica mediterranea 'Golden Lady'
gold-leaved "Irish heath"

Erica x darleyensis
Strybing Arboretum San Francisco

Erica ciliaris 'Aurea'
"Dorset heath" in England

Erica cinerea 'Pallas'
hardy cv. of Holland

Erica sitiens
in Duesseldorf Bot. Gard. Germany

Erica melanthera *in hort.*
(canaliculata), "Christmas heath"

Erica regia, *"Royal heath"*
Kirstenbosch Bot. G., So. Africa

Erica terminalis *(stricta)*
"Corsican heath" in Seattle, Wash.

Erica lusitanica
"Spanish heath", in Sevilla

Erica 'Wilmorei', *in California*
"Prince of Wales heather"

Erica tetralix
"Bog heath" in Scotland

Erica vagans
"Cornish heath" in Dortmund Bot. G.

Erica taxifolia, *in Cape Town*
"Double pink heath"

Erica baccans, *"Berry heath"*
in Kirstenbosch Bot. G., So. Africa

Erica mammosa *(So. Africa)*
Kew Bot. Gardens, England

Erica speciosa
in Cape Prov., So. Africa

Gaultheria procumbens
"Wintergreen" of E. No. America

Gaultheria shallon, *"Salal"*
from Alaska to California

Kalmia hirsuta, in So. Carolina
"American laurel"

Kalmia angustifolia
"Sheep laurel" in California

Kalmia latifolia
"Mountain laurel" in Tennessee

Kalmia angustifolia 'Rubra'
in Rhineland Garden Center, Germany

Gaylussacia baccata *in autumn color*
"Black huckleberry" (Newfoundland to Georgia)

Gaylussacia brachycera *in Virginia*
"Box huckleberry" with ripening fruit

Kalmiopsis leachiana, *small evergreen*
in the Siskiyou Mountains, Oregon

Leucothoe davisiae, *"Sierra laurel"*
Mountains of Central California

Pieris floribunda, *of Virginia*
"Mountain andromeda" in young foliage

Lyonia ferruginea *(Andromeda)*
handsome evergreen with young leaves, in So. Carolina

Lyonia lucida, *"Fetterbush"*
Virginia to Florida and Louisiana

Lyonia mariana, *"Staggerbush"*
in swampy areas of Southeast U.S.

x Ledodendron 'Arctic Tern'
at Chelsea Flower Show London

Ledum groenlandicum
"Labrador tea" in Montreal Bot. G.

Ledum palustre
"Wild rosemary" in Germany

Leiophyllum buxifolium
"Sand myrtle" in New York Bot. G.

Leucothoe axillaris
"Coast leucothoe" in Virginia

Leucothoe fontanesiana 'Rainbow'
in Los Angeles Arboretum

Leucothoe populifolia
"Fetterbush" in So. Carolina

Leucothoe racemosa
"Sweetbells" in Louisiana

Leucothoe fontanesiana
(Andromeda catesbaei hort.)

Pernettya furens
in Duesseldorf Bot. Garden

Pernettya mucronata 'Rosea'
in Los Angeles Arboretum

Pernettya mucronata 'Alba'
Magellan reg. of Chile

Pieris forrestii *(Himalayas)*
with scarlet young foliage

Phyllodoce empetriformis
"Mountain heath" in Oregon

Oxydendrum arboreum
"Sourwood" in Skylands Arb., N.J.

Pieris japonica 'Variegata'
"Variegated andromeda"

Pieris japonica *(Japan)*
"Lily-of-the-Valley bush"

Pieris formosa 'Wakehurst'
Kew Bot. Gardens, England

Menziesia pilosa
"Minnie-bush" in Georgia

Menziesia purpurea
"Mock azalea" of Japan

Arbutus menziesii
"Madrone" fruiting in California

Rhododendron obtusum 'Hinocrimson'
late season Kurume azalea

Rhod. (Kurume) 'Hinodegiri'
"Mist-of-the-Rising-Sun" azalea

Rhododendron 'Coral Bells'
"Kirin", early Kurume azalea

Rhododendron 'Polar Bear'
hardy Beltsville azalea

Rhod. indicum *(macranthum)*
"Satsuki azalea" in Japan

Rhododendron 'Southern Charm'
Southern indica azalea as standard

Rhodod. simsii 'Mad. Petrick'
Belgian Indica azalea, early fl.

Rhodod. 'Sweetheart Supreme'
Pericat azalea

Rhodod. 'Rose Pericat'
(simsii x kurume)

Rhodo. 'Peggy Ann' *(Azalea)*
(kurume x kaempferi)

Rhodo. simsii 'Ambrosiana'
early "Indica azalea"

Rhodo. simsii 'Hexe'
dwarf Indica azalea

Rhodod. simsii 'Leopold-Astrid'
Picotee Indica azalea

Rhodod. simsii 'Eri Schaeme'
early Indica azalea

Rhodod. simsii 'Euratom'
compact Indica azalea

Rhododendron 'Snow'
white Kurume azalea

Rhod. simsii 'Reinhold Ambrosius'
"Indica azalea", grafted plant

Rhodod. simsii 'Triumph'
Belgian Indica azalea, grafted

Rhododendron aberconwayi
of Eastern Yunnan, China

Rhododendron albiflorum
Banff Nat'l. Park, Alberta

Rhododendron atlanticum
"Coast azalea" in Delaware

Rhododendron auriganum
on Eastern Highlands, New Guinea

Rhododendron dalhousiae
in the Himalayas of Sikkim

Rhododendron bakeri
from Cumberland Mts. of Kentucky

Rhododendron 'Boule de Neige'
early bloomer (France 1878)

Rhododendron calophytum *(China)*
in Victoria Garden, Hong Kong

Rhododendron carolinianum
Blue Ridge Mts. in No. Carolina

Rhododendron catawbiense
"Mountain rosebay" in Tennessee

Rhododendron hirsutum
"Hairy Alpine rose" in Tirol Alps

Rhododendron ferrugineum
"Alpine rose", Grindelwald, Switz.

Rhododendron austrinum
"Florida flame azalea"

Rhododendron chapmanii
in N.W. Florida habitat

Rhododendron 'Dexter hyb.'
at Winterthur Gardens, Delaware

Rhododendron fastigiatum
of Yunnan, China

Rhododendron fortunei *(E. China)*
Royal Botanic Gardens, Kew

Rhododendron flammeum
"Oconee azalea" in Georgia

Rhododendron canescens
"Piedmont azalea" (No. Carolina to Texas)

Rhododendron prunifolium
"Plum-leaved azalea" in Savannah, Georgia

Rhododendron calendulaceum
"Flame azalea" in Great Smoky Mountains of No. Carolina

Rhododendron prinophyllum *(roseum)*
"Mayflower azalea", from Québec to Virginia and Okla.

Rhododendron lochmium *from Szechwan, China
in col. Royal Bot. Gardens Kew, England*

Rhododendron macrophyllum
"California rose-bay" (Brit. Columbia to California)

Rhododendron kiusianum *(obtusum japonicum)*
"Kiushima azalea" near Nagasaki, Japan

Rhododendron keiskei
from the mountains of Honshu to Kyushu

Rhododendron 'Kaempferi hybrid'
(obtusum x kaempferi) in N. Jersey

Rhododendron 'Roseum elegans'
popular hardy catawba hybrid

Rhododendron kaempferi
"Torch azalea" in Japan

Rhododendron luteum
"Pontic azalea" in New Jersey

Rhododendron japonicum
"Azalea mollis" in hort.

Rhododendron fortunei 'Duke of York'
Longwood Gard., Kennett Sq. Penna.

Rhododendron lochae
mountains of Queensland, Australia

Rhododendron maximum
"Great laurel" of Southeast U.S.

Rhododendron 'Mollis hyb.'
Longwood Gardens, Pennsylvania

Rhododendron russatum
"Royal Alp rhodod." of Yunnan

Rhodod. jasminiflorum *(Malaya)*
Kew Botanic Gardens, England

Rhododendron impeditum
in Alpine Bot. Garden, Germany

Rhod. periclymenoides 'Album'
"Honeysuckle azalea" in Manitoga, N.Y.

Rhodod. indicum 'Balsaminiflorum'
"Balsam azalea" in Kyoto, Japan

Rhododendron lacteum *(China)*
at Los Angeles Arboretum

Rhodod. stenophyllum
on Mt. Kinabalu, Borneo

Rhod. linearifolium macrosepalum
"Spider azalea" at Chelsea, London

Rhododendron macgregoriae
from mountains of New Guinea

Rhododendron 'Loderi' *(fortunei hyb.)*
in Royal Botanic Gardens Kew, England

Rhododendron 'Bagshot Ruby' *(thomsonii hyb.)*
at Chelsea Flower Show, London

Rhododendron rigidum *(Yunnan 2500-3000 m)*
in Kew Bot. Gardens, England

Rhododendron 'Anthony Waterer'
(Knap Hill hybrid)

Rhododendron arboreum *(Himalayas)*
"Tree rhododendron" at Strybing Arboretum, San Francisco

Rhododendron simsii *(Azalea indica hort.)*
from the Yangtse Valley, E. China

Rhodod. obtusum hybrid *(Kurume)*
in Deer Park of Nara, Japan

Rhododendron obtusum 'Amoenum'
(Azalea amoena) in Kew Bot. G.

Rhododendron periclymenoides
(Azalea nudiflora) in Virginia

Rhododendron mucronatum
(Azalea ledifolia alba) of Japan

Rhododendron mucronulatum
February bl., in Rutherford, N. Jersey

Rhododendron occidentale
"Western azalea" in Oregon

Rhododendron ponticum
"Pontic azalea" in England

Rhododendron radicans
"Rockmantle azalea" of Tibet

Rhododendron schlippenbachii
"Royal azalea" (Manchuria)

Rhododendron arboreum, *a Tree rhododendron
with prayer flags, in the Sikkim Himalayas*

Rhododendron ferrugineum, *"Alpine rose"
on Mt. Jungfrau, Bernese Alps, Switzerland*

Rhododendron indicum, *"Satsuki azaleas"
in Tiger Balm Gardens, Hong Kong*

Rhododendron obtusum *'Kurume' group in var.
"Kirishima azalea" in temple garden, Kyoto, Japan*

Rhododendron vaseyi
"Pink-shell azalea" (No. Carolina)

Rhododendron viscosum
"White swamp azalea" in Virginia

Rhododendron yakushimanum
in the mountains of Kyushu, Japan

Rhododendron yunnanense
in Kew Bot. Gardens, England

Rhododendron forrestii repens
creeping, in Volksgarten, Duesseldorf

Rhododendron makinoi
on mountains of Honshu

Rhododendron hyb. 'Pink Pearl'
in Portland, Oregon

Rhododendron 'Trilby'
at Longwood Gardens, Pennsylvania

Rhododendron 'Harvest Moon'
(Exbury-Knap Hill azalea)

Rhododendron canadense *(ERIC.)*
"Rhodora" in Pocono Mts., Penna.

Rhododendron planecostatum
from Equatorial North Borneo

Rhododendron 'Mrs. G. W. Leak'
Koster hybrid in Kew Bot. Gardens

Rhododendron arborescens
"Sweet azalea" in Pennsylvania

Vaccinium macrocarpon *(ERIC.)*
"Cranberry" blooming in N.Jersey

Zenobia pulverulenta *(ERIC.)*
"Dusty zenobia" in Georgia

Acalypha wilkesiana 'Macafeana'
"Copperleaf" in Nuku Hiva, Polynesia

Acalypha wilkesiana cv. 'Godseffiana'
in Brooklyn Bot. Garden, N.Y.

Acalypha hispida *(EUPH.)*
"Chenille plant" in New Guinea

Breynia disticha 'Roseo-picta'
"Snow bush" on Moorea, Polynesia

Cnidoscolus chayamansa *(EUPH.)*
"Tread-softly" in Mexico

Eucommia ulmoides *(EUCOM.)*
"Hardy rubber tree" (C. China)

Aleurites fordii *(EUPH.)*
"Tung-oil tree" (C. Asia)

Aleurites moluccana
"Candlenut" of the South Pacific

Eucryphia glutinosa *(EUCR.)*
showy flowering tree of Chile

Antidesma bunius *(EUPH.)*
"Bignay" planted in Florida

Bischofia javanica *(EUPH.)*
"Toog tree", Fairchild Gard. Miami

Croton insularis *(EUPH.)*
"Cascarilla" in Queensland

Codiaeum 'Norwood Beauty'
"Croton" in Brooklyn Bot. Garden

Codiaeum 'Imperialis' *(Appleleaf)*
Wellington Bot. G., New Zealand

Codiaeum 'Fred Sander'
in Bot. Garden Essen, Germany

Codiaeum 'Gloriosum superbum'
"Autumn croton" at Roehrs Nursery

Codiaeum 'Aucubifolium'
on Nuku Hiva, Polynesia

Codiaeum variegatum 'Rubrum'
in Palm Beach, Florida

Croton alabamensis
a true croton of C. Alabama

Euphorbia leucocephala
"Flor de Niño", Montego, Jamaica

Euphorbia marginata
"Snow-on-the-Mountain" in Germany

Euphorbia characias *(So. Europe)*
Kew Botanic Gardens, England

Euphorbia characias wulfenii
in Los Angeles Arboretum, Calif.

Euphorbia cyparissias
"Cypress spurge" in Germany

Euph. epithymoides *(polychroma)*
"Cushion euphorbia" in Romania

Euphorbia griffithii *(Himalayas)*
Stockholm Bot. Garden, Sweden

Euphorbia griffithii 'Fireglow'
col. Pamela Harper, Virginia

Euphorbia myrsinites
"Myrtle euphorbia" in Yalta, Crimea

Euphorbia paralias
"Sea spurge" in Madeira

Euphorbia palustris
in Leyden Bot. Garden, Holland

Euphorbia 'Annette Hegg Supreme'
"Poinsettia" for Christmas

Euphorbia pulch. plenissima
"Double poinsettia" in Venezuela

Euphorbia pulcherrima
with wired branches, Beijing, China

Euphorbia pulcherrima 'Praecox' *by the wayside
at La Vera, Tenerife, Canary Islands*

Euphorbia fulgens *(jacquiniiflora)*
"Scarlet-plume" of Mexico

Euphorbia pulcherrima 'Rosea'
"Pink poinsettia" at Roehrs, N.J.

Euphorbia pulcherrima 'Lemon drop'
from Ecke Ranch, California

Euphorbia pulcherrima 'Alba'
white poinsettia for Christmas

Euphorbia cotinifolia, *in flower*
"Hierba mala" of Mexico

Euph. heterophylla graminifolia
in Bermuda Botanic Garden

Euphorbia heterophylla
"Mexican Fire plant"

Jatropha integerrima
"Peregrina" in Havana, Cuba

Euphorbia pilosa *(villosa)*
Duesseldorf Bot. Garden, Germany

Hippomane mancinella
"Manzanillo" on Curacao, W.I.

Homalanthus populifolius
"Queensland poplar"

Hura crepitans
"Sandbox tree" in Venezuela

Jatropha curcas
"Barbados-nut" in Miami, Florida

Mallotus philippensis
"Monkey-face tree" in Taiwan

Macaranga grandifolia *(male inflor.)*
"Coral tree" in Foster Garden Honolulu

Manihot esculenta
"Tapioca" in Brazil

Pedilanthus brachypetalus
"Canary-bird bush" in Mexico

Ricinus communis
"Castor-oil plant" (Trop. Africa)

Sapium sebiferum
"Chinese tallow-tree" in Hawaii

Petalostigma pubescens
ornamental tree of Queensland

Phyllanthus arbuscula
Jardim Botanico, Rio de Janeiro

Phyllanthus acidus
"Gooseberry tree" in Honolulu

Castanea sativa
"Spanish chestnut", in Italy

Quercus castaneifolia
(Iran to Caucasus)

Castanea dentata
"American chestnut"

Castanopsis stellata-spina
on Kosyun Peninsula, Taiwan

Fagus grandifolia
"American beech" in Virginia

Fagus sylvatica
"European beech" in Germany

Fagus sylvatica 'Pendula'
"Weeping beech" with fruit

Fagus sylvatica 'Pendula'
tree in Brooklyn Bot. Garden, N.Y.

Fagus sylvatica 'Zlatia'
with yellow foliage, from Serbia

Fagus sylvatica 'Purpurea'
"Blood beech", Dortmund Bot. Garden

Fagus sylvatica 'Purpurea'
"Purple beech" at Kew G. England

Fagus sylv. 'Roseo-marginata'
Nymphenburg Bot. Garden, Munich

Lithocarpus densiflorus
"Tanbark oak" in Seattle, Oregon

Lithocarpus amygdalifolia
fruiting in Taiwan

Lithocarpus henryi
with male catkins, in China

Nothofagus antarctica
in Santiago, Chile

Nothofagus fusca *(N. Zealand)*
"Red beech" in Surrey, England

Nothofagus menziesii
"Silver beech" with nuts, N. Zealand

Quercus acutissima
"Sawtooth oak" of Korea

Quercus agrifolia
"California live oak"

Quercus alba
"White oak" in Rhineland, Germany

Quercus coccinea
"Scarlet oak" in Virginia

Quercus dentata *as bonsai*
"Daimyo oak" in Brooklyn Bot. G.

Quercus falcata
"Spanish oak" in Louisiana

Quercus ilex
"Holly oak" in Los Angeles Arbor.

Quercus incana
"Bluejack oak" in Nashville, Tenn.

Quercus laurifolia
"Laurel oak" in Tampa, Florida

Quercus marilandica
"Blackjack oak", New York Bot. G.

Quercus macrocarpa
"Bur oak" in Quail Bot. Gard., Calif.

Quercus nigra
"Water oak" in Delaware

Quercus nuttallii
(Mississippi to Texas)

Quercus prinus
"Basket oak" in Virginia

Quercus pontica
"Armenian oak" w. male catkins

Quercus phellos
"Willow oak" in Mobile, Alabama

Quercus robur, *mature tree*
"German oak" in Alpine Bavaria

Quercus robur, *with acorns*
"English oak" in London

Quercus palustris
"Pin oak" in Autumn

Quercus palustris
on High St., E. Rutherford, N.J.

Quercus kelloggii, *at 1500 m*
"Calif. black oak" near San Diego

Quercus mongolica
"Mongolian oak" in China

Quercus rubra, *with acorns*
in Pennsylvania habitat

Quercus rubra, *"Red oak"*
street tree, Grafenberg, Germany

Quercus petraea, *historic oak*
Kew Bot. Gardens, near London

Quercus petraea
"Durmast oak" in Eastern France

Quercus virginiana
"Southern live oak" in Louisiana

Quercus suber, *"Cork oak"*
bark-removed, in So. Spain

Quercus suber, *showing bark*
Quail Bot. G., Encinitas, Calif.

Quercus velutina *(FAG.)*
autumn color in Virginia

Quercus velutina, *lobed foliage*
"Black oak" (Maine to Texas)

Quercus lobata, *with acorns*
"Valley oak" in California

Berberidopsis corallina *(FLAC.)*
"Coral Chile vine", in Valparaiso

Hydnocarpus anthelmintica
"Chaulmoogra tree" in Thailand

Hydnocarpus castaneus *(FLAC.)*
ornamental fruit in Taiwan

Idesia polycarpa *(FLACOURT.)*
"ligiri tree" of So. Japan

Azara dentata *(FLACOURT.)*
flowering evergreen of Chile

Olmediella betschleriana *(FLAC.)*
"Guatemala holly", in San Pasqual

Xylosma congestum *(FLAC.)*
"Shiny xylosma" in Escondido, Calif.

Orphium frutescens *(GENT.)*
"Sticky flower" in Encinitas, Calif.

Garrya elliptica *(CARYOPH.)*
"Silk tassel" in Oregon

Chironia baccifera *(GENT.)*
"Christmas berry" in Cape Town

Lechenaultia biloba *(GOOD.)*
in King's Park, Perth, W. Austral.

Lechenaultia superba
"Barrens lechenaultia", S.E. of Perth

Lechenaultia tubiflora
in Albany District, W. Australia

Ginkgo biloba *(GINKG.)*
"Maidenhair tree" in Shanghai

Ginkgo biloba 'Gold Maiden'
in San Marcos, California

Ginkgo biloba 'Fastigiata'
"Sentry ginkgo" in New Jersey

Calophyllum inophyllum *(GUTT.)*
"Kamani" on Moorea, Polynesia

Clusia rosea, *female flower*
"Fat pork tree" on St. Thomas

Clusia rosea, *open fruit*
"Balsam apple" in Florida

Corylopsis spicata *(HAM.)*
"Spike winter hazel" of Shikoku

Corylopsis pauciflora
"Buttercup winter hazel" in Oregon

Corylopsis veitchiana
"Chinese winter hazel" in England

Fothergilla gardenii
"Witch alder" in Virginia

Fothergilla major
"Featherbush" in Cologne, Germany

Fothergilla monticola
"Alabama featherbush"

Hamamelis virginiana
"Witch hazel" in New Jersey

Hamamelis x intermedia 'Jelena'
in Netherlands Arboretum

Hamam. x intermedia 'Arnold Promise'
in Arnold Arboretum, Mass.

Hamamelis japonica
"Japan witchhazel" in New York Bot. G.

Hamamelis japonica
autumn-fruiting in Germany

Hamamelis mollis, *March-bloom*
in Brooklyn Bot. Garden, New York

Mesua ferrea *(GUTT.)*
"Ceylon ironwood" in Singapore

Kielmeyera variabilis *(GUTT.)*
Jardim Botanico, Rio de Janeiro

Loropetalum chinense *(HAM.)*
from Southeast China

Disanthus cercidifolius *(HAM.)*
Autumn foliage, in Kyushu, Japan

Liquidambar styraciflua *(HAM.)*
with horny fruit in New York

Liquidambar styraciflua
"Sweet gum" in Germany

Rhodoleia championii *(HAM.)*
in Botanic Garden Hong Kong

Liquidambar styraciflua 'Palo Alto'
Autumn foliage, in California

Parrotia persica *(HAMAMEL.)*
"Persian ironwood" in France

Aesculus californica
"Chapparel buckeye" in Portugal

Aesculus glabra arguta
"Texas buckeye" in Kew Bot. G.

Aesculus x carnea, *"Horse-chestnut"*
Strybing Arboretum, San Francisco

Aesculus x carnea 'Briotii'
Kew Botanic Gardens, near London

Aesculus hippocastaneum
in old Visby, Gotland, Sweden

Aesculus hippocastaneum
"Horse chestnut" in Dalmatia

Aesculus pavia *(splendens)*
"Red buckeye" in Illinois

Aesculus octandra
"Yellow buckeye" in Des Moines, Iowa

Aesculus sylvatica *(neglecta)*
in Ashville, No. Carolina

Hypericum androsaemum
"Tutsan" forming fruit, in England

Wigandia caracasana *(HYD.)*
Lisbon Bot. Garden, Portugal

Aesculus parviflora *(HIPP.)*
"Dwarf horse-chestnut" (Alabama)

Hypericum beanii *(HYP.)*
"St. John's-wort" in California

Hypericum empetrifolium
on Mykonos, Greece

Hypericum calycinum
"Rose of Sharon" in Cologne

Hypericum fasciculatum
"Sandweed" in No. Carolina

Hypericum 'Rowallane'
University Bot. Garden, Los Angeles

Hypericum frondosum
"Golden St. John's-wort"

Hypericum galioides
from Delaware to Texas

Hypericum inodorum 'Elstead'
from Surrey, England

Hypericum kalmianum
in Chicago, Illinois

Hypericum x moserianum
Strybing Arboretum, San Francisco

Hypericum leschenaultii
Wellington Bot. G., New Zealand

Hypericum kouytchense
from Western China

Hyper. x moserianum 'Tricolor'
in Los Angeles Arboretum

Hypericum reptans
"Creeping St. John's-wort"

Hypericum patulum *(China)*
in Cologne Botanic Garden

Hypericum olympicum
Int'l. Hort. Exhib., Munich

Erythroxylum coca
"Cocaine" in Perú

Pterocarya fraxinifolia *(JUGL.)*
"Wingnut" in Frankfurt Bot. G.

Gonocaryum pyriforme *(ICAC.)*
Botanic Garden Bogor, Java

Conradina canescens *(LAB.)*
coastal Florida to Alabama

Colquhounia coccinea *(LAB.)*
from Himalayas (foreground right)

Prostanthera nivea *(LAB.)*
"Australian mint-bush"

Phlomis cashmeriana *(LAB.)*
in Munich Bot. Garden, Germany

Hermannia althaeifolia *(BYTT.)*
"Honey-bells" of So. Africa

Pterocarya stenoptera *(JUGLAND.)*
"Chinese wing-nut" of Eastern and C. China

Carya laciniosa *(JUGLAND.)*
"Shellbark hickory" or "King-nut" in Pennsylvania

Carya tomentosa *(JUGLAND.)*
"Mockernut hickory" for edible nuts, in Virginia

Lindera benzoin *(Ontario to Texas)*
"Spice bush", berries for culinary use

Ballota pseudodictamnus *(LAB.)*
Woody perennial of Crete

Salvia microphylla neurepia *(LAB.)*
"Cherry sage" of Mexico

Lindera obtusiloba *(LAURAC.)*
in Governor's Garden, Williamsburg, Virginia

Sassafras albidum *(LAUR.)*
"Sassafras", with pendant fruit (E. No. America)

Salvia microphylla (LAB.)
"Baby sage" of Mexico

Salvia leucophylla
"Purple sage" in So. California

Salvia leucantha
"Mexican sage" in Encinitas

Westringia rosmariniformis (LAB.)
"Coast rosemary" of Queensland

Cinnamomum zeylanicum (LAUR.)
"Cinnamon tree" in Sri Lanka

Cinnamomum camphora (China)
"Camphor tree" in California

Decaisnea fargesii (LARD.)
"Blue-pods" in Rhineland, Germany

Laurus nobilis (LAUR.)
"Bay-tree" in Bruges, Belgium

Laurus nobilis, in flower
true "Laurel" in Barcelona, Spain

Lindera benzoin *in flower*
New York Botanical Garden

Lindera obtusiloba
flowering in Williamsburg, Virginia

Lindera strychnifolia
in Hangchow Bot. Garden, China

Neolitsea sericea
in Seoul, Korea

Persea borbonia
"Florida mahogany"

Umbellularia californica
"California laurel" in Encinitas

Sassafras albidum
autumn color in Virginia

Sassafras albidum
with aromatic leaves

Eusyderoxylon swageri
"Ironwood" in Bogor Bot. G., Java

Shepherdia argentea *(ELAEAG.)*
"Buffalo berry" in South Dakota

Couroupita guianensis *(LECYTH.)*
"Cannonball-tree" in flower

Couroupita guianensis
fruiting in Summit, Panama

Lecythis zabucajo *(LECYTH.)*
"Paradise nut" in Rio de Janeiro

Acacia armata *(LEG.)*
"Kangaroo thorn" in Sydney

Acacia complanata
Brisbane Bot. Garden, Queensland

Acacia drummondii
Jardin Bot. Les Cèdres, France

Acacia farnesiana
"Popinac" in Antigua, W. Indies

Acacia karroo *(LEGUM.)*
"Sweet-thorn" in the Transvaal

Acacia nilotica
"Gum Arabic tree" in India

Acacia pendula, *"Myala"*
in San Diego Zoo, Calif.

Acacia retinodes *(So. Australia)*
"Everblooming acacia"

Acacia cultriformis
"Knife acacia" (Queensland)

Acacia longifolia mucronata
"Narrow Sydney wattle"

Acacia spaerocephala
"Mexican mimosa"

Acacia longifolia
"Sydney golden wattle"

Acacia latifolia *(No. Australia)*
"Broadleaf acacia" in California

Acacia baileyana
"Golden mimosa" in Los Angeles

Acacia drepanolobium, *"Whistling-thorn"*
on the Rift Valley Desert, Kenya

Acacia abyssinica, *flat-topped acacia*
in arid Somalia, East Africa

Acacia decurrens, *"Green wattle"*
in Adelaide Botanic Garden, South Australia

Acacia baileyana *(New South Wales)*
"Golden mimosa" in San Diego, Calif.

Acacia podalyriifolia *(Queensland)*
"Pearl acacia" in Quail Bot. G., Encinitas, California

Acacia saligna, *with curved phyllodes*
"Weeping wattle" in King's Park, Perth, W. Australia

Albizia julibrissin
"Mimosa tree" in Rutherford, N.J.

Adenocarpus complicatus
on Cap Ferrat, France

Albizia distachya
"Plume mimosa" in W. Australia

Albizia lebbeck, *on Rarotonga*
"Woman's-tongue tree"

Albizia lebbeck, *with pods*
in Beguia, West Indies

Amherstia nobilis, *in Sri Lanka*
Peradeniya Botanic Gardens

Amorpha canescens
"Lead plant" in Arizona

Amorpha fruticosa
"False indigo" in Louisiana

Apoplanesia cryptopetala
in Caracas, Venezuela

Bauhinia monandra *(Myanmar)*
Fairchild Trop. Garden, Miami

Bauhinia blakeana
"Hong Kong orchid tree"

Bauhinia variegata
"Mountain ebony" in Honolulu

Bauhinia corniculata
"White camel's-foot" of Brazil

Bauhinia kochia *(Malaya)*
Singapore Botanic Garden

Bauhinia petersiana *(E. Africa)*
Royal Botanic Gardens, Sydney

Bauhinia punctata *(galpinii)*
"Pride of the Cape" in Kirstenbosch

Bauhinia purpurea *(India)*
in Bahamas Botanic Garden

Bauhinia tomentosa
"St. Thomas tree" in Goa

Brownea grandiceps
"Rose-of-Venezuela"

Brownea macrophylla *(Colombia)*
Foster Botanic Garden, Honolulu

Bauhinia acuminata
Mahé Bot. Garden, Seychelles

Butea monosperma *(frondosa)*
"Flame of the forest" in Hawaii

Bossiaea rhombifolia
in Cairns, North Queensland

Bossiaea rosmarinifolia
in the Grampians, E. Australia

Brya ebenus *(Cuba)*
"West Indian ebony" in Havana

Caesalpinia echinata
Quail Bot. G., Encinitas, Calif.

Caesalpinia ferrea *(Brazil)*
"Leopard tree" in Brisbane B.G.

Calliandra emarginata *(Mexico)*
"Miniature powder-puff" in Florida

Calliandra haematocephala 'Alba'
Mughal Gardens, Agra, India

Calliandra haematocephala
St. Vincent Bot. G., W. Indies

Calliandra guildingii
"Trinidad powderpuff tree"

Calliandra houstoniana
(So. Mexico to Honduras)

Calliandra "inaequilatera" *hort.*
in Quail Bot. G., Encinitas, Calif.

Calliandra portoricensis
(West Indies to Panama)

Calliandra schultzei
in Paramaribo, Surinam

Calliandra tweedii
Uni. of Calif. Bot. G. Los Angeles

Caesalpinia gilliesii *(Argentina)*
"Bird-of-paradise shrub" in Arizona

Caesalpinia pulcherrima flava
"Peacock flower" in the Maldives

Caesalpinia pulcherrima
"Barbados pride" in Mysore, India

Campylotropis macrocarpa
(Lespedeza) in England

Caragana arborescens *(Siberia)*
"Pea tree" flowering in Russia

Caragana arborescens, *with pods*
in Montreal Bot. Garden, Canada

Caesalpinia spinosa
"Tara" in bloom, San Diego

Calliandra surinamensis
in Tahiti Botanic Garden

Castanospermum australe
"Moreton Bay chestnut" in Calif.

Cassia x hybrida, *"Rainbow shower" (LEG.)*
official tree of Honolulu, Hawaii

Cassia fistula, *"Golden shower" of India*
in Jardim Botanico Rio de Janeiro

Delonix regia, *the "Flamboyant" (LEG.)*
on Nuku Hiva, Marquesas, South Pacific

Idria columnaris, *the curious "Boojum tree"*
on arid Sierras of Baja California, Mexico

Cassia javanica
"Appleblossom shower" on Kauai

Cassia fistula *with pendant beans
in Mughal Gardens, Agra, India*

Cassia roxburghii *(Sri Lanka)
Fairchild Trop. Gardens, Miami*

Senna alata *(Cassia)*
"Candle bush" in San Diego, Calif.

Senna auriculata *(Cassia)*
in arid Saudi Arabia

Senna excelsa *(Cassia floribunda)*
"Crown-of-gold tree" in Florida

Senna biflora *(Cassia)*
in Mysore, South India

Senna fruticosa *(Cassia)*
at Lake Toba, Sumatra

Senna laevigata *(Trop. America)
Nymphenburg Bot. G., Munich*

Senna pendula
(Cassia floribunda in Calif.)

Senna candolleana *in California*
(Cassia bicapsularis in Calif. hort.)

Senna corymbosa *(Cassia)*
in Santa Cruz, Tenerife

Senna aciphylla *(Australia)*
Quail Bot. Gard., Encinitas, Calif.

Senna artemisioides *(Cassia)*
"Silver cassia" in Fallbrook, Calif.

Senna didymobotrya *(C. nairobensis)*
"Popcorn bush" in Vista, Calif.

Senna leptophylla *(Cassia)*
"Gold medallion tree", Los Angeles B.G.

Cassia moschata
"Bronze shower tree"

Senna surattensis *(Cassia glauca)*
"Scrambled eggs", in Marquesas Isl.

Senna multijuga *(W. Indies)*
"November shower" in Singapore B.G.

Senna septemtrionalis
Cassia floribunda in Taiwan

Senna siamea *(Cassia)*
"Kassod tree" in Sénégal

Senna speciosa *(Cassia)*
in Durban Bot. Garden, Natal

Senna tomentosa *(Cassia)*
Univ. Bot. Garden, Mexico City

Senna spectabilis *(Cassia)*
"Popcorn bush" in Vista, California

Coronilla emerus *(France)*
"Scorpion senna" in Cap Ferrat

Coronilla valentina glauca
Kew Bot. Gardens, near London

Coronilla vaginalis
in the Alps of Austria

Ceratonia siliqua *in flower*
"Carob tree" in California

Cercidium floridum *(torreyanum)*
"Palo verde" near Tucson, Arizona

Cercidium floridum
blooming in Sonora, Mexico

Cercidium sonorae
South Coast Bot. Gard., Los Angeles

Cercis chinensis
"Chinese redbud" in Brooklyn, N.Y.

Cercis canadensis
"Eastern redbud" in No. Carolina

Cercis occidentalis
"California redbud"

Cercis siliquastrum
"Judas tree" in Gibraltar

Cercis siliquastrum alba
nursery-grown in Dallas, Texas

Colvillea racemosa, *"Colville's glory"*
a brilliant tropical flowering tree, in Madagascar

Cercis reniformis
"Love tree" of Texas and New Mexico

Cercidium floridum *(torreyanum)*
"Blue palo verde" in Gila Bend, Arizona

Cercidium microphyllum
"Palo Verde" on the Sonoran desert, Arizona

Cercis canadensis, *"Eastern redbud"*
spring-blooming near Birmingham, Alabama

Cytisus decumbens
"Prostrate broom" in Andalucia, Southern Spain

Chorizema cordatum *(Australia)*
"Heartleaf flame pea" in Calif.

Chorizema ilicifolium
"Holly flame pea" on French Riviera

Cladrastis lutea *(Virgilia)*
"American yellow-wood"

Colutea arborescens
"Bladder senna" in France

Crotalaria agatiflora
"Canarybird bush" in Escondido, Calif.

Crotalaria laburnifolia
"Queensland bird-flower"

Cytisus monspessalanus
"Teline" in San Francisco, Calif.

Cytisus battandieri *(Morocco)*
Frankfurt Palmengarten, Germany

Cytisus x kewensis
at Kew Bot. Gardens, England

Cytisus multiflorus
"White Spanish broom" at Kew

Notospartium glabrescens
December bloom in Christchurch, N.Z.

Cytisus x praecox
"Warminster broom" in England

Cytisus scoparius
"Scotch broom" in Edinburgh

Cytisus scoparius 'Andreanus'
"Goldfinch broom" (Normandy)

Cytisus x racemosus
Longwood Gard., Pennsylvania

Cytisus scoparius 'Pendulus'
Kew Botanic Gard., England

Cytisus nigricans
"Spike broom" in England

Genista sagittalis
"Winged broom" in Greece

Genista tinctoria
"Dyer's greenwood" in England

Genista pilosa
in Duesseldorf Bot. G., Germany

Genista lydia *(Syria)*
in Kew Bot. Gardens, England

Genista sylvestris *(dalmatica)*
along Adriatic coast of Croatia

Genista hispanica, "Spanish broom"
in the Pyrenées of Northern Spain

Dalbergia sissoo *(India)*
"Indian rosewood" in Florida

Dalbergia balansae
"So. China rosewood" in Hong Kong

Dorycnium hirsutum
"Canary clover" of So. Europe

Erythrina variegata orientalis
in Jogyakarta, C. Java, Indonesia

Erythrina velutina
on Dominica, in the Antilles

Erythrina princeps *(lysistemon)*
"Kaffir boom" in Zimbabwe

Erythrina poeppigiana
"Mountain immortelle" in Venezuela

Erythrina montana
col. by Dr. A. Lau, in Mexico

Erythrina falcata
in Organ Mountains of So. Brazil

Ebenus cretica *(Greece)*
in Lisbon Bot. G., Portugal

Erinacea pungens *(Spain)*
"Hedgehog broom" at Kew G., England

Gliricidia sepium *(C. America)*
"Madre de cacao" in Cali, Colombia

Delonix regia
"Flamboyant" in Madagascar

Delonix regia *(Poinciana)*
in Chichen Itza, Yucatán

Erythrina crista-gallii
"Coral tree" in Uruguay

Erythrina x bidwillii
"Florida coral-bean" in Sarasota

Erythrina coralloides *(Mexico)*
"Naked coral-tree" in Huntington Bot. Garden

Erythrina humeana *(So. Africa)*
"Natal coral-tree" (true species)

Erythrina coralloides
at San Diego airport

Erythrina caffra *(South Africa)*
"Kaffirboom coral tree" in Calif.

Gleditsia triacanthos *(LEG.)*
"Honey-locust" in New York

Gleditsia triac. inermis aurea
"Thornless honey-locust" in Calif.

Gled. triac. inermis 'Sunburst'
"Golden honey-locust" in Boston, Mass.

Gleditsia triacanthos
with long sugary pods

Cytisus x praecox 'Hollandia'
in Boskoop, Netherlands

Cytisus purpureus *(LEG.)*
"Purple broom" on Gotland, Sweden

Plectranthus aethiopicus *(LAB.)*
Quail Bot. G., Encinitas, Calif.

Inga edulis *(quaternata) (LEG.)*
"Ice-cream beans" in Panama

Labichea punctata *(LEG.)*
showy Australian evergreen

Laburnum alpinum
"Scotch laburnum" in London

Laburnum x watereri *(tree)*
Botanic Garden Essen, Germany

Laburnum x watereri *(close-up)*
(alpinum x anagyroides)

Laburnum x watereri 'Vossii'
du Pont Winterthur G., Delaware

Laburnum anagyroides
"Golden chain" in the Rhineland

x Laburnocytisus adamii
curiosity with yellow and purple fl.

Indigofera gerardiana
"Himalayan indigo" of India

Indigofera tinctoria
"Indigo" at Floriade, Amsterdam

Indigofera incarnata
"Chinese indigo" in Sydney Bot. G.

Lespedeza bicolor
"Shrub bush clover" of Japan

Lespedeza thunbergii *(Korea)*
"Bush clover" in Munich Bot. G.

Lotus maculatus
"Parrot's-beak" on Tenerife

Leucaena glauca, *with beans*
"Tamarindillo" in Colombia

Leucaena glauca (leucocephala)
"Wild tamarind" on Guam Is.

Leucaena retusa
in the Apache Mts., of West Texas

Gymnocladus dioica
"Kentucky coffee tree"

Lysiloma candida *(Mexico)*
on Cabo San Lucas, Baja California

Liparia spherica
"Mountain dahlia" of So. Africa

Lonchocarpus violaceus
"Lance-pod" of Trinidad

Maniltoa gemmipara *(New Guinea)*
at Mandai Nurs. Singapore

Mucuna bennettii
"New Guinea creeper" in Fiji

Platylobium obtusangulum
in Melbourne, Victoria

Myroxylon balsamum pereirae
source of balsam of Perú

Medicago arborea *(Portugal)*
"Moon trifoil" in Bot. G. Lisbon

Sabinea carinalis
"Carib-wood" in Hawaii

Oxylobium lanceolatum
"Golden shaggy pea" (W. Australia)

Mimosa pudica
"Sensitive plant" in Brazil

Olneya tesota
"Desert ironwood" in Tucson, Arizona

Pongamia pinnata *(Trop. Asia)*
"Karum tree", or "Poonga-oil tree" in Florida

Maackia amurensis
summer-flowering tree of Manchuria and Korea

Prosopis glandulosa *(juliflora)*
"Honey mesquite" in the desert near Tucson, Arizona

Robinia hispida
"Rose acacia" flowering in Alabama

Robinia neomexicana
Western locust in summer bloom near Albuquerque

Parkinsonia aculeata
"Jerusalem-thorn" in San Diego

Parkinsonia aculeata *in Calif.*
"Mexican palo verde", Imperial Valley

Prosopis glandulosa, *with beans*
"Mesquite" at Gila Bend, Arizona

Petteria ramentacea
with fragrant flowers, in England

Haematoxylon campechianum
"Bloodwood tree" in Yucatán

Peltophorum pterocarpum *(Malaya)*
"Yellow flame tree" in Penang

Pithecellobium ligustrinum
with ornamental fruit, in Venezuela

Pithecellobium ligustrinum
"El Orore" of Caracas, by J. Hoyos

Piptanthus nepalensis
Kew Botanic Gardens, England

Robinia pseudoacacia
"False acacia" in Pennsylvania

Pterocarpus indicus *with seedpods*
"Burmese rosewood" in Seychelles

Pseudarthria hookeri
in Valley of 1000 Hills, Zululand

Robinia kelseyi
"Alleghany moss" (No. Carolina)

Robinia x ambigua
at New York Bot. Garden

Podalyria calyptrata
"Sweet pea bush" of So. Africa

Robinia viscosa *(grafted plant)*
in Palmengarten Frankfurt, Germany

Robinia fertilis
in Blue Ridge Mts., No. Carolina

Pultanaea costata
"Bush pea" (Eastern Australia)

Samanea saman *(LEG.)*
"Rain tree" in Honolulu

Descurainia bourgaeana *(CRUC.)*
on Pico Teide, Tenerife

Spartium junceum *(LEG.)*
"Spanish broom" in Gran Canaria

Sophora arizonica *(LEG.)*
"Arizona mountain laurel"

Schotia brachypetala *(LEG.)*
"Tree fuchsia" in Zululand

Saraca indica *(LEG.)*
"Asoka tree" in Mysore, India

Sesbania grandiflora *(LEG.)*
"Vegetable hummingbird" (Puerto Rico)

Sesbania punicea
in Northern Argentina

Sesbania tripetii
"Scarlet wisteria" in California

Tipuana tipu
"Rosewood" in Bolivia

Tamarindus indica
at Royal Palace, Bangkok

Tamarindus indica
"Tamarind tree" in California

Sophora secundiflora
"Mescal-bean" in Texas

Sutherlandia frutescens
"Balloon pea" in the Transvaal

Templetonia aculeata
"Pink coral-bush" (Australia)

Sophora microphylla
"Maori kowhai" (New Zealand)

Sophora japonica
"Japanese pagoda tree"

Sophora japonica 'Tortuosa'
in Somerset Arboretum, N.J.

Dracaena draco *(AGAV.)*
"Dragon tree" in San Diego Zoo

Cordyline australis *(AGAV.)*
in Christchurch, New Zealand

Beaucarnea recurvata intermedia
Seaport Village, San Diego

Yucca brevifolia *(AGAV.)*
"Joshua tree" on the Sonora desert

Yucca elephantipes
"Spineless yucca" in Vista, Calif.

Yucca rostrata *in flower*
in Marathon, Texas habitat

Yucca filamentosa *(flaccida)*
"Adam's-needle" in N. York Bot. G.

Asparagus retrofractus *(LIL.)*
"Zigzag shrub" in Durban, Natal

Danae racemosa *(LIL.)*
"Alexandrian laurel" in England

Ulex parviflorus *(LEG.)*
spiny *"Ajonc de Provence"*

Ulex europaeus
"Gorse" in Wellington, N. Zealand

Virgilia divaricata *(LEG.)*
"Keur-broom" of So. Africa

Ruscus hypoglossum *(LIL.)*
Valley of the Kings, Luxor, Egypt

Ruscus aculeatus, *"Butcher's broom"*
with tiny flowers on cladodes

Ruscus aculeatus, *female plant
with fruit (Kew Bot. G., England)*

Brighamia citrina *(LOBEL.)*
"Tree lobelia" of Kauai, Hawaii

Lobelia rhynchopetalum *(Trop. Africa)*
Duesseldorf Bot. G., Germany

Reinwardtia indica *(LIN.)*
"Yellow flax" in California

Buddleia asiatica, *"Butterfly bush"*
in Mughal Gardens, Agra, India

Buddleia nivea
"Snowy buddleia" of Western China

Buddleia davidii var. alba
"White summer lilac" in Germany

Buddleia cordata
in Rio de Janeiro Bot. Garden

Buddleia davidii 'Royal Red'
Strybing Arboretum, San Francisco

Buddleia alternifolia
"Fountain buddleia" in California

Buddleia globosa *(Perú)*
"Orange-ball tree" in England

Buddleia madagascariensis
in Heraklion, Crete

Buddleia x weyeriana 'Sungold'
in Boskoop, Holland

Eucryphia lucida 'Rosea'
in Kew Bot. Gardens, England

Eurcyphia lucida
"Leatherwood" of N.W. Tasmania

Desfontainea spinosa (LOG.)
from Chile and Perú

Nicodemia diversifolia hort.
"Indoor oak" in Bot. G. Berlin

Strychnos nux-vomica (LOG.)
"Strychnine tree" in Hong Kong

Lafoensia vandelliana (LYTH.)
showy flowering tree of Brazil

Cuphea lanceolata 'Firefly'
during Floriade 82 Amsterdam

Cuphea ignea (LYTH.)
"Cigar flower" (Mexico)

Rubus tricolor (ROS.)
in Kew Bot. Gardens, England

Lagerstroemia indica *(LYTH.)*
"Crape-myrtle" in Brooklyn Bot. G.

Lagerstroemia indica 'Petite Snow'
"Dwarf crape-myrtle" in San Diego

Lagerstroemia speciosa
"Rose of India" in Tahiti

Lagerstr. indica 'Petite Pinkie'
at Los Angeles Arboretum

Illicium anisatum *(ILLIC.)*
"Star anise" near Taipei, Taiwan

Illicium floridanum
"Purple anise" in Louisiana

Lythrum salicaria *(LYTH.)*
"Purple loosestrife" in Rhineland

Lythrum virgatum 'Rose Queen'
in Arnold Arboretum, Massachusetts

Illicium anisatum 'Variegatum'
"Variegated anise" in England

Liriodendron tulipifera
"Tulip tree" at New York Bot. Gard.

Liriodendron tulipifera 'Arnold'
columnar tree in Los Angeles

Liriod. tulip. 'Aureo-marginatum'
"Variegated tulip tree" in Boskoop

Drimys winteri
"Winter's bark" in Buenos Aires

Magnolia acuminata
"Cucumber tree" in Ontario

Magnolia campbellii
in Domain of Auckland, N. Zealand

Magnolia hypoleuca *(obovata)*
"Japanese magnolia"

Magnolia macrophylla, *in Kentucky*
"Great-leaved magnolia"

Magnolia fraseri, *in Virginia*
"Ear-leaved umbrella tree"

Magnolia denudata *(heptapeta)*
"Yulan" in Hangchow, So. China

Magnolia denudata
Spring in E. Rutherford, N.J.

Magnolia denudata
fragrant flowers, conspicua in hort.

Magnolia grandiflora, *w. seedpods*
in San Diego, California

Magnolia grandiflora
"Southern magnolia" in N. Orleans

Magnolia liliiflora *(quinquepeta)*
in Botanic Garden, Hong Kong

Magnolia kobus
"Kobus magnolia" in Virginia

Magnolia kobus *(China)*
in Hangchow Bot. Garden, Chekiang

Magnolia x soulangiana 'Verbanica'
late-blooming, in New Jersey

Magnolia sprengeri
from Hupeh and Honan, China

Magnolia sprengeri var. diva
in Bot. Garden Essen, Germany

Magnolia wilsonii
in Longwood Gardens, Pennsylvania

Magnolia sinensis
in Kew Bot. Gardens, England

Magnolia salicifolia
"Anise magnolia" of Honshu

Magnolia sieboldii, *"Oyama"*
Dortmund Bot. Garden, Germany

Magnolia tripetala
in the Ozark Mts. of Oklahoma

Magnolia cylindrica
in Copenhagen Bot. Garden, Denmark

Magnolia virginiana
at Princeton University, New Jersey

Magnolia x soulangiana
"Saucer magnolia" in N. Jersey

Magnolia liliiflora *(quinquepeta)*
Royal Bot. Gard. Kew, England

Magnolia liliiflora 'Nigra'
Auckland Bot. Gard., New Zealand

Michelia figo *(Magn. fuscata)*
"Banana shrub" in Hangchow, China

Magnolia stellata
"Star magnolia" in New York Bot. G.

Magnolia stellata 'Waterlily'
Greenbrier Farms, Norfolk, Virginia

Manglietia fordiana *(So. China)*
scented flowers, in Hong Kong

Michelia champaca *(Himalayas)*
"Orange champak" in Bot. G., Sydney

Michelia doltsopa
in Khatmandu, Nepal

Malpighia glabra *(MALP.)*
"Acerola", Quail B. G. Encinitas, Calif.

Galphimia glauca *(MALP.)*
"Gold shower thryallis" in Florida

Spachea elegans *(MALP.)*
"Soufrière tree" in St. Vincent, W.I.

Tetracentron sinense *(MAGN.)*
Dortmund Bot. Garden, Germany

Abutilon auritum *(MALV.)*
in Brisbane Bot. G., Queensland

Abelmoschus manihot *(Hibiscus)*
"Musk-mallow" in Hawaii (MALV.)

Abutilon pictum 'Thompsonii'
"Spotted flowering maple" (Guatemala)

Abutilon megapotamicum 'Variegatum'
"Weeping Chinese lantern"

Abutilon fraseri
Sydney Bot. Garden, Australia

Abutilon x hybr. 'Souv. de Bonn'
"Variegated flowering maple"

Abutilon x hybridum 'Old Rose'
"Parlor maple" in Rhineland Bot. G.

Alyogyne huegelii *(Hibiscus)*
"Blue hibiscus" in California

Gossypium sturtianum
"Desert rose" of North Australia

Gossypium herbaceum
"Levant cotton" in Los Angeles Arb.

Hibiscus moscheutos
"Rose mallow" in Louisiana

Goethea cauliflora
in Heidelberg Bot. Garden

Goethea strictiflora
Andromeda Gardens, Barbados

Hibiscus fragilis
in Bot. Garden Mauritius

Hibiscus rosa-sinensis
"Chinese hibiscus" on Moorea

Hibiscus rosa-sin. 'Butterball'
in Escondido, California

Hibiscus rosa-sin. 'Hula Girl'
in Honolulu, Hawaii

Hibiscus rosa-sin. 'Cooperi'
in Barbados, West Indies

Hibiscus rosa-sin. 'Calif. Gold'
Tropic World, Escondido

Hibiscus rosa-sin. 'Cherie'
hyb. from Odense, Denmark

Hibiscus mutabilis
"Cotton rose" in Alabama

Hibiscus diversifolius
Kirstenbosch Bot. G., So. Africa

Hibiscus bifurcatus *(Brazil)*
Jardim Botanico, Rio de Janeiro

Hibiscus rosa-sin. 'Brilliant'
in San Diego, California

Hibiscus rosa-sin. 'Fijian Pink'
in Fiji Botanic Garden, Suva

Hibiscus rosa-sin. 'Scarlet'
on Nuku Hiva, Marquesas

Hib. rosa-sin. 'Crown of Bohemia'
Nurseryland of Escondido, Calif.

Hibiscus rosa-sin. 'White Wings'
prolific bloomer, in California

Hib. rosa-sin. 'Florida Sunset'
in St. Petersburg, Florida

Hibiscus rosa-sin. 'Lucky-me'
Bermuda Bot. Garden, Hamilton

Hib. rosa-sin. 'Punta Gorda Gold'
in South Florida

Hibiscus rosa-sinensis 'Reef'
Quail Bot. Gard., Encinitas

Hibiscus rosa-sin. 'Santana'
Hines Nurs., Santa Ana, Calif.

Hibiscus rosa-sin. 'Lemon Glow'
Andromeda Gardens, Barbados

Hib. rosa-sin. 'Lawrence orange'
in Barbados, West Indies

Hibiscus rosa-sin. 'Tiki'
grafted plant, of Hawaii

Hibiscus rosa-sinensis 'Fiesta'
pat. Monrovia Nurs., Azusa, Calif.

Hibiscus schizopetalus
"Fringed hibiscus" in Bahamas

Hibiscus schizopetalus 'Pagoda'
"Flora en flora" in Colombia

Hibiscus syriacus 'Coelestis'
Cologne Botanic Gard., Germany

Hibiscus syriacus 'Helene'
at Don Roehrs Nursery, N. Jersey

Hibiscus syriacus *(Althaea)*
"Rose of Sharon" in Bonsall, Calif.

Hibiscus syriacus 'Monstrosus'
large flowers, in Germany

Hibiscus syriacus 'Morning sky'
Don Roehrs Nursery, N. Jersey

Hibiscus tiliaceus
"Mahoe" on Moorea, So. Pacific

Hibiscus tetrandra
Bot. Garden Duesseldorf, Germany

Hibiscus syriacus 'Woodbridge'
Notcutt of Suffolk, England

Hoheria lyallii
in Southern Alps of N. Zealand

Lagunaria patersonia
"Pyramid tree" in New So. Wales

Lavatera assurgentiflora
"Malva rosa" in Chula Vista, Calif.

Lavatera olbia 'Rosea' *(MALV.)*
"Tree lavatera" (Portugal)

Montezuma speciosissima *(MALV.)*
"Hibiscus tree" in Puerto Rico

Malvaviscus arboreus mexicanus
"Turk's cap" in Durban, Natal

Pavonia hastata *(MALV.)*
Quail Bot. Gard., Encinitas, Calif.

Plagianthus regius *(MALV.)*
"Ribbonwood" of New Zealand

Thespesia populnea *(MALV.)*
"Portia tree" in Florida

Heterocentron elegans *(MEL.)*
"Spanish shawl" in Guatemala

Heterocentron mexicanum
from Sinaloa, Mexico

Heterocentron macrostachyum
in Munich Botanic Garden

Medinilla astronoides
in Singapore Bot. Garden

Medinilla magnifica *(MELAST.)*
"Rose grape" in Java, Indonesia

Melastoma candidum
(Taiwan and Philippines)

Miconia hookeriana *(MELAST.)*
from Eastern Perú rainforest

Monochaetum bonplandii *(MELAST.)*
along Rio Canaima, Venezuela

Tibouchina urvilleana *(MELAST.)*
"Glory-bush" in Los Angeles Arbor.

Cedrela angustifolia *(MELIAC.)*
"Cedro roseo" in Colombia

Cedrela australis *(Toona)*
Royal Bot. Gardens, Sydney

Aglaia formosana *(MELIAC.)*
with edible fruit, in Taiwan

Cedrela odorata *(MELIAC.)*
"West Indian cedar" in Hawaii

Cedrela sinensis *(Toona)*
"Chinese mahogany" in Taiwan

Cedrela sinensis 'Tinted Sky'
in Quail Bot. G. Encinitas, Calif.

Sandoricum indicum *(MELIAC.)*
"Santol tree" in Seychelles

Lansium domesticum *(MELIAC.)*
"Lady fingers" of India

Swietenia mahagoni *(MELIAC.)*
"Mahogany" in Antigua Bot. G.

Turraea obtusifolia *(MELIAC.)*
"So. African honeysuckle"

Greyia radlkoferi *(MELIANTH.)*
"Mountain bottlebrush" in San Diego

Greyia sutherlandii *(So. Africa)*
"Natal bottlebrush" in habitat

Melia azedarach umbraculifera
"Texas umbrella" in San Antonio

Melia azedarach *"Indian lilac"*
in Bermuda Bot. Garden, Hamilton

Melia azedarach umbraculifera
"China berry" in San Francisco

Melia indica, *"Margosa tree"*
sacred to Hindus, in Colombo, Sri Lanka

Melia indica *(Antelaea or Azadirachta)*
"Neem tree" or "Pride of India" in Calcutta

Melia indica *(MELIAC.)*
Herbarium New York Bot. Garden

Melianthus major *(MELIANTH.)*
"Honey-bush" in Cape Town, S. Africa

Cocculus laurifolius *(MENISP.)*
"Platter-leaf" in Leucadia, Calif.

Ficus aspera *(parcellii)*
"Clown fig" in Berlin-Dahlem

Cudrania tricuspidata
"Silkworm-thorn" of China

Cecropia palmata *(Brazil)*
"Snakewood tree" in Bahia

Ficus benjamina 'Exotica'
in Rockefeller Center, New York

Ficus elastica 'Decora'
"Wideleaf rubber plant"

Ficus auriculata
"Ornamental fig" in India

Ficus elastica 'Decora Honduras'
variegated with cream at Roehrs

Ficus benj. 'Splendens variegata'
Bermuda Bot. Garden, Hamilton

Ficus benj. 'Exotica variegata'
GRUGA Garden, Essen, Germany

Radermachera sinica *(BIGN.)*
flowering tree in Leucadia, Calif.

Ficus monckii, *"Higueron"*
epiphytic strangler in Argentina

Dammaropsis kingiana
in the Finisterre Mts., New Guinea

Ficus altissima *(MORAC.)*
"Council tree" in Malaya

Ficus benghalensis
"Banyan tree" in Calcutta

Ficus elastica
"India rubber tree" in Cape Town

Ficus benjamina
"Weeping fig" in Vista, California

Ficus benjamina, *as standard*
twist-stemmed (Costa Nurs., Florida)

Ficus benjamina, *buttressed tree*
in Foster Bot. Garden, Honolulu

Ficus elastica 'Variegata'
"Variegated rubber plant"

Ficus deltoidea (diversifolia)
"Mistletoe fig" in Germany

Ficus foveolata (Myanmar)
in GRUGA Bot. Garden, Essen

Ficus pretoriae (Transvaal)
"Wonderboom" in San Pasqual, Calif.

Ficus salicifolia
"Willow-leaf fig" as bonsai

Ficus macrophylla
"Moreton Bay fig" in New Zealand

Ficus microcarpa 'Milky stripe'
"Varieg. Indian laurel" in Taiwan

Ficus maxima (mexicana hort.)
in Homestead, Florida

Ficus microcarpa nitida
"Indian laurel" in California

Ficus religiosa
sacred "Bo-tree" of India

Ficus retusa, *standard tree
in Old Town, San Diego*

Ficus rubiginosa *(Australia)
"Rusty fig" in Encinitas, Calif.*

Ficus irregularis *(celebensis)
in Botanic Garden, Singapore*

Ficus lyrata *(pandurata)
"Fiddleleaf fig" (Trop. W. Africa)*

Ficus padifolia *(pertusa)
in Puerto Escondido, Oaxaca, Mex.*

Ficus nekbudu *(utilis)
"Zulu fig" in Encinitas, Calif.*

Ficus microcarpa nitida 'Hawaii'
in Rhineland garden center

Ficus petiolaris
"Blue Mexican fig" in Mazatlan

Ficus rubiginosa 'Variegata'
in Oceanside, California

Ficus triangularis
"Sweetheart tree" of Trop. Africa

Ficus palmeri
from Baja California, Mexico

Maclura pomifera
"Osage-orange" in Oklahoma

Ficus benghalensis krishnae
"Sacred fig tree" in Benares, India

Ficus mysorensis *(India)*
in San Diego Zoo

Morus alba *(non-fruiting)*
"White mulberry" in Escondido

Morus nigra, *"Black mulberry"*
(Horticultural Soc. of New York)

Streblus ilicifolius
in Singapore Bot. Garden

Ravenala madagascariensis *(MUS.)*
"Traveler's tree" in Bangkok

Moringa pterygosperma *(MORING.)*
"Horse-radish tree" on St. Thomas

Comptonia peregrina *(MYRIC.)*
"Sweet fern" in Virginia

Eremophila sargentii *(MYOP.)*
"Emu-bush" of West Australia

Eremophila maculata
"Spotted Emu plant" in Vista, Calif.

Myristica fragrans *(MYRIST.)*
"Nutmeg tree" in Trinidad

Myoporum platycarpum
"Sugar wood", in Adelaide, So. Australia

Myoporum laetum *(MYOP.)*
flowering in Palma de Mallorca

Myoporum laetum *(New Zealand)*
"Mouse-hole tree" in California

Myrica cerifera *(MYRIC.)*
"Wax-myrtle" in New Jersey

Myrica californica
"California bayberry"

Ardisia humilis *(MYRS.)*
Brooklyn Bot. Garden, New York

Ardisia mamillata *(So. China)*
Munich Bot. Garden, by J. Bogner

Ardisia crenata 'Variegata'
in Warrimoo, N.S.W., Australia

Ardisia crispa *(crenulata)*
by Feng Chi Ho in Taiwan

Jacquinia barbasco *(armillaris arb.)*
"Bracelet-wood" at Fairchild G., Miami

Hymenandra wallichii *(India)*
Nymphenburg Bot. Garden, Munich

Myrsine africana *(MYRS.)*
"African boxwood" in California

Ardisia crenata *(MYRS.)*
"Coral berry" in Longwood G., Penna.

Agonis flexuosa *(W. Australia)*
"Peppermint tree", King's Park, Perth

Callistemon citrinus *(lanceolatus)*
"Bottlebrush" in Sydney, N. So. Wales

Callistemon phoeniceus
"Fiery bottlebrush" in W. Australia

Callistemon rigidus *(MYRT.)*
Los Angeles Arboretum, Arcadia

Callistemon viminalis
"Weeping bottlebrush" in Florida

Calothamnus chrysantheros *(MYRT.)*
"Clawflower" in Perth, W. Australia

Chamelaucium pauciflorum
"Wax flower" of Western Australia

Chamelaucium uncinatum *(MYRT.)*
"Geraldton waxflower" in San Diego

Eucalyptus deglupta
"New Guinea gum" in So. Miami

Eucalyptus citriodora
"Lemon gum" in California

Eucalyptus camaldulensis
in Old Bot. Garden, Cape Town

Eucalyptus caesia *(W. Australia)*
"Silver Princess" in Los Angeles

Eucalyptus citriodora
flowering in Queensland

Eucalyptus cladocalyx
King's Park, Perth, W. Australia

Eucalyptus cinerea
"Silver dollar" in San Marcos

Eucalyptus calophylla
"Red gum", Los Angeles Arboretum

Darwinia fascicularis
"Heath plant" in Sydney Bot. G.

Eucalyptus ficifolia *(S.W. Australia)*
"Red-flowering gum" in San Diego

Eucalyptus erythrocorys
"Red cap gum" in Vista, Calif.

Eucalyptus globulus
"Blue gum" in Monterey, California

Eucalyptus grandis *(Queensland)*
"Rose gum" in Rainbow, California

Eucalyptus gunnii *(juv. foliage)*
"Cider gum" planted in Germany

Eucalyptus macrocarpa
with floral buds, in Encinitas, Calif.

Eucalyptus polyanthemos
"Red box" in Melbourne, Victoria

Eucalyptus pulverulenta
"Money tree" in San Pasqual, Calif.

Eucalyptus x rhodantha
"Rose mallee" (Los Angeles Arboretum)

Eucalyptus maculata
"Spotted gum" in Los Angeles Arbor.

Eucalyptus sideroxylon 'Rosea'
blooming in San Marcos, Calif.

Eucalyptus sideroxylon
"Red ironbark" in Queensland

Eucalyptus torquata
"Coral gum" (Anderson Nurs., San Diego)

Eucalyptus viminalis
"Manna gum" in Vista, Calif.

Eucalyptus viminalis, *fruiting*
Adelaide Bot. Garden, So. Australia

Eucalyptus rudis
"Desert gum" painted by Stan Kelly

Feijoa sellowiana, *in flower*
"Pineapple guava" in Uruguay

Hypocalymma angustifolium
"White myrtle" of Western Australia

Kunzea baxteri *(W. Australia)*
crimson-stamened flowers

Kunzea baxteri
Quail Bot. Garden, Encinitas, Calif.

Kunzea pulchella *(W. Australia)*
"Granite kunzea", Los Angeles Arbor.

Leptospermum petersonii
"Lemon-scent tea tree" in Sydney

Leptospermum laevigatum
"Australian tea tree"

Leptospermum scoparium
"New Zealand manuka" in Auckland

Leptospermum scoparium fl. pl.
"Double-fl. tea tree", Fallbrook, Calif.

Leptospermum scop. 'Ruby Glow'
double-flowered, in California

Myrciaria cauliflora *(unripe fruit)*
"Jaboticaba" in Encinitas

Melaleuca nesophylla
"Western tea-myrtle" in San Diego

Melaleuca quinquenervia
(M. leucadendron in hort.)

Melaleuca quinquenervia
"Cajeput tree" in La Jolla, Calif.

Rhodomyrtus tomentosa
"Rose myrtle" in Palm Beach, Florida

Syzygium malaccense *(Eugenia)*
"Rose apple" in Rio de Janeiro

Melaleuca leucadendron *(true spec.)*
"Paper bark" in Queensland

Syzygium kusukusense
along Sun-Moon Lake, Taiwan

Psidium guineense
in Fairchild G., Miami, Florida

Syzygium jambos
"Malay rose-apple" in Encinitas, Calif.

Myrtus communis, *"Myrtle tree"*
Pala Indian Mission, Calif.

Metrosideros excelsus *(tomentosus)*
"Pohotukawa" in New Zealand

Luma apiculata *(Myrtus luma)*
"Temu" of Chile and Argentina

Myrtus communis
"Greek myrtle" in bloom

Myrtus communis 'Microphylla'
"Dwarf myrtle", a bridal tradition

Luma apiculata *(Myrtus luma)*
in Palmengarten, Frankfurt

Regelia velutina *(S.W. Australia)*
"Barren's regelia" near Hopetoun

Myrtus communis 'Variegata'
"Varieg. myrtle" in Brooklyn Bot. G.

Myrtus pubescens *(Argentina)*
in Frankfurt Palmengarten

Syzygium paniculatum *as pyramid*
Charlottenburg Palace, Berlin

Syzygium paniculatum *(Eugenia)*
"Brush cherry" in San Diego Zoo

Eugenia aggregata *(MYRT.)*
"Cherry of Rio Grande"

Tristania conferta 'Albomarginata'
in Warrimoo, New South Wales

Tristania conferta *(MYRT.)*
"Brisbane box" in Queensland

Tristania conf. 'Aureo-variegata'
in San Diego nursery, Calif.

Davidia involucrata *(NYSS.)*
"Dove tree" in Brooklyn Bot. Garden

Hypocalymma robustum *(MYRT.)*
"Swan River myrtle" of W. Australia

Pisonia alba *(NYCTAG.)*
"Lady-love" in Sri Lanka

Nyssa aquatica (NYSS.)
"Cotton gum" in Louisiana

Camptotheca acuminata (China)
Quail Bot. Garden, Encinitas, Calif.

Pisonia umbellifera 'Variegata'
"Birdcatcher tee", Wellington, N.Z.

Ouratea groussordyi (OCHN.)
Caracas Bot. Garden, Venezuela

Ochna atropurpurea (OCHN.)
Kew Bot. Gardens, England

Nyssa sylvatica (NYSS.)
"Black tupelo" in Maryland

Schurmansia henningsii (OCHN.)
in Wongan, New Guinea

Ochna kirkii (OCHN.)
"Micky-mouse plant" in Honolulu

Ochna serrulata
"Birdseye bush" in Natal

Ximenia americana *(OLAC.)*
"Sour plum" in El Salvador

Abeliophyllum distichum *(Korea)*
Brooklyn Bot. Garden, New York

Chionanthus virginicus
"American fringe tree" in Delaware

Chionanthus retusus
"Chinese fringe tree"

Forsythia x intermedia
"Border forsythia" in New Jersey

Fors. mandshurica 'Vermont Sun'
Brooklyn Bot. Garden, N.Y.

Forsythia ovata
"Korean forsythia"

Forsythia suspensa
"Weeping bells" of China

Forsythia viridissima 'Bronxensis'
miniature of New York Bot. Garden

Fraxinus americana
Franklin Arboretum, New Jersey

Fraxinus americana *(female)*
"White ash", with winged fruit

Fraxinus chinensis
"Chinese ash" in Bot. G. Sydney

Fraxinus excelsior
"European ash" in Rhineland

Fraxinus excelsior 'Aurea'
"Golden ash" from Holland

Fraxinus holotricha
National Arboretum, Washington

Fraxinus ornus
"Flowering ash" of Hungary

Fraxinus paxiana
"Himalaya ash", in Bot. G. Essen

Fraxinus holotricha 'Moraine'
in Los Angeles Arboretum

Fraxinus anomala
"Single-leaf ash" in Colorado

Fraxinus uhdei
"Evergreen ash"in Vista, Calif.

Fraxinus retusa
"Chinese ash" in Kwangtung

Fraxinus pennsylvanica 'Summit'
"Green ash" of Stillwater, Minnesota

Jasminum grandiflorum *(Syria)*
"Spanish jasmine" in Damascus

Jasminum polyanthum
"Pink jasmine" from Yunnan

Jasminum officinale
"Poet's jessamine" of Kashmir

Jasminum humile
in Lisbon Bot. Garden, Portugal

Jasminum humile 'Revolutum'
fragrant "Italian jasmine"

Jasminum rex *(Sri Lanka)*
"King jasmine" in Peradeniya

Jasminum nudiflorum
"Winter jasmine" in Brooklyn Bot. G.

Jasminum mesnyi *(primulinum)*
"Primrose jasmine" in California

Jasminum didymum
in Royal Bot. Garden, Sydney

Jasm. sambac 'G. Duke of Tuscany'
at Kew Bot. Gardens, England

Jasminum sambac
"Arabian jasmine" in California

Jasminum multiflorum
"Star jasmine" in Sarasota, Florida

Jasminum nitidum *(ilicifolium)*
"Angelwing jasmine" in Tahiti

Jasminum floridum
"Showy jasmine" in San Diego

Ligustrum amurense
in Bergianska Bot. G., Sweden

Ligustrum japonicum
"Japanese privet" (Los Angeles Bot. G.)

Ligustrum japonicum 'Texanum'
"Waxleaf privet" in S. Marcos, Calif.

Ligustrum jap. 'Rotundifolium'
Botanic Garden Essen, Germany

Ligustrum jap. 'Silver Star'
"Silver-star privet" (Monrovia Nurs.)

Ligustrum lucidum
in Parque Retiro, Madrid, Spain

Ligustrum ovalifolium
"California privet" in New York

Ligustrum vulgare
"Common privet" in Germany

Ligustrum ovalifolium 'Aureum'
"Golden privet" in Sydney, Austral.

Phillyrea decora *(Osmanthus)*
"Lanceleaf linden" in California

Olea europaea 'Manzanillo'
"Black olive" cv. of Spain

Oxydendrum arboreum *(ERIC.)*
"Sourwood" in Brooklyn Bot. Garden

Osmanthus heterophyllus 'Varieg.'
varieg. "False holly" in Calif.

Osmanthus armatus *(OLEAC.)*
"Chinese osmanthus"

Osmanthus americanus
"Devilwood" in Alabama

Ligustrum 'Vicaryi' *(OLEAC.)*
"Vicary privet" in England

Osmanthus fragrans
"Sweet olive" in San Diego

Osmanthus fragrans
in Kweilin, on Li River, China

Osmanthus x fortunei
in Williamsburg, Virginia

x Osmarea burkwoodii
in Hillier Arboretum, England

Osmanthus delavayi *(W. China)*
in Longwood Gardens, Pennsylvania

Syringa pinnatifolia *(W. China)*
Duesseldorf Bot. Garden, Germany

Syringa meyeri
Willow-wood Arboretum, N. Jersey

Syringa x chinensis
Planting Fields Arb., Oyster Bay, N.Y.

Syringa oblata, *"Early lilac"*
Planting fields Arboretum, L.I., N.Y.

Syringa patula
"Manchurian lilac"

Syringa microphylla 'Superba'
"Littleleaf lilac" (Brooklyn Bot. G.)

Syringa pubescens *(No. China)*
Willow-wood Arbor., Gladstone, N.J.

Syringa vulgaris 'Alba'
in Duess.-Grafenberg, Germany

Syringa vulgaris
"Lilac" blooming in Wyoming

Syringa pekinensis
near Beijing, No. China

Syringa x persica
"Persian lilac" (Brooklyn Bot. G.)

Syringa vulgaris 'Ludwig Spaeth'
Willow-wood Arboretum, New Jersey

Syringa reticulata mandschurica
"Amur lilac" in Pennsylvania

Syringa x prestoniae 'Elinor'
Canadian hybrid, Ottawa 1928

Syringa vulgaris 'Alba plena'
double-fl. lilac, in Germany

Fuchsia boliviana
Bot. Garden Darmstadt, Germany

Fuchsia arborescens *(paniculata)*
"Tree fuchsia" of Mexico

Fuchsia fulgens *(Mexico)*
at Floriade Exhib., Amsterdam

Fuchsia magellanica *(Chile)*
"Hardy fuchsia", Auckland, N. Zealand

Fuchsia 'Autumnalis' *hort.*
Furuta garden, Rainbow, Calif.

Fuchsia microphylla *(Mexico)*
at Amsterdam Floriade 1982

Fuchsia wytywskii *(So. America)*
Quail Bot. Gard., Encinitas, Calif.

Fuchsia triphylla *(Haiti)*
Auckland Univ. Bot. G., N. Zealand

Fuchsia splendens *(Guatemala)*
Cap Ferrat Bot. Garden, France

Fuchsia hybr. 'Dollar Princess'
floriferous pot plant cv.

Fuchsia x hybrida 'Golondrina'
at Castle Egeskow, Funen, Denmark

Fuchsia triphylla 'Bonstedt'
"Honeysuckle fuchsia"

Oxalis hedysaroides 'Rubra'
"Fire-fern" of Ecuador

Paeonia lutea *(PAEON.)*
"Tree peony" of Tibet

Hauya heydeana *(ONAGR.)*
in Duesseldorf Bot. Gard., Germany

Paeonia suffruticosa, *"Moutan"*
Gotland Bot. G., Visby, Sweden

Paeonia suffruticosa 'Angelet'
peach tree peony in New York

Paeonia suffruticosa 'Vesuvian'
crimson tree peony in Brooklyn B. G.

Pandanus tectorius *(PAND.)*
"Pandanus palm", Moorea, So. Pacific

Pandanus utilis
"Screw pine" in Cape Town

Pandanus leram
"Nicobar breadfruit" on Ceylon

Dendromecon rigida harfordii
"Island tree poppy" in Calif.

Piper magnificum *(PIP.)*
"Lacquered pepper tree" of Perú

Piper imperialis
Selby Bot. Gard., Sarasota, Florida

Pimelia floribunda *(PIM.)*
"Rice flower" of Western Australia

Hymenosporum flavum *(PITT.)*
"Sweetshade" in Queensland

Pittosporum viridiflorum *(PITT.)*
"Cape pittosporum", San Pasqual, Calif.

Pittosporum rhombifolium
"Queensland pittosporum" in Calif.

Pittosporum tobira *(Japan)*
"Mock-orange" on Mallorca, Spain

Pittosp. tobira 'Wheeler's Dwarf'
miniature, in Los Angeles

Pittosporum colensoi
"Black mapou" of New Zealand

Pittosp. colensoi 'Variegatum'
Botan. Garden GRUGA, Essen

Pittosp. colensoi 'Marginatum'
Auckland Bot. G., New Zealand

Pittosporum ralphii
Nymphenburg Bot. Gard., Munich

Pittosporum tenuifolium
"Kohuhu" in Wellington, N.Z.

Pittosp. tenuifolium 'Variegatum'
Essen Bot. Garden, Germany

Plat. x acerifolia, *w. seed-balls*
"London plane" in Oceanside, Calif.

Platanus occidentalis
"American sycamore" in Philadelphia

Platanus orientalis *(PLAT.)*
"Oriental plane" in Budapest, Hungary

Pittosp. eugenioides 'Variegatum'
"Tarata" in Auckland Bot. G., N.Z.

Pittosporum undulatum *(PITT.)*
"Victorian box" in Melbourne

Platanus racemosa
"Calif. sycamore" in Rancho Bernardo

Pittosp. crassifolium 'Variegatum'
Auckland Univ. Bot. G., N. Zealand

Pittosporum crassifolium
"Karo" at Del Mar Expo, Calif.

Pittosporum daphniphylloides
in Tropic World, Escondido, Calif.

Pittosporum tobira, *"Mock-orange" of Japan
as flowering tree, in Catania, Sicily*

Eucalyptus citriodora *of Queensland (MYRT.)
picturesque "Lemon gum", Sunset Ranch, Vista, Calif.*

Platanus orientalis, *Oriental planes in April
as pollarded trees along the Rhine, Duesseldorf, Germany*

Platanus x acerifolia *(x hispanica) in Summer
London planes on shore of Lake Lucerne, Switzerland*

Plumbago indica *(coccinea)*
"Scarlet leadwort" (E. Indies)

Plumbago auriculata *(capensis)*
"Cape leadwort" in San Diego

Polygala x dalmaisiana
"Sweet-pea shrub", S. Pasqual, Calif.

Cantua buxifolia *(Perú)*
"Sacred flower of the Incas"

Ceratostigma willmottianum
"Chinese plumbago" in Sydney B. G.

Leptodactylon californicum *(POLEM.)*
"Prickly phlox" in Monterey, Calif.

Polygala virgata *(POLYGAL.)*
"Milkwort" in Cape Prov. So. Africa

Homalocladium platycladum *(POLYGON.)*
"Ribbon bush" in Sydney Bot. Garden

Triplaris surinamensis *(POLYGON.)*
"Long John" in Surinam

Coccoloba rugosa *(POLYG.)*
"Ortegon" on Luquillo, Puerto Rico

Coccoloba pubescens *(grandifolia)*
"Moralin" (W. Indies to Guyana)

Eriogonum grande rubescens *(POL.)*
"Red buckwheat" in Encinitas, Calif.

Triplaris caracasana *(POLYG.)*
"Palo Maria" in Venezuela

Banksia ashbeyi *(PROT.)*
near Shark Bay, W. Australia

Banksia media *(W. Australia)*
"Southern Plains banksia"

Conospermum stoechadis *(PROT.)*
"Smoke-bush" in W. Australia

Dryandra sessilis *(PROT.)*
"Parrot bush" of S.W. Australia

Embothrium coccineum *(PROT.)*
"Chilean fire-tree" in England

Grevillea banksii
"Scarlet grevillea" of Queensland

Grevillea aquifolium
"Holly grevillea" in Melbourne

Grevillea robusta
"Silk-oak" in New Zealand

Grevillea juniperina
"Juniper grevillea" in Sydney Bot. G.

Grevillea 'Noellii'
California hybrid, in Vista

Grevillea thelemanniana
"Spider-net grevillea" in W. Austral.

Grevillea rosmarinifolia
"Rosemary grevillea" (New So. Wales)

Grevillea 'Canberra'
Tropic World, Escondido, Calif.

Lambertia formosa
"Honey flower" or "Mountain devil"

Banksia speciosa *(W. Australia)*
"Showy banksia", King's Park, Perth

Banksia grandis, *sawtooth leaves*
"Bull banksia" near Perth, W. Austr.

Leucadendron argenteum *(So. Afr.)*
"Silver tree" in Cape Town

Leucadendron daphnoides
from Cape Prov., So. Africa

Leucadendron discolor *(Cape Prov.)*
"Sunshine bush" at Hout Bay

Leucadendron globosum *(So. Afr.)*
"Gold-tips" in Santa Cruz, Calif.

Hakea victoriae *(W. Australia)*
"Royal hakea", King's Park, Perth

Lomatia tinctoria *(Tasmania)*
in Duesseldorf Bot. G., Germany

Leucospermum reflexum
"Rocket pincushion" in Nelson, N.Z.

Mimetes cucullata *(S.W. Cape)*
in Kirstenbosch Bot. Garden

Lomatia myricoides*(Victoria)*
"River lomatia" in Melbourne

Embothrium wickhamii *(Oreocallis)*
"Satin oak" in Noumea, N. Caledonia

Leucospermum nutans
"Nodding pincushion" in Cape Town

Protea grandiceps *(So. Africa)*
"Peach protea" in Kirstenbosch B.G.

Macadamia integrifolia
flowering in Kona, Hawaii

Protea longiflora
Duesseldorf Bot. Garden, Germany

Protea magnifica *(speciosa)*
"Brown-beard protea" in Johannesburg

Serruria florida *(So. Africa)*
"Blushing bride" in Pretoria Bot. G.

Protea eximia (latifolia)
"Ray protea" in Cape Town

Protea barbigera (So. Africa)
"Queen protea" in Cape Prov.

Protea cynaroides (PROT.)
"King protea" in San Diego

Protea neriifolia
"Pink mink" in Encinitas, Calif.

Protea repens (mellifera)
"Sugar-bush", in Cape Prov., S. Afr.

Telopea speciosissima (PROT.)
"Waratah" in Queensland

Stenocarpus sinuatus (PROT.)
"Wheel of fire" in Bot. G. Los Angeles

Xanthorhiza simplicissima (RAN.)
"Shrub yellow-root" in Virginia

Pomaderris elliptica (RHAMN.)
"Kumeraho" (Tasmania)

Ceanothus arboreus
Strybing Arboretum, San Francisco

Ceanothus coeruleus *(Mexico)*
in Tucson, Arizona

Ceanothus crassifolius
Royal Bot. Gardens Kew, England

Ceanothus integerrimus *(Calif.)*
"Deer bush" in Sequoia N. Park

Ceanothus griseus *(Calif.)*
"Wild lilac" in Sierra Nevada

Ceanothus fendleri
"Redroot" in South Dakota

Ceanothus thyrsiflorus
"Blue blossom" in Oregon

Ceanothus cyaneus 'Sierra Blue'
"California lilac" in Encinitas

Ceanothus papillosus roweanus
"Wart-leaf ceanothus" in Santa Barbara

Punica granatum *(PUN.)*
"Pomegranate" on Algarve, Portugal

Punica granatum 'Legrellei'
"Harlequin" of flowers

Punica granatum 'Flore pleno'
double flowers, Los Angeles Arbor.

Punica granatum 'Nana'
"Dwarf pomegranate" in California

Punica granatum 'Variegata'
Parque Eduardo, Lisbon, Portugal

Punica granatum 'Wonderful'
"Fruiting pomegranate" in California

Ceanothus americanus *(RHAMN.)*
"New Jersey tea" in New York

Ceanothus dentatus
Royal Bot. Gardens Kew, England

Ceanothus x delilianus
in Santa Barbara, California

Ceanothus thyrsiflorus prostratus
at Chelsea Flower Show, London

Hovenia dulcis *near Philadelphia*
"Japanese raisin tree"

Paliurus spina-christii
"Jerusalem-thorn" in Italy

Rhamnus imeretinus
"Caucasus buckthorn"

Rhamnus alaternus 'Arg.-variegata'
"Variegated buckthorn" in Calif.

Rhamnus alpinus fallax
"Alpine buckthorn"

Rhamnus catharicus
"Spiny buckthorn" in Germany

Rhamnus frangula, "Alder buckthorn"
in Nymphenburg Bot. G., Munich

Rhamnus frangula 'Columnaris'
"Tall-hedge buckthorn" of Ohio

Phylica pubescens *(RHAMN.)*
"Featherhead" on Cape of Good Hope

Sageretia minutiflora *(RHAMN.)*
in Colonial Williamsburg, Virginia

Zizyphus mauritiana *(RHAMN.)*
"Indian jujube" in So. Florida

Amelanchier canadensis *(ROS.)*
"Downy service-berry" in Québec

Amelanchier laevis
"Allegany service-berry" in N. Jersey

Amelanchier asiatica
"Sugar plum" of Japan

Amelanchier spicata
"June-berry" in So. Dakota

Aronia arbutifolia *(ROS.)*
in Arnold Arboretum, Mass.

Aronia arbutifolia
"Choke-berry", eaten by Indians

Chaenomeles japonica *(Cydonia)*
"Jap. dwarf quince" in N. Jersey

Prunus ilicifolia *(Mexico)*
"Holly-leaf cherry" in Baja Calif.

Chaen. x superba 'Boule de Feu'
superb French hybrid 1916

Chaenomeles speciosa
"Flowering quince" in California

Chaen. speciosa 'Falconnet Charlet'
in New York Botanical Garden

Coton. glaucophyllus 'Albo-varieg.'
in Warrimoo, N. So. Wales, Australia

Cotoneaster adpressus praecox
"Creeping cotoneaster" in England

Cotoneaster conspicuus
"Wintergreen cotoneaster" in Virginia

Coton. racemiflorus royleanus
in Edinburgh Bot. Garden, Scotland

Serissa foetida *(RUB.)*
at German Hort. Expo Duesseldorf

Cotoneaster salicifolius
"Willow-leaf cotoneaster" in bloom

Cotoneaster salicifolius
with fruit, in Western China

Cotoneaster henryanus *(ROS.)*
with long-lasting fruit, in Calif.

Cotoneaster divaricatus
"Spreading cotoneaster" in Vancouver

Coton. x watereri 'Cornubia'
Univ. Bot. Garden, W. Los Angeles

Cotoneaster lacteus
"Red cluster-berry" in England

Cotoneaster bullatus
fruiting in Munich Bot. Garden

Cotoneaster glaucophyllus
"Bright-bead cotoneaster" (China)

Cotoneaster horizontalis *(China)*
"Rock cotoneaster" in New Jersey

Cotoneaster x watereri 'Pendulus'
with pendant branches, in Germany

Cotoneaster franchetii
in Palma de Mallorca, Spain

Cowania mexicana
"Cliff-rose" in Zion Nat. Park, Utah

Crataegus aestivalis
"May haw" in Tennessee

Crataegus flava
"Summer-haw" (Virginia to Florida)

Crataegus viridis
"Green hawthorn" in Missouri

Crataegus pedicellata
(New England to Illinois)

Crat. monogyna 'Rosea pendula'
in Edinburgh, Scotland

Crataegus crus-galli
"Cockspur thorn" in flower

Crataegus crus-galli
American hawthorn w. 8 cm thorns

Crataegus crus-galli
with edible fruit, in Ontario

Crataegus monogyna
"Single-seed hawthorn"

Crataegus monogyna
spring-flowering in France

Crataegus x prunifolia
in Munich Bot. Garden, Germany

Crataegus irrasa (in Munich)
is prob. Rosa sweginzowii

Crataegus laevigata 'Paulii'
"Rotdorn" (double-fl.) in Germany

Crataegus laevigata *(oxyacantha)*
"English hawthorn" or "Weiss-dorn"

Cydonia oblonga *(Turkey)*
flowering in Bermuda Bot. G.

Eriobotrya deflexa
"Bronze loquat" in San Diego

Eriobotrya japonica
"Loquat" flowering in Florida

Exochorda giraldii *(China)*
"Pearl-bush" in Beijing

Exochorda korolkowii
"Turkestan pearlbush" in England

Exochorda x macrantha 'The Bride'
low form, in Northern California

Exochorda racemosa *(grandiflora)*
in Princeton Nurs., New Jersey

Fragaria vesca
"European strawberry" in Munich

Holodiscus discolor
"Cream-bush"in Brit. Columbia

Kerria japonica *(China, Japan)*
"Japanese rose" in Boskoop, Holland

Kerria japonica 'Pleniflora'
"Double-fl. kerria" in New York

Rubus rosifolius 'Coronarius'
"Mauritius raspberry" in Brooklyn

Malus coronaria
"American crab-apple" in N. York

Heteromeles arbutifolia
"Christmas berry" in Escondido

Heteromeles arbutifolia
"Toyon" in fl., San Marcos, Calif.

Malus floribunda
"Japan. crab-apple", Brooklyn Bot. G.

Malus x atrosanguinea
"Carmine crab-apple" in May

Malus x arnoldiana
Arnold Arboretum, Mass.

Malus baccata 'Jackii'
Strybing Arboretum, San Francisco

Mespilus germanica
"Medlar" flowering in England

Malus baccata *in bloom*
"Siberian crab-apple"

Malus floribunda 'Scheideckeri'
in Strybing Arbor., San Francisco

Malus floribunda 'Scheideckeri'
in autumn color, with fruit

Malus pumila *(domestica)*
apple in fl., Bornholm, Denmark

Malus ioensis
"Prairie crab-apple" in Nebraska

Malus halliana *(Japan, China)*
Bot. Gard. Duesseldorf, Germany

Malus sieboldii *(Japan)*
"Toringo crab" in Kyushu

Malus x purpurea *('Lemoinei')*
May-blooming in Péronne, France

Malus sargentii *(Japan)*
in Princeton, New Jersey

Malus x purpurea 'Eleyi'
"Blood-apple" on Long Isl., N.Y.

Malus spectabilis
"Chinese flowering apple" in Cologne

Malus spectabilis 'Riversii'
large double flowers, in England

Malus 'Van Eseltine'
Park Seeds, Greenville, S. Carolina

Neillia sinensis *(C. China)*
Arnold Arbor., Jamaica Plain, Mass.

Neillia longiracemosa
at Hillier Arboretum, England

Neviusia alabamensis
"Snow-wreath" in Willowwood Arb., N.J.

Photinia x fraseri 'Robusta'
"Redleaf photinia" in Sydney

Photinia glabra
"Japanese photinia" in Kyushu

Photinia serrulata
"Chinese photinia" in California

Photinia villosa
"Oriental photinia" in Korea

Lyonothamnus floribundus *(asplen.)*
"Catalina ironwood" in Chula Vista

Physocarpus opulifolius
"Nine-bark" in Virginia

Potentilla davurica 'Beesii'
English cv. of seed from Tibet

Potentilla fruticosa
"Shrubby cinquefoil" in California

Potentilla fruticosa 'Tangerine'
No. Ireland cv. of Chinese seed

Prunus cerasifera 'Atropurpurea'
"Pissard plum" in Brooklyn Bot. G.

Prunus cerasifera 'Thundercloud'
"Purple-leaf plum", in Oregon

Prunus cerasifera 'Atropurpurea'
"Purple cherry plum" in New Jersey

Prunus armeniaca *(Turkestan)*
"Apricot" flowering in California

Prunus caroliniana
"Carolina cherry laurel"

Prunus cerasifera 'Vesuvius'
South Coast Bot. Garden, Los Angeles

Prunus cerasus 'Montmorency'
"Sour cherry" in bloom, N. Jersey

Prunus domestica *(So. Europe)*
"Italian plum" in N. Jersey Spring

Prunus dulcis *(amygdalis)*
"Almond" in Mycaene, Greece

Prunus fruticosa
"European dwarf cherry"

Prunus glandulosa *(Japan)*
"Dwarf flowering almond"

Prunus glandulosa 'Sinensis'
"Double almond" in Brooklyn Bot. G.

Prunus laurocerasus
"English laurel" in California

Prunus laurocerasus 'Otto Luyken'
low-growth, in the Rhineland

Prunus laurocerasus 'Schipkaensis'
hardier form of "Cherry laurel"

Prunus lyonii *(California)*
"Catalina cherry" in Oceanside

Prunus maritima
"Beach plum" in Delaware

Prunus mahaleb
"St. Lucie cherry" in Italy

Prunus persica 'Rubra-plena'
"Double-fl. peach" in Pretoria, S. Afr.

Prunus persica, "Flow. peach"
for Chinese New Year, Hong Kong

Prunus serrulata (Japan)
"Flowering cherry" in Washington

Prunus persica 'Alboplena', "Double-flowered white peach"
October-blooming in Pretoria, Transvaal, S. Africa

Prunus x yedoensis, "Yoshino cherry" of Japan
in April bloom at National Arboretum, Washington

Prunus persica, ornamental peach
as "Good-luck plant" in Hong Kong

Prunus serrula (W. China)
with glossy red bark, in England

Prunus serrulata 'Kwansan'
"Japanese flowering cherry" in N.J.

Prunus padus
"European bird-cherry"

Prunus serotina
"Wild black cherry" in Vermont

Prunus serrulata 'Amanogawa'
columnar cherry, Arnold Arb., Mass.

Prunus subhirtella
"Higan cherry" in Brooklyn Bot. G.

Prunus triloba *(plena)*
"Flowering almond"

Prunus mume, *"Japan apricot"*
in Sankei En, Yokohama

Prunus persica 'Elberta'
"Elberta peach" in bloom

Prunus serrulata 'Shidare-Sakura'
"Oriental cherry" in Boskoop

Prunus triloba 'Multiplex'
"Double-flowering almond"

Pyrus calleryana 'Bradford'
autumn color in Virginia

Pyrus calleryana 'Bradford'
"Bradford pear", in California

Pyrus calleryana 'Bradford'
April flower in Rutherford, N.J.

Pyrus kawakami, *September fl.*
Escondido shopping center, Calif.

Pyrus kawakami, *in October*
Lawrence Welk Village, California

Pyrus kawakami, *with fruit*
"Evergreen pear" in Taiwan

Pyrus salicifolia 'Pendula'
"Weeping willow-leaf pear"

Pyrus communis 'Bartlett'
"Bartlett pear" flower in Oregon

Pyrus x Lecontei 'Kieffer'
"Kieffer pear" fl. in N. Jersey

Pyracantha coccinea 'Lalandei'
"Laland firethorn" in N. Jersey

Pyracantha coccinea
"Scarlet firethorn" in Germany

Pyracantha fortuneana 'Cherri-Berri'
Hines Nurs., Santa Ana, Calif.

Pyracantha fortuneana 'Graberi'
"Chinese firethorn" in San Diego

Pyracantha koidzumii 'Santa Cruz'
prostrate hyb. in California

Pyracantha koidzumii 'Victory'
"Red firethorn" in Los Angeles

Raphiolepis indica
"Indian hawthorn" in La Jolla, Calif.

Raphiol. x delacourii 'Enchantment'
P. Harper garden, Seaford, Virginia

Raphiolepis umbellata
"Yeddo hawthorn" in California

Rhodotypos scandens
"Jetbead" of Japan

Raphiolepis ind. 'Enchantress'
Monrovia Nurs., Azusa, Calif.

Rosa banksiae
"Lady Banks rose" in Dallas, Texas

Rosa canina, *"Dog rose"*
in Jura Mts., Weissenburg, Bavaria

Rosa rugosa plena
near Innsbruck, Austrian Alps

Rosa centifolia, *"Moss-rose"*
in Jena, Thuringia, Germany

Rosa damascena, *"Damask rose"*
source of attar of roses

Rosa foetida, *"Fox rose"*
naturalized Austria to Spain

Rosa moschata nepalensis
"Musk rose", Tenbury Wells, England

Rosa chinensis 'Judy Fischer'
miniature in Somerset, N. Jersey

Rosa chinensis 'Minima'
"Pygmy rose" in Switzerland

Rosa chinensis 'Mutabilis'
Bermuda Bot. Garden, Hamilton

Rosa chinensis 'Viridiflora'
"Green rose" in Somerset Arb., N.J.

Rosa rubrifolia, *(glauca)*
"Redleaf rose" in E. France

Rosa chinensis 'Rise & Shine'
miniature, Somerset Arb., N.J.

Rosa chinensis 'Nozomi'
ground miniature, in Virginia

Rosa multiflora *(polyantha)*
"Baby rose", Hort. Expo. Munich

Rosa rubiginosa 'Magnifica'
"Hedge rose" in Germany

Rosa x floribunda 'Moulin Rouge'
in Visby Bot. G., Gotland, Sweden

Rosa x floribunda 'Fashion'
Dortmund Bot. Garden, Germany

Rosa x floribunda 'Nordlicht'
in Romberg Park, Dortmund

Rosa x floribunda 'Rumba'
Poulsen bicolor, Denmark

Rosa x floribunda 'Shocking Blue'
tea-rose-like, in Holland

Rosa x floribunda 'Show Biz'
in Somerset Arboretum, New Jersey

Rosa x floribunda 'Vogue'
Jackson & Perkins Nurs., Calif.

Rosa x mult. 'Margo Koster Supreme'
Polyantha rose of Boskoop

Rosa x multiflora 'Cecil Brunner'
"Sweetheart rose" in Bermuda

Rosa x grandifl. 'Queen Elizabeth'
Visby Bot. Gard. Gotland, Sweden

Rosa hugonis *(C. China)*
"Father Hugo rose" in Boston

Rosa nitida
"Shining rose" in Connecticut

Rosa palustris
"Swamp rose" in Arkansas

Rosa xanthina 'Canarybird'
Chelsea Flower Show, London

Rosa pimpinellifolia *(spinosissima)*
"Scotch rose", in Edinburgh

Rosa sweginzowii, *with fruit*
Nymphenburg Bot. G., Munich

Rosa villosa, *"Apple rose"*
in Essen Bot. Garden, Germany

Rosa x odorata 'Yankee Doodle'
"Hybrid tea" at Somerset Arb., N.J.

Rosa x odorata 'Double Delight'
everbl. bicolor H.T., S. Marcos, Calif.

Rosa x odorata 'Joseph's Coat'
bicolor H.T. in San Diego

Rosa x odorata 'Chicago Peace'
bicolor H.T. of Wheaton, Illinois

Rosa x odorata 'Fragrant Cloud'
Somerset Rose Garden, N. Jersey

Rosa x odorata 'Red American Beauty'
Longwood Gardens, Pennsylvania

Rosa x odorata 'Madras'
Hybrid Tea rose in Somerset Arb.

Rosa x odorata 'Revue'
large English H.T. in Holland

Rosa x odorata 'Oregold' *(H.T.)*
Wayside Gardens, So. Carolina

Rosa x odorata 'La France' *(H.T.)*
"Remontant rose", Somerset Arbor., N.J.

Rubus odoratus *(Central U.S.)*
"Flowering raspberry" in Michigan

Rubus parviflorus
"Thimbleberry" in Alaska

Rubus ulmifolius 'Bellidiflorus'
"Double-flowered blackberry"

Sorbaria arborea
"False spiraea" of China

Sorbaria aitchisonii *(Kashmir)*
Royal Bot. Gardens, Kew, England

Sorbus mougeotii *in Switzerland*
"Alpine mountain ash"

Sorbus americana *w. fruit*
in Vancouver, Brit. Columbia

Sorbus americana *in flower*
"American mountain ash"

Sorbus sambucifolia *(No. Japan)*
"Elder mountain ash" in Boston, Mass.

Sorbus intermedia, *in Stockholm*
"Swedish white beam"

Sorbus aucuparia, *flowers*
in Christiansund, Norway

Sorbus aucuparia *with fruit*
"European mountain ash"

Sorbus aria *(Europe, Asia Minor)*
"Chess apple" in Germany

Sorbus alnifolia
"Korean mountain ash" in England

Spiraea thunbergii *in April*
"Bridal-wreath" in New Jersey

Spiraea x brachybotrys
Nymphenburg Bot. Garden, Munich

Spiraea japonica 'Alpina'
"Daphne spiraea" in California

Spiraea x bumalda 'Lime Mound'
Los Angeles Flower Show

Spiraea tomentosa
"Steeplebush" in Montreal

Spiraea x revirescens
Botanic Garden Munich, Germany

Spiraea nipponica 'Snow Mound'
"Tosa spiraea" (Mts. of Japan)

Spiraea bullata *(japonica 'Bullata')*
"Japanese dwarf spirea" in Kyoto garden

Spiraea x bumalda 'Anthony Waterer'
"Dwarf rose bridal wreath" in Los Angeles Bot. Garden

Spiraea x concinna
Nymphenburg Bot. Gard., Munich

Spiraea prunifolia
"Shoe-button spiraea" in Oregon

Spiraea x arguta
"Foam of May" in England

Spiraea media *(E. Europe)*
April blooms, in Vienna, Austria

Spiraea menziesii
"American spiraea" in Oregon

Spiraea salicifolia
"Queen of the meadow" in England

Spiraea latifolia
"Meadowsweet" in Ontario

Spiraea x billiardii
in Saalfeld, Thuringia, Germany

Spiraea x vanhouttei
"Bridal wreath" in New Jersey

Stephanandra incisa *(flexuosa)*
in Osaka Bot. Garden, Japan

Stephanandra incisa 'Crispa'
"Lace leaf" in Franklin Lakes, N.J.

Stephanandra tanakae *(Japan)*
"Kana Utsugi" of Honshu Mts.

Bouvardia ternifolia 'Rosea'
"Trompetilla" at Roehrs, N.J.

Bouvardia ternifolia
in Jardin Botanico Mexico City

Bouvardia longiflora
"Sweet bouvardia" of Mexico

Adina rubella *(So. China)*
in New York Botanical Garden

Morinda parvifolia
"Indian mulberry" in Vietnam

Luculia grandifolia
with fragrant flowers, in Bengal

Burchella bubalina
"Wild pomegranate" (So. Africa)

Hamelia patens
"Fire bush" in Hong Kong

Genipa americana
"Marmalade box" in Venezuela

Carphalea kirondron *(RUB.)*
"Rubia" in Manila, Philippines

Coffea arabica *in bloom (RUB.)*
"Arab. coffee" in Luanda, Angola

Mitriostigma axillare *(RUB.)*
at Logee's, Danielson, Conn.

Alberta magna *of Natal (ROS.)*
in Kirstenbosch Botanical Garden, near Cape Town

Gardenia nitida *of Tropical West Africa (RUB.)*
intensely fragrant flowers, near Lagos, Nigeria

Stranvaesia davidiana *(RUB.)*
"Chinese stranvaesia" in California

Coprosma x kirkii *(New Zealand)*
dwarf shrub, in Fallbrook, Calif.

Coprosma repens 'Marginata' *(RUB.)*
"Mirror plant" in Wellington, N.Z.

Gardenia jasminoides 'Veitchii'
"Everbloom. gardenia" of florists

Gardenia taitensis
"Symbol flower" on Moorea, Polynesia

Gardenia jasminoides 'Prostrata'
"Miniature gardenia" in N. Zealand

Gardenia thunbergia *(Natal)*
Kirstenbosch Bot. G. near Cape Town

Gardenia jasminoides 'August Beauty'
at Monrovia Nurs., Azusa, Calif.

Ixora borbonica *(Enterospermum)*
Jardin Botanique 'Les Cèdres', France

Mussaenda erythrophylla
"Ashanti blood" in Uganda

Mussaenda frondosa *(E. Indies)*
Royal Bot. Gard., Sydney, Australia

Mussaenda erythroph. 'Doña Luz'
near Lake Toba, Sumatra

Ixora coccinea *(E. Indies)*
"Flame of the woods" in Florida

Ixora chinensis 'Lutea'
"Chinese ixora" in Colón, Panama

Ixora chinensis *(So. China)*
on St. Thomas, Virgin Islands

Ixora odorata *(Madagascar)*
in Bot. Garden Rio de Janeiro

Ixora coccinea 'Compacta'
at World Trade Center Singapore

Ixora finlaysoniana
at Hindu temple, Madras, India

Ixora macrothyrsa *(duffii)*
"King ixora" in Acapulco, Mexico

Ixora undulata *(Bengal)*
Royal Bot. Gardens Kew, England

Ixora javanica 'Lutea'
Port Moresby Bot. G., New Guinea

Pavetta opaca *(So. Africa)*
"Christmas bush" in Cape Town

Pavetta revoluta
Kew Botanic Gardens, England

Pinckneya pubens
"Fever tree" in Georgia

Posoqueria longiflora
"Colombian jasmine" in Cali

Posoqueria fragrantissima
"Brazil tree jasmine" (by Linden)

Portlandia grandiflora
"Glorias floridas de Cuba"

Psychotria rubra
"Wild coffee" in Taiwan

Randia macrantha
in Singapore Botanic Garden

Rothmannia capensis *(Gardenia)*
"Scented cups" in Durban, Natal

Rondeletia odorata *(W. Indies)*
Cologne Bot. Garden, Germany

Pentagonia macrophylla rubra
Hirose Gardens, Hilo, Hawaii

Warscewiczia cocc. 'David Auyong'
in Port of Spain, Trinidad

Aegle marmelos *(India) (RUT.)*
"Bael fruit" at Foster G., Honolulu

Tricalysia dubia *(RUB.)*
"Mountain coffee" in Taiwan

Warscewiczia coccinea *(RUB.)*
in Papeari Bot. Garden, Tahiti

Boronia heterophylla
"Red boronia" in Perth, W.A.

Boronia megastigma *(RUT.)*
"Scented boronia" in W. Australia

Calodendron capense *(RUT.)*
"Cape chestnut" in Los Angeles Arb.

Choisya ternata
"Mexican orange" in California

Choisya mollis
"White sapote" in Arizona

Casimiroa edulis, *fl. and fruit*
"White sapote" in Bermuda Bot. G.

Adenandra uniflora *(Diosma)*
"China flower" in San Francisco

Eriostemon myoporoides
"Longleaf waxflower" in Melbourne

Coleonema pulchrum *(Diosma)*
"Pink breath of Heaven" in Calif.

Correa alba, *"White correa"*
Royal Botanic Garden, Sydney

Correa pulchella
in Adelaide, So. Australia

Correa x harrisii
"Australian fuchsia" in Oregon

Citrus limon 'Meyer' *(RUT.)*
"Meyer lemon" in Vista, Calif.

Poncirus trifoliata *(RUT.)*
flowering in New York City

Poncirus trifoliata
with fruit, in the Rhineland

Geijera parviflora *(RUT.)*
"Wilga" flowering in Los Angeles

Geijera parviflora
"Austral. willow" setting fruit

Physocarpus opulifolius *(ROS.)*
"Nine-bark" in fruit, Tennessee

Ptelea trifoliata *(RUT.)*
"Hop tree" (Ontario to Texas)

Correa reflexa *(speciosa)* *(RUT.)*
"Native Austral. fuchsia" in Calif.

Ravenia spectabilis *(RUT.)*
"Tortugo" in Havana, Cuba

Orixa japonica *(Japan)*
"Kokusagi" in Honshu Mts.

Evodia henryi *(C. China)*
in Somerset Arbor., New Jersey

Evodia hupehensis *(C. China)*
"Bee-bee tree" in Kent, England

Severinia buxifolia *(Taiwan)*
"Box-thorn" in Redland, Florida

Murraya sumatrana
with edible fruit, in Taiwan

Murraya paniculata
"Orange-jessamine" on Tonga

Skimmia japonica, *female plant*
Rutgers Farm, New Brunswick, N.J.

Skimmia japonica 'Teufel's Dwarf'
in Portland, Oregon

Skimmia reevesiana
self-fertile, in Los Angeles

Phellodendron chinense *(RUT.)*
"Chinese cork-tree" in Philadelphia

Phellodendron lavallei
"Japan cork tree", Somerset Arb., N.J.

Phellodendron amurense
"Amur cork" in New York Bot. G.

Zanthoxylum americanum *(RUT.)*
"Prickly ash" in Nebraska

Meliosma rhoifolia *(Taiwan)*
"Varnishtree-leaved meliosma"

Meliosma veitchiorum *(SAB.)*
Royal Bot. Gard. Kew, England

Populus alba, *"White poplar"*
Arnold Arboretum, near Boston, Mass.

Populus balsamifera 'Aurora'
"Varieg. balsam poplar" in Cornwall

Populus fremontii *(SALIC.)*
"Western cottonwood" in Calif.

Populus x canadensis 'Regenerata'
whisk-shaped, in E. France

Populus tremula, *"Europ. aspen"*
in Bot. Garden Berlin-Dahlem

Populus tremuloides
"Quaking aspen" in Kanab, Utah

Populus tremuloides, *autumn color*
Zion National Park, Utah

Populus x canadensis
"Carolina poplar" in New York

Populus x canadensis
(deltoides x nigra) in Oregon

Populus nigra, *close-up*
"Black poplar" in Holland

Populus nigra 'Italica' *(tree)*
"Lombardy poplar" in France

Populus nigra 'Italica'
autumn color in Australia

Salix babylonica, *with fruitlets*
Brooklyn Bot. Garden, New York

Salix babylonica
"Weeping willow" in Singapore

Salix babylonica, *young tree*
juvenile stage, in Escondido, Calif.

Salix alba 'Tristis' *(close-up)*
"Yellow weeping willow" in France

Salix alba 'Tristis'
Nordpark, Duesseldorf on Rhine

Salix caprea 'Pendula'
"French pussy-willow" w. catkins

Salix daphnoides
"Violet willow" in England

Salix x sepulcralis *(chrysocoma)*
"Golden weeping willow" in Holland

Salix caprea 'Pendula'
grafted standard, in Germany

Salix discolor, *"Pussy-willow"*
Norfolk Bot. Garden, Virginia

Salix gracilistyla
"Rose-gold pussy willow"

Salix hastata, *in Austria*
"Halberd-leaved willow"

Salix lanata, *"Woolly willow"*
Vatnahalsen near Flam, Norway

Salix chilensis *(humboldtiana)*
Valle del Cauca, Colombia

Salix retusa
"Dwarf willow" in Austrian Alps

Salix matsudana 'Tortuosa'
branchlets w. twisted leaves

Salix matsudana 'Tortuosa'
"Dragon-claw willow" of Korea

Salix repens rosmarinifolia
"Creeping willow" in Darmstadt Bot G.

Koelreuteria elegans *(SAP.)*
with seed capsules, in Miami

Koelreuteria elegans
"Shrimptree" in San Diego

Koelreuteria bipinnata
"Chinese flame tree" in Calif.

Santalum ellipticum *(SANT.)*
"Hawaiian sandalwood" on Maui

Koelreuteria paniculata
forming seed pods, in Vista, Calif.

Koelreuteria paniculata
"Golden rain-tree", in New York

Cupaniopsis anacardioides *(SAP.)*
"Carrotwood" in Los Angeles Arb.

Dodonaea viscosa *(SAPIND.)*
"Hopseed bush" in Escondido

Dodonaea viscosa 'Purpurea'
"Purple hop-bush" in Calif.

Litchi chinensis *(SAPIND.)*
"Lychee-nut" in Quail Bot. G., Calif.

Harpullia arborea *(SAPIND.)*
"Puas" at Fairchild Bot. G., Miami

Mimusops commersonii *(SAPOT.)*
"Spanish cherry" in Madagascar

Exbucklandia populnea *(HAM.)*
in Penang Bot. Garden, Malaya

Sapindus drummondii
"Soap-berry" in Arizona

Sapindus mukorossii *(SAPIND.)*
"Soap-nut" in Taichung, Taiwan

Ungnadia speciosa *(SAPIND.)*
"Texan buckeye" in Sonora

Chrysophyllum oliviforme
''Satin-leaf fruit'' in So. Florida

Chrysophyllum cainito *(SAPOT.)*
"Star-apple" in Costa Rica

Pouteria campechiana *(SAPOT.)*
"Egg-fruit" on Grand Cayman Is.

Carpenteria californica *(SAX.)*
"Tree anemone" in Fresno, Calif.

Xanthoceras sorbifolium *(SAP.)*
"Chinese buckeye" in N. Jersey

Bauera rubioides *(SAX.)*
"Wiry bauera" in Melbourne

Deutzia gracilis *(SAX.)*
"Slender deutzia" of Japan

Deutzia x elegant. 'Rosalind'
June-flowering in Ireland

Deutzia x magnif. 'Staphyleoides'
Lemoine cultivar in France

Deutzia scabra *(Japan)*
"Mayflower bush" in Germany

Deutzia x rosea
in Baltimore, Maryland

Deutzia scabra 'Pride of Rochester'
in Arnold Arboretum, near Boston

Deutzia scabra 'Candidissima'
Quail Bot. G., Encinitas, Calif.

Deutzia scabra 'Plena'
"Maruba Utsugi" in Kyushu

Dichroa febrifuga *(Himalayas)*
Royal Bot. Gard. Kew, England

Escallonia x exoniensis 'Frades'
"Pink princess" in California

Escallonia bifida
"White escallonia" in Argentina

Escallonia rubra *(Chile)*
"Red escallonia" in England

Escallonia laevis *(Brazil)*
South Coast Bot. G., Los Angeles

Escallonia x langleyensis
"Appleblossum escall." in Ireland

Hydr. paniculata 'Grandiflora'
"Peegee hydrangea" in California

Hydrangea macrophylla 'Merveille'
Easter bloom, at Roehrs, N. Jersey

Hydrangea heteromalla
Nymphenburg Bot. Garden, Munich

Hydrangea macrophylla 'Mariesii'
M.-Gladbach Bot. G., Rhineland

Hydrangea macroph. 'Tricolor'
at Logee's, Danielson, Conn.

Hydrangea macrophylla 'Otaksa'
historic "Hortensia" in Japan

Hydrangea macrophylla serrata
"Tea-of-heaven" in Korea

Hydrangea aspera *(Himalaya)*
"Lace-caps" in Boskoop, Holland

Hydrangea paniculata *(Japan)*
"Panicle hydrangea" in Germany

Hydrangea involucrata 'Hortensis'
double-flowered, in England

Hydrangea quercifolia
"Oakleaf hydrangea" in Georgia

Hydrangea arborescens
"Hills of snow" in New York

Schizophragma hydrangeoides
"Jap. hydrangea vine" in Kyushu

Itea ilicifolia *(W. China)*
"Hollyleaf sweetspire" in England

Itea virginica
"Virginia willow" in Delaware

Philadelphus coronarius
"Sweet mock-orange" in N. Jersey

Philadelphus inodorus
El Greco garden, Toledo, Spain

Philad. x lemoinei 'Belle Etoile'
Lemoine Nurs., Nancy, France

Philadelphus x virginalis
"Virginal mock-orange" in France

Philad. lewisii californicus
"Wild mock-orange" in Encinitas

Ribes alpinum *(Europe)*
"Mountain currant" in Norway

Ribes aureum *(Western U.S.)*
"Golden currant" in San Francisco

Ribes odoratum
"Buffalo currant" in So. Dakota

Ribes glaciale *(Himalayas)*
Darmstadt Bot. G., Germany

Ribes petraeum *(Europe)*
"Rock currant" in Swiss Alps

Ribes speciosum *(California)*
"Fuchsia -fl. gooseberry" at Kew G.

Ribes sanguineum
"Winter currant" in B. Columbia

Bowkeria gerrardiana *(Natal)*
Strybing Arbor., San Francisco

Galvezia juncea *(Mexico)*
near Cabo San Lucas, Baja Calif.

Galvezia speciosa *(SCROPH.)*
"Bush snapdragon" in San Diego

Hebe ochracea *(New Zealand)*
(Veronica armstrongii) in England

Hebe pimeloides 'Glaucocoerulea'
in Hillier Arboretum, England

Hebe decumbens *(SCROPH.)*
"Ground hebe" in Fairfield, Conn.

Hebe diosmaefolia *(Auckland, N.Z.)*
at New York Flower Show

Hebe menziesii *(New Zealand)*
in Strybing Arbor. San Francisco

Isopogon anemonifolius *(PROT.)*
"Cone-flower" (enlarged) in Australia

Calceolaria pavoni
in Rio Urubamba Valley, Perú

Lamourouxia rhinanthifolia
on Monte Alban, Oaxaca, Mexico

Paulownia tomentosa *(China)*
"Empress tree", Longwood G., Pa.

Mimulus aurantiacus *(Diplacus)*
"Sticky monkey fl." in Oregon

Mimulus longiflorus
near Santa Barbara, So. California

Russelia equisetiformis
"Fountain pl." in the Seychelles

Hebe buxifolia 'Variegata'
"Varieg. boxleaf" in Holland

Hebe buxifolia *(N. Zealand)*
"Boxleaf veronica" in California

Hebe speciosa
"Napuka" on No. Island, N.Z.

Hebe macrantha *(SCROPH.)*
on mountains of So. Island, N.Z.

Sutera microphylla *(SCROPH.)*
So. Afr. "Wild phlox" in Munich B.G.

Leucophyllum frutescens *(SCROPH.)*
"Texas ranger" along Rio Grande

Hebe elliptica 'Variegata'
Chelsea Physics Garden, London

Isoplexis sceptrum *(SCROPH.)*
"Yellow foxglove" of Madeira

Hebe salicifolia *(N. Zealand)*
"Willowleaf hebe" on So. Island

Quassia amara *(SIMAR.)*
"Bitter-wood" of Surinam

Ailanthus altissima *(SIMAR.)*
"Tree of Heaven" in Brooklyn, N.Y.

Ailanthus altissima erythrocarpa
in Albert Park, Auckland, N.Z.

Brugmansia x candida *of hort.*
Quail Bot. Gard., Encinitas, Calif.

Brugmansia candida fl. pl.
"Floripondio" of Perú

Brugmansia aurea *(Perú)*
Dahlem Bot. Garden, Berlin

Brugmansia arborea
South Coast Bot. G., Los Angeles

Brugmansia chlorantha *(Datura)*
Tuebingen Bot. Gard., Germany

Brugmansia x insignis
(suaveolens x versicolor)

Brugmansia sanguinea *(Perú)*
Quail Bot. Gard., Encinitas, Calif.

Brugmansia suaveolens *(Brazil)*
"Angel's trumpet", Essen B.G. Germany

Brugmansia versicolor *(mollis)*
in Guayaquil, Ecuador

Brunfelsia pauciflora 'Macrantha'
"Yesterday and today" in California

Brunfelsia pauciflora 'Eximia'
Royal Bot. Gard. Kew, England

Brunfelsia pauciflora calycina
"Morning, noon, and night"

Brunfelsia americana
"Lady-of-the-night"

Brunfelsia australis
"Kiss-me-quick"

Brunfelsia paucif. calyc. 'Floribunda'
"Yesterday, today and tomorrow"

Cestrum aurantiacum
"Orange cestrum" in Guatemala

Cestrum diurnum
"Day-jessamine" on Barbados

Fabiana imbricata *(Chile)*
in Lisbon Bot. Garden, Portugal

Cestrum elegans *(Mexico)*
"Flor del soldado" in Veracruz

Cestrum 'Newellii'
in Hillier Arboretum, England

Cestrum nocturnum
"Night jessamine" on Tonga Isl.

Cestrum nocturnum
developing fruit, in California

Cestrum parqui *(Chile)*
in Avila Park, Lisbon

Iochroma coccineum *(Perú)*
Quail Bot. Gard., Encinitas, Calif.

Iochroma cyaneum *(Colombia)*
"Violet bush" in San Diego

Iochroma warscewiczii *(Perú)*
Royal Bot. Garden Sydney, N.S.W.

Juanulloa aurantiaca
"Guacamaya" in Veracruz, Mex.

Lycium carolinianum *(enlarged)*
"Christmas berry" in Florida

Lycium halimifolium *(barbarum)*
"Matrimony shrub" in Virginia

Solanum aviculare
"Kangaroo apple" in Queensland

Solanum incanum
in Arta Mountains, Somalia

Solanum macranthum *(Brazil)*
"Potato tree" in Mysore, India

Solanum wendlandii *(Costa Rica)*
"Potato vine" in California

Solanum marginatum *(Ethiopia)*
Strybing Arboretum, San Francisco

Solanum quitoense *(Ecuador)*
"Furry fruit" in Encinitas, Calif.

Solanum atropurpureum *(Argentina)*
Tuebingen Univ. Bot. G., Germany

Streptosolen jamesonii
"Marmalade bush", Monterey, Calif.

Nicotiana glauca *(So. America)*
"Tree tobacco" in Oceanside

Nicotiana glauca, *as tree*
overlooking Haifa, Israel

Solanum mammosum
"Nipple fruit" in Java

Solanum melongena ovigerum
"Egg-tree", St. Petersburg, Florida

Solanum pseudocapsicum *(Madeira)*
"Jerusalem cherry" in Los Angeles

Solanum rantonnetii *(Paraguay)*
"Blue potato bush" in S. Barbara

Solanum uporo *(So. China)*
ornamental tomato in Kwangtung

Solanum muncatum, *in flower*
"Melon tree" in California

Solanum sodomeum *(Mediterr.)*
"Dead Sea apple", Cap Ferrat, France

Solanum martii *(SOLAN.)*
Jardim Botanico Rio de Janeiro

Vestia lycioides *(Chile) (SOLAN.)*
at Chelsea Flower Show, London

Staphylea colchica *(STAPH.)*
"Bladdernut" of the Caucasus

Staphylea colchica 'Coulombieri'
Nymphenburg Bot. Gard., Munich

Stachyurus praecox *(STACH.)*
Sankei-En Garden, Yokohama

Staphylea pinnata
"European bladdernut"

Staphylea trifolia
"American bladdernut"

Staphylea holocarpa *(STAPH.)*
"China bladdernut" in England

Brachychiton rupestris
"Queensland bottle tree" in Brisbane

Brachychiton acerifolius
"Flame bottle-tree", Vista, Calif.

Brachychiton acerif., *w. foliage*
Royal Botan. Garden Sydney

Brachychiton bidwillii
Los Angeles Arboretum, Arcadia

Brachychiton discolor
"Queensland lacebark"

Brachychiton populneus *(Australia)*
"Kurrajong" in Piraeus, Greece

Cola acuminata *(W. Africa)*
"Cola-nut tree" in Nigeria

Brachychiton australis *(Queensland)*
"Broadleaf bottle tree" in Cairns

Herrania nitida *(Brazil)*
J. Bogner, Munich Bot. Garden

Dombeya elegans *(Réunion)*
Fairchild Trop. Garden, Miami

Dombeya burgessiae, *"Rose Mound"*
U.S.D.A. Research Sta., So. Miami

Dombeya pulchra *(So. Africa)*
Quail Bot. Garden, Encinitas

Dombeya tiliacea *(Natal)*
South Coast Bot. G., Los Angeles

Dombeya wallichii *(Madagascar)*
in Botanic Garden, Munich

Pterospermum littorale
"Champa tet" in Thailand

Firmiana simplex *(Vietnam)*
"Phoenix tree" in S. Pasqual, Calif.

Fremontodendron californicum
"Flannel bush" in Santa Cruz, Calif.

Fremontodendron mexicanum
"San Diego flannel bush"

Sterculia apetala
fruiting in Acapulco, Mexico

Sterculia ceramica *(Celebes)*
"Fairchild's sterculia", in Miami

Sterculia foetida
"Indian almond" in Honolulu

Pterostyrax hispida *(STYR.)*
"Epaulette tree" in Japan

Halesia diptera *(STYR.)*
"Snowdrop tree" in Tennessee

Halesia carolina
"Carolina silver-bell"

Styrax obassia *(STYR.)*
"Fragrant snow-bell" of Japan

Styrax japonica
"Japanese snow-bell" in England

Halesia monticola
"Mountain silver-bell" in New York

Symplocos lucida *(SYMPL.)*
"Sweet leaf" in Taiwan

Symplocos paniculata
"Sapphire berry" in England

Symplocos sumuntia
"Himalaya sweetleaf"

Symphorema luzonicum *(SYMPH.)*
"Molawin-baguin" (Philippines)

Theobroma cacao *(STERC.)*
"Cacao-tree"in Trinidad

Tamarix gallica *(TAMAR.)*
"French tamarisk" in France

Tamarix aphylla, *"Athel tree"*
in Devil's Playground, Arizona

Tamarix chinensis
"Salt cedar" near Van Horn, Texas

Tamarix ramosissima *(pentandra)*
"Flowering cypress" in N. Zealand

Camellia japonica
near Kweilin, Li River, S.W. China

Camellia japonica, *rose form*
Hangchow Bot. G., Chekiang, China

Camellia sasanqua 'Showa-no-Sakae'
(C. hiemalis) in Santa Ana, Calif.

Camellia sinensis var. assamica, *the "Assam tea"*
Tamil women picking leaves in Nuwara Eliya, Sri Lanka

Camellia sinensis var. bohea, *the "Chinese tea"*
Chu Teng Fin commune, Hangchow, Chekiang, China

Camellia sinensis *(Thea)*
"Tea plant" with fragrant flowers

Camellia sasanqua 'Yuletide'
December-blooming in Vista, Calif.

Camellia sasanqua 'Jean May'
at Tropic World, Escondido, Calif.

Camellia japonica 'Debutante'
('Sara Hastie') of So. Carolina

Camellia japonica
'Elegans' (chandleri)

Camellia japonica
'Rosedale Beauty' (California cv.)

Camellia japonica 'Pink Perfection'
(syn. 'Frau Minna Seidel')

Camellia japonica 'Purity'
corsage flower, formal type

Camellia japonica
'William S. Hastie' rose-form

Camellia japonica 'Jordan's Pride'
('Herme'), formal type

Camellia japonica 'Col. Firey'
('C. M. Hovey'), formal type

Camellia reticulata
"Temple flower" of China

Camellia oleifera (China)
"Tea-oil bush" in Hong Kong

Camellia japonica
'Pearl Maxwell', large formal

Gordonia lasianthus
"Black laurel" in Alabama

Camellia sasanqua 'Bonanza'
semi-peony form, in Vista, Calif.

Camellia sasanqua 'Shishi-Gashira'
Monrovia Nurs., Azusa, Calif.

Camellia tsai *(W. China)*
Duesseldorf Bot. Garden, Germany

Eurya japonica, *true species*
"Hi-Sakaki" in Japan

Cleyera japonica, *"Sakaki"*
with leaves entire, in Fallbrook, Calif.

Cleyera japonica 'Variegata'
as Eurya jap. varieg. in Belgium

Eurya japonica, *with fruit*
by Feng-Chi Ho, Pingtung, Taiwan

Camellia japonica 'Elegans Splendor'
anemone form, Monrovia Nurs., Calif.

Camellia sasanqua
"Sunlight camellia", Bot. G. Sydney

Franklinia alatamaha *(THEAC.)*
in Brooklyn Bot. Garden, New York

Franklinia alatamaha
"Franklin tree" in Los Angeles

Stewartia ovata *(THEAC.)*
"Mountain camellia" in Virginia

Stewartia pseudo-camellia
"Japanese stewartia" in New Jersey

Stewartia sinensis *(China)*
Royal Bot. Gardens Kew, England

Stewartia monadelpha
"Tall stewartia" in California

Vellozia candida *(VELL.)*
in Espirito Santo, Brazil

Ternstroemia gymnanthera *(THEAC.)*
in Los Angeles Arb., California

Deherainia smaragdina *(THEO.)*
Nymphenburg Bot. Garden, Munich

Daphne odora 'Marginata'
"Winter daphne" in San Diego

Daphne cneorum
"Garland daphne" in England

Daphne collina *(Italy, Crete)*
grown in Medford, Oregon

Daphne x burkwoodii
Burkwood Nursery, Kingston on Thames, England

Daphne arbuscula *(Slovakia to Ukraine)*
Summer-blooming in Connecticut, by Pamela Harper

Daphne giraldii *(N.W. China)*
Skinner Nursery, Manitoba, Canada

Daphne mezereum, *with fruit*
"February daphne" in New York

Daphne x burkwoodii 'Carol Mackie'
"Varieg. daphne", Somerset Arb., N.J.

Daphne retusa *(THYMEL.)*
Duesseldorf Bot. Garden, Germany

Dais cotinifolia *(THYMEL.)*
"Pompon tree" in Cape Town, S. Afr.

Clavija eggersii *(THEOPH.)*
Selby Bot. G., Sarasota, Florida

Jacquinia pungens *(THEOPH.)*
"Cudjoe wood" of Guatemala

Gnidia polystachya *(THYM.)*
Spring-flowering in So. Africa

Dirca palustris *(THYM.)*
"Leatherwood" in Virginia

Pimelia ferruginea *(THYM.)*
"Rice-flower" in W. Australia

Grewia caffra *(TILIAC.)*
"Star-bush" in San Diego, Calif.

Platytheca verticillata *(TREM.)*
in Melbourne, Victoria

Sparmannia africana *(TIL.)*
"Indoor linden", Carinthia, Austria

Edgeworthia papyrifera *(THYM.)*
"Paper bush" in Hangchow Bot. G.

Edgeworthia papyrifera
on West Lake, Hangchow, China

Sparmannia africana 'Variegata'
Quail Bot. G., Encinitas, Calif.

Sparmannia africana *in fl.*
in Nice, Côte d'Azur of France

Trochodendron aralioides *(TROCH.)*
"Wheel tree"in Seoul, Korea

Turnera aurantiaca *(TURN.)*
in Botanic Garden Singapore

Turnera ulmifolia
"W. Indian holly", Brooklyn Bot. G.

Turnera ulmifolia elegans
"Sage rose" in Kew Bot. Gardens

Tilia x moltkei *(Berlin hyb.)*
Munich Bot. Garden, Germany

Tilia x moltkei
in Brooklyn Bot. Garden, N. York

Tilia petiolaris *(S.E. Europe)*
"Pendant silver linden" in Vienna

Tilia tomentosa *(Hungary)*
"Silver linden" in Rutherford, N.J.

Tilia platyphyllos
"Summer linden" in Lund, Sweden

Tilia platyphyllos
"Big-leaf lime" at Kew G. England

Tilia tomentosa, *fol. and flower*
"Silver linden" in Oregon

Tilia mongolica, *w. inflorescence*
"Mongolian lime" in Helena, Mont.

Tilia mongolica, *small tree*
graceful ornamental, in Germany

Tilia americana
"American linden" in England

Tilia americana
"Bass-wood" in Virginia

Tilia dasystyla
Nymphenburg Bot. Garden, Munich

Tilia cordata, *inflor.*
"Littleleaf linden" in Oregon

Tilia cordata
Bern Bot. Garden, Switzerland

Tilia x europaea
"Common lime" in London

Tilia x euchlora
Royal Bot. Gard. Kew, England

Tilia x euchlora, *inflor.*
"Crimean linden" in Munich

Tilia japonica, *w. inflor.*
"Japan linden" in Kyushu

Ulmus americana
"American elm" in Somerville, N.J.

Ulmus alata
"Winged elm" in Virginia

Ulmus alata
"Small-leaf elm" in New York

Celtis laevigata, *with leaves not toothed*
"Mississippi hackberry" in New York Bot. Garden

Ulmus americana, *showing toothed leaves*
"White elm" or "American elm" in Denver, Colorado

Celtis laevigata, *buttressed trunk*
"Sugar berry" in Virginia

Ulmus glabra *(scabra)*
"Scotch elm" in Edinburgh

Celtis occidentalis
"Nettle tree" in Pennsylvania

Ulmus parvifolia *(ULM.)*
"Chinese elm" in Kyushu, Japan

Ulmus parvifolia, *with fruit*
"Evergreen elm" in Vista, Calif.

Ulmus thomasii
"Rock elm" in Nebraska

Zelkova serrata 'Variegata'
in Martha's Vineyard, Mass.

Zelkova serrata 'Village Green'
at Tropic World, Escondido, Calif.

Zelkova serrata *(ULM.)*
"Sawleaf zelkova" in Kyoto, Japan

Ulmus x hollandica 'Wredei'
"Golden elm" in the Rhineland

Callicarpa americana *(VERB.)*
"French mulberry" in Virginia

Callicarpa bodinieri giraldii
"Beauty berry" in Bot. G. Berlin

Callicarpa dichotoma *(China)*
"Purple beautyberry" in Virginia

Caryopteris x clandonensis
"Bluebeard" in San Francisco

Clerodendrum bungei *(China)*
South Coast Bot. Gard., Los Angeles

Clerodendrum foxii *hort.*
in St. Petersburg, Florida

Clerodendrum fragrans pleniflorum
"Glory tree" in Hong Kong

Clerodendrum inerme *(India)*
"Indian privet" in Bombay

Clerodendrum minahassae *(Java)*
on Bequia Isl., West Indies

Clerodendrum myricoides *(So. Afr.)*
Kirstenbosch Bot. Gard., Cape Prov.

Clerodendrum ugandense
"Blue wings" in Fallbrook, Calif.

Clerodendrum speciosissimum
"Glory bower" on St. Thomas, V.I.

Clerodendrum x speciosum
Jardim Botanico, Rio de Janeiro

Clerodendrum paniculatum
"Pagoda flower" in Kandy, Sri Lanka

Holmskioldia sanguinea citrina
"Mandarin hat plant" in Florida

Clerodendrum wallichii *(India)*
Fairchild Trop. Garden, Miami

Clerodendrum trichotomum
"Glory bower" in Brooklyn Bot. G.

Holmskioldia sanguinea *(China)*
Fortin de las Flores, Veracruz

Gmelina hystrix
"Hedgehog" in Kew Bot. Gardens

Gmelina philippensis
in Andromeda Gardens, Barbados

Duranta repens, *with fruit*
"Pigeonberry" in Martinique

Duranta repens 'Variegata'
in Singapore Botanic Garden

Duranta repens, *in bloom*
"Sky-flower" in Miami, Florida

Lantana camara 'Radiation'
brilliant spreader, in San Diego

Lantana camara *(Mexico)*
"Lakana" in Honolulu, Hawaii

Lantana montevidensis *(Uruguay)*
"Trailing lantana" in Arizona

Lantana camara 'Variegata'
"Yellow sage" in Miami, Florida

Lantana camara 'Mutabilis'
Pala Mission, San Diego County

Nyctanthes arbor-tristis
"Tree-of-sadness" in Mysore, India

Paulownia tomentosa *(SCROPH.), "Princess tree"*
in Dubrovnik, Adriatic coast of Croatia

Tectona grandis *(VERB.), "Teakwood tree"*
at Zamboanga University, on Mindanao, Philippines

Guaiacum officinale *(ZYG.), "Lignum-vitae tree"*
in Charlotte Amalie on St. Thomas, Virgin Islands

Lantana camara 'Festival' *(VERB.), a brilliant "Bush lantana"*
at Indian Mission Pala de San Antonio, California

Vitex agnus-castus *(VERB.)*
"Chaste tree", Andromeda G., Barbados

Guaiacum officinale *(ZYG.)*
Jardin Botanico, Caracas, Venezuela

Stachytarpheta mutabilis *(VERB.)*
Brisbane Bot. Garden, Queensland

Petrea arborea *(VERB.)*
"Queens' wreath" in Trinidad

Vitex lucens *(New Zealand)*
"Puriri" at Lake Taupo, No. Island

Leea coccinea *(Burma)*
"Indian holly" in Rangoon

Leea rubra *(Java)*
as decor. pl. in Philadelphia, Pa.

Guaiacum sanctum *(ZYG.)*
"Palo de Vida Santo" in Miami

Larrea tridentata *(ZYG.)*
"Creosote bush" in Tucson, Ariz.

Mangifera indica 'Haden'
cv. of Coconut Grove, Florida

Mangifera indica 'Joe Welch'
Waimanalo Exper. Sta., Hawaii

Annona cherimola *(ANNON.)*
"Cherimoya" in Vista, Calif.

Anacardium occidentale
"Cashew-nut" on Oahu, Hawaii

Harpephyllum caffrum *(ANAC.)*
"Kaffir plum", Palm Beach, Florida

Pistacia vera *(ANAC.)*
"Pistachio nut" in Bonsall, Calif.

Annona squamosa *(ANNON.)*
"Sugar apple" in Rio de Janeiro

Annona muricata, *"Soursop"*
on Nuku Hiva, Marquesas

Kigelia pinnata *(BIGN.)*
"Sausage tree" in Honolulu

Crescentia cujete *(ANACARD.)*
"Calabash tree" in So. Florida

Spondias cytherea *(dulcis)*
"Otaheite apple" in Tahiti

Spondias purpurea *(ANAC.)*
"Spanish plum", Rio Orinoco, Venezuela

Corylus colurna *(BETUL.)*
"Turkish hazelnut" in Princeton, N.J.

Carissa grandiflora *(macrocarpa)*
"Natal plum" in Vista, Calif.

Spondias mombin *(venulosa)*
"Hog-plum" in Caracas, Venez.

Corylus maxima
"Giant filbert" in Oregon

Corylus avellana, *incl. nuts*
"European hazel", in Rhineland

Corylus cornuta *(BETUL.)*
"Beaked filbert" in Ontario

Adansonia digitata *(BOMB.),* "Baobab" or "Monkey-bread"
ancient giant with fruit, in Sénégal, West Africa

Diospyros kaki *(EBEN.),* "Persimmon tree" fruiting
at the Ming Tombs, near Beijing, North China

Spondias purpurea *(ANAC.),* "Ciruela" or "Red mombin"
at Canaima, near Angel Falls, Guayana, Venezuela

Citrus sinensis 'Valencia' *(RUT.),* "Valencia orange"
summer-fruiting near Winter Garden, C. Florida

Ananas comosus 'Smooth Cayenne'
Pineapple plantation on Maui, Hawaii

Sambucus nigra *(CAPRIF.)*
"European elderberry" in Copenhagen

Semecarpus gigantifolia *(ANAC.)*
"Varnish tree" in Taiwan

Helianthus tuberosus *(COMP.)*
"Jerusalem artichoke" in Minnesota

Goniothalamus amuyon *(ANNONAC.)*
(syn. Uvaria). in So. Taiwan

Canarium pimela *(BURS.)*
"Chinese black olive" in Hong Kong

Cucumis metuliferus *(CUCURB.)*
ripe "Kiwano fruit" in California

Cucumis metuliferus
"Horned melon" in Transvaal habitat

Licania platypus *(Mex. to Colombia)*
"Sansapote" in W. Palm Beach, Florida

Carica x pubescens *(CARIC.)*
"Babaco" in Encinitas, Calif.

Carica papaya 'Oblonga' *(CARIC.)*
female tree, in Singapore Bot. G.

Asimina triloba *(ANNON.)*
"Pawpaw", fl. and fruit, in Virginia

Durio zibethinus *(BOMB.)*
"Durian" in Jogyakarta, Java

Pachira aquatica *(BOMB.)*
"Guiana chestnut", Encinitas, Calif.

Parmentiera edulis *(BIGN.)*
"Guajilote" in Palm Beach, Florida

Cordia sebestena 'Aurea' *(BORAG.)*
"Orange Geigertree" on Aruba

Terminalia catappa *(COMBRET.)*
"Tropical almond" in Tahiti

Ochrosia marianensis *(APOC.)*
Islands of Micronesia

Diospyros digyna *(Mexico)*
"Black sapote" in Cuernavaca

Diospyros ebenum *(EBEN.)*
"Ebony" in Sri Lanka

Diospyros kaki 'Mexican cv.'
"Chocolate persimmon" in California

Diospyros kaki 'Fuyu'
non astringent fruit, in Japan

Diospyros kaki 'Hachiya'
superior "Persimmon" in Vista, Calif.

Diospyros vaccinioides
"Dwarf persimmon" in Hong Kong

Dillenia indica *(DILL.)*
"Elephant apple" in Panama

Licania platypus *(CHRYS.)*
"Monkey-apple" (Mexico to Colombia)

Muntingia calabura *(ELAEAG.)*
"Capulin cherry" in El Salvador

Tamarindus indica *(LEG.)*
"Tamarind" with beans, in Florida

Ceratonia siliqua *(LEG.)*
"St. John's-bread" in San Diego

Malpighia glabra *(MALP.)*
"Acerola" in San Juan, Puerto Rico

Syzygium samarangense *(MYRT.)*
"Java apple", Durban Bot. G., Natal

Euphoria longan *(Nephelium)*
"Longan" in Vista, Calif.

Cola nitida *(STERCUL.)*
"Cola nut", Mahé B.G., Seychelles

Actinidia chinensis *(ACTIN.)*
"Chinese gooseberry", in N. Zealand

Actinidia chinensis
"Kiwi" fruit grown in California

Carica papaya, *female tree*
"Papaya" on Rarotonga, So. Pacific

Monstera deliciosa *(ARAC.)*
"Mexican breadfruit" in maturity

Cereus 'Peruvianus hybrid' *(CACT.)*
"Peruvian apple" in San Diego

Opuntia ficus-indica *(Mexico)*
"Nopal" bearing Tuna fruit

Ipomoea batatas *(CONVOLV.)*
"Yam" harvest, Bontoc, Philippines

Arachis hypogaea *(LEG.)*
"Peanut" harvest in New Guinea

Arachis hypogaea
"Groundnut" in Brazil habitat

Rheum rhabarbarum *(POLYG.)*
"Rhubarb" in Germany

Solanum muricatum *(SOLAN.)*
"Pepino dulce" fruit of Ecuador

Cucurbita moschata *(CUC.)*
"Canada squash" or "Cushaw"

Citrullus lanatus 'Family Fun'
Watermelon at Ball's, W. Chicago

Cucumis melo cantalupensis
Cantaloupe melon

Cucurbita pepo melopepo
Banana squash in California

Cucurbita maxima 'Butternut'
Winter butternut squash

Cucumis melo inodorus
"Honey-dew melon" in Autumn

Cucurbita maxima *(immature)*
Winter pumpkin in W. Chicago

Cucurbita pepo 'Funny Face'
Winter pumpkin for Hallow'een

Cucumis sativus
Cucumber at G. Ball, W. Chicago

Sechium edule, "Chayote"
Quail Bot. Gard., Encinitas

Phyllanthus acidus *(EUPH.)*
"Gooseberry tree" in Honolulu

Arbutus unedo *(ERIC.)*
"Strawberry tree", in Vista, Calif.

Diospyros virginiana *(EBEN.)*
"American persimmon" in Virginia

Vaccinium macrocarpon *(ERIC.)*
"American cranberry" in New Jersey

Vaccinium corymbosum
"Highbush blueberry" in Delaware

Vaccinium vitis-idaea
"Lingon-berry" in Sweden

Arctostaphylos columbiana
"Manzanita" in Bryce Canyon, Utah

Arctostaphylos uva-ursi *(ERIC.)*
"Bearberry" in South Dakota

Vaccinium vitis-idaea minus
"Mountain cranberry" in Alaska

Elaeagnus philippinensis *(ELAEAG.)*
"Lingaros" ripening in San Diego

Antidesma bunius *(EUPH.)*
"Bignay" in Ft. Lauderdale, Fla.

Flacourtia indica *(FLAC.)*
"Governor's plum" in Hawaii

Castanea sativa *(FAGAC.)*
"Spanish chestnut" in Toledo

Castanea molissima, *with fruit*
"Chinese chestnut" in New York

Fagus sylvatica *(FAGAC.)*
"European beech" in Switzerland

Dovyalis caffra *(So. Africa)*
"Kei-apple" in San Diego Zoo

Dovyalis hebecarpa *(FLAC.)*
"Ceylon gooseberry" (Waimanalo, Oahu)

Dovyalis x hybrida
"Tropical apricot" in Redland, Fla.

Garcinia mangostena *(Malaya)*
"Mangosteen" in Kuala Lumpur

Garcinia dulcis *(GUTT.)*
in Kebun Raya, Bogor, Java

Garcinia dulcis
"Gurka" fruit in Indonesia

Garcinia spicata *(India)*
Fairchild Trop. G., Miami, Fla.

Pinus edulis *(PIN.)*
"Pinyon-nut", Grand Canyon, Ariz.

Mammea americana *(GUTT.)*
"Mamey-apple" in Jamaica

Garrya tomentosa *(Southeast U.S.)*
"Mocker-nut hickory" in Florida

Carya cordiformis *(JUGL.)*
"Bitter-nut" in Louisiana

Carya illinoinensis *(pecan)*
"Pecan-nut" in Vista, California

Persea americana 'Hass' *(LAUR.)*
"Alligator pear", Escondido, Calif.

Persea americana 'Fuerte'
"Mexican avocado" or "Aguacate"

Persea americana 'Reed'
"Guatemalan avocado"

Morus alba *(China)*
"White mulberry" in Kwangtung

Morus nigra *(MORAC.)*
"Black mulberry" in Bonsall, Calif.

Artocarpus altilis *(MOR.)*
"Breadfruit tree" in Tahiti

Bertholletia excelsa *(LEC.)*
"Brazil-nut" w. shelled fruit

Ficus carica 'Mission' *(MOR.)*
"Black fig" in Santa Barbara

Ficus carica 'Kadota'
"White fig" in Vista, Calif.

Feijoa sellowiana 'Nazemetz'
superior cv. in Bonsall, Calif.

Feijoa sellowiana *(MYRT.)*
"Pineapple guava" of Uruguay

Noronhia emarginata *(OLEAC.)*
"Madagascar olive" in Miami

Carya ovata *(JUGL.)*
"Shagbark hickory" in Virginia

Juglans nigra *(JUGL.)*
"Black walnut" in Kentucky

Juglans regia
"English walnut" in California

Olea europaea *(OLEAC.)*
"Olive" with ripe black fruit

Brosimum alicastrum *(MOR.)*
"Breadnut tree" in Honolulu

Marlierea edulis *(MYRT.)*
"Cambuca", Bot. G. Rio de Janeiro

Artocarpus altilis *(MOR.), "Breadfruit tree"*
descendant of tree by Capt. Bligh 1793, St. Vincent, W.I.

Musa acuminata, *"Dwarf banana"*
in the Orotava valley of Tenerife, Spain

Artocarpus heterophyllus, *"Jackfruit"*
bearing cauliflorous fruit in Mahé, Seychelles

Olea europaea, *ancient Olive tree*
in garden of Gethsemane, Jerusalem

Psidium littorale *(lucidum hort.)*
"Yellow strawberry guava"

Psidium littorale longipes
"Purple strawberry guava" in Calif.

Psidium guajava *(W. Indies)*
"Apple guava", in Honolulu

Eugenia uniflora *(Guayana)*
"Surinam cherry", Ft. Lauderdale, Fla.

Syzygium malaccense *(Malaya)*
"Malay apple" in Bot. Gard. Penang

Eugenia aggregata *(Brazil)*
"Cherry of the Rio Grande" in Calif.

Syzygium paniculatum *(Eugenia)*
"Brush cherry" of Queensland

Acmena smithii
"Lilly pilly" in Encinitas, Calif.

Syzygium jambos *(S.E. Asia)*
"Rose apple" in San Diego

Musa acuminata 'Hapai'
curious banana, in Waimanalo, Hawaii

Musa 'Fehi' *(troglodytarum)*
"Cooking banana" in Tahiti

Musa acuminata 'Dwarf Cavendish'
in Cuernavaca, Mexico

Myrciaria cauliflora *(MYRT.)*
"Jaboticaba" in Ft. Lauderdale, Fla.

Musa x paradisiaca normalis
"Plantain" for cooking, in Panama

Musa x paradisiaca sapientum
"Paradise banana" as grown in Java

Averrhoa carambola *(OXAL.)*
"Star-fruit" at Fairchild G. Miami

Myrica rubra, *of Kwangtung*
"Chinese strawberry tree"

Averrhoa bilimbi
"Cucumber tree" of Malaya

Phoenix dactylifera
Date palms along Nile, Egypt

Borassus flabellifer
"Palmyrapalm" in Sénégal

Phoenix dactylif. 'Deglet Noor'
protected dates, in Palm Springs

Cocos nucifera 'Golden Malay'
at Univ. of Florida, Davie

Cocos nucifera 'Dwarf Green'
disease resistant, in Recife, Brazil

Cocos nucifera 'Dwarf Samoan'
in the Kingdom of Tonga, So. Pacific

Elaeis guineensis, *"Oil palm"*
palm oil fruit, in No. Sumatra

Salacca edulis
"Snake-skin fruit" of Java

Salacca edulis, *"Salac palm"*
Los Baños Arboretum, Philippines

Cocos nucifera, *Coconut fruits on way to market on the Klongs of Bangkok, Thailand*

Phoenix dactylifera 'Deglet Noor', *"Daughter of Light" Algerian dates in Coachella Valley, California*

Metroxylon sagus, *"Spineless sago palm" source of sago flour in Botanic Gardens Singapore*

Hyphaene schatan, *the "Gingerbread palm" producing edible red fruit, in Madagascar*

Amelanchier x grandiflora *(ROS.)*
"Apple service berry"

Passiflora edulis *(PASS.)*
"Purple granadilla" in San Diego

Passiflora edulis fa. flavicarpa
"Yellow passion fruit" in Hawaii

Fragaria x ananassa *(ROS.)*
"Strawberry" of gardens

Fragaria vesca *(Eurasia)*
"Woodland strawberry" in Thuringia

Pereskia aculeata *(CACT.)*
"Barbados gooseberry" (W. Indies)

Rosa canina, *"Dog-rose"*
with fruits, in the Rhineland

Rosa rugosa *(ROS.)*
"Ramanas rose" in England

Rosa moyesii 'Geranium'
with hip-fruit, in Munich Bot. Garden

Pandanus odoratissimus *(PAND.), "Screw-pine"*
female tree w. fruit, Kota Kinabalu, No. Borneo

Punica granatum *(PUNIC.), fruiting pomegranate*
Container-grown, in Forbidden City, Beijing, China

Punica granatum 'Wonderful', *"Giant pomegranate"*
in Autumn, at Quail Bot. Gard., Encinitas, Calif.

Coccoloba uvifera *(POLYG.), "Sea-grape"*
along beach in Tahiti, French Polynesia

Ziziphus jujuba *(RHAMN.)*
"Chinese date" in Sicily

Ziziphus jujuba 'Lang'
"Jujube" at Del Mar Expo., Calif.

Hovenia dulcis *(RHAMN.)*
"Japan raisin tree" in New York

Casasia clusifolia *(RUB.)*
"Seven-year apple" in Miami

Ziziphus mauritiana
"Indian jujube" at Fairchild G.

Parinari macrophylla *(ROS.)*
"Gingerbread plum" in Sénégal

Chaenomeles cathayensis *(ROS.)*
Quince fruit used for preserves

Macadamia tetraphylla *(PROT.)*
"Rough-skin nut" in Encinitas, Calif.

Macadamia integrifolia *(ternifolia)*
"Queensland nut" in Vista, Calif.

Eriobotrya japonica
"Loquat" in Fallbrook, Calif.

Prunus spinosa
"Blackthorn" fruit in Thuringia

Crataegus pubescens
"Mexican hawthorn" in Encinitas

Cydonia oblonga 'Pineapple' *(1899)*
Luther Burbank cv., Santa Rosa, Calif.

Malus pumila 'Boskoop'
Winter apple of Holland (1856)

Cydonia oblonga 'Apple-form'
"Apple-quince" in Saalfeld, Thuringia

Cydonia sinensis *(China)*
Univ. Bot. Garden, Los Angeles, Calif.

Chaenomeles japonica
"Japan quince" in Kyoto

Prunus dulcis *(amygdalus)*
"Sweet almond" in Encinitas, Calif.

Malus pumila 'Anna' *(Israel)*
early fruiting, in Bonsall, Calif.

Malus pumila 'Golden Delicious'
late fruit, in Grafenberg, Germany

Malus pumila 'Winesap'
late variety, in Seattle, Washington

Malus pumila 'Cox Orange' *(1830)*
harvested in April, in New Zealand

Malus pumila 'Jonathan'
October apple of New York

Malus pumila 'Jonagold'
N.Y. origin, grown in Holland

Malus pumila 'McIntosh'
hardy Canadian apple, in Ontario

Malus pumila 'Winter-banana'
Sept. fruiting in Leucadia, Calif.

Malus pumila 'Granny Smith'
May harvest in So. Chile

Malus pumila 'Golden Delicious' *(sylvestris) (ROS.)*
apples along the Rhône, Canton Valais, Switzerland

Pyrus x Lecontei 'Kieffer' *(Oriental pear hyb.)*
"Kieffer pear", century old, in E. Rutherford, N.J.

Pyrus x pyrifolia 'Chojuro' *(ROS.) (China)*
"Apple-pears" at the market of Kamakura, Japan

Coffea arabica *(RUB.),* "Arabian coffee"
mountain coffee bearing fruit, near San Jose, Costa Rica

Malus hupehensis *(China)*
"Tea crab-apple" in England

Malus floribunda 'Scheideckeri'
"Crab-apple" in N. Jersey Autumn

Malus baccata
"Siberian crab" in Malmoe, Sweden

Prunus 'Plumcot' *(plum x apricot)*
Tropic World, Escondido, Calif.

Prunus padus, *in Germany*
"European bird-cherry"

Prunus virginiana
"Choke cherry" in Princeton, N.J.

Prunus avium 'Early French'
"Sweet cherry" in Burgundy

Prunus cerasus 'Montmorency'
"Sour cherry" in New Jersey

Prunus cerasus austera
"Morello cherry" in Germany

Prunus armeniaca 'Moorpark'
"Moorpark apricot" in New Jersey

Prunus armeniaca 'Royal'
"French apricot" in Los Angeles

Prunus domestica var. cerea
"Mirabelle" (small fruit) with nectarine

Prunus salicina 'Satsuma'
"Japanese plum" in Vista, Calif.

Prunus domestica *(Europe)*
"Italian plum" in Bavaria

Prunus salicifolia *(C. America)*
"Capulin cherry" in Encinitas, Calif.

Prunus avium 'Windsor'
"Black oxheart cherry", in New York

Prunus avium 'Black Tartarian'
"Mazzard cherry" of Russia

Prunus avium 'Bing'
"Bing sweet cherry" in Oregon

Prunus persica 'Bonanza' *(Calif.)*
genetic dwarf peach in Del Mar

Prunus persica 'Golden Jubilee'
free-stone peach, E. Rutherford, N.J.

Prunus persica 'Sim's Cling'
"Cling peach" in Escondido, Calif.

Prunus persica 'Elberta'
free-stone "Elberta peach" in Calif.

Prunus persica 'Santa Rosa'
free-stone peach in Vista, Calif.

Prunus persica nucipersica
sweet California "Nectarine"

Prunus salicina 'Great Yellow'
Japan plum (P. Thomson, Bonsall, Calif.)

Prunus domestica 'Green Gage'
"Reineclaude" in England

Prunus persica 'Ventura'
free-stone peach in Merced, Calif.

Nephelium lappaceum *(SAPIND.), "Rambutan"*
on the Saigon market of Ho Chi Minh, City, Vietnam

Citrus maxima *(RUTAC.), "Pomelo"*
at the market of Jericho, in the Jordan Valley

Citrus x paradisi 'Ruby Blush', *"Pink grapefruit"*
in great cluster, on Sunset Ranch, Vista, California

Citrus reticulata, *"Mandarin orange" in glazed pot*
in China commune of historic Hangchow, Chekiang Prov.

Rubus idaeus *(ROS.)*
Red raspberry, Darmstadt, Germany

Rubus fruticosus
"European blackberry" in Holland

Rubus x loganobaccus cv. 'Boysen'
"Boysen berry" in Vista, Calif.

Rubus ursinus
"Pacific dewberry" in Oregon

Rubus phoenicolasius *(China)*
"Wine berry" in Essen Bot. Garden

Rubus laciniatus 'Prof. Rudloff'
"Thornless blackberry" in Bot. G. Essen

Rubus ursinus 'Thornfree'
"Black pearl dewberry"

Rubus chamaemorus
"Cloudberry" in Flam, Norway

Rubus x loganobaccus *(ursinus hyb.)*
"Logan-berry" in Seattle, Washington

Pyrus communis 'Bartlett'
"Bartlett pear" in Oregon

Pyrus comm. 'Doyenne du Comice'
winter pear in No. California

Pyrus comm. 'Max Red Bartlett'
early pear of Western Washington

Pyrus communis 'Lincoln'
August ripening in Bonsall, Calif.

Pyrus communis
"European pear" in Austrian Alps

Pyrus x Lecontei 'Kieffer'
Oriental pear hyb. in N. Jersey

Mespilus germanica
"Medlar" mystic fruit in So. England

Pyrus x pyrifolia 'Nashi'
"Japan pear" at Los Angeles Arbor.

Pyrus x pyrifolia 'Chojuro'
"Asian pear" in Visalia, Calif.

Coffea arabica *(Ethiopia)*
"Arabian coffee" in São Paulo, Brazil

Coffea canephora *(W. Trop. Africa)*
"Robusta coffee" as house plant

Coffea liberica *(RUB.)*
"Liberian coffee" in Trinidad

Casimiroa edulis var. 'Suebelle'
"White sapote" in Vista, California

Casimiroa edulis var. 'Vernon'
Quail Bot. Garden, Encinitas, Calif.

Casimiroa edulis *(RUT.)*
"Mexican apple" in So. Florida

Aegle marmelos *(RUT.) (India)*
"Bael fruit" in Benares

Prunus dulcis cv. 'Texas'
"Mission almond", Escondido, Calif.

Genipa americana *(RUB.)*
"Marmalade box" in Venezuela

Citrus aurantium, *"Bitter Seville orange"*
at the Alcazar of Cordoba, Andalusia, Spain

Citrus sinensis, *the "Sweet orange" of Vietnam*
in the Royal Palace Garden, Rabat, Morocco

Citrus maxima pyriformis, *"Shatian pomelo"*
in Yangshuo, Li River, Kwangsi Prov., China

Citrus reticulata, *the "Mandarin orange" of China*
in Botanic Garden of ancient Hangchow, Chekiang

Citrus aurantium, *"Sour orange"*
wrinkled fruit in Tobago Bot. G., W.I.

x Citrofurtunella mitis
"Calamondin" in Redland, Florida

x Citrofortunella floridana
"Limequat" in Chula Vista, Calif.

Citrus limetta, *"Sweet lime"*
Quail Bot. Garden, Encinitas, Calif.

Citrus aurantifolia 'Bearss'
"Bearss lime" in Escondido, Calif.

Citrus aurantifolia
"Key lime" on St. Vincent, W. Indies

Catesbaea spinosa
"Lily-thorn" in Santiago, Cuba

Citrus x limonia, *"Rangpur lime"*
"Otaheite orange" in Chula Vista, Calif.

Citrus aurantium 'Myrtifolia'
"Myrtleleaf orange" in Redland, Fla.

Citrus limon 'Meyer'
"Meyer lemon" in Vista, Calif.

Citrus 'Dweet', *a Tangor*
(Orange x Tangerine) in Florida

Citrus limon 'Eureka'
"Acid lemon" in Santa Barbara

Citrus maxima, *"Shaddock"*
in Kota Kinabalu, No. Borneo

Citrus x nobilis 'Temple'
"Temple orange" in Orlando, Florida

Citrus microcarpa *(So. China)*
"Four-seasons tangerine" in Hong Kong

Citrus 'Minneola', *a Tangelo*
at Redland Fruit Exp. Sta., Florida

Citrus paradisi 'Marsh seedless'
"Grapefruit" near Yuma, Arizona

Citrus limon 'Ponderosa'
"Wonder lemon" in San Luis Rey, Calif.

Clausena excavata *(RUT.)*
"Curvedleaf wampee" in So. Taiwan

Clausena lansium
"Wampi" in Ft. Lauderdale, Florida

Carissa grandiflora 'Fancy' *(APOC.)*
"Natal plum" in Santa Monica, Calif.

Nephelium lappaceum *(SAP.)*
"Rambutan" in Singapore

Blighia sapida *(SAPIND.)*
"Aki tree" in Montego, Jamaica

Melicoccus bijugatus *(SAP.)*
"Spanish lime" in Palm Beach, Fla

Citrus taiwanica *(RUT.)*
"Formosan orange" in Hengchun

Triphasia trifolia *(RUT.)*
"Limeberry" in Palm Beach, Florida

Pometia pinnata *(SAPIND.)*
"Langsir" on Nuku Hiva, Polynesia

Citrus sinensis 'Valencia'
Summer orange in Vista, Calif.

Citrus sin. 'Washington Navel'
Winter orange in Riverside, Calif.

Citrus reticulata 'Owari'
"Satsuma mandarin" in No. Florida

Mimusops elengi *(SAPOT.)*
"Spanish cherry" on Cayman Isl.

Fortunella hindsii *(So. China)*
"Dwarf kumquat" on Barbados

Citrus reticulata 'Clementine'
"Algerian tangerine" in Florida

Fortunella margarita *(RUT.)*
"Nagami kumquat" in Vista, Calif.

Citrus reticulata 'Dancy'
Tangerine near Tucson, Arizona

Fortunella japonica
"Marumi kumquat" in Oneco, Florida

Capsicum annuum 'Red Chile'
"Chili pepper" at Ball, W. Chicago

Capsicum annuum grossum
Sweet "Italian bell pepper"

Solanum melongena esculentum
"Black egg-plant" or "Aubergine"

Brassica oleracea gongyloda
"Kohlrabi" or "Stem-turnip"

Lycopersicon lycop. cerasiforme
"Cherry-tomato" or "Basket tomato"

Lycopersicon lycopersicum
"Tomato" or "Love apple"

Physalis peruviana *(SOLAN.)*
"Goose-berry tomato" of So. America

Physalis ixocarpa *(Mexico)*
"Tomatillo" in Vista, Calif.

Solanum quitoense *(Ecuador)*
"Furry fruit" or "Naranjillo"

Solanum tuberosum *(So. Am. Andes)*
White potato w. young growth

Abelmoschus esculentus *(MALV.)*
"Okra" producing edible pods

Vicia faba *(LEGUM.)*
"Broad bean" in Bavaria

Chrysophyllum cainito *(SAP.)*
"Satin-leaf" in Redland, Florida

Chrysophyllum cainito
"Star-apple" in Manila, Philippines

Synsepalum dulcificum *(SAP.)*
"Miracle fruit" in Lagos, Nigeria

Pouteria campechiana *(SAP.)*
"Canistel" near Havana, Cuba

Pouteria campechiana
"Egg-fruit" in Palm Beach, Fla.

Cyphomandra betacea *(SOL.)*
"Tree tomato" in Vista, Calif.

Pouteria sapota *(Mexico)*
"Mamey sapote" on Grand Cayman, W.I.

Pouteria sapota, *"Marmalade plum"*
at Fruit Exper. Sta., Palm Beach

Manilkara zapota *(Achras)*
"Sapodilla", Fairchild Bot. G. Miami

Ribes sativum *(SAX.)*
"Garden currants" in N. Jersey

Ribes sativum 'White Versailles'
"White currants" in the Rhineland

Ribes rubrum *(W. Europe)*
"Northern red currants" in Bavaria

Ribes uva-crispa *(grossularia)*
"English gooseberry" in Britain

Ribes nigrum
"Black currant" in Finland

Ribes x nidigrolaria
"Josta berry" in Cologne, Germany

Vitis vinifera 'Golden Muscat'
"Yellow muscatel" in No. California

Vitis vinif. 'Muscat of Alexandria'
espalier-grown in New Jersey

Vitis vinifera 'Blue Burgundy'
red-wine grape in Switzerland

Vitis vinifera 'Silvaner'
along Danube, near Vienna, Austria

Vitis vinifera 'Thompson Seedless'
Table and Raisin grapes in No. Calif.

Vitis vinifera 'Riesling'
European wine-grape, along Moselle

Vitis vinifera 'Black Alicante'
Dessert grape under glass in N. Zealand

Vitis x labruscana 'Steuben'
"Fox grape", in Dansville, New York

Vitis x labruscana 'Himrod'
New York seedless grape, in Missouri

Vitis x labruscana 'Catawba'
hardy American grape in Michigan

Vitis x labruscana 'Concord'
favorite American garden grape

Vitis rotundifolia 'Cowart'
southern Muscadine grape in Georgia

Vitis vinifera 'Red Flame' *(VIT.), seedless grape*
June 1986 harvest, in Indio, Coachella Valley, Calif.

Theobroma cacao *(STERC.), "Chocolate tree"*
with cauliflorous fruit, near Ibadan, Nigeria, W. Africa

Durio zibethinus *(BOMB.), "Durian" fruit*
with the author, in the Holy Forest of Sangeh, Bali

Litchi chinensis *(SAPIND.), "Lychee" fruit*
harvest time in Kwangtung Prov., China

Text Synopsis for Plants Illustrated
their Family, Origin, and Common Names

Combination Text-Index: Numerals at end of each listing indicate page numbers to plant illustrations, a short-cut to easier finding of photographs.

Plant Names other than species, in conformance with the International Code of Nomenclature, are generally distinguished as follows:

Names of Hybrids: Generic names of bigeneric hybrids, and Latinized specific names of hybrids derived from two species, are as a rule preceded by the x mark;

Cultivar names (horticultural sports or varieties, hybrids with fancy names and clonal selections) start with a capital initial letter, and are enclosed within single quotation marks (');

Names of uncertain standing, or where incorrectly used in horticulture, are shown in double quotes ("), and/or are followed by the abbreviation "hort".

Terms of measurement are generally given according to the International Metric System. Conversions to the Old English terms are:

1 centimeter (cm) = 0.4 inch; 2½ cm = 1 inch; 10 cm = 4 inches
1 metre (m) = 40 inches (or 3.28 feet); (1 cm = 10 mm; 1 m = 100 cm; 1 foot = 30 cm)
1 gram (g) = 0.035 oz; 1 kilogram (kg) = 2.2 lbs.; 1 liter (1) = 1.06 quarts; 4 liters = 1.06 gal.

Temperature Conversion: Degrees Fahrenheit vs. Centigrade.
Freezing point zero deg. Centigrade = 32 deg. Fahrenheit (F.)
Boiling point 100 deg. Celsius (C) = 212 deg. Fahrenheit (F.)

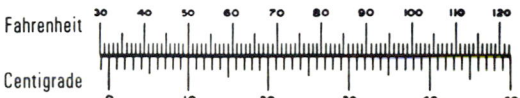

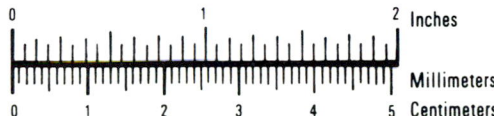

CLIMATE ZONES for PLANT HARDINESS.

The use of a Climate map is very much disputed. Gardeners know that the actual extremes in freezing weather can kill a living plant — unless protected by snow or otherwise. However, practically every garden book and nursery catalog includes such maps, which may be useful in HORTICA also, if only as a general guide.

The Hardiness Zone rating indicates the limit of probable cold tolerance of plants. Zones follow isothermal lines of EXTREME minimum temperatures as recorded or expected each winter across the country, modified by factors such as elevation, wind-chill, snowcover or the lack of it, and degrees of precipitation.

Minimum Temperatures possible

ZONE	down to
1	— 52°C (-58°F)
2	— 46°C (-50°F)
3	— 40°C (-40°F)
4	— 34°C (-30°F)
5	— 29°C (-20°F)
6	— 23°C (-10°F)
7	— 18°C (0°F)
8	— 12°C (10°F)
9	— 7°C (20°F)
10	— 1°C (30°F)
11	8°C (46°F)
12	18°C (64°F)

PLANT DESCRIPTIONS with Photo Index and Climate Zones

ABELIA   *Caprifoliaceae*

chinensis (China), "Glossy abelia"; deciduous shrub to 2 m with opposite ovate, toothed leaves 4 cm long: the funnel-shaped small, fragrant white flowers 2 cm long in terminal panicles. *Zone 7. p. 672*

'Edouard Goucher' (grandiflora x schumannii); semi-evergreen shrub, lower and lacier than grandiflora, 1-1½ m high; small lilac-pink tubular flowers with orange throat. *Zone 5.   p. 672*

floribunda (Mexico), "Mexican abelia"; evergreen shrub 1-2 m high, with arching wiry, downy red branches; ovate, glossy green 3 cm leaves; from the ends of twigs the showy pendulous trumpet flowers 4 cm long, reddish purple with white throat. *Zone 8.   p. 672*

x grandiflora (chinensis x uniflora) (China), "Glossy abelia"; attractive half-evergreen shrub with opposite ovate, glossy leaves; terminal clusters of small bellshaped fragrant flowers white flushed pink, 2-3 cm long, free-blooming and very popular. In Autumn the foliage turns bronze to purplish. *Zone 5.   p. 672*

ABELIOPHYLLUM   *Oleaceae*

distichum (Korea), "White forsythia"; deciduous shrub 60-90 cm high, with square, twiggy branches and opposite ovate, abelia-like leaves to 8 cm long; flowers white with orange center 2 cm across, sweetly fragrant, blooming between January and April, from last year growth. *Zone 6.   p. 806*

ABELMOSCHUS   *Malvaceae*

esculentus (Tropic Asia), "Okra", "Gumbo" or "Lady's finger"; herbaceous annual related to Hibiscus, with rather stout, bristly stem and branches to 2 m long; leaves palmately lobed or compound, to 30 cm across; large axillary white or yellow flowers, purple in center and 8 cm across; grown for the 5-angled cylindric green pods 10-20 cm long, harvested before fully ripe and woody, made into the well-known gumbo soup of the South. Seeds are very frost-sensitive. *Zones 10-11.   p. 940*

manihot (syn. Hibiscus) (China, Japan, India), "Musk mallow"; woody perennial or subshrub to 3 m high, with stout, prickly stems; the leaves palmately deeply 3 to 7-lobed or parted, the lowest to 45 cm long, the lobes slender-pointed, and toothed; showy flowers 15-18 cm across, the corolla sulphur yellow, usually having brown-purple center, blooming Summer and Autumn; prickly 5-angled capsule, resembling Okra, containing musk-scented seeds, yielding perfume, and used medicinally. *Zone 7.   p. 780*

ABIES   *Pinaceae (Coniferae)*

alba (Cent. and So. Europe), "Silver fir" or "European silver fir"; evergreen tree 30 to 50 m high, with straight trunk having gray bark, scaly when old; branches horizontal in tiers, the branchlets brown pubescent; leaves 3 cm long, glossy dark green above and notched at apex, silvery bands beneath; cylindric cones to 15 cm long, usually erect on trees, brown when mature. *Zone 5.   p. 584, 585*

balsamea (Labrador to Alberta and Virginia), "Balsam fir"; stately pyramidal conifer 15-25 m high, with slender trunk, smooth grayish-brown with many resin bumps; stout branches ascending; needles spreading upward 2-3 cm long, and notched at apex, lustrous dark green above and 2 white bands beneath, strongly scented when bruised; cylindrical cones 5-7 cm long, and very resinous. Sometimes trained as dwarf bonsai in Japan. Favored as long-lasting Christmas tree in United States. *Zone 3.   p. 584, 587*

bracteata (California), "Bristle-cone fir"; pyramidal tall tree 30-60 m high, with spreading lower branches and slender crown; flat, stiff needle-like leaves spine-pointed, 4-6 cm long, shining green; broad white lines beneath; female cones erect, roundish and bristly, 10 cm long. *Zone 7.   p. 584*

concolor (Colorado to Arizona and Mexico), "White fir"; noble timber tree 25 to 50 m tall, of symmetrical pyramidal habit, and with gray bark; branches horizontal in tiers; flat bluish-green, stiff needles 5 to 8 cm long; purplish glaucous, cylindric, erect cones to 14 cm long. *Zones 3-7.   p. 584, 585*

concolor 'Violacea'; very handsome cultivar having the long, stiff needles a striking silvery blue and very glaucous; usually grown in gardens as a compact evergreen bush. *Zone 4.   p. 585*

grandis (Brit. Columbia to California and Montana), "Grand fir"; evergreen pyramidal tree 50 m to 100 m tall, probably the tallest of all firs; dense with lateral branches; the smooth branchlets olive green, set with double row of needles 3-5 cm long in flat plane, glossy green above with two white stomatic bands beneath, aromatic when bruised; erect cylindric cones to 10 cm long. Needs cool moist climates. Wood valuable for timber and pulp. *Zone   p. 586*

koreana (Korea), "Korean silver fir"; evergreen tree to 15 m high, having sparry branches, the branchlets with stiff needles 2 cm long, glossy green above when young, round and notched at apex in adult stage, and arranged all around branch; erect cones cylindrical 8 cm long, violet-purple. *Zone 5.   p. 585*

lasiocarpa (Alaska to New Mexico), "Alpine fir"; stately evergreen pyramidal tree to 20 m and 30 m high, having whitish bark; grayish horizontal branches, with branchlets reddish pubescent; needles to 3 cm long, densely arranged, glaucous bluish-green, and stomata on both surfaces; purple cones cylindric, 5-10 cm long. *Zone 3.   p. 587*

magnifica (Oregon and California), "Red fir" or "California red-fir"; magnificent evergreen tree from U.S. Western mountains, to 60 m or more high, at altitudes 2000 m to 3500 m in California; branchlets red-downy, the leaves 4-sided, 3 cm long, glaucous green, densely arranged, horizontal in lower level, the inner ones curving upward; large cylindrical, upright cones, 15-20 cm long, light brown when mature. The name red-cedar refers to its red-brown bark and the reddish timber used in construction and for pulp. *Zone 6. p. 586*

nordmanniana (Greece, Caucasus, Armenia), "Caucasus fir" or "Nordmann fir"; vigorous pyramidal fir 10 to 40 m tall, with gray dark cracked into squares; branches horizontal in dense tiers; thick-set with flat, grooved needles, rounded or notched at apex, shining bluish-green, 2-3 cm long, with silvery bands beneath; resinous erect, green cones 20 cm long. *Zone 5.   p. 585, 586*

pinsapo (So. Spain), "Spanish fir"; bold evergreen tree of pyramidal habit from the Sierra Nevada in So. Spain at 1500 m, where it grows to 30 m and more high; the bark is rather smooth and light brown, the rigid angular branches have short stiff 1 cm needles grayish green and are arranged all around the twigs; the winter buds are resinous; upright conical brownish cones 8-12 cm long. Twigs crushed in water yield a form of soap. *Zone 7.   p. 586*

pinsapo 'Glauca' (France 1860), "Blue Spanish fir"; beautiful French clone descended from the parent trees at home in the mountains of So. Spain; grooved red-brown shoots, with rigid needles to 2 cm long, glaucous blue-green, arranged radially around branchlets; the cones cylindric, 10-12 cm long, purplish brown, carried upright. *Zone 7.   p. 585*

procera (nobilis) (Washington to No. California), "Noble fir"; handsome soft-wooded pyramidal evergreen tree to 50 m high, as found in Western mountains incl. Yosemite National Park, having horizontal branches, radially arranged in whorls, with branchlets reddish-pubescent, the dense needles 3 cm long, bluish-green above, and facing upwards; the showy cylindric cones are carried upright, to 25 cm long, becoming purplish brown. *Zone 6.   p. 585*

procera 'Glauca', "Blue noble fir"; best known form of the Noble fir, rivalling the best of the blue spruces, with its beautiful silver-blue needles; best grafted with leader scions. *Zone 6.   p. 586*

veitchii (Japan: Mts. of Honshu), "Shirabe fir"; evergreen pyramidal tree to 25 m high, having densely pubescent branchlets, with soft leaves crowded, 2-3 cm long, dark glossy green above and grooved, silvery beneath, covering sides and upper part of shoot; cylindric cones to 8 cm long, turning brown. *Zone 4.   p. 585*

ABRONIA   *Nyctaginaceae*

umbellata (Coastal California to Brit. Columbia), "Coast sand verbena"; perennial creeper spreading wide with flexible branches, small ovate, opposite leaves minutely pubescent and sticky; the flowers with corolla-like calyx rose-pink and white-eyed, in 5 cm clusters. *Zone 8.   p. 317, 460*

villosa (Nevada to Arizona and Baja California), "Desert sand verbena"; very similar to A.umbellata; prostrate perennial or annual of arid regions, with trailing, sticky branches, small broad-ovate, finely pubescent grayish leaves 3-4 cm across and clusters of showy little flowers having corolla-like calyx 2 cm across, purplish rose with white eye. *Zone 9.   p. 317, 460*

wootonii (New Mexico, Arizona), "Sand verbena"; herbaceous perennial of arid regions, with spreading branches, having opposite elongate, fleshy leaves, and clusters of fragrant 2½ cm trumpet flowers pink outside and white inside, blooming May to September. Not related to true Verbena. *Zone 9.   p. 317*

ABUTILON   *Malvaceae*

auritum (Old World Tropics); curious evergreen shrub with broadly peltate leaves having eared base, about 20 cm long, the surface corrugated by primary palmate veins and lateral veinlets, finely toothed along margins; the inflorescence in small terminal clusters of flowers with yellow corolla and displaying whitish filaments. Seen in col. Brisbane Bot. Garden. *Zone 10.   p. 780*

fraseri (Western Australia), "Lantern bush"; tomentose shrub 2 to 4 m high, with cordate ovate leaves crenate at margins; flowers 3-4 cm dia., pinkish in bud, when open with petals creamy yellow and crimson in center, followed by fruit of numerous rounded seed carpels. *Subtropic. Zone 10.*   p. 780

x hybridum 'Old Rose'; a good strain of "Flowering maple" or "Parlor maple"; strong grower of sturdy habit, with soft-woody branches, and maple-like lobed, or unlobed leaves; the cup-shaped flowers 3-4 cm long, a good rich rose, blooming 12 months of the year. Excellent both as pot plant and for the garden. *Zone 10.*   p. 781

x hybridum 'Souvenir de Bonn' (darwinii x striatum etc.), "Variegated flowering maple"; herbaceous shrub to 1½ m high, with soft, long-stalked, maple-like leaves a grayish green bordered in creamy-white; bell-shaped flowers salmon veined with crimson. *Zones 10-11.*   p. 71, 781

megapotamicum (So. Brazil), "Trailing abutilon"; slender-branched sub-shrub to 2 m high, with woody, wire-like arching twigs; leaves arrow-shaped, sometimes lobed, 4-6 cm long; pendulous lantern-like flowers, with tubular inflated red calyx, and yellow petals nearly closed. *Zone 10.*   p. 283

megapotamicum 'Variegata' (Brazil), "Weeping Chinese lantern"; evergreen shrub of lax, graceful habit; the slender, drooping branches with small, arrow-shaped, crenate leaves fresh-green, with ivory to yellow variegation, and small pendulous flowers lemon-yellow with lantern-like red calyx. *Zone 10.*   p. 780

pictum 'Thompsonii' (Guatemala), "Spotted flowering maple"; herbaceous shrub with slender branches; soft, maple-shaped leaves deeply 5-7 lobed, the middle lobe narrowed at base, dark green with chartreuse-yellow mottling; bell-like orange-salmon flowers; leaves not pubescent. *Zone 10.*   p. 780

ACACIA   *Leguminosae*

abyssinica (Ethiopia and Somalia); characteristic flat-topped tree to 6 m high, with corky, yellowish bark, which peels off in papery strips, branching from near base and spreading wide, and covered by short spines; bipinnate evergreen leaves with linear leaflets; axillary yellow flower heads 3-6 together; fruit pods 8-12 cm long. Photographed in the Arta Mts. of Somalia. *Zones 9-10.*   p. 745

armata (paradoxa) (Australia), "Kangaroo thorn"; dark green, densely branched erect shrub, to 3 m, with stems ribbed and bristly, dense phyllodia half-ovate, to 2½ cm long; flowers rich yellow in 1 cm globose heads, close to stem; willingly blooming for Easter, in the Northern hemisphere, even as a small pot plant indoors. In habitat from Queensland to Western Australia. *Zone 9.*   p. 743

baileyana (New So. Wales), "Golden mimosa"; handsome spreading tree, to 10 m, with branches often pendulous, very leafy with fern-like bipinnate, glaucous, bluish-silvery leaves; the fluffy bright yellow, fragrant, globose flower heads massed in great sprays of clustering racemes, blooming in the Northern Hemisphere January into April; in Australia, June to August. *Zones 8-9.*   p. 744, 745

complanata (New So. Wales and Queensland); interesting phyllodinous acacia photographed with the colorful red inflorescence mostly in bud; the leathery leaf-like obovate 6 cm phyllodes arranged along flexuous branches in opposite horizontal ranks; a handsome evergreen shrub. *Zone 10.*   p. 743

cultriformis (New So. Wales, Queensland), "Knife acacia"; bushy shrub to 2 m, or more, with stiff, spirally set, triangular phyllodia silvery-gray and glaucous; small fluffy, bell-shaped yellow flowers in long, arching racemes forming a terminal panicle, during February-April. *Zone 10.*   p. 744

decurrens (New South Wales to Tasmania), "Green wattle"; tree 18 m and upwards, densely leafy; leaves bipinnate, 8-12 cm long, green; flowers yellow, fragrant, in numerous globose heads 5 mm dia., forming large panicles. *Subtropic. Zone 9.*   p. 745

drepanolobium (Kenya; Rift Valley; Uganda, Sudan), known in arid regions of Africa as "Whistling thorn" or "Black-galled acacia". Low tree with horizontal twigs forming a flattened top, bark blackish, with long straight white spines to 8 cm long; deciduous, bipinnate, glaucous leaves, and fragrant creamy-yellow flower heads; large hollow, black galls form at base of spines, said to be caused by ants who hollow them out, and when wind blows through the holes in the galls it sounds like a whistle. *Arid-subtropic. Zones 9-10.*   p. 745

drummondii (Western Australia); free-blooming shrub to 3 m, with shoots furrowed, downy, and bipinnate leaves 5 cm long; main divisions 2 or 3, each with 2-6 pairs of oblong leaflets, smooth, pale bluish-green; flowers lemon-yellow, in dense cylindrical, drooping spikes to 3 cm long, in March-April. *Zone 10.*   p. 743

farnesiana (found in Australia, Africa, Asia, also Mexico and Texas), "Popinac" or "West Indian blackthorn"; thorny shrub or small tree to 6 m, much grown on the Riviera for the perfume obtained from the flowers; zigzag branches with glabrous bipinnate leaves, and very sweet scented globose flower heads 1 cm dia., 1-3 in each leaf axil; February-March blooming. Photographed in Antigua Bot. Garden, West Indies. *Zone 8.*   p. 743

karroo (South Africa), "Sweet thorn" or "Mimosa"; widespread tree found in many parts of So. Africa to Zimbabwe; 4-6 m high with round crown; globular yellow flower heads; the branches with sharp, long needle-spines; leaves pinnate with leathery, narrow linear leaflets. *Zones 9-10.*   p. 743

latifolia (No. Australia), "Broadleaf wattle" or "Bush acacia"; attractive flowering shrub with glaucous leaflike stems to 15 cm long and 5 cm wide; the cylindrical flower heads, in loose spikes, to 5 cm long, yellow. *Zone 10.*   p. 744

longifolia (Australia, Tasmania), "Sydney golden wattle"; handsome evergreen tree to 10 m, of willowy, spreading habit, with the arching branches with long, linear, leather dark green phyllodia to 15 cm; the bright yellow, small globose flowers in thin risps along stem during February-March, rather short-lived. *Zone 9.*   p. 744

longifolia floribunda hort.: see retinodes

longifolia mucronata (S.E. Australia), "Narrow Sydney wattle"; small spreading tree with lightly drooping branches having narrow linear, stiffly thick phyllodia only 5-8 cm long, and the lemon-yellow flowers in long, 3 cm cylindrical, fluffy spikes along the stem, March blooming. *Subtropic. Zones 9-10.*   p. 744

nilotica (Trop. Africa), "Gum-Arabic tree"; large arid-regions tree becoming 25 m tall, the spreading branches set with straight needle-spines to 8 cm long; bipinnate leaves having small linear leaflets; axillary yellow, ball-shaped floral heads; linear seed pods 15 cm long; widely naturalized in India, where it supplies the local tanbark, a substitute for gum arabic. *Zone 10.*   p. 744

pendula (E. Australia), "Weeping myala"; very ornamental evergreen tree to 10 m high, with pendulous branches, resembling weeping willow, the leaf-like phyllodia linear 5-8 cm long, often curved outward, and attractively silver gray; flowers yellow in globose fluffy heads in clusters, often forming dense cylindric panicles. *Zone 10.*   p. 744

podalyriifolia (Queensland), "Pearl acacia"; tall, silvery-gray pubescent shrub to 3 m, set with ovate, silvery glaucous phyllodia; flowers in axillary racemes, 5-10 cm long, carrying up to 20 globose 1 cm heads of light yellow stamens; November to January blooming. *Zone 10.*   p. 745

retinodes, in California nurseries as longifolia floribunda, and commonly planted on the Riviera as A. "floribunda"; (South Australia), the "Everblooming acacia"; dense, upright tree to 8 m, having most of its foliage toward the ends of its branches, with narrow linear, dark green phyllodia to 16 cm long, and small ½ cm globular light yellow, fragrant flowers in loose, clustered racemes 15-25 cm long, blooming constantly from February nearly all year. *Zone 9.*   p. 744

saligna (W. Australia), "Weeping wattle"; wide-spreading large shrub or small tree with linear green phyllodes to 30 cm long on willowy branches, densely set with golden-yellow ball-shaped flower heads in racemes. The Cape-Flats near Cape Town, South Africa are a never forgotten sight when in bloom there in September, having been naturalized in moist areas, in South Africa's Spring. *Zone 10.*   p. 745

sphaerocephala (Mexico); "Mexican mimosa"; tree with bipinnate, feathery leaves, armed with hollow, horn-like, ant-tenanted thorns; globose flower-heads yellow. *Arid-subtropic. Zone 10.* p. 744

ACAENA   *Rosaceae*

buchananii (New Zealand: South Island), "Spine-nuts" or "Sheep-burr"; low evergreen perennial with prostrate stems and rooting with short erect branchlets 10 cm high; attractive because of its dense, jade-green, gray-silky alternate pinnate leaves; the 11-13 leaflets deeply toothed; inflorescence in interesting prickly, petal-less globular heads 2-3 cm dia., and furnished with showy 1 cm yellowish to coppery spines. *Zone 6.*   p. 491

microphylla (New Zealand), "Red-spine sheepburr"; low evergreen perennial, spreading to form mats 5 cm high, smooth bronzy-green leaves alternate pinnate to 5 cm long, similar to roses; showy inflorescence with petal-less flowers in close heads and with red stamens, blooming during Summer, and subtended by colorful crimson spines, which remain on the developing prickly, burr-like fruit. *Zone 7.*   p. 491

ACALYPHA   *Euphorbiaceae*

hispida (sanderi) (New Guinea, India), "Chenille plant"; showy tropical shrub 3 to 5 m high, with broad ovate, bright green, hairy leaves with crenate margins to 25 cm long; bright red flowers in long pendant spikes resembling foxtails, 30 to 45 cm long. *Zone 11.* p. 719

hispida 'Pendula', "Firetails"; charming dwarf form received from Aloha Exotics, Haleiwa, Hawaii, and grown as a potted plant in California; probably orignally grown as a seedling, it is a small darling, abundantly blooming when about 25 cm high and as wide or more; petite in every way, small ovate 5 cm leaves, and little rose-red 5-8 cm floral spikelets at tips of the thin branches. *Zone 11.* p. 61

wilkesiana 'Godseffiana' (heterophylla) (New Guinea), "Lance copper-leaf"; profuse shrub to 3 m high, bushy and dense with drooping branches, and ragged, pendant leaves reduced to long narrow, ribbon-like blades glossy green, and with pale yellow, wavy margins, to 30 cm or more long and 3 cm wide. *Zone 10.* p. 719

wilkesiana 'Macafeana' (New Hebrides or Vanuatu), "Copper-leaf"; robust, branching shrub dense with red ovate leaves marbled crimson and bronze, margins serrate; the slender flower spikes are red. *Zone 10.* p. 61, 719

wilkesiana 'Tricolor'; spectacular color variegation in the foliage, shades of green with cream, pink, orange and red. *Humid-tropical.* *Zone 11.* p. 61

ACANTHOPANAX   Araliaceae

sieboldianus (pentaphyllus) (Eleutherococcus), "Five-leaf aralia"; dioecious evergreen shrub to 2 m or more high, with slender arching stems covered by short prickles; compound leaves usually of 5 obovate leaflets, sometimes 3 or 7 each 3 to 6 cm long, glossy beneath and toothed; small starry, greenish-white flowers in globose clusters; small black fruit. *Zone 5.* p. 646

trifoliatus (Himalayas, Mts. So. China, Philippines, Taiwan); scandent shrub to 7 m high, the slender stems with recurved small spines; leaves compound of 3 ovate leaflets, 4-8 cm long, and lightly toothed; terminal inflorescence of small greenish-white flowers. *Zone 7.* p. 646

ACANTHUS   Acanthaceae

balcanicus (longifolius) (Greece, Yugoslavia) "Bear's breech"; ornamental perennial, 75-90 cm high with deeply lobed leaves almost pinnate, not spiny; floral spike 30 cm long, with spiny bracts and rosy, irregular tubular flowers with broad hooded lip. *Zone 9.* p. 339

mollis (So. Europe), "Greek acanthos"; outstanding, decorative perennial herb with large, glossy, lobed leaves to 40 cm long and 25 cm wide, hairy on the surface, cordate at base, not spiny; flowers white or lilac, with expanded 3-lobed lower lip, in showy spikes to 50 cm long, blooming in August. *Zone 9.* p. 17, 339

spinosus (Zander) (spinosissimus in Hortus) (So. Europe: Dalmatia, Greece; Asia Minor), "Classic acanthos"; fairly hardy perennial on lime stone soils, to 70 cm high, leaves glossy green, irregularly deeply lobed, the segments with spines; flowers in dense spikes, with corolla white to purplish. The acanthus leaf is much sculptured in classical Greece, such as on the marble capital of Corinthian columns. *Zone 8.* p. 629

ACCA sellowiana (Zander): see FEIJOA (Hortus 3)

ACER   Aceraceae

barbatum (Virginia to Florida and Texas), "Southern sugar maple" or "Florida maple"; handsome deciduous tree to 15 m high, having grayish to purplish twigs; leaves 3- to 5-lobed, 3-9 cm long, glaucous and pubescent beneath; flowers greenish-yellow, with long beard from throat; winged fruit to 3 cm long. *Zone 7.* p. 632

buergerianum (China, Japan), "Trident maple"; deciduous small tree to 8 m high, of low spreading growth, with very attractive 3-lobed glossy, rich green leaves 8 cm wide, glaucous beneath. Beautiful in autumn colors varying from yellow to orange and red. Decorative patio tree and favorite Bonsai subject. *Zone 6.* p. 632

campestre (Europe to Turkey, Caucasus, Iran), "Hedge maple"; dense shrub or round-topped tree to 8 m high or more; twigs pubescent to corky; leaves normally deeply 5-lobed, 5-10 cm wide, on red petioles, exuding milky juice; greenish flowers in upright hairy clusters; the fruit with wings spreading horizontally. May be sheared, and is used for hedges; autumn-color clear yellow. *Zones 5-9.* p. 632

davidii (China), "David maple"; deciduous tree to 15 m high, having bark striped white; smooth twigs with ovate-oblong leaves 8 to 20 cm long and unevenly toothed but not lobed, reddish-downy on veins; of pretty red color as they unfurl, then turning green, the autumn-color is yellow, red and purple; yellowish flowers in pendant racemes to 10 cm long; the fruit with wings spreading outward. *Zone 6.* p. 632

ginnala (Japan, Korea, E. Siberia, No. China), "Amur maple" or "Fire maple"; extremely hardy tree to 6 m high, or large spreading shrub, with twigs purple when young; small ovate leaves 8 cm long, lightly 3- to 5-lobed with middle lobe longest; fragrant yellowish-white flowers in small clusters; winged fruits turning red in Summer; autumn foliage is beautifully scarlet-red. *Zone 2.* p. 632

griseum (W. China), "Paperbark maple"; large very ornamental shrub or tree to 8 m or more high, with red-brown bark, peeling in thin papery flakes, revealing the new orange-red bark; the shoots woolly at first, with leaves compound of 3 leaflets, silvery beneath, and turning rose and orange in Autumn; flowers in pendant clusters, the downy fruitwings spreading wide. *Zone 5.* p. 632

japonicum 'Aconitifolium' (Japan), "Fernleaf fullmoon maple"; showy cultivar with spectacular large dark green leaves deeply divided, the oblanceolate 9-13 segments pinnately cut or toothed along margins, becoming rich ruby crimson in Autumn; usually grafted, and growing into gracefully branched small tree. *Zone 5.* p. 633

japonicum 'Aureum' (Japan), "Golden fullmoon maple"; strikingly colorful deciduous tree usually grown as a bush with spreading branches, the large roundish deeply lobed leaves 8-14 cm long, a vivid pale yellow into Summer. *Zone 5.* p. 633

x neglectum (x zoeschense) (campestre x lobelii); resembling A. campestre in habit, forming dense shrubs and ideally suited for hedges; the twigs softly downy when young, the foliage on milky petioles; the leaves 3 to 5-lobed, dark green and 8-12 cm wide; lends itself to shearing. *Zone 5.* p. 633

negundo 'Flamingo'; beautiful Box-elder of compact, bushy habit, with colorful pinnate foliage, the red petioles carry 3 to 5 ovate leaflets irregularly toothed, the blades glaucous green and richly splashed and bordered cream; also tinted rose or red. Rare beauty, photographed in Holland, but also seen in col. Wayside Gardens, So. Carolina. *Zones 4-8.* p. 633

negundo 'Odessanum' (negundo auratum Rehder) (Ukraine 1890), "Gold box elder"; robust deciduous tree 20 m high, with open crown, smooth shoots bearing beautifully variegated pinnate foliage; the ovate leaflets edged or blotched golden-yellow in sunlight. *Zone 3.* p. 633

negundo 'Variegatum' (New England to California and Guatemala), "Variegated box elder" or "Ash-leaved maple"; deciduous shrub or small tree with handsome variegated foliage; distinctive pinnate leaves with 3 to 5 or more toothed leaflets, fresh green with broad cream-white margins; flowers appear before leaves. Photographed on Lago Maggiore, Switzerland. *Zones 2-8.* p. 633

palmatum (Japan, Korea), "Japanese maple"; attractive deciduous small tree or shrub to 8 m or more, with membranous leaves deeply 5-9 lobed, in forms green to crimson; flowers purple. Frequently dwarfed and trained in containers as 'Bonsai' in Japan. *Zone 5.* p. 626, 634

palmatum 'Atropurpureum', "Red Cutleaf Japanese maple"; favorite color-form in garden plantings; handsome saw-toothed leaves of rich crimson-purple or coppery bronze, deeply divided into lanceolate lobes; propeller-like winged fruit. *Zones 5-9.* p. 626-634

palmatum 'Bloodgood'; small gracefully branched tree, also grown as a bushy shrub, with the deeply divided new foliage brilliant red, changing to dark crimson through the season; deciduous. *Zones 5-9.* p. 633

palmatum 'Crimson Queen' (dissectum cv.), "Laceleaf Japanese maple"; small tree usually grown as low shrub with spreading branches; the interesting reddish leaves palmately dissected into long, narrow segments, doubly lobed or cut along sides, creating a delicate weeping effect; the older foliage 8-14 cm wide, turning blackish-red toward Autumn, until they drop in Winter. Usually grafted for propagation. *Zone 5.* p. 634

palmatum 'Dissectum' ('Viride'), "Threadleaf Japan maple"; weeping branches with large bright green leaves, finely cut into narrow segments and toothed or lobed along sides. *Zone 5.* p. 634

palmatum 'Laciniatum', "Lacy Japanese maple"; handsome small tree to 8 m high, very popular in gardens when grown as bush; smooth red shoots with attractive foliage 12 cm across, the leaves palmately compound or deeply cut into 5 to 11 lanceolate segments, doubly toothed, yellowish-green in Summer, but turning red in Autumn; flowers purplish-red, in pendulous clusters; the seed-wings spreading horizontally. *Zone 5.* p. 632

palmatum 'Sangokaku' (also spelled 'Senkaki'), "Coral-bark maple"; a rare Japanese cultivar of slender habit; finely and deeply cut light green, delicate leaves, carried in contrast on striking red branches. Photographed at North Haven Gardens, Dallas, Texas. *Zones 5-8.* p. 633

pensylvanicum (E. No. America: Québec to Wisconsin, so. to Georgia), "Striped maple" or "Moose-wood"; deciduous tree 5 to 10 m high, having bark striped with white lines; large leaves with 3 long-pointed lobes, 12 to 20 cm across, and crenate at margins; yellow flowers in pendulous racemes 10-15 cm long; fruit wings spreading. *Zone 3.* p. 632

platanoides (Europe to Turkey and Iran), "Norway maple"; round-headed deciduous tree to 20 m or more high; smooth branches with 5-lobed, glossy 10-18 cm leaves, the lobes sharply pointed; small greenish yellow flowers before the foliage, followed by attractive fruit with spreading wings. Standard street tree in America. Zone 3.   p. 635

platanoides 'Columnare', "Columnar Norway maple"; erect form with close-packed branches remaining low; leaves smaller than the species, reddish when juvenile, later green; in Autumn colored golden-yellow to a beautiful red. Zone 3.   p. 635

platanoides 'Crimson King' ('Nigrum'), "Crimson King maple"; striking ornamental deciduous tree, introduced in France 1946, and patented in U.S., of open habit, with spreading branches; the delicate glossy 5-lobed foliage deep rich maroon-red, its vivid color retained throughout the growing season or until leaves drop. Zone 8.   p. 634

platanoides 'Drummondii', "Variegated Norway maple"; elegant tree, having 5-lobed leaves light green, strikingly variegated creamy-white, primarily inside of margins. Zone 4.   p. 635

platanoides 'Schwedleri', "Schwedler maple"; outstanding cultivar found 1864 in Silesia; showy tree, with attractive 3-lobed 15 cm leaves; young growth rich crimson-purple in Spring and early Summer, gradually turning green; ruby-red color may be maintained by hard pruning in alternate Autumns. Zone 5.   p. 634

pseudoplatanus (Europe and W. Asia), "Sycamore maple"; large handsome tree to 30 m high with immense rounded crown; the bark is shed in small scales; smooth branches with maple-like, green 5-lobed leaves 10-18 cm wide, and coarsely toothed, glaucescent beneath; yellow-green flowers in pendulous racemes to 12 cm long; the nut-wings spreading until leaves drop. Zone 5.   p. 634

pseudoplatanus 'Purpureum', "Purple sycamore"; ornamental form with lobed leaves purple on underside; photographed in garden of Castle Burgh, Thuringia. Zone 5.   p. 635

rubrum (Eastern Canada to Florida, west to Minnesota and Texas), "Red Maple" or "Canadian maple"; magnificent, round-headed fast-growing deciduous tree 15 m or more high, with grayish bark and smooth branches; the leaves 3 to 5-lobed, 8-15 cm across, lustrous dark green above, glaucous and lightly downy beneath, turning brilliant scarlet in Autumn in frosty areas; bright red flowers in clusters in March-April, appearing before foliage; winged fruit on pendulous stalks. Most popular shade tree in the U.S. Zone 3.   p. 635

saccharinum 'Laciniatum' (species from Québec to Florida and Okla.), "Silver maple"; graceful tree with gently pendant branches, and leaves deeply 5-lobed, 8-12 cm wide, green above and silvery white beneath, the segments cut again; good yellow color in Autumn; flowers greenish, without petals, in small clusters. Zone 3. p. 635

saccharum (No. America to Texas), "Sugar maple"; deciduous tree with silver-gray bark; leaves 10-15 cm dia, distinct with 3 to 5 lobes and deep rounded sinuses; flowers without petals, appearing before leaves; striking autumn foliage in colder regions, turning golden-yellow to bright crimson. The sap yields sugar or syrup. Zone 3.   p. 635

tataricum (S.E. Europe, Asia Minor), "Tatarian maple"; deciduous shrub of bushy habit, or wide-spreading tree to 8 m high; the smooth branches with broadly ovate leaves 5-10 cm long, doubly serrate but not lobed except when young; greenish-white flowers in erect clusters; the fruit-wings reddish in late Summer. Zone 4.   p. 635

ACEROLA: see MALPIGHIA

ACHILLEA   *Compositae*
ageratum (So. Europe: Balkans), "Sweet yarrow" or "Sweet Nancy"; aromatic perennial to 40 cm high, having woody base, forming dense silvery rosette, with oblong, crimped leaves 3-5 cm long; small yellow ray-flowers in compact rounded heads 5 cm across, July to September blooming. Zone 7.   p. 369

filipendulina (Asia Minor, Caucasus), "Fern-leaf yarrow"; stiff, erect perennial herb 1-1½ m high; fragrant, hairy leaves finely dissected; small flowers, June to September blooming, in large, flat clusters to 10 cm across, all yellow. The yarrow tea made from leaves and flowers is effective with stomach disorders; good for cuts and wounds when applied externally. Dried cut flowers hold their color indefinitely. Zone 3.   p. 369, 525, 527

filipendulina 'Coronation Gold'; perennial to 1 m high, with finely cut, ferny leaves with a strong, spicy odor; the domed terminal flower clusters are huge and 12 cm or more across, of numerous small flowers bronzy yellow. Zone 4.   p. 369

millefolium (Europe to W. Asia; natural in No. America and Australia), "Common yarrow" or "Milfoil"; rhizomatous perennial 15 to 60 cm or more high, with leaves lacily divided fern-like; the stems

with branched, loose clusters of small white or pinkish flowers, blooming July to December. Popular as a ground cover and for its drought resistance, for its cut flowers, and the strongly aromatic foliage. Zones 2-9.   p. 369, 527

millefolium 'Rosea', "Rosy milfoil" or "Pink yarrow"; a charming color variation of this popular garden perennial, with feathery almost evergreen leaves, aromatic when crushed; the inflorescence with its numerous small rose-red flowers in umbels, blooming in Summer; used by florists in cut-flower bouquets. Zones 2-9.   p. 526

nobilis (No. Greece), "Thessaly yarrow"; erect hairy perennial, with bipinnately dissected leaves; the stems branching into several dense floral clusters of pure white ray-flowers, in June-July. Zone 7.   p 369

ptarmica 'The Pearl' (species from Europe to Caucasus to Siberia), "Sneezeweed"; old-fashioned favorite rhizomatous perennial 50 cm high, very floriferous, with double white, button-like 2 cm flowerheads like miniature pompons, borne in loose clusters, and blooming successively from June to October. Zone 4.   p. 369

taygetea (Mountains of Greece); herbaceous perennial to 50 cm high, with silvery-green leaves pinnately dissected; bright primrose-yellow flowers in close terminal clusters 5-10 cm across, in June-September. Excellent as cut flowers. Zone 5.   p. 369

tomentosa (C. Europe to W. Asia), "Woolly yarrow"; vigorous herbaceous perennial to 25 cm high, forming dense mats; woolly, dissected fern-like foliage is nearly evergreen at base, and aromatic when crushed; large clusters of small blossoms, with ray-flowers bright yellow, from July to September. Zones 2-7.   p. 369

ACHIMENES   *Gesneriaceae*
andrieuxii (Hortus): see Eucodonia andrieuxii (A. Lau)
cettoana (So. Mexico); rhizomatous stiff-hairy plant to 30 cm high; lanceolate leaves in whorls 6 cm long; flowers violet-purple with slender tube and spreading petals. *Humid-tropical.* Zone 11.   p. 61

erecta (coccinea in hort.), (Mexico, Jamaica, Panama); first cultivated species imported to England in 1778); herbaceous plant of neat miniature habit with thickened scaly underground stolons, trailing stems 10-45 cm with 2-3 crenate, hairy leaves together, and small axillary flowers intense bright scarlet, borne in profusion from late August into Winter. Zone 11.   p. 65

ACHRAS zapota: see MANILKARA zapota (Hortus)

ACHYRANTHES herbstii: see IRESINE herbstii

ACIDANTHERA   *Iridaceae*
murieliae (bicolor var.) (Gladiolus) (Ethiopia), "Peacock orchid"; cormous plant with flat, linear leaves, in appearance between Gladiolus and Ixia; about 60 cm high; nodding fragrant flowers 4-5 cm across, with long tubes and spreading petals, creamy-white with purple star in center. The variety murieliae is stronger growing than type. Zone 9.   p. 223

ACMENA   *Myrtaceae*
smithii (Eugenia) (E. Australia), "Lilly-pilly"; evergreen tree to 18 m high; with thickish ovate leaves to 9 cm long, unfolding in rich bronze; terminal clusters of small snow-white flowers, followed by showy edible, pinkish or purple small berries. Zone 10.   p. 918

ACOELORRHAPHE   *Palmae*
wrightii (syn. Paurotis) (So. Florida, West Indies, C. America), "Everglades palm"; cluster palm at home in the Everglades swamps, with slender trunks to 12 m, covered by red-brown matting and bases of leaf stalks; palmate nearly round leaves 60-90 cm dia., divided more than halfway, with stiff segments light green above, silvery beneath, and split at apex; young plants have entire leaves not divided. *Tropical.* Zones 10-11.   p. 108

ACOKANTHERA   *Apocynaceae*
oblongifolia (spectabilis) (So. Africa), "Wintersweet"; evergreen shrub or small tree to 5 m high, with narrow-oval, leathery, glossy leaves 8-12 cm long, and showy clusters of sweetly-scented, 2 cm pure white flowers in dense clusters. The plant is poisonous. Zone 10.   p. 640

ACONITUM   *Ranunculaceae*
fischeri (carmichaelii) (No. China to Kamtschatka), "Aconite" or "Monk's hood"; showy herbaceous perennial with leafy stems 1 m and more high; the thin leaves 5-15 cm wide, cordate at base and divided, the division deeply 3-lobed; the inflorescence in a terminal, loose raceme of pale blue to violet-purple flowers having an arched helmet and small beak 4 cm high or more, blooming in August-September. Plant is poisonous but has been used medicinally. Zone 3.   p. 484

henryi (No. China), "Autumn monkshood"; striking perennial to 1½ m or more high, sinuous and branched in upper part, partially pubescent; the leaves 5-15 cm wide, mostly deeply 3-parted; the blue-purple flowers typically like monks-hood 4-5 cm high, topped by rounded 2 cm helmet, and a short beak in front; blooming July to September. *Zone 4.* p. 484

lycoctonum (No. Europe to E. Asia), "Wolfsbane"; herbaceous perennial to more than 1 m high, with stem leaves deeply 5-7 parted, the divisions 3-lobed; the yellow to cream flowers tubular, each with narrow protective helmet, blooming July-August. *Zone 3.* p. 484

napellus (No. Europe: Sweden etc.), "Helmet flower"; the "Garden monks-hood", from which the drug aconite is extracted; erect perennial with slender stem to 1 m or more high, having leaves palmately cut into narrow segments; the characteristic violet or blue flowers featuring a broad helmet with a beak-like visor, to 5 cm long and borne in loose raceme, blooming late Summer. Extremely poisonous. Goes completely dormant in Winter. *Zones 3-8.* p. 484

ACONTHOPANAX   *Araliaceae*

trifoliatus (Himalayas, Mts. So. China, Philippines, Taiwan); scandent shrub to 7 m high, the slender stems with recurved small spines; leaves compound of 3 ovate leaflets, 4-8 cm long, and lightly toothed; terminal inflorescence of small greenish-white flowers. *Zone 7.* p. 646

ACORUS   *Araceae*

calamus (No. and C. Europe, Temp. Asia, S.E. Canada, U.S.A.), "Sweet flag"; robust water-loving perennial herb of marshlands, to 2 m high; creeping rhizome containing aromatic cells, with iris-like leaves arranged in flat, shingled fans, the linear grass-green leaves parallel-veined, 2 cm wide and with thick midrib; the inflorescence on a cylindrical spadix 5-10 cm long thickly covered with minute greenish-yellow perfect flowers. The candied rhizome was an old-time confection. Rhizomes contain aromatic oil, extracted for drug-bitters, aiding in correcting digestive problems. *Zones 5-10.* p. 325, 525

calamus 'Variegatus' (N. Hemisphere), "Sweet flag"; bog plant with flat, iris-like leathery leaves, green with broad, white, lengthwise variegation. *Zones 6-10.* p. 325

gramineus (Burma, Philippines, So. China, Japan); small water-loving rhizomatous perennial with flat, narrow-linear, grass-like leaves to 40 cm or more long, 5-10 mm wide, grass-green and of thin-leathery texture, forming thick tufts; small 5 cm spadix in catkin form, yellowish-green, eventually setting small green berries containing 2-3 seeds. *Zones 5-8.* p. 325

gramineus 'Variegatus' (Japan), "Miniature sweet flag"; handsome water-loving perennial 20-30 cm high, with creeping rhizomes and tufted, linear, flat, leathery leaves, light green and white, spreading fan-like. *Warm temperate. Zones 8-9.* p. 559

ACRIOPSIS   *Orchidaceae*

javanica (Spathoglottis trivalvis) (Burma, Sumatra, Philippines); small tropical epiphyte with egg-shaped 5 cm pseudobulbs bearing 2-5 fleshy, linear leaves 20 cm long; arching inflorescence of numerous 2 cm yellow-green flowers having purple lip. *Zone 12.* p.81

ACROCLINIUM roseum: see HELIPTERUM roseum

ACROCOMIA   *Palmae*

intumescens (Brazil); bold feather palm with trunk smooth and swollen in lower part, toward top armed with rings of stout spines; dense spiny crown of feathery fronds gracefully arching, the leaflets glossy green and pendulous. *Zones 11-12.* p. 99

ACROSTICHUM   *Polypodiaceae (Filices)*

danaeifolium (excelsum) (Trop. America), tall "Swamp-fern"; with pinnate fronds 1-4 m high, with most or all of the pinnae fertile and bearing spores, on mature fronds. *Humid-tropical. Zones 10-12.* p. 128

ACROTRICHE   *Epacridaceae*

aggregata (Queensland), "Ground-berry"; low, rather sprawling evergreen shrub growing to 40 cm high in sunny location; with small stiff, pungent, needle-like leaves; the flowers in axillary clusters, the tubular corolla with 5-lobed limb; forming glossy red berries on underside of branchlets. *Zone 9.* p. 698

ACTAEA   *Ranunculaceae*

pachypoda (syn. alba), (Nova Scotia to Georgia, west to Minnesota and Missouri), "Gull's eyes"; herbaceous perennial to 50 cm high, with compound leaves, the ovate leaflets sharply toothed; and terminal pyramidal clusters of white flowers, having long slender tube; the main attractions of this plant are its handsome though poisonous fruits, which are white or reddish berries having a purple spot at the tip, blooming May and June. *Zone 3.* p. 483

rubra (E. Canada to Penna. and So. Dakota), "Red baneberry" or "Snakeberry"; bushy perennial 30-60 cm high, with compound leaves in threes, the leaflets ovate and toothed; the creamy-white flowers followed by clusters of handsome, shining cherry-red, but poisonous berries to about 2 cm long. *Zone 3.* p. 483

ACTINEA: see HYMENOXYS

ACTINIDIA   *Dilleniaceae (Actinidiaceae in Hortus 3)*

arguta (Japan: Hokkaido to Kyushu; Manchuria, Korea), "Tara vine, "Yang-tao" or "Saru Nashi"; woody scandent shrub, the branches filled with spongy pith; thin broad-ovate leaves to 10 cm long, undulate or serrate at margins; inflorescence axillate with small 2 cm white flowers, followed by pendant greenish-yellow, edible berries 2½ cm dia. *Zone 5.* p. 275

chinensis (China, Taiwan); "Chinese gooseberry" or "Kiwi vine"; partially deciduous woody vine twining to 10 m, sparsely furnished with large 12 to 20 cm, rough, corrugated ovate leaves, dark green above, white velvety beneath; small 3-4 cm flowers cream turning to yellow in August, followed about November, in the Northern hemisphere, by pendant ovoid, fuzzy brownish fruit 4-5 cm diameter; delicious to eat, with acid, gooseberry-like flavor; male and female flowers usually on separate plants. *Zones 9-10.* p. 275, 909

kolomikta (Japan, Manchuria, China), "Kolomikta vine"; shrubby twining vine to 5 m, grown for their attractive foliage; the long-stalked heart-shaped leaves 8-12 cm long, variegated green with white or pink, some are all white, others with red, more so on male plants; for colorful arbor, trellis or wall-covering; cup-shaped white, axillary flowers; yellow or greenish fruit on female plants. *Zone 5.* p. 275, 636

ACTINOPHLOEUS: see PTYCHOSPERMA

ADANSONIA   *Bombacaceae*

digitata (across Trop. Africa), the giant "Baobab" or "Sour gourd" or "Monkey-bread-tree"; one of the largest trees in the world, thought to become more than 2000 years old, and while only to 18 m tall, the swollen trunk attains a diameter of more than 10 m, is of pulpous wood without growth rings. Leaves deciduous, digitately compound with leaflets 12 cm long; large 18 cm solitary, scented, pendulous white flowers with purplish stamens; oblong, woody, hairy fruit 30 cm long, which also earns it the name "Dead rat-tree". *Zones 9-11.* p. 207, 208, 667, 669, 905

ADENANDRA   *Rutaceae*

uniflora (Diosma) (So. Africa), "China flower"; small evergreen shrub with erect slender branches, 1 cm lanceolate leaves, and solitary flowers 3 cm wide, the 5 petals white with a deep rose streak, anthers brown-purple; late Spring. *Zone 10.* p. 860

ADENIA   *Passifloraceae*

olabuensis (Modecca) (Madagascar), "Spider tree"; curious tropical shrub with slender branches and unusual leathery, peltate, palmately lobed leaves nearly reduced to a skeleton of ribs, glossy gray-green with silvery-cream variegation in central areas; axillary yellow bell-shaped flowers. *Zone 11.* p. 79

ADENIUM   *Apocynaceae*

obesum (coetanum) (E. Africa: Tanzania, Kenya, Uganda), the "Desert rose"; spreading succulent bush 2 m high, with thick, fleshy, twisted base and short branches; deciduous obovate, fleshy leaves glossy dark green with pink midrib, 8 cm long, when young sometimes with minute hairs; numerous showy, 5 cm flowers with spreading petals pinkish edged with carmine or all carmine-rose. *Arid-tropical. Zones 10-11.* p. 151

swazicum (Transvaal, Swaziland, Mozambique), "Impala lily"; succulent bush of arid areas, with short obovate, thick leaves; showy flowers in terminal clusters, white or pink with blood-red eye. *Zone 10.* p. 151

swazicum flore pleno; "Double Impala lily"; seen at Grigsby's Nursery in Vista, California; having showy flowers about 5 cm across, almost entirely rose-pink marked with occasional stripes of white, and an inner row of short petals deep rose. *Zone 10.* p. 151

ADENOCARPUS   *Leguminosae*

complicatus (commutatus) (Portugal, Spain, S.W. France and So. Italy); low deciduous shrub 30-80 cm high, dense with slender branches; leaves compound of 3 obovate leaflets 6-12 mm long; flowers in erect terminal clusters, the corolla golden-yellow, the standard streaked red and silky outside, blooming May-June. *Zone 9.* p. 746

ADENOPHORA   *Campanulaceae*

bulleyana (W. China), "Lady bells"; summer-blooming herbaceous perennial, with erect stem, to 50 cm high; ovate stem-leaves to 8 cm long and serrate at margins; branched inflorescence on wiry stalks, 2 cm bell-flowers pale blue. *Zone 6.* p. 352

confusa (W. China), "Purple lady-bell"; handsome perennial, with rigid erect stem to 1 m or more, having sessile leaves 8 cm long; toward apex a spire of nodding, purplish-blue cupflowers 2-3 cm long, in late Summer. *Zone 4*.   *p. 352*

takedae (howozana) (Japan: Honshu), "Japanese ladybell"; thick-rooted perennial with pendant, branched wiry stems, having long smooth, linear to narrow-ovate leaves 7 to 15 cm long; terminal racemes of violet-blue, cup-shaped flowers 2-3 cm long, blooming in Autumn. *Zone 6*.   *p. 352*

ADHATODA cydoniifolia: see MEGAKEPASMA

ADIANTUM   *Polypodiaceae (Filices)*

capillus-veneris (found around the world), "Venus-hair"; creeping rhizomes produce an abundance of delicate, 2-3 pinnate fronds, the variable segments deeply lobed, with veins leading into teeth; half hardy. *Zone 9*.   *p. 128*

hispidulum (Australia, New Zealand), "Australian maidenhair"; handsome species with 2-3 pinnate fronds, forked at base, borne on long wiry, hairy stalks, the leaflets almost stalkless, thin-leathery, arranged along axis; veins running into teeth. *Zone 10*.   *p. 128*

macrophyllum (Trop. America); showy fern with creeping rhizome, the pinnate fronds 30-40 cm long on shiny, black-brown stalks, the lower pinnae of barren frond 5-10 cm long, ovate, toothed, papery, yellow-green; reddish when young; the fertile leaflets narrower. *Humid-tropical. Zones 11-12*.   *p. 128*

pedatum (No. America), "American maidenhair"; hardy outdoors, and equally useful in the greenhouse, with fronds to 60 cm high, the purplish stalks forked fan-like, each pinnate branch set with neat rows of papery, pea-green leaflets. *Zones 3-9*.   *p. 129*

raddianum (cuneatum) (Brazil), "Delta maidenhair"; an old greenhouse favorite because of its tolerance, sturdiness and simple elegance of the dark green fronds with many small, firm leaflets having a wedge-shaped base, with veins running into sinus between lobes. *Humid-tropical. Zones 11-12*.   *p. 129*

tenerum (Florida, Bermuda, W. Indies, Mexico, Venezuela), "Fan maidenhair"; good potplant with graceful fronds of good texture, 30 to 90 cm long, pink when young, later fresh-green, the fan-shaped leaflets growing large and lacily lobed. *Zones 11-12*.   *p. 129*

trapeziforme (Mexico and W. Indies south to Brazil); delicate looking, yet bold-growing "Giant maidenhair" with slowly creeping rhizome and large 2-pinnate fronds 30 to 60 cm long, on black stems, the stalked trapezoid leaflets to 5 cm long and brilliant green. *Zones 11-12*.   *p. 129*

venustum (Nepal); distinct species of dwarf habit, from the Himalayas as 2100 m altitude; from creeping rhizome spring rather rigid light green 3-4 pinnate fronds 15 to 30 cm long, carried on shiny black stalks. *Zone 10*.   *p. 129*

ADINA   *Rubiaceae*

rubella (So. China); attractive shrub to 3 m high; small opposite evergreen ovate leaves 3 cm long; globular flower heads with protruding long styles, and sweetly scented. *Zone 7*.   *p. 854*

ADLUMIA   *Fumariaceae*

fungosa (Ontario to Michigan and Carolina); "Climbing fumitory" or "Mountain fringe"; high-climbing biennial vine with weak stems; thin bipinnate leaves; graceful clusters of pinkish to pale purple 2 cm flowers from June to October. *Zones 3-8*.   *p. 277*

ADONIDIA: see VEITCHIA

ADONIS   *Ranunculaceae*

amurensis (Manchuria, Japan), "Amur adonis"; charming herbaceous perennial to 40 cm high, with stem leaves 8-15 cm long, cut into linear segments; flowers typically golden-yellow, 5 cm across, but varying in color to white, rose or striped bright red, appearing before leaves are fully developed, in early Spring. *Zone 3*.   *p. 484*

annua (aestivalis and autumnalis) (So. Europe and Mediterran. reg., Asia Minor), "Pheasant's eye"; handsome annual with taproots; branched stems 10-40 cm high, with ferny 3-pinnate leaves; scarlet to dark red cupped flowers 2-3 cm across, having black center, summer-blooming. *Zone 9*.   *p. 484*

flammea (So. Europe to Asia Minor), "Flame adonis"; highly attractive annual 20-50 cm high, with leaves deeply dissected into narrow linear segments; the beautiful cup-shaped flowers 3-5 cm across, bright orange-red to scarlet, with deep purple eye in center; blooming May to July. *Zone 9*.   *p. 484*

vernalis (Cent. and So. Europe to Caucasus and Siberia), "Spring adonis"; very attractive herbaceous perennial 20-40 cm high, the lower leaves reduced to scales, the upper leaves finely divided into linear segments and forming dense rosettes; large yellow flowers to 8 cm across blooming in March to May or later. *Zone 3*.   *p. 484*

ADROMISCHUS   *Crassulaceae*

festivus (Cape Prov.), "Plover eggs"; fascinating clustering succulent with cylindric or thick spatulate leaves 3-4 cm long, flattened toward the crested apex, silvery green marbled maroon; purplish flowers on 30 cm stalk. Photo shown on p. 182 may be the very similar A. cooperi, according to Paul Hutchison of Tropic World, Escondido, Calif. *Zone 10*.   *p. 182*

maculatus (rupicola of hort.) (So. Africa: Cape Prov.), "Calico hearts"; dwarf succulent rosette of few flat leaves to 4 cm long and 3 cm wide, almost round or obovate, gray-green heavily blotched with brown-purple and along margins, the edge a silvery line; flowers tipped red-white. *Arid-subtropic. Zone 10*.   *p. 182*

AECHMEA   *Bromeliaceae*

caudata variegata (Billbergia forgetii) (Brazil); big sparry rosette of rich green stiff leaves broadly banded creamy-yellow; bold inflorescence with white-mealy stem and panicle of yellow bracts and golden-yellow flowers. *Tropical. Zone 10*.   *p. 44*

chantinii (Venezuela, Amazonas, Amazonian Perú), "Amazonian zebra plant"; colorful open rosette of hard olive-green leaves with pronounced pinkish-gray cross-bands; inflorescence on branched spike with tight red bracts tipped yellow, subtended by red bract leaves. *Zone 11*.   *p. 43*

dichlamydea var. trinitensis (Trinidad); handsome, majestic epiphyte with gray-green leaves 50-80 cm in length; long, many-branched, scandent inflorescence a rainbow of color, with pink, arching stalk and flattened lateral spikes bright coral, with densely shingled, blue bracts tipped with black-purple; flowers white with lilac, and deep blue berries. *Zone 10*.   *p. 43*

fasciata (Billbergia rhodocyanea) (Rio de Janeiro), "Silver vase"; stocky rosette of leathery green leaves covered with gray scales and richly tigered silver-white; blackish spines; durable inflorescence in rose-colored globose heads with blue flowers. *Zone 10*.   *p. 43*

fernandae (No. Brazil: Amazonas, Guyana); showy terrestrial in spreading rosette, 30 to 40 cm high, with leaves very long and 5 cm wide, green with underside reddish, serrate with marginal spines; spectacular erect globular inflorescence to 14 cm dia.; the shingled bracts bright red, the flowers greenish-yellow. *Zone 11*.   *p. 44*

fulgens (Pernambuco), "Coral berry"; loose rosette of stiff green leaves dusted gray; inflorescence in showy panicles with oblong red berries tipped with purple flowers. *Zone 11*.   *p. 44*

mariae-reginae (Costa Rica), "Queen aechmea"; robust rosette of broad, gray-green, leathery leaves, recurved and with toothed edge; stout spike with pendant, delicate pink bract leaves, topped by cylindrical head of red-tipped berries and violet flowers. *Zone 10*.   *p. 44*

mertensii (Trinidad, Guyana, Venez., Colombia, Perú, No. Brazil), "China-berry"; epiphytic open rosette with few green leaves to 60 cm long, covered with white scales especially beneath, and having marginal spines; slender stalk with rose bracts, the inflorescence many-flowered, bipinnate with yellow or red petals, fruit blue. *Zone 10*.   *p. 43*

miniata discolor (Brazil); open rosette of soft-leathery olive-green leaves, pale red reverse; inflorescence a paniced spike of orange-red rounded berries tipped by pale blue flowers. *Zone 11*.   *p. 44*

mulfordii (Gravisia fosteriana) (Atlantic coast of southeastern Brazil); large plant with stiff leaves; tall branched spikes of orange-red bracts, yellow flowers. *Zone 10*.   *p. 43*

nudicaulis (Mexico and West Indies to Brazil); stiff tubular rosette of few, variable gray-green leaves to 40 cm long, armed with sharp teeth; arching slender red stalk carries a colorful inflorescence of rosy bract leaves and pinkish-yellow floral bracts and yellow flowers. *Zone 10*.   *p. 43*

phanerophlebia (So. Brazil); tightly closed rosette in habitat growing both epiphytic or on rocks; broad, rigid leaves to 50 cm long, grayish-green and prominently marked with numerous silvery cross-bands, the margins armed with spines; erect inflorescence with rosy-red bracts and blue flowers. *Zone 10*.   *p. 43*

pineliana (S.E. Brazil); small, shapely rosette in soft tones of gray and rose with copper lining, red-brown teeth at margin; inflorescence an upright stem covered with scarlet bracts topped with brush-like head having yellow flowers. *Zone 10*.   *p. 43*

sphaerocephala (Ae. gigantea) (Brazil); giant terrestrial rosette of stiff, thorny leaves 1 to 3 m long; the floral stalk clothed in red bracts, carrying an unusual tight globular, spiny head; producing dark blue flowers. *Zone 10*.   *p. 46*

tillandsioides 'Marginata'; attractive epiphytic rosette of narrow leathery, grayish leaves variegated along the margins by broad white bands, armed with spines; inflorescence with serrated floral bracts green, yellowish or red; flower petals yellow, followed by berries first white, then blue. The species is from Guyana and Venezuela. *Zone 10*.   *p. 43*

AEGLE   Rutaceae

marmelos (India), "Bael fruit" or "Holy fruit"; small spiny tropical tree 3 m high, with slender branches, the foliage divided into 3 slender leaflets with crenate edges; flowers with 4 or 5 narrow petals and showing numerous stamens; fruit is globular or pear-shaped, 5 to 10 cm dia., and covered with smooth, hard gray or yellow rind which contains orange, sweet aromatic pulp in 8-16 cells with seeds. The fruit pulp is used for drinks and conserves; the flowers are made into perfume in India. *Zones* 10-11.   p. 859, 934

AEGOPODIUM   Umbelliferae

podagraria 'Variegatum', (Europe, natur. in No. America), "Bishop's weed" or "Goutweed"; coarse perennial herb 35 cm high, with creeping rootstock; compound herbaceous, wrinkled leaves divided into three parts, milky-green with irregular cream-white margins; flowers white; attractive hardy border plant for the garden in shady places. *Zones* 3-9.   p. 516

AEONIUM   Crassulaceae

arboreum 'Schwarzkopf' ('Zwartkop' in Holland), "Black Tree aeonium"; striking decorative variety with coppery to deep purple leaves. The species Ae. arboreum is Mediterranean from Morocco and Portugal east to Crete; an erect bold succulent to 1 m high, little branching, topped by a flaring 20 cm rosette of spatulate light green, fleshy leaves, fringed white at margins; flowers golden-yellow. According to Backeberg, the var. atropurpureum turns green in Winter; the black clone 'Schwarzkopf' remains glossy brown-purple. *Zone* 10.   p. 180

arboreum 'Variegatum'; very handsome variegated cultivar of the green-leaved species from Morocco; erect thick succulent stem to 1 m high, topped by a rosette 15 cm across of thin fleshy spatulate leaves and ciliate (white-hairy) along edges; in the cultivar 'Variegatum' broadly margined creamy-white and glossy surface; inflorescence 30 cm high, with flowers golden-yellow. *Zone* 10.   p. 180

ciliatum 'Rubrum' (Sempervivum) (Canary Islands: Palma, Tenerife); shrubby succulent to 1 m high, the branches bearing large rosettes of smooth, obovate leaves to 10 cm long, ciliate at margins, and beautifully colored deep maroon-red; pubescent inflorescence to 30 cm long with greenish-white flowers. *Zone* 10.   p. 191

domesticum variegatum: see AICHRYSON x domesticum

haworthii (Tenerife), "Pin-wheel"; bushy plant with short woody branches bearing rosettes 6 to 8 cm across, of thick, obovate-acute gray-green leaves with ciliate, red margins; small flowers pale yellow flushed rose, on inflorescence 10-12 cm long. *Zone* 10.   p. 180

hierrense (Canary Isl.: Hierro); swollen unbranched silvery stem to 50 cm high, topped by a rosette 60 cm across; narrow lanceolate, smooth glaucous blue leaves 15-30 cm long, and suffused with purple; this surmounted by a tremendous, pubescent inflorescence 40 cm high, bearing pale pink flowers on its branches. *Zone* 10.   p. 181

lindleyi hort. (Canary Isl.: Tenerife); miniature succulent widely branched, to 30 cm high, with roundish-rhomboid to wedge-shaped pubescent grayish-green fleshy leaves 1 to 2 cm long, in loose rosettes on thin flexuous stems; small 1 cm starry flowers lemon-yellow. Photo shown on p. 184 could be Aichryson. *Zone* 10.   p. 184

percarneum (Canary Islands: Gran Canaria); succulent shrub to 1 m high, the erect branching stem bearing handsome rosettes of flat, obovate pointed, fleshy leaves, light green and grayish, tinged with red toward apex, 8-10 cm long; panicles of soft flesh-pink flowers. *Zone* 10.   p. 181

tabuliforme (Tenerife), "Saucer plant"; circular, plate-like rosette to 60 cm across, of small spatulate leaves arranged flat like shingles, fresh green, margins ciliate; flowers yellow in pyramidal inflorescence. *Zone* 10.   p. 181

undulatum (pseudotabuliforme) (Gran Canaria), "Green platters" or "Saucer plant"; handsome silvery-stemmed succulent shrub, to 2 m high, suckering near base, and topped by shapely rosettes 30 to 40 cm across, of broad-spatulate shining olive-green leaves, margins finely ciliate; bright yellow flowers in dense inflorescence to 50 cm high. *Zone* 10.   p. 182

AERIDES   Orchidaceae

odorata var. major (virens) (Java), "Foxtail orchid"; handsome, free-growing epiphyte with 2-ranked, bright green fleshy, broad leaves, and waxy peach-pink flowers with yellow horns, very fragrant, on long, drooping racemes (April-July). *Tropical. Zone* 12.   p. 82

AERVA   Amaryllidaceae

persica (tomentosa) (Egypt: Sinai Desert; Somalia, Djibouti); semi-woody perennial of arid deserts, seen in the Arta Mts. of Djibouti; erect branches densely white-hairy, with oval, gray pubescent leaves 4-5 cm long; flowers white, fleecy, in dense woolly spikes. *Zone* 10.   p. 340

AESCHYNANTHUS   Gesneriaceae

obconicus (Malaya), "Basket plant"; tropical epiphyte with slender pendant stems with opposite, glossy elliptic green leaves to 10 cm long; waxy flowers dark red, covered with soft hairs. *Zone* 11. p. 62

radicans (parvifolius) (Himalayas); "Lipstick vine"; trailer similar to grandiflorus, with deep glossy green lanceolate leaves 10 cm long; flowers scarlet, tipped yellow, the corolla 2½ cm long and scarcely contracted. *Tropical. Zones* 10-11.   p. 315

AESCULUS   Hippocastanaceae

californica (California), the "California buckeye" or "Chapparal buckeye"; native to dry slopes of the Sierras; small deciduous tree 3 to 6 m or more high; silvery branches with rich green leaves digitately compound of 5 to 7 leaflets 8 to 15 cm long, finely toothed and with prominent ribs; showy erect, cylindrical clusters of fragrant white flowers tinged with rose and protruding stamens; large pear-shaped green fruits. Striking in spring when creamy, fragrant plumes appear like a giant candle. Buckeye nuts were eaten by Indians after carefully roasting and leaching them. *Zone* 6.   p. 736

x carnea (hippocastaneum x pavia) (Midwestern U.S.), the "Red horse-chestnut"; ornamental flowering tree 10 to 15 m high; large compound leaves of 3 to 7 leathery green leaflets 8-15 cm long, with prominent ribs and serrate margins; in April-May a mature tree bears hundreds of 20 cm plumes of soft pink to red flowers, in center a yellow eye; brown prickly fruit 4 cm dia. *Zone* 4.   p. 736

x carnea 'Briotii', "Ruby horse-chestnut"; superb cultivar with dark green foliage, and floral panicles larger than the parent, the flowers with petals bright scarlet to blood-red; ornamental fruit soft-spiny. Originated in gardens of Trianon Palace, France 1858. *Zone* 4.   p. 736

glabra arguta (Kansas to Texas), "Texas buckeye"; a shrub form of glabra, also known as Ae. arguta, to 2 m high, with deciduous leaves palmately compound of 7-11 narrow lanceolate leaflets 6-12 cm long, doubly toothed at margins; yellowish-green flowers in erect pyramidal clusters, in late Spring. The species glabra is the Ohio buckeye, wide spread in Central U.S., growing as tree to 10 m high, having larger leaves of 5-7 leaflets and erect elongate floral panicles to 18 cm long. The timber can be used for pulp. *Zone* 3.   p. 736

hippocastaneum (Balkan Peninsula; naturalized in C. Europe), "Horse chestnut"; big, deciduous tree to 30 m high, having handsome leaves palmately compound of 5 to 7 coppery corrugated leaflets 10-25 cm long; large erect 20-30 cm panicles of small white flowers blotched with red. Photographed along the ancient 10 Century walls of Visby, Gotland. *Zone* 3.   p. 736

octandra (flava) (Penna. to Georgia, Kansas and Texas), "Yellow buckeye"; deciduous tree 20 m or more high, trunk to 1 m dia., the bark finely broken into flat scales; handsome leaves compound of 5 oblanceolate leaflets 8-18 cm long, having contrasting yellowish midrib, and finely toothed; small yellow 1 cm flowers in upright clusters 10-15 cm long, in late May and June. Leaves and nuts are reported poisonous if eaten. The timber is used for wood pulp. Named "Buckeye" because of the eye-like markings on the nuts. *Zone* 3.   p. 736

parviflora (Georgia and Alabama), "Bottlebrush buckeye" or "Dwarf horse-chestnut"; shrub to 5 m high; leaves with 5-7 leaflets; inflorescence a tall pyramid of small, fragrant, tubular white flowers, displaying protruding white stamens tipped with red anthers, blooming early Summer. Spreading by underground stolons. *Zone* 5.   p. 737

pavia (Illinois to No. Carolina and Texas), "Red buckeye"; deciduous shrub or small tree to 4 m high; rather refined foliage with 5-7 leaflets 8-14 cm long, and dainty salmon-red flowers in large pyramids 10 to 25 cm tall. *Zone* 5.   p. 736

sylvatica (neglecta georgiana) (No. Carolina to Tennessee and Georgia); handsome deciduous tree to 6 m or more high, with palmately compound leaves of 5 broad-obovate leaflets 10-16 cm long, finely serrate at margins, yellowish-green beneath; the inflorescence in showy clusters; flowers with unequal pale yellow petals marked with red veins, sometimes entirely red; globose fruit 3 cm across, usually one-seeded. *Zone* 5.   p. 736

AETHIONEMA   Cruciferae

coridifolium 'Warley Rose', (type from Asia Minor), "Stonecress"; small perennial subshrub 15-20 cm high, with small fleshy, linear, glaucous leaves edged in pink; the flowers to 1 cm dia., deep pink, in terminal racemes; rosy-purple in the species of Turkey and Lebanon. *Zone* 9.   p. 406

grandiflorum (pulchellum) (Turkey to Iran), "Persian stonecress"; loosely spreading perennial, with usually undivided branches, 30-50 cm long; ovate, glaucous 3 cm leaves, and soft pink flowers 3 cm across, in dense terminal clusters, in May to August. *Zone* 7. p. 406

AGAPANTHUS *Liliaceae (Amaryllidaceae Hortus)*
africanus (Cape of Good Hope), "Blue African lily"; summer blooming plant with tuberous rootstock, often grown in tubs, with basal strap-like evergreen leaves to 2 cm wide; funnel-shaped flowers pale porcelain-blue with darker center and margins, up to 30 in large umbels, on erect stalks. *Subtropic. Zones 9-10.* p. 231
africanus 'Minor', "Peter Pan lily"; a diminutive form of the "African lily"; fresh green basal strap leaves; inflorescence on slender stalk 50 cm high, with trumpet flowers pale porcelain-blue. *Zone 10.* p. 231
campanulatus (So. Africa: Natal), "Bell agapanthus"; compact plant with leaves shorter, narrower, and more erect than in A. orientalis; deciduous; flowers sky-blue, 3 cm across, bell-shaped, spreading at mouth, on stalk 45 cm high. *Zone 10.* p. 231
orientalis (Praecox), (So. Africa: E. Cape), "Oriental agapanthus"; handsome perennial herb to 1 m or more high, with thick, fleshy tuberous roots, producing evergreen tufts of soft, recurving strap-shaped leaves 5 cm wide; floral stalks carry large umbels of up to 110 flowers in various shades of blue. *Zones 8-10.* p. 231

AGAPETES *Ericaceae*
serpens (Pentapterygium) (E. Himalayas, Khasias); epiphytic shrub 60-90 cm high, from a tuberous rootstock, with slender pendant stems, small lanceolate 2 cm leathery leaves, and tubular nodding flowers bright red with darker markings. *Zone 7.* p. 698

AGASTACHE *Labiatae*
foeniculum (anethiodora) (C. No. America, Korea and Venezuela), "Anise hyssop" or "Licorice mint"; scented herbaceous perennial, with age to 80 cm high; ovate leaves to 8 cm long, serrate at margins, often with violet sheen; inflorescence in cylindric spikes 10 cm long, with small bilabiate flowers, the 1 cm corolla blue; a honey plant for bees. Dried leaves steeped in water can be substituted for anise seed in bakery and cookies. The dried herbage also makes aromatic tea. *Zones 3-9.* p. 530

AGATHEA coelestis: see FELICIA amelloides

AGATI: see SESBANIA

AGATHIS *Araucariaceae (Coniferae)*
australis, (palustris) (New Zealand: North Island), the famous "Kauri pine"; stately timber tree rising like a gray, straight column to 30 and 50 m high, with dia. of trunk recorded at 7 m, the thick bark peels off, tending to throw off epiphytes; leaves on young trees sparse, linear-oblong, bronze-green, to 6 cm long; the adult leaves oval 1-3 cm long; 8 cm erect ovoid cones. Produces kauri gum from resin. *Subtropic. Zones 9-10.* p. 572
robusta (Queensland), "Queensland kauri"; massive, resinous evergreen tree to 50 m high, with variable leaves; juvenile leaves waxy dark green; adult leaves elliptic and stiff-leathery, to 10 cm long; female cones ovoid, 10-12 cm long and 10 cm dia. *Zones 9-10.* p. 572

AGAVACEAE, a family newly listed in Hortus 3, which transferred 20 genera formerly AMARYLLIDACEAE and LILIACEAE (incl. Agave, Beaucarnea, Beschorneria, Cordyline, Dasylirion, Doryanthes, Dracaena, Furcraea, Manfreda, Nolina, Phormium, Polianthes, Sansevieria, Yucca).

AGAVE *Agavaceae*
americana (Mexico; naturalized in So. Europe), "Century plant" of "American aloe"; large, loose open, trunkless rosette of spreading, broad and thick-succulent, glaucous gray-green leaves 2-2½ m long, sharply bend downward above the middle, with brown hooks at margins, and ending in a spiny point; yellowish flowers fragrant at night, on a tall branched inflorescence to 8 m high, produced when plant is 10 years or more old. *Arid-subtropic. Zone 8.* p. 149
americana 'Marginata', "Variegated century plant"; handsome large rosette with the broad, laxly recurved, glaucous gray leaves having showy, broad yellow margins. *Zones 9-10.* p. 149
angustifolia 'Marginata' (wilsonii, caribaea) (W. Indies), "Variegated Caribbean agave"; beautiful, freely suckering, densely formal rosette with stiff-erect, short, sword-shaped leaves to 50 cm long, bluish-gray with broad white marginal bands and little brown spines. Inflorescence to 3 m high with pyramidal panicle dense with 5 cm greenish flowers and forming abundant bulbils. *Zone 10.* p. 69, 150
atrovirens (So. Mexico: Oaxaca), "Pulque agave"; large stemless rosette producing offsets; stout, fleshy smooth leaves spreading to 2 m long and 25-30 cm wide, concave above, keeled convex beneath, dull dark green or blackish, margins wavy with small spines on horny base. Main source of pulque drink. Massive inflorescence 8 to 10 m high, with pyramidal panicle dense with greenish-yellow flowers 10 cm long. *Zone 10.* p. 150

attenuata (Mexico: Hidalgo), "Dragon-tree agave"; rosette, on 1 m stem when old; leaves to 1 m long, wide in the middle, narrow at base, smooth, without teeth, gray-green; the beautiful inflorescence with greenish-yellow flowers in 3 m spikes gracefully arching, occasionally producing bulbils. *Zone 10.* p. 149
barbadensis (Lesser Antilles: Barbados, also Antigua); stemless rosette rarely suckering; widely lanceolate leaves 1½ to 2 m long, dull dark green, the margins reddish and spiny and a blackish terminal spine; inflorescence 5 to 6 m high, the spreading branches, after blooming, forming numerous plantlets. *Zone 11.* p. 150
cerulata (Baja California); symmetrical rosette with leaves to 35 cm long, deeply concave, gray or gray-green, hollow-grooved toward tip, terminal spine gray-brown; marginal spines brown later gray about 2½ cm apart; inflorescence to 3 m high, flowers yellow, on slender panicle. *Zone 10.* p. 148
ferdinandi-regis, (nickelsii) (N. E. Mexico), "King agave"; beautiful solitary, globose rosette with triangular, pointed leaves, dark green with converging white lines, usually terminated by three spines; fewer leaves 12 to 20 cm long, and less compact than victoriae-reginae. *Zone 10.* p. 150
filifera (Mexico: Hidalgo, San Luis Potosi), "Thread agave"; many-leaved rosette of narrow, stiff, bright green leaves, white lines along edge which splits into loose filaments. Leaves 20-25 cm long. Inflorescence to 2.5 m high, with dense spikes of small green-yellow flowers. *Arid-tropical. Zone 10.* p. 148
franzosinii (Mexico); trunkless rosette similar to A. americana, but more imposing and beautifully colored silvery-gray or bluish-gray; leaves rough, to 2½ m long and 30 cm wide, blackish marginal hook spines; inflorescence to 12 m high, branched with many yellowish flowers. *Zone 10.* p. 148
neglecta (U.S.: Trop. Florida); stoloniferous stemless rosette 3 to 4 m dia., glaucous gray recurving, concave leaves thick at base, to 2½ m long and 15 cm wide, prickly at lower margins and spine at apex; inflorescence 3 to 6 m high, the upper part branched and with greenish flowers, followed by abundant maroon-dotted bulbils. *Zone 10.* p. 150
parryi huachucensis (Southern Arizona); beautiful compact, slow-growing rosette, sending out stolons forming colonies; the tight cabbagey heads impress each cupped leaf firmly on its enclosing mate in beautiful pattern; leaves 30 cm wide and to 65 cm long, broader than the type, thick at broadest part, beige-green to glaucous blue-green, with coarse brown or black hooked marginal teeth; inflorescence stalks to 7 m tall, with greenish-yellow flowers in heavy panicles. *Zone 10.* p. 148
parviflora (Sonora, Chihuahua, Arizona), "Little princess agave"; striking small rosette dense with stiff leaves 10 cm long, having white lines above, the margins with white threads toward tip, lower part dentate; gray-brown terminal spine. Inflorescence to 1 m high, with glaucous, red-tinged flowers. *Zone 10.* p. 148
schidigera (Mexico); "Feather agave"; large rosette of narrow linear, incurving or spreading leaves, light green, to 50 cm long, at margins fine splitting threads; inflorescence 3½ m high, with brown-red flowers. *Zone 9.* p. 148
sebastiana (Mexico: Baja California, Isla Cedros); handsome short-stemmed rosette to 1 m dia., concave leaves stiffly erect, 20 to 60 cm long and to 12 cm wide, glaucous blue with horny margins; striking inflorescence 2 to 3 m high of dense clusters of yellow flowers. *Zone 10.* p. 149
sisalana (Mexico: Yucatán), "Sisal-hemp"; large rosette forming 1 m trunks, developing offsets; with straight and stiff, sword-shaped leaves to 1½ m long and 10 cm wide, matte gray-green, or green, with horny edge and occasional deformed teeth, keeled beneath, and with small black-brown terminal spine; branched inflorescence to 6 m high, with greenish, odoriferous flowers. Young plants will form as suckers on the ground as well as on the flowering stalk, and plantlets or bulbils rise vegetatively from the floral bracts, according to observations I made in Tanzania. *Arid-tropical. Zone 10.* p. 150
victoriae-reginae (No. Mexico: Nuevo Leon, Coahuila, Morelos), "Queen agave"; shapely dense, many-leaved rosette with keeled, dark green leaves about 15 cm long, white margin and abrupt point, and short, blunt, terminal spine. Inflorescence a tall spike to 2 m or more high, with pale green to creamy flowers. *Zone 10.* p. 150

AGERATUM *Compositae*
houstonianum, "Floss-flower"; the popular garden bedding plant, 25 cm high, a compact horticultural form of Mexican origin; bushy herbaceous perennial grown as an annual, with tassel-like heads of clear blue tubular florets, carried nicely above the fresh green, small foliage. From seed, or occasionally cuttings. *Zone 10.* p. 368
houstonianum 'Nordmeer'; very attractive small German cultivar of compact habit, with full clusters of massed rose-pink flowers; ideal as a bedding plant. *Zone 10.* p. 368

AGLAIA   *Meliaceae*

formosana (elaeagnoides var.); medium sized evergreen seashore tree with trunk to 30 cm dia., the branches with milky sap; all parts covered by silvery scales; the leaves odd-pinnate having 3 to 5 pairs of leathery, obovate leaflets 6-8 cm long; inflorescence in clusters of very small yellowish, fragrant flowers, followed by fleshy, scarlet-red edible fruit. *Zone 10.*   p. 787

AGLAONEMA   *Araceae*

commutatum (Philippines, Sri Lanka), "Silver evergreen"; durable plant with leathery, oblong-lanceolate leaves deep green with markings of silver-gray, 20 cm or more long; waxy-white spathe; berries yellow to red. *Humid-tropical. Zone 11.*   p. 19

commutatum 'Medio-pictum' (Malaysia); sturdy cultivar boldly variegated with greenish-white dominating central area of otherwise green leaves; inflorescence with erect spadix and pale green spathe. *Zone 12.*   p. 20

commutatum picturatum (Jervis) (E. Luzon, Philippines); admirable variety of open habit, with oblong ovate leaves shining metallic aluminum above, green beneath. *Zone 12.*   p. 20

commutatum picturatum 'Fat Jade' (Luzon) "Mutton-fat ever-green"; very handsome cultivar with broad leaves, variegated pale lemon, overlaid with silvery sheen. *Zone 12.*   p. 21

commutatum 'Treubii' (Celebes); slender plant with narrow, leathery, bluish-green leaves attractively marked with silver-gray; petioles marbled. *Zone 12.*   p. 19

x commutatum 'White Rajah'; highly variegated, compact cultivar, with contrasting silvery white feathering over dark green foliage. By some taxonomists considered a variation of A. 'Pseudobracteatus'. *Zone 12.*   p. 19

costatum 'Foxii magnificum', "Spotted evergreen"; low plant with broad, leathery, shiny leaves richly variegated or marbled creamy-white; slow growing. Photographed in Bermuda Botanic Garden. *Zone 12.*   p. 20

crispum (Schismatoglottis roebelinii) (Malaya), "Painted drop-tongue"; large and showy, ovate-pointed, leathery leaves medium grayish-green, largely variegated with silver. *Zone 12.*   p. 19

linearifolium (Philippines); unusual plant in Sarian Nursery, Makati, Manila, of compact habit, and long narrow linear, fleshy leaves coppery green. *Zone 11.*   p. 20

marantifolium (Borneo); handsome species of compact habit; broad-lanceolate leaves with midrib and margins glossy dark green, the central area richly overlaid with silvery gray. Photographed in Kota Kinabalu, North Borneo. *Zone 12.*   p. 19

modestum (simplex) (Kwangtung), "Chinese evergreen"; with durable, leathery, waxy-green leaves, ovate-acuminate and, to some extent, pendant, on a slender cane. Spathe green, spadix cream. *Zone 11.*   p. 19

modestum 'Medio-pictum' (pat. as 'Shingii'), "Mandalay plant"; sport of A. modestum (Mahaffey, Apopka, Florida about 1967); attractive and sharply distinct variegation of the leaf color, with yellowish chartreuse or apple-green and ivory along center, abruptly changing to dark green around outer edge of leaf, on variegated petioles; excellent ornamental plant with stock cane and of compact habit, freely branching; ovate-pointed, leathery glossy foliage, with leaves 12-25 cm long; of good keeping qualities. *Zone 12.*   p. 19

philippinense 'Cebu'; bold plant with broad, lanceolate leaves shiny coppery green, having pale midrib and occasional variegation on stiff, reddish petioles. *Zone 12.*   p. 21

philippinense 'Nocturne' (Philippines); in col. of Los Baños Arboretum, on Luzon; of robust habit, with large leaves silvery green, and marbled or splashed with creamy-green. *Zone 12.*   p. 20

philippinense var. stenophyllum 'White Lance' (Luzon, Philippines); curious cultivar photographed at Sarian Nursery, Makati, Manila; stiff linear, recurved leaves, dark green with silver bands; petioles cream-white. *Zone 12.*   p. 20

pictum (Sumatra); dainty plant with broad-ovate, velvety leaf bluish-green with irregular patches of silver gray. *Zone 12.*   p. 20

'Pseudo-bracteatum', (commutatum cv.) "Golden evergreen"; colorful, free-growing mutation or hybrid, with long, showy leaves deep green variegated with light green and yellow, center largely cream-white; stem white and marbled green; cupped, waxy, greenish-white spathe, and cream spadix. *Zone 12.*   p. 19

'Silver King' (nitidum 'Curtisii' x pictum 'Tricolor'); striking, excellent hybrid of lush habit, freely suckering; 20 to 35 cm leaves almost entirely silver-gray; petioles marked silver. *Zones 11-12.*   p. 19

'Silver Queen'; very ornamental and satisfactory decorative plant, from the same Florida hybrid complex as A. 'Silver King', with leaves narrower, about 22 cm long and 3 to 5 cm wide; green with gray marbling in feather pattern, petioles more green; freely branching and suckering, for bushy effect, and of excellent keeping qualities. *Zones 11-12.*   p. 19

simplex metallica (Malaysia); rosette of spreading, broad ovate cordate leaves of fleshy texture, deep waxy green, the surface corrugated by depressed veins; in collection of Mandai Orchids, Singapore. Ident. by Dr. T. Croat, Missouri Bot. Garden. *Zone 12.*   p. 21

'Whorl' (Philippines); very handsome cultivar, photographed in the collection of the Los Banos Arboretum, on Luzon; broadly lanceolate leaves with attractive zebra pattern of silver alternating with bluish-green. *Zone 12.*   p. 20

AGONIS   *Myrtaceae*

flexuosa (W. Australia), "Willow-myrtle"; graceful evergreen shrub or tree to 12 m, ultimate branches pendulous, shoots wiry, often long and slender; willow-like linear leaves 5-15 cm long; the fragrant white flowers in globose clusters, pink at base. The foliage emits a scent of peppermint when bruised. *Zones 9-10.*   p. 797

AGROSTIS   *Gramineae*

capillaris (Eurasia, No. Africa), "Tall bent grass"; perennial with erect stems to 60 cm high; narrow, threadlike, short leaves having rough margins; inflorescence of open clusters with spikelets pale to purplish. *Zone 7.*   p. 570

stolonifera var. palustris (Newfoundland to Alaska, Eurasia), "Creeping bent grass"; perennial grass with a sprawling and rooting base; the narrow leaves flat and only 6 mm wide; stems ascending bearing oblong panicle with small purplish spikelets. The subspecies palustris is a marsh plant requiring much moisture. *Zone 3.*   p. 570

tenuis (Europe, natural in Canada and U.S.), "Bent grass" or "Colonial Bent"; a low, especially fine-leaved, dense-clustered perennial grass spreading by stolons or surface runners, but no rhizomes; blades rich green and flat, 2-3 mm wide; needs much care and cutting, feeding, watering and disease control, and is used on golf course greens. *Temperate, but planted in California.* p. 568, 569

AICHRYSON   *Crassulaceae*

x domesticum 'Variegatum' (Aeonium domesticum cv.) (Canary Isl.), "Youth and old age"; succulent intermediate between sedum and sempervivum; freely branching rosettes with rounded thin fleshy leaves light green with white margins, to 5 cm dia.; flowers yellow. *Subtropic. Zone 10.*   p. 182

AILANTHUS   *Simaroubaceae*

altissima (China, naturalized in U.S.), "Tree of Heaven"; rapid-growing deciduous tree to 15 m high; stout branches carry odd-pinnate leaves to 75 cm or more long, occasionally with purple leafstalk, and divided into 13 to 25 lanceolate leaflets to 12 cm long, entire at margins except for one to three large basal teeth with oil bearing glands on each side; inconspicuous greenish-yellow flowers are followed by clusters of handsome red-brown winged fruit. A tree for adverse conditions, the "Tree that grows in Brooklyn", introduced west to California during the gold rush. *Zone 4.*   p. 876.

altissima erythrocarpa; handsome ornamental form of slower growth and with foliage darker green than the type, the pendant winged fruit a showy bright red. *Zone 4.*   p. 876

AJUGA   *Labiatae*

pyramidalis (Europe to Caucasus), "Bugle weed"; rhizomatous perennial herb with branches 5 to 30 cm long, with stolons produced late in season; obovate leaves faintly toothed, to 10 cm long; flowers pale blue or violet in compact elongate clusters, the corolla 2 cm long, in May-July. Good rockgarden plant. *Zones 7-10.*   p. 431

reptans (Europe, Asia Minor, to Caucasus), "Carpet bugleweed"; popular perennial groundcover practically evergreen, spreading by runners; lustrous round-crenate leaves 5-10 cm long, dark green in the species, milky green with bronze and purple in var. purpurea; flowers blue or white, blooming from May to June. *Zones 3-9.*   p. 315, 431

reptans 'Variegata' (Europe), "Variegated carpet-bugle"; interesting groundcover with ovate basal leaves to 10 cm long, glossy green to coppery, prettily flecked and mottled with cream to rose. *Zones 5-9.*   p. 315

AKEBIA   *Lardizabalaceae*

quinata (China, Korea, Japan), "Chocolate vine"; hardy shrubby twiner, evergreen in warm climate, with digitately compound leaves of usually 5 oblong leaflets 8-12 cm long; fragrant flowers in racemes, the males 6 mm pale purple; female flowers 3 cm wide, with 3 cupped chocolate-purple petal-like sepals. *Zone 5.*   p. 314

ALBERTA   *Rubiaceae*

magna (Natal); evergreen shrub to 8 m high, with willowy reddish branches and leathery, oblanceolate opposite leaves 12 cm long; erect terminal panicles of brilliant crimson flowers with long silky tubular corolla. *Zone 10.*   p. 855

ALBIZIA   *Leguminosae*

distachya (lophantha) (S. W. Australia), "Plume Mimosa"; fast-growing shrub or tree to 6 m high, semi-evergreen; bipinnate foliage dark velvety green, fern-like; flowers greenish-yellow in fluffy, 5 cm spikes. *Zone 9.*   p. 746

julibrissin (Iran to Japan), "Silk-tree" or "Mimosa"; deciduous tree to 12 m high, with large, fern-like, bipinnate leaves to 45 cm long, and terminal clusters of flowers with long, conspicuous, pink stamens arranged like fluffy tassels. *Zone 7.*   p. 746

lebbeck (Tropics of the Old World), "Women's tongue"; tree to 25 m high, with bipinnate leaves 8-22 cm long; flowers yellowish-white, in globose heads of stamens 2 cm wide, forming a terminal panicle 6 cm across; fruit bean-like to 30 cm long, rattling in the wind when ripe. *Tropical. Zone 10.*   p. 746

ALBUCA   *Liliaceae*

nelsonii (crinifolia) (Natal), "Sentry-in-the box"; lovely bulbous perennial with concave basal leaves bright green; inflorescence on stout stalk to 1½ m long, carrying spike-like raceme of white flowers typically with 3 inner petals curved inward cup-like, while linear 3 outer petals swing outward; a green or red stripe down back of each segment. *Zone 10.*   p. 231

ALCEA   *Malvaceae*

rosea (Althaea chinensis) (Asia Minor to E. Asia), "Garden hollyhock"; tall, straight, leafy-stemmed, hairy perennial in China, grown as biennial in gardens, to 2 m or more high, with rough leaves 5 to 7-angled; single or double flowers 8-12 cm across, in long spike, red, rose, pink, yellow or white, blooming July to September; an old favorite garden plant. *Zones 2-10.*   p. 457, 469

rosea plena, "Double hollyhock"; very handsome variety, in col. Kew Bot. Gardens, England, having stately spires dense with crimson-red 6-8 cm flowers, filled with extra petals resembling double roses. *Zone 5-10.*   p. 457

rosea 'Rubra', "Red hollyhock"; handsome, very stately garden biennial 1½ m or more high, with hairy, palmately lobed leaves; forming tall stalks the second year, topped by spike-like racemes of showy, crimson-red flowers 7-10 cm across, in late Summer. *Zone 3-10.*   p. 457

ALCHEMILLA   *Rosaceae*

mollis (vulgaris major in hort.) (Carpathians to Caucasus), "Lady's mantle"; herbaceous perennial to 40 cm high, with horizontal rootstock, producing a clump of long-stalked grayish leaves shallowly lobed; floral stalks bearing clusters of numerous small chartreuse to yellowish flowers to 1 cm across, blooming late Spring into Summer. *Zone 4.*   p. 492

vulgaris (xanthochlora) (Europe, Greenland, Labrador), "Lady's mantle"; perennial hairy herb with stout horizontal rootstock producing a clump of handsome kidney-shaped, gray-pubescent, 10-12 cm leaves toothed and shallowly, palmately lobed, green beneath; small yellowish-green flowers in feathery panicles. Old time herb used medicinally. *Zone 3.*   p. 540

ALEURITES   *Euphorbiaceae*

fordii (C. Asia), "Tung oil tree" or "China wood-oil tree"; large tree to 12 m high, with broad cordate, leathery leaves 15-20 cm long, showing the yellow ribs; flowers white with red veins, to 3 cm long; the squarish fruit is source of tung-oil. *Zone 9.*   p. 720

moluccana (Moluccas and South Pacific Is.), a "Candle-nut" or "Varnish tree"; large tropical tree to 10 or 12 m high, with long-stalked, ovate-pointed, or lobed pale green foliage 10-20 cm long, white downy above, rusty-pubescent beneath; small whitish flowers in large clusters; the green, rough fruit 5 cm dia., containing 1 or 2 jet-black seeds which are polished and made into jewelry; also oil is extracted for varnish or for lamps. *Zone 10.*   p. 720

ALLAMANDA   *Apocynaceae*

cathartica (So. America: Brazil), "Golden trumpet"; robust shrubby, tropical clamberer with whorled, long, leathery, glossy leaves to 12 cm long; large wax-like, funnel-shaped golden flowers 6-8 cm across. With its showy flowers one of the most satisfactory summer bloomers in a sunny location. The cultivar flore pleno, seen at Mandai, Singapore, has flowers with double petals. *Zone 11. p. 263.*

cathartica 'Hendersonii', (So. America: Guyana), "Golden trumpet-vine"; vigorous climber with sturdy vines to 15 m long, with milky sap and leathery elliptic 15 cm leaves in whorls; extra large, golden-yellow trumpet flowers 10 cm across. *Zone 10.*   p. 263

violacea (Brazil), "Purple allamanda"; weak, slender climber, branches hairy, with ovate leaves 8-12 cm in a whorl, downy above, hairy beneath; funnel-shaped flowers rosy-pink with purple throat, in axillary cymes. *Zone 10.*   p. 263

ALLIUM   *Liliaceae (Amaryllidaceae in Hortus 3)*

aflatunense (Iran, C. Asia), "Ornamental onion"; robust very decorative bulbous plant to 1 m or more high, with 6-8 narrow strapshaped glaucous leaves; stiff floral stalk topped by globular umbel of starry flowers having light purple segments, with darker nerve. *Zone 5.*   p. 232

ampeloprasum (porrum) (Europe, No. Africa, Asia), "Leek"; biennial with poorly developed sectional bulb, and cultivated for the edible branched leaf bases, and grown since ancient Egyptian times; fleshy linear leaves 30-60 cm long and 4 cm wide, flat and folded lengthwise to keeled; inflorescence of small rose-pink to whitish flowers in globose umbels 10 cm across, sometimes with bulbils, on stalks 1 to 2 m high, blooming July-August. A popular kitchen vegetable. *Zones 4-8.*   p. 538

ascalonicum (A. cepa group) (Syria, Asia Minor), "Shallots"; onion-like bulbous plant, very popular in Europe, the bulb differing from the common onion in being made up of numerous sections or cloves, each of which can be used for planting; leaves cylindric awl-shaped, shorter than floral stalk which is to 30 cm high, topped by roundish clusters of pink or lilac flowers, sometimes containing bulbils. These cloves are milder tasting than common onions, and are used in seasoning of food. *Zone 8.*   p. 538

cepa (Iran and Asia Minor), the "Persian onion" or "Garden onion"; large biennial bulbs, with membranous skins and edible; leaves cylindrical and hollow, and used in culinary seasoning; floral stalks to 1 m bearing dense heads of lilac to greenish-white flowers with long stamens. *Zone 9.*   p. 232, 538

cernuum (New York to Carolina and Calif.), "Wild onion" or "Lady's leek"; clustering elongate bulbs, with several linear, flat leaves to 1 cm wide; floral stalk 30 to 60 cm high, topped by umbels of small nodding purplish-rose flowers. The strongly flavored bulbs may be eaten if boiled. *Zone 3.*   p. 232

christophii (albopilosum) (Asia Minor to Iran), "Stars of Persia"; an ornamental onion with strap-shaped leaves 4½ cm wide, grown for its hugh ball-like showy 20 cm umbels of starry lilac flowers with metallic sheen. *Zone 4.*   p. 232

fistulosum (Siberia), "Welsh" or "Spanish onion"; 45 cm high; clustered bulbs with hollow, cylindrical leaves about same length as hollow swollen stalk, topped by white flowers in head-like globose umbel. Used for seasoning, and as a leek in Asia. *Zone 3.*   p. 232

flavum (S.W. Europe to W. Asia), "Yellow onion"; bulbous species with narrow leaves; lustrous fascinating inflorescence of bright yellow bell-shaped flowers in loose umbels, subtended by two long bracts, on stalk to 50 cm long, during Summer. *Zone 5.*   p. 232

giganteum (Himalayas), "Giant ornamental onion"; striking bulbous perennial to 1 m or more high when in bloom; glaucous green, fleshy basal leaves 6 to 8 cm broad; stiff floral stalks carry a spectacularly showy, dense globular head 10 to 20 cm dia., consisting of myriads of bright lilac-purple, starry flowers with extended stamens; long-lasting as cut blooms. *Zone 5.*   p. 232, 235

karataviense (U.S.S.R.: Turkestan), "Turkestan onion"; bulbous plant with two very broad, flat leaves to 12 cm across, blue-green tinged with rose, and short stalks carrying a dense 8 cm globe of white flowers with purple midrib like delicate rosy stars, and long stamens; spring-blooming. The flower heads are dried and used in floral arrangements. *Zone 5.*   p. 232

moly (S.W. Europe), "Lily leek" or "Golden garlic"; attractive small decorative species, with clustered bulbs, blue-green flat leaves 2½ cm wide; showy flowers starlike, bright yellow, in 8 cm umbels. *Zone 6.*   p. 232

narcissiflorum (S.W. Italian Alps); striking bulbous perennial forming clusters from rhizome with flat, narrow basal leaves; floral stalk 30 cm long, bearing clusters of showy 2 cm rosy bell-flowers, at first nodding, later erect, during Summer. *Zone 5.*   p. 233

neapolitanum (Mediterranean reg.); "Daffodil garlic" popular bulbous plant to 45 cm high, suitable for pots, with slender linear, keeled leaves, loose-spreading, and large starry, fragrant white flowers with colored stamens, becoming papery, in few-flowered umbels to 8 cm across; Spring. *Zones 7-9.*   p. 233

obliquum (Tien Shan Mts., N.W. China); floriferous bulbous herb on short rhizome, forming clusters, with hollow cylindric leaves from base; the leafy floral stalk 60 cm or more tall, topped by globes of small greenish-yellow flowers. *Zone 5.*   p. 233

oreophilum (ostrowskianum) (Turkestan); ornamental bulbous herb with 2 to 3 glaucous, linear-oblong leaves; floral stalk 20 to 30 cm long, topped by umbel of beautiful carmine-rose bell flowers, in late Spring. *Zone 4.*   p. 233

pulchellum (carinatum) (S. Europe, W. Asia); bulbous herb with thin, semi-cylindric, channelled leaves; floral stalk 40 to 60 cm high, topped by loose clusters of nodding purplish-rose, bell-shaped flowers, subtended by two very long bracts. *Zone 6.*   p. 233

rosenbachianum (Turkestan), "Ornamental onion"; very showy spherical, feathery inflorescence carmine-rose, 8 cm across, on stiff stalk 60 cm long; 2-3 fleshy leaves to 5 cm wide, from elongate bulb. Excellent for drying of flowers in floral arrangements. *Zone 5. p. 233*

sativum (So. Europe to S.W. Asia, India), "Garlic"; herbgarden plant grown since ancient times, for their bulbs, which within their membranous skin divide into several parts or cloves; these are used in cooking or flavoring for their pungent aroma; narrow linear leaves from base, and a floral stalk to 60 cm high, topped by a loose cluster of pinkish flowers and usually bearing bulbils. Cultivated as an annual. *Zones 2-9.*   p. 233, 538

schoenoprasum (Siberia, No. North America), culinary "Chives" or German "Schnittlauch"; hardy tufted, clustered bulbs with onionlike hollow but thin green leaves to 45 cm high, tipped by round heads of rose-purple flowers. Use: fresh leaves in soup, salads, omelet, hamburgers, for a mild onion flavor. *Zones 3-9.*   p. 234, 538

senescens (montanum, tuberosum) (Europe to Siberia, Nepal to China, Japan), "Chinese chives"; bulbs on a stout rhizome forming clusters of two-edged flat, linear leaves normally lightly twisted; floral stalk to 60 cm high bearing small clusters or rosy flowers during Summer. *Zone 3.*   p. 233

senescens glaucum (Europe); curious form of small habit, having curved, flat gray-blue, glaucous leaves all rising from a central point and curving in the same direction; clusters of pink flowers bloom on straight stalk. *Zone 6.*   p. 233

sphaerocephalum (W. Europe, to Iran), "Round-head garlic"; leaves channelled; flowering stalks to 1 m high, leafy in lower third; flowers dark purple, bell-shaped, in dense globular heads. *Zone 5.*   p. 234

stipitatum (Central Asia); very vigorous, showy species with solitary blackish bulb, strap-shaped bright green leaves rough hairy beneath; stout floral stalk to more than 1 m high, bearing large globular umbels of rosy-violet, fragrant flowers having spreading segments and long filaments, during Summer. *Zone 5.*   p. 234

subhirsutum (No. Africa, So. Europe Asia Minor); floriferous bulbous herb with narrow linear leaves 1 cm wide, and ciliate margins; floral stalks to 40 cm high, topped by spreading clusters of starry white flowers. *Zone 8.*   p. 234

suworosii (C. China); showy ornamental onion, with blue-green sword-shaped basal leaves to 3 cm wide; stiff-erect floral stalks to 60 cm high, topped by globose heads 5 to 8 cm wide, dense with small lilac-purple flowers. *Zone 5.*   p. 234

triquetrum (So. Europe), "Triangle onion"; small bulbs with linear, keeled leaves, and 3-angled stalk to 30-40 cm high, bearing clusters of large white bell-flowers 2 cm long, with segments keeled green or rose, pendant on one side. *Zone 8.*   p. 234

tuberosum (S.E. Asia), "Chinese chive" or "Oriental garlic"; ornamental species with elongate bulbs growing on stout rhizome; 4 to 9 slender basal leaves, not hollow, but keeled on back; floral stalks 50 cm high, topped by dense clusters of small, fragrant white flowers, the segments with greenish nerve; summer-blooming. Excellent in dried floral arrangements. Leaves used in salads, in scrambled eggs and cole-slaw for mild garlic flavor. *Zone 4.*   p. 234, 538

unifolium (Coastal ranges, California, Oregon); charming ornamental with lateral rhizomes from the bulb producing bulblets on their tips; the leaves narrow-linear and flat; floral stalks 30 to 50 cm, bearing loose clusters of pretty, rose-pink 1 cm flowers with spreading, ovate segments. *Zone 5.*   p. 234

ursinum (Scotland to Spain, East to Asia Minor, Caucasus, Siberia), "Bear's garlic" or "Gypsy garlic"; strongly scented bulbous herb with short rhizome; lanceolate basal leaves 50 cm wide; 3-angled floral stalks 30 cm high, topped by few-flowered umbel of white blooms; segments 1 cm long. *Zones 4-8.*   p. 234

ALLOPHYTON mexicanum (Hortus 2):
see TETRANEMA roseum (Hortus 3)

ALLOPLECTUS capitatus: see CORYTOPLECTUS

ALLUAUDIA   *Didiereaceae*
comosa (S.W. Madagascar); succulent shrub 2 to 6 m high, dividing into several erect branches these set with pairs of long thin 4 cm thorns; small fleshy obovate leaves to 2½ cm long. Toward upper parts a series of lovely soft pink flowers develops out of axils. *Zone 11.*   p. 194

ALNUS   *Betulaceae*
cordata (Corsica; So. Italy), "Italian alder": handsome ornamental tree to 15 m high, forming shapely crown with angled shoots; dense glossy green foliage, the blades broad ovate with cordate base, 10 cm long, and brownish axil tufts beneath; male catkins 8 cm long, in clusters appearing in Spring before leaves; female cones erect, usually in threes, 3 cm long. *Zone 5.*   p. 658

glutinosa (Europe to Siberia, No. Africa), "Black alder" or "European alder"; deciduous tree 15 to 25 m tall, with sparse branches forming conical crown; rough brown bark which cracks into vertical scales; sticky, glutinous shoots with broadly roundish to obovate leaves to 10 cm long, crenate along margins; unisexual

flowers in catkins, the cylindrical and pendulous appear before the foliage, the females are ovoid and cone-like, 2 cm long. Ideal to grow in wet soils, but subject to canker. *Zone 3.*   p. 657

glutinosa 'Laciniata' (France 1819), "Cutleaf European alder"; French mutation of the Black alder, attractive because of its deeply pinnately lobed leaves, giving the tree a fine ferny texture; the foliage is sticky when young. *Zone 3.*   p. 657

hirsuta (Manchuria and No. Japan), "Manchurian alder"; handsome, vigorous deciduous tree of pyramidal habit to 20 m high, with broad-ovate leaves 15 cm long, dull green above, reddish downy beneath, crenate or shallowly lobed at margins, 9-12 pairs of veins very prominent; fruit cone-like 2 cm long. *Zone 4.*   p. 657

incana (No. Asia, Europe; introd. in No. America), "Speckled alder" or "Grey alder"; shrub or tree to 20 m high, at home in wet places, with young branches covered by gray down; the leaves ovate, 5-10 cm long, coarsely toothed gray-glaucous beneath, veins prominent in 9-12 pairs; male catkins 5-10 cm long in clusters; 2 cm fruit. *Zone 2*   p. 657

incana 'Laciniata' (Scandinavia); handsome form having erect willowy, reddish twigs with gray-green leaves cut into pointed lobes on each side. *Zone 2.*   p. 657

oregona, sometimes spelled oregana (syn. rubra) (Alaska to California), "Red alder" or "Oregon alder"; small pyramidal tree 10-15 m high, with branches lightly pendant; young shoots angled and dark red, bearing ovate leaves to 15 cm long, toothed along margins, smooth above but rusty-hairy beneath, the surface with 15-20 pairs of sunken veins; male catkins 15 cm long and a charming red, the 3 cm cones on orange-red stalks. *Zone 4.*   p. 658

rhombifolia (Western No. America), "White alder" or "Western alder"; tall tree 20-30 m high, with slender branches pendulous at ends; the leaves oblong ovate or rhombic 10 cm long, serrate at margins, green above and downy beneath, having 7-9 pairs of depressed lateral veins; male catkins 15 cm long, and small 2 cm cones. At home along streams. *Zone 5.*   p. 657

ALOCASIA   *Araceae*
cuprea 'Vera', "Copper caladium"; tropical Asian herb with large fleshy, peltate-cordate leaves, waxy, dark metallic green, the veins depressed and deep coppery-purple; purple beneath in the species; the cultivar 'Vera' photographed in Manila, Philippines more green. *Humid-tropical. Zone 12.*   p. 21

korthalsii (thibautiana) (Borneo); stocky plant with sagittate leaf olive-grayish-green, primary veins broadly silver, and veinlets gray; purple beneath. *Zone 12.*   p. 21

macrorrhiza (Malaya, Sri Lanka), giant "Elephant's ear"; to 4½ m high, with thick trunk, large 60 cm broadly shield-shaped, sagittate, fleshy leaves waxy green, with prominent ribs and wavy margins. *Zone 11.*   p. 21, 646

macrorrhiza 'Variegata' (East Indies), "Giant variegated alocasia"; light green leaves strikingly blotched and mottled with white. *Zone 11.*   p. 646

micholitziana 'Cherie Darian'; beautiful California cultivar of the species from the Philippines, having sagittate, sturdy leaves wavymargined, the blades a satiny blackish-green with contrasting white ribs. *Zone 12.*   p. 21

plumbea (indica metallica) (India east to Micronesia and Java); handsome foliage plant of robust habit, 1 m high or more, with thick rhizome appearing above ground; the stiff, deep brown-purple, vaginate petioles carry showy, shield-like broad-sagittate leaves 30 to 50 cm long, rich metallic green quilted, the reverse coppery green with red-brown ribs; short stalked inflorescence near base, with white spathe and slender spadix. *Zone 11.*   p. 646

sanderiana (Philippines), "Kris plant"; tuberous plant with graceful, sagittate leaf shining metallic, silver-green with grayish-white ribs; margins deeply lobed and white; reverse purple. *Zone 12.*   p. 21

ALOCASIA: see also COLOCASIA, CYRTOSPERMA, XANTHOSOMA

ALOE   *Liliaceae*
aculeata (Transvaal); loose rosette almost stemless; very fleshy, bluish leaves, broad lanceolate to 60 cm long and 12 cm wide, concave above and rounded beneath, and set with reddish teeth; branched inflorescence to 1 m high, multi-flowered with lemon-yellow cylindric blooms to 4 cm long. *Zone 10.*   p. 196

acutissima antanimorensis (Madagascar: Tuléar); branching succulent shrub, smaller than the species; the sprawling stems 1 cm dia., crowded with fleshy leaves concave above and recurving, 20 cm long, coppery green and margins with dry spines; tubular 2 cm red flowers in branched pyramidal racemes. *Zone 11.*   p. 196

africana (Transvaal), a "Spiny aloe"; a very pretty tree aloe, good compact rosette when young, though reaching 4 m or more in its habitat, the glaucous bluish leaves are hard and brown-spined at the margins, recurring and to 70 cm long; flowers yellow, tipped green, in striking pyramidal racemes. *Arid-subtropic. Zone 10.* p. 197

arborescens (So. Africa, Malawi); "Candelabra aloe"; handsome spreading rosette with sword-like, fleshy tapering leaves to 60 cm long, glaucous pale bluish-green, edged with yellow horny teeth; on stems reaching 4½ m; flowers coral-red, in dense pyramidal racemes. *Zone 10.* p. 197

bainesii (So. Africa to Mozambique); striking tree, known by the Zulus as "Kalane Enkula", "The Big one"; to 20 m high, with trunk to 2 or more thick and head to 6 m across, one of the largest of the genus; sword-shaped green leaves 60-90 cm long, leathery and concave, with small, marginal prickles; flowers salmon-pink tipped with green, in dense terminal raceme. *Zone 10.* p. 115, 197

barbadensis (vera in hort.) (Ethiopia, So.Arabia, E. Africa to Cape Verdes, Canary Isl., Madeira), the "Barbados aloe", "True aloe" or "Medicine plant"; widely cultivated, short-stemmed, suckering rosette with fleshy, dagger-shaped, channeled leaves to 60 cm long, gray-green and glaucous; spotted when young; edged with soft pale spines; nodding, cylindrical, yellow flowers on spike-like inflorescence to 1 m high. According to Pickering Chronology, Boston 1879: A. perfoliata vera (Linnaeus, 1753). A. officinalis (Forsk.), A. Vulgaris (Lamarck, 1783). Dioscorides in 60 A.D. wrote about its use medicinally in Greece and Egypt since ancient times. Introduced by European colonists to the West Indies. The jellied pulp inside the leaves is used to heal cuts and sore burns; also found in cosmetic lotions and medicinal creams; internally taken as a purgative. *Zone 10.* p. 199, 534

bellatula (C. Madagascar); densely clustering stemless rosettes sprouting from roots, the narrow channeled leaves to 15 cm long and 1 cm wide at base, keeled on reverse, rough-warty on surface and spotted white, and horny-toothed along margins; inflorescence to 60 cm high, with coral-red flowers. *Zone 11.* p. 196

camperi (eru) (Eritrea, Nubia, No. Kenya); branching rosette with stem 45 cm high; very fleshy, arching leaves to 75 cm long, concave above, glossy dark green striped with white, and red teeth; the 'Green form' with only faint markings; salmon-red flowers in branched racemes. *Zone 10.* p. 197

ciliaris (So. Africa: E. Cape), "Climbing aloe"; weak, branching and scrambling stems with open spirals of not very fleshy, 15 cm leaves, dark green with white teeth along the edge; flowers scarlet with green tips, on inflorescence to 30 cm long. *Zone 10.* p. 196

dichotoma (Cape Prov. to Namibia), "Dragon-tree aloe"; bold arborescent succulent rosette with broad fleshy leaves 25 cm or more long, glaucous green edged in brownish-yellow and with triangular teeth; growing into monstrous trees to 9 m high, with branches forking dichotomously on a smooth trunk; short, branched inflorescence of flask-like flowers canary yellow. *Zone 10.* p. 197

divaricata (S.W. and W. Madagascar); arborescent xerophyte of arid Madagascar, with erect slender trunk to 3 m or more high, later branching from base shrub-like; linear-lanceolate recurving succulent gray-green leaves to 65 cm long, spirally arranged; the margins with reddish teeth; inflorescence with numerous scarlet-red flowers. Rich in juice which dries yellow, and marketed for medicinal purposes by the East India Company since 1630. (Reynolds). *Zone 11.* p. 196

dorotheae (Tanzania); dense succulent rosette, branching from base, the concave lanceolate leaves spreading outward with recurving tips, to 15 cm long, colored coppery red over green, and with whitish marginal teeth; erect raceme of cylindrid red flowers. *Zone 10.* p. 196

elgonica (East Africa: Kenya); succulent shrub forming several stems to 1 m high, topped by open rosettes of grayish-green lanceolate leaves to 40 cm long, lightly channelled along center, and with marginal spiny teeth; branched inflorescence 60 cm high, with orange-scarlet 4 cm flowers in pyramidal racemes. *Zone 10.* p. 196

eru 'Maculata' hort: see camperi

ferox (So. Africa), "Ferocious aloe"; bold rosette, developing a stem to 5 m high, with broad, fleshy leaves bronzy green, to 1 m long, hollow above, curved and warty beneath, margins with brown-red teeth; flowers orange-red, dense in striking pyramidal racemes 50-80 cm long. The Zulus use it as an unguent, and for stomach troubles. *Zone 10.* p. 197

harlana (Ethiopia); handsome stemless robust rosette to 60 cm high, with lanceolate leaves spreading wide and decurving, beautiful when young; the glossy surface dark green and striped or marbled lengthwise with creamy pale green, the margins with sinuate horny teeth; the leaves with age to 50 cm long. Photo pg. 199 taken at Seaborn Del Dios Nursery, Escondido, Calif. *Zone 10.* p. 199

haworthioides aurantiaca (C. Madagascar); clustering stemless, dense 3-5 cm rosette of dark green leaves to 4 cm long, closely set with soft, pale spines; simple inflorescence to 30 cm high, with flowers orange, red in the species. *Zone 11.* p. 199

marlothii (Botswana, Transvaal, Natal, Kenya); attractive tree with single trunk, to 5 m high; leaves to 75 cm long and 18 cm wide, in open rosette, pale glaucous blue or greenish, concave and very spiny with short thick purplish-brown thorns; flowers red-orange, in erect pyramidal racemes. I did, however, find a double-headed old tree in the northern Transvaal. *Zone 10.* p. 199

nobilis (So. Africa: Cape Prov.), "Gold-tooth aloe"; attractive, robust succulent rosette to 25 cm across, with broad-ovate, green leaves, overlaid with copper in bright sun, concave above and rounded beneath with keel; prominent curved, horny yellow thorns along margins and on reverse; showy inflorescence 80 cm high, with racemes of red-orange flowers. Good commercial pot-plant. *Zone 10.* p. 199

plicatilis (So. Africa: Cape Prov.), "Fan aloe"; small forking tree to 5 m high, with closely packed, linear, fleshy 30 cm leaves of even width arranged in two ranks, tip rounded, pale glaucous blue with translucent yellow margin; large cylindric, 5 cm scarlet flowers in loose spike. *Zone 10.* p. 199

polyphylla (So. Africa: Drakensberg; Basutoland), "Spiral aloe"; striking low rosette 30-40 cm dia., dense with fleshy, broad leaves relatively short, but becoming 20-30 cm long, pale glaucous green and with a strong, red-brown tip; the foliage spirally arranged and overlapping; branched inflorescence bearing salmon-pink flowers. A succulent of unique beauty whether large or small, with its leaves regularly arranged as in shingles on a roof, in clockwise or counter-clockwise coils. Somewhat difficult in cultivation; in habitat at 2,400 m they are often under snow. *Zone 9.* p. 198

rauhii (Madagascar: Tuléar); handsome short-stemmed open rosette forming clusters, gray-green succulent, lanceolate leaves 10 cm long, with numerous light markings, and occasional white marginal teeth; tubular red flowers with pale tips in branched raceme. *Zone 11.* p. 196

saponaria (Cape Prov., Transkei, Natal, Transvaal), "Soap aloe"; short stemmed, suckering rosette with fleshy, broad lanceolate leaves 15-20 cm long, bluish-green marked with yellow-green elongate blotches arranged in transverse bands; margins with large cream to brown thorns; flowers red to salmon and yellow, on branched inflorescence 60 cm more tall. The native Xosas and Fingos use the leaf gel or sap to heal wounds. *Zone 10.* p. 198

striata (S.W. Africa, Cape Prov.), "Coral aloe"; large rosette, nearly stemless, of broad fleshy leaves almost 60 cm long, pale glaucous gray faintly striped, the hard margins pink and without spines; branched inflorescence to 1 m tall, with clusters of pendulous coral-red flowers 3 cm long. *Zone 10.* p. 198

thraskii (S.E. Africa: Natal to Zululand); trunkforming, to 2 m or more high, with dense rosettes of clasping, recurving concave leaves to 1½ m long, darkish green slightly glaucous, tapering rapidly to long tip; and with fine brown thorns at margins; flowers light orange, in beautiful many-flowered racemes. *Zone 10.* p. 197

variegata (Cape of Good Hope), "Partridge breast"; beautiful succulent to 30 cm high with triangular blue-green leaves arranged in 3 ranks and painted with oblong white spots in irregular crossbands, the margins horny and white-warty; tubular flowers salmon-red, in loose racemes. *Zone 10.* p. 198

vera: see barbadensis

vulgaris LAM.: see barbadensis MILL.

wickensii (No. Transvaal); group-forming stemless rosette with leathery, tapering, rather erect leaves glaucous green to olive, to 60 cm long; dark marginal spines; branched inflorescence 1 m or more high, with yellow flowers. *Zone 10.* p. 197

ALONSOA *Scrophulariaceae*
warscewiczii (Peru), "Mask flower"; bushy herbaceous shortlived perennial 60 to 90 cm high, grown for its attractive scarlet-red or cinnabar winter-blooming flowers 1 cm or more in dia., 2-lipped and carried on brownish stems with fresh green, toothed leaves. *Zone 10.* p. 501

ALOYSIA *Verbenaceae*
triphylla (Lippia citriodora) (Argentina, Chile), "Lemon-verbena"; branching sub-shrub to 3 m high with angular, wiry shoots, and 8 cm lanceolate, smooth leaves in whorls of 3 or 4, lemon-scented; the small reddish-white flowers in graceful pyramidal spikes and very fragrant; summer-blooming. Use: leaves in finger bowls, teas, sachet, perfumes. One of the most fragrant plants in the garden; deciduous in Autumn. *Zones 8-10.* p. 541

ALPINIA *Zingiberaceae*
haenkei (Catimbium) (Philippines: N.E. Luzon), "Erect shell ginger"; very handsome rhizomatous perennial with broad leathery leaves along stiffly erect stems, topped by a lovely pyramidal, spike-like inflorescence of shell-shaped, waxy white flowers, orange-yellow

with red markings inside on lower lip. More attractive in gardens than Shell ginger (A. zerumbet) because its growth habit is smaller and its stems are more upright. *Zone 11.*   p. 520

purpurata (South Seas from Moluccas to New Caledonia and Yap), "Red ginger"; ornamental perennial herb with leafy stems ranging from 2-5 m, each ending in a showy inflorescence, with a flower spike brush-like to 30 cm long, consisting of numerous large, boat-shaped bright red bracts each with a small white flower, normally erect but drooping if long; new plants germinate among the flower bracts. *Tropical. Zones 10-11.*   p. 520

purpurata 'Rosea' (So. Pacific: Solomon Isl.), "Jungle Queen" or "Pink ginger"; beautiful cultivar now grown in Hawaii and the area of Tahiti; majestic tropical perennial 2 to 4 m high, from spreading underground rhizomes, with sturdy stems having 30 cm leaves arranged along upper stalk, topped by showy, erect spike-like inflorescence of shell-pink bracts, covering inconspicuous 3 cm white flowers, between Spring and late Autumn; old stalks die back after blooming, but new rooted plants sprout among the whithered bracts. *Tropical. Zone 11.*   p. 520

sanderae (New Guinea), "Variegated ginger"; very attractive ornamental ginger of dwarf habit, having creeping rhizome and clustered, leafy stems about 45 cm high; the lanceolate leaves arranged somewhat in 2 ranks, pale green, edged and obliquely banded from the center to the margin with pure white. With age growing to 2 m high, but seldom blooming, and having unremarkable flowers. *Humid-tropical. Zones 11-12.*   p. 520

zerumbet (speciosa or nutans in hort.) (China, Japan), "Shell ginger"; majestic rhizomatous plant forming dense clumps of leafy, arching canes to 4 m high, with smooth, long-bladed, leathery leaves arranged in 2 rows; the striking fragrant, porcelain-textured flowers with bell-shaped, waxy-white calyx, the corolla white flushed with pink and tipped with red and yellow lip, in dense racemes to 30 cm long, becoming nodding. *Zones 10-11.*   p. 520

ALPINIA: see also HEDYCHIUM

ALSOPHILA australis: see SPHAEROPTERIS cooperi

ALSTROEMERIA   *Alstroemeriaceae (Amaryllidaceae)*
aurantiaca (Chile), "Lily of the Incas"; herbaceous perennial with fibrous roots from egg-shaped tubers which are attached to a common stem; showy, floriferous plant blooming in Summer, with leafy floral stem nearly 1 m high; lanceolate leaves, and terminal clusters of beautiful azalea-like flowers about 4 cm across, orange with two upper segments streaked with orange-red, the outer ones tipped with green; long-lasting as cut flowers. *Zones 7-10.*   p. 341

aurantiaca 'Cyprus'; showy color variant with large yellow flowers tinted apricot, toward center deep yellow and lined with purple. *Zones 7-10.*   p. 340

ligtu (Chile), "Inca Lily"; herbaceous perennial with thin linear 8 cm leaves along 45 cm flowering stem; the flowers with spreading perianth segments pinkish, streaked with purple, and a touch of yellow, to 5 cm wide. Very long lasting as cut flowers. *Zone 9.* p. 341

pelegrina (No. Chile, Perú), "Lily of Lima"; 40 cm high, with short, lanceolate leaves on stems, the numerous 5 cm lily-like flowers with spreading segments outside lilac, spotted and lined with red-purple inside. Horticultural forms in various colors. *Zone 10.*   p. 341

ALTERNANTHERA   *Amaranthaceae*
ficoidea 'Amoena' (Telanthera) (Brazil), "Parrot-leaf"; small, bushy herb of robust growing habit with broad lanceolate leaves, brownish-red and carmine, to orange; small whitish flower. *Zones 10-11.* p. 340

ficoidea 'Aurea-nana' "Yellow calico plant"; a pretty horticultural variety of slightly more open habit; bushy little plant with its small 2½-4 cm spoon-shaped leaves prettily variegated pale yellow and fresh green. The green counterpart in carpet-bedding to the red A. bettzickiana, and kept in shape by shearing. *Zones 10-11.*   p. 340

ficoidea 'Bettzickiana' ('Magnifica') (Brazil), "Red calico plant"; dwarf, clustering herb to 15 cm high, with twisted 3-5 cm leaves narrow and spatulate, glowing maroon-red, blotched and colored with salmon, cream and deep green; small whitish flowers in leaf axils; ideal for carpet-bedding. *Zones 10-11.*   p. 309, 323, 340

ALTHAEA   *Malvaceae*
officinalis (Europe to Siberia, Asia Minor, natural. in coastal Conn. to Virginia), "Marsh mallow" or "White mallow"; gray-velvety perennial marsh-plant, with stiffly erect stems 1 to 2 m high, and broad ovate leaves prominently veined, mostly pointedly lobed; flowers 3-5 cm across, bluish or pale rose, usually in leaf axils, in July. *Zone 5.*   p. 457
rosea: see ALCEA rosea
syriacus: see HIBISCUS syriacus

ALYOGYNE   *Malvaceae*
huegelii (Hibiscus) (So. and W. Australia), "Blue hibiscus" or

"Lilac hibiscus"; erect, tomentose shrub to 2 m high, with small, deeply 3 to 5-lobed, dark green, coarse-hairy leaves, and numerous small, single, rosy-purple or lilac flowers with spreading petals 5-8 cm across. *Zone 9.*   p. 781

ALYSSUM   *Cruciferae*
heldreichii (Greece), "Greek stone-cress"; prostrate herbaceous perennial with long, thin-wiry branches, creeping over the ground or pendant, and furnished with slender, linear leaves; the small yellow flowers in dense, showy terminal clusters, producing a mass of color. *Zone 7.*   p. 406
maritimum: see LOBULARIA maritima
markgrafii (Albania, Yugoslavia), "Madwort"; low, bushy herbaceous perennial to 30 cm high, the stems softly hairy, with narrow 2 cm leaves; tiny 1 cm yellow flowers in dense clusters, forming mounds of bright color. *Zone 8.*   p. 406
montanum (Europe to Syria), "Mountain alyssum"; herbaceous perennial 10-25 cm high, with prostrate stems forming dense clusters; evergreen, gray-pubescent, obovate to linear leaves; small yellow, fragrant flowers in short clusters, from April to August. *Zone 3.*   p. 412
podolicum: see SCHIVARECKIA podolica
saxatile (Zander): see AURINIA saxatilis (Hortus 3)
serpyllifolium (S.W. Europe, No. Africa), "Thymian madwort"; low herbaceous perennial to 15 cm high, spreading with procumbent branches, forming many non-flowering rosettes; small gray-hoary, 2 cm ovobate leaves; small yellow flowers in short racemes. *Zone 9.*   p. 406
wulfenianum (Europe: S.E. Alps); gray-pubescent perennial with fleshy prostrate branches, commonly low and compact, only 30 cm high; set with silvery, thick elliptic leaves; the small yellow flowers fragrant, with notched petals, in short clusters, during Summer. *Zone 6.*   p. 406

ALYXIA   *Apocynaceae*
ruscifolia (Australia: New So. Wales, Queensland), "Sea-box"; straggling evergreen shrub to 2 m, with small 2-3 cm oval leaves glossy green, their margins turned under, and set in whorls; small white flowers with 5 windmill petals, in terminal clusters, followed by orange berries. *Zone 10.*   p. 266

AMARANTHUS   *Amaranthaceae*
caudatus (So. Asia), "Love-lies-bleeding"; stout herbaceous plant to 1 m or more high, with long, ovate green leaves turning reddish in Autumn, and showy inflorescence of pendant, tail-like branched spikes of tiny red flowers. *Tropical. Zones 10-11.*   p. 339
cruentus (paniculatus) (Tropics), "Prince's feather"; magnificent large bush 1-2 m high, with dense foliage, and the plumy inflorescence with side branchlets spreading and nodding, rich blood-red; photographed on the Greek island of Rhodes. *Zones 10-11.*   p. 339
tricolor (gangeticus) (E. Indies), "Joseph's coat"; vigorous, erect plant with ovate, pointed leaves brilliantly colored in shades of red, green and yellow; especially the summer growth. *Zone 10.*   p. 340

x AMARCRINUM   *Amaryllidaceae*
memoria-corsii (Amaryllis belladonna or Brunsvigia rosea x Crinum moorei); this intergeneric hybrid was originally made as x Crindonna corsii, with better blooms than A. belladonna; very pretty, pink, erect funnelform, somewhat fragrant flowers with recurving segments, borne in clusters on 1 m stems. *Zone 8.* p. 209

AMARYLLIS   *Amaryllidaceae*
belladonna (Brunsvigia rosea) (So. Africa), the "Cape belladonna" or "Belladonna lily", the "true" Amaryllis; a bulbous plant also known as "Naked lily" because the lovely trumpet-shaped, lily-like clear rosy-pink fragrant flowers, 10 cm long, appear in clusters on solid, reddish 60 cm stalks, bare and ahead of the new strap-like leaves, in South Africa before the rains from February to April; in the Northern Hemisphere in August; forming clumps. *Subtropic. Zone 9.*   p. 209
punicea, reticulata, vittata: see under HIPPEASTRUM

AMELANCHIER   *Rosaceae*
asiatica (Temp. E. Asia, Japan, Korea, China), "Sugar plum"; graceful deciduous tree to 10 m high, with ovate leaves 3-8 cm long, finely toothed and covered by loose down; white flowers 3 cm across, having linear petals, in woolly, pendant clusters, blooming in May, sweetly fragrant; small blue-black fruit resembling black currant. *Zone 5.*   p. 829
canadensis (Québec to Georgia), "Downy service berry" or "Shad-bush", inhabiting swampy areas of E. No. America; deciduous shrub or tree to 10 m or more high, with gray bark attractive in Winter; in early Spring a wealth of white flowers cover the tree as the young gray felty leaves unfold, 3-9 cm long; the 3 cm wide blooms are followed by berry-like 1 cm edible, maroon-red sweet fruit; the foliage turns a vivid yellow and red autumn color. *Zone 4.*   p. 829

x grandiflora (arborea x laevis), "Apple serviceberry" or "Sugarplum"; small deciduous tree to 8 m high, with broad pointed leaves, cordate at base; pure white flowers 3 cm wide, in early May; the fruits are orange to red, berry-like, similar to Crataegus, with blueberry flavor, used by early settlers in bakery and preserves. *Zone 4.* *p. 922*

laevis (Canada, so. to Georgia, Ohio and Iowa), "Allegany service-berry"; deciduous shrub or tree 8-12 m high, with branches stiffly erect; the leaves oval-pointed, to 8 cm long, toothed nearly to base, purplish when young; white flowers 3 cm across, the petals narrow and spreading, blooming in April; berry-like 2 cm purplish-black fruit. Foliage turns red in Autumn. Widely distributed in Eastern U.S. *Zone 3.* *p. 829*

spicata (Québec to Ontario, Penna. to So. Dakota), "June-berry"; stoloniferous shrub spreading by suckers at the base and forming thickets, with stems to 1½ m high; ovate leaves 3-5 cm long, toothed at margins; white flowers 2 cm wide, in erect silky clusters, in June. *Zone 5.* *p. 829*

AMHERSTIA   Leguminosae
nobilis (India, Burma or Myanmar), "Queen of flowering trees"; one of the showiest, most striking tropical trees when in flower; 10-20 cm high, with dark green pinnate leaves, unfolding brownish-pink from drooping clusters. Inflorescence in graceful racemes 60-90 cm long, pendulous from every branch, with 20 cm flowers, with bracts, stalks, sepals and smaller petals vermillion-red, the larger petals red with white base and tipped with yellow; long protruding anthers red also. *Zones 10-11.* *p. 746*

AMIANTHIUM   Liliaceae
muscitoxicum (E. No. America: New York to Florida), "Fly poison" of "Crow-poison"; bulbous herb to 1 m high, with linear leaves to 50 cm long; erect pyramidal 12 cm racemes dense with small white flowers, in early Summer; fruit 3-horned. Bulb lethal if eaten; cattle and sheep are frequently poisoned by consuming the foliage. *Zone 5.* *p. 238*

AMOMUM cardamomum: see ELETTARIA cardamomum

AMORPHA   Leguminosae
canescens (Manitoba to Louisiana and New York), "Lead plant"; shrubby plant with angled stems 1 m or more high, the compound odd-pinnate leaves gray-downy, having 15 to 45 elliptic leaflets 2 cm long; inflorescence in cylindrical spikes to 15 cm long, with small purplish-blue flowers, in July to September. *Zone 2.* *p. 746*

fruticosa (Conn. to Minnesota, to Florida, Louisiana), "False indigo"; shrubby plant to 4 m high, with pinnate leaves having 11-25 elliptic bristle-tipped leaflets 2-4 cm long and finely pubescent; flowers purplish-blue in clustered spikes, 7-15 cm long. *Zone 4.* *p. 746*

AMORPHOPHALLUS   Araceae
campanulatus (E. Indies, New Guinea); a giant aroid with tuber 25 cm thick, dark green solitary lobed leaves pinnately cut; inflorescence with ovate spathe 20 x 25 cm, fleshy and funnel-shaped below, green spotted white, purple inside. *Zones 11-12.* *p. 205, 219*

koratensis (Thailand); collected by J. Bogner of Munich Botanic Garden; curious tuberous plant requiring rest; tuber depressed globular, forming inflorescence following dormancy period; the hooded spathe 10-12 cm long, outside below green, upper part purplish; enclosing the erect spadix. *Zone 11.* *p. 219*

rivieri (Hydrosme) (Vietnam), "Devil's tongue" or "Leopard palm"; curious tuberous plant with a 1 m flower-spike which carries the large, reddish spadix and calla-like green and purple spathe, and with unpleasant odor; the foliage, appearing after flowering, is on a single, rose-marbled stalk with 3 palm-like branches bearing numerous elliptic segments. *Tropical. Zone 11.* *p. 22, 205, 219*

titanum (Sumatra); "Titan arum"; giant tuberous plant and a great curiosity with flowers on a 2 m yellow spadix surrounded by the crisped 1 m spathe purple inside, green outside and with disagreeable odor; 4½ m leaves on 3 m leaf stalk. *Zone 12.* *p. 22*

AMPELOPSIS   Vitaceae
aconitifolia (No. China, Mongolia), "Monks-hood-vine"; luxuriant tendril-climbing shrub with thin stems, and fresh green leaves, both sides deeply dissected and divided, leaflets to 8 cm long; fruiting with colorful berries bluish, turning yellow or orange in Autumn. *Zone 4.* *p. 298*

brevipedunculata (N.E. Asia), "Porcelain-berry" of Mongolia; tendril-climbing woody rambler with slender stems, cordate-ovate leaves to 12 cm long; with 3 coarsely toothed lobes; clusters of fruit opposite leaf axils, the pea-size berries changing color from pale lilac to yellow to porcelain-blue, making a colorful show in Autumn. *Zone 4.* *p. 298*

brevipedunculata 'Elegans' (heterophylla) (Manchuria, Japan), "Colored grape-leaf"; attractive climber with blood-red, hairy branches and thin forking vines, variable leaves simple, 3-lobed or 5-lobed, bluish-green and prettily variegated with milky-green, creamy-white and rose. *Zone 7.* *p. 298*

AMPELOPSIS: see also PARTHENOCISSUS

AMSONIA   Apocynaceae
hirtella (Cochise County, Arizona, to W. Texas), "Western Blue star"; arid area perennial 25 to 75 cm high, dense with narrow leaves; the branches topped by starry flowers having 5 narrow lobes, pale blue to nearly white, spreading from corolla tube 2 cm long. *Zone 9.* *p. 340*

tabernaemontana (Mass. to Texas), "Blue star"; herbaceous perennial with milky sap, to 60 cm or more high, forming clumps; alternate thin, ovate leaves; the small, starry flowers 1 cm long, pale blue and hairy outside, in late Spring. *Zone 4.* *p. 341*

AMYGDALUS: see PRUNUS dulcis

ANACARDIUM   Anacardiaceae
occidentale (West Indies), the "Cashew-nut tree"; evergreen spreading tree to 12 m high, with obovate leathery leaves 20 cm long; numerous small fragrant flowers yellowish-pink; the fruit a kidney-shaped nut borne on a pear-shaped yellow or red fleshy receptacle. Juice from shell around seed can burn skin. *Zone 10.* *p. 636, 637, 903*

ANACYCLUS   Compositae
depressus (Morocco); summer-flowering perennial herb with usually prostrate stems with lacy, pinnately cut leaves and terminal flower heads to 5 cm across, with ray-flowers dark-red on back, white above. *Zone 6.* *p. 368*

radiatus (Anthemis) (Mediterr. region); bushy herbaceous perennial, to 50 cm high, thinly hairy; the wiry branches with finely divided leaves, and freely blooming with daisy-like flowers, 3-4 cm across, the ray-petals yellow above and purplish beneath. *Zone 8.* *p. 368*

ANAGALLIS   Primulaceae
monelli (linifolia) (Mediterr. region, Spain), "Flaxleaf pimpernel"; perennial with woody base in mild climate habitat, otherwise grown as annual; 25-50 cm high, with spreading 4-angled branches often rooting at nodes; ovate to oblong 3 cm leaves, usually in threes; attractive flowers 2 cm across, normally blue but variable to rose, and reddish beneath, blooming June to September. *Zone 9.* *p. 478*

ANANAS   Bromeliaceae
bracteatus tricolor (striatus); open rosette of relatively broad colorful leaves predominantly cream-yellow with coppery green center; marginal spines red. *Tropical. Zone 12.* *p. 45*

comosus (sativus) (Bahia, Mato Grosso), "Pineapple"; large formal terrestrial rosette of stiff, tapering and spiny-edged leaves grayish to bronze green, gracefully arching; violet flowers borne in dense heads with tufts of leaves, producing the edible fleshy fruit. *Tropical. Zone 11.* *p. 45*

comosus 'Porteanus' (comosus hyb.), "Golden rocket"; large and stiff rosette with olive-green leaves acquiring a reddish color, and having a broad creamy-yellow center band on upper surface. *Zone 11.* *p. 45*

comosus 'Smooth Cayenne'; elegant rosette of broad recurving, gray-green leaves, the margins smooth and spineless; the large golden-yellow to brown-red fruit of luscious, sweet flavor; topped in time by another dense, smaller rosette of leaves. The 'Smooth Cayenne' was brought to Hawaii from Guyana in 1886 where it developed the big plantations, producing commercial pineapple 14 to 20 cm or more long. *Zone 11.* *p. 906*

ANAPHALIS   Compositae
margaritacea (No. America, East Asia to Japan), "Pearly Everlasting"; attractive, rhizomatous perennial to 50 cm high; stems set with linear leaves 10 cm long, white-tomentose beneath; branched terminal clusters of small 1 cm white flowers embedded in bracts pearly white; ideal for dried bouquets. For everlasting, they are picked before maturity, dried and dyed various colors. *Zone 4.* *p. 370*

triplinervis (Himalayas), "Everlasting"; robust mountain perennial with stout, tomentose stems to 50 cm high; narrow-oblong, gray-pubescent leaves 8 cm or more long; small white ray-flowers in loose clusters; for moist sites. *Zone 3-9.* *p. 370*

yedoensis (cinnamomea or margaritacea var.), (Japan), "Japanese everlasting"; vigorous gray-woolly perennial, with erect stems, bearing linear-lanceolate leaves, and branched terminal clusters of small white, globular flowers. *Zone 6.* *p. 370*

ANCHUSA　*Boraginaceae*

azurea (E. Mediterranean to Caucasus), "Italian alkanet" or "Summer forget-me-not"; hairy perennial to 1½ m, with alternate lanceolate leaves to 45 cm long in the lower ones; the inflorescence on erect leafy-stem with funnel-shaped flowers bright blue, 2 cm across, in Summer-Autumn; fairly hardy Zone 5.　　　　　p. 342

caespitosa (Crete), "Alkanet"; small tufted perennial to 10 cm high, with narrow linear leaves; wide open flowers blue with white tube, blooming during Summer. Zones 9-10.　　　　p. 342

capensis (So. Africa), "Cape forget-me-not" or "Bugloss"; herbaceous perennial, also grown as annual or biennial; 25 to 50 cm high, with narrow-lanceolate leaves, coarse-hairy; erect floral stalks with scattered clusters of vivid blue 1 cm summer-flowers margined with red. Zone 10.　　　　　　　　　　　　p. 342

myosotidiflora: see BRUNNERA macrophylla

sempervirens: see PENTAGLOTTIS sempervirens

ANCISTROCACTUS　*Cactaceae*

uncinatus (Ferocactus, Hamatocactus), (So. Texas, New Mexico, Arizona, No. Mexico), "Hook cactus"; small globular to ovoid cactus to 15 cm high, with turnip-like root; prominent tubercles or knobs bearing reddish spines, the lower ones hooked and 10 cm long; carmine-red flowers to 3 cm across. Zone 9.　　　　p. 158

ANDROMEDA　*Ericaceae*

catesbaei hort.: see LEUCOTHOE fontanesiana

ferruginea: see LYONIA ferruginea (Zander)

floribunda: see PIERIS floribunda

glaucophylla (No. North America), "Downy andromeda"; low evergreen shrub 30-50 cm high, with glaucous stems, and linear leaves to 6 cm long, white-tomentose beneath, and with edges rolled under: small white flowers with globular corollas look like tiny berries. Found in bogs from Manitoba to Virginia. Zone 2.　　　　p. 699

japonica 'Marginata': see PIERIS jap. 'Marginata'

polifolia (Europe,, No. E. Asia, No. North America), "Bog rosemary"; low evergreen shrub 30-50 cm high, with creeping root-stock or rhizomes, spreading easily; leaves linear 2 cm long, glaucous beneath; flowers pale pink to whitish, 1 cm long, in terminal clusters, blooming May to July. Zone 2.　　　　　　　　p. 699

ANDROSACE　*Primulaceae*

primuloides 'Chumbyi' (Hortus: sarmentosa var.) (Himalayas), "Rock jasmine"; low perennial with woody base, spreading by runners forming dense rosettes; obovate leaves 5 cm or more, covered with silky silvery hairs; the pretty flowers, resembling primula, deep pink, 2 cm across in long-stalked clusters, blooming June-July. Considered cv. of primuloides by Beckett; var. of sarmentosa in Zander. Zones 3-7.　　　　　　　　　　　　　　p. 478

sarmentosa (watkinsii) (Himalayas), "Rock jasmine"; subshrubby, variable perennial, spreading by flexuous brown stolons to 15 cm long; the somewhat leathery, ovate 2 to 4 cm leaves in rosettes, covered with silvery hairs when young; small 1 cm rose-pink flowers in clusters on 12 cm stalks, blooming May-June. Zones 3-6.　　p. 478

strigillosa (Sikkim Himalayas); low tufted perennial to 30 cm high, covered with silky-white hairs; obovate leaves to 8 cm long, with hard apex, in rosettes, rising from rhizome; 1 cm flowers rose-pink to purple, resembling primrose, in clusters on long floral stalk. Zone 6.　　　　　　　　　　　　　　　　　p. 478

ANEMONE　*Ranunculaceae*

alpina (Pulsatilla alpina) (Mountains of Spain to Italy, Balkans to Caucasus), "Alpine windflower"; herbaceous mountain perennial with thick taproot or rhizome, forming clusters of soft-hairy stems 10-40 cm long; the largest basal leaves several times divided into fernlike segments; the showy white flowers to 6 cm across, with yellow stamens in center, blooming in May. Zone 6.　　p. 484

blanda (S.E. Europe, Greece to Taurus Mts. in Asia Minor), "Windflower" or "Greek Anemone"; choice low perennial 10 to 20 cm high, with tuberous rhizomes wide-spreading with new shoots appearing each Spring over the surrounding area; the ferny leaves hairless, deeply lobed and cleft; the charming daisy-like flowers with pale or sky-blue petal-like sepals pubescent on outside, and yellow anthers, 5 cm across; March-April blooming. Zones 6-9.　p. 261

blanda 'Atrocaerulea'; with dark blue varying to ageratum-blue flowers, one of the many color varieties of A. blanda from Greece and the Taurus Mts. in Asia Minor, a small herb to 15 cm high with tuberous rhizome; compound and cut leaves, and solitary flowers 5 cm across. Zone 6.　　　　　　　　　　　p. 261

blanda 'Radar', "Royal windflower"; striking carpet-forming tuberous perennial, with showy daisy-like flowers carmine-red and contrasting white center area and yellow stamens; seen in Keukenhof Gardens, of Lisse, Holland, blooming early May. Zone 6.　p. 260

canadensis (Labrador to Québec to Brit. Columbia, south to Maryland and Colorado), "Meadow anemone"; perennial to 50 cm

high, from tuberous rhizome; stem usually branched, with soft-hairy, deeply 3-parted toothed leaves; the starry white flowers 3-4 cm across, on long stalks, in May. Zone 3.　　　　　p. 261

coronaria (So. Europe to Cent. Asia), the Biblical "Lily of the fields"; attractive perennial with tuberous roots, finely divided leaves both basal and sessile along the erect, hairy stalk which bears the large, solitary, poppy-like, 6 cm flowers, the showy sepals in combinations of red, blue, yellow, white; in Spring. I photographed the variety coccinea, with its glowing crimson-red flowers, blooming in March in habitat amongst the ancient temple ruins of Pergamon, above the Asiatic coast of Turkey. Zone 7.　　　　p. 261

coronaria 'De Caen', (coronaria x pavonina), a "Poppy anemone"; florists anemone with single flowers consisting of large round segments, in colors from white to pink, red, purple to deep blue; center black, 6-8 cm across; blooming early Spring. Subtropic. Zone 9.　　　　　　　　　　　　　　　p. 261

coronaria 'St. Brigid'; a popular strain of florists tuberous-rooted "Poppy-anemones" for indoor flowering in late Winter and Spring; hybrid derived from coronaria, fulgens, and hortensis; colorful flowers with several rows of petals in shades of brilliant red, rose, purple, violet, and white; not hardy. Subtropic. Zone 9.　p. 261

x fulgens (annulata) (hortensis x pavonina), "Flame anemone" or "Scarlet windflower"; striking natural hybrid to 30 cm high from tuberous roots, with showy platter-shaped flowers scarlet to vermilion-red and white center area, the stamens violet, in early Spring. Zone 6.　　　　　　　　　　　　　p. 261

halleri (Pulsatilla) (Alps to Crimea); small alpine silky-hairy tap-rooted perennial to 30 cm high, forming mounds, the ferny, finely dissected foliage developing after flowers; lilac-purple blooms appear in Spring, followed by fuzzy fruitheads. Zone 5.　　　p. 261

hupehensis (China), "Dwarf Japanese anemone"; long-lived fibrous-rooted perennial with graceful branching stems 50 cm or more high; dark green, soft-hairy, 3-5 lobed leaves; semi-double flowers white, also pink or rose, 5-8 cm across, blooming September-October. Zone 5.　　　　　　　　　　　　p. 485

hupehensis japonica (China, Japan), "Japanese anemone"; very popular clump-forming garden perennial with stems 30-150 cm or more high, the leaves trifoliolate; leaflets 3-lobed, toothed, flowers 5-7 cm dia., soft lilac-rose, in bud flashed crimson; late Summer. Zone 6.　　　　　　　　　　　　　　　p. 485

hupehensis 'Splendens'; beautiful perennial for autumn color, with large rose-pink flowers to 8 cm across, on slender branches to 90 cm high, set with deeply lobed leaves. Zone 6.　　　p. 485

magellanica (So. Chile and Patagonia), "South American wind-flower"; small perennial resembling multifida, 15 cm high, with much divided basal leaves, partially hairy; flowers having petal-like creamy-white sepals 2-3 cm across. Zone 4.　　　　p. 485

multifida (globosa) (E. Canada and Maine, to Alaska, so. to Dakota and New Mexico); small flowers in globose silky heads, subtended by petal-like white sepals 1 cm long, on slender stalks 15-30 cm high, in June; perennial with erect rootstock, and basal leaves several times divided, the wedge-shaped segments with linear lobes. Zone 3.　　　　　　　　　　　　p. 485

nemorosa 'Allenii' (Eurasia), "Wood anemone"; handsome perennial to 25 cm high, with slender woody rhizome, bearing 3-parted leaves, the segments 3-5 divided again; the flowers with pale, bluish-purple sepals 2 cm long; white in the species; blooming in March. Zone 3.　　　　　　　　　　　　p. 485

occidentalis (Alaska, Brit. Columbia to Montana and Sierra Nevada), "Old man of the mountains"; handsome hairy alpine perennial 10-60 cm high, with thick, vertical roots, the silky, ferny basal leaves 5-8 cm wide divided into threes and dissected again into linear segments; solitary flowers of white sepals 2-3 cm long, occasionally tinged purple, in May to August; the styles of the pistils become long feathery tails pointing down, forming a shaggy beard. Zone 3.　　　　　　　　　　　　　　　p. 485

pulsatilla (Pulsatilla vulgaris) (W. Europe to Ukraine), "Pasque flower"; free-flowering perennial 30 cm high, from black fibrous rootstock; with leaves dissected like a feather and silky-hairy; solitary bell-shaped flowers blue to purple, to 6 cm across and yellow stamens, in Spring; interesting ornamental fruitheads develop from blooms, the spherical gray fluffy balls carrying seed with each feathery style. Zone 5.　　　　　　　　　　　　　　p. 261, 486

rivularis (Himalayas of No. India; Sri Lanka), "Windflower"; perennial 30-60 cm high, with turnip-shaped rhizome, forming a woody base; the 3-parted leaves lightly hairy, with wedge-shaped segments, the lobes again cut and toothed; the floral heads 3-4 cm across, the petal-like sepals normally white, varying to blue; anthers yellow; blooming May-June. Zone 7.　　　　　p. 486

sylvestris (Europe, Siberia), "Snowdrop anemone"; charming perennial 15 to 45 cm high, spreading by stolons; basal leaves 3 to 5 parted, pubescent beneath; the fragrant flowers of 5 satiny-white sepals toothed at apex, 5-6 cm across, in April; followed by woolly white fruit. *Zones 4-8.*　　　　　　　　　　　　　　　*p. 485*

tuberosa (New Mexico, Utah, Arizona to E. California), "Tuber Anemone"; attractive small perennial with tuberous rhizome, basal leaves of 3 finely cut leaflets; stems to 25 cm high, bearing solitary daisy-like flowers with sepals 15 mm long, white or suffused with rose. *Zone 6.*　　　　　　　　　　　　　　　　　　　　　　*p. 262*

vitifolia 'Robustissima' (Nepal Himalaya); handsome perennial 50-75 cm high, with large 3-7 lobed leaves, white-woolly beneath; flowers soft pink 5-8 cm across, white in the species; the anthers copper colored; July blooming. *Zone 5.*　　　　　　　　*p. 486*

ANEMONELLA　　*Ranunculaceae*

thalictroides (Anemone) (Maine to Florida), "Rue anemone"; tuberous-rooted perennial to 25 cm high; with compound leaves rising from the roots; the leafy floral stalk bearing loose clusters of small flowers of flaring white or purplish sepals, in May and June. The tuberous roots are edible. *Zone 5.*　　　　　　　　　*p. 262*

ANEMONOPSIS　　*Ranunculaceae*

macrophylla (Japan), "False anemone"; herbaceous perennial with underground rhizome, stems 60-90 cm high; the long-petioled, compound leaves to 25 cm across, the leaflets 5-10 cm long and sharply toothed; nodding flowers 3-4 cm across, with rose to pale violet petaloid sepals; July-blooming. *Zone 6.*　　　　*p. 486*

ANEMOPAEGMA　　*Bignoniaceae*

chamberlaynii (Brazil); vigorous climbing tropical shrub with leaves of 2 leaflets to 16 cm long, and sometimes a terminal tendril; flowers funnelform 6-8 cm long, in pendant clusters, the tube constricted near base, bright yellow in throat with purple or white. *Tropical. Zone 10.*　　　　　　　　　　　　　　*p. 268*

ANEMOPSIS　　*Saururaceae*

californica (Sierras of California, Nevada, W. Texas; Mexico), "Yerba Mansa" or "Apache beads"; interesting herbaceous perennial 40-50 cm high, with long-stalked oblong basal leaves, cordate at base; the minute flowers on a conical spadix, subtended by a whorl of petal-like white bracts around base, together resembling a single, anemone-like flower, on stalk bearing a solitary leaf; March to September. *Zone 8.*　　　　　　　　　　　　　　　*p. 477*

ANETHUM　　*Umbelliferae*

graveolens (Peucedanum) (Europe, W. Asia), "Dill"; popular annual or biennial aromatic herb 60 to 90 cm high, with leaves finely divided into thread-like segments, on greenish-white stems; small yellow flowers in large clusters. As a culinary herb with strong odor, the leaves are used to flavor cottage cheese, potato salad, tuna, and chicken salad. Seeds are added to apple pies, bread, soup and poultry, also for pickling cucumbers. *Zone 10.*　　　　　*p. 543*

ANGELICA　　*Umbelliferae*

archangelica (Europe, Asia), "Archangel" or "Wild parsnip"; aromatic biennial herb to 2 m, leaves twice divided into threes; small white flowers in large clusters 25 cm across. Truly a popular garden plant. The young leaves are used in cooking fish; the blanched stalk is eaten like celery, roots and stems are used in flavoring liqueurs, or boiled in sugar water for a tasty cordial; tender stems and petioles are often candied; seeds add flavor to soups and stews. *Zones 5-9.*　　　　　　　　　　　　　　　　　　　　　*p. 543*

ANGIOPTERIS　　*Marattiaceae (Filices)*

evecta (Japan to Australia and Madagascar), "Mules-foot fern"; fleshy, robust fern from swampy places, developing a stout stem, the bipinnate leaves on swollen stalk may grow to 5 m long, the linear-oblong pinnae are succulent, dark green, and finely toothed. *Humid-subtropic. Zones 10-11.*　　　　　　　　　　　　　　*p. 128*

ANGRAECUM　　*Orchidaceae*

sesquipedale (Europ. Gardenflora 84):
see MACROPLECTRUM (Hortus, Zander)

superbum (eburneum) (Madagascar); epiphyte with very thick leaves on stems to 1 m high; flowers upside-down on stout spike, sepals and petals green, the broad lip ivory-white with green spur, (Dec.-March). *Tropical. Zone 12.*　　　　　　　　　*p. 81*

ANGULOA　　*Orchidaceae*

clowesii (Andes of Colombia), "Cradle orchid"; magnificent terrestrial growing on damp rocks; the pseudobulbs bearing 2 to 4 plaited leaves; beautiful cup-shaped fleshy, golden-yellow flowers with whitish lip, to 8 cm long, very fragrant. *Subtropic. Zone 11.*　　*p. 81*

uniflora 'Rosea' (virginalis) (Cordilleras of Perú to Colombia); terrestrial of bold habit, with plaited leaves; the solitary, waxy, cupped 6 cm flowers candy-scented, white in the species, but a dainty pink in the var. 'Rosea'. *Subtropic. Zone 10-11.*　　　　　　*p. 81*

ANIGOZANTHOS　　*Haemodoraceae (Amaryllidaceae)*

flavidus (S. W. Australia), "Yellow kangaroo paw"; odd perennial herb with thick rootstock; smooth lanceolate leaves; the inflorescence 1-1½ m high, with large woolly flowers having a long bent tube yellowish green, tinged red, 4 cm long, and with blue petals. *Arid-subtropic. Zones 9-10.*　　　　　　　　　　　　*p. 423*

flavidus rubrum (W. Australia); red form of the yellow-flowered species, seen in King's Park, Perth, having corolla tubes bronzy red and entirely covered by brownish-red, bristly hairs, the pointed, spreading petal tips violet-blue, displaying golden stamens. *Zone 10.*　　　　　　　　　　　　　　　　　　　　*p. 423*

manglesii (Western Australia), known in Australia as "Kangaroo paw"; rosette of onion-like leaves with erect, striking inflorescence 1 m tall with red-hairy stem topped by racemes of yellowish-green, woolly 8 cm tubular flowers, red at calyx, with dark green lines, the lip reflexed and tipped blue. *Arid-subtropic. Zones 9-10.*　　　*p. 423*

pulcherrimus (W. Australia), "Golden kangaroo paw"; rhizomatous perennial to 1 m or more high, with velvety branches, the leaves linear and sickle-shaped, covered by starry wool; the 3 cm flowers in branched clusters rich yellow, with dense reddish bristles. *Zone 10.*　　　　　　　　　　　　　　　　　　　*p. 423*

rufus (Southwestern Australia), "Red kangaroo paw"; curious perennial with stiff woody stems to 1 m high, linear basal leaves; the branched inflorescence with red velvety tubes and starry petals pinkish to purple. *Arid subtropic. Zones 9-10.*　　　　*p. 423*

viridis (W. Australia), "Green kangaroo paw"; small clustering perennial from the South Stirlings region, to 60 cm high, with linear leaves 30 cm long in tufts; inflorescence in branched clusters with flowers to 6 cm long, emerald green at apex, greenish or yellowish toward base. *Zone 10.*　　　　　　　　　　　　　　*p. 423*

ANISODONTEA　　*Malvaceae*

capensis hort. (Malvastrum capense) (So. Africa), "Busy Lizzie"; branching subshrub to 1 m high, with small, deeply lobed or dissected leaves; the inflorescence axillary on erect stalk, with attractive flowers to 5 cm across, the petals spreading in a cup-shaped whorl, light purple toward apex, deep crimson at center base, blooming early Summer. The plant photographed in Germany may be the similar *A. scabrosa* (Hortus). *Zone 10.*　　　　　　　　　　　*p. 457*

ANNONA　　*Annonaceae*

cherimola (Andes of Perú and Ecuador), the "Cherimoya", a custard apple; woody tree to 8 m high, briefly deciduous, with sappy branches and large, luxuriant, leathery leaves 25 cm long, dull green with pale veins, velvety on back; fragrant fleshy flowers 3 cm long, directly from woody branches, yellow or brown-tomentose outside, whitish with purple spot inside; followed by large green conical fruit, 12 cm or more long, containing large black seed, the skin looking like overlapping scales or knobby warts; the creamy-white flesh, tasting like custard or bananas, and is eaten with a spoon; ripening Winter into Spring. For best success flowers are hand-pollinated. *Subtropic. Zone 10.*　　　　　　　　　　　　　　　　　　　　*p. 903*

muricata (West Indies), the "Soursop"; evergreen tropical fruit tree 6 m high, widely planted and liked in Latin America; dark shiny green, leathery, obovate leaves 10-15 cm long; large yellowish flowers with 6 fleshy petals spreading 5 cm across; big ovoid or irregular oblong, pendulous fruit is the largest of the annonas, 15-20 cm long and weighing as much as 3 kilos, deep green and covered with short fleshy spines. The pulp is like white cotton from which a pleasing drink, custard, or chilled sherbet is made in tropical America; in season June through November or longer. *Tropical. Zones 9-10.*　　　　　　　　　　　　　　　　　　　　*p. 903*

squamosa (C. America, West Indies), "Sugar apple" or "Sweet-sop"; tropical fruit tree to 6 m high, partially deciduous with thin-leathery bluish-gray, soft oval leaves 15-20 cm long; small greenish fleshy 2 cm axillary flowers followed by ovoid, grayish-beige fruits 8 cm long, covered with large prominent knobs, divisions falling apart much broken up by its separable sections (carpels), ripening in August to Winter; the flesh is sweet, custard-like but very perishable. Greatly liked in markets from the West Indies to Rio de Janeiro. *Tropical. Zone 10.*　　　　　　　　　　　　　　　　*p. 903*

ANODA　　*Malvaceae*

cristata (Texas to Mexico, West Indies to So. America), "Snow cup"; herbaceous perennial, often grown as annual, with stems more or less bristly, to 1 m or more high; leaves variable, unlobed and arrow-shaped, also palmately 3 to 7-lobed and toothed; axillary flowers blue, purple or white, 5 cm across, during Summer and Autumn. *Zone 10.*　　　　　　　　　　　　　　*p. 456*

ANTELAEA azadirachta　　(Zander):
see MELIA azedarach (Hortus 3)

ANTENNARIA *Compositae*
 dioica ('Nyewood') (North Temp. and Arctic zones), "Pussy-toes" or "Mountain everlasting"; low, spreading perennial 15-30 cm high, with basal rosette of lanceolate 4 cm leaves, white-woolly especially beneath; long-stalked heads of small pink flowers. *Zone 4.*   p. 370

ANTHEMIS *Compositae*
 arvensis (Europe, No. Africa, Asia Minor, naturalized in E. No. America), "Dog camille" or "Corn Chamomile"; wide-spread annual herb to 20 cm high, with small, finely divided ferny leaves, grayish-green and scented; white, daisy-like ray-flowers, and a cushion of yellow disc-flowers, blooming May to August. *Zone 9.*   p. 370
 nobilis (Linnaeus, Hortus 2 and hort.): see CHAMAEMELUM nobile (Hortus 3)
 sancti-johannis (Bulgaria), "Dog fennel" or "St. John's camomile"; much-branched, gray-pubescent perennial, spreading and forming tufts 30-90 cm high, the leaves pinnatisect, with toothed lobes; showy floral heads 5 cm across, with rays vivid orange. *Zones 3-8.*   p. 370
 tinctoria (Europe, W. Asia, sparingly natural, in No. America), "Golden marguerite" or "Yellow camomile"; aromatic biennial or short-lived perennial, about 40 cm high; leaves finely dissected and downy beneath; floral heads to 5 cm wide, with deep yellow center cushion, and yellow ray-flowers fading to near white. Petals yield a dye for cloth. *Zones 3-8.*   p. 370, 524

ANTHERICUM *Liliaceae*
 comosum: see CHLOROPHYTUM comosum
 liliago (So. Europe), "St. Bernard lily"; perennial herb with fleshy roots; tufted basal leaves linear and channeled, to 45 cm long; 60 cm slender stalk with racemes of white flowers to 3 cm across, spreading segments and curved style. *Zones 6-9.*   p. 443
 mandaianum: see CHLOROPHYTUM comosum 'Mandaianum'

ANTHRISCUS *Umbelliferae*
 cerefolium (S.E. Europe to Caucasus, natural. in Québec to Penna.), "Salad chervil"; popular annual herb related to carrot, to 50 cm high, with feathery, bipinnate leaves on furrowed stalks; small white flowers in clusters opposite the leaves, during June. While the roots have been reported as edible, it is the leaves that have been used earlier by the ancient Syrians as boiled vegetable, and to modern times as an aromatic potherb similar to parsley as garnish or in salads and soups. *Zones 5-10.*   p. 542

ANTHURIUM *Araceae*
 andraeanum (S.W. Colombia), "Tailflower"; erect plant with long-lobed, heart-shaped, green leaves; the showy, cordate spathe, 10-12 cm long, waxy, coral-red, puckered; the pendant spadix tipped yellow with white band marking the zone where stigmas are receptive. *Humid-tropical. Zone 12.*   p. 23
 andraeanum rhodochlorum; a robust form with giant, deeply cordate, salmon-red spathe 20 cm or more long, and in which lobes or tip are green. *Zone 12.*   p. 22
 bakeri (Costa Rica); on short stem, strap-like, leathery, elliptic, lanceolate leaves, deep green, with stout midrib; spathe and spadix green; spathe when in fruit to 20 cm long, bearing red berries. *Tropical. Zone 12.*   p. 23
 brownii (Andes of Colombia); Birdsnest type anthurium; on short stem; leaves broad-ovate, to 1 m long and 50 cm wide, glossy dark green, undulate at margins, veins yellowish; lanceolate spathe 12 cm long, purplish-green, spadix purplish. *Zone 11.*   p. 22
 clarinervium (Mexico), "Hoja de Corazon"; a dwarf, ornamental species found growing in the clay of the Chiapas mist forest; dark green, velvety, heart-shaped leaves with clear, silvery-gray veins; similar to A. crystallinum, but more diminutive, with leaves 12-20 cm long; spathe reddish-green. *Tropical. Zone 12.*   p. 23
 crystallinum (Colombia, Perú), "Crystal anthurium"; strikingly beautiful tropical foliage plant; from the central crown with thick-fleshy roots rise wiry petioles, circular in cross-section, carrying the large decorative, heart-shaped, velvety leaves of stiff-leathery texture, glistening emerald green with contrasting network of white veins, 25 to 45 cm long, with basal lobes overlapping, acutely angled at the thickened juncture; long-stalked inflorescence with slender yellowish-green spadix and linear green spathe, followed by red-purple berries. *Humid-tropical. Zone 12.*   p. 23
 x ferrierense (andraeanum x ornatum), "Oilcloth flower"; robust climber with lobed, heart-shaped leaves; ovate-cordate, rosy spathe waxy-smooth, carried upright, and erect spadix white to rose; willing bloomer. *Humid-tropical. Zone 12.*   p. 23
 hookeri (Guyana, W. Indies), "Birdsnest anthurium"; symmetrical rosette resembling birdsnest, with broad, obovate, grass-green leaves 60 cm long; spathe green. *Humid-tropical. Zone 11.*   p. 22
 huegelii (Venezuela, Trinidad); seen in col. Bermuda Bot. Garden; similar to A. hookeri, differs in having leaves rounded at base; bright

green with midrib and lateral veins pale yellow, margins not undulate; spathe 10 cm long; spadix purple. *Zone 12.*   p. 22
 macrolobum (dentatum hort.) (Mato Grosso, Brazil); robust plant with large, leathery, green, sagittate leaf with 5-7 pointed lobes; spathe green. *Zone 12.*   p. 23
 pariense (Venezuela); plant with slightly pendulous leaves; petioles to 40 cm long; leaf-blade oblong-elliptic, to 60 cm long and to 16 cm wide, upper surface glossy dark green, glaucous beneath; floral stem 60-110 cm, with reflexed purple spathe 15-17 cm long; the sessile purple spadix 20-26 cm long. *Tropical. Zone 12.*   p. 22
 scherzerianum (Costa Rica), "Flamingo flower"; leathery plant with lanceolate, green leaves; the long-lasting inflorescence having a golden-yellow spadix spirally twisted, subtended by a showy, broadly ovate, brilliantly scarlet spathe 6 to 10 cm long. *Humid-subtropic. Zone 12.*   p. 23
 veitchii (Colombia), "King anthurium"; unusual plant with pendant, showy leaves to 1 m long, cordate at base, rich metallic green; curved lateral veins sunken, giving a quilted look; pale midrib. Inflorescence with narrow green spathe. Beautiful but difficult. *Humid-tropical. Zone 12.*   p. 23
 warocqueanum (Colombia), "Queen anthurium"; climbing species with showy, long tapering, velvety leaves to 1 m long; deep green with ivory veins; small spathe green to yellowish. *Humid-tropical. Zone 12.*   p. 23

ANTHYLLIS *Leguminosae*
 montana (Mts. of Spain to Alps and Balkans), "Alps anthyllis"; handsome perennial to 30 cm high, forming mats, with pinnate leaves, the oblong leaflets white-silky; inflorescence in dense clusters of rose-pink tubular flowers 2 cm long. *Zone 5.*   p. 440

ANTIDESMA *Euphorbiaceae*
 bunius (India, Malay Arch.), "Bignay"; evergreen tropical tree to 15 m high; elliptic leathery laurel-like leaves 8 to 18 cm long, shining green; inconspicuous green flowers in erect slender spikes to 20 cm long, followed by small 1 cm edible berries, current-like, of tart taste and juicy. *Zone 10.*   p. 720, 913

ANTIGONON *Polygonaceae*
 guatimalense (Guatemala, So. Mexico, introduced in W. Indies and So. Florida), "Coronilla" or "Flor de San Miguel"; perennial tendril climber from tuberous roots; the flexuous branches with thick, cordate leaves to 12 cm long, and hairy; the lovely small rose-pink flowers in graceful slender, axillary racemes. *Zone 10.*   p. 290
 leptopus (Mexico), "Coral vine" or "Flor de Mayo"; showy tendril climber, with edible tuberous roots, slender zigzag stems bearing arrow-shaped, light green 10 cm leaves and axillary racemes of bright rose-pink flowers with deeper center. *Tropical. Zone 10.*   p. 290

ANTIRRHINUM *Scrophulariaceae*
 majus (So. Europe, No. Africa), "Floral snapdragon"; 60 cm or more high, normally summer-flowering, erect herb, with leafy terminal spikes of very showy, curious sac-shaped, bilabiate flowers of many colors and shades, velvety red to pink, yellow or white, yellow mouth closed but forced open by the bees. Also known as "Dragon-jaws". *Zone 9.*   p. 501
 majus 'Royal Carpet', "Dwarf snapdragon"; lovely F 1 cultivar of compact habit, 20 to 30 cm high; excellent carpet-bed strain in bright colors, grown from seed, as annual or biennial; very vigorous, and blooming from early Summer to Autumn. *Zone 9.*   p. 501

ANUBIAS *Araceae*
 afzelii (lanceolata) (West Equatorial Africa, Zaire, Guinea), "Water aspidistra" or "African cryptocoryne"; bog plant along tropical rivers; creeping rhizome giving rise to petioles 25-40 cm long, bearing long-stalked lanceolate, dark green, leathery leaves 10-25 cm long and 6-12 cm wide; inflorescence with waxy spathe green and slender, folded around yellowish spadix half-covered with male and half by female flowers. *Zone 12.*   p. 22

APHELANDRA *Acanthaceae*
 chamissoniana (Brazil), "Yellow pagoda"; erect plant with closely set, thin, slender, pointed leaves, silver-white area along midrib and veins; flowers clear yellow; bracts yellow with green tips. *Tropical. Zone 10.*   p. 17
 sinclairiana (Central America, Panama, Darien), "Coral aphelandra"; compact plant with limp, ovate leaves rich glossy-green; pale, depressed veins; inflorescence clustered, the cupped bracts orange-coral, the corolla rosy-pink. *Tropical. Zone 10.*   p. 17
 squarrosa var. louisae (Brazil), "Zebra plant"; compact growing plant with shiny, emerald green, elliptic leaves and prominent, white veins; bright yellow flowers, tipped green, on fleshy, terminal spikes of long-lasting, waxy, golden bracts; fall blooming. *Tropical. Zone 10.*   p. 17

tetragona (W. Indies, So. America); straggling plant to 1 m, with broadly ovate, green leaves; inflorescence in clustered spikes terminal or axillary; slender tubular, bright scarlet flowers 5-8 cm long. *Tropical. Zone 10.* *p. 17*

APIOS *Leguminosae*
americana (tuberosa) (Québec to Florida, Colorado and Texas), "Ground-nut" or "Potato-bean"; tuberous-rooted twining herb, the roots with strings of tubers; pinnate leaves with 5-7 leaflets to 8 cm long; conspicuous fragrant brownish-purple 2 cm flowers. The tubers are edible when cooked and were eaten by the Indians; also by Pilgrims during first year in New England. *Zones 3-9.* *p. 277*

APIUM *Umbelliferae*
graveolens dulce (No. and So. America, Eurasia, Australia, and New Zealand), "Celery"; strongly-scented leafy biennial vegetable, also grown as annual, 50 cm high; the leaves are pinnate to 3 times divided or toothed, the bitter, fresh-green leaflets are broad and to 4 cm long, on rather watery-succulent petioles; greenish-white flowers in low umbels. The usually blanched leaf stalks are a popular vegetable cooked in meats, poultry and soups, or eaten fresh as spicy ingredient of various salads. The species graveolens is grown as "Celery-root" or "Knob-celery", forming large rounded, edible roots, which are cooked, peeled and sliced for salad. *Zones 3-9.* *p. 544*

APOCYNUM *Apocynaceae*
androsaemifolium (Canada to Mexico), "Spreading Dogbane"; herbaceous perennial with wide-spreading branches to 1 m or more; opposite ovate green leaves 5-8 cm long, pale beneath; bell-shaped flowers in small clusters, pinkish with rose stripes; throughout Summer. *Zone 4.* *p. 341*

APONOGETON *Aponogetonaceae*
distachyus (So. Africa), "Cape pondweed" or "Water hawthorn"; aquatic herb with tuberous rootstock, the linear-oblong, bright green solid, 4 cm leaves floating on the water; stalked inflorescence in two opposing spikes of tiny white flowers of sweet fragrance. *Zones 9-10.* *p. 326*

APOPLANESIA *Leguminosae*
cryptopetala (Mexico to Venezuela), "Palo de Arco"; interesting small ornamental tree 3-6 m high, with short trunk and spreading branches; pinnate leaves of 13-21 leaflets; white flowers lined with maroon in pendant elongate clusters, inflorescence changing to rose, blooming in September-October in Venezuela habitat; the fruit a pubescent capsule containing a single seed. *Zone 10.* *p. 747*

x APOROPHYLLUM *Cactaceae*
'Star Fire' (Aporocactus x Epiphyllum); beautiful Johnson bigeneric hybrid between Orchid cacti and Rat-tail cacti, normally epiphytic and ideally suited for baskets. This and simiar hybrids are free-flowering, earlier than orchid cactus and bloom at odd times. The slender stems are ribbed and pendant but may be trained on a trellis. The large rose-red flowers are flushed scarlet outside. *Subtropic. Zone 10.* *p. 154*

APTENIA *Aizoaceae*
cordifolia (Mesembryanthemum) (So. Africa), "Baby sun rose"; low succulent creeper of the eastern coastal deserts; freely branching with prostrate or pendant branches, small soft-fleshy cordate, fresh green leaves to 2½ cm long, covered with glands, later gray; small 1 cm rosy-purple flowers. The cultivar 'Red Apple', widely planted as groundcover in California, has glowing crimson-red flowers to 2 cm across. *Arid-subtropic. Zones 9-10.* *p. 144, 301*

AQUILEGIA *Ranunculaceae*
caerulea (Rocky Mts. of Montana to New Mexico), "Colorado columbine"; very popular garden perennial 30-60 cm high, having fibrous roots; thin basal leaves twice divided into threes; the interesting, lovely flowers with sepals spreading 5-8 cm across, whitish but tinged light or deep blue and yellow; limb of petals white, spurs straight or curved outward, to 5 cm long and tipped green; April to July. State flower of Colorado. *Zones 2-9.* *p. 486*
chrysantha (Arizona, New Mexico), "Golden columbine"; striking perennial to 1 m or more high; the basal leaves bi-ternate, or divided into threes and divided again; the most attractive flowers 5-8 cm across, the sepals pale yellow tinged pink, the petals deep yellow, shorter than sepals, the slender spurs 5 cm long; May to August. Important parent of the long-spurred garden hybrids. *Zone 3. p. 486*
flavescens (canadensis flavescens) (No. America: E. Canada to Montana, Texas), "Yellow columbine" of the Rocky Mts.; perennial to 60 cm high, the thin, dark green foliage near base usually 2 or 3 times divided; the nodding flowers have sepals yellowish or tinged red, the petals lemon-yellow or cream; spurs 2 cm long; blooming May-July. *Zone 2.* *p. 486*

formosà (Alaska to Montana and California), "Sitka columbine"; branched perennial with stems 60-90 cm high, basal leaves twice triple-divided; flowers pendant, more or less pubescent, red with yellow tips, to 4 cm wide, blooming May to August. *Zone 2.* *p. 486*
saximontana (Colorado, Utah), "Colorado columbine"; small perennial 10 to 20 cm high, with bluish, crinkled thin leaves twice divided into threes; the interesting flowers have blue sepals, limb of petals yellowish, and hooked blue spurs, appearing in April. *Zone 4.* *p. 485*
vulgaris (Europe, No. Africa, Canary Is.), "European crowfoot" or "European columbine"; popular garden perennial 40-70 cm high, with glossy green leaves twice divided; nodding violet-blue flowers with spreading sepals to 5 cm wide, the spurs strongly hooked, blooming May to July. There are many color variations found or created over the long garden history. *Zone 3.* *p. 486*

ARABIS *Cruciferae*
alpina rosea (Mountains of Europe: Arctic to Alps), "Mountain rock-cress"; charming variety forming mounds, covered with masses of little 2-3 cm rose-pink flowers, blooming late Spring. *Zones 4-9.* *p. 407*
alpina 'Variegata', a variegated-leaf form of the "Mountain rock-cress" native in the European Alps; low, densely clustering and slowly creeping perennial with green, pubescent obovate, crenate leaves 3-8 cm long, attractively edged in ivory-white; small white flowers. *Zones 4-9.* *p. 407*
caucasica (albida) (S.E. Europe to Iran), "Wall rock-cress"; herbaceous spreading perennial forming rosettes 15-25 cm high, sometimes grown as an annual; leaves obovate and white-pubescent, 3-8 cm long; spring-blooming with small white, fragrant flowers in loose clusters. Similar to A. alpina but having sagittate stem leaves and larger petals. *Zone 3.* *p. 314, 407*
ferdinandi-coburgii 'Variegata' (Bulgaria); small herbaceous perennial, forming a gray-green cushion; oblanceolate leaves 2 to 7 cm long, finely hairy on both surfaces, and prettily margined with creamy-white, arranged into rosettes; small white flowers in long stalked clusters, 8-10 cm high, spring-blooming. *Zone 6.* *p. 407*

ARACHIS *Leguminosae*
hypogaea (Brazil), the "Peanut vine" or "Ground-nut"; annual herb 30-45 cm high with compound leaves of two pairs of oval leaflets, without tendrils; yellow flowers of two kinds: one set pea-like, showy and sterile, the others fertile, on recurving stalks which touch the ground and penetrate into it where the fertilized ovary ripens into the peanut, an oily, edible seed covered by an oblong thin-woody capsule. *Subtropic. Zone 10.* *p. 910*

ARACHNANTHE: see ARACHNIS

ARACHNIODES adiantiformis (Zander): see RUMOHRA (Hortus)

ARACHNIS *Orchidaceae*
flos-aeris (moschifera) (Malaya, Java, Borneo), "Spider orchid"; epiphytic; slender stems to 4 m, with scattered narrow leaves and erect spike of 10 cm blooms, greenish-yellow, heavily blotched red-brown, more so in basal flowers; musk-scented, (Summer). *Humid-tropical. Zone 12.* *p. 81*

ARALIA *Araliaceae*
californica (Brit. Columbia to California), "Elk-clover"; shrubby perennial 2-3 m high, with stout stems from roots with milky juice, having bipinnate leaves, the leaflets doubly toothed, 15-30 cm long; small whitish flowers in terminal panicles 45 cm long; followed by red berries, becoming black in ripening. *Zone 8.* *p. 653*
chinensis (South China), "Chinese angelica"; deciduous shrub or small tree to 10 m; with prickly stems and large leaves to 1 m long, divided into 5-15 toothed leaflets; inflorescence in huge clusters of small white flowers, followed by black berries. *Zone 5.* *p. 647*
elata (Japan, Korea, N.E. China), "Japanese angelica" or "Angelica tree"; deciduous tree to 15 m high, with spiny branches, bipinnate leaves 60-120 cm long, the oval leaflets to 12 cm, pubescent on veins beneath when young and prickly; small whitish flowers borne in numerous clusters forming a large panicle; purple berry-like fruits. Often mistaken for A. spinosa. *Zone 3.* *p. 647*
elata 'Variegata' (Manchuria, Korea, Japan), "Variegated Angelica tree"; ornamental deciduous shrub or tree to 15 m, with spiny branches and prickly petioles; decorative bipinnate foliage to 1 m long, the ovate, pubescent leaflets toothed, milky green and splashed or bordered with white; small whitish flowers in numerous clusters forming a large panicle; berry-like black fruit. *Zone 3. p. 647*
elegantissima: see DIZYGOTHECA elegantissima
japonica: see FATSIA japonica

nudicaulis (No. Amer., Asia and Malay Penins.), "Wild sarsaparilla"; perennial herb to 40 cm high, growing from an aromatic rhizome, with compound leaves 2 to 3-pinnate of ovate rugose leaflets; finely serrate; small greenish-yellow flowers in globular clusters at apex of floral stalk rising from the roots; fruit black. The rhizome is used as substitute for the drug sarsaparilla. Zone 3.   p. 343

papyrifera: see TETRAPANAX papyriferus
sieboldii: see FATSIA japonica
spinsoa (U.S.: New York to Florida and Texas); deciduous tree to 10 or more meters, known as "Devil's walkingstick"; with very spiny, slender trunk and large bipinnate leaves 60-90 cm long, the ovate leaflets prickly; flowers whitish, fruit black. Zone 5.   p. 647

ARALIA: see also POLYSCIAS, DIZYGOTHECA, FATSIA, TETRAPANAX

x ARANDA   Orchidaceae
'Christine' (Arachnis hookeriana 'Luteola' x Vanda 'Hilo Blue'); robust, floriferous bigeneric hybrid and ideal for shipping as cut flower; waxy flowers about 5 cm across, mauve-pink mottled and shaded carmine-red. Tropical. Zone 12.   p. 81

x ARANTHERA   Orchidaceae
'Anne Black' (Arachnis x Renanthera); seen at Mandai Orchids, Singapore; vandaceous epiphytic hybrid of compact habit, with sturdy stems, clothed by oblanceolate leaves in ranks; arching inflorescence of showy fiery-red spider flowers marked yellow. Zone 12.   p. 82

ARAUCARIA   Araucariaceae (Coniferae)
angustifolia (brasiliana) (So. Brazil), the "Paraná pine"; characterizes the landscape in cooler parts of Sao Paulo and Paraná with wide spreading heads; 5 cm needles stiff and deep green; male cones 8-10 cm long and 2 cm dia. Zone 10.   p. 572

araucana (imbricata) (Mts. of So. Chile, No. Patagonia), the so-called "Hardy monkey puzzle" tree; 15-30 m high, with resinous bark and whorled branches; sharp-pointed, ovate, thick-leathery, dark green leaves 3-5 cm long, densely and uniformly arranged around shoot. Habitat in Chilean Andes at 1900 m. Warm-temperate. Zones 7-8.   p. 571, 572

bidwillii (Queensland), "Bunya-Bunya" or "Monkey-puzzle"; dome-shaped tree to 45 m high; the horizontal branches with thick-leathery, dark glossy-green spine-tipped leaves showing depressed parallel veining and mostly toward branch ends; the juvenile leaves narrow sickle-shaped to 5 cm long and primarily in one or two ranks; adult stage needles shorter, spiral and over-lapping; female cones huge, 8 to 12 cm long and resembling pineapples. The big seeds inside highly prized as food by the aborigines. Subtropic to Tropical. Zones 8-10.   p. 571, 572

columnaris (cookii) (New Caledonia), the "Cook pine"; so named because Capt. Cook discovered it on the Isle of Pines; in silhouette appearing like tall pines, with somewhat leaning trunks, said to grow as high as 60 m; difficult to distinguish from A. heterophylla as young trees in their curved, needle-like leaves; very symmetric with about 5 branches radiating around the trunk in each tier, and each branch triangular in shape; later the Cook pine develops into a narrower column than heterophylla, and on its branchlets bears overlapping more numerous, scale-like sharp-pointed leaves 1 cm long; the female cones are ovoid and 8-10 cm in Zone 10.   p. 572

cunninghamii (New So. Wales), "Hoop pine"; majestic evergreen tree to 60 m high; the juvenile leaves are short, needle-like and bluish-green, 2 cm long; adult stage leaves awl-shaped to lanceolate, incurved and overlapping; the male cones 5-8 cm long and 2 cm dia., female cones ovoid, 6-10 cm long and to 6 cm across. Zones 8-9. p. 512, 572

excelsa: see A. heterophylla
heterophylla (excelsa in hort.) (Norfolk Is.), "Norfolk Island pine"; evergreen tree to 70 m high, from the South Pacific; when juvenile very formal with branches parallel to the ground, in tiers of bright green, soft, awl-shaped needles; best Araucaria for the home. Subtropic. Zone 10.   p. 36, 571, 577

ARAUJIA   Asclepiadaceae
sericifera (So. Brazil), the "Cruel plant" or "Bladder flower"; prodigious woody twiner resembling Stephanotis, with several forms of leaves, mostly oblong, 5-10 cm long, green above, white felted beneath; salver-shaped flowers 3 cm across, white or pinkish-tawny and fragrant, fast fading; the seed pods explode with the characteristic silk of the asclepiads. Biologically interesting because the flowers are able to trap insects. Zone 10.   p. 267

ARBUTUS   Ericaceae
menziesii (British Columbia to Baja California, Mexico), "Madrone"; characteristic evergreen shrub or tree from 6 to 30 m high, with smooth, reddish bark peeling in flakes; leathery, glossy

green leaves, oval or elliptic to 15 cm long; grape-like clusters of small white or pinkish bell-shaped flowers 5 mm long, followed in Autumn by brilliant orange to scarlet-red, pebble-skinned, 1 cm berries, lasting all Winter unless eaten by birds. Zone 7.   p. 708

unedo (So. Europe, etc.), the "Strawberry-tree"; small evergreen tree with rough, shreddy bark, sticky-hairy branches, oblong, shiny, toothed 10 cm leaves, and small white, or pinkish, bell-like flowers in drooping panicles; strawberry-like, orange-red fruit edible but without particular flavor. Subtropic. Zone 8.   p. 912

ARCHONTOPHOENIX   Palmae
cunninghamiana (Australia: Queensland, N.S.W.), "Seaforthia palm" or "Piccabeen palm"; tall feathery palm with slender trunk not enlarging below except at surface of ground; the gracefully arching fronds to 3 m long; broad leaflets dark green on both sides, 8-10 cm wide; pendulous inflorescence with lilac flowers; the coral fruit less than 2½ cm. In the California nursery trade erroneously as Seaforthia elegans; in Florida nurseries as Pytchosperma elegans. Subtropic. Zones 10-11.   p. 99

ARCTOSTAPHYLOS   Ericaceae
columbiana (Coastal Brit. Columbia to No. California), "Manzanita"; hard-wooded, often arborescent shrub to 3 m high, usually shorter, with twisted chocolate-brown branches; leathery ovate leaves 6 cm long; smnall white or pink flowers; fruit like little apples green to bright red; eaten by the Indians. Zone 7.   p. 912

edmundsii (Monterey County, California), "Little Sur manzanita"; low evergreen shrub 10 to 60 cm high, of flat habit, and bronze new growth; with prostrate, crooked woody branches that may spread 4 m wide; with roundish ovate, rigid leathery leaves 3 cm long, light green with reddish margins; waxy small soft pink urn-shaped flowers, in March-April; fruit brown. Zone 9.   p. 700

insularis var. pubescens (California: Santa Cruz Is.), "Island manzanita"; spreading evergreen 2 m or more, the crooked branches with dark red bark; bright green oval, 3-4 cm leaves gray pubescent; waxy white bell-like nodding flowers in large clusters; yellow-brown fruit nearly globose, like tiny apples. Indians chew the fruit to quench thirst. Zone 8.   p. 700

manzanita (C. California to Oregon), "Manzanita"; evergreen shrub 1 m or more high, with crooked, straggling branches, having smooth, chocolate-brown bark; stiff-leathery, ovalish leaves gray-green and 6 cm long; charming little urn-shaped waxy white or pinkish flowers 1 cm long, in pendant clusters, followed by fruit first white then red-brown, resembling miniature apples or manzanitas. Jelly is made from the fruit. Zone 7.   p. 699

uva-ursi (California north to Alaska), "Bearberry" or "Trailing manzanita"; a popular ground-cover in Pacific Northwest; prostrate spreading branches and rooting as it creeps to 5 m; bright glossy green, leathery leaves 2-3 cm long, turning red in Winter; flowers white tinged pink; bright red fruit. The mealy berries are eaten raw, but quite palatable and nourishing when cooked. Zones 2-7.   p. 699, 912

ARCTOTHECA   Compositae
calendula (South Africa), "Cape weed"; evergreen perennial, rapid-running ground-cover, less than 30 cm tall; gray-green divided leaves; daisy-like flowers yellow, 3-4 cm across. Subtropic. Zones 9-10.   p. 312, 369

ARCTOTIS   Compositae
acaulis (So. Africa: Cape Prov.), "African daisy" or "Bush arctotis"; stemless perennial with thick, branching rhizome; leaves pinnately lobed, 15-20 cm long, in rosettes; white-woolly beneath, and with rough surface; daisy-like blooms to 10 cm across, on stalks to 15 cm long, disc purple, and ray-flowers rich yellow above, coppery beneath. Zone 9.   p. 370

breviscapa (So. Africa), "Yellow African daisy"; short-lived herbaceous perennial usually grown as annual, with spreading branches; the leaves oblong and variously lobed or cut, white-woolly beneath; daisy-like flowers 5 cm across, the disc-flowers brown, ray-flowers orange-yellow near base, becoming lighter toward tips, and coppery beneath. Zone 10.   p. 371

fastuosa: see VENIDIUM fastuosum
stoechadifolia (Hortus 3): see A. venusta (Zander 84)
venusta (stoechadifolia grandis hort.) (So. Africa), "Blue-eyed African daisy"; a tall growing subshrubby perennial, sometimes grown as an annual, 75 cm high, with spreading stems becoming woody; obovate, toothed, gray-hairy leaves to 15 cm long; ray flowers cream-white, tinted red underneath, in 8 cm heads with shiny blue-black centers. Zone 10.   p. 371

ARDISIA   Myrsinaceae
crenata (crispa of hort.) (Japan), "Coral berry"; smooth evergreen shrub to 2 m; waxy, deep green, leathery elliptic leaves with undulate

crisped margins to 15 cm long, having 12-18 pairs of lateral veins; small 1 cm white or pink flowers; clusters of attractive and long-lasting glossy coral-red berries. Very popular as a houseplant with an abundance of brilliant fruit during Winter. *Zone 9.* p. 78, 797

crenata 'Variegata', "Variegated coral-berry"; colorful Australian cultivar, a dense bush with elliptic or obovate leathery green leaves vividly variegated creamy-white, primarily along marginal areas; a beautiful ornamental. *Zone 10.* p. 796

crispa (crenulata) (So. China, Taiwan, Japan); usually confused with A. crispa in hort., but the true crispa is a decoration bush with longer, narrow oblanceolate leaves to 20 cm long, and having about 8 pairs of lateral veins on twigs pubescent when young, the margins not crisped as in A. crenata; clusters of small white flowers 8 mm across, followed by glossy, brilliant red and long-lasting berries. *Zone 10.* p. 796

humilis (Malaysia); evergreen shrub to 3 m high, with softly leathery, lanceolate leaves 5-12 cm long, and umbels of small rose-pink flowers; 1 cm fruit flattened-globular, first red then black. *Zone 10.* p. 796

mamillata (So. China); compact subshrub with hairy, semi-herbaceous stems; ovate leaves 5-10 cm long, dark glossy green and thickly covered with raised dots, each with a single hair; flowers in axillary clusters, white, tinged rose, 5 cm long; small 1 cm rosy-red fruit. *Zone 10.* p. 796

ARECA *Palmae*
catechu (Malaysia to Polynesia), the famed, graceful "Betel-nut palm"; a very slender, erect, dioecious palm with solitary trunk, 10 to 30 m high and 5-12 cm dia.; relatively small crown of pinnate fronds 1-2 m long, with many broad, rather soft pinnae irregularly notched at apex, the upper ones united; fragrant white flowers; fruit olive shaped to 5 cm long, reddish-orange, and housing the grooved betelnut. Much cultivated for the nut which is chewed with lime and wrapped in the leaf of Piper betel, as a mild stimulant. *Tropical.*
Zones 11-12. p. 101, 539

ARECA: see also CHRYSALIDOCARPUS

ARECASTRUM romanzoffianum (Hortus):
see SYAGRUS romanzoffiana (Genera Palmarum 1987)

ARENARIA *Caryophyllaceae*
grandiflora (Portugal to Czechoslovakia), "Sandwort"; mat-forming hairy perennial, the creeping branches with 2 cm linear, bristle-tipped, leathery leaves; small white flowers 3 cm across. *Zone 5.* p. 310

montana (Portugal to France), "Mountain Sandwort"; small pubescent perennial with short grass-like linear or oblong 2 cm leaves, the slender floral stalks to 20 cm high, bearing clusters of white flowers with petals 2 cm long. Ideal for planting between stepping stones or use as grass substitute. *Zone 5.* p. 360

rigida (So. Ukraine to Romania and Bulgaria), "Bulgarian sandwort"; subshrubby perennial with densely intertwining branches; linear basal leaves to 12 cm long, stem leaves broader and shorter; the inflorescence in clusters of 2 cm white to pinkish flowers. *Zone 5.* p. 360

stellata (Hortus 3): see MINUARTIA stellata (Zander)

tetraquetra 'Granatensis' (Pyrenees and Sierra Nevada of Spain); "Sandwort"; cushion-forming perennial with tiny gray-green leaves only 3 mm long, hairy at base; small 1 cm flowers. *Zone 7.* p. 360

verna (caespitosa) (Spain to No. Russia), "Irish moss"; cushion-forming perennial, to 5 cm high, moss-like and used in California as lawn substitute: leaves linear to 2 cm long, grayish green; small pinkish-white starry flowers. Needs more moisture than lawn; gets lumps if crowded. *Zone 3.* p. 569

ARENGA *Palmae*
obtusifolia (Java, Sumatra); majestic feather palm to 10 m tall; trunk to 30 cm dia., bearing a dense crown of glossy dark green pinnate fronds to 5 m long; linear pinnae to 1 m, with squared or cleft tips; inflorescence 60 cm long, the male flowers maroon; 5 cm fruit. *Zones 11-12.* p. 101

pinnata (saccharifera) (Malaya), the "Common sugar palm"; important economic palm to 12 m high, with robust solitary trunk covered with black fibers; erect, pinnate leaves to 6 m or more, the leaflets dark green above, whitened underneath, and with jagged apex. When pierced, the young inflorescence yields sugary sap. *Tropical. Zones 11-12.* p. 99

ARGEMONE *Papaveraceae*
corymbosa (Arizona, Utah, to Mohave Desert), "Argemony"; short-lived perennial, photographed at the South Rim of Grand Canyon; densely leafy, 30-40 cm high, with prickly stems and foliage, the blades stiff-leathery and pinnately deeply lobed; clusters of white

flowers to 9 cm across, subtended by horned sepals, blooming March to May, followed by spiny fruit. The species is distinguished by its orange sap. *Zone 8.* p. 463

platyceras (Mexico to So. America), "Prickly poppy"; robust, spiny annual or short-lived perennial 30-70 cm high, with bluish-glaucous leaves, the lower ones deeply lobed with weak spines, higher up sinuate and clasping; showy white flowers 5-12 cm across, blooming August-September; and followed by densely prickly and crested capsules. *Zone 9.* p. 463

ARGYREIA *Convolvulaceae*
nervosa (speciosa) (India), "Elephant creeper" or "Silver Morning-glory"; elegant, robust climber reaching up to 8 m; woody stems with large, overlapping, cordate, rich green leaves prominently nerved and silvery silky beneath, 15 to 30 cm wide; showy deep rose flowers with flaring limb, 5-8 cm long, violet in throat, white-hairy outside, the base enveloped by a large white-hairy calyx. *Tropical. Zones 10-11.* p. 273

ARIOCARPUS *Cactaceae*
scapharostrus (Mexico: Nuevo Leon), "Rock cactus"; small star-like succulent rosette to 10 cm across with overlapping leaf-like pointed boatshaped gray-green tubercles sharply 3-angled and 5 cm long; from the apex small 4 cm violet-rose flowers. *Zone 10.* p. 162

trigonus elongatus (Mexico), "Living star"; similar to trigonus, with longer narrow, numerous leaves; in center a cluster of yellow flowers with dark eye. A. trigonus is a hard, fleshy rosette of numerous erect and spreading leaflike grayish green tubercles; the root is turnip-like. *Arid-tropical. Zone 10.* p. 154

ARIOPSIS *Araceae*
peltata (India); small tuberous tropical herbaceous plant some-what of the habit of Caladium; ovoid tuber 4 cm thick, producing pale green, peltate rounded leaves thin in texture, to 15 cm long by nearly as wide, spathe ovate cup-shaped hooding the cone shaped spadix. Flowering before leaves, following dormancy. *Zone 10.* p. 24, 327

ARISAEMA *Araceae*
dracontium (Québec to Florida, west to Texas, Mexico), "Green dragon" or "Dragonroot"; tuberous herbaceous perennial forming clusters of corms, each with one leaf, from 30 cm to a mature 90 cm tall; the blade divided into 5 to more than 12 segments, each 10 to 15 cm long; the inflorescence with spathe green, the spadix erect, slender, and tail-like; berries orange-red. *Zone 4.* p. 219

flavum (Mediterranean to Himalayas); tuberous herb; small tuber to 3 cm dia., forming two leaves pedately divided, on 30 cm leafstalk; 9 to 11 segments 5-10 cm long; inflorescense with small green, ovoid tubular spathe, deep purple inside, with green veins. *Zone 9.* p. 24

triphyllum (E. No. America), "Jack-in-the-pulpit"; tuberous wood-land herb to 1 m, with usually a pair of trifoliate ovate leaflets to 18 cm long; the erect spadix is surrounded by the green spathe or "pulpit", striped with purple inside, its tip arched forward; berries red. *Warm temperate. Zone 4.* p. 24

ARISTOLOCHIA *Aristolochiaceae*
chessmanniana (Malaysia); tropical twining shrub with leathery glossy green leaves broadly kidney-shaped to elongate, with base deeply cordate; the unusual waxy flowers having flaring basal portion or calyx white with crimson markings, and the upturned lid fluted or tubular blackish-maroon. In col. Singapore Botanic Garden. *Zone 11.* p. 267

clematitis (Europe to Asia Minor, Caucasus, naturalized New York to Ohio), "Birthwort"; clambering herbaceous perennial 50 to 100 cm high, with broadly cordate leaves to 10 cm long, and small 3 cm tubular, yellow flowers terminating in a slender point, blooming late Summer. Once cultivated in herbgardens to aid childbirth. *Zone 6.* p. 267

elegans (littoralis) (Brazil), "Calico flower"; graceful climber with kidney-shaped leaves, and flowers a yellowish, inflated tube and expanded cup rich purplish-brown inside with white markings, to 8 cm across. *Tropical. Zones 10-11.* p. 266

grandiflora var. sturtevantii (West Indies, C. America, So. America), "Swan Flower"; woody tropical climber to 3 m with downy, heart-shaped leaves, and very large downy flowers up to 50 cm long, with tails 1 m long under favorable conditions; yellowish-green inflated tube, and flaring limb deep purplish-crimson, veined and spotted yellow. *Zones 10-11.* p. 270

tricaudata (Mexico); small bush with straggling branches, wrinkled ovate leaves 12-20 cm long; flowers creamy-white, each with three long dark brown-purple twisted tails. *Zone 10.* p. 343

trilobata (West Indies to So. America), "Dutchman's pipe"; evergreen tropical twiner to 3 m; the leaves deeply trilobed into obovate segments; curious large pitchers, the basal portion inflated and bent at right angles, pale green to beige and overlaid with a netted design of brown; terminal lid red-brown and extending into long reddish twisted tail. *Zones 10-11.* p. 267

ARMERIA Plumbaginaceae

juniperifolia (caespitosa) (Spain), "Juniper thrift"; diminutive cushion-shaped, tufted perennial 15 cm high, with rosettes of small 3 cm awl-shaped leaves; very floriferous with pink flower heads on stiff 5-8 cm stalks. *Zone 5.* p. 318

juniperifolia 'Ardenholme', "Rose juniper thrift"; beautiful Scandinavian cultivar with larger heads of flowers darker rose and more fully double, about 3 cm across, beginning to bloom in May and on through Summer. *Zones 5-9.* p. 471

maritima (Maritime Europe, Asia Minor, No. Africa, Pacific Coast of No. America, Chile), "Sea pink", "Ladies cushion" or "Thrift"; cushion-forming small perennial, dense with narrow-linear, grass-like, one nerved, rich green basal leaves to 12 cm long; the small flowers in globular heads to 2 cm dia., on wiry stalks, vivid purplish-rose varying to pink or white, freely blooming Spring into Autumn. *Zones 4-9.* p. 471

maritima 'Alba', "White Ladies cushion"; attractive color variant to 30 cm high, forming cushions of grass-like linear leaves, and long-stalked globular 2-3 cm heads of small white flowers, interspersed with narrow bracts, freely blooming June to August. *Zone 4.* p. 470

maritima 'Vindictive'; excellent English cultivar seen in Kew Bot. Gardens near London; small perennial forming grass-like mounds of rich green linear leaves, and a display of globe-shaped floral heads of vivid deep rose, tipped with white. *Zone 4.* p. 318

pseudarmeria (Portugal), "Pinkball thrift"; small perennial to 30 cm high, forming tufts, resembling A. maritima but with broader, lanceolate leaves 2 cm wide, distinctly 5-7-nerved; small white to rose-pink flowers in dense globular heads 4-5 cm dia., blooming during July-August; the most popular broadleaved garden "Thrift". *Zones 6-7.* p. 471

ARMORACIA Cruciferae

rusticana (Cochlearia) (S.E. Europe, natur. in No. America), "Horseradish"; pungent deep-rooted strong-growing perennial forming stems to 60 cm high, the large lower leaves oblong, with rounded teeth; white flowers in terminal cluster, in May. Popular as condiment plant; the fresh fleshy roots are grated for use as relish to flavor meats or seafood. Photo shows a variegated leaf form in Brooklyn Botanic Garden. *Zone 4.* p. 525

ARNEBIA Boraginaceae

pulchra (Echioides longiflorus in Hortus) (Asia Minor, Armenia to Caucasus and East), "Prophet flower"; alpine low growing perennial to 25 cm high, with dark green oblanceolate leaves, and trumpet-shaped yellow flowers 3 cm long, having spreading lobes and a purple spot at base of sinus between the spreading lobes, in clusters during April and May. *Zone 4.* p. 342

ARNICA Compositae

chamissonis var. foliosa (Wyoming and Colorado to California and Canada), "Leafy arnica"; aromatic rhizomatous perennial 25-50 cm high; oblong-lanceolate lower leaves toothed at margins, 15 cm long; showy flowers 5 cm across, with raised brownish cushion center, and rays rich yellow; blooming July-September in Rocky Mountains. *Zone 4.* p. 371

montana (Cent. Europe to Scandinavia), "Mountain arnica"; aromatic, rhizomatous perennial herb 30 to 50 cm high, with lanceolate, smooth basal leaves 12 cm long; stem leaves smaller; large flowers to 5 cm across, with yellow ray-florets encircling the prominent anthers, blooming in July. Economically important because it yields the tincture of arnica, applied externally against skin inflammation and bruises. *Zone 6.* p. 524

ARONIA Rosaceae

arbutifolia (Eastern U.S.), "Chokeberry"; stoloniferous shrub to 2 m or more high, forming colonies to 4 m wide, the young growth tomentose; leaves oblanceolate to 10 cm long, smooth above and tomentose beneath; charming pink flowers in showy clusters blooming in April-May; small 1 cm bright red berry-fruit hangs on a long time; with foliage also providing red autumn color. *Zone 4.* p. 829

ARRABIDAEA magnifica: see SARITAEA magnifica

ARRHENATHERUM Gramineae

elatius bulbosum (Europe to W. Asia), "Tuber oatgrass"; tuberous-rooted perennial grass, with stems to 40 cm or more high; flat, soft leaf blades 1 cm wide, fresh green with white margins, sometimes known as 'Variegatum'; floral panicle pale green or purplish. *Zone 3.* p. 558

ARTABOTRYS Annonaceae

siamensis (Thailand), "Climbing ylang-ylang" or "Tail-grape"; evergreen shrub climbing by means of flower stalks hardening into hooks; lanceolate leathery leaves to 15 cm long; the blooms are orange-yellow and intensely fragrant, and consist of 3 sepals and 6 petals to 5 cm long, in clusters, followed by bunches of grape-like fruit. *Zone 10.* p. 264

ARTEMISIA Compositae

abrotanum (S.E. Europe to Asia Minor), "Southernwood"; aromatic subshrub to 2 m high, freely branched, with finely divided green, feathery, intensely lemon-scented leaves; the nearly globular, nodding small yellowish-white flowers in loose clusters. The fragrant leaves are used in perfumery, and as moth repellent. *Zone 5.* p. 526

absinthium (Europe to Kashmir), "Wormwood" or "Absinthe"; herbaceous perennial with a woody rootstock, to 1 m, with lobed leaves green and nearly glabrous above, white with cottony down beneath; yellowish flower heads, 5 mm across. Dried leaves employed medicinally. Used in making absinth liquor, and in compounding bitters. Culinary for seasoning of meats. *Zone 3.* p. 526

arborescens (Mediterranean region), aromatic "Wormwood"; shrubby perennial to 1 m with finely divided silvery-hairy leaves; small 1 cm bright yellow flower heads in leafy clusters. *Subtropic. Zone 9.* p. 371

camphorata (So. Europe, No. Africa), "Camphor-scented artemisia"; subshrubby perennial to 60 cm high, woody at base; the green leaves 3-8 cm long, finely divided into threadlike segments; small 1 cm globular, yellow flower heads, in branched clusters, in September-October. Grown in herbgardens for its odor of camphor. *Zone 7.* p. 526

dracunculus (Europe), "Tarragon" or "Estragon"; hardy herbaceous perennial to 1-½ m high, with green linear leaves scented like anise, to 15 cm long; panicles of whitish 1 cm flowers. Use: in salads, steaks, and other cookery; yields flavor to pickles. *Zones 5-10.* p. 526

frigida (Wisconsin to Arizona, Washington and Alaska), "Wormwood" or "Fringed sage"; silky-downy perennial subshrub 25-40 cm high, the branches prostrate and spreading, forming mats; the soft grayish leaves 2 to 6 cm long, finely cut into threadlike segments; small globose, 5 mm yellow flowerheads in leafy clusters. Popular for its aromatic, silvery foliage. *Zone 2.* p. 526

lactiflora (China, India), "White sagebush", "Ghost plant" or "White mugwort"; herbaceous perennial to 1½ m high; erect, deeply grooved stems, with pinnate leaves to 20 cm long; inflorescence in large feathery sprays in cream-colored tiny heads. *Zone 3.* p. 371

lanata (pedemontana) (Austrian Alps to Dolomites), "Woolly wormwood"; subshrubby perennial of tufted habit often only 5 cm high, with downy leaves palmately cut into linear segments; the inflorescence in spikes to 20 cm long; the small flower heads with yellow florets. *Zone 5.* p. 371

ludoviciana (albula) (Brit. Columbia to Michigan and Texas), "Silver King artemisia" or "Western sage"; herbaceous aromatic perennial with rhizomatous roots, to 90 cm high; linear silvery gray leaves 10 cm long, white-woolly beneath; 3 cm grayish-white flower heads in dense, branching clusters. The handsome foliage is used in fresh or dry arrangements. *Zone 9.* p. 371, 526

schmidtiana 'Nana' (Japan), "Silver-mound"; rhizomatous spreading, aromatic perennial to 30 cm high in the species, or to 15 cm in 'Nana'; the 5 cm finely divided foliage covered with silvery white silky hairs, the uppermost leaves linear; small white or yellow flowerheads not showy, in pyramidal panicles. Popular because of its silvery, scented foliage. *Zones 4-9.* p. 312, 525

stelleriana (N.E. Asia, naturalized in E. No. America and Europe), "Beach wormwood" or "Dusty miller"; popular ornamental perennial to 60 cm high, woody at base, and densely covered with soft white down; leaves pinnately lobed, 5-10 cm long; small yellow flower heads crowded in dense, slender racemes. One of the best gray foliage plants in gardens. *Zone 3.* p. 371

vulgaris (Europe, natural. in E. No. America), "Mugwort"; rhizomatous perennial with woody base; purplish stems to more than 1 m high; the leaves are fragrant, to 10 cm long, pinnately divided into oblong segments, dark green above and white-downy beneath; small reddish to yellow-grayish flower heads in terminal compound clusters, in Autumn. The dried aromatic leaves are excellent for seasoning. Used in England to flavor homemade beer, instead of hops. *Zone 3.* p. 526

ARTHROPODIUM Liliaceae

cirrhatum (New Zealand); tufted perennial herb with fleshy roots to 1 m high; numerous spreading flexible, lanceolate, light green, clasping leaves grayish beneath, with a narrow translucent edge and parallel veins, to 60 cm long; clusters of white flowers 3 cm across. *Subtropic. Zone 9.* p. 447

ARTOCARPUS Moraceae

altilis (communis, incisa) (Malaysia to Tahiti), the "Breadfruit tree"; milky-juiced tree to 20 m high, with handsome huge, deeply lobed, leathery leaves to 50 cm long or more, luxuriantly green with yellowish veins; large round or ovoid prickly fruit to 20 cm dia., yellow when ripe, tasting like bread when baked; or like sweet potato when cooked. As a result of reports by Capt. Cook, Captain Bligh was given the task of bringing the nutritious breadfruit from Tahiti to the British Antilles. In 1792, on his second voyage, he took 2500 young trees, sprouted from roots, to Jamaica, and these are now widely planted in the West Indies. *Tropical. Zone 10.* p. 915, 917

heterophyllus (integrifolia) (India to Malaya), the "Jackfruit" or "Jakfruit"; interesting tropical tree to 15 or 20 m high related to the breadfruit, with milky juice; glossy oblong leaves, lobed on younger branches; remarkable for its enormous fruit dangling directly from the trunk and biggest branches of the tree. This fruit is one of the largest in the world, 1/3 to 1 m long and weighing up to 18 kg.; a green knobby soft-spiny rind encloses a soft sweet or acid pulp of unpleasant odor, and is eaten raw or cooked, the seed roasted or cooked, in tropical Southeast Asia. *Zones 10-11.* p. 917

ARUM Araceae

italicum (Europe, No. Africa), "Italian arum"; robust, tuberous plant with hastate, fresh green leaves with whitish veining; spathe green, white inside with reflexed purple limb; the berry-like, fleshy fruit turns scarlet-red as the foliage withers and disappears. *Subtropic. Zone 7.* p. 24, 220

maculatum (England to S.E. Europe and No. Africa), "Lords and ladies" or "Aaron's staff"; fleshy tuberous herb 30 cm high, with arrow-shaped leaves, usually black-spotted, withering in Summer; long-stalked spathe 15-25 cm long pinched at the middle, light green and purple-spotted or margined, longer than the spadix; end of July, on stiff-erect stalks, the ripening berries turn scarlet-red. All parts poisonous. *Subtropic. Zones 7-8.* p. 219

palaestinum (sanctum) (Israel, Syria, Afghanistan), "Solomon's-lily", "Black calla"; tuberous plant with arrow-shaped, green leaves, followed by flower spike with dark spadix, and spathe green outside, black-purple within and the tapering limb. *Subtropic. Zone 9.* p. 24

ARUNCUS Rosaceae

dioicus 'Kneiffii' (sylvester cv.) (Eurasia, No. America), dwarf "Goat's beard"; perennial 60-90 cm high, with 2-3 times pinnate feathery leaves; tall stalks bearing elongate clusters of slender branches, dense with tiny creamy-white flowers, male and female on different plants. Flowering late Spring. *Zone 4.* p. 492

ARUNDINARIA Gramineae

alpina (Mountains of Africa), "Mountain bamboo"; hollow-stemmed bamboo to 15 or more metres high, spreading densely but not in clumps from woody rhizomes; the culms 5-10 cm thick, turning yellow with age; the linear leaves to 20 cm long. I photographed this species in the bamboo forest at 2,430 m on the Kivu border of Zaire, typical gorilla country. *Zone 10.* p. 546

amabilis (So. China, No. Vietnam), the "Tonkin cane bamboo"; grown commercially in Kwantung Prov. and Kiangsi; a noble rhizomatous bamboo spreading densely, and held in high esteem because of its straight, slender stems only slightly tapering, 1 to 5 cm dia. and reaching to 10 m or more in height, in mature canes rarely interrupted by branches and therefore widely used for fishing rods, hop poles, plant stakes and fine handicrafts; the thin-leathery, oblong lanceolate leaves to 25 cm or more long, dark green above, glaucescent beneath and showing transverse venation, on twigs pendant when mature. *Zones 9-10.* p. 546, 549, 551

anceps (Sinarundinaria) (India: Himalayas to 2500 m); clump-forming hardy bamboo to 4 m high, with slender erect or arching canes 2 cm dia., first purplish then changing to greenish-yellow or brown; the stem sheaths mottled; leaves 4-10 cm long, narrow to linear; very attractive species, similar to Fargesia nitida. *Zone 7.* p. 548

falconeri (transferred to Chimonobambusa falconeri by Dr. T. Soderstrom, Smithsonian Washington) (Himalayas); handsome clump-forming bamboo with dark green culms from 8 to 20 m high, and to 5 cm thick, at nodes forming clusters of branches; the leaves to 10 cm long, pale green and finely toothed, glaucous beneath. Photographed in Kew Gardens, London. Used in India for fishing rods and to make baskets. *Zone 8.* p. 548

fastuosa: refer to SEMIARUNDINARIA (Zander)
graminea of hort.: see POGONATHERUM paniceum
murielae hort.: see FARGESIA murielae
pumila (Sasa pumila hort.) (Japan); dwarf bamboo or woody grass spreading by rhizomes, with slender stems to 60 cm; narrow leaves 15 cm long, bright green and slightly hairy on both sides. *Zones 6-8.* p. 548, 556

pygmaea (Japan: Honshu, Kyushu), "Pygmy bamboo"; small hardy bamboo to 30 cm high, spreading by underground rhizomes and forming groundcover; bright green, slender, zigzag cylindric stems, purple and flattened at top; prominent purple internodes; narrow lanceolate leaves 12 cm long and pubescent. *Zones 4-8.* p. 548

variegata (Sasa fortunei, Pleioblastus) (Japan), "Dwarf white-stripe bamboo" or "Miniature bamboo"; I photographed this plant in Brazil, and consider it the most attractive small bamboo in cultivation; its growth habit is low to 1 m high, with gracefully arching branches and leaves 12 cm long, much broader than pygmaea, strikingly banded white; the underside, unlike pygmaea, is finely pubescent. *Zones 6-10.* p. 549

viridi-striata (syn. auricoma) (Pleioblastus viridi-striatus) (Japan); a small fairly hardy running bamboo to 1 m high, slender stems purplish-green, with leaves 4 to 15 cm long x 3 cm wide, finely toothed and pubescent beneath, usually striped yellow in Spring. Known in hort. as Bambusa argentea. *Zone 7.* p. 548

viridistriata 'Aurea', "Gold bamboo"; very highly colored small bamboo, seen in Sunshine Gardens, Encinitas, California, having large leaves attractively colored a warm creamy-yellow. *Zones 8-9.* p. 554

ARUNDO Gramineae

donax (Mediterranean region, naturalized in Southern U.S.), "Giant reed"; one of the largest grasses, and resembling bamboo, to 6 m or more high, perennial with woody stems; two-ranked flat green leaves to 60 cm long and 8 cm wide and with rough margins; inflorescence in slender, greenish or purplish plumes. *Zone 7.* p. 564

donax 'Versicolor' (So. Europe), the "Variegated giant reed"; majestic perennial grass, 2 m high, with knotty rootstock and stout stems almost woody; arching ribbon-like leaves gray-green striped creamy-white, to 60 cm long, alternately arranged on canes, and topped by showy plume-like panicles at first reddish, then white. Very impressive with its bold, bamboo-like leafy canes; quite ornamental in containers. *Zone 7.* p. 564

ASARINA Scrophulariaceae

antirrhiniflora (Maurandya) (Texas, California, Mexico); perennial vine with thin stems climbing by means of coiling petioles, halberd-shaped 3 cm leaves, and showy, axillary, trumpet-shaped 2 cm purple flowers white in throat and belly. *Zone 10.* p. 296

barclaiana (Maurandya) (Mexico); bright-flowered perennial climbing by coiling petioles, somewhat woody at base, with halberd-shaped leaves, axillary irregular trumpet-shaped purple flowers 4-8 cm long, downy outside; in various color forms from deep purple to rose or white; tube greenish; Summer. *Zone 10.* p. 296

erubescens (Maurandya) (Mexico); "Creeping gloxinia"; strongly vining, hairy plant with alternate, triangular, toothed, downy leaves and twining flowerstalks, bearing large, 8 cm trumpet-shaped blossoms having broad green sepals and carmine-rose corolla with pale throat spotted rose, blooming into November. *Tropical. Zones 10-11.* p. 321

roseiflora (Maurandya) (Zacatecas, Mexico); tender creeping herbaceous plant with white-pubescent rounded, fleshy leaves, crenate or lobed at margins; showy tubular flowers with spreading lobes delicate rose-pink. Rediscovered by A. Lau at El Salto, Monte Escobado, Zacatecas, Mexico 1984. *Zone 11.* p. 500

ASARUM Aristolochiaceae

europaeum (No. Europe to Russia), "Wild ginger"; woodland perennial with aromatic rhizomes, 12 cm high, having glossy ever-green, kidney-shaped or heart-shaped leaves to 8 cm dia., and forming dense clusters; small 2 cm bell-shaped flowers greenish-purple or brownish. *Zone 6.* p. 342

europaeum variegatum (niponica at Kew), "Variegated wild ginger"; very attractive form, with its ovate-cordate to heart-shaped dark green leaves low to the ground, and prettily splashed with silver around central areas. *Zone 7.* p. 342

hartwegii (So. Oregon to California), "Asarabacca" of the Sierra Nevada; handsome low perennial having stout rhizome, forming tufts with evergreen, leathery leaves to 12 cm across, cordate-ovate in outline, and the bluish-green blade beautifully mottled and banded silvery white; small 1 cm flowers brownish-purple. *Zone 7.* p. 342

shuttleworthii (Virginia to Alabama), "Mottled wild ginger"; a stemless, rhizomatous "Wild ginger" with 1-2 attractive kidney-shaped, soft-leathery 8 cm leaves, dark green with silvery green marbling; resin-scented flowers near ground-level, mottled violet. *Zone 6.* p. 342

ASCLEPIAS Asclepiadaceae

curassavica (Trop. America), "Blood-flower"; showy perennial to 1 m with woody base, stems with milky sap; oblanceolate leaves 5-15 cm long, the flowers in umbels with reflexed, 5-parted corolla brilliant red-purple, exposing the crown of 5 orange horned hoods. *Tropical. Zones 9-10.* p. 343

incarnata (E. No. America to Colorado), "Swamp-milkweed"; perennial milky herb to 1 m; long-lanceolate, rough leaves, and showy clusters of small rose-pink flowers; the fruit containing seeds with long silk. *Temperate*. Zone 3.   *p. 343*

physocarpa (South Africa), "Butterfly flower"; white-hairy shrubby perennial to 2 m; linear to lanceolate leaves 10 cm long; axillary inflorescence with white corolla and 4-angled hood; curious yellow-green, inflated bristly seedpods 6 cm dia. *Zone 10.*   *p. 654*

syriaca (cornutii) (E. Canada to Kansas) "Common milkweed"; milky perennial with creeping rootstocks, the branches to more than 1 m high; oblong leaves to 20 cm long, pubescent beneath; flowers in drooping axillary umbels with purplish corolla; the large seedpods split open, displaying flat seeds with attached tuft of silky hairs, which are carried by the wind. *Zone 3.*   *p. 343*

tuberosa the "Red butterfly-weed"; a red colorform of the usually orange-flowered type, native from Maine to Arizona, perhaps the showiest of milkweeds, a perennial with rough-hairy stalks 1 m high, lanceolate, thickish, rugose leaves 5-15 cm long, and numerous small flowers in terminal umbels usually bright orange, with 5-parted reflexed corolla lobes. *Zones 3-10.*   *p. 343, 523*

ASIMINA   Annonaceae
triloba (Annona) (New York to Florida and Texas), "Pawpaw" or "Northern banana tree"; very ornamental, deciduous tree of pleasing pyramidal shape, to 10 m high, or large shrub branching from the base, having dark gray bark, the young shoots red-brown pubescent, with large pendant, obovate leaves 10-25 cm long; axillary bisexual flowers with or before foliage, of 6 unequal petals dull purple, the outer ones to 3 cm long; ovoid yellow fruit 5-15 cm long, containing the sweet edible, banana-like creamy pulp of delicious taste. *Frost-hardy.* Zone 5.   *p. 638, 907*

ASPARAGUS   Liliaceae
asparagoides myrtifolius (Medeola) (Cape of Good Hope), the tuberous-rooted "Baby smilax" used for wedding decorations, etc.; graceful twining vine with threadlike stems and dainty, fresh, glossy green, little ovate "leaves" 2-5 cm long, usually allowed to climb on strings for cutting. The apparent "leaves" are actually expanded leaf-like branchlets (cladophylls); the true leaves are minute and scale-like. *Zone 10.*   *p. 282*

densiflorus cv. 'Myers' (So. Africa), "Plume asparagus"; showy tuberous rooted plant dense with stiffly erect, plume-like branches 60 cm or more high, the dense needle-like 1 cm cladodes or "foliage" rich green; small white axillary flowers. *Zone 10.*   *p. 143, 443*

densiflorus 'Myriocladus' (So. Africa: Natal), "Zigzag asparagus"; erect much branched sinuous shrub to 1½ m high, from swollen roots; woody gray stems with zigzag branches, the cladodes (branches simulating leaves) threadlike 1-2 cm long, in dense clusters, bright green. *Subtropic.* Zones 9-10.   *p. 442*

densiflorus cv. 'Sprengeri' (Natal), "Sprengeri fern"; much branched from tuberous roots, scarcely climbing, the fluffy branchlets set with soft, fresh green needles, the true leaves reduced to thorns; small fragrant flowers white, followed by bright red berries. *Subtropic.* Zones 9-10.   *p. 143, 443*

falcatus (Sri Lanka, So. Africa), "Sickle thorn"; widely climbing on zigzag woody stems to 11 m; branches straw-colored, slender and with rigid spines; the clustered, firm, bright green leaves narrow-linear and sickle shaped, 8 cm long; the numerous small flowers sweetly fragrant. *Zone 10.*   *p. 282*

officinalis (Europe, Asia, No. Africa, natural. locally in No. America), "Common asparagus" or Garden asparagus"; important perennial vegetable, growing from rhizomes, sprouting annual flexible herbaceous stems to 1½ m high, much branched and feathery, without spines, having clusters of thin cladodes, or flattened branches functioning as leaves; small greenish-white axillary, drooping flowers, followed by bright red 1 cm berries. Amongst the most valuable of early vegetables, and young fleshy spears are cut below ground level. Appreciated since Roman times for more than 2000 years. *Zones 3-10.*   *p. 442*

retrofractus (macowanii) (So. Africa), "Zigzag shrub"; shrubby plant with beige-gray woody stem to 2 m long, with stiff, thorny zigzag twigs at angles, bearing dense bundles of curved needle-like cladodes (branchlets) bright green; true leaves reduced to scales; small white flowers. *Subtropic.* Zones 9-10.   *p. 143, 282, 771*

setaceus (plumosus of hort.) (So. Africa), "Fern-asparagus"; climber with lacy, fern-like, rich green fronds of needle-like branchlets, arranged on a horizontal plane, on thin wiry stems with sharp prickles. Widely known as "Plumosus" as florists' green, and as popular house plant. *Zone 8.*   *p. 282*

ASPERULA   Rubiaceae
nitida puberula (Mts. of C. Greece); floriferous cushion-forming perennial with woody base, having rough square stems; the leaves

needle-like, 1-1½ cm long, in whorls of four, along branches topped by charming rose tubular flowers to 1 cm long, with spreading lobes, in July-August. *Zone 7.*   *p. 494*

odorata: see GALIUM odoratum

tinctoria (Europe, to the Ural), "Dyer's woodruff"; straggling perennial 30-50 cm high, with reddish roots, and purplish, procumbent stem; the leaves linear to ovate, in whorls of 3 to 6; the flowers red in bud, opening white in branched inflorescence, June-blooming. Dye is extracted from the roots; an old herb garden favorite in Europe. *Zone 6.*   *p. 542*

ASPHODELINE   Liliaceae
lutea (Mediterranean Reg.), "Jabob's-rod", "Yellow asphodel" of the ancient Greeks; perennial with fleshy roots; stems to 1 m high, with leaves linear and needle-pointed; inflorescence a slender pyramid with yellow, fragrant, starry flowers 2 to 3 cm across. Differs from Asphodelus by having leafy stalks. *Zones 6-9.*   *p. 443*

ASPHODELUS   Liliaceae
albus (Portugal to Greece), "Greek asphodel"; elegant tuberous-rooted perennial herb with linear, 3-angled basal leaves, and 60 cm stalks bearing cylindric raceme of white to pale pink funnel-shaped flowers 2 cm long. *Zone 9.*   *p. 236*

cerasiferus (ramosus) (Portugal, Spain, So. France), "Asphodel"; robust perennial to 1½ m high, with tuberous roots; basal narrow, soft-fleshy channeled leaves to 40 cm long, prominently keeled; stout floral stalks bearing long, much branched racemes of white flowers 2½ cm long. *Zone 8.*   *p. 236*

microcarpus (Canary Island to Asia Minor), "Asphodel"; clustering perennial herb with tuberous roots; rosette of broad, fleshy foliage; inflorescence on branched stalks to 1 m high, bearing starry white 2 cm flowers with purple line on each petal. *Subtropic.* *Zones 9-10.*   *p. 236*

ASPIDISTRA   Liliaceae
elatior (lurida) (China), "Cast-iron plant" or "Parlor palm"; old-fashioned tough-leathery foliage plant with thick roots and blackish-green, shining oblong basal leaves to 75 cm long, narrowed to a channeled stalk; purple bell-shaped flowers at the surface of the ground. Ideal for cool, unfavorable locations, very tolerant of neglect. *Subtropic.* Zone 10.   *p. 68*

ASPIDIUM falcatum: see CYRTOMIUM falcatum
phegopteris: see THELYPTERIS phegopteris
tsus-simense: see POLYSTICHUM tsus-simense

ASPLENIUM   Polypodiaceae (Filices)
antiquum (So. Japan); birdsnest-type rosette densely arranged with surrounding leaves narrow lanceolate, thin-leathery glossy fresh green, with prominent reddish midrib, and with wavy margins. *Zone 9.*   *p. 129*

bulbiferum (New Zealand, Australia, Malaya), "Mother fern"; with wiry pinnate fronds, having grooved black stem; the pinnae fresh green, and much larger than viviparum and not as deeply lacily cut, the segments becoming linear only when spore-bearing; bulbils or plantlets are produced on upper surface of frond. *Humid-subtropic.* Zone 10.   *p. 129*

daucifolium (viviparum) (Mauritius), "Mother fern"; tufted plant with dark green, finely lacy, arching fronds on firm stems, the little threadlike linear segments giving rise to tiny bulblets from which develop little plants. *Humid-tropical.* Zones 11-12.   *p. 129*

monanthemum (Madeira, Azores, So. Africa, So. American Andes to Chile, Hawaii); handsome evergreen species densely tufted with pinnate fronds 30-50 cm long, and having 20-40 horizontal, sessile 2 cm pinnae each side, on polished brown stalks; small bulbils are produced at the axils of the lowest pair of leaflets. *Zone 11.*   *p. 130*

nidus (nidus-avis) (India to Queensland and Japan), the "Birdsnest fern"; great epiphytic rosette of simple oblanceolate, stiffly spreading, shining, friendly green fronds anywhere from 30-90 cm long, of thin leathery texture with prominent blackish midrib and wavy margins, rising from a crown densely clothed with black scales. One of the most interesting and attractive of ferns for pots, keeping surprisingly well but should be kept steadily moist and warm, or new fronds may become deformed; avoid drafts; tolerates poor light to 25 fc. *Humid-tropical.* Zones 10-11.   *p. 131*

nidus 'Fimbriatus', "Feathery birdsnest"; a curious mutation; rosette with stiffly erect, glossy bright green leaves, pinnately but irregular deeply lobed nearly down to the midrib; a tropical epiphyte and interesting indoor fern. *Zone 11.*   *p. 131*

platyneuron (Maine to Colorado and Texas, So. Africa), "Ebony spleenwort"; small evergreen fern, spreading with tufts of erect pinnate fronds to 40 cm long and 5 cm wide, the pinnae faintly serrate, and with eared, hastate base. Resembling Christmas fern, Polystichum acrostichoides. *Zones 3-8.*   *p. 130*

simplicifrons (Queensland); tropical epiphytic fern with long linear, entire fronds of somewhat leathery texture, 30 to 40 cm long and 2-3 cm wide, margins slightly undulated; spore masses not quite to midrib or edge. *Zones 11-12.* p. 129

trichomanes (Temp. U.S., Europe, Mts. of Asia), "Maidenhair spleenwort"; exquisite small hardy evergreen fern, forming tufts of arching pinnate fronds to 25 cm long and 2 cm wide, the deep green pinnae rounded and slightly toothed. *Zones 3-8.* p. 130

ASTER Compositae

ageratoides (trinervius) (E. Asia: Japan to India), "Noyama-Kingiku" in Japan; perennial with spreading stolons and forming bushes; small gray-pubescent, ovate leaves 6-8 cm long; small daisy-like flowers 3-4 cm across, with yellow center cushions and white ray-florets, blooming October-November. *Zone 6.* p. 372

x alpellus (alpinus x amellus), "Hardy aster" or "Michaelmas daisy"; leafy-stemmed hybrid perennial 25-50 cm high, with large single flowers, having orange center disk subtended by bluish-rose ray-flowers, in Summer and Autumn. *Zone 4.* p. 372

alpinus (Mts. of Europe to Siberia, Alaska to Colorado), "Alpine aster" or "Rock aster"; lovely small perennial of spreading habit, 15-25 cm high, with 5 cm lanceolate basal leaves; leafy branches carry solitary, showy 5 cm flowers with purplish-rose or purple rays. *Zone 3.* p. 372

amellus (France to W. Asia), "Italian aster"; sturdy rhizomatous, hairy perennial to 60 cm high; branching stems with oblong leaves, and multitudes of violet, yellow-centered flowers 5 cm across, occasionally white or pink, blooming July-August; very drought-resistant. *Zone 3.* p. 372

dumosus 'Prof. Anton Kippenberg', "Pillow aster"; popular and proven autumn-blooming European cultivar forming low mounds to 40 cm high, with light blue flowers having yellow cushion center. The species dumosus is a very floriferous rhizomatous perennial native to Eastern No. America. *Zone 3.* p. 372

ericoides (Québec, Maine to Dakota and New Mexico), "Myrtle aster" or "Heath aster"; floriferous, charming rhizomatous perennial, spreading and forming mounds, to 30 cm or more high, having basal leaves spoon-shaped, the stem-leaves narrow-linear, 3-8 cm long; numerous dainty 2 cm daisy-like floral heads, with ray-flowers lilac-pink, also white or blue, blooming from July to October. *Zone 3.* p. 372

x frikartii (amellus x thomsonii); showy much branched hybrid perennial to 60-90 cm high, with solitary floral heads 5 to 8 cm across, and fragrant; the ray-florets lavender-blue. *Zone 5.* p. 372

linariifolius (Québec to Maine and Florida, west to Wisconsin and Texas), "Savoryleaf aster"; beautiful perennial with short root-crown; rough, downy stems 50 cm high set with stiff, needle-like leaves and terminating with floral heads of yellow center cushions, subtended by purplish-pink reflexed ray-flowers, September blooming. *Zone 4.* p. 372

novae-angliae (Canada and Northern U.S.), "New England aster"; showy robust perennial, much branched 90-150 cm high, from thick rhizome; stem-clasping lanceolate, hairy leaves 5-12 cm long; terminal clusters of large 4-5 cm flowers with rays violet or pink, blooming September-October. *Zones 2-9.* p. 373

novae-angliae 'Harrington Pink'; excellent color variation with lovely 4-5 cm flowers semi-double, having 40-50 linear, salmon-rose rays arranged around orange center disc, the foliage typically with stiff hairs; autumn-blooming. *Zone 3.* p. 373

novi-belgii (E. No. America), "New York aster"; rhizomatous perennial to 1½ m high, with narrow, smooth leaves; stiff stems topped by full clusters of bright blue-violet ray-flowers 3 cm across, disc flower yellow. *Zones 4-9.* p. 373

pringlei (pilosus var.), in hort. trade as A. ericoides, (Maine to N.J., Pennsylvania to Wisconsin), "September-herb" or "September-kraut" in Germany; low, herbaceous perennial 30-50 cm high, having numerous fibrous roots, with stiffish base and dense with threadlike spreading branches; basal leaves lanceolate, the stem leaves narrow linear, on lateral shoots needle-like 5-20 mm long, these branchlets tipped by solitary daisy-like flowers of numerous very narrow-linear ray-florets spreading 25 mm across, and centered by yellow cushion, blooming September-October. Also used as cutflower known as Monte Cassino. *Zone 3.* p. 381

radula (Swamps of Newfoundland, Canada to W. Virginia), "Atlantic aster"; rhizomatous perennial 50 cm to 1 m or more high, with leafy stems, the oblong leaves to 10 cm long and serrate at margins; flowers 3-4 cm across, violet or lavender-rose. *Zone 2.* p. 372

spectabilis (Massachusetts to So. Carolina), "Seaside aster"; herbaceous perennial, spreading rapidly by underground stolons, or rhizomes; the stems 30-50 cm high; firm and thickish, elliptic leaves, usually persistent; inflorescence in leafy-bracted clusters of bright violet or lilac flowers 4 cm across, blooming July-October. *Zone 5.* p. 373

ASTER: see also CALLISTEPHUS

ASTERISCUS Compositae

maritimus (Odontospermum) (Mediterran. reg.: Greece to Portugal), "Gold coin"; small soft subshrubby perennial with spreading branches, covered by silky wool, forming tufts to 25 cm high; oblanceolate to spoon-shaped, usually rough-hairy leaves; flower-heads bright orange-yellow to 4 cm across, having about 30 ray-petals around center cushions, blooming April to October. *Zone 9.* p. 467

sericeus (Odontospermum) (Canary Islands); "Star-flower"; handsome dwarf shrub dense with small rosettes of silky-hairy, obovate green leaves 4-5 cm long; in the apex of branches nestle the pretty, thistle-like golden-yellow heads 4 to 8 cm across, the large cushions of disc flowers surrounded by the spreading ray-florets. *Zone 9.* p. 373

ASTILBE Saxifragaceae

x arendsii 'Fanal' (involving davidii, thunbergii, chinensis x japonica); excellent garden hybrid to 65 cm tall, with much divided bronzy, ferny, tiny vivid garnet-red flowers in plume-like, feathery racemes on slender wiry stalks, blooming Mid-summer. *Zone 6.* p. 496

chinensis (China, Japan), "Chinese astilbe"; showy, robust perennial 50 to 80 cm high, with divided foliage, the glossy leaflets resembling elm leaves 4 cm long, crenate at margins; the branched floral stalks thickly clothed with brown hairs, and bearing loose elongate clusters of slender spikes dense with small rosy or white flowers, during July-August. *Zone 6.* p. 496

chinensis 'Pumila' (China), "Dwarf Chinese astilbe"; small clump-forming perennial to 30 cm high, with herbaceous leaves compound of obovate leaflets lobed or serrate at margins; the inflorescence in slender spires of minute 2 mm raspberry-pink flowers, in lateral, cylindric spikes, in late Summer; ideal for rock-gardens. *Zone 6.* p. 496

chinensis taquetii (East China); giant perennial to 1 m or more high with compound leaves of corrugated ovate leaflets lobed along margins; the striking inflorescence in masses of feathery spires dense with lateral spikes of tiny magenta-rose flowers, blooming in late Summer. *Zones 4-9.* p. 496

fortunei (W. China), "Goat's-beard"; clump-forming perennial curious with inflorescence pendant; small lavender pink flowers in dense lateral spikes, blooming during early Summer; compound leaves with ovate, crenate leaflets. *Zone 5.* p. 496

glaberrima 'Saxatilis' hort. (A. japonica terrestris) (Japan: Kyushu); dwarf rhizomatous, clump-forming perennial herb, 10-15 cm high, with leaves much dissected, tinted bronze; tiny flowers white or pink, in feathery plumes, blooming during Summer. *Zone 6.* p. 495

japonica (Japan); florists "Spiraea" or "Silver-sheath"; showy clump-forming, robust herbaceous perennial to 60 cm high, the fern-like basal leaves twice divided into 3 broad leaflets; the fluffy inflorescence in branched plumes dense with small creamy-white flowers, carried well above the foliage, beginning late Spring. Easily used for forcing in pots for Easter by florists. *Zone 5.* p. 53, 496

x japonica 'Deutschland'; popular florists "Spiraea", 60 cm high, a cultivar by Arends with long, graceful, pure white spreading plumes of tiny flowers, early blooming; excellent for forcing. *Zone 5.* p. 496

x japonica 'Koblenz' (Rhineland); striking cultivar of compact habit to 50 cm high, with dark pinnate leaves; beautiful fluffy plumes dense with small, dark salmon-red flowers, blooming in July. *Zone 5.* p. 496

simplicifolia (Japan: Honshu), "Star astilbe"; small rhizomatous perennial 15 to 25 cm high, with simple ovate, glossy leaves 8 cm long, deeply cut or serrate along margins, coppery red when young; small white, starry flowers in slender clusters, during June-July. *Zone 6.* p. 495

thunbergii (astilboides) (Japan), "Ostrich feather"; attractive herbaceous perennial with basal leaves 3 times divided into three slender leaflets; white A. japonica has leaves twice divided into three; the handsome inflorescence with arching wiry stalk bearing lateral pendant, feathery racemes of tiny flowers, having slender petals, first white but changing to pink with maturity, blooming May to Summer. *Zone 6.* p. 496

ASTILBOIDES tabularis (Zander): see RODGERSIA (Hortus 3)

ASTRANTIA Umbelliferae

major (Spain to Caucasus), "Masterwort"; herbaceous perennial to 60 cm or more high, with mostly basal leaves, deeply lobed, the segments sharply toothed; small white to rose tubular flowers subtended by purplish bracts, in dense branched clusters 2-3 cm across, terminally on purple stalks, blooming in June. Good garden subject along waterside. *Zone 6.* p. 516

ASTRIDIA Aizoaceae
herrei (So. Africa: Namaqualand; Namibia); succulent shrub about 30 cm high, having woody roots; branches at first 2-edged; sickle-shaped leaves velvety gray-green and margined red to 8 cm long, and joined at base; large shiny red flowers, pale on reverse. *Zone 10.* p. 144

ASTROPHYTUM Cactaceae
asterias (No. Mexico to Texas), "Sand dollar"; low, dome-formed succulent to 8 cm wide, with a star-shaped depression; green tinged coppery and covered with white scales, the areoles tufted with white wool; flowers yellow with red throat 4 cm across. *Zone 10.* p. 153

capricorne (No. Mexico), "Goat's horn"; hard green globe to 25 cm high, with some silver marking, 7 to 8 ribs with contorted spines; speading yellow flower with red throat 6 cm across. *Zone 10.* p. 153

myriostigma (C. Mexico), "Bishop's cap"; handsome small globe when young, with usually 5 prominent ribs, spines absent, covered with small white spots; with age becoming elongate, variable with 6 or more ribs, to 60 cm high; flowers yellow, 4 to 6 cm across. *Arid-subtropic. Zone 10.* p. 153

ornatum (Mexico: Hidalgo and Querétaro), "Monk's hood"; attractive hard plant subglobose or cylindric with 8 prominent spiral folds, green and beautifully marked with silvery spots, talon-like spines; with age becoming 25 to 35 cm high; large lemon-yellow flowers 7 to 9 cm broad. *Arid-subtropic. Zone 10.* p. 153

'ornatum x asterias', in col. New York Botanic Garden 1984; robust hybrid semi-cylindric approx. 20 cm high, having spines as in A. ornatum and the liberal felty areoles and markings of A. asterias; flowers pale yellow. *Zone 10.* p. 154

ASYSTASIA Acanthaceae
gangetica (India, Malaysia), "Coromandel"; herbaceous perennial with trailing and rooting or clambering stems; the opposite, small ovate, fresh green, thin leaves 3-8 cm long; on one-sided racemes, the soft-textured bell-shaped flowers with flaring petals 2-3 cm across, orchid pink flushed with purple, and pale throat. *Tropical. Zones 10-11.* p. 306

ASYSTASIA; see also MARIPA and PSEUDERANTHEMUM

ATHANASIA Compositae
crithmifolia (So. Africa), "Coulter bush", also known as "Klaas Louw Bos" in So. Africa; pungent-scented shrub to over 1 m high, densely branched, with narrow linear leaves only 1 mm wide, divided toward apex into 3 little fingers; blooming in Mid-spring with golden-yellow flowers in flat clusters. Very ornamental with its decorative foliage and colorful blooms. *Zone 9.* p. 688

ATRHOTAXIS Taxodiaceae (Coniferae)
laxifolia (Tasmania), "Tasmanian cedar"; evergreen dioecious tree 9 m or more high, of bushy habit when young, the slender, rather pendant branchlets with very short, awl-shaped glossy yellowish-green needles pressed to the shoot as in A. cupressoides; spiny cones are 2 cm wide. Allied to Cryptomeria. *Zone 9.* p. 610

ATHYRIUM Polypodiaceae (Filices)
filix-femina (Europe, Asia, No. America), "Lady fern"; hardy fern with tufted, graceful feathery fronds with brownish stalks, scaly below, the leaflets deeply toothed and bright green. *Zones 3-8.* p. 131

filix-mas: see DRYOPTERIS

niponicum pictum (in hort. as A. goeringianum pictum), also listed as Dryopteris niponicum (Japan, Korea), "Miniature silver fern" or "Japanese painted fern"; attractive small tufted fern with pretty, variegated fronds to 40 cm long, spear-shaped, and pinnate, the segments toothed, the stalks wine-red, and a band of gray down through the frond. Winter-hardy, but deciduous outdoors in cold climate. *Zones 5-9.* p. 131

pycnocarpon: see DIPLAZIUM pycnocarpon

ATRIPLEX Chenopodiaceae
hortensis 'Rubra' (Asia Minor, natural. in Europe and No. America), "Mountain spinach" or "Orach"; ornamental as well as useful leafy annual, to more than 1 m high, with arrow-shaped foliage about 12 cm long, blood-red and on purple stems in cv. 'Rubra'; small purplish flowers, in Summer; used medicinally for soothing inflammations since 16th century. *Zone 9.* p. 367

hymenelytra (Deserts of California to Utah and New Mexico; Sonora); "Desert holly"; compact white scurfy shrub to 1 m high, with persistent silvery rhombic or rounded leaves 4-5 cm long and deeply toothed; small green flowers dioecious; the staminate in long spikes, the female or pistillate in short spikes with entire fruiting bracts 1 cm long; inhabiting arid regions, photographed in Death Valley, California. *Zone 9.* p. 684

ATROPA Solanaceae
belladonna (Europe to India), the "Deadly nightshade" or "Belladonna"; perennial herb to 1 m, with ovate leaves to 15 cm; bell-shaped nodding, axillary 2½ cm flowers purplish-red, blue calyx enlarging to form a shining red 1 cm berry, very poisonous. The sap yields the drugs atropine and belladonna. Atropine is used to enlarge the pupil of the eye. *Zone 6.* p. 511, 541

AUBRIETA Cruciferae
deltoidea (Sicily, Greece to Asia Minor), "Purple rock-cress"; popular mat-forming perennial herb to 15 cm high, dense with small 2 cm obovate, hairy leaves; very floriferous with pretty, 4-petaled, purplish-red flowers 2 cm across, in April to June. *Zones 5-9.* p. 314, 407

deltoidea 'Cobalt'; free-blooming cultivar seen at the Royal Botanic Gardens Kew, in England, forming a low carpet practically covered with 2 cm flowers varying from vivid deep blue and changing to pale lilac, during Spring. *Zone 6.* p. 407

deltoidea 'Red Cascade'; exciting cultivar seen in Holland, producing cascading masses of small red-purple flowers, varying to pink or near-white, during Spring and early Summer. *Zones 4-9.* p. 407

deltoida 'Variegata' (astrolata); strikingly beautiful cultivar, spreading low to form cushions; the 2-4 cm elliptic leaves especially handsome with cream-white borders; 4-petaled flowers 2 cm across, vivid red-purple. *Zones 5-9.* p. 407

kotcheviana (kotschyi) (Iran); herbaceous perennial with prostrate branches, forming tufted mounds; small obovate or wedge-shaped leaves, coarsely toothed and gray-hairy; floriferous with numerous pretty light purple or lilac pink 2 cm flowers, blooming April to June. *Zone 6.* p. 407

AUCUBA Cornaceae
japonica (Himalayas to Japan), "Japanese laurel"; handsome dioecious evergreen shrub to 5 m high, having flexible branches dense with large decorative ovate leaves to 20 cm long, of thick soft-leathery texture, glossy rich green and toothed above the middle; small purple flowers, followed on female plants by clusters of glossy red, very attractive berries, effective all Winter and into Spring. *Zone 7. p. 692*

japonica 'Dentata'; photographed in Kew Gardens, London; handsome evergreen bush, with glossy green leaves smaller than the species, and irregularly toothed at margins. *Zone 7.* p. 692

japonica 'Picturata', also known in horticulture as "Goldiana"; the "Golden laurel"; mutant with large leaves almost entirely golden-yellow and with only the margins light green and occasionally dotted yellow 15-18 cm long. A truly showy colorform although more easily subject to leafscorch or spotting from wetness, due to the absence of chlorophyll. *Zone 8.* p. 692

japonica 'Variegata' (Himalayas to Japan), "Gold dust tree"; evergreen shrub with opposite shining leathery elliptic leaves to 18 cm long, dark green blotched yellow, and toothed above middle; purple flowers; the female plants with scarlet berries. *Warm-temperate. Zone 8.* p. 60, 692

AURINIA Cruciferae
saxatilis (Alysssum saxatile) (C. and S.E. Europe to Turkey), "Basket of gold" or "Golden tuft alyssum"; popular rockgarden perennial forming mats 15-30 cm high; having woody roots and silvery gray foliage; clusters of small, bright golden-yellow flowers in Spring. *Zones 4-8.* p. 314, 406

AVENA Gramineae
sativa (Mediterranean reg.), "Common oats"; tufted grass-like annual to 1 m or more high, the oats of agriculture, with narrow leaves to 30 cm long; the inflorescence on erect stalks, branched toward apex; the branchlets carrying pendulous fruit of oats. Widely cultivated as feed for horses and as cereal food, primarily in cool, moist climates. *Zone 6.* p. 567

sempervirens: see HELICTOTRICHON sempervirens

AVERRHOA Oxalidaceae
bilimbi (Malaysia, Philippines), "Bilimbi"; "Cucumber tree"; known as "Kamias" to Filipinos; tropical evergreen tree to 5 m high, having odd-pinnate leaves of 23 or more leaflets; flowers red-purple, borne cauliflorous on the trunk or branches and displaying fertile stamens; the cylindric-oblong fruit 10 cm long and greenish-yellow, cucumber-like, obscurely 5-angled; the juicy flesh is edible but of sour, acid taste; generally cooked with sugar for juices or jam. The foliage is sensitive to touch. *Zone 10.* p. 919

carambola (India to China), the "Star-fruit", "Carambola tree" or "Oxalis tree"; evergreen 5-10 m high, with pinnate leaves of 5-9 leaflets which close when touched or at night; small fragrant flowers white marked with purple; the fleshy drooping 10 to 15 cm fruit ribbed, yellowish-brown, quince-scented and edible, sweet-tart in flavor, star-shaped in cross-section. *Zone 10.*   *p. 919*

AYLOSTERA: see REBUTIA

AZADIRACHTA indica (Everett):
   see MELIA indica (Corner: Trees of Malaya)

AZALEA: botanically Rhododendron, which see. Linnaeus himself established the genus Azalea in 1735, and in addition 1753 the genus Rhododendron. As then understood, Azaleas were deciduous in North America with funnel-shaped flowers having 5 stamens; Rhododendron evergreen, with 10 stamens. Salisbury in 1796 combined them both under Rhododendron. Yet, in horticulture the name Azalea is firmly fixed.
   amoena: see Rhododendron obtusum 'Amoenum'
   indica of hort.: see Rhododendron x simsii
   ledifolia alba: see Rhododendron mucronatum
   nudiflora: see Rhododendron periclymenoides
   pontica L.: see Rhododendron luteum

AZARA   *Flacourtiaceae*
   dentata (Chile); woody evergreen shrub or tree-like, to 3 m high, with downy reddish branchlets; broad-elliptic leaves to 3 cm long, glossy green above, downy beneath, and toothed at margins; flowers of numerous yellow stamens, but lacking petals, in branching clusters, blooming in June, and sweetly fragrant. *Zone 8.*   *p. 732*

AZOLLA   *Filices (Salviniaceae)*
   filiculoides (Washington State, Mexico, So. America), "Mosquito fern" or "Fairy moss"; free-floating aquatic fern, resembling miniature selaginellas; branching with tiny green leaves appressed and imbricate, 2 mm long, larger than caroliniana, with long hair-like roots at each forking of branches. *Humid subtropic. Zones 7-9.*   *p. 326*

BABIANA   *Iridaceae*
   purpurea (Cape Province), "Purple baboon flower"; cormous plant, 15 cm high, with strongly ribbed leaves; long stalks with spike of light purple, 4 cm dia. flowers. *Subtropic. Zone 9.*   *p. 222*
   rubrocyanea (Cape Prov.), "Wine-cup babiana"; cormous herb with stems 15-20 cm high; sword-shaped leaves to 10 cm; 5-10 flowered spike with green bracts; bicolor fragrant blooms 5 cm dia., the spreading petals lavender blue to tips, lower part rich crimson as in a cup; Spring. *Zone 9.*   *p. 222*
   stricta (So. Africa), "Upright Cape Flower", a "Baboon flower"; low cormous herb with hairy sword-shaped pleated leaves and freesia-like fragrant flowers, 5 cm across, pale to mauve blue; winter blooming. Known as Baboon flower because the bulb-like parts are a favored food of the baboons. *Subtropic. Zone 8.*   *p. 222*

BACCHARIS   *Compositae*
   glomeruliflora (Swamps No. Carolina to Florida and W. Indies); dioecious shrub 2 m or more high, with leathery, light green, spatulate to obovate leaves to 5 cm long, usually toothed above the middle; floral heads yellowish, clustered in leaf axils, blooming in Autumn. Foliage and flowers are resinous. *Zone 9.*   *p. 688*
   pilularis (Oregon and California), "Coyote brush" or "Chaparral broom"; evergreen dioecious shrub with mostly prostrate brown-barked branches, in time building up to 1 m high and 2 m spread; of dense habit with obovate gray-green, leathery leaves serrate at margins, to 4 cm or more long; small yellowish flowers at tips of lateral branchlets; female plants produce cottony seeds. Inhabitat from So. Oregon to the Coast Ranges of San Diego County.
Zones 8-10.   *p. 688*
   pilularis 'Twin Peaks', "Dwarf coyote bush", valuable California cultivar of moderate growth rate; evergreen prostrate shrub forming good ground cover in dry climate; small 2 cm toothed, leathery dark green leaves; small yellowish flower heads. Widely planted in California landscaping. *Arid-subtropic. Zones 8-10.*   *p. 314*

BACKEBERGIA   *Cactaceae*
   militaris (Mexico: Guerrero, Michoacan); tree-like branching cactus to 10 m high, with columns having 9 to 11 ribs; gray 1 cm needle spines tipped black; developing brown woolly cephalium cap at or near apex of branches; cylindric greenish flowers 4 cm across. *Zone 10.*   *p. 159*

BAILEYA   *Compositae*
   multiradiata (Calif. to Texas), "Desert marigold"; attractive white-woolly perennial or annual, to 40 cm high, the twiggy branches with small divided leaves; floral heads 5 cm across, of numerous yellow ray-flowers. Poisonous to sheep. *Zone 7.*   *p. 367*

BALLOTA   *Labiatae*
   pseudodictamnus (Greece, Crete, Rhodes); white-woolly perennial subshrub with woody base, to 60 cm high, the spreading branches with opposite rounded, silvery pubescent leaves, about 3 cm across; small white flowers with numerous purple spots, in distant whorls. *Zone 8.*   *p. 740*

BALLYA   *Commelinaceae*
   zebrina (Trop. East Africa); small succulent trailer with small ovate, clasping leaves velvety hairy, bronzy green with pale stripes lengthwise, flowers pale mauve. *Zones 10-11.*   *p. 310*

BALSAMORHIZA   *Compositae*
   sagittata (So. Dakota and Colorado w. to Brit. Columbia, So. California), "Oregon sunflower" or "Balsam root"; showy perennial tap-rooted herb to 60 cm high, with arrow-shaped basal leaves 20-50 cm long, white-tomentose beneath while young; solitary large yellow flowers 6-10 cm across, from May to August.
Zones 3-9.   *p. 374, 375*

BAMBUSA   *Gramineae*
   arundinacea (India to Malaysia; widely planted in Florida), "Giant thorny bamboo"; large clumping bamboo 20 to 40 m high, from thick, woody rootstock; with hollow stems 15 to 18 cm dia., the joints 25-45 cm apart; zigzag green and glossy when young, becoming straight and golden-yellow with age and having toward top a profusion of graceful leafy branches, the lower branchlets are bearing spines; leaf blades to 20 cm long; large floral panicle, but plant will die after fruiting. Young shoots are edible though bitter, appearing in Autumn. *Zones 9-10.*   *p. 546*
   beecheyana (Dendrocalamus latiflorus hort.) (South-eastern China), "Beechey bamboo", sometimes known as Sinocalamus beecheyanus; a large running, non-hardy timber bamboo, developing thick, bright green culms to 12 m high and 10 cm thick, later turning yellow; with age and weight gracefully arching; 6 to 10 heart-shaped leaves grouped on a twig, 10-22 cm long and to 4 cm wide. This bamboo is one of the important sources of edible bamboo sprouts, cooked and eaten in China and elsewhere. *Zones 9-10.*   *p. 546, 550*
   dolichoclada (Taiwan), "Chosihi chiku"; giant tropical bamboo to 20 m high, forming clumps; having green or gray culms to 10 cm dia.; the leaves are 15 cm long and 2½ cm wide; rarely cultivated in U.S. Photographed in Bot. Garden Singapore. *Zones 9-10.*   *p. 548*
   dolichoclada 'Stripe' (Leleba dolichoclada) (Taiwan); similar to dolichoclada but culms yellow-green with deep green stripes.
Zones 9-10.   *p. 548*
   glaucescens (multiplex) (Vietnam), "Hedge bamboo"; a variable woody grass becoming 12 m high, the green reedlike hollow stems bearing graceful twigs with many very small leaves, fern-like, 3-15 cm long, glabrous deep green, silver-blue beneath, and with a ring of hair at base of leaf; the older culms become 3 cm or more thick. Ideally suited for hedging, as plants form branchlets from base and up, and can easily be trimmed to shape. *Zone 9.*   *p. 549*
   glaucescens 'Alphonse Karr' (syn. B. nana Suochiku) (Japan), "Fernleaf bamboo"; large and attractive hedge bamboo much like the type, however the culms and branches are bright yellow irregularly striped with vivid green and the culm sheaths have yellowish stripes; 7-12 m high. *Zone 9.*   *p. 549*
   glaucescens 'Silver stripe' (argenteostriata hort.), "Silver hedge bamboo"; cultivar having culms between internodes narrowly striped with yellow, the leaves yellowish or variegated white. *Zone 9.*   *p. 549*
   guadua (Guadua angustifolia), (Panama, Jamaica, Colombia, Venezuela, Brazil to Argentina); a giant non-hardy timber bamboo with culms to 20 m or even 30 m tall, and 10-20 cm thick, widely arched above; the internodes hollow with wood 2 cm or more thick, higher up the branches usually thorny, leaves oblong lanceolate 16 up to 20 cm long. Used much for timber in South America, also by opening large culms out flat in place of sawn boards of wood. Locally cut into sections to use instead of flower pots. The largest American bamboo. *Zone 10.*   *p. 550, 553*
   longispiculata (India; Burma, now Myanmar); attractive ornamental species forming clusters to 15 m high; the culms to 8 cm dia., solid green except for some creamy-white vertical lines; the leaves 20-30 cm long and 6 cm wide, with 24 or more nerves; erect inflorescence to 35 cm long and having 6 to 12 flowered spikelets. Planted in Puerto Rico and California. *Zone 10.*   *p. 549*
   malingensis (dissimulator hort.) (China: Hainan Isl.), "Maling bamboo"; clustering species forming imposing clumps 8-10 m high; with straight green culms 4-6 cm dia., near base often zigzag; branches emerge from basal nodes upward; narrow lanceolate leaves 7-14 cm long, sparsely hairy beneath. The culms are strong and are used for frames of farmhouses and making farm appliances.
Zone 10.   *p. 549*
   multiplex in hort., is Bambusa glaucescens (Hortus)

nananae (Arundinaria disticha) (Japan), "Dwarf fernleaf"; very decorative small species with running rootstock, smooth erect, reed-like purplish canes; the leaves in pairs, bunched together toward top. *Zone 9.*   *p. 549*

oldhamii (Sinocalamus), in nurseries as Dendrocalamus latiflorus; (China), "Giant timber bamboo" or "Male bamboo"; large bamboo to 18 m high, forming open clumps; erect canes 9 cm dia., pale green with dense foliage 8-20 cm long, on pendant branchlets. Very ornamental and widely planted in Southern U.S. and in Taiwan. *Zone 9.*   *p. 549*

textilis, (So. China; Kwangsi, Kwangtung), "Wong Chuk"; a handsome subtropical species forming compact clumps of thin-walled but tough culms with long internodes, very straight to 15 or more m tall and 5 cm thick, with nodding tips; 6-10 branches at nodes, with attractive foliage 15-20 cm long, and to 2½ cm wide. These straight, light and tough canes are split and used extensively for weaving of baskets; hardy to -10°C. *Zones 9-10.*   *p. 547, 551*

tulda (India); giant tropical bamboo, to 20 m high, forming clumps, with strong, straight culms 8-10 cm dia.; the stem sheaths triangular, and brown-hairy on outside; leaves to 25 cm long and 3 cm wide. Resembles tuldoides but culms are longer and more straight, making it the most useful tropical bamboo for construction in U.S.; excellent for furniture and as split bamboo, also used for paper pulp. *Zone 10.*   *p. 550*

tuldoides (S.E. China), "Punting pole bamboo"; used to push junks on Chinese rivers; handsome semi-hardy clump bamboo with rigid, straight culms to 18 m high and 8 cm dia.; the broad, rich green leaves to 22 cm long, and green reverse. Because of its strong wood, it is used in China for many industrial purposes. *Zones 9-10.*   *p. 547, 550*

ventricosa (China), "Buddha's belly bamboo"; so called because of the characteristic dark olive culms swollen between internodes, especially in potgrown clumps; otherwise may grow 15 m high; leaves to 18 cm long. Planted adjacent to Palaces and Buddhist Temples in China where I have photographed them. *Zone 9.*   *p. 550, 551, 556*

vulgaris (Java, and wild in tropical regions of E. and W. Indies, Africa, C. and So. America), "Feathery bamboo"; widely grown ornamental bamboo because of its attractiveness and large size; forms open clump with spreading rhizomes, arching culms 15-24 m high and 10-12 cm thick, hollow with thin walls, glossy green at first later yellow banded lengthwise or all yellow, the joints covered wtih deciduous brown hairs; dark green leaves 15-22 cm long borne on branches on the upper part of the stem. *Zone 10.*   *p. 550, 551, 556*

vulgaris 'Vittata', "Greenstripe bamboo"; handsome cultivar with the thick yellow culms striped or banded lengthwise with green, the stems hollow and 4-5 cm thick and to 5 m high; the lateral branches with yellow stem and leaves bright green both sides 15-20 cm long and 2-4 cm wide. The species vulgaris has culm plain green. *Zone 10.*   *p. 550, 557*

BAMBUSA: see also DENDROCALAMUS, PHYLLOSTACHYS, PSEUDOSASA, SASA

BANKSIA   *Proteaceae*

ashbeyi (Northwest Australia); woody evergreen shrub from Shark Bay, to 5 m tall and wide, with vicious, hard, bluish leaves 25 cm long and 3-5 cm wide, cut each side into triangular lobes; the showy floral cones silky gray dense with gold and scarlet styles, 12-18 cm long. *Zone 9.*   *p. 821*

grandis (Western Australia), known as "Bull banksia"; handsome and curious tree 3 to 10 m high, with sparry branches, and un-believable leaves 30 cm long, green to grayish and stiff as metal, deeply cut out to the midrib by alternating teeth like a big-edged saw, richly brown-felted at first; yellow bottle brush flowers 20-30 cm long. My photographs are of typical leaves from trees growing near Perth. *Zone 8.*   *p. 823*

media (W. Australia); bushy, woody shrub, with spatulate, stiff leaves deeply serrate at margins, cylindrical and grayish beneath; inflorescence cone-like, dense of styles light yellow to red-brownish. *Subtropic. Zone 9.*   *p. 821*

speciosa (Western Australia), "Showy banksia"; spectacular spreading shrub 2-3 m tall; thick woody branches with long narrow, green to grayish stiff-leathery leaves to 30 cm long, cut to the midrib into triangular saw teeth; showy inflorescence of curving yellow styles tipped green, silvery in bud. *Subtropic. Zone 9.*   *p. 823*

BAPTISIA   *Leguminosae*

australis (Pennsylvania to Tennessee and Indiana), "Blue false indigo"; very handsome perennial to 1½ m high, and forming huge clumps with spreading branches; compound leaves with oblong, bluish-green leaflets 5-8 cm long; the pea-like, two-lipped flowers 3-4 cm long, lovely indigo blue, in 20-30 cm racemes, summer-blooming, and very attractive to butterflies. *Zones 4-9.*   *p. 440*

perfoliata (So. Carolina to Florida), "Catbells" or "Gopher weed"; curious perennial to 60 cm high, with wiry branches bearing leathery, bluish-glaucous leaves 8-20 cm across, the blades almost circular, plate-like, with stem seemingly growing through the center, and the tiny creamy-yellow flowers nestling in the middle, in April to August. *Zone 8.*   *p. 440*

tinctoria (Podalyria) (Mass. to Florida and Minnesota), "Wild Indigo" or "Rattleweed"; herbaceous bushy perennial 60-90 cm high, with erect stems from underground rhizomes; compound leaves of 3 obovate leaflets 2 cm long; the bright yellow pea-like flowers along the terminal branches. The dry pods are used by children as rattles. Cultivated in Colonial times for its blue dye, but its sap is not as satisfactory as true indigo, Indigofera. *Zone 5.*   *p. 440*

BARBACENIA   *Velloziaceae*

elegans (Vellozia) (Natal); bushy plant with hard, linear-lanceolate leaves to 20 cm long, and starry flowers lilac in bud, white when open, on slender stalks. *Zone 11.*   *p. 78*

BARBAREA   *Cruciferae*

verna (Europe, natural. in No. America), "Early winter cress" or "Upland cress"; herbaceous perennial or biennial to 60 cm high, starting as basal rosette of leaves pinnately cut; the following year forming the stems bearing racemes of small 1 cm yellow flowers in early Spring, followed by linear 4-angled pods containing many seeds. The leaves are used for seasoning and for salads. *Zone 3.*   *p. 528*

BARKLYA   *Leguminosae*

syringifolia (Queensland, New So. Wales), "Gold-blossom tree"; evergreen Australian tree 3 to 15 m high, having dense crown; leaves triangular-ovate 10 cm long, palmately veined; showy golden-yellow pea flowers in pendulous racemes to 22 cm long, forming terminal clusters. *Zone 10.*   *p. 654*

BAUERA   *Saxifragaceae*

rubioides (Queensland to So. Australia, Tasmania), "Wiry bauera"; attractive soft evergreen shrub 60 cm to 2 m high, with 3-parted heathlike toothed foliage 1-2 cm long in a ring, on stems rough wiry and scrambling; stalked pink or white cup-flowers 2 cm wide. *Zone 9.*   *p. 869*

BAUHINIA   *Leguminosae*

acuminata (India, Burma or Myanmar, Malaya, China), "Orchid tree"; tropical shrub to 2 m high, with smooth two-lobed leaves and showy white flowers 5-8 cm across, with spreading petals and prominent stamens; summer-blooming. *Zones 10-11.*   *p. 748*

blakeana, "Hongkong orchid tree"; apparently a sterile hybrid; to 5 m high, with twisted stem, leaves of two jointed leaflets and showy large orchid-like flowers of 5 spreading unequal petals carmine-rose to burgundy, with the fifth petal striped purple. As seen in Queensland, these orchid trees provide a gorgeous show for at least 5 months. *Subtropic. Zones 9-10.*   *p. 747*

corniculata (forficata) (Brazil), 'White camels-foot'; tree to 6 m high, with stems leaning at an angle, the top flattened; leaves deeply lobed; flowers white with narrow petals. *Subtropic. Zone 10.*   *p. 747*

kochia (Malaya), "Malayan orchid tree"; floriferous evergreen shrub with flexuous branches, thin broad oval leaves, and flowers in showy clusters, soft pink, tinted with rose and red on spreading obovate petals. *Zones 10-11.*   *p. 747*

monandra (Burma or Myanmar), "Pink orchid"; small ornamental tree sometimes called "Jerusalem date" or "Butterfly flower"; deciduous in Winter; produces great quantities of big flowers and seldom without blossoms; flower orchid-like, white flushed rose, lip yellow marked red, changing to pink after 24 hours; leaves notched at apex. *Tropical. Zone 10.*   *p. 747*

petersiana (E. Africa: Mozambique); straggling shrub with branches spreading, and stiff ovate, lightly lobed leaves; white flowers with narrow petals having crinkled margins, spotted purple at base, to 6 cm long and with red stamens, on red stalklets. *Zone 10.*   *p. 747*

punctata (galpinii) (Trop. Africa to Transvaal), "Pride of the Cape" or "Red Bauhinia"; floriferous spreading shrub to 3 m, with scandent branches; the bi-lobed, pale green leaves 4-8 cm long, divided at apex usually halfway, the showy flowers 6 cm across, in small clusters, the spoon-shaped 5 petals brilliantly red, blooming during Summer. *Zones 9-10.*   *p. 747*

purpurea (India, Burma or Myanmar, Vietnam), the "Butterfly tree" or "Purple bauhinia"; small tree 2-6 m high, with broad thin-leathery leaves cleft about one third; fragrant flowers reddish-purple; with petals not overlapping, marked and shaded in other tones. *Tropical. Zones 9-10.*   *p. 747*

tomentosa (India, Sri Lanka, China, Africa), "Bell-bauhinia" or "St. Thomas tree"; shrub 2-4 m with drooping branches, hairy except 3 cm leaves above and which are two-lobbed; flowers bell-shaped and pendant, lemon-yellow with 5 overlapping petals, one with purple splash at base. *Zones 9-10.*   *p. 747*

variegata; in horticulture sometimes as B. purpurea (India, China), the "Purple orchid tree" or "Mountain ebony"; small semi-deciduous tropical tree 4 to 8 m high, also grown as a shrub with multiple stems, with curious foliage; the thin-leathery leaves connate or cleft beyond the middle, 8-10 cm long, dull green; gorgeous 9 cm axillary flowers like a cattleya orchid, carmine-rose, the petals with dark purple center stripe, the broad lip lined with crimson, fan-like; blooming January to May. *Subtropic. Zone 10.*   p. 747

BEAUCARNEA   *Agavaceae (Liliaceae)*
gracilis (Nolina) (Tehuacán, Mexico), "Bottle palm" or "Pony tail"; curious, stout xerophytic tree to 10 m, with swollen base and branching; at apex each with a rosette of narrow, grayish-glaucous leaves ½ to 1 m long and 1 cm wide; clusters of small, off-white to reddish flowers. *Arid-tropical. Zone 10.*   p. 195
recurvata (Nolina) (Veracruz, Mexico), "Pony-tail"; tree-like plant with tall trunks to 10 m high, swollen at base, topped by a rosette of linear, pendulous, concave, green leaves to 2 m long, rough and thin-leathery, but not spiny-toothed; panicles of small whitish flowers. A succulent which can store a year-long water supply; related to Yuccas. *Arid-tropical. Zone 10.*   p. 69, 117
recurvata intermedia (Nolina) (S.E. Mexico, Yucatán), "Dwarf pony tail"; a more compact growing form of this curious species, with short, fissured trunk from swollen base, at home in the Maya region of the Mexican Southwest; the slender, glossy olive-green leaves gracefully arching and recurving and less than 1 m long; with age freely branching and terminally bearing huge, showy clusters of densely packed small white flowers; followed by 3-winged fruit capsules. The variety mostly planted in So. California. *Zone 10.*   p. 771
stricta (So. Mexico: Puebla, Oaxaca), "Izote" in Oaxaca; xerophytic tree, trunk with rough bark and swollen base, popularly known as "Elephant's-foot", slowly growing with age to 6 or 8 m high, topped by rosette of long linear, keeled, glaucous leathery and flexible leaves to 60 cm long, having yellowish margins; inflorescence in clusters of pale flowers. *Zone 11.*   p. 117

BEAUMONTIA   *Apocynaceae*
fragrans (murtonii) (Vietnam); "Trumpet flower"; scandent shrub with vining woody branches; large ovate, thick, brittle leaves 20 cm long, with sticky white sap; large white cupflowers with pointed lobes, very fragrant. *Tropical. Zones 10-11.*   p. 266
grandiflora (India: Himalayas), "Heralds-trumpet"; woody twiner or small tree with opposite, ovate leaves to 20 cm long, young shoots tinted rose and rusty-haired; large, fragrant, showy trumpet-shaped 12 cm flowers with 5 twisted lobes, white, with dark throat, in terminal cymes. *Subtropic. Zone 10.*   p. 264

BEFARIA   *Ericaceae*
glauca (Bejaria) (Mountains of Venezuela, Colombia), "Rose of the Andes"; handsome evergreen shrub 1 to 2 m high, from 2000 to 3000 m elevation; the branches angled, and crowded with leathery, oblong leaves 4-6 cm long, gray-green beneath; flowers of 6-7 spreading petals, salmon-rose with purple sheen, and long protruding pistil. *Zone 9.*   p. 701
racemosa (Florida, Cuba, Mexico to So. America), "Tarflower" or "Fly-catcher"; interesting evergreen shrub to 2 m high, with leathery elliptic leaves 5 cm long; showy slightly fragrant flowers 5 cm across, having wide-spreading oblanceolate white petals tipped with pink, giving the blooms a spidery look; the buds and calyxes are sticky and catch flies. *Zone 10.*   p. 701

BEGONIA   *Begoniaceae*
x cheimantha 'Dark Lady Mac', "Dark Christmas begonia"; a desirable color form, and welcome variant of the old-reliable 'Lady Mac'; bushy plant with the rounded, satiny foliage overcast with burnt copper; the 4 cm flowers a deep carmine-rose, forming a large bouquet during early Winter. *Tropical. Zone 12.*   p. 40
x cheimantha 'Lady Mac', a popular "Christmas begonia"; the bushy plant covered in Winter with masses of clear pink and smallish but long-lasting flowers; popularly called "Busy Lizzie". B. x cheimantha is an old hybrid group of socotrana x dregei introduced in France 1891 as 'Glorie de Lorraine'. *Humid-tropical. Zone 12.* p. 40
x cheimantha 'Marina', "Scandinavian winter begonia"; Danish sport of Solbakken, with deep rose, durable flowers larger than 'Solfheim' but not quite as dark, and contrasting nicely with the yellow anthers; of medium growth habit with rich green, medium leaves; flowers October on to December and later. *Humid-tropical. Zone 12.*   p. 40
chlorosticta ('Kew species') (Sarawak); handsome fibrous cane begonia of Borneo; with angelwing, oblique ovate leaves sea-green, covered with silvery or light green markings; flowers pink. *Humid-tropical. Zone 12.*   p. 37

'Christmas Candy' ('Firebird') (B. semperflorens x Argentine sp.); very showy floriferous cane begonia, similar to B. coccinea, photographed in a hanging basket in Vista, California; slender stems arching by the weight of waxy, oblique ovate leaves 10-12 cm long, glossy green; pendulous clusters of semi-double flowers salmon-rose. *Zone 11.*   p. 37
'Cleopatra' (Maphil x Black Beauty), "Mapleleaf begonia"; lovely hybrid distinguished by its translucent maple-leaf nile-green with chocolate-red areas toward margin; rhizomatous; clusters of perfumed pink flowers. *Tropical. Zone 12.*   p. 40
coccinea (rubra) (Orgaos-Brazil), "Angelwing begonia"; tall, bamboo-like canestem to 4 m high with thick ovate leaves glossy green spotted silver, and edged red; drooping clusters of coral-red flowers blooming constantly. *Tropical. Zone 11.*   p. 37
conchifolia rubrimacula (Costa Rica), "Zip begonia"; miniature rhizomatous species, with petioles brown-fuzzy; waxy green, rounded, cupped peltate leaves, having red sinus spot in center; the margins slightly scalloped; veins brownish beneath; clusters of small whitish flowers. *Tropical. Zone 11.*   p. 37
decora (Assam, Vietnam, Malaya); lovely little plant with a creeping, hairy rhizome and oblique-ovate, plushy-brown leaves sharply etched with chartreuse veins, underside red with green veins, edges finely toothed; large rose-pink flowers borne high over foliage. *Tropical. Zone 12.*   p. 39
x erythrophylla 'Bunchii', "Curly kidney-begonia"; rhizomatous, decorative mutant, with the fleshy leaves lighter green, red-tinged, and ruffled and crested at the margins, the lobes rise and meet. *Subtropic. Zone 11.*   p. 40
evansiana; see B. grandis
'Exotica' hort. (brevirimosa at Kew Gardens) (Baiyer River, New Guinea); magnificent, fibrous-rooted begonia with erect, reddish canes and large, oblique-ovate, corrugated leaves of shiny, iridescent taffeta in crimson on deep green, pale green beneath, both sides sparsely covered with short, red bristles, margins densely and irregularly toothed; red hairs on petioles and brown hairs on stems. Semi-dormant in Winter. *Tropical. Zone 12.*   p. 39
floccifera (India); small clustered, rhizomatous plant with thick oval leaves 8 cm or more across, dark green; covered with yellowish hair when young; flowers white. *Tropical. Zone 11.*   p. 42
foliosa var. miniata (fuchsioides of hort.) (Mexico), "Fuchsia begonia"; fibrous-rooted plant with slender arching stems 60-90 cm high, very small oblique-ovate toothed leaves to 4 cm long, waxy dark green; nodding fuchsia-like red flowers. *Tropical. Zone 10.*   p. 42
goegoensis (Sumatra), "Fire-king begonia"; low growing gem on creeping rhizome, silky leaves round peltate, puckered, dark olive-green with lighter veins, reddish beneath; pink flowers. *Humid-tropical. Zone 12.*   p. 41
grandis (evansiana) (China, Japan), "Hardy begonia"; tuberous species, with bulbils forming in leaf axils; stands some frost; on erect stems 30-60 cm high, the olive green, ovate leaves veined purple beneath; 3-4 cm flowers pink. Winter-hardy in parts of Canada. *Warm temperate. Zone 7.*   p. 38, 220, 344
haageana: see B. scharffii
hemsleyana (China); a distinctive rhizomatous species with medium green, palmately compound dentate leaves; thinnish rhizomes somewhat erect; rose-pink flowers during Summer. *Zone 11.*   p. 38
heracleifolia nigricans (Mexico), "Star begonia"; handsome, rhizomatous plant smaller than sunderbruchii, the palmately lobed leaves blackish-green with contrasting pale green area along main veins. *Tropical. Zone 11.*   p. 40
x hiemalis 'Rieger's Yellow'; winter-flowering Elatior begonia with large single blooms in soft yellow with salmon sheen. May be planted outdoors during Summer, with sufficient moisture and light shade, blooming naturally in Autumn. *Zone 10.*   p. 41
x hiemalis 'Rieger's Schwabenland' (1964 Pat.); robust plant with pointed, oblique leaves metallic deep green, and large, glowing scarlet flowers to 5 cm dia., with contrasting yellow stamens. The new German Rieger "Elatior" strain is distinguished by its bushy, free-growing and floriferous habit, with flowers in vivid new colors of superior keeping quality, blooming for 8-10 weeks even in the home, normally in Fall-Winter. *Humid-subtropic. Zone 10.*   p. 41
incana hort.: see B. peltata
limmingheiana (glaucophylla) (Brazil), "Shrimp begonia"; trailing with slender stems; glossy light green leaves with wavy margin, 8-12 cm long; coral-red flowers; good for baskets. *Tropical. Zone 11.*   p. 42, 309
longimaculata (Perú); attractive small fibrous species 15-25 cm high, found by J. Bogner of Munich Bot. Garden; with arching reddish branches; on short petioles the oblique lanceolate leaves 8-11 cm long

to 3 cm wide, the upper surface shiny reddish olive-green with elongate silvery markings between the primary veins, wine-red beneath; flowers whitish with yellow anthers. *Zone 12.* p. 37

manicata 'Aureo-maculata', "Leopard begonia"; robust plant with stout, ascending rhizome; the large waxy, fleshy green leaves are 10 to 20 cm long, smooth and toothed, and blotched yellow or ivory, and occasionally rose-red; reddish beneath; characteristic collar of red bristles at top of leaf stalk; flowers pink. The species is from Mexico. *Tropical. Zone 11.* p. 38

x margaritae (echinosepala x metallica); bushy fibrous plant with soft-hairy, small, ovate-pointed and toothed, quilted leaves, faded bronze green, veins purple beneath; flowers bearded pink. *Tropical. Zone 11.* p. 38

masoniana (Indochina or China, introduced from Singapore), the "Iron cross begonia"; one of the most beautiful begonias in cultivation, spectacular rhizomatous plant of robust habit, with white-hairy, reddish stems and large roundish, firm, puckered leaves nile-green, marked with contrasting, bold pattern of brown-red, the older leaves overlaid with silver, and covered with bristly red hair and red-ciliate, 15-18 cm across; waxy flowers greenish-white with maroon bristles on back; flowering March-May. *Tropical. Zone 12.* p. 41

metallica (Bahia), "Metallic-leaf begonia"; bushy, fibrous-rooted, hairy plant with broad-ovate pointed leaves metallic olive-green and depressed purple veins, red-veined beneath; showy pink hirsute flowers. *Tropical. Zone 11.* p. 38

olsoniae (vellozoana hort.) (Brazil); lush, low, rhizomatous species, with large fleshy leaves in changeable colors bronze to green, contrasting with striking ivory veins; flowers whitish, outer edge sometimes rosy. *Tropical. Zone 11.* p. 39

'Orange-rubra' (dichroa x Coral rubra); cane-stemmed; large leaves obliquely ovate, of the angelwing type, smooth green, silver spotted when young; lacquered orange-red flowers. *Tropical. Zone 11.* p. 38

paulensis (Brazil); large orbicular, peltate, hairy, quilted leaves waxy, fresh-green with pale veins which are red beneath; rhizomatous; bright red, bearded flowers. *Tropical. Zone 11.* p. 39

peltata (incana hort.) (Mexico); thick-stemmed plant woolly white with scurf; fleshy peltate, white-tomentose leaves; drooping white flowers. *Zone 10.* p. 38

platanifolia (Brazil); shrubby plant 30-50 cm high, with near-woody stems, and large, deeply lobed and incised leaves, waxy rich green with occasional pale marbling, 20 cm long, somewhat hairy beneath on the red veins; numerous small white flowers. *Subtropic. Zone 10.* p. 42

rajah (Malaya); charming, dwarf, rhizomatous species with reniform roundish, rich reddish-green, bullate, silky leaves and contrasting veins of yellow-green; under surface dull red; flowers pink. *Humid-tropical. Zone 12.* p. 40

rex 'Comtesse Louise Erdoedy' (rex Alex. von Humboldt x argenteo-cupreata); first spiralled form (1883), known as "Corkscrew begonia"; large oblique-ovate, red hairy leaves light olive-green zoned with silvery rose; one or both basal lobes spirally curled. *Tropical. Zone 11.* p. 39

rex 'Curly Fireflush', "Spiral begonia"; a beautiful curly, erect mutant with the same striking red velvet leaves as 'Fireflush', the basal lobe twisted into a spiral. *Humid-tropical. Zone 12.* p. 39

rex 'Helen Teupel'; diadema hybrid; bushy plant with long leaves sharply lobed, center and margin dark fuchsia-red, metallic green along veins, silvery pink areas between. Probably the best of the lacy diadema hybrids. *Tropical. Zone 11.* p. 40

rex 'His Majesty' (English hybrid 1903); long-pointed and lightly notched leaves maroon with a broad silver zone, overlaid with pinkish-purple. *Tropical. Zone 12.* p. 40

rex 'Princess of Hannover'; smoky velvet, pea green leaves with broad silver zone and a double spiral at the base; the entire surface covered with tiny pink hair. *Zone 11.* p. 39

rex 'Yuletide'; spectacularly colored leaf with reddish-black center, a well defined middle zone vivid ruby-red, outer zone with spots of red, forest green and silver, leaf edge blackish; to 20 cm long. *Tropical. Zone 11.* p. 40

x richmondensis; (fuchsioides x semperflorens seedling); floriferous, fibrous-rooted plant with red stem and medium oblique-ovate, waxy green leaves with bronzy overtone and dentate edge, reddish beneath, 8 to 10 cm long; flowers dainty pink. *Tropical. Zone 11.* p. 42

rufosericea (Brazil); strong, shrubby species, with elliptic gray-green leaves 15 cm long, dentate at margins, and thickly covered with red hairs; flowers pink with red hairs. *Zone 12.* p. 42

scharffiana (Brazil); compact, spreading, densely white-hairy, fibrous-rooted species with red stems; broad ovate leaves, olive-green, red beneath; pale pink hirsute flowers. Of smaller habit than scharffii. *Subtropic. Zone 10.* p. 42

scharffii (haageana) (Brazil), "Elephant-ear begonia"; lovely, rugged, white-hairy plant with fibrous roots, and big 25 cm ovate leaves larger than scharffiana, brownish yellow-green with red veins, and red beneath; large pinkish flowers with beards (hirsute) in clusters. Parent of many velvety beauties. *Subtropic. Zone 10.* p. 42

schmidtiana (Brazil); miniature fibrous-rooted begonia with reddish, hairy stems and oblique, heart-shaped, olive-green, hairy, toothed leaves, beneath reddish with green margin; hirsute flowers in pale pink. *Tropical. Zone 12.* p. 42

x sementacea hort. (Brazil); compact rhizomatous plant; distinctive foliage iridescent grayish-green with a network of silver veins; flowers white, flushed pink. *Zone 11.* p. 39

semperflorens (cucullata hookeri), "Wax begonia"; fibrous-rooted perennial originally from Brazil, but the derivatives in cultivation are grouped under B. x semperflorens cultorum, or "Wax begonias"; fibrous-rooted, glabrous and more or less succulent plants with fleshy, oval leaves, and usually rose-red flowers in axillary clusters. Very popular as summer bedding plants; grown as an annual in colder climates. *Subtropic. Zone 10.* p. 344, 613

semperflorens 'Fiesta'; green-leaved, strong-growing wax begonia with many large scarlet-red flowers set in center with a yellow, double stamen cluster like a tuft of gold. *Zone 10.* p. 40

semperflorens fl. pl. 'Lady Frances', (originally 'Lucy Lockett'), "Rose begonia"; endearing and enduring plant, popular in Milwaukee, with waxy, mahogany-red leaves and a profusion of ruffly camellia-type flowers fully double bright pink, with white ovary but without prominent back petals, in constant bloom. *Subtropic. Zone 10.* p. 40

semperflorens 'Luminosa'; compact variety with flowers soft scarlet, and light green waxy leaves with ciliate red border, turning deep red-brown if grown in full sun. *Subtropic. Zone 10.* p. 40

semperflorens 'Susie'; red-leaved "Wax begonia"; shapely fibrous begonia seen in Frankfurt Bot. Garden, Germany, with leaves a glowing deep bronze-red, and contrasting large rose-pink flowers. *Zone 10.* p. 344

sutherlandii (Natal); slender tuberous plant with drooping branches; lance-shaped, serrate, crisped leaves bright green with red veins; flowers orange. *Subtropic. Zone 9.* p. 38

thelmae (Brazil); scandent trailing species long known as 'Brazil species'; small roundish or oblique-oval somewhat cupped leaves olive-green with pale ribs, margins brown shaggy and lightly crenate, reddish beneath; flowers white. *Zone 11.* p. 38

'Tom Ment'; large angelwing begonia with waxy, oblique-ovate leaves, dark olive-green and blotched with silver; flowers pinkish-white and rose. *Tropical. Zone 11.* p. 41

x tuberhybrida, or "Tuberous begonia"; sturdy hybrids of Andean species, with watery stems and brittle, pointed leaves; large, single and double, waxy flowers, white, yellow, orange or red, during Summer; the male flowers 8-15 cm across. *Humid-subtropic. Zone 10.* p. 249

x tuberhybrida multiflora 'Maxima', "Dwarf tuberous begonia"; strain developed by crossing the large camellia-flowered type with multiflora; compact plants with rigid stems and dark foliage, covered with many medium-sized double blooms, red, rose, yellow, white, 5 to 6 cm dia. Ideal for bedding. *Humid-subtropic. Zone 10.* p. 41

tuberhybrida pendula plena ('Lloydii'), the "Basket begonia"; drooping stems with narrow leaves, and numerous small double pendulous flowers produced from a single tuber; red, rose, salmon, white, yellow; derives its pendant habit from B. boliviensis. *Humid-subtropic. Zone 10.* p. 41, 220

tuberhybrida 'Rubro-marginata'; magnificent color combination of fully double flowers 12 cm across, white edged or variegated with crimson-red. *Humid-subtropic. Zone 10.* p. 220

x tuberhybrida 'Triumph' (Rosebud); double flowers white in center, and margins red 8 to 10 cm dia. *Humid-subtropic. Zone 10.* p. 41

vareschii (Venezuela); attractive suberect, fibrous-rooted plant with green stems and red internodes 2 cm apart; leaves oblique-lanceolate 5 to 7 cm long, crenate along margins, upper surface green with silvery-cream veins, light green beneath; flowers white. *Tropical. Zone 12.* p. 42

BELAMCANDA *Iridaceae*
chinensis (China), "Leopard flower"; rhizomatous perennial about 1 m high, with flat leaves arranged fan-like; branching wiry stalks bear graceful sprays of beautiful flowers 5-6 cm across, orange-yellow, spotted crimson. *Warm temperate. Zones 5-9.* p. 425

BELLIS *Compositae*
perennis (W. Europe, Asia Minor), "English daisy" or "Common daisy"; low perennial rosette, with obovate 3-6 cm leaves flat on the ground; very pretty, small 2 cm flowers with usually white rays around the bright yellow, female disc, blooming May-June. *Zone 3.* p. 373

perennis florepleno (W. Europe, Asia Minor), "English daisy"; low perennial with obovate fleshy leaves in tufts; the short flower heads 3 cm across, with several layers of white to rosy florets. Temperate. Zone 3. *p. 373*

BELOPERONE   Acanthaceae

guttata (Justicia brandegeana Hortus 3) (Mexico), "Shrimp plant"; wiry stems with ovate, hairy leaves; white flowers beneath showy, overlapping, reddish-brown bracts, in drooping terminal spikes. Zone 11. *p. 630*

guttata lutea; attractive variety also known as "Golden Queen" or "False hops"; herbaceous bush, shrubby with age, to 1 m high; the branches thin, with softly hairy ovate leaves to 8 cm long; flowers in terminal, arching spikes to 15 cm long, the shingled bracts greenish-yellow; and white corolla deeply two-lipped. Zone 11. *p. 630*

BELVISIA   Polypodiaceae (Filices)

platyrhynchon (Philippines); rosette of erect glaucous, oblanceolate leaves 50-65 cm long, 4 cm wide, the spore masses located toward apex on underside. Zone 11. *p. 130*

BERBERIDOPSIS   Flacourtiaceae

corallina (Chile), "Coral Chile vine"; low evergreen, scrambling shrub with long cordate, smooth, toothed leaves to 8 cm long; tubular crimson flowers in pendant clusters, followed by small berries. Zone 10. *p. 731*

BERBERIS   Berberidaceae

amurensis (Siberia, Manchuria), "Manchurian barberry"; deciduous shrub to 2 m or more high, densely branched with angled shoots, covered by 3-parted spines; obovate leaves 6 cm long, toothed at margins; yellow flowers in showy pendulous racemes 10-25 cm long, followed by red fruit. Zone 2. *p. 654*

darwinii (Chile, Argentina), "Darwin's barberry"; evergreen shrub to 2 m high, with stems dark brown and covered by 3 to 5-parted spines; small 2 cm rigid, oblong leaves having 2 or 3 coarse teeth each side, lustrous dark green above, paler beneath; flowers orange-yellow to red in pendulous racemes of 10 to 30 blossoms; blue glaucous black fruit. Zone 7. *p. 654*

empetrifolia (Cordilleras of So. Chile to Patagonia); small evergreen alpine shrub 20-30 cm high, with red-brown branches; dark green linear 2-3 cm leaves spiny at apex, and margins rolled under; axillary flowers with tubular corolla and spreading limb golden-yellow, followed by black berry-like fruit. Zone 5. *p. 654*

julianae (China: Hupeh); popular Chinese evergreen of vigorous dense habit, to 2 m high, having yellow branches covered by stout 3-parted spines; obovate 8 cm leaves lustrous green above, and with numerous spiny teeth along sides; clusters of yellow flowers, followed by oblong black fruit, covered with heavy waxy white bloom. Zone 5. *p. 654*

koreana (Korea), "Korean barberry"; deciduous shrub to 1½ m high; dark red branches covered with 3 to 7-parted spines; oval or ovate dull green leaves 4-7 cm long, and edged by numerous spiny teeth; the foliage turning deep red in Autumn; glossy red obovoid fruit in beautiful pendant clusters. An excellent barrier plant. Zone 5. *p. 654*

linearifolia (Chilean Andes); dense evergreen shrub to 1 m or more high, with mature branches yellow, deeply grooved and partially spiny; obovate leaves 3 cm long, glaucous gray beneath; flowers orange or crimson, followed by ovoid blue-black fruit. Most beautiful when in profuse bloom. Zone 7. *p. 654*

x mentorensis (julianae x thunbergii), "Mentor barberry"; (Wayside Gardens, Ohio 1924); very decorative shrub, similar to but more upright than B. thunbergii, to 2 m high, evergreen except in coldest regions; the angled branches are brown and smooth; elliptic leaves 2-4 cm long, with occasional spines along sides; flowers yellow, followed by dull dark red ellipsoid fruit. Very spectacular with scarlet foliage in autumn coloring. Zone 5. *p. 655*

x notabilis (heteropoda x vulgaris); deciduous tall-growing shrub with furrowed branches, and obovate ovate finely toothed leaves; very floriferous with small bright yellow flowers, in elongate clusters; dark red, glaucous fruit. Zone 6. *p. 655*

pinnata: see MAHONIA pinnata

x stenophylla (darwinii x empetrifolia) (England 1860), "Rosemary barberry"; tall evergreen shrub to 3 m high, with gracefully arching thin branches; small 2 cm narrow-elliptic, dark green leaves tipped by short spine; golden-yellow flowers in small clusters in May, followed by blue-black berries. Beautiful hybrid, useful for a clipped hedge. Zone 5. *p. 655*

thunbergii (Japan), "Japanese barberry"; vigorous deciduous shrub of dense, compact growth to 1½ m high, with branches dark red and spiny; rhomboid-ovate fresh green leaves 2 cm long, glaucous

gray beneath; very floriferous with flowers yellow inside, reddish outside; elliptic fruit bright shining red. Beautiful with autumn foliage, widely planted as a very thorny yet handsome hedge. Zone 4. *p. 655*

thunbergii 'Atropurpurea', "Purple Japan barberry"; beautiful cultivar with leaves purplish to bronzy-red, changing in late Autumn to vivid carmine; an ideal and very handsome hedge plant. Zone 4. *p. 614, 655*

thunbergii 'Crimson Pigmy' (atropurpurea nana), a miniature form of the "Japanese barberry" from Japan; spiny shrub, deciduous in cold areas, to 40 cm high and 70 cm wide, with slender arching, spiny branches dense with roundish leaves 2-3 cm long, when mature bronzy blood-red, new leaves bright red when grown in sun; bead-like bright red berries along the branches in Autumn. Zone 4. *p. 621*

verruculosa (Mahonia) (China), "Warty barberry"; evergreen shrub to 1 m or more high, with yellow, warty branches covered by fine hairs; obovate-elliptic leaves 2 cm long, lustrous green above, usually white beneath, and with 2-4 short spinelets along each side; solitary 2 cm yellow flowers followed by ovoid blue-glaucous black fruit. Attractive with its arching branches and bronzy autumn foliage. Zone 6. *p. 655*

vulgaris (Scandinavia to S.E. Europe, Asia Minor), "European barberry" or "Common barberry"; deciduous shrub of upright habit, with yellow arching, spiny branches, to 2 m high; obovate leaves to 6 cm long, dull green to purple above, and numerous teeth along margins; pendulous clusters of small yellow flowers, followed by ovoid vivid red berries. Widely planted, especially in Europe, but unfortunately subject to rust. Beautiful in scarlet autumn colors. The gardeners of colonial times made jellies and drinks from the edible fruits. Zone 3. *p. 655*

vulgaris 'Atropurpurea', "Redleaf barberry"; strikingly beautiful color variation with dense, nearly shingled deciduous foliage vivid crimson to red-purple; very common in gardens. Zone 3. *p. 655*

BERCHEMIA   Rhamnaceae

racemosa (Japan and Taiwan), "Rattan vine" or "Japanese supplejack"; twining deciduous shrub, with alternate, ovate leaves to 6 cm long, having conspicuous parallel veins; greenish-white flowers in 15 cm panicles, followed by 1 cm red fruit, maturing black. Zone 6. *p. 320*

BERGENIA   Saxifragaceae

cordifolia (obcordata) (Siberia), "Heartleaf bergenia"; stout herb with thick rootstock, forming clumps, with roundish heart-shaped soft-leathery, shining grass green leaves, veins lighter, to 30 cm across, margins slightly crenate but not hairy, base cordate, petiole channeled; flowers clear rose in dense nodding cymes partly hidden between the foliage. Zones 2-9. *p. 497*

crassifolia (Siberia, Mongolia), "Winter begonia" or "Siberian tea"; ornamental perennial herb more or less evergreen with thick, woody rootstock, and large fleshy obovate leaves to 20 cm long, shining green and with the blade extending down the leafstalk; flowers rose-pink or lilac, with purple eye, in clusters above the foliage in Spring. Popular in California where it blooms January-February. Zones 3-10. *p. 497*

purpurascens (Himalayas to W. China, Burma), "Himalaya bergenia"; perennial herb with large fleshy, broad oval leaves to 25 cm long, glossy green with depressed yellow ribs, and suffused with purple; carmine-red nodding flowers 2-3 cm across, blooming in Spring. Zone 6. *p. 497*

BERTHOLLETIA   Lecythidaceae

excelsa (Amazonian South America), "Brazil nut"; tropical evergreen tree to 30 m high, with oblong leathery leaves to 50 cm long, wavy along margins; small cream-white to yellow flowers in spike-like racemes, the corolla with six petals and a hooded mass of stamens; the globose cannon-ball like, thick-shelled fruit is 12 cm dia., holding 12-24 seeds packed like orange segments, and known as the Brazilnut. After the fruit has fallen, it is sliced open with a machete. Zone 10. *p. 915*

BERTOLONIA   Melastomataceae

marmorata (Ecuador); beautiful herbaceous plant with quilted ovate leaves velvety moss-green, painted silvery-white along the parallel veins, purple beneath; purple flowers. Tropical. Zone 12. *p. 76*

pubescens hort.: see TRIOLENA pustulata (Hortus, Zander)

BETONICA macrantha: see STACHYS grandiflora

BETA   Chenopodiaceae

vulgaris cicala (dracaenifolia) (Atlantic coast of Europe, Mediterr. reg. to Russia), "Swiss chard" or "Leaf-beet"; ornamental of the Cicla group, which does not develop swollen rootbase or beet; biennial or annual 50 cm or more high, with large herbaceous puckered leaves to 40 cm long, green in the species used as kitchen vegetable, but with contrasting blood-red midrib and stout crimson petioles in the var. cicala; flowers greenish. *Zone 9*.   *p. 367*

BETULA   *Betulaceae*
alba in hort.: see B. pendula or papyrifera

albo-sinensis (Cent. and W. China), "Chinese paper birch"; ornamental tree to 30 m high, interesting because of its unique bright orange to orange-red bark peeling off in sections; ovate leaves 5-8 cm long, yellowish-green above, and jaggedly toothed at margins; female catkins 3-4 cm long. *Zone 5*.   *p. 658*

alleghaniensis (Newfoundland, so. to Georgia and Tennessee), "Yellow birch"; a tree of moist woodlands, to 30 m high, with yellowish-gray to red-brown bark, flaking off in thin strips; ovate leaves 12 cm long, serrate at margins and with 9-11 pairs of sunken veins; oblong fruit cones 2-3 cm long. Foliage turns yellow in Autumn. A valuable timber tree. *Zone 3*.   *p. 658*

ermanii (N.E. Asia, Korea and Japan), "Gold birch"; tree 18-25 m high, with orange-brown bark on young branches, changing to grayish-white when older and flaking; the warty shoots with triangular-ovate leaves to 10 cm long, light green beneath and toothed at margins; female cones 3 cm long. *Zone 4*.   *p. 658*

lenta (Maine to Alabama), "Cherry birch" or "Sweet birch"; tree to 25 m high, with bark nearly black, not peeling but in old trees fissured into thick plates; the shoots at first silvery hairy but soon smooth; leaves ovate and slender pointed, 5-12 cm long. The young twigs and bark are aromatic, and the chief source of oil of Wintergreen. *Zone 3*.   *p. 658*

maximowicziana (Japan to Kuriles), "Monarch birch"; vigorous tree to 30 m high, with grey-white to orange thinly-flaking bark, loosely branched with warty red-brown shoots; leaves linden-like very broad and 8-15 cm long, the base cordate; the surface corrugated with sunken veins in 10-12 pairs, sharply toothed at margins; male catkins drooping, 10-12 cm long: female cones 5-6 cm, nutlet with brown wings. Largest leaves of all birches, beautiful in golden-yellow autumn color. *Zone 2*.   *p. 661*

nana (No. Asia, No. Europe, Alaska), "Arctic dwarf birch" or "Polar birch"; miniature prostrate shrub only 20-50 cm high, the woody branches spreading laterally; roundish leaves 10-15 mm dia., crenate at margins, glossy green above, coloring yellow to red in Autumn; female catkins erect. Inhabiting wet places, and seen on Spitzbergen above the Arctic Circle growing under melting snow. Suitable for rockgardens. *Zone 1*.   *p. 661*

nigra (Massachusetts to Florida and Kansas), "Black birch" or "River birch"; graceful pyramidal tree to 30 m high, with reddish-brown bark peeling off in papery flakes; typically found along stream beds; leaves broad ovate or rhombic to 8 cm long, whitish beneath; cylindric female catkins 3-4 cm long. *Zone 4*.   *p. 658*

papyrifera (alba) (Labrador to Minnesota), "Canoe birch" or "Cluster birch"; the most wide-spread native birch in North America; tall tree to 30 m high; slender trunks with bark a vivid warm white, flaking and papery; ovate leaves to 10 cm long, coarsely serrate; male catkins to 10 cm long. Usually forming multistem clusters. *Zone 2*.   *p. 659, 660*

papyrifera fa. grandis, "Paper-bark birch"; large tree becoming to 40 m tall with massive trunk to 1 m dia.; most conspicuous white birch, the bark chalk-white peeling in thin papery flakes, typically dividing into numerous straight erect branches some 3 to 4 m up the main stem, into open spreading crown; the deciduous foliage also more robust and larger than the species; truly a magnificent specimen, as seen in col. Munich Bot. Garden. *Zone 2*.   *p. 659*

pendula (verrucosa or alba hort.) (Europe and Asia Minor), "European birch" or "White birch"; stately deciduous tree to 20 m tall; bark white and flaking off in layers; branches usually pendulous; leaves angular-ovate to 6 cm long; tiny flowers in catkins. As grown by nurseries often sold in cluster-form. *Zone 2*.   *p. 660*

pendula 'Dalecarlica' (So. Sweden), "Silver birch" or "Cutleaf white birch"; deciduous tree with weeping branches; lively-green leaves deeply lobed and cut into narrow, pointed segments. *Zone 3*.   *p. 660*

pendula 'Gracilis' ('Laciniata'), "Cut-leaf European birch"; very elegant tree, especially where planted solitary and for accent; generally of pyramidal habit but with ultimate branch ends gracefully arching and pendulous; the leaves lacily dissected and fern-like. *Zone 3*.   *p. 659, 660*

pendula 'Purpurea' (verrucosa 'Purpurea'), "Purple European birch"; handsome deciduous tree with glistening white trunk, interrupted by occasional black rings; the branches are pendulous with small serrate 4 cm broad ovate leaves, lustrous, vivid purple turning bronzy in Autumn, and creating a lovely contrast with the snowy bark. *Zone 2*.   *p. 660*

pendula 'Tristis' (verrucosa tristis), "Slender European birch" or "Weeping birch"; elegant columnar tree with branches opening wide and arching, except for the always erect central shoot; terminal branchlets pendant, closely set small ovate-pointed leaflets 4 cm long and toothed along margins, fluttering in the breeze from threadlike petioles as so many little ferns. *Zone 2*.   *p. 660*

pendula 'Youngii', "Young's weeping birch"; dome-shaped form of irregular habit, having branches extremely pendulous from the upper part of the crown, and without a leader; the branchlets very thin and threadlike, the leaves wedge-shaped, long-pointed and doubly serrate. Usually grafted near apex, handsome as a solitary garden subject. *Zone 3*.   *p. 661*

platyphylla var. japonica (Japan, No. China), "Japanese white birch"; attractive tree to 18 m high, forming clusters of straight trunks, covered with ruffled white bark, the branches warty; leaves triangular and slender-pointed 4-7 cm long, and finely toothed at margins; fruit-catkins 5 cm long. *Zone 5*.   *p. 661*

populifolia (Nova Scotia to Delaware), "Gray birch"; small graceful tree to 9 m with chalky gray-white trunk and narrow crown; leaves glossy green on both sides, triangular-ovate to 8 cm long; male catkins 5-8 cm. *Zone 4*.   *p. 659, 661*

populifolia 'Pendula', "Weeping Grey birch"; small graceful tree to 10 m high, with chalk-white to grayish bark, developing an open roundish crown; the branch-ends arching to pendulous, with triangular-pointed glossy leaves 7-10 cm long, some with cordate base, lobed and toothed along margins; female catkins 2-3 cm long. *Zone 4*.   *p. 661*

pubescens (Europe to Siberia), "English white birch"; deciduous tree to 15 m high, having attractive white bark, eventually peeling, with age becoming rugged and dark at base; the branchlets pendant and soft-hairy, with ovate leaves 4 to 5 cm long, coarsely toothed along margins; cones cylindrical. Similar to B. pendula, but without warts on the shoots. *Zone 3*.   *p. 661*

pumila (E. No. America to Montana and Brit. Columbia), "American Swamp birch"; deciduous shrub 1 m or more high, with felty brown shoots; small rounded leaves 2-3 cm across, the margins sharply toothed, downy on both surfaces especially while young; female cones to 25 mm long; inhabiting wet places. *Zone 3*.   *p. 661*

raddeana (Caucasus); small tree or shrub with silvery grey bark, the shoots covered by velvety down, the leaves broadly ovate and 5 cm long, hairy on veins; female catkins 2-3 cm long, the lobes of scales erect. *Zone 5*.   *p. 658*

BIARUM   *Araceae*
tenuifolium (abbreviatum) (So. Europe, Mediterranean); from an oblong-cylindric tuber 3 cm long, rise linear-lanceolate to spoon-shaped, entire leaves, appearing after the inflorescence; cylindrical spathe tube pale, the lanceolate blade extending the spathe 15-25 cm long, dark purple inside; the spadix long and very slender lengthening into a pendant appendix. *Zone 9*.   *p. 24*

BIDENS   *Compositae*
aristosa (Eastern U.S.: New Jersey to Virginia and Texas), "Bearded Beggar-ticks" or "Bur marigold"; herbaceous perennial or annual, densely branched and from 25 cm to more than 1 m high; 15 cm leaves pinnately divided into narrow segments; golden-yellow flowers with ray-florets 2 cm long, blooming late Summer-Autumn. *Zone 4*.   *p. 374*

ferulifolia (So. Arizona and Mexico), "Fern-leaved beggar-ticks"; annual or biennial herb about 50 cm high, the thin branches with leaves 5-15 cm long, bipinnately divided into linear segments; floral clusters of small 2 cm, bright yellow flowers, in Autumn. *Zone 9*.   *p. 374*

BIFRENARIA   *Orchidaceae*
harrisoniae (Brazil); sturdy epiphyte; 4-angled pseudolbulbs with a solitary leathery leaf; large fleshy, 8 cm flowers, the sepals and petals yellowish, tinged with red, the lip violet-red with yellow hairy callus, (March-May). *Subtropic. Zone 11*.   *p. 82*

BIGNONIA   *Bignoniaceae*
capreolata (Virginia, Florida, Louisiana), "Crossvine" or "Trumpet flower"; evergreen climbing shrub to 15 m with leaves of 2 ovate leaflets, each to 15 cm long; funnel-form flowers 5 cm across, yellow and brown-red, the flaring limb golden yellow, anthers cream with reddish line on each. *Warm temperate. Zone 7*.   *p. 266*
cherere: see DISTICTIS buccinatoria
ignea: see PYROSTEGIA venusta
jasminoides:see PANDOREA jasminoides
violacea hort.: see CLYTOSTOMA callistegioides

BIGNONIA   see also ANEMOPAEGMA, CAMPSIS, CLYTOSTOMA, CYDISTA, DISTICTIS, PANDOREA, PYROSTEGIA, SARITAEA, TABEBUIA, TECOMA, TECOMARIA

BILLARDIERA   *Pittosporaceae*
longiflora (Australia: Tasmania, Victoria, N.S. Wales), "Purple apple-berry"; interesting small evergreen shrub with twining branches, bearing narrow leathery green leaves to 5 cm long; the greenish-yellow, blue-tipped 2-4 cm bell-flowers are suspended singly from the slender branches in Spring; later the oblong purple 2 cm berries adorn the plant during Summer. *Zones 9-10.*   p. 290

BILLBERGIA   *Bromeliaceae*
forgetii hort.: see AECHMEA caudata variegata
nutans (So. Brazil, Uruguay, Argentina), "Queen's tears" or "Indoor oats"; slender rosette of narrow, silvery bronze foliage, forming clusters. An arching flowerstalk bears the nodding inflorescence of rosy bracts and green flowers edged violet—a teardrop forming on the stigma. Very tolerant. *Subtropic. Zone 10.*   p. 44
pyramidalis concolor (thyrsoidea) (Brazil), "Summer torch"; rosette shaped like a birdsnest, broad, glossy, apple-green leaves; showy but short-lived inflorescence, stem mealy-white, and head of large red bracts and crimson-red flowers tipped purplish, with blue stigma. *Tropical. Zone 10.*   p. 46
rhodocyanea: see AECHMEA fasciata
venezuelana (Venezuela), "Giant urn plant"; bold tubular plant with attractive coppery leaves marked with pronounced crossbands of silver; margins toothed; inflorescence with rosy bracts, sepals white farinose, and petals yellow-green. *Zone 10.*   p. 46

BIOTA orientalis: see THUJA orientalis

BISCHOFIA   *Euphorbiaceae*
javanica (trifoliata) (Trop. Asia: Java), "Toog tree"; dioecious ornamental evergreen tree to 25 m high, somewhat deciduous, with large alternate compound leaves of 3 ovate, fleshy leaflets deep green to bronzy, minutely toothed; small greenish flowers without petals, and reddish pea-size fruit on female trees, ripening the following year. *Zone 10.*   p. 720

BISMARCKIA   *Palmae*
nobilis (Madagascar); majestic, dioecious fan-palm with great trunks to 60 m high, large crown with gray-green palmate, rigid leaves 3 m across, the stalk streaked with scurfy white; 3 cm plum-like brown fruit on female trees, in huge clusters. *Tropical. Zone 11.*   p. 102

BIXA   *Bixaceae*
orellana (West Indies), "Lipstick-tree" or "Annatto-tree"; a showy small evergreen tree 6-10 m high, with broad, smooth, heart-shaped ovate leaves to 18 cm long; 5 cm regular flowers pink; the fleshy fruit spiny and source of orange henna or Annatto dye made from its pulp. The foliage was reddish where I have seen them growing in East Africa. *Tropical. Zones 10-11.*   p. 523, 666

BLANDFORDIA   *Liliaceae*
grandiflora (Australia: So. Queensland and Blue Mts. or New So. Wales), "Christmas bells"; beautiful fibrous-rooted, rhizomatous perennial to 1 m or more high, with 2-ranked linear leaves mostly basal, to 40 cm long; showy funnelform to nearly bell-shaped flowers 5-6 cm long, red from base, changing to yellow toward lobed apex, pendant in terminal clusters; in Summer. *Zone 10.*   p. 444

BLECHNUM   *Polypodiaceae (Filices)*
brasiliense (Brazil, Perú); coarse rosette growing on a scaly trunk to 1 m high; the leathery green fronds deeply pinnatifid, widest in the upper third, the midrib broad, with pinnae overlapping and wavy, and coppery when young. *Humid-tropical. Zone 11.*   p. 131
capense (South Africa); robust fern with stout rootstock, clothed with large scales; pinnate fronds of two different forms (dimorphic); sterile leaves to 1 m long, the pinnae 8 to 30 cm, toothed at margins; fertile fronds 15 cm long, with narrow linear, well spaced pinnae. *Zone 10.*   p. 128
gibbum (Lomaria) (New Caledonia); graceful, symmetrical rosette, developing a trunk to 1½ m high; with broad, thin-leathery, arching pinnate fronds to 1 m long, the shining green pinnae are long and narrow, and almost threadlike on the fertile fronds. *Humid-tropical. Zones 11-12.*   p. 131
penna-marina (South Temperate Regions, New Zealand, So. Australia and Antarctic), "Sea-feather"; small pinnate fern on wide-creeping rhizomes clothed with rusty scales; barren fronds 10-20 cm long with short pinnae rounded at tip, fertile fronds on stalks to 30 cm long, pinnae narrower and more distant. *Zones 3-8.*   p. 130
spicant (Alaska to California, Europe, Asia), the "Deer-fern"; from a stout, short-creeping rhizome rise the pinnate fronds 25 cm to more than 1 m long; the shorter sterile leaves in each crown surrounding the taller fertile fronds; evergreen. *Zones 1-8.*   p. 130

BLETIA   *Orchidaceae*
hyacinthina of hort.: see BLETILLA striata
reflexa (Sonora, Mexico to Panama); variable terrestrial species with small pseudobulbs bearing 2 or more lanceolate folded leaves to 75 cm long; tall inflorescence of purplish-rose flowers 8 cm across. *Zone 11.*   p. 87

BLETILLA   *Orchidaceae*
striata, better known in horticulture as Bletia hyacinthina (Vietnam, So. China, Japan), "Hyacinth orchid"; handsome terrestrial orchid 30-60 cm high, growing leafy stems from tuberous rhizomes, bearing 3-5 rather thin plaited leaves; light purple flowers with trilobed lip lined by deep purple ridges; the blooms are 3 to 5 cm across, usually not fully opening, in terminal clusters on erect leafless stalk, rising from the center of the new shoots, mostly in June-July. A good orchid for Summer on the patio. Easy to grow and fairly winter-hardy to Zone 6 with protection. *Warm temperate. Zone 9.*   p. 75, 81, 259

BLIGHIA   *Sapindaceae*
sapida (West Africa: Guinea), the "Aki"; large ornamental, tropical fruit tree from West Africa but very common in the West Indies where it was introduced in slave days; 10-12 m high, with compound leaves of 3 to 5 pairs of glossy green oblong leaflets each about 15 cm; greenish-white fragrant flowers; the attractive oblong, ribbed fruit is orange with red cheeks, 8-10 cm long, triangular in cross-section with leathery red shell which opens when ripe, exposing firm white, nut-flavored pulp; wholesome food when ripe, eaten raw, fried or boiled; the seed coat is poisonous. *Tropical. Zones 9-10.*   p. 938

BOERLAGIODENDRON: see OSMOXYLON (Dr. Frodin)

BOLTONIA   *Compositae*
asteroides 'Snowbank' (New York to Georgia), "White boltonia"; aster-like perennial with erect, leafy stems to 1½ m high; pale glaucous oblanceolate to linear leaves to 12 cm long; small 2 cm flowers, white in this cultivar, lilac or purple in the species, in August-September. *Zone 4.*   p. 374

BOMAREA   *Amaryllidaceae*
multiflora (Colombia, Venezuela), "Tetona"; attractive vine with oblong leaves 10 cm long, and dense many-flowered umbels; corolla about 3 cm long with outer segments tinged red, inner reddish-yellow spotted claret-brown. *Tropical. Zone 10.*   p. 316

BOMBAX   *Bombacaceae*
buonopozense (angulicarpum) (West Africa to Nigeria, Cameroon), "Gold Coast bombax"; tropical deciduous tree to 35 m high, the massive trunk set with large conical spines; the branches in whorls, spreading angularly and wide; leaves pinnate having 5-9 oblong leaflets to 16 cm long; showy axillary flowers with waxy, crimson-red petals 8 cm long, blooming when leafless; oblong 5-angled 10-15 cm capsules. *Zones 10-11.*   p. 667
ceiba (malabaricum) (India to Indochina), "Red silk-cotton" or "Red kapok tree", in India known as Salmalia or "Simal", the tree under which Buddha is said to have been born; big soft wooded tree 25 to 30 m high, with buttressed, spiny trunk 2½ m dia.; palmate leaves with 5-7 leaflets; huge orange-scarlet fleshy flowers of 5 petals, overlaid with glowing crimson, 20-28 cm across; in the center orange filaments with blackish stamens, from 3-lobed, black-brown, leathery calyx cup; usually blooming leafless, as seen in Delhi, India. *Tropical. Zone 10.*   p. 667
ellipticum: see PSEUDOBOMBAX ellipticum

BORAGO   *Boraginaceae*
officinalis (So. Europe, No. Africa), the "Borage"; luxuriant, hairy Mediterranean herb 30-60 cm high, with quilted, coarse oblong leaves, 9-15 cm long, gray-green and stiff-hairy; beautiful sky-blue, nodding, starry flowers 2 cm across, attractive to bees. The leaves are edible and taste like cucumbers, and may be used for iced drinks, salads, pickling, or cooked to flavor soups and stews. Grown as an annual in cold climates. *Zones 9-10.*   p. 342, 527

BORASSODENDRON   *Palmae*
machadonis (Thailand to Malaya); solitary fan-palm to 8 m high, with a very irregular, shiny dark green crown; rough trunk with persistent leaf bases; fronds in spiralling ranks, the petioles with sharp edges; blades roundish, 1 m across with strong midrib; some divisions deeply cut. Male inflorescence to 1½ m faintly fragrant; female inflorescence to 60 cm long; blue-green fruits 10 cm dia. *Zones 11-12.*   p. 100

BORASSUS   *Palmae*
flabellifer (India, Burma, Malaya), the widely cultivated and fabled "Palmyra palm" or "Toddy palm" of India where it finds hundreds of uses, for food, black timber, sugar and toddy; trunk

20-30 m tall sometimes swollen above the middle, to 1 m thick; rounded head of palmate gray-green leaves to 3 m across rather folded, rigid and with stiff tips, the stalk with horny thorns. Female trees with big 12-20 cm edible fruit yellow to brown and black. The intoxicating toddy is taken from the dense flower spikes. *Tropical.* *Zones 11-12.*   *p. 101, 920*

BORONIA   *Rutaceae*

heterophylla (W. Australia), "Red boronia"; much branched, smooth evergreen shrub to 2 m, with linear leaves 5 cm long, simple or pinnate; small bell-flowers rosy-red, 1 cm dia., not opening widely. *Zone 10.*   *p. 859*

megastigma (Western Australia), "Scented boronia"; slender, hardwooded, evergreen 60 cm shrub with downy shoots; sessile, fresh-green, needle-like leaflets having transparent dots; small 1 cm, sweetly scented, axillary flowers with globose brown-purple corolla, yellow inside, in Spring. *Zone 10.*   *p. 859*

BORZICACTUS   *Cactaceae*

celsianus (Oreocereus) (Andes of Bolivia, Perú, Chile), "Cotton tree" or "Old man of the Andes"; growing in clumps, creeping when young, later upright to 1 m, areoles with long white hairs and long thin red spines; dark red flowers 10 cm long. *Subtropic.* *Zones 9-10.*   *p. 154*

hendriksenianus var. densilanatus (Oreocereus ritteri) (So. Perú); beautiful, snowy column to 10 cm dia., forming colonies, to 1 m high; green body, with 10 ribs, hidden by long silky, silvery hairs; short yellowish needle spines; red flowers 7 cm long. *Zone 10.*   *p. 154*

madisoniorum (Submatucana in Backeberg; Matucana in Zander 84) (N.E. Perú); small solitary globe, with age elongating to 25 cm high and 10 cm dia., grayish-green with rough surface, the 7 to 12 ribs not high; when older becoming knobby around areoles; occasional spines to 6 cm long, lightly curved; slender funnel-shaped flowers 8-10 cm long, orange-red and covered with brownish hair. Backeberg does not agree with the transfer by Kimnach and Hutchison to Borzicactus as in Hortus 3, maintaining that Submatucana is different. Photo pg. 154 taken at Harry Johnson in Fallbrook, California labelled Matucana madisoniorum. *Zone 10.*   *p. 154*

tuberculatus (Submatucana) (Rio Maranon, Perú); small handsome dark green columnar cactus with about 18 shallow ribs, broken into pointed tubercles, these topped by white-woolly areoles each subtended by some 10 straw-colored needle spines; from the top appear pretty rose-pink trumpet flowers with spreading outer petals. *Zone 10.*   *p. 154*

BOSSIAEA   *Leguminosae (Fabaceae)*

rhombifolia (Queensland); densely branching shrub to 2 m high; small elliptic, hard-leathery leaves with prominent midrib, 1 cm wide, arranged appressed to brownish branches; colorful butterfly flowers on short stalks, clustering near branch ends, yellow with red-brown near center, the wings tinged with red. *Zone 10.*   *p. 748*

rosmarinifolia (Grampians of Eastern Australia); small flowering shrub to 1 m high; narrow leaves 2½ cm long; pretty yellow pea-flowers with dark red keel. *Zones 9-10.*   *p. 748*

BOSWELLIA   *Burseraceae*

carteri (So. Arabia, Somalia, India), "Frankincense tree" or "Weihrauch" of the Hebrews, "Salai" in India; evergreen tree 3 to 6 m high, treasured since ancient times for its aromatic resin; at home in arid deserts, and related to the terebinth; forming gnarled and knotty reddish trunks; leaves unequally pinnate, the ovate leaflets serrate; star-shaped, white or green flowers tipped with rose. The resinous gum exudes in form of brittle, glittering drops, having a bitter taste, and gives off a stong balsamic odor when warmed or burned. This incense was used in the sacrificial service of the Temple by the Hebrews, and by the Egyptians for embalming, and still is the most important incense resin in the world. It is obtained by making incisions in the bark of living trees. *Arid-Tropical.* *Zone 10.*   *p. 539, 668*

hildebrandtii (elegans) (Kenya), "Francincense"; curious tree of the high African savanna, with age to 6 m high; in cultivation much smaller, seen at Grigsby's Nursery in Vista, California in dwarfed form, with swollen woody base, and slender, flecuous branches, having pinnate leaves 6-10 cm long, the small oblong leaflets pubescent; creamy-yellow flowers in small clusters 3 cm long, appearing before the leaves; red triangular, pear-shaped fruit 2 cm long. The stem yields a marketed gum, and an incense valued by the native people. *Zone 10.*   *p. 529*

BOTRYCHIUM   *Ophioglossaceae (Filices)*

dissectum obliquum (E. Canada to So. Carolina and Missouri), "Grape fern"; rhizomatous evergreen fern to 45 cm high, the some-what fleshy fronds compound in three divisions, of which each is 1-2 pinnate; the fertile leaves an erect panicle-like blade with sessile sporangia in grape-like clusters. *Zones 2-7.*   *p. 128*

BOUGAINVILLEA   *Nyctaginaceae*

braziliensis hort.; as known in the California nursery trade and elsewhere, is probably B. spectabilis; usually a plant with bracts in shades of purple, from rose-purple to distinct deep blue-purple. *Tropical. Zones 9-10.*   *p. 286*

x buttiana (peruviana x glabra), the clone 'Mrs. Butt' is widely popular as 'Crimson Lake'; a vigouous, pubescent woody clamberer with large recurved spines, broader and thicker ovate leaves than glabra; blooming in big panicles, with the insignificant flowers subtended by corolla-like, showy cordate bracts of bright crimson, cascading in masses of color from late Winter to Summer. Requiring sun; tolerates drought. Keep cool in Winter. Propagate by cuttings from ripened wood. *Tropical. Zone 10.*   *p. 75, 286*

x buttiana 'Barbara Karst' (peruviana x glabra clone); rather bushy grower with cascading masses of large brilliant red floral bracts borne almost continually, blooming at an early age. Very popular in California gardens. *Tropical to subtropic. Zone 10.*   *p. 286, 615*

x buttiana 'Gerry's Orange' ('San Diego Red' x 'Barbara Karst'); beautiful hybrid of compact habit. with flowers presenting an open face of bracts in glowing salmon-rose flushed and tinted with golden-orange. *Zones 10-11.*   *p. 286*

glabra (Brazil), "Paper flower"; strong woody rambler with bright green, smooth leaves slender pointed and with narrow base; flower clusters smaller than spectabilis, the branchlets with acute purplish-pink bracts in threes, blooming in Summer; more compact than spectabilis. *Tropical. Zone 10.*   *p. 286*

spectabilis (Brazil), "Paper flower"; free ranging canes often with stout spines, not as bushy and compact as B. glabra; leaves more or less ovate, velvety hairy beneath; bracts usually light brick-red or purple 5 cm long; calyx with many spreading short hairs. *Tropical. Zone 10.*   *p. 286*

spectabilis 'Cherry Blossom'; strikingly beautiful evergreen tropical climber, with its great clusters of charming double blooms, dense with circles of petal-like bracts rich rose-pink toward tips, and white to pale green at base and center, reminding of apple-blossoms. *Zones 10-11.*   *p. 287*

spectabilis flore pleno, "Double bougainvillea"; vigorous tropical evergreen with rambling branches forming dense bush, profusely covered by masses of blooms, each filled with petal-like bracts of glowing carmine-rose. *Zones 10-11.*   *p. 287*

spectabilis 'Louis Wathen'; grown in Peradeniya, Ceylon, with magnificent masses of double-bracted flowers in shades of soft salmon-orange; flowers lacking star-like limb. *Tropical.* *Zones 10-11.*   *p. 286*

spectabilis 'Manila Magic Pink'; (Pat. Monrovia Nurs., Calif.); one of the showiest cultivars brought from the Philippines; handsome huge flower clusters of double bracts, frilly pink and carmine-rose. *Tropical. Zones 10-11.*   *p. 286*

spectabilis 'Raspberry Ice'; very ornamental compact evergreen bush, spreading to 1 m, with thin rambling branches, densely covered by milky-green ovate leaves to 6 cm long, boldly variegated along margins with creamy-yellow; the floral bracts magenta-red. *Zones 10-11.*   *p. 287*

spectabilis 'Rosea'; very floriferous tropical clambering shrub, with masses of blooms having showy spreading bracts in soft rose-pink. *Zone 11.*   *p. 286*

spectabilis 'Rubra plena'; floriferous cultivar with branches loaded down by the weight of flowers with fully double, carmine-red bracts. *Tropical. Zone 10.*   *p. 281*

BOUTELOUA   *Gramineae*

gracilis (oligostachya in Zander) (Wisconsin to Alberta, so. to Mex.), "Mesquite grass" or "Mosquito grass", also "Blue grama"; attractive perennial forming clusters to 60 cm high, with mostly basal, arching leaves, more or less flat, 12 cm long and 3 mm wide; inflorescence a one-sided spike with numerous purplish spikelets. Pasture grass in Mexico. *Zone 5.*   *p. 559*

BOUVARDIA   *Rubiaceae*

longiflora (Mexico: San Luis Potosi to Oaxaca), "Sweet bouvardia" or "Flor de San Juan"; beautiful fall-to-winter-flowering shrub 1 to 1½ m high, with woody and flexible branches, opposite, smooth, fresh-green leaves 2-4 cm long and bearing toward the tip clusters of waxy, salver-form, fragrant flowers having long, slender, 6 cm tubes opening into lobes of purest white. The commercial cultivar 'Humboldtii' is of more compact habit, and larger flowers, valued by florists as cut flowers for their intense scent, and exquisite waxy blooms. *Zones 9-10.*   *p. 854*

ternifolia (triphylla) (Mexico, Texas), "Scarlet trompetilla"; straggling shrub with thin, woody branches; the whorled, ovate, pubescent leaves opposite on the branchlets, which are terminated by clusters of 3 cm, tubular flowers of fiery scarlet-red, blooming most of the year; horticultural varieties are 'Christmas Red' and 'Fire Chief'. *Subtropic. Zones 9-10.*   *p. 854*

ternifolia 'Rosea', "Pink trompetilla"; attractive cultivar with clusters of slender tubular flowers 3-4 cm long, tipped by 4 flaring segments a vivid soft pink. Popular in commercial floriculture as cut flower. *Zones 9-10.* p. 854

BOWIEA *Liliaceae*
volubilis (Schizobasopsis) (So. Africa), "Climbing onion"; grown as a curiosity; succulent, light green bulb, to 20 cm dia., above ground, sending up a twining fresh-green branched stem with few linear deciduous leaves; small greenish-white flowers. *Subtropic. Zone 10.* p. 204

BOWKERIA *Scrophulariaceae*
gerrardiana (So. Africa: Natal); erect evergreen shrub 1-3 m high, shoots finely downy; ovate sessile leaves in whorls of three, toothed at margins, 10-15 cm long, dull green; two-lipped satiny white calceolaria-like flowers 2 cm wide, dotted red inside; inflorescence sticky. *Zone 8.* p. 874

BRACHYCHITON *Sterculiaceae*
acerifolius (New S. Wales, Queensland), "Flame bottle tree"; to 30 m high, resembling Trevesia but without thorns; the attractive, glossy green, palmate leaves deeply 5-7 lobed, to 30 cm across, on long petioles; 2 cm flowers without corolla, but a rich-red, bell-shaped calyx. *Subtropic. Zones 9-10.* p. 883
australis (trichosiphon) (Queensland, No. Australia), "Broad-leaf bottle-tree"; subtropic deciduous tree with swollen trunk, to 12 m high; leaves 5 to 7-lobed 20 cm long; narrow white 2 cm bell-flowers in short racemes, not showy; leaves drop when in bloom. *Zone 10.* p. 883
bidwillii (Sterculea) (Australia: Queensland), "Kurrajong"; tropical evergreen shrub or tree 3 to 9 m high, softly downy throughout; the deeply tri-lobed leaves velvety on both sides 8-15 cm long; rose-red bell-flowers among the upper leaves 3-4 cm across, calyx pale red; the woody ovoid fruit consists of 5 pod-like sections, with seeds inside. *Zones 9-10.* p. 883
discolor (No. Australia, Queensland, New So. Wales), "Queensland lace bark" or "White kurrajong"; ornamental tree to 20 m or more high, deciduous in cooler regions, with leaves broadly heart-shaped, irregularly 3-5-7-lobed, 10-20 cm across, yellowish tomentose beneath; 5 cm rose-colored bellflowers in terminal spikes, forming a carpet of pink beneath at end of Summer. The white timber is soft but dries hard and is used for shingles, or for shields of the Aboriginals. *Zones 9-10.* p. 883
populneus (Sterculia diversifolia) (Australia: Victoria, to Queensland, No. Terr.), "Kurrajong"; handsome upright-growing tree to 20 m with bottle-shaped trunk; shining 8 cm leaves which vary considerably in shape, from ovate poplar-like, to deeply cut into linear segments; showy bell flowers in profusion, yellowish-white spotted brown, reddish inside; followed by 8 cm boat shaped pods. *Zone 9.* p. 883
rupestris (Sterculia) (Queensland), the peculiar "Queensland bottle-tree"; semi deciduous, 6-15 m high, with a huge bottle-shaped trunk 3½ m dia., and storing water; the spreading branches with variable blackish-green leaves lanceolate or palmately divided, 16 cm long; tomentose bell-shaped flowers. *Tropical. Zones 9-10.* p. 883

BRACHYCOME (Brachyscome in Zander) *Compositae*
iberidifolia (Western and So. Australia), "Swan River daisy"; charming herbaceous annual 30 to 40 cm high, densely branching with thin, flexible stems; feathery green leaves dissected into linear segments; at the top with masses of daisy-like flowers 2 to 3 cm across, the raised centers blue to purplish, ray-petals normally purplish-rose, but also white, blue or deep purple (spelled Brachyscome in Zander). *Zone 10.* p. 373
multifida (E. Australia: Queensland to Victoria), "Rock daisy" or "Cutleaf daisy"; low perennial 15-25 cm high, spreading wide by underground stolons; divided leaves on wiry branches; and flowers 3-4 cm across, having broad, mauve-pink or lilac rays around pale yellow center disc, blooming year-round. *Zone 9.* p. 373

BRAHEA *Palmae*
armata (Erythea) (Mexico: Baja California), "Mexican blue palm"; stout fan-palm to 12 m; the trunk naturally covered by a dense petticoat of dead leaves; stiff, palmate fronds waxy-blue in heavy crown, deeply cut into many segments, 1-1½ m across, the petiole armed with curved white spines; handsome arching spadices to 5 m long. *Tropical. Zone 11.* p. 101
brandegeei (Erythea) (Mexico: Baja California), "Daughter of the West", or "Hesper palm"; tall, sturdy fan palm to 30 m or more tall, comparatively slender trunk with persistent leaf bases; heavy crown of green, palmate leaves 1-1½ m dia., on long petioles heavily armed with recurving spines; blade divided in center, segments deeply split, waxy white beneath; shiny brown, 1 cm fruit. *Tropical. Zones 10-11.* p. 100

dulcis (Erythea) (So. Mexico), "Rock palm" or "Palma dulce"; a true Brahea: medium-sized, variable fan palm, forming erect trunks to 6 m tall, or procumbent on the ground, sometimes in clusters; upper part covered with old leaf-bases; palmate fronds very stiff, 1 m or more across, deeply cut into about 50 segments, green above, bluish glaucescent beneath; petiole edged with small teeth; small yellow fruit in large pendant clusters. *Tropical. Zone 11.* p. 100

BRASSAIA actinophylla(Hortus):
    see SCHEFFLERA actinophylla (Dr. D. Frodin 86)

BRASSAVOLA *Orchidaceae*
digbyana (Rhyncholaelia) (Honduras), "Lady of the Night"; white-mealy epiphyte, in habit resembling cattleya, the pseudobulb bearing a solitary, rigid, glaucous leaf; large, showy, fragrant flower, the narrow petals and sepals greenish-white, tinged purple, the rounded lip cream-white with green throat, fringed at the margin with a long beard, (May-July). *Tropical. Zone 11.* p. 82
glauca (Laelia) (Mexico, Guatemala); small, bluish-gray epiphyte with slender pseudobulbs bearing a stiff, glaucous leaf; fragrant flowers with linear sepals and petals white, often tinted green, the large lip cream-white sparsely marked with pink, (Dec.-March). *Tropical. Zones 11-12.* p. 82
nodosa (Jamaica, Costa Rica, Colombia to Surinam), "Lady of the night"; epiphyte with stemlike pseudobulbs bearing a solitary, stout, channeled leaf; flowers solitary or in clusters, linear sepals and petals greenish-yellow and broad, pointed, white lip, (Sept.-Dec.). *Tropical. Zones 11-12.* p. 82

BRASSIA *Orchidaceae*
allenii (Panama); pseudobulbless epiphyte with stiff vandaceous, overlapping foliage and showy flowers having long narrow tapering sepals and petals cinnabar red, greenish-yellow toward base, and a broad, almost square yellow lip and spotted brown in front of the white callus. (Spring). *Tropical. Zone 11.* p. 82
maculata (W. Indies, Guatemala); epiphyte with single-leaved pseudobulbs, and erect spike with waxy flowers, the narrow sepals and petals pale greenish-yellow barred with brown, the white lip marked red-brown, (April-Oct.). *Tropical. Zones 11-12.* p. 82
verrucosa (Mexico, Guatemala, Honduras, Venezuela), "Queen's umbrella"; vigorous epiphyte with pseudobulbs bearing 2 oblong leaves; arching, wiry flower stems with long threadlike, 12 cm sepals greenish-yellow, 8-12 cm long, spotted at base with purple, as are the petals; the finely brown-warty lip white. *Tropical. Zones 11-12.* p. 82

BRASSICA *Cruciferae*
hirta (Sinapis alba in Zander) (W. Asia, naturalized in No. America), "White mustard"; annual herb 30-80 cm or more high, having leaves with 2 or 3 pairs of blunt lobes, bright green and usually hairy, sometimes spotted violet; vivid yellow flowers 1-2 cm long, to 50 or more in racemes, followed by 2-edged fruit 4 cm long, containing the mustard and oil producing pale yellow seeds; grown in Europe and California as a crop. *Zone 6 as annual.* p. 528
napus (Mediterranean reg.), "Rape"; glaucous annual or biennial herb of economic importance, to more than 1 m high, with lightly bristly lower leaves deeply 2-lobed each side; the upper leaves lanceolate; very floriferous with elongate racemes of light yellow flowers in Spring; pods to 10 cm long, containing the seed used for oil and as bird feed. Widely sown in America as forage and cover crop. *Zone 6 as annual.* p. 528
oleracea acephala; very popular for outdoor planting in Japan and China, also grown in pots for ornament, and known as "Flowering cabbage"; thick-leaved, glaucous perennial, a form descended from the European type; with spreading leaves forming a green rosette which with the advent of colder weather develops in its center striking shades of ivory to rose, imitating a showy flower. Good commercial cultivars are 'Red Crown' (Kokan) deep green with purplish center and purple ribs; and 'White Ripple' (Ginpa) ivory-white on green. *Warm-temperate. Zones 6-8.* p. 205, 409
oleracea acephala crispa, the "Flowering kale"; a biennial grown as an ornamental pot plant, reported to be a hybrid between "Flowering cabbage" and ordinary Kale, forms a big rosette of large frilled and fringed foliage, glaucous-green in the younger stage, but in Autumn as the season advances and they are kept cold, remarkably beautiful colors begin to appear with the center blossoming forth in shades of ivory, yellow, rose and purple. These plants are used as Christmas and New Year's pot plants in Japan, and have equally been used in flower arrangements in New York. *Warm-temperate. Zones 6-8.* p. 408, 409
oleracea gongyloda (Old World), "Kohlrabi" or "Stem-turnip"; biennial gourmet vegetable to 50 cm high, or more when flowering; from woody base the short stem is swollen with the leaf petioles, forming a depressed globular fleshy knob 8-10 cm dia., which is

cooked and widely served as a kitchen vegetable in Northern Europe; the leaves are soft-fleshy, fiddle-shaped and glaucous green; yellow flowers in large clusters. *Zone 8.*   *p. 940*

oleracea laciniata, "Miniature flowering kale"; very handsome variety of the ornamental kale, all glaucous silvery bluish-gray, the large obovate basal leaves deeply lobed; the higher foliage attached to the lengthening floral stem are pinnately cut into lacy lobes, and becoming smaller toward apex. *Zones 6-8.*   *p. 408*

x BRASSOCATTLEYA   *Orchidaceae*
lehmannii; hybrid with smallish pink sepals and petals, but an exceptional large bearded lip, light purple, deeper purple in throat and with yellow lines. *Humid-tropical. Zone 11.*   *p. 83*

BREYNIA   *Euphorbiaceae*
disticha 'Roseo-picta' (nivosa) (Phyllanthus), known as "Snow bush" or "Leaf-flower" because the little 2-3 cm oval, papery leaves are attractively mottled or variegated green, white and pink, looking like flowers, with red stems and petioles. Interesting tropical shrub to 2 m high, at home on South Pacific Islands. *Zone 10.*   *p. 720*

BRIGGSIA   *Gesneriaceae*
muscicola (Bhutan, Tibet, Yunnan); stemless perennial herb with thick rhizome, native in high mountain areas; dense rosette of fleshy ovate, crenate leaves white-velvety above, 6-8 cm long; pendant bell-shaped flowers 2 cm long, yellowish outside, golden-yellow inside. *Zone 11.*   *p. 62*

BRIGHAMIA   *Lobeliaceae*
citrina (endemic on Kauai, Hawaii), "Alula" or "Tree lobelia"; unique woody plant, with swollen trunk, bearing toward apex a tuft of succulent, deep green obovate leaves 30 cm or more long, the midrib ivory-white, and arranged as in a rosette; from the axils appear the slender tubular flowers, having pure white flaring lobes. *Tropical. Zone 11.*   *p. 200, 772*

BRIMEURA   *Liliaceae*
amethystina (syn. Hyacinthus or Scilla) (Pyrenees of Spain); small hyacinth-like bulbous herb to 25 cm high, with 6-8 linear leaves to 20 cm long; inflorescence in a loose raceme of small light blue nodding bell-flowers. *Zone 6.*   *p. 257*

BRIZA   *Gramineae*
maxima (Mediterr. region; escaped to Calif. and Texas), "Rattle-snake grass"; very ornamental annual or perennial grass 30-60 cm high, with linear leaves, and arching floral stalks bearing attractive cone-like bronze-colored fruit clusters, resembling the tails of rattlesnakes, to 8 cm long, and gracefully dangling on threads. Ideal in dried arrangements. *Zones 8-10.*   *p. 559*

media (Europe, Asia Minor, Caucasus; naturalized from Ontario to Michigan), "Quaking grass"; deciduous ornamental perennial grass to 60 cm high, also known as "Shakers" in Britain, spreading by creeping rhizome; the stiff, slender culms arching at tip; the narrow leaves 1 cm wide and 15 cm long; inflorescence, produced June to August, a loose panicle of scattered floral spikelets, first greenish then beige, and which shake at slightest breeze. *Zones 4-8.*   *p. 559*

BRODIAEA   *Amaryllidaceae*
elegans (Oregon, California), "Harvest brodiaea"; perennial with brown crocus-like fibrous-coated corm; 2 to 5 narrow grasslike leaves rounded underneath; funnelform rosy-violet flowers in clusters on cylindric stalk to 40 cm long. *Zone 8.*   *p. 210*

hyacinthina: see TRITELEIA hyacinthina
laxa: see TRITELEIA laxa
pulchella: see DICHOLOSTEMMA pulchellum

BROMELIA   *Bromeliaceae*
balansae (Brazil, Argentina), "Pinuela"; large and vicious terrestrial rosette used for fencing; stiff green leaves to 1½ m long, with dangerous hook spines facing both directions; center turning red before bloom; flowers white, in paniculate inflorescence forming branches of small, ovoid orange-yellow fruit with pineapple flavor. Easily confused with B. pinguin, but balansae has broad sepal tips, pinguin needle-like tips and loose inflorescence. *Subtropic. Zones 9-10.*   *p. 45*

karatas (West Indies); large terrestrial rosette 60 cm high and to 3 m across, of numerous concave, linear lax leaves to 2 m long x 5 cm wide, dangerously armed with sharp-pointed marginal spines; inflorescence in a dense contracted panicle deep in the center, with pink flowers surrounded by scaly bracts. *Zone 10.*   *p. 45*

pinguin (W. Indies, So. America), "Pinguin"; bold basal rosette of many spreading rigid, light green leaves 1½-2 m long, 3 cm wide, armed with large hooked brown spines; flowers with reddish petals, needle-like sepal tips and white-tomentose at apex, in erect mealy panicles shorter than leaves, and more loosely arranged than B. balansae. *Tropical. Zone 10.*   *p. 45*

serra 'Variegata'; known as "Heart of flame"; large showy plant but dangerously spiny, the spreading leaves grayish-green with broad ivory margins; when flowering, center turns bright red, and spike with red bract-leaves and maroon flowers. Produces orange-colored fruits. Inflorescence globose, unlike the elongate inflorescence of balansae. *Tropical. Zone 10.*   *p. 45*

BROSIMUM   *Moraceae*
alicastrum (Mexico, Cent. America, West Indies), "Breadnut tree"; evergreen tropical shrub or tree, in gardens 2 m high, but may reach 30 m, with trunk to 1 m dia., and having gray bark; the crown broad and dense, with bright green lanceolate, leathery leaves; flowers unisexual in globose heads; the fruit is edible, subglobose, yellow to orange, containing a single 12 mm seed. Milky juice extracted from the plant is used medicinally for asthma patients. The fruit is cooked and eaten in the West Indies. *Zones 10-11.*   *p. 916*

BROWALLIA   *Solanaceae*
speciosa (Colombia), "Amethyst flower" or "Sapphire flower"; attractive herbaceous perennial with shrubby base, and sprawling slender branches; small glossy, fresh green leaves; profusely blooming with dark purple flowers to 5 cm across, pale lilac beneath. Graceful in hanging baskets, usually grown as annual. *Subtropic. Zone 10.*   *p. 511*

viscosa (pulchella) (Perú), "Bush violet"; herbaceous tropical plant usually grown as annual, 30-60 cm high, sticky-hairy on its younger growth, with ovate rough-hairy leaves 4 to 6 cm long; flowers bluish-purple with pale yellow eye, with whitish tube, or all white, 2 cm long, during Summer. *Zone 10.*   *p. 511*

BROWNEA   *Leguminosae*
grandiceps (Venezuela), "Rose of Venezuela"; handsome tropical tree to 20 m high, with stout, hairy branchlets; even-pinnate, leathery leaves to 11 pairs of leaflets, reddish when young; dense flower heads nearly globose, 20-25 cm across, scarlet-red. *Zone 10.*   *p. 748*

macrophylla (Panama, Colombia); small tree to 10 m; branches and petioles brown-hairy; pinnate leaves with 3-6 pairs of leaflets to 30 cm long; flower heads on trunks and branches 20-25 cm across, orange-scarlet. *Tropical. Zone 10.*   *p. 748*

BRUCKENTHALIA   *Ericaceae*
spiculifolia (S.E. Europe: Balkans, N.W. Asia Minor), "Spike-heath"; small evergreen erica-like shrub 15-25 cm high, downy young growth, crowded with tiny linear, ciliate leaves 3-6 mm long; small bell-shaped, 4-lobed magenta-pink flowers 3 mm long in terminal racemes, in Summer. *Zone 5.*   *p. 700*

BRUGMANSIA   *Solanaceae*
arborea (Peruvian Andes), "Tree datura"; small, pubescent tree to 3 m high, with soft-hairy, ovate leaves; the nodding, trumpet-shaped flowers not over 18 cm long, white with green nerves and recurving pointed lobes, the long green calyx spathe-like, tapering to one tip. *Tropical. Zone 10.*   *p. 877*

aurea (Perú); sparry shrub with brittle, woody branches; large corrugated leaves 30-40 cm long; handsome pendant flowers 15 cm long, calyx with 2 to 4 lobes, and corolla a rich apricot-yellow. Seen at Botanical Gardens in Ghent (Belgium), Dortmund and Tuebingen (Germany). *Tropical. Zone 10.*   *p. 877*

x candida (arborea x versicolor) (Datura); large pendant white flowers 20 cm or more long; commonly in cultivation as Datura arborea. *Zone 10.*   *p. 877*

candida flore pleno (Datura) (Perú, Chile), "Floripondio"; this aristocrat of Tree datura photographed in col. Quail Botanic Garden, Encinitas, Calif.; robust tree-like with pendant large pubescent leaves and heavy white trumpet flowers often double with extra petals inside the corolla, at base a single green, ovate spathe. *Zone 10.*   *p. 877*

chlorantha (Peruvian Andes); free-blooming shrub with broad ovate, wavy leaves, and fragrant yellow, pendulous flowers; tubular calyx with 5 teeth, corolla funnel-shaped; August-October; prickly fruit. *Tropical. Zone 10.*   *p. 877*

x insignis (Brugmansia suaveolens x versicolor); magnificent hybrid with beautiful large trumpet flowers 20 cm long, whitish at base and flushed with pink toward margins and the upturned spurs a glowing crimson-rose. *Tropical. Zone 10.*   *p. 877*

sanguinea (Perú); showy tropical shrub becoming 4 to 5 m high, the brittle branches with clustered, long-ovate soft-hairy foliage 16 cm long, and carrying the weight of large pendulous 25 cm trumpets like so many bells, flesh pink to orange-red toward apex, with yellow veins, calyx with two or more pointed lobes. *Tropical. Zone 10.*   *p. 877*

suaveolens (Brazil), "Angel's trumpet"; tree-like shrub to 5 m high, with heavy canes large, lanceolate, 30 cm leaves, oblique at the base, glabrous green, thin and quickly wilting; the large, nodding, funnel-shaped flowers with a tubular, 5-toothed calyx and a fragrant white corolla to 30 cm long. *Tropical. Zone 10.*   *p. 877*

versicolor (mollis) (So. Ecuador: Guayaquil); large shrub or small tree 2-4 m high, with sparry, brittle branches, and big oblong-elliptic, soft pubescent leaves; showy flowers like large hanging trumpets 30 cm or more long, with spathe-like calyx; the thin constricted tube expanding to the reflexed petal-lobes, pinkish and turning apricot-peach with age, fragrant in the evening. *Zone 10.* p. 877

BRUGUIERA *Rhizophoraceae*
   conjugata (gymnorhiza) (Africa, Malaya and India to So. China and Pacific), "Oriental mangrove" or "Many-petaled mangrove"; spreading shrub with jointed branches, sending out aerial stiltroots into shallow water of tropical tidal shores and lagoons, forming dense interconnected tangles; large shiny green, thick-leathery pointed leaves on erect brown branches; pink, yellow or red flowers with 10 or more calyx lobes and short woolly petals. *Tropical.* *Zones 10-11.* p. 333

BRUNFELSIA *Solanaceae*
   americana (West Indies), "Lady of the night"; evergreen tropical shrub to 2 m high, the leathery leaves oval to obovate, 8-10 cm long; exquisite flowers white, fading to pale lemon-yellow with age, usually solitary, with a slender tube to 10 cm long and spreading limb to 6 cm across; very fragrant, especially at night; blooming in Spring and Summer. *Zone 10.* p. 878
   australis (Franciscea latifolia) (Argentina, Paraguay, So. Brazil), "Kiss-me-quick" or "Paraguay jasmine"; shrub 60-90 cm high, with broad, leathery, obovate leaves to 10 cm long, slightly pubescent beneath; flowers pale violet with white eye at first, changing in a day or so to white, and very fragrant; blooming freely in Winter and early Spring. *Zones 9-10.* p. 878
   pauciflora calycina (Franciscea) (Brazil), "Morning-noon-and-night"; handsome spreading shrub with long lanceolate, shining vivid-green leaves and large 6 cm salver-shaped flowers with wavy margins, rich dark purple changing to pale lavender, blooming successively throughout the year. *Tropical. Zone 10.* p. 878
   pauciflora var. calycina 'Floribunda', "Yesterday, today and tomorrow"; floriferous evergreen shrub with spreading branches; dark green, long elliptic, leathery leaves and large, 5 cm rich violet to lavender flowers with small white eye, quickly fading to white, blooming from January to July. *Zones 9-10.* p. 878
   pauciflora 'Eximia' (compacta); small evergreen, of quite compact habit and more profusely flowering than B. pauciflora 'Floribunda'; the corollas with spreading lavender petals. *Zone 9.* p. 878
   pauciflora 'Macrantha' (Franciscea), "Yesterday-and-today"; showy cultivar, most tender, slender growing, and with larger leaves to 20 cm long and 6 cm wide; flowers very large, purple with lavender zone bordering white throat, 5-10 cm across, blooming variously through the year. *Zone 10.* p. 878

BRUNNERA *Boraginaceae*
   macrophylla (syn. B. or Anchusa myosotidiflora) (Caucasus to Siberia), "Siberian bugloss" or "Heartleaf brunnera"; herbaceous perennial 30-45 cm high, with kidney-shaped or ovate-cordate leaves; small, starry blue flowers during Spring. *Zone 4.* p. 342

BRUNSVIGIA x rosea hort.:
   see x AMARCRINUM memoria-corsii

BRYA *Leguminosae*
   ebenus (Aspalanthus) (Cuba, Jamaica), "West Indian ebony"; hard-wooded deciduous shrub to 2 m, or tree up to 6 m high, with fissured bark; leaves compound of ovate leaflets to 15 mm long, and clustered; deep orange-yellow pea flowers with standard 1 cm long; fruit ripening brownish and covered by whitish hairs and 1-seeded. *Zone 10.* p. 748

BRYOPHYLLUM: see KALANCHOE

BUCIDA *Combretaceae*
   buceras (Florida, West Indies to Panama), the "Black olive"; handsome tropical evergreen tree becoming 18 m high; as a younger shrub of very symmetrical growth habit, and sculptured shape, with branches laterally in tiers; small leathery obovate leaves 5-8 cm long, at the end of twigs; insignificant greenish flowers lacking petals, displaying long stamens; followed by small ovoid 1 cm black berries. *Zone 10.* p. 688

BUDDLEIA (BUDDLEJA) *Loganiaceae*
   alternifolia (China); deciduous shrub becoming 3-6 m high, with gracefully pendulous branches bearing alternate, lanceolate green leaves to 10 cm long, gray-scurfy beneath; 6 mm flowers lilac-purple, in dense racemes, on last year's growth, blooming June-July. May be trained into multiple-stemmed small tree resembling Weeping willow. *Zone 5.* p. 773

asiatica (India, So. China), "Butterfly bush"; evergreen shrub 1-2 m high, with narrowly lanceolate leaves 12-20 cm long, white downy beneath, on round stems; sweet scented white flowers in long panicles, during Winter and Spring; grown under glass as a cutflower. *Zone 9.* p. 773
   cordata (Mexico: Chihuahua to Chiapas and Oaxaca); tropical evergreen shrub 4-6 m high; the leaves ovate to narrow lanceolate 8-30 cm long, usually cordate at base, loosely tomentose beneath; flowers pale lavender to light purple, in large elongate, terminal panicles. Photographed in col. Jardim Botanico, Rio de Janeiro. *Zone 10.* p. 773
   davidii (Buddleja L.) (China), "Butterfly bush" or "Summer lilac"; deciduous, strong growing shrub to 4 m with 4-angled downy shoots and long lanceolate, toothed leaves white-felted beneath; fragrant flowers lilac with orange eye, in slender panicles, in July to October. Widely grown in American gardens, it freezes to the ground in areas of winter cold, but will bloom on new growth. 'Royal Red' is a superior Ohio hybrid with red-purple flowers in showy spikes to 30 cm or more long. *Zone 5.* p. 773
   davidii alba, "White butterfly bush" or "White summer lilac"; white-flowering form of this free growing, spreading and showy bush, the hardiest species of all cultivated Buddleias. The sweet-scented blooms are very attractive to butterflies seeking sweet nectar. *Zone 5.* p. 773
   globosa (Chile, Perú), "Globe butterfly bush" or "Orange-ball tree"; semi-evergreen shrub 3-5 m high, with loosely felted branches, opposite lanceolate leaves 10-25 cm long, wrinkled above, tawny-felted beneath; orange-yellow flowers in long-stalked, globe-shaped terminal heads blooming in May, and sweetly scented. *Zone 7.* p. 773
   indica (Hortus, Zander): see NICODEMIA diversifolia as in hort.
   madagascariensis (Madagascar); evergreen tropical shrub of tall, lax habit to 6 m high, with branches downy, 12 cm lanceolate leaves dark green above, pale-woolly beneath; orange-yellow flowers in slender terminal panicles, in Winter. Cultivated in Mediterranean Region. *Zone 10.* p. 773
   nivea (Western China), "Snowy buddleia"; handsome deciduous shrub 2-3 m high, with shoots densely white-woolly, the lanceolate leaves 10-25 cm long dark green above, white felty beneath, becoming pale brown; toothed along margins; the small flowers in spike-like panicles 15 cm or more long, with corolla lilac to purple, so white-woolly outside that only the petal tips show color; blooming August-September. *Zone 8.* p. 773
   x weyeriana 'Sungold' (davidii x globosa); handsome hybrid of vigorous habit, originating in Boskoop, Holland, with flowers vivid orange and yellow, shaded pink outside, in ball-shaped heads arranged in long panicles on the young wood, in Summer. *Zone 7.* p. 773

BUGLOSSOIDES *Boraginaceae*
   purpureo-caeruleum (France to Russia, Asia Minor); procumbent perennial, from dense rhizome, spreading 50 cm wide; lanceolate leaves 3-8 cm long; wide-cupped flowers 2 cm across, first purple then changing to blue, in terminal clusters. *Zone 7.* p. 342

BUGULA *Ectroproctaceae*
   species (off English and Norman coasts), the "Airfern" or "Neptune plant", as sold in department stores; a curious fern-like plume to 30 cm long, by early naturalists (Rondelet 1558) considered as of the nature of plants and grouped as a Zoophyte or "Sea plant", at a time when sea coral was regarded as a "Stony plant". Now recognized to be a lowly moss-animal of the genus Bugula, it is found growing under water on rocks or floating wood. The fan-like structure is produced by the labor of invertebrate polyps which build colonies, skeletal cases of gelatinous material of their own secretions, originally a translucent brownish gray, but dyed a luminous green and sold for decoration like lacy ferns, never requiring water or soil. p. 208

BUININGIA *Cactaceae*
   aurea (Brazil), collected by Glass & Foster N.E. of Minas Geraes; curious globular to elongate cactus to 40 cm high and 6-7 cm dia., having 12 or more snaking ribs, light olive-green at their ridges set with brilliant golden spines; woolly at top, easily forming offsets from base. *Zone 10.* p. 154

BULBINELLA *Liliaceae*
   floribunda (robusta) (So. Africa); showy perennial with fleshy roots, linear basal leaves, and tall 75 cm spikes of small flowers a shining daffodil yellow or orange; resembling miniature kniphofia; dormant in Summer. *Subtropic. Zones 9-10.* p. 444

gibsii (Chrysobactron) (New Zealand), "Cat's tail"; moist-climate perennial to 50 cm or more high, with long-linear, recurving leaves 3 cm wide, the small 1-2 cm yellow flowers in cylindric racemes. *Zones 9-10.* p. 444

hookeri (setosa) (Chrysobactron in N.Z.) (New Zealand), "Maori onion"; perennial with tuberous roots, linear leaves to 30 cm long, and small 2 cm bright yellow flowers in erect racemes on stalks to 1 m high. *Zones 9-10.* p. 444

BULBOPHYLLUM   Orchidaceae

ornatissimum (cirrhopetalum) (Sikkim Himalaya, Philippines); pretty, dwarf epiphyte, with small ovoid pseudobulb and leathery 15 cm leaf; lateral stalk bearing an umbel of flowers 8-10 cm long, yellowish or pale purplish-brown striped and netted with dark purple, lip crimson-purple; Autumn. *Zone 11.* p. 81

purpureorhachis (Megaclinium) (Zaire), the "Cobra orchid"; a sinister-looking, fantastic epiphyte from inner Africa, with clustered pseudobulbs and paired, rigid leaves to 15 cm long: the curious inflorescence 30 cm long, stalk a singular flattened green axis, densely spotted and overlaid with deep red, the tiny 1 cm deep brown flowers, borne in a single row on the flat sides; blooming August into Winter. Snake-like in appearance, this is a striking curiosity plant in collections. *Tropical. Zone 12.* p. 98

BUNIUM   Umbelliferae

bulbocastanum (Sium) (France to Yugoslavia), "Groud chestnut"; perennial with tuberous, edible roots, forming numerous erect stalks, with narrow leaves, topped by branched clusters of small white flowers, during June-July. *Zone 7.* p. 544

BUPHTHALMUM   Compositae

salicifolium (France to Yugoslavia), "Willowleaf oxeye" or "Oxeye daisy"; showy herbaceous perennial to 60 cm high, with willow-like narrow, white-hairy leaves 8-20 cm long; solitary yellow ray-flowers 5 cm wide, blooming in Summer. *Zone 4.* p. 374

speciosum: see TELEKIA speciosa

BURCHELLIA   Rubiaceae

bubalina (So. Africa), "Wild pomegranate"; evergreen shrub 2-3 m high, with leathery, dark green, glossy leaves; tubular-inflated flowers 2-3 cm long, coral red; as buds, they are covered with silky hairs glistening in the sun. *Zone 10.* p. 854

BURSERA   Burseraceae

microphylla (S.W. Arizona, Sonora, Baja California), "Elephant tree" or "Copal"; curious xerophyte growing slowly into tree, with aromatic succulent trunk to 3 m high; the limbs soft spongy and containing a milky, resinous sap; the little pinnate leaves are 4 cm long, evergreen or deciduous; small greenish-yellow flowers in clusters, appearing before the leaves. *Arid-subtropic. Zone 10.* p. 668

simaruba (Elaphrium) (So. Florida, West Indies, C. America), "West Indian birch", "Gumbo-limbo" or "American balsam tree"; deciduous tropical tree 6 to possibly 18 m high, with soft-wooded trunk to 1 m dia., red-brown bark peeling in thin sheets; branches spreading wide; pinnate leaves with 7-11 lanceolate leaflets 4-14 cm long; sweet-scented greenish or yellowish flowers, in close clusters, before leaves; 3-valved fruit containing 3-5 nuts. *Zone 10.* p. 668

BUTEA   Leguminosae

monosperma (frondosa) (India), "Flame of the forest"; tropical semi-evergreen tree to 15 m, with crooked trunk, twigs pubescent; leaves of 3 leathery leaflets, silky beneath; flowers bright orange-red 3 to 5 cm across, appearing before the foliage. *Zones 10-11.* p. 748

BUTIA   Palmae

capitata (Cocos australis) (Brazil, Uruguay, Argentina), "Jelly palm"; short, stocky, rather coarse palm, slowly reaching 5 m, with thick trunk, covered with persistent leafbases; the long pinnate bluish-gray leaves stiffly recurving, whitish underneath, spiny at base; tough pinnae often 2-3 together; orange fruit with edible pulp. *Subtropic. Zones 10-11.* p. 101

BUTOMUS   Butomaceae

umbellatus (Eurasia, naturalized in N.E. No. Amer.), "Flowering rush", or "Water gladiolus"; rush-like perennial bogplant to more than 1 m high; the rootstock producing tiny tubers; narrow linear leaves 50-100 cm long; attractive rose-colored 2 cm flowers having red pistils, in clusters on floral stalks more than 1 m tall. *Zone 5.* p. 328

BUXUS   Buxaceae

balearica (Mallorca, Sardinia, Spain), "Spanish boxwood"; evergreen shrub or small tree to 8 m high, with 4-angled branches; glossy green, leathery elliptic leaves to 5 cm long, tapered at base; of very slow growth. Provides valuable timber. *Zone 8.* p. 670

harlandii (microphylla) (China); handsome evergreen boxwood, a shrub of compact habit, dense with downy branchlets; leathery narrow obovate leaves glossy green, 2-3 cm long. Ideal for use as low hedge. Found in Hongkong 1858; photographed in Brooklyn Bot. Garden 1984. *Zone 7.* p. 670

microphylla 'Compacta' (Japan), "Dwarf Littleleaf boxwood"; dense rounded twiggy cultivar of the Littleleaf box, also called Kingsville Dwarf of Maryland 1940, of compact growth, with small leaves, growing to 30 cm high and 1 m across in 50 years; hardy in Ontario, but leaves have a tendency to turn brown in Winter. *Zone 5.* p. 670

microphylla japonica (Japan), "California boxwood" or "Japanese little-leaf boxwood"; evergreen densely branching shrub to about 2 m high, the wiry shoots with small 1 to 2 cm obovate leathery leaves closely set, and a glossy bright green to deep green. Clipped into hedges, or globes, pyramids or other topiary shapes in containers. Tolerates the dry heat of a California patio, and alkaline soil, but not fully frost-resistant. *Warm temperate. Zone 6.* p. 613, 614, 626, 670

microphylla japonica 'Nana', "Dwarf California boxwood"; miniature cultivar about 20 cm high, popular in California garden centers, and used for low edging. *Zone 6.* p. 670

microphylla koreana (Korea), "Korean boxwood"; dwarf evergreen shrub 40-60 cm high, dense with downy shoots; small leathery, obovate leaves 1-2 cm long, notched at apex; small male and female flowers without petals, in axils and terminal. Used for low hedging and borders, lending itself to shearing, and recommended for colder regions, being hardy to Zone 4. p. 670

sempervirens (Europe, No. Africa, Asia Minor), "Common boxwood" or "English boxwood"; winter-hardy evergreen shrub or tree 2 to 5 m high, much used for sheared hedges or topiary; of dense habit, with quadrangular branches, small leathery obovate leaves lustrous dark green, 2-3 cm long; small axillary flowers without petals. *Temperate. Zone 5.* p. 613, 624, 670

sempervirens 'Angustifolia'; "Narrowleaf English box"; handsome cultivar of dense, upright habit, with stiff-leathery leaves elongate narrow elliptic to 5 cm long; ideally suited for fancy hedging, as seen in Parque Eduardo VII, in Lisbon, Portugal. *Zone 6.* p. 615, 670

sempervirens 'Suffruticosa'; the "Edging box", permanently dwarf and dense variety used for centuries to edge beds and in formal gardens; leaves mostly obovate and smaller than the species, usually 1-2 cm long; can be propagated by division. *Zone 5.* p. 616, 621, 670

BYBLIS   Byblidaceae (Carnivorous plants)

gigantea, (Western Australia); from swampy, sandy places of the Swan River near Perth; semi-shrubby plant 30-50 cm high, with woody rhizome; a stem with several branches long filament-like yellow-green leaves 10-20 cm long, clothed with numerous mucilage glands, secreting viscous glue to hold and eventually digest insects; large rosy or violet flowers. *Subtropic. Zones 10-11.* p. 202

CAESALPINIA   Leguminosae

echinata (Trop. America), "Brazilwood"; tropical tree with prickly trunk, pinnate leaves with many rhombic leaflets; yellow flowers in dense pyramidal panicles; followed by handsome woody, curved red bean pods. The heartwood yields red dye. *Zone 10.* p. 748

ferrea (E. Brazil), "Leopard tree"; tall shrub or tree to 15 m high, with unarmed trunk and branches; bipinnate leaves of 3-4 pairs of pinnate leaflets; the inflorescence in dense terminal clusters of small yellow flowers, followed by thick seedpods 8 cm long. *Zone 10.* p. 748

gilliesii (Poinciana) (Argentina, Uruguay), "Bird-of-paradise shrub"; straggling shrub or small tree to 8 m high with bipinnate leaves to 20 cm long, having 9-11 pinnae each with numerous small leaflets; terminal inflorescence with 5 flaring golden-yellow petals 3-4 cm across, and displaying long red stamens; widely distributed throughout the Tropics of the world. *Zone 10.* p. 750

pulcherrima (Poinciana) (W. Indies and other Tropics), "Dwarf poinciana" or "Pride of Barbados"; prickly, glabrous shrub to 5 m high, with delicate bipinnate, mimosa-like leaves with small rounded leaflets; very gaudy orange-red flowers with 5 crisped, golden-edged petals and red stamens, 6 cm long; fruits are 10 cm flat green pods; widely planted in the Tropics. Photo taken at the Palace Gardens in Mysore, South India. *Zone 10.* p. 750

pulcherrima flava (Poinciana) (East Africa, widespread in Tropics), "Peacock flower"; spiny, handsome-flowered bush to 5 m; with bipinnate fern-like leaves and bright yellow flowers. *Zone 10.* p. 750

spinosa (Western So. America), "Tara"; attractive spiny shrub or small tree from desert regions; thorny branches with bipinnate evergreen leaves, the 8 or more pairs of oval leaflets glossy green and leathery, 5 cm long, on thorny rachis; pyramidal inflorescence with small yellow flowers turning rose, and sweetly fragrant, in long, erect pyramidal racemes. The seed pods yield tannin. *Zone 10.*   p. 750

CALADIUM   *Araceae*
bicolor (Trinidad, Guyana, Brazil), "Heart of Jesus"; tuberous, stock plant with sagittate-ovate, firm leaves mostly green, red veins and scattered white spots; variable; spathe green, top white to yellow. The most important parent of most of our present horticultural forms. *Tropical. Zones 11-12.*   p. 219

x hortulanum, "Fancy-leaved Caladium"; tuberous herbs with membranous leaves varying from 15-30 cm long, mostly beautifully marked in many colors and patterns, on slender petioles; widely hybridized; the larger peltate-heartshaped leaves have C. bicolor blood; the lanceolate strap-leaved hybrids go back to C. picturatum. *Humid-Tropical. Zone 12.*   *Cultivars see listed below:*

'Ace of Hearts'; beautiful leaf, center area transparent-rose to crimson, moss-green toward margin; strong, blood-red ribs.   p. 25

'Candidum', "White caladium"; showy, white leaf traced with dark green veins and green border; delicate, yet a good keeper. Ideal for Easter; 20-30 cm foliage.   p. 219

'Elizabeth Dixon'; showy leaves basically deep green but more or less variegated white, more so in center where there is a flush of transparent pink; main ribs crimson.   p. 25

'E.O. Orpet'; lanceolate strapleaf, almost leathery; a glossy, bright red, shading to blood-red with narrow green border; low habit, and good keeper.   p. 25

'Frieda Hemple'; top red variety, bushy, compact and sturdy; medium size leaves clear bright red with primary ribs scarlet, the outer edge deep green.   p. 25

'Hortulania'; entire leaf transparent, almost shimmering, pink or rose, with narrow green border; veins scarlet; very showy.   p. 25

'Macahyba'; large, showy leaves, the center area transparent with marbling of white to rose, scattering out into the moss-green blade reticulated with occasional yellow-green; primary ribs crimson to purple.   p. 25

'Marie Moir', "Blood spots"; a beautiful variety because of its simplicity, pure white with a network of green tracings, and dark green ribs, and a sprinkling of showy blood-red blotches.   p. 25

'Mrs. F.M Joyner'; a rich looking, bushy plant with large white leaves changing into pinkish, overlaid with a network of bold red veins and a narrow green edge; good keeper.   p. 25

'Mrs. W.B. Halderman', "Coloradium"; beautiful cultivar with medium leaves more lightly variegated than 'Gen. W.B. Halderman'; translucent rose with red along veins; green along margins.   p. 219

'Scarlet Beauty'; bushy plant with large leaves mainly transparent rosy-red, main veins red, outer edge deep green.   p. 25

'Scarlet Pimpernelle'; large leaves bright carmine-rose, mottled grayish-green, outer area straw colored, heavy red ribs.   p. 25

'Triomphe de l'Exposition'; bushy plant with smaller leaf yellowish-green with scarlet veins shooting star-like from the red center; blue stem.   p. 25

'White Queen'; stunning introduction with pure white, lightly crinkly leaves contrasted by clear crimson primary veins, with a tracing of green laterals and a fine deep green edge.   p. 25

lindeni (Xanthosoma) (Colombia), "Yautia"; ornamental, evergreen herb growing from rhizome; showy, arrowshaped, thin-leathery leaves with hastate base, 20 cm long, matte-green with grayish sheen, and silver-white veins. *Tropical. Zone 12.*   p. 24

lindenii 'Magnificum' (Xanthosoma), "Indian kale"; horticultural form of X. lindenii (Colombia), differing by having its yellowish to deep-green leaves beautifully and broadly veined cream to white, and with pale line just inside of margin. This ornamental, evergreen herb, growing from rhizome, with its showy, arrow-shaped, thin-leathery leaves, is one of the most beautiful of warm greenhouse exotics. *Tropical. Zone 11.*   p. 219

macrotites (Brazil, Bolivia); robust tuberous plant forming clusters; stiff petioles measuring to 1 m, vaginate toward base; leaves arrow-shaped about 50 to 100 cm long, rich green with prominent ribs; the bold inflorescence with rolled, cream-colored spathe, inflated and green at base, and concealing the slender white spadix. *Zone 10.*   p. 24

CALAMAGROSTIS   *Gramineae*
x acutiflora (arundinacea x epigeios), German Karl Foerster hybrid of Eurasian species, "Feather Reed grass"; very ornamental perennial grass to 1½ m high, spreading by underground creeping rhizomes; slender, deciduous stems with rough, dull green, narrow grass-like channeled leaves, and long, beautiful lance-shaped inflorescence turning purplish-rose, during Summer. *Zone 5.*   p. 559

CALAMINTHA   *Labiatae*
grandiflora (So. Europe to Asia Minor), "Calamint"; herbaceous aromatic, bushy perennial to 50 cm high, the branches at base decumbent then erect, with ovate leaves 5-8 cm long, rounded at base, and coarsely toothed; the flowers pink and purplish, with tubular corolla 4 cm long, in loose racemes, blooming early Summer. *Zone 6.*   p. 434

CALAMUS   *Palmae*
fasciculatus (Malaysia); seen in Singapore Botanic Garden; interesting tropical feather palm having several slowly elongating slender, striped stems densely covered with long cream spines; the fronds pinnate with broad thin-leathery leaflets, some variegated with white. *Zone 12.*   p. 100

scipionum (Malaysia), "Malacca rattan"; non-climbing "Malacca canes" forming thickets; very spiny, twisting cane-stems, with very long internodes as much as 1½ m apart, making them suitable for walking-sticks and furniture use; large leathery, glossy green pinnate leaves. *Humid-tropical. Zone 12.*   p. 100

CALANTHE   *Orchidaceae*
furcata (Philippines); evergreen terrestrial, with plaited green leaves in a rosette; the flowers in dense raceme on 1 m, erect spike, white turning blue; the lip resembles a dancing girl, (June-Aug.). *Tropical. Zones 11-12.*   p. 84

x vestita 'Baron Schroeder' (regnieri x vestita); well known terrestrial (1894), with deciduous pseudobulbs, and long arching spray of flowers with orchid pink petals and sepals, the lip winged and with dark purple. *Tropical. Zone 11.*   p. 84

x vestita 'William Murray' (vestita x williamsii); terrestrial hybrid with graceful spray of large flowers from alongside the pseudobulb, petals white and lip carmine-red with darker throat, (Winter fl.). *Tropical. Zones 11-12.*   p. 82

CALATHEA   *Marantaceae*
bella (kegeliana hort.) (Brazil); very ornamental plant with glossy leathery, broad ovate leaves on wiry petioles, the coloring mainly gray with a feather design of dark green radiating from the midrib. *Humid-tropical. Zone 12.*   p. 72

ecuadoriana (tigrina hort.) (Ecuador); striking ornamental species, in the col. of Longwood Gardens, Kennet Square, Penna.; large showy leaves velvety deep green with contrasting silvery white ribs and along outer margin. *Zone 12.*   p. 72

insignis in hort.: is C. lancifolia (Dr. Helen Kennedy)

lancifolia (insignis hort.) (Brazil), "Rattlesnake plant"; very pretty, bushy species with narrow, tapering, almost linear stiffly erect foliage wavy at the margins, yellow-green with lateral ovals alternately large and small of dark green; underside a showy maroon red; while slow growing at first, I have seen it measure 60 cm or more as growing in Brazil. *Humid-tropical. Zone 12.*   p. 71

lindeniana (Brazil); vigorous plant to 1 m high, broad oval leaves deep green, with a feathery, pale olive zone either side of midrib and near the border, a darker zone between, purple underneath except near midrib. *Humid-tropical. Zone 12.*   p. 71

makoyana (Minas Geraes), "Peacock plant"; bushy plant 20-40 cm high stunningly beautiful on both sides of its oval 15-20 cm leaves, the surface with a feathery design of opaque, olive-green lines and ovals alternately short and long in a translucent field of pale yellow-green; this pattern of lines and ovals is purplish-red beneath. *Humid-tropical. Zone 12.*   p. 71, 459

metallica 'Undulata' (Brazil); large plant with oblique-oblong pointed leaves 40 cm x 16 cm, corrugated undulate throughout the blade to the margins, the surface iridescent satiny-silky forest green with paler midrib, royal purple beneath. *Tropical. Zone 11.*   p. 72

ornata 'Roseo-lineata'; long narrow-ovate, unequal-sided, metallic olive-green leaves, 15-20 cm long, later stage to 60 cm; in the juvenile stage nicely marked with closely-set pairs of rosy-red lateral stripes, later turning white in older leaves; purple beneath. *Tropical. Zone 12.*   p. 71

picturata 'Argentea' (Venezuela); dwarf plant similar in habit to vandenheckei but with short-stalked leaves almost entirely shining silver except for a border of dark green; wine-red beneath. *Tropical. Zone 11.*   p. 72

roseo-picta (Brazil); low plant with short-stalked, large 22 cm rounded, unequal-sided leaves dark olive-green above with red midrib and narrow zone of bright red near margin, changing to silver-pink when old; underside purple. *Tropical. Zone 12.*   p. 71

stromata: see CTENANTHE stromata

veitchiana (Ecuador, Perú), "Peacock plant"; strikingly beautiful plant from the Jivaro country; with large, stiff-leathery, glossy leaves to 30 cm long, obliquely broad-ovate, in four different shades of green with a peacock-feather design outlined in yellow-green, encircling brownish-green halfmoons which adjoin the pale bluish-green feathered center zone; marginal area bright green; the peacock-feather design outlined in red over bluish-green underneath also. *Humid-tropical. Zone 12.*   *p. 71*

warscewiczii (Costa Rica); heavy plant to 75 cm high, with short-stalked, oblong leaves undulate at margins, velvety deep green except for yellow-green midrib feathering into pale green lateral veins; underside wine-red. Inflorescence a short spike with tubular, leathery white bracts, white flowers. *Tropical. Zone 12.*   *p. 72*

zebrina (Rio, São Paulo), "Zebra plant"; bold, vigorous plant to 1 m high, with magnificent, thin leaves deep velvety green, the midrib and lateral veins pale or yellow-green, purplish beneath. *Tropical. Zone 12.*   *p. 71*

CALCEOLARIA   *Scrophulariaceae*

crenatiflora 'Grandiflora' (herbeohybrida), "Pocketbook plant"; herbaceous cultivar derived principally from C. crenatiflora which grows in the cool Andes of Chile and north, developed for use as potplants, with thin, fresh-green leaves, and clusters of showy, membranous flowers, 5-8 cm across, distinguished by a large inflated lower lip resembling a handbag, 6 cm or more across, in shades of yellow or red, often brilliantly spotted or tigered orange-red to maroon, blooming in Spring. *Humid-subtropic. Zone 10.*   *p. 54*

crenatiflora 'Maxima' (herbeohybrida hort.), "Pocketbook plant" of Chilean parentage; popular as florist's potted plant; rather delicate cool temperature herbaceous perennial grown as biennial from seed or cuttings, to 40 cm high, fresh green, ovate, crinkled leaves to 15 cm or more long; striking inflated, pouch-like flowers 6 cm or more wide, in various colors, usually yellow with brown, normally blooming April-May, but primarily grown in greenhouses timed for Easter and Spring; best at cool temperatures. *Zone 10.*   *p. 501*

crenatiflora 'Multiflora nana'; a herbaceous herbeohybrida form of dwarf, bushy habit, ideal as a potplant, with thin ovate, toothed and quilted leaves, and clusters of numerous, smallish pouch-like flowers, 3 to 5 cm across, most often yellow or orange or red, usually spotted or tigered with crimson. Spring-blooming. Needs protection from hot sun, and prefers cool situations. *Zone 10.*   *p. 501*

integrifolia (rugosa) (Chile), "Chilean pouch flower" for outdoor beds; shrubby perennial of bushy habit, with woody, hairy stems, small, wrinkled, toothed 10 cm leaves, and clusters with masses of small 1 cm pouch-flowers, yellow to red-brown; grown popularly for outdoor garden beds. The cultivar 'Gold Bouquet' produces large clusters of 2 cm flowers entirely golden-yellow. *Zone 9.*   *p. 501*

pavonii (Perú); shrubby perennial we found on the slopes to Machu Picchu in the Peruvian Andes Mts., with rough ovate leaves, and 3-4 cm flowers rich yellow, with inflated pouch. *Humid-subtropic. Zones 9-10.*   *p. 875*

CALENDULA   *Compositae*

officinalis (So. Europe), "Pot-marigold"; popular annual herb 30-40 cm high originating in So. Europe; with fleshy entire, brittle and clammy leaves not scented, on sticky stalks; the large double flowers 8 cm or more across, closing at night, in apricot, also shades of orange, lemon or golden-yellow in other named varieties. Excellent, long-lasting cutflower developing largest blooms if disbudded and grown cool. Their normal outdoor season is from June to frost, however, with a cool greenhouse or wintergarden, pot-marigolds may be had in bloom in the dark of Winter; for Christmas from August sowings. Flower petals are used to make dyes and color food; florets serve medicinally as anti-emetic. *Zones 9-10.*   *p. 377, 525*

officinalis 'Pacific'; "Pacific Beauty" strain favored in So. California and other areas of hot climate because of its better resistance to summer heat; branching herbaceous annual 25-50 cm high, with slightly sticky, aromatic leaves; large 10-12 cm double flowers glowing orange, and very showy in gardens. *Zones 9-10.*   *p. 377*

CALIBANUS   *Agavaceae*

hookeri (Eastern and Central Mexico); curious, caudiciform xerophyte with bulb-shaped rounded, woody base 30-40 cm dia., and to 25 cm high, covered by thick fissured, corky bark, topped by clusters of slender leathery leaves fountain-like; branched 50 cm inflorescence with inconspicuous flowers. Named after Shakespeare's monster 'Caliban'. According to Dorothy Dunn in 'California Garden' Sept. 1989, there are reports from Mexico of plants as big as a Volkswagen in the wild, with an immense caudex bearing monocarpic tufts of grass-like leaves, dying after flowering. *Zone 10.*   *p. 195*

CALLA   *Araceae*

palustris (Atlantic No. America, No. Europe, Lapland, Siberia), the "Water-arum", or "Wild calla"; bog-aquatic with creeping or floating stems or rhizomes with heart-shaped 15 cm leaves; the inflorescence with 5 cm spathe green outside, white inside and thread-like stamens; forming clusters of red berries. *Zone 2.*   *p. 325*

CALLIANDRA   *Leguminosae*

emarginata ('Minima' in hort.) (Mexico, Guatemala), "Miniature powder-puff"; shrub or small tree to 5 m high, with evergreen leaves compound of several uneven leaflets to 5 cm long; small inflorescence a globular head of red stamens 5 cm across. *Zone 10.*   *p. 749*

guildingii (Trinidad and St. Vincent), "Trinidad powderpuff tree"; rambling tropical shrub or tree to 10 m; the bipinnate leaves, with one pair of pinnae, each with 3-4 pairs of narrow leaflets; floral heads with small greenish-white petals, and showy compound bundles of crimson-red stamens to 8 cm long. *Zone 10.*   *p. 749*

haematocephala (Inga pulcherrima) (So. Brazil), "Pink powder puff"; rambling shrub to 5 m, with evergreen, bipinnate, silky leaves and powder-puff-like balls of conspicuous dark crimson stamens 6 to 10 cm across, blooming mostly from December to April. *Zone 10.*   *p. 749*

haematocephala 'Alba' (Bolivia), "White powder-puff"; evergreen sprawling shrub or small tree to 5 m high, with bipinnate leaves, having narrow, oblong leaves, with the terminal leaflets largest, to 9 cm long; showy floral heads 5 cm dia., the small corolla reddish, and a dense puff of long white stamens, tinted red toward apex, blooming Winter into Spring. *Zone 10.*   *p. 749*

houstoniana (So. Mexico to Honduras); slender tropical shrub to 3 m high, covered by rusty hairs; the leaves composed of 7-12 pairs of pinnae, each with 40-50 pairs of linear leaflets 1 cm long; floral heads clustered along raceme-like inflorescence, with long 5 cm purplish stamens emerging in clusters; bristly brown fruit 10 cm long. *Zone 10.*   *p. 749*

"inaequilatera" in hort. (bot. prob. haematocephala) (Ecuador, Bolivia), "Red powder puff"; evergreen shrub to 5 m high, with leaves divided into two pinnate branches, each with numerous leathery, ovate leaflets; beautiful globose inflorescence larger and more dense than tweedii, with showy, silky bright red stamens 4-5 cm long. *Zone 10.*   *p. 749*

portoricensis (caracasana) (Central America); evergreen tropical shrub to 2½ m, with shoots grooved, downy; leaves bipinnate; flowers white in globose heads, the long white stamens spreading like a woolly powder puff 5 cm dia. *Zone 10.*   *p. 749*

schultzei (Venezuela, Surinam); rambling tropical evergreen shrub, with leaves divided into pinnae, each with numerous lateral, oblong leaflets; the striking inflorescence in dense clusters of long white to pink stamens, tipped with red. *Zone 10.*   *p. 749*

surinamensis (Surinam); spreading shrub to 3 m high or woody climber resembling an inverted umbrella, with pinnate leaves always in forked pairs, smothered with pretty, pink brush-like flower heads composed of numerous long, threadlike, silky stamens reddish in the upper part and white below, 6 cm long. *Zone 10.*   *p. 750*

tweedii (Inga pulcherrima) (So. Brazil), "Flame-bush"; shrub with bipinnate leaves, each leaf with 2-7 pairs of pinnae, each of which with numerous linear leaflets 6-8 mm long, silky when young; the inflorescence showy with its semi-globular heads of crimson-red stamen-bundles, 5 to 7 cm broad; somewhat cold resistant. *Zones 9-10.*   *p. 749*

CALLICARPA   *Verbenaceae*

americana (Virginia to Texas; West Indies), "French mulberry" or "American beauty-berry"; deciduous shrub to 2 m high, with downy shoots, and lanceolate leaves 10-15 cm long, displaying elevated lateral ribs, white or rusty tomentose beneath; bluish flowers during June-July; very popular in Southern gardens because of its bright purple berries in dense clusters, profusely produced along branches in early Autumn. *Zone 7.*   *p. 897*

bodinieri var. giraldii (Cent. to No. China), "Beautyberry"; handsome deciduous to evergreen shrub to 3 m high, with lanceolate-pointed leaves 12 cm or more long, matte-green above and corrugated by depressed lateral veins, finely toothed at margins, and pubescent beneath; small lilac flowers in axillary rounded clusters, displaying yellow anthers in July, followed by shining violet berries. *Zone 6.*   *p. 897*

dichotoma (E. and Cent. China, Japan), "Purple beautyberry"; deciduous shrub 1 to 2 m high, with downy shoots, bearing ovate pointed or obovate leaves to 10 cm long, toothed at sides; small pink flowers in July, followed by crimson to purplish-violet berry-like fruit in clusters along stem. *Zone 5.*   *p. 898*

CALLIOPSIS bicolor: see COREOPSIS tinctoria

CALLIRHOE   *Malvaceae*
 involucrata (Missouri to Wyoming, so. to Texas), "Poppy mallow"; beautiful sprawling, herbaceous soft-hairy perennial 30-60 cm high, with roundish leaves, palmately deeply cut into 5-7 segments; solitary flowers 5-6 cm across, deep crimson-red with white eye, but variable to light red, blooming Spring to early Summer. *Zones 3-7.*   p. 456

CALLISIA   *Commelinaceae*
 fragrans (Spironema, or Trad. dracaenoides) (Oaxaca); fleshy rosette sending out long runners with young plants, fresh glossy-green lanceolate clasping leaves turning reddish-purple in strong light, margins smooth and pale green; fragrant white flowers. *Zones 10-11.*   p. 308
 repens (Tradescantia minima in hort.) (Texas to Argentina), "Turtle vine"; vigorous grower with long pendant slender vines, closely shingled with waxy, fresh-green, ovate leaves 2-3 cm long; insignificant small axillary flowers with 3 sepals and 3 tiny white petals, and prominent stamens, toward end of stems. Popular in hanging baskets in California. *Zones 10-11.*   p. 52, 308
 repens 'Bolivian Jew' (South America), "Afro-plant" or "Mini turtle plant"; small self-branching creeper, or pendant in hanging baskets, with thin vines and diminutive 1-2 cm, glossy green ovate or roundish leaves; the tiny white flowers from axils of leaf-like bracts. *Zones 10-11.*   p. 308

CALLISTEMON   *Myrtaceae*
 citrinus (lanceolatus) (Metrosideros floribunda) (New South Wales), "Bottle-brush"; tree-like shrub of sparry, bare habit, with hard, heavy wood, sun-loving and drought resistant; the silky twigs with rigid, long-linear 8 cm leaves and cylindrical flower spikes with masses of brilliant crimson brush-like stamens with dark yellow anthers, out of a grayish, felted calyx. *Zone 8.*   p. 797
 phoeniceus (W. Australia), "Fiery bottle-brush"; bushy shrub to 2½ m; the branches grayish, thick and smooth; narrow oblanceolate leaves to 10 cm long; inflorescence in rich scarlet bottle brushes with stamen bundles tipped dark red. *Zone 9.*   p. 797
 rigidus (New South Wales), "Stiff bottle brush"; erect, sparse, rigid shrub or small tree to 6 m; leaves sharp-pointed, gray-green or purplish, red floral brushes to 10 cm long; very drought tolerant. *Zone 9.*   p. 797
 viminalis (New South Wales), "Weeping bottle brush"; shrub or small tree with pendulous branches, 6 to 10 m high; leaves narrow linear, light green 15 cm long; dense spikes of scarlet-red stamens. *Zone 8.*   p. 797

CALLISTEPHUS   *Compositae*
 chinensis (China), "China aster"; annual herbaceous plant with corrugated deeply toothed leaves; solitary showy flower heads 12 cm across, with ray-petals usually light purple, disc yellow. *Subtropic. Zone 10.*   p. 374

CALLITRIS   *Cupressaceae (Coniferae)*
 columellaris (glauca) (Western Australia), "White cypress pine"; densely branched evergreen 12 to 20 m high, the branchlets in thick clusters of fine filiform sprays of greenish-blue to glaucous appressed leaves, the free tip a short incurved point; globose female cones with woody scales separating nearly to base at maturity. *Zone 10.*   p. 573
 rhomboidea (cupressiformis) (S.E. Australia, Tasmania), "Port Jackson pine" or "Cypress pine"; evergreen tree 10-20 m high, or occasionally shrubby, densely branched; branchlets finely divided, covered by scaly cypress-like bright green or glaucous leaves; female cones globular, with short prickly protuberances. *Zone 9.*   p. 573

CALLUNA   *Ericaceae*
 vulgaris (Europe, Asia Minor), "Heather"; very popular small evergreen flowering shrub to 50 cm high, widespread in Europe and covering large moor areas from North Germany to Scotland, with peaty soils; the slender branches with diminutive scale-like overlapping leaves; the inflorescence in spires to 20 cm long, of lilac-rose flowers 6 mm long, blooming July to October. Calluna are distinguished from Erica in having the colored showy part of the flower, its calyx, 4-parted to base, the smaller corolla cup inside, whereas in Erica the flower is not divided, except for apex lobes. *Zone 4.* p. 701

CALOCARPUM mammosum: see POUTERIA sapota

CALOCEDRUS   *Cupressaceae (Coniferae)*
 decurrens (W. Oregon to Baja California), "California incense cedar"; large coniferous evergreen tree to 30 m or more high, of stiff columnar outline, erect branches with flattened branchlets, scale-like dark green leaves in fours, the lateral pair keeled and overlapping the facial pair; cylindric cones 2 cm long, of 6 scales in 3 pairs, brown when ripe. *Zones 6-9.*   p. 573

 formosana (Libocedrus) (Taiwan), "Formosa incense cedar"; large evergreen coniferous tree to 10 m high, endemic in the mountains of C. Taiwan, similar to C. macrolepis, but with shorter leaves; female cones 2 cm long, on short, flattened branchlets similar to those of sterile branchlets. Wood is valuable in cabinet and furniture making. *Zone 9.*   p. 573
 macrolepis (So. China, Yunnan, Burma), "Incense cedar"; large pyramidal evergreen tree to 30 m high, having white, scaly bark; flattened short-jointed branchlets with spiralled scaly leaves in fours, glaucous beneath, and ending in spine-like teeth; elliptic cones 2 cm long with 6 scales. *Zone 9.*   p. 573

CALOCEPHALUS   *Compositae*
 brownii (Australia), the "Cushion-bush" or "Barbed-wire plant"; rigid, white-woolly dwarf shrub about 30 cm high, with tiny alternate, linear silvery-gray leaves, and round terminal clusters of yellow composite tubular flowers. In habitat from Western Australia to Tasmania. *Zone 9.*   p. 689

CALOCHORTUS   *Liliaceae*
 ambiguus (watsonii var.) (Arizona, New Mexico), "Mariposa lily" of arid Indian country; striking bulbous perennial with grass-like leaves along slender floral stalk, topped by showy bell flower with pinkish or bluish-gray petals and sepals, marked purple near base. *Zone 6.*   p. 237
 caeruleus (Sierra Nevada, No. Calif.) "Cat's-ear" or "Beaver-tail grass"; low bulbous perennial, with erect or flexuous stem to 15 cm long, with linear leaves, and topped by flowers open bell-shaped, the petals bluish, 2 cm long, hairy above center, lined and marked dark blue, inner segments covered and fringed with hairs; July blooming in the Sierras. *Zone 7.*   p. 237
 gunnisonii (Dakota to Montana, Arizona), "Butterfly tulip" or "Sego lily"; charming bulbous perennial 15 to 40 cm high, with linear leaves along slender floral stem; bell-like flowers open wide, 5 to 8 cm across, the petals pale lilac with purple bands below middle, and bearded with glandular hairs. *Zones 4-9.*   p. 237, 444
 kennedyi (Deserts: S.W. Unit. States to Sonora, Mex.) "Desert Mariposa"; beautiful bulbous perennial, with narrowly linear, glaucous basal leaves, and simple leafy floral stems 10 to 25 cm high, topped by one or more showy flowers, the petals 3-4 cm long, orange or red inside, usually with brown spot at base. *Zone 8.*   p. 237
 lyallii (Pacific Northwest to Brit. Columbia), "White Mariposa lily"; low bulbous perennial 15-20 cm high; linear leaves basal and along flexuous stem; flowers terminal, with spreading triangular petals, white or tinged purple, fringed by long hairs, and with purple crescent inside, in June. *Zone 5.*   p. 237
 nuttallii (Dakota to Utah and Arizona), "Lilac Sego lily"; State flower of Utah; elegant bulbous perennial 20 to 40 cm high; glaucous fleshy linear leaves, reduced along stem; erect open bell-shaped flowers having 3 prominent petals to 4 cm long, white tinged with lilac and purple at base, and hairy in lower half; June blooming. *Zones 3-8.*   p. 237
 splendens (Cent. California to No. Baja Calif.), "Lilac mariposa"; stems branching, 40-60 cm high, not very bulbiferous; basal leaves to 15 cm long, stem leaves reduced; flowers terminating the branches, open bell-shaped with petals 3-5 cm long lilac rose, hairy to middle, spring-blooming. *Zone 6.*   p. 237
 venustus (California), "Mariposa lily" or "Butterfly tulip"; showy bulbous perennial with linear basal leaves; stiff, branched floral stalk 10 to 30 cm high, sometimes to more than 1 m; topped by very handsome bell-shaped flowers to 10 cm across, in various colors white to yellow, red or purple, and red blotch in center. *Zone 9.*   p. 237
 weedii (So. California: San Diego), "Weed's mariposa"; striking bulbous perennial 30-50 cm high, with stiff branching stem; linear basal leaf 40 cm long; the bell-shaped erect flowers orange-yellow, the petals 3-4 cm long, bearded with long yellow hairs. *Zone 8.*   p. 237

CALODENDRUM   *Rutaceae*
 capense (So. Africa to Zambia), "Cape chestnut"; tall, semi-evergreen tree to 18 m, with oval 15 cm, ruffled leaves, and very conspicuous when it bears its large clusters of dainty pinky-mauve flowers; the five slender and recurving petals marked with crimson, measuring 8-10 cm across; of 10 pale pink stamens, five resemble thin petals and are spotted with red; the brown fruits are knobby and split to release the seed. *Zone 10.*   p. 859

CALONYCTION   *Convolvulaceae*
 album (Ipomoea alba), (American and other Tropics), the legendary tropical "Moon-flower"; perennial twiner related to morning-glories (Ipomoea), but blooming at night instead of in sunshine; stems more or less prickly, with milky juice, climbing to 5 m

high; cordate, smooth leaves 15 cm long, and large salver-shaped flowers 12-15 cm wide, pure white, and fragrant, opening toward evening and closing in the morning. *Tropical. Zones 10-11.*   p. 273

CALOPHYLLUM   *Guttiferae*
inophyllum (native on shores of the Indian and Western Pacific Oceans), the "Beauty leaf", "Kamani" or "Alexandrian laurel"; handsome, low-branching crooked or leaning tree such as the one I photographed on Moorea in French Polynesia; to 20 m high, with rough gray bark, and shiny green, leathery, oblong leaves 8-20 cm long and with yellow midrib; the white flowers suggest orange blossoms and are very fragrant; the 3 cm green fruit in pendulous clusters; thin leathery skin covers a bony shell, containing an oily kernel yielding "dilo oil", used medicinally and for lights. *Tropical. Zone 10.*   p. 733

CALOTHAMNUS   *Myrtaceae*
chrysantheros (W. Australia), "Claw flower"; dense shrub to 1½ m, with thick brown stems often corky; long pencil-like thin dark green leaves 5-10 cm long; the inflorescence an axillary group of stout crimson stamen bundles feathering at apex into slender filaments; seen at King's Park, Perth. *Subtropic. Zone 9.*   p. 797

CALOTROPIS   *Asclepiadaceae*
gigantea (Iran, Tibet, India, China), the "Crown plant"; lush shrub with white glaucous stem containing milky juice; large obovate leaves 15-20 cm long covered with white down, and with pale veins; axillary inflorescence clusters of star-like flowers lavender to purple, with a crown of 5 narrow, fleshy scales. Sacred to Hanuman, the Monkey-god, in India. *Arid-tropical. Zone 10.*   p. 654

CALTHA   *Ranunculaceae*
leptosepala (Alaska to Alberta, so. to Oregon and New Mexico), "Meadow-bright"; low perennial of wet areas forming clumps 15 cm high, with oval-cordate leaves crenate at margins; 3 cm flowers having 6-12 white sepals tinted blue, in June-July. *Zone 3.*   p. 337
palustris (Labrador, Canada, Alaska, south to Tennessee; Eurasia), "Marsh marigold" or "Cowslip"; fleshy perennial marsh plant with hollow stems 20-50 cm high, the heart-shaped leaves to 20 cm wide; and bright yellow 5 cm flowers resembling butter cups. *Zone 3.*   p. 337
palustris ssp. minor, "Dwarf marigold" or "King-cup"; diminutive variety seen in Kew Gardens, England, with masses of glossy green kidney-shaped, lobed leaves, and pretty, golden-yellow cup-like flowers. *Zone 3.*   p. 337

CALYCANTHUS   *Calycanthaceae*
floridus (Virginia to Florida), "Carolina allspice"; old favorite deciduous shrub 2-3 m high, with very aromatic wood; ovate leaves 8-12 cm long, densely downy beneath; fragrant flowers 5 cm wide, the sepals and petals red-purple, tinged brown, during Summer. *Zone 5.*   p. 671

CAMASSIA   *Liliaceae*
cusickii (N.E. Oregon), "Camass"; prolific perennial having large clustered bulbs; basal, rather succulent glaucous decumbent leaves 2-4 cm wide and to 50 cm long; floral stalks to 1 m, with pyramidal racemes of pale blue 3 cm starry flowers; capsules subglobose. *Zone 5.*   p. 236
leichtlinii (Brit. Columbia to California); bulbous herb with tough linear basal leaves and tall stalks to 120 cm high, with terminal bracted racemes of dark blue to creamy flowers 2½ cm long, having star-like spreading segments, the withered remains tightly clasping the seed capsules. *Zones 4-5.*   p. 236
quamash (esculenta) (Pennsylvania to Georgia, California and north to Alberta), "Common camass" or "Bear grass"; bulbous herb with linear basal leaves, and floral stalks to 1 m high, bearing starry flowers in shades from light to deep blue. The bulbs of Camass were cooked and eaten by the Indians. *Zones 4-5.*   p. 236
quamash alba (esculenta hort.), "Indian hyacinth"; lovely variety seen in Morristown, New Jersey, having pyramidal racemes of starry flowers glistening white, in late Spring. *Zone 6.*   p. 236
scilloides (Pennsylvania to Minnesota, so. to Georgia and Texas), "Atlantic camass" or "Indigo squill"; most attractive spring-flowering bulb; narrow keeled grass-like basal leaves to 60 cm long; inflorescence to 75 cm high bearing 6 to 10 pale blue starry flowers 2 cm dia. with yellow anthers, in May-June. *Zone 5.*   p. 236
scilloides alba, "Wild hyacinth", as seen in Arizona; exquisite colorform with pyramidal spires of starry flowers having 6 waxy-white segments and prominent bright yellow anthers. *Zone 6.*   p. 236

CAMELLIA   *Theaceae*
japonica (Mountains of Japan and Korea), the "Common camellia"; a fine ornamental evergreen tree to 12 m high, well-shaped with woody branches and dark green, glossy, leathery, ovate leaves to

10 cm long, finely toothed; axillary flowers 4 to 12 cm across, variably single to double, white, pink, red, or variegated and listed under various cultivar names. *Zone 7.*   p. 887
japonica 'Colonel Firey' (C. M. Hovey); compact grower with twisted, narrow, dark green leaves, and perfectly formal, very double, large flowers of brilliant crimson, blooming midseason to late. *Zone 8.*   p. 888
japonica 'Debutante' (Sara Hastie); originating in South Carolina; this is a shapely, fast-growing beauty, ideal pot plant; early and free-flowering, with exquisite, full peony-form, firm, small 4-6 cm flowers of clear rose-pink, from October to January and later. *Zone 8.*   p. 888
japonica 'Elegans' (chandleri); an old variety; wide-spreading tree with long, glossy foliage and very large flowers of the peony type, 10 cm across, variegated cherry-red with white, borne in profusion in late January. *Zone 7.*   p. 888
japonica 'Elegans Splendor'; very attractive large flowers of the anemone type, soft pink edged with silky white, the petals deeply crenate along margins, blooming midseason; a choice sport of C. jap. 'C. M. Wilson'. Photographed in col. Monrovia Nurseries, Azusa, California. *Zone 8.*   p. 889
japonica 'Jordan's Pride' (Herma); free-blooming, dependable variety with large formal semi-double 8 to 10 cm flowers of soft shell pink, irregularly bordered deep pink and bordered white, occasionally altogether pink (midseason to late; Janury to March). *Zone 8. p. 888*
japonica 'Pearl Maxwell'; large formal, double flowers soft shell pink; looks like a glorified 'Pink Perfection' (midseason to late). *Zone 8.*   p. 888
japonica 'Pink Perfection'; popular variety of symmetrical, vigorous growth; small, well-formed double, rather flat flowers of delicate shell-pink, free flowering from November-April. Earlier name: 'Frau Minna Seidel.' *Subtropic. Zone 8.*   p. 888
japonica 'Purity'; well-known variety of slender habit, free-blooming while quite young, with glossy, pointed leaves, and exquisite white, double flowers of the formal type, of porcelain texture and long lasting. November-April. *Zone 8.*   p. 888
japonica 'Rosedale Beauty'; outstanding trademarked hybrid, profusely blooming with big double, formal flowers, crimson-red about 10 cm across; of vigorous growth and compact habit with broad, dark green leaves (midseason). *Zone 8.*   p. 888
japonica 'William S. Hastie'; outstanding variety of slender habit with long pointed, dull green foliage, and freely bearing large, perfect, rose-form flowers of brilliant crimson, from February-April. *Subtropic. Zone 8.*   p. 888
oleifera (China), "Tea-oil bush"; freely flowering shrub to 6 m high, with young branches brown-hirsute; leathery leaves elliptic to obovate, minutely toothed, 5-8 cm long; single flowers white, drooping quickly; larger, thicker leaves than sasanqua, also larger fruits. Cultivated in China for the "tea-oil". *Zone 9.*   p. 888
reticulata (China), "Temple flower"; sparry shrub to 6 m high, with scattered rigid foliage having prominent veins; large single flowers 8 to 12 cm and more across, vivid rosy-red, with wavy petals, blooming in February. *Zones 8-9.*   p. 888
sasanqua (China, Japan), "Sasanqua camellia" or "Sunlight camellia"; evergreen shrub of loose habit and with branches pubescent when young; small, thin-leathery leaves elliptic and toothed, shining dark green and hairy on the midrib above; very floriferous with small, 4-5 cm single, slightly fragrant blossoms white in the type, with 5 or more petals and with yellow stamens, but running into many forms semi-double, white, pink to cherry-red; more hardy than japonica, but the flowers shed easily; October-April. Winter-hardy in So. New Jersey. *Warm temperate. Zone 7.*   p. 889
sasanqua 'Bonanza'; beautiful grafted cultivar in California, of low, spreading habit; showy flowers double peony or semi-double, rich rose accented crimson-scarlet, and where visible, by contrasting bright yellow stamens. Photographed in Ganter Nursery, Vista, Calif. *Zone 7.*   p. 889
sasanqua 'Jean May'; low evergreen bush of compact habit, with erect branches and exceptionally glossy green leaves; lovely relatively large double flowers soft shell-pink tinted with rose, to about 6 cm across. *Zone 7.*   p. 877
sasanqua 'Shishi-Gashira'; vigorous Japanese cultivar with spreading branches with dark foliage and semi-double bright rose-pink flowers 6 cm across; ideal in hanging baskets; free blooming. *Zones 7-8.*   p. 79, 889
sasanqua 'Showa-No-Sakae'; charming Japanese form of compact habit with small 6 cm dark green leathery leaves on willowy branches; semi-double peony form; lovely soft rose-pink 5-6 cm across. *Zone 7.*   p. 889
sasanqua 'Yuletide'; striking flowering plant for the winter season; erect bushy plant with dark green small foliage finely crenate; brilliant fiery red to maroon single blooms 5-6 cm across, shaped like

cups, in the center a nest of bright yellow stamens in charming contrast; flowering from Autumn on into the Christmas season. *Warm temperate. Zone* 7. *p. 887*

sinensis (S.W. China, Yunnan), "Tea plant"; evergreen, tree-like shrub to 10 m high, with alternate, waxy, thin-leathery, elliptic leaves 5-10 cm long, finely serrate, and small, white, fragrant flowers; makes a handsome plant for tubs; where I have seen tea cultivated in Sikkim, Sri Lanka, Java, or Japan, the bushes are kept low for women to pick each tender tip every 3 weeks, and gentle heating, rolling and fermenting produces the aromatic black tea of commerce; fruit a woody capsule. *Zone* 9. *p. 887*

sinensis var. assamica (No. India, Assam, Myanmar, Thailand, Vietnam, Sri Lanka), "Assam tea"; similar to C. sinensis, but leaves larger, 7-15 cm long, thinner and slightly toothed; growing tree-like if not kept trimmed; extensively cultivated in the more tropical regions. *Zones 10-11.* *p. 887*

sinensis var. bohea (China: Yunnan to Chekiang Prov.), "Chinese tea"; compact growing shrub 1 to 2 m high, cultivated on tea plantations in cooler climate; the elliptic leaves are leathery, 5 to 12 cm long, dark glossy green; small, nodding, white flowers 2 cm across. This variety has been cultivated for 1300 years, producing 3 crops a year from March to October; the young, top 2 to 3 leaves are picked, and dried at 70°C (160°F), but not fermented, to yield the famous aromatic "Green tea" of China and Japan. Tea as beverage is valued world-wide as a stimulant due to its caffeine content, and, as I was told in China, "refreshes the mind". *Subtropic. Zone* 9. *p. 887*

tsai (W. China); bushy evergreen shrub, with strong, arching branches, more or less appressed pubescent; small lanceolate leaves slender-pointed, 7-9 cm long and toothed at margins, glossy green above, lightly hairy beneath, and undulate along sides; white 2-3 cm flowers, having 5 petals, and very free-blooming. *Zone* 6. *p. 889*

CAMISSONIA: see OENOTHERA

CAMPANULA   *Campanulaceae*

aucheri (Armenia, Caucasus, Iran); diminutive hardy perennial forming clump, 10-12 cm tall, with spatulate pubescent leaves 5-8 cm long; erect violet to pale blue bell-flowers. *Zone* 5. *p. 352*

bellidifolia (Caucasus), "Caucasus bell-flower"; tufted herbaceous perennial forming rosette of ovate, crenate leaves; several erect leafy stems bearing showy, cup-shaped flowers 3 cm long, deep violet-purple, and white in center. *Zone* 5. *p. 352*

calamenthifolia (Greece), "Greek bellflower"; grayish pubescent, short-lived perennial, having rosette of basal leaves, and radiating deflexed branches 20 cm long, the small stem-leaves ovate 2 cm long; numerous solitary, erect, white or blue flowers 2 cm across, and tomentose outside. *Zone* 7. *p. 352*

carpatica (Czechoslovakia, Poland, Hungary); "Carpathian harebell"; charming small mound-forming herbaceous perennial 20-30 cm high, spreading with thin leafy branches, the ovate leaves 3-5 cm long; the solitary wide-cupped flowers 4-5 cm across, purplish-blue with pale center, blooming in Spring to Summer. *Zone* 4. *p. 352*

carpatica 'Alba', "Carpathian bellflower" or "Tussock bellflower"; compact leafy tufts to 20 cm high, with stems branching and spreading; smooth bright green leaves 3 cm long, and toothed; erect, open cup flowers 3-5 cm across, pure white, blooming late Spring. *Zone* 4. *p. 352*

cochleariifolia (European mountains); excellent low-growing perennial, with underground runners sending up dense mats of small, fan-shaped leaves, and floral stalks 10-15 cm high, free-blooming with bell flowers varying from pale blue to sky blue. *Zone* 6. *p. 355*

elatines (No. Italy), "Star of Bethlehem"; freely branching herbaceous perennial forming mounds; the slender, trailing stems with sharply toothed, cordate ovate 3 cm leaves; very floriferous with starry white, 2 cm flowers, in Spring to Summer. *Zones 6-8.* *p. 355*

elatines garganica (C. garganica Zander) (So. Italy), "Adriatic bellflower"; low mat-forming herbaceous spreader with small wrinkled, ovate, lightly hairy leaves to 3 cm long; small starry 2 cm flowers light blue, usually with white eye; in June. *Zones 6-8.* *p. 309, 353*

elatines garganica 'Major'; cultivar of vigorous sprawling habit, with relatively large, starry purplish-blue flowers 2-3 cm across, blooming early Summer. *Zones 6-8.* *p. 309*

glomerata (Europe, Temperate Asia), "Danesblood" or "Clustered bellflower"; charming erect perennial to 1 m high; the leafy stems with lanceolate foliage to 10 cm long, and topped by dense clusters of funnel-shaped smallish flowers rich purple. *Temperate.* *Zone* 3. *p. 353*

hegielia (Asiatic Turkey); charming small bellflower found in habitat hidden on the ancient temple ruins of Apollo, near Priene in Anatolia; lanceolate, white-felty, toothed basal leaves, smaller on ascending stem, crowned by loose cluster of large purplish-pink flowers 4-5 cm long. *Zone* 6. *p. 354*

isophylla (Italy), "Falling stars"; slender trailer with thin stems and small cordate leaves, literally covered by star-shaped, pale violet flowers 3 to 4 cm dia. *Subtropic. Zone* 9. *p. 351, 357*

isophylla 'Alba' (Italy), "Star of Bethlehem"; dainty trailer for hanging basket; small green ovate toothed leaves on thin stems, and white star-like, saucer-shaped flowers 3-4 cm across. *Zone* 9. *p. 352*

lactiflora ('Molyneux') (Caucasus), "Milky bellflower"; branching perennial to 1 m or more high; basal leaves 12 cm long, serrate at margins, the leafy floral stem topped by terminal cluster of milk-white or pale blue cupped flowers with wide-spread lobes to 3 cm across, blooming June to August. *Zone* 5. *p. 353*

medium (So. Europe, naturalized from Britain to Austria), "Canterbury bells"; popular garden biennial, to 1 m high, with basal rosette of obovate, roughish leaves to 25 cm long; inflorescence on leafy erect stalk bearing bold raceme of large inflated, bell-shaped flowers 5 cm long, in shades or rose or blue, also white, in Spring and Summer. *Zones 4-9.* *p. 353*

medium 'Alba' (So. Europe, France), "Canterbury bells"; hairy biennial with tall branched stem bearing numerous large bell-shaped flowers pure white. *Warm temperate. Zones 4-9.* *p. 353*

medium 'Calycanthema', "Cup-and-saucer"; striking biennial of Italian descent, having inflorescence with calyx lobes enlarged and petaloid, or petal-like, forming a saucer, which together with the rose to purple bell-like petals give the appearance of a double flower, to 8 cm across. *Zones 4-9.* *p. 353*

medium 'Calycanthema caerulea' (So. Europe), "Cup and saucer"; bellflower with double blooms clear violet-blue, in erect terminal clusters, seen summer-blooming in the Rocky Mts. of Colorado. *Zone* 4. *p. 353*

medium 'Rosea', "Pink Canterbury bells"; as grown at the Dahlem Botanic Garden in Berlin, with showy bells a soft rose pink. *Zone* 4. *p. 353*

patula (Carpathian Mts., Central and So. Europe); roughly hairy biennial much branched with slender, angled stems 25-75 cm high; obovate basal leaves in crowded rosette, the stem leaves linear; erect funnel-form flowers 3 cm across, bluish-purple in open clusters, in Autumn. *Zone* 3. *p. 354*

persicifolia (S.E. Europe: Balkans); "Peach-leaved bellflower"; very popular perennial 60-90 cm high with clusters of erect leafy stems; the basal leaves are smooth, 10-20 cm long; the stem-leaves shorter and shaped like peach-leaves; open cup-shaped flowers blue, pink or white, blooming July-August. *Zones 3-9.* *p. 354*

portenschlagiana (muralis) (Croatia), "Dalmatian bellflower"; bushy perennial herb 15-20 cm high, densely branching and forming mounds; sharply pointed leaves 3-5 cm long, partially evergreen; small bluish-purple funnel-form flowers not lobed beyond middle, 2-3 cm across. *Zone* 4. *p. 355*

poschkarskyana (No. Yugoslavia), "Serbian bellflower"; sprawling perennial herb of vigorous growth, 10-15 cm high, the weak stems trailing to 50 cm, and set with broad, cordate-ovate leaves; and small 3 cm lilac-blue funnel flowers having lobes flaring wide. *Zone* 4. *p. 355*

punctata (Siberia, Japan); hardy perennial 45 cm high, with underground running root-stock, ovate toothed leaves to 12 cm long; nodding bell flowers creamy-pink, dotted purple inside, 6 cm long; Summer. *Zone* 4. *p. 354*

rotundifolia (Europe to Siberia, Labrador to Alaska, No. America) "Harebell" or "Bluebells-of-Scotland"; dainty perennial herb forming loose rosettes of leaves and stolons; the basal leaves roundish and crenate; stem leaves grass-like, narrow linear; cupped flowers with spreading lobes, lavender blue and 2 cm long, in June-August. *Zones 3-9.* *p. 354*

rupestris (tomentosa hort.) (Greece, Turkey), "Silky bellflower"; handsome short-lived perennial forming a basal rosette of gray, hairy oval leaves; prostrate stems with silky gray foliage, spreading to 30 cm long, bearing lavender-blue bells 2 cm long, borne singly along branches. *Zone* 7. *p. 355*

sarmatica (Caucasus) "Sarmatian bellflower"; mound-forming, hairy perennial, with grayish-green hastate-ovate lower leaves to 8 cm long, usually toothed; floral stems 25-50 cm high, bearing nodding pale blue bell-flowers to 3 cm long, in mid-summer. *Zone* 5. *p. 355*

thyrsoides (Alps of Europe to Balkan Mts.); beautiful small, monocarpic rosette with basal lanceolate leaves to 20 cm long; from center rises the hollow, leafy floral stalk 15 to 40 cm high, bearing cylindric, bracted spike of bell-shaped cream or yellowish flowers 2½ cm long, in July-August. After fruiting the plant will expire. *Zone* 5. *p. 354*

trachelium (Europe to Asia Minor, Siberia), "Nettle-leaf bellflower" or "Coventry-bells"; rough-hairy perennial or biennial, to 50 or 80 cm high with angled stems; lower leaves cordate-ovate to triangular, and toothed at margins; cup-shaped, blue-purple flowers having bristly calyx, autumn-blooming. *Zone* 4. *p. 354*

CAMPHORA: see CINNAMOMUM

CAMPSIS *Bignoniaceae*
   grandiflora (chinensis) (China, Japan), "Chinese trumpet-creeper"; climbing by aerial rootlets; related to Bignonia but without tendrils and with opposite leaves, pinnate, deciduous; the 7-9 ovate leaflets toothed; terminal clusters of large funnel-shaped orange and scarlet flowers 6 cm across. *Zones 7-9.*   *p. 268*
   radicans (Pennsylvania to Florida and Texas), "Trumpet-vine"; high climber to 12 m by means of aerial roots; pinnate leaves with 9-11 oval leaflets partially pubescent; trumpet-shaped flowers in terminal clusters, orange with scarlet limb, 5 cm across. *Warm temperate. Zone 6.*   *p. 268*
   x tagliabuana (grandiflora x radicans); vigorous shrubby climber intermediate between parents, with large pinnate leaves clinging by means of aerial roots; blooming in late Summer in a showy display of trumpet-like salmon-red flowers. *Zones 7-10.*   *p. 664*
   x tagliabuana 'Mad. Galen'; excellent horticultural cultivar, a clinging shrubby vine to 8 m long, the pinnate leaves with corrugated ovate leaflets, crenate at margins; clusters of large wide-open funnel-flowers 8 cm across, rich orange-red and deep crimson in center. *Zones 6-10.*   *p. 268*

CAMPTOSORUS *Polypodiaceae (Filices)*
   rhizophyllus (Quebec to Minnesota and Georgia), "Walking fern"; small evergreen fern, with lanceolate leaves to 24 cm long, cordate at base tapering to a slender apex, often rooting at tip. *Zones 3-6.*   *p. 130*

CAMPTOTHECA *Nyassaceae*
   acuminata (China); quick-growing deciduous tree to 25 m, with ovate, glossy green, corrugated leaves to 15 cm long; small flowers with long white stamens, in clusters, developing into the curious pale yellow winged fruit. *Zone 7.*   *p. 805*

CAMPYLOTROPIS *Leguminosae*
   macrocarpa (Lespedeza) (No. and C. China); deciduous shrub 1 to 2 m high; trifoliate leaves with oblong or elliptic, bristle-tipped leaflets 2-5 cm long, silky beneath; small purple flowers 1 cm long in dense racemes, blooming August-September; silky 2 cm seed pods. *Zone 5.*   *p. 750*

CANANGA *Annonaceae*
   odorata (Burma to Malaya and Australia), "Ylang-ylang" or "Perfume tree"; charming tropical tree with crooked trunk, to 25 m tall, and pendant brittle branches; oblong pointed, soft-leathery foliage 12-20 cm long; large axillary clusters of peculiar greenish-yellow flowers with long lanceolate drooping, twisted petals of soft-leathery texture 5-10 cm long, and intensely fragrant, strongest in early morning. The flowers are worn for their perfume or used in leis as in Tonga; and distilled for their fragrant essential oil in perfume. *Tropical. Zone 10.*   *p. 640*

CANARIUM *Burseraceae*
   album (So. China, Vietnam), "Chinese white olive"; evergreen resinous tree usually 6-9 m high, but occasionally to 18 m, with rounded crown; the trunk covered by whitish bark; large pinnate leaves of 11-15 leaflets to 8 cm long; small white flowers in clusters, during May; followed in October by egg-shaped fruit to 3 cm long, containing a bony, pointed stone inside. The fruits are esteemed in Hongkong and So. China as a condiment, or as a side dish either fresh or salted. *Zone 9.*   *p. 523*
   pimela (S.E. China: Kwangtung; Hongkong), "Chinese black olive"; handsome evergreen tree to 16 m high, with red-brown scaly bark and spreading crown; large pinnate leaves 45-60 cm long, compound of 15-21 leathery, ovate-pointed leaflets; small flowers with cup-shaped trilobed calyx and 3 to 5 whitish petals, blooming in May, followed in Autumn by 4 cm ovoid fruit, changing from green to purplish-black, resembling the European olive, and used preserved for culinary purposes. *Zones 9-10.*   *p. 906*
   vulgare (commune) (Malaysia, Java), "Java almond"; large buttressed tree with gray bark; leaves 30 cm or more long, have 3-5 pairs of oval leaflets and one at tip; small yellowish-white flowers with separate sexes; the fruits are ovoid, somewhat 3-sided blue-black nuts each with one kernel which is edible raw or roasted with almond flavor. *Tropical. Zone 10.*   *p. 669*

CANISTRUM *Bromeliaceae*
   cyathiforme (So. Brazil, Rio de Janeiro); epiphytic or terrestrial open rosette of broad green leaves 50 cm or more long, mottled with dark spots, and edged with soft teeth; showy inflorescence in basket shape with rigid outer bracts brilliant red, flower petals yellow, carried on reddish stalk. *Zone 11.*   *p. 45*

CANNA *Cannaceae*
   edulis (W. Indies, So. America; cult. in Queensland), "Edible canna" or "Achira"; tropical arrowroot 1-3 m high, with thick, tuber-like rhizomes which are edible; stout purplish stalks with oblong pointed leaves to 50 cm long, and topped by unusual inflorescence of spike-like racemes of flowers having reddish sepals, yellowish petals and short red lip. Rhizomes are used as food by Indians of the Andes; grown in Queensland for the starch. *Zones 8-10.*   *p. 358*
   generalis 'Cleopatra'; a fancy cultivar from Texas, with flower heads 20 to 25 cm across, huge yellow petals with contrasting red spots and others solid red; foliage green with purple streaks and also leaves solid purple on same spike. *Tropical. Zones 10-11.*   *p. 359*
   x generalis 'Felix Ragout'; charming cultivar of compact habit, and large flowers a pleasing soft yellow with salmon tint. *Zones 9-11.*   *p. 359*
   x generalis 'Hercules'; vigorous tropical perennial with thick rhizome sprouting large, broadly lanceolate coppery green leaves, at base and along erect floral stem, 1 m or more high, topped by clusters of large orange-salmon flowers to 12 cm across. *Zones 9-11.*   *p. 357*
   generalis 'King Humbert', "Bronze garden canna"; striking perennial tropical herb with thick branching rootstocks and large bronze-red leaves, with a showy truss of large orange-red flowers; to 1 m high. In frost free climates these canna hybrids may be left outdoors all year, but in colder regions they must be lifted and stored inside over Winter. *Zones 9-11.*   *p. 359*
   generalis 'Lucifer'; spectacular plant of dwarf habit to 60 cm high, with deep green foliage; bicolored flowers Chinese-red with bright yellow margins. *Tropical. Zones 10-11.*   *p. 359*
   x generalis 'Pfitzer Dwarf Red'; showy cultivar of small habit, the stout stem with broad rich green leaves, topped by cluster of brilliant scarlet-red flowers, blooming from July to frost. Ideal for bedding, or in tubs for porch and roof gardens. *Zones 9-10.*   *p. 359*
   x generalis 'Pfitzer Dwarf Salmon'; handsome compact yet vigorous German cultivar to 80 cm high, with flowers a lovely bright rosy-salmon. *Zones 9-10.*   *p. 359*
   generalis 'President', an old "Garden canna"; variety with large green leaves and a terminal cluster of large and showy scarlet flowers; to 1 m high. *Tropical. Zones 9-11.*   *p. 357, 359*
   x generalis 'Rosamond'; beautiful cultivar to 1 m high, with glossy green foliage, topped by showy flowers vivid scarlet and margins of yellow, the reverse golden and tinted with red; the buds yellow. *Zones 9-11.*   *p. 359*
   generalis 'Striata'; foliage green and beautifully striped with cream in feather fashion and midrib; margins red; flowers orange-red. *Tropical. Zones 10-11.*   *p. 359*
   indica (Trop. America), "Indian shot"; perennial herb of slender habit to 1 m or more, with thick rootstock and green stem; lanceolate leaves 20-60 cm long, and bright red flowers to 8 cm long, the lip orange spotted with red. *Zone 10.*   *p. 358*
   indica hybrids: see CANNA x generalis
   iridiflora (Perú), "Iris-flowered canna"; rhizomatous perennial to 3 m tall; lanceolate leaves ½-1 m long, woolly beneath at first; flowers rose, in racemes, the nodding corolla 6-12 cm long. *Tropical. Zones 9-10.*   *p. 358*

CANNABIS *Cannabaceae*
   sativa (Russia, Asia Minor, India), "Hemp-plant", "Marijuana" or "Hashish"; handsome annual herb to 3 m tall; large long-stalked digitate leaves of 5-7 leaflets to 15 cm long, coarsely toothed and grayish-green; flowers small, dioecious, the males with 5 sepals and 5 drooping stamens, in axillary panicles, the females in spikes. Cultivated in India for the fiber (hemp) used in rope-making. The resin which exudes from the dried leaves when smoked, has a powerful narcotic effect, especially from the flowering tops of the female plants which are rich in the drug marijuana. Cultivation in the U.S. is controlled by the Federal Marijuana Tax Act of 1937 and must be registered with the Federal Bureau of Narcotics. *Zones 9-10.*   *p. 356*

CANTUA *Polemoniaceae*
   buxifolia (Perú, Bolivia, No. Chile), "Sacred flower of the Incas"; beautiful flowering, dense bush which I saw growing 2½ m high in Puna climate at 4000 m in the Cordilleras of Bolivia; the woody shrubs with small buxus-like leaves; colorful, pendant, 8 cm tubular flowers, pale green calyx, yellow tube striped red, the lobes inside rosy-red, outside crimson. *Zones 9-10.*   *p. 820*

CAPANEA *Gesneriaceae*
   grandiflora (Campanea hort.) (Panama); scaly rhizomatous epiphytic shrub, found by Dr. J. Folsom of Texas, in Chiriqui Prov.; brown-hairy stem 50 cm to 2 m long, with opposite hairy, toothed,

elliptic leaves; bell-shaped corolla 2-3 cm wide, creamy-white with purple spots inside, covered by glistening hairs. The flowers are pollinated by bats. Zone 11.   *p. 61*

CAPPARIS *Capparaceae*

floribunda (Taiwan), "Caper bush"; evergreen shrub slightly scandent; ovate, glossy green leathery leaves 5-12 cm long; white flowers with 4 sepals, followed by clusters of berry-like, reddish-orange fruits. Zone 10.   *p. 671*

micracantha (Burma, Malaysia, Indonesia, Philippines), "Caper-thorn"; evergreen shrub 1 to 4 m high, with thorny trunk and twigs, forming thickets; bark grayish and finely fissured, the branches curving outward, and twigs hanging; oblong leaves 8-15 cm long, dull yellowish-green, having 8-11 pairs of prominent lateral veins; feathery white flowers in rows of 2 to 6, the upper petals turning purple; nearly globular fruit 5 cm wide, green turning red, containing numerous black seeds in the pulp, and edible. Zone 10.   *p. 671*

spinosa (So. Europe, Egypt), the "Caperbush"; straggling spiny, deciduous shrub to 1 m high, with thick roundish or ovate leaves to 5 cm long on flexible branches; white flowers 2-3 cm long, red outside, with large ovary, and prominent red stamens, solitary in leaf axils, and fading before noon; the fruit a berry. The pungent flower buds are pickled and sold as "Capers". Zone 9.   *p. 523*

CAPSICUM *Solanaceae*

annuum conoides 'Fiesta', an ornamental "Christmas pepper" or "Cone pepper"; small tropical shrub originally from South America, but grown as an herbaceous annual pot plant; much branching, the twigs dense with narrow lanceolate, fresh green leaves, and bearing a multitude of small white flowers; followed by an abundance of slender, waxy, tapered miniature peppers, first cream then scarlet-red, 5-8 cm long, beginning in September, to Christmas. Tropical. Zone 10.   *p. 511*

annuum 'Fips', "Christmas pepper", seen in the Trial fields of Geo. Ball, W. Chicago; small ornamental pepper of compact habit, to 18 cm high, with glossy green leaves, topped by erect waxy 2-3 cm cones of fruit, in colors changing from white to yellow then brilliant red in Autumn. Zone 10.   *p. 57*

annuum grossum, the "Italian bell-pepper", also known as "Sweet-pepper"; stout plant about 60 cm high, little branched, with large turgid leaves 10-12 cm long; white flowers, and producing large oblong, puffy fruit wrinkled on the sides, and lacquered red; the "Green Bell-pepper" is waxy dark green, and of a mild flavor. Cooked as vegetable, stuffed with meat, or eaten fresh in salads. Zones 10-11.   *p. 940*

annuum 'Holiday Cheer' of Mexican heritage, "Spanish pepper"; herbaceous or subshrubby ornamental of bushy habit, with glossy green lanceolate leaves; small whitish or greenish flowers, followed by small rounded fruit first white, later turning red toward Winter. Zone 10.   *p. 511*

annuum 'Holiday Time', "Christmas pepper"; ornamental herbaceous plant of bushy habit, with rich green, somewhat succulent ovate leaves; the small whitish flowers in axils and apex of main stem or its branches; followed by glossy, conical fruit 3-4 cm long, first creamy-yellow then ripening to scarlet-red in time for the Christmas holidays. Much grown as potted plant by florists. Zone 10.   *p. 511*

annuum 'Long Cayenne' (Trop. America), "Long Cayenne pepper"; herbaceous bush, perennial or woody in tropical climate, with narrow, fresh green leaves; white flowers; pendant fruits tapering and slender pointed, dark green, maturing to red, 15 to 30 cm long wrinkled at maturity. This culinary or Spanish pepper is pungent and fiery hot in cookery, much favored in Mexican food. Dried, pulverized fruit produces the medicinal drug Capsaicine, used to stimulate nerves. Zone 10.   *p. 543*

annuum 'Red Chile' (Trop. America), "Chili pepper"; much-branched subshrub 50 cm to 1 m high, with glossy green ovate leaves; small white flowers having 5-lobed corolla; grown primarily for its slender conical fruit 6 cm long, coloring from green to scarlet-red, enclosing in its waxy skin the spicy-hot, peppery substance and seeds used in culinary seasoning for its pungent flavor. Zones 10-11. *p. 940*

chinensis (Brazil, Honduras), "Papaya chili" or "Tabanero"; shrubby plant with twiggy branches, small spatulate or ovate leaves, and small starry flowers; grown by the Maya Indians, producing odd-shaped, nearly globular chili fruits scarlet-red, 3 to 5 cm dia., ridged outside; of pleasant taste with mild pungent chili flavor. Photographed in Quail Bot. Garden, Encinitas, Calif., collected in Copan, Honduras. Zone 10.   *p. 543*

frutescens var. Tabasco (Mexico), "Tabasco pepper"; shrubby perennial 1 to 2 m high, with angled stems, bearing ovate, slender-pointed leaves 8-15 cm long; small starry greenish or yellowish-white flowers at nodes, followed by slender conical, erect fruit 4 cm long, first yellow then crimson-red, late maturing. The fruit is very hot and pungent in flavor and is used in commercial production of extremely spicy culinary Tabasco sauces in Louisiana and adjacent Gulf states. Zone 10.   *p. 543*

frutescens 'Wirri-wirri' (Guyana), hot pepper of Barbados; smooth herbaceous perennial subshrubby bush, dense with ovate leaves; small greenish-white flowers, followed by pungent globular cherry-like fruit, first cream ripening to glossy, brilliant red and borne abundantly. Amerindians were brought to Barbados by the first settlers about 1625 to assist with their agriculture; they introduced this pepper to make the potent pepperwine as condiment with soups and fish, using only 2 or 3 drops at a time; the fruits are soaked in sherry or rum for several months. Zones 10-11.   *p. 543*

CARAGANA *Leguminosae*

arborescens (Siberia, So. Russia, Manchuria), "Siberian pea tree"; very hardy deciduous shrub or tree to 6 m high; leaves pinnate, with oblong leaflets in 3 to 6 or more pairs, 2-3 cm long; 2 cm yellow flowers pea-like in elongate clusters, blooming in May; followed by pendant slender pods containing 2-3 seeds. Zone 2.   *p. 750*

CARALLUMA *Asclepiadaceae*

praegracilis (Transvaal); clustering succulent with stems to 10 cm high, bluish-green with long spine-like knobs; ochre-yellow star-shaped flowers with red-brown spots and long 3 cm tails; blooming at base of plant. Arid-subtropic. Zone 10.   *p. 151*

CARDAMINE *Cruciferae*

trifolia (C. Europe to Italy and Yugoslavia), "Bitter cress" or "Cuckoo flower"; rhizomatous perennial or annual about 15 cm high, the lower branches creeping like roots; the leaves trifoliolate, consisting of 3 cm, dark green, wedge-shaped leaflets, lightly toothed and purplish beneath; flowers white or pink, clawed and with broad limb, blooming March to May. Zone 7.   *p. 408*

CARDIOCRINUM *Liliaceae*

giganteum (Lilium) (Himalayas, S.E. Tibet), "Heart-lily"; immense lily-like plant 2 to 4 m high, with principal bulb dying after fruiting, but perennial by offset bulbs, which will bloom in 4 years; stem with broad, heart-shaped foliage to 30 cm or more long; toward apex a pyramidal raceme of white, fragrant funnel flowers to 15 cm long, tinged green, and purple stripes inside, during Summer. Zone 7.   *p. 238*

CAREX *Cyperaceae*

conica 'Variegata' (Japan, So. Korea), "Miniature variegated sedge"; attractive perennial forming tufts 20-50 cm high, with strap-shaped recurving, leathery stiff leaves 2-3 cm wide, dark green and bordered ivory-white; the inflorescence in feathery white clusters, blooming Spring into Summer. Zone 8.   *p. 558*

foliosissima 'Albo-mediana' (elegantissima) (Sakhalin, to Japan); grass-like tufted plant with elegant, flat leaves bright green having a white stripe near each margin, of stiff-erect habit, 30 cm high. Zone 8.   *p. 558*

morrowii 'Variegata' (Japan), "Variegated sedge grass"; attractive, tufting, grass-like plant with narrow-linear, 6 mm wide concave leaves recurving, very colorful ivory-white to pale yellow, edged with green margins. Zones 6 -10.   *p. 558*

pendula (Europe, No. Africa to W. Asia), "Drooping sedge"; handsome grass-like perennial forming tufts from stout rhizomes, with stems 60 cm or more high, arching at the top; the lower leaves without blades; upper leaves having pendant blades 1-2 cm wide, yellow-green above, glaucous beneath, and somewhat keeled; long drooping spikes, the upper male and to 10 cm long; the 4-5 lower, female spikes pendulous. Zone 7.   *p. 569*

plantaginea (Eastern Canada to Alabama), "Plantain sedge"; tufted perennial 30-60 cm high, with bladeless purple sheaths rising from old bases; leaves of sterile rosettes 2-4 cm broad and evergreen; small inflorescence from sheathing purple bracts. Zones 3-7.   *p. 558*

riparia (Europe to Siberia, Asia Minor); perennial waterside sedge with creeping rhizome and forming tufts; solid stems 3-angled and rough, to 1 m or more high; leafy floral stems topped by unisexual flowers in cylindrical spikes. Zone 4.   *p. 329*

CARICA *Caricaceae*

papaya (Colombia), "Melon tree"; dioecious succulent tree to 8 metres high, with leaves digitately 7-lobed; flowers greenish-yellow, the hanging fruits to 30 cm long resembling a melon and with sweet almost peach-like flavor. In tropical plantations, only female seedlings are planted for fruit production; these are recognized by their split mainroots, while male seedlings have a straight tap root. Papaya fruits twice yearly in Tahiti, in December-January and in July. Tropical. Zones 10-11.   *p. 909*

papaya 'Oblonga'; a "Papaya" cultivar with oblong, gourd-like fruit to 30 cm long born on female trees; the fine-flavored fruit is eaten like a melon, or may be baked like squash, stewed or candied. *Tropical. Zones* 10-11.   *p. 907*

x pubescens (x heilbornii) (Ecuador and Colombia), "Mountain papaya" or "Babaco", also known as "Bush melon of the Andes"; according to latest research a natural hybrid involving Carica pubescens, pentagona and stipulata, known as C. x heilbornii, at home in the subtropic valleys of the Andes between 1500 to 2500 m alt.; the unique hardy papaya is a dwarf tree to 2½ m high, having stout stem and bearing a crown of palmately lobed, pubescent leaves at top; pistillate flowers green at base and reflexed white lobes; heavily producing oblong elliptic, 5-ribbed, aromatic fruit 10 cm or more long, ripening deep yellow to orange. Being seedless, it is eaten juicy flesh and rind, tasting like pineapple and banana; may also be cooked with sugar. Propagated by tip cuttings. Photographed in col. Quail Botanic Garden, Encinitas, California. *Zone* 10.   *p. 907*

CARISSA   Apocynaceae

grandiflora (macrocarpa) (So. Africa: Natal), "Natal plum"; woody shrub to 9 m, armed with massive forked spines, lustrous green, ovate leaves, and large 5 cm white, fragrant flowers; big plum-like scarlet fruit to 5 cm long, and edible. *Zone* 9.   *p. 614, 640, 904*

grandiflora 'Fancy' (C. macrocarpa cv.), "Dwarf Natal plum"; dense evergreen shrub usually of low, bushy habit, but may grow up to 2 m high without trunk; the flexible, tangled branches set with sharp 3 cm forked spines and lacquered rich green, thin-leathery leaves; showy axillary fragrant white, starry flowers; the luscious scarlet-red globose to ovoid fruit 4-6 cm long, thin-skinned with milky juice, and the flesh with the quality of sweet cranberry flavor. Excellent garden ornamental. *Zone* 10.   *p. 640, 938*

macrocarpa: see C. grandiflora (Hortus)

CARLINA   Compositae

acanthifolia (Pyrenees to Greece, and W. Asia), "Acanthus thistle"; monocarpic perennial rosette of thistle-like spiny-toothed leaves, to 30 cm long, pinnately cut, and velvety white-hairy beneath; the inflorescence solitary and sessile in center of rosette, to 15 cm across, the head of tubular flowers yellow, surrounded by chaffy petal-like bracts like an everlasting flower; dying after fruiting. *Zone* 7.   *p. 377*

acaulis (Spain to Greece), "Silver thistle"; stemless perennial thistle with spiny leaves 15 cm long, in a rosette, very deeply incised; solitary heads with silvery bracts, spreading to 12 cm across. *Temperate. Zone* 6.   *p. 375, 377*

acaulis simplex (caulescens of gardens) (Europe), "Westher thistle"; perennial variety with taller stems 15-60 cm high, bearing 1 to 6 flower heads 10 cm or more wide, the central florets often reddish, and spreading bracts silvery. *Zone* 6.   *p. 377*

marianus hort.: see SILYBUM marianum

vulgaris (Europe to Caucasus and Siberia), "Gold thistle"; unique stiff biennial 20 cm or more high; spiny thistle-like toothed leaves 8-12 cm long, lobed at margins, and cottony beneath; flower heads purple, the narrow linear papery outer bracts silvery and spreading. *Zone* 5.   *p. 377*

CARLUDOVICA   Cyclanthaceae

palmata (Colombia, Ecuador, Perú), "Panama hat plant"; stemless plant to 2-3 m high, with friendly green, fan-shaped, palm-like leaves to 1 m long, usually cut into 4 parts, the lobes cut again; used for making of hats. *Tropical. Zone* 12.   *p. 116*

CARNEGIEA   Cactaceae

gigantea (Cereus) (So. Arizona, No. Mexico), "Giant saguaro"; tall tapering column to 18 m, or even 20 m, branching with age, the branches erect; close-ribbed; the 12 to 24 ribs with strong light brown spines; white flowers 10 cm long, being nocturnal they will slowly open during the night, and are fully open at daylight. One of largest tree-like cacti known. *Arid-subtropic. Zone* 9.   *p. 154, 159, 169*

CARPANTHEA   Aizoaceae

pomeridiana (mesembryanthemum pomeridianum) (S.W. Cape Prov.); annual branching succulent to 30 cm high, the stems and inflorescence covered with shaggy white hairs; spatulate-lanceolate leaves 4-10 cm long, united at base; showy golden-yellow flowers 4 to 7 cm across. *Zone* 10.   *p. 144*

CARPENTERIA   Saxifragaceae

californica (No. California), "Tree anemone"; handsome evergreen flowering shrub of the foothills of the Sierra Nevada; slow-growing to 2 m or more; the new branches purplish, with long-elliptic, thick-leathery leaves to 10 cm long, glossy dark green above, whitish beneath; large anemone-like pure white flowers 4-8 cm across, and pleasantly fragrant. *Zone* 8.   *p. 869*

CARPHALEA   Rubiaceae

kirondron (Rubia ornamentale) (introduced to the Philippines from Madagascar in 1957), popularly known as "Rubia"; handsome, floriferous shrub to 2 m or more high, dense with willowy branches; opposite ovate or lanceolate glossy green leaves 6 to 12 cm long, the midrib ivory to reddish; the showy inflorescence in globular heads 8 to 10 cm across, of flowers with velvety, linear, glowing red, petaloid bracts or sepals, and tiny white 4-lobed white corolla under 1 cm across, on long protruding slender red tube, and blooming the year round. *Zone* 10.   *p. 855*

CARPINUS   Betulaceae

betulus (Europe to Iran), "European hornbeam"; deciduous shrub or tree to 20 m high, with smooth gray trunk, densely branching and bearing ovate-pointed leaves to 12 cm long, corrugated by 12-14 pairs of ribs, the margins sharply toothed, with hairy tufts in their axils beneath; fruit catkins 5-10 cm long, subtended by 3-lobed bracts. Very popular in Europe for hedges and trimmed avenues or arbors, since it stands shearing well. *Zone* 5.   *p. 613, 614, 619,662*

betulus 'Quercifolia'; attractive shrub with glossy green leaves deeply incised and lobed, resembling foliage of oaks, the prominent veins beige-brown. Photographed in Bunter Garten, M. Gladbach, Rhineland. *Zone* 5.   *p. 622*

caroliniana (Maryland to Florida, Illinois and Texas), "American hornbeam" or "Iron-wood", occasionally called "Blue beech"; slow-growing tree 8 to 12 m high, with twisted gray trunk, freely branching 1 m or so from base; oval-pointed leaves to 10 cm long, undulate at margins, and often doubly-toothed, veins depressed in 10-14 pairs, with surface corrugated; catkins 5-10 cm long, with flaring bracts. The wood is useful and very tough. *Zones* 2-9.   *p. 622*

japonica (Japan), "Japanese hornbeam"; hardwooded deciduous small tree of the birch family, to 12 m high, with smooth gray bark, spreading branches with lanceolate leaves 5-10 cm long and more or less two-ranked; the male flowers in pendant catkins, blooming before the leaves unfold; ribbed nutlets sheltered by leaflike bracts in attractive, drooping clusters. Often used as dwarfed bonsai tree with contorted trunk in Japan. *Zone* 4.   *p. 662*

CARPOBROTUS   Aizoaceae

acinaciformis (Cape Prov.: Cape Town), "Purple Hottentot fig"; robust succulent with spreading branches; saber-shaped gray-green leaves 9 cm long, keeled beneath; carmine-purple flowers to 12 cm across, opening at mid-day. *Zone* 10.   *p. 144*

edulis (So. Africa), "Hottentot-fig"; creeping, freely growing, branching succulent, often planted as a sand-binder along subtropical seashores; branches angled, to 1 m long, with long linear 3-angled fleshy, grass green or glaucous leaves 8-12 cm long, keel minutely serrate; large flowers 8-10 cm across with narrow, silky rays opening with the warming sun, yellow or purple; large fruits edible. In South Africa, I have observed the purple form primarily on the cool Cape Peninsula, the yellow in the glaring hot Karroo. *Arid-subtropic. Zone* 10.   *p. 144, 301*

CARRUANTHUS   Aizoaceae

ringens (Cape Prov.); handsome tufting succulent with fleshy rhizome; smooth obovate gray-green, boat-shaped leaves to 6 cm long, knobby at upper margins; solitary flowers to 5 cm across, the yellow florets reddish outside. *Zone* 10.   *p. 144*

CARUM   Umbelliferae

carvi (Europe to Russia, No. India, natural. in No. America), "Caraway"; perennial, biennial or annual herb with thick root, and hollow stem 30-50 cm high, the leaves in juvenile plants divided into broad, lobed sections, in maturity 15-25 cm long, and bipinnately cut into narrow-linear or threadlike segments; small white or pinkish flowers with deeply notched petals, in irregular clusters, June-July blooming; the smooth aromatic fruit contains the pungent seed, which has been used since ancient Egyptian times in culinary art, to mix with bread, to flavor meats and confections; in Holland with cheese; also distilled for liqueur. *Zone* 3.   *p. 542, 544*

CARYA   Juglandaceae

cordiformis (amara hort.) (Hicoria), (Québec to Florida, Louisiana), "Bitternut" or "Pignut"; symmetrical deciduous tree to 30 m high, with flaking bark; bright yellow winterbuds; odd-pinnate leaves compound of 5-9 lanceolate leaflets 8-15 cm long, the lower surface downy; the nuts nearly globose, 2-3 cm long, thin-shelled and bitter to the taste, the husk grayish and 4-valved. *Zone* 4.   *p. 914*

illinoiensis (pecan) (Indiana to Alabama, Texas and Mexico), the "Pecan nut"; handsome partially deciduous hard-wooded tree to 25 m high, planted by the millions in the South for their delicious nuts; Thomas Jefferson brought the first pecans from the Mississippi Valley to George Washington where he planted them at Mt. Vernon, Virginia in 1775. Wide-spreading, with grayish, deeply furrowed bark and graceful pinnate foliage; thin-leathery fresh green, crenate leaflets with yellow midrib 10 to 15 cm long; the male flowers in pendulous catkins, the female flowers in terminal spikes, producing clusters of oblong, fleshy fruit 4-8 cm long which split into 4 sections exposing the thin-woody shell containing the edilbe, wrinkled sweet-tasting kernel; ripening in Autumn. *Warm-temperate. Zone 5.* p. 914

laciniosa (New York to Oklahoma), "Shellbark hickory" or "King nut"; deciduous tree to 30 m or more high, having shaggy bark falling off in long sections; the branches containing solid pith; odd-pinnate leaves 30-60 cm long, the 7 or 9 leaflets narrow-lanceolate and downy beneath; the long slender male catkins pendulous; the fruit is the largest of the hickory nuts, usually solitary, with woody rind containing thick shells with yellowish flavorful nuts. *Zone 4.* p. 740

ovata (Québec to So. Florida and Texas), "Shagbark hickory"; deciduous popular tree 25-35 m high, having shaggy bark falling away in flakes; odd-pinnate leaves 20-35 cm long, with 5-7 oblong-pointed, corrugated leaflets; male catkins in threes, to 12 cm long; white, thin-shelled 4-angled ellipsoid nuts of sweet taste. *Zone 4.* p. 916

pecan: see C. illinoiensis

tomentosa (Mass. to Florida), "Mockernut hickory"; rugged, handsome, long-lived tree to 30 m high, with deciduous, pinnate leaves 20-30 cm long, composed of 7-9 leaflets; male inflorescence in long, slender pendulous catkins from the leaf axils, the females in terminal spikes, forming pear-shaped brown fruit 5 cm long, containing thick shell which splits into sections, the edible kernel inside, but very small, "mocking" people as hardly worth the trouble to open the woody shell. *Zone 4.* p. 740, 914

CARYOPTERIS *Verbenaceae*

x clandonensis (mastacanthus x mongholica), "Bluebeard"; deciduous shrub of Japanese and Chinese parentage, with opposite lanceolate, toothed leaves 5-9 cm long, underside and stalks gray-white; bright blue flowers with 5-lobed corolla including one larger fringed one. *Zone 5.* p. 898

CARYOTA *Palmae*

mitis (Burma, Malaya, Indonesia), "Clustered fishtail palm"; with numerous suckers growing up in clusters; green-gray trunks 7 m high topped by dense tufts of irregularly bipinnate dull green leaves, the pinnae fan-shaped, jagged at apex and many veined, nodding at the tips; fruit blackish-red. *Tropical. Zone 11.* p. 101

urens (Himalayas, India, Burma, Ceylon, Malaya), "Wine palm" or "Fishtail"; I remember these majestic, solitary palms giving special character to the beautiful, verdant landscape of the mountains of Ceylon; glossy gray trunk more than 30 m high, topped by bipinnate, arching leaves with thick wedge-shaped, loosely spaced segments; yields wine. *Tropical. Zone 11.* p. 99, 101

urens 'Nepal variety', "Mountain fishtail"; a compact growing variation from seed collected in the higher valleys of the Nepal Himalayas, more cold resistant than the tropical parent species; favored in California landscape planting. Photographed in Quail Bot. Garden, Encinitas, California. *Zones 10-11.* p. 101

CASASIA *Rubiaceae*

clusifolia (So. Florida, Bahamas, W. Indies), "Seven-year apple"; evergreen shrub to 3 m, bushy or tree-like; oblong, glossy leaves to 15 cm long, in clusters at branch tips; star-like white flowers to 4 cm across; very fragrant; ovoid fruit 8 cm long, green to brown to blackish when ripe; licorice-flavored, edible, but not tasty; fruit almost always present on the plant. *Tropical. Zone 10.* p. 924

CASIMIROA *Rutaceae*

edulis (Mexico, C. America), the "White sapote" or "Mexican apple"; fast-growing tropical fruit tree to 15 m high, treasured by the Aztecs; shiny green leathery leaves, palmately compound of 5-7 leaflets 12 cm long; small greenish or whitish flowers; the handsome apple-shaped fruit to 10 cm dia. pendant on long stalks, yellow-green with thin waxy glaucous cover; the edible soft and juicy, creamy flesh very sweet resembling mango, and with fragrant aroma, but may have a bitter after-taste. The seeds are used medicinally in Mexico to induce sleep. Planted in South Florida and So. California in several good-flavored varieties; eaten fresh or in sherbets. *Zone 10.* p. 860, 934

edulis 'Suebelle', "White sapote"; a favored cultivar of medium size for the home garden, because of its sweet, rich, soft pulp and small seeds; ripening most in November, turning yellow; fruit has musky sweet flavor and does not keep long. Nearly everbearing close to the Pacific Coast in So. California. *Zone 10.* p. 934

edulis var. 'Vernon'; a superior cultivar of the "Sapote" or "Mexican apple"; usually grafted, producing luscious golden-yellow fruit of better flavor than the species; having juicy flesh similar to custard, combining taste of banana and pears and of unusual sweetness, also containing several large seeds. In season from July to January. *Zone 10.* p. 934

CASSIA *Leguminosae*

aciphylla, alata, artemisioides, auriculata, biflorus, candolleana, corymbosa, didymobotrya, excelsa floribunda, fruticosa, laevigata, leptophylla, marilandica, multijuga, nitida, septemtrionalis, siamea, speciosa, spectabilis, surattensis, tomentosa — are transferred to SENNA. (N.Y. Bot. Garden, also U.S. Herbarium, Smithsonian, Washington)

bicapsularis: see SENNA candolleana

fistula (India, Sri Lanka), "Golden shower" or "Pudding pipe tree"; beautiful tree of moderate size to 10 m high, leaves with leaflets in 4 to 8 pairs, 5-15 cm long; fragrant flowers golden-yellow, in drooping racemes to 30 cm long, resembling huge bunches of grapes. *Zones 10-11.* p. 751, 752

floribunda of hort.: see SENNA excelsa (Fairchild)

glauca: see SENNA surattensis

x hybrida (fistula x javanica), "Rainbow Shower"; beautiful hybrid tree 10 m high, almost evergreen, and the landmark of Honolulu; very spectacular, with showy masses of flowers from cream to orange and red, dominating the landscape from March to August almost obscuring the luxurious pinnate foliage. *Tropical. Zones 10-11.* p. 751

javanica (nodosa) (Indonesia), "Appleblossom shower"; low tree to 6 m high, with wide-spreading crown; pinnate leaves with obtuse, 5 cm leaflets; flowers of short duration, with petals at first pale red, changing to dark red, then paling again, blooming March-April; pendant cylindric brownish seedpods to 60 cm long. *Zones 10-11.* p. 752

moschata (leiandra) (Panama, Colombia), "Bronze shower tree"; showy flowering tree to 20 m; leaves pinnate with 10-18 pairs of leaflets 3-5 cm long; pendant racemes to 25 cm long, of yellow flowers becoming brick-red with age; briefly deciduous before blooming in March. Photographed near Tehuantepec, Mexico. *Zone 10.* p. 753

nairobensis: see SENNA didymobotrya

roxburghii (marginata) (Sri Lanka, South India), "Red cassia" or "Ceylon senna"; large, showy, spreading tree to 6 m high, with hard brown bark deeply cracked; dense ranks of pinnate leaves having 16 to 20 pairs of oval leaflets along a willowy axis; the arching branches beautifully set with masses of axillary flowers salmon-rose. *Zones 10-11.* p. 752

CASSINIA *Compositae*

fulvida (New Zealand), "Yellow cassinia"; evergreen densely branched shrub to 2 m high; leaves crowded, linear to ovate 2 cm long with margins recurved, green and sticky above, yellow tomentose beneath; floral heads to 5 cm across and rounded; small white flowers in July. *Zone 9.* p. 688

CASSIOPE *Ericaceae*

lycopodioides (Northeast Asia, Japan, Alaska); floriferous miniature evergreen shrub only 3-5 cm high, creeping with threadlike branches, spreading 30-80 cm and forming mats; tiny green 2 mm leaves imbricate in 4 rows; solitary axillary nodding bell-flowers 2 cm long, pale blue to whitish, blooming April-May. *Zone 2.* p. 700

mertensiana (Montana, No. Calif., Alaska), "White heather"; tufted evergreen Erica-like shrub 15-25 cm high, the small 1 cm leaves imbricate in 4 rows on the thin branches; charming little white to pinkish bell-flowers to 1 cm long, nodding on short stalks, blooming April-May in England, but seen in flower in July-August in the Rocky Mountains in Banff National Park near Lake Louise, Alberta. *Zone 2.* p. 700

CASTANEA *Fagaceae*

dentata (E. No. America: Maine to Mississippi), "American Chestnut"; majestic deciduous tree to 30 m high, with furrowed bark; long 12-25 cm leaves serrate with bristle teeth; the catkins 10-20 cm long, and the acorns to 6 cm wide, with burr enclosing 2-3 nuts, which are edible and sweet. However, most of this species have died out because of the chestnut bark disease or blight. The resistant C. mollissima is a good substitute. *Zone 4.* p. 726

molissima (China, Korea), "Chinese chestnut"; deciduous tree to 20 m high, with branchlets short-pubescent; lanceolate leaves 8-15 cm long, coarsely serrate at margins, and soft-pubescent beneath, at least along veins; fruiting burs 6 to 10 cm dia., and covered with long hairy spines, usually containing 2-3 nuts, in September to November, and which are tasty eaten fresh, salted or roasted, also used in salads, pies and desserts. Blight resistant. *Zone 5.* p. 913

sativa (So. Europe, No. Africa, Asia Minor), "Spanish chestnut" or "Marone"; the edible chestnut, introduced by the Romans to cultivation; large deciduous tree to 30 m; reddish branches with lanceolate leaves 12-20 cm long, glossy green and with coarse spreading teeth; male flowers in white catkins; the female flowers at base of male catkin, followed by spiny fruit 5-6 cm dia. containing to 3 nuts, of pleasant flavor especially when freshly roasted. *Zones 5-9.* p. 726, 913

CASTANOPSIS *Fagaceae*

stellata-spina (Taiwan); handsome evergreen tree, midway between Castanea and Quercus; ovate-lanceolate leaves 15-25 cm long; fluffy clusters of creamy-yellow flowers; globular spiny fruit encloses 2-3 nuts. *Zone 8.*   p. 726

CASTANOSPERMUM *Leguminosae*

australe (New So. Wales), "Moreton Bay chestnut"; evergreen tree 12-18 m; leaves 30-45 cm long; leaflets 10-15, ovate to oblong, pointed, 8-12 cm long; flowers orange-yellow in axillary racemes 10-15 cm long; fruit a pod 20 cm long, spongy inside, containing seeds as large as a Spanish chestnut and which are eaten when roasted. *Zone 10.*   p. 750

CASTILLEJA *Scrophulariaceae*

chromosa (Oregon and Calif. to Wyoming and New Mexico), "Painted-cup" or "Indian paint-brush"; striking perennial 20-40 cm high, covered by stiff gray hairs, with narrow lanceolate leaves 6-8 cm long, partially 3-5 parted on upper stems; the segments linear; beautiful flowers with floral bracts and calyx green at base, tipped with scarlet; the 3 cm corolla green with crimson margins, blooming depending on local climate between April to August. *Zone 3.* p. 503

coccinea (No. America: Canada so. to Texas, east to New England), "Scarlet paintbrush"; hairy perennial or biennial to 60 cm high, basal leaves obovate to 8 cm long, stem leaves 3-5 lobed; floral bracts brilliant scarlet, corolla pale yellow, to 3 cm long, blooming between April and August. Difficult to cultivate because it is by nature parasitic, deriving most of its food from the roots of other plants. *Zone 3.*   p. 503

CASUARINA *Casuarinaceae*

cunninghamiana (E. Australia and Pacific Isl.), "River She-oak"; stately tree 10-15 m high, brown bark and stout erect branches, usually all the way to the ground, resembling a pine tree; the branchlets joined like Equisetum, and set with scale-like leaves, in adult growth normally in whorls; the petal-less inflorescence unisexual with male and female flowers separate, the females subtended by bracts, forming small 12 mm fruit cones. Valuable timber tree. *Zone 9.*   p. 681

equisetifolia (No. Australia, Queensland), the "Horse-tail tree" or "Australian pine"; hardwooded tree to 25 m high, with pendulous branches swaying in the breeze; wirelike branchlets with apparently leafless twigs, the leaves reduced to scales and suggesting the horsetail (Equisetum). Adaptable as a patio tree, or the sunny, airy greenhouse, when sheared into compact shapes or imaginative topiary forms. *Tropical. Zone 9.*   p. 681

nobilis (Borneo), "Borneo Ru-tree"; elegant pine-like tree of open habit, with bushy branchlets thin and string-like 10-15 cm long, jointed and set with scales; seen in col. Singapore Botanic Garden. *Zone 10.*   p. 681

CATALPA *Bignoniaceae*

bignonioides (Georgia, Florida, Mississippi), the "Indian-bean" or "Southern catawba"; tree 8-18 m high, of rounded, spreading habit, with ovate leaves 15-25 cm long, pale green, downy beneath; inflorescence a broad erect panicle with bell-shaped flowers, and spreading, frilled lobes, white, with two yellow stripes and purple spots, 5 cm across. *Zone 4.*   p. 663

ovata (China; natural. in E. No. America), "Chinese catawba"; interesting tree 6-8 m high, with spreading branches; the leaves opposite, heart-shaped and 12-25 cm long, sometimes lobed, hairy on veins beneath; the inflorescence of creamy-white flowers stained with orange and spotted purple, 3 cm long, in clusters 10-25 cm long; the interesting fruit pods are pendant, bean-like, to 30 cm long. *Zone 4.*   p. 662

speciosa (Indiana to Arkansas and Texas), "Western catawba", "Northern catalpa" or "Cigar tree"; pyramidal tree 15-30 m high, with massive trunk; large ovate, slender-pointed leaves 15-30 cm long, densely pubescent beneath; showy clusters of flowers with corolla white, spotted purple or brown, 6 cm across, the lobes frilled; blooming late June, earlier than bignonioides. Valuable timber tree, used for posts and telephone poles etc., long-lasting in soil. Recommended for dry hot areas. *Zones 4-9.*   p. 663

CATANANCHE *Compositae*

caerulea (Southwest Europe), "Cupid's-dart"; herbaceous perennial or annual, to 60 cm high, with oblanceolate, very hairy 25 cm leaves mostly basal; beautiful flowers 5 cm wide with rays of papery texture, light blue or white, with dark center; suitable for drying. *Zones 5-9.*   p. 374

CATASETUM *Orchidaceae*

roseum (Mexico: Oaxaca); a small, very pretty epiphyte with short pseudobulbs and deciduous leaves; numerous showy and long-lasting, cupped, star-like waxy flowers on short, pendant raceme, cream flushed rose, petals and lip fringed with rosy hairs; lip greenish inside (early Spring). *Tropical. Zones 11-12.*   p. 82

CATESBAEA *Rubiaceae*

spinosa (Cuba, Bahamas), "Lily-thorn"; spiny tropical evergreen shrub to 4 m high, with small leathery leaves in clusters; the sharp 3 cm spines above the leaf axils; flowers funnel-shaped with a very long tube, 8-15 cm long, gradually widening; the corolla pale yellow, drooping; orange-yellow fruit, 3 cm dia. and edible; cultivated in South Florida. *Zone 10.*   p. 936

CATHA *Celastraceae*

edulis (Arabia, Ethiopia), "Khat tree" or "Arabian tea"; evergreen shrub or small tree to 3 m or more high; on fruit-producing growth the pendant, willowy branchlets, with opposite, glossy green, leathery, elliptic leaves 5-10 cm long, finely toothed at margins; clusters of small white flowers develop at leaf axils; fruits a small leathery capsule. The dried leaves or tender shoots are chewed by Moslems as a favorite daily stimulant; also brewed as tea. *Arid-tropical. Zone 10.*   p. 680

CATHARANTHUS *Apocynaceae*

roseus (Vinca rosea) (Java to Brazil), "Madagascar periwinkle"; erect, fleshy plant with oblong leaves glossy green with white center vein; showy 4 cm flowers rosy-red with purple throat. *Tropical. Zone 10.*   p. 341

roseus 'Bright Eyes' (Vinca rosea); a "Rose periwinkle" of compact habit, very prolific bloomer with pretty white flowers having a bright red spot in center. *Tropical. Zone 10.*   p. 18

roseus 'Purple Eyes'; handsome cultivar in California horticulture; shapely bush branching from base becoming woody; the leafy stems topped by showy flowers 4-5 cm across, pink with deep purple center. *Zone 10.*   p. 341

CATIMBIUM: see ALPINIA

CATTLEYA *Orchidaceae*

citrina (Mexico), "Tulip cattleya"; beautiful epiphyte with silvery, globular pseudobulbs and strap-shaped leaves; the fragrant, bell-like flowers are borne singly and pendant, bright lemon-yellow, lip edged white and crisped, (April-June). *Tropical. Zones 11-12.*   p. 82

dowiana (Costa Rica), "Queen cattleya"; epiphyte with stout pseudobulbs bearing solitary leaves, and beautifully colored, fragrant flowers widely used for hybridizing, the crisped petals golden-yellow, the sepals yellow shaded buff, and a great, frilled lip deep crimson-red streaked with old gold, (May-August). *Humid-Tropical Zones 11-12.*   p. 93

'Enid' (warscewiczii x mossiae); robust, elegant hybrid with big, purplish-mauve flowers of firm texture, the lip overlaid with purple, yellow in the throat; blooming at various times, often twice a year. *Tropical. Zone 11.*   p. 83

forbesii (Brazil), a "Cocktail orchid"; clustering epiphyte, and a sight to see it nesting in small trees, loaded with medium-size flowers, the sepals and petals yellow-green, lip white outside, yellow streaked with red inside, borne on stem-like 2-leaved pseudobulbs, (May-October, and various). *Tropical. Zones 11-12.*   p. 84

granulosa (Guatemala and Brazil); free-growing species with slender terete 2-leaved stems 40-50 cm high, and olive-green, fleshy 10 cm flowers spotted with brown, the spreading lip white dotted with purple, (August-September). *Tropical. Zones 11-12.*   p. 83

intermedia (Brazil); epiphyte with 2-leaved, slender, cane-like pseudobulbs; slender flowers to 12 cm, usually 3-5 together in clusters, pale rose, with middle lobe of lip purple and crisped, (April-November). *Tropical. Zone 11.*   p. 83

labiata (Trinidad, Brazil); epiphyte with pseudobulbs bearing a solitary leathery leaf, the showy flowers 15-18 cm across, 3-7 in a cluster, sepals and petals bright rose, the latter broad and wavy, large lip deep velvety-crimson, throat marked yellow, (August-November). *Zones 11-12.*   p. 83

mossiae (Venezuela), "Easter orchid"; epiphyte with pseudobulbs bearing solitary leaves; the handsome flowers 12-15 cm dia., 3-5 or more in a cluster, blush or light rose, large frilled lip crimson and rose with golden-yellow markings, often on a suffused white ground, (March-June.) *Tropical. Zone 11.*   p. 83

'Priscilla alba' ('Enid' x lueddemanniana); old English hybrid 1926; with elegant flowers, sepals and petals pure white, the lip frilled and with purple, inside rich golden-yellow. *Tropical. Zones 11-12.*   p. 83

rex (labiata var.) (Perú); distinctive Andean epiphyte with 1-leaved pseudobulbs, and striking flowers 12-15 cm across, sepals white tinged primrose, petals creamy-white and wavy, lip crimson with yellow in upper throat and frilled, (Summer). *Tropical. Zone 11.* p. 83

trianaei (Colombia), "Christmas orchid"; epiphyte forming 1-leaved pseudobulbs, with showy flowers to 17 cm dia., 2-3 together, sepals and broad wavy petals rose, the frilled lip purple-crimson with yellow throat, (December-March). *Tropical. Zones 11-12.*   p. 84

CAVANILLESIA   *Bombacaceae*

platanifolia (Panama, Colombia), the "Quipo"; tall tropical tree to 30 m high; the thick, smooth grayish trunk with soft wood of lighter weight than balsa; large 5 to 7-lobed leathery leaves, deciduous before blooming; small flowers with 5 narrow red petals 2 cm long, the longer stamens in clusters; hard spindle-shaped orange-colored ornamental fruit with 5 wings, 6-8 cm dia., very attractive on bare branches. *Zone* 10.   *p. 667*

CEANOTHUS   *Rhamnaceae*

americanus (Maine to So. Carolina, w. to Texas), "New Jersey tea"; small deciduous shrub to 1 m high, with ovate, finely toothed, 3-veined leaves 5-9 cm long, matte green above and downy beneath; small white flowers densely borne in a series of oblong clusters from the terminal leaf-axils of the current year's growth, blooming profusely in June. During the Revolutionary war its leaves were used as substitute for tea. *Zone* 4.   *p. 827*

arboreus (Islands of California coast), "Feltleaf ceanothus" or "Catalina mountain lilac"; floriferous evergreen shrub or small tree to 6 m high, having scaling bark; ovate or roundish oval leaves 5-10 cm long, strongly 3-veined, lustrous green above and densely downy beneath; small pale blue flowers, in densely pyramidal clusters to 10 cm long, blooming July-August, and sweetly fragrant. *Zone* 9. *p. 826*

coeruleus (candolleanus) (Mexico, Guatemala); evergreen shrub or small tree to 6 m high, with oblong ovate leaves 3-9 cm long, and having 5 prominent veins, and finely toothed; rusty-tomentose beneath; multitudes of small blue flowers, varying to white, in huge clusters. *Zones* 9-10.   *p. 826.*

crassifolius (So. California, Arizona, Baja Calif.), "Hoary-leaf ceanothus"; arid-area shrub to 2 m high, with stiffly erect branches; deciduous or semi-evergreen leaves broadly ovate or cordate 3-8 cm long and 3-veined, dull glaucous green, and somewhat fleshy, white-hairy beneath; flowers white to light blue, forming large clusters to 30 cm long, during early Summer. *Zone* 9.   *p. 826*

cyaneus 'Sierra blue' (So. California), "San Diego ceanothus" or "California lilac"; evergreen shrub or small tree to 8 m or more high; ovate 3-veined leaves 6 cm long, lustrous green above, smooth beneath; pale to bright blue flowers in columnar cluster 12 cm long, in June-July. *Zone* 8.   *p. 826*

x delilianus (americanus x coeruleus); floriferous hybrid very popular on the Pacific coast especially in the Santa Barbara area; evergreen bush with ovate leaves 3-8 cm long; profusely blooming in April with erect conical clusters of small pale blue flowers, varying to darker shades. *Zone* 7.   *p. 827*

dentatus (California); evergreen shrub to 2 m high, with round, downy shoots, small alternate ovate leaves 1-2½ cm long, the margins recurved, bright green above and densely gray-downy beneath; vivid blue to pale flowers in dense cylindric clusters, blooming in May. *Zone* 9.   *p. 827*

fendleri (So. Dakota to Wyoming, Arizona and No. Mexico), "Red-root"; small deciduous spiny shrub to 50 cm high, sometimes procumbent; small 3 cm elliptic 3-veined leaves, gray-green and downy beneath; flowers white or tinted mauve, in erect terminal clusters, during June-July. *Zones* 5-8.   *p. 826*

griseus (No. California), "Wild lilac"; low spreading shrub or upright to 2½ m; scandent branches with shiny dark green, corrugated leaves 3-5 cm long, gray-hairy beneath; violet-blue flowers. Inhabiting the Sierra Nevada. *Zone* 7.   *p. 826*

integerrimus (California), "Deerbush"; densely branched shrub to 4 m high, from the Sierra Nevadas, with alternate bright green ovate leaves to 5 cm long, having smooth margins; flowers white but occasionally pale blue or pink. Photographed in Sequoia Nat'l. Park, Central California. *Zone* 8.   *p. 826*

papillosus roweanus (Cent. to So. California), "Wart-leaf ceanothus"; floriferous evergreen shrub 1-2 m high, with short lateral branches; the downy shoots with pinnately veined, narrowly oblong leaves 2-5 cm long, shining green above, pubescent beneath, the margins turned under; the small flowers light blue, gathered in flattened clusters, and covering the rounded bush in great profusion. *Zone* 9.   *p. 826*

thyrsiflorus (Oregon to California), "Blue blossom ceanothus"; hardy evergreen shrub or tree to 8 m high; the angled shoots with alternate 3-veined oval leaves 3-5 cm long, shining green above, downy on veins beneath; small pale blue flowers in dense elongate clusters, blooming May-June. *Zone* 8.   *p. 826*

thyrsiflorus prostratus (Oregon to California), "Blueblossom"; evergreen shrub or small tree in the species, but of low spreading or creeping habit in the subspecies prostratus; alternate oblong glossy green leaves 2 to 5 cm long and finely toothed; flowers pale to deep blue, in small clusters, blooming April-June. *Zone* 8.   *p. 828*

CECROPIA   *Moraceae*

palmata (West Indies to So. America), "Snakewood tree"; fast growing tree with soft wood and hollow stems, having milky sap; large corrugated leaves 7 to 11-lobed to the middle or more, 30 cm or more across, underside white tomentose; small flowers in dense spikes. *Zone* 10.   *p. 790*

CEDRELA   *Meliaceae*

angustifolia (odorata) (Colombia), "Cedro rosao"; semi-evergreen tropical tree to 25 m high, at home in the Rio Cauca area, with pinnate leaves of 10-22 lanceolate leaflets, partially deciduous; small white, fragrant flowers, followed by brownish fruit capsules opening into 5 valves. Timber is valued for construction and plywood. *Zone* 10.   *p. 787*

australis (Toona) (New S. Wales, Queensland, New Guinea), "Australian red-cedar"; large rainforest tree 15 to 30 m high, partially deciduous, with pinnate leaves 30 cm long, of 10-20 lanceolate leathery leaflets, opening bronze; the inflorescence in large trusses of small white or pink flowers of honey-scented fragrance. The timber is valued for its beautiful red-fissured wood. (For inflorescence, see photo Exotica 4.) *Zone* 10.   *p. 787*

odorata (West Indies to So. America), "West Indian cedar" or "Cigar-box cedar"; tall aromatic timber tree 30 m high with buttressed base and smooth trunk 1-2 m dia.; pinnate leaves with 8 pairs of lanceolate leaflets; small yellowish flowers, followed by leathery fruit 4 cm long. The reddish heartwood is used in making cigar boxes. *Zone* 10.   *p. 788*

sinensis (Toona sinensis or Ailanthus flavescens) (China), "Chinese mahogany" or "Chinese toon"; ornamental deciduous tree to 15 m or more high, resembling Ailanthus altissima; with shaggy bark peeling in strips; odd-pinnate leaves 30-60 cm long, having about 10-24 lanceolate leaflets to 12 cm long, corrugated with depressed veins and pubescent beneath; the inflorescence in pendulous clusters 30 cm long, of small whitish or greenish-yellow flowers and sweetly fragrant; fruit a capsule enclosing winged seeds. *Zone* 6.   *p. 788*

sinensis 'Tinted Sky'; attractive cultivar of vigorous growth, and pinnate foliage tinted pink and copper; very decorative in difficult urban plantings. *Zone* 6.   *p. 788*

CEDRUS   *Coniferae: Pinaceae*

atlantica (Morocco, Algeria), "Atlas cedar"; slow-growing, large evergreen tree to 30 m high, with wide-spreading branches; stiff, bluish-green needle-shaped, 4-angled leaves to 2½ cm long, softer than C. libani, clustered on short stout, lateral spurs; ovoid male cones erect, 8 cm long; female cones smaller. *Zone* 6.   *p. 588*

atlantica 'Aurea' (reputed origin Boskoop 1900) "Golden Atlas cedar"; wide-spreading branches; the lateral spurs dense with thin, glaucous, grayish-green needles, liberally dusted golden-yellow at tips. Normally propagated by grafting, to any other cedar understock. *Zone* 7.   *p. 588*

atlantica 'Glauca' (No. Africa), "Blue Atlas cedar"; unusually attractive tree of open habit with spreading branches having upright leading shoots with rigid needles in whorls on lateral branches, glaucous bluish-silver. *Zone* 6.   *p. 586, 587*

atlantica 'Glauca pendula', "Weeping blue cedar"; a variety of weeping habit, with the lateral pendulous branches drooping like a bluish curtain 3 m or more from limbs. To attain such height it is grafted to a 2-3 m standard, and the branches are trained horizontally. Originated near Paris, France, about 1870. *Zone* 6.   *p. 587, 624*

deodara (Himalayas), "Deodar cedar"; outstandingly graceful, tall tree to 60 m high, of pyramidal habit, with branches and leading shoots pendulous; slender, needle-thin leaves to 4 or 5 cm long, dark bluish-green, attractive barrel-shaped cones to 10 cm long, carried upright. *Zone* 7.   *p. 586*

deodara 'Compacta' ('Descanso Dwarf'), California cultivar known as "California Christmas tree"; slow-growing dense pyramid with stiff, sharp spine-tipped silvery-bluish needle bundles. *Zone* 6.   *p. 588*

libani (Syria, Lebanon), "Cedar of Lebanon"; aristocratic conifer; when young with branches erect; tufted needles, very stiff and sharp, on short lateral shoots, to 2 cm long, green or glaucous; with age trees will branch and grow from 15 to 30 m high, with spreading branches horizontal and fan-like, the cones to 10 cm long. *Zone* 5. *p. 577, 586*

libani 'Nana', "Dwarf Lebanon cedar"; desirable cultivar of more compact habit than the species, with shorter branches, and slow-growing, the secondary branches arching downward, dense with 2 cm needles dark green. *Zone* 6.   *p. 588*

CEIBA   *Bombacaceae*

rivieri (Mountains of Rio), "Silk cotton"; deciduous tree usually growing tight against another tree for support, and throwing roots around its host; flowers glowing ruby-red. *Tropical. Zone* 10. *p. 666*

CELASTRUS   Celastraceae

orbiculatus (China, Japan), "Oriental bittersweet"; deciduous scandent or twining shrub to 10 m or more; the branches spiny when young; leaves broad-obovate or rounded, to 12 cm long, crenate at margins; small greenish flowers in axillary clusters, the male and female blooms usually on separate plants; fruit in globose capsules. *Zone 4.*   p. 681

scandens (Québec, so. to No. Carolina and New Mexico), "American bittersweet"; deciduous twining shrub up to 6 m; smooth obovate leaves to 10 cm long; the male and female inflorescence usually on separate plants; small yellow flowers in clusters followed on pistillate (female) blooms by 1 cm 3-valved capsules which split open when ripe revealing the yellow inner surface and the bright scarlet seeds; very attractive in late Summer; however, the foliage is poisonous if eaten. *Zone 2.*   p. 681

CELMISIA   Compositae

coriacea (New Zealand), the "Mountain daisy"; noble rosette, at home along the Southern Alps and to the Fiordland, with stiff-leathery sword-like leaves 30-60 cm long, beautifully covered with silver skin above when young, later dark green and shining; beneath dense with silvery wool; large daisy-like ray-flowers 8-10 cm across, white with golden center, on woolly stalks. *Warm-temperate. Zone 7.*   p.377

hookeri (So. Island, New Zealand), "Otago daisy"; large tufted perennial rosette of arid Otago, the sword-shaped leathery leaves 20-50 cm long, dark green above and densely white tomentose beneath; floral heads 8-10 cm across, on stalk 30 cm long, of tubular disc-flowers, the daisy-like ray-florets 3 cm long. *Zone 8.*   p. 377

prorepens (New Zealand: South Island), "N.Z. Alpine daisy"; stout perennial herb creeping by stolons, rooting at nodes, and forming rosettes at ends of branches; obovate leaves 5-9 cm long, wrinkled on both sides; white flowers 3-4 cm across, on sticky 20 cm stalks. *Zone 9.*   p. 374

CELOSIA   Amaranthaceae

argentea plumosa, the "Feather celosia" or "Burnt plume"; herbaceous annual about 1/3 m high in bushy types, with fleshy stem and fresh green ovate leaves; the branches terminated by dense erect spikes of feathery plumes, highly colored fiery red as in 'Fiery Feather', or yellow such as in 'Golden Feather'; developing best in high, humid heat with plenty of sunshine. *Tropical. Zones 10-11.*   p. 339

argentea plumosa 'Apricot Beauty'; handsome horticultural cultivar, very floriferous with erect spike-like racemes of salmon-rose flowers, during Summer. *Zones 10-11.*   p. 339

argentea plumosa 'Flame', "Burnt plume"; herbaceous annual from Tropical Asia with fresh green ovate leaves, and with stem and branches terminated by dense chaffy spikes highly colored as fiery red plumes. *Tropical. Zones 10-11.*   p. 339

cristata (E. Indies), "Cockscomb", one of the most spectacular summer-flowering annuals; a tropical fleshy herb 30 cm or more high with succulent stem and big fresh-green or sometimes bronzy lanceolate leaves; the inflorescence in showy stiff, cockscomb-like velvety fans 15 to 25 cm wide, often contorted and fluted; most effective in glowing crimson, but available also in yellow or orange color forms. Large flower heads develop best during hot, humid Summer. *Tropical. Zones 10-11.*   p. 339

CELTIS   Ulmaceae

laevigata (Indiana to Florida, Texas, Mexico), "Sugarberry" or "Mississippi hackberry"; ornamental tree to 25 m high, with gray trunk; lanceolate thin leaves usually deciduous, to 10 cm long, the margins normally entire, with axil tufts beneath; small inconspicuous flowers, followed on female trees by orange-red to black 1 cm fleshy stone fruit. *Zone 5.*   p. 896

occidentalis (Québec to No. Carolina and Alabama), "Common Hackberry" or "Nettle tree"; large tree to 40 m high; ovate leaves 5-12 cm long, glossy green above and paler beneath, the margins toothed, and base unequal-sided; orange-red to dark purple globose 1 cm fruit. Much planted because of its resistance to smoke and tolerance of poor soils. *Zone 3.*   p. 896

CENTAUREA   Compositae

cineraria (Senecio candidissima) (Sicily), "Dusty miller"; small perennial densely covered with white matted wool; leaves pinnately parted into broad lobes in maturity; inflorescence golden-yellow. *Zone 7.*   p. 376

cyanus (Europe, Near East), "Cornflower" or "Blue-bottle"; herbaceous Winter biennial or Summer annual with stiff stems, narrow gray-green leaves, and flower heads 3-4 cm across, usually sky-blue. *Subtropic. Zone 8.*   p. 378

cyanus purpurea "Purple cornflower" or "Bachelor's button"; annual or biennial field herb 50 cm or more high, with narrow,

cottony-hairy leaves, and slender stalks carrying floral heads to 4 cm across, with small center disk and broad, purple ray-flowers, summer-blooming. *Zone 8.*   p. 378

dealbata (Iran to Caucasus), "Persian centaurea"; perennial to 50 cm high, with handsomely cut leaves to 30 cm long, white-velvety beneath; interesting solitary globose floral heads 5-6 cm across, having fringe of rose-purple outer petals, the center cushion lighter. *Zones 3-9.*   p. 376

gymnocarpa (Italy: Capri), "Velvet centaurea"; perennial 50-80 cm high, with white felt-like leaves more finely divided than Senecio cineraria, to 20 cm long; purple flower heads. *Subtropic.* *Zone 8.*   p. 376

macrocephala (Armenia to Caucasus), "Globe centaurea"; conspicuous perennial to 80 cm high, with stiff, hollow stem, set with rough, deeply cut and lobed leaves, up to 30 cm long; showy floral head solitary, rather globose, the floral rays threadlike, golden-yellow. *Zone 3.*   p. 378

maritima: see SENECIO cineraria

montana (C. Europe to Asia Minor), "Mountain bluet"; creeping perennial 30 to 50 cm high, the stems with oblanceolate cobwebby leaves; the floral heads to 7 cm wide, with marginal flowers much enlarged and ray-like, violet-blue. *Zone 3.*   p. 378

ragusina (Crete); half-hardy subshrub 60 cm or more high, with silvery stems and foliage covered with fine white hairs, the fleshy, oblong leaves deeply lobed, to 12 cm long; bright yellow flower heads without spreading florets. *Zone 9.*   p. 376

scabiosa (C. Euorpe to Caucasus and So. Asia); herbaceous perennial to 1 m or more high; basal leaves oblanceolate to 25 cm long, pinnate or toothed; soft hairy, smaller stem-leaves; flowers 5 cm across, with globose central head, and filament-like ray-florets rose-purple. *Zone 6.*   p. 378

triumfettii (Centr. and So. Europe), "Knapweed"; stoloniferous perennial to 50 cm high, the ovate leaves softly white-hairy on both sides; solitary floral heads to 6 cm across, the ray-flowers enlarged and blue or red-purple. *Zone 6.*   p. 378

CENTAURIUM   Gentianaceae

scilloides (Erythraea mussonii), (England to coast of Portugal, Azores), "Centaury"; miniature herbaceous perennial forming tufts 5-8 cm high; the prostrate branches with fleshy, 1 cm light green, shining leaves usually concave; numerous rose-pink starry flowers in June to September. *Zone 8.*   p. 415

CENTRANTHUS   Valerianaceae

ruber (Europe, No. Africa), "Red valerian"; attractive perennial to 1 m, with ovate, glaucous leaves 10 cm long; small fragrant, carmine-red flowers in dense terminal clusters during Summer. *Zones 4-9.*   p. 517

ruber 'Albus' (Kentranthus), "Jupiter's beard"; handsome color variation of this herbaceous perennial, with bluish glaucous leaves, sometimes toothed; the fragrant white flowers 1-2 cm long, scattered along stem or in dense terminal clusters. *Zones 6-9.*   p. 517

CENTRATHERUM   Compositae

muticum (intermedium hort.) (Brazil), "Brazilian button flower"; herbaceous bush with serrate leaves, bearing at the ends of branches long-lasting, bluish-lavender, fluffy button flowers 2½ cm across, over a long blooming period. *Zone 10.*   p. 374

ruber 'Atrococcineus', "Fox's brush"; very pretty color form seen in Eastern Germany, very floriferous with flowers deep crimson-red, in terminal clusters and along the stiffly erect stems, blooming during Summer. *Zones 4-9.*   p. 517

CENTROSEMA   Leguminosae

virginianum (U.S.: N. Jersey to Florida, Texas; Trop. America, Africa), "Butterfly pea" or "Conchita"; twining or scandent perennial herb, with pinnate leaves of 3 ovate leaflets to 5 cm long; showy whitish to light purple flowers curiously growing upside-down, with broad standard 3 cm wide, and spurred near base. *Zones 6-10.*   p. 277

CEPHALANTHUS   Rubiaceae

occidentalis (E. to W. No. America, Mexico, W. Indies) "Button bush"; waterside shrub to 5 m high, deciduous in cold climate; glossy green lanceolate leaves to 15 cm long; small flowers in creamy-white to pinkish 3 cm globes, with the prominent pistils protruding, giving them a bristly look, during Summer. *Zone 4.*   p. 337

CEPHALARIA   Dipsacaceae

alpina (Scabiosa) (W. Alps of Italy to Greece), "Alpine cephalaria"; handsome perennial with velvety stems 1½ m or more high; the leaves pinnately dissected; flowers sulphur-yellow in lacy heads, scabiosa-like, 3 cm across, in Summer. *Zone 3.*   p. 414

CEPHALOCEREUS   *Cactaceae*
alensis (Mexico), "Woolly torch cactus"; slender columns to 6 m high, branching from base; 12 to 14 ribs with raised knobs, bearing brownish needle-shaped spines; flowering region (cephalium) lateral or terminal, characteristically developing areas of white wool; small bell-shaped purplish flowers nocturnal. *Zone 10.*   p. 159
palmeri (Pilosocereus) (E. Mexico: Tamaulipas), "Woolly torch cactus"; tree type to 8 m; slender columns, dark green, glaucous and bluish when young; 7-9 rounded ribs, white-hairy at top; flowers purplish, to 7 cm long. *Arid-tropical. Zone 10.*   p. 155
royenii (West Indies); strong columns to 6 m high branching near base, to 8 cm thick, bluish-green, with 7-11 ribs, the areoles with white hair tufts, and long, light brown spines; shell-pink tubular flowers 5 cm long, brownish outside; 5 cm globose fruit with red flesh. *Arid-tropical. Zone 11.*   p. 161
senilis (Mexico: Hidalgo), "Old man cactus"; slender column to 6 m or more high, and to 30-40 cm thick, closely ribbed, and covered with long gray hairs; nocturnal flowers rose-colored, to 9 cm long. *Arid-tropical. Zones 9-10.*   p. 157

CEPHALOPHYLLUM   *Aizoaceae*
alstonii (Cape Prov.: Karroo), "Red spike"; striking succulent forming dense cushions of erect, and glaucous green leaves 7 to 10 cm long, and usually angled-cylindrical; showy flowers ruby-red, 5-8 cm across. According to Herre of Stellenbosch, the "Diamond" among the Mesembryanthemums. Known also as Cylindrophyllum in hort. *Arid-subtropic. Zone 10.*   p. 144

CEPHALOSCHEFFLERA blaneoi:
see SCHEFFLERA angustifolia

CEPHALOTAXUS   *Cephalotaxaceae (Coniferae)*
fortunei (China), "Chinese plum-yew"; vigorous evergreen usually in bushform, 8-10 m high, resembling Taxus, but with larger foliage; long, pendant branches with needle-like leaves in 2 ranks, 5-8 cm long, dark green above, silvery beneath; oblong fruit with fleshy covering 3 cm long, olive-green to purple. *Zones 7-8.*   p. 572
harringtonia (Japan), "Harrington plum yew"; shapely evergreen, to 10 m high, with two-ranked narrow needles, dark green, 3-5 cm or more long; small oily, greenish fruit, purple when ripe. *Zone 6.*   p. 572

CERASTIUM   *Caryophyllaceae*
alpinum lanatum (Arctic, No. America and Europe, Alps), "Alpine chickweed" or "Mouse-ears"; mat-forming perennial to 10 cm high, covered with long crisp, tangled hairs; the woolly leaves in small rosettes near tips of branches; 3 cm white flowers in June-August. *Zone 2.*   p. 360
arvense (Europe except far North; naturalized in No. America), "Field chickweed"; clustering perennial herb to 30 cm high, the branches procumbent, rooting at nodes; opposite linear leaves 2 to 5 cm long; small white flowers 2 cm across, from April to June. *Zone 3.*   p. 360
arvense 'Compactum' (Europe), "Starry grasswort"; small Alpine rockgarden plant, a low, compact form of the species, covered with numerous small white, starry flowers. *Zone 3.*   p. 360
boissieri (Spain); mat-forming perennial, less woolly than tomentosum, 10-30 cm high; small sessile ovate leaves on creeping stems, and starry white, 2 cm flowers, in June. *Zone 6.*   p. 360
tomentosum (Mts. of Italy, to Sicily), "Snow-in-summer"; white-woolly perennial, forming mats from many underground stems; lanceolate 3 cm leaves; 2 cm white flowers in June. Much used in rockgardens. *Zone 4.*   p. 360

CERATONIA   *Leguminosae*
siliqua (Eastern Mediterranean reg.), "St. John's bread" or "Carob"; evergreen tree 12-15 m high, with stout trunk and rounded head of branches; leaves pinnate, 15-30 cm long with 6-12 leathery, glossy green oval leaflets 3-7 cm long; flowers in cylindrical racemes to 15 cm long; fruit on female trees are woody brown pods 12-30 cm long, the pulp of which is sweet and much valued in So. Europe as animal food, or for chewing and eaten since ancient times, having a high sugar content. *Zones 9-10.*   p. 755, 909

CERATOPTERIS   *Parkeriaceae (Filices)*
cornuta (Trop. Africa to Indonesia, No. Australia), a "Floating Staghorn fern" of tropical waters; aquatic fern with leafstalks containing air to buoy the plant above water, with roots often extending into the mud below; sterile succulent leaves 10-15 cm long, pinnate or bipinnate; fertile leaves larger and 4 to 5 pinnately divided. *Humid-tropical. Zone 11.*   p. 329

CERATOSTIGMA   *Plumbaginaceae*
plumbaginoides (W. China), "Blue plumbago" or "Dwarf plumbago"; low wiry-stemmed perennial 15-40 cm high, the reddish branches angled and slightly bristly; the obovate glossy green leaves 5 to 8 cm long; flowers vivid purplish-blue, 2 cm across, having short tube, August-September blooming. *Zones 5-10.*   p. 472
willmottianum (W. China), "Chinese plumbago"; low spreading shrub to 1½ m high, with angled branches; obovate dull green leaves 5 cm long, bristly on both sides; salver-shaped flowers 2 cm across; limb sky-blue with white eye and with rosy tube; summer-blooming. *Zones 8-10.*   p. 820

CERATOZAMIA   *Cycadaceae: Zamiaceae*
mexicana (Mexico), "Mexican horncone"; palm-like cycad with stiff pinnate glaucous and hairy leaves borne in a whorl on a short hairy trunk, to 2 m high; with up to 150 leathery leaflets, the stalks spiny; the flowers in cones. *Tropical. Zones 10-11.*   p. 114

CERCESTIS   *Araceae*
taiensis (Ivory Coast); tropical plant with creeping root-stalk sprouting young shoots; dark green, ovate leaves 12-15 cm long with lateral silvery bands, on 6-9 cm petioles; short floral stalk bearing green spathe. *Zone 12.*   p. 24

CERCIDIPHYLLUM   *Cercidiphyllaceae*
japonicum (China, Japan), "Katsura tree"; excellent shade tree 20-30 m high, with wide-spreading branches from usually several trunks forming from the base; the reddish branchlets with deciduous roundish or broad ovate leaves 5-10 cm long, dark green above and glaucous beneath, becoming orange or scarlet in Autumn; the small inconspicuous flowers appearing before the foliage, on short spurs. *Zone 4.*   p. 684

CERCIDIUM   *Leguminocae*
floridum (torreyanum) (Arizona to Mexico), "Blue Palo verde" of the desert; deciduous small bush or tree to 10 m; spiny blue-green branches with finely divided, bipinnate foliage which drops early; in Spring masses of small bright yellow 2 cm flowers. *Arid-subtropic. Zone 9.*   p. 755, 756
microphyllum (So. California, Arizona, Sonora), "Palo Verde" or "Foothill palo verde"; xerophytic shrub of arid regions, 5 m or more high, multi-stemmed from the base, having spiny bright green or yellow-green woody branches; the tiny pinnate pubescent leaves having 4-8 pairs of minute leaflets, appear only for a very short time, then dry up and disappear; pale yellow flowers, with upper petal white, cover the tree in April-May, followed by the long pods having several bulges. Palo verde means "Green stick" to the Mexicans, a good description for the bare green stems. *Zone 9.*   p. 756
sonorae (Mexico: Sonora), "Sonora Palo Verde"; small deciduous tree with trunk and spiny branches green, spreading horizontally, forming a flat crown, all surfaces covered by a coating of wax; foliage sparse with pinnate leaves; the 2 cm yellow flowers in small clusters along the branches; the fruit is an oblong bean-like legume. *Zone 9.*   p. 755

CERCIS   *Leguminosae*
canadensis (New Jersey to Florida and west to Texas), "Eastern red bud"; deciduous tree to 12 m, with leaves rich green, broadly ovate to 10 cm across; small 2 cm rose-pink flowers grown in great profusion on bare twigs and branches. Not native in Canada. *Zone 4.*   p. 755, 756
chinensis (Cent. China), "Chinese Judas tree"; deciduous tree to 12 m or more high, but in gardens usually shrubby; glossy green leaves deeply cordate, 8-12 cm long; very floriferous with masses of purplish-pink pea-flowers appearing before the foliage in mid-May; the Autumn foliage is vivid yellow. *Zone 6.*   p. 755
occidentalis (California), "California redbud"; deciduous shrub or multi-stemmed tree to 5 m high, with kidney-shaped leaves, notched at top and wider than long, to 7 cm across; handsome flowers with reddish tube and flaring lobes pink, 1-2 cm long, in dense clusters, blooming April-May on previous year's growth, on bare wood; fruit 8 cm long. *Zone 8.*   p. 755
reniformis (Texas, New Mexico), "Love tree"; beautiful floriferous, deciduous small tree, in habitat to 12 m; leaves ovate to kidney-shaped 5-10 cm wide and of leathery texture; glorious inflorescence on bare branches before foliage, with flowers deep rose, 12 mm long, usually in clusters, in Spring. *Zone 8.*   p. 756
siliquastrum (So. Europe and the Orient), "Judas tree" or "Redbud"; deciduous tree to 12 m, usually smaller and more shrubby; leaves deeply cordate, 6-10 cm wide, glaucous green; pea-flowers bright purplish-rose 1-2 cm long, in clusters of 3 to 6, produced in immense quantities directly from branches young and old, often appearing before the leaves. *Zone 7.*   p. 755
siliquastrum alba, "White Judas tree"; large tree-like deciduous shrub with pea-like flowers in this variety pure white. Photographed in Dallas, Texas nursery during Summer while with foliage, but blossoms still hanging on past their prime. *Zone 8.*   p. 755

CEREUS   *Cactaceae*

hexagonus (Colombia), "South American blue column"; tall tree type to 15 m, branching near base; glaucous blue-green fleshy columns, with 4-6 high ribs, and few spines; white flowers 20-25 cm long; reddish fruit to 12 cm. Planted as windbreaks along coffee plantations. *Tropical. Zones 10-11.*   *p. 177, 622*

peruvianus (C. Brazil); thought to be the true species; sparry tree type with branching slender columns, powdery blue, to more than 3 m high, usually with 7 ribs, and tan spines; white flowers to 16 cm long. *Zone 9.*   *p. 155*

'Peruvianus hybrid', "Peruvian apple"; the commonly cultivated tree-cereus in the hort. trade; fleshy columns 6-9 ribbed, to 12 m high, glaucous bluish-green, free branching; variable, usually the older portions with long brown spines, upper or younger sections often nearly spineless; showy nocturnal flowers to 24 cm long, open into day, the inside petal white to greenish, outside tinged with copper; the crimson-red fruit is edible, and about 8 cm dia. *Tropical. Zone 10.*   *p. 69, 155, ,910*

peruvianus 'Monstrosus', "Curiosity plant"; an irregular growing monstrose form constantly forming new heads; glaucous bluish, slow growing but always retaining its habit. *Zone 10.*   *p. 155*

CEREUS: see also Carnegia, Cephalocereus, Echinocereus, Espostoa, Hylocereus, Lophocereus, Myrtillocactus, Nyctocereus, Pachycereus, Selenicereus, Trichocereus

CEROPEGIA   *Asclepiadaceae*

haygarthii (Natal), "Wine-glass vine"; twining, succulent stem with small ovate leaves; flower like a fluted wineglass with bent stem, cream with specks of maroon, covered by maroon parachute; from center rises a maroon stalk topped by red knob, sparsely covered by white hair. *Subtropic. Zones 10-11.*   *p. 151*

CEROXYLON   *Palmae*

quindiuense (Venezuela, Colombia: Antioquia), "Andean Wax-palm"; majestic very tall palm, at home in high valleys of the Central Andes to an altitude of 3000 m; the straight, slender trunk 60 m or more high, covered with silvery gray wax, smooth except for prominent rings from old leafscars; crown of graceful, pinnate fronds 5 m or more long, the rigid, dark green leaflets pendant, and powdery white beneath; large pendulous clusters of brown fruit 3 cm long. The wax is used in making candles and polish. *Subtropic. Zones 11-12.*   *p. 100*

CESTRUM   *Solanaceae*

aurantiacum (Guatemala); rambling or half-climbing shrub with matte green ovate leaves 5-8 cm long, and leafy pyramidal clusters of bright orange-yellow 2½ cm flowers with reflexed lobes. *Subtropic. Zones 9-10.*   *p. 878*

diurnum (W. Indies), "Day jessamine"; tropical evergreen shrub or small tree to 5 m, sometimes scandent; leathery oblong leaves 10-12 cm long; flowers in clusters, fragrant by day, shaped like miniature trumpets, 2-3 cm long, white with a touch of green; glossy black fruit. *Zone 10.*   *p. 878*

elegans (purpureum) (Mexico), "Red cestrum" or "Flor del soldado"; rambling evergreen shrub to 3 or more metres, with soft-hairy branches and ovate leaves to 10 cm long; the flowers in nodding clusters, slender tubular corolla with spreading lobes, glowing wine-red. *Zones 9-10.*   *p. 879*

'Newellii' (possibly hyb. of Mexican C. elegans x fasciculatum), by Newell of Norfolk, England; handsome evergreen tropical shrub to 2 m or more high, with sparry branches; glossy green ovate leaves with depressed veins, 12 cm or more long; beautiful smooth, bright crimson tubular flowers 2-3 cm long, in long-stalked clusters, very free-blooming. *Zones 9-10.*   *p. 879*

nocturnum (West Indies), "Night jessamine" or "Queen of the Night"; evergreen shrub to 2 or 3 m high with wiry, brownish branches; shining, thin-leathery, 8 to 15 cm ovate leaves, and small, greenish or creamy-white, slender tubular flowers with pointed lobes, intensely perfumed at night; fruit a succulent berry in grape-like pendant cluster. *Zones 9-10.*   *p. 879*

parqui (Chile), the "Willow-leaved jessamine"; partially deciduous shrub 2-4 m high, with lanceolate leaves 5-12 cm long, and greenish-yellow tubular flowers 3-4 cm long, with spreading lobes, in profuse clusters, intensely fragrant at night. *Zones 9-10.*   *p. 879*

CETERACH   *Polypodiaceae (Filices)*

officinarum (C. and So. Europe to Asia, South Pacific and Africa), the "Scale-fern"; small tufted xerophyte, rhizome covered with black hairs, the pinnate or lobed fronds 15 cm long, thick-leathery, dark green and smooth above, underneath dense with yellow-brown scales. Photographed on Easter Island. *Zones 7-11.*   *p. 130*

CHAENOMELES   *Rosaceae*

cathayensis (Lagunaria) (Cent. China); deciduous or semi-ever-green shrub to 3 m high, stiffly erect, sparsely branched and spiny; the elliptic leaves sharply toothed, each tooth with an awn-like tip; the charming flowers white or pink, 3 cm across, followed by abundant dull green globose or ovoid fruit 10 cm or more long, hard and of bitter taste but used to make excellent jellies. *Zone 5.*   *p. 924*

japonica (Japan: Honshu), "Dwarf Japanese quince"; discovered in the mountains of Hakone; dwarf evergreen shrub of wide-spreading habit, to 1 m high, spread to 2 m, with short spines; glossy green, leathery, spoon-shaped leaves, crenate at margins; orange-scarlet to blood-red flowers 3-4 cm dia., appearing in early Spring in clusters at the joints of one-year-old wood; followed sometimes by fragrant, gnarled apple-shaped, yellowish fruit to 4 cm dia.; flushed with red in sun; the flesh is aromatic and excellent in preserves. *Zones 4-9.*   *p. 616, 830, 925*

sinensis: see CYDONIA sinensis

speciosa (lagenaria) (earlier name Cydonia japonica) (China cult. in Japan), known as "Japanese Flowering quince" in hort.; deciduous shrub to 3 m high, of dense habit, more or less spiny, with sharply toothed, glossy green, ovate leaves; 4-8 cm long; flowers typically scarlet-red, 3-5 cm wide; varieties also have white, pink or semi-double blooms. *Zone 5.*   *p. 627, 830*

speciosa 'Falconnet Charlot'; vigorous French hybrid about 1900, with flowers a lovely pink tinged with rose, and semi-double; fruits large and similar to a small apple. Photographed in col. New York Bot. Garden. *Zone 4.*   *p. 830*

x superba cv. 'Boule de Feu' (japonica x speciosa); beautiful, vigorous French hybrid 1916; thorny shrub to 2 m high, and densely branched, the young branchlets covered with coarse felt; ovate leaves 3-8 cm long; very floriferous with large, 4-5 cm wide-open carmine-red flowers, early March-April blooming. *Zone 4.*   *p. 830*

CHAMAECEREUS   *Cactaceae*

silvestri, (sylvestri) (Argentina: Tucuman to Salta), "Peanut cactus"; little clusters of short cylindric, fresh green branches to 15 cm long, with soft white spines; flowers to 4 cm long, orange-scarlet. C. silverstri (Speg.) in Britton and Rose, Backeberg, Zander; C. sylvestri in Hortus 3. *Zone 10.*   *p. 155*

CHAMAECYPARIS   *Cupressaceae (Coniferae)*

funebris (Cupressus) (China), "Mourning cypress" or "Chinese weeping cypress"; handsome evergreen coniferous tree to 20 m high, with arching branches bearing long branchlets pendulous by their weight; the small scale-like leaves light green or grayish, pressed close to shoot; globose cones to 2 cm wide, of 8 scales, the outer coat bearing resin tubercles. Planted in cemeteries along Mediterranean. *Zone 8.*   *p. 573*

lawsoniana (Oregon to N.W. California), "False cypress" or "Port Orford cedar"; stately evergreen tree of pyramidal habit, to 60 m tall, with reddish bark, the branchlets flattened frond-like, scale-like leaves closely appressed, steel-blue with white lines beneath. Male flowers reddish, females greenish-purple; small 8 mm cones, first green, becoming brown, their scales with low ridges. The wood is one of the most important commercial timbers. *Zone 5.*   *p. 574*

lawsoniana 'Columnaris glauca', "Blue column cypress" hort.; superb slender pyramidal conifer stiffly erect, and dense with flattened branchlets silvery bluish-green; very robust and ideal next to walls of homes or for accent in gardens. *Zone 5.*   *p. 574*

lawsoniana 'Glauca', "Blue false cypress"; very desirable cultivar of conical habit with branchlets spreading and of fine steel-blue coloring. *Zone 6.*   *p. 573*

lawsoniana 'Lanei', "Golden false cypress"; very handsome English cultivar of columnar growth, to 5 m high, with thin, flat branchlets the brightest golden-yellow, especially toward tips. *Zone 6.*   *p. 573*

lawsoniana 'Stewartii'; handsome cultivar originated about 1900 in Bournemouth, England; robust tree of pyramidal habit to 10 m high, with branches and branchlets spreading outward; the shoots tipped golden-yellow while young, the base more green; the drooping leaf tips give plant an elegant appearance. Fairly resistant to leaf burn. Widely popular in Europe, U.S. Pacific Coast; also New Zealand. *Zones 5-8.*   *p. 574*

nootkatensis 'Pendula' (Pacific coast to Alaska), "Weeping Alaska cedar" or "False cypress"; beautiful conifer to 30 m high, with fissured bark, spreading branches; leaves closely appressed on pendulous branchlets; cones 1 cm across, reddish-brown. *Zone 4.*   *p. 573*

obtusa (Japan), "Hinoki cypress"; coniferous, slow-growing evergreen tree to 30 m or more high, having red-brown bark, shed in long narrow strips; handsome with glossy dark green, scale-like leaves lined white beneath, in flat, fan-like branchlets. Cones 2 cm dia., orange-brown when ripe. Important commercial wood in Japan. *Zone 4.*   *p. 574*

obtusa 'Aurea', "Golden false cypress"; attractive form with young shoots and leaves golden-yellow, becoming greener when maturing. *Zone 4.*   *p. 574*

obtusa 'Compacta'; dwarf but broadly spreading form, dense with branchlets covered by appressed, scaly needles; slowly growing in height over many years. Zone 4. *p. 574*

obtusa 'Nana', "Dwarf Hinoki cypress"; compact, slow-growing form and very dwarf, suitable for the rock-garden, balcony boxes, and dishgardens, growing usually sideways and flat-topped, the branchlets open fan-shaped dull dark green. Wyman cites a miniature 30 years old as measuring only 15 cm high. Zone 5. *p. 574*

obtusa 'Nana Gracilis', "Dwarf Hinoki cypress"; widely grown Dwarf Hinoki of low habit and spreading to 1 m across; lustrous dark green foliage in flat fan-like, cupped fronds. Usually offered in nurseries as C. obtusa nana, but according to Wyman it is faster growing than the true 'Nana', becoming more than 1 m high in 30 years, while 'Nana' could be only 15 cm high. Zone 5. *p. 574*

obtusa 'Pygmaea', "Pygmy Hinoki cypress"; handsome dwarf cultivar, ideally suited for low hedges, even with age rarely over 60 cm high; the branches borne horizontally with branchlets fan-shaped and covered by scale-like bronzy green foliage. Zone 5. *p. 613*

obtusa 'Tetragona aurea' (Retinispora), "Dwarf golden retinispora"; shrubby, with irregularly arranged tufted, golden-leaved 4-angled branchlets. Zone 5. *p. 574*

pisifera 'Boulevard' ('Cyanoviridis'), "Blue Sawara cypress" or "Blue moss cypress"; exquisite dwarf evergreen, a mutation of C. pisif. 'Squarrosa': fine-textured, soft plume-like, dense foliage of silvery-blue needles, with age forming irregular rounded cones; very suitable for flower boxes. The parent species C. pisifera of Japan is a large tree to 40 m high, with reddish-brown bark; the foliage in flattened branchlets with scale-like leaves appressed in 4 ranks; small cones 1 cm dia. and brown when mature; known as Retinispora in hort. Zone 3. *p. 575*

pisifera 'Filifera aurea' (Retinispora hort.), "Threadleaf cypress" or "Golden mop"; coniferous shrub of unique appearance, with a dense mass of golden-yellow threadlike branchlets weeping gracefully downward at the tips, growing to 3 m high. Zone 4. *p. 575*

pisifera 'Plumosa aurea' (Retinispora) (Japan), "Plume false cypress"; colorful conifer forming a dense and broad conical bush 5-10 m high, with erect, prickly branches; the feathery twigs clothed by short soft needles vivid golden-yellow in Spring, reverting to green later. With age when more tree-like, will shed lower branches. Zone 3. *p. 575*

pisifera 'Squarrosa' (Retinispora in hort.) (Japan), "Moss cypress"; attractive coniferous bush which may reach 10 m height unless trimmed of the most vigorous growths; the juvenile-type foliage is feathery and soft, dense with glaucous blue-gray appressed needles in pairs or whorls of four. Zone 3. *p. 575*

CHAMAEDAPHNE   Ericaceae

calyculata (Arctic regions of Europe, Asia, America), "Leatherleaf"; evergreen shrub to 1½ m high, with ovate leaves 5 cm or more long, scale beneath and lightly serrate; inflorescence an elongate leafy raceme, with 1 cm urn-shaped white corollas, pendulous along axis, blooming April to June. Zone 2. *p. 700*

CHAMAEDOREA   Palmae

costaricana (C. America), "Showy bamboo palm"; a clustering palm of great beauty, with bamboo-like dark green canes to 3 or even 6 m high, furnished from bottom to top with graceful pinnate fronds, to 50 cm long, each with about 40 pinnae, solid green, not glaucous, and tipped by a pair of broad-obovate leaflets as in a fishtail; long-stalked inflorescence bearing globular fruit. Tropical. Zone 11. *p. 102*

elegans (Collinia) (Mexico), "Parlor palm"; small graceful, relatively fast grower with thin stem to 3 m, 3 times as high as Neanthe bella and eventually forming clusters; pinnate leaves loosely spirally arranged, broadly lanceolate, thin-leathery segments dark green; good keeper in shady locations; fruit yellow to white. Tropical. Zones 11-12. *p. 77, 102*

erumpens (Honduras), "Bamboo palm"; suckering dwarf palm, forming bushy, erect clusters of thin, bamboo-like reed-stems, loosely furnished down to the base with short pinnate, drooping leaves, the segments are broad, almost papery, dark green and recurved; a good keeper when well established. Tropical. Zones 11-12. *p. 77, 102*

metallica, introduced in hort. as tenella (Mexico), the "Miniature fishtail"; one of the smallest of palms, slowly developing a stiff stem to 1 m high, and which bears a rosette of broad, entire leaves forked only toward apex. Tropical. Zone 11. *p. 77, 102*

seifrizii (graminifolia) (Mexico; Yucatán), "Reed palm"; small stoloniferous palm with clustering slender cane-like stems alternately furnished near the top with broadly spreading pinnate fronds, their pinnae long and narrow and spaced apart, giving the plant a lacy appearance; withstands some cold. Tropical. Zone 11. *p. 77, 102*

stolonifera (brachypoda in hort.) (So. Mexico), "Climbing fishtail"; stoloniferous small palm with slender, rattan-like canes 2 cm thick,

clambering to 2 m high; the broad, plaited leaves undivided except for a fishtail-like cleft at apex. Tropical. Zone 11. *p. 102*

CHAMELAUCIUM   Myrtaceae

pauciflorum (Western Australia); widely distributed small Waxflower bush to 60 cm high, with diminutive 1 cm leaves borne in pairs along the stem; the charming waxy flowers occur singly but in great profusion, the corollas with 5 spreading lobes are at first white, but changing to red when matured. Zone 9. *p. 797*

uncinatum (Western Australia), the "Geraldton wax-plant"; a heather-like shrub 1½-2 m high or more, with tiny linear needle-like, fresh green leaves hooked near apex; the nodding branches with masses of waxy 15 mm pink or lilac flowers in Spring, of long-lasting quality. Zone 9. *p. 797*

CHAMAELIRIUM   Liliaceae

luteum (Mass. to Ontario and Michigan, so. to Florida), "Blazing-star", "Fairy-wand" or "Rattlesnake root"; handsome unisexual perennial with tuberous roots, the female plants more leafy and taller than male plants; basal leaves spear-shaped to obovate, 10-15 cm long, the stem leaves lanceolate, deep glossy green; stem of female plants to 90 cm high, bearing slender, arching spires to 30 cm long, of small creamy-white flowers, racemes on male plants are shorter and more dense. Zones 3-8. *p. 444*

x CHAMAELOPSIS   Cactaceae

'Firechief' (Chamaecereus x Lobivia); striking bigeneric hybrid by Harry Johnson of California; small olive-green finger-like, 9 to 10 ribbed columns bearing needle spines and white radials, forming clusters; free-blooming with brilliant flame-red flowers to 8 cm across. Arid-subtropic. Zone 10. *p. 157*

CHAMAEMELUM   Compositae

nobile (Anthemis nobilis) (W. Europe, Azores, No. Africa), "Roman Camomile" or "True Camomile"; aromatic perennial or biennial herb to 30 cm high, with very fragrant, finely segmented leaves; the daisy-like flowers 3-4 cm across, and sweetly scented, the ray-florets white and conical disc yellow and with receptacle hollow inside. The dried floral heads are used medicinally as healing tea; also in skin cream and hair rinses. Known as "Genuine Camille" in Germany. Zones 4-10. *p. 524*

nobile 'Lutea' (Anthemis nobilis Hortus 2) (Europe and Mediterr. region), "Chamomile"; aromatic branched perennial to 30 cm high, with downy stems and pinnately 2-3 times divided leaves to 5 cm long; daisy-like flowers yellow, to 3 cm across. Zone 7. *p. 310*

CHAMAEROPS   Palmae

excelsa hort.: see TRACHYCARPUS fortunei

humilis (Mediterranean, So. Europe, No. Africa), "European fan palm"; usually dwarf, clusterforming, sometimes to 6 m in arborescent forms; trunk rough, clothed with fiber; tough leaves relatively small, stiff and folded, with many narrow segments nearly to the base, on spiny, flat stalks; small red-brown fruit. Subtropic. Zones 8-9. *p. 103, 104*

CHAMOMILLA: see MATRICARIA

CHASMANTHE   Iridaceae

aethiopica (So. Africa); cormous plant with flat, gladiolus-like linear basal leaves and erect spike of reddish-yellow flowers with curved tubular 6 cm corolla, the large upper lobe hooded and contracted below middle. Zones 9-10. *p. 223*

floribunda (Trop. and So. Africa), "Pennants"; herb with bulblike corms, to 90 cm high; two-ranked linear leaves to 3 cm wide; many-flowered erect inflorescence, the tubular curved bloom 5 cm long, two-lipped with upper segment orange-red, lower segments greenish. Zones 9-10. *p. 223*

CHASMANTHIUM latifolium (Hortus):
see UNIOLA latifolia (Zander)

CHEILANTHES   Polypodiaceae (Filices)

gracillima (Brit. Columbia to California), "Lace-fern"; a tiny rock-fern with bipinnate, bronzy green, thin-leathery fronds 5 to 10 cm long, brown-woolly beneath, margins recurved, on brown stalks, forming dense tufts. Zone 6. *p. 132*

lanosa (tomentosa) (Connecticut to Virginia and Arizona, Mexico), "Hairy Lip-fern"; small rock fern to 25 cm high, growing from spreading rhizomes, the lacy 15-20 cm fronds are twice pinnate and woolly, rusty hairy; called lip fern because of the pronounced lip under the margin of each pinnae. Zones 6-9. *p. 131*

CHEIRANTHUS   Cruciferae

x allionii: see ERYSIMUM x allionii

cheiri (Erysimum) (So. Europe), "English wallflower"; woody perennial to 70 cm high, but grown as a biennial, blooming in Spring;

sweetscented flowers on terminal racemes like stocks, but in yellow-brown shades; narrow leaves slightly pubescent, 8 cm long. Subtropic. *Zone 9.*   p. 408

cheiri flore pleno, "Double wall-flower"; attractive biennial or perennial, often grown as an annual pot plant; having elongate clusters of flowers in shades of coppery yellow to mahogany red, spring-blooming and very fragrant. Not tolerant of dry heat, it prefers moist-cool climate like England or the Pacific Northwest. *Zone 9.*   p. 408

cheiri lutea, "Yellow wall flower"; a color variation with showy flowers lemon-yellow. *Zone 9.*   p. 408

CHELIDONIUM   Papaveraceae

majus (Europe, W. Asia to Iran), "Celandine" or "Swallow-wort"; perennial herb to 60 cm high, with erect, brittle, hairy stems having orange-colored juice; lobed leaves; single yellow 2 cm flowers in clusters. *Zone 4.*   p. 466

CHELONE   Scrophulariaceae

lyonii (Great Smoky Mts. of Carolina, Tenn.), "Turtle-head"; herbaceous perennial to 75 cm or more high, with attractive ovate, bronzy green, corrugated leaves 10-16 cm long; unusual turtle-like flowers 3 cm long, purplish-rose with lower lip bearded yellow, blooming late Summer. *Zone 3.*   p. 501

obliqua (Maryland to Florida and Mississippi), "Snake-head"; floriferous herbaceous perennial to 60 cm high, with lanceolate leaves 5-20 cm long; the leafy stems with loose clusters of deep rose bell-flowers 3 cm long, the lower lip bearded pale yellow, blooming in Summer. *Zone 7.*   p. 502

CHENOPODIUM   Chenopodiaceae

ambrosioides (Blitum) (Trop. America, natural. in U.S., Europe, Asia), "Epazote herb", "Mexican tea" or "American wormseed"; coarse weedy annual herb, or perennial in mild climate, strongly scented; with slender stems to 1 m high; narrow, lanceolate leaves to 12 cm long, usually coarsely toothed along margins; small greenish flowers in dense axillary or terminal spikes, from July to September. Cultivated for its essential oil, used for medicinal properties; excellent culinary for Mexican bean and rice dishes; beneficial as tea for stomach disorders. *Zones 6-10.*   p. 526

CHIASTOPHYLLUM   Crassulaceae

oppositifolium (Cotyledon simplicifolia hort.) (W. Caucasus), "Moss rose"; creeping forest perennial with roundish-ovate succulent leaves coarsely crenate 4 cm long; the inflorescence a pendulous raceme 30 cm long, of tiny 4 mm yellow campanulate flowers. *Zone 10.*   p. 181

CHILOPSIS   Bignoniaceae

linearis (saligna) (Texas to Nevada, Calif. and Mexico), "Desert willow" of "Flowering willow"; graceful shrub or small tree 3-6 m high, inhabiting arid regions of the Southwest, evergreen in mild climates, but deciduous in colder area; dense branches with willow-like, narrow-linear leathery leaves 8-12 cm long; terminal cluster of very showy trumpet-flowers with corolla 5 cm long, usually rose-pink but variable, the throat with yellow stripes and lobes curly, blooming in May. *Zone 7.*   p. 663

CHILOSCHISTA   Orchidaceae

lunifera (Sikkim to Burma or Myanmar); dwarf leafless epiphyte with entangled masses of roots, from the center of which rise graceful, pendant inflorescences bearing leaflike bracts and small 2 cm yellow flowers spotted with purple. *Zones 11-12.*   p. 85

CHIMONANTHUS   Calycanthaceae

praecox (fragrans) (China), "Wintersweet"; deciduous shrub to 3 m high, blooming early Winter from November on to March in the Northern Hemisphere, long preceding the foliage; waxy extremely fragrant flowers to 3 cm wide, with outer sepals and petals yellow, inner petals smaller and brown-purple; followed by the lustrous green lanceolate leaves 8-15 cm long. *Zone 7.*   p. 671

CHIMONOBAMBUSA   Gramineae

marmorea (Arundinaria) (Japan), "Marbled bamboo"; bushy dwarf bamboo with creeping rootstock, used in California for outdoor planting, 2 m or more high, and forming dense bush; slender coppery-yellow stems 2 cm dia. with squarish knobs and marbled purplish-black; green leaves 6-8 cm long, 1 cm wide. *Zone 9.*   p. 549

quadrangularis (Bambusa) (So. China, Taiwan), "Square bamboo"; handsome running bamboo 3 to 5 m high, with square, coppery, hollow canes, 2 cm thick, wide-spreading and forming dense clusters; leaves 5-15 cm long, 2 cm wide, green with parallel veins, corrugated lengthwise. A favorite in gardens because of its quadrangular culms. *Zone 9.*   p. 552

CHIONANTHUS   Oleaceae

retusus (China), the "Chinese fringe-tree"; deciduous small tree 3-6 m high with elliptic 10 cm leaves downy beneath, and numerous small white flowers with 4 narrow petals in showy pendulous panicles; dark blue fruit. *Zone 5.*   p. 806

virginicus (Pennsylvania to Florida and Texas), the "American fringe-tree"; deciduous tree to 10 m, with oblong leaves to 20 cm, veins downy beneath; white flowers with usually 4, sometimes 5-6 narrow linear 2½ cm petals, in drooping panicles; dark blue fruit. *Zones 4-9.*   p. 806

CHIONODOXA   Liliaceae

luciliae (gigantea) (Asia Minor, Crete), "Glory-of-the-snow"; early spring-blooming, small bulbous plant to 20 cm high, related to Scilla, with narrow basal leaves and attractive, waxy, funnel-shaped flowers expanded star-like, to 4 cm across, of an intense blue, shading to white in the center, in early Spring. *Zone 4.*   p. 238

nana (cretica), (E. Mediterranean: Crete), low bulbous herb forming colonies; from mountains of Crete; spreading narrow leaves to 18 cm long; floral stems usually 1 per bulb, to 20 cm high, bearing 1-3 small, pale lilac flowers with white central zone, in Spring. *Zone 8.*   p. 238

sardensis (Asia Minor), "Glory-of-the-snow"; bulbous herb to 15 cm high, with rolled channeled leaves, and all-blue flowers with spreading lobes 1 cm long, and white filaments in center, on nodding stemlets, 3 to 6 on each short stalk, in early Spring. Subtropic. *Zone 4.*   p. 238

CHIRANTHODENDRON   Bombacaceae

pentadactylon (syn. Cheirostemon platanoides) (Mexico, Guatemala), "Mexican hand-flower", "Monkey-hand tree" or "Manitos"; tree to 30 m high, with large cordate, 3 to 7 lobed leaves to 30 cm long, green above, tomentose beneath; strange flowers with 5 cm deep red waxy calyx, from the center of which extends a handlike appendage, complete with "finger-nails". Subtropic. *Zone 9.*   p. 666

CHIRITA   Gesneriaceae

lavandulacea (Malaya), "Hindustan gentian"; erect, branching, rather succulent plant with large ovate, soft hairy, opposite leaves with toothed margins, and whorls of axillary flowers with white pouchlike corolla tube and spreading limb of pale lavender blue, marked yellow in throat. *Humid-tropical. Zone 11.*   p. 63

CHIRONIA   Gentianaceae

baccifera (Southern Africa: Namaqualand to Natal and Cape), "Christmas berry"; ornamental subshrub to 60 cm high with opposite linear leaves on angled branches, and terminal cymes of rose-pink or red salver-shaped flowers with narrow tube and spreading limb 2 cm across, blooming Sept.-January in So. Hemisphere; scarlet-red berries. Photographed on Table Mountain during January. *Zone 10.*   p. 732

CHLIDANTHUS   Amaryllidaceae

fragrans (Andes of Perú to N.E. Argentina), "Perfumed fairy lily"; bulbous plant with basal strap-shaped sheathing leaves, and fragrant yellow 8 cm trumpet flowers, appearing before the leaves, in umbels on solid stalks; Summer. Subtropic. *Zones 8-9.*   p. 209

CHLOROPHYTUM   Liliaceae

comosum 'Mandaianum'; Manda cultivar 1915, a small Spider-plant with narrow dark green leaves 10-12 cm long and 1 cm wide, featuring a bright yellow stripe instead of white center stripe; ideal basket plant. *Zone 11.*   p. 68

comosum 'Variegatum' (Anthericum), "Green-lily" or "Walking anthericum"; large rosettes of arching, fresh green, linear leaves 25-40 cm long, 2-3 cm wide, having margins edged in white; long racemes appearing from the center will first bloom with small white flowers, then develop tufts of leaves with aerial roots. Subtropic. *Zone 10.*   p. 68, 444

comosum 'Vittatum' (C. elatum vittatum) (Cape of Good Hope), "Spider plant"; low clustering rosette with channeled narrow-linear, recurving leaves, dark green banded white in center; successive plantlets develop from the long flowering racemes which become pendant if used in baskets; leaves only 10-20 cm long, 1 cm wide. *Subtropic. Zone 10.*   p. 68, 562

CHOISYA   Rutaceae

mollis (Santa Cruz County, Arizona; No. Sonora); small ever-green shrub with palmately compound leaves; the leaflets narrow to narrow lanceolate, to 4 cm long, the midrib depressed; waxy-white flowers with wide spreading ovate petals. *Zones 9-10.*   p. 860

ternata (Mexico), "Mexican-orange"; evergreen shrub to 3 m high, with lustrous, yellow-green trifoliolate leaves, held toward the end of the branches, each leaflet to 8 cm long, and forming fans giving the plant a dense, massive look; fragrant white flowers 3 cm across, like small orange blossoms, in clusters above the foliage; fruit of 8-10 cm dia., leaves are strongly scented when bruised. *Zones 8-10.*   p. 860

CHONEMORPHA   *Apocynaceae*
penangensis (Malaya), "Woodvine"; spectacular climbing shrub developing into lianes on tropical trees; large corrugated leaves wedge-shaped at base, and to 25 cm long; blooming profusely with fragrant white to pinkish flowers having 5 broad petals spreading 8 cm wide.   p. 264

CHORISIA   *Bombacaceae*
insignis (Perú, N.E. Argentina), "White floss-silk tree" or "Drunken tree"; big tree to 15 m high, with fat, flask-shaped green trunk to 2 m thick, big spines on the younger trunk and branches, the sparry branches with palmately compound leaves of 5-7 obovate, waxy green leaflets 6-8 cm long and usually toothed near apex; beautiful, lily-like, large waxy flowers to 14 cm long, with undulate petals at first yellow with purple markings toward base, later fading to cream or white. *Subtropic. Zones 9-10.*   p. 667

speciosa (Brazil, No. Argentina), "Floss-silk tree"; large tree about 15 m high, its trunk usually studded with stout sharp thorns, digitately compound toothed leaves, and showy, variable, usually pinkish 5-petaled flowers; pear-shaped fruits containing silky floss on the seeds. *Zones 9-10.*   p. 667

speciosa 'Majestic Beauty'; a medium size Floss-silk tree, offered as grafted cultivar in California nurseries (1976); more evergreen than the species which blooms usually during the brief leafless stage in Winter; bright green thornless trunk; in Autumn the spectacular, showy flowers with flaring, crisped petals 10 to 13 cm across, rosy-carmine with white center. *Zone 9.*   p. 667

CHORIZEMA   *Leguminosae*
cordatum (Western Australia), "Heartleaf flame pea"; low evergreen sprawling shrub with age to 1 m or more high, with weak, wiry branches, and small leathery, cordate 4 cm leaves sharply toothed and spine-tipped; showy pea flowers red-orange with a yellow blotch, and purplish keel, blooming from Winter into late Spring. *Zone 10.*   p. 757

ilicifolium (W. Australia), "Holly flame pea"; handsome low evergreen shrub with slender branches forming dense bush, with oblong-ovate stiff-leathery leaves 2 to 5 cm long, glossy deep green and spiny-toothed at margins; the pea-like flowers orange streaked with red, spotted yellow at base, the wing petal crimson; blooming as a small plant into Summer. Photographed at Cap Ferrat, France. *Zones 9-10.*   p. 757

CHRYSALIDOCARPUS   *Palmae*
lutescens (Areca) (Madagascar), "Butterfly palm"; with slender, graceful, yellowish stems, forming an attractive clump to 8 m tall, with pinnate foliage nearly to the base; the narrow, thin-leathery pinnae glossy yellow-green and well spaced, on yellow, willowy, furrowed stalks; fruit violet-black. *Tropical. Zones 11-12.*   p. 77, 103

CHRYSANTHEMUM   *Compositae*
argenteum (Tanacetum argenteum) (Asia Minor); attractive clump-forming perennial 10-15 cm high, the leaves twice pinnately divided 3-4 cm long, and clothed with silvery hairs; solitary flower heads ringed by white ray-florets. *Zone 7.*   p. 380

balsamita (W. Asia), "Costmary"; aromatic herbaceous hardy perennial 60 cm or more high, with oblong, serrate leaves 12-25 cm long; small 1 cm flower heads yellow with tiny white rays, in large clusters; persistent plant grown for its sweet-smelling foliage, sometimes called "Lavender" and also known as "Mint geranium". Used in teas, ale, salads, meats, poultry and soups. Pioneers placed leaves in their books to deter silver-fish. *Zones 4-9.*   p. 527

carinatum (Morocco), "Tricolor mum" or "Annual marguerite"; beautiful herbaceous plant sparsely branched, 40 to 80 cm high, with ferny, fleshy grayish-green foliage, pinnate or bipinnate into short linear segments; colorful inflorescence with large heads 6 to 8 cm across; the tubular disc-flowers forming purple cushion; ray-flowers white, yellow, vivid red or two-tone purple, at base yellow and forming a contrasting ring around center; blooming late Summer. *Subtropic. Zones 9-10.*   p. 378

cinerariifolium (Tanacetum cinerar. hort.) (Croatia), "Dalmation pyrethrum" or "Tansy"; glaucous, tufted perennial to 40 cm high, the silvery leaves pinnately cut into narrow segments; the daisy-like flowers 3-4 cm across, the disc-flowers yellow, and a dense circle of ray-flowers white. The dried inflorescence is the primary source of the insecticide powder Pyrethrum. *Zone 8.*   p. 378

coccineum (Pyrethrum roseum) (Caucasus, Iran), the "Pyrethrum" of gardens or "Painted daisy", perennial to 60 cm, with fern-like bipinnatifid vivid green foliage, and showy-daisy-like flower heads in shades of red, also pink, lilac and white, with yellow disc, blooming May-June. Used as an old source of the powdered insecticide pyrethrum, as found in the wild in the mountains of S.W. Asia, collecting the flowers for drying and powdering. The less hardy species Chrys. cinerariifolium or Dalmatian pyrethrum shown on pg. 378, has lately become the main source of the insect powder made from the dried inflorescence. *Zones 4-9.*   -p. 524

coccineum 'Rubrum' (Brenda), "Red Painted daisy"; very popular summer-blooming perennial with large flowers 6 cm across, the ray-florets velvety deep crimson arranged around the center cushion. *Zone 4.*   p. 368

coronarium (Mediterrn. region and Portugal), "Crown-daisy"; floriferous bushy annual or short-lived perennial, to 80 cm high; leaves bipinnately parted into smooth, sharply toothed segments; showy terminal heads of yellow flowers 3-4 cm across, sometimes semi-double, in July to September. Much grown in the Orient, for the young leaves, used as culinary greens; flower heads are also eaten in Japan. *Zone 10.*   p. 375, 379

corymbosum (Tanacetum) (Europe to Caucasus); stout clump-forming perennial 30-90 cm high; the bipinnately dissected, typical leaves of Tanacetum are to 15 cm long; floral heads 3-5 cm wide, daisy-like, with yellow disc, and white ray-flowers, summer-blooming. *Zone 6.*   p. 379

frutescens (Canary Islands), "White marguerite"; bushy branching herbaceous plant with lacy, divided grayish-green leaves, and single white flowers 4-6 cm across, with yellow disc. *Subtropic. Zone 9.*   p. 379

frutescens chrysaster, "Boston yellow daisy"; form with fleshier stem; fresh green, divided leaves, and lemon-yellow rays heavier and not as free flowering as the type. *Subtropic. Zone 9.*   p. 379

frutescens 'Mary Wootten'; a famous "Tree-marguerite" named after a lovely Miss New Zealand; (Pink Beauty x Mrs. Sanders); 5-6 cm flowers, pleasing rose-pink, the high cushion center with the outer fringe darker, center more soft pink; very desirable in this color range; blooming over a long period. *Subtropic. Zone 9.*   p. 379

hosmariense (Leucanthemum hosmariense) (Morocco); rhizomatous spreading, bushy perennial to 30 cm high, the stems with appressed silvery hairs; lower leaves 3-parted to 7 cm long, and white-tomentose; floral heads on 15 cm stalks, with yellow disc flowers and white ray-florets. *Zone 8.*   p. 380

indicum (Dendranthema indicum in China) (China: Hongkong to Beijing; Japan), "Chinese chrysanthemum"; stoloniferous, much branched perennial 50-90 cm high, the thin stems with soft leaves to 8 cm or more long, pinnately cleft or lobed, gray-felty beneath; floral heads to 3 cm across, with center cushion deep yellow, and circle of ray-flowers lighter yellow, blooming in Autumn — one of the parents of garden and florists "Mums". *Zone 6.*   p. 378

leucanthemum (Leucanthemum vulgare) (Europe to Caucasus; naturalized in No. America), "Oxeye daisy"; rhizomatous perennial, with wide-spreading rootstock, not over 60 cm high; basal leaves in rosette, and pinnately lobed; stem leaves oblong and sessile; floral heads 4-5 cm across, having yellow disc and white ray-florets. *Zone 3.*   p. 379

macrophyllum (Tanacetum) (Hungary, Macedonia to Caucasus), "Tansy chrysanthemum"; erect, rhizomatous perennial 60 cm or more high, the 20 cm pubescent leaves pinnately divided into coarsely toothed segments; many-flowered clusters of small 1 cm blooms having yellow disc and cream-white ray-florets during June-July. *Zone 6.*   p. 380

x maximum (Pyrenees), "Shasta daisy" or "Daisy chrysanthemum"; robust perennial, 50-100 cm high; rigid stems with coarse, leathery lanceolate leaves toothed at margins; large flat flowers 6-10 cm across, with golden yellow center cushion, ringed by white ray-florets; blooming July to October; long-lasting as cut flowers, sometimes dyed by florists. *Zones 4-9.*   p. 379

x maximum 'Aglaya' (x superbum); a large-flowered "Shasta daisy"; robust, hardy perennial to 75 cm and more high, often grown as biennial; with lanceolate, serrate, deep green foliage, the stems topped by large 8 to 10 cm marguerite-like white flowers with a double row of frilled ray-flowers, and a white and yellow anemone center cushion; late Summer blooming; popular on the Pacific Coast. *Zones 5-9.*   p. 379

x morifolium (hortorum), the "Florists' chrysanthemum"; known in slang as "Mum"; cultigen of Chinese origin and cultivated in China and Japan for 3000 years; perennial herb ½-1 m or more high, and much-branched, with succulent stems becoming woody, and strong-scented lobed leaves gray pubescent; flowers in showy terminal heads of various colors except blue, the florets modified by long cultivation into petal-like marginal ray-flowers and small, usually tubular disc-flowers forming center cushions; developed into several groups such as single, cascade, anemone (with center cushion), pompon (globular), decorative (aster-like), spider, incurved, and large exhibition; their growth habit is regulated by pinching, or chemical growth retardant. *Warm temperate. Zone 8.*   p. 57, 376

x morifolium 'Bonaffon', "Incurved type"; well-known pot plant variety, with numerous medium-large deep lemon-yellow flowers of good lasting quality, on wiry stems, and with foliage of good substance. *Zone 8.*   p. 57, 376

x morifolium 'Carnelia', large "Anemone" type 8 cm flowers with broad, flattened petals rusty red with golden undertones and eye, and green center cushion, reverse yellow; good pot plant of stiff habit. Normally blooms Nov. 20 in latitude 40-45, North. *Zone 8.*   p. 376

x morifolium 'Cascade'; floriferous and freely branching perennial with slender woody stems, which in the Orient are tied to wires and bamboo canes for decoration, trained to cascade downward; the small 4 cm single flowers with ray-petals in shades of yellow, pink or bronze. *Warm-temperate. Zone 8.*   p. 311

x morifolium 'Daisy White'; "Daisy Mum"; a low garden perennial of the traditional type of Japanese chrysanthemum, symbolic of elegance and beauty; large white, single flowers, or also other colors in this Japanese strain, autumn-blooming. *Zones 4-9.*   p. 380

x morifolium 'Decorative incurved'; typical of the commercial type "Mum" as grown in pots for Thanksgiving; compact plant with firm foliage and large heads of flowers with waxy petals incurved, and long-lasting. *Zone 9.*   p. 57

x morifolium 'Delaware', "Incurved formal type"; a typical good commerical, free branching pot plant with firm foliage and semi-incurved, deep amaranth-red bleaching to bronze; reverse yellow. *Zone 8.*   p. 376

x morifolium 'Golden Cascade'; "Daisy-cascade"; commercial "Cascade" variety of the single daisy type, very floriferous with light yellow ray-petals around a golden-yellow center disc 4 cm dia.; earlier than 'Jane Harte'; its dense habit with long wiry branches is equally adaptable to training to forms as well as broad bushy globes (Oct 30). *Zone 8.*   p. 380

x morifolium 'Illini Bonbon', "Cushion anemone"; small but attractive "Anemone" of short, bushy habit ideal for pots, the stiff stems with massive clusters of 4 cm flowers of daisy-like flat petals lemon-yellow, surrounding a high center cushion of golden-yellow tubular petals. *Zone 8.*   p. 376

x morifolium 'Indianapolis Yellow', large "Incurved"; dependable type, assuring good buds and elegant flowers, with rich yellow petals in part tubular, bleaching to pale yellow with age, but of long-lasting quality; a rather tall variety for pots, very vigorous. *Zone 8.*   p. 376

x morifolium 'Peggy Ann Hoover'; attractive "Spider" mum of the "Fuji" type, large fine mauve pink flowers with thread-like tubular petals, a tint of pale yellow in center; thin-necked but wiry stems and good in pots. *Zone 9.*   p. 58

x morifolium 'Princess Ann'; "Decorative" type, and excellent pot plant of compact, shapely growth habit with firm foliage and substantial flowers 10 cm across, broad-petalled, peach-pink slightly darker in center, paling to light pink at edges. *Zone 8.*   p. 58

x morifolium 'Sassy' (indicum hyb.), "Dwarf garden mum"; attractive perennial of compact habit, to 20 cm high, spreading from base, and ideal for edging or small pots; with masses of small 3 cm golden-yellow pompon flowers, staying neat without pinching, and blooming in Autumn until frost. *Zone 5.*   p. 379

x morifolium 'Shimo-Bashira', an excellent Japanese "Cascade" variety whose name means "Spiny frost"; with several layers of pure white florets making this a "double" form; 3 cm flowers. *Zone 8.*   p. 376

x morifolium 'Songster', "Spider mum"; attractive spidery flowers of the "Fuji" type; large blooms with linear thread-like tubular petals, yellow in bud, but fading to cream when open, and radiating around the golden center cushion. *Zone 8.*   p. 380

x morifolium 'Spoon-type'; freely branching perennial with stems becoming woody; flowers 8-10 cm across with tubular ray-petals opening into a cupped spoon, in shades of pink, yellow or white. In the Orient the stems are tied to wire rings for best display. *Warm-temperate. Zone 9.*   p. 375

x morifolium 'Turner'; an old "Exhibition Incurved" type of showy chrysanthemum, producing large globular, vivid yellow flowers, with loosely incurved broad petals, usually grown on a long single stem. In England, such types, when disbudded, have produced giant heads 20 to 25 cm dia., normally blooming Nov. 10 and grown mainly for cut flower purposes. *Zone 8.*   p. 380

x morifolium 'Yellow Princess Ann'; favorite "Decorative"; mutation of 'Princess Ann' with deep yellow decorative flowers, of good keeping quality. *Warm temperate. Zone 8.*   p. 58

multicaule (Algeria); smooth, glaucous annual, or short-lived perennial in mild climates; much branched to 30 cm high; the leaves fleshy and variable from pinnately dissected to linear; the flowers 6 cm across, with disc and ray-flowers golden-yellow, solitary on long stalks, in July-August. Popular in California gardens. *Zone 10.* p. 380

myconis (France: Provence to Mediterr.), "Yellow marguerite"; smooth perennial, grown as annual in colder climate; ascending stems 15-50 cm high, with angled branches; wedge-shaped or obovate leaves sharply toothed, the stem leaves linear and clasping; long-stalked floral heads 3-4 cm across, with golden-yellow ray-florets, in April to June. *Zones 8-9.*   p. 381

paludosum (No. Africa), "Miniature Shasta daisy"; old-fashioned, short lived, leafy perennial 25 cm or more high, once favored in Victorian gardens, grown from seed as annuals in colder climate; deeply lobed leaves strongly scented; single flowers with high yellow center cushion, and broad white ray-flowers arranged around it, 3-4 cm across, blooming in mid-summer. *Zones 9-10.*   p. 381

parthenium (Tanacetum praealtum, Matricaria capensis) (S.E. Europe to Caucasus), "Feverfew"; old-fashioned erect bushy, aromatic perennial 30 to 60 cm high, once favored in Victorian gardens as cut flower; the leafy stems with strongly scented foliage to 8 cm long, more or less deeply cut or lobed; in Summer a profusion of small heads of yellow floral discs fringed by short white rays, 2 cm across. Dried flowers are used medicinally, made into tincture against fever. *Zone 6.*   p. 403

parthenium flore pleno (Matricaria eximia), "Double feverfew" or "Button flower"; very pretty variation, with numerous white, globular flower heads densely filled with white ray-florets, button-like, 2-3 cm dia. *Zone 6.*   p. 381

parthenium 'Roseum' (Matricaria caucasica), "Pink feverfew"; color variation with button-like 2 cm double flowers a lovely rosy-pink; herbaceous perennial 30-40 cm high, having leaves pinnately lobed; very popular as cut flower. *Zone 6.*   p. 381

ptarmiciflorum (Canary Isl.), "Silver lace"; white tomentose, subshrubby plant to 50 cm high, with lacy, silvery leaves bipinnately parted; inflorescence with white rays, 3 cm across. *Zones 9-10.*   p. 380

segetum ('Prado') (Greece to S.W. Asia, naturalized in W. and No. Europe), "Corn marigold" or "Yellow Boy"; very handsome herbaceous plant, grown as an annual from seed; 50-60 cm high, with scattered, glaucous oblong leaves more or less stem-clasping, and coarsely cut; large floral heads 5 cm across, with deep brownish central disc, ringed by golden-yellow ray-flowers, notched at tip; blooming June-August. *Zones 9-10.*   p. 381

segetum 'Orient Star' (Europe to W. Asia), "Star of the Orient" or "Corn marigold"; showy annual to 60 cm; deeply lobed foliage; large 6 cm flowers yellow with dark center. *Zones 9-10.*   p. 381

x spectabilis (C. carinatum x coronarium); bushy herbaceous hybrid with deeply lobed or pinnately cut green leaves, and attractive single flowers, having golden-yellow central cushion, and spreading lemon-yellow ray-florets, deeper yellow toward base. *Zone 10.* p. 381

vulgare: see TANACETUM vulgare

weyrichii (Japan), "Japanese daisy"; low rhizomatous perennial 15-30 cm high, spreading by stolons; the lower leaves fleshy, roundish, palmately 5-cleft or parted; the upper leaves lobed or linear, and entire; floral heads 4-5 cm across; ray-flowers white or pink, ringed around the yellow disc. *Zone 6.*   p. 381

CHRYSOBACTRON hookeri (in N.Z.):   see BULBINELLA

CHRYSOCOMA   *Compositae*
coma-aurea (So. Africa); evergreen subshrub to 60 cm with small linear leaves, and erect branches successively branching, and terminating in yellow roundish 1 cm heads composed only of disc flowers. Photographed in habitat on Table Mountain, above Cape Town, So. Africa. *Zone 9.*   p. 688

CHRYSOGONUM   *Compositae*
virginianum (Pennsylvania to Florida and Louisiana), "Golden-star"; low herbaceous hairy perennial, almost stemless, about 15 cm high, later branching and elongating, forming a semi-evergreen ground cover; the opposite ovate leaves are toothed at margins; numerous small yellow flowers 4 cm across, blooming Spring to Autumn. *Zone 6.*   p. 382

CHRYSOPHYLLUM   *Sapotaceae*
cainito (C. America), "Star apple" or "Caimito"; handsome ornamental evergreen tree and also a fruit tree, to 15 m high, with gracefully pendant branches; elliptic leaves 15-18 cm long, shining rich

green above, and silky coppery-brown underneath; small purplish-white flowers, followed by the smooth roundish fruit 5-8 cm dia., with green or black-purple skin and sweet white flesh, star-shaped in transverse sections. Seeds are also edible. *Tropical.* *Zone 10.* *p. 868, 941*

oliviforme (So. Florida, W. Indies, trop. America), "Satinleaf fruit"; tropical evergreen tree to 10 m high; leathery lanceolate leaves 8-15 cm long, densely reddish-tomentose beneath; small white flowers, followed by shining red to purplish-black fruits 3 cm long, containing 1 seed, but of insipid taste. *Zone 10.* *p. 868*

CHRYSOPSIS *Compositae*

mariana (New York to Florida and Texas), "Maryland Gold-aster"; floriferous silky-hairy perennial, spreading by stolons, 40-60 cm high; oblanceolate leaves to 20 cm long, smaller along branches; numerous yellow flowers 4 cm across, the central disc with minute bristles, called pappus; blooming in Autumn. *Zone 5.* *p. 382*

villosa (Wisconsin to Brit. Columbia, so. to Texas and Calif.), "Golden aster"; herbaceous tap-rooted gray-hairy perennial, 30 cm or more high, with creeping stems woody at base; narrow oblong, bristly leaves; the inflorescence branched with yellow floral heads 2-3 cm across, July to September. *Zones 4-9.* *p. 382*

CHRYSOTHAMNUS *Compositae*

nauseosus (Brit. Columbia to Colorado and Utah), "Rabbit brush"; floriferous aromatic shrub 2 m high, branching from the base; felty leaves strongly scented, linear thread-like or oblanceolate, to 6 cm long, covered by whitish hairs; inflorescence in dense trusses of golden-yellow flowers, similar to Solidago, or Goldenrod, in great profusion, late Summer. *Zone 3.* *p. 689*

CHRYSOTHEMIS *Gesneriaceae*

pulchella (Trinidad); erect succulent herb producing tubers with age; large fleshy opposite, rough-bristly, puckered 15 cm leaves shiny bright green, with crenate margins; the flowers in the leaf axils are small, bristly 1 cm tubes buttercup-yellow with red stripes and markings inside, but curiously interesting for the cluster of large flame-red calyces which appear well before the blossoms and keep long afterwards, giving the plant a colorful appearance over a long period. Blooms in Spring; allow to go dormant when too tall. *Humid-tropical.* *Zone 11.* *p. 62*

CHUSQUEA *Gramineae*

coronalis (Centr. America); beautiful clump-forming bamboo 3 to 7 m high, with slender canes 2 cm dia., gracefully arching to the ground under the weight of dense green foliage; thin branchlets in whorls around culm nodes, with light green 5 cm leaves, adding cascades of fluffy greenery most attractively; unique decorator planted in tubs. *Zone 10.* *p. 552*

CHYSIS *Orchidaceae*

aurea (Mexico, Colombia, Venezuela); bright colored epiphyte with spindle-like stems bearing 3-5 deciduous leaves; the thick-waxy 5 cm flowers closely clustered in short raceme, petals reddish-buff with golden-yellow edges and base, throat yellow marked red. (March-Aug.). *Humid-tropical.* *Zones 11-12.* *p. 83*

CIBOTIUM *Dicksoniaceae (Filices)*

chamissoi (menziesii in hort.) (Hawaii), "Man fern" of the islanders; with a short, stout, fibrous trunk, and handsome, massive, tripinnate fronds, delicate, glossy nile-green and of a smooth leathery-hard texture, on stalks covered with blackish woolly hair. *Humid-tropical.* *Zone 11.* *p. 127*

schiedei (Mountains of Mexico and Guatemala), "Mexican treefern"; favorite decorator of florists, when grown in tubs; with shapely crown of graceful, light green fronds, thin-leathery and dainty yet durable, lacy tripinnate, and glaucous beneath; will eventually, over many years, form a fibrous trunk to 5 m high. *Humid-tropical.* *Zone 11.* *p. 126*

CICERBITA plumieri: see LACTUCA plumieri

CICHORIUM *Compositae*

intybus (Britain to So. Europe, No. Africa, W. Asia), "Common Chicory" or "Blue sailors"; wide-spread perennial with thick roots, stiff stems 60 cm to more than 1 m high; leaves at base oblanceolate, to 20 cm long, bristly-hairy beneath; axillary flower heads bright sky blue, with ray-flowers spreading 3-4 cm across, sometimes varying to pink or white, and frequently seen as a weed in Europe. The foliage has been used for greens; the root a substitute for, or as additive to coffee. *Zone 6* *p. 529*

CIMICIFUGA *Ranunculaceae*

racemosa (Massachusetts to Ontario, Georgia to Missouri), "Bugbane" or "Snake root"; herbaceous woodland perennial with leafy stem 1-2½ m high; having compound and ferny, astilbe-like foliage with leaflets 3-10 cm long; in Summer this plant will send up tall spires of fragrant white flowers. The root is used medicinally as a sedative. *Zone 3.* *p. 487*

CINCHONA *Rubiaceae*

officinalis (Colombia to Perú), "Lojas quinine", formerly known as "Jesuits bark"; small tree with rough bark; lanceolate leathery leaves to 10 cm long; clusters of 2 cm salverform flowers, deep pink; the fruit a capsule opening from base. The bark is stripped on young trees, and yields the quinine of commerce, used in anti-malarial medicine. *Tropical. Zone 10.* *p. 539*

CINERARIA candidissima hort.: see SENECIO leucostachys

maritima 'Diamond': see SENECIO cineraria

CINNAMOMUM *Lauraceae*

camphora (China, Japan), "Camphor tree"; handsome evergreen tree to 12 m high or more, with dense crown of shiny, dark green leaves 5-12 cm long; when crushed, the leaves have the odor of camphor; tiny, fragrant yellow flowers, followed by berry-like small black fruit. Linens stored in camphor-wood containers keep well. When distilled or boiled, the chopped wood, roots and leaves yield an aromatic white, volatile gum that is used medicinally and for perfume. *Zone 9.* *p. 534, 741*

cassia (Indo-China, Burma or Myanmar, So. China), "Cassia-bark-tree"; evergreen tree to 10 m or more high, with opposite leathery, lanceolate leaves to 15 cm long; clusters of small yellowish flowers. Cultivated in S.E. Asia to Indonesia as the source of one of the oldest spices, known since biblical times; the aromatic bark is stripped from young trees to be used in medicine and for cinnamon-like flavoring. *Zones 9-10.* *p. 534*

zeylanicum (Sri Lanka, S.W. India), "Cinnamon tree"; small evergreen tree to 10 m high; glossy green, leathery ovate leaves to 18 cm long, 3-nerved from base; the young growth with foliage strikingly crimson-red with white veins; small yellowish flowers. Dried bark yields the commercial spice cinnamon. *Tropical.* *Zone 10.* *p. 537, 741*

CIRRHOPETALUM: see BULBOPHYLLUM

CIRSIUM *Compositae*

edule (Oregon to Brit. Columbia, south to Arizona), "Edible thistle"; biennial or short-lived perennial, with stout purple, hollow stem to 2 m high; lower leaves to 40 cm long, pinnately divided and spine-tipped; the stem-leaves smaller, and stiff-spiny; floral heads 4 cm across, with tubular, purplish-rose petals, armed with spiny bracts. The young, stripped stems were eaten by the Indians. *Zones 6-9.* *p. 382*

japonicum (Cnicus) (Japan: Honshu to Kyushu), "Japan thistle"; showy perennial to 1 m or more high; obovate basal leaves to 30 cm long, pinnately cut or lobed, and spiny-toothed; stem-leaves cleft and clasping; floral heads 3-4 cm across, subtended by sticky, spine-tipped bracts, and rose-pink petals arranged in lovely globes. Much used as cut flowers. *Zone 6.* *p. 382*

spinosissimum (Alps of Switzerland and Austria; Apennines), "Alpine thistle"; Alpine perennial to 50 cm high, the stems densely leafy; spiny-toothed leaves to 15 cm long, pinnately parted; floral heads with pale yellow flowers, clothed in feathery bracts. Seen in habitat on the slopes of Jungfrau Peak in the Swiss Alps. *Zone 5.* *p. 382*

CISSUS *Vitaceae*

antarctica (Rhoicissus) (New So. Wales), "Kangaroo vine"; attractive plant with shrubby base and flexuous, slowly climbing, tomentose branches, the elegant, firm leaves almost leathery, bright shining green to a deep metallic shade, and light brown veins, the base cordate, and margins sinuately toothed, becoming 15 cm long; a good keeper. *Subtropic. Zones 9-10.* *p. 298*

discolor (Java, Cambodia), "Rex begonia vine"; beautiful dendril-climber, with thin angled, dark red veins and petioles, the strikingly colored, oblong-cordate, quilted leaves to 15 cm long, the sunken network of veins moss-green, with elevated ridges painted shimmering silver, and the center variegated violet and red-purple with velvet sheen; toothed margin and reverse glowing maroon. *Tropical. Zones 11-12.* *p. 298*

hypoglauca (Victoria, New So. Wales), "Watervine"; pendulous or climbing shrub without tendrils, to 5 m or more; leaves divided into 5 oblong, leathery leaflets with some teeth along margins, polished bronzy green, each 4-8 cm long. *Subtropic. Zone 10.* *p. 298*

rhombifolia (Vitis, Rhoicissus) (West Indies, No. So. America), "Venezuela treebine" or "Grape-ivy"; scandent, herbaceous plant with vine-like, flexuous, brown-hairy branches having coiling tendrils, and compound leaves of 3 rhombic-ovate, stalked, thin-fleshy leaflets 3-10 cm long, wavy-toothed, the glabrous surface fresh green to metallic deep green and with brownish veins and petioles, pubescent underneath; the young growth covered with white hairs. Small flowers with 4 petals, unlike Rhoicissus which have 5-7 petals. Tropical. Zone 10. *p. 299*

rhombifolia 'Ellen Danica'; excellent, vigorously growing grape-ivy; mutation of 'Jubilee' (Nielsen-Denmark) found in Odense about 1965; of bushy habit with foliage divided and larger than the species, the leaflets like deeply lobed and incised oakleaves, rich glossy green, on brownish branches. Suitable for larger containers or for pyramids. Subtropic. Zone 10. *p. 79, 299*

striata (Vitis) (Chile), "Miniature grape-ivy"; cute little plant with thin reddish shoots climbing by tiny tendrils, dense with small, palmately compound leaves to 4 cm across, with 5 obovate leaflets toothed toward the apex, bronzy green above with pale midrib, and wine-red beneath. Has been listed in Europe as Vitis orientalis. Zone 10. *p. 300*

CISSUS: see also Piper, Parthenocissus, Rhoicissus, Tetrastigma

CISTUS   *Cistaceae*

algarvensis: see HALIMIUM ocymoides

x hybridus (x corbariensis), hybrid of populifolius x salviifolius, (Mediterranean reg.), "White rockrose"; bushy hybrid shrub, 50 cm to 1 m or more high, evergreen in mild climate, with gray-green crinkly, ovate leaves 5 cm long, downy all over, and fragrant on warm days; flowers 3 cm across, white with yellow centers, summer-blooming, and widely grown in California gardens. Zone 7. *p. 686*

incanus (villosus) (Corsica to Crimea), "Rock rose"; low shrub to 1 m, with small, rugose, ovate leaves, and large crepy rose-pink flowers 6 cm dia., in late Spring. Found resistant to brush fires in So. California. Zone 8. *p. 685*

ladanifer (Portugal), "Laudanum" or "Gum cistus"; compact bush 1 m high, with rugose, fragrant leaves to 10 cm; large 3 cm flowers, carmine-pink with crimson spots. Zone 8. *p. 685*

monspeliensis (So. Europe, No. Africa), "African rock-rose" or "Southern rock-rose"; small soft-hairy flowering shrub to 1 m high, with sticky branches; lanceolate leaves to 4 cm long, much wrinkled above, densely tomentose beneath; white flowers 3 cm across, having 3 sepals; summer-blooming. Zone 8. *p. 685*

x purpureus (ladanifer x villosus), "Orchid rock-rose"; flowering evergreen shrub to 1 m or more high, with sticky-hairy twigs; dark green, rough leaves 3-5 cm long, gray-hairy beneath; showy purple, crepy flowers 6-8 cm across, yellow at base with maroon blotch on each petal. Zone 8. *p. 685*

salviifolius (S.E. Europe), "Sageleaf-rock-rose"; low spreading shrub to 60 cm high, photographed amongst ancient Greek ruins on the island of Rhodes; with small gray-green rugose leaves 3 cm long, and flowers like wild roses, with white or pinkish petals of crepy texture, with yellow spots in base, 4 cm across; blooming very profusely in Spring. Subtropic. Zone 9. *p. 685*

x CITROFORTUNELLA   *Rutaceae*

floridana (Citrus aurantiifolia x Fortunella japonica) "Limequat"; hybrid of Mexican lime x Kumquat; low evergreen shrub to 2 m high, but usually grown as dwarf in containers, dense with oval-ovate leaves 5-8 cm long; waxy flowers white or streaked with pink, followed by attractive ovoid, golden-yellow fruit the size of an olive, borne nearly year-round; very ornamental as miniature orange tree, but fruits may be used as substitute for limes in drinks. Zones 8-10. *p. 936*

mitis (Citrus maderensis hort.) (Philippines), "Calamondin"; a small, spineless tree with upright slender branches dense with broad-oval, leathery leaves on narrowly-winged petiole; small white, fragrant flowers borne singly at the tips of twigs; small 3 to 4 cm round fruit somewhat flattened, deep orange-yellow, loose skinned. Probably a hybrid of lime with kumquat; strongly acid, pleasant flavor like lime; season Nov.-Dec., but occasionally everbearing. Popularly grown in pots for Christmas. Fruit, including rind is used for making marmalade. Subtropic. Zones 9-10. *p. 58, 936*

CITRULLUS   *Cucurbitaceae*

lanatus 'Family Fun', "Watermelon"; annual, long-running hairy herbaceous vine of tropical Africa heritage, having deeply pinnately lobed leaves on stems with branched tendrils; yellow flowers 3 cm across, followed on female blooms by large oblong vegetable fruit about 40 cm long, the rind green and banded silver, the very juicy sweet flesh rich in water content, also usually holding numerous flat black seeds. The crisp flesh is very refreshing eaten fresh, especially when chilled. Zone 10. *p. 911*

CITRUS   *Rutaceae*

aurantifolia (Malaya, India), the "West Indian Lime", "Mexican lime" or "Key lime"; small thorny tree to 5 m tall, having twiggy branches; with aromatic small 6-8 cm glossy green, oval leaves;

waxy-white, fragrant, axillary flowers; small oval, green to greenish-yellow fruit 3 to 5 cm dia. usually in clusters; smooth, thin-skinned with very acid seedy pulp; used in drinks, on seafood or in preserves. Subtropic. Zone 10. *p. 936*

aurantifolia 'Baerss'; round-headed, vigorous tree, a California seedling cultivar, with some thorns, to 8 m high, but usually grown as dwarf 3 m high; the white flowers followed by thin-skinned fruit nearly lemon-size, green but turning yellow when ripe, very juicy and acid and without seeds. Hardier than the Mexican lime and more ornamental. The fruit is used for culinary purposes, for juice, to flavor drinks; also known as "Bartender's lime". Zones 9-10. *p. 936*

aurantium (Vietnam), "Sour Seville orange" or "Bitter orange"; vigorous tree with slender-pointed leaves on broadly winged petioles; large fragrant, white-waxy flowers; fruit orange when ripe, of tart taste; in Curacao the wrinkled peel of unripe fruit is used for its aromatic oils to flavor the famous liqueur. Subtropic. *p. 541, 935, 936*

aurantium 'Myrtifolia' (China), "Myrtleleaf orange"; dwarfish, thornless tree with dense, deep green, stiff, little 2 cm leaves; waxy flowers and small, sour, bright orange fruits; while blooming in April in the northern hemisphere, I remember the strikingly impressive sight of these trees in Uruguay and Argentina in October, when literally covered with fragrant white flowers. Subtropic. Zone 10. *p. 936*

'Dweet' (Orange x Tangerine) (reticulatta x sinensis), "Tangor"; dwarf tree to 2½ m of open habit; fruit globe-shaped 6-7 cm dia., with orange skin; seedy, but packed with sweet juice. Subtropic. Zone 10. *p. 937*

limetta (E. Meditterran. reg.), "Sweet lime" or "Greek lime"; a small evergreen subtropic bush with thick-leathery, ovate 4 to 10 cm leaves; small white waxy flowers; the globular fruit is typically lime-like green to yellowish, 4-5 cm in dia., but reportedly sweeter in taste than the Mexican lime. Somewhat surrounded by mystery. I was able to find and photograph this species in col. Quail Bot. Garden, Encinitas, California. Zones 9-10. *p. 936*

limon 'Eureka' (Los Angeles seedling 1858), "Acid lemon"; medium size tree, open and spreading, almost thornless; large dark green leaves; fragrant waxy white flowers; oblong fruit with protruding apex, lemon-yellow, 8 cm or more long; very juicy and acid. Subtropic. Zones 9-10. *p. 937*

limon 'Meyer' (hybrid of lemon with sweet orange), "Meyer lemon" or "Dwarf Chinese"; semi-dwarf, spreading tree, nearly thornless, with small leaves, often grown in pots as it produces sweetly-scented, lavender to white flowers while young, and bears good-looking, roundish lemons of table quality, 6-7 cm long furnishing excellent acid juice almost the year round; of somewhat sweeter or milder flavor than the typical Eureka lemon. Zones 9-10. *p. 861, 937*

limon 'Ponderosa' (Maryland hybrid 1887), "American wonder-lemon"; ornamental tree 2½-3 m high, often grown in tubs; with irregular branches and short, stout spines, large oblong leaves on short petioles nearly wingless; the large waxy flowers white; the somewhat pear-shaped, enormous fruit lemon-yellow, almost 12 cm long, weighing 1 kg, and while edible, its juice is sour. Zones 9-10. *p. 937*

x limonia (otaitensis) (limon x reticulata), "Lemandarin", "Otaheite orange" or "Rangpur lime"; small evergreen tree to 2 m high, with thorny irregular branches, the short spines stiff and stout; matte-green ovate oval leaves toothed at margins; flowers tinged red in bud, white inside, followed by numerous depressed globose or globular fruit 5-6 cm dia., with thin yellowish to reddish-orange rind, somewhat rough but loose, holding 8-10 juicy segments of insipid, acid taste, and containing many seeds. Formerly much grown in greenhouses as a seasonable potted plant, known in hort. as C. taitensis, as a small bush 40 cm high, very ornamental with numerous golden fruit sold for the Christmas holidays. Zone 10. *p. 936*

maxima (grandis), the "Shaddock" or "Pummelo", probably from So. China, Malaya and Polynesia; tender tropical spiny tree to 9 m, with angular twigs and large oval 10-20 cm leaves slightly pubescent beneath, the petiole widely winged; large white flowers; fruit 15 cm large and pale yellow, the acid flesh coarse-grained and separating readily. Zones 9-10. *p. 931, 937*

maxima pyriformis (S.W. China, Kwangsi), "Shatian pomelo"; gigantic shaddock fruit in pear-shaped form 15-20 cm long, with temptingly orange-yellow rind, widely cultivated in the bizarre dragon mountain region along the Li-jiang River, in Kwangsi Prov. of Southwest China; sold in the market of Yangshuo, as gifts for important holidays such as New Year. The somewhat dry sections are peeled and eaten fresh. Zones 9-10. *p. 935*

microcarpa (So. China), "Four-season tangerine"; possibly hybrid of Mandarin x Fortunella; depressed globose fruit 3 cm dia., with thin peel and with intensely acid pulp; very juicy and refreshing in desserts. Photographed at Kadoorie Farms, Taipoo, Hongkong. Zone 10. *p. 937*

'Minneola' (Tangelo) (Grapefruit x Tangerine) (reticulata paradisi); reddish-orange fruit about 8 cm dia., with smooth skin and elongate neck, few seeds, unusual exotic tangy flavor and very juicy. Flavorful hybrid of Dancy mandarin with Florida grapefruit 'Duncan'. This has become the most important commercial Tangelo in California. Zones 9-10. *p. 937*

mitis: see CITROFORTUNELLA mitis

x nobilis 'Temple' (reticulata x sinensis), a beautiful, highly flavored, juicy "Tangor" (tangerine x sweet orange hyb.) originated in Florida; loose-skinned mandarin-type orange maturing January to Spring; 7 to 9 cm dia. with reddish-orange peel and flesh; bushy, thorny tree with medium-size leaves and waxy white, fragrant flowers; bearing freely when very young, ideal for the home garden and lending itself to culture in tubs; more tender than sweet orange. *Subtropic.* Zones 9-10. *p. 937*

x paradisi 'March Seedless', "Seedless grapefruit"; important commercial, white-fleshed grapefruit of the West. Needs 18 months to ripen. Large light yellow fruit to about 12 cm dia., with few or no seeds, and big glossy leaves. This very juicy fruit ripens in No. California in May to August; further south November to June; likes hot Summers; excellent for eating and juice. *Zones 9-10. p. 937*

x paradisi 'Ruby Blush', "Pink grapefruit"; large fruit with orange skin blushing pink; deep pink flesh and quite mildly sweet tasting in flavor. Best in desert heat to color well. *Subtropic.* Zones 9-10. *p. 931*

reticulata (Southeast Asia), "Mandarin orange"; small spiny tree with slender branches; lanceolate leaves; flowers white and fragrant; fruit deep orange-yellow depressed globose, to 8 cm dia.; loose thin skin, sweet pulp. *Subtropic. Zones 9-10. p. 931, 935*

reticulata 'Clementine', "Algerian tangerine"; tree to 4 m high, of open habit, with slender branches hanging under weight of fruit; fruit deep orange-red with glossy surface, 5-6 cm dia., apex depressed, skin loose; tender melting flesh. Ripens in late Fall, then hangs on for months. *Subtropic. Zones 9-10. p. 939*

reticulata 'Dancy', "Dancy tangerine"; small tree of spreading growth with thin branches and twig-like shoots becoming pendulous; narrow dark green leaves, and bright orange colored fruits to 8 cm with zipper-skin, peeling easily and segments easy to separate, but rather seedy. *Subtropic. Zones 9-10. p. 939*

reticulata 'Owari' (Japan), "Satsuma mandarin" or "Unshin"; early ripening fruit October-December, medium size 5-6 cm, depressed globose, smooth, loose thin skin, pulp acid-sweet. Does well in cooler climate. *Subtropic. Zones 9-10. p. 939*

sinensis (Kwangtung, Vietnam), "Sweet orange"; tree to 10 m high with regular branches, flexible spines, dark green, ovate, leathery leaves on narrow-winged petioles; fragrant, waxy-white flowers smaller than aurantium, the nearly round fruit golden-yellow with sweet pulp; the Navel orange belongs here. *Zones 9-10. p. 75, 935*

sinensis 'Valencia' (Spain), "Valencia orange"; large vigorous tree to 10 m high, fuller growing than Washington Navel, with regular branches and rounded top; flexible slender spines sometimes absent; dark shining green, ovate, leaves narrowly winged; waxy-white, sweetly fragrant flowers; fruit nearly globose, golden-yellow 7-8 cm dia., and with sweet pulp, late season ripening March to July and lasting on the tree for months, improving in sweetness. It is the most widely planted juice orange in the world. Known in California since 1876, it had its origin in Spain under the name "Naranja tarde de Valencia". *Subtropic. Zones 9-10. p. 905, 939*

sinensis 'Washington Navel' or 'Bahia', from Brazil, "Winter orange"; excellent, large commercial sweet orange, early-ripening, and seedless, to 8 or 10 cm dia., from November to April (Valencia from March to Nov.); best adapted to California and Arizona climate and produces low yield and poor fruit in tropical regions; it derives its name from the characteristic rudimentary secondary fruit imbedded in the apex of the primary fruit, and which serves as a trademark; yellow to deep orange in color, and easy peeling; flowers in large clusters, waxy-white and sweetly fragrant. *Subtropic. Zone 9. p. 939*

taitensis hort.: see C. x limonia

taiwanica (Taiwan), "Formosan orange"; small evergreen tree in Hengchun Tropical Botanic Garden in Southern Taiwan, with broad ovate, leathery leaves; fragrant white flowers, and very handsome richly orange-colored rounded fruit having distinct pointed apex; the flesh is juicy and tart-sweet to the taste when fully ripe. Zone 10. *p. 938*

CLADANTHUS *Compositae*
arabicus (Anthemis) (So. Spain, Morocco); strongly aromatic annual herb to 1 m high, with finely divided leaves, and heads of yellow ray and disc-flowers, 6 cm across. Zone 9. *p. 382*

CLADRASTIS *Leguminosae*
lutea (kentukea, tinctoria; Virgilia lutea) (Penna. to So. Carolina and Oklahoma), "American yellow-wood"; ornamental deciduous tree 6 to 15 cm high, with smooth gray bark and rounded crown; large odd-pinnate leaves to 30 cm long, the 7-11 leaflets broadly ovate to 12 cm long; fragrant wisteria-like 3 cm white flowers, in pendulous clusters during June. Popular in Southern States as street tree. Zone 4. *p. 757*

CLARKIA *Oenotheraceae*
amoena (Godetia) (California to Brit. Columbia), "Farewell-to-spring"; showy herbaceous annual to 80 cm, with linear leaves, and satiny flowers 5 cm across, in shades of purplish-carmine or rose-pink in loose clusters; day-blooming. Zone 9. *p. 461*

amoena plena (Godetia) (California to Brit. Columbia), double "Farewell-to-spring" or "Satin flower"; slender annual, branching herb, 30-75 cm high with narrow leaves, often with smaller ones in the axils; profuse with double flowers 2½-5 cm wide, the satiny petals lilac-crimson or reddish-pink; July-October. Zone 9. *p. 461*

amoena whitneyi (Godetia grandiflora), "Satin flower"; of N.W. California origin; sprawling, low, leafy, summer-blooming annual to 30 cm or more; with stout stem and lanceolate leaves to 5 cm long; satiny 5-6 cm flowers looking up, petals pinkish with central carmine spots; also in other colors, rosy red to white. *Subtropic.* Zone 9. *p. 461*

purpurea viminea (Washington to Arizona; Baja California), "Orchid godetia"; showy herbaceous perennial, usually erect, to 80 cm high, with narrow-lanceolate leaves 6-8 cm long; beautiful flowers with fan-like petals 3 cm long, glowing wine-red, but varying to pink or lavendar, and displaying conspicuous cream stamens, blooming April-June. Zone 7. *p. 460*

unguiculata 'Rosea plena' (elegans), "Mountain garland"; the species is from the Sierra Nevada of California; tall garden annual to 1 m high, ovate to lanceolate leaves, and showy flowers on erect, reddish-glaucous stems; single in the species, double carmine-rose in this form of plena, 5 cm across, from July to October. *Subtropic.* Zone 9. *p. 461*

CLAUSENA *Rutaceae*
excavata (lunulata) (Murraya burmanni) (India, Burma, Philippines, So. China, Indonesia), "Curvedleaf wampee"; deciduous or semi-evergreen tropical shrub or small tree, with young branches downy; the leaves pinnate with sickle-shaped leaflets 3 cm long; white flowers with prominent stamens, followed by pendant ovoid fruit 2 cm dia., the skin orange and tinted with red; the pulpy flesh is tasty and sweet to eat, holding one seed. Zone 10. *p. 938*

lansium (So. China, Malaysia, Sri Lanka), "Wampi"; evergreen tropical tree to 10 m high, having flexible branches, dense with pinnate leaves 15-30 cm long, having up to 9 ovate dark green leaflets; white 2 cm flowers in pendant racemes to 40 cm long, blooming in June; followed by closely packed globular or ovoid orange-yellow fruit the size of grapes; translucent yellow skin holds jelly-like flesh with a refreshing aroma and holding several seeds; eaten as a dessert when fully ripe, or for fruit drinks. May be grafted on Citrus. Zones 10-11. *p. 938*

CLAVIJA *Theophrastaceae*
eggersii (Trop. So. America); curious evergreen tropical shrub or small tree, 3 m or more high, producing at the tops of stems a cluster of leathery, oblanceolate leaves 30-50 cm long; inflorescence of yellow fragrant flowers in axillary pendant racemes; later producing red berry-like fruits. Photographed in col. Selby Bot. Garden, Sarasota, Florida. Zone 10. *p. 892*

CLAYTONIA *Portulacaceae*
sibirica: see MONTIA sibirica
virginica, (So. Canada to Eastern U.S. and west to Texas), "Virginia Spring beauty"; succulent spring-blooming perennial to 30 cm high, from globose corm; narrow-linear leaves 12 cm long, on stem topped by loose clusters of starry pinkish flowers, each petal with veins of deep rose. Zone 6. *p. 260*

CLEISOSTOMA *Orchidaceae*
paniculatum (Taiwan); a charming dwarf, terrestrial orchid which I photographed in Taipei growing in a terracotta bowl; long-linear glossy green leaves and branching, wiry stems bearing a cascade of small waxy flowers 1 cm dia., with light brown sepals and petals, the lip yellow, densely set on pendant racemes. Zone 11. *p. 84*

CLEISTOCACTUS *Cactaceae*
baumannii (Argentina, Paraguay), "Scarlet bugler"; thin, ribbed column to 2 m high and 3 cm dia., clambering and branching at base, covered with white or brown spines; flowers scarlet, 6-7 cm long. *Arid-subtropic.* Zone 10. *p. 155*

hyalacanthus of hort. (Argentina: Jujuy); branching slender columns to 1 m high, with 12 ribs deeply furrowed, topped by gray areoles, and densely covered by bristly, creamy spines; light red flowers to 4 cm long. Photo on pg. 156 is of plant shown at Del Mar Floral Exhib., and appears different from photo of this species in EXOTICA 4 pg. 650. *Zone 10.*   p. 156

jujuyensis (No. Argentina), "Argentine Silver torch", the "False strausii" according to Backeberg; handsome columns to 1 m high and 4-6 cm dia., branching from base; about 20 low ribs, the areoles white-hairy and set with slender needle spines; light red flowers 4 cm long. *Zone 10.*   p. 155

smaragdiflorus (Argentina, Uruguay, Paraguay), "Firecracker cactus"; slender, erect stems with 12-14 ribs, 5 cm thick, 2 m high, later leaning; closely set yellow areoles and numerous thin yellow to brown spines very sharp; 5 cm flowers orange-red, green inside but remaining closed; small round fruit 1½ cm dia. *Arid-subtropic. Zone 10.*   p. 155

strausii (Bolivia), "Silver torch"; slender, light green, clustering, many-ribbed column to 2 m high and 6 cm thick, covered with bristle-like white spines, central spine pale yellow; flowers red, to 9 cm long. *Arid-subtropic. Zone 10.*   p. 155

CLEMATIS   *Ranunculaceae*

alpina (No. Europe, Siberia); woody deciduous climber to 2 or 3 m high, with compound, toothed leaves, and nodding bell-shaped flowers of usually 4 sepals each 3 cm long, violet-blue, in Spring. *Zone 4.*   p. 293

armandii (West and So. China); vigorous evergreen climber with vines that may spread 20 m or more; compound leaves of 3 lanceolate leathery leaflets 8-12 cm long; fragrant white flowers 5-6 cm dia., in axillary clusters, blooming on wood of the previous year. *Zone 7.*   p. 293

chrysocoma (S.W. China: Yunnan), "Gold-wool clematis"; scandent deciduous shrub, vining 2-3 m high; and dense yellow-pubescent compound leaves of 3 lobed corrugated leaflets; white or pinkish flowers of 4 oval sepals, 4 cm across, on growth made the previous year. *Zone 6.*   p. 294

crispa (Virginia to Florida and Texas), "Blue jasmine" or "Curly clematis"; shrubby climber to 3 m, with pinnate leaves of 5-9 ovate leaflets, entire or 3 to 5-parted; solitary nodding, bell-shaped, fragrant flowers 5 cm or more long, the pale calyx cylindrical, the upper half purple and spreading and wavy at margins. *Zone 5.*   p. 293

florida bicolor ('Sieboldii') (China); desirable woody climber reaching 2-4 m high, semi-evergreen in mild climates; the foliage twice 3-leaved with 3 to 5 cm leaflets; cream-white flowers 5-8 cm across, of 5-8 sepals, a green stripe on back, and center packed with conspicuous purple sterile stamens. *Zone 5.*   p. 294

hyb. 'Alice Fisk'; large flowers with elliptic petaloid sepals pale lilac, shaded deeper purplish toward undulate, wavy margins, July-blooming in Dortmund Bot. Garden, Germany. *Zone 5.*   p. 293

hyb. 'Andrew'; very free-blooming hybrid with smallish flowers lilac-rose to pale lavender, the sepals occasionally marked with purple lines, blooming in July, as seen in col. Romberg Arboretum in Westphalia. *Zone 5.*   p. 292

hyb. 'Barbara Dibley' (patens group); large flowers to 15 cm across, having 5-7 overlapping sepals purple with magenta central band, later becoming pale lilac along margins, blooming May-June. Similar to 'Nelly Moser', but more floriferous. *Zone 5.*   p. 293

hyb. 'Countess of Lovelace' (patens group 1876); striking inflorescence with double flowers, the sepals densely shingled in 6-7 series, 15 cm across, lavender-blue, but becoming lighter in final stage of bloom; in Autumn flowers are single; season May-June and Autumn. *Zone 5.*   p. 293

hyb. 'Duchess of Edinburgh' (C. florida hyb. Jackman before 1877); excellent vigorous climber with vines to 3 m, the leaves of 3 leaflets; pure white, fragrant flowers 10-15 cm dia., fully double rosettes of many pointed sepals and striking yellow stamens; blooming May-June and again September. *Zone 5.*   p. 292

hyb. 'Ernst Markham' (vitifolia hyb.); very floriferous 1926 cultivar; large flowers 10 to 15 cm dia. vivid petunia-red with velvet sheen, blooming from July to September on wood formed the current year. *Zone 4.*   p. 291

hyb. 'Etoile de Malicorne'; French hybrid, having flowers spreading 15 to 20 cm wide, the broad petal-like sepals lilac-rose and purplish-red center band, blooming May and late Summer. *Zone 4.*   p. 291

hyb. 'M. Koster'; large-flowered hybrid seen blooming in July at Romberg Arboretum, Dortmund, having 5 spoon-shaped petal-like sepals purplish-rose and white center band on each blade. *Zone 5.*   p. 292

hyb. 'Mrs. N. Thompson'; English bicolor hybrid growing 3 to 4 m high, with 10-15 cm flowers having petal-like sepals with a

central bar of crimson-red, and the marginal areas carmine changing to purple, blooming May-June, and September. *Zone 5.*   p. 291

hyb. 'Percy Picton'; star-shaped single flowers with elliptic sepals mauve-pink and lighter shading, the filaments straw-yellow and dark stamens; July blooming in Germany. *Zone 5.*   p. 292

hyb. 'Proteus' (syn. 'The Premier') (Clem. florida hyb.); large double flowers with elliptic petaloid sepals, pink shaded lilac-rose, and yellow anthers; single flowers on young growth. *Zone 5.*   p. 292

hyb. 'Titania' (M. Johnson 1952); fantastic flowers 20-22 cm across, having 6-8 lanceolate, overlapping petaloid white sepals with a central band of purple lines, and undulate along margins, the anthers violet-purple. *Zone 5*   p. 292

hyb. 'Ville de Lyon' (French viticella hybrid, Morel 1899); vigorous vine spreading 4 m or more, bearing beautifully rounded flowers of carmine-red, shading to crimson around the margins, to 15 cm across and of velvety texture, the stamens a contrasting yellow; blooming June to September. *Zone 4*   p. 291

hyb. 'Voluceau'; French hybrid, with large showy flowers having broad oval sepals rich rose-purple; similar to 'Rose Cardinal' but becoming increasingly deeper purple; the anthers yellow. *Zone 5.*   p. 293

integrifolia (S.E. Europe); erect subshrub to 1 m high, with thin, ovate leaves 5-10 cm long, and violet-blue flowers edged in white, and 3-4 cm long, with yellow stamens; June-August. *Zone 3.*   p. 487

x jackmanii; the jackmanii group (lanuginosa x hendersonii) is one of the best of "Virgin's bowers" for size of flower, vigorous in growth, and profuse in bloom; climber to 3 m, with pinnate or 3-foliolate leaves; flowers 10-15 cm across, rich purple, and long-lasting, in July to October; fairly hardy. *Warm temperate. Zones 4-9.*   p. 291

x jackmanii 'Purpurea'; handsome color form with large flowers, the petaloid sepals velvety deep violet-purple. *Zone 4.*   p. 291

lanuginosa 'Mad. Moser'; floriferous hybrid similar to 'Nellie Moser' with star-like flowers having pure white sepals spreading wide, and dark stamens, blooming in July. *Zone 4.*   p. 292

lanuginosa 'Nellie Moser'; an old reliable favorite (1897); free-blooming hybrid with C. patens; growing to 2 m high; large flowers 18 cm or more across, usually having 8 sepals, pale mauve-pink, and with a carmine-red bar down the middle of sepals; blooming throughout early Spring into Summer, first from the buds of last year's growth, followed by a second crop from new growth. *Zone 4.*   p. 291, 294

lanuginosa 'President' (hybrid by Noble about 1875); large handsome flowers 15 cm across, of 6-8 petaloid sepals deep violet and a lighter purple center band, paler beneath and striped, blooming June-July and again October. *Zone 4.*   p. 291

lanuginosa 'Ville de Paris' (Christen 1885); very large flowered European hybrid, to 15 cm across, the obovate sepals rosy-crimson and marbled in the center area with white, borne on new wood; flowering June to July. *Zone 5.*   p. 291

x lawsoniana 'Henryi' (lanuginosa x patens); stunning, vigorous climbing hybrid with leaves in threes; tremendous size flowers 15-20 cm across, having 6-8 broad, overlapping white, ribbed sepals accented by cream band, blooming from June through September. *Zones 3-9.*   p. 292

macropetala (China, Siberia), "Downy clematis"; deciduous climber with angled shoots to 1 m high; downy leaves 2 to 3-pinnate with leaflets crenate or lobed; solitary nodding flowers with narrow sepals spreading 6-10 cm wide, violet-blue or varying to pink, in May-June. *Zones 4-9.*   p. 293, 294

montana 'Tetrarose' (Boskoop 1960), "Anemone clematis"; deciduous woody climber having leaves of 2-3 toothed leaflets, derived from the species montana of W. China, which has small white fragrant flowers 3-5 cm across, turning pink. The form 'Tetrarose' is a tetraploid with larger flowers 8 cm dia., in soft lilac-pink. Developed as a result of Colchicine injection into its tissues, changing the chromosomes in the plant; foliage bronze. *Zone 6.*   p. 292

paniculata (true species, of New Zealand), "Puawhananga" of the Maoris; magnificent evergreen climber to 6 m, in habitat cascading over shrubs and trees with festoons of 10 cm starry white flowers, in Spring, followed in Autumn by fluffy silken balls of seed-heads; the foliage in juvenile stage trifoliate with 5 cm leaflets, the adult form shining green leaves are thick-leathery and 8 cm long. *Zone 5.* p. 294

paniculata hort. (maximowicziana of Japan and Korea); evergreen climber to 10 m high, with compound leaves of 3-5 oval or ovate leathery leaflets 3-10 cm long; the inflorescence in masses of fragrant white flowers 3 cm wide with 4 linear sepals; followed by a curious matted constellation of spidery seed pods. The botanical status of this species is confused and uncertain, by Wyman and Hortus mentioned as probably a variety of C. dioscoreifolia. The true paniculata is from New Zealand. *Zone 5.*   p. 294

recta (So. and C. Europe to Temp. Asia), "Ground clematis'; herbaceous perennial 60 cm to 1 m or more high; basal leaves to 15 cm long, pinnate into 5-9 leaflets, or deeply lobed; multitudes of fragrant white flowers 2-3 cm across, borne in axillary and terminal clusters during June to September. *Zone 3.* p. 487

tangutica (No. China, Mongolia), "Golden clematis"; deciduous climber with glaucous green, pinnate or bipinnate toothed leaves, and nodding flowers with golden-yellow petal-like sepals to 5 cm long June-July followed by silvery plumed seed heads. *Zone 3.* p. 293

virginiana (Nova Scotia to Kansas), the "Woodbine" or "Virgin's bower"; deciduous vine to 6 m, with leaves coarsely toothed or lobed, and small 2½-cm flowers white, in leafy panicles; the male and female flowers on separate plants; Aug.-Sept. *Zone 4.* p. 294

CLEOME   *Capparaceae*

hassleriana (arborea hort.) (S.E. Brazil, Argentina), "Spider plant"; thinly pubescent erect, strongly scented annual to 1 m high; compound leaves of 5-7 leaflets generally with pairs of spines at base; flowers in bracted clusters, rose-pink but fading to whitish by noon; protruding stamens 6 cm long. *Zone 10.* p. 358

spinosa (pungens) (W. Indies to Venezuela), "Spiny Spider flower"; pubescent strong-scented annual with spiny stem, palmately compound leaves, and large rose-purple flower clusters having long spidery stamens. *Tropical. Zone 10.* p. 358

CLERODENDRUM   *Verbenaceae*

bungei (China); erect-growing shrub with wiry branches to 2 m high, with large, broadly ovate, quilted leaves to 30 cm long and coarsely toothed, dark green on the surface; fragrant flowers rosy-red in a head-like cluster 10-20 cm across, blooming from June to September. *Subtropic. Zones 9-10.* p. 898

foxii hort.; magnificent shrub, in the Florida nursery trade, resembling C. paniculatum; glossy green, corrugated foliage of various shapes, in the center a tall erect inflorescence fountain-like, with masses of outwardly spreading, slender tubular scarlet flowers. *Subtropic. Zone 10.* p. 898

frangrans pleniflorum (China, Japan), "Glory tree"; shrubby plant with stiff stems covered with white hairs; broad ovate, opposite leaves light green and hairy on the surface, green beneath; with margins toothed; the fragrant, 2 cm flowers in a dense terminal cluster, delicate peach-white and fully double, calyx purplish-red. *Subtropic. Zones 9-10.* p. 898

inerme (India: Bombay), the "Indian privet"; evergreen branching shrub with hard-leathery, small boxwood-like shiny deep green leaves, and small white flowers with purple stamens; indigenous to mangrove areas near Bombay, and planted at the Hanging Gardens of Bombay, trained over wire frames, into topiary shapes of animals; sheared every 2 weeks. *Tropical. Zones 10-11.* p. 628, 898

minahassae (Malay Arch., Indonesia); evergreen tropical shrub or small tree, with elliptic or obovate leaves to 20 cm long; the very attractive inflorescence consisting of vivid scarlet-red, fleshy calyces, subtending the pretty white flowers with their slender curving tubular corolla and spreading lobes, which are followed by blue fruits. Much planted in So. Florida. *Zones 10-11.* p. 898

myricoides (Trop. and So. Africa); dense shrub to 2 m, with spoon-shaped oval, matte-green leaves 6-9 cm long, crenate at margins; the pretty flowers light lavender-blue with violet on lip, and long curling stamens. *Subtropic. Zones 9-10.* p. 898

paniculatum (E. Trop. Asia), "Kashmir bouquet" or "Pagoda flower"; robust bush with broad, shining green, 5-lobed leaves, and showy terminal conical panicles to 30 cm high, of scarlet-red flowers. *Tropical. Zones 10-11.* p. 899

speciosissimum (fallax) (Java, Sri Lanka), "Glory bower"; a magnificent shrub I remember from the mountains of Java and Ceylon, the 30 cm flower clusters a blaze of fiery scarlet above white-pubescent, heart-shaped foliage, on white-hairy, angled stems to 1 m high. *Tropical. Zone 10.* p. 899

x speciosum (splendens x thomsonae); shrubby plant of semi-erect habit with scandent branches, dark green glossy leaves, and terminal clusters of flowers having a pinkish calyx and deep crimson corolla shaded violet, blooming in Summer. *Tropical. Zone 10.* p. 899

splendens (W. Africa: Senegambia to Angola); twining shrub with large, oblong or elliptic, corrugated, leathery leaves to 15 cm between which show large clusters of brilliant scarlet 2 cm flowers. *Tropical. Zone 10.* p. 296

thomsoniae (Trop. West Africa), "Bleeding heart vine"; twining evergreen shrub, climbing to 4 m, with ovate, quilted, glossy, papery leaves to 12 cm long, deep green; showy flowers in forking clusters, the inflated calyx pure white changing to pink, corolla deep crimson; spring-blooming. Often grown under the synonym C. balfouri, but this has larger flowers. *Tropical. Zone 10.* p. 296

trichotomum (Japan); "Harlequin glory-bower"; hardy shrub or tree 3 to 6 m high, deciduous in colder regions, with pithy, downy branches and dark green ovate leaves to 20 cm long, downy beneath; in upper leaf axils the clusters of small white, fragrant flowers with spreading petals 4 cm across, from inflated, fleshy crimson-red calyx; small blue berries. *Warm temperate. Zone 6.* p. 899

ugandense (Uganda to Zimbabwe), "Blue wings'; smooth climbing shrub to 3 m high; bright green elliptic or obovate leaves 10-12 cm long, toothed at margins; flowers to 3 cm long, calyx lobes crimson, corolla with 3 lobes pale blue and 1 lobe violet-blue, filaments purple and anthers blue resembling small butterflies. *Tropical. Zones 10-11.* p. 898

wallichii (India); handsome evergreen shrub of dense habit, 2-3 m high; the narrow lanceolate leaves 12-18 cm long, glossy rich green with depressed veins and wavy at margins; the inflorescence a gracefully pendant cluster on thin-wiry red stalks, flowers white with red calyx and prominent, curving stamens. *Subtropic. Zone 10.* p. 899

CLETHRA   *Cleathraceae*

acuminata (Virginia to Alabama), "Cinnamon clethra" or "White alder"; tall deciduous shrub with cinnamon-brown bark, to 6 m high; thin elliptic 8 to 20 cm leaves primarily at ends of branches; treasured for its nodding densely pubescent spike-like racemes 10-20 cm long of small white flowers, and its ornamental bark; the foliage turns yellow to orange in Autumn color. *Zone 5.* p. 687

alnifolia (Maine to Florida), "Sweet pepperbush" or "Summer-sweet"; deciduous shrub to 3 m high, with young branches downy, the obovate leaves 10 cm long and serrate at margins; the inflorescence in erect spike-like racemes to 15 cm long, of small white flowers, sweetly fragrant, in late Summer; the foliage coloring attractively yellow and orange in Autumn. *Zone 3.* p. 686

alnifolia 'Rosea', "Pink Summersweet"; charming color variation, with flowers pale pink in showy cylindric clusters, seen blooming in Brooklyn Botanic Garden during late Summer. *Zone 3.* p. 687

arborea (Madeira), "Lily-of-the-Valley tree"; beautiful small evergreen tree to 8 m, with rusty-pubescent young shoots; glossy bronzy green elliptic leaves 8 to 10 cm long; at tips of branches the lovely erect inflorescence in spikes of ranked nodding, waxy bell-flowers creamy-white and sweetly fragrant. *Subtropic. Zone 9.* p. 687

barbinervis (Japan), "Cinnamon clethra" or "Japanese clethra"; deciduous coarse shrub or tree to 8 m high; oblanceolate or obovate leaves 8-15 cm long, and serrate at margins, pubescent when young; very attractive inflorescence of small fragrant white flowers in terminal spike-like racemes 10-15 cm long, held out horizontally and gracefully arching downward, in Summer to Autumn. *Zone 5.* p. 687

monostachya (Cent. China), "China alder" or "Chinese Summersweet"; handsome deciduous shrub or small tree to 6 m high, with thin, smooth lanceolate leaves 6-12 cm long, woolly beneath, and serrate at margins; the inflorescence a spike-like raceme 12 to 20 cm long, of creamy-white small flowers at ends of branches, in July-August. *Zone 5.* p. 687

CLEYERA   *Theaceae*

japonica (Ternstroemia; Eurya in hort.) (Temp. E. Asia), "Sakaki" in Japan; decorative evergreen shrub or small tree, the smooth branches dense with ovate and obovate leathery leaves 7 to 11 cm long, not toothed along margins, dark glossy green above, lighter beneath; small bisexual axillary flowers white turning yellow, oblong, thick petals 1 cm long, blooming June-July; fruit pea-sized black berries. Cultivated in Japan for centuries, and cut branches are used on the altar of Shinto temples. *Zones 7-8.* p. 889

japonica 'Variegata' (Japan, Korea); very neat evergreen bush of slow growth, the oblique-elliptic above-pointed, leathery leaves 6-10 cm long, having entire, smooth margins, the surface shiny, dark and milky-green, beautifully variegated creamy-white from the margin toward the center, decoratively arranged and densely overlapping on willowy, spreading branches and woody stems; an excellent keeper. *Zones 8-9.* p. 889

CLIANTHUS   *Leguminosae*

puniceus, (New Zealand), "Parrot's-bill" or "Red kowhai"; evergreen scandent shrub to 3½ m; leaves pinnate; flowers in axillary clusters on a pendulous stalk wholly brilliant red; keel canoe-shaped, 6 cm long. *Subtropic. Zone 9.* p. 277

CLIFTONIA   *Cyrillaceae*

monophylla (Louisiana to Florida and Georgia), "Buckwheat bush"; evergreen shrub to 8 m high, dwelling in swampy areas; leathery oblanceolate leaves glossy green 6-8 cm long, glaucous beneath; elongate clusters of white, fragrant flowers, attracting bees. *Zone 8.* p. 329

CLINOPODIUM   *Labiatae*

coccineum (Calamintha) (Georgia, Alabama, Florida), "Calamint"; aromatic subshrubby perennial 30-90 cm high, the square stems dense with small ovate, leathery leaves 2 cm long; funnel-shaped, lobed scarlet flowers with corollas 3-4 cm long, in Summer and Autumn. *Zone 8.*   *p. 431*

CLINTONIA   *Liliaceae*

umbellulata (New Jersey to Georgia, Ohio to Texas), "Speckled wood lily"; rhizomatous perennial 20 to 40 cm high, with oblong pointed, deep green leaves to 30 cm long, forming basal rosettes; small white flowers spotted with green and purple, in terminal cluster on leafless stalk, May-blooming; followed by black berries. *Zone 4.*   *p. 445*

uniflora (C. California to Brit. Columbia), "Bride's bonnet"; small herbaceous perennials of the Sierra Nevada region, to 20 cm high, with spreading rhizomes; ground-level basal, obovate and lanceolate leaves to 15 cm long; starry white flowers with 6 spreading petals, usually solitary, May to July blooming; followed by blue berries. *Zone 7.*   *p. 445*

CLITORIA   *Leguminosae*

ternatea (Pantropic: Panama to India and Moluccas), "Butterfly pea"; tropical annual or biennial slender twiner with pinnate leaves, and pea-like solitary, showy flowers 5 cm long with broad, fan-like lip narrowing to the base, bright blue with beautiful markings in the throat, blooming all Summer. *Tropical. Zones 10-11.*   *p. 278*

CLIVIA   *Amaryllidaceae*

x cyrtanthiflora (C. miniata x C. nobilis); handsome hybrid to 60 cm high, with rich green, fleshy basal leaves; the inflorescence a dense umbel of narrow, drooping tubular flowers, with inner segments broader than the outer, rich salmon-pink flushed rose. *Zone 10.*   *p. 209*

miniata (Imantophyllum) (Natal), "Kafir lily"; bulb-like plant with fleshy roots, with long, waxy, strap-like, arching leaves; broad, fleshy bell-shaped, erect, orange-red flowers to 8 cm long, yellow toward center, in stiff umbels. *Subtropic. Zone 10.*   *p. 209*

miniata 'Citrina'; seen at Chelsea Flower Show, London; attractive cultivar with large flowers pale lemon-yellow, shaded deeper at base of segments. *Zone 10.*   *p. 209*

nobilis (So. Africa), "Greentip Kafir lily"; inflorescence with many drooping, narrow, funnel-shaped flowers salmon-red with green tips. *Subtropic. Zones 9-10.*   *p. 209*

CLUSIA   *Guttiferae*

rosea (W. Indies, Panama, Venezuela), "Balsam apple" or "Fat pork tree"; evergreen tree 6 m or more high, growing naturally on rocks or epiphytic on other trees; with obovate thick leathery, deep green, opposite leaves to 20 cm long, without lateral veins; large rose flowers with fleshy petals, 5 cm across; globose greenish-yellow fruit of 8 cm dia., splitting open in numerous sections and revealing scarlet pulp with many seeds, eaten by bats. *Zone 10.*   *p. 733*

CLYTOSTOMA   *Bignoniaceae*

callistegioides (Bignonia violacea in Calif. hort.) (Brazil, Argentina), "Argentine trumpet vine"; climbing shrub with opposite leaves with one pair or 3 entire leaflets, the axis extending into simple tendril; large funnel-shaped flowers to 8 cm long, in pairs, with spreading lobes, lavender and streaked violet. *Zones 9-10.*   *p. 269*

CNICUS   *Compositae*

benedictus (Carbenia or Carduus) (Portugal, Mediterr. reg. and Near East), "Blessed thistle"; annual or biennial to 60 cm high, with large leaves 15 cm long, pinnately spiny-lobed, the blades are blotched with white, the veins prominently ivory; the thistle-like floral heads with tubular yellow flowers and spreading linear, spiny bracts. *Zone 8.*   *p. 382*

CNIDOSCOLUS   *Euphorbiaceae*

chyamansa (Mexico to Caribbean and Brazil), "Chaya" or "Tread softly"; succulent shrub to 2 m high, clothed with stinging hairs; the leaves deeply 3-lobed, 8-10 cm wide, the segments irregularly indented or toothed, on fleshy petioles; small white flowers in conical clusters. "Chaya" leaves are eaten as a vegetable in the Caribbean area. *Zone 10.*   *p. 720*

COBAEA   *Polemoniaceae*

scandens (Mexico), "Monastery-bells"; attractive climber with pinnately compound leaflets terminating in a branched tendril used for climbing, and with large bell-shaped flowers to 5 cm long, having a violet calyx, corolla greenish, then violet. *Subtropic.* *Zones 9-10.*   *p. 290*

COCCOLOBA   *Polygonaceae*

pubescens (grandifolia) (Trop. America), "Moralin"; great tree to 25 m high, with woody stems and giant round, leathery, sessile leaves to 1 m across, fresh green and with sunken veins, the margins turned down, with rusty hairs beneath, especially on the prominent ribs. *Zone 11.*   *p. 821*

rugosa (Puerto Rico), "Ortegon"; handsome, now rare tropical tree from the slopes of Sierra Luquillo in Puerto Rico; with trunk usually unbranched except for spreading crown; large leathery, sessile cordate leaves nearly round, 30-50 cm across, wrinkled with sunken ribs; showy cylindric spike-like inflorescence red, followed by reddish fruit. *Zones 10-11.*   *p. 821*

uvifera (South Florida, W. Indies), the familiar "Sea-grape"; along sandy tropical shores, a good decorative shrub or tree to 6 m with flexuous branches and stiff-leathery, rounded leaves to 20 cm across, glossy yellowish to olive-green, with prominent crimson-red veins on young growth, later changing to ivory; the flowers white; fruits purple, to black when ripe, resembling bunches of grapes, used for jelly. *Zone 10.*   *p. 80, 923*

COCCULUS   *Menispermaceae*

laurifolius (Himalayas), "Platter-leaf"; decorative, sparry shrub to 5 m high, with wiry green branches and alternate stiff-leathery, ovate to narrow-elliptic leaves 12-15 cm long, shining forest green, concave with prominently raised yellow-green parallel veins. *Zone 8.*   *p. 789*

COCHEMIEA   *Cactaceae*

poselgeri (Baja California), "Long hook cactus"; sprawling cylindric plant with numerous stems, to 2 m long and 4 cm thick, bluish-green, with conical warts, and white-woolly in axils, reddish radials and solitary hooked central spine; small, glossy scarlet flowers 3 cm long. *Arid-tropical. Zone 10.*   *p. 157*

COCHLIODA   *Orchidaceae*

rosea (Andes of Perú); epiphyte with flattened pseudobulb 8 cm long, solitary linear soft leaf; inflorescence gracefully arching, to 40 cm long, 4 cm flowers dark rose-red. *Subtropic. Zone 11.*   *p. 86*

COCHLIOSTEMA   *Commelinaceae*

odoratissimum 'Striatum' (jacobianum); large epiphyte of the habit of a billbergia, 30-75 cm high; oblong lanceolate leaves to more than 1 m long, and 10 cm wide, rich green above and with white length-stripes, purplish-red with violet lines beneath, sheathing at the base and forming a rosette; numerous beautiful, deep violet-blue flowers of three petals and large white claw, and leaf-like hairy yellow-green sepals with reddish tip. The species is native from Nicaragua to Ecuador. *Tropical. Zone 11.*   *p. 52*

COCHLOSPERMUM   *Cochlospermaceae*

religiosum (Burma or Myanmar, to India), "Silk-cotton tree"; soft-wooded tree to 6 m high, with trunk to 40 cm or more dia., covered by smooth, ash-colored bark; much branched with obovate leaves 3 to 5-lobed, green above and gray-downy beneath, 8-10 cm across, but deciduous during dry or hot season; the showy flowers of spreading petals and sepals are brilliant golden-yellow, displaying numerous stamens, 8 cm across, blooming on bare branches preceding the foliage; the dark brown pods measure 5-8 cm dia., and contain numerous seeds, embedded in soft silky wool. This cotton is used for stuffing pillows. Source also of an important gum used industrially. *Zone 10.*   *p. 687*

vitifolium (Mexico, Central America, So. America), "Buttercup tree"; highly ornamental deciduous tree, with 5-lobed, toothed leaves to 30 cm dia.; attractive golden-yellow flowers to 10 cm across appear before the leaves. *Tropical. Zone 10.*   *p. 687*

COCOS   *Palmae*

australis: see BUTIA capitata

nucifera (Indian Archipelago), "Coconut palm"; widely spread into all tropical regions, especially along the sea where its curving-erect swaying trunks, to 30 m high, leaning toward the water, and topped by majestic crowns of glossy, feathery fronds are a feature of tropical shores; producing its edible nuts inside a large yellow-brown, tough, fibrous husk, 20-30 cm long. This "Tree of life" is of greatest economic importance in most tropical regions; the meat of the coconut is dried into copra, used to manufacture palm-oil, fats and soap. *Zones 11-12.*   *p. 103, 207, 921*

nucifera 'Dwarf Green' (Malaya), "Green Malay coconut"; a strain brought in from Malaysia having shorter trunk and starting to produce its green fruit earlier (3 years on) than the larger species; also has been found more resistant to the "lethal yellowing", a bacterial fungus, spread by deadly microbes, an epidemic disease that has killed 6 million coconuts in Florida and the Caribbean since 1970. *Zone 11.*   *p. 920*

nucifera 'Dwarf Samoan' (Marquesas); a dwarf growing coconut forming stout but short trunk, to 8 m high, and bearing fruit larger and more rounded than that of C. nucifera typica; begins to bear at 5 years from planting seed while var. typica takes 8-10 years; husk color either green or red, with average 550 gram of fresh meat per nut against the normal 350 gram in the type coconut. *Tropical.* Zones 11-12. *p. 104, 920*

nucifera 'Golden Malay', "Dwarf coconut"; originated from seedlings of the dwarf King-coconut from the Andaman Islands; more diminutive and more slender-trunked than 'Dwarf Samoan', and smaller-fruited (yellow, green, or red); starts producing in about three years, in time 100 or more nuts per year as against 30 or 40 of the common coconut palm, and has a trunk so low that the clusters may need props. *Zones 11-12.* *p. 920*

plumosa hort.: see under SYAGRUS romanzoffiana

CODIAEUM *Euphorbiaceae*
variegatum pictum (So. India, Sri Lanka, Malaya, Sunda Isl.); "Crotons" are beautiful tropical shrubs 2 to 3 m high, with highly ornamental leaves, thick leathery, glabrous, ovate to linear, entire or lobed, or spirally twisted, 10-30 cm long, variegated in beautiful colors, the green and yellows of the leaves later often change to shades of red; small female and male flowers on separate plants, the latter with white petals; developed into many varieties and hybrids; some of the better known cultivars are listed below. *Tropical. Zones 10-12.*

'Appleleaf'; bushy plant with small ovate, colorful leaves 8-10 cm long, vari-colored with yellows, salmon shades and red. Zones 11-12. *p. 60*

'Aucubifolium' (C. variegatum pictum cv.) (Polynesia); bushy plant with small elliptic thin leathery leaves 6-10 cm long, bright glossy green blotched and spotted yellow, resembling in leafshape and coloring a miniature Aucuba. *Zones 10-11.* *p. 721*

'Craigii' (1910); attractive plant with stiff, deeply trilobed leaves, bright green with yellow veins. *Zones 11-12.* *p. 60*

'Fred Sander' (1910); yellow stems with leaves distinctly 3-lobed, yellow central area and fresh green margins, soft stem often yellow; delicate and susceptible to checks. *Zones 11-12.* *p. 721*

'Gloriosum', "Autumn croton"; an excellent hybrid, fast growing yet tough, and colors well; the large oval glossy leaves are rich green with yellow veins when young, later olive-green to maroon with veins golden-yellow to red. *Zones 11-12.* *p. 60*

'Gloriosum superbum', "Autumn croton"; dependable variety with long leathery leaves lobed near the apex, nicely variegated according to age of leaf with yellow veins and margins changing to autumn-color and crimson; the blade fresh green to almost red-black; good keeper. *Zones 11-12.* *p. 721*

'Imperialis' (Appleleaf in hort.); small, compact plant and good keeper, with simple, elliptic leaves almost entirely colored yellow, shading to peach and turning rose and red, green midrib and apex turning metallic purple. *Zones 11-12.* *p. 721*

'Norwood Beauty' (C. variegatum pictum cv. 1924); small and tough 3-lobed leaves of the oakleaf type, dark green with bronze to brown-red and rosy edge, yellow in vein areas, 15-20 cm long. Zones 10-11. *p. 721*

variegatum 'Rubrum'; large and showy semi-oakleaf with the center totally a glowing salmon-rose, and extending out between the coppery green. *Zones 11-12.* *p. 721*

CODONOPSIS *Campanulaceae*
ovata (Kashmir and Pakistan), "Bonnet bellflower" or "Asia bells"; small perennial 15-30 cm high, lower part of stems spreading, upper erect, with ovate hairy leaves 2 cm long; solitary bell-shaped flowers with flaring lobes, pale blue with darker veins, 3-4 cm long. From the Western Himalayas at 3000 to 4200 m altitude. *Zone 5.* *p. 355*

COELOGYNE *Orchidaceae*
cristata (Nepal, Himalayas); small easy-growing epiphyte with branching rhizome forming mats of fleshy pseudobulbs with thin twin leaves; large 8-10 cm crystalline, fragrant flowers in drooping clusters, snow-white with five golden-yellow, fringed keels down the middle of the lip. (Feb.-April). *Humid-subtropic. Zone 10-11.* *p. 84*

dayana (Borneo, Sumatra), "Necklace orchid"; decorative epiphyte with pseudobulbs having 1-2 narrow leaves; pendulous racemes 1 m long, loosely many-flowered; 6 cm flowers with narrow lemon-yellow sepals and petals, and broad, lobed lip blotched with chocolate and with white keels. *Tropical. Zone 12.* *p. 83*

flaccida (Nepal, Himalayas); epiphyte with dark green twin leaves; the small flowers in graceful pendulous racemes and of heavy odor, cream-white with lip having brownish streaked side lobes and yellow in middle. *Zones 10-11.* *p. 83*

pandurata (Borneo, Sumatra), "Black orchid"; straggling epiphyte with large pseudobulbs and shining leaves; the large flowers to 10 cm, in pendulous sprays 60 cm long and very fragrant, sepals and petals lovely green, lip greenish-yellow with black raised ridges, (May-July). *Tropical. Zone 12.* *p. 83*

parishii (So. Burma: Moulmein); small epiphyte with squarish pseudobulbs and several 8 cm flowers resembling small pandurata, with slender pointed sepals and petals pale nile-green, the crested lip marked with black (Spring). *Tropical. Zone 12.* *p. 86*

COFFEA *Rubiaceae*
arabica (Ethiopia, Angola), "Arabian coffee"; evergreen shrub to 5 m high, with willowy branches bearing shining dark green, ornamental, elliptic foliage to 15 cm long, and wavy at the margins; the pure white, fragrant flowers, in axillary clusters at the base of leaves, are followed by brilliant crimson, pulpy, 1½ cm berries containing the two seeds or "beans", which are roasted into coffee. Superior type of 'Blue Mountain' coffee, grown at higher altitudes or cool climates. C. arabica is the "Brazilian coffee" grown in Sao Paulo state since 1727. *Subtropic. Zone 10.* *p. 855, 927, 934*

canephora (robusta) (Zaire), "Robusta coffee"; vigorous, small evergreen tree of luxuriant habit, 4 m or more high, with willowy branches furnished with large ovate-elliptic, sharp-pointed leaves 8-20 cm long, shining dark green and distinctly corrugated or wavy between the veins; the axillary fragrant flowers pure white, later developing large brownish-red berries and containing a pair of coffee beans; not as exquisitely flavored as C. arabica but a better producer in the tropics. *Tropical. Zones 10-11.* *p. 541, 934*

liberica (West Africa: Liberia), "Liberian coffee"; more robust than arabica, with longer, wider obovate, shining leaves to 30 cm long, and with a shorter point; flowers in a dense cluster of 15 or more; fruit black 2 cm long; a chief source of coffee, thriving in hot climates where C. arabica will not grow well. *Tropical. Zone 11.* *p. 934*

COIX *Gramineae*
lacryma-jobi (Trop. Asia), "Job's tears"; perennial or annual grass 1-2 m high, with leaves 30-50 cm long, sword-shaped and with prominent midrib; the stems curiously jointed, grown for the interesting female spikelets which develop the peculiar beads 4 cm dia., hard and shining pearly white, containing the kernel; young green seeds are source of the cereal food adlay in East Asia. *Zone 10.* *p. 530*

COLA *Sterculiaceae*
acuminata (Trop. Africa, Togo to Angola), "Cola-nut tree"; evergreen tree 16 m or more high, with obovate leathery leaves 10-20 cm long; starry pale yellow flowers 3 cm across; fruit 15 cm long, star-shaped and woody, resembling a horse-chestnut, consisting of several podlike segments each containing 8 seeds, which, when boiled in water, provide the bases of cola beverages; seed bitter and is a stimulant when chewed. *Zones 10-11.* *p. 883*

nitida (Trop. W. Africa), "Cola nut"; evergreen tree to 20 m high, with glossy green, obovate leaves 15-20 cm long; small flowers with yellow calyx; orange colored leathery fruit 2 cm dia., enclosing the caffeine-holding seed or cola nut, which is chewed by Africans; also used commercially in cola-flavored beverages. *Tropical.* *p. 909*

COLCHICUM *Liliaceae*
autumnale (Europe, No. Africa), "Autumn crocus" or "Meadow saffron"; with long tubed lilac-violet flowers resembling slender-stemmed goblets with segments spreading to 10 cm wide, and produced from the corms without foliage in August-September; the basal leaves to 25 cm long and 4 cm wide, appearing the following Spring. Widely planted for naturalizing in gardens or woods. The corms are poisonous, and the alkaloid colchicine is extracted from them, used in treatment of gout and rheuma. The flowers of Colchicum have 6 stamens, while the very similar Crocus have only 3 stamens. *Zone 5.* *p. 238, 526*

cilicicum (byzantinum) (Taurus Mts. of Turkey), "Byzantine autumn crocus"; floriferous cormous perennial, having about 5 broadly strap-shaped dark green leaves to 25 cm long; in Autumn with up to 20 lilac-rose flowers from one corm, to 8 cm across, a cream-colored keel on back, and with golden-yellow anthers. *Zone 6.* *p. 238*

speciosum (Caucasus, Asia Minor), "Showy autumn crocus"; magnificent cormous perennial, with tulip-like flowers 10 cm or more wide, first cream with lilac, then gradually deepening to crimson-purple with white throat, typically with 6 anthers; profusely blooming in Autumn; leaves in Spring 8-10 cm wide and to 40 cm long, then fading away slowly during Summer. *Zone 5.* *p. 238*

COLEONEMA *Rutaceae*
pulchrum (Diosma) (So. Africa), "Pink breath of Heaven"; evergreen heath-like shrub 1 to 2 m high, with long, slender branches;

filiform long-pointed leaves 2 to 3 cm long, and having 2 lines of dots beneath; rose-pink flowers 2 cm wide, solitary in the upper leaf axils, the petals recurved, and color deepening to red toward base. *Zone 10.*   *p. 860*

COLEUS   *Labiatae*

blumei (Java), "Painted nettle"; gorgeous herbaceous foliage plant having succulent, square stems, with very decorative foliage; the opposite, generally ovate leaves 10 to 15 cm or more long, now grown in many cultivars beautifully painted and variegated in brilliant colors; the inflorescence in a spire of small lilac-blue flowers with two-lipped corolla. *Tropical. Zone 11.*   *p. 61*

blumei 'Brilliancy', "Flame-nettle"; horticultural cultivar of the "Painted nettle" from Java, a soft but showy-leaved herb with square, succulent stems and blue flowers; the leaves of 'Brilliancy' are boldly crimson-red, marked gold on finely crenate edge. *Tropical. Zone 11.*   *p. 431*

blumei 'Verschaffeltii' (Java), "Painted nettle"; most beautiful variety with large, glowing crimson-red leaves, 10 to 20 cm long, purple in center, and narrow, nile-green border, underside purplish-red also; stems and petioles white to purple; flowers pale blue. *Tropical. Zone 11.*   *p. 431*

pumilus 'Red Trailing Queen'; robust creeper with small, broad-ovate leaves, the center purple-carmine, outer zone deep blood-red, broad border of dull green into lobes. *Tropical. Zones 10-11.*   *p. 340*

pumilus 'Trailing Queen', (rehneltianus); a popular commercial cultivar densely branching especially if pinched, with somewhat large 4-6 cm, ovate leaves chartreuse to emerald green along margins, prominently overlaid and marbled with brownish-purple, carmine center near base. *Tropical. Zones 10-11.*   *p. 316*

scutellarioides (Malaya, No. Australia); strikingly beautiful herbaceous perennial with succulent, square stems, and broad ovate-cordate, shield-shaped leaves 15-20 cm long, and crenate at margins; the blades deep green, and richly patterned palmately with cream and rosy-red mainly along vein areas. Seen in col. Nymphenburg Bot. Garden, Munich. *Zone 11.*   *p. 431*

COLLINIA: see CHAMAEDOREA

COLLOMIA   *Polemoniaceae*

grandiflora (Brit. Columbia to So. California, east to Rocky Mts.); garden annual 40-80 cm high, branching with leafy stems; the lanceolate leaves to 10 cm long; the small flowers cream to salmon-yellow or reddish, in dense half-round clammy heads, in late Summer. *Zone 9 as annual.*   *p. 472*

COLOCASIA   *Araceae*

esculenta (Hawaii and Fiji), "Elephant's ear", "Yam", or "Taro"; soft, fleshy herb with edible tuber and large peltate, quilted leaf to 1 m, bright, satiny green. A popular vegetable in the West Indies; the tubers, which are 8-40 cm long and to 20 cm thick, are also a staple food in South China, and known as "Yam" in Hong Kong. *Zone 9.*   *p. 26, 325*

esculenta 'Illustris' (antiquorum hort.) (E. Indies), "Black caladium"; the soft, peltate, heart-shaped leaves are spring-green in vein areas, the balance brownish-purple which shows through to grayish reverse; stems green or violet. *Zone 11.*   *p. 26*

COLQUHOUNIA   *Labiatae*

coccinea (Himalayas); gray-downy shrub to 2 m high, with semi-woody, 4-angled branches; ovate-elliptic to cordate leaves 7-15 cm long, white-felted beneath; spiral clusters of tubular flowers scarlet-red to orange, the tube 25 mm long, blooming August to October. *Zone 7.*   *p. 739*

COLUMNEA   *Gesneriaceae*

arguta (Panama); epiphytic trailer with dense pendulous strands covered with maroon bristles and densely set, waxy, ovate, very sharp pointed leaves; wide open, large salmon-red flowers marked yellow during the leafless state in its native habitat. *Zone 11.*   *p. 62*

arguta 'Merkur'; horticultural hybrid by Magne Haualand, Stavanger, Norway 1976; of more compact growth habit, and featuring smooth leaves, and large yellow flowers, blooming over a long period from May to October. *Zone 11.*   *p. 62*

arguta 'Sirius' (verecunda cv. x arguta); worthy commercial hybrid by Haualand, Stavanger, Norway, valuable because of its upright rather than trailing growth habit, 20 to 25 cm high, with smooth leaves, and large bilabiate crimson-rose flowers, blooming over a long season. *Zone 11.*   *p. 62*

brenneri (Trichantha) (Ecuador); epiphytic plant with flexuous fleshy, brownish stems covered by thin-bristly hairs; the waxy, brittle green leaves long ovate, and pubescent especially on the red ribs beneath and along the lightly crenate margins; flowers on hairy stalks,

the corolla slender tubular to 5 cm long, creamy-yellow and striped with red, the small spreading lobes edged in purple. *Zone 11.*   *p. 61*

hirta (Costa Rica), "Goldfish plant"; epiphytic creeper with rooting stems covered with red hairs; small ovate, red-satiny leaves; vermillion-red, bilabiate flowers marked with orange, solitary from axils; smaller than gloriosa but more floriferous. *Humid-tropical. Zone 11.*   *p. 61*

microphylla (diminutifolia) (Costa Rica), "Goldfish vine"; soft trailing plant with tiny rounded or broad-elliptic, coppery hairy leaves, and relatively very large, spread-open bilabiate flowers 6-8 cm long, burnt-red with yellow along bottom of tube, similar to gloriosa but smaller. *Humid-tropical. Zone 11.*   *p. 62*

microphylla 'Variegata'; a variegated-leaf Goldfish vine, with long pendulous branches, dense with paired 2 cm ovate leaves prettily bordered creamy-white; the solitary two-lipped flowers to 8 cm long, scarlet-red with yellow patch at throat. *Zone 11.*   *p. 315*

minor (teuscheri) (Trichantha minor Dr. H. Wiehler) (Ecuador); rambling creeper with long threadlike vines set with lance-shaped blackish-green leaves shiny above and hairy beneath; from the leaf axils the very unusual tubular 5 cm flowers dark purple, with 4 stamens, the calyx a feathery cluster of carmine bristles, and the face of the corolla contrasting yellow and black, with 5 curious yellow horns at the mouth; blooming for 4 months, starting in Summer. *Humid-tropical. Zone 12.*   *p. 65*

purpureovittata (Trichantha Dr. H. Wiehler) (Perú); wide-spreading gesneriad with long, flexible, hairy branches; long lanceolate, fleshy, wrinkled leaves with unequal sides, 10-14 cm long, glossy deep green, dark red underneath; pendulous tubular flowers yellow with purple stripes; followed by red berries. *Zone 11.*   *p. 65*

COLUTEA   *Leguminosae*

arborescens (France to No. Africa), "Bladder senna"; vigorous bushy shrub to 4 m high, with downy shoots, bearing odd-pinnate leaves to 15 cm long, having 9-13 obovate leaflets 5 cm long, notched at apex and silky beneath; interesting flowers yellow, having standard petal marked with red, the wings as long as keel, blooming successively from June to September; fruit an inflated bladder-like pod 8 cm long. *Zone 5.*   *p. 757*

COLVILLEA   *Leguminosae*

racemosa (Madagascar), "Colville's glory"; spreading, showy tree to 15 m, with fern-like bipinnate foliage and robust, curving whips of branches bearing masses of pendant floral racemes to 60 cm long; brilliantly fiery-red flowers with yellow stamens, opening from burnt-red berry-like buds; the round seed pods to 15 cm long. *Tropical. Zones 10-11.*   *p. 756*

COMBRETUM   *Combretaceae*

fruticosum (Trop. America), "Burning bush"; large woody climber with corrugated elliptic leaves, and showy terminal orange-scarlet spikes 10-12 cm long, with one-sided brushes of long, protruding orange stamens. *Zone 9.*   *p. 689*

COMMELINA   *Commelinaceae*

coelestis (Mexico), "Dayflower" or "Blue spiderwort"; a rank creeper with soft fleshy, obliquely ovate leaves glossy green, purple when older, especially underneath, on hairy purplish stems; flowers sky-blue, 3 cm across, open only mornings of sunny days. *Zone 10.*   *p. 368*

COMPTONIA   *Myricaceae*

peregrina (Nova Scotia to No. Carolina and Michigan), "Sweet fern"; aromatic fern-like deciduous shrub to 1½ m high, with branch-lets and foliage pubescent; leaves narrow linear oblong to 12 cm long, deeply pinnately notched; the male flowers in short catkins; the females forming burr-like capsule subtended by awl-shaped bracts. *Zone 2.*   *p. 795*

CONGEA   *Verbenaceae*

tomentosa (India), "Shower orchid"; climbing shrub with opposite ovate entire, 8 cm leaves hairy beneath; white flowers subtended by lilac leaf-like, hairy bracts. *Tropical. Zone 11.*   *p. 296*

CONOCARPUS   *Combretaceae*

erectus (Seashores, Trop. America, and W. Africa), "Button mangrove"; prostrate shrub or tree from mangrove swamps, with leathery ovate leaves to 10 cm long; flowers greenish, followed by purplish fruit clusters. *Humid-tropical. Zone 10.*   *p. 688*

CONOPHYTUM   *Aizoaceae*

auriflorum (So. Africa: Cape Prov.); mat-forming low succulent with thick conical bodies ½ cm across, dark green with reddish on sides; small golden-yellow flowers. *Arid subtropic. Zone 10.*   *p. 153*

CONOSPERMUM *Proteaceae*
  stoechadis (Northwest Australia), "Smoke-bush"; curious multi-stemmed shrub to 1½ m high, with stiff foliage resembling pine needles 7-12 cm long; the inflorescence of white-woolly or grayish flowers 6 mm long, along terminal branches of the many rigid stems. *Zone 9.*   p. 821

CONRADINA *Labiatae*
  canescens (Florida to Alabama); much branched low shrub 30-90 cm high, from coastal pinelands; small 1 cm pubescent leaves linear-spoon-shaped; small clusters of pale purple flowers in upper leaf axils. *Zone 8.*   p. 739

CONSOLEA rubescens: see OPUNTIA rubescens

CONSOLIDA *Ranunculaceae*
  ambigua (Delphinium ajacis) (Mediterran. reg.), "Rocket lark-spur"; soft-hairy annual larkspur 30-60 cm high, with 3-cleft leaves divided into linear segments; the branches terminating in spike-like racemes of violet, rose or blue flowers having slender 2 cm spur, from June to August. *Zone 9 as annual.*   p. 487
  orientalis (Delphinium ajacis) (So. Europe, No. Africa, W. Asia), "Oriental larkspur"; very popular garden annual with erect branches to 75 cm high; the leaves divided into numerous threadlike segments; the handsome inflorescence of violet, purple, or pink flowers, in stately spires, blooming June to August. *Zone 9 as annual.*   p. 487
  regalis (Centr. Europe to Turkey), "Regal larkspur"; showy annual to 1 m or more high, freely branching, with leaves finely dissected into narrow-linear lobes; flowers in elongate clusters of lovely semi-double blooms in rose, pink or deep blue, or also white, during Summer. *Zone 9 as annual.*   p. 487

CONVALLARIA *Liliaceae*
  majalis (Europe, Temp. Asia), "Lily-of-the-valley"; very popular small perennial herb to 20 cm high, with horizontal, slender creeping rhizomatous rootstock; the upright sectional parts called pips, each with 2-3 basal, fresh green lanceolate leaves, forming clusters; the floral stalk with nodding little bells of sweetly fragrant, waxy, white flowers 1 cm wide, normally May-blooming. *Temperate.* *Zones 3-9.*   p. 238, 445

CONVOLVULUS *Convolvulaceae*
  althaeoides (Mediterranean reg.); deciduous perennial "Bind-weed", with twining stem to 1 m; leaves shining silvery; palmately divided into narrow segments in the upper leaves, the lower ovate-cordate; large rose or lilac flowers, 4 cm across, during April-June. *Zone 10.*   p. 404
  mauritanicus (No. Africa; Spain), "Ground-morning-glory"; twining perennial covered with soft white hair; small ovate leaves and 2½-5 cm flowers lilac-blue or violet, and yellow anthers. Valid name in Zander is C. sabatius. *Zone 7.*   p. 405
  tricolor (Sicily, Spain), "Dwarf morning-glory"; charming annual to 30 cm high; spreading, hairy branches with dark green, narrow-ovate leaves; the colorful flowers platter-like 5 cm across, normally tricolored, and quite variable in contrasting shades of pink, white, purple with yellow throat, opening only when the sun shines. An old summer garden plant. *Subtropic. Zone 10.*   p. 405
  tricolor 'Royal Ensign'; spectacular "Glorybind" with large platter-like cup flowers 5-6 cm across, deep purple and displaying a contrasting white star around the center of the corolla. *Zone 10.*   p. 405

COPERNICIA *Palmae*
  prunifera (cerifera) (N.E. Brazil: Ceara), "Carnauba wax palm"; beautiful fan palm 8 to 12 m tall, famous as wax palm; the light green palmate fronds are firm and erect, to 1½ m broad, divided to the middle in about 60 segments, with a waxy covering furnishing the wax of commerce; the petioles are armed with strong teeth; bisexual flowers in clusters; brown 2 cm fruit. *Tropical. Zones 11-12.*   p. 104

COPIAPOA *Cactaceae*
  laui (Chile: Esmeralda); clustering miniature globe 1 to 3 cm dia., completely covered with low olive-green knobs, from the white-woolly areoles spread tiny pale radial spines; at apex a woolly cephalium gives rise to glistening yellow flowers. *Zone 11.*   p. 162

COPROSMA *Rubiaceae*
  x kirkii (acerosa x repens) (New Zealand); scrambling or suberect dwarf shrub to 50 cm high, dense with silvery branches and closely-set narrow gray leaves 1-3 cm long, and little greenish-white flowers; translucent, oblong 1 cm fruit, speckled with red. With its mounding dense habit an ideal groundcover or rockgarden plant. *Zone 9.*   p. 855
  x kirkii variegata (acerosa x repens) (williamsii hort.) (New Zealand), "Silvery birdsnest"; handsome scrambling shrubby peren-nial to 50 cm or more, with long straight, stiff branches spreading outward, and densely set with narrow, linear leaves 3 cm long, lime-green prettily margined creamy-white. *Zones 8-10.*   p. 321, 494
  repens 'Marginata' (baueri) (New Zealand), "Mirror plant"; evergreen densely leafy dioecious shrub to 6 m high, with opposite, roundish, soft-leathery leaves 6-8 cm long, bright green and glossy as if varnished; small flowers greenish, the berries on female trees orange-yellow; planted in Southern California along the seashore because of its resistance to salt spray. *Zone 9.*   p. 855

COPTIS *Ranunculaceae*
  occidentalis (Brit. Columbia and Washington to Montana), "Goldthread"; low evergreen perennial herb 15-30 cm high, from slender rhizome; palmately divided basal leaves on petioles 5-15 cm long, the leaflets trilobed almost to middle, and toothed at margins; small white or yellow flowers, having narrow white, deciduous sepals, and fleshy petals tubular at apex on short stalks; primary habitat in Rocky Mts., blooming April-May. *Zones 3-7.*   p. 488

CORALLOBOTRYS *Ericaceae*
  acuminatus (Agapetes) (Assam, Bhutan, Eastern Himalayas); tropical evergreen growing epiphytic, with branches 60 to 100 cm long; ovate leathery glossy green leaves 10 cm or more long; beautiful tubular flowers vivid coral-red tipped yellow, in pendant clusters. *Zone 11.*   p. 701

CORDIA *Boraginaceae*
  elaeagnoides (Mexico: Guerrero to Chiapas), "Gueramo", "Ocote" or "Bocote"; striking flowering tree 6-10 m high, dense with erect leafy branches; the thin-leathery foliage ovate-pointed 8-16 cm long; the showy inflorescence in terminal clusters of starry creamy-white flowers 2 cm across. Photographed in Zihuatanejo, near Ixtapa, So. Mexico. Photo may be of the similar C. alliodora according to Dr. Barnaby of New York Botanical Garden. *Zone 10.*   p. 668, 669
  sebestena (Florida Keys, Bahamas, West Indies to Barbados), "Geiger tree"; small evergreen tropical tree to 8 m, with rough brown bark; dark green, oval leaves 8 to 20 cm long, with pale veins, in clusters at ends of branches; flowers to 5 cm across, brilliant orange-scarlet, quilted and ruffled and of a crepy texture; small white 2 cm fruit sweet and edible. *Zone 10.*   p. 668
  sebestena 'Aurea', "Orange geiger tree"; variety with orange-yellow flowers, edible whitish 2 cm fruit. *Zone 10.*   p. 907

CORDYLINE *Agavaceae*
  australis (New Zealand), "Dracaena indivisa" of florists; palm-like tree to 12 m high, with single erect stem crowned by a dense cluster of flat and narrow, arching leaves tough-leathery, bronzy green with fresh green midrib, 6-8 cm wide in maturity; fragrant white flowers, following which the head will fork. Small plants in pots grown from seed by florists have slender leaves only 1-2 cm wide. Known as "Grass palm", or in New Zealand as "Cabbage tree"; an ancient monocot. Roots are typically white in Cordyline (yellow in Dracaena). *Zone 10.*   p. 115, 771
  fruticosa (Polynesia); similar to Cordyline terminalis 'Ti', but of stockier habit, thicker cane and broader, oblanceolate leaves glossy green to bronze. *Tropical. Zones 11-12.*   p. 116
  indivisa (New Zealand), "Palm lily"; slender tree to 8 m high, usually with single, flexible stem, with a large head of sessile, flat, tough leaves, matte-green with raised orange midrib, glaucous blue beneath, to 20 cm or twice as wide as australis; not branching after flowering. *Subtropic. Zones 9-10.*   p. 116
  rubra 'Bruantii'; form with gracefully recurved, coppery red leaves, of this Australian, slender tree-like species, intermediate between terminalis and stricta, growing to 5 m; leaves continually ascending, closely set, narrow oblanceolate and thick, normally dull green, reddish reverse when young, prominent midrib, on broad grooved petiole. *Subtropic. Zone 10.*   p. 116
  stricta (Drac. congesta) (Queensland, New So. Wales); tree-like, with slender stem to 4 m high, occasionally branched; narrow clasping leaves sword-shaped, leathery, matte-green with rough edges, in-conspicuously toothed, narrowing toward a constricted base; young growth reddish. *Subtropic. Zones 9-10.*   p. 116
  terminalis (India, Malaysia to Polynesia), "Red tree of kings"; a commercial "Red dracaena" with rather slender, leathery, sword-shaped leaves in a cluster of erect habit, on a cane to 3 m high; the normal leaves are copper-green shading into red, the young winter growth intense rosy-crimson; flowers lilac-tinted, in panicles, followed by red berries. *Tropical. Zone 12.*   p. 116
  terminalis 'Liliput'; short, compact cultivar with broad leaves, bronzy green edged in rose, the upper leaves primarily carmine-pink. *Tropical. Zone 11.*   p. 70
  terminalis var. 'Ti' (Taetsia fruticosa) (Hawaii to New Guinea), "Tree of kings" or "Hawaiian good luck plant"; palm-like, robust, with slender cane to 4 m high, topped by a cluster of oblong leaves to 60 cm

long spirally arranged, smooth, flexible and plain green; this foliage is used for hula skirts; sections of cane will sprout young plants. Tropical. Zones 11-12.   p. 116, 208

COREOPSIS   *Compositae*

auriculata (Virginia to Florida), "Eared tickseed"; handsome stoloniferous herbaceous perennial 30-45 cm high, forming clumps, with spreading branches, 5-10 cm spatulate leaves; flowers 3 to 6 cm across, the petals fringed at apex, bright yellow with darker lines. Zone 4.   p. 383

grandiflora (Missouri to Kansas, so. to Florida and New Mexico), "Tickseed"; herbaceous perennial to 60 cm or more high, often grown as biennial; the branches with long linear leaves, some pinnately cut; floral heads to 6-8 cm across, with disc orange, the yellow ray-flowers sterile. Zone 7.   p. 399

grandiflora 'Sun baby'; (lanceolata cv.), seen in Germany as 'Sonnenkind'; perennial 30-50 cm high, forming clumps, with slender leaves, entire or pinnate, and beautiful large flowers 6 cm across, the ray-florets golden-yellow with a crimson blotch at base and fringed at apex. Zones 5-9.   p. 383

lanceolata (Ontario to Florida and New Mexico), "Lance tickseed"; robust perennial to 60 cm or more high, forming clumps; leaves simple or pinnately lobed, mostly along stems; very floriferous with long-stalked bright yellow flowers 6 cm across, during Summer. Zone 4.   p. 383

maritima (So. California, Baja California, Mexico), the "Sea dahlia"; perennial to 1 m, with leafy hollow stems, divided leaves, and long-stalked 8 cm daisy-like flower heads vivid yellow, in Autumn. Zone 9.   p. 383

tinctoria, "Calliopsis" in hort. (Minnesota to Arizona), "Plains tickseed"; herbaceous summer-flowering perennial or biennial 60-90 cm high, with pinnately divided leaves, and beautiful long-stalked flowers 3-4 cm across, with toothed yellow florets having crimson base, disc brownish-purple. Zones 4-8.   p. 383

verticillata (Maryland to Florida, w. to Arkansas), "Arkansas tickseed" or "Threadleaf coreopsis"; branched perennial 50-75 cm high, spreading twice as wide; the leaves palmately parted into pinnate fern-like linear segments; flowers golden-yellow, 5 cm across; during Summer. Zones 3-9.   p. 383

CORIANDRUM   *Umbelliferae*

sativum (Asia Minor, No. Africa), "Coriander" or "Chinese parsley"; popular aromatic annual herb, 40-80 cm high; fern-like, shining green leaves several times divided into linear segments, the lower leaves with ovate sections; small white flowers in short-stalked clusters. The strong-smelling foliage is widely used in Chinese or Mexican cooking; the seeds become fragrant when dry, and are added for seasoning sausage and for pickling, also in confectionary; ground seed to flavor gingerbread, cookies and pastries. Zones 7-9.   p. 544

CORNUS   *Cornaceae*

alba 'Albo-marginata' (No. China), "Red-bark dogwood"; deciduous flowering shrub to 3 m high, grown for its red winter twig color, and the leaves margined with white; blooming in late May with small yellowish-white flowers in clusters; followed by white or light blue berries in Autumn. Zone 4.   p. 692

alba 'Argenteo-marginata' (Siberia, No. China, No. Korea), "Tatarian dogwood"; handsome, dense bush to 3 m, with red stems; elliptic leaves, to 12 cm long, milky green heavily bordered and variegated with cream. Zone 2.   p. 692

alternifolia (Nova Scotia to Minnesota, s. to Alabama, and Missouri), "Pagoda dogwood"; beautiful deciduous tree to 6 m high, with horizontal branches; alternate ovate leaves 12 cm long, glaucous and hairy beneath; small yellowish-white flowers in dense clusters, in June; berries blue-black. Zone 3.   p. 692

canadensis (No. America: Newfoundland to Alaska, W. Virginia; E. Asia), "Bunch berry"; woody perennial herb with creeping rootstock, to 25 cm high with whorled leaves 8-10 cm long; purplish flowers in dense heads surrounded by 4 white petal-like bracts; the bright red berries are edible. Zones 2-8.   p. 406

capitata (Himalayas); attractive evergreen tree dense with leathery 10 cm elliptic leaves, reverse grayish and finely pubescent, on willowy branches; inconspicuous flowers subtended by fleshy, 4 cm sulphur-yellow bracts; fruit puckered strawberry-like, salmon-red to crimson. Zone 8.   p. 693

controversa (China, Japan), "Giant dogwood"; large deciduous tree 10 to 20 m high, characteristically spreading wide, with branches horizontal in tiers; alternate lustrous green ovate leaves 12 cm long, whitish beneath; small white flowers in flattish clusters 16 cm across; globose blue-black fruit 1 cm dia. Zone 5.   p. 692

florida (Maine to Florida and Texas), "Flowering dogwood"; popular deciduous flowering tree to 12 m high, with spreading branches, and blooming on bare wood, the small inconspicuous yellow flower cluster surrounded by 4 large, gleaming petal-like white bracts 4-6 cm long, notched at apex, turning pink with age; the 8-12 cm ovate green leaves will turn red in late Autumn; berry-like fruit scarlet. Temperate. Zone 4.   p. 693

florida 'Cloud Nine' (Plant Patent); outstanding for its free-blooming habit, literally a cloud of white-bracted flowers at an early age; opening creamy-yellow, then becoming pure white, and practically hiding the foliage. Compact and slower growth than the species. Photographed at North Haven Garden in Dallas, Texas; offered by Wayside Gardens. Zone 6.   p. 694

florida 'Rainbow' (Plant patented); beautiful small tree densely branched, very attractive with its colorful foliage variegated bright yellow and green during Spring and Summer, gradually changing to brilliant scarlet, shades of lavender and rich purple; large white-bracted flowers before leaves in early Spring. Zone 6.   p. 693

florida 'Rubra' (Maine to Florida and Texas); attractive deciduous tree to about 10 m high, with ovate leaves 10-15 cm long and small greenish flowers in dense heads, subtended by 4 large showy, notched rosy, petal-like bracts; white in the species florida; fruit red. Zone 6.   p. 693

florida 'Sweetwater'; handsome cultivar seen in col. New Jersey Agric. Experiment Sta., New Brunswick; distinguished by flowers with deep red bracts, followed by glossy red fruit. Zone 4.   p. 693

florida 'Welchii', "Tricolor dogwood"; strikingly beautiful cultivar with colorful foliage variegated white, pink, yellow and rose, over green, turning nearly red in Autumn; blooms are sparse; glossy red berries in axillary clusters. Foliage tends to burn in hot sun. Zone 5.   p. 693

hessei (N.E. Asia); small deciduous shrub 50 cm high; leaves narrow obovate 3-4 cm long, dark green but changing to deep violet in Autumn; white flowers in small clusters 4 cm across, in June to August; bluish-white pea-size fruit. Zone 4.   p. 694

kousa (Japan, Korea), "Kousa dogwood" or "Japan dogwood"; shrub or small tree to 6 m; leathery oval leaves 10 cm long, with yellow veins and glaucous beneath; inflorescence with globular green head, subtended by 4 petal-like narrow bracts creamy-white; followed by pendant, strikingly handsome, fleshy red fruit with puckered rind, 2-3 cm dia. and edible. Zone 5.   p. 693

macrophylla (Himalayas, China, Japan), "Largeleaf dogwood"; attractive large deciduous tree to 15 m high, with very decorative opposite lanceolate leaves 10-18 cm long, lustrous green above, glaucous and with appressed hairs beneath, veins in 6-8 pairs; blooms creamy-white 2-3 cm across, in rounded clusters, late-blooming in July-August, followed by berry-like fruit. Zone 6.   p. 694

mas (C. to So. Europe, Asia Minor, Armenia, Caucasus), "Cornelian cherry"; highly desirable, deciduous twiggy bush or small tree to 5 m or more high with age and care, very early blooming before the leaves in February-March, the small yellow flowers enclosed in 4 downy, yellowish bracts; followed by the ovate 10 cm leaves, at first green, later turning yellow and reddish in Fall; Autumn color is enhanced by the elongate glossy vivid red fruit which is edible and loved by birds, and also made into preserves. Zone 4.   p. 528, 694

nuttallii (Brit. Columbia to No. California), "Pacific dogwood"; spectacular flowering tree 5 to 25 m high, often encountered in Sequoia National Park and the Sierra Nevada, blooming on bare branches, the flowers with 4 to 6 or 8 glistening white bracts 4-6 cm long, later turning pink, around a center cluster of tiny flowers; the downy foliage 8-12 cm long and glaucous beneath. Zone 7.   p. 694

officinalis (Japan and Korea), "Japanese Cornelian cherry"; deciduous small tree to 5 m high, similar to C. mas but more tree-like, with small yellow flowers in clusters, appearing before the foliage in early Spring; elliptic leaves to 12 cm long; oblong red fruit. Distinguished by having patches of reddish down at the vein axils beneath. Zone 5.   p. 694

sanguinea (Europe), "Blood-twig dogwood" or "Pegwood"; deciduous shrub to 4 m high, with branches dark red, more so in Winter; leaves ovate 8-10 cm long, thinly hairy on both surfaces, red in Autumn; strongly scented flowers with white petal-like bracts in clusters 5 cm wide, June-blooming, followed by black, bitter fruit. Zone 4.   p. 694

sericea (stolonifera) (E. No. America), "Red Osier dogwood"; deciduous shrub 2 m high, creeping by stolons with bark on the arching branches attractively red, and very colorful in Winter; broad lanceolate leaves 5-10 cm long, dark green above and showing contrasting veins, glaucous beneath; floral bracts yellowish white, in 3-5 cm clusters in May-June; followed by white berries. Branchlets often root when they touch the ground. Zone 2.   p. 694

suecica (N.W. Europe to N.E. Asia, N.E. Canada to Alaska), "Dwarf cornel"; charming low subshrub 10-20 cm high, with underground rhizomes sending up shoots, with foliage deciduous; ovate leaves to 3 cm long, 5 or 7-veined, in pairs; the clustered inflorescence surrounded by 4 large white bracts; each true flower consists of 3 small brown-black petals and stamens, in June-July, followed by ovoid red fruit. *Zone 2.* p. 694

COROKIA *Cornaceae*
cotoneaster (New Zealand), "Golden koroko" or "Zigzag bush"; slow-growing stiff evergreen shrub to 3 m high; the numerous slim, nearly black branches contorted and so interlaced as to make an intricate, bizarre pattern; the little 2 cm leaves dark green above, white-tomentose underneath; tiny yellow, starry 1 cm, jasmine-like flowers in Spring to Summer, followed by small bright yellow to red fruits. Thrives in containers, best in sun. *Zone 9.* p. 691

CORONILLA *Leguminosae*
emerus (Central and So. Europe), "Scorpion senna"; deciduous shrub to 3 m, with angled shoots, unequally pinnate leaves with 2 to 4 pairs of obovate 3 cm leaflets; yellow 2 cm flowers with long claws, the standard petal marked with red. *Zone 6.* p. 754

vaginalis (C. Europe, Alps to Balkans); low, procumbent subshrub 20 cm high with pinnate leaves, their usually 7-9 leaflets bluish-gray-green and arranged in 3-6 pairs; the flowers with petals golden-yellow, the upper lip oval, and sweetly fragrant. *Zone 6.* p. 754

valentina glauca (S.E. France west to Albania); deciduous shrub to 1 m or more high, with pinnate leaves having 2 to 3 pairs of glaucous ovate 2 cm leaflets; clusters of deep yellow pea-flowers 25 mm long, with claws of petals nearly as long as calyx, blooming mainly in April; pendant 5 cm fruit pods. *Zone 8.* p. 754

varia (Europe to Syria, Asia Minor, natural. in Northeast U.S.), "Crown vetch"; straggly herbaceous perennial to 60 cm high, with flexuous branches; compound leaves of about 11-25 narrow leaflets; pinkish to white pea-like flowers in clusters, blooming June to November; erect long-beaked fruit. *Zone 3.* p. 440

CORREA *Rutaceae*
alba (S.E. Australia), "White correa"; evergreen shrub 1 m or more, with leathery oval leaves buxus-like, 3 cm long, woolly beneath; small white 2 cm bell-flowers split into 4 petals; resistant to salt-spray. *Zones 9-10.* p. 860

x harrisii (speciosa hybrid), "Australian fuchsia"; evergreen shrub with opposite simple, downy leaves, and nodding, tubular 3 cm flowers scarlet-red with protruding stamens and yellow anthers. *Zone 10.* p. 860

pulchella (South Australia); attractive small evergreen shrub to 60 cm or more high; concave leathery, glossy elliptic leaves 2-3 cm long; pendant tubular pinkish-red flowers, the corolla lobes arching outward; yellow anthers protruding; blooming April-May. *Zones 9-10.* p. 860

reflexa (speciosa) (So. Australia to Queensland, Tasmania), known in Australia as "Native fuchsia"; evergreen shrub to 1 m; small 2 cm ovate leaves tomentose beneath; beautiful tubular 4 cm flowers red with green tips. *Zones 9-10.* p. 861

CORRYOCACTUS *Cactaceae*
kraussii (Chile, Bolivia); branching succulent shrub of the Andes, to 3 m high, with slender columns 10 or more cm thick, having 8 to 10 ribs variedly covered with spines; yellow funnel flowers 5-6 cm long, diurnal. *Zone 10.* p. 161

CORTADERIA *Gramineae*
richardii (Agrostis conspicua or Arnudo conspicua) (New Zealand), "Plumed tussock grass"; magnificent perennial grass with rigid, erect culms 2½ to 3 m high, the leaves linear and serrate, mostly basal, and topped by showy elongate inflorescence 50 cm long, bearing spikelets with light brown, glossy bracts (glumes) on its branches, the weight of which causing them to droop to one side; the flower heads are silvery or yellowish and vary according to habitat, blooming in Summer; plants are either female or bisexual. *Zone 8.* p. 559

selloana (argentea) (Argentina), the "Pampas-grass"; gigantic tufted grass 2-3 or even 6 m high, forming great clumps; the leaves 1-3 m long and 2 cm wide, with rough edges; female spikelets borne in panicles; beautiful silvery-white, silky plumes to 1 m long. The plumes can be dried for indoor decoration. *Zones 7-8.* p. 559

CORTUSA *Primulaceae*
matthioli (Mts. of C. Europe to Japan, No. China); hairy herbaceous perennial to 30 cm high, with basal leaves rounded heart-shaped and lightly lobed; inflorescence in small clusters of flowers with nodding, bell- to funnel-shaped rosy-pink 2-3 cm corollas, turning violet as they age; the 5 lobes reflexed; July blooming. *Zone 6.* p. 478

CORYDALIS *Fumariaceae*
aurea (No. America: Québec to Minnesota), "Golden corydalis"; densely branching annual or biennial 15 cm high, with bipinnate glaucous leaves divided into linear lobes; golden-yellow, 2 cm flowers with blunt spur, pendant in short racemes, in late Spring to Summer. *Zone 6.* p. 414

cava (Cent. Europe), "Fumewort"; attractive perennial 15-30 cm high, from hollow tuberous roots; fern-like foliage, divided into wedge-shaped segments; flowers lilac to purple, with upper petal rolled back, horizontal on long, erect raceme, in March to May. *Zone 6.* p. 414

lutea (Europe: So. Alps to Mediterranean), "Yellow corydalis"; very ornamental small perennial, sometimes grown as annual, 20-30 cm high, with wide-spreading branches; fern-like foliage, twice divided into 3 sections, the segments wedge-shaped and glaucous beneath; the flowers golden-yellow, 2 cm long, pendant, and with straight spur, blooming May to August. *Zone 5.* p. 413

ochroleuca (Italy, Yugoslavia, Greece); very handsome herbaceous perennial 30 cm high, without tuber; many-stemmed with leaves much divided into obovate segments, glaucous on both surfaces, on winged petioles; inflorescence on axillary racemes, dense with pendant pale yellow flowers 2-3 cm long, in June to September. *Zone 8.* p. 414

CORYLOPSIS *Hamamelidaceae*
pauciflora (Japan: Honshu), "Buttercup winter hazel"; spreading deciduous shrub to 2 m high; broadly ovate leaves 3-8 cm long, bristle-toothed along margins; small 25 mm scented yellow flowers, several together, blooming early in March-April before the leaves appear. *Zone 6.* p. 733

spicata (So. Japan), "Spike winter hazel"; deciduous shrub from Shikoku Isl., to 2 m high with branches silky when young; popular in gardens because of its very early bloom, before foliage; leaves ovate-roundish to 10 cm long, with 6-7 pairs of lateral veins; charming with flowers in pendulous elongate racemes 8 cm long, the corollas yellow subtended by greenish bracts, and sweetly fragrant. *Zone 6.* p. 733

veitchiana (W. China), "Chinese winter hazel"; deciduous shrub 1½ to 2 m high, early blooming on bare, reddish branches; with fragrant, primrose-yellow flowers displaying red-brown anthers, in large clusters; ovate to elliptic leaves 8 cm long. *Zone 6.* p. 733

CORYLUS *Betulaceae*
avellana (Europe, North Temp. Zone), "European filbert" or "Hazel-nut"; popular woody shrub 4-6 m high, with willowy branches forming dense thicket; ovate, slender pointed leaves to 10 cm long, showing prominent ribs, pubescent beneath; male catkins to 6 cm long; the tasty, edible 2 cm nuts in partially hidden husks are highly valued in commerce for their pleasant taste; the twigs are used for basketry. *Zone 3.* p. 662, 904

avellana 'Contorta', "Twisted hazel"; a definite curiosity of erect, moderate growth, with branches densely intertwined and twisted like a screwdriver; the ovate leaves 5-10 cm long, slender pointed. Found in English hedgerow in 1863. *Zone 3.* p. 662

colurna (S.E. Europe and Asia Minor), "Turkish filbert" or "Turkish hazelnut"; deciduous monoecious tree to 20 m or more high, of very ornamental appearance, with scaling bark; the leaves broad and cordate, 12 cm long, pubescent on veins beneath, the margins toothed or lightly lobed; male catkins 8 cm long; the female flowers developing edible nuts in very hard shells, 2 cm long, clustered 3-6 together, imbedded in fringed, downy husks. *Zone 4.* p. 904

cornuta (rostrata) (Québec to Saskatchewan, south to Georgia and Missouri), "Beaked filbert"; deciduous shrub to 3 m high; ovate and obovate leaves to 10 cm long, cordate at base, and closely toothed; the edible nuts enclosed in a bristly husk, ending in a cylindrical beak 3 cm long. *Zone 2.* p. 904

maxima (S.E. Europe); tall deciduous shrub 3 to 6 m high with lightly hairy shoots; the leaves broadly cordate and roundish, 8-14 cm long, toothed and shallowly lobed at sides, the numerous veins depressed on surface; purplish beneath; the edible nuts deeply enclosed by the tubular, much lobed husk. Produces large nuts much used in commerce; in cultivation since ancient times. *Zone 5.* p. 904

maxima 'Purpurea' (S.E. Europe), "Purple filbert" or "Blood-hazel"; very ornamental shrub or small tree to 8 m high, with leaves broadly cordate or ovate 8-12 cm long, toothed and shallowly lobed, richly colored blackish red throughout the season; the large nuts are fully enclosed in a tubular husk, twice as long as in C. avellana; the catkins are also red. *Zone 4.* p. 662

CORYNOCARPUS *Corynocarpaceae*
laevigata (New Zealand), the "Karaka" of the Maori, and "New Zealand laurel"; handsome evergreen tree 6-15 m high, with laurel-like glossy green leaves 8-16 cm long; tiny 5 mm white flowers in clusters, followed by orange, edible fruit 4 cm long, but its seed is very poisonous. *Zone 10.* p. 695

CORYPHA   Palmae

umbraculifera (Sri Lanka, So. India), the "Talipot palm"; slow-growing to 30 m high, with straight trunk and a great crown of fan-shaped, plaited bright green leaves about 4 m wide, on spiny stalks; pyramidal terminal inflorescence of creamy-white flowers, the small olive-colored fruit appears when palm is 25 to 80 years old; after fruiting the tree will die. *Tropical. Zones 11-12.*   p. 104

CORYPHANTHA   Cactaceae

bella: see ESCOBARIA bella (Zander)

cornifera (Mexico: Hidalgo); pale green, small globe or short-cylindric, to 12 cm high, woolly at top, with short, broad grooved knobs, set with all radials yellowish tipped red; flowers lemon-yellow tinged red, to 5 cm across. *Zone 10.*   p. 156

henricksonii (Escobaria) (Mexico: S.E. Chihuahua); from large tuberous root rises a column to 8 cm high, with grooved elevated tubercles typical of Coryphantha; these topped by a symmetrical spine arrangement, spreading star-like; lavender-pink flowers rise from older axils. *Zone 11.*   p. 162

laredoi (Escobaria) (Sierra de Parras, Coahuila, Mexico); small globes 4 to 5 cm dia., becoming elongate, forming rounded clusters, the areoles white-woolly, and densely set with a net of long white needle-spines, and shorter radials; wide open star flowers purplish-red. *Zone 10.*   p. 156

potosiana (clavata) (syn. Mammillaria) (San Luis Potosi, Mexico); small robust globular to elongate body, 8 cm dia., with turnip-like root; gray-green spiralled knobs topped by tricolored stout curved spines yellow to brown-red and dark crossbands; small 2 cm flowers purplish-red with cream margins. *Zone 10.*   p. 162

vivipara (from Manitoba and Alberta to Kansas, Colorado, Texas), "Spiny stars"; olive-green globes 5 cm thick, clustering, dense with high woolly nipples covered with spreading white radials and central spines; purplish-rose 3 cm flowers. *Temperate. Zone 3.*   p. 162

CORYTOPLECTUS   Gesneriaceae

capitatus (Alloplectus) (Colombia, Venezuela), "Velvet alloplectus"; erect, 4-angled red tomentose stem to 60 cm with large velvety, olive-green, ovate leaves, reddish beneath; dense clusters of bright yellow flowers with red sepals. *Tropical. Zone 11.*   p. 62

COSMOS   Compositae

atrosanguineus (Mexico), "Black cosmos"; tuberous perennial to 1 m high, usually grown as an annual; with odd-pinnate leaves; beautiful flowers 4 cm across, of glowing deep blood-red ray-florets ranged around red disc; blooming July to October. *Zone 10.*   p. 383

bipinnatus (Mexico to Brazil), "Garden cosmos"; showy summer and fall-blooming annual that may grow to 2 m and more, of open branching habit, with light green bipinnate leaves finely cut into lacy segments, and daisy-like heads 5 to 8 cm across, with broad petal-like ray-flowers in white, shades of pink, rose, lavender, purple or crimson, with tufted yellow centers. *Tropical. Zone 10.*   p. 383

sulphureus (Mexico to Brazil), "Yellow cosmos" or "Mexican aster"; herbaceous annual to 1 m or more high, with leaves deeply cut; large flowers to 8 cm across, having yellow discs and golden-yellow or orange ray-florets. *Zone 10.*   p. 383

COSTUS   Zingiberaceae

igneus (Brazil), "Fiery costus"; stout leafy stems maroon with 15 cm leaves green above, reddish beneath, spirally arranged; large 6 cm flowers deep orange. *Tropical. Zone 11.*   p. 80

malortieanus (zebrinus) (Costa Rica), "Stepladder plant"; showy, suckering plant with stout stalks to 1 m high in spirals, with broad, recurved, fleshy leaves to 30 cm long, bright emerald green, banded lengthwise with dark zones and covered with glistening hair; flowers yellow marked with red. *Tropical. Zone 11.*   p. 80

pulverulentus (sanguineus) (C. America), "Violet spiral flag"; beautiful "Spiral flag" with coppery green stems clasped by wine-red petioles bearing in spiral order, the gracefully recurving, oblique-elliptic, fleshy leaves of shimmering velvet-bluish-green, marked with a central band of silver, thin gray lines, and a zone of yellow-green toward the margin; deep blood-red beneath. *Tropical. Zone 12.* p. 80

speciosus (India, Malaysia), "Spiral ginger" or "Crepe ginger"; perennial herb with heavy rootstock; clustering, slender reed-like, green, leafy stems to 3 m long, growing upward in loose spirals or drooping in graceful curves, set in spiral order with fresh green, oblanceolate, glossy, succulent, slender-pointed leaves, silky beneath, to 20 cm long; flowers in dense spike, white with yellow center and red bracts. *Tropical. Zones 10-11.*   p. 520

speciosus 'Marginatus', "Variegated spiral ginger"; very ornamental cultivar, having its glossy, oblanceolate leaves prettily bordered with creamy-white. *Zone 11.*   p. 520

spicatus (West Indies), "Indian head ginger"; stout perennial herb with leafy stems to 2½ m tall; smooth, thick ovate leaves to 15 cm; club-like cylindrical inflorescence of overlapping red bracts, and yellow flowers. *Tropical. Zone 11.*   p. 520

stenophyllus (Costa Rica); tall clustering plant 2 m or more high, with bamboo-like canes green with dark section rings, and long linear leaves; the inflorescence on separate low stalks from the base, the yellowish flowers emerging from a striking cone of brilliant scarlet, imbricated bracts. Photo by J. Bogner of Munich Bot. Garden; see Exotica 4 p. 2132. *Zone 11.*   p. 520

COTINUS   Anacardiaceae

coggygria (Rhus cotinus) (So. Europe to Asia), "Smoke tree" or "Venetian sumac"; deciduous bushy shrub to 5 m high and wide; roundish 4-8 cm leaves, bluish-green in Summer, turning yellow to orange-red in Autumn; the inflorescence in large puffs of tiny greenish blossoms. *Zone 5.*   p. 636

coggygria 'Rubrifolius' (S.E. Europe), "Purple Venetian sumac"; ornamental shrub, having 8 cm leaves dark purple, later partially paling to green; the inflorescence in much branched clusters 20 cm long, of small white flowers, their hairy reddish fruit-stalks creating a "smoky" effect. *Zone 5.*   p. 636

obovatus (Rhus cotinoides) (Tennessee to Alabama and Texas), "American smoke tree"; shrub, or small tree to 10 m high with obovate leaves 15 cm long; floral clusters not showy, but foliage colors brilliant red in Autumn. *Zone 5.*   p. 636

COTONEASTER   Rosaceae

adpressus praecox (W. China, Szechwan), "Creeping cotoneaster"; slow-growing dwarf deciduous shrub to 25 cm high, and to 40 cm across; small 2-3 cm rounded leaves, wavy at margins; small pinkish flowers, followed by pearl-like orange-red fruit; an excellent rockgarden plant. *Zone 4.*   p. 830

apiculatus (W. China), "Cranberry cotoneaster"; spreading evergreen shrub with tiny roundish dark glossy green leaves set with solitary, pink flowers all along the sparry, woody branches, followed by red berries, retained well into Winter; an excellent groundcover. *Zone 4.*   p. 320

bullatus (Western China); deciduous shrub to 2 m or more high in habitat, with black-brown bark but with a tendency to remain low forming a cushion; dense with ovate or oblong leaves 5-8 cm long, dark green and bullate above, and downy beneath; flowers rosy-white in clusters, their petals soon falling, but with their brilliant red fruit this is a most handsome species. *Zone 5.*   p. 831

congestus (pyrenaicus hort.) (Himalayas), "Pyrenees cotoneaster"; small evergreen resembling microphyllus, but more dwarf; with short stubby branches, very dense with congested leaves and forming mounds; small 1 cm pinkish flowers in June, followed by bright red berries. *Zone 6.*   p. 320

conspicuus (Tibet), "Wintergreen cotoneaster"; very pretty species when in bloom with white flowers and crimson anthers 15 mm across, in June; followed by brilliant red 1 cm berries persisting during most of Winter, all against a dense background of small 1 cm oval deep green leaves on prostrate or wide-spreading branches; similar to microphyllus but taller. *Zone 6.*   p. 830

dammeri (humifusus) (C. China: Hupeh), "Bearberry cotoneaster"; low, prostrate evergreen with rooting branches and forming dense mats; leathery round-ovate leaves 2-3 cm or more long, dark green and shining above, pale beneath; small white flowers with red stamens, from leaf axils, followed by bright red berry-like fruit. *Zones 5-9.*   p. 320

dammeri radicans (China), "Dwarf bearberry"; evergreen depressed creeping shrub, with small, ovate, corrugated, leathery 1 cm leaves; small white flowers, wax-red berries. One of the best as a groundcover. *Zone 5.*   p. 319

dammeri 'Skogholm'; excellent Swedish cultivar, possibly hybrid with C. rotundifolius, introduced by Skogsholmen Arboretum in Malmoe 1950; vigorous evergreen groundcover 30 cm or more high but trailing 3 m wide, the branches curving downward with tips rooting when touching ground; elliptic leaves to 3 cm long, glossy dark green; white 1 cm flowers, followed by matte red 6 mm fruit. *Zone 5.*   p. 320

divaricatus (China), "Spreading cotoneaster"; popular shrub with spreading branches, dense with dark green oval 2 cm leaves turning orange to red in Autumn, and usually deciduous; pink flowers, followed by glossy, oblong red fruit. *Zones 5-9.*   p. 320, 614, 831

franchetii (W. China, Burma); evergreen shrub to 3 m high, fountain-like, with arching branches; thickish, ovate leaves 3 cm long, dull green above; pink flowers, followed by 3 cm scarlet fruit in clusters. *Zone 6.*   p. 832

glaucophyllus (China), "Bright-bead cotoneaster"; evergreen erect arching shrub to 2 m, with oval 5 cm gray-green leaves, closely set; flowers pinkish followed by 1 cm dull red fruits. *Zone 7.* p. 831

glaucophyllus 'Albo-variegata' (serotina); low prostrate evergreen shrub with oval or ovate leathery, 3-5 cm glossy green leaves prettily splashed and variegated creamy-white. Photographed in Bewley Garden, Warrimoo, New So. Wales. *Zone 9.* p. 830

henryanus (Central China: Hupeh); semi-evergreen shrub to 4 m high, with arching branches; leathery, grayish lanceolate, wrinkled leaves 5-12 cm long; numerous white flowers in axillary clusters, followed by dark red ovoid berries, effective in Autumn. Evergreen in mild climate. *Zone 7.* p. 831

horizontalis (China), "Rock cotoneaster"; low, semi-evergreen shrub spreading horizontally over rocks, branching herring-bone-like, and set with dark glossy green, leathery, rounded leaves, 5-12 mm long, small pinkish flowers and later, with coral-red fruit. *Zone 4.* p. 320, 832

lacteus (parneyi) (W. China: Yunnan), "Red cluster-berry"; evergreen to 2 m or more, with arching branches, leathery, corrugated leaves to 5 cm long, deep green above, white-hairy beneath; small white flowers in clusters; followed by long-lasting red fruit. *Zone 7.* p. 831

microphyllus (Himalayas, W. China), "Rockspray cotoneaster"; ornamental low evergreen shrub spreading to 5 m, in an entangled mass of twigs, with lustrous leathery, 1 cm ovate leaves, gray-pubescent beneath; small white flowers, followed by a shower of scarlet berries in Autumn. *Zone 5.* p. 319

microphyllus 'Cochleatus', "Snail cotoneaster"; an excellent clone of more compact habit, with branches prostrate and arching downward, snail-like, and occasionally rooting, the glossy leaves white-pubescent beneath and spirally arranged; small white flowers May-June, followed by red berries. *Zone 5.* p. 319

racemiflorus var. royleanus (W. Asia to Himalaya); deciduous shrub to 2 m high in the species, lower in this variety, with arching branches pubescent when young; the leaves oval to elliptic 2-3 cm long, glossy green above, whitish beneath; small white flowers in clusters along branchlets. *Zone 3.* p. 830

salicifolius (W. China, Szechwan), "Willowleaf cotoneaster"; popular evergreen or semi-deciduous shrub 3 m high, gracefully arching with willow-like narrow lanceolate leaves 4-8 cm long, rugose above and white-felted beneath; flowers white in hairy clusters 5 cm across, and with red anthers, blooming in June; followed by bright red berry-fruits. *Zone 6.* p. 831

x watereri 'Cornubia' (frigidus x henryanus x salicifolius); tall in mild climate evergreen shrub to 6 m high and wide; oval leaves 8-12 cm long, corrugated and with red veins; white flowers; large red fruit in profuse clusters. Rothschild-Exbury hyb. England 1930. *Zone 7.* p. 831

x watereri 'Pendulus' (frigidus x henryanus); low growing, with spreading branches more or less pendant, rooting readily where touching the ground and forming good carpets; as seen in Germany. *Zone 7.* p. 832

COTYLEDON   Crassulaceae

ladismithiensis (Cape Prov.: Karroo), "Club's paws"; attractive branching succulent 30 cm high, with small and thick-fleshy leaves yellowish-green and covered with white hair, 5 cm long, apex claw-like and maroon; shiny flowers pale yellow tinged apricot, darker outside. This species is from Ladismith in the Little Karroo; there is another town in South Africa spelled Ladysmith, Natal. *Subtropic. Zone 10.* p. 181

macrantha (E. Cape Prov.); showy and beautiful succulent to 1 m high, much grown on the Riviera; stout stem with erect branches, dense with fleshy, fresh green obovate, concave leaves edged in red, to 10 cm long; inflorescence on stiff stalk with inflated tubular, nodding flowers intensely red, inside greenish. *Zone 10.* p. 181

simplicifolia: see CHIASTOPHYLLUM oppositifolium

undulata (Cape Prov.), "Silver crown"; beautiful succulent to 50 cm high, with opposite, broad wedge-shaped leaves covered with silver-gray bloom, 8-12 cm long, the crimped apex pure white; inflorescence long-stalked, bearing a cluster of pendant, tubular orange-yellow flowers 2½ cm long, reddish near apex. *Zone 10.* p. 182

COUROUPITA   Lecythidaceae

guianensis (Guyana), the "Cannonball-tree"; tall, soft-wooded, deciduous tree to 15 m high, with armed branches; obovate, serrate 30 cm leaves, and fragrant 12 cm waxy flowers rose-colored inside, orange-yellow outside, borne on the tree-trunk on tangled stems, later followed by the large round 15-20 cm brownish fruits. *Tropical. Zones 10-11.* p. 743

COWANIA   Rosaceae

mexicana (Utah and California to Mexico), "Cliffrose" or "Quinine bush"; dense shrub to 2 m or more high, with aromatic bark; leathery, pinnatifid leaves, and sticky; cream-colored flowers 2-3 cm across, followed by interesting feathery, papery fruit; at home also in Grand Canyon Nat'l Park; Arizona. *Zone 5.* p. 832

CRAMBE   Cruciferae

cordifolia (Caucasus), "Colewort"; striking large herbaceous perennial 1-2 m high; basal, fleshy leaves cordate, to 60 cm across, lightly lobed and toothed; the upper leaves along the stout stems ovate; white 1 cm flowers in great, much branched clusters, in June-July. *Zone 6.* p. 408

maritima (Coast of No. Europe to Black Sea), "Sea kale" or "Scurvy grass"; stocky perennial to 1 m or more high, with thick root and stout stems; basal leaves fleshy, to 60 cm long, lobed or wavy and crenate, glaucous and quite brittle; small white flowers in large terminal cluster, blooming May-June. Grown for succulent edible spring shoots. *Zone 5.* p. 408

CRASSULA   Crassulaceae

alstonii (Cape Prov. and Namibia); small succulent to 10 cm high, slowly clustering, with thick-round gray-green leaves 2 cm broad in four ranks tightly appressed like shingles, and curved inward; stalked clusters of tiny white flowers. *Zones 10-11.* p. 182

arborescens (So. Africa: Namaqualand to Natal), known commercially as argentea or "Silver dollar" or "Silver jade plant"; heavy, branching succulent growing tree-like with thick trunk to 3 m high, the robust branches with boldly fleshy, broad obovate, opposite leaves 4-6 cm long, united at the base, silver gray with reddish dotting and contrasting red margin; starry flowers white, turning pink. Slow growing and rarely blooming. *Arid-subtropic. Zone 10.* p. 183

argentea of 1778 and arborescens of hort.: see C. ovata of 1768

arta (Cape Prov.); small succulent column 10 cm high, of glaucous green, fat triangular opposite leaves with projecting gray markings, 1-2 cm long, arranged in 4 dense rows; flowers pale yellow, suffused with pink. *Zone 10.* p. 181

coccinea (Zander): see ROCHEA coccinea (Hortus)

corymbulosa 'Campfire' ('Flame'); erect-growing plant with gray-green, triangular leaves to 5 cm long, densely shingled in 4 ranks, shorter and more separated upward on floral stalk; inflorescence 30 cm long with red tubular trumpet flowers. The species is from S.E. Cape Prov., So. Africa, and has white blossoms. *Zone 10.* p. 183

falcata (Rochea) (Cape Prov. to Natal), "Scarlet paintbrush" or "Propeller plant"; handsome succulent with wide, flattened and sickle-shaped curved leaves 8-12 cm long, arranged like parallel shingles, rough gray-green, and sending up fleshy stalk with showy terminal cluster to 12 cm across, of bright crimson flowers. *Subtropic. Zone 10.* p. 181

grisea (So. Africa: Namaqualand); small succulent to 15 cm high, the fleshy stem branched from base and upward, dense with thick, lanceolate leaves 3 cm long, and with round keel beneath; tiny white flowers in flat-topped inflorescence. *Zone 10.* p. 182

hemisphaerica (Namibia), "Arab's turban"; small round plant 3-5 cm dia., forming cushions; the rounded leaves are close together, overlapping and curving downwards, dark gray-green and finely fimbriate at edges; inflorescence to 20 cm high, in terminal cluster of tiny white flowers. *Zone 11.* p. 182

'Jade Necklace' (falcata x marnieriana); small succulent shrub, branching from base, having numerous slender erect or arching columns to 20 cm high, the short ovate grayish-green, thick leaves 2 cm long, densely shingled along the wiry stem; at the apex small clusters of starry white flowers. *Zone 10.* p. 183

lactea (Natal, Transvaal), "Tailor's patch"; succulent subshrub 30-60 cm high, with broad, flat, basally united broad-ovate leaves 6 cm long, smooth dark green and spotted white at margins; flowers white and fragrant, in a paniculate cyme. *Zone 10.* p. 183

lycopodioides (Namibia: near Luederitz Bay), "Skinny fingers" or "Toy cypress"; first erect, later spreading lycopodium-like with string-like brittle branches covered tightly with scale-like pointed leaves 4 mm long, in 4 ranks, fresh yellowish-green; minute whitish flowers. *Zone 10.* p. 183

'Morgan's Beauty' (C. mesembryanthemopsis x falcata); charming little clustering plant, dense with irregularly wedge-shaped thick 3-4 cm leaves, covered with pearly gray puckers, bearing a tight cluster of rosy-salmon fragrant flowers with yellow anthers, lasting a long time. Hybrid by Dr. M. Morgan, Richmond, Calif. *Subtropic. Zone 10.* p. 182

ovata (of 1768) (argentea hort. of 1778) (Cape Prov., Natal), known as C. arborescens, the "Jade plant", in the trade, and so listed in Loudon's Encyclopedia of Plants (England 1836); freely-branching or

forking succulent growing to 3 m; leaves spatulate, thick-fleshy, 4-6 cm long, upper surface convex, lower flat, glossy jade-green, turning reddish in the sun, edged red; an old house plant; with age blooming with clusters of small starry, pinkish-white flowers. Crassula argentea (as in Hortus 3): Toelken gives priority to C. ovata (Miller 1768), with synonyms argentea (1778), portulacea (1786), obliqua (1789). (Cactus & Succulent Journal, May 1981). In California horticulture long as C. arborescens hort. C. ovata in Zander 1984. *Subtropic*.
Zone 10.   p. 58, 183

ovata 'Minima variegata' (argentea cultivar of hort.); highly variegated miniature mutation seen in Old Town nursery, San Diego, California; the succulent fleshy leaves 2-3 cm long, largely creamy-white suffused with rose toward margins, and some remnants of milky-green. Not vigorous. *Zone 11*.   p. 182

perforata 'Marginata', "Variegated necklace vine"; very colorful sport of the green-leaved species from the Karroo of South Africa; freely branching and rambling with thin wiry stems, the opposite triangular 1 to 2 cm leaves somewhat thin and recurved, bluish-green with ciliate edges, and margins prettily bordered in ivory-white; small yellow flowers. *Subtropic. Zone 11*.   p. 182

picturata (Cape Prov.: Steynberg Div.); attractive low, stemless rosette with leaves arranged in 4 rows as in a cross, elongate boat-shaped 2-4 cm long, grayish with dark green spots and ciliate margins; small white flowers in clustered inflorescence 5 cm high.
Zone 10.   p. 184

portulacea 'Gollum' ('Hobbit' mutation of convoluta); very curious small succulent with glossy olive-green, club-like leaves 4-5 cm long, curving upward from stem, and with rounded or convex apex; margins reddish. *Zone 10*.   p. 181

pseudolycopodioides hort. (Namibia), "Princess pine"; similar to lycopodioides but more vigorous and freely branching, leaves rich green and spread away from stem which is lax and rambling.
Zone 10.   p. 183

rubicunda of hort.: see ROCHEA coccinea

streyi (South Africa: So. Natal); interesting succulent species resembling peperomia; fleshy reddish stems, branching from base, set with pairs of soft flexible, thin leaves obovate in outline, somewhat cupped, 4-6 cm long and connected at stem, wine-red on reverse; clusters of small white flowers. *Zone 11*.   p. 183

teres (So. Africa and Namibia), "Rattlesnake"; dwarf clustering plant with glaucous cylindric columns, to 10 cm high and 2 cm dia.; closely appressed, glaucous green leaves, having a pale-translucent margin, which gives them a glazed appearance; small fragrant white flowers clustered at apex. *Zone 11*.   p. 183

CRATAEGUS   Rosaceae

aestivalis (So. Carolina to Texas), "May Haw"; deciduous shrub or tree 5-9 m tall, fissured bark red-brown; leaves elliptic 2-7 cm long, crenate at margins, tomentose when young; small white flowers; fruit depressed globose, red at maturity, to 15 mm dia. *Zone 7*.   p. 832

crus-galli (Québec to Michigan, so. to No. Carolina), "Cockspur thorn"; thorny deciduous tree to 10 m high, the wide-spreading branches furnished with straight spines 5-8 cm long; thin-leathery obovate leaves 4-8 cm long, and toothed at margins, turning orange and scarlet in Autumn; inflorescences in large clusters of 2 cm white flowers turning pink, having red anthers in center, and blooming in June; near globular 15 mm fruit dull red, persisting into March. Useful for clipped hedges. *Zone 4*.   p. 833

flava (Virginia to Florida), "Summer haw" or "Yellow-fruited thorn"; deciduous slow-growing shrub or small tree to 6 m high, with scaly bark, and flexuous thorny branches, soft downy when young; ovate or elliptic leathery leaves 2-5 cm long; small white 2 cm flowers displaying red anthers, followed by pyriform 2 cm yellow fruit having firm flesh; of culinary use in jellies. *Zone 5*.   p. 832

irrasa (Québec to New York and Michigan); arborescent shrub spreading into thickets, or up to 4-5 m, with thorny branchlets. Leaves ovate to elliptic 3-5 cm long, serrate and deeply divided into 4-5 pairs of lobes; white flowers 15 mm wide, in clusters; oblong fruit bright red, spindle-shaped 3-4 cm long. *Zone 3*.   p. 833

laevigata (oxyacantha) (Europe, North America, W. Asia), "English hawthorn", in cultivation since ancient times; spiny deciduous, hard-wooded shrub or small tree 2 to 5 m high; twiggy branches with thorns 2½ cm long; glossy 4 to 5 cm lobed leaves, toothed at margins; pretty white flowers in Spring, followed in late Summer by clusters of small red fruit, resembling a miniature apple, edible and sometimes used in jellies. Known in Germany as "Weiss-dorn" for its white blossoms, occasionally rose. *Zone 4*.   p. 833

laevigata 'Paulii' (oxyacantha cv.); very popular cultivar with large clusters of very double crimson-scarlet flowers, widely planted in Western Europe, known locally as "Double-flowered Red-thorn". Introduced in Waltham Cross, England 1866 as 'Paul's Scarlet', in Germany as monogyna 'Kermesina plena', the genuine "Rot-dorn".
Zone 4.   p. 833

monogyna (France to Yugoslavia, No. Africa, Asia), "Single-seed hawthorn"; deciduous, very thorny tree to 10 m high, usually much smaller; leaves rich green and more or less deeply 3 to 7 lobed; not turning to autumn colors; single white 2 cm flowers in axillary clusters, distinct in having one style only and with red anthers, in June; ovoid insipid fruit 1 cm long, containing one stone. Good subject for hedges.
Zone 4.   p. 618, 833

monogyna 'Rosea pendula'; handsome European cultivar seen in Edinburgh, Scotland, with gracefully arching branches, profusely bearing charming single flowers of soft pink, concave petals.
Zone 5.   p. 832

oxyacantha: see C. laevigata

pedicellata (New England to Ontario and Illinois); thorny deciduous tree to 8 m high, with broad-elliptic to ovate leaves partially toothed or sharply lobed toward apex, 5-8 cm long; white flowers 2 cm across, in downy clusters, and reddish anthers; followed by bright red ovoid fruit 6 mm dia. *Zone 5*.   p. 832

x prunifolia (crus-galli x macrantha); deciduous shrub or small tree to 6 m high, often leafy to ground level; having prominent spines 3 to 8 cm long; the broad-ovate leaves to 9 cm long, vivid green, and crenate along margins; white flowers 2 cm across, with pink anthers in rounded clusters, June-blooming; rich crimson glossy globular fruits in Autumn. *Zone 6*.   p. 833

pubescens (Mexico), "Mexican hawthorn" or "Tejocote"; deciduous shrub or small tree to 10 m high, with scarce pubescence and few thorns; elliptic to obovate, glossy green leaves 3 to 9 cm long, serrate at margins; white 2 cm flowers displaying numerous stamens and pink anthers; fruit short pear-shaped to globose, 3 cm dia., yellow shading into orange and dotted; long persisting; edible, with juicy flesh. Photographed in Quail Botanic Gardens, Encinitas, Calif.
Zone 7.   p. 925

viridis (Virginia to Florida, Illinois to Texas), "Green hawthorn"; deciduous tree to 12 m high, with 3-4 cm thorns; elliptic and ovate leaves 6 cm long, of thin texture and smooth except for hairy tufts beneath; clusters of small 1 cm white flowers, followed by orange-red berry-like fruit. *Zone 4*.   p. 832

CRATEVA   Capparaceae

roxburghii (Crataeva Linn.) (Sri Lanka, India to Indochina), "Garlic pear" or "Indian Dalur"; deciduous small tree to 3 m high, with leaves of 3 lanceolate reddish leaflets 5-10 cm long; showy white flowers changing to yellow, with long pinkish stamens, blooming before or with the new leaves; large round or oblong orange-colored edible fruit 6-7 cm long, containing many hard, curiously horseshoe-shaped seeds within the pulp. *Zone 10*.   p. 671

CREMNOPHILA   Crassulaceae

nutans (Sedum) (Mexico: Morelos); smooth succulent rosette 6-10 cm across, with basal rhombic, turgid leaves having rounded margins and keeled beneath, to 7 cm long, grayish with coppery tints; the inflorescence 15-20 cm high, a nodding cluster of small yellow flowers. *Zone 10*.   p. 184

CREPIS   Compositae

aurea (Alps to So. Italy and Balkans), "Yellow hawksbeard"; rhizomatous perennial to 30 cm high; leaves all basal, oblanceolate, 4-lobed and wavy along margins; flowers orange, with spreading linear rays, in Autumn. *Zone 6*.   p. 384

rubra (So. Italy, Dalmatia to Greece, Turkey), "Pink hawksbeard"; tap-rooted annual 25-40 cm high, basal leaves oblanceolate, to 15 cm long, pinnately lobed, or toothed, softly hairy; long-stalked flowers pink or white, daisy-like, 3-4 cm across; blooming quickly from seed, in Autumn. *Zone 6*.   p. 384

CRESCENTIA   Bignoniaceae

cujete (Trop. America), the "Calabash tree"; small tree to 12 m high, with sparry, spreading branches; simple oblanceolate usually clustered leaves to 15 cm long, borne in groups of 2 or more on spurs from axillary buds on thick gray branchlets; flowers bell-shaped 5-8 cm long, yellow with brownish markings; interesting are the melon-like smooth, yellow to black fruit 12-30 cm or more dia., like a hard-shelled gourd, on its trunk and older branches; like gourds they can be tied around their girth as they mature to produce unusual forms, for making into cups or other vessels in tropical lands.
Zone 10.   p. 663, 904

CRINDONNA memoria-corsii: see x AMARCRINUM

CRINODENDRON   Elaeocarpaceae

hookerianum (Chile), "Lantern tree"; interesting evergreen tree to 8 m high, usually with several trunks; narrow lanceolate leathery leaves 5-12 cm long, hairy along main veins beneath; beautiful pendant urn-shaped or lantern-like rich crimson-red flowers, with petals curving inward, 3 cm long; wonderful as garden shrub, hardy as far North as Scotland, blooming May-June in North. Hemisphere.
Zone 6.   p. 697

patagua (Tricuspidaria lanceolata) (Chile), "White lily-tree" or "Flowering oak"; evergreen tree 6 to 10 m or more high, with leathery elliptic leaves 3 to 8 cm long, dark green above, gray beneath, and with toothed margins; the charming, nodding, waxy flowers cup-shaped, with petals white, not curving inward, 2 cm long, followed by leathery red fruit capsules. *Zone 10.* p. 697

CRINUM *Amaryllidaceae*

amabile (Sumatra), "Giant spider lily"; large bulbous plant with neck to 30 cm long, crowned by rosette of fleshy leaves shaded purple, 10 cm wide and 1 m long; robust floral stalk bearing fragrant flowers with red tube, and red down center of the white segments 12 cm long. *Tropical. Zone 10.* p. 211

americanum (Florida to Texas), "Swamp-lily"; bulbous plant with 6-10 arching leaves 4-5 cm wide; 45-60 cm stalk bearing umbel of fragrant, creamy-white flowers with greenish tube, linear segments, and purplish anthers; in Winter and Spring, usually preceding leaves. *Zone 9.* p. 211

asiaticum (Trop. So. Asia, Melanesia), known as "Poison-bulb"; showy, large rosette with bulb-like roots, very decorative alone for its numerous broad, sword-like, fleshy, yellow-green leaves 8-12 cm wide, with broad clasping base, center rib depressed, 1-1½ m long; the white waxy flowers between foliage, with narrow, pointed petals inside purple-red; Melanesian maidens wear these fragrant blooms in their black hair. *Tropical. Zones 9-10.* p. 211

augustum (amabile hort.) (Mauritius, Seychelles), "Queen Emma lily"; sturdy plant with bulb sometimes 15 cm thick and 30 cm neck; many leaves 8-10 cm broad; numerous fragrant flowers on 1-1½ m stalk, the lanceolate segments deep wine-red outside, lighter inside. *Tropical. Zone 10.* p. 211

bulbispermum (capense, longifolium) (So. Africa); probably the most common Crinum, with relatively narrow leaves and funnel-form flowers white, flushed rose, with curved tube 10 cm long, to 12 blooms in umbels. *Zones 8-9.* p. 211

erubescens (So. Mexico, C. America, to Brazil); attractive bulbous plant related to americanum but larger; thin strap-like foliage; salver-form flowers with spreading segments 5 to 8 cm long, white inside, keeled bright wine-red outside, on long tube and with bright red filaments, in umbels on stalks 60 cm long; blooming Mid-summer to Autumn. *Zone 10.* p. 210

macowanii (Transvaal, Natal, Zimbabwe); large bulb to 20 cm thick with persistent strap-shaped fleshy leaves to 1 m long and 10 cm wide; lily-like white flowers tinged purple, greenish on tube, 10 cm long, in umbels. *Zone 9.* p. 210

moorei (So. Africa: Natal), "Longneck swamp lily"; herbaceous plant from a large bulb with stem-like neck to 30 cm; broad and thin, smooth-edged, somewhat wavy, bright green leaves 60-90 cm long; showy, lily-like, soft rose bell-shaped fragrant flowers 12 cm or more across, very attractive with pink filaments, 6 to 8 blooms to a cluster, on stout stalk, during Summer; free bloomer. *Zone 9.* p. 211

x powellii (bulbispermum x moorei), "Powell's swamp lily"; a spectacular old English hybrid (1732), with globose bulb, carrying abundant, decorative foliage, about 20 sword-shaped leaves to 120 cm long; a 60-90 cm firm floral stalk appears in Summer, crowned by a cluster of up to 10 trumpet-shaped flowers 10 cm long, generally deep rose, and opening in succession; blooming at a time when there are few other bulbous plants of its stature or beauty in flower. Slightly hardy. *Subtropic. Zones 8-9.* p. 211

x powellii 'Roseum'; handsome evergreen variety with long recurving, glossy green leaves; stiff erect stalks carrying clusters of soft pink trumpet flowers. *Subtropic. Zone 9.* p. 211

CROCOSMIA *Iridaceae*

x crocosmaeflora (Crocosmia aurea x Tritonia pottsii), known in horticulture as "Montbretia"; a popular hybrid much cultivated as cut flower and widely planted in mild climate gardens; charming cormous plant with 4 soft light green, sword-shaped leaves 2 cm wide on either side of the floral stalk, with many parallel ribs; branched sprays 50 cm or more high, with curved funnel flowers in long one-sided spikes, the waxy corolla 3-4 cm long, with segments flaring wide and a flaming orange-crimson, lasting a long time on the plant or 2 weeks and more as cut flowers; somewhat winter-hardy with protection. *Subtropic. Zones 8-9.* p. 223

masoniorum (Tritonia) (So. Africa: Transvaal), "Golden swan tritonia"; magnificent cormous herb forming clumps of ribbed, sword-shaped basal leaves 75 cm long and 5 cm wide; branched arching stems bearing two-tiered spike-like clusters of starry flowers glowing orange-scarlet, 4 cm across, and blooming July or August; similar to Tritonia crocosmaeflora, the "Montbretia" of gardens, but with broader foliage, broader flower segments of deeper red, and inflorescence more pendant. Goes dormant during Winter. Not winter-hardy. *Subtropic. Zones 8-9.* p. 223

pottsii (So. Africa: Natal, Zululand), the "Slender tritonia"; this species resembles the garden montbretia, T. crocosmaeflora, but the flowers are more narrow and are a rich crimson; each flower has a curved slender tube about 4 cm long with 6 short petals which do not open very wide; the flower spike has numerous flowers open at the same time and buds continue to open in Mid-summer; lateral spikes spring from the main stalk, growing to nearly 1 m tall, subtended by the bluish-green leaves. *Subtropic. Zones 9-10.* p. 223

CROCUS *Iridaceae*

chrysanthus 'Blue Pearl' (chrysanthus: Bulgaria to Greece and Asia Minor), "Snow Crocus"; bulbous herb having stiff fibers at apex of 2 cm corm; sprouting 4-6 keeled, narrow leaves to 30 cm long, appearing after bloom; flowers 10 cm long, usually yellow in the species; cv. 'Blue Pearl' lavender outside, white inside and yellow throat; in late Winter. *Zone 4.* p. 224

etruscus (species origin Toscana, Italy); leaves very narrow, appearing with the flowers; freely blooming in early Spring, the blossoms 10 cm long, lilac shading to purple, yellow in throat. *Zone 4.* p. 224

flavus (aureus) (Yugoslavia to Turkey); cormous plant forming 6-8 narrow-linear leaves appearing with the flowers, these cup-shaped orange-yellow to 16 cm high and blooming late Winter into Spring. Excellent for naturalizing in gardens. *Zone 4.* p. 225

medius (Maritime Alps of S.E. France, No. Italy); showy species with scarlet stigmas and deep lilac petals, expanding widely; flowers to 25 cm long; 3-4 leaves appearing after autumn blooming. *Zone 6.* p. 224

niveus (Mts. of South Greece); robust plant with 4-6 leaves appearing with the flowers; blooms pale lilac or white with some green veins, to 24 cm long, throat yellow, in late Autumn. *Zone 7.* p. 224

sativus (Italy to Greece and Asia Minor), "Saffron crocus"; distinguished bulbous herb with globular depressed corm, forming many grass-like leaves after bloom; large fragrant flowers bluish-lilac, veined purple inside; spreading segments to 5 cm long, anthers orange-yellow, the divided stigma brilliant scarlet. Widely cultivated commercially in Spain where the flowers are collected in baskets into October, to produce the costly saffron. Since ancient times, the stigmas are separated and dried or dehydrated into the finished golden threads of saffron. Formerly used medicinally in teas, it is also treasured as a spice for flavoring and coloring in cooking and baking. The vivid yellow robes of Buddhist monks are traditionally dyed with saffron. *Zone 6.* p. 225, 528

sieberi (Greece, Crete); winter-blooming small cormous species with basal grass-like leaves; showy erect flowers with 3 cm segments spreading, varying from lilac to white, darker streaked outside, anthers and stigmas orange; in late Winter to Spring. *Zone 7.* p. 225

speciosus (S.E. Europe to Turkey and Iran), "Autumn-flowering crocus"; cormous plant with 4-5 grass-like, linear leaves, appearing after blooming; the short-stalked flowers with spreading segments 5-6 cm long, the petals bluish-lilac feathered with purple veins inside, blooming September-October. *Warm-temperate. Zones 6-7.* p. 225

speciosus albus; autumn-blooming variety with flowers crystallic white, the spreading segments 5 cm long; the filaments white, and anthers orange. *Zone 6.* p. 224

tomasinianus (Hungary to Dalmatia); leaves appearing with or shortly after flower; blooms lilac to purple with white throat, to 14 cm long, in early Spring. *Zone 5.* p. 224

tournefortii (Greek Islands); cormous species with 3-4 leaves appearing before or with the blooms; flowers soft rosy-lilac and yellow in throat, always open at night; the tube 5 cm long, the anthers white and branched style scarlet; in Autumn. *Zone 9.* p. 225

vallicola (Caucasus), "Autumn crocus"; attractive cormous herb; grass-like leaves to 25 cm long, with an obscure white band; buff floral tube 10 cm long, and wide-spreading pale cream petals 60 cm long veined internally with several purple lines, and orange spots in throat. *Zone 5.* p. 223

vernus 'Giant Purple', large-flowered "Dutch crocus", developed from the species at home in Austria and Italy; well-known for early spring-blooming in gardens; lovely cupped flowers 20 cm or more high, glowing purple with orange stigmas. Dutch hybrids tend to naturalize and return the following year better than species. *Zone 4.* p. 224

vernus 'Orange'; early spring-blooming Dutch hybrid with substantial flowers glowing orange-yellow; the linear leaves rich green with white center band. *Zone 4.* p. 225

vernus 'Pickwick'; "Dutch crocus" with beautiful oval blooms pale silver-lilac with purple stripes, to 24 cm high, orange stigma inside, in Spring. Ideal for bowls. *Zone 4.* p. 224

vernus 'Purpureus'; showy Dutch hybrid with sturdy flowers rich purple outside, inside shading to lilac and white toward base; contrasting red stigma; linear leaves with ivory center band. *Zone 4.* p. 225

CROSSANDRA *Acanthaceae*

infundibuliformis (undulaefolia) (India), "Firecracker-flower"; shrubby plant with glossy, ovate leaves; showy salmon-red tubular flowers with split limb, in angled, bracted spike. While grown in our greenhouses as a small 10 cm potplant, I have seen these in India and Ceylon as an ever-blooming 1 m bush. *Tropical. Zone 11.* p. 17

CROTALARIA *Leguminosae*

agatiflora (ageratifolia) (Trop. E. Africa), "Canary-bird bush", "Rattle-box", "Lion's claw"; shrub to 1 m high, with green branches; leaves 3-foliolate, consisting of 3 ovate leaflets 8 cm long; flowers very large, pale greenish-yellow, pointed keel dull brownish-purple at tip, 4 cm long; fruits are small pods with seeds which rattle in the wind. *Zone 10.* p. 757

juncea (India to Australia), "Bengal hemp" or "Sunn-hemp"; branching annual herb with silky-downy stems 1 m or more high; linear-oblong leaves to 10 cm long, downy beneath; flowers rich yellow and pea-like with reflexed banner-petal, 4 cm across, in terminal racemes, blooming August-September. Sunn-hemp is cultivated for its fiber to make ropes, canvas, and paper, used for thousands of years, as reported in Sanskrit literature. *Zone 10.* p. 440

laburnifolia (Australia), "Queensland bird-flower"; interesting shrub 2 m or more high with leaves of 3 ovate to oblong leaflets 3-4 cm long; bird-like greenish-yellow pea-flowers 4-5 cm long, hanging by their beaks to the stems. *Zone 10.* p. 757

CROTON *Euphorbiaceae*

alabamensis (C. Alabama); evergreen shrub 2-3 m tall, with grayish-white bark, to 6 cm thick; oblong leaves with silvery scales or rusty, the upper to 5 cm long; floral racemes 2 to 5 cm long, with numerous staminate flowers; pistillate flowers with scaly tubular petals pale pink. *Zone 9.* p. 721

insularis (Queensland), "Cascarilla"; attractive small semi-evergreen tree to 5 m high, branching closely to ground, dense with small ovate, glossy green leaves, changing to red in Autumn before falling, but are followed throughout the year by young foliage; small nonconspicuous whitish flowers in attractive cylindric racemes. *Zone 10.* p. 720

CROTON of hort.: see CODIAEUM

CRUCIANELLA *Rubiaceae*

stylosa 'Rubra' (stylosa: Iran, Asia Minor to Caucasus), "Crosswort"; low perennial 15-20 cm high, also grown as annual, with prostrate, 4-angled leafy branches; leaves narrow-lanceolate 6-9 in a whorl, and having revolute, thorny-hairy margins; the inflorescence in ball-shaped heads 2 cm dia., of tiny rose-red tubular flowers with 5 spreading lobes, blooming June-August. *Zone 8.* p. 494

CRYPTANTHUS *Bromeliaceae*

beuckeri (Brazil), "Marbled spoon"; irregular rosette of flat, thin leathery spoon-shaped leaves with slender point, rich green marbling on pale green; flowers whitish. *Tropical. Zone 12.* p. 44

bivittatus minor(roseus pictus in hort.; bivittatus atropurpureus according to H. Luther, Florida) (Brazil), "Rose-stripe star"; flattened, small, star-like terrestrial rosette satiny olive-green with two pale bands, overcast with salmon-rose, turning coppery red in strong light; finely toothed, 10 to 15 cm dia. *Zone 11.* p. 44

bivittatus tricolor; handsome large rosette of narrow lanceolate, stiff leathery leaves to 20 cm long, olive-green with cream-white marginal bands tinged rose, crisped and wavy along sides. *Humid-tropical. Zone 11.* p. 49

zonatus 'Zebrinus' (fuscus), "Zebra plant"; strikingly beautiful form with bronzy purple long wavy leaves, the pronounced silvery to beige crossbanding resembling those of a zebra. C. zonatus is from Pernambuco, a rosette to 45 cm across. *Tropical. Zone 12.* p. 44

CRYPTOCEREUS *Cactaceae*

anthonyanus (Chiapas), "Anthony's rick-rack"; nightblooming climber of the rain forest, using aerial roots; unusual deeply lobed stems looking like fish bones; flowers intensely fragrant, lasting but a single night, beautifully colored burning red with cream-yellow petals. *Tropical. Zone 11.* p. 176

CRYPTOCORYNE *Araceae*

albida (Burma); tropical rhizomatous plant growing in warm 23 to 28° C shallow water; long-stalked lanceolate, light green quilted leaves 7-12 cm long and 1-1½ cm wide; a 7-10 cm spathe with twisted tube, opening into long lanceolate blade white or yellowish with purple spots. *Zone 12.* p. 26

aponogetifolia (usteriana) (Philippines: Luzon); tropical aquatic growing in fresh water, from creeping rhizomes with long stolons; leaves submersed or floating, narrow-elliptic, 12-50 cm long, dark

green and blistered above; inflorescence with 6 cm twisted spathe, purple inside. *Zone 11.* p. 327

cordata 'Rosanervis' (Malaya; Borneo; Java) "Water trumpet"; beautiful tropical bog plant with creeping rhizome; the leaves to 10 cm long, olive-green, reddish-purple beneath; in mature stage broadly elliptic or cordate; in the juvenile phase usually seen in aquaria, it has leafblades oblong-lanceolate; spathe 20 cm long, the tube pale rose, recurved blade purple and inside yellow. The cv. 'Rosanervis' in col. Munich Bot. Garden has leaf blades veined with rose. *Zone 11.* p. 326

pondederiifolia (West Sumatra); tropical waterside herb with creeping rhizome; light green ovate leaves 6-12 cm long, on 10-20 cm green petioles; short inflorescence with spathe tubular at base, opening wide, yellow to reddish inside. *Zone 12.* p. 26

CRYPTOGRAMMA *Polypodiaceae (Filices)*

crispa (Arctic, No. Europe and adjacent No. Asia); "European parsley fern" or "Rock brake"; small tufted fern spreading by runners; densely clustered leaves 2 to 4 pinnate, 5-10 cm long, the fertile fronds with tips of pinnae inrolled; deciduous in cold winter climate. *Zones 2-8.* p. 131

CRYPTOMERIA *Taxodiaceae (Coniferae)*

japonica (Japan and C. China), "Japanese cedar"; graceful evergreen tree of pyramidal habit and somber appearance to 50 m tall, with reddish-brown bark peeling in strips; the branches spreading and slightly pendulous, clothed with short 1-2 cm needle-like green leaves turning brownish in Winter; roundish female cones globose 2 cm dia. *Zone 6.* p. 607, 612, 628

japonica 'Bandai Sugi'; most unusual dwarf cultivar of very irregular, broadly conical habit, with variously sized foliage, some on strong leaders, others in tightly packed clusters of miniature foliage, creating an artistic effect; in Winter the needles turn greenish-brown. *Zone 6.* p. 612

japonica 'Dacrydioides' (1867 cv.); handsome evergreen tree, while young of compact, shrub-like habit; branches slender, with short, stiff bronzy green, closely arranged needles, 6-8 mm long, partly smaller and scale-like in older trees. *Zone 5.* p. 612

japonica 'Lobbii' (Japan: Kyushu); compact pyramidal tree 20-30 m high, densely branched, branches shorter than the species, slightly decurving; longer, pointed branchlets with leaves sickle-shaped and densely set, directed forward, 1 cm long, flat and glossy light green, not changing color in Winter. *Zone 5.* p. 612

CRYPTOSTEGIA *Asclepiadaceae*

grandiflora (Mascarene Islands, Mauritius), "India rubber-vine" or "Purple allamanda"; scandent tropical shrub with willowy, climbing branches, bearing opposite, glossy green soft-leathery leaves with ivory midrib, 10 cm long; large bell-shaped flowers 5 cm across, white inside, and reddish-purple outside, changing with age to pink. Cultivated in India for rubber-yielding latex; plants however are poisonous. *Tropical. Zones 10-11.* p. 267

CRYPTOSTYLIS *Orchidaceae*

arachnites (Malaya, Sumatra, Java); curious tropical terrestrial orchid having fleshy rhizome creeping under the surface; the rising ovate leaves to 20 cm long, handsome with a network of darker veins; erect inflorescence to 60 cm tall, bearing numerous spidery flowers, sepals and petals greenish, the lip with purple. *Zone 12.* p. 87

CTENANTHE *Marantaceae*

sp. 'Burle Marx' (Stromanthe amabilis hort.) (Brazil); handsome small tropical ornamental of compact habit; short vaginate petioles hold the broad-oval or obovate, leathery leaves 12-15 cm long, waxy deep green with silver-green feather design on surface, purple on underside. *Zone 11.* p. 72

oppenheimiana 'Tricolor', (Brazil) "Never-never plant"; very colorful tufted variety with narrow leaves, highly variegated white over green and silver-gray, their wine-red underside in vivid contrast, and showing through the surface. *Tropical. Zone 12.* p. 72

stromata (Brazil); attractive low bushy plant of stiffish, thin-leathery foliage; leaves broad oblong, 10-12 cm long, with squared-off apex, silver-gray with dark green herring-bone pattern; reverse deep purple. *Tropical. Zone 11.* p. 72

CUCUMIS *Cucurbitaceae*

melo var. cantalupensis hort. (reticulatus group) (W. Africa), "Cantaloupe melon"; herbaceous annual vine with trailing tendrilled rough-hairy stem; the leaves deeply lobed to kidney-shaped or round-ovate; yellow flowers 3 cm across; the female blooms develop the showy globular to oblong fruit 15-25 cm long, having hard rind slightly ribbed with corky surface, the firm flesh bright orange and musk-scented, juicy sweet and delicious when eaten fresh. *Zone 10.* p. 911

melo var. inodorus, "Honey-dew melon"; soft hairy herbaceous annual with prostrate vines; large, roundish, angled leaves; yellow flowers followed by smooth-skinned globular fruit to about 20 cm dia., with silvery-cream to pale green rind; crisp, usually green to white, very juicy flesh of delicious sweet flavor when fully ripe, and holding numerous flat seeds. A favorite eaten fresh for desserts. *Zone 10.* *p. 911*

metuliferus (Transvaal), "Kiwano fruit", "Horned cucumber" or "Horned melon"; sticky-hairy, tendril-climbing annual, with leaves broadly ovate-cordate or heart-shaped, more or less trilobed and toothed; the flowers yellow as in melons; the curious fleshy, oblong fruit is green with silvery design, 8-12 cm long, orange-red when ripe, and covered by bold spines; the inside with many flat seeds, imbedded in greenish jellied flesh, which is eaten together with the seeds, combining the tastes of banana and limes. *Zone 10.* *p. 906*

sativus (W. Trop. Asia), the "Cucumber"; rough-hairy annual trailing or tendril-climbing vine with herbaceous, lobed leaves; male and female yellow flowers 2-3 cm across; cylindric oblong edible fruit smooth or prickly, green with pale marbling; used for salads and pickles. The pictured cultivar 'Patio Pik' (Geo. Ball, W. Chicago 1973) is adapted for growing on trellis in containers on the patio, for both ornamental and culinary purpose. *Tropical. Zone 11.* *p. 911*

CUCURBITA   *Cucurbitaceae*

ficifolia (Trop. America), "Figleaf gourd" or "Malabar gourd"; tender ornamental herbaceous, long-running vine, perennial in warm climates, with kidney-shaped leaves sinuate or lobed along margins; yellow flowers, followed by large rounded fruit to 30 cm long, olive-green with pale mottling and white stripes; the white flesh is not very tasteful; seeds are black. *Zone 10.* *p. 276*

maxima (So. America origin), "Squash"; tendril-bearing herbaceous, running vine, slightly prickly, with large, orbicular, lobed leaves, rough to the touch; yellow flowers with soft corolla, the female flowers producing the vegetable squash. The "Winter butternut squash" is of very curious, oblong flask-shape, 25 cm long, the skin cream-colored, flesh deep orange, and of excellent flavor. Winter squash ripens in Autumn and Winter, and is commonly eaten when baked. *Zone 10.* *p. 911*

moschata, "Canada squash" or "Cushaw"; a squash with ornamental and edible fruit of variable shapes, rounded, oblong, or crookneck; with soft-hairy leaves more rounded than C. pepo; herbaceous annual, spreading with tendril bearing vining and rooting stem, the leaves cordate at base; flowers yellow with crinkled corolla, and spreading lobes; the fruit on angled stalk, ripening in Autumn and Winter, with its yellow flesh is used for culinary purposes, normally cooked or pickled, also used in canning. *Zone 10.* *p. 910*

pepo (Trop. America), "Winter squash" or ornamental "Gourd"; herbaceous annual with prickly vines and harsh, rugose lobed leaves and yellow flowers; producing hard-shelled, so-called winter squash with woody rinds and firm, close-grained, fine-flavored flesh, and used for baking and pies. They come in various shapes, such as the cv. 'Langeniformis' or 'Bottle gourd', about 30 cm long, grown as an ornamental, very much so in Japan, draped over trellis or bamboo frames. *Zone 10.* *p. 285*

pepo 'Funny Face', "Autumn pumpkin"; ideal for Halloween; handsome large orange-colored globose pumpkin-squash weighing 5 to 10 kg (about 10-20 lbs), ripening in Autumn, and growing from a rough vine with furrowed stems; the leaves ovate-triangular, often deeply lobed; flowers are yellow. The soft flesh inside the fruit makes delicious pies; the black seeds are used medicinally, and are edible when roasted. The hard shells are carved into funny faces or Jack-o-lanterns lighted by candles in advent of All Saints. Photographed in California end of October. *Zone 10.* *p. 911*

pepo melopepo (Trop. America), "Banana squash" or "Bush pumpkin"; bush variety of various shapes, turban, warted and banana, as in the var. melopepo or the "Banana squash"; with curved cylindric, pale yellow fruit 30-40 cm long, ripening Summer and Autumn; photographed in Vista, California. *Zone 10.* *p. 911*

pepo 'Pyriformis' (ovifera), pear-shaped "Ornamental gourd"; herbaceous spreading vine with typically yellow flowers, and very hard-shelled, mostly ornamental fruit, as distinguished from the white-flowered Lagenaria; gourds come in many different shapes and colors, such as Pear, Bottle, Banana or Turban. They will grow in zones 3 and 4 during Summer, but may not ripen in time before frost. *Zone 10.* *p. 276*

CUDRANIA   *Moraceae*

tricuspidata (China, Korea, Japan), "Silkworm thorn" or "Vanicria"; deciduous tree to 6 m high, with thorny branches but smooth young shoots; ovate or obovate leaves 4 to 8 cm long, sometimes 3-lobed at apex; small green flowers in globose clusters, followed by orange-red, edible berries of 3 cm dia. The foliage has been used as food for silkworms. *Zone 6.* *p. 790*

CUNILA   *Labiatae*

origanoides (mariana) (E. No. America), "American dittany" or "Sweet horsemint"; aromatic herbaceous perennial 20-40 cm high, with ovate leaves 2-6 cm long, crenate along margins; small purplish-pink flowers in whorls toward apex of branches. Used for seasoning in culinary dishes. *Zone 5.* *p. 532*

CUNNINGHAMIA   *Taxodiaceae (Coniferae)*

lanceolata (China), "China fir", or "Mao Chia" in Taiwan; when visiting China, I confused this handsome tree with Araucaria bidwillii which it closely resembles, but the glossy dark green 6 cm needles are narrower, more close, and finely serrate. Picturesque evergreen 10 to 25 m high, with heavy trunk, stout whorled branches and drooping branchlets; interesting brown cones 3-4 cm across. *Warm Temperate to Subtropic. Zone 7.* *p. 609*

CUNONIA   *Cunoniaceae*

capensis (So. Africa), "African red alder"; small evergreen tree with pinnate, leathery glossy green leaves with toothed margins, on reddish petioles; dense feathery axillary racemes of white flowers; attractive cool house decorator. *Subtropic. Zone 9.* *p. 695*

CUPANIOPSIS   *Sapindaceae*

anacardioides (anacardiopsis) (Australia: New So. Wales), "Tuckeroo" or "Carrot-wood"; evergreen tree to 10 m high; pinnate leaves with 5-10 obovate, leathery leaflets to 15 cm long; small white flowers in axillary clusters; fruit a 3-lobed capsule 2 cm dia. *Subtropic. Zone 9.* *p. 867*

CUPHEA   *Lythraceae*

ignea (platycentra) (Mexico, Jamaica), "Cigar flower"; low herbaceous subshrub with slender stems, lanceolate leaves and solitary axillary flowers having a slender, bright scarlet calyx 2½ cm long, with white mouth and dark ring at end, without petals. *Zone 10.* *p. 774*

lanceolata ('Firefly') (procumbens) (Mexico), "Lanceleaf cigar-flower"; attractive subshrub with sticky-hairy stems to 1 m or more high; opposite hairy, lanceolate leaves to 8 cm long, prominently veined beneath; small but showy, pretty flowers having 6 petals, violet or purple in the species, crimson-red in 'Firefly', and yellow inside, the stamens with red beards. *Zone 10.* *p. 774*

CUPRESSOCYPARIS   *Cupressaceae (Coniferae)*

'Leylandii' (Chamaecyparis nootkatensis x Cupressus macro-carpa), "Leyland cypress"; very ornamental with red stems, and striking green, flattened branchlets; cones 1½-2 cm dia. Fast growing bigeneric hybrid widely planted in Europe, with age as evergreen tree to 25 m tall, of dense pyramidal habit. *Zone 5.* *p. 575*

leylandii 'Castle Wellan', "Golden Leyland cypress"; strong growing, upright form densely branching, minimizing the need for trimming; the new growth golden-yellow. *Zones 6-9.* *p. 575*

CUPRESSUS   *Cupressaceae (Coniferae)*

arizonica (Arizona, Mexico), "Arizona cypress"; evergreen tree to 12 m high, having rough bark; the erect branches dividing into slender branchlets covered by small scale-like, glaucous green to bluish leaves; female cones to 3 cm across and glaucous. Much planted in Southwest U.S., being tolerant of arid conditions. Also popular as small plants in dish-gardens. *Zone 7.* *p. 575*

arizonica columnaris (So. Arizona, Mexico); stately evergreen conifer of erect, pyramidal habit, elegantly branched outward, the trunk covered by rough, resinous bark; the branches dense with slender twigs, sheathed by small appressed bluish scales. *Zone 8.* *p. 575*

cashmeriana (Himalayas, Tibet), "Kashmir cypress"; considered the most beautiful and elegant of all cypresses, with graceful weeping branchlets of silvery gray-green, from a pyramidal tree to 5 m or more high; the cones to 2 cm dia., greenish to brown, with scales tipped by recurved spine. *Zones 8-10.* *p. 576*

funebris: see CHAMAECYPARIS funebris

glabra (arizonica bonita) (Cent. Arizona), "Smooth Arizona cypress"; coniferous tree of arid region, to 20 m high; shedding its outer bark annually and revealing the thin, cherry-red inner bark; branches erect and closely arranged; the branchlets irregularly divided into prickly sprays; leaves scale-like, in 4 ranks closely overlapping and bluish-glaucous; small cones 2 cm wide, of 6-8 scales. *Zone 7.* *p. 575*

goveniana (Monterey County, Calif.), "Gowen cypress"; elegant coniferous tree to 6 m or more high, cone-shaped when young; with gray bark becoming rough; branches and branchlets red-brown; scale-like, appressed bright green leaves, fragrant when crushed; globose female cones 2 cm dia.. *Zone 9.* *p. 576*

lusitanica (Mexico, Guatemala, Costa Rica), "Mexican cypress"; evergreen tree to 30 m, with red-brown bark splitting in long strands;

branches widely spreading, with branchlets more or less pendulous; small appressed, pointed needles glaucous green; cones 1 cm dia. and glaucous. *Zone 8.*   *p. 619*

macrocarpa (California), "Monterey cypress"; beautiful evergreen tree to 20 m high, pyramidal when young and with bright green opposite, linear needles; spreading and picturesque in old age, and with leaves appressed and scale-like; the globular brown female cones 3 cm dia. *Zone 7.*   *p. 576, 577*

macrocarpa 'Aurea', "Golden Monterey cypress"; New Zealand cultivar, handsome evergreen with branches of horizontal habit and golden foliaged. *Zone 9.*   *p. 576*

macrocarpa 'Goldcrest'; golden leaf cultivar of delicate appearance, originated in Cornwall, England; much used in Europe for indoors or patios, in tubs; often grown in form of standards, as seen in Holland. *Zone 8.*   *p. 576*

sempervirens (So. Europe, W. Asia, No. India), "Mediterranean cypress"; the classic conical cypress of the Greek and Roman writers, with very short branches, usually, but not always forming a dense, narrow column slowly to 20 m or more high; the stout branchlets with scale-like leaves dark green with grayish cast in 4 ranks; small 3 cm woody cones. Esteemed for formal effect because of its stiff, picturesque outline. Suitable in containers for warm, sunny places; cool in Winter. *Subtropic. Zones 7-9.*   *p. 576, 579, 616, 624*

sempervirens 'Fastigiata' hort., 'Pyramidal Italian cypress"; according to Hortus, possibly synonymous with 'Stricta'; slender candle-like columns to 15 cm high, with bluish-green needles, seen along roadside in subtropic Thessaly, Northern Greece. *Zone 8.*   *p. 577*

sempervirens 'Glauca', "Blue Italian cypress"; slender columnar evergreen to 20 m high, of symmetrical narrow habit and bluish coloring is well suited to tall buildings and roadside use, also as tubbed specimen in patios. *Zones 7-9*   *p. 576*

sempervirens 'Stricta', "Columnar Italian cypress"; branches densely erect, forming a slender, dark green pyramid, to 20 m high; very much a feature of the Mediterranean landscape. *Zone 7. p. 576*

CURCULIGO   *Amaryllidaceae or Hypoxidaceae*
latifolia (Malacca), "Palmgrass"; herbaceous plant with tuberous rhizome, bearing folded curving leaves to 60 cm long and 12 cm wide; inflorescence of creamy-yellow flowers near the ground on short stalks. *Zone 10.*   *p. 210*

CURCUMA   *Zingiberaceae*
aeruginosa (Thailand: Burma, now Myanmar); tropical perennial with tuberous root, short leafy stem, and interesting inflorescence, appearing before the leaves, a spike to 20 cm long with fleshy shingled bracts, red on upper half and greenish on lower, the nesting flowers yellow; sessile, lance-shaped leaves 50-90 cm long. *Zone 11.*   *p. 522*

roscoeana (Burma, now Myanmar), "Hidden lily"; robust, perennial herb with tuberous roots, sending up 6-8 long-stalked, lanceolate, ribbed, handsome leaves with dark green nerves; the inflorescence a splendid spike about 20 cm long, with cone-like, showy bracts gradually changing from green to vivid scarlet-orange; corolla yellow, with rich golden lip. *Tropical. Zone 11.*   *p. 521*

CURMERIA wallisii: see HOMALOMENA wallisii

CURRANIA dryopteris and **robertiana** (Zander): see GYMNOCAPPIUM

CURTONUS   *Iridaceae*
paniculatus (Antholyza) (Transvaal, Natal), known as "Pleated leaves" in South Africa; cormous plant with distinct and decorative foliage, arranged in flat tufts and growing stiffly to nearly 1 m, tapering toward both ends, 8 cm wide and deeply knife-pleated and a pleasant green; tubular flowers deep rusty or orange-red on zigzag spikes; blooming in South Africa's Autumn February-March, in the Northern Hemisphere in August-September; dormant during Winter. *Zone 9.*   *p. 223*

CUSSONIA   *Araliaceae*
holstii (E. Africa: Kenya), "Cabbage tree"; small shapely tree with slender stem and handsome leathery foliage deep glossy green, stalked ovate leaflets with crenate margins, palmately compound and carried on long wiry petioles. *Zone 9.*   *p. 647*

paniculata (So. Africa), "Cabbage tree"; evergreen small tree forming rosette of heavy fleshy leaves palmately compound, the 7-12 grayish leaflets 15-30 cm long, having serrate and lobed margins, and covered with silvery bloom; on single trunk to 3 m high. *Subtropic. Zone 9.*   *p. 651*

spicata (Transvaal), "Spiked cabbage tree"; evergreen tree with handsome leathery leaves palmately compound of 5 to 9 leaflets, each 8 to 12 cm long; the smooth, grayish-green segments dentately cut or lobed again, and arranged in flat rosettes. *Zone 9.*   *p. 647*

CUTHBERTIA   *Commelinaceae*
rosea (Tripogandra rosea or Tradescantia rosea) (Coastal regions No. Carolina to Florida); perennial forming tufts to 50 cm high, with zigzag stems; narrow, almost grass-like leaves; stalks 40 cm long bearing bright rose or pink flowers, 4 cm across. *Zone 8.*   *p. 368*

CYANOTIS   *Commelinaceae*
somaliensis (Somalia), "Pussy ears"; succulent little creeper with linear, clasping, glossy green leaves covered with soft white hair, 3-4 cm long; flowers purple and orange. *Zones 10-11.*   *p. 308*

CYATHEA   *Cyatheaceae (Filices)*
arborea (mountains of Puerto Rico to Jamaica), "West Indian treefern"; slender treefern to 15 m high, with mostly bare brown trunk, the upper part covered with pale brown scales, and crowned by bipinnate, finely toothed, ample fronds soft-textured, fresh green, paler below, and without spines. Very graceful in appearance. *Humid-tropical. Zone 11.*   *p. 127*

medullaris: see SPAEROPTERIS medullaris

spinulosa (China: Kwangtung Prov.); graceful small treefern with slender trunk covered with black-brown fiber; fine-feathered rich green fronds of firm texture. *Subtropic. Zones 10-11.*   *p. 126*

CYBISTAX   *Bignoniaceae*
donnell-smithii (Tabebuia) (Mexico, Guatemala), "Primavera" or "Gold tree"; magnificent deciduous tree to 20 m tall, with smooth gray trunk; leaves palmately compound with 5-7 leaflets to 25 cm long; when the foliage has fallen, masses of golden-yellow blooms crowd branch ends, a most beautiful sight; the flowers are bell-shaped and crepy, 3 cm long. *Tropical. Zone 10.*   *p. 663*

CYCAS   *Cycadaceae*
circinalis (India, Madagascar, New Guinea), "Fern palm"; palm-like tree with stout trunk to 3½ m or more high, topped by a graceful rosette of stiff-glossy leaves pinnately divided, the leaflets flat on edges; male and female inflorescence on separate plants. I have seen colonies of this species in the Bulolo highlands in New Guinea, at 1200 m in tall Kunai grass. *Tropical. Zone 11.*   *p. 113*

media (No. Australia, Queensland), "Australian nut palm"; slender trunk to 6 m high, reported to be one of the tallest of the cycads; topped by a handsome crown of fronds, 1 m or more long, shorter than circinalis, with numerous flat leaflets, narrowed to a spiny tip; the scales of male cones tapering into long spines. *Tropical. Zone 11.*   *p. 113*

revoluta (So. Japan to Java), "Sago palm"; dioecious palm-like tree slowly forming hulking trunk to 3 m or more high, usually solitary but sometimes branched, topped by a terminal crown of stiff, deep glossy green, feathery pinnate fronds 1 to 2 m long; the leathery leaflets are spine-tipped and rolled down at margins; the petal-less flowers are in terminal clusters; brown-woolly carpels, in female trees, contain orange fruit, covering nut-like poisonous seeds. *Subtropic. Zones 9-10.*   *p. 113*

taiwaniana (Taiwan); seen in thickets near Tohol; elegant rosette of spreading pinnate fronds from bulbous base, the angled rachis (axis) of the leaf set with well-spaced glossy green narrow linear, stiff pinnae in one plane; male or female cones on separate plants. *Zone 11.*   *p. 114*

CYCLAMEN   *Primulaceae*
coum (orbiculatum) (S.E. Europe, Balkans to Syria and Anatolia); small cyclamen 8-15 cm high, from 4 cm tuber, early spring-blooming, from December on in mild climate; leaves green or marbled above, red-purple underneath, beginning to appear in Autumn as the temperatures drop; nodding flowers 2 cm long, carmine-rose, with basal purple blotch; the floral stalks coil spirally at fruiting time, as do other species. *Zone 7.*   *p. 260*

hederifolium (neapolitanum) (So. Europe, France to Greece), "Baby cyclamen"; lovely little plant to 15 cm high, with black, flattened tuber, green, angled leaves lightly marked, and tiny, sweet-scented flowers appearing in late Summer, mostly before the foliage, rosy-lavender with deep carmine blotch at eared base, the stalks coiling when with seed pod. Hardy in New York as well as Texas. *Zones 5-8.*   *p. 260*

persicum (indicum) (Greece and Mediterranean islands to Syria), "Persian cyclamen"; charming low, fleshy herb with large, hard tuberous roots; heart-shaped basal leaves in a rosette, prettily patterned with silver; and long-stalked solitary nodding, fragrant flowers, with purplish-rose flaring corolla lobes elegantly reflexed. Growth rests during Summer, losing foliage with reduced moisture. *Zones 9-10.*   *p. 53*

persicum 'Pearl of Zehlendorf' (Berlin 1907); the favorite color form, with elegant flowers vivid salmon-red, deeper toward eye, shading to lighter salmon at margins, free-blooming during Winter. *Zone 10.*   *p. 53, 260*

persicum 'Rose of Marienthal' (Stoldt-Wandsbek 1881); very popular large-flowered "Florists cyclamen" developed in Germany, of robust habit, beautiful gray-bluish leaves painted with silver, and 6 cm blooms soft rose with carmine-red eye, winter-blooming. *Zone 10.*   *p. 260*

x persicum 'Swiss Dwarf'; diminutive persicum x purpurascens cultivar, with attractive foliage marked silver; flowers on slender stems with petals 3 cm long; developed in Switzerland for lilliputian effect as house plant. *Subtropic. Zone 10.*   *p. 56*

purpurascens (europaeum) (Alps of France to Carpathian Mts.), "Alpine violet"; charming small garden cyclamen to 15 cm high, with small tuber, rooting all over; the evergreen leaves beautifully traced with silvery pattern; blooming late Summer and Autumn with very fragrant 2 cm flowers rose-pink with crimson at base. Should never dry out. *Zone 6.*   *p. 260*

repandum (So. France to Rhodos, E. Mediterran. reg); charming little cyclamen to 12 cm high, with small tuber rooting from lower surface; waxy leaves broadly cordate, marbled or not above and red-purple beneath; elegant, fragrant 3 cm flowers carmine-rose, in early Spring. *Zone 7.*   *p. 260*

CYCLANTHUS   *Cyclanthaceae*
bipartitus (Guyana), "Splitleaf cyclanthus"; stemless, palm-like herb with milky juice, forming clumps; the decorative leathery, broad-ovate, quilted leaves 1 m or more long, having two primary, deeply depressed veins, forked at apex; in mature stage divided to base, carried on petioles 1 to 2 m long; the curious, fragrant inflorescence is unisexual, tiny male and female flowers on a spadix in alternate whorls, subtended by several cream-white spathes. *Zone 11.   p. 464*

CYCNOCHES   *Orchidaceae*
ventricosum (Guatemala), "Swan orchid"; striking epiphyte; stout pseudobulb with arching raceme of sweet-scented, waxy flowers greenish-yellow, a white lip, and an arched slender column resembling a swan's neck, (July-Nov.). *Humid-tropical. Zone 12.*   *p. 86*

CYDISTA   *Bignoniaceae*
aequinoctialis (W. Indies to Mexico, C. America and Brazil), "Garlic vine"; scandent shrub climbing by tendrils, with shiny leathery, obovate, dual leaves to 15 cm long, and with clusters of funnelform flowers a pretty rose with white throat. Erroneously called "Garlic vine" in Florida, its leaves are not garlic-scented; the true "Garlic-scented vine" is Pseudocalymma alliaceum. *Tropical. Zone 10.*   *p. 268*

CYDONIA   *Rosaceue*
japonica: see CHAENOMELES japonica
oblonga (No. Iran, E. Turkey), "Fruiting quince"; sparry, thornless tree to 6 m high, deciduous in colder regions; with attractive ovate 5-10 cm leaves, dark green above and whitish tomentose beneath; yellow in Autumn; 5 cm, white to pink flowers at young branch tips; the fruit apple-like, greenish-yellow, somewhat wrinkled, and covered with light brown felt, 6 cm or more dia. and showing a woody calyx. The large, fragrant fruits are inedible when raw, being quite acid and harshly astringent when uncooked, but used for making jams and jellies. For flowering quince, see Chaenomeles. *Zone 4.   p. 834*

oblonga 'Appleform'; attractive ornamental as well as fruiting shrub or small tree, of Persian heritage; bold dark green leaves with white-felty underside, on twisted branches; Spring-blooming with masses of white or pinkish flowers; followed by apple-shaped quince fruit having golden-yellow skin and dark yellow fine-grained flesh of aromatic flavor, ripening late August; edible after cooking; makes good jellies. *Zones 4-9.*   *p. 925*

oblonga cv. 'Pineapple', "Pineapple quince"; one of the improved quince seedling varieties developed by Luther Burbank in California in 1899; roundish, light golden fruit, covered with white felt; tender white flesh of pineapple flavor; becoming soft as an apple upon cooking. *Zones 4-9.*   *p. 925*

sinensis (Pseudocydonia) (China), "Chinese quince"; small spine-less tree to 6 m high, usually deciduous, with ovate leaves 8 to 10 cm long; the 4 cm flowers with pink petals having white base, emerging after the foliage; dark yellow ovoid fruit 6 to 10 cm long, used for stewing, marmalade or jelly. Not as winter-hardy as Chaenomeles. *Warm temperate. Zone 6.*   *p. 925*

CYLINDROPHYLLUM speciosum hort.:
see CEPHALOPHYLLUM alstonii

CYMBALARIA   *Scrophulariaceae*
muralis (Linaria cymbalaria) (Germany, France, Switzerland; naturalized in Britain and No. America), "Kenilworth ivy"; creeping, perennial, herbaceous ground cover naturalized in Ontario to Pennsylvania, an old-fashioned basket-plant, with thread-like stems rooting at the nodes, small kidney-shaped, fresh green, waxy leaves irregularly lobed, purplish beneath; tiny lilac-blue flowers with yellow throat, like miniature snapdragons. *Zones 3-8.*   *p. 322*

pallida (Linaria) (Mts. of Italy), "Pale pennywort"; small creeping perennial herb with trailing rhizomes and pubescent, rooting branches; the 2 cm leaves kidney-shaped or round and lobed, and soft-hairy; purplish-rose flowers with yellow throat. *Zone 8.   p. 322*

CYMBIDIELLA   *Orchidaceae*
rhodochila (Madagascar); epiphyte often classified as Cymbidium; almost always growing together with Platycerium; the folded leaves grow from the axils of the older ones creating a braided effect; floral stalks from base of pseudobulbs, to 1 m high, bearing 20 or more yellowish-green flowers, with brownish spots on petals, and crimson lip with yellow stripe (Autumn). *Tropical. Zone 12.*   *p. 89*

CYMBIDIUM   *Orchidaceae*
'Flirtation' (pumilum x 'Zebra'); attractive, semi-miniature; flowers 5 cm, pale pink to greenish-ivory, and striped orchid, lip white and blotched maroon. *Subtropic. Zone 11.*   *p. 86*

x insigne (Hybrid); beautiful terrestrial of Vietnam parentage with globose pseudobulbs sheathed by narrow strap-shaped, glaucous green leaves to 1 m long; strong erect 1 m raceme of numerous fleshy, long-lasting 8 cm flowers, sepals and petals pale rose, lip white flushed and marked with crimson and yellow. (Feb.-March). *Zones 10-11.*   *p. 84*

lancifolium (Himalayas at 2000 m; India to Japan, south to Malaysia); charming, terrestrial forest dweller of low habit; spindle-shaped pseudobulbs clothed with 3 to 5 ribbed thin-leathery leaves 20 cm long; stiff-erect stalks bearing inflorescence 30 cm high of scattered, fragrant and long-lasting flowers 4 to 5 cm across, greenish-cream with purple spots, the lip white boldly marked with maroon, blooming in Spring and early Summer. *Subtropic. Zone 11.   p. 86*

pumilum (China: Yunnan); dwarf terrestrial with linear leaves to 30 cm long; small waxy flowers 3 cm across, reddish-brown and yellow. *Subtropic. Zone 11.*   *p. 86*

'Show Girl The Bride'; superior hybrid seen at the New York Flower Show 1984; typical of the many primary or secondary hybrids involving parents such as x alexanderi, eburneum or insigne, developed in horticulture; bold terrestrial 1 m or more high, with thick pseudobulbs bearing stiff linear leaves; erect branched inflorescence with waxy 10 cm flowers rosy-pink with purple markings of good keeping quality both in pots or as cut flower. *Zones 10-11.   p. 84*

CYMBOPOGON   *Gramineae*
citratus (Andropogon) (India, Sri Lanka), "Lemongrass" or "Fever grass"; densely tufted perennial grass to 2 m high, the narrow, hard lemon-scented leaves 1 to 2 cm wide and to 80 cm long, rough-edged and flexuous; the inflorescence a loose cluster of somewhat nodding branches, bearing the spikelets with minute flowers, the joints long-haired, almost concealing the spikelets. Cultivated in Florida for the aromatic lemon-grass oil; very popular in tropic countries as beverage plant; leaves are delicious as an iced tea. *Zones 9-10.*   *p. 530*

CYNANCHUM   *Asclepiadaceae*
vincetoxicum (Vincetoxicum) (Europe to Himalayas), "Cruel plant"; herbaceous perennial 50-75 cm high, with erect or scrambling branches; narrow lanceolate leaves to 12 cm long; axillary clusters of small 1 cm greenish-white flowers. *Zone 6.*   *p. 343*

CYNARA   *Compositae*
cardunculus (Mediterr. reg. to Portugal), "Cardoon"; thistle-like perennial to 1 m or more high; leaves gray-green above, whitish-tomentose beneath, pinnately cut or lobed at sides, and with thorny apex, to 30 cm long; globular spiny floral head bristly with purple disc-flowers, cultivated for its edible root and thickened leaf stalks. *Zone 9.*   *p. 384*

scolymus (So. Mediterranean reg., Canary Islands), the "Arti-choke" or "Globe artichoke"; robust ferny-looking perennial of irregular, fountain-like form, to 1 m or more high; silvery green leaves deeply dissected and somewhat spiny, white cottony beneath; heads with purple disc-flowers resembling a thistle, 15 cm across with a nest of fleshy scales beneath. The fleshy buds are cut before they open, and are edible when cooked. Flowers may be cut for fresh or dried arrangements. *Subtropic. Zone 8.*   *p. 384*

scolymus glauca, "Blue artichoke"; handsome horticultural se-lection for its ornamental glaucous blue leaves, dissected and spiny at margins, the thistle-like floral heads with feathery, rose-colored disc-flowers in numerous attractive globes. *Zone 8.*   *p. 384*

CYNODON *Gramineae*

dactylon (Warm regions of both Hemispheres), "Bermuda grass" or "Devil's grass"; perennial grass with creeping stolons and rhizomes, spreading aggressively; the green or grayish-green leaf-blades are flat and short, 4 mm wide, on basal shoots often 2-ranked; very heat tolerant; can be grown from seed, rhizomes or sprigs. Several excellent hybrid strains with unusually fine, thread-like foliage merely 2 mm wide, have been developed for lawn-planting in Florida and California. *Tropical to Subtropic. Zones 7-10.* p. 568, 569

CYNOGLOSSUM *Boraginaceae*

amabile (E. Asia), "Chinese forget-me-not"; popular gardenplant from dry areas, blooming profusely throughout Summer with small 2 cm blue flowers; hoary biennial to 50 cm high, with lanceolate leaves 5-20 cm long. *Zone 9.* p. 346

nervosum (Himalayas), "Great hounds-tongue"; hairy herbaceous perennial or biennial to 75 cm high, with narrow lanceolate leaves to 20 cm long and distinctly veined; flowers in one-sided arching racemes, with 2 cm funnel-shaped blue corolla, in early Summer. *Zone 5.* p. 346

CYPERUS *Cyperaceae*

albostriatus (diffusus or laxus) (Mauritius), "Broadleaf umbrella plant"; compact bushy plant sending out runners with suckers which are used for propagation; sturdy, 3-angled stalks with a crown of broad, matte-green, rather rough leaves and long, pale brown spikelets. *Tropical. Zone 10.* p. 328

albostriatus 'Variegatus', "Striped umbrella palm"; compact-growing variety having its broad green leaflets striped and banded pale yellow or cream. *Topical. Zone 11.* p. 328

alternifolius (Madagascar, Kenya), "Umbrella plant"; clustering perennial bogplant with ribbed stalks to 1 m high, bearing a crown of bright green, leaf-like bracts around a head of small green flowers. I have seen this also along the Athi River in Kenya. *Tropical. Zone 10.* p. 328, 558

papyrus (Egypt), "Egyptian paper plant" or "Papyrus"; a stately plant for pools, with stout dark green stalks to 2 m high, topped by brush-like umbel of drooping, threadlike leaves. Along the shores of Lake Victoria in Africa I have seen them 5 m tall. Used in Egypt for making "papyrus" since 2750 B.C. *Tropical. Zones 9-11.* p. 338

CYPHOMANDRA *Solanaceae*

betacea (So. Brazil), the "Tree-tomato" or "Tamarillo"; tree-like shrub somewhat woody, to 3 m, with heart-shaped ovate 30 cm soft-hairy, fleshy leaves, and fragrant 1 cm flowers in pendulous raceme, the 5-lobed corolla greenish-pink with a dark stripe on back of each segment; the egg-shaped, edible, reddish 8 cm fruit resembling a tomato in looks and flavor. *Subtropic. Zones 9-10.* p. 941

CYPRIPEDIUM *Orchidaceae*

acaule (Newfoundland to Alberta, Alabama, No. Carolina), "Pink ladyslipper"; deciduous terrestrial of the temperate zone, with two light green plaited leaves 20 cm long and parallel-veined; large solitary flowers with hairy sepals and petals greenish-brown, the divided, pouch-like lip rose veined with crimson. (May-June). *Temperate. Zone 3.* p. 85, 464

calceolus (Europe, No. America, No. Asia), the "Yellow lady-slipper" of Eurasia; hardy terrestrial with short rhizome and stems to 60 cm, with deciduous plicate (folded) leaves; at the apex usually 1-3 showy fragrant flowers with narrow petals green and marked purple, the yellow lip shaped like a large pouch, and 12-15 cm long; blooming May-July. *Zone 4.* p. 85, 464

calceolus pubescens (No. America: N. Scotia to Minnesota, so. to Alabama), "Yellow ladyslipper"; terrestrial orchid with leafy stem bearing 1-2 flowers, the broad leaves deciduous, soft-hairy, sepals and petals purplish-brown to green, petals more or less twisted, the rounded pouch yellow veined with red. (April bl. in south, Aug. in north). *Temperate. Zone 4.* p. 464

candidum (Ontario to Missouri, Kentucky), "Small white lady-slipper"; rigidly erect terrestrial 15 to 35 cm high; several folded leaves along stem; solitary flowers spreading to 10 cm wide, sepals and petals greenish-yellow and spotted purple, the pouch waxy-white, slightly fragrant. (April-June). *Zone 5.* p. 85

cordigerum (alpinum) (Kashmir, Nepal, Himalayas); terrestrial perennial to 60 cm high, with leafy stems; the foliage broad elliptic, deeply ridged lengthwise; flowers having lemon-yellow sepals, and white pouch with purple spots; Summer. *Zone 10.* p. 85, 464

japonicum (Japan, China); curious rhizomatous terrestrial, the large fan-shaped, ribbed twin leaves to 15 cm long, with veins radiating to margins; solitary 6 cm flowers, sepals greenish spotted red, petals whitish, lip white stained with crimson; Summer. *Zones 10-11.* p. 85

reginae (Canada to Missouri), "Showy ladyslipper"; beautiful deciduous terrestrial to 75 cm tall, densely hairy, stems leafy, bearing

1-2 flowers, the ovate sepals and petals white, or flushed rose, the round pouch white or pink striped with rose, to 10 cm long; sweetly fragrant. (June-Aug.). *Zones 3-4.* p. 85, 464

speciosum (macranthon) (Japan); hardy terrestrial with 3 to 4-leaved stems; folded elliptic foliage to 30 cm long, bright glossy green; attractive solitary flowers, the large dorsal sepal and narrow petals rose, and inflated lip white flushed pink, similar to macranthum which has rich purple flowers. Transferred to C. macranthon in Europ. Gard. Flora 1984. *Zone 4.* p. 85

CYRILLA *Cyrillaceae*

racemiflora (Virginia to Texas, West Indies, Mexico, E. So. America), "Leatherwood" or "Titi"; handsome smooth shrub 1 m or more high, in warm climate occasionally as tree to 10 m tall, with red bark, oblanceolate leathery, glossy green leaves 4 to 12 cm long, deciduous in eastern No.America, turning orange and scarlet in Autumn; evergreen in West Indies; it bears graceful, slender racemes of small white flowers in late Summer, and loved by bees. *Warm-temperate to Tropical. Zones 7-10.* p. 695

CYRTANTHUS *Amaryllidaceae*

mackenii (Natal), "Ifafa lily"; bulbous herb with linear leaves 30 cm long, and umbels on 30 cm stalks with pure white fragrant flowers having a 5 cm long curved tube and 6 spreading lobes. *Subtropic. Zones 8-9.* p. 211

purpureus: see VALLOTA speciosa (Hortus)

CYRTOMIUM *Polypodiaceae (Filices)*

falcatum (Japan, China, India, Celebes, Hawaii) the "Holly-fern"; with handsome pinnate fronds on brown scaly stalks, the leathery, shining dark green leaflets are ovate, slender pointed and very durable under adverse conditions. *Subtropic. Zones 8-10.* p. 132

falcatum 'Rochfordianum', "Fringed Holly fern"; the cultivar mostly grown in greenhouses at present, its habit is more robust, the fronds broader and fuller, and the large leathery, glossy leaves are serrate and wavy at the margins. *Zone 10.* p. 132

CYRTOPODIUM *Orchidaceae*

andersonii (Brazil, W. Indies); bold terrestrial and on rocks, with long pseudobulbs and tall 1 m branching spikes of yellow flowers tinged with green, and rich yellow lip. (Spring bl. but saw it bloom near Rio, in September). *Tropical. Zone 11.* p. 84

CYRTOSPERMA *Araceae*

merkusii var. chamissonis (Southeast Asia); robust rhizomatous plant to 2½ m high; large glossy green, wrinkled, sagittate leaves 50 to 70 cm long and wide, on spiny petioles to 2 m long; spathe much longer than spadix. *Zone 11.* p. 26

CYRTOSTACHYS *Palmae*

lakka (Malaya, Borneo, Pacific Islands), "Sealing wax palm"; known as "Maharaja palm" in the Philippines; beautiful feather palm, clustering with slender, glossy green trunks to 5 m high and 8 cm thick; very handsome with their 60 cm long scarlet-red leaf bases sheathing the base of the crown of fronds; the leaves pinnate on scarlet petioles, the numerous leaflets dark green above, glaucous beneath; small 1 cm black fruit from red stalk. *Zones 11-12.* p. 104

CYSTOPTERIS *Polypodiaceae (Filices)*

bulbifera v. crispa (regia) (Connecticut, N. Jersey), "Crested berry bladder-fern"; small rock-dwelling fern, found in Connecticut, to 30 cm high, with tri-pinnate fronds having fan-shaped crisped leaflets, bearing green fleshy bulblets on lower surface, soon dropping off to form new plants. Leaves wither at first frost. *Zone 5.* p. 128

fragilis (Temp. No. Hemisphere, south to Chile), "Brittle fern"; graceful little hardy fern of delicate texture, with bipinnate fronds 10-20 cm long, on petioles shorter than blade. *Zones 3-6.* p. 130

CYTISUS *Leguminosae*

battandierii (Algeria, Morocco); deciduous, vigorous, silvery shrub, to 5 m high, with drooping branches; leaves large, 3-foliolate, leaflets soft, silvery-pubescent especially beneath, 5-9 cm long; flowers in cylindrical racemes, 8-12 cm long, bright yellow and fragrant. *Zone 9.* p. 757

decumbens (France, Spain to Yugoslavia), "Prostrate broom"; dwarf deciduous shrub to 20 cm high with prostrate branches; small obovate leaves 2 cm long, and lightly hairy; axillary flowers with bright shining yellow corolla covering the sprawling plant in multitudes during May-June or even into August; followed by small 3 cm bean-like fruit. *Zone 5.* p. 756

x kewensis (ardoini x multiflorus), "Kew broom"; low-growing, procumbent Kew Garden hybrid 1891, to 30 cm high, with soft-pubescent deciduous leaves, variably compound of 3 leaflets, or simple 1 cm narrow-elliptic leaves; creamy-white or pale yellow pea-flowers 15 mm long, axillary on slender arching branches, in late Spring. *Zone 6.* p. 757

monspessulanus (Teline monsp. or Genista candicans) (Mediterr. reg. Portugal and Azores, Canary Isl. west to Greece and Asia Minor); evergreen densely branched shrub to 3 m high; leaves of 3 obovate leaflets softly pubescent beneath, 2 cm long; vivid yellow pea-flowers in small clusters on the furrowed young branchlets, and sweetly fragrant; blooming April-June. Zones 9-10.   p. 757

multiflorus (albus) (Spain, Portugal, No. Africa), "White Spanish broom"; popular deciduous shrub to 3 m high, with grooved branchlets; the lower leaves with 3 leaflets, toward apex simple and leaf oblong 1 cm long, silky pubescent; very floriferous with pure white pea-flowers in leaf axils, blooming May-June. The variety incarnatus has corollas flushed pink. Zone 6.   p. 758

nigricans (C. Europe to No. Italy), "Spike broom"; erect deciduous shrub 1 to 2 m high, dense with straight stems, and leaves usually of 3 leaflets to 25 mm long; inflorescence in slender terminal racemes of 1 cm light yellow flowers, blooming into July and August. Plant turns black when dried out. Zone 5.   p. 758

x praecox (multiflorus x purgans), "Warminster broom" (England 1867); showy early-blooming hybrid, deciduous but with green stems all Winter, 1-2 m high, with nearly linear leaves mostly simple, 2 cm long, but dropping early. Very free-blooming, with axillary, pale yellowish 1 cm flowers during May. Zone 5.   p. 758

x praecox 'Hollandia'; bushy cultivar 1 m or more high, covered with handsome flowers rosy-purple, the keel margined with creamy-white. Zone 5.   p. 762

purpureus (Austrian Alps to Yugoslavia), "Purple broom"; deciduous small shrub to 60 cm high, with procumbent branches; leaves compound of 3 obovate leaflets 2 cm long; axillary flowers purple and pink with tubular calyx, blooming in May; the fruit a small 2 cm pod. Zone 6.   p. 762

x racemosus (canariensis x maderensis magnifoliosus), "Florists' genista"; a hybrid favored over canariensis because of its smaller, darker green leaflets, and shorter, more numerous racemes with flowers deep yellow, set closely on terminal racemes; longer-lasting blooms than canariensis. Zones 9-10.   p. 758

scoparius (Britian to Sweden to So. Europe), "Scotch broom"; very floriferous deciduous shrub to 2½ m high, having green stems throughout Winter; with pubescent young shoots, small leaflets to 1 cm long; flowers axillary with bright, shining yellow corolla; May-June blooming. Naturalized in Eastern U.S. Zone 6.   p. 758

scoparius 'Andreanus' (fulgens in hort.), "Goldfinch broom"; dense shrub with broom-like, green branches, sparsely covered with tiny, deciduous leaves, but in Spring changing into a sea of strikingly beautiful, bilabiate 1 to 1½ cm flowers, golden-yellow with crimson-red wings. Found wild in Normandy 1884. Zone 6.   p. 758

scoparius 'Pendulus'; a cultivated form of prostrate habit, photographed in col. Kew Botanic Gardens, England; with arching green branches; tiny 1 cm deciduous leaves, and flowers having corolla a shining bright yellow, during May. Zone 6.   p. 758

DABOECIA   *Ericaceae*

cantabrica (No. Portugal, Spain, to W. Ireland), "Irish heath" or "Connemara heath"; evergreen, heath-like small shrub 30-60 cm high, with narrow elliptic leaves 1 cm long, shining green above, white-tomentose beneath; urn-shaped 1 cm flowers in racemes to 15 cm long, the corollas white in cv. 'Alba', or rose-purple in cv. 'Purpurea', June to September-blooming. Zone 5.   p. 700

DACRYDIUM   *Podocarpaceae (Coniferae)*

cupressinum (New Zealand), known as "Rimu" by the Maori or "Red pine"; tall forest tree to 30 m, with cypress-like branchlets and overlapping scale-like leaves when mature; very interesting while juvenile when the branchlets are like Lycopodium and pendulous, and the needles soft and awl-shaped; the nuts are seated on a fleshy red receptacle. This tree with its long, gracefully weeping bronzy green branches is in habitat in both North and South Island. Zone 6. p. 606

franklinii (Tasmania), "Huon pine"; decorative evergreen tree to 30 m high, with short branches supporting the long pendulous branchlets, resembling a weeping cypress; small dark green, scale-like leaves 3 mm long, appressed to twigs thread-like; cones very small with fleshy appendage attached. The fragrant red wood is used for furniture; also yields Huon pine-wood oil. Zone 7.   p. 606

DACTYLORHIZA   *Orchidaceae*

foliosa (Orchis maderensis) (Madeira, Portugal); beautiful terrestrial orchid with keeled lanceolate green leaves; the inflorescence in a cylindric showy spike 8-12 cm long, dense with small purple flowers having trilobed lip. Zones 9-10.   p. 86

DAHLIA   *Compositae*

coccinea (So. Mexico), "Acocotli" or "Dalia del campo"; splendid tuberous plant usually low-growing; fresh green, serrate pinnate leaves; the velvety, brilliantly colored ray-flowers in a single series, 6-8 cm across, varying from scarlet through orange to yellow; the

central disc-flowers are yellow. The tubers were a popular food in the time of the emperor Montezuma, who greatly loved them. Subtropic. Zone 9.   p. 221

imperialis (Mexico), a "Tree-dahlia"; tree-like 2-6 m tall, with tuberous roots, few woody stalks mostly solid and 4-grooved; compound leaves lacy; flowers 10-15 cm across; florets white, tinged purple near base, disc yellow. Subtropic. Zone 9.   p. 384

pinnata, parent of Garden dahlias:
CLASSIFICATION:

SINGLE: Blooms with single row of ray-florets having flat margins, surrounding a center disc.

DECORATIVE: Very double blooms showing no disc, with floral rays broad and usually rounded at tips (Formal), or having long outer rays, pointed and twisted with margins turned under (Informal).

CACTUS: Full-double flowers showing no center disc, and the long pointed florets straight with margins turned under (Revolute).

ANEMONE: Blooms with one or more rows of outer rays and center cushion of massed tubular florets.

POMPON: Blooms with densely packed florets into smallish ball of globular form, the petals boat-shaped and relatively short.

COLLARETTE: Blooms having single outer row of broad petals, usually flat, and one more row of shorter inner florets usually in a different color, forming a collar around the center cushion.

pinnata (variabilis) hybrid, the "Garden-dahlias", originally from Mexico, but now in about 14 groups, with thousands of named clones; herbaceous bush 1½-2 m tall, with tuberous roots, stout semi-woody stalks, turgid leaves 5-foliolate, fresh-green above, grayish beneath; showy flower heads in many horticultural forms, sizes and colors, originally purple, but now also in white, yellow, salmon, bronze, red, pink, violet. Subtropic. Zone 9.

pinnata 'Casey'; formal decorative type; carmine-rose tipped white. Zone 9.   p. 221

pinnata 'Collarette'; semi-double bicolor type; outer petals maroon-red, inner circle with white. Zone 9.   p. 221

pinnata 'Fairie'; "Pompon dahlia" rose-pink with pale pink tips. Zone 9.   p. 221

pinnata 'Figaro'; single-flowered, bright red. Zone 9.   p. 221

pinnata 'Garnet Spoon'; showy anemone type flower; bright red oblanceolate spoon-like outer petals, lined with white toward center cushion. Zone 9.   p. 222

pinnata 'Informal Decorative'; a selected cultivar with heads of ray-flowers only; rays irregularly arranged, broad and twisted or pointed, margins usually turned under. Subtropic. Zone 9.   p. 235

pinnata 'Mignon'; dwarf single; open-centered; petal-like florets crimson-red with pale markings. Zone 9.   p. 221

pinnata 'Schweizerland'; formal decorative type; striking color combination with outer petals white, toward center blood-red, about 10 cm across. Zone 9.   p. 221

pinnata 'Siegerland'; cactus-flowered type, yellow at base, but heavily overlaid with orange-scarlet. Zone 9.   p. 222

pinnata 'Summer Smile'; formal decorative type; broad petals blood-red, with contrasting white tips. Zone 9.   p. 222

pinnata 'Unwin's Dwarf' ("Mignon"); dwarf growing strain suitable for growing as a compact pot plant, producing 6 cm and 8 cm double and semi-double blooms in colors red, salmon, yellow, and lavender; usually grown from seed but forming small tubers; blooming first year in cool climate. Zone 9.   p. 221

DAIS   *Thymelaeaceae*

cotinifolia (So. Africa), "Pompon tree"; delightful small tree to 6 m; obovate leaves 8 cm long; the lovely pompon clusters of lilac-pink tubular 15 mm fragrant flowers measure 8 cm in dia., and cover the tree in profusion in Spring. Photographed in Kirstenbosch Bot. Garden, near Cape Town. Subtropic. Zone 10.   p. 892

DALBERGIA   *Leguminosae*

balansae (Hongkong, Kwangtung), "China Rosewood"; large deciduous tree to 12 m high, with rough, cracked bark, and spreading crown; long, pinnate leaves having 5-12 pairs of elliptic leaflets to 4 cm long plus one single terminal one; flowers small and pea-like, white or pale lavender, blooming May or June; the fruit is an elongate pod 10-15 cm long, long-stalked and pendant, becoming pale brown and woody. Zones 9-10.   p. 759

sissoo (India: Bengal, naturalized in Florida), "Sissoo tree" or "Indian rose-wood"; tropical tree 15 to 25 m high, with light, fissured bark; deciduous during dry season; alternate-pinnate leaves having 5 ovate leaflets 8 cm long on zigzag rachis; small pea-like labiate flowers yellowish-white, very fragrant, displaying 9 stamens united, blooming in axillary clusters. The true Rosewood is very hard, and important timber in India, used for furniture, carvings, wheels and boats. Zones 9-10.   p. 759

DAMMAROPSIS   *Moraceae*
kingiana (New Guinea); extraordinarily interesting small branch-ing tropical tree about 3 to 5 m high which I collected in the Finisterre Mountains; very decorative with great leaves at first ovate, later much broader and 60 cm long, turgid, leathery, deeply corrugated, the margins undulate, deep glabrous green above, with red ribs when young, later changing to ivory, and pale beneath, petioles red; large pineapple-like brown fruit. *Zone 10.*   *p. 791*

DAMNACANTHUS   *Rubiaceae*
indicus (E. Asia); dense shrub 60 to 120 cm high, having slender branches armed with long needle-like spines; lustrous ovate spine-tipped leaves 1-2 cm long; axillary trumpet-shaped white flowers with 5 lobes, followed by scarlet-red berries. *Zone 6.*   *p. 699*

DANAE   *Liliaceae*
racemosa (Syria to Iran), "Alexandrian laurel"; branched, ruscus-like evergreen shrub to 1 m, with modified branches or cladodes resembling lanceolate leathery leaves, dark glossy green, to 10 cm long; the actual leaves scale-like; small white flowers followed by 1 cm red berries. *Zone 7.*   *p. 771*

DANTHONIA   *Gramineae*
decumbens (Europe, No. Africa), "Oat grass"; perennial grass forming open clusters of culms about 60 cm high, bearing few-flowered spike-like panicles and long green, linear leaves near base; the slender inflorescence with reddish spikelets. *Zones 6-8.*   *p.559*

DAPHNE   *Thymelaeaceae*
arbuscula (Slovakia, Hungary, Carpathians, Rumania); dwarf prostrate evergreen shrub to 15 cm high, similar to cneorum, but with dark green lanceolate 2 cm leaves revolute, or rolled under at margins; flowers in terminal clusters rose-pink, the corolla tube 2 cm long with spreading lobes, and downy at calyx, blooming in June or longer. *Zone 6.*   *p. 891*
x burkwoodii (caucasica x cneorum); very vigorous and freely blooming deciduous hybrid shrub, evergreen in mild climate, originated as a seedling 1935 by Burkwood in England; growing 50 to 75 cm high and densely bushy; lanceolate leaves 3 cm long, deep green and long remaining on branches; creamy-white 2 cm flowers changing to pale rose, blooming May-June, and very fragrant. *Zone 5.*   *p. 891*
x burkwoodii 'Carol Mackie', "Variegated daphne"; this beautiful cultivar was discovered in Carol Mackie's New Jersey garden, as a mutation of D. x burkwoodii 'Somerset'; its charmingly shingled rich green leaves margined by a contrasting gold band; in addition, in May and June, it's star-shaped, fragrant soft pink flowers add to a display of superb beauty. Distributed by Wayside Gardens, Hodges, So. Carolina, and photographed at Somerset Arboretum, New Jersey. *Zones 5-8.*   *p. 891*
cneorum (Spain, France, Germany to Balkans and Russia), the "Garland-flower"; low evergreen shrub to 30 cm high, with trailing branches to 1 m wide; small 2½ cm leaves shiny dark green and with sharp point, and carmine-rose flowers deliciously perfumed, in clusters, in early Spring, blooming again in Autumn in southern mild areas. *Zone 4.*   *p. 891*
collina (sericea in Zander) (Italy, Sicily, Crete, Asia Minor); bushy evergreen shrub to 1 m high; obovate leaves to 5 cm long, pubescent beneath; flowers deep rose 1 cm across, in dense clusters, blooming May-June, and sweetly fragrant. *Zone 7.*   *p. 891*
giraldii (N.W. China), "Giraldi daphne"; handsome deciduous small shrub to 60 cm or more high, with oblanceolate 6 cm leaves crowded toward apex of erect branches; slightly fragrant flowers in terminal heads, having golden-yellow calyx, the floral lobes spreading, blooming in May; followed by ovoid scarlet berries in July. *Zone 3.*   *p. 891*
mezereum (Europe to Caucasus, Asia Minor, Siberia); deciduous shrub to 1 m high, with oblanceolate thin leaves 2½ to 8 cm long, vivid green, grayish beneath, usually appearing after bloom; the flower light carmine and very fragrant; known as "February daphne", it begins to flower early before leaves come out, into March-April. The scarlet-red fruit is ornamental but poisonous, as in all Daphnes, and so are the leaves. *Zone 4.*   *p. 891*
odora 'Marginata' (japonica) (Japan, China), "Winter daphne"; evergreen shrub 1 m or more high, with leathery elliptic leaves to 8 cm long, glossy green, the margins attractively bordered with creamy-yellow; small 2 cm flowers with corolla tube white, toward apex and lobes soft pink to rose-purple, in showy terminal clusters in late Winter and early Spring, and extremely scented, the most fragrant of all Daphne. *Zone 7.*   *p. 891*
retusa (W. China); evergreen shrub of compact habit, to 1 m high, with leathery oblanceolate leaves 8 cm long, generally notched at

apex, glossy green above; flowers in rounded terminal clusters, purplish-pink outside, white and tinted purple inside, 2 cm across, blooming May-June; followed by oval red fruit 2½ cm long. More tolerant of garden conditions than most Daphne. *Zone 6.*   *p. 892*

DARLINGTONIA   *Sarraceniaceae (Carnivorous Plants)*
californica (California, Oregon), "Cobra plant"; carnivorous bog plant with hollow, light green pitchers, equipped inside with downward pointed hairs entrapping insects; the top is hooded and has trans-lucent windows, and a cobra-like, purple-spotted forked tongue; nodding flowers purple. *Zones 7-9.*   *p. 203*

DARMERA peltata (Zander): see PELTIPHYLLUM peltatum

DARWINIA   *Myrtaceae*
fascicularis (New So. Wales), "Australian heath plant"; very floriferous heath-like shrub to 2 m high, and densely branched; crowded with stiff narrow-linear, sharply pointed leaves; flowers variously white to rose or red, in small heads between terminal needles, the stamen with globose black anthers. *Zone 10.*   *p. 798*

DASYLIRION   *Agavaceae*
longissimum (Nolina longifolia in Hortus 3) (Mexico), "Mexican grass-tree" or "Junquillo"; stemless xerophyte with swollen base, to 3 m high, forming dense bundle of narrow-linear, stiffly erect olive-green leaves without ribs, 1 m or more long; inflorescence a narrow cluster of small whitish flowers. *Arid-subtropic. Zone 8.*   *p. 566*
serratifolium (S.E. Mexico); dense rosette with stout stem, narrow wiry, grass-like, green leaves to 1 m long, 2-3 cm wide; margins set with vicious spines; apex divided and with feathery tufts of hairs; white flowers in dense clusters. *Zone 9.*   *p. 116, 566*

DATURA   *Solanaceae*
inoxia (meteloides hort.) (syn. wrightii) (Texas to California, Mexico), "Indian apple"; perennial to 1 m cultivated as an annual, grayish-pubescent, with ovate leaves, and erect, 5-lobed, funnel-shaped flowers 20 cm long, white tinged with violet, and fragrant; round fruit 5 cm dia., with long spines. *Zone 7.*   *p. 511*
metel florepleno (S. W. China), "Horn-of-plenty"; herbaceous bush to 1 m or more high, with ovate, thin leaves downy when young; inflorescence erect, trumpet-shaped, with 1 or more inner corollas, whitish to purple, to 20 cm long. *Subtropic. Zone 9.*   *p. 511*
stramonium (Mexico to No. America), "Jimson-weed" or "Thorn-apple"; annual herb 1-1½ m with pointed, lobed green leaves; erect funnel-shaped flowers 10 cm long, white or violet; ball-shaped fruit very spiny. Roots, leaves and seed very poisonous. *Zone 10   p. 511*

DATURA arborea, aurea, x candida, x insignis, sanguinea, suaveolens, versicolor (Zander):   see BRUGMANSIA (Hortus)

DAVALLIA   *Polypodiaceae (Filices)*
fejeensis (Fiji Islands), "Rabbit's foot fern"; a name referring to its brown woolly, creeping rhizomes, from which rise the graceful durable fronds on wiry stems, more finely cut than solida. *Humid-tropical. Zones 11-12.*   *p.132*
fejeensis 'Plumosa' (Polynesia); a dainty, dwarf variety with fresh-green, more finely cut, 4-pinnatifid, plume-like, pendulous fronds of long-lasting character. *Humid-tropical. Zones 11-12.*   *p. 132*
griffithiana (India, So. China); epiphytic fern with creeping rhizomes, covered with glistening white scales; wiry fronds 3-4 pinnatifid into well spaced segments, with the ultimate leaflets deeply toothed; not deciduous. *Humid-tropical. Zone 11.*   *p. 132*
mariesii (bullata) (Japan), "Ball fern"; long creeping, flexible, slender, light brown, hairy rhizomes with uniformly small, 4-pinnate, finely lacy yet tough fronds; I saw them in Japan trained into many shapes, such as balls, pillars, bells, animals, monkeys and dolls; deciduous in cool climates. *Humid-tropical. Zones 10-11.*   *p. 132*
trichomaniodes (Malaya), D. "canariensis" of horticulture; "Squirrel's-foot fern"; small creeping rhizome covered with pale brown scale; wiry gray stalks bearing rather leathery fronds 15-22 cm long, 4 times pinnate, with leaflets overlapping, the final pinnae cut into strap-shaped segments. More durable than fejeensis, seldom fertile. *Humid-tropical. Zones 11-12.*   *p. 132*

DAVIDIA   *Nyassaceae*
involucrata (Western China), "Dove tree"; deciduous tree to 15 or 20 m, with rounded crown; cordate leaves vivid green 8-15 cm long; small clustered, red anthered flowers are carried by two large unequal, creamy-white bracts, the larger 15 cm long. When in bloom, the tree gives the effect of white doves resting among green leaves. *Zone 6.*   *p. 804*

DECAISNEA   *Lardizabalaceae*
fargesii (W. China), "Blue pods"; deciduous shrub to 4 m high, with blue-glaucous branches, compound feathery leaves light green

above, bluish beneath; 2½ cm pendulous flowers yellowish-green; blue, cylindrical, edible fruit, being fleshy blue pods, from the inconspicuous female flowers. *Zone 5.* p. 741

DECUMARIA   *Saxifragaceae*

barbara (Virginia to Florida and Louisiana), "Woodvamp" or "Climbing hydrangea"; deciduous woody vine, clinging by aerial rootlets; opposite elliptic, lustrous 5-10 cm leaves; inflorescence in round-topped, 10 cm terminal clusters of small white, all-fertile flowers. *Zone 6.* p. 296

DEHERAINIA   *Myrsinaceae*

smaragdina (Trop. Mexico); evergreen shrub with hairy branches; 10 cm lanceolate toothed leaves smooth above, soft-hairy beneath; deep green wheel-shaped 5 cm flowers primrose-like, between the foliage. *Zone 10.* p. 890

DELONIX   *Leguminosae*

regia (Poinciana) (Madagascar), the "Flamboyant", "Royal poinciana" or "Mohur tree"; a regal flowering tree and one of the showiest; widely planted in the tropics; wide-spreading and to 15 m high; finely subdivided, ferny leaves often fall before blooming time; brilliant 8-10 cm flowers scarlet-red with broad cream lip marked red; followed by flat, woody black pods to 45 cm long. *Tropical.* *Zones 10-11.* p. 751, 761

DELOSPERMA   *Aizoaceae*

aberdeenensis (Cape Prov.: Karroo); densely branched low shrub with small 2 cm succulent gray-green leaves, flat above and rounded below; flowers with light purple ray-petals. *Zone 10.* p. 145

'Alba' (So. Africa), "White iceplant" or "Disneyland iceplant"; dwarf, spreading succulent groundcover rooting freely from stems; small fleshy, 2 to 3 cm boat-shaped angled leaves forming a dense grayish-green carpet; the little glistening white 1 to 1½ cm flowers not very showy. *Dry subtropic.* *Zones 9-10.* p. 144

cooperi (So. Africa: Orange Free State); prostrate freely branching subshrub; soft-fleshy linear, subcylindrical leaves about 5 cm long, very floriferous with terminal silky, purple flowers to 5 cm dia. *Zone 9.* p. 145

sutherlandii (So. Africa: Transvaal, Natal); low succulent rosettes branching and hugging the ground; thin-fleshy lanceolate leaves grayish-green, somewhat keeled, to 8 cm long; showy rose-purple flowers 4-6 cm across, the ray-petals white at base, forming a contrasting eye. *Arid-subtropic.* *Zone 10.* p. 145

tradescantioides (So. Africa: Cape Prov., Natal, Transvaal); freely branching low succulent, resembling tradescantia, creeping and rooting at the nodes; leaves light green, ovate with flat or furrowed surface, to 3 cm long; white flowers 1,5 cm dia. *Zone 10.* p. 144

DELPHINIUM   *Ranunculaceae*

ajacis: see CONSOLIDA ambigua

elatum (Pyrenees to Siberia), "Candle larkspur"; winter-hardy perennial herb to 2 m high, the branches upright, large leaves palmately 5-7 parted; inflorescence in dense spike-like racemes 30 cm long, of 2-3 cm flowers sky blue or purple, with curved spurs, blooming during Summer. *Zone 3.* p. 487

elatum 'Klingsor'; excellent selection of the British Round-table strain of cultivars of compact habit, displaying dense terminal spike-like racemes of deep purplish-blue flowers, during Summer. *Zones 4-6.* p. 487

elatum 'Pacific hybrid'; a race of showy, mainly seed-grown short-lived perennials with candle-like spikes of semi or double flowers on long stems 1 to 2 m tall; they range in color from white through pink and purple to blue, blooming early Summer. *Zones 3-8.* p. 487

exaltatum (Pennsylvania and Ohio to Alabama), "Tall larkspur"; nearly smooth, fibrous-rooted perennial 60 cm to 1 m high or more, the lower leaves 3 to 5-parted; the stem leaves 3-parted into lanceolate segments; inflorescence branched at base, with long racemes of blue or purple flowers 2-3 cm long, characteristically long-spurred, blooming in Summer. *Zones 4-7.* p. 488

grandiflorum (chinense) (Siberia, No. China), "Siberian larkspur"; lovely perennial, often grown as annual, blooming first year from early-sown seed; 40-80 cm high; leaves palmately divided into narrow segments; inflorescence in racemes of showy flowers in shades of blue, violet or whitish, blooming July-August, followed by 3-angled, winged seed. The handsome cv. 'Blue Mirror', photographed in Fallbrook, Calif., has large 5 cm flowers vivid gentian-blue, with long spur in back. *Zones 3-9.* p. 488

nelsonii (So. Dakota and Idaho, so. to Arizona); slender perennial with brittle stems 15-40 cm high; deeply 3 to 5-parted leaves with lobes divided into narrow segments and covered by fine gray down;

crowded bright blue flowers 3 cm long, the two upper petals are white with blue lines; a slender spur in back; April to July bloom. *Zones 3-8.* p. 488

orientale (Zander): see CONSOLIDA orientalis (Hortus)

DENDRANTHEMA morifolium as in Floras of China and Russia, is referred to CHRYSANTHEMUM morifolium (Zander)

DENDROBIUM   *Orchidaceae*

bigibbum (Queensland to New Guinea), "Cooktown orchid"; showy epiphyte having stems to 40 cm long, in upper part with leathery 12 cm leaves; from the apex of pseudobulbs an arching inflorescence of 6 to 12 flowers to 5 cm across, rich rosy-magenta. Floral emblem of Queensland. *Tropical.* *Zone 12.* p. 85

densiflorum (Himalayas, Burma); beautiful epiphyte with tall, stout cane-like 4-sided pseudobulbs bearing 3-5 leathery leaves; the flowers golden-yellow with velvety orange-yellow lip, in dense, pendant trusses, from near the top of either old or young growth. (March-May). *Tropical.* *Zones 11-12.* p. 86

farmeri var. albiflorum; variety with sepals and petals creamy-white, and orange-yellow disc on lip. D. farmeri is from the Himalayan region; a compact epiphyte with club-shaped pseudobulbs tipped by leathery leaves; pendulous clusters of 5 cm flowers with rose petals. *Tropical.* *Zone 11.* p. 89

fimbriatum (Himalayas, Burma, Vietnam); tall epiphyte with cane-like stems with numerous leaves topped by loose clusters of flowers, deep yellow with fringed lip rich orange and velvet-like, a large blood red blotch at base of lip, in the variety oculatum, (March-April). *Tropical.* *Zones 11-12.* p. 86

infundibulum (So. Burma); an epiphyte of great beauty with black-haired cylindric stems to 60 cm long and 2-4 showy flowers 8-10 cm across from the upper joints, snow-white with orange-yellow stain in the throat, (May-Aug.). *Tropical.* *Zones 11-12.* p. 86

johnsoniae (macfarlanei) (New Guinea); noble epiphyte with erect cylindric, 2-3 leaved pseudobulbs bearing terminal racemes of large 10-12 cm flowers pure white except for 3-lobed lip marked purple; Summer. *Tropical.* *Zones 11-12.* p. 86

nobile 'Albiflorum' (Himalayas, Assam, Yunnan); popular epiphyte with large fragrant 8 cm flowers produced in twos and threes from nodes of 2-yr. pseudobulbs, sepals and petals white, lip white with deep velvet crimson throat, (Jan.-June). *Tropical.* *Zone 11.* p. 86

phalaenopsis (bigibbum var.) (Queensland, New Guinea, Timor); a most beautiful epiphyte with stiffly slender canes 60-90 cm tall, bearing leaves in 2 ranks, and long, arching chain-like sprays of large, neatly draped 8 cm flowers, the sepals pale magenta with reticulated darker nerves, petals rose, much larger; lip dark purplish-red; blooming variously, mainly in Spring, sometimes also in Fall to November. *Tropical.* *Zone 12.* p. 89

DENDROCALAMUS   *Gramineae*

asper (Java, and Myanmar or Burma), "Rebong" or "Rough dendrocalamus"; giant tropical clumping bamboo forming large clusters of strong culms 15 to 30 m high, and to 20 cm dia., and covered by dense brown hairs; large pale green sheaths, thick and hard, soon falling; leaves are 15-40 cm long and rough above. Because the wood is strong and durable, it is used much as structural lumber, especially for building of houses in Java. The young shoots are edible, and appear during Summer and Autumn. *Zone 9.* p. 552

giganteus (Burma or Myanmar; Sri Lanka, Malaya), "Giant Bamboo"; this tropical giant of the tribe, largest of all bamboos, grows to 35 m high with stem 25 cm or more in diameter, thin-walled, joints to 40 cm apart; later developing branches with large leaves to 50 cm long borne in graceful masses toward the top. The young emerging culms, growing at the rate of 45 cm a day, were an instrument of torture and death to prisoners of war in Ceylon, pushing through their bodies when they were tied down to the ground in a bamboo grove. In temperate climate for the large conservatory only. Widely planted in Southeast Asia and used for building, water-sprouting or plant pots. *Tropical.* *Zones 10-11.* p. 553

latiflorus (Sinocalamus) (D. strictus hort.) (Taiwan, Kwangtung, Vietnam), "Tim Chuk" or "Sweet bamboo"; handsome tropical and subtropical giant bamboo, with thick-walled culms to 20 m high and 12-20 cm in dia., and of a striking glossy, golden-yellow coloring, forming clusters; the leaves rather large 15-25 cm long and 3-5 cm wide, rounded at base. Widely grown in Kwangtung for its excellent edible shoots, usually cured, pickled and then used in soup or as relish. *Zones 6-9.* p. 550

pendulus (Malaysia); very handsome clump-forming tropical bamboo 6 m or more high, with clusters of slender culms 2-3 cm dia., and gracefully arching toward apex, and distinguished by fine, fern-like foliage; photographed in Bot. Gardens Singapore. *Zones 10-11.* p. 552

DENDROCHILUM *Orchidaceae*
glumaceum (Platyclinis) (Philippines), "Foxbrush"; small cluster-ing epiphyte with lovely arching slender spikes of scented 2-ranked flowers, sepals straw-white and greenish-yellow lip. *Tropical.* *Zone 11.* p. 88

DENDROMECON *Papaveraceae*
rigida harfordii (California: Santa Cruz and Santo Rosa Isl.), "Island tree poppy"; small rounded shrub to 2 m high, or tree to 6 m, with yellowish-white bark; spreading branches with roundish to oblong leaves 3-10 cm long, blue-glaucous and of thick texture; golden-yellow flowers 5-7 cm wide and fragrant, blooming April-June. Ideal in arid subtropic area of California. *Zone 9.* p. 816

DENDROPANAX *Araliaceae*
trifidus (Gilibertia) (Japan), "Kakure mino"; small evergreen tree with gray-brown branches and thick green branchlets; shiny green, ovate leaves 7-12 cm long, 3-nerved, sometimes 2 or 3-lobed or 3 to 5-cleft; small yellow-green flowers in clusters, followed by black berries. *Zone 7.* p. 647

DENNSTAEDTIA *Polypodiaceae (Filices)*
punctilobula (Nova Scotia to Georgia), a "Fragrant fern" or "Hay-scented fern"; hardy fern with hairy, creeping rhizome; bipinnate fronds to 1 m long, deeply cut, with pinnae coming to long slender points, and pleasantly fragrant. Often planted in the wild garden. *Zones 3-8.* p. 133

DENTARIA *Cruciferae*
diphylla (E. Canada to Minnesota, south to So. Carolina), "Toothwort" or "Crinkle-root"; herbaceous perennial with creeping scaly rhizome, to 30 cm high, and forming many rosettes; related to Cardamine; erect stem with leaves of 3 ovate, toothed leaflets; small white trumpet flowers with purple outside, clustered on short stalks, blooming March to June. *Zone 3.* p. 410

DERRIS *Leguminosae*
involucrata (Queensland), "Jewel vine"; woody climber with odd-pinnate leaves; the inflorescence in axillary racemes of charming, small pale purple flowers. The crushed roots and stems contain the insecticidal Rotenone, also used as fish poison. *Zone 10* p. 278

DESCHAMPSIA *Gramineae*
caespitosa (Greenland to Alaska, so. to No. Carolina, west to California; Eurasia), "Tufted hair-grass" or "Tussock grass"; very ornamental evergreen perennial with slender culms to 1 m high, forming clumps; leaves mostly basal, flat or folded; beautiful feathery inflorescence with huge clusters to 50 cm long, the nodding branches bearing spikelets toward the ends, ranging from silvery to greenish-yellow or tinted purple, in June to August. One of the most graceful of all grasses. *Zone 5.* p. 559

DESCURAINIA *Cruciferae*
bourgaeana (Sisymbrium; Spartocytisus nubigenus) "Hierba pajonera" or "Retama del Teide", endemic in Tenerife on Pico Teide 1600-2200 m; floriferous dense shrub of rounded form to 2 m high or more, covered entirely by masses of yellow flowers in showy clusters, over small, lobed foliage. *Zone 9.* p. 769

DESFONTAINEA *Loganiaceae*
spinosa (Chile, Perú); evergreen shrub to 3 m, with pale, shining branches; ovate, ilex-like 3-6 cm leaves glossy dark green with spiny margins; 3 cm tubular flowers scarlet with yellow lobes, blooming late Summer. *Zone 7.* p. 774

DEUTZIA *Saxifragaceae*
x elegantissima 'Rosalind' (purpurescens x sieboldiana); Donard cv. 1 to 1,5 m high, with fragrant 2 cm flowers dark carmine-rose, in clusters; deciduous shrub with erect slender branches; ovate leaves 5-8 cm long, serrate at margins. *Zone 5.* p. 869
gracilis (Japan), "Mayflower shrub" or "Slender deutzia"; attrac-tive floriferous winter-hardy deciduous shrub of low habit, about 1 m high or sometimes more, with slender branches, wide-spreading or arching; lanceolate leaves with star-like hairs above, serrate at margins, to 6 cm long; masses of pure white 2 cm flowers in open simple or compound clusters, blooming outdoors in Spring. *Zone 5.* p. 869
x magnifica 'Staphyleoides' (scabra x vilmoriniae) Lemoine cv.; robust, deciduous shrub with erect brown branches; ovate leaves 4-6 cm or more long, toothed at margins; showy panicles of large 2,5 cm white flowers with long deflexed petals, reminding of Staphylea, blooming in June. D. magnifica has double flowers filled with additional petals. *Zone 5.* p. 869
x rosea (gracilis x purpurascens) (France); handsome compact shrub with flaking bark, to 1,5 m high, having arching branches; cup-shaped white flowers 2 cm wide, soft rose-pink outside, in short

clusters, blooming in Mid-May to June; ovate leaves toothed at margins and slightly pubescent. *Zone 5.* p. 869
scabra (Japan, China), "Mayflower bush"; widely cultivated flowering shrub, especially in the double-flowered variety known as 'Pride of Rochester'; with arching branches, the shreddy bark reddish-brown; oval, hairy leaves deciduous; and large white flowers pinkish outside, the clusters spire-like and 8-12 cm long, June-July blooming. *Zone 5.* p. 869
scabra 'Candidissima', selected cultivar (Europe 1872), "White Mayflower bush"; deciduous erect shrub, 3-4 m high, with red-brown bark, peeling late; dark green ovate leaves 8-10 cm long, toothed at sides; double pure white flowers in beautiful erect cylindric racemes, in late June. *Zone 5.* p. 870
scabra 'Plena' (Japan: Honshu to Kyushu), "Maruba-Utsugi" in Japan; deciduous shrub to 2½ m high; hollow, woody branches with opposite ovate-pointed, rough, thinly pubescent leaves 6 to 10 cm long and finely serrate margins; very floriferous with slender racemes of small lacy, double flowers 1 cm long, white inside and tinged with rose outside. One of the latest to bloom. *Zone 5.* p. 870
scabra 'Pride of Rochester' (New York hyb. 1893), "Double Mayflower bush'; deciduous erect shrub 2 m or more high; somewhat pendant branches with brown bark; ovate leaves 5-10 cm long; charming flowers densely double of small petals, white inside, outside striped rose, blooming in early Summer. *Zone 5.* p. 870

DIANELLA *Liliaceae*
caerulea (New South Wales), the "Blue flax-lily"; rhizomatous perennial about 60 cm high, with fibrous roots; long linear, sheathing, keeled, rough-edged leaves from the base and in two ranks along the erect stalk, bearing the inflorescence in branched panicles of blue flowers, with deep yellow anthers, followed by blue berries. *Zones 9-10.* p. 444, 564

DIANTHUS *Caryophyllaceae*
x allwoodii (caryophyllus x plumarius), "Cottage pinks" or "Allwood pinks"; handsome perennial 20-50 cm high, forming tufts of firm, linear, blue-gray leaves; very pretty flowers with fringed petals, 4-5 cm across, white with red eye, also in various bright colors, pink, red, or bicolored, mostly semi-double. Good garden plant. *Zones 3-9.* p. 361
alpinus (Switzerland to Greece and Russia), "Alpine Pink"; smooth clustering perennial to 20 cm high; short leaves are hidden by a profusion of rose-purple flowers during late Spring, the 2 cm wedge-shaped petals are bearded and fringed at apex. *Zone 3.* p. 362
armeria (Centr. and So. Europe to No. Iran; naturalized in E. No. Amer.), "Deptford pink"; pubescent biennial also grown as annual, to 40 cm high; leaves linear to lanceolate, finely hairy; branched in-florescence of small carmine-rose flowers marked with white and purple, the bearded petals 1 cm long. *Zone 6.* p. 361
barbatus (So. and S. Eastern Europe to So. Russia and East), "Sweet William" or "Bunch pink"; popular garden perennial better treated as a biennial; from some seed also annual; smooth herb 45-60 cm high with green flat and broader leaves than most Pinks; the sturdy stem with 3 cm flowers in large bracted heads, the spreading petals fringed and calyx bearded, in colors from white, pink, rose, red, purplish to bi-colored, blooming from June to August; winter-hardy. *Zones 5-9.* p. 361
caryophyllus (So. Europe to India), "Carnation" or "Clove pinks"; tufted glaucous perennial plant of stiff habit, with bluish linear leaves, the flowers showy, double, dentate, in many colors, and spicy-fragrant. Usually grown as biennial. Occasionally hardy to Zone 5. *Subtropic to Warm temperate. Zones 8-10.* p. 361
caryophyllus chorus, "Clove pinks"; variety with pendant stems used for hanging baskets, as seen in Hardangerfjord, Norway; deep red, double flowers. *Subtropic. Zones 8-10.* p. 361
caryophyllus 'Mini Queen'; a special race of cut-flower car-nations with tall, erect, wiry stems 30-50 cm long, each carrying several medium size 4-5 cm fully double, spicily fragrant flowers deep rose with white edges, the petals fringed; (photographed at the Scandinavian Flower Show, Malmoe, Sweden, October 1970). *Warm temperate. Zones 8-10.* p. 361
caryophyllus 'Pink Sim', florist's "Carnation"; superb cultivar, grown under glass as cut flower crop at Longwood Garden, Kennett Square, Pennsylvania and elsewhere; long-stemmed large flowers 10-12 cm across, soft pink and fully double with fringed petals. *Zones 8-10.* p. 361
chinensis (Cent. and E. China, Japan), "Rainbow pink" or "Chinese pink"; very attractive biennial or short-lived perennial, also grown as annual; freely branching with erect stalks 30-50 cm high, set with linear leaves, and topped by solitary, showy flowers having fringed petals, in colors such as carmine-rose with white margin, to 3 cm across or more; also rosy-lilac, red or white, and bicolors; very popular for garden beds. *Zones 7-10.* p. 362

chinensis 'Heddewigii' (China, Japan), "Rainbow pink"; blue-green tufted biennial; flowers in velvety colors and markings and petals much cut and frilled; typically carmine-red with white eye. Usually grown as annual in this strain, blooming first year from seed. *Warm temperate. Zones 7-10.* p. 362

chinensis 'Heddewigii Baby Doll'; charming dwarf horticultural cultivar, practically covered by lovely cupped flowers 5 cm across, rose-pink with light center, the margins of petals fringed. *Zones 8-10.* p. 362

chinensis 'Pink Charm'; low-growing cultivar with narrow-lanceolate leaves, and large, showy flowers vivid rose-pink, with a deep purple ring around center, the upper margins of petal lobed and fringed. *Zones 8-10.* p. 362

chinensis 'Queen of Hearts', "Chinese pinks"; biennial, 15-50 cm high, with narrow leaves; stems branching at top, with 3 cm fringed single flowers, scarlet-red. *Warm temperate. Zones 8-10.* p. 362

chinensis 'Snowfire'; very attractive bushy biennial, grown as annual, to 20 cm high, covered with fringed flowers white with red center. *Warm temperate. Zones 8-10.* p. 362

deltoides (Europe to Temp. Asia), "Maiden pink"; clustering perennial forming mats of green foliage, with leaves very small and narrow; floral stalks forked, 10-30 cm high, with flowers red or pink, and petals spreading 2 cm wide. *Zone 4.* p. 360

gratianopolitanus (caesius) (Great Britain, Central Europe), "Cheddar pinks"; bushy perennial forming mounds, with blue-gray foliage; weak stems to 30 cm long with very fragrant pink blooms 2 cm wide, petals toothed. *Warm temperate. Zone 5.* p. 363

knappii (W. Yugoslavia, Hungary); pubescent perennial to 40 cm high, spreading and forming loose mats; gray-green leaves finely downy, linear-lanceolate and 3-nerved; bright sulphur-yellow flowers spotted purple near base, in June. *Zone 6.* p. 360

plumarius (Italian Alps to Dalmatia and East), "Cottage pinks" or "Feather carnation"; attractive mat-forming perennial much planted in rock-gardens; dense with waxy, glaucous-blue, linear leaves; the floral stalks usually branched, 20 to 30 cm high, and topped by sweetly scented, semi-double or double flowers 2-4 cm across, the petals deeply fringed, in colors rose to purple or white. *Warm temperate. Zones 3-10.* p. 361

plumarius 'Her Majesty', "Feather carnation"; striking cultivar, seen in col. New York Bot. Gardens, with lovely soft pink flowers feathered and deeply cut and fringed. *Zone 5.* p. 361

pungens hort. (E. Pyrenees of Spain); beautiful clustering perennial 5 to 20 cm high, woody at base, the branches with rigid leaves 2 cm long, the lovely flowers soft pink with petals 2 cm long and prettily fringed at margins. *Zone 7.* p. 362

seguieri (N.E. Spain, Pyrenees to Germany, Italy and Czechoslovakia), "Bearded pink"; related to D. chinensis; clustering perennial with creeping sterile and flowering stems, 20-40 cm high, forked and topped by fragrant, summer-blooming flowers having rose-pink 2 cm petals spotted white at base, fringed and bearded; flat linear, firm leaves. *Zone 7.* p. 362

sylvestris (Spain to So. Alps, and Greece), "Wood pinks"; densely clustering perennial to 30 cm high, with stiff, narrow linear, green basal leaves, 3-10 cm long; pale pink to rose flowers with notched petals, usually without scent. June to August. *Zone 6.* p. 360

DIASCIA *Scrophulariaceae*

barberae (So. Africa: W. Cape Prov.), "Twinspur"; annual with spreading square branches, to 50 cm high, having opposite ovate leaves to 4 cm long, toothed at margins; attractive rose-pink 2 cm flowers, yellow in throat, in terminal raceme. Frequently grown as potted plant. *Zone 9.* p. 503

rigescens (So. Africa: E. Cape), "Twinspur"; handsome perennial or annual of somewhat shrubby growth, to 50 cm high; with ovate, toothed leaves; terminal inflorescence of pyramidal dense spikes of warm coppery pink flowers, the corolla having 2 spurs. *Zone 6.* p. 503

DICENTRA *Fumariaceae*

eximia (Mts. of New York to Georgia), "Fringed bleeding-heart" or "Turkey corn"; interesting, sturdy perennial 30-50 cm high, forming clumps from short, fleshy rhizome; the compound leaves are pinnately lobed and feathery, mostly basal; the curious flowers are pink or purplish and heart-shaped, the outer petals spreading, nodding on stalks to 30 cm high, and blooming during Summer. *Zone 3.* p. 413

eximia 'Alba', "White Turkey-corn"; charming dwarf cultivar, seen June-blooming in Germany, with clusters of pendant flowers pure white. *Zone 3.* p. 415

formosa (Fumaria) (Brit. Columbia to California), "Western bleeding-heart"; charming perennial 30-40 cm high, forming tufts; the compound leaves all basal, pinnately divided into broad segments; the interesting flowers purplish-rose pendant from curving stalks, their corollas 2 cm long, with two outer petals spreading apart, and enclosing the inner two; blooming May to September. *Zone 4.* p. 413

spectabilis (Japan), "Bleeding-heart"; very popular garden perennial with fleshy rootstock, 30-60 cm high, with leathery, divided leaves, and arching stalks bearing pendulous, heart-shaped, rosy flowers 4 cm long, the white inner petals protruding, and blooming May-June. *Temperate. Zone 4.* p. 415

spectabilis 'Alba', "White bleeding-heart"; exquisite cultivar with arching racemes of pendulous waxy, snow-white flowers, rising from a rosette of firm, divided leaves, during early Summer. *Zone 4.* p. 415

DICHELOSTEMMA *Amaryllidaceae*

pulchellum (Brodiaea pulchella) (Oregon to Baja California and W. Utah), "Blue dicks" or "Wild hyacinth"; cormous perennial with chiefly basal leaves 2 cm wide, keeled beneath; floral stalk to 60 cm; flowers 2 cm long, with petals violet, subtended by purplish spathe bracts. *Zones 6-9.* p. 209

DICHONDRA *Convolvulaceae*

micrantha (repens) (West Indies), known as "Lawn-leaf"; used as a grass substitute in California; low herb creeping close to the ground and rooting, with close-matting stolons; small, rounded or kidney-shaped fresh green, silky leaves to 1-2 cm across, tightly overlapping; the little flowers greenish-yellow; seeds freely. *Subtropic. Zone 10.* p. 312, 569

DICHORISANDRA *Commelinaceae*

thyrsiflora (Brazil), "Blue ginger"; tall canes to 1 m or more, bearing rosettes of broad lance-shaped, glossy green leaves with purplish reverse, umbrella-like, topped by a huge raceme 15 cm long of brilliant, deep electric-blue flowers with yellow anthers. *Tropical. Zone 10.* p. 368

DICHROA *Saxifragaceae*

febrifuga (Himalaya to China); evergreen hydrangea-like shrub 1-2 m high, shoots and inflorescence downy; opposite lanceolate leaves 10-20 cm long, coarsely toothed and with ribs depressed; flowers white outside, bright blue inside, in terminal clusters; small berry-like blue fruit. *Zone 7.* p. 870

DICKSONIA *Dicksoniaceae (Filices)*

antarctica (Australia, Tasmania), "Tasmanian treefern"; tree fern with woody trunk to 15 m high, covered with matted aerial rootlets, fronds to 2 m long, 3 pinnate, dark green with hard lanceolate toothed segments which are turned down at the margins, and a network of straw-colored veins. *Humid-subtropic. Zones 10-11.* p. 126, 127

squarrosa (New Zealand), "Westland treefern"; a medium-sized tree-fern to 6 m high, the slender black trunk clothed with leafbases, crown with fronds nearly horizontal, 2-3 pinnate, to 2½ m long, dull, dark green and stiff-leathery, and harsh to the touch; on black-brown stalks clothed when young by long brown, stiff hairs. *Humid-subtropic. Zones 10-11.* p. 126

DICLIPTERA *Acanthaceae*

suberecta (Justicia, Jacobinia) (Uruguay); spreading low, herbaceous pubescent plant with small ovate, velvety 6 cm green leaves; downy 2-lobed flowers 3 cm long, reddish-orange, in small clusters. *Zone 10.* p. 629

DICTAMNUS *Rutaceae*

albus (fraxinella) (So. Europe to Palestine and China), "Dittany", "Gasplant", or "Burning bush"; aromatic perennial 60 to 90 cm or more high; the stems with pinnate leaves of 9 to 11 ovate, toothed leaflets scented of lemon-peel; irregular flowers 4 cm across, the 5 petals white or rosy, with purplish lines and long curving stamens. The volatile oil exuding gas-like from the foliage and inflorescence during warm evenings is easily ignited by a match or extreme heat. By some authorities believed to be the bush "that burned with fire" of the Bible (Moldenke). *Zone 4.* p. 495

albus 'Rubra' (So. Europe to No. China), "Burning bush" or "Red gas plant"; beautiful color variant, with flowers having spreading petals rose-red and purple lines lengthwise, blooming early Summer; followed by seed pods which are poisonous as is the plant. *Zone 4.* p. 495

DICTYOSPERMA *Palmae*

album (Mauritius), the "Princess-palm"; handsome feather-palm to 10 m, the slender, dark gray trunk with numerous vertical cracks, topped by a crown-shaft and the graceful pinnate fronds to 4 m long; the drooping leaflets shiny green with pale veins; the last undeveloped leaf always stands up in the center and unfolds from its binding as from a needle; fragrant reddish flowers at an early stage. *Tropical. Zones 11-12.* p. 104

DIDIEREA   *Didiereaceae*
trollii (S.W. Madagascar); weird xerophytic succulent with thick arms waving in all directions forming tangled twigs, eventually forming trunks with horizontal branches; stems covered with convex tubercles with short shoots whose tips bear 5 thin thorns; fleshy leaves 1-2 cm long; cyathia greenish-yellow. *Arid tropical.* *Zone 11.*   *p. 193*

DIDISSANDRA   *Gesneriaceae*
morganii (Malaya); curious tropical perennial with thick woody rootstock; basal rosette of glossy deep green, fern-like, leathery leaves deeply lobed along sides; flowers with cylindrical tube and a two-lipped and spurred white corolla colored purplish-red above. *Zone 12.*   *p. 67*

DIDYMOCHLAENA   *Polypodiaceae (Filices)*
truncatula (Aspidium) (Tropics of South America, Africa, Polynesia); terrestrial fern, resembling Adiantum in younger stage, later with bipinnate fronds densely tufted, to 1½ m long, the leaflets nearly rectangular, 1-2½ cm long, thin-leathery, glossy green, and the margins irregularly crenate or sinuate. *Tropical. Zone 11.*   *p. 133*

DIEFFENBACHIA   *Araceae*
amoena (Colombia, Costa Rica); sturdy, thick-stemmed species with large, oblong-pointed, glabrous leaves, deep green and marked with cream-white bands and blotches along veins. *Zone 12.*   *p. 27*
amoena 'Tropic Snow' (syn. 'Tropical Topaz' or 'Hi-Color'); beautiful Florida (Chaplin) mutation of very compact habit; showy leathery foliage glossy deep green highly variegated from center with cream and nile-green. *Tropical. Zone 12.*   *p. 27*
'Camilla'; outstanding Danish mutation of D. 'Exotica Perfection', similar to D. 'Marianne'; of smallish, compact, sturdy habit and freely self-branching; highly colored ovate, slender-pointed leaves primarily creamy-yellow with lighter veins, bordered in rich green, 20 to 25 cm long. *Zone 12.*   *p. 27*
'Candida'; handsome cultivar from Holland, of very compact habit, branching from base, dense with highly variegated foliage; broadly lanceolate leaves stiffly erect, splashed and marbled cream over fresh green. *Zone 11.*   *p. 27*
'Exotica Perfection'; a Florida selection of compact habit, the smallish leaves 15-20 cm long, broadly bordered with deep matte-green and of leathery feel; highly variegated greenish-ivory. Excellent keeper as a house plant. *Tropical. Zone 12.*   *p. 27*
maculata (picta) (Brazil), "Spotted dumbcane", in Latin America as "Cucaracha"; glossy, grass-green, oval leaves with cordate base and ivory-white marbling and blotching; petioles dotted pale green; spathe greenish; found growing wild by the writer at the confluence of the Solimoes and Rio Negro in Amazonas. *Tropical. Zone 12.*   *p. 27*
maculata 'Rudolph Roehrs' (Roehrs cultivar, named by the author 1937), "Gold dieffenbachia"; a striking mutant having oblong pointed 25-30 cm leaves almost entirely yellow or chartreuse, with ivory-white blotches, and only the midrib and border dark green. Both beautiful and showy, and proven an excellent house plant. *Tropical. Zone 12.*   *p. 27*
'Wilson's Delight'; handsome, bold plant; wide, fleshy leaves deep green with broad, cream-white midrib, the cream fanning out into the lateral veins. *Tropical. Zone 12.*   *p. 27*

DIERAMA   *Iridaceae*
pendulum (So. Africa), "Angel's fishing rods"; cormous plant to more than 1 m high, with long rigid linear basal leaves; the floral stalk arching with a raceme of showy nodding pink bell-flowers 3 cm long; summer blooming. *Zone 9.*   *p. 225*
pulcherrimum (So. Africa: Cape to Transvaal), "Wand flower" or "East London harebell"; pretty, cormous herb about 1½ m high, with basal long-linear, narrow, rigid leaves; blooming on branched, pendant spikes, the 3 cm funnel-shaped flowers bright purple or blood-red, in Autumn. *Subtropic. Zone 9.*   *p. 225*

DIERVILLA   *Caprifoliaceae*
florida; referred to Weigela, as all large-flowered Diervilla. (Kruessmann)
sessilifolia (Virginia to Georgia and Alabama), "Bush honey-suckle"; deciduous suckering shrub to 1½ m high, with arching branches, the branchlets 4-angled; leaves lanceolate to 15 cm long; inflorescence in clusters of small sulphur-yellow flowers. *Zone 5.*   *p. 672*

DIETES   *Iridaceae*
bicolor (Moraea) (So. Africa: E. Cape), "Yellow wild iris"; tufts of evergreen, stiff and light green leaves growing to 60 cm and only 1 cm wide; the erect, branching floral stalk with most attractive flowers 5 cm across, with 3 inner petals clear lemon-yellow, and 3 round, flat petals blotched orange and maroon-black near base; summer blooming. October-November in So. Africa. *Zones 8-10.*   *p. 426*

grandiflora (So. Africa: E. Cape to Natal), "Large wild iris"; rhizomatous perennial with creeping rootstalk, to 1 m or more high; sword-shaped leaves in flat fan; big flowers to 10 cm across, with large white to pinkish petals and purple band in center. *Zones 9-10. p. 426*
vegeta (Moraea iridioides) (So. Africa: E. Cape, Natal), "African iris"; lovely, free-blooming rhizomatous, clustering plant with linear, dark green basal leaves arranged fan-like from creeping root stock; on long branching stalks the somewhat fleeting, iris-like flowers 5-8 cm across, white tinged with blue, and yellow on outer petals, the crest of style marked with blue; summer-blooming. Widely planted in California where it seems to be in bloom all year. *Zones 8-10. p. 426*

DIGITALIS   *Scrophulariaceae*
grandiflora (ambigua) (C. Europe, Balkans, So. Russia, W. Siberia), "Yellow foxglove"; hairy perennial with lanceolate toothed, veiny leaves, the nodding tubular 5 cm flowers pale ochre-yellow marked with brown inside. *Zone 3.*   *p. 502*
lutea (S.W. and Cent. Europe, to Italy, and Morocco), "Straw foxglove"; bushy perennial to 60 cm or more high, with lanceolate leaves; the stems terminating in branched 1-sided racemes of yellow to whitish flowers having 3 cm corolla, the upper lip 2-parted, and blooming during July. *Zone 6.*   *p. 502*
x mertonensis (grandiflora x purpurea); true-breeding English tetraploid hybrid by Innes, 1925, with dark green leaves; inflorescence in spires 80-100 cm high of large pendant flowers, having corollas 6 cm long, with lighter apex, blooming May to June. *Zone 5.*   *p. 502*
purpurea (W. Europe), "Foxglove"; biennial with wrinkled leaves in rosettes and on the erect ½-1 m showy spike of dense, bell-shaped, bilabiate, nodding flowers, purple, varying to white, with dark purple spots, edged white inside, 8 cm long, in Summer. Dried leaves are principal source of the drug digitalis. *Zone 4.*   *p. 502*
purpurea 'Alba', "White foxglove"; color variant with a spike of white 8 cm bell-flowers, yellow in throat. *Zone 4.*   *p. 502*
purpurea 'Excelsior hyb.'; excellent hybrid strain of robust habit, biennial with spikes dense with big bell-shaped flowers exposing the interior mottling; in various colors cream, pink, carmine, or purple, blooming early Summer. *Zone 4.*   *p. 502*
purpurea 'Rosea'; handsome variant with tall erect spikes of large pendant bell flowers, the corolla deep rose, and soft pink at spreading apex, mottled dark red inside. *Zone 4.*   *p. 502*
sibirica (E. Asia); herbaceous biennial or short-lived perennial, with downy, lanceolate leaves; the inflorescence on leafy stalks to 1 m high, bearing slender 1-sided racemes of yellowish-white trumpet flowers 2-3 cm long, the corolla tube swollen at base and netted with brown, blooming July-August. *Zone 3.*   *p. 502*

DILLENIA   *Dilleniaceae*
indica (India to Java and Philippines), "Elephant apple"; handsome tree to 12 m high, usually evergreen but may lose foliage in dry season; very ornamental, large oblanceolate, thick leaves 30-40 cm long, bright light green above and strongly pinnately depressed-veined; rough beneath, and margins toothed; fragrant magnolia-like white flowers with golden stamens. Globose, acid fruit to 10 cm dia., edible when fresh; used in curries and jellies. *Tropical. Zone 10.*   *p. 695, 908*

DIMOCARPUS longan (Zander):
see EUPHORIA longan (Hortus)

DIMORPHOTHECA   *Compositae*
ecklonis: see OSTEROSPERMUM ecklonis
sinuata (aurantiaca in hort.) (So. Africa), "Rain Cape marigold"; beautiful freely branching perennial in mild climate, grown as annual in cold regions, to 30 cm high, with oblanceolate 8 cm leaves along stems, coarsely toothed; inflorescence 3-4 cm across, with disc-flowers yellow, and ray-florets orange-yellow, and violet at base. *Zone 10.*   *p. 384*

DIONAEA   *Droseraceae (Carnivorous Plants)*
muscipula (Carolinas), "Venus fly trap"; carnivorous perennial rosette of damp mossy places, with leaves 3-12 cm long; in the upper part the two halves of a leaf are turned upward and equipped with long teeth which close traplike when entered by flies; the small 2 cm white flowers in clusters on tall stalks. *Warm temperate. Zone 8.*   *p. 203*

DIONYSIA   *Primulaceae*
involucrata (Pamir-Altai, Russia); alpine perennial related to Primula, forming dense cushions; fragrant 1½ cm leaves toothed at margins, with raised veins, to 1½-2 cm long; rose-pink flowers with yellow eye. *Zone 5.*   *p. 341*

DIOON   *Cycadaceae: Zamiaceae*
edule (C. Mexico, Nuevo Leon), "Virgin's palm"; palm-like plant from the hot open country, closest to the fossil cycads, with stiff

pinnate leaves 1-2 m long, and having spiny tips, the young petioles are covered with white wool; edible seeds borne in cones to 30 cm long. *Tropical. Zone 11.*   *p. 113*

purpusii (Puebla, Oaxaca, So. Mexico); stout, short trunk, crowned with numerous stiff and ascending pinnate leaves to 1 m or more, pinnae 5-10 cm long, sharp-pointed usually with 1-3 spinelike teeth on the upper margin; male cones 15-20 cm, ovate female cones 45 cm long, with woolly bract. *Zone 11.*   *p. 113*

spinulosum (Mexico: Veracruz, Yucatán), "Giant dioon"; treefern-like plant from the rain forest, with tall trunks to 15 m high and slender, the spreading pinnate leaves to 2 m long in noble rosette, spiny teeth at margins. *Zone 11.*   *p. 113*

DIOSCOREA   *Dioscoreaceae*

discolor (Surinam), "Ornamental yam"; tall climbing plant with beautiful broad, heart-shaped leaves having long basal lobes, dark olive-green marbled light green and silver-gray, veins carmine to silver, reverse purple. *Tropical. Zone 11.*   *p. 277*

elephantipes (Testudinaria) (Cape Prov., Natal, Transvaal), "Elephant's foot" or "Hottentot-bread"; curious-looking partially exposed tuber to 90 cm across, the bark divided into corrugated angled knobs and from which rises the annual vining stalk bearing heart- or kidney-shaped leaves and greenish-yellow flowers with dark spots. *Subtropic. Zone 10.*   *p. 204, 277*

macrostachys (Testudinaria) (Mexico), the "Tortoise plant"; large, knobby woody, chocolate-brown tuber 20 cm or more across, resting above the soil and looking like a horny turtle, its coat broken into numerous angled plates; sprouting slender, asparagus-like shoots becoming vine-like, 1 m or more high, with alternate leaves and small axillary greenish-yellow flowers; grown as a curiosity in greenhouse. *Arid-tropical. Zones 10-11.*   *p. 204*

quaternata (Pennsylvania to Florida, west to Oklahoma), "Wild yam"; tuberous-rooted perennial, with stems at first erect, then twining upward counter-clockwise; cordate-ovate corrugated leaves with parallel veins, to 15 cm long; small greenish flowers, and pendant winged seed capsules. *Zone 5.*   *p. 277*

DIOSMA pulchra: see COLEONEMA pulchrum
uniflora: see ADENANDRA uniflora

DIOSPYROS   *Ebenaceae*

digyna (ebenaster) (Mexico, C. America), "Black sapote" or "Chocolate-pudding tree"; evergreen tree to 20 m, with alternate, simple elliptic leaves, glossy dark green; small fragrant, whitish flowers; globular fruit 10 cm dia., olive green becoming dark; soft chocolate-brown flesh. Popular fruit in Mexico. Photographed in Borda Gardens, Cuernavaca, Morelos. *Zone 11.*   *p. 908*

ebenum (India, Sri Lanka), "East Indian ebony" or "Makassar ebony"; large evergreen tropical tree with smooth branchlets, elliptic, glossy green leaves 5 to 15 cm long; male flowers 3 to 15 together, female blossoms solitary, producing small 2 cm fruit. Wood is jet-black, sometimes streaked with yellow, very heavy and strong, the best ebony of commerce. Fruit is edible, borne on female trees. *Zone 10.*   *p. 908*

kaki (Japan, China), "Kaki" or "Japanese persimmon"; a well-known fruit tree of the Orient; bushy, deciduous tree 8 to 12 m high, with brownish branches, broad ovate leathery leaves 8-20 cm long and shining green above, pubescent beneath; 4 cm flowers yellowish-white; on female trees the depressed globose glowing red fruit 8 cm dia., with custard-like orange flesh; especially piquant and delicious when served frozen, with a taste like fruity sherbert. Reported frozen at minus 10 deg. C. *Zones 8-9.*   *p. 627-905*

kaki 'Fuyu', "Japanese persimmon"; with firm-fleshed fruit, like a flattened apple; orange-colored and non-astringent, even when not ripe; ready in late Autumn. Self-fertile fruiting without assistance of pollinating trees. *Zone 8.*   *p. 908*

kaki 'Hachiya'; large conical, somewhat pear-shaped, very large fruit to 10 cm dia., of high quality, skin deep red; nearly seedless, with delicious yellow, jelly-like flesh slightly astringent; ripens in Autumn. *Subtropic. Zone 9.*   *p. 908*

kaki 'Mexican cv.' ('Tamopan'), "Chocolate persimmon"; popular variety similar to D. 'kaki', but with smaller, elongate turban-shaped fruit having very sweet, brown streaked flesh, in taste non-astringent when fully ripe. *Zone 10.*   *p. 908*

vaccinioides (So. China to Malaysia), "Dwarf persimmon"; low much branched evergreen shrub with rigid branches to 1 m high, the young growth rusty-pubescent; small leathery, glossy leaves 2 cm long; small white, 4-petalled axillary flowers in May; oval-pointed shiny black 2 cm fruit holding 2-4 brown seeds; edible when fully ripe. A good hedge plant resembling Buxus or also Vaccinium. *Zones 10-11.*   *p. 908*

virginiana (Connecticut to Florida and Texas), "American persimmon" or "Possum apple"; deciduous tree 20 to 30 m high,

having rugged bark and rounded crown, the branches often slightly pendulous; dense foliage with ovate leaves 8-15 cm long, shining green above; bell-shaped flowers, with greenish-yellow corolla, tipped by 4 recurved lobes; the female blooms followed by numerous oblong fruit 3 to 5 cm dia., yellow with red cheek. To become edible, fruit must be fully ripe and soft, usually after first hard frost. *Zone 5.*   *p. 912*

DIPELTA   *Caprifoliaceae*

floribunda (Central and West China); deciduous shrub 2 to 5 m high, with peeling bark; ovate, slender-pointed leaves 10 cm long; charming bell-shaped flowers 3 cm long, the corolla pink with orange-yellow throat and sweetly fragrant. *Zone 6.*   *p. 672*

DIPHASIASTRUM complanatum (Zander):
see LYCOPODIUM complanatum (Hortus)

DIPLACUS glutinosus: see MIMULUS aurantiacus

DIPLADENIA (Zander 84) referred to MANDEVILLA (Hortus 3)

DIPLAZIUM   *Polypodiaceae (Filices)*

lanceum hort.: see PYRROSIA lingua

pycnocarpon (Athyrium) (Québec to Kansas, Georgia and Louisiana), "Glade fern"; hardy tufted fern with pinnate fronds 1 m or more long, bright green changing to bronze in Autumn; the taller fertile leaves have narrower pinnae. *Zones 3-8.*   *p. 133*

DIPSACUS   *Dipsacaceae*

sylvestris (W. Europe to Ukraine, Asia Minor), "Teasel"; thistle-like, prickly perennial or biennial to 2 m high; basal leaves oblanceolate with crenate margins, stem-leaves usually united at base, prickly on underside and along margins; pale lavender flowers in a spiny, cylindric head 5 cm long; of ornamental value in dried floral arrangements. *Zone 3.*   *p. 414*

DIPTERONIA   *Aceraceae*

sinensis (C. China); deciduous tree to 10 m high, bearing handsome opposite leaves 20-30 cm long, with odd-pinnate serrate leaflets; upright panicles of whitish flowers with 5 sepals longer than petals; the seed subtended by ovate or nearly orbicular cupped wings, in large clusters, green at first, later turning red-brown. *Zone 6.*   *p. 636*

DIRCA   *Thymelaeaceae*

palustris (New Brunswick to Minnesota, so. to Florida), "Rope-bark" or "Atlantic Leatherwood"; deciduous shrub 1-2 m high, with flexible branches having tough bark; obovate leaves 3-6 cm long, pale green above, and glaucous beneath; flowers yellowish, not as conspicuous as those of Forsythia, blooming March-April. Pliable shoots have been used for basket making by the Indians. *Zone 4.*   *p. 892*

DISA   *Orchidaceae*

uniflora (grandiflora) (So. Africa), "Pride of Table Mountain"; terrestrial rosette of shining, lanceolate leaves with tuberous root-stock, and producing an erect, leafy spike to 60 cm high with a lax cluster of showy flowers to 10 cm across, the helmet-shaped dorsal sepal red outside, inside lighter, veined with crimson and shaded with yellow, the lower sepals vivid scarlet, lip small, (Jan.-April). *Subtropic. Zone 11.*   *p. 89*

DISANTHUS   *Hamamelidaceae*

cercidifolius (Japan: Kyushu), "Maruba-No-Ki"; tree-like deciduous shrub to 5 m high, branching from near base; leaves rounded to ovate 10 cm across, palmately 5 to 7-lobed, bluish-green and somewhat leathery, most beautiful in its brilliant autumn coloring, becoming wine-red with orange tints; flowers dark purple 2 cm across, having linear petals, but not showy, blooming in Fall. *Zone 6.*   *p. 735*

DISCHIDIA   *Asclepiadaceae*

nummularia (Queensland, Papua, Borneo); epiphytic succulent vine growing on small trees, starting out with small fleshy, round leaves less than 2½ cm dia., and called "Thruppence" in New Guinea; later forming large pear-like, hollow, angled bulbs glaucous-gray, harboring ants. *Zones 10-11.*   *p. 270*

rafflesiana (Malaya, New Guinea), "Malayan urn vine"; epiphytic climber with oddly thick-fleshy oval leaves formed into pitchers; the mature, 8-10 cm, opposite leaves are pear-like, hollow, purplish inside, in habitat frequented by ants; yellowish flowers in umbels. *Tropical. Zone 11.*   *p. 270*

DISCOCACTUS   *Cactaceae*

silicicola (Brazil: Mato Grosso); small globular cactus to 5 cm high, with bristly woolly mass at apex, the numerous ribs knobby and with small spines; large white nocturnal, fragrant flowers. Of weak growth, and difficult on their own roots, therefore often grafted in cultivation. *Zone 11.*   *p. 156*

DISPORUM   Liliaceae

flavum (col. in Korea), "Fairy bells"; handsome perennial with creeping rootstock, with bambus-like, rigid stems 60-90 cm high; the ovate leaves very ornamental, soft-leathery, having parallel depressed veins, and with silky sheen beneath; the lovely pendant, lemon-yellow Mandarin bells 3 cm long. Young shoots spear up each Spring.
Zones 4-8.   p. 447

sessile 'Variegatum' (Japan, China), "Japanese Fairy bells"; attractive rhizomatous woodland perennial to 60 cm high, with alternate lanceolate green leaves to 15 cm long, handsomely lined and margined with white; the bell-shaped flowers white, 3 cm long, spring-blooming. Zones 4-9.   p.447

DISSOTIS   Melastomataceae

rotundifolia (plumosa) (Trop. W. Africa: Sierra Leone to Zaire); handsome tropical perennial woody at base, with slender procumbent 4-angled branches with bristly nodes; leaves broadly ovate, to 4 cm long, 3-veined and hairy; the showy flowers purplish rose, to 5 cm across. Zone 11.   p. 460

DISTICTIS   Bignoniaceae

buccinatoria (Phaedranthus; Bignonia cherere) (Mexico), "Blood trumpet"; vine with showy flowers which I first saw, smothered with blooms, around the Union Buildings in Pretoria, South Africa; rough-leathery oval leaves and axillary clusters of large trumpet-shaped waxy flowers with flaring lobes, crimson-red with scarlet sheen, and yellow throat, 5 cm across. Subtropic. Zones 9-10.   p. 268, 270

x riversii (Phaedranthus, Tecoma, Bignonia) (buccinatoria x laxiflora); tendril-climbing woody vine, with paired obovate leaves, shining green; showy large flowers with spreading petals 6-8 cm across, rosy purple with white throat. Tropical. Zone 10.   p. 268

DIZYGOTHECA   Araliaceae

elegantissima (transferred to Schefflera by D. Frodin, Baileya 1989) (Aralia) (New Caledonia), "False aralia" or "Fingerleaf aralia"; graceful shrub, forming small tree to 8 m high; slender stems and branches mottled cream; in juvenile stage with threadlike, narrow lobed segments metallic red-brown; in mature stage as tree the leaflets are much wider. Tropical. Zone 11.   p. 36

elegantissima 'Castor'; a compact growing, freely branching cultivar seen in Germany, with palmately compound leaves, the leathery leaflets broader than the species, purplish-green with ivory-white midrib. Tropical. Zone 10.   p.647

veitchii (Schefflera) (New Caledonia, Vanuatu); slender shrub with leathery, palmately compound, dainty leaves dark coppery green, the little segments long-elliptic and with pink ribs, the margins crisped; in maturity stage found on older specimen, the leaves are larger with much broader leaflets having margins wavy-undulate. Referred to Schefflera by Dr. David Frodin of New Guinea University. Zone 10.   p. 647

DODECATHEON   Primulaceae

hendersonii (Vancouver Is. to California), "Sailor caps" or "Mosquito bills"; handsome perennial 15-40 cm high, with obovate fleshy, 15 cm leaves in basal rosette; nodding, cyclamen-like flowers, with reflexed 2 cm corolla lobes purplish red, revealing dark red filaments and anthers margined yellow; blooming February to May. Zone 8.   p. 478

meadia (pauciflorum) (Manitoba to Pennsylvania and Texas), "Shooting-star"; small perennial herb to 50 cm high, with wavy-margined basal leaves, and nodding cyclamen-like flowers with reflexed corolla lobes, rose with white base and long purple anthers, blooming April-June. Zone 3.   p. 478

pulchellum (So. Alaska and W. Canada, Kansas, California and New Mexico), "Southern shooting star"; handsome small herbaceous perennial to 50 cm high, forming rosettes of oblanceolate leaves to 25 cm long; the interesting flowers usually in clusters on long stalks, the purplish-red corolla lobes are reflexed, displaying yellow pollen, and blooming May-June. Zone 5.   p.478

DODONAEA   Sapindaceae

viscosa (Arizona to W. Indies), "Hopseed-bush"; fast-growing evergreen bush to 5 m high, with many upright branches, narrow willow-like 10 cm green leaves; small whitish flowers in short clusters; the straw-like pinkish winged seed capsules were used as hops by early settlers. Subtropic. Zone 9.   p. 867

viscosa 'Purpurea', "Purple hop-bush"; introduced from New Zealand; a rich bronze-purple leaved cultivar, the color deepening in Winter; best coloring in full sun. Subtropic. Zone 9.   p. 867

DOLICHANDRONE in Florida and California hort.:
see MARKHAMIA lutea

DOLICHOS   Leguminosae

lablab (Trop. Africa: Egypt), "Hyacinth-bean"; woody perennial climber with purple stems, usually grown as an annual; leaves of 3 ovate, purplish-green leaflets 8 to 15 cm long, and veined with purple, rosy-lilac 2 cm butterfly flowers in loose racemes, standing out from the foliage; followed by velvety, bean-like pods 6 cm long. Tropical. Zone 10.   p. 278

DOLICHOTHELE: see MAMMILLARIA

DOMBEYA   Sterculiaceae (Byttneriaceae in Hortus)

burgessiae (Kenya to Natal), "Wedding flower" or "Rose-mound"; palmately veined, broad cordate leaves to 20 cm long, the surface corrugated and with contrasting yellow veins; charming pale pink flowers with red veins, 3 cm across, in large clusters. Tropical. Zone 10.   p. 884

elegans ((Réunion); slender branched, smooth tropical shrub, with broad cordate leaves to 12 cm long, serrate at margins and palmately veined; smallish flowers in attractive dense clusters, soft pink. Zones 10-11.   p. 884

pulchra (South Africa); attractive subtropical tree, with simple, palmately veined, lobed leaves, and bearing at branch tips showy clusters of beautiful white or pinkish flowers, 5 to 6 cm across, and rose-red in center, the 5 petals usually overlapping and forming a saucer. Zones 9-10.   p. 884

tiliacea (natalensis) (S.E. Africa: Natal), "Heartleaf dombeya"; small tree to 8 m, with gray-brown bark; soft leaves cordate-ovate, to 9 cm long, irregularly toothed; pretty white flowers with crimson red center, 3 cm across, in showy clusters though often hidden between the foliage. Subtropic. Zones 9-10.   p. 884

wallichii (E. Africa, Madagascar); tropical evergreen tree to 10 m, with large 30 cm, lobed, herbaceous leaves matte-green, densely hairy beneath; showy bell-like flowers with flat, spreading petals salmon-rose to scarlet, in dense hanging heads. Zones 10-11.   p. 884

DONATIA   Donatiaceae

nova-zelandiae (Tasmania, New Zealand), "Cushion plant"; beautiful Alpine perennial forming cushions to 1 m across; densely branched herb with crowded stems to 10 cm high, the branches covered with white hairs, the thick imbricate, glossy leaves 1 cm long; small fleshy white 1 cm flowers. Zone 9.   p. 329

DONAX   Marantaceae

gradis (cannaeformis) (Malaysia to Solomon Isl.); rambling tropical perennial, seen in Malacca rain-forest; branches to 3 m long, with ornamental oblique-oblong leaves to 20 cm long, clustered at end of slender branches; inflorescence in panicles with pairs of small flowers. Zone 11.   p. 72

DOODIA   Filices: Polypodiaceae

caudata (New Zealand: North Isl., also Australia, Polynesia), "Hacksaw-fern" or Maori "Moki-moki"; handsome small fern on short rhizome, bearing numerous pinnate fronds on black stalks, 10 to 30 cm long; the barren fronds shorter and more drooping; the fertile fronds stiffly erect with single row of sori along midrib. Zone 10.   p. 141

DORONICUM   Compositae

cordatum (columnae) (S.E. Europe to W. Asia), "Leopard's-bane"; herbaceous perennial 25-60 cm high, with leaves cordate-kidney-shaped or ovate; yellow flowers 5 cm wide, with spreading threadlike ray-florets, blooming during Spring. Zone 5.   p. 385

plantagineum (W. Europe), "Plantain leopard's bane"; excellent garden perennial forming clumps, to 75 cm high with broad-ovate leaves, toothed at margins; daisy-like bright yellow flowers to 8 cm across, during May. Foliage will disappear in Summer. Very satisfa tory in cut flower arrangements. Zone 3.   p. 385

DOROTHEANTHUS   Aizoaceae

bellidiformis (Cleretum) (Cape Prov.), "Livingstone-daisy"; small annual herb branching from the root; short, fleshy obovate leaves, rough-puckered, to 8 cm long; masses of daisy-like flowers in colors red purple, salmon, straw-yellow, yellow, lavender, white or white with red tips, opening to the sun. Arid-subtropic. Zone 10.   p. 145, 301

DORSTENIA   Moraceae

argentata (Santa Catarina, Brazil); erect, small plant with a downy purple stem and lanceolate leaves to 12 cm long, dark green at margins while the main area, in the center, is metallic silver; the small male and female flowers crowded on a concave receptacle, margined with purple tubercles. Zone 11.   p. 459

crispa (Somalia, Kenya); curious succulent from dry regions; thick-fleshy stems 12 to 40 cm tall, with swollen base 4 cm thick; the branches pale brown and covered with tubercles and bearing leaf-scars; small, narrow obovate, turgid leaves 4-7 cm long, tinted coppery and with curly, dentate margins; receptacles are round stellate, 2 cm across, the margins with 8 to 10 spreading bracts. Zone 10.   p. 200

yambuyaensis (Zaire); erect, bristly herb with oblanceolate leaves to 15 cm long, shining green above, pale and dull beneath, and irregularly toothed; the green receptacle angularly rounded, almost 2½ cm across, the winged margins with rays to 10 cm long. *Tropical. Zone 12.* *p. 459*

DORYANTHES *Agavaceae*
excelsa (New South Wales, Queensland), the "Globe spear-lily"; bold rosette of numerous succulent sword-shaped leaves to 2 m long; and a leaning inflorescence to 4½ m long, the heavy head of 10 cm flowers with divided perianth segments crimson-red outside, pale inside, and with green bracts. *Subtropic. Zone 10.* *p. 150*

DORYCNIUM *Leguminosae*
hirsutum (Cytisus lotus) (So. Europe), "Canary clover"; perennial subshrub to 60 cm high, the hairy branching stems from woody base and normally dying back in Winter; leaves compound of 5 obovate leaflets to 3 cm long; pea-like flowers 2 cm long, from June to September, having corolla white with rose lines and purple keel. *Zone 4.* *p. 759*

DOUGLASIA *Primulaceae*
laevigata (Cascade Mts. of Washington, Oregon); densely leafy, low perennial 6 cm high, forming tufts; small ovate, fleshy 2 cm grayish-green leaves in rosettes; attractive bright rose flowers having funnel-form corollas 1 cm across, and crested in the throat, borne in clusters, in Spring and Autumn. *Zone 6.* *p. 479*

DOVYALIS *Flacourtiaceae*
caffra (So. Africa), "Kei-apple"; dense thorny shrub to 5 m; wiry branches with one large stiff spine to each node; leaves shiny green; small yellowish flowers; yellow 3-5 cm fruit with yellow flesh of apricot flavor; eaten fresh or in preserves. *Subtropic. Zone 10.* *p. 913*

hebecarpa (Aberia gardneri) (Sri Lanka, India), "Ceylon-gooseberry"; decorative evergreen growing into a small dioecious tree to 6 m high; the alternate ovate, undulate, 10 cm papery leaves glossy green with metallic sheen, and rosy midrib, grayish beneath; the thin wiry branches set with scattered 1 cm needle-like thorns; small greenish flowers, followed by 2½ cm purple fruit with edible pulp. *Zone 10.* *p. 913*

x hybrida (abyssinica x hebecarpa), "Tropical apricot"; natural hybrid in Florida; large spreading shrub to 5 m, light green ovate leaves 8-10 cm in length, on long drooping branches, some with thorns; small greenish flowers; 3 cm globular fruit with velvety brownish skin and soft melting flesh of apricot flavor. *Zone 10.* *p. 913*

DOXANTHA: see MACFADYENA

DRABA *Cruciferae*
arabisans (Newfoundland to Ontario and New York); bushy perennial 20-50 cm high, with numerous erect stems; basal leaves clustering, narrow and 4 cm long; stem-leaves scattered, smaller and toothed; small white flowers in elongate clusters. *Zone 3.* *p. 410*

carinthiaca (siliquosa) (Pyrenees to Alps and Carpathian Mts.); clustering perennial to 15 cm high, with many stems 12 cm long, forming rosettes of small 1 cm ovate, hairy leaves, ciliate at margins and single-toothed at apex; small white flowers, in elongate clusters, May-blooming in New York. *Zone 5.* *p. 410*

pyrenaica: see Petrocallis pyrenaica

sibirica (Siberia, Caucasus; Greenland); popular vigorous prostrate perennial quickly forming rosettes of large oblong, soft green leaves, from which rise stems 15 cm long, bearing clusters of small, bright yellow flowers, blooming both in Spring and Autumn. *Zone 3.* *p. 410*

DRACAENA *Agavaceae (Liliaceae)*
americana (Honduras to Panama); the only cultivated species native in America, a slender tree with swollen base resembling Yucca, trunk to 7 m high topped by a rosette of long, glossy-green, thin strapleaves clasping the stem; panicles of white flowers followed by orange fruit. *Zones 11-12.* *p. 116*

congesta: see CORDYLINE stricta

deremensis 'Compacta', "Dwarf bouquet" or "Calypso Queen"; very compacted, dense rosette or bundle of thin-leathery lanceolate, corrugated dark green, shiny leaves; introduced from Puerto Rico and Florida 1973; very attractive as a pot plant. *Tropical. Zone 11.* *p. 70*

deremensis 'Janet Craig'; green sport of warneckii, a rosette of freer, larger growing habit, similar to fragrans but more erect and stiff, with dark green, lustrous, wavy-margined leaves, corrugated lengthwise; of excellent keeping qualities. *Zone 11.* *p. 70*

deremensis 'Skunky'; colorful patented mutation of D. 'Warneckii' by Roy Krieser of Manitowoc, Wisconsin 1974; sturdy plant of compact habit and with thick, smooth dark green leaves having a striking broad white central band throughout the blade; true to color in propagation. *Zone 11.* *p. 70*

deremensis 'Souvenir de Aug. Schryver'; beautiful Belgian cultivar, 1970; a symmetrical, wide-spreading rosette of soft-leathery, lanceolate leaves, deep glossy green in center with broad creamy-white margins. *Tropical. Zone 11.* *p. 69*

deremensis 'Warneckii' (Trop. Africa), "Striped dracaena" attractive house plant for dark locations; branching stout canes to 5 m high, covered with sessile, sword-shaped, leathery leaves, fresh green streaked milky-green in center, and bordered by a translucent white band on each side inside the narrow bright green edge, 25-40 cm long. *Tropical. Zone 11.* *p. 70*

draco (Canary Isl.), "Dragon tree"; forming large trees to 20 m, with monstrous trunks of 4½ m dia., decorative as young plants with crowded rosette of sessile, sword-shaped, thick fleshy leaves, smooth to glaucous green, translucent edges, outlined in red if in the sun; flowers greenish. Superstition believes that the dark red, resinous substance exuding from leaves and trunk is "dragon's blood". *Subtropic. Zone 10.* *p. 115, 117, 207, 771*

fragrans 'Massangeana', "Cornstalk plant"; an old-fashioned robust house plant with its rosette of rich green, laxly arching leaves broadly striped and banded light green and yellow down the center, 30 to 60 cm long and 10 cm wide. The species is native in Nigeria, W. Africa, growing tree-like with age with slender yellowish trunks, to 6 m high; inflorescence in cluster of fragrant yellowish flowers. *Tropical. Zone 11.* *p. 69, 117*

fragrans 'Victoriae', "Painted dragon lily"; beautiful, slow-growing conservatory plant with gracefully pendant, wide, soft-leathery leaves green streaked silvery-gray in center, bordered by contrasting broad margins of cream to clear golden-yellow. *Humid-tropical. Zone 12.* *p. 117*

godseffiana (surculosa) (Zaire, Guinea), "Gold-dust dracaena"; small shrubby plant with spreading, wiry stems bearing thin-leathery, elliptic leaves in pairs or whorls of three, glossy deep green, irregularly spotted yellow, maturing to white; greenish-yellow flowers followed by red berries. *Tropical. Zone 11.* *p. 68*

goldieana (So. Nigeria, 900 m), "Queen of dracaenas"; the most spectacular dracaena in cultivation, but requiring humid-warm conditions to thrive; I remember a branched specimen 3 m high in Pará, its slender canes furnished with leathery foliage from bottom to top; the ovate, glossy deep green, long-stalked leaves strikingly marked with crossbands of pale green, maturing to almost white. Flowers in a dense spiral head, fragrant white, opening at night. *Humid-tropical. Zone 12.* *p. 69*

indivisa hort.: see CORDYLINE australis

marginata (gracilis) (Madagascar), "Madagascar dragon tree"; a favored decorator; tree-like, with branching slender trunk, growing to 5 m high, each cane topped by a dense terminal rosette of thick-fleshy, narrow linear clasping leaves 40 cm long, rigidly spreading horizontally, shiny deep olive-green prettily edged in red. The flexuous canes have the tendency to grow snaky and twisted, giving a branched specimen very artistic appearance. Slow and durable. *Tropical. Zones 11-12.* *p. 69, 117*

marginata 'Tricolor', "Rainbow tree"; magnificent cultivar found in Japan, developed in Puerto Rico and Florida (1973); multi-colored fountain of leaves striped cream between green and with rosy-red margins; bright light for most intense glow. *Tropical. Zone 12.* *p. 68*

reflexa (Hortus, Zander): see PLEOMELE reflexa

sanderiana (Cameroons, Zaire), "Ribbon plant"; neat, very durable, little rosette, erect on slender cane until becoming too heavy, with narrow lanceolate, elegantly twisted leaves, deep green somewhat milky, and with broad marginal bands of white. *Tropical. Zone 11.* *p. 68*

DRACOCEPHALUM *Labiatae*
nutans (E. Russia to Siberia), "Dragonhead"; bushy herbaceous, pubescent perennial or biennial 30-70 cm high; the stems dense with ovate leaves 2-5 cm long, and coarsely crenate; small 2 cm purplish-blue flowers having 5-toothed calyx, the upper tooth larger than the others, and set in distinct whorls in spike-like terminal raceme, in early Summer. *Zone 3.* *p. 432*

prattii (W. China), "Chinese dragonhead"; herbaceous perennial to 90 cm high, with ovate leaves 5 cm long, the lower ones petioled higher up on stems sessile; the purplish-blue flowers having toothed calyx and 3 cm corolla, arranged in dense whorls forming a pyramidal raceme; summer-blooming. *Zone 5.* *p. 432*

DRACONTIUM *Araceae*
changuango (Venezuela), "Serpent cup"; tuberous plant with dormancy period; leaf blade divided, medium green, on rough, spotted petiole 30-50 cm long; the bold, purple, cupped spathe 7-10 cm long, hairy inside; black purple spadix. *Zone 12.* *p. 26*

DRACOPHYLLUM   *Epacridaceae*

secundum (New So. Wales), "Dragonheath"; evergreen shrub to 60 cm with 5-10 cm linear-lanceolate leaves, the bases clasping and hiding stem; flowers on slender cylindrical spikes, with 1 cm tubular white corolla. *Zone 9.*   *p. 698*

traversii (New Zealand), "New Zealand grasstree"; handsome small tree found on South Island, of candelabrum-like habit, sparry very hard woody branches, and thick-leathery, stiff-recurving linear concave leaves deep bronzy, glossy green, with bases clasping and tips curling, in rosettes at branch-ends; the inflorescence in brownish terminal clusters. *Subtropic. Zone 9.*   *p. 698*

DRACOPIS   *Compositae*

amplexicaulis (Rudbeckia) (Kansas to Georgia and Texas), "Coneflower"; striking herbaceous annual 50-80 cm high, with lower leaves oblong spoon-shaped, the upper ones ovate, stem-clasping and glaucous; the remarkable flowers with prominent, long protruding cone-like brown disc, subtended by obovate yellow rays 3 cm long, in July. *Zone 4.*   *p. 385*

DRACUNCULUS   *Araceae*

vulgaris (Arum dracunculus) (Mediterranean), "Dragon arum"; tuberous herb with pedately dissected, bright green leaves with 13-15 segments; spathe tube purplish-white striped purple, the purple blade 30 cm long, deeper at margin; spadix tipped purple also; offensive odor in bloom. *Subtropic. Zone 9.*   *p. 26*

DRIMIOPSIS   *Liliaceae*

kirkii (Zanzibar); bulbous plant with lax, strapshaped, keeled, fleshy leaves narrowing toward base, pale blue-green with marbling of dark blotches; white flowers on short spike in July. *Tropical. Zone 11.*   *p. 70*

DRIMYS   *Magnoliaceae*

winteri (Mexico to Argentina), "Winter's bark"; evergreen tree to 8 m, with aromatic bark and reddish branches; the leathery elliptic-oblong leaves glaucous beneath, and 15-20 cm long, also very aromatic; as are the pretty milk-white starry flowers 3 cm across, and fragrant of jasmine. The bark had been used medicinally in the 16th Century as treatment for scurvy amongst sailors. *Zone 9.*   *p. 776*

DROSANTHEMUM   *Aizoaceae*

floribundum (Cape Prov.), "Rosea ice plant"; cushion-forming succulent creeping and freely branching with 1 cm light green cylindrical leaves thickened toward apex; producing a great profusion of pale pink daisy-like flowers 2 cm across. *Zones 9-10.*   *p. 145, 301*

hispidum (S.W. Africa: Namibia; Cape); succulent shrub to 60 cm high, freely branching, more than 1 m wide; branches at first erect, later some falling down and rooting, slender, gray-brown skinned, and covered with rough white hairs; cylindrical light green to reddish leaves 2 to 2½ cm long, covered by translucent pimples; very floriferous with beautifully silky-shining deep purple ray-flowers to 3 cm across. *Arid-subtropic. Zones 9-10.*   *p. 145*

speciosum (Cape Prov.); shrubby succulent with inclined branches, tiny 16 mm fleshy leaves curved upwards, semi-cylindrical, blunt, fresh green, set with crystalline blisters; masses of beautiful 5 cm daisy-like flowers glowing brownish to orange-red, greenish in center. *Subtropic. Zones 9-10.*   *p. 145*

DROSERA   *Droseraceae (Carnivorous Pl.)*

aliciae (So. Africa), "African Sundew"; low basal rosette of fleshy, obovate wedge-shaped leaves 2-4 cm long, covered by hair-like tentacles exuding droplets of glue from their tips, reacting and bending to entrap insects when touched by them; the floral stalk to 20 cm high, glandular pubescent in upper part. *Zone 10.*   *p. 203*

binata (dichotoma) (S.E. Australia, New Zealand), "Twin-leaved sundew"; small perennial 15 cm high, with long-stalked leaves deeply divided into two linear lobes with sensitive glandular hairs discharging sticky fluid to hold and digest insects. Will go dormant in wintery habitat, where above-ground growth will dry up and re-emerge next season. *Subtropic. Zones 10-11.*   *p. 202*

capensis (So. Africa), "Daily-dew"; perennial 15 cm high with linear oblong, blunt leaves tapered toward base, and densely furnished with hairs giving off sticky sap attracting insects, whereupon the sensitive hairs curve inward acting as a trap until the fluid digests their body. *Subtropic. Zone 11.*   *p. 202*

pedata (E. Australia); small perennial herb similar to binata, of wet habitats; long petioles rising from the roots and bearing forked tentacle-like linear leaves to 15 cm long, set with glandular hairs; the tips reddish and discharging sticky fluid, capable of holding and digesting insects; flowers white. *Zones 11-12.*   *p. 202*

rotundifolia (Canada so. to Florida, w. to Montana and Calif., Europe incl. Britain, No. Asia), "Roundleaf sundew; small flat rosette with 2-5 cm petioles, holding spoon-like leaves fringed with glandular-

tipped red hairs which exude sticky dew-like fluid; insects are attracted, and become enmeshed in the closing tentacles and are eventually digested; flowers are white. *Zones 3-8.*   *p. 202*

DRYANDRA   *Proteaceae*

sessilis (Southwest Australia), "Parrot bush" or "Holly-leaf dryandra"; evergreen shrub with rigid, upright branches 2 to 5 m and more high; leathery leaves ilex-like and set with sharp spines; at apex of branches the showy inflorescence consisting of a flattened cushion of creamy-yellow stamens held by a cup of overlapping bracts; an excellent honey plant. *Zone 9.*   *p. 821*

DRYAS   *Rosaceae*

octopetala (Northern Latitudes, Greenland to Alaska), "Mountain avens"; evergreen creeping plant shrubby at base, with elliptic 2 cm leaves, white-tomentose beneath; white 3 cm flowers; the feathery fruit on long stalk. Photographed in Longyearbyen, on Spitzbergen, above the Arctic Circle, in early July. *Zone 2.*   *p. 492*

x suendermannii (drummondii x octopetala) (Sweden); floriferous, prostrate evergreen perennial with woody base and alternate undivided, ovate leaves; attractive flowers yellow in bud, white when opening and 3 cm across, blooming during Summer. *Zone 6.*   *p. 492*

DRYNARIA   *Polypodiaceae (Filices)*

quercifolia (Polypodium) (So. India, Queensland, Fiji), "Oak-leaved fern"; growing on trees and rocks, with a thick, brown, woody rhizome, having stalkless brown, bluntly lobed barren fronds and long-stalked deeply pinnate rigid fertile fronds with brown veins, the pinnae cut to center. *Humid-tropical. Zones 11-12.*   *p. 133*

DRYOPTERIS   *Polypodiaceae (Filices)*

arguta (Polystichum strigosum in Calif. hort.) (Brit. Columbia to California), "Coastal woodfern"; spreading fern with long stalks, bearing bipinnate herbaceous fronds, 25-90 cm long, the pinnae well separated on thin wiry rachis. *Zones 6-10.*   *p. 139*

austriaca (dilatata) (No. America, Europe, Siberia, Caucasus, E. Asia), "Shield fern"; large tufted, hardy fern with 2 to 3-pinnate leaves to 1 m long, abruptly pointed; the pinnae in 10-15 pairs, the lowest segments spiny-toothed. *Zones 3-7.*   *p. 133*

erythrosora (China, Japan), "Autumn fern"; tufted wood-fern with underground creeping stem, scaly stalks bearing 30-45 cm pinnate fronds of firm though papery texture, the leaflets lobed; the spore masses with bright red covers when young. *Zones 5-8.*   *p. 133*

filix-mas (Athyrium) (England and throughout Europe; No. America from Greenland to So. America, Perú; Lapland to Japan; Himalayas to Malaysia; Azores to Africa), the "Male fern"; one of the commonest of ferns, densely tufted; crowns with scaly stalks bearing handsome bipinnate fronds ½-1 m long, the spear-shaped dark green leaflets of papery texture, pale beneath; very variable; nearly evergreen, hardy. Has medicinal properties. *Zones 3-8.*   *p. 133*

filix-mas crispa cristata (Nephrodium) (Britain: Cornwall); beautiful variety with dark green, pinnate fronds to 1 m long, bending from the weight of their large, many times branched, and crispy terminal tuft or crest, the lobed leaflets also ending in smaller crests ringing the outline of the frond with a border of crispy crests. *Zones 7-9.*   *p. 133*

goldiana (E. No. America: N. Brunswick to Minnesota, Virginia, Tenn.), "Giant wood fern"; massive but deciduous fern with rugged dark green pinnate leaves in large crowns, 1 m or more long, the pinnae deeply cut and toothed; developing croziers covered with shaggy scales. *Zones 3-8.*   *p. 134*

marginalis (spinulosa) (E. United States), "Marginal shield fern"; tufted fern with scaly stalks and bipinnatifid fronds to 45 cm long, the segments cut to axis and with hairy teeth. Photographed in Gordon Foster's Garden, Sparta, N.J. *Zone 3-8.*   *p. 133*

wallichiana (Aspidium) (Nepal, China, Taiwan, Japan: Kyushu), "Wood fern"; stout rhizome topped by rosette of large erect pinnate fronds 1-2 m long; the pinnae horizontally spreading, thin-leathery and lobed, the stalks brown and scaly. *Zones 6-8.*   *p. 134*

DUCHESNEA   *Rosaceae*

indica (India), "Mock strawberry"; perennial herb with trailing branches rooting along the ground, bright green three-parted leaves; 2 cm yellow flowers followed by strawberry-like 2 cm red fruits of insipid taste; used as ground cover in California, and for hanging baskets. *Zones 5-10.*   *p. 319*

DUDLEYA   *Crassulaceae*

brittonii (Mexico: Coastal Baja California); low rosette 10 to 50 cm dia., on short stem with numerous lanceolate leaves, rounded at base, glaucous silver gray, and tipped red, later bluish; pale yellow flowers in clustered inflorescence on stem 25-70 cm high. *Arid-tropical. Zone 10.*   *p. 184*

candida (Mexico: Coronado Isl. off Baja Calif.); clustering rosettes to 20 cm dia., with sharply pointed, thick lanceolate leaves to 10 cm, beautifully covered with silvery-white glaucescence; flowers greenish-yellow, on branched inflorescence to 50 cm tall. *Zone 10.* p. 184

farinosa (syn. Cotyledon, and many others) (Coast of No. California to So. Oregon); attractive rosette to 10 cm across, succulent, narrow-oblong, green or white-mealy leaves, and short-pointed; floral stem to 30 cm bearing double, starry, pale yellow flowers. *Zone 9.* p. 184

greeneae (Cotyledon greenei) (California: Islands of San Miguel to Catalina); variable species with numerous synonyms; open rosettes to 40 cm across, on stout stem, branching and forming clumps to 1½ m wide; 15-50 mealy gray-green oblanceolate succulent leaves to 11 cm long, branched inflorescence 1 m tall with pale yellow flowers. *Zone 10.* p. 184

pachyphytum (Mexico: Cedros Isl.); a very desirable succulent found by Dr. A. Lau of Cordoba, Mex. in 1980, one of the finest of the genus; small clustering rosette of unusually thick, three-sided leaves to 4 cm long, heavily coated with white powdery farina and tinged with rose. *Zone 11.* p. 184

virens (Coast of So. California), "Alabaster plant"; succulent, branching rosette with spreading strap-shaped green leaves, 5 to 25 cm long, covered with white glaucescence, reddish toward tips; small yellowish flowers on tall leafy stalk. *Subtropic. Zone 10.* p. 184

DURANTA   *Verbenaceae*

repens (Florida, West Indies, Mexico, to Brazil), "Sky flower" or "Pigeon-berry"; small tree to 6 m, occasionally spiny and with drooping 4-angled branches; ovate 10 cm leaves; small flowers with cylindrical corolla and spreading limb lilac-blue, followed by orange-yellow berries. *Tropical. Zone 10.* p. 900

repens 'Variegata', "Sky flower"; spreading willowy branches with thin-leathery, opposite leaves 8 cm long, glossy green and attractively bordered with creamy-white; clusters of lilac flowers followed by the 6-10 mm yellow berries. *Zones 10-11.* p. 900

DURIO   *Bombacaceae*

zibethinus (Borneo, and widespread in Malaysia), the "Durian"; medium to large tropical evergreen tree to 25 m high, famous for its edible fruit; long ovate, shiny dark green, leathery leaves 10-16 cm long; white flowers with prominent stamens 5 cm long, are clustered in the branches; the green ovoid fruit becomes 20-30 cm long, with a stout spiny covering enclosing a creamy delicious, but unpleasant-smelling pulp, and is produced from the woody branches. Favorite aphrodisiac in S.E. Asia. *Zone 11.* p. 907, 944

DUVERNOIA   *Acanthaceae*

adhatodoides (So. Africa); tropical shrub to 3 m high, with opposite elliptic leaves to 20 cm long; the inflorescence spike-like, having 2-lipped fragrant white corolla 3 cm long, with purple marking on throat and lower lip. *Zone 10.* p. 629

DYCKIA   *Bromeliaceae*

fosteriana (Paraná), "Silver and gold dyckia"; very ornamental small rosette in a dense whorl of stiff silvery-purple arched leaves with silver spines; inflorescence a spike of rich orange flowers. *Subtropic. Zone 10.* p. 153

DYMONDIA   *Compositae*

margaretae (Southern Cape, So. Africa); colorful low evergreen forming rosettes by branching from the base and planted as ground cover; the leaves are long lanceolate and glossy green, the underside is white-woolly with edges of the leafblades turned up; the inflorescence is of showy yellow composite flowers; seen at Kirstenbosch Bot. Garden. *Zone 9.* p. 689

DYSSODIA   *Compositae*

tenuiloba (Thymophylla) (Texas and adjacent Mexico), "Dahlberg daisy" or "Golden fleece"; bushy annual or spreading short-lived perennial herb to 30 cm high; small pinnate, ferny leaves with bristle-tipped segments; daisy-like floral heads of golden-yellow ray-flowers, blooming for several months. *Zone 8.* p. 310, 385

EBENUS   *Leguminosae*

cretica (Crete and Greek Isles); evergreen shrub to 1 m high; leaves of 3 or 5 leaflets, linear-oblong 2-3 cm long; flowers purplish-red, having obcordate standard petal streaked with dark lines, and closely grouped in axillary cylindric spikes to 10 cm long. *Zone 10.* p. 760

ECCREMOCARPUS   *Bignoniaceae*

scaber (Chile), "Glory flower"; scrambling bush climbing to 4 m high, with lobed bipinnate leaves, the leaflets to 3 cm long; inflated tubular flowers orange-scarlet, 3 cm long, in clusters. Sometimes grown as annual, blooming first year. *Subtropic. Zones 10-11.* p. 270

ECHEVERIA   *Crassulaceae*

agavoides (Urbinia) (San Luis Potosi), "Moulded wax" or "Lipstick"; solid starlike rosette with rigid fleshy leaves triangular pointed, glossy pale apple-green, 3 to 9 cm long, margins frequently reddish, spinetipped; flowers reddish tipped yellow on arching pink floral stalk to 50 cm long. *Zone 9.* p. 186

chihuahuaensis (Mexico); large suckering, formal rosette densely composed of thick-fleshy obovate short-pointed keeled leaves, to 4 cm long, glaucous silvery flushed purplish-red toward apex, inflorescence on 20 cm stalk, with bell-flowers red inside. *Zone 10.* p. 186

crenulata 'Pettycoat'; very interesting hybrid rosette 30 cm or more across, with thick-fleshy fan-shaped leaves silvery glaucous blue, prettily frilled and purple along the broad upper edge; inflorescence a tall raceme of yellow to red flowers. E. crenulata is from Cuernavaca, So. Mexico. *Zone 11.* p. 185

crenulata 'Valentine'; a beautiful hybrid "Scallop echeveria", seen at Dick Wright Nursery, De Luz, California; large succulent rosette about 25 cm across, of obovate concave leaves like polished wax, glaucous and overlaid with purple, at upper margins prettily undulated. *Zone 11.* p. 185

derenbergii (So. Mexico: Oaxaca), "Painted lady"; charming small, globe-shaped clustering rosettes 3 to 6 cm across, of numerous thick leaves pale green, glaucous with waxy silvery-blue bloom and tipped red; flowering freely on short 8 cm stems, golden-yellow with orange, incurved raceme. *Tropical. Zone 11.* p. 185

'Desmetiana' hort. (So. Mexico), "Fancy hen-and-chicks"; an old-time carpet-bedding plant in Europe, close to peacockii or a synonym for it; elegant blue-glaucous rosette 10-15 cm dia., with incurving leaves tipped with rose, floral stalk to 30 cm high, bearing one-sided raceme of scarlet-red flowers. *Subtropic. Zone 10.* p. 185, 323

'Doris Taylor' (setosa x pulvinata), "Woolly rose"; very handsome, robust rosette to 12 cm across, with glossy deep green, obovate leaves tipped red, and beautifully covered with white hair. *Tropical. Zone 11.* p. 184

elegans (Hidalgo), "Mexican snowball"; like small balls of ice 3 to 6 cm long, opening into beautiful clustering rosette of spoon-shaped leaves waxy glaucous pale blue, with white translucent margins; flowers coral-rose with yellow tips, on arching pink stalk 10-20 cm long. *Zone 10.* p. 186

'Festival' (harmsii x carminea); an excellent hybrid for cut flower purposes, grown at Wright Nursery, De Luz, Calif.; erect floral stalks about 50 cm high bearing slender spike-like racemes of scarlet flowers tipped with yellow; the base with pubescent narrow lanceolate leaves. *Zone 10.* p. 185

gibbiflora (So. Mexico); forming a heavy stem crowned with a large rosette of spoon-shaped glaucous leaves 12-30 cm long, pale metallic green tinted pink and edged red; branched inflorescence 60 cm tall, with clusters of 30-50 flowers red outside, yellow within. *Zone 11.* p. 185

gibbiflora 'Mauna Loa'; spectacular, robust succulent rosette to about 25 cm across, the thick-fleshy glaucous bluish leaves overlaid with copper, the upper edge densely wavy or pleated and tinged in red. *Zone 11.* p. 185

'Haageana' (agavoides x pulchella?), "Fruit cups"; fleshy open rosette 12 cm across, of obovate pointed, rather broad leaves keeled beneath, light green with a rough rugose white surface, tips slightly edged and flushed carmine, short, branched inflorescence with rosy flowers tipped yellow. *Zone 11.* p. 185

x imbricata (glauca x gibbiflora metallica); "Hen-and-chicks"; an old popular hybrid long grown in California gardens; clustering saucer-like rosettes of broad obovate, spiny-tipped, glaucous bluish-gray leaves, 10-15 cm or more across; bell-shaped flowers dull orange-red. *Zone 9.* p. 186

x kirchneriana (carnicolor x derenbergii); attractive small hybrid rosette 8-10 cm across, of densely shingled thick-fleshy short-obovate, spine-tipped silvery glaucous leaves; inflorescence with yellow and red cup-flowers. *Zone 11.* p. 186

lindsayana (Mexico); beautiful stemless rosette rather flat, of obovate, thick-succulent leaves 5-9 cm long, keeled beneath, glaucous grayish-green with red pointed tips; inflorescence on 50 cm stalks, with crimson-rose flowers, yellow at tips and inside. Described by E. Walther, San Francisco 1959. *Zone 10.* p. 184

listida (prob. Mexico); handsome open succulent rosette in col. New Jersey Cactus & Succulent Soc.; spreading oblanceolate, concave leaves to about 12 cm long, olive-green overlaid with coppery red. *Zone 10.* p. 184

peacockii (So. Mexico), "Peacock echeveria"; lovely symmetrical, dense rosette of numerous cupped, oblanceolate fleshy leaves richly covered with silvery-blue glaucescence, edged and tipped with red; rose-red flowers glaucous outside; the favorite for carpet-bedding in Europe. *Tropical. Zone 11.* p. 185

pulidonis (E. Mexico); small succulent rosette, branching at base, with 25 or more obovate, spoon-shaped, smooth leaves to 5 cm long, and spur-tipped, light green with red margins; inflorescence of yellow flowers with reddish points. *Zone 10.*   p. 186

secunda glauca (Valley of Mexico), "Blue hen-and-chickens"; popular small saucer-shaped rosette 10 cm across, forming offsets, obovate leaves, always bluish glaucous, sometimes red-edged, the apex with short red spine; slender 20-30 cm floral stalk bearing raceme of bright red flowers tipped yellow. *Zone 9.*   p. 186

shaviana (E. Mexico); beautiful rosette 10 to 20 cm across, spatulate, rather thin succulent leaves with upturned tips, glaucous blue with bright red or white wavy edges; tall glaucous inflorescence to 30 cm high, with flowers pink outside, orange inside. *Tropical. Zone 11.*   p. 186

ECHINACEA   *Compositae*
purpurea (Rudbeckia) (Ohio to Louisiana and Georgia), "Purple cone-flower"; coarse, rough-hairy perennial herb to 1 m or more; lower leaves ovate and coarsely toothed; the leafy stems crowned by showy flowers to 15 cm across, the ray-flowers purplish-pink, in center a cone-like brown-purple disc. *Zones 4-9.*   p. 385

ECHINOCACTUS   *Cactaceae*
grusonii (C. Mexico), "Golden barrel"; growing into a giant globe of 90 cm dia., light green, closely ribbed, covered with golden spines; yellow flowers imbedded around top, opening in sun, to 5 cm across. *Arid-tropical. Zone 10.*   p. 158

ECHINOCEREUS   *Cactaceae*
dasyacanthus hort. (Hortus 2 and Backeberg Lex.): see E. pectinatus neomexicanus (Hortus 3).

fasciculatus (Mamillaria fasciculata, Backeberg) (So. Arizona, N. Sonora), "Pitaya"; clustering with elongate cylindric stems to 45 cm high and 8 cm dia., having 8-18 ribs, densely set with long white needle spines; red-purple flowers 6 cm across. *Zone 9.*   p. 156

nivosus (Mexico: S.E. Coahuila); cluster-forming small columns to 12 cm high and to 5 cm dia., covered by stiff glassy, snow-white spines tipped black; wide-open magenta-red flowers to 4 cm across. *Zone 10.*   p. 162

panamesiorum (Mexico: Zacatecas); collected by Dr. A. Lau of Fortin de las Flores in 1979 near Monte Escobedo; handsome small clustering columnar new species 15 to 25 cm high and 7 cm thick, 12 to 14 green ribs bearing pale yellow radial spines and long central spines; pretty rose-pink flowers 7 cm across; small greenish-yellow 2 cm fruit. *Zone 10.*   p. 157

pectinatus var. neomexicanus (dasyacanthus) (Arizona, New Mexico to W. Texas; Mexico), "Rainbow cactus"; small cylindric, hard and closely ribbed xerophyte to 30 cm high and 10 cm dia., densely stiff-spined in rainbow-like zones of straw-yellow, purple, tan, red-brown and amethyst, spines pointing out and downward; funnel-shaped flowers mostly yellow, also varying to red, 8 to 10 cm long. *Arid-subtropic. Zone 9.*   p. 157

pentalophus (So. Texas, Mexico); cylindric branches sprawling and ascending to 12 cm long and 3 cm thick, green, with 4-6 warty ribs, and white areoles; large round flowers lilac or pink with reddish-violet, 8 to 12 cm across. *Arid-subtropic. Zone 10.*   p. 156

reichenbachii var. perbellus (W. Texas, S.E. Colorado to New Mexico), "Lace cactus"; colorful globe or short-cylindric, to 10 cm high, closely ribbed olive-green, radial spines shaded from reddish to nearly white; flowers iridescent light purple, 4 to 6 cm long. *Zone 9.*   p. 157

ECHINODORUS   *Alismataceae*
macrophyllus (muricatus) (Colombia to Guyana), "Sword plant"; tropical perennial aquatic herb, spreading by runners; broad ovate-cordate or lance-shaped leaves to 50 cm long, on long, erect stalks; branched inflorescence to 1 m high, with white flowers; lateral vines from base will form new plants. *Zone 11.*   p. 325

palaefolius (Trop. America), "Mexican sword-plant"; tropical aquatic plant growing in shallow water, with fleshy petioles bearing very broad cordate, almost round leaves with ribs prominent; large branched inflorescence of white flowers, having 3 petals. *Zone 11.*   p. 325

ECHINOFOSSULOCACTUS   *Cactaceae*
arrigens (Central Mexico), "Brain cactus"; elongate globular plant to 13 cm high and 8-10 cm thick, having about 24 narrow, undulate bluish-green ribs set with curved yellow spines, the apex topped by woolly felt; 2½ cm flowers purple down center of petals, white outsides. *Zone 10.*   p. 156

ECHINOMASTUS unguispinus (Zander):
see NEOLLOYDIA unguispina (Hortus)

ECHINOPS   *Compositae*
ritro (E. Europe: Russia), "Globe thistle"; handsome, thistle-like perennial to 1 m or more high, with white-woolly stems; leaves to

20 cm long, pinnately dissected into lanceolate, spiny-toothed segments, white-downy beneath; globular inflorescence 4-5 cm dia., densely compound of bristly bluish flowers. *Zone 5.*   p. 385

ECHINOPSIS   *Cactaceae*
multiplex (So. Brazil), "Easter lily cactus"; small barrel to 20 cm high and 15 cm thick, forming clusters; dark green, close-ribbed, with sharp brown spines; long, erect funnelformed pink or rosy flowers to 25 cm long. *Arid-subtropic. Zone 9.*   p. 156

ECHIOIDES longiflorum: see ARNEBIA pulchra

ECHIUM   *Boraginaceae*
fastuosum (Canary Isl.), "Pride of Madeira"; gray-hairy shrubby perennial ½ to 2 m high, with narrow lanceolate leaves covered with soft white hair, and deep blue, bell-shaped flowers with protruding red stamens, on one-sided spikelets formed in cylindrical inflorescence. *Subtropic. Zone 10.*   p. 349

lycopsis (plantagineum) (S.W. England to So. Europe), "Purple viper's bugloss"; tap-rooted biennial herbaceous plant to 50 cm high, covered by stiff white hairs, ovate leaves appressed hairy; showy flowers first red but changing to purplish-blue or mauve. *Zone 8.*   p. 349

simplex (giganteum in hort.) (Tenerife), "Tower of jewels"; striking herbaceous tap-rooted biennial, 2-3 m high, with magnificent fleshy, grayish, lanceolate leaves in dense rosettes, becoming shorter toward apex; the elongate stem terminating in a massive pyramid of small white, bell-shaped flowers. Seen in col. of Botanic Garden Orotava, on Tenerife, Spain. *Zone 10.*   p. 349

vulgare (Europe, No. Africa, Asia Minor, naturalized in E. No. America), "Blue thistle" or "Blue-devil"; herbaceous top-rooted perennial 30-80 cm high, covered with bristly white hairs; linear lanceolate leaves 5 to 15 cm long, having prominent midrib; flowers axillary or in terminal clusters, usually first pink, then changing to blue. Contact with the bristly hairs causes dermatitis. *Zone 8.* p. 349

wildpretii (syn. bourgaeanum) (Canary Islands), "Pride of Tenerife"; herbaceous soft-felty biennial to 1 m or more high, often unbranched, developing successive rosettes of numerous narrow-lanceolate leaves upward, terminating in pyramids dense with rose-red flowers, displaying long protruding red stamens, and arranged in showy spires. *Zones 9-10.*   p. 349, 357

EDGEWORTHIA   *Thymelaeaceae*
papyrifera (Himalayas to China), "Paper-bush" or "Mitsumata"; strikingly beautiful deciduous shrub to 2 m high, seen in February bloom in gardens of Chekiang Prov. of Central China; the stocky branches tipped by dense clusters of vanilla-scented flowers, the corolla-like calyx tubes 3-4 cm long, silky outside and golden-yellow inside and at flaring lobes; the subsequent lanceolate leaves 12 cm long. Used in So. Japan as a source of soft, tough paper. *Warm temperate. Zone 7.*   p. 893

EHRETIA   *Boraginaceae*
tinifolia (Yucatán, Mex., West Indies), "Bastard cherry" or "Capulin"; tropical evergreen shrub or tree to 10 m or more high, with dense crown and smooth bark; glossy green, ovate leaves to 12 cm long; inflorescence of small white flowers in 15 cm clusters, followed by 6 mm cherry-like edible red or purple fruit. Photographed at the Maya ruins of Chichen-Itza, Mexico. *Zone 9.*   p. 668

EICHHORNIA   *Pontederiaceae*
azurea (Brazil), "Peacock hyacinth"; aquatic herb rooting in shallow water, and sending flexuous runners across its surface, with fleshy stalks not inflated, fresh green, waxy leaves rounded or obovate, 12 cm dia.; terminal spikes of showy flowers, lilac-blue with purple center, the two lower petals fringed. *Humid-tropical. Zones 10-11.*   p. 336

crassipes (speciosa) (Piaropus) (Trop. and Subtrop. America), "Water hyacinth"; small aquatic plant usually floating, with bluish, feathery roots, and runners forming clumps, the roundish, glossy green leaves 5-15 cm long, in rosettes, on petioles much inflated at base causing them to stay afloat; clusters of large, lilac flowers with yellow center surrounded by blue blotch and purple stripes. Naturalized in Florida, Portugal and Trop. Africa. *Zones 9-10.* p. 336

ELAEAGNUS   *Elaeagnaceae*
angustifolia (So. Europe, W. Asia), "Russian olive" or "Oleaster"; willow-like deciduous shrub or tree 5-6 m high, forming a crooked trunk with shredding bark; the spiny branches covered by glistening silvery scales when young, arching downward and set with decorative narrow-oblong leaves 6-10 cm long, matte green above, silvery beneath; small fragrant flowers 1 cm long, in leaf axils, with bell-shaped corolla yellow inside, silvery outside, followed by oblong sweet, mealy 2 cm fruit glossy red. *Zone 2.*   p. 692, 696

commutata (E. Canada, so. to Minnesota and Utah), "Silverberry"; deciduous shrub to 4 m high, with unarmed stems, spreading by stolons; the lanceolate leaves silvery above and underneath, 4-10 cm long and undulate at margins, on reddish branchlets; flowers yellow, silvery outside and fragrant, in late Spring; fruit a 1 cm silvery berry with dry mealy flesh. *Zone 2.* p. 696

x **ebbingei** (macrophylla x pungens), "Ebbinge's silverberry"; handsome hybrid, originated in Holland; shrub to 3 m high, evergreen in mild climate, with spineless branches, covered by brown scales; elliptic leaves to 10 cm long, shining green above, silvery scaly beneath; axillary small white flowers, in clusters; the autumn fruit is red. *Zone 7.* p. 696

x **ebbingei 'Gilt edge'**; outstanding small hort. mutation, evergreen as planted in California and other mild regions; its branches furnished with large leathery leaves, deep green usually in center, but strikingly variegated or bordered with golden-yellow; the bright coloring is retained during the life of the foliage. Photographed at the Chelsea Flower Show in London 1984. *Zone 7.* p. 696

multiflora (Japan, China), "Cherry elaeagnus"; deciduous shrub 2-3 m high, occasionally semi-evergreen; the young branches covered by red-brown scales; ovate leaves 6 cm long, smooth green above, and silvery beneath; the axillary flowers yellowish-white, their corollas or slender tube 2 cm long and segments spreading wide at apex, April-blooming and sweetly fragrant; pendulous red fruit 2 cm long, of pleasant acid flavor. *Zone 4.* p. 696

philippinensis (Philippine Islands), "Lingaros"; evergreen tropical shrub to 3 m or more, with drooping branches, long ovate leaves 10 cm long, silvery underneath and with undulate margins; small axillary flowers; glossy red, edible berries 1 cm dia., dense along woody branches. *Zone 10.* p. 913

pungens (Japan, China), the "Silver berry" or "Thorny elaeagnus"; slow-growing brown-stemmed evergreen shrub of rather rigid, angular sprawling habit of growth, usually spiny, to 2-5 m high; leathery oval grayish-green leaves with rusty-brown tinting, 3-8 cm long and with wavy edges and silvery beneath; the surface is covered with silvery scales reflecting sunlight which give the plant a special sparkle; white, fragrant flowers. *Warm temperate. Zone 7.* p. 697

pungens 'Maculata' (Japan); very colorful large leaves, with the normally green blades golden-yellow mainly in center, but varying to almost entire leaf or variegated irregularly in other parts and occasionally entirely green; seen in Cologne Bot. Garden, Germany. *Zone 7.* p. 697

pungens 'Variegata' (Japan, China); evergreen brown-stemmed shrub with leathery oval, wavy margined, green leaves painted yellow, primarily along margins, young surface covered with silvery scales, silver beneath; white fragrant flowers. *Zone 7.* p. 696

umbellata (Himalayas, China, Korea, Japan), "Autumn elaeagnus"; deciduous shrub 4-5 m high, in mild areas semi-evergreen; wide-spreading branches often spiny, silvery or covered with brown scales; lanceolate leaves 10 cm long, and silvery beneath; tiny 1 cm flowers in leaf axils funnel-shaped, creamy-white inside, and sweetly fragrant, blooming May-June; small berry-like fruit 1 cm wide, silvery at first, then red. *Zone 3.* p. 696

ELAEIS *Palmae*
guineensis (Trop. West and C. Africa), "African oil-palm"; feather-palm to 18 m or more tall, with ringed trunk crowned by graceful pinnate fronds to 5 m long, the ridged narrow leaflets green on both sides; male and female flowers in separate clusters on the same tree; the ovoid red to black 4 cm fruit in large clusters of 200-300; source of palm-oil. *Tropical. Zones 11-12.* p. 104,920

oleifera (Costa Rica to Venezuela and Guyana), "American oil palm"; showy feather palm to 12 m or more high, with slender trunk occasionally procumbent; topped by a handsome crown of pinnate leaves to 3 m long, the many leaflets in one plane and pendant, dark glossy green; oily-fleshy 2½ cm red fruit, a source of palm-oil. *Zones 11-12.* p. 103

ELAEOCARPUS *Elaeocarpaceae*
grandiflorus (philippensis) (Burma or Myanmar, to Indochina, Java); handsome evergreen tree with stout spreading branches; leathery lanceolate leaves 8-15 cm long; silky white to pale yellow flowers, in pendant small clusters, usually among upper leaves; followed by large olive-like fruit on red floral stalks. *Zone 9.* p. 697

hainanensis (Hainan, in So. China Sea), "Hainan elaeocarpus"; small evergreen tree to 9 m high, with brownish, striped branches; lanceolate, alternate leaves to 12 cm long, toward apex of branchlets; interesting greenish-white flowers 4 cm long, subtended by pinkish bracts, several to a cluster. *Zone 10.* p. 697

kirtonii (New So. Wales, Queensland), "Pigeon-berry ash" or "Illawara ash"; evergreen tree to 30 m tall; leaves lanceolate 10-20 cm long, toothed at margins; flowers of spreading and incurved lanceolate, pinkish petals; small berry-like ovoid fruit to 2 cm long, hard inside. *Zone 9.* p. 697

reticulatus (Queensland, New So. Wales, Victoria), "Blueberry ash"; bushy shrub or tree, in habitat to 15 m high, with grayish bark;

lanceolate leaves to 10 cm long, conspicuously veined, and serrate; flowers white, in showy elongate racemes; small blue fruit. *Zone 9.* p. 698

ELETTARIA *Zingiberaceae*
cardamomum (Amomum) (India, Sri Lanka, Java), "Cardamom" or "Malabar cardamom"; aromatic perennial herb with creeping root-stock, and clustering leafy stems which can attain 3 m, but usually grown in horticulture as a durable foliage plant 60 cm high; linear-lanceolate, leathery leaves 12-18 cm long or more, deep dull green, and finely hairy, giving off, when rubbed, a spicy fragrance; flowers in cone-like spikes beneath the foliage, the white corolla 2 cm long, the lip blue with white stripes and a yellow margin. Widely cultivated in S.E. Asia. The fruit is a capsule and its seed is the spice cardamom, used for pungent flavoring in baking of cakes; extensively used in Asian, Indian and African cooking; also in medicine for stomach and nerve stimulation, largely in India. *Zone 10.* p. 545

ELEUTHEROCOCCUS sieboldianus (Zander):
see ACANTHOPANAX sieboldianus (Hortus)

ELLEANTHUS *Orchidaceae*
capitatus (West Indies, Mexico to Perú); terrestrial of the habit of Sobralia, with leafy, slender reed-stems 30 cm or more; thin but stiff leaves prominently length-ribbed ending in two short points; terminal heads of rose-purple flowers; April-June. *Tropical. Zone 11.* p. 87

ELSHOLTZIA *Labiatae*
stauntonii (No. China), "Mint shrub"; semi-woody perennial to 1 m or more high, with downy shoots partially dying back in Winter; aromatic leaves ovate-elliptic to 12 cm long, crenate at margins; cylindric 10-20 cm spikes of purplish-pink two-lipped flowers, in Autumn. *Zone 7.* p. 443

ELYMUS *Gramineae*
arenarius (No. and N.W. Europe to No. Asia), "European dune grass", "Wild rye" or "Lyme grass"; aggressive stoloniferous, deciduous perennial spreading by long rhizomes and forming colonies; with flat grass-like, glaucous-gray leaves 1-2 cm wide and 60 cm long, rigid and sharply pointed; erect stems to 1 m or more high, the inflorescence a compact spike to 40 cm long, having sessile 4-flowered spikelets metallic blue, becoming buff with age. Used for borders and erosion control. *Zone 4.* p. 562

racemosus (Leymus) (S. Siberia), "Volga wild rye" or "Corn grass"; annual or perennial grass to 1 m high, with thick rhizomes; elongate linear leaves mostly at base, having rough surface; dense fruit-spike slender cylindric 15-20 cm long and 2 cm thick, without awns, or bristles. *Zone 5.* p. 567

EMBOTHRIUM *Proteaceae*
coccineum (Chile and Argentina), "Chilean fire-tree"; evergreen suckering bush 2 m or tree 5 to 15 m high; lanceolate leaves 12 cm or more long, dark glossy green; striking cluster of crimson-scarlet tubular flowers with corolla 4 to 5 cm long, separating into recurving linear segments, enclosing the anthers but exposing the protruding style topped by yellow stigma; blooming May-June. *Zone 8.* p. 821

wickhamii (Oreocallis) (New Caledonia, Queensland), "Satin oak"; magnificent tropical evergreen shrub dense with long oval, leathery concave, waxy leaves, the inflorescence a striking flat brush of brilliant orange-red filaments tipped with yellow. I photographed this tropical bush, 2 m high, near Noumea. *Zone 10.* p. 824

EMILIA *Compositae*
javanica (sagittata) (Pantropic), "Flora's paintbrush"; showy erect annual to 60 cm or more with elliptic leaves on winged stalks; flower heads loosely clustered, 2 cm dia., without rays, scarlet-red. *Tropical. Zone 10.* p. 385

ENCELIA *Compositae*
californica (Coastal California, and Baja California, Mexico), "Brittle bush"; perennial woody at base, 90-100 cm high, strong scented with hoary, lanceolate leaves 3-5 cm long; the flowers 6 cm across, with disc flowers purple, and ray-florets yellow. *Zone 9.* p.384

farinosa (So. California to Utah and New Mexico), "Brittlebush" or "Incienso"; arid-climate shrub, dense with stiff branches to 1½ m high, with silvery-green ovate, pubescent leaves 6 cm long; inflorescence daisy-like with both disc and ray-flowers yellow in early Spring, when very conspicuous in the deserts. The fragrant resin exuded from the stems was used as incense by the Spanish padres. Photographed in Death Valley, California. *Zone 10.* p. 688

ENCEPHALARTOS *Cycadaceae*
arenarius (So. Africa); handsome rosette of twisted leaves, glaucous blue with recurved apex, tips divided into spine-like sharp points, the margins of the rigid leaflets toothed. *Subtropic. Zones 10-11.* p. 114

lehmannii (So. Africa), "Blue-leaved cycad"; thick trunk to 1 m or more high, crowned by a mighty rosette of elegant, recurving fronds about 1 m long, the glaucous blue-green leaflets 16-18 cm long, with spiny tip and marginal spines. *Subtropic. Zone 11.*   *p. 114*

villosus (Natal); short underground trunk almost globular and woolly, spreading with leaves to 2 m long, erect in young growth, later outward; leaflets are green and spiny at edges; male cones are bright yellow 60 cm long. *Zone 11.*   *p. 113*

woodii (So. Africa: Zululand); large cycad with massive trunk reaching 6 m tall, topped by a majestic crown of 50 or more gracefully arching fronds 2 m or more long, the dense linear leaflets are bright green and to 20 cm long, armed with a few spiny teeth; male cones slender cylindric to more than 1 m long. *Zone 11.*   *p. 113*

ENCYCLIA   *Orchidaceae*

baculus (Epidendrum pentotis) (C. America, Brazil); stiff epiphyte with long spindle-shaped pseudobulbs and 2 leaves, the large waxy, very fragrant flowers back to back in pairs on short stem, tapering fleshy sepals and petals greenish-white, lip white with purple (Mar.-July). Genus transferred from Epidendrum to Encyclia (European Garden Flora, Cambridge 1984). *Tropical. Zone 11.*   *p. 87*

citrina: (Zander) see CATTLEYA citrina (Hortus)

cochleata (Epidendrum) (W. Indies, C. America), "Cockle-shelled orchid"; epiphyte with pear-shaped, usually 2-leaved pseudobulbs and erect cluster of curious upside-down flowers, the narrow greenish-white petals and sepals grouped together, the shell-shaped lip black-violet with yellow lines, (Nov.-Feb., and various). *Zone 11.*   *p. 87*

cordigera (Epidendrum atropurpureum) (Mexico to Panama, W. Indies, Brazil), "Spice orchid"; handsome epiphyte with pear-shaped pseudobulbs bearing 2-3 long leaves, stout racemes of 5-8 cm flowers having sepals and petals chocolate with incurved green tips, often tinged with purple, large white lip with crimson center. Photo shown is cv 'Lionet'; the species usually is more white, (Dec.-June). *Tropical. Zone 11.*   *p. 87*

fragrans (Epidendrum) (W. Indies, C. America, Brazil); stocky epiphyte with compressed pseudobulbs with solitary leaf; the waxy, fragrant flowers in short clusters, sepals and petals creamy-white, narrow linear and curled, the heart-shaped pointed lip white, lined red-purple, (Feb.-Aug.). *Tropical. Zone 11.*   *p. 87*

mariae (Epidendrum) (So. Mexico); excellent little epiphyte; small pear-shaped pseudobulbs with 1-2 leaves, topped by clusters of several large waxy flowers with greenish-yellow sepals and petals, and very broad, wavy white lip with green throat, (Summer). *Tropical. Zone 11.*   *p. 87*

oncidioides (Epidendrum) (C. America to Brazil); stately epiphyte with spindle-shaped bulbs bearing 2-3 straplike leaves; arching inflorescence to 1 m long with many 4 cm flowers bronzy yellow, lip marked red, (June). *Tropical. Zone 11.*   *p. 87*

prismatocarpa (Epidendrum) (Costa Rica, Panama), "Rainbow orchid"; beautiful robust epiphyte with flask-shaped pseudobulbs bearing 2 leaves; and erect spike of brightly colored, waxy, long-lasting flowers, sulphur-yellow blotched maroon, lip marked rosy-red, (May-June). *Tropical. Zone 11.*   *p. 87*

radiata (Epidendrum radiatum) (Mexico); epiphyte with short spindle-shaped pseudobulbs and 2-3 stiff leaves; compact clusters of fleshy cream-white flowers, broad white lip with radiating purple lines, (May-June). *Tropical. Zone 11.*   *p. 87*

ENDYMION   (Hortus 3): see HYACINTHOIDES (Zander 84)

ENKIANTHUS   *Ericaceae*

campanulatus (Japan); deciduous shrub to 8 m with 4-angled whorled branches, red when young; serrate, elliptic leaves turning brilliant red in Autumn; bell-shaped yellow flowers with red veins; the berries orange-yellow. *Zone 5.*   *p. 699*

cernuus rubens (Japan); very ornamental deciduous shrub 2-4 m high, with obovate leaves 5 cm long, crenate at margins; flowers in nodding clusters, with bell-shaped rich red corollas 1 cm long, prettily frilled, white in the species; blooming late Spring, and followed by vivid scarlet-red berries. *Zone 5.*   *p. 699*

perulatus (Japan); "White enkianthus"; much-branched deciduous shrub to 1½ m high, with smooth, reddish young shoots; oval, serrate leaves to 5 cm long; pendulous flowers in terminal clusters, urn-shaped 1 cm white waxy corolla with recurved lobes, blooming before foliage; followed by glossy red fruit. *Zone 5.*   *p. 699, 700*

ENSETE   *Musaceae*

maurelii (Musa) (Ethiopia), "Black banana"; symmetrical plant with the decorative habit of ventricosum; rosette of sturdy, broad, dark-complexioned leaves, deep green suffused with blackish-red above, with brown-purple midrib and margins, purplish-brown beneath. *Tropical. Zones 11-12.*   *p. 122*

ventricosum (Musa ensete) (Moist Central and E. Africa), "Abyssinian banana"; to 12 m, stout solitary pseudostems, not

stoloniferous, conspicuously swollen at the base, bearing erect broad leaves to 6 m long in a cluster, banana-like, and dying after fruiting. Leaves bright green with red midrib and purple edge, on short red stalks. Erect inflorescence with dark red bracts and whitish flowers. Used as shapely centerpiece in summer beds. Have seen this at alt. 1500 m on Mt. Kilimanjaro (Tanzania), and at 2300 m in Kikuyu country of Kenya. *Zones 10-11.*   *p. 122, 459*

ENTEROSPERMUM borbonicum: see IXORA borbonica

EOMECON   *Papaveraceae*

chionantha (E. China), "Snow poppy"; small herbaceous perennial 30 cm or more high, with spreading rhizome; cordate-kidney-shaped, fleshy leaves to 10 cm wide, the margins shallowly lobed; white, short-lived flowers 4-5 cm wide, in terminal clusters, on erect stalk. *Zone 7.*   *p. 466*

EPACRIS   *Epacridaceae*

impressa (Tasmania, Australia), "Victoria heath"; evergreen shrub 1-1½ m high with erect, downy shoots, small leaves 2 cm long; tubular flowers pale yellow with red hairs at base, 2-3 cm long. The floral emblem of the state of Victoria. *Zone 9.*   *p. 698*

longiflora (New South Wales) "Australian fuchsia"; heath-like shrub 1 m or more, with downy shoots and closely-set, sharply pointed leaves 1-2 cm long; pendant slender tubular flowers 3-4 cm long, rosy-crimson with white tips. *Subtropic. Zone 9.*   *p. 698*

EPHEDRA   *Ephedraceae*

distachya (So. Europe to W. Asia), "Joint fir"; prostrate dioecious shrub of peculiar appearance, with slender, dark green jointed stems somewhat like equisetum, to 60 cm long, its leaves are small scales; the small flowers are not ornamental, but the berry-like rose-red fruit formed by two fleshy bracts are attractive. Cultivated as a source of the drug ephedrine. *Zone 6.*   *p. 528, 698*

EPIDENDRUM   *Orchidaceae*

The segregate genus ENCYCLIA is being recognized for those species with short, fat pseudobulbs, as opposed in the typical EPIDENDRUM having long stem-like pseudobulbs. Epidendrum atropurpureum, cochleatum, fragrans, mariae, oncidioides, pentotis, prismatocarpus, radiatum: see ENCYCLIA (European Gardenflora, Cambridge 1984).

EPIDENDRUM   *Orchidaceae*

brassavolae (Guatemala); epiphyte with small pear-shaped, 2-leaved pseudobulbs, the waxy, spidery 10 cm flowers in erect clusters; narrow sepals and petals yellowish-brown, the heart-shaped lip white, narrowing to a purple point; sweet-scented in evening. *Zone 11.*   *p. 89*

ciliare (W. Indies, C. America, Brazil); strong epiphyte with oblong, compressed pseudobulbs with 1-2 leathery leaves; the inflorescence an erect cluster of waxy, fragrant flowers with long linear, greenish-yellow sepals and petals and a lobed and fringed white lip spotted yellow, (Dec.-Jan., Sept.). *Tropical. Zone 11.*   *p. 88*

x o'brienianum (evectum x radicans), "Butterfly orchid"; slender reed-stems with aerial roots and alternate leaves like in ibaguense, and extending into long stalks with showy clusters of brilliant carmine-red flowers, with bright yellow on the crested lip (Spring-Summer). *Tropical. Zones 11-12.*   *p. 89*

parkinsonianum (falcatum) (Mexico); pendulous epiphyte with tiny cylindrical pseudobulb and a solitary thick, linear leaf, 1-2 spidery, waxy flowers, the narrow sepals and petals greenish-yellow, lip trilobed, side lobes wing-like, midlobe narrow, white with yellow throat, (June-Aug.). *Tropical. Zones 11-12.*   *p. 89*

stamfordianum (Honduras, Guatemala, Venezuela, Colombia); beautiful epiphyte with spindle-shaped pseudobulbs with 2-4 leaves, the inflorescence a lax panicle to 60 cm long from the base of the bulb, with fragrant 3 cm flowers yellow spotted bright red, lip fringed, (Feb.-May). *Tropical. Zone 11.*   *p. 88*

EPIGAEA   *Ericaceae*

repens (Newfoundland to Florida), the "Trailing arbutus"; small evergreen creeper with woody, hairy, rooting stems, ovate 8 cm, deep green leathery leaves, and clusters of very fragrant, bell-shaped flowers with green sepals and flesh-colored corolla, in early Spring. *Zone 3.*   *p. 701*

EPIGENEIUM   *Orchidaceae*

lyonii (Sarcopodium, Dendrobium) (Philippines); handsome small epiphyte from the mountains of Luzon, with angular pseudobulbs each with two leaves; pendant inflorescence with beautiful star-like flowers 8 cm across, crimson-red in center fading to a delicate pink near tips, and very fragrant. Spelled Epigenium in Hortus 3. *Zone 11.*   *p. 87*

EPILOBIUM   *Oenotheraceae (Onagraceae)*

angustifolium (Chamaenerion), (No. Temp. hemisphere), "Fireweed" or "French willow"; shrubby perennial to 2 m, with lanceolate, grass-green, 12 cm leaves; with undulate margins; 3 cm flowers rose to purple, or white in var. album. Seen at Rochford's Nurseries in England. *Zone 3.* p. 461

canum (Zander): see ZAUSCHNERIA californica (Hortus)

hirsutum (Europe to Asia, No. Africa, natural. in U.S.), "Willow-weed"; rhizomatous meadow perennial, softly downy, to 1 m or more high; opposite, lanceolate leaves 5-10 cm long, stem-clasping; flowers regular, with purplish-rose corolla 3-4 cm across, summer-blooming. *Zone 3.* p. 460

EPIMEDIUM   *Berberidaceae*

alpinum var. roseum (Europe: So. and E. Alps, to Balkans), "Alpine epimedium"; low perennial 15-25 cm high, spreading by underground stems; the attractive compound evergreen leaves are reddish in Spring; the peculiar flowers have red sepals, and light yellow, slipper-like petals, blooming May-June. *Zone 3.* p. 347

grandiflorum (Japan, Korea, Manchuria), "Bishop's hat"; herbaceous perennial to 25 cm high, spreading from rhizome; pinnately compound leaves with ovate, leathery leaflets, attractively bronze in Autumn; the inflorescence in clusters of rosy-red flowers with long deflexed spurs, during Spring. *Zone 5.* p. 346

grandiflorum album (macranthum) (Japan, Korea, Manchuria), "Japanese barrenwort"; variety with spurred flowers pure white, 3-5 cm across. *Zone 5.* p. 347

grandiflorum 'Rose Queen', "Longspur epimedium"; showy cultivar with large crimson-rose flowers having distinctive, projecting, long spur tipped with white; pinnate foliage with ovate leaflets serrate at margins. *Zone 5.* p. 347

x rubrum (alpinum x grandiflorum); attractive perennial hybrid with compound leaves reddish-bronze when they appear in Spring, later prettily margined in red; flowers 3 cm across, crimson-rose outside, the inside slipper-like and yellow, and with appressed spur. *Zones 6-8.* p. 346

x youngianum (diphyllum of Japan x grandiflorum of Korea); low rhizomatous perennial to 25 cm high, with somewhat woody base, and spreading branches; the compound leaves usually thrice pinnate with ovate, finely toothed leaflets to 8 cm long; small bell-shaped nodding, pale pink flowers in clusters, spring-blooming. *Zone 5.* p. 346

x youngianum 'Niveum', "Snowy epimedium"; low perennial with creeping underground rhizomes sending up compound leaves which stay evergreen during Winter; the 8 cm leaflets very handsome, from light green in Spring, taking on reddish-bronze tints but leaving a pale network along the veins; small white, starry 2 cm flowers. *Zone 5.* p. 347

x EPIPHRONITIS   *Orchidaceae*

veitchii (Epid. radicans x Sophronitis grandiflora); attractive small bigeneric hybrid with reed-type stems with alternative leaves, topped by clusters of fiery red 2½ cm flowers with a golden-yellow center on the lip, (Spring to Fall). *Subtropic. Zone 11.* p. 87

EPIPHYLLUM   *Cactaceae*

chrysocardium (Marniera) (Mexico: Chiapas), "Corazón de Oro" or "Golden heart"; an interesting species growing at the base of trees, with bright green, flat stems cut into narrow segments like fishbones, and looking more like a fern; very large white flowers 20 cm across, noted for their beautiful golden filaments; night-blooming, with unpleasant odor. *Tropical. Zone 11.* p. 176

hyb. 'Grace Ann'; striking large-flowered "Orchid cactus" with flattened green branches; showy rosy-red flowers of waxy texture, shading to pink toward tips, 15 cm or more across. There are thousands of named hybrids bursting forth with huge blossoms of great beauty to 20 cm or more across, in iridescent colors from purple to red, pink, yellowish, white, or multi-colored, hybridized from such usually epiphytic genera as Heliocereus, Nyctocereus, Hylocereus, and Selenicereus, blooming over a long period. *Humid-tropical. Zone 11.* p. 176

laui (Mexico: Chiapas); vigorous, rampant vining Orchid cactus found by Dr. A. Lau in the Maya forest near Tumbala at 2200 m alt., So. Mexico 1975; day-blooming in character unlike most other Epiphyllums; wide-spreading succulent stems, the basal section roundish, extending to the flattened portion, 5-7 cm wide with prominent midrib, shining green, and crenate or undulate along sides; very floriferous with large flowers of pleasing shape, the inner tepals pure white, contrasting with the linear, concave yellow and orange outer tepals, 7 to 9 cm long. *Zone 10.* p. 176

oxypetalum (latifrons) (Mexico to Brazil), "Pond-lily cactus" or a "Queen of the night"; the best nightblooming cactus for the home, grows large, branches usually flat and thin, waxy green and deeply crenate; large fragrant white flowers 12 cm across, reddish outside. *Tropical. Zone 11.* p. 176

phyllanthoides: see NOPALXOCHIA

EPIPREMNUM   *Araceae*

aureum (Scindapsus aureus) (Solomon Islands), "Devil's ivy", known commercially as "Pothos"; fleshy vine climbing tall by rootlets; juvenile leaves broad ovate, waxy, dark green with yellow variegation, 8-10 cm long; mature leaves to 60 cm long, the blades becoming lobed or slashed; bisexual flowers on short spadix within the boat-shaped spathe. (Birdsey 1962 to Raphidophora; Bunting 1964 to Epipremnum). *Tropical. Zone 12.* p. 28, 265

pinnatum (Malaya through Java to New Guinea); prolific tropical climber with large, oblong leaves pinnately parted into regular segments, and tiny pinholes appearing as silvery dots along midrib. The juvenile leaves are entire, oblique-ovate. *Humid-tropical. Zone 11.* p. 31

EPISCIA   *Gesneriaceae*

cupreata (Colombia), "Carpet plant"; tropical creeper, rooting at joints, with soft-hairy, oval, wrinkled leaves almost entirely a metallic copper, faintly marked silver; small solitary flowers with short corolla tube yellow-tinged below, the lobes orange-scarlet, and yellow with red spots inside. *Humid-tropical. Zone 12.* p. 63

lilacina (Costa Rica), "Blue flowered teddy-bear"; a beautiful blue-flowered species also known as 'Fannie Haage' and 'Variegata'; pubescent creeper with dark coppery, rough-puckered 5 to 10 cm leaves decorated with a prominent fishbone pattern of silvery green; large flowers of lavender-blue, 3 to 4 cm long, good grower, but sensitive to cold. *Humid-tropical. Zone 12.* p. 63

reptans (fulgida, coccinea) (Brazil, Guyana, Surinam, Colombia), "Flame violet;"; tropical pubescent creeper with broad ovate, quilted, brown-green leaves and bright silvery green veins, margins crenate; flowers with long blood-red corolla tube with fringed edges and pink inside. *Humid-tropical. Zone 12.* p. 63

EPITHELANTHA   *Cactaceae*

micromeris (Texas, N. Mexico), "Button-cactus"; group-forming tiny globes usually 1-2 cm dia., but may grow to over 5 cm; depressed on top; small tubercles in spirals almost entirely covered by flattened white spines; pinkish flowers. Of weak growth habit, and in California seen grafted on Trichocereus trichogonus. *Zone 10.* p. 158

EQUISETUM   *Equisetaceae*

arvense (No. Hemisphere), "Common horsetail"; leafless perennial herb of ponds and wet areas, having whorls of succulent green leafless branches, and a terminal yellowish cone; very persistent. *Zone 4.* p. 329

giganteum (So. America), the "Giant horsetail"; a remnant of ancient vegetation; rush-like tropical perennial with rhizomatous rootstock, at home in moist places; erect hollow jointed stems to 4 m high, without proper foliage, the leaves reduced to sheaths at the joints; the sterile branches are fresh green, set in whorls, and pendant from the joints. During the Carbon Age, the equisetums were forming gigantic forests, through millions of years turning into coal. Belonging to the fern-allies, they bear no flowers, but spores in a cone-like spike. *Zone 10.* p. 329

hyemale (No. America, Europe, Asia), "Horsetail"; "Scouring rush" name implying that its tough, wiry, rough stems are used for polishing and scrubbing. Furrowed, evergreen, jointed hollow stems to 1 m or more high, with scale-like pointed leaves, clustered at the joints in whorls. A fern-ally without flowers, but with cone-like spikes bearing spores. Equisetum represents a single living genus of a complex group that thrived during the Coal age more than 300 million years ago. As an indoor plant will grow immersed in water. *Zones 3-10.* p. 329

maximum (telmateia) (Europe, Asia Minor, California to Alaska), "Dutch rush"; interesting evergreen perennial of marshy areas; sterile grooved, hollow stems 1-2 m high and with joints at intervals, sprouting whorls of lateral, 4-angled fresh green branches for dense effect; fertile stem about 30 cm high, topped by spore-bearing cones, 5-8 cm long. *Zones 4-8.* p. 329

ERANTHIS   *Ranunculaceae*

hyemalis (Europe: France to Hungary), "Winter-aconite"; small tuberous perennial herb 10 to 15 cm high, basal leaves roundish and 7-parted, leaves on flower stem broad-linear; solitary 4 cm sessile flowers, bearing 5-9 bright yellow petal-like sepals, in very early Spring. *Zone 5.* p. 262

EREMOCHLOA   *Gramineae*

ophiurides (S.E. Asia and China), "Centipede grass"; warm season grass creeping by thick, leafy stolons with short nodes; forming dense clump of coarse-textured arching lanceolate leaves; stems depressed or ascending to 10 cm high; inflorescence spike-like with short spikelets. Also known as "Lazy man's grass" because needs little care and infrequent mowing, and is widely grown on sandy soils of Southeastern States. The upright stolons resemble a centipede. *Zone 7.* p. 570

EREMOPHILA *Myoporaceae*

maculata (N.E. Australia to New So. Wales), "Spotted Emu bush"; floriferous evergreen shrub to 2 m or more high, with rigid, downy branches; the narrow oblong leaves to 4 cm long; solitary axillary flowers toward apex of stems, the 3 cm corolla pink, changing to red toward front, spotted yellow inside, the upper lip erect, lower lobes reflexed, stamens protruding. *Zone 10.* p. 795

sargentii (Western Australia), "Emu-bush"; attractive small evergreen shrub to 1 m high, with densely clustered sticky leaves; prolific with masses of pale purple flowers during Spring. *Zone 10.* p. 795

EREMURUS *Liliaceae*

elwesii (Turkestan), "Desert candle"; stately perennial from the steppes of Central Asia, with fleshy, narrow basal leaves 75 cm long, and strong spike-like racemes 2 m or more, with numerous stalked flowers having spreading segments, pink with deeper center stripe; May-blooming. *Zone 6.* p. 445

himalaicus (N.W. Himalayas), "Himalayan desert-candle"; stout perennial 1 to 1¹⁄₂ m high, with heavy fiborus roots; the smooth, bright green strap-shaped, somewhat succulent leaves to 40 cm long, forming rosette-like clusters; inflorescence in tall cylindrical spike-like racemes dense with starry white flowers, displaying orange anthers, usually blooming in June. Very popular in American gardens. *Zones 3-10.* p. 445

x isabellinus (warei) (olgae x stenophyllus); beautiful hybrid of Central Asian parentage, one of the Shelford crosses 1902, 1¹⁄₂ m or more high, with rosettes or tufts of narrow linear leaves; the inflorescence in impressive spike-like racemes dense with bright yellow flowers, on wire-stiff stalks, blooming June-July. This hybrid strain also produced blooms in other colors, in pink, copper and white. *Zones 4-10.* p. 445

olgae (Turkestan), "King's spear"; stately perennial to 1¹⁄₂ m high, with tufting linear, recurved leaves 30 cm long, rough along margins; lovely white or pink starry flowers 3 cm across, displaying long stamens, and densely clustered in a cylindric raceme, blooming during June and July. *Zone 6.* p. 445

stenophyllus (bungei, aurantiacus) (Iran), "Afghan desert candle"; with stately flowering stalk 1 m high, dense with 1 cm flowers having narrow, spreading segments bright golden-orange; basal rosette of firm linear leaves 30 cm long, from thick fibrous roots. *Zone 6.* p. 445

ERICA *Ericaceae*

arborea (Mediterr. region, Canary Isl., Tenerife), "Tree heath"; evergreen tall shrub or small tree to 6 m high, the branches with young shoots hairy; leaves needle like in whorls of three, 8 mm long; inflorescence in elongate clusters 25 to 45 cm long, of globular bell-shaped, fragrant white flowers 6 mm long, the corolla with spreading lobes, winter- or spring-blooming. Source of briar root used for making smoking pipes. *Zone 7.* p. 701

baccans (So. Africa), "Berry heath"; erect shrub 1-1¹⁄₂ m high, tiny linear bluish-green leaves; the globular bell-flowers, mostly in terminal fours, deep rose, the 6 mm corolla narrowed at throat; Winter-Spring. *Subtropic. Zone 9.* p. 704

canaliculata (Zander, Kruessmann):
see E. melanthera hort. (Wyman)

carnea (Alps to So. Europe), "Spring heath" or "Snow-heather"; tolerant to limestone, a low bush to 30 cm high, with prostrate branches, tiny needle-like leaves, and rosy-red flowers in short, one-sided racemes during January to May, depending on location. Has been offered as "Scotch heather" by nurseries, but this name should be properly applied to Calluna, which is hardier, has scale-like leaves, and flowers having a colored, 4-parted calyx. *Zone 5.* p. 701

carnea 'Alba', "White heath"; lovely small cultivar, of low, bushy habit, very floriferous with masses of pure white flowers, which in mild region will bloom from January into Spring. *Zone 5.* p. 701

carnea 'Springwood White'; very vigorous cultivar, spreading rapidly, producing a multitude of white flowers tinted with pink, in more or less 1-sided erect racemes, in February-March; outstanding white color-form. *Zone 5.* p. 702

cerinthoides (So. Africa); a brilliant species with erect branches, leaves 4-6 in a whorl, ciliate; flowers in a close terminal cluster, the belled corolla 2¹⁄₂-3 cm long, fiery crimson, blooming May-October. *Zone 8.* p. 702

ciliaris 'Aurea' (W. Europe), "Dorset heath"; small evergreen subshrub to 30 cm high, with prostrate branches; leaves in whorls of three, narrow needle-like, and handsomely gold-tipped; inflorescence in terminal racemes to 12 cm long, of rosy-red flowers 1 cm long, blooming Summer to Autumn. *Zone 7.* p. 702

cinerea (Norway to Italy), "Twisted heath" or "Bell heather"; small evergreen 25-50 cm high, with lustrous green, strongly recurved needles in threes along the slender branches; lovely rosy-purple ovoid flowers blooming June to September. The foliage will turn to orange and bronze in Autumn. *Zone 5.*

cinerea 'Pallas' ('Pallida' hort.); hardy cultivar of Holland 1970; vigorous bushy plant to 35 cm high, with glossy green leaves in whorls; very floriferous with masses of lilac-pink flowers, blooming June to September. *Zone 5.* p. 702

x darleyensis (carnea x mediterranea); vigorous hybrid evergreen to 1 m high; the needle-like leaves usually in whorls of four, with margins strongly turned under; very attractive flowers having urn-shaped inflated corolla pale pink 1 cm long, the calyx greenish-white or tinted pink, blooming November to May; a most valuable of hardy Ericas. *Zone 6.* p. 702

'Felix Faure' (hyemalis hybrid), "French heather"; branching evergreen of low, compact habit to 30 cm high; bright green needles; tubular flowers 3 cm long, purplish-orange with whitish tips. *Subtropic. Zone 9.* p. 702

gracilis (So. Africa), "Rose heath"; bushy shrub with small light green linear leaves, the side shoots loaded with terminal clusters of tiny globose rosy flowers (Winter). *Subtropic. Zone 10.* p. 57, 701

hyemalis (So. Africa), "French heather"; spreading bush to 60 cm producing tall, tapering racemes of tubular rose-pink flowers 2-2¹⁄₂ cm long, and tipped with white, winter blooming. Possibly form of summer-fl. perspicua. *Subtropic. Zone 8.* p. 702

lusitanica (W. Europe), "Spanish heath" or "Portugal heath"; erect, densely branched shrub to 4 m high, with hairy young shoots, scattered linear 6 mm needle-leaves pale green; multitudes of white flowers along lateral twigs, stamens and stigma pink, blooming March to May. *Zone 8.* p. 703

mammosa (So. Africa); tall shrubby plant to 1 m, the little needle-like leaves in fours, or scattered; tubular flowers pendulous in a dense cluster, corolla 2 cm long, reddish-purple, blooming July to October (Autumn). *Subtropic. Zone 10.* p. 704

mediterranea 'Golden Lady' (purpurescens), "Irish heath"; dense upright heath 1-3 m high, with tiny 1 cm needle-like leaves in four's; ovoid urn-shaped lavender pink flowers 5 mm long, with black anthers. The cv. 'Golden Lady' has golden-yellow leaves. *Zone 8.* p. 702

melanthera hort. (caniculata) (So. Africa), "Christmas heather" or "Blackeyed heath"; compact shrub to 60 cm high, with downy shoots and tiny linear leaves; the small globular flowers delicate pale rose with prominent black anthers, blooming in Winter. Kruessmann and Zander refer this to E. caniculata. *Subtropic. Zone 9.* p. 57, 703

regia (Cape Prov.), the "Royal heath"; striking heath of straggling habit 60-90 cm high but bearing lovely glossy sticky flowers with inflated tubular, waxy corolla 2 cm long, rich crimson-red; the small appressed needle-leaves fresh green. The photo shown is probably E. regia var. variegata, their bicolored corollas crimson with white base, and popular in cultivation. *Subtropic. Zone 9.* p. 703

sitiens (So. Africa: Cape Prov.); free-blooming heath, normally to 60 cm high, but the thin wiry branches become pendant from the weight of masses of blooms, their inflated sepals light pink. *Zone 8.* p. 703

speciosa (So. Africa: Cape Prov.); sparry heath 60-120 cm high, the short, plump needles close to stems; long tubular curved flowers to 3 cm long, and sticky, crimson-red with yellow tips. *Subtropic. Zone 10.* p. 704

taxifolia (Cape Prov.); small shrub to 30 cm high, known as the "Double pink heath" because its small flowers appear to be double; the jar-shaped deep pink corolla, tipped red, is half concealed, like petticoats, by broad pink sepals; in clusters on the branchlets; linear leaves 3-sided. *Subtropic. Zone 9.* p. 703

terminalis (stricta) (So. Europe), "Corsican heath"; bushy shrub to 1 m or more high, dense with slender, stiff branches, clothed by linear 1 cm leaves finely ciliate; flowers in small terminal clusters; urn-shaped corollas rosy-pink, tipped by recurved lobes, blooming June to November. *Zone 8.* p. 703

tetralix (W. Europe, natur. in E. No. America), "Bog heath" or "Crossleaf heath"; very hardy evergreen to 50 cm high, with woolly, grayish foliage on prostrate branches, the leaves in fours, glaucous beneath; flowers in dense terminal clusters, with 6 mm rose-pink cylindric urn-shaped corollas, blooming June-October. Known as "Glockenheide" in Germany. Yields yellow dye used in Scotland. *Zone 3.* p. 703

vagans (W. Europe), "Cornish heath"; low evergreen shrub to 30 cm high, with spreading branches; small bright green needle-leaves in whorls of four or five; flowers in leafy racemes to 15 cm long, having purplish-pink urn-shaped corollas, displaying protruding stamens, blooming July to October. Very popular in American gardens. *Zone 7.* p. 703

'Wilmorei', "Prince of Wales heather"; a grand old large-flowered hybrid well-known since 1835, probably E. perspicua but with swollen tubes and more bushy; showy spikes with stiff linear leaves in threes, and tubular rosy flowers 4 cm long, prettily tipped with white; blooming Winter to Spring; very showy and with long-lasting flowers. *Subtropic. Zone 9.* p. 703

ERIGERON   *Compositae*

alpinus (Alps to Balkans; Lebanon to Caucasus), "Alpine flea-bane"; coarsely hairy perennial to 25 cm high; basal leaves oblanceolate, stem leaves linear; daisy-like flowers 4 cm across, outer disc-flowers female, the slender ray-flowers spreading, pink or purple, during Summer. *Zone 5.*   p. 386

danelium (col. Bermuda Bot. Garden); herbaceous perennial to 50 cm high, with clusters of small, 1 cm white flowers having greenish center disc; lanceolate 6 cm glossy green leaves on erect stems. *Zone 8.*   p. 386

flettii (Washington: Olympic Mts.), "Olympic fleabane"; small herbaceous perennial to 15 cm high, from a stout, branched root-crown; stems soft-hairy, with small leaves; the basal foliage larger, to 5 cm long; solitary floral heads to 4 cm across, with numerous white ray-florets, ranged around the yellow center disc. *Zone 5.*   p. 386

glabellus (Alaska, so. to Colorado and Wisconsin), "Alaska fleabane"; fibrous-rooted perennial or biennial, 20-50 cm high; basal leaves oblanceolate 15 cm long, and persistent, the stem-leaves mostly linear; floral heads in clusters, 5 cm across, of numerous ray-florets white, pink or blue, ranged around yellow disc; June-blooming. *Zone 3.*   p. 386

glaucus (Coastal California to Oregon), "Beach aster" or "Seaside daisy"; sprawling, rather succulent perennial 15-30 cm high, with short, thick rhizome, and forming clusters; pale green oval, glaucous leaves, contrast attractively with the floral heads, to 5 cm across, the golden center disc ringed with lilac or purple ray-florets, appearing from May on. *Zone 3.*   p. 386

x hybridus; involved hybrid incl. atticus and aurantiacus; bushy perennial; leafy-stemmed to 60 cm high; many large heads 5 cm across, with lilac-blue ray-petals and yellow disc. Erigeron hybrids have various colors, incl. violet, pink, purple. *Zone 5.*   p. 386

x hybridus roseus (atticus x aurantiacus); floriferous hybrid to 60 cm high, with lovely bloom having broad, double ray-florets in soft rose-pink frilled at margins, during Summer. *Zone 5.*   p. 386

pinnatisectus (Mts. of Wyoming, Colorado, New Mexico), "Rocky Mountain fleabane"; small tufted perennial 10-20 cm high, with pale green, pinnately cleft leaves mostly basal, on bristly petioles, crowned by light blue, daisy-like flowers 2 cm wide, in Summer. *Zone 3.*   p. 386

pulchellus (Maine to Minnesota, Georgia to Texas), "Robin's plantain"; fibrous-rooted attractive biennial or short-lived hairy stemmed perennial, to 50 cm high, spreading by stolons; basal leaves oblanceolate and toothed, to 12 cm long, stem-leaves shorter; daisy-like flowers 4 cm across, the numerous ray-florets white, blue or pink, April-June. This species may be identical with E. bellidifolius. *Zone 3.*   p. 386

speciosus (Pacific coast to Montana, N. Mexico), "Ray-aster" or "Fleabane"; free-blooming perennial to 75 cm high, with narrow, smooth leaves; purple daisy-like flowers, 4 cm across, the ray-petals threadlike in 2 or more rows. *Warm temperate. Zones 4-8.*   p. 385

unalaskensis (Aleutians, Alaska); low perennial with woody base from barren rocks of Unalaska Island in the Bering Sea, to 15 cm high, having grayish ovate leaves; the flowers daisy-like 3 cm across, with prominent yellow to brown central disc, ringed by pale purple ray-florets. *Zone 2.*   p. 385

ERINACEA   *Leguminosae*

pungens (Anthyllis) (So. France, Spain, Algeria, Tunisia), "Hedge-hog broom" or "Branch-thorn"; small bushy shrub 30-50 cm high, with rigid green branches intricately twisted and spine-tipped; linear-oblong leaves to 2 cm long, soon deciduous; flowers pale violet 3 cm long, blooming in Spring; small 2 cm silky hairy oblong pods. *Zone 9.*   p. 760

ERINUS   *Scrophulariaceae*

alpinus (Mts. of C. Europe, Spain, Italy, and Austria), "Alpine liverbalsam"; floriferous herbaceous perennial to 15 cm high, forming tufts, with 2 cm hairy, spoon-shaped leaves, deeply toothed; small purple to rose or white flowers 2 cm across, the corollas with notched lobes, in terminal clusters, blooming March to June. *Zone 4.*   p. 503

ERIOBOTRYA   *Rosaceae*

deflexa (Taiwan), "Bronze loquat"; woody evergreen 2 m or more high, with obovate wrinkled leaves 12-25 cm long, bright coppery when young and rusty hairy, serrate at margins; small white flowers; 2 cm fruit not edible. *Zone 9.*   p. 834

japonica (China), "Chinese loquat" or "Japan plum"; symmetrical evergreen tree to 10 m high, with noble decorative thick foliage, 15-30 cm long obovate, glossy green on the surface, strongly ribbed, and toothed, the underside and stalk rusty-woolly; fragrant white flowers, and pear-shaped yellow to orange edible fruit 3 to 8 cm long, ripe in January to April, of pleasant, sprightly flavor. The combined sweet rind with tart pulp make it suitable for preserves and candy-making. *Zones 7-10.*   p. 834, 925

ERIOCACTUS: see NOTOCACTUS (Hortus, Zander)

ERIOCEREUS martinii (Zander): see HARRISIA martinii (Hortus)

ERIOGONUM   *Polygoniaceae*

grande rubescens (Channel Isl.; So. California), "Red buck-wheat"; subshrubby plant to 1 m high, with leafy stems, the leaves spatulate or ovate 3-8 cm long, green above and white-hairy beneath, wavy and revolute at margins; small rose-red flowers in dense clusters. *Zone 10.*   p. 821

ovalifolium (Brit. Columbia to Arizona), "Wild buckwheat"; low subshrubby perennial 10 cm high, forming mats; leaves in dense white-woolly rosettes of oval blades 2 cm long; tiny creamy-white to bright yellow flowers in dense globular clusters, blooming June-July. *Zone 8.*   p. 475

umbellatum (Washington to California and Wyoming), "Sulphur flower"; spreading, low perennial of the Sierras and Rocky Mts., with branches from woody base, to 30 cm high; the ovate leaves green above and woolly beneath; small daisy-like flowers bright yellow, or varying to cream, in leafy-bracted clusters. *Zone 7.*   p. 475

ERIOPHORUM   *Cyperaceae*

angustifolium (polystachion) (Europe, Asia, No. America), "Common cotton grass"; perennial bog-pool plant; creeping rhizome with stems not tufted, 15-60 cm high; grass-like channeled leaves 6 mm wide, to 3-angled toward apex; the fluffy, white fruit heads, more than one on drooping stems. *Zone 3.*   p. 328

latifolium (Europe, Asia Minor, Caucasus, Siberia to No. America), "Broadleaved cotton-grass" tufted, non-running deciduous perennial to 60 cm high, with channelled leaves 30 cm long, broader than E. angustifolium, 3-angled above middle; the leafy stems hollow and sharply angled; very attractive inflorescence culminated by large showy seedheads with cotton-like, silky white threads. *Zones 3-7.*   p. 558

vaginatum (No. Hemisphere: Norway, Britain and Arctic Region), "Arctic cotton grass" or "Hare's tail"; perennial bog plant 25-45 cm high, forming dense tufts of short threadlike, 3-angled leaves; inflorescence on long wiry stalks topped by white cottony-bristly fruiting heads. *Zone 2.*   p. 328

ERIOPHYLLUM   *Compositae*

lanatum (Brit. Columbia to Oregon, and Montana), "Woolly sunflower" or "Woolly eriophyllum"; perennial 25-50 cm high, with alternate, woolly-tomentose leaves divided into 3-7 segments; flowers yellow in daisy-like heads 3-4 cm across, resembling miniature sunflowers. *Zone 5.*   p. 387

ERIOSTEMON   *Rutaceae*

myoporoides (E. Australia), "Longleaf wax flower"; beautiful evergreen shrub 60-120 cm high; aromatic narrow lanceolate leaves 5-10 cm long, having midrib depressed; blooming abundantly with axillary clusters of waxy-white flowers, pink beneath and in bud, blossoming in August, early Spring in Victoria to Queensland. *Zone 10.*   p. 860

ERIOSYCE   *Cactaceae: Echinocactanae*

ceratistes (Chile); large globular cactus, in habitat above Santiago de Chile; olive-green body to 50 cm dia. with 20 ribs, to 30 when older, divided into knobs of which each bears numerous curving, reddish to blackish spines 3 cm long, densely covering the surface; in a circle around the top appear the bell-shaped red flowers 3 to 4 cm long, and enveloped in a matting of white wool. *Zone 10.*   p. 162

ERITRICHIUM   *Boraginaceae*

elongatum (Oregon to Utah, Montana, Colorado, New Mexico), "Alpine forget-me-not"; low perennial herb forming cushion-like mats, with small 1 cm overlapping leaves, softly hairy; lovely 6 mm blue flowers, with yellow crests in throat. *Zone 3.*   p. 347

ERODIUM   *Geraniaceae*

chamaedryoides (Mallorca, Corsica), "Alpine geranium"; mat-forming, dainty herbaceous perennial to 8 cm high, small cordate leaves 1 cm across, wavy and crenate at margins; flowers white with red veins, throughout Summer. *Subtropic. Zones 7-9.*   p. 314

x kolbianum (macradenum x supracanum), (Spain); small perennial of Pyrenees heritage, to 30 cm high, with soft-hairy, bipinnate leaves; lovely flowers white to soft pink, the two upper petals marked with purple at base; Summer. *Zone 6.*   p. 419

manescavii (Pyrenees), "Heron's-bill"; herbaceous stemless perennial 30-60 cm high, with all basal, pinnate leaves 15 cm long, the segments toothed or divided again; showy flowers to 5 cm across, purplish-red, in branched clusters, summer-blooming. *Zone 6.*   p. 418

pelargoniflorum (Asia Minor: Anatolia); shrubby, hairy perennial to 30 cm high, with heart-shaped, lightly lobed, green basal leaves, pubescent above; flowers white, two upper petals spotted brown-purple. *Zone 6.*   p. 419

petraeum (Pyrenees of Spain), "Cliff heronbill"; spreading herbaceous perennial to 15 cm high, with softly hairy, all-basal pinnate leaves 8-15 cm long, the ovate leaflets lobed; lovely flowers soft pink and veined with red. *Zone 6.*   *p. 314*

ERVATAMIA: see TABERNAEMONTANA (Hortus 3, Zander 84)

ERYNGIUM   *Umbelliferae*

agavifolium (Argentina); handsome clustering evergreen rosettes to 2 m high, of leathery-succulent, sword-shaped leaves to more than 1 m long, and spiny along margins, the lower leaves deflexed; the bracted inflorescence is somewhat thistle-like with tiny greenish flowers mostly concealed by spathe-like brownish bracts in heads 5 cm long; during Summer. *Zone 8.*   *p. 515*

alpinum (Europe: Maritime Alps to Balkans), "Alpine thistle"; handsome perennial 60 to 80 cm high, with rich green leaves lobed or palmately cut; the inflorescence with blue or white flowers in cone-like heads, subtended by ray-like silvery bluish bracts. *Zone 3.*   *p. 515*

bourgatii (Medit. region, Spain, Pyrenees), "Eryngo"; clustering perennial forming numerous stems 30-60 cm high, with roundish basal leaves palmately 3-parted, the lobes dissected or forked; the inflorescence with cone-like head, hiding small bluish flowers amongst bristles, and subtended by a ring of spiny-tipped linear bracts; June to August. *Zone 6.*   *p. 515*

bromeliifolium (Mexico); perennial rosette of fleshy olive-green, channelled leaves edged by large thorny teeth; tall stalk to 2 m, with thistle-like inflorescence of bluish flowers. Photographed outdoors in July at the Botanic Garden, Strasbourg, France. *Zone 6.*   *p. 515*

giganteum (Armenia to Caucasus), "Ivory thistle"; handsome spiny biennial or short-lived perennial to 1 m or more high; ovate, heart-shaped basal leaves, and crenate, clasping 3-lobed stem-leaves; attractive terminal inflorescence in conical heads of small blue flowers, subtended by a circle of rigid, long-toothed ivory-white bracts, in July-August. Being of monocarpic character, the plant normally expires after producing fruit, but frequently self-sowing. *Zone 5.*   *p. 515*

planum (S.E. Europe to Asia Minor and Kashmir), "Noble bristle"; handsome perennial freely branching with slender stems, 30 to 80 cm high; the lower leaves oval-heart-shaped; stem leaves 3-5 parted and toothed; the small blue flowers in ovoid heads 2 cm long, subtended by narrow, rigid bracts in a whorl, during Summer. *Zone 5.*   *p. 515*

ERYSIMUM   *Cruciferae*

x allionii hort. (Cheiranthus x allionii, Erys. hieraciifolium, E. asperum), "Siberian wallflower"; subshrubby biennial or short-lived perennial 40-70 cm high, with mid-green narrow lanceolate leaves 8 cm long; 4-petaled flowers deep orange mixed with mahogany, 2 cm across, in large clusters, blooming Spring to Summer. Prob. hyb. of E. ochroleucum x perofskianum, England 1846. According to Wyman this is E. asperum of Ohio to Texas. *Zone 6.*   *p. 420*

x allionii 'Aurantium', "Golden wallflower"; lovely biennial of compact habit, with large 2 cm golden-yellow flowers of 4 sepals and 4 petals, in large clusters. *Zone 6.*   *p. 410*

linifolium ('Bowles Mauve') (Pyrenees of Spain), "Alpine wallflower"; clustering, evergreen perennial with many ascending stems 15-40 cm long, from a root-like rhizome; linear-lanceolate green or white leaves; small 2 cm purple to violet flowers in elongate racemes, blooming May to July. *Zone 6.*   *p. 410*

scoparium (Cheiranthus scoparius) (Canary Isl.: Tenerife), "Teide wallflower"; bushy subshrub about 50 cm high, branching at woody base; slender erect broom-like stems with linear leaves; at apex the small pale lilac flowers with spreading petals. *Zone 9.*   *p. 695*

ERYTHEA: see BRAHEA (Hortus 3)

ERYTHRINA   *Leguminosae*

x bidwillii (crista-galli x herbacea), "Florida coral-bean"; handsome deciduous, thorny subshrub forming many canes, to 3 m or more high, with leaves of 3 leaflets, and erect inflorescence of crimson-red curved flowers, blooming intermittently between April and November. *Zone 10.*   *p. 761*

caffra (humeana hort.) (E. Cape Prov., Natal), "Kaffirboom coral tree"; large spreading, deciduous, tree to 25 m, trunk and branches with hooked thorns; pointed leaflets in three's, spade-shaped; tubular nectar-filled flowers more than 3 cm long, in a spreading spike, brilliant cinnabar-scarlet fading to purple; protruding stamens give a whiskery look; blooming late January into April. Widely planted in California. *Zone 10.*   *p. 761*

coralloides (corallodendrum) (Arizona to Mexico), "Coral tree"; tree to 6 m with woody stems prickly or unarmed; leaves of 3 broad leaflets; flowers with standard never opening, deep scarlet, in long racemes, appearing after leaves fall. *Zone 10.*   *p. 761*

crista-galli (Brazil to Uruguay and Argentina), "Coral tree"; small spiny tree to 10 m high, with trifoliolate leaves on thorny petioles, and

showy butterfly flowers deep scarlet-red, in dense racemes, usually produced before the leaves, but may bloom 3 times a year. Spent flowers should be removed. *Zones 9-10.*   *p. 761*

falcata (So. Brazil, Argentina, Bolivia, Perú); magnificent tropical tree with bright coral-scarlet flowers; I will never forget the breathtaking sight of these leafless trees in red, blazing against the azure blue sky of the Organ mountains in the dry landscape of Minas Gerais in Brazil. Tree to 15 m high, with scattered prickles on branches, and partially evergreen; trifoliate with leathery leaflets, usually dropped before blooming, brilliant waxy flowers with falcate, curved keels in massed pendant clusters normally in late Spring. *Zones 9-10. p. 760*

humeana (So. Africa), "Natal coral tree"; semi-evergreen shrub or tree; may grow to 10 m, but begins to bear its bright crimson-red blooms when 1 m high; flowers in long-stalked clusters at branch ends and inclined to be pendant or arching; blooming Mid-summer to November; foliage with 3 broad leaflets. *Zone 10.*   *p. 761*

montana (Mexico: Zacatecas, Durango, Jalisco); interesting subshrub from the Sierra Madre, with unarmed herbaceous stems to 60 cm high; compound leaves having leaflets 4-12 cm long; the showy inflorescence with erect cluster of fleshy, tubular curved corolla 5-7 cm long, varying from salmon-rose to amber and purplish. In So. Mexican habitat areas of frost the tops of stems are regularly killed. *Zones 9-10.*   *p. 760*

poeppigiana (So. America: Venezuela), "Mountain immortelle"; very showy deciduous tree to 20 m high, with trunk dividing from near base, flowering in clusters on bare spiny branches or appearing together with foliage; corolla with wings chestnut-red with purplish edge, the large standard orange-red 3-6 cm long and deflexed, the keel petals united; leaves 20 cm long, having 3 rhombic-ovate leaflets, dropping in Spring just before blooming. *Zone 10.*   *p. 760*

princeps (lysistemon) (Transvaal, Zululand, Zimbabwe, Natal), "Kaffirboom"; spectacularly showy deciduous, thorny tree to 12 m with gray branches; leaves after bloom, the obovate leaflets arranged in three's; large tube-shaped, bright salmon-scarlet flowers, in large compact clusters reminding of a coxcomb. *Zones 9-10.*   *p. 760*

variegata var. orientalis (indica picta) (India, Malaysia, Australia); a beautiful variegated-leaved bushy tree with black spines to 15 m high, and partially deciduous, the large leaves to 15 cm long and composed of 3 broad-ovate or triangular leaflets, fresh glossy-green, strikingly variegated cream to golden-yellow along the primary veins; waxy flowers brilliant crimson-red, 6 cm long, in Winter to Spring. *Zones 10-11.*   *p. 760*

velutina (Antilles, Dominica to Venezuela); tropical tree to 10 m high, with spreading, spiny branches, having leaves of 3 obovate leaflets, which are deciduous when blooms appear; flowers in large terminal clusters, with corolla brilliant red, in form pea-like except for standard petal much longer, and appearing like a tiger claw; fruits are black pods containing red seed lined with black. Very showy when in bloom Mid-winter into Spring. *Zone 10.*   *p. 760*

ERYTHRONIUM   *Liliaceae*

americanum (Nova Scotia to Florida), "Trout-lily", also known as "Dogtooth-violet"; bulbous herb to 25 cm high, producing offsets; with two lanceolate basal leaves 15 cm long, dotted and mottled with brown and white; solitary 5 cm flowers bright yellow with spreading, recurved segments, blooming April to June. The bulbs were cooked by the Indians as a vegetable. *Zone 3.*   *p. 240*

'Golden Torch'; hybrid seen at Keukenhof Gardens in Holland blooming in May, having broad bluish-green leaves marked with silver, and graceful rich yellow flowers resembling small lilies, the petals reflexed, and spreading 6 cm across. *Zone 5.*   *p. 240*

grandiflorum (Brit. Columbia, Montana, Oregon, Utah), "Avalanche lily" or "Glacier lily"; beautiful cormous perennial, with green-elliptic leaves to 15 cm long; lily-like flowers variable, usually bright golden-yellow with recurved petals 4 cm long. I photographed this plant in July, breaking through the melting snow, in Glacier National Park, Montana. *Temperate. Zone 5.*   *p. 240*

montanum (Oregon, Washington, Brit. Columbia), "Dog-tooth violet" of Alpine meadows; having lanceolate, mottled leaves to 15 cm long; the 30 cm floral stalk carrying one or several white flowers orange at base inside, the segments recurved. *Zone 6.*   *p. 240*

'Pagoda' (tuolumnense x revolutum); cormous hybrid seen at Keukenhof Gardens in Holland, blooming in May; broad lanceolate pairs of basal leaves with pale markings; floral stalk 40 cm high, bearing lemon-yellow flowers 5 cm across, and a brown ring in center. *Zones 5-8.*   *p. 240*

revolutum 'White Beauty', "Great Fawn lily"; vigorous, attractive cultivar with broad foliage veined silver gray, the floral stalk 15-40 cm long, often bearing several snow-white flowers with chocolate-zoned center, the deflexed segments 4 cm long. The species is from No. California to Brit. Columbia. *Zone 6.*   *p. 240*

tuolumnense (Cent. California), "Coast Fawn-lily" or "Adder's tongue"; handsome small perennial from membrane-coated corms; broad-lanceolate, glossy green basal leaves to 30 cm long; floral stem bearing one to several lily-like golden-yellow flowers 3 cm long, greenish at base, during Spring. *Zone 7.* p. 240

ERYTHRORHIPSALIS *Cactaceae*

pilocarpa (Brazil: Rio, São Paulo), "Bristle-tufted twig-cactus"; attractive branched epiphytic cactus, at first erect, later pendant, slender cylindrical purplish-green stems, with joints clustered by whorls or alternate branches grooved, closely set by areoles with appressed, whitish hair-like bristles; small 2½ cm white to pale yellow, fragrant flowers, also set with bristles; 12 mm red fruit. *Zone 11.* p. 160

ERYTHROXYLUM *Erythroxylaceae*

coca (Eastern Andes), "Cocaine plant"; densely leafy shrub to 4 m, obovate leathery leaves to 6 cm; small 1 cm yellowish flowers, followed by small ovoid reddish berries. Coca leaves mixed with lime are chewed daily by the Indians of the Andes for a powerful stimulant at high altitudes. *Subtropic. Zones 9-10.* p. 739

ESCALLONIA *Saxifragaceae*

bifida (montevidensis, floribunda hort.) (Brazil, Paraguay, Uruguay, Argentina), "White escallonia"; tall, broad evergreen shrub 2-3 m or small tree to 8 m high; glossy leathery elliptic leaves 4-8 cm long; cream-white flowers in terminal clusters, the petals short-clawed and reflexed, blooming late Summer-Autumn. *Zone 9.* p. 870

x exoniensis 'Frades' (rosea x rubra), "Pink princess escallonia"; medium-size evergreen shrub to 2 m high; glossy green ovate leaves 4 cm long; prolific rich crimson-rose flowers in terminal clusters in Spring through Summer. *Zone 8.* p. 870

laevis (organensis) (So. Brazil: Organ Mts.), "Pink escallonia"; sturdy ornamental evergreen, bushy shrub to 2 m, with angled branchlets; obovate firm bronzy green, toothed leaves to 8 cm long, often red-margined; small 1 cm fragrant, rosy flowers apple-blossom-like, in dense terminal clusters; blooming in Autumn. *Zone 8.* p. 870

x langleyensis (rubra x virgata), "Appleblossom escallonia"; dense evergreen with sprawling, arching branches 1-3 m high; small obovate or oval leaves about 2-3 cm long, with tiny resin glands beneath; pinkish-white flowers from pink buds, blooming all Summer. *Zone 7.* p. 870

rubra (Chile), "Red escallonia"; evergreen shrub 3-5 m high, with reddish twigs having sticky, glossy green, lanceolate leaves 4-8 cm long, serrate at margins; small 2 cm rose-red flowers in loose clusters, the 2 cm petals with long claws united in a tube, blooming July-August or longer. *Zone 8.* p. 870

ESCHSCHOLTZIA *Papaveraceae*

californica (California, Oregon), "California poppy"; soft herb with gray-green, 3-pinnatifid leaves and large showy, poppy-like 6-8 cm flowers, bright yellow with orange-red base, opening in the sun; widely naturalized in southern Chile where I noted them climbing even into the Andes. *Subtropic. Zones 9-10.* p. 468

ESCOBARIA *Cactaceae*

bella (Coryphanta bella in Hortus) (Rio Diablo, Texas); clustering small globular to cylindric body 6 to 8 cm high, with raised knobs tipped star-like by white radial spines and brown central needles; rose-pink 2 cm flowers. *Zone 9.* p. 160

vivipara (Zander): see CORYPHANTHA vivipara (Hortus 3)

ESPOSTOA *Cactaceae*

lanata (No. Perú, Ecuador), "Peruvian old man" or "Soroco"; from arid mountains at 1200 to 2250 metres; a small and very attractive column when young, with 20 to 30 ribs beautifully covered with cottony, snow-white hair; with age the trunk becoming thicker, to 20 cm dia., and branching with numerous wide-spreading arms, each to 15 cm dia., and to 5 m high; flowers whitish, 4-5 cm long, borne out of the cephalium wool on one side of the stem; the 3 to 4 cm carmine-red juicy fruit is sweet and eaten by the Indians. *Arid-subtropic. Zone 10.* p. 157, 159

melanostele (Pseudoespostoa, Binghamia) (W. Perú); interesting with its white-woolly head when small, growing into gray-green columns 2 m high and 10 cm dia., usually branching, having about 25 tubercled ribs, densely covered by small spines; white flowers 5 cm long. *Zone 10.* p. 162

EUCALYPTUS *Myrtaceae*

caesia (Western Australia), the "Gungurru" or "Silver Princess"; handsome small, graceful tree of weeping habit 5 to 7 m high; wood, leaves and seed pods beautifully coated with waxy, silvery white powder; gray-green lanceolate leaves contrast with the red stems; bark white and mottled, curling when older; dusty rose-pink flowers; seed capsules shaped like silver bells. *Zone 9.* p. 798

calophylla (W. Australia), "Marri" or "Red gum"; round headed large tree 30-50 m high, with rough, flaky bark; broad lanceolate, beautiful leaves 10-18 cm long, deep green; large showy heads of white stamen flowers, sometimes rose or red; the large urn-shaped capsules to 3 cm dia. *Arid-subtropic. Zone 9.* p. 798

camaldulensis (rostrata) (Australia), "River red gum"; wide-spreading tree 25-40 m high; smooth bark, red when young, later grayish and mottled; gracefully weeping branches with long slender leaves; unimportant white to pale yellow flowers in drooping clusters, followed by pea-sized seed capsules. *Zone 8.* p. 798

cinerea (cephalophora) (New So. Wales, Victoria), "Silver dollar tree"; small glaucous tree, with brown-red, willowy branches bearing pairs of sessile leaves rigid, stiff-leathery and silvery glaucous, rounded like a silver coin, to 8 cm across, in the juvenile stage; later when 2 m or more high the leaves become ovate to lanceolate, with yellow midrib; used by florists as cut branches; often preserved with glycerine; creamy-white flowers in the axils of the upper leaves and covered by a waxy coating, in Spring. *Zone 9.* p. 798

citriodora (Queensland), "Lemon-gum"; one of the most graceful of trees to 25 m, with smooth powder-white to pinkish trunk; branches pendant with long 8-20 cm sickle-shaped leaves, golden-green and lemon-scented; white flowers in clusters. Older specimen are designer's trees, very picturesque with bare trunks. Oil has been distilled from leaves. *Zone 9.* p. 798, 819

cladocalyx (South Australia), "Sugar gum"; slender tree to 25 m high, having attractive white or tan-colored bark very smooth after flaking in upper part of trunk; alternate glossy narrow to broad-lanceolate leaves, the juvenile stage distinctive elliptic or circular, green on reddish twigs; inflorescence in pendant clusters of rose-pink flowers with white stamens, blooming in habitat January and February; the 1 cm fruit urn-shaped and ribbed. *Zone 9.* p. 798

deglupta (New Guinea, Indonesia, Philippines), "New Guinea gum" or "Mindanao gum"; noble tall tree, with trunk displaying a striking coloring as the bark peels, revealing a beautiful spectrum of browns, yellows, grays, greens, pinks and reds; handsome dark olive, lanceolate foliage on pendulous branches. *Zone 9.* p. 798

erythrocorys (W. Australia), "Red-cap mallee" or "Illyarie"; beautiful small tree 3 to 8 m high; white smooth bark, peeling in thin flakes; thick shiny green narrow sickle-shaped leaves 10-18 cm long; the inflorescence with bright scarlet caps which drop off to reveal yellow stamen flowers. *Zones 9-10.* p. 799

ficifolia (S.W. Australia), "Scarlet flowering gum"; slower growing, ornamental tree to 15 m high, with dark and furrowed bark, thick lanceolate green leaves with yellow midrib; well known for its showy masses of flowers having massed bright scarlet stamens and dark red anthers. *Zone 9.* p. 799

globulus (Tasmania, Victoria), "Tasmanian blue gum"; a pretty plant when small, with shoots and clasping cordate leaves a glaucous blue, but rapidly growing into a gigantic tree to 60 m high, with bluish-white, smooth trunk; the leaves becoming long and lustrous dark green, 15 to 30 cm long; the creamy-white stamen flowers are rich in nectar; the seed pods are covered by a wide flat disc which pops off when seed is ripe. Much used for windbreaks in California; its foliage contains aromatic oil used for medicinal purposes. *Zone 9.* p. 799

grandis (Queensland and New So. Wales), "Rose gum"; tall, straight tree to 60 m high, and trunk with gray bark, reaching a dia. of 2 m, becoming smooth higher up; large leaves narrow-lanceolate and glossy green; the inflorescence in clusters of 4-10 rosy stamen flowers with conical bud cap; glaucous fruit pear-shaped. *Zone 9.* p. 799

gunnii (Tasmania, South Australia), "Cider gum"; occasionally planted outdoors in So. England and the Rhineland in Germany; ornamental tree to 30 m tall, with green and white bark, deciduous in cold climate; leathery leaves glaucous blue, rounded to oblong in juvenile stage, 2-5 cm wide; in adult stage lanceolate, greenish to 10 cm long; small creamy-white stamen flowers in clusters of two or three. *Subtropic. Zone 8.* p. 799

macrocarpa (Western Australia), "Mottlecah", "Rose of the West", or "Blue-bush"; curious sprawling shrub to 5 m; the stiff stems closely set with broad ovate, silvery blue, clasping leaves in ranks, 12 cm long and to 8 cm broad; flat-topped fluffy flowers with short filaments usually crimson-red in clusters directly from leaf axils; the large gray conical bud cap is most distinctive; the woody seed-goblet 5 cm across is the largest fruit of the genus. *Zone 9.* p. 799

maculata (Queensland to Victoria), "Spotted gum"; dignified tall tree with single trunk branching to make wide head, 20-30 m high; pearl-gray bark mottled dark red to violet; glossy dark green lanceolate leaves; whitish puffy flowers in clusters to 8 cm wide; small urn-shaped capsules. *Zone 9.* p. 800

polyanthemos (Victoria, New So. Wales), "Red box"; tree to 45 m high, with persistent bark on lower part; the slender, sparry, glaucous branches with distantly spaced attractive leathery leaves almost round in juvenile stage, to ovate 5-10 cm long in maturity, glaucous bluish gray and edged all around with purple; white stamen flowers rich in nectar, in Spring and Summer; bud cap conical, and rounded fruit. *Zone 9.*   *p. 799*

pulverulenta (New So. Wales), "Moneytree"; straggling tree to 10 m high, with smooth white bark, peeling in small flakes, interesting with leaves opposite, rounded in the juvenile stage, and attractive bluish-silver; adult leaves oval or kidney-shaped to 8 cm across; axillary flowers of white stamens 3 cm across; small 1 cm seed capsules very silvery glaucous. The handsome coin-shaped foliage of young trees is widely used in floral arrangements. *Zone 9.*   *p. 799*

rhodantha (W. Australia), "Rose Mallee"; ornamental sprawling shrub to 4 m, with horizontal branches densely set with clasping, sessile leaves in lovely glaucous blue, 5-10 cm long and nearly round; showy inflorescence of long bright crimson-red stamens tipped yellow, looking like small brushes. *Zone 9.*   *p. 799*

rudis (W. Australia), "Desert gum"; robust upright, spreading, often weeping tree 15-20 m high; with rough, dark gray, persistent bark; juvenile leaves broad ovate and silvery, mature leaves lance-shaped 10-15 cm long and more green; white flowers in clusters, not showy; small 1 cm capsules. *Zone 8.*   *p. 800*

sideroxylon (Queensland to Victoria), "Red ironbark"; graceful medium-sized tree to 25 m, with furrowed, non-shedding, red to nearly black trunk; slim blue-green leaves turn bronze in Winter; fluffy flowers creamy-white in pendulous clusters; seed capsules goblet-shaped. *Zone 9.*   *p. 800*

sideroxylon 'Rosea'; lovely color variant with showy stamen flowers soft pink, profusely blooming December to June in U.S.; medium sized tree 6 to 15 m high, with hard blackish bark, deeply furrowed and persistent; slim blue-green leaves turn bronze in Winter; goblet-shaped seed capsules. *Zone 9.*   *p. 800*

torquata (Western Australia), "Coral gum"; small aromatic tree 4 to 8 m high, usually forking into multiple trunks, with willowy light brown stems, and blue-grayish-green leathery, lanceolate leaves; blooming at an early age, the coral-red buds covered by long pointed caps open to pink stamens, flowering profusely during Mid-summer in Australia; fruit is a small urn-shaped capsule. *Zone 10.*   *p. 800*

viminalis (S.E. Australia), "Manna gum"; picturesque tall spreading tree to 50 m high, with beautiful smooth whitish trunk, the rough cover peeling in ribbons; drooping willow-like branches with narrow 10-20 cm leaves; little white flowers in threes on long, open pendant clusters; small 1 cm seed capsules. Bark yields manna, eaten by aboriginals; the leaves form the principal food of Koala bears. *Zone 9.*   *p. 800*

EUCHARIS   *Amaryllidaceae*
grandiflora (amazonica) (Urceolina) (Andes of Colombia), "Amazon lily"; bulbous plant with broad, basal leaves narrowed into petioles; umbels of fragrant white flowers with spreading segments, 5 to 8 cm across. *Tropical. Zones 9-11.*   *p. 209*

EUCODONIA   *Gesneriaceae*
andrieuxii (Achimenes); compact and shapely, hairy little plant with scaly rhizomes, forming rosette of quilted ovate leaves; from the leaf axils rise numerous 5 cm stalks bearing the small, pretty violet flowers, their pure white throat lined with purple dots giving a bicolor effect and looking like miniature gloxinias. *Zone 11.*   *p. 63*

EUCOMIS   *Liliaceae*
autumnalis (undulata) (So. Africa), "Pineapple flower"; bulbous plant 25 cm high, with broad, undulated bright green leaves to 8 cm wide, with tough margins and keeled beneath, thin and spreading, plain green; the inflorescence on cylindric stalk with dense head of bright green 2 cm flowers crowned by a tuft of small leaves; August. *Subtropic. Zone 9.*   *p. 239*

bicolor (Natal); "Pineapple-lily"; robust herb to 60 cm high, with globose bulb; rosette of oblong plain green leaves crisped at margins; spotted stalk with dense pyramidal cluster 8-10 cm long of pale green flowers, petals with distinct purple edges; blooming in late Summer. *Zone 9.*   *p. 239*

comosa (punctata) (So. Africa), the "Pineapple-flower"; interesting bulbous rosette with large attractive lanceolate dark green leaves to 30 cm or more long, mottled purple underneath; fragrant, star-shaped flowers greenish-white with purple center, 2 cm across, in cylindric raceme topped by a tufted crown of leafy bracts; in late Summer. *Zone 9.*   *p. 239*

EUCOMMIA   *Eucommiaceae*
ulmoides (Cent. China), "Hardy rubber-tree"; deciduous elm-like tree to 20 m or more high, with ovate-oblong leaves 8-20 cm long, serrate at margins, exuding strings of rubber when torn apart;

inconspicuous flowers before or with the foliage, the anthers brown. Interesting because this is the only frost-hardy tree capable of yielding rubber from leaves, bark and trunk, but not commercially economical. The bark is used medicinally in China. *Zone 5.*   *p. 720*

EUCRYPHIA   *Eucryphiaceae*
glutinosa (Chile); showy flowering tree, evergreen or partly deciduous, 4-8 m high, with leaves pinnately compound of 3 to 5 oval leaflets 2-6 cm long, toothed at margins, and shining dark green; showy flowers 6 cm across, consisting of 4 white to pinkish petals, and yellow anthers. *Zone 8.*   *p. 720*

lucida (N.W. Tasmania), "Leather wood"; slender evergreen tree normally 8-10 m high, in Australian habitat to 25 m tall; downy shoots with leathery oblong leaves having rounded apex, to 8 cm long, shining green above, glaucous beneath, and resinous; cupped axillary pure white flowers to 5 cm across, holding a nest of white to purplish stamens, summer-blooming and sweetly fragrant. *Zones 7-10.*   *p. 774*

lucida 'Rosea'; charming color form found in the rain forest of N.W. Tasmania, having flowers soft pink slightly stained with crimson in center; trees planted in Britain have a long bare trunk, with their flowers high up, blooming June to September, but nearly hidden by their evergreen foliage. *Zones 7-10.*   *p. 774*

EUGENIA   *Myrtaceae*
aggregata (Myrciaria edulis in hort.) (Brazil, Argentina), "Cherry of the Rio Grande"; evergreen tropical shrub or small tree to 5 m high, the bark on older trunks peeling in thin layers; narrow-elliptic, leathery leaves to 8 cm long and dark glossy green; solitary flowers in opposite pairs, with white petals and protruding stamens; followed by fleshy, edible, obovoid berries to 3 cm long, at first orange-red, ripening to a glossy maroon-red, with cherry-like flavor, also used for pies. *Zone 10.*   *p. 804, 918*

jambos: see SYZYGIUM jambos
longipes: see PSIDIUM littorale var. longipes
malaccense: see SYZYGIUM malaccense
myrtifolia hort.: see SYZYGIUM paniculatum
smithii: see ACMENA smithii

uniflora (Brazil, Guayana), "Surinam cherry"; small glabrous tree to 8 m high, with glossy, ovate, 5 cm leaves, and fragrant white flowers; producing distinctive grooved, round fleshy fruit deep crimson, edible and of spicy flavor. *Tropical. Zone 10.*   *p. 918*

EUODIA   (as in Zander):   see EVODIA (Hortus)

EUONYMUS   *Celastraceae*
alata (Temp. E. Asia), "Winged spindle tree"; deciduous shrub 2-3 m high, of stiff, open growth, with branches showing 2-4 corky wings; dark green elliptic leaves 5 to 8 cm long, arranged in flat plane, coloring to brilliant scarlet in Autumn; small yellowish flowers, and purplish fruit partially covered by fleshy orange shield. *Zone 4.*   *p. 681*

alata 'Compacta', "Dwarf winged euonymus"; ideally suited for hedges; dense shrub to 1 m high, with branches spreading to 3 m wide, of roundish shape, flattened on top; the dark green, elliptic leaves coloring scarlet-red in Autumn. Introduced by Adams, Springfield, Mass., about 1926. *Zone 4.*   *p. 620*

americana (New York to Florida and Texas), "Strawberry bush" or "American spindle tree"; deciduous woodland shrub 2 m high, with straggling branches; lanceolate leaves 10 cm long and lightly toothed; small greenish-purple flowers in June; peculiar deep rose warty fruit cracking open in Autumn showing the scarlet seed inside; the foliage colors red preceding Winter. *Zone 6.*   *p. 681*

europaea (Europe, W. Asia), "European spindle tree"; vigorous deciduous shrub or small tree to 6 m high, with lanceolate leaves to 8 cm long, lightly crenate at margins and with prominent veins; small 15 mm greenish-white or yellowish flowers, followed by curious light red, fleshy capsules, bursting open to reveal the orange-coated seed. *Zone 3.*   *p. 681*

fortunei (Cent. and W. China), "Wintercreeper"; evergreen subshrub, or climbing by rootlets, with small 2 cm roundish leaves of leathery texture to larger ovate size in the maturity stage, crenate at margins; small greenish flowers in clusters, followed by pinkish fruit capsules with seed. *Zone 6.*   *p. 681*

fortunei 'Colorata', "Purple-leaf winter creeper" from China; evergreen sprawling shrub with elliptic leaves, deep green or milky-green and cream, 3-5 cm long, turning deep purple in Fall; small greenish flowers. *Zone 5.*   *p. 309, 682*

fortunei 'Elegans' (vegeta aurea); handsome winter-creeper with broad ovate leathery leaves bordered or almost entirely creamy-yellow. *Zone 5.*   *p. 682*

fortunei 'Emerald n'Gold'; attractive and vigorous rambling shrub to 1½ m high with leaves margined yellow, sometimes flushed pink, to reddish in Winter; introduced 1926 in Worcester, Mass. as 'Emerald n'Gold'. *Zone 5.*   *p. 682*

fortunei 'Gracilis' ('Variegata') (Japan, Korea), "Silver-edge creeper"; low spreading evergreen shrub climbing by rootlets; small oval, serrate leaves gray-green, variegated and edged white, tinted pink, to 5 cm long in the juvenile stage, but becoming more elongate, 6-10 cm long in the maturity stage, obovate to oblanceolate in outline, after climbing a tree. Zone 6. *p. 682*

fortunei 'Kewensis' (minima); handsome miniature ivy, low evergreen with slowly creeping wiry branches, distantly set with leathery elongate leaves 1-4 cm long, deep bluish-green and a silver-gray central band. Zone 6. *p. 309, 682*

fortunei 'Minima variegata'; smaller foliage than 'Gracilis'; low creeper with ovate leaves edged creamy-white, 3-4 cm long, a charming groundcover. Photographed in col. New York Botanical Garden. Zone 6. *p. 682*

fortunei radicans (Cent. Japan, So. Korea), "Creeping euonymus"; evergreen shrub creeping or climbing by rootlets, with small, leathery, deep green leaves 2-3 cm long, margins serrate. *Temperate.* Zone 5. *p. 309*

fortunei vegeta (Central and Western China), "Big-leaf winter creeper"; low, spreading shrub to 1½ m high, or climbing by rootlets; leaves ovate to 5 cm long; orange seeds in little hat-boxes. Zone 5. *p. 682*

hamiltoniana yedoensis (China, Japan); deciduous shrub 3-4 m high, becoming more woody and tree-like to 12 m tall, with sparry flexuous branches; lanceolate or ovate elliptic leaves 6-12 cm long, and finely serrate at margins, dull green but coloring red-brown in Autumn; small greenish flowers with purple anthers, followed by clusters pendant with pink berry-like capsules. Zone 5. *p. 682*

japonica (Japan), "Japanese spindle tree"; dense evergreen shrub to 5 m high, with erect willowy branches closely set with opposite small leathery oval leaves 2½-6 cm long, obscurely toothed, glossy dark green; small greenish-white flowers. Zone 7. *p. 683*

japonica 'Albo-marginata' (So. Japan); this "Silver-leaf euonymus" has somewhat smaller, narrower leaves milky-green bordered with creamy-white. Zone 7. *p. 683*

japonica 'Argenteo-marginata' (Japan), known as "Silver Queen"; leaves oval, glossy fresh green to silvery, with broad white marginal variegation, 4-5 cm long. Zone 7. *p. 683*

japonica 'Argenteo-variegata' (Japan); leaves oval, glossy, silvery-green with cream-white variegation, 2-3 cm long; attractive small, bushy evergreen of compact habit. Zone 7. *p. 683*

japonica 'Aureo-marginata'; compact bush with colorful oval 4-5 cm leaves, deep green with yellow margins. Seen in Germany, grown as handsome standard tree with sheared globular crown, a decorative container plant for the patio. Zone 7. *p. 683*

japonica 'Medio-picta', "Goldheart euonymus"; erect branches with very colorful elongate oval leaves 5-6 cm long, waxy fresh green at margins, golden-yellow in the center and down the petiole and stem. Zone 7. *p. 683*

japonica 'Microphylla' (pulchella) (Japan), "Boxleaf euonymus"; dense little, stiff erect shrub 30-50 cm high, with closely arranged tiny, toothed leaves deep green. Very formal in appearance, usually trimmed as low hedge or border. Zone 6. *p. 683*

japonica 'Yellow Queen'; evergreen bush of compact habit, having flexible, erect branches, densely set with handsome oval-ovate leathery leaves 4-5 cm long, the center waxy green, and broadly bordered golden-yellow. Zone 7. *p. 683*

latifolia (Algeria, S.E. Europe to Iran), "Broadleaf euonymus"; deciduous or semi-evergreen shrub or tree 3-6 m high, with ovalish leaves 8-12 cm long, finely toothed; small greenish flowers 1 cm across in clusters, followed by pendulous 4 to 5-winged bright red capsules, the seed coat orange. Zone 5. *p. 684*

phellomana (No. and W. China); deciduous shrub 2-4 m high, the branchlets 4-angled with conspicuous corky wings; ovate leaves to 12 cm long, serrate at margins, and strongly net-veined beneath; small greenish flowers with purple anthers; 4-lobed rose-red fruit, the seed coat deep red. Zone 4. *p. 684*

sachalinensis (planipes) (N.E. Asia); deciduous shrub to 4 m high, with broadly obovate leaves 8-12 cm long, crenate at margins; handsome 5-angled carmine-red fruit capsules, splitting open to reveal the fleshy orange aril (coat) covering the seed; profuse in showy pendant clusters. Zone 5. *p. 684*

EUPATORIUM *Compositae*

coelestinum (New Jersey to Florida, Texas, W. Indies), "Blue boneset" or "Hardy ageratum"; herbaceous perennial to 60 cm high, with thin ovate, coarsely toothed leaves; numerous small flowerheads resembling ageratum, light blue to violet, in compact cluster, in late Summer. Zones 5-10. *p. 387*

purpureum (Eastern U.S.), "Sweet Joe-Pyeweed"; fragrant herbaceous perennial with stems 1 to 3 m tall, bluish at nodes; elliptic

leaves in whorls, to 20 cm long, and scented of vanilla when bruised; showy rounded clusters of small purplish flowers, in Autumn. Zone 4. *p. 387*

riparium (Mexico), "Mexican mist-flower"; subshrubby perennial with woody base, 30-60 cm high; the spreading or pendant branches reddish, with opposite oblong lanceolate leaves 5-10 cm long, toothed along margins; clusters of 20 or more small white flowers. Zones 9-10. *p. 387*

EUPHORBIA *Euphorbiaceae*

aeruginosa (Transvaal: Olifant River Valley); handsome slender columns to 30 cm high, branch from a usually buried caudex; branches subcylindric and lightly 4 to 5-angled about 1 cm thick, milky bluish-green, contrasting with the coppery brown spine-shields from which rise a pair of thorns; very attractive in late Winter when the upper portions are lined with vivid yellow cyathia. Zone 11. *p. 193*

ammak 'Variegata' (So. Arabia parentage); interesting arid-climate tree, the green species in habitat to 10 m high; the ascending branches dark green, mostly 4 to 5-angled wing-like, to 15 cm dia., the angles knobby and set with thorns; glossy green oblanceolate leaves, early deciduous; the handsome cultivar 'Variegata' in col. Grigsby, Vista, Calif. has leaves beautifully variegated and margined with ivory-white. Zone 11. *p. 192*

canariensis (Canary Islands), "Hercules club" or "African cereus"; large cactus-like succulent branching from the base, to 10 m high; the stems 5, 4 or 6 angled, brownish fresh green, the sinuate angles set with black spine-pairs; small yellow flowers; poisonous. The Eastern hemisphere parallel to Western hemisphere cactus. *Subtropic.* Zone 10. *p. 69, 193*

candelabrum (erythraeae) (Ethiopia, Sudan, Uganda); massive candelabra-like tree to 10 m high, at home in the Nile basin, with 4-angled yellowish-green branches 8 to 10 cm thick, constricted to joints, the angles wavy-toothed and set with spines; commonly used as living fences. *Arid-tropical.* Zone 10. *p. 193*

caput-medusae (So. Africa: Cape Prov.), "Medusa's head"; short, partly buried globose stem to 20 cm dia., forming clumps, with many snake-like gray-green branches 3-5 cm thick, densely knobbed and with tiny leaves at the growing tips. *Arid-subtropic.* Zone 10. *p. 192*

characias (Spain to Greece); interesting subshrub with woody base and pithy stems to 1 m or more high, the blue-green narrow lanceolate leaves to 10 cm long, in close spirals; the inflorescence of small yellow or greenish cupflowers in cylindrical heads. Zone 8. *p. 722*

characias wulfenii (vaneta) (Dalmatia, Yugoslavia); commonest form, with large, broader clusters of more yellow cupflowers; evergreen subshrub fairly drought-resistant, to 1 m high, the narrow strap-shaped leaves recurving from base and along floral stalk. Zone 8. *p. 722*

cotinifolia (caracasana sanguinea hort.) (West Indies, Mexico to Venezuela and Perú), "Hierba mala"; ornamental, somewhat succulent shrub or small tree 1 to 6 m high; wiry purplish-red branches set with thin-fleshy ovate leaves 5-12 cm long, wine-red when young, metallic blue-green when mature, red veins and prominent midrib, and abounding in acrid, milky juice; whitish inflorescence. Used as fish-poison. Zone 10. *p. 724*

cyparissias (Europe, naturalized in Eastern U.S.), "Cypress spurge"; small subshrub to 30 cm high, with slender branches containing milky sap, from creeping rootstock, the narrow linear leaves needle-like, 3 cm long; terminal inflorescence triangular in many-rayed clusters, yellowish when young, becoming reddish. Zone 3. *p. 722*

epithymoides (polychroma) (E. Europe to Ukraine), "Cushion euphorbia" or "Yellow spurge"; subshrubby, showy perennial to 30 cm high, forming an attractive bush, with dark green, oblong leaves, and inflorescence with yellow bract-leaves subtending the cyathia or small cupflowers, in showy clusters. Zone 4. *p. 722*

fianarantsoae (Madagascar); small succulent subshrub to 20 cm high, the cylindrical branches about 2 cm thick, the thorns arranged in 8 rows; elliptic 2-3 cm leaves at ends of stems, green with red margins; inflorescence of 2 to 3 creamy cyathia. Zone 11. *p. 193*

fulgens (jacquinaeflora) (Mexico); "Scarlet plume"; leafy shrub with slender thin-wiry branches gracefully arching, the small leaves narrow lanceolate, and the flowers in brilliant terminal sprays of small petal-like orange-scarlet bracts. *Tropical.* Zones 11-12. *p. 723*

'Giant Christ-thorn', "Giant California Christ-thorn"; a phenomenal flowering plant; the result of 25 years of hybridizing by Ed Hummel of Carlsbad, California, involving E. milii bojeri, breonii and lophogona; a swollen, stout grayish stem to 6 cm thick, with long brown thorns; toward the apex with bluish-green leathery leaves 20-25 cm long and, arranged as a giant bouquet, strong stalks bearing the clustered inflorescence with firm, large bracts 2 to 5 cm across, larger than a silver dollar, in glowing cerise-pink with salmon sheen. Slow-growing. *Tropical.* Zone 11. *p. 60, 192*

grandicornis (Natal to Kenya), "Cow horn euphorbia"; thorny branching succulent to 2 m, of interesting shape, the green to gray-green branches 3-angled, to 15 cm thick, irregularly constricted, angles wing-like with horny margins. *Arid-tropical.* Zone 11. p. 60, 192

griffithii (Himalayas of Bhutan, So. Tibet); attractive subshrubby perennial, with creeping rhizomes, forming slender stem 60 cm high; lanceolate leaves having pink midrib; broad, headlike clusters of small cyathia, subtended by showy floral leaves orange-red to glowing carmine-red; seen in Bergianska Botanic Garden near Stockholm, blooming in June. Zone 5. p. 722

griffithii 'Fireglow'; rhizomatous or subshrub to 90 cm high of Himalayan origin; long-lanceolate leaves with pink midrib; inflorescence in clusters 5-10 cm across, with showy brick-red bracts. Zone 5. p. 722

heterophylla (Illinois to Perú), "Annual poinsettia", or "Mexican fire plant"; noted annual with variable green leaves linear, ovate or even fiddle-shaped, the upper ones red at the base, bract-like, surrounding the little flowers. Zone 10. p. 724

heterophylla graminifolia (Montana to Florida, Central America), "Paint-leaf" or "Mexican fire plant"; also known as "Annual poinsettia"; annual or biennial branching herb to 1 m high, with bright green ovate or variable leaves in the species, linear in graminifolia, at the ends of branches; tiny flowers in terminal clusters, surrounded by bract-leaves scarlet at the base and blotched with white. Zone 10. p. 724

ingens (Natal, Transvaal, Mozambique, Zambia), a giant "Candelabra tree" to 10 m high, trunk 5 to 6- angled, 15-18 cm dia.; the leafless branches succulent, constricted into joints, dark green, 4-angled, 8-12 cm thick, winged and wavy; the ridges with black spines; rudimentary inflorescence with yellowish cyathia. In habitat in the bush-veld of northern Transvaal, I noted that seedlings in their juvenile stage up to 1½ m are beautifully marked with silver. *Arid-tropical.* Zone 10. p. 193

lactea (India, Sri Lanka), "Dragon bone-tree" or "Candelabra cactus"; cactus-like plant growing like a candelabra to 5 m high, the branches 3-4 angled and 3 to 5 cm dias., distantly but deeply scalloped and black-spined, dark green with greenish-white band down the center; minute rounded, deciduous leaves. Used in India medicinally, as a hot jam, for rheumatism. *Tropical.* Zone 11. p. 194

lactea 'Cristata', "Elkhorn" or "Frilled fan"; an intricately monstrose form with fan-shaped crested branches forming a snaky ridge or crowded cluster, attractively green marked silver-gray. *Tropical.* Zone 11. p. 60, 194

lathyrls (Tithymalus) (So. Europe), "Mole-plant" or "Gopher purge"; annual or biennial to 1 m with blue-glaucous stiff erect branches, densely leafy when young, in two opposite ranks as in a cross, long linear leaves 8-10 cm long, the floral ones ovate; small flowers subtended by large green bracts, in May-June; the caper-like seeds are poisonous; keeps gophers and moles away because of the acrid taste of the spreading root system. Zone 9. p. 527

leucocephala, "Flor de Nino"; attractive shrub 2-3 m high, often seen from the West Indies to So. Mexico, Guatemala and Costa Rica, with pinkish stems bearing narrow oblanceolate, channeled leaves and a profusion of small yellow flowers literally obscured by masses of small, obovate white bracts 2-4 cm long. *Tropical.* Zone 11. p. 721

loricata (So. Africa: Cape Prov.); spiny, branching shrub to 1 m high, the fleshy cylindric branches 5 cm thick, with somewhat spiralling high ribs, these broken into dense prominant knobs; linear leaves to 8 cm long, clustered toward apex of columns; inflorescence green, somewhat spirally tuberculate and with well developed leaves. Zone 10. p. 194

mammillaris 'Variegata', "Indian corn cob"; a beautiful cultivar which I photographed in California at Los Angeles Plant Company, Vista; the notched columns are largely greenish-white marked fresh green and tinted pink, with buff spines. The green species is from So. Africa. *Subtropic.* Zone 11. p. 60

marginata (variegata) (Plains of Minnesota, Dakota to Texas), "Snow-on-the-mountain" or "Ghost-weed"; hardy pubescent annual to 60 cm high; numerous branches with glaucous gray-green ovate to oval soft-fleshy leaves, 3-8 cm long with milky sap, the upper ones white-margined; inflorescence in umbels with showy bract-leaves 6-8 cm long, and having striking, broad white border, and small white flowers in September; long lasting. Zone 10 as Annual. p. 721

milii 'Albiflora' (splendens) (W. Madagascar), "White Crown of thorns"; xerophytic spiny shrub with slender scandent woody stems to 2 m long, the spreading branches about 1 cm dia., grooved and armed with spines; obovate 4 cm leaves dull green, deciduous, and soon falling if disturbed or too dry; flower bracts soft salmon-red with pale center in the species, but pure white in the cultivar 'Albiflora' as seen in Duesseldorf, W. Germany. May be trained against trellis or wire frame; very cheerful when in bloom at Easter time; good house plant for warm location. From stem cuttings. *Tropical.* Zone 11. p. 192

milii var. imperatae (Madagascar), "Mini-Christ-thorn"; small, very bushy shrub to 50 cm high, with slender woody, brown stems not swollen at the base, the spines rather distant; leathery roundish or obovate leaves 1-2 cm long; the flower bracts red or yellow. *Tropical.* Zone 11. p. 192

myrsinites (So. Europe to Crimea and Asia Minor), "Myrtle euphorbia"; branching succulent with prostrate then ascending thick, yellow stems densely shingled with sessile ovate, fleshy leaves bluish-glaucous, in whorls or spirals; umbels of yellow flowers, in greenish cyathias or cups, subtended by yellow bracts. Zone 5. p. 722

neohumbertii (Madagascar); small succulent column with 5 angles, densely set with soft brown spines; the fleshy moss-green obovate leaves 15-25 cm long, in a rosette on top, but soon deciduous; and crowned by a cluster of colorful flower-like cupped cyathia. Zone 11. p. 193

palustris (Europe to C. Asia, Siberia); subshrub with erect stems 1-2 m high, clothed by stalkless elliptic leaves 4-8 cm long; yellow-bracted flowers in showy terminal clusters 10-15 cm wide; thrives in wet soil and is suitable for bog gardens. Zone 3. p. 722

paralias (Madeira and Mediterranean reg.), "Seaside spurge"; succulent shrub 40-60 cm high, branching from base, the slender pyramidal columns dense with series of shingled small ovate, dark green leaves, resembling a Lycopodium. Zone 10. p. 194, 722

pilosa (villosa hort.) (Europe), "Yellow spurge"; subshrubby, similar to epithymoides with softly hairy stems to 50 cm high; succulent elliptic and ovate leaves, and showy clusters of yellow cyathia subtended by greenish rounded bracts. Zone 6. p. 724

polychroma (Zander): see E. epithymoides (Hortus 3)

pulcherrima (So. Mexico), "Poinsettia" or "Flor de Noche Buena"; branching shrub to 3 m high, with woody trunk and milky juice, ovate leaves, deciduous when disturbed or resting, the terminal shoots forming dark red-velvet, lanceolate bract leaves, surrounding the tiny yellowish flowers during the short-day period of year. Buds will be initiated about Sept. 21-25 at latitude 40-45 deg. north, provided the night temperature is below 18°C. This means total darkness for 14 hours during 10 weeks, each night from 5 pm to 7 am. Zones 10-11. p. 208, 723

pulcherrima 'Alba'; compact, willowy plant with grayish-green leaves having pale veins; floral bracts creamy-white. Zone 11. p. 59, 723

pulcherrima 'Annette Hegg' (Norway 1964), "Christmas poinsettia"; durable variety of compact habit; freely branching; wiry stems; ovate leaves long lasting; blooms early; does well at temperate 16°C; develops broad, smooth bracts vivid medium red, even under low winter light intensity. *Tropical.* Zone 10. p. 59

pulcherrima 'Annette Hegg Supreme'; introduced 1970, a bright red sport of 'Dark Red Hegg', with the most brilliant crimson-red color of the multiflower types, especially under artificial light; the bracts very substantial, and of larger size than 'Annette Hegg', forming stars with close-in center, according to my measuring in our green houses, of 40 cm across at Christmas time. *Tropical.* Zones 10-11. p. 723

pulcherrima 'Eckespoint' (Paul Ecke 1967); strain of striking diploid hybrids of medium height, characterized by stocky growth, strong self-supporting stems, vigorous oakleaf foliage and a close-in circle of lush bracts lightly crinkled. The variety 'C-1 Red' has bracts intense scarlet-red with rosy sheen, and is ideal for Christmas bloom. Needs some warmth, feeding, and attention to moisture to best hold foliage. *Tropical.* Zones 11-12. p. 59

pulcherrima 'Henriette Ecke', "Double poinsettia"; sported in 1927 in Hollywood, blooming early December, and with broader vermilion horizontal bracts and "double" crown. *Tropical.* Zone 10. p. 59

pulcherrima 'Lemon-Drop' (Eckespoint cv.) (Paul Ecke Ranch 1989); true yellow-bracted F-1 seedling; slow growing of short compact habit, with dark green foliage; blooming very early, starting Thanksgiving in late November, forming bright golden-yellow bracts spreading to 25 cm across; ideal for small size 8 to 12 cm pots. Zone 11. p. 723

pulcherrima plenissima, "Double poinsettia"; wild in Mexico; large shrub with flexible branches and grayish-green leaves producing a striking inflorescence composed of a circle of vermilion-red lanceolate bracts, as well as a bushy central head of smaller bracts, transformed from flowers; normally blooms in late Winter. Needs high intensity tropical sun for best double crown. *Tropical.* Zones 10-11. p. 723

pulcherrima 'Praecox', "Poinsettia"; variety of very compact habit, used for outdoor planting in Spain and the Canary Islands. Zone 10. p. 723

pulcherrima 'Rosea', "Pink poinsettia"; sparry plant with pale green ovate leaves, green petioles and veins, and full, but smallish heads of fleshy, obovate bracts of delicate rose, with darker veining; flowering early. The cultivar 'St. Louis' is a sport of the pink poinsettia. 'Ecke Pink' is a clone of 'Rosea'. *Zones 11-12.* *p. 723*

punicea (West Indies; Jamaica, Cuba, Bahamas); tree-like to 9 m high, the branches with leaf-scars and with obovate, sharp-pointed leaves toward the ends, glaucous beneath; terminal clusters of flower cyathia subtended by bright crimson-red bract-leaves 8 cm long. *Tropical. Zone 11.* *p. 193*

squarrosa (Cape Prov.); dwarf succulent with deep green branches, sometimes 3-5-angled 15 cm long, the ridges toothed and set with pairs of short reddish spines; toward upper part furnished with linear leaves, soon deciduous; inflorescence green. *Zone 10.* *p. 194*

tirucalli (Uganda, Zaire, Zanzibar), "Milk bush", "Elephant bush" or "Pencil tree"; with age forming tree to 10 m high, branches cylindrical and pencil-thick, glossy green and bursting with poisonous milk; narrow deciduous leaves. *Tropical. Zone 10.* *p. 192*

xanti (Mexico: Baja California, from Playa Santa Catarina south to Cabo Region); smooth succulent shrub to 2 m high, freely branching with slender pencil-thick limbs; often densely interwoven; at internodes 2-8 cm apart 3-6 elliptic leaves to 3 cm long; attractive terminal inflorescence of white or pink florets circling the yellow cyathia; planted in Fallbrook, California as protective hedging. *Zone 9.* *p. 194, 619*

xylophylloides (Madagascar); dense shrub with round trunk to 2 m high, green branches more or less in whorls, compressed and flattened or 2-angled and jointed, about 15 cm long, slightly toothed; minute leaves deciduous. *Zone 11.* *p. 194*

EUPHORIA *Sapindaceae*

longan (Nephelium) (India to So. China), "Longan" or "Dragon's eye"; evergreen fruit tree to 10 m; pinnate leaves with thick-leathery, lanceolate leaflets 15 cm long; small creamy-white flowers, followed by clusters of russet-brown globose fruit 2½ to 3 cm dia., with white sweetly juicy flesh covering large black seed. Ripe in July-August, they are eaten fresh or in salads. *Zone 10.* *p. 909*

EURYA *Theaceae*

japonica (Cleyera) (Japan, Taiwan to Himalayas), "Hi-Sakaki"; small evergreen shrub or tree reaching to 10 m high, having rough gray bark, with elliptic, smooth, leathery leaves 5-10 cm long, typically finely toothed at margins; small axillary flowers a greenish-white, less than 1 cm across, with unpleasant odor; small black berries on female trees; not to be confused with Cleyera japonica (see Hortus 3). *Warm temperate. Zone 7.* *p. 889*

japonica of Belgian hort.: see CLEYERA japonica

EURYALE *Nymphaeaceae*

ferox (Tropical and Subtropical India to China and Japan), "Prickly water-lily"; a widespread aquatic perennial with large circular floating bright glossy green leaves 1 to 2 m across, very spiny and with inflated bubbles, and spiny-ribbed beneath; small 5 cm flowers green outside, purplish-red within, barely above the water and short-lived; the seeds are edible when roasted. Much at home in rice paddies in the Orient; stunning in the conservatory pool. *Humid-tropical. Zones 10-11.* *p. 333*

EURYCLES *Amaryllidaceae*

sylvestris (amboinensis) (Pancratium) (S.E. Asia, No. Australia); bulbous plant with roundish leaf 20-25 cm across, the blade with depressed parallel veining, connected by thin cross-nerves; amaryllis-like flowers with long tube and spreading lanceolate segments white, on stalk 30-45 cm long. *Zone 10.* *p. 210*

EURYOPS *Compositae*

acraeus (evansii) (So. African Mts.), "Silver euryops"; handsome subshrubby perennial of the Drakensberg Mts., branching to form a rounded evergreen bush to 60 cm high, densely leafy, the leathery pinnately divided foliage silvery gray; bright yellow, daisy-like flowers 3-4 cm across. *Zone 8.* *p. 387*

pectinatus (So. Africa), the "Resin bush"; shrubby, free blooming perennial with thick green leaves covered by white pubescence, pinnatifid and cut into narrow segments, strongly scented when bruised; daisy-like flowers with firm, pretty ray-flowers vivid yellow, surrounding a yellow disc, 5 cm across; blooming nearly year-round. *Subtropic. Zone 10.* *p. 387*

EUSTOMA *Gentianaceae*

grandiflorum (Lisianthus russelianus hyb.) (Nebraska to Colorado, New Mexico), "Prairie gentian"; attractive, showy biennial or annual with erect stems 60-90 cm high; opposite oblong 8 cm leaves, and branched clusters of bell-shaped pale purple flowers 5 cm long, the base inside purple, summer-blooming. *Zone 8.* *p. 417*

EUSYDEROXYLON *Lauraceae*

swageri (laurifolia in Zander) (Borneo, Sumatra, Philippines), "Ironwood of Borneo"; large tropical evergreen tree, with massive trunk and reddish bark, and heavy crown, the branches developing dark red aerial roots, called "hunger roots" in poor soil; leathery elliptic leaves 20-30 cm long; small inconspicuous axillary flowers, followed by large woody fruit, variably 8-15 cm long, cylindrical, or nearly spherical, grooved down the sides, and containing one big seed. Locally called "Belian", the timber is valued as very strong, durable wood. *Zone 10.* *p. 742*

EUTERPE *Palmae*

edulis (Brazil), "Assai palm" or "Palmito" in the Mato Grosso; slender feather palm with graceful trunk to 30 m high, topped by prominent crown shaft and the crown of arching pinnate fronds 2 to 3 m long, dense with drooping, thin, plaited leaflets, on scaly rachis; small round fruit. A most delicate palm, with trunks containing pulp which is eaten in Paraná. *Tropical. Zone 11.* *p. 102*

globosa (in Puerto Rico): see PRESTOEA montana

EVODIA *Rutaceae*

henryi (Zander: Euodia) (Hupeh, Cent. China); deciduous tree 6 to 10 m high, with handsome odd-pinnate foliage compound of 5-9 oblong-ovate to lanceolate leaflets 6-10 cm long, undulate along margins and lightly glaucous beneath; small pinkish flowers in flat-topped clusters 8 cm across; small red-brown fruit-capsules with splitting sections having slender beak. *Zone 6.* *p. 862*

hupehensis (Euodia) (Cent. China), "Bee-bee tree"; deciduous tree with age 15 m or more high, having odd-pinnate aromatic leaves of 5 to 9 elliptic leaflets to 12 cm long; small fragrant 1 cm white flowers in broad pyramidal clusters, in August; followed by colorful reddish fruits, having a slender hooked beak, which split open to display lustrous black seeds. *Zone 5.* *p. 862*

EVOLVULUS *Convolvulaceae*

arbuscula (glomeratus) (Brazil); low, spreading herbaceous perennial or subshrub, to 40 cm high, with slender branches; oval or obovate leaves 4 cm long, silvery-hairy on both sides; lovely bright blue, wide-open, 3 cm flowers have a white star in center, blooming from leaf axils or terminally, lasting only a day, but new flowers seem to appear every morning. Popular in Europe for hanging pots. *Zones 10-11.* *p. 404*

EXACUM *Gentianaceae*

affine (Socotra Is.), "Persian violet" or "Mexican violet"; bushy little herbaceous, free-flowering biennial with waxy, stalked, ovate leaves and tiny, wide open, bluish-lilac, star-like, fragrant flowers 1 cm across, with pretty eye of deep yellow stamens. *Tropical. Zone 11.* *p. 59, 417*

affine flore pleno, "Double Persian violet"; charming, very floriferous densely leafy biennial with waxy green 3 cm leaves, and literally covered with small globular, 1 cm double flowers lilac-blue. Short-lived perennial in mild climates. *Zone 11.* *p. 417*

EXBUCKLANDIA *Hamameliaceae*

populnea (Symingtonia populnea) (E. Himalaya and Sumatra); ornamental evergreen tropical tree with leathery glossy green ovate-cordate leaves palmately nerved, 10-15 cm long, veins and lower surface reddish; petioles to 8 cm long; small unisexual pinkish flowers in showy clusters. Photographed in Botanic Garden Penang. *Zone 10.* *p. 868*

EXOCHORDA *Rosaceae*

giraldii (N.E. China), "Pearlbush"; deciduous shrub to 3 m or more high, with spreading branches, the branchlets, leafstalks and veins pink or red; obovate leaves 3 to 6 cm long; showy white flowers 3 cm across, blooming in May. *Zone 5.* *p. 834*

korolkowii (C. Asia, Turkestan to China), "Turkestan pearlbush"; smooth deciduous shrub 3-4 m high, of erect growth; ovate and obovate leaves 3-8 cm long, yellowish to gray beneath; white flowers 3-4 cm across, with 25 prominent stamens, blooming in April-May. *Zone 6.* *p. 834*

x macrantha 'The Bride' (korolkowii x racemosa); low Pearl-bush hybrid to 1 m high and as broad; deciduous shrub with roundish, 3-5 cm leaves, blooming with new, expanding foliage; the floral buds pearl-like, in great profusion, opening to dainty flowers of spreading obovate petals a snowy white, in late April. *Zone 5.* *p. 834*

racemosa (grandiflora) (Eastern China); deciduous shrub to 3 m high, of rounded bushy habit, with slender red-brown branchlets; leaves narrowly obovate, 4-8 cm long; flowers white, 3-4 cm wide in showy erect clusters, the petals rounded but narrowed to a claw at base and with 15 stamens. *Zone 4.* *p. 834*

EXOGONIUM *Convolvulaceae*

bracteatum (Ipomea) (Trop. and subtrop. America, West Indies, Mexico and Florida), "Jicama" in Sonora, "Flor de Candelaria" in

Guerrero; perennial woody-stemmed twining vine; ovate-cordate leaves, 6-9 cm long; showy inflorescence somewhat similar to Bougainvillea, having 5 large sepals carmine-red and funnel-shaped tubular corollas 3-4 cm long, often blooming without foliage; large watery, sweet roots often eaten raw or cooked in Mexico. *Zones 10-11.*   *p. 273*

FABIANA   *Solanaceae*
  imbricata (Chile, Perú), "Perú Falseheath"; heath-like shrub to 2 m or more; imbricate scale-like juniper-type foliage; small white 1 cm bells in pendant racemes, blooming in June; at home where Summers are cool. *Zones 8-9.*   *p. 878*

FAGOPYRUM   *Polygonaceae*
  esculentum (Central Siberia, Manchuria), "Buck-wheat"; agricultural annual herb with purple stems to 1 m high, the leaves ovate triangular, to 8 cm long; small white flowers in axillary clusters during Summer, sweetly fragrant and attractive to bees. Buckwheat flour is made from the large 3-cornered seeds. Important cover crop in farming, plowed under when plants are young and succulent. *Zone 9 as annual.*   *p. 540*

FAGUS   *Fagaceae*
  crenata (sieboldii) (Japan: Hokkaido to Kyushu), "Buna" or "Japanese beech"; tall deciduous tree to 30 m high, forming a rounded crown; leaves ovate-rhomboid 5 to 8 cm long, shallowly notched; fruit cups with long bristles. An important forest tree in Japan; it is to the credit of the patience of a Japanese bonsai fancier having created a miniature Buna landscape 30 years old, from such a normally large tree.   *p. 627*
  grandifolia (Eastern No. America), "American beech"; ornamental deciduous tree to 30 m high, suckering from the base and with light gray bark; ovate-oblong leaves to 12 cm long, coarsely toothed and having 9-15 pairs of veins (vs. 5-9 pairs in F. sylvatica); the seed is enclosed in a downy, prickly husk. Very attractive with foliage in reddish-bronze autumn-colors. *Zone 3.*   *p. 726*
  sylvatica (Central and So. Europe), "European beech" or "Redbeech"; excellent large ornamental shade tree to 30 m or more tall, with smooth gray bark, the ovate, deciduous leaves are shining green above, 8-10 cm long, with 5-9 pairs of veins, and lightly serrate toward apex, turning reddish-brown in Autumn; the 4-lobed, prickly capsules hold 2-3 triangular, sweet, edible beech-nuts inside. *Zone 4.*   *p. 726, 913*
  sylvatica 'Pendula' (Europe to Caucasus), the "Weeping beech" or "European beech"; great ornamental deciduous tree to 30 or 40 m high, with smooth gray trunks and wide-spreading limbs, often horizontal, and pendulous branches with lustrous green, ovate leaves remotely toothed, 8-12 cm long, turning reddish in Autumn; the female flowers producing triangular nuts with sharp edges, enclosed in a 4-lobed spiny husk. *Zone 4.*   *p. 726*
  sylvatica 'Purpurea' (Europ. Garden Flora 1989) ('Atropunicea' or 'Atropurpurea'), "Blood beech" or "Purple beech"; formerly known as 'Atropunicea' but changed to 'Purpurea' in 1976, according to Kruessmann, for Bloodbeech grafted in Holland which perpetuate best foliage color. Magnificent giant deciduous tree 30-50 m high, most ornamental with glossy leaves blood-red or coppery purple; ideal as solitary specimen for best effect in the landscape; great in spacious city parks and near reflecting water. *Zone 5.*   *p. 727*
  sylvatica 'Roseo-marginata', "Variegated European beech"; handsome cultivar with deciduous, rather firm purple leaves edged pale pink. Seen in col. Nymphenburg Botanic Garden, Munich, Germany. *Zone 5.*   *p. 727*
  sylvatica 'Zlatia'; natural var. found in Serbia 1890, of normal growth but with leaves first golden-yellow very lustrous, later yellowish-green; possibly form of F. moesiaca *Zone 4.*   *p. 726*

FALLOPIA aubertii (Zander):
  see POLYGONUM aubertii (Hortus)

FARGESIA   *Gramineae*
  murielae (Sinarundinaria or Arundinaria murielae; also known in hort. as Thamnocalamus spathaceus) (Mts. of Western China), "Umbrella bamboo"; handsome ornamental bamboo to 4 m high, with straight, slender culms first bright green, and finally yellow, covered by deciduous straw-colored stem-sheaths; toward top stems are arching gracefully under the heavy weight of foliage; the rich green leaves 6-12 cm long; closely related to F. nitida, which is distinguished by its purple canes. Widely planted in Europe. *Zone 5.*   *p. 548*
  nitida (Arundinaria or Sinarundinaria) (Korea, China), "Hardy blue bamboo"; running bamboo with slender canes 3 to 6 m high, forming robust clumps, the stems purplish-black and very hollow, only 1 cm thick, and leafless the first year; branchlets dense with leaves bright green above, glaucous beneath, to 18 cm long, the margins bristly on one side. Photographed in Bot. Garden Copenhagen. Widely grown in Europe. *Zones 5-9.*   *p. 548*

  spathacea (Thamnocalamus spathaceus or Sinarundinaria sparsifolia) (W. China: Sechuan Prov.), "Chinese mountain bamboo" or "Umbrella bamboo"; medium-sized hardy bamboo to 5 m high, from high altitude regions at 3000 m or more, formerly considered identical with F. murielae, but according to the Chinese botanist Li, and so recorded by the American Bamboo Society in 1989 as separate from murielae, widely grown in Europe; slender hollow culms, forming clusters of branchlets from internode, the canes arching under weight of narrow lanceolate foliage 9-15 cm long and to 1 cm wide; the culm sheaths are pale brown with rounded apex; the principal food of the pandas in China. *Zone 5.*   *p. 557*

FASCICULARIA   *Bromeliaceae*
  pitcairniifolia (Chile); stiff, spreading terrestrial rosette with spiny leaves to 50 cm long; the inner rosette will color strikingly crimson-red at flowering time; petals of corolla are blue. *Zone 10.*   *p. 48*

x FATSHEDERA   *Araliaceae*
  lizei, "Ivy tree", "Miracle plant" or "Botanical wonder"; bigeneric hybrid between Fatsia japonica 'Moseri' and Hedera helix hibernica, the "Irish ivy". Evergreen shrub combining characters of both parents, growing erect over 2 m high if the woody stem has support; leathery leaves 5-lobed, similar to English ivy but larger, often 12-20 cm wide, dark lustrous green. Small light green flowers in dense clusters. *Zone 9.*   *p. 36, 648*

FATSIA   *Araliaceae*
  japonica (Aralia sieboldii) (Japan), "Japanese aralia"; evergreen shrub 2-4 m high, with leathery, palmately lobed leaves 15-40 cm wide, dark, shining green, the broad lobes pointed and toothed; tiny stamen flowers milky white, in terminal panicles. *Zone 8.*   *p. 648*
  japonica 'Marginata'; grown by Oakhurst Gardens in California, a cultivar with large deeply lobed leaves grayish or milky-green prettily edged in ivory-white. *Zone 10.*,   *p. 35*
  japonica 'Variegata'; very showy mutant having the palmately lobed, medium green leaves more or less edged or variegated cream-white, especially the leaf tips. Photographed in Sydney, Australia. *Zone 10.*   *p. 648*

FAUCARIA   *Aizoaceae*
  tigrina (So. Africa: Cape Prov.), "Tiger jaws"; ferocious-looking small succulent with opposite, thick, keeled or boat-shaped, gray-green leaves 3-5 cm long, and marked with numerous white dots; margins armed with stout recurved teeth so that the leaf-pairs resemble a gaping jaw. Large golden-yellow sessile flowers 5 cm across. *Arid-subtropic. Zone 10.*   *p. 153*

FEIJOA   *Myrtaceae*
  sellowiana (Acca) (So. Brazil, Paraguay, Uruguay, No. Argentina), "Pineapple guava"; small tree to 5 m high, dense with whitish-felted branches and small thick 6 cm oval, opposite leaves waxy dark green above and lightly rugose, midrib white, white to brown-tomentose beneath; flowers with fleshy petals white tomentose outside, purplish inside, and dark red stamen; green edible fruit tinged red, with guava flavor. *Zone 9.*   *p. 800, 916*
  sellowiana 'Nazemetz', "Pineapple feijoa"; selected cultivar grown in California, with larger, thicker fruit 8-10 cm long, and of a special sweet flavor. *Zone 9.*   *p. 916*

FELICIA   *Compositae*
  amelloides (Agathea coelestis) (So. Africa: Cape Prov.), "Blue daisy" or "Blue marguerite"; beautiful shrubby herb to 1 m high, with opposite, obovate leaves and daisy-like flowers 3-4 cm across, with sky-blue florets and yellow disc, on long stalks. *Zone 9.*   *p. 387*
  amelloides 'Variegata', variegated-leaved "Blue daisy"; low spreading, shrubby plant with small green leaves prettily bordered with white; flowers sky-blue with yellow center; an attractive ground-cover in climates such as California. *Subtropic. Zones 9-10.*   *p. 387*
  amoena (So. Africa), "Bush felicia"; attractive herbaceous plant, perennial and subshrubby in mild climate, or annual in colder regions, to 40 cm high, covered with soft hairs; opposite small elliptic or linear leaves; and long-stalked flowers having blue or light purple ray-florets around yellow center cushion. *Zone 9.*   *p. 387*
  fruticosa (So. Africa), "Aster bush"; much branched shrub to 75 cm high, with crowded, small linear leaves; 3 cm aster-like heads with purplish-blue ray-flowers and yellow disc. *Subtropic. Zone 9.*   *p. 689*

FENESTRARIA   *Aizoaceae*
  aurantiaca (Cape Province), "Window plant"; clustering succulent with club-like gray-green glaucous leaves 6 cm tall, the pearly flat top whitish and with translucent windows; flowers golden-yellow 3-6 cm across. *Arid-subtropic. Zone 10.*   *p. 146*
  rhopalophylla (aurantiaca var. alba) (S.W. Africa), "Baby toes"; tufts of cylindrical, succulent leaves thicker above and bearing a

translucent "window" at top; flowers white, 3 cm across; wants dry conditions, in sandy soil with lots of lime. *Arid-subtropic.* Zone 10. *p. 153.*

FEROCACTUS Cactaceae

diguetii var. carmenensis (Isla Cerralvo, Gulf of California, Mex.); handsome cactus of W. Mexico, barrel-shaped when young, elongating to 1 m high and 40 cm dia. with age, having to 40 high ribs, covered by spines 3-4 cm long; flowers around apex 3½ cm long, yellow with red in center. Zone 10. *p. 158.*

glaucescens (C. America), "Blue barrel cactus"; solitary or clustering blue glaucous globe to 40 cm thick; 11 to 13 ribs bearing yellowish spines to 4 cm long; yellow 3 cm flowers around apex. Zone 10. *p. 158.*

macrodiscus (Mexico: San Luis Potosi to Oaxaca), "Visnaga"; a depressed globular barrel cactus to 45 cm dia., with yellow to reddish recurved radial spines and long stout needle spine; funnel-shaped flowers from top, 5 cm long, petals rose with red central band. Zone 10. *p. 158.*

peninsulae (horridus) (So. Baja California), "Fish-hook cactus"; globular when young becoming cylindric to 2½ m high; dark glaucous green, with 12-30 thick, notched ribs, the spines red, tipped yellow, one long central spine hooked at tip; flowers yellow to red, 6 cm long. Zone 10. *p. 158.*

stainesii var. pringlei (Mexico: Coahuila); massive globular cactus becoming cylindric to 2 m or more high and 60 cm dia., with approx. 18 high ribs, their low knobs densely covered by pale brown spines; flowers around apex coppery rose (yellow in the species). Zone 10. *p. 158.*

wislizenii (emoryi) (Sonora, Texas, Arizona); robust globe when young, becoming cylindric to 2½ m high, matte grayish-green with 13-25 thick, notched high ribs with woolly tufts and clusters of thin but hard curving spines crimson to gray; showy yellow flowers orange in center, 6 cm across. Zone 10. *p. 158.*

FERRARIA Iridaceae

crispa (undulata) (So. Africa: S.W. Cape), "Spider flower" or "Orchid-iris"; cormous herb to 40 cm high, allied to Tigridia, with stiff flat bluish-green leaves passing into ovate bracts; the branched leafy zigzag stalk bearing fascinating, curious, fragrant flowers 4-5 cm across, the 6 broad petals with crisped margins appearing orchid-like, basically green and cream but edged and spotted velvety brown, and with orange pollen; opening only for one day in Spring; dormant late Summer. Zones 9-10 *p. 223.*

FERULA Umbelliferae

chiliantha (Rhodes, Turkey), "Gold giant fennel"; robust herbaceous perennial with thick hollow stem to 5 m high; lower leaves soft, divided into linear segments; upper leaves reduced to inflated sheaths clasping stem. The orange-yellow flowers in spectacular rounded umbels. Zone 6. *p. 515.*

communis (S. Europe to Syria), "Giant fennel"; robust perennial with hollow stems to 4 m high, having thick roots, and handsome, large foliage dissected into narrow-linear, flaccid segments; the bold, branched inflorescence in clusters of small greenish-yellow flowers, the lateral, male umbels long-stalked; blooming in late Spring. Zone 7. *p. 516.*

FESTUCA Gramineae

cinerea 'Blue-silver' (S.E. France to Italy, centr. Germany), "Silver fescue"; attractive evergreen perennial grass 30 cm or more high, forming dense cluster of narrow, arching leaves of bluish-silver; the feathery white inflorescence in pyramidal spikes. Zone 7. *p. 560*

elatior (arundinacea in Zander) (Europe to W. Asia, natural. in meadows of New York and west to California), "Reed" or "Meadow fescue"; robust perennial grass forming clusters without rhizomes, the leaves 30 cm long and 1 cm wide; flat fruiting clusters with many branches and spikelets. Cultivated as forage grass. Zone 3. *p. 570*

ovina (Northwest U.S., New Mexico; Eurasia, No. Africa), "Sheep fescue"; robust perennial grass of cooler regions, with stiff, slender culms erect or spreading, 30-50 cm high, forming clusters; narrow-linear leaves often rough; the inflorescence spike-like with lateral few-flowered branchlets. Cultivated as meadow and forage grass. Zones 4-7. *p. 560*

ovina glauca (No. Temp. Europe and Asia), "Blue fescue"; perennial low tufted ornamental grass with thread-like, linear leaves rolled inward or circular, 15-20 cm long, silvery blue glaucous and almost wiry-stiff; evergreen. Zone 5. *p. 570*

rubra (Canada to Georgia and Mexico, Eurasia, No. Africa), "Red fescue"; a fine-leaved creeping clustering perennial, with reddish or purplish base; soft dark green, slender leaves only 20 cm high, stems topped by branched panicles of 3-10 flowered spikelets pale green or glaucous or tinged purple. Used as lawn grass in blends with bluegrass. Zones 3-8. *p. 570*

scoparia (Pyrenees), "Bearskin grass"; mound or carpet-forming perennial grass, developing dense small tufts of soft, brilliant green leaves, unlike most other Festucas; spreading with short rhizomes; leafblades inrolled, to 15 cm long, stiff and ending in a sharp point; inflorescence an elongate panicle, with spikelets first green, becoming reddish-brown. Zone 4. *p. 560*

FIBIGIA Cruciferae

clypeata (So. Tyrol, Italy to S.W. Asia); erect herbaceous rough-hairy perennial 30-50 cm high; lower leaves oblong and occasionally toothed, and covered by gray hairs; the stem leaves linear; the flowers yellow, 3 cm long, in clusters toward end of branches; the blooms are followed by flat, coin-like seed pods which are quite ornamental and are used as dried material for floristic arrangements. Zone 9. *p. 408*

FICUS Moraceae

altissima (Assam to Malaya, Java and Phillipines), the "Lofty fig" or "Council tree"; magnificent banyan-tree with silvery gray bark and branches spreading to 20 m wide, dense with leathery, smooth oval or ovate leaves 10 to 20 cm long, and veins ivory to reddish; profuse with attractive axillary 2 cm fruit varying from yellow-orange to scarlet-red. Widely planted in tropical North America as a shade tree, a marvel of beauty with its striking red fruit on slender branchlets. Zone 10. *p. 791*

aspera (parcellii) (South Pacific Islands), "Clown fig"; tropical shrub or small tree with sparry branches bearing large oblong, slender pointed leaves to 20 cm long, toothed, rough hairy, grass-green and milky-green, wildly variegated and marbled ivory-white; even the pear-like fruits are variegated white. Zone 11. *p. 790*

auriculata (roxburghii) (India), "Ornamental fig"; low, spreading tree to 6 m high, very showy for its large foliage on slender woody branches, the light brown petioles covered with white hairs; big papery, rounded and toothed, slightly glossy leaves to 40 cm long, their surface covered with a fine pubescence, and with depressed veins; when young an attractive mahogany-red. Big flat-globose figs are borne on the stems. Not a house plant as foliage easily catches red spider and drops. Zone 10. *p. 790*

benghalensis (India, Sri Lanka), "Banyan tree"; large tropical tree; to 30 m high, the top spreading by aerial roots which become secondary trunks; leathery leaves ovate or elliptic, to 20 cm long, dark green, with yellow-green veins, on pubescent stem; round red fruits. Zones 10-11. *p. 791*

benghalensis krishnae (India, Pakistan), the "Sacred fig tree"; probably a form of benghalensis; small tree sacred to the Hindu god Krishna, said to have folded its leaves into cups to collect drops of dew, when the god was thirsty in the desert; leathery, irregularly cupped, deep green leaves with raised ivory ribs, finely pubescent inside, on grayish branches. Very interesting collection plant because of its curious leaves. Zones 10-11. *p. 794*

benjamina (India, Malaya), the graceful "Weeping fig"; a beautiful tropical tree of dense growth, forming aerial roots, and with branches of somewhat pendant habit; the pendulous, shining deep green leaves long ovate, slender pointed 8-10 cm long; small round fruit blood-red when ripe. One of the most attractive tubbed decorators for tropical effect, preferring smallish containers, and rejoicing in warmth and good light, 40 fc. and up to 500 fc. (400 to 5000 lux), the more light the more leaves. Allow surface to become dry, then water. The name benjamina is the Latinized form of the Sanskrit name for banyan. Zones 10-11. *p. 73, 74, 624, 791*

benjamina 'Exotica' (Java, Bali), "Java fig"; especially graceful, weeping form with slender, arching branches, and smaller, rather narrow and pendulous glossy green, leathery, oblique 9-12 cm leaves, which are given special charm by the coquette twist of their slender tip; small red berries; thrip-proof. I have seen large trees of this variety quite common in Bali. Good indoor decorator tub plant but needs at least 50 fc (500 lux) of light; some leaves may drop at first when temperature changes, or a tree is moved to air-conditioning. *Tropical.* Zone 10. *p. 73, 790*

benjamina 'Exotica variegata'; willowy tropical evergreen with elegant long-elliptic and obovate slender-pointed leaves almost completely creamy-yellow, the remaining green overlaid with glaucous silver. Zone 11. *p. 790*

benjamina 'Splendens variegata'; beautiful highly variegated and very decorative form, seen in col. Bermuda Botanic Garden; freely branching tropical evergreen with flexible, willowy twigs gracefully arching downward; the small ovate to obovate glossy green, leathery leaves splashed and broadly bordered with cream and milky-silver, and very ornamental. Zone 11. *p. 790*

benjamina 'Variegata', "Variegated mini-rubber"; handsome cultivar grown in Florida and California; charming as bushy little tree, with slender brownish stem and small elliptic leaves 6-8 cm long, glossy light green, prettily margined and variegated with ivory-white. *Tropical.* Zone 11. *p. 74*

carica 'Kadota', "White fig"; broad, irregular, deciduous shrub or tree much planted from California to Texas for its sweet, pear-shaped greenish-yellow fruit; leaves thick, rough above, deeply 3-5 lobed and with palmate veining. The species is at home in the Mediterranean region and Asia Minor, grown since earliest times for its tough-skinned honeyed fruit. *Zone 8.*   *p. 915*

carica 'Mission', "Black Mission fig"; medium large pear-shaped fruit with purplish-black skin and light strawberry-colored flesh; it has excellent flavor and good both to eat as fresh and as dried fruit. *Subtropic. Zones 7-9.*   *p. 915*

deltoidea (diversifolia) (India, Malaya, Java), "Mistletoe fig"; woody shrub with small obovate, hard leaves 5 cm long, dark green with brown specks above, pale beneath; liberally bearing small yellowish fruit lined with gray. *Zone 10.*   *p. 792*

elastica (India, Malaya), "India rubber plant"; durable old houseplant but grows into large trees to 30 m high, and rooting from the branches; young plants erect, with brown woody stem and thick-leathery oblong leaves glossy deep green, to 30 cm long, the young leaves enclosed in a rosy sheath; yielding latex-bearing milky sap. *Tropical. Zones 9-10.*   *p. 75, 791*

elastica 'Decora', "Wideleaf rubber plant"; superb commercial seedling, originated about 1950, and introduced from Belgium; of bold habit, larger and much broader, heavier leaves, 25-35 cm long, deep glossy green, with prominent lateral depressed veins, at right angles to the ivory midrib which is red beneath, the sheath at the growing tips is red. *Tropical. Zone 10.*   *p. 74, 790*

elastica 'Decora Honduras'; colorful vigorous Cent. American cultivar of compact habit; large soft-leathery glossy green leaves with cream variegation or mottling, the ribs pale yellow, tinted pink; branches and young sheaths reddish. *Zones 10-11.*   *p. 790*

elastica 'Decora tricolor' (England); seen at Rochford Nurseries near London; beautiful as a decorative pot plant with broad, colorful gray-green leaves variegated cream, white and pink, with prominent red ribs. *Zone 11.*   *p. 74*

elastica 'Variegata'; the common "Rubber plant" in variegated form, the leathery leaves are usually variegated gray and edged in creamy-yellow, coloring variable. *Zone 11.*   *p. 792*

foveolata (So. China, Taiwan, Burma or Myanmar); scandent tropical shrub, with young branchlets pubescent, pendant with leaves lanceolate 10-15 cm long, the veins creamy-yellow and margins undulate. *Zone 10.*   *p. 792*

irregularis (celebensis, neriifolia hort.) (Celebes, Moluccas); small willow-like tree of graceful weeping habit, with linear lanceolate leaves 7 to 12 cm long and 2 cm wide, resembling oleander; tiny axillary globular fruit 4 mm dia., green with brown flecks. *Zones 10-11.* *p. 793*

lyrata (pandurata) (Trop. West Africa, Liberia to Togo or Tokoin), "Fiddleleaf plant"; close headed tree to 12 m high, with large, thick-leathery leaves 30 to 60 cm long, fiddle-shaped, wide rounded apex, deep waxy green, quilted and wavy, with attractive yellow-green veins, on woody stem; fruits with white dots. *Zone 11.*   *p. 75, 793*

macrophylla (Queensland, New South Wales), the "Australian banyan" or "Moreton Bay fig"; large tree with ovate to broad oblong leathery leaves blunt at apex, to 25 cm long and 10 cm wide, cordate at base, glossy green with pronounced ivory veins, shiny light green underneath, netted. *Zone 10.*   *p. 792*

maxima (mexicana hort.) (Mexico: Sinaloa to Oaxaca and Yucatan), "Copoy"; robust, densely branching decorative tree to 20 m high, with wiry, erect branches; narrow lanceolate leathery leaves 8-20 cm long, shiny deep green, tips lightly twisted, reverse green; receptacles green, 2 cm dia. *Zone 10.*   *p. 792*

microcarpa 'Milky Stripe' (nitida cv.), "Variegated Indian laurel"; tropical evergreen, highly variegated with waxy ovate-pointed leaves milky-green heavily margined or variegated cream; smaller fruit than benjamina. *Zone 11.*   *p. 792*

microcarpa nitida (nitida in hort.) (Malaya), "Indian laurel"; attractive, glabrous thick-topped banyan tree forming aerial roots and buttressed trunk in habitat; with erect branches and small, rubbery, elliptic leaves 10 cm long, waxy, nice green and very smooth; can be shaped into pyramids and standards resembling a true laurel. Good tub plant; also widely used as a containerized street tree in our Southwest. In the interior of buildings this sun-lover requires 50 fc. to 500 fc. (500 to 5000 lux); the more light, the more leaves it can hold. *Subtropic. Zone 10.*   *p. 74, 792*

microcarpa nitida 'Hawaii', "Variegated Indian laurel"; attractive ornamental mutation ideal for decoration indoors; bushy tropical evergreen dense with glossy green, elliptic 8 cm leaves prettily bordered and variegated creamy-white. *Zone 11.*   *p. 74, 793*

monckii (Argentina), "Higueron"; epiphytic strangler fig, of similar habit as Ficus aurea of Florida; oblong glossy leaves 8-15 cm long, 5-6 cm across; yellow subglobose fruit 1 cm or more. Viable seed may be deposited by a bird in a crevice in the bark of a host tree or palm, there to germinate and sprout as an epiphyte, forming cord-like roots encircling its host to finally strangle it. *Zone 11.*   *p. 791*

mysorensis (So. India, Burma or Myanmar); large tree with twigs tomentose becoming glabrous; large leathery, rich green, ovate leaves to 30 cm long, glossy under the loose pubescence, and with pale yellowish veins; fruit orange-red; tolerates some frost. *Zone 10.*   *p. 794*

nekbudu (utilis) (Trop. Africa), "Zulu fig"; large forest tree, young growth pubescent; fresh green leathery leaves thick, oval to obovate, 15-40 cm long, rounded at both ends and with pretty, yellow ribs; small globular greenish to beige fruit 2 cm dia., covered with white felt, densely set toward apex of branches. Good examples of their shapely form are the old specimens in front of the Capitol in San Juan, Puerto Rico. *Zone 10.*   *p. 793*

nitida: see F. microcarpa nitida (Dr. Condit)

padifolia (pertusa) (So. Mexico to Costa Rica), "Plum-leaf fig" or "Nacapuli"; handsome tropical tree, varying from small size to large specimen to 30 m high, forming an immense crown of dark green foliage from usually numerous trunks; one of the strangler figs, forming aerial roots as a banyan; dark green, ovate leaves 4-12 cm long; the globular fruit is tinged red and of sweet taste, eaten by children and birds. *Zone 10.*   *p. 793*

palmeri (Baja California, Mexico); a magnificent xerophytic, desert-climate tree to 20 m tall, growing on rocky cliffs as a strangler fig; base swollen and bulbous; cordate 15 cm leaves soft-leathery grayish-green with ivory ribs, velvety beneath; small yellowish figs. *Zones 9-10.*   *p. 794*

pandurata: see F. lyrata

parcellii: see F. aspera

petiolaris (jaliscana) (Mexico), "Blue Mexican fig"; small tree to 1¾ m high, developing very wide, swollen base; attractive, heart-shaped, leathery, wavy leaves with long pointed tip, metallic blue-green, to 15 cm wide, with ivory pink to showy red veins and petioles. *Arid-tropical. Zone 11.*   *p. 793*

pretoriae (Transvaal), "Wonderboom"; big, ornamental evergreen tree 12 m tall or more; the spreading branches bend down and take root developing into new trees; leathery lanceolate leaves 20 cm long; fruits orange-red. Grown in Holland from seed as an attractive pot plant. *Zones 9-10.*   *p. 792*

pumila (repens, stipulata) (China, Japan, Australia), "Creeping fig"; freely branching creeper with small, obliquely cordate, dark green leaves less than 3 cm long, clinging to walls by roots like ivy and then flattened; fruiting branches erect, with stiff, much larger, oblong leaves to 10 cm long. *Zone 11.*   *p. 284, 625, 626*

pumila 'Marginata', "Variegated creeping fig"; seen at Fortmann Nursery, Ratingen, Germany; attractive miniature creeping fig having small roundish 2-3 cm leaves, dark green and neatly edged with white. *Zone 12.*   *p. 74*

religiosa (India), "Bo-tree"; sacred to Hindus and Buddhists, and under which Buddha received enlightenment; large glabrous tree to 30 m high, with gracefully pendant, thin, bluish-green leaves about 15 cm long, heart-shaped with tail-like driptip, ivory or pinkish veins, on slender branches; purple fruit. *Zones 10-11.*   *p. 626, 793*

retusa (So. China, Macao, Philippines), "Chinese banyan"; shapely tree with dense foliage, the branches first ascending but becoming pendulous, with small leathery 8-10 cm leaves broadly obovate and waxy; ideal for shaped standards as decorator trees growing in tubs. *Subtropic. Zone 10.*   *p. 73, 75, 793*

retusa 'Variegata', "Variegated Chinese banyan"; handsome and sturdy cultivar, seen in Del Dios nursery in California, with broad obovate leaves 8 cm long, glossy green with ivory-white variegation and margins. *Zone 11.*   *p. 74*

roxburghii: see F. auriculata

rubiginosa (australis) (New South Wales, Queensland), "Rusty fig"; broad tree, spreading by means of aerial roots like the banyan; small leathery 8-15 cm leaves oval or elliptic, rusty-pubescent beneath. *Zones 9-10.*   *p. 793*

rubiginosa 'Variegata'; a pretty miniature rubber plant with graceful branches and small, egg-shaped, deep green, leathery leaves richly marbled and edged yellowish-cream; tomentose during juvenile stage only. *Zones 10-11.*   *p. 794*

sagittata 'Variegata' (radicans), "Variegated rooting fig"; attractive variegated creeper much grown under glass, with lanceolate, grayish-green 5-8 cm leaves irregularly marked with creamy-white, the variegation beginning at the margin. *Tropical. Zone 11.*   *p. 284*

salicifolia (subulata Hortus 3) (Guyana), "Willow-leaf fig"; tropical evergreen shrub or tree with dense branches, closely set with willow-like, narrow lanceolate, leathery leaves 3 to 10 cm long, the margins recurved. Because of its small foliage, trained as miniature bonsai in shallow bowls. F. salicifolia of the hort. trade is subulata, which is from Eastern Asia, with larger leaves to 25 cm long. *Zones 10-11.*   *p. 792*

triangularis (Trop. Africa); small evergreen ornamental tree with curious triangular, thick-fleshy, dark green leaves 6 cm long, the margins rolled down; masses of small 1 cm greenish-beige berries are growing cauliflorous directly from the woody branches. *Zone 10.*   *p. 794* triangularis 'Variegata', (diversifolius in German hort.) "Sweet-heart tree"; very handsome broadleaf evergreen bush with lax or pendant willowy branches; the thick-leathery, waxy, triangular, heart-shaped or obovate leaves 5 to 8 cm long and broad, beautifully variegated deep green to milky-gray, from the margins inward with contrasting creamy-white. *Tropical.* Zone 11.   *p. 74*

FILIPENDULA   *Rosaceae*

palmata (Siberia), "Meadowsweet"; herbaceous perennial re-sembling spiraea, 60 to 90 cm high, with large palmately lobed leaves, white-tomentose beneath; small rosy flowers fading to pale pink, in terminal cluster on leafy stalks, during July. *Zone 3.*   *p. 492*

rubra (Penna. to Minnesota, so. to Georgia), "Queen of the Prairie"; very handsome herbaceous perennial 60-80 cm or more high, with leaves irregularly pinnate, and large lobed terminal leaflet; showy inflorescence dense with tiny peach-pink flowers during June. *Zone 3.*   *p. 492*

ulmaria 'Plena' (Europe, Asia, natural. E. No. America), "Queen-of-the-meadow"; handsome perennial 60 cm to more than 1 m high, the furrowed stems with pinnate leaves 30 cm or more long, having serrate ovate lateral leaflets and 3-5 lobed terminal leaflet, white-tomentose beneath; small creamy-white double flowers, dense in branched racemes, in June to August. *Zone 3.*   *p. 492*

vulgaris flore pleno (hexapetala) (syn. Spiraea filipendula) (Europe, W. Asia), "Double dropwort"; tuberous-rooted perennial 60-90 cm high, with smooth, fern-like, pinnately lobed leaves to 25 cm long; the inflorescence very ornamental with double-white flowers 2 cm across, usually reddish outside, in loose clusters during June-July. *Zone 3.*   *p. 492*

FIRMIANA   *Sterculiaceae*

simplex (platanifolia) (E. Asia: Okinawa to Vietnam), "Phoenix tree" or "Chinese parasol tree"; large semi-deciduous tree to 20 m high, with smooth trunk; decorative leaves palmately 3-5 lobed to 30 cm across, with contrasting yellow ribs; flowers without petals, but with showy yellow calyx 2 cm across; fruit opening into 5 papery sections displaying seeds. *Subtropic.* Zone 9.   *p. 884*

FITTONIA   *Acanthaceae*

verschaffeltii (Perú), "Mosaic plant"; a pretty tropical ground-cover; low, creeping herb with hairy, rooting stems and colorful oval 8-10 cm leaves dark olive-green and entirely covered with a network of deep red veins. Although the leaves are somewhat papery they are fairly sturdy. Small yellow green-bracted flowers. *Tropical.* *Zone 11.*   *p. 18*

FLACOURTIA   *Flacourtiaceae*

indica (Trop. Asia, Madagascar), "Governor's plum" or "Ramontchi"; fruit-bearing shrub or tree to 8 m high; the branches with long slender spines and ovate, glossy green, toothed leaves to 8 cm long, partially deciduous; small yellowish flowers in leaf axils, followed by the globose maroon-red fleshy fruit to 2 cm diameter tipped with short radiating styles; the juicy, edible pulp surrounding several flattened stones. *Tropical.* Zones 10-11.   *p. 913*

FOCKEA   *Asclepiadaceae*

edulis (South Africa); milky-juiced succulent forming massive edible tubers from 15 lbs to possibly 50 lbs, sprouting from its top a few slender leaf-bearing stems. *Zone 9.*   *p. 204*

FOENICULUM   *Umbelliferae*

vulgare (So. Europe, found by Darwin in Argentina), "Fennel" or "Sweet anise"; aromatic herbaceous short-lived perennial, grown as annual; when mature with branching stems 1 m or more high; feathery leaves several times pinnate into linear or awl-shaped segments; yellowish flowers in large clusters, in late Summer. The lacy foliage is used in salads and teas; seeds are adding flavor to cooked food, and unpleasant-tasting medicines; distilled as oil for soaps and perfumes. *Zone 3.*   *p. 542, 544*

FORSYTHIA   *Oleaceae*

x intermedia (suspensa x viridissima), "Border forsythia"; European hybrid about 1880; deciduous shrub known as "Golden bells"; is amongst the earliest bloomers in the Spring about April, but frequently forced as cut branches for late January; the showy, rich yellow blossoms appearing before the leaves; flowers 4-parted into oblong, spreading corolla lobes 2 cm long, in successive clusters on long whip-like branches, leaves to 12 cm long, often trifoliolate. The cultivar 'Spring Glory' is a branch sport found in Ohio 1930, more floriferous and with larger flowers 5 cm across, of lighter primrose-yellow. *Zone 4.*   *p. 620, 806*

mandshurica 'Vermont Sun'; very frost-hardy clone selected by University of Vermont, and photographed in col. Brooklyn Botanic Garden; vigorous deciduous shrub with erect branches, with blooms in clusters arranged at intervals along bare stems; flowers larger than the species, in vivid golden-yellow. *Zone 3.*   *p. 806*

ovata (Korea), "Korean forsythia"; deciduous shrub 1 m or more high, with spreading pithy branches; ovate leaves to 6 cm long, serrate at margins; small axillary flowers to 2 cm long, bronzy yellow or amber, blooming somewhat irregular but earlier than other species, usually February-March. *Zone 4.*   *p. 806*

suspensa (China), "Weeping forsythia"; large deciduous shrub to 3 m high, with branches arching downward; the stems with hollow pith, and leaves 5-10 cm long, often lobed or divided into 3 leaflets, and toothed; showy flowers golden-yellow, usually clustered, the corolla lobes 2 cm long and spreading, blooming March-April, though not as freely as intermedia. *Zone 5.*   *p. 806*

viridissima cv. 'Bronxensis'; very dwarf miniature shrub to 50 cm high, a clone found at New York Botanical Garden in 1939, with twiggy branches, and leaves 2-3 cm long, blooming profusely at an early age with small flowers in vivid yellow appearing in April; ideal for the rockgarden. *Zone 5.*   *p. 806*

FORTUNELLA   *Rutaceae*

hindsii (Hong Kong, Kwangtung), the "Wild Kumquat" or "Dwarf kumquat"; ornamental, small spiny tree, with leathery green, oval-obovate leaves, and nearly round, small 2 cm orange-red fruit of 3-4 cells, edible but not very juicy. *Zones 9-10.*   *p. 939*

japonica (Citrus madurensis) (South China), "Marumi kumquat"; small shrub usually spiny, with elliptic leaves; white flowers; small round fruit 3 cm dia., deep orange; edible with sweet rind and acid juice. *Subtropic.* Zone 9.   *p. 939*

margarita (Kwangtung), "Nagami kumquat"; small, vigorous, bushy citrus, often grown as a standard in tubs, with slender, erect, angled branches, long-pointed, shining dark green leaves, fragrant white flowers, and small, rather persistent, oblong, golden-orange fruit of 3 cm dia., with finely-flavored pulp, produced prolifically in Oct.-Jan. and longer. The sweet fruit is used for preserves. *Subtropic.* *Zones 9-10.*   *p. 58, 939*

FOSTERELLA   *Bromeliaceae*

penduliflora (Lindmania) (N.W. Argentina); terrestrial rosette of spreading linear-lanceolate soft leaves with smooth edges, satiny grayish-green and a faint yellow-green stripe down the middle; tall 30 cm wiry stalk having branched inflorescence, bearing to one side small white flowers. *Zone 11.*   *p. 46*

FOTHERGILLA   *Hamamelidaceae*

gardenii (Virginia to Georgia), "Witch alder"; deciduous low shrub 60-90 cm high, with slender, crooked stems, the young shoots white-hairy; early blooming before the foliage appears; the flowers in short cylindric spikes, fragrant and consisting of some 24 bundled white stamens or filaments and yellow anthers, without petals; obovate to oblong leaves 5 cm long, turning orange-red in Autumn. *Zone 5.*   *p. 734*

major (U.S.: Georgia), "Featherbush"; beautiful deciduous shrub to 3 m high; coarsely-toothed witchhazel-like leaves to 10 cm long, glaucous and pubescent beneath; white, fragrant flowers without petals borne in dense terminal heads in which the white stamens are the conspicuous part, flowering with the leaves. Foliage turns brilliant scarlet in Autumn. *Zone 5.*   *p. 734*

monticola (No. Carolina to Alabama), "Alabama featherbush"; excellent deciduous shrub more spreading than F. major, to 2 m high; leaves broad ovate, green not glaucous beneath, to 10 cm long; flowers with the foliage, in conspicuous spikes of bundled white filaments or anthers, without petals, very beautiful in spring bloom, and again with orange foliage in Autumn. *Zone 5.*   *p. 734*

FOUQUIERIA   *Fouquieriaceae*

diguetii (peninsularis) (Baja California and Western Sonora); much branched xerophytic shrub to 3 m high, the numerous spiny stems set with small rounded, succulent leaves, later deciduous; the flowers in 15 cm pyramidal clusters, with 2 cm red tubular corollas. *Zone 10.*   *p. 195*

fasciculata (Mexico: Durango to Queretaro and Hidalgo), "Teocotillo"; xerophytic shrub or tree to 4 m, forming thick caudex; obovate leaves 2 to 3 cm long, on slender branches; narrow panicle of red flowers. *Zone 10.*   *p. 204*

splendens (N. Mexico, Arizona, So. California), the "Ocotillo" of the desert; a xerophytic shrub with many whip-like gray, furrowed basal stems, to 6 m; rigid spines bear clusters of small oval, deciduous leaves in their axils; and at the very tips of branches the brilliant red flowers in showy racemes to 25 cm long. *Arid-subtropic.* *Zone 9.*   *p. 195*

FRAGARIA   *Rosaceae*

x ananassa (1766) (chiloensis x virginiana), the "Garden straw-berry"; a herbaceous perennial with large white flowers, and big delicious red fruit, produced in Spring. The late fruiting or everbearing varieties also include F. vesca blood, and these produce some berries from early Spring to late Autumn. *Zones 4-10.*   *p. 922*

chiloensis (Coastal Alaska to California and So. America), "Sand strawberry"; ground cover forming low mats, with rooting runners; leaves of 3 leaflets, with toothed margins; 2 cm white flowers followed by bright red, seedy fruit 2 cm dia., attracting birds. *Zones 4-10.* *p. 319*

vesca (No. Europe, Temp. Asia, also No. America), "European strawberry" or "Woodland strawberry"; herbaceous subshrub with woody base and thick rootstock, to 30 cm high; sending out arching, rooting runners; leaves compound of 3 oblique ovate leaflets to 6 cm long, with quilted blade, serrate at sides, glaucous and silky beneath; bisexual white flowers 2 cm across, followed by the pendulous aromatic, sweetly tasting red fruit, with white flesh, everbearing through the season from June to late Autumn. *Zones 5-6. p. 834, 922*

FRANCISCEA: see BRUNFELSIA

FRANCOA   *Saxifragaceae*
ramosa (Chile), "Maiden's-wreath" or "Bridal-wreath"; stalked perennial to 1 m, with basal, lobed, crinkled leaves coarsely toothed, and showy, pubescent spikes of white 2½ cm flowers with 4 petals; used as cut flowers. Evergreen in mild regions. *Zones 8-10.*   *p. 497*

FRANKLINIA   *Theaceae*
alatamaha (S.E. United States), "Franklin tree"; beautiful shrub or small tree to 8 m high, first found in Georgia in 1765, possibly at home in China; deciduous, thin-leathery glossy green, obovate leaves to 15 cm long, finely toothed at margins, and turning scarlet in Autumn; large, showy waxy white flowers 10 cm across and displaying big bundles of prominent golden orange stamens, blooming in late Summer over a long period, larger than Gordonia and daintily fragrant. *Temperate. Zone 5.*   *p. 890*

FRAXINUS   *Oleaceae*
americana (Nova Scotia, south to Florida, west to Texas), "White ash"; vigorous, rapid-growing tree to 40 m high, with fissured bark; glossy shoots bearing large odd-pinnate leaves 20-40 cm long, of 5-7-9 lanceolate 10-15 cm leaflets, pale glaucous beneath, providing purple to yellow autumn-color; small flowers without petals, the pistillate blooms on female trees producing fruit of one-seeded nutlets with 3-5 cm wing at apex, carried in long pendant clusters. *Zone 3. p. 807*

anomala (Colorado, Utah to California), "Single-leaf ash"; deciduous, usually multi-stemmed tree to 6 m high, of vase-like habit, with slender, square shoots lightly winged; unique with foliage reduced to mostly one broad roundish-ovate leaflet to 6 cm long, dark glossy green; flowers without petals; small 2 cm obovate fruit, with rounded wing surrounding the seed. Distinct by its simple leaves and angular branches. *Zone 6.*   *p. 808*

chinensis (China), "Chinese ash"; deciduous tree to 15 m high, having odd-pinnate leaves 12-20 cm long, of 5-9 lanceolate or oval leaflets to 10 cm long, light green beneath and downy at primary veins, shallow toothed at margins; flowers without petals; lanceolate winged fruit on female trees 4 cm long, in pendant clusters. *Zone 6.*   *p. 807*

excelsior (Europe, Asia Minor), "European ash"; large deciduous tree 30-40 m high, with furrowed bark; the winter-buds black; odd-pinnate leaves of 7-11 lanceolate or ovate leaflets 5-12 cm long, dark green above, lighter beneath and with main-rib downy, toothed along margins; the numerous oblong winged fruit in pendant clusters; petal-less flowers before foliage. Wood is used for general carpentry. *Zone 3.*   *p. 807*

excelsior 'Aurea', "Golden ash"; handsome variant from Holland 1807; with older bark distinctly yellowish, and young branchlets yellow, especially noticeable during the leafless stage in Winter; the foliage is at first yellowish-green, changing later to yellow. The tree has a tendency to form numerous branches from near the base. *Zone 5.*   *p. 807*

holotricha (S.E. Europe, Balkans to Danube Delta); deciduous tree of upright habit, to 12 m high, covered with soft down; the odd-pinnate leaves 15-25 cm long, of 9 to 13 ovate to lanceolate leaflets 8 cm long, sharply toothed at sides; the inflorescence with petal-less flowers, and pendant clusters of winged fruit. *Zone 5.*   *p. 807*

holotricha 'Moraine'; handsome tree of neat symmetrical form, a variant of broader, ellipsoid habit than the species, found in Romania as seedling, with its pinnate foliage longer retained on the tree, and producing very few seeds, and turning uniform bright yellow in Autumn. Good lawn tree, as the leaves dry up and shrivel before they fall. *Zones 6-9.*   *p. 807*

ornus (So. Europe, Hungary to W. Asia), "Flowering ash"; handsome round-headed deciduous tree to 18 m high, with smooth gray bark, interesting because it is a species which produces showy flowers having petals, these are heavily scented and have a white corolla, the linear segments 6 mm long in dense clusters; the narrow-oblong fruit 3 cm long; odd-pinnate leaves 12-20 cm long with usually 5

or 7 ovate, lightly toothed leaflets. Very attractive when in bloom during mid-May. Sweet-tasting Manna is obtained from the sap. *Zone 5.*   *p. 807*

paxiana (China: Hupeh and Szechwan), "Himalaya ash"; handsome deciduous tree 12-18 m high, with rusty winterbuds; leaves odd-pinnate 25-35 cm long, having 7-9 lanceolate toothed leaflets; the inflorescence, appearing with or after foliage, is attractive because it has flowers with petals, these are creamy-white, and carried in showy pyramidal clusters 20 cm long, in June; small linear 3 cm fruit. *Zone 6.*   *p. 807*

pennsylvanica 'Summit' (Eastern No. America); handsome tree to 20 m high, a clone introduced by Summit Nurseries of Stillwater, Minnesota; of upright habit, with strong central leader; odd-pinnate leaves glossy green, having 5-9 ovate leaflets 8-14 cm long and finely toothed; small yellow flowers in erect clusters, the stamens shorter than the 4 petals, blooming May-June; the clone 'Summit' is female and produces many seeds. Golden autumn foliage. *Zone 3.*   *p. 808*

retusa (S.E. China: Kwantung), "Chinese ash"; tender shrub or small tree to 8 m high, with gray young branches, the odd-pinnate leaves having 3-7 soft-leathery broad-ovate leaflets 5-15 cm long, with veins elevated; the inflorescence in dense pendant clusters of flowers having white petals; the oblong fruit 3 cm long. Related to F. mariesii but having leaflets stalked, often dentate, and with large calyx. *Zone 9.*   *p. 808*

uhdei (Mexico), "Evergreen ash" or "Shamil ash"; charming evergreen to semi-evergreen tree to 15 m high, with widely spreading crown and pendulous branches; odd-pinnate leaves with 5-9 lanceolate leaflets glossy deep green, the margins with fine teeth; petal-less flowers in pendant clusters to 18 cm long; elliptic 3 cm fruit. Very popular in California; also planted along the Paseo de la Reforma, Mexico City. *Subtropic. Zone 9.*   *p. 808*

FREESIA   *Iridaceae*
x hybrida; large-flowered hybrid of such South African species as refracta and armstrongii; bulb-like corms with linear leaves, and very fragrant, firm, funnelform flowers on bent wiry spikes, creamy-white through orange to lilac-blue; August blooming unless forced. *Subtropic. Zone 9.*   *p. 226*

x hybrida 'Ballerina'; large-flowered Dutch hybrid with substantial, waxy white trumpets tinted pink, growing from bulblike corms. *Zone 9.*   *p. 229*

x hybrida 'Czardas'; striking cultivar with flowers bright scarlet-red and contrasting golden-yellow in lower part of tube; very floriferous. *Zone 9.*   *p. 226*

x hybrida 'Stockholm Red'; brilliant funnel flowers of firm texture, vivid crimson-red, carried more or less erect over rich green linear leaves. *Zone 9.*   *p. 226*

x hybrida 'White Swan'; superb hybrid very floriferous with fleshy funnelform flowers a shimmering snow-white, on firm stems. *Zone 9.*   *p. 226*

refracta (So. Africa), "Common freesia"; cormous species and parent of many hybrid cultivars; with few 2-ranked green linear leaves 15 cm long; flexuous usually branched floral stalks to 30 cm or more, bearing 5-8 creamy to greenish-yellow flowers, 4 cm long and very fragrant. *Zone 9.*   *p. 226*

FREMONTODENDRON   *Sterculiaceae (Bombacaceae in Hortus 3)*
californicum (Fremontia) (California), "Flannel-bush"; evergreen shrub or small tree to 3 m, dark green leathery roundish or lobed 3 cm leaves with felt-like covering beneath, lemon-yellow flowers of showy saucer-like nearly circular calyx without petals, 3 cm wide, in late Spring, making a gorgeous show of color in the mountains of southern and central California. *Zone 9.*   *p. 884*

mexicanum (Fremontia) (San Diego and Baja California), "Southern flannel bush"; evergreen shrub or small tree to 6 m, with spur-like branches bearing 5-lobed leaves, dark green above and covered with felt beneath, 4-8 cm long, flowers star-shaped with showy orange-yellow calyx to 9 cm across, but without petals; black seeds. *Subtropic. Zone 9.*   *p. 884*

FREYCINETIA   *Pandanaceae*
cumingiana (Philippines); woody tropical tree-climbing screwpine with flexuous stems, alternately set with stiff-leathery, narrow lanceolate, sharp-pointed green leaves 11-14 cm long; the curious inflorescence with red bracts. *Zone 11.*   *p. 284*

funicularis (insignis) (Indonesia: Java); a beautiful climbing screwpine with long flexuous stems; sword-shaped leathery leaves glossy green with very few minute marginal spines; the terminal inflorescence very showy, with large triangular bright red bracts and cylindric yellow spadices in center. Female plants will produce cone-like, many-seeded multiple fruit. *Zones 10-11.*   *p. 284*

javanica (Java), "Climbing pandanus"; slender climbing shrub with stems rooting onto the bark of trees, and pandanus-like branches with spirally arranged, narrow, glossy green, toothed leaves; in the mountains of Java whole trees are covered with this rambler, its pendant branches tipped by bright orange, bracted flowers, greenish outside, with green spadix. The variety *expansa*, shown on p. 284, was collected by J. Bogner of Munich Bot. Garden in Sumatra, and has broader leaves. *Zones 10-11.* p. 284

multiflora (Philippines), "Climbing pandanus"; climbing tropical shrub with slender rooting stems becoming pendant from trees; sessile leathery, black-green, linear lanceolate keeled leaves, and showy terminal inflorescence with glowing salmon-rose bracts, and rosy spadix. *Tropical. Zones 10-11.* p. 284

FRITHIA Aizoaceae
pulchra (Transvaal), "Purple baby toes"; pretty, clustering rosette similar to Fenestraria, with club-like succulent gray leaves under 3 cm high, the flat top with translucent windows; carmine-purple flowers with white center. *Subtropic. Zone 10.* p. 146

FRITILLARIA Liliaceae
amoena; small bulbous plant with sessile long ovate leaves glaucous green along stalks 12 cm high, topped by pale yellow bells. Photographed in Alpine Garden of Duesseldorf Bot. Garden. *Zone 6.* p. 241

atropurpurea (Oregon, No. California to New Mexico and Dakota); bulbous perennial, its stem to 60 cm high, set with narrow leaves, and topped by usually several open bell-flowers with segments 2-cm long, dull purple-brown, spotted yellow and white. *Zones 5-8.* p. 241

imperialis (Iran, W. Himalaya), "Crown Imperial"; simple-stemmed stout, strong-smelling herb to 1 m, with scaly bulb, lanceolate leaves, with some in a terminal whorl above the nodding 5 cm flowers, with 6 veined segments brilliant red, borne on a stiff-erect, purple-spotted stalk. *Zone 5.* p. 241

imperialis 'Aurora', "Orange Crown Imperial"; color variation of this imposing bulbous perennial, with a rosette of leaves, and a stout purplish stalk bearing a ring of reddish to bronzy crimson bell-flowers 5 cm long, topped by a tuft of leaves, in Spring. *Zone 5.* p. 241

imperialis 'Lutea', "Yellow Crown-Imperial"; cultivated garden form with pendant flowers yellow with orange shading. Photographed in New Hope, Pennsylvania. *Zone 6.* p. 241

imperialis 'Lutea maxima'; striking cultivar blooming in Holland in early May, with robust, stiff-erect floral stem topped by a crown of spreading leaves, and below them a circle of large pendant, lemon-yellow bell-flowers 4-5 cm long. *Zone 6.* p. 241

involucrata (Maritime Alps of France and Italy); Alpine perennial from small globular bulb; stem to 40 cm high, with linear leaves; toward apex the solitary to several, narrow bell-shaped flowers 3-4 cm long, dull purple, tessellated yellow, the nectary black. *Zone 5.* p. 241

meleagris (Britain, Norway, C. Europe to Caucasus), "Checkered-lily" or "Snake's head"; bulbous perennial to 45 cm high, with scattered linear to oblanceolate glaucous leaves along middle of stem; usually solitary bell-shaped 5-8 cm flowers, purple with white checkering, or white with green network of veins. *Warm temperate. Zones 3-8.* p. 241

persica (libanotica) (Iran, Turkey, Israel, Jordan); robust perennial, having spindle-shaped bulb to 5 cm thick; stout stem 20 to 150 cm high, with alternate lanceolate glaucous leaves 10 cm long; toward apex a raceme of usually violet-blue narrow bell-shaped flowers with segments 2 cm long, and slightly scented. *Zones 5-8.* p. 241

pudica (Brit. Columbia to Utah), "Yellow bell" or "Yellow fritillary"; bulbous perennial with stem to 30 cm high, with narrow lanceolate leaves along it; and toward apex 1 to 3 pendant bell-flowers 2 cm long, the segments yellow or orange, tinged with purple. *Zone 4.* p. 240

verticillata (Cent. Asia, China, Japan); early spring-blooming bulbous perennial, sometimes forming tiny bulblets; stem to 60 cm high, set with linear-lanceolate leaves 10 cm long, the upper ones with tendril-like tips; toward apex several cup-shaped pendant flowers 3 cm long, white or yellow flecked with green outside, purplish inside. *Zone 6.* p. 240

FUCHSIA Onagraceae
arborescens (Mexico, Guatemala, Costa Rica); small tree to 6 m or more high, with smooth, woody branches red when young; lanceolate, bright green leaves in three's, to 25 cm long; small 1 cm flowers in dense erect panicles resembling lilac bloom, pinkish-purple, followed by blue-black berries. *Zone 10.* p. 814

'Autumnalis' hort.; colorful shrub, with reddish branches and large ovate leaves salmon-pink and light yellow, shaded blood red on young growth; veins red; seen in col. Tok Furuta, of Univ. of California at Riverside. *Zone 10.* p. 814

boliviana (Perú to Boliva and Argentina); handsome branched, bushy shrub to 1 m high and evergreen in sheltered indoors, in habitat to 6 m high; decorative softly hairy elliptic leaves 5-18 cm long, corrugated by numerous depressed veins and a red midrib; striking inflorescence of long tubular trumpet flowers crimson-red to 7 cm long, the calyx tubular, sepals spreading and petals erect, pendant in dense clusters. The fruits are edible as in all fuchsias, and cultivated in ancient times by the Incas. *Zone 10.* p. 814

fulgens (Mexico); robust shrub to 1 m high, with red branches and large, broadly ovate, green leaves, and numerous, brilliant 8 cm flowers in nodding clusters, the long cylindrical tube vivid red with short, only slightly spreading lobes, greenish at tips, the short corolla scarlet-red, (Summer). *Zone 10.* p. 814

hyb. 'Dollar Princess'; an old floriferous pot and basket variety still in cultivation after 50 years, medium small but full plant and small, compact flowers 3 to 4 cm long, with densely double violet-purple corolla and carmine reflexed sepals. *Zone 10.* p. 815

hyb. 'Golondrina' (1941); vigorous grower and ideally suited to training as standard; masses of slender, pendulous single flowers, the long reflexing sepals light red, the corolla deeper carmine-red. *Zone 10.* p. 815

hyb. 'Winston Churchill'; excellent commercial potplant of compact habit and a willing bloomer, with dark green leaves and large round flowers with salmon-red sepals, and deep purplish-blue, fully double petals, on stiff stem, (Spring). *Subtropic. Zone 10.* p. 54

magellanica (Perú, Chile, to Tierra del Fuego), known as the "Hardy fuchsia"; bushy perennial plant growing into a shrub 2 m high, and with support on walls to 6 m, arching branches with small ovate leaves to 5 cm long, wavy-toothed at margins, and pendulous slender flowers with purplish-red calyx lobes longer than the purple-blue petals; deciduous in severe cold climate, when tops die back. Attractive to hummingbirds. *Zones 6-10.* p. 814

microphylla (Mexico); low evergreen bush to 60 cm high, larger in habitat to 2 m; spreading wiry branches, with small oval or obovate leathery leaves lightly toothed, 2 cm long; charming little axillary flowers, with funnel-shaped 1 cm scarlet calyx tube having pointed lobes and deep red, toothed petals, blooming in Autumn. *Zone 10.* p. 814

procumbens (New Zealand), "Trailing fuchsia"; creeping, branching plant with slender stems, roundish 1-2 cm crenate leaves, forming mats; tiny erect, 2 cm flowers with calyx tube pale orange and reflexed purple calyx lobes, petals absent; followed by bright red small berries. Good basket plant. *Subtropic. Zone 10.* p. 316

splendens (Mexico, Guatemala); much branched shrub to 2 m, shiny 12 cm, corrugated leaves ovate-cordate, pale green, toothed; flowers drooping, rather short, about 3 cm long, crimson-red, tipped green, base swollen, compressed above, and with prominent stamens. *Zone 10.* p. 814

triphylla (West Indies: Haiti); bushy shrub to 60 cm high, with downy shoots, ovate to obovate, bronzy, toothed leaves to 8 cm long, purplish beneath; nodding 3 cm flowers in terminal racemes, the spreading tube cinnabar-red, the short corolla vivid coral-red. *Zone 10.* p. 814

triphylla 'Gartenmeister Bohnstedt', the "Honeysuckle fuchsia"; a pretty descendant of this little West Indian shrub, with dark metallic green, purple veined leaves, red-purple beneath, and lustrous, slender tubular flowers of salmon-rose with inner petals orange-scarlet, on purple stems, in terminal, nodding clusters, blooming during Winter over a long period of time. (1906). *Humid-subtropic. Zone 10.* p. 815

wytywskii (So. America); very handsome species from southernmost So. America, from col. University of California Bot. Garden at Berkeley; low shrub with lustrous green ovate leaves, and cluster of pendant tubular flowers to about 6 cm long, the waxy corolla scarlet-red; seen blooming in Quail Bot. Garden, Encinitas during August. *Zone 8. ?* p. 814

FUNKIA: see HOSTA (Zander, Hortus)

FURCRAEA Agavaceae
foetida 'Striata' (gigantea), "Mauritius hemp" or "False agave"; spectacularly showy, variegated open rosette of broad, sword-shaped fleshy leaves 45-60 cm long, sharp-pointed and with occasional marginal spines; highly colored with stripes and broad bands of ivory and milky-green over rich green. The green species is from Brazil and is cultivated in Mauritius and Tanzania etc. for its fiber. Branched inflorescence to 9 m high, with flowers milky-white inside, greenish outside. *Tropical. Zones 10-11.* p. 152

macdougallii (Fourcroya) (Mexico: Oaxaca); solitary tree to 8 m or more high, with massive trunk to 20 cm dia., in habitat densely sheathed by pendant old foliage and topped by a showy rosette of massed fleshy, linear leaves 2 m long, toothed along margins; branched inflorescence 8 m high, with pendant whitish flowers. *Zone 10.* p. 151

selloa marginata (Colombia), "Variegated false agave"; succulent rosette, forming trunk. Leaves sword-like, more than 1 m long, narrowed toward base, thin and flexible, glossy green with broad cream margins, armed with vicious curved brown teeth. *Tropical. Zone 10.*   *p. 152*

GAILLARDIA   *Compositae*

aristata (Minnesota to Brit. Columbia), the "Blanket flower"; flower garden hardy perennial 60-90 cm high, more or less rough-hairy, with narrow, gray-green foliage to 12 cm long; colorful flower heads 8-10 cm across, the ray-florets red with yellow tips. The plants in cultivation are called G. 'Grandiflora', which may vary in colors, in warm shades of red and yellow with orange or maroon, from June until frost. *Temperate. Zone 3.*   *p. 389*

x grandiflora hybrid of aristata x pulchella; perennial with gray-green foliage more vigorous than the native species and blooming early from seed; flower heads 8-10 cm across, orange-yellow with blood red toward blackish center cushion. *Zones 4-10.*   *p. 389*

x grandiflora 'Mandarin' (aristata x pulchella), "Blanket flower"; gorgeous perennial similar to aristata but more vigorous and easier to grow, often blooming first year from seed; to 1 m high, with rough, gray-green foliage, and showy flowerheads 8-10 cm across, the ray-petals maroon-red tipped with yellow, blooming in Summer. *Zone 4.*   *p. 389*

GALANTHUS   *Amaryllidaceae*

elwesii (Asia Minor), "Giant snowdrop"; spring-blooming bulb to 30 cm high, 2-3 basal narrow linear leaves 20 cm long, glaucous; solitary nodding, bell-like flowers 3 cm long, the 3 long, spreading outer segments white, the 3 short inner segments green at base and tips. *Zone 4.*   *p. 212*

nivalis (France east to Caucasus), "Common snowdrop"; early spring-blooming bulb with 2-3 narrow basal leaves and solitary white 2 cm flowers, the short inner segments green on sinus. *Warm temperate. Zones 2-3.*   *p. 212*

nivalis 'Flore pleno', "Double-flowered snow drops"; charming early spring bloomer, with greenish-white flowers having several rows of the shorter inner green segments; the white wide-spreading outer petals tend to close in cool weather. *Zone 3.*   *p. 212*

GALAX   *Diapensiaceae*

urceolata (aphylla) (Virginia to Alabama), the "Beetle-weed"; evergreen perennial herb with basal, tufted thin-leathery leaves to 12 cm across, heart-shaped to nearly round, waxy green with crenate red margins and prominent netted veins, on thin-wiry petioles; small white flowers in a dense, spike-like raceme, 30-50 cm high, June-July. The leaves are widely used by florists. *Zones 3-6.*   *p. 413*

GALEANDRA   *Orchidaceae*

stangeana (Brazil); semi-terrestrial orchid with long club-like pseudobulbs bearing narrow folded leaves in upper part; the inflorescence in terminal racemes of showy flowers with waxy brownish sepals and petals, the flaring lip pale rose. *Zone 11.* *p. 88*

GALEGA   *Leguminosae*

officinalis (So. Europe, Asia Minor), "Goats rue"; bright green herbaceous perennial to 1 m, with pinnate leaves, and racemes of 1 cm purplish-blue pea-flowers similar to Wisterias, in Summer. Used medicinally, and also as feed for livestock. *Zones 3-8.*   *p. 440, 535*

GALIUM   *Rubiaceae*

odoratum (Asperula) (Europe, No. Africa, Asia), "Sweet wood-ruff" or "Waldmeister"; fragrant perennial 15-25 cm high, spreading to form a good groundcover, with whorls of glossy green, bristle-tipped elliptic leaves to 4 cm long on delicate square stems, and small starry 4-petaled white flowers in loose clusters, blooming May-June. The sweet-scented leaves and tips are used in German May-wine and liqueurs, also in apple juice; dried leaves in sachets to scent linens. *Zones 4-8.*   *p. 544*

schultesii (Europe), "Bedstraw"; vigorous and persistent herba-ceous perennial 60-80 cm high, similar to G. boreale, with linear leaves along stems in whorls of fours at joints; small white, fragrant flowers in dense terminal clusters, during Summer. *Zone 3.*   *p. 495*

GALPHIMIA   *Malpighiaceae*

glauca (Thryallis) (Mexico to Panama), "Gold shower thryallis"; handsome bush of open habit, 1 to 1½ m high, with scandent branches, opposite thin-leathery, oblong bluish glaucous leaves to 5 cm long, and small 2 cm yellow flowers in showy, elongate clusters. Very floriferous evergreen for the warm greenhouse or conservatory. *Zones 8-10.*   *p. 780*

GALTONIA   *Liliaceae*

candicans (So. Africa), "Giant Summer hyacinth"; beautiful bulbous plant to 1 m high, with flat, linear leaves and showy white fragrant flowers, 4 cm long, nodding like little bells in tall, loose clusters; Summer. *Subtropic. Zones 8-10.*   *p. 239*

GALVEZIA   *Scrophulariaceae*

juncea (Baja Calif., Sonora, Mexico); erect much branched shrub with slender stems to 2 m high; nodes 2-10 cm long; narrow leaves to 1 cm long; flowers tubular in pairs or threes, the slender corolla bright red 2-3 cm long, 3-lobed with lower lip reflexed, and tawny pubescent inside; fruit an ovoid capsule 1 cm long. Blooming February to October in arid areas from Ensenada to the Cabo San Lucas region islands. *Zone 9.*   *p. 874*

speciosa (Islands off So. California, Mexico to Ecuador), "Bush snapdragon"; evergreen shrub spreading 1 to 2 m across, somewhat less in height, but can lean on other shrubs and reach higher; young growth herbaceous with leaves elliptic to ovate 3 cm long; attractive trumpet-shaped 2-lipped flowers vivid scarlet-red, 3 cm long, cluster-ing toward tips of branches, blooming heaviest in Mid-spring; suitable for arid areas. *Zones 9-10.*   *p. 874*

GAMOLEPIS   *Compositae*

chrysanthemoides (So. Africa: Eastern Cape to Natal), "Daisy bush"; subshrubby perennial 60-90 cm high; smooth green leaves pinnately parted, the divisions lobed and fern-like; the daisy-like flowers 4-5 cm across, with bright yellow ray-florets around the deep yellow center cushion. *Zone 9.*   *p. 390*

tagetes (Psilothonna), "Golden edging daisy"; desirable garden plant because of its prolific bloom; slender branching annual 10-25 cm high, with wiry branches; leaves having linear lobes; daisy-like flowers 3 cm across, the ray-florets lemon-yellow around the deep yellow center. *Zone 9.*   *p. 390*

GARCINIA   *Guttiferae*

dulcis (Philippines, Java to Malaysia, Molucca Is.), "Gourka"; tropical fruit tree to about 6 m high, with slender lanceolate leaves 15 cm or more long, bright glossy green above, pale beneath; flowers creamy-white with incurved petals, appearing globular, February blooming; smooth, thick-skinned fruit bright yellow, in size like an apple, containing watery pulp surrounding the seed, of aromatic tart taste when eaten fresh; high in vitamin C. Also used in preserves. Much planted in Borneo and Java. *Zones 10-11.*   *p. 914*

mangostana (Malaya), the "Mangosteen"; important tropical fruit tree 6 to 10 m; in Peradeniya, Sri Lanka are magnificent specimens to 30 m high; the opposite, dark green and leathery elliptic foliage is 15 to 25 cm long; purple or yellow-red male flowers with fleshy petals are 4 cm across; the brilliant purplish-crimson fruit, measuring 6 to 8 cm dia., with rind and edible segments like an orange, yellow juice and with large flat seeds; at the base with 4 persistent sepals. The white delicious pulp has a flavor between a grape and peach. Fruit usually ripens in Peradeniya in July or August, but differs according to season. *Tropical. Zones 10-11.*   *p. 914*

spicata (India and Sri Lanka, Taiwan); tropical tree to 12 m high, with smooth dark brown bark showing minute horizontal cuts; wide-spreading branches in whorls, forming dense canopy; thick-leathery elliptic dark green leaves to 20 cm long; small 1 cm flowers twice a year in the axils of fallen foliage; globose to ovoid orange-colored fruit 4 cm dia., the soft pulp containing the seed. *Zone 10.*   *p. 914*

GARDENIA   *Rubiaceae*

jasminoides 'August Beauty'; evergreen 1 to 2 m high, of bushy habit, with lustrous rich green foliage; large fragrant, velvety white double blooms from May through November in California. *Zones 8-10.*   *p. 856*

jasminoides 'Fortuniana' (syn. florida) (So. China), "Cape jasmine"; robust shrub with strong woody branches rather sparry, large, shining dark green, leathery, quilted leaves, and big 10 cm, fragrant, waxy-white flowers of heavy substance, turning creamy-yellow with age, Spring and Summer; the yellow fruit is eaten in China. *Tropical. Zone 11.*   *p. 75*

jasminoides 'Prostrata' (radicans florepleno) (Taiwan, Japan), "Miniature gardenia"; dwarf, shrubby plant with spreading, rooting branches, narrow, 5-8 cm pointed leaves and small, solitary, ir-regularly double, white flowers, very fragrant. *Zones 10-11.*   *p. 856*

jasminoides 'Veitchii', "Jasmine rose" or "Everblooming gar-denia"; double-flowering form of the Chinese species, of compact, bushy habit, dense with smaller, shining green leaves, and while the sweetly fragrant, pure white flowers average only 8 cm in dia., they are extra double and willing to bloom from January to May; often laden with buds and flowers. *Zone 11.*   *p. 54, 856*

nitida (Trop. West Africa: Sierra Leone, Guinea, Ghana, Nigeria); evergreen smooth shrub or small tree 1 to 3 m high, the slender, grayish spreading branches with opposite, oblong-lanceolate leaves shining green and wavy, 8 to 10 cm long; the pure white, waxy flowers with long slender corolla tube, and the 7 narrow petal segments reflexed like birds in flight, and very fragrant, but lasting only one day. *Zones 10-11.*   *p. 855*

radicans fl. pl.: see G. jasminoides 'Prostrata' (Hortus 3)
rothmannia: see ROTHMANNIA capensis (Hortus)

taitensis (Society Islands: Tahiti), the charming "Symbol flower" or "Tiare tahiti"; considered the most beautiful flower of the islands; evergreen bush some 2 m high, with dark and glossy obovate 10 cm foliage with creamy midrib; the fleshy salver form waxy flowers of 6-8 linear petals arranged like a pin-wheel, 4-5 cm across, snow-white, incomparably scented, blooming in the evening and lasting several days; Tahitians put a blossom behind the ear as a symbol, collecting it in the bud. *Zones 10-11*. *p. 856*

thunbergia (So. Africa: Natal); robust evergreen 2-3 m high, with woody branches, leathery, glossy green, broad-elliptic 10-15 cm leaves; large 8-14 cm long-tubed, waxy-white single flowers of 8-9 petals overlapping shingle-like, 6-10 cm across; very fragrant. *Zones 10-11*. *p. 856*

GARRYA   *Garryaceae*

elliptica (Coast of Cent. California to Oregon), "Silk-tassel"; interesting evergreen shrub or small tree to 4 m high, very vigorous, with young branches downy; the thick-leathery, oblong-ovate leaves 5-10 cm long, very undulate or crisped along margins and tomentose beneath; very ornamental for its long pendant string-like male catkins 8-30 cm long, appearing from November to February; the fruits are silky berries. *Zone 8*. *p. 732*

GASTERANTHUS   *Gesneriaceae*

atratus (Besleria) (W. Ecuador); compact cloud forest terrestrial of rather succulent habit, with fleshy stems and deeply bullate or puckered, unequal-sided ovate, thick leaves 12 to 17 cm long, the surface deep green and waxy, overlaid with metallic black patina, the margins crenate, and underside reddish-purple; flowers tubular with long spur, to 7 cm long, lemon-yellow and marked with maroon stripes *Zone 11*. *p. 63*

GASTERIA   *Liliaceae*

gracilis 'Variegata' (Natal parentage); charming succulent mini-rosette of tongue-shaped recurving leaves 6-8 cm long dark green with numerous whitish dots, lined and margined with white, the surface rough, and keeled beneath. *Zone 11*. *p. 198*

liliputana (Cape Province), a miniature "Ox-tongue"; attractive, suckering miniature, smallest of the genus, with first two-ranked, later spirally arranged, thick, short-stubby, keeled leaves 4-6 cm long, dark green and glossy, mottled nile-green, and horny along margins; tiny red flowers on 10 cm stalk. *Arid-subtropic. Zone 10*. *p. 198*

rawlinsonii (So. Africa: Cape Prov.); strange succulent with elongate stem having tongue-shaped, gray-green channelled leaves to 15 cm or more long, arranged alternately distichously on one plane along its length, the margins with small teeth; inflorescence of red to green balloon-shaped flowers. *Zone 10*. *p. 196*

GASTORCHIS   *Orchidaceae*

luteus (Phaius luteus: Lecoufle, France) (Madagascar); rare terrestrial similar to Phaius, on occasion growing on pandanus trees; elongate stem-like pseudobulbs set with folded, ribbed foliage; erect inflorescence bearing a raceme of waxy flowers of peach-cream, the lip blotched with crimson. *Tropical. Zone 12*. *p. 90*

GAULTHERIA   *Ericaceae*

procumbens (Québec to Manitoba and Minnesota, south to Georgia, Alabama), "Checkerberry" or "Wintergreen"; vigorous decorative, creeping evergreen woodland shrub of the Eastern U.S., 8-15 cm high; lustrous green elliptic leathery leaves 2-3 cm long and bristly at margins toward apex; nodding waxy-white bell-flowers urn-shaped, followed by berry-like red fruit, which is edible having the peculiar wintergreen flavor. *Zone 3*. *p. 704*

shallon (W. No. America: Alaska to California), "Salal" or "Lemon leaf", a "Florist's greens"; low evergreen shrub to 1 m high in sun, in shade to 3 m, densely spreading and forming thickets, as in the Redwood forest along the Pacific coast; the decorative foliage oval, 8-10 cm long, leathery bright green and with depressed ribs; white or pinkish bell-like flowers on reddish stalks; edible black fruits resembling large huckleberries, but are bland in flavor. *Zone 6*. *p. 704*

GAURA   *Onagraceae*

lindheimeri (Louisiana, Texas; Mexico); erect perennial to 1 m or more high, stems with lanceolate leaves 4-10 cm long, toothed at recurved margins; flowers white, turning rose, 4 cm across, in spike-like racemes, from July to October. *Zone 5*. *p. 461*

GAYLUSSACIA   *Ericaceae*

baccata (Eastern Canada, south to Georgia, and Iowa), "Black huckleberry", not to be confused with Vaccinium; low shrub to 1 m high, with deciduous foliage on branches sticky when young; the leaves oval 3-5 cm long, richly colored red in Autumn; nodding flowers in clusters, the corolla with 5 spreading, red lobes, during May-June, followed by shining black berries, edible and deliciously sweet. *Zone 2*. *p. 705*

brachycera (Delaware to Tennessee), "Box huckleberry"; creeping evergreen low shrub to 50 cm high, forming mats; ovate leathery leaves to 2½ cm long, finely toothed; small white or pinkish flowers, with urn-shaped corolla striped and tipped with red, 4 mm long; the somewhat pear-shaped berry-fruit first pale, turning blue-black; edible but insipid or tasteless. *Zone 5*. *p. 705*

GAZANIA   *Compositae*

maritima (So. Africa), "Sea gazania"; handsome rhizomatous perennial, with leathery, pinnately lobed, silvery gray leaves about 10 cm long; the vivid yellow flowers 4 cm across. Seen in col. Nymphenburg Bot. Garden, Munich, Germany. *Zone 9*. *p. 388*

nivea (krebsiana) (So. Africa); small, spreading plant from thick, woody rhizome; crowded silvery leaves, much divided and white-hoary; daisy-like flowers golden-yellow. *Subtropic. Zone 9*. *p. 388*

pavonia var. hirtella (So. Africa: Little Karroo); low plant with small pinnate leaves, silver gray beneath; large daisy-like flowers deep orange, with white and brown peacock design at the base of each floret, forming a ring around center. *Subtropic. Zone 9*. *p. 388*

pinnata (S. Africa: Cape Prov.); herbaceous perennial spreading with prostrate branches, having milky juice; the foliage very variable, usually pinnately parted, or lanceolate, 8-20 cm long, white-woolly beneath; the daisy-like flowers to 8 cm across, having ray-florets orange-yellow with dark basal spot, around the deep yellow center cushion. *Zone 9*. *p. 388*

rigens (splendens in hort.) (So. Africa), "Treasure flower"; handsome rhizomatous perennial, with decumbent branches, spreading to 50 cm long, smooth or hairy; the leaves narrow lanceolate to 20 cm long; long-stalked daisy-like flowers to 8 cm across, the ray-florets bright yellow to orange, ranged around the brownish-yellow center cushion. Seen and photographed in col. Kirstenbosch Bot. Garden near Cape Town. *Subtropic. Zone 9*. *p. 388*

rigens 'Aztec', "Goldband treasure flower"; beautiful cultivar of the clumping type, with long narrow green leaves, silky-white underneath; medium size 8-10 cm flowers, their ray-florets orange along margins, and broad carmine-red bands down center, marked blackish at base. *Zone 9*. *p. 389*

rigens 'Aztec Queen', "Aztec treasure flower"; gorgeous clump-forming cultivar with large flowers 8-10 cm across, the multi-colored white and pink ray-florets flaring with yellow and maroon, deep purple at base, in the center the gold-yellow cushion. *Zone 9*. *p. 388*

rigens 'Copper King' (splendens hort.); clumping plant with gray leaves and exceptionally large flowers 8-10 cm across, deep orange with chestnut brown and violet. *Subtropic. Zone 9*. *p. 388*

rigens 'Fiesta Red' (splendens), "Treasure flower" of So. African origin; rhizomatous perennial cultivar, forming clumps, with long narrow dark green leaves, silvery tomentose beneath; and strikingly beautiful daisy-like blooms 6 cm across, the ray-flowers vivid orange and a red center band; dark purple around base. *Zone 9*. *p. 312, 389*

rigens 'Gold Nuggets'; beautiful hybrid involving G. rigens and others; with small foliage, forming clumps; short-stalked large, showy daisy-like flowers 5 to 8 cm across, rich yellow with black at base of each ray; a dazzling color display during peak of bloom in late Spring and early Summer, in mild climate. *Zone 9*. *p. 388*

rigens leucolaena (uniflora hort.) (Natal), "Trailing gazania"; grows to same height as rigens, but spreads rapidly by long, trailing stems; foliage is clear silvery gray. The yellow, orange, white or bronze 4 cm flowers bloom in profusion. *Zone 9*. *p. 312, 389*

rigens fa. splendens; possibly a hybrid; free-blooming, tall-growing to 45 cm; narrow spoon-shaped leaves silky-white beneath; large heads of orange or yellow ray-flowers each black at base with a white spot, forming a pretty ring around the dark disc. *Zone 9*. *p. 390*

rigens 'Sun Gold'; handsome cultivar seen in col. Los Angeles Arboretum; clump-forming, dense with narrow lanceolate leaves, and showy flowers, entirely bright yellow. *Zone 9*. *p. 389*

GEIJERA   *Rutaceae*

parviflora (So. Australia to New So. Wales), "Wilga" or "Austral. willow"; evergreen shrub or hardwooded small tree 3 to 8 m high, having sweeping branches with gracefully drooping, narrow, willow-like leaves 8-10 cm long, aromatic when crushed; blooming Winter and Spring with pendant clusters of small white to cream flowers; followed by fruit of shiny black seeds. *Zone 8*. *p. 861*

GEISSORHIZA   *Iridaceae*

rochensis (Cape Prov.), "Wine-cups"; a very pretty small cormous herb 15-22 cm high, with long-linear, ribbed, basal leaves; wiry stalks bear several wide cup-like flowers 3 cm across, the outer area satiny violet-blue, the base crimson, both colors separated by a thin white line. *Subtropic. Zone 9*. *p. 229*

GELSEMIUM   *Loganiaceae*

sempervirens (Virginia to Florida, Texas and Central America), "Carolina yellow jessamine" or "False jasmine"; sparry evergreen shrub with scandent or clambering brown branches reaching to 6 m; leathery glossy green ovate-lanceolate, opposite leaves 4 to 10 cm long; small flaring trumpet flowers 3 cm dia., yellow and sweetly fragrant like a tea rose blooming from December into Summer and later. *Warm temperate. Zone 7.*   p. 283

GENIPA   *Rubiaceae*

americana (Mexico to Perú and Brazil), "Marmalade box"; evergreen tropical tree to 10 m high, with smooth oblong obovate leaves 12-25 cm long; silky-white or pale yellow flowers 3 cm across, in axillary clusters; large greenish-white fruit 8 cm across, full of dark purple juice and rather acrid pulp; used in tropical America as a preserve called Genipot, and for making marmalade and drinks by Indians. *Zone 10.*   p. 854, 934

GENISTA   *Leguminosae*

hispanica (No. Spain, So. France, No. Italy), "Spanish gorse" or "Spanish broom"; very spiny deciduous small shrub 40-60 cm or more high, branchlets densely white-hairy; simple 1 cm leaves, the upper ones linear, lower down lanceolate; flowers pea-like, bright yellow in showy clusters terminating leafy shoots, blooming in profusion during June-July. *Zone 6.*   p. 759

lydia (spathulata) (E. Europe to Balkans; Anatolia, Syria); popular rockgarden plant especially in Great Britain; very free-flowering shrub to 60 cm high, with branches spine-tipped, and simple leaves linear or elliptic; yellow pea-flowers in profuse bloom during May and June, creating a mass of color. *Zone 7.*   p. 759

pilosa (Europe: Sweden, Italy, Balkans), "Sand broom" or "Silky-leaf woodwaxen"; prostrate shrub from 8 to 60 cm high, with procumbent silky-hairy shoots, forming a mat of interwoven rooting branches; simple oblong to elliptic 2 cm leaves hairy beneath; yellow pea-flowers silky outside, in short clusters on long stalks, blooming late Spring to July. *Zone 6.*   p. 759

sagittalis (Spain, Italy, Greece to W. Asia), "Winged broom"; deciduous prostrate shrub to 30 cm high, with inflorescence to 60 cm, having corky winged, and occasionally rooting evergreen branches; ovate, hairy leaves to 15 mm long; pea-like flowers in erect terminal racemes, with corollas yellow, and silky-hairy calyx, in June-July; develops into good groundcover. *Zone 5.*   p. 758

sylvestris (dalmatica) (S.E. Europe: Yugoslavia), "Dalmatian broom"; small spiny shrub to 20 cm, with slender green stems, the leaves simple, linear to narrow-lanceolate 1 cm long; profuse with deep yellow pea-flowers, the corolla with ovate standard, in terminal racemes to 10 cm long, blooming May-July; small flat, ovoid seedpod with curved beak. *Zone 6.*   p. 759

tinctoria (Europe and W. Asia, natural. in No. America), "Dyer's greenweed"; bushy deciduous shrub from a low 30 cm to 1 m high, with slender, striped branches, the small foliage bright green, elliptic-ovate to 3 cm long; flowers in dense terminal leafy racemes, the corolla rich yellow, blooming during Summer; followed by narrow-oblong seed-pods. The blossoms are used to produce a yellow dye. *Zone 2.*   p. 759

GENTIANA   *Gentianaceae*

acaulis (kochiana) (Europe: Alps and Pyrenees), "Blue gentian" of the Swiss Alps; very pretty low, tufted perennial to 10 cm high with narrow elliptic leaves and solitary 5-6 cm funnel-shaped flowers deep blue, in Spring. *Temperate. Zone 3.*   p. 416

angustifolia (Western Alps to Pyrenees), "Gentian"; slender-stemmed, stoloniferous Alpine perennial to 10 cm high, forming tufts; elliptic basal leaves 5 cm long, stem-leaves shorter; stalked, solitary 5 cm flowers funnel-shaped, deep sky-blue, pale inside, July blooming. *Zone 5.*   p. 416

asclepiadea (Alps of So. Europe; Caucasus), "Willow gentian"; tall perennial with arching leafy 60 cm stems, light green ovate leaves, and solitary, bell-shaped 4 cm flowers dark blue with pale stripes, and spotted purple inside. *Zone 5.*   p. 416

bavarica (Northern Alps), "Bavarian gentian"; small tufted perennial to 15 cm high, forming mats; short 1 cm obovate, thick basal leaves, stem leaves rounded; solitary saucer-shaped, deep blue flowers 2 cm across, with spreading obovate lobes, and funnel-shaped calyx; blooming July-August. *Zone 5.*   p. 416

clusii (acaulis var.) (Alps of E. France to Italian Dolomites, east to Yugoslavia), "Stemless gentian"; handsome species photographed in the Dolomites at 2000 m alt.; basal rosette of leathery, rich green, elliptic leaves with distinct center vein; flowers solitary without or very short stalk, the funnel-shaped corolla 5-6 cm long, deep blue with pale throat spotted green, blooming June to September. *Zone 4.*   p. 416

cruciata (C. Europe to W. Siberia, Caucasus, Asia Minor), "Cross gentian"; herbaceous, leafy perennial 15 to 40 cm high, with ovate,

3-nerved, 12 cm leaves forming rosettes; small flowers in terminal and axillary clusters, the bell-shaped corolla bluish-green to deep blue, 2-3 cm long, in Summer. *Zone 5.*   p. 416

cruciata var. phlogifolia (Eastern Europe to Carpathian Mts.); leafy perennial 30-45 cm high, with basal leaves 10 cm long, stem leaves shorter, and having rough margins; blue flowers in dense, mostly terminal heads, bell-shaped 2 cm long, July-blooming; differs from cruciata by the rounded corolla lobes. *Zone 5.*   p. 416

farreri (N.W. China: Kansu, to Tibet), "Kansu gentian"; stoloniferous, almost prostrate perennial having wiry branches dense with short linear leaves, and terminal large bell-flowers 6 cm long, the corolla sky-blue and marked white inside, and yellowish bands outside, blooming late Summer. *Zone 6.*   p. 417

germanica (Gentianella) (Alps to Italian Dolomites), "German gentian"; interesting perennial found in the Dolomites at 2800 m elevation, with branched, leafy stems to 30 cm high; basal leaves arranged in rosettes; the purple to lilac or whitish flowers 3 cm across, having a tubular, lacy-ciliate crown in center, and blooming from May to October. *Zone 6.*   p. 416

lutea (Pyrenees, Alps, Balkans, Asia Minor), "Yellow gentian"; leafy perennial 1-1½ m tall, ovate leaves blue-green; 2½ cm flowers in whorls on erect stalks, yellow, veined or spotted. *Temperate. Zone 5.*   p. 417, 421

parryi (Mts. of Wyoming, Colorado, Utah, Montana), "Rocky Mountain gentian"; herbaceous perennial with clustered, leafy stems, about 30 cm high; thick-fleshy, succulent oblong leaves 4 cm long, with rough margins; flowers in terminal or axillary heads, the blue corollas bell-shaped 3 cm long, in August-September. *Zone 4.* p. 416

scabra (No. China, Manchuria), "Rough gentian"; leafy perennial to 30 cm high, the ovate leaves in many pairs, having rough midrib and margins; flowers several in terminal clusters, with bell-shaped corolla dark blue, to 4 cm long, in August. *Zone 5.*   p. 416

septemfida (Asia Minor to Caucasus and Iran), "Crested gentian"; perennial with leafy stems 30 cm or more high, ovate, 5 to 7-nerved leaves 4-8 cm long; clustered bell-flowers 5 cm long, bluish-purple, summer-blooming. *Zone 3.*   p. 417

septemfida lagodechiana (Eastern Caucasus); prostrate, leafy perennial, with slender stems 20-40 cm long; cordate to ovate 3 cm leaves; solitary deep blue funnel flowers 4- cm long, pale outside and spotted green, autumn-blooming. Differs from septemfida by the branched floral stalks, short calyx tube with lobes contracted at base. *Zone 3.*   p. 416

sino-ornata (Yunnan, Tibet), "Chinese gentian"; prostrate perennial spreading by rooting stolons, dense with thin, pale green, lanceolate leaves 3 cm long; very ornamental with large, bright blue trumpet flowers 6 cm long, paler at base, and banded with purple, blooming from July to severe frost. *Zone 5.*   p. 416

thermalis: see GENTIANOPSIS thermalis

tibetica (Himalayas); robust mountain perennial 60 cm high, from a basal rosette of fleshy, broad lanceolate leaves to 30 cm long, the stem-leaves forming a tube around the stem, the uppermost enclosing the inflorescence; the numerous flowers at apex greenish-white and tubular funnel-shaped. *Zone 6.*   p. 417

verna (Europe: Alps and Pyrenees), "Spring gentian"; very pretty low, tufted perennial to 10 cm high with narrow elliptic leaves and solitary 5 cm, funnel-shaped flowers deep blue, in Spring. Found in Swiss Alps to 3500 m alt. *Temperate. Zone 5.*   p. 417

GENTIANELLA   *Gentianaceae*

diemensis (Australia: New So. Wales and Tasmania); low, floriferous subshrubby alpine perennial of Mt. Kosciusko Nat'l Park above tree-line, in New South Wales; forming tufts of narrow linear, grass-like leaves; the cupped star-flowers white, the petals lined with purple. *Zone 6.*   p. 424

GENTIANOPSIS   *Gentianaceae*

thermalis (Gentiana elegans or thermalis) (Arizona to Wyoming and Canada), "Fringed gentian"; slender annual or short-lived perennial to 30 cm high, with obovate basal leaves, and solitary bell-flowers, having deep blue corolla streaked lighter blue, 5 cm long and with 4 beautifully fringed lobes. *Zone 8.*   p. 417

GERANIUM   *Geraniaceae*

argenteum (Italy: Alps to Apennines), "Silver-leaved cranesbill"; small biennial or perennial to 12 cm high, with leaves nearly all basal, white-silky on both surfaces, 5 to 7-parted into linear segments; showy flowers 3 cm across, pink with darker veins, in June-July. *Zone 8*   p. 418

cinereum (Pyrenees of Spain); small perennial to 15 cm high, with deeply 5 to 6-lobed leaves, white-glaucous and finely hairy; large pink flowers with red stripes, 2 cm across, throughout Summer. *Zone 6.*   p. 418

dalmaticum (Yugoslavia); perennial similar to macrorrhizum, but smaller, having stems more slender, the roundish leaves deeply lobed and pale beneath; small clusters of lovely 2 cm flowers with rose-pink petals; foliage turns red and yellow in Autumn. *Zones 4-10.*   *p. 419*

endressii (Pyrenees); beautiful mountain perennial to 40 cm high, with palmately divided firm leaves, the lobes sharply toothed at margins; floral stalks each bearing two light rose flowers faintly veined, 1 cm across, during Mid-summer. *Zone 6.*   *p. 418*

grandiflorum hort. (himalayense: Hortus 3) (Sikkim); branching perennial 30 cm high, with roundish ample leaves deeply 5-lobed and toothed; the 4 cm flowers characteristic with 5 equal petals and 10 stamens, lilac with purple veins. Zander 1984 lists as G. meeboldii. *Zone 3.*   *p. 418*

macrorrhizum (Italy to Balkans), "Bigroot geranium"; attractive aromatic perennial with long, thick roots; hairy, forked stems woody at base, to 50 cm high; the leaves palmately 5-lobed, on long petioles, the lobes toothed at apex; terminal, branched inflorescence of bright purple flowers 2½ cm across, in May to July. *Zone 4.*   *p. 418*

maculatum (Maine to Georgia and Kansas), "Wild geranium" or "Spotted geranium"; handsome perennial of open habit about 45 cm high, with hairy, forked stem; leaves palmately 3 to 5-parted, the broad segments spotted and deeply toothed; purplish-rose 3 cm flowers blooming May to Summer. *Zone 4.*   *p. 418*

maderense (Madeira); robust perennial to 1 m high, having stout stem, densely set with long-stalked leaves, the petioles reddish and to 50 cm long; leaf blades 30 cm dia., palmately dissected and lobed; the branched inflorescence bearing numerous flowers 4 cm across, carmine-pink with violet center. *Zone 9.*   *p. 419*

malviflorum (Mediterranean reg.); tuberous-rooted perennial to 45 cm high; the broad, hairy leaves divided into 7-9 narrow, dentate lobes; flowers purplish-rose, the petals lobed at apex, and striped with red. *Zone 8.*   *p. 419*

palmatum (anemonifolium) (Canary Isl., Madeira); charming perennial to 40 cm high; the leaves palmately divided at base, the lobes pinnately arranged and toothed, fern-like, on long petioles; the pretty, purplish-rose flowers marked with crimson-red in center; July to September blooming. *Zone 9.*   *p. 419*

platypetalum (ibericum var.) (Caucasus to Armenia, Iran); handsome perennial 30 to 60 cm high, the leaves roundish in outline, deeply 5-7 parted, the lobes rhombic and dentate; inflorescence clustered, with flowers 4 cm across, light to dark purple, the petals shaded and lined violet toward base. *Zone 3.*   *p. 419*

psilostemon (armenum) (Armenia); clustering perennial to 75 cm high, the lower leaves 15-20 cm wide, deeply divided, with segments lobed again fern-like; the branched inflorescence with flowers rich red, 3 cm across, and with black spot at base, summer-blooming. *Zone 5.*   *p. 418*

renardii (Caucasus Mts.); attractive clump-forming perennial 15-30 cm high, the velvety olive-green leaves palmately 5-lobed and silvery-silky beneath; loose clusters of pale pink flowers having violet veins, blooming Mid-summer. *Zone 6.*   *p. 418*

sanguineum (Europe to Caucasus, Armenia), "Blood-geranium"; handsome perennial to 50 cm high, wide-spreading with trailing, white-hairy, slender branches; opposite, roundish leaves 6 cm across, deeply lobed and toothed, turning blood-red in Autumn; flowers deep purple to nearly crimson, 4 cm across, blooming May to August in profusion. *Zones 4-10.*   *p. 419*

subcaulescens (cinereum var.) (Italy to Balkans, Lebanon); small almost stemless perennial forming mounds, with hairy, glaucous deeply lobed leaves, and 3 cm flowers bright rose with red center, blooming June-July *Zone 7.*   *p. 418*

sylvaticum (No. Europe to W. Siberia, Asia Minor), "Woods cranesbill"; perennial with creeping rootstock, to 75 cm high; leaves roundish, 12 cm across, palmately divided into 7 obovate sections, cut and toothed at apex; rosy-purple flowers 2 cm across, bearded on claw; June-July blooming. *Zone 5.*   *p. 419*

wallichianum (Temp. Himalayas); prostrate herbaceous perennial, with purplish stems covered by silky hairs; the broad-cordate leaves 5-lobed, the lobes broadly wedge-shaped, pointed and silky-hairy; lovely 5 cm flowers light purple with white center, blooming August-September. *Zone 6.*   *p. 418*

GERBERA   *Compositae*

jamesonii (Transvaal), "African daisy" or "Transvaal daisy"; herbaceous tufted perennial with pinnately lobed leaves very woolly beneath; long-lasting flowers 8-10 cm across, daisy-like with slender, usually orange-flame colored florets, but also in shades from brick-red to yellow and white; blooming May to frost in North Lat., in So. Africa habitat November to May. *Zones 8-10.*   *p. 389*

x jamesonii hybrida (jamesonii x viridifolia), "Giant African daisy"; superior perennial hybrid strain developed since 1888 at the Cambridge Botanic Garden, continued by Veitch in England and Vilmorin in France, also Haage in Erfurt, Germany 1891; resulting in elegant, large flowers to 12 and 15 cm across, in colors red, bronze, yellow and white, on stiff stalks to 60 cm or more long. Long lasting as a cut flower. *Zone 9.*   *p. 389*

GESNERIA   *Gesneriaceae*

cuneifolia (Pentarhaphia reticulata) (Cuba, Puerto Rico, Hispaniola), "Firecracker"; low-growing rosette of leathery, glossy grass-green, long wedge-shaped leaves with toothed margins; and tubular somewhat bottle-shaped flowers burning red, yellow inside, borne singly on short stalks. *Humid-tropical Zone 12.*   *p. 66*

GEUM   *Rosaceae*

coccineum (So. Europe, Asia Minor), "Scarlet avens"; perennial herb, with pinnate or lyrate basal leaves, the large roundish terminal leaflet rough-hairy, corrugated and with crenate margins, 8-12 cm across; the erect floral stalks with small leaves, to 50 cm or more high, topped by glowing red flowers, 3 cm dia., in center an orange-yellow stamen cluster; spring-blooming; followed by bristly fruit. *Zone 6.*   *p. 493*

quellyon (chiloense hort.) (Chile), "Chilean avens"; charming floriferous herbaceous perennial 25-50 cm high; leaves rounded in outline, lobed or divided into 3 segments, the terminal lobe crenate; long-stalked flowers 3-4 cm across, brilliant scarlet or copper colored, the filaments orange or red, blooming May-July; followed by feathery fruit. *Zone 6.*   *p. 493*

triflorum (Ontario to Illinois, Nebraska and Montana), "Avens"; herbaceous perennial of the Western prairies, 20-40 cm high, soft-hairy; basal leaves pinnate with leaflets cut and toothed; the flowers often 3 on branched stalk, with sepals purple, the petals straw-colored to purplish, oblong and not spreading, to 5 cm long, July-blooming; feathery in fruit. *Zone 6.*   *p. 493*

GIBASIS   *Commelinaceae*

schiedeana (geniculata) (Jamaica); in hort. trade as Tradescantia multiflora, the "Tahitian bridal veil"; small free-branching creeper with string-like stem, narrow shining olive-green 2½ to 5 cm leaves purplish beneath; tiny white flowers. *Tropical. Zone 11.*   *p. 308*

GIBBAEUM   *Aizoaceae*

dispar (Cape Prov.); cluster-forming growth of 2 unequal succulent oval leaves somewhat keeled, gray-green with velvety touch; flowers lilac-pink, 2½ cm across. *Zone 10.*   *p. 153*

GIGANTOCHLOA   *Gramineae*

apus (Bambusa apus) (India to Java); large tropical bamboo to 20 m high, forming clusters of stiff green canes to 10 cm diameter, densely covered with hairs; the culms with straw-colored, deciduous sheaths; large pendant, lanceolate leaves 30 cm long, very decorative. Used for structural purposes in S.E. Asia; young shoots are edible. *Zone 10.*   *p. 552*

verticillata (Bambusa) (Malacca, Malaya to Java); majestic clump-forming tropical bamboo, with rhizomes producing dense clusters of culms 15 m or more high, and 10-12 cm dia., nodding at apex; the internodes green, at first with dark hairs, later smooth; clusters of branchlets from joints; the leaves large and with prominent parallel veins, about 20 cm long; important source of building material and edible shoots in Malaysia. *Zone 10.*   *p. 552*

GILIA   *Polemoniaceae*

aggregata: see IPOMOPSIS aggregata

capitata (Brit. Columbia to Calif. and Idaho), "Globe gilia"; attractive annual to 60 cm or more high, with 10 cm leaves twice pinnate into linear segments; funnel-flowers light blue, with 2 cm corollas, in dense clusters topping the floral stalk, blooming during Summer. *Zone 8.*   *p. 466*

micrantha: see LINANTHUS androsaceus (micranthus)
multiflora, rubra: see IPOMOPSIS multiflora

GILIBERTIA trifida: see DENDROPANAX trifidus

GILLENIA   *Clethraceae*

trifoliata (Spiraea trifoliata hort.) (New York, Ontario, Michigan to Alabama), "Indian physic" or "Bowman's-root"; woodland perennial 60-80 cm high; compound leaves of 3 toothed leaflets; longstalked, star-shaped white flowers 2½ cm across in loose clusters; after petals drop, the persistent calyx enlarges and becomes red and very decorative. *Zone 4.*   *p. 367*

GINKGO   *Ginkgoaceae*

biloba (China), the "Maidenhair-tree"; deciduous resinous tree to 40 m high; perhaps the most ancient existing flowering plant, sole survivor of an extinct race of the carbon age. Woody trunk with gray, corky bark, and broad fan-like leathery grayish-green leaves 5-8 cm across, with parallel veining; flowers without petals in catkins, male and female on separate trees; grown in pots as dwarfed bonsai in Japan. The kernels or ginkgo nuts are much eaten in the Orient. *Temperate. Zone 4.*   *p. 733*

biloba 'Fastigiata' (S.E. China), "Sentry Maidenhair"; an elegant, space-saving cultivar, with branches growing stiffy erect, forming a narrow pyramidal or columnar head; the fan-shaped green leaves 3 to 10 cm wide, turning yellow in Autumn, and create a golden carpet where they fall. Leaf shape and veining resemble Maidenhair fern (Adiantum). Ginkgo were formerly classified amongst the Conifers, but now considered of a more ancient order. *Zone 4.*   p. 733

biloba 'Gold Maiden'; very handsome form with the broad, fan-like leathery leaves golden-yellow over green, in sunny contrast against a blue California sky. *Zone 5.*   p. 733

GLADIOLUS   *Iridaceae*
byzantinus (communis ssp.) (Mediterr. region); robust cormous perennial herb to 90 cm high, forming 3 to 5 basal sword-shaped leaves; stiff leafy floral stems bearing loose multiflowered spikes of purple blooms, the lower 3 segments having central white line. *Zone 8.*   p. 227

x colvillei (cardinalis x tristis and others), "Coronado hybrid"; striking gladiolus of small habit to 75 cm high, with branching stems bearing 6-8 graceful flowers each, to 6-8 cm across, white with crimson-red elliptic design on upper segments; stamens white. *Subtropic. Zone 8.*   p. 227

communis (Mediterr. region to Caucasus), "Sword lily"; perennial with cormous base and sword-shaped leaves, parent of many garden hybrids; in its native habitat with leafy stems to 60 cm high, carrying loose spikes of bright purple bell-flowers, the flaring segments 6 cm long. May to July blooming in Europe. *Zone 8.*   p. 227

x hortulanus (South Africa), "Painted lady" or "Garden gladiolus"; strong floriferous plant, descendent of numerous So. African species including natalensis and primulinus; bulb-like corm with basal flattened, sword-shaped leaves in ranks; showy wide-open funnel-flowers with rounded petals, 10 cm or more across, in wide color range white, buff, yellow, orange, salmon, reds, rose, purple; on stiff fleshy spike 60 to 90 cm long, the buds opening flower after flower, and an excellent long-lasting cut flower. *Subtropic. Zone 9.*   p. 227

x hortulanus nanus 'D'Artagnan', "Butterfly gladiolus"; of dwarf habit, with 50 cm spikes bearing 6 to 10 smallish but very attractive flowers to 6 cm across, white with blood red blotches on lower segments. One of many named cultivars originated in Holland, and widely used as cut flowers in Europe. *Subtropic. Zone 9.*   p. 227

murieliae: see ACIDANTHERA murieliae

segetum (Mediterranean reg.), the "Corn-flag"; slender plant 40-50 cm high, with 2-4 leaves 30 cm long; flowers on zigzag stalks, in loose clusters, funnel-shaped with flaring segments bright purplish-rose, 4 cm across face, inside with white central line outlined in violet. *Zone 8.*   p. 227

tristis (Natal); "Marsh-Afrikander" cormous plant 60 cm high, with 3 terete, ribbed leaves; fragrant curved tubular trumpet flowers yellowish-white with purplish on the keels, in a loose, strongly one-sided spike; Summer. *Zone 8.*   p. 227

GLAUCIDIUM   *Ranunculaceae*
palmatum (Japan: Hokkaido, Honshu; also China), "Shirane" of the mountains; attractive perennial with unbranched stem from short, thick rhizome, bearing 2 or 3 kidney-shaped leaves 10-30 cm across, 4 to 7 lobed to middle and toothed; showy flowers with rose to pale mauve petal-like sepals to 5 cm long, during April-May. *Zone 6.*   p. 488

GLAUCIUM   *Papaveraceae*
corniculatum (Europe, S.W. Asia), "Horned poppy" or "Sea poppy"; handsome biennial or annual herb, 25-40 cm high, with orange-colored sap, the oblong, hairy leaves lobed or divided; large 6 cm poppy-like red flowers, often with black in center, blooming in June to August. *Zone 9.*   p. 466

flavum (W. Europe, Mediterr. area to Turkey), "Horned poppy"; glaucous annual, biennial or perennial with wiry stems 60 cm or more high; basal leaves pinnate and hairy, higher up lobed, and sessile; delicate yellow or orange poppy-like flowers 5 cm across, summer-blooming; followed by bristly pods 30 cm long; the seeds yield illuminating oil. *Zone 9.*   p. 467

GLECHOMA   *Labiatae*
hederacea, better known as Nepeta hederacea (Europe, Asia), naturalized in North America, "Gill-over-the-ground"; small, lively creeper useful as ground cover or for baskets, the hairy, kidney-shaped leaves light green, crenate at the margins, 2-4 cm across, and rooting at the nodes; small light blue flowers. *Temperate. Zone 3.*   p. 315

hederacea 'Variegata' (Nepeta), "Variegated ground-ivy"; very attractive small mat-forming herbaceous spreader, with thin, string-like creeping or pendulous stems, opposite little rounded leaves 4 cm across, milky green, with scalloped margins, and more or less variegated toward outer edge. An ideal and charming basket plant. *Zones 3-10.*   p. 315

GLEDITSIA   *Leguminosae*
triacanthos (Eastern U.S.), "Honey locust"; formidable deciduous tree to 40 m high, covered by stiff single or 3-branched spines 10 cm long; with spreading branches; pinnate leaves consisting of oval leaflets in 10-14 pairs, some bipinnate; foliage turns yellow in Autumn; the flowers inconspicuous, followed on fruiting trees by elongate curling seed pods to 40 cm long. *Zone 4.*   p. 762

triacanthos inermis, "Thornless honey-locust"; rapidly growing medium sized deciduous tree to 20 m high, of more slender, open habit than the species, with upright and arching branches, bearing rather small pinnately compound finely divided leaves creating a light, airy effect; similar to the species but almost entirely without thorns. The var. **aurea** has leaves tinted yellow and coppery especially in Autumn. Very popular as a satisfactory deeply-rooted street tree. The patented cultivar 'Shademaster' is a vigorous variety to 10 m or more high, of more upright growth with dark green foliage, and long-lived. *Zone 4.*   p. 762

triacanthos inermis 'Sunburst', "Golden thornless honey locust" (Patented 1954); excellent graceful, deciduous shade tree with growth to 12 m high, the golden tipped fern-like foliage is especially prominent during the early growing season. To maintain true strain, perpetuating thornless habit, and male trees without seed pods which may be unwanted, young wood is grafted and budded on understock of G. triacanthus. *Zone 4.*   p. 762

GLIRICIDIA   *Leguminosae*
sepium (Central America, Colombia), "Madre de cacao"; ornamental tropical tree to 9 m, with pinnate leaves; clusters of flowers pinkish-lilac with white in profusion before the leaves; pods to 12 cm long; a favorite shade tree for coffee and cacao plantations. *Zone 10.*   p. 760

GLOBULARIA   *Globulariaceae*
cordifolia (So. Europe: Pyrenees to Balkans), "Heartleaf globularia"; prostrate evergreen subshrubby perennial forming mounds to 15 cm high, with much-branched stems; basal rosettes of obovate leathery, dark green leaves 3 cm long; lacy blue globular floral heads 3 cm dia., the flowers arranged around a dark central cone, and having upper lips divided into linear lobes; May-June blooming. *Zone 9.*   p. 423

nudicaulis (alpina) (Pyrenees of Spain to Alps and Yugoslavia), "Globe daisy"; evergreen perennial 25 cm high, with thick rootstock; obovate glossy green, leathery basal leaves to 20 cm long in rosettes; floral stalks topped by small globular heads 4 cm dia., composed of tiny blue flowers around central disc, blooming June-July. *Zone 9.*   p. 423

trichosantha (E. Bulgaria, Turkey, Crimea, Asia Minor), "Syrian globularia"; herbaceous perennial to 20 cm high, with rooting stolons forming clusters; obovate leathery basal leaves bluish-green, forming rosettes; floral stalks with linear leaves; and bearing solitary heads 2 cm across of small light blue flowers, around the deep blue crown-disc; May-June blooming. *Zone 7.*   p. 423

GLORIOSA   *Liliaceae*
rothschildiana (Kenya, Uganda), "Glory lily"; a climbing "Lily" with tuberous roots, the fresh green, lanceolate leaves prolonged into tendrils; striking flowers with broad, recurved petals crimson-scarlet, golden-yellow toward base; blooms early Spring on, but can be flowered anytime. I remember this growing north of Mombasa, clambering over coastal jungle. *Tropical. Zone 11.*   p. 242, 282

simplex (virescens, plantii, greenei) (No. Uganda, Mozambique, Zaire, Fernando Po), a dwarf "Glory lily"; with broader petals, not crisped, and which I first saw in Surinam where, in the shade of trees, it is a clear yellow, while in sunlight, the petals turn orange; summer-blooming. *Tropical. Zones 10-11.*   p. 282

superba (India, Sri Lanka), "Crisped glory lily" or "Malabar gloriosa"; tall vining herb blooming late Summer to Fall only, flowers are smaller, with narrow but crisped petals, to 8 cm long, first green, then yellow, changing to orange-red; at its best into Autumn. *Tropical. Zone 10.*   p. 239, 281, 282

GLOTTIPHYLLUM   *Aizoaceae*
fragrans (Mesembryanthemum) (Cape Prov.); low succulent forking with fleshy, twisted, tongue-shaped leaves flat on top, keeled beneath, 6-8 cm long; flowers 8-10 cm across, shining golden-yellow and sweetly scented. *Arid-subtropic. Zones 9-10.*   p. 146

linguiforme (So. Africa), "Green tongue leaf"; small, branching succulent with tongue-shaped, soft-fleshy leaves 5 to 8 cm long, glossy green; ray-flowers golden-yellow. *Zones 9-10.*   p. 146

GLOXINIA: see SINNINGIA

GLYCERIA   *Gramineae*
maxima 'Variegata' (aquatica hort.) (No. temp. zones of Europe and Asia), "Manna grass"; handsome waterside or aquatic, deciduous perennial, spreading by stolons; erect, smooth culms to 1 m or more

high; the showy leaves to 50 cm long and 5 cm wide, brilliantly striped with white or pale yellow; the inflorescence a branched, elongate panicle, green tinged yellow or purple, during June to August. Amongst finest of variegated garden grasses. *Zone 5.* p. 560

GLYCINE *Leguminosae*
clandestina (Australia, except North. Ter.), "Twining glycine"; woody-stemmed climber to 1 metre or more; compound leaves of 3 leaflets; from the upper axils rises the inflorescence, in clusters of up to 20 lovely lavender to purple pea flowers, followed by straight, narrow pods. *Zones 9-10.* p. 278
multijuga: see WISTERIA floribunda

GLYCYRRHIZA *Leguminosae*
glabra (C. Europe, Spain, Mediterranean reg.), "Licorice" or "Sweet-wood"; perennial with sweet, woody rootstock inside yellow and which furnishes licorice; erect stem to 1½ m high with vivid-green pinnate leaves 20 cm long; small pale blue pea-flowers in axillary raceme. Used to flavor cough medicines and candy. Cultivated by the ancient Egyptians. *Zone 9.* p. 530

GLYPTOSTROBUS *Taxodiaceae (Coniferae)*
lineatus (pensilis) (S.E. China), "Chinese water pine"; small deciduous buttressed tree, usually at water's edge, with brown, split-barked trunk; coniferous needles linear and flat on sterile branches, scale-like on fertile ones; 2 cm ovoid cones. *Zone 4.* p. 612

GMELINA *Verbenaceae*
hystrix (Philippines), "Hedgehog"; spiny climbing shrub with habit of bougainvillea; elliptic leaves 8 cm long, glaucous beneath; large yellow flowers obliquely 2-lipped bell-shaped, in 8 cm cones with large reddish purple bracts. *Tropical. Zones 10-11.* p. 899
philippensis (philippinensis) (Philippines) "Bulang" or "Snap-dragon tree"; interesting tropical tree, partially deciduous, 8 to 20 m high, with long-petioled ovate leaves to 10 cm, smooth beneath; flowers brownish-yellow, 2-3 cm across, in pendant cones 30 cm long, composed of shingled triangular purplish bracts which shield the emerging flowers. *Zones 10-11.* p. 899

GNIDIA *Thymelaeaceae*
polystachya (carinata) (So. Africa); graceful evergreen shrub to 2 m high, the stems appressed hairy; linear leaves 1-2 cm long; orange-yellow to rose flowers densely packed in rounded clusters, their corolla tube hairy, the limb 1 cm across, blooming in Spring. *Zones 9-10.* p. 892

GODETIA: see CLARKIA

GOETHEA *Malvaceae*
cauliflora (Brazil); evergreen shrub 45 cm high; erect woody stems with large decorative oval leaves; flowers minute but their waxy calyx showy with 4-6 segments yellowish and scarlet-red, developing from leafless stems or old wood. *Zone 10.* p. 781
strictiflora (Brazil); small tropical shrub with long-ovate, crenate leaves tinted red; the inflorescence axillary or directly out of woody stems, with bracts 2 cm long and beautifully glowing crimson, longer than the white petals. *Zone 10.* p. 781

GOLDFUSSIA anisophyllus: see STROBILANTHES anisophyllus

GOMPHRENA *Amaranthaceae*
globosa (India), "Globe amaranth"; erect annual branching herb with elliptic leaves ciliate at edge, and strawy clover-like flower heads which, if cut just before maturity, are "everlasting", retaining their color, usually white, to purple, for a long time. *Tropical. Zone 10.* p. 340

GONIOLIMON *Plumbaginaceae*
tataricum (Statice tataricum, Limonium) (So. Europe to Caucasus), "Shore lilac"; gorgeous feathery mound of tiny rose-pink flowers, carried on multiple branchlets, rising 50 cm or more and spreading 1 m wide from the woody base of this evergreen perennial, having tufted leathery basal leaves to 15 cm long, blooming in July. *Zone 5.* p. 472

GONIOPHLEBIUM subauriculatum (Zander): see POLYPODIUM subauriculatum (Hortus 3)

GONIOTHALAMUS *Annonaceae*
amuyon (Uvaria) (So. Taiwan, Philippines); small evergreen tree or shrub to 5 m high; smooth leathery elliptic leaves to 12 cm long; flowers axillary or above leaf-scars, yellowish green and sweetly fragrant, having 6 petals and displaying numerous stamens; orange-yellow ellipsoid 12 mm edible, sweet fruit containing 1 or 2 seeds which can be used medicinally. *Zone 10.* p. 906

GONOCARYUM *Icacinaceae*
pyriforme (Indonesia, Moluccas, Java); small tropical tree 5-12 m high, with alternate leathery broad-elliptic leaves edged white, about 10 cm long; small white flowers in pendant racemes 20 cm long; globular to oblong stone-fruit 5 cm thick, turning shining orange-red when ripe; beautiful with its numerous brilliantly colored fruit. *Zones 10-11.* p. 739

GORDONIA *Theaceae*
lasianthus (No. Carolina to Mississippi), "Black laurel"; tall evergreen tree to 30 m high; with leathery elliptic, dark green and glossy leaves to 15 cm long, serrate in upper half; axillary, solitary flowers white, 6 cm across and with prominent yellow anthers. *Zones 7-9.* p. 888

GOSSYPIUM *Malvaceae*
herbaceum (Arabia, Asia Minor), "Levant-cotton"; annual little-branched subshrub to 1 m, with thin-leathery, palmately 5-7 lobed leaves, and showy yellow flowers with purple center; capsular fruits or "bolls" whose seed coats bear fleece or lint, furnishing cotton of commerce. *Zone 10.* p. 457, 781
sturtianum (No. Australia), "Desert rose"; tropical evergreen shrub 1-2 m high, having many black-tubercled stems, with rounded and ovate leaves; the flowers hibiscus-like, 8-10 cm across, pale lilac or mauve with red-purple center; followed by small ovoid fruit capsules. Floral emblem of the Northern Territory. *Zone 10.* p. 781

GRAMMATOPHYLLUM *Orchidaceae*
scriptum (measuresianum) (Moluccas); attractive epiphyte of relative small size in the genus, with stem-like ribbed pseudobulb some 60 cm high bearing strap-shaped leathery leaves, and basal raceme 60-90 cm long with many 8 cm waxy flowers, the spreading oblong sepals and petals canary yellow blotched all over with brown and gold, (Summer). *Tropical. Zone 12.* p. 89

GRAPTOPETALUM *Crassulaceae*
bellum (Zander): see TACITUS bellus, as in Hortus 3
paraguayense, also known by its synonym Sedum weinbergii (Mexico), "Ghost plant" or "Mother-of-pearl plant"; branching succulent loose rosette forming thick stem and fleshy, broad 5-8 cm leaves flat and somewhat recurved on surface, keeled beneath, amethyst-gray with silvery bloom; branched inflorescence with 2 cm white flowers. The foliage has a subtle opalescent blending of colors, but the leaves are brittle and drop easily when handled. *Arid-subtropic. Zones 9-10.* p. 186.

GRAPTOPHYLLUM *Acanthaceae*
pictum (hortense) (South East Asia), "Caricature plant"; dense evergreen shrub to 2½ m high, with leathery elliptic leaves 10-15 cm long, deep green variegated creamy-white along central area; crimson-red flowers. *Tropical. Zone 10.* p. 18, 629

GRATIOLA *Scrophulariaceae*
officinalis (Europe to Asia), "Herb of grace"; herbaceous perennial, related to Mimulus, to 30 cm high; narrow-lanceolate leaves, mostly on the numerous stiff-wiry stems, bearing a multitude of small white, tubular flowers, having 2-lipped corolla, the upper lip notched, the lower 3-cleft, during May. *Zone 6.* p. 508

GREIGIA *Bromeliaceae*
sphacelata (Chile); large clustering terrestrial plant with narrow strap-like, soft-leathery, decurved leaves 3 cm wide, and 1 to 2 m long, glossy green, the margins serrate with brown spines; inflorescence in heads near base with greenish bracts and rose flowers; fruit a large white berry, edible and tasting like apple. *Zone 10.* p. 48

GREVILLEA *Proteaceae*
aquifolium (Victoria, New South Wales), "Holly grevillea"; evergreen shrub 1 to 3 m high, spreading 2 to 5 m wide; dense with rigid holly-like leaves to 8 cm long, armed with spines on triangular lobes; the showy inflorescence on short terminal branches, forming a one-sided green toothbrush-like raceme with long curved styles protruding in glowing crimson-red. *Zone 9.* p. 822
banksii (Queensland), "Scarlet grevillea"; small tree 4½-6 m high, hairy branches with pinnate leaves to 25 cm long, segments linear and white-silky beneath; bright coral-red flowers downy outside, in dense, one-sided clusters. *Zone 10.* p. 822
'Canberra' (juniperina x rosmarinifolia); handsome Australian hybrid shrub to 2 m or more high, of erect habit; the slender branches with narrow linear leaves 2-3 cm long; the flowers rich coral-red with lightly curved corolla tube and reflexed style column; primarily spring-blooming. *Zone 9.* p. 822
juniperina (sulphurea) (New South Wales, Victoria), "Juniper grevillea"; bushy shrub to 2 m high, with sharp-pointed linear needle-leaves, 2-3 cm long; the inflorescence is silky-hairy with pale yellow suffused with orange-red tubular flowers having reflexed lobes, in terminal clusters, the curving styles scarlet and tipped with yellow, blooming May-June. *Zone 9.* p. 822

'Noellii' (rosmarinifolia cultivar of California origin); low evergreen shrub to about 1 m high and spreading as wide; with fine needle-like green foliage on graceful branches; leaves 2-3 cm long; curious pink flowers with cream-white corolla, blooming in Spring. More compact than rosmarinifolia. *Zone 8.* p. 822

robusta (Queensland, New South Wales), "Silk oak"; daintily lacy, ornamental plant while small, but growing into a mighty tree 45 m high; silvery downy shoots with fern-like, green leaves, 2-pinnate into finely lobed segments silky-haired, giving them a grayish appearance; flowers golden-yellow to coral-salmon in one-sided racemes to 10 cm long. *Zone 9.* p. 822

rosmarinifolia (New Caledonia, New South Wales), "Rosemary grevillea"; evergreen densely branched shrub to 2 m high, the branchlets thin-wiry, with slender needle-like leaves to 3 cm long, dark green above and gray beneath, reminding of Rosemary; flowers mostly axillary, red with pink in curved corolla 2 cm long; very variable in coloring. Used in California for hedges. *Zone 9.* p. 822

thelemanniana (W. Australia), "Orange spider-flower"; showy shrub with bipinnate silky, bluish leaves divided into linear segments; flowers with rosy-red tube and yellowish-green recurved lobes, and long, curving 2½ cm red style. *Zone 9.* p. 822

GREWIA　　Tiliaceae

caffra (So. Africa), "Lavender star-bush"; spreading evergreen shrub to 2-3 m high, dense with small oval waxy, moss-green leaves with finely crenate margins, 6-8 cm long; charming starry flowers soft lavender pink with prominent yellow stamens in center, 4 cm across; larger and more perfectly shaped flowers than the similar G. occidentalis. *Subtropic. Zone 10.* p. 892

GREYIA　　Melianthaceae

radlkoferi (Transvaal), "Mountain bottle brush"; bushy shrub to 12 m; with big, fleshy-herbaceous, downy, bronzed foliage, deeply toothed; terminal erect raceme of glossy scarlet-red, cup-shaped flowers. *Subtropic. Zones 9-10.* p. 788

sutherlandii (Natal, Transvaal), "Natal bottle-brush"; small tree with deciduous, broad, deeply toothed, smooth leaves to 8 cm; inflorescence brush-like, bright scarlet, with conspicuous purplish-red filaments. *Zones 9-10.* p. 788

GRINDELIA　　Compositae

chiloensis (Argentina), "Gum plant"; clammy biennial or perennial with woody base, to 60 cm high; obovate leaves to 10 cm long, serrate at margins; flowers to 8 cm across, the disc orange-yellow, and ray-florets bright yellow; covered before opening with thick sticky varnish; blooming July, August. *Zone 9.* p. 390

GRISELINIA　　Cornaceae

littoralis (New Zealand), "Kupuka tree"; evergreen shrub or tree 6 to 15 m high, with leathery, broadly ovate, glossy green leaves 5-10 cm long; the minute petalled flowers 5 mm across, the males yellow, females green, in clusters 8 cm long, blooming November to January in New Zealand; the fruit is a greenish berry. *Zone 7.* p. 695

GUADUA angustifolia is now BAMBUSA guadia (Soderstrom Smithsonian 1985 and Stover)

GUAIACUM　　Zygophyllaceae

officinale (West Indies, N. So. America), "Lignum-vitae tree"; to 10 m high, with trunk of very hard, heavy, greenish-brown, resinous wood; glossy pinnate leaves with 5 cm leaflets in 2 to 3 pairs; small blue flowers at ends of twigs. *Zone 10.* p. 901, 902

sanctum (So. Florida, W. Indies, Mexico, to No. South America), "Palo de Vida Santo" or "Lignum vitae"; ornamental evergreen shrub or small tree, sometimes to 8 m high, of very hard, resinous wood; handsome glossy green, opposite, pinnate leaves to 10 cm long, the leathery leaflets oval, and smaller than in G. officinale; at branchtips large clusters of felty blue flowers, followed by angled 2 cm orange-yellow fruit. The commercially valuable wood is dark brown with black streaks, and is so heavy that it sinks in water. *Tropical. Zone 10.* p. 902

GUNNERA　　Haloragidaceae (Gunneraceae)

chilensis: see G. tinctoria

magellanica (Patagonia, Falkland Is.); low, stoloniferous perennial 12 cm high forming carpets; leaves orbicular or reniform, forming cups, and with margins crenate, on long petioles; small greenish flowers on nearly globose heads, the female spikes very short and hidden amongst leaves. *Zones 9-10.* p. 330

manicata (So. Brazil), "Prickly rhubarb"; the largest species with huge leaves to 2 m across, palmately lobed, more kidney-shaped than chilensis; hard, rough puckered, light green with buff veining, on thick light brown stalks with thorn-like prickly hairs. *Subtropic. Zones 8-10.* p. 330

tinctoria (chilensis) (scabra) (Chile, Patagonia, Ecuador, Colombia), "Chilean rhubarb"; large perennial herb with creeping

rhizome and dark green hard, puckered leaves to 1½ m diameter, palmately and deeply cut into pointed and toothed lobes, on reddish stalks with fleshy green spines; the inflorescence spikes with branches short and thick, while they are long in manicata. *Zones 7-10.* p. 330, 425

GUZMANIA　　Bromeliaceae

conifera (Caraguata) (Perú and Ecuador); showy rosette growing epiphytic or terrestrial in rainforest 1500 m alt.; green leaves 60-80 cm long, covered both sides with gray-brown scales; inflorescence elongate cylindric to 10 to 20 cm long, dense with bright red bracts tipped yellow; flowers yellow. *Zone 11.* p. 46

lingulata 'Major' (Broadview), "Scarlet star"; magnificent clone of a plant collected in Ecuador; epiphytic rosette of smooth, metallic green leaves, from the center of which rises the bold inflorescence of recurving, glossy-leathery bracts in vivid scarlet-red, its center with short waxy, incurved red bracts tipped yellow, and white flowers; the scape leaves typically red at base. *Tropical. Zone 11.* p. 44

monostachia (tricolor) (W. Indies, C. America, to Brazil), "Striped torch"; formal rosette of thin-leathery bayonet shaped yellow-green leaves; inflorescence a stiff spike with bracts salmon-red striped brown, and white flowers. *Tropical. Zone 11.* p. 46

sanguinea (crateriflora) (C. America, Trinidad, Colombia, Ecuador); stout, compact, rather flat rosette with broad, thick leaves 30 cm long, scaly at base, the inner leaves ruby-red from the middle up to the apex, the lower part yellow and chartreuse at flowering time; the flowers a slender yellow tube with spreading white lobes, in a center cup. *Tropical. Zone 11.* p. 44

zahnii (Colombia, Panama); very ornamental plant with strap-like, papery, olive-green leaves pencil-striped maroon-red, the center tinted pink to coppery red; strong branched inflorescence with pink to yellow bracts and white flowers. *Tropical. Zone 12.* p. 44

zahnii 'Tricolor'; striking cultivar seen in Denver Botanic Garden, Colorado, has leaves almost entirely creamy-white flushed with red, and green at margins. *Tropical. Zone 12.* p. 46

zamorensis: see VRIESEA

GYMNANDRA:　　see LAGOTIS

GYMNOCACTUS　　Cactaceae

subterraneus var. zaragosae (Neolloydia in Hortus 3) (Mexico: Tamaulipas, Nuevo Leon); small club-shaped cactus from turnip-like root, to 5 cm long and 3 cm dia., vivid green; warty tubercles topped by areoles with long white, woolly hairs and star-like white radial spines; and upward pointed black needle spines; the apex densely covered with light wool; rose-violet 3 cm flowers. *Zone 11.* p. 162

viereckii major (Thelocactus) (Mexico: Tamaulipas); clustering small rounded bodies to 7 cm dia., bluish-green; the low tubercles in 15 to 18 rows, set with stout brownish needle spines; dense white-woolly at apex; 2 cm flowers a delicate rose. *Zone 10.* p. 162

GYMNOCALYCIUM　　Cactaceae

denudatum (So. Brazil to Argentina), "Spider cactus"; broad globe to 15 cm dia., deep green, with 5-8 very broad, notched ribs, spidery, curved yellowish spines; flowers white or pale rose. *Arid-subtropic. Zone 10.* p. 160

guerkeanum (Bolivia); small globular body approx. 5 cm dia., divided into elevated knobs, each topped by a circle of recurved yellowish spines; greenish to yellow glossy flowers, 4 cm across, emerge from apex. *Zone 9.* p. 160

mihanovichii (Paraguay), "Plain chin cactus"; grayish-green, depressed little globe to 6 cm thick, with 8 triangular, notched ribs and banded with maroon, straw-colored spines; free-flowering chartreuse. *Arid-subtropic. Zone 10.* p. 160

mihanovichii friedrichii 'Rubra'; the novel "Red cap", "Oriental moon", "Hibotan"; strikingly colorful red (or yellow) small globe; variant with chlorophyll-poor body; for better growth and survival usually grafted on night-blooming Hylocereus undatus. *Arid-subtropic. Zone 10.* p. 160

GYMNOCARPIUM　　Polypodiaceae (Filices)

dryopteris (Currania) (Québec to Florida, Europe, Asia, Labrador to Alaska), "Oak fern"; at intervals from creeping rootstock rise bipinnate leaves 15-30 cm long and triangular in outline, formed by two broadly deltoid pinnae having a common junction with bipinnate upper section. *Deciduous. Zones 2-8.* p. 134

robertianum (Thelipteris robertiana in Oxford Bot. Garden; Currania rob. in Zander 84) (North Temp. reg.: No. North America, Europe), "Limestone fern" or "Northern Oakfern"; small woods-fern with slender, widely creeping rhizomes, and 2-3 pinnate triangular fronds 20 cm long. *Zones 3-8.* p. 141

GYMNOCLADUS　　Leguminosae

dioica (East and Central U.S.), "Kentucky coffee tree" or "Nicker tree"; picturesque deciduous tree to 25 m high, with pinnate and bipinnate leaves 50-80 cm long and leaflets 3 to 6 cm long; dioecious flowers greenish-white, female clusters 20-30 cm long, males 6-10 cm long, in June; fruit pods 20 cm long. The seeds have been used as coffee substitute. *Zone 4.*   *p. 764*

GYNANDRIRIS   *Iridaceae*
sisyrinchium (Iris) (Portugal and Mediterr. region to Centr. Asia), "Spanish nut"; handsome cormous perennial herb with linear leaves, the corms covered with soft fibers; the floral stalks to 40 cm high; inflorescence with flowers in clusters, produced in succession, the blossoms having 6 petal-like segments, blue-purple with white markings and a yellow ridge on claw. *Zones 9-10.*   *p. 228*

GYNURA   *Compositae*
aurantiaca (Java), the popular "Velvet plant"; a beautiful tropical herbaceous plant with stout stems and fleshy, broad-ovate, serrate 12 cm leaves densely velvety with violet or purple hairs and deeper purple veins; orange disc-flowers. *Tropical. Zone 11.*   *p. 61*

x sarmentosa (aurantiaca x bicolor), "Purple passion vine"; twiner with reddish stem, lanceolate leaves with wavy-toothed or shallowly lobed margins, and covered by purple hairs; wine-red beneath; small orange flower heads in clusters at ends of branches. In Europe (Hay-Synge Blumenbuch 1973) as G. procumbens (Lour.) Merr.; in Hortus 3 as G. aurantiaca cv. 'Purple Passion'. *Zone 11.*   *p. 60*

GYPSOPHILA   *Caryophyllaceae*
elegans (Caucasus), "Annual Baby's breath"; annual bushy herb with forking stems to 50 cm high; narrow lance-shaped leaves 8 cm long; clusters of profuse small white or rosy 2 cm flowers. Popular garden plant providing fresh cut flowers. *Zone 9.*   *p. 363*

paniculata (Central and Eastern Europe to Central Asia), "Chalk-flower" or "Baby's breath"; perennial, much branched with thin, wiry stems to 1 m high; narrow leaves, and with hundreds of tiny white flowers. Used in flower arrangements. *Temperate. Zone 4.*   *p. 363*

paniculata 'Bristol Fairy' (Ehrlei) Cuming 1928, "Florists double baby's breath"; widely used in the florist trade in cut flower arrangements or as dried material; excellent rhizomatous cultivar more robust, to 90 cm high, and earlier than flore-pleno, and also larger blooms; the 1 cm double white flowers in greater clusters, July-August blooming. In horticulture usually grown grafted on seedlings. *Zones 4-9.*   *p. 363*

paniculata flore pleno, "Double baby's breath"; perennial with thick roots or rhizome, the generally 4-angled stems freely branching with thin, wiry twigs forming billowing bushes 50-100 cm high, set with narrow glaucous blue-green leaves 6 cm long; small double flowers white or sometimes pinkish, in loose clusters. Popularly used in cut flower arrangements, or for dried bouquets by bundling and hanging up the floral clusters to preserve. *Zone 4.*   *p. 363*

repens (Pyrenees of Spain to the Alps and Carpathians), "Creeping Baby's breath"; prostrate perennial much branched from creeping rhizome, with numerous stems to 25 cm high; narrow linear 2 cm curved leaves, topped by profuse clusters of small 2 cm pale purplish flowers, June to July. *Zone 4.*   *p. 363*

repens 'Rose Beauty', "Pink Baby's-breath"; rhizomatous perennial to 25 cm high, dense with wiry branches and curved 3 cm leaves; the inflorescence multi-flowered with pretty pink blossoms 15 mm across. *Zone 4.*   *p. 358*

HABENARIA   *Orchidaceae*
clypeata (Mexico: Chihuahua to Vera Cruz and Oaxaca), "Rein orchid"; tuberous-rooted terrestrial orchid, with basal lanceolate, deciduous leaves; the inflorescence on a leafy floral stalk with white flowers. *Zone 10.*   *p. 88*

HABERLEA   *Gesneriaceae*
ferdinandi-coburgii (Bulgaria); tufted perennial rosette with spatulate, leathery leaves in a rosette, deeply toothed, and umbels of tubular, 5-lobed, nodding, lilac flowers with broad upper lip, spotted yellow and violet in throat. *Temperate. Zone 7.*   *p. 63*

rhodopensis (Thrace of Greece and Turkey); small perennial rock-garden plant, forming rosettes of evergreen leaves, the soft-hairy obovate blades to 8 cm long, coppery green and wrinkled, with crenate margins; the primrose-like pale lilac flowers 2 cm long, carried in small clusters on long stalks, blooming late Spring. Best grown in shady crevices among rocks. *Warm temperate. Zone 7.*   *p. 63*

HABRANTHUS   *Amaryllidaceae*
tubispathus (Zephyranthes robusta) (Argentina); small bulbous herb to 22 cm high, with recurved linear leaves, appearing after blooms; flowers rose, to 8 cm long, with short greenish tube. *Subtropic. Zone 9.*   *p. 210*

HACKELIA   *Boraginaceae*
floribunda (Lappula) (Montana to Brit. Columbia and California), "False forget-me-not" or "Stickseed"; herbaceous rough-hairy perennial or biennial 25-80 cm high, with narrow lanceolate thin-hairy

---

leaves, basal and along stems; at apex with clusters of small 1 cm light blue flowers blooming after snow melts, in June-July in habitat; nuts from ovary 7 mm wide, edged with barbed prickles. *Zone 3.*   *p. 348*

HAEMANTHUS   *Amaryllidaceae*
albiflos (So. Africa), "White paint brush"; bulbous plant to 30 cm high, fleshy, wide evergreen leaves with ciliate margins, the inflorescence of white flowers in heads 5 cm across. *Subtropic. Zone 9.*   *p. 212*

katherinae (Scadoxus multiflorus katherinae) (Natal), "Blood flower"; robust bulbous plant branching from offsets, the soft-fleshy fresh green sword-shaped leaves with channeled midrib running into channeled petiole, separate solid stalk bearing umbrella-shaped head of star-like flowers with salmon petals and long red stamens. Revised to Scadoxus by D. Snijman 1984. *Subtropic. Zone 9.*   *p. 212*

katherinae 'King Albert' (Scadoxus) (katherinae x puniceus), "Blood lily" or "Catherine wheel"; beautiful hybrid of So. African species, a robust bulbous plant with broad scarlet-red flowers having long, thread-like stamens in globular heads, 12-18 cm in dia., on a separate thick stalk. *Subtropic. Zones 9-10.*   *p. 212*

multiflorus (Trop. Africa), "Salmon blood lily"; bulbous plant with leaves on short spotted petioles; the showy inflorescence, separate from foliage, forming a perfect ball with up to 100 flowers, 8-12 cm across, coral-pink to red, crimson at base of narrow petals with long extended stamens tipped yellow. *Subtropic. Zone 9.*   *p. 212*

HAEMARIA   *Orchidaceae*
discolor dawsoniana (Anoectochilus) (Ludisia in Zander) (Malaya), "Jewel orchid"; vigorous terrestrial with creeping, branching rootstock and fleshy, ovate, gorgeous leaves of blackish red-green velvet with a network of coppery red veins, wine-red beneath, 5-8 cm long; small, waxy white flowers, with yellow center, in terminal raceme, (Oct.-Feb.). *Tropical. Zone 12.*   *p. 89*

HAEMATOXYLUM   *Leguminosae*
campechianum (Yucatán, W. Indies), "Bloodwood Tree"; fast-growing spiny shrub or tree to 8 m, with gnarled trunk; small pinnate leaves, the glossy leathery, obcordate leaflets in 2 to 4 pairs, 2-3 cm long; narrow clusters of small yellowish flowers with prominent stamens. *Zone 10.*   *p. 767*

HAKEA   *Proteaceae*
victoriae (Western Australia), "Royal hakea"; magnificent, colorful sparry tree 3-4 m high, with broad, rigid leaves 5 to 10 cm across, densely shingled, and with sharp spines along margins, light glossy green beautifully veined and variegated with yellow and into red, the base golden-yellow and looking like big flowers; pinkish blooms among the foliage. *Zone 10.*   *p. 823*

HAKONECHLOA   *Gramineae*
macra 'Variegata' (syn. Phragmites macer) (Japan: Honshu); strikingly beautiful deciduous hardy perennial to 30 cm high, spreading by slowly creeping rhizomes; erect slender, wiry culms bright green; narrow leafblades 20 cm long and 1 cm wide, variegated white and yellow, with little green and a tinge of rose. *Zone 6.*   *p. 550*

HALESIA   *Styracaceae*
carolina (W. Virginia, so. to Florida, Tennessee and Texas), "Wild olive" or "Carolina silverbell"; floriferous deciduous tree to 10 m or more high, with spreading branches; leaves ovate oblong or lanceolate, to 10 cm long, minutely toothed and starry-downy beneath; very attractive pendant bell-flowers pure white, 2 cm long, in clusters on last year's wood, spring-blooming as the leaves appear. *Zone 6.*   *p. 885*

diptera (So. Carolina to Tennessee and Texas), "Snowdrop-tree"; popular small deciduous tree to 10 m high, having wide-spread branches; elliptic to obovate leaves 6-12 cm long; very pretty pendant bell-flowers pure white 2½ cm long, divided to near base, blooming in June; not very floriferous, but quite hardy. *Zone 5.*   *p. 885*

monticola (Mountains of No. Carolina to Georgia), "Silverbells"; or "Snowdrop tree"; charming deciduous tree, with age to 20 m tall; in late Spring the lovely white or pinkish bell-shaped 2 to 3 cm flowers hang from graceful branches just as foliage begins to appear; oval leaves are finely toothed and 10-15 cm long; interesting 4-winged brown fruit persists for long time. *Zone 5.*   *p. 885*

x HALIMIOCISTUS   *Cistaceae*
sahucii (Cistus salviifolius x Halimium umbellatum) (So. France); low bigeneric evergreen to 45 cm high, a natural hybrid in the wild, having characters intermediate between Cistus and Halimium; with white-pubescent linear-lanceolate leaves 2-3 cm long; pretty white flowers 3 cm across, blooming in June. *Zone 6.*   *p. 686*

HALIMIUM   *Cistaceae*
lasianthum (Helianthemum formosum) (So. Spain, So. Portugal, Morocco); low evergreen with densely spreading branches, to 50-

80 cm high, soft white-hairy; obovate 3 cm 3-nerved leaves, and very beautiful wide-open golden-yellow flowers 3 cm across, each petal with crimson spot near base, blooming beginning in May. Zone 9.   p. 686

ocymoides (Cistus algarvensis) (Spain, Portugal); low evergreen shrub 60-90 cm high, the slender branches with white silky hairs; obovate 3-nerved gray-tomentose leaves 2-3 cm long; long-stalked bright yellow flowers 3 cm across, each petal marked by black-brown at base, June-blooming. Zone 8.   p. 686

HAMAMELIS   *Hamamelidaceae*
x intermedia 'Arnold Promise' (Arnold Arboretum 1963); superb cultivar, with autumn foliage a rich red and yellow; sulphur yellow flowers with linear petals red inside, intensely fragrant and blooming in early Spring. Zone 4.   p. 734

x intermedia 'Jelena' (japonica x mollis); large deciduous shrub with erect branches; oval leaves to 17 cm long and 12-15 cm wide, having cordate base, turning beautiful autumn color from orange to scarlet-red; flowers in showy clusters, the ribbon-like petals yellow tinted with copper and rose, 2 cm long and twisted, the center cup wine-red; a spectacular color form. Zone 4.   p. 734

japonica (China, Japan), "Witch-hazel"; deciduous shrub reaching 10 m with broad-ovate, toothed 10 cm leaves, unequal at base, and stellate-hairy when young; flowers yellow in roundish heads on the leafless branches, slightly scented, the 4 rose petals linear, and reddish bracts; in January-March. Zone 5.   p. 734

mollis (W. China), "Chinese witchhazel"; very popular deciduous shrub or small tree to 10 m high, with ovate or orbicular leaves to 15 cm long, toothed at margins; flowers very fragrant, with linear petals deep golden-yellow 2 cm long, the calyx red-brown, early blooming in January-February on bare branches; the largest blooms in the group. Zone 6.   p. 734

virginiana (macrophylla) (E. No. America), "Witch hazel"; common in the woods of Eastern U.S.; tall deciduous shrub or small tree to 5 m high; obovate leaves 8-15 cm long, coarsely toothed at margins; the yellow, ribbon-like flowers appear in time when leaves have turned yellow and begin to drop in October, the last woody plant to bloom in New England. Zone 4.   p. 734

HAMATOCACTUS uncinatus (Zander):
see ANCISTROCACTUS uncinatus (Hortus)

HAMELIA   *Rubiaceae*
patens (Florida, W. Indies to Bolivia), "Fire bush"; evergreen shrub or small tree to 8 m, gray pubescent; elliptic leaves 15 cm long; tubular flowers scarlet-red, 2-3 cm long, in one-sided raceme. Zone 10. p. 854

HAPLOPAPPUS   *Compositae*
glutinosus (Chile, Argentina), "Chilean daisy"; mat-forming clustering perennial to 30 cm high; the woody branches with sticky lobed or divided leaves, and terminal daisy-like flowers 3 cm dia. with bright yellow rays. Zone 6.   p. 310

HARDENBERGIA   *Leguminosae*
comptoniana (W. Australia), "Lilac vine" or "Wild sarsaparilla"; evergreen woody liane twining to 3 m high; compound leaves of 3 to 5 glossy, lanceolate leaflets to 12 cm long; racemes of purplish-rose pea-flowers, the standard tipped pink, and deep purple in throat. Zone 9.   p. 278

HARPEPHYLLUM   *Anacardiaceae*
caffrum (So. Africa: E. Cape, Natal, Transvaal), "Kaffir-plum"; attractive evergreen tree to 12 m with pinnate, glossy deep green leathery leaves, the leaflets lanceolate, slightly curved, to 6 cm long, and wavy-margined; small white or greenish flowers in clusters; the female tree bears edible plum-like fruit. Zone 10.   p. 636, 903

HARPULLIA   *Sapindaceae*
arborea (Philippines), "Puas"; tropical tree with thin, green pinnate foliage; green-petaled flowers; the fruit in coppery red capsules 4 cm dia., with large black seeds inside. Zones 10-11. p. 868

HARRISIA   *Cactaceae*
martinii (Eriocereus) (Argentina), "Moon cactus"; nightblooming, much branched, clambering vine, 4-5 angled, with needle-like pale spines; large white flowers 20 cm long, tinged with red; small spiny red fruit. Zone 10.   p. 160

HAUYA   *Onagraceae*
heydeana (elegans) (So. Mexico, Guatemala); attractive evergreen tropical shrub with wiry, scandent branches 2 m or more high, and waxy elliptic leaves; showy star-flowers 4 cm across, with red sepals and white petals, changing to pink and red during a three-day period. Zone 10.   p. 815

HAWORTHIA   *Liliaceae*
cooperi (So. Africa), "Window haworthia"; curious rosette having fleshy, boat-shaped leaves purplish-green to brownish, 3-5 cm long,

with transparent ciliate edges and window-like, translucent apex; small white with green flowers in simple raceme 40 cm high. Zone 10.   p. 198

fasciata (So. Africa: Cape Prov.), "Zebra haworthia"; very attractive commercial, small erect rosette 5-8 cm across, forming offsets, of slender tapering somewhat incurved leaves dark green, with large white warts in neat connected cross bands; small tubular, whitish-green flowers in loose raceme. Subtropic. Zone 10.   p. 198

limifolia (Africa: Swaziland), "Fairy washboard"; exquisite small rosette 8-10 cm across; leaves triangular pointed, the upper surface concave, dark green-brown, on both sides with 15-20 transverse ridges. Arid-subtropic. Zone 10.   p. 199

setata var. major (Cape Prov.); beautiful formal, succulent rosette 5 cm dia., dense with triangular light green leaves, transversed by dark longitudinal lines, margins and keels with long porcelain-white bristles, and a long transparent one at apex. Zone 10.   p. 198

truncata (Cape Prov.: Little Karroo), "Clipped window plant"; most unusual "Window plant" with succulent leaves 2 cm long, oval in cross-section, arranged in 2 ranks, dark green-brownish and rough-warty, apex of each leaf flat as if cut off, and translucent. Subtropic. Zone 10.   p. 199

HEBE   *Scrophulariaceae*
buxifolia (Veronica) (New Zealand), "Boxleaf veronica"; rounded evergreen shrub of symmetrical habit eventually to 1½ m high, with branches erect; dense with small buxus-like 2 cm obovate leaves lustrous deep green, of thick texture; small white, starry flowers with 4 spreading petals, 2 cm across, in dense clusters, during Summer. Zone 8.   p. 875

buxifolia 'Variegata' (Veronica) (New Zealand); dense evergreen bush resembling euonymus, with small, soft, 2 cm obovate leaves, opposite and overlapping, dark, waxy green with gray, variegated cream-white from the margin inward; small white flowers in closely packed spikes. Subtropic. Zone 9.   p. 875

decumbens (Veronica) (New Zealand), "Ground hebe"; small decumbent shrub to about 50 cm high, with purplish-black shoots; small succulent 2 cm grayish evergreen leaves with red margins, set attractively in shingled ranks; white 1 cm flowers in dense, short racemes near tips of the distinctive shiny-black shoots, blooming during Summer. Not tolerant of excessive heat. Zone 7.   p. 874

diosmaefolia (New Zealand); evergreen shrub from the Auckland area, to 1½ m or more, dense with small 2½ cm shingled glossy linear leaves; white to pale lavender star-flowers in terminal clusters. Zone 9.   p. 874

elliptica 'Variegata' (Veronica decussata) (Tierra del Fuego, Falkland Isl., Chile, New Zealand); the green species is a much branched evergreen shrub or a tree to 6 m high, with opposite, soft leathery and quilted, obovate leaves to 3 cm long, having pyramidal racemes dense with rich red-purple, fragrant flowers, feathery with their prominent stamens. The attractive cultivar 'Variegata' has its dense foliage broadly margined with creamy-white. Zone 9.   p. 876

macrantha (Veronica) (New Zealand); stout shrub from Mts. of South Island to 1600 m amongst Alpine vegetation, to 2 m tall, in cultivation to 60 cm high; with ovate toothed thick glossy leathery leaves 3 cm long; snow-white flowers 2 cm across in clusters, the corolla with broad oval petals arranged like a saucer, and very attractive. Zone 7.   p. 876

menziesii (New Zealand); evergreen shrub of spreading habit, may reach to 1½ m high; narrow closely spaced rigid leathery 2 cm shiny bright green leaves, toothed at margins; white flowers tinged blue in showy clusters, during Summer. Zone 7.   p. 874

ochracea (armstongii in hort.) (Veronica) (New Zealand); evergreen shrub to 1 m high, often branching fan-like; slender shoots in the adult stage densely clothed with ochre-yellow appressed, overlapping, tiny 1 mm roundish leaves; white flowers in terminal clusters. Zones 7-8.   p. 874

pimeloides 'Glaucocoerulea' (Veronica) (species from South Island New Zealand); evergreen shrub to 60 cm high; small leathery sessile, obovate leaves 1-2 cm long, glaucous blue with purplish margins; flowers lavender to purple 1-2 cm across, blooming during Summer. Zone 7.   p. 874

salicifolia (New Zealand), "Evergreen veronica" or "Willowleaf veronica"; evergreen shrub to 3 m with shining, lanceolate leaves 15 cm long, and variable flowers densely packed in erect slender cylindrical racemes 10 to 15 cm or more long, lilac tinged white to bluish-purple, blooming June to August. Zone 7.   p. 876

speciosa (Veronica) (New Zealand: North Island), "Napuka" or "Showy veronica"; robust, evergreen shrub with spreading, angled branches dense with opposite, thick, oblong leaves glossy dark green and downy on the midrib above, 5-8 cm long; the small purple-crimson flowers in dense axillary racemes opposite near tips of branches, summer blooming. Subtropic. Zone 10.   p. 875

HECHTIA   Bromeliaceae

glomerata (Mexico); dangerous low rosette of fleshy, glossy green recurved leaves, on occasion turning entirely red, and with silvery white reverse, to 40 cm long, and armed with vicious spines; sending out creeping off-shoots; flower petals white. *Zone 10.*   *p. 47, 152*

HEDERA   Araliaceae

canariensis (Azores, Canaries, Morocco), "Algerian ivy"; robust creeper, or climbing by roots; burgundy-red twigs and petioles with glossy, fresh green, leathery leaves broadly ovate and quite flat, even recurved, shallowly lobed and usually with slender main lobe; covered with grayish-white scales, to 15 cm wide. *Subtropic. Zones 8-10.*   *p. 302*

canariensis 'Arborescens variegata', the "Ghost tree ivy"; so called because of the ghostly trembling of the pendant foliage in a breeze; arborescent or fruiting form of the variegated Algerian ivy, its ovate, hard leaves with cream variegation on light green or gray; fruit black. An excellent, very durable, but slow-growing decorative plant in containers, for the sunny window or the patio, the beautiful variegated foliage stiff as if varnished. Propagated from half-hard cuttings. *Subtropic. Zone 9.*   *p. 35, 303, 648*

canariensis 'Gloire de Marengo'; long cultivated in Europe under this name, this is probably identical with H. canariensis 'Variegata' or one of its color forms. The relatively large leaves are usually 3-lobed, green in the center changing to milky gray, then white to cream to yellowish in irregularly variegated areas, mostly along the margins; stems and petioles red. *Subtropic. Zone 9.*   *p. 303*

canariensis 'Variegata' (maderensis), known as 'Gloire de Marengo' and "Hagenburger's" commercially; very colorful with the thin-leathery leaves in the center fresh green to slate-green, joined by a zone of blue or gray-green, and marginal variegation of creamy-white, 6-12 cm long. *Subtropic. Zones 9-10.*   *p. 267, 302*

colchica (Caucasus to Iran), "Persian ivy"; a bold woody climber with juvenile leaves thick-leathery, somewhat heart-shaped, dark dull green, to 25 cm long, occasionally lightly lobed. *Zone 5.*   *p. 303*

colchica 'Dentato-variegata' (Caucasus, Iran), "Variegated Persian ivy"; twigs pea-green with large, leathery, green leaves broadly ovate to 25 cm long, lightly lobed and remotely toothed, with dense, scaly pubescence, and broad cream-white margin. *Warm temperate. Zone 6.*   *p. 302*

helix (Europe, Asia, No. Africa), "English ivy"; root climbing vine with juvenile leaves 5-lobed, glossy forest green, with creamy veins, 6-12 cm wide, and somewhat cupped; this species has 4-12 stellate hairs covering the foliage, mostly underneath, seen through a magnifying lens; in the arborescent stage leaves are unlobed, the fruit black. *Temperate. Zones 5-9.*   *p. 303, 323, 614*

helix 'Abundance'; slow trailer, and bushy, with broad and large 10 cm 4-5 to 7-lobed variable leaves dark green with pale veins, some are wavy in the sinus, some have 2-pointed apex. *Zone 7.*   *p. 302*

helix 'Adam'; photographed at Rochford's Nurseries near London, England; a vigorous freely branching ivy with small, rather dainty, distinctly 5-lobed leaves 4 cm long, fresh green with white edges. *Zone 7.*   *p. 304*

helix 'Albany', "Albany ivy"; selfbranching from strongly flattened (fasciated) twigs with leaves sharply 5-lobed, to 9 cm long, rich green to purplish-green with pale veins; purplish beneath. *Zone 6.*   *p. 302*

helix 'Arborescens'; the arborescent form of the "English ivy", in adult, flowering stage more shrubby and only slowly climbing, usually on trees, with woody branches having cordate to elongate leathery leaves usually not lobed; producing clusters of small greenish flowers and berry-like black fruit. *Zone 5.*   *p. 303, 648*

helix 'Baltica' (Latvia), "Baltic ivy"; clinging vine similar to English ivy but the leathery foliage not so large and more cut, whitish veins; very hardy. *Temperate. Zones 4-7.*   *p. 304*

helix 'California Fan', (Calif. clone); wiry stems self-branching, with broad, leathery green 7-lobed, 4-5 cm pleated leaves medium-large, lobes ovate and the sinuses wavy; branchlets starting in axils of main stems. *Zones 7-10.*   *p. 303*

helix 'Chicago variegated'; small leaves with irregular variegation giving blotched or marbled effect over whole leaf with more cream than green, some leaves altogether green, others only margined with white; popular in Australia and Europe as an indoor house plant. *Zone 6.*   *p. 302*

helix 'Conglomerata' (English clone 1871), "Japanese ivy"; slow growing shrubby, prostrate spreading contorted stems closely crowded with small undulate and frilled 2-4 cm leaves dark green and stiff, with green veins. *Zone 6.*   *p. 304*

helix cristata 'Curlilocks'; sport with young growths sprouting from every axil of the crested leaves resulting in densely bushy vines. *Temperate. Zone 7.*   *p. 302*

helix 'Deltoidea'; dark green leaves leathery with pale veins, cordate to shield-shaped, somewhat like 'Scutifolia' but longer and narrower leaves, and lobes of mature size leaves overlap at base; from Laurenson of New Zealand. The young stage is known as "Sweetheart ivy". *Zone 6.*   *p. 302, 303*

helix 'Diamant'; low miniature, photographed at the German National Show in Hamburg 1973; graceful, flexuous branches set evenly with several 1½-2½ cm leaves, obscurely 3-lobed and all about equal size, with milky green center and creamy-white variegation and edging. *Zone 7.*   *p. 304*

helix 'Discolor' (marmorata minor), "Marmorata ivy"; robust, old-time variety with wiry twigs and the small, scattered, leathery leaves deep green mottled or spotted with white. *Zone 7.*   *p. 302*

helix 'Erecta' (conglomerata erecta or congesta) (Japan); similar to conglomerata but the stout twigs grow more erect, the leaves are more broadly triangular pointed and not undulate, dark green with whitish veins, and rigidly arranged opposite each other, 2-4 cm long; non-climbing. *Zone 6.*   *p. 304*

helix 'Fluffy Ruffles'; unusual ivy with scattered roundish 4-6 cm leaves very much undulate and crested at the margins; quite self-branching. Very attractive as an indoor potted plant. *Zone 7.*   *p. 303*

helix 'Garland'; compact, bushy variety with medium-large leaves mostly shallow to deeply trilobed, lightly corrugated and pleated, causing the sinuses to become wavy. *Zone 7.*   *p. 302*

helix 'Glacier', "Glacier ivy"; good vining growth combined with nicely variegated, small, triangular, leathery leaves of several shades of green down to gray, with white marginal areas and pink edge, 3 to 5 cm long. Popular house plant and in baskets; outdoors in California. *Zones 7-9.*   *p. 305*

helix 'Goldheart', "d'Oro di Bogliosco"; a superb small leaved ivy from Italy with slender pink vines, and neat, pointed 3-5-lobed, leathery, green leaves splashed in the middle golden-yellow and cream, 4-6 cm long, on reddish petioles. Generally holds its variegation well when climbing, but creeping on the ground may revert to green. *Zone 7.*   *p. 305*

helix 'Hahnii' (Hahn's Self-branching), in California hort. as 'Hahnii'; a bushy clone of the Pittsburgh ivy, the first of the self-branching mutations of the English ivy, typical with pointed leaves lighter green and thinner, only 5-6 cm long; constant forking near the growing tips will develop into dense matting. Favorite for indoors, window-boxes, baskets, or outdoor beds, especially in mild climate. *Zones 6-9.*   *p. 305*

helix 'Hahn's Variegated'; probably the best grower of the small albinos; long vines with silver-gray, leathery leaves and narrow white edge turning reddish. *Zone 7.*   *p. 302*

helix 'Harald', "White and green ivy" or "Improved Chicago variegata"; a medium small-leaved yet robust, variegated clone favored in Europe because its 4 to 6 cm, 3 to 5 shallowly lobed leaves, somewhat rounded, are mostly green but not gray in the center, broadly margined creamy-white; also quite durable as a house plant. *Zone 7.*   *p. 305*

helix 'Heise Denmark'; attractive Scandinavian self-branching miniature, of bushy, compact habit; purplish branches with tri-lobed leaves 3-5 cm wide, green and gray-green highly variegated creamy-white, mainly along margins. Very suitable as a pot plant or in terrariums. *Zone 8.*   *p. 302*

helix hibernica (Ireland); the "Irish ivy" is the largest of the helix varieties, growing more dense and vigorous than the "English ivy" with roundish leaves to 12 cm across, dull green with pale green veining. *Zones 6-8.*   *p. 306*

helix hibernica 'Variegata'; creeping vine with firm broad leaves similar to English ivy, shallowly 3-5-lobed, dark green with irregular cream-white variegation and mottling; veins milk-white. *Temperate. Zone 7.*   *p. 306*

helix 'Ivalace'; lovely mutation with vines to 20 cm long, with self-branching characteristics resulting in close growth, the 5-lobed, dark green leathery 4-6 cm leaves with upcurled, crimped margins creating a lacy appearance. *Zone 7.*   *p. 305*

helix 'Jubilee'; tiniest of the variegated leaf forms, self-branching; the little snubnosed leaves friendly light green, gray and white, and quite irregular. *Warm temperate. Zone 8.*   *p. 306*

helix 'Maculata'; this may be a slow-growing, variegated form of hibernica, the Irish ivy; the leaves are roundish, shallowly 5-lobed, rather flat and fleshy, and the yellow-green mixed with dark green beautifully variegated white or cream. *Temperate. Zone 7.*   *p. 306*

helix 'Mandaiana variegata'; striking mutant of 'Manda's Crested', a New Jersey cultivar; of compact habit, with 5-8 cm roundish leaves having crisped and undulate margins; highly variegated jade-green with creamy-white and rosy edge, on reddish stalks. *Zone 7.*   *p. 305*

helix 'Manda's Crested'; attractive plant with star-shaped, jade-green leaves 5-8 cm across, and having rosy edge, the long lobes fluted and undulate, on straight, upright, reddish stalks. *Warm temperate. Zone 7.*   *p. 305* helix **'Needlepoint'**; dwarf plant self-branching from leaf axils, with twigs upright when young, the tiny elongate leaves usually slender 3-lobed, 4 cm long, arranged in ranks and facing one side. Zones 6-9. *p. 306*

helix **'Parsley crested'** (cristata); long vining variety called "Parsley ivy" because the small, leathery, medium green, 5-lobed 4-6 cm roundish leaves are minutely frilled and crimped on margins. Zone 7. *p. 306*

helix **'Pittsburgh fa. Patricia'**; sport of 'Pittsburgh', an excellent Philadelphia cultivar; dense self-branching ivy with medium-sized leathery leaves to 3-6 cm wide and long, usually remotely 5-lobed, and prettily curled in at sinuses. A good keeper and favorite in a 13 cm pot, with its neatly draped reddish branches. Better keeper indoors than the "Pittsburgh ivy". *Warm temperate. Zone 7.* *p. 305*

helix **'Ripples'**; pendant branches heavily loaded with medium-large roundish foliage irregularly lobed, the margins more or less curled or crested. Zone 7. *p. 306*

helix **'Schafer'**; German cultivar; miniature self-branching, close-jointed with triangular leaves 3-4 cm long, tri-lobed with central lobe longest, sharply pointed; bluish to milky green beautifully bordered with creamy-white. Zone 8. *p. 306*

helix **'Shamrock'**, "Shamrock ivy" or "Cloverleaf"; wiry plant with red stems and tiny, bright to rich green, leathery 3-4 cm leaves having 3 lobes more or less of same size, side lobes folded forward alongside the center segment. Popular house plant or in baskets in Europe. Zone 7. *p. 304*

helix **'Star'**; shapely self-branching, bushy variety, leaves 5-pointed, star-shaped with slender finger-like lobes. Zone 7. *p. 306*

helix **'Telecurl'**; vigorous, bushy self-branching red-stemmed plant with interesting 5-7-lobed leaves 4-5 cm long, the main lobe deeply cut to base and recessed, the adjoining lateral lobes overlapping or ruffled. Probably derived from the Pittsburgh ivy, or its mutation 'Merion Beauty' (see EXOTICA). Zone 7. *p. 304*

helix **'Triton'**; very curious leaf, narrow palmate 7-9 cm long and 3-4 wide, leathery deep green deeply cut into slender, pointed segments, with prominent veins running fan-like; from the collection of W. Freeland, Columbia, So. Carolina. Zone 7. *p. 304*

helix **'238th Street'**; this maturity stage arborescent ivy produces, in addition to flowering twigs, stiff, viny, green shoots with unlobed, waxy green leaves, spreading horizontally, and which stay green in Winter; flower greenish-cream, fruit green to black. First seen in the Bronx, New York City. *Warm temperate. Zone 6.* *p. 305*

helix **'Zorgvlied'**; exhibited during Floriade, Amsterdam 1982; very handsome clone of compact habit, forming dwarf trees, covered with narrow lanceolate, lustrous deep green leaves having cream veins and wavy margins, topped by branched clusters of small greenish flowers. Zone 6. *p. 303*

nepalensis (Himalayas, Afghanistan and W. China); climbing vine with scaly red-brown stems; dark green leaves 3 to 5-lobed on sterile, juvenile stems, in the fertile, adult stage lanceolate, leathery and pendant, 6-10 cm long, only obscurely lobed on flowering branches; fruit yellow to orange, as frequently seen in habitat or Southern Europe. Zones 8-9. *p. 306*

HEDYCHIUM   *Zingiberaceae*

coccineum (Himalaya, Burma, Ceylon), "Scarlet ginger-lily"; robust perennial herb with suckering rootstock and leafy stems to 2 m high, long, stiff leaves to 50 cm long, smooth green above, bluish beneath; the scarlet-red flowers with long corolla tube and pink filament, dense on a stout spike. *Topical. Zone 11.* *p. 521*

coronarium (Himalayas into China), "Butterfly lily"; also known as "Garland flower", this "White ginger" is most popular in Hawaii and used for leis because of the sweet perfume of its broad-petaled, pure white flowers, showing a yellow heart on their lip, and appearing from behind a green, waxen bulb of scale-like bracts in terminal clusters, on robust, leafy canes to 2 m long, the leaves silvery-haired beneath. *Subtropic. Zone 10.* *p. 521*

flavescens (coronarium flavescens) (Indian Himalayas), "Cream ginger"; robust perennial herb with leafy stems to 2 m high, from stout rhizomes; leathery, lanceolate leaves 30 cm or more long; at apex a cluster of fragrant creamy flowers with yellow in base, and long red stamens. (see Neal: In Gardens of Hawaii). Zone 10. *p. 521*

flavum (Indian Himalayas), "Yellow ginger"; luxuriant green herb with leafy canes to 1½ m high; long, glabrous, slender pointed leaves almost 60 cm long and sheathing, alternate along the stem in 2 rows, bearing on its summit a head of shingled green bracts from which appears a broad cluster of heavily perfumed flowers, yellow with orange patch and cream stamens; threaded into leis in Hawaii. Zone 10. *p. 521*

gardnerianum (No. India), "Kahili ginger"; beautiful, desirable species growing in the Himalayas to 2500 m, of stiff habit, canes to 1½ m high, leaves to 45 cm and powdery-white beneath when young; the delightfully fragrant flowers in elongate, open terminal spikes to

45 cm long, and from a cylindrical cone of green bracts appear the yellow flowers having long, conspicuous, bright red filaments. Zone 10. *p. 80, 521*

greenei (Alpinia) (Bhutan); beautiful ginger with stout leafy canes ½-2 m high, with heavy leaves to 25 cm long and a dense terminal head of large, fiery orange-red flowers with dark red lip and red filament. Zone 10. *p. 521*

HEDYOTIS   *Rubiaceae*

caerulea (Houstonia) (Nova Scotia to Québec and Wisconsin, so. to Georgia), "Bluets" or "Quaker Ladies"; attractive small herbaceous perennial 8-15 cm high, forming tufts, with ovate leaves 2 cm long in basal rosette; charming small waxy star-flowers 1 cm across, various in white or porcelain blue with yellow eye, beginning in June. Zone 3. *p. 495*

HEDYSARUM   *Leguminosae*

coronarium (So. Europe, W. Mediterr. reg.), "French honeysuckle"; showy perennial or biennial 1 m or more high; the leaves odd-pinnate with 3-7 pairs of elliptic leaflets; fragrant, winged pea-flowers deep red, in branched clusters, summer-blooming. Zone 3. *p.443*

HEIMERLIODENDRON brunonianum 'Variegatum':
see PISONIA umbellifera 'Variegata'

HELENIUM   *Compositae*

autumnale (Québec to Florida, west to Brit. Columbia and Arizona), "Common sneezeweed"; stout perennial to 1½ m high, with winged stems and strong branches; alternate narrow-lanceolate leaves 8-12 cm long; flowers to 5 cm across, with bronze yellow rays lobed at apex, the disc brownish-yellow, blooming August to October. Zone 3. *p. 390*

autumnale 'Waltraut'; beautiful German cultivar, to 1 m high, with showy flowers 6-8 cm across, having rounded brownish center cushion, elongating to prominent cone, and ringed by broad ray-florets heavily toned gold-brown, the apex lobed and contrasting yellow. Zone 4. *p. 390*

bigelovii 'Moerheim Beauty' (California), "Sneezewort"; floriferous perennial to 80 cm, with unbranched stems forming a clump; lanceolate leaves sparsely hairy; floral heads 6 cm across, the disc cushion brownish, ray-flowers yellow in the species, brownish-orange in the cultivar; blooming July-September. *Subtropic. Zone 8.* *p. 390*

hoopesii (Rocky Mts. of Wyoming to N. Mexico and C. California), "Orange sneezeweed"; perennial to 1 m high, from rhizome; lanceolate, rather thick leaves to 30 cm long; large flowers to 8 cm across, the ray-florets bright orange, June to September; a valued cut flower. Zone 3. *p. 390*

HELIAMPHORA   *Sarraceniaceae (Carnivorous Plants)*

nutans (Guyana), "Sun pitcher"; carnivorous rosette from the moist Roraima savannah, with funnel-shaped pitchers hairy inside, forming an insect trap of the pitfall type; leaves are red-veined; the delicate nodding flowers white. *Humid-subtropic.* Zones 10-11. *p. 202*

HELIANTHEMUM   *Cistaceae*

apenninum var. roseum (syn. rhodanthum carneum) (W. Europe, Asia Minor), "Apennine sun-rose"; small shrub to 40 cm high; arching branches with linear oblong, grayish-green leaves 3 cm long, covered with silky white hairs; small flowers 3 cm across, white in the species, deep rose in var. roseum, June-blooming. Zone 6. *p. 685*

canum (W. and So. Europe, Armenia, Asia Minor, N.W. Africa), "Sun-rose"; dwarf, densely branched shrub to 15 cm high and 30 cm wide; lanceolate gray-white foliage lightly hairy, 2 cm long; very floriferous with clear yellow flowers 2 cm wide, in terminal clusters, June-blooming. Zone 6. *p. 685*

lasianthum: see HALIMIUM lasianthum

nummularium (Europe, Atlas Mts. of Morocco, Asia Minor to Caucasus), "Yellow sun-rose"; low evergreen or semi-evergreen shrub 30-50 cm high, dense with spreading branches; the ovate leaves 3-5 cm long, silvery tomentose beneath; attractive flowers 3 cm across, resembling wild roses, usually yellow but varying to white or pink, profusely blooming early Summer, after which they should be trimmed to bloom again same year. Zone 6. *p. 687*

nummularium 'Cupreum' (Europe, Asia Minor), "Red sun-rose"; beautiful semi-shrubby plant to only 30 cm high, but spreading 60 cm wide or more; oblong leaves 2-5 cm long, green above, gray beneath, and silky-hairy; profusely blooming with flowers brilliant coppery red 25 mm across; yellow in the species, blooming June-July in Northern zones, in April-June in California; the blossoms lasting only one day, but buds continue to open. Zone 6. *p. 686*

nummularium 'Rubro-plenum', "Double sun-rose"; beautiful display of rose-red, double flowers 3 cm across, peeking above the gray-green lanceolate foliage 5 cm long; carried on low, shrubby plant 45 cm high. Zone 6. *p. 685* nummularium 'Wisley Pink' (parentage So. Europe, Mediterran. reg.), "English rock-rose" or "Sun rose"; small evergreen or semi-evergreen shrub to 60 cm high, with gray, ovate leaves; charming large 3-5 cm pink flowers, form of normally yellow-flowered species; very floriferous and showy. *Zone 6.* p. 685

HELIANTHOCEREUS huascha (Backeberg):
see TRICHOCEREUS (Hortus 3)

HELIANTHUS   *Compositae*

annuus (Western United States), the "Common sunflower"; coarse stiff-hairy annual with stout straight stalk to 5 m tall, rarely branched, and leafy with large ovate, rough hairy, toothed foliage to 30 cm long, and topped by tilted, immense heads sunlike to 30 cm or more across in cultivation, large disc of yellow tubular rays and blackish bracts, the large outer ring of florets orange-yellow. The white seed is used as food, as birdfeed, and furnishes oil. Wild on the prairies the flowers are only 8-15 cm across.
Zones 3-9 as Annual. p. 391

annuus 'Autumn Beauty'; striking horticultural annual plant to 2 m high, with herbaceous, rich green broad-ovate leaves, and beautiful flowers 15 cm across, the rich yellow sterile florets painted with copper and crimson at base, forming a blood-red zone around the mahogany brown fertile center cushion disc.
Zones 4-10 as Annual. p. 391

annuus flore pleno, the "Double sunflower" or "Cut-and-come-again"; annual; a dwarf form 1-1½ m high, with golden-yellow chrysanthemum-like fully double flowers about 10 cm across, the rays very dense and largely serrated at tips; excellent as cut flower.
Zones 3-9 as Annual. p. 391

annuus nanus, "Dwarf sunflower"; of smaller habit than the species, to 1 m high, smaller leaves and flowers 15 cm across, with deep yellow florets framing the brownish disc.
Zones 3-10 as Annual. p. 391

annuus 'Russian Giant'; superb horticultural achievement as the largest annual sun-flower with floral heads 40 cm or more across, the vivid golden-yellow florets encircling the broad blackish disc.
Zones 3-9 as Annual. p. 391

grosseserratus (Dakota to Oklahoma, Colorado and Texas), "Sawtooth sunflower"; clustering perennial of the Western prairies, with erect, leafy stem from 1 m to 4 m tall; the lanceolate leaves coarsely toothed, green above and woolly beneath; numerous yellow flowers 3-8 cm across, both on axillary stalks along upper stems, and in terminal clusters at apex, in July to October. *Zone 3.* p. 391

laetiflorus (Kansas, Nebraska, Colorado), "Showy sunflower"; perennial of the high prairie; 15 cm to 2 m tall, with usually paired leaves; variable flowers, dark brown or yellow disc and yellow ray-flowers, 4-6 cm across. *Temperate. Zone 4.* p. 391

x multiflorus (annuus x decapetalus), double "Cut-and-come-again"; very ornamental perennial to 2 m high, with broad-ovate leaves to 20 cm long, stiffly-hairy; showy floral heads to 12 cm across, single with disc, or double with extra rows of bright yellow florets, autumn-blooming. *Zone 5.* p. 391

salicifolius (Missouri to Oklahoma and Texas), "Willow-leaved sunflower"; leafy perennial to 2 m or more high; very ornamental with stems having grass-like, linear glaucous foliage 20-30 cm long; inflorescence in clusters of flowers 5 cm across, the ray-florets golden-yellow, and the disc purplish-brown, in Autumn. *Zones 3-9.* p. 390

tuberosus (Nova Scotia to Manitoba, south to Florida, Louisiana and Texas), "Jerusalem artichoke"; robust tuberous perennial with rigid erect stems to more than 3 m high, the ovate, opposite leaves 10-20 cm long, rough above, and on winged petioles; terminal sunflower-like floral heads 5-8 cm across, with deep yellow rays encircling the discs, in Autumn. The large, starchy, irregular root tubers are edible, called the weight-watchers potato, yet rich in carbohydrates and valuable diabetic food containing insulin; delicious when roasted or boiled. May be dug through Autumn and Winter. *Zone 4.* p. 527, 906

HELICHRYSUM   *Compositae*

angustifolium (Mediterran. region), "White-leaf everlasting" or "Curry plant"; perennial aromatic subshrub to 30 cm high, with strong curry fragrance; white-downy, threadlike leaves 4 cm long; numerous small yellow flower-heads in terminal clusters, from June to August. Since the 16th century, recommended to put between woolens to keep out moths. *Zone 9.* p. 524, 527

arenarium (Europe to Siberia, C. Asia, Mongolia), "Northern everlasting"; herbaceous perennial with somewhat woody base; the branches 15-30 cm high; white-woolly leaves narrow spoon-shaped, 5 cm long; small 1 cm yellow flowers in terminal clusters, August blooming. Used medicinally, and also for decorative purposes. *Zone 2.* p. 392

bellidioides (belloides) (Gnaphalium) (New Zealand), "Im-mortelle"; much branched perennial with trailing stems to 50 cm;

obovate leaves white-woolly beneath; 2 cm flowers yellow with brown disc. *Zone 7.* p. 392

bracteatum (Australia), "Strawflower"; popular annual herb with narrow leaves and stalks of solitary flowers, their discs enclosed by straw-like colored bracts, 3-4 cm across, in shades from white through yellow to red, and suitable for drying. *Subtropic. Zone 9.* p. 392

graveolens (Greece to S.W. Asia, incl. Crimea); half-hardy herbaceous perennial to 40 cm high, with base rather woody, freely branching; linear-oblong leaves to 8 cm long, having 2 distinct veins, and densely near-white-woolly; small yellow floral heads terminating leafy stems in flattish clusters. *Zones 8-9.* p. 392

lanatum (tianshanicum of hort.) (So. Africa), "Flannel everlasting"; remarkable subshrubby perennial, with woody base, 30-50 cm high; oblanceolate, sessile stem-leaves to 8 cm long, thickly covered with soft flannel hairs, the inflorescence in terminal clusters, consisting of several small, bright yellow floral heads. *Zone 9.* p. 392

milfordiae (So. Africa: Natal, Basutoland), "Lesotho immortelle"; cushion-forming perennial rosettes of oblong 1 cm leaves; attractive solitary daisy-like white flowers 3 cm across, the surrounding bracts tipped crimson. *Zone 9.* p. 392

orientale 'Sulphur Light' (S.E. Europe, Asia Minor); an "Everlasting", hardy perennial subshrub with woody base and erect, leafy flowering shoots, 15-40 cm high, leaves gray-hairy 3-8 cm long; papery 1-2 cm flower heads lemon-yellow with orange center in terminal clusters; late summer-blooming. *Zone 5.* p. 392

petiolare (petiolatum) (Gnaphalium lanatum) (So. Africa), "Licorice plant", an "Immortelle"; shrubby perennial with woolly stems and vine-like shoots; oval white-woolly leaves to 4 cm across; 1 cm flower heads with yellow disc flowers and cream-white bracts. *Subtropic. Zone 9.* p. 392

roseum (W. Australia), annual "Immortelle"; freely branching annual to 30 cm high, densely furnished with linear leaves to 8 cm long; the floral heads globose, with petal-like pink bracts, white toward base, around the yellow center disc. *Zone 9.* p. 392

selago (New Zealand), "Everlasting"; small densely branched evergreen shrub 15-35 cm high, resembling cupressus, the slender branches closely set with 5-10 mm triangular leaves, shingled or appressed to shoots, glossy green outside, and convex, woolly inside; small floral heads with white bracts. *Zone 10.* p. 690

HELICONIA   *Musaceae*

bihai (W. Indies, Brazil, New Caledonia, Samoa), "Wild plantain" or "Firebird"; large perennial herb to 5 m high, long-stalked, oblong, smooth-textured, pointed, green leaves having a pale midrib and raised lateral veins; greenish-yellow flowers clustered in the axils of large, stiff boat-shaped, crimson-red, flattened bracts with pointed tip, and arranged in two ranks, on erect inflorescence. *Tropical. Zone 11.* p. 120, 459

bihai 'St. Vincent'; Andromeda Gardens, Barbados clone of bihai with inflorescence variously pure yellow to brownish-red. *Zones 11-12.* p. 120

brasiliensis (Brazil), "False bird-of-paradise"; clustering perennial with long-stalked leathery leaves green above, pale beneath, to 60 cm long; lanceolate scarlet bracts, 6-10 cm long; flowers pink to purple. *Tropical. Zones 11-12.* p. 121

caribaea (West Indies: Martinique), "Wild plantain"; huge perennial with large leaves 90 cm or more long and rounded at base resembling bananas but arranged in two ranks, the striking inflorescence is carried erect between the foliage, being a series of large, fleshy boat-shaped, pointed, stiff bracts holding water, and compacted shingle-like on two alternate series, waxy golden-yellow with keel and tip greenish. *Tropical. Zones 11-12.* p. 120

humilis (Trinidad, Brazil), "Lobster's claw"; related to H. bihai, but with leaves shiny green, and smaller, salmon-red, boat-shaped bracts changing into green toward tip, and ridge of greenish-yellow; flowers yellowish-white. *Tropical. Zone 12.* p. 121

lanceana (So. Brazil); tropical perennial very similar in habit to H. psittacorum; clustering with long-stalked broad-lanceolate, leathery leaves, and colorful erect inflorescence with boat-shaped, long-pointed, glossy red bracts holding the small canary-yellow flowers. *Zones 11-12.* p. 120

lingulata (Bolivia); found in the foothills of the Eastern Cordilleras near Santa Cruz; tall-growing clustering tropical perennial, with broadly lanceolate leaves on long petioles; the inflorescence in erect spikes with boat-shaped, long-pointed coral-red spathes cradling the small creamy flowers. *Zone 11.* p. 121

longiflora (Panama), "Coral plantain"; tropical rainforest perennial of moderate height, with broad-ovate oblong leathery leaves, partially clothing the erect floral spike topped by a clustering inflorescence composed of slender boat-shaped waxy, soft coral-rose bracts having pink tips, and enclosing the small flowers. *Zones 11-12.* p. 121

marginata (Venezuela); plant to 2 m tall, with erect, narrow lanceolate leaves; inflorescence pendulous 30-40 cm long, the red bracts bordered with yellow; flowers yellow. *Tropical. Zones 11-12.*   p. 120

mariae (C. America: Venezuela, Colombia), the "Beefsteak heliconia"; big plant to 5 m tall, with hanging inflorescence 25 to 80 cm long, having overlapping scarlet-red bracts with pink flowers. *Tropical. Zone 12.*   p. 121

pendula (collinsiana) (Guatemala); robust tropical perennial with lush growth to 3 m tall, big banana like foliage dull green, on thick petioles; the striking inflorescence pendant below the leaves, with spreading bracts crimson-red and covered with waxy powder, yellowish toward tips; cream flowers. *Tropical. Zone 12.*   p. 121

psittacorum (coast of Guyana; Brazil), "Parrot flower"; tufted perennial with long-stemmed, narrow lanceolate, leathery, rich green leaves and a stalked inflorescence of shining orange, long-pointed bracts tipped red, and greenish-yellow flowers with black spots near apex. *Tropical. Zones 11-12.*   p. 120

rostrata (Perú), "Hanging lobster-claws"; beautiful tropical herb 1 to 3 m high, with banana like, leathery, green leaves; magnificent pendant inflorescence of alternating bracts, each 6-10 cm long, scarlet-red tipped with cream to yellow. *Tropical. Zone 12.*   p. 121

schiedeana (Mexico: Veracruz); tall clump-forming perennial to 2 m high, with long-stalked narrow-oblong leaves, usually slashed from the margins; the erect tall inflorescence on a red floral stalk with folded, sharp-pointed bracts red with greenish-yellow tips, distantly spaced along the rachis; out of the little boats peek yellow flowers, followed by the prominent clusters of fruit, first green then blue. *Humid-tropical. Zones 11-12.*   p. 122

spectabilis 'Edwardus Rex'; richly colored, robust plant with large showy leaves of an intense, deep red with coppery sheen, more so underneath, especially the veins and stalks. *Tropical. Zone 12.*   p. 122

subulata (Argentina); sole Heliconia native to Argentina, found 1976, and welcomed in gardens of Buenos Aires; clustering perennial with large broad leaves, and erect inflorescence of maroon-red boat-shaped, slender pointed bracts holding small yellow flowers. *Zones 10-11.*   p. 122

wagneriana (Costa Rica, Panama); clump-forming tropical perennial, with stems to more than 1 m and long banana-like, but leathery leaves 1-2 m long, 30 cm wide; erect inflorescence with up to 20 folded bracts in 2 ranks and overlapping, light red shading to dark crimson, tips green; white flowers *Zones 11-12.*   p. 121

HELICTOTRICHON   *Gramineae*
sempervirens (Avena) (W. Mediterran., France), "Blue oat grass"; perennial 60 cm or more high, forming tufts without stolons; narrow leaves at base to 30 cm long, recurving and glaucous blue; stems to 90 cm long, holding flower clusters well above foliage in Summer; evergreen in mild climate. *Zone 5.*   p. 560

HELIOCEREUS   *Cactaceae*
speciosus (Central Mexico: Mexico City region), the "Sun cactus" because of its large and showy, day-flowering, bright rose or scarlet flowers 15 cm across, with a lovely steel blue sheen; 3 to 5-ribbed, 4-angled or flattened stems erect or clambering, 3 to 5 cm thick, freely branching; the spines all alike. *Tropical. Zone 11.*   p. 179

HELIOPSIS   *Compositae*
helianthoides (scabra) (Eastern U.S., Ontario), "Orange sunflower"; bushy perennial to 1½ m high, smooth ovate leaves; flowers 6-8 cm across; disc brownish-yellow, ray-flowers orange-yellow. *Temperate. Zone 3.*   p. 393

helianthoides 'Incomparabilis' (Eastern U.S.), "Ox-eyes"; perennial 1 m high, with rough-textured ovate foliage, and 8 cm flowers with brownish disc and semi-double with several rows of orange-yellow ray-flowers. *Temperate. Zone 4.*   p. 393

helianthoides scabra (New York to N. Mexico), "Rough oxeye"; perennial similar to helianthoides, but having rough-hairy leaves; flower heads fewer, and ray-florets light chrome yellow, around brownish disc, but variable in colors, blooming in August. *Zone 3.*   p. 393

helianthoides scabra 'Golden Plume'; handsome cultivar, to 1 m high, with pairs of opposite, ovate, rough-textured leaves, toothed at margins, and heavy floral heads 6 cm wide, with double rows of orange-yellow ray-flowers, in late Summer. *Zone 4.*   p. 393

HELIOTROPIUM   *Boraginaceae*
arborescens (peruvianum) (Perú), "Heliotrope"; fleshy perennial to 1 m high, with small 3 to 8 cm ovate wrinkled leaves and large flat clusters of small 1 cm purple flowers, very sweetly fragrant of vanilla. *Tropical. Zone 10.*   p. 350

HELIPTERUM   *Compositae*
manglesii (W. Australia), "Swan River everlasting" or "Sunray";

slender much branched annual to 50 cm high, with ovate, glaucous leaves 3-10 cm long; floral heads 3-4 cm across, with yellow disc, surrounded by bright rose or pink bracts. Adaptable to drying and use as winter bouquets. *Zone 10.*   p. 393

roseum (Acroclinium) (W. Australia), "Rose sunray" or "Everlasting"; annual strawflower to 60 cm, smooth linear leaves; solitary heads 5 cm across, usually rose colored. *Subtropic. Zone 10.* p. 393

HELLEBORUS   *Ranunculaceae*
cyclophyllus (S.E. Europe: Greece); stemless deciduous perennial, with leaves to 40 cm across, palmately divided into 7-9 mostly forked segments bright green above, and prominent veins beneath, on petioles to 30 cm long; sweet-scented, saucer-shaped yellow-green flowers 6 cm across, the sepals overlapping, and with yellowish anthers; blooming April-May. *Zone 7.*   p. 489

foetidus (W. and So. Europe), "Bear's-foot hellebore"; wintergreen subshrub to 60 cm high, with leafy stems; the leathery foliage dark shining green, cut birdfoot-like into 7-10 narrow, toothed segments; nodding, cup-shaped flowers creamy-green to 3 cm across, the petal-like inner sepals marked red-brown, the tubular nectaries funnel-shaped; blooming late Winter. *Zone 6.*   p. 489

lividus corsicus (Corsica), "Corsican hellebore"; evergreen, rather woody stem-forming perennial with glaucous 45 cm stems; bluish-green, thick-leathery 3-parted leaves borne near bottom of plant; nodding 5 cm cup-shaped flowers yellowish-green, in profuse clusters; early Spring. *Zone 7.*   p. 489

niger (Europe: Alps, Italy, Balkans), the most popular, beautiful "Christmas-rose", known since the 16th century; a wintergreen stemless perennial to 30 cm high, with palmately divided leathery, olive-green leaves; solitary flowers with white or greenish-white, later pinkish petal-like sepals, 4 to 7 cm across, blooming late Autumn or with beginning of Christmas season into Spring, sometimes under snow. *Zones 4-8.*   p. 489

orientalis 'Atropurpureus' (W. Asia: Black Sea area, Armenia), the "Lenten-rose"; handsome evergreen, stemless perennial, to 45 cm high, with basal leaves palmately divided; 5 cm flowers dark purple outside, purplish-rose inside, spring-blooming. This may be a orientalis x niger hybrid. *Zone 5.*   p. 489

viridis occidentalis (Ireland to Yugoslavia), "Green hellebore"; stemless hardy perennial with deciduous palmate leaves of 7-11 green leaflets; stalk with 5-6 cup-shaped nodding flowers 4 cm across, bright green, the petal-like sepals wide, and yellow-green nectaries. February-blooming. The var. occidentalis has leaves larger than the species. *Zone 6.*   p. 489

HELONIOPSIS   *Liliaceae*
orientalis (Japan, Korea, Sakhalin), "Shojobakama"; attractive rhizomatous perennial to 30 cm or more high; the lustrous oblanceolate, somewhat fleshy leaves 15 cm long, forming basal rosettes; the inflorescence, on purplish stalks, in clusters of rose flowers, changing to purple, blooming April-June; ascending in Japan to the Alpine zone. Curiously, when leaftips touch the grounds, young plantlets will develop from tiny buds on leaf tips. *Zone 5.* p. 445

HELXINE soleirolii: see SOLEIROLIA soleirolii

HEMEROCALLIS   *Liliaceae*
aurantiaca (China), "Golden summer daylily"; perennial with fleshy, tuberous roots; evergreen, sturdy strap-shaped leaves 60-90 cm long, 3 cm wide; fragrant, early-blooming bright orange flowers 10 cm long, opening for one day in the morning and closing in the evening. Day-lilies otherwise known as "Poor man's orchids", are one of the most popular and satisfactory, long-lasting garden perennials. The evergreen varieties are at their best in mild climates, such as the American South and So. California, displaying green foliage year-round; in severe cold climate, beyond their hardiness limits, their otherwise evergreen leaves become shabby or freeze completely. Hemerocallis are also a gourmet vegetable in China, they have been used for centuries in cuisine, as all parts are edible including early leaves, the small tubers, and buds or flowers. *Zone 6.*   p. 446

citrina (China), "Citron daylily"; night-blooming, with fragrant, pale yellow tubular funnel-shaped flowers 12 cm long, tinged brown outside, clustering on short branches at top of wiry stalks to 1 m long, blooming July-August; vigorous perennial with fleshy roots, and strap-shaped, dark green leaves 75 cm long. This species is in the ancestry of many excellent yellow and fragrant garden varieties. *Zones 2-8.*   p. 446

forrestii (S.W. China); small spring-flowering Day-lily to 40 cm high, perennial with fleshy roots, and narrow 45 cm basal leaves recurving toward ends; trumpet-shaped sulphur-yellow flowers having narrow segments, and glistening silvery inside, 8 cm long, not fragrant, several in clusters, on branched slender stalks. *Zone 7.*   p. 446

fulva (Europe; Asia to China; naturalized in E. United States), "Orange daylily" or "Tawny daylily"; popular garden perennial, vigorously forming clumps by spreading fleshy rhizomes, 60-90 cm high; dense with deciduous narrow linear leaves 60 cm long; the showy flowers wide-funnel-shaped 12 cm long, orange to deep copper, marked and striped crimson inside, the wavy petals with an apricot band; not fragrant; blooming Mid-summer.

Zones 3-10. *p. 446*

hybrida 'Bonanza'; "Bicolor daylily" of dwarf habit, 40 cm high, with large flowers flaring to 15 cm wide, having spectacular bicolor pattern orange-yellow with maroon-red star toward center; July to September blooming. Zones 5-10. *p. 446*

hybrida 'Royal Flare'; magnificent and very vigorous, free-blooming modern tetraploid hybrid, having rounded flowers 12-15 cm across, vivid salmon-rose with reflexed petals tinted coppery red and a white line down center; an early season bloomer 50 cm high.

Zones 5-10. *p. 446*

lilio-asphodelus (flava) (Siberia to Japan), "Tall yellow day-lily"; deciduous, vigorous perennial herb with spreading rhizomes; linear basal leaves 60 cm long and weak, arching, branched stalks 60-90 cm high with lily-like lemon-yellow, fragrant flowers spreading 9 cm; May to July. Popular in California. Zones 4-10. *p. 446*

lilioasphodelus 'Ewen'; beautiful color form seen in Fortin de las Flores, Vera Cruz, Mexico, with showy coppery red flowers, the petals flaring wide and recurved, having orange-yellow line down center inside. Zones 8-11. *p. 446*

minor (E. Siberia to China, Korea and Japan), "Grassleaf daylily"; small perennial to 45 cm high, forming dense clumps of narrow, grass-like, deciduous leaves; blooming sparsely during late Spring, with starry, light yellow fragrant flowers 10 cm long, tinted brown outside. Zone 3. *p. 446*

HEMIGRAPHIS   Acanthaceae

alternata (colorata) (Java), "Red ivy"; prostrate tropical herb with stringy, rooting branches and opposite, broad-cordate, puckered and toothed leaves 6 to 10 cm long, shimmering silvery violet, underneath red-purple; terminal heads of small white flowers between large bracts. Tropical. Zone 11. *p. 306*

HEMIONITIS   Polypodiaceae (Filices)

palmata (Tectaria incisa) (West Indies, Brazil); handsome tropical terrestrial fern with stout rhizome, giving rise to broad, thin-leathery fronds 50 cm or more long, rich green but covered with reddish pubescence; palmately lobed at base, the upper terminal lobe pinnately cut into wide segments tapering to a point or merely with rounded lobes, the surface puckered and the margins wavy. Subtropic. Zones 10-11. *p. 135*

HEPATICA   Ranunculaceae

americana (Nova Scotia to Manitoba, and Florida), "Liver-leaf"; low perennial herb to 15 cm; leaves with 3 rounded lobes on shaggy-hairy petioles; solitary 2 cm flowers with petal-like sepals lavender-blue passing into white; blooming before new leaves.

Zones 4-9. *p. 488*

nobilis (Europe: Romania), "European liver-leaf"; small, silky-hairy perennial with short rhizome, very similar to H. americana; ovate, trilobed leaves with cordate base, purplish beneath; floral stalks to 15 cm high, bearing attractive pale lilac flowers 3 cm across, blooming early Spring. Zone 4. *p. 488*

HERACLEUM   Umbelliferae

laciniatum (villosum; or stevenii in Zander) (S.W. Asia, Caucasus), "Cow parsnip"; floriferous biennial or short-lived perennial with stems reaching to 3 m high or more, the leaves deeply cut and toothed; white tomentose beneath; the tiny white 5-petalled flowers terminally in large flat clusters, followed by prickly fruit. Zone 3. *p. 515*

mantegazzianum (S.W. Asia to Caucasus), "Giant hogweed" or "Cartwheel flower"; imposing biennial, or monocarpic, short-lived hairy perennial with robust, purple spotted, ridged stem 2 to 4 m tall, having leaves to 1 m long tripartite to trifoliate, dull green with pale ribs beneath, toward apex bipinnate or serrate; topped by a compound inflorescence of several umbels to 15 cm wide, the white flowers 2 cm across in huge branched clusters, during Summer. Zone 6. *p. 515*

sphondylium (Europe; east to Siberia, naturalized in No. America), "Common Cow-parsnip"; robust perennial or biennial herb to 2 m or more high, with trisected leaves of 5-9 toothed segments, white-tomentose beneath; the inflorescence in large flat floral clusters, to 50 cm across, consisting of numerous tiny white or greenish flowers. Not a general ornamental but ideal for moist soils. Caution: Dermatitis has been contracted from touching it. Zone 3. *p. 384*

HERMANNIA   Byttneriaceae (Sterculiaceae)

althaeifolia (Cape Prov. So. Africa), "Honey bells"; evergreen downy shrub 60 cm to 1 or more high, with angled spreading branches; small 3 cm obovate leaves, shallowly toothed; beautiful

mostly pendant bell-flowers with corolla 2 cm long, yellow or orange, and forming leafy clusters to 30 cm long, during Summer.

Zone 10. *p. 739*

HERNANDIA   Hernandiaceae

bivalvis (Queensland), "Grease-nut"; handsome shrub or tree 6-12 m high, with scaly or furrowed bark; shiny green, broadly ovate leaves 6-15 cm long, partially deciduous during dry season; cream-colored flowers 2 cm across, borne in threes, the female bloom flanked by two males; most interesting for its striking display of pendant lantern-like fruit, enclosed by 2 or 3 inflated orange-red bracts, holding the hard seed, and filled with colorful dye; the soft greasy timber has been used on the brakes of horse-drawn vehicles. Photo by Ellison, Nowra, N.S.W., Australia. Zones 9-10. *p. 697*

HERNIARIA   Caryophyllaceae

glabra (So. Europe, No. Africa, Turkey to C. Asia), "Green carpet"; low, dense groundcover forming thick carpets and hugging the ground; hairy perennial with gray-green to bright green oval leaves 4-12 mm long, ciliate at margins; tiny insignificant greenish-white flowers. Used in California for rockeries and between stepping stones; turns bronzy in Winter. *Warm temperate.*

Zone 6. *p. 310, 360*

HERRANIA   Sterculiaceae

nitida (Brazil, Perú); evergreen shrub, with leaves palmately divided into 5 elongate-obovate light green leaflets 15-23 cm long and 6-7 cm wide, on 15 cm petioles; interesting red flowers 5 cm long; ellipsoid furrowed, yellowish fruit 6 cm long and about 4 cm thick. Zone 10. *p. 883*

HERSCHELIA   Orchidaceae

graminifolia (So. Africa), "Blue Disa"; lovely small terrestrial orchid seen on Table Mountain, Cape Town; subterranean tubers give rise to 4-6 grass-like basal leaves; the inflorescence on a reedy stalk to 60 cm high, with fragrant flowers 3 cm long; the sepals bright blue, lip white and edged with blue. Zones 10-11. *p. 88*

HESPERALOE   Agavaceae (Liliaceae)

parviflora (Texas to Mexico), "Western aloe" or "Red yucca"; evergreen yucca-like cluster-forming rosette of hard, recurving, channeled leaves to 1 m long, and 2½ cm wide, linear, thick and leathery, bright green lined with gray, and white coiling threads hanging from the corky margin; branched slender stalks to 2 m long, with racemes of small, nodding, waxy, bell-like 2½ cm flowers salmon-red outside, yellow inside. Zone 9. *p. 195, 447*

HESPERANTHA   Iridaceae

vaginata (So. Africa), "Evening flower"; charming small cormous species, with curled basal leaves; the showy cupped flowers golden-yellow, with blackish markings opening toward evening, and very fragrant. Zone 9. *p. 229*

HESPERIS   Cruciferae

matronalis (So. Europe, east to Siberia; natural. in No. America), "Dame's violet" or "Sweet rocket"; branched perennial to 80 cm high, partially hairy, with lanceolate, toothed 10 cm leaves, and 2 cm flowers lilac to purple, varying to white, in loose clusters; fragrant in evening; blooming late Spring to Summer. In former times used medicinally. Zone 3. *p. 410, 526*

HESPEROCALLIS   Liliaceae

undulata (So. California to Arizona), "Desert lily" of the Sonoran desert region; bulbous, leafy-stemmed herb to 60 cm high, the leaves linear and crisped or undulate at margins; raceme of short-lived trumpet-shaped fragrant flowers 6 cm long, the segments white with green stripe on back. Zone 8. *p. 246*

HETERANTHERA   Pontederiaceae

dubia (graminea) (U.S.A, Mexico, Cuba), "Water star-grass"; aquatic plant with stems submerged in water, or floating on the water surface, or creeping on wet ground; linear green leaves 6-12 cm long; spidery yellow flowers carried above the water. *Humid-subtropic.*

Zone 10. *p. 336*

reniformis (Pennsylvania to Argentina), "Mud-plantain"; aquatic perennial with underwater branches, rooting at joints; the submersed leaves lanceolate, the above water small reniform or kidney-shaped leaves on long stems, rich green with yellow base; sparse flowers, white or pale blue on 10 cm stalks. Zones 8-10. *p. 336*

HETEROARIDARUM   Araceae

annae (Sarawak, Borneo); small ornamental aroid of moist-tropical locations; from a very short stem with cord-like roots rise vaginate petioles, having long free sheath, bearing narrow, long elliptic, deep green leathery leaves to 25 cm long, arranged in two ranks, midrib very strong and lateral veins parallel; the handsome inflorescence with fluted, creamy-white spathe green at base, and club-shaped yellowish spadix. The plant collected by J. Bogner of Munich Bot. G. was later described as Aridarum. Zone 12. *p. 26*

HETEROCENTRON Melastomataceae

elegans (Heeria; Schizocentron) (Highlands of So. Mexico, Guatemala and Honduras), "Spanish-shawl" or "Crimson creeper"; low evergreen subshrub with slender spreading branches, rooting at nodes; ovate leaves 15 mm long; numerous solitary crimson-red flowers 2-3 cm across, forming a floral shawl over the ground. *Zone 10.* p. 786

macrostachyum (roseum in Standley; Lasiandra) (Mexico: Veracruz, Oaxaca to Chiapas; Honduras), "Perla de Cuba" or "Perl flower"; small evergreen shrub 60-100 cm high, with 4-angled branches; opposite elliptic 5 cm leaves, and clusters of bright rose flowers of 4 spreading petals 8 mm long, blooming Autumn into Winter. *Zone 10.* p. 786

mexicanum (Mexico: Durango to Sinaloa and Guerrero); tropical subshrub of the Sierra Madre, with erect stems partially herbaceous; elliptic or oblong leaves 3-7 cm long, appressed bristly; inflorescence with red branchlets topped by flowers having red calyx, opening with 4 obovate white or pink petals to 8 mm long, framing a prominent cluster of greenish stamens. *Zone 10.* p. 786

HETEROMELES Rosaceae

arbutifolia (Photinia) (California, Baja California), "Toyon" or "California holly"; also known as "Christmas-berry"; evergreen drought-resistant shrub or multiple trunk tree of the Sierra Nevada foothills, 3 to 8 m high, with leathery, recurved, shining leaves to 10 cm long; small white 1 cm flowers, followed by masses of bright red, long persistent berries through Winter; a striking ornamental. *Zone 9.* p. 835

HEUCHERA Saxifragaceae

x brizoides; charming hybrid coralbells (H. americana x sanguinea); floriferous herbaceous perennial 60 cm high, with rounded evergreen basal leaves lobed along margins; in May slender stalks rise to unfurl with a terminal one-sided raceme of small bell-shaped flowers of coral-rose, or occasionally white, to 5 mm long, lasting in bloom into Summer. *Zones 4-9.* p. 497

cylindrica (Brit. Columbia to No. California, east to Alberta, and Wyoming), "Alumroot"; tufted perennial 50 to 75 cm high, with roundish-cordate leaves, shallow-lobed and undulate; the inflorescence spike-like, dense with small waxy flowers having yellow-green to cream petals, during Summer. *Zones 3-7.* p. 497

rubescens (alpicola) (Oregon to So. Calif., Utah, Colorado); small rockdweller of the Sierra Nevada, forming tufts, with thick, roundish or kidney-shaped leaves; the inflorescence a series of open, one-sided clusters of small flowers with pinkish, green-tipped sepals, on wiry, scandent stalks to 40 cm long, in May to July. *Zone 3.* p. 497

sanguinea (Arizona, Mexico), "Coral bells"; attractive herbaceous perennial 30-50 cm high, with a tuft of rounded, lobed leaves 3-5 cm across, having silver markings; slender stalks bear airy racemes of small bell-shaped 1 cm flowers, bright rose-red; winter-hardy. Seen in the Swiss Alps as a potted plant. An important garden favorite, blooming from May on. *Zones 3-9.* p. 497

x HEUCHERELLA Saxifragaceae

tiarelloides (Heuchera x Tiarella); beautiful French intergeneric perennial of vigorous habit, spreading by stolons; pretty, golden-green, mostly roundish and lobed leaves 8-10 cm long; the inflorescence on wiry stalks 40 cm long, dense with small bell-shaped flowers 1 cm long, having carmine-rose calyx, and pale pink petals, blooming during May-June, and often again later. *Zone 4.* p. 497

HIBBERTIA Dilleniaceae

cuneiformis (Candollea) (Western Australia), "Button flower"; evergreen shrub to 3 m high, with leathery oblong leaves 2-4 cm long, toothed at margins; showy, rich yellow, solitary flowers 4 cm, among the crowded upper foliage. *Zone 10.* p. 695

scandens (Australia; New South Wales, Queensland), "Guinea goldvine"; shrub with trailing stems, and ovate leaves 8 cm long, silky beneath; beautiful, deep yellow flowers, to 5 cm across. *Subtropic. Zone 10.* p. 275

HIBISCUS Malvaceae

bifurcatus (Brazil); handsome tropical evergreen shrub, photographed in col. of Botanic Garden, Rio de Janeiro, having large and decorative leaves nearly round, lobed or cordate at base, showing contrasting veins spreading palmately; single yellow flowers 6-8 cm across, the 5 petals with ridged surface, tinted orange, and with bold black-purple base, framing the forked column. *Zone 10.* p. 782

cannabinus (Trop. Africa to India), "Kenaf" or "Indian hemp"; spiny annual, to perennial in mild climates, to 2 m or more tall; the upper leaves palmately 3-7 lobed, the lower foliage heart-shaped; large yellow flowers with crimson center, 8-15 cm across; bristly round 2 cm fruit, grown for its jute-like fiber. *Zone 10.* p. 456

coccineus (Coastal marshes of Georgia, Alabama and Florida), "Scarlet Rose-mallow"; handsome perennial to 2 m or more high, with

bluish-green leaves palmately parted into 5-7 toothed segments, on erect reddish stem; solitary, showy flowers in upper leaf axils, the glowing rose-red petals spreading in a whorl, to 15 cm across, and displaying staminal column. *Zone 7.* p. 456

diversifolius (Trop. E. Africa to Pacific), a tropical "Mallow"; prickly shrub 2 m high, with leaves varying from round to angular to deeply three to five-lobed; flowers 15 cm dia., yellow to purplish with blackish-red center. *Zone 10.* p. 782

fragilis (Mauritius); tropical evergreen shrub, with ovate, turgid leaves, soft downy beneath; charming smallish flowers about 10 cm across, coppery salmon petals lined or tinted with red above, the erect very prominent staminal column rising from center. *Zone 10.* p. 781

huegelii: see ALYOGYNE huegelii

moscheutos (Mass. to Michigan, so. to Florida and Alabama), "Rose mallow" or "Wild cotton"; evergreen perennial subshrub 1-2 m high, with hairy stems, and broadly ovate hairy leaves to 15 cm long, green above, white pubescent beneath; showy solitary flowers from leaf axils, the corolla 10-15 cm across, usually soft rose with crimson center, blooming August-September. *Zone 5.* p. 781

moscheutos 'Disco Belle' (Japan), "Dwarf rose-mallow"; superb dwarf hybrid by Sakata of Yokohama; perennial of compact branching habit, to 50 cm high, with large hairy leaves, and huge, beautiful flowers to 25 cm across, light to rosy-red with dark crimson center; white in another cultivar; blooming Summer into Autumn and covering the plant like an umbrella. *Zones 6-9.* p. 457

moscheutos 'Southern Belle'; "Giant Rose-mallow"; garden hybrid 80-120 cm high; serrate leaves, white-downy beneath; flowers pink, crimson-red, or white with red center; blooms extremely large, to 25 cm or more across, in late Summer. *Zones 5-9.* p. 457

mutabilis (South China), "Confederate rose" or "Cotton-rose"; fast-growing shrubby bush becoming tree-like where planted in the tropics and subtropics; green stems becoming woody, the large 3 to 5-lobed leaves 10-20 cm wide, dull green and rough pubescent; toward branch ends the showy axillary flowers 10-12 cm across, opening white or rose in the morning with crimson center and a divided maroon column; by evening the flower becomes deep red. In colder areas the plant is deciduous. *Subtropic. Zone 8.* p. 782

rosa-sinensis (Trop. Asia), "Chinese hibiscus" or "Tropical hibiscus"; magnificent flowering shrub of vigorous habit, to 3 m high; glossy green, serrate leaves, and mostly very large 5-petaled flowers from white to yellow and red to magenta. Hibiscus are among the most showy flowers of the tropics, especially the Chinese hibiscus, which is the state flower of Hawaii where some 5000 varieties are known. Raw flowers are eaten there to aid digestion. In Tahiti, a flower worn over the right ear shows that one is looking for a mate. Blossoms of most varieties remain open for one day only, unfolding early in the morning and dying after closing near sunset, but in good sunlight are almost everblooming, especially if given liberal watering and nourishment. Much used as flowering shrubs and hedges in tropical gardens. Chinese hibiscus are also wonderful container plants for pots or tubs indoors, or on the summer patio, preferring some rest, and cutting back in Winter; need lots of food and water when growing, to support adequate foliage and prodigious bloom. *Zones 9-10.* p. 622, 782

rosa-sinensis 'Brilliant', also known as 'San Diego Red'; vigorous evergreen tropical shrub to 5 m high, having willowy branches, dense with firm glossy green ovate leaves, strongly toothed at margins; free-blooming with showy, vivid crimson-red flowers about 10 cm across, the petals having frilled margins, and blooming throughout most of the year. *Zone 10.* p. 782

rosa-sinensis 'Butterball'; tropical evergreen shrub of bushy habit 1-2 m high, with flowers fully double, having spreading petals frilled and wavy in clear lemon-yellow. *Zone 10.* p. 782

rosa-sinensis 'California Gold'; shapely bush of robust habit to 2 m high, with fresh green, broad ovate leaves, and medium large, firm, single flowers golden-yellow, with crimson-red center, blooming with the sun. Very popular in California gardens. *Zones 9-10.* p. 782

rosa-sinensis 'Cherie'; bushy Danish hybrid (Nielsen 1960), of compact habit, with flowers bright orange-yellow or light beige, and crimson-purple in center, the margins of petals wavy. *Zone 10.* p. 782

rosa-sinensis 'Cooperi' (E. Indies), "Checkered hibiscus"; ornamental shrub mainly grown for its colorful foliage, the narrow-lanceolate leaves are metallic green and brightly variegated and marbled with dark olive, white, pink and crimson; small scarlet flowers. *Zone 10.* p. 615, 782

rosa-sinensis 'Crown of Bohemia'; bushy evergreen shrub to 3 m high; charming with double golden-yellow flowers; petals change to orange and carmine toward base; of long-lasting quality. *Zone 10.* p. 783

rosa-sinensis 'Fiesta' (Monrovia Nurs. pat.); very impressive cultivar with striking single flowers to 16 cm across, the center a white zone framed with red, from there streaking upward on petals and changing to bright orange toward apex, crinkled along margins; in the middle of corolla a prominent staminal column; evergreen bush of vigorous growth eventually 2 m high, with excellent green foliage. Similar to H. 'Single orange' as offered by some California garden centers. Zone 10. p. 784

rosa-sinensis 'Fijian Pink' (Fiji); tropical evergreen bush, profusely blooming with single flowers pale pink, having contrasting, deep maroon-red center, with long protruding staminal column, the petals prettily frilled. To add vigor and height, the plant photographed in Suva Botanic Garden had been grafted. Zone 10. p. 783

rosa-sinensis 'Florida Sunset'; dense evergreen bush, with glossy, rich green foliage, and showy flowers of exquisite coloring, 10 cm or more across, the central area blotched or streaked with crimson-red, toward the frilled margins creamy-yellow to ivory. Zone 10. p. 783

rosa-sinensis 'Hula Girl'; of compact growth, to 2 m; large single flowers 15 cm across, yellow to salmon with bold crimson center and purple lines; prolific blooms; the blossoms may remain open several days. Zone 10. p. 782

rosa-sinensis 'Lawrence orange'; vigorous erect evergreen bush, dense with small foliage, and very free-blooming with a profusion of 8-10 cm single flowers vivid rosy-orange, shading to red in center, the margins lacily frilled. Photographed in col. Andromeda Gardens, Barbados. Zones 10-11. p. 784

rosa-sinensis 'Lemon Glow'; tropical cultivar of compact habit, with medium size flowers vivid pale yellow, except for purplish lines and streaks at base of petals, surrounding the staminal column. Photographed on the Caribbean island of Barbados. Zones 10-11. p. 784

rosa-sinensis 'Lucky-me'; fascinating large flowers, with broad recurving petals of firm texture, glossy crimson-red, transversed by elevated ridges or veins of white. Seen in col. Bermuda Botanic Garden, Hamilton. Zones 10-11. p. 783

rosa-sinensis 'Punta Gorda Gold'; exquisite flowers with broad, recurved crepe-like petals lemon-yellow tinted deep orange, and with purplish-red base, ringing the pistillate column. Zones 10-11. p. 783

rosa-sinensis 'Reef'; delicate-looking, exquisite beauty with overlapping, shingled broad petals glowing crimson in central part, and creamy-white toward undulate, frilled margins. The plant photographed at Quail Botanic Garden in Encinitas, California, had been grafted on H. 'President', a more vigorous understock for better growth under less than ideal tropical situations. Zones 10-11. p. 783

rosa-sinensis 'Santana'; lovely mutant of low habit, evergreen bush to 120 cm high, with single flowers of medium size 10 cm across orange-red except for the pinkish-cream marginal area of petals. Zones 10-11. p. 71, 784

rosa-sinensis 'Scarlet'; a cultivar very floriferous with single, medium-large flowers in blazing scarlet-crimson, 10-12 cm across, and bold staminal column, blooming with the sun from early Spring into late Fall and through the Winter if kept light and warm; its strong habit with its glossy foliage lends itself to training into attractive tree-like semi-standards. Zones 9-10. p. 783

rosa-sinensis 'Tiki'; attractive exotic Hawaii cultivar with large single flowers vivid yellow, shading to apricot-salmon inside, and a contrasting maroon-red center at base of long staminal column. The plant photographed in col. Quail Bot. Garden, Encinitas, Calif., was grafted on the more vigorous H. 'President', a robust single red. Zones 10-11. p. 784

rosa-sinensis 'White Wings'; large flowers with linear, spreading petals 9 cm long, freely separated to base, white with contrasting feathery crimson base, and long red staminal column. Willing grower of spreading habit, to 4 m high, and profuse with blooms. Zones 9-10. p. 71, 783

schizopetalus (Trop. E. Africa), "Fringed hibiscus" or "Japanese lantern"; glabrous evergreen shrub to 4 m high, with slender drooping branches, and smooth, ovate-elliptic, toothed leaves; the showy orange-red flowers, hanging from slender stalks, to 8 cm across, the petals deeply slit and recurved, and a long projecting pendulous staminal column. Zone 10. p. 784

schizopetalus 'Pagoda' (Colombia), "Flora en flora"; curious mutant from Colombia, with bright red flowers, the tubular column of united stamens white, the style developed into a petaloid secondary cluster of frilled petals resembling a miniature rose. Zone 10. p. 784

syriacus (East Asia), "Rose of Sharon" or "Shrub althaea"; deciduous shrub or small tree to 3 m; leaves to 8 cm long, triangular or three-lobed and coarsely toothed; flowers single or double, 6-8 cm across, rosy-lavender with purple center, but also other shades including white, summer-blooming June to September; and beloved by bees. Zone 5. p. 784

syriacus 'Coelestis'; a form of "Shrub-althaea" with flaring bell-like single flowers in a shade of delicate mauve-blue with darker eye, 9 cm across. Zone 5. p. 784

syriacus 'Helene'; attractive triploid hybrid, seen in col. Cologne Bot. Garden, Germany; with white-pubescent branches, and trilobed deciduous leaves, the segments toothed at margins; showy flowers arranged along upper part of stem, the broadly campanulate corolla 8 cm across, white with crimson center, valued for its late-season blooming August-September. Zone 5. p. 784

syriacus 'Monstrosus'; showy cultivar of robust habit, to 2 m high, with trilobed leaves 5-10 cm long; very large single flowers, the petals white and tinted pink, crimson-purple at base, jagged and ruffled at margins; blooming June-September, on young shoots. Zone 5. p. 785

syriacus 'Morning sky' ('Sky-blue'); vigorous Rose of Sharon with erect branches, and rich green, lobed leaves; the flowers broadly cup-shaped, opening wide, bluish-lavender with contrasting purple eye; blooming late Summer. Zone 5. p. 785

syriacus rubis 'Woodbridge', introduced by Notcutt of Suffolk 1928 and admired in many gardens; densely leafy rounded bush with lobed foliage; producing a multitude of flowers rated among the largest in the species, to 10 cm across; the open campanulate corolla rich carmine-rose deepening to magenta-red inside, and with red-purple eye. Zone 6. p. 785

tetrandra; interesting evergreen shrub, seen in col. Duesseldorf Botanic Garden, Germany; narrow elliptic glossy green leaves; small yellow flowers 3 cm across, with 5 obovate petals lightly lobed or squared at apex; blooming in May. Zone 10. p. 785

tiliaceus (Althaea) (Trop. Asia and Polynesia), "Cotton-wood" or "Mahoe"; evergreen tropical crooked shrub or much branched tree to 4 m or more, with large cordate, matte-green leaves, white-hairy beneath; 8 cm flowers open lemon-yellow with or without brown-red base inside, later in the day they change to orange and by night to red. In Polynesia, the fiber of its inner bark is used for ropes or tapa cloth. Zone 10. p. 785

trionum (So. Europe, W. and C. Asia, E. and So. Africa), "Flower-of-an-hour"; bushy annual with leaves deeply divided into coarsely toothed lobes; cupped 8 cm flowers sulphur-yellow or white with velvety purple center. Subtropic. Zone 10. p. 456

HIERACIUM   *Compositae*

aurantiacum (No. Europe, Poland, Russia, Romania; natur. in E. No. America), "Orange hawkweed" or "King-devil"; stoloniferous perennial 30 to 50 cm high, covered with long, spreading hairs; green leaves oblanceolate, bearing milky juice, to 20 cm long, mostly in basal rosettes; inflorescence in long-stalked clusters, with floral heads 3 cm across, the ray-florets orange or red, ranged around the yellow disc, in June to September. Of striking color, but apt to become troublesome, spreading rapidly by rooting, leafy runners. Zone 6. p. 394

bombycinum (Pyrenees of Spain), "Hawkweed"; perennial to 40 cm high, forming a flat rosette of soft, obovate grayish-green leaves to 8 cm long and silvery pubescent; spreading by underground stems; the floral heads on long stalks, attractive with numerous yellow ray-florets, to 4 cm across, throughout the Summer. Zone 4. p. 394

maculatum (West and Cent. Europe), "Devil's paintbrush"; spreading perennial of basal rosettes, with broad-ovate leaves, wavy-toothed and spotted purple; reddish hairy stems to 40 cm, also leafy, and topped by clusters of yellow flowers; the ray-florets toothed; blooming Summer to Autumn. Zone 6. p. 394

villosum (Europe: Alps to Carpathian Mts.), "Shaggy hawkweed"; handsome spreading perennial to 60 cm high, the oblong silvery glaucous leaves silky pubescent; the attractive wide open flowers of many bright yellow ray-florets to 5 cm across, blooming June to August. Zone 5. p. 394

HILLIA   *Rubiaceae*

parasitica (West Indies to Trop. So. America); tropical epiphytic straggling shrub dwelling on trees, having thick ovate leaves to 10 cm long; large white starry flowers with corolla tube 8-10 cm long, the six long slender lobes with margins rolled under and tinted pink. Zone 11. p. 298

HIPPEASTRUM   *Amaryllidaceae*

'Leopoldii hybrid' (Amaryllis), a Dutch "Amaryllis"; the leopoldii hybrids are considered the finest class of fancy flowering amaryllis in pots, the result of breeding H. leopoldii from Perú with reginae and other species; large flat, open-faced flowers generally 20 cm but even to 30 cm across, with roundish, overlapping segments, and short tubes. Hybrid clones come in a wide range of colors, from deep glowing red, clear scarlet, orange-red, light rose, and white with stripes or finally, all white. Tropical. Zone 10. p. 56, 213

'Papilio' (Argentina), "Butterfly amaryllis" (Wayside Gard. introduction 1986); exotically different from other amaryllis, with flaring flowers 10 x 15 cm wide, the white background tinged soft green, and handsomely variegated with radiating areas and stripes of maroon-red, carried on 60 cm floral stalks above the glossy evergreen leaves. Zones 9-10. p. 213

puniceum (H. equestre) (West Indies and Mexico to Brazil), popularly known as the "American belladonna" or "Barbados lily"; a smaller-flowered amaryllis with bulb having brown scales and short neck, narrow strap-shaped, pointed waxy green leaves 2 to 3 cm wide, and long round stalk bearing 2 or more obliquely trumpet-shaped flowers of 12 cm dia. and 10 cm long, salmon-red, with center creamy-whitish with greenish bands, an oblique feathery corona in base; stamens when straight larger than stigma; an old-fashioned flowering houseplant almost continuously in bloom. *Tropical.*
Zones 9 -10.   *p. 213*

reticulatum 'Striatifolium', "Stripe-leaf amaryllis"; an interesting variety of this bulbous Brazilian plant because of its strap-shaped dark green leaves having a prominent ivory-white midrib; the lily-like flowers are rose-pink lined with darker rose. *Tropical.*
Zone 10.   *p. 213*

vittatum (Peruvian Andes), "Striped amaryllis"; large bulb producing trumpet-shaped flowers white with purple stripes; fairly broad, pointed petals; stalks hollow; strap-shaped leaves appearing with or after flowers. *Zone 9.*   *p. 213*

'Vittatum hybrid', commercial "Dutch Amaryllis", developed from species of the Peruvian Andes; large bulb producing spectacular trumpet-shaped flowers to 15 cm across, several on a hollow stalk, most often scarlet-red with white; strap-shaped leaves appearing with or after bloom, in late Winter; parentage includes H. leopoldii, reginae, aulicum, solandriflorum, reticulatum. *Tropical.*
Zone 10.   *p. 213*

vittatum 'King of the Striped'; striking amaryllis cultivar seen at Keukenhof Gardens in Holland 1985, with showy flowers 20 cm dia., having crimson-red bands and stripes alternating with white.
Zone 10.   *p. 213*

HIPPOMANE   *Euphorbiaceae*
mancinella (W. Indies), "Manzanillo"; large spreading shrub with milky, poisonous sap, leaves shining green, ovate, 8 cm long; flowers inconspicuous; the fruitlike little green apples; very ornamental and prominent along the shores of Curacao. *Tropical. Zone 10.*   *p. 724*

HIPPOPHAE   *Elaeagnaceae*
rhamnoides (Europe; Caucasus, Iran, Siberia), "Sea-buck-thorn"; spiny shrub, very hardy, to 10 m high, covered with silvery scales; narrow willow-like, thin-leathery leaves; inconspicuous yellow flowers, and masses of bright orange-yellow 1 cm fruit, staying on all Winter.
Zone 3.   *p. 695*

HIPPURIS   *Hippuridaceae (Haloragidaceae)*
vulgaris (No. America, No. and C. Europe, No. Asia, Patagonia), "Mare's-tail"; perennial species suggestive of a horse-tail or a slender needle-tree, but aquatic or as marsh plant; the trailing stems to 1 m long when floating or rooting in the mud, erect and unbranched above water; the linear leaves in whorls, 1-2 cm long. Tolerates water temperature down to 10°C. Hibernates during Winter.
Zones 6-10.   *p. 331*

HOFFMANNIA   *Rubiaceae*
ghiesbreghtii 'Variegata', "Variegated taffeta plant'; delicate form with its long perfoliate leaves variegated and mottled on the quilted surface with cream and pink over milky green and bronze; red beneath. *Tropical. Zone 12.*   *p. 79*

refulgens (Chiapas), "Quilted taffeta plant"; beautiful, low, herbaceous plant with the short-jointed, red stem hidden by the broadly obovate, heavily quilted leaves almost fleshy, iridescent-velvety coppery purple, shading to greenish, with bluish or light green ribs and red-hairy, red margin; wine-red beneath; flowers pale red. *Humid-tropical. Zone 12.*   *p. 79*

HOHENBERGIA   *Bromeliaceae*
stellata (Brazil, Venezuela); loose rosette of green leathery leaves, finely toothed; inflorescence a long leaning spike with alternate clusters of red bracts with purple flowers. *Tropical. Zone 11.*   *p. 46*

HOHERIA   *Malvaceae*
lyallii (glabrata) (New Zealand), "Mountain lace-bark"; deciduous shrub or small tree to 6 m high, from the Southern Alps of New Zealand; white-pubescent in all parts; bright green, leathery, ovate-cordate leaves 5-10 cm long, and jaggedly toothed; pure white flowers 3 cm across, in small axillary clusters, displaying numerous stamens, blooming June-August. *Zone 7.*   *p. 785*

HOLCUS   *Gramineae*
mollis 'Albo-variegatus' (Europe, Algeria), "Velvet grass" or "Creeping soft grass"; attractive variegated deciduous grass with rhizomes forming tufts of erect culms to 30 cm high, very effective in gardens during Spring and Summer; the hairy leaves striped green and white, to 20 cm long; branched oblong inflorescence with two-flowered bisexual spikelets during July-August. *Zone 5.*   *p. 560*

HOLMSKIOLDIA   *Verbenaceae*
sanguinea (Himalayas), "Chinese-hat-plant" or "Cup-and-saucer plant"; subtropical, straggling shrub attaining 10 m, with slender-pointed ovate leaves to 10 cm long, and curious flowers having scarlet tubular corolla 2 cm long, and a spreading bell-shaped, orange calyx. Widely grown for its odd and beautiful blossoms. *Subtropic.*
Zone 10.   *p. 899*

sanguinea citrina (Himalayas, China), "Mandarin's hat"; attractive color form with cup-and-saucer flowers having yellow corolla, usually set in axillary clusters along branches. *Zone 10.*   *p. 899*

HOLODISCUS   *Rosaceae*
discolor (Brit. Columbia to Montana, and So. California), "Cream-bush" or "Ocean spray"; deciduous shrub to 4 m high, with gracefully arching branches; ovate leaves to 8 cm long, with sunken veins, and shallowly lobed or toothed along margins; small creamy-white flowers in large feathery clusters 20 cm long, blooming in July.
Zone 5.   *p. 834*

HOMALANTHUS   *Euphorbiaceae*
populifolius (Ceylon to Pacific Is., E. Australia), "Queensland poplar"; attractive bushy shrub or small tree 2 m or more high, with soft, broad-ovate glaucous leaves 5-10 cm long, on slender stalks, coppery while young; the foliage turning to rich red in Autumn; the flowers pale green and yellow, the males and females separate; bark and leaves yield black dye. *Zones 9-10.*   *p. 724*

HOMALOCLADIUM   *Polygonaceae*
platycladum (Muehlenbeckia) (Solomon Isl.), "Ribbon bush" or "Tapeworm plant"; odd curiosity plant with perfectly flat, jointed, fresh green stems and small, lanceolate leaves; leafless in the blooming stage, with small greenish flowers at alternate joints; in the tropics making round canes to 4 m long. *Zones 10-11.*   *p. 820*

HOMALOMENA   *Araceae*
wallisii (Curmeria) (Colombia), "Silver shield"; low, compact, leathery plant with broad, oval, reflexed leaves 12-18 cm long, dark olive-green and beautifully blotched with yellowish-silver, translucent-silvery edge. *Tropical. Zone 12.*   *p. 30*

HOMERIA   *Iridaceae*
breyniana (collina) (S.E. Cape, So. Africa), "Cape tulip"; cormous plant to 45 cm high; usually one basal leaf only but others along floral stem, these concave and to 60 cm long; very fragrant 4 cm flowers variable salmon-pink or yellow, lasting only a day and closing at night.
Zone 9.   *p. 226*

breyniana 'Aurantiaca' (S.W. Cape, So. Africa), "Orange Cape tulip"; natural variety less robust in habit, with orange flowers. Homeria corms are covered with a loose outer skin.
Zone 9.   *p. 226*

HOODIA   *Asclepiacadeae*
rosea (So. Africa, Botswana), "African hat plant"; clustering cactus-like succulent to 30 cm high with leafless circular grayish-green stems branching from the base, ribs about 14, dense with tubercles armed with pale brown spines; the spectacular flowers have a saucer-shaped flat corolla 8 cm across, rosy to cinnamon and covered with thin hairs. Keep dry and warm in Winter. *Arid-subtropic.*
Zones 10-11.   *p. 151*

HORDEUM   *Gramineae*
nodosum (West. U.S. Pacific States to Alaska, Rocky Mts.), "Barley grass"; stiffly erect perennial grass forming clusters, with narrow linear leaves; erect stems to 60 cm or more high, topped by slender fruit spikes. Cultivated as fodder in agriculture; also quite ornamental. *Zone 4.*   *p. 567*

vulgare (Sativum distichum) (Temp. Eurasia), "Barley grain" or "Nepal barley"; hardy annual grass of importance in agriculture, with flat leaves, and stems to 1 m high, topped by mostly erect fruiting spikes filled with seeds, and tipped by awns to 15 cm long; the fruit is furrowed along the face and 1 cm long. Widely cultivated for the grains, as cereal and source of malt in brewing beer. *Zone 4.*   *p. 567*

HOSTA   *Liliaceae*
amanuma (Japan); miniature perennial species seen in col. Palmengarten, Frankfurt, Germany 1984; bushy clustering rosette of broad, ovate-cordate, matte-green leaves 10-15 cm or more long, having parallel depressed ribs; from the base rise slender, purple floral stalks bearing small whitish trumpet flowers tinted lilac to purple, blooming June-July. *Zone 6.*   *p. 447*

crispula (Japan), (syn. H. fortunei var. marginato-alba, H. coerulea); elegant plant densely tufted, slow growing but forming large groups; elliptic long-pointed leaves with 7-9 veins, matte-green above, bordered white, and undulate; glossy beneath, 20 cm long; 5 cm lavender flowers, on stalk to 90 cm long. *Warm temperate.*
Zones 5-8.   *p. 448*

decorata 'Marginata' (Japan: Honshu); clustering perennial plantain-lily of compact habit, with oval green leaves 15-20 cm long, bordered with white, 4-5 pairs of lateral veins, on winged petioles; dark lilac to violet pendant 5 cm flowers with striped segments, on stalks to 60 cm high, exceeding foliage; spreading by underground stolons; Hosta leaves are deciduous during dormant period. In most American nurseries known as 'Thomas Hogg'. *Zones 4-9.* p. 447

elata 'Praeflorens' (Japan); handsome, robust perennial to 90 cm or more high, clustering with decorative broad-ovate leaves to 25 cm long, dark green and with cordate base, 8-10 depressed nerves each side of midrib; bluish-lavender funnel-flowers 6 cm long, in dense clusters topping the slender purplish stalk, June-blooming, earlier than the species. *Zones 3-7.* p. 448

fortunei (Japan: Honshu), the "Tall-cluster plantain-lily" or "Giant plantain-lily"; broad leaves about 20 cm long, cordate at base, dark green to bluish-green slightly glaucous, with 10-12 nerves either side of midrib, grayish beneath; funnel-shaped flowers white flushed lavender, 5 cm long, in elongate clusters, the scapes much taller than foliage, to 60 cm or more high, summer-blooming. *Zones 3-9.* p. 448

fortunei 'Albo-picta'; handsome deciduous perennial forming clusters of near rosettes, with very decorative, thin-leathery leaves to 20 cm long, the margins dark green but entire central area primrose-yellow to cream; the surface corrugated by depressed, darker veins. *Zones 4-9.* p. 448

fortunei 'Aureo marginata';compact cultivar, with corrugated, broad ovate-cordate leaves, rich green, and bordered with yellow along margins, turning to cream in Summer. *Zones 4-9.* p. 448

fortunei 'Rugosa', "Crinkled plantain-lily"; rosettes of somewhat fleshy leaves, oblong nearly rounded in outline and cupped, with cordate base, on thick petioles, the blades matte-green, and corrugated or crinkled, and glaucous beneath. *Zones 4-9.* p. 448

lancifolia (japonica) (Japan), "Narrowleaf plantain-lily"; vigorous, clustering perennial, with narrow, tapering lanceolate glossy green leaves 12 cm long, having 3 to 4 depressed nerves either side of midrib, on long slender petioles; funnel-shaped 3-4 cm flowers pale lavender, with spreading segments, on 60 cm stalks. *Zones 3-9.* p. 447

lancifolia 'Albo-marginata', "White-rim plantain-lily"; handsome horticultural variety, elegant with slender, trim green leaves prominently corrugated by depressed parallel ribs, and prettily edged ivory-white. *Zones 4-9.* p. 447

plantaginea (grandiflora) (Japan, China), "Fragrant plantain-lily"; bold plant with large ovate-cordate green leaves 25 cm long, 7-9 veins either side of midrib, stalk with incurved wings; large white, 10 cm trumpet-like, ascending fragrant flowers in short racemes, but above foliage. August-September blooming. *Zones 3-9.* p. 448

plantaginea cv. 'Honey Bells' (plantaginea x lancifolia); robust horticultural variety of rather flat, rosette-like habit, with large, grass-green leaves to 25 cm long, and fragrant, lavender to lilac bell-flowers on 90 cm stalks. *Zones 4-9.* p. 447

rectifolia (Japan, Sakhalin), "Giant funkia"; vigorous perennial, forming large clusters of corrugated, somewhat leathery, mid-green leaves, broad-ovate in outline, to 30 cm long, on channelled, winged petioles to 40 cm long; the trumpet-shaped flowers lilac to violet, 5 cm long, in erect racemes to 30 cm long, blooming July. *Zones 3-8.* p. 449

sieboldiana (albomarginata hort.) also listed in catalogs as H. glauca, the "Seersucker-plantain-lily"; large rhizomatous perennial to 75 cm high; giant roundish to ovate 25-40 cm leaves with many deeply depressed veins, bluish-green on surface, glaucous blue beneath and occasionally margined white; deciduous during dormant season; nodding 4 cm trumpet flowers white tinged lilac, in clusters above foliage, midsummer-blooming. *Zones 3-9.* p. 449

sieboldiana 'Elegans', "Giant blue hosta"; beautiful horticultural variety with huge, puckered bluish-gray leaves, rather rounded, and with cordate base, to 40 cm long; the flowers are pale lavender to white, on 45-60 cm stalks in July-August. *Zones 3-9.* p. 449

sieboldiana viridis; robust showpiece variety with large corrugated leaves all satiny green; the whitish to pale lilac tubular flowers in dense erect racemes, blooming late Spring to early Summer. *Zones 3-9.* p. 449

sieboldiana 'Williams' ('Frances Williams'), "Gold circle hosta"; beautiful cultivar to 90 cm high, with large, broad-ovate leaves having cordate base, the center bluish-gray and wrinkled, and a variable edging of golden-yellow, to 40 cm long; the lavender or pale purple flowers in dense heads, partially hidden by the foliage; late summer-blooming. A favorite classic of the Hosta Society. *Zones 3-9.* p. 449

tardiflora (lancifolia var., syn. sparsa) (Japan), "Autumn plantain-lily"; close to lancifolia; low-growing dwarf variety, forming mounds 15-30 cm high, with almost leathery, lanceolate long pointed, dark green leaves; 3-4 cm flowers pale purple with darker veins, late-blooming. *Zones 3-9.* p. 448

'Thomas Hogg'; of American hort., bot. prob. clone of H. decorata; attractive compact, clustering perennial with broad ovate leaves to 20 cm long, prettily edged by broad white margins, and grayish beneath; the violet flowers carried well above foliage, on stalks to 60 cm long. *Zones 4-9.* p. 448

tokudama (Japan), "Todukama" of Honshu Isl.; handsome clustering perennial of low habit, with rounded leaves 15 by 20 cm dia., the blades glaucous green and wrinkled above, bluish beneath, cupped saucer-like and leathery; floral stalks 30-50 cm long, topped by short, dense racemes of white or pale purple 4 cm flowers, blooming in Summer. Very popular in Japanese gardens. *Zones 3-8.* p. 449

undulata 'Univittata' (Japan), "Wavy leaf shade lily" or "Snow feather funkia"; very pretty perennial forming low clusters of elegant, rich green, ovate, sharp-pointed leaves 15 cm long, splashed through the middle with creamy-white; the blade typically twisted and undulate, abruptly narrowed into winged petiole; funnel-form, pale purple flowers 5 to 6 cm long, having recurved segments, the anthers purple, clustered in tall racemes on floral stalks to 1 m long, blooming late Spring to Summer. *Zones 4-9.* p. 449

ventricosa (caerulea) (E. Asia), "Bell funkia" or "Blue plantain lily"; bushy plant with broad ovate-cordate, ribbed green leaves 20 cm long; tall many-flowered raceme on stiff stem to 1 m long; the flowers with expanded tubular corolla 5 cm long, dark lavender to nearly blue, striped white inside; in May. *Zones 3-9.* p. 449

venusta (Japan and Korea), "Pretty plantain lily", "Otome-giboshi"; petite perennial 15 to 30 cm high, the most widely planted of the real dwarf species; thin-leathery, lance-shaped mid-green leaves to 6 cm long and shiny beneath; the funnel form 4 cm flowers pale purple, a few to a cluster, on hollow stalk 10-30 cm long, summer-blooming. *Zones 3-8.* p. 449

HOUSTONIA caerulea (Zander):
see: HEDYOTIS caerulea (Hortus)

HOUTTUYNIA　　　*Saururaceae*
cordata (Himalaya to Japan); pungent-scented swamp perennial to 40 cm high, with creeping rootstock; 6-10 cm cordate-pointed leaves richly coloring in Autumn, and red beneath; tiny petal-less flowers subtended by 4 white petal-like bracts. *Zone 6.* p. 495

HOVENIA　　　*Rhamnaceae*
dulcis (Japan, China to Himalaya), "Japanese raisin tree"; interesting deciduous tree to 10 m high, with oval leaves 10-16 cm long; small greenish flowers in terminal or axillary clusters; after blooming the red fruit stalks are swelling, containing a sweet red pulp, which is eaten, especially in Japan. *Zone 5.* p. 828, 924

HOWEA (HOWEIA)　　　*Palmae*
belmoreana (Kentia) (Lord Howe Island), "Sentry palm"; handsome feather palm to 8 m, with pinnate leaves erect and then arching downward, the segments crowded, narrower than forsteriana, first upward then gracefully pendant and slender-pointed, on reddish stalks; fruit yellow-green. *Subtropic. Zone 11.* p. 108

forsteriana (Kentia) (Lord Howe Isl., near Australia), "Paradise palm"; elegant, sturdy decorator, widely used by florists because of its good keeping qualities; graceful pinnate fronds growing successively larger on slender stalks, the well-spaced, waxy deep green pinnae leathery and durable; with age forming a robust trunk 20 m high; yellow-green, olive-shaped fruit, in heavy clusters, in successive 4-strand racemes; the seed requiring about 4 years to ripen after first flowering. *Subtropic. Zone 10-11.* p. 77, 105

HOYA　　　*Asclepiadaceae*
bella (paxtonii) (India), "Miniature wax plant"; dwarf, shrubby plant with flexuous branches first upright, later drooping, the small, thick leaves ovate, deep green; flowers waxy-white with purple center. *Tropical. Zone 11.* p. 266

carnosa (Queensland, So. China), called "Wax plant" because of the waxy, wheel-shaped, fragrant, pinkish-white flowers 2 cm across, with a red, star-shaped crown in pendant umbels; root climbing vines with elliptic fleshy-waxy leaves 8 cm long. *Subtropic. Zone 10.* p. 266

carnosa 'Variegata', "Variegated wax plant"; ornamental variety with the fresh green to bluish leaves broadly bordered creamy-white and even pink; more variegated than 'Marginata'. *Tropical. Zones 10-11.* p. 266, 267

lacunosa (Malaysia); tall twiner with thin, rooting stems; long-elliptic leaves; velvety, fragrant flowers greenish-yellow. *Zone 11.* p. 266

multiflora (Malacca in Malaya), "Shooting stars"; stout, smooth climber with elliptic, leathery leaves 8 cm long; magnificent inflorescence a dense cluster of starry straw-colored flowers tipped brown; silky inside. *Tropical. Zones 10-11.* p. 267

polyneura (Himalayan reg.), "Fishtail hoya"; broad ovate, opposite glossy green leaves with darker veins, 6-8 cm long; waxy flowers like white stars, corona bronzy red. *Subtropic.* *Zone 10.* p. 267

HUDSONIA   Cistaceae

ericoides (Nova Scotia to No. Carolina), "Golden heather" or "Beach heather"; twiggy low heath-like evergreen with spreading branches and forming mounds to 20 cm high, with green scale-like, awl-shaped leaves 1 cm long, and covered with fine down; small bright yellow flowers 1 cm wide, borne along the twigs. *Zone 3.* p. 686

HUERNIA   Asclepiadaceae

reticulata (So. Africa: Cape Prov.); clustering succulent 5-10 cm high, stems with 5 acute, toothed angles, coppery green mottled with red; plate-like flowers 5 cm dia., yellow reticulated with red; fleshy blackish-red crown. *Arid-subtropic. Zone 10.* p. 151

HUMULUS   Moraceae (Cannabaceae)

japonicus 'Variegatus' (scandens) (Temp. E. Asia), "Japanese hops"; ornamental rough-stemmed, tall twining perennial, with serrate leaves deeply 5-7-lobed, rugose surface in shades of green, yellow and splashed with white; small flowers in cone-like, bracted spikes; useless for the brewing of beer. Generally grown as an Annual. *Warm temperate. Zone 7.* p. 284

lupulus (Eurasia), "European hops"; vigorous rough-stemmed, tall-climbing woody perennial with 3 to 5-lobed, rough leaves coarsely toothed; flowers greenish-yellow, the males small in loose clusters; the female plants bearing their flowers in imbricated green cones or "hops" which are stripped and used in brewing of beer. *Zone 3.* p. 284, 540

HUNNEMANNIA   Papaveraceae

fumariifolia (Mexico), "Mexican tulip-poppy"; erect perennial or annual 60-90 cm high, woody at base, grown as annual; glaucous 3-parted leaves 5-10 cm, with linear segments, and long-stalked yellow flowers 5-8 cm across, of four concave petals. *Zone 10.* p.467

HURA   Euphorbiaceae

crepitans (West Indies, Costa Rica, So. America), "Sandbox-tree", or "Monkey-dinner-bell"; great tree to 30 m; the trunk and branches spiny, with poisonous milky juice; large hairy, poplar-like ovate, toothed leaves to 60 cm long; small red flowers without petals; the hard-shelled, ribbed 8 cm fruit bursts with loud noise when ripe, ejecting its seed. *Zone 10.* p. 724

HUTCHINSIA   Cruciferae

alpina (Pyrenees of Spain, to Alps and Balkans), "Alpen-cress"; miniature Alpine perennial to 10 cm high, with dark green, dissected 2 cm fern-like foliage, covered by masses of small, pure white flowers in 3 cm clusters, blooming May-July. *Zone 6.* p. 410

HYACINTHOIDES   Liliaceae

hispanica (Endymion hispanicus, Scilla campanulata) (Spain, Portugal to Morocco), "Spanish bluebells"; clustering perennial plant, from bulbs renewed yearly; strap-shaped linear basal leaves to 30 cm long; very floriferous with erect cylindrical raceme to 50 cm high, loosely set with bell-shaped blue or purplish flowers having blue anthers, in Spring. *Zone 5.* p. 239

non-scripta (syn. Scilla nutans in hort.; Endymion) (W. Europe), "English bluebell" or "Wood hyacinth"; popular perennial in Europe, bushy with narrow linear leaves 20-40 cm long; floral stems to 45 cm high, bearing one-sided raceme of bell-shaped, fragrant blue flowers 2 cm long, with cream anthers, in late Spring; in contrast to Scilla, new bulblets are formed each year. *Zone 6.* p. 239

HYACINTHUS   Liliaceae

orientalis hybrids, known as the "Dutch Garden Hyacinths", derived from the species native from Greece to Asia Minor and Syria; bulbous perennials to 30 cm high, with glossy green, strap-shaped fleshy basal leaves, and producing on succulent stalks showy spike-like racemes dense with intensely fragrant, waxy bell-flowers, in many named cultivars in colors white, pink, red, purple, blue and yellow, blooming outdoors in temperate climate from mid-April to May; bulbs planted in gardens are reasonable frosthardy to Zone 6, with mulch protection. Very popular for indoor forcing, using large-size bulbs in pots, to bring into bloom from December on.

'Anne Marie'; a Dutch garden hyacinth; bulbous plant with glossy green, fleshy, strap-shaped leaves and producing showy spike-like raceme of fragrant, waxy, delicate soft, clear pink flowers 3 cm long; heads smallish, but fine for earliest forcing. *Zone 7.* p. 242

'Blue Jacket'; large heads of single dark blue flowers, with small purple stripe; excellent for Spring forcing. Early to Mid-season. *Zone 6.* p. 242

'Carnegie'; an excellent late-blooming Dutch hyacinth of robust, compact habit with large and full heavy heads of pure white, waxy

flowers; a favorite for flowering in pots especially if Easter is late, while the ivory-white 'L'Innocence' is recommended for an early Easter. *Late. Zone 6.* p. 242

'Delft Blue', a "Dutch hyacinth"; excellent for Easter flowering in pans; large 3-4 yr. bulbs will produce a full spike of bright porcelain-blue flowers of rich fragrance, mid-season to Late. *Zone 6.* p. 54, 242

'Lady Derby'; splendid large pyramidal head of very fragrant, large waxy bell-flowers vivid rose-pink, for mid-season blooming. *Zone 6.* p. 242

'Ostara'; robust Dutch garden hyacinth with large, heavy spikes of medium sized, 3 cm porcelain-blue or violet-purple waxy flowers on pale center, suitable for both early and Easter flowering in pots; an improvement of the old favorite, pale blue 'Bismarck'. Early to Mid-season. *Zone 6.* p. 242

'Pink Pearl'; an excellent, vivid pink hyacinth, often with two spikes per bulb; the trumpet-shaped flowers are more loosely set, the stout stalks are brittle as in all hyacinths, and leaves are linear. Early. *Zone 6.* p. 242

HYDNOCARPUS   Flacourtiaceae

anthelmintica (Thailand), "Chaulmoogra tree"; evergreen tree to 15 m, with thin, leathery narrow leaves; flowers with numerous stamens; fruit 6 cm dia., a hard shell covered with brown velvet; the seed containing oil for treatment of skin diseases or leprosy. *Tropical. Zone 10.* p. 731

castaneus (Taiwan); large evergreen tree to 20 m high; leathery lanceolate leaves 11-13 cm long and 3-4 cm wide, glossy green with yellow midrib; flowers white, followed by globose, rust-brown fruit 7-10 cm in dia., very ornamental. *Zone 10.* p. 731

HYDRANGEA   Saxifragaceae

anomala petiolaris (Japan), "Climbing hydrangea"; deciduous woody climber, clinging by aerial rootlets, spreading 20 m or more on walls or trees; ovate leaves to 12 cm long, serrate at margins; the showy inflorescence in large clusters of flowers, the sterile ones along margins showy with enlarged white calyx lobes 3 cm across, blooming in June. *Zone 5.* p. 296

arborescens (New York to Louisiana), "Hills-of-snow"; shrub 10-25 cm high, with bright green ovate leaves 10-20 cm long, and small fertile flowers dull white, in rounded terminal clusters to 15 cm across; few sterile blooms. *Zone 4.* p. 872

aspera (syn. sargentiana) (Himalayas to 2300 m, China, Taiwan, Sumatra, Java), "Lace-caps"; shrub to 2 m or more, of stiff habit, with downy branches; slender-pointed 10-22 cm, toothed leaves with harsh surface, gray-downy underneath; 3-4 cm sterile flowers with 4-6 blue or white petals. *Zones 8-10.* p. 871

heteromalla (xanthoneura) (Himalayas: No. India, Nepal, Bhutan, Tibet, No. China), "Table hydrangea" or "Bretschneider hydrangea"; handsome floriferous shrub to 2 m high, much branched with downy shoots; ovate leaves 10-20 cm long, finely toothed and covered by close white hairs beneath; the inflorescence a flat-topped cluster to 30 cm across, of sterile and fertile flowers; the sterile blooms white and 2-3 cm wide, in June-July. *Zone 5.* p. 871

involucrata 'Hortensis' (Japan); free-blooming shrub 1-2 m high, all bristly-hairy; leaves roundish-ovate 10-20 cm long and finely toothed; floral clusters 8-15 cm across, enclosed in bud stage by several ovate bracts; sterile flowers along margins white or bluish, in 'Hortensis' with silver pink double flowers, in August-September. *Zone 7.* p. 872

macrophylla 'Chaperon Rouge' (Red Ridinghood), also known as 'Chapeau Rouge' (Red Cap), "French hortensia"; superb French (Mouillere 1951) cultivar of compact habit, with smallish dark green foliage on stiff-erect stem, which bears a large firm, rounded head dense with flowers in vivid, pure rosy-crimson to clear carmine, depending on degree of temperature and pH of soil; ideal pot plant, medium-early. *Warm temperate. Zone 7.* p. 55

macrophylla 'Kuhnert' (1926) (Gartendirektor Kuhnert), "Snow-ball"; an old freely branching variety easily becoming tall, with small toothed foliage and medium size flower-heads normally rose, but mostly grown as a good blue; not as showy as 'Enziandom', but a ready forcer and good keeper, responding willingly to aluminum treatment with a clear sky-blue and cream center, to corn-flower-blue. *Warm temperate. Zone 7.* p. 55

macrophylla 'Mariesii'; old variety used for outdoor planting, of robust habit, with broad leaves, and flat flower clusters with numerous insignificant fertile flowers, the marginal, pink sterile flowers very large 5-8 cm across. *Zone 6.* p. 871

macrophylla 'Merveille' (1927), "French hortensia"; robust vigorous, mid-season variety of excellent keeping qualities, with stout stem not requiring staking, firm foliage and large heads of big round, carmine-rose flowers of good texture; lend themselves also to coloring into blue or lilac; the showy calyces hold well after forcing. Deciduous in cold climate. *Zone 7.* p. 871

macrophylla 'Otaksa', "Big leaf hydrangea"; formerly well-known old "Hortensia", in cultivation for about 100 years, one of the first to be tried for pot forcing but later used for planting outdoors; a hybrid Japanese clone of Thunberg's original H. macrophylla, forming the foundation for the modern race of pot-flowered hydrangeas. 'Otaksa' is of dwarfer habit than the type species, yet vigorous, with obovate, short-pointed leaves rather thick and smooth, the rounded heads of blooms partly with insignificant fertile flowers, and showy 4 cm sterile ones with obovate, entire petals, pink or blue. However, it flowers only on 2nd year wood, and only if buds were not hurt by early cold. Zones 5-6. p. 871

macrophylla 'Sensation'; striking cultivar seen at German Nat'l. Garden Expo Duesseldorf 1987; shapely "Hortensia" with showy heads of carmine-rose flowers bordered with contrasting white. Zone 8. p. 56

macrophylla serrata (Japan and Cheju Is., Korea), "Tea of Heaven"; deciduous shrub to 2 m or more high, evergreen in mild climate; often pubescent with appressed hairs; ovate leaves to 15 cm long, variously and closely toothed; inflorescence large and showy, consisting of several clusters dense with small fertile and sterile flowers white or blue, in Summer. Zone 6. p. 871

macrophylla 'Tricolor' ('Variegata'); colorful cultivar of the "Lace-caps" group; bushy shrub branching from base, with woody to stiff-fleshy canes bearing broad ovate leaves, attractively variegated green, gray and pale yellow; large flattened floral clusters of small greenish fertile flowers in center, and large sterile pale pink to white blooms along outer rim. Zone 7. p. 871

paniculata (S.E. China, Japan, Kuriles), "Panicle hydrangea"; floriferous deciduous shrub or small tree 4 to 8 m high, with ovate leaves 8-15 cm long and toothed, often in threes on vigorous plants, bristly on veins beneath; inflorescence in showy erect pyramidal clusters 15 to 40 cm long, with outer flowers sterile 2-3 cm across, white turning purplish; the small fertile blossoms yellowish. Zone 4. p. 871

paniculata 'Grandiflora' "Peegee hydrangea"; the commonest hardy hydrangea in cultivation; tree-like shrub 2½-8 m high, with elliptic leaves pubescent beneath; the small fertile flowers yellowish, the larger showy outside, sterile flowers white changing to purplish, in panicles to 38 cm long, in large masses for Mid-summer bloom. This showy deciduous cultivar was introduced from Japan; similar to the species but floral clusters more conspicuous, with nearly all flowers sterile. Zone 4. p. 871

quercifolia (Georgia to Florida and Mississippi), "Oakleaf hydrangea"; shrub to 2 m, with stout brown-woolly branches, deeply 3-7 lobed 20 cm leaves, dull green above, pale downy underneath; pyramidal 30 cm panicles of white sterile 2-3 cm flowers turning purplish, and small fertile ones; fairly hardy. Zone 6. p. 872

HYDRASTIS *Ranunculaceae*

canadensis (Vermont to Ontario and Minnesota, so. to Alabama), "Goldenseal" or "Orangeroot"; low herbaceous perennial with hairy stems to 30 cm high, from thick yellow rhizome; basal leaves to 20 cm across, palmately 3 to 9 lobed, the lobes entire or serrate; small greenish-white flowers 2 cm across, having petal-like sepals in May-June; followed by clusters of bright red, berry-like fruit, nested sessile to upper leaves. Ground roots are used medicinally. Zones 3-8. p. 488

HYDRIASTELE *Palmae*

microspadix (Australia); clustering unarmed fan palm dense with slender canes, found in humid forest; the rather small, pinnate fronds having divisions with squared-off apex; similar to Ptychosperma; flowers monoecious on same plant. Zone 11-12. p. 104

HYDROCHARIS *Hydrocharitaceae*

morsus-ranae (Europe to Siberia, No. Africa, Australia), "Frog's bit"; floating aquatic herb with fine, silky roots; long-petioled cordate-orbicular, fleshy leaves 5 cm dia., in rosettes; pretty, white flowers with broad petals 2 cm across. Not generally used in aquariums. Zone 4. p. 331

HYDROCLEYS *Butomaceae*

martii (Trop. America), tropical "Pond poppy" or "Water key"; aquatic perennial with prostrate underwater-stems, rooting at nodes; the roundish-cordate or kidney-shaped leaves rising above the water; poppy-like yellow flowers. Zone 10. p. 328

nymphoides (C. America to Argentina), "Water poppy"; perennial water plant with floating leaves, broadly heart-shaped or almost round, leathery-pulpy, and glossy green; everywhere in the leaves and stalks are airy tissues that causes them to float; beautiful flowers shining yellow with red center, 4-5 cm wide. *Humid-tropical.* Zone 10. p. 328

HYDROPHYLLUM *Hydrophyllaceae*

capitatum (Brit. Columbia, Alberta, so. to Oregon, Colorado),

"Cat's breeches"; herbaceous perennial 20-50 cm high, and grayish pubescent; leaves to 12 cm long, pinnately parted into 5-7 divisions, often cleft again; flowers purplish to white, in dense clusters, in early Summer. Zone 5. p. 332

HYDROSME rivieri: see AMORPHOPHALLUS rivieri

HYDROTHRIX *Pontederiaceae*

gardneri (Brazil); tropical, densely branching underwater aquatic, with thin wiry branches, and feathery or sessile whorls of linear leaves; at tips of branchlets the small, 5-petaled starry whitish bloom. These flowers are cleistogamous, with self-pollination effected before petals expand. Zone 11. p. 336

HYLOCEREUS *Cactaceae*

undatus, known in horticulture as Cereus triangularis (Brazil), "Honolulu queen"; one of the largest night-blooming cereus; epiphytic, deep green 3-angled clamberer of 5 cm dia.; white flowers nearly 30 cm long, blooming one night. Edible red fruit. Used as understock for grafting of Gymnocalycium, Rhipsalis or Zygocactus, for better root system. *Tropical.* Zone 11. p. 161

HYLOMECON *Papaveraceae*

japonica (East Asia: Japan), "Japanese poppy"; herbaceous perennial 30 cm high, with odd-pinnate leaves, the ovate leaflets toothed, and 3-8 cm long; golden-yellow flowers 5 cm across, blooming in June. Zone 6. p. 466

HYMENANDRA *Myrsinaceae*

wallichii (N.E. India); interesting small tropical evergreen bush to 1 m high, with fleshy stem; large obovate succulent leaves to 25 cm long, dark green; beautiful flowers with wheel-shaped 5-parted pink corolla in lateral clusters. Collected by J. Bogner of Munich Bot. Garden in Assam. Zones 10-11. p. 796

HYMENOCALLIS *Amaryllidaceae*

caribaea (Lesser Antilles); tropical summer-flowering "Spider lily" with globose bulb, a dozen leaves in several ranks, narrowing at base, and solid scape bearing an umbel of elegant fragrant white flowers with toothed crown and long linear segments, green outside at base. This may be H. pedalis from South America, naturalized in Florida and the West Indies. *Tropical.* Zone 10. p. 214

expansa (Trop. America); tropical bulbous plant with long, glossy green strap-shaped leaves, grooved down center; spidery flowers pale green, more or less tri-cornered, with long narrow linear segments; November-blooming. Zone 10. p. 214

'Festalis' (Ismene) (H. narcissiflora x Elisena longipetala from Peru); beautiful flowers with large white central crown recurved and frilled at margins, the narrow-linear outer petals cream-white. Zone 9. p. 214

littoralis (Polynesia: Marquesas; So. America), "Crown beauty"; a "Spider lily" which I photographed on the South Pacific Island of Nuku Hiva; tropical bulbous plant with broad leaves, and very spidery, pure white, waxy flowers, with 8-10 cm tube and long, threadlike segments, in the center a wavy-edged cup or corona. *Tropical.* Zone 10. p. 214

narcissiflora (Ismene calathina) (Andes of Perú, Bolivia), "Peruvian daffodil"; bulbous plant with strap-shaped leaves; umbels of large, fragrant, white flowers, crown funnel-shaped, lobes fringed. *Subtropic.* Zones 8-9. p. 214

speciosa (W. Indies), "Winter spice"; evergreen flowering plant with big bulb; the thick-fleshy, dark green oblanceolate leaves on tapering, channeled petioles; from the center rises a flattened, glaucous stalk crowned by a cluster of fragrant, spidery pure white flowers with long greenish tube and linear segments 5 cm long, a distinctive inner cup bearing the long anthers. *Tropical.* Zone 10. p. 214

HYMENOCYCLUS:

see MALEPHORA (Zander) (MALEOPHORA [Hortus])

HYMENOSPORUM *Pittosporaceae*

flavum (Queensland, New South Wales), "Sweetshade"; graceful evergreen shrub or tree to 15 m high, of open habit, with shining light green, leathery leaves 8-15 cm long; clusters of honey-scented bright yellow flowers 3 cm wide, blooming Spring into Summer. Zone 10. p. 816

HYMENOXYS *Compositae*

acaulis glabra (Actinea herbacea) (Ontario to Ohio, Illinois); spreading perennial to 30 cm high, forming tufts; basal, narrow-linear, grass-like leaves silky-hairy, 5 cm or more long; floral heads 5 cm across, with vivid yellow ray-florets and yellow center disc. Zone 3. p. 393

grandiflora (Actinea) (Alpine Idaho and Montana, to Utah and Colorado); stout, woolly mountain perennial to 40 cm high, branching near base, with lower leaves dissected into linear lobes, upper leaves linear and entire; showy solitary floral heads to 8 cm across, with orange-yellow bracts encircling the brownish central cushion. *Zone 3.*   *p. 393*

HYOPHORBE   Palmae

lagenicaulis (Mascarena) (Mascarene Isl.), "Bottle palm"; grotesque, solitary palm to about 4 m high, the trunk very fat and bulging at base and quickly tapering upward, like a flask, topped by few heavy pinnate, arching fronds, 1-2 m long, the leaflets erect and rigid, yellowish-green, the bases forming a prominent crown-shaft. *Tropical. Zones 11-12.*   *p. 106*

HYPERICUM   Hypericaceae (Guttiferae)

androsaemum (Europe, W. Asia), "Tutsan"; vernacular name from the French toute saine or heal-all; the wine-colored juice of the ripening fruits has for centuries been attributed medicinal properties; semi-evergreen subshrub to 1 m high, with angled branches; leaves broad-ovate 10 cm long; small flowers with yellow petals and greenish sepals, blooming June to August; the developing berry-like fruit is a capsule first red then black, forming from the base of the ovary. *Zone 6.*   *p. 737*

beanii (patulum henryi) (China, Japan), "St. John's-wort"; semi-evergreen spreading shrub to 1 m or more high, with 2-edged, purplish branches, stiff-leathery oblong leaves 6-8 cm long, glaucous beneath; the showy bowl-shaped flowers bright golden-yellow, 6 cm wide, the sepals elliptic-pointed with long silky stamens spreading to form a ring at base of ovary; photographed in Leucadia, California. *Zone 6.*   *p. 737*

calycinum (S.E. Europe, W. Asia Minor), "Rose of Sharon"; stoloniferous evergreen subshrub with large golden-yellow flowers, to 5 cm across; short ovate, rough leaves, dense. *Zones 6-8. p. 315, 737*

cerastoides (S.E. Balkans), "Rhodope St. John's-wort"; procumbent perennial subshrubby herb with branches to 25 cm long; opposite oblong or ovate 3 cm leaves; bright yellow flowers 6 cm across, the petal-margins black-dotted; blooming June to August. *Zone 6.*   *p. 424*

empetrifolium (S.E. Europe, Greece to Asia Minor); low evergreen, beautiful shrub 30 to 40 cm high, often prostrate, with angled branches; the 1 cm linear leaves usually in whorls of three; bright yellow flowers 2 cm across, the short sepals edged with black glands, blooming July to September. *Zone 7.*   *p. 737*

fasciculatum (No. Carolina to Mississippi and Texas), "Sandweed"; evergreen subshrub to 1 m or more high, the stems with spongy bark, and numerous 4-angled branchlets; linear leathery leaves 2 cm long, usually in axillary clusters; flowers with 1 cm bright yellow petals and linear sepals 4 mm long, blooming Spring and Summer. *Zone 8.*   *p. 737*

formosum (W. No. America: Brit. Columbia to Montana, Calif. and Texas), "St. John's-wort"; rhizomatous perennial to 40 cm high, with small, rough 3 cm leaves; small yellow flowers dotted at tip with violet glands, 3 cm across, blooming June to August. *Zones 3-9.*   *p. 424*

frondosum (So. Carolina to Tennessee and Texas), "Golden St. John's-wort"; beautiful deciduous shrub, evergreen in mild climate, of dense habit 1 m or more high, with 2-winged branches; ovate bluish glaucous leaves to 8 cm long; charming orange-yellow flowers 5 cm across, with sepals leaf-like and shorter than petals, and filled with a veritable fountain of deep yellow stamens, blooming July-August; fruit a red, pointed capsule. *Zone 5.*   *p. 737*

galioides (Delaware, to Florida and Texas); evergreen bushy subshrub 60-90 cm high, with rounded branches, dense with small elliptic leaves 3-5 cm long, floriferous with light yellow flowers, the corolla 2 cm across with flaring petals and linear sepals, displaying numerous golden stamens and 3 stigmatic styles; blooming July to October; the fruit a conic, ridged capsule. *Zone 7.*   *p. 738*

hirsutum (villosum) (Europe to Caucasus, Siberia), "Hairy St. John's-wort"; subshrubby perennial with erect rounded stems to 1 m or more high; short branches covered by yellowish hairs; opposite oval, pubescent leaves; inflorescence in pyramidal clusters of pale yellow flowers 2 cm across. *Zone 5.*   *p. 424*

inodorum 'Elstead' (Mediterr. region parentage); compact English cultivar of inodorum, with attractive salmon-red fruits. Arching shrub with opposite ovate leaves; small pale yellow flowers in terminal clusters. *Zone 5.*   *p. 738*

kalmianum (Québec to Illinois); evergreen shrub to 1 m high, having twisted branches, dense with narrow lanceolate, glaucous leaves 3 to 6 cm long; handsome golden-yellow flowers 3 cm across, blooming in August; quite winter-hardy. *Zone 3.*   *p. 738*

kouytchense (W. China); semi-evergreen shrub to 1 m or more high, much branched and partially prostrate; the branchlets red and with 4 lines; elliptic-ovate leaves to 8 cm long, glaucous beneath; flowers 6 cm across with spreading yellow obovate petals and sepals ovate; the stamens in 5 indistinct bundles and with 5 styles; blooming in Autumn. *Zone 5.*   *p. 738*

leschenaultii (Malaya); handsome tropical ornamental shrub 2-3 m high usually evergreen but deciduous in colder climate; obovate leathery leaves 4-6 cm long, glaucous beneath; large cupped, clear yellow flowers with concave petals, to 8 cm across, displaying the numerous stamens. *Zones 9-11.*   *p. 738*

x moserianum, (calycinum x patulum), "Gold flower"; evergreen shrub or perennial to 1 m tall where winters are mild; grows as hardy perennial in cold-winter areas; forms mounds, with arching, reddish stems; leaves 5 cm long, bluish beneath; large cup-shaped golden-yellow blooms 6 cm across. *Zones 5-9.*   *p. 738*

x moserianum 'Tricolor' (patulum x calycinum); striking low-growing deciduous shrub to 60 cm high, with arching reddish branches; the silvery green, elliptic-ovate leaves 5 cm long, edged creamy-white and tinted pink to red; glaucous beneath; showy golden-yellow flowers during July-October. A beautiful English cultivar since 1887. *Zones 7-10.*   *p. 738*

olympicum (polyphyllum hort.) (S.E. Europe, Asia Minor); attractive upright, ascending subshrub to 40 cm high; the sessile glaucous, elliptic-oblong leaves 3-4 cm long; the flowers in branched clusters, with corolla vivid yellow tinted pink outside, pointed, opening wide to 6 cm across, blooming in Summer. Photographed at Int'l. Hort. Expo, Munich, Germany 1983. *Zone 7.*   *p. 739*

patulum (China: Szechwan; Himalaya, Japan); evergreen shrub 1 m or more high, with branches lined or 2 to 4-angled; ovate leaves 6 cm long, glaucous beneath; flowers golden-yellow, 4-5 cm across, having ovate sepals shorter than the roundish petals; the stamens in bundles, forming a ring at base of ovary; 5 styles, blooming July-September. *Zone 6.*   *p. 738*

reptans (W. China to Himalayas); vigorous low shrub 10 cm high, with prostrate spreading thin branches rooting as they creep along ground; thin oval, tiny light green leaves 2 cm long; pretty, bowl-shaped yellow-golden flowers 3 cm across, tinged crimson outside, blooming in Autumn. Ideal for rockgardens. *Zone 7.*   *p. 738*

'Rowallane' (hookerianum 'Rogersii' x leschenaultii) (Ireland 1932); evergreen bush of straggly growth to 2 m high, with glossy green, ovate leaves 5-7 cm long, and handsome bowl-shaped golden-yellow flowers 8 cm across, profuse in late Summer and Autumn. *Zone 7.*   *p. 737*

HYPHAENA   Palmae

schatan (Madagascar); robust fan palm from dry habitats; the straight trunk with old leaf-scars, topped by a rounded crown of rigid palmate fronds, the stiff reddish petioles armed with strong teeth, and extending for some distance into the leaf itself, which is known as costa-palmate; the female trees bear pendant clusters of attractive, large red fruit 5-7 cm long, with edible fleshy interior. *Zone 11.*   *p. 921*

thebaica (Upper Egypt, Sudan, Yemen, Kenya, Tanzania), "Dhoum palm" or "Gingerbread palm"; botanical wonder with its repeatedly forked habit, to 15 m high; the slender trunk and branches smooth like a cordyline, each branch end tipped by a rosette of smallish, stiff, green fan-leaves, the blade 60-75 cm long, deeply cut to the middle, on spiny petiole. The orange edible fruit tastes like gingerbread. Although palms normally are not hosts to epiphytic orchids, I have often seen Ansellias growing in the forks of their branches in East Africa. *Tropical. Zones 11-12.*   *p. 107*

HYPOCALYMMA   Myrtaceae

angustifolium (W. Australia), "White myrtle"; small much-branched shrub to 1 m high, the gray, angled slender shoots with narrow linear leaves 3 cm long; stalkless flowers 8 mm across, white or pink with purple center, and long protruding stamens, set in pairs in leaf axils along upper stem. *Zones 9-10.*   *p. 800*

robustum (Western Australia), "Swan River myrtle"; smooth, evergreen shrub to 1 m with stiff 2½ cm linear leaves having thick midrib; axillary tiny flowers with 5 petals rich pink and numerous protruding red stamens, forming long leafy spikes; blooming in Spring. *Zone 9.*   *p. 804*

HYPOCYRTA selloana: see NEMATANTHUS fissus

HYPOESTES   Acanthaceae

aristata (So. Africa), "Ribbon bush"; perennial herb of erect habit to 1 m high, with downy ovate leaves 8 cm long, entire; downy 3 cm tubular flowers rose-purple with short lobes striped and spotted purple or white. *Zone 10.*   *p. 339, 631*

phyllostachya (sanguinolenta) (Madagascar), "Freckleface"; herb with soft, downy, small leaves green with rosy-red marking, 4-6 cm long; flowers lilac. *Zone 11.*   *p. 17*

HYPOXIS   Hypoxidaceae

angustifolia (Transvaal, So. Africa), "Star flower"; stemless herbaceous perennial 30-50 cm high, with corm-like rhizome, forming rosettes of narrow, arching, keeled leaves; clusters of starry yellow flowers 4-5 cm across, blooming early and Mid-summer. *Zone 10.*   *p. 424*

hirsuta (Maine, so. to Florida and Texas), "Star grass" or "Yellow star grass"; rhizomatous perennial to 30 cm high, having long, grass-like leaves; short, leafless floral stalks bearing bright yellow, star-like flowers of 6 segments, 3 cm across, in early Summer. _Zone 4. p. 424_

mexicana (Arizona, Mexico), "Gold-eye grass"; small plant at home in mountains of So. Arizona to Durango, Mexico; corm-like underground rhizome bearing grass-like leaves, and flowering stem with cluster of small stars green outside and yellow inside; in Autumn. _Zones 7-8._   p. 210

stellata (Spiloxene capensis) (So. Africa), "White star-grass"; cormous herb with basal, keeled, grass-like 30 cm leaves; the small star-like flowers white inside, green-keeled outside, on few-flowered stalks. _Zone 10._   p. 424

HYSSOPUS   _Labiatae_
officinalis (So. and E. Europe to Asia), "Hyssop"; aromatic sub-shrubby perennial 30-60 cm high, with square branches, and linear-lanceolate leaves to 4 cm long; bilabiate flowers in whorls along terminal branches, the bluish-violet corolla to 2 cm long, varying to pink or rose. Foliage with somewhat bitter, persistent aroma, is widely used as perfume base, second only to lavender. Also grown for medicinal use. _Zone 3._   p. 530

HYSTRIX   _Gramineae_
patula (Asperula hystrix) (Québec to Dakota, Oklahoma), "Bottle-brush grass"; handsome deciduous perennial grass to more than 1 m high, and forming tufts; rigid bamboo-like, brownish culms; flat green leaves to 15 cm long; inflorescence in September-October, with curious stiff, showy pink flowers in a bristly spike 15 cm long, with spikelets in horizontal pairs. Dried spikes used in bouquets. _Zone 5._   p. 560

IBERIS   _Cruciferae_
amara (W. Europe), "Rocket candytuft"; very handsome, erect branching annual 15-30 cm high, with thickish oblanceolate leaves 8-10 cm long, and large white, fragrant flowers on racemes that lengthen with age, summer-blooming, and used as cut flowers. _Zone 8._   p. 411

sempervirens (So. Europe), "Evergreen candytuft"; charming, almost evergreen perennial wide-spreading subshrub to 30 cm high, with linear, glossy green 3-4 cm leaves, and 4 cm clusters of small white flowers, blooming in May. Very popular for edging in garden beds. _Zones 4-9._   p. 411

sempervirens 'Snowflake', "Snowflake candytuft"; superior cultivar of this almost evergreen mound-forming perennial, selected because of its more compact habit and large white flowers, borne in showy clusters in late May, lasting a long time. _Zones 5-9._   p. 314

umbellata (Mediterranean region), "Globe candytuft"; hardy annual herb 15-40 cm high, with narrow mid-green leaves 8 cm long, and pale purple, pink or white flowers in 5 cm clusters. _Warm temperate. Zones 9-10._   p. 411

IBERVILLEA   _Cucurbitaceae_
lindheimeri (Maximowiczia ammocodon) (Texas to California and Sonora), "Balsam gourd" or "Herba de Vibora"; dioecious vine forming thickened tuber-like rootstock extending above ground; the stems thin and flexuous growing to 3 m long, bearing unbranched tendrils and dissected, small green leaves 3 to 5 cm long, the segments deeply lobed and toothed; small 1 cm flowers yellow and striped with green; red 3 cm berries. _Zones 9-10._   p. 276

sonorae (Maximowiczia) (No. Mexico); climbing plant with heavy, bottle-shaped base, the fissured bark grayish-white and corky; several stems 2-3 m long; 3-lobed leaves 4-10 cm long; small hairy yellow flowers; ovoid fruit 3-5 cm long, red when ripe. _Arid-subtropic. Zones 9-10._   p. 276

sonorae peninsularis (Maximowiczia) (Mexico: Baja California); from thickened tuberous rootstock rise tendril-climbing perennial vines, longer than in sp. sonorae, and non-glaucous, hispid leaves having 3 to 5 deeply dissected lobes; greenish-yellow flowers followed by spectacularly ornamental, globular orange fruit with thin rind. Male and female flowers are on separate plants. _Zone 10._   p. 276

IBOZA   _Labiatae_
riparia (Moschosma) (So. Africa), "Misty plume bush"; stout, musk-scented perennial subshrub to 1½ m, with 4-angled stems, broad ovate, toothed leaves, and numerous small flowers creamy-white with dark anthers in erect, plumy panicles. _Subtropic. Zone 9._   p. 432

IDESIA   _Flacourtiaceae_
polycarpa (So. Japan, China, Korea), "Iigiri tree"; small deciduous attractive tree to 15 m high, with handsome cordate leaves 15-25 cm long on red petioles, dark green above and glaucous beneath; the yellow-green flowers are sweetly fragrant; male clusters 12-15 cm long; the female blooms followed by roundish 1 cm fruit bright orange-red in large panicles; very ornamental until frozen. _Zone 6._   p. 731

IDRIA   _Fouquieriaceae_
columnaris (Arizona to Sonora and Baja California, Mexico), "Boojum tree"; bizarre xerophytic desert tree with soft swollen, often hollow trunk to 15 m or more high, tapering to apex, spreading spiny branches and obovate, deciduous leaves 2 cm long; small yellow flowers in panicles. In habitat found in many curious shapes, and described as "Telegraph pole" or "Upside-down carrot". _Arid-subtropic. Zones 9-10._   p. 195, 751

IGUANURA   _Palmae_
wallichiana (Malay Peninsula); showy rainforest palm with big entire leaves 1 m or more long, pink when young, on a stem to 2 m long. In juvenile stage the fronds show some divisions. _Tropical. Zones 11-12._   p. 104

ILEX   _Aquifoliaceae_
x altaclarensis (aquifolium x perado), "Altaclara holly"; ever-green shrub with purplish bark; hybrid resembling the English holly but the stiff-leathery, 11 cm elliptic leaves are larger, thinner, and flatter at the margin which has more numerous and more regular spiny teeth, and slightly glossy. _Zone 6._   p. 643

x altaclarensis 'Lawsoniana' (varieg. form of hendersonii); colorful evergreen shrub with young branches red-brown; 6-8 cm ovate leaves green liberally splashed with creamy-yellow, and partially spiny at margins; a most beautiful yellow-colored form. _Zone 6._   p. 643

amelanchier (dubia) (S.E. Virginia to Georgia and Louisiana), "Sarvis holly" or "Swamp holly"; low woody shrub to 2 m high, more or less deciduous; thin ovate or lanceolate leaves 5-10 cm long, very rough beneath; male inflorescence staminate, the female flowers in axils, followed by dull red 1 cm berries. _Zone 6._   p. 642

aquifolium (Europe, No. Africa, W. Asia), "English holly"; ever-green tree to 12 m or more; alternate leathery, ovate leaves shining, and with coarse spiny teeth along wavy margins; small unisexual flowers whitish, followed by scarlet-red berries on female trees, being borne on previous year's growth. _Zone 6._   p. 643

aquifolium balearica (Mediterranean reg., No. Africa), "Mallorca holly"; evergreen shrub with elliptic or obovate thick leaves deep glossy green, 6-8 cm long, the margins entire or with occasional spines; fruiting profusely with coral-red berries on female plants, ripening in September and persisting into March; very handsome and ideal in a hedge 50 cm high. _Zone 7._   p. 622

aquifolium 'Marginata', "Variegated English holly"; attractive horticultural form with black-green waxy leaves having ivory margins, silvery in places, especially on the underside. _Zone 6._   p. 84

x attenuata 'Fosteri' (cassine x opaca), "Topel holly"; closely branched evergreen pyramidal shrub, with obovate or oblanceolate light green, rather flat leaves 4 to 10 cm long, sometimes toothed near apex; small clustered scarlet berries on female plants in profusion every year. A good plant for mild regions. _Zone 7._   p. 643

cassine (Virginia to Florida and Texas), "Dahoon holly"; evergreen shrub of small tree to 10 m high; willowy and erect branches with obovate, thick-leathery, smooth leaves 4-10 cm long, somewhat boat-shaped and only slightly toothed near apex, silvery pubescent beneath; small globular scarlet berries, varying to yellow. _Zone 7._   p. 643

cornuta (Eastern China), "Chinese holly" or "Horned holly"; evergreen shrub of dense bushy growth, to 3 m high; recurved shining green, leathery leaves 8-10 cm long, nearly rectangular with pro-nounced spines at the 4 corners and at the tip of each leaf; large bright red, long-lasting berries. Female plants have the ability to produce fruit without the use of pollen. _Zone 7._   p. 644

cornuta 'Burfordii'; handsome globose form of "Chinese holly", originated in Atlanta, Georgia; having pendant branches; the squarish, glossy dark green leaves entire along sides but spine-tipped at apex; fruiting heavily with large clusters of scarlet berry-like fruit. Excellent ornamental for planting in mild climate Southern states. _Zones 6-9._   p. 644

cornuta 'Rotunda', "Dwarf Chinese holly"; compact, densely branched form of low mounding growth, with smallish, spiny leaves. Ideal small hedge; of outstanding appearance in sun or shade. _Zones 6-9._   p. 644

crenata (Japan), "Japanese holly"; stiff evergreen to 6 m, with smooth, dark green, oval leaves 6 cm long, sharply pointed and sparsely toothed; small black berries on female plants. _Zone 6._   p. 615, 643

crenata 'Helleri', "Heller's Japanese holly"; handsome robust dwarf evergreen of densely branched, mounding growth, to 30 cm high; quite small dark green elliptic leaves 1-2 cm long; of female descent. _Zone 6._   p. 644

crenata 'Hetzii', "Hetz's Japanese holly"; medium size evergreen, vigorously growing, and densely erect branching with large oval, glossy green, convex, bullate leaves. _Zone 6._   p. 644

crenata 'Mariesii'; miniature evergreen shrublet with annual growth under 3 cm; the leathery leaves orbicular or broadly ovate, 1 cm wide. Very popular in Japan. Zone 6.   p. 644

crenata 'Microphylla', "Small-leaved Jap. holly"; popular low evergreen shrub, dense with twisted branches, the small leathery, lustrous dark green oblong leaves 1-2 cm long, faintly toothed. Widely used for hedging and topiary, and may be trimmed to shape; also good bonsai subject. Zone 6.   p. 643

decidua (Illinois to Florida and Texas), "Possum haw"; deciduous shrub usually 2 to 3 m high, or small tree reaching to 10 m, with smooth gray branches bearing dull green obovate leaves 3-6 cm long, bluntly toothed and with downy midrib; bright orange-red, globose 1 cm fruit in great profusion, holding into Winter, after foliage has dropped. Zone 6.   p. 644

glabra (Nova Scotia to Florida and Texas), "Gallberry" or "Inkberry"; excellent native evergreen shrub 3 to 6 m high, with ascending angular, downy branches; leathery obovate, flat leaves 3-6 cm long, glossy green above, toothed toward apex; flowers white, the males clustered, the female ones axillary, producing small 1 cm usually globose black fruit. Staminate plants keep the green foliage color in Winter better than the female plants. Zone 3.   p. 644

x koehneana (aquifolium x latifolia); small-leaved, compact evergreen shrub or small tree, having young shoots purplish, the leathery glossy green foliage ovate-lanceolate, the margins undulate and spiny; large red, berry-like fruit. Photographed in col. Rutgers University Experimental Farm, New Brunswick, N.J. Zone 6.   p. 645

laevigata (So. Maine to Georgia), "Smooth winterberry"; deciduous holly, of shrubby habit 2-3 m high, with smooth branches; the leaves oval-ovate 3-6 cm long and wedge-shaped at base, and toothed at margins, lustrous green above and glabrous beneath, unlike verticillata which are dull green; vivid scarlet fruit on female plants. Zone 4.   p. 645

latifolia (E. China, Japan), "Luster-leaf holly" or "Tarajo"; elegant robust evergreen holly tree to about 15 m high, with stout, smooth branches, and large thick-leathery, oblong ovate leaves 6 to 18 cm long, lustrous, shining green above, toothed with black spines; red fruit in small clusters. Often planted in Temple gardens.
Zone 7.   p. 645

x meserveae 'Blue Girl' (rugosa x aquifolium); evergreen shrub to 1 m high, with branches spreading or erect; leathery ovate blue-green leaves toothed at margins, on blue-purple shoots. Similar to 'Blue Boy' but plants produce a profusion of bright red berries.
Zone 4.   p. 643

opaca (Massachusetts to Florida and Texas), "American holly"; evergreen, spreading tree to 15 m, with stiff, elliptic or obovate leaves dull green above, yellowish beneath, to 9 cm long, and with large spiny teeth; small red fruit, usually solitary, borne on the current year's growth, developing on female trees. Zone 5.   p. 645

paraguariensis (So. Brazil, Paraguay), "Yerba-de-Mate"; small evergreen tree with oblong, wavy-toothed, leathery leaves, 10-15 cm long; forked clusters of small greenish-white flowers in leaf axils; berries red; the dried, powdered leaves contain caffeine and produce the South American favorite, "Mate" or "Paraguay tea", of somewhat bitter taste reminding of quinine, but giving a stimulating effect.
Subtropic. Zone 9.   p. 523, 645

pedunculosa (China, Japan), "Long-stalked holly"; smooth evergreen shrub or small tree to 5 m high, with slender branches; bearing laurel-like oblong ovate, thin-leathery leaves 4-8 cm long, dark glossy green, usually not toothed; globose fruit pendant on long stalks bright red, sometimes yellow, on female trees. Zone 5.   p. 645

pernyi (China); evergreen sparry shrub to 6 m with willowy branches dense with closely ranked, small 5 cm quadrangular-ovate leaves glossy black-green, with 1 to 3 spines on each side and a larger terminal one; berries red, in clusters. Zone 6.   p. 645

rotunda (Japan, China, Korea, Vietnam, Taiwan), "Kurogane holly"; smooth evergreen tree to 18 m high, forming massive trunk; leathery obovate, dark green, glossy leaves 4-8 cm long and with smooth margins; small white flowers; dense clusters of glossy scarlet-red 1 cm berries on female trees. Zone 7.   p. 645

serrata (Japan, China), "Japanese winterberry" or "Fine-tooth holly"; large dioecious shrub to 5 m high, liberally branching at base; the shoots usually downy; deciduous thin ovate or oblong leaves 3-8 cm long and finely toothed at margins; very showy with small red fruit profusely borne into Winter. Zone 5.   p. 646

verticillata (No. America: Newfoundland to Texas), "Winterberry"; wide-spread deciduous dense shrub 2 to 5 m high, smooth or slightly hairy; obovate leaves to 10 cm long, dull green above, the margins saw-toothed; 1 cm berries red or yellow, on female plants.
Zone 3.   p. 645

vomitoria (Virginia to Florida and Texas), "Yaupon"; dioecious or partially monoecious evergreen to 8 m with obovate, shiny green, leathery leaves 4 cm long, slightly toothed; small light red berries, in clusters. A bitter tea, cassine, may be prepared from the dried leaves.
Zone 7.   p. 621, 646

wilsonii (China, Taiwan, No. Burma); small evergreen tree to 8 m; thick-leathery obovate, glossy olive-green leaves to 6 cm long and with acute tip, the margins smooth; glossy, crimson-red berries on female plants. Zone 7.   p. 646

ILLICIUM   *Magnoliaceae (Illiciaceae)*

anisatum (religiosum) (Japan: Honshu to Kyushu; Taiwan, China), "Star anise"; shrub or small tree; wood and leaves very aromatically fragrant; leaves 5-10 cm long; flowers with numerous linear petals, pale greenish-yellow, without fragrance. In Japan the powdered bark is mixed with resin and used to burn as incense. Much planted in Buddhist temple gardens. Zone 8.   p. 775

anisatum 'Variegatum', "Variegated anise"; very attractive evergreen shrub, with obovate, aromatic leaves 10 cm long, glossy green and overlaid with glaucous sheen, variegated creamy-white primarily along margins; very decorative. Zone 10.   p. 775

floridanum (Florida to Louisiana), "Purple anise" or "Florida anis-tree"; handsome evergreen tree to 3 m high, with aromatic elliptic-lanceolate leathery leaves 8 to 15 cm long; the very showy flowers maroon-red, with their more than 20 narrow petals spreading 5 cm wide, the stamens cradled in their midst, blooming in May.
Zone 9.   p. 775

IMANTOPHYLLUM: see CLIVIA (Hortus 3, Zander)

IMPATIENS   *Balsaminaceae*

balsamina rosea plena, "Rose balsam"; annual herbaceous plant, with succulent knotty stem to 60 cm tall, and fleshy, lanceolate leaves to 15 cm long; the charming variety rosea plena with soft baby pink double flowers shaped like a rose-bud, peeking out between the dark green foliage. The species balsamina is from India to China.
Zones 10-11.   p. 344

glandulifera (roylei) (India to China), "Jewel-weed"; tall herbaceous plant with reddish succulent stem, large ribbed leaves on long petioles; flowers in clusters, toward top of stem, inside pink and outside red and with short spur. Tropical. Zones 10-11.   p. 344

hawkeri (New Guinea, Sunda Isl.); herbaceous species with branching, purple stem to 50 cm high; dark green, quilted leaves with red midrib, 10-12 cm long and finely toothed; showy flower scarlet-red with white eye, but variable, 4- cm across and with red spur. Collected by the author on expedition at Chimbu in the Eastern Highlands of New Guinea 1960. Zone 10.   p. 345

'New Guinea hybrid'; magnificent ornamental herbaceous plants, the results of much hybridization of several New Guinea species such as hawkeri and linearifolia, collected between 1960 and 1970, and further crossed with species from Java and Celebes likewise having 32 chromosomes; the best selections are commercially segregated into several series and many named cultivars, all forming spreading bushes 25 to 40 cm high, with each succulent branch topped by a beautiful rosette of frequently corrugated ovate leaves 8-15 cm long, in a riot of color and variegation, usually creamy-yellow along center with green, serrate margins and red to milky-white ribs; showy spurred flowers 3-7 cm across, in shades from crimson to scarlet, red, orange, salmon, pink, chartreuse, purple or blush white. Ideal for shade gardens, as summer annual or as house or basket plants in Winter. Zone 11.   p. 37

'New Guinea Lollipop'; developed by Longwood Gardens, Pennsylvania; of sturdy habit, with firm lanceolate leaves, and large coral-rose flowers. Zones 10-11.   p. 345

'New Guinea Starfire' hawkeri cv., by Iowa State University; handsome hybrid of compact habit, with firm stems; waxy foliage, deep coppery green with central area creamy-yellow to pink; flowers orange-rose. Zones 10-11.   p. 345

'New Guinea variegata'; colorful mutation with leaves beautifully edged and variegated with white; flowers rosy-red. Shown at Del Mar Hort. Expo., California 1982. Zone 11.   p. 345

oliveri (sodenii) (Trop. E. Africa), "Giant touch-me-not"; large growing, fleshy herb with long, oblanceolate, succulent leaves olive-green with prominent, pale midrib, edged with coarse bristles; large spurred flowers a delicate lilac-pink. Tropical. Zone 10.   p. 344

repens (Sri Lanka), "Creeping impatiens"; small trailer with creeping fleshy red branches and alternate small round or kidney-shaped, ciliate leaves 2 cm wide, waxy deep green, purplish beneath, on long red petioles; golden-yellow hooded flowers with brownish net-like striping, and curved spur. Tropical. Zone 11.   p. 344

walleriana (sultanii, holstii) (Tanzania to Mozambique); fibrous-rooted perennial with watery-succulent, branching stems to 50 cm high; fresh green ovate, toothed leaves 3 to 8 cm long; and waxy flowers 3-4 cm dia., with upturned, long slender spur, usually carmine-rose, but variable in color to red, pink or white in nearly continuous bloom. Collected by the author in the cloudforest on Mt. Kilimanjaro, Tanzania (1960). Zone 10.   p. 345

walleriana cultivars, well known as "Sultana", "Busy Lizzie" or "Patient Lucy"; diploid clones and hybrids developed in horticulture, resulting in various type and colors, with rose to red, salmon or white flowers 3-5 cm across; forming densely branched, rounded mounds with glossy green leaves, 15-30 cm high, and blooming from early Summer until late Autumn. Very popular for garden planting or planted in pots and baskets, and grown as annuals. *Zones 10-11.*   p. 345

walleriana 'Elfin', "Liliput miniature sultana"; succulent dwarf self-branching F-1 hybrid only 15 to 20 cm (6-8 in.) high, having small deep green foliage, blooming almost continuously, with multitudes of smaller flowers 3-4 cm across. *Zone 11.*   p. 37, 345

walleriana 'Futura', "Patient Lucy"; semi-dwarf vigorous yet compact commercial strain of F-1 hybrids, 20-30 cm high, with large carmine-red flowers 5 cm across; also in other colors, rose, pink or white. Tropical annual or perennial. *Zone 11.*   p. 37

walleriana 'Minima', "Creeping Buzy Lizzy"; freely branching low succulent, perennial in frost-free areas; the somewhat watery stems prostrate along the ground; ovate-pointed deep green leaves 3-5 cm long, and small carmine-rose, spurred flowers. *Zone 11.*   p. 315

walleriana 'Red Ripple', "Star sultana"; charming cultivar, grown as an annual from seed; bushy, compact plants 25-30 cm high, with happy-green to bronzy foliage, and prolific blooms of red with white star pattern. Tropical. *Zones 10-11.*   p. 345

walleriana 'Rosette', "Rose-type impatiens"; double and semi-double, of compact habit, ideal for growing as potted plant. *Zones 10-11.*   p. 345

walleriana 'Variegata' (sultanii 'Variegata'), "Variegated patient Lucy"; long, tapering leaves gray-green, irregularly bordered white; flowers carmine-red. Tropical. *Zone 11.*   p. 37

IMPERATA   *Gramineae*
cylindrica 'Rubra' (Japan; natural. in Mediterranean reg.), "Japanese blood grass"; colorful ornamental perennial forming clusters from rhizomes, with culms 1 m or more high in the species, shorter in cv. 'Rubra'; leathery, flat leaves ruby-red, green at base, the color remaining intense during growing season; leaf-sheaths cylindrical; inflorescence an oblong elliptic or fan-shaped panicle of slender hairy spike-like racemes of lateral spikelets. *Zone 6.*   p. 561

INCARVILLEA   *Bignoniaceae*
delavayi (W. China, Yunnan, Tibet), "Hardy gloxinia"; herbaceous perennial to 50 cm high, with fleshy pinnate leaves, the 15 or more crenate leaflets alternately arranged; curious two-lipped, tubular flowers bright rose-red with yellow throat and spreading segments, 4 to 6 cm long and wide. *Warm temperate. Zones 6-10.*   p. 344

mairei (grandiflora) (Tibet to Nepal, W. China); herbaceous perennial with pinnate leaves 15 cm long, the lateral ovate leaflets 3 cm long and crenate at margins; the showy trumpet flowers with yellow tube and crimson lobes spreading 10 cm across, and whitish inside. *Zone 7.*   p. 344

INDIGOFERA   *Leguminosae*
gerardiana (India), "Himalayan indigo"; graceful, shrubby perennial to 2 m high, or more in mild climates, but cut back to ground level in cold areas, then 60-120 cm high; odd-pinnate leaves 5-10 cm long, the oval leaflets gray-hairy or glaucous beneath; purplish-rose flowers in dense racemes to 15 cm long, during Summer; the fruits are small dry pods. *Zone 7.*   p. 440, 763

incarnata (decora) (Japan, China), "Chinese Indigo"; deciduous shrub 50 cm high, with attractive pinnate leaves of 3-6 pairs of leaflets 6 cm long; inflorescence wisteria-like in pendant racemes of rose-pink flowers with pale standard, showy. Used in the manufacture of permanent blue-colored indigo dye by extracting it from the herbage. *Zone 5.*   p. 763

tinctoria (N.W. China), "Indigo"; subshrub 1-2 m high, with long pinnate leaves having 10 or more pairs of obovate leaflets, hairy beneath; pea-like flowers with pale standard petal and red wings and keel, in axillary racemes blooming in July. Grown in warm countries as a source of the clear blue indigo dye produced from cut branches. *Zone 10.*   p. 763

INGA   *Leguminosae*
edulis (quaternata) (C. and So. America), "Ice cream beans" or "American St. John's-bread"; tropical tree to 15 m, with broad crown and gray bark; pinnate leaves glossy dark green, the leaflets separated by winged axis; flowers with long white stamens and brown-hairy corolla; long 4-angled pods contain edible, sweet white pulp, and split open when ripe. *Zones 10-11.*   p. 762

pulcherrima: see CALLIANDRA tweedii

INULA   *Compositae*
britannica (England), "English elecampane"; herbaceous perennial spreading with basal rosettes of narrow lanceolate leaves; lightly indented, and pubescent beneath; floral heads to 5 cm across, on slender stalks, the ray-florets vivid yellow, narrow linear, surrounding the large golden-yellow center cushion; July-August; at home in humid grasslands. *Zone 6.*   p. 394

ensifolia (C. Europe to Caucasus), "Sword-leaf inula"; attractive perennial to 30 cm high, forming clumps; the erect branches with linear or narrow-lanceolate, many-nerved, sessile leaves to 10 cm long; floral heads 3-4 cm across, with yellow ray-florets, tireless blooming from July-September. *Zone 4.*   p. 394

helenium (Centr. Asia), "Elecampane"; robust perennial to 2 m high; basal leaves 40 cm long, velvety-hairy beneath and toothed at margins; the furrowed stems with clasping ovate leaves, and topped by showy floral heads to 10 cm across, with narrow, bright yellow rays around the contrasting raised brown and yellow center cushion; blooming July-September. *Zone 3.*   p. 394

hookeri (Sikkim Himalayas); herbaceous perennial to 60 cm or more high, sparingly branched; the leaves oblong-lanceolate, to 10 cm long, and minutely toothed, long-hairy beneath; floral heads 7-10 cm wide, the ray-florets light yellow with a touch of green, surrounding the yellow to brown central cushion; slightly scented, and blooming August to October. *Zone 5.*   p. 394

macrocephala (S.E. Europe to Armenia); soft-hairy perennial to 60 cm or more high; broad-ovate leaves minutely toothed on robust stems; toward apex the branched inflorescence of showy flowers to 15 cm across, the yellow ray-florets narrow linear; the central disc yellow to brown, blooming July-August. *Zone 6.*   p. 395

magnifica (Eastern Caucasus); robust perennial to 2 m tall, with ridged, black-purple stems; ovate, toothed leaves, hairy beneath, to 30 cm long; floral heads 15 cm across, with numerous narrow ray-florets golden-yellow, and central disc corollas yellow, tipped orange. *Zone 5.*   p. 395

orientalis (Asia Minor to Caucasus), "Caucasian inula"; hairy perennial 40 to 60 cm high, with petioled basal leaves, and oblong, sessile stem-leaves to 15 cm long; floral heads to 8 cm across, with orange-yellow, wavy ray-florets, and yellow to brown center disc, blooming June-August. *Zone 3.*   p. 394

IOCHROMA   *Solanaceae*
coccineum (Perú); robust tropical evergreen shrub with downy shoots; and soft herbaceous green, flaccid leaves 8-12 cm long; clusters of pendant lovely, tubular bell-shaped flowers carmine-red, 5 cm long, near apex of branches. *Zone 10.*   p. 879

cyaneum (tubulosum) (Colombia), the "Violet bush"; hairy tropical shrub 1 to 2 m high, with soft herbaceous, thinly downy, long elliptic 12 cm green leaves; axillary pendulous clusters of lilac-purple cylindric-tubular flowers 4½ cm long, pale lavender at the toothed mouth, and blooming during Summer from June on. Ideal for the patio, as they love fresh air. *Zone 10.*   p. 879

warscewiczii (Trop. America: Perú); handsome spreading shrub with pubescent shoots, and large herbaceous, ovate leaves with depressed ribs; from the apex a cluster of charming pendant flowers 5 cm long with balloon-like calyx and lavender-blue tubular corolla striped dark blue; photographed at Royal Botanic Garden, Sydney. *Zone 10.*   p. 879

IONOPSIDIUM   *Cruciferae*
acaule (Portugal), "Diamond flower"; charming, petite annual resembling a violet in miniature, 8-12 cm high, and spreading over the ground; small roundish or 3-lobed leaves; little bell-shaped flowers lilac or white tinged violet; normally summer-blooming, but can flower in Winter when grown in pots indoors. *Zone 9.*   p. 411

IPHEION   *Amaryllidaceae*
uniflorum (Brodiaea, Leucocoryne) (Argentina), "Spring-star-flower"; small cormous herb with onion-like odor, grass-like leaves, and solitary, star-shaped 2 to 4 cm flowers with spreading petals white tinged with blue, opening in bright weather. *Zone 8.*   p. 212

uniflorum 'Wisley Blue' (England); charming cultivar 15 to 22 cm high, with showy 3 to 4 cm Star-flowers delicate lavender-blue, over areas of white, and opening in bright weather. *Zone 8.*   p. 212

IPOMOEA   *Convolvulaceae*
alba (Hortus): see CALONYCTION album (Zander)

batatas (prob. Trop. America), "Sweet Potato vine"; in the Southern U.S., commonly called "Yam"; an economic as well as a hanging basket plant, trailing perennial with deeply rooted yellow-brown tuberous roots, the long vines are stem-rooting, with milky juice, the variable leaves ovate, angular or digitately lobed; tubular flowers spreading widely, pinkish-lavender; the tubers are often grown in water, provided they have not been previously cured. A food plant of great economical importance in the tropics; the tubers when cooked or baked become mealy, similar to potatoes, but are more sweet in taste with white or yellow flesh. *Zones 8-10. p. 222, 350, 910*

cairica (palmata) (Old World Tropics, also No. New Zealand); rampant perennial high climber with slender, threadlike stems; palmately compound leaves of 5 segments; very attractive lilac-pink flowers with purple eye, 5 cm across. *Tropical. Zones 10-11.*   p. 273

carnea fistulosa (crassicaulis) (Brazil); large straggling herbaceous plant, becoming woody, climbing when finding support, the stems with milky juice; leaves heart-shaped to 15 cm long, soft hairy beneath; funnel-shaped pinkish flowers with ruffled margins, 6 cm across, singly or in pairs. *Tropical. Zones 10-11.*   p. 273, 691

carnea fistulosa alba (Trop. So. America); an exquisite color form of this bold, woody-stemmed tropical climber, with fresh green cordate leaves and large wide-open, pure white flowers, seen in col. Botanic Garden Singapore. *Zones 10-11.*   p. 273

carnea fistulosa var. 'Goodetlii'; scandent with stem becoming woody and spreading; leaves ovate with cordate base; showy pinkish-white flowers with purple in throat, 6-7 cm across. *Zone 10.*   p. 691

coccinea (Hortus): see QUAMOCLIT coccinea (Zander)

crassicaulis hort.: see I. carnea fistulosa

digitata (mauritiana) (Pantropic); slender perennial climber to 10 m, with tuberous roots; the leaves palmately 5 to 7 parted, the sinus between lobes acute; broad bell-flowers carmine-pink with darker eye, to 8 cm across. *Tropical. Zones 10-11.*   p. 274

holubii (Turbinia or Merremia) (So. Africa); curious xerophyte with large swollen, woody brown bulbous caudex, from its apex springs the finely divided foliage. *Arid-subtropic.* *Zone 10.*   p. 204, 222

horsfalliae (W. Indies), "Morning glory", or "Princess vine"; twining winter-flowering perennial with palmately lobed leaves, the showy, 6 cm waxy-glossy, bell-shaped flowers deep rich rose or red. *Tropical. Zone 10.*   p. 274

x multifida (coccinea x quamoclit), "Cardinal-climber"; climbing with twining branches, the leaves palmately divided into 7 to 15 slender segments, to 12 cm across; handsome funnel-shaped flowers 5 cm long, glowing crimson with white eye; usually grown as annual. *Zone 10.*   p. 274

murucoides (Mexico: Michoacan to Oaxaca), "Morning-glory tree"; sparry tree or large shrub, with oblong-lanceolate leaves, 15-20 cm long, white-woolly beneath, on tomentose branchlets; large crepy, ruffled flowers, 6-10 cm across, pure white and apparently night-blooming, fading to creamy-yellow in the morning. *Tropical. Zones 10-11.*   p. 691

nil (Pharbitis) (Old World Tropics), "Imperial Japanese morning-glory"; floriferous hairy perennial; rank tendril-climbing vine, with yellow-green, 3-lobed leaves 10-15 cm wide; showy axillary, funnel-form flowers about 10 cm wide, blue-purple or rose. Can be grown as a bushy pot plant for the cool, sunny window as in Japan, where plants are pinched back every second or third leaf to prevent climbing, resulting in large blooms all Summer and Fall; blooms open in morning and fade late afternoon. *Zone 10.*   p. 274

pauciflora (arborescens) (Mexico: Sonora to Morelos and Veracruz), "Casahuate tree" or "Palo blanco"; large shrub or small tree of dense habit, with smooth white bark; glossy green, heart-shaped leaves, downy beneath; large and showy white flowers 5-8 cm across, with frilled margins and red centers. *Tropical. Zone 10.*   p. 691

pes-caprae (Sandy beaches, Pantropic), "Beach morning-glory"; creeper on sandy shores, fleshy oval, fresh green leaves 10 cm long; flowers purplish-pink with carmine center. *Tropical. Zone 10.*   p. 312

purpurea (Pharbitis) (Trop. America), "Common morning-glory"; widely naturalized; annual twiner with 12 cm cordate-ovate leaves and large funnel-shaped flowers deep purple with pale tube, opening from early morning until about 10 a.m.; garden forms in white, pink, carmine-blue, striped, or double. *Tropical. Zone 10.*   p. 274

purpurea caerulea; attractive blue-purple flowers patterned with rosy lines radiating from orange center. *Zone 10.*   p. 274

purpurea kermesina; striking variety, having flowers crimson-red with purplish-black blotches on petals; seen on Atlantic Island of Madeira. *Zone 10.*   p. 274

quamoclit (Quamoclit pennata) (Trop. America: naturalized in Southern U.S.), "Cypress-vine"; twining herb to 6 m, with wiry stems and pinnate leaves, the lobes cut into threadlike segments; flowers scarlet, with slender tube and flaring 5-lobed limb, 5 cm long; usually grown as an annual. *Zone 10.*   p. 274

tricolor (rubro-caerulea) (Pharbitis) (Trop. America); perennial climber usually grown as annual, having cordate leaves; large purplish-blue, trumpet-shaped flowers to 10 cm dia. with tips red before opening, the tube white. The cultivar 'Heavenly Blue' has flowers dark sky-blue, to 12 cm across. *Zone 10.*   p. 274, 285

tuberosa: see MERREMIA tuberosa

woolcottiana (arborescens Zander) (Mexico), "White morning-glory tree"; scandent shrub or small tree 4-6 m high, the branches and foliage velvety pubescent; leaves cordate-oval; showy white flowers with flaring segments spreading 6-8 cm wide. *Zone 10.*   p. 691

IPOMOPSIS   *Polemoniaceae*

aggregata (Gilia) (Brit. Columbia, California, east to Rocky Mts.), "Scarlet gilia"; striking biennial or short-lived perennial to 60 cm high,

similar to rubra but more dwarf, with 5 cm leaves pinnately dissected into linear segments; the inflorescence on slender hairy stalk bearing toward apex a succession of fiery red, fragrant flowers 3-4 cm long, having narrow corolla lobes reflexed; blooming June to September. *Zones 6-9.*   p. 471

aggregata macrosiphon (Gilia) (Pima County, Arizona), "Sky rocket"; charming variety with larger flowers pink, the slender tubes 4-5 cm long, the spreading segments reflexed, with stigma protruding. *Zone 9.*   p. 471

multiflora (Gilia) (New Mexico, Arizona, Nevada), "Sky rocket"; small downy perennial 10-30 cm high, with leaves variously pinnately divided or entire and threadlike; the trumpet-shaped purplish-blue flowers 2-3 cm long, having projecting stamens, are carried in pendant clusters on leafy stalks. *Zone 8.*   p. 466

rubra (Gilia) (So. Carolina to Florida and Texas), "Texas plume" or "Standing-cypress"; remarkable biennial or perennial to 2 m high, dense with leaves divided needle-like; numerous trumpet-shaped scarlet flowers, 4 cm long, yellow dotted with red inside. *Zones 8-10.*   p. 471

IRESINE   *Amaranthaceae*

herbstii (Achyranthes verschaffeltii) (So. Brazil), a "Beefsteak plant"; bushy tropical herb with waxy 2 to 6 cm leaves almost round, and notched at tip; glowing purplish-red and traced with light red veins. The ornate foliage coloring is brought out best in good sunlight. A bedding or border plant where red is required. Small woolly flowers not showy. *Tropical. Zone 10.*   p. 340

lindenii 'Formosa' (reticulata), the "Yellow blood-leaf"; very attractive, colorful form with broader, pointed 5-8 cm leaves yellow with light green area between veins; stems and petioles red. Charming for carpet bedding and as a window plant. *Tropical. Zone 10.*   p. 340

IRIS   *Iridaceae*

Perennial herbs with sword-like, flat leaves, and roots generally rhizomatous, although some species are bulbous; mostly spring-blooming into early Summer. Horticulture describes the flowers as having "falls", the outer 3 parts or sepals, which are usually pendant; the inner parts or upright petals are called "standards". Irises are divided into several classes:

Bulbous — having a bulbous root rather than rhizomes.

Bearded — the basal half of the "fall" has filaments or tufts of hairs on center base.

Beardless — the falls are smooth and have neither crests nor hairs.

Crested — the falls have a central serrated ridge or crest.

Juno — bulbous iris with thick fleshy roots from the base when dormant.

Onocyclus — with reddish rhizomes bearing stolons; one flower to spathe.

Regelia — stolons rising from main rhizome, and 2-3 flowers per spathe.

Reticulata — bulbous iris with netted covering on the bulb.

Xiphium — bulbous species known as Spanish, Dutch, or English iris, having large erect standards, and no fleshy roots at base of bulb during resting stage.

aucheri (Turkey to Syria and Iraq), (Juno section); lovely species, characteristically having bulbs with several persistent fleshy, tuberous roots attached (Juno); inflorescence to 20 cm high, the blue flowers lined with yellow, early blooming in the axils of the lanceolate foliage. *Zone 9.*   p. 228

bucharica (Turkestan); (Juno group: bulbs with tuberous fleshy roots); robust bulbous species to 35 cm high; the flowers with creamy-white standards and 5 cm pendant outer segments or falls; these falls with golden-yellow blotch and yellow central ridge; channeled leaves lanceolate, glaucous on underside. Excellent for rockgarden. *Zone 5.*   p. 228

chamaeiris (pumila in hort.) (So. Europe to Italy, So. France and Spain), "Crimean iris"; rhizomatous small bearded iris to 25 cm high, with 4-6 broad, sword-shaped leaves to 15 cm long, slightly glaucous, forming tufts; the spathes with 1-2 flowers, with oblong petals 2 cm wide, dull blue-purple, varying to yellow or white, the beard white, tipped bright orange; standards erect and clawed, the margins crisped; blooming April-May. *Zone 5.*   p. 427

cristata (Maryland to Georgia and Missouri), "Crested iris"; beautiful dwarf iris 10-15 cm high, with rhizomes creeping along the ground; sword-shaped leaves arranged distichously, but dying down in Autumn; short stalks bearing spathes with 2 lilac flowers 3-4 cm across, the falls with central white patch along which run 3 crisped ridges down the claw, bordered by yellow and purple markings; early summer blooming, and variable in colors. *Zone 4.*   p. 428

crocea (spuria aurea) (Kashmir); rhizomatous perennial, with stout stalks 1 m or more high, above the sword-shaped 60 cm leaves;

the spathes with 2-3 bright golden-yellow beardless flowers, deeper than in I. monnieri; the crisped falls to 9 cm long, in June. Zone 3. *p. 428*

cycloglossa (Juno sect.) (Turkey, Afghanistan); stout species photographed blooming early March amongst ancient Greek temple ruins of Miletus, Turkey; Juno-type bulbs with persistent tuberous roots bear narrow leaves and branched floral stem 50 cm or more high, topped by scented flowers light blue, blotched yellow on the circular pendant falls. Zones 7 -8. *p. 229*

douglasiana (California, Oregon); dwarf, rhizomatous plant 15-30 cm high, with narrow lanceolate, evergreen leaves equalling or surpassing stems; flowers variable, lilac purple to cream, outer segments oblanceolate and 2 cm wide, inner standards clawed; beardless. Zone 8. *p. 428*

ensata (Thunb. 1794) (syn. kaempferi Sieb. 1858) (earlier name biglumis) (Himalayas of C. Asia, China, Korea, Japan), "Japanese iris" of hort., also as "Sword-leaved iris"; primary parent of the beardless Iris kaempferi hybrids of hort., cultivated in Japan for 500 years; rhizomatous species with floral stalks 40-60 cm high, and forming tufts; flat, glaucous, firm leaves with prominent midrib, 60 cm or more long; flowers 1 to 3 in a cluster, varying from white to dark rose, marked with yellow and green veins, the petals without beards, all oblanceolate, to 7 cm long; blooming April-May. Zone 5. *p. 426*

x ensata (kaempferi hyb. of hort.) "Japanese iris", cultivated in Japan as I. ensata hortensis; magnificent rhizomatous perennial 60 cm high, with sword-like leaves having marked midrib; stiff floral stalks topped by showy ruffled, beardless flowers purple marked with yellow, or in various other colors, often 15 cm or more across in some cultivars; the blooms are characteristic with 3 sepals or outer 3 parts and called the falls, usually pendant and about 8 cm long; the inner parts or upright petals are called standards; the falls are smooth with neither crest nor beards. Zones 4-10. *p. 332*

x ensata 'Better Yet' (kaempferi hyb. of hort.); fancy beardless Japanese iris, with short, erect violet-purple standards, the large falls or outer segments spreading wide, pale lilac and faintly lined with purple. Zones 4-10. *p. 427*

x ensata 'Housah' (kaempferi); very exotic beardless, rhizomatous cultivar, seen at Harrison's, New Zealand; the large flowers with all petals rather open and flat, violet-purple from margins inward, and white feather design from center, the base inside orange. Zones 4-10. *p. 427*

x ensata 'Violet' (kaempferi hyb. of hort.); rhizomatous beardless cultivar, growing by the waterside in Palmengarten Frankfurt, of slender habit and with flowers vivid violet-purple and white in center, blooming in early July. Zones 5-10. *p. 332*

flavissima hort. (humilis) (Czechoslovakia, Austria, Hungary to Russia), "Gold beard iris"; small bearded, rhizomatous iris, with branched floral stalks to 12 cm high; the few linear leaves tufted; flowers with standards short, the outer petals, or falls oblong, 4 cm long, bright yellow, veins with brown, and an orange beard; May-blooming. Zone 6. *p. 427*

florentina (x germanica var.) (So. Europe), "Florentine iris" or "Orris"; charming intermediate bearded perennial of slender habit, with white flowers showing traces of blue on the "falls" or outer, pendant segments, and having an orange beard attached to center; the leaves are grayish-green, 30-50 cm long; blooming in May. This species is one of the iris producing from the dried rhizomes the powder Orris, used since ancient times in perfumery; widely cultivated in Tuscany, Italy. Zone 6. *p. 531*

x fulvala (I. brevicaulis x I. fulva), "Louisiana iris"; attractive rhizomatous, beardless hybrid of Southern U.S. parentage forming clusters of long linear, arching leaves; the flowers with short standards, the outer segments narrow and 5 cm long, light purple with deep violet-purple center bands, spreading wide, on zigzag floral stems to 75 cm high. The Louisiana iris group of native American inter-specific hybrids, recognized about 1920 as found in the Mississippi Delta, having blooms in various colors; well adapted for areas with hot, humid Summers. Zone 6. *p. 428*

x germanica (probably Mediterranean); of barbata x elatior hybrid origin, now as a class of "Common bearded iris"; rhizomatous, with flat glaucous leaves to 45 cm long; tall stems 60-90 cm, forked, with fragrant flowers, the outer segments bright purple, the claw white with brownish veins; beard yellow, the erect inner segments deep lilac; May. Zones 4 -9. *p. 427*

x germanica 'Beverly Sills'; tall bearded class, with gorgeous lacy, flaming pink blooms with flaring falls; excellent pink iris for the garden, and very popular. Zones 4-9. *p. 427*

x germanica 'Lilacina', "Bearded iris"; compact garden cultivar with large pale lilac flowers, the outer petals bearing yellow beard. Zones 4-9. *p. 427*

x germanica 'Old Melodies'; showy bearded iris to 1 m high, seen at Harrison's, New Zealand; large flowers with erect standards nearly

white, but outer, reflexed petals vivid purple showing a pattern of violet lines over white areas at base. Zones 4-9. *p. 427*

x germanica 'Wiener Walzer'; tall bearded iris with branched stalks topped by handsome flowers with frilled white petals prominently bordered rich violet. Zones 4-9. *p. 427*

gracilipes (Japan), "Slender iris"; beautiful, petite crested iris, with creeping rhizome forming clusters, to 25 cm high; the arching glossy green leaves linear, sword-shaped 30 cm long; branched, slender floral stalks with dainty ruffled, lilac flowers, the perianth tube funnelform, and obovate falls 3 cm long with deeper veins, and yellow crest around central white area; blooming May-June. Zone 6. *p. 426*

gracilis (goniocarpa) (Sikkim Himalayas, Nepal, Tibet to S.W. China); a pretty little miniature, as photographed in col. Kew Bot. Garden, England, and found in the Himalayas at 400-500 m alt.; rhizomatous perennial to 30 cm high forming tufts of linear leaves; spathes with single, delicate, bearded flowers 6 cm across, with standards as well as outer segments held horizontally and wide open, blue-purple, the blade tipped yellow. Zone 2. *p. 428*

graminea (C. and So. Europe, to Caucasus); rhizomatous species with two edged stem, its narrow 30-90 grass-like leaves often surpassing the 1-2 fragrant flowers, with pendant segments creamy-white veined purple, the erect standards more purple. Zone 6. *p. 332, 426*

histrioides 'Major' (Iriodictyum) (Armenia) (Reticulata group), "Harput iris"; dwarf bulbous species only 6 to 12 cm high, the 4 cm angled leaves appearing with or after blooms in early Spring; large flowers vivid royal-blue, 7 cm across, the outer falls with white center and golden ridge. Zone 5. *p. 228*

japonica (Central China, Japan), "Fringed iris"; charming semi-hardy rhizomatous perennial 40 to 75 cm high, with broad sword-shaped, glossy evergreen leaves carried in a fan on a short bamboo-like stem; the lacy flowers borne on branched stalks; individual blooms 5 to 8 cm across, pale lilac with conspicuous yellow crest, orange markings and dark blue shadings. *Warm temperate.* Zone 8. *p. 428*

kaempferi hybrid of hort.: see I. x ensata

laevigata 'Alba' (E. Asia, China, Japan), "Japanese swamp-iris" or "Rabbit-ear iris"; rhizomatous perennial to about 60 cm high, similar to kaempferi but the flat, glaucous leaves lacking distinct midrib; flowers beardless and bright blue in the species, white in cv. 'Alba'; usually 3 blooms in each spathe. Zone 5. *p. 332*

laevigata 'Albo-variegata'; very attractive rhizomatous water-side perennial, having its glaucous leaves strikingly variegated and splashed with creamy-white; beardless flowers deep blue. Zone 5. *p. 332*

laevigata 'Regal' (species of Japan and Korea), "Rabbit-ear iris"; elegant beardless rhizomatous cultivar of the blue-flowered species having lovely blooms with petal standards lilac-purple, and outer segments 6 cm long, with reflexed broad apex vivid royal-purple and without beard on the white keel. Zone 4. *p. 429*

laevigata 'Variegata' (Japan), "Variegated rabbit-ear"; lovely perennial swamp iris seen along ponds in Japanese gardens, with the long leaves margined white, and beardless flowers clear blue, in early Summer. Zone 5. *p. 429*

macrosiphon (No. California, Oregon), "Tube iris"; miniature rhizomatous perennial 10 to 25 cm high, forming colonies; linear leaves 30 cm long, finely ribbed and deflexed; the beardless flowers usually blue-purple, but sometimes lavender, yellow or cream; outer segments obovate, with white markings, to 6 cm long; May-blooming. Best in Pacific Northwest climate. Zone 8. *p. 429*

melitta (S.E. Europe, Balkans to Asia Minor), "Konotope" or "Toad iris", the smallest of the dwarf bearded iris to 12 cm high, with rhizomes forming tufts; tiny red-edged sickle-shaped leaves about 8-12 cm long, lying flat on the ground; delicate, fragrant flowers smoky brown with red-brown veining, the falls with white beard tipped blue; the standards larger than the outer petals; blooming April-May, and also again in Autumn. Related to I. pumila but spathes are more rigid. Zone 5. *p. 426*

orientalis (spuria ochroleuca) (Greece to Syria), "Oriental iris"; handsome rhizomatous perennial to 90 cm high, closely related to I. sibirica but stem and foliage of equal height; dark green, sword-shaped, firm leaves 3 cm wide; purple spathes with 2-3 clustered flowers having erect purple standards and reflexed beardless falls to 5 cm wide, white with yellow centers, the rounded apex bluish-purple; May-June blooming. Zone 4. *p. 428*

orientalis sulphurea (spuria group) (Asia Minor), "Yellow-banded iris"; beautiful form with elegant beardless flowers having erect pale yellow standards, and reflexed, broad outer segments golden-yellow on the broad roundish apex, on stiffly erect stalks 80 cm high, blooming early Summer. Zone 4. *p. 428*

pallida (odoratissima) (Italy: So. Tyrol, to Yugoslavia), "Orris" or "Sweet iris"; very handsome rhizomatous, bearded iris to 90 cm high, with flat leaves silvery glaucous, differing from the green of

I. germanica, arranged fan-like, 60 cm long; the branched floral stems each bearing 2-3 flowers, fragrant and lavender-blue, the outer segments with white beard tipped yellow, blooming in June, and carried well above the foliage. One of the irises grown for the powdered dry rhizome Orris, used in perfumes. Zone 6.   p. 429

pallida 'Variegata' (So. Tyrol), "Variegated orris"; attractive fan of flat leaves light or milky green edged in cream; flowers lavender-blue with brown, beard white, tipped yellow. Temperate. Zone 6.   p. 429

pseudacorus (Europe to Asia Minor and W. Siberia), "Yellow flag" or "Water flag"; showy rhizomatous perennial of wet areas, to 1 m or more high, having sword-shaped bluish-green leaves; beardless bright yellow flowers, the outer segments 5 cm long, often violet veined. Zone 5.   p. 332

pumila (Centr. Europe to S. Russia and Asia Minor); attractive dwarf species to about 20 cm high, forming clusters from thick tuber-like rhizomes; stems very short; the leaves sword-shaped and somewhat glaucous; 5-6 cm solitary, bearded flowers usually in shades of purplish-blue but may vary to cream or yellow, bearded on keel; blooming in April. Zone 5.   p. 229

pumila hybrid, "Dwarf bearded iris", of robust habit, forming clumps from rhizomes; compact, to 25 cm high, with broad, concave bluish-green leaves; huge flowers with petals 6-8 cm long, in various colors, from wine-red to lilac and blue, also yellow and cream, blooming almost before the leaves appear in early Spring. Very popular in rockgardens. Zone 5.   p. 426

reticulata (Russia, Caucasus, Iran), "Netted iris"; enchanting dwarf iris 15 cm or more high, a favorite early-blooming plant typical for this species for its reticulated or netted bulb, with leaves linear and slightly ribbed or rounded almost rush-like, 20-25 cm long; and a single scented flower raised on a long tube, deep violet, veined and spotted with orange, the erect standard petals 6 cm long. Zone 5.   p. 229

reticulata 'Cantab', charming Bowles hybrid; stemless bulbous plant, having scented flowers light blue or flax colored with orange blotch on petals. Zone 5.   p. 229

reticulata 'Joyce'; of dwarf habit, with large scented, medium-blue flowers; for borders or rockgardens, multiplying rapidly. Early blooming and can be forced for Christmas. Zone 5.   p. 229

sibirica (Cent. Europe, Russia, Turkey), "Siberian iris"; tufting rhizomatous perennial, with hollow floral stem 60-120 cm high, much taller than the linear leaves; subtended by the spathes are 2-3 beardless flowers, usually lilac-blue or blue-purple, occasionally white, the broad outer segments 3-6 cm long, with white central area; June blooming. Parent of many forms and hybrids. Zone 4.   p. 429

sibirica 'Perry's Blue', "Siberian iris" (beardless); slender cultivar with hollow stalks 60-120 cm high, bearing 2-3 flowers lilac-blue, the reflexed outer petals 2 cm long, white and with a pretty design of violet lines and white rays. Zone 4.   p. 426

sisyrinchium (Zander): see GYNANDRIRIS (Hortus 3)

spuria (Sweden to Spain, Greece, to Caucasus), "Butterfly iris"; vigorous rhizomatous perennial to 60 cm high, with linear arching glaucous leaves 30 cm long, forming tufts; erect, branched stalks with 1 to 3-flowered spathes topped by fragrant, beardless blooms having erect blue-purple standards, and spreading spoon-shaped outer segments 4 cm wide, lilac, streaked with blue and white, but variable, and parent to many garden varieties; in season June-July. Zones 2-3.   p. 428

tectorum (China and Japan), "Roof iris", grown on thatched roofs of Japanese homes; rhizomatous plant 30 cm high, with thin, pale green, sword-shaped leaves; the wiry stalks bearing 2-3 flowers, bright lilac or blue-purple with darker veins, the segments 5 cm long, wavy-margined and with deeply serrate white crest streaked violet; blooming May-June. Zone 5.   p. 426

tectorum 'Alba' (China and Japan), "White roof-iris"; charming cultivar only 30 cm high, with leaves arching sideways; above them the flowers spreading wide, all segments white with occasional purple edging, and crests deeply cut on outer petals. Zone 5.   p. 429

tingitana (xiphium var.) (Morocco), "Tangiers iris"; stout bulbous species to 60 cm high with leaves sheathing stem, and distinctly nerved; large flowers violet varying to white, the outer segments (falls) roundish, to 7 cm long, lilac with pale lines, and yellow ridge; spring-blooming. Zone 7.   p. 229

verna (Pennsylvania to Kentucky and Georgia), "Dwarf iris" or "Violet iris"; dwarf rhizomatous perennial, similar to pumila but beardless; floral stems to 15 cm high; firm linear, glaucous leaves to 15 cm long when in bloom and elongating with age; the pretty flowers to 5 cm across, the erect standards violet-blue and white, the outer segments bright lilac-blue, with broad basal patch of orange rayed with white; April-May blooming. Zone 5.   p. 429

versicolor (Labrador to Manitoba, so. to Virginia), "Blue flag" or "Poison flag"; the common wild iris of E. No. America; rhizomatous perennial 60-90 cm high, forming clusters of firm glaucous, sword-shaped leaves; the floral stalks often branched, bearing wine-purple

flowers having perianth-tube funnel-form, the outer segments or falls to 8 cm long, white and greenish or orange at base, blooming May-June. Zone 3.   p. 429

'Wedgwood', "Forcing iris", a most important "Dutch iris"; bulbous hybrid of the No. African I. tingitana and the "Spanish iris", xiphium; sword-like leaves and stiff spike with striking violet-blue flowers, the outer segments or "falls" lavender and marked with yellow; much grown under glass. Very early April-flowering. Zones 6-8.   p. 228

xiphioides (latifolia hort.) (Pyrenees), in hort. as "English iris", brought back by English sailors from Spain, (xiphium group); bulbous species with narrow, channeled leaves; floral stem to 50 cm high, bearing 2-3 flowers, lavender with yellow patch on falls, but varying from blue to white, blooming June-July, later than xiphium. Zones 5-7.   p. 228

xiphioides 'Montblanc'; bulbous "English iris" producing showy white flowers, the falls or deflexed outer segments with light yellow at base and tinted pale lavender toward wavy margins. Zones 6-7.   p. 228

xiphioides 'Queen of the Blues'; a "Dutch iris" photographed in Palmengarten, Frankfurt, Germany in summer bloom; flowers violet-blue with a patch of white on the falls or deflexed segments of the outer whorl of petals. Zones 6-7.   p. 228

xiphium (So. France, Portugal, Spain, No. Africa), "Spanish iris"; bulbous species to 60 cm high, the glaucous leaves channeled and nearly cylindrical; showy flowers to 10 cm across, with falls or outer segments nearly oval, blue-purple and yellow blotch at center base. Parent with tingitana of the "Dutch iris" hybrids. Zones 7-8.   p. 228

xiphium hybrid, known as "Dutch iris"; large-flowered bulbous hybrid group 45-60 cm high, a class resulting from breeding in Holland of the "Spanish iris"; I. xyphium (from Spain, Portugal, No. Africa), and known for their brilliant colors with strong contrasts, and numerous flowers, in purple, blue, bronze yellow, white. Dutch Iris have larger flowers, and flower 2 weeks earlier (June) than the Spanish, and lend themselves to cool forcing. The cultivar 'Ideal' is similar to 'Wedgwood' but flowers deeper violet-blue, with orange patch on falls. Grown under glass as cut flower. Zones 7-8.   p. 229

ISATIS   Cruciferae
tinctoria (Europe to W. Asia), "Dyer's woad" or "Asp-of-Jerusalem"; biennial to 1 m high, with thin, wiry branches; smooth lanceolate leaves 10 cm long, the stem-leaves clasping, all glaucous; small yellow flowers in branched, scattered clusters, June blooming. Formerly grown for the blue dye, obtained from the leaves. Zone 7.   p. 411

ISLAYA flavida (Zander, Backeberg):
    see NEOPORTERIA islayensis (Hortus 3)

ISMENE: see HYMENOCALLIS (Hortus 3)

ISOLEPIS gracilis: see SCIRPUS cernuus

ISOLOMA: see KOHLERIA

ISOPLEXIS   Scrophulariaceae
sceptrum (Canary Islands, Madeira); shrubby plant to 2 m high, close to Digitalis, its stiff stalk with thick, shining leaves 15 cm long, lance-shaped and sharply toothed; tubular flowers with long upper lip, yellow with darker veins, closely packed in an erect raceme 12 cm long; not 2-lipped as in canariensis. Zone 10.   p. 876

ISOPOGON   Proteaceae
anemonifolius (prostratus) (Australia, N. So. Wales, Queensland), "Drumsticks" or "Cone-flower"; subtropic shrub 1 to 2 m high, having downy young shoots; the leaves 2 to 3 times pinnately divided or lobed, to 10 cm long, the segments linear are sharp-pointed and flat, the whole tapering to a long stalk; yellow elongate cone-like or tubular flowers densely packed in a solitary globose terminal head, 3 cm across, in Spring. Zone 10.   p. 874

ISOTOMA fluviatilis: syn. of LAURENTIA fluviatilis (Hortus 3)

ITEA   Saxifragaceae
ilicifolia (W. China), "Hollyleaf sweetspire"; evergreen shrub (4 m) with 5-12 cm ovate, spiny-toothed leaves like holly but thinner, dark glossy green; tiny greenish-white flowers in arching and pendulous racemes foxtail-like, to 38 cm long. Zone 7.   p. 872

virginica (New Jersey to Florida and Louisiana), "Virginia willow" or "Sweetspire"; deciduous shrub 2-3 m high, having many erect red stems branched at top; leaves usually oblong to 10 cm long, bright green above, slightly hairy beneath; often bright red in Autumn; small fragrant, creamy-white flowers in erect showy, cylindric downy racemes to 15 cm long, on leafy twigs, in June-July. Prefers moist soil. Zone 5.   p. 872

IXIA   Iridaceae
crocata: see TRITONIA crocata

maculata (So. Africa), "Golden ixia"; slender cormous plant to 60 cm high with grass-like leaves conspicuously ribbed; attractive, brilliantly colored flowers normally yellow, but varying to white, marked with red or purple, on wiry stems; spring-blooming. *Zones 8-10.* p. 230

maculata var. ornata (So. Africa: Cape Prov.), "African corn-lily"; small cormous plant, with sword-like leaves folded flat; thin-wiry, straight erect stalks 30-50 cm high, carry a series of 12 to 18 charming cup-shaped flowers of 6 waxy concave petals, spreading 3 cm across, the center with blackish-purple eye, and a carmine-red band on the keel of 3 outer segments. The species maculata has yellow flowers, white in the variety ornata. Ixias have been widely hybridized; photo on pg. 230 shows the hort. cultivar 'Nelson'. *Zones 8-10.* p. 230

polystachya hybrid (So. Africa: Cape Prov.), "Corn lily"; cormous herb to 60 cm high, with smooth linear basal leaves to 1 cm wide; inflorescence on wiry stalks bearing elongate clusters of small, long-lasting, slightly fragrant white flowers having flaring segments, yellow toward base. *Zones 9-10.* p. 230

speciosa (So. Africa), "Red corn lily"; small cormous herb with folded, flat leaves arranged iris-like; wiry stalks 15-30 cm long bearing on one side a row of deep crimson flowers having 6 segments, 3 cm across. *Subtropic. Zones 9-10.* p. 230

IXIOLIRION *Amaryllidaceae*

tataricum (montanum) (So. Russia, C. Asia), "Tartar lily" or "Siberian lily"; attractive small lily-like plant from the Steppe of Southern Russia to Afghanistan with ovoid bulb 3 cm dia.; 3 to 8 broadly linear, mostly basal, persistent leaves, and clusters of long-lasting 4-5 cm lilac flowers with spreading segments; filaments, style and stigma violet, the anthers white, on wiry, leafy stalks 30-45 cm long; blooming Spring to June, and becoming dormant in Autumn. *Zone 7.* p. 210

IXORA *Rubiaceae*

borbonica (bot. Enterospermum); a beautiful tropical foliage plant somewhat resembling a croton, from the Indian Ocean Isle of Reunion; branching shrub with stiff-leathery narrow-lanceolate leaves about 25 cm long, in bluish or mossy-green, mottled with pale green; the midvein a bold salmon-red; small whitish flowers. With age, leaves are longer and less colorful. *Zones 11-12.* p. 856

chinensis (So. China, Malaya); small tropical evergreen shrub 1 m or more high, with rich green, firm, obovate leaves 10 cm long; waxy tubular flowers with spreading lobes orange-red, varying to yellow and white, in dense clusters, blooming constantly throughout the year in warm climates. *Zone 10.* p. 857

chinensis 'Lutea' (So. China, Malay peninsula), "Yellow Chinese ixora"; evergreen bush to 1 m or more high; oblong corrugated leaves 5-7 cm long; slender tubular flowers 2½-3½ cm long, with flaring lustrous creamy-yellow lobes, in large, showy clusters. *Zone 10.* p. 857

coccinea (East Indies), "Flame of the woods"; evergreen, tropical, flowering shrub to 2 m or more, with sparry branches; opposite, sessile, short leathery leaves 4-10 cm long, and clusters of dark scarlet, tubular flowers with spreading lobes. *Zone 10.* p. 618, 857

coccinea 'Compacta' (Malaysia); miniature tropical evergreen to 40 cm high, seen in Singapore; with small dark green, sessile leaves, cordate-ovate in outline, and clasping the stem; vivid carmine-rose to red tubular flowers, dense in showy clusters. Ideal as a colorful low hedge or for edging. *Zones 10-11.* p. 857

finlaysoniana (Thailand); attractive tropical evergreen shrub or small tree to 5 m high, dense with glossy green, leathery, oblanceolate leaves to 15 cm long; small pure white, waxy 4-lobed flowers in large clusters 10 cm across, of haunting fragrance. *Zones 10-11.* p. 857

javanica 'Lutea' (Malaysia), "Yellow ixora"; tropical flowering shrub or small tree to 6 m high; ovate pointed corrugated leaves 10-20 cm long, often cordate at base; inflorescence in clusters dense with waxy flowers, their corollas apricot-yellow, changing to salmon-red. Frequently grown as a house plant. *Zones 10-11.* p. 857

macrothyrsa (duffii in hort.) (Sumatra), "King ixora"; large tropical flowering shrub freely branching, and a prolific bloomer, with oblong lanceolate deep green leaves to 30 cm long and slender-pointed, the 2 cm flowers rosy-red, becoming tinged crimson with age, in large striking clusters. *Zone 10.* p. 857

macrothyrsa 'Super King'; probably hybrid of I. coccinea var. fraseri x macrothyrsa (duffii); vigorous free-blooming, very showy evergreen shrub with stout, cane-like branches with large leathery leaves, bearing 15 cm ball-shaped clusters of brilliant orange-scarlet flowers tinted cinnamon, 1-3 cm across. *Tropical. Zone 11.* p. 78

odorata (Madagascar); tropical evergreen shrub to 1 m high, dense with leathery green lanceolate leaves to 30 cm long; terminal clusters of ray-like slender tubular flowers 8-10 cm long, pinkish with red base, very fragrant. *Zone 10.* p. 857

undulata (Bengal); tropical evergreen to 1 m high, elliptic, undulate leaves with slender points; flowers coral-red, sometimes white in dense, showy clusters. *Zones 10-11.* p. 857

JACARANDA *Bignoniaceae*

mimosifolia (acutifolia) (Brazil), "Mimosa-leaved ebony" or "Sharp-leaved jacaranda"; semi-evergreen tropical tree 8 to 20 m high, with lacy, bright green, bipinnate foliage to 45 cm long, lightly downy. In early Spring the leaves drop, following which appear the big 20-30 cm erect clusters of trumpet-like 5 cm lavender-blue flowers, with silky, inflated tubular corolla. In the juvenile stage an attractive house plant because of its fern-like foliage. *Zone 10.* p. 666, 669

obtusifolia (filicifolia) (Venezuela, Guyana), "Green ebony"; graceful tree to 18 m high; feathery leaves to 40 cm long, with many pairs of leathery 2 cm leaflets, shining above and glaucous beneath; bluish-purple flowers to 5 cm long usually borne on old leafless branches; the ovary with white hairs. Ovary smooth in rhombifolia. *Zone 10.* p. 665

JACOBINIA *Acanthaceae*

carnea (Justicia in Hortus) (Brazil), "Flamingo plant"; upright plant with ovate, grayish-green, satiny leaves on reddish stem, and magnificent terminal head of arched clear rose, 5 cm flowers. *Zone 10.* p. 17, 629

carnea 'Alba' (Justicia in Hortus); beautiful color variant, with inflorescence appearing as in a burst of glistening white, 2-lipped flowers in terminal cluster. Photographed in col. Posada Lomas, Fortin de las Flores, Veracruz, Mexico. *Zone 11.* p. 629

ghiesbrechtiana: see JUSTICIA, as in Hortus 3
suberecta: see DICLIPTERA (Hortus 3)

JACQUINIA *Theophrastaceae*

barbasco (armillaris arborea in hort.) (W. Indies), "Bracelet-wood"; attractive small evergreen shrub or tree to 3 m or more, with thick-leathery, grayish-green obovate leaves; terminal clusters of fragrant white inconspicuous flowers, followed by conspicuous glossy bright orange-red berries. *Zone 10.* p. 796

pungens (arborea) (Mexico, Guatemala), "Cudjoe wood"; evergreen shrub or small tree to 4 m high, with 6 cm leathery, long-elliptic leaves; small scarlet-red cup flowers opening star-like, in clusters; small orange fruit. *Tropical. Zone 10.* p. 892

JASIONE *Campanulaceae*

montana (jankae) (Europe to Asia Minor; naturalized in Northeast U.S.), "Sheeps-bit-scabious"; variable, usually biennial herb, with slender branches 30 cm or more high, linear or lanceolate leaves 4 cm long and toothed, clustered at base; flowers in long-stalked globose heads, 3 cm across, pale blue; summer-blooming. *Zone 5.* p. 355

perennis (laevis) (S.E. Europe to Balkans), "Shepherd's scabiosa"; attractive perennial herb, to 50 cm high, with oblanceolate lower leaves 10 cm long, branching with leafy stems topped by globular, bracted heads of feathery blue flowers 5 cm dia. *Zone 6.* p. 354

perennis 'Rosea' (So. Europe); lovely color variation with feathery, spherical heads of flowers dense with narrow petals pink in center base and tipped pale blue. *Zone 6.* p. 354

JASMINUM *Oleaceae*

didymum (No. Queensland, North. Territory and So. Pacific Islands); tropical scandent shrub, seen in Sydney Botanic Garden, blooming in February; wiry branches with elliptic to obovate glossy green thin-leathery leaves about 8 cm long; creamy-white trumpet flowers, the corolla having 5 flaring lobes. *Zone 10.* p. 809

floridum (China, Japan), "Showy jasmine"; evergreen or partially deciduous sprawling shrub; glossy green leaves divided into 3 to 5 leaflets; clusters of golden-yellow, scentless 2 cm flowers. *Zone 8.* p. 809

grandiflorum (Kashmir, Himalayas), "Poets jasmine", also known as "Spanish jasmine"; straggling tender bush with slender, angled branches, opposite, pinnate leaves of usually 7 small leaflets, and showy white, fragrant flowers, reddish beneath, commonly in clusters; June-October blooming. *Zones 9-10.* p. 808

humile (Nepal Himalayas to Tiber, Afghanistan to Yunnan); semi-evergreen or evergreen erect shrub to 2 m high, or even tree-like to 6 m; with weak branches, the leaves trifoliolate to sometimes 7 ovate leaflets 5 cm long; yellow flowers with 2 cm corolla tube often fragrant, in terminal clusters, blooming June-July. *Zones 7-9.* p. 808

humile 'Revolutum' (So. European clone), "Italian jasmine"; frost-tender evergreen shrub of spreading habit, with strong, angled branches; alternate, large leaves with 3 to 7 thick leaflets revolute at the edges, 2-6 cm long and dull green; lemon-yellow flowers 2½ cm across, larger than the species and fragrant, in axillary and terminal clusters from June to September. *Zone 10.* p. 808

mesnyi (primulinum) (China), "Primrose jasmine"; free-flowering, evergreen, rambling shrub up to 5 m if trained, with 4-angled, glabrous branches, opposite trifoliolate leaves with small, 3-5 cm lanceolate shining green leaflets and showy, single or semi-double, solitary yellow flowers with darker center, to 4 cm across, in Spring. *Warm temperate. Zone 8.*   p. 287, 809

multiflorum (pubescens) (China, India), "Snowy jasmine" or "Star-jasmine"; popular, wide-spread tropical jasmine, prized for centuries in the Orient, especially India; vigorous, freely spreading, downy shrub; cordate, dull green leaves 5 cm long, hairy beneath; pure white, star-like, sweetly scented flowers, borne in clusters at the ends and along the often drooping branches. *Zone 10.*   p. 809

nitidum (So. Pacific: Admiralty Isl.); known in Florida hort. as J. ilicifolium, in California hort. as magnificum; the "Angelwing jasmine"; semi-vining small evergreen shrub with shiny dark green leaves ovate with tapering tip, 6 cm long; large 4 cm windmill-like glistening white flowers with lanceolate petals and long calyx teeth, purplish in bud, and sweetly fragrant. *Zone 10.*   p. 809

nudiflorum (No. China) "Winter jasmine"; deciduous twiggy, nearly erect shrub with 4-angled stiff branchlets bearing small opposite, deep glossy green foliage of 3 little ciliate 15 mm leaflets, solitary, yellow, axillary flowers; in late Winter and early Spring. *Zone 5.*   p. 909

officinale (floribundum) (Himalayas to Iran, Nile region, Africa), "Poet's jasmine" or "Free-flowering jessamine"; rambling bush with 7-9 pinnate leaves to 6 cm long, and white fragrant 2 cm flowers having broader lobes only half as long as the tube, in axillary and terminal clusters. Flowers are distilled for essential oil used in perfumes. *Zones 7-9.*   p. 808

parkeri (Himalaya of N.W. India); small prostrate shrub to only 35 cm high; stems green with tiny pinnate 3 cm leaves of usually 5 leaflets; relatively large solitary flowers 1½ cm wide, clear yellow; forming low mounds and suitable for rockgardens. Also grown in California. *Zones 7-9.*   p. 318

polyanthum (Yunnan), "Pink jasmine"; freely blooming, shrubby plant rapidly climbing, and reaching up to 6 m with red, glabrous branches having small pinnate leaves of 5-7 lanceolate leaflets; early in the year it produces masses of deliciously scented flowers white inside and rosy outside, beginning to bloom in late Winter if grown inside. *Zones 8-9.*   p. 287, 808

rex (Southwest Thailand), "King jasmine"; outstanding glabrous climbing or scandent evergreen shrub with young branches green, round and wiry; simple, rigidly hard opposite leaves broad-ovate, dark green, 10-20 cm long; large pure white, salver-shaped flowers without scent, 5 cm or more across, during Winter, usually in 2-3 flowered clusters. Very showy in bloom. *Zones 10-11.*   p. 809

sambac (Arabia, India), "Arabian jasmine"; woody shrub clambering to 2 m high, with firm, broad elliptic, dark green leaves, opposite or in threes, to 8 cm long; 3 cm flowers in clusters, gardenia-white but turning purple as they fade, and very fragrant, blooming from early Spring to late Autumn. *Zone 10.*   p. 287, 809

sambac 'Grand Duke of Tuscany' (trifoliatum), "Gardenia jasmine"; a button-flowered form from Italy with large, 3-4 cm tightly double, gardenia-white blooms that won't drop off, of a penetrating sweet fragrance; waxy, quilted, oval leaves in whorls, on stiff pubescent stems; flowers more fully double than 'Maid of Orleans' and slower growing. *Zone 10.*   p. 809

JATROPHA   *Euphorbiaceae*

cathartica (Texas and Mexico along the Rio Grande), "Jicamilla"; caudex-forming xerophyte developing big bulbous base, and fleshy compound, glaucous green leaves containing milky latex, the segments folded and wavy at margins; the starry inflorescence in clusters on short stalks, coral-red. *Zone 9.*   p. 204

curcas (Trop. America), "Barbados-nut" or "Physic nut"; tree to 5 m bearing seeds which are used for their oil; leaves lightly 3-5 lobed, resembling ivy; small yellowish-green flowers. *Zone 10.*   p. 724

integerrima (Cuba), "Peregrina"; evergreen shrub to 1 m, with milky sap, more or less 3-lobed leathery, glossy green leaves, and clusters of red flowers. *Tropical. Zone 10.*   p. 724

JOVELLANA   *Scrophulariaceae*

violacea (Chile); tender subshrubby perennial 1 m or more high, with hairy brown branches; the ovate deep green leaves 3 cm long, toothed or lobed at margins, evergreen in mild regions; inflorescence in terminal clusters of 2 cm flowers creamy-white or pale lilac with purple spots, blooming during Summer. *Zone 9.*   p. 503

JOVIBARBA   *Crassulaceae*

arenaria (Jacobsen: Jovisbarba) (Sempervivum arenarium), (Eastern Alps); small light green globular rosette 1-2 cm across, forming tiny offsets on horizontal stems and spreading; the little succulent bodies dense with light green lanceolate leaves flushed red outside; floral stem to 12 cm high with pale yellow flowers. *Zone 5.*   p. 191

heuffelii (Sempervivum), (S.E. Europe: Yugoslavia to Rumania); "Live-forever"; open succulent rosettes 6-10 cm wide, from thick rhizome, dividing at the center to multiply; leaves generally red toward apex and with spine-like tip; floral stalk to 20 cm high, with pale yellow flowers. *Zone 5.*   p. 191

hirta (Sempervivum hirtum) (S.E. Europe: Dolomites to Carpathians); clustering, somewhat open succulent rosettes 3-5 cm wide, forming small globular offsets, leaves olive-green, occasionally tinted brown toward apex outside, and bristly; small 1 cm pale yellow flowers on stalk 10-20 cm high. *Zone 5.*   p. 191

JUANULLOA   *Solanaceae*

aurantiaca (Perú), known as "Guacamaya" in Mexico; evergreen shrub 1-2 m high, growing epiphytic in habitat; branches covered with felt; oval-pointed leathery matte dark green leaves 5-12 cm long; axillary pendant tubular flowers toward ends of branches, orange corolla in large, fleshy, angled calyx, in forked racemes. *Tropical. Zone 10.*   p. 879

JUBAEA   *Palmae*

chilensis (spectabilis) (Andes of Chile), "Syrup-palm" or "Chilean wine-palm"; massive feather-palm with trunk usually swollen and to 1 m thick and 12-24 m high, crowned by spreading pinnate fronds 2-4 m long; the numerous green pinnae in pairs, standing out in different directions, and split at apex; the short thick petioles covered with brown fibers at base. The sap of the trunk yields syrup. *Subtropic. Zone 9.*   p. 105

JUBAEOPSIS   *Palmae*

caffra (South Africa), "Cliffhangers"; along rivers in Pondoland, E. South Africa; trunk short, possibly to 6 m, bearing stiff, pinnate fronds, the leaflets with unequal tips. Fruits are walnut size. *Subtropic to Tropic. Zone 11.*   p. 105

JUGLANS   *Juglandaceae*

nigra (Massachusetts to Texas), "Black walnut"; great tree reaching 45 m with thick trunk; pinnate leaves 30-60 cm long and toothed; tiny male flowers in hanging catkins, the female ones in small erect clusters; petals absent; the hairy 5 cm black fruit nearly round, containing the hard-shelled wrinkled, edible nut. *Zone 4.*   p. 916

regia (S.E. Europe, W. Asia), "English walnut" or "Persian walnut"; deciduous tree to 30 m high, with silvery gray bark; large odd-pinnate leaves; flowers in drooping catkins; edible fruit a furrowed nut within a thick-woody, globular husk. *Zones 6-9.*   p. 916

JUNCUS   *Juncaceae*

effusus 'Spiralis' (Eurasia, No. America, Australia, New Zealand and S. Africa), "Bog rush" or "Corkscrew rush"; tufted marsh perennial, with pliant yellow-green arching stems to 1 m long, in dense tussocks, curiously twisted in cv. spiralis; bearing small clusters of brownish-green flowers at tips. The fibrous stems are used to make mats, such as the tatami in Japan. *Zone 6.*   p. 330

JUNIPERUS   *Cupressaceae (Coniferae)*

chinensis (China, Mongolia, Japan), "Chinese juniper"; erect pyramidal evergreen tree to 20 m high, or sometimes dense with short branches, and leaves of two kinds on the same tree; juvenile in three's, awl-shaped, glaucous above; adult type scale-like in four's, in opposite pairs; glaucous brown, fleshy, berry-like fruit; winter-hardy. Subject in Japan for training into dwarfed bonsai, growing in shallow containers. *Zone 4.*   p. 578

chinensis 'Blue Point', "Teardrop juniper"; decorative evergreen with slender erect branches, the branchlets dense with soft blue-green foliage; the natural broad pyramidal shape retained with age, requires little pruning. *Zone 4.*   p. 578

chinensis 'Emerald Green'; slender columnar cultivar, quite elegant in habit with branches filled in nicely along central trunk; the adult age twigs covered by appressed scale-leaves in bright green; small globular, light brown cones. Suitable for containers. *Zone 4.*   p. 578

chinensis 'Globosa' (China, Mongolia, Japan), "Dwarf Chinese juniper"; dense, subglobose form of the normally quite tall, dioecious evergreen species; slow-growing and remaining compact; the crowded, stringy branchlets clothed with scale-like, densely appressed, grayish-green leaves. Chinese nurserymen skillfully train them as dwarf Ming trees by twisting steel wire around stem and branches to form into picturesque shapes. The small Penjing tree shown on p. 627 was growing in a 12 cm clay dish and measuring overall only 15 cm high. *Zone 4.*   p. 627

chinensis 'Hetzii' (glauca), "Hetz blue juniper"; robust evergreen shrub with branches spreading outward fountain-like; the foliage light frost-blue, with juvenile stage leaves needle-like tipped with spines; in adult stage as appressed scales. *Zone 4.* *p. 578*

chinensis 'Pfitzeriana', "Pfitzer juniper"; evergreen dense shrub broadly spreading, to 2 m high and 3 m across; the branches more or less horizontal, with scale-like awl-shaped, gray-green, sharp-needled foliage; dioecious with male catkins and female berry-like cones on separate plants. Widely planted in California. Originated at Spaeth Nurseries, Berlin 1899. *Zones 4-9.* *p. 578*

chinensis 'Pfitzeriana aurea' ('Aureo-Pfitzeriana' in Hortus), "Golden Pfitzer juniper"; sport of Pfitzeriana, with young foliage a beautiful golden-yellow, especially when grown in heavy claysoils as in Illinois. *Zone 4.* *p. 578*

chinensis 'Pfitzeriana glauca', "Blue Pfitzer juniper"; this differs chiefly from the Pfitzer juniper in that the foliage is silvery blue-gray and not green; with age, this evergreen shrub will grow to 2 m high and spread 3 to 5 m wide. *Zone 4.* *p. 578*

chinensis 'Procumbens nana', "Dwarf Jap. Garden juniper", as offered in the California nursery trade; of very compact habit, slowly spreading, with short 1 cm needles of glaucous silvery appearance. *Zones 5-10.* *p. 311, 578*

chinensis sargentii (Japan: Sakhalin); excellent procumbent variety spreading to 3 m wide and 60 cm high, with whorled gray-green or bluish scale-like needles; on younger shoots awl-shaped or linear with white bands below. A favorite for Bonsai culture in Japan. *Zone 4.* *p. 627*

chinensis 'Torulosa' ('Kaizuka') (Japan), "Hollywood juniper", "Twisted juniper", or "Dragon Chinese Juniper"; very artistic irregular growing juniper to 5 m high, branching with an appealing twisted effect; the tiny imbricated scaly leaves rich green on brown stem, the cordlike branchlets somewhat flattened and contorted; cones berry-like 5-7 mm dia., at first blue-glaucous, dark brown later. Fairly winter-hardy. Very decorative as container plant. *Zones 5-9.* *p. 578, 579, 626*

communis (No. America, Eurasia), "Common juniper"; dense coniferous shrub or tree to 15 m, reddish bark peeling off; branchlets triangular, leaves awl-shaped 1½ cm long, with white band above; the small 5 mm fruit cones on female plants are green the first year, the second year brown or bluish-black, and are an essential ingredient of gin and genever. Used culinarily for seasoning meat, venison, and sauerkraut. The early settlers have roasted fruit as substitute for coffee. *Zone 2.* *p. 528, 580*

communis alpina (saxatilis) (No. Europe, Alps, No. Asia, No. America), "Mountain juniper" or "Dwarf juniper"; prostrate evergreen shrub from high elevations, to 75 cm high, branches rising and growing sideways, the leaves mostly needle-like, bluish-green, in Autumn purple. Also known as var. saxatilis, montana, nana, sibirica. *Zone 2.* *p. 580*

communis depressa 'Aurea', "Rheingold juniper"; beautiful dwarf bush, with dense rising branches starting in Spring with bright yellow foliage, then changing to yellow-bronze; to 30 cm high, the juvenile leaves prickly. *Zone 5.* *p. 580*

communis 'Echiniformis' (comm. hemispherica); dwarf evergreen, slow-growing, irregularly mound-forming bush, to 15 cm high, dense with small dark green, prickly leaves; a collector's specimen for rockgardens. *Zone 4.* *p. 580*

communis hibernica (Rehder) (stricta), "Irish juniper"; brought to American from Ireland 1836; pyramidal evergreen tree forming narrow silvery columns to 4 m high; the branchlets dense and erect, leaves scale-like glossy green, becoming bronzy in Winter; slow growing. Similar to suecica, but leaves shorter and less spreading. *Zone 3.* *p. 580*

communis 'Hornibrookii'; low prostrate creeper with upturned branches, excellent for the rockgarden where it will spread to more than 1 m, and 25 cm high; the needle-like leaves are short and prickly, with a twist that shows the white bands along the inner keel. *Zones 4-9.* *p. 311*

communis 'Prostrata'; low spreader of horizontal habit similar to 'Hornibrookii', but is much more vigorous and strong-growing, having the same small prickly leaves and dainty look. *Zone 4.* *p. 311*

conferta 'Blue Pacific', "Shore juniper"; excellent low groundcover to 30 cm high, with creeping branches spreading to 2 m; the needle-like foliage soft blue-green and tolerant of seashore conditions, as is the species, growing along the sea in Japan. *Zones 7-10.* *p. 311, 580*

davurica 'Expansa variegata' (squamata x expansa cv.) (Siberia), "Daurian juniper"; robust low evergreen shrub 75 cm high and wide-spreading to nearly 2 m; rigid horizontal branches, dense with prickly branchlets of juvenile foliage, mixed with scale-like adult stage green leaves variegated creamy-white. *Zone 4.* *p. 580*

excelsa 'Stricta' (S.E. Europe to Asia), "Greek juniper"; pyramidal dense conifer to 20 m, with scale-like leaves bluish-green; female cones glaucous, purplish, berry-like. *Zone 7.* *p. 580*

horizontalis 'Andorra compact', "Andorra juniper"; a low growing American mutant by Andorra Nursery Philadelphia 1916; flat-topped, robust cultivar to 50 cm high, from the old 'Plumosa'; evergreen spreader dense with slender branchlets; gray-green foliage turning a peculiar lilac-bronze during Winter. The species horizontalis is widespread from E. Canada and Maine west to Alaska, and south to the Rocky mountains of Wyoming; procumbent to 30 cm high with long trailing branches, the leaves scale-like and typically bluish; female cones 1 cm dia. glaucous blue-black. *Zones 4-7.* *p. 581*

horizontalis 'Bar Harbor' (Maine), "Creeping juniper"; sturdy, selected clone of the species native in Northeast U.S.; low creeper to 30 cm high, and spreading 2-3 m, and a good groundcover; the needle-like foliage steel blue turning to wine-red in Winter. *Zones 4-9.p. 311*

horizontalis 'Blue Chip'; beautiful low, creeping juniper to 30 cm high, the spreading, prostrate branches dense with ranks of evergreen scale and needle leaves of vivid silver blue color, forming superior groundcover or mounds; glaucous blue-black female cones 1 cm dia. *Zones 4-9.* *p. 307, 579*

horizontalis 'Glauca', "Blue creeping juniper"; the species ranges from Nova Scotia to Alaska, south to N.J. and Montana; the blue form found by Arnold Arboretum; procumbent evergreen shrub very flat growing and forming mats; leaves needle or scale-like, glaucous blue. Much used in cemetery planting in Europe. *Temperate. Zones 3-8.* *p. 581*

horizontalis 'Prince of Wales', introduced from Canada, but planted as far south as California; very low creeping evergreen forming dense mat 10-15 cm high and spreading 2 m wide; foliage soft apple green, acquiring a purple tint in Winter; very hardy. *Zones 3-10.* *p. 311*

horizontalis 'Wiltonii', "Blue rug juniper"; excellent dwarf, the most prostrate and slowest growing of the blue horizontalis, to only 15 cm high, selected from the species in Maine 1914; intense silver blue, very glaucous foliage varying from scale-like to all needle-like, becoming purplish glaucous in Winter. *Zone 4.* *p. 581*

osteosperma (utahensis) (Montana to New Mexico and California), "Utah juniper"; woody evergreen shrub to tree 6 m high, the trunk short with bark peeling in strips; scale-like leaves in threes overlapping, yellowish-green; female cones to 2 cm long, red-brown and glaucous. Adapted to high desert. *Zones 5-8.* *p. 579*

recurva (Sikkim Himalayas, S.W. China), "Himalayan juniper"; erect evergreen tree from 10 to 30 m high, having graceful pendulous branches. The picture on pg. 581 shows a prostrate form photographed in Nymphenburg Bot. Garden, Munich, as low shrub with branches trailing, having awl-shaped leaves in whorls of three, and overlapping, gray-green and lined white above; female cones brown to purple. *Zone 7.* *p. 581*

recurva var. coxii (Burma), "Drooping juniper"; graceful evergreen tree with weeping branches to 25 m high, from the Highlands of Burma; normally smaller in gardens usually to 3 m high; the juvenile-type green needles are so closely appressed to twigs that these look like pendulous threads. The durable aromatic timber is valued in Burma and China for making of coffins. *Zone 8.* *p. 581*

rigida (Korea, Japan), "Needle juniper"; graceful pyramidal evergreen tree to 10 m high, with pendulous branchlets; the leaves rigid, needle-like to 2 cm long, yellow-green and having silvery band above; female cones glaucous brownish-black 1 cm dia. There is also a low, prostrate form. *Zone 6.* *p. 581, 627*

sabina 'Tamariscifolia' (So. Europe), "Tamarix juniper"; low spreading evergreen to 40 cm high but 2 m wide, with branches arching out from the center carrying the upward-facing branchlets, with short awl-shaped bluish-green needles, scale-like near the top; fruit brownish glaucous blue; maturing to dark green; a favorite for groundcover in California. *Zones 4-10.* *p. 311, 581*

scopulorum 'Blue Heaven' ('Blue Haven'); excellent commercial cultivar of the "Colorado Red cedar" or "Rocky Mountain juniper"; tall-growing pyramidal trees from Brit. Columbia to Arizona and Texas; this form is of compact habit, to 6 m tall, with appressed scale-like leaves strikingly silver blue; the cones nearly globular 6 mm dia., glaucous blue. *Temperate,* but widely planted in California. *Zones 5-9.* *p. 581*

scopulorum 'Gray Gleam', silvery form of "Colorado red-cedar", a male form not producing berries; vivid gray-green foliage; narrow, very symmetrical column, slow growing, durable, very regular requiring no trimming, and remaining attractive all year, keeping its silver coloring also during Winter. *Zone 5.* *p. 582*

scopulorum repandens, "Weeping red-cedar"; unique variety with gray-green branches growing outward and pendulous from a red-barked trunk. *Zone 5.* *p. 582*

scopulorum 'Tolleson's Weeping' (pendula); remarkable evergreen with red-brown bark, growing upright but with branches arching, and the silvery bluish-gray, string-like foliage hanging gracefully as if weeping, with artistic effect, in landscape planting in California. *Zones 5-9.* *p. 582*

squamata (recurva squamata) (No. India and Tibet to Taiwan), "Singleseed juniper"; low spreading, or erect evergreen shrub, with leaves in threes, awl-shaped or needle-like 1 cm long, silvery mainly beneath; ovoid cones 1 cm long, black when ripe. Zone 5.　　p. 582

squamata 'Blue Carpet'; handsome evergreen of low, spreading habit, covered by needle-like foliage an intense silver blue; seen in Germany and also in California. Zones 4-10.　　p. 311

squamata 'Blue Star'; attractive dwarf form of irregular growth forming mounds to 1 m high; the steel blue needles suggest twinkling stars. Dutch cultivar originating from a witches broom on J. squam. 'Meyeri'. Zone 4.　　p. 582

squamata 'Prostrata' (Brit. Columbia to Arizona), "Rocky Mountain juniper"; low form with prostrate branches spreading horizontally and forming dense mat; the linear bluish-green needles to 1 cm long, in bundles of threes. Zones 4-9.　　p. 311, 582

virginiana (Eastern No. America), "Eastern Red-cedar" or "Pencil-cedar"; widely popular evergreen tree juniper, to 30 m high, usually pyramidal, later spreading with age; the bark red-brown, shredding in long strips; branches densely arranged, the final branchlets divided into fine spray; juvenile leaves awl-shaped in pairs, the adult scale-like in 4 ranks, closely appressed and glaucous; dioecious with cones in female tree blue-black 1 cm dia. Excellent timber tree; very hardy. Zone 2.　　p. 582

virginiana 'Canaertii'; originating in Belgium about 1865; of compact pyramidal habit, with cord-like branchlets of dark green foliage; profuse bluish glaucous fruit on female plants; very hardy. Zone 2.　　p. 582

virginiana 'Columnaris', "Pyramid red-cedar"; excellent erect tall-growing narrow columnar form, dense with dark green branchlets of mostly appressed scale-like leaves. Zone 3.　　p. 583

virginiana 'Skyrocket'; very narrow cylindric columnar form of the Eastern red-cedar; lustrous silver blue foliage held close together on tight branches. Originally found growing wild in U.S. 1949, and propagated in Indiana. Zone 4.　　p. 582

JURINEA　　*Compositae*
alata (Caucasus); biennial or perennial, to 1 m high, the stems winged in lower part; basal leaves 15 cm long, lanceolate or fiddle-shaped, gray-hairy beneath; thistle-like floral heads globular, 3 cm dia., of tubular purplish-blue flowers and with several rows of feathery, rough bristles. Zone 5.　　p. 390

JUSTICIA　　*Acanthaceae*
aurea (umbrosa) (Mexico, C. America); bushy shrub with angled stems, grayish-green, lanceolate leaves 20-30 cm long; bilabiate, curving flowers in dense terminal bouquet; corolla 5 cm long, clear yellow. Subtropic. Zone 10.　　p. 629

betonica (Jacobinia) (Trop. Asia, South Pacific), "White shrimp plant"; handsome bush photographed in Tonga; opposite, corrugated ovate leaves; the stems terminated by slender bracted spikes, the bracts white with green veining; flowers white to bluish. Humid-tropical. Zone 11.　　p. 629

brandegeana: see BELOPERONE guttata (Zander)

carnea: see JACOBINIA as in Zander

ghiesbreghtiana (Jacobinia) (Mexico); bushy subshrub to 1½ m high, with leathery leaves ovate-lanceolate, smooth bright green; slender tubular orange-red bi-lobed flowers 3-4 cm long in loose terminal clusters. Zone 11.　　p. 629

KAEMPFERIA　　*Zingiberaceae*
brachystemon (Tanzania: Usambara Mts.), "Dwarf ginger lily"; tropical clustering plant with tuberous roots, forming rosettes of light green, elliptic leaves 10-15 cm long, with depressed veins, appearing before blooms; the showy flowers rising from base light blue with white eye, 4-5 cm across. Tropical. Zones 10-11.　　p. 522

galanga (India); rhizomatous, stemless herb with aromatic, edible tubers and opposite, horizontally spreading, fleshy, roundish, to oblique-ovate leaves shiny green; flowers with two violet bands on lip. Tropical. Zone 11.　　p. 80

grandiflora (Kenya); erect herb with tuberous rhizome bearing a rosette of stalked, shining fresh green, unequal sided, lanceolate leaves with depressed veins, and light blue flowers, appearing before the foliage. Tropical. Zone 11.　　p. 80

pulchra (E. Tropical Asia: Burma), "Pretty resurrection lily"; attractive tropical rhizomatous herb with broad, corrugated leaves flat to the ground, a gray band in peacock design over the bronze blade; large 4 cm light purple flowers with broad petals and narrow translucent lip, white eye in center. Tropical. Zone 12.　　p. 80

roscoeana (pulchra) (Burma), "Peacock plant"; stemless plant with fleshy rhizome and wide, fleshy leaves spreading horizontally, beautiful like shining bronzy chocolate taffeta, iridescently veined and zoned pale green like a peacock tail, purplish and shining gray beneath; fleeting flowers pale purple with white eye, appearing day after day in Summer. Humid-tropical. Zone 12.　　p. 80

KALANCHOE　　*Crassulaceae*
beharensis (So. Madagascar), "Elephant ear", "Felt-buch" or "Napoleon's hat"; woody succulent shrub with knobby, spiny branches to 3 m high, and large, broadly arrow-shaped, lobed leaves to 40 cm long, rich green but densely rusty-haired above, silver-haired beneath and on leaf stalks; branched inflorescence with urn-shaped flowers yellowish, violet inside. Arid-tropical. Zone 10.　　p. 187

blossfeldiana 'Tom Thumb', "Flaming Katy"; a dwarf clone, and very compact "Christmas kalanchoe"; with bronzy foliage, and covering itself during late Winter with masses of bright red flower clusters. To encourage initiation of buds, place the plant outside for the Summer. If flowers are wanted earlier than usual, daylight should be restricted to between 9 or 10 hours during July and August (in the Northern hemisphere), by covering the plant with black paper or a box; for Christmas flowering short-day treatment from early September until buds show. Zone 11.　　p. 58, 187

daigremontiana (Bryophyllum) (Madagascar), "Devil's back-bone"; easy-growing robust, erect plant with fleshy, tricornered brownish-green leaves to 20 cm long, nicely arched and producing plantlets from the serrate margins, reverse gray flecked purple; 2 cm bell flowers gray-violet, pendant in tall inflorescence. Zone 10. p. 187

fedtschenkoi (Bryophyllum) (Madagascar), "Purple scallops"; bushy succulent with wiry branches erect or creeping to 30 cm long; small fleshy leaves notched at apex 2-5 cm long, metallic green and delicately glaucous amethyst, edged purple; 2 cm flowers brownish rose, on 20 cm inflorescence. Zone 10.　　p. 187

fedtschenkoi 'Marginata', "Aurora Borealis plant"; an attractive sport which I first photographed in Mr. Orpet's garden in Santa Barbara, California, the pale bluish-gray leaves beautifully margined creamy-white flushed with pink. Tropical. Zone 11.　　p. 188

gastonis-bonnieri (Madagascar), "Life plant"; loose, fleshy plant with large, lanceolate leaves, pale to coppery green with darker spots, glaucous white, especially young growth, brownish margins as if stitched and toothed; forms young plantlets on tips of foliage. Flowers with corolla tube pale pink, in clustered inflorescence 30 cm high. Zone 10.　　p. 188

'Grandiflora hybrid'; a striking, compact-growing cultivar with large clusters of 2 cm flame-scarlet blooms, of a type that won't close overnight as the blossfeldiana varieties tend to do. A number of good hybrids have been created involving blood of K. grandiflora, blossfeldiana, flammea and others. The photo on pg. 187 is of a young, pinched plant in 6 cm pot, normally larger and grown under the name 'Surprise' in U.S., but appears identical with the late blooming Swiss 'Grob's Triomphe du Chef', a large-flowered stock succulent plant of vigorous habit, with shiny rich green, crenate leaves, and long-lasting leathery blooms; normally spring-blooming, but winter-flowering can be induced by short-day treatment. Zone 11.　　p. 187

'Grandiflora marginata'; attractive cultivar seen in Germany, grown as a dwarfed plant, having foliage with contrasting white margins around crenate edges. Zone 11.　　p. 54

laciniata (glaucescens) (Africa, India, Java, China, Brazil), "Christmas tree kalanchoe"; free-growing, variable succulent with erect stem to 1 m, oblong or lanceolate leaves, the upper ones lobed, or pinnatisect; fragrant flowers yellow, orange, pink, or red, to 1 cm dia., in terminal branched inflorescence. Zone 10.　　p. 187

manginii (Madagascar), "Madagascar wax-bells"; shrubby succulent having wiry branches, loosely set with small 2½ cm thick-fleshy, obovate leaves waxy olive-green, and bearing pendant flask-like flowers 3 cm long, orange-red with green calyx. Zone 11. p. 187

marmorata (Ethiopia, Eritrea), "Pen-wiper"; stout plant with fleshy, broad obovate leaves pinkish to bluish-green, dusted glaucous blue and blotched purple on both sides, 10 cm long, margins scalloped; flowers white, in clusters of 6-8 cm tubular flowers. Arid-tropical. Zone 11.　　p. 188

pinnata (Bryophyllum) (India, Africa, and other trop. regions), "Air plant"; also known as "Miracle-leaf" or "Curtain plant", because young plantlets are produced from the leaves, even if broken off, and pinned to window curtains; stout hollow stem to 1 m high, with fleshy foliage 5 to 20 cm long, grayish-green and tinged with red, at first undivided oval oblong and notched, in later stages divided into 3 to 5 scalloped leaflets; nodding greenish inflated bell-flowers tinted purple. Arid-tropical. Zone 10.　　p. 187, 206

teretifolia (bentii, kewensis) (India, Arabia, Madagascar); tree-like succulent with shrubby base, stem to 1 m high, corky with age; thick cylindrical gray-green leaves, to 35 and 40 cm long, occasionally forked at tips; clusters of light yellow flowers jasmine-like. Zone 10.　　p. 187

tomentosa (pilosa) (C. Madagascar), "Panda plant"; strikingly beautiful succulent with erect branching stem and soft fleshy spoon-shaped leaves 6 to 10 cm long, entirely clothed in dense white felt, apex dentate and the teeth marked brown; erect whitish flowers with light brown stripes, carried in branched inflorescence on pubescent stalk, to 50 cm tall. Arid-tropical. Zone 10.　　p. 188

tubiflora (verticillata) (Bryophyllum) (Madagascar), "Chandelier plant"; slender erect succulent with pinkish-brown stem with many almost cylindric, pinkish leaves blotched purplish, 3 to 12 cm long; young plants forming at tips; flowers red, in compact clusters. *Arid-tropical. Zone 11.* p. 188

KALMIA *Ericaceae*
angustifolia (E. No. America), "Sheep-laurel"; erect evergreen to 1 m high, of thin, open habit; leathery, fresh green, 6 cm lanceolate leaves usually opposite; small 1 cm saucer-shaped flowers purplish-rose, in axillary clusters, along terminal part of previous season's growth. Also known as "Lamb's-kill"; the foliage is poisonous when eaten as in all Kalmias. *Zone 2.* p. 704
angustifolia 'Rubra'; handsome evergreen cultivar similar in habit to species, but with flowers vivid crimson to deep red-purple, in numerous showy clusters. *Zone 2.* p. 704
hirsuta (So. Carolina to Florida and Alabama), "American laurel"; evergreen, much branched decorative shrub 30-60 cm high, the young shoots hairy; with oblong pointed leaves; saucer-shaped wide-open flowers 2 cm across, the angular lobed corolla lavender to light purple with center whitish, blooming during Summer. *Zone 8. p. 704*
latifolia (E. No. America), "Mountain-laurel" or "Calico bush"; thicket-forming evergreen shrub to 3 m or more high, with leathery elliptic, glossy green leaves and large terminal clusters of beautiful pink saucer-shaped flowers marked with purple. *Zone 4.* p. 704

KALMIOPSIS *Ericaceae*
leachiana (Oregon); small evergreen shrub 25-40 cm high, dense with woody stems and small leathery, deep green elliptic leaves 1 cm long and somewhat cupped; little rose-colored flowers with red-fleshy calyx; blooming March to May. *Zone 6.* p. 705

KALOPANAX *Araliaceae*
pictus (Japan, Kuriles, Korea, China), "Castor aralia"; deciduous tree to 25 m high, with thick grayish branches and stout spines; thin-leathery, smooth, dark green leaves palmately lobed, 15-30 cm across; the margins finely serrate and brown pubescent beneath; small whitish flowers in umbels, followed by blue-black berries. *Zone 4.* p. 648

KENNEDIA *Leguminosae*
rubicunda (Australia: Victoria, N.S.W., Queensland), "Coral-pea"; strong-growing bean-like twiner, the young growth covered with silky brown fur; variable palmate-trifoliate leaves, the leaflets ovate, 5-8 cm long; red pea-shaped, pendulous axillary flowers in pairs, a long standard, or upstanding petal, reflexed upward. *Subtropic. Zone 10.* p. 278

KENTIA of hort.:   see HOWEA

KENTIOPSIS *Palmae*
oliviformis (New Caledonia); lofty feather palm, with elegant pinnate fronds, gracefully recurving, the broad leaflets glossy green and leathery. *Tropical. Zones 11-12.* p. 105

KENTRANTHUS: see CENTRANTHUS (Hortus)

KERRIA *Rosaceae*
japonica (West and Central China, cult. in Japan), "Japanese rose"; widely planted deciduous shrub to 2 m high, with twiggy, typically green branches; ovate, corrugated leaves 3-5 cm long and doubly toothed; showy single golden to orange-yellow flowers 4-5 cm across, solitary on lateral branchlets, blooming April-May. *Zone 4.* p. 835
japonica 'Pleniflora', "Double Japanese rose"; deciduous shrub 2 m or more high, ovate, doubly-toothed leaves 5 cm long; flowers golden-yellow, fully double in this cultivar, 5 cm across. *Zone 4.* p. 835

KERRIODOXA *Palmae*
elegans, handsome fan palm seen in Phuket, Thailand; solitary trunk topped by a crown of near circular fronds nearly 2 m across on slender petioles, the blade neatly folded and divided along outer margin into pointed segments; large 3 cm fruits in pendant clusters. *Zones 11-12.* p. 105

KETELEERIA *Pinaceae (Coniferae)*
fortunei (Abies fortunei) (Taiwan, S.E. China); handsome evergreen, symmetrical coniferous tree to 25 m high, with wide-spreading branches; young branchlets orange-red with linear flat leaves 4-5 cm long, spiny pointed on young tree, green and ridged on both surfaces; cylindric cones 10-16 cm long, purple when immature, later with scales expanding. *Zone 7.* p. 588

KIELMEYERA *Guttiferae*
variabilis (So. Brazil); handsome small tree with milky sap; large oval, glossy green, leathery leaves 12-15 cm long; terminal racemes of beautiful white flowers 5 cm across, with crisped petals and center cushion of yellow stamens. *Tropical. Zone 10.* p. 735

KIGELIA *Bignoniaceae*
pinnata (Trop. Africa: Sudan, Uganda, Kenya, Zimbabwe, Transvaal, Mozambique), "Sausage-tree"; spreading tree to 15 m, with pinnate leaves, and pendant racemes of large, showy flowers with curved tubular-flaring corolla orange-yellow at base, the 6 cm corrugated lobes blood-red; on reverse striped yellow; a curiosity mainly because of the cylindric, pale brownish-gray fruit 30-45 cm long, hanging on a cord often to 1 metre long; the Kikuyu make beer with this fruit, adding sugar water and honey. *Tropical. Zone 10.* p. 664, 668, 903

KINGIELLA *Orchidaceae*
philippinensis (Philippines); small tropical epiphyte with short stems bearing leathery oblong leaves to 20 cm long; erect inflorescence like a miniature phalaenopsis; multiple small pale yellow flowers 1-2 cm across, flushed purple at trilobed lip. *Zones 11-12.* p. 88

KIRENGESHOMA *Saxifragaceae*
palmata (Japan: Kyushu); herbaceous perennial to 1 m, with thin, roundish-cordate, palmately lobed, hairy, toothed leaves to 17 cm long on purple stems; trumpet-shaped, nodding flowers yellow, 10 cm long. *Zone 5.* p. 498

KLEINIA: see SENECIO

KNAUTIA *Dipsacaceae*
arvensis (Scabiosa) (Europe to Siberia and Caucasus, No. Africa; natural. in E. No. America), "Blue buttons"; perennial with soft-hairy stem to 1 m high, the stem-leaves gray-green, pinnately cut into narrow segments; flowers lilac with linear rays, in scabiosa-like heads, in May to September. *Zone 4.* p. 414

KNIPHOFIA *Liliaceae*
tuckii (ensifolia variant) (So. Africa: Transvaal), "Dwarf torch-lily"; showy low-growing and handsome perennial, to 60 cm high, forming tufts, the narrow leaves having rough edges, 2 cm wide; the rigid floral stalks topped by club-like inflorescence, dense with 2 cm tubular flowers; the younger unopened corollas are vivid red near top, the older lower blooms change to yellow. *Zones 7-10.* p. 451
uvaria (Tritoma) (So. Africa), "Torch lily"; stout perennial herb with thick roots, clumps of long grass-like basal leaves, and a showy poker-like 1 m spike of nodding tubular flowers, the upper ones in bud scarlet-red, and lower ones yellow, 4 cm long; summer-blooming. *Zones 6-10.* p. 451
uvaria praecox, "Red-hot poker"; showy, floriferous variety forming impressive clusters of narrow sword-shaped leaves, with masses of orange-red flowers in spikes of medium height. Seen in col. of Strybing Arboretum, San Francisco. *Zones 7-9.* p. 451
uvaria 'Royal Standard'; a robust "Poker plant" with rhizomatous roots forming clusters of narrow-linear basal leaves, and stiff floral stems 1 m or more high; the inflorescence in long spike-like dense racemes of tubular flowers, the lower open corollas 5 cm long and yellow, and those toward apex while in bud are vivid red. *Zone 7.* p. 451

KOCHIA *Chenopodiaceae*
scoparia (S.E. Europe, Temperate Asia), "Summer cypress", "Belvedere cypress" or "Fire bush"; showy, densely branched, ornamental annual, with its formal globe or columnar shape resembling Cupressus, 1/2 to 1 m high; a subshrub with numerous narrow, partly almost threadlike leaves 5 cm long, fresh green. The tiny green axillary flowers are insignificant. *Warm temperate. Zones 9-10.* p. 367
scoparia 'Childsii' (So. Europe to Japan), "Bold Summer cypress"; improved strain with larger foliage, remains green throughout season; this cypress-like annual herbaceous shrub of globular or pyramidal shape is of robust habit to 1½ m high. *Zones 9-10.* p. 367
scoparia trichophylla, "Burning bush"; a variety of this cypress-like annual, or short-lived perennial in mild climate, having its ferny leaves, normally fresh green and tipped with silver, change to purplish-red and burgundy in Autumn. *Zones 9-10.* p. 367

KOELERIA *Gramineae*
glauca (C. Europe to C. Asia), "Blue hair grass"; tufted ornamental perennial grass with slim stems to 50 cm high, and bulbous at base; narrow linear leaves glaucous above and pubescent beneath; elongate inflorescence pyramidal with 2-3 flowered spikelets silvery glossy and very attractive. *Zones 5-7.* p. 560

KOELREUTERIA *Sapindaceae*
bipinnata (integrifolia) (S.W. China: Yunnan), "Chinese flame tree"; handsome deciduous tree to 12 m or more high, with broad

head, the young branches and twigs with numerous pores; leaves to 50 cm long, with 7 to 12 shiny green leaflets, broader than elegans; 5 cm flowers bright yellow with purple spot at base, in large terminal cluster in Summer, followed by beautiful salmon-colored seed capsules 6 cm long, separating into 3 papery segments. Zone 8.   p. 867

elegans (formosana) (Fiji), "Chinese rain tree" or "Shrimp tree" (in Florida); spreading, flat-topped tropical tree 6-15 m high; bipinnate leaves to 45 cm long with 9 to 16 leaflets narrow ovate and lustrous green, later turning yellow before dropping; small fragrant, yellow flowers; fruit a capsule separating into 3 rosy-salmon papery segments. Zone 9.   p. 867

paniculata (China, Korea, Japan), "Golden raintree"; deciduous tree 3-12 m with pinnate leaves, the thin ovate leaflets coarsely toothed and notched, and showy panicles to 45 cm long, of fragrant irregular yellow flowers in Summer, followed by attractive lantern-like papery seed pots of buff coloring. Zones 6-9.   p. 867

KOHLERIA   Gesneriaceae

bogotensis (Isoloma pictum) (Colombia); erect tropical herb with velvety dark green to brownish-tinged, ovate leaves, pale along the veins, not bordered with reddish hairs; nodding 3-4 cm flowers red above shading to yellow at the swollen lower side of tube, the lower lobes yellow marked deep crimson. Tropical. Zone 11.   p. 64

'Eriantha hybrid' (Isoloma hirsutum multiflorum), "Tree gloxinia"; robust plant more floriferous than the species and with more prominently inflated orange-red corolla tube and large, spreading limb, throat and lower lobes yellow and all marked red. Tropical. Zone 11.   p. 64

x sciadotydaea (Sciadocalys digitaliflora x Tydaea warscewiczii); a larger growing upright hybrid of stout habit with ovate, white-downy, green leaves and large flowers with hairy purplish-red tube and spreading limb, the lower lobes greenish-yellow dotted and lined with violet-purple. Tropical. Zone 11.   p. 65

KOLKWITZIA   Caprifoliaceae

amabilis (W. China: Hupeh), "Beauty-bush"; showy deciduous shrub to 4 m high, with opposite, broad-ovate leaves 3-8 cm long, somewhat hairy above, and crenate at margins; twin 2 cm bell-shaped flowers pink with yellow throat, spring-blooming, followed by bristly fruit. Zone 4.   p. 672

KOPSIA   Apocynaceae

singaporensis (Ochrosia) (Malaysia); tropical evergreen tree to 8 m high, with conical crown, the bark silvery brown becoming flaky; broad-ovate dark green, thin-leathery leaves 10-20 cm long; starry white flowers in loose clusters. Zone 11.   p. 640

KRAINZIA longiflora (Backeberg):
see MAMMILLARIA longiflora (Hortus)

KUNZEA   Myrtaceae

baxteri (W. Australia); evergreen heath-like shrub to 1 m or more high, with stiff branches, the young growth soft-hairy, and dense with narrow linear 1 cm leaves; the inflorescence in bottlebrush fashion, having small red petals but showy with their crowded stamens crimson-red, tipped by yellow anthers; similar to Callistemon. Zone 9.   p. 801

pulchella (sericea) (W. Australia), "Granite kunzea"; handsome evergreen shrub 1 to 3 m high, dense with small 1-2 cm obovate, gray-silky leaves; the inflorescence in short bottlebrushes of long crimson-red stamens. Distinguished from the related Leptospermum by stamens longer than petals; from Callistemon by the persistent calyx; from Melaleuca by stamens free and not in bundles. Zone 9.   p. 801

LABICHEA   Leguminosae

punctata (Australia); handsome shrub with alternate leaves compound of 3 or 5 leaflets; attractive flowers almost orchid-like, having 4 large, nearly equal obovate petals vivid yellow, marked at base with violet, in terminal clusters; oblong flat pods containing 2 seeds. Zone 10.   p. 762

x LABURNOCYTISUS   Leguminosae

adamii, hybrid originated 1825 in France; curious tree from a graft of Cytisus purpureus on Laburnum anagyroides, with foliage similar to laburnum, but smaller, producing two different flowers in nodding racemes, mostly the yellow Laburnum anagyroides, springing from the outer tissues, and then the purplish blooms of Cytisus purpureus, bursting through from the inner tissues of the branches. Zone 6.   p. 763

LABURNUM   Leguminosae

alpinum (So. Europe), "Scotch laburnum"; deciduous tree to 10 m high; smooth branches with leaves having 3 green 2 cm leaflets; inflorescence in pendulous racemes 40 cm long of numerous pea-like yellow flowers in mid-May, two weeks later than anagyroides; more upright and of stiffer growth. Zone 4.   p. 763

anagyroides (vulgaris) (C. and So. Europe), "Golden chain tree" or "Bean tree"; poisonous but beautiful tree to 10 m high; leaves of 3 leaflets to 8 cm long; pendant inflorescence 15-25 cm long, of deep yellow 2 cm flowers, in late Spring; followed by bean-shaped downy pods 5 cm long, containing the extremely toxic black seeds. Zone 5.   p. 763

x watereri (alpinum x anagyroides), "Golden chain"; small ornamental deciduous tree to 10 m high, with trifoliolate leaves, and long pendulous, very showy, 40 cm racemes of rich yellow, fragrant flowers; considered to be superior to both parents when in bloom, the corollas larger than alpinum. Zone 5.   p. 763

x watereri 'Vossii', very floriferous form, found in Holland 1875, and presently considered the most important laburnum in horticulture; tree of vigorous but slender habit; trifoliolate leaves to 10 cm long, with elliptic leaflets glossy deep green; the showy inflorescence in pendulous racemes to 50 cm long of vivid yellow pea-like flowers in June, and sweetly fragrant; producing a minimum of seed, with only 1 or 2 in each pod. Zone 5.   p. 763

LACHENALIA   Liliaceae

aloides (tricolor) (So. Africa), "Tricolor Cape cowslip"; dainty hyacinth-like bulbous plant to 30 cm high, with two broad linear lanceolate spreading, fleshy leaves dark green and spotted purple; bright, colorful nodding waxy tubular flowers 2½ cm long, the outer segments yellow tipped green, inner ones scarlet-red at tip, much exceeding the outer, on erect fleshy stalk; spring-blooming. Subtropic. Zone 9.   p. 239

pustulata (So. Africa); attractive bulbous plant about 30 cm high; lanceolate fleshy leaves 15 to 25 cm long; 2 cm bell-flowers whitish or tinged red, in a dense spike-like raceme. Zone 9.   p. 239

LACTUCA   Compositae

plumieri (Cicerbita) (Europe: Pyrenees, W. Alps, Black Forest), "Mountain lettuce"; stout perennial to 1 m or more high, the leaves to 40 cm long, broadly fiddle-shaped and pinnately cut and toothed, glaucous beneath; floral heads of 3 cm blue-purple flowers, in large spreading terminal clusters, during Summer. Zone 6.   p. 388

LAELIA   Orchidaceae

anceps (Mexico, Honduras), known in horticulture as "Amalia"; handsome epiphyte with egg-shaped, angled pseudobulbs to 12 cm high, usually single-leaved, topped by long wiry stems to 1 m high, bearing small clusters of slender, variable 8-10 cm flowers, sepals mostly lilac-rose, the petals slightly darker, lip purplish-crimson with yellow throat, (Nov.-Feb.) Tropical. Zones 11-12.   p. 88

cinnabarina (Brazil); charming epiphyte of compact habit with cylindric tapered 12-25 cm pseudobulbs and usually single leaved; flower stalks 30-60 cm high, with clusters of 5-8 cm flowers bright orange-red, lasting 6 weeks (March-May, Nov.). Tropical. Zones 11-12.   p. 88

purpurata oculata (Brazil); grand, robust epiphyte with tall, club-shaped pseudobulbs 30 cm or more, and a long, dark green, solitary leaf; the elegant flowers in clusters and fragrant, 12 cm or more across, the narrow sepals and slender petals glistening white, sometimes flushed pink, large lip white, marked purple with pale yellow throat striped crimson. Tropical. Zones 11-2.   p. 88

rubescens (acuminata) (Mexico), "Flor de Jesú"; dwarf epiphyte with oval, flattened pseudobulbs with solitary leaf; a wiry stem to 45 cm tall bearing a small cluster of 5 cm lilac-mauve flowers, lip lemon-white with purple throat, and fragrant. (Sept.-March). Tropical. Zones 11-12.   p. 88

tenebrosa alba (Brazil: Bahia); beautiful epiphyte distinctive for the color of its large 14-18 cm flowers, sepals and petals coppery green, the lip white; furrowed stems with solitary leaf (May-July). Tropical. Zones 11-12.   p. 88

x LAELIOCATTLEYA   Orchidaceae

canhamiana alba (L. purpurata x C. mossiae reineckeana); excellent intergeneric hybrid of robust habit; free blooming with clusters of large elegant flowers, sepals and petals ivory or pure white, with deep violet-purple frilled lip edged white, and a golden throat, (Feb.-June). Tropical. Zones 11-12.   p. 90

hassallii alba 'Majestica' (L.C. Britannia x C. warscewiczii); charming bigeneric hybrid with glistening white sepals and broad wavy petals, and bright purplish-violet lip, yellow in the throat and frilled (Spring). Tropical. Zones 11-12.   p. 90

LAFOENSIA   Lythraceae

vandelliana (Brazil); showy tropical evergreen tree to 10 m high, with leathery elliptic, short-stalked leaves; the curious inflorescence of flowers having globose red, lobed calyx and showy, red-brown corolla of petals spreading wide, and displaying the long stamens. Zone 10.   p. 774

LAGENANDRA *Araceae*

insignis (ovata) (Cryptocoryne) (W. India, Sri Lanka); large tropical waterside plant with thick, creeping rootstock, bearing rosette of lanceolate, fleshy leaves matte grass green, nearly 1 m long with stalk; spathe short and thick-fleshy covered with coarse purplish-red scales. *Humid-tropical. Zone 12.* p. 30

lancifolia (Cryptocoryne) (Sri Lanka); rhizomatous tropical river-side or bog plant; sprouting petioles from 20 cm to 1 m long, bearing lanceolate leathery, 10 cm leaves, dark green above, paler and marked with white beneath; thick-fleshy purplish 5 cm spathe. *Tropical. Zone 12.* p. 30

LAGENARIA *Cucurbitaceae*

siceraria 'Clavata' (Old World Tropics), "White-flowered calabash gourd"; long-running, tender annual vine, with cordate-ovate leaves; white flowers; smooth, pendant fruit, hard-shelled when ripe, 30-40 cm long. *Tropical. Zone 10.* p. 276

LAGERSTROEMIA *Lythraceae*

indica (Japan, Korea, China), the "Crape myrtle"; handsome flowering tree to 10 m high, foliage falling annually, the elliptic leaves 2 to 6 cm long; at branch tips the gorgeous clusters of frilled, though scentless flowers pink or purple and resembling crepe-paper, blooming profusely all Summer and Fall from August to October; best in hottest or sunniest season. In old trees the bark flakes off to reveal a smooth pinkish inner bark. *Zone 7.* p. 775

indica 'Petite Pinkie',™ "Dwarf crape-myrtle"; handsome compact growing form with clear pink flowers offered by Monrovia Nurseries of Azusa, California, the trade-marked 'Petite' strain is very floriferous with blooms in large clusters, and rich green foliage having a bronze tint while young; vigorous cultivars of upright habit, usually shrubs to 2 m high, but in mild climates and with age may reach up to 5 m. *Zone 7.* p. 775

indica 'Petite Snow'™; another selection of dwarf crape myrtle from the trade-marked 'Petite' strain in California, a shrub of compact habit and free-blooming with clusters of snow-white flowers, and a welcome addition to the smaller garden, usually not over 2 m high. *Zone 7.* p. 775

speciosa (India to Australia), "Rose of India" or "Queen's crape myrtle"; in Hawaii as the "Giant crape myrtle"; a beautiful flowering tree to 20 m high; thin-leathery ovate leaves 25 cm long, and clusters of large, very showy flowers with frilled petals, to 8 cm across; colors usually mauve to purple, but in Tahiti have seen trees with flowers in gorgeous clear rose. *Tropical. Zone 10.* p. 775

LAGOTIS *Scrophulariaceae*

stolonifera (Gymnandra) (Caucasus); seen blooming in June in col. Bergianska Bot. Garden near Stockholm; a herbaceous perennial with stout creeping rootstocks, to 40 cm or more high, the leaves pinnately lobed, basal leaves clustered, stem leaves becoming smaller upward; the near-white or bluish flowers in congested cylindric spikes. A special plant for the cool, moist Alpine rockgarden. *Zones 4-7.* p. 444

LAGUNARIA *Malvaceae*

patersonii (New South Wales, Queensland), the "Pyramid-tree"; of symmetrical pyramid shape, evergreen, 6-15 m high; the young growth scurfy; thick, ovate 10 cm leaves white-scaly beneath; 6 cm axillary, bell-shaped flowers rosy-pink, with 5 recurved petals; capsule fruits (see TROPICA p. 624). *Zone 9.* p. 785

LAGURUS *Gramineae*

ovatus (Mediterran. reg. to Canary Is.), "Rabbit-tail grass"; beautiful annual grown for its flowers which resemble rabbit tails; with green culms, to 60 cm high when blooming; velvety green, flat leaves 20 cm long; cylindric inflorescence pale pink becoming beige, softly hairy and silky, 3-6 cm long. Escaped to Eastern U.S. and California; ideal in dried bouquets. *Zone 9.* p. 562

LAMARCKIA *Gramineae*

aurea (Mediterran. reg.), "Goldentop grass"; loosely tufted annual with culms to 40 cm long, erect or arching; soft narrow-linear leaves to 1 cm wide; curious inflorescence an elongate panicle of glossy yellow to purplish fruiting spikes, very ornamental and used in dried bouquets. Naturalized in Texas and So. California. *Zone 9.* p. 561

LAMBERTIA *Proteaceae*

formosa (New So. Wales), "Honeyflower" or "Mountain devil"; tall evergreen shrub to 3 m high, with erect branches dense with linear leaves to 5 cm long, the margins recurved and pale beneath; the showy inflorescence erect bell-shaped 5 cm long, holding up to 7 scarlet-red tubular flowers with protruding styles. *Zone 10.* p. 822

LAMIASTRUM *Labiatae*

galeobdolon 'Variegatum' (Québec, C. and E. Europe, to Urals), "Yellow archangel"; rampant creeper with square threadlike, rooting stems covered with appressed pale hairs; nettle-like, opposite, crenate leaves 3-5 cm long, deep green and rugose, prettily zoned and painted with silver; two-lipped yellow flowers, the lower lip marked red. *Temperate. Zone 4.* p. 315, 432

LAMIUM *Labiatae*

galeobdolon: see LAMIASTRUM galeobdolon

maculatum (No. Europe, Russia, Iran), "Spotted dead-nettle"; perennial herb with erect square rooting reddish stems, opposite, small 5 cm ovate leaves with crenate margins, rugose and short-hairy, matte-green with broad silver band down the middle; small hooded, axillary flowers carmine-red. Young leaves are boiled and eaten as greens in Sweden. An old medicinal herb used to stop bleeding as a styptic. *Zones 2-8.* p. 316, 432, 529

LAMOUROUXIA *Scrophulariaceae*

rhinanthifolia (Mexico); striking woody shrub 1-1½ m high with stiff, sharply spined leaves; the inflorescence candelabra-like with tubular scarlet, pubescent flowers 4-5 cm long; photographed on Monte Alban, Oaxaca, So. Mexico. *Subtropic. Zone 9.* p. 875

LAMPRANTHUS *Aizoaceae*

aureus (Mesembryanthemum) (Cape Prov.), "Orange ice plant"; succulent creeper with brown-barked branches, leaves shortly connate, sides convex, 5 cm or more long, narrowing to a point, fresh green, with transparent dots; large 5 cm flowers deep, shining orange with yellow center. Naturalized in So. California. *Subtropic. Zones 9-10.* p. 146, 301, 307

conspicuus (Cape Prov.); succulent shrub with stout, creeping branches, fleshy, 3-angled linear, incurved leaves crowded at ends of branches to 8 cm long, green, often dotted and with red point at end; 5 cm daisy-like flowers purple-red, with cream centers. *Zone 10.* p. 146

haworthii (So. Africa: Cape Prov.); freely branching, shrubby succulent, with slender woody, brown-skinned stems; semi-cylindrical 4 cm leaves light green with gray bloom; light purple ray-flowers to 7 cm across, opening at noon. *Zone 10.* p. 147

multiradiatus (roseus in hort.) (Cape Prov.: Table Mountain), "Pink ice plant"; spreading succulent, with compressed 3-angled, linear leaves 3 cm long, covered with translucent spots, and large soft pink flowers 4 cm across, becoming deeper toward base, and with yellow in center. *Arid-subtropic. Zones 9-10.* p. 146

productus (Cape Prov.: Karroo), "Purple ice-plant"; freely branching, shrubby succulent to 75 cm or more high, and forming mounds, with bundles of bluish to coppery cylindric leaves 3-4 cm long on brown-purple stems; the large 4 to 5 cm flowers with glistening purple rays, opening to the warming sun; very floriferous, and popular for planting on steep banks in California. *Arid-subtropic. Zones 9-10.* p. 147, 301, 307, 618

roseus (Hortus 2): see L. multiradiatus (Hortus 3)

spectabilis (Mesembryanthemum spectabile) (So. Africa: Cape Prov.), "Red ice plant"; somewhat woody perennial, branching with long prostrate reddish flowering stems; succulent keeled leaves 2-5 cm long, glaucous gray-olive; the 4-5 cm flowers gleaming in brilliant color, normally purplish, and with longer leaves. The color forms in the California trade as L. spectabilis are probably hybrids such as the pictured "Red ice plant" in shining crimson; other colors available are pink or rose. Beautiful flowering plants in Spring and Summer. *Arid-subtropic. Zones 9-10.* p. 147, 307

tricolor (Transvaal), "Copper ice plant"; low creeper with small linear, succulent, glaucous leaves; masses of brilliantly colored daisy-like heads of ray-flowers brick-red to crimson toward apex, with whitish button in center. *Arid-subtropic. Zone 10.* p. 147

LANSIUM *Meliaceae*

domesticum (India, Malaysia), "Lady's fingers"; evergreen tropical tree to 15 m high, having trunk deeply fluted and reddish-brown bark; leaves 30-40 cm long, of 5 to 7 large alternate, stalked leaflets 12-20 cm long; small yellow flowers densely arranged in erect hairy spikes, occasionally from the trunk; the round or oblong brownish fruit to 5 cm wide, containing seeds and sweet white pulp, commonly planted in Malayan villages. *Zone 10.* p. 788

LANTANA *Verbenaceae*

camara (West Indies), "Shrub verbena", "Lakana" in Hawaii; freely blooming tropical shrub to 3 m high, with thin-woody, angled branches sometimes prickly, and ovate, scented, toothed, rough-bristly leaves; with stiff-erect, small but showy 3-4 cm heads of verbena-like flowers, changeable, usually opening pink or yellow, becoming red or orange, and several color combinations may be found on the same plant; summer-blooming; followed by clusters of small glossy black berries. *Zones 9-10.* p. 78, 900

camara 'Festival'; low dense cultivar with woody, spreading, thin branches, usually quite brittle, with rather rough, opposite ovate,

3-5 cm leaves; profusely blooming with attractive rounded clusters of small flowers in pink, orange and yellow, from Spring to Autumn. Evergreen in frost-free areas. *Zones 9-10.*   p. 324, 901

camara 'Mutabilis', "Shrub verbena"; tropical evergreen prickly shrub to 1 m or more high, with variable flowers opening white, quickly changing through yellow, lilac and rose to blue, in globose clusters; known from Hawaii; photographed in Pala Mission, California. *Zones 9-10.*   p. 900

camara 'Radiation'; floriferous evergreen shrub with brittle branches, 1 to 1¹/₂ m high and wide with age, having ovate, scented leaves 6-8 cm long, serrate at margins and with rough surface; the rounded bush literally covered by showy clusters of 16 mm flowers ranging from yellow to rich orange and vivid scarlet, blooming Summer into Autumn. Lovely as a staked patio plant. *Zones 9-10.*   p. 900

camara 'Variegata', "Yellow sage"; attractive cultivar of smallish, compact habit, with leaves richly splashed and variegated with creamy-white especially from margins inward; flowers primarily yellow, in clusters having the outer blooms becoming purplish, the inner ones orange. A charming foliage plant in pots. *Zones 10-11.*   p. 900

montevidensis (sellowiana) (Uruguay), "Trailing lantana" or "Polecat geranium"; small, downy, spreading shrub with weak, vine-like, pendant branches, used as a ground cover or in baskets; small ovate, rough leaves, a profuse bloomer Winter and Summer, with pretty 3 cm heads of rosy-lilac flowers. *Subtropic.* *Zones 9-10.*   p. 324, 900

LAPAGERIA   *Liliaceae*
rosea (Chile), "Chile bells"; showy vine with alternate ovate, leathery leaves, and many large 8 cm pendulous axillary bell-shaped flowers, rich rosy-crimson, spotted white inside; summer-blooming. *Subtropic. Zone 10.*   p. 283

LAPEIROUSIA   *Iridaceae*
laxa (cruenta) (Anomatheca) (Transvaal), "Woodland painted petals"; miniature cormous plant with flat narrow basal leaves, the small flowers on a one-sided wiry raceme, long 4 cm tubes with spreading lobes bright orange-red and blood-red border; summer-blooming. *Subtropic. Zones 8-9.*   p. 231

LARIX   *Pinaceae (Coniferae)*
decidua (Europe), "European larch"; deciduous coniferous tree 30 to 50 m high; pyramidal while young, but old trees have a large trunk and wide-spreading branches; young terminal shoots are gray and furrowed; leaves of long shoots 2-3 cm long; those of short shoots 30 to 40 bundled together; male flowers yellow, in long heads; females red or white, 1 cm long; cone ovoid 3 cm long, brown. Wood is of excellent quality. *Zone 2.*   p. 586, 588

kaempferi (leptolepis) (Japan), "Japanese larch" or "Kara-matsu"; deciduous coniferous tree to 30 m high, with linear needle-like leaves arranged spirally on the young shoots and clustered on the short spurs, light or bluish-green; cones 3-4 cm long, when mature, with brown scales spreading and recurved; can be grown in pots and trained into miniature bonsai. *Zone 4.*   p. 588, 589

laricina (E. Canada to Alaska, south to Maryland), "American larch" or "Tamarack"; very cold-hardy, rather thin deciduous coniferous trees 10-12 m or more high, with slender smooth branch-lets often pendulous and glaucous; light green thin leaves triangular in sections 2-3 cm long, in bundles on short spurs, turning yellow in Autumn; very small ovoid cones 1-2 cm long. *Zone 1.*   p. 588

LARREA   *Zygophyllaceae*
tridentata (California to Texas and Mexico), "Creosote bush"; evergreen balsam-scented bush to 3 m high, with resinous foliage, creosote-scented; the leathery 1 cm leaves divided into two tiny crescents; small solitary yellow flowers blooming irregularly all year, followed by white berry-fruit. Flower buds are eaten like capers when pickled. Attractive straggling or rounded bush in arid deserts of the Southwest. *Zone 8.*   p. 902

LASIA   *Araceae*
concinna (Borneo); tropical bog plant, with thick stem lying on the ground; leaves on long erect stalk, with a basal spiny sheath; the young leaves sagittate, in adult stage pinnately divided; long spathe twisted. *Zone 11.*   p. 326

LATANIA   *Palmae*
loddigesii (Mauritius), "Blue latan palm"; handsome fan palm 15 m tall, with rough, slender trunk, bearing a large crown of numerous palmate, rigid blue-gray leaves to 1 m across, the deeply cut segments fuzzy beneath, the petioles and leaf veins colored orange. *Tropical. Zones 11-12.*   p. 106

lontaroides (borbonica, commersonii) (Mauritius), "Red latan"; robust, rapid-growing fan palm to 16 m, with gray trunk swollen at base, bearing a large crown of numerous handsome thick leaves

palmate fan-shaped, gray-green, and deeply cut, 2-2¹/₂ m across; the segments edged with tiny sawteeth, veins and margins tinged with red, fuzzy beneath; the stalks colored orange, thorny when young, the rachis extending into the leaf for 45 cm or more. Highly ornamental. Loves warmth and moisture with good drainage. *Tropical. Zones 11-12.*   p. 105

LATHYRUS   *Leguminosae*
clymenum articulatus (E. Mediterranean, Asia Minor, No. Africa), "Wild pea"; attractive rambling annual with tendril climbing stems, linear leaflets, and clusters of 2-4 purple flowers with rose-colored wings; narrow leaflets bluish-gray. *Subtropic.* *Zone 10.*   p. 279

grandiflorus (So. Europe), "Everlasting pea" or "Two-flowered pea"; climbing perennial to 2 m, with 4-angled (not winged) branches, ovate leaflets in pairs; lovely purplish-rose pea-flowers 3 cm across, 2 to 3 on each stalk; beans cylindric. *Zone 5.*   p. 279

latifolius (So. Europe), "Perennial pea"; perennial becoming rampant, climbing by tendrils to 3 m or more, with branches strongly winged; ovate leaflets 10 cm long, in one pair; large and showy rose-pink flowers 3-4 cm wide, in large clusters; fruit to 12 cm long. Widely naturalized in U.S. *Zone 4.*   p. 279

latifolius 'Albus' (So. Europe); a color form of the perennial "Everlasting pea" in large racemes of pure white flowers. *Zone 4.*   p. 279

luteus aureus (gmelinii in Zander) (Taurus Mts. of Turkey), "Yellow wild pea"; herbaceous perennial 30-80 cm high, with branched, angled stems; leaves pinnate with ovate leaflets in 3-5 pairs, glaucous beneath; the erect racemes of pea-flowers brownish-apricot colored or shaded old gold; bright yellow in the species; blooming early Summer. *Zone 6.*   p. 442

odoratus (So. Italy, Sicily), "Sweet pea"; annual, tendril-climbing herb with brittle, winged stems, paired oval leaves, and large, sweetly fragrant, butterfly-like 4 cm flowers originally purple, but now hybridized into many delicate pastel tints, beloved by gardeners and the florists trade. *Zone 10.*   p. 279

odoratus carnea (Sicily), "Salmon Sweet pea"; beautiful variety with masses of flowers rich salmon-rose, as seen luxuriating in the Holy city of Benares, along the River Ganges in tropical India. *Zone 10.*   p. 279

odoratus 'Rosea'; florists' "Sweet pea" cultivar with fragrant rose-pink flowers to 5 cm across. Grown as annual vine in cool northern greenhouses as cut flowers for winter-bloom beginning November to Christmas, into Spring, planted into ground beds, and climbing up cotton strings, as recalled by the author from early experience in South Dakota. Outdoor sowings succeed best where the climate is not excessively hot. *Zone 10.*   p. 279

rotundifolius (Anatolia: Taurus Mts.), "Persian everlasting pea"; perennial climber, branched with winged stems; roundish leaflets in one pair; long floral stalks with clusters of brick-red to rose-colored flowers. *Zone 6.*   p. 279

tuberosus (Europe, W. Asia), "Earth-nut pea" or "Dutch mice"; tuberous-rooted perennial climber or trailer with 4-angled branches to 1 metre or more, oblong leaflets in one pair, 4 cm long; flowers rose-pink, 3-4 on long floral stalks. The small tubers are edible. *Zone 5.*   p. 279

vernus 'Roseum' (Europe to Siberia and Asia Minor), "Spring vetchling"; herbaceous perennial forming small bush 30-60 cm high, the flexuous stems with pinnate leaves having 2-3 pairs of ovate, shining leaflets; small, nodding pea-flowers, very floriferous in massed racemes, the corollas soft rose-pink; purple and blue with red veins in the species; April-May-blooming. *Zone 5.*   p. 442

LAURENTIA   *Lobeliaceae (Campanulaceae)*
fluviatilis (Isotoma) (So. Australia, New Zealand), "Blue star creeper"; low prostrate perennial forming mats; small rounded 1 cm rich green leaves; masses of little light blue star flowers. Used as groundcover in California. *Subtropic. Zone 9.*   p. 317

LAURUS   *Lauraceae*
nobilis (Asia Minor, naturalized in So. Europe), "Sweet bay" or true "Laurel"; evergreen, pyramidal aromatic tree to 10 m high, very leafy, with elliptic, stiff thin-leathery leaves dark green and lightly crimped, 3-8 cm long, and small, inconspicuous greenish-yellow flowers followed by blue-black berries; much grown in tubs and clipped into formal shapes, mainly in Belgium. The leaves are used in cooking and seasoning; the essential oil from the fruit is used in perfumery. *Zone 9.*   p. 73, 537, 624, 628, 741

LAVANDULA   *Labiatae*
angustifolia (syn. officinalis or L. spica in hort.) (Mediterr. region), "English lavender"; aromatic subshrub with square stems 60-90 cm high, having narrow linear semi-evergreen leaves white tomentose when young; 12 cm spikes of fragrant purple-blue flowers in late

Summer. Use: medicinal; in perfumes, soaps, sachets, moth prevention; the fragrance remains in the flowers for years. Zone 5. *p. 529, 530*

dentata (Spain, Mallorca, So. France), "French lavender"; charming subshrubby, aromatic perennial 30 to 90 cm high, forming mounds, with square, gray-tomentose shoots, dense with attractive, ovate, grayish, toothed leaves 3 cm long, white-hairy when young; and a profusion of lavender-blue flowers, not strongly scented, in dense terminal spikes, during July-August. Zones 9-10. *p. 432, 530*

dentata 'Vera', "Green-toothed lavender" or "Green dentata"; green leaved form of the "True lavender"; blooming nearly year-round in mild climate with dense spikes of purplish flowers. Zones 9-10. *p. 530*

lanata (Sierra Nevada of So. Spain), "Woolly lavender"; aromatic sub-shrubby perennial 40-60 cm high, similar to L. angustifolia, but densely white-woolly; narrow oblanceolate leaves 1 cm wide; inflorescence on 4-angled stems, terminal in a spike to 8 cm long, of very fragrant, violet-purple flowers 1 cm long, in July to September. An outstanding perfume herb, retaining its haunting scent over a long period when cut and dried. Zone 6. *p. 530*

officinalis: see L. angustifolia

stoechas (So. France to Portugal), "Spanish or French lavender"; gray-tomentose tender perennial shrub to 90 cm high, with gray-green linear leaves 3 cm long, and spikes of dark purple flowers. Use: flowering tips for perfumes, scented sachets; young tips for flavoring in jellies and beverages. Zone 9. *p. 529*

viridis (Madeira), "Green Fire"; aromatic herbaceous perennial to 50 cm high, very bushy with leafy stems, the foliage narrow and gray pubescent; corolla greenish tipped purple, from dense pyramidal terminal spikes, subtended by green bracts, blooming in June. Known from Madeira since 1777. Zone 9. *p. 432*

LAVATERA *Malvaceae*

arborea (Coasts of W. Europe, Canary Isl., Mediterr.), "Tree mallow"; tree-like biennial softly hairy all over, 2-3 m high, with robust, brownish stem, and large, fleshy leaves 3 to 9 lobed, and crenate at margins; attractive flowers 5 cm across, in axillary clusters, light purple, with deep violet lines and center; blooming Summer into Autumn. Zones 8-9. *p. 458*

assurgentiflora (So. California to Baja Calif.), "Malva rosa"; woody shrub from the Channel Islands, 2 to 5 m high, with twisted gray trunk and branches, the leaves palmately 5 to 7-lobed, and cordate at base, 8-15 cm wide, white-hairy beneath; deciduous in cold climate; axillary flowers 6-8 cm across, the petals deep cherry-red with darker veins, and having long narrow claw; the staminal tube usually downy, July-blooming. Zone 10. *p. 785*

cachemiriana (Kashmir, Himalayas), "Kashmir tree mallow"; soft-pubescent herbaceous plant to 1½ m or more high, the lower, long-stalked leaves roundish with several lobes, the upper leaves sessile and sharply lobed; axillary flowers delicate pink, to 8 cm across, the petals notched at apex, summer-blooming. Zone 8. *p. 458*

olbia 'Rosea' (W. Mediterran. to So. France), "Tree lavatera"; handsome perennial subshrub to 2 m high; the leaves velvety hairy, lower ones to 15 cm long and 5-lobed; uppers smaller, 3-lobed or entire; the flowers 6 cm across, with outer calyx joined, and the heart-shaped petals soft rose in the cultivar, purple in the species, blooming June to September. Zone 9. *p. 458, 786*

thuringiaca (Cent. and S.E. Europe to Russia, Caucasus), "Saxon mallow"; hairy herbaceous perennial to 1 m high and wide; leaves cordate ovate, or 3 and 5-lobed, to 8 cm long; flowers 4-5 cm across, axillary or in loose terminal clusters, having petals purplish-pink, deeply notched, blooming during Summer. Zone 4. *p. 458*

trimestris (Mediterranean Reg. to Portugal), "Tree-mallow"; rough-hairy annual herb 1-2 m high, with lower leaves nearly round, upper ones angled or trilobed and toothed; showy axillary, solitary saucer-like flowers 6-10 cm across, rosy with darker veins. The cultivar **'Silver cup'** has petals blended with white; July to October blooming. Zones 8-9. *p. 458*

LAYIA *Compositae*

platyglossa (California), "Tidy-tips"; charming annual with thin leafy branches, to 30 cm high; the linear leaves divided or entire; lovely yellow flowers 5 cm across, with rays having cream-colored edges, seen blooming as conspicuous field plant in California during March through May. Zone 9. *p. 393*

LECHENAULTIA *Goodeniaceae*

biloba (Western Australia), "Blue lechenaultia"; evergreen shrub of straggling habit, 60 to 90 cm high; bi-lobed flowers clear blue, 2 cm across, with wedge-shaped petals; soft needle leaves to 2 cm long, on slender stems. One of the most beautiful West Australian plants. Zone 10. *p. 732*

superba (Western Australia), "Barrens lechenaultia"; slender shrub to 70 cm high, with soft needle-like leaves 1-2 cm long; showy flowers tubular 2-3 cm long with spreading lobes, crimson-red. Zone 10. *p. 732*

tubiflora (formerly Leschenaultia) (Western Australia); low evergreen, prostrate shrub dense with small 1 cm narrow linear leaves; most beautiful erect tubular 2-3 cm flowers with white base and red petal tips. In habitat from Albany to Moora, W. Australia. Zone 10. *p. 732*

LECYTHIS *Lecythidaceae*

zabucajo (Guyana, Brazil), "Paradise nut" or "Sapucaya nut"; known in commerce also as cream nuts, better tasting and more delicious than the better known Brazil nut; tropical oak-like tree with 18 cm leathery elliptic leaves; creamy-white flowers hidden by the magnificent foliage; the huge curious seed pods are 20 cm long, with an opening at one end where the monkeys can reach the 8 cm edible nut. Photographed in Boa Vista, Rio de Janeiro. Zone 10. *p. 743*

LEDEBOURIA *Liliaceae*

socialis (Scilla violacea) (So. Africa), "Silver squill"; small suckering bulbous plant with swollen base, attractive because of its variegated foliage; strap-like fleshy leaves olive-green 5-10 cm long, with silver blotching and banding, glossy wine-red beneath; small green and blue flowers on slender racemes to 15 cm high, in Winter. Subtropic. Zones 10. *p. 248*

x LEDODENDRON *Ericaceae*

'Arctic Tern' (Ledum glandulosum and Rhododendron trichostomum); evergreen low shrub more broad than high, slow growing to 50 cm; thin elliptic leaves 2-5 cm long, ciliate at margins, matte green above, pale beneath; tiny white 1 cm flowers in dense pyramidal racemes. Seen at Chelsea Flower Show London 1984. Zone 6. *p. 706*

LEDUM *Ericaceae*

groenlandicum (Greenland to New Jersey and across Canada), "Labrador tea"; floriferous evergreen shrub to 1 m high, favoring boggy areas; with rusty-hairy young branches; ovate or narrow-oblong leaves to 5 cm long, dark green above, rusty tomentose beneath; small 1 cm white flowers in dense clusters, blooming late Spring. The leaves are aromatic when bruised, and were used as substitute for tea. Zone 2. *p. 706*

palustre (C. Europe to No. Asia), "Wild rosemary" or "Crystal tea"; erect evergreen shrub to 1 m high, with young branches brown-hairy; elliptic to linear green leaves 3 cm long, rusty tomentose beneath; attractive pinkish or white 5-petalled flowers 12 mm across, displaying 7-11 conspicuous stamens, in dense terminal clusters. Zone 5. *p. 706*

LEEA *Leeaceae*

coccinea (Burma), "Indian holly"; willowy shrub with long, 3-pinnate leaves of scattered, lanceolate, glossy green leaflets, with margins wavy or recurved and dentate; the small flowers in a large, flat-topped cluster, scarlet-red in bud, the spreading corolla lobes pink; starts flowering when small. Zone 10. *p. 902*

rubra (India, Burma, Malaya); evergreen shrubby herb with dark bronzy, pinnate foliage, and clusters of flowers opposite the leaves, brick-red; when open the petals are pink inside, red outside; the fruit a small berry. Tropical. Zone 10. *p. 902*

LEIOPHYLLUM *Ericaceae*

buxifolium (U.S.: New Jersey to Florida), the "Sand-myrtle"; low evergreen shrub to 20 cm with tiny 2 cm glossy leathery leaves, and small flowers of 5 spreading petals, with white corolla tipped pink, in terminal clusters. Zone 5. *p. 706*

LEMAIREOCEREUS:
see STENOCEREUS (Europ. Garden Flora 1989)

LEMNA *Lemnaceae*

minor (Temperate and Subtropical No. Hemisphere), "Duckweed"; small floating perennial aquatic herb without stems, and consisting of one minute frond or thallus to 6 mm long and one unbranched root; they cohere by their edges in two's and three's, and new fronds will grow out of the edge of old ones; in Autumn they fall to the bottom of a pool and rise in the Spring. Used as food by fish and water birds. Zones 4-9. *p. 331*

LEONOTIS *Labiatae*

leonurus (So. Africa), "Lion's ear"; tall perennial to 2 m high, with light green, soft pubescent, crenate, elliptic leaves; the 2-lipped, orange-red, downy flowers 6 cm long, in dense showy whorls, during Winter. Subtropic. Zone 10. *p. 432*

LEONTOPODIUM   *Compositae*

alpinum (Alps, Pyrenees, Himalaya), "Edelweiss"; low tufted white-woolly perennial herb to 30 cm high, creeping by rhizomes, having lanceolate and linear leaves; the striking inflorescence, so well beloved by mountain climbers in the Alps, is a constellation of small 6 mm yellow flowers, surrounded by the showy silvery-felty, linear bracts arranged to form stars 4-8 cm across. *Zone 4.*   p. 395

souliei ('Mignon') (China: Yunnan, Szechuan, Tibet), "Chinese edelweiss"; stoloniferous perennial, forming mats; with linear leaves gray-silky above, and silvery-hairy beneath; leaflike bracts form a white woolly star enclosing the tiny yellow flowers. *Zone 4.*   p. 395

stoechas (China: Szechuan), "Miniature edelweiss"; lovely small relative to the Alpine edelweiss; low, spreading perennial with gray-woolly linear leaves to 5 cm long, forming dense mats; silky-white inflorescence of star-like floral bracts 3 cm across, and more diminutive than the Alpine species. *Zone 5.*   p. 395

LEPIDIUM   *Cruciferae*

fremontii (So. Arizona), "Desert alyssum"; subshrubby perennial to 60 cm high, at home in Joshua Tree National Monument, having many thin-wiry whitish, smooth branches; leaves mostly 3-5 cm long, with or without narrow lobes; small white flowers in dense clusters in branched inflorescence, March to May. *Zone 7.*   p. 411

sativum (Egypt and W. Asia, escaped in No. America), "Garden cress", "Pepperweed" or "Upland cress"; herbaceous plant usually annual, to 50 cm high; smooth green leaves rounded or irregularly divided to 6 cm or more long; small white flowers in upright racemes in June. A piquant salad plant for its tasty leaves, also used for its pungency in vegetables and meats. Eaten by the Persians since 400 BC; introduced to England 1548. *Zone 9 as Annual.*   p. 527

LEPISMIUM paradoxum (Zander):
see RHIPSALIS paradoxa, as in Hortus 3

LEPTOCARPUS   *Restionaceae*

similis (New Zealand: Rotorua, Chatham Is.); rush like perennial bog plant, with creeping rhizome covered by brown scales, leaves reduced to bract-like sheaths, on culms 50 to 150 cm high. *Zone 9.*   p. 336

LEPTOCLADODIA elongata (Zander):
see MAMMILLARIA elongata (Hortus 3)

LEPTODACTYLON   *Polemoniaceae*

californicum (Gilia) (California), "Prickly phlox"; low subshrub to 1 m high, with densely spreading branches; the leaves alternate, palmately divided into 3 to 9 narrow, stiff and hairy segments; charming salverform flowers rose-pink or white 3 cm across, the spreading lobes sometimes toothed, blooming late Winter to Summer. *Zone 10.*   p. 820

LEPTOSPERMUM   *Myrtaceae*

laevigatum (S.E. Australia, Tasmania), "Australian tea tree"; large shrub to 10 m, forming picturesquely twisted gray-brown trunks; fine-textured leathery oval leaves 3 cm long; small white flowers 2 cm wide. *Zone 9.*   p. 801

petersonii (citratum) (New South Wales), "Lemon-scented tea tree"; evergreen shrub or tree 6 m high, with linear 3-5 cm lemon-scented leaves, and yielding aromatic oil; small white flowers, between the foliage. *Zone 9.*   p. 801

scoparium (Australia, New Zealand), "Manuka" or "Tea-tree"; an attractive flowering shrub which may grow to 6 m high, the young growth silky, dense with tiny rigid sharp pointed leaves under 1 cm, dotted with fragrant oil glands; and numerous small white or rosy axillary flowers amongst the foliage, in Summer. *Zone 9.*   p. 801

scoparium flore plenum, "Double-flowered tea tree" of New Zealand; aromatic, pubescent shrub; rigid branches set with short needle-like, pungent leaves, and pretty flowers having a double circle of rose-pink petals and darker red in center. *Zone 9.*   p. 801

scoparium 'Ruby Glow', "New Zealand tea tree"; excellent cultivar of compact habit, with age growing to 2 m or more; tiny dark needle-like foliage, and semi-double, crimson-red flowers with dark center, 2 cm across, blooming in great profusion. *Zone 9.*   p. 801

LESPEDEZA   *Leguminosae*

bicolor (Japan), "Shrub bush clover"; floriferous shrub to 2 m or more high, with trifoliolate leaves of 3 oval or obovate bristle-tipped leaflets 3-5 cm long; pale rose to purple flowers pea-like, in erect axillary racemes, blooming August-September. *Zone 5.*   p. 764

thunbergii (Desmodium) (Japan, Korea, Manchuria), "Bush clover", "Miyagino-Hagi" in Japan; shrub to 2 m or more high; the leaves of 3 ovate leaflets 3-5 cm long; pea-like flowers rose-purple, in pendant clusters, blooming in Autumn. *Zone 5.*   p. 764

LESPEDEZA: see also CAMPYLOTROPIS

LEUCADENDRON   *Proteaceae*

argenteum (Leucodendron in Hortus 3) (So. Africa), "Silvertree"; beautiful, eye-catching tree to 10 m high, the branches dense with clasping, pointed leaves to 15 cm long, thickly covered with silvery pubescence which glistens like shining silver in the sun; globular flower heads yellow; fruit heads large and heavy. *Zone 10.*   p. 823

daphnoides (So. Africa: Cape Prov.); handsome compact shrub to 1 m high, of delicate appearance; narrow leaves becoming quite red around the flower head; the globular terminal inflorescence like a ball of golden-yellow stamens on male plants, surrounded by chrome-yellow bract leaves. *Zone 10.*   p. 823

discolor (Cape Prov.), "Sunshine bush" or "Flame gold-tips"; striking, erect evergreen shrub, with narrow, gray-hairy leaves, and blooming at the tips of each branch; the flowers with obovate golden-yellow bracts tinged with red, in bright mahogany-red, cone-shaped inflorescence in the male plant, on the female plant the bracts are flushed with green. *Zone 9.*   p. 823

globosum (So. Africa); attractive, very floriferous woody bush, seen in col. Santa Cruz Botanic Garden, California; leathery elliptic leaves along the stout branches, which are topped by a showy inflorescence which is a nest of canary-yellow obovate bracts holding a fluffy cushion of masses of tiny golden-yellow flowers and their anthers on male plants. *Zone 9.*   p. 823

LEUCAENA   *Leguminosae*

glauca (leucocephala in Zander) (Trop. America, naturalized elsewhere in tropics), "White popinac" or "Wild tamarind"; evergreen tree to 9 m with brown stems; feathery leaves 2-pinnate; leaflets in 10 to 20 pairs, glaucous beneath; flowers creamy-white in globose, fluffy heads about 3 cm across, stamens 3 times as long as petals; bean-like flat seed pods 15 cm long, edible while young. The flat seeds are used to make bracelets. Planted in coffee plantations as shade trees. *Zone 10.*   p. 764

retusa (Texas, New Mexico); arid region unarmed shrub, with age growing into tree 8 m high; with bipinnate, feathery leaves, having 2 to 5 pairs of pinnae, the leaflets linear to oblong in 4-8 pairs; small 2 cm white, globose floral heads, and slender seed pods to 25 cm long. *Zones 8-10.*   p. 764

LEUCANTHEMUM: see CHRYSANTHEMUM

LEUCHTENBERGIA   *Cactaceae*

principis (No. to C. Mexico), the "Prism cactus" or "Agave cactus"; to 20 cm high, a very different type of small cactus with a parsnip-like root and the elongated tubercles looking like triangular fleshy grayish-green leaves as in Agave but with the tips cut off and bearing grayish wool and angular papery spines; fragrant yellow, silky flowers near the center 9 cm long, borne at the tip of new tubercles. *Arid-tropical. Zone 10.*   p. 160

LEUCOCORYNE   *Amaryllidaceae*

ixioides (odorata) (Chile), "Glory-of-the-sun"; originally in the Liliaceae family but now included with the Amaryllidaceae; small bulbous plant, with many linear basal leaves, and stalks 30-45 cm bearing umbels of lavender fragrant flowers with 1 cm tube and flaring lobes pale blue to light purple. *Zone 9.*   p. 210

LEUCOCRINUM   *Liliaceae*

montanum (Oregon, No. Calif. to So. Dakota, Nebraska, New Mexico), "Sand lily" or "Star lily"; lovely stemless perennial with deep-seated rhizome and fleshy roots; basal linear leaves 10-15 cm long; the funnel-shaped, pure white, fragrant flowers displaying yellow anthers, and rising from the rhizome in clusters, 10 cm long, blooming in Spring but lasting only for a day. *Zones 4-7.*   p. 450

LEUCOGENES   *Compositae*

leontopodium (Helichrysum) (New Zealand), "New Zealand edelweiss"; native mainly in South Island mountains, from Canterbury southward; silvery-downy perennial, woody at base, to 20 cm high, having prostrate branches; the 2 cm ovate leaves overlapping in rosettes; small 2 cm flowers with white ray-florets and deep yellow center disc. *Zone 8.*   p. 395

LEUCOJUM   *Amaryllidaceae*

aestivum (Europe, No. Africa), "Giant snowflake" or "Summer snowflake"; small, bulbous plant with basal leaves; nodding, bell-shaped, white flowers tipped green, the 6 segments of even length; in late Spring. *Zone 4.*   p. 210

autumnale (Mediterr. region), "Autumn snowflake"; small bulbous herb, forming clumps with very narrow leaves developing after flowers; the hollow floral stalks to 15 cm long, topped by nodding little 12 mm white bells tinged with red, in loose clusters, in late Summer. *Zones 5-6.*   p. 210

vernum (Cent. Europe), "Spring snowflake"; charming small bulbous herb to 30 cm high, narrow linear basal leaves; the nodding solitary bell-flowers white, tipped with green, 2 cm long, in early Spring. *Temperate. Zone 4.*   p. 210

LEUCOPHYLLUM   *Scrophulariaceae*

frutescens (texanum) (Texas: Rio Grande Valley), "Texas sage" or "Texas ranger"; evergreen, loose-growing shrub 1 to 3 m high, with pale gray shoots; gray-green obovate leaves 2-3 cm long, silvery white-woolly beneath; axillary flowers with trumpet-shaped corolla to 3 cm across and a lovely rosy-lavender, bursting into bloom following Summer rains. *Zone 8.*   p. 876

LEUCOSPERMUM   *Proteaceae*

nutans (So. Africa: S.W. Cape), "Nodding pincushion"; beautiful bush about 1 m high, of low spreading shape, dense with small 8 cm tough-leathery, concave, gray-green sessile leaves, and a showy, symmetrical inflorescence, the flowers curled tightly in the center like a pincushion, 10 cm across, with long curving, waxy styles varying in color from yellow to orange, or pinkish; the heads sometimes nodding to one side, and lasting for about one month. *Zone 9.*   p. 824

reflexum (So. Africa), the "Rocket-pincushion"; strikingly beautiful gray-downy shrub which can become 4 m high; the branches densely and regularly set with small obovate silvery leaves 6 cm long and becoming shorter toward the brilliant terminal head of salmon tubular flowers with yellow base, exceeded by the showy 8 cm long, threadlike glossy scarlet styles and stigmas, which become reflexed and look like a rocket with red streamers. *Zone 9.*   p. 823

LEUCOTHOE   *Ericaceae*

axillaris (Andromeda) (Virginia to Florida and Mississippi), "Coast Leucothoe"; evergreen shrub 1 m to 2 m high, dense with crooked and arching branches, with elliptic, leathery leaves 3-10 cm long; urn-shaped white flowers with 5 lobes in lateral racemes 8 cm long, April-May blooming; similar to L. fontanesiana but less hardy. *Zone 6.*   p. 706

davisiae (Mts. of Cent. California to Oregon), "Sierra laurel"; beautiful evergreen shrub to 1 m high, with ovate-oblong lustrous dark green leaves 2-6 cm long; the inflorescence in showy, erect, somewhat arching spike-like racemes 15 cm long, of nodding urn-shaped waxy-white flowers, in June. *Zone 6.*   p. 705

fontanesiana (Andromeda catesbaei) (Eastern U.S.: Virginia to Georgia), "Drooping leucothoe"; excellent evergreen shrub to 2 m with glossy dark green, leathery lanceolate leaves, the young branches red; small cylindrical 6 mm white waxy flowers in crowded clusters; the foliage turns a beautiful bronze color in Autumn; very popular in American gardens. *Zone 4.*   p. 706

fontanesiana 'Rainbow'; colorful cultivar with its shining dark green leaves striped and blotched with pink, and spotted white; the young growth coppery red and yellow. Introduced 1949 by Girard, Geneva, Ohio. *Zone 5.*   p. 706

populifolia (So. Carolina to Florida), an evergreen "Fetterbush"; vigorous shrub to 4 m high, with spreading and arching branches; ovate to lanceolate, leathery leaves 3-10 cm long; flowers in axillary clusters, with cylindric urn-shaped white corolla 1 cm long, the sepals fringed with minute hairs; during May-June. *Zone 7.*   p. 706

racemosa (Mass. to Georgia and Florida, west to Louisiana), "Sweet bells"; erect deciduous shrub 1 to 4 m high, with firm ovate leaves 2-6 cm long and pubescent beneath; the inflorescence very charming, with white flowers hanging bell-like along terminal, more or less horizontal slender twigs, in late Summer. *Zone 5.*   p. 706

LEUZEA   *Compositae*

centauroides (Centaurea) (Mediterranean reg. to Pyrenees); striking perennial to 75 cm tall, with robust, stiff stems clothed by alternate, deeply lobed or pinnate leaves 15 to 20 cm long, deep green except for contrasting ivory midrib; the striking, thistle-like inflorescence 5 cm across, consisting of a cone-like head of bracts and tubular corollas purplish-carmine. *Warm temperate.*
Zones 7-9.   p. 395

LEVISTICUM   *Umbelliferae*

officinale (So. Europe; natural. N. Jersey to Virginia and New Mexico), "Lovage"; aromatic herbaceous perennial to 2 m high, the ferny leaves several times pinnate, the outer segments toothed; small greenish-yellow flowers in compound clusters, subtended by narrow bracts. Grown for centuries for its aromatic seeds used in confections and in cordials; leaves and stems give a celery flavor to soups and salads; blanched leafstalks and stems make a fragrant tea; sliced roots preserved in honey are a delicacy. *Zones 6-10.*   p. 544

LEWISIA   *Portulacaceae*

cotyledon (No. California, So. Oregon); beautiful rosette forming mats, with thick, starchy roots, and spatulate fleshy, green 8 cm leaves; lovely flowers of rose petals veined deep red and spreading wide to 3 cm across, in late Spring. Often difficult, needing excellent drainage. *Warm temperate. Zone 7.*   p. 200

cotyledon howellii (California, Oregon); small perennial forming rosettes of fleshy, brittle, oblanceolate or variable leaves crisped or fine-toothed at margins; the 4-5 cm flowers with spreading sepals and petals rose-pink changing to white along margins, in clusters on stalks to 15 cm high. *Zone 7.*   p. 477

milleri hyb.; in col. Duesseldorf Bot. Garden, Germany; low subshrubby perennial resembling L. cotyledon, with branches spreading wide; thick-fleshy obovate leaves, and free-blooming with numerous pretty flowers soft pink, and a purplish-red center band down each petal. *Zone 7.*   p. 477

nevadensis (Sierras of California to Washington and Rocky Mts.); small fleshy perennial to 10 cm high, with thick, starchy roots, and deciduous obovate to narrow needle-like leaves to 6 cm long, in basal rosette; white to pinkish flowers 4-5 cm across, on short 5 cm stalk, in Summer, lasting only short time. *Zone 5.*   p. 477

rediviva (Western U.S.), "Sand rose" or "Bitter-root", state flower of Montana; perennial herb with fleshy rootstock; linear, fleshy leaves 3 cm long, deciduous after blooming, large solitary flowers rose or white with red veins, 3 cm long, on 5 cm stalks. Roots were important as Indian food. *Zone 4.*   p. 477

tweedyi (Rocky Mts. to Washington and Brit. Columbia); beautiful evergreen mountain perennial forming tufts from very thick, reddish root, with oblanceolate fleshy to leathery leaves 10 cm long; on 10 cm floral stalks the large, charming flowers 5 to 8 cm across, having salmon-pink petals, blooming Spring to Summer; most attractive species for the cool Summer garden. *Zone 5.*   p. 477

LEYCESTERIA   *Caprifoliaceae*

formosa (Himalayas), "Himalaya-honeysuckle"; vigorous shrub to 2 m, with glaucous hollow branches, ovate leaves 5-18 cm long, grayish-downy beneath; the tubular 5-lobed 2 cm purplish flowers from between showy purple bracts, in drooping spikes, followed by red-purple berries in Autumn. *Zone 7.*   p. 675

LIATRIS   *Compositae*

aspera (Ontario to So. Dakota and Texas), "Gay-feather"; coarse perennial to 2 m high, the stout stems short-hairy and rough, the stiff leaves lanceolate or rhombic, to 30 cm long, the upper leaves linear; inflorescence small 3 cm heads of purple, exclusively disc-flowers, surrounded by many incurved, papery greenish bracts.
Zone 4.   p. 395

elegans (Texas to South Carolina and Florida), "Blue blazing star"; perennial herb 1 m or more high, with basal tufts of narrow, grassy leaves to 10 cm long; in Summer pushing up leafy stalks, topped by narrow plume of small elongate, fluffy rosy-purple flower heads.
Zone 7.   p. 395

punctata (Mass. to Alberta, so. to Kansas and Texas), "Western gay-feather"; striking erect perennial to 75 cm high, from underground tuberous roots; with stiff, 10 cm linear leaves angled upward from the stems, and marked by numerous dots; the spike-like inflorescence consisting of small 2 cm purple heads composed of only disc-flowers, blooming throughout Summer. *Zone 3.*   p. 396

spicata (callilepsis hort.) (Long Island to Michigan, so. to Louisiana), "Gay-feather"; floriferous clustering perennial 1 m or more high, with narrow linear leaves to 40 cm long; the inflorescence in showy 15 to 30 cm spikes of small 2 cm purple heads of all disc-flowers, summer-blooming. *Zones 3-9.*   p. 396

spicata 'Alba', "White gay-feather"; charming clustering cultivar about 90 cm high, from cormous base, dense with linear, grass-like leaves, and erect spike-like inflorescence to 40 cm long with pristine white flower heads. *Zone 4.*   p. 396

LIBERTIA   *Iridaceae*

chilensis (formosa) (Chile); perennial with short, creeping rhizome; basal leaves linear, rigid and dark green 15-45 cm long; floral stem 80-120 cm with some reduced, sheathing leaves; the inflorescence in many clusters along terminal axis, the small flowers with inner petals white or pale yellow, the outer segments greenish-brown; spring-blooming. *Zone 8.*   p. 425

grandiflora (New Zealand), "New Zealand iris"; perennial herb with short creeping rhizome and fibrous roots; numerous linear leaves crowded at base of stem, 2-ranked and rigid; tall stems to 1 m with 2½ cm flowers clustered in axils toward top, white, the outer segments greenish; summer-blooming. *Zone 10.*   p. 425

pulchella (New Zealand, Tasmania, So. Australia, New Guinea); robust perennial to 25 cm high, with long rhizome, forming tufts of grass-like but leathery, linear leaves to 15 cm long; inflorescence in clusters of small 1 cm white flowers, arranged toward apex, in April-May. *Zone 10.*   p. 425

LIBOCEDRUS: see CALOCEDRUS

LICANIA   *Chrysobalanaceae*

platypus (So. Mexico to Panama, Colombia), "Sansapote" or "Monkey apple"; stately tropical tree 30-50 m high, having rounded crown of thick branches, the bark dark purplish or brown; the deciduous leaves are narrow elliptic to lanceolate 10-30 cm long, having thick midrib sunken above; new foliage red-purple and showy; abundant small fragrant flowers having protruding stamens, followed by obovoid 12-20 cm long fruit with thin brownish, warty rind; the flesh is edible and pumpkin-scented, orange-yellow, sub-acid or sweet flavored and containing one flattened seed. Fruit is eaten raw but not too highly regarded. *Zone 10.*   *p. 906, 908*

LICUALA   *Palmae*

grandis (New Britain Isl. near New Guinea), "Ruffled fan palm"; very attractive small fan palm with slim solitary 3 m trunk, topped by plaited bright green leaves almost round, lobed and toothed along the continuous margin, on slender, thorny petioles; glossy crimson fruit. *Tropical. Zone 12.*   *p. 105*

peltata (India: Bengal); clustering fan palm with slender trunks to 5 m, leaves orbicular appearing as if peltate, 120-150 cm across, divided into wedge-shaped, ribbed segments. *Tropical. Zone 12.*   *p. 105*

spinosa (Malaya to Java), "Spiny licuala palm"; clustering fan-leaf, densely suckering palm forming compact tufts with a mass of foliage from top to bottom, with age to 4 m tall; glossy green leaves parted to the center into plaited segments ending abruptly in a toothed apex as if cut off, the rigid petioles armed with curved black thorns; fruit lustrous red. *Tropical. Zones 11-12.*   *p. 105*

LIGULARIA   *Compositae*

dentata (Senecio clivorum) (China, Japan), "Golden-ray"; stout herbaceous perennial to 1 m or more high, with long-stalked rounded or kidney-shaped leaves 30-40 cm across, sharply toothed at margins; showy floral heads 6-12 cm wide, of yellow ray-flowers and brown discs, summer-blooming. *Zone 5.*   *p. 396*

hodgsonii (Mts. of Hokkaido, Sakhalin, Kuriles), "Togebuki"; herbaceous perennial, similar to L. dentata, but of smaller habit; stout rhizome; stems 30-80 cm long; basal leaves kidney-shaped to 27 cm wide and toothed; floral heads 4-5 cm across, cobwebby hairy, and with orange ray-florets, in July-August. *Zone 3.*   *p. 396*

przewalskii (Senecio) (No. China), "Rocket ligularia"; handsome perennial, 100-150 cm tall, with creeping rootstock; purple stems and large, deeply cut leaves; small yellow flowers in long spike to 45 cm long. *Temperate. Zone 4.*   *p. 396*

stenocephala (China, Japan, Taiwan); perennial with numerous tufting dark purple stems, 1 m or more high; basal leaves arrow-shaped, to 25 cm long, and with angled lobes; slender columnar inflorescence dense with small yellow heads having 5-12 disc-flowers and 1-3 ray-florets 2-3 cm long, June-September blooming. *Zone 4.*   *p. 396*

tussilaginea 'Aureo-maculata' (L. kaempferi or Farfugium japonicum) (Japan), "Leopard plant"; with large rounded, green, smooth leaves blotched yellow and cream, 10 to 15 cm long; light yellow daisy-like flowers. *Zones 6-9.*   *p. 396*

wilsoniana (Central China), "Giant groundsel"; sturdy herbaceous perennial, with floral stem up to 1½ m high, the ornamental basal leaves leathery, rounded kidney-shaped with cordate base, to 40 cm wide, bronzy green above, and blood-red beneath, on hollow petioles; spike-like racemes dense with golden-yellow flowers 3 cm across, in July-August. *Zone 6.*   *p. 396*

LIGUSTRUM   *Oleaceae*

amurense (No. China), "Amur privet"; deciduous or semi-evergreen, erect shrub to 5 m high, with firm ovate or oblong-oval leaves 6 cm long, pubescent on midrib beneath; small white 1 cm flowers in 5 cm clusters, blooming June-July. Somewhat similar to California privet, L. ovalifolium, but with leaves less lustrous, and more frost-hardy in cold climate. *Zone 3.*   *p. 810*

japonicum (Japan, Korea), the "Japanese privet"; fast growing evergreen bush to 3 or even 6 m high, with spongy leathery, rich dark glossy green ovate, short-pointed leaves 4-10 cm long, on minutely downy twigs; small white flowers in terminal clusters, and black berries. Widely planted in Southern States and confused with L. lucidum, but japonica has leaves more glossy with raised nerves beneath while in lucidum they are sunken. Popular for hedges. *Zones 7-9.*   *p. 75, 617, 618, 619, 810*

japonicum 'Rotundifolium'; handsome evergreen of compact habit to 1½ m high, having short stiff branches, with glossy green leaves nearly round and 6 cm long, very closely set; small white flowers in clusters shorter than the species. An excellent hedge plant. *Zones 7-9.*   *p. 810*

japonicum 'Silver Star', patented Texanum cultivar; handsome compact, dense evergreen bush of slow growth; oval spongy-leathery leaves with deep green centers and edged in creamy-silver. Offered by Monrovia Nurseries, Azusa, California. *Zones 7-9.*   *p. 810*

japonicum 'Texanum', the "Wax-leaf privet"; a favorite evergreen cultivar 2-3 m high, with glossy, thick-leathery dark green, broad-

ovate-acuminate leaves 6-9 cm long, somewhat wavy; ideally suited to shaping by trimming, and an enduring decorator under unfavorable conditions. *Zones 7-9.*   *p. 810*

lucidum (China, Korea, Japan), the "Glossy privet" of the South, or "White-wax tree" in China, planted widely in the southern states; dense leafy evergreen shrub to 10 m high, with glossy, dark green, thick-leathery, ovate leaves 8-15 cm long, on flexible, glabrous branches; white flowers in long panicles followed by black berries. Blooming in August, later than the Japanese privet; the foliage is leathery but without the spongy feel of L. japonicum. *Zones 8-9.*   *p. 616, 810*

ovalifolium (Japan), widely known as the "California privet"; densely branching half-evergreen shrub of erect habit to 4 m high, and much used for hedging including planter boxes for the sidewalk restaurants of New York, where it is quite hardy; the willowy, fast growing shoots are either evergreen, or if the leaves fall off during cold Winters, quickly cover themselves anew with oval and ovate, rich green smooth leaves 3-7 cm long; summer-blooming, if not trimmed back, with erect panicles of white flowers, followed by shining black berries. *Zone 5.*   *p. 618, 810*

ovalifolium 'Aureum', ('Aureo-marginatum'), "Golden privet"; outstanding color form, with narrow oblong and ovate leaves to 6 cm long, the green center completely surrounded with the yellow, glossy above and pale beneath, neatly arranged along willowy stems; more or less evergreen in mild climate. *Zone 6.*   *p. 810*

'Vicaryi' (vulgare x ovalifolium 'Aureum'), "Vicary golden privet"; handsome shrub of erect habit, to 4 m high, originated in England before 1920; having leathery golden-yellow oblong to elliptic leaves, holding its foliage until late season; evergreen in mild climate; flowers white. *Zone 5.*   *p. 811*

vulgare (W. Europe to No. Africa, Asia Minor), "Common privet"; vigorous shrub to 5 m high, deciduous in cold climate, densely branched, the willowy stems with lanceolate leaves 4-6 cm long, narrower than in L. ovalifolium, and not as glossy; small white flowers in erect clusters, and heavily scented, blooming early Summer; followed by large clusters of glossy black berries. *Zone 4.*   *p. 810*

LILIUM   *Liliaceae*

amabile 'Enterprise', "Korean lily"; stiff erect stems to 1 m or more, with lanceolate leaves, and nodding Turk's cap flowers, with waxy recurved petals 6 cm long, brilliant red, spotted with black, in late Spring. *Warm temperate. Zones 4-8.*   *p. 243*

auratum (Japan), "Goldband-lily"; tall erect, leafy stalk from a scaly bulb, to 2 m, with flaring, fragrant trumpet-flowers 25 cm across, white, spotted with crimson, each segment with a central yellow stripe. *Zone 5.*   *p. 243*

x aurelianense (henryi x sargentiae), "Aurelian lily"; hardy tall-stemmed lily, closely set with narrow green leaves; horizontal fragrant flowers to 12 cm across, yellow-orange, the petals tending to recurve. *Zone 4.*   *p. 243*

canadense (Nova Scotia to Virginia, Ohio and Alabama), "Meadow lily" or "Canada lily"; widely native in No. America; stem 50 to 150 cm tall, with lanceolate leaves usually whorled; beautifully graceful bell-shaped, pendant flowers orange-yellow to red, spotted purplish-brown and 8 cm across, during Summer. New bulbs produced annually at end of stolons. *Zones 3-8.*   *p. 245*

candidum (S.W. Asia), "Madonna lily"; lovely bulbous plant 1 m high, with numerous leaves becoming successively shorter, the trumpet-shaped flowers delicately fragrant, pure waxy white, the upper ones erect, the lower drooping, 8 cm long, June blooming. Much used in churches and cemeteries, and cultivated for several 1000 years. *Zone 5.*   *p. 243*

cernuum (Korea, No. China, Siberia); perennial from scaly bulb, to 1 m high, 1-6 flowers in racemes, 4-6 cm long, purplish-pink with wine-purple spots and fragrant; petals strongly reflexed. *Temperate. Zones 3-8.*   *p. 242*

concolor (China: Manchuria; Korea, Japan), "Star lily"; charming miniature; the small scaly bulbs freely forming bulblets; wiry, green to purplish stem 30 to 60 cm high, sparsely furnished with narrow-linear leaves, and topped by clusters of small star-shaped flowers 6 cm across, the recurving segments glossy scarlet-red or occasionally orange-yellow, often spotted with minute blackish dots or lines toward base; stamens red; early summer-blooming. *Warm temperate. Zones 5-8.*   *p. 243*

'Connecticut King'; a Mid-Century hybrid derived from Asiatic species, of medium height, typically with outward facing flowers, the wide-spreading segments lemon-yellow, marked with green. *Zone 5.*   *p. 244*

'Enchantment'; very popular, vigorous Mid-Century hybrid, derived from Asiatic species by Jan de Graaff of Oregon, to 1 m or more high; the sturdy leafy stems bearing clusters of upward facing showy flowers 14 to 16 cm across, the spreading reflexed, waxy segments brilliant orange-red with scattered maroon spots, and displaying darker stamens, during June-July. *Zones 5-9.*   *p. 244*

hansonii (Japan, Korea), "Japanese Turk's cap"; excellent garden plant to more than 1 m high, with elliptic leaves in whorls; inflorescence in a loose raceme, the firm flowers fragrant, their waxy segments spreading 7 cm across and reflexed, orange-yellow and spotted purple, in late Spring. *Zone 4.*   p. 243

henryi (Yunnan, W. China); very vigorous plant producing enormous purple bulbs, and flexible, arching stem 2 m or more tall, crowded with lanceolate leaves; toward apex a raceme of up to 20 trumpet flowers 10 cm across, deep orange spotted brown, the segments reflexed, and conspicuous reddish anthers; August-blooming. Known as a "Stem-rooting lily", with underground stem bearing roots which produce small bulblets. *Zone 5.*   p. 244

x hollandicum (x umbellatum), "Candle-stick lily"; an old Japanese hybrid of bulbiferum x maculatum, rarely over 60 cm high, very pleasing, with showy, upright, large cup-shaped flowers of glowing scarlet, or similar shades, 10 cm long, and dense, broad-linear leaves. *Zones 5-8.*   p. 242

'Imperial Crimson', an "Empress lily" of the Oriental hybrids, fantastic strain of magnificent, vigorous lilies raised by Oregon Bulb Farms, involving blood of L. auratum, speciosum, japonicum and rubellum; tall, leafy, wiry stalks 1½-2 m high carrying giant, rather flat, firm flowers 20 cm across, the petals gently curling back, white along margins but toward the middle changing to pink with red spotting, the center of each segment intense crimson; blooming in August. *Warm temperate. Zones 5-9.*   p. 245

lancifolium (tigrinum) (Japan, Korea, E. China), "Tiger lily"; handsome bulbous plant 1 m or more high; the purplish, hairy stem with alternate lanceolate leaves to 16 cm long, and forming bulbils in axils; showy nodding, firm flowers 12 cm across, the reflexed segments bright orange-red, spotted purple-black, and prominently protruding filaments with red anthers. *Zone 3.*   p. 243

'Limelight' (Aurelian Trumpet hyb.), derived from Asiatic species; bold and vigorous, tall lily to 1½ m, the stems with narrow leaves; fragrant flowers funnel-shaped to 20 cm across, lime-yellow. Summer-blooming. *Zones 4-8.*   p. 244

longiflorum 'Ace', Oregon clone of the "Croft Easter lily" complex; prolific bloomer of rather short, compact habit, dark shining green foliage on husky green stem about 45 cm above pot, toward the apex of which appear buds and flowers one above the other, unlike Croft which are all in one cluster; the firm-textured, fragrant white trumpets are generally shorter (12-14 cm long) and usually better bud-count; and force well from a slow start; best for late Easter bloom. Blooming Mid-summer in outdoor garden. Propagation from scales. *Zones 7-8.*   p. 245

longiflorum 'Nellie White', worthy selection of breeding stock made by J. White of Langlois, Oregon 1955; similar to L. 'Ace' but midseason, used by florists for forcing as pot plant for early Easter; of medium height, sturdy and of heavy substance; flowers horizontal with trumpets 16-18 cm long. *Zone 8.*   p. 54

maritimum (Coastal No. California), "Coast lily"; from scaly bulb rises the leafy stem 30-60 cm high, foliage oblanceolate to 8 cm long; 1 to 5 horizontal funnel-form flowers deep orange-red, the recurved segments 3 cm long, spotted maroon inside. *Zone 8.*   p. 244

martagon (Europe and W. Asia to Mongolia), "Martagon lily" or "Turban lily"; stately and interesting hardy lily very popular in Europe; the purplish stem to 1½ m or more high, with oblanceolate leaves in whorls; at apex a raceme of many flowers of heavy texture, 5 to 7 cm across, the segments strongly recurved, purplish with pink; stamens long exserted. *Zone 4.*   p. 243

martagon album, "White Turk's cap"; attractive variety 1 m or more high, the stem green and enriched by whorls of broad leaves; and toward apex with numerous Turk's cap flowers having a ring of turned-under segments glistening white and protruding yellow anthers. *Zone 5.*   p. 244

monadelphum (Caucasus, Iran), "Caucasian lily"; bold species to 1½ m high, the stem with alternate oblanceolate leaves, and topped by raceme of many nodding, fragrant flowers 12 cm across, the reflexed segments golden-yellow, tinged or spotted purple, early blooming. *Zone 4.*   p. 244

parryi (So. California to So. Arizona), "Lemon lily" from the San Gabriel to San Jacinto Mountains; slender stem 60 to 120 cm high, with alternate or whorled leaves, rising from a scaly rhizomatous bulb, the horizontal flowers solitary to 25 in a raceme, funnel-form 10 cm long, very fragrant, clear lemon-yellow, occasionally spotted maroon, the anthers brown. *Zone 7.*   p. 245

parvum (C. California, Nevada to Oregon), "Sierra lily" or "Alpine lily"; Alpine species of the high Sierra Nevada, with rhizomatous scaly bulb; the stem 40 to 150 cm high, the leaves alternate or in whorls; ascending funnel flowers bright orange to dark red, spotted maroon, the segments 3 cm long. *Zone 4.*   p. 245

pensylvanicum (dauricum) (Silberia, Mongolia, Manchuria, Korea, Japan), "Candlestick-lily"; about 1 m high, with erect flowers to 12 cm wide, the spreading elliptic segments orange-red spotted with purplish-black; early to bloom. *Zone 3.*   p. 244

'Prosperity' (tigrinum x hollandicum) Mid-Century hybrid; compact plant 50 cm or more high, slender stalk with papery foliage, 12 cm flowers outward facing with firm segments, lemon-yellow with brown spots. *Zones 5-8.*   p. 242

pumilum (tenuifolium) (China), "Coral lily"; to 50 cm high, with wiry stem, numerous linear leaves; fragrant nodding flowers, 5 cm dia., waxy scarlet, with reflexed segments. *Warm temperate. Zones 5-8.*   p. 242

regale (W. China: Szechwan), "Regal lily"; bulbous plant with wiry, purplish stem to 2 m high, covered with numerous, short, narrow leaves and topped by a cluster of fragrant, trumpet-shaped, white flowers with recurved tips, pale purple outside and with yellow throat, 15 cm long, during Summer. *Zones 4-9.*   p. 243

speciosum rubrum (Japan), "Japanese lily"; wiry purplish stem to 1 m or more high, with scattered, lanceolate leaves, and sweetly fragrant; nodding flowers to 15 cm wide, with reflexed petals having wavy margins, rose-pink flushed carmine and with purple spots, in large clusters, during August-September, one of the last to bloom in gardens. *Zone 5.*   p. 245

superbum (E. Canada to Missouri), "American Turk's-cap"; superb lily, 1 to 2½ m tall; stem carries 15-20 orange-scarlet flowers spotted purplish-brown, 10 cm across; segments strongly reflexed, leaves in whorls along stalk. *Zone 5.*   p. 245

szovitsianum (monadelphum var.) (Trans-Caucasus, So. Shore Black Sea), "Caucasus lily"; beautiful plant with alternate leafy stem to 1 m or more high, topped by a raceme of to 20 nodding flowers, the recurving yellow segments spotted with brown and 10 cm long; anthers brown (yellow in monadelphum); valued for its early June blooming. *Zone 4.*   p. 245

x umbellatum: see L. x hollandicum

washingtonianum (Sierra Nevada, Calif. to So. Oregon), "Shasta lily" or "Washington lily"; from the foot of Mt. Shasta, a very fragrant lily from scaly bulb, the stem 60 to 150 cm high, having leaves in whorls, and a raceme of horizontal funnel flowers which open white then fade to lilac-purple, the segments to 9 cm long. The **var. minus** has fewer and smaller flowers. *Zone 6.*   p. 245

LIMNANTHES   *Limnanthaceae*
douglasii (California, Oregon), "Meadow-foam"; small sprawling annual herb with lacy pinnatifid yellowish-green leaves; a profusion of fragrant 2½ cm flowers, with 5 spreading petals white or pinkish with yellow base, in early Spring. *Zone 9.*   p. 316, 455

LIMONIUM   *Plumbaginaceae*
latifolium (Rumania to So. Russia), "Wideleaf sea lavender"; outstanding perennial with woody base, the elliptic leaves all basal, to 25 cm long, the ornamental inflorescence on wiry stalks to 60 cm long, very much branched into clusters of small spikelets with tiny bright lilac flowers, blooming May to July. *Zones 3-10.*   p. 472

latifolium 'Violetta', "Violet sea lavender"; very pretty colorform with dense inflorescence of small 6mm violet flowers, late summer-blooming, in large clusters; evergreen perennial 30-50 cm high. *Zones 3-10.*   p. 472

sinuatum (Mediterranean reg.), "Statice" or "Sea-lavender"; biennial or perennial to 60 cm high, with tufted, lobed leaves to 10 cm long, and panicles of numerous small, clustered flowers with blue calyx and yellowish-white corolla, on winged branches; used as an "everlasting" when cut. *Subtropic. Zone 8.*   p. 472

suworowii (Zander): see PSYLLIOSTACHYS suworowii (Hortus)

LINANTHUS   *Polemoniaceae*
androsaceus (Gilia micrantha) (Coast Range of Calif.), "Trumpet gilia"; attractive annual 30-40 cm high, the leaves palmately 5-9 parted into slender lobes, partially spine-tipped; the flowers with slender corolla tube 3 cm long, pink or white, in clusters; August-blooming. *Zone 9.*   p. 472

montanus (Sierra Nevada, California), "Mustang clover"; charming ornamental annual 10-60 cm high; leaves 5-11 divided into linear lobes 2-3 cm long and edged with fine hairs; the lovely rose-pink flowers with yellow eye, and a crimson spot near base of each spreading petal; blooming May to August in the Sierras at higher elevations. *Zone 8.*   p. 472

LINARIA   *Scrophulariaceae*
maroccana 'Fairy Bouquet' (Morocco, natural. in Northeast U.S.), "Spurred snapdragon"; charming annual to 30 cm high, with slender branches and linear leaves; the inflorescence in large fluffy clusters of spurred flowers resembling miniature snapdragons, purple in the species of Morocco, but larger and in various colors, especially soft shades of pink with white throat in the 'Fairy Bouquet' strain, June-blooming. *Zone 9.*   p. 503

pallida: see CYMBALARIA pallida

purpurea 'Canon Went' (So. Europe parentage), "Toadflax"; vigorous herbaceous glaucous perennial or annual 60-80 cm high, the slender stems with linear leaves, terminated by racemes of small 1 cm flowers, purple in the species, but pink in the cv. 'Canon Went'; the corolla with the incurved spur, the lower lip bearded white; blooming in Summer. Zone 5.   *p. 503*

LINDELOFIA   *Boraginaceae*
longiflora (Himalayas); herbaceous perennial to 50 cm high; the leaves narrow lanceolate, 8-25 cm long, basal and on leafy stems, topped by racemes of vivid blue cylindric flowers 2 cm long, blooming May to August. Zone 6.   *p. 347, 348*

LINDERA   *Lauraceae*
benzoin (Ontario to Texas), "Spice bush"; aromatic deciduous shrub; leaves entire, obovate, 5-12 cm long; fragrant flowers greenish-yellow, small, opening before the foliage during March and April in dense clusters; oblong red 1 cm berries used as substitute for culinary Allspice. Zone 4.   *p. 740, 742*
obtusiloba (Mts. of China, Korea, Japan); deciduous shrub or tree 6 to 8 m high; broad-ovate leaves to 15 cm long, usually 3-lobed and having 3 white nerves from base, partially downy beneath; yellow flowers densely packed in silky clusters, opening before leaves in March-April; globular fruit 1 cm dia., red to black. Zone 6.   *p. 740, 742*
strychnifolia (China); aromatic evergreen shrub with ovate soft-leathery leaves 4-6 cm long, glaucous beneath, pubescent while young; unisexual flowers without petals; fruits berry-like. Zone 9.   *p. 742*

LINDHEIMERIA   *Compositae*
texana (West Texas), "Star daisy"; erect, rough-hairy branched annual 30-60 cm high, with toothed, spoon-shaped basal leaves, and stem-leaves lanceolate, the 4 to 5 ray-flowers golden-yellow to cream, to 3 cm across. Zone 8.   *p. 397*

LINGMANIA chungii: see BAMBUSA tuldoides

LINNAEA   *Caprifoliaceae*
borealis (Brit. Columbia to No. California and Idaho), "Western twin-flower"; forest creeper with somewhat woody stems; leaves suborbicular 1-2 cm long; from the axils a pair of short-stalked funnel-flowers 15 mm long, rose-colored; ovoid fruit. Zone 3.   *p. 270*

LINUM   *Linaceae*
arboreum (Crete to Anatolia), "Greek flax"; small spreading subshrubby perennial 30 cm or more high, with 4 cm obovate, glaucous leaves; the thin branches topped by numerous clear yellow 4 cm flowers, blooming in May. Zones 9-10.   *p. 454*
austriacum (Austrian Alps and Southeast), "Austrian flax"; freely branching herbaceous perennial with erect stems 30-60 cm high; small linear leaves, and terminally with many soft-blue, delicate flowers 2 cm across, during June-July. Zone 3.   *p. 454*
capitatum (Italy to Balkans and Asia Minor), "Flax"; vigorous herbaceous perennial to 50 cm high, with fine green obovate leaves; the wiry stems topped by clusters of vivid deep yellow flowers 3 cm across; photographed blooming in May. Zones 8-9.   *p. 454*
flavum (Germany to Russia), "Golden flax"; floriferous, somewhat woody perennial to 60 cm high, with narrow-lanceolate leaves; the numerous stems topped by multiple branched heads of golden-yellow 3 cm flowers, from June to August. Plants grown as "Yellow flax" may be Reinwardtia indica. Zones 6-10.   *p. 454*
grandiflorum (North Africa), "Flowering flax"; floriferous, densely branching erect annual herb to 75 cm tall; thin leafy stems with alternate linear, grass-green foliage, toward apex with masses of showy 5-petaled flowers 3 cm across, glowing red with white center, summer-blooming, opening to the sun. Zones 9-10.   *p. 454*
grandiflorum 'Rubrum', "Scarlet flax"; striking color form seen at the Red Fort in Delhi, India, very free-blooming with masses of delicate, bright crimson-red flowers under the Indian sun in early Spring. Zone 10.   *p. 454*
perenne (E. Europe to W. Asia), "Perennial blue flax"; upright perennial to 60 cm high, with linear leaves, lower part of stem usually leafless; the cupped, shortlived flowers deep chicory-blue, 3 cm across, blooming May to September in California; a very popular garden plant. Zones 5-10.   *p. 454*

LIPARIA   *Leguminosae*
spherica (So. Africa), "Mountain dahlia"; striking very leafy shrub of stiff habit, to 2½ m; leaves crowded and overlapping, 4-5 cm long; flowers in showy terminal heads to 10 cm wide, subtended by numerous bracts in a confused mass, bright yellow or orange. Zones 9-10.   *p. 764*

LIPARIS   *Orchidaceae*
liliifolia (New England west to Minnesota, south to Alabama), "Large twayblade"; hardy bulbous orchid with broad basal twin leaves

which sheath the erect, angled floral stalk bearing a loose terminal raceme of showy purple flowers with broad lip. Zone 4.   *p. 90*

LIPPIA:
citriodora: see ALOYSIA triphylla (Zander)
nodiflora of hort.: see PHYLA nodiflora

LIQUIDAMBAR   *Hamamelidaceae*
styraciflua (Connecticut to Florida and Mexico), "American Sweet gum"; attractive tree, deciduous in colder climate, to 20 m or more high, with furrowed bark and corky wings on twigs, the leaves maple-like and deeply cut into 5-7 lobes, 8 to 15 cm wide, deep glossy green, but turning purple, yellow or deep red in Autumn; flowers inconspicuous, but the dangling spiny fruits add ornament in Winter; small greenish-yellow flowers. Zone 5.   *p. 735*
styraciflua 'Palo Alto'; a striking California cultivar with rich green foliage turning orange to bright crimson in Fall. This small tree is usually grafted to maintain its pyramidal habit and distinctive foliage colors. Zone 6.   *p. 735*

LIRIODENDRON   *Magnoliaceae*
tulipifera (Mass. to Florida and Mississippi), the noble "Tulip tree"; becoming 60 m high, with curious lobed, almost square deciduous leaves to 12 cm each way, and bell-shaped flowers to 10 cm across, greenish-yellow with orange at base, and displaying the very prominent stamens; very fragrant, blooming in June. Zones 4-9.   *p. 776*
tulipifera 'Arnold', dubbed "Yellow poplar" in California; columnar form, usually grafted, growing quite tall, having many short ascending branches, with deciduous lobed leaves to 12 cm long and wide, turning butter-yellow in Autumn; the cup-shaped greenish-cream with yellow flowers somewhat resemble wide open tulips. Zones 4-9.   *p. 776*
tulipifera 'Aureo-marginatum', "Variegated tulip-tree"; very handsome cultivar of bushy habit, having its lobed green foliage liberally variegated and splashed or bordered with yellow or cream; quite ornamental, as seen in Boskoop, Holland. Zone 7.   *p. 776*

LIRIOPE   *Liliaceae*
graminifolia (Japan, China), "Grassy lily-turf"; rhizomatous perennial with narrow green, grass-like linear leaves to 40 cm long and ½-1 cm wide, tapering to slender point; flowers cup-shaped, light violet, almost white. Zone 6.   *p. 565*
muscari (Japan, China), the "Big blue lily-turf"; evergreen perennial to 60 cm high; deep green, leathery leaves to 45 cm long and 2 cm wide, from a clump of roots and tubers, the erect deep violet flowers in closely packed heads mostly not exceeding foliage; fruit black. Zone 6.   *p. 565*
muscari 'Variegata' (exiliflora?) (Japan, China), "Variegated lily-turf"; tufting, grass-like perennial with firm linear leaves to 45 cm long, rich green with yellow margins and bands; the little lilac flowers carried erect on purple spikes. Zone 6.   *p. 565*
platyphylla (China, Japan), "Lily-turf"; robust clustering perennial plant 30 cm or more high, with long linear, thin-leathery leaves, and tall cylindrical inflorescence of pale purple flowers. Zone 7.   *p. 565*
spicata (China, Vietnam), "Creeping lily turf"; grass-like stemless perennial 20-30 cm high, spreading by underground rhizomes and forming mats, with arching linear leaves to 40 cm long and 1 cm wide and having translucent teeth along margins; small pale lilac-to near-white tubular flowers spike-like on erect stalks above foliage, during July-August. Evergreen in colder regions until late Winter. Zone 4.   *p. 565*

LISIANTHUS russellianus: see EUSTOMA grandiflorum

LITCHI   *Sapindaceae*
chinensis (Nephelium litchi) (So. China), the "Lychee nut"; round-topped evergreen fruiting tree, 6 to 12 m high, with spreading branches; leaves compound with 2-4 pairs of shiny leathery, ovate leaflets 8-16 cm long; small flowers with greenish-white sepals, no petals, followed by the round, juicy red fruit, enclosed in brittle warty shell, 2 to 3 cm in dia., according to variety, in pendant clusters, looking like strawberries hanging from the end of the twigs. Opened with fingernails, the firm, whitish pulp is exposed, delicious to the taste and mildly acid. The dried fruit called "Litchi nut" and with sweeter taste, is eaten like a raisin. Very popular in China. Subtropic. Zones 9-10.   *p. 868, 944*

LITHOCARPUS   *Fagaceae*
amygdalifolia (Quercus amygd.) (Mts. of Taiwan), "Formosa tanbark"; large evergreen tree with straight trunk, often buttressed; leathery, lanceolate leaves having lateral veins distinct on both surfaces, grayish underneath; the inedible acorn nuts enclosed in a rounded capsule of 25 mm dia., having interesting puckered surface. Zone 9.   *p. 727*
densiflorus (Oregon, California), "Tanbark oak"; evergreen tree 20-30 m high, of conical habit, the branchlets thickly covered with

white wool while young; elliptic leaves 12 cm long, lustrous green and of hard texture, downy beneath, having 12-14 parallel ribs, each ending in a sharp tooth; male catkins semi-erect; 2-3 acorns partially enclosed by a shallow cup; at home in moist habitats. Zone 7.
p. 727

henryi (China); evergreen tree 15 m or more high, with rounded crown, the branches smooth except when young; narrowly oblong, leathery leaves 10-20 cm long, shining green; the male inflorescence in feathery white catkins, the female flowers clustering along a stout spike developing into the flattened-globose acorn nuts embedded in a thin, shallow cup. Zone 9.
p. 727

LITHODORA   *Boraginaceae*
diffusa (Lithospermum hort.) (So. Europe, Morocco); dwarf subshrubby perennial 15 to 30 cm high, forming mounds; with dark green linear hairy leaves; cupped 2 cm flowers clear glistening blue, striped with purple, blooming over a long period. Zone 5.
p. 342

diffusa 'Heavenly Blue' (Lithospermum diffusum hort.) (So. Europe, Morocco); low-growing, prostrate or creeping rough-hairy evergreen subshrub 20 cm high, forming broad matting; hairy stems with small oblong 1 cm dark green leaves; small 1 cm funnel-shaped flowers deep gentian blue striped with purple, in bracted clusters, blooming Spring and Summer. Zone 6.
p. 347

rosmarinifolia (Lithospermum rosmarinifolium) (So. Italy, Sicily, Algeria), "Gromwell" or "Rosemary-leaf puccoon"; shrubby evergreen perennial 30-60 cm high, with glossy green narrow, furrowed leaves; inflorescence of bright blue flowers lined with white, 2 cm across, in terminal clusters, blooming Mid-winter. Zone 9.
p. 668

LITHOPS   *Aizoaceae*
bella (So. Africa), "Pretty stoneface"; small succulent plant with two thick leaves united, except for fissure across top and resembling pebbles which they mimic; brownish-yellow with darker markings; fragrant white flowers 3 cm across. Arid-subtropic. Zone 10.
p. 153

dorotheae (Cape Prov.); beautiful clump-forming cleft stone 2½ cm high, pale dove-gray, the deep green translucent top windows are deep gray with blood-red reticulated tracings; yellow ray-flowers from fissure. Zone 10.
p. 148

LITHOSPERMUM   *Boraginaceae*
canescens (Ontario to Georgia and Texas), "Hoary Gromwell" or "Indian-paint"; hairy perennial with leafy stem, to 50 cm high, from rootstock which is used to make red dye; one-sided inflorescence with 2 cm tubular orange-yellow flowers, blooming April to June. Zone 3.
p. 347

diffusum (Royal hort.): see LITHODORA diffusa (Hortus, Zander)

rosmarinifolium (Royal Hort.): see LITHODORA rosmarinifolia (Zander)

LITTONIA   *Liliaceae*
modesta (Natal, Transvaal), "Climbing lily"; tuberous herb with climbing, flexuous leafy stem similar to Gloriosa, to 2 m; bright shining green leaves ending in a tendril, and axillary bell-shaped flowers rich orange, 3 cm long. Subtropic. Zone 10.
p. 246

LIVISTONA   *Palmae*
australis (Queensland, New South Wales, Victoria), "Australian cabbage palm"; with slender, ringed trunk to 25 m or more, when younger covered with brown leaf bases and brown fiber; dense crown of soft-leathery palmate fronds rounded in outline, 1-1½ m across, divided to middle into narrow glossy green segments with yellow central nerve, and without threads between; the petiole with stout curved spines; the rib extends to 10 cm into base of leaf. Subtropic. Zones 10-11.
p. 106

benthamii (Queensland); stately fan palm in col. Singapore Botanic Garden; with palmate leaves split nearly to base into narrow-linear segments and carried on slender, toothed petioles. Zone 11.
p. 106

chinensis (South China), the formerly widely grown "Latania borbonica" of horticulture, "Chinese fan palm"; spectacular, large fan palm with thick trunk that may grow to 10 m high, but extending in spread sideways to a diameter of 8 m, with gigantic, glossy, fresh green, plaited leaves more broad than long, to 2 m wide, cut halfway into many narrow, one-ribbed segments which are split again, the tips will hang like a fringe; petioles armed with small spines when the palms are young, usually disappear later; fruit metallic blue. Long popular in Europe and America in parlors, hotels and winter gardens before the advent of Howeias. Satisfied with medium-warm conditions but requiring lots of water and big space. Subtropic. Zones 10-11. p. 106

LLOYDIA   *Liliaceae*
serotina (Mts. of Europe, Asia, No. America from Alaska to Oregon, Montana and New Mexico), "Alp lily" of the Arctic-alpine zones; fibrous-coated bulb with creeping rootstock; several lanceolate leaves, and slender stems to 15 cm high, bearing flowers usually solitary, with spreading segments creamy-white, veined with purple, 1-2 cm long. Zone 1.
p. 246

LOASA   *Loasaceae*
acanthifolia (Chile); stinging, yet handsome plant, perennial in mild climate, grown as annual elsewhere; to 1 m or more high, covered with bristly hairs; the fleshy 10 cm, dark green leaves pinnately deeply cut and cordate at base, the lobes toothed and pointed; charming 3 cm yellow flowers with 5 recurved petals, displaying stamens and nectar scales from deep yellow center; summer-blooming. Zone 10.
p. 455

LOBELIA   *Lobeliaceae (Campanulaceae in Zander)*
cardinalis (Québec to Minnesota, Florida and Texas), "Cardinal flower"; striking, short-lived perennial to 1 m high, with purplish stems, oblong leaves 10 cm long; brilliant scarlet flowers 3-4 cm long, in bracted racemes, blooming July to September. Zones 2-8. p. 455

erinus (So. Africa: Cape); attractive herbaceous annual, developing dense bushes of threadlike stalks 10 to 25 cm high; tiny narrow, toothed leaves green in shade but turning purplish-bronze in sun; topped by a profusion of vivid purplish-blue flowers with white eye, 2 cm across, blooming during Summer. Parent of many hort. cultivars, very popular as bedding plant in gardens. Zone 10. p. 455

erinus 'Pendula' (So. Africa), "Balcony lobelia"; herbaceous perennial in habitat, but usually grown as annual; thin trailing branches are developed into a pendulous form in this cultivar; the stems dense with small 2 cm linear, serrate leaves, and terminal racemes of vivid purplish-blue 2 cm flowers having a white throat. Zone 10.
p. 317

erinus 'Rosamonde' (compacta cv.); showy annual of So. African heritage; floriferous, very bushy herbaceous plant, to about 10 cm high, usually grown as an annual for garden beds or edging, blooming from late May to September; fresh glossy green little elliptic to linear leaves, the uncounted thin, leafy branches topped by masses of appealing 2 cm flowers a deep cherry-red with white eye. Zone 10.
p. 455

erinus 'Sapphire' (pendula cv.), "Edging lobelia"; an excellent cultivar of low habit, partially trailing with branches spreading or pendulous, with multitudes of relatively large flowers shining medium blue tinted purple, with white eye, blooming from late May to September. Zone 10.
p. 455

rhynchopetalum (Trop. Africa); very attractive large rosette from woody base, with oblanceolate fleshy leaves 40-50 cm long, rich green with prominent center band of creamy-white; blooming with age, having beak-petaled flowers. Seen in col. University Botanic Garden, Duesseldorf, Germany. Zone 10.
p. 772

siphilitica (Maine to So. Dakota and Louisiana), the "Great lobelia" or "Blue cardinal flower"; hardy perennial 50-75 cm high, with oval to lanceolate, toothed leaves; erect racemes dense with bluish-purple flowers 2-3 cm long, in Autumn. Zones 5-8.
p. 455

splendens (fulgens) (Mexico), "Mexican lobelia"; slender branching perennial to 60 cm or more high, with narrow lanceolate leaves to 10 cm long, sometimes colored bronze; the stiff wiry stems bearing toward apex small clusters of scarlet flowers 4 cm long, the corolla lobes flaring wide; blooming late Summer. Widely used as cut flower in Europe. Zone 8.
p. 456

tupa (Chile); perennial 2-2½ m high, with erect leafy, thick stem; oblong, toothed leaves white downy and wrinkled; large downy 5 cm flowers blood-red, the corolla-lobes united at tips, in terminal spike-like raceme. Zone 9.
p. 456

LOBIVIA   *Cactaceae*
cylindrica (Argentina: Cordoba), "Cob cactus"; small, deep green cylindrical plant 12 cm high with 11 ribs, bristling with whitish radials and brown needle spines; the large 5 cm flowers pale canary yellow outside, the inside petals deeper orange-yellow and spreading outward like a star. Arid-subtropic. Zone 10.
p. 162

famatimensis (No. Argentina to 3000 m elev.); small oval or elongated body to 15 cm high, with some 20 notched ribs somewhat spiral, and many yellowish short spines; 4 cm flowers varying from yellowish to deep red as in var. nigricans. Arid-subtropic. Zones 9-10.
p. 163

huascha rubiflora: see TRICHOCEREUS huascha rubiflora

marsoneri (Northern Argentina: Los Andes); small clustering gray-green globes to 8 cm high, with short white radial spines; topped by large orange-yellow flowers tinted with red, to 6 cm across. Zone 10.
p. 163

x LOBIVIOPSIS   *Cactaceae*
'Aurora' (Lobivia x Echinopsis); striking Paramount bigeneric hybrid; small globes with numerous ribs tipped by white glochids and

sand-colored spiny hairs; very floriferous with long semi-double trumpet flowers 6 cm across, beautiful salmon-rose. *Zone* 10.   *p. 163*
'Red Riding Hood', (Lobivia x Echinopsis); charming Pygmy Paramount hybrid by Harry Johnson, Bonsall, Calif., clustering with small globes 6 to 8 cm dia., very floriferous with beautiful intense glowing red 4 cm flowers looking like little hoop skirts.
Zone 11.   *p. 163*

LOBULARIA   *Cruciferae*
maritima (Alyssum) (Mediterranean reg.), "Sweet alyssum"; a much branched little perennial, usually grown as an annual, 10-30 cm high; with linear leaves, and many small 5 mm pure white, very fragrant flowers blooming a long time. Very popular in summer garden beds. *Subtropic. Zone* 9.   *p. 411*
maritima 'Oriental Nights'; lovely small Sweet alyssum with clusters of flowers in several shades of pale lilac to purple, and of haunting fragrance. *Zone* 9.   *p. 411*
maritima 'Royal Purple'; fancy Sweet alyssum cultivar pot-grown as annual in California, with branches trailing, and flowers deep royal purple. *Zone* 9.   *p. 411*

LOCKHARTIA   *Orchidaceae*
acuta (Costa Rica to Trinidad), "Braided orchid"; small epiphyte with stem densely clothed with little shingled leaves folded flat, and axillary stalked, tiny flowers lemon-yellow marked with red (Summer). *Tropical. Zone* 12.   *p. 90*

LODOICEA   *Palmae*
maldivica (seychellarum) (Seychelles Isl. in the Indian Ocean), the "Coco-de-Mer"; slow-growing solitary fan palm to 30 m high, and trunk 30 cm dia., the large palmate fronds in dense crown on 4 m petioles, the deep glossy green blade 6 m long, cut ⅓ into segments whose ends are drooping; the female trees bear the famous "double coconuts", immense dark brown, woody fruits weighing to 20 kg., 45 cm long, taking 6 years to mature, the nut inside two-lobed or "double". *Tropical. Zone* 12.   *p. 108*

LOLIUM   *Gramineae*
perenne (Europe, No. America), "Perennial ryegrass"; perennial grass of medium-coarse appearance, with reddish base, flat, glossy green leaf blades mostly 15-25 cm long if not mowed; 3 mm wide; usually grown as sod from seed, in improved varieties such as the pictured "Penn Blue" sold in California nurseries, and easy to grow, and inexpensive. *Temperate. Zone* 5.   *p. 570*

LOMARIA gibba: see BLECHNUM gibbum

LOMATIA   *Proteaceae*
myricoides (Victoria, New So. Wales), "River lomatia"; much branched shrub 2-4 m high, with narrow leaves 10-20 cm long, partially toothed toward apex; small clusters of creamy-white flowers with flaring, narrow lobes. *Zone* 9.   *p. 824*
tinctoria (Tasmania); floriferous small shrub to 60 cm high, spreading by underground suckers and forming broad bushes; the leaves pinnate or bipinnate, the divisions narrow linear and 15-20 cm long; flowers sulphur-yellow and 2 cm across, in erect elongate racemes to 25 cm long. *Zone* 9.   *p. 823*

LOMATIUM   *Umbelliferae*
martindalei (Mts. of Brit. Columbia to Cascades of Oregon); short-stemmed herbaceous perennial to 30 cm high, with thickened roots, and leaves pinnately divided into toothed segments or rounded lobes; small lemon-yellow or white flowers, in compound clusters, the stalks often lying on the ground. *Zone* 6.   *p. 516*

LONAS   *Compositae*
annua (Italy, N.W. Africa), "Yellow ageratum"; annual, branching herbaceous plant, to 30 cm high, with leaves finely divided into linear segments; the slender stems topped by flat clusters of small 1 cm yellow flowers. *Zone* 9.   *p. 397*

LONCHOCARPUS   *Leguminosae*
violaceus (Trinidad, Tobago), "Lance-pod" or "Spanish ash"; handsome small tree to 15 m high, with pinnate, fresh green foliage, having 3-6 pairs of ovate leaflets; axillary racemes 25 cm long of rose-purplish flowers, turning whitish outside with age.
Zones 10-11.   *p. 765*

LONICERA   *Caprifoliaceae*
x americana (caprifolium x etrusca), natural hybrid; vigorous twining climber, widely cultivated in Europe; deciduous obovate leaves to 8 cm long, glaucous beneath; fragrant yellow flowers, purplish outside, 5 cm long, in whorls at end of branches.
Zone 6.   *p. 271*
x brownii (hirsuta x sempervirens), "Scarlet trumpet honeysuckle"; beautiful winter-hardy deciduous twiner; thin-woody stems with broad-ovate leaves downy and glaucous beneath; striking

clusters of glowing red, slender tubular flowers 4 cm long with mouth somewhat 2-lipped; evergreen in warmer climate. *Zone* 3.   *p. 271*
x brownii 'Dropmore Scarlet'; popular deciduous climber to 3 m, from Dropmore Exper. Sta. in Manitoba, Canada; very floriferous with all red flowers including corolla inside, blooming May to October, in pendulous clusters. *Zone* 3.   *p. 271*
x brownii 'Fuchsioides'; deciduous hardy climber becoming very dense with thin branches covered by opposite glaucous leaves and bearing terminal clusters of colorful slender tubular flowers, scarlet outside. *Zone* 3.   *p. 271*
caprifolium (Europe to W. Asia), "Italian woodbine" or "Sweet honeysuckle"; twining shrub to 6 m or more, with paired leaves bluish-green beneath, the upper roundish leaves united at base; beautiful fragrant yellowish-white, two-lipped flowers 5 cm long, tinged purple outside, in late Spring. *Zone* 5.   *p. 271*
dioica (Québec to Carolina and Iowa), "Wild honeysuckle"; climbing shrub with smooth branches, the leaves varying from oblong to broad ovate 5-12 cm long, glaucous beneath, the uppermost pairs united into a rhombic disc; tiny 2 cm greenish two-lipped flowers, followed by clusters of glossy crimson-red berry-like fruit.
Zone 3.   *p. 271*
flava (Southeast U.S. west to Okla.), "Yellow honeysuckle"; handsome native climbing shrub, with elliptic leaves to 8 cm long, smaller and united at base toward branch ends, glaucous beneath; the fragrant trumpet-shaped 3 cm two-lipped flowers salmon-yellow in whorls, in late Spring. *Zone* 5.   *p. 271*
fragrantissima (China), "Winter honeysuckle"; semi-evergreen bushy shrub 2-3 m high, with spreading branches; ovate leaves 3-6 cm long, bluish-green beneath; evergreen in mild climate; flowers 2 cm across, creamy-white, and very fragrant, in axillary pairs, appearing usually before the foliage in early Spring, where deciduous.
Zone 5.   *p. 672*
heckrottii (americana x sempervirens), "Gold-flame honeysuckle"; popular vine or small shrub with opposite, blue-green leaves 5 cm long; beautiful two-lipped flowers coral-pink to carmine-red outside, yellow inside, 4 cm long, blooming throughout Summer. *Zone* 5.   *p. 271*
hildebrandiana (Burma, Thailand, So. China), "Burmese honeysuckle" or "Giant honeysuckle"; evergreen climber, the woody stem reaching 18-24 m; ovate 15 cm leaves, and axillary, fragrant, creamy-white flowers deepening to orange-red, the corolla 10-15 cm long with two-lipped limb. *Subtropic. Zones* 9-10.   *p. 272*
japonica (Japan, Korea, China), "Japanese honeysuckle"; vigorous shrub with clambering branches; oval, deep green leaves, deciduous in coldest regions; bilabiate, white flowers set in pairs in leaf axils, and sweetly fragrant. *Zone* 5.   *p. 272*
japonica 'Aureo-reticulata' (brachypoda), "Yellow-net honeysuckle"; attractive evergreen twiner with wiry stems and small ovate leaves veined and netted bright yellow; fragrant flowers white, tinged purple. *Zone* 6.   *p. 272*
japonica 'Halliana' (Japan); extremely forceful shrubby vine, much planted in No. America because of its vigorous habit of growth; ovate leaves along wiry branches, and terminal clusters of bilabiate white flowers changing to yellow; the upper lip divided to middle. *Zone* 4.   *p. 272*
japonica 'Variegata', "Gold and silver flower"; colorful cultivated variety with wiry red-brown branches having pairs of small opposite, oval leaves prettily marbled and variegated green and yellow.
Zone 6.   *p. 272*
korolkowii 'Zabelii' (Turkestan), "Blue-leaf Honeysuckle"; deciduous or semi-evergreen shrub to 4 m high, with broadly ovate leaves 2-3 cm long, bluish-green beneath usually in the species; two-lipped flowers in pairs, rose or sometimes white, to 2 cm long, in late Spring; fruit bright red. *Zone* 5.   *p. 673*
maackii (Manchuria, Korea); deciduous wide-spreading shrub to 5 m with ovate 8-10 cm downy leaves, and fragrant bilabiate white flowers fading to yellowish, the corolla 2 cm long, in pairs.
Zone 2.   *p. 673*
morrowii (Japan), "Morrow honeysuckle"; dense bush with twiggy branches spreading wide, to 2 m high, usually deciduous, sometimes evergreen; the elliptic leaves gray-green, 5 cm long, pubescent beneath; two-lipped white flowers in pairs changing to yellow, in late Spring; followed by dark red fruit. *Zone* 3.   *p. 673*
nitida 'Baggesen's Gold', "Yellow box-honeysuckle"; very handsome shrub with branches spreading outward, closely ranked with small roundish leaves; beautifully colored golden-yellow during Summer. *Zone* 7.   *p. 673*
nitida 'Elegant', (pileata fa. yunnanensis) (Central and West China), "Box honeysuckle"; twiggy evergreen shrub 1 m high with arching branches, the shining leaves nearly round or ovalish 2 cm long; creamy-white flowers lightly fragrant; followed by blue fruit. Excellent for clipped hedges. *Zone* 7.   *p. 673*

periclymenum (Europe to No. Africa and W. Asia), "English woodbine"; climbing shrub very common in Europe, with grayish-green ovate leaves 3-8 cm long; showy two-lipped flowers yellowish to white, 5 cm long, in whorls, and sweetly fragrant; fruits red. Zone 5.   p. 272

periclymenum 'Belgica', "Dutch woodbine"; Dutch cultivar of the serotina group, blooming earlier than the type; the more attractive whorls of fragrant tubular bilabiate flowers are deep purplish-red in bud and creamy-white on the lip; very vigorous and shrubby in growth, readily covering an area of 5 m or more and beautiful on espalier or pergola, and evergreen with thickish leaves in mild climate. Zone 5.   p. 272

periclymenum serotina; beautiful variety differing from periclymenum in having showy flowers dark purple outside, yellow inside. Zone 5.   p. 272

periclymenum 'Serotina Winchester', "Purple woodbine"; excellent cultivar of vigorous habit, climbing to 5 m; the leaves are deciduous in severe cold climates; a profusion of sweet-scented flowers, rich purple-red in bud or on the long tubes, and the expanded lobes soft yellow, blooming into late Autumn. Zone 5.   p. 272

pileata (China), "Privet honeysuckle"; very handsome shrub of low spreading habit, to 1 m high, evergreen especially in younger plants, later often deciduous depending on climate; glossy green leathery leaves to 3 cm long, ovate or obovate, in two ranks along purplish twigs; fragrant tubular flowers yellowish-white, having 5 oblong lobes, followed by shining purple berry-fruit. Popular for low hedging, with stiff horizontal branches. Zone 6.   p. 618, 673

rupicola (Himalaya, Tibet), "Rock cherry"; low deciduous or semi-evergreen shrub of dense habit, with intertwining prostrate branches; oblong dark green leaves to 3 cm long, pale beneath; fragrant flowers pink in axillary pairs, followed by glossy red to purple berries. Zone 3.   p. 673

sempervirens (Connecticut to Florida and Texas), "Trumpet honeysuckle"; showy straggling very hardy deciduous vine, evergreen in warmer zones; opposite ovate leaves 6-8 cm long, glaucous beneath and united at base; at ends of branches dense conspicuous clusters of slender trumpet-like flowers 5 cm long, usually orange-yellow varying to scarlet, yellow inside, during Summer; red fruit. Zones 3-8.   p. 271

standishii (China); semi-evergreen woody shrub to 2½ m high, with bristly shoots, ovate-oblong leaves 5-10 cm long, ciliate at margins, and prickly beneath; creamy-white bilabiate flowers in axillary pairs, blooming early Spring, or November to March in mild areas, and delightfully fragrant; followed by red fruit. Zone 6. p. 674

tatarica (Russia to Turkestan), "Tatarian honeysuckle"; upright, vigorous deciduous shrub to 3 m high, with ovate leaves 3-6 cm long, glaucous beneath; fragrant white or pinkish flowers in axillary pairs, of rather spidery appearance with spreading linear to obovate lobes, blooming May-June; followed by red or yellow fruit. Zone 3.   p. 673

x tellmanniana (L. sempervirens x tragophylla), "Coral honeysuckle"; floriferous climbing shrub, deciduous in cold climates; the flexuous, thin woody stems set with glaucous, ovate leaves, the upper ones united at base; beautiful flowers deep yellow to salmon-rose, 5 cm long, in clusters. Zone 5.   p. 270

xylosteum (Europe to C. Asia, Caucasus), "Fly honeysuckle" or "Hedge cherry"; bushy deciduous shrub to 3 m high, having downy shoots, with broad obovate leaves 6 to 8 cm long, pale green and soft-hairy beneath; two-lipped flowers yellowish-white, often suffused with red, in axillary pairs, blooming late Spring; berry-like fruit deep red. Zone 5.   p. 674

LOPEZIA   *Onagraceae*

hirsuta (lineata) (Mexico), "Mosquito-flower"; shrubby plant 30-90 cm, with hairy stems and serrate ovate leaves, the small winged red flowers with 5 petals, the 2 upper ones bent away from center disclosing an apparent drop of honey, actually a glossy piece of hard tissue which deceives flies. Tropical. Zone 10.   p. 460

LOPHOCEREUS   *Cactaceae*

schottii (Sonora, Arizona, Baja California), "Totem pole" or "Senita"; moss-green column 8 cm thick, with 5-9 acute ribs, the areoles set with small clusters of white wool, and short black spines; night-flowering red 3 cm blooms. The monstrose form L. mieckleyanus grows more slender, with irregular smooth ribs. Arid-subtropic. Zone 10.   p. 161

schottii 'Monstrosus,' "Monstrose totem"; very peculiar yet attractive form consisting of a short column entirely composed of large, smooth knobs or remnants of ribs with spineless areoles, waxy moss-green. Arid-subtropic. Zone 10.   p. 161

LOPHOPHORA   *Cactaceae*

williamsii (So. Texas, Mexico south to Querétaro), the famous "Mescal" or "Peyote" of the ancient Mexicans, because of its powerful exhilarating and narcotic properties; small depressed globe

to 8 cm dia., freely sprouting laterally, bluish-green, 5-13 low and wide ribs, tubercles white tufted; small 2 cm flowers pink to white. Venerated as a god by certain Indians in Mexico, at sacrifices or religious rites. Arid-subtropic. Zone 10.   p. 160

LOROPETALUM   *Hamamelidaceae*

chinense (S.E. China); free-blooming, evergreen shrub to 3 m high or more, the twiggy branches brown with starry down; the oval leaves 4 to 6 cm long; flowers white with strap-shaped petals 2-3 cm long. March-April blooming. The white petals and evergreen leaves distinguish this from Hamamelis. Zone 7.   p. 735

LOTUS   *Leguminosae*

berthelotii (peliorhynchus) (Cape Verde, Canary Isl.), "Winged pea"; silvery-haired shrub spreading along the ground with straggling branches, having pinnate, grayish foliage of threadlike leaflets, and butterfly-type scarlet flowers. Subtropic. Zone 10.   p. 317

corniculatus (Europe, No. Asia, naturalized in E. No. America, also Pacific Coast), "Birds-foot tree-foil"; perennial to 60 cm often procumbent, foliage with 3 to 5 leaflets, and small 2 cm flowers bright yellow fading to orange, the standard striped red, blooming June to August. Sometimes grown for forage. Zone 5.   p. 442

maculatus (Canary Islands), "Parrot's beak"; low evergreen shrub with prostrate, pubescent branches; grayish foliage alternate and divided into linear needle-like segments; the attractive winged pea-flowers 4 to 5 cm long, vivid orange-yellow tipped by slender brown beak. Subtropic. Zone 10.   p. 764

tetragonolobus (Tetragonolobus purpureus) (So. Europe, Mediterr. reg. to Transcaucasus), "Winged pea" or "Asparagus pea"; trailing annual, with branches to 40 cm long; pinnate leaves with ovate, 2 cm leaflets; 2 cm flowers purplish red, singly or twin, in leaf axils, in June to August; the pea-like pods 4-angled with wings, to 8 cm long. The young fruit is edible; the ripe seed is used as coffee substitute. Zone 10 as Annual.   p. 442

LUCULIA   *Rubiaceae*

grandifolia (tsetensis) (India, Bhutan); dense ornamental shrub to 6 m, with deep green ovate, corrugated leaves with reddish midrib 30-40 cm long, and showy clusters of tubular waxy flowers with spreading limb pure white, to 3 cm long. Zones 9-10.   p. 854

LUDISIA   (Zander):   see HAEMARIA (Hortus)

LUDWIGIA   *Onagraceae*

sedioides (Trop. America), "False loose-strife"; small perennial of ponds and marshes; plant spreading 7-10 cm across; rhombic 1 cm leaves with crenate margins, on long reddish petioles; bright yellow flowers to 1 cm dia. Ludwigias are shedding lower leaves at beginning of Winter, especially in heated aquariums. Zones 10-11.   p. 327

LUFFA   *Cucurbitaceae*

aegyptica (cylindrica) (Egypt, Arabia eastward), the odd "Vegetable sponge," "Dishcloth gourd" or "Sauna sponge," is produced by a fast growing tropical climber of the cucumber family; 4-angled stems pull themselves up by coiling tendrils,the rough-hairy herbaceous angled or lobed green leaves cucumber-like, 10-15 cm wide; separate male and female 8 cm flowers golden-yellow; when pollinated the pistillate flowers produce the swollen cylindric fruit to 60 cm long, which may be eaten when young, but the ripe yellow fruit contains the sponge-like fiber that is washed and dried, and marketed for scrubbing, stimulating massage and skin care. Tropical. Zones 10-11.   p. 276

LUMA   *Myrtaceae*

apiculata (Eugenia, Myrtus luma, Amomyrtus), (Chile, Argentina), "Temu"; densely branched evergreen shrub or tree 2 to 5 m high, with golden-brown bark; small sharp-tipped ovate leaves 2-3 cm long; 2 cm flowers cream-white suffused with pink; small black berries. Zone 9.   p. 803

LUNARIA   *Cruciferae*

annua (biennis) (Europe: Sweden, etc.), a biennial variously known as "Silver dollar", "Honesty", "Moonwort" or "Satin flower"; to 1 m high, with toothed ovate leaves, erect stems with violet to white flowers, followed by moon-shaped seed pods opening to papery satiny, translucent discs to 5 cm long, which are cut and used for lasting winter bouquets. Temperate. Zone 6.   p. 412

rediviva (Europe), "Perennial honesty" or "Silver-leaf"; herbaceous perennial 60 cm or more high; ovate leaves more sharply toothed than L. annua, and bearing smaller, white or purplish flowers, sweetly fragrant, in May-June; the flat, papery-white seed-pods oblong, narrowed at both ends. Zone 6.   p. 412

LUPINUS   *Leguminosae*

arboreus (California), "Tree lupine"; striking subshrubby plant to 2 m or more high, and densely branched; compound leaves with 5-12 oblanceolate leaflets 6-8 cm long; fragrant sulphur-yellow flowers in spike-like racemes to 40 cm long, in March to June in California. *Zones 8-10.* p. 441

hartwegii (Mexico); showy lupine, perennial in warm climates, but grown from seed as annual in colder zones; 60-90 cm high, with palmately compound leaves of 7-9 leaflets, covered by shaggy pubescence; the inflorescence striking tall spires dense with flowers in shades of blue with whitish keel, varying to white, rose, or red, and blooming July to September or October, in racemes 30-50 cm long. *Zone 10 or Annual.* p. 441

luteus (W. Mediterr., Portugal), "Yellow lupine" of Europe; attractive small short-lived perennial to 60 cm high, usually grown as annual; densely soft-hairy, with palmately compound leaves of 7-11 narrow oblanceolate leaflets; large bright yellow, fragrant flowers in whorls forming pyramidal racemes, blooming June-July. Much grown as fodder for livestock. *Zones 6-9.* p. 441

perennis (Eastern No. America), "Sundial lupine"; charming herbaceous minutely hairy perennial to 60 cm high; the long-stalked lower leaves palmately compound, of 7-11 oblanceolate leaflets; flowers sky-blue varying to pink or white, having standard with white center, and carried in bold racemes, blooming late Spring to early Summer. *Zones 3-8.* p. 441

polyphyllus (Brit. Columbia to No. California), "Washington lupine"; beautiful, stout perennial to 1 m or more high, with palmately compound leaves having 10 or more obovate leaflets to 15 cm long, and silky-hairy underneath; the inflorescence in showy spike-like racemes 20 to 60 cm long, dense with pea-like bluish or purple flowers, blooming from June to September. There are many colorforms including pink and white. *Zones 4-9.* p. 441

polyphyllus hyb.; perennial typical of the successful breeding of horticultural cultivars widely popular in gardens, with magnificent spires to 50 cm long, packed with flowers from blue to rose, and bicolor variegated with white, blooming from early Summer into Autumn. *Zones 4-9.* p. 441

regalis 'Castellan' (Russell hybrid); strikingly handsome herbaceous perennials, 60-90 cm high, the result of hybridizing L. polyphyllus (Wash. to Calif.) with the tree-lupine arboreus; this strain has massive spikes of pea-like flowers in many colors; pink, salmon, red, white, yellow, violet; leaves digitately compound. *Zones 5-9.* p. 441

texensis (Texas), "Texas blue bonnet"; silky-hairy annual 30 cm high, a roadside plant in Texas, with palmate leaves of usually 5-6 narrow, rather fleshy leaflets; flowers dark blue, with white or yellow on standards, and wings not inflated, in showy pyramids, blooming in early Summer. *Zone 10 as Annual.* p. 441

LURONIUM   *Alismataceae*

natans (Elisma natans) (W. Europe to Russia and Carpathians), "Floating spoons"; perennial bogplant with two types of leaves, submersed and floating; from the rootstock (Stodola p. 176) grows a rosette of ribbon-shaped leaves 40 cm long; the small floating leaves are obovate or oval to only 3 cm long; small white flowers also float on water surface. *Zone 5.* p. 334

LUZULA   *Juncaceae*

nivea (Pyrenees, Alps, Italy, C. France), "Snowy wood rush"; stoloniferous perennial forming tufts, with stems 30-60 cm high; semi-evergreen narrow linear, soft flat basal leaves 30 cm long; white to rusty-brown flowers in nodding terminal clusters during Spring. Good groundcover. *Zone 5.* p. 564

LYCASTE   *Orchidaceae*

aromatica (Mexico to Honduras); dwarf epiphyte with oval pseudobulbs having 1-2 dark green, elliptic leaves; flower stalks clustered, each with a solitary, fragrant, waxy blossom, to 15 cm high, sepals greenish-orange, petals golden-yellow, the concave lip golden-yellow dotted red. (April-Oct.) *Tropical. Zone 11.* p. 90

cruenta (Guatemala, Mexico); epiphyte with 2-3 leaved pseudobulbs and small 5 cm, long-lasting, individually stalked flowers, sepals greenish-yellow, petals deep golden-yellow, lip orange-yellow with blood-red throat, (March-April, and longer). *Tropical. Zone 11.* p. 90

skinneri (virginalis) (Mexico, Guatemala, Honduras), "Nun orchid"; handsome profusely flowering epiphyte with large pseudobulbs, each with 2-3 broad, plaited leaves to 60 cm long; large, waxy, solitary flowers to 15 cm across, rose-pink, shaded carmine-rose in the center, lip whitish, thickly spotted with rose and crimson, (Nov.-May). *Subtropic. Zone 11.* p. 90

LYCHNIS   *Caryophyllaceae*

alpina (Vicaria) (No. Europe, Alps to Pyrenees; Greenland to Quebec), "Campion" or "Catchfly"; clustering smooth Alpine and Arctic perennial to 30 cm high; the rosette of basal leaves linear to spoon-shaped; inflorescence in clusters of up to 20 rose-colored flowers each 1 cm across, occasionally white, in June to August. *Zone 2.* p. 363

x arkwrightii (chalcedonica x haageana); very handsome spreading Maltese Cross hybrid perennial 30-40 cm high, with bronzy ovate to lanceolate leaves, and beautiful vivid scarlet-red flowers of 5 petals deeply notched at apex 3 cm across, blooming Mid-summer. *Zone 3.* p. 363

chalcedonica (So. Russia to Siberia; natur. in E. No. America), "Maltese-cross", "Scarlet lightning" or "London-pride"; popular sturdy garden perennial because of the showy terminal heads of multiple brilliant scarlet flowers, 60 cm high on finely hairy, leafy stems; blooming June-July; the ovate leaves are 5-10 cm long, the flowers with deeply lobed petals 2 cm wide. *Zone 3.* p. 363

coeli-rosa (Silene) (Mediterranean region, Canary Islands), "Rose of Heaven" or "Viscaria"; colorful summer-blooming annual herb 30 to 80 cm high, with wiry, leafy stems, the narrow-linear foliage gray-green; the branches topped by multitudes of single, saucer-shaped flowers 2 to 3 cm across, in various colors, carmine-red with blood-red eye, blue-purple, lavender, pink or white. *Subtropic. Zone 9.* p. 364

coeli-rosa 'Loyalty' (Silene coeli-rosa), "Blue viscaria"; profusely blooming cultivar with dainty lavender-blue flowers; a charming annual bedding or border plant for the sunny summer garden. *Subtropic. Zone 9.* p. 364

coronaria (Mediterranean reg. to Cent. Asia), "Mullein pink" or "Rose campion"; striking white-woolly biennial or short-lived perennial with branched stems to 1 m; leafy non-flowering stalks at base, with oblong leaves 3-10 cm long; flowers glowing crimson-red, 3 cm across. In Asia, the foliage is cooked as vegetable. *Zones 4-9.* p. 364, 525

flos-jovis (Western Alps), "Flower-of-Love"; attractive white-tomentose perennial, with rosette of lanceolate basal leaves, and stiff erect leafy stems to 90 cm high; terminal clusters of purplish-red flowers, the petals 2-lobed, blooming May-July. *Zone 5.* p. 364

x haageana (coronata x fulgens of China), "Haage's campion"; handsome hybrid perennial to 30 cm high; the stems with clasping ovate leaves, and branching toward apex, bearing numerous orange-scarlet or crimson flowers 4-5 cm across, with lobed petals, in early Summer. *Zone 5.* p. 364

viscaria (Europe to Turkey, cent. Asia and Siberia), "German catchfly"; tufting perennial to 50 cm high, with grass-like linear leaves mostly basal; the inflorescence in clusters of several flowers 2 cm across, rose-pink to dark purple, the petals lightly notched; late Spring to early Summer. *Zone 4.* p. 364

viscaria 'Splendens Plena', "Double German catchfly"; neatly clustered perennial, 30-50 cm high, with mostly erect, narrow-lanceolate leaves, and long-stemmed terminal inflorescence of clustered carmine-rose, double flowers. *Zone 4.* p. 364

LYCIUM   *Solanaceae*

carolinianum (So. Carolina to Florida and Texas), "Christmas-berry" or "Boxthorn"; thorny shrub 30-150 cm high, with widely branched erect stems; thick-fleshy spatulate leaves 2 cm long; small lilac or white 5-lobed, funnel-shaped, axillary flowers, followed by bright red globose berries 8-12 mm long; quite showy. *Zone 9.* p. 880

halimifolium (barbarum) (So. E. Europe and W. Asia, natural. in E. No. America), "Matrimony shrub"; thorny shrub with arching, spiny, gray-green thickish branches to 3 m high; lanceolate leaves to 6 cm long; small 15 mm lilac-purple flowers blooming late June with stamens protruding, followed by oval, scarlet fruit 2 cm long. *Zones 6-9.* p. 880

LYCOPERSICON   *Solanaceae*

lycopersicum (esculentum) (Andean So. America), "Tomato" or "Love apple"; tender hairy-bristly, scented perennial grown as annual in temperate regions, erect to decumbent, spreading 3 m wide; large pinnate leaves having leaflets to 8 cm long, coarsely toothed; short clusters of yellow flowers; very juicy, thin-skinned globular fruit usually 5-10 cm dia., eaten fresh, in salads, or cooked. Closely related to the potato, Solanum tuberosum. I have proved this relationship by successfully grafting a tomato on a sprouting potato, a combination known as 'Potomato'. *Zone 10.* p. 940

lycopersicum (esculentum) cerasiforme, the "Cherry-tomato"; in cultivation since the 16th century, and before by the Incas of western South America, their native home; fleshy herb with strong-smelling, pinnately compound, hairy foliage, small yellow flowers, and long clusters of globular red or yellow fruit 2-3 cm in dia., during the hot season, and used for ornament or in the kitchen. *Zone 10.* p. 940

LYCOPODIUM   *Lycopodiaceae*

clavatum (Asia, Europe; No. America: Greenland to Alaska, Oregon to No. Carolina), "Running pine" or "Staghorn clubmoss"; moss-like, with wide-ranging creeping rhizomes rising with forked upright leafy branches resembling deer antlers, 3-15 cm high, the many-ranked linear leaves bristle-tipped. *Zones 3-8.* p. 142

complanatum (Alaska to Labrador, so. to Wash., Montana, Ontario, Maine; Temp. Eurasia), "Ground cedar"; wide-creeping branching with erect flattened stems, divided and spreading presenting a spidery look, the tiny glaucous leaves in 4 ranks. Zones 3-6. *p. 142*

obscurum (Newfoundland to Alaska, south to Montana, Pennsylvania, Alabama), "Ground pine", also known as "Princess pine"; evergreen moss-like herb, allied to the ferns; main stem creeping horizontally, sending up aerial branches 10-25 cm high, like miniature pine-trees, the branches covered by dark green scale-like leaves and topped by club-shaped spikes producing spores. Bound together into little Christmas trees and sold by florists as "Mystery plant". Zones 2-8. *p. 142*

squarrosum (Polynesia, Trop. Queensland), the "Rock tassel" or "God's-strings"; a difficult epiphyte often found growing on rocks, branched flexuous yellow-green, arching stems set with grass-green narrow ovate needle-hard, sessile leaves like a spruce tree. Zones 11-12. *p. 142*

LYCORIS   *Amaryllidaceae*
radiata (China, Japan), "Red spider lily"; formerly sold as Nerine sarniensis or N. japonica; bulbous plant 45 cm high, good grower with liner basal leaves with silver band along middle, and disappearing before the flowers which are borne in an umbel, the recurved and crisped petals bright scarlet-red and edged with gold, the long stamens curving upward; late fall-blooming and hardy. *Warm temperate. Zones 7-8.* *p. 213*
radiata of hort.: see also NERINE sarniensis
squamigera (Japan), "Magic lily" or "Resurrection lily"; bulbous herb with leaves 2½ cm wide, the fragrant flowers 7 cm long, in umbels, petals separated and a pretty lilac-pink, yellow in base, the long stamens turned up; hardy. *Warm temperate. Zones 5-6. p. 213*

LYGODIUM   *Schizaeaceae (Filices)*
japonicum (Japan to Himalayas and No. Australia), "Climbing fern"; with twining, threadlike stems bearing pretty, pleasing green, pinnate, papery leaflets, the sterile pinnae with lobed segments (pinnules); the fertile pinnae narrow, 3-times divided. *Humid-subtropic. Zones 9-11.* *p. 142, 277*

LYONIA   *Ericaceae*
ferruginea (Andromeda) (Coastal So. Carolina to Florida); handsome evergreen to 5 m high, with leathery oval to obovate leaves 3-6 cm long, rusty-scaly especially beneath; axillary clusters of nodding flowers with globular urn-shaped corolla white, the calyx segments also brown-scaly, blooming February-March. Zone 7. *p. 705*
lucida (Virginia to Louisiana), "Fetterbush"; dense evergreen bush 1-2 m high, with 3-angled branchlets; leathery ovate leaves to 8 cm long, glossy green above and black-dotted beneath; axillary clusters of white cup-shaped flowers tinged with pink, tipped with 5 tiny pointed reddish lobes, in June-July. Zone 6. *p. 705*
mariana (Pieris) (Rhode Island to Arkansas and Florida), "Staggerbush"; deciduous shrub of wet areas, 1-2 m high, with slender branches, and ovate or obovate thin leaves to 10 cm long, coloring red in Autumn; axillary clusters of flowers, with cup-shaped corolla white or pinkish, blooming profusely from June into Summer. Zone 5. *p. 705*

LYONOTHAMNUS   *Rosaceae*
floribundus var. asplenifolius (California: Santa Catalina Is.), "Catalina Ironwood"; inhabiting Catalina, Santa Cruz Is. and other islands off California coast; slender hard-wooded evergreen tree 10-16 m high, with reddish shreddy bark, smooth branches, and narrow elliptic, leathery leaves 8-20 cm long, minutely toothed or entire; small white 1 cm flowers in wide terminal clusters to 15 cm across, blooming May-July. Leaves are linear in the typical species; broader in var. asplenifolius. Zone 9. *p. 838*

LYSICHITON   *Araceae*
americanum (sometimes spelled Lysichitum; Zander: L. americanus) (W. No. America: Alaska to Montana), "Skunk cabbage"; swamp herb of the temperate zone; oblong leaves 25-60 cm long, succeeding flowers, from thick rootstocks; spathe to 15 cm long, boat-shaped, pale yellow; ill-scented. Zones 4-9. *p. 325*

LYSILOMA   *eguminosae*
candida (Mexico: So. Baja California), "Palo blanco"; unarmed tree to 7½ m high, with often several trunks having smooth white bark; bipinnate leaves with white floral spikes and yellow stamens, followed by elongate flat beans 8-15 cm long, the valves thin and papery. The bark is much used locally for tanning. Photographed at Cabo San Lucas. Zone 10. *p. 764*

LYSIMACHIA   *Primulaceae*
barystachys (Japan, Korea, Manchuria), "Loosestrife" or "Nojitora-no-o" in Japan; herbaceous perennial, with erect, slender stems

to 60 cm high; alternate narrow-lanceolate leaves covered with appressed hairs, glaucous beneath; small white flowers in dense terminal arching, spike-like raceme, blooming July-August. Zone 5. *p. 479*
clethroides (China, Japan), "Gooseneck loose-strife"; erect, little branched herbaceous perennial to 1 m, with ovate, hairy leaves 8-15 cm; small 1 cm bell-shaped white flowers with spreading petals, dense in slender pyramidal spikes, in late Summer. Zone 3. *p. 479*
ephemerum (So. France to Spain); herbaceous perennial with slender erect stems to 90 cm high; glaucous linear-lanceolate, opposite leaves 10-15 cm long, joined at base; small white flowers tinged with purple, in long slender terminal racemes, in Summer. Zone 7. *p. 479*
nummularia (C. Europe and Britain, nat. in E. No. America), "Creeping Jennie" or "Creeping Charlie", "Moneywort"; prostrate perennial creeper, with herbaceous dull light green, rounded leaves to 2½ cm long, in pairs along a threadlike, squarish, pink stem, forming rootlets opposite the axils; flowers bright yellow 2 cm across, winter-hardy. *Warm temperate. Zone 5.* *p. 319*
punctata (S.E. Europe, Asia Minor), "Yellow loose-strife"; erect perennial hairy herb, branches in three's, 30-60 cm high, with ovate leaves, and starry 3 cm yellow flowers in axillary whorls. Zone 5. *p. 479*
vulgaris (No. Europe to Asia; natural. in No. America), "Garden loosestrife"; bushy, vigorous perennial with slender, leafy stems to 1 m or more high; the leaves whorled or opposite lanceolate, 8-12 cm long; bright yellow flowers dotted orange, 2 cm across, in leafy clusters, during Summer. Zone 5. *p. 479*

LYTHRUM   *Lythraceae*
salicaria (Europe, Asia, N.W. Africa; natural. in Eastern No. America), "Purple loosestrife"; downy perennial subshrub of wet places, to 2 m high; 10 cm lanceolate leaves; flowers red-purple in long leafy spikes, blooming all Summer. Zone 4. *p. 775*
salicaria 'Flame' ('Stichflamme') (species from Eurasia, naturalized in No. America), "Rose loosestrife"; erect shrubby perennial of marshland, with stiff 4-angled stems 50-150 cm high, clothed by willow-like lanceolate leaves 5-12 cm long; inflorescence in spike-like raceme of purplish-rose flowers, variable in colors; summer-blooming. Zone 4. *p. 456*
virgatum 'Rose Queen' (parentage Europe and Asia); attractive shrubby perennial to 1 m high, smooth and without downy hairs, having narrow-ovate to lanceolate leaves, the numerous 4-angled stems topped by showy cylindric, leafy racemes of usually paired rose-red flowers, blooming profusely June to August. Related to L. salicaria but shorter, more smooth, daintier and quite popular. Zone 3. *p. 775*

MAACKIA   *Leguminosae*
amurensis (Manchuria, Korea); summer-flowering shrub or tree to 15 m or more high; odd-pinnate leaves 20-30 cm long, having 7-11 ovate leaflets to 8 cm long; dull white flowers in cylindric racemes at apex of branches, blooming in August; legume fruit 5 cm long. Zone 4. *p. 766*

MACADAMIA   *Proteaceae*
integrifolia (ternifolia in Calif. hort.) (N.E. Australia), "Smooth-skinned macadamia" or "Queensland nut"; handsome subtropic, evergreen tree to 18 m high; glossy green leathery, lanceolate leaves 10-30 cm long, normally arranged in whorls of three, occasionally four; adult stage mostly smooth-margined leaves, sometimes lightly toothed, but not spiny; small creamy-white flowers in long, pendant racemes; the pistils of the flowers develop into a glossy green, smooth-skinned husk which splits open at maturity, releasing an extremely hard-shelled 3 cm brown nut holding a kernel of nutritious firm white flesh, not quite as sweet as M. tetraphylla, but highly regarded and eaten fresh, roasted, salted, or chocolate-covered. Fruit ripens between November and April, generally dropping to the ground; best if stored in a dry area. Thrives in coastal area of California, and widely planted commercially in Hawaii, where the nuts are processed for shipping. Zone 10. *p.824, 924*
tetraphylla (Queensland, New South Wales), "Rough-skin macadamia" or "Macadamia nut"; evergreen sub-tropical tree to 15 m high, of open habit, with stiff, dark branches; long, pointed, spiny, ilex-like to lanceolate leaves to 30 cm long, normally four to a whorl; flowers are generally pink, in long drooping clusters; the fruit is a rough, pebbly husk, splitting open to release a hand-shelled nut 2-3 cm dia., the kernels are slightly sweeter in taste than integrifolia; they may be dried after cracking the shell and stored in a dry place for several months; best for inland California. Zone 10. *p. 924*

MACARANGA   *Euphorbiaceae*
grandifolia (Philippines), "Coral tree"; growing into a tree 5 m or more high, with rosettes of large peltate pointed, leathery leaves

prominently veined, to 60 cm across; small petal-less flowers, the males on elongate axis in panicles. Dioecious species, with male and female flowers on separate plants. Zone 10.   p. 725

MACFADYENA   Bignoniaceae
unguis-cati (Doxantha) (West Indies to Argentina), "Cats-claw"; tropical woody vine high-climbing into trees, with opposite leaves each with a pair of leaflets separated by a tendril split into 3 claws; leaflets are thin, oval-pointed, to 8 cm long; funnel-form, allamanda-like lobed flowers, rich yellow, to 10 cm wide, borne profusely in short clusters normally in Spring, often also in Autumn.
Zones 9-10.   p. 268

MACHAERANTHERA   Compositae
tanacetifolia (Aster) (Alberta to So. Dakota, so. to Mexico), "Tahoka daisy"; biennial herb, often grown as annual, to 60 cm high, densely leafy and often sticky; the ferny foliage to 8 cm long, mostly pinnately parted; the aster-like flowers 6 cm across, with purple or violet ray-florets, and yellow center disc, summer-blooming.
Zone 3.   p. 398

MACHAEROCEREUS gummosus (1920)
transferred to Stenocereus (1978)

MACLEANIA   Ericaceae
insignis (Mountains of Veracruz to Guatemala); scandent shrub with tuberous base; the slender branches dense with glossy 5 cm leaves, reddish when young; charming waxy, tubular flowers bright scarlet with apricot tips, 4 cm long. Subtropic. Zones 9-10.   p. 277

MACLEAYA   Papaveraceae
cordata (China, Japan), "Coral plume poppy"; excellent vigorous perennial with leafy stems 1-2 m high, spreading from fleshy roots; large bronzy green leaves to 20 cm wide, palmately lobed, and grayish-white underneath; the small cream to pinkish flowers lacking petals, in showy plume-like, elongate panicles, in July-August.
Zone 3.   p. 467
microcarpa (Bocconia) (Cent. China), "Plume poppy"; stout perennial to 2 m tall, with stiff stems containing yellow sap, from fleshy roots forming colonies; the handsome leaves at base and upward deeply lobed, leading toward the pyramidal inflorescence of tiny bronzy, petal-less flowers in plume-like clusters, in early Summer.
Zone 3.   p. 467

MACLURA   Moraceae
pomifera (Midwest U.S., Oklahoma, Arkansas and Texas), "Osage-orange" or Bow-wood"; vigorous deciduous tree with orange bark, milky sap and dense branches with spines 3 cm long; the alternate leaves ovate slender-pointed, 3-10 cm long, dark glossy green; the small staminate greenish flowers are inconspicuous; the pistillate female blooms are clustered in large bundles forming an orange-like green decorative ball of fruit of rough texture 8 cm across, containing unhealthy milky juice. Planted as spiny hedge difficult to penetrate. Zone 5.   p. 794

MACROPLECTRUM   Orchidaceae
sesquipedale (Angraecum) (Madagascar), "Star of Bethlehem"; epiphyte with stems to 1 m, densely 2-ranked leaves; thick-fleshy flowers to 18 cm dia., ivory-white, with long spur; largest in the genus, (Nov.-March). Tropical. Zone 12.   p. 90

MACROZAMIA   Cycadaceae: Zamiaceae
communis (New South Wales); elegant palm-like cycad, dioecious with stems to 2 m tall, but often underground; pinnate fronds more or less erect, to 2 m long, with up to 130 pinnae each to 40 cm long, the lower ones spine-like; cylindric male and female cones 45 cm long, on separate plants. Zones 10-11.   p. 114
moorei (Queensland, New South Wales); large plant with stem underground or to 1 m high; fronds 2 m long, pinnae spreading and directed forward, the lower ones progressively spine-like; cones cylindrical, the female salmon-pink inside.
Subtropic. Zone 11.   p. 114

MAERUA   Capparidaceae
kirkii (Kenya), known as "Mupopotwe" on the Tsavo Desert; arid region shrub or small tree to 5 m high, with erect branches; ovate oblong leathery leaves to 10 cm long and having rough surface, pubescent beneath; showy flowers greenish-white with black centers, the petals shorter than sepals, in dense clusters; small 1 cm fruit.
Zone 10.   p. 672

MAGNOLIA   Magnoliaceae
acuminata (Ontario to Georgia and Louisiana), "Cucumber tree"; vigorous deciduous tree to 30 m high, at first erect, later spreading, with ovate leaves to 26 cm long, smooth green or sometimes tomentose beneath; the somewhat smallish flowers appearing with or

after the new foliage, the corolla with spreading petals greenish-yellow to yellow, to 8 cm long, blooming late Spring; purplish-red fruit 10 cm long. Zone 4.   p. 776
campbellii (Sikkim); deciduous Himalayan tree 10 to 30 m high, with elliptic-oblong leaves to 30 cm long, glaucous beneath; 15-25 cm cup-shaped fragrant flowers before the leaves, pink outside deep rose inside, early-blooming in February-March. Zone 8.   p. 776
cylindrica (China: Anhwei Prov.); deciduous shrub or small tree to 9 m high, with oblong obovate leaves to 15 cm, dark green and showing distinct veins; flowers before foliage, similar to M. denudata, the obovate petals white and a soft pink center band, and 10 cm long; fruit cylindrical 5-7 cm long. Zone 5.   p. 778
denudata (heptapeta; conspicua in hort.) (Eastern and Southern China), "Yulan" or "Lily tree of China"; deciduous shrub or tree 2 to 12 m high, blooming early Spring on bare, crooked branches; erect bell-shaped flowers creamy-white, to 12 cm across, and lightly fragrant; soft-hairy foliage obovate, 8 to 15 cm long. A lovely sight when bursting forth in glistening brilliance, and widely planted near temples in China. Zone 5.   p. 777
fraseri (Mts. of Virginia to Georgia, Alabama), "Ear-leaved umbrella tree"; deciduous tree to 15 m high, with thin oblanceolate leaves to 40 cm long, cordate at base; the large white flowers with obovate petals spreading to 25 cm across and sweet-scented, blooming in May-June when the plant is with foliage; rose-red, cone-like fruit. Zone 5.   p. 776
fuscata: see MICHELIA figo
grandiflora (Carolina to Florida and Texas), the "Southern magnolia"; noble evergreen pyramidal tree to 30 m high, with decorative thick-leathery, rich-green ovate oblong leaves to 20 cm long with shining surface and rusty tomentose beneath; large and beautiful 20 cm cup-shaped flowers creamy-white and fragrant; blooming June and September; rust-brown cone-like fruit. Zone 7.   p. 777
heptapeta (Hortus 3):
   see M. denudata (European Garden Flora 1989, Zander)
hypoleuca (obovata) (Kurile Is. to Japan), "White-leaf Japanese magnolia"; handsome, exotic-looking deciduous tree 15 to 30 m high, with leathery, obovate leaves 20-40 cm long, glaucous green above and bluish-white beneath; the fragrant flowers, appearing after foliage has developed in June, are very decorative, having corolla of 6-9 obovate petals, white with crimson filaments in center, 15-20 cm long. Better than tripetala which has smaller flowers not fragrant.
Zone 5.   p. 776
kobus (So. Japan, Korea), "Kobus magnolia"; deciduous tree to 10 m or more high, shrubby in habit, with smooth branches and soft-hairy winter buds; obovate oblong leaves 8-12 cm long; flowers appearing before foliage in April, the corolla with 6 or more flaring petals creamy-white 10 cm across, marked purple at base; pink fruit 10 cm long. While of vigorous growth, it is slow to bloom until older; but used as understock for grafting. Zone 4.   p. 777
liliiflora (quinquepeta) (China), "Lily magnolia"; deciduous shrub to 4 m high, with obovate leaves to 20 cm long, pale beneath; flowers appearing before foliage, bell-shaped, purple outside, white inside to 10 cm long, blooming April to June. Zone 6.   p. 777, 779
liliiflora 'Nigra' (syn. x soulangiana 'Nigra') "Purple lily magnolia"; this color form of the Chinese species has flowers 10-12 cm long with fleshy petals deeper, vivid purplish-red outside and lighter inside; mainly growing in bush form, having leaves 10-16 cm long; the beautifully colored flowers appear over a period of several weeks, starting late May or early June with the foliage. Zone 6.   p. 779
macrophylla (Kentucky to Florida and Louisiana), "Great-leaved magnolia"; deciduous tree to 18 m high, very exotic-looking having the largest leaves and flowers of all hardy magnolias; the corrugated leafblades are 40-60 cm or even 90 cm long, the creamy-white flowers 30 cm across, with a purple blotch at base, and sweetly fragrant, blooming after foliage in May-June; large 8 cm ovoid rose-colored fruit. Zone 5.   p. 776
quinquepeta (Hortus 3):
   see M. liliiflora (Europ. Garden Flora 1989)
salicifolia (Japan: Mountains of Honshu, Kyushu), "Anise magnolia"; densely branched deciduous pyramidal tree to 10 m high, with narrow aromatic leaves resembling willow, to 10 cm long, scented of anise when crushed, glaucous beneath; white flowers with 6 narrow petals spreading 12 cm wide, sometimes purplish at base, and appearing in April-May before the foliage and sweetly fragrant.
Zone 5.   p. 778
sieboldii (Japan, Korea), "Oyama magnolia"; wide-spreading deciduous shrub or small tree to 10 m high; broad-elliptic or obovate leaves 10-15 cm long, showy prominent veins, dark green above, glaucous and downy beneath; medium-sized distinctly fragrant flowers 10-15 cm across, the waxy-white cupped petals cradling the deep crimson stamens, blooming with the foliage in late Spring and Summer. Zone 6.   p. 778

sinensis (China: W. Szechwan), "Chinese magnolia"; deciduous shrub or small tree to 6 m high; oval-oblong leaves 8-16 cm long, bright green above, silvery-pubescent beneath; the lemon-scented, saucer-shaped pendant flowers to 10 cm across, with the foliage in June, the corolla white with red staminal cone in center; pendulous 8 cm carmine-rose fruit. Zone 7. *p. 778*

x soulangiana (hybrid of M. denudata x liliiflora), both from China; the "Saucer magnolia" is common in cultivation and one of the showiest spring-flowering small trees to 5 m high; obovate deciduous 15 cm leaves and solitary 15 cm flowers white, tinged purplish-rose outside, blooming ahead of foliage; cross made by one of Napoleon's retired soldiers about 1820 and now widely planted across Europe and North America. Zone 5. *p. 779*

x soulangiana 'Verbanica'; cultivar with large cup-shaped flowers 15 cm across, purplish and pink, from long slender buds; blooming before leaves, later than M. soulangiana. Zone 5. *p. 777*

sprengeri (Western China); pyramidal deciduous tree from Hupeh and Honan, to 20 m high, with yellowish young shoots; dull green oblong leaves 12-18 cm long, downy on veins beneath; showy saucer-shaped white flowers, streaked with pink inside, to 20 cm across, blooming early Spring, appearing before foliage; cone-shaped red fruit to 20 cm long. Zone 7. *p. 778*

sprengeri var. diva (W. China: Szechwan), "Diva magnolia"; handsome variety 5 to 10 m high, with deciduous obovate leaves 10-16 cm long, and beautiful erect flowers 20 cm across, the corolla of 12 or more petals dark rose outside, and soft pink inside with thin rose lines, blooming in March to April, and sweetly fragrant. Zone 7. *p. 778*

stellata (halliana) (Japan), "Star magnolia"; deciduous, much branched shrub to 8 m high; dull green obovate 12 cm leaves; fragrant white flowers with narrow petals, spreading 8 cm across, later reflexed, and appearing before the foliage in early Spring; red fruit; fairly hardy. Zone 5. *p. 779*

stellata 'Waterlily'; handsome cultivar introduced by Greenbrier Farms, Norfolk, Virginia about 1939, possibly a hybrid of stellata x soulangiana; densely branched shrub of more erect habit than stellata; the inflorescence with rose-pink buds, when open white; the petals longer, wider, and partially recurved or twisted. Zone 7. *p. 779*

tripetala (tetrapetala) (Pennsylvania to Oklahoma), "Umbrella magnolia"; small open-headed deciduous tree with large lanceolate leaves to 50 cm long, crowded at end of branches, giving an umbrella-like effect; large creamy-white flowers with obovate petals, to 25 cm across, followed by rosy fruit, blooming May or June, after foliage has fully developed. Zone 4. *p. 778*

virginiana (glauca) (Massachusetts to Texas), "Sweet-bay magnolia"; large deciduous shrub, or tree to 20 m with smooth branches and hairy buds, half evergreen in the subtropics, with elliptic 12 cm leaves glaucous gray beneath; 8 cm very fragrant flowers with the foliage, the cupping fleshy petals creamy-white, in May-June. Zone 5. *p. 778*

wilsonii (Western China); vigorous deciduous shrub or small tree to 8 m high, with brown-haired young growth; the oblong leaves 8-15 cm long, silky beneath; saucer-shaped fragrant flowers 8-10 cm wide, appearing with the foliage, the corolla with usually 9 incurved petals white, and rich red stamens in center, blooming May-June. Related to M. sinensis. Zone 7. *p. 778*

MAHONIA   Berberidaceae

aquifolium (Brit. Columbia, Oregon to No. California), "Barberry", "Oregon grape" or "Holly mahonia"; handsome hardy evergreen thornless shrub to 1 m or more, with flexible stems and pinnate leaves with spiny-toothed, leathery leaflets 8 cm or more long, glossy dark green, the young foliage a pretty bronzy red; lemon-yellow flowers in dense clusters, followed by blue-black, edible berries with glaucous bloom. Very durable, hardy in So. New England. Zone 6. *p. 614, 656*

bealei (China), "Leatherleaf mahonia"; distinctive evergreen shrub with stout, erect woody stems, to 4 m high, carrying horizontal leaves 25 cm long, with 7-15 thick-leathery, broad leaflets as much as 12 cm long, bluish-green with yellow at base; underneath, glaucous green veins, the margins with a few large teeth, on red petioles; fragrant yellow flowers in spike-like clusters followed by powdery blue berries; fairly winter-hardy. Zone 6. *p. 656*

darwinii: see under BERBERIS
koreana: see under BERBERIS

lomariifolia (China: Yunnan), "Chinese holly grape"; evergreen shrub with erect woody, bamboo-like stem with rosette of long pinnate leaves, the hard leathery, holly-like, undulate 9 cm leaflets olive-green with lighter veins, with pointed spiny lobes, set in pairs on long wiry axis to 30 cm long; showy spike-like erect racemes dense with numerous small yellow flowers; followed in Autumn by purplish-black fruit. Zone 7. *p. 656*

x media (M. japonica x lomariifolia); ornamental hybrid cultivar of medium height, with stiff erect stems, and long pinnate leaves gracefully arching; the up to about 13 thin-leathery leaflets ovate to lanceolate, slender-pointed, and lightly crenate along margins; flowers in small clusters on terminal racemes. Zone 7. *p. 656*

pinnata (Berberis pinnata) (California to Mexico), "Cluster mahonia"; robust evergreen shrub to 3 m and more high, related to broad M. aquifolium, but pinnate leaves of 7-13 leaflets which are dull green not lustrous, spiny-toothed along sides, and overlapping; the pale yellow flowers in clustered racemes 6-8 cm long, followed by ovoid black fruit covered with blue glaucescence. Zone 7. *p. 656*

repens (Berberis) (Brit. Columbia, No. California, East to Rocky Mountains), "Creeping mahonia"; small spreading evergreen creeping by underground stolons or stems, 30 cm or more high, dull bluish-green leaves have 3-7 spine-toothed leaflets, turning bronze in Winter; yellow flowers in 8 cm clusters followed by dark blue, powdery berries. Zone 5. *p. 656*

trifoliolata (Berberis trifoliata) (Texas, New Mexico to Cent. Mexico), "Trileaved holly-grape"; evergreen shrub to 2 m or more high; the curious leaves consisting of 3 thick leaflets to 5 cm long, ovate in outline but often deeply indented with lobes pointed and spine-tipped; inflorescence in clusters of 3-6 yellow flowers, followed by ovoid red fruit; used in jellies. Zone 8. *p. 656*

verruculosa: see under BERBERIS

MAIANTHEMUM   Liliaceae

bifolium (Europe, Siberia, Kuriles, E. Asia to Korea), "Two-leaved Solomon's seal"; small woodland perennial 10-20 cm high, with slender rhizomes, long-creeping; stems 8-15 cm long, each bearing two membranous leaves, ovoid-deltoid with cordate base, 2-5 cm long; floral racemes with about 20 small white flowers, blooming May-July; small globose berry-fruits 5 mm dia. Zones 4-8. *p. 450*

canadense (Newfoundland to So. Dakota and Tennessee), "Canada mayflower"; low perennial woodland creeper 8-15 cm high, with stems bearing 2-3 alternate sessile, cordate-ovate leaves; and terminal raceme of tiny white fragrant flowers, in May; followed by light red berries. Zones 3-8. *p. 450*

kamschaticum (dilatatum) (Alaska to Idaho and Cent. Calif.; E. Asia), "False-lily-of-the-valley"; low herbaceous perennial, spreading by creeping rhizomes, to 25 cm high; lustrous, deep green leaves broad ovate to kidney-shaped with cordate, deep sinus, 10-20 cm long; tiny white 1 cm flowers in small clusters, blooming May-July; followed by red fruit. Zones 2-8. *p. 450*

MAJORANA hortensis: see ORIGANUM majorana

MALAXIS   Orchidaceae

latifolia (India, Malaysia, So. China, Australia), "Adder's mouth"; interesting terrestrial orchid, with clustered 10 cm pseudobulbs bearing 4-5 lanceolate leaves to 25 cm long; the erect 15 cm inflorescence in a dense column of small 1 cm flowers yellow-green and tinted purple. Zone 12. *p. 90*

MALCOLMIA   Cruciferae

maritima (Cheiranthus maritimus) (Mediterr. region to Greece; Albania), "Virginian stock"; bushy annual, 20-30 cm high, with spreading branches; the leaves elliptic, on broad petioles; small 4-petaled flowers 15 mm across, varying from lilac to rose, or white, with green eye, followed by long, slender fruit. Zone 9. *p. 412*

MALEPHORA   Aizoaceae

latipetala (Hymenocyclus) (Cape Prov.); creeping woody perennial with succulent keeled leaves to 3 cm long, glaucous blue to reddish; buds purplish-red opening into daisy-like flowers variably orange-red or yellow. Zone 10. *p. 146*

luteola (Hymenocyclus) (So. Africa), "Yellow trailing ice plant"; spreading succulent, forming dense cushions to 30 cm high; short gray-green leaves cylindrical or flattened on top; bright yellow flowers 3-4 cm across but blooming sparsely. Arid-subtropic. Zones 9-10. *p. 146*

MALLOTUS   Euphorbiaceae

philippinensis (Taiwan, India to So. China, Philippines to N.S.W.), "Monkey-face tree"; small evergreen tree, young leaves and inflorescence rusty pubescent; leaves oblong-elliptic 6-20 cm long, globular capsules, densely covered with red powdery glands. Zone 10. *p. 725*

MALOPE   Malvaceae

trifida (grandiflora) (Spain, No. Africa); attractive annual to 1 m high with broad ovate leaves, dentate at margins; axillary flowers salver-shaped, 4-8 cm dia., pink or rose-colored with purple lines spreading out from center, the petals reflexed, and surrounded by 3 heart-shaped bracts; blooming throughout the Summer. Zone 9. *p. 458*

MALPIGHIA   *Malpighiaceae*

glabra (So. Texas to So. America), "Barbados cherry"; known in Puerto Rico and Mexico as "Acerola"; shrub or small tree to 4 m, with shining green ovate, leathery 8 cm leaves; pretty flowers carmine-rose with fimbriate petals, 1 cm across, followed by small 1 to 2 cm cherry-like edible fruit, of acid flavor and high in Vitamin C (Ascorbic acid), and ranking as its richest known natural source. Can be made into high-vitamin jelly or fruit juice. *Zones 9-10.*   p. 780, 909

MALUS   *Rosaceae*

x atrosanguinea (halliana x sieboldii) (China); handsome, floriferous "Crab-apple"; a small tree with purplish twigs and ovate, deciduous, glossy leaves finely serrate, covered in Spring with masses of rosy-carmine flowers 3 cm wide, with narrow petals, not fading to white, followed by small, yellow and dark red apples. *Zone 4.* p. 835

x arnoldiana (baccata x floribunda); excellent hybrid with flowers up to 5 cm across, pink outside and to white inside when open, while in bud a lovely rose to red; the fruits are very attractive yellow miniature apples. *Zone 4.*   p. 835

baccata (Siberia, China), "Siberian crab apple"; deciduous tree to 15 m high, with hard branchlets, and small 4-6 cm ovate leaves; 3 cm fragrant white flowers; pale yellow waxy fruit; trained into dwarfed bonsai trees in Japan. Hardiest of all crab-apples, and a source of fruit-jellies and preserves in very cold regions. *Zone 2.*   p. 836, 928

baccata 'Jackii' (Korea 1915); a superior variety forming broad head with wide elliptic leaves and pure white flowers to 4 cm across; charming little 1 cm apples glossy red and very ornamental. Seen at Strybing Arboretum, San Francisco. *Zone 2.*   p. 836

coronaria (Ontario to Wisconsin, No. Carolina to Texas), "American crab apple"; deciduous much-branched tree to 10 m high; ovate leaves coarsely toothed, 5-10 cm long, soon smooth; flowers white, tinted rose, 3 cm wide, and deliciously fragrant, blooming in clusters May-June; followed by depressed globular, rosy fruit, of harsh and acid taste. *Zone 4.*   p. 835

floribunda (Japan), "Showy crab apple" or "Japanese crab"; introduced from Japan 1862, it is still one of the best ornamental crab-apples; very floriferous with rose or red floral buds opening to pink inside, 3 cm across, displaying united pistils, typical of Malus; fragrant, and blooming mid-May; round-headed deciduous tree to 10 m high, ovate serrate leaves 4-8 cm long; yellowish globose fruit very decorative little apples in Autumn. *Zone 4.*   p. 835

floribunda 'Scheideckeri' (floribunda x prunifolia); beautiful "Flowering crab-apple"; of pyramidal habit to 6 m high with ovate leaves 3-5 cm long, and large, semi-double, 3-4 cm flowers of delicate rose-pink to pale tinged pink, borne with great profusion in large clusters during May, followed by small 2 cm yellow to reddish tart fruit, used for jellies. *Zone 4.*   p. 836, 928

halliana (Japan, China); small deciduous tree 4-6 m high, with purple branchlets; elliptic leaves to 8 cm long, dark green to purplish; lovely bright rose flowers 3 cm across, single or semi-double, having 5-8 petals, and blooming in May; small ovoid dull red or purplish fruit. *Zone 5.*   p. 836

hupehensis (China, Assam), "Tea crab-apple"; deciduous tree to 8 m high, with stiff, spreading branches; ovate-oblong leaves 5-10 cm long and finely toothed; fragrant white or pinkish flowers 3 cm across, and sepals purplish, in small clusters blooming May-June; globose 1-2 cm fruit, greenish-yellow with red cheek, its calyx falling away, and edible, made into jelly. Very picturesque with its fan-shaped habit, especially in Spring with deep pink buds. *Zones 4-8.*   p. 928

ioensis (Minnesota to Missouri and Kansas), "Prairie crab-apple"; a handsome American crab-apple to 10 m high with downy branchlets, and ovate leaves 8-10 cm long; beautiful flowers with concave petals, soft pink, the corolla to 5 cm across displaying a central clustering of purple stamens, during May-June, and scented of violets; followed by miniature yellowish apples. The popular 'Bechtel crab' is a double-flowered form of this. *Zone 2.*   p. 836

pumila, (Europe and W. Asia), "Common apple"; round-headed deciduous tree to 12 m high, with oval, leathery leaves 5-10 cm long, and flowers white or light pink, 3-5 cm across, appearing with first foliage, and followed by its large depressed globular edible fruit, with firm, tart-sweet flesh. Similar to M. sylvestris, the Crab-apple, but rarely thorny. Kruessmann refers the cultured modern market apples to M. silvestris var. domestica; Zander lists these apples as M. domestica. Hortus holds M. domestica a synonym of M. pumila. *Zone 3.*   p. 836

pumila 'Anna' (from Israel); an excellent apple photographed at Paul Thomson's, Bonsall, California; beautiful yellow fruit overlaid with red; of firm crisp textured flesh; producing well in subtropical climate. *Warm temperate. Zones 6-9.*   p. 926

pumila 'Boskoop', a superior winter apple originating in Boskoop, Holland 1856; vigorous deciduous fruit tree with spreading crown; the primary branches quite horizontal; flowers medium early, and very frost-sensitive to late freezes; blooming on one-year branchlets; fruit depressed globular, medium to large-sized, yellow-green and rugose overlaid with red; with crisp flesh of sweet-tart flavor; for harvest October-November; a popular favorite in Europe. *Zones 4-7.* p. 925

pumila 'Cox Orange' (Pippin) (England 1830); heavily, hearty bearing tree with medium sized fruit greenish-yellow, having firm crisp and tender flesh, very juicy and aromatic. A fine dessert apple. *Zones 6-8.*   p. 926

pumila 'Golden Delicious'; excellent multi-purpose apple with golden-yellow skin and crisp, firm, aromatic flesh, ripening in late Summer. Most important cultivar in U.S.; originated in West Virginia. Flesh becomes softer with storage. *Zones 4-8.*   p. 926, 927

pumila 'Granny Smith' (Australia); old-time Australian favorite proven to be a consistent producer of large 8 cm very green apples, spotted white, with a fresh tart flavor, excellent for eating fresh, juices or wine-making; outstanding keeper, in cold storage for 6 months, becoming sweeter. Best adapted for mild climate not less than Zone 6, ripening there in early November; available in Chile in May. *Zones 6-9.*   p. 926

pumila 'Jonagold' (Geneva, New York Exper. Sta.); triploid hybrid between the crackling tart 'Jonathan' and the creamy sweet 'Golden Delicious'; heavy producer of apples 8-10 cm dia., yellow-green skin overlaid with coppery red; the flesh is cream-colored, crisp and juicy, of excellent taste and good keeping quality, ripening Mid-September in Zone 6. Eating appeal amongst the best. *Zones 5-8.*   p. 926

pumila 'Jonathan' (New York); very productive widely adapted early-bearing tree with glossy bright red fruit, and snappy crisp flesh, juicy and with rich flavor, one of the top varieties produced in the Central States. *Zones 4-8.*   p. 926

pumila 'McIntosh'; very productive, famous and most popular apple introduced from Ontario, Canada about 1870; dependably bearing crops annually and very hardy; the flat-topped fruit 8 cm dia., the thin skin yellow with bright red blush; white-fleshed, crisp and juicy, one of the best eating varieties, ripening late September. *Zones 3-7.*   p. 926

pumila 'Winesap'; popular apple originating in Kansas; vigorous tree quite winter-hardy, bearing medium-size early fruit abundantly, in color yellow with red coat; solid flesh of subacid, sweet winey taste, aromatic and a good keeper; an all-purpose bruise-resistant apple, now mainly grown in Northwest. Ripens mid-October in Zone 6. Excellent for apple-cider. *Zones 4-8.*   p. 926

pumila 'Winter Banana'; a semi-tropic large, beautiful apple of pale color with red blush and waxy finish; distinctive, tangy aroma. Accepts mild Winters; needs pollenizer. Ripening September-October. *Zones 7-9.*   p. 926

x purpurea ('Lemoinei') (atrosanguinea x pumila); valued and popularly planted for the deep purple color of its blooms, to 3 cm across, later turning pale; said to be the darkest of all crab-apples, seen near Orleans in the Peronne of Central France blooming in early May; tree to 8 m high, with small 2-4 cm ovate leaves, the flowers single or semi-double, followed by small purplish fruit. *Zone 4. p. 837*

x purpurea 'Eleyi', "Blood-apple" or "Jay Darling", U.S.A. (Hesse), cultivar 1920; large shrub to 6 m high, with wide-spreading branches; the ovate leaves reddish when unfolding, later dark green with red midrib, dark purple in Autumn; flowers 3½ cm across deep wine purple, darker than the type; the fruit ovoid, and a beautiful wine red, 3 cm dia., on slender stalks. *Zone 4.*   p. 837

sargentii (Japan); probably the lowest of all crab-apples; deciduous shrub to 2½ m high, with pure white, fragrant flowers; the horizontal branches with ovate leaves 3-8 cm long, often 3-lobed on young branchlets; the blooms 3 cm wide, with petals overlapping in clusters, flowering in May; the pendant little apples bright red. *Zone 4. p. 837*

sieboldii (Japan: Mountains of Honshu, Kyushu), "Toringo crab"; deciduous shrub to 4 m high, with spreading, gracefully arching branches; leaves ovate, 3-6 cm long, and finely toothed; bright pink 2 cm flowers, fading to near white, blooming in April; small fruit red to brownish-yellow, the calyx falling away. *Zone 5.*   p. 836

spectabilis (Cult. in China), old-fashioned "Chinese flowering apple" or "Crab-apple"; deciduous tree to 8 m high, with dark green ovate or elliptic leaves 5-8 cm long; flowers bright pink, to 5 cm across; globose yellow fruit 2½ cm across, of sour taste. *Zone 4.*   p. 837

spectabilis 'Riversii', "River's crab-apple"; valued cultivar with larger flowers 4-5 cm across, rose-pink and very double with 9 to 20 petals, very showy in dense clusters, blooming in May, bearing green to yellow fruit in alternate years. Originated in England 1872. *Zone 4.*   p. 837

'Van Eseltine' (arnoldiana x spectabilis plena), "Double-flowering apple"; deciduous tree with branches of very erect habit; large 4 cm double flowers rich rose-pink and white inside, red in bud; small 2 cm yellow fruit with red cheeks. Very striking when in bloom. Originated 1941 by New York State Exper. Sta., Geneva, N.Y. *Zone 4.*   p. 837

MALVA   *Malvaceae*

alcea (Europe; natural. in Eastern U.S.), "Hollyhock mallow"; perennial to 1 m or more high, the light green basal leaves kidney-shaped and shallowly lobed; the stems hairy, and with leaves palmately divided into 5 narrow segments; flowers of 5 petals light purplish-rose, 5 cm across, in terminal and axillary clusters, blooming early Summer. Zone 4.   p. 457

moschata (Britain to Italy, No. Africa; natural. in No. America), "Musk mallow"; herbaceous perennial with leafy branches 60-80 cm high, the lower leaves kidney-shaped, higher up generally 5-lobed with each lobe jaggedly divided again; the delicate, showy flowers lilac-rose or bluish, 4-5 cm across in axillary and terminal clusters, blooming June-July and followed by interesting, bristly seedpods. Zones 3-9.   p. 458

sylvestris (Mediterran. reg. to Himalayas), "High mallow" or "Algiers mallow"; robust biennial to 1 m, with rounded lobed leaves; rosy-purple flowers with darker stripes, to 4 cm across. *Warm temperate.* Zones 7-9.   p. 458

verticillata crispa (Eurasia, natural. in No. America), "Curled mallow"; very decorative biennial, or annual, branching with erect stems to 1 m or more high, the leaves kidney-shaped 5 to 7-lobed and beautifully crisped; flowers 2-3 cm across, in dense axillary clusters, the white to pinkish petals striped with deep crimson-red; blooming Summer to early Autumn. Used as a salad plant. Zone 6.   p. 458

MALVASTRUM **capense** of hort.:   see ANISODONTEA

MALVAVISCUS   *Malvaceae*

arboreus mexicanus, (Mexico), "Turk's cap"; tall tropical shrub more or less hairy, with narrow ovate, toothed leaves, narrower than the species; flowers hibiscus-like 3 cm long, with scarlet corolla, but which do not open, and with protruding staminal column. Zone 10.   p. 786

MAMILLOPSIS   *Cactaceae*

senilis (Mexico: Chihuahua to Oaxaca); carpet-forming globular to oblong bodies to 20 cm long and 6 cm dia., shiny fresh green; with conical tubercles hidden by white spines, their axils with white hairs and bristles; flowers 6 cm across, red with orange-yellow inside. Zone 10.   p. 162

MAMMEA   *Guttiferae*

americana (West Indies, So. America), the "Mammee apple" or "South American apricot"; handsome tropical tree 10 to 20 m high, with a broad crown of shiny leathery, oval leaves 10-20 cm long; fragrant white 2 cm male and female flowers; in Spring the large globose, russet-brown fruit 8 to 20 cm dia., with rough, bitter skin and orange, apricot-flavored pulp surrounding 1 to 4 round seeds; the pleasantly sweet flesh is eaten raw or cooked; the juice also makes a refreshing drink. *Tropical.* Zone 10.   p. 914

MAMMILLARIA (MAMILLARIA in Backeberg)   *Cactaceae*

albicans (Baja California: Isla Santa Cruz); small columnar cactus, branching and ascending to 20 cm high and 6 cm thick; the conical tubercles in up to 21 spirals, the axils with wool and bristles, and densely covered with interlocking whitish spines; pinkish-white flowers 2 cm dia. *Arid-subtropic.* Zone 10.   p. 164

aureilanata (C. Mexico: San Luis Potosi); attractive small dark green globe to 8 cm dia., with elevated knobs in up to 13 spirals, covered with yellow hair-like spines; small 2 cm rose-purple flowers around the woolly crown. Zone 10.   p. 164

bachmanii (Mexico); handsome elongate globe to 18 cm dia., covered by up to 21 spirals of conical knobs, bearing light brown spines; white-woolly in axils and a ring of small 2 cm deep rose flowers; carmine-red fruit. Zone 10.   p. 164

baxteriana (pacifica) (Baja California Sur, Mexico); elongate globe to 10 cm dia., olive-green with high nipples densely armed with long cream needle spines tipped black; 2 cm flowers yellow marked red. Zone 10.   p. 164

brauneana (N.E. Mexico: Tamaulipas); usually solitary small gray-green globe to 8 cm dia., with pyramidal knobs in up to 34 spirals, white-woolly in axils; hair-like white radials, and awl-shaped central spines reddish; around the apex a ring of small rose flowers purple in center. Zone 10.   p. 165

bravoae (Mexico: Guanajuato); beautiful small globe 6 cm high, glossy bright green, tubercles arranged in dense spirals, almost hidden by spines and wool, radials white, stiff centrals; tiny 1 cm carmine-rose flowers in a ring around apex. Zone 11.   p. 166

bucareliensis (Cent. Mexico: Guanajuato); small depressed bluish-green globe 5 cm high and 8 cm dia., with 4-angled cones in spirals; short radials and stiff central spines tipped black; rose-purple flowers 2 cm across. Zone 10.   p. 165

camptotricha (Pseudomammillaria, Dolichothele) (Mexico: Querétaro), "Birdsnest cactus"; small clustering globes to 5 cm high,

fresh green, with extended nipples and long yellow bristle-like spines often twisted; flowers white, greenish outside, hidden in axils. *Arid-tropical.* Zone 10.   p. 164

candida (Mammilloydia) (C. Mexico: San Luis Potosi), "Snowball cactus"; an exquisite 15 cm globe closely tubercled and covered with a multitude of pure white radial spines; clustering 2 cm flowers rose-colored. *Arid-tropical.* Zone 10.   p. 164

centricirrha (magnimamma) (C. Mexico), "Bird's foot" or "Mexican pincushion"; clustering globe, to 10 cm, dark green and milky, with large conic tubercles topped with 3-5 recurved horn-colored spines; 2 cm carmine-red flowers from near apex. According to Backeberg and Hortus, the very similar M. magnimamma has cream-colored flowers. *Arid-tropical.* Zone 10.   p. 165

cerralboa (Mexico: Isla Cerralboa, Gulf of California); seen in extremely arid area habitat, elongate bodies to 15 cm long, 6 cm thick, clustering erect and prostrate, yellowish-green, with multiple small cones, densely covered with yellowish spines; small 1 cm flowers, prob. white. Zone 11.   p. 163

chionocephala (Mexico: Coahuila, Durango); symmetrical, globular plant to 12 cm dia., slowly becoming branched, dark green but the milky tubercles nearly hidden by bristly straw-white radials and short central spines tipped black; 2 cm rose flowers in a ring around apex, followed by glossy crimson-red fruit. *Arid-subtropic.* Zone 10.   p. 165

ebenacantha (Mexico); attractive small depressed globe, with olive-green 4-angled high tubercles tipped by short stiff spines, in upper part with white-woolly cephalia, and a ring of rose-red small flowers. According to Backeberg, insufficiently known. Zone 10.   p. 166

elegans (Mexico: Distrito Federal); lovely elongate globe 5 cm dia., glaucous green, densely tubercled and covered with fine white bristle-like radials and contrasting brown needle-like central spines; small flowers carmine-red, followed by a ring of red fruit 2 cm long. *Arid-subtropic.* Zone 10.   p. 163

elongata (Mexico: Hidalgo), "Golden stars"; small, clustering cylinders to 3 cm thick, light green; tubercles in spirals and covered with yellow, interlacing radial spines; small white flowers. *Arid-tropical.* Zone 10.   p. 174

elongata 'Cristata' "Brain cactus"; beautifully crested form with many snaking ridges, growing larger with age, handsomely covered with golden-yellow spines. For best survival and growth, crests are usually grafted on column cactus. Zone 11.   p. 164

eriacantha (Mexico: Veracruz, Jalapa); small cylindric column to 15 cm high and 5 cm thick, occasionally branching; emerald green conical knobs in up to 13 spirals, with axils woolly and covered by yellow needle spines; canary yellow 2 cm flowers. Zone 11.   p. 164

fasciculata: see ECHINOCEREUS fasciculatus

fragilis (gracilis var.) (Mexico: Hidalgo), "Thimble cactus"; little oblong stem branching toward top, to 8 cm high, bright green, knobs with white radial spines; tiny flowers cream, pinkish outside. *Arid-tropical.* Zone 10.   p. 166

geminispina (bicolor) (C. Mexico: Veracruz to Hidalgo), "Whitey"; small club-shaped plant 8 cm dia., becoming cylindric and clustering; glaucous, with prominent knobs topped by white radials and needle-like white, black-tipped central spines; small 2 cm red flowers in a ring around snowy apex. *Arid-tropical.* Zone 11.   p. 166

glassii var. ascensionis (No. Mexico: Nuevo Leon), col. by Glass and Foster 1971 near Ascension; attractive small white-spined heads 2½ cm thick, forming clusters; reminiscent of M. bocasana; flowers pale pink with red center, larger than the species. Zone 10.   p. 167

glassii var. nominis-dulcis (Mexico: Nuevo Leon); col. by A. Lau at 2700 m alt.; diminutive 2-3 cm globe densely covered by fine, hair-like white radials, and hooked brown-red central spines; small starry 2 cm light purple flowers around apex. Zone 10.   p. 166

gracilis pulchella (Mexico: Hidalgo); slender cylindric fresh green columns to 10 cm high and 2 to 3 cm thick, freely branching and forming mounds; the axils partially woolly and densely covered with bristly spines; small yellowish flowers. Zone 10.   p. 165

hahniana (Mexico: Guanajuato, Querétaro), "Old lady cactus"; attractive little globe, 10 cm dia., rich green with long and curly snowy-white hair-like bristles and red-tipped spines; 2 cm flowers violet-red. *Arid-tropical.* Zone 10.   p. 165

herrerae (Mexico: Querétaro); attractive cylindric globe, seldom suckering, to 4 cm dia., densely covered with appressed white, hair-like radials, and short erect needle-spines; small 2 cm purple flowers. *Arid-tropical.* Zone 11.   p. 166

huizilipochtli (Mexico: Tomellin Canyon); ferocious-looking small globe, collected by A. Lau; the spherical body entirely covered by circles of white radials, while long curved brown tipped central spines present a formidable defense; small carmine-rose flowers from upper axils. Zone 10.   p. 166

longicoma (Mexico: San Luis Potosi); robust small globe 5 cm wide, tubercles dense with hair-like and silky whitish radials, the central spines brown, some with hooks; flowers white suffused with rose. *Arid-tropical. Zone 10.*   p. 165

longiflora (Krainzia) (No. Mexico: Durango); small globe 5 cm dia. and to 6 cm high, solitary or clustering, the conical tubercles in 5 and 8 spirals; the radial spines bristle-like pubescent, red-brown central spines partially ferociously hooked 15 mm long; carmine-rose flowers. *Zone 10.*   p. 166

longimamma (Dolichothele) (C. Mexico), "Finger-mound"; interesting plant of globular shape to 10 cm high but consisting almost entirely of cylindrical knobs to 5 cm long, deep green and soft-fleshy, tipped with scattered soft pale spines; flowers yellow to 6 cm across. *Arid-tropical. Zone 10.*   p. 156

louisae (Mexico: Baja California); small globular to elongate body to 3 cm high, having fibrous roots, at home near Socorro; the conical tubercles tipped with white wool and pale spines; relatively large white flowers lined with purple, 4 cm across. *Zone 11.*   p. 163

magnimamma of hort. see M. centricirrha (red-flowered). The true and similar M. magnimamma has cream flowers; according to Britton-rose 1923, this species also known as Neomammillaria magnimamma, together with 65 other synonyms.

martinezii (So. Mexico: Oaxaca); handsome small cylindric plant to 14 cm high, close to albilanata, entirely covered with white-wooly axils and pale brown spines tipped brown, longer than albilanata, as well as dense straw-white radials topping the neatly spirally arranged conical tubercles; small 1 cm rosy flowers in a ring around wooly apex. *Zone 11.*   p. 166

melanocentra (Texas, New Mexico; No. Mexico: Nuevo Leon, Coahuila); globe to 16 cm high and 9 cm thick and glaucous green, pointed tubercles pyramidal, set with needle-like, starry spreading spines pale yellow to black; 2 cm flowers pinkish-red. *Zone 9. p. 166*

multiseta (Mexico: Puebla); globular to elongate small cactus, usually solitary, to 12 cm high and 8 cm dia., olive-green with 4-angled pyramidal knobs, white-woolly in axils and bearing numerous bristle-spines and few brown-tipped needle spines; small bell-shaped rose flowers. *Zone 10.*   p. 167

nejapensis (Mexico: Oaxaca); beautiful elongate clustering globe to 15 cm high, with fresh green, prominent nipples tipped with white-woolly tufts, and sets of stout glistening white spines, red-brown at the extreme tip, the axils also filled with white wool especially near apex; yellow flowers shaded with red-purple. The curious crested form shown on pg. 205 is an old plant in California, with contorted ribs in shape of a smiling face and which the grower called "Smiling Jack". *Arid-tropical. Zones 10-11.*   p. 205

oteroi (So. Mexico: Oaxaca); profusely clustering, low globular cactus 3 to 4 cm dia. and 2 to 3 cm high, dull green slender tubercles tipped by white-woolly areoles and spreading pale spines; small flowers with pale pink petals having cerise midband. *Zone 11. p. 166*

parkinsonii (C. Mexico: Hidalgo to Querétaro), "Owl's eyes"; clustering small depressed globe or elongate to 20 cm high and to 8 cm thick, glaucous green, tubercles neatly arranged and topped by white radials and prominent central spines tipped brown; flowers yellowish with brown-pink center, 2 cm long; 1 cm scarlet fruit. *Zone 10.*   p. 164

parkinsonii cristata; a clustered old plant partially becoming deformed into fasciations and developing crests shaped like a down-turned mouth, accented by the straw-colored spines, giving rise to the name "Sadsack" in this particular plant 25 cm across; photographed at Crestview Nursery, Carlsbad, California. *Arid-tropical. Zone 10-11.*   p. 205

pennispinosa (Mexico: Coahuila); solitary small globe 3 cm dia. and 3 cm high, longer if grafted; the axils with some wool, and knobs densely set with distinct pale orange-yellow hooked spines, these covered with fuzzy hairs; flowers white with red bands. *Zone 10.*   p. 167

prolifera haitiensis (Haiti), "Little candles"; cluster-forming small dark green globes or elongate to 6 cm long and 4 cm dia., covered by rounded or conical knobs, dense with pale bristle-spines and hairy needle spines; 1 cm cream-colored flowers; fruit coral-red. *Zone 10.*   p. 167

saboae var. saboae (N.W. Mexico: Chihuahua); exquisite true miniature cactus, found on the Sierra Madre Occidental at about 2000 m altitude; clustering 2½ cm globes covered with 2-3 mm all radial spines; showy delicate rose-pink flowers crocus-like with slender tubes. *Zone 11.*   p. 166

spinosissima (Mexico: Morelos, Puebla, Michoacan, Guerreo); solitary globular bluish-green body, later columnar to 30 cm long and 10 cm dia.; the conical knobs densely set with pale bristle-spines and some needle spines; the axils with wool, 2 cm rose-red flowers around the bristly apex. *Zone 10.*   p. 167

tegelbergiana (Mexico: Chiapas); beautiful, perfect little globe about 8 cm dia., dense with small dark green tubercles, completely clothed with interlacing, thin white radials and stouter central spines tipped black-brown; the axils toward apex filled with white wool; small flowers rosy-red in a ring around apex. *Arid-tropical. Zone 11.*   p. 167

verhaertiana (Mexico: Baja California); club-shaped to 5 cm dia., later becoming cylindric and 30 cm long, branching from the base and forming colonies; rounded green nipples, woolly in axils and tipped by numerous interwoven white radials and long brownish needle spines; small rosy flowers tipped white. *Zone 10.*   p. 167

winteriae (No. Mexico: Nuevo Leon, near Monterrey); depressed globe to 10 cm wide, with large dark green 4-angled fleshy knobs, the axils with white wool, grayish radials some short, others long needle-like and tipped brown; flowers sulphur-yellow outside and variegated red inside. *Zone 10.*   p. 167

zeilmanniana (Mexico: Guanajuato), "Strawberry cactus"; choice small globe 7 cm high, glossy green, with high cylindrical knobs covered by long white interlaced, soft radials, and reddish central spines, one hooked; 2 cm flowers bright violet-purple. *Arid-tropical. Zone 10.*   p. 167

MAMMILLOYDIA candida (Zander):
see MAMMILLARIA candida (Hortus 3)

MANDEVILLA   *Apocynaceae*
x amabilis (Dipladenia x amoena) (splendens hybrid); woody twiner, having large corrugated, oblong leaves containing milky sap; very showy flowers 8-10 cm across, opening blush pink but changing to deep rose; very floriferous. *Zone 10.*   p. 264

x amabilis 'Alice du Pont' (Dipladenia) (formerly 'Splendens hybrid'); grown by Longwood Gardens (Baileya March 1962), a hybrid apparently derived from M. splendens, glabra, and superba. Woody climber growing to perhaps 10 m long; leaves opposite, dark green, rugose, lustrous, oblong-elliptic, 12-20 cm long; inflorescence a raceme from alternate leaf axils, with large blossoms, funnel-shaped to 12 cm dia., dawn pink with darker throat, turning dark rose. *Tropical. Zones 10-11.*   p. 264

boliviensis (Dipladenia) (Bolivia), "White dipladenia"; free-blooming shrubby climber with slender branches; shining green oblong, slender pointed 5-8 cm leaves; and 5 cm funnel-form flowers white, with orange-yellow throat, in axillary racemes. *Subtropic. Zone 10.*   p. 264

laxa (suaveolens) (Argentina, Bolivia), the "Chilean jasmine"; woody vine with opposite, thin-leathery, ovate-cordate leaves 8-15 cm long, bright green and smooth, purplish to grayish beneath, on brownish wiry twining stems covered by rough warts; pure white funnel-shaped flowers 5 cm across and deliciously fragrant, in racemes of 6-8 or more, in Summer. *Subtropic. Zones 9-10.*   p. 264

sanderi (Dipladenia) (So. Brazil), "Rose dipladenia"; woody shrub of compact habit, with wiry stems having milky sap; small leathery 4-5 cm ovate leaves glossy green, bronzy beneath; the 6-8 cm flowers rose-pink with pure yellow throat. A beautiful climber, blooming throughout the year in good light, even as a smaller, shrub-like plant; requires copious watering when growing, with good drainage. The cv. 'Red Riding Hood' as offered by California nurseries is a sturdy plant only slowly vining, with flowers rich rosy-red. *Zones 9-10.*   p. 264

splendens (Dipladenia) (S.E. Brazil); woody twiner with stems finely hairy, and with milky sap; opposite, thin-textured leaves broadly elliptic, to 20 cm long; clusters of showy flowers 8-10 cm across, in a lovely rose-pink. *Tropical. Zones 10-11.*   p. 264

MANDRAGORA   *Solanaceae*
officinarum (So. Europe), "Devil's apples" or "Mandrake"; herbaceous perennial steeped in superstition, with thick spindle-shaped tuberous roots often divided into two leg-like parts; the large wavy, ovate leaves to 30 cm long grow from the tips of the roots; bell-shaped, yellowish or purplish 3 cm flowers cradled in the foliage, followed by the juicy berries supposedly poisonous. During the Middle Ages associated with witchcraft, and considered an aphrodisiac. The roots contain the alkaloid hyoscyamine, which doctors have used as an anaesthetic drug in medicine. *Zone 8.*   p. 543

MANETTIA   *Rubiaceae*
inflata (bicolor) (Paraguay, Uruguay), "Firecracker plant"; twining herb with threadlike stems, thin-fleshy, green, ovate leaves and attractive solitary, 2 cm, tubular, waxy flowers from the axils, flask-like and vivid yellow, the lower part of the tube densely covered with bright scarlet bristles, giving the appearance of a red corolla tipped yellow. *Subtropic. Zone 10.*   p. 296

MANGIFERA   *Anacardiaceae*
indica (No. India, Burma, Malaya), the "Mango" tree; with large, spreading, evergreen crown, 18-30 m high, and grown for its delicious fruit all over the tropics; leathery, lanceolate leaves to 40 cm long; small pinkish flowers in terminal panicles, followed by large, variably

yellow to reddish sweet-fleshy fruit averaging 12 cm long, containing the large adhering stone. *Tropical. Zone 10.* p. 636

indica 'Haden', a "Mango"; good commercial tropical cultivar with large 10 cm fragrant fruit, of good quality, greenish to red and covered with silvery glaucescence; low fiber content. Originated in Coconut Grove, Florida. *Zone 11.* p. 903

indica 'Joe Welch'; beautiful large mango fruit 10-15 cm long, yellow with red cheeks, and very sweet flesh. Very frost-sensitive. *Tropical. Zone 11.* p. 903

MANGLIETIA *Magnoliaceae*
fordiana (So. China: Hong Kong); evergreen tree 7-15 m tall, with gray bark smooth except for leaf scars; the lanceolate thick leathery leaves 10-16 cm long; scented flowers white, tinged pink, the sepals and petals similar, arranged in 3 rings of three, cup-shaped but later spreading; followed by the cone-like fruit, turning purplish and eventually split open. *Zone 9.* p. 779

MANIHOT *Euphorbiaceae*
esculenta (Brazil: Goias), "Tapioca" or "Manioc"; evergreen bush to 3 m high, with milky juice and long tuberous roots; leaves deeply parted into 3-7 lobes, 35 cm wide; flowers without petals. The sturdy, tuberous, edible roots yield tapioca, cassava and starch. The poison in the roots is destroyed by cooking. A most important root-crop in tropical cultivation. *Tropical. Zone 10.* p. 725

MANILKARA *Sapotaceae*
zapota (Achras) (C. America), "Sapodilla" or "Chicle tree"; evergreen tree to 20 m with milky sap; obovate leaves to 40 cm long; small white flowers; fruit ovoid to 15 cm long, russet-orange, with reddish, sweet, edible flesh. Usually made into jelly or marmalade. From the kernels of the seed, a candy confection is made in Costa Rica. *Zones 10-11.* p. 941

MANILTOA *Leguminosae*
gemmipara (New Guinea); handsome tree 5-20 m high, with short trunk, large pinnate leaves of leathery shining leaflets; when in new flush hanging limply on the young shoots, white or pink in color; white flowers in large globular clusters, subtended by red bracts. *Zones 10-11.* p. 765

MARANTA *Marantaceae*
arundinacea 'Variegata' ('Phrynium micholitzii') (Mexico to So. America), "Arrow-root"; erect herb to 1 m high, with starchy roots and forking, zigzag branches; in this variegated form having the narrow lance-shaped, light green, papery leaves prettily variegated or margined with white; variegation passing through the leaf, showing underneath. *Tropical. Zone 10.* p. 459

leuconeura erythroneura (Brazil: Estado do Rio), the beautiful "Red-veined prayer plant" from the Organ Mts. near Petropolis; a low-growing herbaceous plant, the foliage more or less horizontal with the ground; 10 to 12 cm leaves obovate, on short winged petioles, patterned with a herringbone design of carmine-red veins over light yellow-green to dark velvety olive-green, jagged silvery green along center; reddish beneath except green along center; flowers whitish with purple eye. *Tropical. Zone 12.* p. 71, 459

leuconeura kerchoveana (Brazil) "Prayer plant" or "Rabbit's tracks"; low-growing plant with 15 cm oval leaves mostly hugging the ground, and folding upward in the evening; the surface is vivid to pale grayish-green, more pronounced along the midrib and feathering along the veins, with a row of chocolate, later dark green, blotches on either side; blotched red beneath; small flowers white, striped purple, in a raceme. *Tropical. Zone 11.* p. 71

MARCGRAVIA *Marcgraviaceae*
paradoxa (Puerto Rico), "Bejuco de palma"; epiphytic climber of the rainforest, forming two stages; the stem-rooting juvenile, with small ovate leaves appressed to the tree bark; later the maturity stage with larger leathery, long-elliptic 12 cm leaves on woody, pendent stems, and forming curious green and red club-like inflorescence in circular clusters. The name is often confused with an aroid, Monstera dubia in the juvenile stage of shingled leaves. *Tropical.*
Zones 10-11. p. 283

rectiflora (Cuba, Hispaniola, Puerto Rico), "Shingle plant"; climbing epiphytic shrub; the sterile shoots with small 2 cm leaves clinging shingle-like to tree bark; the mature, freely pendant fruiting branches with 12 cm lanceolate, leathery leaves, tipped by greenish inflorescence, followed by globular fruit capsules. *Tropical. Zone 10.* p. 283

MARIPA *Convolvulaceae*
passifloroides (Asystasia) (Trop. America); rambling clamberer with glossy ovate leaves; flowers open bell-shaped with purple flushed with pink, 5 cm across. *Tropical. Zones 10-11.* p. 275

MARKHAMIA *Bignoniaceae*
lutea (as Dolichandrone in Florida and California hort.) (Trop.

Africa: Ghana, Nigeria, Cameroon); beautiful evergreen tree to 8 m high, with rough, blackish bark; pinnate leaves of 7-11 glossy green leaflets to 18 cm long, and a profusion of large clustered 6 cm trumpet flowers with flaring lobes, golden-yellow lined with red. *Zone 10.* p. 665

MARLIEREA *Myrtaceae*
edulis (Brazil), "Cambuca"; evergreen fruiting tree with spreading branches; obovate corrugated, leathery glossy green leaves 15-20 cm long, with pale veins and lightly pubescent beneath; the globular, edible fruit orange-yellow 3-4 cm dia., in the shape of a pomegranate. *Tropical. Zone. 10.* p. 916

MARNIERA chrysocardium (Backeberg): see EPIPHYLLUM (Hortus)

MARRUBIUM *Labiatae*
incanum (Italy, Sicily to Balkan Pen.), "Silver horehound"; bitter-aromatic, white-woolly perennial 40-70 cm high, with opposite ovate, suede-textured leaves 5 cm long, crenate at margins; the small white, two-lipped flowers in whorls along axils of branches, in late Summer. Grown for its handsome foliage. *Zones 4-10.* p. 434

vulgare (W. Asia, So. Europe, No. Africa, Canary Isl., natural. in No. America), "Horehound"; bitter-aromatic white-woolly perennial 50-90 cm high, with opposite round-ovate leaves 4-5 cm long, crenate at margins; the small two-lipped whitish flowers appear in axillary clusters from June to August. The annual stems and leaves are dried and used in herb tea; also in candied confections and for cough medicines. *Zone 3.* p. 531

MARSILEA *Marsileaceae (Filices)*
drummondii (W. Australia), "Water-clover"; aquatic perennial tufted herb with creeping rhizome rooting at nodes, and floating 4-parted clover-like leaves 8 cm dia., the fan-like leaflets covered with whitish hairs, and with wavy margins, on long slender stalks; the bean-like spore cases or fruiting bodies at the base of leaf stalks. *Subtropic. Zone 10.* p. 326

vestita (Southern U.S. and West Indies), "Cinquefoil"; rhizomatous under-water or swamp fern with 4-parted silky, wedge-shaped leaves, floating in deep water or erect on land or shallow water. *Zones 10-12.* p. 128

MASCARENA (Zander): see HYOPHORBE (Hortus 3, Dransfield)

MASDEVALLIA *Orchidaceae*
infracta (Brazil, Perú); small tufted epiphyte with spatulate leaves but without pseudobulbs; the flowers of fantastic shape, the prominent sepals extending into long tails, upper sepal whitish shaded yellow, lower sepals violet-purple inside and tails yellow, (May-July). *Tropical. Zones 11-12.* p. 91

militaris (ignea) (Colombia); clustering species with rigid leaves to 10 cm long, stalked at base; handsome inflorescence, a long stalk 35 cm tall with solitary flowers 6 cm across, bright cinnabar-red, the dorsal sepal prolonged into linear tail (Summer). *Subtropic. Zone 11.* p. 91

veitchiana (Andes of Perú to 4000 m); a most beautiful species with densely tufted leathery, dark green leaves linear oblong and shining, and a wiry stalk bearing 1 or 2 showy, bright orange-scarlet flowers to 15 cm long, the dorsal sepal with long tail, the tailed lateral sepals partly grown together, closely studded with purple hairs (May-July). *Humid-subtropic. Zones 10-11.* p. 91

MATRICARIA *Compositae*
capensis hort.: see CHRYSANTHEMUM parthenium
maritima: see TRIPLEUROSPERMUM maritimum (Hortus)
recutita (M. chamomilla) (Chamomilla recutita) (Europe to No. Asia; natural. in E. No. America), "Sweet Chamomile" or "German Camomile"; prolific annual herb 30 to 75 cm high, with sweetly scented foliage of apple flavor, twice pinnate leaves 6 cm long, finely divided into linear segments; the floral heads 3 cm across, having white ray-florets encircling the raised yellow cushion disc, which is not hollow. The flowers are used medicinally in herbal tea against digestive disorders; externally for sores and inflammation. *Zone 6 as Annual.* p. 524, 527

MATTEUCCIA *Polypodiaceae (Filices)*
orientalis (Japan, Kuril, Korea, China to Sikkim Himalaya), "Oriental Ostrich fern"; stout rhizome bearing pinnate fronds, the sterile leaves longer than the fertiles, 30-50 cm long, on scaly stalks; 8-20 pairs of flat, smooth pinnae lobed at margins. Deciduous in cold climates. *Zones 6-8.* p. 134

pensylvanica (No. America, Newfoundland to Alaska, to Virginia, So. Dakota and Br. Colombia), "American ostrich fern"; largest fern in Temperate No. America, having leathery pinnate fronds possibly 2-3 m long, under favorable conditions, on stalks with green 4-angled rachis; sterile fronds leafy, longer than fertile leaves, forming a vase-like crown. *Zones 2-8.* p. 134

struthiopteris (Onoclea) (E. No. America, No. Europe to Caucasus), "Ostrich fern"; crown of elegant pinnate fronds 1-1½ m long, from erect rootstock; the fertile pinnae contracted and short, growing from the middle of crown. *Zones 3-8.* p. 134

MATTHIOLA *Cruciferae*
   incana, "Stocks" or "Gilliflower"; short-lived perennial, well-known for its spicy-sweet fragrance, by origin a semi-shrubby plant, usually grown as a biennial and lately as annual (10-14 weeks); at home around the Mediterranean from the Canary Islands to Asia Minor; cool-temperature plant highly developed, with brittle stems and grayish pubescent leaves, the popular branching stocks in the trade as 'Giants of California' or 'Imperial stocks', 45-60 cm high, with spike-like clusters of mostly double, quite fragrant flowers 3 cm wide, in many pastel or vivid colors from rose, apricot and red to blue, violet, lavender, even canary yellow and white. Normally blooming from April to Fall in cool climate. *Zone 9.* p. 412
   incana 'Rosea', "Imperial stocks"; one of the many color forms, soft pink, and a good commercial cultivar, to 60 cm high. *Zone 9.* p. 412
   incana 'Rubra'; excellent color variation of the old-fashioned garden "Stocks", with sweet-scented crimson-red, single flowers, in long racemes, produced on sturdy plants, growing as perennial where photographed in Durban, Natal, So. Africa. *Zone 9.* p. 412
   sinuata (Britain to Greece), "Greek gilliflower" or "Sea stocks"; short biennial or perennial subshrub 20-60 cm high, with white-felted gray leaves deeply lobed; small clusters of purple flowers, 2½ cm across, sweet-scented at night, and blooming March to June. *Zone 8.* p. 412

MATUCANA: see BORZICACTUS (Hortus 3)

MAURANDYA: see ASARINA

MAURITIA *Palmae*
   flexuosa (Brazil, Venezuela), "Ita palm"; tall fan palm of the floodlands of the Amazon, with smooth trunks to 40 m high, and 50 cm dia., sometimes swollen; large crown of palmate deep green leaves of rigid texture to 3 m across, cut almost to base, drooping at tips; oblong fruit 8 cm long, covered with reddish scales, in heavy clusters. *Zone 12.* p. 109

MAXILLARIA *Orchidaceae*
   picta (Brazil); epiphyte with ovoid pseudobulbs, each with 1 or 2 thick, strap-shaped leaves; the individual fragrant flowers yellow streaked and dotted purple and chocolate inside, petals incurved, lip white spotted purple. (Oct.-Aug.). Tropical. *Zones 11-12.* p. 91
   punctata (Brazil); small epiphyte with ovoid pseudobulbs, solitary lanceolate leaf; flowers on short stalk, 6 cm across, light yellow, the lip with purple lines. Tropical. *Zones 11-12.* p. 91
   tenuifolia (Mexico); small clustering epiphyte; flattened pseudo-bulbs at intervals on ascending rhizomes, topped by solitary, linear leaves almost hiding the small, individually stalked, strongly scented flowers, sepals and petals dark rusty red, lip spotted blood-red on yellow base, (Dec.-June). Tropical. *Zones 11-12.* p. 91

MAYTENUS *Celastraceae*
   boaria (Chile), "Mayten tree"; evergreen shrub 3 m high, with time growing into a tree to 10 m, with graceful spreading and pendant branches; the leathery leaves lanceolate 3-5 cm long, grayish-green and glistening in the sunlight; small 1 cm greenish-yellow flowers in axillary clusters; fruit a leathery 1 to 3-celled capsule, containing the seeds covered by scarlet aril or fleshy coat. Planted as street tree in So. California and Florida. *Zone 9.* p. 684
   dryandri (Catha dryandra), "Madeira bittersweet"; evergreen shrub 1-2 m high, with leathery oblanceolate leaves, crenate at margins, and soft-downy beneath; small white 5-petalled flowers blooming in Mid-winter; followed by leathery fruit capsules. *Zone 10.* p. 684
   pittieri (No. Venezuela), "Zapatero"; evergreen shrub or small tree from the humid tropical forest, 3 to 6 m high; leathery, lanceolate alternate leaves 3-7 cm long, crenate at margins; small axillary greenish flowers, in habitat blooming April-May; fruit as small leathery, yellow capsule, opening by two valves, shielding the fleshy pale salmon seed coat (aril). Graceful as street tree, planted along avenidas of Caracas. *Zone 9.* p. 684

MAZUS *Scrophulariaceae*
   reptans (Himalayas), "Wart flower"; tiny mat-forming herb to 5 cm high, rooting at nodes, with toothed obovate 3 cm leaves, and purplish-blue bilabiate flowers, the lower lip spotted white, yellow and purple. *Zone 6.* p. 322

MECONOPSIS *Papaveraceae*
   betonicifolia (W. China: Yunnan, Tibet; Burma), "Blue poppy"; charming perennial, or monocarpic if flowered as a biennial; to 1 m or more high, with ovate leaves to 15 cm long, lightly notched at margins,

whitish-glaucous beneath; flowers sky-blue or purplish, 5 cm across, and with conspicuous yellow stamens in center, June-August blooming. Very popular in Britain. *Zones 6-7.* p. 466
   cambrica (aurantiaca) (W. Europe), "Welsh poppy"; small cool-summer perennial to 50 cm high, with tufted rootstock; basal leaves to 15 cm long, pinnately divided, the segments crenate; solitary flowers yellow to orange, 8 cm across, in June to October. *Zone 6.* p. 466
   grandis (Nepal, Sikkim, Himalayas), "Asiatic poppy"; perennial with erect, bristly stems to 1 m or more high; basal and lower leaves oblanceolate, to 20 cm long, entire or toothed; vivid blue flowers to 12 cm across, in upper leaf axils or on terminal stalks. *Zone 6.* p. 466
   napaulensis (E. Himalayas to W. China), "Satin poppy"; handsome monocarpic biennial or short lived perennial 2 m or more high, basal leaves in rosette to 50 cm long, pinnately cut or lobed and covered by reddish bristles; upper leaves sessile, entire or lobed; poppy-like flowers to 8 cm across, rose-red, sometimes purple or blue, solitary in upper leaf axils. *Zone 6.* p. 467
   regia (Nepal Himalaya), "Royal poppy"; beautiful herbaceous perennial or monocarpic biennial to 1 m or more high, covered by soft silvery hairs; basal winter-rosette of leaves narrow elliptic, to 40 cm long, the leaves on branched stems lobed; toward apex the long-stalked yellow poppy-flowers to 8 cm across, blooming in June. *Zone 6.* p. 467
   x sheldonii 'Branklyn' (betonicifolia x grandis); superb British hybrid of Himalayan heritage, with larger, vivid sky-blue flowers 12-15 cm across, on stalklets in upper leaf axils; perennial with basal winter-rosettes of bristly leaves, and leafy stems to 120 cm high. *Zone 6.* p. 467

MEDICAGO *Leguminosae*
   arborea (Mediterran. reg., Portugal), "Moon trifoil" or "Medick"; evergreen dense shrub to 4 m high, usually much smaller, with new branches white-hairy; leaves compound of 3 obovate leaflets 2 cm long and silky beneath; golden-yellow flowers pea-like in short clusters, opening gradually from May to September; the fruit a flat, spiral pod. *Zone 10.* p. 765

MEDINILLA *Melastomataceae*
   astronoides (Malaya); interesting tropical shrub seen in col. Botanic Garden Singapore, having large, broad-ovate, thick-leathery leaves about 25 cm long, with depressed yellow veins, palmately arranged; the inflorescence a pyramidal cone of densely packed tubular flowers, rose-pink except for the spreading white corolla lobes at apex. *Zone 11.* p. 787
   magnifica (Philippines, Java), "Rose grape"; gorgeous tropical evergreen shrub to 2 m high, with angled woody branches and large, opposite, sessile, thick-leathery leaves to 30 cm long and with ivory midrib; striking inflorescence in a pendulous panicle to 30 cm long, of carmine-red flowers with purple anthers and great showy pink bracts. *Zone 11.* p. 78, 787

MEEHANIA *Labiatae*
   urticifolia (China, Japan, Korea), "Creeping mint"; low stoloniferous herbaceous perennial with usually trailing, 4-angled stems, the opposite triangular to cordate, toothed leaves to 10 cm long; blooms on one-sided spikes to 12 cm long, with trumpet-shaped blue-purple flowers 4-5 cm long, in April-May. *Zone 4.* p. 316

MEGAKEPASMA *Acanthaceae*
   erythrochlamys (Adhatoda cydoniifolia) (Venezuela), "Brazilian red-cloak" or "Red justicia"; showy tropical shrub to 3 m high, with appressed reddish hairs; stout stems with broad ovate leaves 12 to 30 cm long, dark green with pink midrib; inflorescence with conspicuous crimson bracts and two-lipped white flowers. *Zone 10.* p. 630

MEGACLINIUM purpureorhachis:
   refer to BULBOPHYLLUM purp. (Hawkes)

MELALEUCA *Myrtaceae*
   leucadendron (Australia, New Caledonia, Malaya), "Paper bark"; slender tree to 10 m, its undulate trunk with papery white bark, peeling off in broad strips; lanceolate 10 cm rigid bluish-green leaves, softly downy when young, with prominent veining and bearing masses of honey-laden cream fragrant flowers in fluffy terminal spikes 8-15 cm long; the long stamens may be variable whitish, greenish-yellow, pink or purple; a very resistant tree in arid areas, and blooming June to October. The leaves have up to 7 longitudinal veins, in contrast to M. quinquenervia which is often seen in horticulture as M. leucadendron (leucodendron). *Zone 9.* p. 802
   leucadendron in hort.: see M. quinquenervia
   nesophylla (W. Australia), "Western tea myrtle"; shrub or small tree to 6 m high, with thick spongy bark, peeling in long strips; the branches dense with narrow oblong 2-3 cm leaves; branchlets tipped by globular heads of rose-pink or lilac staminal flowers 2-3 cm across. *Zones 9-10.* p. 802

quinquenervia (E. Australia, New Guinea), "Cajeput tree", often sold as M. leucadendron; evergreen tree with thorny green trunk to 12 m; pendulous branches with narrow, stiff, pale green leaves 5-10 cm long, the young foliage covered with silky pubescence; fluffy flowers lemon-white, occasionally purple, with bundles of long stamens in short spikes. The leaves of this species have 5 longitudinal veins, in contrast to M. leucadendron which have up to 7 veins. *Zone 9.* p. 802

MELAMPYRUM *Scrophulariaceae*
nemorosum (Europe: Pyrenees to Alps and north), "Cowwheat"; charming woodland perennial or annual of semi-parasitic character, with opposite, ovate leaves; the stems bearing terminal inflorescence of colorful flowers, 2-3 cm long, having purple bracts, hairy red calyx, and corolla orange-yellow toward apex, blooming June to August; photographed in Thuringia Forest. *Zone 5.* p. 504

MELANDRIUM rubrum: see SILENE dioica

MELANTHIUM *Liliaceae*
virginicum (N.Y. to Indiana, Florida and Texas), "Bunchflower"; stout plant with thick rootstock; erect stem to 1½ m high, and narrow leaves 30 cm long; many small greenish-cream flowers in a much branched panicle, held above the foliage, in July. *Zone 5.* p. 246

MELASTOMA *Melastomataceae*
candidum (Taiwan to Southeast Asia and Philippines); shrub to 3 m high, with nearly cylindrical, brown-scaly branches; oblong-ovate leaves 12 cm long, with up to 7 longitudinal veins, and bristly above; very showy, fragrant flowers, the flaring petals white or pink, 4-8 cm across, the calyx gray-hairy; summer-blooming. *Zone 10.* p. 787

MELIA *Meliaceae*
azedarach (Azadirachta; Antelaea azadirachta) (No. India, Himalayas, China), "Bead-tree", "China-berry", "Indian lilac"; spreading, partially deciduous tree to 20 m, naturalized in Europe and Southern U.S.; handsome pinnate and bipinnate foliage 25 to 80 cm long, with flat, lanceolate toothed leaflets 4-8 cm long, in lower part of tree also tripinnate; clusters of fragrant, 2 cm pale lavender flowers with purple stamens in loose panicles, blooming April-May in Southern U.S., in India throughout the year; followed by green to brownish but poisonous 2 cm berries usually during a brief leafless stage. In India seed extract has been found to have insecticidal properties, primarily against locusts, and has been proven effective also against other insects by the U.S. Dept. of Agric. in tests since 1979. The two species Melia azedarach and indica are confused in literature, but both are authenticated in Corner, Wayside Trees of Malaya, and followed up by my personal visits to habitats and collections in India. *Zones 8-10.* p. 789
azedarach umbraculifera, "Texas umbrella tree"; tree of weeping appearance, with foliage drooping from spreading branches giving an umbrella effect; ideal to provide shade and especially suited to hot and arid areas. *Zone 7.* p. 789
indica (Azadirachta indica) (India, Sri Lanka to Indonesia, Java), "Nim" or "Neem tree" or "Pride of India", "Margosa" on Ceylon; stately tropical tree to 8 m high, forming bushy crown, partially evergreen, and sacred to Hindus; bark gray, becoming ridged and flaky with age; leaves pinnate 20-40 cm long, with 9 to 15 or more light green ovate-lanceolate, thin leaflets 8-10 cm long, usually toothed at sides and distinctly curved backwards; small white fragrant flowers 1 cm across, widely spaced along communal stalk, a few opening each day; followed by round or ovoid 2 cm fruit, green and ripening to yellow, pulpy inside and containing seed. A strongly aromatic oil is obtained from the seed, much valued in native medicine. *Zones 9-10.* p. 789

MELIANTHUS *Melianthaceae*
major (South Africa), "Honey bush"; evergreen semi-woody shrub having widely creeping roots and herb-like stems erect to 3 m high or sprawling, with striking pinnate foliage 20-30 cm long, the deeply serrate, soft-fleshy leaflets in pairs, glaucous green above, grayish beneath; strong-scented when bruised. Reddish-brown 3 cm flowers in dense racemes secreting honey. *Zone 10.* p. 789

MELICA *Gramineae*
nutans (uniflora) (Europe to S.W. Asia), "Nodding melic grass" or "Pendant pearl grass"; robust perennial to 60 cm high, with thin rhizomes; angular stems loosely clustered and slender; bright green lanceolate leaves flat or rolled, to 20 cm long, short-hairy on upper surface; inflorescence with purplish spikelets in arching, loose racemes. *Zone 6.* p. 560

MELILOTUS *Leguminosae*
alba (Eurasia, natural. in No. America), "White sweet clover" or "White melilot"; aromatic biennial of the Old World, growing to the size of a small bush to 1 m high or more; leaves of 3 leaflets 3-4 cm long and faintly toothed, scented when dry; small 1 cm

white flowers in slender racemes, blooming May to September, and of sweet fragrance, attractive to bees for its sweet nectar. *Zone 3.* p. 442

MELICOCCUS *Sapindaceae*
bijugatus (Melicocca) (Cent. America, West Indies), "Spanish lime"; a tropical tree to 20 m high, with grayish bark and spreading branches; handsome light green evergreen foliage, the leaves alternate pinnate having 4-6 leaflets 10 cm long; small fragrant flowers with 4-5 petals; on female trees followed by round or ellipsoid green fruit 2-3 cm dia., with leathery green skin; the juicy pulp is yellowish-pink translucent, popular locally eaten fresh, especially by children, having spritely acid flavor, and a good thirst quencher. *Zone 10.* p. 938

MELIOSMA *Sabiaceae*
rhoifolia (Taiwan), "Varnish-tree-leaved meliosma"; evergreen tree of medium size, with odd-pinnate foliage of lanceolate leaflets variably 5-15 cm long; small flowers in terminal clusters, followed by globose 5 mm fruit. *Zone 9.* p. 863
veitchiorum (Cent. to West China); deciduous tree 7 to 10 m high with stiff-erect branches; leaves pinnate, 40-80 cm long, with 9-10 long-elliptic leaflets; fragrant yellow flowers 5 mm dia., in pendant racemes, blooming in May; berry-like black fruit. *Zone 6.* p. 863

MELISSA *Labiatae*
officinalis (Europe, Asia), "Lemon balm"; aromatic herbaceous perennial to 60 cm high; square stems with ovate toothed leaves fragrant of lemon when bruised, 5-8 cm long; small light yellow or white two-lipped flowers in axillary clusters, in July. Use: fragrant leaves in tea, fruit drinks, salads, stews, also distilled for a most refreshing perfume. Used since ancient times as tranquilizer and medicine to induce sleep; also to calm stomach disorders. *Zones 4-10.* p. 532

MELITTIS *Labiatae*
melissophyllum (C. Europe to Ukraine), "Bastard balm"; aromatic herbaceous perennial with stem 30-40 cm high; the ovate hairy and wrinkled 5 cm leaves are fragrant, the axillary clusters of two-lipped flowers with bell-shaped green calyx, and 2 cm corolla creamy-white spotted pink or purple; attractive to bees, and planted in herb gardens for the pleasant fragrance of its dried stems and foliage. *Zones 6-7.* p. 430, 531

MELOCACTUS *Cactaceae*
intortus (Cactus inaguensis) (West Indies); known as "Turk's cap" in reference to the tall, cylindric cephalium on top of mature plants, its white-woolly head setting off the red bristles making it look like a Turk's cap. Barrel-shaped plant to 1 m tall, with 14-20 ribs and yellow or brown stout spines; small pink flowers 2 cm long; 2-3 cm red fruit. *Arid-tropical. Zone 11.* p. 161
matanzanus (Cuba), "Melon-cactus"; small dome-shaped plant to 8 cm high; deep green, 8-9 rounded ribs, yellowish clusters of recurved spines; at apex a "Turk's cap" of white wool and red bristles; small 2 cm flowers rose-pink. *Arid-tropical. Zone 11.* p. 163
maxonii (Guatemala); depressed little globe, to 15 cm high, fresh green, with notched ribs, and strong recurved yellow to reddish radial spines; flowers rose-red 2 cm long; scarlet-red fruit at top of woolly apex. *Zone 11.* p. 168

MENTHA *Labiatae*
x gentilis 'Variegata' (arvensis x spicata), "Scotch mint"; aromatic perennial 30-50 cm high, with reddish branches, and ovate green leaves to 6 cm long, irregularly variegated with milky-white lines and blotches, the margins sharply toothed; flowers pale purple. The sweet-scented spearmint oil is extracted from the green form. *Zone 5.* p. 532
piperita (Europe incl. Britain), "Peppermint"; herbaceous strong-scented perennial 30-60 cm high, with spreading stolons on square reddish stems and numerous runners, the dark green toothed leaves 10 cm long, containing pungent or pepper-like oil; flowers purple, in terminal spikes, autumn-blooming. Use: leaves for tea and flavoring liqueurs and candy; oil in menthol. *Zones 3-9.* p. 531, 532
piperita var. citrata (Europe), "Orange bergamot mint" or "Lemon mint"; smooth perennial with ovate leaves having depressed veins and crenate margins, the young foliage purplish; autumn-blooming with small purple flowers in terminal spikes; the leafy branches have a characteristic lemon fragrance when crushed; real nice as an evening tea. *Zones 3-9.* p. 532
pulegium (Europe to W. Asia), "English pennyroyal" or "Flea mint"; creeping herbaceous perennial, with pungent, minty scent; shiny green, oval leaves 2 cm long; small lavender-purple flowers in circles or separated whorls along the stem, blooming in August. Very popular because of its delightful fragrance. Used in cookery to flavor sauces with its strong minty aroma; also to make tea for coughs and colds. Once known as Flea mint, having been used as a flea and fly repellent since Middle Ages. *Zone 7.* p. 532

requienii (Corsica), "Corsican mint"; small creeping and spreading herb used for ground cover, with very tiny round, stalked, bright green leaves 1 cm dia., strongly peppermint-scented; flowers pale purple, tiniest in cultivation, in loose whorls, during July-August. Popular as the fragrant "Creme de Menthe plant". Zone 7.　　p. 532

spicata (Europe), "Spearmint"; aromatic perennial 60 cm high, spreading by leafy stolons; square stems with smooth light green leaves 6 cm long and purple flowers in dense terminal spikes. Use: leaves to flavor cold drinks and tea, chewing gum, jelly; valued for its essential distilled oils. Zone 3.　　p. 531

spicata 'Variegata' (Europe), "Variegated spearmint"; ornamental form branching with 4-angled stems, bearing opposite, oval leaves 5 cm long, with crinkled surface, and more or less variegated with creamy-white along margins; small lilac flowers in whorls along terminal spires, in August. Attractive as a sweet pot herb.
Zones 5-10.　　p. 532

suaveolens 'Variegata' (rotundifolia) (So. and W. Europe), "Pineapple mint" or "Variegated apple-mint"; freely branching aromatic perennial, with pubescent oval, crinkly leaves 5 cm long, irregularly variegated creamy-white along edges; inflorescence of pink or whitish flowers in small spikes, during Summer. Much cultivated sweet herb, and used for flavoring jellies, custards, ice cream, stewed fruits, salads, and teas. Zones 5-10.　　p. 532

MENTZELIA   Loasaceae
asperula (Mexico: Sonora; also Arizona), "Stickleaf"; procumbent annual of the Sonoran Desert region, spreading with stems 10-40 cm long; the dark green, fleshy, ovate leaves 10-15 cm long, toothed or lobed at margins, and covered with barbed, spinelike hairs; lovely wide-open flowers, with 1 cm yellow petals, shaded red toward base. Zone 10.　　p. 455

MENYANTHES   Gentianaceae
trifoliata (Temp. No. hemisphere), "Bog-bean"; waterside perennial fleshy herb with creeping root stocks, olive-green trifoliolate leaves and small 1 cm white flowers with recurved petals and beard-like purplish stamens; bog-plant. Zone 3.　　p. 331

MENZIESIA   Ericaceae
pilosa (Mts. of Pennsylvania to Alabama), "Minniebush" or "Allegheny menziesia"; deciduous shrub 60 cm to 2 m high, with obovate leaves to 5 cm long, hairy above and on midrib beneath; nodding urn-shaped flowers in small terminal clusters, the corolla creamy-white, blooming May-June. Zone 4.　　p. 708

purpurea (Japan), "Mock-azalea"; deciduous shrub 1-2 m high, with mainly obovate leaves to 3 cm long and sprinkled with bristles; rather pretty nodding cup-flowers with red corolla 2 cm long, tipped by 5 short lobes, in small clusters, during May-June; probably the best of the genus. Zone 6.　　p. 708

MERREMIA   Convolvulaceae
holubii: see IPOMOEA holubii
tuberosa (Ipomoea) (India), "Wood-rose" or "Ceylon morning-glory"; perennial viner with 20 cm leaves digitately parted into 5-7 narrow lobes; funnel-form yellow flowers, the globular fruit ultimately a woody pod, when ripe opens and which with its persistent large, rounded leathery sepals form the "Wooden" rose some 8-10 cm across; used for decoration, especially in Hawaii. Tropical. Zones 10-11.　　p. 275

umbellata (Operculina), (Mexico: Sinaloa); herbaceous climber, with undivided wrinkled, lanceolate leaves to 10 cm or more long; flowers with pear-shaped calyx and wide-open deep yellow, platter-like corolla. Zone 10.　　p. 275

MERTENSIA   Boraginaceae
longiflora (Brit. Columbia to Montana, so. to California), "Small bluebells" or "Lungwort"; small perennial to 30 cm high, with tuberous roots, forming tufts of rather succulent, oblanceolate blue-green leaves 5-8 cm long; the inflorescence on stiff stalks, in clusters of pendant tubular lavender-blue flowers 2-3 cm long. Shortly after blooming the plant becomes dormant. Zone 3.　　p. 349

virginica (New York to Tennessee and Kansas), "Virginia Blue-bells"; vigorous herbaceous perennial with clustered stems to 60 cm high; oblong elliptic leaves to 20 cm long; the inflorescence in branched one-sided nodding racemes of trumpet-shaped lavender-blue 3 cm flowers, in early Summer. Zone 3.　　p. 348

MERYTA   Araliaceae
sinclairii (New Zealand), "Puka tree"; small evergreen tree with oblong, entire, leathery leaves crowded at ends of branches; blade glossy green with irregular margin, pale, prominent veins, up to 50 cm long; petioles striped brown. Subtropic. Zone 10.　　p. 648

MESEMBRYANTHEMUM: most species formerly listed under this genus are now referred to segregate genera in the Aizoaceae, including Aloinopsis, Aptenia, Argyroderma, Carpobrotus,
Cephalophyllum, Cheiridopsis, Conicosia, Conophytum, Delosperma, Dorotheanthus, Drosanthemum, Faucaria, Fenestraria, Gibbaeum, Glottiphyllum, Hereroa, Hymenocyclus, Lampranthus, Lithops, Oscularia, Pleiospilos, Rhombophyllum, Ruschia, Trichodiadema.
conspicuum: see LAMPRANTHUS conspicuus
cordifolium: see APTENIA cordifolia
crystallinum (Cryophytum) (So. Africa, S.W. Africa; carried off to the shores of California), the California "Ice plant"; annual branching succulent with soft-fleshy stems creeping close to ground; spatulate soft-fleshy leaves 2-5 cm long, grayish-green, thickly covered with crystal-clear bubbles filled with watery fluid and looking like ice-crystals; the starry flowers 1-3 cm across, translucent white tinted lavender. Subtropic. Zone 10.　　p. 147
deltoides: see OSCULARIA deltoides
pomeridianum: see CARPANTHEA pomeridiana
spectabilis: see LAMPRANTHUS spectabilis

MESPILUS   Rosaceae
germanica (W. Europe to Iran), "Medlar" or "Mispel"; mystic small deciduous tree to 6 m, sometimes spiny, often of crooked, quaint habit; oblong leaves to 12 cm long; 3-5 cm white flowers; fruit apple-shaped, brown, 3-5 cm dia., open at top; edible after frost, or made into preserves. Emperor Charlemagne ordered its culture in 800 A.D. Zone 5.　　p. 836, 933

MESUA   Guttiferae
ferrea (India, Thailand, Malay Pen.), "Ceylon ironwood"; handsome tropical evergreen tree to 12 m high; elliptic to narrow-lanceolate leaves to 15 cm long, glaucous beneath, deep red while young; fragrant white flowers 8 cm across, displaying in center a cushion of golden-yellow stamens, in July-August; ovoid 5 cm fruit. The hard wood is used for cabinet work. Zone 10.　　p. 735

METASEQUOIA   Taxodiaceae (Coniferae)
glyptostroboides (Central China: Hupeh), "Dawn redwood"; this "Fossil-age conifer" has been found growing to 30 m high, by Chinese botanists near Chungking (1941) after having been thought extinct; handsome, monoecious, moisture loving tree with reddish bark, symmetric branches and soft textured, deciduous light green needles, two-ranked on horizontal plane; small, nearly globular brown cones, 2 cm dia. Zones 5-8.　　p. 610

METROSIDEROS   Myrtaceae
excelsus (tomentosus) (New Zealand), "Pohotukawa" or "New Zealand Christmas-tree"; handsome tree 10 to 20 m, with spreading branches; oval-pointed, leathery shining green leaves 5-10 cm long, the flowers in terminal clusters of showy brilliant scarlet stamens, exceeding the small petals; blooming at Christmas time during December-January (in N.Z.). Zone 10.　　p. 803

METROXYLON   Palmae
sagus (Indonesia, Philippines, Malaya), "Spineless sago palm" of commerce; tall growing monocarpic feather palm to 12 m high, with smooth trunk becoming 40 cm thick; the pinnate fronds erect and gracefully arching, to 6 m long, the numerous leaflets glossy green; dull yellow 5 cm fruit; flowering only once, with tall branching inflorescence at apex, then leaves fall and tree dies. The trunks contain the edible flour-like sago, extracted from the pith-like center, and the staple food for millions of people in the Far East. Similar to M. rumphii, but sagus does not have spines on the flower stalk. Tropical. Zones 11-12.　　p. 108, 921

MICHELIA   Magnoliaceae
champaca (Himalayas), "Orange champak" or "Fragrant champaca"; tall evergreen tree with smooth gray trunk; narrow ovate, shiny, wavy leaves 20-25 cm long; orange-yellow flowers with 15-20 sepals and petals, 5 cm dia., and intensely fragrant, blooming much of the year and often mentioned in Indian poetry. Champaca oil is distilled from the blooms. Zone 9.　　p. 779

doltsopa (E. Himalayas, Nepal, Tibet, Yunnan); evergreen tree to 25 m high in habitat, with thin-leathery, elliptic leaves 15 cm long; the flowers fragrant and magnolia-like, 8 cm long, having waxy white to yellowish petals, tinged green at base. A timber tree in the Himalayas. Zone 9.　　p. 779

figo (Magnolia fuscata) (South China), "Banana shrub"; evergreen shrub to 3 m high, with velvety brown-hairy twigs and buds; the thick, broad-oval leaves 5 to 10 cm long and shiny green; waxy flowers strongly banana-scented, 3 cm across, with petals creamy-yellow and edged with purple. Very popular in China because of their fragrance, the flowers are also used to perfume hair oil and tea. Zone 8.　　p. 779

MICONIA   Melastomataceae
calvescens (magnifica) (Mexico), "Velvet-tree"; tropical foliage plant with woody stem and beautiful, long ovate, thin leaves to 75 cm

long, velvety green with the sunken primary ribs ivory, and a network of pale green secondary veins; reddish-purple beneath. Flowers insignificant. A show piece for the humid greenhouse. *Tropical. Zone 12.*   *p. 80*

hookeriana (Cyanophyllum) (E. Perú); handsome tropical shrub with large opposite 3-nerved, elliptic leaves to 30 cm long, with a rugose and wrinkled, velvety surface, deep olive-green with broad silvery band following the midrib and branching laterally; the underside hairy and bluish-gray; flowers pale red-brown. *Zone 11.   p. 787*

MICROBIOTA   *Cupressaceae (Coniferae)*
decussata (in Hortus as Platycladus orientalis 'Decussatus') (S.E. Siberia); low evergreen, flat-topped shrub with crowded, spreading branches, small opposite leaves, mostly scale-like; species is unisexual, the female plants with berry-like fruits having almost woody scales that break apart when mature. *Zone 4.*   *p. 583*

MICROLEPIA   *Polypodiaceae (Filices)*
strigosa (speluncae of hort.) (Japan, China, Trop. Asia, Polynesia); robust fern with stout creeping rhizome bearing wiry brown stalks and lacy bipinnate fronds 30-90 cm long, the oblique pinnae dentate, olive-green, thin but hard and somewhat glossy. *Humid-subtropic. Zones 10-11.*   *p. 134*

MILIUM   *Gramineae*
effusum 'Aureum' (Québec to Minnesota; Eurasia), "Millet grass" or "Bowle's golden grass"; deciduous perennial with creeping rhizomes forming tufts, and culms 50 cm to more than 1 m high when blooming; flat linear leaves 30 cm long, gracefully arching, bright yellow or nile green; inflorescence in loose clusters of spikelets in drooping pairs with yellow flowers in early Summer; attractive for dried arrangements. *Zone 5.*   *p. 562*

MILLA   *Liliaceae*
biflora (S.W. United States to Guatemala), "Mexican star flower"; cormous plant to 30 cm high, with thin grass-like leaves; starry flowers waxy white, to 6 cm across. *Subtropic. Zone 9.*   *p. 246*

MILLETIA   *Leguminosae*
reticulata (China), "Evergreen wisteria"; woody-stemmed climbing vine related to Wisteria; with odd-pinnate evergreen leaves, the thin-leathery lanceolate leaflets to 8 cm long; stout floral racemes to 20 cm, dense with purplish-rose pea-flowers of 5 petals, in late Summer. *Zone 8.*   *p. 278*

MILLINGTONIA   *Bignoniaceae*
hortensis (Burma), "Indian cork tree"; graceful tropical evergreen tree to 25 m high, with deeply cracked, spongy, cork-like bark; leaves opposite, unequally pinnate, with elliptic, crenate leaflets 3-5 cm long; long tubular, waxy flowers 8-10 cm long, pinkish-white, night-blooming and deliciously fragrant, in great profusion during the early hot months. The bark produces an inferior grade of cork. *Tropical. Zone 10.*   *p. 664*

MILTONIA   *Orchidaceae*
candida (Brazil); beautiful epiphyte with flattened, pear-shaped, two-leaved pseudobulbs; large, waxy, 8 cm flowers in loose, erect clusters, sepals and petals chestnut-brown tipped and barred with yellow, lip white tinged rose near base (Aug.-Nov.). *Tropical. Zones 11-12.*   *p. 91*
schroederiana (Costa Rica); bold epiphyte with ovoid pseudobulbs and fresh green fleshy, obovate leaves to 25 cm long; fragrant, waxy flowers chestnut-brown, marked and tipped with yellow, the lip purplish-rose at base, white in front (Summer). *Zone 11.   p. 93*
'Storm' (Mokadem x Piccadilly); small "Pansy orchid" with light green, strap-shaped leaves, and lovely large flowers spreading 9 cm, dark blood-red with velvety texture and a yellow-brown face outlined in white, blooming in Spring and again in Autumn. *Tropical. Zones 11-12.*   *p. 91*
vexillaria 'Volunteer' (Miltoniopsis); very floriferous form, with flowers lavender pink veined purple, and a distinct pattern with a white eye stained in the center with deep yellow (May). Parentage Ecuador. *Zone 11.*   *p. 91*

x MILTONIDIUM   *Orchidaceae*
'Aristocrat' (Miltonia schroederiana x Oncid. leucochilum); clustering plant with flattened pseudobulbs and strap-shaped leaves; inflorescence in loose arching racemes of small waxy flowers with narrow sepals and petals basically yellow but almost completely overlaid with deep maroon, the lip white with purple base (Autumn). *Tropical. Zones 11-12.*   *p. 91*

MILTONIOPSIS vexillaria (Zander):
see MILTONIA vexillaria as in Hortus 3

MIMETES   *Proteaceae*
cucullatus (S.W. Cape), "Scarlet bottlebrush"; in collection Kirstenbosch Botanic Garden; woody shrub with stiff, obovate

leaves, grayish-green, covered with velvety hairs and edged in red; pinkish flowers in terminal heads, subtended by showy, scarlet bracts. *Zone 9.*   *p. 824*

MIMOSA   *Leguminosae*
pudica (Brazil; naturalized in tropics), "Sensitive plant"; short-lived, spiny subshrub, 60-90 cm high; remarkable because of the ability of its pinnate leaves to go to sleep at the slightest touch, causing the leaflets to close and the petiole to fall; the flowers resemble little purplish puffs. An ubiquitous weed throughout the tropics, and it is thought that its mechanism is actuated by heat. I have seen it not only in Brazil, but in the West Indies where it is called "Mori-Vivi", through Africa, and in Vietnam where it is known as the "Shame plant". Propagated from seed. *Zone 10.*   *p. 206, 765*

MIMULUS   *Scrophulariaceae*
aurantiacus (Diplacus glutinosus) (Oregon, California), "Monkey flower"; branching shrub with narrow, leathery leaves toothed and turned down at the margins and sticky to the touch, pubescent beneath; the showy orange-salmon flowers 3 cm long, having notched, spreading lobes giving the effect of a monkey-face. *Subtropic. Zone 8.*   *p. 875*
bigelovii (Mojave County, Arizona to Colorado and California); beautiful annual of western deserts, 5 to 25 cm high, densely downy, with clammy oblong-pointed 3 cm leaves; showy trumpet flowers 3 cm long, with crimson-red corolla marked purple in throat, blooming April to June. *Zone 9.*   *p. 504*
cardinalis (Oregon to No. Mexico; Utah, Arizona), "Scarlet monkey flower"; sticky-hairy herbaceous perennial 30-100 cm high, with clammy, oblong leaves to 10 cm long, stem-clasping and sharply toothed; strongly two-lipped flowers with scarlet to yellowish-red corolla, the upper lobes reflexed, displaying prominent stamens; blooming June to August. *Zone 4.*   *p. 504*
cupreus (S. Chile), "Chilean monkey flower"; compact summer-blooming annual to 20 cm high, with smooth, herbaceous leaves 4 cm long, toothed at margins; 4 cm open bell-flowers with spreading lobes, with a pretty face, yellow and boldly blotched with deep blood-red, the throat with crimson spots; other color variations are also seen. *Zones 9-10.*   *p. 504*
guttatus (luteus) (Alaska to Mexico), "Monkey flower"; smooth perennial plant to 45 cm high, leaves nearly oval with small marginal teeth, to 15 cm long; pretty two-lipped yellow flowers, 4 cm across, with two red marks at mouth; summer-blooming. *Zone 5.   p. 504*
guttatus 'Malibu Orange'; handsome California cultivar, having showy flowers with spreading lobes vivid orange-red, spotted or tinted with copper; perennial to 50 cm high, with small oval to ovate leaves; may also be grown as annual. *Zone 8.*   *p. 504*
lewisii (British Columbia to California and Utah), "Pink monkey flower"; clammy-hairy herbaceous perennial to 75 cm or more high, with sessile, ovate 8 cm toothed leaves; bilabiate 5 cm flowers pink or rosy-red with spreading lobes. Photographed in habitat of Glacier National Park, Montana. *Zone 2.*   *p. 504*
longiflorus (Diplacus) (Coastal S. California to Baja California, Mexico); floriferous much-branched sticky shrub to 1 m high, with lanceolate leaves to 8 cm long, pubescent beneath; flowers vary from cream to orange-yellow, the corolla with wavy lobes. *Zone 9. p. 875*
luteus (Chile), "Golden monkey flower"; smooth herbaceous perennial to 25 cm high, with hollow branches rooting when touching the ground; ovate or oblong, toothed leaves 3 cm long, and with prominent nerves; flowers with yellow corolla 3-4 cm long, spotted with red, blooming in Summer. *Zone 8.*   *p. 504*
moschatus (Montana to California), "Musk-plant"; spreading, sticky-hairy perennial with musky odor, sessile ovate leaves, and pale yellow flowers dotted and splashed brown, 2 cm long. *Zones 3-8.*   *p. 504*
tilingii (Brit. Columbia to Montana, Arizona and California); mat-forming perennial with smooth stems spreading 20-40 cm; toothed leaves usually ovate 3 cm long and somewhat slimy; yellow trumpet flowers with corolla 3-4 cm long, its opening partially closed by the ridges on the lower lip, which are spotted brown; July to September. *Zones 3-8.*   *p. 504*

MIMUSOPS   *Sapotaceae*
commersonii (Madagascar), a "Spanish cherry"; dense evergreen tropical tree with milky sap, handsome obovate, leathery, glossy green leaves with yellow midribs; axillary small fragrant white flowers, followed by long-stalked pendant globular greenish to yellow fruit 3 cm dia., with yellow, edible pulp of mild flavor. *Zone 10.   p. 868*
elengi (India, Malaysia), "Tanjong" or "Medlar"; tropical evergreen tree to 10 m or more high, with leathery oblong, pointed leaves 10 cm long; fragrant flowers white, 2 cm across; oblong glossy orange-yellow fruit with mealy yellow flesh, grooved along on side, 3 cm long, and edible, though of astringent taste, containing one black seed. Children string the fallen petal-stars into necklaces. *Zones 10-11.*   *p. 939*

MINA *Convolvulaceae*
lobata (Quamoclit; Ipomoea versicolor) (Mexico), "Star-glory"; annual twining herb vigorously climbing to 6 m with leaves deeply 3-lobed 8 cm across; brilliant boat-shaped baggy 5-angled flowers fiery scarlet-red when in bud, when opening changing to creamy-yellow and orange; stamens and style protruding; borne on one side of long-stalked axillary racemes. *Tropical. Zone 10.*   *p. 275*

MINUARTIA *Caryophyllaceae*
stellata (Alsine parnassica) (Mts. of Greece and So. Albania), "Greek sandwort"; miniature perennial bush 15 cm or more high, branching from woody base, the narrow oblong leaves glaucous green; inflorescence in loose clusters of pretty pale yellow flowers 3 cm across, deeper yellow in center; seen June-blooming in the Alpine section, Duesseldorf Bot. Garden, Germany. *Zone 6.* *p. 364*

MIRABILIS *Nyctaginaceae*
jalapa (Perú), "Four-o'-clock" or "Marvel-of-Peru"; deep-rooted, bushy, tuberous perennial herb 60-80 cm high, usually grown as an annual; with smooth, ovate leaves and large fragrant flowers 5 cm long, opening in late afternoon, closing in morning, in shades of red, yellow and white, often striped, blooming profusely in late Summer. *Subtropic. Zones 9-10.*   *p. 283, 460*
longiflora (Mexico), "Umbrellawort" or "Sweet four o'clock"; evergreen herbaceous bush to 1 m high, with pubescent cordate ovate leaves; clusters of white fragrant flowers with long tubular, corolla-like 10-12 cm calyx, opening after sunset. Perennial in warm climate; grown as annual in colder areas. *Zone 9.*   *p. 463*
multiflora (Utah to No. California, Colorado, Arizona, Texas), "Umbrellawort"; handsome herbaceous, deep-rooted plant widely branching, 30 to 80 cm high, perennial in mild climate but grown as annual in colder zones; thick fleshy, ovate gray-green, downy leaves to 8 cm long; lovely purplish-rose flowers with corolla tube to 6 cm long, blooming April to September. *Zone 5.*   *p. 460*

MISCANTHUS *Gramineae*
floridulus (Japan, Pacific Isl.), "Giant miscanthus"; robust perennial to 3 m high forming clumps; pale glaucous green, arching leaves to nearly 1 m long, and 3 cm wide; inflorescence in pyramidal white plumes with bristly spikelets, in Autumn. *Zones 5-8.*   *p. 561*
sinensis (Japan to Thailand), "Eulalia grass" or "Japanese Silver grass"; excellent ornamental perennial grass of robust habit, forming large clumps of culms to 2 m or more high; the flat leaves mostly basal, serrate at margins and gracefully arching; inflorescence a showy elongate feathery panicle of spikelets surrounded by silky whitish or purplish hair, enduring throughout the Winter in protected area. *Zone 5.*   *p. 561*
sinensis 'Variegatus', "Variegated eulalia grass"; very attractive form with the flat green leaf-blades striped or margined with ivory-white, holding well through Winter. *Zone 5.*   *p. 561*
sinensis 'Zebrinus', "Zebra grass"; highly ornamental perennial cultivar with gracefully arching, narrow leaves prettily zoned or banded with white or yellow, and areas alternating with green; the inflorescence very showy with large feathery plumes of white. *Zone 5.*   *p. 561*

MITCHELLA *Rubiaceae*
repens (E. No. America), "Partridge berry"; low evergreen creeper with thin, rooting stems to 30 cm long; tiny 2 cm oval, shining dark green leathery leaves often with white lines; twin white flowers with 4 spreading lobes, and fiery-red 1 cm berries characterized by having two navels. *Zones 3-8.*   *p. 321*

MITRIOSTIGMA *Rubiaceae*
axillare (Gardenia citriodora) (So. Africa); evergreen bush to 1 m high, sometimes growing prostrate; willowy branches with opposite glossy green, leathery, lanceolate leaves 10 cm long; very floriferous with sweetly fragrant, axillary clusters of small waxy, trumpet-shaped flowers 1-2 cm long, pink outside, white inside. *Zone 10.*   *p. 855*

MOLINIA *Gramineae*
altissima (arundinacea var. in Zander) (Europe, Asia), "Tall moorgrass"; clump-forming perennial with slender, rigid culms to 2½ m tall, and narrow, arching foliage, deciduous in cold climate; coloring beautifully yellow to reddish in Autumn; slender white, cylindrical floral panicles with small 2-5 flowered spikelets, in Winter dying above ground; newly sprouting in Spring. *Zone 6.*   *p. 561*
caerulea (Europe to W. Siberia, Caucasus, Asia Minor), "Moor grass"; tuft-forming perennial grass, dense with narrow linear leaves 1 cm wide and 10 to 40 cm long, tapering to a fine point; inflorescence a sparse elongate panicle variably purplish to brown or green, with short spikelets; very winter-hardy. *Zone 2.*   *p. 561*
caerulea 'Variegata', "Variegated moor grass"; ornamental garden cultivar, forming dense tufts of leaves and culms spreading outward fountain-like; the blades prettily striped cream with green. *Zones 4-9.*   *p. 561*

MOLTKIA *Boraginaceae*
x intermedia (M. petraea of Yugoslavia x M. suffruticosa of Italy); hoary perennial subshrub to 30 cm high; much branched, with linear leaves along stems, white-tomentose beneath; pendant terminal clusters of 2 cm tubular, 5-lobed flowers purplish-blue. *Zone 6.*   *p. 348*

MOLUCCELLA *Labiatae*
laevis (Syria), "Bells of Ireland"; old-fashioned herbaceous annual interesting because its 60 cm stalks are closely set with whorls of the oversized, light green, bell-shaped calyx in which nestle the little pinkish, bilabiate, fragrant flowers, in late Summer. *Subtropic. Zone 9.*   *p. 433*

MONADENIUM *Euphorbiaceae*
torreyi (Tanzania); unusual, tree-like succulent, with erect spiny trunk 3 cm or more thick, branching laterally and bearing alternate fleshy, deep green oblanceolate leaves about 10 cm long, their margins and apex serrate; long-stalked inflorescence with clusters of tubular white flowers. *Zone 11.*   *p. 194*

MONARDA *Labiatae*
didyma (Québec to Georgia and Texas), "Bee balm" or "Oswego tea"; aromatic perennial to 1 m high, with square stems, mint-scented ovate leaves 10 cm long, roughly hairy and finely toothed; striking two-lipped flowers, arranged in circular clusters, corolla vivid scarlet, 3 cm long, during Summer. Makes a spicily scented tea; used in some oils and perfumes to mask odor of ill-smelling chemicals; attractive to bees and hummingbirds. *Zones 4-9.*   *p. 433, 531*
didyma 'Croftway Pink', "Pink bee balm"; very attractive English cultivar, freely blooming with large clusters of rose-pink flowers; irresistible to hummingbirds; the 15 cm leaves have strong, pleasant odor of mint. *Zone 4-9.*   *p. 433*
fistulosa (Québec to Brit. Columbia, so. to Virginia, west to Arizona), "Wild bergamot"; robust perennial to 1 m or more high; lanceolate leaves to 10 cm long, generally pubescent; rosy-lavender flowers, with corolla 3 cm long; the surrounding bracts whitish or purple, carried in terminal whorls, and blooming in Summer. *Zones 3-10.*   *p. 433*
punctata (New York to Florida, Louisiana and Texas), "Horsemint"; pubescent herbaceous perennial or biennial to 75 cm high, with lanceolate leaves 10 cm long, somewhat serrate at margins; the showy inflorescence of 2 cm yellowish and purple corollas in headlike whorls, axillary or on terminal shoots. *Zone 6.*   *p. 433*

MONARDELLA *Labiatae*
linoides (viminea) (California, Nevada, Arizona); perennial 30-40 cm high, with semi-woody, silvery pubescent stems; small 3 cm leaves, hairy underneath; rosy-lavender flowers with two-lipped corolla 2 cm long surrounded by greenish bracts, in clusters along terminal shoots, summer-blooming. At home on the Mohave Desert to the Sierra Nevada. *Zone 8.*   *p. 433*
macrantha (So. California to Baja), "Large-flowered monardella"; handsome small perennial 15-30 cm high, spreading by creeping rhizomes; with somewhat leathery, ovate leaves 4 cm long; showy flowers with red-orange to scarlet corollas to 5 cm long, displaying protruding stamens in dense clusters subtended by purplish bracts, blooming early Summer. *Zones 9-10.*   *p. 467*

MONOCHAETUM *Melastomataceae*
bonplandii (syn. sericeum) (Venezuela, Guayana to Perú); attractive evergreen tropical shrub, photographed in Canaima rain forest, Southern Venezuela near Angel Falls; the slender silvery-hairy, brittle branches with elongate-ovate leaves transversed by 3 or 4 depressed longitudinal lines; with purplish-rose flowers 3-4 cm across, freely blooming from February on. *Zone 11.*   *p. 787*

MONOPYLE *Gesneriaceae*
grandiflora (Panama: Darien); straggling rough-hairy cloudforest terrestrial to 60 cm high, with slender branches; oblique ovate or lanceolate green to purple leaves 12-18 cm long, the margins serrate; flowers trumpet-like with flaring lobes, bordered lilac-purple, the center white, yellow inside tube. *Zone 11.*   *p. 64*

MONSTERA *Araceae*
decursiva: see RHAPHIDOPHORA decursiva
deliciosa (Philodendron pertusum) (So. Mexico, Guatemala), "Ceriman" "Mexican breadfruit"; stout, woody-stemmed, close-jointed tree-climber forming long hanging, cord-like aerial roots, with large, thick, leathery leaves, glossy green, to 1 m, pinnately cut and perforated with oblong holes; bisexual spadix and boat-shaped, white spathe; cone-like, edible fruit with pineapple aroma. When fully ripe, the scented white pulp is eaten; unripe fruit is reported poisonous. The long-jointed, rapid-climbing juvenile stage with smaller, less perforated leaves is known as Philodendron pertusum in hort. *Tropical. Zones 10-11.*   *p. 28, 29, 265, 910*

deliciosa borsigiana (Cordoba, Mexico); vining type with smaller, glossy leaves with pinnate lobes widely and evenly separated, few, if any holes; the leafstalk is wrinkled where it joins the leaf. *Tropical. Zone 11.* *p. 28*

pertusa (adansonii) (Panama, Guyana), "Windowleaf"; lush climber with soft-textured, unequal-sided leaves perforated and pinnatisect; a poor keeper, from tropical lowland forests. *Tropical. Zone 11.* *p. 31*

MONTANOA *Compositae*
grandiflora (Honduras), "Teresita"; warm-climate flowering shrub to 4 m high, with stout pithy stems, and opposite foliage to 30 cm long, the broad, rough-textured leaves deeply palmately lobed; charming double flowers with ray-florets creamy-white, and shaped like wide-open roses in large tight, rounded clusters. *Tropical. Zone 10. p. 689*

speciosa (mexicana) (Mexico: Morelos), "Daisy tree"; sparry shrub with woody, pithy branches; large, opposite rugose leaves deeply indented or lobed, 20-25 cm long; at the apex a cluster of floral heads, with white, sterile ray-flowers surrounding the protruding yellow central disc of fertile, bisexual flowers. *Zone 9.* *p. 689*

MONTBRETIA of hort.:   see CROCOSMIA x crocosmiiflora

MONTEZUMA *Malvaceae*
speciosissima (Thespesia grandiflora) (Puerto Rico), "Hibiscus tree"; showy evergreen tree to 15 m; slender woody branches with heavy cordate, leathery leaves to 25 cm long, glossy green; large 15 cm waxy flowers, glossy crimson-red, heavily veined, and with protruding style. *Zone 10.* *p. 786*

MONTIA *Portulacaceae*
sibirica (Claytonia) (Alaska to California, Utah, Montana), "Siberian purslane"; small rather succulent annual or perennial herb 15 to 40 cm high, the basal leaves rhombic-ovate on long petioles; small starry flowers 2 cm across, white with pink lines, in May to September. *Zone 3.* *p. 478*

MONTRICHARDIA *Araceae*
arborescens (Guyana); tree-like aroid, growing by the side of tropical rivers, with glossy-leathery, broad sagittate leaves 20-30 cm long, deep green with pale veins, on slender thorny canes. Photo shown on pg. 30 is the true species in col. Munich Botanic Garden. *Zone 12.* *p. 30, 327*

linifera (Brazil); tropical tree-like herb growing in wet places and along rivers; robust, fleshy stems 1 to 4 m high, with leathery, waxy green, hastate arrow-shaped leaves 20 cm long, more cordate than M. arborescens; spathe oblong, slender-pointed, 20 cm long, green outside, inside white. *Zones 11-12.* *p. 30, 338*

MORAEA *Iridaceae*
iridioides: refer to DIETES vegeta

huttonii (spathacea) (Transvaal, Natal), "Butterfly iris"; cormous perennial herb forming large clump of long green leaves growing up to more than 1 m high; fragrant flowers at tips of erect stems, standing above the foliage; blooms are bright yellow with deeper patches at the base of the 3 outer segments; similar to spathulata with which it has been confused, but flowers are smaller, 4 cm across. *Zone 9.* *p. 226*

ramosissima (ramosa) (So. Africa), "Branching moraea"; cormous herb with flowers similar to Iris but in clusters; basal narrow leaves bearing cormlets in axils; much branched leafy floral stems 90 cm high, topped by clusters of fragrant yellow flowers having blue basal markings, opening in succession. *Zone 9.* *p. 226*

MORINA *Dipsaceae*
longifolia (Nepal), "Whorl-flower"; thistle-like perennial to 1 m with furrowed stem and pinnatifid, spiny-toothed leaves about 30 cm long; the 3 cm tubular flowers in crowded whorls in upper leaf-axils, at first white, turning delicate pink and finally crimson, and subtended by spiny-toothed bracts. *Zone 5.* *p. 414*

MORINDA *Rubiaceae*
parvifolia (Philippines, Vietnam to So. China), "Indian mulberry"; more or less climbing shrub with pubescent branchlets; oblong leaves 4-5 cm long; scented creamy flowers in globose head; fruit an orange-colored composite capsule. *Zone 10.* *p. 854*

MORINGA *Moringaceae*
pterygosperma (oleifera) (India to Malaysia), "Horseradish tree"; deciduous tree to 10 m high, with much divided 2 to 3-pinnate fern-like leaves to 50 cm long; panicles of 2 cm white fragrant flowers, followed by 3-6-angled pendulous pods to 45 cm long; seeds are roasted and eaten; the roots taste like horseradish. *Zone 10.* *p. 795*

MORUS *Moraceae*
alba (China), "White mulberry"; deciduous tree to 25 m high; ovate, corrugated leaves 10 cm or more long, coarsely toothed, glossy green above; small flowers in drooping catkins; berry white to

blackish-purple, with insipid, sweet juice. Photo on p. 794 is of a non-fruiting budded clone of California nurseries. *Zone 6.* *p. 794, 915*

nigra (West Asia), "Black mulberry"; large shrub or tree to 10 m high, with rough, dull green broad-serrate 20 cm leaves, crenate at margins; flowers in drooping catkins; luscious edible red to black berries somewhat hidden on underside of branches. Has the largest and juiciest fruit of the mulberries. *Zone 7.* *p. 794, 915*

MUCUNA *Leguminosae*
bennettii (New Guinea), "New Guinea creeper"; striking vine with glossy green, compound leaves on woody, twining stems, and long axillary pendant racemes of sickle-shaped, claw-like, waxy, fiery scarlet flowers; probably the most showy of all tropical climbers. *Zones 10-11.* *p. 765*

MUEHLENBECKIA *Polygonaceae*
axillaris (New Zealand), "Wire plant"; creeping low evergreen shrub about 10 cm high, dense with vining, wire-like branches sprawling to form mats 30 cm across; tiny roundish leaves 1 cm wide; small greenish flowers borne in the axils of the foliage. *Zone 7.* *p. 570*

complexa (New Zealand), "Wire vine" or "Maidenhair-vine"; twining, threadlike, purplish-brown, wiry stems furnished with scattered, tiny round, fresh-green 1-2 cm leaves; flowers greenish-white, in small spikes; a graceful basket plant. *Subtropic.* *p. 318*

platyclada: see HOMALOCLADIUM platycladum

MUNTINGIA *Elaeocarpaceae (Tiliaceae)*
calabura (Trop. America), "Panama berry", "Capulin cherry" or "Calabur"; tropical downy tree to 10 m high, with wide-spreading drooping branches bearing oblique oblong, rough leaves 12 cm long, serrate, and arranged in one plane; single or paired white 2 cm flowers, followed by globose red 2 cm berries of pleasant taste. The fruits must be allowed to ripen on the tree at which time they have a unique sweet flavor that is relished by children and also birds. The leaves are used for tea. *Zones 10-11.* *p. 908*

MURRAYA *Rutaceae*
paniculata (exotica in hort.) (India), "Satinwood" and "Cosmetic bark tree"; related to M. exotica but more tree-like with strong and durable light yellow wood, and bark which is the source of a cosmetic; pinnate leaves of 3-9 obovate, glossy green leaflets, 6 cm long; the large strongly scented 5-petaled white blooms in few-flowered clusters, and worn in the hair for their beauty and fragrance by the women of the East Indies. Also known as "Orange-jessamine". *Zone 10.* *p. 541, 862*

sumatrana (Indonesia, Taiwan), "Mock orange"; evergreen tropical shrub to 2 m or more high; odd-pinnate foliage with 3-5 leaflets glossy green, 3-8 cm long; small white fragrant flowers, followed by conical edible red fruit 2-4 cm long. *Zone 10.* *p. 862*

MUSA *Musaceae*
acuminata (cavendishii or nana in hort.) (So. China), "Dwarf banana", also known as "Dwarf Jamaica"; shapely stoloniferous plant of compact habit, to 1½-3 m high, with short pseudo-stem formed of sheathing leaf petioles, and dense rosette of oblong, glaucous green, leathery leaves with satiny sheen, blotched with red when young, on short stout petioles; produces edible, smallish but deliciously fragrant yellow, 12 cm fruit; stands more cold than most bananas; good tub plant. *Zones 10-11.* *p. 123, 917*

acuminata 'Dwarf Cavendish' (cult. in So. Mexico), "Ladyfinger banana"; a triploid cultivar, also known as M. nana; very popular dwarf banana 2 m or more high, with leaves 120 cm long and 60 cm wide; the fruits are yellow and only 12 cm long, the pulpy flesh is whitish to yellow and deliciously sweet when eaten fully ripe; an ideal exotic plant container grown for the terrace and patio. *Zone 10.* *p. 919*

acuminata 'Hapai' (Waimanalo, Hawaii); curious form of the Dwarf Jamaican banana, bearing small fruit of pleasing flavor, densely packed standing erect inside the crown of leaves and partially within the trunk formed of leaf bases, and maturing there. Photographed in Waimanalo, Hawaii, and known there as May'a hapai. *Zone 11.* *p. 919*

basjoo (Southern Japan: Liu-Chiu archipelago), "Japanese fiber-banana"; cluster-forming to 4 m or more, slender reddish pseudo-stem bearing shining thin leaves to 3 m long, bright green on both sides; arching inflorescence with yellowish flowers under reddish bracts; followed by bunches of 30 to 60 curved fruits, 8 cm long. Grown for its fiber in Japan. *Subtropic. Zones 10-11.* *p. 123*

coccinea (Vietnam: Cochin), "Flowering banana"; showy flowering plant to 1½ m high and stoloniferous, with green pseudo-stems topped by spirally arranged, long-stalked, bright green leaves and erect flowering head with flaming fiery-red bracts yellow at tips and yellow flowers. Small fruit orange-yellow 5 cm long, and with white flesh. *Tropical. Zones 11-12.*   *p. 122*

ensete: see ENSETE ventricosum

Fehi (troglodytarum) (No. New Guinea), "Cooking banana"; tree-like, stoloniferous plant to 7 m high; stem cylindrical formed of sheathing leaf-petioles, with violet sap; broad shining green leaves 2 m long, 60 cm wide, often windblown into shreds; inflorescence erect, the flowers hidden under colored bracts; small, angled fruit in large erect clusters, orange, 12-15 cm long, and eaten only after cooking: used also fried for the popular banana chips. *Zone 11.*   *p. 919*

x paradisiaca (x sapientum; acuminata x balbisiana) (India, Sri Lanka), "Common banana"; tree-like herb to 7 m high, with spirally arranged green leaves with reddish midrib, becoming frayed or broken by the wind, forming a slender trunk by their sheathing bases; flowers yellow, bracts violet, and the well-known, yellow, edible fruit, about 20 cm long; after fruiting the stem dies but is replaced by new suckers. A very complex hybrid group, widely grown in Central America and West Indies; the well-known "Chiquita" banana probably belongs here. *Zones 11-12.*   *p. 123*

x paradisiaca 'Champa', "Lady-fingers"; a slender banana bush seen in England, with pendant bunches of smaller size, finger-like fruit with thin skin, but with meat deliciously mild and tasty and of almost buttery consistency. *Tropical. Zone 11.*   *p. 123*

x paradisiaca 'Koae'; probably an Hawaiian bud mutation triploid of some Maoli banana of the Pacific; this most beautiful variegated-leaf banana is named after the Koae bird with "hair prematurely graying"; the leaves are striped or banded white and very light green on dark green, laterally; the midrib, petiole and trunk alternating white and green, even the immature fruit is variegated, but ripens to yellow, is short and roundish, with yellow flesh. *Tropical. Zone 11.*   *p. 80*

x paradisiaca normalis (x sapientum; acuminata x balbisiana) (parentage India, Sri Lanka, Malaysia), "Plantain"; a cooking banana with generally seedless fruits; sometimes gigantic stoloniferous herbaceous plants, as seen in Panama, to 30 m high; stems cylindrical formed by leaf basis, extending into large oblong green, thin-leathery blades to 150 cm long; the inflorescence with male flowers and bracts persisting; the fruit cylindric to 30 cm long, not particularly sweet and needing to be cooked. This is the plant almost universally cultivated in the Tropics for food. Ripening without conversion of their starch to sugar. *Zone 11.*   *p. 919*

x paradisiaca var. sapientum (cult. in Java), "Paradise banana" a clone of the paradisiaca hybrid complex, cultivated in the Malaysian tropics, and seen in Java, Indonesia; luxuriously large productive species, characteristic with male flowers falling early, and yielding great bunches of yellow three-sided and seedless fruit to 12 cm or more long, edible without cooking. *Zone 11.*   *p. 919*

sumatrana (Sumatra), "Blood banana"; desirable plant to 2½ m high, not as tall as zebrina, leaves shorter and to 40 cm wide, on short petioles, deep grayish-green blotched with dark wine-red, and red beneath as well, but losing this coloring with age; more tolerant to winter chills. *Tropical. Zone 12.*   *p. 122*

velutina (Assam), "Ornamental banana"; dwarf species to 2 m or more high, slender, with pinkish in stem, petioles and into midrib, leaves 1 m long and 30 cm wide; erect inflorescence with red bracts, pale yellow flowers and small, red velvety fruit. *Tropical. Zones 11-12.*   *p. 122*

MUSCARI   *Liliaceae*

armeniacum (Yugoslavia to Greece, Asia Minor), "Grape hyacinth"; spring-blooming bulbous plant to 20 cm high, suitable for forcing in pots; with narrow channelled basal leaves appearing in Autumn; and delicate spires of nodding, urn-shaped fragrant, 1 cm flowers azure-blue, tipped white. *Zone 5.*   *p. 246*

botryoides (So. Europe to Asia Minor), "Common grape hyacinth" or "Starch hyacinth"; charming hardy bulbous flowering herb to 25 cm, soft-fleshy linear, glaucous leaves; the erect stalks with pretty spike-like racemes of tiny fragrant globose blue flowers with white teeth, in early Spring; a favorite in gardens. *Zone 4.*   *p. 246*

comosum (France to So. Russia, Greece, Asia Minor), "Tassel hyacinth"; interesting bulbous perennial, seen in habitat at the ancient Greek temples on Delos; fleshy, strap-shaped basal leaves to 40 cm long; the floral stalk 45 cm high, bearing a loose spike-like raceme of many small urn-shaped 1 cm blue flowers with pale tips, in April. *Zone 5.*   *p. 246*

racemosum (neglectum) (France, S.W. Europe and Asia Minor), "Meadow hyacinth"; small bulbous spring-blooming plant to 20 cm high; with stiff, fleshy, linear leaves, and small fragrant dark purplish-blue flowers, fading to yellowish. *Zone 6.*   *p. 246*

MUSSAENDA   *Rubiaceae*

erythrophylla (Zaire), "Ashanti blood"; beautiful tropical spreading shrub or rambler with roundish ovate, bright green, silky-hairy,

soft leaves, and tiny 1 cm creamy-white flowers with cushion of blood-red felt in center, each having appended one large, odd, ovate 10 cm showy sepal of rich vermilion-scarlet with parallel dark veining, which cover the bush almost entirely by their masses. *Zones 10-11.*   *p. 856*

erythrophylla 'Doña Luz' (Sumatra, Malaysia); charming color form with bracts rich rose, and contrasting deep red borders. *Humid-tropical. Zones 11-12.*   *p. 856*

frondosa (roxburghii) (E. Indies, Malaysia); semi-shrubby tropical evergreen, with dull green, large broad-ovate, corrugated leaves, orange-yellow star-flowers, subtended by ovate bracts of pure white. *Zone 11.*   *p. 856*

MUTISIA   *Compositae*

spinosa (Chile and W. Argentina); subshrubby vine with branches to 6 m long, elliptic 6 cm leaves, notched at apex and ending in a tendril, occasional teeth along margins; the floral heads 6 cm across, the disc-flowers yellow, and obovate ray-flowers pale pink. *Zones 9-10.*   *p. 310*

MYOPORUM   *Myoporaceae*

laetum (New Zealand), the "Ngaio" or "Mouse-hole tree"; vigorous evergreen tree or shrub of exceptionally fast growth to 10 m high and 6 m spread, forming a dense, billowing mass of dark green; older growth stiff-woody, young shoots flexible, with lanceolate or elliptic 8-10 cm soft-leathery, glossy leaves having translucent oil glands; clusters of 1 cm flowers white with purple markings; small purplish fruits. Favours the seashores in New Zealand and is very salt-resistant. *Zones 9-10.*   *p. 618, 795*

parvifolium (Australia, Tasmania); low evergreen shrub spreading along the ground, and used as ground cover in California; leathery, linear leaves densely set 1-3 cm long, with crenate margins; small white honey-scented flowers. *Subtropic. Zone 9.*   *p. 317*

platycarpum (New So. Wales to Western Australia), "Sugar-wood"; evergreen shrub 3 to 6 m high, exuding a sweet sugary substance; narrow pointed leaves 2 to 7 cm long, lightly toothed; small white star-flowers followed by flattened fruits. *Zones 9-10.*   *p. 795*

MYOSOTIS   *Boraginaceae*

alpestris (Mts. of Europe, No. America), "Alpine Forget-me-not"; low, densely tufted perennial herb 8-20 cm high, covered with appressed hairs; with lanceolate leaves, and pretty flowers azure-blue with small yellow eye, the flat limb 1 cm across. *Zones 3-8.*   *p. 350*

scorpioides (palustris) (Britain to Siberia, naturalized in No. Amer.), "Water Forget-me-not"; herbaceous perennial, prostrate with angled branches to 40 cm long, and forming mats; leaves oblanceolate; small 1 cm bright blue flowers with yellow, pink or white eye, in one-sided clusters, blooming Spring to Autumn. *Zone 5.*   *p. 350*

sylvatica (Europe, No. Asia), "Forget-me-not"; small tufted perennial herb with oblong leaves, and racemes bearing the appealing little sky-blue flowers with yellow eye, and 1 cm across. Often listed as alpestris. Usually grown as annual. *Temperate. Zone 6.*   *p. 350*

sylvatica 'Blue Globe' (Blaue Kugel); in hort. commonly as M. alpestris; very compact, mound-like German hort. cultivar, with masses of light blue flowers; used as an annual bedding plant. *Zone 4.*   *p. 350*

MYRCIARIA   *Myrtaceae*

cauliflora (So. Brazil to Paraguay and N.E. Argentina), "Jaboticaba"; curious tropical tree to 5 m or more high, with leathery, ovate leaves 10 cm long; small white flowers develop cauliflorous from the trunk and twisted woody branches, followed by shiny globose 2-3 cm black to purple fruit, which is of sweet flavor and tasting somewhat like grapes; also used for making jelly. *Zone 10.*   *p. 801, 919*

MYRICA   *Myricaceae*

californica (Washington to California), "California bayberry"; slender evergreen shrub to 5 m high or taller as a tree; narrow oblanceolate leaves 10 cm long, of lustrous bronzy color; small petal-less greenish flowers in short catkins, followed by female pistillate plants by purple 4-6 mm berries thinly covered with wax in Autumn. *Zone 7.*   *p. 796*

cerifera (New Jersey to Florida and Texas), "Wax myrtle"; evergreen or partially deciduous bayberry shrub or tree to 10 m high, with aromatic foliage; the leaves obovate 4-10 cm long, toothed toward apex, and resin-dotted; the inflorescence of small whitish flowers in arching cylindric racemes; the small berry-like gray fruit covered by a waxy coat, are borne on pistillate plants in dense clusters along the stem. The wax is made into fragrant candles. *Zone 6.*   *p. 796*

rubra (Japan, So. China, Korea, Philippine Islands), "Chinese strawberry tree"; small tree with obovate leathery leaves to 12 cm long; small flowers in short spikes; succulent edible fruit deep red-purple, to 3 cm dia. *Subtropic. Zone 10.*   *p. 919*

MYRIOPHYLLUM *Haloragidaceae*
 aquaticum (proserpinacoides) (Chile, Uruguay), "Parrot's feather"; fresh-water aquatic herb used for oxygenating the water; normally rising about 15 cm above the surface, with whorled feathery leaves on shoots from a creeping rhizome-like stem in mud on the bottom of pond or aquarium. *Zone 10.* p. 331

MYRISTICA *Myristicaceae*
 fragrans (Indonesia: Moluccas), the "Nutmeg tree"; evergreen, dioecious, 10-18 m high, with willowy green branches, and leathery, yellowish olive-green ovate, aromatic leaves 5-12 cm long, bluish beneath; axillary pale yellow flowers; the yellow pear-like fleshy 5 cm fruit opens by two valves and showing red pulp—the spice—which surrounds a brown, hard-shelled seed; the kernel of the seed is nutmeg, borne on female trees. *Tropical. Zone 10.* p. 537, 795

MYROXYLON *Leguminosae*
 balsamum pereirae (Cent. and So. America), "Balsam of Perú"; tropical tree to 10 m high, with slender pendant branches; odd-pinnate leaves of 9-13 ovate leaflets glossy green; fragrant whitish pea-like flowers in small axillary clusters; fruit 8 cm long, often curved. *Zone 10.* p. 765

MYRRHIS *Umbelliferae*
 odorata (Europe: Pyrenees east to Caucasus), "Myrrh" or "Sweet cicely"; aromatic herbaceous perennial 60 to 80 cm high, with edible carrot-like fleshy roots; fern-like, sweet-scented, 2-3 times pinnate leaves; small whitish flowers in compound clusters, followed by strongly ribbed, jet-black shining fruit. The seeds have a spicy licorice flavor, and are used in liqueurs; long used in England and Germany as a culinary herb, the leaves for seasoning in soups, stews, or as salad, going back to Roman times. *Zone 4.* p. 544

MYRSINE *Myrsinaceae*
 africana (So. Africa, Arabia, to C. China), "African boxwood"; shrubby bush resembling boxwood but more graceful, to 1 m, with angled, downy, red shoots, dense with small rounded, shiny dark green, 1 cm leaves finely serrate; tiny pale brown axillary flowers and purplish-blue berries. *Zone 9.* p. 796

MYRTILLOCACTUS *Cactaceae*
 geometrizans (So. Mexico: San Luis Potosi to Oaxaca), "Blue myrtle" or "Blueberry cactus"; branching tree type to 4 m high; smooth, slender columns six-ribbed, 8 to 10 cm dia., glaucous powder-blue; with practically no spines; small 3 cm diurnal flowers greenish-white; berry like, edible blue fruit. *Arid tropical.* p. 161

MYRTUS *Myrtaceae*
 communis (Mediterran. reg.), "Greek myrtle"; evergreen shrub to 4 m high, loosely leafy with leathery, rather broad-ovate 5 cm leaves, dark lustrous green, spicy when bruised; fragrant white flowers with numerous stamens, and purple-black berries. This plant has been revered since ancient times as sacred to Venus, the goddess of love of the Romans. The fruit is eaten by the moderns as by the ancient Athenians. Dried flower buds and fruit used as spice in Tuscany. *Zones 8-10.* p. 537, 617, 803
 communis 'Microphylla', "Dwarf myrtle"; the compact form grown by European plantsmen in pots and sheared into little globes as houseplant; densely leafy shrub with brown twigs and small, needle-like, shining black-green leaves 2 cm long and starry white flowers of aromatic fragrance. Bridal wreaths and sprigs of myrtle have been traditionally worn at weddings. *Zones 9-10.* p. 803
 communis 'Variegata', "Variegated myrtle"; small evergreen shrub with leathery, pointed, green leaves 2-3 cm long, attractively variegated or margined with creamy-white. *Zone 10.* p. 803
 luma: see LUMA apiculata (Zander) (AMOMYRTUS in Hortus)
 pubescens (Argentina); dense evergreen shrub with small leathery, ovate leaves 3 cm long, and showy axillary flowers with numerous pure white feathery stamens protruding, subtended by white petals flaring wide. *Zone 10.* p. 803

NANDINA *Berberidaceae*
 domestica (China, Japan), "Heavenly bamboo"; attractive shrub usually low, but to 2½ m, slender cane-like stems with 2 to 3 pinnate leaves, the ultimate leaflets narrow; turning red in Fall; small white flowers in large panicles, followed by bright red berries; fairly hardy. *Zone 7.* p. 657
 domestica 'Compacta', "Dwarf Heavenly bamboo"; more compact growing than N. domestica; fine bright green, lacy foliage on erect stems turns a brilliant red coloring in Autumn and into Winter. *Zone 7.* p. 620
 domestica filamentosa, "San Gabriel nandina"; curious form seen in Pepper-tree Nursery, San Marcos, California, having apparent leafless woody branches, with leaves reduced to colorless to pinkish needles or ribs, in great feathery clusters. A curiosity like the String

nandina, N. dom. longifolia 'Ito' seen in a Japanese nursery and shown in TROPICA. *Zone 10.* p. 657
 domestica 'Nana'; charming small, compact form of low, bushy habit, the dense foliage with ovate leaflets glowing crimson or rose in the younger growth and in autumn color. Photographed in the Domain Garden, Auckland, New Zealand. *Zone 9.* p. 657

NARCISSUS *Amaryllidaceae*
 asturiensis ('Minimus') (Spain, Portugal); perfect miniature of a large trumpet daffodil but only 5-10 cm high; flower deep yellow, shaded green, the mouth of the 1 cm long trumpet wavy; early blooming; leaves glaucous. *Zones 5-7.* p. 216
 bulbocodium (So. France to Morocco), "Petticoat daffodil"; distinct variable small species with slender, almost threadlike leaves to 38 cm long, exceeding the blooms; solitary flowers bright yellow, the tubular funnel-shaped crown to 2½ cm long, on stalk 10-20 cm high. The popular variety **conspicuus** grows only 10-15 cm high, with deep yellow flowers. *Zones 6-8.* p. 216
 cyclamineus (Portugal, Spain); interesting small species 20 to 30 cm high, the narrow linear leaves with deeply grooved keel; deep yellow flowers singly on slender stalk, 3 to 5 cm long, the crown narrow, and the short outer corolla segments folded back, reminding of cyclamen. *Zone 7.* p. 216
 cyclamineus 'February Silver', a hybrid of N. cyclamineus from Portugal with a "Trumpet" type blossom; compact "Pot narcissus" about 25 cm high, with narrow linear leaves, and smallish but numerous flowers having creamy-yellow perianth segments spreading 5 cm across, and yellow trumpet, crenate at mouth. Normally early blooming, this pretty hybrid is ideal for pots from Valentine to Easter. *Warm temperate. Zone 7.* p. 215
 dubius (So. France), (N. juncifolius x papyraceus); natural hybrid with narrow, glaucous leaves and clusters of a few white starry flowers 2-3 cm wide. *Zone 7.* p. 216
 x incomparabilis 'Gold Medal'; a true, short pot daffodil; outstanding large-flowered trumpet variety almost exactly like 'King Alfred' except that it is more stocky and shapely in pots for Spring, the large 9 cm flowers clear yellow with richer colored trumpet, carried on solid stalks 30 cm high, 2 to 3 to a bulb; late blooming. *Warm temperate. Zone 4.* p. 215
 x incomparabilis 'Gustav Mahler' (N. poeticus x pseudo-narcissus); beautiful large-cupped daffodil ideal for culture in pots for Easter; flat linear leaves 30 cm long; the showy solitary flowers 8-10 cm wide with vivid yellow segments, and corona cup contrasting scarlet-red. *Zone 5.* p. 216
 jonquilla (simplex) (So. Europe to No. Africa), "Jonquil"; a miniature clustering daffodil to 30 cm tall, with slender, narrow channeled leaves, and numerous stalks bearing 2-3 pretty, small 4 cm flowers with long tube spreading into 6 segments and small cup, rich yellow and very fragrant; free-flowering in Spring and very striking. *Temperate. Zones 4-7.* p. 216
 jonquilla 'Baby Moon'; miniature rockgarden plant only 20 cm high, free-blooming with sweet-scented slender-tubed flowers light buttercup-yellow, and flaring petals. *Zone 4.* p. 216
 jonquilla 'Minnow'; rockgarden miniature jonquil with reed-like leaves; the slender floral stalk topped by sweet-scented rich yellow flowers, the spreading petals obovate rounded, and with short corona cup. *Zone 4.* p. 215
 jonquilla 'Tittle Tattle' (1953); charming small "Jonquil" to 25 cm high, the saucer-shaped flowers with wide-spreading overlapping yellow petals and short cup shaded orange, blooming relatively late and lasting for 3 weeks into early Summer. *Zone 4.* p. 215
 poeticus (Spain, through the Alps, to Greece), "Poet's narcissus"; clustering bulbous plant 25-45 cm high, with narrow gray-bluish leaves and two-edged stalks with solitary, very fragrant flowers glistening white tinted yellow at base, the small, yellow corona with crisped edge; Mid-spring. Very cold-hardy. *Zones 4-5.* p. 215, 249
 poeticus 'Actaea', "Pheasant's eye"; attractive cultivar 45 cm high; flowers with large flat, pure white petals spreading 7 cm, and yellow center cup like an eye, broadly margined scarlet; derived from N. poeticus, the "Poet's narcissus" from France to Greece. Mid- to late Spring. *Warm temperate. Zone 5.* p. 216
 poeticus 'Praecox'; clustering with narrow erect leaves, and large sweet-scented flowers, the flaring segments glistening white, surrounding the small cup yellow inside. *Zone 5.* p. 215
 pseudonarcissus (Europe: France), "Daffodil" or "Trumpet narcissus"; the classic daffodil, a spring-blooming bulbous herb with narrow linear basal leaves, 30-45 cm long; yellow flowers with prominent frilled trumpet 5 cm long, and spreading segments; easy to naturalize in gardens. *Zone 5.* p. 215
 pseudonarcissus 'King Alfred' (Trumpet type), "Lent lily"; spring-flowering, bulbous plant with basal leaves; large, solitary, golden-yellow, trumpet flowers spreading 8-10 cm wide; very sub-

stantial, with strong stem, an outstanding florists forcing and pot "daffodil"; probably the best-known cultivar derived from the W. European species N. pseudo-narcissus. *Zones 4-10.*   p. 56

tazetta (canaliculatus) (Mediterran. reg., Asia Minor, to Japan), "Polyanthus narcissus"; popular, variable species late Winter (Jan.-Feb.) blooming; with 4-6 narrow leaves 2 cm dia.; 25-35 cm stalks carrying clusters of sweetly-scented flowers, flaring segments white, 3-5 cm across, the short cup yellow. *Zone 8.*   p. 216

tazetta 'Geranium', "Poetaz narcissus"; showy cultivar carrying several fragrant blooms on each floral stem; the flowers larger than the species, with widespread, broad white petals, and short, fringed orange cup. *Zone 7.*   p. 216

tazetta var. orientalis (China), "Chinese sacred lily" or "Joss-flower"; a sweet little miniature of the "bunch-flowered" class, to 30 cm high, with flat, strap-shaped, bluish-green foliage; stiff stalks carry clusters of small, white flowers 3 cm across, with short yellow corona cup, and daintily fragrant. During a stay in Shanghai, I have seen this "Polyanthus" narcissus happily blooming on window-sills during February, growing in glazed bowls filled with water and pebbles. *Subtropic. Zone 8.*   p. 215

tazetta papyraceus (Canary Is., Portugal, So. France, Italy), "French Paper white"; well-known very early variety widely used for Christmas or early Winter indoor forcing; having narrow-linear leaves, and floral stalks to 45 cm high, tipped by clusters of small white, starry flowers, spicily scented. *Zone 8.*   p. 215

tazetta 'Ziva strain' (Israel), "Israeli paper-white"; a superior strain of vigorous growth and abundant in flowering; tall stems to 40 cm high, bearing numerous broad-petaled flowers of purest white, heavily fragrant. Very early and used for forcing. *Zone 8.*   p. 216

triandrus (Spain, S.W. France), "Angel's tears narcissus"; lovely native of the Pyrenees area, 15 to 30 cm high, with rush-like, cylindrical leaves channeled above; slender floral stalks bear the nodding blossoms 3 cm long, the flaring petals and coronas white. *Zone 4.*   p. 216

triandrus 'Silver Chimes'; charming hybrid of N. triandrus and tazetta, having the best attributes of both parents. Clusters of 6 or more small blossoms with shimmering creamy-white overlapping petals and cups pale yellow, blooming late; 25 cm high; strap-like dark green foliage. *Zone 6.*   p. 214

NARTHECIUM   *Liliaceae*
ossifragum (N.W. Europe, incl. Britain), "Bog asphodel"; herbaceous perennial to 30 cm high, with stout rhizome base; narrow iris-like leaves basal and on stem, rigid and strongly ribbed; small yellow flowers in a continuous raceme, in June. *Zone 6.*   p. 260

NASTURTIUM   *Cruciferae*
officinale (Europe, W. Asia), "Watercress"; aquatic perennial naturalized in streams in No. America; with much branched stem, sometimes short and creeping or floating in shallow water, in marshes, or sometimes along the shore as bushes; with small pinnate leaves of 3-9 ovate leaflets; tiny white flowers in racemes. The pungent leaves are eaten as a salad; high in vitamins. *Zone 4.*   p. 527

NASTURTIUM: see also RORIPPA

NAVIA   *Bromeliaceae*
arida (Venezuela); primitive mountain xerophyte of the "Lost world"; handsome small rosette with leathery, oblanceolate leaves covered with silvery scales and finely toothed at margins, the inner circle a glowing crimson; the sessile, nest-like inflorescence vivid yellow tipped red-purple. *Subtropic. Zone 10.*   p. 48

splendens (Venezuela, Guyana); small xerophytic, flat rosette living on rocks, and forming stems to 20 cm long; leaves to 37 cm long, strap-shaped with crisped margins and small spines; the inflorescence a barely stalked rounded nest-like head with white-scaly red bracts and yellowish flowers. *Zone 11.*   p. 47

NEILLIA   *Rosaceae*
longiracemosa (thibetica) (W. China: Sikiang); rare deciduous shrub 2-3 m high, with angular, pubescent young branches; slender-pointed, elliptic, often 3-lobed leaves 4-10 cm long; attractive tubular pink flowers with whitish petal tips, in dense racemes 5-15 cm long, in May-June. *Zone 5.*   p. 837

sinensis (China), "Chinese neillia"; handsome deciduous shrub to 2 m high, of dense growth, with light green ovate leaves 5-8 cm long, corrugated by sunken veins, and sharply toothed at margins; pretty pinkish-white tubular flowers, tipped pink and with red calyx, in nodding racemes 6 cm long, in May-June. *Zone 5.*   p. 837

NELUMBO   *Nymphaeaceae*
nucifera (Nelumbium nelumbo) (Trop. East Asia to N.E. Australia), "East Indian lotus"; large, aquatic, stemless plant symbolic of perpetual life in Buddhism; long, milky, prickly petioles bear shield-like leaves above the water, 30-50 cm across and more; and bold

stalks with large, delicate pink flowers of a haunting fragrance; the petals soon fall leaving the prominent, flat-topped receptacle bearing edible seed. *Tropical. Zones 10-11.*   p. 338

NEMATANTHUS   *Gesneriaceae*
fissus (Hypocyrta selloana), (Brazil); fibrous-rooted, robust plant with fleshy, oblong, deep green, hairy leaves with reddish midrib, purplish beneath; axillary, deep red, downy, long cylindric flowers with ventricose throat. *Humid-tropical. Zone 11.*   p. 64

NEMESIA   *Scrophulariaceae*
strumosa (So. Africa), "Cape jewels"; floriferous, densely branching annual to 60 cm high, with opposite, sessile, linear, dentate leaves, and erect racemes of attractive, bilabiate flowers, with a pouch at base, 3 cm across, and bearded throat, borne in great profusion from June to Dec., in white, yellow, rose, orange, crimson, with spotted throat. *Subtropic. Zone 10.*   p. 505, 507

versicolor (S.E. Cape Prov. to Namaqualand, Namibia), "Spurred nemesia"; attractive annual, or short-lived perennial becoming subshrubby, 15-30 cm high, with lanceolate to linear leaves 5 cm long; flowers in branched clusters, with spurred corolla 2 cm long, in various colors from orange-yellow to white or lilac, summer-blooming. *Zone 10.*   p. 505

NEMOPANTHUS   *Aquifoliaceae*
mucronatus (Ilex canadensis) (Nova Scotia to New England, Virginia, Minnesota), "Catberry" or "Mountain holly"; stoloniferous shrub 1 to 3 m high, with purplish branches when young, later ashgray; thin ovate leaves dull bluish-green 3-6 cm long, turning a colorful yellow in Autumn; attractive light red 1 cm berries in late Summer. *Zone 3.*   p. 646

NEMOPHILA   *Hydrophyllaceae*
menziesii (insignis) (California, Oregon), "Baby-Blue-eyes"; dainty soft-hairy annual, spreading herb to 20 cm high, with pinnatifid leaves, summer-blooming with light blue flowers 3 cm across, usually with white center. *Subtropic. Zone 10.*   p. 424

NEOFINETIA   *Orchidaceae*
falcata (Angraecum falcatum) (Japan, Korea); lovely miniature epiphyte 8-15 cm high, with leathery linear light green, keeled leaves arranged in 2 ranks; freely blooming with clusters of pure white, waxy flowers 3 cm across, having a slender spur 5 cm long, and blooming in Summer; intensely fragrant, mostly at night. *Subtropic. Zone 11.*   p. 90

NEOLITSEA   *Lauraceae*
sericea (Japan, Korea, China, Taiwan); handsome evergreen tree to 6 m high; lanceolate, leathery leaves 8-18 cm long with distinct pattern of yellow veins, white beneath; clusters of yellow flowers in Autumn; small 15 mm oblong red fruit. *Zone 7.*   p. 742

NEOLLOYDIA   *Cactaceae*
conoidea (Coryphantha, Echinocactus) (Texas to C. Mexico: Zacatecas); small clustering globe to 10 cm high, with short straw-colored spines; pretty, silky flowers 6 cm across, carmine-rose with deeper center and reflexed petals. *Arid subtropic. Zone 10.*   p. 168

unguispina v. laui (Echinomastus) (Mexico: Chihuahua, Zacatecas); solitary small globe to 10 cm high and 7 cm dia., having woolly apex, and covered entirely with circular gray spine clusters, some stout spines strongly deflexed; 2 cm greenish flowers with reddish center. *Zone 10.*   p. 168

NEOMARICA   *Iridaceae*
bicolor (Brazil), "Walking iris"; vigorous tropical iris-like plant with perennial rootstalk, the broad, fresh-green leaves arranged like fans; from their sheathing base rise stout stalks bearing at an angle the attractive, if fleeting flowers lavender-blue, 10 cm across, the center segments yellow with brown cross-lines, their tips marked with blue. *Subtropic. Zone 10.*   p. 430

caerulea (So. Brazil), "Twelve apostles"; beautiful iris-like plant 60 cm high, with large 10 cm flowers having outer petals bright sky-blue, the center petals pale and marked with yellow and brown; unforgettable sight when I first saw such a field of blue on the Serra do Mar above Santos in São Paulo state. Flowers carried on clear stem not clasped by leaves, as on northiana. *Subtropic. Zone 10.*   p. 430

longifolia hort.: see TRIMEZA caribaea

northiana ('Marica') (Brazil), "Walking iris"; perennial herb to 90 cm high, with flat, glossy green leaves arranged like fans with a leaf-like spike bearing fragrant 10 cm flowers, followed by young plants from the same point, bending down and rooting; white outer petals marked brown at base, recurved inner segments tipped violet with base striped brown and yellow. Popularly known as "Twelve apostles" because twelve leaves are said to form before one turns brown. *Zones 9-10.*   p. 430

NEOPANAX arboreum:
see PSEUDOPANAX arboreus (Dr. Frodin)

NEOPORTERIA *Cactaceae*

islayensis (Islaya flavida) (So. Perú); handsome species at first globular, to 10 cm dia., later elongate and 25 cm high, having up to 25 interrupted ribs; gray radials and stout central spines; the crown white woolly, from its center the 2 cm yellow flowers. Sometimes grafted for faster growth. *Zone 10.*   *p. 168*

nidus senilis (Northern Chile), "Birdsnest"; globular, later elongate stem with up to 18 ribs, densely covered with matted white or darker spines; 3 cm flowers half open, carmine-rose. The var. senilis has softer spines than the species, with larger flowers. Sometimes grafted on Cereus for better growth. *Zone 10.*   *p. 168*

rapifera (Chile); robust globular to elongate species with turnip-like root, 10 cm thick, the dark green high ribs broken into prominent knobs, these set with slender needles; from near top the small rosy flowers, white in center. *Zone 10.*   *p. 168*

NEOREGELIA *Bromeliaceae*

ampullacea (Brazil: Espirito Santo and Guanabara); small tubular rosette 12 cm high found growing on rocks along the coast of Brazil; hard, channeled and recurving leaves to 12 cm long, glossy olive-green with irregular brown-purple cross-bands or spots, purple teeth at margins; clustered at base of vase the white flowers tipped with purple, lasting one day only; plant sends out long stolons, branching freely, and ideal in a hanging pot. *Zone 10.*   *p. 47*

carolinae 'Marechalii', "Blushing bromeliad"; dwarf variety with flattened metallic leaves; at flowering time the inner leaves are brilliant rosy-crimson, remaining so for six months or more, flowers lilac. The species N. carolinae is an open rosette with leathery leaves 30 cm long, having toothed margins; the central cup holding the inflorescence is filled with water in its Brazilian habitat and, as recently discovered, will trap and digest insects. *Tropical. Zone 11.*   *p. 201*

carolinae 'Meyendorffii' (Karatas); broad rosette of flat olive-green leaves with coppery tinting; at flowering time the inner leaves turn a dark maroon; flowers lilac deep in center. *Tropical. Zone 11.*   *p. 47*

carolinae 'Tricolor' (Brazil), "Striped blushing bromeliad"; very attractive variety with the glossy green leaves having ivory-white lengthwise bands becoming rose-tinted in good light; at flowering time they become shorter and carmine-red; flowers violet-purple edged white. *Tropical. Zone 11.*   *p. 47*

compacta (Nidularium) (Rio de Janeiro); open terrestrial rosette from the coastal Restinga of S.E. Brazil; firm broad leaves to 25 cm or more long, bronzy green, toward base and into nest rich crimson-red; inflorescence deep in center. *Zone 11.*   *p. 48*

concentrica (Nidul. acanthocrater) (Rio de Janeiro); stiff, fresh green or reddish rosette with purple blotches and black spines; when in flower the center leaves are purplish-carmine with blackish tips, blue flowers deep in center. *Zone 11.*   *p. 48*

marmorata (Brazil: São Paulo, Paraná), "Marble plant"; bold rosette of thick-leathery broad leaves to 30 cm long, 8 cm wide, glossy yellowish-green to grass-green heavily blotched and marbled with blood-red, the margins spiny; the inner center brownish-red; numerous white flowers. *Tropical. Zone 11.*   *p. 50*

olens (Brazil); variable epiphytic rosette of leaves 30 cm long, the outer silvery green without spots and finely toothed, the inner shorter blades glowing crimson-red; the inflorescence deep in the center, flowers blue. *Zone 11.*   *p. 47*

NEPENTHES *Nepenthaceae (Carnivorous Pl.)*

ampullaria (Malaya to New Guinea); contrary to others, this species grows mostly on the ground, and I have collected it in wet savannahs in Malaya where the little rounded green pitchers grow in matted clusters hidden by moss or clay. *Humid-tropical.*
Zone 12.   *p. 201*

x coccinea (distillatoria x mirabilis); a very satisfactory old hybrid (1882), with gracefully pendulous flask-shaped pitchers pale yellowish-green, richly splashed with red-brown, the ring around the top lined with maroon, and with ciliate wings in back; inside bluish with red spots. We have found this plant very willing to produce its colorful pitchers, more so on young branches. *Humid-tropical.*
Zone 12.   *p. 201*

madagascariensis (S.E. Madagascar); terrestrial tropical pitcher plant found near Tolagnaro, formerly Fort Dauphin, with fleshy lanceolate leaves, which carry from their tips on extended, coiled stalks graceful small yellow pitchers with raised lid colorfully spotted with maroon. *Zone 12.*   *p. 201*

maxima (Celebes, Borneo, N. Guinea); slender, high-climbing species with colorful pitchers; the lower ones flask-shaped, the upper ones funnel-shaped, pale green and heavily marbled wine-red. *Humid-tropical. Zone 12.*   *p. 201*

x mixta (maxima x northiana), a "Pitcher plant"; large funnel-shaped pitchers to 30 cm long, yellow-green occasionally marked crimson, increasingly toward the ribbed rim. *Humid-tropical.*
Zone 12.   *p. 201*

rafflesiana (Sumatra to Borneo); straggling climber on low trees of the open savannah; the lower pitchers are urn-shaped, the upper large funnel-form, greenish-yellow marked purplish-brown; I have collected pitchers of giant size as long as 25 cm or more, in Johore state, Malaya. *Humid-tropical. Zone 12.*   *p. 201*

'Superba' (sedenii x hookeriana); vigorous epiphyte with long soft-leathery, deep green leaves, and variable pitchers 15 cm or more long, some urn-shaped, later funnel-shaped, yellow-green blotched with wine-red, the glossy ribbed rim with wine-red and crimson, inside spotted red, the lid striped red, the fringe in back with red hairs.
Humid-tropical. Zone 12.   *p. 201*

NEPETA *Labiatae*

cataria (Europe to Asia; natural. in No. U.S. and So. Canada), "Catnip"; popular aromatic mint-scented perennial, gray-pubescent with square stems 60-80 cm high; hoary ovate leaves, deeply lobed at base, 8 cm long; small 1 cm whitish to light purple flowers in whorls toward apex of floral stalk, from July to Autumn. A good mint-scented herb tea is brewed from dried leaves, used to soothe the nerves. Cats like the fragrance of the dried leaves and blossoms, better than fresh ones. *Zones 3-9.*   *p. 531*

x faassenii (mussinii x nepetella), "Catmint" or "Persian ground-ivy"; sprawling herbaceous perennial to 45 cm high, originated in Copenhagen Botanic Garden before 1939; valued for its attractive silvery green foliage; the little ovate, rugose leaves 3 cm long, with margins crenate; small tubular, two-lipped flowers are lavender-blue, in whorls forming a pyramidal inflorescence; blooming Spring and Summer. In horticulture often confused with N. mussinii. Cats love to roll in this herb and eat from it. *Zone 4.*   *p. 434, 531*

mussinii (racemosa) (Caucasus, Iran), "Catmint"; low, mat-forming herbaceous perennial to 25 cm high, with spreading, pros-trate branches, the ovate, short-pubescent gray-green leaves 3 cm long, and crenate at margins; more cordate than x faassenii; the lilac-blue 1 cm flowers in loose terminal racemes. *Zone 4.*   *p. 434*

NEPHELIUM *Sapindaceae*

lappaceum (Malaysia), "Rambutan" or "Hairy litchi"; large ever-green tropical fruit tree to 12 m high, similar to litchi, with leaves compound of 5-7 pairs of oblong leaflets each 10 cm long, shining dark green; small pubescent flowers with cleft calyx, but without petals, in axillary panicles or from branch tips; the fruits in clusters of ten or twelve are oval, 5 cm long, crimson-red and covered with soft fleshy spines; the outer covering is thin-leathery, easily torn off, exposing the white, juicy flesh; the flavor is somewhat acid like a grape; very popular in Malaya and Vietnam. *Zones 10-11.*   *p. 931, 937*

longan: see EUPHORIA longan

NEPHROLEPIS *Polypodiaceae (Filices)*

biserrata 'Furcans' (Cuba to Brazil, Africa, Hong Kong to Queensland), "Fishtail fern"; massive fern with long arching pinnate fronds, the segments widely spaced, broad, leathery yellow-green, and forked toward their tips. *Humid-tropical. Zones 11-12.*   *p. 135*

cordifolia (tuberosa), (Trop. Asia to N. Zealand, also Jamaica, Chile), the "Erect sword fern"; clustering fern bearing tubers on the roots; the dark green pinnate fronds are 60 cm long and slender and of narrow linear form, the short pinnae bearing many sori; blackish stalks with hair-like scales. *Zones 10-11.*   *p. 134*

duffii (cordifolia var.) (New Zealand, Polynesia), "Pigmy sword fern"; densely crowded, compact fern with brown downy scales at base, the erect wiry stalks sometimes forked, and closely set with tiny rounded, toothed, leathery 1-2 cm leaflets. *Humid-subtropic.*
Zones 10-11.   *p. 134*

exaltata (Florida to Brazil, Africa, So. Asia, Australia), "Sword-fern"; tufted plant with simply pinnate, rather stiff, fresh green fronds which can continue to grow in length almost indefinitely, to 1 m or more, and bearing sori beneath; the rootstock sending out threadlike runners which produce buds, giving rise to new plants. *Zones 9-10.*   *p. 135*

exaltata 'Bostoniensis', the "Boston fern", a variety found in Boston in 1894, and an old time house plant; rich green fronds simple pinnate, larger and wider than the basic species, to 1 m long; the leaflets not lobed and nearly flat, more graceful and pendant; entirely without fertile spores; therefore propagation by division or runners. Still a favorite for decoration, appreciating good light, 25 fc. (250 lux) minimum, or better 100 fc. (1000 lux), but not burning sun; not too warm, and all the atmospheric moisture possible. Air too dry favors white scale, brown scale, white fly and mealy bugs. Active growth is fairly fast from May to October. Tolerates air conditioning but dislikes cold drafts of air. *Tropical. Zone 11.*   *p. 135* exaltata 'Bostoniensis compacta', "Dwarf Boston fern"; long used as a house plant, of more compact habit, the wide simply pinnate fronds fresh green and spreading; freely clustering and usually not over 30 cm high. *Tropical. Zone 11.*   *p. 135*

exaltata 'Whitmanii', a sport of 'Barrowsii', old fashioned "Lace-fern"; of open habit, the broad, light green fronds are relatively short and arching, or pendant when older, the segments deeply and evenly cut and not bunched; tripinnate, with small segments, leaves up to 45 cm long. *Humid-tropical. Zone 11.*   *p. 135*

pendula (cordifolia pendula) (Pantropic); cultivated in England since 1841; according to Carl Christensen in 1906 a var. of N. cordifolia; Johnson 1917, a form of N. exaltata; commanding attention because of its extraordinary pendulous fronds which may become 2 to 3 m or more long; growing epiphytic on trees or rocks; a stoloniferous base gives rise to odd-pinnate, sturdy leaves, the sickle-shaped leaflets glossy green and 4-6 cm long, on brown-fuzzy threadlike rachis, eventually bending over and growing downward like long green ribbons. *Zones 10-11.*   *p. 135*

NEPHTHYTIS of hort.:   see SYNGONIUM

NEPTUNIA   *Leguminosae*
oleracea (prostrata) (Tropics of Southeast Asia and elsewhere), "Water-mimosa"; aquatic plant with long floating or anchored roots, branching stems with dark green bipinnate leaves, lightly sensitive to touch; yellow flower heads. *Tropical. Zones 10-11.*   *p. 332*

plena (flava) (Trop. America, Trop. Asia), "Sensitive water mimosa"; creeping or floating aquatic perennial with shrubby, long pendant branches forming water roots; touch-sensitive, bipinnate leaves with 2 to 4 pairs of grass-green leaflets; the underwater stems are thickened and white-spongy, full of air cells, enabling them to float; flowers bright yellow. The leaves are sensitive and fold when touched. *Zone 11.*   *p. 327*

NERINE   *Amaryllidaceae*
bowdenii (So. Africa), a "Spider lily"; bulbous plant 45 cm high, with glossy green linear basal leaves rather thick; large umbels of beautiful soft pink flowers with a darker line on each segment, recurved at apex; blooming before foliage. *Subtropic. Zone 9. p. 218*

sarniensis (So. Africa); sometimes in hort. as Lycoris radiata, the "Guernsey lily"; bulbous herb with strap-shaped basal leaves and funnel-form, crimson flowers with green, crisped segments, and protruding stamens not as long as in L. radiata, appearing in long-stalked clusters before the foliage; numerous hybrids have been developed, in various colors from white and pink to red. *Subtropic. Zone 9.*   *p. 218*

undulata (So. Africa); bulbous plant forming narrow linear strap-shaped basal leaves to 35 cm long, usually appearing before flowering; the 25 cm floral stalk topped by umbels of 8 to 12 spidery blooms, the undulate narrow segments 2 cm long, pale to flesh-pink. *Zone 9.*   *p. 218*

NERIUM   *Apocynaceae*
oleander (Mediterranean), "Common oleander" or "Rose bay"; evergreen shrub from 2-6 m high, often used in tubs, with willowy branches set with pairs or whorls of linear-lanceolate, leathery leaves, and flowers in terminal cymes, rosy-red to crimson. All parts are poisonous if eaten. *Subtropic. Zone 8.*   *p. 18, 641*

oleander 'Album', "Sister Agnes oleander"; large flowered cultivar with white flowers; favored by So. California nurseries because the single varieties have a way of "cleaning" themselves, or "shed" their faded blooms. *Zone 8.*   *p. 641*

oleander 'Carneum florepleno'; known in the trade as 'Mrs. Roeding', somewhat weaker in growth and with a slightly weeping habit, the long branches loaded with double salmon-pink blossoms; having a tendency to "hang on". *Subtropic. Zone 8.*   *p. 18*

oleander 'Cherry'; handsome cultivar with large single flowers 6 cm across, deep pink shading to rose-red, in large clusters, free-blooming and popular in So. California. *Zone 9.*   *p. 641*

oleander 'Petite Pink'; small, compact grower to approx. 1 m high; free-blooming with simple, soft shell-pink flowers. *Zone 9.*   *p. 18, 641*

oleander 'Roseum', "Pink oleander"; charming color form pro-fuse with single rose-pink flowers. *Zone 8.*   *p. 641*

oleander 'Sealy Pink'; robust evergreen, sun-loving scented shrub with lovely large, single flowers soft pink; a very charming cultivar offered in California nurseries. *Zone 8.*   *p. 641*

NERTERA   *Rubiaceae*
granadensis (depressa) (Andes, to Cape Horn, New Zealand, Tasmania), "Coral-bead plant"; mat-forming, creeping groundcover with tiny, broad-oval, leathery, opposite leaves and inconspicuous, greenish flowers in June, followed by the attractive, pea-size, translucent, orange-red berries. I have collected this species along cold Milford Sound, in the Fiordland of New Zealand growing on

dripping rocks, frozen stiff in Winter—as well as in the mountains of New Guinea at 2,100 m under rippling water, in company of sphagnum moss. *Warm temperate. Zone 9.*   *p. 58*

NEVIUSIA   *Rosaceae*
alabamensis (Alabama), "Snow-wreath"; interesting deciduous shrub 2 m high, and spreading wide; ovate leaves to 8 cm long, toothed and sometimes lobed at margins; inflorescence uniquely exquisite of flowers without petals, and feathery with a fountain of spreading long white stamen filaments, blooming April-May. Photo-graphed in col. Willowwood Arboretum, New Jersey. *Zone 5.*   *p. 837*

NICANDRA   *Solanaceae*
physalodes (Perú, but escaped in U.S. and Amer. Tropics), "Apple-of-Perú" or "Shoo-fly plant"; short-lived herbaceous perennial popularly grown as annual; 60 cm to 1 m or more high, with ovate, undulate leaves to 30 cm long, wavy-toothed or lobed at margins; axillary flowers 3-4 cm across, lavender to deeper blue, blooming July to September. *Zone 9.*   *p. 512*

NICODEMIA   *Loganiaceae*
diversifolia hort. (Buddleja indica in Zander) (Madagascar), "Indoor oak"; free growing bush with woody stems and thin-leathery quilted leaves with lobed and undulate margins, looking remarkably like an oak-leaf, the surface has an iridescent, metallic blue sheen, with bronzy petioles. *Zone 10.*   *p. 774*

NICOLAIA   *Zingiberaceae*
elatior, long known in horticulture as Phaeomeria magnifica (Amomum) (Indonesia), the magnificent "Torch ginger"; gigantic herb forming clumps of robust, stiff, arching canes to 6 m high, with alternate, pointed leaves to 60 cm long in 2 ranks; the striking inflorescence of large, torch-like heads of brilliant red, formed of innumerable waxen bracts, on separate leafless stems 2 m high or more, subtended by red basal bracts, margined white, forming a nest for the red cone, brightened by yellow-margined lips of the small red flowers. *Tropical. Zone 11.*   *p. 521*

NICOTIANA   *Solanaceae*
africana (S.W. Africa); curious tropical perennial with gray-green, oblong leaves, irregularly lobed; erect blackish stem terminating in slender, branched cluster of small creamy-white flowers, having curved tube and spreading lobes. *Zone 10.*   *p. 512*

alata (affinis) (Brazil, Uruguay, Paraguay), "Jasmine tobacco"; tender herbaceous perennial with sticky-hairy stalks to 1½ m high, set with large 10-25 cm, pubescent, ovate, soft leaves, terminated by loose racemes of long, trumpet-shaped flowers pale purple or white within, yellowish outside, closing in cloudy weather, and with a sugar-sweet perfume at night. The cv. 'Nicki White' as seen in Geo. Ball's trial fields in West Chicago: very floriferous, base-branching, bushy plant to 40-50 cm high with showy, pure white tubular flowers with lobes spreading wide, and fragrant in evening, blooming throughout Summer. *Zone 10.*   *p. 512*

glauca (Argentina, Bolivia, Paraguay), "Tree-tobacco" or "Indian tobacco"; erect, glaucous shrub, tree-like, to 6 m high, with broad, long-petioled bluish leaves 12-45 cm long; tubular, salverform flowers in loose clusters, open during daytime, first greenish, later yellow. Naturalized in California. *Zone 9.*   *p. 881*

tabacum (West Indies, South Pacific), "Common tobacco"; herbaceous clammy-hairy plant growing to 1½ m high, perennial in mild climate, closely furnished with huge, membranous, pale green leaves 30-50 cm or more long, and used in the manufacture of tobacco; loose terminal clusters or rosy, funnel-shaped, fragrant flowers 3 cm across, open during daytime. *Zone 9.*   *p. 512*

tabacum macrophylla, "Large-leaf tobacco" of commerce; short-lived herbaceous perennial, clammy-hairy, and somewhat woody at base, to 2 m tall, usually grown as biennial or annual; large ovate, thin leaves to 40 cm or more long; tubular rosy flowers 4-6 cm long, with flaring lobes sweetly scented and open during day, blooming in Summer. *Zone 10.*   *p. 512*

NIDULARIUM   *Bromeliaceae*
acanthocrater: see NEOREGELIA concentrica

fulgens (S.E. Brazil), "Blushing cup"; showy rosette with numerous flattened shiny leaves pea-green with dark mottling and conspicuous spines; inflorescence cup in center bright crimson tipped nile-green, flowers blue. *Tropical. Zone 11.*   *p. 51*

innocentii (Karatas) (So. Brazil); bold open rosette of broad oblanceolate leaves 25 cm long, metallic green above and tinted purple, especially toward base, deep wine-red underneath, the margins finely spiny; at blooming time a dull crimson center cup of shorter leaves forms a nest for white flowers. *Tropical. Zone 11.*   *p. 50*

NIEREMBERGIA *Solanaceae*

hippomanica (Argentina), "Dwarf cupflower"; compact herbaceous perennial 15-20 cm high, densely branched, with linear to spoon-shaped leaves 2 cm long; flowers with tubular bluish corolla having 5 lobes flaring 2 cm wide, summer-blooming. Zone 9. *p. 512*

hippomanica violacea (Argentina), "Cup flower"; lovely herbaceous plant to 40 cm high, freely spreading with thin erect, hairy stems having needle-like leaves; bearing numerous wide bell-shaped flowers 2 cm dia., purplish-blue with violet lines and yellow eye. Zone 7. *p. 322*

hippomanica violacea 'Purple Robe'; very floriferous low perennial dense with tangled thin, leafy branches, covered with a multitude of cupflowers darker purple than violacea, and more freely blooming, June to September. Zone 7. *p. 512*

repens (rivularis) (Uruguay to Andes of Chile), "White cupflower"; popular herbaceous perennial with creeping stems, rooting and forming mats 10 to 15 cm high; the leaves oblong to spoon-shaped 3 cm long; charming cupped flowers creamy-white to pale lilac, with yellow throat, 3 to 5 cm across, during Summer; often treated as an annual in cold regions. Zone 7. *p. 512*

scoparia (frutescens) (Uruguay, Argentina), "Tall cupflower"; subshrubby perennial, close to hippomanica, but 50 to 90 cm tall, much branched and set with small 2-5 cm spoon-shaped to linear leaves; cup-shaped flowers 3-4 cm across, having delicate blue corollas changing to nearly white at margins; normally during Summer; grown as annual in pots, blooming almost continuously. Zone 7. *p. 512*

NIGELLA *Ranunculaceae*

damascena (So. Europe), "Love-in-a-mist" or "Devil-in-the-bush"; annual ornamental herb to 45 cm, with leaves pinnately cut into threadlike segments; showy flowers 3 cm dia., white or light blue, with prominent green pistils united at base. Zone 10. *p. 488*

hispanica 'Persian Jewels'; a "Fennel flower" with striking lavender blooms to 6 cm across, marked with purple, or in other colors such as pink, blue or white, prominently displaying red stamens during Summer, followed by handsome seedpods; annual herb to 50 cm high, with finely dissected leaves. The species is from So. France, Spain and No. Africa. Zone 10. *p. 488*

sativa (Mediterran. reg. to Caspian Sea), "Nutmeg flower" or "Fennel flower"; popular annual herb to 40 cm high, rather hairy with finely cut leaves of spreading segments; solitary pretty, bluish flowers to 4 cm across, followed by inflated pods containing pungent seed, spicy to the taste, and used for seasoning of bread and cakes in Israel, and going back to ancient Egyptian times. Seeds contain some poison and should be used sparingly. Zone 10. *p. 488, 542*

NIPHAEA *Gesneriaceae*

oblonga (Mexico), a "Snowwort" from Chiapas and collected by Thos. MacDougall in 1961 (Gloxinian Nov. 1970); attractive herbaceous species with scaly rhizomes, growing to 30 cm high, with fleshy red stem and several pairs of 10 cm, rugose leaves with depressed red veins and toothed margins; flowers with white corolla 4 cm across, carried on slender red stalks. Zone 11. *p. 64*

NOLANA *Nolanaceae*

paradoxa (acuminata, napiformis hort.) (No. Chile), "Bluebird nolana" or "Chilean bellflower"; beautiful procumbent usually pubescent perennial of the Atacama Desert in No. Chile, 15-20 cm high, often grown as annual; with fleshy, ovate leaves 6 cm long, very showy flowers 5 cm across, the outer lobes sky-blue or darker, the funnel inside white, and yellow toward base, blooming during Summer; but seen blooming in Chile in October, their Spring. Zone 10. *p. 460*

NOLINA *Agavaceae*

bigelovii (Dasylirion) (California, Arizona, Sonora), "Bear grass"; leaves in large numbers arranged in a symmetrical way, their margins shredding away in brown fibers; with striking tall plumy panicles of uncounted whitish-green minute flowers standing far above the leaves 2-3 m high. Arid-subtropic. Zone 9. *p. 566*

tuberculata: see BEAUCARNEA recurvata

NOPALXOCHIA *Cactaceae*

ackermannii (Epiphyllum) (Mexico: Chiapas, Oaxaca 2000-2700 m), a species "Orchid cactus"; in habitat mostly epiphytic, with flattened green branches, sometimes 3-angled, the angles notched (crenate); large and showy funnel-form flowers glowing red 10 cm or more across; good flowering plant. Tropical. Zone 11. *p. 176*

phyllanthoides (Epiphyllum) (Mexico); an old, free-flowering house plant widely grown under the name "Deutsche Kaiserin" (German Empress); an epiphyte from Puebla state at 1700 m; densely bushy with flattened, pendant, crenate branches bearing a profusion of day-flowering, long-lasting, carmine-rose flowers of medium size, 5 cm across, 10 cm long and with pale blue tips and short tube; a lovely

basket plant. According to Backeberg "Deutsche Kaiserin" may actually be a hybrid of Nop. (Epiphyllum) ackermannii with Nop. phyllanthoides. Tropical. Zone 11. *p. 176*

phyllanthoides 'Pink Nightie'; an excellent 'German Empress' cultivar seen at Dick Wright Nursery in De Luz, Fallbrook, California, with larger, substantial flowers with petals of deeper rose, suffused over pale pink inside; crenate branches of firm habit, and said to be disease-resistant. Zone 11. *p. 176*

NORONHIA *Oleaceae*

emarginata (Malagasy Rep.), "Madagascar olive"; tropical evergreen tree, with paired, leathery 15 cm leaves dark green with cream midvein; clusters of fragrant yellow flowers from leaf axils, with thick 4-parted corolla; purplish fruit 3 cm dia., with sweet-tasting edible pulp, enclosing a large seed. Tropical. Zones 10-11. *p. 916*

NOTHOFAGUS *Fagaceae*

antarctica (Southern Chile, Argentina), "Antarctic beech"; ornamental 5 m high, in habitat growing into tree 30 m tall; deciduous or evergreen depending on climate; the leaves oval and small 15-20 mm long in juvenile stage, later 3 cm and ovate, the margins undulate and crenate; the fruit a 4-lobed husk containing 3 small acorn nuts. Zone 8. *p. 727*

fusca (New Zealand), "Red beech" of N.Z.; handsome evergreen tree of slender growth to 30 m high, with old trunks furrowed and to 2 m dia., the branchlets downy and zigzag on young trees; the ovate leaves glossy green 2-4 cm long, lightly downy, with incurved teeth at margins; the male flowers bell-shaped, in September to January in Southern Hemisphere; female inflorescence producing 4-lobed capsule containing pubescent nuts. Zone 8. *p. 727*

menziesii (New Zealand), "Silver beech"; larger evergreen tree with silvery bark, to 30 m high; small leathery leaves dark green and shining, 2 cm long, ovate or rounded, the margins crenate; produces downy nuts, 2-3 winged. Subtropic. Zone 9. *p. 727*

NOTHOPANAX *Araliaceae*

filicifolia (Aralia, Polyscias) (South Sea Islands), "Fernleaf aralia" or "Angelica"; evergreen shrub with flexuous stems and leathery but variable leaves, bright green and with purplish midrib, pinnate with leaflets cut into narrow lobes; fern-like in younger plants, broader and entire when older. According to Dr. David Frodin, a specialist on Malaysian Araliads, my photos, taken in Singapore Bot. Garden, show a form of the variable Polyscias filicifolia. Zone 10. *p. 36, 650*

laetus: see PSEUDOPANAX laetus

NOTOCACTUS *Cactaceae*

crassigibus (So. Brazil: Rio Grande do Sul), "Ball cactus"; small globe resembling Gymnocalycium; the dark green raised knobs set with a radial of decurved spines; from the crown a bouquet of immense 7 to 10 cm satiny yellow flowers, centered by red stigmas. Zone 10. *p. 168*

herteri (Uruguay: Dept. Rivera); small light green globe to 15 cm dia., having about 20 high ribs notched into nipples, these topped by radiating needle spines; ringed toward apex by showy carmine-rose 4 cm flowers, pale in center. Zone 10. *p. 169*

leninghausii (Eriocactus) (So. Brazil), "Golden ball"; attracive, smallish clustering, cylindrical column, to 1 m high and 10 cm thick, close-ribbed, covered with soft golden hair; flowers yellow at top, 4 cm long. Beautiful, and of easy growth. Arid-subtropic. Zone 10. *p. 169*

magnificus (Eriocactus) (So. Brazil: Rio Grande do Sul); handsome deep green 12-15 cm globe with 12 high ribs covered along their crest by woolly white areoles and brown needle spines; showy yellow 6-8 cm flowers from the crown. Arid-subtropic. Zone 10. *p. 169*

mammulosus (Brazil to Uruguay and Argentina), "Lemon ball"; simple plant nearly globose, to 8 cm thick, shining green, with 18-25 high ribs, and yellowish to reddish spines from recesses on the knobs; fragrant yellow flowers to 4 cm long, appearing at an early stage. Arid-subtropic. Zone 10. *p. 168*

scopa (Brazil, Paraguay), "Silver ball"; globular to cylindrical, 25 to 45 cm high, closely ribbed and nearly covered with short, soft-hairy white radials and long brown needle-spines; 4 cm flowers silky canary yellow, deeper in center. Arid-subtropic. Zone 10. *p. 169*

uebelmannianus (Brazil: Rio Grande do Sul); rare small depressed globular "Ball cactus", seen in col. Bermuda Botanic Garden 1983; the glossy olive-green body 7 cm dia. cut into broad notched ribs; from the depressed surface of each knob with woolly areoles the radial spines spread star-like; near the crown a ring of shining red flowers 5-6 cm across. Zone 10. *p. 169*

NOTONIA petraea: see SENECIO jacobsenii

NOTOSPARTIUM *Leguminosae*

glabrescens (New Zealand: South Island), "Southern broom"; curious much branched shrub to 2 m, or small round-headed tree to 10 m high, leafless except as young plant, with several trunks;

branches ascending or pendulous; showy rose-pink flowers flushed with purple and with darker lines, having round standard, and wings shorter than the keel. Beautiful during December bloom in New Zealand habitat. *Zones 9-10.* *p. 758*

NUPHAR   *Nymphaeaceae*
advena (New England to Texas and Mexico), "Cow lily" or "Spatterdock"; rhizomatous pond perennial, with thick and more or less erect leaves usually above water surface, oval deeply cordate at base, 30 cm across; globose yellow flowers 4 cm across, well above the water. Common in streams and ponds in Eastern U.S. *Zone 4.* *p. 334*
luteum (Europe, Temp. Asia), "European pond-lily"; aquatic plant with stout rootstock creeping in the mud; large rounded leaves, some submerged, others floating or standing erect above the water, to 30 cm across; small yellow flowers slightly above the water or floating. *Zone 4.* *p. 334*

NYCTANTHES   *Verbenaceae*
arbor-tristis (Southeast Asia, India), "Tree-of-sadness"; tropical tree or shrub 3-6 m high, with 4-angled red branches spreading wide; cordate, slender pointed leaves to 12 cm long and rough to the touch; the flowers are white and intensely fragrant, the corolla tube orange, tipped by 5-8 lobes, blooming July; the fruit an orbicular capsule 2 cm dia. The fallen blooms are collected in India and used in perfumery, and yield an orange dye. *Zone 10.* *p. 900*

NYCTOCEREUS   *Cactaceae*
serpentinus (Mexico), a "Queen of the night", or "Snake cactus"; slender erect or clambering night-bloomer; cylindric many-ribbed stems, to 5 cm thick, deep green; woolly areoles and white to brownish spines; large white, sweet-scented funnel-form nocturnal flowers to 25 cm long, blooming into daylight; edible red fruit. *Tropical. Zone 10.* *p. 169*

NYMPHAEA   *Nymphaeaceae*
alba (Eurasia, No. Africa, Palestine to Kashmir), "European white water-lily"; robust hardy water lily, with leaves red when young, crowded on rhizome; white flowers 8-12 cm across with yellow stigmas, open nearly all day, and floating on the water. All growth not persistent during cold Winter, except for thick rhizome. *Zone 6.* *p. 335*
caerulea (Egypt to C. Africa), "Blue lotus of Egypt"; tender, day-blooming water lily, with large leathery, floating leaves glossy dark green, and light blue, faintly scented flowers with numerous narrow petals, 8-15 cm across, borne well above the water. *Humid-tropical. Zones 10-11.* *p. 335*
callicantha (Uganda to Namibia); tropical equatorial water-lily with roundish-ovate leaves green above, purplish beneath; found floating on the waters of Lake Victoria; the smallish pink flowers carried above the water level. *Zone 11.* *p. 334*
candida (No. and Arctic Europe, to Siberia; Spain); winter-hardy, rhizomatous water-lily similar to N. alba but smaller; roundish, floating leaves about 20 cm across and cleft to leafstalk; summer-blooming, with flowers of pure white petals and yellow stamens, 8 cm across, and resting on the water. Deciduous during Winter. *Zone 4.* *p. 335*
capensis (So. Africa), "Cape blue waterlily"; subtropical day-blooming water-lily of robust, luxuriant habit, with sinuate leaves; stiff stems carry large flowers 15-20 cm across, sky-blue with pale center, fading to nearly white. *Subtropic. Zone 10.* *p. 335*
x chromatella (mexicana x alba); free-blooming, century-old hardy water lily with floating leaves, much blotched with brown, rising above the water when crowded; flowers bright yellow with concave petals and yellow stamens, floating on the water. *Zone 8.* *p. 78*
colorata (Trop. Africa: Dar-es-Salaam); lovely pygmy tropical day-bloomer; from erect rhizome the vigorous, abundant foliage dark green, 25 cm dia.; light blue broad-petalled 10 cm flowers with darker center; develops clusters of tiny tubers; excellent for tub culture. *Tropical. Zones 10-11.* *p. 335*
x daubeniana, a tropical viviparous "Pygmy water lily"; for confined spaces, very free blooming with small, fragrant, light blue flowers carried well above the water; young plants develop at the junction of petiole and leaf; possibly a hybrid of micrantha and caerulea. *Humid-tropical. Zones 10-11.* *p. 335*
'Director George Moore' (Missouri Bot. Garden 1941); superb day-flowering tropical, tuberous waterlily, with smallish 10-20 cm dark green floating leaves occasionally speckled, profusely blooming with deep rich purple, fragrant flowers 15 cm or more across, and a golden center, carried well above the water surface. Propagates freely from tubers. *Zone 11.* *p. 334*
gigantea (New Guinea, Queensland), "Giant water-lily" or "Australian waterlily"; big leathery, glossy green leaves 50 cm dia.; flowers carried well above water surface, light blue with broad petals, tipped dark blue and with yellow center, 15-30 cm across; day-

blooming for 7 days, and remaining open from the fourth day; very fragrant. *Tropical. Zone 10.* *p. 334*
lotus dentata (Egypt, Sierra Leone), "White lotus of Egypt"; robust, tender night-blooming species with smooth leaves 30-50 cm across; fragrant white flowers 12-25 cm dia., remaining open until noon. *Humid-tropical. Zones 10-11.* *p. 334*
odorata (So. Canada and Eastern U.S.), "Fragrant water-lily"; beautiful, very fragrant aquatic perennial, having rounded rather thick leaves 10-25 cm dia., with a slit to center where attached to the petiole, and resting on the water, green above and purplish beneath; the lovely scented, 8-15 cm flowers are white, floating on the water surface; the waxy petals are open only during morning hours, in summertime; native in ponds and quiet rivers. *Zone 3.* *p. 333*
'Pink Sensation'; perennial water-lily, with rhizome living through the Winter even under ice, with round, smooth-edged leaves; fragrant flowers rich pink, opening to the sun, and remaining open for 2 or 3 hours after other blooms have closed, from May until frost. *Warm temperate. Zone 6.* *p. 335*
rubra (India), "India red waterlily"; beautiful tropical night-blooming species, remaining open until nearly noon; flowers deep carmine-red 15-25 cm across; floating leaves red bronze and crisped, 30-50 cm dia. *Humid-tropical. Zone 11.* *p. 334*
satellata (India to S.E. Asia, Malaya), "Blue lotus of India"; excellent tropical water-lily, its floating round, peltate leaves having margins dentate and crisped, and lavender-blue beneath; lovely flowers 8-16 cm across, pale blue, varying to pink, as seen in Sydney Botanic Garden. *Zone 10.* *p. 335*
x virginalis; hardy natural hybrid (prob. alba x candida), ideal for pools to 1 m deep; slightly fragrant, showy flowers to 25 cm across, white with prominent rich yellow stamens, floating on the water; an excellent bloomer. *Zone 6.* *p. 335*

NYMPHOIDES   *Gentianaceae*
humboldtiana (Limnanthemum) (Trop. America), "Floating heart"; aquatic perennial with stout rootstock, sending up long threadlike petioles bearing fleshy floating leaves, with runners developing from leafstalks, the leafblades orbicular, to 15 cm across; interesting white flowers with yellow center, the 2 cm lobes fringed at margins. Suitable for aquariums. *Zone 11.* *p. 331*
indica (Pantropic: S.E. Asia, S.W. China, Australia, So. Japan, Trop. Africa), "Water snowflake" or "Floating heart"; perennial aquatic herb with kidney-shaped floating leaves to 20 cm across; fimbriate (fringed) flowers white with yellow center. *Humid-tropical. Zones 10-11.* *p. 334*
peltata (Europe, Asia, naturalized in U.S.), "Yellow floating heart" or "Water-fringe"; fresh-water aquatic perennial, resembling miniature water-lily, with roundish-cordate floating leaves 10 cm across, the margins toothed and crisped; yellow flowers 3 cm across, having fringed lobes, carried well above water surface, from Spring to Summer. Suitable for cool temperature aquariums. *Zones 6-10.* *p. 331*

NYPA   *Palmae*
fruticans (Philippines, Malaya, India, to Australia), "Nypa" or "Nipa palm"; low, shrubby palm usually growing with base more or less submerged in brackish water; trunk-like rootstock forming colonies with age, the pinnate fronds erect-recurving and rigid, 3-9 m tall, the leaflets 1-1½ m long, folded, and shiny bright green, grayish beneath; large compound fruit near base, to 30 cm dia., and consisting of a clump of carpels, each enclosing a seed kernel. The immature seeds are eaten fresh or are made into sweetmeat. The juice from the flower spathes produces an alcoholic brew, or sugary syrup. *Humid-tropical. Zones 12.* *p. 111*

NYSSA   *Nyssaceae*
aquatica (Virginia to Florida, Missouri to Texas), "Cotton gum"; deciduous tree from river swamps, to 30 m high, the shoots red; ovate-oblong leaves 10-30 cm long, their margins entire or toothed, shining above, pale and pubescent beneath; small yellow-green flowers; dark purple fruit 3 cm long; a plant favored by bees. *Zone 4.* *p. 305*
sylvatica (Maine to Ontario, Michigan, Delaware to Florida and Texas), "Black tupelo", "Pepperidge" or "Sour gum"; excellent ornamental, deciduous tree to 30 m high, with somewhat pendulous branches, and ovate or obovate leaves 8-12 cm long, which turn to brilliant red and yellow in autumn-color; small greenish-yellow flowers, followed on female trees by 1 cm ovoid berry-like blue-black fruit. *Zone 4.* *p. 805*

OCHNA   *Ochnaceae*
atropurpurea (So. Africa), a "Mickey-mouse plant"; ornamental small shrub to 2 m high, with leathery ovate leaves sharply toothed; flowers yellow with dark purple calyx, when in fruit displaying shining black seed cases. *Zone 10.* *p. 805*

kirkii (Trop. S.E. Africa), "Mickey-mouse plant"; evergreen smooth shrub with leathery oblong, finely toothed 5-8 cm leaves on woody branches; flowers bright yellow, the 5 petals soon falling, the glossy calyx lobes turning a glowing red and later the red to shining black fruit, this peculiar inflorescence looking like a fairy-tale Mickey Mouse. *Zone 10.* *p. 805*

serrulata ('multiflora') (Natal), "Birdseye bush"; woody shrub to 1½ m high with hard leathery, narrow-elliptic leaves to 12 cm long, serrate glossy green at the margins; the flower corolla yellow but quickly falling, the sepals at first greenish then turning bright red and persistent; interesting black berry-like fruit seated on a red receptacle. *Zone 10.* *p. 805*

OCHROSIA   *Apocynaceae*

marianensis (Pacific Islands, Micronesia); small tree with milky sap; whorled leathery leaves, long oblanceolate and glossy green; small white flowers; red flattened fruit with edible seeds. *Tropical. Zones 10-11.* *p. 907*

OCIMUM   *Labiatae*

basilicum (Trop. Asia, Africa, Pacific Isl.), "Sweet basil"; pretty, aromatic annual herb to 60 cm high, with light green, broad leaves 8-12 cm long, and small white flowers. Use: the scented leaves for culinary seasoning of fish, meats, game, salads, stews, with spicy, clove-like flavor. Reported to repel flies and mosquitoes. *Zone 10.* *p. 532, 533*

basilicum 'Purpurascens', "Dark opal basil"; very handsome color form of this popular aromatic herb so widely used for culinary purposes; erect reddish branches 40 to 50 cm high, bearing long-petioled ovate leaves, crenate along margins, and of rich purple color; small pink flowers in whorls at intervals along terminal stalk, blooming in Summer. Excellent as potherb. *Zone 10.* *p. 533*

gratissimum (India to Vietnam, Malaysia), "Tree basil" of "Hobokbok"; aromatic shrub to 2 m or more high, with broad-ovate, scented leaves 5-10 cm long, and toothed along margins; small pale yellow flowers in slender, dense racemes. Grown in the kitchen gardens of Cochinchina. *Zones 7-10.* *p. 533*

sanctum (India), "Sacred basil" or "Clove basil"; aromatic annual herb, with pubescent purplish stems, and opposite, oblong pointed leaves 4-5 cm long; purple flowers in spike-like racemes to 20 cm long. This plant with its scented leaves is held sacred by the Hindus in the temples of India. The only basil to self-sow in So. New England. *Zone 10.* *p. 533*

ODONTADENIA   *Apocynaceae*

speciosa (hoffmansegiana in Bot. Garden Singapore) (Costa Rica, Trinidad, Guayana, Brazil); tropical woody vine closely related to Mandevilla, with leathery dark green oblong corrugated leaves 15 cm long; and bearing large showy clusters of bright yellow funnel-shaped flowers tinged with orange, 8 cm across, and delicately scented. *Zone 11.* *p. 265*

ODONTOGLOSSUM   *Orchidaceae*

'Alispum' (Alorcus x crispum); typical of many of the hybrids originated so successfully in England 80 years ago, featuring beautiful, large, rounded, 8-10 cm flowers with white base, blotched, barred or spotted brown, mauve, purple or crimson, and with crisped margins, (bl. various). *Humid-subtropic. Zone 11.* *p. 92*

crispum (Colombia); very handsome epiphyte with stout, two-leaved pseudobulbs, and arching racemes of daintily crisped, waxy star-shaped 9 cm flowers of pure white, the lip yellow at base and blotched reddish toward front; variable, (Feb.-April). *Humid-subtropic. Zone 11.* *p. 92*

grande (Rosioglossum) (Guatemala, Mexico), "Tiger orchid"; very beautiful epiphyte of compact habit; an easy grower, with thick, two-leaved pseudobulbs, and erect, 30 cm stalks with large 12-15 cm flowers, sepals yellow barred with brown, petals half reddish-brown, tips yellow, lip cream spotted with brown, (Aug.-March). *Humid-tropical. Zone 11.* *p. 93*

insleayi (Mexico); noble epiphyte with two-leaved compressed pseudobulbs, and an erect stalk with 5-10 cm flowers with oblong sepals and petals greenish-yellow transversely banded with chestnut red, the spoon-shaped lip bright yellow with a border of crimson spots, (Aug.-Sept., Dec.-Jan.). *Humid-subtropic. Zone 11.* *p. 92*

laeve reichenheimii (Miltonia) (Mexico to Panama); attractive variety; epiphyte with compressed two-leaved pseudobulbs and slightly branched racemes of 5 cm fragrant flowers, with narrow sepals and petals yellowish-green barred with purplish-brown, lip light purple without claw; willing bloomer, (Spring). *Humid-subtropic. Zone 11.* *p. 92*

pulchellum (Guatemala), "Lily-of-the-valley orchid"; dainty epiphyte with dark green pseudobulbs topped by 2-3 grass-like leaves, and clustering; erect racemes with small waxy, sweetly fragrant 2-3 cm flowers of crystalline white with yellow crest, (Dec.-May). *Humid-subtropic. Zone 11.* *p. 92*

rossii (Mexico, Guatemala); pretty epiphyte of dwarf habit, with one-leaved pseudobulbs, delicate though wiry inflorescence with star-like, 5-8 cm flowers, linear sepals white, barred with brown, crisped petals, and lip white with yellow crest, (Feb.-April). *Humid-subtropic. Zone 11.* *p. 92*

williamsianum (Rosioglossum) (Mexico to Costa Rica); tropical epiphyte similar in habit to O. grande, with shorter and broader pseudobulbs, and flowers with more yellow and less red-brown blotching; spring-blooming. *Zone 11.* *p. 90*

ODONTOSPERMUM: referred to ASTERISCUS (Hortus 3)

OENOTHERA   *Onagraceae*

berlandieri (speciosa 'Childsii') (Texas; Mexico), "Mexican evening primrose"; small arid area, hairy perennial, bushy with slender branches to 15 cm long, rising from underground stolon; small ovate leaves, lobed or toothed at margins; charming cupped flowers rose-pink, 4-5 cm across, blooming in early Summer. *Zone 7.* *p. 463*

biennis (E. No. America), "Evening primrose" or "German rampion"; popular wild garden biennial 30-120 cm high, with hairy green basal, lanceolate leaves in a rosette, 10-30 cm long, finely toothed; the upper leaves ovate; light yellow flowers 4 cm wide, in terminal racemes, opening in the afternoon and remaining open during evening, aging old gold. The fleshy roots are eaten as a vegetable, and the shoots in salads. *Zone 4.* *p. 462*

brevipes (Camissonia) (deserts of California, Nevada, Utah, Arizona); small evening-flowering perennial with hairy stems 10 cm high; the leaves mostly near base, forming a rosette; blades variously shaped, often ovate, with veins red on underside; golden-yellow flowers in small clusters, with petals to 2 cm long, blooming March to May. *Zone 5.* *p. 461*

caespitosa (No. Dakota to Texas and California), "Twisted evening primrose"; short-lived perennial or biennial herb to 1 m high, with woody roots; pubescent, narrow oblong leaves, sinuate and lobed at margins; fragrant white flowers aging pink, 5-8 cm across, and opening in the evening; April to September. *Zone 5.* *p. 460*

clavaeformis (Death-Valley of East. California); annual xerophytic herb 20 to 50 cm high, with leaves in a basal rosette 10 to 20 cm long, broad ovate blades crenate or lobed and somewhat succulent; white flowers 2 cm across, tinted yellow and often red-brown at throat, in terminal clusters, day-blooming. *Zone 6.* *p. 461*

deltoides (howellii) (Deserts of So. California and Arizona), "Desert evening primrose"; small evening-blooming Winter or Spring annual 15-30 cm high, with narrow-lanceolate, entire or pinnate leaves to 8 cm long; flowers white, aging pink, 4-8 cm or more wide, and staying open well into the next morning. Photographed in col. New York Bot. Garden. *Zone 9.* *p. 462*

erythrosepala prob. a hookeri hybrid; evening-blooming perennial or biennial 1 m or more high, with stout reddish stems; undulate and more or less crinkled stem-leaves; flowers yellow, but changing to orange-red in age, 5 to 8 cm across; in Summer and Autumn. According to Royal Hort. Dict. originated in England about 1850. *Zone 8.* *p. 462*

fruticosa (Eastern U.S.), "Sundrops"; day-blooming perennial 30-50 cm high, with reddish stems, lance-shaped leaves, and yellow flowers nearly 5 cm wide. *Zones 4-9.* *p. 463*

hookeri (Texas to California, north to Colorado and Washington), "Night-candle"; majestic perennial with erect stems to 2 m high, with narrow lanceolate leaves 10-15 cm long; showy golden-yellow flowers 6 cm across, opening in succession toward apex during the night and blooming until late morning, and aging orange. *Zone 6.* *p. 462*

laciniata (mexicana) (Maine to So. Dakota, so. to Texas and Arizona), "Pale evening primrose"; evening-blooming, perennial in mild climate, annual in colder regions; branches decumbent or erect, 30 cm or more long, more or less hairy; leaves lanceolate or pinnately divided; flowers in leaf axils, with pale yellow petals, drying pink, 2 cm long; in April to October. *Zones 3-9.* *p. 461*

missouriensis (Central U.S.), "Ozark evening primrose"; perennial evening-flowering garden plant to 30 cm high, with woody base; hairy lanceolate leaves to 10 cm long; showy bell-shaped yellow flowers nearly 10 cm wide. *Temperate. Zone 4.* *p. 463*

neomexicana (Arizona and New Mexico); day-blooming perennial sundrops 30-60 cm high, from arid region habitats; the lanceolate leaves are 5 cm long, wavy-margined or toothed and downy; showy flowers 6 cm across, creamy-white but turning pink in aging; normally blooming in July-August, but seen in flower in So. California during October. *Zones 8-9.* *p. 462*

perennis (pumila) (Canada to Missouri and Georgia), "Canada sundrops"; freely blooming day-flowering perennial with slender branches 20-60 cm high, beginning with a rosette of oblanceolate leaves 5 cm long; inflorescence forming on short 5 cm stalk, gradually elongating and continuing to flower with yellow blooms 2 cm across, in loose raceme, nodding in bud; July. *Zones 3-8.* *p. 462*

pilosella (Ohio to Missouri and Arkansas, also Ontario), "Prairie sundrops"; small day-blooming perennial 15-50 cm high, covered with straight hairs; obovate and lanceolate leaves to 10 cm long; the numerous diurnal yellow flowers 3-5 cm across, conspicuously veined, June-blooming. *Zone 4.*   *p. 462*

speciosa (Kansas to Texas), "Showy white sundrops"; lovely day-blooming perennial or annual to 40 cm high, from underground rhizome; leaves lanceolate hairy or pinnately divided; showy white flowers becoming rose-pink, 3-6 cm across, nodding while in bud, in upper leaf axils, blooming early Summer. *Zone 5.*   *p. 462*

speciosa grandiflora, "Great white sundrops"; handsome day-blooming perennial forming widespread bushes 60 cm high; finely hairy, with elliptic entire or lobed leaves; very floriferous with large white flowers 5-7 cm across, changing to pink, blooming early Summer. *Zone 5.*   *p. 462*

tetragona fraseri (glauca) (Eastern U.S.), "Sundrops"; charming day-blooming perennial freely branching, 40 to 60 cm high; pubescent reddish stems with bluish-green, narrow-lanceolate leaves and toothed at margins; bright golden-yellow cupped flowers 3-5 cm across, during Summer, opening from colorful red buds. Very similar or related to Oe. fruticosa. *Zone 3.*   *p. 463*

OLEA   *Oleaceae*
europaea (E. Mediterran. reg.), "Olive tree" or "Black olive"; small, sparry, evergreen tree with stiff-leathery, narrow lanceolate leaves gray-green above, silvery scurfy beneath; flowers yellowish-white and fragrant; oblong 3 to 4 cm fruit green turning shining black when ripe; used for its valuable oil, and is eaten as pickled fruit. *Subtropic. Zone 9.*   *p. 537, 623, 916, 917*

europaea 'Manzanillo'; a Spanish cultivar of the Black olive; evergreen tree of lower habit, with multiple trunks, and rounded head and distinctive gray-green foliage, bearing choice edible fruit. Excellent decorative tree and grown in standard form in California nurseries. *Zone 8.*   *p. 811*

OLEARIA   *Compositae*
albida (New Zealand), "Coastal tree-daisy"; evergreen shrub 2-3 m high, or small tree to 6 m in habitat; leathery ovate leaves 3-10 cm long, white-felted beneath; floral heads white, in terminal and axillary clusters 5-8 cm across, the ray-flowers with 3-6 florets, summer-blooming. *Zone 9.*   *p. 690*

ilicifolia (New Zealand), "Hollyleaf daisy" or "Hakeke" (Maori); spreading evergreen shrub or small tree 3-5 m high, having a musky scent; rigid leathery, oblong leaves to 10 cm long, with margins undulate and toothed, yellowish-hairy beneath; floral heads fragrant, daisy-like, in dense clusters 5-10 cm across, the ray-flowers white. *Zone 9.*   *p. 690*

nummulariifolia (New Zealand), "Daisy-bush"; woody shrub 1 to 3 m high, of dense growth, with sticky shoots closely set with rounded thick, shining leaves 1 cm long, topped by small flowerheads with yellowish florets. *Zone 9.*   *p. 690*

stellulata (New So. Wales, Tasmania), "Tasmanian daisy-bush"; shrub to 1¹/₂ m with oblong or lanceolate leaves to 8 cm with toothed margins, white tomentose beneath; heads of white ray-flowers and yellow discs, in leafy clusters. *Zone 9.*   *p. 690*

stellulata 'Pink form', "Pink daisy-bush"; evergreen bush, with leathery leaves 6-8 cm long, the margins serrate, and white-felted underneath; inflorescence in loose clusters of charming starry flowers with linear ray-florets rose-pink. *Zone 9.*   *p. 690*

OLMEDIELLA   *Flacourtiaceae*
betschleriana (Guatemala), "Guatemala holly" or "Manzanote"; ornamental evergreen, dioecious small tree to 6 or 8 m high, dense with alternate stiff-leathery, dark green, long elliptic leaves 10 to 15 cm long, spiny-toothed at margins, somewhat like English holly (Ilex); inconspicuous flowers with numerous stamens but without petals; female trees produce hard-shelled, flattened orange-sized fruit to 8 cm dia., but inedible. *Subtropic. Zone 9.*   *p. 732*

OLNEYA   *Leguminosae*
tesota (California, Arizona to W. Mexico), "Desert ironwood"; arid region shrub or tree-like, with many stems to 8 m high; leaves pinnate having 4-12 pairs of oblong gray-pubescent leaflets 2 cm long; inflorescence in small clusters of pea-like pale purplish-rose flowers, the petals 1 cm long; hairy 6 cm fruit with black seeds. *Zone 9.*   *p. 766*

OMPHALODES   *Boraginaceae*
cappadocica (Asia Minor), "Navel-seed"; herbaceous perennial from creeping rhizome, to 25 cm high; ovate and lanceolate leaves to 10 cm long, covered by silky hairs, and showing prominent lateral veins; small 1 cm flowers blue with white centers. *Zone 6.*   *p. 349*

nitida (lusitanica) (Spain, Portugal), "Navelwort"; sturdy perennial to 50 cm high, with narrow, oblong-lanceolate leaves, hairy underneath; small 1 cm flowers blue with white centers, in erect, loose racemes, during Spring. *Zone 7.*   *p. 349*

verna (Europe: S.E. Alps, Italy to Romania), "Creeping forget-me-not"; herbaceous perennial to 20 cm high, the main stems prostrate but flowering tips ascending, the leaves ovate; pretty blue flowers 2 cm across, and marked with white, in Spring. *Zone 6.*   *p. 349*

ONCIDIUM   *Orchidaceae*
concolor (Brazil); lovely little epiphyte with 2-3 leaved flattened pseudobulb and cluster of large flowers 4-5 cm across, lemon-yellow and large yellow lip, (Oct.-May). *Subtropic. Zone 11.*   *p. 92*

flexuosum (Brazil, Paraguay), "Dancing doll orchid"; beautiful little epiphyte with 1-2-leaved pseudobulbs, and dainty, thin-wiry sprays of small "dancing doll"-like golden-yellow flowers with center marked deep red, (Oct.Aug.). *Tropical. Zones 11-12.*   *p. 92*

forbesii (Organ Mts. of Brazil); handsome epiphyte with compressed pseudobulbs and solitary leaf; many-flowered panicles of waxy, showy 5-6 cm blooms with crisped petals rich chestnut brown and broken golden borders, (Mar.-April, Oct.-Nov.). *Zone 11.* *p. 94*

kramerianum (Ecuador, Colombia); beautiful epiphyte with small round pseudobulbs bearing a solitary leaf; flower stalks to 75 cm long and round, with several very curious, highly colored flowers in succession, the long narrow dorsal sepal and petals chocolate-brown, lateral sepals broad, orange-red mottled with yellow, lip lemon-yellow bordered red-brown, (March-May, Nov.-Dec.). *Tropical. Zones 11-12.*   *p. 94*

lanceanum (Trinidad, Guyana), "Leopard orchid"; strikingly beautiful epiphyte with minute pseudobulbs, broad and thick, brown-spotted, solitary leaves and erect spikes with large, vanilla-scented flowers, the fleshy sepals and petals yellow shaded green, blotched with chocolate-brown, the large lip violet at base, rose in front, (May-Aug.). *Tropical. Zones 11-12.*   *p. 92*

longipes (Brazil); small epiphyte densely clustered with 3 cm pseudobulbs, bearing usually two linear, leathery leaves to 20 cm long; inflorescence of numerous long-lasting flowers 3 cm across, pale red-brown streaked with yellow, the lip yellow. *Zones 11-12.* *p. 94*

papilio (Trinidad, Venezuela, Brazil, Perú), "Butterfly orchid"; epiphyte with small pseudobulbs bearing a single leaf mottled purplish-brown; the large, unusual flowers developing successively on flat stalks to 1 m long, dorsal sepal and petals long linear, reddish-brown marked with yellow, lateral sepals oblong, brown barred with yellow, lip yellow with brown border. *Tropical. Zones 11-12.*   *p. 92*

sphacelatum (Mexico to Honduras), "Golden shower"; prolific epiphyte with elongate, flattened pseudobulbs of 2-3 leaves; the branched, loose inflorescence to 1¹/₂ m long, with many small, yellow flowers, marked with brown, 2 to 3 cm across, (Feb.-Sept.). *Tropical. Zones 11-12.*   *p. 92*

splendidum (Guatemala); handsome stout epiphyte with short pseudobulbs bearing a single stiff-fleshy, mahogany leaf, and erect, 1 m spike with large substantial flowers, 5 cm across, small sepals and petals yellow barred with brown, the large lip golden-yellow, (Dec.-Feb.). *Tropical. Zones 11-12.*   *p. 92*

uniflorum (Brazil); small epiphyte of bushy habit; the short inflorescence with 1 or 2 waxy flowers, sepals and petals greenish-yellow shaded brown, lip bright yellow, (April to December). *Tropical. Zones 11-12.*   *p. 94*

ONOCLEA   *Polypodiaceae (Filices)*
sensibilis (Newfoundland to Louisiana, Siberia, Japan), called "Sensitive fern" because the herbaceous barren fronds are sensitive to cold or if cut, and fold their leaflets face to face; handsome sterile fronds of glaucous pale green pinnae with undulate, lobed margins; underground creeping rhizome; hardy. *Temperate. Zones 3-7.*   *p. 135*

ONOPORDUM   *Compositae*
acanthium (C. and So. Europe, W. Asia and Siberia), "Cotton thistle" or "Scotch thistle"; handsome thistle-like perennial 1-2 m or more high, occasionally annual; white-tomentose throughout; oblong or ovate leaves lobed, toothed, and spiny, the lower ones to 60 cm long; the inflorescence with bristly heads to 5 cm across, the outer bracts cobwebby, flowers purple. *Zone 5.*   *p. 397*

nervosum (arabicum) (Spain), "Ornamental thistle"; coarse, thistle-like herb, 2-3 m high, with lobed, white-hairy leaves and spiny; flowers rose-purple within bracted head, 5 cm across. *Zone 7. p. 397*

ONOSMA   *Boraginaceae*
albo-roseum (Turkey, Asia Minor), "Pink gold drops"; small perennial to 20 cm high, with woody base, and stiff erect stems; the obovate leaves are densely hairy with conspicuous midrib; blooms are velvety-hairy on outside, to 3 cm long, white changing to rose and bluish-pink. *Zone 6.*   *p. 350*

echioides (Spain to Greece, W. Asia), "Golden drops"; hairy, much branched herbaceous subshrub 40 cm high, with gray obovate or linear leaves to 10 cm long, covered with bristly yellow hairs; and nodding tubular 2 cm yellow flowers. *Zone 7.*   *p. 350*

tocuensis (S.E. Europe), "Hungarian gold-drops"; small subshrubby perennial similar to O. echioides but with more broadly long-lanceolate gray-bristly leaves, and pendant tubular flowers pale-yellow. *Zone 6.* p. 350

OPHIOPOGON   Liliaceae

intermedius 'Argenteo-marginatus' (India, Sri Lanka, China), "Silvery mondo grass"; lovely tufted bulbous evergreen plant with leathery, narrow linear leaves to 60 cm long and 2 cm wide, deep green with pure white edging, and gracefully recurving; flowers white or lilac; mat-forming. *Zone 9.* p. 565

jaburan (Japan), "White lily-turf"; evergreen sod-forming tufting perennial, with cord-like roots; linear strap-like, thick-leathery, dark green leaves to 60 cm long, and pure white, drooping flowers in long racemes, on flattened stalk. *Zone 7.* p. 562

japonicus (Japan, Korea), "Snake's beard"; evergreen perennial 15-30 cm high, forming low tufts of narrow linear, grass-like, but leathery, blackish-green leaves gracefully arching, with long underground stolons and the roots tuber-bearing; small, pale lilac flowers. Popular groundcover in mild climate gardens. *Zones 7-10.* p. 565

japonicus 'Kyoto Dwarf' (Japan), "Dwarf mondo grass"; lawn-forming stemless perennial with long underground stolons; tufted, recurving leaves only 4 cm high, dark green; small pale lilac flowers. Seen planted at old Imperial Palace in Kyoto, dating from 780 A.D. *Zone 8.* p. 565

planiscapus nigrescens, in hort. as "arabicus" (So. Japan), the "Black dragon"; small grass-like clustering plant 10-15 cm or more high, with narrow linear, leathery, curving leaves 4-6 mm wide, arranged in opposite ranks, at first bright green and glossy, later almost black; lavender flowers followed by black berries. Very attractive as a somber groundcover. *Zone 8.* p. 565

OPHRYS   Orchidaceae

fuciflora (arachnites) (Spain to Albania, No. Africa), "Bee orchid"; terrestrial with leafy stems, to 40 cm high; stout, broad leaves; the stalk with several flowers, the sepals and petals velvety white or pink; large lip dark brown with white center, and a shining eye-like knob each side of column. *Subtropic. Zone 11.* p. 93

speculum (So. Europe, to Greece), "Mirror of Venus"; miniature terrestrial 10-25 cm high, with tuberous rhizome producing a leafy stalk with remarkable 3 cm flowers, sepals pale green outside and light brown within, the shorter petals violet-brown, brown fringed lip with disc a steel blue glassy mirror edged in gold and margined maroon, (Spring). *Subtropic. Zone 11.* p. 91

OPHTHALMOPHYLLUM   Aizoaceae

schlechteri (Cape Prov.); stemless dwarf succulent with cylindric body 3 to 4 cm high and cleft at top, matte-green to reddish, all over set with tiny pale dots; white flowers 2.5 cm across. *Zone 10.* p. 153

OPLISMENUS   Gramineae

hirtellus 'Variegatus' (Panicum variegatum) (W. Indies), "Basket grass"; weak, creeping grass, rooting at nodes, with flowering culms generally erect; the rather broad, lanceolate, thin leaves daintily striped white and pink, 4-6 cm long. *Zone 10.* p. 569

OPUNTIA   Cactaceae: Opuntieae

arbuscula (Arizona, Sonora), "Pencil cholla"; dense succulent, much branched miniature shrub becoming 1 m high; the pencil-size olive-green joints 1 cm thick and 10 cm long, with prominent warts and long needle-spines; small 3 cm flowers bronze to yellowish; club-shaped fruit. *Arid-subtropic. Zone 10.* p. 170

basilaris (S.W. United States, No. Mexico), "Beaver tail"; growing in clumps, broadly obovate fleshy pads a bluish-coppery color, 12-20 cm long, almost spineless; large pale purple flowers 5 to 8 cm across, variable to rose or yellow. *Arid-subtropic. Zones 7-10.* p. 170

bergeriana (naturalized in Italy, of American origin); clambering and branching, or erect tree-like to 4 m high, developing trunk to 40 cm dia.; fleshy bluish-green joints narrow-oblong to 20 cm long; areoles distant with some gray wool and usually 2-3 stiff spines; bell-shaped crimson-red 5 cm flowers; fruit red. *Zone 10.* p. 170

brasiliensis (Brazil, Argentina, Bolivia), "Tropical tree-opuntia"; tree-like, to 4 m high; trunk and branches cylindrical, the terminal joints flat and leaf-like, to 10 cm long, glossy fresh green, with few spines; pale yellow flowers. A good and attractive house plant because of its tropical origin, resembling a miniature tree even as a young plant. *Subtropic. Zone 10.* p. 172

cholla (Mexico: Baja California); a true "Cholla cactus" seen on arid Isla Cerralvo, forming masses of scrambling, cylindric joints to 25 cm long, deeply notched into prominent oblong knobs, with few spines; pink flowers 3 cm across, followed by proliferous red fruit 5 cm long; *Zone 10.* p. 171

chrysacantha (Mexico: Hidalgo); bushy plant with orbicular to obovate pads 12 to 20 cm long, bluish-green; large areoles filled with brown wool; spreading yellowish spines; flowers lemon-yellow, 5-6 cm long; fruit purple. *Zone 10.* p. 170

dillenii (S.E. U.S., W. Indies, Spanish Main), "Tuna"; either low spreading, or tall branched, the long fleshy, flat joints bright green when young, glaucous bluish later, and stout orange-yellow spines; flowers yellow, and edible red fruit. *Subtropic. Zone 10.* p. 170

elata (Brazil, Paraguay), "Orange tuna"; erect bush to 2 m with fat obovate, waxy smooth pads to 25 cm long, rich green with brown-purple blotches around areole; occasional straw-colored to gray needle spines; 5 cm flowers orange-yellow. *Subtropic.* *Zone 10.* p. 170

erinacea ursina (California), the famous "Mojave Grizzly bear" of hidden reaches of the high Mohave desert; forms low clumps with oblong, thick, grayish-green flattened joints 10 to 15 cm long, densely covered with glistening white, threadlike spines usually 10 to 15 cm long, and I have seen them in the Mohave as long as 25 cm. Flowers may be red or yellow, 6 cm across. *Arid-subtropic. Zones 7-9.* p. 169

falcata (Consolea) (Haiti), a "Tree opuntia"; tree-like, with stout, straight, spiny brown trunk to 1½ m long, when older, and a heavy crown of thick-fleshy, oblong flat joints sickle-shaped, 20-30 cm long and 8 cm wide, glossy rich green, with raised knobs especially on margins, nearly spineless; flowers red turning orange. *Tropical.* *Zone 11.* p. 171

ficus-indica (Trop. America: prob. Mexico), the "Indian fig" or "Nopal"; a flat-jointed cactus that may grow bushy, or with woody stems to 3 m or more high; widely spread into warm-climate countries and cultivated for its pear-shaped juicy, orange-red fruit 6-8 cm long, called Tuna, which is peeled and the pulp eaten in salads, raw or cooked for its flavor and food value, from Mexico to Spain and Southern Italy and Eastward. The oblongish flat joints are green or glaucous bluish from 30 cm to almost 60 cm long, in some forms spineless but with irritating yellow bristles; the flowers are yellow to 10 cm across. These are monstrous plants, but durable with sculptured and exotic decorative effect. *Arid-tropical.* *Zone 10.* p. 171, 910

ficus-indica 'Burbank's Spineless', "Spineless Indian fig"; a lightly glaucous bluish-green, tree-like form to 4 m, with long flattened joints almost 60 cm long, with yellow flowers and edible orange Tuna fruits. A cultivar selected by Luther Burbank for its almost total absence of spines. *Arid-subtropic. Zone 10.* p. 171

fragilis (Wisconsin to Brit. Colombia and south to Texas and Arizona), "Pigmy tuna"; low spreading plant not over 5 cm high, with fresh green, roundish or cylindrical joints very fragile, dropping off easily; small white areoles and brownish spines; pale yellow flowers. Also found as far north as Cache Creek, Alberta. *Temperate.* *Zone 3.* p. 172

fulgida (So. Arizona to No. Mexico), "Jumping cholla"; cylindrical joints 3-5 cm thick and 10-20 cm long, with age becoming tree-like 1 to 4 m tall, the branches of sparry habit; the raised knobs densely covered with glistening white spines; pink flowers 2 cm across. *Arid-subtropic. Zone 10.* p. 171

galapageia (Galapagos Islands); a jointed succulent becoming tree-like with stems 45 cm thick and 2 m long; the elongate pads dark green to bluish-green, to 40 cm long, covered with golden-brownish needle spines; small 2½ cm yellow flowers, and small fruit. *Tropical.* *Zone 11.* p. 171

humifusa (compressa) (Ontario; Mass. to Montana, so. to Florida and E. Texas); low and spreading succulent with grass-green pads, almost smooth, oblong to 12 cm long, with few spines; yellow flowers 5-8 cm across. *Temperate. Zones 6-9.* p. 170

imbricata (arborescens) (Colorado to Mexico), "Chainlink cactus"; tree-like to 3 m; slender, woody joints 8 to 20 cm long, cylindric and strongly tubercled; small deciduous leaves; stiff brown sheathed spines; flowers purple, 7 cm across; yellow fruit. *Zones 6-9.* p. 170

juniperina (Arizona to New Mexico, north to Colorado and Utah), "Apache grizzly-bear"; spreading low along ground, with flat obovate or oval green pads to 12 cm long, having long 4 cm needle spines from upper areoles; lemon-yellow flowers, 3 cm red fruit. *Zone 9.* p. 171

microdasys (No. Mexico south to Zacatecas); called "Bunny ears" because of the young pads appearing ear-like at the apex of the older ones; plant low with rounded and flat, fleshy joints to 15 cm long, satiny green and set with neat rows of yellow to light brown tufts of barbed bristles which rub off easily and are painful to the skin; 4-5 cm flowers yellow. *Zones 9-10.* p. 170, 172

microdasys rufida (Texas, No. Mexico), "Cinnamon-cactus" or "Red bunny-ears"; bushy plant to 2 m high, eventually forming trunk; fleshy pads 8-15 cm long, velvety grayish-green covered with tufts of short brown bristles (glochids), which rub off easily and cause itching under the skin; 5 cm orange-yellow flowers. Will rot if too wet. *Arid-subtropic. Zones 9-10.* p. 172

phaeacantha (Texas to Calif. and No. Mexico, also into So. Colorado and Utah); "Prickly pear" of the Southwest; widespread sprawling species, with orbicular to obovate flat pads 10 to 30 cm long to 20 cm wide, bluish-green, covered with distant areoles and strong spines; showy orange-yellow flowers 5 cm across; pear-shaped reddish fruit. *Zones 6-10.*   *p. 171*

polyacantha (Brit. Columbia and Alberta, Dakota to Arizona); prostrate, spreading prickly-pear with rounded, thin joints 5-10 cm wide, close-set areoles and deflexed spines; flowers mostly yellow, 5 cm across. *Temperate. Zones 3-9.*   *p. 172*

rubescens (Consolea) (West Indies), "Ornamental Tuna"; tree-like to 6 m tall, with woody trunk to 15 cm thick; branching with glossy green, oblong thin and flat joints to 25 cm long, usually nearly spineless; yellow to red 2 cm flowers, reddish fruit. *Zone 11.*   *p. 171*

schickendantzii (No. Argentina), "Lion's tongue"; shrub-like and much branched, elongate, warted, flattened, rather thin and narrow joints to 20 cm long, fresh green with reddish spines; yellow flowers 4 to 5 cm across. *Arid-subtropic. Zone 10.*   *p. 172*

subulata (Chile, Argentina), "Eve's pin cactus"; tree-like to 4 m high, the branches smooth cylindrical bright green, with persistent, long fleshy pin-like leaves to 10 cm long, but few spines; flowers red-orange or greenish-yellow. Very attractive as a small clustering succulent plant. *Zones 9-10.*   *p.170*

tuna (West Indies to Jamaica); growing to 1 m high, with light green flat joints rounded to obovate and 15 cm long, brownish around the areoles, and pale yellow spines, 5 cm flowers yellow tinged with red, and red fruit. *Zones 10.*   *p. p.172*

violacea santa-rita (gosseliniana var.) (Texas to Arizona), "Blue blade" or "Dollar cactus"; handsome branching bush to 2 m, with flat joints rounded in outline, to 20 cm across, bluish to coppery purple, with glochids but few spines; yellow flowers 8 cm across, red at base inside. *Arid-subtropic. Zones 9-10.*   *p. 172*

vulgaris (monacantha) (So. Brazil to Argentina), "Irish mittens"; tree-like to 2½ m, flattened fleshy, glossy green joints 10 to 30 cm long, almost spineless; flowers yellow, the unripened fruit will root and grow forming little ears, and offered as "Eared buds". *Subtropic. Zones 10.*   *p. 172*

ORBEA variegata (Zander):   see STAPELIA variegata (Hortus)

ORBIGNYA   *Palmae*
martiana (Attalea) (So. America); majestic armed feather palm with solitary massive trunk bearing very erect pinnate leaves to 10 m long with stiff dark green leaflets; flowers yellow; 5 cm nuts in grape-like clusters. *Zones 11-12.*   *p. 112*

ORCHIS   *Orchidaceae*
maderensis (Hawkes): see DACTYLORHIZA foliosa (Europ. Gardenflora)
morio (W. Europe, Asia Minor, Siberia), "Salep orchid" or "Green-winged orchid"; tuberous terrestrial to 40 cm high; bluish-green lanceolate 15-20 cm basal leaves; inflorescence in a loose spike with flowers to 2 cm, the sepals purplish arching over the greenish petals to form a helmet, lip purple with dark spots. *Zone 9.*   *p. 91*

OREOCALLIS wickhamii (Lord):   see EMBOTHRIUM

OREOCEREUS: see Borzicactus

OREODOXA regia:
see ROYSTONEA regia (Genera Palmarum 1987)

OREOPANAX   *Araliaceae*
capitatus, also known as nymphaeifolius (Mexico, C. America, West Indies); small evergreen tree having glossy green, broad ovate, leathery leaves very variable, juvenile stage having peltate base, adult obtuse or cordate, on slender stalks. *Zone 9.*   *p. 651*

ORIGANUM   *Labiatae*
majorana (Majorana hortensis) (S. Europe, No. Africa, S.W. Asia), "Sweet marjoram"; bushy, half-hardy perennial, 25 cm high, sweet-scented, with furry gray-green foliage; white flowers with green bracts. Use: leaves used for flavoring in cooking vegetables, stews, beef, chicken, sausage. Often grown as annual. *Zones 8-10.*   *p. 533*

pulchellum (S.E. Europe, Asia Minor), the "Showy marjoram"; small subshrub with woody base 30 to 50 cm high, with gray-hairy, ascending stems; small 2 cm opposite ovate, sessile leaves; toward the tips the showy rose-pink flowers in nodding head-like spikes; both a decorative blooming plant, and also economic uses in seasonings, such as for pizza and other Italian dishes. *Zones 5-10.*   *p. 533*

vulgare (onites) (Europe to Cent. Asia, natural. in Eastern U.S.), "Pot marjoram" or "Oregano"; aromatic pubescent perennial or subshrub to 75 cm high, with ovate leaves to 4 cm long, larger than of Sweet marjoram; purplish flowers in 5 cm clusters or whorls, during July-August. Long planted in the herb-garden for flavoring in cooking, stuffings, soup, sausages, and in salads. Should harvest leaves before blooming. Not considered as good as Sweet marjoram. *Zone 3.*   *p. 533*

vulgare 'Aureum' (Europe), "Golden marjoram"; very ornamental form, with opposite thick-fleshy, ovate leaves to 4 cm long, tinted yellow or golden-orange; flowers lavender-pink. Very attractive in the herb garden or as potherb with its distinctive aroma. *Zone 5.*   *p. 532*

ORIXA   *Rutaceae*
japonica (Japan, Korea, China), "Kokusagi"; handsome deciduous shrub 2-3 m high, with graceful spreading branches; aromatic scented, obovate lustrous green leaves 5-12 cm long; small 1 cm inconspicuous dioecious green flowers in short racemes, borne on last year's growth, blooming in April; brown fruits with black seeds. A fine foliage plant. *Zone 5.*   *p. 862*

ORNITHOCEPHALUS   *Orchidaceae*
bicornis (Panama), "Mealybug orchid"; miniature epiphyte 5-6 cm high with bright green leaves spreading and overlapping fan-like; small greenish flowers with white petals and waxy greenish lip, (Winter and various). *Tropical. Zones 11-12.*   *p. 95*

ORNITHOGALUM   *Liliaceae*
arabicum (Mediterran. reg.), "Star of Bethlehem" or "Arabian star"; bulbous plant with pale green, thick basal leaves 30-45 cm long and 2½ cm wide; stalk 30-60 cm high with a cluster of 2½ cm fragrant, white flowers, with black pistil; in Summer. *Zone 8.*   *p. 247*

caudatum (So. Africa), "False sea-onion"; an old-fashioned window-sill plant, with ovate, green bulb to over 10 cm thick, usually showing above the soil, 5-6 basal strap leaves and a stalked pyramidal raceme 45-90 cm long with 50-100 small white flowers with petals having a green median stripe. The filament is wide at base (narrow in Urginea); the narrow channeled leaves 4 cm wide, and form a tube at base. Also known as "Healing onion", or "Meerzwiebel", crushed leaves are tied over cuts and bruises; also used as cooked syrup with rock-candy, against colds. *Subtropic. Zone 8.*   *p. 247*

montanum (Sicily to Israel and Turkey), "Snowflake"; small bulbous plant to 20 cm high, with basal lanceolate leaves, and short, flattened head of a few long stalked starry white flowers, the outside of each petal with a median green band. *Subtropic. Zone 8.*   *p. 247*

nutans (Europe, S.W. Asia), "Nodding Star-of-Bethlehem"; bulbous plant to 60 cm, forming underground bulblets; with flaccid, strap-shaped basal leaves 1 cm wide; starry nodding flowers white inside, green with white margins outside, to 5 cm across, in Spring. *Zone 5.*   *p. 247*

saundersiae (So. Africa), the "Giant chincherinchee"; tall-growing bulbous perennial 1-2 m high; broad, sword-shaped basal leaves to 60 cm long; 2½ cm flowers grouped in a flat-topped cluster on long erect stalk, each bloom with 6 spreading, creamy petals and prominent black center. *Subtropic. Zone 8.*   *p. 247*

thyrsoides (So. Africa: Cape Peninsula), "Chincherinchee" or "Wonder flower"; spring-blooming, (October in the Southern hemisphere); tender bulb with fleshy lanceolate leaves and strong 60 cm racemes with numerous long-lasting flowers having spreading segments, to 5 cm across, white with buff eye. *Subtropic. Zone 8.*   *p. 247*

umbellatum (Mediterranean), "Star-of-Bethlehem" or "Summer snowflake"; small spring-blooming bulb with grass-like leaves veined with white, and 15 cm stems with clusters of numerous star-like flowers, satiny-white inside, green striped white outside, 3 cm across. *Zone 5.*   *p. 247*

ORONTIUM   *Araceae*
aquaticum (Atlantic No. America), "Golden club"; aquatic perennial growing in ponds or along streams, with fleshy rootstocks and leaf-stalks 25-50 cm long, the parallel-veined, oblong, dark green leaves floating or ascending, 15-30 cm long; long bright yellow, club-like spadix, and small inconspicuous spathe, on white, 60 cm stalks. *Warm temperate. Zone 7.*   *p. 326*

OROSTACHYS   *Crassulaceae*
iwarenge fa. 'Fuji'; variegated cultivar from Japan; beautiful succulent rosette 12-15 cm across; persistent through Winter; obovate leaves milky green with broad cream bands along sides; later pushing up a tall spike to 35 cm high with small white flowers. *Warm temperate. Zone 9.*   *p. 188*

japonicus (erubescens var.) (N.E. China, Korea, W. Japan); starry succulent rosette with fleshy narrow pointed leaves to 3 cm long, yellowish-green, extending upward into a spike with inflorescence to 10 cm long; flowers whitish-pink. *Warm temperate. Zone 7.*   *p. 191*

OROYA   *Cactaceae*
peruviana (neoperuviana) (C. Perú); attractive small globe to 15 cm dia., from the Andes at 3,800 m; depressed on top, dark green, with 12-23 low rounded ribs, slightly notched into tubercles, these with yellowish areoles, and 2-5 brown central spines if present; 3 cm pink flowers yellow at base, and red at tip; reddish fruit. *Zone 9.*   *p. 168*

ORPHIUM   *Gentianaceae*

frutescens (So. Africa), "Sticky flower"; shrubby perennial to 60 cm, with narrow-linear, leathery, light green leaves, and showy, shining rosy, star-like flowers 4 cm dia. *Subtropic. Zone 10.*   p. 732

ORTHOSIPHON   *Labiatae*

stamineus (spicatus, grandiflora hort.) (Trop. Asia); erect herbaceous plant to 60 cm high, with coarsely toothed, ovate leaves glaucous beneath; the inflorescence in crowded whorls at ends of branches; bilabiate tubular flowers 3 cm long, pale lilac-blue and with long protruding stamens. *Tropical. Zone 10.*   p. 434

ORTHROSANTHUS   *Iridaceae*

laxus (Western Australia), "Morning iris"; perennial with woody rootstock to 60 cm high, with iris-like mostly basal leaves, forming tufts; the inflorescence in spike-like clusters topping the erect stalks, with delicate pale blue to lavender flowers 3 cm across, each open successively beginning in the morning, but lasting only a few hours; in sunny weather they fade by noon; blooming in Spring.
Zone 10.   p. 430

multiflorus (Sisyrinchium cyaneum) (W. Australia), "Purple morning flag"; photographed in col. of Orotava Bot. Garden on Tenerife; tufting perennial with long-linear, leathery leaves, inflorescence on stiff-erect stalks 30-45 cm high, the sky-blue flowers 2½-4 cm across, in elongate clusters, opening one at a time, mostly during morning, and blooming Spring-Summer. *Zones 9-10.*   p. 430

ORYZA   *Gramineae*

sativa (S.E. Asia), "Rice"; annual tropical waterside grass, to 1 m high, with flat elongate leaves; fruiting panicle drooping, producing the yellow rice kernels; of great economic importance in tropic regions, there yielding to 3 crops a year. The grains are white when polished for commerce. *Zone 10.*   p. 567

OSCULARIA   *Aizoaceae*

deltoides (Mesembryanthemum) (So. Africa: Cape Prov.), "Pink fig marigold"; spreading shrubby succulent with short, triangular, keeled, blue-gray leaves, to 1 cm long, toothed; free-blooming with soft pink 1 to 2 cm flowers. *Zone 10.*   p. 147

OSMANTHUS   *Oleaceae*

americanus (No. Carolina to Mississippi and Mexico), "Devilwood" or "American olive"; elegant evergreen to 15 m high, with leathery, glossy green, lanceolate leaves to 18 cm long, showing a prominent yellowish midrib; lovely small creamy-white flowers in short clusters, very fragrant; dark blue berry-fruits. *Zone 6.*   p. 811

armatus (China), "Chinese osmanthus"; attractive and shapely evergreen shrub to 5 m high, with holly-like narrow elliptic, leathery, glossy green leaves having ivory midrib, 16 cm long, the margins with spines, slow-growing and with stiff reddish branches; tiny white, fragrant flowers. *Zone 7.*   p. 811

x burkwoodii (Zander): see x OSMAREA burkwoodii (Hortus)
decorus (Zander): see PHILLYREA decora (Hortus)
delavayi (Siphonosmanthus) (Yunnan); broadly spreading shrub to 2 m high, with arching, downy branches, small elliptic, leathery leaves to 3 cm long, sharply toothed at margins, dark glossy green; small tubular, pure white, fragrant flowers in axillary and terminal clusters. *Zone 7.*   p. 812

x fortunei (fragrans x heterophyllus); handsome Japanese hybrid to 4 m high, popular in the South and on the West Coast for its evergreen holly-like foliage; the ovate glossy green, leathery leaves 6-10 cm long, armed with large triangular spine-tipped teeth; small white flowers in axillary clusters and sweetly fragrant; very attractive, with blue-black berries in Autumn. *Zone 7.*   p. 812

fragrans (Olea) (Himalayas, China, So. Japan), "Sweet olive"; small tree to 10 m high, with wiry twigs and holly-shaped, stiff-leathery, olive-green leaves to 10 cm long, finely toothed at margins; the small white flowers in clusters, strongly and deliciously fragrant. The dried blossoms are used in China to mix with their tea to add aroma. *Zones 8-9.*   p. 537, 627, 811

heterophyllus 'Variegatus' (ilicifolius var.), "False holly"; extremely attractive, slow-growing, dense evergreen shrub resembling variegated holly but a better keeper; the spiny, glossy-leathery leaves somewhat smaller, 4 to 6 cm long, fresh green to bluish-gray-green, edged and variegated creamy-white, tinted pink when young; should be grafted on privet for best growth. The green-leaved species is from Japan and Taiwan. *Zone 7.*   p. 811

x OSMAREA   *Oleaceae*

burkwoodii (Osmanthus delavayi x Phyllyrea decora); evergreen hybrid shrub 2-3 m high, with dark green ovate to elliptic leaves 3-5 cm long, the margins entire or sparsely toothed and with lustrous surface; the flowers ivory-white with corolla 4-lobed, in showy clusters during April-May, and sweetly scented. *Zone 6.*   p. 812

OSMOXYLON   *Araliaceae*

boerlagei (Boerlagiodendron eminens) (Philippines: Mindanao); evergreen tree 5-10 m high, glabrous throughout; large leaves to 60 cm long, palmately 10-14 lobed, lobes reaching nearly to base, irregularly toothed and coarsely incised, shining green on both sides. *Tropical. Zone 10.*   p. 648

'Miagos' (Boerlagiodendron) (Philippines); curious tropical tree with large leathery leaves palmately divided into numerous narrow, linear segments; very showy inflorescence of densely clustered orange-yellow flowers in terminal clusters. Photographed in col. Los Baños Arboretum, on Luzon, Philippines. *Zone 10.*   p. 648

OSMUNDA   *Osmundaceae (Filices)*

cinnamomea (E. No. America, Mexico to Brazil, E. Asia), "Cinnamon-fern"; coarse but attractive deep fibrous rooted fern with large crowns of 1½ m fronds, the fertile fronds 2-pinnate and becoming brown as spores mature; its fibrous roots are used as a growing medium for orchids in pots or baskets. *Humid-subtropic to Temperate. Zones 3-9.*   p. 126

claytoniana (E. No. America, Himalaya, China), "Interrupted fern"; decorative fern forming crown of pale green, pinnate fronds 30-60 cm long, from massive root stock; the pinnae deeply lobed and papery; the fertile fronds quite erect and distinct in having the spore-bearing, very much contracted leaflets about halfway up the stalk, exceeded above by more normally flat, barren pinnae.
Zones 3-8.   p. 126

regalis (No. America, Europe, Siberia, Japan, China, India, So. Africa, etc.), "Royal fern", also known as "Flowering fern"; rootstock with blackish-brown fibrous roots developing a spongy clump of great thickness; the bipinnate, fresh green, papery fronds ½ to 2 m long on firm, naked stalks. The leaves bearing spores have their fertile portion in the upper part of the frond transformed into brown panicles full of spores, resembling an inflorescence of "flowers" borne above the foliage. *Zones 3-8.*   p. 126

OSTEOSPERMUM   *Compositae*

ecklonis (Dimorphotheca) (South Africa), "Cape marigold"; perennial subshrub 60 cm to 1 m high, with narrow, toothed leaves to 10 cm long; prolific with large daisy-like flowers 6 to 8 cm across, in the center a blackish-blue disc, the broad ray-florets white on surface, purplish beneath, and closing at night. *Subtropic.*
Zones 9-10.   p. 397, 689

ecklonis 'Buttermilk' (Dimorphotheca) (chrysanthemifolia x ecklonis); beautiful hybrid seen at Chelsea Flower Show in London; the ray-florets cream and shading to primrose yellow and copper toward apex, and ringed around the blue-black center disc.
Zone 10.   p. 397

ecklonis 'Whirligig'; striking cultivar seen in England at Notcutt's Nursery, Suffolk, but since also introduced to horticulture in So. California; the flower like a fairy-wheel with the linear pale lilac ray-florets constricted in the middle to a thread and ending at apex in a circular, spoon-like blade, and all the rays encircling the blue-black center disc. *Zone 10.*   p. 397

fruticosum (Dimorphotheca) (So. Africa: Cape, Natal), "Trailing African daisy" or "Burgundy mound"; semi-shrubby plant spreading rapidly by trailing, rooting branches; small fleshy leaves with several points; large ray-flowers to 5 cm across, lilac above, fading nearly white by second day, deeper purple beneath, and dark purple center cushion; excellent ground cover for sunny, mild climate.
Zones 9-10.   p. 307, 312

fruticosum 'Album', "Trailing African daisy"; horticultural variety with flowers white, 5 cm across; very floriferous. *Subtropic.*
Zone 9.   p. 397

fruticosum 'Burgundy Mound' (Dimorphotheca); a popular cultivar in So. California, with ray-flowers deep royal-purple, fading to pale lilac on second day and ranged around the purplish-brown center cushion. *Zones 9-10.*   p. 397

OSTRYA   *Betulaceae*

carpinifolia (So. Europe and Asia Minor), "European hop hornbeam"; deciduous small tree to 18 m high, with gray bark, the branches forming an open, roundish crown; downy shoots with ovate leaves 5-10 cm long, having to 15 pairs of depressed veins, margins toothed; interesting with its pendant elongate fruit-clusters.
Zone 7.   p. 663

virginiana (Eastern No. America, Ontario to Texas), "American hop hornbeam" or "Ironwood"; slow-growing tree to 15 m high, with dark brown bark; the leaves oblong-lanceolate 5 to 12 cm long, sometimes cordate at base; attractive because of its bladder-like pendant fruit clusters resembling hops, throughout all Summer.
Zone 4.   p. 663

OTACANTHUS   *Scrophulariaceae*
 coeruleus (Brazil); perennial herb to 80 cm high, with stems often woody at base; leaves 8-10 cm long in pairs along stem on winged petioles, elliptic, serrate, having pleasant aroma; tubular flowers in clusters, corolla 5 cm long, with tube curved downward; limb divided into two lobes, violet-blue with white throat. *Zone 10.*   *p. 505*

OTATEA   *Gramineae*
 acuminata (syn. Yushania aztecorum) (So. Mexico), "Mexican weeping bamboo"; beautiful clumpforming bamboo 3-6 m high, with more solid than hollow, flexuous culms 3-4 cm dia., bending under the weight of its ferny foliage fountain-like, the abundant pendant, narrow-linear lacy leaves 15-18 cm long; very ornamental, and suitable for tubs. *Zone 9.*   *p. 554, 556*

OTHONNA   *Compositae*
 parviflora (So. Africa: Cape Prov.); semi-woody mountain perennial, with thick fleshy oval leaves, basal and along stems; dense, showy clusters of small yellow flowers at ends of branches, with tubular sterile disc-flowers ringed around the fertile petal-like ray-flowers, blooming December-June in habitat, the So. African Summer. *Zone 9.*   *p. 398*

OURATEA   *Ochnaceae*
 groussordyi (Venezuela); attractive small evergreen shrub with thin-leathery elliptic leaves 8-10 cm long; the inflorescence in tight clusters usually at the end of short lateral branchlets; the buds enclosed by brown calyx, flowers when open rich yellow, 3 cm across. *Zone 10.*   *p. 805*

OURISIA   *Scrophulariaceae*
 macrophylla (New Zealand: North Island), "Mountain foxglove"; herbaceous rhizomatous perennial with floral stalks 30-50 cm high, with elliptic-ovate bright green leaves 4-10 cm long; the 2 cm white flowers having short tube, yellow-haired in throat, the lobes rounded, the upper two rather smaller, and carried in several 3-8 flowered, superimposed whorls; blooming January-February in New Zealand, July in Northern hemisphere. *Zone 7.*   *p. 506*

OXALIS   *Oxalidaceae*
 acetosella (No. Europe to Siberia, Caucasus to Japan), the "European wood-sorrel" or "Cuckoo-bread"; stemless perennial 8 cm high, with scaly rhizome, producing long-stalked leaves 2 cm dia., with 3 obcordate, slightly hairy leaflets; 2 cm flowers with oval petals white with rosy veins; half the size of O. oregana. *Zone 5.*   *p. 258*
 adenophylla (Chile), bulbous "Shamrock"; hardy stemless perennial 10-15 cm high, from a roundish, bulb-like base; long-stalked leaves in basal rosette, with 12-22 obcordate leaflets 1 cm long, glaucous grayish-green; 2½ cm flowers lilac-pink with deeper veins and orange throat and with blackish-red spots at base of each of 5 petals; solitary or in umbels. *Warm temperate. Zone 7.*   *p. 258*
 bowiei (purpurea) (So. Africa), "Giant pink clover"; stemless plant with thickened roots and scaly bulbs, the fleshy, long-stalked leaves with 3 large, obcordate, waxy, light green segments; strong flower stalks to 30 cm long, topped by a cluster of giant, rosy-carmine flowers, during Summer and Fall. *Zone 9.*   *p. 259*
 braziliensis (Brazil); bulbous plant without stem, 8-15 cm high, with stalked bright green basal leaves having 3 bluntly obcordate leaflets 1 cm long and wide; flowers 2½ cm dia., bright rosy-red with darker veins, and yellow in throat; in Winter and Spring. One of the "Shamrocks" sold by florists. *Zone 10.*   *p. 258*
 crassipes (So. America), "Lady's sorrel"; compact evergreen plant from thick rhizome, with leaves of 3 leaflets cut ⅓ their length, dotted with rust-brown spots beneath; floral stalks 15 cm or more, bearing clusters of small pink flowers, occasionally white, blooming at all seasons and popular in California. *Zones 8-9.*   *p. 258*
 deppei (esculenta; Ionoxalis) (So. Mexico), "Lucky clover"; bulbous plant with edible tuber, large leaves having 4 truncate segments (cut off straight at the apex) 4 cm long, and crossed by a purplish-brown zone; flowers rosy-red with yellow base. Attractive pot plant for winter bloom. *Subtropic. Zone 9.*   *p. 258*
 enneaphylla (Patagonia, Falkland Is.), "Scurvy-grass"; herbaceous plant from horizontal rhizome with thick, fleshy scales; leaves with 9 to 20 obcordate leaflets, in two series or whorled, gray-green and pubescent, on 8 cm stalks; large white, as in var. alba, or pale rose, fragrant flowers about 3 cm across. *Zone 7.*   *p. 258*
 hedysaroides 'Rubra' (Colombia, Venez., Ecuador), "Firefern"; beautiful plant with erect, shrubby, wiry stem and thin, fern-like foliage of glowing, satiny wine-red, each petiole with 3 stalked ovate leaflets which are sensitive to the touch; many, little, bright yellow flowers in attractive contrast to the showy leaves. Subshrub to 1 m tall. *Tropical. Zone 11.*   *p. 259, 815*
 hirta (So. Africa); winter-blooming plant with branching leafy pubescent stem from a large brown tuber, at first erect but becoming procumbent; with feathery foliage of 3 small spatulate leaflets nearly

sessile, alternate and scattered; axillary flowers deep rose with yellow tube, and silky sepals. *Subtropic. Zone 9.*   *p. 259*
 oregana (Washington to California), a "Woodsorrel" sometimes sold as "Irish Shamrock"; 8-20 cm high; from rhizome rise stalks with large bright green, hairy leaves; the 3 obcordate leaflets 2½-5 cm wide; flowers white or rose veined with purple, yellowish at base. *Zone 8.*   *p. 258*
 pes-caprae (cernua) (So. Africa), "Bermuda buttercup"; perennial with thickened roots and deep scaly bulbs, with many basal, long-stalked leaves of 3 obcordate leaflets hairy beneath; nodding bell-shaped bright yellow flowers 2½-4 cm across, in Spring; a weed in Bermuda and Florida and other mild districts. *Subtropic. Zone 9.*   *p. 259*
 purpurea (variabilis) (Cape Prov.), "Cape oxalis"; low growing perennial 8-12 cm high, spreading by bulbs and rhizome-like roots, and large clover-like leaves of 3 leaflets, and with very pretty rose-red flowers 3 cm across, between November and March in California. *Zone 9.*   *p. 259*
 purpurea 'Grand Duchess'; low, spreading bulbous perennial with succulent, fresh green foliage 6-8 cm across, of three ciliate leaflets not notched, on rosy-red stalks pubescent with soft white hair, barely topped by large and showy, pretty flowers to 5 cm dia., bright rose with yellow base, winter-blooming in the sun. Popularly grown as a house plant in pots. *Zone 9.*   *p. 258*
 purpurea 'White Duchess'; lovely color variation of the South African species, as seen growing in Quail Bot. Garden, Encinitas, California; spreading bulbous perennial with leaves of 3 fleshy leaflets, and bowl-shaped flowers pure white, centered by yellow stamens. *Zone 9.*   *p. 259*
 regnellii (Perú, Bolivia, Brazil to Argentina); in horticulture sometimes as "rubra alba", shapely, freeblooming perennial with tuberculate rhizome and grass-green leaves with 3 deltoid, thin, finely ciliate segments, the apex as if cut off almost straight across, and with slender white flowers. *Zone 10.*   *p. 259*
 rubra ("rosea") (Brazil), "Window box oxalis"; freeblooming tuberous perennial often used for hanging baskets, with thick erect stalk, long hairy petioles and 3 coppery green obcordate hairy leaflets; clusters of rosy flowers with red veins, opening to the sun. Winter-blooming as a house plant. *Zone 8.*   *p. 259*

OXERA   *Verbenaceae*
 pulchella (New Caledonia); climbing shrub with opposite oblong leathery leaves to 12 cm long, and trumpet-shaped 4-lobed white flowers 5 cm in length, with conspicuous calyx and long protruding stamens. *Tropical. Zone 10.*   *p. 298*

OXYCOCCUS macrocarpos: see VACCINIUM macrocarpon

OXYDENDRUM   *Ericaceae*
 arboreum (Illinois to Florida, Louisiana), "Sourwood"; deciduous tree usually to 6 m high in gardens, in habitat to 25 m; lanceolate, corrugated thin leaves to 20 cm long; attractive inflorescence in pendant racemes 25 cm long, of small downy white flowers in late Summer; foliage beautifully colored in shades of red in Autumn. *Zone 5.*   *p. 707, 811*

OXYLOBIUM   *Leguminosae*
 lanceolatum (West. Australia), "Golden shaggy pea"; handsome shrub 2 m or more high; leaves compound usually of 3 lanceolate leaflets 5-10 cm long; showy erect clusters of yellow to orange and red bell-shaped flowers. *Zone 10.*   *p. 765*

OXYPETALUM   *Asclepiadaceae*
 caeruleum (Argentina); twining subshrub with heart-shaped oblong, hairy leaves; attractive 2½ cm flowers having 5 linear blue lobes, and inside with darker blue, fleshy corona, in axillary clusters. *Zone 10.*   *p. 343*

OYEDAEA   *Compositae*
 verbesinioides (Trop. So. America); tall branching perennial subshrub, with grayish, ovate leaves, having cream primary veins; spreading clusters of flowers with brownish cushion, and scattered yellow ray-flowers, 5 cm across. *Tropical. Zone 10.*   *p. 398*

OZOTHAMNUS   *Compositae*
 rosmarinifolius (Helichrysum) (Tasmania), "Rosemary-everlasting"; charming densely branched bushy shrub, in habitat to 2 m high, the shoots white-woolly; firm linear leaves to 3 cm long, dull green above, beneath whitish to brown-felty; small white floral heads, red in bud. Used for dried floral arrangements. *Zone 9.*   *p. 690*

PACHIRA   *Bombacaceae*
 aquatica (So. America), the "Guiana chestnut" or "Oje"; large tropical tree with palmately compound leaves of 5-7 leathery-oblong leaflets 8-20 cm long; large flowers with narrow pinkish petals 10-15 cm long, which drop off and expose numerous long white stamens;

the large green or brown woody ovoid five-valved fruit is 10-30 cm long, containing rounded seeds, without floss; these can be eaten raw or roasted. Known in Hawaii as the "Malabar chestnut".
Zones 10-11.
p. 907

PACHYCEREUS Cactaceae
pringlei (Mexico: Sonora, Baja California), "Mexican giant"; one of the most massive cacti, stout branching tree to 11 m high and 1 m thick at base, the olive-green columns to 40 cm dia., with 10-16 prominent but rounded ribs, closely studded by large oval areoles with short white or grayish wool especially toward apex, numerous ash-gray radials and 1-3 long central spines at first reddish, afterwards gray; bell-shaped flowers 10 cm long, greenish-red outside, white inside. Arid-tropical. Zones 10-11.
p. 177

PACHYPHYTUM Crassulaceae
werdermannii (N.E. Mexico: Tamaulipas); small subshrub to 25 cm high, dense with ovate, thick succulent leaves 3-10 cm long, waxy glaucous and suffused with amethyst pink; clusters of 1 cm flowers whitish with red. Zone 11.
p. 188

PACHYPODIUM Apocynaceae
lamierei (lamerei) (Madagascar: Fort Dauphin), "Madagascar palm" or "Club-foot"; weird succulent, a thick, spiny gray column 1-3 m high and scarcely branched; at the base spindle-shaped, the pinkish spines 3 cm long; toward the top the spirally arranged strap-like leathery 20 cm leaves, dark shining green with white midrib; small funnel-shaped white flowers. A member of the queer vegetation prevailing in Southern Madagascar. Arid-tropical. Zone 11.
p. 151
succulentum (Cape Prov.: Namaqualand); curious succulent shrub having short, thick bulb-like caudex with tuberous roots, from which rise several slender thorny stems, first erect then tending to be arching down or prostrate, bearing fleshy lanceolate leaves and pretty flowers about 4 cm across, the 5 spreading petals pink and lined with red. Zone 11.
p. 151

PACHYSANDRA Buxaceae
procumbens (Kentucky to Florida and Louisiana), "Alleghany spurge"; herbaceous subshrubby perennial, evergreen in mild regions, deciduous in cold climate; with stems at first trailing then erect, to 25 cm high; leaves broad-ovate, to 8 cm long, and mottled with gray; small starry flowers greenish-white or purplish, in spike-like clusters, appearing in Spring before the foliage. Zone 5.
p. 348
terminalis (Japan), "Japanese spurge"; low evergreen perennial herb spreading by means of creeping rootstocks, with fleshy obovate leaves grouped whorl-like, coarsely toothed toward apex and 3-8 cm long; terminal spikes of greenish-white flowers. Warm-temperate. Zone 5.
p. 309, 348

PACHYSTACHYS Acanthaceae
lutea (Perú), "Lollypops"; introduced in Europe as Beloperone "Super Goldy"; semi-woody plant 25 cm or more high with lanceolate, depressed-veined herbaceous, matte dark green leaves; contrasting with a striking, erect inflorescence of hops-like, shingled, orange-yellow bracts, bursting with creamy-white flowers in late Summer. Tropical. Zone 10.
p. 17

PACHYSTEGIA Compositae
insignis (New Zealand), "Marlborough rock-daisy"; evergreen erect shrub 1 to 2 m high, with leathery, obovate oblong leaves to 16 cm long, silky white-hairy beneath; daisy-like heads to 8 cm across, with central fruiting flower yellow, and lateral, sterile rays pure white, on long stalks. Zone 9.
p. 689

x PACHYVERIA Crassulaceae
haagei, "Jewel plant"; Intergeneric hybrid of Pachyphytum x Echeveria; compact star-like hard rosette of short fleshy, boat-shaped leaves flat on top, bluish-green dipped in purplish-red toward apex and bluish glaucous, about 6 cm long; flowers yellow and orange-red. Possibly P. glauca. Subtropic. Zone 10.
p. 188

PAEONIA Paeoniaceae (Ranunculaceae)
lactiflora (albiflora sinensis) (China), the "Chinese garden peony"; hardy perennial with roots a collection of narrow tubers; herbaceous leaves, twice compound; stems to 1 m high; large fragrant flowers, 10-12 cm across, typically white, but varying to shades of rose-pink or red; blooming late Spring. Hundreds of named cultivars have been derived from this species. Zone 3.
p. 465
lactiflora 'Edmund Steichen'; splendid garden peony, seen in col. Brooklyn Bot. Garden, having large semi-double cupped flowers with glowing crimson-red, silky petals, wavy at apex, and showy yellow stamen bundle in center. Zone 5.
p. 465
lactiflora 'Festiva Maxima' (Siberia, China, Japan), "Double-flowered peony" or "Chinese peony"; outstandingly beautiful hardy perennial herb to 1 m high, with spindle-shaped dahlia-like tuberous roots; large ornamental, herbaceous, compound leaves, and magnificent rose-type fragrant flowers to 15 cm across, having double

incurved white petals with pink sheen; blooming normally in our gardens in late May or early June. Zone 5.
p. 465
lactiflora 'Grace Root'; very appealing cultivar seen in col. Brooklyn Bot. Garden; large semi-double flowers having soft rose-pink, silky petals, changing to contrasting white at base. Zone 5.
p. 465
lactiflora 'Requiem' (lactiflora x macrophylla); free blooming cultivar with medium-size waxy white single flowers, showing a center cushion of yellow stamens; early-blooming. Zone 5.
p. 465
lutea (W. China, Tibet), "Yellow tree peony"; picturesque deciduous shrub to 1½ m high, with robust woody stems, and long-stalked compound leaves twice divided into three, the leaflets deeply lobed, dark green above, glaucous beneath; showy yellow cup flowers to 8 cm wide, the petals concave framing a conspicuous disc of yellow stamens, blooming in June. Zone 6.
p. 815
mascula (So. Europe: France, Austria; No. Africa to Caucasus), "Southern peony"; herbaceous perennial 60-90 cm high, with lower leaves twice divided into 9-16 elliptic leaflets 4 cm long, hairless on underside; upper leaves once divided; cup-shaped rose-red flowers 8-14 cm across, blooming in June. Zone 6.
p. 464
mascula arietina (peregrina) (E. Europe to Asia Minor), "Turkish peony"; herbaceous perennial to 1 m or more high, with reddish leaves much divided, its 12-15 leaflets hairy beneath; showy flowers 10-15 cm across, with magnificent silky, rose to deep red petals, May-blooming. Zone 5.
p. 464
mlokosewitchii (Cent. Caucasus), "Caucasian peony"; elegant perennial with stout stems 40-60 cm high, the leaves are hairless on the dark bluish-green surface, and of 3 divisions each of 3 oval leaflets; the beautiful rich yellow flowers 10-12 cm across, have about 8 concave petals and purple stigma, blooming in May; an excellent garden plant. Zone 5.
p. 464
mollis (prob. Siberia), "Siberian peony"; small herbaceous perennial with mostly twice divided leaves, each division having 3 narrow-lanceolate leaflets glaucous and densely white-hairy beneath; stems rigidly upright, 30-45 cm high; very floriferous with smallish single, cup-shaped red flowers about 8 cm across, and showy yellow pistils in center; seen late May-blooming in Kew Bot. Gardens, England. Zone 3.
p. 465
officinalis (France to Albania), "Peasant's-peony" or "Piney"; compact bush with twice compound, herbaceous leaves, the leaflets cut into narrow elliptic segments 10 cm long; very decorative single flowers, rich crimson-red to 12 cm across, with red filaments, and yellow stamens; blooming late May. Requires chilling period to initiate flower buds. Zone 5.
p. 465
suffruticosa (Moutan) (W. China, Tibet, Bhutan); the beautiful "Chinese tree-peony"; highly developed and admired in China for centuries; woody perennial, branching and becoming 2 m tall, with bipinnate leaves; showy flowers 12 cm or more across, red to white with purple center; usually grafted. Zones 5-8.
p. 465, 815
suffruticosa 'Angelet', "Tree peony"; beautiful tree-peony of Chinese heritage; deciduous shrub with picturesque woody stems, to 2 m high; large divided bluish-green leaves; very showy flowers 12-15 cm across, with ruffled petals orange-yellow and crimson-red at base. Zones 5-8.
p. 815
suffruticosa 'Vesuvian', "Red tree-peony"; deciduous shrub with woody stems and compound foliage; large semi-double to double flowers glistening crimson-red, the petals undulate and crisped. Developed from species at home in China to Tibet. Zones 5-8.
p. 815
tenuifolia (Rumania to Caucasus); perennial herb with creeping rootstock and leafy stem 30-60 cm high, dark green fern-like leaves lobed 3-pinnately into linear segments; deep crimson, cup-like flowers 8-10 cm across, blooming late May. Zone 5.
p. 465

PAEPALANTHUS Eriocaulaceae
costaricensis (Costa Rica); tropical perennial bog plant, with sword-shaped concave, green to bronzy leaves set as in a dense rosette; from the center rise stiff stalks topped by compact globular heads of minute flowers with dry corolla. Zone 10.
p. 327
itatiaiensis (Brazil), "Pipewort", inhabiting wet ground; perennial herb with tufts of narrow lanceolate leaves, rushlike; from the base rise long wiry floral stalks, each topped by a rounded head of minute flowers. Zones 10-11.
p. 327

PAGIANTHA Apocynaceae
dichotoma (So. India, Sri-Lanka, So. China), "Forbidden fruit of India"; large evergreen shrub dense with shiny green, leathery, ovate leaves to 20 cm long; very exotic with waxy white flowers 4 cm across, their 5 long linear petals curved sickle-shaped windmill-like, twisted and with margins turned under, and very sweetly fragrant; orange-yellow oblong, ribbed fruit 10-12 cm long, opening along seams, displaying scarlet pulp, holding seeds which are a medicinal purgative and a poisonous narcotic. Also known as Tabernaemontana.
Zones 10-11.
p. 640

PALISOTA   Commelinaceae

barteri (Fernando Po); dark green rosette with spreading, stalked elliptic glossy leaves having parallel veins, and edged with hairs; flowers purplish, near base, followed by a dense cluster of showy orange-red, pointed berries. Tropical. Zone 11.   p. 52

pynaertii 'Elizabethae' (W. Equatorial Africa); ornamental leafy rosette becoming large; the thin-leathery oblanceolate, stalked foliage 20-50 cm long and spreading; glossy rich green surface, with feathered pale green or cream center-band, and reddish hairs along margins; in the center a dense cone of small white flowers, followed by attractive purplish berries. Tropical. Zone 11.   p. 52

PALIURUS   Rhamnaceae

spina-christi (So. Europe to No. China), "Christ-thorn" or "Jerusalem-thorne"; large shrub or tree to 6 m, branches armed with twin spines, and ovate, 3-veined leaves 3 cm long, finely toothed, alternate in 2 ranks; small greenish-yellow flowers; 2 cm fruit brownish-yellow; cultivated more for religious interest than as ornamental. Zone 7.   p. 828

PANAX   Araliaceae

pseudoginseng (ginseng) (Korea, Manchuria), "Ginseng"; herbaceous perennial to 60 cm high, growing from thick, spindle-shaped and forked roots; leaves palmately compound, of 3 to 7 ovate leaflets serrate at margins; small yellowish-green flowers in globular clusters, followed by berry-like red fruit. The aromatic roots are used in China as drug in medicine and are of bittersweet taste. Considered an aphrodisiac throughout the Orient. Zone 5.   p. 343, 523

quinquefolius (Aralia quinquefolia) (Québec to Minnesota, so. to Georgia and Oklahoma), "American ginseng"; deciduous perennial herb to 45 cm high, with tuberous aromatic, spindle-shaped root, often forked; leaves compound, handlike, of usually 5 stalked, toothed leaflets to 12 cm long, the basal pair smallest; small greenish-white flowers in clusters, appearing in June, and followed by bright red berries. The roots were exported to China, and have been used in the Orient medicinally for centuries, supposedly aiding rejuvenation of the body. Zone 3.   p. 523

PANCRATIUM   Amaryllidaceae

maritimum (Spain to Syria), "Sea daffodil"; showy, bulbous plant; 5-7 cm bulb with dense reddish skins; the basal evergreen, persistent, linear leaves gray-green, to 75 cm long; white, fragrant flowers with tube 8 cm long and linear segments 4 cm long, and with large crown inside; summer-blooming. Zone 8.   p. 214

PANDANUS   Pandanaceae

baptistii (tectorius var.) (New Britain Isl. near New Guinea), "Blue screwpine"; very decorative, symmetrical plant with stiff channeled leaves spirally arranged, gracefully arching, and tapering to a long point, blue-green with several yellow center stripes, without thorns at the margins. Tropical. Zones 11-12.   p. 124

lamprocephalus (Sararanga sinuosa) (Solomon Islands); seen in col. Lae Botanic Garden, New Guinea; tropical low altitude "Pandanus palm" similar to P. brosimus of New Guinea mountains, but more graceful, with slender stilt-root trunk topped by a spiral rosette of arching serrate leaves. Zone 12.   p. 124

leram (Sri Lanka), "Nicobar bread-fruit"; large tree dividing into numerous twisting branches and supported by stilt-roots; topped by long pendant bluish-green, prickly leaves arranged in spirals; notable for its large ovoid fruits made up of many wedge-shaped 12 cm drupes (ripened ovary) containing sugar and starch, and nut-like seeds, edible when roasted. Tropical. Zone 11.   p. 124, 816

odoratissimus (along coasts of Hawaii, Polynesia to Vanuatu, Queensland, Monsoon Asia), the "Hala screw-pine" or "Walking tree"; forming groves, but favoring the seashores; picturesque tree branching into twisted woody and flexuous, ringed stems to 6 m high, and with straight, supporting aerial roots as if standing on stilts; the thin-leathery, pliable sword-shaped leaves arranged spirally are grayish-green 1 m or more long, with white marginal teeth; flowers on male trees fragrant; brownish 20 cm fruit on female trees looks like a pineapple, containing the nut-like, edible seeds. Tropical. Zones 11-12.   p. 125, 923

papuanus (New Guinea), "Papua screwpine"; majestic tree to 12 m high, with massive trunks having stilt-roots toward base; branching with age into several spiral rosettes of long-linear, drooping leaves, having serrate margins. Zones 11-12.   p. 125

pristis (Madagascar); clustering rosette 2 to 4 m high, dark green glossy leathery foliage with prominent pale spines, the leaves spreading out horizontally and recurving beyond the middle; beginning to flower when 1 m high. Growing on limestone in habitat. Tropical. Zone 12.   p. 124

pygmaeus (graminifolius) (Madagascar, Mauritius); low spreading shrub to 60 cm high, sending out from the base numerous horizontal, stilt-rooting branches with long narrow-linear, rich glossy green

leaves spirally along the stem, the margins and keels with whitish spines, glaucous beneath. Zone 12.   p. 124, 566

sanderi: see P. tectorius sanderi (Dr. B. Stone, 1986)

tectorius (Southern trop. Asia to Polynesia), a "Pandanus palm"; widely cultivated for its economic values, especially the pendulous clusters of edible seed; slender, branching, 6 m tree with flexuous trunk supported by brace-roots, light green fibrous leaves pendant above the middle, with small green teeth. Tropical. Zone 11.   p. 816

tectorius var. novo-caledonicus (syn. odoratissimum) (New Caledonia); a South Pacific screwpine similar to P. tectorius but not as robust, with shorter leaves; female tree produces woody multiple cone-like fruit holding the edible seeds within. Zones 11-12.   p. 124

tectorius sanderi (Moluccas, Polynesia); a handsome, very ornamental screwpine with short green stem, but suckering freely with great spiralling rosettes of magnificent long leaves, glossy green largely variegated with ivory-white to yellow, green band toward finely spiny margins, with age breaking above the middle and laxly pendant. Tropical. Zones 11-12.   p. 124

utilis (Madagascar), a useful as well as ornamental "Screw pine"; spiral rosette of long curving, strap-like, thick-leathery leaves to 2 m long and 10 cm wide, keeled beneath, deep olive-green with showy red spines; with age becoming a branching tree to 18 m high, with stilt-like brace roots; the leaves are used for making hats and baskets. Tropical. Zone 11.   p. 124, 816

veitchii (Polynesia), "Variegated screwpine"; shapely and attractive house plant; rosette of thin-leathery, recurving leaves to 8 cm wide, narrowing to a long point, shining light to deep green lined and broadly margined with creamy-white, the edges and keel beneath with small spines; with age developing stilt-like, thick aerial roots. Tropical. Zones 11-12.   p. 75, 124

PANDOREA   Bignoniaceae

jasminoides (Bignonia) (New So. Wales, Queensland), "Bower plant" or "Bower of beauty"; tall flowering climber with compound leaves feather-fashion, of 5 to 9 glossy green elliptic leaflets 3-5 cm long; the Tecoma-like trumpet flowers 6 cm long, opening to 5 crepy lobes; pinkish-white streaked with pink or red inside of throat. Subtropic. Zones 9-10.   p. 269

PANICUM   Gramineae

clandestinum (No. America: S.E. Canada to Florida and west to Texas), "Panic grass"; robust perennial forming dense clumps, with branched stems 60-120 cm high; the lanceolate green leaves 10-20 cm long, and sheaths usually stiffly hairy; the terminal panicle with elliptic spikelets. Zones 3-8.   p. 563

variegatum hort.: see OPLISMENUS hirtellus 'Variegatus'

virgatum (Oplismenus) (E. Canada to Florida, west to Wyoming and Arizona), "Switch-grass"; rhizomatous perennial forming dense clusters 1½-2 m high; narrow linear flat, arching leaves 30-60 cm long, gold orange in Autumn; inflorescence in open panicles 50 cm long, with short spikelets; profuse flower clusters very ornamental, creating dense buff-brown masses held above foliage. Zone 5.   p. 563

PAPAVER   Papaveraceae

anomalum (Cent. China); herbaceous, near stemless perennial, with leaves all basal, 10 cm long and twice pinnately divided and glaucous; flowers solitary on red-bristly stalks 40 cm long, orange-yellow varying to white with yellow center, 4 cm across; the petals crisped at margins; blooming in June. Zone 5.   p. 468

aurantiacum (Switzerland), "Yellow Alpine poppy"; miniature alpine annual photographed at Schynige Platte Alpine Garden near Interlaken; deeply divided glaucous leaves, and large yellow flowers, about 4 cm across, seen blooming in late August. Zone 5.   p. 468

burseri (alpinum hort.) (Europe: Alps, Carpathians), "Alpine poppy"; tufted mountain perennial 15-30 cm high with glaucous, finely divided basal leaves, and bristly-hairy stalks 10 to 25 cm long with solitary white to yellowish flowers, 3 cm across. Zone 5.   p. 468

dubium (Europe to Greece, W. Asia, natural. in S.E. America), "Greek poppy" or "Long-headed poppy"; showy, bristly-hairy annual to 60 cm high; basal leaves pinnately dissected, stem-leaves finely divided and ferny; the numerous branches literally covered by vivid scarlet-red delicate poppy flowers 5 cm across, the petals often with blackish spot at base, but variable; at home in arid climate on the Greek island of Delos. Zone 9.   p. 469

nudicaule (Arctic to Colorado), "Iceland poppy"; perennial grown as annual in warmer regions; divided leaves with coarse pubescence; hairy stems 30-50 cm high; flowers cup-shaped 3-8 cm across, fragrant, sometimes double; white or cream with yellow at base, salmon, orange, pink, rose to scarlet-red. Much planted for summer bloom in Japan. Temperate. Zones 2-9.   p. 468, 469

orientale (Mediterranean to Iran), "Oriental poppy"; a showy perennial with milky-colored juice and white-hairy sparsely leafy stem to 1 m high, the thick, green leaves pinnately dissected and toothed, and large 10-15 cm flowers scarlet with black spot in the base, followed by an ornamental glaucous capsule; summer-blooming. Short-lived in warm winter climate. *Zones 2-7.* p. 468, 469

orientale 'Flore Pleno', "Double oriental poppy"; vigorous beauty with showy, very double flowers in shades of rose and pink, literally bursting with countless narrow-linear, convex petals resembling the so called cactus dahlias for unusual effect in the summer garden. *Zones 2-7.* p. 468

orientale 'Mary Finan'; striking cultivar in the summer garden, with giant flowers to 18 cm across, the petals deeply fringed and cut into linear segments, vivid scarlet-red and with black blotch at base. *Zones 2-7.* p. 470

radicatum (Arctic Europe), "Arctic poppy"; charming clustering perennial, 10-20 cm high, containing milky juice, and with persistent leafbases; the leaves basal and pinnately lobed or cut; floral stalk with reddish hairs, bearing solitary flowers 4-5 cm across, varying from white to yellow or even pink; photographed on Arctic Spitzbergen of Norway at 79 deg. North Latitude, blooming during the brief Summer after the surface ice has melted. *Zone 2.* p. 468

rhoeas (Europe, Asia, natural. in No. America), "Corn poppy"; the well-known Field poppy common in European grain farms; herbaceous annual to 80 cm high, the branches with bristly hairs; ovate leaves irregularly lobed or pinnate, to 15 cm long; the silky flowers 5 to 7 cm across, on long, hairy stalks; petals normally deep glowing red, often with black blotch at base. *Zone 9 as Annual.* p. 470

somniferum (S.E. Europe and W. Asia), "Opium poppy"; glaucous annual herb, occasionally short-lived perennial from deep roots, in mild climate such as So. Italy, 60 cm or more high; ovate leaves mostly basal, 8-12 cm long, with wavy, toothed margins; large, showy flowers to 10 cm across, on long, hairy stalks, with silky petals normally white having purple design at base, but varying to pink, red or purple, blooming during Summer; the fruit is a globose capsule which is notched while unripe to extract the milky juice which is dried into crude opium. Illegal to cultivate in U.S.A. Its derivative morphine is used medicinally. Dried seeds are flavoring bakery goods. *Zones 9-10.* p. 470, 538

somniferum 'Danebrog', "Fringed opium poppy"; beautiful, very ornamental Scandinavian cultivar to 90 cm high, with deeply cut and serrated bluish leaves, and huge flowers having petals glowing crimson, changing to white toward base, the margins lacily fringed; blooming July to October. *Zone 9.* p. 470

somniferum paeoniaeflorum, "Peony-flowered poppy"; very showy variety with large 10 cm rosy-red to pink double flowers, frilled throughout with lacily cut petals; the glaucous bluish leaves strongly toothed at margins, seen blooming in Portugal in late May; the large seedpods are suitable for winter decoration. *Zone 9.* p. 470

PAPHIOPEDILUM   *Orchidaceae*

bellatulum (Burma, Thailand); dwarf terrestrial with fleshy dark green leaves mottled with pale green, purple beneath; solitary 5-8 cm waxy flowers on very short stalk, shell-shaped, creamy-white, covered with raised spots and blotches of purple-maroon, (April-Sept.). *Tropical. Zones 11-12.* p. 94

callosum (Thailand, Vietnam); colorful terrestrial with leaves tessellated bright green on deep green, and large 9-10 cm flowers with greenish petals deflexed and strap-like, purple at tip and with several black warts, the dorsal white lined with purple and green veins, and a brown-purple pouch. *Tropical. Zones 11-12.* p. 94

fairrieanum (fairieanum in Hortus 3) (Himalayas, Bhutan, Assam); dwarf terrestrial with pale green leaves and uniquely pretty flowers; dorsal white, greenish at base and with purple lines, petals similar, sickle-shaped, pouch green flushed red and veined with purple, (July-Jan.). *Tropical. Zone 11.* p. 94

x harrisianum (villosum x barbatum); distinct hybrid with large 6-8 cm sinister, very dark vibrant deep wine-red, waxy flower having dorsal greenish-yellow and white striped with red; leaves mottled light and dark green, (Summer). *Tropical. Zones 11-2.* p. 94

insigne (Cypripedium) (Nepal, Assam), terrestrial "Lady slipper"; growing on rocks in the Himalayas at 2000 m; small plant with green leaves, soon forming tufts; the flowers waxy, dorsal yellow-green with purple spots at base, white at apex, petals yellowish-green veined with brown, slipper reddish-brown, (Oct.-March). *Subtropic. Zone 11.* p. 93

insigne 'Sanderae' (Assam); desirable form with flowers of a beautiful primrose-yellow, except the upper part of the dorsal which is pure white, (Winter). *Subtropic. Zones 11-12.* p. 94

irapeanum (Cypripedium) (Mexico); showy terrestrial found near Mitla, Oaxaca, with broad pale green foliage, the branched floral stalk with ovate leaves, and golden-yellow flowers to 10 cm across, the inflated lip stained red inside. *Zones 11-12.* p. 94

lawrenceanum (No. Borneo); robust terrestrial with long leaves brightly mottled pale green, and bold flowers, dorsal white with shining purple stripes, greenish at base, the horizontal petals greenish, shaded purple and black-warted, lip brown-purple, (April-Aug.). *Tropical. Zones 11-12.* p. 94

lowii (Sarawak, Borneo); beautiful large epiphyte on trees or limestone rocks, with straplike, light green leaves and stalks to 1 m, with 2 to 6 hairy flowers 8 to 10 cm across, dorsal greenish with purple stripes, the narrow, obovate petals greenish-yellow blotched brown and purple-tipped; pouch coppery green with purple lines, (Feb.-July). *Tropical. Zones 11-12.* p. 94

x maudiae (Cypripedium) (callosum x lawrenceanum); beautiful and highly desirable hybrid with marbled leaves yellow-green and bluish-gray; the usually single flowers with a white dorsal striped with green, the slender petals greenish closely lined with green, pouch yellowish-green, (April-Aug.). *Tropical. Zones 11-12.* p. 93

PARAHEBE   *Scrophulariaceae*

lyallii (Veronica) (New Zealand: South Isl.); very floriferous perennial subshrub with woody base; branches prostrate and rooting at nodes below; small 1-2 cm thick-leathery ovate or deeply lobed leaves; white or pink flowers 1 cm dia., in erect slender-stalked racemes; found growing near Milford Sound. *Zone 9.* p. 382

PARAMONGAIA   *Amaryllidaceae*

weberbaueri (Perú), known to the Quechua Indians as "Cojomaria"; deciduous bulbous plant related to Hymenocallis (Ismene), with 6-8 two-ranked glaucous strap-shaped leaves to 75 cm long, developing with or after the bloom; floral stalks 60 cm high topped by solitary yellow flower 16 cm across, suggesting a daffodil. *Zone 9.* p. 218

PARINARI   *Rosaceae*

macrophylla (Sénégal, Guinea), "Gingerbread plum" or "Seabeam"; evergreen tropical shrub or small tree, with thickly brown-pubescent branches; large oblong ovate leathery leaves to 12 cm long, cordate at base, green above, downy beneath; irregular white flowers, displaying numerous stamens, in terminal racemes, blooming February; the fruit roundish to pear-shaped 6-8 cm long, containing pulpy flesh and edible. *Zone 10.* p. 924

PARIS   *Liliaceae*

polyphylla (Himalayas); herbaceous perennial with creeping rhizomes, to 90 cm high; oblong-lanceolate leaves to 15 cm long, 4 to 9 in a whorl, on short petiole; the inflorescence leafy; flowers to 10 cm or more across, with yellow threadlike, spreading petals subtended by greenish, leaflike lanceolate sepals, early to late summer-blooming; followed by berry-like, fleshy brilliant scarlet fruit. *Zone 7.* p. 450

PARKINSONIA   *Leguminosae*

aculeata (Trop. America to Cape Verde Is.), "Jerusalem thorn" or "Mexican palo verde"; small spiny ornamental tree, with narrow bipinnate, fern-like foliage; small yellow flowers sweet-scented, in loose racemes; 12 to 18 cm pods constricted between the seed. *Zones 9-10.* p. 767

PARMENTIERA   *Bignoniaceae*

cereifera (Panama), "Candle tree"; interesting small tree with rough bark; the leaves with winged petiole and 3 obovate leaflets; bell-shaped, curved white flowers to 8 cm long; curious with cylindrical fleshy, greenish-yellow fruit pendant direct from old woody branches 30 cm to 1 m long, with apple-like odor, and resembling wax candles. *Tropical. Zone 10.* p. 664

cujete: see CRESCENTIA (Hortus, Zander)

edulis (Mexico, Guatemala), "Guajilote tree"; tropical tree of dense, thorny growth to 10 m high, with ovate leaves; large, funnel-form flowers greenish-yellow; oblong, grooved greenish-yellow fruit 10-15 cm long, edible but of poor quality. *Zone 10.* p. 907

PARNASSIA   *Saxifragaceae*

fimbriata (Alaska to S. Colorado), "Bog-stars"; showy herbaceous perennial 15-30 cm high, with kidney-shaped basal leaves strikingly hooded at base, 4-5 cm long; stem-leaves clasping; interesting white flowers 3 cm across, with petals fringed on lower sides. *Zone 3.* p. 475

PARODIA   *Cactaceae*

ayopayana (Bolivia: Puente Pilatos); small fresh-green globe 9 cm dia., sprouting from base, with 12 or more angled, notched ribs; the knobs with white-woolly areoles, and stiff needle spines in all directions; deep yellow 2 cm flowers. *Zone 10.* p. 173

borealis (Bolivia: La Paz area); handsome small grayish-green demi-globe 4 cm dia., with about 13 notched ribs, these set toward apex with white wool, and erect brownish needle spines; 2 cm golden-yellow flowers from crown. *Zone 10.* p. 173

echinus (Bolivia: La Paz Canyon); attractive light green elongate globe to 25 cm high, found in the Cordilleras East of La Paz at 3600 m alt.; 11 to 16 angled ribs, toward upper part neatly covered with white-woolly areoles and pale yellow spines; at apex orange-yellow flowers. *Zone 10.*   *p. 173*

mairanana (E. Bolivia: Santa Cruz); very attractive miniature olive-green demi-globe to 6 cm dia., found in the Eastern Cordilleras at 1500 m; about 14 spiraling ribs set in upper part with white-woolly areoles and short spines; white-hairy orange-yellow flowers. *Zone 10.*   *p. 173*

nivosa (Notocactus nivea hort.) (No. Argentina: Salta); attractive small species, at first globular, later oblong to 15 cm high and 8 cm dia., the ribs dissolved into light green conical knobs, densely covered by snowy areoles, and long white needle spines; brilliant scarlet 5 cm flowers at apex. *Zone 10.*   *p. 173*

ocampoi (Bolivia: Cochabamba); impressive small semi-cylindric dark green miniature, to 7 cm high and 6 cm dia., sprouting from base forming cushions; 15 or more angular ribs set with gray areoles and short spines; toward crown densely white-woolly, and yellow flower from apex. *Zone 10.*   *p. 173*

penicillata (No. Argentina: Salta); at first globular, to 12 cm dia., later elongate to 70 cm long, the fresh green body with 17 spiralled ribs broken into knobs, the areoles woolly and densely covered by long thin spines; small bell-like red flowers near top. May become pendant with age. *Zone 10.*   *p. 173*

ritteri (Eastern Bolivia); globular when young, with age columnar to 50 cm high and 10 cm dia., grass green; 15-21 ribs at first with knobs, less so later; the upper areoles white, set with numerous curving spines to 4 cm long; from the apex rises a flower reddish outside, yellow within. *Zone 10.*   *p. 173*

sanguiniflora (No. Argentina: Salta), "Red Tom Thumb"; solitary little soft green globes woolly on top, to 6 cm dia., with spiralled tubercles set with bristly white radials and brownish central spines, one hooked; numerous flowers a silky blood-red, to 4 cm across. *Arid-subtropic. Zone 10.*   *p. 173*

subtilihamata (Bolivia: Prov. Sud-Cinti); rare species found near Salitra at 2400 m alt., small green globe 4-7 cm dia., having depressed spiny apex; usually 11 spiral ribs, in young plants with pronounced knobs, the areoles white-felty, covered by thin spines, some hooked; flowers silky rose-red with yellow margins, open for one week; reddish fruits. *Zone 10.*   *p. 174*

PARONYCHIA   *Caryophyllaceae*

kapela serpyllifolia (Pyrenees of Spain to Alps of Austria), "Nailwort" or "Chickweed"; low mat-forming perennial herb to 15 cm high, the small oblong 5 mm ciliate leaves crowded and two-ranked; profusely covered by small white flowers tinted rose, in 2 cm clusters, subtended by silvery bracts. *Zone 5.*   *p. 365*

PARROTIA   *Hamamelidaceae*

persica (No. Iran, Caucasus), "Persian ironwood"; deciduous tree to 5 m with 10 cm oval leaves coarsely toothed above middle, green but turning to brilliant autumn colors; flowering before foliage; dense clusters of flowers without petals surrounded by brown-hairy bracts, and protruding, pendant stamens with red anthers. *Zone 6.*   *p. 735*

PARTHENOCISSUS   *Vitaceae*

henryana (Ampelopsis) (China), "Silver-vein creeper"; ornamental, vigorous, tall climber with young branchlets 4-angled, the divided tendrils clinging by adhesive tips, grape-like leaves of 5 slender, oblanceolate, thin-fleshy leaflets, toothed above middle, dull olive-green with broad silver band following midrib and feathering into lateral veins, reddish beneath, 6-8 cm long. Sometimes known as "Cissus gongyloides." *Zones 8-10.*   *p. 300*

inserta (quinquefolia vitacea) (Québec to Arizona and Mexico); known in California greenhouses as "Cissus sicyoides", a miniature Virginia creeper, and grown there on treefern poles, an attractive decorative plant, with lustrous deep green, palmately compound leaves, 4 to 10 cm long; the 5 leaflets lanceolate, glossy and deeply toothed; vines climbing by tendrils without discs; fruit bluish-black. Covering walls of buildings, aided by wires, in the Zona Rosada in Mexico City. *Zones 4-9.*   *p. 299*

quinquefolia (Ampelopsis, Vitis) (U.S.: New England to Florida and Texas), "Virginia creeper" or "American ivy"; vigorous climber with smooth stems having tendrils with 5-12 branches; sticky-tipped; large palmate foliage with usually 5 coarsely toothed dull green leaflets 4-15 cm long, glaucous beneath, turning crimson-red in Autumn; small blue-black berries; frost-hardy. *Temperate to Subtropic. Zones 3-9.*   *p. 299*

quinquefolia 'Engelmannii'; cultivar having smaller leaflets than the species; compound leaves on reddish petioles, the 5 lanceolate leaflets to 12 cm long serrate at margins, dark green above and blue glaucous beneath, turning dark red in Autumn; excellent for draping over stone walls and over trellis. *Zone 3.*   *p. 299*

tricuspidata (Vitis veitchii) (Japan, China), "Boston-ivy", "Woodbine" or "Japanese ivy"; popular, quick-growing deciduous climber

attaching itself to walls and houses by their sticky-tipped tendrils; densely shingled, variable smallish foliage, mostly broadly ovate irregularly lobed and toothed, or trifoliolate, 5-12 cm wide; when adult occasional large leaves are produced 15-25 cm across; the shining green color changes to autumn shades of crimson; small blue berries. *Warm temperate. Zone 4.*   *p. 299, 323*

tricuspidata 'Lowii', (England 1907); attractive seedling clone, dense with 5 to 7-lobed leaves, often forked and resembling a butterfly, each wing with about 3 main lobes; the bronzy green changing to red in Autumn. *Warm temperate. Zone 5.*   *p. 299*

tricuspidata 'Veitchii' "Japanese ivy"; juvenile form of the species; of compact, dense habit in climbing and covering entire walls; small glossy green leaves roundish to trilobed, 5 cm or more across, purplish when young. *Zone 4.*   *p. 300*

PASPALUM   *Gramineae*

notatum (W. Indies, Mexico, So. America), "Bahia grass"; perennial lawn grass spreading by rhizomes; although coarser than Zoysia or Bermuda, is widely planted in Florida and the Deep South for its toughness and ability to thrive in sandy soil and disease resistance; leaf blades flat or folded, 5 mm wide, green or grayish-green. Usually established by seed; photo shows the trade-named "Argentine Bahia", which is a finer-leaved strain. *Subtropic. Zone 9.*   *p. 569*

PASSIFLORA   *Passifloraceae*

alata (E. Brazil to N.E. Perú); climbing vine with 4-angled and winged branches; simple ovate leaves to 15 cm long; handsome and fragrant flowers 10-12 cm across, the sepals green outside and crimson-red inside, petals white beneath and red on surface; the corona variegated red, white and purple. The yellow fruit to 12 cm long, is edible. *Zone 10.*   *p. 288*

x alato-caerulea (pfordtii) (alata x caerulea), "Showy passion flower"; free-blooming hybrid well-known because of its large and showy, fragrant, axillary, 10 cm flowers with sepals white, petals pink, and a fringed crown purple, white and blue; with trilobed leaves. *Tropical. Zone 10.*   *p. 288*

amethystina (Brazil); luxuriant climber with very slender stem, smooth leaves deeply 3-lobed, 10 cm wide; flowers 7 cm across, lapis-lazuli blue, corona rays deep purple. *Tropical. Zones 10-11.*   *p. 288*

aurantia (Tacsonia mixta) (New Guinea to Vanuatu or New Hebrides); vigorous climber with glossy green, deeply 3-lobed leaves; lovely starry flowers with rosy, convex petals, and blood-red corona; photographed in the rainforest in the mountains of S.E. Papua. *Tropical. Zone 11.*   *p. 288*

caerulea (Brazil), a showy tendril-climbing "Blue passion flower"; religious symbol to early missionaries who saw in its greenish-white petals the 10 apostles at the crucifixion, in the blue, white and purple rays of the corona the crown of thorns, in the 5 anthers the wounds, the 3 stigmas the nails; cords and whips in the coiling tendrils of the vine, and in 5-lobed leaves the cruel hands of the persecutors. The 6-10 cm flowers keep best floating on water. *Zones 9-10.*   *p. 288*

coccinea (Trop. So. America), a "Red passion flower"; climbing with grooved purplish downy stems, leaves 8-15 cm long, ovate and coarsely crenate; free-blooming with flowers of medium size, with glowing scarlet petals, red sepals yellowish outside, the crown filaments deep purple, pink to white base; ovoid yellow or orange fruit 5 cm dia., and edible. *Tropical. Zone 9.*   *p. 289*

'Coral Glow' (manicata x jamesonii x mollissima); beautiful California hybrid; vigorous climber with trilobed leaves, and very floriferous with large coral-pink flowers, blooming throughout the year. *Zone 10.*   *p. 289*

coriacea (So. Mexico to Perú), "Bat-leaf vine"; vigorous climber with red stems, interesting mainly because of its hard to being brittle, transversely oblong-peltate leaves, more broad than long like a butterfly, blue-green blotched with silver gray; small 2½ cm flowers in clusters, with pale green petals, a yellow ray-crown, and purplish-chocolate base. *Tropical. Zones 10-11.*   *p. 288*

edulis (Brazil), the "Purple granadilla"; sturdy climber with angular stems, large 15 cm leaves deeply lobed, with wavy edges; 6 cm white flowers, its corona white, banded with purple, mostly summer-blooming; the 8 cm aromatic, edible fruit thickly purple-dotted and quite ornamental; widely grown in warm climates for its delicious flavor in beverages, fruit salads, sherbets, also jam and marmalade; fruiting in Spring and Autumn. *Zones 10-11.*   *p. 922*

edulis flavicarpa, "Granadilla" or "Yellow passion fruit"; a form with its edible, sweet fruits maturing yellow, as grown commercially in Hawaii and New Zealand. *Zones 10-11.*   *p. 288, 922*

'Imperatrice Eugenie' (alata x caerulea); famous hybrid; tendril-climbing, with deeply 3-lobed rich green leaves; flowers 50% larger than caerulea, measuring 10-16 cm across; white sepals, rosy-purple petals, ray-crown purple and white. *Tropical. Zones 10-11.*   *p. 289*

manicata (ignea) (Colombia, Ecuador, Perú) "Scarlet passion flower"; strong climber, with angled stems, finely downy; leathery,

3-lobed, toothed leaves to 10 cm wide; flowers 10 cm across, vivid scarlet with tiny blue crown; fruit yellowish-green. *Zone 10.* *p. 289*

mollissima (Tacsonia), "Banana passion fruit"; according to Hortus, from the Andes of So. America; but on expedition in the New Guinea highlands, I found this species at the remote Chimbu Pass, beyond Goroka; rambling tropical tendril climber, with deeply 3-lobed leaves, and flowers 8 cm across on long tube, a lovely pink with pale center; pendant oblong 8 cm fruit yellow, insipid taste when eaten. *Zone 10.* *p. 289*

ornithoura (Costa Rica); scandent tropical shrub, with strange leathery leaves forked into two narrow blades like scissors, a band of silver down the length of each linear lobe; flowers unusual with green, orange and purple parts. *Zone 11.* *p. 288*

palmeri var. sublanceolata (Mexico: Campeche to Baja California), "Sandia de la pasión"; low rambling shrub 50 cm high and spreading to 120 cm wide, broad-ovate leaves lightly 3-lobed; flowers with sepals and petals white overlaid with rose, 6 cm across, corona filaments purple and white. The species P. palmeri according to Standley has petals and sepals all white. *Zone 10.* *p. 289*

platyfolia (El Salvador); robust climber with deeply lobed leaves; flowers with sepals and petals white and purple, filaments barred dark purple; produces delicate edible, orange-colored, large fruit. *Zone 10.* *p. 289*

quadrangularis (Trop. America), "Giant granadilla"; robust climber with winged stems and oval leaves, much grown in the tropics for its edible fruit, which is oblong, 12-25 cm long, yellowish-green and pulpy; 8-12 cm fragrant flowers with oval, white sepals, reddish petals, and crown with 5 rows of white and purple rays. *Tropical.* *Zones 10-11.* *p. 289*

racemosa (princeps) (Brazil), a "Red passion-vine"; climbing by tendrils, with deeply 3-lobed or occasionally ovate leaves; 10 cm flowers in pendulous racemes, the narrow petals rosy-crimson and spreading, the fringed crown with outer rays purple tipped white, the short inner rays red. *Tropical. Zone 10.* *p. 289*

seemannii (Trop. America); robust tendril climber, with smooth, broad ovate leaves 5-12 cm long, lighter below; large flowers blue and white to 10 cm across; oblong fruit 5 cm dia. *Tropical. Zones 10-11.* *p. 288*

suberosa (Costa Rica); scandent shrub of vigorous growth, with trilobed leathery leaves, the middle lobe much larger, and veins a contrasting yellow; small 2-3 cm greenish-white flowers in elongate clusters, the corona white with purple. *Zone 10.* *p. 290*

trifasciata (Venezuela, Brazil, Perú), "Three-banded passion vine"; ornamental climber with wiry stems and broad, beautifully colored, lightly 3-lobed leaves, satiny olive to deep bronze green with 3 broad, pink to silvery green zones along the purple veins, and purple beneath; small, fragrant, yellowish flowers 3 to 4 cm across; globose 2½ cm fruit. *Tropical. Zone 11.* *p. 290*

violacea (Brazil, Paraguay, Bolivia), "Purple passion flower"; tall climber with trifoliate leaves, the segments occasionally lobed again, gray-green beneath; fragrant 10 cm, pretty flowers pendant from long stalks, sepals pinkish-lilac, petals violet, crown with violet and white rays. *Tropical. Zone 10.* *p. 290*

vitifolia (Tacsonia) (Nicaragua to Perú), "Crimson passion flower"; climber with rusty-downy stems and grape-like leaves, coarsely toothed; showy, 10-15 cm flowers orange-scarlet to blood-red, with bristle-tipped sepals, outer rays of corona bright red, the shorter, inner ones pale red; shy bloomer. *Tropical. Zone 10.* *p. 290*

PATERSONIA *Iridaceae*

glabrata (Australia: Queensland, N. So. Wales, Victoria), "Australian native iris"; handsome perennial herb with short rhizome, forming clumps of narrow, strap-shaped leaves which are deciduous; floral stalks 15-30 cm high, bearing fragile flowers about 6 cm across, usually light purple to deep blue; spring-blooming. *Zone 10.* *p. 430*

PATRINIA *Valerianaceae*

triloba (Japan); hardy perennial to 40 cm, hairy at nodes and on stalks; leaves heart-shaped, palmately 3-5-lobed to entire, lower ones coarsely serrate; small flowers golden-yellow, in branched clusters to 10 cm across. *Zone 6.* *p. 516*

PAULOWNIA *Scrophulariaceae as in Zander*
(Bignoniaceae in Hortus 3)

tomentosa (China), "Empress tree"; deciduous, hairy tree 12-20 m tall, resembling Catalpa, with horizontal branches; light green, cordate leaves 12-30 cm long; flowers before leaves, forming upright clusters of trumpet-shaped, fragrant flowers of lilac-blue with dark spots and yellow stripes inside, 5 cm long. *Warm temperate. Zone 5.* *p. 875, 901*

PAUROTIS wrightii in hort.:
transferred to ACOELORRHAPHE wrightii (Hortus)

PAVETTA *Rubiaceae*
opaca (So. Africa), "Christmas bush"; photographed in Kirsten-bosch Botanic Garden, Feb., 1977; evergreen shrub to 3 m; glossy dark green lanceolate foliage; large clusters of sweetly fragrant white flowers with long ivory styles, blooming in Summer. *Zone 10.* *p. 858*

revoluta (obovata) (So. Africa); neat evergreen bush to 1 m, with glossy green, rounded leaves; sweetly scented white flowers with long protruding white styles. *Zone 10.* *p. 858*

PAVONIA *Malvaceae*

hastata (So. America, natural. in Southern U.S.); bushy evergreen shrub to 2 m high, with woody branches, finely gray-hairy; long-stalked lanceolate leaves to 5 cm long and lightly toothed; axillary bell-shaped flowers 3 cm long, the corolla crimson-red, variable to rose; summer-blooming. *Zones 9-10.* *p. 786*

PAXISTIMA *Celastraceae*

canbyi (Mts. of Virginia and West Virginia), "Cliff-green" or "Mountain-lover"; low evergreen shrub to 30 cm high, forming densely branched mounds; narrow oblong leaves only 2 cm long; small white flowers. Very ornamental with its beautiful bronze autumn color. *Zone 5.* *p. 686*

PEDICULARIS *Scrophulariaceae*

groenlandica (Labrador to Brit. Columbia and Calif.), "Elephant-heads"; interesting herbaceous perennial to 60 cm high, with leaves 15 cm long, pinnately divided; the curious inflorescence of light to dark purple flowers, having corolla with upper lip compressed into decurved beak 2 cm long; summer-blooming. *Zones 3-7.* *p. 441*

PEDILANTHUS *Euphorbiaceae*

brachypetalus (Mexico), "Canary-bird bush"; interesting shrub with milky juice; succulent branches bearing alternate, deciduous leaves; small flowers borne in red, fleshy bracts; the fruit a 3-lobed capsule. *Zone 10.* *p. 725*

tithymaloides 'Variegatus' (carinatus cv.) (W. Indies), "Zigzag plant"; branching succulent bush with milky juice, with age to 1 m high; gray-green, fleshy stems bent with each waxy, pale green, ovate leaf, 6 to 10 cm long, highly variegated white and tinged carmine-red; terminal inflorescence red. *Tropical. Zone 11.* *p. 195*

PELARGONIUM *Geraniaceae*

crassicaule (Southwest Africa), "Succulent geranium"; a succulent species with thick, fleshy stems to 15 cm high, and small, pubescent, lobed leaves; flowers white, the upper petals spotted purple. *Subtropic. Zone 9.* *p. 195, 422*

crispum (So. Africa), "Lemon geranium"; mildly lemon-scented shrub with rigidly erect branches to 80 cm high, reddish petioles, and tiny round, crinkled, satiny green leaves 2 cm across, lobed and crisped, often held close to stem; used in finger bowls, or hung in closets; small lavender flowers, the upper 2 petals deeper purplish-pink. *Zone 10.* *p. 529*

x domesticum, "Martha Washington geranium" or "Regal geranium"; complex hybrids involving P. grandiflorum and other species; soft-hairy brittle stems, to 50 cm or more high; toothed leaves 5-8 cm across; large showy flowers 3-6 cm, in clusters in colors white, pink, red, purple, the two upper petals with dark blotches and veins. *Subtropic. Zone 10.*

x domesticum 'Circus Day'; a premium cultivar with big heads of very large flowers rosy-pink, the upper petals deep pink with velvety brown-black blotch flushed with salmon. *Zone 10.* *p. 420*

x domesticum 'Easter Greeting'; popular early and long-blooming variety; rosy-carmine flowers 6 cm across, each petal with a long black blotch. *Subtropic. Zone 10.* *p. 55*

x domesticum 'Frilly Aztec'; striking California cultivar with large clusters of showy flowers white to pale pink, having petals fringed and lobed at apex, the inside of corolla beautifully painted crimson-red. Seen at Kartuz Greenhouses, Vista, California, summer-blooming. *Zone 10.* *p. 422*

x domesticum 'Gay Nineties'; good commercial cultivar with large 6 cm frilled flowers with crimson eye. *Zone 10.* *p. 420*

x domesticum 'MacKay'; well-shaped commercial plant with flowers dark salmon-pink, and crimson blotches in center. *Zone 10.* *p. 420*

x domesticum 'Mrs. Mary Bard'; compact grower and early bloomer, with medium-size flowers pure white, striped purple at base of petals. *Zone 10.* *p. 60*

x glaucifolium (gibbosum x lobatum), the "Black-flowered geranium"; shrubby perennial with large glaucous leaves pinnately lobed and ruffled; long-petioled 4 cm flowers striking dark maroon edged with gold, and sweetly fragrant in the evening. *Zones 9-10.* *p. 422*

graveolens (Cape Prov.), old fashioned "Rose geranium"; bushy plant with deeply lobed leaves appearing gray-green because of their covering of soft white hair; small blooms lavender-pink marked purple. The rose-scented leaves are used in cookery, sachet, and for making perfume; also used as a source of fragrant commercial geranium oil, distilled from plant. *Zone 9.* *p. 422, 530*

graveolens 'Lady Plymouth', "Variegated rose geranium"; a lower growing and less vigorous mutant of graveolens, with lobed leaves quite small and deformed looking but more white variegation and less green than 'Grey Lady Plymouth'. Zones 9-10.   *p. 529*

graveolens x tomentosum, "Lemon Rose geranium"; very fragrant hybrid, covered with silky white hairs; the grayish, fleshy leaves palmately divided into narrow elliptic lobes irregularly toothed and undulate along margins. Ideal as a pot-herb, strongly scented of rose and mint. Zone 10.   *p. 530*

x hortorum (So. African origin), "Zonal geranium" or "Garden geranium"; as grown by commercial nurseries today, these are of complex hybrid origin, largely derived from P. zonale and inquinans, familiar as potplants, in window boxes or in garden beds. Succulent stems 30-50 cm high with rounded or kidney-shaped leaves 6-10 cm across, often colorfully zoned or variegated; the flowers varying from 3-5 cm across, in showy clusters, with petals nearly equal, in many vivid colors, primarily scarlet-red, purple, soft pink or salmon, pure white, or bicolor, also double-flowered and miniatures; in many fancy-named cultivars. Subtropic. Zone 10.   *p. 421*

x hortorum 'Carefree Scarlet'; all-American selection as an outstanding color-form of a new F1 hybrid or heterosis seed strain of single and double garden geraniums by Pan-American Seed Co.; grown directly from seed, and available also in shades of pink and red, also bicolors and white. Geraniums from seed are not as early as those propagated from cuttings, but begin to bloom in June-July and are at their best from August to October. Seed has to be started warm at a constant 21-24°C; for early bloom in mid-May sow beginning of January; grow with all the light or sun possible, keep warm to initiate buds, then intermediate or cool, although they tolerate high summer temperatures. Zone 10.   *p. 420*

x hortorum 'Happy Thought', "Butterfly geranium"; old English mutant (1877) of vigorous medium-large habit, with attractive, gaily colored leaves bright green painted cream-yellow in center, in shape of a butterfly, and zoned with splashes of brown; single 3-4 cm flowers glowing carmine-red, scarlet on upper petals, in clusters 8 cm across. Zone 10.   *p. 422*

x hortorum 'Irene'; good commercial, bushy plant with fine, zoned foliage, and free-blooming with semi-double red flowers close to American Beauty cerise. Introduced 1942 and progeny of many excellent named varieties. Subtropic. Zone 10.   *p. 56*

x hortorum 'Madame Salleron', "Carpet-bed geranium"; a unique, old French hybrid which I remember my father using in fancy carpet bedding; small plant sprouting multiple short branches from the base, with little papery, crenate leaves glistening gray-green with white border on long, thin petioles; rarely blooming, with small salmon-red flowers. Zone 10.   *p. 420*

x hortorum 'Mr. Wren'; a very striking variety with single, 4 cm bright red flowers edged in white, but not very freely produced, on strong plants. Zone 10.   *p. 420*

x hortorum 'Mrs. Strang', "Tricolor geranium"; beautiful multi-colored foliage silvery green zoned with black-maroon and red, edged with gold and canary yellow. Subtropic. Zone 11.   *p. 56*

x hortorum 'New Porter'; fascinating cultivar of exceptionally prolific growth habit forming large well-shaped plants in containers, covered with large clusters 12-15 cm across of single flowers vivid scarlet-red; photographed in Vista, California 1973. Zone 10.   *p. 53*

x hortorum (zonale) 'Olympic Red' (Ricard x Radio Red); popular commercial geranium of early-blooming, free-flowering and branching habit; beautifully zoned leaves and large heads of semi-double, fiery red flowers each 3-4 cm across. Zone 10.   *p. 420*

x hortorum 'Salmon Irene'; bushy and vigorous "Zonal geranium" with good foliage and large clusters of semi-double soft salmon-rose flowers. Zone 10.   *p. 422*

x hortorum 'Salmon Supreme'; distinctive commercial variety of the French type, more vigorous than 'Poitevine' and a freer bloomer but of the same fine, large semi-double flowers of clear light salmon-pink. Zone 10.   *p. 420*

x hortorum 'Velma', "Tricolor geranium"; gaily-colored, very compact geranium with small tricolored foliage, the rounded, near waxy leaves grayish-green in center, surrounded by a rosy-red zone and bordered in creamy-yellow; single salmon 3 cm flowers; of stronger growth, larger leaves than Mrs. H. Cox. Zone 11. p. 60, 420

'Lumière du Matin' (peltato-zonale hyb.); floriferous French hybrid with long creeping or pendant stems and waxy green, ivy-leaf type foliage; similar to 'Ville de Paris' but with single flowers crimson-red; very successful in sun-starved, cool regions; ideal for window boxes and containers outdoors. Zone 10.   *p. 422*

x nervosum, "Lime geranium"; lime-scented; an old English hybrid (1820), of bushy growth, with small rounded, green leaves having sharply toothed margins, 3-4 cm across, and lightly ruffled; showy clusters of lavender flowers. Zone 10.   *p. 529*

peltatum (Eastern South Africa), called the "Ivy geranium", because of the ivy-like, pointed 5-lobed leaves which are fresh green,

waxy and rather succulent, 5-8 cm across, on trailing, zigzag branches; flowers normally single and rose-carmine, but now highly hybridized into many types and colors with single or double flowers, in rounded clusters, in white, pink, rose, red and lavender; the 2 upper petals usually blotched or striped; Ivy geraniums are ideally suited for hanging baskets, window boxes, patio containers or as groundcover. In So. Africa, the acid leaves are eaten. Zone 10.   *p. 307, 323*

peltatum 'Amethyst', "Giant ivy-geranium"; robust hybrid originated in Dresden, Saxony; stems of exceptional sturdiness, with age lending themselves to training on stakes, forming woody trunks, carrying bushy heads with waxy, fresh green leaves and large and showy semi-double flowers 6 cm across, vivid amethyst purple and deep crimson markings. Seen grown in containers in the formal gardens of Charlottenburg Palace, Berlin. Zone 10.   *p. 57, 314, 421*

peltatum 'Mexico', bicolor "Ivy geranium"; striking cultivar seen in Germany 1976; free growing with long branches; fresh green waxy, lobed leaves, and large double flowers with petals white in center, red around the margins. Zone 10.   *p. 422*

peltatum 'Variegatum', "Variegated ivy geranium"; charming variety with silvery green waxy foliage, having margins beautifully bordered with creamy-white. Subtropic. Zone 10.   *p. 60*

'Prince Rupert variegatum', also known as "French lace"; lemon-scented; habit of P. crispum but bushier and more prolific, the small lobed and crisped leaves are light green and prettily edged in white. Zone 10.   *p. 420*

tomentosum (Cape of Good Hope), "Peppermint-geranium"; strongly scented species of sprawling habit, with large, soft velvety, emerald green leaves, triangular-heartshaped, shallowly lobed, 8-10 cm wide, with a felt-like covering of white hairs; small, fluffy white flowers. The peppermint-scented leaves are used to give mint flavor to jellies, desserts and other culinary arts. Zone 10.   *p. 420, 530*

tricolor (violareum) (So. Africa), "Viola geranium"; odd species with low spreading branches; long-stalked powdery-gray ovate, toothed leaves; and pansy-faced flowers, with lower petals white, the two upper petals ruby red with dark blotch. Nice in baskets and hanging pots, blooming in Spring and Summer. Subtropic. Zone 9.   *p. 420*

'Ville de Paris' (peltato-zonale hyb.), "Strassbourg geranium"; color form of this new French hybrid race, introduced about 1965; profusely blooming ivy-leaf type geranium with thin-leathery leaves, and 3-4 cm single flowers with narrow-linear or obovate petals glowing carmine-rose with blood-red stripes, in small clusters but forming a blanket of color with cascades to 1 m long, during summertime, even in sun-poor regions such as Northern Europe, where it has become immensely popular in window boxes and outdoor urns. Zone 10.   *p. 422*

PELLAEA   *Polypodiaceae (Filices)*
bridgesii (California, Oregon to Idaho), "Cliff brake" found in the Sierra Nevada; small rock-loving fern with tufted, leathery pinnate leaves to 30 cm long, the pinnae oval-oblong, on glossy brown petioles to 20 cm long. Zones 9-10.   *p. 136*

rotundifolia (New Zealand), "Button fern"; small rock-loving fern with creeping rhizome and pubescent stems, fronds nearly uniform, and staying near ground; simple pinnate, evenly spaced leaflets, round when young, later oblong, dark green and waxy leathery. Humid-subtropic. Zone 10.   *p. 136*

viridis macrophylla, better known in horticulture as Pteris adiantoides; variety with bipinnate fronds to 45 cm high, having thin-leathery leaflets much larger and broader than in the species, although less in number on each pinna, and resembling Holly-fern, but leaves are not as leathery. Used in small fern-dishes as a "Table-fern". From S.E. Africa. Humid-subtropic. Zones 10-11.   *p. 136*

PELLIONIA   *Urticaceae*
pulchra (Vietnam; Cochin), "Satin pellionia"; attractive fleshy creeper hugging its support or pendant from a basket, with pinkish stems and stipules, obliquely oval leaves light green to grayish, entirely covered with a network of blackish or brownish veins, pale purple beneath on gray. Tropical. Zone 12.   *p. 76*

PELTANDRA   *Araceae*
virginica (Maine to Florida and Missouri), "Arrow arum"; hardy aquatic perennial herb with thick fibrous roots and large bright green, firm arrow-shaped leaves 15 to 75 cm long, on long sheathing petioles; undulate, fleshy, greenish-white spathe to 20 cm long; the spadix with female flowers in lower third; male, staminate flowers on upper two-thirds. Temperate. Zones 4-8.   *p. 326*

PELTIPHYLLUM   *Saxifragaceae*
peltatum (Oregon, California), "Umbrella plant"; perennial bog plant, similar to Saxifraga; stout rhizome, with 30-60 cm hairy petioles supporting large roundish peltate, lobed leaves with toothed margins,

often 30 cm across; the flowers on erect hairy stalks appearing before the leaves, with numerous pinkish or white blooms in April. *Zone 5.* p. 337

PELTOPHORUM   Leguminosae
pterocarpum (Malaysia to Australia), "Yellow flame tree"; stately tree to 15 m, with heavy luxuriant, bipinnate foliage to 60 cm long; large erect panicles of round, rust-colored buds opening into orange-yellow fragrant flowers 4 cm across. *Zone 10.* p. 767

PENNISETUM   Gramineae
alopecuroides (E. Asia to E. Australia), "Chinese fountain grass"; showy ornamental perennial, with culms to 1 m high; slender linear, rough leaves to 60 cm long; the dark green sheaths rounded; floral plumes 15 cm long, with silvery rose spikelets along axis. *Zones 5-9.* p. 562

orientale (W. Asia to India), "Orient fountain grass"; tufted deciduous perennial with short rhizomes; slender culms 20-90 cm high, and having bearded nodes; leafblades narrowly linear with pointed tips; beautiful arching spike-like inflorescence to 40 cm long of silky, purplish spikelets. *Zones 7-9.* p. 563

setaceum (No. Trop. Africa, Ethiopia, Arabia), "Fountain grass"; perennial ornamental grass to 1 m or more high, forming clusters; the numerous rough, narrow leaves to 50 cm long; bristly cylindric floral spikes of fruit heads to 30 cm long, creamy-white to pink or rose. Often grown as annual from seed sown in late Summer. *Zone 7.* p. 563

setaceum 'Atrosanguineum', "Blood grass"; striking dense bush with leathery leaves wine-red to purplish, and masses of very ornamental, gracefully arching tail-like pink to purplish plumes. *Zone 7.* p. 563

setaceum 'Cupreum', "Red fountain grass"; perennial grass with simple stems 1 m high, forming clumps; narrow arching leaves 60 cm long, reddish-brown, and copper-colored spikes. *Zone 7.* p. 563

villosum (Africa: Ethiopia; escaped in Mich., Texas and California), "Feathertop"; perennial in habitat; grown as annual in cold climate or short-lived perennial in warmer regions; tufts of narrow linear leaves; and culms to 60 cm long; the elongate flower-heads peek out from the foliage like pink feather dusters, 10 cm long, with bristles longer than the spikelets. *Zone 8.* p. 563

PENSTEMON   Scrophulariaceae
barbatus (Utah to Mexico), "Scarlet beard-tongue"; smooth perennial to 2 m high, with glaucous stems and narrow lanceolate leaves; tall racemes of elongate two-lipped scarlet trumpet flowers 3 cm long, blooming June-August. *Zone 3.* p. 505

campanulatus (pulchellus) (Mexico and Guatemala); perennial to 60 cm high, with clammy-hairy stems; leaves linear to narrow lanceolate, to 10 cm long, with small teeth along margins; bell-shaped flowers 3-4 cm long, with rosy-purple, inflated corolla, densely bearded near apex, in erect terminal racemes. August-blooming. *Zone 8.* p. 506

campanulatus 'Evelyn'; popular English cultivar to 50 cm high, with narrow lanceolate leaves, to 10 cm long; flowers inflated tubular or bell-shaped with flaring lobes, 3 cm long, soft pink with white tips, and bearded at apex, in terminal clusters, blooming in June. *Zone 7.* p. 506

eriantherus (Nebraska and Dakota to Brit. Columbia), "Dakota beard-tongue"; pubescent perennial 20 to 40 cm high, with narrow-lanceolate leaves; flowers in compact clusters, with bell-shaped corollas pink and lined with purple, showing conspicuous sterile stamens extended beyond the opening and bearded with long, yellowish hairs, blooming June and July. *Zone 3.* p. 506

fendleri (W. Kansas to Arizona and Sonora); erect perennial to 45 cm high, with leathery, glaucous, ovate leaves 5 cm long; the inflorescence in slender, interrupted terminal racemes, with leaflike bracts in lower part; the bluish-pink flowers with thin tubular corollas 2 cm long, the stamens bearded at apex; blooming April-July. *Zone 4.* p. 506

fruticosus (scouleri) (Brit. Columbia to Oregon, Alberta and Wyoming), "Bush penstemon"; floriferous perennial with woody base, forming dense bush to 40 cm high, with lanceolate leathery leaves 5 cm long; the inflorescence in airy clusters of purplish-rose 3 cm flowers, the lower lip yellow-bearded; blooming in Kew Gardens in late May. *Zone 4.* p. 505

x gloxinioides, "Garden penstemon"; hybrid of Mexican P. hartwegii; strong herbaceous perennial with lance-shaped leaves and dense spikes of large, gloxinia-like, bell flowers to 5 cm long, in many brilliant colors, especially reds, blooming late Summer to Autumn. *Zone 6.* p. 505

x gloxinioides 'Fire King'; brilliant red trumpets carried in a raceme along slender stalk, the throat white. *Zone 6.* p. 505

hartwegii (gentianoides hort.) (Mexico and Guatemala); showy, short-lived perennial to 80 cm or more high, with purple stems; the leaves narrow-lanceolate; inflorescence terminal on leafy branches, of pendant flowers deep rose, varying to red, the corolla funnel-shaped, 5 cm long and white-bearded near mouth, blooming in June. Originating in cooler regions of Mexico, and a parent of many garden hybrids. *Zone 9.* p. 505

heterophyllus (Coastal Mts. of California), "Chaparral penstemon"; handsome subshrubby perennial with woody base, 30-60 cm high, with linear or narrow-lanceolate leaves to 5 cm long; bell-shaped flowers 4 cm long, with inflated purple-lilac corolla tinted with pink; blooming April-July. *Zone 9.* p. 506

hirsutus 'Pygmaeus'; dwarf form of species from Maine to Virginia and Wisconsin; perennial to 60 cm high, covered with fine hairs; stem-leaves lanceolate, to 10 cm long and toothed; slender tubular flowers 3 cm long, with corolla pale purple, the throat nearly closed, and the barren stamens bearded near apex. *Zone 3.* p. 506

parryi (Arizona to Sonora, Mexico); glaucous perennial 60 cm to more than 1 m high with age, with whitish stems; clasping lanceolate, leathery leaves to 12 cm long; showy inflorescence with rose-purple bell-flowers 2 cm long, the inflated corolla with protruding stamens yellow-bearded; blooming March to June. *Zone 9.* p. 506

rupicola (Washington to No. California), "Cliff penstemon"; downy perennial having woody base, the branches prostrate and forming mats, leafy with small 2 cm ovate leaves of thick texture; terminal clusters of carmine-rose flowers 3-4 cm long, the 2-lipped corolla bearded at throat, blooming in May. *Zone 6.* p. 506

smallii (No. Carolina and Tennessee); bushy herbaceous perennial to 1 m high or more; with ovate basal leaves, serrate at margins; stem leaves lanceolate to triangular, to 12 cm long; purplish-pink flowers 3-4 cm long, with corolla striped white inside, and yellow-bearded on lower lip; blooming May-June. *Zone 7.* p. 505

PENTADENIA   Gesneriaceae
zapotelana (Ecuador); subshrub with firm branches; alternate oval-elliptic leaves having lightly crenate margins, purplish-brown at apex beneath; axillary small tubular flowers orange-yellow. *Zone 11.* p. 64

PENTAGLOTTIS   Boraginaceae
sempervirens (Anchusa in hort.) (France to Spain, Portugal), "Evergreen Alkanet"; hairy herbaceous perennial 30-80 cm high, with basal leaves broadly ovate; leafy stems with axillary racemes of rich blue, cup-shaped flowers in Spring and Summer. *Zone 7.* p. 348

PENTAGONIA   Rubiaceae
macrophylla rubra (El Llano, Panama); striking tropical evergreen developing tree-like, with erect stems bearing showy ornamental broad-elliptic leaves of firm texture, 30-40 cm long, glossy olive-green on surface, and glowing ruby red underneath, the ribs depressed and surface corrugated. Seen in Hawaii as beautiful specimen 4 m high. *Zone 11.* p. 859

PENTAPTERIGIUM: see AGAPETES

PENTAS   Rubiaceae
lanceolata (Trop. Africa, Arabia), "Egyptian star-cluster"; herbaceous flowering plant to 40 cm high with woody base, downy branches and soft or limp, ovate, bright green, hairy leaves, with sunken veins, 5-15 cm long, the tubular flowers in showy clusters, hairy in the throat, purplish-rose, and with spreading lobes, 2 cm across. *Zone 10.* p. 495

PEPEROMIA   Piperaceae
argyreia (sandersii) (Brazil), "Watermelon peperomia"; attractive rosette, almost stemless, with deep red petioles bearing fleshy, broad peltate-pointed, concave leaves 8 to 10 cm across, glossy fresh green to bluish, painted with showy bands of silver radiating from their upper center, pale beneath; minute flowers in long, whitish catkins. *Tropical. Zone 12.* p. 76

arifolia litoralis (São Paulo); compact rosette with hard, flat, cordate leaves dark green with lustrous silver bands between the primary veins, looking like a shining shield. *Tropical. Zone 11.* p. 76

asperula (Hawaii); low succulent spreading from base, forming rosettes with thick, ovate, boat-shaped light green 5-8 cm leaves of rough surface, and pale up to margins; long-stalked inflorescence of several whitish spikelets of tiny flowers. *Tropical. Zone 11.* p. 198

caperata (Brazil), "Emerald Ripple"; sturdy, very useful little species with short, branching stem developing dense clusters of roundish, heart-shaped or peltate leaves deeply corrugated and quilted like a washboard, waxy forest green, the valleys tinted chocolate, the ridges often grayish, reverse pale green, the pink petioles striped red; the slender flowering catkins greenish-white. *Tropical. Zone 12.* p. 76

clusiifolia (West Indies), "Red-edged peperomia"; stocky, slow-growing plant with thick-fleshy, rather oblanceolate, concave leaves, 8-15 cm long, metallic olive-green with broad, red-purple margin, light green beneath except for the purple midrib. *Tropical. Zone 11.* p. 76

columella (columnaris) (Perú); interesting succulent, spreading from base with snake-like decumbent to erect cylindric, fleshy dark green columns 8-12 cm long, and to 2 cm thick; the sides covered by elevated knobs, spirally arranged, their glassy surface with translucent windows. *Zone 11.*   *p. 198*

fraseri 'Variegata' (resedaeflora cv.), "Variegated Mignonette peperomia"; striking California mutation of the green species from Ecuador and Colombia; low rosette of small quilted, round cordate leaves frosted dull green in center, and broadly variegated cream toward margins, red-ribbed beneath; the inflorescence on tall red stalks topped by fluffy white flowerspikes resembling mignonette. *Zone 12.*   *p. 76*

graveolens (Trop. South America); small and pretty succulent, branching and spreading from base; the flexuous red stems with petioled thick fleshy, spoon-like leaves, to 6 cm long, concave and dark glossy green above, the reverse red-purple up to curled margins. *Zone 11.*   *p. 199*

magnoliifolia 'Rainbow', "Tricolor Pepperface"; colorful, robust Florida mutation; large fleshy obovate-elliptic leaves 10-12 cm long, glossy fresh green, broadly banded with cream toward margins and tinted red at edges, on brownish stem. *Zone 11.*   *p. 76*

obtusifolia 'Variegata', "Variegated peperomia"; beautiful, small, succulent plant with pale stems blotched bright red; alternate, rounded or obovate-elliptic, waxy leaves, light green variegated with milky green, and from the margin inward, a broad area of creamy-white. *Tropical. Zone 11.*   *p. 76*

pernambucensis (Brazil), "Birdsnest peperomia"; unusual tropical rosette of stiff upright, leathery lanceolate, green leaves 10-15 cm long, eventually forming a small vase, on red petioles; the inflorescence on red floral stalks topped by bottlebrush-like clusters of small white flowers. *Zone 11.*   *p. 76*

puteolata (Perú), "Parallel peperomia"; gorgeous hanging plant with angled stems and slender, lanceolate, leathery leaves 10 cm long, waxy dark green with 5 contrasting, yellowish, subtranslucent, parallel veins depressed on the surface and raised on the light green reverse. *Tropical. Zone 12.*   *p. 76*

scandens 'Variegata', "Philodendron peperomia"; colorful, scandent, semi-erect, fleshy creeper with small cordate leaves gracefully slender-pointed, light green to milky green, irregularly bordered with creamy-white, on red petioles and reddish stems. Somewhat rank in growth, but useful for baskets. *Tropical. Zone 11.*   *p. 318*

verschaffeltii (Alto Amazonas), "Sweetheart peperomia"; a beautiful shapely plant which I rediscovered on the upper Amazon; a short-stemmed rosette of fleshy, oval-heartshaped leaves 10 cm long, similar to marmorata but basal lobes not overlapping, and alternate on short branching stem, the waxy surface is bluish-green with broad silver bands between the recessed yellowish veins, on petioles red with dots, (Ill. Hort. 1869). *Tropical. Zone 12.*   *p. 76*

PERESKIA   *Cactaceae*

aculeata (Venezuela to Mexico), "Barbados gooseberry" or "Lemon vine"; leafy shrub with flexible, woody stems not jointed, straggling and climbing; waxy green, ovate leaves 8 cm long, the areoles with needle-like spines; lemon-scented flowers creamy-yellow to pinkish, 3 to 4 cm across; small 2 cm yellow edible fruit resembling goose-berries, agreeable to eat fresh, or made into preserves. Widely used in the West Indies. *Tropical. Zone 10.*   *p. 922*

grandifolia (grandiflora) (Rhodocactus) (Brazil), a "Rose cactus"; a shrub or tree to 4 m with very spiny trunk, the elliptic fleshy waxy, rich green leaves to 15 cm long; flowers like wild roses rose-pink, 3-4 cm across, in terminal clusters. *Tropical. Zone 10.*   *p. 179*

PERILEPTA dyeriana (Zander):
see STROBILANTHES dyerianus (Hortus)

PERILLA   *Labiatae*

frutescens (India, Himalayas, to E. Asia), "Shiso" of Japan; herbaceous annual 40-80 cm high, grown for its handsome foliage, with pubescent, thick fleshy, 4-angled stem; the wrinkled opposite leaves broadly ovate, 6-15 cm long, greenish or purplish, and toothed at margins; the small white flowers in terminal spikes. *Zone 10 as annual.*   *p. 433*

frutescens 'Atropurpurea' (Japan), "Black nettle"; very decorative color form with its ornamental foliage very deep purple to nearly black, and very popular as showy bedding plant in parks of China and Japan. *Zone 10 as annual.*   *p. 433*

frutescens 'Atropurpurea crispa' (India, China, Japan), "Frilled nettle" or "Fancy fringe"; very ornamental annual coleus-like herb to 1 m with 4-angled stem, and with colored foliage; sharply toothed, bullate leaves 5-12 cm long, a showy purplish-brown or bronzy; small white flowers. Leaves may be used as vegetable or for flavoring. *Zone 10 as annual.*   *p. 433, 532*

PERISTERIA   *Orchidaceae*

elata (Costa Rica, Panama, Colombia), "Dove orchid", or "Holy Ghost orchid", national flower of Panama; vigorous, handsome epiphyte also growing terrestrial, with ovoid pseudobulbs bearing 3-5 plaited leaves to 1 m long; inflorescence tall, erect, to 1½ m high, with fleshy, waxy white, very fragrant, 6 cm flowers, almost globose, the column with its wings resembling a dove, (Aug.-Oct.). *Tropical. Zones 11-12.*   *p. 93*

PERITYLE   *Compositae*

crassifolia (vulgaris) (Baja California: Isla Ceralvo), "Rock-daisy"; small xerophytic marguerite with silvery pubescent leaves; small 3 cm daisy-like flowers having white ray-florets around the yellow center cushion. Seen and photographed in rocky, arid habitat East of La Paz, alongside the dried bones of a pelican. *Zone 10.*   *p. 398*

PERNETTYA   *Ericaceae*

furens (Cent. Chile); handsome evergreen shrub to 1½ m high, with spreading branches and stiff pubescent young twigs; elliptic to ovate leathery leaves to 5 cm long, bristly hairs above and beneath; beautiful urn-shaped white to pinkish, waxy flowers 1 cm long, in very decorative axillary clusters, in May; red-brown berry-like fruit, which is toxic if eaten. *Zone 8.*   *p. 707*

mucronata (So. America; Magellan region to Chile), "Chilean myrtle" or "Chilean pernettya"; bushy little evergreen shrub becoming ½-1 m high, with woody branches densely set with small stiff glossy green 2 cm ovate leaves lightly toothed, and tipped by a sharp translucent spine; numerous tiny urn-shaped nodding white or pink flowers in late Spring, followed on female plants by little 1 cm stalked, depressed globose berries, persistent through the Winter; depending on variety these may be white, pink, or brilliant red. Very pretty for tubs or window boxes, but note that berries are poisonous. More fruit is set if more plants are grouped together. *Warm temperate. Zones 6-7.*   *p. 58*

mucronata 'Alba' very similar to species, but female plants bearing pretty 1 cm berries waxy-white. *Zone 7.*   *p. 707*

mucronata 'Rosea' (Chile and Argentina), "Chilean pernettya"; small evergreen shrub to 50 cm high, the woody branches from underground runners, bearing stiff lustrous little leaves throughout Winter, having turned bronzy red; bell-shaped white to pinkish flowers; but loved and grown for its colorful fruit which is pink in 'Rosea'. However, individual plants will not fruit well by themselves, although the flowers are bisexual, several varieties should be grown together to insure cross-pollinations and best fruit set. *Zone 7. p. 707*

PEROVSKIA   *Labiatae*

abrotanoides (Turkestan to Afghanistan), "Russian sage"; much branched, twiggy, semi-woody perennial, more or less covered with white or gray, starry hairs, to 1 m or more high; with deeply cut or dissected leaves; the inflorescence spike-like with small blue flowers. *Zone 6.*   *p. 434*

atriplicifolia (W. Pakistan), "Azure sage"; deciduous semi-woody perennial 1 m to 1½ m high, with a sage-like scent, the shoots and inflorescence white-downy; small ovate, 3 cm leaves, toothed at margins; little 1 cm, two-lipped lavender-blue flowers, in a series of opposite spikes, in August-September, charming for its late bloom. *Zone 6.*   *p. 434*

PERSEA   *Lauraceae*

americana (W. Indies, Guatemala and Mexico), the "Avocado" tree; also called "Alligator pear"; a round-headed tropical and subtropical tree 6 to 10 m high or more, spreading wide with large leathery, elliptic or oval 10-20 cm leaves, glaucous beneath; and small 6 mm greenish flowers, forming in Winter. The Avocado tree grows fast in well-drained soil containing humus, beginning to bear when 4 to 8 years old, the large fleshy apple or pear-shaped edible fruit, for which it is usually cultivated, is about 10 cm across with green or purplish skin, its flesh is buttery and of high nutritional value rich in vitamins and containing 7 to 23% fat; it is served in salads. The cultivar **'Fuerte'** belongs to the "Mexican race" which includes the hardiest types (Persea drymifolia x americana); fruit 10 cm long, dull green, with flesh cream-yellow; season Nov. to Summer in California. More frost-resistant than 'Hass' or 'Reed'. *Zone 10.*   *p. 915*

americana 'Hass'; excellent avocado pear of warm climate background; large evergreen spreading tree bearing big dark purple superior pear-shaped fruit, with thick, pliable pebbly skin, easy to peel; a favorite in Southern California, and having delicious flavor, rich in buttery aromatic flesh, enclosing a hard woody seed stone; ripening Spring to October. *Zones 10-11.*   *p. 915*

americana 'Reed', "Guatemalan avocado"; very narrow, upright tree to 8 m high, producing huge round fruit with smooth, buttery flesh, ripening July to September; very frost sensitive tropical cultivar; bearing most years, fruiting at a young age. *Zone 11.*   *p. 915*

borbonica (Delaware to Florida), "Red bay" or "Florida mahogany"; handsome evergreen tree to 12 m high, inhabiting swamplands, with leathery, lanceolate leaves to 15 cm long, glaucous beneath; flowers hairy and not showy, but the 15 mm blue-black fruit on red stalks is interesting. The leaves are good for culinary seasoning. *Zone 7.* p. 742

PETALOSTIGMA   *Euphorbiaceae*
pubescens (Queensland), "Quinine bush"; small ornamental tree to 5 m high, forming trunk 45 cm dia. with age; of pleasing shape with rounded, spreading canopy; slow growing, having dark, scaly bark; small ovalish glossy green, leathery leaves; orange-red globular fruit, covered by fine hairs. *Zone 10.* p. 725

PETASITES   *Compositae*
hybridus (vulgaris) (Europe, No. and W. Asia; natur. in E. No. America), "Butter-bur" or "Bog rhubarb"; stoloniferous perennial, with large, roundish or kidney-shaped leaves 50 cm or more across, white cobwebby beneath, on long petioles, appearing with or after blooming; the inflorescence in clusters of white or purplish heads, in March to May. *Zone 4.* p. 398

PETREA   *Verbenaceae*
arborea (Trinidad, Guyana, Venezuela), "Queen's wreath tree"; shrub or low tree to 8 m high, cordate-elliptic leaves to 15 cm long; axillary raceme of purplish-blue flowers, calyx with 5 linear lobes, the inner corolla with oval petals. *Tropical. Zones 10-11.* p. 902

volubilis (racemosa) (Mexico to Panama), "Purple wreath"; one of the most beautiful of tender twiners, climbing perhaps 10 m high, with woody or wiry stems, ovate to long lanceolate brittle-hard, rough leaves to 20 cm long, and showy racemes of lovely, star-like flowers of long, lilac-blue sepals and small violet corolla; primarily in March-April. *Tropical. Zones 10-11.* p. 298

PETROCALLIS   *Cruciferae*
pyrenaica (Draba pyrenaica) (Pyrenees to Alps and Carpathian Mts.); herbaceous Alpine perennial 5-10 cm high, densely tufted and forming cushions; the shoots downy, with tiny wedge-shaped leaves, toothed at apex; small white, fragrant flowers, changing to lilac-pink, in sparse clusters, blooming May-June. Ideal for limestone rock-gardens. *Zone 6.* p. 413

PETROCOSMEA   *Gesneriaceae*
kerrii (Thailand, Vietnam), "Hidden violets"; low, flattened rosette from the jungle floor, with long-pointed, cordate, quilted leaves rather thick and fleshy, velvety green, attractively covered with white hairs, on brown petioles and with crenate margins; small violet-like flowers with upper petals cream-yellow, lower petals white, several to a short stalk usually hidden between or under the arching foliage. *Zone 11.* p. 64

PETRORHAGIA   *Caryophyllaceae*
saxifraga 'Flore pleno' (Tunica) (C. and So. Europe to C. Asia), "Coat flower" or "Tunic flower"; low, spreading herbaceous perennial 15-25 cm high woody at base, the stems thin and wiry; small 1 cm linear leaves with marginal bristles; flowers in profusion, similar to Dianthus but smaller, white or pink, 15 mm across; double in 'Flore pleno'. *Zone 5.* p. 364

PETROSELINUM   *Umbelliferae*
crispum (Europe, W. Asia), "Parsley"; hardy biennial herb 15-30 cm high, with scented, much divided, rich green, curly leaves looking like miniature celery; small greenish-yellow flowers, in compound clusters. Great in culinary use since ancient Greek and Roman times; the spicy leaves are used for flavoring in cooking and as garnish for salads; rich in iron and vitamins. An ideal potherb. *Zones 3-10.* p. 544

PETTERIA   *Leguminosae*
ramentacea (Yugoslavia); deciduous shrub 1-2 m high, with leaves of 3 leaflets; fragrant laburnum-like yellow flowers 2 cm long, in dense, erect racemes. *Zone 7.* p. 767

PETUNIA   *Solanaceae*
x hybrida 'All Star'; eye-catching bedding or window box petunia to 30 cm high, with showy single flowers having white star pattern over crimson-red background. *Zone 10.* p. 513

x hybrida 'California Giant'; herbaceous plant with small oval leaves, dwarfed by giant single flowers ruffled toward the margin, 10-15 cm across, in shades from white, rose, orchid, purple, combined with showy centers in contrasting colors or designs; desirable potplant for Mother's Day. *Tropical. Zone 10.* p. 55

x hybrida fl. pl. 'Caprice' (Grandiflora); compact plant with clear carmine-rose flowers densely double with frilled petals pale beneath, 8 cm across, early flowering; a named variety of the Panamerican strain, which also comes in white, lavender, purple, or variegated forms, all of which make superb potplants. *Zone 10.* p. 55, 513

x hybrida grandiflora 'Bingo'; huge bicolor flowers up to 12 cm across, richly variegated wine-red and white in shape of a star; part of the blooms are only 8 cm in dia., but are equally colorful; of compact habit. *Tropical. Zone 10.* p. 55

x hybrida 'Happiness' (Grandiflora); showy F1 hybrid of compact habit, with large single rose-pink flowers 8-12 cm across, early blooming; used for bedding, patio containers and in hanging baskets. *Zone 10.* p. 513

x hybrida multiflora 'Summer Fun'; F1 hybrid, a smaller-flowered, but free-blooming compact bedding type, in unusual shade of bright yellow, 5 cm across. (Geo. Ball, W. Chicago, 1976) *Zone 10.* p. 513

x hybrida 'Royal Cascade' (Grandiflora), "Balcony petunia"; favorite early-blooming hanging basket and window box plant producing huge 8-10 cm single flowers in rich velvety purplish-blue, very floriferous, on long branches. *Zone 10.* p. 513

violacea (Brazil, Uruguay, Argentina, natural. in U.S. zone 8); herbaceous plant to 25 cm high, sticky-pubescent with ovate leaves to 8 cm long; single flowers purplish-rose shading to violet toward center, 4-6 cm across, during Summer. *Zone 8.* p. 513

PHACELIA   *Hydrophyllaceae*
campanularia (Colorado to So. California: Mohave), "California bluebell"; bristly-hairy annual to 50 cm high, with elliptic, coarsely toothed leaves on long petioles; bell-shaped, bright blue flowers for spring and summer bloom. *Zone 9.* p. 424

PHAEDRANASSA   *Amaryllidaceae*
carmiolii (Costa Rica), "Queen lily"; bulbous plant with 1 to 3 stalked oblanceolate, fleshy leaves to 38 cm long, appearing at blooming time, and showy nodding, curved tubular 5 cm flowers crimson at base, greenish toward segmented apex, and with protruding stamens, clustered on 60 cm stalk. *Zones 9-10.* p. 214

PHAEOMERIA speciosa: see NICOLAIA elatior (Zander)

PHAIUS   *Orchidaceae*
luteus: see GASTRORCHIS luteus

tankervilleae (grandifolius) (No. India, So. China, Malaysia to No. Australia), "Nun's orchid"; charming, robust terrestrial from grassy savannahs, with plaited leaves on stout pseudobulbs, and erect spikes to 1 m high with spreading, fleshy flowers, sepals and petals light brown, silvery white behind, lip rose with darker throat, (Feb.-April). *Tropical. Zone 11.* p. 95

PHALAENOPSIS   *Orchidaceae*
amabilis (Malaya, Sunda Isl.), "Moth orchid"; exquisite epiphyte without pseudobulbs; fleshy, light green, deflexed leaves, and a pendant spray of flowers, glistening snowy-white, except for its yellow crest spotted with red, (Oct.-Jan.). *Tropical. Zone 12.* p. 95

'Doris' ('Elizabethae' x 'Katherine Siegwart'); a tetraploid of excellent keeping quality; magnificent sprays of heavy-textured flowers 10-12 cm across, glistening white; derived from P. amabilis and rimestadiana parentage (Duke Gardens). *Tropical. Zone 12.* p. 93

equestris (Philippines); epiphytic miniature, with leathery coppery green oval leaves to 20 cm long; inflorescence arching or pendant, dense with small pale rose flowers 2 cm across, the lip magenta and spotted red. *Zones 11-12.* p. 93

lueddemanniana (Philippines); compact epiphyte with pale green, fleshy leaves, and short racemes with thick, waxy flowers whitish and beautifully marked with cinnamon-brown and bars of amethyst; stalks often bearing offshoots, (May-June and various). *Tropical. Zones 11-12.* p. 95

x rothschildiana (schilleriana x amabilis); old James Veitch hybrid with leaves dark green mottled with silvery gray; well-rounded, dainty flowers in large sprays, with white petals, the sepals pale sulphur, tinted with rosy-pink, the lobed lip spotted with purple. *Tropical. Zone 12.* p. 95

schilleriana (Philippines), "Rosy moth orchid"; beautiful epiphyte with flat roots and long, flat, tongue-like leaves transversely blotched with silvery gray, purplish-red beneath; arching, branched inflorescence with delicate, 5-8 cm flowers of dainty rose in varying tints, (Feb.-May). *Tropical. Zone 12.* p. 95

PHALARIS   *Gramineae*
arundinacea picta (variegata) (No. America, Eurasia), "Ribbon grass" or "Canary grass"; attractive rhizomatous perennial with glaucous culms 60 cm to more the 1 m high, resembling a short bamboo; the narrow-lanceolate leaves striped and margined creamy-white, to 30 cm long; the inflorescence terminal with flattened spikelets and flowers typical of grasses. *Zone 4.* p. 563

PHANERA   *Leguminosae*
kockiana (syn. Bauhinia) (Borneo: Sarawak); woody tropical climber, becoming large and bushy; ovate leaves 6 to 10 cm long, not bifid, waxy light green, and prominently showing three parallel main

veins; beautiful flowers with wide-spread petals scalloped at margins, 3½-4 cm across, and vivid orange to brilliant scarlet. *Zones 10-11.*   *p. 285*

PHARBITIS (Zander): see IPOMOEA 'Nil' and purpurea (Hortus)

PHASEOLUS   *Leguminosae*
   caracalla (Zander): see VIGNA caracalla (Hortus)
   coccineus (Trop. So. America), "Scarlet runner bean"; an ornamental bean; deep green leaves, and bright scarlet flowers held well above the foliage, blooming over a long period and followed by the 20 cm beanpods; when ripe the 2½ cm seed is mauve-pink spotted and striped with black. Grown as perennial in the Tropics; as annual from seed in areas with frost. *Zone 10.*   *p. 278*

PHELLODENDRON   *Rutaceae*
   amurense (China, Japan), "Amur cork"; slow-growing deciduous tree to 12 m, interesting with corky bark; branchlets with pinnate leaves, 5-13 ovate leaflets 10 cm long, glossy above, glaucous beneath; greenish pubescent flowers; black, berry-like fruit on female trees. Good shade tree with wide-spreading crown, but male trees should be planted to avoid bothersome berry-drop. *Zone 3.*   *p. 863*
   chinense (Cent. and W. China), "Chinese cork tree"; deciduous aromatic tree 8-10 m high, dioecious with sexes on separate plants; the young branchlets red-brown; handsome odd-pinnate foliage to 40 cm long, with 7-13 spongy lanceolate leaflets 7-14 cm long, dark yellowish-green above, light green and pubescent beneath; small yellowish-green flowers in dense racemes 6 cm long; globose black fruit 9 mm dia. *Zone 5.*   *p. 863*
   lavallei (Japan), "Japanese cork tree"; deciduous tree 3 to 10 m or more high, having corky bark; with branches purplish-brown; odd-pinnate foliage having 5-15 lanceolate leaflets to 10 cm long, dull yellow-green above; small greenish-yellow flowers in loosely grouped clusters 8 cm wide; berry-like black, juicy fruit. *Zone 5.*   *p. 863*

PHILADELPHUS   *Saxifragaceae*
   coronarius (So. Europe, Italy to Asia Minor, Caucasus), "Sweet mock orange" or "False jasmine"; very popular deciduous shrub to 3 m high, having arching branches and forming rounded bush; ovate leaves 6-8 cm long and distinctly toothed; flowers creamy-white 3-4 cm across and very fragrant, blooming in June. *Zone 4.*   *p. 872*
   inodorus (Pennsylvania to Alabama), "Scentless mock-orange"; very decorative deciduous shrub 2-3 m high, having branches arching to the ground; leaves 4-10 cm long, nearly entire at margins and the only mock-orange having foliage glossy on both surfaces; showy white flowers 4 to 6 cm wide, with overlapping petals, blooming in June, but only faintly fragrant. Photographed in the garden of El Greco, in romantic Toledo, Spain. *Zone 5.*   *p. 872*
   x lemoinei 'Belle Etoile' (coronarius x microphyllus) (Lemoine, Nancy, France); attractive hybrid shrub to 2 m high, having gracefully arching branches, dense with ovate-pointed leaves; showy star-shaped very fragrant single white flowers with maroon centers, 5-6 cm dia., in May-June. *Zone 5.*   *p. 872*
   lewisii (N.W. No. America), "Wild mock-orange"; deciduous shrub to 3 m high; ovate leaves 6 cm long, stiff-hairy and with occasional teeth; large white, satiny flowers 4 to 5 cm across and fragrant. State flower of Idaho. The subspecies californicus from Central California is a larger form, with broader floral petals and is more drought tolerant, blooming May to July. *Zone 7.*   *p. 873*
   x virginalis (lemoinei x nivalis) (Lemoine 1909), "Mock orange"; showy floriferous, deciduous shrub to 2 m or more high, with curved branches, the brown bark peeling; leaves ovate to 8 cm long, pubescent beneath; double white highly fragrant blooms 5 cm across, in 3-7 flowered clusters; late Spring and Summer. *Zone 5.*   *p. 873*

PHILLYREA   *Oleaceae*
   decora (Osmanthus decorus) (Asia Minor), "Lanceleaf linden"; evergreen shrub of stiff, neat habit to 3 m high, with leathery, oblong-lanceolate leaves glossy dark green to 12 cm long and having prominent midrib; small pure white flowers in axillary clusters, in May; followed usually on female plants by oval 12 mm blue-black stone-fruit in Autumn; resembling Portugal laurel, Prunus lusitanica. *Zone 6.*   *p. 811*

PHILODENDRON   *Araceae*
   andreanum - juv. stage of P. melanochrysum which see
   bipennifolium 'Variegatum' (panduraeforme varieg. in hort.) "Variegated fiddle leaf"; species from So. Brazil, a climber with unusual leaves to 25 cm long, shaped like a violin, the basal lobes extended, central lobes narrowed toward middle, of leathery texture, dull olive-green. Very decorative trained to poles. The cv. 'Variegatum' with leaves largely variegated with cream. *Zone 12.*   *p. 30*
   bipinnatifidum (Rio to Mato Grosso); stout tree with a formal head of upright, waxy green, stiff leaves to 1 m long, bipinnate with 10-12 segments each side of prominent midrib, the lobes are narrow,

and lobed again, with long lobe at apex; spathe chestnut-brown; pale yellow berries; tender. *Tropical. Zone 11.*   *p. 31*
   erubescens (Colombia), "Blushing philodendron"; clamberer rooting at every joint, with arrow shaped, 25 cm waxy leaves bronzy green edged red, wine-red beneath; petioles green with red, occasionally winged. *Tropical. Zone 11.*   *p. 265*
   x evansii (selloum x speciosum); semi-selfheading, showy plant with large sagittate, dark green glossy leaves like elephant's ears, to 1 m long or more, the blade undulate, margins lightly lobed and wavy; young growth pinkish beneath. One of the most beautiful of all arborescent philodendrons; tolerant of both hot climate and chilly nights. *Tropical. Zone 11.*   *p. 29, 265*
   laciniatum (pedatum) (Ter. Ampa, Brazil; Guianas and Venezuela); epiphytic on trees, or climbing on rocks; smooth petioles carry the broad leathery leaves with depressed ribs, usually cut into 5 broad lobes, center segment largest; spathe greenish. *Zone 11.*   *p. 28*
   leyvae (serratum in Calif. hort.) (Colombia); slowly climbing species dense with glossy, deep green deflexed leaves 40-50 cm long, relatively narrow and irregularly lobed or cut. *Zone 11.*   *p. 28*
   melanochrysum known in juvenile stage as **andreanum**, (Colombia, Costa Rica), "Black gold" or "Velour philodendron"; beautiful climber from the moist coastal forests, with oblong-sagittate, iridescent, velvety leaves 20 to 70 cm long, nearly black-olive and shimmering with copper, and bordered by translucent margins, the veins ivory-white. *Humid-tropical. Zone 12.*   *p. 31*
   panduraeforme: see P. bipennifolium
   pertusum hort.: see MONSTERA deliciosa
   pinnatifidum (Venezuela, Amazonas); selfheader growing tree-like, with leathery leaves pinnately parted, the lobes well apart with wide sinus, metallic green, veins sunken; the channeled petioles spotted red. *Tropical. Zone 11.*   *p. 31*
   'Pluto'; very ornamental selfheading cultivar originated and meristem-cultured in Florida; leaves about 50 cm long, carried on stiff petioles; similar to P. undulatum, but more deeply lobed or incised in adult stage; an excellent, compact decorator substitute for P. selloum, stretching less under indoor conditions. *Zone 11.*   *p. 28*
   rugosum (Ecuador); climbing species, collected in Puyo, Prov. Pastaza; pale brown stems forming aerial roots; from short internodes the 40 cm petioles carry medium green, ovate cordate leathery leaves to 35 cm long, with rugose surface and translucent margins. Inflorescence with basally constricted 10 cm spathe, red below, pink toward apex; spadix cream. *Zone 11.*   *p. 30*
   scandens oxycardium (Puerto Rico to Jamaica and Central America), known in horticulture as "cordatum"; pre-Linnaean as hederaceum. The most popular and widely sold vining Philodendron, known as "Heartleaf philodendron" or "Parlor ivy", or simply "Cordatum vine". A tall tropical, rapid climber by aerial roots, with glossy deep green, broadly heart-shaped, soft-leathery leaves in juvenile stage 10-15 cm long; in maturity or flowering stage to 30 cm long. In habitat when very young the foliage is apparently velvety, from observations I made in Costa Rica. This species may be used in many ways, as a cascading vine in pots, baskets, window boxes, or room dividers; or it may be trained against support, preferably on mossed poles, bark slabs, or milled treefern pillars. *Tropical. Zone 11.*   *p. 31, 265*
   seidelii (Brazil: Mucuje, Bahia); very decorative species collected by A. Seidel of Corupá, Santa Catarina; slow growing with firm triangular deeply lobed leaves 30 to 40 cm long, the primary ribs a contrasting yellow. *Zone 10.*   *p. 30*
   selloum (S.W. Brazil), "Lacy tree-philodendron"; selfheader, tree-like or scandent on trees. In the moist forests of western Parana I have seen it growing epiphytic, sending down aerial roots to strike the ground. The lush, dark green, pendant 60 cm leaves are bipinnate with short lobe at tip; juvenile leaves are merely lobed; spathe greenish-white. *Tropical. Zone 11.*   *p. 28, 29*
   sellowianum (Brazil); fast growing selfheader with deeply cut leaves which stand considerable cold. According to Robert Blossfeld in São Paulo, similar to bipinnatifidum, but has green seed pod sheaths instead of black ones. *Tropical. Zone 11.*   *p. 31*
   tweedianum (Argentina, Paraguay, Uruguay, So. Brazil); unusual species found by Dr. E. Pingatore in Northern Argentina, forming several trunks into dense bush; sagittate triangular leaves with rounded basal lobes, 30 cm long, margins undulate; spathe greenish. *Zone 10.*   *p. 29*
   undulatum (Paraguay); a smaller selfheader, and I have seen these small trees in the dry savannahs of Paraguay, the sagittate wavy and lobed leaves somewhat cupped, carried on erect stalks; with age forming massive trunks. *Tropical. Zone 11.*   *p. 28*
   verrucosum (Costa Rica, Colombia), "Velvet leaf"; long-vining, with delicate, undulate, heart-shaped leaves to 60 cm long, shimmering velvety, dark, bronzy green; pale green vein areas and margins emerald green, salmon-violet beneath; petioles red and covered with

green hairs; showy inflorescence with spathe an ovoid rose-purple tube 8 cm long, densely white-hairy and with white margin, and enclosing the slender spadix. Gorgeous. *Tropical. Zone 12.* p. 31

PHINAEA   Gesneriaceae
multiflora (C. America); true miniature gesneriad less than 3 cm high; with rhizomatous roots; opposite, ovate leaves green with white veins, and with toothed margins, covered with soft white hair; from the leaf axil the solitary tiny white flower. From Ruth Katzenberger, New York (Gloxinian, March 1957). *Zone 11.* p. 64

PHLEBODIUM aureum (Zander):
see POLYPODIUM aureum (Hortus)

PHLOMIS   Labiatae
cashmeriana (Kashmir to Turkey, Pakistan, Afghanistan); attractive subshrub to 60 cm high, with white-woolly stems; ovate leaves to 20 cm long, white-hairy beneath; the interesting flowers in long-stalked clusters, their corollas pale lilac, 3 cm long, having downy upper lip, blooming during Summer. *Zone 9.* p. 739
chrysophylla (Lebanon, Asia Minor), "Jerusalem sage"; sub-shrubby perennial 60-90 cm high, covered with appressed golden hairs, the felty leaves broadly ovate, 4-6 cm long; the tubular, two-lipped, hooded 2-3 cm flowers golden-yellow, in whorls or twins in axils of rigid, spine-tipped bracts. *Zones 9-10.* p. 434
fruticosa (Mediterr. region, w. to Sardinia), "Jerusalem sage"; old-time subshrubby perennial garden plant to 1 m or more high, with wooly branches, the hairs usually yellowish; the oblong leaves 5-10 cm long, green above and white-hairy beneath, yellow flowers 3 cm long, in tight, ball-shaped whorls at ends of branches, blooming in early Summer. Evergreen in mild climates. *Zones 6-10.* p. 435
russeliana (viscosa) (Turkey: Anatolia), "Sticky Jerusalem sage"; beautiful subshrubby, pubescent perennial to 1 m or more high, with ovate, wrinkled leaves 10 cm or more long, green above and hairy beneath, cordate at base; the flowers with sticky calyx and hairy, slightly 2-lipped yellow corolla 2½ cm wide, in showy whorls at regular intervals toward apex of stems, blooming during Summer. *Zones 6-10.* p. 435
tuberosa (E. Europe, Russia, to C. Asia), "Lion's heart"; vigorous, deciduous perennial, with purplish stems to 1½ m high, the roots with small tubers; heart-shaped to obovate, wrinkled crenate leaves to 20 cm long; the flowers purplish-rose or pink, the upper lip very hairy with white fringe, in clustered whorls spaced along upper part of erect branches, blooming during Summer. *Zones 4-8.* p. 435

PHLOX   Polemoniaceae
austromontana (Oregon to Calif. and Idaho, Arizona); low perennial forming clumps 10-15 cm high, having awl-shaped 3 cm leaves sharp at tip; very free-blooming with 5-petaled pink or lavender flowers faintly fragrant, May to July. *Zone 6.* p. 473
bifida (Michigan to Kansas, Texas), "Sand phlox"; perennial with woody base and creeping rhizome, forming tangled mound of leafy branches 10-25 cm high; light green, narrow leaves to 5 cm long; interesting lilac to light purple flowers 2 cm wide, with petals bifid, or deeply cleft into two lobes; blooming April-May. *Zone 4.* p. 474
carolina 'Miss Lingard' (suffruticosa) "Thickleaf phlox", or "Carolina phlox"; old favorite summer-flowering perennial 60 cm high, derived from the purple species at home from Ohio to Florida; showy panicles of salverform fragrant flowers white with pale pink center, blooming tirelessly from May to October. *Zones 3-9.* p. 474
diffusa (Oregon to Utah, So. Dakota); prolific perennial with prostrate branches, to 15 cm high; linear 2 cm leaves; 2 cm flowers pink or white. *Temperate. Zone 3.* p. 474
divaricata (Québec to Michigan, Georgia, Alabama), "Wild sweet William" or "Wild blue phlox"; spreading perennial from rhizome, creeping along surface and rooting at nodes, giving rise to numerous finely downy stems 15 to 40 cm high, with elliptic leaves 5 cm long, and leaflike bracts which surround the base of the loosely clustered pretty, bluish or lavender flowers, 4 cm across, from April to June. *Zone 3.* p. 474
douglasii (Washington, Oregon to Montana); dwarf perennial forming tufts 5-15 cm high, with awl-shaped 1-2 cm leaves from a somewhat woody base; small whitish flowers, varying to pink or lavender, the corolla with 2 cm tube, blooming May to June or even into August. *Zone 4.* p. 474
douglasii 'Crackerjack'; excellent cultivar, seen at Chelsea Flower Show in London, producing a profusion of flowers vivid rosy-red, from late May to June. *Zone 4.* p. 473
drummondii (Texas), "Dwarf annual phlox"; dwarf branching, pretty annual with fresh green, small lanceolate leaves; flat, terminal clusters of brightly colored, salverform, 2½ cm flowers in shades of rose-red; cultivars in white, buff, pink, red, purple, and blue, with colorful eyes; attractive little plant for garden planting and in pots. *Zone 9 as annual.* p. 473

lutea (No. Mexico); low herbaceous biennial or short-lived perennial, or annual with stems becoming prostrate, giving rise to branches 6-8 cm high, with narrow-linear leaves, and bearing tagetes-like yellow flowers to 3 cm across, blooming July into October. *Zone 10.* p. 474
nivalis (subulata var.) (Virginia to Alabama), "Trailing phlox"; low perennial to 30 cm high, with decumbent branches forming mounds, similar to subulata; the 1-2 cm leaves awl-shaped or linear, densely set on the thread-like branches; attractive pink flowers 2 cm across, the corolla lobes entire or shallowly notched, varying to lilac or white; blooming March to May. *Zone 7.* p. 473
ovata (Penna. to Indiana, so. to Alabama), "Mountain phlox"; showy perennial with underground stem, bearing leafy decumbent branches, the usually ovate leaves 10-15 cm long, forming low mats; the floral stalks 40 cm long, topped by flat clusters of rose-purple or occasionally pink 2-3 cm flowers, in June-July. *Zone 3.* p. 473
paniculata (U.S.: New York to Arkansas), "Summer phlox"; herbaceous perennial phlox, to 1 m, with lanceolate leaves, the leafy stems topped by panicles of large 2½ cm purple flowers; varying in colors white, salmon, scarlet, lilac, in Summer and Autumn; hardy. *Zones 3-9.* p. 473
paniculata 'Starfire'; superb perennial garden phlox of bushy habit, and with dome-shaped clusters of broadly open flowers 2-3 cm across, vivid rose-red with petals changing to soft pink on broadest part, blooming during Summer. *Zones 3-9.* p. 473
stansburyi (So. Utah); attractive creeping, downy perennial 10-40 cm high, at home in the Zion National Park region of Utah; having narrow lanceolate leaves to 8 cm long; very floriferous with white or pink flowers, the corolla 3 cm long, blooming April to June. *Zone 4.* p. 474
stolonifera (Pennsylvania to Georgia), "Creeping phlox"; low perennial 12-30 cm high, producing creeping stolons at base; oblong leaves to 10 cm long, smaller on stems; flowers 2-3 cm across, light purple, in terminal clusters, during April-May. *Zone 3.* p. 474
subulata (New York to Maryland, west to Michigan), "Moss pink" or "Creeping phlox"; mat forming herbaceous semi-evergreen perennial with semi-woody branches densely spreading 15 cm; stiff linear 2 cm leaves, and small clusters of 2 cm flowers variously red-purple, pink, or white, blooming March through May. *Zones 3-9.* p. 318, 473
subulata 'Atropurpurea'; excellent cultivar forming mounds literally covered with masses of vivid rose-purple, starry flowers showing dark purple eye in center. *Zones 3-6.* p. 473
woodhousei (austromontana group) (Arizona); attractive small perennial 10-15 cm high, woody at base, with thick, elliptic leaves to 5 cm long; the numerous lovely little purple or pink flowers, often streaked in center, and with notched petals, blooming Spring and Autumn in Grand Canyon habitat. *Zone 6.* p. 474

PHOENIX   Palmae
canariensis (Canary Islands), "Canary Islands date palm"; stately feather palm widely planted in subtropical regions as an ornamental; compact, robust and stiff when young, with age forming thick, straight trunks, becoming 15 m high, with arching pinnate leaves 6 m long, the short stalk armed with yellow spines, the leaflets glossy green, in various directions; on female trees small yellow fruit in large clusters. *Subtropic. Zones 9-10.* p. 77, 106
dactylifera (Arabia, No. Africa), the fruiting "Date palm" of Egypt and North Africa, and its descendants in the Coachella Valley in the California desert; a massive tree becoming 30 m high, dense with stiff pinnate fronds spiny at the base, with narrow rigid folded pinnae in double rows when older, bluish-glaucous, to 45 cm long and sharp-pointed; following pollination, female trees will set delicious oblong edible fruit in great, heavy clusters. *Zones 10-11.* p. 107, 920
dactylifera 'Deglet Noor', "Algerian date"; fondly known by the Arabs as "Daughter of Light"; a favorite variety of date palm cultivated in California for its excellent large and meaty, "semi-soft" fruit, which packs and keeps well; each female tree producing, after artificial pollination, 90-120 kg of dates a year, on irrigated land, where the trees "have their feet in water and their heads in fire", according to an Arab saying; to produce good fruit, just hot days are not good enough, and the desert climate of the Coachella Valley, in interior So. California near the Mexican border, with temperatures of 40°C at night and to 52°C in daytime suits them best. I remember the custom of spraying my bed with a water hose, before going to sleep at night, while living in Palm Springs, before the advent of air-conditioning. *Tropical. Zones 10-11.* p. 920, 921
reclinata (Trop. Africa from Sénégal to Natal), "Sénégal date palm"; a leaning date palm somewhat resembling Cocos, in habit, and which will live in the subtropics; solitary trunks 12 m high, or shorter if allowed to cluster, the pinnate lustrous green leaves rather stiff and curving downward; small red fruit. *Tropical. Zones 10-11.* p. 107
roebelenii (humilis loureiri) (Assam to Vietnam), "Pigmy date palm"; very graceful both as a miniature potplant or when with

slender, rough 4 m trunk, topped by a dense round crown of feathery leaves, the pinnae narrow and folded and dark green, glossy when rubbed; berry-like black fruit in large clusters; female trees often clustering. *Tropical. Zones 11-12.*   *p. 77, 106*

sylvestris (India, Nepal), "East Indian wine palm"; stout erect palm to 18 m tall, with rough trunk, and arching pinnate, grayish-green or glaucous fronds 3-4 m long, with rigid, somewhat clustered leaflets, on spiny stalk; olive-like 2 cm reddish fruit. In India, this palm is a valuable source of sugar, each tree yielding 7 to 8 pounds annually; the sap produces not only sugar, but also wine and toddy, and is tapped from the apex of the trunk. *Tropical. Zones 11-12.*   *p. 106*

PHOENOCOMA   *Compositae*
prolifera (Cape Prov.); small rigid shrub to 60 cm; hard scale or needle-like leaves; flower heads with leathery ray-petals white, pink or rose. *Subtropic. Zone 9.*   *p. 690*

PHORADENDRON   *Loranthaceae*
californicum (Mohave Desert, California; Arizona so. to Sonora), "California mistletoe"; woody parasite or "Tree-thief", with slender branching stems, the leaves reduced to thin short scales; floral spikes densely set with small globular sessile, fleshy berries rosy-pink and fragrant. Parasitic on desert shrubs such as Prosopis. *Zones 8-9.*   *p. 206*

juniperinum (U.S. Southwest, Arizona); another mistletoe, parasitic on coniferous trees such as juniper and cedar, mimicking the character of their host with their thick cylindric, jointed stems, having imbricated leaves that are reduced to yellowish or gray-green scales; tiny straw-colored berries. Commonly seen at Grand Canyon, Arizona. *Zones 7-9.*   *p. 206*

PHORMIUM   *Agavaceae*
colensoi 'Tricolor', "Mountain flax"; large clusters of arching, leathery, green strap-leaves colorfully variegated lengthwise with irregular banding of cream to golden-yellow, the margins reddish; inflorescence a tall panicle with long twisted seed capsules. *Subtropic. Zone 10.*   *p. 117*

tenax (New Zealand), "New Zealand flax"; large tufting plant with two-ranked, tough leathery leaves which may grow to 3 m long, dark or brownish-green with reddish margin, clasping at base, and splitting at apex; flowers dull red in tall panicle. Seen in New Zealand growing even in the cold water of glacial lakes. Very dramatic and tolerant as container plant. *Zone 9.*   *p. 117, 566*

tenax 'Variegatum', "Variegated flax"; attractive variant with the usually brownish-green leaves striped and margined with creamy-yellow and white. *Subtropic. Zone 10.*   *p. 566*

tenax 'Yellow Wave'; beautiful variation exhibited at New York Flower Show 1986. Showy plant with long, arching leaves 4 cm wide, dark green with broad creamy-yellow band lengthwise down the center. *Zone 10.*   *p. 117*

PHOTINIA   *Rosaceae*
arbutifolia: see HETEROMELES arbutifolia (Hortus)

x fraseri (glabra x serrulata), "Redleaf photinia"; colorful evergreen to 3 m, with glossy leaves to 12 cm long, new growth a showy bronzy red; small white flowers, having petals bearded inside. *Zone 7.*   *p. 621*

x fraseri 'Robusta'; handsome clone of vigorous habit, with leaves similar to P. serrulata, thick leathery, oblong to obovate and glossy green in maturity, but very attractive in young foliage with the blades a flaming salmon-rose to coppery red. Originated at Hazlewood Nursery, Sydney, Australia. *Zone 8.*   *p. 838*

glabra (Japan: Honshu to Kyushu), "Japanese photinia" or "Kaname-mochi"; handsome evergreen shrub or small tree of broad, dense growth 3 to 5 m high; lustrous green, obovate leaves 7 to 12 cm long, coppery red when young; broad clusters of small white, hawthorn-scented flowers, their petals bearded inside, followed by red berries later turning black. *Zone 7.*   *p. 838*

serrulata (China), evergreen shrub or tree to 12 m high; oblong leaves to 20 cm long, dark and shining above, yellowish-green beneath; inflorescence of white flowers to 15 cm across, followed by clusters of small red berries. *Zone 7.*   *p. 838*

villosa (China, Korea, Japan), "Oriental photinia"; deciduous small tree to 5 m high; new foliage pale gold with rosy tints, bright red in Fall, hairy beneath; small 2 cm white flowers; bright red 2 cm fruits. *Zone 5.*   *p. 838*

PHRAGMIPEDIUM   *Orchidaceae*
x grande (Selenipedium) (longifolium x caudatum), "Spiralled lady-slipper"; plant similar to caudatum but flowers with tail-like, spiralled petals shorter, at the base yellowish-white, changing to carmine-red, dorsal pale yellow veined green, waxy pouch greenish-yellow spotted red inside, (Summer). *Humid-subtropic. Zone 11.*   *p. 95*

vittatum (Selenipedium) (Brazil), a "Mandarin orchid"; of terrestrial habit, with flowers greenish and overlaid or striped with

brown, the long narrow petals twisted and undulate at margins; slipper-like lip light brown outside. *Humid-tropical. Zones 11-12.*   *p. 95*

PHUOPSIS   *Rubiaceae*
stylosa (Caucasus, Iran, E. Turkey); clump-forming, pungent perennial herb to 25 cm high, with spreading branches, developing mats; leaves in whorls of 6-7, narrow elliptic 2 cm long, having spiny-ciliate margins; slender-tubed pink flowers with 5 lobes in dense heads. *Zone 5.*   *p. 495*

PHYGELIUS   *Scrophulariaceae*
aequalis (Transvaal), "River bells"; herbaceous pubescent perennial to 1 m high, with dark green, oval soft leaves 12 cm long, on winged, square stems; flowers scarlet or dusky rose, with straight or slightly curved tubes and flaring limbs, yellow inside, 3-5 cm long. *Zone 10.*   *p. 508*

capensis (So. Africa), "Cape fuchsia"; subshrubby plant 1-2 m high, with herbaceous, angled, purple branches; opposite, smooth, crenate leaves to 12 cm long and panicles of tubular, coral-scarlet flowers 5 cm long, pendulous from horizontal stalks, blooming in Summer. Perennial in Pacific Northwest. *Zone 7.*   *p. 508*

capensis 'Moonbells' (capensis x aequalis), "White Cape fuchsia"; beautiful subshrubby perennial 1 to 2 m high, with ovate or lanceolate leaves to 12 cm long, toothed along margins; the charming pendant trumpet-flowers 6-8 cm long creamy-white with flaring lobes, the corollas somewhat curved; carried in clusters on horizontal branches; summer-blooming. *Zone 8.*   *p. 508*

PHYLA   *Verbenaceae*
nodiflora rosea (Tropics and Subtrop. incl. southern U.S.), "Frog fruit" or "Cape weed"; herbaceous creeping perennial with branches rooting at nodes, and forming mats; obovate leaves to 5 cm long; rose-colored trumpet-flowers. *Zones 9-10.*   *p. 322*

PHYLICA   *Rhamnaceae*
pubescens (So. Africa: Cape Prov.), "Featherhead"; xerophytic shrub 1 m or more high, of heath-like habit, with densely set linear leaves 2-3 cm long, whitish-woolly beneath; floral heads 3-5 cm across, having narrow, spreading bracts, feathered with white silky hair, and normally without petals. *Zone 10.*   *p. 829*

PHYLLANTHUS   *Euphorbiaceae*
acidus (So. Asia), "Otaheite" or "Gooseberry tree"; handsome tree to 10 m high and grown for its edible fruit; leaf-like phyllodia ovate to 8 cm long, two-ranked on twigs; small reddish flowers; yellow 2 cm fruit 6-8 ridged, clustered on the trunk and older branches of female plants, and made into preserves. *Tropical. Zone 10.*   *p. 725, 912*

arbuscula (speciosus) (Jamaica); shrub or tree to 6 m high, with lanceolate leaf-like branchlets (phyllodia) 5-8 cm long and 2¹/₂ cm wide, arranged in two ranks on a branch, appearing like pinnate leaves; tiny yellow flowers with whitish calyx in pendent racemes. *Zone 10.*   *p. 725*

PHYLLITIS   *Polypodiaceae (Filices)*
scolopendrium (Scolopendrium vulgare) (Europe, Madeira, E. No. America), "Hart's-tongue fern"; rhizomatous, hardy fern with stout rhizome and long straight or curved strap-shaped leathery fronds 15-45 cm long, pale yellow-green to bright green, quilted and undulate at margins; spore masses in thick strips at right angles to the bold midrib, running into a short black stalk. *Zones 3-7.*   *p. 136*

scolopendrium 'Crispum' (plicatum), "Crisped deer-tongue"; attractive fern with long narrow, strap-like light green fronds nicely and regularly undulated and wavy, 30 cm long by 2-3 cm wide, crested at the base, on stalks covered with hair-like brown scales. *Zones 5-8.*   *p. 136*

PHYLLOCACTUS: see EPIPHYLLUM

PHYLLODOCE   *Ericaceae*
empetriformis (No. California to Brit. Columbia and Alaska), "Mountain heath"; low heath-like evergreen 15-20 cm high, spreading to form mats, with linear needle-like 1 cm leaves; inflorescence in terminal clusters of little bell-shaped rosy-purple flowers, in early Spring to Summer, according to Latitude. *Zone 5.*   *p. 707*

PHYLLORHACHIS   *Gramineae*
sagittata (Trop. Africa), "Aquatic bamboo"; ornamental bamboo-like clustering perennial which I found growing in the tropical pool at Munich Botanic Garden; thin reed-stems 50-80 cm high, set with leathery rich green, lanceolate leaves corrugated lengthwise, and with stem-clasping base. *Zones 10-11.*   *p. 554*

PHYLLOSTACHYS   *Gramineae*
aurea (China), the "Golden bamboo" or "Fish pole bamboo"; popular tall woody grass with wide-ranging rhizomes; hollow canes flattened on one side, to 4 m or more high and 3 cm thick, brilliant yellow, the internodes at the base very short; quite straight and stiffly

erect, very hard and bonelike when matured, and used for fishing poles; leaves usually 5-10 cm long and long-pointed, light green, and glaucous beneath. Normally hardy around New York City. Young shoots appearing in Mid-spring are edible. Crowded joints at base are characteristic. Ideal for screening and hedging. *Zones 7-10.* p. 552

aureosulcata (China), "Yellow-groove bamboo"; invasive, very hardy running bamboo 8 to 10 m high; culms 1½ to 3 cm dia., with yellow groove in otherwise green culms; the internodes very prominent, mealy above and below; sometimes growing in zigzag manner; leaves occasionally striped yellow, to 20 cm long; on branches with 3-5 leaves, to 15 cm long. Mild flavored edible shoots. Grown along W. front of Capitol in Washington; but known to have survived in So. Vermont. *Zones 6-8.* p. 556

bambusoides (China), "Giant timber-bamboo" or "Madake"; one of the largest and most valuable "hardy" timber bamboos, with green culms to about 20 m high, thick-walled and more than 12 cm dia., grooved on side, striped or yellow in some forms; two unequal branches off each branch-bearing node, oblong pointed leaves 6 to 15 cm long, having patches of silky hairs at base; culm-sheaths greenish to reddish. Very versatile in its uses, especially for construction, and its strength is exceeded only by the Tonkin cane (Arundinaria amabilis). Hardy north to about Norfolk, Virginia. *Zones 7-9.* p. 554, 555

bambusoides 'Allgold' (Ph. sulphurea hort.) (China, Japan), "Yellow running bamboo" or "Moso bamboo"; a fairly hardy running bamboo 4-9 m high, culms yellow or green and 5-8 cm thick; leaves to 12 cm long and 2 cm wide, glaucous beneath, on purple petioles. Very handsome with arching yellow canes, and effective in containers in entryways or the patio. Hardy in the Pacific Northwest, or Washington D.C., tested to -18°C (Zero F.) *Zones 7-9.* p. 553

makinoi (China, Taiwan), "Taiwan madake"; hardy bamboo to 18 m tall, with wide-ranging rhizomes; yellowish-white culms to 8 cm dia., forming branches from hollow internodes; the stems leaning sideways and somewhat zigzag; firm leaves 10 cm long. *Zone 7.* p. 552

nigra (So. China), "Black bamboo"; graceful black-culmed bamboo to 8 m high, the culms 3-5 cm thick, green at first later speckled then all black; slim branchlets with small leaves commonly 8 cm long, culm-sheaths greenish to buff; thin-walled; hardy to about Norfolk, Virginia, and where temperatures do not go below -20°C. *Zones 7-9.* p. 554, 555

nigra var. henonis (So. China, much grown in Japan), "Hachiku" or "Henon bamboo"; handsome giant hardy bamboo to 15 m high, with spreading rhizomes forming loose clusters of culms to 8 cm diameter, green when mature, rough to the touch, and covered with gray, waxlike coating, bending gracefully under the weight of their foliage, the wood turning yellowish with age; leaves 12 cm or more long. Successfully planted in glass-enclosed Atrium of the IBM Bldg. in New York. *Zone 7.* p. 553

pubescens (heterocycla fa.) (China), "Moso bamboo" or "Noble bamboo" in Japan; most handsome ornamental canes, to 20 m or more high, tallest of the hardy running bamboo type, and most popular bamboo grown in China; culms to 12 cm dia. near base, pale green and densely velvety at first, the stem sheaths greenish-buff, with brown hairs; leaves to 12 cm long. Commercially the most important species in China, used to make furniture, scaffolding; the spring-shoots are edible when boiled. Difficult to propagate. *Zone 8.* p. 555

viridi-glaucescens (Bambusa viridiglaucescens) (China); medium-sized hardy running bamboo to 10 m high, with very straight, green to yellowish culms 5 cm thick, and farinose, or covered with white powder; stem-sheaths pale green spotted brown; leaf blades narrow, to 10 cm long, with numerous parallel nerves, bright green but glaucous beneath. The young spring-shoots are edible, and even tasty when raw. *Zone 7.* p. 554

vivax (China: Sichiang Prov.), "Elegant bamboo"; very handsome and vigorous giant hardy bamboo to 20 m high, with running rhizomes spreading wide; the culms golden-yellow ringed with green at each node and 4-12 cm diameter, sprouting lateral branches from the nodes; narrow-lanceolate leaves 10-20 cm long, with patches of hairs at base, and drooping from side branches and massed toward top; similar to P. bambusoides but the wood is somewhat thin and not strong enough for construction use. Young shoots are mild-flavored and can be eaten fresh. *Zone 8.* p. 554

PHYSALIS *Solanaceae*

alkekengi (franchetii) (Japan), "Chinese lantern plant" or "Winter cherry", known since the 12th century; herbaceous perennial with creeping underground stems, often grown as an annual, 1 m high, with large ovate leaves, inconspicuous axillary yellowish flowers; the calyx, after fertilization, becomes inflated like a lantern, 5-6 cm long, bright orange-red, enclosing the scarlet berry-like fruit; when cut in Fall the lanterns will keep for a long time, in everlasting bouquets. *Zones 3-9.* p. 514

ixocarpa (Mexico; natural. in E. No. America), "Mexican husk tomato", "Tomatillo" or "Jamberry"; ornamental annual or perennial herb with erect or decumbent branches to 1 m or more; alternate ovate or rhombic leaves 8 cm long; bright yellow flowers 2 cm across, with brown blotches in throat; followed by the bladder-like capsule 3 cm dia., frequently split by the enlarging purple, sticky, cherry-like fruit; cultivated for food in Mexico; cooked or made into jelly. *Zone 10.* p. 940

peruviana (Perú), "Cape-gooseberry" or "Gooseberry tomato"; perennial, hairy plant with square stems 60-90 cm high; heart-shaped leaves with wavy-toothed margin; 1 cm flowers with bell-shaped, light yellow corolla inside spotted with purple, and violet anthers; fruit purplish in the species, yellow and edible in var. edulis, enclosed in the inflated pale calyx. The aromatic fruit with acid-sweet flavor is used in salads fresh, or in marmalade. *Zone 10.* p. 940

PHYSOCARPUS *Rosaceae*

opulifolius (Québec to Tennessee and Michigan), "Ninebark"; spiraea-like deciduous shrub to 2 m high, having bark separate in many thin layers; rounded leaves to 8 cm long, cordate and lightly 3-lobed; small white 1 cm flowers tinged with pink, dense in rounded clusters, at end of branchlet of previous year, the stamens purplish in June; the seed capsules remain on plants all Winter. *Zone 2.* p. 838, 861

PHYSOPLEXIS (Zander): see PHYTEUMA (Hortus)

PHYSOSTEGIA *Labiatae*

virginiana (Eastern U.S.), "False dragonhead" or "Obedience"; stoloniferous perennial to 1 m high, with opposite lanceolate leaves, and irregular bell-shaped flowers rose-purple, borne in a dense pyramidal, terminal cluster, or occasionally in the axils of leaves, during late Summer into Autumn. *Zones 4-9.* p. 435

virginiana 'Violacea'; color form of the "Virginia lion's-heart", with columns of showy flowers having bell-shaped corollas violet-rose, 3 cm long, inflated at the mouth. *Zones 4-9.* p. 435

PHYTEUMA *Campanulaceae*

comosum (Physoplexis) (Southern Alps, Dolomites), "Horned Rampion"; small Alpine perennial with tufted, pendant stems to 15 cm long; lanceolate leaves serrate at margins; short-stalked clusters of rose-purple or lilac flowers inflated below, to 3 cm long, during July. *Zone 5.* p. 356

humile (Southern Alps: Italy, Switzerland), "Dwarf horned rampion"; dwarf Alpine herbaceous perennial only 12 cm high, forming tufts; the lower leaves lanceolate; stem leaves shorter and ovate; blue flowers in terminal clusters. *Zone 6.* p. 356

nigrum (Eastern France: Alsace), "French rampion"; herbaceous perennial with erect stems 20 to 30 cm high; leaves ovate to lanceolate along stalk; branched inflorescence with oval heads dense with small violet or blue flowers, summer-blooming. *Zone 6.* p. 356

PHYTOLACCA *Phytolaccaceae*

americana (decandra) (Maine to Florida; Mexico), "Poke-weed"; herbaceous perennial with fleshy, poisonous roots, to 3½ m high, strong-smelling; 15 cm lanceolate leaves becoming purple in Autumn; white flowers in long raceme, and dark purple berries filled with crimson, poisonous juice; hardy. *Zone 3.* p. 470

PICEA *Pinaceae (Coniferae)*

abies (excelsa) (North and Central Europe), "Norway spruce"; evergreen coniferous forest tree to 45 m high, of pyramidal habit, reddish-brown scaly bark, and whorled branches, the usually pendulous branchlets with linear 4-angled, shiny dark green needles 2 cm long, spirally arranged; pistillate flowers bright purple; drooping slender light brown cones 10-17 cm long, very decorative. *Zone 2.* p. 589, 590, 597, 614

abies 'Acrocona', "Dwarf weeping spruce" (Uppsala 1870); slow-growing evergreen tree more dwarf than the species, different also in having the ultimate branchlets arching downward or pendulous, quite attractive with its shiny dark green needles; interesting in addition, having its curious and very large cones carried on the tips of the main branches. *Zone 3.* p. 590

abies 'Columnaris'; tall evergreen tree of columnar habit, with branches spreading or horizontal, but short, the flexuous branchlets dense with glossy, dark green needles. *Zone 2.* p. 590

abies 'Diffusa' (origin Kew Gardens); very dwarf English cultivar developing into dense conical or globose forms, with twisted flexuous branches close together, the soft, thin needles light green and curved 6-9 mm long, packed into a tight cover of foliage. *Zone 3.* p. 590

abies 'Echiniformis', "Prickly hedgehog"; handsome dwarf, slow-growing form, with close angular branches and somewhat flat-topped; dense 1 cm rigid, prickly needles dark green, and tipped with spines. *Zone 3.* p. 592

abies 'Nidiformis', "Bird's-nest spruce"; dwarf spruce, remaining low, with branches radially arranged in tiers, growing first erect but then gracefully curving outward and horizontal, spreading wide, leaving in the middle around the stem a depression somewhat resembling a birdsnest of glossy green 1 cm needles; attractive in Spring when the brown buds burst in bright fresh green. *Zone 4.*   *p. 590*

abies 'Pendula', "Weeping spruce"; robust, very erect tree of narrow pyramidal habit, with stiff pendant branches falling close to the trunk, each tier well separated from the next, the lowest spreading horizontally over the ground. *Zone 2.*   *p. 590*

alcoquiana 'Howell's Dwarf' (bicolor); handsome dwarf cultivar of the Alcock spruce of Japan; the species is a coniferous evergreen tree to 25 m tall, densely branched, with branchlets yellow or red-brown; the needles rhombic in cross-section, and 2 cm long, with white bands on all 4 angles. *Zone 5.*   *p. 590*

breweriana (So. Oregon and No. California), "Siskiyou spruce"; very decorative, distinctive evergreen tree to 30 m tall, with gray, flaky bark; short branches divided into long whip-like, pendulous branchlets sometimes 2 m or more long, the young shoots hairy; slender, flattened needles to 3 cm long, surrounding the axis, dark green above, and several lines of grayish stomata beneath; oblong cones to 10 cm long, brown when ripe and the scales open. *Zone 6.*   *p. 590*

engelmannii (Brit. Columbia to New Mexico), "Engelmann spruce"; excellent evergreen tree to 50 m high, with resinous, scaly bark, densely branched, with handsome glaucous, bluish-green, soft foliage 2-3 cm long, surrounding the shoot; broadly cylindric cones 5-8 cm long, green tinged red when young; thin scales with toothed margins. *Zone 3.*   *p. 591*

glauca (across Canada and No. U.S.), "White spruce"; drought resistant evergreen forest tree largely in Canada, to 20 m or more high, with spreading stout branches and having grayish-brown, scaly bark; the smooth branchlets usually pendant, densely set with curved 4-angled bluish-green needles 2 cm long, surrounding the shoot; cylindric cones to 6 cm long, hanging from near the branch tips, the scales with entire margins. *Zone 2.*   *p. 591*

glauca albertiana 'Pyramidalis', "Dwarf Alberta spruce"; slow-growing, pyramidal form of Alberta spruce, with 4-sided, leaves bluish-green, very crowded and spirally arranged, more dense above than below; small cylindric cones 3-5 cm long. *Zone 3.*   *p. 591*

glauca 'Conica' (albertiana cv.) (Canadian Rockies), "Dwarf Alberta spruce"; evergreen of compact conical or pyramidal habit, very dense, to 2 m high, branches erect and stiff; the branchlets thin, with needles set radially, nearly round, 1 cm long, light glaucous green. *Zone 3.*   *p. 591*

glauca 'Densata' (South Dakota), "Black Hills spruce"; slow-growing, dense symmetrical tree of great hardiness; the linear needles glaucous green on upper side, to 1 cm long; cylindrical cones to 6 cm long, green to light brown. *Zone 2.*   *p. 591*

glauca 'Echiniformis', "Hedgehog spruce"; slow-growing, valuable dwarf spruce forming cushions only about 5 cm high, with very glaucous blue, prickly leaves arranged radially, resembling a hedgehog; originated from a witches' broom; a treasure for the rockgarden, or growing in a pot on the balcony. *Zone 5.*   *p. 591*

glehnii (Japan, Sakhalin), "Sakhalin spruce"; slow-growing evergreen tree, with age 10-30 m high, with dense crown, having red-brown bark, turning white as it flakes off; young shoots reddish and hairy, with leaves 4-angled to 1-2 cm long, dark blue-green, densely arranged; cones cylindric 5-8 cm long, with glossy brown, leathery scales lightly toothed. Dwarfed and grown as bonsai in containers in Japan, as seen at Osaka Hort. Expo. *Zone 4.*   *p. 591*

omorika (Yugoslavia), "Serbian spruce"; handsome tree of tapering, spire-like shape, habitually narrow and erect, to 35 m high; bark reddish-brown, the branches short, with flattened 2 cm leaves dense and horizontally arranged, pointing downward on the sides, scanty beneath, dark green above, and two white stomatic bands below, separated by prominent midrib; egg-shaped 6 cm cones, dark brown when mature. *Zone 5.*   *p. 591*

x omorika 'Gnome' (x mariorika); striking German dwarf conical hybrid form, dense with bluish cylindrical 1 cm needles having sharp and prickly points, from a multitude of twisted branchlets, and resulting in a perfect shape, not requiring shearing. According to Welch, an interspecific hybrid of Picea mariana x omorika. Photographed in col. Dortmund Bot. Garden, Germany. *Zone 4.*   *p. 591*

orientalis 'Aurea' (Caucasus and Asia Minor heritage), "Golden Oriental spruce"; pyramidal tree with spreading or ascending branches; young branchlets slightly pendulous; the needles on upper side densely set, to 1 cm long, glossy green in the species, in this cultivar needles golden-yellow; nodding cylindrical cones 5 to 9 cm long. In its Caucasus habitat the species is a graceful tree to 50 m high. *Zone 5.*   *p. 592*

orientalis 'Aureospica', "Gold-spike Oriental spruce"; elegant pyramidal tree with spreading branches, dense with glossy green

needles, on the tips of slender young branchlet a beautiful golden-yellow, though much of the color is lost during Summer. *Zone 5.*   *p. 592*

pungens (Wyoming, Colorado, Utah, New Mexico), "Colorado spruce" or "Blue spruce"; noble pyramidal tree broad at base, to 30 m tall; horizontal branches with stout branchlets, needles 4-angled, stiff, sickle-shaped, bluish-green, to 3 cm long, with spiny point, arranged radially around twig; oblong light brown cones 5-10 cm long. *Zone 2.*   *p. 589, 592*

pungens 'Argentea', "Silver Colorado spruce"; beautiful cultivar dense with branches literally covered by slender, stiff needles encircling the twigs, and practically glistening silvery bluish-white; choice in any garden planting. *Zone 3.*   *p. 592*

pungens 'Glauca', "Blue spruce"; truly elegant coniferous tree with horizontal branches in regular tiers along the erect trunk; the branchlets dense with stiff 2-3 cm curved needles glaucous blue-green; handsome pendant brown cones 10 cm long. Often sold in nurseries as P. kosteriana, but not as intense blue. *Zone 3.*   *p. 592*

pungens 'Koster', "Koster's blue spruce"; world-famous cultivar first distributed by Koster (Boskoop, Holland 1885); forming magnificent pyramids with branches in whorls; stiff, curving needles distinct silvery-glaucous blue, 2-2½ cm long, dense on orange-brown branchlets. According to Wyman, Picea pungens 'Koster' is form of pungens 'Pendens'. *Zone 3.*   *p. 589*

sitchensis (Alaska to South California), "Sitka spruce"; very ornamental evergreen forest tree along the Pacific Coast, up to 50 m or more high, with broad conical crowns, probably largest of the spruces; closely branched, with massive trunk and having wide-spreading buttresses, and scaling bark; light brown young shoots surrounded by flattened stiff, spine-tipped needles silvery white above, rounded and glossy green beneath; cylindric cones 5-10 cm long. Prominent timber tree in the Pacific Northwest. *Zone 6.*   *p. 592, 603*

PIERIS   *Ericaceae*

floribunda (Virginia to Georgia), "Fetterbush"; rounded evergreen shrub 1½-2 m high with hairy branches, elliptic leathery leaves and ciliate; little 6 mm urn-shaped white flowers specked with tiny black bristles; drooping in erect terminal panicles, blooming in mass from March to May. The young foliage emerges a lovely salmon-red. *Zone 4.*   *p. 705*

formosa 'Wakehurst' (species from E. Himalayas); handsome evergreen shrub to 4 m high or taller; similar to japonica but larger in all parts; glossy green, lanceolate leaves 15 cm long, beautifully red in young growth; very floriferous with somewhat pendant 12 cm racemes of waxy white flowers, the corolla 9 mm long, subtended by green sepals. *Zone 7.*   *p. 707*

forrestii (formosa) (Himalayas), "Chinese pieris"; handsome evergreen shrub 2-3 m high, oblanceolate leaves to 12 cm long; the young foliage fiery red; flowers in pendant terminal clusters, with corolla and sepals or calyx lobes both white, blooming in April. Sometimes called "Flame-of-the-Forest" because of its brilliant scarlet foliage. *Zone 7.*   *p. 707*

japonica (Andromeda) (Japan), "Lily-of-the-valley bush"; evergreen shrub to 3 m high; with glossy green, leathery leaves 5-8 cm long, in dense whorls; small waxy white 1 cm urn-shaped flowers in pendulous long-lasting clusters, the calyx lobes tinted red. *Temperate.* *Zone 5.*   *p. 707*

japonica 'Variegata' in horticulture as "Andromeda", the "Lily-of-the-valley bush"; compact evergreen shrub slowly growing to 1½ m or more, the gnarled woody branches with leathery leaves 5 to 8 cm long, glossy green edged with creamy-white; loaded in Spring with pendant terminal clusters of waxy white, urn-shaped flowers, the calyx lobes tinted red; winter-hardy. *Zone 5.*   *p. 707*

PIGAFETTA   *Palmae*

filaris (Indonesia: Celebes, Moluccas); very handsome, solitary-growing spiny feather palm, with ringed trunk; the base of crown and petioles densely covered with erect hairs; the beautiful pinnate fronds spreading with long leaflets rich green. David Fairchild considered Pigafetta his favorite palm. Photographed at Dr. Darian's palmarium, Vista, California. *Tropical. Zone 12.*   *p. 108*

PILEA   *Urticaceae*

cadierei 'Minima', "Miniature aluminum plant"; a darling cultivar of dwarf, freely branching habit with pink stems and 4-5 cm elliptic pointed, succulent, quilted leaves much smaller than the species, deep olive-green with raised areas covered with silver, and with crenate margins. The species is native in Vietnam. *Zone 12.*   *p. 78*

depressa (Puerto Rico), "Miniature peperomia"; freely branching, low, succulent creeper with tiny 6 mm roundish obovate, fleshy leaves, light pea-green and glossy, with the apex crenate, opposite and dense on thin green stems, rooting at nodes where touching the ground. *Tropical. Zones 10-11.* p. 322

forgetii (spruceana), "Angelwings"; lovely species from Perú; freegrowing, small ornamental herb, dense with somewhat fleshy, deeply quilted, broad-oval leaves 6-8 cm long, metallic bronze to blackish-green with raised silver bands, wine-red beneath; the tiny rosy flowers clustered closely in the axils of foliage. *Tropical. Zone 12.* p. 78

involucrata (West Indies, Panama, No. South America), "Panamiga"; freely spreading ornamental herb, dense with oval, somewhat fleshy, deeply quilted leaves to 6 cm long, coppery green above, wine-red beneath; tiny rosy flowers closely clustered. *Tropical. Zone 12.* p. 78

mollis (Costa Rica, Colombia), "Moon Valley green"; charming tropical plant similar to 'Moon Valley' which is probably a mutant heavily overlaid with brown; in the species mollis the foliage is deeply quilted like a carpet and a soft light emerald green, and covered with white hairs; veins olive-green. *Tropical. Zone 11.* p. 78

nummulariifolia (West Indies to Perú), "Creeping Charley"; low creeping herb; thin, reddish branches rooting at the nodes, with small circular 2 cm quilted, crenate leaves, corrugated and hairy, light friendly green, paler beneath; tiny flowers. *Tropical. Zone 11.* p. 322

'Silver Tree' (Caribbean), "Silver and bronze"; a copyrighted name 1957 by Mulford for this species from the Caribbean area; herbaceous branching plant with white-hairy stalks, quilted ovate leaves having depressed veins and crenate margins, bronzy green, with broad silver band along center, silver dots on sides; reddish beneath. *Tropical. Zone 12.* p. 78

spruceana: see P. forgetii

PILEOSTEGIA *Saxifragaceae*

viburnoides (Himalayas to Taiwan); evergreen climbing shrub with clinging vines to 8 m or more; elliptic, entire leaves to 12 cm long; the freely borne small white, all-fertile flowers in terminal clusters during late Summer. Closely resembling climbing hydrangea. *Zone 7.* p. 296

PILOSOCEREUS (as in Backeberg)

see CEPHALOCEREUS (Hortus 3)

PIMELEA *Thymelaeaceae*

ferruginea (W. Australia), "Rice flower"; pretty shrub to 1 m, dense with opposite, 1 cm ovate sessile leaves in 4 ranks, and with silky-hairy deep pink flowers in round heads. *Zone 10.* p. 892

floribunda (Western Australia), "Rice flower"; dainty shrub to nearly 1 m high, with soft ovate leaves 3 cm long; inflorescence in heads 6 cm wide; starry white flowers silky-pubescent and slightly scented, blooming from July to October in Australia. *Zone 10.* p. 816

PIMENTA *Myrtaceae*

dioica (officinalis) (Jamaica to C. America), "All-spice"; small tree to 12 m high, with oblong feathery, aromatic leaves to 16 cm long, small white flowers, followed by clusters of small green to brown pleasantly spicy 1 cm pea-sized berries; these are picked green and dried and called "All-spice" because they seem to have the combined flavors of cinnamon, nutmeg and cloves, and are used for seasoning of food. *Tropical. Zone 10.* p. 537

PIMPINELLA *Umbelliferae*

anisum (Greece to Egypt), "Common anise"; aromatic annual sprawling herb to 50 cm high, with basal leaves compound, the leaflets deeply toothed or lobed, stem-leaves more finely cut; small yellowish-white flowers in loose clusters. The sweet scent of licorice exudes from the plant; the feathery leaves are used for seasoning salads, fish, poultry and other foods; the flowers, dried and powdered to flavoring muscatel and vermouth; the sweet and spicy licorice seeds are most popular as additive to European liquors; also for flavoring cakes and cookies. Used medicinally since 1500 B.C. *Zone 9.* p. 542

major 'Rosea' (W. Europe to Caucasus, No. Africa), "Rose anise"; herbaceous perennial to 1 m or more high, with fern-like, pinnate leaves, the broad 3-5 cm membranous leaflets lobed or toothed; small rose-pink flowers in handsome flat terminal clusters, in June-July. Formerly used medicinally for digestive problems; also to break up kidney and bladder stones. *Zone 6.* p. 545

PINANGA *Palmae*

geonomaeformis (Philippines); seen in col. Makiling Arboretum, Los Banos; small tropical featherpalm with slender cane-like stems from branching rootstock, 1-2 m high, with short, pinnate leaves of few broad lanceolate leaflets. *Zones 11-12.* p. 100

PINCKNEYA *Rubiaceae*

pubens (So. Carolina to Florida), "Fever tree" or "Georgia bark"; small tree to 6 m high, evergreen in habitat, with opposite hairy branches; elliptic, opposite leaves 10-20 cm long; inflorescence of yellowish tubular corollas, subtended by large leaf-like pink calyx lobe or sepal, 5 cm long, the stamens protruding; blooming May-July. The bark contains cinchonin, used in treatment of intermittent fevers. *Zone 8.* p. 858

PINGUICULA *Lentibulariaceae (Carnivorous Plants)*

caudata (bakeriana or moranensis) (Mexico), "Tailed butterwort"; carnivorous flattened rosette from moist bogs, with fleshy obovate pale green leaves which are sticky with a digestive fluid which will attract and capture insects, gradually absorbing them; flowers carmine, with long spur. *Humid-subtropic. Zones 10-11.* p. 202

vulgaris (N. No. America, Europe, Asia), "Butterwort"; small rosette to 15 cm across, with oblong obtuse, succulent leaves greasy to the touch from a sticky glandular fluid which holds and digests insects; flowers purple. *Temperate. Zones 3-7.* p. 202

PINUS *Pinaceae (Coniferae)*

aristata (Mts. of California to Rockies of Colorado), "Bristle-cone pine" or "Hickory pine"; small coniferous tree to 3 m or more high, sometimes shrubby with short trunk and densely crowded branches; the branchlets yellowish-brown and reddish pubescent; needles in bundles of five 3-5 cm long, dark green tipped with resin drops of pitch, and lasting several years; cylindric cones 8-10 cm long, each scale bearing a prickle. Very attractive as dwarf specimen, probably the slowest growing of all pines; a specimen found in Nevada is believed to be 4900 years old. *Zone 5.* p. 593

armandii (Mountains of W. China, Taiwan), "Armand pine"; evergreen conifer to 20 m high, with spreading branches and pale greenish-gray bark; thin flaccid needles in bundles of five, 8 to 15 cm long, fresh green; pendulous cones 10 to 20 cm long, of woody, reddish-brown scales. *Zone 5.* p. 593

bungeana (N.W. China), "Lace-bark pine"; attractive but rare species, in habitat 20-30 m high, but in cultivation often bushy with several main trunks; especially valued for its beautiful bark which is flaky with plates which eventually expose a white trunk with red blotches in old specimen; winter buds spindle-shaped 1 cm long, and resinous; stiff needles in threes, and 10 cm long, lasting 3-4 years, emitting oil when bruished; ovoid cones 8 cm long. *Zone 4.* p. 593

canariensis (Canary Islands), "Canary Island pine"; picturesque exotic tree to 30 m, with drooping branchlets; very long, string-like, pendant needles, glossy green, in bundles of 3, to 30 cm long; ovoid 20 cm female cones; the candle-like young inflorescence shown on pg. 593 is tipped by male flowers. *Zone 8.* p. 593, 595

cembra (Alps of Europe to No. Asia), "Swiss Stone pine" or "Russian cedar"; excellent landscape pine of tightly pyramidal habit, with dense branchlets when young; old trees heavily branched in habitat, to 25 m high; in gardens with slow growth of regular conical shape, neatly furnished to ground level with foliage; the stiff needles, holding to the branches for up to 5 years, are short (5-8 cm), dark green and in bundles of five; ovoid cones to 10 cm long, the scales not opening when ripe. *Zone 2.* p. 593

cembra 'Aurea', "Russian cedar"; slow growing cultivar with bundles of 5 needles, attractively yellow at its best during Winter. *Zone 4.* p. 593

cembroides (Arizona, Mexico), "Pinyon pine" or "Mexican stone pine"; shrub or small tree with gnarled, scarred trunk, and twisted branches; the dark green needles stiff and generally curved, in bundles of 3, but occasionally 2, 4, or 5; small cones 3 cm dia. The edible seeds (pinons), are eaten by Indians in Mexico. *Zone 7.* p. 593

contorta (Alaska to California), "Shore pine"; conifer varying from a shrub to a stunted looking flat-topped small tree, or even to a forest giant of up to 70 m tall in the mountains; but all have short, stiff, twisted dark green needles in pairs of two, to 5 cm long, lasting 3-8 years; ovoid 5 cm cones, with thin brown scales prickly at apex. At sea-level or in cultivation usually small, with branches short and crooked. An attractive garden subject. *Zone 7.* p. 593

coulteri (California mts., to N.W. Mexico), "Big-cone pine"; outstanding coarse-looking coniferous tree to 25 m high, with branches spreading wide, having ridged, light brown bark; the stout curved needles in threes, 15 to 30 cm long, glaucous green with stomata on each of 3 surfaces, living 2-3 years, densely arranged at ends of branches; characteristic huge drooping cones to 35 cm long, and weighing 2 kg or more, the brown woody scales spreading for grand effect. *Zone 8.* p. 594

densiflora 'Pendula', "Weeping Japanese red pine"; very prostrate pine that can be left to trail along the ground, or first trained upwards to form a trunk before letting it revert to its weeping habit, creating an attractive specimen, as I have seen it in Hangchow, South China; willowy branches with bluish-green needles in pairs, to 12 cm long, and very ornamental in the garden. Needles are brittle and will snap. *Zone 5.* p. 594

densiflora 'Umbraculifera' (Japan), "Tanyosho" or "Japanese Umbrella pine"; probably the best-known cultivar of the Japanese red pine, which in habitat grows to 30 m high. The Tanyosho pine is a low form, slowly growing to 4 m high, shaped flat-topped with the spreading branches covering downward as ribs in an umbrella; stiff green needles 8 cm long, in pairs; small 5 cm cones. Excellent for tubs and rockgardens, where the reddish bark adds to its exotic effect. Zone 5.   p. 593

echinata (New York to Florida, Kansas and Texas), "Shortleaf pine" or "Yellow pine"; large tree to 30 m high, having slender trunk with rough furrowed bark, and pendant branches; the young shoots green, the slender needles usually in pairs but sometimes in threes and fours, lasting two to five years, 8-12 cm long and dark bluish-green, margins finely toothed; ovate cones several together, 5 cm long, with spreading brown, spiny scales. The timber is of considerable commercial value. Zone 6.   p. 594

edulis (cembroides var.) (Wyoming to Texas, California to No. Mexico), "Pinyon pine" or "Two-leaved nut pine"; compact short-needle pine, ideal in gardens, to 2 m high or more; the rather stout needles usually in pairs, but occasionally single or in threes, and 5 cm long; the name edulis refers to the 2 cm edible, nut-like seeds that are carried in knobby rounded cones 6 cm in dia., and which are valued as delicious food by Indians of the Southwest. Zone 5.   p. 594, 597, 914

x eldarica (halepensis x brutia), "Afghanistan pine" or "Desert pine"; excellent arid climate pine forming symmetrical pyramid with long blue-green needles; very handsome as seen in California Nurseries. Zone 6.   p. 594

elliottii (So. Carolina to Florida and Mississippi), "Slash pine" or "Swamp pine"; forest tree of the coastal plains, to 30 m high; threadlike, thin needles in pairs of threes, to 20 cm long; 15 cm cones broad-ovate when open. Yields timber, turpentine. Zone 8.   p. 594

excelsa hort.: see P. wallichiana (Hortus)

glabra (So. Carolina to Florida and Louisiana), "Cedar pine"; large tree to 30 m or more high, with reddish-brown bark, having intermediate branches between the regular whorls, forming a broad crown; winter buds brown and ovate-pointed; needles in pairs, 8 cm long, and lightly twisted, lasting 2-3 years; solitary 5 cm cones on short stalks, pointing backwards, and having dark yellow flexible scales. Closely related to echinata but having pairs of leaves constant. Zone 7.   p. 594

halepensis (Portugal to Afghanistan), "Aleppo pine" or "Jerusalem pine"; characteristic pine of rugged character, older trees irregular and round-topped, 15-25 m high; soft needles in two's, to 10 cm long, light green; oblong reddish cones to 8 cm. Yields turpentine. Zone 8.   p. 594, 597

jeffreyi (So. Oregon to Baja California), "Jeffrey pine"; pyramidal tree 30-60 m high, with open branches and cinnamon-brown bark; thin bluish-green needles 12-25 cm long, in bundles of three, dense on glaucous branchlets; male flowers reddish; large hollow-base ovoid cones 12-30 cm long. Picturesque forest tree related to ponderosa, but with stiffer leaves and larger cones; also in habitat in Yosemite Nat'l. Park on the Sierra Nevada. Zone 5.   p. 596

kochiana (Turkey), "Turkish Scotch pine"; robust tree of pyramidal habit, with reddish trunk and erect brown branches, furnished attractively by stiff leathery, dark green needles in somewhat scattered pairs, about 6 cm long or more. Photographed in col. Pacific Tree Farms, Chula Vista, California. Zone 7.   p. 598

leucodermis (heldreichii) (Italy, Balkan Penins.), "Bosnian red-cone pine"; handsome high-mountain tree, in habitat to 30 m tall, having grayish, flaky bark, and closely branched; young shoots glaucous, dense with dark green, erect and rigid needles 5-8 cm long, their margins finely toothed, and lasting 5-6 years; ovoid 6-8 cm cones solitary or a few together, nearly black when mature, composed of narrow scales; the gray seed with long wing. High mountain species allied to P. nigra, but more compact with shorter, erect leaves. Zone 6.   p. 596

maximinoi (tenuifolia) (Western Mexico); handsome subtropical pine to 30 m high, densely branched, and featuring thin, flexible needles in clusters of five, attractively arching and pendulous 20 to 28 cm long, spreading like fountains; oblong cones with thin, flexible scales. Zone 8.   p. 596

monophylla (Utah, California to Mexico), "Single-leaf pinyon"; handsome low tree 5 to 15 m high, conical in shape while young, with age the trunk will branch, and forms a flat-topped, picturesque crown; bark 2 cm thick, divided into narrow, flat ridges; the needles are usually solitary, but sometimes in pairs, stiff and stout, incurved gray-green 3-4 cm long; cones broadly ovoid, to 6 cm long, having brown woody scales. Primary habitat Wasatch Mts. in Utah and Sierra Nevada. Zone 6.   p. 601

montezumae (Mexico, Guatemala), "Montezuma pine"; tall tree to 40 m, with spreading crown and rough bark; long stiffish needles 16 to 24 cm long, in bundles of five, spreading or drooping, green or bluish-green, the margins finely toothed; variable cones 6-24 cm long, usually conical. Subtropic. Zone 9.   p. 598

monticola (Brit. Columbia to California), "Western white pine"; attractive tree 20 m high, in favorable habitat to more than 50 m, with open crown to pyramidal with age; winter buds broad-cylindric, narrowing to a point and with close scales; blue-green leaves in bundles of 5, white-banded beneath, 8-10 cm long, densely arranged and lasting 3-4 years; light brown, slender, soft cones pendulous, 12-25 cm long, with thin, resinous scales opening when ripe. Valuable timber tree. Zone 8.   p. 601

mugo (montana) (Mts. of Central and S.E. Europe), "Mugho pine" or "Swiss mountain pine"; low prostrate shrub or shrubby coniferous tree 4 m or more high, with long stiff and twisted needles in bundles of two, 2½-8 cm long, dark green; variable ovoid, brown cones 2½-6 cm long. Zone 2.   p. 596

mugo 'Compacta' (Europe), "Dwarf mountain pine" or "Dwarf mugho"; popular cultivar of low, globular shape, and densely branched, and somewhat prostrate; the stiff dark green needles in pairs, more or less twisted, 3-4 cm long; very useful in rockgardens. Zone 3.   p. 596

nigra (Corsica to So. Europe, Turkey, and Asia Minor), "European Black pine"; pyramidal forest tree 12 to 40 m high, blackish-gray, deep fissured bark, rather dense and uniform in habit, becoming flat-topped with age, the branches in regular whorls; slender needles dark green, 10-16 cm long in pairs, more flexible than in var. nigra; ovoid, glossy brown cones 5-8 cm long. Needles will crush and never snap cleanly. A tree of strong character, and smoke tolerant. Occasionally used for dwarf Bonsai training. Zone 6.   p. 596, 627

nigra var. nigra (austriaca) (C. Europe), "Austrian pine"; slow growing mountain tree with black bark, a geographical habitat variety of the Black pine, dark and scruffy in appearance, to 35 m high, but usually much smaller in cultivation, having broad and heavy branches; the curved dark needles thick and rigid, 8-12 cm long in pairs, separated in short blackish bunches; light brown cones 5 to 8 cm long. Zone 4.   p. 596

nigra 'Hornibrookiana'; very ornamental dwarf cultivar originated as a witches' broom of Austrian pine in Rochester, New York; growing slowly into a roundish, ground-hugging evergreen to about 60 cm high; rigid dark green, twisted needles in pairs, with creamy young shoots standing erect as candles. Usually propagated by grafting. Zone 4.   p. 596

palustris (U.S.: Virginia to Florida and Mississippi), "Southern pine" or "Longleaf yellow pine"; large coniferous tree 25-30 m high, with threadlike, graceful dark green needles to 45 cm long, arranged in clusters of three; cylindric 25 cm cones. Cut branches are frequently used for decoration. Source of timber for ships, bridges and pulp wood; also tapped in the Southern U.S. for resin, to yield turpentine. Zone 7.   p. 598

parviflora (pentaphylla) (Japan: Honshu, Kyushu), "Japanese white pine"; very ornamental tree to 20 m high, pyramidal when young; if older with long horizontal spreading branches forming flattened crown; the bark gray-brown; slender bluish-green needles 3-6 cm long, in bundles of five often tufted at branch ends; cones ovoid 8-10 cm long, the scales opening wide; adopted in Japan for the culture of Bonsai, or dwarfed trees, and I have seen them 3 centuries old less than 60 cm high; often grafted on P. thunbergii, the black pine for dwarfing. Zone 5.   p. 598, 627

parviflora 'Glauca'; attractive cultivar of slow growth, with silvery blue, twisted needles in clusters of five, and accented by blue-white stomatic bands on the inner side of each leaf, the reverse being green. Ideally suited for small gardens and trained as bonsai. Zone 5. p. 598

pentaphylla: see P. parviflora

pinaster (Mediterranean region), "Cluster pine" or "Maritime pine"; attractive tree of rapid growth, first conical, with age losing lower limbs but with wide crown formed by clusters of spreading branches, displaying the handsome though rough brown-red, deeply fissured bark; the stiff, dark green needles are two in a sheath, 12-20 cm long, lasting 3 years; cones single or several together, 10-20 cm long, remaining closed for years. Very adapted to seaside planting. For many years the main supplies of resin, extracted from the trunk by tapping. Zone 7.   p. 598

pinea (So. Europe and Turkey), "Italian stone pine"; the characteristic broad and flat-topped pine of the South Italian landscape, 15 to 26 m high; with stiff, bright to gray-green needles in two's, 10 to 20 cm long; in juvenile stage, needles are short, 3 cm long and silvery glaucous; the cones are 12 cm long. The seeds are eaten in the Mediterranean region. Very picturesque in the landscape with the branches all clustered at the top. Handsome decorator, when container grown; takes heat and drought. Frequently used as Christmas tree. Zone 8.   p. 595, 597, 598

ponderosa (Brit. Columbia to Baja California, So. Dakota to Texas), "Western yellow pine" or "Ponderosa pine"; majestic tree to 50 or 70 m high, with red bark to nearly black, fissured into large plates, branches spreading; needles in bundles of three, densely crowded on branchlets, 12-26 cm long, dark green; ovoid cones 8-15 cm long, shining brown. *Zone 5.* p. 599, 600

pseudostrobus (So. Mexico, Central America), "False Weymouth pine" or "Guatemala pine"; very handsome evergreen tree to 30 m tall, allied to P. montezumae but with smooth bark and glaucous young shoots; the needles in bundles of five, 20 to 30 cm long, slender, glaucous green and gracefully pendant; curved cones to 15 cm long. *Zone 9.* p. 599, 600

pungens (New Jersey to Georgia), "Prickly pine" or "Table mountain pine"; typically flat-topped tree of moderate size, to 10 m or more high, with irregular, spreading branches; young shoots green, turning brown; needles in pairs, occasionally three, 6-8 cm long, stiff and often twisted, lasting 3 years; curious cones ovate to 8 cm long, having thick, pointed spine-tipped scales, and remaining on branches for many years. *Zone 6.* p. 600

radiata (California), "Monterey pine"; legendary tree of the California coast, 24-40 m high, with irregularly open crown, becoming wind-blown and characteristically one-sided where exposed to ocean winds; thick dark brown bark on old trees; needles in bundles of three, in dense clusters 10-14 cm long; fresh green; nut-brown cones 7-14 cm long, 5-6 cm broad, in sessile clusters. *Zone 7.* p. 599, 600

resinosa (Eastern Canada to Pennsylvania and Minnesota), "American Red pine" or "Canadian Red pine"; massive tree to 30 m high, with large head of branches very ornamental featuring reddish bark and limbs; the winter buds are resinous with tips of many scales free; needles are glossy dark green, in pairs, 12-15 cm long, finely toothed and flexuous but will snap cleanly when bent backwards, and lasting 4 years; unarmed ovoid cones 6 cm long and light brown. Timber is of good quality. *Zone 2.* p. 599, 600

rigida (N.E. North America, south to Georgia), "Pitchpine"; widespread conifer 10 to 25 m high, with open crown; bark on younger trees thin and broken into plate-like scales, on older trees irregularly fissured; stout horizontal branches, the branchlets with dark green needles in bundles of three, 12 cm long, stiff and spreading; the ovoid cones 6 to 10 cm long. *Zone 4.* p. 600

roxburghii (longifolia) (Himalayan foothills), "Emodi pine" or "Indian longleaf pine"; decorative graceful tree when young, with long, drooping foliage; later broad, with round top, to 50 m high in habitat; arching needles in bundles of three, shining green, to 30 cm long; ovoid cones to 18 cm, the scales reflexed. Similar to Canary Island pine. *Subtropic. Zone 9.* p. 600

sabiniana (California foothills), "Digger pine" or "Nutpine"; open-growing tree 15-25 m high, dividing into several secondary trunks, and widely spreading branches; closely arranged cylindric winter buds are resinous with fringed scales; the bluish-green needles are slender, flaring or pendulous, three in each sheath, and 20-30 cm long, lasting 3 years; ovoid cones 15-25 cm long, remaining on the tree several years, after the open, light brown resinous scales have dropped their edible seeds. *Zone 6.* p. 600

strobus (Newfoundland and Manitoba south to Georgia), "White pine" or "Weymouth pine"; well-known, widely distributed graceful conifer 30 m or more high, fast-growing and ornamental, with a smooth, gray bark when younger, and a feathery effect because of its thin, soft needles in bundles of five, and bluish-green; the pendant cones long cylindrical, often curved and very resinous, 8-15 cm long. Used in Japan for training as dwarfed Bonsai in containers. *Zone 3.* p. 601

strobus 'Nana', "Dwarf white pine"; excellent rockgarden subject of compact growth habit, with needle clusters so close as to hide the inner branches, forming a low bush. Propagation is by grafting on a P. strobus seedling. *Zone 3.* p. 601

strobus 'Pendula', "Weeping white pine"; very decorative cultivar with long spreading branches; the lateral branchlets are gracefully pendulous, and show off the blue-green needles to great advantage. Propagated by grafting. *Zone 3.* p. 601

strobus 'Variegata', "Tiger pine"; rare cultivar, of compact habit, with grayish bark and ascending branches; the lateral branchlets featuring needles green at base, but mainly entirely yellow in dense clusters. *Zone 6.* p. 601

strobus fa. 'Witches' broom', "Dwarf Eastern white pine", originated as witches' broom at Arnold Arboretum, Jamaica Plain, Mass., photographed 1970; dense bushy growth from an adult Weymouth pine, caused by a parasitic fungus or virus; when cut off from branches to propagate, it will normally retain the parent character, except to be more dwarf and bushy, and needles reduced in size. Numerous dwarf conifer forms in horticulture owe their origin to propagations from witches' brooms. *Zone 3.* p. 597

sylvestris (No. Europe, W. Asia; natural. in N.E. U.S.), "Scots" or "Scotch pine", "Scotch fir"; widely grown European tree 20 m or more high, having beautiful reddish trunk, the bark peeling off in thin, papery layers; conical and dense in habit when young; later open and rather picturesque; typically with bluish-green, stiff twisted needles,

two in a sheath, varying in length, 3 to 10 cm long; oblong cones 6-8 cm long. Important timber tree in Europe. *Zone 2.* p. 602

sylvestris 'Nana', "Dwarf Scotch pine"; low, densely rounded bush with short horizontal or ascending branches; the stiff twisted, glaucous needles in pairs; the winter growth buds are 1 cm long, oblong pointed, having lanceolate fringed scales. Very suitable for the rockgarden. *Zone 3.* p. 602

sylvestris 'Watereri'; slow-growing blue form tending toward columnar or rounded habit, of old English origin, sometimes sold as 'Nana'; the silvery-white stomata on young leaves give the foliage a charming variegated effect. *Zone 3.* p. 602

taeda (U.S. East coast New Jersey to Florida, west to Texas), "Loblolly pine"; forest tree 30 to 50 m high, with red-brown, deeply fissured bark, and having branches irregularly spreading; long 15-25 cm needles bright green, lasting 3-4 years, in bundles of three, their margins finely toothed; cones narrow egg-shaped, 8-12 cm long, with scales spine-tipped. The wood yields timber and is used for pulp. *Zone 6.* p. 595

thunbergiana (thunbergii) (Coastal Japan and Korea), "Japanese black pine"; handsome spreading tree 8 to 30 m high, resembling, and perhaps a form of the Austrian pine but quicker growing; with somewhat shorter, darker green leaves 6-18 cm long, the sharp-pointed stiff needles in pairs, of irregular habit, and featuring long white buds. May be pruned; excellent in planters and as Bonsai; carefully thinned out in Japan gardens. *Zone 4.* p. 595, 601, 603, 611, 626

torreyana (So. California, Coastal San Diego), "Torrey pine" or "Soledad pine"; picturesque tree from along the Pacific coast, to 12 m high, of broad, open irregular habit, especially when exposed to Ocean winds; gray-green to dark needles in bundles of five, 20-30 cm long, tufted near the ends of shoots, lasting several years; ovoid cones to 15 cm long, having woody scales; the seed kernels are edible. *Zone 8.* p. 601, 602

virginiana (New York to Georgia and Alabama), the "Scrub-pine" or "Jersey pine"; normally a pyramidal tree 9-12 m high, with short trunk sometimes forked, with thin brownish bark, the branches crowded in irregular whorls; twisted, grayish-green needles in pairs, 5 cm long; oblong cones 5-7 cm long. The photo in EXOTICA 4, pg. 847, shows a prostrate seedling form from a "Witches' broom" photographed at the Arnold Arboretum in Boston 1970. *Zone 5.* p. 601

wallichiana (griffithii; excelsa hort.) (Himalayas: Bhutan), "Himalayan white pine", "Bhutan pine" or "Tearful pine"; beautiful wide-spreading tree 15 to 40 m tall, with horizontal branches, and pendant branchlets; young shoots glaucous; winter buds cylindric, having resinous scales; leaves 5 in a sheath, lasting 3 to 4 years, the youngest erect, older gracefully deflexed downward, 12 to 20 cm long, glaucous green and of soft texture; the cylindric cones are pendulous, 15 to 30 cm long, remaining on branches for several months after shedding their seed. Particularly attractive during Spring, with young growths standing erect, later opening out into needles. *Zone 5.* p. 602

PIPER *Piperaceae*

betle (Bali, E. Indies), "Betel-leaf"; commonly used in Indonesia and India for chewing with betel-nut; stems trailing; and in Bali I have seen it climbing high on trees, with foliage in neat ranks, the leaves are fleshy, broadly heart-shaped 8-15 cm long, dark green with depressed veins; flowers in stalked catkins, opposite of the leaves. *Tropical. Zone 11.* p. 287

imperialis (Trop. America); beautiful ornamental pepper photographed in col. Selby Botan. Garden, Sarasota, Florida; with succulent stem, bearing large decorative leaves, heart-shaped in outline, about 20 cm long, of fleshy texture and having white primary rib, and undulate along margins. *Zone 11.* p. 816

magnificum (bicolor) (Perú), "Lacquered pepper-tree"; beautiful tropical, erect branching foliage plant with corky stem and winged, clasping leafstalks bearing large, fleshy, quilted, oval leaves lacquered forest-green of a metallic sheen, with ivory veins and edge, wine-red beneath, 15-20 cm long. *Zone 11.* p. 80, 816

nigrum (Malabar coast, Malaya, Java), "Black pepper"; tropical climber with flexuous stems dense with leathery, glossy blackish-green, ovate or elliptic leaves, 12-15 cm long, and bearing long clusters of green berries turning first red, then black. Black pepper is obtained from the dried unripe fruit; when its skin is removed, the product is white pepper. Once a rare spice, it is now the most important pungent culinary seasoning. *Zone 11.* p. 540

porphyrophyllum (Cissus) (Indonesia), "Velvet cissus"; strikingly beautiful climber without tendrils, stems red with lines of white bristles; the roundish-cordate, recurved, 8-10 cm quilted leaves, velvety moss-green with yellow veins, and pink markings mainly along the veins, wine-red underneath. *Tropical. Zones 11-12.* p. 287

sylvaticum (Burma), "Silver cissus"; attractive, ornamental vine, with tiny-wiry stems, and heavy, leathery, ovate leaves more or less with cordate base, corrugated between the sunken dark veins, dark steel green, the raised areas covered with stippled silver, and with metallic pink sheen. *Tropical. Zone 11.*   *p. 287*

PIPTANTHUS   *Leguminosae*
nepalensis (laburnifolius) (Himalayas of Nepal and Sikkim); semi-evergreen shrub or small tree to 3 m high; leaves with 3 lanceolate leaflets 8-15 cm long, silky at first, dark green above, glaucous beneath; bright yellow flowers 3-4 cm long, in erect bracted racemes, blooming in May; seedpods 8-12 cm long. *Zone 8.*   *p. 767*

PIQUERIA   *Compositae*
trinervia (Stevia serrata) (C. America, Haiti), florists' "Stevia serrata"; to 80 cm high, grown for its profuse winter bloom; shrubby herb with narrow, glossy leaves 8 cm long, and small fragrant, white disc-flowers; used in cut flower arrangements. *Zone 10.*   *p. 398*

PISONIA   *Nyctaginaceae*
alba (morindifolia) (Philippines, Sri Lanka), "Lettuce tree" or "Lady-love"; evergreen tropical tree of medium size, to 7 m high, with greenish-yellow or yellow-white foliage looking like lettuce, the thin leaf blades lanceolate and corrugated 10-30 cm long, undulate at margins; clusters of tiny greenish-white flowers, and 2 cm long-stalked fruit from female blooms. Cooked leaves are eaten as a vegetable. *Zone 10.*   *p. 804*
umbellifera 'Variegata' (Heimerliodendron brunonianum 'Variegatum') (New Zealand), "Bird-catcher-tree"; showy sport of the "Para-Para" tree 6 to 15 m high and native from Tahiti and the Marquesas to New Zealand and Australia, with oblong foliage to 40 cm long, having very sticky ribs, on short, robust petioles, and slightly angled stem; the glossy leaves are marbled in two shades of green, edged with warm cream to almost white; unfolding young growth has a tinge of red at edge and midrib; clusters of inconspicuous greenish flowers. The seed pods are covered with a sweet gum which attracts birds. *Zone 10.*   *p. 805*

PISTACIA   *Anacardiaceae*
atlantica (Canary Is., Mediterranean reg.), "Mt. Atlas mastic tree" or "Pistache"; semi-evergreen ornamental tree to 18 m tall; odd-pinnate leaves of 7 to 11 leaflets; small flowers without petals, followed on female trees by berry-like fruit first red, later purple when ripe, 1 cm dia. *Arid subtropic. Zone 9.*   *p. 638*
chinensis (China, Taiwan, Philippine Isl.), "Chinese pistache"; rapid growing deciduous tree having umbrella-like crown, to 15 m or more high; with pinnate or odd-pinnate leaves lightly downy, 25 cm long, normally having 6-10 pairs of glossy green leaflets, turning vivid crimson in Autumn; male and female inflorescence axillary on separate plants, the small flowers without petals, in clusters; berry-like 1 cm fruit first red and finally blue. Used as understock for grafting of P. vera. *Zone 7.*   *p. 638*
vera (Syria), "Pistachio nut"; widely planted throughout the Mediterranean region and Northern India; spreading tree to 10 m high, partially deciduous and suited only for dry regions where the olive grows; the leaves of 1 to 5 pairs of thick, oval leaflets, and an extra one at the tip; tiny brownish-green flowers unisexual, without petals on female trees; clusters of oblong red fruit, 2-3 cm long, becoming wrinkled; inside the husk a stone contains the pistachio kernel, of rich taste, and used for flavoring cake and candy. The nuts are prepared in brine while still in the shell and are also favored for eating and nibbling. *Subtropic. Zone 9.*   *p. 903*

PISTIA   *Araceae*
stratiotes (Trop. America), "Water lettuce"; water-floating leaf rosettes 10-15 cm across, bright green and velvety, hairy, with hanging roots; small green flowers hidden between leaves. Apparently naturalized in other parts of the tropical world, I have seen them colonizing lagoons and rivers in West Africa, in Kenya and Uganda, and along the upper Nile. *Tropical. Zones 10-11.*   *p. 330*

PITCAIRNIA   *Bromeliaceae*
andreana (Colombia: Choco); small terrestrial, with leafy stems to 20 cm long; recurving, narrow lanceolate leaves, green and speckled with silver dots above, heavily frosted beneath with white scales; inflorescence with orange petals tipped with yellow. *Tropical. Zone 12.*   *p. 50*
bifrons (Lesser Antilles, Barbados); terrestrial or rock-dwelling rosette photographed on St. Vincent, W.I., with broad, laxly pendant leaves to 70 cm long, beneath with brownish scales; erect floral stalk with grayish bracts and dark red flowers. *Zone 11.*   *p. 48*
flammea var. floccosa (E. Brazil: Bahia to Santa Catarina); rock-dwelling or terrestrial rosette, with bulbous-thickened base; narrow linear leaves to 1 m long and 2 cm wide, scaly beneath and without spines; unbranched slender inflorescence with red flowers 3 cm long. *Tropical. Zone 10.*   *p. 47*

PITHECELLOBIUM   *Leguminosae*
ligustrinum (lanceolatum) (Mimosa) (Mexico to No. South America), "El Orore", "Timuche" in Mexico); handsome evergreen tree to 5 m high or more, widespread in Mexico from Veracruz to Chiapas, south through Cent. America to Venezuela; trunk and branches armed with short stout spines; bipinnate leaves with 2 pinnae, each having 2 oblong thick leaflets 4-8 cm long, bright green; inflorescence in showy erect spike-like raceme of small white flowers with white stamens protruding; fruit a flat legume 10 cm long, much curved and contorted. *Zone 10.*   *p. 767*

PITTOSPORUM   *Pittosporaceae*
colensoi (New Zealand), "Black mapou"; evergreen shrub or small tree to 10 m high, forming densely leafy canopy; with bark dark gray to nearly black; leathery glossy green elliptic leaves to 12 cm long, and having prominent yellowish midrib; solitary flowers deep purplish-red 2 cm long, with petals recurved; fruit in 3-valved globose woody capsules black in maturity. *Zone 10.*   *p. 817*
colensoi 'Marginatum'; elegant and popular cultivar dense with gray-green leaves 6 cm long irregularly bordered with white, the margins flat and smooth; reddish flowers; photographed at Auckland University Botanic Garden. *Zone 10.*   *p. 817*
colensoi 'Variegatum'; highly attractive color form dense with leathery elliptic and oblique-ovate leaves 8-10 cm long, variegated and bordered creamy-yellow, the margins highly undulate. *Zone 10.*   *p. 817*
crassifolium (New Zealand), "Karo" or "Turpentine tree"; shapely evergreen shrub or small tree 5-10 m high, of dense erect habit, with lustrous green obovate leaves 4 to 10 cm long, of fleshy to leathery texture, the margins thickened, and covered beneath with pale brown or whitish felt; small deep purple flowers with narrow petals, in terminal clusters, the males up to 10 in each, females up to 5, followed by 3-valved fruit capsules. *Zone 9.*   *p. 818*
crassifolium 'Variegatum'; very attractive cultivar seen in col. Auckland University Botanic Garden, New Zealand; evergreen shrub dense with fleshy obovate leaves 4 cm long, the blades milky-green neatly bordered ivory-white, lightly pubescent. *Zone 10.*   *p. 818*
daphniphylloides (W. China, Taiwan); ornamental evergreen shrub or small tree 3 m high, in habitat to 10 m; handsome evergreen lanceolate leathery leaves 10-20 cm long; small 1 cm creamy-yellow, fragrant flowers in globose clusters combined into large terminal cluster, blooming April to July; small 1 cm globose, wrinkled red fruit. *Zones 9-10.*   *p. 818*
eugenioides 'Variegatum'; New Zealand cultivar having attractive long-elliptic, leathery leaves grayish-green, with wavy ivory-white margins. The species P. eugenioides is a decorative evergreen growing into a tree to 12 m high, with narrow, glossy green foliage 10 cm long, and small yellow flowers scented like honey. *Zones 9-10.*   *p. 818*
ralphii (New Zealand: North Island); distinctive evergreen shrub 3-5 m high, with obovate leathery leaves varying from small 5 cm to 12 cm long, the underside and stalks thickly covered by white and brownish wool; small dark red flowers in terminal clusters, the anthers yellow. Confused in hort. with crassifolium, but has broader leaves and 9-12 pairs of secondary veins. *Zone 10.*   *p. 817*
rhombifolium (E. Australia), "Queensland pittosporum" or "Diamondleaf pittosporum"; evergreen 10 m or more high, used as a street tree in So. California, with glossy green leathery rhomboid or oblique ovate leaves 6-10 cm long, irregularly toothed; very floriferous with clusters of white 1 cm blooms followed by bright orange berries with Mid-winter. *Zone 9.*   *p.817*
tenuifolium (New Zealand), "Kohuhu"; handsome evergreen tree 5-10 m high, with bark nearly black; membranous obovate leaves 3-6 cm long, shiny light green and with sinuate, wavy margins; fragrant flowers with black-purple petals 1 cm long, followed by 2-3-valved woody fruit capsule; variable species. Related to P. colensoi but with leaves generally smaller and thinner, also more strongly undulate. *Zone 10.*   *p. 620, 817*
tenuifolium 'Variegatum' (New Zealand), "Variegated Kohuhu"; evergreen shrub or small tree, with gray bark; elliptic thin-leathery leaves 2-5 cm long, grayish-green with undulate, cream-white margins tinted pink; small purple flowers. *Zone 10.*   *p. 817*
tobira (China, Japan), "Mock orange"; tough, evergreen shrub to 3 m high, branching into a rather flat-topped, shapely bush, with thick-leathery obovate, convex, dark lustrous green leaves to 10 cm long, arranged in dense pseudowhorls, and with terminal clusters of small, creamy-white flowers, very fragrant. *Zone 9.*   *p. 79, 817, 819*
tobira 'Variegatum', "Variegated mock-orange"; attractive variegated form with leathery leaves slightly thinner, milky or grayish-green raggedly margined creamy-white; the little, fragrant flowers resembling orange-blossoms. *Subtropic. Zone 10.*   *p. 78*

tobira 'Wheeler's Dwarf'; miniature form of tobira; very compact low mound to 60 cm high, of glossy, dark green foliage. *Zones 9-10.* *p. 817.*

undulatum (Australia), "Sweet pittosporum" or "Victorian-box"; loosely branching tree growing to 12 m high, with soft-leathery, long elliptic or oblanceolate leaves to 15 cm long, lightly pendant, and with wavy margins, dark green; sweetly fragrant white flowers from May to July, followed by ovoid brownish fruit. *Zone 9.* *p. 818.*

viridiflorum (So. Africa: Transvaal), "Cape pittosporum"; yellow erect upright woody evergreen shrub to 3 m, or a tree to 6 m high with obovate leaves to 10 cm; thin leathery semi-glossy, grayish-green leaves with pale midrib; dense clusters of greenish-yellow flowers, jasmine scented; slow growing. *Zone 10.* *p. 816.*

PITYROGRAMMA   *Polypodiaceae (Filices)*

chrysophylla (calomelanos aureo-flava) (So. America, West Indies), a "Gold fern"; of graceful habit, with wide-spreading tripinnate, somewhat fleshy fronds to 60 cm long, dull green above, thickly covered with golden-yellow, waxy powder on the underside, carried on purplish-brown channeled stalks; the young shoots also waxy golden-yellow. *Humid-tropical. Zone 11.* *p. 136.*

PLAGIANTHUS   *Malvaceae*

regius (betulinus) (New Zealand, Australia), "Ribbonwood"; graceful dioecious evergreen tree to 15 m or more high, covered by soft down, the leaves in juvenile plants ovate to 3 cm long, in adult stage of tree much longer, to 8 cm, crenate or lobed along margins; the small dull-white flowers in large clusters. *Zone 10.* *p. 786.*

PLANTAGO   *Plantaginaceae*

major (Europe to Asia), "Cart-track plant" or "Broadleaved plantain"; stout perennial of all basal leaves, arranged in clustering rosettes, broad ovate, corrugated and parallel-veined, to 15 cm or more long; tiny flowers in slender spikes on stalks to 40 cm long. Vigorously spreading by seed or suckers, it can become an unwelcome lawn weed. *Zone 3.* *p. 471.*

major rosularis, "Rose-Plantain"; interesting variety having floral spike replaced by a rose-like rosette of little spoon-shaped, concave green leaflets 10 cm across, carried on a firm stalk rising from the basal rosette of broad, corrugated leaves. *Zone 3.* *p. 471.*

major 'Rubrifolia' (macrophylla purpurea), "Redleaf plantain"; handsome clustering perennial rosette, with wrinkled leaves tinted and colored copper to purplish-red, 12-18 cm long. *Zone 5.* *p. 471.*

PLATANUS   *Platanaceae*

x acerifolia (x hybrida, or x hispanica in Zander) (occidentalis x orientalis), "London plane"; magnificent deciduous tree to 40 m high, with a tall clean trunk freely scaling in late Winter; forming a rounded crown; the attractive leaves deeply palmately 3-5 lobed and 12-25 cm wide, the lobes triangular and coarsely toothed; bristly fruit-balls 3 cm dia., pendant usually in pairs. Most popular street tree in London, withstanding urban pollution. Common in No. America; may be sheared into shapes. *Zone 3.* *p. 623, 818, 819.*

occidentalis (Maine to Minnesota, Florida and Texas), "Eastern Sycamore", "American plane" or "Buttonwood"; large deciduous tree 30-50 m high, with broad, open head, its bark creamy-white, later flaking; shiny green leaves 3 or 5 lobed but not deeply cut, 12-22 cm wide, and with large teeth along sides, pale beneath; fruitballs 3 cm wide, less bristly than P. orientalis, and usually borne singly. Subject to parasitic canker causing die-backs of branchlets, and P. x acerifolia should be planted instead. *Zone 4.* *p. 818.*

orientalis (S.E. Europe and W. Asia), "Oriental plane"; handsome deciduous tree to 30 m high, usually with short grayish or greenish trunk, the bark knobby and peeling in large flakes, and an immense crown of branches; the leaves maple-like, deeply 5 or 7 lobed, the segments with smaller lobes or teeth, downy at first, later glossy green, 10-20 cm wide; bristly fruit balls 2 to 6 on a pendant stalk. Name often applied to P. x acerifolia. Wood is used for pulp. *Zone 6.* *p. 818, 819.*

racemosa (So. California and Baja Calif.), "California sycamore"; vigorous semi-deciduous tree, 15-30 m high, often dividing into secondary and irregular trunks, with attractive patchy light brown bark; rather thick leaves 10-20 cm long, deeply divided palmately in 3-5 pointed lobes, and tomentose beneath; the bristly fruitheads in Winter hang 2 to 7 together in pendant clusters. *Zone 7.* *p. 818.*

PLATYCERIUM   *Polypodiaceae (Filices)*

andinum (E. Perú, E. Bolivia), "American staghorn"; this sole So. American, subandine species is a large epiphyte with mighty erect, lobed barren fronds, and much forked long pendant fertile leaves to 3 m long, with long ribbon-like lobes, and sporangia placed at third fork back. *Tropical. Zones 11-12.* *p. 137.*

bifurcatum (alcicorne hort.) (E. Australia, New Guinea, New Caledonia, Sunda Isl.), the common "Staghorn fern"; easy growing epiphyte freely producing young plants on its roots; the basal fronds are kidney-shaped, in old specimen lobed; the usually laxly pendant, leathery, grayish dark green fertile fronds to 1 m long are thinly covered with white, stellate hairs, and usually twice long forked; soral patches only on distal segments, being the tips of the ultimate forks. Sterile fronds round, but feathered on back. Reverse silvery or green. Known as "Elkhorn" in Australia. On Mt. Boss, New South Wales, at 900 m this species tolerates -9°C cold, rainfall is 320 cm yr.; near Sydney they are found growing between 240-450 m altitude. *Subtropic. Zones 9-11.* *p. 137.*

bifurcatum cv. 'Netherlands' (alcicorne 'Regina Wilhelmina'); from Holland, with soft-leathery fertile fronds broader than the type, well divided into numerous lobes, and the habit of growth is with bright green fronds in all directions star-like. *Subtropic. Zones 10-11.* *p. 137.*

coronarium (biforme) (Burma, Thailand, Malaysia, Java, Philippines), "Crown staghorn"; a glorious epiphyte of which I have seen immense clusters growing high in trees of the rainforest in Malaya, the long, fresh green pendulous fronds are to 4 m long, several times widely forked, and the narrow lobes gracefully twisted; the thick barren fronds are tall and lobed; spores are curiously borne on a separate fertile reniform disc. *Tropical. Zone 12.* *p. 137.*

grande (Philippines); this true species is rare and restricted to the Philippine Islands; a noble epiphyte with vivid green sterile fronds erect and outward-spreading; the leathery, pendant fertile fronds in mature specimen to 1 m long; smaller in habit, but otherwise similar to P. superbum (grande of hort.), except that these fronds consist of two primary divisions, each forked again and spreading into numerous lobes, the two wide main sinuses each bearing a soral patch (P. superbum has only one spore-patch on each fertile frond). *Zone 12.* *p. 137.*

holtumii (Thailand); large epiphytic fern from Monsoon forests; the sterile frond spreads circular fan-like, shallow-lobed at margins; the fertile fronds with two lobes, one smaller and elevated, the other larger and pendulous, to 1 m long; both lobes have spore patches, but differing from P. wilhelminae-reginae by not having little frills around the bud. Photographed in Singapore Botanic Garden. *Zone 12.* *p. 136.*

ridleyii (Malaya, Borneo, Sumatra); epiphyte at home in high trees, allied to coronarium, but more compact; rounded basal fronds mostly appressed to the support; normal frond rather erect, fresh green 30-60 cm long, about 5 times irregularly forked in pairs and sterile, but one branch sometimes carrying at its base a concave fertile lobe bearing the sporangia; the divisions are characteristically short and wide-spreading. The existence of this species is discussed in Baileya Sept. 64. *Tropical. Zone 12.* *p. 136.*

stemaria (aethiopicum) (W. Africa to Madagascar), "Triangle staghorn"; curious species with basal fronds convex and elongated into lobes; the triangular grayish-green fertile fronds to 45 cm long, thick-leathery, with prominent ribs, and divided twice, the main fork spreading wide, with a sinus, around which follow the spore masses; the underside densely covered with silvery white felt. *Tropical. Zones 11-12.* *p. 136.*

superbum (grande of hort. and in Hortus 3) (Queensland, New South Wales, Eastern Malaysia, Java), "Regal elkhorn"; magnificent epiphytic fern forming a great crown of sterile fronds, glossy vivid green, with dark venation, the upper lobes double forked and staghorn-like, gracefully flaring outward; pendulous pairs of thick-fleshy, fertile fronds, several times divided, appear with age, holding between them in the rounded sinus of the first fork a single wedge-shaped disc bearing the sporangia. Mature specimen with fan-like sterile fronds spread to 1 m; drooping fertile fronds may become 1½ m long. It may take 20 years of age before spores are first produced. I have found P. superbum as far south as New South Wales at 600 m, where the temperature ranges from 3 to 49°C, on Stinging trees as hosts. According to Prof. Hoshizaki of U. of Calif., the species superbum from Australia, long known in cultivation as P. grande, has one spore patch in the main fork of the fertile fronds, whereas the rare P. grande from the Philippines has three main divisions bearing a spore patch on each of the two sinuses. *Tropical. Zones 10-12.* *p. 137.*

wandae (wilhelminae-reginae) (New Guinea), "Queen elkhorn"; with large crown of feathered sterile fronds spreading 1½ m; not as deeply lobed as grande but fuller; the long, gracefully pendant fronds to 2 m long, in pairs each with 3-4 long lobes, flanked on both outsides by one or two sets of separate big, obliquely broad-triangular spore-blades; glossy dark green above, silvery beneath, with prominent dark veins; lettuce serration at base; young growth covered with silvery scales. I have found this species widespread from southern Papua near sea level to the forbidding mountain ranges of northern New Guinea, at 1,100 m. P. wilhelminae-reginae in Hortus 1976; Zander 1984-transferred to P. wandae (Barbara Joe Hoshizaki, Los Angeles 1975). *Tropical. Zones 11-12.* *p. 137.*

wilhelminae-reginae: see P. wandae
willinckii (Java), "Silver staghorn"; a distinct epiphyte with uneven, forked basal leaves and densely silvery-pubescent fertile fronds, erect at first, later completely pendant, very narrow and several times forked into long slender lobes, sporangia-bearing at tips. *Tropical. Zones 11-12.*   p. 137

PLATYCLADUS orientalis (Hortus 3):
see THUJA orientalis (Zander 84, Europ. Gardenflora, Cambridge 1986)

PLATYCLINIS: see DENDROCHILUM

PLATYCODON   *Campanulaceae*
grandiflorus (Japan, No. China), "Balloon flower" because of balloon-like buds; excellent garden perennial of erect habit to 60 cm tall, the stems with 10 cm ovate leaves, glaucous blue beneath, branching into floral stalks bearing open bell-flowers 5-8 cm across, usually violet-blue, varying to lilac or white, summer-blooming year after year. Completely dormant and deciduous during Winter, even in mild climate California. *Zones 3-9.*   p. 356
grandiflorus 'Mariesii', "Dwarf balloon flower" or "Japanese bell flower"; striking erect perennial having fleshy roots; more dwarf in habit than the species, to only 45 cm high, the inflorescence in bud balloon-like, opening into showy, wide open bell-flowers to 7 cm across, in shades of shimmering blue to lilac or pink. Dormant during Winter. *Zones 4-10.*   p. 356
grandiflorus 'Semi-plenus', "Double balloon flower"; showy perennial with erect stems bearing large semi-double blue flowers, with greatly expanded corolla having an extra inner row of segments in vivid blue. *Zone 6.*   p. 356

PLATYLOBIUM   *Leguminosae*
obtusangulum (E. Australia, Tasmania); handsome shrub to 1 m or more high, with ovate to triangular leaves to 3 cm long, and showy broad pea-flowers 3 cm wide, orange-yellow with crimson-red center, the keel and wings small. *Zone 10.*   p. 765

PLATYSTEMON   *Papaveraceae*
californicus (Utah, Arizona, California), "Cream cups"; flowering annual herb to 30 cm high, forming dense bushes; with linear leaves, and cream-yellow flowers 3 cm across, solitary on long stalks, in Spring. *Zone 9.*   p. 466

PLATYTHECA   *Tremandraceae*
verticillata (galioides) (S.W. Australia); dainty small shrub 30-60 cm high; the slender stalks with soft needle-leaves 12 mm long, are arranged tier above tier like spokes of a wheel; delicate light purple flowers 2½ cm across, blooming in Spring. *Zone 10.*   p. 892

PLECTRANTHUS   *Labiatae*
aethiopicus (E. Africa); bushy subshrub to 1½ m high, with corrugated, broad ovate leaves 8-15 cm long, sharply serrate at margins; terminal inflorescence of clustered racemes with 10-15 mm bilabiate tubular flowers, the corolla light purple, autumn-blooming in California. *Zone 10.*   p. 762
australis (nummularius) (Australia, Pacific Islands), the "Swedish ivy"; in California horticulture as "Creeping Charlie"; vigorous creeping perennial herb with small leathery, thickish, metallic green, waxy leaves almost round, 3-6 cm across and deeply crenate, glaucous gray-green beneath and with purplish veins; small white two-lipped flowers in spikes. A tough trailer tolerating abuse; good for hanging pots or wall containers. *Tropical. Zone 10.*   p. 316
ciliatus (Transvaal); low, mat-forming creeper, with fleshy, ovate, crenate leaves 5-8 cm long, matte green and slightly rugose, and with purple veins; small 2 cm whitish, bilabiate flowers in erect racemes. *Zone 10.*   p. 435
coleoides 'Marginatus' (tomentosus), "Candle plant"; low, bushy plant dense with opposite, ovate, hairy herbaceous, 5-8 cm leaves dark green and grayish, the crenate and scalloped margins creamy-white; 4-angled stem; flowers white with purple; the type is from the Nilghiris (So. India). *Subtropic. Zone 10.*   p. 435
ecklonii (Zululand, So. Africa), "Purple spur-flower"; showy perennial becoming 1 m or more high, with four-sided stem, and large fleshy leaves, broadly ovate with corrugated, rough surface, serrate at margins, and prominent red veins underneath; large attractive inflorescence of mauve to purple flowers in branched clusters, autumn-blooming. *Zone 10.*   p. 434
'Variegated' Mintleaf (prob. madagascariensis cv, from S.E. Africa), in hort. also as "minima" and "Iboza"; pretty creeper with brownish, hirsute stems; small 3-4 cm fleshy, crenate leaves milky-green bordered white, strongly mint-scented; white flowers flushed lilac. Ideal for baskets. *Subtropic. Zone 10.*   p. 432, 435

PLECTRITIS   *Valerianaceae*
congesta (Brit. Columbia to No. California); floriferous annual to 50 cm high, freely branched, with ovate leaves 5 cm long; small 1 cm

pinkish to rose flowers, in dense terminal clusters, the corollas two-lipped and spurred at base, blooming April-June. *Zone 8.*   p. 516

PLEIOBLASTUS: see ARUNDINARIA

PLEIONE   *Orchidaceae*
bulbocodioides (yunnanensis) (Taiwan, Yunnan, Tibet), "Indian crocus"; charming small terrestrial or growing on rocks, with annual flattened, warted 2 cm pseudobulbs, deciduous at blooming time, the lanceolate leaves plicate; showy flowers to 8 cm across, on short stalk, bright rose, the fringed lip white and blotched purple. *Zones 10-11.*   p. 95

PLEIOSPILOS   *Aizoaceae*
magnipunctatus (So. Africa: Karroo), "Stone-plant"; low succulent forming clumps to 8 cm high, with pairs of stone-like, tapering leaves 3 to 7 cm long, wide in the middle and somewhat boat-shaped, green with dark dots; flowers with golden-yellow rays 4 to 5 cm across. *Zone 10.*   p. 147
purpusii (So. Africa: Cape Prov.), "Living rock-cactus"; beautiful low succulent forming growths of 2 to 4 fleshy green leaves 5 to 7 cm long flattened and 3 cm wide in center, covered with numerous darker dots; showy sessile rayed yellow flowers to 9 cm across. *Zone 10.*   p. 147

PLEOMELE   *Agavaceae*
angustifolia honoriae (Solomons, Torres Straits); beautiful ornamental with willowy, scandent stems densely clothed with clasping flexible-leathery, lanceolate leaves 15-25 cm long, shining grass-green with distinct ivory-yellow borders, and turning metallic red in the sun. *Tropical. Zone 12.*   p. 118
reflexa (Dracaena) (Madagascar, Mauritius, India), "Malaysian dracaena"; ornamental rosette of densely clustering short and narrow, leathery leaves, deep glossy green, without midrib, wavy and reflexed, persistently clasping the willowy, self-branching stem, to 3½ m high if given support; I have noticed them widely used in India and Thailand as a most satisfactory pot plant; flowers whitish. *Tropical. Zones 11-12.*   p. 118
reflexa 'Song of Jamaica'; a color variation seen at Sarian greenhouses, Makati, Philippines; sturdy ornamental plant dense with leathery lanceolate leaves bluish-green, variegated with length stripes or bands of lemon yellow and cream. *Zone 11.*   p. 70
reflexa 'Variegata' (South India, Ceylon), "Song of India"; a beauty I fell in love with when I first saw it in Ceylon; a tropical evergreen; self-branching with slender, flexuous stems eventually becoming scandent to 3 m long, densely furnished with clasping, narrow lanceolate, leathery leaves 12 cm long, beautifully margined by two wide bands of golden-yellow or cream and framing the green center; very slow-growing. *Tropical. Zone 12.*   p. 70, 118

PLUMBAGO   *Plumbaginaceae*
auriculata (capensis) (So. Africa), "Cape leadwort"; straggling, shrubby perennial with small oblong, scattered leaves 5 cm long, and wiry racemes of salver-shaped, azure-blue flowers having a very slender tube 3 cm long, and phlox-like lobes. *Zones 9-10.*   p. 820
indica (coccinea, rosea) (Malaysia), "Scarlet leadwort"; showy, semi-scandent subshrub, with wiry, zigzag stems, ovate-elliptic leaves to 10 cm long; and long terminal racemes of scarlet-red salver-shaped flowers 3-5 cm long. *Zones 10-11.*   p. 820

PLUMERIA   *Apocynaceae*
obtusa (Hispaniola, Cuba, Yucatán Penin.), "Temple tree" or "Lirio de la Costa"; small evergreen tree to 8 m high, the heavy oblanceolate, dark green leaves with milky sap, to 18 cm long; large white, waxy flowers with spreading petals, 5 to 7 cm across and with yellow center, intensely fragrant. *Zone 10.*   p. 641
rubra (acuminata) (Mexico to Ecuador), "Frangipani tree" or "Flor de Mayo"; large, waxy, single blossoms carmine-rose with yellow eye, very fragrant; thick, soft branches with latex-like, sticky juice, dark-green leaves, shedding in dry season. *Zone 10.*   p. 641
rubra acutifolia (Mexico), the "West Indian jasmine", and the "Temple tree" of India; leaves wedge-shaped; flowers waxy white with yellow throat, sweetly fragrant, funnelform. *Zone 10.*   p. 641

POA   *Gramineae*
pratensis (Eurasia, No. Africa, natural. in No. America), "Kentucky bluegrass"; the most popular lawn grass in the cooler states of U.S. north of Tennessee; perennial 30-50 cm high, spreading by underground creeping rhizomes; bluish-green, soft leaves; inflorescence in branched clusters with 3-5 flowered spikelets. Bluegrass can be established from seed or matted sod; it is a fine-textured grass that forms a dense turf for golf courses and athletic fields and for pasture in moist regions. *Zone 3.*   p. 570

PODALYRIA   *Leguminosae*
calyptrata (So. Africa); "Sweet pea bush"; much branched shrub to 3 m high; shoots and 5 cm obovate leaves downy; clusters of

pea-like flowers pale rose to purple, the standard petal 2 cm long; floral bracts very wide, united to a cap over the buds, soon deciduous; fruit a woolly legume 3 cm long. *Zone 10.*   p. 768

PODOCARPUS   *Podocarpaceae (Coniferae)*
elongatus (spinulosus) (Western Africa), "African yellow-wood"; coniferous evergreen tree to 20 m high, with gracefully pendant branches, densely pinnate, with long, leathery, narrow-linear, tapering leaves, bright green; short male catkins, and globose crimson fruit. *Zone 9.*   p. 605
falcatus (So. Africa), "Oteniqua yellow-wood"; evergreen tree rather loose in habit, to 30 m high, with thin brown bark, shed in scales or strips; the long, narrow, grayish-green needles usually spirally arranged 5 cm long; male catkins often in threes; seed fruit globose, 1 cm dia., glaucous green. Yields non-resinous yellow timber. *Zone 10.*   p. 606
gracilior (Kenya, Uganda, Ethiopia), "African fern pine"; subtropical coniferous tree to 18 m high, common on the slopes of Mt. Kenya at 2,100 to 2,800 m; a valuable timber tree; graceful willowy branches with long, narrow-lanceolate, needle-like leathery leaves glossy deep green, to 10 cm long on young trees, and loosely arranged; 6 cm long and dense on older specimen; glaucous, purple berries. This may be the same as the cultivated P. "elongata" as grown in California nurseries. *Subtropic. Zone 9.*   p. 605
henkelii (enciculare hort.) (Transvaal, Natal), "Long-leaved yellow-wood"; luxuriant rounded tree dense with glossy, deep green, pendant or recurving leaves 12 to 15 cm long; male catkins cylindrical and erect from leaf axils. *Subtropic. Zone 9.*   p. 605
latifolius (So. Africa); ornamental evergreen of stiff-erect habit, on older trees the bark shredding in long strips, to 30 m tall; needle-like rigid-leathery, deep green leaves 4-6 cm long; globose 2 cm fruit glaucous green. *Zone 10.*   p. 606
macrophyllus (chinensis) (China, Japan), "Buddhist pine"; dioecious coniferous tree to about 12 m high, with horizontal branches, and numerous crowded leafy twigs, the leathery, deep green, narrow, linear-lanceolate leaves needle-like 8-14 cm long as seen in China; with a single midrib prominent on both sides; male, axillary flowers resembling catkins; on female trees the berries bluish-purple. *Zone 7.*   p. 605, 611, 624
macrophyllus 'Maki' (China), a compact "Southern yew"; popular evergreen shrub; for hedges in the southern states and grown as a superb decorative container plant in the North; lends itself well to shearing and shaping; as a tree attaining 15 m in this variety with rather erect branches, dense with waxy, blackish-green, linear lanceolate leaves spirally arranged, 4-8 cm long and about 1 cm wide, with distinct midrib; pale green beneath. Male flowers in 4 cm catkins; the fleshy oval fruit on female trees glaucous purple. *Zone 7.*   p. 605, 624
milanjianus (Uganda), "African yellow-wood"; evergreen forest tree to 25 m high, with thin, pale brown bark, cracking and peeling in long narrow strips; leathery long-linear leaves, scented like yew; male cones catkin-like, flesh-pink; globose 1-2 cm fruit glaucous, and attached to large fleshy, scarlet receptacle. *Zone 9.*   p. 605
nagi (China, Japan, Taiwan), "Broadleaf podocarpus"; tall conifer to 30 m high, with smooth, purplish bark, elegant spreading branches and slender, semi-pendant branchlets having shiny green, rigid-leathery, elliptic leaves to 2½ cm wide; very durable decorator but not as dense as macrophyllus. *Zone 9.*   p. 606
neriifolius (China to New Guinea), "Oleander pine"; evergreen tree to 20 m or more tall, of straggly growth; lance-shaped, leathery leaves to 15 cm long, glossy green above, somewhat glaucous beneath, with raised midrib both sides. *Zone 10.*   p. 606
salignus (Chile), "Willowleaf pine"; evergreen tree 15 to 20 m high, with numerous, irregularly arranged branches; slender, pendant willowy branchlets set alternately with scattered, narrow-lanceolate, glossy green leaves of leathery texture, 6-12 cm long; small 3 cm male catkins in clusters; seeds on dark purple fleshy base. *Zone 10.*   p. 606
totara (New Zealand); the "Totara" is a lofty, coniferous timber tree, to more than 30 m high, and 5-7 m girth; with small needle-like leaves 1-2 cm long, spiny-pointed, and rigid-leathery, bronzy green; fruit is a small nut set on a fleshy, crimson base. *Zone 9.*   p. 606
wallichianus; handsome tropical evergreen tree of dense habit, with broad, lanceolate leathery leaves 15-20 cm long in opposite pairs on flexible, pendant branches. Photographed in col. Singapore Botanic Garden. *Zone 10.*   p. 605

PODOPHYLLUM   *Berberidaceae*
hexandrum (emodi) (Himalayas), "May-apple"; perennial woodland herb with creeping rootstock and thick roots, and peltate, palmately lobed leaves on fleshy stalks 15-30 cm high, and white, waxy flowers to 4 cm across, followed by 5 cm red, edible fruit. *Warm temperate. Zone 6.*   p. 346

peltatum (Québec to Florida and Texas), "American mandrake"; herbaceous perennial with creeping rhizome and thick fibrous roots, 30 to 40 cm high; the peltate leaves palmately 5 to 9-lobed, to 30 cm across, and resembling a webbed foot; solitary white flowers 5 cm across, followed by ovoid, orange to scarlet fruit 3-5 cm long, edible with sweet, slightly acid flavor, ripe in July. *Zone 3.*   p. 347

PODRANEA   *Bignoniaceae*
ricasoliana (Tecoma violacea) (So. Africa), "Port St. Johns creeper"; showy evergreen climber with pinnate, deep glossy green leaves divided into 7-11 ovate, thin leaflets 5 cm long, with toothed margins; flowers with inflated calyx and trumpet-like corolla pinkish-lavender with red veining, 5 cm long and opening 6 cm wide into 5 rounded lobes, on blackish petioles. *Subtropic. Zone 10.*   p. 269

POGONATHERUM   *Gramineae*
paniceum (Saccharum paniceum; Arundinaria graminea hort.) (So. China, Malaya, N.E. Australia), "Cat grass", "German bamboo", or "Miniature bamboo"; dwarf relative of the sugarcane, clustering woody perennial 40-50 cm high; thin, wiry, yellow canes, set with linear-lanceolate, grass-like leaves 6-8 cm long; the stems topped by small whitish floral spikelets; grown as a houseplant in Europe. *Zones 10-11.*   p. 556

POINCIANA pulcherrima: see CAESALPINIA pulcherrima

POLEMONIUM   *Polemoniaceae*
caeruleum (Europe, Asia), "Jacob's ladder"; vigorous herbaceous perennial with hollow, angled stems 25 to 75 cm high; pinnate leaves of up to 27 elliptic leaflets arranged as in a ladder; small, cup- or bell-shaped normally blue flowers 2 cm long, in terminal racemes, blooming late Spring to Summer. *Zone 3.*   p. 475
carneum (syn. amoenum) (Calif.: San Francisco to Olympic Mts., Washington); densely branched perennial 40-80 cm high, with pinnate leaves 4 cm long; practically covered with lovely lavender-pink flowers 2-3 cm across; seen blooming late May at Kew Bot. Gardens, England, when it was with the name P. amoenum. *Zone 7.*   p. 466
foliosissimum (Wyoming to Arizona), "Greek valerian"; rhizomatous perennial with woody base; hairy branches 30-75 cm high; pinnate, ladder-like leaves on winged leaf stalk; bell-shaped flowers 2 cm long, pale violet, white or blue, in loose clusters, summer-blooming. *Zone 4.*   p. 475
pulcherrimum (Mts. of Alaska to California, Wyoming), "Skunk-leaf"; clustering herbaceous perennial 10-25 cm high, clammy-hairy, with mostly basal pinnate leaves; small 1 cm open bell-flowers usually light blue to purplish with yellow throat and tube, in late Spring to Summer. *Zone 3.*   p. 475
reptans (New Hampshire to Georgia, Alabama, Minnesota), "Creeping polemonium"; attractive rhizomatous perennial, with branched stem 20-50 cm high; pinnate leaves having ovate leaflets 5 cm long; bell-shaped light blue or white flowers 2 cm long, in loose clusters, blooming Spring to Summer. *Zone 3.*   p. 475

POLIANTHES   *Agavaceae (Amaryllidaceae)*
tuberosa (Mexico), the famed "Tuberose"; widely cultivated in the tropics where it is esteemed for the purity and powerful fragrance of its blooms as a cut flower and in gardens; a beautiful summer- or fall-blooming herb having a bulb-like tuberous rootstock covered with the broadened bases of the grass-like, channeled leaves; the leafy floral spikes are wiry and ½ to 1 m high, bearing numerous funnel-shaped waxy white flowers 4-6 cm long, in pairs. The tuberose may be had in flower throughout most of the year by potting bulbs in succession, taking 4 to 5 months to bloom; grow warm but keep dry until the leaves appear, then water freely, dry off after blooming when foliage turns yellow. *Tropical. Zone 9.*   p. 217
tuberosa flore pleno, "Double-flowered tuberose"; the form usually found in cultivation; the fragrant flowers are enlarged by extra rows of pure white petals inside for fuller and more showy effect. *Zones 9-10.*   p. 217

POLYALTHIA   *Annonaceae*
longifolia pendula (India), the "Asoka tree" or "Mast tree" in India; a lofty evergreen, graceful column of symmetrical pyramidal growth 15 m or more tall, with willowy, weeping pendulous branches, long narrow lanceolate leaves to 20 cm long, shiny green with undulate margins; in Spring the tree is covered with delicate, star-like pale green flowers with wavy petals, followed by the ovoid black 2 cm fruit, loved by bats and flying foxes. It is held in great esteem by Hindus, and planted near their temples. *Tropical.*
Zone 10.   p. 637, 638

POLYGALA   *Polygalaceae*
x dalmaisiana (oppositifolia x myrtifolia), "Sweet-pea shrub"; evergreen shrub to 2 m high or more, with small ovate to linear leaves

to 3 cm long; flowers purplish or rosy-red, blooming almost continuously. Photographed in October in San Pasqual, Calif. *Zone 9.*   p. 820

senega (Québec to Alberta, south to Georgia), "Seneca snakeroot"; herbaceous perennial with several stems 15-30 cm high, from a thick rootstock; the lanceolate leaves 5 cm long and rough at margins; small white or greenish flowers in cylindric racemes. The dried roots are used medicinally. The long leaves in background of photo pg. 541 are Liatris. *Zone 3.*   p. 541

virgata (So. Africa: Cape Prov.), "Milkwort"; floriferous shrub or small tree to 5 m high, with twiggy branches; the narrow leaves 5-8 cm long; flowers in terminal clusters, purplish or pink, having roundish wings and crested keel. *Zone 9.*   p. 820

POLYGONATUM   *Liliaceae*

commutatum (New England to Georgia, Nuevo Leon, Mex.) "Great Solomon's seal"; graceful rhizomatous perennial with fleshy underground roots; arching stems 60 cm to 2 m high, and furnished with alternate lanceolate leaves about 15 cm long; toward upper part with pendant bell-shaped, yellowish-green or white flowers 2 cm long, on 2-10 flowered stalks, in May or June; followed by shining blue-black berries in Autumn. *Zone 3.*   p. 450

jacquinii; a "Solomon's seal", seen in col. Kew Botan. Gardens 1984; rhizomatous perennial, with arching, leafy stems 1 m high, the broad-ovate leaves glossy green, and cordate at base; small white bell-flowers in clusters on axillary stalks, blooming late May in England. *Zone 7.*   p. 450

multiflorum (Temp. Europe, No. Asia), "Solomon's seal"; charming perennial herb with creeping rootstock; leafy stems to 1 m high; smooth, clasping ovate leaves; greenish-white nodding flowers 2 cm long, and bluish-black fruit. *Zones 2-7.*   p. 450

odoratum 'Variegatum' (japonicum) (Japan), "Variegated Solomon's seal"; charming perennial with arching, angled stems to 50 cm or more high, set with alternate, lanceolate 10 cm leaves deep green, attractively margined and striped creamy-white; toward apex the fragrant white bell-flowers to 3 cm long, tipped with green, dangling in pairs from short stalklets, in late Spring; followed by blue-black berries in Autumn. *Zone 4.*   p. 450

POLYGONELLA   *Polygonaceae*

americana (So. Carolina to New Mexico), "Jointweed"; perennial with subshrubby base, the flexuous stems to 90 cm or more high, with narrow 3 cm leaves; the attractive branched inflorescence of many small white or pinkish flowers from jointed axis, in elongate clusters. *Zone 7.*   p. 475

POLYGONUM   *Polygonaceae*

affine (Nepal Himalayas), "Himalayan Fleece flower"; spreading, evergreen perennial 15-30 cm high, with mainly basal oblanceolate leaves to 10 cm long, finely serrate, deep green and becoming bronzy in Winter; small bright rose flowers consisting only of calyx and 5 sepals, in dense spikes to 8 cm long, blooming in August. *Zone 3.*   p. 475

aubertii (Fallopia) (W. China and Tibet), "Fleece-vine" or "Silver lace vine"; twining perennial vine rapidly spreading 10 m during season, covering walls and link fences; leaves ovate 6 cm long, deciduous in cold climate; small fragrant, greenish-white flowers in foamy sprays, in late Summer. *Zones 5-10.*   p. 290

bistorta (No. Europe to Asia), "Snakeweed"; clustering perennial to 60 cm high, with mostly basal lanceolate leaves to 15 cm long, glaucous beneath; the handsome inflorescence of tiny pink or white flowers in cylindric spikes, on broadly winged stalks; in late Summer. *Zone 3.*   p. 476

campanulatum (Himalayas), "Alpine bistort"; hairy perennial with creeping base, and branching, slender reddish stems 60-90 cm high; small pale pink to white flowers in forking clusters, blooming in Summer. *Zone 8.*   p. 476

capitatum (Himalayas: No. India), "Knot-weed"; pretty perennial with trailing branches, the wiry, rooting brownish stems set with small alternate elliptic leaves 4 cm long, indistinctly crenate, matte-green with pale or light brown midrib and prominent, acute-angled design in brown-purple; the small pink flowers in globular heads. *Subtropic. Zone 9.*   p. 318

carneum in hort. (paleaceum) (Himalayas); perennial much branched bush, with narrow lanceolate, concave leaves; very floriferous with cylindric pokers shorter than in bistorta, of small deep pink flowers, blooming in June-July. *Zone 6.*   p. 476

cuspidatum (Reynourtia japonica) (Japan), "Japanese fleece flower" vigorous deep-rooted perennial to 2 m or more high, the hollow, jointed stems curving outward; ovate or roundish leaves to 12 cm long; inflorescence dioecious, with small greenish-white flowers, in axillary feathery clusters to 10 cm long, blooming July to October. The young shoots are often cooked like asparagus stems. *Zone 3.*   p. 476

cuspidatum compactum 'Femina', "Japanese knotweed"; dwarf form of more compact habit, to 60 cm high; dark green, broad ovate leaves wavy or crisped at margins, to 5-12 cm long; the inflorescence is dioecious, male and female flowers on separate plants, the little greenish-white blossoms in feathery clusters in male plants; female flowers have no stamens and develop by sepals enlarging over the ovary and turning red. *Zone 4.*   p. 476

orientale (India to Australia, naturalized in No. America), "Prince's feather"; handsome garden annual with robust branching stem to 1 m or more high; large ovate pointed leaves to 25 cm long, and beautiful pendulous cylindric spikes to 10 cm long, dense with small rose flowers, in Autumn. *Zone 10 as annual.*   p. 476

vacciniifolium (Himalayas), "Rose carpet knotweed"; vigorous perennial creeper with branches trailing and rooting along the ground; ovate 2 cm leaves, and spike-like erect racemes to 8 cm long, of small rosy flowers during late Summer. *Zone 7.*   p. 318

viviparum (No. America, Alaska, to Asia and Europe to Arctic), "Serpent grass"; handsome perennial 10-40 cm high, with slender rootstock, the narrow to oblong leaves mostly basal, 20 cm long, and glaucous beneath; small pink or white bell-flowers on reddish stalks in slender pyramidal racemes to 8 cm long, and bearing tiny purple bulbils on lower part; blooming June to August. *Zone 2.*   p. 476

weyrichii (Sakhalin), "Sakhalin knotweed"; robust perennial to 1 m or more high, with hairy stems, and broad ovate leaves to 20 cm long, dull green and rough above, white-hairy beneath; small greenish-white flowers in feathery terminal clusters, in July to September. *Zone 3.*   p. 476

POLYPODIUM   *Polypodiaceae (Filices)*

aureum (Phlebodium) (W. Indies to Brazil, Australia); named "Hare's foot fern" because of the stout creeping rhizomes clothed with bright rusty brown hair-like scales, the wiry stalks bearing bold, metallic light green, thin-leathery fronds, lobed with broad linear pinnae, separated by a rounded sinus and not cut to center; epiphytic. *Humid-tropical. Zones 10-11.*   p. 138

aureum 'Mandaianum', "Crisped blue fern"; a beautiful crested form having graceful bluish glaucous fronds of broad, pendulous, wavy pinnae with margins irregularly lobed, crisped and lacerated. (Manda 1912). *Humid-tropical. Zones 11-12.*   p. 138

bifrons: see SOLANOPTERIS bifrons

interjectum (West and Central Europe), "Lacy wall-fern"; possibly stable hybrid of P. vulgare x australe; small evergreen fern forming tufts from creeping rhizomes; graceful dissected bipinnate fronds, softer and broader in outline than P. vulgare, to 30 cm high. *Zones 5-8.*   p. 138

phyllitidis (Campyloneuron) (So. Florida, Bermuda, So. Brazil), "Strap fern"; found in the swampy Florida Everglades; strap-shaped entire, thin-leathery, glossy fresh green, brittle-stiff fronds 30-90 cm long, and to 10 cm wide, more or less waxy, born stalkless on short creeping rhizome, clothed with brownish scales. *Zones 10-11.*   p. 138

polypodioides (Delaware to Florida and Texas, Trop. America, So. Africa), "Resurrection-fern"; epiphytic on trees, a small, interesting creeping fern, with thin, wiry rhizomes, bearing small leathery, pinnate fronds 5-15 cm long, matte grass-green, the alternate pinnae with small brown, scaly dots evenly dispersed on the grayish reverse; the fronds curl and fold when dry. *Warm temperate to tropical. Zones 7-11.*   p. 138

punctatum (polycarpon) (New South Wales, Natal, Angola, Guinea), "Climbing birdsnest"; singular-looking, succulent fern with stout rhizome and stalkless, thick-fleshy, yellow-green, simple fronds to 1 m long, gradually narrowed on both ends and irregularly indented or undulate at margins. Usually epiphytic. *Tropical. Zones 11-12.*   p. 138

punctatum 'Grandiceps' (irioides grandiceps), "Fish-tail"; clustering fern with odd-shaped, thick leathery, almost succulent, waxy yellow-green fronds 30-60 cm high with prominent midrib, and tips forking to points or broad crests. Very curious, yet attractive and durable house plant. *Humid-tropical. Zones 11-12.*   p. 138

scouleri (Coastal B. Columbia to California), "Leathery polypody"; cliff-dwelling or on mossy surfaces, small fern with creeping rhizomes, bearing few pinnate, leathery fronds of triangular outline, 15 to 40 cm or more long, on chaffy stalks; the 4 to 14 pairs of broad pinnae bear clusters of spore capsules beneath. *Zones 9-10.*   p. 138

subauriculatum 'Knightiae' (Australia), "Lacy pine fern"; an excellent, slow growing and durable basket fern, with glossy yellow-green, pinnate fronds at first upright, later pendulous and to 1 m long, the linear pinnae deeply serrate and sliced into narrow, pointed lobes. The species is native in No. India, Malaya to Queensland. *Zone 11.*   p. 138

virginianum (Labrador to Alberta, so. to Georgia), the hardy, practically evergreen "American wall-fern"; growing on rocks, by creeping rhizomes, with pinnate leathery fronds to 25 cm long and having wavy segments, on wiry stalks. Like P. vulgare but rhizomes not sweet to the taste, and leaves smaller. *Zones 2-8.* p. 139

vulgare (Newfoundland to Alaska, Alabama; Eurasia), "Common polypody" or "Adder's fern"; ornamental, hardy evergreen fern, often epiphytic, growing on walls, roofs or trees; mat-forming on stout, rusty-scaly rhizomes, straw-colored stalks bearing 15-30 cm pinnate fronds, the papery leaflets toothed and wavy. *Temperate. Zones 1-8.* p. 139

POLYSCIAS Araliaceae

balfouriana, in some collections as scutellarium; (Aralia) (New Caledonia), "Dinner plate aralia"; leafy, bushy tropical shrub in habitat to 8 m high, branching with willowy stems; the large leathery somewhat concave leaves variable but at first entire, later usually of 3 rounded, coarsely toothed glossy green leaflets to 10 cm across, often with white margins, on bronzy stems speckled gray. *Tropical. Zone 10.* p. 36, 649

balfouriana 'Pennockii', "White aralia"; attractive cultivar by Pennock's, Puerto Rico; the waxy leaves olive-green with pronounced vein areas of creamy-white. *Tropical. Zone 10.* p. 35

crispatum (Brazil), "Chicken gizzard", "Geranium-leaf aralia", or "Dark green Papua" in Philippines; bushy evergreen of compact habit, with pinnate leaves; the small leathery, deep glossy green leaflets roundish or triangular in outline, quilted and irregularly indented, lobed or deeply cut to base, the lateral ones often overlapping, the margins with scattered teeth. Common hedge plant in the Philippines. *Tropical. Zone 10.* p. 649

filicifolia (Nothopanax) (Pacific Islands), "Fernleaf aralia"; very ornamental tropical evergreen to 2 m high, with smooth, usually purple and flexible stems; the foliage pinnate and having purplish petioles, the glossy green leaflets very variable, to 15 cm long, more or less shallow or deeply lobed, or cut into narrow segments; in older plants much broader to nearly entire. Widely used for hedges in Florida and Tropics worldwide. *Zone 10.* p. 650

filicifolia 'Golden Prince' (Nothopanax, Aralia); charming cultivar with fern-like pinnate leaves glossy rich green and suffused with golden-yellow in upper part of plant, the midrib purple. Seen in col. Foster Botanic Garden, Honolulu. *Zone 11.* p. 650

fruticosa (Nothopanax) (Polynesia, Malaysia, India), "Ming aralia" or "Parsley panax"; evergreen shrub 1½-2½ m high, with spotted, willowy branches, and very feathery leaves irregularly 3-pinnately cut, to 30 cm long, the segments spiny-toothed, often edged with white. *Zone 10.* p. 649

guilfoylei (Polynesia), "Wild coffee"; aromatic evergreen bushy shrub to 2 m or more, the erect flexible branches smooth and gray; pinnate foliage 20-50 cm long, with usually 5-7 leaflets shining green, often with white margins, and more or less toothed; small flowers in large, branched umbels. This species is very variable and many different leaf-forms are found throughout the Pacific and Malaysian area. *Tropical. Zone 10.* p. 649

guilfoylei 'Crispa', 'Blackie' or 'Amazonica' as grown in Florida nurseries; compact bush of sinister appearance, the pinnate leaves with coarsely puckered leaflets, glossy blackish or bronzy green, the margins with soft teeth. *Zone 10.* p. 650

guilfoylei 'Laciniata', "Lace-leaf papua" of Polynesian origin; small evergreen shrub somewhat resembling 'Victoriae' but with thin-leathery, grayish-green leaflets larger and with jagged margins, feathery and very dainty in appearance. *Tropical. Zone 10.* p. 649

guilfoylei 'Marginata', "Silver edge wild coffee"; handsome ornamental evergreen, as seen planted at World Trade Center in Singapore, the somewhat pendant pinnate leaves consisting of usually 7 leaflets bluish-green distinctly edged with white and a touch of red at margin. *Zone 11.* p. 36

guilfoylei 'Quercifolia', "Oakleaf panax"; sturdy form with glossy deep green, thin-leathery pinnate leaves on reddish petioles; the leaflets irregularly shallow or deeply lobed. *Zone 10.* p. 36, 649

guilfoylei 'Quinquefolia', "Celery-leaved panax"; a variety grown in Florida, with its hard-leathery leaves more or less irregularly cut into five divisions or lobes, deep coppery olive-green. *Zone 10.* p. 649

guilfoylei 'Variegata'; colorful variant, having pinnate leaves highly variegated and splashed creamy-white, contrasting with the dark green in its leaflets. Photographed in col. of New York Bot. Garden. *Zone 11.* p. 649

guilfoylei 'Victoriae' (Polynesia), "Lace aralia"; charming tropical evergreen dense with slender, willowy branches and grayish-green, thin-leathery, lacy, bipinnate leaves, the small, pendant, feathery segments toothed and bordered white. Lovely small foliage plant enjoying warmth and moisture, with its tasseled variegated foliage the most exquisite of the variegated leaf forms. *Tropical. Zone 10.* p. 35

ornata 'Aurea' (Nothopanax ornatum); very ornamental tropical foliage plant, with pinnate leaves 30-60 cm long, having 11-17 narrow-lanceolate leaflets of thin-leathery texture, undulate and toothed

along margins; the younger foliage is creamy-yellow. The species is probably from So. America, but is widely planted in gardens of the tropics; my photo was taken in Surabaya, Java. *Zone 10.* p. 650

ornata 'Wavy Pam'; tropical evergreen shrub with flexible slender stems, having very decorative, large pinnate foliage, gracefully arching or pendant; the 11 or more leathery leaflets glossy deep green, in this cultivar prominently undulate along sides. Photographed in Gutierrez garden, Hemet, California. *Zone 10.* p. 650

paniculata (Gilibertia) (Mauritius to Polynesia), "Wild coffee"; erect smooth evergreen shrub; leaves pinnate, 15-25 cm long, usually with 7 oblong leaflets of which the terminal one is largest, leathery and glossy green. *Zone 10.* p. 649

paniculata 'Aurea' (Gilibertia); very handsome ornamental tropical evergreen with long pinnate foliage gracefully arching, its 9 leaflets glossy green contrasting with a feathery veining of golden-yellow. *Zones 10-11.* p. 650

paniculata 'Variegata' "Variegated Roseleaf"; attractive variegated form of the species from Mauritius; willowy shrub with pinnate, pendant leaves to 30 cm long, including petiole, and usually having 9 leaflets 8-14 cm long, leathery and acutely serrate, deep green and richly splashed with cream and greenish-white, glossy on both sides. *Tropical. Zones 10-11.* p. 650

scutellaria (Nothopanax) (Java), "Panax" or "Saucer panax"; large decorative shrub with heart-shaped to oval, saucer-like leaves simple or with 2-5 leaflets 5-12 cm dia. margins wavy. In Malaysia young leaves are cooked as a vegetable. *Zone 10.* p. 650

POLYSTACHYA Orchidaceae

affinis (bracteata) (Sierra Leone to Zaire, Angola, Uganda); handsome epiphyte having clustered disc-shaped pseudobulbs 5 cm dia., bearing leathery elliptic twin-leaves to 20 cm long; the many-flowered pubescent inflorescence arching or pendulous, the blossoms 2 cm across, golden-yellow, striped with brown, and covered with orange hairs. *Zone 12.* p. 97

pubescens (Transvaal, S.E. Africa); robust epiphyte with crowded, fleshy pseudobulbs bearing two short leaves; from the apex the erect 12 cm floral stalk with sweetly fragrant, waxy, inverted 2 cm flowers golden-yellow, the lip with red markings, (Spring). *Zones 11-12.* p. 97

POLYSTICHUM Polypodiaceae (Filices)

acrostichoides (No. America: Nova Scotia to Texas), "Christmas fern" or "Dagger-fern"; hardy evergreen leather fern, with tufted pinnate fronds similar in appearance to Nephrolepis; 30-60 cm long and 5-10 cm wide, thin-leathery and bright glossy green; green, stiff axis, brown near base, and covered with brown scales, on short creeping, underground rootstock; the 24-30 pairs of pinnae oblique-halberd-shaped and finely serrate; spores set toward apex of frond. *Zones 3-8.* p. 139

aculeatum (Europe, E. Asia and So. America), "Prickly shield fern"; rosette of rigid, dark green, bipinnate leaves 30-60 cm long, on brown-scaly rachis. *Zones 3-8.* p. 139

adiantiforme: see RUMOHRA adiantiformis

braunii (Newfoundland to Northeastern U.S. and Wisconsin); deciduous hardy fern, with beautiful, lustrous deep green, leathery, bipinnate fronds to 1 m long, the petiole and rachis covered with long brown scales; sporangia in round dots beneath pinnae. *Zones 3-6.* p. 139

capense: see RUMOHRA adiantiformis

coriaceum: see RUMOHRA adiantiformis

lonchitis (Aspidium) (Alaska to Ontario and Greenland, Montana to No. Carolina, No. Europe), "Northern holly fern"; rock-dwelling evergreen fern of northern latitudes, with pinnate fronds 25-50 cm long, the dark green leathery 3-4 cm pinnae spiny-toothed. *Zones 2-7.* p. 139

munitum (Aspidium) (Alaska to Montana and California), the "Western sword-fern" or "Giant holly-fern"; handsome hardy evergreen fern, common in the Muir Woods near San Francisco, growing in the shade of the great redwood trees; gracefully arching pinnate fronds to more than 1 m long, on brown-hairy stalks, the rich green, glossy pinnae of leathery texture and with fine sharp teeth. *Zones 4-8.* p. 139

setiferum, sometimes spelled setigerum (Trop. and Temp. Zones of both hemispheres), the variable, low growing "Hedge-fern"; feathery pinnate fronds 30-60 cm long, covered with brown hair-like scales, borne on shaggy, stout stalks; the fresh green pinnae close together, and deeply lobed; frost-hardy and winter-green; much planted in shaded rock gardens. *Temperate to subtropic. Zones 5-10.* p. 140

setiferum 'Proliferum' (viviparum) (Australia), "Filigree fern"; tufted fern, scaly at base, the fleshy, brown-woolly stalk bearing the pinnate, light green fronds, the pinnae deeply cut or lobed, and bud-bearing, giving rise to young plantlets. *Zones 7-10.* p. 140

strigosum in Calif. hort.: see Dryopteris arguta

tsus-simense (Aspidium); from the island of Tsus-sima in the Straits of Korea; dwarf and shapely tufted fern suitable for terrariums, with small leathery, lanceolate, dark green fronds, 15-30 cm or more long, bipinnate in the lower part, the segments becoming gradually smaller toward the slender point and sharply toothed. *Subtropic.* Zone 10.   p. 139

POMADERRIS   *Rhamnaceae*
elliptica (New Zealand, Tasmania), "Kumeraho"; evergreen shrub to 2 m or more high, the shoot and foliage gray with starry down; oval or ovate leaves 5-10 cm long, white tomentose beneath; flowers in flat clusters, with light yellow petals, blooming May-June. Zone 10.   p. 825

POMETIA   *Sapindaceae*
pinnata (Malaysia to Polynesia), "Langsir"; luxuriant evergreen tree with glossy green pinnate leaves 20 cm or more long, the large corrugated leaflets in a dozen or more pairs; tiny greenish flowers hanging in long panicles, followed by nearly globular fruit with brownish rind 3 to 5 cm dia.; the seeds are edible when roasted. Photographed on Nuku Hiva, Marquesas. *Tropical.* Zones 10-11.   p. 938

PONCIRUS   *Rutaceae*
trifoliata (North China), "Hardy orange"; small, stiff-growing spiny deciduous tree to 4 m, dark green flattened branches and long stout spines 6 cm long; blooms in Spring on bare branches in axils of large spines; white flowers opening flat, to 5 cm across; trifoliate leaves, with thin-leathery shining green leaflets, on winged petiole; small orange-like, aromatic fruit to 5 cm dia., with acid pulp; fairly hardy north to Philadelphia and New Jersey. Zone 6.   p. 861

PONGAMIA   *Leguminosae*
pinnata (Trop. Asia and Australia), "Karum tree" or "Poonga-oil tree"; an ornamental tree in Southern U.S.; to 12 m high, with odd-pinnate leaves of 5-7 shining ovate leaflets to 10 cm long, having strong odor when bruised, pink when unfolding; pea-shaped flowers pale lilac, pink or occasionally white, having broad standard or banner petal and blunt keel of petals cohering at their tips; sickle-shaped woody pods containing seed, which furnish oil. Zone 10.   p. 766

PONTEDERIA   *Pontederiaceae*
cordata (Nova Scotia to Florida and Texas south), "Heartleaf pickerel-weed"; aquatic perennial herb to 1 m, with thick parallel-veined long-stalked leaves from a rootstock, heart- or arrow-shaped to 25 cm long; blue flowers in spikes; used in ponds and water-gardens. Zones 3-9.   p. 336
lanceolata (Southeast U.S.), "Pickerel-weed"; aquatic similar to P. cordata but with leaves generally lanceolate; the floral spikes shorter, with tiny blue flowers thinly hairy. *Warm temperate.* Zone 7.   p. 336

POPULUS   *Salicaceae*
alba (Europe to Siberia, natural. in No. America), "White poplar" or "Silver-leaved poplar"; wide-spreading deciduous tree to 30 m high, having smooth gray bark and soft white wood, spreading by root suckers; foliage lustrous dark green above, silvery-white felted beneath, broadly ovate on short shoots 4-5 cm long and margins wavy, on young trees and strong leading branches 8-12 cm long and 3 to 5-lobed, with each lobe triangularly toothed. Female trees produce clusters of small pods which open and discharge a cotton-like fluff. Zone 3.   p. 863
balsamifera 'Aurora', "Balsam poplar" in variegated form; handsome English cultivar from Cornwall, having foliage cream-white with green blotches in center; derived from the No. American species also known as P. tacamahaca or candicans, widespread from Labrador to Alaska, south to New York to Oregon; very hardy deciduous tree to 30 m or more high, with sticky buds and broadly ovate leathery leaves 5-12 cm long, giving off a balsam-like aroma while unfurling in Spring; sucker growth leaves may be 30 cm long. Wood used for plywood and paper pulp. Zone 2 (?).   p. 863
x canadensis (deltoides x nigra), "Carolina poplar"; robust deciduous tree of upright character, to 40 m or more high, widely planted in the past, but now barred in communities where its vigorous roots tend to clog the drains, and also lift pavements; the leaves are triangular ovate, to 10 cm long, serrate and ciliate at margins; male catkins 7 cm long. Zone 4.   p. 864
x canadensis 'Regenerata' (deltoides x nigra) (French cultivar 1814); older trees develop a fairly straight trunk with somewhat spreading branches, not typically pyramidal but rather of whisk-shaped or whorled character; bark is an attractive light gray, with young growth brown; foliage triangular and light green. Very popular in France. Zone 5.   p. 864
fremontii (California, Arizona), "Cottonwood"; round-topped tree to 25 m high or more; glossy green leaves broadly rhombic triangular 4-10 cm wide; catkins 5-10 cm long; female trees become

objectionable because of the plentiful cottony fluff discharged from their capsules. Related to P. deltoides but with wider leaves lacking glands at base and distinct by their large rounded teeth. Suitable for planting in dry areas. Zone 7.   p. 863
nigra (Europe, W. Asia), "Black poplar"; deciduous tree to 30 m tall, with dia. of trunk to 1½ m or more; bark deeply furrowed, often with knobby burs near base; trunk short, with wide-spreading branches; shoots yellowish with reddish sticky buds; leaves triangular or ovate, 5-12 cm long, green on both sides, and toothed along margins. Zone 2.   p. 864
nigra 'Italica', "Italian poplar" or "Lombardy poplar"; striking tree of columnar habit, to 30 m or more high, the branches appressed and growing directly upward; usually male; the leaves broadly ovate to near triangular wedge-shaped, and with slender tip, smaller than the species, 5-8 cm long, on reddish petioles; short-lived tree, widely planted in America for two centuries; fast growing, making a good screen, but often develops canker at the top, leaving the top dead and becoming unsightly. Zone 2.   p. 864
tremula (Europe, No. Africa, Asia Minor, Caucasus, Siberia, China), "European aspen"; deciduous tree to 20 m or more, forming an open crown, and suckering; leaves thin, grayish-green and roundish, to 8 cm long, 5 cm long on short interior twigs, margins with large teeth; woolly at first, later smooth, on flattened petioles; male catkins 5 to 10 cm long, in February. Notable for the nearly constant trembling of the foliage. Zone 2.   p. 864
tremuloides (Labrador to Alaska, Missouri to Sonora and Baja California), "Quaking aspen"; deciduous tree 6-20 m tall, with grayish-white trunk; dainty, light green round or ovate leaves to 8 cm long, and which tremble in slightest air movements; turning golden-yellow in Autumn; flowers in drooping catkins, appearing before the leaves. Zone 1.   p. 864

PORPHYROCOMA   *Acanthaceae*
pohliana (lanceolata) (Brazil); beautiful herbaceous plant with opposite, lanceolate leaves 12-15 cm long, rich green with contrasting cream-yellow veining; the inflorescence in cone-like spike with large crimson-red overlapping bracts, 2-lipped tubular flowers purple. *Tropical.* Zone 10.   p. 18

PORTEA   *Bromeliaceae*
petropolitana (Coastal S.E. Brazil); shapely rosette of shiny yellow-green leaves broadened at base and with blackish spines; erect stem with dense panicle or orange-pink ovaries and sepals and white-lavender petals. *Tropical.* Zone 10.   p. 47

PORTLANDIA   *Rubiaceae*
grandiflora (West Indies), "Glorias floridas de Cuba"; shiny tropical evergreen shrub 3-4 m high, with elliptic, leathery leaves, and large white, solitary bell-shaped flowers 12 cm long, reddish inside, very fragrant at night. Zone 10.   p. 858

PORTULACA   *Portulacaceae*
grandiflora (Brazil), "Rose-moss"; succulent herb with low spreading branches, scattered, cylindrical leaves and colorful, sun-blooming flowers 3 to 4 cm across, in rose, red, purple, yellow, or white, surrounded by whorls of leaves and tufts of hairs; grown as an annual. Plants self-sowing. *Arid-tropical.* Zone 11.   p. 200,477
oleracea (prob. India, but common in Southeast U.S.), "Purslane"; fleshy annual or perennial herb to 15 cm high, spreading with succulent branches and forming mats; spatulate to oval glossy green leaves 3 cm long, bright yellow flowers 2 cm across, in June-July. In Europe eaten as greens or in salads; older plants as potherbs or for pickling. Zone 9.   p. 542
oleracea cv. 'Belgica'; also known in horticulture as 'New Guinea species'; excellent succulent basket plant with pendant branches tipped by showy, silky salmon-rose flowers 4 cm across, almost everblooming. Zone 10.   p. 79, 319
oleracea cv. 'Wildfire' (origin prob. India), "Flowering purslane"; endearing low creeping succulent with flexuous soft branches spreading 15-30 cm wide, dense with fleshy short 3 cm obovate, glossy olive-green leaves and forming mounds; at branch ends the showy 4 cm flowers, like silky cups, in vivid colors rose, cerise, orange or yellow, closing on cloudy days, in the shade, and evenings. Ideal for hanging baskets. Usually grown as an annual. Zone 10.   p. 200, 319, 477
pilosa 'Hortualis', "Shaggy garden purslane"; ornamental cultivar of the species from No. Carolina to Mexico, having larger flowers than pilosa; fleshy trailing herb having stems with tufts of white, shaggy hairs; succulent cylindrical or boat-shaped leaves 2 cm long; red-purple flowers 2-3 cm across, opening to the full sun, and closing at night. Zone 9.   p. 477

PORTULACARIA   *Portulacaceae*
afra 'Macrophylla' (So. Africa), "Giant elephant bush"; handsome succulent neatly branching from thick brown-red stem, the

fleshy, glossy green obovate leaves to 3 cm long, much bigger though fewer than the species. Grown by Los Angeles Plant Co., Vista, California. *Subtropic. Zone 10.* *p. 198*

POSOQUERIA *Rubiaceae*
   fragrantissima (Brazil), "Brazil tree jasmine"; interesting tropical evergreen tree, with yellow branches, handsome oblong ovate leaves shining green, and main veins a contrasting yellow; pendant white flowers with slender tube 15 cm long, the narrow segments at apex deflexed, and intensely fragrant. *Zones 10-11.* *p. 858*
   longiflora (French Guiana to Colombia), "Colombian jasmine"; evergreen tropical shrub to 2 m high, at home in the lovely Valle del Cauca; narrowly oblong leaves to 20 cm long; the inflorescence of slender tubular white corollas 15 cm long, tipped by flaring lobes; heavily fragrant. *Zone 10.* *p. 858*

POTAMOGETON *Potamogetonaceae*
   natans (lucens) (Europe, Asia, Africa, No. America, New Zealand), "Pondweed"; most common species of pondweed, usually occuring in standing waters of ponds; long underwater stems develop linear phyllodes in Spring; toward top there are floating leaves; broad ovate-cordate or oval, to 12 cm long; the inflorescence in small brownish cylindric spikes. *Zone 6.* *p. 334*

POTENTILLA *Rosaceae*
   abla (Cent. Europe to Caucasus), "Cinquefoil" or "Five-fingers"; beautiful low, spreading perennial to 25 cm high, with palmate leaves of 3 to 7, but usually 5 lanceolate leaflets, at first silvery-silky beneath, later smooth and glaucous, 6 cm long; toothed at apex; white flowers to 3 cm across, in loose clusters, the petals obovate, longer than the silky, slender-pointed sepals; blooming late Spring. *Zone 5.* *p. 493*
   arbuscula hort.: see under P. davurica
   atrosanguinea (argyrophylla var.) (Himalayas), "Himalayan cinquefoil"; beautiful herbaceous perennial to 40 cm high, having silky, white-hairy, tripartite leaves with toothed margins, growing in mounds, and bearing sprays of showy flowers 2-3 cm across, scarlet-red into center, and yellow along outer margin. Photographed in Saalfeld Alpinum, East Germany, Summer 1980. *Zone 5.* *p. 493*
   davurica 'Beesii' (syn. arbuscula, fruticosa, glabrata) "Bush cinquefoil"; deciduous shrub to 1 m or more high, of broad habit, with leaves gray on both sides and silky-hairy; bright yellow flowers 2-3 cm dia., blooming from July into Autumn. English cultivar of seed from Tibet. *Zone 2.* *p. 838*
   fragiformis (Siberia to Aleutians and Alaska), "Strawberry cinquefoil"; perennial herb 12-20 cm high, spreading from thick rhizome, with strawberry-like, soft-hairy palmate leaves of 3 obovate, toothed leaflets; yellow flowers 2-3 cm across, in a few clusters, during July-August. *Zone 2.* *p. 493*
   fruticosa (North Temp. Zones), "Bushy cinquefoil" or "Golden hardhack"; perennial forming mats of dense woody growth, to 1 m high; small pinnate leaves, and bright yellow flowers to 3 cm across, blooming throughout Summer. This versatile species may be found high in the Himalayas, but also in Southern California gardens. *Zones 2-9.* *p. 321, 493, 838*
   fruticosa 'Tangerine' (No. Ireland cultivar from Chinese seed) (Donard); handsome shrub of low habit with pinnate leaves usually of 7 small elliptic leaflets; the showy flowers are 3 cm wide, beautifully colored coppery yellow to vivid salmon-rose-red. *Zone 4.* *p. 838*
   glabrata (Zander): see P. davurica, as in Hortus 3
   heptaphylla (E. Europe), "Seven-fingers"; mound-forming herbaceous perennial to 60 cm high, with pubescent stems from a rosette of foliage; the leaves palmate but dissected into 7 oblanceolate leaflets, instead of 5 as in the similar P. crantzii; flowers yellow, 3 cm across, blooming late Spring. *Zone 5.* *p. 493*
   nepalensis (Western Himalayas), "Nepal cinquefoil"; vigorous perennial to 60 cm high, spreading wide; palmate leaves with 5 obovate, toothed leaflets 3-6 cm long; attractive rose-pink flowers with purple base, 2-3 cm across, the petals wavy, and twice as long as the purplish sepals, blooming July-August. This species has given rise to several red-flowered hybrids. *Zone 5.* *p. 493*
   recta 'Warrenii' (recta: Cent. and So. Europe, natural. E. No. America), "Sulphur cinquefoil"; perennial herb with velvet-hairy stems 30-50 cm high, palmate basal leaves with 5-7 downy oblanceolate leaflets 3-10 cm long crenate or lobed along margins; large bright yellow flowers 3 cm across, profusely blooming June-August. *Zone 3.* *p. 494*
   rupestris (W. Europe to Asia Minor and Siberia), "Prairie tea"; perennial downy herb with erect reddish branches 15-45 cm high; pinnately cut and toothed, green, hairy basal leaves, and 1-2½ cm white flowers with rounded petals, in loose clusters in late Spring. *Zone 4.* *p. 494*
   x tonguei (P. anglica x nepalensis), "Tormentilla cinquefoil"; hybrid perennial forming mounds 10-20 cm high, with sprawling stems

to 30 cm long; dark green basal leaves palmately divided into 3-5 coarsely toothed leaflets 3 cm long; 2 cm flowers having yellow petals with red base, longer than the sepals, blooming July to September. *Zone 6.* *p. 494*
   tridentata (Greenland to Wisconsin, so. to Georgia), "Three toothed cinquefoil" or "Wineleaf cinquefoil"; herbaceous perennial groundcover, woody at base, and evergreen in milder areas; dark green, lustrous leaves having 3 oblong leathery leaflets to 2 cm long, and toothed at apex; small white flowers. *Zones 3-9.* *p. 320*
   verna (W. Europe), "Spring cinquefoil"; dainty, bright green, tufted creeper to 15 cm high; leaves divided into 5-7 toothed leaflets; rich yellow flowers 15 mm wide, in Spring and Summer. Good groundcover in California. *Zone 6.* *p. 321, 494*

POTERIUM *Rosaceae*
   obtusum: see SANGUISORBA obtusa (Hortus)
   sanguisorba (minor) (Europe, W. Asia, natural. in Eastern No. America), "Burnet"; smooth, glaucous perennial 15-45 cm high, with pinnate basal leaves, the leaflets 1-2 cm long; stem leaves in pairs or whorls, triangular and toothed at apex; small greenish 1 cm flowers in dense heads, during June-July. The leaves are edible and have a cool cucumber-like flavor and are used in salads, soups, cold drinks; in vinegar or in French dressing. *Zone 3.* *p. 542*

POTHOS aureus of florists: see EPIPREMNUM aureum

POUTERIA *Sapotaceae*
   campechiana (Lucuma nervosa) (Cuba to Mexico and Panama), "Canistel", "Egg-fruit" or "Ti-es"; evergreen tree with milky sap, normally to 6 m high, but may reach 15 m; the spreading branches have leathery, bright green, oblanceolate leaves 10 to 20 cm long, clustered near ends of twigs; inconspicuous greenish-white flowers in the axils of new foliage, followed in Autumn by edible fruit of sweet, musky flavor, ovoid in shape with a sharp point, 5 to 10 cm long, covered by papery, orange-yellow skin; contained inside the soft flesh are 1 to 3 large brown, glossy seeds. *Tropical. Zone 10.* *p. 869, 941*
   sapota (Calocarpum mammosum or sapota, Lucuma mammosa) (Mexico to No. South America), "Mamey sapote" or "Marmalade plum"; a favorite fruit in the West Indies and C. America; handsome open tree 10 to 20 m high, with milky juice; similar to Sapodilla, but partially deciduous, with larger, obovate leaves 10 to 30 cm long, shining green, mostly near ends of branches; small whitish, insignificant flowers, followed by elliptic-pointed fruit 8 to 20 cm long, during early Summer; the rough scaly, reddish-brown skin covering orange-red, sweet, edible pulp, and usually one large seed. *Zones 9-10.* *p. 941*

PRATIA *Lobeliaceae* or *Campanulaceae*
   angulata (New Zealand), "Creeping half-flower" or "Pa-Nake-Nake" of the Maori; creeping herb rooting at nodes and forming low mats; slender stems with thin 7 mm roundish leaves coarsely toothed; white flowers 2 cm long with 3 of the 5 petals broader and facing to one side. The genus Pratia is under Lobeliaceae in Hortus; with Campanulaceae in Royal Hort. and Zander. Somewhat winter-hardy. *Zones 9-10.* *p. 317, 455*

PRESTOEA *Palmae*
   montana (Euterpe globosa) (West Indies: Cuba, Puerto Rico, to Grenada), the "Mountain palm" or "Palma de Sierra" as it is known in the Luquillo mountain region of Puerto Rico; handsome palm to 12 m high, with ringed trunk bearing rather few, broad pinnate fronds to 2½ m. *Tropical. Zone 11.* *p. 108*

PRIMULA *Primulaceae*
   alpicola (S.E. Tibet, Bhutan, Sikkim), "Moonlight primrose"; hauntingly beautiful perennial to 50 cm high, with oblong elliptic 5-15 cm leaves, rugose on surface, and crenate at margins; fragrant, funnel-shaped flowers 1 cm long, with spreading lobes normally yellow, but varying to creamy-white or purple, in two superimposed clusters, in May-June. *Zone 5.* *p. 479*
   aurantiaca (W. China: Yunnan), "Candelabra primrose"; shapely perennial to 25 cm high, forming rosettes of oblanceolate, fleshy leaves with wrinkled surface, 20 cm long, toothed at margins, tapering to winged petiole; the narrow bell-shaped, reddish-orange flowers with flaring lobes, 2 cm across, in 2-6 superimposed whorls, on stiff brownish 25 cm stalk. *Zone 7.* *p. 479*
   auricula (Alps and other mountains of Europe), "Alpine auricula"; hardy perennial herb, with thick obovate, persisting leaves to 10 cm long and spiny at margins; the bell-shaped, fragrant flowers 2½ cm across, in clusters of 3 to 20 on long stalk, basically yellow, but in nature in several other colors red-brown, mauve and purple. *Zone 3.* *p. 480*
   auricula hybrid, "Auricula primrose" of gardens; beautiful color form with flowers having center of corolla yellow, and contrasting violet on outer petals, 3 cm across, in clusters of numerous blossoms,

rising from the handsome rosette of evergreen leaves, during Spring. Widely hybridised resulting in many bicolor forms. *Zone 3.* p. 480

beesiana (W. China: Szechwan, Yunnan); sturdy waterside primrose 35-40 cm high, with stiffish oblanceolate leaves to 25 cm long, arranged in clustering rosettes; flowers rose-red with yellow eye and orange tube, 2 cm across, in several whorls along stiff erect stalk, blooming early Summer. *Zone 6.* p. 480

x briscoei hort. (japonica x bulleyana); small perennial rosette of leathery, obovate leaves; salmon-rose flowers in umbels on erect stalk 30 cm high. *Zone 7.* p. 480

x bulleyana (W. China: Yunnan), "Yunnan candelabra"; vigorous perennial to 75 cm high, forming tufts of rosettes with lanceolate, undulate leaves 15-30 cm long, and toothed at margins; flowers deep orange, 2 cm across, with spreading notched lobes, in several superimposed whorls on stout 60 cm stalk, summer-blooming. *Zone 7.* p. 479

burmanica (Burma, China), (Candelabra group); shapely perennial to 60 cm high, forming rosettes of oblanceolate leaves to 25 cm long, tapering to a winged petiole; stiff floral stalk bearing one or more whorls of flowers, superimposed one above the other, the purplish-crimson corolla 2 cm across, and having small yellow eye, blooming in June. One of the best in the Candelabra Section, including on Pacific Coast. *Zone 6.* p. 480

capitata (Sikkim Himalayas to Tibet), "Purple-head primrose"; interesting mountain perennial to 40 cm high, with basal rosette of oblanceolate leaves to 12 cm long, white-mealy beneath, and tapering to winged petioles; long-stalked, dense floral head of small bell-shaped violet flowers around the outer circles, the center with white filaments, blooming April-May. *Zone 6.* p. 480

cockburniana (W. China: Szechwan), (Candelabra group); herbaceous perennial 40 cm high, the broad, fleshy leaves having cordate base, to 15 cm long, wrinkled on surface and dentate along margins; the inflorescence of nodding flowers creamy-yellow to orange, tinged with red, 2 cm across, in usually 1-3 superimposed clusters, blooming in June. *Zone 7.* p. 480

denticulata (Afghanistan to W. China), "Globe primrose"; hardy perennial 30-50 cm high; with thin broadly lance-shaped basal leaves, usually white-powdery and dentate and narrowed into winged petioles; the flowers in dense heads, pale purple with yellow eye, 2 cm across, the clusters surrounded by small leafy bracts; spring-blooming. *Zone 5.* p. 482

elatior (Europe to Iran), "Oxlip primrose"; perennial rosette to 20 cm high, of fresh green, broad-ovate, wrinkled leaves 8 cm long, on winged petioles; charming light to rich yellow flowers 2-3 cm across, the corolla subtended by hairy tubular, 5-angled yellowish calyx, in one-sided clusters on stalks 10-20 cm long, from March to May. *Zone 5.* p. 481

elatior pallasii (Ural Mts. to Caucasus and Iran); variety differing in having leaves oblong and wrinkled, the petioles scarcely winged; sulphur-yellow corollas with lobes recurved and subtended by narrow calyx tube; very showy in long-stalked clusters. *Zone 5.* p. 481

florindae (Himalayas of S.E. Tibet), "Giant cowslip" or "Tibetan primrose", (Sikkimensis sec.); vigorous herbaceous perennial to more than 1 m high, clustering with shining green basal leaves broadly oblong, 20 cm long, on reddish petioles extending 20 cm from base; stalks to 90 cm high, with bright sulphur-yellow, pendant, funnel-shaped fragrant flowers 2 cm across, making a great show from June to August, flourishing best by the waterside. *Zone 5.* p. 480

frondosa (C. Bulgaria, Balkans), "Balkan primrose", (Farinosae section); charming small herbaceous perennial to 15 cm high, with obovate leaves 5 to 10 cm long, densely covered with white-waxy coating beneath; very floriferous with clusters of lovely rose-pink, open bell-shaped flowers 15 mm across, tinted yellow and purple in center; spring-blooming. *Zone 6.* p. 480

helodoxa (W. China, Burma), "Amber primrose"; herbaceous perennial to 60 cm high, with oblanceolate basal leaves to 35 cm long; fragrant flowers dark amber-yellow, 2-3 cm across, and having mealy cream calyx, arranged in several umbels, one above the other, on tall stalks, blooming in Summer. *Zone 7.* p. 481

japonica (Japan, Taiwan), "Japanese candelabra primrose"; very popular perennial in American gardens; to 60 cm high, with ovate 15-20 cm leaves in clustering rosettes; stout floral stalks bearing several floral clusters one above the other, dense with purplish-red flowers 2-3 cm across, variable in color, and often with yellow eyes; blooming May-July. *Zones 5-8.* p. 481

juliae (Caucasus: Georgia); clustering, rhizomatous small perennial to 8 cm high, with winged petioles bearing thin, puckered, cordate leaves; and nearly sessile rosy to crimson flowers 2½ cm across, with red eye; hybrids come with white flowers, and with crisped leaves. *Zone 5.* p. 481

kisoana (Honshu, Japan), "Kakko-so" in Japan; charming small perennial to 20 cm high; from short rhizomes the roundish leaves 5-10 cm dia., lobed along margins, covered with soft reddish hairs;

floral stalks 10-15 cm long, topped by umbels of deep rose flowers 2-3 cm across, the corolla lobes deeply notched. *Zone 6.* p. 482

malacoides (Yunnan, China), "Fairy primrose" or "Baby primrose"; small, bushy herbaceous plant with numerous light green, smallish, papery leaves, white-hairy beneath, and toothed at margins; several straight stalks, bearing small 2 cm flowers in successive umbels above each other, lavender or rose-pink to crimson-red or white, flowering late Winter-Spring. *Subtropic.* *Zone 9.* p. 481

melanops (China: S.W. Szechwan); herbaceous perennial to 35 cm high, with neat rosette of obovate leaves crenate at margins, mealy-white or yellow beneath, the base tapering to broad winged petiole; slender trumpet flowers light purple with black eye, 2 cm across and sweetly fragrant, clustering on white-mealy 20 cm stalk. *Zone 5.* p. 482

obconica (Hupeh, China), "German primrose"; winter-blooming pot-primrose with fresh green, brittle, broad-cordate leaves sparsely covered with irritating hairs, and showy umbels of large flowers in pastel shades of rose-pink, lavender, lilac to carmine-red, or even white; with greenish eye, 4-5 cm across. *Subtropic.* p. 56, 483 *Zone 10.*

odorata; in col. Duesseldorf Bot. Garden, Germany; handsome perennial rosette of leathery, wrinkled leaves with crenate or wavy margins; small fragrant, carmine-rose flowers with white eye, on stout, farinose or pubescent stalks. *Zone 6.* p. 481

x polyantha 'Crescendo', excellent cv. of the hybrid group of P. vulgaris probably with veris and elatior the hardy "Polyanthus primrose", "Lady's fingers" or "English primrose"; popular in American gardens and blooming in early Spring; clump-forming perennial 20-30 cm high with long wrinkled, obovate leaves narrowed into winged petioles; the 4-5 cm flowers sweetly fragrant like roses, brilliant scarlet with contrasting yellow eye, borne in clusters well above foliage; (those of vulgaris are solitary). Bred for hardiness, lacking in most polyanthas. *Zones 3-8.* p. 481

x polyantha 'Pacific Giants' (elatior hyb.) "Polyanthus primrose"; very popular hybrid strain involving P. elatior, vulgaris and veris; perennials to 30 cm high, often treated as annuals; fresh green, obovate basal leaves tapering to winged petioles; large and showy flowers 5-7 cm across in brilliant shades of blue, red, pink, yellow, or white, usually with yellow center, in clusters on tall stalks, blooming from Spring onward. *Zones 5-8.* p. 481

pulverulenta (China: Szechwan), "Silverdust primrose"; a floriferous waterside perennial to 90 cm high, spreading with rosettes of oblanceolate mealy-white basal leaves to 30 cm long; the silvery stalks bearing a succession of tiered whorls of purple flowers with eye deeper red, in June. *Zone 5.* p. 482

rosea (Caucasus, Afghanistan, Himalayas), "Kashmir primrose"; small alpine perennial 12 to 15 cm high in bloom; open bell-shaped rose-colored flowers having yellow eye, 2 cm across, blooming in April; leaves not fully developed until after flowering, the blades obovate, lobed and toothed at margins. *Zone 5.* p. 482

secundiflora (Himalayas, east to Yunnan), "Sideflower primrose"; sturdy perennial rosette of fleshy, oblanceolate leaves to 30 cm long incl. petiole, finely toothed, yellow-mealy beneath while young; floral stalk 30-50 cm high, white-mealy toward apex, and bearing clusters of funnel-shaped deep rose-red flowers 2 cm across, in May-June. *Zone 5.* p. 483

sieboldii (Kyushu to Hokkaido; Siberia) (cortusoides group), "Sakkura-so"; attractive small bog-garden primrose, with white-pubescent wrinkled, ovate cordate leaves lobed and toothed at margins, 20 cm long incl. petiole; flowers normally rosy-purple with white eye, to 4 cm across, varying in color incl. white, blooming late May to June. *Zone 4.* p. 482

sikkimensis (Himalayas); hardy, strong growing perennial with 12 cm wrinkled, obovate leaves in a rosette; the small yellow flowers nodding, 3 cm wide, with powdery calyx, in clusters on 60 cm stalks, in May-June. *Zone 6.* p. 483

veris (officinalis) (No. and C. Europe, Russia), "Cowslip"; spring-blooming, clustering perennial with wrinkled, oblanceolate leaves and masses of small, fragrant, golden-yellow flowers 2 cm across, in umbels on 30 cm stalks. *Zone 5.* p. 483

vialii (littoniana) (China: N.W. Yunnan, S.W. Szechwan), "Orchid primrose"; remarkable beauty; rhizomatous perennial to 60 cm high, with lanceolate basal leaves hairy on both surfaces; the small 1 cm orchid-pink flowers in striking dense 12 cm spike and very fragrant, the unopened calyx bright scarlet, blooming June-July. *Zone 8.* p. 483

vulgaris (acaulis) (W. and So. Europe), the "English primrose"; hardy perennial, to 15 cm high, with oblong, wrinkled basal leaves and crinkled margins; numerous solitary 2½-4 cm flowers individually on slender stalks, usually sulphur-yellow, blotched with dark yellow near eye; colorforms in white, purple, blue, rose, and red. *Zone 5.* p. 482

vulgaris 'Rubra' (acaulis hort.); vigorous garden cultivar forming low rosette of broad, fleshy leaves wrinkled on surface, from the center of which rise the beautiful short-stalked solitary flowers 4-5 cm across, vivid crimson-red with large yellow eye, blooming in Spring. Some horticultural strains may occasionally have 2 or 3 blooms on a floral stalk. *Zone 5.* *p. 482*

PRITCHARDIA   *Palmae*

pacifica (Fiji, Tonga, Samoa), "Fiji fan palm"; impressive with slender, clean trunk 9 m tall, to 30 cm in dia., the numerous short-stalked palmate fronds forming a large round crown to 2½ m across, the leaves 1 m wide, bright glittering olive-green and deeply folded, very leathery, covered with brownish-white fuzz when young, only lightly cut at apex; the 1 m stalk unarmed, with brown fiber at base; 1 m spadix amongst foliage, with brownish fragrant flowers, and 1 cm lustrous blue-black fruit. *Tropical. Zone 11.* *p. 112*

PROSOPIS   *Leguminosae*

glandulosa (juliflora var.) (Kansas to N.E. Mexico), "Honey-mesquite"; large shrub to 10 m, with deep roots, branches crooked, spines to 3 cm long; leaves bipinnate, with small leaflets bright green; small yellowish flower heads; long, somewhat curved fruit, with seeds made into flour by Indians of the desert. Flowers attractive to honey bees for their sweet nectar. *Zone 7.* *p. 766, 767*

PROSTANTHERA   *Labiatae*

nivea (New So. Wales, Victoria), "Australian mint-bush"; beautiful evergreen shrub to 2 m high, with opposite linear leaves to 4 cm long, the margins incurved; spotted with resinous glands and strongly scented of mint; 2 cm flowers snow-white, pink, or tinged light blue, in large leafy sprays; spring-blooming. *Zone 10.* *p. 739*

PROTEA   *Proteaceae*

barbigera (So. Africa: S.W. Cape Prov.), "Queen protea" or "Giant woolly-beard"; most handsome, sparry evergreen shrub 1½ m high; white-hairy, light gray-green, oval, leathery leaves 15 cm long, undulate and hairy at margins; the beautiful, large inflorescence to 20 cm across, balls resembling pine cones; the outer bracts soft pink or rose, tipped with fine silvery white hairs, and surrounding a soft mass of white woolly flowers which become black-violet in the raised center of the flower heads. *Zone 9.* *p. 825*

cynaroides (So. Africa), "King protea"; characteristic, showy shrub ½-1½ m high, with varying thick-leathery stalked leaves 5-12 cm long edged red, on woody red stem; the true flowers packed in large 20 cm heads surrounded by numerous shingled series of stiff-leathery bracts as in a cup, white to delicate pink and silvery silky-downy, (Summer). *Zones 9 10.* *p. 825*

eximia (latifolia) (So. Africa), "Ray protea"; large-flowered protea from the S.W. Cape mountains; a dense shrub to 2½ m high, with broad oval, red-edged silvery leaves to 9 cm long, densely clasping and clothed around the upright branches, topped by the flower heads 12 cm long, with deep rose spoon-shaped bracts fringed with white silky hairs, the cup is filled with a mass of flowers tipped with old rose bristles. *Zone 9.* *p. 825*

grandiceps (So. Africa), "Peach protea"; most beautiful neat, dense shrub from the high Cape mountains; its elliptic, leathery, 12 cm highly decorative grayish leaves edged in red, and arranged closely and regularly on woody branches; the 10 cm flower head with 7 or 8 whorls of incurving rosy-salmon or coral bracts arranged like in an artichoke, and with soft white hairs. *Zone 9.* *p. 824*

longiflora (S.W. Cape Prov.); sparry shrub to 3 m high, with sessile elliptic leaves to 10 cm long; the bisexual inflorescence on branches with greenish-white bracts cradling the numerous whitish and pink flowers with their long stamens and pistils. *Zone 9.* *p. 824*

magnifica (speciosa) (So. Africa), "Brown-bearded protea"; robust shrub to 1 m high, with stout woody branches and woolly shoots; leathery oblong leaves 3-12 cm long, the margins thickened and wavy; the showy floral heads 12 cm wide, with brownish-tipped silky-hairy bracts creamy-white, in 7-8 series; the small dark true flowers in center. *Zone 9.* *p. 824*

neriifolia (So. Africa: Cape), the "Pink mink" or "Oleander-leaved protea"; large floriferous bush to 3 m high, with long narrow linear, leathery leaves, and a showy terminal inflorescence 12 cm long, of cupping, shingled bracts pale salmon to deep rose with silvery sheen, the tips white and incurving and bearded with purplish-black, set off against the mass of tawny-colored little flowers within the head. *Zone 9.* *p. 825*

repens (mellifera) (So. Africa: Cape), "Sugarbush" or "Honey-protea"; a shapely evergreen one cannot help admiring when travelling down the Cape Peninsula; large rounded bush to 3 m, its woody branches with dense whorls of silvery glaucous, leathery, elliptic leaves 8-12 cm long; terminal inflorescence, 12 cm long, of shingled, smooth, shiny and silky, sticky bracts, varying in color from white to nearly red. In the early morning these cupped heads are half filled with nectar which the early colonists boiled into syrup in the absence of sugar. *Zone 9.* *p. 825*

PRUNELLA   *Labiatae*

grandiflora (S.E. Europe, to Caucasus), "Self-heal"; spreading herbaceous perennial 30 cm high, forming mounds of ovate, ever-green leaves, often toothed; blooming during Summer with long-stalked clusters of pretty flowers having lobed corolla 3 cm long, with whitish tube and lips rosy-violet. *Zone 5.* *p. 436*

vulgaris (Mediterran. reg. to C. Asia; widely naturalized in No. America), "Heal-all"; herbaceous perennial, to 60 cm high, with prostrate or ascending, pubescent 4-angled branches; ovate or lanceolate 5 cm leaves, usually toothed and often purplish; the 2-lipped pink or purple 2 cm flowers in terminal clusters, during July to September. Widespread as a weed in lawns. Cultivated in herb gardens for its historic use as folk medicine for the cure of tonsilitis. *Zone 3.* *p. 436*

PRUNUS   *Rosaceae*

amygdalus: see P. dulcis

armeniaca (Turkestan to Manchuria, natur. in Asia Minor), "Apricot"; small tree with reddish bark and smooth twigs; ovate leaves 5-8 cm long; flowers before the leaves, pinkish-white; yellow sweet edible fruit flushed with red, with ridge on one side, 3-4 cm dia. *Zone 4.* *p. 839*

armeniaca 'Moorpark' (China), "Moorpark apricot"; small round-crowned tree with reddish bark and smooth twigs; leaves subcordate 5-8 cm long; 2 cm flowers pinkish, before the leaves; large smooth pubescent fruit yellow flushed with red, 5 cm dia., excellent rich flavor, ideal for home garden. *Zones 6-9.* *p. 929*

armeniaca 'Royal' ('Blenheim') "California apricot"; medium to large 3-4 cm fruit yellow to orange-yellow, aromatic orange flesh; California standard commercial variety. Delicious sweet fruit nearly identical to 'Blenheim' of England. *Zones 7-9.* *p. 929*

avium 'Bing' (Oregon 1875), "Bing cherry"; this famous cultivar is a vigorous wide-spreading tree, producing heavy crops of one of the best sweet cherries of consistently large size fruit with glossy deep mahogany-red, firm mealy yet juicy flesh, ripening midseason. Delicious for table use, and excellent for canning. *Zones 6-8.* *p. 929*

avium 'Black Tartarian' (Russia), "Mazzard cherry"; popular purple-black oxheart cherry, with fruit not as large as 'Bing', but thick and sweet; glossy red to dark purple skin; very productive in large clusters; softens quickly when picked; one of the earliest to ripen. Needs pollinizer, as all sweet cherries, but any other variety of sweet cherries will bring results. *Zone 3.* *p. 929*

avium 'Early French' (Rhone Valley, Eurasia, natural. in No. America), "Sweet cherry"; cultivated in warm vineyard areas of Southern France; medium size deciduous tree with high crown; early to bloom, followed by clusters of 2 cm cherries having dark crimson to near-black skin, holding soft, juicy flesh of high sugar content, ripening early in season. Important commercial fruit for table use, but also as preserves and for liqueur. *Zones 5-8.* *p. 928*

avium 'Windsor', "Black oxheart cherry"; sweet cherry tree of vigorous upright growth freely producing one of the best dark cherries, with firm pinkish flesh and almost black skin; large and juicy, delicious to eat fresh; ripening late July in New York State. *Zone 3.* *p. 929*

caroliniana (No. Carolina to Texas), "Carolina laurel", "Cherry laurel" or "Mock-orange"; native evergreen cherry-laurel to 15 m or more, dense with glossy green, thin-leathery, obovate leaves 5-10 cm long, occasionally with teeth; small creamy-white flowers, followed by small 1 cm shining black fruit. *Zone 8.* *p. 839*

cerasifera 'Atropurpurea' (pissardii) (Balkans to C. Asia), "Pissard plum" or "Purple-leaf plum"; ornamental deciduous shrub or small tree to 8 m; ovate leaves 4-8 cm long, dark purple becoming greenish-bronze in late Summer, margins crenate; white flowers, and small red plums of sweet taste, and known as "Cherry plums". Planted in California for its colorful foliage. *Zone 4.* *p. 839*

cerasifera 'Thundercloud' (Oregon 1937), improved P. pissardii, "Purple leaf plum"; prob. the best of the purple flowering plums, with rich dark foliage; handsome tree to 6 m high, with rounded crown; flowers light pinkish to white; sometimes producing small red cherry plums. *Zone 4.* *p. 839*

cerasifera 'Vesuvius'; developed by Luther Burbank before 1929; small round-headed deciduous tree with twiggy, slender ascending and spreading branches; leaves are large and deep purplish-red, and remain so through the season; light pink flowers appear in early Spring. *Zone 4.* *p. 839*

cerasus var. austera (S.E. Europe, W. Asia), "Morello cherry", "Schatten-morelle"; a self-fertile variety known as "Sour cherry"; round-headed tree to 6 m high, suckering at base; elliptic ovate leaves 5-8 cm long, shining green and finely toothed; flowers white or pinkish 2-3 cm across, blooming in May together with new unfolding foliage; glossy red to blackish fruit with soft, acid-tart red flesh and juice, and roundish stone. Used for cakes and preserves. *Zone 3.* *p. 928*

cerasus 'Montmorency', "Sour cherry" or "Sweet-tart cherry"; preferred variety with small 1½ cm bright red, soft, sweet-tart fruit, richly filled with tasty red juice; slender deciduous tree 6-8 m high. *Zone 3.*   *p. 839, 928*

domestica (Eurasia), "Garden plum" or "Italian plum"; small unarmed deciduous tree 6-9 m high, with dull green ovate leaves 10 cm long, serrate at margins; whitish or pinkish flowers 2 cm dia., before the leaves; ovoid violet juicy fruit with yellowish sweet flesh, containing elliptic free, non-cling stone. *Zones 4-9.*   *p. 839, 929*

domestica var. cerea (insititia) (Europe to W. Asia), "Mirabelle"; a small freestone fruit, oblong or nearly round, 3 cm dia., yellow to greenish, sometimes lightly tinted red; the juicy flesh similar to Green Gage plum, of aromatic, spicy-sweet flavor as eaten fresh; also for preserves and to make brandy. A characteristic deciduous tree with brown bark, drooping, toothed leaves, and white flowers, cultivated since ancient times; widely grown in France. *Zone 6.*   *p. 929*

domestica 'Green Gage' (italica) (France), "Reine Claude"; old French variety, with smooth globular, green to yellowish fruit shaded or streaked with bronzy red; the flesh is amber and very sweet and juicy, embedding a large stone, ripening in August; trees are medium-size and self-pollinating; very popular in the European countryside, for eating fresh, or as preserves. *Zone 6.*   *p. 930*

dulcis (amygdalus) (W. Asia), the "Almond"; deciduous peach-like tree 6-10 m high, with gray bark; lanceolate firm, shining leaves, finely serrate; large, showy 3 cm pink flowers with red center, appearing before the leaves; fruit a compressed stone-fruit with hard flesh, 4 cm long, splitting open at maturity and freeing the pitted kernel (almond). Limited to areas with less frost than tolerated by peach; in U.S. confined mainly to California. *Zone 6.*   *p. 839, 925*

dulcis cv. 'Texas', "Sweet almond" or "Mission almond"; cultivar more hardy than species; tree to 10 m high, with broad crown, the twigs smooth, bearing lanceolate leaves 8-12 cm long, thinly toothed at margins; blooming before the foliage, with white to pinkish flowers 3 cm across; the oblong, 6 cm flattened fruit is green and dry when ripe but inedible, finally splitting to expose the nut which is pitted for its sweet-tasting kernel, the important almond, grown worldwide in subtropic regions, including California, in many cultivars; uses in bakery or chocolate, fresh or roasted. *Zones 5-8.*   *p. 934*

fruticosa (Cent. Europe, Siberia), "European dwarf cherry"; densely spreading deciduous shrub 1 m or more high, forming mounds, with obovate, dark glossy green leaves 2-5 cm long, bluntly toothed at sides; pretty white flowers with flaring lobes, blooming in May; small 1 cm dark red round fruit of harsh taste. Cultivated in Europe over 3 centuries, often grafted high on P. avium as standards, with branches pendant. Valued for its hardiness. *Zone 3.*   *p. 840*

glandulosa (Japan, China), "Dwarf flowering almond"; small deciduous shrub to 1½ m high, very beautiful when in bloom along the many short branches covered with 1 cm single white or pink flowers, in May; the ovate, toothed leaves 3-10 cm long; small fruit nearly round and dark red. *Zone 5.*   *p. 840*

glandulosa 'Sinensis' (China), "Double-flowered almond"; strikingly handsome Chinese shrub just covered with showy clusters of double pink flowers in Spring; the leaves darker than the species; widely used for early forcing in greenhouses in No. Europe. *Zone 6.*   *p. 840*

ilicifolia (Alta California to Baja California), "Holly-leaf cherry" or "Evergreen cherry"; dense evergreen shrub or small tree 2 to 8 m high, with shiny green, leathery ovate leaves 3-5 cm long, toothed and crisped at margins; small white 1 cm flowers in erect cylindric racemes, July-blooming; berry-like fruit ovoid, first red then ripening to purplish-black, with thin, sweetish pulp. *Zones 6-9.*   *p. 830*

laurocerasus (S.E. Europe to Iran), "English laurel" or "Cherry laurel"; decorative, quick growing, evergreen bush with smooth, pale green shoots and broad, handsome, leathery, dense foliage, dark glossy green, oblong-pointed, to 15 cm long; small, white flowers, and dark purple fruit. *Zone 6.*   *p. 840*

laurocerasus 'Otto Luyken'; excellent cultivar by Hesse, and used in German landscaping as a very compact form of English laurel; short and bushy 50 cm high, the foliage dense and glossy dark green, to 10 cm long and 2-3 cm wide, slender pointed; free-blooming with spikes of white flowers in May; winter-hardy in C. Europe. *Zone 6.*   *p. 618, 840*

laurocerasus 'Schipkaensis', a hardier form of "Cherry laurel"; from the Schipka Pass in Bulgaria; with narrower glossy green leaves 5-11 cm long, only faintly toothed, on handsome yellow-green branches. *Zone 6.*   *p. 840*

lyonii (integrifolia) (Isl. off California), "Catalina cherry"; bushy evergreen tree 4 to 8 m high, with gray-brown bark becoming fissured; glossy green, oblong ovate leaves 3-8 cm long; small white flowers in axillary racemes, followed by red to dark purple, almost black ovoid fruit 2 cm long. Very ornamental because of its dark glossy foliage. *Zone 8.*   *p. 840*

mahaleb (Europe to W. Asia), "St. Lucie cherry" or "Rock-cherry"; deciduous tree to 10 m high, with spreading crown; leaves rounded to broad-ovate 2-6 cm long, having short abrupt point, and crenate at sides; fragrant white flowers in showy clusters, in April-May; followed by ovoid, nearly black fruit. Seedlings used as understock for grafting cherries. Aromatic wood is made into pipestems. *Zone 5.*   *p. 840*

maritima (Coastal Maine to Delaware), "Beach plum"; straggling deciduous shrub 2 to 3 m high, with ovate to obovate leaves 3-6 cm long; white flowers 2 cm across, blooming in great mass of elongate erect racemes in May; the 2 cm red fruit is edible, with tart, acid flesh; used for jams and jellies. *Zone 3.*   *p. 840*

mume (China and Japan), "Japanese apricot"; deciduous tree to 10 m, with thin green twigs; ovate 4-10 cm leaves; flowers before foliage, 3 cm dia., white or pinkish with red eye, and sweetly fragrant; the yellow or greenish 3 cm fruit is edible although bitter, and used to make liquor. *Zone 6.*   *p. 842*

mume 'Alboplena', "Double-flowered Japanese apricot"; seen in China as dwarfed Penjing, usually grown in shallow terracotta bowls; with small white flowers semi-double and fragrant, appearing in late Winter long before foliage. *Zone 6.*   *p. 625*

padus (Europe to Japan), "European bird cherry"; deciduous tree to 15 m high, having peeling bark, and downy branchlets, with obovate or oval leaves 8-12 cm long, finely toothed, and dull dark green above; small 1 cm white, fragrant flowers having petals toothed, dense in pendant racemes, blooming in May; small ovoid black cherries of bitter, astringent taste loved by birds. The wood is used for furniture and interior work. *Zone 3.*   *p. 842, 928*

persica (Amygdalus) (China), "Peach tree" or "Good-luck peach" for the Chinese New Year; normally a bushy tree, but trained by pruning and starving into dwarf forms in Japan and China, with masses of solitary, delicate pink flowers in advance of the lanceolate foliage, early in Spring. *Warm temperate. Zones 5-8.*   *p. 208, 842*

persica 'Alboplena', "Double-flowered white peach"; wide-spreading multi-trunk tree, covered at time of bloom with multitudes of pure white, fully double flowers in Spring, which was October in the Southern Hemisphere, when photographed in Pretoria, Transvaal. *Zone 5.*   *p. 841*

persica 'Bonanza' (California origin); genetic dwarf peach; one of the oldest and widely known dwarf peach trees of compact growth to 2 m high; showy pink semi-double flowers, followed by medium to large size fruit, the skin orange with red blush, covering firm sweet flesh with melting body, very aromatic in taste; freestone in character, and ripening early in season. *Zones 5-9.*   *p. 930*

persica 'Elberta', "Elberta peach"; medium to large yellow freestone peach, skin blushed red; high quality; midseason; needs winter chill. Originated in Georgia 1970; a favorite for home gardens, self-fruitful tree of medium size, often grafted on Siberian rootstock; a leading commercial, juicy processing peach for canning; good shipper. *Zones 5-9.*   *p. 842, 930*

persica 'Golden Jubilee'; a standard variety of freestone peach originating in New Jersey but also grown in California; fruit of medium size with firm yellow flesh of fair flavor; skin yellow and mottled bright red; early, ripening 3 weeks before 'Elberta'. *Zone 5.*   *p. 930*

persica nucipersica (syn. var. nectarina) (China); a "Nectarine" popular in California; small deciduous tree, with long-lanceolate, finely toothed leaves 8-15 cm long; charming pink or red flowers to 3 cm across, blooming before the foliage appears in Spring; the good-looking fruit 5-8 cm in dia., the glossy skin basically orange-yellow but tinted red on the side exposed to the sun, very juicy and sweet; the stone deeply furrowed, fruiting from April to June. *Zone 5.*   *p. 930*

persica 'Rubra plena', "Double flowering peach"; small deciduous tree, blooming before the foliage appears in Spring, then literally covered with masses of brilliant carmine-red blossoms having double petals, 3 cm across. *Zone 5.*   *p. 841*

persica 'Santa Rosa', "Freestone peach"; freestone peach for Southern California; medium size with yellow flesh, fruiting in August. *Zones 6-10.*   *p. 930*

persica 'Sim's Cling'; large clear yellow cling peach of good canning quality; flesh yellow to the pit; late August. Very satisfactory in So. California. *Zones 5-9.*   *p. 930*

persica 'Ventura' (California), "Freestone peach"; medium sized attractive yellow freestone peach with smooth skin tinted wine-red; firm flesh slightly acid-sweet; good producer; requiring only minimal chilling period. *Zones 6-9.*   *p. 930*

'Plumcot' (armeniaca x salicina); a hybrid of plum with apricot, photographed at Tropic World, Escondido, California; slender deciduous tree with ovate leaves glossy green; very attractive when in rose-pink bud, followed by globular stone-fruit about 5 cm dia., vivid red to purplish, lightly wax-coated; the thin skin enclosing delicious, juicy flesh of rich tart-sweet taste. *Zones 6-9.*   *p. 928*

salicifolia (C. America), "Capulin cherry" or "Tropical cherry"; small tree to 10 m, with obovate leaves toothed at margins, glaucous beneath; white flowers; sweet-tasting globular fruit 2 cm dia., maroon-purple with green flesh somewhat bland in flavor. *Subtropic. Zones* 8-10. *p. 929*

salicina 'Great Yellow' (China), "Great yellow plum" or "Japan plum"; small smooth tree to 7 m high; obovate, pointed leaves, serrate at margins; 2 cm white flowers; sweet fruit yellow or light red, 5-6 cm dia. *Zones* 6-9. *p. 930*

salicina 'Satsuma' (Japan), "Japanese plum"; improved by Luther Burbank, Santa Rosa, Calif.; upright deciduous tree, bearing medium-sized round fruit with dull red skin, with juicy, sweet red flesh of mild flavor; freestone with small pit. Used for desserts and preserves. *Zones* 6-9. *p. 929*

serotina (Nova Scotia to No. Dakota, south to Florida and Texas), "Black cherry" or "Rum cherry"; handsome tree to 25 m high, with gracefully arching branches, having dark brown outer bark, and aromatic inner cambium; lustrous, peach-like lanceolate shining green leaves to 15 cm long, having hard incurved teeth along sides; small 1 cm fragrant white flowers in cylindric racemes to 15 cm long; cherry fruits red to purple-black, astringent to sweet of taste. *Zone* 3. *p. 842*

serrula (W. China); striking tree to 10 m high, with beautiful glossy red-brown mahogany colored trunk and branches, the bark later flaking; the young branchlets finely pubescent; lanceolate leaves 4-10 cm long and finely toothed, having 9-15 pairs of veins; small white flowers in late April, followed by oval red fruit. *Zone* 5. *p. 841*

serrulata (E. Asia), "Japanese flowering cherry"; deciduous tree to 20 m, with shining ovate leaves 6-10 cm long, serrate at margins; double white flowers with or before foliage, early to Mid-May; followed by small black fruit. *Zone* 5. *p. 841*

serrulata 'Amanogawa'; small picturesque deciduous tree of stiff columnar habit, 6 to 8 m high; glossy leaves ovate-pointed with serrate margins; fragrant light shell pink flowers 4 cm across, single or semi-double, medium-late, slightly fragrant. *Zone* 5. *p. 842*

serrulata 'Kwansan' (properly 'Sekiyama') (Japan), "Japanese double flowering cherry"; deciduous tree to 12 m high, with glossy reddish bark and stiffly ascending branches, ovate leaves with bristly teeth, turning reddish in late Autumn; large double, deep rose-pink flowers 5 cm across of up to 30 petals, in pendant clusters of 2 to 5, blooming late in Spring, usually before foliage. The nomenclature of these ornamental cherries is highly confused, having been hybridized and cultivated in Japan for centuries. *Zone* 5. *p. 841*

serrulata 'Shidare Sakura' (prob. from China, cult. in Japan), "Oriental flowering cherry"; small tree with broad crown, 3 m or more high; in Autumn with foliage golden-yellow; flowers in bud rose, when opening to near white, semi-double, 5 cm dia., the petals fringed at tips, in pendant clusters, late blooming to June. *Zone* 5. *p. 842*

spinosa (Cent. Europe to Siberia, No. Africa), "Blackthorn" or "Sloe"; densely branched deciduous, spiny shrub 2-3 m high, suckering from the base, with black shoots; small obovate 3 cm toothed leaves; profusely blooming in Spring before the foliage, with white flowers; followed by waxy, blue-black berries; they are picked after frost and are of astringent flavor, but are primarily used to make, with sugar, delicious fruit juice; also in flavoring of liqueur. *Zone* 4. *p. 925*

subhirtella (Japan), "Higan cherry" or "Rosebud cherry"; early-blooming deciduous shrub or tree 8-12 m high, with ovate slender-pointed leaves 4-8 cm long, sharply toothed at margins, downy on veins beneath; single flowers rose-pink to nearly white, 3 cm across, in showy pendant clusters in April; ovoid 1 cm black cherries in early Summer, hidden by the foliage. *Zone* 5. *p. 842*

triloba (plena) (China), a graceful shrub or tree to 5 m high, known as "Double flowering almond"; often grown as a small standard and forced; with serrate, deciduous leaves, the dainty, double pink flowers flushed with rose 2-3 cm across, unfolding ahead of the foliage from tight round buds set closely along woody branches of last year's growth, in Spring. Usually grafted as standards. *Zone* 5. *p. 842*

triloba 'Multiplex' (China), "Double flowering almond", deciduous shrub or tree-like to 3 m high; blooming with exceptionally large double pink flowers 4 cm across, before foliage appears in Spring. *Zone* 5. *p. 842*

virginiana (Newfoundland to W. Canada, No. Carolina and Kansas), "Choke cherry"; deciduous shrub or small tree to 4 m high, with elliptic to obovate leaves 5-12 cm long, finely toothed at sides; blooming with the unfolding foliage; white flowers in dense pendant clusters, followed in early Summer by the lustrous, juicy dark red 1 cm fruit of rather acid astringent, harsh taste; but used for wine-making, pies and jellies, and also relished by birds and eaten by the bears in Rocky Mountain region. *Zone* 2. *p. 928*

x yedoensis (Japan), "Yoshino cherry"; multi-trunked, wide-spreading tree to 15 m high, with broadly ovate dark green leaves 6-12 cm long, and sharply toothed; profuse single flowers soft pink becoming white, 2½ cm across, slightly fragrant, and early blooming

March-April, usually before leaves; small black, bitter fruit. These are the single-flowered cherries around the Tidal Basin, Washington, D.C. *Zone* 5. *p. 841*

PSEUDANANAS   *Bromeliaceae*
sagenarius (Ananas sagenaria) (Paraguay, Brazil, Bolivia); robust terrestrial, forming thickets by sending out underground stolons; larger than ananas, with stiff, strap-like leaves to 120 cm long, shiny coppery green and with barbed spines at margins; the succulent, flattened inflorescence with spiny pink bracts and lavender flowers; edible fruit but without the topknot of the true pineapple. *Zone* 11. *p. 47*

PSEUDARTHRIA   *Leguminosae*
hookeri (Trop. So. Africa, Zululand); sparry shrub to 2 m high, the branches and petioles covered by beige hairs; trifoliolate leaves with fleshy ovate, pubescent leaflets 8-10 cm long; racemes of small bilabiate, rose-purple flowers 1 cm long, the broad lip light lavender. Photographed in the Vally of 1000 Hills, and checked in Kirstenbosch Bot. Gardens. *Zone* 10. *p. 768*

PSEUDERANTHEMUM   *Acanthaceae*
alatum (Mexico), "Chocolate plant"; low growing herb with copper brown papery leaves, 8-10 cm long, on flat, winged petioles, silver blotching near midrib; gray beneath; small salverform, purple flowers in racemes. *Tropical. Zone* 10. *p. 18*

atropurpureum 'Variegatum' (Polynesia); colorful woody ever-green shrub with dense erect branches; attractive waxy, elliptic leaves 10-15 cm long, variegated coppery purple with rose, gray-green, yellow and white; small rose-purplish flowers with red markings at branch tips. *Zone* 10. *p. 630*

graciliflorum (Asystasia chelonoides hort.) (Penang, Sri Lanka, India); scandent tropical subshrub to 1 m or more high, the straggling branches with elliptic 10 cm leaves; the flowers in elongate terminal clusters, the corolla slender tubular with flaring rose-purple lobes. *Zone* 10. *p. 630*

kewense (South Pacific, Solomon Islands); low tropical subshrub, with herbaceous, broad ovate leaves glossy purple above, corrugated with veins depressed and green beneath; flowers in spike-like clusters, the corolla tube slender and 3 cm long, the flaring lobes white and fringed with hairs. *Zone* 11. *p. 630*

reticulatum (New Hebrides), "Yellow-vein eranthemum"; tropical shrub with attractive lanceolate smooth foliage, slightly fleshy, green with reticulation of golden-yellow veins; 3 cm flowers with wine-purple in throat, and dots of same color on lower lip. *Zone* 11. *p. 630*

sinuatum hort. (longifolia) (New Caledonia); shrubby plant with linear leaves 8 cm long, olive-green mottled with gray, the margins deeply scalloped, purplish beneath; white flowers in terminal racemes, 3 cm across, freely spotted rosy-lavender. *Zone* 11. *p. 631*

PSEUDOBOMBAX   *Bombacaceae*
ellipticum (Mexico: Jalisco, Veracruz to Yucatán), the "Shaving brush"; a large soft-wooded tree with green trunk; the large deciduous leaves of 5 leaflets finger-like, wine-red when young, later dark green; the flower buds composed of 5 purplish petals stuck together, later bursting open and revealing a bundle of delicate, silky rose-pink stamens 8 cm long, tipped with golden anthers. *Tropical. Zones* 10-11. *p. 667*

PSEUDOCALYMMA   *Bignoniaceae*
alliaceum (Guyana, Brazil), "Garlic vine" or the true "Garlic-scented vine"; ornamental woody climber with leaves of two ovate, leathery leaflets 10 cm long, with or without tendril between them, the leaf-tips curling downward; 5-lobed flowers 6 cm across, light purple with creamy throat, in clusters. Crushed leaves and blooms have a faint garlic odor. *Tropical. p. 269*

PSEUDOLARIX   *Pinaceae (Coniferae)*
amabilis (kaempferi) (Chrysolarix amabilis) (E. China), "Golden larch"; deciduous conifer 15 to 20 m high, often almost as wide at base, with spreading branches, pendulous at tips; linear needles 4-6 cm long, mainly clustered in tufts, bluish-green, turning golden-yellow in Autumn; pendant 8 cm cones resembling flowers, which will scatter in the Fall and drop. *Zone* 5. *p. 602*

PSEUDOMAMMILLARIA camptotriche (Zander):
   see MAMMILLARIA

PSEUDOPANAX   *Araliaceae*
'Adiantifolius' (lessonii x crassifolius) (New Zealand); robust shrub of flexible stems with spatulate lobed, leathery green leaves; small whitish flowers in heavy cluster. *Subtropic. Zone* 9. *p. 651*

arboreus (Neopanax) (New Zealand), known as "Five fingers"; evergreen tree with palmately compound leaves, the stalked segments leathery, dark green with coarsely serrate margins, pale center veins, and brownish stem. *Zone* 9. *p. 651*

ferox (New Zealand), "Lancewood"; interesting slender evergreen tree to 6 m high, with variable, thick and stiff leaves 15 to 50 cm long, linear, later obovate, chocolate-brown with pale brown midrib; margins jaggedly toothed. *Zone 10.*   p. 651

laetus (Neopanax) (New Zealand); willowy shrub to 3 m high, with slender, smooth branches and fine leathery leaves palmately compound usually of 5 broad elliptic leaflets; very attractive with purplish-red petioles and midribs; robust, tough and vigorous. *Zone 9.* p. 651

lessonii (New Zealand), "False panax"; small evergreen tree with palmately compound leaves, the segments are obovate, shining and leathery, toothed toward apex. *Zone 10.*   p. 651

lessonii 'Goldsplash', "Gold panax", a decorative California mutant, multi-stemmed and bushy, with palmately compound leathery leaves, the usually 5 obovate leaflets to 10 cm long, dark green with yellow variegation along ribs. *Zone 10.*   p. 36

PSEUDOPHOENIX   *Palmae*
sargentii (Florida, Mexico, Honduras), "Cherry palm"; tropical feather palm with solitary trunk to 8 m tall, topped by a crown of handsome pinnate fronds to 3 m long, the leaflets in several planes and in groups of 2 to 6 at the middle; the fleshy cherry-like fruit is red. *Zone 12.*   p. 109

PSEUDOSASA   *Gramineae*
japonica (Bambusa Metake) (Japan), the "Female arrow bamboo" or "Hardy Metake bamboo"; a running bamboo of moderate size; with hollow round stems 2 to 4 m high and to 1½ cm dia., from creeping rootstocks, with broad deep green foliage 10-30 cm long, glaucous beneath. Fairly hardy in New Jersey, where it has flowered; withstanding freezing to -18°C. One of the best for decoration in tubs, holding leaves better than other species; for cool bright rooms; keep moist. *Zones 7-10.*   p. 556

PSEUDOTSUGA   *Pinaceae (Coniferae)*
menziesii (douglasii, taxifolia) (Brit. Columbia to California), "Douglas fir"; graceful tree to 60 m high, pyramidal when young, the crown very broad in older trees, with trunk to 4 m in dia., bark brown, fissured into broad ridges; the spreading branches slightly pendulous; needles shining dark green 2-3 cm long, and smelling of camphor; cones pendulous, elongate to 10 cm long, 3-4 cm dia. A major timber tree on the Pacific Coast. *Zone 6.*   p. 603, 604

PSIADIA   *Compositae*
trinerva (Mauritius); handsome evergreen shrub to 1½ m high, with glossy green, lanceolate leaves to 12 cm long, having 3 prominent parallel veins depressed; showy terminal clusters of small fragrant white flowers. Photographed in Sydney Bot. Garden, Australia. *Zone 10.*   p. 690

PSIDIUM   *Myrtaceae*
guajava (W. Indies, Mexico to Perú), "Apple guava", "Tropical guava" or "Common guava"; small branching tree, reaching 9 m; 4-angled branchlets with light green, elliptic, corrugated leaves, hairy beneath; large white fragrant flowers, and producing edible, globose yellow, sweet flavored fruit 4-8 cm dia., used for making jam, jellies and salads, but usually eaten fresh. *Zone 10.*   p. 918

guineense (Trop. America), "Guyana guava"; evergreen shrub or small tree to 6 m high; oblong leathery leaves to 12 cm long, rusty hairy beneath; fragrant white flowers; large luscious-looking red to yellow fruit 4 cm dia., slightly acid to the taste. *Zones 9-10.* p. 802

littorale (lucidum in hort.) (Brazil), "Yellow Strawberry guava" or "Cattley"; evergreen shrub or small tree to 6 m high, with glossy green, leathery, obovate leaves 5-10 cm long; small white 2 cm flowers displaying numerous stamens, followed by juicy oval-pointed 3 cm fruit with sulphur-yellow skin, and flesh with many seeds imbedded in a tart sweet resinous pulp. Eaten fresh, in salads, or made into jellies; high in Vitamin C. Ripens from June to August. *Zone 9.*   p. 918

littorale longipes (cattleianum hort.) (Brazil), "Purple Strawberry guava"; dense shrub to 7½ m high, smooth branches with obovate, leathery leaves 5-8 cm long; white flowers with many stamens, and 4 cm berry-like purplish-red fruit with strawberry flavor. *Subtropic.* *Zone 9.*   p. 918

PSILOTBONNA tagetes (Eliovson):   see GAMOLEPIS tagetes

PSITTACANTHUS   *Loranthaceae*
americanus (Mexico: Sinaloa, Veracruz, Yucatán, Chiapas; C. America, W. Indies), "Parrot flower" showy parasite on hardwood trees; green leaves 6-10 cm long; clusters of bright red flowers. *Zones 10-11.*   p. 208

PSYCHOTRIA   *Rubiaceae*
rubra (Taiwan), "Wild coffee"; small tropical evergreen shrub, with oblanceolate leaves 8-18 cm long, shining green, with veins depressed; glossy scarlet-red berries, resembling coffee beans. *Zone 10.*   p. 858

PSYLLIOSTACHYS   *Plumbaginaceae*
suworowii (Limonium) (C. Asia to Iran and Israel), "Sea lavender"; annual herb with oblanceolate leaves 15 cm long; inflorescence in spikelets 40 cm long, with funnel-form flowers rosy-purple. *Zone 9 as annual.*   p. 472

PTELEA   *Rutaceae*
trifoliata (New York, Ontario, so. to Florida and Texas), "Stinking ash" or "Hoptree"; aromatic tree to 6 m high, having chestnut-brown bark; deciduous trifoliolate scented leaves; the elliptic dark green leaflets 6-15 cm long and usually finely toothed; small greenish-white flowers in 8 cm clusters during June; 1-2 seeded fruit densely clustered, each with circular wing, and used as substitute for hops. *Zone 4.*   p. 861

PTERIDIUM   *Polypodiaceae (Filices)*
aquilinum (Worldwide, both Temperate and Tropic), the "Bracken" or "Eagle-fern"; coarse-looking fern with wide-creeping, underground rhizomes; the black-polished stalks carry the great tri-pinnate, feathery fronds to more than 1 m long and 75 cm wide in cool climates, immense and to 3 m high in the tropics; the pinnae are bright green and somewhat tough in texture, and sometimes pubescent. *Zones 3-10.*   p. 140

PTERIS   *Polypodiaceae (Filices)*
adiantoides of hort.: see PELLAEA viridis macrophylla

cretica 'Childsii'; handsome cultivar with its pinnate fronds consisting of broad, fresh green leaflets prettily frilled, lobed, or wavy along margins. *Humid-tropical. Zones 10-11.*   p. 140

ensiformis 'Victoriae', "Victoria fern" or "Table fern"; an elegant, graceful little fern with both the short, broad sterile fronds and the abundant, erect, slender fertile fronds having leaflets beautifully banded white, bordered by a wavy margin of rich green. *Humid-tropical. Zone 11.*   p. 140

tremula (New Zealand, Tasmania, New South Wales), "Australian bracken"; robust grower, with large, attractive, bright green, herbaceous, broad, 3-4-pinnate fronds to 1 m high and spreading; lower pinnae often compound, upper segments linear and finely crenate, on stiff brown stems. I have found this species in northern New South Wales, growing to 1 m high, in dry forest gullies. *Zones 10-11.*   p. 140

PTEROCARPUS   *Leguminosae*
indicus (India to China, Malay Arch., Philippine Isl.), "Narra tree" or "Burmese rosewood"; tropical tree 10 to 25 m high; leaves odd-pinnate with 5-9 ovate leaflets to 10 cm long; yellow pea-flowers in axillary racemes, blooming in May; interesting silky orbicular seed pods 5 cm across, very ornamental. The durable red wood, streaked with black, is valued for furniture. *Zones 10-11.*   p. 768

PTEROCARYA   *Juglandaceae*
fraxinifolia (Caucasus, Iran), "Caucasian wing-nut"; large multi-stemmed Asiatic deciduous tree to 30 m high, with compound leaves, the oblong leaflets 5-12 cm long; unisexual green flowers, the male catkins short, the females longer and pendulous, 30-50 cm long and very attractive when in bloom in early Summer; the nuts with rounded wings. *Zone 5.*   p. 739

stenoptera (E. and C. China), "Chinese wingnut"; interesting deciduous tree to 30 m high, with branches containing sections of pith; the leaves odd-pinnate, 20-40 cm long, having 11-23 oblong-elliptic leaflets, each 6 to 12 cm long and toothed, the axis winged between each pair of leaflets; female catkins 20-30 cm long, the fruit with oblong wings and 2 cm nutlet in long racemes. *Zone 5.*   p. 740

PTEROCEPHALUS   *Diapensiaceae*
parnassi (perennis) (Mountains of Greece), "Teasel winghead"; spreading, deep-rooted small perennial 8-10 cm high, forming broad cushion; dense with elliptic or fiddle-shaped leaves 3-4 cm long, crenate at margins and covered by gray pubescence; small soft purplish-pink flowers in tight heads, blooming Spring and Summer. *Zone 6.*   p. 413

PTEROSPERMUM   *Sterculiaceae*
littorale (Thailand), "Champa tet"; tropical tree with younger growth covered by scales or star-shaped stellate hairs; leathery, lobed leaves alternate on the twigs and in two ranks; interesting flowers axillary or terminal, having calyx splitting along side into 5 linear lobes, the five petals white or yellow and wavy; fruit a large leathery capsule splitting into 5 parts, and containing many winged seeds. *Zones 10-11.*   p. 884

PTEROSPORA   *Pyrolaceae*
andromedea (Brit. Columbia to Mexico, east to Michigan and Penna.), "Giant bird's-nest" or "Pinedrops"; curious herbaceous plant parasitic on roots, developing stout, clammy-pubescent, reddish

stem with a scaly base substituting for leaves; small white to red flowers having united petals, and forming small vase, in a long, terminal raceme, with stalk 90 cm long; blooming during Summer. Difficult to grow, as are most parasites. *Zones 3-9.*   *p. 483*

PTEROSTYRAX   Styracaceae

hispida (Japan, China: Szechwan, Hupeh), "Epaulette tree"; deciduous tree to 12 m high in habitat, in gardens usually as vigorous shrub about 5 m high, with spreading branches; ovate leaves wedge-shaped at base, 8 to 20 cm long, downy beneath; fragrant white flowers in attractive pendulous slender clusters 10-20 cm long, blooming June-July; fruit spindle-shaped, 10-ribbed and densely bristly. *Zone 5.*   *p. 885*

PTYCHOSPERMA   Palmae

caryotoides (New Guinea: Port Moresby area); clustering tropical feather palm to 6 m tall, with slender green-ringed trunks, seen in New Guinea Univ. Botanic Garden near Port Moresby; the pinnate fronds with stiff leaflets partially jagged or split at tips. *Zone 12.*   *p. 109*

elegans (Seaforthia elegans) (Queensland), "Solitaire palm"; handsome solitary feather palm to 6 m tall, with gracefully slender trunk, topped by 6 to 8 rather short pinnate fronds 1 to 2 m long; about 20 pairs of bright green pinnae, cut off and jagged at apex; bushy, white, fragrant flowers, and small bright red fruits. *Tropical.* *Zone 11.*   *p. 109*

macarthurii (Actinophloeus, Kentia) (New Guinea), "Hurricane palm"; suckering feather palm with several slender grayish trunks to 8 m high; pinnate leaves in a sparse crown, the pinnae glossy green and rather soft, with the apex jagged and toothed as if bitten off; fruit bright red. *Tropical. Zones 11-12.*   *p. 109*

PUERARIA   Leguminosae

phaseoloides (Phaseolus) (Himalayas to China and Malay Arch.), "Tropical Kudzu"; wide-spreading twiner to 8 m or more, with brown-hairy stems; leaves of 3 leaflets, each to 15 cm long, and with matted hairs beneath; and flaring pea-flowers lavender-rose. *Zone 11. p. 280*

PULMONARIA   Boraginaceae

angustifolia (E. Europe to Caucasus), "Blue lungwort" or "Blue cowslip"; bristly-hairy perennial to 30 cm high, with creeping rootstock; long-stalked basal leaves narrow-lanceolate; inflorescence in clusters of funnel-shaped purplish-blue flowers 2 cm long, in Spring. *Zone 4.*   *p. 351*

longifolia (W. Europe), "English lungwort"; spring-flowering hairy perennial, 30 cm high, the ovate-lanceolate leaves bristly-hairy and spotted white; trumpet flowers blue-purple, in dense terminal heads. *Zone 5.*   *p. 351*

officinalis (Europe), "Blue lungwort" or "Jerusalem sage"; handsome perennial herb 15-30 cm high, with colorful, bristly basal leaves liberally splashed with silvery-white; funnel-form flowers first pink, turning red-purple or blue. Dried leaves formerly used in medicine. *Zone 3.*   *p. 525*

saccharata (So. Europe), "Lungwort" or "Bethlehem sage"; clustering perennial herb with creeping rootstock, 30-40 cm high, with stalked ovate basal leaves, bristly hairy, dark green, freely spotted and blotched with silvery-white; clusters of funnel-shaped flowers first rose then blue; fairly hardy. *Zone 4.*   *p. 351*

saccharata 'Mrs. Moon' (picta); handsome cultivar, popular because of its large rose-pink flower buds and showy gentian-blue flowers; the olive-green foliage richly spotted with silver. *Zone 4.*   *p. 351*

PULSATILLA (Zander):   see ANEMONE (Hortus)

PULTANAEA   Leguminosae

costata (Grampians of Australia), "Bush pea"; evergreen shrub to 1 m high, and spreading 2 m wide; ovate-pointed, smooth green leaves, having prominent longitudinal veins beneath; very attractive orange-yellow pea-flowers with prominent violet eye inside, displayed in terminal clusters during Spring and Summer. *Zone 10.*   *p. 768*

PUNICA   Punicaceae

granatum (S.E. Europe to Himalayas), "Pomegranate"; deciduous shrub or small tree becoming 6 m high, with shining oblong leaves 2 to 8 cm long; flowers orange-red, with crumpled petals, the calyx purple, and with its lobes persistent on the developing edible fruit, growing as large as an orange, outside deep yellow to red, inside the membrane-covered sections contain numerous small seeds which are imbedded in the juicy crimson, fleshy pulp, of delicious, somewhat acid flavor; fruit going back in ancient Oriental history; Solomon sang of it in the Old Testament, and Theophrastus described it in 300 B.C. as a valuable fruit. The juice is used in making grenadine syrup, as well as a refreshing, aromatic drink. *Zone 7.*   *p. 827, 923*

granatum 'Florepleno' "Double-flowering pomegranate"; attractive cultivar with large double flowers crimson-red, 4-6 cm across; very fascinating as an exotic patio plant. *Zone 9.*   *p. 827*

granatum 'Legrellei'; popular, free-blooming, ornamental form of the pomegranate tree, distinguished by its fully-double, showy flowers of coral-red, striped yellowish-white along margins, and pendant at the end of wiry branches, dense with lanceolate, wavy-margined, glossy leaves. *Zone 9.*   *p. 827*

granatum 'Nana' (Iran to Himalayas), "Dwarf pomegranate"; a miniature version of the pomegranate tree, in form of a shrub to 2 m high, with shining vivid green, narrow leaves and scarlet flowers 3-4 cm long, with salmon calyx at end of thin branchlets, producing small orange-red fruit to 5 cm dia. with hard rind and juicy, edible pulp; attractive as a small potplant. *Zone 9.*   *p. 827*

granatum 'Variegata'; handsome form with large semi-double or single flowers 6-8 cm across in pastel shades of salmon-rose suffused with pink and variegated white toward margins, against a background glossy dark green foliage. *Zone 9.*   *p. 827*

granatum 'Wonderful', "Fruiting pomegranate"; favorite form in California for fruit production, of fountain-like habit, grown as a shrub 2 m high, or medium size tree 3-5 m, deciduous or semi-evergreen, with glossy green, leathery oval leaves 3-8 cm long; orange-red single flowers 6-10 cm wide, followed by burnished red fruit 10-12 cm dia., with delicious juicy pulp, in Autumn. *Zone 7.*   *p. 827, 923*

PUSCHKINIA   Liliaceae

scilloides (Lebanon, Asia Minor to Caucasus), "Striped squill"; lovely small early spring-blooming bulbous perennial related to Scilla, to 15 cm high; linear strap-shaped leaves from base; the robust floral stalk topped by 6 or more waxy, pale porcelain blue flowers, the segments with a darker greenish-blue median stripe and unlike Scilla, joined at base bell-like before opening flat, 2 to 3 cm wide. Requires winter rest. *Zone 4.*   *p. 247*

scilloides libanotica (Syria, Lebanon), "Small striped squill"; spring-blooming bulbous plant with ice-blue flowers smaller than scilloides, and having a crown of united stamens sharply toothed. *Zone 5.*   *p. 247*

PYCNANTHEMUM   Labiatae

virginianum (Maine to No. Dakota, to Georgia, Oklahoma), "Mountain mint"; aromatic much-branched herbaceous perennial to 90 cm high, with pungent, mint-like odor when crushed; ovate and lanceolate leaves 6 cm long, serrate at margins; inflorescence in axillary and terminal clusters of small bilabiate, pinkish flowers, subtended by leafy, smooth bracts. *Zones 4-8.*   *p. 438*

PYRACANTHA   Rosaceae

coccinea (S.E. Europe and Asia Minor), "Scarlet firethorn"; evergreen round-headed thorny shrub to 2 m or small tree to 5 m high, with dense leafy branches; leathery oval-pointed, glossy green leaves 3-6 cm long; small 1 cm white flowers, blooming in June; followed by showy clusters of scarlet-red berries. Widely planted as hedges. *Zone 6.*   *p. 844*

coccinea 'Lalandei', a robust cultivar of the "Firethorn" from So. Europe and Asia Minor; evergreen, woody, thorny shrub to 2 m high, with oval oblong, shiny, leathery, dark green leaves, finely toothed; the numerous small, white flowers followed by dense clusters of waxy, orange-red berries. Deciduous in coldest zones. *Zone 5.*   *p. 844*

fortuneana (crenato-serrata) (West and Cent. China) "Chinese firethorn"; thorny shrub to 5 m high, evergreen in milder regions; leathery obovate leaves 3-8 cm long, crenate-serrate at margins, and green beneath; small white, fragrant flowers, followed by scarlet berries. Very effective as a spiny barrier hedge. *Zone 7.*   *p. 621*

fortuneana 'Cherri-Berri', a beautiful California firethorn by Hines Nurseries in Santa Ana; dense evergreen shrub of vigorous habit, fast growing to 3 m high, and nearly as wide, with lustrous dark green, oblanceolate leaves 6 cm long; multitudes of dainty white flowers in Spring are followed by showy clusters of large shiny cherry-red fruit which will remain through the Winter; ideal for barriers or espaliers. *Zone 6.*   *p. 844*

fortuneana 'Graberi' (crenulata yunnanensis), "Chinese firethorn"; this evergreen shrub from China has been developed into outstanding forms such as 'Graberi', a vigorous grower with 6 cm long, narrow, oblanceolate, thick-leathery leaves rounded at the apex, and great clusters of large orange-red berries somewhat appressed to stem, from September to Winter. *Zone 6.*   *p. 844*

koidzumii (formosana) (China: Taiwan), "Formosa firethorn"; evergreen shrub of upright habit, to 4 m high, dense with leafy branches; young twigs reddish and pubescent; leathery obovate leaves 3-5 cm long; big clusters of small white flowers; the flattened berry fruit rounded at apex, vivid orange-scarlet, lasting into Winter. Widely used for hedges, and also trained as pyramids or topiary. *Zone 7.*   *p. 619*

koidzumii 'Santa Cruz' (crenato-serrata cv.); low evergreen with prostrate branches spreading from base to 2 m across; produces good crops of coral-red berries. Kept below 1 m high by pinching out occasional upright shoots, thus forming dense ground cover. *Zone 7.*   *p. 844*

koidzumii 'Victory' (crenato-serrata cv.), an excellent "Red firethorn"; robust evergreen shrub of Chinese (Taiwan) origin, becoming spreading to 3 m with thorny, rambling branches and deep green leathery foliage; very ornamental as a smaller container plant bearing large clusters of glistening brilliant, scarlet, long-lasting 1 cm berries into Winter and for Christmas, coloring late. Small white, fragrant flowers in May, on spurs along wood of last year's growth. Timely decorator for the Christmas season, the branches often trained into pyramids or against trellis. Not as frost-hardy as P. coccinea. Zone 7.   p. 844

PYROLA   Pyrolaceae

asarifolia (E. Canada west to Brit. Columbia, south to New Mexico), "Pink wintergreen"; small evergreen perennial to 30 cm high, spreading with underground stolons; thin-leathery, shining green, kidney-shaped or broad ovate leaves to 5 cm long; the waxy, light purple flowers 2 cm across, in pyramidal racemes, on stalks to 40 cm long, in June to August. Zones 3-8.   p. 483

PYROSTEGIA   Bignoniaceae

venusta (Bignonia ignea) (Brazil, Paraguay), "Flame vine" or "Flaming trumpet"; gorgeous flowering woody vine high-climbing by tendrils over fence and rooftops, with leaves of 2 or 3 ovate leaflets; red-orange slender-tubed flowers 8 cm long, in heavy clusters hanging brilliantly from eaves or arbors. Tropical. Zone 10.   p. 266, 269

PYRROSIA   Polypodiaceae (Filices)

lingua (Cyclophorus; Diplazium lanceum in hort.) (Japan, China, Vietnam, Taiwan), "Tongue fern"; creeping fern close to Asplenium, with thin scaly rhizome; stalked lanceolate, wavy, tomentose leaves 22 cm long, covered with gray felt beneath, becoming pendant; in horticulture as Diplazium lanceum. Humid-subtropic. Zones 10-11.   p. 140

longifolia cristata (Malaysia to Queensland and Polynesia); epiphytic fern on old trees; hanging strap-like fleshy fronds 40 to 100 cm long, with gray undersurface are quite distinctive; growing from long creeping rhizomes. The variety cristata has forked tips. Tropical. Zones 11-12.   p. 140

PYRUS   Rosaceae

calleryana 'Bradford' (China); vigorous deciduous tree to 10 m or more high, a clone from Chinese seeds introduced by U.S. Plant Introduction Sta., Glenn Dale, Maryland. Free-blooming, with masses of 3 cm white flowers in April; autumn foliage yellow to orange-red in colder areas. More erect and narrower than the species, with upswept branches and without spines; an excellent and very handsome tree, very popular from Coast to Coast; grafted trees are widely planted along streets. Zones 5-9.   p. 843

communis (Europe and W. Asia), "European pear" or "Winter pear"; grown in America since the earliest settlement; large long-lived deciduous, hardy tree with oval or ovate, dark green leathery leaves; flowers 3 cm across, white sometimes tinged pink, appearing with the first foliage; fruit pyriform and edible, with gritty cells, in many sweet-tasting varieties. Dwarf pears or espaliers can be obtained by grafting on quince. Seedlings are used commercially as rootstocks for grafting European pear cultivars. Zone 4.   p. 933

communis 'Bartlett'; standard summer pear, a major commercial pear of European descent for midseason, September harvest, and favored for milder areas of New England southward and the Pacific Coast; medium to large thin-skinned yellow fruit, very sweet and tender, buttery, of rich and musky flavor, for eating and also for canning; it takes summer heat provided there is adequate cold in Winter; in cold climate it sets poorly without a pollinator. Zones 5-7.   p. 843, 933

communis 'Doyenne du Comice' (France), "Comice pear"; late season fruit, large, yellow with crimson, fine sweet and buttery, juicy aromatic flesh; successfully fruited in Southern California by Paul Thomson of Bonsall. Vigorous tree, with minimal chilling requirement for setting fruit; considered as probably the best winter pear. Zones 5-8.   p. 933

communis 'Lincoln'; a pear grown successfully in Bonsall, So. California by Paul Thomson; medium sized light brown fruit in large bunches, ripening in August. Zones 5-9.   p. 933

communis 'Max Red Bartlett' (Washington); bud sport of Bartlett, bearing handsome medium-size pears basally yellow-green and striped brownish red, changing to lustrous bright red when picked; early harvest. Occasionally some branches will revert to produce green fruit. Attractive in red autumn-coloring of foliage. Zones 5-8.   p. 933

kawakami (Taiwan), "Evergreen pear"; subtropic shrub or tree to 10 m high, evergreen in California, partially deciduous in colder zones; branchlets drooping, at end the large glossy, leathery, obovate leaves to 10 cm long or more; fragrant white flowers appear like sheets in masses from late Winter into early Spring, followed by small

inedible fruit, seldom seen. Willowy young branches are often fastened to trellis for ornamental espalier. Zone 9.   p. 843

x Lecontei 'Kieffer' (communis x pyrifolia) (Europe, W. Asia), "Kieffer pear tree"; long-lived deciduous tree, with rough bark, leathery, ovate leaves 3-6 cm long; 3 cm flowers with first leaves, white or tinged pink; fruit medium to large greenish-yellow, gritty in texture; requires winter chill. Old-fashioned oriental hybrid pear, for colder regions. Originated in Philadelphia about 1850. Zone 3.   p. 843, 927, 933

x pyrifolia 'Chojuro' (China, natural. in Japan), "Apple pear", "Sand pear" or "Oriental pear"; vigorous ornamental hybrid tree to 15 m high, with leathery green ovate leaves 8-12 cm long, similar to pears, beautifully colored in Autumn; snowy-white 3 cm flowers in Spring, followed by roundish to oblique-oblong fruit having medium brown, russeted, thick skin, the flesh white and very hard, mildly sweet but bland in taste; should be allowed to ripen on the tree to develop their distinctive flavor. Zone 6.   p. 927, 933

x pyrifolia 'Nashi' (pyrifolia x ussuriensis) (N.E. Asia, China), "Japanese pear" or "Nihon Nashi"; a Japanese cultivar exhibited at the Los Angeles Arboretum; large round apple-shaped fruit with red-brownish over green skin, the flesh hard and gritty, but while sweet and juicy to the taste, it lacks the typical pleasing flavor of pears; midseason harvest. Characteristic of the Japanese pear are its large, shining green ovate leaves to 12 cm long; the flowers are white, appearing just before or with the leaves; the tree itself grows to about 15 m high; it is less hardy than P. communis. Zone 6.   p. 933

salicifolia 'Pendula' (S.E. Europe, Caucasus, Armenia), "Weeping Willowleaf pear"; deciduous tree 5-8 m high, with gracefully arching and pendant branches; handsome willow-like leaves to 10 cm long, at first with silvery-white down, later smooth and glossy; pure white flowers 2 cm across, with red anthers in center, in rounded clusters, blooming in April. Zone 4.   p. 843

PYXIDANTHERA   Diapensiaceae

barbulata (Diapensia) (New Jersey to So. Carolina), "Pixie moss" or "Flowering moss"; evergreen, moss-like perennial shrublet, creeping with branches to 30 cm long and only about 3 cm high, having sessile, oval 1 cm leaves; small 1 cm white or pinkish flowers, practically covering the foliage from March to May. Zone 7.   p. 414

QUAMOCLIT   Convolvulaceae

coccinea (Ipomoea) (Penna. to New Mexico, Arizona), "Star ipomoea" or "Scarlet star-glory"; half-hardy annual twining herb to 2 m or more, with leaves cordate or sagittate at base, to 15 cm long; scarlet flowers with yellow throat 3 cm long, and fragrant; differing from Ipomoea by the shape of the corolla tube and cup-shaped limb, and long stamens. Zone 10.   p. 273

lobata (Zander): see MINA lobata (Hortus)
pennata (EXOTICA): see IPOMOEA quamoclit (Hortus 3)
vulgaris (Zander): see IPOMOEA quamoclit, as in Hortus 3

QUASSIA   Simaroubaceae

amara (Surinam), "Bitterwood" or "Palo blanco amara"; tropical shrub or small tree to 8 m, with odd-pinnate leaves to 25 cm long, rachis conspicuously winged, 3-7 elliptic leaflets 15 cm long; inflorescence a raceme of slender crimson flowers 5 cm long. Zone 10.   p. 876

QUERCUS   Fagaceae

acutissima (Korea, Japan, China), "Sawtooth oak"; excellent wide-spreading, deciduous tree to 15 m high, with glossy, lanceolate foliage 8 to 18 cm long, bright green above and beneath, but with axil tufts of downy hairs; 12 to 16 pairs of veins, each ending in a bristle-like tooth; the acorns 2 cm long, a cup partially enclosing the nut, covered by slender scales. The bark produces a fine dye. Zone 6.   p. 728

agrifolia (California), "California live oak"; great, picturesque wide-spreading tree to 30 m high, more or less evergreen; with rough black bark, and long, persistent, dark green, hard-leathery, oval convex leaves scalloped or lobed, and with spiny teeth, 8 cm long, light green and glossy beneath; the conical 2 cm acorns partly enclosed in the silky cup. Subtropic. Zone 9.   p. 728

alba (U.S.: Maine, Minnesota, to Florida and Texas), "White oak"; magnificent deciduous, round-headed hardwood tree 30 m high; stout trunk to 2 m thick, with light gray bark; obovate 5-9-lobed leaves to 22 cm long, bright green above, glaucous beneath; 2 cm acorns enclosed 1/4 in woody cup; foliage turning wine-red in Autumn. Zone 4.   p. 728

castaneifolia (Iran, Caucasus); magnificent deciduous oak to 25 m high, with wide-spreading branches; the lanceolate leaves chestnut-like, 10-18 cm long, deeply toothed along margins; lustrous green above, grayish and downy beneath; acorns 2-3 cm long, partially enclosed by shaggy cup. Zone 6.   p. 726

coccinea (Maine to Florida and Missouri), "Scarlet oak"; very colorful and popular deciduous tree to 25 m high, with lustrous, bright green leaves 8-15 cm long, deeply 7 or 9-lobed, the lobes with bristle-tipped teeth; the acorns 25 mm long, partially enclosed by the rounded cup. Widely planted because of the glorious, long-lasting scarlet autumn color of its foliage. *Zone 4.* p. 728

dentata (Japan), "Daimyo oak"; deciduous tree to 25 m high, large ovate leaves 10 to 30 cm long, the margins lobed, pubescent beneath; cup partially enclosing a nut. Produces tan bark. Trained in Japan into dwarfed Bonsai shapes. *Zone 5.* p. 728

falcata (New Jersey to Florida and Texas), "Southern Red oak" or "Spanish oak"; elegant deciduous tree to 25 m high, with rounded crown, and obovate, deeply cut green leaves to 18 cm long, gray and downy beneath, its autumn color orange to brown; the acorns with base enclosed in a shallow cup. *Zone 6.* p. 728

ilex (No. Spain, France, Mediterr. region), "Holly oak"; evergreen densely leafy tree to 20 m high, with branches spreading wide; small spiny-toothed often holly-like leathery leaves to 8 cm long, dark shining green above, gray-felted beneath; ovoid acorns 2 cm long, in cup enclosing about half of nut. One of the finest of evergreen trees, popular for hedges in Southern Europe. Suitable for shearing into high hedges. *Zone 8.* p. 728

incana (Southeast U.S.), "Bluejack oak"; deciduous shrub or low tree to 8 m high, with oblong, dark green leaves 10 cm long, usually without or only occasional teeth, gray tomentose beneath; the nuts with base enclosed in cup. *Zone 8.* p. 728

kelloggii (Mts. of Oregon and California), "California black oak"; handsome deciduous, dense tree 25 m high, with stoutly spreading branches; attractive firm leaves 8-15 cm long, similar to those of Red oak, dark shining green above, divided about halfway into sharply dentate lobes, attractive with yellow bristle-tipped ribs; the oblong acorns two-thirds enclosed in the cup. Photographed on Mt. Cuyamaca, Calif. at 4660 ft. (about 1500 m) altitude. *Zone 8.* p. 730

laurifolia (Virginia to Florida and Louisiana), "Laurel oak"; semi-evergreen tree to 20 m high, dense with obovate lustrous green leaves to 15 cm long, occasionally lightly lobed; the acorns solitary or in pairs, in a saucer-shaped cup. Used as a street tree in Southeast U.S. *Zone 7.* p. 728

lobata (California), the "Valley oak" or "California white oak"; large and mighty deciduous tree of inland California, reaching 25 m or more and equal spread; the massive trunk and twisted limbs with ashy gray, checkered bark; deeply lobed leathery green leaves 8-10 cm long; the female flowers developing the acorn nuts, 4-5 cm long. *Zone 9.* p. 731

macrocarpa (Nova Scotia to Pennsylvania and Texas), "Bur oak" or "Mossy-cup oak"; majestic member of the White oak group, to 25 m or more high; with deciduous leaves deeply 5 to 7-lobed, 10 to 30 cm long, the terminal segment largest, grayish pubescent beneath; the large 3 cm acorn rests in a spiny cup the rim of which is thickly fringed with threadlike curling scales which explain its common name "Mossy-cup". *Zone 2.* p. 729

marilandica (New York to Florida, west to Nebraska and Texas), "Blackjack oak"; deciduous tree 6-15 m high, with a spreading crown of branches; the handsome obovate leaves broadening toward apex and dividing into several rounded lobes, dark polished green above, and brown tomentose beneath; the 2 cm acorns partially enclosed by a cup. The curiously shaped leaves turn brown or yellow in Autumn. *Zone 6.* p. 729

mongolica (E. Siberia, N.E. China, Korea), "Mongolian oak"; handsome deciduous tree to 30 m tall, with foliage crowded at end of branches; dark green blades obovate oblong 10-20 cm long, along the margins indented, with 7-10 broad, obtuse teeth, of firm texture, and showing contrasting creamy-yellow ribs; ovoid 2 cm acorns enclosed one-third by a thick cup with keeled scales overlapping and forming a short fringe. *Zone 5.* p. 730

nigra (Delaware to Florida and Texas), "Water oak"; deciduous or semi-evergreen tree to 25 m high, of symmetrical rounded shape, with obovate bluish-green leaves 8-10 cm long, very variable in shape, occasionally lobed at apex; small acorns, with lower third in shallow cup. Popular street tree in the Southern United States; retaining its foliage until January. *Zone 6.* p. 729

nuttallii (Missouri to Mississippi and Texas), "Nuttall's oak"; deciduous tree to 25 m tall, with leaves deeply 5 to 7-lobed though not as deep as palustris; the lobes tapering to points or teeth along margin; acorn-cup enclosing about half the ovoid nut 25 mm long. Inhabiting wet places and woods. *Zone 7.* p. 729

palustris (Mass. to Delaware and Arkansas), "Pin oak"; a most beautiful tree, of densely leafy, graceful growth, with spreading branches, 20 m or more high, having rough bark; deciduous foliage deeply 5 to 7-lobed and toothed, of firm texture and glossy green both surfaces except for tufts of hair in the vein-axils beneath, and 10-15 cm long, changing to brilliant red in Autumn; often planted as street tree. *Zone 4.* p. 730

petraea (Europe to W. Asia, Caucasus), "Winter oak" or "Durmast oak"; stately deciduous tree to 45 m high, similar to Q. robur, but with trunk continuing erect and pushing through the crown; also having longer petioles and cupped fruit almost sessile; handsome oblanceolate leaves relatively large, 10-14 cm long, with shallow, rounded lobes, lustrous green and of firm texture, with stellate hairs, distinctly along midrib beneath, on long yellow petiole. The tree photographed in Kew Botanic Gardens is from seed brought from Verdun 1916. *Zone 5.* p. 730

phellos (New York to Florida and Texas), "Willow oak"; distinctive deciduous tree to 20 m high, with slender branches densely leafy; the blades light green, narrow-oblong 5-15 cm long and of thin texture, turning yellow in Autumn; acorns shallowly seated in their cups. *Zone 5.* p. 729

pontica (Armenia, Caucasus), "Armenian oak"; noble shrub-like, deciduous small tree 3-6 m, often more broad than high, with ribbed branchlets; distinct bright green obovate leaves 10-16 cm long, with yellow midrib, corrugated by numerous lateral veins, coarsely toothed, and glaucous beneath; attractive slender pendant male catkins; ovoid acorns half seated in the cup. Notable for its silky winterbuds and elegant foliage. *Zone 8.* p. 729

prinus (Delaware to Florida and Texas), "Basket oak" or "Chestnut oak"; large deciduous tree to 30 m tall, with obovate leaves to 18 cm long, having depressed veins, and coarsely toothed at margins, dark glossy green above, and finely downy beneath; the acorns to 3 cm long, the lower part enclosed by short-stalked cup; foliage turns rich crimson. Furnished important wood, and tanbark. *Zone 4.* p. 729

robur (Europe, Africa, W. Asia), "English oak" or "German oak"; majestic deciduous tree with short trunk, having rather irregular or fissured bark, to 30 or even 50 m high, forming open, broad head; firm obovate leaves 8-12 cm long, glossy green and deeply round-lobed along sides; cup enclosing half of nut. Steeped in history and legend, this oak has been widely planted in Europe, and trees in England are estimated to be 1000 years old. *Zone 6.* p. 729

rubra (borealis; maxima) (Québec to Carolina and Iowa), "Red oak"; widely grown deciduous tree to 25 m tall, of pyramidal habit in younger stage, forming short massive trunk with furrowed bark; handsome leaves 10-20 cm long, deeply cut halfway to middle, the lobes sharply toothed and spine-tipped, and with yellowish ribs; turning vividly red in autumn-color; the nuts one-third enclosed by supporting cup. Widely planted street tree. *Zone 3.* p. 730

suber (So. Spain, Portugal, No. Africa), the "Cork oak"; an evergreen related to our California "Live oak", to 15 m or more high, with broad round-topped head and thick, deeply furrowed bark which is spongy and possessing elastic properties; shining dark green, ovate 4 to 8 cm leathery leaves with toothed margins, grayish-tomentose beneath. Their lightweight bark is removed in sections around the Western Mediterranean for use in insulation and other economic purposes, and trees are selected in rotation or when ready for the stripping of their grayish bark down to the cambium layers about every 8 to 10 years, following which it grows back again without seriously harming the tree. A curiosity plant which may be grown in containers. *Subtropic. Zones 7-10.* p. 731

velutina (Maine to Florida and Texas), "Black oak"; very large tree 30 to 50 m high, with deciduous leaves 12 to 30 cm long, glossy green and of firm texture, having 5-7 bristle-tipped lobes; ovoid acorns 2 cm long, half enclosed in short-stalked cup having fringe-like border. An extract made from the dried inner bark is used to make bright yellow dye; bark also yields tannin. Beautiful red foliage in Autumn. *Zone 4.* p. 731

virginiana (Virginia to Georgia, west to Mexico), "Southern live oak"; imposing tree to 20 m high, with massive trunk and branches spreading wide, evergreen in the Deep South or in mild regions, deciduous within the colder limits of Zone 7; leathery oval leaves 5-12 cm long, dark shining green above, white with down beneath, occasionally with teeth toward apex; nuts 1/3 enclosed in cup, with appressed thin scales. Most beautiful of American evergreen oaks, widely planted in the Gulf Coast states. *Zone 7.* p. 730

QUIABENTIA   Cactaceae

chacoensis (No. Argentina: Chaco Austral); spiny shrub of the Chaco region, similar to Pereskiopsis, having lanceolate later deciduous succulent leaves 7 cm long, light olive-green with pale margins; thin spines from the axils; flowers red. *Zone 11.* p. 174

QUISQUALIS   Combretaceae

indica (Burma to Philippines), "Rangoon creeper"; tropical clambering shrub with liana-like, vining, woody stems; soft, light green, pubescent leaves, and beautiful, drooping, fragrant flowers having slender green tube 8 cm long, with petals red when in bud, opening white but later changing to pink and crimson-red; very fragrant. *Tropical. Zones 10-11.* p. 273

RADERMACHERA   Bignoniaceae

sinica (Stereospermum radermacherii) (China, India), "China doll"; small evergreen tree to 4 or 6 m high in habitat, branching from the base; newly popular as an indoor decorative plant, dense with bipinnate leaves, the 5 to 8 cm ovate-pointed leaflets glossy dark green, margins toothed in juvenile stage; bignonia-like tubular flowers in panicles, pale yellow, 10 cm long, with 5 spreading lobes. *Zone 10.* *p. 36, 664, 791*

RAFFLESIA *Rafflesiaceae*

tuan-mudae (Sabah, Borneo); terrestrial parasite growing on underground roots of tropical trees, found on Mt. Kinabalu at 1000 m alt.; very spectacularly showy, fleshy, circular flower 26 cm across on the forest floor, maroon-red with contrasting white blotches, and yellow central ring. *Zone 12.* *p. 206*

RAMONDA *Gesneriaceae*

myconii (syn. pyrenaica) (Pyrenees); small alpine perennial with toothed, deep green, softly hairy, wrinkled 6 cm leaves in a rosette; showy violet or rosy-lavender flowers with broad, overlapping lobes and yellow eye, spreading 2 cm wide. (Spelling Harold Moore.) *Warm temperate. Zone 7.* *p. 63*

RANDIA *Rubiaceae*

macrantha (Africa: Sierra Leone); climbing evergreen shrub or small tree 3-9 m, with obovate membranous leaves slightly hairy beneath; solitary fragrant, pale yellow flowers with long corolla tube gracefully pendant, to 30 cm long, and spreading limb, in June. *Zone 11.* *p. 858*

RANUNCULUS *Ranunculaceae*

aconitifolius (Mts. of C. Europe to Russia), "Aconite buttercup" or "Fair maids of France"; handsome perennial with tuberous roots, having glossy green 3 to 7-parted leaves, and producing branched stems to 50 cm high, bearing loose clusters of small white flowers 2-3 cm across. *Zone 5.* *p. 262, 490*

acris flore pleno (Eurasia), "Meadows buttercup"; hairy herbaceous perennial 20 to 80 cm high, with roundish, lobed or deeply cleft leaves, segments wedge-shaped; yellow flowers to 3 cm across, in the form flore pleno with additional petals to form double blooms, sometimes known as "Yellow bachelor's buttons". *Zone 3.* *p. 489*

asiaticus (S.E. Europe, Syria, Iran), "Persian buttercup"; slender perennial with tuberous roots; alternate leaves, divided into narrow segments, on erect stalks, each bearing 1-4 flowers, usually double; many various colors, the wild type yellow; cultivated varieties white, yellow, orange, pink, scarlet, crimson, (Spring). *Subtropic. Zone 8.* *p. 262*

asiaticus 'Sakata dwarf', "Florists' Ranunculus"; superb Japanese double-flowered strain of dwarf habit, fully double in shades of yellow, orange, cream, rose, and red, 6-8 cm across. *Zone 8.* *p. 262*

eschscholtzii (High mts. of Alaska to Calif. and New Mexico), "Crow-foot"; charming low, herbaceous perennial to 15 cm high, as photographed in the Canadian Rockies, with rounded leaves 3 cm across, deeply 3-cleft and lobed; flowers with silky yellow sepals tinged lavender, and longer yellow petals, blooming July-August. *Zone 2.* *p. 489*

ficaria (Europe to W. Asia, naturalized in No. America); "Lesser Celandine"; perennial to 15 cm high, with fleshy, tuberous roots; glossy green ovate cordate 5 cm leaves; the branched stems usually decumbent bearing 3 cm deep yellow flowers, during April to May. Foliage disappears during Summer. *Zone 5.* *p. 262*

gramineus (So. Europe), "Grassy buttercup"; smooth herbaceous perennial 15-30 cm high, from fibrous roots; leaves linear-lanceolate and glaucous; vivid yellow flowers to 3 cm across, blooming April to June. *Zone 6.* *p. 489*

lanuginosus (Denmark to So. Europe, Russia to Caucasus), "Bachelor's buttons"; erect woodland perennial 30-100 cm high, the stem covered with reflexed hairs; ovate or hand-shaped leaves 3-5-lobed and toothed; numerous golden-yellow flowers, blooming May-June. *Zone 5.* *p. 490*

lingua (Britain to Siberia), "Buttercup" or "Greater spearwort"; perennial bog or waterside plant with dense fibrous roots, and forming stolons, creeping in the mud; stems to 50 cm high and hollow; leaves linear to lanceolate, to 25 cm long; rich yellow flowers 5 cm across. *Zone 3.* *p. 337*

montanus (geranifolius) (Pyrénées to Alps and Caucasus), "Mountain buttercup"; beautiful low herbaceous perennial to 15 cm high, spreading from creeping rootstocks; rounded or 3-5-parted basal leaves and sessile stem-leaves; the cupped, vivid yellow flowers 3 cm across, having hairy sepals and a hooked beak, blooming May to July; a variable species. *Zone 5.* *p. 490*

repens (Eurasia, natural. in No. America and New Zealand), "Creeping buttercup"; herbaceous perennial 15 cm or more high, spreading by runners rooting at joints; the leaves divided into 3 wedge-shaped segments, lobed at apex; yellow flowers 2-3 cm wide, having hairy sepals, and 5 petals, with curved beak in back, blooming May to August. *Zone 3.* *p. 490*

RAOULIA *Compositae*

australis (lutescens, hookeri) (New Zealand), "Silvermat patch plant"; moss-like ground cover, a prostrate perennial forming mats to 1 m across, dense with tiny 3 mm white-woolly green leaves imbricate in 5 series; small 2 mm glassy-looking sub-funnel flowers with white florets. *Zone 8.* *p. 312*

RAPHIA *Palmae*

australis (South Africa); robust feather palm, usually forming several trunks; arching pinnate fronds 5 m or more long, the leaflets dark glossy green; enormous flowerstalk with branched inflorescence and large fruit. Trunks will die after flowering, but new suckers will form from base. Photographed in Singapore Botanic Garden. *Zones 11-12.* *p. 111*

RAPHIDOPHORA or RHAPHIDOPHORA *Araceae*

decursiva (Ceylon to Indochina); tree-climber with stem stiffly scandent; large, glossy, dark green leaves pinnately divided to midrib to 60 cm long; decorative, but slow and stubborn, and not easy to train. *Tropical. Zone 11.* *p. 31*

RAPHIOLEPIS *Rosaceae*

x delacourii 'Enchantment' (indica x umbellata); very handsome evergreen hybrid shrub to 2 m high; leaves obovate pointed, 4-10 cm long, toothed above their middle, broader than indica and thinner than umbellata; beautiful flowers 2 cm across, blooming Spring and Summer; soft pink in 'Enchantment'; carmine-rose in 'Delacourii'. *Zone 7.* *p. 844*

indica (So. China), "Indian hawthorne"; attractive, dense evergreen shrub to 1½ m high, with alternate, shining leathery, lanceolate, 8 cm leaves bluntly toothed, and loose clusters of small pink flowers blooming intermittently from February to August, more profusely through Winter. *Zone 7.* *p. 844*

indica 'Enchantress', "India-hawthorne" or "Pink hawthorn"; charming evergreen shrub to 1½ m high; dark green, leathery elliptic leaves to 8 cm long, bluntly toothed at margins; large pretty flowers appleblossom-like, rosy-pink with white eye, 2½ cm across, in loose clusters, carried in profusion from late Winter to late Spring and into Summer; dark blue berries follow. A compact-growing form of the species indica which has smaller white flowers tinged with pink and comes from South China. *Zone 7.* *p. 845*

umbellata (ovata) (Japan), "Yeddo hawthorn" or "Roundleaf hawthorn"; evergreen shrub 2-3 m high, with thick-leathery, broad-ovate to rounded leaves 4-8 cm long, finely toothed and revolute at margins; fragrant white flowers 2 cm across in dense hairy clusters, blooming in June; small pear-shaped 2 cm blue-black fruit. *Zone 8.* *p. 844*

RAUVOLFIA *Apocynaceae*

caffra (No. Nigeria, West Trop. Africa), "Quinine tree"; small to large evergreen tree, with age reaching 20 m; broadly lanceolate leaves to 20 cm long, with numerous lateral nerves, and arranged in pairs or whorls, on 4-angled branches; small 6 mm white flowers. Used in medicine as alkaloid drug for nervous disorders. *Zone 10.* *p. 642*

tetraphylla (Trop. America); evergreen shrub to 2 m high, with milky sap; branches with 4 unequal leaves in a whorl, to 20 cm long; small creamy-white flowers with slender tube, followed by glossy red berries 1 cm dia., having medicinal properties. *Zone 10.* *p. 642*

RAVENALA *Musaceae (Strelitziaceae)*

madagascariensis (Madagascar), "Travelers tree"; striking tree with palm-like trunk to 30 m high, topped by leathery, banana-like leaves with pale midrib, arranged like a fan on long petioles, and sheltering the great flower bracts with white blooms and sky-blue seed; the cup-shaped leaf bases hold healthy drinking water for thirsty travelers. *Tropical. Zones 11-12.* *p. 123, 125, 795*

RAVENEA *Palmae*

rivularis (Ranevea) (Madagascar); elegant feather palm to 25 m high, having solitary white trunk slightly swollen near center; bearing a crown of self-cleaning pinnate, pendant fronds 1½ m long; the petiole is covered with white cottony down; produces small red fruit. *Zones 11-12.* *p. 102*

RAVENIA *Rutaceae*

spectabilis (Lemonia) (Cuba), "Tortugo"; small evergreen tropical shrub to 60 cm high, with leaves of 3 glossy, elongate leaflets; beautiful salver-shaped deep scarlet-red flowers 3 cm across during July-August. *Zone 10.* *p. 861*

REBUTIA *Cactaceae*

albiflora (Aylostera) (So. Bolivia: Tarija, Rio Pilaya); miniature rounded 2 cm bodies entirely covered by fine brownish spines; freely branching and forming cushions; exquisite 3 cm flowers, the petals glistening white with rose midline. *Zone 11.* *p. 174*

cajasensis (heliosa var.) (Bolivia); floriferous small globe in Harry Johnson col., California, having spiralling ribs divided into conical knobs, and covered almost entirely by red-brown needle spines; from near apex rise trumpet flowers with flaring scarlet-red petals. *Zone 11.*   p. 174

calliantha (krainziana var.) (Northern Argentina); small globe with spiralling knobbed ribs and depressed apex, and covered by white spines; showy flowers 4 cm across, the narrow petals a vivid crimson-red. *Arid-subtropic. Zone 10.*   p. 174

fiebrigii (Aylostera) (Bolivia, 3600 m alt.), "Crown cactus"; attractive small glossy green, 6 cm dia. depressed globose to elongate clustering plant; spiralled tubercles, with white hairlike spines; yellowish to vermilion-red flowers. *Arid-subtropic. Zone 10.*   p. 175

glomeriseta (Sulcorebutia) (Bolivia: Cochabamba, Sucre); small globes to 6 cm dia., spreading from base and forming clusters, the knobs in about 20 spirals, areoles brown or white, densely covered by interlaced bristle spines; 2½ cm golden-yellow flowers, blooming over a long period. *Zone 11.*   p. 175

heliosa (Bolivia ?); miniature delicate globes, with ribs divided into multitudes of knobs, tightly covered with small silver-gray spines; clustering and very floriferous with showy flowers about 3 cm across, the broad petals shimmering salmon-rose. Seen at P. Hutchison's Tropic World, Escondido, California, where it was grafted on Myrtillocactus for better growth. *Zone 11.*   p. 174

marsoneri (No. Argentina: Jujuy); light green, flattened globular body to 5 cm across; the knobs topped by small whitish radial spines; large flowers 4 to 5 cm dia., golden-yellow, inside shaded orange. *Zone 10.*   p. 175

minuscula (N.W. Argentina: Tucuman); tiny bright green flattened globe to 5 cm dia., and becoming tufted; tubercles in many spirals, very small whitish spines; bears its scarlet-red flowers freely, 6 cm long, lasting several days. *Arid-subtropic. Zone 10.*   p. 175

narvaecense (N.W. Argentina to So. Bolivia); small depressed globe 10 cm spread, densely covered with silvery spines; beautiful pale purple colored flowers, magenta outside, emerge from lower sides. *Zone 10.*   p. 175

nivea (Bolivia); choice small globes, in col. Harry Johnson, California; the entire body with spiralling tubercles, densely covered by white areoles and silvery-white hairlike bristles; showy salmon-scarlet flowers from the sides. *Zone 10.*   p. 175

senilis (No. Argentina, Chile), "Fire crown"; depressed clustering, bluish globe, to 25 cm high, but usually very small; spiralled tubercles, covered with interlocking white to yellow hairlike spines; red flowers 3½ cm across. *Arid-subtropic. Zone 10.*   p. 174

spegazziniana (Aylostera) (No. Argentina: Salta); short cylindrical green stems to 3½ cm thick, freely branching and forming mounds; white-woolly areoles along the ribs, and short yellowish spiny; multitudes of wide-open scarlet-red flowers 4 cm across. *Zone 10.*   p. 174

violaciflora (Northern Argentina: Salta), "Rosy crown cactus"; low globe with sharp needle spines, very tiny and barely 3 cm dia.; the flowers relatively large 3 cm long, a beautiful rose-purple. *Arid-subtropic. Zone 10.*   p. 175

RECHSTEINERIA: see SINNINGIA (Zander, Hortus)

REEVESIA   *Byttneriaceae*
  thyrsoidea (Southeast China to Java); small evergreen tree 5-8 m high, with leathery, glossy green, lanceolate leaves to 12 cm long; terminal clusters of sweet-scented creamy-white flowers, the corolla having 5 spreading petal-lobes, and displaying long staminal column, blooming late Winter. *Zone 10.*   p. 671

REGELIA   *Myrtaceae*
  velutina (grandiflora) (Southwest Australia), "Barrens regelia"; strikingly beautiful shrub with erect branches; needle-like 15 mm gray-silky leaves, densely set in 4 ranks along slender shoots; inflorescence in showy terminal clusters of vividly scarlet staminal flowers to 4 cm across, blooming in Spring. *Zone 10.*   p. 803

REHMANNIA   *Gesneriaceae (formerly Scrophul.)*
  elata (angulata) (C. China), "Foxglove gloxinia"; perennial herb with a rosette of soft, irregularly lobed, obovate leaves; a sticky-hairy, leafy stalk with showy, large, bilabiate flowers having corolla 6 cm long, rosy-red with yellow throat and spotted purple. Previously included with the foxgloves (Digitalis), family Scrophulariaceae. *Zone 7.*   p. 64, 508

REINECKIA   *Liliaceae*
  carnea 'Variegata' (China, Japan), "Fan grass"; tufting perennial with creeping rhizome and broad, arched, grass-like, channeled 30 cm leaves arranged with military precision alternately to left and right in two orderly ranks, fresh-green strongly banded white; fragrant flesh-pink flowers. Usually grown as indoor plant. *Zone 9.*   p. 564

REINWARDTIA   *Linaceae*
  indica (trigyna) (No. India), "Yellow flax"; bushy, shrubby plant to 1 m high, with obovate, membranous, dark green leaves, and large, golden-yellow, cupped flowers 3-5 cm across and very showy. *Zone 8.*   p. 772

RENANTHERA   *Orchidaceae*
  monachica (Burma), "Fire orchid"; colorful epiphyte with stiff leafy stems, short mottled leaves and an arching raceme of orange-yellow, spreading flowers 3 cm across, marked with blotches and bars of fiery-red, (April). *Tropical. Zones 11-12.*   p. 95

RESEDA   *Resedaceae*
  luteola (Mediterr. region, Canary Islands), "Dyer's rocket"; herbaceous biennial with hollow stems to 1 m or more high; the basal leaves narrowly oblanceolate to 8 cm long; the inflorescence in dense racemes of small flowers with yellowish sepals and petals. Formerly cultivated as source of deep yellow dye. *Zone 10.*   p. 491

  odorata (No. Africa, Egypt), "Mignonette"; branching annual or short-lived perennial 25-40 cm high, at first upright but becoming spreading, with oblanceolate leaves and yellowish-white, inconspicuous flowers having contrasting saffron-red anthers, in pyramidal, terminal racemes; much loved for their sweet fragrance. *Zones 9-10.*   p. 491

  odorata 'Goliath', "Giant mignonette"; European cultivar seen at Cologne Federal Garden Expo; aromatic annual or perennial herb larger than the species, having spatulate leaves 8-10 cm long, and large conical racemes of sweetly fragrant, yellow-white flowers, summer-blooming. Cultivated for its essential oil used in perfumes. *Zone 10.*   p. 540

RESTREPIA   *Orchidaceae*
  elegans (Andes of Venezuela and Colombia); small epiphyte to 30 cm high; stems in tufts, with fleshy leaves 10 cm long; showy flowers 4 cm long, sepals and upper petals threadlike, lateral sepals united and boat-shaped, yellow brown with maroon spots. *Subtropic. Zone 11.*   p. 97

  guttulata (Andes of Venezuela to Ecuador); miniature epiphyte with stems 5 cm high, and in tufts, with solitary leaves; the conspicuous flowers, having upper sepals and the petals linear, greenish-white with crimson line, lateral sepals united into a boat shape, greenish-yellow with purple spots. *Subtropic. Zone 11.*   p. 95

RETINISPORA: see CHAMAECYPARIS

REYNOUTRIA japonica (Zander):
  see POLYGONUM cuspidatum (Hortus 3)

RHABDADENIA   *Apocynaceae*
  biflora (So. Florida, West Indies, Mexico, Central America), "Rubber vine"; shrubby evergreen gradually twining; opposite leathery, ovate leaves to 8 cm long; the trumpet flowers with 5 flaring overlapping petals white and flushed with pink, 5 cm across. *Zone 10.*   p. 266

RHAMNUS   *Rhamnaceae*
  alaternus 'Argenteo-variegata' (So. Europe), a variegated "Buckthorn"; bushy shrub with twiggy, beige-brown stem; obovate 6 cm leaves, attractively colored green in center, margins ivory-white, slightly toothed; small greenish flowers, followed by bluish-black fruit. *Zone 7.*   p. 828

  alpinus fallax (S.W. Europe, East Alps, Balkans to Greece), "Alpine buckthorn"; deciduous mountain shrub to 3 m high, with handsome ovate firm leaves 5-12 cm long, having numerous sunken veins; small greenish-yellow flowers in little clusters, blooming August to October. *Zone 5.*   p. 828

  catharticus (Europe, Asia), "Common buckthorn" or "Rhine berry"; vigorous deciduous shrub or small tree to 6 m high, characteristic with short branchlets tipped by stiff spiny thorn; ovate or oval leaves 3-6 cm long; small green flowers clustered in lower leaf axils; the fruits are small black berries. The bark is used medicinally as a laxative; also planted for clipped hedges. *Zone 3.*   p. 828

  frangula (Europe, No. Africa, Asia, escaped East U.S.), "Alder buckthorn"; very ornamental deciduous shrub or small tree to 5 m high, the branchlets downy, with obovate leaves 4-8 cm long, glossy green and having 8-9 pairs of prominent veins; small greenish flowers in axillary clusters in June; 2-seeded berries red, ripening to purplish-black, and eaten by birds. *Zone 2.*   p. 828

  frangula 'Columnaris' (Ohio), "Tall-hedge buckthorn"; excellent shrub of columnar growth-habit, and favored as a hedge plant because its handsome foliage needs no shearing on the sides. Introduced by Cole Nursery, Painesville, Ohio. *Zone 2.*   p. 828

  imeretinus (Caucasus, Asia Minor), "Caucasus buckthorn"; deciduous shrub to 3 m high, with stout branches and elliptic leaves 10-25 cm long, having 24 or more pairs of veins depressed above, the margins toothed, downy on both sides; small green flowers in axillary clusters. Most handsome of buckthorns, foliage turning bronze red in Autumn; small 6 mm black fruit. *Zone 6.*   *p. 828*

RHAPIS   *Palmae*
   excelsa (flabelliformis) (So. China), "Large lady palm"; miniature fan-palm with bamboo-like canes 3½ m or more, the thin stems densely matted with coarse fiber, forming clumps from underground suckers, the leathery leaves glossy green divided into 3-10 broad segments; widely used in China and Japan as a durable potted palm. *Subtropic. Zone 11.*   *p. 109*
   humilis (So. China), "Slender lady palm"; clustering stems thinner and more graceful than excelsa, less vigorous, likewise covered with dark brown fibers; the deep green palmate leaves more slender and divided into 9 to 20, narrower segments. *Subtropic. Zone 11. p. 109*
   subtilis (Thailand, Laos); diminutive tropical palm in col. Rhapis Garden, Gregory, Texas, the "Siamese lady palm"; clustering with thin canes 50 cm to 2 m high, covered by woven brown fibers; small durable palmate leaves of thin-leathery texture, divided into 2-4 segments 8-15 cm long, down to juncture with petiole. *Zone 12.*   *p. 109*

RHAZYA   *Apocynaceae*
   orientalis (S.E. Europe, Asia Minor); small shrub 25 cm high, closely related to Vinca, with dark green elliptic leaves to 6 cm long, with pale mid-vein; small 2 cm clustered flowers pale lavender suffused with pink toward tip of petals and small white blotch at each side of base of petals; late Summer. *Zone 9.*   *p. 340*

RHEKTOPHYLLUM   *Araceae*
   mirabile (Nephthytis picturata) (Nigeria, Cameroon, Zaire); creeping and climbing aroid sending out long rooting internodes; the large thin-leathery, arrow-shaped, hastate leaves 20-30 cm long, dark green between the veins, variegated silvery-cream in form of a fern-leaf, becoming green in older leaves; the maturity-stage leaves broad heart-shaped in outline, 30-50 cm long and deeply sliced into broad, obtuse, glossy green segments; the 10 cm spathe green outside, red-purple inside. *Tropical. Zone 12.*   *p. 32*

RHEUM   *Polygonaceae*
   officinale (W. China), "Medicine rhubarb"; robust perennial with thick, somewhat woody rhizome; large roundish leaves, palmately 5 to 7-lobed, and to 1 m across; the inflorescence branched, on leafy stalk to 2 m or more high, with small white to greenish flowers in dense clusters, during Summer. Roots and rhizome are used medicinally. *Zone 5.*   *p. 540*
   palmatum (Tibet, W. China), "Chinese rhubarb"; stout perennial herb with woody rhizome, 1½ m high; large, palmately lobed leaves on cylindrical stalks; flowers deep red in large cluster. Used medicinally for stomach and digestive disorders. *Zone 5.* *p. 540*
   rhabarbarum (undulatum) (Manchuria, Siberia), "Garden rhubarb"; stout perennial herb with thick, somewhat rhizomous roots, clump-forming; half-round, smooth green or red stalks to 75 cm long, bearing large gray-green, wavy, wrinkled, round-cordate ovate leaves 30-40 cm across; showy inflorescence of greenish-white small flowers, in lateral clusters from stout central stalk to 1½ m tall. Parent of several hybrids of garden rhubarb. The succulent, acid-tasting stalks are edible and prepared as fruity compote or pie, the leaf blades however are poisonous. *Zone 3.*   *p. 540, 910*

RHEXIA   *Melastomataceae*
   mariana (Maryland to Texas), "Maryland Meadowbeauty"; slender bristly perennial 30-60 cm high, with fleshy roots, and 6-angled stem; the opposite elliptic, bristly leaves are 3 cm long, prominently 3-5-veined and crenate; the rosy or white 4-petaled flowers 4-5 cm across, in small clusters; blooming Summer and Autumn. *Zone 6.* *p. 435*

RHIPSALIDOPSIS   *Cactaceae*
   gaertneri (Schlumbergera, Epiphyllopsis) (So. Brazil), the "Easter cactus"; bushy epiphyte with stiffish spreading branches of long flattened joints, dull green with purplish crenate margins, a few bristles at apex; star-like regular flowers, deep scarlet, the ovaries angled; spring-blooming. *Tropical. Zone 11.* *p. 59*
   x graeseri 'Rosea' (Epiphyllopsis) (gaertneri x rosea); a free-blooming hybrid which I first saw in Brazil where it flowered in their Spring (Sept.), while in the Northern Hemisphere it blooms in March, indicating its being influenced by day-length; wide open, star-shaped regular flowers clear pink with double row of broad petals, flushed deep rose in center. *Tropical. Zone 11.*   *p. 58*

RHIPSALIS   *Cactaceae*
   baccifera (cassutha hort.) (Florida to Perú to Brazil, Ceylon and trop. Africa), "Mistletoe cactus"; growing on trees or rocks hanging in many strands to 3 m; branches thin-cylindrical, 2-3 mm thick, somewhat bristly when young; flowers cream; with mistletoe-like white

fruit, as have many Rhipsalis. In Africa, this is found on Lake Kivu, and I have seen them in eastern Kenya, and the Usambara Mts. of Tanzania. *Tropical. Zones 10-11.*   *p. 179*
   capilliformis (E. Brazil), "Old man's head"; epiphytic cactus with long, branching cylindrical, string-like, hanging stems 3 mm thick; many cream-colored flowers of 8 mm dia. along sides. *Tropical. Zone 11.*   *p. 179*
   houlletiana (S.E. Brazil: Rio, São Paulo, Minas Geraes), "Snowdrop cactus"; high altitude epiphyte with leaflike hanging, flat and thin branches to 2 m long, 3 to 5 cm wide notched at margins; 2 cm flowers cream with red eye. *Zones 10-11.*   *p. 179*
   paradoxa (São Paulo), "Chain cactus"; hanging in clusters to 1 m with many aerial roots, glossy green branches 3 to 4-winged, 2 cm thick, and zigzag links; flowers white, 2 cm across, and red fruit. *Zone 10.*   *p. 179*
   quellebambensis (Perú), "Red mistletoe"; epiphytic cactus with pendant thin cylindric branches, dull green with occasional purple markings and lightly grooved, 3 to 5 mm thick; glossy carmine-red berry-like fruit at the tips. *Tropical. Zones 10-11.*   *p. 179*

RHIZOPHORA   *Rhizophoraceae*
   mangle (Florida, W. Indies to So. America), the "American mangrove" or "Red mangrove", so common along the shores and bayous of the Florida Keys; growing into small trees; producing many trunks or rooting shoots forming dense thickets by the many arching aerial roots; thick-leathery opposite, dark green leaves 5 to 15 cm long; yellow, long-stemmed flowers with 4 calyx lobes and 4 narrow hairy, pale yellow petals; fruit 3 cm long; before dropping into the wet soil, the fruit usually germinates and develops a root 30 cm long. *Humid-tropical. Zone 10.*   *p. 333*
   mucronata (Sri Lanka and Eastern Tropics), "Four-petaled mangrove"; moderate-sized spreading tree inhabiting lagoons and tidal tropic seashores, with many aerial props forming dense and difficult tangles and stilt roots; shiny green, thick-leathery, small oval leaves, and leathery 2 cm yellowish flowers; fruit bearing one seed. Interestingly the seed germinates long before fruit is ripe, and its root gradually projects out of the fruit like a long green finger; when fruit is ripe the seedling drops into the mud and begins to sprout immediately. *Zones 10-11.*   *p. 337*

RHODOCACTUS grandifolius (Backeberg):
   see PERESKIA (Hortus, Zander)

RHODOCHITON   *Scrophulariaceae*
   volubile (Mexico: Oaxaca), the "Purple bell-vine"; graceful vine climbing to 3 m assisted by coiling petioles, similar to Asarina but more vigorous, and usually treated as a tender annual; alternate heart-shaped downy leaves to 8 cm long, and pendulous flowers 5 cm long with tubular corolla dark blood-red and spreading bell-like calyx pale reddish, on red stems; June. Habitat Cerro de Polon 2400 m. *Zone 10.*   *p. 297*

RHODODENDRON   *Ericaceae*
   aberconwayi (E. Yunnan, China); evergreen shrub to 2 m or more high, with elliptic, brittle leaves 5-8 cm long; showy inflorescence with clusters of cup-shaped or saucer-like flowers 3-4 cm wide, the corolla a lovely pinkish-white and speckled with red; blooming in May; distinct by the unusual shape of its blooms. *Zone 7.*   *p. 710*
   albiflorum (Brit. Columbia to Alberta, Oregon and Colorado); deciduous shrub to 2 m high, with glossy green elliptic leaves 3-6 cm long, crenate at margins, somewhat rusty pubescent; bell-shaped nodding white flowers 2 cm wide, having 5 lobes, June-July blooming. *Zone 5.*   *p. 710*
   'Anthony Waterer' (Knap Hill hyb.); very floriferous, deciduous shrub, an early introduction around 1870 by A. Waterer of Knap Hill Nursery, of Woking, England; involving R. gandavense, calendulaceum, arborescens and molle; leaves 6-8 cm long, and large wide-open flowers, the corolla cream, tinged with rose, 5 to 8 cm across. The Knap Hill group includes many gorgeous azaleas of brilliant colors from white and pink to orange and red, as many as 18-30 blooms in a single cluster; blooming before foliage. *Zones 5-6. p. 715*
   arborescens (Mts. of Pennsylvania to Georgia and Alabama), "Sweet azalea"; unusually fragrant, deciduous shrub to 3 m or more high, with bright green, obovate leaves 3-8 cm long; tubular funnelform flowers white with lobes flaring to 5 cm across, and sweetly scented, the stamens protruding, the style red; blooming early Spring, after foliage appears. Leaves turn a dark glossy red in Autumn, and are aromatic when dry. *Zone 5.*   *p. 719*
   arboreum (Himalayas), "Tree rhododendron"; evergreen tree to 15 m high, with leathery, lanceolate leaves 20 cm long, green and glossy above, silvery beneath; flowers scarlet with darker spots, 5 cm across, in large clusters. Photographed in habitat in the Sikkim Himalaya forest near Darjeeling. *Zone 7.*   *p. 715, 717*

atlanticum (Delaware to So. Carolina), "Coast azalea"; deciduous low shrub to 60 cm high, vigorously spreading by stolons; obovate and elliptic leaves to 6 cm long; fragrant flowers with funnelform white or pinkish corolla, the lobes flaring and recurved, flushed crimson, generally preceding the foliage. Zone 6. *p. 710*

auriganum (N.E. New Guinea); strikingly colorful epiphytic evergreen which we collected in the Finisterre Mts. at 2100 m alt. near the frost line; clusters of large 12 cm trumpet-shaped flowers with fleshy, yellow tube and salmon-rose petal-lobes; small elliptic, leathery leaves. Zone 10. *p. 710*

austrinum (Florida to Mississippi), "Florida flame azalea"; handsome Gulf Coast deciduous shrub to 3 m high, with elliptic leaves to 10 cm long, and softly pubescent; showy funnelform flowers 3 cm long, faintly fragrant, usually yellow, but with forms varying with red corolla tubes; blooming before or just after foliage unfolds. Zone 6. *p. 711*

'Bagshot Ruby' (thomsonii hybrid) by A. Waterer of Knap Hill Nursery, England; handsome evergreen, rounded bush, with excellent foliage, and striking clusters of large blood-red flowers with white center; photographed at the Chelsea Flower Show, London, in bloom May 1984. Zone 6. *p. 715*

bakeri (Kentucky to Georgia and Alabama), "Cumberland azalea"; deciduous shrub 2 m or more high, related to R. calendulaceum but smaller, and later to bloom; obovate leaves 5 cm long; the flowers, appearing after the foliage, are striking in color, the funnelform corolla vivid red, but may vary to orange or yellow, 5 cm across, blooming June into July. Zone 6. *p. 710*

'Boule de Neige' ("Snowball") (caucasicum x catawbiense hyb.) (France 1878); spring-blooming white, the buds pink; handsome rounded broadleaf evergreen of dense compact habit; for many years a favorite garden plant because of its glistening white blooms, very early in the season. Zones 5-8. *p. 710*

calendulaceum (Ohio to Penna. and Georgia), "Flame azalea"; the most showy of American azaleas, a deciduous shrub to 3 m high, with elliptic leaves 5-8 cm long, downy beneath; abundantly blooming in early June after the new foliage has fully unfolded; flowers predominantly bright yellow, but varying to orange and tinted with red, 5 cm across, in showy clusters of brilliant colors. Zone 5. *p. 712*

calophytum (W. Szechwan); noble evergreen tree, in cultivation to 3 m high, in China habitat found to 15 m tall; oblong to lanceolate leathery leaves to 30 cm long; strikingly colored flowers 8 cm across, white to rose-pink, with dark crimson blotch at base, very beautiful when blooming in March-April. Zone 6. *p. 710*

canadense (Rhodora) (No. America: Newfoundland to Pennsylvania); attractive deciduous shrub which can be seen in profuse bloom in the Pocono Mountains of N.E. Pennsylvania in May and June; the clustered flowers 4 cm wide, with 2-lipped corolla rosy-lavender with darker purple tips; the foliage follows after blossom time, the oval leaves 3-5 cm long, downy beneath. Much loved as reflected in New England poetry of Emerson. Zone 2. *p. 719*

canescens (No. Carolina to Florida and Texas), "Hoary azalea" or "Piedmont azalea"; deciduous shrub with few branches, to 5 m high; obovate leaves to 10 cm long, gray-pubescent beneath; funnelform flowers deep pink to near white, spreading 3-4 cm wide, during Spring, blooming before or just after foliage unfolds, southernmost in March, on Long Island, N.Y. around May. Zone 7. *p. 712*

carolinianum (No. Carolina), "Carolina rhododendron"; handsome evergreen from the Blue Ridge Mountains, to 1 m or more high, with oval-obovate leaves 4-8 cm long, densely covered with dark brownish scales beneath; excellent for its funnel-shaped rosy-purple flowers 3-4 cm across, in Mid-May. Zone 5. *p. 710*

catawbiense (Eastern U.S.: Virginia to Georgia), "Mountain rose-bay"; excellent evergreen to 3 m or more high, with shining, leathery elliptic leaves 15 cm long; flowers in clusters, lilac-purple, 6 cm across, blooming late Spring to July. Because of its frost-hardiness, much used for hybridizing. In their habitat in the Great Smoky Mountains they cover large areas; very popular in gardens, and valued because of their handsome foliage. Zone 5. *p. 711*

chapmanii (N.W. Florida); beautiful flowering evergreen from sandy coastal pinelands, to 2 m high, with erect rigid branches bearing obovate leaves, and rose-pink blooms, their corolla 3 cm across, the pale pink lobes crisped and flaring, in late Spring. Zone 7. *p. 711*

'Coral Bells' (Azalea) (Kirin); favorite selection of the "Kurume" hybrids, small-flowered evergreen azaleas originated on Kyushu Island (So. Japan) during the Meiji era (1868-1912), from species involving Rhododendron obtusum, kaempferi and kiusianum; this charming cultivar is of low habit, densely branched, with small shiny, fresh green leaves; early blooming with a multitude of bell-shaped 3 cm hose-in-hose flowers of dainty silver-pink, deepening to coral-pink in center. Zone 7. *p. 56, 708*

dalhousiae (Himalayas of Bhutan and Sikkim); elegant broadleaf evergreen 2 m or more high, often epiphytic, with bristly branchlets,

the leaves oblanceolate to 15 cm long, white-scaly beneath; fragrant flowers with waxy white funnel-shaped corolla tinged rose, its 5 lobes spreading 8-10 cm wide; blooming May-June. Zone 9. *p. 710*

'Dexter hybrid' (primarily fortunei x decorum background); beautiful evergreen hybrids incorporating the attractive fragrant flowers and clear colors of R. fortunei from China; fairly winter hardy. The cultivar photographed at du Pont Winterthur Gardens in Delaware, is distinguished by its brilliant crimson flowers, blooming in May. Zone 6. *p. 711*

fastigiatum (Yunnan); attractive small evergreen to 1 m high, with narrow 1 cm leaves, densely scaly on both surfaces; inflorescence in small terminal clusters, the corolla 12 mm long, with spreading lobes purplish-rose. Zone 7. *p. 711*

ferrugineum (Mountains of C. Europe), "Alpine rose"; shrubby evergreen, sometimes to 1 m high, with 4 cm elliptic, leathery leaves with rusty scales primarily beneath, the margins rolled under; waxy salmon-rose flowers to 2 cm long. Zone 4. *p. 711, 717*

flammeum (Azalea speciosum) (So. Carolina, Georgia), "Oconee azalea"; deciduous shrub to 2 m high, having hairy branchlets, furnished with obovate leaves to 6 cm long, the margins ciliate and pubescent beneath; showy funnelform flowers to 5 cm wide, variable from light red to orange, shaded scarlet. Zone 7. *p. 711*

forrestii repens (repens in hort.) (Yunnan, Burma or Myanmar, Tibet), "Creeping rhododendron"; prostrate evergreen, creeping shrub of slow growth unless grafted, to 40 cm high, the lowest branches rooting on the ground; small leathery oval leaves 5-7 cm long; bright scarlet to crimson, waxy bell-shaped flowers 4 cm long; of striking beauty when blooming as seen in Germany in early May. Zone 7. *p. 718*

fortunei (E. China); introduced by Robert Fortune to England 1856, from the mountains of Chekiang, Kiangsi, Hupeh and Kwantung; vigorous wide-spreading broadleaf evergreen to 9 m high in habitat, forming a dense bush; leaves 10-20 cm long and to 8 cm wide; fragrant flowers funnelform, with pale lilac to pink corolla 8 cm across, variable to cream, blooming in May. Parent of many good hybrids. Zone 6. *p. 711*

fortunei 'Duke of York' (fortunei x 'Scapio'); handsome evergreen hybrid with long elliptic leaves, and showy clusters of mauve-pink flowers 8-9 cm across, colored cream-yellow toward center; young shoots will form while still in bloom. Zone 6. *p. 713*

'Harvest Moon' (Exbury-Knap Hill azalea 1938) (mollis x gandavense x calendulaceum); large fragrant flowers amber-yellow, whitish in some areas of the wide-spreading petals, in very showy clusters. Zone 7. *p. 718*

hirsutum (Alps of So. Cent. Europe), "Hairy Alpine rose"; evergreen low bush to 80 cm high, dense with oval to elliptic fresh green, leathery leaves 2-3 cm long, scaly beneath; similar to R. ferrugineum, but leaf margins, calyx and floral stalk are all bristly-hairy; small waxy funnel-shaped flowers 10-12 mm long, deep rose to nearly scarlet, blooming during Summer. Zone 6. *p. 711*

impeditum (China: Yunnan), "Cloudland rhododendron"; low evergreen rockgarden plant 15 to 50 cm high, dense with twiggy branches; small 1 cm ovate leaves, scaly on both surfaces; daintily fragrant flowers with flaring lobes 25 mm wide, pale purplish-blue, showing 10 protruding purple stamens; very freely blooming in May. Zone 4. *p. 714*

indicum (lateritium) (Japan), "Satsuki azalea", "Macranthum azalea"; low evergreen or semi-evergreen densely branched shrub, seldom to 2 m high, and lending itself to dwarfing as bonsai; small 2½-3 cm lanceolate, slightly hairy leaves with finely toothed margins; large funnelform flowers 8 cm across, bright red or rosy with crimson marking in throat, June blooming unless forced; hardy. This is not the Azalea (Rhod.) "indica" of florists, which is a group name for many large-flowered tender hybrids derived from Azalea (Rhod.) simsii, the so-called "Belgian indica", forced in greenhouses during Winter and Spring in many named cultivars in a wide assortment of lovely colors. Zone 6. *p. 708, 717*

indicum 'Balsaminiflorum' (Azalea rosaeflora), "Balsam azalea" introduced from Japan 1877; very low form only 10 cm high, dense with bristly shoots, ovate leaves 15-25 mm long, and fully double flowers salmon-rose, blooming in Summer. A choice rockgarden evergreen. Zone 6. *p. 714*

indicum 'Shinnyo-no-tsuki' ('Moon of the Real Moon') (Azalea); a spectacular hybrid with large single flowers of 7 cm dia., white, with broad crimson border, May flowering, and developed as one of the 'Satsuki' (Fifth Moon) race of azaleas for beauty of leaves and flowers both, from the Japanese species indicum (lateritium). Zone 6. *p. 628*

japonicum (Azalea mollis in hort.) (No. and Cent. Japan), "Japanese azalea"; very hardy deciduous shrub to 2 m high, with oblanceolate leaves 5-10 cm long; broadly funnelform flowers 5-8 cm across, the corolla with spreading lobes, soft-rose to salmon-red, or yellow, blooming in late May. Mostly grown as Azalea mollis, and a parent of a beautiful race of garden hybrids. Zone 5. *p. 713*

jasminiflorum (Malaya); attractive evergreen shrub often epiphytic, with obovate, leathery leaves 2½-6 cm long; large terminal truss of slender tubular waxy white flowers 4 cm long and with flaring lobes, filaments pink. *Zone 11.*   p. 714

'Jean Marie de Montague'; excellent evergreen griffithianum cultivar suitable for Easter forcing indoors; compact, shapely plant budding well with firm, solid heads of bell-shaped flowers to more than 8 cm across, glowing bright crimson and very charming with wavy petals; smallish, dull-green elliptic foliage. Beautiful color for the outdoor garden on the Pacific Coast, but not bud-hardy enough in the northern Atlantic States. *Zone 7.*   p. 55

kaempferi (Japan), "Torch azalea"; well-known deciduous or semi-evergreen shrub to 2 m or more high, loosely branched; elliptic or ovate leaves 6 cm long, pubescent on both sides; attractive funnelform flowers to 5 cm across, the corolla deep rose or vivid orange-red, blooming preceding foliage. Parent of numerous garden hybrids. *Zone 5.*   p. 713

'Kaempferi hybrid', "Torch azalea"; (cultivar of Japanese species, prob. obtusum and kaempferi); tall deciduous bush to 2½ m high, elliptic, rough textured leaves 6 cm long, pubescent on both sides; flowers 4 cm across, brilliant orange-red, blooming before leaves. *Zone 5.*   p. 713

keiskei (Japan: Mts of Honshu and Kyushu); evergreen shrub to 2 m high, low and compact when young, but becoming straggly with age; lanceolate leaves 6 cm long; the inflorescence in clusters of few wide bell-shaped flowers 3-5 cm wide, the 5-lobed corolla is clear lemon-yellow, blooming April-May. Valued in the Northern U.S. and Canada because it is, according to Don Wyman, the only yellow-flowered evergreen rhododendron hardy in the North. *Zone 5.*   p. 712

kiusianum (obtusum japonicum) (Cent. So. Japan), "Kiushima azalea"; low evergreen shrub to 70 cm high, densely clothed by small ovate leaves; flowers with funnelform corollas salmon-red to rose, 3 cm across, characteristic with brown anthers (yellow in obtusum), blooming in May-June. *Zone 6.*   p. 712

lacteum (China: Yunnan); handsome evergreen shrub or tree-like, 5 to 8 m tall, from the mountains of S.W. China at 3500 m alt.; with ovate leaves 10-20 cm long, 6-8 cm wide, base often cordate, beige-felted beneath; flowers vivid yellow, with 5 lobes spreading 5 cm across, blooming April in habitat. Photographed in col. Los Angeles Arboretum. *Zone 8.*   p. 714

lateritium: see R. indicum

ledifolium album: see R. mucronatum

linearifolium macrosepalum (Japan), "Spider azalea"; strikingly different evergreen seen at the Chelsea Flower Show London 1984, having flowers with corolla dissected into spidery linear segments of rose-lilac color, each lobe to 3 cm long, blooming in May, and sweetly fragrant; stems very hairy and to 1 m or more long, with downy, narrow leaves 5-8 cm long. *Zone 7.*   p. 714

lochae (Queensland); the only known Australian rhododendron, found on Bellenden Ker mountain above 1500 m, not far from tropical Cairns; evergreen shrub often epiphytic, usually grown as a dwarf plant; small leathery broad elliptic leaves 5-8 cm long, dark glossy green; and hanging bells of waxy 4-5 cm flowers deep rosy-crimson with salmon sheen. *Subtropic. Zone 10.*   p. 713

lochmium (glaucophyllum, davidsonianum hort.) (China: W. Szechwan); flowering evergreen shrub to 3 m high, having straggling branches, with oblanceolate leaves 6 cm long, brown scaly beneath; funnelform flowers 3-4 cm long, the corolla pink, spotted with red, prominent stamens protruding; very floriferous. *Zone 6.*   p. 712

'Loderi' (fortunei x griffithianum); excellent evergreen hybrid, typical of a group of these parents, originated by Sir Edmund Loder of Sussex in 1901; large rounded bushes to 6 m high, dense with oblong leaves 15-25 cm long, covered by masses of fragrant flowers 18 cm across, in large clusters, white to shell pink, according to cultivar, and very popular in gardens. *Zone 7.*   p. 715

luteum (Azalea pontica) (E. Europe to Caucasus), "Pontic azalea"; deciduous winter hardy shrub to 4 m high spring-flowering before foliage; leaves rugose and partly hairy; showy flowers 5 cm across, golden to orange-yellow and very fragrant. *Zone 5.*   p. 713

macgregoriae (highlands of New Guinea at 1500 to 2000 m); straggly evergreen mountain shrub with clustered elliptic leaves; charming little waxy flowers 2 cm across, creamy-white with orange center. *Subtropic. Zones 9-10.*   p. 205, 714

macrophyllum (Brit. Columbia to Cent. California), "California rosebay"; popular evergreen flowering shrub from along the Pacific Coast, to 3 m high, the Western counterpart of R. catawbiense; with handsome elliptic leathery leaves to 25 cm long; the inflorescence with showy corollas rose-pink to light purple, spotted with brown and to 6 cm across, blooming in June. *Zone 6.*   p. 712

makinoi (metternichii var.) (Japan: Mts. of Honshu), "Hosoba-Shakunage"; strikingly beautiful rose flowers with bell-shaped corolla

3-4 cm wide, pale pink in center, in large clusters, blooming May-June; evergreen shrub to 2 m high, with woolly branches, and lanceolate leaves 20 cm long. *Zone 6.*   p. 718

maximum; the species is North American, from Nova Scotia to Alabama; an evergreen shrub to 12 m high, with glossy green leaves 25 cm long, tomentose beneath; the bell-shaped 5 cm flowers are pale rose and spotted with green, in large terminal clusters, blooming June into Summer. *Zone 3.*   p. 713

'Mollis hybrid' (japonicum x molle); the hybrid cultivar shown is typical of this group, according to Beckett, originating in Belguim, starting with selection of R. japonicum, later crossed with R. molle, a species from E. China, producing similar plants but with larger flowers with more varied and intense coloring, primarily pink and vivid rose, or yellow; deciduous shrub 1-3 m high, with erect branches, oblanceolate leaves 5-15 cm long, gray velvety beneath; the flowers appearing before the foliage, 5-6 cm across, blooming May-June. *Zone 6.*   p. 713

'Mrs. G.W. Leak' (Koster and Zonen 1934); outstanding hybrid of compact habit, with lanceolate evergreen leaves and huge conical clusters of strikingly beautiful pale pink flowers, with contrasting dark crimson center, the corolla open funnel-shaped 12 cm or more across, for mid-season bloom. *Zone 7.*   p. 719

mucronatum (Azalea indica alba or ledifolia alba) (Japan), "Snow azalea"; spreading semi-evergreen or evergreen shrub to 2 m high; corrugated elliptic leaves 6 cm long; funnel-shaped fragrant white flowers with flaring lobes 5 cm across, blooming in May. According to Wyman, it is the hardiest of white-flowered evergreen azaleas. *Zone 5.*   p. 716

mucronulatum (Azalea) (N.E. Asia, China to Korea), "Korean azalea"; very early-blooming shrub to 2 m, with erect branches, deciduous or half evergreen, the narrow leaves 3-8 cm long; bell-like flowers appearing before leaves, rose-purple, to 4-5 dia., in profusion between January and April. *Zone 4.*   p. 716

obtusum (Azalea) (Japan), "Kirishima azalea" and parent of the Kurume group: spring-blooming evergreen becoming dense and bushy, 1 m or more high; leathery elliptic leaves 2-3 cm long, glossy dark green; small funnelform flowers carmine-rose with darker eye, 2½ cm across. Developed into numerous popular garden varieties. *Zone 6.*   p. 717

obtusum 'Amoenum' (Azalea amoena) (Japan), "Kirishima"; densely branched evergreen to 1½ m high, with small dark green glossy leaves 2-3 cm long; very floriferous with hose-in-hose double flowers brilliant magenta-red, in clusters, blooming Mid-May. *Zone 6.*   p. 716

obtusum 'Hino-crimson' ('Amoenum' x 'Hinodegiri'); Kurume type evergreen similar to Hinodegiri but while its growth is more compact, it is an improvement over the Hinodegiri in that its single flowers are a clear crimson-red without bluish overtones; late bloomer, fairly hardy. *Zone 6.*   p. 708

obtusum 'Hinodegiri' (Mist-of-the-Rising-Sun); an old favorite bushy evergreen 'Kurume' azalea, to 1 m high, fairly hardy, with glossy foliage and small 3 cm single flowers vivid carmine-red; late blooming Mid-May. *Zone 6.*   p. 708

obtusum hybrid (Japan), "Kurume" or "Hiryu Azalea"; group of evergreen hybrid azaleas 30 to 60 cm high, derived from various forms of R. obtusum, originating in Japan, of more compact form, smaller foliage and flowers than the R. simsii group of hybrids, both widely used by florists as greenhouse plants in pots for winter and spring forcing; the Kurumes are also planted much in gardens although not all of them are reliably winter-hardy north of Zone 7; flowers may be single, semi-double and double, 2 to 4 cm wide, and range in colors from white to pink, salmon, red and light purple, blooming in May. *Zones 6-7.*   p. 716

obtusum japonicum: see R. kiusianum

occidentale (Oregon to No. California), "Western azalea"; handsome deciduous shrub to 3 m and more, with rough, obovate leaves 3 cm long; funnelform flowers 3 cm across, pale pink to purple, blooming late May. *Zone 7.*   p. 716

'Peggy Ann' (Roehrs-Bauman hyb.); one of the loveliest azalea creations the bees have brought about, between Kurume hybrids and kaempferi; small 4 cm wide open hose-in-hose flowers, with two rows of white petals edged in rosy-pink like apple blossoms; late blooming; fairly hardy. *Zone 7.*   p. 709

periclymenoides (R. nudiflorum or Azalea nudiflora in hort.) (Maine to So. Carolina and Tenn.), "Pinxter-bloom" or "Wild honeysuckle"; deciduous shrub to 3 m high; sparry, slender branches with elliptic leaves to 8 cm long, lightly scented; funnelform flowers with corollas 3 cm across, the tube rose and flaring narrow lobes pink, displaying long protruding stamens, blooming April into May. *Zone 3.*   p. 716

periclymenoides 'Album' (Azalea nudiflora alba) (Maine to So. Carolina, Tennessee), "Honeysuckle azalea"; deciduous shrub 1 to

2 m or more high, with bristly hairy branches; elliptic to obovate leaves 3-10 cm long, vivid green above; inflorescence in clusters of funnel-shaped flowers 3 cm wide, with flaring lobes, pink in the species, white in this cultivar. Zone 4. p. 714

'Pink Pearl' (1897); an English evergreen hybrid derived from the large-flowering griffithianum of Sikkim and the hardy catawbiense; a shapely plant with very large trusses of good-textured, rose-pink flowers with darker shading and spotted maroon in throat; good for early forcing. Zone 7. p. 718

planecostatum (North Borneo); small equatorial shrub with broad-ovate leathery leaves, and waxy tubular red flowers, covered with fine pubescence; collected by J. Bogner of Bot. Garden Munich. Zone 10. p. 719

'Polar Bear' (Firefly x Snow); a 'Beltsville' hardy evergreen type azalea suitable for late blooming, small-flowered 4 cm, floriferous, pure white, hose-in-hose with flaring petals; shining green foliage. Zone 6. p. 708

ponticum (Azalea pontica hort.) (Spain, Portugal, Balkans, Asia Minor, Caucasus), "Pontic azalea"; vigorous evergreen shrub or tree-like to 8 m high, with glossy dark green elliptic leaves 10-20 cm long; blooming in June, with purplish-pink or purple single flowers 5 cm across. The pointed, glossy leaves distinguish this species from catawbiense. Used for trimmed hedges in Britain, and as understock for grafting better hardy rhododendrons. Zone 6. p. 716

prinophyllum (Azalea roseum hort.) (Québec and Maine to Illinois, Virginia to Oklahoma), "Piedmont azalea" or "Mayflower azalea"; deciduous flowering shrub to 2 m or more; elliptic or obovate leaves to 6 cm long, soft-downy beneath; spicy-fragrant funnelform blooms appearing with the foliage, whitish to pink or deep rose, 4 cm across, during May. Zone 3. p. 712

prunifolium (Georgia and Alabama), "Plumleaved azalea"; excellent deciduous ornamental 2 m or more high, obovate or oblong leaves to 12 cm long, ciliate at margins, on reddish shoots; funnelform flowers vivid orange to rich red, 3-4 cm wide, blooming after foliage unfolds, in July-August, latest of the season. Zone 7. p. 712

radicans (calostrotum) (Tibet, Burma or Myanmar), "Rockmantle azalea"; prostrate evergreen shrub forming low mats to 15 cm high; small 1-2 cm elliptic, rich green leaves; charming rose to purple flowers 2 cm wide, with flaring petals, usually solitary, downy and scaly outside; an attractive dwarf rockgarden plant. Zone 6. p. 716

repens hort.: see R. forrestii repens

rigidum (China: Yunnan); evergreen very floriferous shrub 1 to 2 m high, with oblanceolate leaves 4 to 6 cm long, scaly on both surfaces; clusters of funnel-shaped flowers, with corolla 5-lobed, pale rose with crimson markings, 3 cm long, blooming in May; in habitat growing on rocks at 2500 to 3000 m altitude. Zone 6. p. 715

'Rose Pericat' (x Simsii x Kurume 1931); one of the best "Pericat" azalea hybrids, of robust bushy growth, dark foliage and 6-7 cm pleasing clear pink double flowers with salmon sheen, center lacy and with red lines in throat, outer petals form a star; early. Zone 8. p. 709

'Roseum elegans'; old cultivar known for its hardiness, bred with R. catawba, a good evergreen species from mountainous regions of Virginia to Georgia; compact globular bush with leathery decurved, olive-green leaves, a heavy budder with numerous clusters of rosy-lilac flowers of good substance, 7 cm across, deeper at margins, and pale in the center, marked with purple spots on upper petals; mid-season blooming; very reliable and popular hybrid introduced by Waterer 1851. Zone 4. p. 713

russatum (China: N.W. Yunnan), "Royal Alp rhododendron"; excellent small, very floriferous evergreen shrub 60-120 cm high, with elliptic 3 cm leaves scaly on both surfaces, rusty-brown beneath; small but numerous blue-purple flowers with white throat, with 5 lobes spreading 3 cm wide, April-May blooming. Needs cool Alpine conditions and moisture. Zone 5. p. 714

schlippenbachii (Manchuria, Korea, Japan), "Royal azalea"; exquisitely beautiful deciduous azalea; shrub to 5 m high, with pubescent branchlets with obovate 6 to 12 cm leaves in whorls; beautiful funnelform flowers with flaring lobes to 9 cm across, pale pink to soft rose, April-May blooming and sweetly fragrant. Foliage turns orange to crimson in Autumn. Zone 4. p. 716

simsii (Azalea) (Yangtse Valley, E. China and Taiwan); evergreen or half-evergreen shrub to 1 m or more high, the branchlets appressed-hairy; leaves are dimorphic, having two differect characters: spring-leaves elliptic to ovate 5 cm long; summer-leaves oblanceolate or obovate, to 3 cm long; beautiful wide-open funnelform single flowers 5-6 cm across, the corollas rose-red to glowing crimson, during late Spring. Parent of the widely known "Belgian indica azaleas", grown by florists under glass, and forced to bloom from Christmas to Easter. Zone 9. p. 715

'SIMSII HYBRIDS' or "Belgian Indica azalea"; descendents of Rhododendron simsii native in moist-warm subtropical South China, Yunnan and along the Yangtse; deep rosy-red, to 4 m high. These hybrids were developed primarily for their large and showy double flowers, principally in Belgium, for forcing and flowering in pots; they are usually grafted on understock of 'Phoenicea concinna' for better growth and longer life; not winter hardy in cold climate.

x simsii 'Ambrosiana' (1948) ('Mad. Petrick' x 'Reinhold Ambrosius'); superb early flowering azalea; German hybrid easily forced for Christmas; vigorous grower with obovate glossy leaves and 7½ cm double flowers like little roses, glowing crimson-red. Zone 9. p. 56, 709

x simsii 'Eri' (Eric Schaeme) (1930), sport of Azalea 'Paul Schaeme'; dense habit with flowers double with small rosette in center, vivid salmon-rose, variegated and margined white; early. Zone 9. p. 709

x simsii 'Euratom'; a dwarf simsii azalea hybrid similar to 'Hexe' but with frilled flowers, vivid crimson with glistening hose-in-hose funnels, on plant of compact habit with broad, dark green foliage. Zone 9. p. 709

x simsii 'Hexe' (Azalea) (1888) (simsii x obtusum amoenum); excellent late season potplant, very free-blooming and of dwarf but even habit, with dark green leaves, and long lasting, smallish, 5 cm flowers a glowing crimson coming alive under light, the hose-in-hose petals frilled. Zone 9. p. 709

x simsii 'Leopold-Astrid' ('Picotee'); azalea hybrid 1933; sport of 'Vervaeneana'; a lovely improvement over 'Albert-Elizabeth', with very pretty, 8 cm double flowers white with pink, and bordered in a rich salmon-red, the margins daintily frilled; mid-season. Zone 9. p. 709

x simsii 'Madame Petrick' (Azalea indica hort.) (1901); not a strong grower but is known for its dependably early bloom and forces readily for Christmas; double flowers medium large and a bright carmine-rose. Zone 9. p. 709

x simsii 'Reinhold Ambrosius' (1930); beautiful German "Indica azalea" hybrid for early forcing in pots to bloom during winter-time; silky, soft rosy-red, wide open double flowers 7 cm across, with silky sheen, for mid-season January, February bloom indoors, and long lasting. Zone 9. p. 709

x simsii 'Triumph' "Belgian indica" azalea 1923, (Mad. Aug. Haerens x Lentegroet); strong grower, budding readily and early blooming; the double flowers are crimson-red and beautifully frilled, holding their fresh color for a long time. Zone 9. p. 709

'Snow'; popular "Kurume" azalea; willing grower with rich green, glossy foliage covered by masses of small 3 cm pure white, hose-in-hose flowers with freely spreading petals; early and mid-season. Zone 7. p. 709

'Southern Charm'; a typical, excellent "Southern indica" azalea, sport of 'Formosa', a phoeniceum hybrid; tall evergreen shrub with large 9 cm single flowers carmine-rose with red spots, the petals rounded and half free; rough-hairy 6 cm elliptic leaves. Sun tolerant and vigorous; mid-season bloom. This group of azaleas may be trimmed and trained into standard or poodle shapes. Zone 8. p. 708

stenophyllum (North Bornea: Sabah); most unusual exotic evergreen species often growing epiphytic or as lanky shrub with slender stems to 1 m long on Mt. Kinabalu in Tropical Borneo; leathery narrow linear, glossy green leaves 5-10 cm long and 3 mm wide; flowers nodding, with funnel-shaped waxy corolla to 3 cm long, orange-scarlet to bright red; collected by Dr. Weber of Vienna at 1500 to 3000 m altitude, blooming to December. Zone 11. p. 714

'Sweetheart Supreme' (1931); probably the best liked of 'Pericat' hybrids, of strong spreading, irregular growth; the buds are rosy-pink unfolding like a dainty sweetheart rose, opening flat to starlike 5 cm flowers with successively smaller circles of delicate pink petals toward center; mid-season. Zone 8. p. 709

'Trilby'; excellent evergreen Van Ness hybrid of dense, compact habit, with numerous medium-large flowers per head, rich deep crimson spotted with black in throat; thick-leathery leaves dark green and pointed; good for Easter forcing. (Queen Wilhelmina x Stanley Davies.) Zone 7. p. 718

vaseyi (North Carolina), "Pink-shell azalea"; deciduous shrub to 5 m high, with elliptic-oblong leaves 5-10 cm long, and lightly bristly; flowers in clusters of 4 to 8, with corolla rose-pink, 3-4 cm across, deeply 5-lobed; the upper 3 segments spotted red and grouped together, blooming April-May, before the new foliage unfolds. Zone 5. p. 718

viscosum (Maine to So. Carolina), "White swamp azalea"; spicy fragrant white-flowering deciduous azalea to 3 m or more high, blooming in June-July after all the new foliage has fully developed; the leaves are lanceolate, to 6 cm long, and turn orange to bronze in Autumn; beautiful white, fragrant flowers having long 5 cm tube and narrow lobes spreading wide, sticky viscose outside. Zone 3. p. 718

yakushimanum (metternichii var.) (Mountains of Kyushu), "Yakushima-Shakunage"; handsome rounded evergreen of compact habit to 75 cm high, with young silvery growths, dark glossy green lanceolate leaves to 8 cm long, tomentose beneath; erect clusters of bell-shaped flowers first pink, becoming white, the corolla 5-lobed 5 cm across, blooming in May. *Zone 6.*   *p. 718*

yunnanense (So. China: Yunnan); evergreen or partially deciduous shrub to 3 m high, with lanceolate and oblanceolate leaves 4 to 8 cm long, slightly hairy; clusters of white or pinkish flowers having flaring lobes spreading 5 cm wide, spotted crimson inside, blooming during May; valued for its profuse and never failing blossoming. *Zone 7.*   *p. 718*

RHODOHYPOXIS   *Hypoxidaceae*

baurii (baueri) (So. Africa), "Red star"; charming small perennial herb with short rhizome and fleshy roots; glaucous 8-10 cm ribbed basal leaves with spreading silky hairs; rose-red flowers 2-3 cm across, solitary in leaf axils on 10 cm stiff stalk; for a cool, sunny location. *Zones 8-10.*   *p. 425*

baurii pictus; color variation seen at Chelsea Flower Show, London 1984, having flowers with the six white petals prettily lined with crimson-red and tinted rose. *Zones 8-10.*   *p. 425*

baurii var. platypetala (So. Africa); lovely color variation from the mountains of N.W. Cape and Natal, and grown in California, where it blooms in June-July; small perennial 10 cm high, the stiff leaves are silky hairy; and flowers pure white, or white tinted with rose, 3 cm across, blooming in So. Africa during October to January. Hardy in England. *Zones 8-10.*   *p. 425*

RHODOLEIA   *Hamamelidaceae*

championii (Hong Kong); a small evergreen tree with reddish stem and petioles, glossy dark green, ovate, thick-leathery leaves, glaucous beneath; nodding 6 cm flowers with rosy petals in bracted heads. *Subtropic. Zones 9-10.*   *p. 735*

RHODOMYRTUS   *Myrtaceae*

tomentosa (India, Malaya, Philippines), "Rose myrtle" or "Hill guava"; evergreen shrub, sometimes a small tree to 3 m, nearly all parts densely downy; obovate, leathery leaves 3-8 cm long, having 3 prominent veins; small axillary rosy flowers 3 cm wide, with pink stamens and downy outside; tiny 1 cm ovoid, berry-like purple fruit, pleasantly flavored. *Zone 10.*   *p. 802*

RHODORA canadensis: see RHODODENDRON canadense

RHODOTHAMNUS   *Ericaceae*

chamaecistus (Rhododendron chamaecistus) (Swiss and Austrian Alps), "Dwarf Alpine-rose"; low evergreen shrub to 30 cm high, dense with small leathery obovate 1 cm leaves; flowers with shell-pink corolla, spreading 2-3 cm across, displaying dark brown anthers, in April-May. *Zone 6.*   *p. 699*

RHODOTYPOS   *Rosaceae*

scandens (Japan, China), "White Kerria" or "Jetbead"; twiggy deciduous shrub 1-2 m high in cult., to 5 m in habitat; the greenish-brown branches with ovate leaves 5-8 cm long, doubly toothed, silky-hairy beneath; white flowers to 5 cm across, solitary at end of branchlets, having 4 petals and 4 toothed sepals, from May to July; very ornamental pea-size shining black fruit, persisting all Winter. *Zone 5.*   *p. 845*

RHOEO   *Commelinaceae*

spathacea 'Vittata' (discolor) (Mexico), "Oyster plant", "Moses-in-the-cradle" or "Variegated boat-lily"; fleshy rhizomatous rosette of stiff waxy lance-shaped, metallic dark green leaves, striped lengthwise with pale yellow and tinted red, vivid glossy purple beneath; in the leaf-bases, little white flowers are peeking from boat-shaped bracts. *Subtropic. Zone 11.*   *p. 52*

RHOICISSUS   *Vitaceae*

capensis (Vitis) (So. Africa), "Evergreen grapevine"; strong clambering vine with globular ground tubers; brown-hairy, somewhat woody stems, and long-stalked, thickish leathery, metallic green, glossy leaves nearly round or kidney-shaped, to 20 cm across, deeply lobed and wavy-toothed, rusty-tomentose beneath and at the margin; red-black glossy fruit. *Subtropic. Zones 9-10.*   *p. 299*

rhomboidea: see CISSUS rhombifolia (Zander)

RHOMBOPHYLLUM   *Aizoaceae*

nelii (Hereroa) (So. Africa), "Elkhorns"; clustering small succulent with spreading, gray-green leaves 2 to 2½ cm long, two-lobed at apex; flowers yellow, 4 cm across. *Arid-subtropic. Zone 10.*   *p. 148*

RHOPALOBLASTE   *Palmae*

ceramica (hexandra, elegans) (Malaysia, Java, Solomon Isl., New Guinea); graceful tropical fan palm 4 to 10 m tall, solitary or clustering, the slender, ringed trunk bearing a noble crown of arching pinnate fronds 2 to 3 m long, with numerous soft, pendulous leaflets; small ovoid orange-yellow to red fruit. *Zone 12.*   *p. 108*

RHOPALOSTYLIS   *Palmae*

baueri (Norfolk Is.); spineless feather palm to 15 m tall; clean-looking, ribbed trunk bearing an elegant crown of 3 m pinnate leaves, often larger than sapida, the leaflets stiff and glossy green; flowers white, followed by 2 cm red-brown fruit. *Zone 11.*   *p. 108*

sapida (New Zealand, Norfolk Is.), the "Nikau palm" also known as the "Feather-duster"; representing the southern limit of palms; attractive palm to 10 m or less high usually with straight trunk strongly ringed, 10-20 cm thick, and topped by a prominent bulbous crown-shaft; the pinnate fronds 1-4 m long, stand stiffly erect in a crown like a brush-like tuft, the erect, channeled leaflets glossy green, with split apex; purplish flowers at base of crown-shaft, and small vivid red fruit. *Subtropic. Zones 10-11.*   *p. 108*

RHUS   *Anacardiaceae*

aromatica (canadensis) (Ontario to Minnesota, south to Florida and Texas), "Fragrant sumac"; low-spreading deciduous shrub to 1 m high, with downy shoots; leaves compound of 3 leaflets 8 cm long, coarsely toothed and downy beneath; small yellowish, sweet scented flowers in dense heads, forming terminal clustered panicles, followed by small globose, hairy fruit. *Zone 3.*   *p. 639*

chinensis 'September Beauty' (species from Temp. E. Asia), "Nutgall tree" or "Chinese Sumac"; coarse growing suckering shrub or tree to 8 m high, with yellowish downy shoots, having alternate compound leaves of 7-13 ovate, toothed leaflets, velvety beneath; small creamy-white flowers in showy feathery clusters to 25 cm long, blooming August-September; small orange-red fruit. *Zone 5.*   *p. 637, 639*

copallina (Eastern U.S.), "Shining sumac"; very ornamental deciduous shrub or tree to 8 m high in the Southern U.S.; decorative pendant pinnate leaves on reddish shoots having 9-21 lanceolate leaflets 5-10 cm long, dark shining green, changing to reddish-purple; small greenish flowers in large terminal, compound clusters, in July to September; hairy crimson fruit. Beautiful autumn color. Source of Tannin. *Zone 4.*   *p. 639*

diversiloba (Brit. Columbia south to Baja California), "Poison oak"; extremely poisonous shrub 2 m or more high, occasionally climbing, similar to the Poison ivy of the East, but more shrubby; the leaves, compound of 3 leaflets glossy green, each rounded-lobed similar to oak leaves; small greenish-white flowers in axillary clusters, followed by berry-like whitish fruit. *Zone 6.*   *p. 639*

glabra (E. N. America), "Scarlet sumac" or "Vinegar tree"; ornamental deciduous shrub or tree to 6 m tall, with red woody stems; long feathery, bipinnate leaves, the 11-31 lanceolate, toothed leaflets 5-12 cm long, becoming bright red in Autumn; greenish flowers in dense clusters; hairy scarlet fruit. *Zone 2.*   *p. 639*

ovata (Arizona to California, Baja California), "Sugarbush"; evergreen shrub of the Southwest deserts, to 3 m high, rarely a tree; spreading branches with glossy leathery leaves 4-8 cm long, usually entire and trough-shaped; small white or pinkish flowers in dense clusters, in Spring; followed by reddish pubescent, small fruit. Very drought tolerant. *Zone 9.*   *p. 639*

radicans (Toxicodendron) (No. America from Canada to Guatemala), "Poison ivy"; trailing vine or climbing shrub, deciduous in cold climate, supporting itself by aerial roots; compound leaves of 3 ovate or rhomboid leaflets 10 cm long, dull dark green or glossy, and having occasional coarse teeth, lighter green and pubescent underneath; in Autumn turning orange or red; greenish-white flowers, small whitish waxy axillary berries. Weedy in shady gardens and all parts very poisonous to the touch, and especially its sap, causing painful blisters. *Zone 3.*   *p. 638*

typhina (Northeastern No. America), "Staghorn sumac"; deciduous shrub or small tree 4 to 10 m tall, with spreading crown; the twigs densely covered by a velvety brown fur like on deer's antlers; pinnately compound leaves to 60 cm long, with up to 31 odd-pinnate lanceolate leaflets, toothed at margins, and coloring orange to brilliant red in Autumn; on female trees with fuzzy crimson fruit. The bark is a source of tannin. *Zone 3.*   *p. 639*

typhina 'Laciniata', "Lacy velvet sumac"; ornamental multi-stemmed large shrub, or tree to 8 m high; the large decorative densely pubescent leaves bipinnate with 11-31 deeply cut leaflets 12 cm long, giving a ferny effect; hairy crimson fruit. *Zone 3.*   *p. 639*

RHYNCHSPORA — see under RYNCHOSPORA

RIBES   *Saxifragaceae*

alpinum (Mts. of No. and C. Europe to Spain, Italy, Bulgaria, Siberia), "Mountain currant"; deciduous unarmed unisexual shrub to 2 m or more high, densely bushy, with small 2-3 cm ovate leaves usually 3-lobed and toothed, and scattered bristly; small greenish-yellow flowers in erect pyramidal racemes, 20 to 30 on male plants about 6 cm long, less on females; blooming April-May; dark red, sweet edible berries produced on pistillate specimen. *Zone 2.*   *p. 873*

aureum (Washington to Montana, California), "Golden currant"; unarmed, deciduous shrub to 2 m high; the leaves usually 3-lobed and toothed, 2-5 cm wide; small yellow, spicely fragrant flowers in pendant racemes to 5 cm long, in April; followed on female plants by yellow to red to black berries of tart taste. *Zone 2.*   p. 873

glaciale (Himalayas; China: Hupeh, Yunnan, Tibet); deciduous shrub 2 to 4 m high, similar to R. alpinum; young growth reddish; leaves trilobed or 5-lobed, with crenate margins; small flowers purplish-brown, in clusters; fleshy berries scarlet-red, tart in taste. *Zone 3.*   p. 873

x nidigrolaria (R. nigrum hyb. x divaricatum hyb.) "Josta berry", a black currant x gooseberry hybrid; vigorous deciduous shrub to 2 m high, with unarmed branches; ovate leaves glossy green, palmately veined and shallowly lobed; fruiting is on last year's wood, produced in small clusters, berries larger than currants all along the stem; in taste they are slightly sweeter and juicier than black currants; they freeze well and make fine jam and juice. *Zone 4.*   p. 942

nigrum (C. Europe to Siberia, Caucasus, Himalayas), "Black currant"; unarmed shrub 1-2 m high; the leaves are 5-10 cm wide, having a heavy, very distinctive odor, due to yellow glands beneath; the small greenish-white flowers in drooping racemes blooming April-May; followed by glossy black berries, filled with juicy, musky sweet flesh, made into fruit juice and marmalade. *Zone 4.*   p. 942

odoratum (So. Dakota to Texas and Arkansas), "Buffalo currant" or "Clove currant"; unarmed shrub of loose habit to 2 m high, with shiny green or glaucous 3 to 5-lobed firm leaves 2-6 cm wide and large fragrant flowers golden-yellow, the corolla tubular with spreading lobes, followed by black berries on female plants. *Zone 4.*   p. 873

petraeum (Mts. of Europe, No. Africa), "Ornamental currant" or "Rock currant"; deciduous erect shrub to 2 m high with robust brownish branches; tri-lobed leaves to 10 cm wide, margins toothed; small bell-flowers green to reddish, numerous in clusters; acid dark red fruit. *Zone 6.*   p. 873

rubrum (No. Europe, No. Asia), "Northern red currant"; unarmed deciduous shrub to 2 m high, with stiff erect branches, the small leaves palmately veined and lobed; small greenish-brown flowers in racemes, followed by mini grape-like, pendant clusters of glossy, crimson-red berries, very tart-juicy and invitingly tasty when eaten fresh; very popular in Scandinavia. *Zone 4.*   p. 942

sanguineum (Coast reg. of Brit. Columbia to No. Calif.), "Winter currant"; attractive ornamental deciduous shrub 2 to 4 m tall, with pubescent aromatic branches; maple-like 3 to 5-lobed leaves 6-10 cm wide, downy beneath; showy 2 cm flowers deep pink to rose-red; female plants produce glaucous bluish-black 1 cm berries in drooping clusters. Probably the most ornamental of currants. *Zone 6.*   p. 873

sativum (W. Europe), "Red currants"; deciduous shrub to 1½ m, unarmed, with erect canes; palmate, lobed leaves; flowers green or purplish; glossy little, juicy red fruit 5-8 mm dia. in pendant clusters, with tart flavor. Ribes are subject to white pine blister rust disease; cultivation restricted in U.S.A. *Zone 5.*   p. 942

sativum 'White Versailles' (W. Europe); French cultivar with long pendant, grape-like clusters, very attractive with its mini berries translucent amber-yellow; very juicy with tart-sweet flesh; refreshing when eaten fresh because of its aromatic acid-sweet taste; also popular as dessert sweetened with sugar. *Zone 5.*   p. 942

speciosum (Santa Clara Co. of California to Baja Calif., Mexico), "Fuchsia-flowered gooseberry"; handsome subtropic evergreen shrub to 4 m high; the branches gray-brown with 1-2 cm thorns at joints; leaves thick and 3 cm long, 3-lobed and toothed at margins; pendant flowers with narrow purplish-red sepals, red petals in bells, and long protruding anthers; followed on female plants by bristly red fruit. *Zone 9.*   p. 873

uva-crispa (grossularia), "English gooseberry"; low deciduous spiny shrub to 1 m high, with roundish, 5-lobed leaves 2 to 6 cm wide, soft-hairy beneath; small greenish to pinkish flowers, followed by thin-skinned pubescent, globular fruit about 2 cm dia., usually green to yellowish, but in some varieties red, and filled with tasty juicy flesh, tart but sweeter when fully ripe; eaten fresh or for preserves. *Zone 4.*   p. 942

RICHEA   *Epacridaceae*

scoparia (Tasmania), "Austral heather"; interesting bushy shrub to 1½ m high, branching freely from the base; stem clothed with sheathing, shingled narrow leaves to 8 cm long, they are stiff and pointed, set in rosettes and looking like small bromeliads; from the apex the small 1 cm white to pink bell-flowers in erect terminal spires to 30 cm long, followed by dense columns of oval, glossy rose-red berries. *Zone 9.*   p. 698

RICINUS   *Euphorbiaceae*

communis (Trop. Africa), "Castor-oil plant" or "Palma Christi"; striking gigantic tree-like annual herb to 5 m high, or in the tropics where it is widely naturalized, a tree to 12 m; in gardens often planted for foliage effects; from a stout hollow stem, the large handsome peltate leaves, palmately divided into 5 to 11 crenate lobes, 15 to 90 cm across, and with metallic luster; small greenish-white, unimpressive flowers in clusters on long stalks, followed by attractive 3 cm prickly husks covered by brown spines and containing the poisonous seeds, source of castor oil. *Tropical. Zones 10-11.*   p. 528, 725

RIVINA   *Phytolaccaceae*

humilis (laevis) (West Indies, Mexico, So. America), "Rouge plant"; soft-leaved herb to 1 m high, with thin stem and branches; membranous, green, lightly pubescent, ovate foliage, and pendant little sprays of tiny pinkish-white flowers, forming lustrous little berries of bright crimson, soon dropping; used for red dye. *Zones 9-11.*   p. 470

ROBINIA   *Leguminosae*

x ambigua (pseudoacacia x viscosa) (syn. dubia); a hybrid locust tree with sticky shoots and small spines; odd-pinnate leaves having 13-21 elliptic leaflets; pea-like pale pink flowers tinted rose, axillary and in dense racemes. *Zone 6.*   p. 768

fertilis (hispida hort.) (No. Carolina to Georgia); handsome shrub to 2 m high, spreading by stolons producing new stems, with sticky branches; odd-pinnate leaves with 9-15 elliptic leaflets 2-5 cm long; interesting rose-pink flowers 2-3 cm long, partially covered by viscid white hairs, blooming in June; seed pods 5-7 cm long and bristly-hairy. Similar to R. hispida but leaves and flowers smaller. *Zone 7.*   p. 768

hispida (Southeastern U.S.), "Moss locust" or "Rose acacia"; semi-deciduous shrub 2 m or more high, of spreading habit, branches with bright red bristles; leaves divided into 3-6 pairs of leaflets; showy inflorescence in pendant racemes of deep rose flowers each 3 cm long. *Zone 5.*   p. 766

kelseyi (fertilis) (No. Carolina), "Alleghany moss"; shrub or small tree to 3 m or more, with prickly shoots, and odd-pinnate leaves of 9-13 oblong-ovate leaflets to 5 cm long; pea-like 2 cm flowers bright rose and soft pink with broad standard petal 2 cm across, in short clusters, blooming May-June. *Zone 7.*   p. 768

neomexicana (New Mexico, Arizona), "Western locust"; dense shrub to 2 m high, with pinnate leaves of 4-7 pairs of elliptic leaflets 3 cm long; lovely pink flowers in dense pubescent racemes, blooming in Summer; the fruit a legume 10 cm long. *Zone 9.*   p. 766

pseudoacacia (Pennsylvania to Georgia, Iowa and Oklahoma), a slow-growing "Black locust" or "False acacia"; attractive deciduous tree with odd-pinnate foliage on prickly branches, having 7-19 oval-ovate leaflets 2-4 cm long; pendant racemes to 20 cm long, of very fragrant, pea-like white flowers, the standard with a yellow spot at base, to 20 cm long; linear-oblong pods 5-10 cm long. *Zone 3.*   p. 768

viscosa (No. Carolina to Alabama), "Clammy locust"; deciduous tree 9 to 12 m high, with sticky shoots; odd-pinnate leaves to 25 cm long, with 11-25 ovate leaflets densely shingled on axis; 2 cm pale rose pea-flowers, having yellow spot on standard petal, the calyx dark red, in short racemes, blooming in June. The photo taken at Frankfurt Palmengarten, Germany, was of a plant grafted on R. pseudoacacia. *Zone 7.*   p. 768

ROCHEA   *Crassulaceae*

coccinea (Crassula rubicunda) (So. Africa); branched succulent subshrub to 60 cm high, with small pointed, closely set 2½ cm leaves on fleshy stem, green above, red beneath; tubular flowers bright scarlet and fragrant, in beautiful terminal clusters. *Subtropic. Zone 10.*   p. 190

falcata hort.: see CRASSULA falcata (Hortus)

RODGERSIA   *Saxifragaceae*

aesculifolia (C. China); decorative moisture-loving perennial, with deciduous foliage resembling horse-chestnuts, from thick scaly rhizome, 75 cm to nearly 2 m high with age; leaves palmately compound, the ribbed, oblanceolate leaflets 10-25 cm long, toothed along margins; white, brown-tomentose flowers with rounded sepals, in branched clusters on long brown-hairy stalks. *Zone 5.*   p. 498

pinnata (S.W. China: Yunnan); robust perennial to 1 m or more high, with hollow branches first erect, then arching; having odd-pinnate foliage with leathery, corrugated, oblanceolate leaflets to 20 cm long; pendant terminal branched clusters of small flowers reddish outside, and inside white, in July. *Zone 6.*   p. 498

podophylla (Korea, Japan); popular decorative waterside perennial to 1 m or more high, with large basal, palmately compound leaves, the obovate leaflets sharply toothed, 12-25 cm long, light green in Spring, metallic bronze toward Autumn; small yellowish-white flowers, in feathery, branched clusters, in June-July. *Zone 5.*   p. 498

sambucifolia (S.W. China: Yunnan); showy, robust perennial to 1 m high, with large pinnate basal leaves 20-35 cm long, the oblanceolate leaflets in widely separated pairs plus one terminal; small white flowers in dense terminal clusters. *Zone 6.*   p. 498

tabularis (Astilboides) (Manchuria, Korea), "Umbrella leaf"; bushy perennial to 1 m high, with shield-like, peltate leaves 30-60 cm across, the margins lobed or sharply toothed; small white flowers in many-headed inflorescence of numerous small clusters resembling Astilbe, blooming during June. *Zone 5.*   *p. 498*

RODRIGUEZIA   *Orchidaceae*
secunda (Colombia, Panama, Trinidad, Guyana), "Coral orchid"; epiphyte with compressed pseudobulbs and narrow leaves; arching stalks to 30 cm high with rosy flowers usually on one side, (Feb.-Oct.). *Tropical. Zones 11-12.*   *p. 95*

ROHDEA   *Liliaceae*
japonica (Japan, China), "Sacred lily of China"; extremely durable, modest plant with thick rhizome; basal rosette of oblanceolate, arching, channeled or plaited, thick-leathery leaves, to 60 cm long, densely arranged somewhat in two ranks, matte green; white flowers aroid-like in dense spike; fruit a red berry. *Subtropic.* *Zones 9-10.*   *p. 451*
japonica 'Marginata' (Japan), "Sacred Manchu lily"; sheathing, channeled, leathery foliage black-green with white border; a favorite in Japan where hundreds of named varieties are cultivated by fanciers. *Subtropic. Zone 10.*   *p. 70*

ROMNEYA   *Papaveraceae*
coulteri (So. California, Mexico), "Matilija poppy" or "California tree-poppy"; perennial herb to 2½ m tall, with flexuous stems, and pairs of leaves pinnately cut, to 10 cm long; solitary fragrant white, showy flowers 15 to 25 cm across, blooming May to July and later. *Zones 9-10.*   *p. 468*

RONDELETIA   *Rubiaceae*
odorata (West Indies, Panama); evergreen shrub 1-1½ m high, with downy, straggling branches; ovate dark green leaves 5 cm long, in opposite, distant pairs, the margins wavy or turned down, dentate toward apex; clusters of fragrant, tubular flowers with 5 expanding lobes, 1½ cm across, cinnabar-red with conspicuous yellow eye. *Zones 10-11.*   *p. 859*

RORIPPA   *Cruciferae*
sylvestris (Nasturtium) (No. Hemisphere), "Creeping yellow cress" or "Swamp cress"; scrambling perennial bog plant growing near streams, to 45 cm high; leaves deeply cut or pinnate; small yellow flowers in clusters during late Summer. *Zone 5.*   *p. 328*

ROSA   *Rosaceae*
'American Pillar' (Van Fleet 1902) (wichuriana hyb.); robust favorite old rambler climbing to 5 m high; with glossy leathery pinnate leaves, profusely bearing big clusters of large fragrant wide open carmine-rose flowers with white eye; fruit red. *Zone 5.*   *p. 295*
banksiae (China), "Lady Banks rose"; charming climber with vigorous canes rambling to 6 m, very spiny, evergreen foliage; deciduous in cold winters; pretty 3 cm double flowers pale buff-yellow, in large clusters, slightly fragrant; good for arbors, in mild climates. *Warm temperate. Zone 7.*   *p. 295, 845*
x borboniana 'Magna Charta' (1876) "Hybrid-perpetual" rose; long favored for forcing in pots because of its prolific, bushy habit, producing numerous, erect canes with light green foliage, topped by clusters of great, very double, fragrant globular flowers with numerous, carmine-rose petals usually opening more or less at the same time and making a grand show. *Temperate. Zone 7.*   *p. 55*
canina (Europe, W. Asia), "Dog rose" or "Brier"; ancient rose with arching stems to 3 m and strong hooked spines; odd-pinnate leaves with 2 to 3 pairs of toothed leaflets; single flowers pink to white, 4-5 cm across; scarlet fruit, used medicinally, and its pulp makes pleasant mince-meat and jelly. *Zone 3.*   *p. 541, 845, 922*
centifolia (possibly Caucasus, but probably ancient hybrid of R. gallica, moschata, damascena), "Moss rose" or "Provence rose"; robust bush with strong canes armed with scattered spines; pinnate leaves with 5 to 7 ovate leaflets, hairy beneath; the showy, heavy flowers nodding, densely double rich rose, 8-10 cm dia., and sweetly fragrant. Grown in Europe, especially France, as a source of attar of roses, an essential oil distilled from the fresh flowers. *Zone 6.* *p. 845*
chinensis 'Judy Fischer' (var. minima) (Little Darling x Magic Wand 1983), "Miniature China rose"; with dark leathery, bronzy foliage; lovely small rose-pink, double flowers, pointed in bud, and free-blooming, of vigorous bushy habit, not over 25 cm high. *Zone 7.*   *p. 846*
chinensis 'Minima' (roulettii) (China), "Pygmy rose"; well-loved miniature, averaging about 20-25 cm high, vigorous, hardy and long-lived, with appealing 4 cm double flowers of lively rose-pink with pale eye, in continuous bloom; once thought lost to cultivation, it turned up again on the window-sill of a Swiss cottage in 1918. Also known as "Fairy rose". *Warm temperate. Zone 7.*   *p. 846*
chinensis 'Mutabilis' (Correvon 1932); interesting small cultivar; pinnate foliage with oval and elliptic leaflets, and large single flowers sulphur-yellow changing to orange, then red and finally crimson, the

broad petals spreading 5 cm wide. Seen in col. Bermuda Botanic Garden. *Zone 7.*   *p. 846*
chinensis 'Nozomi' (Onodera 68) (Fairy Princess x Sweet Fairy); groundcover miniature rose with beastly thorny branches, but forming truly dense flat mats, very free to bloom with dainty pearl-pink, slightly fragrant; small glossy green pinnate foliage. A plant from England, deserving of a category of its own. *Zone 5.*   *p. 846*
chinensis 'Rise & Shine' (Pat. Moore); superior miniature introduced 1977, valued for its beautiful clear yellow double flowers 4 cm across, produced freely on a vigorous bush 50-60 cm high, blooming continuously for a long time. *Zone 5.*   *p. 846*
chinensis 'Viridiflora' "Green rose"; curious mutation originating 1855 in Charleston, So. Carolina; low evergreen shrub 30-80 cm high; pinnate leaves of 3-5 ovate leaflets to 6 cm long; the inflorescence unusual, in having corolla petals replaced by montrose serrated, narrow, thin green leaves or sepals, and small green sterile "flowers" tinted purple outside, and 5 cm wide. *Zone 7.*   *p. 846*
'Crimson Rambler'; the first hardy rambler hybrid of wichuriana x multiflora (1893); based on an old Chinese garden variety known as "Ten sisters"; a forerunner of many hybrids to come in various colors; pliable clambering stems producing on 1 yr. wood a fine burst of double, but rather small, crimson-red flowers all at once in June; the thin branches rooting where touching the ground; small dark glossy green leaves, subject to mildew. *Zone 5.*   *p. 295*
damascena (Asia Minor), "Damask rose"; old rose of hybrid origin in Asia Minor, introduced to Europe in the 16th Century; shrub 2 m or more high, the branches covered with numerous hooked prickles; the pinnate leaves having 5-7 ovate leaflets convex and often gray-green, downy beneath; large fragrant double flowers pink, varying to red, in July; oblong red, bristly fruit. Source of Attar of roses, distilled from the flowers. *Zone 5.*   *p. 845*
'Double Paul's Scarlet' (1943), 'Fern Roehrs' rose, beautiful, very double sport of 'Paul's Scarlet Climber'; a pillar rose with vigorous canes with deep green, leathery leaves, bearing axillary clusters abundant with large, fragrant, very double flowers 5-7 cm across, with 80-100 rolled, persisting petals, four times the number of the parent, and of a glowing deep scarlet-red with velvety sheen. *Temperate. Zone 5.*   *p. 295*
eglanteria (Hortus): see ROSA rubiginosa (Zander)
Floribunda class: a group of hybrids which was created by inbreeding the 'Multiflora' (rehderiana) with 'Hybrid Tea' ('Odorata') roses; more free-flowering over a longer season, with larger blooms than the 'Multiflora hybrids' and more vigorous.
x floribunda 'Fashion' (Jackson & Perkins 1949); charming 'Crimson Glory' hybrid of bushy habit to 60 cm high; matte, light green foliage; lovely flowers 8 cm dia., loosely double, luminous coral-pink, overlaid with gold; pointed red buds unfold slowly to wide hybrid-tea form; blooming profusely and with delightful rose fragrance. *Zone 5.*   *p. 847*
x floribunda 'Moulin Rouge' (Sanssouci) (Alain x Orange Triumph); upright, very busy cultivar with glossy foliage; medium size double flowers 5 cm across, carmine-red to rose-pink, having 20-25 petals, blooming in clusters; very floriferous as seen on Isle of Gotland, Sweden. *Zone 5.*   *p. 847*
x floribunda 'Nordlicht' (Kordes 1957) (Bergfeuer x Gertrud Westphal); large double, high centered flowers deep cinnabar-red, and slightly fragrant, in small clusters; blooming profusely on vigorous low bush, with leathery foliage. *Zone 5.*   *p. 847*
x floribunda 'Rumba' (Poulsen 1958) ('Masquerade' x 'Poulson's Bedder' x 'Floradora'); vigorous, bushy plant with dark glossy leaves; abundant bloomer with double bicolor flowers (35 petals), cupped, slightly fragrant, center yellow, margins poppy red and of 6 cm dia. *Zone 5.*   *p. 847*
x floribunda 'Shocking Blue' (Kordes 1974) ('Silver Star' seedling); large fragrant flowers resembling tea-rose; pointed buds opening white with margins shaded bluish-purple; shrub of vigorous growth to 60 cm high, with glossy, dark green foliage; beautiful but somewhat tender. *Zone 7.*   *p. 847*
x floribunda 'Show Biz' (Jackson & Perkins Pat.), All-America winner 1985; very free bloomer with large double crimson-red flowers, opening cluster after cluster and holding its color well, and having a flat, open form 8 cm across, with wavy petals for charming character; a bush of compact habit to 90 cm high, dark glossy foliage very mildew resistant and always tidy. *Zone 5.*   *p. 847*
x floribunda 'Vogue' (Jackson & Perkins 1951) (Pinocchio x Crimson Glory); charming double rose of elegant tea-rose form of 25 petals, an ovoid bud opening with corolla recurved, salmon-pink shaded coral, and sweetly fragrant, 8-10 cm across; fine compact bush with glossy foliage. *Zone 5.*   *p. 847*
foetida (Armenia, Kurdistan, Iran to Himalayas), "Austrian brier rose" or "Foxrose"; in gardens since ancient times, brought by the

Moors to Spain in 13 Century; erect shrub 1 m or more high, having few, straight prickles; pinnate leaves with 5-9 leaflets; showy rich yellow, single flowers 5-6 cm across, blooming in June; of unpleasant odor. Naturalized in Austria to Spain. *Zone 5.* p. 845

Grandiflora class; this new group of hybrids approach in size of flowers the Hybrid Teas; developed by breeding of Floribundas with Hybrid Teas; characterized by more flowers per stem, in larger clusters than the HT, and individual stems longer than in the Floribunda, making them suitable for cutting; more nearly ever-blooming, tallish, with erect branches, reaching to 1½ m high.

(Grandiflora) 'Queen Elizabeth'; vigouous hybrid of Hybrid Tea and Floribunda, to 1½ m or more high, with Hybrid Tea type 9 cm flowers borne singly or in long-stemmed candelabras, soft rose-pink and very fragrant; very close to Hybrid Tea roses, this type is valuable for its large number of flowers appearing at one time. *Warm temperate. Zone 7.* p. 55, 848

hugonis (Central China), "Father Hugo rose"; excellent yellow species to 2 m high, vigorous with dark brown stems branching above, and with straight prickles below; foliage pinnate with 7-12 obovate leaflets to 2 cm long; canary-yellow flowers 5 cm across, solitary on short stiff branches, blooming May-June; the fruits are dark scarlet to blackish. *Zone 5.* p. 848

'Mad. Eugene Jacquet' (1916) (wichuriana x multiflora); a free-blooming, symmetrical "Rambler" rose much used for forcing in pots for Easter, the long, rambling canes trained into globes, baskets or on trellis, with fresh green, pinnate leaves and big clusters of small, fragrant, carmine-rose, double flowers on short, axillary branches appearing from the upper parts of winter-hardened canes of the previous season. *Temperate. Zone 5.* p. 295

moschata nepalensis (brunonii) (S.E. Europe to Himalayas), "Himalayan musk rose"; robust clamberer 3 to 8 m up, the stems with hooked spines; pinnate leaves having 5 or 7 leaflets 3-5 cm long; white single flowers 3-5 cm across, and sweetly fragrant, blooming June-July. *Zone 6.* p. 845

moyesii 'Geranium', (W. China), "Moyes rose"; erect shrub to 3 m high, with generally smooth branches having few, straight prickles; leaves odd-pinnate with 7-11 elliptic leaflets, the midrib silky-downy beneath, on prickly stalk; blood-red single flowers 6 cm across, blooming in June; followed by crimson-red flask-shaped fruit 3 cm long, used in making marmalade. The cv. 'Geranium' is of compact habit, with 5 cm, almost scarlet flowers, raised at Wisley, England. *Zone 5.* p. 922

multiflora (polyantha) (Japan, Korea), "Japanese rose" or "Baby rose", as known in hort., usually grown as a small bush, but in time or in habitat clambering up with rank canes to 3 m or more, covered by scattered spines, the pinnate leaves with leathery ovate leaflets to 3 cm long, deciduous in cold climate; freely blooming with white or pink simple flowers 2 cm across, in large clusters in June-July; small globular red fruit. Principal parent of the Polyantha roses. *Zone 5.* p. 846

x multiflora 'Cecile Brunner' (Mignon) (prob. Polyantha x Mad. de Tartas, Pernet 1881), "Sweetheart rose"; exquisite tea-rose type double flowers relatively small, with high pointed buds, opening with outer petals recurved, bright pink on yellow ground and deliciously fragrant; of dwarf, busy growth, with sparse, soft foliage; a well-beloved dainty hybrid of a nostalgic era; photographed on Bermuda. *Zone 7.* p. 847

x multiflora 'Margo Koster' (Sunbeam) (1935); excellent commercial "Baby-rose" (rehderiana), sport of 'Dick Koster', of short compact habit about 30 cm high, and large rather globe-shaped double flowers with incurved petals like 'Dick Koster' but a delicate soft light orange shading to salmon-red in the heart; good pot-forcer for Easter. *Temperate. Zone 5.* p. 55

x multiflora 'Margo Koster Supreme'; excellent Polyantha rose, larger than 'Margo Koster', with globular double salmon-rose flowers forced in pots for Easter; originated by Koster Nurseries, Boskoop, Holland. *Zone 5.* p. 847

x multiflora 'Mothersday' (1949) (Polyantha); excellent "Baby rose" (rehderiana) for pots, sport of 'Dick Koster', well-shaped, of small compact habit, never rambling, with glossy, pinnate leaves and short wiry branches profusely bearing clusters of relatively large, globular flowers of firm texture, deep crimson-red. *Temperate. Zone 5.* p. 55

nitida (Newfoundland to Connecticut), "Shining rose"; small species rose to only 60 cm high, suckering freely; the branches erect and covered with slender prickles and brown bristles; 7 or 9 narrow elliptic leaflets shining dark green, very ornamental and becoming red or purple in Autumn; showy solitary rosy-red single flowers up to 5 cm across, blooming in July; small bristly, scarlet fruit. *Zone 3.* p. 848

x noisettiana 'Maréchal Niel' (1864) (chinensis x moschata); a famous old "Noisette" rose of climbing habit, with long rambling canes which I remember my father training on wires following the ridge of his greenhouse, and from which developed weak, axillary, pendant branches with large, most beautiful, hauntingly fragrant blooms of a delicate pale yellow, resembling a fine Tea rose; not frost-hardy north. *Subtropic. Zone 7.* p. 295

x odorata 'Chicago Peace'; vigorous hybrid-tea rose to 1½ m high; large 12 to 15 cm fully double fragrant flowers of 50-60 petals, with yellow base, shell pink and coral toward margins, sweetly perfumed; glossy deep green leaves; beautiful sport of the famous HT 'Peace', but of darker, richer coloration. Originated in Wheaton, Illinois. *Zone 7.* p. 849

x odorata 'Double Delight' ('Granada' x 'Garden Party') (Pat.); strikingly beautiful bicolor ever-blooming "Hybrid-tea", with huge urn-shaped buds, opening to formal blossoms creamy-white, fully double with margins of outer petals recurved and edged with contrasting rich red, 12 cm across, having a delightful spicy aroma and carried on strong stems; excellent as cut flowers. Introduced by Armstrong Nurs. 1977. *Zone 7.* p. 849

x odorata 'Fragrant Cloud', exquisite "Hybrid-tea" originated in Germany as 'Duft-Wolke' (Math. Tantau 1963); bud ovoid, opening to 12 cm wide, double with 25-30 petals, well formed, coral-rose becoming geranium-red, in clusters of up to 10 blooms, and very fragrant; very vigorous with dark glossy foliage, and free-blooming. Introduced in U.S. Jackson & Perkins 1968. *Zone 7.* p. 849

x odorata 'Joseph's Coat' (Armstrong 1964) ('Buccaneer' x 'Circus'); hybrid-tea with large double flowers 8 cm across, slightly fragrant, yellow and red multicolor; dark glossy foliage; vigorous pillar rose; recurrent bloom. *Zone 7.* p. 849

x odorata 'La France'; world famous as prototype of first Hybrid tea or "Remontant rose" 1867, by Guillot of Lyon; seed parent oriental Tea rose 'Mme. Bravy' x pollen parent occidental Hybrid perpetual 'Mme. Victor Verdier'; elegant, ever-blooming, large flower of 60 petals, silvery-pink, very fragrant. *Zone 7.* p. 849

x odorata 'Madras' (Pat.), "Hybrid-tea" introduced by Jackson & Perkins 1981 Rose of the Year; brilliant cerise-red blooms, with petals outside rose-pink and white, and strong yellow at their base; the flowers measure up to 15 cm across, and have a mild refreshing fragrance; in bloom all season. *Zone 7.* p. 849

x odorata 'Mrs. W.C. Miller' (1909); a dependable old "Hybrid tea" rose of robust habit, and with leathery leaves, used for forcing in pots as it remains stocky, with a thick neck producing elegant, tightly double, dainty pink flowers flushed with rose, the petals are of good substance and unfold gracefully like a true Tea rose, with the same intense fragrance, blooming "monthly" into Autumn. *Temperate. Zone 7.* p. 55

x odorata 'Oregold' (Hybrid tea) ('Piccadilly' x 'Konigin der Rosen'); rich saffron yellow hybrid tea; high-centered double 12 cm blooms of heavy substance, 35-40 petals, with delicate tea fragrance (Tantau; All-America Award 1975). A radiant beauty that fills the garden with sunny brilliance. *Zone 7.* p. 849

x odorata 'Red American Beauty' (hybrid tea) ('Happiness' x 'San Fernando'); vigorous, upright growth, with deep green leaves; ovoid bud; double, fragrant flowers, large to 12 cm dia., deep crimson-red, prolific bloom. (Morey/Jackson & Perkins 1959). *Zone 7.* p. 849

x odorata 'Revue' ('Review') (Berkshire hyb. England); a beautiful hybrid-tea, with very large double flowers 15-18 cm across when open, and having some 50 petals, bright rose along margins, pale pink to white toward base; sweetly fragrant; the foliage matte green, on medium size plant. *Zone 7.* p. 849

x odorata 'Yankee Doodle' (Hybrid tea) ('Color Wonder' x 'Kings Ransom'); tall growing, with massive double blooms (50 petals) peach-pink to orange, yellow reverse, of fruity fragrance; singly on stem tea-rose fashion (Kordes) (All-America Award 1976). *Zone 7.* p. 848

palustris (pensylvanica) (Eastern No. America), "Swamp rose"; stoloniferous shrub to 2 m high, spreading by rhizomes, with slender purplish-brown stem covered by hooked bristles; 5 to 7 or 9 oblong leaflets, finely toothed, on prickly stalk; showy single flowers soft to vivid pink 4-5 cm across, late season blooming July; bright red 1 cm fruit, retained long into Winter. *Zone 4.* p. 848

'Paul's Scarlet Climber' (Rambler) (Paul, England 1916); widely planted, vigorous rambler, with glossy pinnate leaves on stiff canes; medium size semi-double vivid deep scarlet flowers 5-6 cm across, in clusters, profusely blooming in early Summer and ideal on a garden fence or pillar. *Zone 5.* p. 298

pimpinellifolia (spinosissima hort.) (Ireland, but naturalized through Europe and W. Asia), "Scotch rose", "Burnet rose"; deciduous shrub forming patches to 1 m high, spreading from rhizomes; dense with very thorny and bristly slender branches; the leaves with small 1 to 3 cm oval and obovate pinnae, sharply toothed toward apex; flowers creamy-white or pale yellow, rarely pink, variably 3-5 cm across, sweetly scented, during May-June; rounded purplish-black fruit. *Zone 4.* p. 848

'Polyantha': see R. multiflora (Hortus)
roulettii: syn. of R. chinensis 'Minima' which see
rubrifolia (glauca) (Cent. Europe: Pyrenees to Yugoslavia), "Redleaf rose"; very winter-hardy shrub to 2 m high, having few spines; valued for its reddish foliage and purple shoots, but sparsely blooming with rose to purplish single flowers 3-5 cm across, sub-tended by purplish-red sepals, in June; roundish red fruit. *Zone 2*.   p. 846
rubiginosa (Zander) (eglanteria in Hortus) (Europe to W. Asia), "Eglantine" or "Sweetbrier"; dense shrub scrambling to 2 m high, much found as hedgerows or hedges in Europe, the canes covered with hooked prickles; sweet-scented leaves pinnate with small roundish leaflets, pubescent beneath; bright pink single 3 cm flowers, pale in center, followed by beautiful orange to scarlet ovoid fruit (hips) in Autumn. *Zone 4*.   p. 295
rubiginosa 'Magnifica' (Hortus III: eglanteria) (C. Europe, Asia Minor), "Hedge rose"; much used for hybridizing; flowers single or semi-double, bright rose 3 cm dia.; scarlet fruit; thorny canes 1-2 m long; foliage hairy beneath. *Zone 2*.   p. 846
rugosa (W. Asia, China, Japan, Korea), "Turkestan rose", "Japanese or Ramnanas rose"; popular species rose to 2 m or more high, densely bristly and prickly, the leaves pinnate having 5-9 toothed leaflets 3-5 cm long, shining green above and hairy beneath; large fragrant, red or white flowers 6-8 cm across, having reflexed, hairy sepals, June-July blooming; the colorful showy brick-red round fruits or "hips" are 2-3 cm dia. and crowned by erect sepals; often used in preserves and jams. Useful for hedges, with leaves turning gorgeous orange-yellow in Autumn. Resistant to salt spray if planted along ocean shores. *Zone 2*.   p. 541, 620, 922
rugosa plena (No. China, Japan), "Double Turkestan rose"; very hardy rambling shrub, valued because of its showy double flowers purplish-carmine-rose; formerly known on the prairies of Midwest U.S.A. as "Empress of the North". *Zone 2*.   p. 845
spinosissima (Hortus): see R. pimpinellifolia (Zander, Kruessmann)
sweginzowii (N.W. China: Kansu); upright shrub to 3 m or more high, the canes and reddish shoots covered by large 3-angled straight spines, mixed with bristles; few on flowering branches; leaves pinnate with 7-13 toothed leaflets; rose-pink flowers 4 cm across in June; flask-shaped orange-scarlet fruit 3 cm long and bristly. *Zone 6*. p. 848
villosa (Europe to Iran), "Apple rose" or "Hedge rose"; vigorous wild rose with scandent stems covered with slender prickles; leaves with 2 or more pairs of leaflets 2-4 cm long, hairy on both sides; single flowers pink to carmine-rose, 3-5 cm across. Fruit is eaten and used for beverages. *Zone 5*.   p. 848
xanthina 'Canarybird' (parentage China and Japan), "Manchu rose"; prob. hybrid of hugonis x xanthina; charming semi-double flowers 3-5 cm across, lighter yellow than the species; fruit blackish-purple. Photographed at Chelsea Flower Show, London. *Zone 5*.   p. 848

ROSCOEA   *Zingiberaceae*
alpina (Himalayan Region: Kashmir, Nepal); perennial with fleshy roots, and leafy stems 10-20 cm high, the lanceolate light green, fleshy leaves in a loose rosette; short inflorescence terminal with 1 or 2 flowers, calyx green and slit to base, the corolla pink with deep purple upper petal, and with two-lobed lip; summer-blooming. *Zones 9-10*.   p. 522
cautleoides (China: N.W. Yunnan); tall, slender perennial 25-40 cm high, with fleshy roots and leafy stems, the lower part with 2 sheaths; the leaves sessile and lanceolate, glossy green; at top of stem the inflorescence of 4 to 7 large sulphur-yellow flowers 5-8 cm long, the dorsal petal hooded; summer-blooming. *Zone 7*.   p. 522
humeana (China: West Yunnan); perennial herb with thick-fleshy roots, lanceolate parallel veined leaves 10-30 cm long, green and smooth, sheathed at base; stout, short terminal spike with 4 to 8 large trumpet flowers to 10 cm long, purple or blue, the upper bracts veined dark purple. *Zone 8*.   p. 522
purpurea (Sikkim Himalayas); perennial herb with thick-fleshy roots, to 30 cm high; stems with lanceolate sessile leaves; almost hidden in the upper foliage, short-stalked clusters of deep purple flowers 4 cm across, the dorsal petal arching; summer-blooming. *Zones 9-10*.   p. 522

ROSIOGLOSSUM (Zander):
see ODONTOGLOSSUM (Hortus)

ROSMARINUS   *Labiatae*
officinalis (Mediterranean reg.), "Rosemary" or "Garden sage"; evergreen shrub to 1 m or more high, with downy shoots well known as a sweet herb, and grown for its aromatic leaves which are needle-like and grayish, shiny above, white downy beneath, 2-4 cm long; axillary flowers light blue. Leaves fresh or dried have a pleasant, pungent odor and are used for seasoning of meats, oven roasts,

soups, stuffing, or for dressings. Tasty honey is made by bees. *Zones 8-10*.   p. 533, 539, 618
officinalis majorica (Portugal), "Pink rosemary"; attractive variety with green, aromatic foliage, and showy spires of soft pink flowers. *Zones 8-10*.   p. 533
officinalis 'Prostratus', "Creeping Rosemary"; a variety more low and compact growing, with branches having a tendency to grow sideways. *Zones 8-10*.   p. 316

ROTHMANNIA   *Rubiaceae*
capensis (Gardenia rothmannia) (So. Africa), "Scented cups"; attractive evergreen shrub or tree to 3 m with oval, glossy leaves; flowers when in bud are greenish-cream, when open the spreading lobes are ivory-white inside with maroon spots in the throat; sweetly scented; decorative globose, hard green fruit the size of a small orange. *Zone 10*.   p. 858

ROYSTONEA   *Palmae*
elata (Oreodoxa) (South Florida), "Florida royal palm"; majestic feather palm at home in the Everglades, on wet ground; similar to R. regia but taller; smooth gray trunk to 32 m tall, swollen above the middle, graced by a heavy crown of arching plume-like pinnate leaves to 6 m high, the leaflets glossy deep green arranged in several rows, on bright green petiole; long inflorescence with fragrant flowers followed by round, circular 2 cm dark red fruit. *Subtropic. Zone 11*.   p. 110
oleracea (Trinidad, No. South America), the "South American royal palm"; very tall feather palm 30 m or more high, with slender erect, smooth trunk not bulging, bearing the large glossy green crownshaft, and crown of gracefully arching pinnate fronds 3-6 m long, the numerous glossy leaflets attached to rachis in opposite, horizontal rows; fragrant flowers, and small purplish-black fruit. *Tropical. Zones 11-12*.   p. 110
regia (Oreodoxa) (Cuba), "Cuban royal palm"; smooth erect gray trunks somewhat swollen above the middle, to 20 m high or more, with a terminal crown of gracefully arching feathery fronds regularly pinnate, 2-3 m long, the pinnae to 75 cm long and 2 cm wide, bright green and prominently ribbed and arranged in double rows, in 2 planes on either side of the axis. *Tropical. Zones 11-12*.   p. 110
venezuelana (No. South America), "Venezuelan Royal palm"; stately feather palm with smooth, straight gray trunk; the fronds when young on purplish petioles; leaflets broader and more shiny than R. oleracea; smaller in habit with shorter trunk, but relatively large crown. *Tropical. Zone 11*.   p. 110

RUBIA ornamentale hort.:   see CARPHALEA kirondron

RUBUS   *Rosaceae*
calycinoides (Taiwan), "Chinese bramble"; evergreen, trailing subshrub, creeping with prickly branches, rooting along the ground and forming carpet; roundish, lobed and crinkled 4 cm leaves, white-felted beneath; small white flowers similar to those of strawberries, followed by salmon-colored berries. *Zones 7-9*.   p. 321
chamaemorus (No. Canada, Labrador; Arctic Scandinavia), "Cloudberry" in Scandinavia, "Baked apple berry" in Newfoundland; subshrubby or herbaceous perennial 8-25 cm high, with slender, unarmed stem springing from a woody rootstock, or creeping rhizome; 2 to 4 leaves rounded in outline and lightly lobed; solitary white flowers 2-3 cm across; flavorful reddish or orange soft berry-fruit of mild sweet taste, high in Vitamin C, eaten fresh, used for preserves, also made into liqueur. Suitable for the cool moist rockgarden. *Zone 2*.   p. 932
fruticosus (Europe), "European blackberry"; deciduous or semi-evergreen shrub with scandent, angled, usually prickly canes; the leaves compound of 3 or 5 toothed leaflets, glaucous beneath; white or pink 2 cm flowers followed by glossy black berry-fruit, quite sweet and tasty to eat fresh; also used for preserves, and to make the well-known blackberry brandy. *Zone 3*.   p. 932
idaeus (Eurasia), "Red raspberry"; scandent shrub with prickly canes propagated by suckers; leaves with 3 or 5 toothed leaflets; small whitish flowers; deliciously sweet, aromatic red berry fruit. *Zone 3*.   p. 932
laciniatus 'Prof. Rudloff' (Europe), "Thornless blackberry"; trailing shrub with perennial canes, without thorns in this European cultivar; leaves cut into toothed segments, flowers white or pink; juicy black, edible berries. *Warm temperate. Zone 5*.   p. 932
x loganobaccus (ursinus x idaeus) (Pacific Northwest), "Logan-berry" or "Tayberry" in Germany; California hybrid seedling 1881; vigorous rambling shrub, similar in habit to Blackberry, with thin vining annual branches 2-3 m long; leaves compound mostly of 5 leaflets, densely hairy beneath; large white flowers in June-July, self-fruitful on 1 year wood; the impressively large fruit pendant, resembling raspberries in structure but more oblong to 3 cm long, purplish-red and of acid-sweet taste unless fully ripe. Valuable for preserves. *Zone 8*.   p. 932

x loganobaccus cv. 'Boysen' (Oregon to Baja California), "Boysenberry"; vigorous shrub with lightly thorny scandent or trailing branches, the leaves palmately compound of mostly 5 pinnae, densely pubescent beneath; large white flowers followed by purplish-red fruit 3 cm long, changing to reddish-black at maturity, and of sweet taste; borne on canes of previous year's growth. Zone 6. .... p. 932

odoratus (Nova Scotia to Michigan, Georgia and Texas), "Flowering raspberry"; ornamental shrub to 3 m high, with nearly spineless canes, the bark shedding; forming colonies branching from the base; leaves 3-5 lobed, to 25 cm wide and jaggedly toothed, at first soft and velvety beneath; the flowers rose-purple and fragrant, 3-5 cm across, clustered in broad panicles, from July to September; fruit is red but not tasty. Zone 3. .... p. 850

parviflorus (Michigan to Alaska, so. to Mexico), "Thimble berry" or "Salomon berry"; unarmed deciduous shrub to 2 m high, increasing by young canes from the base, and forming dense thickets; 3-5 lobed leaves 10-20 cm across, and irregularly toothed; flowers pure white 3-6 cm wide, in terminal clusters, blooming in June; small red fruit edible but of little flavor, however is used for preserves and jellies. Zone 3. .... p. 850

phoenicolasius (China, Japan, escaped in U.S.), "Wineberry"; deciduous shrub reaching 2-3 m, the stems biennial, covered with colorful red-brown bristles, and arching gracefully, rooting at the tip; the leaves of 3 leaflets cordate-ovate, coarsely toothed, and having purple veins, white-tomentose beneath; flowers whitish or pink, in close clusters; large bristly calyx; small bright red edible sweet berry-fruits. Zone 5. .... p. 932

reflexus (moluccanus) (So. China, Hong Kong), "Trailing velvet plant"; attractive robust, somewhat sparry woody clamberer with rambling stems having occasional thorns, the young growth, petioles and underside of the foliage covered with cinnamon-colored wool; sturdy, pubescent, toothed and lobed leaves 10-20 cm long, vivid emerald green painted with chocolate brown along primary ribs, followed by a zone of splashed silver. Handsome foliage vine especially striking in younger shoots and when kept warm; best planted out but if in pots, then trained on trellis or wire frame. Subtropic. Zone 10. .... p. 295

rosifolius 'Coronarius' (E. Asia), "Mauritius raspberry"; ever-green shrub with prickly, scandent canes 2 m or more long; pinnate leaves, with corrugated leaflets double-serrate, 3-9 cm long; flowers white, 4 cm across, very double in form coronarius; edible red berries, but insipid. Zone 7. .... p. 835

ulmifolius 'Bellidiflorus' (inermis: Zander) (W. Europe), "Double-flowered blackberry"; spreading semi-evergreen shrub 2-3 m high, with purplish downy stems armed with broad prickles; the 3 or 5 leaflets white felted beneath; small pink flowers double, in dense rounded clusters in July and August. Zone 6. .... p. 850

ursinus (Oregon to Baja California), "Pacific blackberry" or "Pacific dewberry"; scandent or vining canes with stout prickles, dull green foliage tomentose beneath and with 3 leaflets; flowers white; edible berries deep red to black, and very sweet; with delicious aroma. Warm temperate. Zone 6. .... p. 932

ursinus 'Thornfree', "Black Pearl dewberry", thornless black-berry of American origin; vigorous shrub with deciduous thornless, scandent canes; remarkably large-fruited, the berries lustrous black when ripe; the juicy flesh is of aromatic taste, about middle of August; excellent for the home garden. Zone 6. .... p. 932

tricolor (China: Yunnan); low evergreen spreading shrub to 30 cm high, deciduous in cold regions, with trailing bristly branches; dark green, cordate, corrugated leaves 8-10 cm long, white-felted beneath; white flowers with purple throat, 3 cm across, blooming July; followed by edible, bright red fruit. Zone 7. .... p. 774

RUDBECKIA　　*Compositae*

fulgida (Pennsylvania to Florida and Texas), "Orange cone flower"; perennial ½-1 m high, with 3-nerved, lanceolate leaves, and typical cone-flowers 8 cm across, with 12-14 orange-yellow rays surrounding the high, cone-like, black-purple disc. Temperate. Zone 3. .... p. 399

fulgida sullivantii (Connecticut to Michigan); showiest, very popular variety, with large flowers to 10 cm across, the rich yellow ray-florets encircling the blackish cone-disc; a robust perennial with ovate, crenate leaves along stems. Zone 3. .... p. 399

hirta 'Double Gloriosa', "Gloriosa daisy"; the tetraploid Gloriosa Double daisy strain has flowers 10-12 cm across, with two or more layers of ray-florets orange-yellow encircling the dark central cone. Warm temperate. Zones 4-9. .... p. 399

hirta 'Gloriosa', a tetraploid strain of the species of Ontario to Florida and Texas, "Gloriosa daisy" or "Black-eyed Susan"; annual or biennial, bristly-hairy, 30-60 cm high; sessile leaves spatulate to lanceolate; solitary flower heads to 15 cm across, with about 14 golden-yellow rays, often orange-red at base, to 5 cm long; and high purple-brown disc of tubular florets. Temperate. Zones 4-9. ...... p. 399

laciniata (Québec to Florida and Arizona), "Cutleaf Cone-flower"; tall perennial to 3 m high, with leaves pinnately divided into toothed or lobed segments; flower heads 10 cm across, with yellow rays soon drooping, and greenish-yellow disc; summer-blooming. Zone 3. .... p. 399

nitida 'Autumn Sun' ('Herbstsonne'), (the species from Georgia to Texas); attractive clustering perennial with stem 1½ m tall; bright green ovate leaves, and showy floral heads 10 cm across, with broad, deep yellow ray-florets, around the raised green to brownish central cone, in late Summer. Zone 4. .... p. 399

purpurea: see ECHINACEA purpurea

triloba (New Jersey to Minnesota, Georgia and Okla.), "Brown-eyed Susan"; herbaceous biennial or perennial to 1½ m high, with thinly hairy cordate-ovate leaves, also trilobed, on rambling branches; the numerous floral heads 6 cm across, with yellow ray-florets around the brown-purple raised disc. Zone 5. .... p. 399

RUELLIA　　*Acanthaceae*

ciliosa (humilis) (So. Carolina to Florida and Texas); hairy herbaceous subshrub to 30 cm high, with ovate rugose 8 cm leaves, ciliate; large 5 cm trumpet flowers variable, blue or white with purple midveins on lobes. Zone 8. .... p. 630

longifolia: see WHITFIELDIA elongata

macrantha (Brazil), "Christmas pride"; bushy plant with erect stems; opposite lanceolate leaves matte dark green, to 15 cm long, veins depressed; large trumpet-shaped flowers carmine-rose, with pale throat lined red. Zone 10. .... p. 630

RUMEX　　*Polygonaceae*

acetosa (Europe, Asia, natural. in No. America), "Garden sorrel" or "Sourdock"; tufting herbaceous perennial to 50 cm or more high, with fleshy succulent long-stalked basal leaves, various from oblong to arrow-shaped 8-15 cm long; small petal-less greenish-pink male flowers, in dense cluster. The leaves are used for salads. Zones 3-10. .... p. 476

scutatus (Europe and Asia), "French sorrel"; low annual or perennial herb with prostrate stems, large fleshy, broad ovate-cordate basal leaves 8-12 cm long, arrow-shaped along stems; small greenish petal-less flowers in clusters. The tender spinach-like leaves have unique sour flavor valued in French cuisine, their sorrel soup, tasty in salads, as sauce for beef, or cooked with cabbage. Zone 7. .... p. 542

RUMOHRA　　*Polypodiaceae (Filices)*

adiantiformis (Polystichum adiantiforme, capense or coriaceum) (So. America, So. Africa, New Zealand, Polynesia), "Leather fern"; a spreading fern in dense clusters with creeping brown rhizome, similar to Davallia, with fresh green fronds to 1 m, thick-leathery, 1-3 pinnate, with oblong segments coarsely toothed. Also known as Aspidium capense or Arachniodes, the "Leather-leaf-fern". Subtropic. Zones 9-11. .... p. 140

RUSCHIA　　*Aizoaceae*

karrooica (Cape Prov.: Karroo); robust, stiff desert shrub 30 cm high, the branchlets with succulent cylindric blue leaves having a recurved spiny point and dotted with green, to 2 cm long; solitary 5 cm flowers with purplish petals having dark purple stripe. Zone 10. .... p. 148

RUSCUS　　*Liliaceae*

aculeatus (England, Mediterranean reg. to Iran), "Butchers broom"; erect shrub with tiny greenish flowers curiously borne along midrib of the ovate, stiff, spiny, leaf-like branches (cladodes); berries bright red, during Winter, borne on female plants. Branches are cut, dried and dyed different colors mostly red, for floral decorations. Zone 7. .... p. 772

hypoglossum (Hungary, Italy, Egypt, Asia Minor), "Mouse-thorn"; evergreen, tufted shrub with creeping rootstock and rigid stems to 45 cm high or more, the flexible, leaflike branches, or cladophylls, narrow and tapering to both ends, 6-10 cm long, and bearing small yellow flowers on their centers. Zones 7-9. .... p. 205, 772

RUSPOLIA　　*Acanthaceae*

seticalyx (Trop. Africa); small straggling shrub, with cylindrical branches; stems and foliage lightly hairy, the leaves are ovate, opposite and corrugated; the flowers in terminal clusters, with tubular corolla and flaring lobes, cinnabar-red and pale beneath. Zone 11. .... p. 631

RUSSELIA　　*Scrophulariaceae*

equisetiformis (Mexico), "Coral plant" or "Fountain plant"; shrubby plant with whip and rush-like, 4-angled stems to 1 m long, arching or pendulous; the normally lanceolate dentate leaves mostly reduced to small scaly bracts on the branches; tubular two-lipped flowers with fiery scarlet-red corolla 3 cm long, in nearly continuous bloom. Subtropic. Zone 10. .... p. 875

RUTA   *Rutaceae*
graveolens (So. Europe), the "Herb-of-grace" or "Common rue"; strongly aromatic subshrub to 1 m high, with 2-3-pinnate leaves, and small starry, yellowish flowers in terminal clusters; cultivated for centuries in herb gardens, and its name was associated with repentance as sprigs of rue were sprinkled on holywater in early Christian ritual. A leaf or two are excellent flavorings in salad dressing. The leaves can cause skin irritations, but are also used for medicinal purposes. *Zone 4.*   p. 543

RYNCHOSPORA — spell RHYNCHOSPORA
Cyperaceae
alba (nervosa) (Trop. America), "Star grass"; very ornamental perennial grass, with leafy stems 30-40 cm high, the narrow, glossy green, keeled, soft leaves 1 cm wide and 25 cm long, ciliate at margins; a wiry stalk topped by showy inflorescence of small white flowers, subtended by horizontally spreading broad bract-leaves silvery white at base, and forming stars. *Humid-tropical. Zone 10.*   p. 329

SABAL   *Palmae*
bermudana (Bermuda), "Bermuda palmetto"; massive fan palm 6 to 10 m or more tall, with large costapalmate fronds to 2 m long, the petiole continuing through the blade as a distinct pronounced midrib as in Sabal. The leaves are used for thatching roofs and for plaiting baskets; distinctive because of its large 2 cm fruit. *Zone 11.*   p. 110
mexicana (Mexico, Guatemala), "Texas palmetto"; robust fan palm with stout, strong trunk; large dark green palmate leaves with a lightly bluish cast, 1 m across, segments cut back about one-third, and with a few long brown fibers; petioles to 1½ m long, smooth dark green with brown margins, concave on the upper side. *Zone 11.*   p. 110
minor (No. Carolina, Florida to Georgia and Texas), the "Dwarf palmetto", Blue palmetto, or "Scrub palmetto"; wide-ranging dwarf fan palm usually without trunk, the rigid palmate leaves 1-1½ m wide, stiff and flat, glaucous or grayish-green, the segments cut halfway or more; fronds generally upright but older blades kink at the junction with petioles, hanging downward and folding; erect inflorescence, black-glossy fruit. *Subtropic. Zones 7-8.*   p. 110
palmetto (Carolina coast to Florida), "Cabbage palm", or "Palmetto"; variable fan palm 6 to 20 m high or more, with stout trunk either almost smooth and brown, or covered with a criss-cross pattern of leaf-bases, slightly curving; the palmate leaves 1-1½ m long, divided into many slender, hanging segments, green or bluish above and gray on the underside, with numerous threadlike fibers; the midrib extending through the blade; white flowers and blackish fruit. *Subtropic. Zones 8-9.*   p. 110

SABINEA   *Leguminosae*
carinalis (Dominica), "Carib wood"; small tree with pinnate leaves, leaflets in 6-8 pairs, 2 cm long; showy flowers crimson-red, to 4 cm long, marked with white at base, and borne directly on wood of branches and trunk. *Zones 10-11.*   p. 765

SACCHARUM   *Gramineae*
officinarum (China, East Indies), "Sugarcane"; very tall stout perennial grass to 4 m high, with solid yellowish-green canes 2-5 cm thick; rich green, arching, clasping leaves to 1 m long, with broad midrib and rough edge; inflorescence in spikelets in large terminal fluffy silky plumes; its sap is a major source of sugar; the fermented and distilled juice becomes a well-known intoxicating drink, otherwise known as rum. *Subtropic to tropical. Zones 9-10.*   p. 568

SADLERIA   *Polypodiaceae (Filices)*
cyatheoides (Hawaii), "Pigmy cyathea"; attractive, vigorous small tree fern forming a trunk 1-1½ m high, and a crown of fleshy, soft-leathery, light green, bipinnate fronds to 1 m long, with neatly regular, linear segments crenate and turned under at edges; leaf stalks stout and fleshy. *Humid-tropical. Zones 11-12.*   p. 141

SAGERETIA   *Rhamnaceae*
minutiflora (No. Carolina to Florida and Alabama); straggling spiny shrub, with tomentose twigs and young foliage; leathery ovate shining leaves 1-5 cm long; inflorescence in slender spikes to 4 cm, of small fragrant whitish flowers; fruit berry-like. *Zone 8.*   p. 829

SAGINA   *Caryophyllaceae*
subulata (W. Europe to Italy and Greece), "Irish" or "Scotch moss" or "Pearlwort"; small mat-forming perennial herb with low, mossy foliage; leaves yellowish-green, linear, awl-shaped to 1 cm long, and bristle-tipped; small white flowers. Planted in California as ground-cover in drier places. *Warm temperate. Zones 5-9.*   p. 365, 568, 569
subulata 'Aurea' (W. and Central Europe), "Golden pearlwort" or "Scotch moss"; low mat-forming grass-like perennial, the creeping branches to 15 cm; the tiny 1 cm needle-like leaves awn-tipped and golden-green; small white flowers. Widely planted in California as lawn-substitute. *Zones 5-9.*   p. 310, 365

SAGITTARIA   *Alismataceae*
latifolia (No. America), "Arrowhead" or "Duck potato"; aquatic perennial with tuberous rootstock, and variable leaves from linear lanceolate to broad, arrow-shaped, blades to 50 cm long; flowers white; freely adapting itself to all sorts of growing conditions. Roots are edible. *Zone 4.*   p. 325

SAINTPAULIA   *Gesneriaceae*
Well beloved small tropical East African herbaceous plants known as "Usambara" or "African violets"; usually symmetrical rosettes of pubescent, spoon-shaped, brittle leaves and basal stalked flowers from the leaf axils; the corolla is flattened and two-lipped, with 5 large rounded lobes; the upper lip is 2-lobed and usually smaller than the 3-lobed lower lip. The primary color is in shades of violet-blue. The first two species S. ionantha and confusa were discovered in Tanzania, then German East Africa in 1892. The first seedlings from one or hybrids from both species began to appear the following year. Since Saintpaulias are also easily propagated vegetatively from leaf cuttings, the miracle of a single somatic or body cell has given rise to thousands of variations and cultivars including pink and white sports, mainly from one species, S. ionantha. These mutants, and further intense hybridizing, have resulted in many different horticultural types and forms including double-flowered and bicolors, most of them named and recorded. In addition, numerous new species have been discovered, some miniatures, others creeping. The relative ease of cultivation in the home, and their simple propagation by leaf cuttings, have made Saintpaulias the most popular house plant in America, well suited to our warm homes. *Tropical.*
ionantha (Tanzania), "African violet", found near Tanga at 30 m and higher, warm-humid; parent with S. confusa of most hybrids; upright species with large flowers a pretty violet-blue, to 2½ cm across, and dark, coppery green, pubescent leaves reddish beneath. On the steep and breezy rocks towering up from the Amboni Caves, north of Tanga, I have seen plants hanging from narrow clefts or footholds surviving the seasonal dry periods by means of rhizomes almost bare of foliage. *Humid-tropical. Zone 12.*   p. 65
ion. 'Blue Peak'; of flat habit; free blooming though short, the double flowers are violet-blue with each fringed little petal daintily edged in white; ovate leaves bronzy green. *Humid-tropical. Zone 12.*   p. 65
ion. 'Delaware'; Optimara strain violet by Holtkamp, Germany 1978; sturdy and shapely rosette with glossy deep green leaves, and long-lasting bright red single flowers, having slightly curled petals and showy yellow stamens in center. *Zone 12.*   p. 65
ion. 'Elfriede' (Rhapsodie strain); one of the successful German (Holtkamp) triploid hybrids characterized by their "Biedermeier" habit of growth forming closed, rather flat rosettes of dark green, firm leaves, and a formal mound of long-lasting, thick-textured, non-dropping blooms; 'Elfriede' has single round, dark blue 4 cm flowers; a prolific bloomer. *Humid-tropical. Zone 12.*   p. 66
ion. 'Loretta'; compact plant with leaves shelving, quilted and rough, blackish forest green; good grower, and free-blooming with delicate pale pinkish-lavender double flowers, dark center. *Zone 12.*   p. 65
ion. 'Morning Glow'; lovely cultivar of compact habit, with lightly ruffled soft-pink single flowers dark rose in center. *Zone 12.*   p. 65
ion. 'Pocono'; low platter-like rosette with waxy cordate leaves; the giant 5 cm single to semi-double flowers of firm substance, purple with fringed pinkish margins. *Humid-tropical. Zone 12.*   p. 65
ion. 'Savannah Sweetheart', typical "holly-leaf, double bright rose"; low rosette with fleshy rich green leaves holly-like curly and ruffled, with margins turned under forming irregular points; free-blooming with heavy, large double flowers 4 cm across, with frilled petals rosy-pink; hanging because of their weight. *Humid-tropical. Zone 12.*   p. 65
'Pixie Blue'; a true miniature shumensis x ionantha hybrid; flat rosette of small leaves and little 2½ cm single flowers pale lilac-blue. *Zone 11.*   p. 65
rupicola (Kenya), an "African violet"; pretty species which I collected north of Mombasa, growing on perpendicular limestone rocks in crevices; when older often hanging by a long, thick rhizome which sustains the plant through the dry seasons; grass green, thinnish, lightly wrinkled, faintly crenate foliage 7-8 cm long, glossy pale silvery green beneath; both short and long hairs erect or slightly bent near top; pretty flowers 3 cm across, wisteria-blue with darker center. *Humid-tropical. Zone 12.*   p. 54, 66

SALACCA   *Palmae*
edulis (Malaya, Java, Bali), the "Salac" or "Snake-skin fruit"; Malaysian feather palm, with multiple trunks mostly subterranean, forming rosettes of tall fronds 5 to 6 m long, on ferociously armed leaf stalks; the leaflets flat in one plane, silvery gray on lower surface, the

back of the rachis with long spines; from the base, the female plants bear attractively ornamental fruit 6 cm long, on flexuous spikes, pear-shaped and shell-like covered with overlapping brown scales, a perfect imitation of snake-skin; enclosed is the yellow edible flesh. Widely cultivated in Java; in Bali on the slopes of the volcano Gunung Agung; sold in markets as buah salac. *Tropical.*

Zones 11-12. p. 112, 920

SALIX *Salicaceae*

alba 'Tristis' (French cv. 1815; S. alba from Europe, No. Africa, Asia; natural. in No. America), "Yellow weeping willow"; deciduous tree to 20 m; branches somewhat spreading; thin pendant shoots distinctly bright yellow; leaves narrow-lanceolate 8-10 cm long, white-silky beneath and finely toothed at sides; small whitish flowers borne in catkins, appearing with the leaves. Twigs are used for wicker work and basketry. *Zone 2.* p. 865

babylonica (China), "Babylon weeping willow"; very handsome deciduous tree 10 to 15 m high, having short, rugged trunk and long pendulous branches, with narrow-lanceolate leaves 12-15 cm long, grayish beneath and finely toothed, on yellow branchlets; catkins appearing with the foliage. Less hardy than other weeping willows, it was first thought to be from Babylon where it was brought to by early caravans. *Zone 6.* p. 865

caprea 'Pendula' (Europe), "Pussy willow" or "Kilmarnock willow"; deciduous small tree with oblong leaves to 10 cm long, gray-pubescent beneath, in cv. 'Pendula' on crooked, drooping, willowy branches; usually grafted on regular species; catkins appear before foliage. The species is also known as "French pussy-willow" beloved for its cut branches with their silky white floral cushions in early Spring. *Zone 4.* p. 865

chilensis (humboldtiana) (Mexico to Central America, Colombia and Chile), "Sauce colorado"; evergreen shrub or columnar tree 15-20 m high, with branches erect or sometimes pendant; the slender branchlets often drooping, with leaves linear-lanceolate to 15 cm long bright green and smooth; the small flowers are followed by fruit capsules containing numerous seeds. Very ornamental as this is the only willow keeping its green foliage for all or most of the year. The columnar form has a habit much like Lombardy poplar. Leaves and sap are used medicinally. *Zone 9.* p. 866

chrysocoma (Zander) see S. x sepulcralis (Hortus, Kruessmann)

daphnoides (Europe to Siberia and Himalayas), "Violet willow"; interesting deciduous tree to 10 m high, with vigorous deep purple shoots covered with white bloom; narrow-lanceolate leaves to 4-10 cm long, glaucous beneath; silvery white oblong male catkins 4 cm long in Spring before or with foliage. Very attractive in Winter with its purple shoots covered by white waxy powder. *Zone 5.* p. 865

discolor (Nova Scotia to Virginia and Missouri), "Pussy willow"; hardy shrub or low tree 3-5-½ m high, with straight willowy purplish-brown branches and 8-10 cm oblong, deciduous leaves, bluish-green beneath; male and female flowers on separate plants, which bloom before the leaves expand; the female catkins are the familiar pussy-willows which can be easily forced by bringing into a warm room in late Winter. The flowers have no petals or sepals, but the series of bracts protecting them form a dense catkin. *Zone 3.* p. 866

gracilistyla (Manchuria, China, Korea, Japan), "Rose-gold pussy-willow"; interesting deciduous shrub 2 m or more high, the gray-downy shoots with oblong to narrow-ovate leaves 5-10 cm long, tapered at both ends, gray-green above and glaucous and silky beneath, characteristic with numerous parallel veins; the showy male reddish catkins to 4 cm long, displaying orange-scarlet anthers, and appearing before foliage, are very attractive. *Zone 5.* p. 866

hastata (Europe to Kashmir), "Halberd-leaved willow"; shrub of bushy habit to 2 m high; young growth glossy and greenish, turning purplish in second year; leaves ovate or obovate, often cordate at base, to 9 cm long, and glaucous beneath; very floriferous with long cylindric white catkins to 5 cm long, blooming in May, appearing with the leaves. *Zone 6.* p. 866

lanata (Arctic and subarctic Europe and Asia), "Woolly willow"; deciduous shrub to 1 m or more high, with shoots thickly covered by soft gray wool; leaves obovate 6-8 cm long, and silvery-hairy on both sides; male catkins 5 cm long, females up to 10 cm long when ripe with scales pinkish, and clothed by silky golden-yellow hairs and anthers. Photographed in Northern Norway at 900 m altitude. Very attractive when in bloom. *Zone 1.* p. 866

matsudana 'Tortuosa', "Dragon-claw willow"; a form of the species from No. China and Korea; small tree with twisted, contorted branches, and wiry pendulous branchlets with curiously twisted linear olive-green leaves 4-8 cm long, grayish glaucescent beneath. *Zone 4.* p. 866

repens var. rosmarinifolia (Europe, Asia), "Creeping willow"; low deciduous shrub up to 1 m high, of dense habit, with narrow elongate ovate leaves to 6 cm long, on arching or pendant willowy branches, the blades channeled and deep green. Often creeping with prostrate stems and ideal for rockgardens. *Zone 4.* p. 866

retusa (Mts. of Cent. and Eastern Europe), "Dwarf willow"; slow-growing prostrate low shrub creeping and self-rooting, with small oval or obovate leaves 1-4 cm long, green on both sides; flowers in miniature 2 cm catkins. *Zone 1.* p. 866

x sepulcralis (Hortus, Kruessmann) (syn. S. x chrysocoma, Zander) (S. alba 'Tristis' x babylonica), "Golden weeping willow"; very popular in Europe; tree to 20 m high, with massive trunk to 1 m dia.; similar to babylonica but more vigorous; thin, pendant yellowish branches with linear leaves glossy green above and glaucous beneath, retaining color until frost. *Zone 5.* p. 865

SALPIGLOSSIS *Solanaceae*

sinuata (Chile, Perú), "Painted tongue"; showy, branching clammy-hairy annual with sinuately toothed leaves and large solitary, 6 cm, funnel-shaped flowers brilliantly colored yellow through scarlet and primrose, and nearly to blue, and with a variation in veining in the wide throat. *Subtropic. Zone 10.* p. 514

SALVIA *Labiatae*

argentea (Mediterranean reg.), "Silver sage"; shaggy biennial to 1 m high; broad ovate leaves to 20 cm long, white-woolly, lobed and wrinkled; the basal leaves stalked, stem-leaves sessile; tubular two-lipped flowers in whorls, with corolla pinkish-white, 5 cm long. *Zone 6.* p. 436

azurea (Carolina to Nebraska and Texas), "Blue sage" or "Ramona"; showy perennial to 1 m or more high, with ovate, wrinkled leaves to 8 cm long, usually downy beneath; inflorescence of small blue flowers in whorls, along terminal branchlets, August-September blooming. *Zone 6.* p. 436

azurea grandiflora (pitcheri) (Minnesota to Texas), "Pitcher's sage"; subshrubby, downy perennial to 1 m or more high, oblong leaves 5-10 cm long; inflorescence denser than the species, of 3 cm tubular flowers gentian-blue, or occasionally white, in whorls along terminal shoots, from early July to Autumn. *Zones 5-10.* p. 436

blepharophylla (Mexico), "Red sage"; striking subshrubby perennial with fleshy stolons, 30 cm high, the ovate, dark green leaves wrinkled with margins crenate or lobed and ciliate; the beautiful 2-lipped flowers scarlet to crimson-red, 2 cm long, the lower lip large, the upper hooded, downy outside. *Zones 9-10.* p. 437

canariensis (Canary Islands); handsome shrubby perennial 1½ m or more high, with white-woolly stems; lanceolate leaves, rough on surface; branched inflorescence with beautiful rosy-purplish flowers, the bell-shaped corolla 2-lipped and with curved hood. *Zone 10.* p. 437

coccinea (So. Carolina to Florida and Texas; Trop. America), "Texas sage"; hairy annual or perennial to 60 cm high, with ovate, toothed leaves to 6 cm long; slender stalks with twiggy racemes of scarlet bilabiate flowers to 2½ cm long. *Zones 8-10.* p. 437

elegans (rutilans) (Mexico), "Pineapple sage"; perennial aromatic subshrub to 1 m or more high, with slender pointed leaves 5-10 cm long, soft-hairy above and toothed at margins; brilliant red bilabiate flowers 3-4 cm long, in distant whorls during Summer. Popular for its fragrant leaves of pineapple scent used in potpourri and to flavor cold drinks such as tea; the red blooms attract hummingbirds. *Zone 9.* p. 534

farinacea (New Mexico, Texas), "Mealy-cup sage"; perennial or annual to 1 m high, forming mounds; gray-green 10 cm leaves with serrate margins; erect, slender spikes of small, violet-blue or lavender flowers. *Subtropic. Zones 8-10.* p. 436

farinacea 'Blue Bedder'; handsome cultivar of compact habit, freely branching, having lanceolate, channeled leaves, remotely crenate; inflorescence with whorls of flowers violet-blue, the short tubular corolla 2 cm long, and white-hairy calyx, often tinged violet. *Zones 8-10.* p. 437

farinacea 'Catima'; handsome cultivar, with tall cylindric spires of deep violet-blue flowers, to 60 cm high, seen blooming in New York Botanical Garden in early September. *Zones 8-10.* p. 438

farinacea 'Victoria'; very elegant cultivar forming handsome bushes, with long-lanceolate, concave leaves, and showy terminal cylindric inflorescences of vivid purple flowers in a succession of small whorls; exhibited during the Floriade in Amsterdam, 1982. *Zones 8-10.* p. 438

fruticosa (Sicily to Greece and Syria), "Greek sage"; white-pubescent, subshrubby perennial 60 to 120 cm high, with simple elliptic, or pinnate leaves having 1-2 pairs of ovate leaflets, gray-white beneath; flowers with purple tubular corollas, and rosy-lilac lobes, 2-3 cm long, in whorls along terminal shoots. *Zone 8.* p. 436

gesneriiflora (Colombia); handsome perennial having woody base, 60 cm to 1½ m high; ovate leaves 3-8 cm long, with rounded teeth and cordate at base, white-hairy beneath; very showy, pendant flowers to 5 cm long, the hairy corolla vivid scarlet, in clusters, July-blooming. *Zone 10.* p. 437

greggii (Texas, Mexico), "Autumn sage"; shrub about 1 m high, dense with small linear-oblong 1 cm leaves dull pale green; 2½ cm flowers carmine or purplish-red, with swollen, bilabiate tube in terminal racemes. *Zone 9*. p. 437

guaranitica (ambigens) (S.E. Brazil to Paraguay and No. Argentina); subshrubby perennial to 1 m or more high, often cultivated as annual, with hairy, 4-angled branches; ovate leaves 5-12 cm long, toothed at margins, green and rough above, paler and pubescent beneath; tubular flowers to 5 cm long, violet-blue with white at base, in branched clusters; blooming September-October. *Zone 8*. p. 437

involucrata (Mexico, Central America), "Rose-leaf-sage"; subshrub to 1 m or more high, with ovate, toothed leaves 12 cm long, the bract-like floral leaves colored; calyx purplish, and 2½ cm rose corolla, in whorls. *Subtropic. Zones 9-10*. p. 438

lavandulifolia (Spain, So. France, N.W. Africa), "Spanish sage"; subshrubby perennial to 50 cm high, with pubescent, leafy stems; narrow, oblong hairy leaves 5 cm or more long and faintly crenate; flowers having usually pubescent red-purple calyx, and 2-3 cm corolla lilac or blue-purple, arranged in whorls along upper part of branches. *Zones 8-10*. p. 438

leucantha (Mexico), "Mexican bush-sage"; subshrubby, aromatic perennial about 60 cm high with woolly branches and narrow wrinkled leaves 15 cm long, white-downy beneath; the woolly flowers with white perianth, and the calyx covered by dense purple felt, in long slender spikes. *Subtropic. Zones 9-10*. p. 438, 741

leucantha purpurea, "Mexican purple sage"; attractive variety with velvety, fragrant leaves, and slender silvery, arching branches ending in spires 15-25 cm long, of flowers having purple-felted calyx, and 2 cm two-lipped corollas rich purple, blooming Summer and Autumn; very drought tolerant. *Zones 9-10*. p. 438

leucophylla (So. California), "Purple sage"; legendary shrub of the American Southwest, accustomed to arid regions, to 1 m or more high, grayish-white tomentose, with rough and crinkly narrow ovate leaves 3-6 cm long and quite aromatic; the inflorescence spike-like in interrupted clusters along terminal stalk, with bluish-lavender corolla 2 cm long, subtended by purplish bracts, blooming May-June. *Zones 9-10*. p. 741

mexicana (Mexico), "Ramona"; perennial to 1 m high, with rugose ovate leaves to 8 cm long, tomentose beneath; deep blue flowers in erect raceme. *Subtropic. Zones 8-10*. p. 438

microphylla (Mexico), "Baby sage"; ornamental subshrub to 1 m high with woody base; small coppery, ovate leaves 2 cm long and a zigzag stalk; showy tubular flowers with corolla 25 mm long, having large lip, deep velvety cherry-red. *Zone 10*. p. 741

microphylla neurepia (grahamii) (Mexico), "Cherry-sage"; handsome shrub 2 m or more high, with aromatic ovate, smooth leaves, toothed at margins, 5 cm long; flowers deep crimson, in whorls or flat clusters. *Zone 9*. p. 740

officinalis (Mediterranean region), "Garden sage"; popular white-woolly perennial subshrub 40 to 60 cm high, with slender lanceolate, gray-green, pebbly leaves 3-6 cm long; light purple or white flowers in terminal racemes of successive whorls during June. Much grown since the Middle ages as an important potherb or spice plant. The foliage has many culinary uses for seasoning poultry, cheese, meats, sausage, tomatoes and fish; also used in domestic medicine and in China brewed for tea. *Zones 5-9*. p. 534

officinalis 'Icterina', "Golden sage"; handsome cultivar with oblong lanceolate, aromatic pubescent leaves beautifully variegated light green and golden-yellow; excellent ornamental for the herb-garden. *Zones 6-10*. p. 534

officinalis latifolia (So. Europe), "Mammoth sage"; robust perennial with grayish aromatic, broad ovate leaves 6-8 cm long, wrinkled on surface and pebbly along margins, much wider than the species; purple flowers 2 cm long, in terminal spikes. Used as herb tea against neck and throat infections, also digestive disorders. *Zones 5-9*. p. 534

officinalis 'Tricolor', "Variegated sage"; attractive variety with gray-green leaves variegated white or yellowish and pink becoming velvety red along margins. *Zones 6-10*. p. 534

patens 'Cambridge blue', "Gentian sage"; colorform of the species at home in the mountains of Mexico; sticky-hairy, half-hardy perennial to 75 cm high, with ovate or arrow-shaped leaves 5 to 8 cm long, crenate at margins; tubular flowers with the bilabiate corolla 5-6 cm long, lilac-blue, having lips gaping wide, in remote whorls along terminal shoots; September blooming. *Zone 8*. p. 438

pratensis (Europe, Morocco), "Meadow clary" or "Meadow sage"; aromatic, pubescent perennial 30-90 cm high, with tuberous roots; the wrinkled, ovate leaves 3 cm long, crenate at margins; the branches toward upper part with showy, pyramidal inflorescence of pink or bright blue 2-lipped 3 cm flowers in whorls arranged spike-like, 40 cm long, blooming June to August. *Zone 5*. p. 436

sclarea (So. Europe), "Clary sage"; hardy biennial 1 m high, with broad-ovate hairy and pebbly gray-green leaves to 22 cm long, floral leaves colored rose and white; the 2 cm flowers whitish-blue in

clusters. Use: flavoring muscatel wine; distilled oil for perfume. Flowers are used in medicines for eye diseases. *Zones 6-9*. p. 534

splendens (Brazil), "Scarlet sage"; a well-known perennial to 90 cm high, usually cultivated as an annual, with ovate, rich green, glabrous leaves on erect spikes bearing showy, scarlet-red flowers 3-4 cm long, with fiery-red calyx, in late Summer. *Tropical. Zone 10*. p. 437

x superba (virgata nemorosa) (sylvestris x villicaulis) sterile hybrid of E. Europe to S.W. Asia parentage; subshrubby perennial with many 4-angled twiggy branches to 1 m high, softly hairy, with ovate gray-green leaves 3-8 cm long; the inflorescence in showy spires of purple to violet flowers, subtended by red bracts conspicuous after blooming; the anthers without pollen. *Zone 6*. p. 437

viridis 'Oxford Blue' (species of S.E. Europe), "Joseph sage"; soft-hairy, herbaceous annual to 50 cm high, with oblong leaves 3-6 cm long, crenulate at margins; the flowers in the species are usually rose or white, but vivid violet and long-lasting in 'Oxford Blue'. *Zone 9*. p. 436

SALVINIA   *Salviniaceae (Filices)*

auriculata (Tropical America), "American floating fern"; small, flowerless, aquatic fern-ally (Cryptogam), floating on water, with 1 cm, oval leaves pale yellowish-green and warty-haired on the surface, set along threadlike floating rhizomes, soon forming clusters. *Humid-tropical. Zones 10-11*. p. 331

natans hort. (rotundifolia) (Europe to Siberia and Malaysia); free-floating aquatic fern without actual roots, broadly oval to rounded, 2 cm long, brown-hairy beneath. The nomenclature status of S. natans vs. auriculata vs. rotundifolia is confused. *Zones 4-10*. p. 331

SAMANEA   *Leguminosae*

saman (Pithecellobium) (West Indies, Central America), the "Rain-tree", "Saman", or "Monkey-pod"; great tropical shade tree to 24 m high, with spreading head like an open umbrella, to 30 m wide; bipinnate or 4-pinnate leaves with oblique ovate or roundish leaflets to 4 cm long, shiny above, downy beneath; small silky-yellow flowers with long pink stamens, white towards lower part, followed by flat pods 15-20 cm long. *Zone 10*. p. 769

SAMBUCUS   *Caprifoliaceae*

callicarpa (California north to Washington), "Pacific red elder"; deciduous shrub 2 m high or tree-like to 6 m, with pithy stems; pinnate leaves of 5-7 obovate, toothed leaflets 5-10 cm long, hairy on midrib beneath; small whitish flowers in round panicles, followed by scarlet fruit in showy clusters. *Zone 7*. p. 674

ebulus (Europe, No. Africa, Asia), "Dwarf elder" or "Danewort"; shrubby perennial 60 cm to 1 m or more high, with stout grooved stems, and 9-13 narrow lanceolate leaflets sharply serrate; small white flowers tinged pink, dense in broad terminal clusters, 8-10 cm across, followed by small black fruit, which yields a blue dye. *Zone 6*. p. 674

nigra (Europe, No. Africa, West Asia), "European elderberry"; deciduous shrub with pithy stems, to 10 m high; pinnate foliage with usually 5 elliptic leaflets 12 cm long; flowers yellowish-white in umbels; edible berries shining black. Elderberry juice when boiled, or in German "Holunder", is an old home remedy against colds and fever. *Zone 5*. p. 674, 906

pubens (Eastern No. America, west to Rocky Mts.), "American red elder" or "Scarlet elder"; shrub from Eastern and Western mountains, 4-8 m high, the stems with red-brown pith; very similar to S. racemosa but with shoots, flowers and floral stalks downy; branches spreading with pinnate leaves of 5-7 lanceolate leaflets 10 cm long; yellowish-white flowers in pyramidal clusters in late Spring, followed by inedible red berries. *Zone 4*. p. 674

racemosa (Europe; Asia Minor to No. China), "European red elder"; vigorous shrub to 4 m high, very popular in gardens of Europe; with stems filled with brown pith; pinnate leaves of 5-7 elliptic leaflets to 8 cm long; tiny flowers yellowish-white in dense ovoid panicles in early May; followed by showy clusters of scarlet berries ripening June-July. *Zone 4*. p. 674

racemosa 'Plumosa aurea', "Golden elder"; handsome cultivated form with pinnate foliage, its leaflets up to 12 cm long, cut nearly to midrib into narrow lobes or teeth, purplish when unfolding, later suffused with golden-yellow. *Zone 6*. p. 674

SANCHEZIA   *Acanthaceae*

speciosa (nobilis) (Ecuador); handsome tropical shrub cultivated for its large lanceolate, soft-leathery leaves to 22 cm long, glossy green with bold, contrasting yellow veins; large yellow flowers with bright red bracts in showy terminal panicle. Foliage tends to become green in older plants. *Zone 10*. p. 631

SANDERSONIA   *Liliaceae*

aurantiaca (So. Africa: Natal), "Christmas-bells", or "Chinese lantern-lily"; tuberous climbing plant 45-60 cm high, with alternate, 10 cm ribbed, lanceolate leaves, often tipped with a tendril, along slender wiry stems; axillary bright orange-yellow, inflated urn-shaped, nodding flowers 2½ cm long, of shiny, papery texture. *Subtropic.* Zone 9. p. 248

SANDORICUM *Meliaceae*
indicum (S. koetjape) (East Indies, Malaysia), "Santol tree"; tropical tree to 40 m or more high, more or less deciduous, with pinkish or grayish bark, peeling in thin flakes; the young foliage purplish, mature leaves trifoliolate with ovate leaflets corrugated by depressed veins; flowers in axillary clusters, corolla of 5 overlapping yellow petals, followed by small fleshy, orange-like fruits of acid-sweet taste. Zone 10. p. 788

SANGUINARIA *Papaveraceae*
canadensis (E. No. America), "Red puccoon" or "Blood root"; small herbaceous woodland perennial 15 cm high, with rhizome and red stems containing blood-red sap; kidney-shaped leaves lobed, and bluish above; lovely white flowers to 8 cm across, in April-May. The red sap was used by Indians as dye. Zone 3. p. 470

SANGUISORBA *Rosaceae*
canadensis (Labrador to Illinois, so. to Georgia), "American burnet"; handsome marshland perennial 1 m or more high, with pinnate leaves of 7-17 lanceolate leaflets 3-10 cm long, serrate at margins; cylindrical floral spikes to 20 cm long, dense with tiny flowers of creamy-white sepals but lacking petals, and long white stamens in male blooms; during Autumn. Dried rhizomes have been used medicinally. Zone 3. p. 494

obtusa (Poterium obtusum) (Japan: Honshu), "Japanese burnet"; herbaceous perennial 1 m or more high, with large pinnate basal leaves having numerous ovate, toothed leaflets to 6 cm long, glaucous beneath; tiny purplish-rose flowers displaying prominent stamens, cylindrical erect or pendant spikes, on long branched stalks, during Summer. Zone 3. p. 494

SANSEVIERIA *Agavaceae*
ehrenbergii (Ethiopia, Kenya, Tanzania), "Blue sansevieria"; plant with leaves to 1½ m long, alternately arranged as in a large fan, concealing the stem; the blue-green foliage above with triangular channel and white papery edge, flat on sides and rounded below. *Arid-tropical.* Zone 11. p. 200

pinguicula (N.E. Kenya); strange species resembling Agave; 5 to 7 broad ovate glaucous green leaves arranged in a rosette, 12-30 cm long and thick-fleshy, the upper side deeply concave, with horny, pale margins, narrowing to a spine-like point. Zone 11. p. 200

trifasciata 'Golden Hahnii' (pat. 1953); very showy plant when fully variegated; a sport of 'Hahnii' with firm, broad-elliptic leathery leaves to 15 cm long, in a low rosette, grayish-green with broad cream to golden-yellow bands alongside the margins, and more or less cross-banded in gray. *Tropical.* Zone 11. p. 200

trifasciata 'Laurentii' (Zaire: Eastern Province), "Variegated snake plant"; leading commercial variety because of its elegant, stiff, sword-shaped leaves to 50 cm or more high, having yellow bands on either side of the deep green, light banded center, forming nicely turned rosettes, soon clustering from the fleshy rhizomes. *Tropical.* Zone 10. p. 68

SANTALUM *Santalaceae*
ellipticum (Hawaii), the "Iliahi" or Hawaiian "Sandalwood"; small evergreen tree with opposite thick, glossy pale green oval leaves 8 cm long; clusters of pink to red flowers with red or green calyx at branch ends or leaf axils, and black berries. Santalum is partially parasitic, sending out roots with sucking organs into the root system of neighboring trees such as Casuarina or Acacia koa, stealing their food. Of economic importance during the height of the sandalwood trade with China mostly from 1810 to 1820, where the wood was used for incense and in making small furniture. *Tropical.* Zone 10. p. 867

SANTOLINA *Compositae*
chamaecyparissus (incana) (Mediterranean), "Lavender cotton"; low shrubby aromatic perennial, 30-60 cm high, with silvery gray tomentose, lacy leaves; yellow fragrant, globular flower heads 2 cm across, during Summer. Planted in carpet-bedding, and pruned for edging in knot-gardens. Leafy stems and flowers are used in the household and placed between clothes as a moth repellent. Also, oil is produced for perfume. Zone 7. p. 398, 529, 539

SANVITALIA *Compositae*
procumbens (Mexico, Guatemala), "Hussars heads"; hairy perennial grown as annual, with wide-spreading trailing stems, ovate leaves to 2½ cm long, and 2 cm heads of flowers having light yellow ray-petals and dark purple disc. *Tropical.* Zone 10. p. 399

SAPINDUS *Sapindaceae*
drummondii (Missouri to Arizona and Mexico), "Soap berry"; deciduous tree to 15 m high, with scaly red bark; leaves pinnate with 8-18 leaflets, obliquely lanceolate 5-8 cm long, and hairy beneath;

small yellowish-white flowers in loose, hairy clusters to 25 cm long; globose fruit first yellow then ripening to black. The Indians made soap from the berries. Zone 5. p. 868

mukorossi (India to Cent. Japan) "Chinese soap-berry", a "Soap-nut"; evergreen, brittle tree to 15 m high, with pinnate leaves to 40 cm long, having up to 13 lanceolate leaflets, smooth beneath and 10-15 cm long; flowers white in large terminal clusters, followed on female trees by fleshy globular orange-red to black fruit 2 cm dia. Fruit is used like soap, and the black seed for beads. Zone 9. p. 868

SAPIUM *Euphorbiaceae*
sebiferum (C. China, Taiwan), "Chinese tallow tree" or "Vegetable tallow"; evergreen tree resembling poplar, to 12 m high, with poisonous milky sap; broad rhombic-ovate, leathery leaves 7 cm long, with ivory midrib, and turning a beautiful yellow to red; small petal-less greenish flowers; the female blossoms followed by 3-parted globular brown fruiting capsules 1½ cm dia. The fatty white wax seed-coating is used in making candles and soap; the wood is made into furniture. Zone 9. p. 725

SAPONARIA *Caryophyllaceae*
caespitosa (Pyrenees), "Soapwort"; small clustering evergreen perennial to 15 cm high, with thick succulent, linear leaves 3 cm long, forming cushions of foliage, covered by masses of rosy flowers, partially enclosed by inflated purplish calyx. Zone 6. p. 365

lutea (S.W. and Central Alps), "Yellow soapwort"; floriferous clustering herbaceous Alpine perennial with woody roots, and thin, hairy branches to 15 cm long; pale green basal leaves narrow lanceolate, the stem leaves linear; inflorescence in loose clusters at apex of stems, flowers yellow, having hairy calyx and protruding violet stamens, July-August blooming. Zone 6. p. 365

ocymoides (Mts. of Spain, France, Switz., Italy), "Rock soapwort"; spreading, many-branched Alpine perennial, ascending to 25 cm high, with sessile ovate 2 cm leaves; inflorescence in masses of bright pink flowers, each with 5 petals, from May to August. Stems and leaves have been used in making soap. Zone 5. p. 365, 526

officinalis (Europe to Asia; naturalized in No. America), "Bouncing bet"; sturdy rhizomatous perennial 50-80 cm high; the straight stems with opposite, elliptic leaves 10 cm long; axillary and terminal inflorescence in clusters of tubular pink flowers 3 cm long, with flaring lobes, blooming throughout Summer, especially at night. The rhizomes have been used in medicine. Zone 4. p. 365

officinalis alba (Europe to Siberia), "White soapwort"; excellent perennial for garden borders, a color variation very floriferous with clusters of flowers in pure white, having narrow lobes spreading, resembling little stars. Popularly called soapwort, because its juice may be used for forming a lather when mixed with water. Zone 4. p. 365

x olivana (caespitosa x pumila); low cushion-forming perennial with narrow linear leaves 3 cm long, summer-blooming with many rose-pink flowers 2 cm across, having hairy calyx, and 5 petals spreading wide. Zone 5. p. 365

SARACA *Leguminosae*
indica (Mysore, India), the "Asoka tree" or "Sorrow-less tree"; dense pyramidal tree, to 10 m tall, pinnate with long narrow, shining, undulate leaflets to 20 cm long; beautiful flower heads rich orange, fragrant, with long crimson stamens; sacred to Hindus and Buddhists, as Buddha is believed to have been born under it. Zone 10. p. 769

SARARANGA sinuosa:
see PANDANUS lamprocephalus (Dr. B. Stone)

SARCOCAULON *Geraniaceae*
pennicillatus (Namibia); peculiar low, fleshy xerophytic shrub with fissured woody bases, covered by resinous coat; spreading with spiny branches; small ferny grayish leaves but soon deciduous; pretty, pale pink flowers 2 cm across. Zone 11. p. 195

SARCOCOCCA *Buxaceae*
hookeriana humilis (China: Himalayas), "Himalayan sweet box"; handsome rhizomatous evergreen shrub to 60 cm high, with lustrous thin-leathery lanceolate or elliptic leaves 5-10 cm long; small white, fragrant flowers displaying bright pink anthers; the fruits are 1 cm black berries. The species is taller to 2 m high. Zone 5. p. 671

ruscifolia (W. China), "Fragrant sweet box"; evergreen shrub to 2 m high, with cane-like branches; attractive lanceolate, leathery leaves 3-5 cm long, lustrous dark green and undulate; the inflorescence axillary in clusters of tiny creamy-white, fragrant flowers; small dark red berry-like fruit. Zone 7. p. 671

SARCODES *Monotropaceae*
sanguinea (Oregon, California), "Snow plant"; curious plant lacking chlorophyll, arising on the forest floor from a thick fleshy mat of roots and living on dead organic matter, 20-60 cm high; bright red

pubescent herbage with fleshy stem and scale-like leaves, the upper strap-shaped and 5-10 cm long; small red flowers in a stout terminal cluster. *Warm temperate. Zones 7-8.*   *p. 208*

SARCOPODIUM lyonii: see EPIGENEIUM lyonii (Zander)

SARITAEA   *Bignoniaceae*
magnifica (Arrabidaea, Bignonia) (Colombia); climbing tropical vine with opposite, bifoliate leaves, obovate leaflets 10 cm long, smooth and leathery; the flowers tubular bell-shaped 8 cm long, mauve to purple, throat yellow. *Tropical. Zone 10.*   *p. 269*

SARMIENTA   *Gesneriaceae*
scandens (repens) (Chile); shrubby plant with creeping, wiry stems, dense with opposite, small fleshy leaves; the numerous small flowers with inflated crimson tubes and spreading lobes; in habitat climbing over trees and rocks, requiring abundant water. Needs 3 months winter rest at 5 to 8°C. to bloom. (Dr. Messick, American Gloxinia Society 1967).   *p. 66*

SARRACENIA   *Sarraceniaceae (Carnivorous Pl.)*
alata (Gulf Coast of Alabama to Texas), "Yellow trumpets"; rhizomatous, carnivorous perennial herb with erect rather narrow trumpets to 75 cm high, green with yellow, reddish in upper part and on the nearly erect lid; creamy-yellow, fiddle-shaped flowers. *Zone 9.*   *p. 203*
flava (Virginia to Florida), "Yellow pitcher plant"; tall and slender tubes to 1 m long, light green with mouth and lid edged yellow-green and crimson throat; large nodding yellow flowers. *Warm temperate. Zones 7-8.*   *p. 203*
leucophylla (Georgia to Miss.), "Fiddler's trumpet"; handsome pitcher plant of the passive type, with slender, long green tubes 40 cm high, toward the inflated apex beautifully marbled with white, the lid white with green veining. *Warm temperate. Zones 7-9.*   *p. 203*
minor (No. Carolina to Florida), "Hooded pitcher plant"; pitchers short and also growing to 60 cm tall, fresh green to purple, with white translucent spots near the yellowish top, the lid arching over mouth, purple-netted inside; flowers pale yellow. *Warm temperate. Zones 8-9.*   *p. 203*
psittacina (in sandy swamps of Georgia, Florida, Alabama and Louisiana), the "Parrot pitcher plant"; low rosette with leaves 5-15 cm long, the tube club-shaped, with an erect, broad obovate, flat wing, green with red and white veins, the inflated top with incurved beak, like a parrot; flowers green and red. *Humid-subtropic. Zone 9.p. 203*
purpurea (Labrador to Maryland and Rocky Mts.), "Sweet pitcher plant"; low, spreading rosettes usually found growing in sphagnum bogs; clustering pitchers erect or prostrate, 6-35 cm long, broadly winged, throat and lid hairy, and beautifully veined crimson; nodding purple flowers. *Temperate. Zones 3-7.*   *p. 201*
rubra (No. Carolina to Florida), "Red pitcher plant"; slender tubular leaves green to reddish-brown, 15-30 cm and more long, the lid forming a hood and veined purple; flowers crimson and fragrant, on elongate stalks. *Warm temperate. Zones 8-9.*   *p. 203*

SASA   *Gramineae*
fortunei: see ARUNDINARIA variegata
palmata (No. Japan, Sakhalin), "Sato chimaki" or "Palmate bamboo"; low running bamboo to 1 m or more high, with hollow stems 2 cm dia., dense with thick-leathery, handsome, lanceolate leaves 20-30 cm long, bright green above, silvery glaucous beneath. Spreading groundcover from underground rhizomes. Evergreen except in severe cold climate. Leaves are used in Japan to wrap pastry and fish. *Zones 6-9.*   *p. 552, 556*
pumila hort.: see ARUNDINARIA pumila (Hortus, Zander)
tessellata (syn. Bambusa) (China); a dwarf "Running" bamboo with creeping rootstocks, and slender culms 3/4-1 m high, short-jointed, with brownish-yellow culm-sheath, and ovate to lanceolate, leathery leaves 8 to 12 cm long and 3-4 cm broad, rich green above, glaucous beneath. *Zones 7-10.*   *p. 556*
variegata: see ARUNDINARIA variegata

SASSAFRAS   *Lauraceae*
albidum (Eastern No. America), "Sassafras"; deciduous tree to 30 m high; leaves 8-15 cm long, variable in shape and size, entire or 3-lobed, glaucous beneath; flowers 5 mm wide, greenish-yellow; fruit roundish-ovoid, dark blue; foliage tinted orange and scarlet in Autumn. Bark and roots yield oil of sassafras, an important flavoring; leaves are used for medicinal tea. *Zone 5.*   *p. 740, 742*

SATUREJA   *Labiatae*
douglasii (Western U.S.) "Yerba buena" or "Oregon tea"; herbaceous perennial with trailing, rooting stems to 50 cm long; small grayish, broad ovate leaves 3 cm long and faintly serrate, dense along branches; axillary white or purplish flowers 1 cm long, in Spring and Autumn. Makes excellent tea, or mixed with other teas. *Zone 4.*   *p. 535*

hortensis (Mediterr. region), "Summer savory"; popular annual aromatic herb to 50 cm high, with erect downy stems, dense with narrow 2 cm leaves; pale lilac flowers in axillary whorls, during April to September. Used to season bean dishes, soups, gravy, and stuffing; excellent addition to salads. Known in German as "Bohnenkraut" or "Beanherb". Good container plant. *Zones 9-10.*   *p. 535*
montana (So. Europe, No. Africa), "Winter savory"; pleasantly aromatic evergreen perennial 20-40 cm high, wide-spreading with thin branches, densely set with stiff linear leaves to 3 cm long, and having bristly margins; profusion of pale pinkish to purple flowers, in axillary whorls, in early Summer, attractive to bees. In culinary use, a very good condiment, not as sweet as S. hortensis, in flavoring food, such as green beans; also used in liqueurs. *Zones 6-10.*   *p. 535*

SAXIFRAGA   *Saxifragaceae*
x arendsii (Germany); varied hybrid group of low, mat-forming habit, involving S. rosacea, hypnoides and caespitosa; small fresh green obovate 3-cleft leaves, resembling miniature ivy; very floriferous with pretty 5-lobed flowers to 2 cm across, in various colors rose with white eye, also red, pale yellow and white; blooming in May. *Zone 4.*   *p. 499*
x boydii (aretioides x burseriana), "Yellow hind"; interesting low hybrid of European parentage forming low cushions of grass-like rosettes 4 cm high; stiff-leathery, bluish-gray linear leaves 1 cm long; attractive lemon-yellow flowers with yellow stamen bundles in center, blooming in Spring. *Zone 6.*   *p. 498*
bronchialis (Urals to No. Asia, Alaska, W. Canada); mat-forming perennial to 20 cm high, with wiry, creeping branches; densely leafy, with stiff linear, pointed leaves 1-2 cm long, ciliate at margins; small starry, yellowish-white flowers spotted with orange, in May. *Zone 2.*   *p. 500*
cortusifolia var. fortunei (Japan: Honshu, Kyushu); attractive woodlands perennial to 40 cm high, with roundish or kidney-shaped leathery, shining green leaves to 10 cm wide, pointedly cut and lobed and red underneath; deciduous in cold climate; spreading to form new plants; white flowers 2 cm long, with toothed petals, the lower ones larger than the uppers, on branched stalks, blooming in Autumn. *Zone 7.*   *p. 500*
x geum (S. hirsuta x umbrosa), "Kidney-leaf saxifrage" of West European parentage; mat-forming rosettes of shiny green, kidney-shaped, leathery leaves 3 cm long, having crenate, corky margins; branching floral stalks to 30 cm long, bearing loose clusters of tiny white flowers, red in center, in early Summer. *Zone 5.*   *p. 500*
hirculus (Europe to Arctic Norway and No. Hemisphere); mat-forming tufts with narrow, waxy, green to bronze leaves; single bell-shaped light yellow flowers marked with orange and purple, to 2 cm across, as photographed above the Arctic Circle at Ny Alesund, Spitzbergen. *Zone 2.*   *p. 499*
hirsuta (geum) (Pyrenees, No. Spain, S.W. Ireland, Scotland); mat-forming, basal rosettes of rounded or kidney-shaped, leathery leaves often red beneath, lightly hairy, the margins crenate; branching stalks with many small white flowers in scattered clusters, in late Spring to Summer. *Zone 3.*   *p. 500*
hostii (Eastern Alps); encrusted succulent rosettes forming clusters, in habitat always growing on limestone, the margins beaded with lime glands; floral stalks to 30 cm high bearing creamy-white flowers in branched panicles, blooming in May. *Zone 5.*   *p. 499*
hypnoides (N.W. Europe), "Moss-rockfoil" or "Eve's cushion"; cushion-forming perennial to 15 cm high, with emerald green leaves finely 3 to 5 cleft, bristle-tipped and with bulbils in axils; very floriferous with 2 cm cream-white flowers in early Summer. *Zone 6.*   *p. 500*
longifolia (Pyrenees of Spain), "Encrusted rockfoil" or "Longleaf saxifrage"; very ornamental formal succulent rosette to 60 cm across, dense with long-linear, spoon-shaped silvery green leaves calcium-encrusted at margins; bearing sprays of white flowers 1 cm across, in leafy clusters 25-50 cm high, during June. *Zone 6.*   *p. 499*
oppositifolia (Arctic and subarctic regions, No. America to Siberia), "Purple saxifrage" or "Redsildre" in Norway; found growing at Longyearbyen on Spitzbergen, Norway, at 70 deg. No. Lat. above the Arctic Circle; cushion-forming, densely matted obovate 2 cm leaves with one limegland; small 1 cm flowers with rose petals, blooming July in habitat. *Zone 2.*   *p. 499*
paniculata (aizoon), (Pyrenees to Alps, Labrador), "Encrusted saxifrage"; evergreen rosettes forming clusters, with silvery obovate, fleshy leaves 4-5 cm long, having margins encrusted with lime; inflorescence a branched panicle to 25 cm high, with small cream-colored flowers to 2 cm across, blooming May-July. *Zone 2.*   *p. 499*
rhomboidea (Brit. Columbia to Alberta, to Rocky Mts. of Colorado); rosette of broad-ovate leaves 6 cm or more long, white pubescent; inflorescence to 30 cm high, on white hairy stalks, with heads dense with white or greenish flowers. *Zone 3.*   *p. 499*

x rosacea 'Kumomaso', in Japan; of European hybrid origin, with ceaspitosa as one parent; evergreen low herbaceous perennial forming moss-like mats 4-6 cm high; rosettes of finely divided fresh green leaves, and literally covered with charming star-like flowers 15 mm across, carmine to crimson-red with white center, spring-blooming. Zone 4.   p. 499

rotundifolia (Alps to Caucasus, Armenia); tufted rosettes with stem to 60 cm high, fleshy, kidned-shaped basal leaves 5 cm across and with crenate margins; starry white 2 cm flowers speckled pink, in loose clusters, blooming early Summer. Zone 5.   p. 498

stolonifera (sarmentosa hort.) (China, Japan), "Strawberry geranium"; loosely tufted perennial spreading near the ground, strawberry-like, by threadlike runners bearing young plantlets; the soft, fleshy, rounded, bristly hairy leaves 3 to 5 cm across, coarsely toothed, deep olive-green with silver gray areas following the veins, densely spotted purple beneath; numerous flowers on erect panicle, white, with 2 petals longer than others. Zones 7-10.   p. 321

stolonifera 'Tricolor' (sarmentosa cv.), "Magic carpet"; beautiful variety smaller and more tender than the type, with leaves dark green and milky green, variegated inward from the margin with ivory-white, tinted pink or even rosy-crimson in younger leaves, with red edging, and purplish-rose beneath; small white flowers on erect panicles. Zone 10.   p. 499

trifurcata (Pyrenees, No. Spain), "Threefork saxifrage"; perennial with woody stems to 20 cm high, evergreen mats formed of small bright green, stiffly erect leaves, divided into 3 prongs, 2 cm across; creamy-white flowers 2 cm dia., in Spring. Zone 6.   p. 500

umbrosa (Europe), "Porcelain flower"; tufting rosettes of thick, leathery, spatulate, gray-green leaves crenate at margins, tinged red beneath, 6 cm long; small, starry, pinkish flowers, 1 cm across, in small clusters, on stalks to 40 cm long, in early Summer. Zone 7.   p. 500

umbrosa aurea (Europe: Britain to Pyrenees), "Golden London-pride"; ornamental, nest-like rosettes to 25 cm high, mound-forming, of thick-leathery, obovate leaves 6 cm long and tapering to petioles, the margins corky or crenulate, and blades variegated with creamy-yellow; starry 1 cm pink or white flowers in loose clusters, during early Summer. Zone 6.   p. 498

x urbium (spathularis x umbrosa) (Europe), "London pride"; similar to umbrosa, but with longer petioles and larger leaves having more pointed and numerous crenations; larger white or pink flowers. Zone 6.   p. 500

SCABIOSA   Dipsacaceae

atropurpurea (So. Europe), "Sweet scabiosa" or "Pincushion flower"; erect annual to 60 cm high, with opposite, lanceolate leaves coarsely toothed; the floral heads pincushion-like to 5 cm across, with usually deep crimson, fragrant flowers, sometimes rose, lilac or white, summer-blooming. Zone 9.   p. 415

caucasica (Caucasus), "Caucasian pincushion"; perennial to 60 cm or more high, with lanceolate, glaucous basal leaves; the stem leaves divided; the floral heads flattish, 5 to 8 cm across, light blue, with a pincushion-like center; blooming June to October. Zone 4.   p. 415

graminifolia (So. Europe, Switzerland), "Grassleaf scabious"; clustering pubescent perennial 25 to 40 cm high, from short, creeping rhizome; grass-like linear, silvery white leaves; floral heads to 5 cm across, with pale lilac to rose flowers, during July-August. Zone 6.   p. 415

lucida (Pyrenees to Alps and Carpathian Mts.), "Pincushion"; perennial 15 to 60 cm high, with silvery leaves linear or finely dissected; rather flat, rose-lilac flowers 3-4 cm across, having pale cushion in center, and blooming June to September. Zone 5.   p. 415

ochroleuca (Europe: Poland, Balkans, Russia), "Cream scabious"; perennial or biennial to 60 cm high, softly white-hairy; basal leaves fiddle-shaped or entire, stem-leaves pinnately divided into ovate segments; small globular floral heads 3 cm across, of primrose yellow flowers, in June to September. Zone 5.   p. 415

SCADOXUS   see HAEMANTHUS

SCAEVOLA   Goodeniaceae

microcarpa 'Mauve Clusters' (Temp. Southern Australia, Victoria, Tasmania), "Fan flower" or "Half-flower"; small scrambling perennial with thin branches, and obovate, finely toothed, fleshy leaves slightly woolly, 3-4 cm long; charming rosy-purple flowers interesting in having their floral petals fan-like to one side, 3 cm long, lined with red, and white at base, blooming throughout the Summer. Ideal in balcony boxes. Zone 10.   p. 315

SCANDIX   Umbelliferae

pecten-veneris (Britain to Italy, Crete, Egypt), "Venus comb" or "Shepherd's needle"; annual to biennial, with leaves 2 to 4 times pinnately divided; small white flowers in loose clusters, blooming April-July, followed by the fruit extending into long linear needle-like beak. Known as a culinary potherb in ancient Egypt, and reported by Theophrastus in Greece, as eaten raw or cooked. Young shoots are used in salads. Zones 6-9.   p. 545

SCHAUERIA   Acanthaceae

flavicoma (Justicia) (Trop. Brazil); tropical shrub 60-120 cm high, with lustrous, ovate leaves to 15 cm long, the midrib and veins pale green or whitish; the trumpet-shaped flowers in terminal cluster, with corolla yellow 4 cm long, upper lip notched, the lower lip 3-lobed, and calyx white. Zone 10.   p. 631

SCHEFFLERA   Araliaceae

actinophylla (Dr. David Frodin, Univ. of New Guinea 1986) (as Brassaia in Hortus 3, Zander) (Queensland, New Guinea, Java), the "Queensland umbrella tree" or "Octopus tree"; an attractive ornamental tub plant in U.S.A.; in Queensland becoming a tall tree 30 m or more high; in New Guinea I have seen them growing epiphytic 30 m up on rainforest trees 5 m high; the sparry, willowy brownish, later woody branches each end at their top with a rosette of successively larger, palmately compound leaves forming umbrella-like symmetrical heads; lacquered green, soft-leathery oblong, stalked leaflets, having about 5 prominent lateral veins each side of the ivory midrib; the young leaves with 3 later 5, in older plants 7 to 12 and 16, to 30 cm long; with irregularly spaced, sparse teeth on juvenile plants, entire on mature stage leaves. Terminal inflorescence of several 1-1½ m straight spikes set with sessile round, dense clusters of honey-laden flowers with fleshy wine-red petals, and which form into the purple fruit. Very satisfactory decorator if kept warm and fairly dry. Tropical. Zones 11-12.   p. 35, 652, 653

albido-bracteata (Philippines), "Starshine schefflera"; handsome ornamental plant found 1977 by Ingwersen of Oceanside, California, growing epiphytic in a tree on Mindanao; tree-like but becoming scandent with willowy, beige-brown stems to 6 m high, long wiry petioles carry the palmately compound striking leaves, 30 cm or more across, consisting of usually 9 to 12 pendant, narrow lanceolate leaflets 12 to 25 cm long, deeply corrugated, of leathery texture and lustrous deep green but tending to defoliate at cool temperatures. May need staking when used as decorator plant. Tropical. Zone 11.   p. 652

angustifolia (Dr. D. Frodin) (Cephaloschefflera blaneoi) (Philippines); a Malaysian tropical evergreen shrub or tree, branching from the base, with slender flexuous stems, handsome palmately compound foliage, with narrow lanceolate, leathery leaflets glossy green and lightly concave, carried on long wiry petioles. Seen in col. Los Baños Arboretum on Luzon. Zone 10.   p. 652

arboricola (Heptapleurum) (Taiwan), "Hawaiian Elf"; freely branching plant of dwarf habit, resembling when young a miniature Schefflera actinophylla; wiry stems flexible and becoming scandent with age; the palmate foliage glossy green, to 15 cm across, arranged in a circle of 7 to 8 soft-leathery leaflets; inflorescence in erect, terminal cluster of orange-red to blackish berries; very charming in appearance and a good decorator plant. Subtropic. Zone 10.   p. 35, 653

arboricola 'Variegata', "Variegated Elf"; a very attractive decorator plant indoors; sport of the Chinese species with highly variegated palmate leaves rich green with ivory-white. Zone 10.   p. 35, 653

digitata (D. Frodin: moorei) (New Zealand), "Seven fingers"; bush or small tree 3-6 m high, densely branching, sometimes growing epiphytic, with thin-leathery leaves palmately compound, 5-10 foliolate obovate leaflets to 17 cm long, dull satiny green above, shiny light green beneath, densely ciliate and undulate at margins, and with yellowish, depressed veins; greenish-yellow flowers in panicles, purplish-black fruit berry-like. S. digitata prefers cool locations and I saw large colonies of this evergreen bush in the chilly southern New Zealand Fiordland, especially near Milford Sound. Zone 10.   p. 652

elegantissima (Baileya Jan. 1989): see DIZYGOTHECA elegantissima as in hort.

elliptica (odorata hort.), (Makiling, Philippines); decorative ornamental tropical plant in habitat growing as terrestrial or epiphyte on trees or rocks; flexible stems, and palmately compound foliage, consisting of about 6-7 leathery oblanceolate, stalked leaflets rich glossy green about 15 cm long. Seen in col. Los Baños Arboretum, Laguna, Philippines. Zone 11.   p. 652

insularum (insularis) (Los Baños, Philippines); bushy tropical evergreen with very decorative foliage; the leaves palmately compound of usually 8 leathery, stalked leaflets, obovate to lanceolate in outline, the surface smooth and rich green with darker ribs. Zone 10.   p. 652

minutifolia (Baguio, Philippines); miniature with green, wiry stems; compound leaves with 5 to 8 glossy green, narrow leaflets 3-6 cm long. According to Dr. David Frodin, this is near S. microphylla. Zone 10.   p. 653

octophylla 'Variegata' (Brassaia), "Variegated umbrella plant"; strikingly colored form of the species of China and Japan, highly variegated and splashed with creamy-white; seen in col. Bermuda Botanic Garden. *Zone 11.*   *p. 652*

polybotrya (Java); slender evergreen tropical shrub, the branches covered with roundish warts; leaves palmately compound of 5-7 leathery ovate leaflets, 15-20 cm long, on 20 cm stalks, swollen at base, deep green with ivory veins; small green flowers in pendant racemes 30 cm long; followed by small berry-like 5-celled fruit. *Zone 10.*   *p. 652*

pueckleri (Tupidanthus calyptratus) (Assam: Khasia Hills; Burma), "Mallet flower"; small ornamental evergreen tree which later becomes a scandent climber to 6 m high; long reddish petioles carry leaves palmately divided into 7 to 9 stalked, undulate, somewhat pendant, obovate to oblanceolate firm-textured, leathery leaflets 24 cm or more long, glossy green above, matte beneath, with about 30 closely spaced lateral veins each side of the reddish to beige midrib; the inflorescence in compound clusters of 2 to 3 cm greenish flowers with fleshy petals, followed by globular fruit containing seeds. A handsome decorator of sturdy character. *Subtropic.*
Zone 10.   *p. 35, 653*

'Starshine': see S. albido-bracteata

venulosa (Heptapleurum venulosum) (Queensland, China, Indo-china, India), a "Starleaf"; branching tree with palmately compound leaves; the 7-8 stalked leaflets lanceolate when young, obovate or elliptic in maturity, soft-leathery, semi-glossy on both sides, to 15 cm long; mature leaves entire, dark green, but lightly toothed in juvenile stage; inflorescence in panicles with whitish flowers, followed by small red fruit. *Zone 10.*   *p. 653*

venulosa erythrostachys (Heptapleurum stelzerianum hort.) (Trop. Asia to Australia), a "Starleaf"; scandent evergreen to 6 m high, inclined to become semi-climbing, forming adventitious roots; leaves alternate, palmate with 6-7 leaflets, oval or ovate, fleshy, to 15 cm long, yellowish-green; globular flowers dark red, in long, pendant raceme. *Zone 10.*   *p. 652*

volkensii (polyscidia) (Tanzania, Uganda); great evergreen tree to 25 m high from mountains at 2200-2700 m, such as growing in the mist-forest belt on Mt. Kilimanjaro at 2700 m. Palmately compound leaves with 5-7 glossy-leathery leaflets to 15 cm long, on willowy branches. *Subtropic. Zones 9-10.*   *p. 653*

SCHINUS   *Anacardiaceae*

molle (Ecuador, Perú), introduced in 1830 by Franciscan missionary fathers to California, at San Luis Rey; "Peppertree" or "California pepper tree"; dioecious evergreen tree with gracefully weeping branches, 6-10 m high, with age developing a rough, gnarled trunk 60-90 cm thick; pinnate, feathery leaves 12-20 cm long, of numerous leathery, linear, deep green leaflets; yellowish-white flowers; on female trees the rosy 6 mm fruit resembling pepper-corns, in pendulous terminal clusters. In Mexico, the fruit is ground for beverages, and made into an intoxicant by fermenting it; the bark is used for tanning skins. *Subtropic. Zones 9-10.*   *p. 207, 637, 638*

terebinthifolius (Brazil, Paraguay), "Brazilian pepper-tree" or "Christmas-berry tree"; ornamental evergreen tree 6-9 m high, of more rigid habit and less pendulous than S. molle, the California pepper tree; broadly spreading with willowy to woody branches densely clothed with pinnate leaves 10-17 cm long, of 5 to 9 broad leathery leaflets, dark glossy green and long-persistent. Small white flowers, followed by bright red berries on female trees, very showy in Winter. *Zone 9.*   *p. 638*

SCHISANDRA   *Magnoliaceae (Schisandraceae)*

rubriflora (syn. grandiflora) (China), "Magnolia vine"; handsome small evergreen, with leathery obovate leaves 5-15 cm long, pale underneath, and toothed at margins; bright red waxy flowers 3 cm across. Photographed in col. Kew Botanic Gardens, England.
Zone 9.   *p. 278*

SCHISMATOGLOTTIS roebelenii:
see AGLAONEMA crispum

SCHIVERECKIA   *Cruciferae*

podolica (Alyssum) (S.E. Europe, the Urals of Russia; Asia Minor); small perennial or biennial, similar to Alyssum, forming mounds 10-25 cm high; silvery, narrow-oblong 1 cm leaves; white flowers in small clusters on leafy stalks, blooming in Spring. *Zone 5.*   *p. 413*

SCHIZANTHUS   *Solanaceae*

pinnatus (Chile), "Butterfly-flower"; herbaceous plant, usually grown as annual, to 60 cm or more high, with fern-like leaves pinnately cut and divided, to 12 cm long; profusely blooming, with peculiar flowers with spreading lobes, to 4 cm across, usually lilac-pink but varying to violet, or whitish with lip marked violet, blooming late Spring to Autumn. Excellent as pot plant on the terrace.
Zone 10.   *p. 513*

retusus (Chile), "Butterfly flower"; herbaceous short-lived perennial, or annual to 1 m, with sticky stems and foliage; leaves finely divided, to 12 cm long; attractive irregular orchid-like flowers along the stalks, flaring wide 4-5 cm across, peach-colored with deep yellow center and lilac on lip. *Subtropic. Zone 10.*   *p. 513*

x wisetonensis, "Poor man's orchid"; beautiful hybrid of pinnatus x grahamii (Chile); bushy herbaceous plant usually to 40 cm high, with slender, sticky branches, pale green, divided leaves, and a profusion of showy, irregular, pansy-like flowers in shades of lilac, purple, pink, carmine, reddish-brown, or white, the upper lip often marked with purple and yellow, blooming Spring or Summer. *Subtropic.*
Zone 10.   *p. 513*

SCHIZOCASIA: see XENOPHYA

SCHIZOPHRAGMA   *Saxifragaceae*

hydrangeoides (Japan), "Japanese hydrangea vine"; scandent deciduous shrub spreading low but later with clinging vine to 10 m high, supporting their stems by aerial roots; leaves broadly ovate 8-12 cm long and coarsely toothed, reddish when young, and with red midrib; small yellowish-white fertile flowers in flattish clusters 15-20 cm broad, subtended by showy marginal flowers consisting of a single large creamy-white sepal 3 cm long, blooming July.
Zone 6.   *p. 872*

SCHIZOSTACHYUM   *Gramineae*

brachycladum (Moluccas); charming small tropical bamboo with erect culms forming open clumps; canes green and yellow, 3-4 cm thick; long lanceolate foliage. Used by the Chinese in celebration of their New Year. *Zones 10-11.*   *p. 557*

sp. 'Finisterre' (Northeastern New Guinea); a giant bamboo with hollow culms 8 to 10 cm dia., turning a polished bright yellow when mature. Long sections of the stems are cut and the dividing sectional cross-walls are rodded out except for the lowest one, and so used by the Melanesian tribes to carry water from the river valleys to their mountain villages. *Tropical. Zones 10-11.*   *p. 557*

zollingeri (Malay Peninsula, Philippines), "Golden bamboo"; elegant tropical species to 3 m or more high, forming dense clumps of stiffly erect, slender canes to 3 cm dia., dark olive-green and largely covered by light brown spathes; the attractive foliage clustered toward apex; the stiffish leaves broadly lanceolate and arranged very attractively toward tips of lateral branches in fan-like fashion.
Zones 10 -11.   *p. 556*

SCHIZOSTYLIS   *Iridaceae*

coccinea (So. Africa), "Kaffir-lily", "Crimson flag" or "River lily"; a beautiful rhizomatous evergreen herb forming clumps to 1 m high; curved narrow green leaves 25 cm long and 1 cm wide; a slender stalk bears 6 to 14 showy scarlet-red flowers like stars 4-5 cm across, with yellow anthers, lasting 4 days, summer-fall-blooming. *Zone 9.* *p. 425*

SCHLUMBERGERA   *Cactaceae*

bridgesii (Epiphyllum truncatum) (Bolivia ?), "Christmas cactus"; branching epiphyte with small glossy green leaf-like joints, crenate and with blunt apex; pendant flowers in December, with flaring petals carmine-red tinged purple in center; angled ovaries. *Tropical.*
Zone 11.   *p. 59, 206*

gaertneri: see RHIPSALIDOPSIS gaertneri

orssichiana (S.E. Brazil), Dr. Ira Slade has named this "Christmas Countess"; clambering epiphyte of the cool Serra do Mar; with flat green joints similar to S. truncata, but broader and thicker, also more deeply notched; the giant 5 by 8 cm flowers with numerous elongate petals white in center and shading to carmine-rose margins and tips, spreading wide and recurving when open, in the center the golden anthers. Dr. Slade has bloomed this in his Greenlife Gardens, Griffin, Georgia in September, January and May. *Zone 10.*   *p. 179*

truncata (Zygocactus truncatus) (Organ Mts., Rio de Janeiro), "Thanksgiving cactus", also called "Crab-cactus"; branching epiphyte with flattened joints 5 cm long, dark glossy green, and having two prominent teeth or claws at apex; Oct.-Nov. blooming with irregular (zygomorphic) scarlet flowers characterized by round ovaries. *Tropical. Zone 11.*   *p. 59, 179*

truncata 'Delicatus' (Zygocactus); variety of upright habit, reluctant to branch, long dark green joints sharply toothed, and with irregular white flowers delicately tinged pink; more rose-pink in good light; the ovaries round; Nov.-Dec. (Winter) bloom. *Tropical.*
Zone 11.   *p. 58*

SCHOMBURGKIA   *Orchidaceae*

undulata (Laelia) (Trinidad, Venezuela, Colombia); bold epiphyte with tall, spindle-shaped, 2-3-leaved pseudobulbs, bearing the 1 m reedy stalk topped by a many-flowered dense raceme, the waxy sepals and petals longer and narrower than crispa, much twisted and crisped, wine-purple with a rosy lip, (Dec.-July). *Tropical.*
Zones 11-12.   *p. 96*

SCHOTIA   *Leguminosae*
   brachypetala (Transvaal, Natal, Zululand), "Tree fuchsia"; notable tree on the dry, ochreous bushveld of the Transvaal, to 12 m high, loaded with pendulous, crowded clusters of glowing deep crimson-red flowers, having 4-lobed leathery calyx and minute petals, with protruding red stamens; pinnate green leaves partially deciduous, dropping most of them before flowering. *Zone 10.*   *p. 769*

SCHURMANSIA   *Ochnaceae*
   henningsii (New Guinea); interesting tropical ornamental evergreen, found in Wongan, N.G., seen in col. Pingatore of Buenos Aires Bot. Garden, Argentina as Schefflera roxo-albida, but identified by David Frodin of New Guinea University; densely branched and with palmate leaves, the glossy green, soft-leathery leaflets lanceolate about 25 cm long and undulate along margins; inflorescence in showy feathery terminal clusters of salmon-rose flowers. *Zone 10.*   *p. 805*

SCIADOPITYS   *Taxodiaceae (Coniferae)*
   verticillata (Central Japan), the "Umbrella pine"; slow growing, very ornamental evergreen to 20 or 30 m high, of pyramidal habit; dense with slender linear, dark green needles 8-15 cm long, with 2 white bands below and deflected in graceful whorls; oblong woody 8 to 12 cm cones. *Zone 6.*   *p. 612*

SCILLA   *Liliaceae*
   campanulata (Endymion in Hortus 3): see HYACINTHOIDES hispanica (Zander)
   hispanica: see HYACINTHOIDES (Zander)
   mischtschenkoana (tubergeniana) (Mountains of N.W. Iran), "Persian blue bell"; choice miniature bulbous plant barely 15 cm high, each bulb producing several stalks with beautiful starry flowers 3 cm across, pale blue with deeper mauve backs and deep blue median line on each segment; blooms appear before leaves. *Zone 5.*   *p. 248*
   non-scripta (nutans) (Endymion in Hortus 3):
see HYACINTHOIDES non-scripta
   peruviana (Mediterranean reg., Madeira), "Peruvian jacinth"; erroneously called the "Cuban lily"; bulbous plant very showy, carrying a dense cluster of small star-like lilac-blue flowers 2½ cm across, with petals edged in rose, blue stamens and yellow pollen, on thick-fleshy stalk, above broad, soft succulent, fresh green leaves; Spring. *Subtropic. Zone 9.*   *p. 54, 248*
   siberica (Russia to Caucasus and Asia Minor), "Siberian squill"; early spring-blooming bulbous perennial to 15 cm high, with 2-5 strap-shaped ascending basal leaves; producing several floral stalks bearing 1-4 nodding bowl-shaped flowers spreading 2 cm across, bright blue with dark central stripe. Very popular for naturalizing forming clusters. *Zone 4.*   *p. 248*
   siberica 'Spring Beauty' ('Atrocaerulea') "Blue squill"; excellent robust clone with particularly bright, deep purplish-blue flowers spreading to 3 cm, multiplying easily from bulblets and seed, forming beautiful blankets of bloom in early Spring. *Zone 4.*   *p. 248*
   violacea: see LEDEBOURIA socialis (Hortus 3)

SCINDAPSUS   *Araceae*
   aureus: is transferred to EPIPREMNUM aureum
   pictus argyraeus (Pothos argyraeus) (Borneo), "Satin pothos"; beautiful creeper with the smaller, cordate leaves satiny, bluish-green with markings and edge of silver; probably the juvenile stage of pictus. *Tropical. Zone 12.*   *p. 34*

SCIRPUS   *Cyperaceae*
   cernuus (Isolepis gracilis) (So. Africa; naturalized in So. Europe); grass-like, graceful tufted plant to 15 cm high, with numerous round, threadlike, fresh glossy green stems becoming pendant, tipped with little white flower heads as in bulrush. *Subtropic. Zones 9-10.*   *p. 558*
   lacustris albescens (Europe to Siberia), "White bulrush"; reed-like waterside perennial with erect cylindric white stems to 1 m or more high, tending to become greener toward tip; nearly without leaves, strap-shaped in streams; small white to brownish spikelets in terminal inflorescence. Used for mat-making and chair-bottoms. *Zone 5.*   *p. 558*

SCLERANTHUS   *Caryophyllaceae*
   uniflorus (New Zealand), "Knawe" of the Maori; moss-like perennial forming low cushion, the linear 1 cm leaves are curved, rather leathery and rigid; tiny flowers consisting of 4 sepals. *Zone 9. p. 367*

SCLEROCARPUS   *Compositae*
   divaricatus (Costa Rica), "Trailing wedelia"; collected alongside the railroad tracks near Puntarenas; delicate little perennial herb; the thin, wiry branches with small, rich green ovate leaves; golden-yellow flowers 3 cm across, with 5 fertile ray-florets around the yellow disc. *Zone 10.*   *p. 401*
   frutescens (Morelos, Mexico); low subshrub with silvery pubescent leaves; dahlia-like 3 cm flowers with 5 broad vivid orange-

yellow ray-petals having purple blotch at base. Photographed at the ancient ruins of Xochicalco in Morelos. *Zone 10.*   *p. 691*

SCOLYMUS   *Compositae*
   hispanicus (S.W. Europe), "Golden thistle" or "Spanish oyster plant"; vicious-looking biennial to 60 cm high, with rigid leaves deeply cut into spiny lobes; the flower heads in leafy spikes, with several rows of yellow, linear ray-florets. *Zone 8.*   *p. 398*

SCORZONERA   *Compositae*
   hispanica (Europe to W. Siberia), "Black salsify" or "Schwarz-wurzel"; perennial 75 cm high, often treated as biennial, with long, fleshy black-skinned taproot; forming slender branches with narrow linear, clasping leaves; yellow floral heads 5 cm across. A root vegetable, the white flesh is of sweet and agreeable flavor. *Zone 6.*   *p. 400*
   humile (Europe), "Salsify" or "Viper's grass"; herbaceous perennial or biennial with long, fleshy black-skinned taproot, forming dense tuft of long linear, grass-like leaves 20 cm long; free-blooming with 3-4 cm yellow, daisy-like flowers, seen May-blooming in England. *Zone 6.*   *p. 398*

SCUTELLARIA   *Labiatae*
   costaricana (mociniana) (Mexico, Costa Rica), the "Scarlet skullcap"; herbaceous shrub of robust habit, to 50 cm high, with purplish-brown square stem, opposite, ovate-cordate, quilted leaves 10 cm long, dark metallic green, thin-leathery, and with crenate margins, grayish-green beneath; striking erect, terminal spikes topped by a dense burst of brilliant scarlet-red long-tubular flowers 4-5 cm long, having orange-yellow lip and showing white stamens; the individual flowers will last only 6-10 days but succeeding clusters of flowers appear from upper leaf axils, extending blooming period from January to July. *Tropical. Zone 11.*   *p. 439*
   indica var. parvifolia (japonica) (China, Japan), "Lilac skullcap"; charming small perennial to 30 cm high, with broadly ovate leaves, shallowly lobed along margins, and cordate at base; beautiful flowers lilac to bluish, the corolla 2-3 cm long, curved tubular and purple inside, in dense clusters. *Zone 10.*   *p. 439*

SEAFORTHIA   *Palmae*
   elegans (of Queensland): see PTYCHOSPERMA
   elegans (in Calif. hort.): see ARCHONTOPHOENIX

SECALE   *Gramineae*
   cereale, "Common rye", the "Rye" of agriculture; ancient cultigen, possibly from the perennial S. montanum of S.W. Asia; in cultivation mainly in No. Europe for centuries as source of rye flour, as cereal, and fodder crop for livestock; grass-like annual with soft, glaucous bluish linear leaves; stalks to more than 1 m high, are bearing arching long-awned (bristly) spikes up to 15 cm long, crowded with seeds. This grain is used in making bread, and rye whiskey. Winter rye is a form sown in Autumn and plowed under as green manure. *Zone 5.*   *p. 567*

SECHIUM   *Cucurbitaceae*
   edule (Trop. America), "Chayote Squash" or "Christophine"; tropical climber to 4 m, with tendril-bearing stems; large tuberous roots weighing to 10 kg., rich in starch and edible yam-like, after cooking; leaves triangular-ovate, 10-20 cm long; flowers yellow, in long racemes, the corolla 5-parted, in June; oblong green fleshy fruit deeply grooved, 10 cm or more long, a culinary vegetable; much planted in warm-climate countries. *Zones 10-11.*   *p. 911*

SEDUM   *Crassulaceae*
   acre (Europe, No. Africa, to W. Asia), "Golden carpet"; widely colonized stonecrop forming moss-like covers; evergreen creeping branches with small succulent, overlapping ovoid 5 mm leaves, and branched clusters of bright yellow flowers, in early Summer. *Zones 3-9.*   *p. 313*
   adolphi (Mexico), "Golden sedum"; small branching rosette of plump, fleshy keeled leaves 4 cm long, waxy yellowish-green with reddish margins; showy inflorescence in large cluster of starry, white flowers. *Subtropic. Zone 9.*   *p. 188*
   aizoon (Siberia to China and Japan), "Aizoon stonecrop"; smooth perennial 30 to 80 cm high, with short rhizome, leafless in Winter; stems with alternate obovate, thin-succulent green leaves 5-8 cm long, toothed in lower part; flat clusters of yellow to orange flowers. *Zone 3.*   *p. 189*
   cauticola (Mountains of No. Japan); hardy, spreading succulent perennial close to S. sieboldii, with prostrate purple stems; the rounded, cupped, fleshy leaves 3 cm long, glaucous bluish-gray and dotted with red; the inflorescence with carmine-rose flowers in loose clusters. *Warm temperate. Zone 6.*   *p. 189*
   dendroideum praealtum (Mexico); large handsome branching succulent to 1½ m or more high; oblanceolate spoon-shaped,

incurving leaves arranged in loose rosette at apex of stems, 5-7 cm long, pale green flushed red at tips; flowers light yellow, in loose inflorescence. *Arid-subtropic. Zone 10.*   *p. 188*

hybridum 'Immergruenchen' (kamtschaticum hyb.); worthy German hybrid forming mats, with evergreen branches spreading to 15 cm; the fleshy leaves oblong, and having crenate margins; clusters of starry yellow flowers, June to August. *Zone 6.*   *p. 313*

kamtschaticum (No. Japan, Korea, No. China, Siberia); attractive succulent perennial spreader, with spatulate leaves 3-5 cm long, toothed toward apex, fresh green with white margins; flower petals yellow with orange centers, in loose inflorescence. *Temperate. Zones 3-9.*   *p. 189*

kamtschaticum var. middendorfianum (E. Siberia, Manchuria), "Orange stonecrop"; smooth perennial with elongate rhizomes sprouting several annual stems 15-30 cm high; fleshy succulent oval 5 cm leaves crenate at upper margins; starry yellow flowers during Summer. *Zone 4.*   *p. 313*

laconicum (Greece, Asia Minor); creeping evergreen perennial with spreading branches lined with small 1 cm succulent ovate leaves alternate or in rosettes; clusters of small starry, yellow flowers. *Zone 7.*   *p. 313*

makinoi (Japan: Honshu to Kyushu); creeping low perennial or biennial succulent, forming mats, the branches rooting at nodes; smooth spatulate roundish thick leaves 2 cm long, glaucous light green; yellow flowers in broad clusters. *Zone 9.*   *p. 189*

morganianum (Mexico: Veracruz), "Burro-tail"; a lovely hanging succulent plant, with tassels of short spindle-shaped leaves yellowish-green covered with silvery blue bloom; terminal flowers pale pink. The heavy branches are quite pendulous and a beautiful sight when grown like long queues; terminal clusters of deep rose flowers. Excellent basket plants. Leaves will root when detached to form plantlets. *Subtropic. Zone 10.*   *p. 190*

nutans: see CREMNOPHILA nutans

oreganum (Oregon to Alaska), "Oregon stonecrop"; attractive creeping succulent with 2 cm obovate leaves in near-rosettes, glossy green tinged with red, or all-red in sunny, hot locations; clusters of starry yellow flowers, fading to pink. *Zone 4.*   *p. 313*

pachyphyllum (Oaxaca), "Jelly beans"; small shrubby succulent with cylindric club-shaped fleshy leaves curved upward, 3-4 cm long, light green and glaucous blue, with red tips; flowers light yellow in dense flat clusters. *Subtropic. Zone 10.*   *p. 188*

pilosum (Umbilicus pubescens) (Mountains of Asia Minor, Armenia, Caucasus); small biennial succulent to 10 cm high, with fat little 2 cm recurving leaves densely shingled along stem, dark green, and ciliate at edges; the stems topped by showy cluster of rose-red, starry flowers. *Zone 8.*   *p. 190*

pluricaule 'Rose Carpet' (parentage Sakhalin, Hokkaido); colorful succulent perennial spreading from fleshy roots, with slender branches to 18 cm long, dense with rounded obovate, grayish 2 cm leaves; vivid rose-pink flowers in terminal clusters. *Zone 6.*   *p. 190*

reflexum (Europe: France to Norway, East to Ukraine); spreading low perennial, with branches dying back during cold Winter; the stems crowded with succulent linear-cylindric gray-green leaves 12 mm long; small yellow flowers in clusters. *Zones 3-9.*   *p. 189*

rubrotinctum (guatemalense hort.) (Mexico), "Christmas cheer"; small branching succulent with thickly clustered, fleshy, club-shaped 2 cm leaves glossy green, turning coppery red in sun; small yellow flowers in clusters. This may be a garden hybrid. *Arid-subtropic. Zone 10.*   *p. 189*

sempervivoides (Asia Minor: Armenia; Caucasus, at 2000 m alt.); pubescent biennial, in sempervivum-like rosettes to 5 cm across, of soft-hairy ovate fleshy leaves purplish, the floral stems forming following Summer, with clusters of crimson flowers. *Zone 9.   p. 189*

sieboldii (Japan), "October plant"; graceful perennial, in cold climates with annual low arching red branches, suitable in rock-gardens or for hanging baskets; flexible stems set with whorls of 3 roundish, notched leaves, glaucous blue changing to copper, 2 cm long, and edged with red; terminal clusters of pink flowers, blooming August into October. *Warm temperate. Zone 7.*   *p. 190, 313*

sieboldii 'Medio-variegatum'; an attractive variegated form with the grayish-green leaves having a cream-yellow center, and stems are pink. *Warm temperate. Zone 9.*   *p. 190*

sordidum (Central Japan); hardy perennial with tuberous roots, forming trailing stems annually, 20 to 40 cm long, with succulent ovate, 4-6 cm leaves; usually dentate at margins, green or bluish glaucous; small greenish-white flowers in rounded clusters. *Zone 5.*   *p. 189*

spathulifolium pruinosum (Northern California: Cape Blanco, to British Columbia), "Capa Blanca"; evergreen branching succulent with stems topped by small rosettes; leaves spatulate 2-3 cm long, glaucous bluish with red margins; flowers yellow, in leafy clusters. Excellent for ornamental planting. *Warm temperate. Zone 8. p. 189*

spectabile (Japan, Korea, Central China), hardy "Live forever" or "Showy sedum"; strong growing, tough winter-hardy perennial succulent 30-60 cm high, freely suckering at base with erect thick fleshy stems and soft leathery, glaucous light green or grayish obovate leaves 6-8 cm long, toothed toward apex, and generally set in twos and threes along the stems, which terminate in large flat clusters of rosy-lavender or red flowers in late Summer. Propagation by division of the rootstock or cuttings. Probably the showiest of Sedums, good for tubs which may be left outdoors during the cold season, with plants going dormant in Winter. *Zone 5.*   *p. 190*

spurium (Caucasus), "Dragon's-blood"; rambling, matforming small succulent with thin, flexible reddish stems set with opposite tiny waxy green, 2½ cm roundish leaves, crenate toward apex, and forming rosettes; flowers red to white; hardy. *Zones 3-9.*   *p. 313*

spurium 'Purple Carpet'; beautiful "Two-row stonecrop" forming a dense carpet; spreading with reddish stems, having opposite succulent leaves, semi-evergreen in cold climate, blooming in late Summer with clusters of crimson-red flowers. *Zones 3-9.*   *p. 313*

suaveolens (W. Mexico: Durango); handsome echeveria-like spreading, succulent rosette 8 cm or more across, of broad-obovate leaves, concave on surface and keeled beneath, bluish-glaucous with reddish margins and spine-like tips; flowers white. *Zone 10.*   *p. 188*

telephioides (No. Carolina to Illinois); succulent perennial with tuber-like thickened roots, forming annual leafy stem 15 to 50 cm long, withering in Autumn; usually alternate obovate fleshy, gray-green leaves to 6 cm long, some with marginal teeth; terminal clusters of small white to pink flowers. *Zone 4.*   *p. 191*

telephium (W. Europe), "European ice plant" or "European live-forever"; robust perennial with thickened carrot-like roots; strong stems erect to 45 cm high, set with oblong-ovate bluish-green soft-leathery, toothed leaves 5-10 cm long and rarely opposite, not in twos and threes as spectabile; in early Autumn each leafy stem is topped by a large cluster of bronzy, rosy or red-purple flowers. Winter-hardy and going dormant. 'Autumn Joy' (Herbstfreude) has coppery rose blooms and is 75 cm high. *Warm temperate. Zone 6.*   *p. 190*

weinbergii: see GRAPTOPETALUM paraguayense

SELAGINELLA   *Selaginellaceae*

emmeliana (pallescens in Hortus 3) (So. America), "Sweat plant"; lacy, small rosette of fern-like, erect, bright green fronds, revelling in high humidity; if allowed to dry the tips will curl and turn brown and won't recover. *Humid-tropical. Zone 12.*   *p. 143*

kraussiana (Lycopodium denticulatum) (South Africa, Cameroons), "Spreading clubmoss"; a charming, moss-like herb with matforming, creeping stems rooting as they grow, with tiny, crowded, bright green, pinnate, scale-like leaves; very useful as a quickly spreading groundcover in terrarium or conservatory. *Humid-tropical. Zones 11-12.*   *p. 143*

kraussiana 'Brownii' (apus elegans) (Azores), "Dwarf clubmoss"; shapely, moss-like cushions of densely clustering, short branches of vivid emerald green, supported by translucent aerial roots; very attractive in terrariums. *Humid-tropical. Zones 11-12.*   *p. 143*

lepidophylla (Texas, Mexico, Perú), "Resurrection plant" or "Rose of Jericho"; flat rosette of densely tufted, branched stems with fairly hard, scale-like leaves, red-brown with age; when the plants dry out the branches curl up into a tight ball, but will unfold to fresh emerald green when placed into water. *Subtropic. Zones 9-10. p. 143*

martensii (Mexico); bold ornamental species, with broad, vivid glossy green, scale-like, fleshy, almost hard leaves on much branched stems, upright at first, later sub-erect or creeping with young growth erect, supported by strong stilt roots. *Zones 11-12.*   *p. 143*

tamariscina (Honshu, Kyushu); evergreen tufted rosette of ribbon-like linear firm fertile fronds green with yellow tip; the tiny scale-like leaves in shingled ranks closely appressed to the flattened axis; forms miniature tree with age. Photographed at an exhibition of Japanese fanciers in Ikeda Park, Tokyo. *Subtropic. Zone 10. p. 143*

SELENICEREUS   *Cactaceae*

grandiflorus (Jamaica, Cuba), "Queen of the night" or "Moon cactus"; climbing epiphyte with large flowers 15-25 cm long, salmon outside, white inside, and blooming by moonlight, with a powerful vanilla perfume, earning it the name "Queen of the night"; the flowers expand at sunset or by moonlight and fade off in the morning; stems with 5-8 ribs 2-3 cm thick, light grayish-green to purplish, climbing by aerial root. *Tropical. Zone 11.*   *p. 176*

SEMECARPUS   *Anacardiaceae*

gigantifolia (Trop. S.E. Asia, Taiwan, to Micronesia, No. Australia), "Varnish-tree"; medium sized tropical tree with oblong lanceolate leaves to 30 cm long, having numerous distinct lateral veins each side of midrib, but reported irritating or poisonous to the touch; small greenish-white flowers, followed by nearly globose, edible nut, purplish-black when ripe, set in a fleshy orange cup being the thickened disc and calyx base; sap of young fruit hardens to a black resin used as an ink or black lacquer, also obtained from incision into the bark. *Zone 10.*   *p. 906*

SEMIARUNDINARIA   *Gramineae*

fastuosa (Japan), the "Narihira bamboo"; stately "running" bamboo with stems to 7-12 m high and 3 cm dia. at base; the culms thin-walled, slightly zigzag, marked with purplish-brown, mostly round but toward top flattened above the internodes; 1-3 upright branches mostly at the upper nodes, with leaves to 17 cm long, dark green and smooth above, grayish and pubescent beneath. Hardy to minus 18° C. *Zone 7.*   *p. 555*

SEMPERVIVUM   *Crassulaceae*

albidum 'Oddity'; curious Oregon mutation, possibly of S. tectorum or hybrid; small succulent tube-like rosette 5-6 cm dia., with smooth grayish-green leaves folded nearly cylindrical, leaving hollow opening at red apex and a purple spur. *Zone 9.*   *p. 191*

arachnoideum (Mountains of So. Europe: Pyrenees to Carpathians), "Cobweb house-leek"; tiny rosettes to 2 cm dia., clustering by stolons and forming mounds, prettily covered by a cobweb of white hairs from tip to tip of leaves; starry 3 cm red and pink flowers. *Temperate. Zone 5.*   *p. 191, 313*

arenarium (Hortus): see JOVIBARBA arenaria (Zander)
ciliatum 'Rubrum': see AEONIUM ciliatum 'Rubrum'
heuffelii: see JOVIBARBA heuffelii
hirtum: see JOVIBARBA hirta

tectorum (Europe), variable species, most widely grown, and known as "Hen-and-chicken" because of the miniature rosettes sprouting from the mother rosette; also called "Roof-houseleek" since it is often found growing on roofs; plant 8-10 cm across with many obovate cuspidate leaves gray-green, lightly tipped brown; 2 cm flowers purplish-red in clusters on floral stalk 20-40 cm high. *Zone 5.*   *p. 191*

SENECIO   *Compositae*

adonidifolius (W. Europe: Pyrenees to So. France), "Pyrenees groundsel"; floriferous, smooth perennial to 45 cm high, branching with erect stems; the stalked deep green, ferny leaves finely pinnately divided into linear lobes; small golden-yellow 2 cm floral heads in dense compound clusters. *Zone 6.*   *p. 400*

articulatus 'Variegatus' (Kleinia) (species of Cape Prov.), "Candle Plant"; succulent with swollen, jointed stems 30-60 cm high, glaucous blue with darker lines, and fleshy leaves deeply lobed; in the cultivar 'Variegatus' suffused with white to pink; flower heads yellowish-white. *Zone 11.*   *p. 180*

bicolor (Spain to Rhodos; Algeria), "Silver cineraria"; ornamental perennial subshrub to 60 cm high, with white-felted branches and leaves, the blades fleshy and broad-cordate, crenate and lobed at margins; branched flattish heads of small yellow flowers with white-woolly bracts, blooming May to August. *Zone 9.*   *p. 403*

cineraria (Cineraria maritima) (Mediterranean), "Silver groundsel"; beautiful, white-woolly perennial to 1 m tall, with thick leaves at first oak-leaved, later pinnately cut, the pinnae well separated and broad, crenate at their broadening apex; inflorescence on beautiful white-felted stalks, in cymes of small 2 cm thistle-like flower heads with short bright yellow rays. Listed in seed catalogs as Cineraria maritima 'Diamond'; much used as a border plant. *Subtropic. Zone 8.*   *p. 376, 400*

confusus (Mexico), "Mexican Flame vine"; colorful trailing vine or scandent shrub with fresh green, fleshy, ovate leaves 4 to 10 cm long, coarsely toothed at margins; striking daisy-like double flame-scarlet flowers in clusters at ends of branches. *Subtropic. Zone 10.*   *p. 273*

x cruentus (hybridus) from the Canary Islands; after much modification and possibly hybridization with S. heritieri and populifolia, have become the widely cultivated "Cineraria" of florists; a showy, herbaceous cool house plant with handsome, triangular-ovate, large turgid leaves rich grass green above, purplish beneath and grouped around a large rounded, and dense truss of starry flowers with variously colored rays from white to shades of pink to red, purple and blue, surrounding the usually purple center cushion; often with white eye. *Humid-subtropic. Zone 11.*   *p. 53*

x cruentus 'Multiflora nana'; medium small-flowered class of low, compact habit; the many smallish, often white-eyed flowers, primarily in bright reds, purples and blues, make up in big showy heads what they lack in individual size; a favorite commercial and widely cultivated group for early spring bloom. *Subtropic. Zone 11.*   *p. 54*

deflersii (So. Yemen, Arabia), "Cucumber plant"; curious clustering succulent, seen at Wright's, De Luz, Calif.; with ovoid oblong stems 10 cm high, narrowed toward both ends, with rounded tops, deep green and set with scattered rudimentary spines, looking very much like a cucumber-pickle; with age may reach 60 cm high. *Zone 10.*   *p. 180*

grandifolius (So. Mexico), "Giant senecio"; semi-woody species 2-4 m high, with erect, stout, purplish stem; large ovate leaves to 45 cm long, coarsely toothed, dark green above, downy beneath; winter flowering with large cluster of yellow heads. *Subtropic. Zone 9.*   *p. 400*

jacobsenii (Notonia petraea) (Kenya, Tanzania); succulent, erect when small, later creeping upwards, with alternate obovate fleshy, sessile nerveless leaves 8 cm long, glossy green, the stems rooting at the joints; flower heads orange. *Arid-tropical. Zones 10-11.*   *p. 180*

kleinia (Kleinia neriifolia) (Canary Islands); succulent shrub up to 3 m high, successively branching, with gray-green stems to 20 cm thick, segmented in yearly growths, the youngest segments to 4 cm thick, light green and waxy-mealy and marked with cross-lines; narrow, thickish, deciduous gray-green leaves to 15 cm long; yellowish flower heads with awl-shaped bracts. *Zone 10.*   *p. 180*

leucostachys (Cineraria candidissima in hort.) (Argentina), a tall-growing "Dusty miller"; shrubby at base but herbaceous as usually grown from cuttings; entire plant white tomentose, slender branches to 60 cm tall with leaves pinnatifid with linear lobes; inflorescence in corymbs with small heads of yellow flowers. This species is known as S. vira-vira according to HORTUS 3. *Zone 9.*   *p. 400*

macroglossus 'Variegatum', "Variegated wax-vine"; very attractive creeper, of which the green type comes from E. Cape Prov., but I found this lovely variegated form in Kenya; densely branching and mat-forming, with small 3-4 cm ivy-like lobed, waxy, thin-succulent leaves with cordate base, green to milky green and bordered or variegated with cream; pretty daisy-like ray-flowers with 12-14 white florets and yellow center. *Subtropic. Zone 10.*   *p. 310*

petasitis (So. Mexico), the "California-geranium"; shrub-like perennial to 2 m high with roundish, wavy-lobed grayish downy leaves 15-30 cm long; 3 cm flower heads in large terminal panicles, the 5-6 ray-florets bright yellow, disc brownish. *Tropical. Zone 9.*   *p. 691*

przewalskii: see LIGULARIA przewalaskii

rowleyanus (So. Namibia), "String of pearls"; creeping thin, flexible stems with adventitious roots forming dense mats; furnished as in a string of beads the globular pointed, succulent leaves shiny pale to dark green, with a translucent stripe, about 1 cm dia.; the flowers cinnamon-scented, without ray-florets, the corolla white and with brownish-violet anthers. *Subtropic. Zone 10.*   *p. 180*

scaposus (So. Africa), "Silver coral kleinia"; low branched succulent with 5 to 8 cm long cylindrical leaves arranged in rosettes, gray marbled olive-green, and silver cobwebby when young; inflorescence of numerous yellow flower heads. *Zone 10.*   *p. 180*

serpens (better known in hort. as Kleinia repens) (So. Africa: Cape Prov.), "Blue chalk sticks"; low succulent branching shrub 20-30 cm high, with fleshy, nearly cylindrical leaves to 3 cm long, grooved above, bluish-gray with blue waxy coating; flower heads pale yellow. Attractive but has a tendency to drop leaves. *Arid-subtropic. Zone 10.*   *p. 182*

webbii (Spain: Gran Canaria); ornamental perennial with erect, succulent, brown-felty stem, clothed by roundish-cordate or reniform leaves, wavy and fine-hairy at margins; at apex a clustered inflorescence of flowers with white ray-florets, arranged around the purplish center disc. *Zone 9.*   *p. 400*

SENNA   *Leguminosae*

aciphylla (Cassia alpinum) (Australia); low, spreading bush available in California nurseries; evergreen pinnate leaves 6 cm long, dense with 20-30 pairs of 15-20 mm needle-like leaflets; and charming vivid yellow axillary flowers 2 cm wide. *Zone 9.*   *p. 753*

alata (Cassia) (Trop. America), "Candle-bush"; short-lived deciduous shrub 1 to 4 m high, with pinnate foliage; 6 to 10 cm leaflets; erect candle-like spikes of golden-yellow flowers; long-blooming into Winter. *Zones 9-10.*   *p. 752*

artemisioides (Cassia) (Queensland to West Australia), "Feathery senna" or "Silvery cassia"; bushy shrub 2-3 m high, covered with silky-gray pubescence, with pinnate leaves 6 cm long, dense with pairs of linear needle-like leaflets, and bright yellow, showy flowers in small clusters, displaying their black anthers. *Zones 9-10.*   *p. 753*

auriculata (Cassia) (Saudi Arabia to So. India and Sri Lanka), "Avaram" or "Tanner's cassia"; tall evergreen shrub to 4 m high, with smooth gray bark; pinnate leaves to 10 cm long, having 8-12 pairs of obovate leaflets; the inflorescence in clusters of yellow flowers 3-5 cm across, followed by thin seed pods 12 cm long. A principal native tanbark of India. *Zones 9-10.*   *p. 752*

biflora (Cassia) (Mexico: Baja Calif. to Chiapas and Yucatán; West Indies), "Flor de San Jose"; tropical shrub to 2½ m high, with erect branches, developing into small tree spreading from short trunk; pinnate leaves of narrow oblong leaflets 3-4 cm long; showy yellow flowers 2-3 cm long in twos, blooming in August; flat fruit pods 5-10 cm long, straight or curved; photographed in Mysore, South India. *Zone 10.*   *p. 752*

candolleana (Cassia bicapsularis in Calif. hort.) (Chile); very floriferous erect shrub to 3 m high, in hort. usually lower, and weak straggling stems, with pinnate leaves having 3 to 5 pairs of obovate or roundish, fleshy leaflets; light yellow flowers with cupped petals in showy terminal clusters, blooming November to February; slender bean-like seed pods 8-16 cm long, containing a single row of seeds; bicapsularis has two rows. Very popular in California. *Zones 9-10.*   p. 753

corymbosa (Cassia) (Argentina), "Flowering senna"; sunloving shrub to 3 m high, with pinnate foliage of 3 pairs of leathery leaflets, and showy clusters of nearly regular, rather cupped flowers of golden-yellow, blooming July into Winter. Sometimes listed as C. marilandica in horticulture. *Zone 8.*   p. 753

didymobotrya (Cassia nairobensis) (Trop. Africa), "Popcorn-bush"; bushy shrub or small tree to 3 m, young shoots and leaves finely downy; leaves 35 cm long; leaflets in 4-18 pairs; inflorescence in erect, showy racemes 15-30 cm long, several borne near end of shoots; very showy with their large cupped golden-yellow flowers. *Zone 10.*   p. 753

excelsa (Cassia floribunda) (E. Brazil), "Crown-of-gold tree"; tall shrub or tree to 10 m, with branchlets softly pubescent; pendant foliage with 10-20 pairs of oblong leaflets 4 cm long; inflorescence in axillary or terminal clusters of fragrant bright yellow flowers. *Zone 10.*   p. 752

fruticosa (Chamaefistula antillana hort.) (Trop. America), "Drooping cassia"; tall scandent shrub 2 to 4 m high; compound leaf with leaflets ovate-oblong, finely pubescent beneath; flowers in terminal and axillary raceme with pale yellow or ochre petals and stamens. *Zone 10.*   p. 752

laevigata (Cassia) (Trop. America, naturalized in Australia and Africa); erect tropical shrub to 1½ m high, leaves pinnate with 2 to 5 pairs of lanceolate leaflets 4-7 cm long and slender-pointed; yellow flowers with corolla to 3 cm wide, in axillary or terminal clusters, blooming during July; cylindric seed pods 5-7 cm long. *Zone 10.*   p. 752

leptophylla (Cassia) (Brazil), "Gold medallion tree"; very ornamental evergreen tree 10 m high, widely planted in Brazil; bearing great quantities of large cupped, golden-yellow flowers 3-4 cm across, in showy heads on long flexuous branches; glaucous leaves pinnate with 8-10 pairs of broad, crenate leaflets. *Zones 9-10.*   p. 753

marilandica (Cassia hebecarpa), (Mass. to Wisconsin and No. Carolina), "Wild senna"; subshrub sending up erect, pithy shoots from a woody rootstock to 1 m; pinnate leaves glaucous beneath, flowers with corolla 1 cm wide, petals yellow, anthers purple, in axillary racemes, blooming in Summer; followed by pods 10 cm long. *Zones 4-8.*   p. 440

multijuga (Cassia) (W. Indies, So. America: Brazil to Guyana), "November shower"; small tree to 6 m high; pinnate foliage with 18-40 pairs of linear-oblong leaflets to 2 cm long; golden-yellow flowers 5 cm dia., in erect dense clusters. Naturalized in Caribbean region. *Zone 10.*   p. 754

nitida (Chamaefistula antillana hort.) (Indonesia: Sumatra), "Climbing senna"; found at Lake Toba in Central Sumatra; tropical evergreen shrub with clambering branches, pinnate leaves having ovate leaflets; inflorescence in dense racemes of waxy pink flowers. *Zones 10-11.*   p. 283

pendula (Cassia floribunda in California hort.) (Trop. America); showy, robust bush to 3 m high, with pinnate leaves, the oval leaflets leathery; erect terminal inflorescence with large cupped golden-yellow flowers 4 cm across. Also known as C. tricuspidata. A member of the C. bicapsularis complex, but S. pendula has beans with seeds arranged in two rows. *Zone 10.*   p. 753

septemtrionalis (Cassia floribunda in Taiwan), "Peanut butter cassia"; evergreen tropical shrub 2 m high, with pinnate leaves having 3-4 pairs of leathery, ovate-pointed leaflets; showy yellow flowers in small terminal cluster; cylindrical seed pods 10 cm long. *Zones 9-10.*   p. 754

siamea (Cassia) (Malaysia, naturalized in W. Africa), "Kassod tree"; tropical tree to 12 m tall; pinnate leaves with leathery leaflets to 8 cm long; inflorescence forming large terminal clusters of yellow flowers 3 cm across. Planted in Africa as shade trees for coffee plantations, and known there as "Coffee senna". *Zone 10.*   p. 754

speciosa (Cassia) (Brazil); large shrub with leaflets in 2 pairs, obliquely ovate, soft-hairy beneath; inflorescence in wide, terminal clusters to 50 cm long, flowers deep yellow, 4-6 cm across. *Zone 10.*   p. 754

spectabilis (Cassia leptophylla in hort.) (Trop. America), "Popcorn bush"; showy spreading tree to 12 m high, with long pinnate leaves, the leaflets lanceolate and bright green; branches bearing spectacular erect 30-60 cm racemes of large beautiful, cupped golden-yellow 4 cm flowers like shining lamps. *Zone 10.*   p. 754

surattensis (Cassia glauca) (Marquesas, India, Sri Lanka), "Scrambled eggs"; tall shrub or tree to 5 m high, shoots angular;

leaves 15-22 cm long; leaflets in 6-9 pairs, very glaucous beneath, 4-6 cm long; flowers in a fine, erect cluster of axillary and terminal racemes 10 cm long; corolla 3 cm across, yellow; flat pods 15-20 cm long. *Zones 9-10.*   p. 753

tomentosa (Cassia) (So. Mexico and Guatemala, W. So. America); evergreen shrub to 4 m high, with hairy branches; pinnate leaves having 6-8 pairs of oblong-ovate leaflets to 5 cm long, yellowish-tomentose beneath; golden-yellow flowers with spreading waxy petals; the fruits are flat pea-pods 12 cm long. *Zones 9-10.*   p. 754

SEQUOIA   Taxodiaceae (Coniferae)
gigantea: see SEQUOIADENDRON giganteum
sempervirens (Oregon and Calif. Coast ranges), "Redwood"; the tallest tree in the world, to 110 m, with red bark, horizontal branches spreading in flat sprays, needles deep green, bluish beneath, and persistent; the female cones 3 cm long. Their knotty burls, cut from trunks, will sprout young growth in a shallow dish of water. *Zones 7-9.*   pg. 206, 607

sempervirens 'Adpressa', "Dwarf redwood"; from the tallest of trees comes one of the finest of our dwarf conifers, with very short 6-8 mm needles, bluntly abbreviated; seen best in Spring and Summer when all growing tips are frosted creamy white, becoming more green in Autumn and Winter; to keep the plant dwarf, all new erect leader shoots having radial type appressed foliage, should be removed promptly. *Zone 7.*   p. 610

SEQUOIADENDRON   Taxodiaceae (Coniferae)
giganteum (California), the famous "Giant sequoia", "Giant redwood" or "Big tree"; at home on the high western slopes of the Sierra Nevadas at an elevation of 1,400 to 1,800 m, where venerable old trees have lived for 5000 years; diameter of trunk to 11 m, and reaching a height of 81 m; the pendulous green shoots are smooth and cord-like; closely covered with spine-like leaf bases, leaves widely awl-shaped, spirally densely arranged closely overlapping, deep green, glaucous when young; grayish hanging cones 5 to 9 cm long. The wood of the Giant sequoia is a beautiful red brown, and extremely durable, never invaded by destructive insects; the fissued bark is divided into cinnamon-brown ridges and to 50 cm thick. Young trees may be grown in pots from small seedlings; it is fairly winter-hardy. *Zone 6.*   p. 610, 611

SERENOA   Palmae
repens (So. Carolina to Florida Keys), "Saw palmetto"; scrubby, variable palm with creeping stems often underground, and forming wide-spread colonies; heads of palmate leaves 1 m across, deeply cut almost to base into 18-24 widely separated rigid, pendant segments, powdery blue-green or bright yellow-green, on thorny petioles; fragrant white flowers, and edible blackish fruit. *Subtropic.* *Zone 9.*   p. 110

SERISSA   Rubiaceae
foetida (Japan, China), "Yellow rim serissa"; dwarf shrub to 60 cm or more high, with small, opposite, elliptic 2 cm leaves dark green; funnelform little 1 cm white flowers. The more popular cultivar 'Variegata' has foliage with margins ivory-white. *Zone 8.*   p. 831

SERRURIA   Proteaceae
florida (So. Africa; Cape Mts.), "Blushing bride"; slender, evergreen shrub to 1½ m high; distinctive feathery foliage finely divided into smooth, needle-shaped segments; nodding inflorescence 5 cm across, consisting of a showy nest of papery petal-like pointed, creamy-white bracts flushed with pink, surrounding the true flowers which appear in a mass of silky pinkish hair. *Zone 9.*   p. 824

SESAMUM   Pedaliaceae
indicum (orientale) (India and elsewhere in Tropics), the "Sesame-oil bush" or "Gingelly oil-plant"; useful herb to 60 cm high, with rough, lanceolate leaves 12 cm long, two-lipped 3 cm pink or white flowers in the leaf axils; followed by 3 cm seed-capsules, with 4 grooves, the source of valuable oil, and the Sesame seed used in oriental baking and cooking for thousands of years. Usually grown as annual from seeds. *Zone 10.*   p. 542

SESBANIA   Leguminosae
grandiflora (Agati) (Trop. Asia to W. Africa), "Vegetable hummingbird" or "Red wisteria"; soft-wooded tree to 12 m; pinnate leaves to 30 cm long, leaflets in 10 to 30 pairs, to 5 cm long; remarkable sickle-shaped red to white flowers 10 cm long, hanging in two's to four's from leaf axils; followed by curling flat beans to 50 cm long. *Zone 10.*   p. 769

punicea (So. Brazil, Uruguay, Argentina, natural. from Florida to Louisiana); evergreen shrub to 1-2 m or more high, with pinnate leaves having 6-20 pairs of narrow leaflets to 3 cm long; pea-like crimson-red 2 cm flowers on short 10 cm racemes; the fruit a 4-angled pod 5-10 cm long, having leathery wings. *Zone 10.*   p. 769

tripetii (No. Argentina and Brazil), "Scarlet wisteria tree"; vigorous deciduous or partly evergreen shrub 2 to 3 m high, with pinnate, almost fern-like leaves, consisting of two ranks of narrow or oval leaflets 3 cm long; the inflorescence in pendant clusters of orange-red pea-like flowers, the standard petal scarlet with yellow spot on claw at base, wings and keel pale; blooming June to October; fruit pods are 4-angled and winged. *Zone 10.*   p. 769

SETARIA   *Gramineae*

italica (Mediterran. reg. to Asia), "Bristle grass" or "Foxtail millet"; ornamental annual 60 cm to 1 m high, branching at base, the flat leafblades to 15 cm long and 1 cm wide; inflorescence in arching cylindric spike-like panicles 10 to 30 cm long, packed with greenish-yellow to purplish bristles. Fruitheads ripen in Autumn. Also grown as a cereal grain or for forage. Sacred in China for more than 4000 years. *Zone 9.*   p. 563

SETCREASEA   *Commelinaceae*

pallida 'Purple Heart' (purpurea hort.) (Mexico); so named because of the striking purple color of this plant in strong sun, aided by a pubescence of pale hair covering the lance-shaped leaves, 6-10 cm long, on fleshy stems, first erect, later creeping; large 3-petaled orchid-colored flowers. *Subtropic. Zone 10.*   p. 308

SEVERINIA   *Rutaceae*

buxifolia (Taiwan, So. China), "Boxthorn" or "Chinese box orange"; spiny evergreen subtropic shrub to 2 m high, dense with leathery buxus-like, ovalish leaves 3-4 cm long and having parallel veins; spring-blooming with terminal clusters of small white flowers, followed by shiny black pea-sized berries containing pulp of insipid flavor. Useful for barrier hedges. *Zone 8.*   p. 862

SHEPHERDIA   *Elaeagnaceae*

argentea (Manitoba to Minnesota, Kansas to Nevada), "Buffalo berry"; very tough and hardy deciduous shrub 4 to 6 m high, with thorny branches; oblong 3 to 5 cm leaves, silvery on both sides; inconspicuous yellowish flowers, followed on female plants by clusters of small 1 cm red berries, which are acid but edible; also made into jelly. The Indians used to dry them and eat them with their buffalo meat. *Zone 2.*   p. 743

SHORTIA   *Diapensiaceae*

galacifolia (Mts. of Virginia to Georgia), "Oconeebells"; delightful rockgarden perennial to 20 cm high, with creeping roots forming mats; evergreen leathery, glossy green, rounded leaves 5-10 cm across, crenate at margins, and becoming bronzy crimson in Autumn; dainty white, funnel-shaped flowers 2½ cm across and turning pink, on red stalks, in Spring. *Zone 4.*   p. 413

soldanelloides (Temp. No. America, Japan), "Fringed galax"; evergreen alpine stemless perennial with creeping roots to 20 cm high, having rounded, cordate leathery leaves 3-5 cm wide, glossy deep green, and toothed at margins; very pretty rose-colored flowers with corolla lacily fringed, spreading 3 cm wide, in April to June. *Zone 5.*   p. 414

SIBTHORPIA   *Scrophulariaceae*

peregrina (Madeira), "Hera terrestre" or "Madeira moneywort"; evergreen hairy, carpeting trailer with slender herbaceous branches rooting at nodes; small round-toothed leaves with scalloped margins; 5 to 8-petaled 1 cm flowers from leaf axils. *Zone 10.*   p. 322

SIDALCEA   *Malvaceae*

malviflora (Oregon, California; Baja Calif.) "Checker mallow" or "Checkerbloom"; twiggy perennial with slender branches, 30-90 cm high; basal leaves roundish, to 8 cm wide, shallowly lobed, and somewhat fleshy; upper leaves more deeply divided and pinnatifid; lilac-pink flowers, also varying to purple or rose, 3-5 cm across, in loose clusters, during Summer. *Zone 8.*   p. 460

SIDERASIS   *Commelinaceae*

fuscata (Tradescantia, Pyrrheima) (Brazil), "Brown spiderwort"; clustering rosette of broad and oblong olive-green leaves to 20 cm long, with silvery center band, and covered with brown hair as is the purple reverse; large lavender-blue flowers at base. *Subtropic. Zone 11.*   p. 52

SILENE   *Caryophyllaceae*

acaulis (Arctic Eurasia, to Alps, Arctic No. America to Québec and Montana), "Cushion pink" or "Moss-campion"; moss-like little perennial forming mats; grass-like leaves 1-2 cm long, covered with small 2 cm purplish-pink flowers, from May to August; a good rockgarden plant. *Zone 5.*   p. 366

californica (So. Oregon to So. California), "California Indian pink"; loosely branching perennial 50 cm or more high, the stems slightly sticky; spring-blooming with showy crimson-red flowers 3 cm wide, the petals cleft and fringed. *Zones 8-10.*   p. 366

caroliniana (New Hampshire to Alabama, Missouri), "Wild pinks"; densely clustered, short-lived perennial, branching from base, 20 cm high; soft pubescent ovate, bluish-green leaves 12 cm long; white to

deep pink flowers with wedge-shaped petals 15 mm long, in early Summer. *Zones 5-8.*   p. 366

coeli-rosa: see LYCHNIS coeli-rosa

colorata (N.W. Africa, So. Europe, S.W. Asia), "Catchfly"; annual 10-30 cm high, with mealy-white stems, obovate to linear leaves 1-3 cm long; flowers with bi-lobed pink petals and white crown. *Arid-subtropic. Zone 8.*   p. 366

compacta (S.E. Europe to S.W. Russia), "Campion"; biennial, or short-lived gray-green perennial to 40 cm or more high; the lower leaves spoon-shaped, in a rosette; stem-leaves ovate; inflorescence in dense terminal clusters of small rose-pink flowers, in June-July. *Zone 6.*   p. 366

dioica (Lychnis, Melandrium rubrum) (Europe to Siberia, naturalized in No. America), "Morning campion"; hairy, coarse biennial or perennial herb to 80 cm high; obovate basal leaves to 20 cm long incl. winged petiole; 8 cm stem-leaves; inflorescence diurnal in loose clusters of 3 cm purplish-red flowers, opening in the morning, during Summer, and called "Daylight Pink". *Zone 5.*   p. 366

laciniata (Mts. of California to New Mexico and Mexico), "Fringed Indian pink" or "Mexican campion"; pubescent perennial to 80 cm high, with linear-lanceolate, sessile leaves to 12 cm long; few-flowered inflorescence with showy blooms having spreading crimson-red petals cleft and fringed. *Zone 8.*   p. 366

maritima (vulgaris ssp.) (Coasts of W. Europe to Murmansk), "Sea campion"; glaucous-blue, tufted perennial with woody rootstock, and ascending branches to 20 cm long, and set with ovate leaves; loose clusters of white flowers 2½ cm wide, having inflated calyx, blooming July to September. *Zone 4.*   p. 366

pendula (Mediterr. reg., So. Russia, Caucasus, Turkey), "Nodding catchfly"; attractive annual plant 10 to 25 cm high, with ovate, pubescent leaves 5 cm long; the inflorescence in loose clusters of rosy-red or white flowers having petals 1 cm long, lobed at apex. Blooming from spring-sowing in July-August, and ideal for gardens. *Zone 8.*   p. 366

SILPHIUM   *Compositae*

perfoliatum (Ontario to So. Dakota, so. to Mississippi), "Cup plant" or "Rosinweed"; coarse perennial herb containing resinous sap, 1 m or more high, with square stems; ovate foliage 15-40 cm long, the bases of upper leaves united, forming a cup around stem holding rainwater; flower head 5-8 cm across, with flaring bright yellow ray-florets around deep yellow cushion, blooming July. *Zones 4-8.*   p. 400

SILYBUM   *Compositae*

marianum (Mediterranean region), "Holy thistle"; thistle-like biennial to 1 m high, with shining dark green leaves netted with white, deeply cut, with spiny lobes; flower heads purple 4-8 cm across. Seen on Delos, Greece as Cnicus benedictus. *Subtropic. Zones 7-10.*   p. 400

marianum compactum (So. Europe, naturalized in Germany and England, also California), "St. Mary's thistle"; attractive, compact variety of "Milk-thistle", so-called because of the milky-white network of veins on the thistle-like leaves. The foliage may be boiled and eaten like spinach. *Zones 7-10.*   p. 377

SIMAROUBA amara: see QUASSIA amara

SIMMONDSIA   *Buxaceae*

chinensis (californica) (Southwest U.S., No. Mexico), the "Jojoba", "Quinine plant" or "Goat-nut"; evergreen boxwood-like shrub from arid hillsides of the Sonoran Desert, and of great economic potential; densely branching, 1 to 3 m high, with opposite dull gray-green, leathery oblong leaves 3 to 5 cm long; inconspicuous axillary flowers, the male yellowish and female pale green on separate plants; the feminine bushes bear edible nuts of hazelnut-like flavor, inside a 3-valved capsule 2 to 3 cm long. The brownish nut-like fruits contain a unique oil, actually about 50% of clear liquid wax possessing valuable chemical qualities similar to sperm whale oil for which it promises to be a desirable and superior substitute, to supply lubrication for precision instruments, also to pharmaceutical, cosmetic and food industries. Frost-sensitive in young stage. *Arid-subtropic. Zone 9.*   p. 523, 671

SINAPIS alba (Zander):   see BRASSICA hirta (Hortus)

SINARUNDINARIA   *Gramineae*
murielae: see FARGESIA murielae
nitida: refer to FARGESIA nitida (Amer. Bamboo Soc.)

SINNINGIA   *Gesneriaceae*

canescens (Rechsteineria leucotricha) (Brazil: W. Paraná); a breathtaking species which I saw when first on exhibition in São Paulo in 1954; huge 30 cm tubers sprouting happily without soil in glazed bowls, the glistening silvery foliage suggesting to me the name "Brazilian edelweiss". Found on cliffs near the waterfall 'Salto

Apucarazinho' at 1100 m, it is called locally "Rainha do Abismo". The stout, densely matted, white, later brown hairy stems to 25 cm high, carry one or two whorls of 3-4 large obovate leaves to 15 cm long, densely covered with shimmering, long silvery white hair, with margins entire or obscurely crenate; slender tubular inflated 3 cm flowers soft rosy-coral, entirely covered outside with silky white hair, the lobes sometimes marked with crimson; blooming Spring and Summer. *Subtropic. Zone 11.*   p. 67

cardinalis (Rechsteineria) (C. America), "Cardinal flower"; brilliantly flowered, tuberous plant with round cordate, emerald green, velvety leaves, topped by large curved, tubular, bilabiate flowers, white downy over brightest scarlet, throat marked purple, 5-8 cm long. *Tropical. Zone 12.*   p. 66

concinna (Brazil); miniature tuberous plant, with stems, stalks and veins red, the small hairy leaves roundish-ovate with crenate margins; 2½ cm flowers purple above, yellowish beneath, and spotted inside the inflated tube. *Tropical. Zone 12.*   p. 67

guttata (Brazil); attractive, rather succulent plant, in cultivation since 1827; with broadly ovate to lanceolate waxy leaves 10 to 18 cm long, somewhat corrugated and with crenate margins, green in center and along ribs; the raised areas overlaid with silvery gray; axillary tubular flowers 3½-4½ cm long, yellow in throat, with expanding limb creamy-white and prettily spotted with purple. *Zone 12.*   p. 66

hirsuta (Brazil); tuberous rosette of broad ovate leaves 6-10 cm long, with a network of sunken veins, covered with white hairs, the margins crenate and purplish beneath; from the center a large bouquet of smallish flowers 3 cm across, lilac-white, violet inside tube and with violet spots on expanded limb. *Humid-tropical. Zone 12.*   p. 67

macropoda (Rechsteineria) (So. Brazil), "Vermillion helmet flower"; charming tuberous herb with unbranched hairy stem 15-22 cm high, bearing opposite, rather thin, rugose, velvety bright green leaves almost round, 8-12 cm broad; small nodding flowers in clusters, the slender 2½-3 cm tubes vermillion-red with the lower lobes marked brown-red; in March-April. *Humid-tropical. Zone 12.*   p. 67

pusilla (Brazil); miniature rosette only 5 cm high, of little, oval, puckered leaves, olive-green with brown veins, hugging the ground; thin stalks are bearing attractive, slender tubular flowers with five spreading lobes, 1 cm across, orchid-colored with darker veins and lemon-yellow throat. *Humid-tropical. Zone 12.*   p. 67

regina (speciosa var.) (Brazil), "Cinderella slippers"; tuberous species related to speciosa, with ovate pointed, bronzy green, red-backed, velvety leaves beautifully patterned with ivory veins; and a profusion of nodding "slipper" type, violet flowers, 4-5 cm long, shorter and more slender than S. speciosa 'Macrophylla'. *Humid-tropical. Zone 12.*   p. 67

speciosa fyfiana, the "Gloxinia" of florists; commercial hybrid strain involving S. crassifolia hort., with erect bell-shaped, regular flowers in white, violet, rose or red, variously variegated or spotted, and with 5-12 lobes. *Humid-tropical. Zone 12.*   p. 53

speciosa fyfiana 'Chicago'; a "Double gloxinia" of the habit of the 7 to 8-petalled frilled 'Switzerland'; produced following meticulous breeding in U.S.; very exciting in having large 9 cm flowers featuring 2 or more rows of frilled petals glowing crimson with crisped white borders, blooming best from Spring to Summer. *Humid-tropical. Zone 12.*   p. 67

speciosa fyfiana 'Defiance'; large leaf "crassifolia" type, medium-large flowers completely dark cerise-red, with crimson sheen, the margins lightly wavy. *Humid-tropical. Zone 12.*   p. 54

speciosa fyfiana 'Emperor Frederick'; a leading commercial hybrid "gloxinia" bred with large upright bell-shaped flowers 8-10 cm across, velvety dark ruby red bordered white, and the typical, over-sized, robust, somewhat brittle, and horizontal leaves of the "crassifolia" class; forming large tubers. *Humid-tropical. Zone 12.*   p. 222

'Tom Thumb' (speciosa x pusilla); the most charming little Baby gloxinia that ever appeared for the pleasure of the gesneriad fancier; in every detail resembling its big brother the florists (fyfiana) gloxinia, except for its diminutive size no larger than an African violet. First of its kind to flower in 6-8 cm pots, and a perfect windowsill plant with little bell-shaped, velvety red blossom edged in white, 4 cm across. The plant is only 10 cm high, and its small ovate, crenate leaves 5 cm long, deep green above, silvery haired beneath; the bell flowers are erect and not oblique and slipper-like as in speciosa. This hybrid was developed by Fischer's in New Jersey. *Humid-tropical. Zone 12.*   p. 67

SIPHOKENTIA   *Palmae*

beguinii, (Molucca Isl.), "Tanis"; slender unarmed feather palm to 10 m high, with pinnate leaves to 1 m long, forming a prominent crownshaft; the pinnae mostly united in juvenile stage, later linear and toothed at apex; inflorescence 50 cm long, flowers cream, and red fruit. *Zone 12.*   p. 111

SISYRINCHIUM   *Iridaceae*

angustifolium (gramineum) (E. Canada to Minnesota, to Florida and Texas), "Blue-eyed grass"; attractive perennial, with basal, bluish-green linear leaves; the flat, winged floral stems 15-30 cm long, usually forking, bearing dainty 2 cm star-like, lilac-blue flowers, featuring a violet-blue ring, or eye, around the center, but lasting only a few hours. *Zone 3.*   p. 430

arizonicum (Cochise County, Arizona; New Mexico); perennial herb to 30 cm high, forming tufts of grass-like linear leaves 1 cm wide; the floral stalks with clusters of small 3 cm cream to orange flowers, blooming in August. Belonging to the "Blue-eyed grasses", but wrongly applied to this species, as the flowers have yellow centers, not blue. *Zone 7.*   p. 430

bellum (Calif.), "California blue-eyed grass"; charming perennial forming clumps, with branching, winged stems 10 to 50 cm long; grass-like linear leaves to 25 cm long; the flowers well clear of bracts, 2-3 cm across, lilac-blue marked with purple, and a blue eye encircling the yellow stamens in center. *Zone 7.*   p. 430

bermudiana (nigrum in English hort.) (Bermuda), "Blue-eyed Susan"; lovely perennial 30-50 cm high, forming tufts of grass-like, linear leaves; the stiff, flattened, winged stems bearing clusters of 6-8 lilac-blue flowers 2 cm across, yellow and blue in center; May-June blooming. *Zones 8-10.*   p. 430

bourgaeanum: see DESCURAINIA bourgaeana

californicum (brachypus) (Hydrastylus) (California, Oregon), "Golden-eyed grass"; clump-forming perennial, with linear, all basal leaves 30 cm long; the curved floral stalks 60 cm long, bearing clusters of starry flowers 3-4 cm across, light yellow with gold-yellow center, opening in succession; during Summer. *Zone 7.*   p. 430

cyaneum: see ORTHROSANTHUS multiflorus

macounii (Brit. Columbia), "Blue-eyed grass"; robust perennial, forming tufts of linear-lanceolate, all basal leaves to 30 cm long; inflorescence on stalks 30-50 cm long, often twisted, with clusters of showy 4-5 cm flowers purplish-blue, and deep violet-blue eye at base. *Zone 7.*   p. 431

macrocephalum (No. Argentina, Bolivia, E. Brazil, Uruguay), "Bolivian blue-eyed grass"; handsome, robust, clump-forming perennial to 1 m or more high, with dark green, linear leaves; starry yellow flowers 2-3 cm across, deeper orange in center, but without blue. Photographed in Kew Bot. Gardens as S. macrocarpum, blooming in May. *Zone 8.*   p. 431

striatum (Marica striata) (Chile, Argentina), "Satin flower", "Yellow-eyed grass" or "Rush-lily"; fairly hardy perennial 30-60 cm high, with short rootstock, and grass-like, 2-ranked glaucous leaves; leafy stalks bearing elongate spikes of pretty flowers 2 cm across, soft primrose-yellow veined with purplish-brown, and opening in sunshine; June-July blooming; an easy grower for a moist-cool location. *Zone 6.*   p. 431

SIUM   *Umbelliferae*

sisarum (Europe, east to Caucasus, Siberia, China, Korea, Japan), "Skirret" or "Suesswurzel" in Germany, in Italy as "Carota bianca"; aromatic perennial to 80 cm high, with clustered tuberous roots; pinnate leaves having toothed leaflets; small white flowers in flat-topped terminal clusters. Grown for the fleshy, edible tuberous roots; when boiled one of the sweetest, most pleasant of roots, much used in French cookery. The Roman Emperor Tiberius demanded these roots as a tribute from the Germans living along the Rhine. *Zone 3.*   p. 545

SKIMMIA   *Rutaceae*

japonica (Japan) "Japanese skimmia"; handsome evergreen, broad compact shrub to 1 m or more high, dioecious, with thick-leathery, elliptic, glossy green leaves 6-10 cm long, clustered at end of branchlets, and tipped by erect clusters of small, creamy-white, fragrant flowers, followed on female plants by coral-red berries, which last for months, during Winter and Spring. *Zone 7.*   p. 862

japonica 'Teufel's Dwarf'; originally from Japan, this dwarf type, also known as 'Dwarf Female', is a selected seedling resembling reevesiana but not as tall and leggy; developed by Teufel-Oregon. *Zone 8.*   p. 58, 862

reevesiana (fortunei) (India, Malaysia, China); decorative small evergreen bush to 50 cm high, with smooth leathery, ovate leaves 5-10 cm long, dark green above, lighter beneath; usually bisexual self-fertile small white flowers; and crimson-red 12 mm ovoid berries. *Zone 9.*   p. 862

SMILACINA   *Liliaceae*

racemosa (Canada: Nova Scotia to British Columbia; U.S.: Georgia to Arizona), "False Solomon's seal", rhizomatous perennial herb 60-90 cm high, with leafy stems, lanceolate leaves 8-22 cm long; numerous small white flowers in terminal panicles; followed by red berries. *Zones 3-8.*   p. 451

stellata (Newfoundland to British Columbia; New Jersey to California), "Star-flowered Lily-of-the-valley"; perennial 30-60 cm high, with lanceolate leaves 5-15 cm long and clasping the stalk, glaucous and mealy beneath; small white flowers to 6 mm long, in dense terminal racemes, followed by 1 cm fruit green with black stripes or black. *Zones 3-6*.   p. 451

SMILAX   *Liliaceae*
   glauca (Massachusetts to Florida and Texas), "Catbrier" or "Wild sarsaparilla"; widely climbing shrub deciduous or partially evergreen; stems squarish-cylindrical with scattered prickles; leaves broadly ovate about 10 cm long, glaucous beneath; inconspicuous fruit silvery blue to black. *Zone 5*.   p. 282
   laurifolia (So. N. Jersey to Florida and west to Texas), "Laurel-greenbrier" or "Bamboo-vine"; evergreen woody vine climbing high, with very prickly stems; leathery elliptic leaves 10-12 cm long, inconspicuous flowers followed by 1-seeded blue-black berries on female plants. *Zone 7*.   p. 282

SMITHIANTHA   *Gesneriaceae*
   'Orange King', "Orange temple bell"; hybrid with beautiful large velvety, emerald green leaves with crenate edge, overlaid with a pattern of red along veins; the flower bells orange-red, yellow beneath, inside yellow with red spots. *Humid-tropical*.
Zone 12.   p. 67

SOBRALIA   *Orchidaceae*
   decora (galleottiana) (Mexico, Guatemala), "Reed orchid"; vigorous terrestrial with slender, reed-like stems to 60 cm high, clothed with scattered, plaited leaves, and bearing large, cattleya-like flowers, of short duration, sepals and petals creamy-white with light rose blush, lip purplish-rose, (April-July). *Tropical*.
Zones 11-12.   p. 96
   macrantha (Mexico to Costa Rica), "Zapatitos"; reed-like terrestrial with stems 1½-2 m high, furnished with plaited, slender pointed leaves and large fragrant 15 cm flowers rich purple and crimson, the broad lip with cream or yellow throat (Summer). *Tropical*. *Zones 11-12*.   p. 96

SOEHRENSIA oreopepon (Zander):
   see LOBIVIA oreopepon (Hortus)

SOLANDRA   *Solanaceae*
   grandiflora (Jamaica, Puerto Rico, Lesser Antilles), "Golden Chalice"; bold woody vine, to 10 m or more; leathery obovate leaves to 20 cm long; large funnel flowers with lobes reflexed, 10-15 cm long, white turning yellow to brownish the second day. *Zone 10*.   p. 297
   longiflora (Cuba, Hispaniola, Jamaica), "Copa de Oro", or "Trumpet plant"; evergreen shrub clambering to 2 m high, woody branches with small hard, oval or obovate leaves on purple petioles, and large, showy, stiff upright, trumpet-like flowers 22-30 cm long, greenish-white, showing purplish-brown venation, contracted at the throat, the limb turned back and frilled. *Tropical*. *Zone 10*.   p. 297
   maxima (nitida, guttata) (Mexico), "Chalice vine" or "Cup-of-gold"; clambering to 6 m or more, with leathery, elliptic, glossy leaves; the large 25 cm long, chalice-shaped flowers with corolla-lobes reflexed and frilled, yellow with purplish stripes. *Tropical*.
Zone 10.   p. 297
   maxima cv. **'Warrimoo'** (New So. Wales); spectacular Bewley cv. from seed; young growth with leaves variegated green with cream, tinted pink and rose; very colorful as a clipped shrub.
Zones 10-11.   p. 297

SOLANOPTERIS   *Polypodiaceae (Filices)*
   bifrons, (Polypodium) (Perú and Ecuador); a very unusual creeping fern with wiry slender rhizomes carrying small oblanceolate deeply lobed, both sterile and fertile fronds but besides, forming curious chestnut-like vessels hollow inside, pocket-like, similar to Dischidia, separate from its leaves. Rare and difficult in cultivation, best trained to a piece of tree fern trunk and hung from a greenhouse rafter; needs warmth and humidity and should be dunked in water daily. *Humid-tropical. Zones 11-12*.   p. 141

SOLANUM   *Solanaceae*
   atropurpureum (Brazil, Uruguay, Paraguay, No. Argentina, Colombia); ornamental erect subshrub 2 m or more high; the branches blood-red with unequal prickles; leaves 15-20 cm long and 5 to 7-lobed, with strong 2 cm prickles; flowers in lateral clusters, having purple corolla on yellow base and 5-lobed; fleshy fruit at first white and ripening to yellow. *Zone 10*.   p. 880
   aviculare (New Zealand, Australia), "Kangaroo-apple"; shrub 1½ to 3 m high, with variable dark green membranous leaves lanceolate or pinnately lobed, 15-30 cm or more long; few violet flowers 2-3 cm across; the rather large 2½ cm ovoid edible berry green or yellow. *Subtropic. Zone 9*.   p. 880

dulcamara (Europe, No. Africa, W. Asia; natural. in No. America), "Deadly nightshade" or "Bittersweet" in Europe; twining perennial with stems 1 to 4 m long, having woody base; ovate or cordate leaves, sometimes lobed, to 10 cm long; small 1 cm violet or whitish flowers spotted green in pendent clusters along branches; followed by the glossy 1 cm scarlet, very poisonous fruit. All parts of the plant are poisonous if eaten raw. Bark of roots and twigs are used medicinally for relief of skin irritation. *Zone 4*.   p. 543
   incanum (coagulans) (Arta Mts. Somalia); stout gray densely pubescent spiny subshrub, with broad oval sinuate lobed leaves; large pale purple flowers, followed by fruit as large as a plum. Photographed on the border of Ethiopia. *Zone 9*.   p. 880
   integrifolium (Tropics: Africa), "Tomato-fruited eggplant" or "Ethiopian eggplant"; spiny annual bush with blackish stems to 1 m high; ovate pubescent leaves sharply lobed; small white flowers; hard, ornamental tomato-like fruit glossy orange to scarlet-red deeply ridged to 6 cm dia., used in California in floral arrangements.
Zone 10.   p. 204
   jasminoides (Brazil), "Jasmine nightshade"; shrubby deciduous twiner with twiggy stems, ovate leaves to 8 cm long, sometimes 2 to 5 parted; star-shaped flowers white tinged blue, 2 cm across, in branching clusters. *Zones 9 -10*.   p. 297
   jasminoides 'Grandiflorum' (Brazil); vigorous smooth-stemmed scandent shrub with branches climbing to 5 m or more, with white flowers tinged blue, larger than the species, and with broader petals.
Zone 10.   p. 297
   macranthum (Brazil), "Brazilian potato-tree"; spiny pubescent shrub or tree to 10 m high, with ovate leaves 30 cm long, sinuately lobed, prickly on veins; flowers cornflower-blue, 3-6 cm across, in racemes paling with age. *Tropical. Zone 10*.   p. 880
   mammosum (C. America), "Nipple-fruit"; a thorny, sparry shrub with few pubescent leaves, and weirdly formed, orange-colored, waxy fruit, large like a tomato, but shaped somewhat like an inverted pear with nipples near base. *Tropical. Zone 11*.   p. 204, 881
   marginatum (North Africa: Ethiopia); spiny white-hairy shrub to 1 m high, with broad ovate, sinuately lobed leaves prickly on both sides, having white margins, and densely white tomentose beneath, to 20 cm long; flowers white lined with blue, 2½ cm across; spiny, yellow fruit. *Subtropic. Zone 9*.   p. 514, 880
   martii (Brazil: Panaceix); handsome small tree with woody trunk, and large, leathery leaves 30 cm long, glossy green with beige colored ribs; between the foliage the white star-flowers hidden in woolly cushions from the axil of the leaf. Photographed at Jardim Botanico, Rio de Janeiro. *Tropical. Zone 10*.   p. 882
   melongena esculentum (India), "Egg plant", "Jew's apple", or "Aubergine"; pubescent prickly herb or shrub, to 1 m high; ovate, angled or lobed leaves 10-20 cm long, woolly beneath; the purplish flowers 3 cm across. The common egg-plant is a warm-weather plant, and popular vegetable usually grown as an annual with edible, shining fruit 15-30 cm long, purple, white, yellowish or striped. It is usually eaten baked or fried, having low calorie, succulent flesh. *Tropical. Zone 10*.   p. 940
   melongena ovigerum (India), "Egg-tree"; pubescent prickly herb to 1 m high, or woody shrub becoming tree-like to 2 m; ovate, angled or lobed leaves 8 to 22 cm long, with starry wool beneath; the purple flowers 2 cm across; white, egg-shaped fruit, 6 cm long, resembling a large hen's egg, turning golden when ripe; edible. *Subtropic.*
Zones 10-11.   p. 206, 881
   muricatum (Perú, Chile), "Pepino dulce" or "Melon pear"; subtropic evergreen subshrub with woody base to about 1 m high, with ovate to long lanceolate, corrugated leaves of thin texture 10-15 cm long; flowers blue to purple, occasionally white with purple dots, with corolla 4 cm across and deeply 5-lobed in long-stalked clusters; the economically important edible fruit pendant, ovoid 10-15 cm long, cream with purple base and splashes, the juicy flesh yellow and aromatic but acrid to sweet when ripe, tasting like an acid cantaloupe. *Zones 9-10*.   p. 881, 910
   pseudo-capsicum (Madeira), "Jerusalem cherry"; robust, shrubby plant with flexible branches dense with lanceolate, turgid-firm, deep green leaves wavy at the margins and smooth beneath, 5-6 cm long, glabrous-smooth, though with velvety feel above; branches smooth or with slight fuzz; small, white, star-like flowers followed by large globular, lustrous orange-scarlet, cherry-like fruit of 1½-2 cm dia.; much grown as an ornamental potplant for Christmas; there is also a yellow fruited strain. *Subtropic. Zone 9*.   p. 57, 881
   quitoense (Ecuador, Colombia, Perú), "Naranjilla" or "Furry fruit"; woody bush with brittle branches to 2 m high; large pubescent ovate leaves prettily lobed and with spiny ribs on reverse, 30-40 cm long, softly woolly; 2-3 cm flowers violet and woolly on outside, white inside; fruit globose, covered with green fur, about 4-5 cm dia., golden-yellow when ripe and fragrant; the juicy pulp contains numerous

seeds; the sweet, slightly tart, green colored juice has a distinct aroma and is used for fruit drinks and flavoring; short-lived about 3 years. *Zones 10-11*.   *p. 880, 940*

rantonnetii (Paraguay, Argentina), "Blue potato tree"; rambling evergreen or deciduous shrub to 2 m high, unarmed and nearly smooth; ovate or oval, bright green undulate leaves to 10 cm long; charming 3 cm flowers dark blue or violet with yellow eye, in clusters blooming throughout the warm Summer and Fall, sometimes nearly all year; the red fruit like small apples. Blooms as small plant but may be grown into treeform by staking, or trained on support as a vine. *Subtropic. Zones 9-10*.   *p. 881*

seaforthianum (So. America), "Star potato vine"; shrubby climber to 3 m with mostly pinnate leaves to 20 cm long; the leaflets unequal; large star-shaped lavender or purple 2½ cm flowers with yellow anthers; scarlet fruit. *Zone 10*.   *p. 297*

sisymbriifolium (Brazil); sticky-hairy, very prickly annual or perennial to 1 m high, with light green leaves deeply and distantly pinnately lobed, and furnished with yellow spines, 3 cm flowers light blue to white; and red fruit. *Zone 9*.   *p. 514*

sodomeum (Mediterranean region), the "Dead-Sea apple", or "Apple of Sodom"; spiny pubescent shrub to 2 m high, with sinuately lobed leaves; flowers violet, 2½ cm across; the berries first white, then green-marbled, to yellow and shining red-brown 2½ cm dia., more or less poisonous. *Zone 9*.   *p. 882*

tuberosum (Peruvian Andes), "White potato"; succulent non-woody annual developing underground edible tubers; pinnately compound foliage to 25 cm long; 2 cm white or bluish flowers in clusters. Large starchy tubers are produced on fleshy roots, and have been cultivated by the Incas of Perú since ancient times. Since introduced to Europe in the 17th Century, potatoes have developed into many improved strains, grown by agriculture in temperate climates as a major source of food, becoming the world's leading vegetable crop. Only moderately tolerant to frost. *Zone 9*.   *p. 262, 940*

uporo (antrhopophagorum) (So. China); an ornamental type of tomato, seen in Kwangtung Prov., China; woody shrub with ovate, hairy leaves and bearing showy globular, soft-fleshy fruit 6 cm dia., ridged at base and colored brilliant scarlet. *Subtropic. Zones 9-10*.   *p. 881*

wendlandii (Costa Rica), "Potato-vine" or "Climbing potato"; shrubby climber, to 6 m, with a few scattered, hooked prickles; variable leaves bright green, the upper ovate or tri-lobed, the lower pinnate or lobed; large lilac-blue flowers 6 cm across, in branched clusters. *Tropical. Zone 10*.   *p. 297, 880*

SOLDANELLA   *Primulaceae*

alpina (Pyrenees, Alps), "Glacier Alpenclock"; dainty, very attractive dwarf alpine perennial to 15 cm high, spreading by rhizomes; leaves basal, rounded kidney-shaped 4 cm wide; reddish floral stalks topped by clusters of pendulous, bell-shaped flowers, 2 cm long, bluish-white with crimson lines inside, the petals sliced and fringed; blooming from April on. *Zone 4*.   *p. 483*

SOLEIROLIA   *Urticaceae*

soleirolii (Helxine) (Corsica, Sardinia), popularly known as "Baby's tears", also as "Mind-your-own-business", "Irish moss", "Corsican curse" and "Japanese moss"; low moss-like creeping herb hugging the ground and forming dense mats or cushions as ground-cover or over pots in subtropical plantings; tiny roundish lush green leaves 6 mm or less across on threadlike intertwining branches, with minute greenish flowers in leaf-axils. *Subtropic. Zone 10*.   *p. 321*

SOLENANGIS   *Orchidaceae*

aphylla (Angraecum) (Mozambique, Madagascar, Kenya, Tanzania); climbing orchid with thin woody stem and long aerial roots; raceme of white, bell-shaped, spurred flowers 3-4 mm dia., brown dots at tips of sepals. *Zone 12*.   *p. 97*

SOLIDAGO   *Compositae*

altissima (Québec to Florida, west to Dakota and Arizona), "Goldenrod"; robust rhizomatous perennial to 2 m high, the gray stems with short hairs; very leafy narrow-lanceolate foliage 15 cm long, pubescent beneath, 3-nerved and rough above; small yellow flower heads in one-sided spreading plumes. *Zones 3-7*.   *p. 401*

canadensis (Newfoundland to Manitoba, Virginia to Colorado), "Canada goldenrod"; very popular, showy rhizomatous perennial of the fields, 1 to 2 m high, with rough-hairy stems; the leaves very narrowly elliptic, 8-15 cm long, and pubescent beneath; small floral heads on one-sided spreading branchlets, forming a broad pyramidal cluster, blooming August to October. *Zones 2-7*.   *p. 401*

nemoralis (Canada to Arizona), "Dyersweed goldenrod"; clump-forming perennial to 1 m high; densely pubescent, narrow ovate, toothed leaves; small yellow flowers in one-sided recurved branches. *Temperate. Zone 3*.   *p. 401*

serotina (gigantea) (Brit. Columbia to Québec, Oregon, Texas to Georgia); perennial to 2 m high, nearly glabrous; leaves oblong lanceolate to 15 cm long, toothed at margins; terminal inflorescence in branched elongate racemes of small rich yellow flowers; blooming July to September. *Zones 2-8*.   *p. 401*

spathulata (Coastal No. California to Oregon and Alaska); stout perennial 20 to 60 cm high, from woolly rhizome, strongly aromatic, basal leaves oblanceolate, to 15 cm long, incl. petiole, crenate at margins; stem-leaves smaller upward, the little yellow flower heads, having only 7-9 short rays, are arranged along the upper branches as an erect spire. *Zones 2-7*.   *p. 401*

virgaurea minuta (minutissima hort) (So. Japan: Kyushu), "Miniature goldenrod"; dwarf perennial 10 to 25 cm high, close-growing and forming mats; the branches with small pinnately veined, ovate leaves; the small yellow flowers 2 cm across, in dense terminal clusters. A mountain variety ideal for rockgardens, blooming July to October. The species virgaurea is from Asia, Europe and No. Africa. *Zone 7*.   *p. 401*

x SOLIDASTER   *Compositae*

luteus (hybridus) (Solidago x Aster) (France 1910), "Hybrid golden rod"; herbaceous perennial producing many erect branches 60-80 cm high, with lanceolate leaves to 15 cm long; terminal clusters of small 2 cm daisy-like flowers with deep yellow disc, and ray-florets yellow changing to cream, in Mid-summer. Very useful as fill-in cut flower. *Zone 3*.   *p. 401*

SOLLYA   *Pittosporaceae*

heterophylla (Western Australia), "Bluebell creeper"; beautiful evergreen climbing shrub strongly twining to 2 m or more; valued for the small brilliant blue 2 cm flowers; leathery lanceolate leaves variably to 5 cm long; excellent cover on low fences or banks. *Zone 10*.   *p. 318*

SOPHORA   *Leguminosae*

arizonica (Coconimo area, Arizona), "Arizona mountain laurel"; evergreen shrub 2-3 m high, with pinnate foliage of many gray-green leaflets; inflorescence with 2-3 cm lavender pea-like flowers in terminal clusters; inhabiting arid regions, and of slow growth. *Zone 9*.   *p. 769*

japonica (China and Korea), "Japanese pagoda tree" or "Chinese scholar tree"; deciduous tree to 25 m high, with corrugated bark; odd-pinnate leaves 15-25 cm long, having 9-17 ovate 3-5 cm leaflets; pea-like 2 cm flowers creamy-white, in loose panicles to 35 cm long; blooming late August-September; the bean-like pods 5-9 cm long. Wood, bark and fruit yield yellow dye. *Zone 5*.   *p. 770*

japonica 'Tortuosa'; picturesque form of the Pagoda tree, of more compact habit and slow growth, dense with handsome shiny pinnate leaves on branches contorted and twisted on trunk green in Winter; ideal for limited space. *Zone 5*.   *p. 770*

microphylla (tetraptera microphylla) (New Zealand), the "Maori Kowhai"; large shrub with pinnate leaves very similar to tetraphylla, but in the main, its leaflets are only 1 cm long; the sulphur yellow flowers 4 cm long, with a calyx of old gold; freely secreting nectar; however, it is also different in going through two distinct stages in its development, at first being a flexuose shrub with yellow, interlacing stems; when 2½-4 m high, a mature form with round leafy head with trunk and straight brown branches. *Zone 9*.   *p. 770*

secundiflora (Texas to Mexico), "Mescal-bean"; evergreen tree of chaparral deserts, to 10 m high; pinnate leaves 15 cm long, leaflets notched at apex; flowers 2½ cm long, violet-blue and violet-scented. The ornamental seed pods are 5 to 20 cm long, but seeds and foliage are said to be poisonous. *Zone 8*.   *p. 770*

SOPHRONITIS   *Orchidaceae*

cernua (Brazil); miniature epiphyte or rockdweller, with tightly clustered pseudobulbs and forming mats; solitary grayish leaf 3 cm long; relatively large 3 cm flowers opening flat, vivid cinnabar-red or burnt-orange, with base of lip yellow, (Autumn). *Tropical. Zones 11-12*.   *p. 96*

coccinea (grandiflora) (So. Brazil); dwarf epiphyte with small pseudobulb and a stiff, 8 cm leaf; large solitary flowers to 8 cm across, showy scarlet with salmon sheen, the throat yellow with red stripes. I will never forget these brilliant spots of red in the chilly rain-forest of the Serra do Mar, (Sept.-Feb.). *Subtropic. Zone 11*.   *p. 96*

coccinea rosea (Brazil); a lovely small epiphyte in the col. of Alvim Seidel, Corupa, Santa Catarina; pseudobulbs smaller and leaves rounder than S. coccinea; flowers not as large and more round, and of a delicate rose-pink, the lip with purple. *Zones 11-12*.   *p. 96*

SORBARIA   *Rosaceae*

aitchisonii (Afghanistan, Kashmir), "False spiraea"; deciduous flowering shrub to 3 m; tall stems with few branches and bright red branchlets; large pinnate leaves of bright green, toothed leaflets to 8 cm long; small white flowers in feathery clusters 25 cm long. *Zone 6*.   *p. 850*

arborea (Central and Western China), "False spiraea"; deciduous shrub to 6 m high, the shoots and leaves finely downy, the pinnate leaves 20-40 cm long, having 13-19 lanceolate leaflets, their veins parallel and deeply impressed; flowers white, in loose pyramidal pendant clusters 30 cm long. *Zone 5.* p. 850

SORBUS *Rosaceae*

alnifolia (Japan, Korea, Manchuria), "Korean mountain ash"; deciduous tree to 18 m high, forming dense rounded crown; the young branchlets red-brown and early pubescent; broad-ovate, simple leaves 5-10 cm long, and having 6-10 pairs of veins; small white flowers in clusters, in May, followed by pea-size yellow and red oval fruit. Very attractive with foliage in orange and red autumn color. *Zone 5.* p. 851

americana (North America), "Missey-moosey" or "American mountain ash"; smooth deciduous shrub or tree to 10 m high, with pinnate leaves to 25 cm long, 13-15 narrow leaflets, with sharp marginal teeth, grayish beneath; small white flowers in terminal clusters, followed by bright red 1 cm berries, loved by birds; edible when thoroughly ripe and mellowed by frost. *Zone 2.* p. 850

aria (Europe, Asia Minor, Caucasus), "White beam" or "Chess apple"; deciduous tree to 15 m high, with twigs tomentose when young; the leaves simple, elliptic or broad-ovate 8 cm long, glossy green above, and 10 or more pairs of sunken lateral veins; white-downy beneath; margins crenate; small white flowers in clusters 10 cm wide, during May; scarlet berries, speckled with brown, in Autumn, but quickly eaten by birds. *Zone 5.* p. 851

aucuparia (Europe, Asia Minor), "European mountain ash"; deciduous tree to 20 m, with narrow crown; gray-brown twigs, pinnate leaves 10-25 cm long, glaucous beneath; small white flowers in dense flat clusters, followed by orange-red 1 cm berries liked by birds; also used to make brandy. *Temperate. Zone 3.* p. 541, 851

intermedia (No. Europe), "Swedish white-beam"; deciduous tree to 10 m; deeply lobed and toothed leaves 10 cm long, gray-hairy underneath; spring-flowering, small white flowers in large clusters 10 cm across, followed by bright red berries. *Zone 6.* p. 851

mougeotii (W. Alps, Pyrenees, Switzerland), "Alpine mountain ash"; deciduous tree or shrub 8 to 30 m high; elliptic simple leaves 10 cm long pinnately lobed with 8-12 pairs of veins, the veins following along lightly lobed margins of leaves, gray-downy beneath; small white flowers having 5 petals, strongly scented, in terminal elongate clusters; the red berries are edible after mellowed by frost; or dried and ground into flour. *Zone 6.* p. 850

sambucifolia (No. Japan, Kuriles, Sachalin), "Elder mountain ash"; deciduous shrub to 2 m or more high, with young shoots pubescent; leaves odd-pinnate, having 9-11 lanceolate leaflets 3-8 cm long, unequal at base, shining green above, light green beneath; inflorescence brown pubescent, of 1 cm white flowers in small clusters, in June; subglobose fruit 1 cm dia., red lightly glaucous, in November. *Zone 2.* p. 850

SORGHUM *Gramineae*

dochna (Holcus) (cult. in Tropics and Subtropics), "Sugar moor-millet" or "Sorghum"; a strong growing grass to 1 m or more high, probably of African descent; long, arching lanceolate leaves, from pithy central stalk and covered with white waxy bloom, topped by club-shaped seedhead, containing grains rich in protein and low in fat; otherwise similar to maize, ground into a meal for porridge and bread. The pith of the stalk contains sweet juice and is used for molasses and syrup. Sorghum is the leading cereal grain in Africa and other warm regions from India, No. China, Iran and So. Europe; the grain is also used for alcoholic beverages. It is grown in America for forage, for livestock and poultry, and distributed in hundreds of varieties with related species. *Zones 7-10.* p. 568

SPACHEA *Malpighiaceae*

elegans (perforata) (Guayana), "Soufriere tree"; interesting small tropical evergreen tree, with narrow lanceolate, leathery leaves glossy green, about 10 cm long, and gracefully pendulous, cylindric racemes 12-15 cm long, dense with small whitish flowers. This species, according to Iris Bannochie of Barbados, was originally collected along the Essequibo in former Brit. Guyana and planted on Mt. Soufriere in St. Vincent where all but one were destroyed during the earthquake and volcanic eruption in 1902. This survivor is now growing in St. Vincent Botanical Gardens but being hermaphrodite had never produced seeds. *Zone 10.* p. 780

SPARAXIS *Iridaceae*

tricolor 'Firebrand' (So. Africa), "Scarlet wandflower" or "Velvet-flower"; dainty cormous plant with linear leaves to 30 cm long; spectacular, large brilliant scarlet flowers 5 cm across, with yellow ring surrounding purple center. *Subtropic. Zone 9.* p. 230

tricolor 'Harlequin', "Harlequin flower"; striking cultivar of this small So. African cormous perennial, with two-ranked basal, narrowly sword-shaped, mid-green leaves; slender, wiry stalks carry several

showy, flat open flowers 4 cm across, the segments vivid orange deepening to crimson and to nearly black, at base a contrasting golden-yellow. A popular cut flower in Madeira during Spring. Other cultivars grown in colors white to yellow and purple. *Subtropic. Zone 9.* p. 230

SPARMANNIA *Tiliaceae*

africana (So. Africa), "African hemp"; much cultivated in German homes, and known there as "Zimmer-Linde", as it resembles a miniature linden tree, with large lobed, light green, soft leaves, 15-25 cm long, white hairy on both sides and on the sparry stems; flowers with white petals and yellow filaments; rapidly growing into a shrub with many trunks, to 6 m high. *Subtropic. Zones 9-10.* p. 79, 893

africana 'Variegata', "Variegated African hemp"; very attractive mutation of this decorative plant so popular as a house plant or tubbed specimen on balconies and patio in Europe; the large light green, soft pubescent leaves irregularly splashed and variegated with creamy-white. *Zone 10.* p. 893

SPARTINA *Gramineae*

pectinata 'Aureo-marginata' (species from New England to Texas), "Prairie cord grass"; showy marshgrass, in variegated form; deciduous perennial to 1½ m or more high, usually less in gardens; narrow arching flat leaves, light green with broad yellow bands along rough margins; rigid or wiry culms, bearing slender inflorescence of one-sided spikelets with bristly flowers. Foliage turns a showy bright yellow in Autumn. *Zone 5.* p. 562

SPARTIUM *Leguminosae*

junceum (Genista) (Mediterranean, Canary Isl.), "Spanish broom"; ornamental shrub, to 3 m, with almost leafless, reed-like branches, the small leaves linear; fragrant, showy yellow, butterfly-like flowers 2 cm long, in loose, terminal racemes. *Zone 7.* p. 769

SPATHICARPA *Araceae*

sagittifolia var. gardneri, "Fruit-sheath plant"; interesting and attractive herb with tuberous rhizome having small, arrow-shaped, membranous leaves, 10-12 cm long, waxy green with contrasting feathered cream band along midrib; inflorescence on stiff stalks with recurved green spathe, and spadix attached along its center. The species sagittifolia is from Bahia, having foliage entirely green. *Zone 12.* p. 34

SPATHIPHYLLUM *Araceae*

blandum (gardneri) (W. Indies, Jamaica, Surinam); robust plant with large, lanceolate, leathery, deep green leaves and sunken veins; spathe spoon-shaped and pointed, pale green; spadix white with elevated knobs. *Tropical. Zone 11.* p. 32

'Clevelandii' (kochii), "White flag", also known as "Peace-lily"; freely branching and free flowering commercial plant close to wallisii but larger in all parts; thin-leathery, glossy green, lanceolate leaves with undulate margin; the inflorescence on reed-like stems with ovate-pointed, white, papery spathe 10-15 cm long, turning apple green with age, and having a green line on back; maze-like spadix white. *Tropical. Zone 10.* p. 32

floribundum (multiflorum) (Colombia), "Snow-flower"; dwarf, compact plant, freely suckering and forming clusters; the matte, satiny green, leathery leaves obovate or elliptic, with pale center band, on broadly winged petioles; small spathe white; short spadix green and white. *Tropical. Zone 10.* p. 32

floribundum 'Mini variegata'; pretty Florida cultivar of dwarf, compact habit, dense with recurving elliptic, leathery leaves 6-8 cm long, green with contrasting ivory center band; inflorescence with narrow white spathe. *Zone 12.* p. 32

'Londonii' (wallisii x 'Mauna Loa'); excellent Florida decorative hybrid of robust habit, 60 cm high; the glossy green leaves featuring undulate margins; the showy inflorescence carried well above foliage, with beautiful white, cupped spathe 15 cm long. *Zone 11.* p. 32

'Mauna Loa'; a diploid hybrid developed by Griffith-Los Angeles, and so far as I could determine in discussing its origin with him, a seedling of S. floribunda x a Hawaiian hybrid, probably S. 'McCoy'; robust plant of compact habit, tending to divide from the base; leaves dark glossy green; very floriferous over an extended period, with pure white spathes 10-12 cm and even 20 cm long in older plants in large pots, somewhat cupping and of soft-leathery texture, slightly scented. We have found the strain variable, leaning toward 'Clevelandii'. *Tropical. Zone 11.* p. 32

patinii (Colombia); graceful plant with papery, narrow oblanceolate, waxy leaves having depressed veins on thin, vaginate petioles; inflorescence on long, thin stems with a pendant, slender, white spathe tipped green; thin spadix green and white. *Tropical. Zone 11.* p. 32

wallisii (Colombia, Venezuela); vigorous plant with glossy green, thin-leathery, oblong-lanceolate leaves; inflorescence on reed-like stems, the ovate spathe white turning green with age, 8-10 cm long; maze-like white spadix; very close to 'Clevelandii' (kochii) but smaller in all parts. *Tropical. Zone 11.*   *p. 32*

SPATHODEA   Bignoniaceae
campanulata (nilotica) (Trop. Africa: West Kenya, Uganda), "African tuliptree", or "Flame of the forest"; spectacularly showy evergreen tree to 20 m high, with odd-pinnate foliage, the leaflets 6-12 cm long; large bell-shaped flowers 8-12 cm long, swollen on one side and 5-lobed, crimson-red with yellow frilled edge, carried facing upwards in terminal clusters. *Tropical. Zone 10.*   *p. 665*

SPATHOGLOTTIS   Orchidaceae
plicata (Malaysia); terrestrial with small corm-like pseudobulbs and grass green plaited leaves, to 1 m tall; erect racemes with 2½-5 cm flowers of rosy-purple, (April-June). *Tropical. Zones 11-12.*   *p. 96*

SPEIRANTHA   Liliaceae
gardenii (convallarioides) (China); robust perennial related to Convallaria, with thick, stoloniferous rhizome; evergreen oblanceolate, rich green leaves to 15 cm long, in basal rosettes; numerous small white, starry flowers in clusters on slender 10 cm stalk, in June. *Zone 7.*   *p. 451*

SPHAERALCEA   Malvaceae
coccinea (Manitoba so. to Texas and Arizona), "Prairie mallow"; attractive perennial of the Rocky Mountain region, to 30 cm high, with thin reclining branches to 60 cm long, small silvery pubescent, deeply cleft leaves to 6 cm long; lovely cupped, brick-red flowers 3-4 cm across, in terminal clusters, during Summer and Autumn; spreading by shoots from the underground woody roots. *Zone 5.*   *p. 460*

SPHAEOPTERIS   Cyatheaceae (Filices)
cooperi (Alsophila australis or Cyathea cooperi) (Tasmania, Australia), "Australian treefern"; a noble treefern, with heavy trunk to 6 m high, with well proportioned, spreading crown even when small, but requiring lots of water; the arching fronds finely divided, metallic green, on rough stalks covered with small pale brown hair-like scales. *Humid-subtropic. Zone 11.*   *p. 126*
medullaris (Cyathea in hort.) (New Zealand, S.E. Australia), the "Black tree-fern" or "Mamaku"; tallest of N.Z. tree ferns to 20 m or more, slender black trunk, at base covered with matted aerial roots, on top a great crown of spreading, curving, feathery fronds 2-6 m long, firm, tripinnate, deep green above, paler beneath; the apex and leaf bases clothed with black scales. *Humid-subtropic.*
Zones 10-11.   *p. 127*

SPIGELIA   Loganiaceae
marilandica (So. Carolina to Texas), "Indian pink" or "Pink root"; attractive perennial with erect stems, 30-60 cm high, having thin-textured ovate-lanceolate leaves to 10 cm long; flowers in one-sided terminal cluster, with trumpet-shaped corollas 5 cm long, glowing red outside, and yellow inside the flaring lobes; July-blooming. *Zone 8.*   *p. 456*

SPILOXENE capensis: see HYPOXIS stella hort.

SPIRAEA   Rosaceae
x arguta (thunbergii x multiflora), "Garland spiraea" or "Foam of May"; most free-blooming of the early spireas, flowering April to Mid-May; white blossoms in small flattened clusters garland-like along arching branches, from a rounded shrub to 2 m high; the leaves obovate 2-3 cm long. *Zone 4.*   *p. 852*
x billiardii (douglasii x salicifolia); deciduous shrub to 2 m high, with broadly ovate leaves 5-8 cm long, gray-tomentose beneath; small purplish-rose flowers, in slender spike-like panicles 10-20 cm long, blooming during Summer. Handsome hybrid originated in France about 1850. *Zone 5.*   *p. 853*
x brachybotrys (canescens x douglasii); one of the best of the taller summer-blooming spireas; vigorous shrub to 2½ m high; ovate leaves 2-3 cm long, sparsely toothed and gray-felted beneath; small bright pink flowers in clusters to 8 cm long and wide, blooming in late June in the area of Boston. *Zone 4.*   *p. 851*
bullata (japonica 'Bullata') (cult. in Japan), "Japanese dwarf spirea"; rusty-hairy shrub to 40 cm high, forming thickets; roundish-ovate leaves to 3 cm long, puckered on surface and toothed and crisped at margins; small deep rose flowers in clusters to 8 cm across, showing pinkish stamens, profusely blooming in July. *Zone 5.* *p. 852*
x bumalda 'Antony Waterer' (japonica x albiflora), "Dwarf rose bridal wreath"; superior deciduous shrub to 80 cm high with showy flat heads 15 cm across of bright carmine-rose flowers in Summer; ovate 4-8 cm leaves occasionally variegated cream and pink. *Zone 5.*   *p. 852*
x bumalda 'Lime Mound' (albiflora x japonica); colorful bush forming dense mounds of slender branches, displaying an array of lemon-yellow ovate, toothed leaves, tinged with bronze when emerg-

ing in Spring; the foliage blending into lime-green when mature, contrasting with clusters of rose-pink flowers in Summer; in Autumn foliage becomes orange-scarlet, on red stems. *Zone 3.*   *p. 851*
x concinna (fastigiata x albiflora); compact shrub 1 m or more high, with pubescent branchlets having ovate, serrate leaves pale green beneath; small pinkish-white flowers in broad leafy clusters. *Zone 5.*   *p. 852*
japonica 'Alpina' ('Nana') (Temp. E. Asia, Japan to Himalaya), "Daphne spiraea" or "Japanese Alpine spiraea"; excellent dwarf to 30 cm high of mound-forming habit; leaves ovate, rich green, 2-4 cm long, smaller than the species; and compound clusters of rose-pink flowers in Summer. *Zone 5.*   *p. 851*
latifolia (E. Canada to Ontario and Michigan, so. to No. Carolina), "Meadowsweet"; vigorous shrub 1-2 m high, with reddish, angled branches, the ovate leaves to 8 cm long and coarsely toothed; flowers white or tinted blue, compound in broadly pyramidal panicles, blooming June to August. Differs from salicifolia in having flowers white, and its smooth character. *Zone 6.*   *p. 853*
media (Austria, Czechoslovakia, Carpathians, Ukraine, Siberia); stiff erect deciduous shrub with orbicular brownish branches, 1-2 m high; leaves ovate 3-5 cm long, toothed toward apex; white flowers in April-May, in numerous dense lateral leafy clusters along branches, forming a near pyramid of snowy bloom. *Zone 5.*   *p. 853*
menziesii (Alaska to Oregon, Idaho), "American spirea"; handsome suckering shrub 1 to 1½ m high, with brown stems, bearing lanceolate leaves 3-8 cm long, serrate above the middle; showy inflorescence of purplish-rose flowers in dense cylindric terminal apparent spikes. *Zone 6.*   *p. 853*
nipponica 'Snow Mound' (tosaensis) (Mts. of Japan), "Tosa spiraea"; deciduous shrub to 1 m or more high, with bluish-green or dark green leaves, almost completely covered in late May with compound clusters of tiny white flowers. *Zone 4.*   *p. 852*
prunifolia (syn. prunifolia plena) (China), "Shoe-button spirea"; beautiful erect shrub to 2 m high, with slender arching branches; the leaves oval-ovate 2-4 cm long, finely toothed and soft-pubescent beneath; white double flowers built up of numerous petals, each individual bloom solitary on a thin stalk 2 cm long, up along the twigs, 30-60 cm long, in May. *Zone 5.*   *p. 852*
x revirescens (amoena x japonica); handsome bushy shrub 1 m or more high; young growth angled and downy; ovate-oblong leaves 5-10 cm long and coarsely toothed, glaucous with brown veins beneath; small rosy flowers in dense flat, downy clusters to 12 cm wide, first blooming in June-July, and again in September if the spent inflorescence is removed. *Zone 5.*   *p. 852*
salicifolia (C. and E. Europe, Siberia to E. Asia), "Willow-leaf spirea", "Queen-of-the-meadow" or "Bridewort"; deciduous shrub 1-2 m high, forming multiple downy stems from suckers; narrow lanceolate willow-like leaves to 8 cm long; the inflorescence of small light rose to near-white flowers in terminal pyramidal racemes 10 cm long, the stamens twice as long as petals. *Zone 5.*   *p. 853*
thunbergii (Japan, China), "Bridal-wreath": bushy deciduous shrub to 1½ m high, with branches wiry and angled; light green leaves narrow lanceolate 3 cm long, and finely toothed; pure white 1 cm flowers with obovate petals, in small clusters, thickly set, wreath-like on gracefully arching twigs, very early blooming in April or May; autumn color of foliage usually orange and scarlet. *Zone 4.*   *p. 851*
tomentosa (Québec to No. Carolina), "Steeple-bush"; small bush to 1 m high, of Eastern No. America, with brown-felted branches, and ovate leaves 4-8 cm long, yellow or gray-tomentose beneath; rose or purplish, flowers densely crowded on erect pyramidal spike-like racemes to 20 cm long, during August-September. *Zone 3.*   *p. 852*
x vanhouttei (cantoniensis x trilobata), "Bridal wreath"; beautiful deciduous, woody shrub to 2 m high, with numerous slender, gracefully arching branches; coarsely toothed leaves bluish beneath, and tiny, white flowers in masses of dense, lacy clusters forming a veritable blanket of snow in May-June. *Zone 4.*   *p. 853*

SPIRANTHES   Orchidaceae
aurantiaca (Stenorrhynchus) (Jalisco, Mexico), "Ladies' tresses"; terrestrial orchid with tuberous roots; fleshy ovate leaves along rising stalk bearing twisted pyramidal inflorescence of showy salmon-orange flowers. *Zone 11.*   *p. 97*
cernua (Nova Scotia to Florida and West), "Nodding ladies' tresses"; terrestrial orchid with tuberous roots, growing in bogs or wet places, to 50 cm high; grass-like linear, basal leaves to 25 cm long; the inflorescence on wiry stalks in densely-flowered spike, the small nodding white blooms sweetly fragrant, in early Summer. Occasionally used in aquaria. *Zone 3.*   *p. 336*

SPONDIAS   Anacardiaceae
cytherea (dulcis in hort.) (Society Islands: Tahiti), "Otaheite apple" or "Ambarella"; smooth gray-barked tropical tree to 20 m high, with bright green pinnate foliage 20-80 cm long, clustered at branch

ends; tiny greenish-white flowers in large clusters; the large ovoid-fleshy fruit with tough orange skin, 5 to 8 cm long, and though unpleasant smelling, has apple-flavored yellow pulp surrounding the fibrous core containing a spiny seed; fruiting October to January. Eaten fresh, or in preserves. *Tropical. Zone 10.* p. 904

mombin (venulosa) (Trop. America), the "Mombin", "Hog plum", "Spanish plum", or "Caja Mirim"; a most important and valued fruit tree in tropical America; a tree to 8 m high, with furrowed bark, and long pinnate leaves 20 cm or more long; small 2 cm purplish-maroon flower clusters, followed by globular or ovoid light brown or purple fruit with soft, yellow flesh, 3 to 4 cm diameter, and when eaten fresh has an acid spicy flavor resembling cashew but less aromatic. Fruit is also boiled or dried. *Tropical. Zone 10.* p. 636, 904

purpurea (Guayana, Venezuela), "Spanish plum", "Ciruela" or "Jocote"; semi-deciduous tropical tree to 10 m high, with leaves compound of 7-23 shortly stalked, elliptic to obovate leaflets to 4 cm long, usually blunt near top and often toothed; small greenish or purplish flowers in axillary culsters along branches, followed by obovoid yellow to red fruit with spicy flesh, nearly acid and containing large seed. Widely cultivated in West Indies. *Zone 10.* p. 904, 905

SPREKELIA   *Amaryllidaceae*

formosissima (Mexico, Guatemala), "Jacobean lily" or "Aztec lily"; beautiful bulbous herb with linear leaves; solitary, showy crimson flower, with a spathe-like bract, appearing in June, before the foliage. *Subtropic. Zone 9.* p. 218

STACHYS   *Labiatae*

byzantina (syn. lanata, olympica) (Turkey, S.W. Asia, Caucasus), "Woolly betony" or "Lamb's ears"; attractive perennial, with erect branches to 1 m high; the soft foliage is densely white-woolly, the thick lower leaves tongue-shaped, to 10 cm long; the floral stalks with many whorls of small purplish flowers in June. Plant is valued most in gardens for its ornamental foliage effect; also used medicinally. *Zones 5-10.* p. 439, 535

grandiflora (macrantha) (syn. Betonica) (Caucasus, Turkey, Iran), "Big betony"; beautiful rosette-forming perennial to 50 cm high, with ovate, hairy leaves 6 cm long, crenate; inflorescence with orchid-purple flowers, in dense whorls, blooming in late Summer. *Zones 4-8.* p. 438

grandiflora 'Superba' (macrantha cv.); outstanding cultivar in col. Nymphenburg Bot. Garden, Munich; its broad-ovate, thick leaves deeply crenate and corrugated by depressed ribs; the showy flowers 4 cm long, with trumpet-shaped vivid rose-pink corollas, in large clusters carried well above the foliage. *Zones 5-8.* p. 439

officinalis (Europe, Asia Minor); aromatic, tufting perennial herb to 50 cm high, known as "Betony"; with ovate-oblong, herbaceous, pubescent, ornamental leaves to 12 cm long, fresh green, quilted and crenate; purple two-lipped flowers in dense whorls forming an oblong spike, blooming July-September. Betony was an invaluable medicinal herb in England, known to the Romans, and used for headaches, liver, and bronchitis; much planted in herbgardens. *Zone 5.* p. 439, 535

olympica (byzantina var.) (S.E. Europe, S.W. Asia), "Woolly betony"; photo taken in Botanic Garden Darmstadt, Germany; variety of A. byzantina, with broader, less hairy aromatic leaves, and heavier spikes of purple flowers. According to Simmons, the whole plants were collected for a flavorful tea, said to have the good qualities of China tea plus virtues of its own. *Zones 6-10.* p. 535

STACHYTARPHETA   *Verbenaceae*

mutabilis (syn. Verbena mutabilis) (Central to So. America); subshrub to 90 cm high; leaves ovate, narrowed to stalk, rough and gray above, green and downy beneath; large crimson flowers changing to rose, sunk in furrows of an erect spike, subtended by awl-shaped bracts; blooming most of the year. *Zone 10.* p. 902

STACHYURUS   *Stachyuraceae*

praecox (Japan), "Spike-tail"; deciduous shrub 2-4 m high, with reddish shoots and willow-like branches; lanceolate, toothed leaves 8 to 15 cm long; small 1 cm bell-shaped flowers pale yellow, borne charmingly in stiffly pendant racemes 10 cm long, like a chain of pearls, in Spring before the leaves; berry-like fruit greenish-yellow with red cheeks. *Zone 6.* p. 882

STANGERIA   *Cycadaceae*

eriopus (Cape Prov., So. Africa); fern-like perennial cycad with underground stem, each bearing 1-4 pinnate leaves to 2 m long; cones silvery-pubescent. *Subtropic. Zone 10.* p. 114

STANHOPEA   *Orchidaceae*

tigrina (Mexico), "El Toro"; from apprentice days in my father's greenhouses have I remembered this fantastic epiphyte as my most impressive orchid; the memory of its large, 15 cm waxy flowers with sepals and petals deep blood-red marked with yellow, an orange-yellow lip blotched with maroon and its ivory horns, together with an

overpowering fragrance of vanilla, haunts me still, (May-July). Valid name may be S. hernandezii. *Tropical. Zones 11-12.* p. 96

wardii (Guatemala, Venezuela), "El Toro"; showy epiphyte with robust inflorescence, the fragrant flowers having yellow sepals and petals, with maroon rings and spots, and in the center two maroon-black eyes, or one large, confluent blotch, in front are two sickle-shaped, light yellow horns, (July-Sept.). *Zones 11-12.* p. 96

STAPELIA   *Asclepiadaceae*

gigantea (Zululand to Zimbabwe), "Giant toad plant"; ribbed, fat stems pale green and velvety, with gigantic flowers to 20 cm or more across, pale yellow with transverse crimson lines, variable in color, with forms more reddish, and covered with purplish or crimson hairs; exuding an offensive odor. *Arid-tropical. Zone 10.* p. 152

hirsuta (Cape Province), "Hairy star-fish flower"; clustering succulent fingers sooty-green, the 10 cm flowers purple-brown with transverse lines of cream or purple, and with the margins ciliate-hairy. *Arid-subtropic. Zone 10.* p. 152

nobilis (Transvaal, Mozambique); branching, tufted, light green stems; flowers star-like, reflexed, reddish purple on back, yellow on face with crimson lines, covered with purple hairs; flowers 15 cm or more across, and with a deep depression in center. *Arid-subtropic. Zone 10.* p. 152

semota lutea (Tanzania); small clustering succulent to 7 cm tall, 4-angled stems grayish-green, with long tubercles tapering to sharp tip; charming little star-flowers 4 cm dia., bright yellow with blood-red center star, and with ciliate margins. *Arid-tropical. Zones 10-11.* p. 152

variegata (Orbea) (Cape Province), the "Star flower" or "Carrion flower"; very showy, fleshy flowers 5-8 cm across, greenish-yellow with purple-brown spots on petals; branching green stems clustering and finger-like. Unfortunately the flowers, like those of other Stapelias, exude a carrion smell to attract flies which, in the hope of finding ripe meat, succeed only in transferring pollen from one flower to another. *Zone 10.* p. 152

STAPELIOPSIS   *Asclepiadaceae*

neronis (So. Africa: Namaqualand); tufted small succulent growth with erect irregularly 4-angled green stems, spotted purple, to 7 cm high, covered by minute hairs; little fleshy urn-shaped 2 cm flowers velvety brown-purple outside. *Zones 10-11.* p. 153

STAPHYLEA   *Staphyleaceae*

colchica (Caucasus), "Bladdernut"; floriferous shrub 3-4 m high, with compound leaves of 3-5 ovate leaflets 6 8 cm long, finely toothed; inflorescence in clusters usually pendulous but sometimes upright; the flowers bell-like 2 cm long and pure white, blooming in May; fruit an inflated capsule to 10 cm long, 2 to 3-lobed. *Zone 6.* p. 882

colchica 'Coulombieri' (French cultivar 1872 from Vitry); in all parts larger than the species, the leaves with 3 to 5 leaflets long pointed, to 12 cm long; flowers white, in clusters more compact than colchica, petals shorter and wider. *Zone 6.* p. 882

holocarpa (Central China), "China bladdernut"; hardy deciduous shrub or tree 3 to 10 m or more high; leaves compound of 3 elliptic to lanceolate leaflets to 10 cm long, and finely toothed, downy on midrib beneath; flowers rose in bud, becoming pure white, 12 mm long, blooming in May before foliage in pendulous 10 cm axillary clusters; pear-shaped fruit 3-5 cm long. *Zone 3.* p. 882

pinnata (C. Europe to So. Italy, Bulgaria, Ukraine), "European bladdernut"; deciduous shrub 2 to 5 m high, with pinnate leaves having 5 to 7 sharply toothed leaflets 6-10 cm long, vivid green, glaucous beneath; white flowers 1 cm long, green at base and the tips tinted red, seated erect on pendulous cluster to 12 cm long, blooming May to June. *Zone 8.* p. 882

trifolia (Eastern U.S.), "American bladdernut"; hardy shrub or small tree to 5 m, bearing opposite compound leaves of 3 leaflets, pubescent underneath; white flowers about 1 cm long, in nodding panicles to 5 cm across, followed by the bladder-like fruit, an inflated capsule grown for ornament. *Zones 3-4.* p. 882

STATICE latifolia: see LIMONIUM latifolium

STATICE tatarica: see GONIOLIMON tataricum

STELLARIA   *Caryophyllaceae*

holostea (Europe to No. Africa and Near East), "Moon flower" or "Stitchwort"; perennial chickweed to 50 cm high, with weak, 4-angled branches brittle at nodes; the lanceolate leaves 3 to 8 cm long, rigid and with ciliate margins; starry white flowers 2 cm across, blooming April to June. *Zone 6.* p. 367

STENOCARPUS   *Proteaceae*

sinuatus (Queensland, New South Wales), "Wheel of fire"; evergreen tree 10-30 m high with leaves either oblong-lanceolate and unlobed or pinnately cut into 1 to 4 pairs of oblong lobes, 30-45 cm long, leathery, glossy light green with pale midrib and lighter beneath; blooming in Summer or Fall; 8 to 10 cm heads of brilliant scarlet flowers tipped with yellow, arranged to resemble a pinwheel, orange-red when young; the inflorescence seeming to explode like fireworks into fiery-red when mature. *Zone 10.*   *p. 825*

STENOCEREUS   *Cactaceae*
gummosus (Machaerocereus: Backeberg, Lemaireocereus: Hortus), "Dagger cactus"; dense bush with cylindric branches 4 to 6 cm thick and 1 m long, 8 to 9 ribs covered by spines, the central spine dagger-like; tubular flowers pink or white; 6 cm edible red fruit. *Zone 10.*   *p. 177*

marginatus (Lemaireocereus, Pachycereus) (Central and So. Mexico), "Organ-pipe cactus"; beautiful column cactus tree-like, or branching from base, to 8 m tall; slender, smooth green stems to 12 cm thick, with 5-7 ribs and gray spines; bell-tubular flowers 5 cm long, red outside, greenish-white inside; globular orange fruit 4 cm dia., with reddish flesh and black seed. Often planted in Mexican villages as a natural fence. *Arid-tropical. Zones 10-11.*   *p. 177, 622*

thurberi (Lemaireocereus) (Arizona; Mexico: Sonora to Baja California), "Arizona organ-pipe"; forbidding-looking columns with 12-17 acute ribs, dark green to grayish, to 20 cm thick, the dense areoles with black cushions and clusters of stiff spines gray to black; branching from the base and becoming 6 m high; purplish flowers 7 cm across, with white margin, nocturnal but may remain open next day; globose edible red fruit 6 cm dia.; Pitahaya are gathered and eaten by the Papago Indians. *Arid-subtropic. Zone 10.*   *p. 161, 177*

STENOCHLAENA   *Polypodiaceae (Filices)*
tenuifolia (palustris of hort.) (India, So. China, Polynesia, So. Africa, Malaysia, Australia), "Liane fern"; tropical epiphytic fern climbing by its slender woody rhizome, which is covered with occasional brown scales, and bearing leathery, pinnate fronds to 1 m long, shining green, finely serrate at margins, coppery when young; as a pot plant likes to climb on tree-fern slabs. Differs from palustris in having slender fertile fronds twice pinnate. *Zones 10 -12.*   *p. 141*

STENOGLOTTIS   *Orchidaceae*
fimbriata (So. Africa); pretty terrestrail orchid with tuberous roots producing a tuft of leaves, and an erect bracted raceme 30 cm high, of small rosy-pink or purple flowers with brown-spotted lip, (Autumn). *Zone 11.*   *p. 97*

STENOMESSON   *Amaryllidaceae*
variegatum (Ecuador, Perú, Chile); tender bulbous plant, with inflorescence arising before the leaves; floral stalk 40-50 cm tall, with tubular funnel-shaped flowers red, the outer segments with green markings. *Tropical. Zone 10.*   *p. 218*

STENORRHYNCHUS aurantiacus (Zander):
see SPIRANTHES aurantiacus

STENOTAPHRUM   *Gramineae*
secundatum (So. Carolina to Florida and Texas), "Saint Augustine grass"; creeping perennial subtropical grass, its branching, compressed stems coarse-textured, with wide blades of dark green, less than 15 cm long; makes a serviceable lawn, fairly pest-free and salt-tolerant; cut 2 to 4 cm high. *Zones 7-9.*   *p. 570*

secundatum 'Variegatum' (So. U.S., Trop. America), "Variegated St. Augustine grass"; very ornamental creeping stoloniferous evergreen grass to 15 cm high, with flattened stems and firm linear leaves prettily banded creamy-white, the tips round. *Zone 9.*   *p. 564*

STEPHANANDRA   *Rosaceae*
incisa (flexuosa hort.) (Japan, Korea), "Cutleaf stephanandra"; graceful deciduous shrub to 2^1/$_2$ m high, with zigzag wiry branches, and small roundish-ovate to triangular leaves 4-6 cm long, irregularly dentate or lobed at margins, often cordate at base; tiny greenish-white flowers in clusters, blooming in June. Valued for its elegant foliage, and bright brown stems in Winter. *Zone 5.*   *p. 853*

incisa 'Crispa' "Lace-shrub"; exquisite shrub 60 to 90 cm high, spreading wide, with branches arching downward; leaves triangular divided into 3 main parts, these lobed again and prettily crisped at margins. Found in Holmstrup, Denmark 1930. Adaptable as a low hedge. *Zone 5.*   *p. 853*

tanakae (Mts. of Honshu, Japan), "Kana-Utsugi"; deciduous shrub of twiggy habit to 2 m high, the slender brown stems arching; with slender pointed, broad ovate leaves 5-12 cm long, often cordate or shallowly 3-lobed at base, and sharply toothed, orange-red in Autumn; small white flowers in lax terminal clusters in June-July. *Zone 6.*   *p. 853*

STEPHANOTIS   *Asclepiadaceae*
floribunda (Madagascar), "Madagascar jasmine" or "Wax flower"; evergreen wiry climber with milky juice, twining to 5 m high, with opposite elliptic, thick-leathery glossy dark green leaves to 10 cm long; producing axillary clusters of very beautiful, exquisite waxy,

white tubular flowers 5 cm wide, and intensely fragrant. A favorite for pots on wire or trellis, for the winter garden, or light, warm window; keep cooler and drier in Winter. Propagate by cuttings. *Tropical. Zones 10-11.*   *p. 268*

STERCULIA   *Sterculiaceae*
apetala (So. Mexico, W. Indies to So. America); tropical tree to 15 m high, with naked trunk and densely leafy crown; long-petioled smooth, leathery 5-lobed leaves cordate at base, 30 cm or more long and wide; flowers without petals, the calyx yellow inside, spotted pink and purple, 2-3 cm long; fruit carpels roundish, containing tomentose seeds. *Zones 9-10.*   *p. 885*

ceramica (Celebes), "Fairchild's sterculia"; interesting large tropical tree with leathery, cordate leaves showing net of palmate yellow veins; inflorescence without petals, but with colored calyx, developing into the peculiar rusty-red fruit, splitting open to display shiny black seed inside. *Zones 9-10.*   *p. 885*

diversifolia: see BRACHYCHITON populneus

foetida (E. Africa to No. Australia), "Indian almond"; tall, noble tropical tree to 20 m high, with gray bark faintly ridged; reddish branches usually horizontal, crowded at end with large, digitate leaves 10-30 cm long and divided into 5-7 leaflets; appearing usually on bare branches, before the new leaves, are the small calyx flowers of crimson and yellow 2 cm long, with offensive odor; the attractive-looking pendant fruit consists of one to five rounded, scarlet, woody sections or pods, each about 8 cm in dia., and gaping open along one line when ripe to reveal 10 to 15 black, oblong seeds 2 cm long. These seeds are oily, pleasant tasting, and are eaten raw or toasted, but will also act as purgative. *Zone 10.*   *p. 885*

STEREOSPERMUM   *Bignoniaceae*
chelonoides (India, So. China, Malaya), "Yellow snake tree"; semi-evergreen tree to 18 m, with pinkish-gray bark; the leaves 40 cm long, divided feather-fashion into 7-13 elliptic leaflets which are paired, with one at tip; fragrant flowers ochre-buff, tinged and lined with red, 3 cm long; snake-like, curved thin fruiting capsules extend to 75 cm. *Tropical. Zone 10.*   *p. 666*

sinica: see RADERMACHERA sinica

STERNBERGIA   *Amaryllidaceae*
lutea (So. Europe, Asia Minor), "Winter-daffodil", or "Lily-of-the-field"; small bulbous herb, with narrow channeled, dark green basal leaves, 15-30 cm long; and bright yellow, crocus-like, funnel-shaped, strong-textured, fragrant flowers 4 cm long, at the end of a stout stalk 10-17 cm high; fall-blooming; fairly hardy. *Zone 7.*   *p. 218*

STEWARTIA   *Theaceae*
monadelpha (Cent. and So. Japan), "Tall stewartia"; large deciduous tree 10 m high in cultivation, to 25 m in habitat; leaves elliptic 5-6 cm long, densely silky on veins beneath; elegant white, cup-shaped flowers relatively small, 3-4 cm across, the anthers and filaments white, blooming July-August. *Zones 7-8.*   *p. 890*

ovata (Virginia, Kentucky to Georgia, Alabama), "Mountain camellia"; deciduous shrub 4-8 m high, having ovate leaves 6-12 cm long, rounded at base and sparingly toothed, lightly downy beneath; flowers cup-shaped, creamy-white 6-8 cm across, prominently displaying white filaments, yellow stamens and orange anthers, blooming July-August; fruit sharply 5-edged, to 2 cm long, containing winged seed. *Zone 5.*   *p. 890*

pseudocamellia (Japan); large shrub or small tree to 7 m or more, of pyramidal habit, the smooth trunk with red bark, prettily mottled beige, brown and gray, peeling off in large flakes; rather thick, elliptic, toothed leaves 5-10 cm long, turning brilliant crimson in Autumn; deciduous in the colder belt around New Jersey; cup-shaped white flowers 6 cm across, with yellow stamens. *Zone 5.*   *p. 890*

sinensis (China), "Chinese stewartia"; evergreen or deciduous small tree to 10 m, with obovate, toothed, leathery leaves 10 cm long; showy white, solitary flowers 5 cm across, with many stamens, and fragrant; young growth fine-hairy. *Warm temperate. Zone 6.*   *p. 890*

STIFFTIA   *Compositae*
chrysantha (Brazil); unusual evergreen shrub to 2 m or more high, with rigid lanceolate leaves; the floral heads very showy, 5-10 cm across, shaving-brush-like, composed of brilliant orange-yellow florets and numerous long pale pinkish-yellow hairs, blooming February to April in Brazil. *Zone 10.*   *p. 691*

STIGMAPHYLLON   *Malpighiaceae*
ciliatum (Brazil), "Golden vine"; slender twiner with threadlike stems, and glabrous, heart-shaped, thin-leathery leaves, oblique at base and with ciliate margins; large 4 cm golden-yellow flowers in clusters of 3-7. *Tropical. Zone 10.*   *p. 283*

STIPA   *Gramineae*
gigantea (Portugal, Spain, Morocco), "Feather grass"; ornamental perennial grass with culms to more than 2 m high; arching narrow

linear leaves with rolled margins 50 cm long; showy inflorescence with loose elongate clusters of golden-yellow spikelets with long bristles, in Summer. Zone 5.   *p. 564*

pennata (S.W. Europe to Asia), "European feather grass" or "Maidenhair grass"; perennial ornamental grass with slender stems 50-80 cm high; narrow leaves with margins turned under; graceful arching inflorescence of feathery yellowish heads. Zone 5.   *p. 564*

STOKESIA   *Compositae*

laevis (So. Carolina to Louisiana), "Stoke's aster"; popular perennial to 60 cm high, with purplish stems white-woolly in upper part; the leaves lanceolate and 20 cm long, spiny-toothed toward base; showy floral heads 5-10 cm across, typically lavender-blue, the outer rays lobed at apex, the innner rays tubular; blooming July to October. Zone 5.   *p. 400*

STRANVAESIA   *Rosaceae*

davidiana (Southwest China), "Chinese stranvaesia"; vigorous evergreen shrub or small tree to 8 m high, with lanceolate leathery leaves 5 to 12 cm long, dark green to a colorful purple and bronze; the small white flowers having concave petals and dark red anthers, in terminal clusters during June, followed by scarlet berry-like fruits at their best in December. Zone 7.   *p. 855*

STREBLUS   *Moraceae*

ilicifolius (S.E. Asia); evergreen tropical tree with crooked branches, the ultimate twigs pendant and containing white latex; handsome alternate, long-ovate leaves about 8-12 cm long, with corrugated surface, and toothed along margins; inflorescence in the leaf axils, having males and females on the same tree, the tiny male flowers in small heads, the female blooms each on long stalks in clusters; the fruit a small berry. Zone 10.   *p. 794*

STRELITZIA   *Musaceae (Strelitziaceae)*

alba (augusta) (Natal), "Great white strelitzia"; palm-like trees of which I have seen extensive groves inland west of Durban, to 10 m high, with woody trunk bearing shining green, leathery leaves 1-1½ m long and arranged fan-like, frequently cut into ribbons by the wind; the curious, large inflorescence on short stalks between the foliage; from a rigid, boat-shaped pointed purplish bract or spathe rises a row of white sepals and petals. Subtropic. Zone 5.   *p. 125*

reginae (Transkei, South Africa), "Bird-of-Paradise"; trunkless, compact, clustering but slow-growing plant to 1½ m high, with stiff-leathery, concave, oblong, bluish-gray leaves having pale or red midrib; strikingly exotic, long-stemmed flowers emerging from the green boat-shaped spathe bordered in red, measuring 12-18 cm in length, and placed at right angles to the stem, giving it the appearance of a bird's head; the flowers which emerge one at a time from the spathe, consist of 3 brilliant orange sepals, standing up like the crest on a bird's head, and 3 shimmering peacock-blue petals, 2 of which are joined together to form an arrow-like nectary. Subtropic. Zones 10-11.   *p. 123, 459*

nicolai (So. Africa), "Bird-of-Paradise tree"; trunk forming, clustering tree to 4 m high, with banana-like, shining green, leathery leaves having an obtuse base, arranged in 2 ranks; inflorescence in boat-shaped, reddish bracts cradling white sepals and light blue petals united tongue-like. Subtropic. Zones 9-10.   *p. 122, 123*

STREPTOCALYX   *Bromeliaceae*

biflorus (Pastaza, Ecuador); showy, open rosette from tropical rainforest at 1300 m; numerous narrow linear leaves to 50 cm long or more, green and lightly scaly, spiny at margins, the inner nest deep red, holding the compound head of inflorescence with pink petals. Zone 10.   *p. 48*

STREPTOCARPUS   *Gesneriaceae*

x hybridus, "Hybrid cape primrose"; complex group of hybrids with a long line of parents including S. dunnii for color, rexii for bushy habit, and wendlandii for stem-length; light green fleshy, quilted leaves; free-blooming with large trumpet-like flowers, in a wide range of color, from white with purple veining, through rose, orchid, mauve, blue to purple. Humid-subtropic. Zone 11.   *p. 66*

phyllanthus (So. Africa); showy tropical plant with a large and fleshy, solitary leaf 20-25 cm long and almost as wide, the surface grayish-green, furrowed by a network of depressed veins, and covered with soft white hair; the inflorescence rises from the leaf base; branched slender stalks carry a pendant shower of flowers pale lavender with yellow center. Photographed at Longwood Gardens, Kennett Square, Pennsylvania. Humid-subtropic. Zone 11.   *p. 66*

rexii (So. Africa), "Cape primrose"; small fibrous-rooted, stemless plant with long narrow, quilted and pubescent leaves in rosette hugging the ground, with several flower stalks bearing trumpets of pale lavender lined with purple in the throat. Humid-subtropic. Zone 11.   *p. 67*

saxorum (Tanzania), "False African violet"; small bushy plant from the cool Usambaras, with fleshy, pubescent, elliptic, 3 cm leaves

in crowded whorls; flowers with white tube and oblique limb of large pale lilac lobes, spreading to 3 cm wide, on long thin stems, blooming over many months. Have seen them clinging to perpendicular, exposed cliffs, at 1100 m in the Usambara Mountains of Tanzania. Humid-subtropic. Zone 11.   *p. 67*

STREPTOSOLEN   *Solanaceae*

jamesonii (Colombia, Ecuador), "Marmalade bush"; rough-pubescent, floriferous, rambling shrub to 2 m high, with small oval, wrinkled leaves 3 cm long on flexuous branches, and terminal clusters of tubular, bell-shaped, orange flowers 3 cm long, in Spring. Tropical. Zone 10.   *p. 881*

STROBILANTHES   *Acanthaceae*

anisophyllus (Goldfussia, Bot. Magazine) (India: Assam; Sey-chelles); tropical shrub to 1 m high, having opposite lanceolate green leaves to 10 cm long on one side of the pair, the opposite only 4 cm, corrugated with depressed veins and toothed; numerous curved tubular 3 cm flowers pale lavender, in terminal heads. Zone 10.*p. 631*

dyerianus (Perilepta) (Burma), "Persian shield"; beautiful tropical herbaceous shrub with magnificent iridescent 15 cm leaves, long-ovate and toothed, purple with silver above and curiously shimmering; glowing purple beneath; pale blue flowers. Best in a moist-warm greenhouse. Humid-tropical. Zone 11.   *p. 18*

STROMANTHE amabilis hort.:
    see CTENANTHE sp. 'Burle Marx'

STROMBOCACTUS (Hortus):   see TURBINICARPUS

STRONGYLODON   *Leguminosae*

macrobotrys (Philippines), "Philippine jade vine"; a most beautiful and striking woody twiner, with large pinnate leaves, best trained over pergola or frame support to allow the large racemes, 30 to 90 cm long, a free display of the curious 8 cm flowers with their slender-pointed, upturned beak, and rolled, recurved standard, colored entirely in an unusual shade of bluish-green jade over yellow-green, the beak a pale blue-green. Tropical. Zone 10.   *p. 280*

STROPHANTHUS   *Apocynaceae*

gratus (West Tropical Africa), "Climbing oleander"; robust clambering evergreen shrub, with opposite leathery, ovate to obovate olive-green leaves somewhat puckered, 10-15 cm or more long, on brown-purple woody stems; the waxy, trumpet-shaped flowers 6 cm diameter, with crinkled lobes, flushed purplish-red outside and pinkish-white inside, and with a prominent pale rose-purple inner crown, blooming late Spring. Zones 10-11.   *p. 266, 642*

speciosus (So. Africa: Cape, Natal, Zululand), "Corkscrew-flower"; rambling evergreen shrub, in habitat climbing into the trees; narrowly oval, leathery leaves to 9 cm long; curious flowers at tip of branches, a wide-mouthed corolla opens into 5 long, 3-5 cm narrow, spirally twisted lobes radiating in all directions, deep yellow with large red spot at base. Subtropic. Zone 10.   *p. 266*

STRYCHNOS   *Loganiaceae*

nux-vomica (India to Malaysia, No. Australia), "Strychnine tree"; evergreen tree to 12 m high, with ovate leaves to 10 cm long, having 5 longitudinal veins; small greenish flowers in terminal clusters, followed by globose 3 cm orange-colored berries, holding the seeds which yield the drug containing the poison strychnine. Zone 10.   *p. 774*

STYLIDIUM   *Stylidiaceae*

adnatum (Southeastern Australia), "Trigger plant"; herbaceous perennial 5-30 cm high; leaves scattered; upper crowded into a whorl-like tuft, linear; sometimes all very narrow, sometimes rather wide to 4 cm long; flowers pink in nearly sessile clusters along rachis. The column of the flower moves like a trigger when touched at base by insects, enabling pollination. Zone 9.   *p. 514*

STYLOPHORUM   *Papaveraceae*

diphyllum (Virginia to Wisconsin and Missouri), "Celandine poppy"; attractive downy perennial to 50 cm high, with thick root, sending up floral stalk bearing cluster of deep yellow flowers of 4 petals, 3 to 5 cm across; the leaves deeply cut, and the segments lobed again; spring-blooming. Zone 4.   *p. 466*

STYRAX   *Styracaceae*

japonica (Japan: Hokkaido to Kyushu; Korea, China, Taiwan, Philippines), "Japanese snowbell" or "Snowdrop tree"; graceful much-branched small deciduous tree to 10 m high; the thin branches strongly spreading horizontally, with elliptic leaves 4 to 8 cm long, gray-felted while young, and turning to red in Autumn; white, faintly fragrant, starry flowers 2 to 3 cm across, in charmingly pendulous clusters, in early Summer; small ovoid fruit, with seeds yielding oil. Zone 5.   *p. 885*

obassia (Japan), "Fragrant snowbell"; deciduous tree to 10 m high, with leaves broadly oval or nearly round, 10-25 cm long, distantly toothed and densely downy beneath; flowers fragrant in slender pendant racemes 15-20 cm long, the corolla pure white and deeply 5-lobed; very handsome but partly hidden by the large foliage. Zone 5.   p. 885

SUBMATUCANA: see BORZICACTUS

SULCOREBUTIA   Cactaceae
   albo-pectinata (Bolivia: Cochabamba); exquisite little clustering globes, about 3 cm dia., entirely covered with interlaced appressed white spines; from the sides rise showy, relatively large flowers with glistening rose-red petals. Zone 11.   p. 175
   rauschii (Bolivia), interesting miniature "Crown cactus"; delicate 3 cm depressed globular body clustering with time, smooth purplish-green, tinted red, the areoles set with jet-black spines; showy purplish-red flowers 3 cm across. Because of weak root-system, they may be grafted for better growth. Zone 10.   p. 165

SUTERA   Scrophulariaceae
   microphylla (Chaenostoma) (So. Africa), "Wild phlox"; low ever-green shrub to 30 cm high, the wiry branchlets with little clustered 1 cm lanceolate leaves, 4-ranked and overlapping; very floriferous with axillary flowers, the spreading corolla light purple and 2 cm across. Zone 9.   p. 876

SUTHERLANDIA   Leguminosae
   frutescens (floribunda) (So. Africa), "Cancer bush" or "Balloon pea"; downy shrub to 1½ m high, with pinnate leaves; the rich scarlet flowers 2-3 cm long in axillary racemes, developing into numerous decorative puffed, papery seed pods. Tea was made from the leaves by the early settlers to try to control cancer. Zones 9-10.   p. 770

SWAINSONA   Leguminosae
   galegifolia (Queensland, New So. Wales), "Swan flower" or "Winter sweet-pea"; ornamental, freely blooming perennial plant; semi-climber with scandent branches, bearing unequally pinnate leaves, and small pea-like flowers in long-stalked showy racemes, deep red, or other shades. Subtropic. Zone 10.   p. 280

SWERTIA   Gentianaceae
   perennis (Alpine regions of Europe to Pyrenees, C. Asia to Japan, Alaska to Calif.); erect herbaceous perennial 15-30 cm high; basal leaves broadly oval 5-15 cm long, narrower along stem; the flowers with corolla 5-parted, blue to white, and 5 cm across, blooming August-September. Zone 4.   p. 418

SWIETENIA   Meliaceae
   mahagoni (Florida Keys and West Indies), "Mahogany"; tropical evergreen tree to 25 m, with dark red hard wood which furnishes the mahogany of commerce for furniture, etc.; dark glossy green, leathery, pinnate leaves to 10-20 cm long with 6 cm leaflets; small white flowers; showy green woody fruit capsule 10 cm dia. Zone 10.   p. 788

SYAGRUS   Palmae
   romanzoffiana (Arecastrum romanzoffianum) (Cocos plumosa) (Bahia to Argentina and Bolivia), "Queen palm"; very handsome with straight smooth trunk to 12 m high and a graceful crown of long arching plumy fronds, the soft, dark shiny green leaf segments pendant above the middle; edible orange fruit. Humid-subtropic. Zones 10-11.   p. 101

SYMINGTONIA populnea: see EXBUCKLANDIA populnea

SYMPHOREMA   Symphoremataceae
   luzonicum (Philippines), "Molawin-baguin" (Tagalog); large creeping shrub similar to Congea, with leathery, smooth elliptic leaves; flowers with purplish spreading bracts and pale blue petals, blooming April-May. Zones 9-10.   p. 886

SYMPHORICARPOS   Caprifoliaceae
   albus (No. America: Alaska to Québec), "Snowberry"; popular deciduous shrub 1 m or more high, with slender woody branches with oval leaves 5 cm long, hairy beneath; pinkish cup flowers, followed in September by decorative snow-white, balloon-like fruit in small clusters. Zone 3.   p. 675
   orbiculatus (vulgaris) (New York to Florida, west to Colorado and Texas), "Indian currant" or "Coral-berry"; popular deciduous shrub of erect habit, 1-2 m high, with wiry stems, and broad ovate, thick leaves to 5 cm long, glaucous and pubescent beneath; small 1 cm bell-shaped pinkish or white flowers in axillary spikes, July to Sept.; berry-like fruit coral-red to purplish in showy clusters. Zone 3. p. 675

SYMPHYANDRA   Campanulaceae
   hoffmannii (Dalmatia), "Ring bellflower"; hairy perennial 25-50 cm high, with obovate, serrate leaves along stems, lower leaves ob-lanceolate 20 cm long; inflorescence in leafy clusters of nodding, white, bell-shaped 3 cm flowers, during July. Zone 5.   p. 356

SYMPHYTUM   Boraginaceae
   asperum (Russia to Iran; naturalized in No. Amer.), "Prickly

comfrey"; herbaceous perennial to 1 m or more high, with thick roots; ovate-elliptic leaves covered with prickly hairs; flowers in pendant terminal clusters, with inflated tubular 2 cm corolla first rose, changing to purple and blue. Zone 5.   p. 351
   caucasicum (So. Russia, Caucasus), "Blue comfrey"; very orna-mental softly hairy perennial, to 50 cm high; lanceolate leaves wrinkled with depressed veins; terminal clusters of 2 cm trumpet flowers first rose then blue, from June to August. Zone 3.   p. 351
   grandiflorum (Caucasus), "Ground-cover comfrey"; perennial herb 20-40 cm high, covered with bristly hairs; ovate or cordate leaves; inflorescence in branching clusters, of creamy-white or pale yellow tubular flowers 2 cm long, spring-blooming. Zone 5.   p. 348
   officinale (Europe, Asia; natur. in No. America), "Comfrey", "Healing herb", or "Boneset"; perennial to 1 m high, with thick tuber-like roots; lanceolate, bristly leaves 15-25 cm long; the nodding flowers are yellowish-white to purple, from June to August. Intro-duced to America as a medicinal plant, and also grown as a potherb. Zones 3-8.   p. 525
   orientale (Asia Minor: Turkey), "Comfrey"; perennial herb to 50 cm high, growing from thick roots; tufted hairy branches, with ovate, pubescent leaves; small white trumpet flowers 2 cm long. Zone 7.   p. 351
   x uplandicum (peregrinum) (asperum x officinale) (Caucasus), "Russian comfrey"; coarse bristly-hairy perennial to 1 m or more, from thick roots; large leaves at base, but upper-leaves smaller and attached to winged stems; trumpet-shaped 2½ cm flowers first rose, changing to blue-purple, in clusters from upper leaf axils. Leaves and root make excellent herbal tea; young foliage good in salads. Zone 5.   p. 351, 525, 527

SYMPLOCARPUS   Araceae
   foetidus (Québec to No. Carolina, west to Minnesota), "Eastern skunk cabbage", or "Pole catweed"; strong smelling perennial swamp herb with thick rhizome; spathe ovoid with incurved summit, 8-15 cm long, purple-brown and green, enclosing the spongy spadix, and partly underground; heart-shaped basal leaves to 1 m long, appearing after the inflorescence, which has a disagreeable odor. Zone 3.   p. 34, 326

SYMPLOCOS   Symplocaceae
   lucida (Laurus lucida) (Japan, Taiwan), "Sweetleaf"; densely branched small evergreen tree with leathery, long elliptic leaves 6-8 cm long, lightly toothed near tip, the midrib raised on both sides; flowers in axillary heads, pale yellow to brownish and 2 cm across, blooming March-April; 2 cm ellipsoid fruit. Zone 8.   p. 886
   paniculata (Himalayas to China, So. Korea and S.W. Japan), "Sapphire berry" or "Asiatic sweetleaf"; deciduous tree 3 to 12 m high, of dense twiggy habit, with ovate leaves 4-8 cm long, but variable, pubescent beneath; small white fragrant flowers 1 cm across, in small clusters during late May, quickly fading; very ornamental because of its unusual bright blue pea-size berries in October, persisting into Winter. Zone 5.   p. 886
   sumuntia (So. China, Himalayas), "Himalaya sweetleaf"; ever-green tree with smooth branches, the young shoots covered by white waxy bloom, later purplish-brown; broadly ovate thick-leathery leaves with veins scarcely visible; the white flowers 3-6 cm long, tubular with spreading lobes, blooming from March through Summer, and sweetly fragrant. Zone 8.   p. 886

SYNANDROSPADIX   Araceae
   vermitoxicus (No. Argentina); handsome aroid from the Andes near Tucumán and Salta; thick tuber with fleshy petioles striped with dark green, carrying sagittate-cordate leaves 20-45 cm long, 15-20 cm wide; showy spathe pale greenish to brownish inside, lined green, 10 cm long; spadix brown-red. Subtropic. Zone 10.   p. 34

SYNGONIUM   Araceae
   podophyllum 'Imperial White'; an "Arrowhead-vine" with arrow-shaped leaves deep bluish-green, and a contrasting network of ivory-white veining. Widely grown in California greenhouses. Tropical. Zone 11.   p. 34, 265
   steyermarkii (Venezuela); curious tropical clamberer with sagittate leaves irregularly lobed or indented, carried on long petioles; the inflorescence in terminal clusters of bird-like waxy white spathes with green apex, enfolding the short spadix. Zone 11.   p. 33

SYNSEPALUM   Sapotaceae
   dulcificum (Pouteria, Planchonella, Sideroxylon) (Ghana, Benin, Nigeria, Cameroon), the "Miracle fruit" or "Miraculous berry"; tropical West African shrub 2-4 m high, with leathery, obovate leaves 10-15 cm long; clustered small axillary flowers, with 5-lobed whitish corolla and narrow tube; followed by oblong, 2 cm glossy red, fleshy fruit containing one seed. Miraculously, after eating the berry, it causes a sour, acid fruit such as citrus-lime, to appear to taste sweet; the Africans chew it to make maize-bread more palatable, and to give sweetness to their sour palm-wine. Tropical. Zones 10-11.   p. 941

SYNTHYRIS *Scrophulariaceae*

reniformis (Washington, Oregon, to San Francisco, California); low rhizomatous perennial 10 to 25 cm high; nearly orbicular leaves to 5 cm across, having pronounced teeth along margins; small 1 cm blue or purplish cupped flowers, in compact clusters; blooming in March-April. *Zone 8.*   *p. 508*

SYRINGA *Oleaceae*

x chinensis (persica x vulgaris), "Chinese lilac" of hort.; beautiful French hybrid since 1777, to 3 m high, with slender, arching shoots; leaves ovate-pointed 4-8 cm long; flowers lilac or purple in long clusters in May; free-blooming and very fragrant. *Zone 5.*   *p. 812*

meyeri (No. China, Korea); small densely branched deciduous shrub 1-1½ m high; the shoots squarish and downy; leaves ovate or obovate to 5 cm long, typical with 2 pairs of longitudinal veins parallel to margins; flowers purplish-violet, in dense clusters blooming May-June, even as a small plant. *Zone 5.*   *p. 812*

microphylla 'Superba' (France 1939), "Little leaf lilac"; small shrub to 2 m high, with roundish-ovate leaves 3-4 cm long, pubescent beneath; flowers pale lilac in the species from China, in 'Superba' vivid deep rose outside and in bud, paleish inside, in lateral erect pyramidal clusters, blooming in May. *Zone 5.*   *p. 812*

oblata (No. China), "Early lilac"; vigorous deciduous shrub to 4 m high, with cordate to kidney-shaped leaves 8-10 cm wide, often with red autumn coloring; the foliage longer in var. dilatata; the inflorescence in large lateral clusters of pinkish lilac to purplish flowers, opening before the leaves have fully developed, with corolla 2 cm across; earliest species to bloom, usually April-May. *Zone 4.*   *p. 812*

patula (syn. palibiniana) (China, Korea), "Manchurian lilac"; very hardy shrub to 3 m high, with ovate-oblong leaves 8 cm long, pubescent on both sides; the flowers fragrant, having corolla 1 cm wide, rosy-lilac outside and white inside, in erect panicles 20 cm long. *Zone 3.*   *p. 812*

pekinensis (No. China); deciduous shrub 3 to 5 m high, with smooth bark, and branches arching outwards; slender brownish twigs, with leaves ovate or lanceolate 5-10 cm long, rich green above, and grayish beneath; flowers yellowish-white, having short corolla tube with anthers protruding, in dense elongate clusters to 15 cm long, blooming in June and fragrant like Ligustrum. *Zone 5.*   *p. 813*

x persica (afghanica x laciniata), "Persian lilac"; popular hybrid and one the smallest lilacs, usually not over 2 m high, of neat, rounded habit, and with very fragrant, pale lilac flowers profusely covering the branches, with leaves only 6 cm long, smaller than vulgaris; blooming in May. *Zone 5.*   *p. 813*

pinnatifolia (W. China); small deciduous shrub, in habitat to 3 m high, gracefully branched, with odd-pinnate leaves 8-10 cm long, of 7-11 ovate leaflets finely ciliate; the flowers white or pale lilac, in axillary clusters in early May. Unique with its leaves pinnate. *Zone 6.*   *p. 812*

x prestoniae 'Elinor' (reflexa x villosa); very hardy Canadian hybrid typically late-blooming, developed in Ottawa 1928; sturdy shrub to 3 m high, of dense habit, with large ovate leaves, glaucous and softly hairy beneath; the colorful flowers pale lavender to rose, in large clusters to 20 cm long, blooming into mid-June, 2 weeks later than vulgaris, and much hardier in cold climate. Very useful for hedges. *Zone 2.*   *p. 813*

pubescens (No. China); handsome lilac valued for its early blooms; deciduous shrub 2 m or more high, with slender angled shoots; the leaves broadly ovate or rhombic 3-7 cm long, dark green above and pubescent beneath; showy inflorescence in erect elongate panicles, usually paired, of fragrant pale purple flowers, very beautiful when blooming in May. *Zone 6.*   *p. 813*

reticulata var. mandschurica (amurensis) (Manchuria), "Amur lilac"; deciduous sparry shrub or small tree to 4 m high; the gray branches with broad-ovate, slender-pointed leaves 5-12 cm long, dark green above, pale or glaucous and reticulate or net-like beneath; flowers white to creamy, in fluffy clusters 10-18 cm long, blooming in June but lacking fragrance. *Zone 4.*   *p. 813*

vulgaris (S.E. Europe), "Lilac" or "Common lilac"; bushy deciduous shrub with crooked woody stems to 3 m or more high, the flexible twigs with opposite, thin ovate leaves to 12 cm long; blooming outdoors in late Spring with terminal or lateral pyramidal clusters of sweetly fragrant small flowers, normally pale purple tinged with violet. Brought to America by the earliest settlers, becoming naturalized in many States; my photo was taken in late June, in Grand Teton Nat'l. Park, Wyoming; elsewhere blooming in May. *Zone 3.*   *p. 813*

vulgaris 'Alba' ('Virginalis'), "White lilac"; very popular color variant of the common lilac, a vigorous shrub freely suckering and sprouting from the base, forming dense clusters of stems; the inflorescence in slender elongate clusters of fragrant flowers with single corollas glistening white. *Zone 4.*   *p. 813*

vulgaris 'Alba plena', "Double flowered lilac"; attractive color form of the Common lilac; robust growing deciduous shrub, with

flexible twigs and simple ovate leaves; the inflorescence in showy lateral pyramidal clusters of small fragrant flowers, the white corolla filled with double layer or curled lobes, blooming in Spring. *Zone 4.*   *p. 813*

vulgaris 'Ludwig Spaeth' (Berlin 1883); very handsome deciduous shrub of medium size, with ovate leaves of firm texture; spring-blooming with a profusion of beautiful deep magenta purple flowers in showy clusters, sweetly fragrant and in vivid color unexcelled. *Zone 4.*   *p. 813*

SYZYGIUM *Myrtaceae*

aromaticum (Eugenia caryophyllata) (Moluccas, Indonesia, Philippines), the "Clove tree"; evergreen tree to 10 m high, with elliptic, glandular dotted, aromatic leaves; yellowish-white tubular flowers 1 cm across, turning red when ripe. The sun-dried flower buds will be black, and are the commercial "cloves" used as culinary spice. *Zone 10.*   *p. 537*

jambos (S.E. Asia), "Malay rose-apple" or "Malabur plum"; evergreen tree to 12 m high, with dark green, lanceolate leathery leaves to 20 cm; greenish-white flowers 5-6 cm across; the popular apple-like fruit cream-yellow to 4 cm long, fragrant of roses, and edible, of a taste between plum and lychee; prized also for making into jellies. *Zone 10.*   *p. 802, 918*

kusukusense (syn. Eugenia) (Taiwan); evergreen tree of medium size, with oblong-elliptic leaves 10-14 cm long and to 4 cm wide, punctate beneath; flower characteristic with numerous prominent stamens; globose bronzy to blackish fruit 2 cm dia. *Zone 10.*   *p. 802*

malaccense (Eugenia) (Malaya), "Rose apple"; beautiful tropical tree 5-12 m high; glossy ovate oblong, leathery leaves 15-30 cm long; showy flowers of many stamens purplish-red, from old wood; pear-shaped red fruit, about 5 cm long, edible raw or cooked and used as preserves. *Zone 10.*   *p. 802, 918*

paniculatum (Eugenia myrtifolia) (Australia), "Brush cherry"; small vigorous shrub which lends itself to shearing into pyramids; slender branches dense with small elliptic foliage vivid red when young, later shining green; fluffy white flowers followed by edible red berries, with pleasantly acid pulp. Very popular as a clipped hedge in California, Mexico and So. Florida.
Zones 9-10.   *p. 616, 617, 621, 804, 918*

samarangense (Eugenia javanica) (Malay Archipelago), "Java apple"; evergreen tree to 10 m; leathery elliptic leaves 15 cm long; white flowers 4 cm across; pear-shaped fruit 4 cm long, white to glossy red; edible, but insipid. *Tropical. Zones 10-11.*   *p. 909*

TABEBUIA *Bignoniaceae*

argentea (Tecoma argentea) (Paraguay); the "Silver trumpet-tree", or "Golden bell"; showy flowering tree with crooked trunk and corky bark, to 8 m high, covering itself in the leafless stage with a profusion of rich yellow trumpet-flowers 5-8 cm long; after bloom appears the foliage, leaves palmately divided into 5-7 narrow leaflets to 15 cm long, and covered with silvery scales; oblong woody dark brown fruit 15 cm long. *Zone 9.*   *p. 666*

avellanedae (ipe) (Paraguay, Argentina); erect trumpet tree to 18 m tall, usually evergreen with palmate leaves of smooth, dark green leaflets 15 cm long; flowers clustered profusely at branch tips, lavender-rose with white throat banded yellow and purple. *Subtropic. Zone 9.*   *p. 665*

chrysotricha (Colombia, Brazil), "Golden trumpet-tree"; semi-evergreen tree to 8 m or more; palmate leaves with 5 leaflets to 10 cm long, the underside with yellowish fuzz; bright yellow trumpet flowers 6 cm long, blooming heaviest in Spring, when leaves drop for brief period. *Subtropic. Zone 9.*   *p. 665*

donnell-smithii: see CYBISTAX

heterophylla (spectabilis) (West Indies); shrub or small tree to 8 m high; palmately compound leaves of 3 to 6 elliptic leaflets to 4 cm long, dark green and thin-leathery; great clusters of inflated tubular flowers 3-4 cm long, carmine-pink outside and on slightly flaring lobes, creamy inside. *Tropical. Zone 10.*   *p. 665*

impetiginosa (Brazil); flamboyant deciduous small tree to 6 m; palmate leaves of 5 oblong to ovate leaflets to 12 cm long; large purplish-pink trumpet flowers with salmon sheen, 5 cm long, white and purple with yellow markings in throat. Blossoms cover bare branch tips in Spring. *Subtropic. Zone 9.*   *p. 665*

pallida hort. (W. Indies, C. and No. America), the "Cuban pink trumpet-tree"; showy flowering tree to 15 m or more high; leaves with 3-5 elliptic leaflets 10-15 cm long, often renewed after blooming; handsome flowers in dense terminal clusters, slender tube with flaring pale lilac-pink limb, yellow in throat, the corolla 6-8 cm long; winter-blooming; the fruit a long pod. *Zone 10.*   *p. 666*

palmeri (Mexico, Guatemala); large deciduous tree to 8 m high; the widespread branches with palmately compound leaves of usually 5 elliptic scaly leaflets 5 to 12 cm long; when the foliage falls, the bare limbs cover themselves with masses of bright pink tubular flowers, 7 cm long, and marked white and yellow, the spreading petals prettily ruffled. Zone 9.   p. 665

rosea (pentaphylla) (Mexico, C. America, Colombia), the "Rosy trumpet-tree"; small to medium winter-flowering tree, partially deciduous, with digitately compound leaves of 3-5 leathery leaflets, simple in young plants; large clusters of showy flaring tubular flowers a pretty lilac-rose. Zone 9.   p. 666

roseo-alba (pallida) (Brazil, Paraguay, Bolivia); small evergreen tree to 8 m high; leaves with 3 or more oval leaflets glossy rich green and leathery; large rose-pink frilled trumpet flowers of crepy texture. Zone 9.   p. 665

serratifolia (Puerto Rico, Trinidad), "Yellow pui" or "Yellow tecoma tree"; spectacularly showy flowering trumpet-tree about 6-9 m high, of densely branched habit, with papery leaves of 4-5 ovate leaflets to 12 cm long; the narrowly funnel-shaped 6 cm flowers in brilliant yellow, an unforgettable sight for the visitor to Puerto Rico, blooming on bare branches before the new foliage. Zone 10.   p. 664

TABERNAEMONTANA   *Apoccynaceae*

corymbosa (Ervatamia) (No. India to Malaya), "Great Rosebay", "Red bay" or "Flower of Love"; evergreen shrub with milky sap to 10 m; obovate leaves 8 to 20 cm long, glossy green and depressed at the veins; sweet-scented creamy-white, waxy gardenia-like 3 cm flowers with flaring, curving petals. The latex is poisonous. Photographed in Mughal Gardens Agra, India. Zone 10.   p. 640

divaricata (Ervatamia coronaria) (No. India), the "Crape jasmine" or "Paper gardenia"; dense evergreen, smooth, gardenia-like bush to 2 m or more high; shiny green, thin-leathery, paired leaves 8-16 cm long; waxy white, nearly scentless tubular flowers with 5 or 6 crinkled lobes spreading to 3-5 cm across. Zone 10.   p. 640

divaricata plena (syn. coronaria plena) (India), "Fleur d'amour" or "Butterfly gardenia"; tropical evergreen shrub to 2 m or more high, dense with flexible branches; handsome glossy green, lanceolate to obovate leaves to 15 cm long; large waxy white flowers 4-5 cm across, fully double with crisped petals spreading from 2 cm tube, and intensely fragrant, especially at night. Zone 11.   p. 640

TACCA   *Taccaceae*

chantrieri (Malaya), "Bat-flower"; curious, bat-like inflorescence both in shape and color, with wide-spreading, wing-like bracts of rich maroon-black, accompanied by long trailing filaments or "whiskers"; the small black flowers are succeeded by heavy berries; corrugated olive-green leaves to 60 cm long, with oblique base. Tropical. Zone 10.   p. 514

TACITUS   *Crassulaceae*

bellus (Graptopetalum bellum) (Mexico: Chihuahua), "Chihuahua flower"; handsome discovery 1972; spreading miniature succulent rosette of small, broad-obovate pointed, glossy coppery green leaves; striking inflorescence of scarlet-red star flowers 2½ to 3½ cm across, having contrasting yellow stamens. Arid-subtropic. Zone 10.   p. 192

TACSONIA: see PASSIFLORA

TAGETES   *Compositae*

lemmonii (Arizona: Sonora), "Arizona marigold"; subshrubby perennial 50 to 100 cm high, with leaves divided into from three to seven lanceolate, toothed segments; loose clusters of showy flowers, with bright yellow 1-2 cm ray-florets encircling brownish discs; August to October blooming. Zone 9.   p. 402

patula 'Gold Rush'; dwarf marigold strain to 25 cm high, the fully double flowers with frilled orange and red center crest, and crimson-red outer guard petals. Tropical. Zone 10.   p. 402

patula 'Naughty Marietta', "Single French marigold"; very pretty single marigold of semi-dwarf habit, to 30 cm high, bushy, with finely netted leaves; 5 cm flowers golden-yellow, painted in the center with a deep red, velvety eye. Tagetes patula are at home in Mexico and Guatemala, strongly scented, and have become very popular as summer garden annuals. Tropical. Zone 10.   p. 402

patula 'Pascal', "Rose de l'Inde"; colorful low annual bush with scented, large single flowers golden-yellow and bold brown-red blotches. Tropical. Zone 10.   p. 402

patula 'Petite Orange', "Dwarf marigold"; compact, bushy annual, extra dwarf to 20 cm high, with fully double flowers 3 cm across. One of the 'Petite series' at Ball's trial grounds in West Chicago. Zone 10.   p. 402

tenuifolia 'Orange Gem', "Striped Mexican marigold"; bushy annual to 50 cm high, with pinnate leaves divided into narrow leaflets; flowers solitary but numerous, to 3 cm across, having few ray-florets orange-yellow, usually with purplish-brown lines toward base. The species tenuifolia is from Mexico south to C. America. Zone 10.   p. 402

TAIWANIA   *Taxodiaceae (Coniferae)*

cryptomerioides (Mountains of Taiwan and mainland China);

evergreen tree, to 50 m in habitat; allied to Cryptomeria, but differing in having foliage of two kinds: juvenile leaves curved awl-shaped 2 cm long, adult leaves scale-like and imbricate; small 2 cm cones. Planted as temple tree in China. Zone 7.   p. 607

TAMARINDUS   *Leguminosae*

indica (Trop. Africa), the "Tamarind tree"; immense, picturesque evergreen tree to 25 m high, important both as an ornamental shade tree and economically for its brown 20 cm pods containing edible fleshy pulp of pleasing acid flavor; feathery pinnate, pendant leaves with leathery leaflets 2 cm long; and pale yellow 2 cm flowers, striped red. Bark, wood, leaves, flowers and seeds are also useful. Tropical. Zone 10.   p. 537, 625, 770, 909

TAMARIX   *Tamaricaceae*

aphylla (No. Africa and E. Mediterr. region), "Athel tree"; evergreen-appearing tree or shrub to 8 m high; reddish bark and with small scale-like sheathing leaves, similar to Casuarina, but with feathery pink flowers in terminal slender racemes 6 cm long, the petals soon falling, blooming Summer-Autumn. Planted as windbreak in Southwest American desert regions with alkaline soils. Zone 8.   p. 886

chinensis (Temp. East Asia), "Salt cedar"; shrub or small tree to 5 m high, with brown bark; the branches very slender, often pendulous, with tiny glaucous sessile 2 mm leaves; small pink flowers in cylindrical racemes, together forming large drooping panicles on current season's growth, in July to September. Naturalized in Southwest U.S. Zone 7.   p. 886

gallica (W. Europe to Himalayas), "French tamarisk"; charming shrub or small tree 5 to 8 m tall, the graceful slender branches bearing small heath-like bluish leaves, deciduous in Winter; white or pinkish flowers in feathery cylindrical racemes 3-5 cm long, in early Summer; at home along the coasts of France and W. Europe. Zone 6.   p. 886

ramosissima (pentandra) (S.E. Europe, Asia), "Flowering cypress", "Salt-cedar" or "Summer tamarisk"; spreading feathery shrub 2-10 m high, with tiny scale-like blue-green leaves; small rose-pink flowers in great plumes on current year's growth. Also known as "Five stamen tamarisk". Zone 5.   p. 886

TANACETUM   *Compositae*

cinerariifolium: see Chrysanthemum cinerariifolium

corymbosum: see Chrysanthemum corymbosum (Zander, Hortus)

praealtum: see Chrysanthemum parthenium

vulgare (Europe to Caucasus), "Common tansy" or "Golden buttons"; a strong-scented perennial herb to 1 m high, with alternate pinnate leaves nearly glabrous, to 10 cm long; clustered yellow flower heads 1 cm dia. Dried leaves are used medicinally; known as a bitter herb used for seasoning in puddings and cakes during Lent, in Britain; stems and leaves are poisonous if eaten fresh. Zone 3.   p. 524

vulgare crispum (Hortus 3) (Chrysanthemum in Zander) (Europe, Asia, naturalized in Eastern U.S.), "Fernleaf tansy" or "Bitter herb"; handsome rhizomatous perennial 60 to 90 cm high, with ferny pinnate, strong-scented foliage to 12 cm long, the leaflets deeply cut; the button-like yellow flowers in flat-topped clusters during Summer. This herb was formerly used medicinally and is reported poisonous if eaten fresh. Used as ornamental garnish. In England cakes with Tansy as the bitterweed are used during Lent. Zone 3.   p. 527

TAPEINOCHILUS   *Zingiberaceae*

ananassae (Malaysia, to Ceram and Queensland), "Giant spiral ginger"; perennial herb related to Costus, to 2½ m high, with bamboo-like canes, bearing leathery 15 cm green leaves arranged spirally; terminal inflorescence of cone-like, hard, recurved crimson bracts 10 cm across, nesting the yellow flowers; an ovoid cone resembling a pineapple, covered with brown bracts on leafless stalk rises directly from the rootstock. Tropical. Zones 10-11.   p. 522

TARAXACUM   *Compositae*

officinale (Temp. Europe to Asia), "Dandelion" or "Blowballs"; herbaceous perennial with milky sap; from stout tap-root rises a basal rosette of soft-fleshy, fresh-green leaves, oblong or spoon-shaped but variously cut, the terminal segment largest; flower heads bright yellow, to 5 cm across, fully double with numerous linear florets, on hollow stalks, blooming all Summer; the seeds are carried in white, feathery globes blown by the wind. A cosmopolitan weed but quite attractive. The bitter leaves are used as greens in salads. Zone 3.   p. 402, 528

TAXODIUM   *Taxodiaceae (Coniferae)*

distichum (New Jersey, Delaware to Florida, west to Texas), the "Bald cypress" or "Swamp cypress", also known as the "Tidewater red cypress"; tall deciduous coniferous tree, becoming 50 m high, with buttressed trunk usually 1-1½ m but sometimes 4 m or more in diameter, usually hollow in old age; the spreading branches with delicate and feather-like light yellow-green 1 cm needles in graceful sprays. At home in cypress swamps and tidewater bayous along the

Gulf of Mexico and the Florida Everglades; this is not only a very decorative tree but valuable as the "Red" or "Yellow cypress" for its durable red or yellow lumber used in greenhouse construction and benches, for boats, piling, shingles, and wherever wood must withstand warm and wet conditions. The base of the tree is flared to help absorb oxygen from the water; it is also known for its curious "Cypress knees", which are modified roots of a very light, soft spongy wood, showing above water. *Zone 4.*   *p. 607, 610*

distichum nutans (ascendens), (Virginia to Florida and Alabama), "Pond cypress"; deciduous coniferous tree of pyramidal habit, smaller than the species; the trunk with broad ridged base, the bark light brown and fissured in old trees; the roots rise above water as knobby cypress knees; needles less abundant, to 1 cm long, delicate fresh green in Spring, later turning yellow to orange-brown in early Winter before shedding the foliage completely. *Zone 5.*   *p. 612*

mucronatum (So. Mexico, Guatemala), "Montezuma cypress"; evergreen tree reaching great dimensions and age, a tree in Chapultepec, Mexico City is 51 m high and 700 years old; the famous tree of Tule near Oaxaca is estimated 4000 years old, with trunk dia. of 12 m and spreading 42 metres. Trunk covered by reddish, shredded bark, with roots often growing in water; needles 1 cm long, partially deciduous, on weeping branches; small 2 cm cones.
Zone 8.   *p. 610, 611*

TAXUS   *Taxaceae (Coniferae)*

baccata (Europe, No. Africa, W. Asia), "English yew"; densely branched evergreen shrub or tree growing slowly to 15 m, with wide-spreading branches forming a broad crown; flat needles dark green and glossy above, paler beneath, 2-3 cm long; female plant bearing fleshy scarlet, cup-shaped berries nearly enclosing a single, poisonous seed. *Zone 6.*   *p. 608, 611, 623*

baccata 'Fastigiata' (stricta) (Ireland), the "Irish yew"; a columnar form of the English yew, found in Ireland in 1780; evergreen tree to 18 m high of very dense pyramidal habit, with blackish-green needles to 3 cm long; female trees with fleshy scarlet, cup-shaped berries (not cones), containing a single seed. Very popular in Europe, but T. cuspidata seems to be superior in colder American regions.
Zone 6.   *p. 608*

baccata 'Repandens', "Flat-top yew"; low-growing bush with nearly prostrate branches spreading wide covering a circle to 4 m diameter; attractive with dark bluish-green needles rather straight, and having a tidy habit of growth. *Zone 5.*   *p. 609*

cuspidata (Japan, Korea, Manchuria), "Japanese yew"; somber evergreen tree to 15 m high, cultivated in a number of horticultural forms; T. cuspidata is the most important of ornamental yews in North America; best for dense bush or formal hedges, as it lends itself to shearing; far hardier than the English yew (T. baccata) and faster-growing; needle-like flat leaves about 2 cm long, suddenly tapering to a sharp point, leathery in texture, blackish-green, 2 yellowish bands below, and with prominent midrib, arranged on one plane along either side of the flexuous branchlets; berry-like scarlet fruit.
Zone 4.   *p. 608, 616*

cuspidata 'Capitata' hort., "Upright Japanese yew"; botanically synonymous with T. cuspidata, but because of its pyramidal habit, American nurserymen have attached the term "Capitata" to the species name in order to distinguish it from the spreading type. There is no mystery about the background of "Capitata" however; all true seed collected in its Japan habitat and imported since about 1910 has produced seedlings of typical pyramidal tree shape, and this character can also be perpetuated if using cuttings from only leader tips of older plants. *Zone 4.*   *p. 608*

cuspidata 'Densiformis' "Dense yew"; finest dense, lightly spreading yew, of dark color, growing more slowly than cuspidata; with branches erect and arching away from center, not forming a pointed cone. *Zone 4.*   *p. 609*

cuspidata 'Green Mountain'; vigorous spreading yew with dense foliage faster-growing than the species; from a cutting taken in 1957 originated a clone of pyramidal shape, requiring little trimming.
Zone 4.   *p. 608*

x media (baccata x cuspidata), "Anglo-Japanese yew"; valued American hybrid, retaining the best features of both parents, of erect bushy habit, hardier than baccata; similar to cuspidata but mature leaves olive-green, more distinctly 2-ranked as in baccata, and spreading. There are numerous cultivars of this hybrid, very popular in America, and the colder regions of Europe. *Zone 5.*   *p. 609*

x media 'Hatfieldii', "Hatfield yew"; male cultivar, long-time favorite, of open pyramidal habit, to 1½ m high, having dense upright branches; the needles spreading in all sides, and colored a rich deep green. *Zone 5.*   *p. 608*

x media 'Hicksii', "Hick's yew"; long-time favorite of upright habit, with dark green glossy foliage, similar to Irish yew but hardier, with several stems from base, most are female producing red berries in Autumn. *Zone 5.*   *p. 608*

TECOMA   *Bignoniaceae*

alata (smithii) (Stenolobium) (prob. hybrid of T. stans var. velutina and Tecomaria capensis) "Trumpet bush"; robust clambering shrub, with leaves pinnate of 11 to 17 leaflets, serrate at margins and to 5 cm long; clusters of funnel-shaped flowers yellow to glowing salmon-rose.
Zones 9-10.   *p. 269*

cherere: see DISTICTIS buccinatoria

mackenii hort.: see PODRANEA ricasoliana

stans (Stenolobium) (West Indies, Mexico to Perú), "Yellow-bells", or "Yellow elder"; ornamental shrub or tree-like to 6 m high; unequally pinnate leaves with serrate oval leaflets to 10 cm long; a profusion of showy 5 cm flowers bright yellow, in pendulous clusters, with funnel-shaped corolla hairy inside, the stamens curved in two pairs; long narrow pod-like fruits. *Zone 9.*   *p. 666*

violacea hort.: see PODRANEA ricasoliana

TECOMANTHE   *Bignoniaceae*

dendrophylla (New Guinea); large woody vine, with dark green leaves 16 cm long, pinnately compound, with 4 paired oblong leaflets and one at apex; attractive flowers with inflated bell-shaped corolla 10 cm long, deep rose to maroon outside and tipped with 5 short lobes, lighter inside, the lobed calyx purple. *Tropical.*
Zone 10.   *p. 269*

speciosa (Three Kings Isl. off N.W. New Zealand); curious woody twiner, discovered 1945, capable of ascending to 10 m, and in habitat growing over tall specimen of Leptospermum trees. Having seen this novel plant in N.Z., I feel it may become a desirable windbreak over fences, and ornamental even without support. The glossy leathery compound leaves are 15-30 cm long, of obovate leaflets; 6 cm trumpet flowers creamy tinged green. *Tropical. Zones 10-11.*   *p. 270*

TECOMARIA   *Bignoniaceae*

capensis (So. Africa to Transvaal and north), "Cape honey-suckle"; rambling, evergreen shrub 2-3 cm high, with leaves of 7-9 ovate, shining green, toothed leaflets to 5 cm long, and bearing bunched masses of curved funnel-form flowers fiery orange-scarlet, 5 cm long, and with protruding stamens. *Subtropic.*
Zones 9-10.   *p. 269, 664*

capensis 'Aurea' (Tecoma), "Gold Cape honeysuckle"; vigorous evergreen shrub or clamberer, with shiny rich green pinnate, corrugated leaves, and clusters of tubular 5 cm flowers with curved corolla vivid golden-yellow with stamens protruding, in Autumn.
Zones 9-10.   *p. 664*

TECOPHILAEA   *Tecophilaeaceae (Amaryll.)*

cyanocrocus (Andes of Chile at alt. 3000 m), "Chilean crocus"; small alpine plant with fibrous-coated cormous rootstock, 2-3 linear bright green basal leaves 8-12 cm long; short-stalked flowers with short tube and long lobes, deep blue veined or suffused with white in throat, the segments 4 cm long; in early Spring. Grown in European rockgardens. *Zone 8.*   *p. 262*

TECTARIA incisa: see HEMIONITIS palmata

TECTONA   *Verbenaceae*

grandis (India to Malaysia and Java), the "Teakwood"; a great tree of Monsoon Asia, to 50 m tall, with quadrangular shoots more or less woolly; leaves arranged in twos or threes, ovate, of leathery texture, 30-80 cm long, rough above, gray or brownish woolly beneath; small white flowers in terminal clusters, the calyx longer than the petals; dry, 3 cm, somewhat globular fruit pale green to brown. The strong, durable wood is valued as highly as mahogany, and used in furniture. *Tropical. Zone 10.*   *p. 901*

TELEKIA   *Compositae*

speciosa (Buphthalmum speciosum) (S.E. Europe to Asia Minor and So. Russia), "Ox-eyes"; strongly scented, robust perennial 60 to 150 cm high; the lower leaves triangular-cordate and sharply toothed, to 25 cm long; the uppers along stem ovate and sessile; showy floral heads to 8 cm across, the disc-flowers yellow, and slender ray-florets orange. July blooming. *Zone 6.*   *p. 401*

TELLIMA   *Saxifragaceae*

grandiflora (Alaska to California), "Fringecups"; rhizomatous herbaceous hairy perennial, with basal leaves rounded or heart-shaped, to 10 cm across, lobed or deeply cut; stem leaves similar; wiry purplish floral stalks to 60 cm high, bearing racemes of small nodding 2 cm flowers greenish-white, becoming reddish in age, the petals pinnately cut. *Zone 4.*   *p. 500*

TELOPEA   *Proteaceae*

speciosissima (New South Wales, Queensland), "Waratah"; striking flowering shrub related to Protea, of erect habit, 3-4 m high, with narrow obovate, leathery leaves toothed in upper part; magnificent terminal inflorescence of coral-red tubular flowers with protruding styles, packed in a dense globose head 8-10 cm across, and subtended by numerous narrow bracts of brilliant crimson. *Zone 10.*   p. 825

TEMPLETONIA   *Leguminosae*
   aculeata (retusa) (South and Western Australia), "Pink coral-bush"; handsome evergreen shrub 1 to 3 m high, with grayish leathery elliptic and obovate leaves 2-4 cm long; showy flowers pea-like, the corolla vivid red fused with pink, 3-5 cm long, for a brilliant Winter and Spring display. *Zone 10.*   p. 770

TERMINALIA   *Combretaceae*
   catappa (Madagascar to Malaysia), "Tropical almond" or "Olive-bark tree"; small or large tree to 25 m high, much planted in tropical countries near sea-shores for ornament and shade; wide-spreading branches arranged in tiers with large obovate, leathery leaves to 30 cm long, becoming red before they fall twice a year; flowers greenish-white in spikes, followed on female flowers by greenish or reddish 2-angled fruit 3-5 cm long, with oil-bearing seed, which can be eaten raw or roasted. *Tropical. Zones 10-11.*   p. 687, 907

TERNSTROEMIA   *Theaceae*
   gymnanthera (India, Malaya, Japan) (Cleyera of S.E. Trade); smooth evergreen shrub or small tree to 10 m; the foliage is spirally arranged and crowded near tips of new growth on red twigs; elliptic glossy-leathery leaves 4-8 cm long, handsome with new growth bronzy-red, later green and purplish; small 2 cm fragrant flowers creamy-yellow; small red-orange fruit splitting to reveal shiny black seeds. *Subtropic. Zones 7-8.*   p. 890

TESTUDINARIA elephantipes (Zander):
   see DIOSCOREA elephantipes (Hortus)

TETRACENTRON   *Magnoliaceae*
   sinense (So. China; Burma or Myanmar); deciduous tree 10-30 m high, with handsome foliage, the blades ovate, 8-12 cm long, furrowed by veins palmate from base, and toothed at margins; the tiny yellowish flowers in slender pendulous spikes 10-12 cm long, in June-July, on short spurs along one-year wood. *Zone 8.*   p. 780

TETRACLINIS   *Cupressaceae (Coniferae)*
   articulata (So. Spain, Malta, Morocco), "Sandarak wood" or "Arar tree"; tender evergreen conical tree 6 to 15 m high, having spreading branches; the branchlets flattened, divided into thin threads covered by scale-like triangular leaves, their tips pointed; solitary 1 cm glaucous cones at end of shoots. The species is tolerant of arid climate, its aromatic hardwood timber is valued for furniture; sandarak resin exuding from trunk is used for varnish. *Zone 9.*   p. 583

TETRAGONOLOBUS purpureus (Zander):
   see LOTUS tetragonolobus (Hortus 3)

TETRANEMA   *Scrophulariaceae*
   roseum (Allophyton mexicanum) (Vera Cruz, Mexico), "Mexican foxglove"; darling little plant with short stem, long obovate, dark green, leathery, flexible leaves glaucous beneath, and angled purplish stalks with clusters of pretty little nodding, trumpet-shaped flowers, orchid-colored with large, lobed, whitish lip and purple-violet throat, blooming from Summer on. *Tropical. Zone 11.*   p. 79

TETRAPANAX   *Araliaceae*
   papyriferus (Aralia) (China, Taiwan), "Rice paper plant"; a small tree to 4 m high, with large, ornamental foliage; the woody trunk and branches filled with white pith used to make paper; the lobed leaves 30 cm across, are covered with white felt while young. *Zone 10.*   p. 651

TETRASTIGMA   *Vitaceae*
   voinierianum (Vitis) (Vietnam), "Chestnut vine"; robust climber with woody stems and clambering, fleshy, brown-hairy branches having coiled wiry tendrils and gigantic, digitate, thick-fleshy leaves with 3-5 shining green, stalked, broad-obovate or oblique leaflets 25 cm long, wavy toothed at margins and pale green, pubescent underneath. *Tropical. Zone 10.*   p. 300

TEUCRIUM   *Labiatae*
   betonicum (Madeira), "Germander"; subshrubby perennial to 50 cm high, having shaggy branches with ovate-oblong leaves 8-10 cm long, crenate at margins and woolly beneath; inflorescence on long stalks, with curved tubular, purplish flowers, in spike-like racemes to 15 cm long, blooming May-August. *Zone 10.*   p. 439
   chamaedrys (Holland to Russia, south to Syria), "Germander"; dwarf rhizomatous, subshrubby perennial 15-40 cm high, with small ovate leaves 2-4 cm long, deeply crenate at margins; bilabiate rose to deep purple flowers 2 cm long, the lower lip spotted white and red, in whorls on leafy spikes, during July to September. This species of the Mint family is popular because of its fragrance, and beloved by bees. *Zones 5-10.*   p. 535, 621

   fruticans (Portugal to Adriatic reg.), "Tree germander"; sub-shrubby perennial to 1½ m high, with small 3 cm boxwood-like revolute leaves, white or reddish-brown hairy beneath; bluish 3 cm 2-lipped flowers along axillary and terminal branchlets, blooming during Summer. Used medicinally for fevers. *Zone 8.*   p. 439
   scorodonia (Norway to Poland, naturalized in Ontario to Ohio), "Wood sage"; small rhizomatous perennial with woody base, the stems 20-50 cm high, and pubescent; leaves triangular-ovate, rough above, and usually cordate at base and crenate at margins; spike-like inflorescence 15 cm long, on branches dense with small 1 cm yellow flowers displaying protruding stamens. *Zones 2-7.*   p. 439

THALIA   *Marantaceae*
   dealbata (So. Carolina to Florida and Texas), "Water-canna"; perennial aquatic or marsh herb, covered with white powder; basal, leathery ovate oblong leaves to 50 cm long and 25 cm wide, on long petioles; inflorescence on leafless stalk 3 m or more high, the small flowers dull violet, in a spreading panicle. *Zone 7.*   p. 330, 332

THALICTRUM   *Ranunculaceae*
   aquilegifolium (Europe, No. Asia), "Columbine meadow-rue"; glaucous herbaceous perennial 60-80 cm high, with hollow stems, and airy foliage 2 or 3 times pinnate; the fluffy flowers in multiple floral heads of white or pinkish sepals and erect purple or pink stamens, and lacking petals, blooming May-July; followed by 3-winged, drooping fruits. *Zones 5-8.*   p. 490
   dipterocarpum (W. China), "Yunnan meadow-rue"; beautiful herbaceous perennial 60 cm to 1 m or more high, with delicate, much divided leaves, the leaflets mostly 3-lobed; nodding bisexual flowers 2 cm across, having petal-like sepals mauve pink, and yellow stamens in large clusters, blooming in August, the last of the various species to bloom. *Zone 4.*   p. 490
   kiusianum (Japan: Kyushu), "Meadow-rue"; low stoloniferous perennial 10-15 cm high, with purplish leaves once or twice divided into 3 ovate, toothed leaflets; small bisexual flowers 1 cm across, lilac-pink sepals and very blue stamens, in large clusters; summer-blooming. *Zone 5.*   p. 490
   rochebrunianum (Japan), "Lavender-mist"; very ornamental glaucous perennial 60-90 cm high, with smooth leaves, bipinnate or divided into segments, suggesting maidenhair; charming flowers without petals but showy lavender-rose sepals and conspicuous yellow stamens, in loose clusters above the foliage; from July into September. *Zone 4.*   p. 490
   speciosissimum (glaucum in hort.) (W. Mediterran. reg., Spain, Portugal), "Dusty meadow-rue"; robust perennial with stout furrowed stems 60 cm to more than 1 m high, conspicuous for its blue-gray, glaucous leaves, 2 or 3 times pinnate, the leaflets to 4 cm wide; numerous small, fluffy flowers of pale yellow sepals, and bright yellow stamens, in dense clusters, blooming July-August. *Zone 5.*   p. 490

THAMNOCALAMUS spathaceus (Europ. Gard. Fl., Zander):
   see FARGESIA murielae (Amer. Bamboo Soc. 1990)

THAPSIA   *Umbelliferae*
   villosa (So. Europe to Portugal), "Gaimão"; robust herbaceous perennial with stem to 1 m or more high, with silky hairy tri-pinnate leaves, the ultimate leaflets with wavy margins and frilled; small yellow flowers in dense clusters, during June-July. *Zone 9.*   p. 516

THAUMATOCOCCUS   *Zingiberaceae*
   daniellii (Trop. W. Africa); rare tropical perennial to 2 m high, with spreading underground rhizomes giving rise to numerous erect, cane-like stems, terminally bearing large ovate, corrugated, leathery leaves; the small inflorescence, forming red fruit, rises directly from the roots on short stalks. Photographed in col. Mandai Gardens, Singapore. *Zone 11.*   p. 522

THEA sinensis: see CAMELLIA sinensis

THECOPHYLLUM sintenisii: see VRIESEA sintenisii

THELOCACTUS   *Cactaceae*
   lophothele longispina (No. Mexico: Chihuahua); clustering small globes, elongating to 25 cm high; to 20 spiralled ribs dissolved into prominent conical knobs set with piercing needle spines 3 cm long; flowers 5 cm across, variably creamy-white to rose-red. *Zone 10.*   p. 177
   McDowellii (Mexico: Coahuila); small depressed pale green globe to 7 cm high, 9-12 cm dia., the spiralled tubercles densely covered by interwoven long white spines; attractive flowers in late Winter at apex of new tubercles, purplish-rose. Collected Glass and Foster between Saltillo and Monterrey. *Zone 10.*   p. 178
   viereckii (Zander): see GYMNOCACTUS viereckii (Backeberg)

THELYPTERIS   *Polypodiaceae (Filices)*
   hexagonoptera (Québec to Minn., so. to Texas and N. Florida), "Broad beech fern"; hardy medium sized terrestrial fern spreading

rapidly from shallow rhizome, deciduous in cold climates; bipinnate light green fronds 25-60 cm long, slightly hairy. *Zones 3-8.* p. 141

noveboracensis (Dryopteris) (E. North America: Newfoundland to Wisconsin, so. to Georgia), "New York fern"; spreading by creeping rhizomes, with pinnate fronds 30-60 cm long, the lobed pinnae becoming shorter and tapering toward both ends of the leaf axis. The leaves are killed by the first frost. *Zones 2-8.* p. 141

phegopteris (Newfoundland to Alaska and Washington, so. to Tennessee Mts.), "Long beech fern"; from slender, creeping, rooting rhizomes rise at intervals the pinnate fronds 20-40 cm long, forming mats; pinnae are lobed, the two basal ones stretch downward. *Zones 2-7.* p. 141

robertiana: see GYMNOCARPIUM

THEOBROMA *Sterculiaceae (Byttneriaceae: Hortus 3)*

cacao (C. America, Trinidad, Guyana) "Cacao-tree"; wide-branching evergreen tree to 8 m high, with attractive, satiny, hard-papery, pendant leaves to 30 cm long; the small, yellowish flowers in axillary clusters, or curiously even cauliflorous from the trunk, succeeded there by the large, ribbed fruit containing bean-like seed which is the source of chocolate. *Tropical. Zones 10-11.* p. 886, 944

THERMOPSIS *Leguminosae*

caroliniana (villosa) (No. Carolina, Georgia, Tenn. to Alabama), "Carolina lupine"; deep-rooted perennial 60-90 cm or more high; leaves of 3 ovate leaflets, glaucous and pubescent beneath; the flowers yellow, in tall spike-like racemes to 25 cm long, blooming June-July; the 5 cm pea-fruit densely hairy. *Zones 3-8.* p. 443

divaricarpa (New Mexico, Arizona, Utah), "Golden pea", also known as "False lupine"; handsome herbaceous perennial 30-60 cm high, with leaves divided into 3 narrow-lanceolate leaflets to 6 cm long; bright yellow pea-flowers in erect racemes, April to July-blooming; followed by flat seed-pods. *Zone 4.* p. 443

montana (Washington to Rocky Mts. of Montana, New Mexico to Colorado), "False lupine"; charming perennial herb to 60 cm high, with trifoliolate leaves, having lanceolate leaflets to 8 cm long, and loose terminal cluster of vivid yellow pea-flowers, in June-July. *Zone 3.* p. 443

THESPESIA *Malvaceae*

populnea (Pantropic), "Portia tree" or "Milo"; tropical tree to 20 m high, with cordate-ovate unlobed leaves 15 cm long or more; solitary bell-shaped flowers 5-8 cm dia., yellow with purple center, fading to orange-yellow and withering into pink during the day. Much grown along the seashores of Hawaii and the Pacific Islands, valued as shade tree. *Zone 10.* p. 786

THEVETIA *Apocynaceae*

ovata (Mexico: Nayarit), "Egg tree" or "Huevo de gato"; tropical evergreen shrub or small tree, with long ovate leaves having pinnate nerves, and undulate at margins; large yellow funnelform flowers with spreading lobes, followed by brilliant scarlet berry-like fruit. Photographed in the tropical rain forest near San Blas, Nayarit. *Zone 11.* p. 642

peruviana (W. Indies, Mexico), "Yellow oleander" or "Be-still tree"; tropical evergreen shrub 2-3 m high with linear, shining green, 10-15 cm leaves, their edges rolled under; large, funnel-shaped lemon-yellow flowers 5-8 cm long, shading to pinkish or orange-apricot, and sweetly fragrant like a tea-rose; blooming anytime, mostly June to November. Takes heat and sun with ample water; may be trained into small tree. Poisonous like their relatives, the oleanders. *Zone 10.* p. 642

thevetioides (yccotli) (Mexico: Michoacán to Veracruz), "Giant thevetia" or "Narciso amarillo"; bushy shrub or small tree to 5 m high, with milky sap; linear dark green leaves 10 cm or more long, with the margins turned under and hairy beneath; large trumpet-like orange-yellow or pinkish-yellow flowers to 9 cm long. *Zone 10.* p. 642

THLADIANTHA *Cucurbitaceae*

punctata (Eastern Asia, Taiwan to Philippines); tuberous-rooted tendril-climbing dioecious perennial, with reniform to cordate-ovate leaves 5-15 cm long; bell-shape flowers yellow, followed on female plants by ovoid fruit 5 cm long, orange or red when ripe. *Zone 10.* p. 276

THRINAX *Palmae*

morrisii (ekmanii, microcarpa) (So. Florida, West Indies, Virgin Islands), "Key palm"; attractive fan palm to 10 m high, with fresh green leaves almost a complete circle to 1 m across, cut into broad segments, but not quite to base. *Tropical. Zones 11-12.* p. 111

parviflora (Florida Keys, Bahamas, Cuba, Haiti, Jamaica), "Florida thatch palm"; slender solitary fan-palm to about 8 m tall, 10-15 cm thick, enlarged at base by root-like growths; 2-edges petioles reddish at base and with hairy fiber; palmate leaves 1 m across, cut halfway to base into about 50 segments and forming almost a complete circle,

green on both sides, joined by radiating prominent yellow ribs; small berry-like, white fruit in large clusters. *Zones 11-12.* p. 111

radiata (Florida, W. Indies, to Honduras), "West Indian thatch palm"; moderately sized unarmed fan palm to 12 m tall, the palmate leaves glossy green and folded, deeply sliced into drooping segments; flowers white; ivory-colored fruit pea-like. *Tropical. Zones 11-12.* p. 111

THRYALLIS glauca (Zander): see GALPHIMIA glauca (Hortus)

THUJA *Cupressaceae (Coniferae)*

occidentalis (E. No. America; Québec to Hudson Bay, New Jersey to No. Carolina, west to Minnesota), "American arborvitae" or "White cedar"; ornamental evergreen tree of pyramidal habit, about 20 m high, with reddish-brown buttressed trunk divided near ground into several secondary stems, the branches densely arranged, flat fan-like, branchlets like fern fronds but with hard scale-like, shingled leaves, needle-shaped when young, dark green above, yellowish-green beneath, with a strong resinous odor; oblong cones erect when young, brown and pendulous when mature, 2 cm long. *Zone 2.* p. 583, 616

occidentalis 'Emerald' ('Smaragd'), "Emerald arborvitae"; valuable introduction from Denmark, with fresh green foliage throughout Winter; of dense growth forming elegant cones; ideal for hedges, adapted to cold regions as also to subtropic So. California. *Zones 3-9.* p. 583

occidentalis 'Fastigiata' ('Columnaris'); narrow columnar arborvitae of dense growth, to 8 m high and 1½ m wide, with short lateral branches as high as the leader; good plant for tall hedges and screens, especially in colder regions; can be trimmed to shape. *Zone 2.* p. 619

occidentalis 'Filiformis' (flagelliformis), "Threadleaf arborvitae"; low and bushy form to 1 m or occasionally more high, with main branches long and whip-like; the slender branchlets in dense clusters; leaves scale-like and rich green, closely pressed to the trailing stems, creating a cord-like effect, and contrasting with the orange-brown wood. *Zone 4.* p. 583

occidentalis 'Gold Tip', "Gold-tip arborvitae"; handsome cultivar seen at Don Roehrs Nursery in New Jersey, as a low evergreen bush, with spreading branches, the rich green fans of foliage tipped golden-yellow. *Zone 3.* p. 583

orientalis (Biota in hort.; Platycladus in Hortus 3; Thuja in Zander and European Gardenflora 1986) (China, Manchuria, Korea), "Oriental arborvitae"; dense conical evergreen usually consisting of several stems; differing from Thuja occidentalis in having branchlets 2-ranked fan-like in a flat, vertical plane; the tiny scaly, juvenile leaves needle-like, glossy yellowish-green; female cones 2 cm long, fleshy, and bluish before ripening. Warm temperate, but widely planted in the Tropics, as far south as Oaxaca, Mexico. *Zone 6.* p. 577, 584, 624

orientalis 'Aurea nana', "Dwarf golden arborvitae"; well beloved old cultivar, grown in gardens for many years; beautiful evergreen of slow growth and compact habit, to 1 m high, a rounded bush that needs no trimming; the foliage in flat fans golden-yellow in Spring, turning brownish in cold Winter. *Zone 6.* p. 584

orientalis 'Elegantissima' (Platycladus), "Golden arborvitae"; columnar form showing bright golden-yellow along the outer edges of the flattened fans of foliage during Spring into Summer. *Zone 6.* p. 583

plicata (No. California to Alaska), "Western arborvitae" or "Giant cedar"; noble pyramidal tree 30 to 60 m high; buttressed trunk with cinnamon-red bark divided into wide ridges; branches horizontal, pendant at the ends, and set with shiny green scale-like leaves in 2 ranks, forming flat, graceful, lacy sprays; erect brown cones 2 cm long. *Zone 5.* p. 584, 616

THUJOPSIS *Cupressaceae (Coniferae)*

dolabrata (Japan), "Broadleaf arborvitae" or "False arborvitae"; handsome evergreen growing into large tree to 30 m high in habitat; in cultivation usually shrub or pyramid of moderate size; branches spreading horizontally and arching downward by the weight of its attractive foliage; the flattened branchlets 1 cm wide, with broad needles dark glossy green, having a white hatchet pattern beneath; female cones 2 cm long, with scales thick woody. *Zone 6.* p. 584

dolabrata 'Aurea', "Lizard tree"; attractive as a young pyramidal bush, with its broad, fan-like leaves showing a pattern of variegation on the glossy scales, especially on the underside, where the leaf scales are tipped golden-yellow, resembling the appearance of a lizard. *Zone 7.* p. 606

THUNBERGIA *Acanthaceae*

alata (So. E. Africa, but naturalized in Tropics), the "Black-eyed Susan"; twining perennial herb, with herbaceous, toothed, triangular ovate leaves to 8 cm long, on winged petioles; funnel-shaped showy flowers 4 cm long, creamy-yellow or orange with or without black-purple throat, blooming late Summer to Autumn. Attractive vine for the cool, light window. Can be grown as an annual from seed. *Subtropic. Zone 10.*   p. 263

battiscombei (Trop. Africa); tropical scrambler often climbing, having ovate elliptic, thin-leathery leaves to 10 cm long, palmately 3 to 5-nerved; purple trumpet flowers with flaring segments and yellow throat, in axillary racemes. *Zone 10.*   p. 263, 631

erecta (Trop. West Africa), "King's mantle"; erect evergreen shrub to 2 m; thin branches with almost glossy ovate leaves 3-6 cm long; axillary trumpet-shaped flowers 6 cm in length, with large violet lobes, and yellow inside tube; July. *Zone 10.*   p. 631

grandiflora (India), "Clock vine"; woody twiner with rough, toothed, ovate leaves; bell-like flowers somewhat two-lipped, lavender-blue; throat white, solitary in the leaf axils. *Tropical. Zone 11.*   p. 263

gregorii (gibsonii) (Trop. Africa), "Orange clock-vine"; perennial herbaceous twiner or creeper, with cordate leaves 6-8 cm long, fresh green and lightly hirsute, on winged petioles; showy flowers bright orange 4 cm across, blooming nearly all year. *Tropical. Zone 10.*   p. 263

laurifolia (India); choice woody twiner with lanceolate leathery leaves to 12 cm long; funnelform flowers, light blue with white throat, to 8 cm across, several to a raceme. *Tropical. Zone 10.*   p. 263

mysorensis (So. India); tall-climbing, vigorous tropical vine from the Nilghiri Mountains; lance-shaped 3-nerved leaves 10-15 cm long; the attractive funnel flowers golden-yellow 5-6 cm across, with yellow and red-brown spreading limb, in long pendant racemes. *Tropical. Zone 10.*   p. 263

THUNIA   *Orchidaceae*
alba (India, Burma, China); robust epiphyte, occasionally becoming terrestrial, with tufted, tapering leafy stems 60 cm high, topped by a nodding raceme of large, pure white flowers to 8 cm across, with white lip inside yellow, striped with orange and shortly spurred and crested, (June-July). *Tropical. Zones 11-12.*   p. 96

THYMOPHYLLA tenuiloba (Zander):
see DYSSODIA tenuiloba (Hortus)

THYMUS   *Labiatae*
capitatus (Coridothymus capitatus) (E. Mediterran. reg. to Turkey and Palestine), "Thymian" or "Headed savory"; subshrubby aromatic perennial bush 12-25 cm high, becoming spiny with dead branchlets, densely hairy; small leathery, 1 cm linear leaves clustered at nodes; cone-like inflorescence of rose flowers 1 cm long, in July to September. The fragrant twigs are used as savory for culinary seasoning; introduced in Britain in 1596. *Zones 6-9.*   p. 536

x citriodorus 'Aureus' (pulegioides x vulgaris), "Golden thyme" or "Lemon thyme" very ornamental subshrub 10-30 cm high, densely branched, with narrow oblong leaves 1 cm long, beautifully colored golden-yellow, the margins turned under and dotted with glands; small 2-lipped pale lilac flowers in oblong heads. The lemon-scented leaves make excellent tea, and are delicious in salads. *Zones 3-10.*   p. 536

glabrescens (Central and S.E. Europe), "Loevyanus thyme"; low mat-forming herbaceous perennial 15-30 cm high, fast growing, with gray, lanceolate leaves 2 cm long; globose terminal inflorescence of small lavender to purple flowers. An aromatic potherb or goundcover. *Zone 6.*   p. 536

herba-barona (Corsica, Sardinia), "Caraway thyme"; aromatic perennial with woody base, and long spreading branches having small ovate, dark green leaves 1 cm long, and dotted with glands; oblong inflorescence of small 1 cm purplish-pink flowers, in June. The caraway-scented leaves are used as culinary herb to flavor vegetable dishes, also sandwiches. *Zones 4-10.*   p. 536

pannonicus (marshallianus) (E. Europe to Balkans, Turkey to Caucasus), "Pannonian thyme"; aromatic perennial with spreading branches from woody base, the stems 10-20 cm high, hairy on 4 sides; herbaceous, narrow leaves 2 cm long; very floriferous with elongate racemes of small purplish-pink flowers, May-blooming. Used for seasoning in cookery. *Zones 5-8.*   p. 536

pulegioides 'Coccineus' (Europe: from Britain to Caucasus), "Coconut thyme"; bushy aromatic subshrubby perennial 10-30 cm high, with 4-sided stems, hairy on the angles; oval but variable dark green leaves 1 cm long; the oblong inflorescence with small bright red flowers; mauve-pink or white in the species. The leaves exude a strong scent of coconut and plants are grown as a potherb. *Zone 6.*   p. 536

serpyllum (Europe, Asia, No. Africa), "Mother-of-thyme" or "Creeping thyme"; prostrate flowering thyme, robust subshrub with rooting stems, bright evergreen oval foliage less than 1 cm long, on reddish stringy branches, with strong aromatic scent; small purplish flowers 1 cm long, blooming Spring into Autumn. Forming dense mats to replace grass and can be walked over without harm, and are soft

and fragrant underfoot. Leaves can be used in seasoning and in pot-pourri. *Zone 3.*   p. 317, 536

villosus (S.W. Spain to Portugal), "Hairy thyme"; small bushy perennial to 25 cm high, with narrow ovate leaves, crenate at margins and pubescent with white hairs; inflorescence in clusters of deep pink flowers, in July-August. The aromatic foliage makes this a good potherb, at hand for culinary seasoning. *Zones 6-9.*   p. 536

vulgaris (serpyllum var. vulgaris) (Portugal to So. France, So. Italy, Greece), the "Common thyme"; aromatic subshrub 20-30 cm high, lemon-scented; white-pubescent stems with small oval, recurved leaves 1 cm long; tiny 6 mm rosy-lilac flowers in May-June. Used as seasoning for soups, chowders, sauces, vegetables, meat, and fish. *Zones 5-10.*   p. 535

vulgaris 'Argenteus' (W. Mediterr. to Italy), "Silver thyme"; excellent rockgarden plant having foliage variegated with silver, and being both very ornamental and having lemon-scented aroma; an ideal potherb. *Zones 5-10.*   p. 536

THYSANOTUS   *Liliaceae*
tuberosus (Australia except Tasmania), "Fringed lily" or "Fringed violet"; beautiful tuberous-rooted perennial, with grass-like basal leaves to 30 cm long, and erect slender stems to 60 cm high, bearing clusters of interesting purple flowers 2 cm dia., during Summer; the 3 outer petals are narrow, the 3 inner petals are broader and conspicuously fringed, becoming twisted as they fade. *Zone 10.*   p. 248

TIARELLA   *Saxifragaceae*
cordifolia (Nova Scotia, so. to Appalachian Mts. to Carolina and Alabama), "Foamflower"; attractive herbaceous downy perennial with broad ovate-cordate leaves to 10 cm wide, with pointed lobes or toothed along margins; hairy floral stalks to 30 cm high, bearing starry white or reddish flowers 1 cm across, in terminal racemes, in April-June; slender spreading stolons from rootstock will form after blooming. *Zone 3.*   p. 501

trifoliata (Alaska to Oregon, east to Rocky Mts.), "False miterwort"; rhizomatous herbaceous perennial, having leaves of 3 rhombic, lobed leaflets, coarsely toothed; floral stalk 15-50 cm high, bearing minute white flowers with threadlike petals, in dense, elongate clusters, blooming late Spring or Summer, after snow. *Zone 3.*   p. 500

wherryi (Virginia to Georgia and Miss.), "False miterwort"; attractive perennial herb 35 cm high, with stolon-less compact rootstock, and basal leaves 8 cm wide, deeply 3 to 5 lobed; very floriferous starry, fragrant flowers white or tinged rose, 1 cm across, with orange anthers, dense in slender racemes, blooming in May-June. *Zone 7.*   p. 501

TIBOUCHINA   *Melastomataceae*
semidecandra: see T. urvilleana
urvilleana (semidecandra) (So. Brazil), "Glory bush"; free-branching, tree-like shrub growing to 8 m high, with 4-angled stems and fresh green, 10 cm ovate leaves densely covered with soft white hairs; large violet-purple flowers 6 cm or more across, blooming over a long period of time. *Zones 10-11.*   p. 787

TIGRIDIA   *Iridaceae*
bicolor (So. Mexico: Oaxaca), "Mexican shell flower"; lovely small bulbous plant, with narrow ribbed leaves, and wiry stalk bearing flowers with white cups having purple apex folded back, the outer lobes flaring, white with purple base. *Zone 10.*   p. 231

pavonia (Mexico, Guatemala), "Tiger flower"; gay summer-blooming bulbs; erect stems with leaflike spathes bearing large brilliantly colored cup-like flowers spotted with yellow and purple in the center, 8 to 15 cm across, the spreading segments red or yellow, lasting only a day but succeeded by others. *Zones 9-10.*   p. 231

TILIA   *Tiliaceae*
americana (Québec, Montana, so. to Virginia to Texas), "American linden" or "Basswood"; great tree to 40 m high, from woodlands of E. No. America, with deeply furrowed bark and rather symmetrical in outline; smooth shoots with coarse leaves 10-20 cm long, roundish ovate, usually cordate at base and sharply toothed, dark dull green above, tufts of down in vein axils beneath; small fragrant yellowish, feathery flowers, subtended by stalked bracts in pendulous clusters in July. Good honey tree, but its coarse appearance and early browning of foliage does not recommend it as very ornamental. *Zone 2.* p. 895

cordata (Europe), "Little leaf linden" or "Winter lime"; very decorative tree 15 to 30 m high, of pyramidal outline, the branches dense with small leaves nearly orbicular, 3-7 cm long, toothed along margins, cordate at base and pointed at apex; brown-felted tufts at vein axils beneath; fragrant flowers in pendant clusters, subtended by bracts 3-8 cm long, in June-July; a good honey tree, widely used for street planting. *Zone 3.*   p. 895

dasystyla (multiflora) (S.E. Europe to Caucasus and W. Asia, Iran); tall tree to 30 m high; the crown broad cone-shaped, on straight trunk; young shoots smooth and red; leaves of firm texture, broad-ovate pointed, and oblique ovate, sharply serrate with bristly teeth, 8-14 cm long, glossy above, white hairy tufts in vein axils beneath; flowers without staminodes, in pendant clusters; globose 1 cm fruit lightly 5-ribbed. *Zone 6.* p. 895

x euchlora (cordata x dasystyla), "Crimean linden"; deciduous tree to 20 m with smooth bark; glossy rounded ovate leaves 10 cm long, serrate at margins; inflorescence in pendant clusters of yellowish flowers, principally stamens, and partially attached linear bract. *Zone 4.* p. 895

x europaea (cordata x platyphyllos), "European linden" or "Common lime"; beautiful tree to 40 m high, cultivated for ages in Europe; the bark of young trees is smooth and gray, the bark of older trunks is thick and deeply furrowed; smooth shoots, with obliquely cordate, ovate leaves 6-10 cm long, dull dark green above and with axillary tufts beneath, short-pointed and sharply serrate at margins; sweetly fragrant, yellowish-white flowers in pendant clusters, displaying prominent staminodes or sterile stamens; the narrow leaf-like floral bracts 6-10 cm long. Delicious tea is prepared from blossoms, an old household remedy for quieting coughs and relieving colds; also promoting respiration; the soft white wood is used for furniture and wooden-ware, easy to work for woodcarvers. *Zone 3.* p. 531, 895

japonica (Japan: Mts. of Honshu, Kyushu), "Japanese linden"; shapely tree to 20 m high, similar to T. cordata but shorter; leaves roundish-ovate 5-8 cm long, with cordate base, bluish and with axil tufts of hair beneath; floral clusters of 4-40 staminate flowers in July; thin-shelled ellipsoid nut-like fruit capsules containing 2-3 seeds. *Zone 6.* p. 895

x moltkei (spectabilis) (americana x petiolaris) (Spaeth-Berlin 1880); robust hybrid "Linden", with loose crown, the branches more or less pendulous; the leaves similar to americana, roundish ovate 10-20 cm long, grayish downy beneath, but without axillary tufts; flowers in downy-stalked clusters; sub-globose ribbed fruit. *Zone 5.* p.894

mongolica (Mongolia and No. China), "Mongolian linden"; small tree to 10 m high of elegant habit, with reddish branches, dense with small deciduous leaves 3 to 5 cm long, broad ovate, often trilobed, with slender tip, the margins coarsely toothed, lustrous green above; glaucescent and having conspicuous vein-axil tufts beneath; clusters of small flowers subtended by 3-4 cm narrow bracts; obovoid downy thick-skinned fruit. *Zone 4.* p.894

petiolaris (tomentosa) (S.E. Europa, W. Asia), "Weeping silver-linden"; round-headed graceful tree to 25 m high, the branches pendulous, tomentose when young; leaves rounded ovate to 10 cm long and obliquely cordate, regularly toothed at margins, lightly pubescent above, white-tomentose beneath; floral clusters of 3-10 whitish, fragrant flowers, blooming July-August; brownish tomentose floral bracts 5-8 cm long; fruit warty with 5 grooves. *Zone 6.* p.894

platyphyllos (Europe), "Big-leaf lime" or "Summer-linden"; superb ornamental tree 30 to 40 m high, having rough bark; the shoots downy, with large roundish ovate leaves, 5-12 cm long and wide, obliquely cordate at base, sharply toothed, and densely downy beneath, especially on veins; flowers yellowish-white 3 to 4 or 6 in pendant clusters, the floral bracts to 12 cm long; pear-shaped or globose 5-angled fruits. Differs from vulgaris and cordate by its downy shoots and leaves. *Zone 3.* p. 613, 622, 894

tomentosa (S.E. Europe, W. Asia), "Silver linden" or "Hungarian silverlinden"; of all the lindens, the most beautiful, with its two-colored leaves green above and silvery white on underside; the blades roundish-cordate, 5-10 cm long and wide, short-pointed and toothed and white-felted beneath; flowers dull white in pendant clusters in July-August; the white fruit 5-angled. The tree is majestic 20-30 m high, broadly pyramidal and having erect branches; trunk is covered by rough bark. Ideal under Southern California conditions. *Zone 5.* p.894

x vulgaris (Zander): see T. x europaea (Hortus)

TILLANDSIA *Bromeliaceae*

aeranthos (syn. dianthoidea) (Uruguay, Argentina, Brazil); branching, caulescent plant to 22 cm with broad but quickly tapering narrow, concave leaves, grayish-green with purplish tinting and silvery scurf; inflorescence spike with 5-20 blue flowers and bracts purplish-rose. *Zone 10.* p. 48

caput-medusae (Mexico to Costa Rica); attractive small rosette with bulb-like base; thick channeled, tapering and twisting leaves glistening with silky-gray hairs; short panicles with pale blue flowers. *Tropical. Zone 11.* p. 50

crispa (Panama, Colombia, Ecuador, Perú); miniature epiphyte 10-25 cm high, with ovoid bulbous base, having brown-scurfy narrow leaves, with undulate margins, green with maroon spots; slender stalk bearing spiked inflorescence with scurfy, red floral bracts and purplish flowers, *Tropical. Zone 11.* p. 49

crocata (So. Brazil, Bolivia, Uruguay, Argentina); small xerophyte growing on rocks, forming stems 20 cm long, with gray-scaly 15 cm leaves in 2 ranks, semi-cylindric and channeled on top; the floral stalk with small green spike and 3-4 yellow flowers. *Zone 11.* p. 50

cyanea (morreniana) (Ecuador: Manabi to Loja Prov.), "Pink quill"; excellent, suckering rosette of linear, channeled leaves with red-brown lines; short spike with broad flattened, clear pink bracts and large violet-blue flowers. *Tropical. Zone 12* p. 50

dyeriana (Ecuador); tropical epiphytic rosette with leaves 4-5 cm wide and 15-20 cm long, green with brown spots, gray-scaly beneath; showy inflorescence pendant to 20 cm long; bracts bright red, arranged pinnately along axis; flowers white and very fragrant. *Zone 12.* p. 49

fasciculata (Florida, W. Indies, C. America), "Wild pine"; epiphytic dense rosette with recurving, hard linear-lanceolate, concave leaves, gray and variably from 25 cm to 1 m long; branched inflorescence with greenish, creamy-yellow or brilliant red bracts, and violet-blue flowers. *Subtropic. Zone 10.* p. 49

flabellata (Guatemala) "Red fan"; beautiful rosette of narrow, recurved leaves fresh green turning red in good light; giving rise to a 60 cm inflorescence branching into flattened spikes arranged fan-like, the bracts vivid red, flowers blue. *Tropical. Zone .* p. 49

flexuosa (aloifolia) (So. Florida to So. America), "Spiralled air plant"; hard rosette with leaves starting off at the base with a twist, broad but tapering, thick leathery, concave, silvery gray over green, with indistinct silver bands outside; 2-ranked inflorescence with rose bracts and white flowers. *Subtropic. Zone 10.* p. 50

imperialis (Mexico: Oaxaca, Puebla, Veracruz), "Christmas candle"; showy epiphyte at home at 1500-2600 m altitude, and largely used by Mexicans at Christmas time to decorate for their "Natividad", because of the festive spirit radiated by the flaming red central inflorescence, looking like a candle or slender cone; remaining in brilliant color through Summer into Winter; flowers purple; the dense, formal rosette of broad, smooth leathery leaves a pleasing light green, about 45 cm long. *Tropical. Zone 11.* p. 49

ionantha (erubescens) (So. Mexico to Nicaragua), "Sky plant"; tufting, miniature rosette only 5-10 cm high with numerous closely overlapping leaves recurving, thick-fleshy, channeled, fresh green but covered on outside with silvery bristles; sessile inflorescence with violet flowers. *Subtropic. Zone 10.* p. 50

leiboldiana (So. Mexico, Guatemala, Costa Rica); epiphytic rosette of lightly arching, green, thin, straplike leaves 15-45 cm long, 2½ cm wide and tapering to a sudden point, lightly scurfy and soft-leathery; inflorescence loosely compound, with large red primary bracts, and narrow, sessile spikes with tubular violet flowers. *Tropical. Zone 11.* p. 49

lindenii (N.W. Perú), "Blue-flowered torch"; attractive, formal rosette of recurved linear channeled leaves 30-40 cm long, green with red-brown pencil lines becoming more prominent toward base; inflorescence a long spike of flattened carmine-rose bracts 10-15 cm long, with large royal-blue flowers distinguished by white eye in center. *Tropical. Zone 12* p. 50

streptophylla (Jamaica), "Twist plant"; dense basal rosette of sharply recurved leathery leaves gradually tapering to a coiling tip; gray-green thickly covered with silvery scurf, turning red-purple in strong light; branched inflorescence with rosy bracts and lilac flowers. *Tropical. Zone 11.* p. 49

usneoides (S.E. United States to Argentina and Chile), "Spanish moss"; growing from trees as silvery gray threadlike masses to 6 m long, densely covered by the gray scales which are a means of receiving and holding atmospheric moisture, and which helps to enable the plant to dispense with roots; small axillary flowers with petals 1 cm long, in changing colors yellowish-green to blue. *Subtropic. Zone 9.* p. 50

utriculata (Florida, W. Indies), "Big wild pine"; rosette of spreading linear leaves 60 cm long, gradually tapering from an ovate base, and recurved top; compound spike with two-ranked green bracts edged red, and erect flowers with greenish-white petals; plant dies after flowering without off-setting. *Subtropic. Zone 10.* p. 49

TIPUANA *Leguminosae*

tipu (So. Brazil, Bolivia, Argentina), "Rosewood" or "Pride of Bolivia"; semi-deciduous, wide-crowned tree to 30 m high; the light green, odd-pinnate fern-like leaves with 6-11 pairs of oval leaflets 3-4 cm long; profuse sprays of golden-yellow or apricot-colored pea-flowers, in profusion during Summer like tiny butterflies; winged pods 6 cm long. A source of rosewood timber. *Zone 10.* p. 770

TITANOTRICHUM *Gesneriaceae*

oldhamii (Taiwan, So. China); erect perennial herb to 1 m high, with fleshy rhizome; rough green, white-hairy toothed, ovate leaves decreasing in size up the elongate stem to the nodding, swollen tubular hairy golden flowers, bold brown-red inside on spreading lobes; scale-like reproductive bodies often replace flowers toward the apex of the inflorescence. *Humid-subtropic. Zone 11.* p. 66

TITHONIA   *Compositae*

diversifolia (Mexico and C. America, but naturalized in Hawaii and Sumatra), "Tree marigold"; clump-forming perennial or shrub to 3 m high, with thin 3-5-lobed leaves, hairy beneath; showy flower heads with broad, orange-yellow ray-florets 6-8 cm dia. on long stalks. *Subtropic.* Zones 9-10.   *p. 402*

rotundifolia (speciosa) (Mexico, Cent. America), "Mexican sunflower"; shrubby annual forming bushes 1 to 3 m high, with ovate crenate leaves 15 cm long, sometimes 3-lobed; on hairy stout blackish stalks, the inflorescence sunflower-like, 8 cm across, a disc ringed by oval florets vivid orange-scarlet, orange beneath; in Autumn. *Tropical.* Zone 10.   *p. 402*

TMESIPTERIS   *Psilotaceae*

tannensis (New Zealand); a primitive plant, in habitat common in forests from sea-level to 950 m usually epiphytic and pendulous on the trunk of tree ferns, occasionally on rocks; rhizomes deep in the mass of fibrous aerial rootlets along the trunks of tree fern, with some as dull green aerial leafy shoots 15 cm or more long, producing sporophylls, or spore-bearing leaves. Zones 10-11   *p. 142*

TOFIELDIA   *Liliaceae*

glutinosa (syn. Triantha) (Eastern No. America to Brit. Columbia, so. to Georgia), "False asphodel"; herbaceous rhizomatous perennial, forming tufts, to 50 cm high; grass-like leaves, at base to 20 cm long, the stem-leaves much shorter; white flowers tinted pink, in dense, showy racemes, on stalks rising from rhizome, and covered with glutinous, sticky glands; June to August blooming. Zones 2-8. *p. 451*

TOLMIEA   *Saxifragaceae*

menziesii (Alaska to California Coast), "Piggy-back plant"; pubescent perennial herb with soft, fresh-green, lobed and toothed ovate leaves to 10 cm across, covered by scattered white bristles, carried in a basal rosette; grown in pots as a curiosity, as it produces young plantlets out of the base of mature leaves, which can be cut off and rooted; small greenish nodding flowers, lined with maroon, in long erect, slender raceme. Zones 7-9.   *p. 205, 500*

TOLPIS   *Compositae*

barbata (Crepis) (So. Europe); annual herb of the Mediterran. region, with lanceolate, toothed leaves containing milky juice; floral heads 3 cm across, with outer ray-flowers light yellow, inner florets red-brown with yellow tips; subtended by awl-shaped bracts; blooming Mid-summer to frost. Zone 9.   *p. 403*

TOONA (Zander): see CEDRELA (Hortus 3)

TORENIA   *Scrophulariaceae*

fournieri (Vietnam), "Wishbone plant"; delicate, small, herbaceous annual to 30 cm high, with ovate, fresh-green, serrate leaves 5 cm long, and scattered, bilabiate, attractive, pale violet flowers lower lip having 3 lobes of velvety deep violet and a yellow blotch in the middle of the lower lobe, blooming almost continuously. *Tropical.* Zone 11.   *p. 508*

TORREYA   *Taxaceae (Coniferae)*

californica (No. California), "California nutmeg"; evergreen tree from the Western slopes of the Sierra Nevada, of pyramidal growth, in maturity rounded, to 20 m high; the smooth shoots are green at first, later brown; stiff leathery and straight needles 4-8 cm long, dark green above, and two bands of glaucous stomata beneath, the apex a sharp spine; seed enclosed in a fleshy plum, green and streaked purple. The leaves have strong aroma when crushed. Deciduous in cold climate. Zone 7.   *p. 609*

nucifera (Japan), "Japanese torreya"; slow-growing evergreen similar to Taxus, to 20 m or more high, but usually as smaller trees, having strong horizontal branches, the young shoots green changing to reddish-brown; small glossy winter buds; aromatic leaves radially arranged, curved, stiff needle-like and 2-3 cm long, dark glossy green above, but beneath with 2 glaucous grooves; the seeds in their fleshy green covering containing oil, are eaten in Japan. Zone 7.   *p. 609*

taxifolia (Florida), "Stinking cedar"; handsome evergreen, bushy when young, growing into a tree to 15 m high; having horizontal or pendant branches in whorls; the yellow-green branchlets with long linear needles glossy dark green, 2-4 cm long, arranged in 2 ranks, but having a disagreeable odor when crushed; the ovoid fleshy fruits are purple, 3 cm long, and borne on female trees. Zone 8.   *p. 609*

TOUMEYA (Zander) see: TURBINICARPUS

TOWNSENDIA   *Compositae*

parryi (Alberta to Idaho and Wyoming); showy tap-rooted biennial, or short-lived perennial, with stalk-like stems, to 30 cm high; obovate basal 10 cm leaves in a rosette, the floral heads 7 cm across, with linear ray-flowers pale blue to violet, ranged around broad orange disc. Zone 3.   *p. 403*

TOXICODENDRON radicans (Zander):
see RHUS radicans (Hortus)

TRACHELIUM   *Campanulaceae*

caeruleum (W. and C. Mediterranean, Europe), "Throatwort"; perennial herb ½-1 m high, with ovate double-toothed, thin leaves 8 cm long; flowers very numerous, in clustered panicles, with slender tubular corolla 2 cm long, violet-blue, the styles protruding. Zone 8.   *p. 356*

TRACHELOSPERMUM   *Apocynaceae*

jasminoides (Rhynchospermum) (So. China, Himalayas), the "Star jasmine" or "Confederate jasmine" of the South; small woody evergreen with wiry stems and milky sap, slowly climbing and twining, with 5-8 cm leathery leaves; small white, star-like 2 cm flowers with wavy lobes. A pretty, free-blooming jasmine for pots and intensely fragrant; can be kept bushy by trimming. *Subtropic.* Zones 9-10.   *p. 265*

lucidum (fragrans hort.) (N.E. India and Nepal); tall evergreen climber, with leathery dark green, obovate elliptic leaves to 12 cm long; very floriferous with clusters of starry white to creamy flowers soft-hairy in throat, the narrow-linear corolla segments spreading 3 cm wide during Summer, and scenting the garden with jasmine fragrance. Zones 9-10.   *p. 265*

TRACHYCARPUS   *Palmae*

fortunei (Chamaerops excelsa hort.) (China, Japan), "Windmill palm"; somewhat hardy, with solitary, shaggy trunk 3-12 m high, covered with a mat of long, dark brown fibers, topped by dense crown of tough fan-shaped dark green leaves 50 to 75 cm across, divided into stiffish, folded segments nearly to base, glaucous beneath, the petioles spineless or lightly toothed; fruit lustrous blue. *Subtropic.* Zones 8-9.   *p. 77, 107, 111, 123*

takil (wagnerianus) (Western Himalayas), "Takil palm"; handsome fan palm of compact habit and slow growth, with short robust trunk clothed with a mat of furry brownish fiber; the stiffly rigid, deeply plaited palmate leaves average 40 cm across, rough dull green on horizontal unarmed petioles; very decorative in small plantings or containers. Trees at Los Angeles Arboretum in Arcadia are about 6 m high, shorter than T. fortunei. *Subtropic.* Zones 9-10.   *p. 111*

TRADESCANTIA   *Commelinaceae*

x andersoniana (virginiana of gardens), "Showy spiderwort"; complex garden hybrid with erect stems 50-75 cm high, with glossy green, long-linear fleshy leaves 15-40 cm long and deflexed; large and showy flowers 4-5 cm across, of 3 sepals, and 3 petals purplish-rose and having undulate margins. Zone 5.   *p. 368*

dracaenoides: see CALLISIA fragrans

fluminensis 'Variegata' (Argentina, Brazil), "Wandering Jew"; lively little creeper rooting at nodes, generally smaller and weaker than albiflora, with shining ovate leaves 4 cm long, fresh green and striped and banded yellow and cream; flowers white. *Tropical.* Zone 11.   *p. 52, 308*

fuscata: see SIDERASIS fuscata

multiflora hort.: see GIBASIS schiedeana

rosea: see CUTHBERTIA rosea

sillamontana (villosa) (N.E. Mexico), "White velvet creeper"; introduced by the trade as Tradescantia 'White Velvet' and 'White Gossamer'; fleshy trailer with clasping ovate leaves in ranks, deep green with parallel veins but entirely covered with fluffy white wool, underside and stems purplish; tripetaled flowers rich orchid colored; erroneously listed as Cyanotis veldthoutiana. *Subtropic.* Zone 11.   *p. 52*

virginiana (Eastern U.S.: Connecticut to South Dakota and Georgia), "Widow's-tears" or "Spiderwort"; creeping perennial succulent herb with linear-lanceolate leaves 10 to 25 cm long, and showy regular flowers having 3 equal, violet-purple or violet petals, 2-3 cm across. *Temperate.* Zone 5.   *p. 308*

TRAGOPOGON   *Compositae*

dubius (Europe, Asia), "Goatsbeard"; clustering perennial up to 1½ m high, the stems with straight, clasping linear leaves, somewhat glaucous; flower heads lemon-yellow, followed by white, feathery globes carrying the seeds on top of hollow stalks. Zone 5.   *p. 403*

porrifolius (S.E. Europe; natural. in No. America), "Salsify" or "Oyster plant"; glaucous tap-rooted biennial or perennial to 1 m high, linear-lanceolate leaves, tapered to slender point, the sheaths inflated; flower head rose or red-purple with flaring rays 10 cm wide, opening in the morning and closing at noon. The long roots are edible and taste like oysters, and are widely cultivated. Zone 7.   *p. 403*

TREVESIA   *Araliaceae*

palmata 'Micholitzii' (Yunnan, China), "Snowflake plant"; small evergreen tree with puckered leaves, 40 cm across or more, palmately lobed, the segments irregularly pinnate, thin-leathery, glossy green and covered with silvery dots, which earned it the name "Snowflake plant"; the petioles are spiny. Dr. David Frodin suggests that this may be T. burckii. Zone 10.   *p. 651*

TRICALYSIA *Rubiaceae*

dubia (Canthium, Diplospora) (Taiwan), "Mountain coffee"; handsome evergreen ornamental tree, with stiff, brown branches, long elliptic leathery leaves, and axillary stalked cherry-like scarlet fruit resembling coffee. *Zone 10.*   *p. 859*

TRICHANTHA minor (Dr. H. Wiehler, Selby Bot. G.): see COLUMNEA minor (F. Batcheller)

TRICHOCENTRUM *Orchidaceae*

tigrinum (Costa Rica, Ecuador); desirable dwarf epiphyte with shining green 10-15 cm leaves on very small pseudobulbs; large flowers 5 cm across, sweet-scented and waxy, with sepals and petals tawny yellow and blotched with brown, the large lip white with two large purple spots near base (May-June). *Humid-subtropic.* *Zones 11-12.*   *p. 96*

TRICHOCEREUS *Cactaceae*

chilensis (Chile: Atacama Prov.); olive-green columnar plant growing into a branched tree to 8 m high, 9 fat ribs when young, later 10-15 and divided into tubercles; set with strong black-gray spines, apex clothed with white-wooly areoles; flowers white, red outside. T. chiloensis in Hortus. *Zone 10.*   *p. 622*

huascha rubriflorus (Helianthocereus Backeberg) (Argentina: Catamarca); fresh green cylindrical stems 6 cm thick, branching from base, to 1¹/₂ m high, 12 to 18 low ribs, the gray areoles with short white radials and long needle spine; flowers 7 cm across; yellow in the species, red in var. rubriflorus. *Zone 10.*   *p. 177*

peruvianus (C. Perú: Matucana), "Peruvian torch-cactus"; branching with stout columns of 20 cm dia. and to 4 m tall, and 8-10 cm thick, dull green, glaucous when young, 6-8 broad and rounded notched ribs, brown spines; large white flowers to 25 cm long. *Tropical. Zone 10.*   *p. 178*

spachianus (W. Argentina), the beautiful "Torch cactus"; short slender columns to 2 m high, close-ribbed, 6 cm thick, clustering, short brown spines; nocturnal flowers white, 20 cm long, blooming into late morning. Widely used as understock for grafting, although T. pachanoi may be preferable. *Subtropic. Zone 10.*   *p. 177*

TRICHOPILIA *Orchidaceae*

suavis (Costa Rica); beautiful small epiphyte with thin pseudobulb and solitary broad leaves; producing clusters of relatively large flowers delicately hawthorn-scented, creamy-white, with large frilled lip, yellow in throat and spotted purplish-rose (Dec.-May, Oct.) *Tropical. Zone 11.*   *p. 96*

TRICHOSANTHES *Cucurbitaceae*

cucumeroides (Japan, Taiwan, China), "Snake-gourd"; herbaceous vine with thick, tuberous root, climbing by tendrils 4 to 5 m; leaves palmately lobed and lightly crenate, finely pubescent beneath; white flowers; the fleshy long-ovoid fruit light gray, with deep green markings turning red. Dried fruit is used as soap substitute. *Subtropic. Zones 9-10.*   *p. 276*

TRICYRTIS *Liliaceae*

hirta (Japan: Kyushu), "Hairy toad lily"; rhizomatous herb to 1 m, hairy all over; leafy stems with ovate foliage, 15 cm long; flowers in clusters, white and spotted purple inside, to 3 cm long. *Zones 5-8.*   *p. 452*

macranthopsis (Mountains of Honshu, Japan), "Toad lily"; attractive perennial with short creeping rhizome; reclining stems 40-80 cm long, with alternate, lanceolate, lustrous leaves 8-18 cm long, and having two basal ears; charming pendulous yellow bell-flowers, 3 to 4 cm long, axillary or terminal, having purplish dots inside, and spurred at base, in August to October. *Zone 5.*   *p. 452*

TRIFOLIUM *Leguminosae*

incarnatum (So. Europe, France to Italy and Hungary, Balkans), "Crimson clover" or "Italian clover"; beautiful annual with slender, hairy stems to 90 cm high; trifoliolate with 3 obcordate leaflets 3-4 cm long; showy ovoid, terminal floral heads bright crimson, 6 cm long, in June-July. *Zone 8.*   *p. 442*

pratense (Europe to C. Asia, natural. in No. America), "Red clover"; widely distributed biennial or short-lived perennial of straggly habit, to 60 cm high; the branches with trifoliolate leaves, having 3 ovate leaflets to 6 cm long, each with silvery white marking across the middle; the deep rose and white globular 3 cm flower heads are bristly with the calyx hairs extending through the corollas; blooming throughout the Summer. Used in agriculture as forage and for crop rotation. *Zone 3.*   *p. 442*

procumbens (dubium, minus) (native in Ireland and elsewhere in Europe; naturalized in No. America), the "Yellow clover", and widely grown as "Irish Shamrock"; popular trefoil with branching creeping stems 15-45 cm long and hued brown; the 3 small leaflets matte satiny green, obovate and obcordate 1 cm long, the terminal one attached by individual stalklets to the petiole, the petioles and stipules being

hairy, unlike in repens which is not hairy and has leaflets rounded at summit; procumbens has canary-yellow or greenish-yellow small flowers 1 cm long, in loose heads, while repens has corolla white or tinged with pink. *Temperate. Zone 6.*   *p. 442*

repens (Europe, widely naturalized in No. America), "White clover" or "Shamrock"; branching perennial herb with creeping stems to 30 cm; digitate leaves of 3 obovate or lightly obcordate leaflets, and small white, fragrant flowers in dense globular heads of 2 cm dia. Planted as forage crop in agriculture. *Zone 3.*   *p. 442*

TRILISA *Compositae*

paniculata (Virginia to Florida), "Carolina vanilla" or "Vanilla plant"; herbaceous perennial with fibrous roots, from 20 cm to more than 1 m tall; the thick basal leaves 6-30 cm long; stems sticky and bristly, bearing large, branched inflorescence with rose-purple flowers, in Autumn. *Zone 7.*   *p. 353*

TRILLIUM *Liliaceae*

cernuum (E. Canada to Wisconsin, Penna. and Georgia), "Nodding trillium"; attractive perennial 15-40 cm high, with pale green rhombic-ovate leaves to 10 cm long, the surface with recessed veins; the small fragrant, nodding 3 cm flowers pinkish or white, blooming in June; the fruit is a deep purple berry. *Zones 3-8.*   *p. 453*

chloropetalum (Washington, Oregon, to Cent. California), "Wake-robin"; spring-flowering woodland perennial with thick, erect rhizome, and stem 30-60 cm high; the whorled leaves rhombic ovate 15 cm long, usually mottled; showy, sweet-scented flowers from center, 10 cm long, the 3 petals greenish-yellow or white, occasionally maroon-red, subtended by 3 green sepals, blooming in May. *Zones 4-8.*   *p. 453*

decumbens (S.E. United States), "Birth-root"; attractive woodland perennial, with short reclining stem, spreading the foliage flat on the ground; often forming mats; the broad ovate leaves are 15 cm long, deep bluish-green, patterned with silvery gray, irregular patches; the flowers have brownish-crimson petals to 5 cm long, blooming March-April in mild climate. *Zones 6-9.*   *p. 453*

erectum (Nova Scotia to Manitoba and Tennessee); an attractive perennial herb of the woods, known as "Stinking Benjamin" or "Squaw-root"; short thick rootstock; solitary stem 30 cm high bearing at top 3 broad ovate, whorled, clasping leaves, topped by a flower of 3 large ovate petals 2¹/₂ cm long, usually deep maroon-red or greenish-purple, longer than the slender-pointed outer sepals; with unpleasant odor; hardy. *Zones 3-8.*   *p. 453*

erectum albiflorum (E. Canada to No. Carolina), "Squawroot"; small color variant, seen in col. Royal Botanic Gardens Kew, England, having flowers white, in midst of the whorl of 3 broad, near triangular leaves, blooming in May; followed by 6-angled dark red fruit. *Zones 3-8.*   *p. 452*

grandiflorum (E. No. America: Québec to Minnesota), the white "Wake-robin"; perennial with solitary stem 30-45 cm high, bearing a whorl of 3 rhombic-ovate leaves, topped by a large petaloid flower pure white, fading to rosy-pink, the 3 corrugated petals to 8 cm long; April-June blooming. *Zones 3-8.*   *p. 453*

grandiflorum flore pleno, "Double wake-robin"; seen in col. Royal Botanic Gardens Kew; an unusual form having the white flowers graced with an extra, inner ring of florets, somewhat resembling gardenias. *Zones 6-8.*   *p. 453*

ovatum (Brit. Columbia to Cent. California), "Coast trillium"; perennial of the Pacific Coast region, to 50 cm high; with 3 rhombic-ovate leaves in a whorl, each to 15 cm long, topping the stem; white flowers 5 cm wide, fading to rose, on 6 cm stalklets. *Zone 8.*   *p. 453*

sessile (New York to Missouri and Mississippi), "Toadshade"; most handsome perennial of shady woods, to 30 cm or more high, with 3 broad-ovate, leathery leaves 8 cm long, wonderfully patterned bluish-green with silver gray, and arranged in a whorl; in the center the brown-purple or maroon wide-spreading flowers, sometimes yellow-green; blooming in Spring, and scented. *Zone 6.*   *p. 453*

undulatum (Québec to So. Carolina and Georgia), "Painted trillium"; beautiful spring-blooming perennial 30 to 50 cm high, with tall reddish stems, and dark green, petioled lanceolate leaves with wavy margins, 15 cm long and set in a whorl; from its center rise the showy flowers, having 3 green sepals, margined red, and 3 crimped petals, white and striped purple at base, 3 cm long; followed by berry-like red fruit. *Zones 3-8.*   *p. 452*

viride (Illinois to Oklahoma and Arkansas), "Woods trillium"; stout perennial to 40 cm high, with fine pubescence on upper part; ovate-pointed leaves to 15 cm long, mottled with silver gray; flowers greenish or yellowish, purplish at the base, 5 cm long. *Zones 3-7.*   *p. 453*

viride luteum (sessile var.) (Mts. of Kentucky to Florida), "Yellow wood trillium"; a form with smooth stems and leaves, 20 cm or more high; the foliage with silver pattern over glaucous green; flowers yellow, faintly scented. *Zones 6-9.*   *p. 453*

TRIMEZA   *Iridaceae*

caribaea (Neomarica longifolia hort.) (Brazil), "Fan iris"; rhizomatous perennial herb to 1 m high with flat, bluish-green sword-shaped leaves; stiff-wiry stalks carry the smallish 5 cm fleeting flowers with ochre-yellow spreading segments, the inner, spoon-like petals spotted brown. *Subtropic. Zone 10.*   p. 231

TRIOLENA   *Melastomataceae*

pustulata (Bertolonia pubescens hort.) (Ecuador); small branching plant; nettle-like, pointed, corrugated leaves with white bristles, emerald green with purplish-brown band down center. In habitat in the humid cloud forests of the Andes. *Zones 11-12.*   p. 459

TRIOSTEUM   *Caprifoliaceae*

perfoliatum (Mass. to Kentucky and Kansas), "Wild coffee" or "Feverroot"; perennial plant to 1 m or more high, with opposite sessile, entire leaves, ovate in outline, to 25 cm long, and corrugated above; purplish flowers 2 cm long, followed by leathery, orange-yellow berry-like fruit, similar to coffee-beans. *Zone 6.*   p. 358

pinnatifidum (Japan, N.W. China), "Tinker's weed"; herbaceous perennial with erect branches to 60 cm or more high, the opposite bristly-hairy, rugose leaves deeply lobed; flowers inside brownish-purple, outside greenish-yellow, in terminal clusters; white berries covered with hair. *Zone 5.*   p. 358

rosthornii (China), "Horse-gentian"; herbaceous perennial, with large opposite sessile leaves of firm texture, lobed margins and corrugated with depressed veins; inflorescence a cluster of small cupped, white flowers. *Zone 7.*   p. 358

TRIPHASIA   *Rutaceae*

trifolia (Malaya?), "Lime-berry"; spiny evergreen ornamental shrub or small tree to 5 m high, with trifoliolate leathery leaves remotely crenate; fragrant white flowers singly in leaf axils, followed by 1½ cm crimson-red berries with edible flesh. *Zones 10-11.* p. 938

TRIPLARIS   *Polygoniaceae*

caracasana (Trop. America: Venezuela and Colombia), "Hormigo" or "Palo Maria"; beautiful tropical flowering tree 6 to 18 m high, with hollow branches inhabited by ants; large elliptic leaves green when mature, but in unfolding are a lovely wine-red; the male and female flowers are on separate trees; the female blossoms cover the tree tops with a mass of crimson-red color, as seen in Venezuela during March; the male blossoms are insignificant. Named Triplaris by Linnaeus because of its 3-parted fruit. *Zone 10.*   p. 821

surinamensis (Guyana, Surinam to Brazil), "Guayabo hormiguero" or "Long John ant tree"; interesting tropical tree to 10 m or even 30 m in Guyana; having hollow branches; the narrow elliptic or ovate leaves of firm texture, to 30 cm long; inflorescence in long pendant spikes with flowers in 2 ranks, the calyx white, and long corolla with spreading segments becoming red when aging. *Zone 11.*   p. 820

TRIPLEUROSPERMUM   *Compositae*

maritimum (Chrysanthemum paludosum hort. or Matricaria maritima) (Europe, natural. in No. America), "Matricary" or "Bridal robe"; short-lived perennial with prostrate branches to 30 cm long; the 8 cm leaves bipinnately cut into linear, fleshy segments; small daisy-like flowers 2-3 cm across, with pure white ray-florets, encircling the golden-yellow center disc. Foliage is strongly scented. *Zone 5.*   p. 403, 524

TRIPTERYGIUM   *Celastraceae*

regelii (Manchuria to Japan and Korea), "Kurozuru"; scandent shrub rambling 2 to 10 m, with deciduous, broad-ovate leaves to 15 cm long, dull green and with veins depressed, crenate at margins, on angled branchlets; small yellowish-white flowers, dense in large pyramidal terminal clusters to 25 cm long; greenish-white fruit 3-angled, each angle with a wing, 2 cm long. May be trained and grown as an upright shrub. *Zone 4.*   p. 684

TRISTANIA   *Myrtaceae*

conferta (Eastern Australia), "Brisbane box" or "Brush box"; stately evergreen tree, in habitat to 40 m or more high, having reddish bark, peeling to show smooth pale cambium beneath; beautiful leathery foliage alternate or whorled, ovate in outline 8-15 cm long; free-blooming with attractive 2 cm white staminal flowers in clusters; followed by woody 3-parted, cup-shaped fruits. Widely planted as a street tree in Sydney and Melbourne. *Zones 9-10.*   p. 804

conferta 'Albomarginata'; very attractive cultivar by Bewley of Warrimoo, New South Wales; with the glossy, vivid green foliage richly variegated and bordered creamy-white, clustered mainly at end of branchlets. *Zone 10.*   p. 804

conferta 'Aureovariegata', "Variegated Brisbane box"; another handsome cultivar with the long glossy leaves mostly variegated golden-yellow in center area, with contrasting rich green retained toward margins; attractive 2 cm creamy-white flowers, blooming in an early stage of young trees. *Zone 10.*   p. 804

TRISTELLATEIA   *Malpighiaceae*

australasiae (Malaysia, Australasia), "Galphimia vine"; climbing shrub with thin-wiry, woody, winding branches, carrying dull green ovate leaves 5-10 cm long; small bright yellow flowers with red stamens in striking racemes. *Tropical. Zone 10.*   p. 283

TRITELEIA   *Amaryllidaceae*

hyacinthina (Brodiaea) (Brit. Columbia to California), "Wild hyacinth"; cormous perennial forming 1 or 2 narrow-linear leaves keeled beneath; slender floral stalks to 40 cm carry clusters of twenty or more small 2 cm flowers in shades of purple or white. *Zones 6-7*   p. 217

laxa (Brodiaea or Ipheion) (California), "Triplet lily" or "Ithuriel's spear"; strong cormous plant 50 cm high, with usually a pair of basal leaves; clusters of funnel-shaped flowers 3 cm long with widespread segments a lovely violet purple with blue anthers. *Zone 7.*   p. 217

TRITHRINAX   *Palmae*

acanthocoma (So. Brazil), "Webbed trithrinax"; fan-palm with solitary trunk to 4 m, 8-10 cm thick, with long spines, and distinctive because of its intricate fibrous web-like covering, formed by leaf bases; palmate leaves to 1 m across, deeply cut into rigid segments which are split at apex, dark grayish-green above, lighter green beneath. *Zone 11.*   p. 111

TRITICUM   *Gramineae*

aestivum (sativum) (of Asiatic origin), "Common wheat" or "Soft wheat" of No. Europe, also grown in U.S. Pacific and Western states, the most important flour grain for bread and cakes, in form of Winter and Spring wheats. Stems erect, freely branching at base, 40-80 cm high, according to cultivar; narrow leaves 40 cm long; erect fruit spikes without or with bristles (awns), somewhat compressed, spikelets with seeds imbricate or somewhat spaced, about 10 cm in length, the grains reddish. *Zone 5.*   p. 567

dicoccon (durum group), "Emmer" or "German wheat"; annual Spring wheat, or biennial as Winter wheat, growing with stiff stems topped by erect spikes bearing ranks of seed grains without noticeable bristles or awns. One of the so-called hard wheats, also known as "Starch wheat" or "Two-grained spelt". Cultivated by the ancient Babylonians, and presently in mountains of Europe on dry soils, for livestock; also as breakfast cereal. *Zone 5.*   p. 567

durum (turgidum) (U.S. Midwest; So. Italy), "Hard wheat" or "Mediterranean wheat"; annual Winter or Spring wheat with solid stems to 1 m high, broad linear, hairy leaves; the fruiting spikes about 10 cm long, holding the short, very starchy, gluten-rich grains, and with long stiff, but brittle awns, or bristles. The ripe seeds are flinty and hard to grind, and the resulting flour is used for noodles, macaroni, pastry, and spaghetti. Primarily grown in arid areas, the Great Plains states of U.S., Russia, Spain and India. *Zone 3.* p. 567

turgidum (Hortus 3): see T. durum (Zander)

TRITOMA: see KNIPHOFIA

TRITONIA   *Iridaceae*

crocata (So. Africa: Natal to Cape), "Flame freesia" or "Kalkoentje"; cormous herb 60 cm high with linear sword-shaped leaves, and wiry stems with expanded bell-shaped flowers tawny-yellow or orange 5 cm wide; somewhat winter-hardy with protection. The cv. 'Incomparabile' has large, silky vivid salmon-rose blooms, in early Summer. *Subtropic. Zones 8-10.*   p. 230

crocata 'Emile McKenzie' (Montbretia); handsome cormous plant of So. African parentage, with narrow leaves fan-like as in freesia, and wiry stalks bearing cup-shaped 4 cm flowers with spreading lobes brilliant orange, painted crimson-red toward base, and arranged around the white central area, blooming in Oct.-Nov. in the Southern hemisphere. *Zones 9-10.*   p. 230

x crocosmiiflora: see CROCOSMIA x crocosmiiflora

pottsii: see CROCOSMIA pottsii (Zander)

rubrolucens (Montbretia rosea) (So. Africa); cormous plant to 60 cm high, with few linear leaves 30 cm long; the inflorescence a branched spike, bearing flowers in two ranks, the floral funnel rose and 5 cm long. *Zone 9.*   p. 230

TROCHODENDRON   *Trochodendraceae*

aralioides (Mountains of Japan, So. Korea, Taiwan), "Wheel tree"; evergreen tree to 20 m; obovate leathery leaves 10 cm or more long, with serrate margins, in clusters at end of branches; small 1 cm green flowers without petals. *Warm temperate. Zone 7.*   p. 893

TROLLIUS   *Ranunculaceae*

asiaticus (Russia, Siberia, Turkestan), "Siberian globeflower"; handsome perennial to 40 cm high, with bronzy green leaves palmately cut into wedge-shaped, deeply lobed or toothed segments; orange-yellow flowers 5 cm across, having 10 spreading sepals and 10 shorter petals, displaying prominent stamens, blooming May-June. *Zone 3.*   p. 491

chinensis (No. China), "Chinese globeflower"; attractive smooth perennial to 80 cm high, with stout, grooved stems; lower leaves kidney-shaped, the upper roundish and 5-parted into broad, toothed segments 8 cm long; flowers on long, 25 cm stalks, with broad incurving golden-yellow sepals 2 cm long, and about 20 narrow linear petals. *Zone 4.* p. 491

x cultorum 'Orange Globe' (europaeus x chinensis and asiaticus); very handsome, bushy hybrid to 90 cm high, with stiff erect stalks and deeply divided leaves; large bowl-shaped orange-yellow flowers blooming May-June. *Zone 5.* p. 491

europaeus (Arctic Europe and Arctic America, Caucasus, W. Siberia), "Globeflower"; popular garden perennial 30-60 cm high, with basal leaves 3-5 lobed, the sessile stemleaves 3 lobed with side lobes deeply cut; the slightly fragrant flowers more or less globular, 3-5 cm across, having 10-15 greenish-yellow sepals and shorter incurved, deeper yellow petals, in June to August. *Zone 4.* p. 491

ledebourii (E. Siberia); perennial globe-flower similar to T. europaeus, but having less foliage, and blooms of only 5 broad sepals; the stems 60-80 cm high, with leaves cleft to base, the segments lobed and toothed; cup-shaped orange-yellow flowers 5-6 cm across, with spreading waxy, veined sepals, and narrow-linear petals, longer than the dark orange stamens, blooming May-July. The photo shown may be a hort. form. *Zone 3.* p. 491

TROPAEOLUM   *Tropaeolaceae*

majus (Perú, Brazil), known as "Nasturtium" or "Indian cress"; quick-growing, pretty, somewhat succulent, glabrous annual herb, climbing by means of coiling petioles to a height of 2-4 m, with waxy peltate leaves, and long-stemmed, fragrant 5-6 cm irregular flowers usually bright orange, sometimes in shades of red, subtended by 5 sepals, of which the upper one is lengthened into a nectar-bearing spur. For culinary use, the flowers and spicy young leaves can be mixed in salads; the unripe seed, when young and green are used for pickling and are an excellent substitute for capers. *Zone 10.* p. 514, 545

majus coccineum, "Red nasturtium"; showy color form seen on the Isle of Rhodes, Greece, with flowers to 6 cm across, brilliant scarlet-red, and golden-yellow in throat; the rather succulent peltate leaves in handsome green contrast. *Zone 10.* p. 514

majus flore pleno, "Double nasturtium"; a favorite form with showy long-spurred, funnel-shaped double flowers 6 cm dia., rich red-orange; leaves are rounded-peltate, 5 cm across, from succulent, twisted stems. Double varieties are propagated from cuttings. *Zone 10.* p. 514

pentaphyllum (E. Bolivia to Brazil, Paraguay, Argentina); handsome climbing perennial from long beaded tubers; the purple stems with long-stalked 5-lobed leaves, and flowers 3 cm long, the petals scarlet tipped green and conical spur red and green, during Summer. *Zone 10.* p. 324

polyphyllum (Chile, Argentina), "Wreath nasturtium"; tuberous-rooted, prostrate or climbing perennial, leafy stems with fleshy divided bluish-gray leaves; yellow flowers streaked with red, and a 2 cm spur. Tubers are edible. *Zone 7.* p. 324

speciosum (Chilean Andes), "Vermillion nasturtium"; climbing perennial to 3 m with fleshy roots; leaves divided into 5-6 leaflets; beautiful flowers to 4 cm long, vivid scarlet-red, yellow at base. *Subtropic. Zones 9.* p. 324

tricolor (Chile), "Tricolored Indian cress"; slender climbing perennial herb with fleshy tubers; leaves circular, of 6 leaflets; curious flowers 2-3 cm long, not wide-mouthed nor spreading limb, but with fiery scarlet spur, purplish calyx lobes or sepals, and bright yellow petals. Very pretty summer-flowering twiner on wire frames, for the sunny cool window. *Subtropic. Zone 8.* p. 324

tuberosum (Andean So. America), "Tuber nasturtium"; high-climbing perennial from large underground tubers; rounded leaves having 5-6 lobes; clusters of attractive flowers 2 cm long, with deep yellow petals and red nectar-bearing spur, in long stalks. Tubers are edible. *Zone 8.* p. 324

TSUGA   *Pinaceae (Coniferae)*

canadensis (E. No. America: Nova Scotia to Alabama), "Hemlock-spruce" or "Canada hemlock"; a very prolific coniferous often branching evergreen tree with slender horizontal branches, to 25 m high, gracefully drooping in age; the flat needles lustrous dark green above, bluish beneath, about 1 cm long mostly arranged in opposite rows on branchlets; small brown pendulous cones. Prefers moisture, sun and wind protection but very tolerant to situations wet or dry, sunny or shade, and may be clipped into dense columns, or hedges. Best grown from seed. The young shoot tips have been used to make tea. *Zone 4.* p. 603, 604, 620

canadensis 'Prostrata', "Cole's prostrate hemlock"; amazing, extremely dwarf clone of the Eastern hemlock, collected by Cole near Mt. Madison, New Hampshire 1929, with branches spreading appressed to ground or rocks; unless trained upward while young, or

grafted to a short standard, with the branches pendant and allowed to take on its natural weeping, spreading out 1 m or more. *Zone 5.* p. 604

caroliniana (Mts. of Virginia to Georgia), "Carolina hemlock"; graceful pyramidal tree to 20 m high; young shoots gray and sparsely hairy; the leaves needle-like, to 2 cm long, dark green and grooved above, and two silvery lines beneath, arranged in two ranks; oblong cones 3-4 cm long, the scales enclosing small winged seed. *Zone 5.* p. 604

heterophylla (mertensiana hort.) (Alaska to California), "Western hemlock"; large decorative pyramidal tree to 60 m or more high, of rapid growth, the largest of the hemlocks; of narrow habit having short pendulous branches; grayish-green, flat leaves 2 cm long, grooved above and finely toothed; small ovoid 2½ cm cones. Will perform best in the Pacific Coast area. Wood is valued for timber and pulp. *Zone 6.* p. 604

mertensiana (Alaska to California), "Mountain hemlock"; large pyramidal tree to 40 m high, densely branched when young; the needles closely arranged around shoot, 2-3 cm long, blue-green and convex on surface, stomata both above and beneath; oblong cones 4-6 cm long, light brown when mature, with scales spreading. *Zone 6.* p. 604

sieboldii (Japan: Mountains of Honshu, Kyushu), "Japanese hemlock"; tall pyramidal evergreen tree to 30 m high in habitat, usually much less in cultivation; short branches spreading horizontally, their young shoots light brown and smooth; with narrow needles glossy green and grooved above and 2 bands of silver stomata beneath, lightly notched at tip, arranged with side leaves longer than those on face, 1-2 cm long; small ovate 2 cm cones. *Zone 6.* p. 597

TULBAGHIA   *Liliaceae*

fragrans (Transvaal), known as "Pink agapanthus"; bulbous-rooted plant with narrow glaucous leaves, and slender stem bearing umbels of 20-40 small tubular, sweet-scented flowers 2 cm long, lavender-purple tinged pink, in late Spring. However, the foliage does not have the garlic odor of T. violacea. *Zone 9.* p. 248

violacea (So. Africa), "Society garlic"; cormous plant with a garlic-like odor; linear channeled, soft-fleshy leaves 30 cm long and 1 cm wide, narrower than T. fragrans; umbels of bright lilac, star-like flowers, the spreading segments with deeper purplish median stripe, 2 cm long, on stems to 60 cm high. Used in salads and soups for its mild garlic aroma. *Zone 9.* p. 248, 538

violacea 'Tricolor', "Tricolor garlic"; handsome cultivar with its fleshy linear leaves variegated lengthwise in green and contrasting cream and bronzy red. *Zone 9.* p. 218

TULIPA   *Liliaceae*

acuminata (W. Asia, Iran), "Turkish tulip"; a garden tulip 25-40 cm high, with flowers of varying colors light yellow to pink, 8-10 cm long, segments all alike, narrowed gradually to a long point. Midseason. *Zones 3-8.* p. 255

batalinii (Bokhara, W. Asia); charming small bulbous plant 15 cm high, with glaucous grass-like linear leaves, and pretty flowers 5 cm long, clear primrose yellow, darker in center; early-blooming. *Zones 3-8.* p. 256

biflora (polychroma hort.) (Ukraine to Crimea, Turkey, Afghanistan), "Two-flower tulip"; interesting small stoloniferous tulip to 20 cm high, with 2-3 linear glaucous leaves 12 cm long; each floral stalk branching to bear usually two, and occasionally more white 4-5 cm flowers, opening flat, with yellow basal coloring and the outer segments tinted crimson, the inner with green median line. *Zones 5-8.* p. 256

chrysantha (Iran), "Golden tulip"; small species to 15 cm high, with recurved, glaucous leaves, and little 3 cm flowers with outer segments pointed, bright yellow, tinted red outside; in April. *Zone 6.* p. 256

clusiana (Portugal to Iraq, Iran, Afghanistan), the "Lady tulip" or "Candystick tulip"; eye-catching species with fragrant solitary flowers, flat star-like when open, white with purple base, the pointed segments 5 cm long, crimson outside; midseason. *Zones 3-10.* p. 256

clusiana var. chrysantha (India, Afghanistan); "Golden lady tulip"; delightful little tulip 15 cm high, blooming in Mid-spring; the starry flowers with inner petals deep yellow, the outer segments yellow with broad rose band on back. *Zones 4-9.* p. 256

dasystemon (Central Asia, Tienshan), "Kuen Lun tulip"; very hardy small tulip, to 18 cm high, with dual lanceolate leaves, and usually several yellow flowers with petals edged white, greenish outside. Very similar to T. tarda. *Zones 4-8.* p. 256

fosteriana (Samarkand, Turkestan, Central Asia); robust bulbous plant to 30 cm or more high; glaucous broadly ovate 20 cm leaves; floral stalk slightly hairy, bearing elegant, pointed glossy flowers opening flat, the petals brilliant scarlet, with black basal blotch inside margined yellow; in early Spring. *Zones 3-7.* p. 255

fosteriana 'Juan'; excellent and compact cultivar with large glossy, beautiful flowers cup-like and yellow at base, the segments orange-scarlet and spreading outward. May-blooming in Holland. *Zones 3-7.*   *p. 255*

x gesneriana hybrids or "Common garden tulips" widely used for garden planting; hybrids of this group are best for early Spring and Easter-flowering in pots, producing elegant flowers 6 to 10 cm long. Derived from T. gesneriana (Armenia, Iran), and inbred with several other species in Asiatic Turkey, So. Russia and Iran, they were brought to Western Europe from 1554 on, reaching Holland sometime after 1573. *Temperate. Generally Zones 3-8.*

gesn. 'Ace of Spades' (Darwin); beautiful large oval-shaped deep purple to near black flowers, carried on strong stem, a very impressive variety. *Zones 3-7.*   *p.252*

gesn. 'Apeldoorn' (Darwin hybrid); large and beautiful long-lasting flowers of noble form, orange-scarlet, their black base outlined in yellow. A favorite cutflower in Europe. *Zones 3-7.*   *p. 53*

gesn. 'Balaleika' (Single late); shapely Cottage tulip with glowing red flowers having contrasting yellow base and black stamens. *p. 250*

gesn. 'Bartigon' (Darwin); popular pot variety known since 1898, with medium large flowers bright cochineal to crimson-red, normally mid-May blooming; but can be forced from Jan. 15 on; 60 cm tall. Darwin flowers have squarish base in profile.   *p. 252*

gesn. 'Black Forest' (Darwin); cheerful variety of sturdy habit, seen at the Spring Tulip Show in Brooklyn Botanic Garden; stiff stems carry cups of carmine-rose flowers with broad white margins. *p. 252*

gesn. 'Blenda' (Triumph); stiff-erect Triumph tulip with cupped flowers, pointed petals, deep rose with white base, early.   *p. 250*

gesn. 'Burgundy Lace' (Fringed); fancy strain of tall tulips having handsome egg-shaped flowers with crystal-like fringe on edge of wine-red petals, May-blooming. *Zones 4-7.*   *p. 254*

gesn. 'China Pink' (Lily-flowered); lovely variety with flowers soft satiny pink, and having white base; points slightly reflexed; very fine for pots. *Zones 4-7.*   *p. 254*

gesn. 'Couleur Cardinal' (Single early); excellent tulip of erect habit, and glowing rich cardinal-red flowers of exceptional keeping quality, in cultivation since 1845; ideal for bedding or Easter forcing. *Zones 3-8.*   *p. 251*

gesn. 'Cream Delight' (Darwin); compact and sturdy single midseason tulip, with large squarish flowers in creamy-yellow tinted with gold; photographed early May in New York. *Zones 3-7.*   *p. 252*

gesn. 'Double early' seen in variety during the Tulip Festival in Keukenhof Gardens, Holland, in early May; striking display of double-flowered tulips of compact habit in various colors yellow to red; very showy and of good keeping quality. *Zones 3-7.*   *p. 251*

gesn. 'Duc van Tol' (Single early); very early blooming tulip of compact habit, only 15 cm high, with glowing deep scarlet flowers opening wide, and displaying contrasting yellow center. For earliest forcing to bloom during Winter, and early flowering in gardens. Originated 1850, hybridized with T. suaveolens. *Zones 3-8.*   *p. 251*

gesn. 'Duc van Tol Aurora' (Single early); early blooming, compact variety with bell flowers opening wide to lovely faces of golden-yellow to salmon, displaying pale center. *Zones 3-8.*   *p. 251*

gesn. 'Duc van Tol Violet' (Single early); striking color variation seen at the Tulip Festival of Keukenhof Gardens in Holland; the flowers violet and tinged with maroon, yellow base inside, and contrasting white along margins. *Zones 3-8.*   *p. 251*

gesn. 'Elsie Eloff' (Cottage); charming May-blooming single tulip with ovoid blossoms pale butter-yellow, ideal for outdoor gardens; since 1949, (single late). *Zones 3-7.*   *p. 253*

gesn. 'Eros' (Double late, Peony tulip); splendid many petalled double flowers peony-like, lovely old rose, 45-60 cm high, in late Spring. *Zones 3-7.*   *p. 250*

gesn. 'Evening Song' (Lily-flowered); elegant form of the late Cottage group, with flowers distinctive in chalice form and slender pointed petals turned outward, glistening crimson-red and a yellow base, in May. *Zones 4-7.*   *p. 253*

gesn. 'Firebird' (Parrot); very showy 1939 sport of the popular 'Parrot Fantasy'; large shaggy flowers with flaring fleshy, lobed petals intense vermilion-red with velvety sheen, and green markings on outside; May-blooming. *Zones 4-7.*   *p. 253*

gesn. 'Flaming Parrot' (Parrot type); unique and striking flowers with fringed and twisted petals spread outward, variegated white with crimson-red bands, on lax stalks 60 cm long; May-blooming.   *p. 254*

gesn. 'Flying Dutchman' (Darwin); stiffly erect midseason tulip with flowers rich vermilion-scarlet, outstanding in any garden planting, seen blooming in early May in New York. *Zones 3-7.*   *p. 252*

gesn. 'Fringed Beauty' (Double early fringed); spectacular floral beauty with double flowers spreading wide open, displaying broad petals of glowing vermilion-red, the margins yellow and fringed. *Zones 4-7.*   *p. 254*

gesn. 'Georgette' (Cottage); floriferous and decorative variety with each stem branching and bearing 4 or more good size and

beautiful flowers with yellow petals suffused with red toward margins, in late Spring, (single late). *Zones 3-7.*   *p. 253*

gesn. 'Ivory Gem' (Cottage), Hillegan 1943; single late tulip of compact habit with sturdy stems, bearing egg-shaped flowers in ivory-white, in May.   *p. 253*

gesn. 'Jeanette Heath' (Cottage); charming 'Single Late' seen at Tulip Festival of Brooklyn Botanic Garden in early May; pretty flowers bluish-white decorated with carmine-red stripes outside. *Zones 3-7.*   *p .253*

gesn. 'Karel Doorman' (Parrot); also known as "Dragon tulip"; large cherry-red flowers mingled with green, and edged with golden-yellow, the perianth segments variously frilled; 40 cm high, late bloomer. *Zones 4-7.*   *p. 250*

gesn. 'Kees Nelis' (Triumph); midseason Triumph tulip about 34-46 cm tall, of somewhat flexuous habit but responding fast to forcing; very striking in dark flame red, edged with orange-yellow. *Zones 3-7.*   *p. 251*

gesn. 'Makassar' (Triumph); dark canary yellow, excellent late-blooming Triumph tulip for Easter pots, about 50 cm tall, with stiff stem and foliage, the cupped flowers 7 cm high, clear yellow; often producing more than one bloom per stalk. *Zones 3-7.*   *p. 250*

gesn. 'Mariette' (Lily-flowered); outstanding May-blooming tulip with slender yet stiff stems to 60 cm high, bearing lovely lily-like rose-pink flowers of satiny texture, and white inside at base. *p. 253*

gesn. 'Merry Widow' ('Lustige Witwe') (Triumph); excellent old midseason tulip known since 1942, very popular as cut flower in Europe, of firm substance, and long lasting, 60 cm tall; glowing deep red, frosted with glistening white at petal edges, April-May.   *p.252*

gesn. 'Nizza' (Peony type); late-blooming large double flowers, the petals yellow alternating with areas or stripes of crimson-red. *p. 254*

gesn. 'Olympic Flame' (Darwin hyb.): 45 cm or more high, striking flowers to 10 cm long, orange-yellow streaked with red; in late Spring. Seen at National Garden Expo in Duesseldorf, Germany 1987. *Zones 3-7.*   *p. 250*

gesn. 'Overdale' (Triumph); robust early-blooming single variety with elegant, pointed flowers cinnabar-red, shaded with purple. *Zones 3-7.*   *p. 251*

gesn. 'Paris' (Triumph); a very colorful, recommended pot variety, deep orange-red, each segment edged with contrasting yellow, on stiff stalks, 45 cm high. *Zones 3-7.*   *p. 250*

gesn. 'Peachblossom' (Double early); superb variety with fully double flowers deep rose, held very erect on sturdy stems.   *p. 251*

gesn. 'Princess Elizabeth' (Darwin); midseason tulip of compact habit and firm texture, having large flowers vivid rose-pink; seen blooming in early May in Brooklyn Botanic Garden.   *p. 252*

gesn. 'Princess Irene' (Single Early); sport of 'Couleur Cardinal'; coral or soft orange with bronze red flaming from base, 45 cm high, in April. *Zones 3-8.*   *p. 250*

gesn. 'Princess Margaret Rose' (Cottage); handsome May-blooming single, to 24 cm high, the long-lasting flowers golden-yellow, the petals on the edges feathered with orange-red, in May. Very pretty in gardens or in bouquets. *Zones 3-7.*   *p. 253*

gesn. 'Queen of Bartigons' (Darwin); outstanding Bartigon sport of great substance, with flowers delicate salmon-pink, and having yellow stamens (in contrast to other Bartigons); blooming in April-May. *Zones 3-7.*   *p. 252*

gesn. 'Queen of Sheba' (Lily-flowered); outstanding type with large flowers having broad, pointed petals lightly reflexed, coppery red with tips and margins of orange-yellow, in May. *Zones 4-7. p. 254*

gesn. 'Red Giant'; an excellent "Triumph" tulip for Easter pots; a group resulting from crosses of "Darwin" and "Early" tulips; large, substantial, long-lasting, deep scarlet flowers, often 2-3 on the stiff robust stem. *Zones 3-7.*   *p. 54*

gesn. 'Rembrandt' (Rembrandt); colorful May-blooming tulips to 55 cm tall, with globe-shaped flowers of the Darwin type, but with "broken" colors, feathered and splashed with vibrant combinations of reds or yellows with white, for a brilliant display.   *p. 254*

gesn. 'Robinea' (Triumph), a superior "Triumph tulip" for Easter flowering; a healthy companion to 'Red Giant', even stockier, 30-36 cm above pot, with firm-fleshy, large flowers deep crimson, often producing more than one bloom per stalk; resistant to "rotting off" or "fire". *Zones 3-7.*   *p. 250*

gesn. 'Rose Beauty' (Triumph); lovely bicolor, deep pink maturing to cherry-red against a white base; the flowers becoming quite large as they mature; 38 cm. *Zones 3-7.*   *p. 250*

gesn. 'Rose Tendre' (Darwin); lovely deep rose cupped flowers, edged with white. Seen at the May Festival in Brooklyn Botanic Garden 1984. *Zones 3-7.*   *p. 250*

gesn. 'Sweet Harmony' (Darwin); a beautiful, giant tulip to 60 cm tall; unique color combination of lemon-yellow, edged ivory-white, embellished by yellow anthers; midseason. *Zones 3-7.*   *p. 252*

gesn. 'Thule' (Triumph); sturdy early-blooming single cupped flower, brilliant crimson-red with yellow borders. *Zones 3-7.* *p. 251*

gesn. 'Topscore' (Triumph); remarkable cultivar developing three or more blooms on each floral stem, to 50 cm high; flowers sparkling geranium-red, in April-May. *Zones 3-7.* p. 250

gesn. 'Ursa Minor' (Single Early); shapely oval medium size flower clear deep yellow, on slender stem, a good commercial pot variety once included with the "Triumphs". *Zones 3-8.* p. 54

gesn. 'Vincent Van Gogh' (Peony-flowered); long-stemmed May-blooming double flowers rounded in outline when open, the flaring petals crimson-red with crisped yellow margins. *Zones 3-7.* p. 254

gesn. 'West Point' (Lily-flowered); graceful May-blooming tulips to 60 cm high, in spring display of GRUGA Garden Expo in Essen, Germany; flowers with outward-curved narrow pointed petals primrose-yellow. *Zones 4-7.* p. 253

greigii 'Oriental Splendor'; colorful cultivar of the all red species from Turkestan; compact bulbous plant with broad 20 cm bluish leaves streaked with brown and gray; beautiful flowers 8 cm long, the petals spreading, crimson-red with broad yellow margins. *Zones 3-7.* p. 255

greigii 'Plaisir'; attractive low plant to 30 cm high, having broad, fleshy leaves bluish-green and striped with brown lengthwise; colorful flowers carmine-red outside, when wide open the petals vermilion-red edged sulphur-yellow, the base inside golden-yellow with black spots. *Zones 3-7.* p. 255

greigii 'Red Riding Hood'; striking early blooming tulip 30 cm high, of sturdy habit, with attractively patterned leaves bluish-green with silvery stripes; the wide open flowers having scarlet petals of silky texture, the base black inside. *Zones 3-7.* p. 255

kaufmanniana (Turkestan), the "Water-lily tulip"; short plant 12-20 cm high, with broad, slightly glaucous leaves, and beautiful, solitary flowers 9 cm long, opening to a waterlily-like flat star; the pointed segments yellowish-white inside with yellow base, outside streaked carmine-red; early blooming. *Zones 4-8.* p. 255

kaufmanniana 'Corona'; pretty water-lily-type flowers with slender petals soft orange with pale margins, painted crimson-red outside and at base inside. *Zones 5-8.* p. 255

kolpakowskiana (Turkestan), "Kolpak tulip"; miniature low-growing species with narrow, glaucous leaves; stalks 15 cm long bearing 1-2 flowers opening flat with pointed segments 5½ cm long, bright yellow, backs with olive and red flush; midseason-early. *Zones 2-7.* p. 256

linifolia (Bokhara), "Slimleaf tulip"; small species to 20 cm high, with goblet-like solitary 5 cm flowers glossy crimson with black-purple bottom; narrow, grass-like foliage; early Spring. *Zones 4-8.* p. 256

montana (Turkestan to Iran), "Mountain tulip"; small species with purplish bulb, producing 3 or 4 linear grass-like, glaucous leaves 10 cm long, and slender 20 cm floral stalk, bearing glossy, deep crimson-red flowers, the petals flaring wide, and with black basal spot. *Zones 4-7.* p. 255

patens (Siberia to Caucasus), "Persian tulip"; dwarf botanical bulbous species to 22 cm high, with 2-3 lanceolate curved leaves, and fragrant yellow 5 cm flowers, the segments opening wide star-like, showing yellow stamens; Mid-spring. *Zone 4.* p. 256

praestans 'Unicum', "Leather-bulb tulip"; attractive variation with its broad glaucous leaves variegated and margined with creamy-white; the species is native to Central Asia, 30-40 cm high, with cup-shaped 6 cm flowers brick-red; bulb is covered by leathery tunic, silky-hairy inside. *Zones 4-7.* p. 257

pulchella (humilis) (Asia Minor), "Red crocus tulip"; miniature tulip to 15 cm high, with 2-3 linear strap-shaped leaves, and producing 1-3 pointed 4 cm flowers opening flat, the waxy segments crimson-red to purple, and a white-margined bluish basal blotch inside. *Zones 4-8.* p. 257

saxatilis (Crete); stoloniferous species to 30 cm high, forming long, narrow, shining green leaves, and stalks with 1-3 cup-shaped fragrant flowers opening flat, the pointed segments 5 cm long, pale lilac with yellow bottom; midseason. *Zones 4-10.* p. 254

sylvestris (Europe to No. Africa, W. Asia), "Florentine tulip"; small meadow-tulip to 25 cm or more high, widely naturalized in Europe, blooming April-May; stoloniferous and forming bulblets; fragrant flowers to 6 cm long, bright yellow or cream, tinged with green outside. *Zones 4-10.* p. 257

tarda (dasystemon in hort.) (Turkestan); small species 15 cm high; rosette of glaucous leaves, the 8 cm stalks bearing 1 to 6 small starry flowers, the 4 cm segments yellow at base, white toward tips, marked green and red on back, the inner segments with green line; May. *Zones 4-8.* p. 257

urumiensis (N.W. Iran); small species, with strap-shaped, dull green leaves; the short 5 cm stem carrying 1-2 flowers first urn-shaped, later spreading star-like, with narrow, pointed yellow petals, the outer segments olive and red outside. *Zones 4-7.* p. 257

TUNICA: see PETRORHAGIA

TUPIDANTHUS calyptratus   (Hortus 3 and in hort.) transferred to Schefflera pueckleri (Frodin, Baileya Jan. 1989).

TURBINA holubii: see IPOMOEA holubii

TURBINICARPUS   Cactaceae
laui (Hortus: Strombocactus; Zander: Toumeya; Britton and Rose: Neolloydia pilispina) (No. Mexico: San Luis Potosi); rare clustering small globe 3 cm dia., the high knobs tipped by white areoles and long curving needle spines; soft pink flowers from near crown. *Zone 10.* p. 178

pseudomacrochele (Hortus: Strombocactus; Zander: Toumeya) (Mexico: San Luis Potosi); miniature clustering globes 2-3 cm dia.; tubercles in 5 oblique rows; yellowish recurved radials neatly covering body; large flowers with white petals having pink central band. *Zone 11.* p. 178

TURNERA   Turneraceae
aurantiaca (Guiana); decorative tropical shrub, with alternate leathery, lanceolate leaves, glossy green and corrugated on surface; yellow flowers in terminal clusters, having 5-parted calyx and 5 sepals, very pretty when in bloom. Photographed in col. Singapore Botanic Gardens. *Zone 10.* p. 893

ulmifolia (W. Indies, Mexico to Argentina), "West Indian holly" or "Sage rose"; pretty herbaceous subshrub ½-1¼ m high, with scandent stems, and alternate narrow-elliptic leaves 8-10 cm long, nettle-like, deep glossy green, white-hairy underneath; axillary golden-yellow, 5 cm flowers with 5 petals, blooming from March to September, opening only in the morning. *Tropical. Zone 10.* p. 893

ulmifolia elegans (Brazil: Recife), "Sulphur alder"; subshrubby perennial to 60 cm high, with downy lanceolate leaves, coarsely toothed, to 10 cm long; showy platter-form flowers 5 cm across, pale to sulphur-yellow, violet in center, blooming during Summer, open mornings only. *Zone 10.* p. 516, 893

TURRAEA   Meliaceae
obtusifolia (So. Africa: Natal, E. Cape), "South African honeysuckle", or "Bluntleaf star-bush"; attractive, broad, slow-growing, more or less evergreen shrub 1-1½ m high, with small obovate, recurved dark green leaves 3-5 cm long; numerous axillary solitary, star-like white flowers with 5 narrow petals, 2½ cm across, and sweetly scented; red berries. *Zones 9-10.* p. 788

TUSSILAGO   Compositae
farfara (Europe to No. Asia; natur. in E. No. America), "Coltsfoot"; herbaceous perennial with underground spreading rhizomes, sending up purplish floral stalks 30 cm high, flowering before foliage appears; the basal leaves roundish-cordate to 20 cm across, lobed and toothed, white-felty beneath; the daisy-like bright yellow blossoms 3 cm across open in early Spring. Fresh foliage is eaten as a vegetable; dried leaves used in cough medicine; lotion helps to heal cuts; tea is drunk to improve poor skin conditions. *Zone 3.* p. 524

TYPHA   Typhaceae
angustifolia (No. and So. America, Europe, Asia), "Narrow-leaved cat-tail"; rush-like waterside perennial of smaller habit than T. latifolia, with stiffy erect canes 1 to 2 m high, covered by sheathing dark green, linear leaves, and topped by ornamental cylindric light brown floral spikes. *Zone 3.* p. 337

latifolia, (No. America, Europe, Asia), "Cat-tail"; decorative aquatic perennial, with creeping rootstock, tall erect unbranched reed-like stems to 2½ m high, the leaves linear, almost flat and glaucous; cylindric flower spike dark brown, 30 cm long, and 3 cm thick; dried for indoor decoration and known in England as "Reedmace". *Warm temperate. Zone 3.* p. 337

TYPHONIUM   Araceae
divaricatum (India, Java, Celebes, Timor, Vietnam, Hong Kong); tuberous aroid with hastate, spear-shaped, glossy light green leaves 5-15 cm long, on slender 10-30 cm petioles; spathe tubular expanding into broad ovate limb, brown-purple inside, to 15 cm long. *Zone 11.* p. 327

TYPHONODORUM   Araceae
lindleyanum (Madagascar, Zanzibar); handsome tree-like, smooth aroid, in habitat growing in warm lowland rivers, and sometimes becoming gigantic, 3-4 m high; forming thick stems 1-3 m long; the large, thick-fleshy, bright green sagittate leaves ½ to 1 m long, with triangular sinus; suberect creamy-white spathe 45-60 cm in length, enclosing golden-yellow spadix to 40 cm long, female in lower part, male toward apex. *Humid-tropical. Zones 10-11.* p. 326

UEBELMANNIA   Cactaceae
pectinifera (Brazil); small globular cactus to 10 cm or more dia., later becoming elongate, with about 15 ribs; at first blackish-brown

tinted purple, later with tiny white scales; small 1/2-11/2 cm spines, blackish near apex, arranged in rows comb-like, the areoles dense along ridges; flowers yellow. *Arid-tropical. Zone 11.*   p. 177

ULEARUM   *Araceae*
viridispadix (*Zomicarpella maculata* hort.) (Brazil); beautiful small aroid spreading from underground rhizome, 10 cm long, with several leaves, roundish or reniform with overlapping basal lobes in juvenile stage; the adult leaf blades sagittate, 8-10 cm long, richly splashed with silver, the main ribs and margins moss-green; inflorescence having small spathe 3 cm long; the 3 cm spadix bearing a few female flowers below, and fertile stamens (staminodes) toward apex. Photographed by J. Bogner of Munich Botanic Garden. *Tropical. Zone 11.*   p. 26

ULEX   *Leguminosae*
europaeus (Western Europe, including Britain), "Gorse", "Whin" or "Furze"; densely spiny shrub to 1 m as seen wild, twice as high in gardens; shoots hairy and stiff, with the leaf-like phyllodes reduced to spines; the golden-yellow 11/2 cm flowers solitary but in profusion, mainly in Spring. Naturalized in Eastern U.S. *Zone 6.*   p. 772

parviflorus (Portugal to So. France), "Ajonc de Provence"; spiny shrub 60-150 cm high, the broom-like stiff branches with narrow leaf-like phyllodes converted into 3-angled spines 1-3 cm long; at ends of branches the yellow flowers, having short wings, the standard and keel longer, blooming February to June. *Zone 9.*   p. 772

ULMUS   *Ulmaceae*
alata (Virginia to Florida, and Texas), "Winged elm" or "Small-leaved elm"; deciduous tree to 15 m high, the trunk and branches with flaking bark, the shoots developing two corky wings; leaves 3-6 cm long, obovate or oblong-ovate, smooth above and downy on veins beneath; inconspicuous bisexual flowers in pendant clusters, appearing before leaves; fruit 1 cm long, with incurved beaks, and covered with long white hairs. *Zone 4.*   p. 896

americana (New Foundland to Florida, west to Rocky Mts.), "American elm" or "White elm"; best of the elms; to 40 m high, of elegant, vase-shaped habit, with open head of branches pendulous at the ends; oval or obovate leaves 8-15 cm long, unequal at base and slender pointed, doubly toothed at margins, rough above and usually downy beneath; inconspicuous flowers in hanging clusters before the foliage; fruit deeply notched, with dense ciliate margins. Autumn color is yellow. Unfortunately many trees have been affected by the Dutch elm disease, caused by a fungus spread by flying beatles, damaging the tree and resulting in the loss of many elms. *Zone 2.*   p. 896

glabra (scabra) (Great Britain to Siberia), "Scotch elm"; large wide-spreading tree to 40 m high, the downy shoots with decorative, obovate or oblong leaves 8-16 cm long, oblique at base, toothed at margins, and occasionally 3-lobed toward apex, rough above and downy beneath, more in up to 20 pairs; inconspicuous flowers before the foliage; downy oval fruit 2-3 cm long. Used as understock for grafting because of its non-suckering habit. *Zone 4.*   p. 896

x hollandica 'Wredei' (carpinifolia x glabra) "Golden elm" and "Dutch elm"; pyramidal seedling tree 1877, suckering from the trunk; large, broadly ovate leaves, usually glossy above, 5-6 cm long, and having to 14 pairs of veins, golden-yellow, deeply double-toothed, and curly. *Zone 4.*   p. 897

parvifolia (China, Japan, Korea), "Evergreen elm" or "Chinese elm"; graceful, open-headed tree to 20 m high, evergreen in mild climates; usually multi-stemmed, dense with ovate leaves small and firm, 2 to 5 cm long or more, glossy grass-green and finely crenate, on pendant, weeping willowy branches with foliage arranged rather flat; blooming in late Summer or Autumn, with inconspicuous greenish flowers. Beautiful tree in California plantings. *Warm temperate. Zones 6-9.*   p. 897

thomasii (Québec to Tennessee and Nebraska), "Rock elm"; large tree of irregularly columnar habit, 20-30 m high, the branches very corky; the buds pubescent; with obovate, large leaves 10-15 cm long, doubly toothed at margins, smooth above but downy beneath; depressed veins in 14 to 20 pairs; flowers in 5 cm racemes, followed by 2 cm oval fruit, completely downy and shallowly notched. *Zone 2.*   p. 897

UMBELLULARIA   *Lauraceae*
californica (California to Oregon), "Myrtlewood" or "California laurel"; strongly aromatic evergreen tree, 15-25 m; leaves alternate, glossy green above, leathery, 5-12 cm long, narrowly oval or oblong, tapered to both ends; flowers yellowish-green in stalked umbels 1 cm wide; fruit roundish 1-21/2 cm long, green becoming purplish. Leaves similar to Laurus nobilis, but not as hard-leathery, and with veins confluent inside margins; foliage of Laurus has veins running to margins. *Zone 7.*   p. 742

UMBILICUS   *Crassulaceae*
rupestris (W. Europe to Canary Isl., East to Egypt.), "Pennywort"; low succulent perennial herb, with tuberous root, forming annual shoots; basal leaves rounded peltate 3-6 cm wide, the upper ones smaller; stem elongating into pyramidal inflorescence to 40 cm high, with tiny greenish flowers. *Zone 6.*   p. 192

UNGNADIA   *Sapindaceae*
speciosa (Texas, New Mexico to Sonora), "Texan buckeye"; deciduous tree to 10 m high; alternate leaves unequally pinnate with 6 or 7 pairs of leaflets about 10 cm long, the terminal one long-stalked; rose-pink flowers having crested claws, borne in lateral clusters and blooming before the leaves; seed capsules 5 cm dia. *Zone 9.*   p. 868

UNIOLA   *Gramineae*
latifolia (Chasmanthium latifolium) (Mass. to Florida, New Mexico), "Wild oats" or "Spike grass"; strong-growing deciduous perennial with culms to 11/2 m high, the grass-like lanceolate leaves to 25 cm long clasping stem; the showy ornamental flower-spikes gracefully pendant with heavy fruitheads, which can be cut and dried in late Summer. *Zone 5.*   p. 562

paniculata (U.S.: Virginia to Florida and Texas, West Indies), "Sea-oats", or "Spike-grass"; ornamental perennial grass growing along coastal sands, with creeping rhizomes, stems to 21/2 m high, with narrow leaves to 40 cm long, and 1 cm wide, rolled inward; the drooping panicle crowded with straw-colored, flat spikelets to 4 cm long, sharply keeled; used in combinations of dry flower arrangements. *Zone 6.*   p. 564

URBINIA: see ECHEVERIA

URCEOLINA   *Amaryllidaceae*
grandiflora (Zander): see EUCHARIS grandiflora (Hortus)
peruviana (Perú), "Urn flower"; interesting low species with small 3 cm bulb; 1 or 2 oblanceolate leaves 15-20 cm long, striated and with reflexed margins; the slender floral stalk rising at base, not from crown of bulb, 20 to 40 cm high, bearing several nodding, tubular-inflated, scented flowers 4 cm long, bright scarlet, blooming in early Summer. *Subtropic. Zone 10.*   p. 217

URGINEA   *Liliaceae*
maritima (Canary Islands to Syria, Brittany, Normandy), the "Sea-onion", or "Squills"; an old house plant, forming a very large ovoid red-brown bulb 10-15 cm thick, partially above ground; 10-20 fleshy, glaucous green strap-shaped leaves 30-45 cm long, wide above the middle, in the Spring, the old leafbases remaining for a time; during the leafless time in Summer, a 30-90 cm long slender stalk bears a short, pyramidal raceme of whitish flowers 11/2 cm wide, each segment with an indistinct green median stripe, the filament is threadlike, anthers green. The bulb furnishes syrup of squills. *Warm temperate. Zones 8-9.*   p. 257

UROSPATHA   *Araceae*
sagittifolia (Trop. So. America: Brazil); rhizomatous aroid from wet forest, with few triangular, hastate leaves 30-50 cm long, the two basal lobes broad and with deep sinus; floral stalk to 60 cm bearing lanceolate spathe 25-30 cm long, yellowish or green, mottled with rosy-red and having long twisted apex, white inside; spadix green. *Zone 11.*   p. 33

UROSPERMUM   *Compositae*
dalechampii (So. Europe, Mallorca); herbaceous plant to 45 cm high, forming a spreading clump to 1 m across; the rough, silvery-gray leaves variously lobed and toothed; floral heads dandelion-like, light or bright yellow, to 4 cm across, and velvety-hairy at base. *Zone 9.*   p. 404

URSINIA   *Compositae*
anethoides (So. Africa), "Dill-leaf ursinia"; shrubby perennial to 60 cm high, having woody branches; the scented leaves pinnately divided into linear segments; showy orange-yellow flowers 4 to 5 cm across, with a dark patch at base of each ray-floret, forming a ring around orange center; rays orange beneath. *Zone 9.*   p. 403

URTICA   *Urticaceae*
dioica (Europe and Asia, widely naturalized in No. America), "Stinging nettle"; herbaceous, dioecious perennial to 1 m or more high, with spreading rootstock and bristly stems, bearing opposite, ovate leaves 12-15 cm long and having crenate margins, covered by minute but very stinging hairs; small greenish flowers in clusters of small spike-like racemes. In Europe, young shoots in Spring are cooked and eaten like spinach; according to Sir Walter Scott, long cultivated in Scotland as pot herb. Very attractive to butterflies. *Zone 3.*   p. 545

UTRICULARIA   *Lentibulariaceae (Carnivorous Pl.)*
inflata (Southern U.S.), "Bladderwort"; aquatic herb forming a whorl of inflated tubes united into a floating raft which support the erect stalk bearing yellow flowers. Insects are sucked into the hollow tubes as a trapdoor opens when its trigger is touched, then closing. *Warm temperate. Zones 9-10.*   p. 202

UVARIA: see GONIOTHALAMUS

UVULARIA Liliaceae

grandiflora (Québec to Georgia and Kansas), "Big merrybells"; charming perennial herb from rootstock, to 50 cm or more high, having green perfoliate membranous leaves, and lemon-yellow flowers with lanceolate segments 4 cm long, nodding bell-like; spring to summer-blooming. Zones 3-8.   p. 452

perfoliata (Québec to Ohio, so. to Florida), "Strawbells" or "Wood merrybells"; rhizomatous perennial 30-50 cm high, with forking stems, bearing membranous oblong, perfoliate leaves encircling branches, 4-8 cm long; pale yellow flowers 2-4 cm long, in Spring to early Summer. Zones 4-9.   p. 452

sessilifolia (Oakesiella) (E. Canada to So. Dakota, so. to Alabama), "Little merry-bells"; widely distributed perennial known as "Wild oats", with forked stems to 30 cm high, bearing lanceolate, sessile leaves to 8 cm long; the axillary, nodding, slender bell-flowers creamy-yellow or greenish, 3 cm long, in Spring and early Summer. Zones 4-8.   p. 452

VACCINIUM Ericaceae

corymbosum (Maine to Florida), "Highbush blueberry" or "Whortleberry"; deciduous dense shrub to 5 m high, with leathery, usually pubescent elliptic leaves to 8 cm long; white to pinkish urn-shaped small 1 cm flowers, followed by the glaucous blue-black edible berries full of sweet, juicy, flesh. Temperate. Zone 3.   p. 912

macrocarpon (Oxycoccus microcarpos) (Newfoundland to Minnesota, south to No. Carolina), large-fruited "Cranberry"; creeping evergreen shrub with ascending branchlets to 80 cm high, forming mats; small oblong 2 cm leaves, whitish beneath; the little flowers bell-shaped, pendant from lateral stalks, the corolla 1 cm long, rose-pink to purplish-red, divided into 4 lobes, blooming June-August, followed by scarlet berry-fruits, of acid taste, the commercially grown Cranberry of Eastern No. America, in several selected forms; inhabiting bogs and swamps. Zone 2.   p. 719, 912

vitis-idaea (Europe, No. Asia), the "Lingonberry" or "Cowberry"; evergreen creeping shrub to 30 cm high, spreading by underground runners; leaves shining dark green 1-3 cm long, the flowers white or pink, 5 mm long in short nodding clusters; edible, sour red berries, like tiny cranberries, and used for preserves. Zone 4.   p. 912

vitis-idaea minus (Newfoundland, Massachusetts to Alaska), "Mountain cranberry"; dwarf evergreen forming dense mats from creeping rhizomes, never over 10-20 cm high; an American variety of the European and Asian lingonberry; very useful as a garden plant, because it displays to advantage, against the lustrous foliage, both its little pink to red bell-flowers, and the glossy scarlet edible berries of tart-sweet flavor. Zones 2-6.   p. 912

VALERIANA Valerianaceae

globulariifolia (Pyrenees); small fragrant, herbaceous perennial 8-20 cm high; oval or ovate lower leaves, stem leaves divided; grooved stem topped by clusters of minute pinkish flowers; ideal for rock-gardens. Zone 8.   p. 516

officinalis (Europe, W. Asia; natural. locally in Canada and No. U.S.), "Valerian"; fragrant-flowered herbaceous perennial to 1 m or more high, spreading by rhizomes; with pinnate leaves having lanceolate, toothed segments; the small flowers white or pink, sweetly scented like heliotrope, in terminal clusters, on erect slender stems, during Summer. The rhizomes yield aetherial oil, the drug Valerian, used as a tranquilizing sedative. Zone 3.   p. 545

VALLOTA Amaryllidaceae

speciosa (purpurea) (So. Africa: Cape Prov.), the "Scarborough lily"; a charming evergreen plant with large brown bulb; strap-shaped bright green leaves 45-60 cm long, the fleshy, hollow ½-1 m stalk carrying a cluster of funnel-shaped bright scarlet, long-lasting flowers 8 cm across, with stamens attached to each petal; blooming from June on. Strong undisturbed bulbs produce several flower stalks in succession. An old, good house plant, but which must be kept moderately moist even during its cool rest period in Winter. Now (1989) considered Cyrtanthus purpureus in South Africa. Subtropic. Zone 10.   p. 217, 235

VANCOUVERIA Berberidaceae

hexandra (Washington to California), "American barrenwort"; rhizomatous perennial herb to 40 cm high, from the Redwood forests of the Pacific coast; compound leaves with ovate, thin leaflets to 4 cm long, deciduous in Winter; white flowers 4 cm across, having 6 petals, in clusters, blooming May-June. Zone 5.   p. 346

VANDA Orchidaceae

coerulea (Himalayas, Assam, Burma), the beautiful "Blue orchid"; with stems 30-90 cm high, two-ranked with 20 cm, strap-type, channeled leaves; the axillary racemes with large round, membranous flowers 5-8 cm across, sepals and petals light blue with a network of deep azure, the small lip blue, (July-Jan.). Humid-subtropic. Zone 11.   p. 97

cristata (Nepal, Burma); curious epiphyte with erect stems bearing 2-ranked leaves having 3 teeth at apex; few-flowered inflorescence with 5 cm flowers, the sepals and petals yellow-green, the lip buff, striped rich purple between 5-7 raised white lines, and with 3 divergent narrow, horn-like lobes at tip; March-July. Zone 11.   p. 98

lamellata (Philippines, Marianas); robust stems very densely leafy, to 50 cm tall, narrow folded leaves and recurved, 20 cm long, and cut at tip; inflorescence with waxy flowers very fragrant, to 3 cm across and long lasting; sepals and petals yellowish or greenish blotched and striped with red-brown; small lip yellow and marked brown. Tropical. Zones 11-12.   p. 98

'Miss Agnes Joaquim' (hookeriana x teres) (Singapore 1893), "Corsage orchid"; terete hybrid, the famous orchid grown in Hawaii for leis and corsages, flowering in succession throughout the year; large 8 cm blooms lasting a long time, sepals white tinged with rose, the larger petals mauve-purple, the broad lip purple, with yellow throat spotted red. Tropical. Zone 12.   p. 98

teres (N.E. India, Upper Burma); showy epiphyte with terete (round) stems and leaves, to 2 m high, climbing trees in hot plains by aerial roots; flowers few but large, to 8 cm across, with sepals white, tinged with rose, the larger petals rose-magenta, lip 3-lobed carmine-red with orange throat, (May-Sept.). Tropical. Zone 12.   p. 97

tricolor (Java); spectacular epiphyte with stems to 1 m long, dense with two ranks of recurving strap-shaped leaves; the inflorescence in lateral racemes of fragrant waxy flowers 5-8 cm across, sepals and petals lemon-yellow spotted with reddish-brown, lip white with purple, (Oct.-July). Tropical. Zone 12.   p. 98

tricolor suavis (Java, Bali); a beautiful variation, with the fragrant waxy flowers having a white base, spotted with blood-purple; in the mountains of Bali, at 1000 m, not far from the temple of Besakih, boys and girls offered me plants in flower in July, one naked boy asking 2 Rupiahs, then 20¢. Tropical. Zone 12.   p. 98

VANILLA Orchidaceae

planifolia (fragrans or aromatica) (Eastern Mexico), "Common vanilla"; tall climbing orchid said to attain a length of 100 m; the light green, cylindrical stem bears 2 ranks of succulent, green, fleshy, elliptic leaves as well as aerial roots; the 5 cm flowers in axillary clusters, sepals and petals greenish-yellow, and wavy-edged lip almost white, deep yellow in throat; its dried seed pod provides vanilla for flavoring, (Dec.-June). Tropical. Zone 12.   p. 98, 540

planifolia 'Marginata'; attractive variety if grown on bark, for ornamental purposes, having nicely draped fleshy leaves of milky green, bordered on each margin by a broad band of creamy-white. Tropical. Zone 12.   p. 98

pompona (lutescens) (Mexico to Panama to Venezuela); a large-leaved climber with heavy cylindrical stem and broad ovate, thick-fleshy, dark green leaves 8-18 cm, with marked veining on the surface; large 15 cm flowers greenish-yellow with bright yellow lip; freer blooming than planifolia. Tropical. Zone 12.   p. 98

tahitensis (Tahiti); cultivated in Tahiti for its "Vanillon" fruit; thick-fleshy clambering stems with sessile short, lanceolate succulent leaves, and starry flowers having rather narrow pale green sepals and petals, the fringed lip white and yellow inside. Zone 12.   p. 98

VEITCHIA Palmae

joannis (Fiji); magnificent solitary feather palm 15 m tall, and in habitat to 30 m; the smooth straight trunk prominently ringed, 25 cm dia., with green crownshaft topped by handsome pinnate fronds gracefully arching, to 3 m long, on short petioles, the dense leaflets lustrous green and prettily pendant, cut off obliquely at their apex; inflorescence from below crownshaft, with red fruit 3 cm long. Tropical. Zones 11-12.   p. 112

merrillii (formerly Adonidia) (Philippines), the "Christmas palm", or "Manila palm"; attractive, erect palm to 6 m high, with rather slender, prominently ringed single trunk; the 1½ m fronds above a glossy green crownshaft in handsome rigidly arching crown; bright green sword-shaped, leathery, broad leaflets many and closely placed, feathered almost to base of petiole; lustrous, attractive red fruit in pendulous clusters below the crown, a striking sight during our winter season. Tropical. Zones 10-11.   p. 112

VELLOZIA Velloziaceae

candida (Espirito Santo, Brazil); tropical woody shrub with tufted fibrous, short, sometimes tree-like stems, branched and leafy at apex; the foliage linear grass-like, rigidly keeled and remotely spine-toothed; flowers pure white, with broad petals recurved and undulate or lobed along margins; conspicuous yellow stamens in bundles, blooming in Summer. Col. A. Seidel, Corupa, Santa Catarina. Zone 10.   p. 890

elegans: see BARBACENIA elegans

VELTHEIMIA Liliaceae

viridifolia (capensis) (So. Africa), "Forest lily"; bulbous plant having broad lance-shaped bright green leaves with undulate margins, and arching; long tubular, nodding flowers to 4 cm long, yellowish-green shading to dusty-red, and spotted, tipped green, on 50 cm long red-spotted stalk; winter-blooming. *Subtropic.* Zone 9.   p. 257

VENIDIUM   *Compositae*
   fastuosum (Arctotis fastuosa of hort.) (So. Africa: Namaqualand), "Cape-daisy", or "Namaqualand-daisy"; showy annual herb 60 cm or more high, cobwebby when young, with small grayish-green leaves irregularly lobed; solitary large, daisy-like flowers 8-10 cm across, with orange florets chocolate-brown at base, appearing as if in two rows, arranged around the flat, shining blackish-purple disc, and opening to the sun. *Subtropic.* Zone 9.   p. 370
   fastuosum 'Exotic' (Arctotis), "Monarch of the Veldt"; handsome annual herb, or short-lived perennial in mildest climates, to 1 m high, with small grayish, lobed leaves, in this cultivar with especially large, vivid orange flowers appearing as if double. Seen in col. Munich Bot. Garden, Germany. Zone 9.   p. 371
   fastuosum 'Phantom' (Arctotis), "Monarch of the Veldt", of So. African origin; superb cultivar seen as planted at the Temple of Luxor, Egypt; very handsome annual with large flowers 10 to 12 cm across, the golden-yellow ray-florets arranged in two distinct rows, the inner cupped and with crimson at base. Zone 9.   p. 403

VERATRUM   *Liliaceae*
   viride (N.E. Canada, to Minnesota and Georgia), "American hellebore", or "Indian poke"; perennial herb 1/2-2 1/2 m high, with thick, very poisonous rhizome; erect leafy stem; clasping, plaited foliage 30 cm long becoming smaller; terminal panicle with numerous small, hairy, yellowish-green flowers to 2 1/2 cm across. Veratrine, a valuable medicine, is extracted from this species and Hellebore powder, to destroy caterpillars, is made from the rhizome. Zones 3-8.   p. 452

VERBASCUM   *Scrophulariaceae*
   blattaria (Europe and C. Asia, natural. in No. America), "Moth mullein"; attractive stately, sun-loving biennial to 1 m or more high; basal leaves ovate, lobed or entire velvety-pubescent and 10-25 cm long, stem leaves shorter; the erect leafy floral stem forming a spire with 2-3 cm flowers rising from leaf axils, the corolla yellow or pink in bud, opening to white with filaments violet pubescent, blooming June to September, unfolding with morning light. Leaves were used medicinally for tuberculosis; flowers in tea to cure colds and coughs. Zones 3-9.   p. 542
   bombyciferum (broussa of gardens or lagurus hort.) (Spain to Turkey, Western Asia Minor); robust biennial to 1 m or more high, entirely covered by felty-white hairs, the basal leaves ovate-oblong to 30 cm long; stem leaves shorter; the stems terminating in dense, branched inflorescence of slender spikes of yellow flowers 2 to 3 cm across, the anthers purple-woolly. Zone 5.   p. 509
   bombyciferum 'Arctic Summer'; excellent cultivar grown in California; herbaceous biennial forming rosettes 30 cm high of furry, silvery green leaves and stems to 2 m tall powdery white, elongating into bold spikes of rich yellow flowers to 3 cm across. Zones 6-9.   p. 509
   caesareum (Asia Minor); robust, compact biennial plant with rough oblanceolate foliage, becoming smaller along floral stalk; funnel flowers lemon-yellow, opening successively along pyramidal spikes. Photographed in col. Kew Botanic Gardens, England 1984. Zone 6.   p. 509
   chaixii 'Album' (Spain to Russia), "Nettle-leaved mullein"; handsome herbaceous bush, usually perennial to 90 cm high, with white-hairy stems; basal leaves ovate-oblong 10-30 cm long, crenate at margins; inflorescence in slender spike-like racemes of showy white flowers 2-3 cm wide, displaying purple-woolly filaments. The species chaixii has yellow corollas. Zone 5.   p. 509
   nigrum (Spain, to Scandinavia, east to Siberia), "Dark mullein"; bushy biennial 60-120 cm high, lightly covered with white hairs; oblong-pointed leaves to 25 cm long; the inflorescence on angled branches in slender pyramidal spike-like raceme, 30-40 cm long, dense with light yellow 1-2 cm flowers, showing filaments with purple hairs, blooming June-October. Zones 3-6.   p. 509
   olympicum (Greece), "Olympic mullein"; densely white-hairy biennial bush 1 m or more high, forming a candelabra of leafy branches, bearing slender spires with bright yellow flowers to 3 cm across, the filament white-woolly, blooming June to September; very handsome with large rosette of gray-felted leaves. Zone 6.   p. 509
   pulverulentum (Europe incl. Britain, to E. Asia), "Hoary mullein"; bushy biennial or short-lived perennial 60-90 cm high, having angled stem, and lanceolate basal leaves 10-25 cm long, coarsely crenate, matted with white-woolly hairs beneath; the inflorescence much branched, with small 2 cm bright yellow flowers in pyramidal clusters, the filaments with white hairs; blooming July-August. Zone 5.   p. 509
   thapsiforme (densiflorum) (Holland, Sweden to Russia), "King's candle"; robust biennial to 1 m or more tall, densely covered with yellow hair; the oblong-pointed basal leaves to 30 cm long, and serrate along margins; the leafy stem dividing into numerous branches

densely set with yellow flowers to 5 cm across, in spikes, with filaments white-bearded, blooming June to August. Zone 3.   p. 509
   thapsus (Europe to Asia), "Common mullein"; tall biennial, to 2 m high, with large white-woolly leaves arranged as in rosette, to 40 cm long; branched inflorescence of numerous spikes of yellow flowers 3-4 cm across, blooming during Summer. Zones 4-8.   p. 509

VERBENA   *Verbenaceae*
   bipinnatifida (So. Dakota to Arizona, No. Mexico), "Dakota vervain"; densely branching perennial to 50 cm high with prostrate stems rooting at nodes and forming mats; having palmately forked or pinnately divided leaves to 6 cm long, with primary veins depressed; lilac-purple flowers 1-2 cm across, varying from pink to violet, blooming throughout the growing season. Zone 3.   p. 517
   bonariensis (patagonica) (So. America, natural. in southern U.S., West Indies); rough-hairy perennial or annual with erect, 4-angled stems to 1 m or more high; narrow lanceolate, clasping leaves to 10 cm long, toothed at margins; the inflorescence branched, bearing clusters of small lilac flowers, varying in color to purple or blue. Zone 8.   p. 517
   canadensis (Ontario, Michigan, so. to Florida, Colorado, Texas), "Rose verbena"; low herbaceous plant with creeping stems, rooting at nodes; perennial in mild climate, otherwise annual; leaves 3-8 cm long, pinnately lobed or divided; flowers carmine-rose, varying to pink, lavender or white, 2 cm across, in showy clusters. Zone 8.   p. 517
   x hybrida 'Springtime' (derived from V. peruviana crossed with other species), "Garden verbena"; handsome cultivar of this very popular group, usually grown as annuals; large pink flowers with deep crimson center, in dense clusters 5-8 cm across, blooming all Summer until frost; attractive leaves lobed or deeply cut, 5-10 cm long. This hybrid class also comes with flowers red, yellowish, white and purple; their growth is frequently decumbent, and they are excellent edging plants. Zones 9-10.   p. 517
   laciniata (Argentina, Chile), "Moss-verbena"; freely branching herbaceous plant, with creeping stems rooting where touching the ground, perennial in mild climates, annual in colder zones; leaves deeply 3-parted or lacily divided, 2-3 cm long; terminal inflorescence of deep rose or lavender flowers in rounded clusters, summer-blooming. Zone 8.   p. 517
   peruviana (chamaedryfolia) (Argentina and Perú to So. Brazil); semi-woody perennial creeper often grown as annual, with prostrate branches rooting at nodes along the ground; small glossy ovate leaves sharply toothed to 5 cm long; and with striking clusters of vivid crimson-red flowers on long stalks. Zone 9.   p. 324, 517
   rigida (venosa) (So. Brazil, Argentina); erect stiff perennial herb 30-50 cm high, with tuberous roots, leafy 4-angled branches, and narrow very rigid lance-leaves 5-7 cm long, sharply toothed, rough to touch; the inflorescence in bracted spikes with purple or magenta flowers 5 mm wide; a bedding plant; tubers may be kept over like dahlias. Zone 8.   p. 518
   tenera (pulchella, or sellowiana hort.), "Sand vervain"; subshrubby perennial, grown as annual in colder climate, to 60 cm high, branching with prostrate stems, rooting at nodes; the hairy 3 cm leaves divided into narrow segments; the inflorescence in terminal flat clusters of lilac-rose flowers. Zone 8.   p. 518
   tenera 'Aphrodite'; attractive cultivar, with dense heads of light crimson flowers, freely produced during Summer. Zone 8.   p. 518
   tenera var. maonettii (So. Brazil to Argentina); semi-shrubby creeping perennial with spreading stems rooting at nodes; hairy leaves finely divided; flat clusters of beautiful 1-2 cm carmine-rose flowers with distinct white margins. Zone 8.   p. 518
   tenuisecta (So. America; natural. from Georgia to Louisiana), "Creeping moss-vervain"; spreading perennial to 30 cm high, with prostrate branches; the leaves 3-4 cm long, finely divided into linear segments; tubular flowers with spreading lobes, in dense clusters, dark pink, but varying to lilac, blue or purple. Zone 8.   p. 518

VERBESINA   *Compositae*
   encelioides (Florida, west to Mexico), "Golden crown-beard" or "Butter-daisy"; annual herb to 1 m high, with grayish-hairy triangular leaves running down the stem, and flowers in solitary heads 5 cm across, the ray-florets golden-yellow, around the orange disc. Zone 10.   p. 404

VERNONIA   *Compositae*
   noveboracensis (Massachusetts to Mississippi), "Iron weed"; herbaceous perennial with stems to 1 1/2 m high, and narrow-lanceolate leaves 10-20 cm long, rough above and sparsely hairy beneath; 30-50 small purple flowers in each head, having long bristles in loose clusters. Zones 4-7.   p. 404

VERONICA   *Scrophulariaceae*
   armstrongii: see HEBE ochracea
   austriaca (teucrium hort.) (S.E. Europe, Asia Minor to Caucasus), "Austrian speedwell"; downy herbaceous perennial 30-60 cm high,

freely branching, with leaves narrow ovate or deeply cut into linear segments; the flowers variably light or dark blue, to 2 cm across. *Zone 6.* p. 510

bachofenii (grandis) (E. Europe); bushy herbaceous perennial, with erect stems to 60 cm high; opposite, lanceolate leaves, toothed along margins; much branched cylindric racemes of small lilac-pink flowers, in July-August. *Zone 5.* p. 510

filiformis (Europe and Asia Minor), "Creeping veronica"; annual or perennial herb with slender threadlike, prostrate branches rooting at nodes; small ovate or roundish leaves 1 cm long; pale blue, cupped flowers 1 cm across, on thin stalklets. A pretty plant but invasive as a weed in lawns, and naturalized in N.E. No. America. *Zone 3.* p. 508

gentianoides (S.E. Europe, Asia Minor, Caucasus, Crimea), "Gentian speedwell"; showy herbaceous perennial 15-50 cm high, with basal obovate, thick leaves in a rosette 3-8 cm long; small 1 cm pale blue flowers in long pyramidal racemes, blooming in June. *Zone 4.* p. 510

incana (No. Asia, Russia), "Woolly speedwell"; striking silvery gray herbaceous perennial 30-50 cm high, with rosettes of lanceolate, pubescent leaves to 10 cm long, lightly crenate; showy terminal spike-like racemes dense with small blue flowers, blooming July. *Zone 5.* p. 510

longifolia (maritima) (C. Europe to W. Asia), "Speedwell"; shrubby perennial to 75 cm or more tall, the stiff, slender branches with opposite, narrow-lanceolate, herbaceous leaves to 10 cm long, serrate at margins; attractive inflorescence of dense, branched spikes of small violet-blue flowers with protruding stamens, in late Summer. *Zone 4.* p. 510

lyallii: see PARAHEBE lyallii

pectinata 'Rosea' (Asia Minor, Syria), "Comb-speedwell"; low evergreen, subshrubby perennial with prostrate branches, forming mats; small obovate white-hairy leaves to 2 cm long, bluntly toothed; flowers purplish-blue with white center in the species, but rose-pink in 'Rosea', in small clusters 8-12 cm high, in May-June. *Zone 5.* p. 510

persica (Europe incl. Britain, W. Asia), "Persian speedwell"; herbaceous annual similar to V. agrestis, to 35 cm high, with procumbent, spreading fleshy branches, to 25 cm long; broadly ovate, toothed 2 cm leaves, and with lovely cupped, light blue flowers with white eye. *Zone 10.* p. 322

prostrata (Holland to Russia, so. to Italy and Spain), "Creeping speedwell"; herbaceous perennial, forming mats with hairy, prostrate branches; small ovate or linear concave leaves 3-4 cm long; pretty, light lavender-blue flowers 1 cm across, in small clusters, in May-June. *Zone 5.* p. 510

sibirica (virginica var.) (N.E. Asia), "Culver's-root"; herbaceous perennial with erect unbranched, downy stems, 60 cm to nearly 2 m high; lanceolate leaves in whorls, 5-10 cm long; very floriferous with numerous slender, spike-like racemes dense with small white or light blue flowers, autumn-blooming. *Zone 3.* p. 510

spicata (No. Europe, Asia), "Cat's-tail speedwell"; popular herbaceous hardy perennial with stems 30-60 cm high; opposite toothed, lance-shaped leaves 4-5 cm long, and bright blue flowers in long, dense racemes at end of stems, with long purple stamens, Summer. *Zone 3.* p. 510

VERONICA: see also HEBE

VERONICASTRUM *Scrophulariaceae*

virginicum (Veronica) (Manitoba to Louisiana and Texas), "Culver's-root"; erect perennial to 2 m or more high; stems with whorls of lanceolate leaves 15 cm long, topped by clusters of floral spikes to 25 cm long with tiny pale blue or white flowers. *Zone 3.* p. 341

VERSCHAFFELTIA *Palmae*

splendida (Seychelles), "Stilt-root palm"; unique feather-leaf palm, beautiful as a slender mature tree, to 25 m tall; trunk to 15 cm dia., spiny when young, and supported by aerial roots at the base; the deep green leaves pinnately veined, quilted and more or less entire, especially when young; green fruit 3 cm dia., carried between leaves. *Tropical. Zone 12.* p. 112

VESTIA *Solanaceae*

lycioides (Chile); handsome evergreen shrub with downy branches, dense with alternate, oblong, smooth leaves 3-5 cm long; axillary nodding tubular flowers pale yellow 4 cm long, with reflexed lobes and protruding stamens. *Zone 9.* p. 882

VIBURNUM *Caprifoliaceae*

acerifolium (E. Canada to Carolina, west to Minnesota), "Maple-leaf viburnum" or "Arrow-wood"; woodland plant of Eastern No. America, erect deciduous shrub to 2 m high; 3-lobed leaves resembling maple, to 12 cm long and coarsely toothed and turning red in Autumn; small flowers creamy-white, in showy clusters 8 cm across; followed by oval fruit first red then turning to purplish-black. *Zone 3.* p. 675

alnifolium (New Brunswick to No. Carolina and Michigan), "Hobblebush" or "American wayfaring tree"; early-blooming deciduous shrub to 4 m high, with shoots scurfy-downy, the leaves broad-ovate or roundish, 10-20 cm long and toothed at margins; conspicuous sterile white flowers on the outside of the flat floral clusters 8-12 cm across, in May-June, followed by berries first red then black. Beautiful with foliage in crimson autumn coloring. The fresh fruit is edible, and used in making jellies. *Zone 3.* p. 676

x bodnantense (ferreri x grandiflorum) (originated in Wales); vigorous deciduous shrub of erect habit, to 3 m or more, with leaves 5-10 cm long, variable from ovate to obovate, lanceolate or oval, with 6-9 depressed pairs of veins; beautiful trumpet flowers in pendant clusters, in buds deep rose, later almost white, and sweetly fragrant; the fruit red. *Zone 7.* p. 677

burejaeticum (Manchuria and No. China); floriferous deciduous shrub to 5 m high, with young branches pubescent, smooth and gray second year; ovate leaves to 10 cm long, having depressed veins and wavy-toothed margins; small white flowers in dense clusters 5 cm across, followed by small bluish-black fruit. *Zone 5.* p. 675

x burkwoodii (carlesii x utile); handsome hybrid of England 1924 where it is semi-evergreen, but evergreen in milder climate such as California; shrub 1-2 m high with glossy green, deeply furrowed leaves to 10 cm long, downy beneath; small pinkish flowers becoming white, in showy dense clusters 10 cm across, spring-blooming, sweetly fragrant. Very popular in American gardens, from New England to California. *Zone 5.* p. 675

x carlcephalum (carlesii x macrocephalum), "Fragrant snowball"; highly valued deciduous shrub to 3 m high, originated in England 1932; ovate leaves deep green with waxy sheen; the small fragrant flowers pinkish, turning white tinged outside with red, in dense globular clusters 12 cm across, the anthers protruding, in Spring. Beautiful with autumn foliage brilliantly colored. *Zone 5.* p. 675

carlesii 'Compactum', "Fragrant viburnum"; a low form of the popular Korean species, deciduous in cold climate, having shoots densely downy, the broad ovate leaves 5-9 cm long and toothed at margins, dull green and soft-hairy beneath; the very fragrant flowers white, strikingly red in bud, in close clusters 5-8 cm wide during Spring, beginning to bloom before the leaves; small oval black fruit. *Zone 4.* p. 675

cassinoides (E. Canada to No. Carolina and Minnesota), "Withe-rod" or "Appalachian tea"; very floriferous deciduous woodland shrub to 3 m high, with scurfy shoots, and ovate leaves 3-12 cm long, obscurely toothed, dull green but changing color in fall; flowers yellowish-white in flat clusters to 10 cm across in June; berry-like edible fruit in interesting color change from green to yellowish, to bright red and finally blue-black. Most beautiful with foliage in brilliant red autumn color. *Zone 2.* p. 675

davidii (China); evergreen shrub 1 m or more high, of compact growth densely branched with warty shoots; glossy green ovate leathery leaves 8-12 cm long, conspicuous with 3 parallel depressed veins; small white flowers dense in flat clusters 8 cm wide, followed by light blue fruit in Autumn. *Zone 7.* p. 676

dentatum (New Brunswick so. to Florida and Texas), "Southern arrowwood"; tall deciduous bush to 5 m high, with smooth branches from base; ovate leaves to 8 cm long and sharply toothed at margins, veins in 6-8 pairs, glossy green above, changing to red in Fall; white 1 cm flowers in clusters to 8 cm across, in May-June; blue-black berry-fruit. Beautiful in red foliage color in Autumn. *Zones 2-8.* p. 676

dilatatum (Mountains of Japan), "Linden viburnum" or "Gamazumi" in Japan; handsome deciduous shrub to 3 m high, with ovate leaves to 12 cm long, very corrugated by lateral veins, toothed along sides and hairy above and beneath; flowers pure white, borne in airy clusters, in June, followed by prolific glossy scarlet-red berries. Very attractive in its striking rusty-red autumn foliage. *Zone 5.* p. 676

farreri 'Candidissimum' (fragrans) (North China), "Fragrant viburnum"; probably the first viburnum to bloom in New England, preceding foliage, with highly scented pure white flowers in small clusters; deciduous shrub to 3 m high; leaves elliptic-pointed to 7 cm long, and sharply serrate at margins; fruit yellow in this cultivar, red and later black in the species. *Zone 6.* p. 677

grandiflorum (Himalayas); robust deciduous shrub to 2 m high, with stout branches; the elliptic leaves 7-10 cm long, having 6-10 pairs of nerves, hairy beneath; charming tubular flowers white flushed with rose, in dense clusters 8 cm across, sweetly fragrant, and blooming in February-March, before foliage; fruit black-purple. *Zone 7.* p. 677

henryi (Central China); evergreen shrub of stiff erect habit to 3 m tall; the thin-leathery ovate or obovate leaves to 12 cm long, dark shining green above, finely toothed at margins; the inflorescence is pyramidal to 10 cm high, of small white flowers during Summer; followed by fruit at first red, ripening to black. *Zone 7.* p. 677

x hillieri (erubescens x henryi); semi-evergreen shrub to 2 m; young foliage coppery, bronze in Winter; cream-white flowers; berries red, later blackish. *Zone 7.*   p. 677

japonicum (Japan: Honshu, Kyushu; Taiwan), "Japanese viburnum"; evergreen bush with stout branches to 2 m high; ovate leathery leaves 10-15 cm long, dark shining green above and numerous black dots beneath; very fragrant white flowers 1 cm wide, closely set in rounded trusses, in June; followed by prolific red berryfruit. *Zone 7.*   p. 676, 679

x juddii (bitchiuense x carlesii); deciduous shrub 2½ m high, with spreading branches, broad-ovate leaves to 9 cm long and hairy beneath; clusters of charming trumpet-shaped flowers, rose-pink in bud but flaring open with white inside, blooming March-April and sweetly fragrant; fruit red to nearly black. Originated at Arnold Arboretum near Boston 1920. *Zone 5.*   p. 677

lantana (Europe to W. Asia), "Woolly snowball"; vigorous floriferous shrub to 5 m high, with downy shoots and leaves 12 cm long, gray-felty beneath; the white flowers are silky outside, in dense and showy clusters to 10 cm across, blooming May-June, followed by 1 cm oblong fruit first red then changing to black; autumn foliage attractively red in some areas. *Zone 3.*   p. 677

lantana rugosum (Europe, West Asia), "Wayfaring tree"; deciduous shrub to 5 m, sometimes tree-like; finely toothed ovate leaves 12-15 cm long, larger than V. lantana and more wrinkled, gray-felted underneath; small white flowers in 10 cm clusters, followed by glossy red, berry-like fruit, becoming black. *Zone 3.*   p. 677

macrocephalum (China), "Chinese snowball"; the largest of the Snowballs; bushy deciduous shrub to 4 m tall, partly evergreen in the U.S. South; scurfy shoots with ovate leaves 5-10 cm long and thinly downy; inflorescence with sterile marginal flowers pure white and 3 cm dia., in dense globular clusters 12 cm across, the most showy in the genus, blooming in May. *Zone 6.*   p. 677

odoratissimum (India to Japan), "Sweet viburnum"; large evergreen shrub to 3 m, with willowy, reddish, rugose branches and opposite, flexible leathery, elliptic leaves glossy dark green, pale midrib and lightly crenate margins; fragrant white flowers in panicles to 15 cm wide, followed by fruit first red, ripening to black. A favorite in Southern gardens. *Zone 9.*   p. 676

odoratissimum 'Irvinii' (Himalayas, India, China, Japan); ornamental red-leaf form of the "Sweet viburnum"; robust evergreen shrub to 6 m high, the species with willowy red, rugose branches, and opposite, flexible leathery, elliptic leaves 10-25 cm long, glossy dark green with pale midrib and lightly crenate margins; small pure white, fragrant flowers in conical clusters. The cultivar 'Irvinii' is an attractive decorative plant in California nurseries with larger leaves 15-28 cm long, bright green to a lacquered maroon-red in the older foliage. *Zone 9.*   p. 678

opulus (Europe, No. Africa, No. Asia), "European cranberry bush"; deciduous shrub 3-4 m high, with opposite 3 to 5-lobed maplelike green leaves, rugose above and pubescent beneath, to 10 cm long, turning red in Autumn; flowers white in stalked clusters, the white marginal flowers sterile, the center filled with fertile flowers producing the scarlet fruit. *Zone 3.*   p. 678

opulus roseum (op. sterile) (Europe, No. Africa, No. Asia), "Common snowball-tree", or "European cranberry-tree"; deciduous shrub 3-4 m high, with 3-lobed, maple-like leaves 5-10 cm long, and coarsely toothed, downy beneath; the white flowers all sterile, and forming round, ball or rose-like terminal heads 5-6 cm across; the foliage turns deep red in Autumn; hardy. *Zone 3.*   p. 678

plicatum (tomentosum) (China, Japan), "Japanese snowball"; deciduous shrub to 3 m high, with 10 cm ovate toothed leaves, pubescent beneath; clusters of white flowers in 2 rows, the outer sterile. *Zone 4.*   p. 678

plicatum 'Roseum' (tomentosum roseum), "Double-file viburnum" or "Pink snowball"; attractive with spreading horizontal branches tipped in May-June by multitudes of ball-shaped clusters dense with sterile flowers first white, deepening to dark rose later; not developing fruit on sterile blooms, but the foliage coloring wine-red in Autumn. *Zone 4.*   p. 679

x pragense (rhytidophyllum x utile); evergreen shrub to 2½ m high, with slender, arching branches; thin-leathery elliptic corrugated leaves 5-10 cm long, glossy green above, white-felted beneath; creamy-white, mostly sterile flowers in terminal clusters. Originated at the city nursery in Prague 1955. *Zone 5.*   p. 678

prunifolium (Connecticut so. to Florida and Texas), "Black haw" or "Sheep-berry"; deciduous shrub or small tree to 5 m high; reddish branchlets with glossy green ovate leaves 4 to 10 cm long; pure white flowers in flattish clusters to 10 cm across, blooming in June; glaucous, blue-black fruit, edible after frost, made into preserves since Colonial times; roots are used medicinally. Foliage beautiful in autumn color of shining red. *Zone 3.*   p. 678

rhytidophyllum (Central and W. China), "Leatherleaf viburnum"; handsome shrub or small tree to 6 m high; with stout branches densely downy; the leaves ovate-oblong 10-20 cm long, deep green above and very wrinkled, gray with thick felt beneath; flowers yellowish-white during May, dense in rounded clusters 10-20 cm across; oval 1 cm fruit red then shining black. Remarkable for its unusual corrugated foliage; semi-evergreen in cold areas, but evergreen in the milder Southern states. *Zone 5.*   p. 678

rigidum (Canary Islands), "Canary Island viburnum"; evergreen shrub 2-3 m high, with young branches pubescent; ovate thin-leathery leaves 5-15 cm long, showing veins recessed, dull green and rough on surface, softly silky beneath; small white flowers densely packed in flattish clusters 8-12 cm across, rather pretty with pink stigmas, blooming early Spring; followed by glossy berries first red then turning black. *Zone 8.*   p. 678

sargentii 'Onondaga' (N.E. Asia), "Sargent cranberry bush"; hybrid of sargentii clones (Kruessmann); deciduous bush of globular shape 2 m high, dark gray branches, with mostly 3-lobed leaves irregularly toothed at margins; the inflorescence with red buds, when open the sterile flowers creamy-white in flat clusters to 12 cm across; autumn foliage reddish. *Zone 4.*   p. 676

setigerum (Cent. and West China), "Tea viburnum"; deciduous shrub to 4 m high, its young branches smooth, with dark green, lanceolate leaves to 12 cm long; white flowers having purple calyx in pendant clusters 5 cm across, developing from the fertile blooms the glossy red fruits. The leaves were used by monks in Japan as substitute for tea. *Zone 5.*   p. 678

setigerum 'Aurantiacum' (China); attractive shrub of special interest because of its coppery fruits, a unique color amongst berried shrubs, borne in pendulous clusters from arching branches. *Zone 5.*   p. 679

sieboldii (Japan: Honshu, Kyushu), "Goma-Ki" (Ohwi); vigorous tree-like deciduous shrub to 5 m or more high, with dark wrinkled but lustrous leaves to 12 cm long, obovate in outline, prominently veined and coarsely toothed, pubescent beneath; inflorescence of small, all-fertile creamy-white flowers in dense clusters 10 cm wide, blooming May-June; from the fertile blossoms develop the small berries, first rose then turning black; when they fall, the remaining red fruit stalks adorn the plant in Autumn. *Zone 4.*   p. 679

suspensum (Japan), "Sadankwa viburnum"; ornamental evergreen shrub 2-4 m high, with shiny dark green, leathery oval leaves crenate toward apex, 5-12 cm long, and clusters of tiny fragrant flowers pinkish to cream-white, March-blooming; small globose red fruit. *Zone 9.*   p. 679

tinus (S.E. Europe, Mediterranean reg.), "Laurustinus"; evergreen thickly branched and luxuriantly leafy shrub, with ovate deep green, stiff-leathery 8 cm foliage with rough underside, on reddish petioles; dense 5 to 8 cm clusters of tiny pinkish-white, very fragrant flowers; blooming May to August; small fruit first blue, later black. Known in Europe as "Laurustinus", where it is one of the most popular durable decorator tub plants, and with its handsome foliage and compact shape ideal for cooler areas, the patio, or roof garden. *Subtropic. Zone 8.*   p. 679

tinus 'Aureo-variegatum', "Golden laurustinus"; discovered in Buenos Aires; grown by Mr. Bewley of Warrimoo, Australia; very handsome form with leathery green leaves bordered and variegated golden-yellow. *Zone 10.*   p. 679

trilobum (Northern U.S., So. Canada), "American cranberry"; the American counterpart of the European V. opulus; deciduous shrub to 4 m high, with broad-ovate usually smooth leaves 12 cm long, tri-lobed and toothed at margins; white flowers in clusters to 10 cm across, the marginal blooms sterile; fruit scarlet-red and edible, turning color in July, and remaining on plant the greater part of Winter. Best in cooler climate gardens. *Zone 2.*   p. 679

wrightii (Japan), "Leatherleaf"; deciduous shrub 2-3 m high, with broadly ovate leaves 5-10 cm long, having 6 to 10 pairs of sunken veins, toothed along margins; white flowers in clusters 10 cm across, followed by handsome 1 cm red fruits from fertile blooms, giving the plant outstanding character in Autumn; in addition the foliage turns brilliant in color late in season. *Zone 5.*   p. 679

VICIA   *Leguminosae*

faba (No. Africa, S.W. Asia), "Broad bean" or "Sow bean"; very leafy annual 60 cm to more than 1 m high, with compound leaves of 2 to 6 somewhat fleshy, elliptic leaflets to 10 cm long; flowers in leaf axils, white with violet blotch, in May to August; thick pea-pods to 20 cm long, containing large seeds used as cooked vegetable when young, the beans of antiquity. Widely grown in cool climate agriculture, as food crop and for forage. *Zone 9 as annual.*   p. 442, 940

VICTORIA   *Nymphaeaceae*

amazonica (regia) (Guyana, Amazon, Bolivia), "Royal water lily"; gigantic, floating, 1½ m fresh green leaves with upturned red edges; projecting air-filled ribs beneath give the leaves good buoyancy, sufficient to support great weight; the fragrant floating flowers are white turning deep rose the following day; at home in quiet "Igarapes" of warm 30° C water. *Humid-tropical. Zone 11.*   p. 333

cruziana (trickeri) (Paraná, Paraguay, No. Argentina), "Santa Cruz water lily"; large perennial aquatic with a thick rhizome, thorny petioles and round, floating leaves not as large as regia but with higher upturned margins to 20 cm high and green; flowers white turning deep pink on second day; requires only moderately warm water. *Humid-subtropic. Zone 10.*   *p. 333*

VIGNA *Leguminosae*
caracalla (Phaseolus) (Trop. So. America), "Snail-flower"; perennial twiner with leaves usually of 3 leaflets, and light purple, fragrant flowers tinted yellow, to 5 cm long and with contorted standard, the keel and wings spirally coiled like a snail shell. Also known as "Corkscrew flower". *Tropical. Zone 10.*   *p. 280*

VINCA *Apocynaceae*
major (S.E. Europe), "Greater periwinkle" or "Blue buttons"; trailing vine with flexible branches to 2 m long, at intervals opposite, oval or ovate leaves 5 cm long, deep green and leathery; axillary funnel-shaped flowers bright lavender-blue, to 5 cm across in Mid-May. Very ornamental in gardens of mild climates. *Zone 7.*   *p. 301*
major 'Variegata' (So. Europe, No. Africa), "Band plant"; trailing evergreen basket plant or for window boxes, with long, thin, wiry vines having opposite, oval, green leaves beautifully edged in cream, to 5 cm long; flowers blue. *Subtropic. Zones 7-9.*   *p. 301*
minor (So. Europe to Asia Minor), "Periwinkle"; trailing evergreen subshrub with glossy dark green, ovate leaves; flowers bluish-purple with white throat, 2 cm dia. *Warm temperate. Zone 5.*   *p. 301*
rosea: see CATHARANTHUS roseus

VINCETOXICUM hirundinaria (Zander):
see CYNANCHUM vincetoxicum (Hortus)

VIOLA *Violaceae*
calcarata (Alps of C. Europe), "Spurred violet"; beautiful small alpine perennial to 10 cm high, with slender stolons creeping below ground; the smooth oval leaves wavy-toothed and forming a basal rosette; showy flowers to 4 cm across, with broad, purplish-violet petals and slender spur, freely blooming from late Spring to August. *Zone 5.*   *p. 518*
canadensis (E. Canada to Rocky Mts., Alabama to Arizona), "Canada violet"; tufting herbaceous perennial, with leafy stems to 30 cm, from thick rhizome; broad ovate leaves with cordate base; sweetly fragrant flowers with white petals, having yellow eye inside, tinged violet outside, and with short spur. *Zones 3-8.*   *p. 518*
canina (No. Europe and Asia to Japan), "Dog violet"; pretty spring-blooming perennial to 10 cm high, from short creeping rhizome; the leaves broad-ovate with cordate base; flowers light purple to blue, with whitish base inside, in April to June. *Zone 5.*   *p. 519*
cornuta (Spain to Pyrenees; natural. W. to So. Europe), "Horned violet"; charming herbaceous perennial to 30 cm high, forming tufts, with ovate leaves, usually cordate at base; flowers like miniature pansies and without fragrance, purplish to violet, having petals to 2 cm long, and with slender spur, blooming June to August. Some larger flowered hort. strains have been developed. *Zones 6-9.* *p. 519*
'Cornuta hybrid' (wittrockiana x cornuta), "Tufted pansy"; herbaceous dwarf perennial, grown as annual or biennial, with smooth oval leaves; small pansy-like flowers deep purple, and having yellow eye in center. Seen in col. Duesseldorf Bot. Garden, Germany. *Zone 6.*   *p. 519*
hederacea (Erpetion reniforme) (New South Wales, Victoria, Tasmania), "Australian violet", "Trailing violet", or "Ivy-leaved violet"; attractive trailing species; the vertical rhizome putting out long, threadlike stolons with well separated tufts of leaves; these kidney-shaped or rounded, 2-4 cm across, fresh green and herbaceous; small 2 cm flowers with petal-tips white, center area violet except for white eye; scarcely spurred. *Subtropic. Zone 9.*   *p. 324*
odorata (Europe to Caucasus, Western Asia), "Sweet violet"; small perennial with stout rhizome putting out rooting runners; long-stalked, deep green leaves round heart-shaped and toothed; the little 2 cm nodding flowers purple to violet-blue with small white eye, sweetly scented, in early Spring. Flowers and leaves are sources of essential oil used in French perfumery and added to liquors; flowers are also candied in violet bonbons. *Zones 6-9.*   *p. 519, 542*
sororia (papilionacea) (E. No. America: Québec to Minnesota and Okla., so. to Carolina), "Woolly blue violet" or "Butterfly violet"; charming small stemless herbaceous perennial 10 cm high, from thick fleshy rhizome, with broad ovate-cordate leaves, usually pubescent; flowers blue or purple but varying to red or white; the petals bear tufts of white hairs. Widely distributed in Northeast U.S. *Zone 3.*   *p. 518*
sororia 'Immaculata', "Pentecost violet"; floriferous cultivar, seen at Federal Hort. Expo in Duesseldorf, Germany 1987; covered with multitudes of pure white flowers 3 cm across, blooming in May. *Zone 4.*   *p. 518*
tricolor (No. Europe to C. Asia), "Wild pansy", "Johnny-jump-up" or "Kiss-me-love"; pretty annual or shortlived perennial, of tufted

habit, to 15 cm high, with ovate, crenate, fresh waxy green leaves; small and cute miniature pansy flowers 1-2 cm across, with faces yellow and purple, blooming April to September. *Zone 4.*   *p. 519*
x wittrockiana (tricolor hybrid with lutea and altaica), also known as V. tricolor hortensis; "Garden pansy" or "Ladies-delight"; widely popular herbaceous garden biennial or shortlived perennial 10-20 cm high; much branched with leafy stems, the lower leaves ovate-cordate, uppers elliptic; large rounded flowers 5-10 cm or more across, according to strain, with flattened petals usually in 3 colors, primarily golden-yellow, violet, blue, crimson-red and brown, apricot, cream or white, also bicolors, and marked by blackish or purple blotches; blooming in the cool Spring, after being planted out on beds in Autumn, maintaining their smooth foliage even under snow. *Zones 6-9.*   *p. 519*
x wittrockiana 'Bambini'; petite flowers with "whiskered" faces in colors from pale pink to yellow and blue or lavender. *Zones 6-9.*   *p. 519*
x wittrockiana 'Illumination'; "Pansies" with friendly faces in shades of orange, copper and ruby-red, freely blooming in early Spring. *Zones 6-9.*   *p. 519*
x wittrockiana 'Majestic Giant'; huge flowers of good substance, to 10 cm across, in bronze or other shades, each bloom with conspicuous dark blotches on lower petals. *Zones 6-9.*   *p. 519*

VIRGILIA *Leguminosae*
divaricata (So. Africa), "Keur-broom"; shrub-like tree to 10 m high, with horizontal branches; evergreen pinnate leaves having 6-10 pairs of leathery, narrow oblong leaflets 3 cm long, pale and tomentose beneath; pea-like mauve-pink flowers 2 cm long, grouped at end of branches, and sweetly fragrant. *Zones 9-10.*   *p. 772*

VISCUM *Loranthaceae*
album (Europe, No. Asia), the Old world "Mistletoe" of legend; parasitic evergreen shrub attached to host trees such as apples, poplars, maples or pines stealing their food; forming pendulous clusters of twiggy little branches of woody texture, dichotomously forked; sickle-shaped grayish-leathery 4-9 cm leaves; berry-like fruit yellowish to translucent white, on female plants. In Europe, cut branches are an invitation to a kiss. *Temperate. Zone 7.*   *p. 206*

VITEX *Verbenaceae*
agnus-castus (So. Europe and Asia Minor; naturalized in southern U.S. and warm areas worldwide), "Chaste tree", "Hemptree" or "Monk's pepper"; aromatic shrub or small tree to 6 m or more high; the branches gray-felted and 4-angled; hemp-like deciduous, palmately compound foliage, pleasantly scented when bruised, the 5 to 7 leaflets narrow-lanceolate, 5 to 10 cm long, dark green above, grayish tomentose beneath; the inflorescence in showy terminal spikes of small fragrant, pale lilac-blue flowers in Autumn; little berry-like stone fruit with pungent, peppery flavor. *Warm temperate. Zones 7-8.*   *p. 902*
lucens (New Zealand: northern No. Island), the "Puriri" or "New Zealand oak"; shrub or tree becoming 20 m high, with strong, oak-like timber; palmately compound leaves of broad-elliptic, folded, leathery, bright glossy green leaflets 8-10 cm long; axillary clusters of pink, trumpet-like flowers with spreading lobes, yellow in throat, and with protruding stamens. Bright red 2 cm fruit resembling small cherries. *Subtropic. Zones 9-10.*   *p. 902*

VITIS *Vitaceae*
coignetiae (Japan); "Crimson glory vine"; handsome, strong-growing vine with heavy foliage brightly coloring crimson in Autumn; leaves large, sometimes 30 cm across, roundish, and shallowly lobed, dull green above and gray or rusty-tomentose beneath; persistent purplish-black berries prettily covered with waxy bloom; fairly hardy. *Zone 6.*   *p. 300*
x labruscana 'Catawba' (Eastern U.S.); an American grape cultivar partially with European (vinifera) blood; strong woody deciduous vine high-climbing by tendrils, in arid region erect shrubby; tomentose on young growth; leaves triangular-ovate, 10-20 cm wide, lightly 3-lobed and shallow toothed, and downy beneath; the fruit in conical clusters, of thick skinned coppery to purplish-black 2 cm berries, sweet or astringent with a musky flavor; ripening late, and an excellent keeper. Used for wine-making and champagne; also eaten fresh and for jellies. *Zones 5-8.*   *p. 943*
x labruscana 'Concord'; a favorite American all-purpose grape, popular in the home garden; very productive with beautiful clusters of blue-black fruit of sweet, delicious taste that ripen in late August; ideal for jam, jellies and preserves, also table use and juice, from coast to coast; self-pollinating. *Zones 4-9.*   *p. 943*
x labruscana 'Himrod'; promising new seedless grape by New York Exper. Sta. Geneva, with superior results in cool climate of Northeast U.S.; large pendant clusters of green to golden-yellow grapes without seeds, very juicy flesh of sweet, delicious flavor,

ripening in early Autumn, disease-free on vigorous vines. Not very satisfactory on the Pacific Coast, with low yield. *Zone 3.*   *p. 943*

x labruscana 'Steuben' (labrusca x vinifera) "Fox-grape"; very best blue-black; tender-sweet with a tempting delicate flavor; long, slender clusters in mid-September from vines that produce full crops after 20° below zero F (-30°C). American labruscana varieties need short season and high elevation growing areas, while European vinifera cultivars need long warm growing season in valley and hillside locations. *Zone 4.*   *p. 943*

riparia (vulpina) (Nova Scotia to Montana, Virginia to New Mexico), "River side grape" or "Frost grape"; vigorous high climber with pithy canes, and rotund fresh green leaves 10-20 cm long, sharply serrate and with pointed lobes along margins; staminate flowers fragrant; fruit in clusters of glaucous black 1 cm berries with acid pulp of sour taste, ripening in September, mostly after frost.
Zone 2.   *p. 300*

rotundifolia (Delaware to Florida, w. to Kansas and Mexico), "Muscadine grape"; large vigorous spreading bush with pithy, warted canes, climbing to 30 m with unbranched tendrils; form orbicular, glossy leaves coarsely toothed at margins and 12 cm long; fruit in clusters of 2 cm dull purple, thick-skinned berries with strongly musky-flavored pulp. Several varieties of grapes have been developed from this species especially for growing in the Southern U.S.
Zone 6.   *p. 300*

rotundifolia 'Cowart' (Southeast U.S.), "Muscadine grape"; one of the best known of all muscadines, this variety is almost 3 cm across; these sweet purplish-black grapes are reported to be the best flavored of all the large fruiting types. No other grape has been shown to be better adapted to the Deep South than the Cowart.
Zones 7-9.   *p. 943*

striata: see CISSUS striata

thunbergii (Japan, China, Korea, Taiwan), "Ebizuru" in Japan; slender-stemmed climber of moderate growth, the branches angled and downy, tendrils occasionally missing; corrugated leaves deeply 3 (or 5) lobed and sharply toothed, 8-15 cm wide, brown-felted beneath, turning red in Autumn; small black fruits. *Zone 6.*   *p. 300*

vinifera 'Black Alicante' (Alicante or Black Tokay) 'Hamburg' type European "Vinous" grape or "Dessert grape"; vigorously vining canes with large, deep green leaves, covered with down underneath looking silvery; the oval fruit thick-skinned, black and covered with dense blue bloom, semi-sweet, with squashy flesh of a strong wine-flavor and earthy; for late season, and an excellent keeper, free-fruiting with large bunches of splendid appearance and weighing 1 to 2½ kg. Foremost variety long used for forcing under glass in northern Europe, and even in U.S.A. where during the time of the great conservatory ranges, it was listed in Roehrs catalogs since 1907. *Warm temperate. Zone 8.*   *p. 943*

vinifera 'Blue Burgundy'; from the Nile Valley, distributed by Phoenicians, Greeks and Romans; luscious medium to large size grapes, with thin red to blue-black skin, enclosing the very sweet and juicy flesh and seeds; ripening September-October; delicious when eaten fresh; most important grape for red-wine making in Switzerland. *Zone 6.*   *p. 942*

vinifera 'Golden Muscat', "Yellow Muscatel grape"; vigorous productive vine; an old cultivar from Asia Minor, cultivated mostly in So. Europe, a favorite in Italy; grows well in coastal areas of California; in colder climate as espalier on a sunny wall; in U.S. grafted on American understock; large fruit green to golden-yellow, with sweet, aromatic muscat flavor, having tender skin and crisp, seeded flesh; excellent table grape, and for raisins; also widely used for making of Muscatel wine. *Zone 6.*   *p. 942*

vinifera 'Muscat of Alexandria'; a European "Muscat" white grape; with a musky or perfumed flavor; large oval berries, with clear skin, rather thick, greenish-yellow; firm, crackling fleshy, exceedingly sweet, in handsome, long-tapering clusters weighing 1-2 kg or more; for late fruiting, and requiring some warmth; will keep in good condition until late Spring. Healthy grower with deeply lobed rugose foliage. Grown under glass in Holland for table use, but also produces Muscatel wine; much used for the popular Muscat raisins of California. *Zone 6.*   *p. 942*

vinifera 'Red Flame', (Thompson Seedless x Red Cardinal); superb new cultivar of red seedless grapes (about 1980), ideal for the South, producing large thin-skinned, spicy fruit of plump, rounded shape and coppery red color with extra crisp texture, and of sugary sweet flavor and excellent when eaten fresh; ripening in California Coachella Valley in June, further north in August. Self-pollinating. *Zones 7-10.*   *p. 944*

vinifera 'Riesling', the "Wine grape", originally believed from the Caucasus region, known in ancient Egypt, and cultivated for centuries; woody deciduous vine moderately climbing by tendrils, with rather thin, scarcely toothed, 3-5-lobed leaves and with intermittent tendrils; small, greenish unisexual flowers in long clusters followed by delicious, fleshy, glaucous green berries, tender and sweet. The

tawny yellow, highly acid 'Riesling' grape is most widely grown in temperate Europe for high production of the best white wines, expecially in the Moselle and Rhine valleys; also cultivated in California where it has become adapted in warmer climate, producing wines of finesse and quality, marketed under the label "Johannisberg Riesling". Less demanding, but more proliferous is the 'Silvaner' grape, grown in Hesse and Franconia. Brought by the Romans to Germany. *Zone 6.*   *p. 943*

vinifera 'Silvaner' (Italy, Austria); widely grown in South Germany, reportedly better in taste than 'Riesling'; bushy shrub with spreading branches, with mid brown woody stems; leaves roundish, mostly tri-lobed, glossy green above, finely toothed; late blooming, followed by medium-large, depressed globose to round berries, greenish-yellow with thick skin, the flesh of sweet taste, ripening end of September; excellent for wine-making of dry-type full-bodied flavor. Grown on sunny, fairly frost-free slopes in Zone 8. *Zones 9-10.*   *p. 943*

vinifera 'Thompson Seedless'; sport of the English white grape, discovered in Sutter County, California, from an Old country budsport (from cutting); leading raisin and table variety; large clusters of medium-sized, elongated greenish-white to light golden seedless berries, ripening in August in California vineyards, and of delicious sweet taste as a table grape. *Zone 7.*   *p. 943*

VRIESEA   *Bromeliaceae*

fenestralis (Brazil), "Netted vriesea"; compact rosette of broad recurved foliage arranged spirally, yellow-green leaves ornamented by numerous dark green lines and network of cross lines, purplish circles underside; sulphur yellow flowers scattered on pale spike. *Humid-tropical. Zone 11.*   *p. 50*

fosteriana 'Seideliana'; handsome formal rosette of olive-green leaves crossed by irregular, narrow yellow bands, center and reverse bronze. Photographed at Botanic Garden Frankfurt, Germany. *Tropical. Zone 11.*   *p. 51*

heliconioides (Guatemala, Costa Rica, Colombia, Brazil, Guyana, Bolivia); striking flowering plant, with rosette of plain, glossy green leaves 20 cm long, suffused with red underneath; the erect flattened inflorescence heliconia-like having lateral triangular boat-shaped floral bracts bright red above the middle, greenish-yellow at the apex; the flowers peeking out with creamy-white petals. *Tropical. Zone 12.*   *p. 51*

heterostachys (Brazil: Minas Gerais to São Paulo); epiphytic rosette of light green leaves 30-40 cm long; elliptic inflorescence to 20 cm long; floral bracts orange-salmon, petals yellow, tipped green. *Zone 11.*   *p. 50*

hieroglyphica (Brazil: Espirito Santo to Paraná), "King of bromeliads"; large epiphytic rosette with broad yellow-green leaves to 60 cm long, beautifully cross-banded with hieroglyphic marks dark green above and purplish-brown beneath; inflorescence a tall branched spike with sulphur yellow flowers. *Humid-tropical. Zone 11.*   *p. 51*

imperialis (Estado do Rio), "Giant vriesea"; gigantic terrestrial rosette which I found growing on the dry west slopes of the Organ Mountains; leathery green leaves to 1½ m long, in good light becoming deep wine-red, and even young plants produce seedling-like suckers at the base; the inflorescence a tall branched spike 2 m or more, the large bract leaves glossy maroon-red, and from which extend the arching bracted spikes with yellow flowers. *Tropical. Zone 11.*   *p. 51*

regina (Brazil: Distrito Federal); giant, bold rosette of regular, elegant beauty; the broad concave, waxy green leaves densely speckled with maroon dots toward base and underneath as well as along margins, pointed apex sharply recurved; inflorescence to 2 m high, with 2-ranked spikes of rose bracts and white to yellow perfumed flowers. *Zone 10.*   *p. 51*

sintenisii (Thecophyllum) (Puerto Rico, Cuba, Haiti, Jamaica); epiphyte of the high cloud forests; shapely rosette of soft-leathery, glossy leaves 25 to 45 cm long, green in shade, but beautifully colored wine-red in bright light; inflorescence a lax spike with showy red bracts, and yellow flowers. *Tropical. Zone 11.*   *p. 51*

splendens (Guyana, Venezuela, Trinidad), "Flaming sword"; broadly funnel-form rosette, both epiphytic and terrestrial, of slender bluish-green leaves 40-80 cm long, marked with broad deep purple crossbands; underneath grayish with the purple bands very bold; flower spike long and sword-shaped with flattened fiery-red bracts and yellow flowers. *Tropical. Zone 11.*   *p. 51*

splendens 'Variegata'; a remarkable cultivar on exhibit at the German National Flower Show in Cologne 1971, with leaves blackish-green cross-banded in sharply contrasting yellow-green to creamy-white. *Tropical. Zone 11.*   *p. 51*

zamorensis (Guzmania, Tillandsia) (So. Ecuador, No. Perú 1000 m elev.); tropical epiphytic rosette of glossy green leaves to

45 cm long, scurfy beneath; the showy inflorescence branched into lateral spikes of appressed coral-red floral bracts, petals yellowish-rose. Zone 10.   p. 46

WALDSTEINIA   Rosaceae

geoides (Hungary to Greece); strawberry-like perennial spreading with creeping rhizome near surface, 5-25 cm high; leaves palmately 3-5 lobed or divided, the lobes coarsely toothed; yellow flowers 2 cm wide showing barely above foliage, blooming April-May.
Zone 6.   p. 492

ternata (Centr. Europe, to Siberia, Japan), "Barren strawberry"; evergreen flat-growing groundcover perennial forming mats, from creeping rhizomes; glossy green leaves with 3 oval leaflets; clusters of small 2 cm yellow flowers followed by strawberry-like but dry hairy fruit. Zones 4-10.   p. 321

WARSZEWICZIA   Rubiaceae

coccinea (Trinidad, C. America to Brazil), "Wild poinsettia"; large tropical shrub to 6 m high, with sparry, woody branches bearing big obovate, corrugated leaves 20-50 cm long; at end of arching shoots the striking elongate inflorescence 30 cm or more long, serving as a rachis (axis) for sessile clusters of small 1 cm orange flowers set at intervals and subtended on both sides by the bract-like crimson-red calyx lobes 8-12 cm long. Photographed at Papeari Botanic Garden, Tahiti. Zone 11.   p. 859

coccinea cv 'David Auyong' (Trinidad cultivar); spectacular tropical rambling shrub, having spreading branches with large corrugated leaves extending into a long rachis carrying a dense row of small yellow flowers sitting along the top, on both sides a dual row of oblong glowing red bracts or calyx leaves. Zone 11.   p. 859

WASHINGTONIA   Palmae

filifera (So. California desert, S.W. Arizona, Baja California), "Desert fan palm" or "Petticoat palm"; in habitat in Agua Caliente canyon, Palm Springs, California; bold solitary, erect fan palm with massive grayish trunk to 1 m thick and 18 to 25 m tall, usually clothed by the densely shingled older leaves and looking like a skirt, unless burnt off; the top with a crown of palmate, gray-green, leathery fronds 2 m or more across, divided more than half-way to base, and with many long threads attached to segments, on thorny, long, green petioles. For dry-hot climate. Subtropic. Zones 8-9.   p. 112

robusta (N.W. Mexico: Sonora, Baja California), the "Mexican fan palm"; more slender than filifera and faster growing, to nearly 34 m tall, the upper part dense with brown dead, and living glossy bright green foliage, the plaited fan-leaves are stiff and lightly cut, to 1¼ m long, and with some fibrous threads in juvenile stage; fruit black-brown. Rarely used as container plant, but much planted in warm-arid climate along avenues and homes for tropical effect in not quite tropical regions. Older tall specimen look scrawny, with relatively small crowns up high. Subtropic. Zones 9-10.   p. 112

WATSONIA   Iridaceae

beatricis (So. Africa), "Bugle lily"; evergreen Watsonia with rich orange-red tubular flowers in great profusion on erect spikes.
Subtropic. Zone 8.   p. 227

pyramidata (rosea) (South Africa), "Pink watsonia"; breathtaking to see a slope in the Hottentot-Holland Mountains, or down the Cape Peninsula, covered in Spring with these rosy-flowered Watsonias; cormous plant 1-1½ m high, having nearly linear basal leaves, and the long, branched spike-like inflorescence carrying showy rose-pink funnel-shaped flowers with curved tube, the spreading lobes to 5 cm across. Subtropic. Zone 8.   p. 235

pyramidata 'Alba' (Lathyrium odoratus) (So. Africa: Cape Peninsula); floriferous hybrid photographed in South Africa blooming in April; trumpet flowers with curved tube glistening pure white.
Zone 8.   p. 227

WEDELIA   Compositae

trilobata (West Indies, North So. America), "Creeping daisy"; prolifically branching herb with slender, flexible trailing stems; elliptic, fresh green, notched and lightly lobed, somewhat fleshy leaves, 5 to 15 cm long; and attractive marigold-like flowers with golden-yellow florets to 3 cm across. A cheerful basket plant or groundcover.
Tropical. Zone 10.   p. 312, 404

WEIGELA   Carpifoliaceae

floribunda 'Variegata'; handsome gold-edged foliage distinguish this cultivar from Japan, seen at the Floriade in Amsterdam; a deciduous shrub with pubescent obovate leaves 7-10 cm long; very floriferous with blooms crowded on lateral branchlets, the funnel-shaped corolla rose-red, to 3 cm long. The cultivar 'Nana variegata' remains shorter and globular. Zone 6.   p. 680

florida (Diervilla) (No. China, Korea); handsome, very popular deciduous shrub 2-3 m high, with spreading branches, broad-elliptic toothed leaves 8-10 cm long; very pretty, funnel-shaped flowers 4 cm

long, with blunt, spreading lobes, deep rose outside, paler inside; in small clusters, profusely on new season stems; fairly hardy.
Zone 5.   p. 680

florida 'Aureo-variegata', "Gold-leaved weigela"; striking mutation with leaves highly variegated and almost totally suffused with tints of pinkish lemon and bright golden-yellow, originated in Bewley's garden, Warrimoo, New So. Wales, Australia. Zone 10.   p. 680

florida 'Bristol Ruby'; deciduous shrub 2 m tall, a color variation of the species from China and Korea; small ovate 10 cm leaves; trumpet flowers ruby red (rose-colored in the species), blooming late Spring. Zone 5.   p. 680

florida 'Eva Ratke'; slow, compact growth; free-blooming carmine-red flowers open to pink inside; pale yellow anthers; blooming over long period. Zone 5.   p. 680

florida 'Foliis purpuriis', "Purple-leaf weigela" or "Java red weigela"; deciduous flowering shrub of dwarf habit to 1 m high, with colorful purple foliage suffused with bronze; the funnel-shaped flowers rose outside at tube, soft pink toward apex and inside.
Zone 5.   p. 680

florida 'Variegata'; attractive cultivar of compact habit, its elliptic green leaves prettily bordered with creamy-white; the lovely funnel flowers soft pink. Seen at the Chelsea Flower Show, London.
Zone 6.   p. 680

maximowiczii (Mts. of Honshu, C. Japan); deciduous shrub to 1½ m or more high, with elliptic or obovate leaves to 8 cm long; flowers with 2-lipped calyx, the upper lip 3-lobed, the 2 lower lobes distinct; corolla tube greenish-yellow, 3 cm long. Seen in col. Munich Bot. Garden, Germany. Zone 6.   p. 680

WEINGARTIA   Cactaceae

hediniana (Gymnocalycium) (Bolivia: Sucre); solitary small elongate globe 6 cm dia., and to 10 cm high, vivid green, the ribs dissolved into high knobs, white-woolly areoles and spreading radial spines, and stiff central spines; the crown covered by white wool, numerous light yellow 3 cm flowers near top. Zone 10.   p. 178

longigibba (Bolivia: Oropeza Prov.); small light green globe to 9 cm dia., later more elongate; about 10-13 ribs divided into high knobs to 4 cm long, bearing yellowish radials and stiff central spines; rich yellow flowers 3-4 cm across. Zone 10.   p. 178

WEINMANNIA   Cunoniaceae

trichosperma (Chile); evergreen shrub to 1½ m high with handsome glossy green, pinnate leaves 8-10 cm long, the leaflets toothed; inflorescence in showy cylindrical racemes of small white flowers, during May. Zone 7.   p. 695

WESTRINGIA   Labiatae

rosmariniformis (Queensland, New So. Wales), "Coast rosemary"; evergreen flowering shrub ½ to 1 m high, dense with small linear, leathery 1-3 cm leaves in whorls; shining green above, hoary and silvery when beneath, the margins turned under; small tubular, axillary white flowers spotted purple; July-blooming. Zone 9.   p. 741

WHITFIELDIA   Acanthaceae

elongata (Ruellia longifolia) (Trop. West Africa); beautiful tropical flowering subshrub to 2 m or more high, on straggling or scandent branches, containing pith; the nodes constricted; elliptic leaves 6-18 cm long; conspicuous inflorescence in clusters, with tubular flowers 5-8 cm long, glistening white and very striking.
Zone 11.   p. 631

WIGANDIA   Hydrophyllaceae

caracasana (urens) (C. America, Venezuela); robust woody shrub or small bushy tree to 3 m high, silky pubescent; the large ovate leaves 40 cm long, covered with glistening, irritating hairs; small violet flowers showy, in gorgeous clusters. Subtropic. Zone 10.   p. 737

WILCOXIA   Cactaceae

albiflora (Mexico); dwarf branching succulent shrub with tuberous roots, the lower twigs woody and 15 cm long, light green and 1 cm thick, covered by tiny areoles and short appressed hair-spines; showy soft pink flowers from near growth tips. Col. Glass and Foster, Calif.
Zone 11.   p. 178

poselgeri (Texas; Mexico: Coahuila); low spiny cactus with tuberous, dahlia-like roots; slender cylindrical dark green stems 60 cm high and 2 cm thick, with 8-10 ribs almost hidden by appressed whitish spines; fragrant pink flowers 4-5 cm long, lasting several days.
Arid-subtropic. Zone 10.   p. 178

WISTERIA   Leguminosae

floribunda (Glycine) (Japan), "Japanese wisteria"; spectacular woody liana with twining stems from right to left, with vines extending 10 m or more; pinnate leaves of 13-19 small leaflets, appearing with the inflorescence in Spring; blooming profusely with beautiful pendulous racemes 20 to 50 or even 120 cm long, of fragrant pea-shaped 2 cm flowers, in shades of violet-blue except for the whitish standards, opening progressively down toward the tip, in late Spring. Very hardy. *Zone 4.*   *p. 280, 281*

floribunda 'Alba' (Glycine) (Japan), "Japanese wisteria"; woody liana with twining stems to 10 m or more long; fresh green pinnate leaves, usually of 13-19 leaflets, and beautiful pendulous racemes 20 to 80 cm long, with fragrant 2 cm flowers, violet-blue in the species; white in cv. 'Alba'. Magnificent when trained over pergolas. *Temperate. Zone 4.*   *p. 285*

floribunda 'Macrobotrys' (multijuga) (Japan); tall-climbing woody vine with glossy green pinnate leaves 25-30 cm long; the showy terminal racemes of 2 cm pea-like, purple flowers, in extremely long, hanging clusters to 1 m long, followed by velvety pods; the most popular of cultivated Japanese wisterias; the flowers appearing before, or with the leaves. *Temperate. Zone 4.*   *p. 285*

frutescens (Glycine) (Virginia to Alabama and Texas), "Southern wisteria"; native American shrub, climbing 6-9 m high; leaves with 9-15 ovate leaflets; inflorescence in dense racemes to 12 cm long, of small 2 cm pale to lilac-purple flowers; flat fruit 10 cm long.
Zone 5.   *p. 280*

frutescens nivea, "White Southern glycine"; color form with odd-pinnate leaves, and compressed elongate clusters of pure white flowers; blooming in June. *Zone 6.*   *p. 280*

sinensis (China), "Chinese wisteria"; deciduous twining woody vine, spreading to 30 m long; pinnate leaves divided into 7 to 13 large leaflets, blooming before leaves, in great pendant clusters to 30 cm long; flowers 3 cm in length, bluish-violet, not fragrant, and all opening simultaneously. Stems are twining from left to right, or counter-clockwise according to T. Everett of New York Bot. Gardens. *Warm temperate. Zone 5.*   *p. 280, 281*

sinensis 'Alba' (China), "White Chinese wisteria"; beautiful cultivar with pendant racemes dense with very fragrant, pure white flowers. May be shaped into tree-form by pruning, not needing support. *Zone 5.*   *p. 285*

venusta (China), "Silky wisteria"; twining woody vine, with odd-pinnate leaves, the 9-13 leaflets velvety-pubescent; floral racemes thin and open, to 15 cm long, with flowers white. *Zone 5.*   *p. 280*

WITTIA   *Cactaceae*

panamensis (Wittiocactus) (Panama, Colombia, Venezuela); small epiphyte having flattened leaf-like branches 25 cm to 1 m long and 3-6 cm wide, with strong midrib; numerous small flowers with ovary and tube carmine-red, and perianth dark blue. *Zone 11.*   *p. 178*

WOODSIA   *Polypodiaceae (Filices)*

obtusa (Nova Scotia to Minnesota, south to the Gulf, Texas and Arizona), "Blunt-lobed woodsia"; rock-loving small tufting fern with bipinnate gray-green fronds 30-40 cm long, the secondary pinnae bluntly lobed. Each season new growth rises from the stubble of past year's petioles. *Zones 3-8.*   *p. 142*

WOODWARDIA   *Polypodiaceae (Filices)*

areolata (Maine to Florida and Texas), "Netted chain fern"; mat-forming from spreading rhizomes, the pinnate fronds to 50 cm long, the pinnae are glossy dark green; the fertile pinnae are narrower and sporangia underneath are arranged like 2 lines of chain links.
Zones 4-8.   *p. 142*

fimbriata (chamissoi) (W. Brit. Columbia to So. Calif. and Arizona), "Giant chain fern"; large terrestrial fern with woody rhizome, bearing pinnate fronds 1 to 3 m long, the herbaceous pinnae deeply lobed; fertile leaves with 2 rows of sori beneath, resembling chains. *Zones 5-8.*   *p. 142*

WRIGHTIA   *Apocynaceae*

religiosa (Holarrhena) (S.E. Asia), "Jasmine tree"; tropical evergreen shrub or small tree; slender branches with opposite broad-ovate leaves; the sweetly fragrant flowers in stalked, branched clusters creamy-white, corolla with slender tube and 5 spreading petals, and in the throat a corona of fringed, overlapping scales; the fruits are slender erect and pot-like. *Zone 10.*   *p. 642*

WULFENIA   *Scrophulariaceae*

carinthiaca (Austrian Alps, to Greece); Alpine perennial, with glossy green, oblong-pointed leaves to 20 cm long, from thick rhizome; finely crenate along margins; inflorescence on slender stalks to 50 cm long, with small violet-blue tubular flowers 2 cm long, in dense clusters, blooming June-August. *Zone 5.*   *p. 508*

WYETHIA   *Compositae*

amplexicaulis (Washington to Montana and Colorado), "Mules-ears"; handsome herbaceous perennial to 1 m high; with glossy green, lanceolate leaves, the basal foliage to 45 cm long, shorter along the stems; floral heads 8-10 cm across, with long yellow ray-florets, blooming early Summer. *Zone 6.*   *p. 404*

angustifolia (Washington to No. California), "Narrow-leaf mules-ears"; showy, tap-rooted perennial with leafy stems 50-80 cm high;

lanceolate leaves 15-60 cm long; sunflower-like floral heads 10-15 cm across, with broad yellow ray-flowers circling the golden center cushion; autumn-blooming. *Zone 9.*   *p. 404*

XANTHOCERAS   *Sapindaceae*

sorbifolium (No. China), "Chinese buckeye" or "Yellow horn"; handsome deciduous shrub 3-4 m high, with pithy branches; pinnate leaves with toothed, bright green leaflets 5 cm long; showy axillary erect clusters of whitish flowers about 2½ cm across, the base of each of the 5 spreading petals first greenish-yellow, then red; fruit a hard green capsule resembling horse-chestnut; fairly hardy.
Zone 5.   *p. 869*

XANTHORHIZA   *Ranunculaceae*

simplicissima (New York to W. Virginia, Florida and Alabama), "Yellow-root"; deciduous shrub 60-90 cm high, from long creeping rootstock, forming a dense mass of foliage; the long-stalked leaves have 3 or 5 deeply lobed and toothed leaflets; the inflorescence a loose cluster of small, starry, deep purple flowers, appearing in March-April before the leaves. Bark and cambium of roots are yellow.
Zone 4.   *p. 825*

XANTHORRHOEA   *Liliaceae (Xanthorrhoeaceae in Zander)*

preissii (Western Australia), the famous "Blackboy" or "Grass tree"; conspicuously dominating the landscape of the interior of the dry West, like the occasional aboriginal one meets; the massive black trunks becoming 60 cm or more thick, the old leaf bases cemented together by black resinous gum; on top a tuft of hard-leathery rigid, reed-like leaves ½-1 m long; the inflorescence a long, candle-like spike, with small flowers, in habitat always opening on the north (sun) side first. *Arid-subtropic. Zone 9.*   *p. 566*

XANTHOSOMA   *Araceae*

atrovirens (Venezuela); sturdy plant forming cylindrical rhizome but no trunk; sagittate leaves to 1 m long, dark green above and gray-green beneath, veins light green, fleshy stalks green; green spathe. *Zone 10.*   *p. 34, 220*

lindenii (Hortus, Zander):
see CALADIUM lindenii (Selbyana 1981)

plowmanii (Brazil); small tuberous plant, normally with resting period or dormancy; 18 to 40 cm petioles bearing soft-hairy leaves, cordate in juvenile stage, in adult stage divided into 5 leaflets; 15-20 cm long; short floral stem with creamy-white spathe and whitish spadix.
Zone 11.   *p. 34*

robustum (C. America, Mexico), "Palma yautia" or "Ape"; large aroid with milky juice; forming a thick short trunk from a rhizome; topped by a cluster of big fleshy, sagittate leaves, on grooved, stout petioles, the blade to 1 m long and 60 cm wide, covered by white powdery coating and showing prominent pale, whitish ribs; inflorescence sweet-smelling, each with a pinkish creamy spathe 15 cm long. In Guatemala young leaves are cooked and eaten, but the roots are said to be poisonous. *Zone 11.*   *p. 33*

XENOPHYA   *Araceae*

lauterbachiana (Schizocasia hort.) (New Guinea); fleshy rosette of stiff lanceolate leaves to 50 cm long with lobed margins and hastate base, metallic bronzy green and paler veins; spathe blade persistent, opening briefly in the middle only, opposite the staminate flowers. *Tropical. Zone 11.*   *p. 34*

XERANTHEMUM   *Compositae*

annuum (So. Europe to Asia Minor, Caspian reg.), "Immortelle"; an excellent garden annual, freely branching, to 60 cm high, with ovate 5 cm leaves; floral heads purple, rose or white, 3-4 cm across, the bracts glossy; blooming July-September. One of the best "everlastings" for drying of flowers used in durable bouquets.
Zone 10.   *p. 404*

XEROPHYLLUM   *Liliaceae*

asphodeloides (New Jersey to Georgia), "Turkeybeard" or "Mountain asphodel"; tall perennial with woody rootstock, 1 m or more high, with basal linear, grass-like, rather stiff leaves 30-40 cm long; the beautiful inflorescence of creamy-white, fragrant flowers 1 cm across, arranged like bursting stars in feathery racemes.
Zone 6.   *p. 454*

tenax (Brit. Columbia to Wyoming and Cent. California), "Bear grass"; impressive perennial of the Rocky Mts. region, 1½ m or more high, with narrow-linear, stiff leaves to 80 cm long near base; small 2 cm creamy-white flowers displaying violet stamens, dense in club-shaped inflorescence to 60 cm long, on tall woody stalk. The leaves are used by the Blackfeet Indians for weaving baskets.
Zones 3-7.   *p. 454*

XIMENIA   *Olacaceae*

americana (El Salvador), "Sour plum"; small shrub of the sub-tropical zone, with leathery ovate leaves; the small yellow fruits are edible, with acid-flavor. *Zones 9-10.*   *p. 806*

XYLOPHYLLA: see PHYLLANTHUS (Hortus)

XYLOSMA *Flacourtiaceae*

congestum (seticosum) (So. China), "Shiny xylosma"; low ever-green shrub with arching branches, in time growing into small tree to 5 m high; the branches with sharp axillary spines; ovate-pointed leathery leaves 6-9 cm long, finely toothed along margins, and glossy green; inconspicuous unisexual flowers; small black berries from female blooms. *Zone 8.* p. 732

YUCCA *Agavaceae*

aloifolia (S.E. United States, West Indies, Mexico), "Spanish bayonet"; tree-forming stiff rosette, becoming 8 m tall, with usually solitary woody trunk; thick-fleshy, sharp-pointed, dagger-like concave leaves to 75 cm long and 6 cm wide, glaucous green, margins faintly toothed but not thread-bearing; cup-shaped flowers creamy-white tinged with purple, in 60 cm clusters. In Puerto Rico, one can see this yucca decorated with egg-shells, a custom carried over from the Carib Indians, and believed to ward off ill fortune; called locally "Mata de Rosa Blanca". *Subtropic and tropical. Zones 9-10.* p. 118, 208

aloifolia 'Tricolor', "Red dagger"; colorful variety with the pungent dagger-leaves margined ivory, partly yellow in the center and with a tinge of red when young. *Subtropic. Zone 11.* p. 68, 118

baccata (Colorado, Arizona, California), "Datil yucca"; heavy succulent rosette of thick, stiff-erect, rough, concave leaves to 90 cm, spine-tipped and with peeling fiber at margins; large white flowers; dried fruit is eaten by Indians. *Warm temperate. Zones 7-8.* p. 118

brevifolia, native to high deserts in Southern California, Nevada, Utah and Arizona, the extraordinary "Joshua tree"; hard to believe but this is related to lilies, growing into a succulent tree to 22 m high, with palm-like trunk to 1⅓ m thick branching into tortuous arms dense with rosettes of short and rigid dagger-shaped leaves; in bloom from February to April with greenish-white 5 cm cup-shaped flowers in dense clusters 30 cm long. Its grotesque silhouette is very characteristic in dry-sunny desert landscapes. *Arid-subtropic. Zones 7-8.* p. 119, 771

carnerosiana (South Texas, No. Mexico) arborescent "Spanish dagger"; stiff succulent, becoming tree-like, with thick trunk, to 5 m tall; rigid, sword-shaped leaves in a terminal rosette, 80 cm long, and 10 cm wide; dense inflorescence with fragrant white flowers. *Arid-subtropic. Zones 9-10.* p. 119

elata (Arizona), the "Soaptree yucca"; tree-forming to 6 m; dense rosettes of narrow-linear spine-tipped leaves 60 cm long and 3 cm wide, yellow-green and smooth, margins white; flowers white in tall inflorescence. *Arid-subtropic. Zone 8.* p. 119

elephantipes (guatemalensis, gigantea) (Mexico, Guatemala), "Giant yucca" or "Spineless yucca"; round-headed "Palm-lily" with trunks springing from a swollen base suckering from below, and branching above with age, reaching 15 m high, topped by rosettes of leaves to 10 cm wide, glossy grass green with rough margins and soft tip; bell-flowers ivory-white, in large clusters. Very decorative and durable in containers; known as Y. gigantea in hort. *Subtropic. Zones 9-10.* p. 119, 771

filamentosa (flaccida) (S.E. United States; Carolina to Florida and Mississippi), "Adam's needle"; bold rosette, nearly stemless, with leathery sword-shaped leaves 75 cm long, bluish-glaucous, and with marginal, curly white threads; pendulous flowers nearly white in tall panicle to 4 m high. *Warm temperate. Zones 5-6.* p. 118, 566, 771

filamentosa 'Variegata', (filumentana in N.Z.); beautiful rosette of broad bayonet-shaped leaves, bluish-green contrasting with cream or white bands along margins. *Subtropic. Zones 8-9.* p. 118

flaccida (No. Carolina to Alabama); from underground stem a clustering rosette of leathery, pliable sword-shaped, bluish glaucous leaves 30 to 50 cm long and with white fiber along margins; less rigid than Y. filamentosa; inflorescence a showy panicle of 4-5 cm white flowers. Sometimes grown as Y. filamentosa in hort. *Zones 6-7.* p. 118

glauca (New Mexico, north to So. Dakota), "Soapweed"; stemless rosette dense with straight narrow-linear, glaucous blue-green leaves 40 to 80 cm long and 2 cm wide; margins with a few white threads; flowers greenish-white. *Zones 3-7.* p. 119, 566

gloriosa (shores of Carolina to Florida), "Spanish dagger"; to 2½ m high, with short, thick trunk topped by dense rosette of sword-shaped, flat glaucous gray-green, rough leaves 5 cm wide, with reddish margins and spiny point; white bell-like flowers striped purple outside. *Subtropic. Zones 8-9.* p. 119

recurvifolia (pendula) (Georgia, Alabama, Mississippi), "Lord's candle"; stem-forming lax rosette of broad, flexible, glaucous dark green leaves 6 cm wide and recurving, large panicle of white flowers. *Warm temperate. Zones 7-8.* p. 119

rostrata (So. Texas and Sonora, Mexico); handsome arborescent "Palmella" from the arid Big Bend area, branching with several woody trunks to 5 m tall, topped by symmetrical rosettes of stiff sword-shaped leaves to 50 cm long, glaucous with yellow margins, about 15 mm wide; white 5 cm flowers in large clusters. *Zones 9-10.* p. 115, 771

schidigera (Mohave Desert, California); shrubby rosette on trunks to 2½ m; leaves sword-shaped to 75 cm long, yellow-green; creamy flowers, tinged with purple. *Arid-subtropic. Zone 8.* p. 119

schottii (Arizona); stem-forming rosette to 5 m high, rarely branched, with concave leaves 45-90 cm tapering to a fine point, the margins without coarse threads; showy panicle with globose white flowers. *Zone 8.* p. 119

thompsoniana (So. Texas, No. Mexico); photographed near Cuatrocienegas, Coahuila; arborescent to 3 m high, with a dense symmetrical rosette of stiffly erect sword-shaped leaves to 30 cm long, having brownish margins; large 6 cm white flowers in tall panicle. *Zones 9-10.* p. 120

torreyi (New Mexico, So. Texas and No. Mexico); tree-like to 6 m high, infrequently branched, with rosettes of rigid leaves to 1 m long, ending in stout terminal spine; the margins thread-bearing; erect clusters of creamy-white flowers. *Zones 9-10.* p. 120

valida (Mexico); handsome robust species forming trunk; the leaves bayonet-like stiff erect, 30 cm or more long, concave and leading to a pale spiny apex, the horny margins set with curling fibers. Seen at Del Mar Hort. Expo, California 1981. *Zone 10.* p. 200

whipplei (Alta California, Baja California), "Our Lord's candle"; stemless rosette of stiff glaucous leaves to 50 cm long, with terminal spine and finely serrate margin; fragrant flowers creamy-white, in clusters on stalk to 4 m tall. *Arid-subtropic. Zones 9-10.* p. 120

YUSHANIA aztecorum is correctly OTATEA acuminata (aztecorum) (European Garden Flora)

ZAMIA *Cycadaceae: Zamiaceae*

fischeri (Mexico); small spindle-shaped trunk, bearing several fern-like pinnate fronds 30 to 45 cm long, with thin-leathery, lanceolate leaflets shiny grass-green, serrate along margins; male cone 4 to 8 cm long, female shorter. *Tropical. Zone 11.* p. 114

pumila (furfuraceae) (Mexico to Colombia), "Jamaica sagotree"; stem more or less tuberous, sometimes branched, bearing a tangled profusion of pinnate leaves 1-1⅓ m long, on prickly stalks, the thick-leathery leaflets oblanceolate 20 cm long, more or less toothed and overlapping, densely brown scurfy beneath, or on both sides when young; male cones 10 cm long, the female ones shorter. An excellent, "different" decorator plant, hard and durable as iron, and of relatively small size. *Subtropic. Zone 11.* p. 114

ZAMIOCULCAS *Araceae*

zamiifolia (Zanzibar; E. Africa); tropical herb with thick, horizontal rhizome, sending up swollen stalks; the pinnately arranged, small, dark, waxy leaves with yellow-green veins; short inflorescence appearing from near base, consisting of boat-shaped, green spathe and short, club-shaped spadix. *Tropical. Zone 11.* p. 30

ZANTEDESCHIA *Araceae*

aethiopica (Calla, Richardia) (South Africa and north), "White calla", "White arum-lily", or as known in South Africa: "Pig-lily"; robust marsh-loving herb with thick rhizome; forming a tuft of fleshy-stalked, glossy green leaves 60-90 cm high, on succulent petioles; a stout basal stalk 1-1½ m high bearing the large, funnel-shaped rolled-flaring waxy white spathe 20-25 cm long, surrounding a bright yellow spadix. To the visitor of the moister parts of the South African Cape it is a common sight to see whole fields of these beautiful callas in bloom during summertime; but I have also seen them at 2,300 m altitude in Kenya. *Subtropic. Zone 10.* p. 33, 220, 338

albo-maculata (So. Africa to Angola), "Spotted calla"; leaves arrow-shaped, green with oblong, white, translucent spots; spathe trumpet-shaped with pointed limb, creamy-white, in throat purple. *Zone 10.* p. 33, 220

elliottiana (So. Africa: Transkei); known as "Yellow calla" and growing from a flattened rhizome; the succulent, cordate, bright green leaves have translucent white spots; the obliquely flaring, tubular spathe is rich yellow, to 15 cm long. *Subtropic. Zone 10.* p. 33, 220

'Green Goddess' ('Green Lily'); very charming flowering plant, probably a cultivar of Z. aethiopica, of luxuriant growth with lush green arrow-shaped leaves, and strong-stalked inflorescence with flaring, fleshy spathe 15-20 cm long, white at base, but moss-green at margins and across apex. *Subtropic. Zone 11.* p. 33, 220

rehmannii (Natal); the shapely "Pink calla" having lanceolate leaves bright green with linear, translucent white spots; the most attractive, charming, pale rosy-purple spathe an obliquely flaring tube lined with cream. *Subtropic. Zone 10.* p. 33

'Striped hybrida'; striking descendants of South African species including Z. aethiopica; flaring spathes in pink, orange-yellow and red, some with contrasting white bands. Photographed at the Indian mercado in Oaxaca, Southern Mexico. *Subtropical. Zone 10.* p. 33

ZANTHOXYLUM   Rutaceae

americanum (fraxineum Zander) (Québec to Dakota, Virginia to Oklahoma), "Prickly ash" or "Toothache tree"; aromatic deciduous shrub 2-3 m high or small tree to 8 m; the young branches with prickles or thorns; odd-pinnate leaves of 5-11 leaflets 3-6 cm long; inconspicuous yellowish-green flowers in axillary clusters in Spring, appearing before the foliage, followed by small black fruit. Dried bark used medicinally. *Zone 3.* *p. 863*

ZAUSCHNERIA   Onagraceae

californica (Epilobium canum) (Coast of California), "California fuchsia"; sub-shrubby perennial with stems 30-90 cm high, evergreen in mild climates; with lanceolate grayish-green 3-4 cm leaves; deep crimson to scarlet funnel-form flowers to 5 cm long, the split lobes at apex yellow inside; August-October blooming. *Zone 9.* *p. 463*

californica latifolia (Oregon to California and New Mexico), "Hummingbird trumpet"; herbaceous perennial of compact habit, 20-40 cm high; alternate lanceolate leaves 4-5 cm long, broader than the species; interesting fuchsia-like tubular trumpet-flowers with 2-cleft scarlet-red petals, 3-5 cm long, displaying long stamen bundles; blooming August-September, and attractive to hummingbirds. *Zone 8.* *p. 463*

ZEA   Gramineae

diploperenne (Oaxaca, So. Mexico), "Perennial corn"; vigorous tall-growing perennial grass 2 m or more high, branching from the base; stiffly erect canes, with narrow leaves along the stem, and topped by the inflorescence of male flowers, being whitish tassels and the females lower and which eventually form the fruit spike known as "ears", holding ranks of edible seed kernels, enclosed by a sheltering husk. Probably one of the widely cultivated cultigen Zea mays. *Zone 9.* *p. 568*

mays (America, prob. Mexico or C. America), the "Indian corn" or "Maize"; its exact origin has been lost in pre-Mayan, Aztec or Incan antiquity; cultivated since and to them the most important food, with the exception of the potato to the Incas in South America; robust, tall annual grass 3 to 4 m high, suckering at base, with jointed, solid stem bearing broad, glossy green, sword-shaped leaves; male flowers in terminal spike with pollen, the female blooms in small clusters borne below the males, their long styles are the showy corn-silk, and producing the ears of edible corn kernels containing starch, heavily sheathed in husks. For farm production, highly refined cultivars have been developed, containing less starch and more sugar. *Tropical. Zone 10.* *p. 568*

mays gracillima (Trop. America), "Decorative maize" or "Broom corn"; robust annual grass of short, compact habit, suckering at base; long sword-shaped fresh green leaves, and stiff canes to 1 m high, bearing a panicle of tiny flowers; an attractive decorative plant in outdoor bed. *Zone 9.* *p. 568*

mays indurata 'Rainbow' (Mexico), "Indian flint corn"; very ornamental with cylindric cobs of multicolored, hard seed kernels, arranged in 10 or more rows, and displayed on occasion of Thanksgiving in North American and Mexican homes. *Zone 10.* *p. 568*

ZEBRINA   Commelinaceae

pendula (Mexico), "Silvery wandering Jew" or "Inch plant"; fleshy trailing plant rooting at joints, small ovate leaves about 5 cm; long, fairly succulent, deep green to purple with two broad, glistening silver bands, vivid purple beneath; flowers rosy-purple. *Tropical. Zone 11.* *p. 52, 308*

ZELKOVA   Ulmaceae

serrata (Planera acuminata) (Japan, Korea), "Sawleaf zelkova"; deciduous elm-like shrub or tree to 30 m high, having attractively flaking gray-brown bark with orange spotting, developing a broad rounded crown; slender branches with ovate leaves 5-12 cm long, sharply toothed; small green flowers. A favorite object in Japan for training into dwarfed Bonsai. Highly resistant to Dutch elm disease, which has claimed so many of its cousin elms. *Zones 5-9. p. 626, 897*

serrata 'Variegata' (Japan), strikingly beautiful color form with slender branches red, and leaves brightly variegated green, white and pink; photographed on Martha's Vineyard, Massachusetts. *Zone 5.* *p. 897*

serrata 'Village Green', "Village Green zelkova"; this popular cultivar is a vigorous straight-trunked tree to 20 m high, with wine-glass shape of American elms; large dark green leaves resembling Ulmus, turning attractively rusty-red in Autumn. Vigorous grower and very cold tolerant. *Zones 5-9.* *p. 897*

ZENOBIA   Ericaceae

pulverulenta (S.E. United States); semi-evergreen shrub to 2 m high; small leathery, elliptic leaves to 8 cm long, glaucous beneath; small 2 cm waxy white, fragrant bell-flowers in Spring. *Zone 5. p. 719*

ZEPHYRANTHES   Amaryllidaceae (Liliaceae)

atamasco (Virginia to Florida and Mississippi), "Atamasco lily"; bulbous plant with narrow strap-like leaves 30 cm long; early spring-blooming, lily-like with flaring lobes, to 8 cm long, white and tinged purple, on 30 cm hollow stalk. *Zones 7-8.* *p. 218*

candida (Argentina: La Plata), "Fairy lily" or "Westwind-flower"; attractive small bulbous plant, with narrow, perennial leaves, and forming clumps; funnel-shaped glossy white flowers 4 cm long, with 6 spreading segments, singly on hollow stalks, and blooming Summer to Autumn. *Warm temperate. Zone 9.* *p. 217*

citrina (Guyana, Trinidad), a "Rain lily"; small bulbous herb with channeled linear, grass-like leaves 20-30 cm long; on hollow stalks the solitary, funnel-shaped lemon-yellow flowers to 4 cm long, during Summer; resting in Winter; somewhat hardy. *Tropical. Zones 9-10.* *p. 218*

grandiflora (Mexico, Guatemala), a pretty "Rain-lily" or "Flower of the westwind"; with flat, linear basal leaves and large, deep rose-pink, funnel-form flower, to 10 cm across, at end of the hollow stalk; blooming through Spring and Summer. Named "Rain-lily" for its habit of blooming anew after each rain. *Tropical. Zone 10.* *p. 217*

lindleyana (San Luis Potosi, Mexico), a "Zephyr lily", also known as "Rainlily"; small bulbous plant with linear leaves to 25 cm long, appearing with or after flowering; floral stalk bearing an erect pale pink corolla. *Zones 9-10.* *p. 217*

rosea (Cuba), "Cuban zephyr-lily"; small bulbous herb forming colonies, with narrow linear leaves arching downward; floral stalk 10-16 cm high, the wide open 3 cm flowers rose with pale center; autumn-blooming. *Zone 10.* *p. 218*

tubispatha (West Indies), "Zephyr lily"; bulbous, with white narrow spreading leaves 1 cm wide, present when blooming; the floral stalks 10-20 cm long, bearing white flowers 3-6 cm long, with spreading petals. *Zones 9-10.* *p. 218*

ZIGADENUS   Liliaceae

fremontii (So. Oregon to No. Baja California), "Star zygadene" or "Star lily"; bulbous perennial to 1 m high; strap-shaped basal leaves 50 cm long, having rough margins; the inflorescence in racemes or clusters of small starry, yellowish-white flowers. *Zones 8-9.* *p. 257*

ZINGIBER   Zingiberaceae

officinale (India to Pacific Isl.), "Common ginger"; slender, reed-like stems to 1 m high, from tuberous rhizomes which are used as a pleasantly flavored rootspice; the scattered, sessile leaves are glossy deep green and narrow, almost grass-like; flowers in dense spike with pale green bracts, yellowish corolla, and purple lip marked yellow. This ginger of commerce is widely cultivated in Tropical Asia, West Indies and Africa; the white ginger is extracted from the rhizomes after scraping the outer rind layers; its camphor-like but pleasant aroma add piquant taste to bakery; the young rhizomes are boiled and steeped in syrup for delicious confectionary. Rhizomes are also used to make ginger ale. *Zones 10-11.* *p. 545*

spectabile (Malaya), "Giant ginger"; robust species shooting up stout, somewhat flattened stems over 2 m high; deep green leaves oblong-lanceolate 20-30 cm long, paler and downy beneath; the flowers yellowish-white, the 2-lobed lip lemon with a black tip, in a loose cylindrical spike 20-30 cm long; the sulphur yellow bracts passing to scarlet, shingled and prettily recurved. *Zone 11.* *p. 521*

zerumbet (India, Malaya to Polynesia), the "Wild ginger", or "Bitter ginger"; well known and widely cultivated tropical ginger with knobbed rootstock at first taste aromatic, then becoming bitter; leafy shoots to 1 m high; the lanceolate, thin leaves 10-20 cm long, more or less hairy beneath; in the late Summer an oblong flowering head, 5-8 cm long, appears on a stalk about 30 cm long, separate from the leaves, consisting of large green to red overlapping bracts, and small yellowish flowers. The leaves and shoots are used as culinary greens in Bengal. *Zones 10-11.* *p. 545*

zerumbet 'Variegata' (India); attractive tropical ginger of low habit, 30-50 cm high, with leafy stems from underground knobby aromatic rootstock; leathery leaves rich grass green and beautifully variegated with cream; the inflorescence in cone-like heads of overlapping fleshy bracts a vivid scarlet-red, with small yellow flowers. Photographed at Botanic Gardens Trinidad. *Tropical. Zone 11.* *p. 522*

ZINNIA   Compositae

angustifolia (linearis) (Mexico), "Narrowleaf zinnia"; low, spreading annual rambler to 20 cm high, with linear, entire leaves, very floriferous with small single, rich yellow flowers, the ray-florets edged with red; 4-5 cm across, summer-blooming. *Zone 10.* *p. 405*

elegans (Mexico), "Youth-and-old-age"; gaily colored annual garden favorite, 50 cm to 1 m high, stiff growing and covered with short hairs; bright green leaves ovalish, clasping the stem; flowers in solitary heads 6-8 cm across in white, pink, rose, red, yellow, orange, purple; distinctly hot-weather plants. *Tropical. Zone 10.* *p. 409*

elegans 'Cherry Ruffles', (Ruffled strain); medium size double blooms, dense with ruffled ray-florets in cherry-red, scarlet, pink, yellow, or white, on long stiff stems to 75 cm tall. Excellent as cut flowers. *Zone 10.* *p. 405*

elegans 'Giant Cactus strain'; popular summer to autumn-blooming annual 30-90 cm high; the species with stem-clasping, opposite, ovate leaves; the robust stems with showy flowers to 12 cm across, the ray-florets variable, in red, rose, tangerine or white. Very much improved in cultivars such as the "Giant cactus flowered", with striking double flowers 12 cm across, the fluted or linear ray-florets in many bright colors, from red to rose, orange, yellow and white. Zone 10.   *p. 405*

elegans 'Peter Pan'; excellent, free-blooming strain with large 6-8 cm semi-double to double flowers on bushy, dwarf plants to 30 cm high, the broad ray-florets in colors of red, yellow, coral-pink, or cream. Zone 10.   *p. 405*

elegans 'Thumbelina' (miniature); extra dwarf zinnia only 15 cm high, very compact and ideal for bedding or window boxes; the bright and colorful semi-double flowers 3 cm across in shades including yellow, salmon, rose or red; blooming all Summer, a rare breeding achievement by Bodgar Seeds, El Monte, California. *Tropical.* Zone 10.   *p. 405*

elegans 'Yellow Ruffles'; free-blooming bushy annual plant 50-75 cm tall, with stiff stems carrying 6 cm double blooms, the yellow ray-florets quilted and ruffled. Zone 10.   *p. 405*

ZIZIPHUS   *Rhamnaceae*

jujuba (Ziziphus hort.) (S.E. Europe to Himalayas, No. India, W. China), "Chinese jujube" or "Chinese date"; slender deciduous to partially evergreen shrub or tree to 10 m high, with spiny, gnarled branches somewhat pendulous; shiny green ovate leaves 3-6 cm long, having 3 prominent veins; small inconspicuous greenish-white flowers in axillary clusters; followed by shiny reddish-brown ovoid edible fruit 3 cm long, of sweet apple-like flavor, resembling dates when candied and dried. Tolerant of arid conditions. Zone 7.   *p. 924*

jujuba 'Lang', "Lang jujuba"; a cultivar of commercial importance, as planted in California for its larger fruit to 5 cm long; usually eaten fresh when still unripe and solid; when fully ripe the fruit may be stored and dried to sweeten, to eat like dates, or may be candied and prepared into preserves, sweet pickles or mincemeat. Zone 7. *p. 924*

mauritiana (India), "Indian jujube"; evergreen shrub or small tree, with the pendant zigzag twigs and undersides of foliage rusty tomentose; the leathery 3-nerved leaves broad-oval, 6 cm long, lacquered rich green above; small greenish-white flowers; fleshy fruit 2-3 cm dia. first green, later brown; edible, with acid taste but usually sweet-pickled, candied or stewed. Zones 9-10.   *p. 829, 924*

ZOYSIA   *Gramineae*

japonica 'Meyer' (Japan, China), the "Korean grass"; subtropical perennial creeping lawn grass widely used in the Southeast, California and Hawaii; mat forming and coarser than tenuifolia; fine grass-like leaves to 4 mm wide and 3-8 cm long; the rootstock sending out numerous tough, wiry runners; slow to establish and taking a long rest period, but in time looking like blue-grass; purplish spikelets 1 cm long. Zones 9-10.   *p. 569*

tenuifolia (Mascarene Islands), the "Mascarene grass" or in Hawaii as "Temple grass"; perennial creeping grass with rich green 2-3 cm leaves threadlike and finer than japonica, and forming a turf; widely planted in California and Hawaii, but as groundcover grass somewhat lumpy; with its fine texture, it makes a beautiful tapestry, especially on slopes. Winter-hardy to -12° C., but turns brown after first frost. Zone 8.   *p. 570*

tenuifolia 'Emerald' (Z. japonica x tenuifolia), "Velvet grass"; creeping warm season hybrid perennial grass, favored in the South for lawns; spreading by above ground stolons and also underground rhizomes; leaves are fine-textured but rather stiff compared to other grasses, forming dense turf highly resistant to wear such as on golf courses; it is also drought tolerant, and more frost-hardy than 'Meyer', also growing faster. Zone 8.   *p. 570*

ZYGOCACTUS: transferred to SCHLUMBERGERA (Hortus 3)

ZYGOPETALUM   *Orchidaceae*

mackayi (So. Brazil: São Paulo); although said to be an epiphyte, I have seen it growing in quantity in red clay on high savannah of the Serra do Mar above Santos; robust species with clustered pseudobulbs and 45 cm leaves having raised veins; erect racemes of beautiful 5-8 cm fragrant, waxy flowers, sepals and petals yellow-green blotched with brown, the large showy lip white, with spots and streaks of blue, (Nov.-June). *Tropical.* Zone 11.   *p. 97*

ZYGOSEPALUM   *Orchidaceae*

labiosum (Zygopetalum rostratum) (Guyana to Amazonas); tropical epiphyte with ovoid pseudobulbs 6 cm long, each topped by 1-2 oblanceolate, plicate 25 cm leaves; floral stalk bearing showy flower to 5 cm across, sepals greenish suffused maroon, petals similar but violet at base, lip white with violet stripes. Zones 11-12.   *p. 98*

Abrams-Ferris: Flora of the Pacific States (Stanford 1960)
Allan: Flora of New Zealand (Wellington 1961)
Arbelaez: Plantas Utiles de Colombia (Bogotá 1947)
Backeberg: Das Kakteen Lexikon (Stuttgart 1966)
Bailey: Hortus Third (New York 1976)
Baileya, Journal of Horticultural Taxonomy (Ithaca 1953-1991)
Beard: West Australian Plants (Perth 1970)
Beckett, Encyclopedia of Garden Plants (London 1984)
Borg: Cacti (London 1956)
Bravo: Las Cactaceas de Mexico (Mexico 1937)
Britton & Brown: Flora of the N.E. United States and Canada
Britton & Rose: The Cactaceae (Washington 1919)
Bruggeman: Indisch Tuinboek (Amsterdam 1948)
Bryan, Bulbs: (Portland, Oregon 1989)
Chabouis: Flore de Tahiti (Paris 1972)
Christensen: Index Filicum (Copenhagen 1906-1933)
Condit: Ficus (Arcadia, Calif. 1969)
Corner: Wayside Trees of Malaya (Singapore 1952)
Dale, Greenway: Kenya Trees and Shrubs (Nairobi 1961)
Den Ouden, Boom: Manual of Cultivated Conifers (The Hague)
Eliovson: South African Flowers (Cape Town 1955)
Encke: Parey's Blumengaertnerei, 2nd Ed. (Berlin 1961)
Engler: Das Pflanzenreich (Leipzig 1900-)
Erikson: Flowers and Plants of Western Australia (Sydney 1973)
European Garden Flora, (Cambridge 1986 etc.)
Everett: Encyclopedia of Gardening (New York 1960)
Fassett: Manual of Aquatic Plants (Madison 1957)
Foster: Bromeliads — A Cultural Handbook (Orlando 1953)
Genera Palmarum (Cornell & Kew 1987)
Graf: Exotica Series 4, 12th Ed. Rev. (E. Rutherford, NJ 1986)
Graf: Tropica, 4th Ed. (E. Rutherford, NJ 1992)
Harrison: Ornamental Conifers (New Zealand 1975)
Harrison: Trees and Shrubs for the Southern Hemisphere
Hawkes: Encyclopedia of Cultivated Orchids (Miami)
Hillier Dict. of Trees & Shrubs (1982)
Hong Kong Shrubs, Trees (Hong Kong 1976)
Hooker: Flora of British India (London 1875-1897)
Hoyos: Flora Tropical Ornamental (Caracas 1978)
Hulme: Wild Flowers of Natal (Pietermaritzburg 1954)
Hutchinson: Flora of West Tropical Africa (London 1958)
Index Kewensis and Supplements (Oxford 1895-1959)
Jacobsen: Das Sukkulenten Lexikon (Stuttgart 1970)
Jex-Blake: Gardening in East Africa (Nairobi 1948)
Johnson's Gardener's Dictionary (London 1846, revised 1917)
Kanehira: Formosan Trees (Fukuoka 1936)
Kelly: Eucalypts (Melbourne 1969)
Kew Bulletin (London 1887-1969)
Kruessmann: Die Laubgehoelze (Berlin 1976-1978)
Kruessmann: Die Nadelgehoelze (Berlin 1955)
Laing and Blackwell: Plants of New Zealand (Auckland 1940)
Lamb: Cacti and Other Succulents (New York 1955)
Le Bon Jardinier, Encyclopedie Horticole (Paris 1964)
Lecomte: Flore Générale de l'Indochine (Paris 1942)
Lee: The Azalea Book (Princeton 1958)
Linnaeus: Species Plantarum (Uppsala 1753)
Lloyd: The Carnivorous Plants (Waltham 1942)
Lord: Shrubs and Trees for Australian Gardens (Melbourne)
Lowe: Ferns, British and Exotic (London 1864)
MacMillan: Trop. Planting and Gardening, Ceylon (London)
Makino: Illustrated Flora of Japan (Tokyo 1967)
Mathias, McClintock: Woody Ornamental Plants of California
McClure: The Bamboos (Cambridge, Mass. 1966)
McCurrach: Palms of the World (Palm Beach 1959)
Menninger: Flowering Trees of the World (Stuart, Florida 1961)
Moldenke: Plants of the Bible (New York 1952)
Moore: African Violets, Gloxinias, and Relatives (New York)
Morton: 500 Plants of South Florida (Miami 1974)
Neal: In Gardens of Hawaii (Honolulu 1948)
North American Flora (New York 1949)
O'Gorman: Mexican Flowering Trees & Plants (Mexico City)
Ohwi: Flora of Japan (Washington 1965)
Padilla: Bromeliads (New York 1973)
Parodi: Enciclopedia Argentina de Agricultura (Buenos Aires)
Pittier: Plantas Usuales de Venezuela (Caracas 1926)
Polunin: Flowers of the Mediterranean (Boston 1966)
Polunin: Guide des Plantes et Fleurs de l'Europe (Paris 1974)
Rehder: Manual of Cultivated Trees and Shrubs (New York)
Rice and Compton: Wild Flowers of the Cape (Kirstenbosch)
Richards: New Zealand Trees and Flowers (Christchurch 1956)
Rickett, New York Botanical Garden: Wild Flowers of the U.S.
Royal Hort. Soc. Dictionary of Gardening
Sanders Orchid Guide and List of Hybrids (St. Albans, 1963)
Schlechter: Die Orchideen (Berlin 1927)
Schneider: Book of Choice Ferns (London 1892-1894)
Small: Flora of the Southeastern U.S. (New York 1913)
Spuy: South African Shrubs and Trees (Johannesburg 1971)
Standley: Trees and Shrubs of Mexico (Washington 1926)
Stodola: Encyclopedia of Water Plants (Jersey City 1967)
Thompson: Begonia Guide (New York 1977)
Weberbauer: El Mundo Vegetal de los Andes Peruanos (Lima)
Western Garden Book (Lane) (Menlo Park, Calif. 1969)
Wyman's Gardening Encyclopedia, New York 1977
Zohary: Plant Life of Palestine (Jerusalem 1962)
Zander: Dictionary of Plant Names, 13th Ed. (Stuttgart 1984)

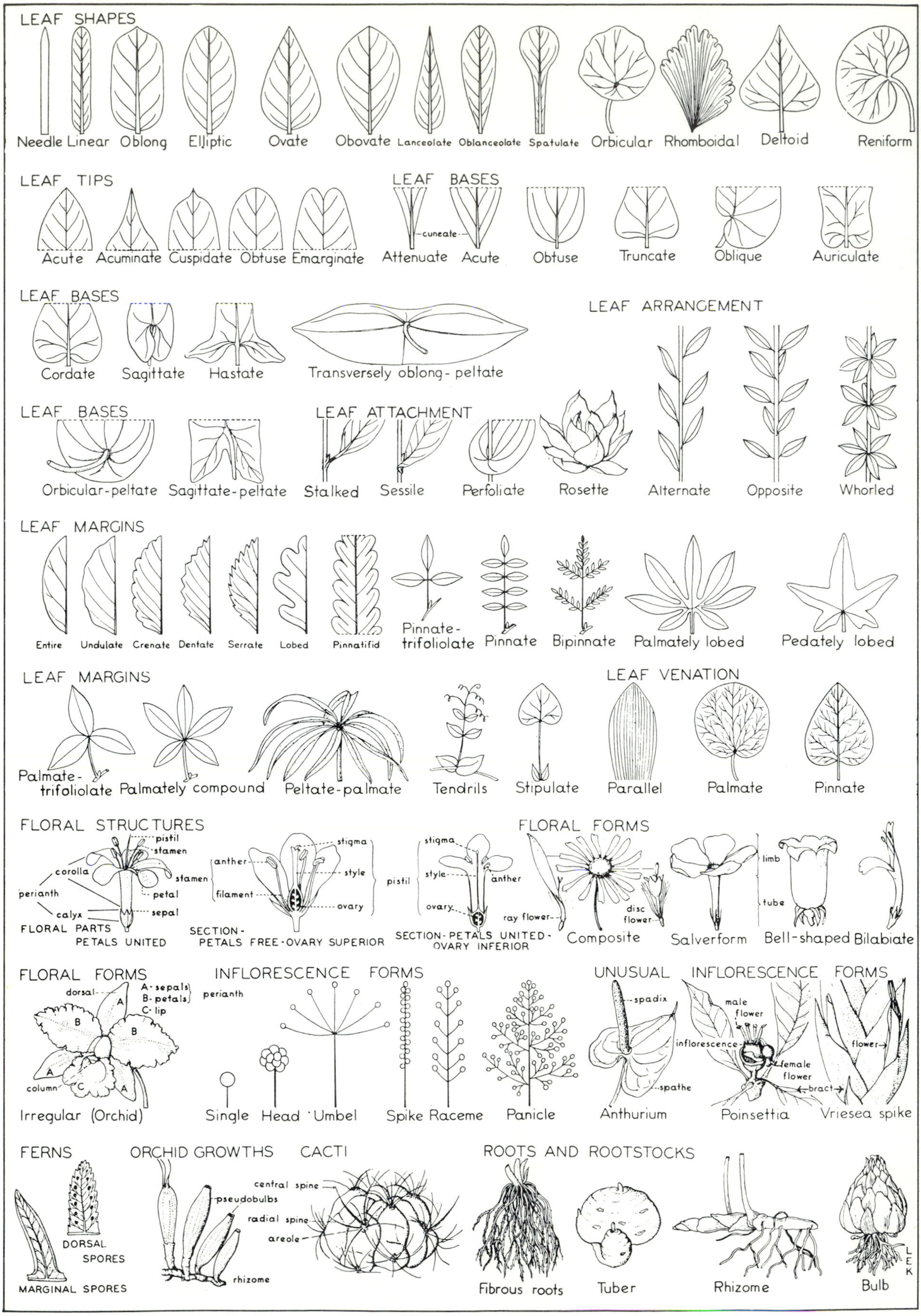

LEAF SHAPES

Needle Linear Oblong Elliptic Ovate Obovate Lanceolate Oblanceolate Spatulate Orbicular Rhomboidal Deltoid Reniform

LEAF TIPS

Acute Acuminate Cuspidate Obtuse Emarginate

LEAF BASES

cuneate Attenuate Acute Obtuse Truncate Oblique Auriculate

LEAF BASES

Cordate Sagittate Hastate Transversely oblong-peltate

LEAF ARRANGEMENT

Rosette Alternate Opposite Whorled

LEAF BASES

Orbicular-peltate Sagittate-peltate

LEAF ATTACHMENT

Stalked Sessile Perfoliate

LEAF MARGINS

Entire Undulate Crenate Dentate Serrate Lobed Pinnatifid Pinnate-trifoliolate Pinnate Bipinnate Palmately lobed Pedately lobed

LEAF MARGINS

Palmate-trifoliolate Palmately compound Peltate-palmate Tendrils Stipulate

LEAF VENATION

Parallel Palmate Pinnate

FLORAL STRUCTURES

pistil
stamen
corolla
stamen
perianth
petal
calyx
sepal

FLORAL PARTS
PETALS UNITED

anther
filament
stigma
style
ovary

SECTION-
PETALS FREE-OVARY SUPERIOR

stigma
style
pistil
anther
ovary

SECTION-PETALS UNITED-
OVARY INFERIOR

FLORAL FORMS

ray flower
disc flower
Composite
Salverform
limb
tube
Bell-shaped
Bilabiate

FLORAL FORMS

dorsal
A
B
A
A
B
A-sepals
B-petals
C-lip
A
column C A
Irregular (Orchid)

INFLORESCENCE FORMS

perianth
Single Head Umbel Spike Raceme Panicle

UNUSUAL INFLORESCENCE FORMS

spadix
spathe
Anthurium

male flower
inflorescence
female flower
bract
Poinsettia

flower
Vriesea spike

FERNS

DORSAL
SPORES
MARGINAL SPORES

ORCHID GROWTHS

central spine
pseudobulbs
radial spine
areole
rhizome

CACTI

ROOTS AND ROOTSTOCKS

Fibrous roots Tuber Rhizome Bulb

L E K

acicular — needle-like

acuminate — tapering to a point

acute — sharply pointed, but not drawn out

adventitious — other than usual place

alternate — arranged along a stem at different levels

anther — pollen bearing top of stamen

apex — the tip of an organ (as a leaf)

apiculate — with short, not stiff point

areole — cushion-like structure out of which can arise spines, branches, and flowers, a characteristic confined to cacti

articulated — jointed, separating freely by a clean scar

asexual — propagates without benefit of sex

attenuate — becoming narrow, tapered

auriculate — with ears at base

axil — the point just above the leaf where it rises from the stem

basal — at the base of an organ

bifid — divided halfway into two

bifurcate — forked

bilabiate — divided into two or equal lips

bipinnate — both primary and secondary divisions with separate leaflets

bipinnatisect — 3 times divided leafblade whose 3 parts are again several times divided

bipinnatifid — twice pinnately cut

bisexual — possessing perfect (hermaphrodite) flowers having both stamens and pistils

blade — the expanded portion of a leaf

bract — modified leaves intermediate between flower and the normal leaves, frequently colored

bristly — bearing stiff strong hairs or bristles

bulb — a growth bud with fleshy scales, usually underground

bullate — blistered or puckered

calyx — outer circle or cup of floral parts (usually green)

campanulate — bell-shaped flower with broad base

carpel — division in a compound fruit (section)

caudex — upright root stock or trunk

caulescent — becoming stalked

cauliflorous — production of flowers or fruit directly out of old wood (Ficus)

cephalium — woolly cap at the apex of cacti

channeled — hollowed out like a gutter

chloroplast — the granules of protoplasm which are of a green color

chromosomes — microscopic rodlike bodies in the plant cell, bearing the hereditary material

ciliate — fringed with eyelash hairs

cladodes — branchlet simulating a leaf, leaf-like (Asparagus)

clasping — leaf surrounding stem

cleft — cut halfway down

column — combined stamens and style into one body (as in orchids)

compound — similar parts aggregated into a common whole

compound leaf — a leaf of two or more leaflets

concave — hollowed out

connate — united

convex — umbrella-like

cordate — heart-shaped

corm — bulb-like but solid; enlarged fleshy base of a stem

corolla — complete circle of petals

corymb — a flat-topped open flower-cluster blooming from the outside in

creeper — a trailing shoot rooting at intervals

crenate — with teeth rounded, scalloped

crested — with elevated and irregular ridge

culm — the peculiar hollow stem or stalk of grasses and bamboo

cultivar — special form originating in cultivation

cuneate — wedge-shaped, triangular

cuspidate — tipped with a sharp and stiff point

cyme — a broad, usually flat-topped flower cluster with center flowers opening first

decumbent — reclining, but summit ascending

deltoid — triangular

dentate — with coarse teeth, usually directed outward

dichotomous — forked, parted by pairs

digitately lobed — fingered and main veining radiating from more than one point

dioecious — unisexual; the male and female reproductive organs in different plants

diploid — having the basic chromosome number twice the number in normal germ-cells, characteristic of a species

disc — (in orchids) rounded structure on lip

dissected — several times cleft into small segments

distichous — two-ranked; in two vertical rows

diurnal — daytime

divided — separated at the base

dorsal — back; in orchids usually a top sepal

downy — clothed with soft short hairs

drupe — ripened ovary containing nuts

elliptical — oblong, with widest point at center

elongate — drawn out in length

emarginate — notched at the end

endemic — native to a restricted region

entire — margin without toothing or division

epiphyte — air-plant; a plant growing on another, but not taking food from its host

F 1 hybrid — first generation hybrid obtained by artificial cross-pollination between two dissimilar parents (F meaning filial), each from a pure line or race, and each bearing hereditary factors (genes), which characteristics will be transmitted, according to their dominant genes, to an F 1 hybrid; as a rule imparting also greater vigor (heterosis).

F 2 generation — second generation from a given cross, usually obtained through self pollination within the F 1 hybrids, and which can then segregate into the various types present in the family lines, according to Mendel's Law.

farinose — covered with a mealiness, or starchy matter

ferns — plants without flowers

fertile — spore bearing or seed bearing

fibrous — with fibers, or thread-like parts

filament — thread-like stalk of an anther or stamen

filiform — thread shaped; very slender

floccose — with locks of soft hair or wool

frond — leaf of fern

funnelform — a tubular flower gradually widening upward and spreading into disc

geniculum — thickened joint or node of a stem

glabrous — smooth, not hairy nor rough

glaucous — covered with a white powder that rubs off

glochid — barbed hair, or bristle, as in cacti

glutinous — sticky

hairy — having longer hairs

haploid — having the basic chromosome number, or half the diploid number characteristic of a species

hastate — halberd-shaped, with basal lobes turned outward, or flared

head — a short dense flower spike

herb — a plant with no persistent stem above ground, usually contrasted with woody plants

herbaceous — non-woody

hermaphrodite — stamens and pistils in same flower

hirsute — hairy, with long rather stiff hairs

hybrid — a plant resulting from a cross between parents that are unlike

hypochil — lower or basal part of the lip in some orchids

imbricated — ovelapping (as tiles on a roof)

inferior ovary — one that is below the calyx leaves

inflorescence — the flowering portion of a plant, or more precisely the mode of its arrangement

insectivorous — plants which capture insects and absorb nutriment from them

intergeneric — hybrid between genera

internode — space between two joints

involucre — bracts surrounding flowers or their support

irregular flower — a flower which cannot be halved in any plane, or in one plane only

laciniate — slashed into narrow irregular pointed lobes

lanceolate — lance-shaped; tapering toward the tip

lateral — from the side

lenticel — lens-like corky elevations on young bark giving vent to breathing pores

lepidote — beset with small scurfy scales

limb — the border or expanded part of corolla (or spathe) above the throat

line — 1/12 of an inch or 1.2 mm

linear — the narrow and flat, margins parallel

lip — the principal lobes of a bilabiate corolla; in orchids a much modified petal

lobe — any projection of a leaf, rounded or pointed

lobed — leaf cut less than halfway to the base

marcottage — airlayering (from Latin mergus)

marginal — at the edge

membranous — thin, semi-transparent

monocarpic — a plant that flowers but once

monoecious — the stamens and pistils in separate flowers but borne on the same plant

mutant — form derived by sudden change from a species

needle-shaped — long, slender and rigid
node — a joint in a stalk where leaves or their vestiges are born
obcordate — inversely heartshaped, the notch being at the apex
oblanceolate — broad end near tip, long tapering toward base
oblique — slanting of unequal sides
oblong — much longer than broad, with parallel sides
obovate — inverted ovate, the broad end upward
obtuse — blunt or rounded at the end
opposite — opposite each other
orbicular — leaf with circular outline
ovary — that part of the pistil which contains the future seed
ovate — a leaf broadest near base, tapering upward
palmate — veins or leaflets radiating from tip of petiole
palmately compound — more than 3 leaflets borne at tip of petiole
palmately lobed — palmately divided leaf not cut to base
panicle — an open and branched flower cluster
parallel — equally distant at every part
parasite — organism subsisting on another living organism
parted — leaf cut ¾ or more
pectinate — comb-like, merely fringed, with spines
pedate — footed; palmately divided or parted
pedicel — stalk of each flower and cluster
peduncle — primary flower stalk
peltate — leaf-blade attached to stalk inside its margin
peltate-palmate — palmate leaf completely circular in outline
pendant — hanging down from its support
perianth — the calyx, or corolla, or both
perfoliate — petiole in appearance passing through the leaf
petal — a flower-leaf
petiole — the supporting stalk of a leaf; leaf stem
petiolate — furnished with a petiole
petiolule — a small petiole
phenotype — of similar physical make-up as the type species, influenced by environment
phylloclade — a flattened branch assuming the function of foliage
phyllode — petiole taking on the form and functions of a leaf
phyllodia — leaf-like stems and no blades (as in Acacia or Epiphyllum)
pilose — shaggy with soft hairs
pinnae — primary division of a pinnate leaf, its leaflets
pinnate — feather formed; separate leaflets arranged along side of leaf stalk; separation complete
pinnatifid — feathered; cut halfway to midrib
pinnatisect — pinnately divided down to the rachis; a feathered leaf cut down to the midrib
pinnule — secondary pinna or segment
pistil — the female organ of a flower, consisting of ovary, style and stigma
pistillate — flower having pistils only; female
plicate — pleated; folded like a fan or ribbed; plaited
pollen — the fertilizing powder contained in the anther
polymorphic — variable as to habit
procumbent — lying along the ground; leaning
prostrate — lying flat on the ground
prothallus — first stage of germination of fern spore into flat shield, bearing the sexual organs
pseudobulb — thickened and bulb-like portion of stem in epiphytic orchids
pubescent — covered with short, soft hairs, downy
punctate — having tiny translucent glands, appearing like dots
raceme — elongated simple inflorescence with stalked flowers
rachis — axis bearing flowers or leaflets
ray — marginal portion or floret of a Compositae flower when distinct from the disc
recurved — bent backward or downward
regular flower — with the parts in each set alike
reniform — kidney-shaped
rhizome — creeping rootstock, on or under the ground
rhombic — irregularly slanting rectangle
rosette — a cluster of leaves radiating in a circle from a center usually near the ground
rosulate — bearing a rosette, or basal cluster of spreading leaves
rugose — covered with wrinkles
runner — a slender prostrate shoot, rooting at the end or at joints
saccate — bag-shaped
sagittate — arrow-shaped, with basal ears turned straight downward or inward
salverform — slender tube abruptly expanded into disk-like limb
saxicolous — living on rock
scabrous — rough or harsh to the touch
scale — usually small, dry leaves or bracts

scaly rhizome — a rhizome with closely appressed, much modified leaves, scale-like in appearance
scandent — climbing, in whatever manner
scape — leafless flower stalk arising from the ground (root)
scorpioid — curved or coiled at the end
segment — one of the divisions into which a plant organ may be cleft
sepal — each segment of a calyx, or outer floral envelopes
serrate — notched like saw; finely toothed
sessile — sitting close, without stalk
setose — covered with bristles
simple leaf — one blade; opposite of compound
single flower — flower with one set of petals
sinuate — with a deep wavy margin, curved
sinus — the curve between two lobes of a leaf
slipper-shaped — tubular ventricose
sori — spore masses (in ferns)
spadix — a fleshy spike bearing tiny flowers as in aroids
spathe — a flower-like bract partly surrounding the inflorescence, often colored or showy
spatulate — oblong, broadly rounded at tip but tapering to narrow base
spike — elongated flower stem, with flowers not stalked
spine — a sharp woody outgrowth from stem
sporangium — a sac producing spores — a spore-case in ferns
spore — in ferns a reproductive cell, somewhat corresponding to seed in flowering plants
spur — a tubular projection from the base of a petal or sepal
stamen — the pollen-bearing or "male" organ
staminate — flower wholly male
stellate — star-form; stellate hairs have radiating branches
stigma — that part of the pistil or style which receives the pollen
stipe — "leafstalk" of a fern
stipule — a leaf-like appendage at base of a petiole
stoloniferous — sending out, or propagating itself by stolons
style — the connecting stalk between the ovary and stigma
sub-cordate — indented a trifle
subtend — to extend under, or be opposite to
subulate — awl shaped, tapering from broad or thick base to a sharp point
succulent — juicy, or storing water in stems or leaves
sulcate — grooved or furrowed
superior ovary — when all petals and sepals are inserted below it
synonym — a name rejected in favor of another
tendril — a thread-shaped shoot used for climbing
terete — circular, rounded in cross section; cylindric and usually tapering
terrestrial — plants growing in the ground
tetraploid — having four sets of chromosomes
thallus — plant body showing no differentiation into distinct members, as stem, leaves and roots
throat — the opening of the flower
tomentose — densely covered with matted wool
transverse — directed across (as on a leaf); crosswise
transversely oblong-peltate — long target-like leaf lying crosswise
trapeziform — no two lines parallel
trifoliate — three-leaved
trifoliolate — with three leaflets, as in clover — commonly, but incorrectly, termed "trifoliate"
triploid — having 3 times the haploid chromosome number
truncate — as if cut off at the end
tube — the united portion of calyx or corolla
tuber — modified underground stem; the thickened portion of subterranean stem, provided with "eyes"
tubercle — a wart-like or knobby projection
tubular — having form of a hollow cylinder
turgid — inflated; swollen
umbel — inflorescence in which flower stalks or cluster arise from same point
undulate — wavy, or wavy-margined
unisexual — of one sex; staminate (male), or pistillate (female) only (see dioecious)
vaginate — sheathed; surrounded by a sheath, usually of leaf stems
ventral edge — belly side
ventricose — swollen on one side
viable — capable of germinating or living
viviparous — producing young, while attached to parent
whorled — leaves in circle around stem (above)
woolly — clothed with long and entangled soft hairs
xerophytic — growing in dry situation, subsisting with little moisture
zygomorphic — can be divided into two symmetrical halves only a single longitudinal plane passing through the axis

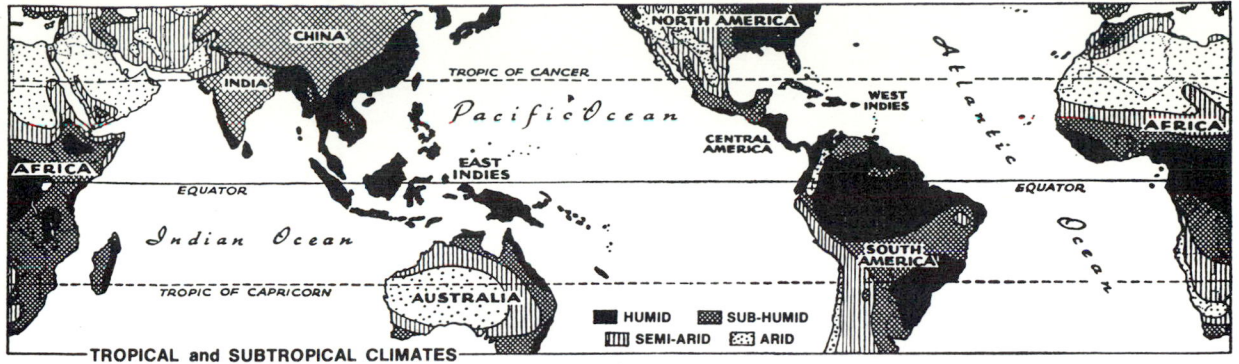

TROPICAL and SUBTROPICAL CLIMATES

HUMID **SUB-HUMID** **SEMI-ARID** **ARID**

PLANT GEOGRAPHY

To give a potential indoor plant the best possible chance of success, we should know something about the climatic backgrounds that prevail in their native habitats. Environment has shaped characteristics in plant types that make them either tolerant or difficult to acclimate when taken into cultivation. If too sensitive it may be best not to try them as a house plant, but many tropicals are far too beautiful not to tempt us to experiment with them just the same.

This is where knowledge of their origin helps us to provide for them those conditions under which such plants feel at home. Each climatic zone has favored and subsequently evolved plant populations that are peculiar to it.

As if by magic carpet, the fascinating world of the Collector of Exotics extending East from the tropics of the Western Hemisphere to subtropical Europe, the vast expanse of Africa and Monsoon Asia and on to Australasia and the islands of the Southern Seas — these are the areas where our house plants were originally found.

Temperature and Rainfall at typical locations in the Tropic and Subtropic Zones.

	LAT. deg.	ELEV. metres	TEMP. °C min.	TEMP. °C max.	RAIN cm
NORTH AMERICA					
California, San Diego	32.7 N	40	2	31	27
Florida, Miami	25.8 N	3	−3	35	140
Mexico, Mexico City	19.2 N	2310	−4	33	60
Mexico, Vera Cruz	19.1 N	16	9	35	172
WEST INDIES					
Cuba, Habana	23.8 N	49	10	35	120
Puerto Rico, San Juan	18.2 N	30	16	34	152
Jamaica, Kingston	18.1 N	7	14	37	82
CENTRAL AMERICA					
Guatemala, Guatemala City	14.3 N	1481	5	32	127
Costa Rica, San José	9.5 N	1147	8	34	177
Panama, Colón	9.2 N	8	19	35	312
SOUTH AMERICA					
Venezuela, Caracas	10.3 N	1043	7	33	80
Venezuela, Ciudad Bolivar	8.9 N	38	19	36	88
Guyana, Georgetown	6.5 N	21	20	33	225
Colombia, Buenaventura	3.5 N	12	23	33	975
Ecuador, Quito (Sierra)	0.1 S	2852	2	26	122
Ecuador, Mendez (Oriente)	2.4 S	698	16	32	255
Brazil, Manaos (Amazonas)	3.0 S	45	19	38	182
Brazil, Rio de Janeiro	22.5 S	64	11	39	108
Brazil, Sao Paulo	23.3 S	820	−2	38	140
Peru, Iquitos (Amazon)	3.7 S	90	18	31	258
Peru, Lima	12.3 S	156	4	32	5
Peru, Cuzco	13.3 S	3452	−2	26	80
Bolivia, La Paz	16.3 S	3660	−3	24	55
Chile, Santiago	33.2 S	520	−4	37	35
Argentina, Buenos Aires	34.3 S	25	−2	40	95
EUROPE					
France, Marseilles	43.1 N	75	−6	38	58
Italy, Palermo (Sicily)	38.1 N	70	3	36	75
Spain, Seville (Andalusia)	37.2 N	30	−5	46	47
AFRICA					
Egypt, Cairo	30.3 N	30	−1	45	3
Cameroon, Douala	4.0 N	10	19	32	395
Equat. Africa, Brazzaville	4.2 S	290	12	38	123
East Africa, Nairobi	1.1 S	1662	2	32	95
Tanzania, Amani (Usamb.)	4.5 S	945	7	30	125
Tanzania, Tanga	5.1 S	30	18	34	153
Madagascar, Tamatave	18.9 S	4	13	38	313
So. Africa, Johannesburg	26.1 S	1754	−5	32	80
South Africa, Cape Town	33.5 S	12	−1	40	63
ASIA					
Israel, Haifa	32.6 N	10	2	38	67
Japan, Nagasaki	32.4 N	133	−5	37	198
China, Yunnan-Fu	25.2 N	1943	−4	33	105
Sikkim, Manjitar, Rangit R.	27.1 N	249	10	35	437
India, Cherrapunji (Assam)	25.2 N	1289	9	32	1065
India, Madras	13.4 N	7	14	45	120
Taiwan, Keelung (Teipei)	20.1 N	10	3	33	337
Burma, Mandalay	21.6 N	76	9	41	82
Philippines, Baguio	16.5 N	1461	8	25	457
Philippines, Manila	14.3 N	14	14	38	200
Thailand, Bangkok	13.4 N	4	11	41	130
Vietnam, Saigon	10.4 N	11	15	40	175
Ceylon, Colombo	6.5 N	7	17	36	200
Borneo, Sandak	5.5 N	3	20	36	300
Sumatra, Toba	2.5 N	1150	14	27	225
Malaya, Singapore	1.2 N	2	18	38	238
Java, Jakarta	6.1 S	8	19	36	180
Java, Bogor	6.6 S	280	18	32	430
New Guinea, Port Moresby	9.3 S	39	20	36	102
AUSTRALASIA					
Hawaii, Honolulu	21.2 N	4	11	32	90
Hawaii, Hilo	19.4 N	12	11	33	342
Fiji Is., Suva	18.8 S	13	14	36	280
Australia, Brisbane	27.3 S	42	2	42	112
New Zealand, Auckland	36.5 S	46	0	32	110

Freezing point zero deg. Centigrade = 32 deg. Fahrenheit (F.).

1 meter (m) = 40 inches (or 3.28 feet).

WORLD CLIMATES and VEGETATION

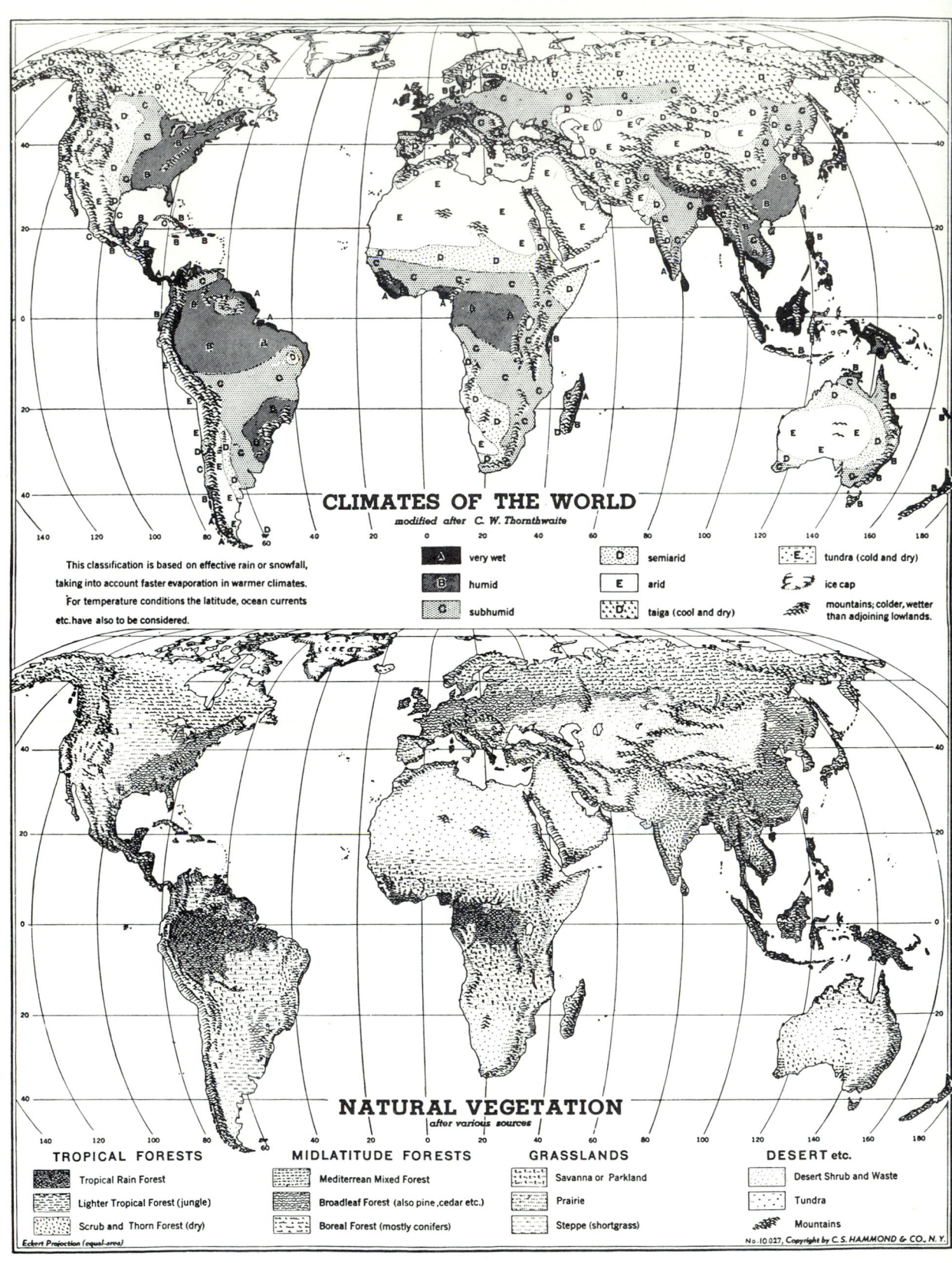

CLIMATES OF THE WORLD
modified after C. W. Thornthwaite

This classification is based on effective rain or snowfall,
taking into account faster evaporation in warmer climates.
For temperature conditions the latitude, ocean currents
etc. have also to be considered.

A very wet	**D** semiarid	**E** tundra (cold and dry)
B humid	**E** arid	ice cap
C subhumid	**D** taiga (cool and dry)	mountains; colder, wetter than adjoining lowlands.

NATURAL VEGETATION
after various sources

TROPICAL FORESTS
- Tropical Rain Forest
- Lighter Tropical Forest (jungle)
- Scrub and Thorn Forest (dry)

MIDLATITUDE FORESTS
- Mediterrean Mixed Forest
- Broadleaf Forest (also pine, cedar etc.)
- Boreal Forest (mostly conifers)

GRASSLANDS
- Savanna or Parkland
- Prairie
- Steppe (shortgrass)

DESERT etc.
- Desert Shrub and Waste
- Tundra
- Mountains

Eckert Projection (equal-area)

No. 10.027, Copyright by C.S. HAMMOND & CO., N.Y.

ON PRONUNCIATION OF BOTANICAL NAMES

Botanical nomenclature is basically Latin, or words adopted from other languages, with Latin endings, and conceived to be understandable internationally. Correctly pronounced and clearly enunciated, the recital of botanical names has a stately and noble sound. However, in the words of L. H. Bailey, there is no standard agreement on rules for the pronunciation of botanical binomials. Many English-speaking people pronounce generic and descriptive specific names simply as if the words were English, in what is known as the Traditional English system.

Alternately there is the Restored Academic, or phonetic pronunciation of classical scholars, which comes close to the manner of speech of the ancient Romans. Their idiom has been conserved through the centuries. The Florentine vernacular Latin of Dante in the 14th Century is the touchstone of modern Italian. Castilian Spanish also is an enhanced but faithful perpetuation of spoken Latin practically unchanged since the 5th Century. Anyone conversant with these languages will have no difficulty to articulate Botanical Latin in the classical tradition.

In spoken Latin, much the same as in Italian and Spanish, also in German or even Japanese, the vowels are pronounced precisely and uniformly: a as in apart; e as in pet; i as in pin; o as in note; u as in full; y in phyllus as in the French rue, the German or Chinese ü. Typical of the clear sound of spoken Latin is the Spanish expression "Te amo!".

Combinations of two vowels, or imperfect diphthongs found in Latin or Greek are enunciated separately as two syllables: aë (ah-eh = Gr. aer, Aërides); ai (ah-ee = eye); au (house); ei (eight); eo (areole); eu (eh-oo = aureus); ie (ee-eh = variegata; oi (oh-ee = deltoides); iu (ee-uu = folius); ue (uu-eh = cruentus); ui (ruin).

Exceptions are the perfect diphthongs or inseparable ligatures æ or ae (in caeruleus, Linnaeus, Caesarea), sounded as one vowel halfway between ah and eh, as in hat or fair, in French père, or the German "Umlaut" ä; œ or oe (in Coelogyne, coelestis) as in the French heureux, also the German or Swedish "Umlaut" ö.

Consonants: In the classical Latin used by Cicero in the first century B.C., the Romans never pronounced C like an English s, or G as j, but always like k and g (in get). By 180 A.D. however, the classical standard was gradually lost, and while C was still being pronounced as k before a, o, u — it changed to sound as z or s before ae, e, i, oe, y. G remained hard before a, o, u — as in Gardenia, but became a soft j as in joy before e and i (Geranium).

Many botanical names or epithets are derived from foreign-root personal or geographical names with Latin endings. To be recognizable, these are best pronounced in the idioms of their source, with accent on the preferred syllable.

The accent for nomenclatural Latin names with two syllables is on the first syllable; in words with several syllables the stress is usually on the next-to-the-last. If in doubt, pronounce all syllables with equal emphasis.

With a background of European schooling, I find it appropriate to use the pleasing phonetics of Continental Latin; those employing the English inflections may have difficulty being understood in non-English speaking areas. However, since English is increasingly a universally understood world language, it may well be employed, wherever found to be more convenient, in the pronunciation of Botanical names. I feel that a language should be our servant, not our master.

Alfred B. Graf

INTERNATIONAL METRIC SYSTEM

Terms of Measurement
   are generally given according to
   the International Metric System.

1 centimeter, or centimetre (cm) = 0.4 inch
   2½ cm = 1 inch
   10 cm   = 4 inches

1 meter, or metre (m) = 40 inches (or 3.28 feet)
   1 cm = 10 mm
   1 m   = 100 cm
   1 foot = 30 cm or 300 millimeters, or millimetres

1 gram (g) = 0.035 oz
   1 kilogram (kg) = 2.2 lbs.

1 liter (l) = 1.06 quarts
   4 liters = 1.06 gal.

Temperature Conversion:
Degrees Fahrenheit vs. Centigrade.
Freezing point
   zero (0) deg. Centigrade = 32 deg. Fahrenheit (F.)
Boiling point
   100 deg. Celsius (C.) = 212 deg. Fahrenheit (F.)

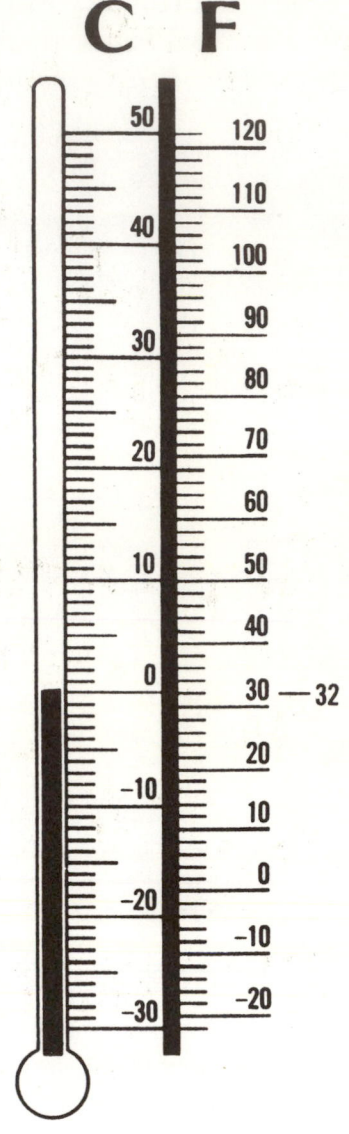

INCHES

CENTIMETERS, or CENTIMETRES